CONFLICT OF LAWS

Fourth Edition

By

Eugene F. Scoles
Max L. Rowe Professor of Law Emeritus
University of Illinois
Dean and Professor of Law Emeritus
University of Oregon

Peter Hay
L.Q.C. Lamar Professor of Law
Emory University

University Professor Emeritus
Technische Universität Dresden

Patrick J. Borchers
Dean and Professor of Law
Creighton University

Symeon C. Symeonides
Dean and Professor of Law
Willamette University
Judge Albert Tate Professor of Law Emeritus
Louisiana State University

HORNBOOK SERIES®

Vincennes University
Shake Learning Resources Center
Vincennes, Indiana 47591-9986

Mat #40149476

West, a Thomson business, has created this publication to provide you with accurate and authoritative information concerning the subject matter covered. However, this publication was not necessarily prepared by persons licensed to practice law in a particular jurisdiction. West is not engaged in rendering legal or other professional advice, and this publication is not a substitute for the advice of an attorney. If you require legal or other expert advice, you should seek the services of a competent attorney or other professional.

Hornbook Series, *Westlaw*, and West Group are trademarks registered in the U.S. Patent and Trademark Office.

ISBN 0–314–14645–8

 TEXT IS PRINTED ON 10% POST
CONSUMER RECYCLED PAPER

Dedicated

to

**Those who have afforded us the rare
opportunity to consider, to contemplate,
and to chronicle our view of this area of the law.**

*

Preface to the Fourth Edition

The conflict-of-laws river continues to flow swiftly. Since the publication of the last edition there have been important developments in the United States, including Supreme Court decisions, as well as internationally, including the promulgation of a new regulation in jurisdiction and judgments in the European Union.

In preparing this edition we have been mindful of the aspects of the book that most readers have found helpful. We have continued to emphasize both interstate and international aspects of the conflict of laws. We have also (we hope) maintained the book's evenhanded character. Particularly in the area of choice of law, the field has taken on a remarkable pluralism of theories. We have attempted to cull those theories and to take from each its valuable insights. Some areas have seen both a theoretical and practical convergence, leading to more predictability and stability. Aware that busy jurists and lawyers who do not specialize in the discipline are anxious for guidance where it can be given, we have endeavored to identify such areas of convergence.

As is inevitably the case with any project this massive, we are indebted to many persons and institutions. In particular, we are grateful for the support that we have received at the various institutions with which we have been affiliated during the preparation of this and previous editions: Albany Law School of Union University, Creighton University School of Law, Emory University School of Law, University of Illinois College of Law, Louisiana State University Law Center, University of Oregon School of Law, Technische Universitat Dresden, and Willamette University College of Law. We are also grateful to our families, who showed remarkable patience during the seemingly endless period that this was a work in progress.

EUGENE F. SCOLES
PETER HAY
PATRICK J. BORCHERS
SYMEON C. SYMEONIDES

Eugene, Oregon
Dresden, Germany
Omaha, Nebraska
Salem, Oregon
Fall, 2004

*

v

WESTLAW® Overview

Conflict of Laws, Fourth Edition, offers a detailed and comprehensive treatment of basic rules, principles, and issues relating to conflict of laws. To supplement the information contained in this book, you can access Westlaw, a computer-assisted legal research service. Westlaw contains a broad array of legal resources, including case law, statutes, expert commentary, current developments, and various other types of information.

Learning how to use these materials effectively will enhance your legal research abilities. To help you coordinate the information in the book with your Westlaw research, this volume contains an appendix listing Westlaw databases, search techniques, and sample problems.

The instructions and features described in this Westlaw overview are based on accessing Westlaw via westlaw.com® and **www.westlaw.com**.

THE PUBLISHER

*

Summary of Contents

	Page
PREFACE	v
WESTLAW OVERVIEW	vii

Chapter

1. Introduction: The Subject Defined and Overview — 1
   I. Definitions—Conflict of Laws—Private International Law — 1
   II. Scope of the Subject — 3

2. The Development and Current State of Approaches to Choice of Law — 5
   I. Introduction — 6
   II. A Brief History of European Private International Law — 9
   III. The American Development Prior to the Conflicts Revolution — 18
   IV. The Scholastic Revolution — 25
   V. The Second Restatement — 58
   VI. The Judicial Revolution — 68
   VII. The Evolution of Principled Rules: A Goal for the Future — 105
   VIII. Conflicts Law Reform in Other Countries — 110

3. Determining the Applicable Law — 119
   I. Introduction — 120
   II. Pervasive Problems — 122
   III. Problems of Federalism: Constitutional Limitations on Choice of Law — 149
   IV. Problems of Federalism: State Law in Federal Courts — 177
   V. Problems of Federalism: Federal Common Law — 208
   VI. International Treaties — 222

4. Domicile — 232
   I. Introduction—The Use of the Domicile Concept in Conflict of Laws — 233
   II. Preliminary Matters Significant in Considering Domicile — 235
   III. Domicile Compared and Defined — 241
   IV. Traditional Requirements for the Acquisition of a Domicile of Choice — 251
   V. Geographic Boundaries of Domicile — 265
   VI. Domicile as Affected by Status — 266
   VII. Analogous Relationships of Corporate Entities — 283

Page

Chapter

5. Basic Considerations in Personal Jurisdiction 284
 I. Introduction 284
 II. The Development of American Jurisdiction 286
 III. Traditional Jurisdictional Relationships 295
 IV. New Jurisdictional Relationships 305
 V. The Need for Statutory Authorization 320
 VI. Other Jurisdictional Issues Compared 324
 VII. Challenging Jurisdiction 329
 VIII. Continuing Jurisdiction 334

6. General Jurisdiction 336
 I. Introduction 336
 II. "Satellite" Bases of Jurisdiction 338
 III. Contacts–Based General Jurisdiction 350

7. Specific Jurisdiction in Tort Cases 360
 I. Introduction 360
 II. Personal Injuries 361
 III. Injuries to Property 373
 IV. Injuries to Reputation 376
 V. Economic Injuries 382

8. Specific Jurisdiction in Contract Cases 386
 I. Introduction 386
 II. Insurance Contracts 389
 III. Franchise and Similar Contracts 392
 IV. Employment and Personal Service Contracts 395
 V. Purchase and Sale Contracts 397
 VI. Construction Contracts 399
 VII. Leases 400
 VIII. Carriage Contracts 401

9. Specific Jurisdiction in Statutory Cases 403
 I. Introduction 403
 II. Environmental Harm 406
 III. Copyright and Trademark Infringement 408
 IV. Patent Infringement 411
 V. Employment–Related Statutory Obligations 414
 VI. Securities and Related Statutes 416
 VII. Private Antitrust and Other Unfair Trade Actions 419
 VIII. Anti–Fraud Statutes 421

10. Special Jurisdictional Problems 423
 I. Introduction 423
 II. Federal Court Personal Jurisdiction 424
 III. Class Actions 444
 IV. Special Problems of Jurisdiction Over Business Associations .. 450
 V. Pendent Personal Jurisdiction 464
 VI. Foreign States and Instrumentalities 469

Page

Chapter

11. Limitations on Jurisdiction ------------------------------- 477
    I. Introduction -- 477
    II. Contractual Limitations on Forum Selection ----------- 478
    III. Forum Non Conveniens ------------------------------- 492
    IV. Immunities From Service ----------------------------- 508
    V. Other Federal Limitations on State Court Jurisdiction --------- 509
    VI. Native American and Indian Country Limitations -------------- 510

12. Procedure --- 518
    I. Notice -- 519
    II. Service Abroad of Documents ------------------------- 523
    III. Taking Evidence Abroad ---------------------------- 529
    IV. Admissibility of Evidence: Testimonial Privilege ----------- 536
    V. Proof of Foreign Law -------------------------------- 543

13. Forming Domestic Relationships---------------------------- 557
    I. Marriage and Other Forms of Domestic Relationships as a
       Problem in the Conflict of Laws ---------------------- 558
    II. Law Governing Recognition of Marriage --------------- 564
    III. Unusual Marriages, Same–Sex Marriages and Unions, Con-
        tractual Domestic Arrangements --------------------- 584

14. Marital Property -- 596
    I. Preliminary Policy Observations --------------------- 596
    II. Immovables -- 602
    III. Movables -- 607
    IV. Subsequent Intentional Property Transactions ---------- 616
    V. The Separate Property and Quasi–Community Property Con-
       cepts -- 618
    VI. Contractual Modification of the Marital Property Regime ----- 621
    VII. Debts -- 623

15. Dissolution of Domestic Relationships and its Consequences---- 627
    I. Interstate Recognition of Dissolution Decrees--------------- 628
    II. Annulment in the United States---------------------- 646
    III. International Recognition of Dissolution Decrees ----------- 648
    IV. Incidents of Divorce Decrees: Support and Custody ------------- 663

16. Legitimation and Adoption--------------------------------- 693
    I. Legitimacy and Legitimation ------------------------- 693
    II. Adoption --- 699

17. Torts --- 709
    I. Introduction --------------------------------------- 711
    II. Choice–of–Law Approaches to Torts in General ----------- 713
    III. From Rules to Approaches to Rules------------------- 785
    IV. Particular Tort Problems --------------------------- 866
    V. Products Liability---------------------------------- 896
    VI. Territoriality and Personality in Tort Conflicts -------------- 942

Page

Chapter

18. Contracts -- 946
      I. Choice of Law by the Parties (Party Autonomy)------------------ 947
      II. Choice of Law in the Absence of Choice-of-Law Agreement ---- 987
      III. Contract Choice-of-Law by Subject Matter ----------------------- 1005
      IV. Choice-of-Law Alternatives -------------------------------------- 1037
      V. Unjust Enrichment-- 1040

19. Property-- 1053
      I. Interests in Land --- 1054
      II. Tangible Movables--- 1072
      III. Intangibles --- 1101

20. Succession -- 1109
      I. Introduction --- 1109
      II. Intestate Succession -- 1110
      III. Testamentary Succession ------------------------------------- 1117
      IV. Family Protection—Forced Shares—Election ------------------- 1133
      V. International Wills -- 1138
      VI. Devises to Aliens -- 1140

21. Trusts and Powers of Appointment ---------------------------- 1142
      I. Trusts -- 1142
      II. Powers of Appointment -- 1154

22. Probate and Administration of Estates -------------------------- 1164
      I. Probate--- 1165
      II. Administration of Estates------------------------------------- 1170
      III. Accounting and Distribution --------------------------------- 1209
      IV. Guardians and Conservators----------------------------------- 1211

23. Corporations, Winding-Up, and Bankruptcy-------------------- 1218
      I. The Law Applicable to Corporations -------------------------- 1218
      II. Bankruptcy --- 1235

24. Recognition and Enforcement of Foreign Judgments and De-
      crees-- 1257
      I. Preliminary Considerations ---------------------------------- 1258
      II. Interstate Recognition of Judgments------------------------- 1272
      III. International Recognition of Judgments --------------------- 1308
      IV. Extralitigious Proceedings, Administrative Determinations,
          and Arbitral Awards -- 1337

PUBLISHER'S APPENDIX: RESEARCHING CONFLICT OF LAWS -------------------- 1345
TABLE OF RESTATEMENT CITATIONS-- 1361
TABLE OF UNIFORM COMMERCIAL CODE CITATIONS -------------------------- 1371
TABLE OF UNIFORM PROBATE CODE CITATIONS --------------------------- 1375
TABLE OF STATUTES AND RULES --- 1377
TABLE OF CASES -- 1397
INDEX -- 1549

Table of Contents

―――――――

		Page
PREFACE		v
WESTLAW OVERVIEW		vii

Chapter 1. Introduction: The Subject Defined and Overview **1**
   I. Definitions—Conflict of Laws—Private International Law 1
  II. Scope of the Subject 3

Chapter 2. The Development and Current State of Approaches to Choice of Law **5**
     I. Introduction 6
    II. A Brief History of European Private International Law 9
        A. From Ancient Greece to Medieval Italy 9
        B. Bartolus and the Italian Statutists 10
        C. The French Statutists 13
        D. The Dutch Contribution: Comity 14
        E. The German Contribution: Wächter and Savigny 15
   III. The American Development Prior to the Conflicts Revolution 18
        A. From "Comity" (Story) to "Vested Rights" (Beale) 18
        B. The First Critics (Cook and Cavers) 22
   IV. The Scholastic Revolution 25
        A. "Governmental Interests Analysis" (Currie) 25
        B. The Lex–Fori Approach (Ehrenzweig) 38
        C. Functional Analyses 43
        D. Value–Oriented Approaches 47
            1. In General 47
            2. The "Better Law" Approach 52
     V. The Second Restatement 58
   VI. The Judicial Revolution 68
        A. The Chronology of the Revolution in Torts and Contracts 68
            1. Introduction 68
            2. The Erosion of the *Lex Loci Delicti* Rule 69
            3. The Erosion of the *Lex Loci Contractus* Rule 74
        B. The Revolution at the Beginning of the 21st Century 79
            1. Introduction 79
            2. Caveats 79
            3. The Methodological Camps 84
            4. Traditional States 86
            5. Significant–Contacts States 98

Page
6. Second Restatement States ---------------------------------- 98
7. Interest Analysis and the Lex Fori Variant --------------- 102
8. Other Modern Approaches ----------------------------------- 104
VII. The Evolution of Principled Rules: A Goal for the Future ------ 105
VIII. Conflicts Law Reform in Other Countries ------------------------ 110

Chapter 3. Determining the Applicable Law --------------------- **119**
I. Introduction -- 120
II. Pervasive Problems -- 122
A. Characterization --- 122
1. Introduction --- 122
2. Subject Matter Characterization ---------------------- 124
3. Connecting Factors ----------------------------------- 126
4. Substance—Procedure Characterization --------------- 127
a. In General -- 127
b. Statutes of Limitation ------------------------------ 129
B. Renvoi --- 138
C. Public Policy -- 142
D. Public Policy—Penal and Governmental Claims ------------ 145
E. Availability of Local Procedure and Remedy ------------- 148
III. Problems of Federalism: Constitutional Limitations on
Choice of Law -- 149
A. Due Process and Full Faith and Credit: From Interest–
Balancing to Contacts ------------------------------------- 149
1. Introduction --- 149
2. The Due Process Cases ------------------------------- 151
3. The Full Faith and Credit Cases -------------------- 160
4. Constitutional Limitations Analyzed ---------------- 165
a. Due Process -- 165
b. Full Faith and Credit ------------------------------ 170
B. Privileges and Immunities, Equal Protection and Commerce --- 171
1. Privileges and Immunities and Commerce Clauses ----- 172
2. Equal Protection ------------------------------------- 176
IV. Problems of Federalism: State Law in Federal Courts ---------- 177
A. The Erie/Klaxon Doctrine: Policy Considerations ------------ 177
B. *Erie*—Problems in Practice -------------------------------- 180
1. Byrd, Hanna and the Federal Rules ------------------ 182
2. Court–Closing Rules ---------------------------------- 188
3. Interstate Forum Shopping --------------------------- 195
a. Interpleader -------------------------------------- 195
b. The 100–Mile Bulge Rule ------------------------- 197
c. Supplemental Jurisdiction ----------------------- 197
d. Federal Transfers -------------------------------- 198
C. Pervasive Erie/Klaxon Problems --------------------------- 201
1. What Is "State Law"? -------------------------------- 201
2. Klaxon and Constitutional Limitations on Choice of
Law --- 205

Page

  V. Problems of Federalism: Federal Common Law 208
     A. The Standard 208
     B. The Federal Interest 212
       1. Government Obligations 212
       2. Contractual Relations With the Government 215
       3. Tort–Related Issues 216
       4. Private Disputes Over Government–Created Rights 218
     C. When Is Federal Common Law Appropriate? 220
 VI. International Treaties 222
     A. In General 222
     B. Multilateral Treaties 223
     C. Bilateral Treaties 226
     D. Conclusion 231

Chapter 4. Domicile **232**
  I. Introduction—The Use of the Domicile Concept in Conflict of
     Laws 233
 II. Preliminary Matters Significant in Considering Domicile 235
     A. Findings, Evidence and Preclusion by Prior Litigation 235
     B. Law Determining or Characterizing Domicile 239
 III. Domicile Compared and Defined 241
     A. Domicile Compared to Nationality—International Con-
       flicts 241
     B. Domicile Compared to Residence, Habitual Residence and
       Other Persistent Relationships 244
     C. Domicile Defined 249
 IV. Traditional Requirements for the Acquisition of a Domicile of
     Choice 251
     A. In General 251
     B. Physical Presence 252
     C. Intent Necessary for Domicile 255
       1. In General 255
       2. Domicile of a Person Having Multiple Homes 257
       3. Intent Distinguished From Motive 259
       4. Freedom to Exercise Choice 260
  V. Geographic Boundaries of Domicile 265
 VI. Domicile as Affected by Status 266
     A. Domicile of Aliens 266
     B. Domicile of Married Persons 269
     C. Derivative Domicile 271
       1. Domicile of Origin 271
       2. Domicile of Minor—General 273
       3. Children Born Out of Wedlock 276
       4. Adopted Children 277
       5. Separated Parents 277
       6. Death of Parent 278
       7. Emancipation 280
       8. Marriage of Minor 281

Page

   D. Capacity to Acquire a Domicile 281
VII. Analogous Relationships of Corporate Entities 283

Chapter 5.   Basic Considerations in Personal Jurisdiction .. **284**
  I. Introduction 284
  II. The Development of American Jurisdiction 286
     A. 1789–1877: Developing Full Faith and Credit Standards ... 286
     B. 1878–1944: Developing Due Process Standards 288
     C. 1945–Present: The Minimum Contacts Test 292
  III. Traditional Jurisdictional Relationships 295
     A. In Rem Jurisdiction 295
     B. Quasi In Rem Jurisdiction 297
     C. Status Jurisdiction 299
     D. In Personam Jurisdiction 300
     E. Continuing Significance of Traditional Categories 301
  IV. New Jurisdictional Relationships 305
     A. Specific Jurisdiction 305
       1. Related Contacts: Distinguishing Specific from General Jurisdiction 305
       2. Purposeful Availment 309
       3. Reasonableness 314
     B. General Jurisdiction 316
  V. The Need for Statutory Authorization 320
     A. State Courts 320
     B. Federal Courts 322
  VI. Other Jurisdictional Issues Compared 324
     A. Notice and Opportunity to be Heard 324
     B. Competence of the Court—Subject Matter Jurisdiction 326
     C. Venue 327
  VII. Challenging Jurisdiction 329
     A. Direct Attacks 329
       1. Federal Court—FRCP 12(b) 329
       2. State Courts 331
     B. Collateral Attacks 332
     C. Limited Appearances 333
  VIII. Continuing Jurisdiction 334

Chapter 6.   General Jurisdiction **336**
  I. Introduction 336
  II. "Satellite" Bases of Jurisdiction 338
     A. Transient Jurisdiction—The Rule of in–State Service 338
     B. Consent 340
     C. Residence, Domicile and Nationality 343
     D. Appearance 345
     E. Jurisdiction by Necessity 348
  III. Contacts–Based General Jurisdiction 350
     A. Distinguished From Specific Jurisdiction 350
     B. Application to Individual Defendants 353
     C. "Continuous and Systematic" Contacts 354

Page

Chapter 7. Specific Jurisdiction in Tort Cases 360
  I. Introduction 360
  II. Personal Injuries 361
    A. Products Liability—The "Stream of Commerce" Test 361
    B. Intentional Torts 367
    C. Negligence 370
    D. Other Strict Liability 372
  III. Injuries to Property 373
    A. Personal Property 373
    B. Real Property 374
  IV. Injuries to Reputation 376
    A. Libel 376
    B. Slander 379
    C. Invasion of Privacy 381
  V. Economic Injuries 382
    A. Interference With Contract and Related Torts 382
    B. Fraud and Related Torts 384

Chapter 8. Specific Jurisdiction in Contract Cases 386
  I. Introduction 386
  II. Insurance Contracts 389
  III. Franchise and Similar Contracts 392
  IV. Employment and Personal Service Contracts 395
  V. Purchase and Sale Contracts 397
  VI. Construction Contracts 399
  VII. Leases 400
  VIII. Carriage Contracts 401

Chapter 9. Specific Jurisdiction in Statutory Cases 403
  I. Introduction 403
  II. Environmental Harm 406
  III. Copyright and Trademark Infringement 408
  IV. Patent Infringement 411
  V. Employment–Related Statutory Obligations 414
  VI. Securities and Related Statutes 416
  VII. Private Antitrust and Other Unfair Trade Actions 419
  VIII. Anti–Fraud Statutes 421

Chapter 10. Special Jurisdictional Problems 423
  I. Introduction 423
  II. Federal Court Personal Jurisdiction 424
    A. Fifth and Fourteenth Amendment Standards 424
    B. Federal Rule of Civil Procedure 4(k) 429
      1. Incorporation of State Long–Arm Statutes 429
      2. The "100–Mile Bulge Rule" 431
      3. Federal Rule 4(k)(2) 433
    C. Admiralty Jurisdiction 435
    D. Bankruptcy Cases 440

Page

E. Removed Cases ------ 442
III. Class Actions ------ 444
  A. Jurisdiction Over Defendants ------ 444
  B. Jurisdiction Over Plaintiffs ------ 446
    1. Opt-out Classes ------ 446
    2. Mandatory Classes ------ 448
IV. Special Problems of Jurisdiction Over Business Associations -- 450
  A. Partnerships and Other Unincorporated Associations ------ 450
  B. Domestic Corporations ------ 453
  C. Foreign Corporations ------ 454
    1. Historical Development ------ 454
    2. Current Jurisdictional Theory ------ 457
  D. Corporate Parent–Subsidiary Relationships ------ 460
  E. Jurisdiction Over Individuals for Corporate or Fiduciary Activities ------ 462
V. Pendent Personal Jurisdiction ------ 464
VI. Foreign States and Instrumentalities ------ 469

Chapter 11. Limitations on Jurisdiction ------ **477**
I. Introduction ------ 477
II. Contractual Limitations on Forum Selection ------ 478
  A. Exclusive and Non–Exclusive Forum Clauses ------ 478
  B. Enforceability in Federal Courts ------ 481
    1. Non–Diversity Cases ------ 481
    2. Diversity Cases ------ 486
  C. Enforceability in State Courts ------ 488
  D. Interpretation and Scope of Forum Clauses ------ 489
  E. Judgment Recognition Issues ------ 491
III. Forum Non Conveniens ------ 492
  A. Introduction ------ 492
  B. Significant Factors in Application ------ 495
    1. Preference for Chosen Forum ------ 495
    2. Availability of Another Forum ------ 496
    3. Other Factors ------ 498
    4. Methods of Application ------ 501
    5. State Practice ------ 502
  C. Federal Transfers ------ 505
IV. Immunities From Service ------ 508
V. Other Federal Limitations on State Court Jurisdiction ------ 509
VI. Native American and Indian Country Limitations ------ 510

Chapter 12. Procedure ------ **518**
I. Notice ------ 519
  A. Method of Notice ------ 519
  B. Opportunity to be Heard ------ 521
  C. Waiver of Notice ------ 522
II. Service Abroad of Documents ------ 523
III. Taking Evidence Abroad ------ 529
IV. Admissibility of Evidence: Testimonial Privilege ------ 536

Page

A. Introduction ----- 536
B. Interstate Conflicts ----- 537
C. International Conflicts ----- 540
D. The Interstate and Convention Approaches Compared ----- 542
V. Proof of Foreign Law ----- 543
  A. The Fact Approach to Foreign Law ----- 543
    1. The Common Law Background ----- 543
    2. Other Legal Systems ----- 546
  B. State Statutes and Uniform Laws ----- 547
  C. Federal Law ----- 549
  D. When Proof Fails: Presumptions and Use of the Lex Fori 553

Chapter 13. Forming Domestic Relationships ----- **557**
I. Marriage and Other Forms of Domestic Relationships as a Problem in the Conflict of Laws ----- 558
  A. Marriage as a Contract and a Status ----- 558
  B. Marriage: Significant Policies ----- 558
  C. Marriage and Other Relationships as an Incidental Question ----- 561
  D. Competing Approaches in Choice of Law: Domicile and Nationality ----- 563
II. Law Governing Recognition of Marriage ----- 564
  A. The Traditional Statement ----- 564
  B. Requirements of Place of Celebration ----- 566
  C. Prohibitions of the Domicile of the Parties ----- 570
    1. Form and Capacity ----- 570
    2. Substantive Prohibition ----- 571
    3. Prohibitions Upon Remarriage After Divorce: Progressive Polygamy ----- 573
    4. Miscegenation ----- 577
    5. "Incestuous" Marriages ----- 578
    6. Non–Age—Consent of Parent ----- 578
    7. Marriage Evasion Legislation ----- 579
  D. Effect in Third State of Marriage Void by Law of Domicile 580
  E. Marriage of Parties With Different Domiciles ----- 581
  F. The Covenant Marriage ----- 583
III. Unusual Marriages, Same–Sex Marriages and Unions, Contractual Domestic Arrangements ----- 584
  A. Unusual Marriages ----- 584
  B. Same–Sex Marriages and Unions ----- 591
  C. Other Partnerships ----- 594

Chapter 14. Marital Property ----- **596**
I. Preliminary Policy Observations ----- 596
  A. Introduction ----- 596
  B. Common Law System ----- 597
  C. Community or Marital Property System ----- 598
  D. Matrimonial Property as Conflict of Laws Issues ----- 599

		Page
II.	Immovables	602
	A. Land Owned at Time of Marriage	602
	B. Land Acquired After Marriage	603
	C. Income From Immovables	606
III.	Movables	607
	A. Movables Owned at Time of Marriage	607
	B. Movables Acquired Subsequent to Marriage	609
	C. Income From Movables	613
	D. Accrual Values: Insurance, Pensions, etc.	613
IV.	Subsequent Intentional Property Transactions	616
V.	The Separate Property and Quasi–Community Property Concepts	618
	A. Characterization of Separate Property	618
	B. Quasi–Community Property	620
VI.	Contractual Modification of the Marital Property Regime	621
VII.	Debts	623

Chapter 15. Dissolution of Domestic Relationships and its Consequences **627**

I.	Interstate Recognition of Dissolution Decrees	628
	A. Introduction	628
	1. In General	628
	2. Domicile and Choice of Law	630
	B. Ex Parte Divorces	633
	1. Full Faith and Credit and the Domicile Requirement: The Williams Cases	633
	2. Domicile and Durational Residence Requirements	635
	C. Inter Partes Divorces	637
	D. The Effect of a Collateral Determination of Invalidity	640
	E. Conclusion and Outlook	645
II.	Annulment in the United States	646
III.	International Recognition of Dissolution Decrees	648
	A. Recognition of Foreign–Country Judicial Divorces in the United States	648
	B. Recognition of Foreign Non–Judicial Divorces in the United States	657
	C. Recognition of U.S. Dissolution Decrees Abroad	662
IV.	Incidents of Divorce Decrees: Support and Custody	663
	A. Divisible Divorce	663
	B. Support Obligations	669
	1. Establishing the Support Obligation by Judicial Decree	669
	2. Enforcement and Modification of Support Decrees	671
	a. Lump Sum Child Support and Claims for Additional Support	672
	b. Modification of Support Decrees	674
	c. Choice of Law for Modification	676
	d. Summary	676
	3. International Recognition	678

Page

C. Child Custody 680
1. Obtaining Custody 680
2. Interstate Recognition and Modification 683
3. International Recognition and Modification 689

Chapter 16. Legitimation and Adoption **693**
I. Legitimacy and Legitimation 693
A. Status 693
B. Inheritance Rights of Legitimate and Legitimated Children 696
C. Inheritance Rights of Illegitimate Children 697
II. Adoption 699
A. Jurisdiction to Decree an Adoption 700
B. Extrastate Consequences of Adoption 703
C. International Adoptions 704

Chapter 17. Torts **709**
I. Introduction 711
II. Choice–of–Law Approaches to Torts in General 713
A. Traditional Approaches: The First Restatement's *Lex Loci* Test 713
1. The *Lex–Loci–Delicti* Rule 713
2. Characterization 722
B. Interest Analysis 726
1. In General 726
2. Interest Analysis and the Lex–Fori Variant in the Courts 728
a. False Conflicts 728
b. True Conflicts 730
c. Unprovided–For Cases 734
d. The *Lex–Fori* Variant 737
3. The "Comparative Impairment" Approach 741
a. The California Version 741
b. The Louisiana Version 749
C. The "Better Law" Approach 752
D. The Most–Significant–Relationship Test and the Second Restatement 759
1. Introduction 759
2. The Case Law 761
E. The New York Experience 770
1. Babcock and Guest–Statute Conflicts 770
2. From *Babcock* to *Neumeier* 772
3. The Neumeier Rules 775
4. Extending the Neumeier Rules to Other Loss–Distribution Conflicts: *Schultz* and *Cooney* 777
III. From Rules to Approaches to Rules 785
A. From Rules to Approaches 785
1. Introduction 785
2. Policy Analysis: A Synthesis 786

Page

a. False Conflicts ----- 786
b. Conflicting Rules: Accommodation ----- 787
c. Resolving the Impasse ----- 787
3. Time for Rules? ----- 789
B. From Approaches to Rules ----- 790
  1. The Distinction between Conduct–Regulation Rules and Loss–Distribution Rules ----- 790
  a. The Origins and Meaning of the Distinction ----- 790
  b. The Difficulties of the Distinction ----- 793
  c. The Usefulness of the Distinction ----- 798
  2. Loss–Distribution Conflicts ----- 799
  a. Common–Domicile Cases ----- 799
  b. Cases Analogous to Common–Domicile Cases ----- 806
    (1) Domicile in states with same law ----- 806
    (2) Pre-existing Relationship ----- 808
    (3) Choice-of-Law Clauses ----- 809
  c. Split–Domicile Conflicts Between the Laws of Two States ----- 812
    (1) True Conflicts ----- 812
      (a) Cases in which the conduct, the injury, and the tortfeasor's domicile are in a state whose law protects the tortfeasor ----- 812
      (b) Cases in which the conduct, the injury, and the domicile of the victim are in a state whose law protects the victim ----- 819
      (c) Cases in which the conduct and the tortfeasor's domicile are in a state whose law favors the tortfeasor, while the injury and the victim's domicile are in a state whose law protects the victim ----- 824
    (2) No–Interest or Unprovided-for Cases ----- 830
  a. The *Neumeier* Pattern ----- 830
  b. The *Hurtado* Pattern ----- 834
  c. Summary ----- 835
  d. Split–Domicile Conflicts Involving Three States ----- 837
  e. Summary and Rules ----- 841
  3. Conduct–Regulation Conflicts ----- 842
  a. Generic Conduct–Regulation Conflicts ----- 842
  b. Summary and Rule ----- 850
  c. Punitive–Damages Conflicts ----- 852
    (1) The Pertinent Contacts and Typical Patterns ----- 853
    (2) Three– or Two–Contact Patterns ----- 854
    (3) Single–Contact Patterns ----- 858
    (4) The Victim's Domicile or Nationality ----- 863
    (5) Summary and Rule ----- 865
IV. Particular Tort Problems ----- 866
A. Injury to Intangible Values ----- 867
  1. Fraud and Misrepresentation ----- 867

Page

2. Unfair Competition --- 868
3. Alienation of Affections ------------------------------- 871
4. Defamation and Invasion of Privacy ------------------ 872
B. Statutory Liability -- 874
1. No–Fault Liability -- 874
a. In General -- 874
b. Law Governing the Tortfeasor's Liability ----------- 879
b. Coverage of the No–Fault Statutes ----------------- 881
2. Workers' Compensation ------------------------------------ 883
a. Workers' Compensation Benefits --------------------- 883
b. Statutory Benefits and Tort Immunity --------------- 886
c. Exclusivity With Regard to Subcontractors and
Their Employees ----------------------------------- 888
d. Mutual Employment for Benefit of Two Employers -- 889
C. Admiralty --- 890
V. Products Liability --- 896
A. In General -- 896
B. Samples From the Case Law -------------------------------- 900
1. Common Denominators --------------------------------------- 900
a. Recent Trends --------------------------------------- 900
b. Pertinent Contacts --------------------------------- 901
c. Typical Patterns ----------------------------------- 903
2. Cases in Which Each State's Law Favors the Local
Litigant (True Conflicts) ----------------------------- 905
a. Cases Applying the Pro–Defendant Law of a Defendant–Affiliated State --------------------------- 905
b. Cases Applying the Pro–Recovery Law of a Victim–Affiliated State -------------------------------- 907
(1) Choice supported by three contacts -------------- 907
(2) Choice supported by two contacts ---------------- 909
(3) Choice supported by a single contact ------------ 912
3. Cases in Which Each State's Law Favors a Litigant
Affiliated With the Other State ----------------------- 918
a. Cases Applying the Pro–Recovery Law of a Defendant–Affiliated State ------------------------------ 919
b. Cases Applying the Pro–Defendant Law of a Victim–Affiliated State -------------------------------- 924
(1) Choice supported by three contacts -------------- 924
(2) Choice supported by two contacts ---------------- 929
(3) Choice supported by a single contact ------------ 933
C. Choice–of–Law Rules -- 934
1. Enacted Rules --- 934
2. Proposed Rules --- 937
3. Common Features and Differences --------------------- 939
VI. Territoriality and Personality in Tort Conflicts ----------- 942

Page

Chapter 18. Contracts ---- **946**
  I. Choice of Law by the Parties (Party Autonomy) ---- 947
    A. General Principles ---- 947
    B. Limitations on Party Autonomy ---- 956
      1. Questions of Interpretation and Construction ---- 956
      2. Validity and Public Policy ---- 957
        a. Public Policy Limitation in General ---- 957
          (1) Which State's Public Policy? ---- 957
          (2) Which Level of Public Policy? ---- 960
          (3) Public Policy and "Mandatory Rules" ---- 961
          (4) "Fundamental Policy" ---- 963
        b. Public Policy in Specific Contexts ---- 966
      3. The Requirement of a "Substantial Relationship" ---- 974
        a. In General ---- 974
        b. Satisfaction of the Requirement: Connecting Factors ---- 977
    C. Second Restatement, § 187 ---- 979
      1. Connection with Chosen Law ---- 980
      2. Public Policy Limitation ---- 982
      3. Validation ---- 982
    D. Section 1–105 of the Uniform Commercial Code ---- 983
  II. Choice of Law in the Absence of Choice-of–Law Agreement ---- 987
    A. The Classic Approach ---- 988
    B. Modern Approaches ---- 991
      1. Overview ---- 991
      2. The Case Law: Issue Identification (Characterization) and Connecting Factors ---- 992
      3. The Choice-of-Law Approaches in the Courts: Summary ---- 1000
  III. Contract Choice–of–Law by Subject Matter ---- 1005
    A. Contracts by Subject Matter ---- 1006
      1. Interests in Land ---- 1006
      2. Sales of Chattels ---- 1007
        a. Interstate Transactions ---- 1007
          i. Restatement and U.C.C. ---- 1007
          ii. Case Law ---- 1007
        b. International Transactions ---- 1009
      3. Insurance Contracts ---- 1011
      4. Suretyship ---- 1016
      5. Contracts for the Repayment of Money Lent ---- 1017
      6. Rendition of Services ---- 1019
      7. Agency ---- 1023
      8. Other Contracts ---- 1030
    B. Contract Issues ---- 1034
  IV. Choice–of–Law Alternatives ---- 1037
  V. Unjust Enrichment ---- 1040
    A. Introduction ---- 1040
      1. In General ---- 1040
      2. Case Categories ---- 1041
    B. Choice–of–Law Alternatives ---- 1042
      1. Preexisting (Contractual) Relationships ---- 1042

Page

2. Voluntary Bestowal of Benefits ----------------------------- 1045
3. Claims Related to Tort --------------------------------- 1047
4. Equitable Remedies ------------------------------------- 1049
5. Extent and Nature of Relief --------------------------- 1051

Chapter 19. Property ------------------------------------- **1053**
   I. Interests in Land --------------------------------------- 1054
      A. Introduction --------------------------------------- 1054
      B. The Situs Rule ------------------------------------- 1056
      C. Contract and Conveyance Distinctions -------------- 1058
         1. Policy Analysis—Capacity ----------------------- 1058
      D. Particular Issues ---------------------------------- 1061
         1. Conveyances: Effect and Construction ----------- 1061
         2. Covenants -------------------------------------- 1063
      E. Equitable Interests -------------------------------- 1064
         1. Generally -------------------------------------- 1064
         2. Equitable Servitudes --------------------------- 1065
         3. Equitable Remedies ----------------------------- 1066
      F. Encumbrances -------------------------------------- 1069
  II. Tangible Movables ------------------------------------- 1072
      A. Policy Considerations ------------------------------ 1072
      B. Chattel Transfers --------------------------------- 1075
         1. Contract and Property Issues ------------------- 1075
         2. Situs and Market Policies ---------------------- 1076
         3. Prescription ----------------------------------- 1078
         4. Removal of a Chattel --------------------------- 1079
      C. Chattel Security ---------------------------------- 1081
         1. Introduction ----------------------------------- 1081
         2. The Uniform Commercial Code -------------------- 1082
            a. Introduction ------------------------------- 1082
            b. Documents, Instruments, and Ordinary Goods --- 1084
            c. Goods Covered by a Certificate of Title ---- 1090
            d. Accounts, General Intangibles and Mobile Goods --- 1091
            e. Chattel Paper ------------------------------ 1096
            f. Minerals ----------------------------------- 1097
            g. Uncertificated Securities and Other Investment
                Property ----------------------------------- 1097
            h. Renvoi ------------------------------------- 1098
         3. Treaties --------------------------------------- 1099
 III. Intangibles --- 1101
      A. Introduction -------------------------------------- 1101
      B. Assignability of Intangible ----------------------- 1101
      C. Assignment of Intangibles ------------------------- 1103
         1. Introduction ----------------------------------- 1103
         2. Assignments for the Benefit of Creditors ------- 1104
         3. Commercial Assignments ------------------------- 1105
      D. Corporate Stock ----------------------------------- 1107

Page

Chapter 20.   Succession 1109
- I. Introduction 1109
- II. Intestate Succession 1110
  - A. Immovables—Land 1110
  - B. Movables 1114
- III. Testamentary Succession 1117
  - A. Introduction 1117
  - B. Wills of Immovables—Land 1118
    - 1. Formal Validity 1118
    - 2. Validity—Testamentary Trusts 1121
    - 3. Construction 1123
  - C. Wills of Movables 1125
    - 1. Validity 1125
    - 2. Restrictions on Charitable Gifts 1128
    - 3. Revocation 1129
      - a. By Instrument or Physical Act 1129
      - b. By Operation of Law 1130
    - 4. Construction 1131
- IV. Family Protection—Forced Shares—Election 1133
  - A. Forced Shares 1133
  - B. Election 1136
- V. International Wills 1138
- VI. Devises to Aliens 1140

Chapter 21.   Trusts and Powers of Appointment 1142
- I. Trusts 1142
  - A. Introduction 1142
  - B. Validity 1143
    - 1. Testamentary Trusts 1143
    - 2. Inter Vivos Trusts 1145
  - C. Administration of Trusts 1149
    - 1. Introduction 1149
    - 2. Qualification of Foreign Trustees 1150
    - 3. Administrative Issues 1151
    - 4. Change in Place of Administration 1153
- II. Powers of Appointment 1154
  - A. Introduction 1154
  - B. Validity of a Power 1155
  - C. Nature and Scope of a Power 1156
  - D. Exercise of Powers 1157
    - 1. Generally 1157
    - 2. Rule Against Perpetuities 1160
    - 3. Exercise by Residuary Clause 1162

Chapter 22.   Probate and Administration of Estates 1164
- I. Probate 1165
  - A. Introduction 1165
  - B. Probate of Will of Movables 1165
  - C. Recognition of Foreign Probate 1166
  - D. Probate of Will of Immovables—Land 1168

Page

II. Administration of Estates -- 1170
   A. Introduction --- 1170
   B. Place and Necessity of Administration ----------------- 1170
      1. Domicile -- 1170
      2. Situs of Tangible Assets ---------------------------- 1171
      3. Chattels Temporarily Present Within a State ------ 1172
      4. Chattels Brought Into a State After Owner's Death ----- 1173
      5. Intangibles -- 1174
      6. Commercial Paper ----------------------------------- 1178
      7. Corporate Stock ------------------------------------- 1180
      8. Life Insurance --------------------------------------- 1182
   C. Powers of Personal Representative Outside Appointing
      State -- 1183
      1. Power to Sue --------------------------------------- 1183
      2. Other Acts -- 1186
      3. Payment to a Foreign Representative ------------- 1189
      4. Transfer of Claim by Personal Representative ----- 1191
      5. Suits Arising Out of Administration --------------- 1192
      6. Actions Against Foreign Representatives ---------- 1194
      7. Privity Between Foreign Representatives ---------- 1200
   D. Creditors' Claims—Proof and Payment -------------- 1206
   E. Spousal and Family Allowances --------------------- 1208
III. Accounting and Distribution ----------------------------- 1209
IV. Guardians and Conservators ------------------------------ 1211
   A. In General --- 1211
   B. Conservators --- 1212
   C. Guardians of the Person ----------------------------- 1216

Chapter 23. Corporations, Winding–Up, and Bankruptcy ---- **1218**
  I. The Law Applicable to Corporations --------------------- 1218
   A. The Law of the Place of Incorporation -------------- 1218
      1. The General Principle ------------------------------ 1218
      2. Special Choice–of–Law Rules --------------------- 1223
      3. Applications of the Incorporation—Rule --------- 1226
   B. Regulation of Foreign Corporations by the Forum --------- 1229
      1. Constitutional Limits ------------------------------ 1229
      2. Qualification Statutes ----------------------------- 1230
      3. Pseudo–Foreign Corporations --------------------- 1232
      4. Piercing the Corporate Veil --------------------- 1233
   C. Dissolution and Winding–Up ----------------------- 1234
  II. Bankruptcy --- 1235
   A. Introduction --- 1235
   B. Interstate Bankruptcy ------------------------------- 1239
   C. International Bankruptcy ----------------------------- 1248
      1. Effect of Foreign Proceedings in the United States ----- 1249
      2. Effect of U.S. Proceedings Abroad -------------- 1252
   D. Insolvency of Related and of Multinational Corporations -- 1253

Page

Chapter 24. Recognition and Enforcement of Foreign Judgments and Decrees..**1257**

   I. Preliminary Considerations 1258
     A. The Policy of Preclusion 1258
     B. Preclusion and the Enforcement of Interstate Judgments 1261
     C. Preclusion and the Enforcement of International Judgments 1264
     D. Methods of Enforcing Foreign Judgments 1268
  II. Interstate Recognition of Judgments 1272
     A. What Constitutes Enforceable Foreign Proceedings 1272
       1. Finality 1272
       2. Equity Decrees: Jurisdiction and Recognition 1273
       3. Foreign Decrees Relating to Land 1276
       4. Nature of the Proceeding 1278
     B. Methods of Enforcing Interstate Judgments 1279
       1. Full Faith and Credit 1279
       2. Recognition and Enforcement by Registration or Summary Proceeding 1282
     C. Defenses to Claim on Sister–State Judgments 1284
       1. Lack of Jurisdiction of Rendering Court 1284
       2. Judgment Obtained by Fraud; Equitable Defenses 1288
       3. The Public Policy of the Forum, Penal Judgments, Tax Judgments, and Lack of a Competent Court 1289
         a. Public Policy 1291
         b. No Competent Court in Recognizing Forum 1293
         c. Tax and Penal Judgments and Claims 1296
       4. Foreign Judgment Not on the Merits 1298
       5. Other Defenses 1302
 III. International Recognition of Judgments 1308
     A. Recognition and Enforcement 1308
       1. Early Approaches and the Hilton Doctrine 1308
       2. Recognition Practice After Hilton and Erie 1310
       3. Foreign Approaches and Their Implications for U.S. Recognition Practice 1315
       4. Federal Preemption by Recognition Treaty 1322
       5. Valuation of Foreign Money–Judgments 1326
     B. Defenses to Claim on Foreign–Country Judgment 1328
       1. Jurisdiction 1329
       2. Foreign Judgment for Taxes or Penalties 1331
       3. Public Policy 1333
       4. International Recognition Treaties and Preclusion 1336
 IV. Extralitigious Proceedings, Administrative Determinations, and Arbitral Awards 1337

PUBLISHER'S APPENDIX. RESEARCHING CONFLICT OF LAWS 1345
TABLE OF RESTATEMENT CITATIONS 1361

Page

TABLE OF UNIFORM COMMERCIAL CODE CITATIONS ---------------------------- 1371

TABLE OF UNIFORM PROBATE CODE CITATIONS -------------------------------- 1375

TABLE OF STATUTES AND RULES --- 1377

TABLE OF CASES --- 1397

INDEX -- 1549

*

CONFLICT OF LAWS

Fourth Edition

*

Chapter 1

INTRODUCTION: THE SUBJECT DEFINED AND OVERVIEW

Table of Sections

		Sections
I.	Definitions—Conflict of Laws—Private International Law	1.1
II.	Scope of the Subject	1.2–1.3

I. DEFINITIONS—CONFLICT OF LAWS— PRIVATE INTERNATIONAL LAW

§ 1.1 The term "Conflict of Laws" describes generally the body of law that aspires to provide solutions to international or interstate legal disputes between persons or entities other than countries or states *as such*. A dispute is considered international or interstate if one or more of its constituent elements is connected with more than one country or state.[1] These elements may include the parties' citizenship, domicile, residence, or other affiliation with a state or country, the location of the events that give rise to the dispute, or the location of the object of the dispute. Thus, a contractual dispute between citizens of different countries or domiciliaries of different states, or a property dispute between domiciliaries of one state regarding assets situated in another state, or a tort resulting from conduct occurring in one state and causing injury in another state are examples of disputes that fall within the scope of this subject.

"Conflict of Laws" is the term primarily used in the United States, Canada and more recently in England, while "Private International Law" is the term used in Continental countries, and by some writers in England, at least since the writings of Westlake.[2] Each of the two terms

---

§ 1.1

1. Hereafter the words "state" or "country" are used interchangeably to denote any country or territorial subdivision thereof that has its own system of private law. Cases involving the laws of more than one state or country are referred to hereinafter as "multistate."

2. Private International Law (1858). See Restatement, Second, Conflict of Laws § 2 (1971); Dicey & Morris, Conflict of Laws 33 (12th ed. by Collins et al., 1993); Kegel, Introduction, International Encyclopedia of Comparative Law, vol. 3: Private International Law 1 et seq. (1986).

reflects different assumptions about the nature and function of this body of law, but neither term is fully descriptive.

The term "Private International Law" may be more descriptive, but also more idealistic, than the term "Conflict of Laws." The word "international" describes the disputes that fall within the scope of this subject, which are international (or interstate) in that they have contacts with more than one country or state. The word "private" echoes the civil-law division between private and public law and signifies that only private-law disputes fall within the scope of this subject. In contrast, public-law disputes of an international character, such as those between sovereign countries or other international-law persons, fall within the scope of the "law of nations" or "Public International Law." Yet, the term "Private International Law" is misleading to the extent it suggests that there exists a distinct body of law universally observed by most nations that provides solutions to multistate private-law disputes. Reality is much different. Besides the few international conventions that avoid or resolve conflicts through substantive or conflicts rules, international law has little to say on the subject. Thus, for the most part, the task of resolving multistate private-law disputes is left to individual countries, subject perhaps to certain mild restraints imposed by international law. Accordingly, conflicts law is essentially *national* law.[3] Similarly, within the United States, conflicts law is, *de facto* and for the most part, *state* law rather than federal law. Although the United States Constitution provides the power to federalize the law of interstate conflicts,[4] this power has been exercised very sparingly. Thus, the initiative for resolving interstate (state/state) *and* international (state/foreign country) conflicts remains with the states, albeit subject to some federal constitutional, treaty, and statutory constraints.

The term "Conflict of Laws" is also not entirely accurate. It seems to assume that, in all cases that have contacts with more than one state or country: (1) each involved state or country has an active or passive desire or claim to have its law applied; (2) these claims "conflict" in the sense of being of roughly equal intensity and validity; and (3) there exists an impartial mechanism of hierarchically superior authority for resolving such conflicts. All three of these assumptions are at least questionable. First, even assuming the propriety of using anthropomorphic terms to describe state objectives, both the hypothesis that a state is "interested" in the outcome of disputes between private persons and the concomitant assumption that the application of its law indeed effectuates that objective are the subject of intense debate; second, not

---

3. See Lipstein, The General Principles of Private International Law, Hague Academy, 135 Recueil des Cours 96, 165–194 (1972–I). The diversity of conflicts law begins with the rejection of the "universalistic" (id. at 119) doctrine of the statutists (infra, chapter 2) and the resulting consideration of conflicts law as part of each state's (country's) own *lex fori* (id. at 192).

See also Kahn–Freund, General Problems of Private International Law, Hague Academy, 143 Recueil des Cours 139, 165 ff. *passim* (1974–III).

4. See the second sentence of the Full Faith and Credit Clause of the United States Constitution. U.S. Const. Art. IV, § 1.

all multistate cases necessarily involve conflicting state claims or interests; and third, even if such conflicting claims are implicated, there is presently no superior impartial authority for assessing their validity, measuring their intensity, or delineating their scope. Since, for better or worse, conflicts law is domestic law, the claims or interests of another state or country can influence the resolution of a multistate dispute only when and to the extent permitted by the conflicts law of the forum. In the final analysis, therefore, it might have been more accurate to speak of accommodating conflicting *reasons* for applying foreign rather than local law, rather than speaking of resolving "conflicts" of law.

In any event, the above nomenclature is well established, both in the United States and (as private international law) in other countries, and is therefore maintained here, even though other terms (such as "law of multistate or transnational problems"[5]) might be technically more descriptive.

II. SCOPE OF THE SUBJECT

§ 1.2 While many conflicts problems can be resolved through negotiation, mediation, or arbitration, most of them end up in litigation. In planning for this eventuality, or when forced to confront it, parties involved in multistate activity should keep in mind three major questions: (1) Where can or should litigation be initiated? (2) Which law will the court apply? and (3) Where can the resulting judgment be enforced? These three questions correspond to the three consecutive phases that comprise the process of judicial resolution of most conflicts problems, namely: (1) jurisdiction; (2) choice of law; and (3) recognition and enforcement of judgments. In the United States and other common-law systems, these are also the three major divisions of the law of Conflict of Laws. The organization of this book follows these three divisions.

In contrast, in civil-law systems, questions of jurisdiction and judgment-recognition form part of "international procedural law" rather than of "private international law." In these systems, private international law deals primarily with choice-of-law problems, although, for historical and other reasons, it often encompasses the law of nationality and citizenship, as well as rules regulating the condition of aliens. Another difference between civil-law and common-law systems is that in the former the law to be applied to a case ordinarily has little to do with a court's jurisdiction, except coincidentally, as in cases dealing with local land or immovables.[1] In the latter systems, jurisdiction and applicable

---

5. See von Mehren & Trautman, The Law of Multistate Problems: Cases and Materials on Conflict of Laws (1965). Ehrenzweig spoke of "Private Transnational Law," a term he derived from Walker, Internationales Privatrecht 13 (5th ed. 1934): Specific Principles of Private Transnational Law, Hague Academy, 124 Recueil des Cours 167, 255 (1968–II).

§ 1.2

1. In fact, the confluence of applicable law and jurisdiction with respect to local land or immovables is more a common-law phenomenon than a civil-law rule. Compare, for instance, with respect to succession the common-law situs rule and the civil-law concept of "universal succession." Infra §§ 19.2, 20.2.

law are also distinct, but as a practical matter they are often intertwined, either because the subject matter is considered local or because certain, especially recently developed, choice-of-law theories favor the application of local law.[2] Finally, with respect to recognition of foreign judgments, civil-law countries tend to have well-established rules usually introduced by statute or treaty. In the United States, states are relatively free[3] to follow a variety of approaches with regard to foreign-country judgments, but are subject to uniform restraints imposed by the United States Constitution's Full Faith and Credit Clause[4] with regard to sister-state judgments.

§ 1.3 The focus of this book is primarily interstate and secondarily international and comparative. In the context of the legal structure of the United States, conflicts problems are addressed primarily in the interstate setting. In addition, international situations are examined, especially when there are significant differences in approach or in result. Both for the treatment of international problems and for enhanced understanding and evaluation of interstate approaches, the discussion frequently draws on the relevant experience of foreign legal systems.

Preceding the consideration of jurisdiction, the book treats a number of problems and topics pervasive of the whole subject. The chapter immediately following addresses the development and current state of conflicts theories. These are primarily relevant for an understanding of the choice-of-law material. However, in view of the considerable latitude of courts in other areas as well, conflicts theory is more than a tool for the resolution of choice-of-law problems. It is also indicative of a legal system's *attitude* and approach to multistate legal problems in general, such as federal-state relations (including Constitutional constraints), the concept of domicile, the identification of false conflicts, and the proper role of local public policy.

2. See infra ch. 2.

3. But see the potential use of bilateral recognition-of-judgment conventions which, as federal treaty law, may supersede contrary state statutory or decisional law under the Constitution's Supremacy Clause. See infra ch. 3.

4. U.S. Const. Art. IV, § 1.

Chapter 2

THE DEVELOPMENT AND CURRENT STATE OF APPROACHES TO CHOICE OF LAW

Table of Sections

		Sections
I.	Introduction	2.1
II.	A Brief History of European Private International Law	2.2–2.6
	A. From Ancient Greece to Medieval Italy	2.2
	B. Bartolus and the Italian Statutists	2.3
	C. The French Statutists	2.4
	D. The Dutch Contribution: Comity	2.5
	E. The German Contribution: Wächter and Savigny	2.6
III.	The American Development Prior to the Conflicts Revolution	2.7–2.8
	A. From "Comity" (Story) to "Vested Rights" (Beale)	2.7
	B. The First Critics (Cook and Cavers)	2.8
IV.	The Scholastic Revolution	2.9–2.13
	A. "Governmental Interests Analysis" (Currie)	2.9
	B. The Lex–Fori Approach (Ehrenzweig)	2.10
	C. Functional Analyses	2.11
	D. Value–Oriented Approaches	
	1. In General	2.12
	2. The "Better Law" Approach	2.13
V.	The Second Restatement	2.14
VI.	The Judicial Revolution	2.15–2.25
	A. The Chronology of the Revolution in Torts and Contracts	
	1. Introduction	2.15
	2. The Erosion of the *Lex Loci Delicti* Rule	2.16
	3. The Erosion of the *Lex Loci Contractus* Rule	2.17
	B. The Revolution at the Beginning of the 21st Century	
	1. Introduction	2.18
	2. Caveats	2.19
	3. The Methodological Camps	2.20
	4. Traditional States	2.21
	5. Significant–Contacts States	2.22
	6. Second Restatement States	2.23
	7. Interest Analysis and the Lex Fori Approach	2.24
	8. Other Modern Approaches	2.25
VII.	The Evolution of Principled Rules: A Goal for the Future	2.26
VIII.	Conflicts Law Reform in Other Countries	2.27

I. INTRODUCTION

§ 2.1 In the adjudication of any case, a court is called upon to effectuate two basic but at times opposing objectives—to achieve justice in the individual case and to protect the interests of society in the integrity of its legal system. Individual justice includes regard for the expectations of the parties and the avoidance of invidious results caused by the application of generally applicable laws to a "hard" case. Societal interests include the furtherance of the policies underlying particular rules of law and concern for uniformity in the adjudication of similar problems to assure predictability and efficiency in the administration of justice. Extended to their extremes, societal needs would best be advanced by rigid rules; conversely, complete justice in the individual case would often call for *ad hoc* decisions.

In the purely single-state setting, legal systems have achieved a remarkable accommodation of these two main objectives, a balance that in Anglo–American law was principally the result of the interplay of law and equity.[1] However, when a case involving foreign (out-of-state) aspects arises, the balance is not so easily achieved since the elements involved will now have multiplied. The choice is no longer one between the literal application of local law or relief through the use of an equitable concept or safety valve. Instead, the problem becomes whether to ignore the foreign element and to treat the case as arising under local law, or to seek an accommodation between the forum and the foreign legal system by giving weight to the foreign element and applying foreign law. The first alternative, if applied in all cases, would lead to forum-shopping by the plaintiff—often to the detriment of the defendant—since more than one state or country often will have jurisdiction. It would also frustrate any attempt to achieve some uniformity of result without regard to the place of suit and, with it, predictability. The second alternative is more attractive but leaves unanswered the questions of why, when, and at what point foreign law becomes relevant and, if more than one foreign law is relevant, which law should be applied. Conflict-of-laws theory thus addresses the questions of *when* and *why* foreign law should be applied and at the same time indicates the particular approach and orientation of a jurisdiction–as open or inward-looking—with regard to foreign-law related problems or issues.

Theoretical concern with problems of the conflict of laws is relatively new in Anglo–American law. The early English cases held that, to be actionable in England, the cause must have arisen there. Thus, cases involving foreign elements were dismissed.[2] Conflicts cases were first recognized in England when the accession of James I in 1603 gave

---

§ 2.1

1. For Continental analogues see generally Schlesinger, Baade, Damaska & Herzog, Comparative Law: Cases, Text, Materials (6th ed. 1998).

2. Anonymous, Year Book 2 Edw. II, S. S. Year Book Series 110 (1308); Sack, Conflicts of Laws in the History of the English Law, 3 Law, A Century of Progress, 1835–1935, 342 ff. (A. Reppy, ed., 1937). This practice had less to do with self-restraint

England and Scotland a single monarch.[3] In 1760, Lord Mansfield rendered a contracts conflicts decision, which was to be followed in 1775 by the first statement of a "rule."[4] In the United States, conflict-of-laws theory received its major, although not first,[5] impetus with the appearance of Joseph Story's *Commentaries on the Conflict of Laws, Foreign and Domestic* in 1834.

In Europe, by contrast, theories about conflicts law date to medieval times[6] and, in the course of several centuries of development, had by 1850 run the gamut of virtually all conceivable approaches. Familiarity with these trends and countertrends of the European experience is highly instructive for the understanding and assessment of current American conflicts theories, which have undergone so much "revolution,"[7] "crisis,"[8] and ferment in the past forty years. Indeed, the neglect of historical antecedents and the failure to consider contemporary for-

than with the English jury system. Because jurors were drawn from the vicinage, i.e., the locale in which the events giving rise to the dispute occurred, and foreign jurors could not be impaneled, foreign cases were not triable in England. Later on, the courts developed the fiction that the foreign locale was somehow situated in England and thus assumed jurisdiction for cases arising abroad. Consistently with this fiction, however, the courts applied English law to these cases. See F. Juenger, Choice of Law and Multistate Justice 22 (1993).

3. Dicey, Private International Law, 28 L.Q. Rev. 341, 342 ff. (1912); R. H. Graveson, Conflict of Laws 34 (7th ed. 1974); F. Harrison, Jurisprudence and the Conflict of Laws 118 ff. (1919). There did exist, prior to this time, merchant courts applying the international *law merchant*. However, cases decided by them were not true conflicts cases since "the law merchant never came directly into conflict with the law of England. . . . [I]n cases to which the law merchant applied, there was only one law. And when, in the sixteenth century, the law merchant was taken over and administered in the courts of common law, it was applied on the theory that it was part of the common law, and not a law foreign to the court." Graveson, supra, at 33–34. See also F. Juenger, supra n. 2 at 23–24 (discussing the practice of maritime courts).

In contrast, Scottish case law shows much earlier concern with foreign law and more frequent reliance on classic Continental sources, beginning in the 17th century, mainly as a result of the Dutch education of many Scottish lawyers. A. Anton, Private International Law 10–11 (1967).

4. Robinson v. Bland, [1760] 2 Burr. 1077, 97 Eng.Rep. 717; Holman v. Johnson, (1775) 1 Comp. 341.

5. See infra § 2.7.

6. From the extensive literature see especially: De Nova, Historical and Comparative Introduction to Conflict of Laws, 118 Recueil des Cours 443 (1966–II); M. Gutzwiller, Le développement historique du droit international privé, 29 Recueil des Cours 289 (1929–IV); M. Gutzwiller, Geschichte des Internationalprivatrechts Von den Anfängen bis zu den grossen Privatrechtskodifikationen (1977); F. Juenger, Choice of Law and Multistate Justice 6–27, 31–46 (1993); A. Lainé, Introduction au droit international privé (2 vols. 1888, 1892, reprinted Verlag Detlev Auvermann KG, Germany, 1970); Lewald, Conflit de lois dans le monde grec et romain, 13 Archeion Idiotikou Dikaiou 30 (1946), reprinted in 57 Revue critique de droit international privé 419 (Pt. 1), 615 (Pt. 2) (1968); Lipstein, The General Principles of Private International Law, 135 Recueil des Cours 96 (1972–I) [revised and reprinted as: Principles of the Conflict of Laws, National and International (1981); subsequent citation are to the original version]; Nadelmann, Some Historical Notes on the Doctrinal Sources of American Conflicts Law, in: Ius et Lex, Festgabe für Gutzwiller 263 (1959); Yntema, The Historic Bases of Private International Law, 2 Am. J. Comp. L. 296 (1953). See also Juenger, American and European Conflicts Law, 30 Am. J. Comp. L. 117 (1982).

7. See Ehrenzweig, A Counter–Revolution in Conflicts Law? From Beale to Cavers, 80 Harv. L. Rev. 377, 379 ff (1966).

8. See Kegel, The Crisis in the Conflict of Laws, 112 Recueil des Cours 95 (1964–II).

eign conflicts theory may have contributed to the "crisis" and "revolution" in American conflicts law. This isolation has at times led to the rediscovery of the wheel.[9] Europeans for their part also did not fully understand modern American developments, and their initial criticism was severe, often scathing, albeit justified in many instances.[10] More recently, European commentators have inquired whether American approaches hold any lessons for Europe,[11] and the several European conflicts codifications of the last twenty years[12] display some of the flexibility first introduced by the American conflicts "revolution."[13] Some American decisions in turn have limited earlier open-ended approaches by adopting a modified, flexible-rule approach.[14]

The following presents a brief and necessarily general introduction to the development of conflicts theory. The intent is to help in the

9. See Nadelmann, *Internationales Privatrecht*: A Sourcebook on Conflicts Theory Analyzed and Reviewed, 17 Harv. Int'l L. J. 657, 669 and 672 (1976) (concerning the *but social* (the social purpose of laws) and "governmental interests" respectively). See also infra § 2.3, at nn.9–10; § 2.6, n.9; § 2.9, nn.2–7; von Mehren, The Contribution of Comparative Law to Theory and Practice of Private International Law, 26 Am. J. Comp. L. (Supp.) 31 (1978).

10. See A. Anton, Private International Law 39 (1967); Heldrich, Internationale Zuständigkeit und anwendbares Recht 129 (1969); Kegel, Crisis, supra n.8; Kegel in F. Juenger, Zum Wandel des Internationalen Privatrechts (113 Schriften der Juristischen Studiengesellschaft, 1974) at 35–44; Vitta, Il principio dell'uguaglianza tra "lex fori" e diritto straniero, 18 Riv. trim. pro. 93 (1964). American criticism is noted subsequently. But see Kahn–Freund, General Problems of Private International Law, 143 Recueil des Cours 139, 245 (1974–III), who regards some of the American developments as *uniquely* American because of the interstate setting from which they arose, thus implying that their importance for *general* conflicts theory is limited and the worldwide criticism overstated. Nevertheless, to the extent that interstate approaches and solutions are applied without differentiation to international cases, American doctrines do have greater than local importance (whatever the reasons for their original emergence) and call for evaluation and critique.

11. See Jayme, The American Conflicts Revolution and its Impact on European Private International Law, in Forty Years On: The Evolution of Postwar Private International Law in Europe, Centrum voor Buitenlands Recht en Internationaal Privaatrecht Universiteit van Amsterdam, 15 (1992); Kropholler, & von Hein, From Approach to Rule–Orientation in American Tort Conflicts in Law and Justice in a Multistate World: Essays in Honor of Arthur T. von Mehren, 317 (Nafziger, & Symeonides, eds. 2002); Siehr, Ehrenzweigs lex-fori-Theorie und ihre Bedeutung für das amerikanische und deutsche Kollisionsrecht, 34 RabelsZ 585 (1970); Siehr, Domestic Relations in Europe: European Equivalents to American Evolutions, 30 Am. J. Comp. L. 37 (1982); Siehr, Da Livermore a Rabel, Tradizione Americana del diritto internazionale privato, 24 Riv. dir. int. priv. e proc. 17 (1988); Vischer, New Tendencies in European Conflict of Laws and the Influence of the US-Doctrine: A Short Survey, in Law and Justice in a Multistate World: Essays in Honor of Arthur T. von Mehren, 459 (J. Nafziger & S. Symeonides, eds. 2002); Vitta, The Impact in Europe of the American "Conflicts Revolution," 30 Am. J. Comp. L. 1 (1982): Zweigert, Some Reflections on the Sociological Dimensions of Private International Law or: What Is Justice in the Conflict of Laws?, 44 U. Colo. L. Rev. 283, 292 ff. (1973), reprinted, in German, in 37 RabelsZ 435, 445 ff. (1973). See also infra § 2.27, n.1.

12. See infra § 2.27.

13. See von Overbeck, Cours général de droit international privé, 176 Recueil des Cours 28 (1982–III) (European courts have sometimes looked to the Restatement, Second, of Conflict of Laws (1971)); E. Vassilakakis, E., Orientations méthologiques dans les codifications récentes du droit international privé en Europe (1987); Vischer, General Course on Private International Law, 232 Recueil des Cours 9 (1992); Vischer, Drafting National Legislation on Conflict of Laws: The Swiss Experience, 41 Law & Contemp. Prob. 131 (1977).

14. See, e.g., Schultz v. Boy Scouts of America, Inc., 65 N.Y.2d 189, 491 N.Y.S.2d

understanding of the current state of American theory and to assess possible future directions.

II. A BRIEF HISTORY OF EUROPEAN PRIVATE INTERNATIONAL LAW

A. FROM ANCIENT GREECE TO MEDIEVAL ITALY

§ 2.2   According to most western authors, the history of private international law begins in Northern Italy in the 12th century. Yet conflicts problems existed, and solutions to them had been devised, in much earlier times. Although the historical record is incomplete, some evidence of such solutions has survived. For example, in 393 B.C., in addressing a court in the Greek island-state of Aegina, the Athenian orator Isocrates (436–358 B.C.) argued that the testament of Thrasylochus should be declared valid because it conformed to both the law of the "testator's fatherland" and the law of the forum.[1] A compact between two Greek city-states signed *circa* 100 B.C. provided that claims arising from torts were to be adjudicated by the courts of the state in which the tortfeasor was domiciled and would be governed by the law of the forum.[2] Similarly, a decree issued in Hellenistic Egypt circa 120 B.C. provided that contracts written in Greek were subject to the jurisdiction of the Greek courts which applied Greek law, whereas contracts written in the Egyptian language were subject to the jurisdiction of the Egyptian courts which applied Egyptian law.[3]

Interestingly, in the last two cases, the question of the applicable law was linked to the question of jurisdiction, and both questions were answered in advance by means of a pre-established rule. In contrast, at the time of the Roman empire, the two questions were detached. Jurisdiction to decide cases with foreign elements, such as disputes involving non-Roman citizens, was vested exclusively in one official, the *praetor peregrinus*, but the question of which law would govern these disputes was not answered in advance. In resolving these disputes, the praetor came up with the idea of crafting an ad hoc substantive rule drawn from the laws of the involved states rather than applying the law of one of those states. Thus, for the first time, multistate disputes were resolved not through a *choice of law*, but rather through the creation and application of a special body of substantive law applicable only to those disputes.

90, 480 N.E.2d 679 (1985) (discussed infra § 17.32).

§ 2.2

1. See Isocrates, *Aegineticus* 19.16. For an analysis of *Aegineticus*, see I. Maridakis, Idiotikon Diethnes Dikaion, 119 *et seq.* (1967). For earlier evidence of the existence of choice-of-law rules dating back to the Sixth century B.C., see Papastathis, Problems of Choice of Law in Sixth Century Greece: Contribution to the Study of the Pre-history of European Private International Law, Revue Hellénique de droit européen 531 (1982).

2. See D. Evrigenis, Idiotikon Diethnes Dikaion, 50–51 (1968); A. Grammatikaki–Alexiou, Z. Papassiopi–Passia, & E. Vassilakakis, Idiotikon Diethnes Dikaion, 6–7(1997).

3. See F. Juenger, Choice of Law and Multistate Justice 7–8 (1993).

The law thus created through this "substantive-law method,"[4] later called the *jus gentium*, was gradually incorporated into the *jus civile* (the law governing relations between Roman citizens), and both laws were eventually "codified" by the emperor Justinian in his Digest in 533 A.D. Because by that time the Roman empire encompassed much of the trading world and because most of the empire's inhabitants had been accorded Roman citizenship, conflicts between Roman and non-Roman laws became far less frequent. Perhaps for that reason, the Digest did not contain any provisions on the subject.

However, by the 12th century, when the Digest was "re-discovered" and expounded upon by the Italian Glossators (1100–1250), the social and economic landscape had changed dramatically. Although all of Italy was by now under the authority of the Digest and the new *jus commune* that was based on it, the city-states of Northern Italy had begun to develop their own local customs and laws (*statuta*), while swearing allegiance to the revived Roman law which remained the over-arching general law. These cities engaged in extensive trade among themselves and with other states. Conflicts of law, therefore, began to emerge again. For example, "[i]f a merchant from Bologna was sued in Modena, should he be judged by the statutes of the former or the latter city?" asked the famous Glossator Accursius. The need to address such questions became increasingly pressing.

B. BARTOLUS AND THE ITALIAN STATUTISTS[1]

§ 2.3 For more than a century, several Glossators and their successors, the post-glossators or Commentators, wrestled with conflicts questions,[2] but one Commentator, Bartolus of Sassoferrato (1313–1357), thought that he had definitive answers. As a loyal and careful Romanist, however, Bartolus recognized that for these answers to have any authority they had to be grounded on Justinian's law. Although Justinian had said virtually nothing on the subject, Bartolus found a way to make it appear that these answers were implicit in Justinian's Code, in fact in

---

4. For the status of this method in contemporary American and foreign conflicts law, see S. Symeonides, Private International Law at the End of the 20th Century: Progress or Regress? 9–12, 18–20 (1999).

§ 2.3

1. On the statutists see especially Meijers, Histoire des principes fondamentaux du droit international privé, 49 Recueil des Cours 543, 549 (1934–III); A. Anton, Private International Law 10–11 (1967); F. Juenger, Choice of Law and Multistate Justice 10–19 (1993); De Nova, Historical and Comparative Introduction to Conflict of Laws, 118 Recueil des Cours 443 (1966–II); Lipstein, The General Principles of Private International Law, 135 Recueil des Cours 96 (1972–I); For comprehensive overviews see Kegel, Fundamental Approaches, in: In-

ternational Encyclopedia of Comparative Law, vol. 3: Private International Law, at 3–4 et seq. (1986); Keller & Siehr, Allgemeine Lehren des internationalen Privatrechts 1–126 (1986); Hatzimihail, Pre-Classical Conflict of Laws: An Essay on the Writing of the History of Private International Law (2002).

2. One Glossator, Magister Aldricus (1170–1200), argued that conflicts problems should be resolved through the application of that law which is *potior et utilior* (better and more useful). See 1 A. Lainé, Introduction au droit international privé, 146, 264 (1888). Eight centuries later, a better-law approach was proposed in the United States. See infra § 2.13.

the very first sentence of it. This sentence provided: *"Cunctos populos, quos clementiae nostrae regit temperamentum, in tali volumus religione versari, quam divinum Petrum apostolum traditisse Romanis[.]"*[3] Literally translated, this sentence states: "All peoples who are subject to our merciful sway, we desire them to live under that religion which the divine apostle Peter has delivered to the Romans."

Obviously, this sentence had nothing to do with secular law, much less conflicts law. It simply expresses the emperor's desire for all peoples under his power to adhere to the Christian religion. But the emperor speaks only of people *under his power*, his "merciful sway," i.e., his jurisdiction, as we would say today. Bartolus read this sentence as a recognition by the emperor/law-giver of a limitation to his own power, and thus as an implicit delineation of the scope of Roman law *vis à vis* foreign law. If Roman law applies only to those under the emperor's sway, then those who are not subject to his authority must be governed by the law of the authority to which they are subject.[4] From this elementary proposition, Bartolus and the Italian post-glossators began to construct principles for delineating the reach of Roman and non-Roman laws and for resolving conflicts between them, as well as conflicts among the laws of the Italian city-states.[5]

The post-glossators are also known as *statutists* because their method of resolving conflicts was based on a classification of local laws (*statuta*) into two categories: "real" and "personal." Real statutes were those that operated only within the territory of the enacting state and not beyond. In contrast, personal statutes operated beyond the territory of the enacting state and bound all persons that owed allegiance to it.[6] The statutists thought that this classification could resolve all potential conflicts because all statutes, both domestic and foreign, belonged to either the one or the other category, leaving neither gaps nor doubts.

Obviously, this was too optimistic, but worse yet was the fact that the criteria the early statutists employed for classifying a statute as real or personal were simplistic and mechanical in that they were based

3. Codex 1.1.1.

4. See Bartolus, *Commentarii in Lex Cunctos Populos*, translated by C. Smith, in 14 Am. J, Leg. Hist. 154, 174–83, 247–75 (1970); For a recent insightful analysis of Bartolus' work, see Hatzimihail, supra n. 1.

5. These "intra-Roman" conflicts presented a more difficult problem for Bartolus. First, he had to answer the question of whether the Digest even permitted the city-states to adopt laws that were at variance with the general law of the Digest. He answered the question affirmatively by stretching the meaning of a provision of the Digest, D.1.3.32, that recognized the authority of local *customs* and, as Bartolus postulated, local *statutes*. He then proposed that conflicts between these statutes be resolved by the same principles of conflicts resolution that he enunciated in discussing

the *Cunctos populos* clause. See Bartolus, *Commentarii in Lex de Quibus*, translated by Smith, supra n.4, at 163–74. By so doing, Bartolus tacitly subscribed to the notion that, by and large, the same principles under which one resolves "international conflicts" can also resolve inter-city or interstate conflicts. Many centuries later, a similar hypothesis came to be accepted in the United States. See infra § 2.13.

6. The French statutists later added a third category of statutes, called "mixed." See infra § 2.4. However, contrary to what this term might connote, it did not really describe a new category of statutes. Rather it encompassed all those personal statutes that, on closer examination, were thought to operate territorially.

solely on the statute's wording. For example, if the statute's first words referred to a person, for instance, by providing that "the first-born son shall succeed to the property," then the statute was personal. If the first words referred to a thing, for instance, by providing that "the property shall pass to the first-born son," then the statute was real. It is therefore not surprising that the early statutists were ridiculed by subsequent authors. This criticism was justified to the extent it referred to the mechanical way in which the statutists classified the various statutes. However, despite this obvious deficiency, the statutists influenced the future direction of private international law for many centuries. In particular, the following features of the statutist methodology may be relevant to contemporary American conflicts law:

a.   The Italian statutists re-introduced the "conflictual method," a method by which multistate disputes are resolved by choosing the law of one of the involved states, rather than by blending those laws and crafting a new substantive rule as the *praetor peregrinus* had done.[7] The conflictual method has remained the dominant method ever since;

b.   The statutists introduced the "unilateral" conflictual method, as distinguished from the "bilateral" or "multilateral" method that was developed later in history. The bilateral method postulates a system of *a priori* choice-of-law rules that designate the cases that fall within the scope of domestic and foreign law, respectively.[8] In contrast, the unilateral method approaches the matter from the other end. It focuses on the conflicting domestic and foreign laws themselves and tries to determine whether the case at hand falls within the intended scope of the one or the other law. The unilateral method has survived the subsequent onslaught of the bilateral method and has enjoyed a certain resurgence both in Europe[9] and in the United States, where it formed the basis of one of the most influential approaches, Brainerd Currie's interest analysis;[10]

c.   In trying to ascertain the intended scope of conflicting laws, the statutists committed the serious error of relying unduly on the wording of the statutes. Since the statutists were little more than grammarians, this error was understandable. However, this was simply a deficiency of interpretative *technique* that could be easily cured through the use of a more enlightened interpretative method that relies on teleology rather than on grammar. Eventually this happened when another Commentator, Guy de Coquille, proposed that the classification of statutes into real or personal should not depend on the wording of the statute, but rather on the presumed and apparent *purpose* of those who enacted it.[11] The

---

7.   See supra § 2.2.

8.   See infra § 2.6. For the status of this method in contemporary American and European private international law, see S. Symeonides, Private International Law at the End of the 20th Century: Progress of Regress? 9–18, 20–21 (1999).

9.   See S. Symeonides, supra n.8 at 13–18.

10.   See infra § 2.9; Symeonides, American Choice of Law at the Dawn of the 21st Century, 37 Willamette L. Rev. 1, 19–39 (2001).

11.   See 1 A. Lainé, Introduction au droit international privé, 303 (1888); F.

similarity of this notion with 20th century approaches that rely on the *policy* of a statute is obvious;

d. The statutist classification of statutes was the first comprehensive, and predictably unsuccessful, attempt to delineate the legislative competence of states. Bartolus, of course, pretended that his delineation was implicit in the supranational law of Justinian's Digest. Yet, by basing his delineation on the wording of state statutes, Bartolus subconsciously subscribed to the opposite and somewhat circular notion: that a state's legislative competence is not fixed from above through a superarching law but rather depends, largely though not exclusively, on the words through which that state has unilaterally chosen to express its assertion of legislative competence. This idea led not only to the realization that private international law is essentially national law, but also to the notion that the "wish" of a state to apply its law, as that wish is expressed in the words or content of its statutes, is an acceptable criterion for resolving conflicts. Again, the similarity of this line of thinking with contemporary American approaches, especially interest analysis, is obvious.

C. THE FRENCH STATUTISTS

§ 2.4 By the 16th century, the intellectual leadership of the statutist school had shifted to France. The French statutists distinguished mainly between "substance" and "procedure" and focused on a sovereign's power to create rights and obligations, i.e. legislative jurisdiction,[1] which was thought not to exist locally in the case of a foreign citizen. The French judge and scholar D'Argentré (1519–1590)[2] added a third category of statutes, that of "mixed statutes," to the Italian classification of statutes into real and personal. "Mixed" questions arose, and required rules, when relationships had contacts with different communities, for instance when a contract was concluded by citizens of different city-states. In the application of "conflicting" mixed statutes, preference was given to the one with the "real" element.

The notion of a "personal law," which follows an individual wherever he goes, still has profound influence in European conflict of laws,[3] for

---

Juenger, Choice of Law and Multistate Justice 19 (1993).

§ 2.4

1. The French statutists thought that legislative jurisdiction depended on such connecting factors as the place of contracting or of the commission of the tort.

2. Another notable French statutist, Dumoulin (1500–1566), is credited with resurrecting the idea of party autonomy, namely the notion that a contract should be governed by the law that the parties have chosen. Dumoulin also extended this notion to cases in which the parties did not make

an express choice. See F. Juenger, Choice of Law and Multistate Justice 17 (1993); Lipstein, The General Principles of Private International Law, 135 Recueil des Cours 96, n.6 at 119 (1972–I). In the United States the principle of party autonomy did not gain explicit acceptance until the adoption of § 187 of the Restatement, Second (1971) and of § 1–105(1) of the U.C.C. See infra §§ 18.8–18.12.

3. Writing about the 19th century Italian school led by Mancini, Professor De Nova states: "[N]otwithstanding the disdainful criticism levelled by the new school at the statutists, it ended up by resurrecting their broad classifications. The main

instance in the form of a rule that nationality may be the *"connecting factor"* for determining the applicable law in matters of status, capacity, and the like.[4] Statutist theory thus categorized legal rules, recognized a division of legislative jurisdiction among territorial governmental units, and accepted implicitly the premise that one unit has the power to legislate with extraterritorial effect subject only to another's ability to block that effect through adoption of an (overriding) real statute. The system envisioned was "international" and "universalistic."[5] This universalism, however, was undermined by D'Argentré's emphasis on the predominance of real statutes, which favored territorialism, with the extraterritorial application of laws the exception.[6] However, the major shortcoming of statutist theory was its failure to explain *why* a territorial unit should accept another's extraterritorial legislation, that is, why one should import the other's law.

This question acquired political dimensions because, in the meantime, Europe had witnessed the emergence of modern nation-states, and the "best-seller" of the time, Jean Bodin's *Six livres de la république* (1576), emphasized the independence of these states and their unrestricted power to make law, i.e., the modern notion of state sovereignty. How could this notion be reconciled with the notion of applying foreign law?

D. THE DUTCH CONTRIBUTION: COMITY

§ 2.5 The Dutch School, identified with the names of Johann Voet (1647–1714) and Ulrich Huber (1635–1694), undertook to answer the above question. The answer given can be synopsized in one henceforth famous word: *comity*. Comity was defined as something between mere courtesy and a legal duty, as derived from the tacit consent of nations and based on mutual forbearance and enlightened self-interest. In a ten-page essay that is reputed to be the most widely read document on our subject and which was the first writing to use the term "conflict of laws," Huber[1] postulated the following axioms:

difference ... was the shift from the 'real' to the 'personal' law, and the substitution of nationality for domicile as the criterion for choosing the latter law." De Nova, Historical and Comparative Introduction to Conflict of Laws, 118 Recueil des Cours 443, at 464–65 (1966–II). For the Mancini Report to the Institut de Droit International in 1874, which was to have such profound effects in establishing the nationality rule, see 1 J. Droit Int. Privé 220–239, 285–304 (1874) and the discussion by Nadelmann, Mancini's Nationality Rule and Non–Unified Legal Systems, 17 Am. J. Comp. L. 418 (1969).

4. See, e.g., Art. 14 of the German EGBGB (1986) retaining nationality as the first connecting factor, in priority order, for the determination of the incidents of marriage. See also infra Chapter 15. For the

reasons underlying the German adoption of the nationality principle see Braga, Staatsangehörigkeit oder Wohnsitzprinzip (1954). For an assessment of the apparent trend away from nationality and toward adoption of domicile or habitual residence as the basis for the "personal law" in Europe, see Bucher, Staatsangehörigkeits-und Wohnsitzprinzip, 28 Schweizerisches Jahrbuch für internationales Recht 76 (1972). For discussion of domicile in American law see infra ch. 4.

5. Lipstein, supra n.2, at 119 (detailing problems with statutist theory).

6. Lipstein, supra n.2, at 121.

§ 2.5

1. Huber's essay is entitled *De conflictu legum diversarum in diversis imperiis* and

(1) The laws of each state have force within its territory but not beyond;

(2) These laws bind all those who are found within the territory, whether permanently or temporarily; and

(3) Out of comity, foreign laws may be applied so that rights acquired under them can retain their force, provided that they do not prejudice the state's powers or rights.

The first two axioms abandon the classification of statutes into real and personal and elevate territorialism into the main operating principle of private international law, a position that remained unchallenged for many generations. The third axiom attempts to explain *why* the forum state will apply the law of another sovereign but not *when*. Neither the vague notion of comity nor the less vague but equally problematic notion of "acquired rights" provides concrete guidance as to the circumstances in which the forum will or will not apply the law of another state. In any event, the comity doctrine formed the cornerstone of Story's celebrated work which, in turn, influenced English and Scottish courts and writers.[2] Story's work influenced European writers—among them Savigny[3]—but his views on comity found little receptivity on the Continent.[4] We return to Story's work below.

E. THE GERMAN CONTRIBUTION: WÄCHTER AND SAVIGNY

§ 2.6 During the 19th century, two German authors published their views which, although diametrically opposed, changed the course and direction of European private international law. The first author was Carl Georg von Wächter, who, it is said, "debunked statutist learning, exposed the vested rights theory's circular reasoning and disparaged the comity doctrine."[1] In a lengthy essay he criticized the uncertainty inherent in the classification of *statuta* and, more importantly, denied that a state's legislative jurisdiction within its own territory could raise an obligation in another state to recognize such legislation

is contained in his work entitled *Praelectiones Juris Romani et Hodierni* (1689). For translations of the essay, see Davies, 18 B.Yb.Int'l L. 49 (1937); E. G. Lorenzen, Huber's De Conflictu Legum, Selected Articles on the Conflict of Laws 136 (1947). For an authoritative historical analysis of the doctrine, see Yntema, The Comity Doctrine, in: 2 Vom Deutschen zum Europäischen Recht, Festschrift für Dölle 65 (1963), reprinted in 65 Mich. L. Rev. 1 (1966) with an introduction by Nadelmann.

2. See A. Anton, Private International Law 13 (1967). A 1760 decision by Lord Mansfield rested on Huber's views. Robinson v. Bland, 2 Burr. 1077, 97 Eng. Rep. 717. See also Anton, The Introduction in the English Practice of Continental Theories on the Conflict of Laws, 5 Int'l & Comp. L.Q. 435 (1956); Davies, The Influence of Huber's *De Conflictu Legum* on English Private International Law, 18 B. Yb. Int'l L. 49 (1937).

3. See Kegel, Story and Savigny, 37 Am. J. Comp. L. 37, 48–49 (1989).

4. Id. at 65–66.

§ 2.6

1. F. Juenger, Choice of Law and Multistate Justice 32 (1993). See also De Nova, Historical and Comparative Introduction to Conflict of Laws, 118 Recueil des Cours 443, 452 (1966–II).

extraterritorially.[2] Describing the judge as an instrument of state legislative will, Wächter argued that, in resolving conflicts disputes, the judge should keep in mind the policies and interests of the forum state rather than notions of comity and other multistate considerations. In Wächter's view, the judge should begin with the substantive law of the forum, and only if that law is found inapplicable should the judge consider the applicability of a foreign law.[3] This emphasis on the law of the forum led some commentators to call Wächter the "outstanding advocate of the lex fori"[4] and others to see him as stepping "backwards towards the early practice of the postglossators" and as falling "back on the learning of the statutists."[5]

These judgments may be too harsh. As Nadelmann[6] has shown, Wächter *proceeded* from the lex fori, perhaps even starting with the "assumption ... that the *lex fori* was the *lex generalis*,"[7] without, however, excluding the potential applicability and relevance of foreign law. Nevertheless, as a matter of practical application—but not theoretical conception—his system was ethnocentric, displaying a "state-orientation ... or localism."[8] Wächter's contribution lies in abandoning the statutist *classification of laws* and in focusing, instead, on *legal relationships* for which an applicable law had to be determined. For him, the starting point for such a determination was the *lex fori*. Although Wächter's approach had no followers in Europe, it bears remarkable resemblance to some approaches developed in the second half of the 20th century in the United States, especially Ehrenzweig's *lex fori* approach and Currie's interest analysis.[9]

The second German author of this period was the great Romanist Friedrich Carl von Savigny (1779–1861). His contribution to private international law was both constructive and decisive.[10] Like Wächter,

2. von Wächter, Über die Collision der Privatgesetze verschiedener Staaten, 24 Archiv für die civilistische Praxis 230 (1841), 25 id. 1 and 200 (1841), and 25 id. 361 (1842). For discussion and translated excerpts see Nadelmann, 13 Am. J. Comp. L. 414 (1964).

3. For modern analyses of spatially or otherwise self-limited forum rules see De Nova, An Australian Case on the Application of Spatially Conditioned Internal Rules, 22 Rev. Hell. 25 (1969); Kelly, Localising Rules in the Conflict of Laws (1974); Sedler, Functionally–Restrictive Substantive Rules in American Conflicts Law, 50 S. Cal. L. Rev. 27 (1976); Kegel, Die selbstgerechte Sachnorm in: Gedächtnisschrift für Albert A. Ehrenzweig 51 (E. Jayme & G. Kegel, eds., 1976); Hay, Comments on "Self–Limited Rule of Law" in American Conflicts Methodology, 30 Am. J. Comp. L. Supp. 129 (1982).

4. A. Ehrenzweig, Conflict of Laws 322 (rev. ed. 1962).

5. Lipstein, The General Principles of Private International Law, 135 Recueil des Cours 96, 133 (1972–I).

6. See supra n.2.

7. De Nova, Historical and Comparative Introduction to Conflict of Laws, 118 Recueil des Cours 443, at 456 (1966–II).

8. Id. at 455.

9. See infra § 2.10 and § 2.9, respectively.

10. Savigny's contribution to conflicts law is contained in the 8th volume of his treatise on Roman law entitled *System des heutigen Römischen Rechts* (1849). This volume was translated into English by William Guthrie, under the title Private International Law, A Treatise on the Conflict of Laws and the Limits of their Operation in Respect of Place and Time (1st ed. 1869, 2d ed. 1880). See also Zweigert, Some Reflections on the Sociological Dimensions of Private International Law or: What Is Justice in the Conflict of Laws?, 44 U. Colo. L. Rev. 283, 284 (1973).

Savigny rejected the statutist doctrine, but unlike Wächter, he rejected both the unilateral approach and the primacy of the *lex fori*. Instead Savigny adopted and perfected the bilateral choice-of-law approach, which up to that time was badly losing the competition with the unilateral approach. Rather than focusing on the conflicting laws and trying to ascertain their intended spatial reach, Savigny began his analysis from the opposite end. He focused on disputes or *"legal relationships,"* and then sought to identify the state in which each relationship has its *"seat,"* or in whose legislative jurisdiction it *"belongs"*:

> It is [the] diversity of positive laws that makes it necessary to mark off for each ... the area of its authority, to fix the limits of different positive laws in respect to one another.... When a legal relation presents itself for adjudication, we seek a rule of law to which it is subject, and in accordance with which it is to be decided.... [11] [The task is to determine] that legal system to which the legal relation belongs according to its particular nature (where it has its seat).[12]

Savigny divided the field into broad categories corresponding to the major divisions of private law (family law, successions, property, contracts, torts, etc.) and then, through "connecting factors," such as domicile, situs, or the place of the transaction or event, identified those inherent characteristics of each legal relationship that place its seat in one state rather another. The result of this classificatory approach was a network of neutral, evenhanded, bilateral choice-of-law rules. These rules placed foreign law on parity with forum law and assigned each legal relationship to one particular state regardless of whether that state had expressed, through statute or otherwise, a wish to apply its law and regardless of the content of that law. Savigny argued forcefully that the objective of these rules should be to ensure "international uniformity of decisions" (*internationaler Entscheidungseinklang*) regardless of forum. Indeed, in Savigny's cosmopolitan and universalist milieu, there was no room for forum protectionism; private international law should not be concerned with promoting the forum's interests as such, but should instead aspire to ensure that each multistate dispute is resolved in the same way regardless of where it is litigated.

Despite the obvious difficulties in assigning a seat for a great number of legal relationships[13] (and the distinct possibility that various legal systems may choose a different assignment),[14] the vistas first

11. Guthrie translation, supra n.10, 1st ed., at 6.

12. Savigny, supra n.10, at 108 (authors' translation).

13. As a matter of fact, however, legal relationships are not infinite but can be reduced to a more limited number of typical situations (tort, contract, status, succession, etc.) for which a "seat" may be identified with the aid of predetermined and unchanging connecting factors (e.g., the decedent's nationality or domicile in succession cases,

lex loci commissi in tort, etc.). See Neuhaus, Savigny und die Rechtsprechung aus der Natur der Sache, 15 RabelsZ 364, 371 (1949). See also infra ch. 18.

14. For example, in succession cases, some systems use the decedent's domicile, while others use the decedent's nationality. One side effect is that conflicts research becomes comparative-law research. See Zweigert, Die dritte Schule im internationalen Privatrecht, Festschrift für Leo Raape 35 (1948); Zweigert, Rechtsvergleichung als

opened by Wächter and then more comprehensively by Savigny charted the future shape of Continental conflicts theory and practice. The focus became the *particular relationship* which, with the help of connecting factors (nationality, domicile, and others), was then localized. The quest for consensus on a universally accepted seat may have failed, but the technique of localizing a legal relationship for the choice of the applicable law has remained. This localization selects the applicable legal *system*. It is "jurisdiction selective,"[15] not "rule selective" (let alone "result selective"), as are most modern American approaches. Recent European doctrine and codifications have adopted some of the flexible techniques of current American theory.[16] This trend will be considered in another section.[17]

III. THE AMERICAN DEVELOPMENT PRIOR TO THE CONFLICTS REVOLUTION

A. FROM "COMITY" (STORY) TO "VESTED RIGHTS" (BEALE)

§ 2.7 As Professor Nadelmann has shown,[1] Huber's ideas on comity were quoted in American cases from at least 1788,[2] and references to Huber and the early English decision in Robinson v. Bland[3] are contained in "all conflicts decisions of the period."[4] A 1797 U.S. Supreme Court case contained a translation of Huber's maxims in a note to the decision,[5] but the most important factor in the spread and acceptance of the comity doctrine was its exposition in Joseph Story's *Commentaries on the Conflict of Laws, Foreign and Domestic* (1834), the first comprehensive conflicts treatise in English.[6] In supporting Huber's comity

---

universale Interpretationsmethode, 15 RabelsZ, 16 (1949).

The *seat* theory led Savigny to a more inclusive system of rules than was the case even in traditional Anglo–American law. With respect to the question whether "property," for purposes of succession, should be a unitary concept (and the applicable law that of the situs) or should be governed by the law of domicile in the case of personal property and by situs law only in the case it was immovable property, Savigny and Story split. Savigny considered the Anglo–American scission as "having remained on a lower level of development." Kegel, Wohnsitz und Belegenheit bei Story and Savigny, 52 RabelsZ 431, 463 (1988) quoting from Savigny, supra n.10, at 298 (authors' transl.). The idea of "universal succession" has been adopted by the Hague Convention of Decedents' Estates (pending). For Story see infra § 2.7.

15. See Kegel in F. Juenger, Zum Wandel des Internationalen Privatrechts 35–44 (113 Schriften der Juristischen Studiengesellschaft 1974).

16. See Joerges, Zum Funktionswandel des Kollisionsrechts (1971), and infra § 2.27.

17. See infra § 2.27.

§ 2.7

1. Nadelmann, Introduction to Yntema, The Comity Doctrine, 65 Mich. L. Rev. 1, 2 (1966).

2. Camp v. Lockwood, 1 U.S. (1 Dall.) 393, 398, 1 L.Ed. 192 (Phila. County, Pa. C.P. 1788).

3. 2. Burr. 1077, 97 Eng.Rep. See also supra § 2.5, n.2.

4. Nadelmann, supra n.1, 2

5. Emory v. Grenough, 3 U.S. (3 Dall.) 369 n. (a), 1 L.Ed. 640 (1797).

6. Story's work was the first comprehensive treatment of the subject in English. However, James Kent, to whom Story dedicated his Commentaries, had addressed many conflicts questions in his general Commentaries on American Law (4 vols.

doctrine,[7] Story wrote this explanation of why one state applies the law of another:

> The true foundation on which the administration of international law must rest is that the rules which are to govern are those which arise from mutual interest and utility, from a sense of the inconveniences which would result from a contrary doctrine, and from a spirit of moral necessity to do justice, in order that justice may be done to us in return.[8]

The influence of Story's work was profound,[9] not only in the United States but also abroad, where it served to reinforce earlier reliance on Huber (in England),[10] revived interest in the doctrine's country of origin (Holland),[11] and influenced both Savigny[12] and French doctrine.[13]

1826–1830). To give only one illustration, Kent had stated that "a contract valid by the law of the place where it is made is valid everywhere *jure gentium*.... If it were otherwise, the citizens of one nation could not contract or carry on commerce in the territories of another. The necessities of commerce require, that acts valid where made, should be recognized in other countries, provided they be not contrary to the independence of nations [do not violate the public policy of the forum] ..." 2 Kent, Commentaries on American Law 364 (1st ed. 1827). Story repeated the rule, citing inter alia to the second edition of Kent's Commentaries. See J. Story, Commentaries on the Conflict of Laws, at 201 (1st ed. 1834). However, by this time, the formulation of the public policy exception had been redefined: "Contracts, therefore, which are in evasion or fraud of the laws of a country, or the rights and duties of its subjects, contracts against good morals, or religion, or public rights, and contracts opposed to the national policy or institutions, are deemed nullities in every country ... although they may be valid by the laws of the place, where they are made." Id. at 204, also citing to Forbes v. Cochrane, 2 B. and Cres. R. 448, 471, 117 Eng. Rep. 450, 459 (K.B. 1824).

The first American book devoted exclusively to conflicts law was S. Livermore, Dissertations on the Questions which Arise From the Contrariety of the Positive Laws of Different States and Nations (1828). For the content and influence of this book, see De Nova, The First American Book on Conflict of Laws, 8 Am. J. Leg. Hist. 136 (1964). This monograph was a concerted attempt to import to the United States the doctrine of the Continental statutists (see supra §§ 2.3–2.5), soon to be abandoned in Europe itself. Although this attempt was unsuccessful, Livermore had some indirect impact on the course of American conflicts law by making available to Joseph Story the otherwise inaccessible Continental conflicts literature. In addition to providing a thorough English summary of this literature in his own book, Livermore donated his entire library of continental writings to the Harvard Law School where then professor Story put them to good use in writing his seminal *Commentaries*.

7. See supra § 2.5.

8. J. Story, Commentaries on the Conflict of Laws, Foreign and Domestic § 35, at p. 34 (1834). See also id. § 38 at p. 37: "[T]he phrase 'comity of nations' ... is the most appropriate phrase to express the true foundation and extent of the obligation of the laws of one nation within the territories of another. It is derived altogether from the voluntary consent of the latter; and is inadmissible, when it is contrary to its known policy, or prejudicial to its interests."

9. For an evaluation of Story's work see Nadelmann, supra n.1; Nadelmann, Joseph Story's Contribution to American Conflicts Law: A Comment, 5 Am. J. Legal Hist. 230 (1961); Lorenzen, Story's Commentaries on the Conflict of Laws: One Hundred Years After, 48 Harv. L. Rev. (1934). See also Nadelmann, Bicentennial Observations on the Second Edition of Joseph Story's Commentaries on the Conflict of Laws, 28 Am. J. Comp. L. 61 (1980).

10. See Dicey, A Digest of the Law of England With Reference to the Conflict of Laws 16 ff *passim* (1st ed. 1896); Graveson, The Comparative Evolution of Principles of the Conflict of Laws in England and in the U.S.A., 99 Recueil des Cours 21, 30 (1960–I); Huber v. Steiner, [1835] 2 Bing. (N.C.) 202.

11. Nadelmann, supra n.1, 5.

12. Kahn–Freund, General Problems of Private International Law, 143 Recueil des

13. See p. 20.

"Comity" sought to reconcile the territoriality (sovereignty) of states with the need to consider foreign law in appropriate cases. The doctrine was generally accepted as an operational theory in the courts during the half century from 1850–1900, and, although references to it can still be found in judicial decisions in the United States,[14] the doctrine was the subject of considerable polemic criticism[15] from the outset. It also suffered from the conceptual difficulty that law was said to be at once territorial, yet entitled to some effect beyond the limits of the territorial sovereign from which it emanated. The critics sought to accommodate the concept of territoriality with the continued need to give recognition to foreign law in appropriate cases by proposing the doctrine of "vested rights," a doctrine that gained considerable influence during the period from 1900 to 1950.

In the United States, the main proponent of the vested-rights doctrine was Joseph H. Beale, the reporter of the American Law Institute's First Restatement of the Conflict of Laws (1934), but the doctrine had European precursors and proponents, especially in Dicey. In Dicey's formulation: "Any right which has been duly acquired under the law of any civilized country is recognized and, in general, enforced by English Courts, and no right which has not been duly acquired is enforced or, in general, recognized by English Courts."[16] Beale's formulation was simi-

Cours 139, at 285 (1974–III); Gutzwiller, Der Einfluss Savignys auf die Entwicklung des Internationalprivatrechts 110 ff. (19 Collectanea Friburgensia, Freiburg, Switzerland, 1923); Kegel, Wohnsitz und Belegenheit bei Story and Savigny, 52 RabelsZ 431, 463 (1988). Wächter, on the other hand, did not become aware of Story's work until his Essay had been finished. Nadelmann, 13 Am. J. Comp. L. 414, 415–16 (1964).

13. J. J. Foelix, Traité de droit international privé, I, n.229 (7th ed. 1981); Kegel in F. Juenger, Zum Wandel des Internationalen Privatrechts (113 Schriften der Juristischen Studiengesellschaft, 1974) at 35–44; Lambert & Xirau, L'Ancetre americain du droit comparé: La doctrine du Juge Story (1947).

14. See, e.g., Yoder v. Yoder, 31 Conn. Supp. 345, 330 A.2d 825, 826 (1974) (recognition of Mexican divorce on the basis of comity); In the Matter of Red Fox, 23 Or. App. 393, 542 P.2d 918 (1975) (divorce decree of Indian tribal court not entitled to recognition under "Full Faith and Credit" but on the basis of comity); Leon v. Numkena, 142 Ariz. 307, 689 P.2d 566 (App.1984). See also infra ch. 24.

15. See A. Anton, Private International Law at 23 (1967); W. Schaeffner, Entwicklung des internationalen Privatrechts § 30, at p. 38 with specific reference to Story (1841, reprinted 1970, Verlag Ferdinand

Keip, Germany): "Where is the beginning of the end of comity? How can *legal questions* be answered on the basis of political considerations which are the most changeable [notions] in the world?" (Authors' translation.)

In Société Nationale Industrielle Aerospatiale v. United States District Court for Southern District of Iowa, 482 U.S. 522, 107 S.Ct. 2542, 96 L.Ed.2d 461 (1987), the U.S. Supreme Court had to rule on the relationship between the Hague Convention on the Taking of Evidence Abroad and the Federal Rules of Civil Procedure applicable to pretrial discovery. In an opinion that drew extensively on an analysis of the comity principle, Justice Blackmun urged that there be a presumption in favor of the primary applicability of the Convention. 482 U.S. at 547, 554–568, 107 S.Ct. at 2557, 2561–68 (Blackmun, J. concurring in part and dissenting in part). The majority, in contrast, concluded that "international comity ... requires ... a more particularized analysis of the respective interests of the foreign nation and the requesting nation than petitioners' proposed general rule would generate." 482 U.S. at 543, 544, 107 S.Ct. at 2555. The decision is discussed infra § 12.9 n.9.

16. Dicey, A Digest of the Law of England With Reference to the Conflict of Laws at 22 (1st ed. 1896). Holland, in his Elements of Jurisprudence (1880), had previ-

lar: "A right having been created by the appropriate law, the recognition of its existence should follow everywhere. Thus an act valid where done cannot be called in question anywhere."[17]

Predictably, this formulation found its way into the (First) Restatement that Beale drafted under the auspices of the American Law Institute. For example, § 384 of the Restatement provides:

> "(1) If a cause of action in tort is created at the place of wrong, a cause of action will be recognized in other states.

> (2) If no cause of action is created at the place of wrong, no recovery in tort can be had in any other state."

In addition to exemplifying Beale's attachment to the vested rights doctrine, the above rule also reflects his adherence to the principle of territoriality.[18] Indeed, territoriality and vested rights were the twin theoretical pillars of most of the rules Beale drafted for the First Restatement. From a structural viewpoint, these rules were mechanical, rigid,[19] and jurisdiction-selecting, attributes that will be discussed

ously stated the theory citing Wächter, supra § 2.6 n.2, in support. The latter had, however, opposed the theory. See Nadelmann, Bicentennial Observations on the Second Edition of Joseph Story's Commentaries on the Conflict of Laws, 28 Am. J. Comp. L. 61, 75 n.60 (1980). In the 6th ed. of Dicey's work, "duly" acquired became acquired "according to the English rules of the conflict of laws," at 11, 12. See also Nadelmann, Some Historical Notes on the Doctrinal Sources of American Conflicts Law, in: Ius et Lex, Festgabe für Gutzwiller 263, 276 ff. (1959). For a view tracing the doctrine to the post-glossators see H. Müller, Der Grundsatz der Wohlerworbenen Rechte im Internationalen Privatrecht (1935). For a French statement of the doctrine, contemporary with Dicey and Beale, see Pillet, Principes de droit international privé 24, 496 (1903). See also Lassalle, Das System der erworbenen Rechte (2d ed. by Bucher 1880).

17. J. Beale, 3 Cases on the Conflict of Laws 517 (1901). The classic judicial formulation is by Justice Holmes:

> But when such a liability is enforced in a jurisdiction foreign to the place of the wrongful act, obviously that does not mean that the act in any degree is subject to the lex fori, with regard to either its quality or its consequences. On the other hand, it equally little means that the law of the place of the act is operative outside its own territory. The theory of the foreign suit is that, although the act complained of was subject to no law having force in the forum, it gave rise to an obligation, an *obligatio*, which like other obligations, follows the person, and may

be enforced wherever the person may be found.

> ... But as the only source of this obligation is the law of the place of the act, it follows that that law determines not merely the existence of the obligation (Smith v. Condry, 1 How. 28, 11 L.Ed. 35), but equally determines its extent.

Slater v. Mexican Nat'l Railroad Co., 194 U.S. 120, 126, 24 S.Ct. 581, 582, 48 L.Ed. 900 (1904).

18. See, e.g., 1 J. Beale, Conflict of Laws 45–46 (1935):

> Law operates by extending its power over acts done throughout the territory within its jurisdiction and creating out of those acts new rights and obligations.... It follows also that not only must the law extend over the whole territory subject to it and apply to every act done there, but only one law can so apply.... By its very nature law must apply to everything and must exclusively apply to everything within the boundary of its jurisdiction.

Compare with Restatement § 1:

> No state can make a law which by its own force is operative in another state; the only law in force in the sovereign state is its own law, but by the law of each state rights or other interests in that state may, in certain cases, depend upon the law in force in some other state or states.

19. An example of the rigid rules of the First Restatement are its sections 377 and 378. Section 377 defined the "place of wrong" as the state "where the last event necessary to make an actor liable for an

later.[20] Despite these deficiencies, however, and despite severe criticisms by commentators, these rules were to dominate American conflicts law for more than a generation. Indeed, many of these rules have been retained,[21] albeit often as only one choice among others, in the Second Restatement of 1971.[22]

B. THE FIRST CRITICS (COOK AND CAVERS)

§ 2.8 Although highly influential in the courts until the 1950s, the vested-rights theory was subject to severe criticism in the literature even at the time of the debates on the formulation of the First Restatement.[1] The principal objections were that the territorial orientation of the vested-rights theory assigned greater weight to foreign than to local law, in effect giving the foreign law extraterritorial force over the local law which was the source of the courts' authority. It was also argued that the traditional American rejection of renvoi[2] might lead to the application of the law of another state even though the courts of that state, employing different criteria for the application of their law, might not have applied it to the case at bar.[3]

The reaction against Beale was led by Walter Wheeler Cook[4] and his "local law theory" which, at least in its underlying premises and

alleged tort" took place; the latter provided that "the law of the place of wrong determines whether a person has sustained a legal injury." These rules were clear and provided predictability but made no allowance for the important possibility that the "place of wrong," apart from being the place of the injury, might otherwise have no other connection with the parties and their relationship. Application of the law of the place of wrong might thus deny recovery when the place of the parties' common domicile might have allowed it, and when denial of recovery might thus place the burden of providing care for the victim on the home state itself. Compare Alabama Great Southern Railroad Co. v. Carroll, 97 Ala. 126, 11 So. 803 (1892) with Babcock v. Jackson, 12 N.Y.2d 473, 240 N.Y.S.2d 743, 191 N.E.2d 279 (1963), on remand 40 Misc.2d 757, 243 N.Y.S.2d 715 (1963). For modern approaches to choice of law in tort see infra ch. 17. For decisions adhering to the traditional approach in tort, see infra § 2.21.

20. See infra §§ 2.8–2.9.

21. For a reconsideration see Dane, Vested Rights, "Vestedness," and Choice of Law, 96 Yale L.J. 1194 (1987).

22. See infra § 2.14.

§ 2.8

1. The classic criticisms are by Cook, The Logical and Legal Bases of the Conflict of Laws, 33 Yale L.J. 457 (1924) and Jurisdiction of Sovereign States and the Conflict of Laws, 31 Colum. L. Rev. 368 (1931); Lorenzen, Territoriality, Public Policy, and the Conflict of Laws, 43 Yale L.J. 736 (1924); Yntema, The Hornbook Method and the Conflict of Laws, 37 Yale L.J. 468 (1928).

2. The use of renvoi calls for referring to the "whole" foreign law, including its conflicts law, and following the latter's reference, if that be the case, to another jurisdiction or back to the forum. See infra § 3.13. In England, Dicey had originally endorsed renvoi but subsequent editions, under different editors, had gradually come to reject it. In apparent recognition of the incompatibility of a rejection of renvoi and adherence to a vested-rights theory, recent editions of Dicey (beginning with the 6th in 1949 and completed by the time of the 8th in 1967) have now abandoned the vested-rights theory. See P. Picone & W. Wengler, Internationales Privatrecht 53–54 n.5 (1974).

3. Beale himself recognized this inconsistency in his discussion of the various rules applying to choice-of-law in contract. See Beale, What Law Governs the Validity of a Contract, 23 Harv. L. Rev. 79, 260 (1909).

4. See supra n. 1. See also Cook, An Unpublished Chapter of the Logical and Legal Bases of the Conflict of Laws, 37 Ill. L. Rev. 418 (1943).

orientation, resembles much of the theories advocated in the last half of the 20th century, particularly by Currie and Ehrenzweig. Paraphrased, the local-law theory denies that the forum accords extraterritorial effect to foreign-created rights. Rather it grants a local-law remedy that approximates the result the foreign law provides. The court applies local law adapted to the needs of justice that the existence of a foreign element creates.[5] In this respect, the local-law theory resembles Ago's idea that the forum in essence creates special *forum* rules for cases with foreign law elements.[6] In contemporary times, this idea reappears in von Mehren's call for "special substantive rules" for conflicts cases.[7]

Cook's emphasis on the *lex fori* marked a drastic departure from the universalistic conception of private international law that characterized earlier generations of American conflicts scholars, including Story. Cook's subliminal message may well have been that the function of conflicts law is not to preserve international order, but rather to carry out local law and policy.

Cook's main contribution to American conflicts law lies less in enunciating a new theory and more in deconstructing the old one: discrediting the traditional choice-of-law methodology and thus, in his words, freeing the "intellectual garden" of conflict of laws of "rank weeds" so that useful vegetables could grow and flourish. He argued that the First Restatement's professed goals of certainty, predictability, and uniformity of result regardless of forum were illusory ideals because of the multitude of escape devices available to and so frequently used by judges. The seemingly simple but excessively broad principles of the first

---

5. See W. Cook, The Logical and Legal Bases of the Conflict of Laws 20–21 (1942):

> The forum, when confronted by a case involving foreign elements, always applies its own law to the case, but in doing so adopts and enforces as its own law a rule of decision identical, or at least highly similar, though not identical, in scope with a rule of decision found in the system in force in another state with which some or all of the foreign elements are connected.... The rule thus "incorporated" into the law of the forum, ... the forum ... enforces not a foreign right but a right created by its own law.

See also the following formulation by Judge Learned Hand:

> [N]o court can enforce any law but that of its own sovereign and, when a suitor comes to a jurisdiction foreign to the place of the tort, he can only invoke an obligation recognized by that sovereign. A foreign sovereign under civilized law imposes an obligation of its own as nearly homologous as possible to that arising in the place where the tort occurs.

Guinness v. Miller, 291 Fed. 769, 770 (S.D.N.Y.1923), affirmed 299 Fed. 538 (2d Cir.1924), affirmed in part, reversed in part 269 U.S. 71, 46 S.Ct. 46, 70 L.Ed. 168 (1925).

6. R. Ago, Teoria del diritto internationale privato (1934). See P. Picone & W. Wengler, Internationales Privatrecht 59 (1974).

7. See von Mehren, Special Substantive Rules for Multistate Problems: Their Role and Significance in Contemporary Choice of Law Methodology, 88 Harv. L. Rev. 347 (1974), discussed infra § 2.11 n.8. The similarity between the two theories is that both contemplate the creation of a rule that did not exist before and its application only to cases with foreign elements. The difference is that while Cook imports the foreign rule *in toto* (although he recasts it in terms of a *lex fori* remedy), von Mehren goes further in that he may import *only part* of the foreign rule and then add to it a part from the forums' rule, thus creating a true hybrid rule similar to the rules produced by the substantive-law method of the *praetor peregrinus*. See supra § 2.2.

Restatement were, in his words, "inadequate," both as descriptions of what the courts were doing and as guides to what the courts ought to do.[8] Conflicts problems are essentially complex, and a simplistic, static system working with preexisting formulae cannot provide solutions to such problems. What was needed instead was "a set of guiding principles, which make provision for as much certainty as may reasonably be hoped for in a changing world, and at the same time provide for not only needed flexibility but also continuity of growth."[9] This anti-fundamentalist statement has much to do with the notion, that later prevailed in American conflicts thought, that an "approach" is preferable to a system of rules.

Although Cook fell far short of articulating any affirmative approach of his own, his writings contained many of the seeds of modern theories. For example, on the basic question of how the forum court should select the foreign law on which to "model" its rule of decision in multistate cases, Cook simply said that "the problem involved is that of legal thinking in general," and that the forum should use "the same method actually used in deciding cases involving purely domestic torts, contracts, property, etc."[10] This resort to the "domestic method" for handling conflicts cases anticipated Brainerd Currie's perception of the choice-of-law process as a method grounded on the "ordinary process of construction and interpretation."[11] Cook's reference to "socially useful" solutions to conflicts problems also anticipated the result-selectivity of many judicial decisions and academic commentators and the notion that "conflicts justice" should not be pursued at the expense of substantive justice.[12] Moreover, Cook's exhortation to consider legislative purposes and policies "before a wise choice *between conflicting rules* can be made,"[13] though reminiscent of older ways of thinking, reveals that like many modern American scholars, Cook thought of the choice-of-law problem as one of choosing between competing rules, not competing jurisdictions in the abstract.

Cook's attack on the traditional theory was continued by Professor David F. Cavers, who at the time shared many of Cook's legal-realist convictions and the same skepticism towards generalizations. In a pioneering law review article, Cavers further exposed the mechanical nature of the traditional methodology, which he compared to a slot-machine programmed to select the applicable law in a "blindfold" fashion, based solely on territorial contacts and without regard to the content of the implicated laws.[14] In Cavers's view, this exclusive reliance on territorial contacts and the insistence on using "jurisdiction-selecting" rules not only prevented a more individualized treatment of conflicts cases, but

8. See Cook, *An Unpublished Chapter,* supra n.4, at 422.

9. Cook, *Logical Bases,* supra n.5, at 97.

10. Id. at 43.

11. See Currie, Selected Essays on the Conflict of Laws, 183–84 (1963) (discussed infra § 2.9).

12. See infra §§ 2.12–2.13.

13. Cook, *Logical Bases,* supra n.5, at 46 (emphasis added).

14. See Cavers, A Critique of the Choice-of-Law Problem, 47 Harv. L. Rev. 173, 178 (1933).

also prevented intelligent choices. After all, Cavers observed, "[t]he court is not idly choosing a law; it is deciding a controversy. How can it choose wisely without considering how that choice will affect that controversy?"[15]

Cavers would settle for nothing less than a complete reversal of the priorities of the choice-of-law process. He argued for a transformation of the choice-of-law process from one of choosing between states without regard to the way each such state would wish to regulate the multistate case at stake, to a process of choosing among the conflicting rules of law in light of the result each rule would produce in the particular case. In this process, territorial contacts would be relegated to a secondary role, and the criteria of selection would be the content of competing laws and their underlying policies, the peculiarities of the particular case, and the need to ensure justice to the individuals involved. Although falling short of articulating a comprehensive methodology to replace the first Restatement, Cavers's analysis provided useful markers on the path on which the quest for alternative methodologies should proceed. More than thirty years later, Cavers returned to the conflicts scene with a set of "principles of preference" for the solution of tort and contract conflicts. These principles are discussed later in this chapter.[16]

IV. THE SCHOLASTIC REVOLUTION[1]

A. "GOVERNMENTAL INTERESTS ANALYSIS" (CURRIE)

§ 2.9 Dissatisfaction with the fixed and thus mechanical rules of the First Restatement produced a number of new suggestions and counter-suggestions, a "revolution" in American conflicts law. Two approaches stand out—Brainerd Currie's governmental-interest theory, and Albert A. Ehrenzweig's lex-fori approach. Both approaches reflect attitudes similar to those of the European statutists of the 14th–16th centuries.[2] As employed in this chapter, the term "statutist" describes

---

15. Id. at 189.

16. See infra § 2.12.

§ 2.9

1. Despite its rhetorical excessiveness, the term "revolution" will be used hereinafter without quotation marks as a convenient shorthand reference to all modern American choice-of-law methodologies. The adjective "modern" is used here in its temporal rather than its qualitative sense.

2. See supra §§ 2.3–2.4; Kahn–Freund, General Problems of Private International Law, 143 Recueil des Cours 139, 245, 246 (1974–III). The term "statutist" has by now acquired a pejorative connotation and has been freely and readily, but often inaccurately, bandied about in the recent battles of the theoretical schools. See, e.g., *Currie*

and *Ehrenzweig* as statutists: Kahn–Freund, supra, at id. (who, however, also sees some relationship between Currie's thinking and that of the followers of Savigny); *Currie* as neo-statutist: Lipstein, The General Principles of Private International Law, 135 Recueil des Cours 96 at 154 (1972–I) and Ehrenzweig, Conflict of Laws 349 (rev. ed. 1962); *Cavers, von Mehren* and *Trautman* as statutists: Ehrenzweig, A Proper Law in a Proper Forum: A Restatement of the Lex Fori Approach, 18 Okla. L. Rev. 340 (1965) as reprinted, with author's additions, in Picone & Wengler, Internationales Privatrecht 324 at 331 n. 25 (1974); *Ehrenzweig* as "Wächter redivivus": Lipstein, supra at 144; distinguishing Wächter and the *lex-fori* theory: Nadelmann, 13 Am. J. Comp. L. 414, 416 (1964).

the classification of *rules of law* to determine their applicability territorially or by their nature, as distinguished from a determination of the applicable law from the viewpoint of the *legal relationship* at issue. As noted earlier, the important shift of focus from classification of rules to consideration of legal relationships was first achieved by Savigny. The First Restatement also sought to assign each *relationship* to its proper law, even if it did so through mechanical rules. Currie and Ehrenzweig, however, proceed from a classification and evaluation of forum and foreign law *qua* law.[3] In this sense, they may be regarded as neo-statutists, returning to an essentially locally-oriented approach that the European development since Savigny had largely abandoned.[4]

Currie's was basically a nihilist view of conflicts law in the traditional sense.[5] He rejected not only the particular choice-of-law rules of the First Restatement, but all choice-of-law rules in general, proclaiming that "[w]e would be better off without choice-of-law rules."[6] To fill the vacuum left by his rejection of choice-of-law rules, Currie resorted, like Cook, to the method of statutory construction and interpretation that courts employ in fully domestic cases. In Currie's words: "[j]ust as we determine by that process how a statute applies in time, and how it applies to marginal cases, so we may determine how it should be applied to cases involving foreign elements."[7] Thus, rather than selecting the applicable law without regard to its content, Currie, like Cavers, focused directly on the content of the substantive laws of the states implicated in the conflict. He argued that the "ordinary process of construction and

---

3. This is also true, in part, with respect to the views advanced by von Mehren and Trautman. See infra § 2.11.

4. See Vitta's characterization of Ehrenzweig's approach as "legeforismo" (lex-forism) in: II principio dell'uguaglianza tra "lex fori" e diritto straniero, 18 Riv. trim. proc. 93 (1964). On the "homeward trend" in modern American approaches see infra § 2.26 n.4.

5. However, it was Ehrenzweig's approach which—unjustly, it would seem—drew the criticism of "desperate nihilism": H. Valladao, Direito Internacional Privado 84 (1968); Evrigenis wrote that Ehrenzweig advocated an "anti-conflicts law" ("anti-matière"): Book Review, 18 Revue Hellénique droit int'l 471, 473 (1965). Both criticisms more accurately describe Currie's approach (see quote accompanying n.6). However, they do not do justice to Ehrenzweig's method, which seeks to elaborate conflicts rules although the source from which he derives them (forum law) virtually assures that they will ordinarily be inward-looking.

6. Currie, Selected Essays on the Conflict of Laws 183 (1963). See also id. at 180, 183: "The rules [of the traditional theory] . . . have not worked and cannot be made to

work. . . . But the root of the trouble goes deeper. In attempting to use rules we encounter difficulties that stem not from the fact that the particular rules are bad, . . . but rather from the fact that we have such rules at all. . . . We would be better off without choice-of-law rules."

7. Id. at 184. By resorting to this "domestic method" Currie was unknowingly importing to this country the debate between nationalism and universalism and between unilateralism and bilateralism that marked the European conflicts scene for centuries. See Symeonides, Revolution and Counter–Revolution in American Conflicts Law: Is There a Middle Ground? 46 Ohio St. L.J. 549, 553–54 (1985). In so doing, Currie was rejecting one fundamental article of faith of European and American multilateralism: that conflicts cases are so different from fully domestic cases as to require a distinctive mode of refereeing that draws from principles superior, or at least external, to the law of the involved states. Indeed, Currie rejected the existence of an overarching legal order that delineates affirmatively and in advance the legislative jurisdiction of each state. He believed that in searching for choice-of-law solutions, the forum should look inward rather than upward. See id.

interpretation" would reveal the policies underlying those laws and would, in turn, determine their intended sphere of operation *in terms of space*.[8]

According to Currie, whenever a case falls within the spatial reach of a law as delineated by the interpretative process, the state from which that law emanates has a governmental interest in applying such law in order to effectuate its underlying purposes. In Currie's words:

> [T]he court should . . . inquire whether the relationship of the forum state to the case at bar–that is, to the parties, to the transaction, to the subject matter, to the litigation–is such as to bring the case within the scope of the state's governmental concern, and to provide a legitimate basis for the assertion that the state has an interest in the application of its policy in this instance.[9]

Despite what the term might imply, a governmental interest is not the unilateral wish of the enacting state to apply its law in a given case. It is rather the result of the judge's evaluation of the reasonableness of this wish in light of the factual elements that connect the enacting state with the case at hand. In Currie's words, an "interest . . . is the product of (a) a governmental policy and (b) the concurrent existence of an appropriate relationship between the state having the policy and the transaction, the parties, or the litigation."[10] And in the words of one of Currie's followers, a state's interest consists in making "effective, in all situations involving persons as to whom it has responsibility for legal ordering, that resolution of contending private interests the state has made for local purposes."[11] Thus, Currie's legal-realist, or perhaps legal-positivist, conception of law as "an instrument of social control"[12] is projected at the interstate level: states do have an interest in the outcome of litigation between private persons, in domestic as well as in conflicts cases.[13] However, in articulating those interests, Currie almost invariably assumed that a state is interested in protecting its domiciliaries only, but not out-of-staters similarly situated.[14]

8. For a critique of this notion, see infra n.51.

9. Currie, *Selected Essays*, supra n.6, at 189.

10. Id. at 621. But see McDougal, Choice of Law: Prologue to a Viable Interest–Analysis Theory, 51 Tul. L. Rev. 207, 212 (1977) ("[A]n interest is not the 'product' of a policy; rather a policy reflects underlying interests. . . . Interests give rise to the promulgation of policies and not vice versa.").

11. Baxter, Choice of Law and the Federal System, 16 Stan. L. Rev. 1, 17 (1963).

12. Currie, *Selected Essays*, supra n.6, at 64 ("Law is an instrument of social control. Recognition of this fact, and emphasis on the economic and social policies expressed in laws, would lead to a fresh and constructive approach to conflict-of-laws problems."). For the influence of American Legal Realism and other philosophical trends on American choice-of-law thinking, see S. Symeonides, An Outsider's View of the American Approach to Choice of Law: Comparative Observations on Current American and Continental Conflicts Doctrine 202–34 (1980).

13. For a critique of this postulate, see infra n.54.

14. For example, in discussing the well-known case Kilberg v. Northeast Airlines, Inc., 9 N.Y.2d 34, 172 N.E.2d 526, 211 N.Y.S.2d 133 (1961) (a case arising out of a Massachusetts air plane crash that resulted in the death of a New York passenger who had bought his ticket and boarded the plane in New York), Currie was quite explicit that New York's pro-plaintiff "no damages ceil-

In Currie's view, when a court confronted with a case with foreign elements is asked to apply the law of another state, the court should first inquire into the policies expressed in the laws of the involved states and into the circumstances in which it is reasonable for each state to assert an interest in the application of these policies. This inquiry may lead to three possibilities which correspond to the three, henceforth well-known if not well-accepted,[15] categories of conflicts: (a) only one of the involved states would be interested in applying its law (the *"false conflict"* pattern);[16] (b) more than one state might be so interested (the *"true conflict"* pattern); or (c) none of the states would be so interested (the "no-interest" pattern or *"unprovided-for* case"). In his later work, Currie recognized a fourth category, what he called an *"apparent conflict,"* which is something between a false and a true conflict.[17] In a

ing" rule was reserved for the benefit of New York domiciliaries only: "New York's policy is not for the protection of all who buy tickets in New York, or board planes there. It is for the protection of New York people." Currie, *Selected Essays*, supra n.6, at 705. See also id. at 691–721. Similarly, Currie thought that a state with a defendant-protecting rule, such as a guest statute or the rule of contractual incapacity involved in Milliken v. Pratt, 125 Mass. 374 (1878), has an interest in applying that rule only for the benefit of defendants domiciled in that state. See Currie, *Selected Essays*, supra n.6, at 724, 785–86, respectively. Currie's reading of state interests as being domicile-oriented caused some critics to observe that Currie's approach "amounts to little more than a complicated way of saying that the law of the domicile governs." Juenger, Conflict of Laws: A Critique of Interest Analysis, 32 Am. J. Comp. L. 1, 39 (1984). It should be noted, however, that while Curried thought that what he called "compensatory" or defendant-protective rules like the ones described above are domicile-oriented, he also thought that conduct-regulating laws, such as traffic laws, operate territorially and bind or benefit everyone within the territory regardless of his or her domicile. See Currie, *Selected Essays*, supra n.6, at 58–61, 69.

15. These categories are neither self-evident nor dispositive. For example, determining whether or not a state is "interested" is something on which reasonable people may disagree. Nevertheless, these terms are useful in providing a common vocabulary and framework for analysis and discussion.

16. False conflicts also include cases in which the laws of the involved states are identical, or different, but produce identical results. However, this aspect of the "false

conflicts" concept does not add much since parties will rarely seek the application of foreign law when it is *identical* with local law, especially when the use of foreign law may leave them with the burden of having to prove it (see infra Ch. 12). Elimination of foreign law in this type of case is said to serve the purpose of guarding against a Constitutional-law objection to the application of the lex fori by an unconnected forum. Lipstein, supra n.2, 155–156. As the discussion in Chapter 3 shows, such instances are rare.

17. In Currie's words, an apparent conflict is a case in which "each state would be constitutionally justified in asserting an interest, but on reflection the conflict is avoided by a moderate definition of the policy or interest of one state or the other," or "a case in which reasonable men may disagree on whether a conflicting interest should be asserted." Currie, The Disinterested Third State, 28 Law & Contemp. Prob. 754 at 763, 764. According to another definition, an apparent conflict is a conflict that appears to be true if all possible interests of the involved states in the abstract are considered, but which may well be false upon a closer investigation of the factual contacts and a more moderate interpretation of the policies involved. See Sedler, The Governmental Interest Approach to Choice of Law: An Analysis and a Reformulation, 25 UCLA L. Rev. 181, 187 (1977). This category is terminologically useful in that it gives a name to the gray area lying between false and true conflicts. However, the practical utility of this category is impaired by the fluidity and manipulability of its outer limits. Currie admits this when he says that "indeed, the three classes of cases [i.e., false, apparent, true] are a continuum with no clear internal boundaries" and when he says that reasonable men may disagree on an apparent conflict. Currie, supra, at 764.

nutshell, Currie argued that, subject only to constitutional restraints,[18] the forum is entitled to and should apply its law to all of the above cases, except a few cases of the first and last categories, as explained below.

Thus, in false conflicts, Currie would apply the law of the only interested state, which in the great majority of cases is likely to be the forum state.[19] This part of Currie's analysis is neither controversial nor controvertible, at least for those who subscribe to the view that consideration of state interests is a proper starting point for resolving conflicts of laws. In contrast to the traditional theory, whose failure to inquire into state interests resulted in randomly sacrificing the interests of one state without promoting the interests of the other state,[20] Currie's solution to a conflict that is admittedly a false one results in applying the law of the interested state, without sacrificing any policies of the uninterested state. In this sense, the concept of a false conflict is an important breakthrough in American choice-of-law thinking and has become an integral part of all modern policy-based analyses.[21]

Currie's solutions to the other categories of conflicts, however, are both questioned and questionable. Under Currie's analysis, the law of the forum necessarily governs in true conflicts[22] because one *may not*

---

18. See infra n.58.

19. False-conflicts analysis examines the underlying policies *both* of forum law and of the other interested state(s), including whether either law is in some way "self-limited." See supra § 2.6 n.3. If the foreign law's policy does not call for its application, forum law will apply. If the policies of both laws call for their application, a "true conflict" exists, and forum law also applies in Currie's view. It is for this reason that Kahn–Freund, supra n.2 at 264, wrote: "Only ... in the court of what Brainerd Currie in his peculiar language called the 'disinterested third state' has the notion of a 'false conflict' an intelligible meaning." This assessment, however, overlooks the principal contribution of this concept to conflict-of-laws methodology—the introduction of policy analysis and the concomitant possibility of conflict avoidance. That Currie's system ultimately breaks down is a result of his approach to, and resolution of, "true conflicts," particularly his refusal to "weigh" policies; it is not due to the recognition—through the "false conflict" concept—that analysis should focus on underlying policies. See also, as illustrations, Handel v. Artukovic, 601 F.Supp. 1421 (C.D.Cal.1985); Abels v. State Farm Fire & Cas. Co., 596 F.Supp. 1461 (W.D.Pa.1984), judgment vacated 770 F.2d 26 (3d Cir. 1985), appeal after remand 694 F.Supp. 140 (W.D.Pa.1988); Pearce v. E. F. Hutton Group, Inc., 664 F.Supp. 1490 (D.D.C.1987) (false conflict determined as a result of interest analysis).

20. See Currie, *Selected Essays*, supra n.6, at 191. See also id. at 589–90.

21. "That this [concept] is by now taken for granted, even by [Currie's] critics, and forms the common denominator of all current choice of law methodologies is no reason to deny him the credit rightfully due to him. Even if this were Currie's only contribution to conflicts theory, it would be sufficient to secure him a permanent position in the conflicts 'Hall of Fame.' " Symeonides, supra n. 7, at 564.

22. A true conflict may arise before an interested or a disinterested forum. In the first situation, Currie would apply the law of the forum for reasons stated in the text. Regarding the second situation, known as the case of a "disinterested forum" (i.e., a true conflict between the laws of states other than the forum), Currie was less categorical, apparently because he assumed that such situations would arise only rarely. He offered some tentative suggestions including dismissal on *forum non-convenience* grounds. If such dismissal is not possible, however, Currie would again apply the law of the forum, at least if that law corresponds with the law of one of the interested states. See Currie, *The Disinterested Third State*, supra n.17, at 765, 777 ff. Alternatively, Currie suggested, "the court might decide the case by a candid exercise of legislative discretion, resolving the conflict as it believes it would be resolved by a supreme legislative body having power to determine which interest should be required to yield."

subordinate the forum's interests to those of another state.[23] Indeed, the very possibility of such a subordination impels Currie to insist that judges should not even attempt to weigh the interests of the two states. His explanation is that judges have neither the constitutional power nor the necessary resources to weigh conflicting governmental interests and to choose between or among them, especially when the forum's interests also are involved. Such a weighing, Currie thought, is a "political function of a very high order . . . that should not be committed to courts in a democracy."[24] For the proud adherent to the common-law tradition that Currie was,[25] this explanation is surprising.[26] It is also inconsistent with the basic tenets of his theory which, in every other respect, assumes an activist judge.[27]

Currie's summary reproduced in P. Hay, R. Weintraub & P. Borchers, Conflict of Laws 500–02 (12th ed. 2004).

23. "In the absence of action by higher authority, each state must be conceded the *right* to apply its own laws for the reasonable effectuation of its own policies." Currie, Comments on Babcock v. Jackson: A Recent Development in Conflict of Laws, 63 Colum. L. Rev. 1233, 1237–38 (1963) (emphasis added). For a judicial endorsement of this notion, see Lilienthal v. Kaufman, 239 Or. 1, 16, 395 P.2d 543, 549 (1964) (discussed further infra § 3.29 n.3). The court stated: "We have, then, two jurisdictions, each with several close connections with the transaction, and each with a substantial interest, which will be served or thwarted, depending upon which law is applied. The interests of neither jurisdiction are clearly more important than those of the other. We are of the opinion that in such a case the public policy of Oregon should prevail and the law of Oregon should be applied; we should apply that choice-of-law rule which will advance the policies or interests of Oregon." 239 Or. at 16, 395 P.2d at 549.

24. Currie, *Selected Essays*, supra n.6, at 182. See also id. (where Currie speaks of the "embarrassment of [a court] having to nullify the interests of its own sovereign)."; id. at 278–79, 357; Currie, The Disinterested Third State, 28 Law & Contemp. Prob. 754, 778 (1963).

25. See Currie, *Selected Essays*, supra n.6, at 627("I am proud to associate myself with the common law tradition.").

26. Indeed, Currie's thesis on this point assumes a conception of the judicial process that does not reflect the realities of the common-law tradition, or at least its American version, in which judges almost routinely engage in evaluating and weighing conflicting social policies. As one observer put it, "[e]ver since conflicts law first developed, courts did precisely what Currie would forbid them to do; no judge has ever been impeached for inventing or applying a choice-of-law rule that sacrifices forum interests." Juenger, Choice of Law in Interstate Torts, 118 U. Pa. L. Rev. 200, 206–7 (1969). See also Ehrenzweig, A Counter-Revolution in Conflicts Law? 80 Harv. L. Rev. 377, 389 (1966): "As far as I can see, all courts and writers who have professed acceptance of Currie's interest language have transformed it by indulging in that very weighing and balancing of interest from which Currie refrained." Currie's response to such observations was sharp and short: "I do not care whether courts undertake to weigh and balance conflicting interests or not," he said, but when they do, "such action can find its justification in politics, not in jurisprudence. . . . [L]et us not delude ourselves with any notion that we can control or predict the process by a juridical science of conflict of laws." Currie, *Selected Essays*, supra n.6, 600–01. See id. at 183, 274 for a more moderate response.

27. For example, according to Currie's own analysis, in order to determine whether the conflict is a false or a true one, the judge must identify and evaluate the interests of the involved states. Whether such an evaluation is qualitatively different, less subjective or politically sensitive, than is a weighing of interests is at least debatable. If judges are empowered and qualified to discharge this task, it is hard to see why they should lose that power the moment they encounter a true conflict. As Cavers put it, in Currie's analysis, "[w]eighing of interests after interpretation is condemned: weighing of interests in interpretation, condoned, not to say, encouraged." Cavers, Contemporary Conflicts in American Perspective, 131 Recueil des Cours 75, 148 (1970). See also Hill, Governmental Interest and the Conflict of Laws: A Reply to Professor Currie's, 27 U. Chi. L. Rev. 463 476–77 (1960); von Mehren, Book Review, 17 J. Legal Ed. 91, 95 (1964).

The same aversion to a judicial weighing of state interests characterizes the "comparative-impairment" theory proposed by Professor William F. Baxter as an addendum to interest analysis for the solution of true conflicts.[28] Rather than weighing interests as such, comparative impairment weighs the *loss* that would result from the subordination of the interest of the one state rather than of the other. However, in so far as the gravity of the loss depends on the strength and importance of the

28. See Baxter, supra n. 11. Baxter agrees with Currie on two points: first, on the process of identifying and resolving false conflicts and, second, on the view that the weighing of governmental interests by courts is not a proper way to resolve true conflicts. See id. at 8, 5–6, 18–19. Echoing Currie, Baxter states that weighing of interests involves super-value judgments that are incompatible with the judge's "non-political status." Id. at 5. Baxter does not, however, accept Currie's view that the application of the *lex fori* is the only possible solution for true conflicts. Rather, Baxter believes that a "normative resolution of real conflicts cases is possible" and that an examination of the basic premises underlying the federal system would reveal "normative principles which could and should serve as a foundation for choice-of-law rules." Id. at 8–9. To that end, Baxter proposes his "comparative impairment" formula. Baxter was later joined in this approach by Professor Harold Horowitz. See Horowitz, Toward a Federal Common Law of Choice of Law, 14 UCLA L. Rev. 1191 (1967); Horowitz, The Law of Choice of Law in California—A Restatement, 21 UCLA L. Rev. 719 (1974). Baxter distinguishes between two types of governmental interests or objectives, namely, the "internal" and the "external." The internal objectives are those that underlie each state's resolution of conflicting private interests in wholly domestic situations. The external objectives are "the objectives of each state to make effective in all situations involving persons as to whom it has responsibility for legal ordering, the resolution of contending private interests the state has made for local purposes." Baxter, supra at 18. In a true conflict, ex hypothesi, this external objective conflicts with the corresponding external objective of a foreign state. Rather than subordinating the external objective of the foreign state to that of the forum, as does Currie's, Baxter would "subordinate, in the particular case the external objective of the state whose internal objective will be least impaired in general scope and impact by subordination in cases like the one at hand." Id. In other words, Baxter would apply the law of that state whose interests would be most impaired if its law were not applied. As Professor Juenger points out, this notion is not new. "Probably without knowing it, Baxter paraphrased Pillet's idea of sacrificing 'the least part possible of ... the law's authority'." F. Juenger, Choice of Law and Multistate Justice, 141 (1993) (quoting Pillet, Théorie continentale des conflits de lois, 2 Recueil des Cours 447, at 472 (1924–I)).

For a judicial application of this approach see Bernhard v. Harrah's Club, 16 Cal.3d 313, 128 Cal.Rptr. 215, 546 P.2d 719 (1976), cert. denied 429 U.S. 859, 97 S.Ct. 159, 50 L.Ed.2d 136 (1976) (discussed infra § 17.17). In this decision, the court applied the California dram shop act to a Nevada tavern owner who had served a California driver who in turn injured the California plaintiff in California. The court reasoned that like cases would occur so rarely that Nevada's interest in protecting local taverns from liability was not significantly impaired, especially when compared to California regulatory and compensatory interest. The result may have been the same under the approach of both the First and the Second Restatement (on the latter see infra §§ 2.14, 17.24–17.28), but consistent use of either of those approaches would have brought results that avoid forum-shopping. On the other hand, use of Currie's approach by Nevada, had the case arisen there, no doubt would have resulted in the application of Nevada law, i.e. no liability on the part of the defendant tavern owner. Similarly, it is open to question whether the Nevada court would have agreed that Nevada's policies would be only minimally impaired by the application of California law; it is not unreasonable to expect that it would have applied its own law. For other applications of the comparative impairment test in California see Offshore Rental Co. v. Continental Oil Co., 22 Cal.3d 157, 148 Cal.Rptr. 867, 583 P.2d 721 (1978); Roesgen v. American Home Products Corp., 719 F.2d 319 (9th Cir.1983) (California); Rosenthal v. Fonda, 862 F.2d 1398 (9th Cir.1988).

For another refinement of Currie's approach see also Sedler, supra n.17.

state interest, it is difficult to avoid the conclusion that comparative impairment does involve a weighing of interests.[29]

In one of his last writings,[30] Currie's recognized that on occasion it may be appropriate for a court to subject the law of either the forum state or the other involved state to a more moderated and restrained interpretation which may lead to the conclusion that one of those states is not as interested as it might appear at first blush. If so, the court should resolve this "apparent conflict"[31] by applying the law of the other state.[32] Currie's insisted, however, that this process of re-evaluating the interests of the two states is qualitatively different from weighing those interests.[33] Whether or not this stretches the meaning of words depends, of course, on the meaning one ascribes to those words.[34]

29. Perhaps the only difference between Baxter's interest-weighing and the one Currie's categorically denounced lies instead in *who* is to do the weighing: in Baxter's ideal scheme (which presupposes the overruling of *Klaxon*), the resolution of conflicts problems and the concomitant interest-weighing is to be done by federal, rather than state, courts. In his words, since "the process of resolving conflicts cases is necessarily one of allocating spheres of legal control among states ... [r]esponsibility for allocating spheres of legal control among member states of a federal system cannot sensibly be placed elsewhere than with the federal government." Baxter, supra n.11, at 22, 23. Federal courts may be expected to discharge that function more impartially than would state courts who, being "active participants in the formulation and implementation of local policies," cannot be impartial in "deciding when those policies will yield and when they will prevail over the competing policies of sister states.... Baseball's place as the favorite American pastime would not long survive if the responsibilities of the umpire were transferred to the first team member who managed to rule on a disputed event." Id.

30. See Currie, *The Disinterested Third State*, supra n.17, at 763, 764.

31. See id.

32. See id. Currie pointed to Bernkrant v. Fowler, 55 Cal.2d 588, 360 P.2d 906, 12 Cal.Rptr. 266 (1961) and People v. One 1953 Ford Victoria, 48 Cal.2d 595, 311 P.2d 480 (1957), both decided by Justice Traynor, as examples of how a court faced with a potential true conflict can subject *its law* to a more restrained or enlightened interpretation and thereby resolve the conflict without having to apply the law of the forum. In both cases, it was the law of the forum that was subjected to this "restrained interpretation." However, in the last and final summation of his theory, Currie's spoke of "[a] more moderate and re-

strained interpretation of the policy or interests of *one state or the other*," Currie's summary supra, n.22 (emphasis added). See Kanowitz, Comparative Impairment and Better Law: Grand Illusions in the Conflict of Laws, 30 Hastings L.J. 255, 266–68 (1978).

33. See Currie, *Selected Essays*, supra n.6, 759 ("[T]here is an important difference between a court's construing domestic law with moderation in order to avoid conflict with a foreign interest and its holding that the foreign interest is paramount. When a court avowedly uses the tools of construction and interpretation, it invites legislative correction of error.... When it weighs state interests and finds a foreign interest weightier, it inhibits legislative intervention and confounds criticism.").

34. Interestingly, even Justice Traynor, see supra n.32, recognized that this process of restraint that Currie's advocated entails interest weighing. See Traynor, Conflicts of Laws: Professor Currie's Restrained and Enlightened Forum, 49 Calif. L. Rev. 845, 855 (1961). See also id. at 853 (noting that "Currie's proscription of interest weighing seems to strike at the heart of the judicial process.")

Although Currie's statements regarding *which* state's interests are to be subjected to a "restrained interpretation" are ambiguous, see supra n. 32, it seems that in most cases this aspect of his analysis presupposes the very kind of judicial discretion that he proscribes. This is clearer if the judge is to *choose between the two interests* in deciding which one to re-evaluate, or if the judge is to subject *both* interests to this re-evaluation. On the other hand, if the judge is to subject only the *forum's* interests to this "restrained interpretation," then this will entail a subordination of those interests, which (in Currie's conception of courts as instruments of state policy) is something judges are not supposed to do. Finally, if

Finally, under Currie's analysis, the law of the forum applies even to the third category of conflicts, the unprovided-for cases, even though in these cases the forum is, ex hypothesi, a disinterested state. Currie's explanation for applying the law of the forum is that "no good purpose will be served by putting the parties to the expense and the court to the trouble of ascertaining the foreign law."[35] However, although practical and seemingly sensible, this explanation overlooks the problem grammarians call a *proteron hysteron*: One cannot know whether the case is in fact an unprovided-for case without first knowing whether the foreign state is in fact uninterested; and one cannot know whether that state is uninterested without first ascertaining the content of its law and identifying the policies underlying it.[36]

In sum, therefore, under Currie's analysis, almost all roads lead homeward.[37] As noted above, Currie's would apply foreign law in only two situations, both of which are comparatively rare: false conflicts in which the forum is not interested, and apparent conflicts in which the judge chooses to subject the law of the forum,[38] rather than that of the foreign state, to a restrained interpretation. In all other cases, Currie's would apply the *lex fori*, to wit: (a) in a false conflict in which the forum is the interested state; (b) in a true conflict in which the forum is one of the interested states; (c) in the no-interest or unprovided-for case; and (d) even in a true conflict before a disinterested forum, if the court cannot dismiss on grounds of *forum non conveniens*.

Currie's defended his forum favoritism with arguments that ranged from the practical to the philosophical.[39] He was unable to convince his critics who, with much justification, have charged that such forum-favoritism rewards forum-shopping[40] and is generally antithetical to the fundamental goals of conflicts law—justice in the individual case and harmony, i.e. uniformity and predictability of decision, among legal systems.[41] In the words of one commentator, "Currie's analysis, which

---

the judge is to subject only the *foreign* interest to this "restrained interpretation," then this would seem to defeat the purpose for which Currie's proposed this re-evaluation (i.e., to rebut accusations that his theory was unduly parochial and forum-oriented).

35. Currie, *Selected Essays*, supra n.6, 156, 152–56.

36. For criticisms of Currie's solutions to unprovided for cases, see, e.g., Twerski, Neumeier v. Kuehner: Where are the Emperor's Clothes? 1 Hofstra l. Rev. 93 (1973); Symeonides, Revolution and Counter–Revolution in American Conflicts Law: Is there a Middle Ground? 46 Ohio St. L.J. 549, 565–66 (1985).

37. With respect to the "homeward trend" of some other modern theories, see also infra § 2.26 n.4.

38. See supra nn. 32, 34.

39. See, e.g., Currie, *Selected Essays*, supra n.6, 89, 93–94, 191, 197, 278–80, 323, 447, 489–90, 592, 627, 697.

40. Currie recognized this possibility: "The conflict of interests between states will result in different dispositions of the same problem, depending on where the action is brought." Currie, supra n.23, at 1243.

41. See Hay, Flexibility versus Predictability and Uniformity in Choice of Law, 226 Recueil des Cours 281 (1991–I); A. Anton, Private International Law at 41–42 (1967):

"In a free society the court's duty is not wholly or even primarily to give effect to state interests [except in the relatively rare cases where local public policy is offended, see infra § 3.15] but rather to balance those interests with such private interests as seek recognition. . . . [I]n the

compels him to give to the forum's law such broad effects, would tend to fasten upon the international and the interstate communities ... a legal order characterized by chaos and retaliation."[42]

Despite the above criticisms, however, Currie's theory dominated choice-of-law thinking in the United States for almost three decades.[43] His "seductive style" of writing "hypnotized a whole generation of American lawyers,"[44] perhaps in the same way that Beale's teachings had indoctrinated the previous generation. While judicial support for Currie's approach has decreased dramatically in recent years,[45] his analysis "still controls the academic conflicts agenda,"[46] even though Currie's "new critics"[47] seem to outnumber his old and new

conflict of laws ... such interest as the state may have in giving effect to its legislative policies must be weighed against the need to give effect to the reasonable expectations of the parties.... The [historic] relative disinterest of the state has enabled the courts to make the warrantable assumption that their own system has no monopoly of legal truth and to adopt an attitude of qualified neutrality towards the substantive laws pressed upon its [sic] attention. Much would be lost if we abandoned this system for one which, through a bias for the *lex fori,* gave primacy to the legislative policies of the state over the need to do justice in the individual case."

Kegel, The Crisis in the Conflict of Laws, 112 Recueil des Cours 95 at 207 (1964–II): "Governmental interests are the own interests of the state. But in conflicts law (as well as in substantive private law) the interests at stake are private and the aim is justice between individuals." See also Kegel, Paternal Home and Dream Home: Traditional Conflict of Laws and the American Reformers, 27 Am. J. Comp. L. 615, 618, 631 (1979). For further critical evaluation see Hill, Governmental Interest and the Conflict of Laws: A Reply to Professor Currie, 27 U. Chi. L. Rev. 463 (1960); Brilmayer, Interest Analysis and the Myth of Legislative Intent, 78 Mich. L. Rev. 293 (1980). See also Federal Ins. Co. v. Fries, 78 Misc.2d 805, 355 N.Y.S.2d 741, 747 (Civ.Ct. 1974): "So we ask whether Pennsylvania's interest in having its law applied to this controversy is greater than New York's? Is New York's greater than Pennsylvania's? Again, I do not know: Neither state, to my mind, has the slightest interest in whose law is applied to this controversy."

42. von Mehren, supra n.27, at 91, 97 n.2.

43. The intense academic interest in Currie's theory is illustrated, *inter alia,* in the many Symposia devoted to interest

analysis. See Symposium on Interest Analysis in Conflict of Laws, 46 Ohio St. L. J. 457 (1985) (contributions by Kozyris, Brilmayer, Sedler, Weintraub, Juenger, Evrigenis, Berman, Zaphiriou, Shreve, Luneburg, and Symeonides); New Directions in Choice of Law: Alternatives to Interest Analysis, 24 Cornell Int'l L.J. 195 (1991) (contributions by Simson, Singer, Brilmayer, and Kramer); Choice of Law: How It Ought to Be, 48 Mercer L. Rev. 623 (Roundtable discussion by David Currie's, Felix, Kay, Knowles, Posnak, Rees, and Sammons; Articles by Borchers, Cox, Juenger, Kay, O'Hara, Ribstein, Reynolds, Sedler, Shreve, Singer, Symeonides, and Weintraub).

44. Korn, The Choice-of-Law Revolution: A Critique, 83 Colum. L. Rev. 772, at 812 (1983).

45. See infra § 2.24.

46. Juenger, Conflict of Laws: A Critique of Interest Analysis, 32 Am. J. Comp. L. 1, at 4 (1984).

47. As Professor Nadelmann has pointed out, governmental-interest talk is not new, nor is severe criticism of it any more novel. Nadelmann, *Internationales Privatrecht*: A Sourcebook on Conflicts Theory Analyzed and Reviewed, 17 Harv. Int'l L.J. 657, at 672 (1976)(citing to de La Morandière's Preface to H. Batiffol, La capacité des étrangères en France I, at ix-xi (1929)). Among Currie's early critics in the United States see the following (in addition to the authors cited elsewhere in this chapter): Hill, supra n.41; Juenger, supra n.26; Rosenberg, Comments on Reich v. Purcell, 15 UCLA L. Rev. 641 (1968); Twerski, supra n.36; von Mehren, supra n.27. For early European criticisms, see Evrigenis, Tendances Doctrinales Actuelles en Droit International Privé, 118 Recueil des Cours 313 (1966); Kegel, The Crisis of Conflict of Laws, 112 Recueil des Cours 91 (1964).

For later American criticisms, see Bodenheimer, The Need for a Reorientation in

defenders.[48] The new critics concur with the old ones and among themselves that Currie's theory is parochial if not chauvinistic, a criticism which has been addressed above.[49] Of the many other criticisms, the following are summarized below:

    (a) that Currie's reliance on the "domestic method of statutory construction and interpretation"[50] was misguided, if not suspect, because this method fails to recognize the differences between domestic and conflicts cases and is inherently biased;[51]

American Conflicts Law, 29 Hastings L.J. 731 (1978); Borchers, Conflicts Pragmatism, 56 Alb. L. Rev. 883 (1993); Brilmayer, The Role of Substantive and Choice of Law Policies in the Formation of Choice of Law Rules, 252 Recueil des cours 9 (1995); Brilmayer, Methods and Objectives in the Conflict of Laws: A Challenge, 35 Mercer L. Rev. 556 (1984); Brilmayer, supra n.41; Ely, Choice of Law and the State's Interest in Protecting its Own, 23 Wm. & Mary L. Rev. 173 (1983); Hay, Reflections on Conflict-of-Laws Methodology: A Dialogue, 32 Hastings L.J. 1644 (1981); Hill, Choice of Law and Jurisdiction in the Supreme Court, 81 Colum. L. Rev. 960 (1981); Juenger, Governmental Interests and Multistate Justice: A Reply to Professor Sedler, 24 U.C. Davis L. Rev. 227 (1990); Juenger, Governmental Interests—Real and Spurious—in Multistate Disputes, 21 U.C. Davis L. Rev. 515 (1988); Juenger, How Do you Rate a Century? 37 Willamette L. Rev. 89 (2000); Juenger, supra n.14; Korn, supra n.44; Kozyris, Reflections on Allstate—The Lessening of Due Process in Choice of Law, 14 U.C. Davis L. Rev. 889 (1981); Rosenberg, The Comeback of Choice-of-Law Rules, 81 Colum. L. Rev. 946 (1981); Singer, Real Conflicts, 69 Boston U. L. Rev. 1 (1989); Trautman, Reflections on Conflict-of-Law Methodology: A Dialogue, 32 Hastings L.J. 1609 (1981); Tushnet, Legal Scholarship: Its Causes and Cure, 90 Yale L.J. 1205 (1981); Twerski, On Territoriality and Sovereignty: System Shock and Constitutional Choice of Law, 10 Hofstra L. Rev. 149 (1981); von Mehren, American Conflicts Law at the Dawn of the 21st Century, 37 Willamette L. Rev. 133 (2000).

48. See, in particular, Kay, Currie's Interest Analysis in the 21st Century: Losing the Battle, But Winning the War, 37 Willamette L. Rev. 123 (2001); Kay, A Defense of Currie's Governmental Interest Analysis, 215 Recueil des Cours 9 (1989–III); Kay, "The Entrails of a Goat": Reflections on Reading Lea Brilmayer's Hague Lectures, 48 Mercer L.Rev. 891 (1997); Posnak, Choice of Law: Interest Analysis and Its "New Crits," 36 Am. J. Comp. L. 681 (1988); Sedler, Interest Analysis and Forum

Preference in the Conflict of Laws: A Response to the "New Critics," 34 Mercer L. Rev. 593 (1984). See also Allo, Methods and Objectives in the Conflict of Laws: A Response, 35 Mercer L. Rev. 565 (1984); Baade, Counter–Revolution or Alliance for Progress? Reflections on Reading Cavers, The Choice-of-Law Process, 46 Tex. L. Rev. 141 (1967); Kay, Testing the Modern Critics Against Moffatt Hancock's Choice of Law Theories—Review Essay, 73 Cal. L. Rev. 525 (1985); Kramer, Interest Analysis and the Presumption of Forum Law, 56 U. Chi. L. Rev.1301 (1989); Sedler, Professor Juenger's Challenge to the Interest Analysis Approach to Choice-of-Law: An Appreciation and a Response, 23 U.C. Davis L. Rev. 865 (1990); Weinberg, On Departing from Forum Law, 35 Mercer L. Rev. 595 (1984); Weintraub, Interest Analysis in the Conflict of Laws as an Application of Sound Legal Reasoning, 35 Mercer L. Rev. 629 (1984).

49. See supra text at nn. 37–42.

50. See supra text accompanying n.8.

51. See, e.g., Brilmayer, supra n.41, at 417 ("[D]omestic interpretation and conflicts interpretation are different enterprises altogether."); Leflar, Choice-of-law Statutes, 44 Tenn. L. Rev. 951, 954 (1977) ("The term 'statutory construction' is no more than a pretentious disguise for application of the court's conflicts law."); Rosenberg, supra n.47, at 947: (By resorting to the domestic method, Currie's "inescapably" implies that "the 'foreign elements' in a case do not call for a distinctive mode of refereeing."). To the extent that these criticisms are directed against Currie's forum favoritism, they have been addressed in the text supra at nn.35–42. However, it must be noted that forum-favoritism is not a necessary ingredient of the use of the "domestic method" in resolving conflicts cases. See Symeonides, supra n.36, at 553 (1985). Symeonides also argues that "[b]esides filling the vacuum left by the collapse of Bealian systematics and taking the magic out of choice of law adjudication, the domestic method of interpretation has enriched the choice of law process by making available to

(b) that the above method is incapable of pinpointing the policies underlying the conflicting rules of law;[52]

(c) that, even if such policies can be ascertained, they cannot help delineate a law's intended territorial reach;[53]

(d) that states do not have an interest in the outcome of disputes between private parties;[54]

it the vast resources of the domestic common law process. It has also introduced functionalism into choice of law thinking, has allowed a more individualized approach to cases, and has tempered the conflictual method by injecting into it considerations of substantive justice." Id. at 554 (footnotes omitted.)

52. See, inter alia, Bodenheimer, supra n.47 at 737; Brilmayer, supra n.41, at 399, 417, 424; Hay, supra n.47, at 1661 (1981); Juenger, supra n.14 at 33–35; Reese, Chief Judge Fuld and Choice of Law, 71 Colum. L. Rev. 548, 559–60 (1971); Rosenberg, Two views on *Kell v. Henderson*: An Opinion for the New York Court of Appeals, 67 Colum. L. Rev. 459, 463–64 (1967). To the extent that it pertains to the ascertainment of *forum* policies, this skepticism may or may not be justified. As one notable conflicts scholar has put it, "[t]he most important lesson taught in the first year of law school is that an intelligent decision to apply or not to apply a legal rule depends upon knowing the reasons for the rule." Weintraub, Interest Analysis in the Conflict of Laws as an Application of Sound Legal Reasoning, 35 Mercer L. Rev. 629, 631 (1984). According to one of Currie's colleagues, "governmental interest analysis is merely one of the many applications of teleological interpretation. It seeks to determine the pertinence of rules of law to multiple-contact cases through an analysis of the purposes behind these rules." Baade, supra n.48, at 149 (1967). Ascertaining the *telos* or purpose of a law is not always easy, although it is more difficult in conflicts cases than it is in ordinary domestic cases. On the other hand, *teleology* has its limits when the rule under interpretation is that of another state, especially a foreign country with a legal tradition, language, and terminology different from our own. See infra § 2.11 nn. 23–26.

53. See Brilmayer, supra n.41, at 393 ("legislatures *have* no actual intent on territorial reach"); Juenger, supra n.14, at 35 ("policies do not come equipped with labels proclaiming their spatial dimension"). For counter arguments, see Kay, *A Defense*, supra n.48, at 117–29; Sedler, Interest Analysis and Forum Preference in the Conflict of Laws: A Response to the "New Crits," 34

Mercer L. Rev. 593, 606–20 (1983); Sedler, Reflections on Conflict-of-Laws Methodology, 32 Hastings L.J. 1628, 1632–35 (1981); Weintraub, supra n.57, at 630–34. See also Symeonides, Revolution and Counter–Revolution in American Conflicts Law: Is There a Middle Ground? 46 Ohio St. L.J. 549, 555 (1985) (arguing that the vitality of the "domestic method" has never depended on proof of *actual* legislative intent or ready labels). Symeonides also argues that, without agreeing with Currie's theory or with his particular inferences about the spatial reach of laws, one could still accept the notion that the spatial reach of laws can best be determined by looking to their purpose, "as long as it is understood that such determination goes at best only half way toward actually resolving a conflicts problem. The second half of the process, in which Currie's insights were much less inspiring, is to actually and rationally accommodate laws with overlapping spatial reach." Id. at 556.

54. See, inter alia, 1 A. Ehrenzweig, Private International Law 63 (1967); P. Graulich, Principes de droit international privé 14 (1961); Borchers, Professor Brilmayer and the Holy Grail, 1991 Wisc. L. Rev. 465, 474; Juenger, supra n.26, at 206 (1969); Kegel, *Crisis*, supra n.41, 180–82; Rheinstein, How to Review a Festschrift, 11 Am. J. Comp. L. 632, at 664 (1962) (arguing that, aside from public-law matters such as currency or taxation, a state does not have an interest in the outcome of litigation between private persons). But see Traynor, War and Peace in the Conflict of Laws, 25 Int'l & Comp. L.Q. 121, 124 (1976): "The concept [of governmental interest] is an old one in other areas of the law, with a respectable place in the law reports of countless jurisdictions. Its honourable history counters those who would debase it to mean identification with the partisan interest of a State involved in litigation as a party, as in actions by or against it with respect to contracts it has made, the torts of its agents, the vindication of its property rights, or the enforcement of its criminal laws. So narrow a definition ignores the objectivity that is basic to the judicial process in all litigation, regardless of whether

(e) that, even if states have such an interest, Currie's reading of interests was unduly narrow, in that: (I) he failed to consider so-called "multistate" interests;[55] (ii) he assumed that a state is interested in protecting only its own citizens, and not out-of-staters similarly situated (the "personal-law principle");[56] and (iii) he neglected the interests of individuals involved in the conflict;[57] and

(f) that Currie's "personal-law principle" is constitutionally infirm,[58] or incompatible with the basic tenets of American federalism, if not morally reprehensible.[59]

or not it has multi-state aspects." For other responses, see Baade, supra n.48, at 148–49; D. Cavers, The Choice of Law Process 100 (1965); Kay, *A Defense*, supra n.48, at 133; A. Shapira, The Interest Approach to Choice of Law, 72–73 (1970); Sedler, supra n.17, at 191–92; Symeonides, supra n.7, at 557–58; By using the unfortunate qualifier "governmental" Currie's facilitated this criticism. According to Juenger, this qualifier was "chosen to reflect [Currie's] view that the pursuit of forum policies in conflict cases is a vital political endeavor with which courts should not interfere." Juenger, supra n.14, at 9; See also Trautman, Reflections on Conflict-of-Law Methodology: A Dialogue, 32 Hastings L.J. 1609, 1614 (1981); "Characterizing these interests as governmental ignores the fact that often the interests involved are individual interests in private ordering. Although these individual interests are respected and often nurtured by governmental authority, the emphasis on the governmental nature of the interest downplays a vast area of law making by individuals and often tends to distort the issue."

55. Currie was unwilling to recognize interests other than those reflected in the domestic laws competing in a given case, or to concede that these interests may acquire a different tenor or intensity in multistate cases. Accordingly, he refused to include in his calculus the so-called "multistate interests"—interests that, though not directly reflected in a state's domestic law, stem from that state's membership in a broader community of states. Despite his stated belief that "[t]he short-sighted, selfish state is nothing more than an experimental model [and that] [n]o such state exists, at least in this country," Currie's, *Selected Essays*, supra n.6, at 616, Currie's specifically dismissed the view that a state should be guided in its choice-of-law decisions by the "needs of the interstate and international system." Id. at 614. The only restraints he recognized were those the federal constitution imposes See infra n.58. For criticisms on this point see Hill, supra n.41, at 489–90; Kegel, *Crisis*, supra n. 41, at 180–82; Rosenberg, *Two Views on Kell*, supra n.52,

at 464; von Mehren, Recent Trends in Choice-of-Law Methodology, 60 Cornell L. Rev. 927, 938 (1975); von Mehren, supra n. 27, at 92–93. For Currie's response, see Currie's, *Selected Essays*, supra n.6, at 186–87. See also Kay, *A Defense*, supra n.48, at 131–33.

56. See supra n.14. For criticism of this principle, see infra nn. 58–59.

57. Currie admitted that he found "no place in conflict-of-laws analysis for a calculus of private interests [because] [b]y the time the interstate plane is reached the resolution of conflicting private interests has been achieved; it is subsumed in the statement of the laws of the respective states." Currie's, *Selected Essays*, supra n.6, at 610. But see Currie's letter to Cavers in Cavers, A Correspondence with Brainerd Currie's, 1957–58, 34 Mercer L. Rev. 471, 488 (1983) ("I shall not admit that I am unwilling to consider the claims of human beings to justice unless I can fit them into the conception of state interests.").

58. See Ely, supra n.47, at 173–78 (1981) (charging that Currie's notion that states are interested in "generat[ing] victories for their own people in a way that they are not interested in generating victories for others," violates the Privileges and Immunities Clause of the Constitution). See also Laycock, Equal Citizens of Equal and Territorial States: The Constitutional Foundations of Choice of Law, 92 Colum. L. Rev. 249 (1992). Anticipating these charges, Currie's proclaimed that this notion is "not vitiated, but rather vindicated" by the Constitution and that his approach, which "counsels the rational, moderate and controlled pursuit of self-interest[,] ... also counsels that self-interest should be subordinated freely, and even gladly, to the constitutional restraints required and made possible by the federal union." Currie's, *Selected Essays*, supra n.6, at 525. Currie's also returned the criticism to supporters of the traditional theory who "because of the compulsion of internationalist and altruist ideals, have guiltily suppressed the natural instincts of community self-interest. The

59. See p. 38.

It may well be that there is more than a kernel of truth in the above criticisms. Some of Currie's critics, however, seem to have focused more on debunking Currie's theory rather than on separating the tenable from the untenable elements of his analysis. It would seem that, even if the latter elements outnumber the former, Currie's overall contribution to the advancement of American conflicts law can still be considered a decidedly positive one, if only because he stirred the stagnant waters of the "dismal swamp."

B. THE LEX–FORI APPROACH (EHRENZWEIG)

§ 2.10   Albert A. Ehrenzweig's theory[1] resembles Currie's in practical result. Although it proceeds from different premises and does not

[traditional theory's] impersonal choice-of-law rules ... are themselves discriminatory at times, and at other times enforce a purposeless self-denial, or an unwarranted intrusion into the concerns of other states." Id. Ultimately, however, Currie's acknowledged the potential for discrimination inherent in his analysis (id. at 185–86), but expressed the confidence that the Equal Protection and Privileges and Immunities clauses of the Constitution would help to control undue protectionism (id. at 123–26, 185, 191, 280, 285), while the Due Process and Full Faith and Credit clauses would help to control excessive forum favoritism (id. at 271, 280–81, 191). As has been pointed out, a major analytical flaw in Currie's system is his equation of the *constitutionally permissible* reach of state law with the quite separate issue of what is an *appropriate choice* between or among conflicting state laws, the application of which is equally permissible. See Siehr, Ehrenzweigs lex-fori-Theorie und ihre Bedeutung für das amerikanische und deutsche Kollisionsrecht, 34 RabelsZ 583, 591 (1970). See also infra § 2.10 nn.28, 30, § 2.14 n.53. In any event, one must wonder whether it is sound policy first to cultivate and nurture protectionism and favoritism and then to depend on constitutional compulsion to curtail it.

59. See, e.g., Cavers's charge that some of Currie's prescriptions are "more appropriate to a tribal system of law than to that prevailing in the American Union." Cavers, *Process*, supra n.54, at 151 n. 29; Bodenheimer, supra n.47, at 738; Brilmayer, supra n.41, at 416; Trautman, supra n.47, at 1615. Currie's anticipated these criticisms when he explained that his analysis did "not imply the ruthless pursuit of self-interest by the states," Currie's, *Selected Essays*, supra n.6, at 185, and did not preclude the possibility of what he called "rational

altruism." Id. at 186. See also id. at 549: "In a federal union such as ours there is no room for the cycle of discrimination, retaliation, and reciprocity. Each state may and should extend the benefits of its laws to foreigners, not merely with the hope but with the assurance that all other states will reciprocate as a matter of course." He strongly condemned, however, what he called "irrational altruism," which in his opinion characterized the traditional approach which "often requires a state to sacrifice its own interest even though the interest of no other state is thereby advanced." Id. at 191. But Currie's never retreated from his basic premise that a state is interested in protecting its own citizens only. Again, one has to wonder whether it is sound policy, first to elevate into a choice-of-law principle the notion that each state should be interested in protecting its own citizens only, and then to depend on "rational altruism" to curtail the inevitable excesses.

§ 2.10

1. Among Ehrenzweig's major works are the following: A. Ehrenzweig, A Treatise on the Conflict of Laws (1962); A. Ehrenzweig, Private International Law v. I (1967), v. II (with Jayme) (1974), v. III (with Jayme) (1977); A. Ehrenzweig, Conflicts in a Nutshell (3d ed. 1974); Ehrenzweig, Specific Principles of Private Transnational Law, 125 Recueil des Cours 170 (1969); Ehrenzweig, A Proper Law in a Proper Forum: A "Restatement" of the "Lex Fori Approach," 18 Okla. L. Rev. 340 (1965) as reprinted, with author's additions, in P. Picone & W. Wengler, Internationales Privatrecht at 324 (1974); Ehrenzweig, The Lex–Fori–Basic Rule in the Conflict of Laws, 58 Mich. L. Rev. 637 (1960). See also

deny the applicability of foreign law in appropriate cases, in the end it is at least as forum-biased as Currie's theory. Ehrenzweig divides the field of conflicts law into two major areas: the settled and the unsettled. The first includes all cases where "true" or "settled" choice-of-law rules have been established by legislative or judicial fiat, while the second encompasses areas where no such rules have been established. Acknowledging that in the United States statutory choice-of-law rules are uncommon,[2] Ehrenzweig defines as "true" or "settled" those rules that "stat[e] the actual 'doing' of the courts rather than merely their language."[3] Accepting these rules as *binding*,[4] Ehrenzweig maintains that choice-of-law theories, his own included, can play a role only in cases that do not fall within the scope of true or settled rules.[5] He summarizes his own theory as follows:

> Unless application of a foreign rule is required by a settled (formulated or nonformulated) rule of choice, all choice of law should be based on a conscious interpretation de lege lata of that "domestic rule" which either party seeks to displace. If that interpretation does not lead either to dismissal of the suit or to the application of a foreign rule, the forum rule, in a proper forum, applies as the "basic," or "residuary" rule, as a matter of "nonchoice."[6]

the bibliography collected in 54 Calif. L. Rev. 1638–48 (1966) and the tributes in Gedachtnisschrift für Ehrenzweig (1976); 62 Calif. L. Rev. 1070 (1974); 97 Juristische Blatter 363 (1976); 39 RabelsZ 1 (1975); 10 Riv. dir. int'le priv. proces. (1974). For the latest succinct statement of Ehrenzweig's theory, see his own summary in Cramton, Currie's & Kay, Conflict of Laws 303–05 (2d ed. 1975). For discussions of his theory, see the Conflict of Laws Round Table: Ehrenzweig's Proper Law and Proper Forum, 18 Okla. L. Rev. 233 (1965). For critical foreign reviews, see De Nova, Book Review, 51 Calif. L. Rev. 461 (1963); Evrigenis, Book Review, 18 Rev. Hellénique 471 (1966); Kegel, The Crisis of Conflict of Laws, 112 Recueil des Cours 91, 208–236 (1964). For favorable reviews, see Jayme, Ausländische Rechtsregeln und Tatbestand inländischer Sachnormen—Betrachtungen zu Ehrenzweigs Datum–Theorie, in Gedächtnisschrift für Ehrenzweig 35 (1976); Siehr, Ehrenzweig's Lex Fori Theorie und ihre Bedeutung für das amerikanische und deutsche Kollisionsrecht, 34 RabelsZ 585 (1970).

2. See Ehrenzweig, Nutshell, supra n.1, at 41–42.

3. Ehrenzweig, Nutshell, supra n.1, at 42. Ehrenzweig further subdivides "true" rules into "formulated" and "non-formulated" or "inchoate." "Formulated" rules are those enacted by statute or articulated by clear, unambiguous precedent. Examples of such rules are: "the lex situs in land cases,

where its application serves the security of title, the lex domicilii in the law of succession, where its application serves the unity of the estate or a testator's expectations; and the 'lex status' in the law of persons, in the rare case in which 'incidents' do not require separate treatment." Id. at 43. "Non-formulated" or "inchoate" rules are those that can be deduced through proper analysis from "settled actual holdings in disregard of language." Ehrenzweig, Private International Law, supra n.1, at 91. Examples of such rules are "the presumption of validity in contracts, trusts, and will cases." Ehrenzweig, Nutshell, supra n.1, at 44. See also Ehrenzweig, Specific Problems of Private Transnational Law, 124 Recueil des Cours 179, 208 (1968–II).

4. Ehrenzweig, A Proper Law in a Proper Forum, supra n.1, at 328: " '[T]rue rules . . . though of course subject to criticism, are binding and thus beyond the reach of any a priori inquiry.' "See also Ehrenzweig, Nutshell, supra n.1, at 45.

5. See Ehrenzweig, A Proper Law in a Proper Forum, supra n.1, at 330: "[T]rue rules must be excluded from any discussion of a priori conflicts doctrine." See also A. Ehrenzweig, Private international law 90 (1967).

6. Ehrenzweig, Private International Law, supra n.1, at 93 (footnotes and cross-references omitted).

Noticeably absent from the above is any consideration of the content or policy of the foreign rule that is sought to be applied in the particular case. Indeed, Ehrenzweig thought that "[n]ever ... will the foreign law be applied by virtue of its own policy alone."[7] Instead, "a foreign interest or policy can become relevant only by virtue of [the forum rule's] interpretation."[8] This interpretation may reveal that the domestic rule of the forum either "expressly declares itself applicable to foreign facts,"[9] or expressly confines itself to local facts,[10] or, as in the vast majority of cases, the rule is simply silent on the question of its spatial operation.[11] In the last case, the court is to determine whether the policies embodied in the domestic rule reflect a legislative intent for the rule of another state to be applied. In the rare case in which the answer is affirmative, then the foreign rule is applied "without regard to any policy or interest of the ... other state which, following its own policy, might very well have found another law applicable."[12] In the much more common case in which the answer is negative, the *lex fori* applies.

Thus, in contrast to Currie's analysis–which always includes consideration, albeit half-hearted, of the policies of the foreign state–[13] Ehrenzweig's analysis remains exclusively focused on the law of the forum.[14] Foreign law applies only when the forum has expressed a wish to import it by adopting one of a handful of "true" choice-of-law rules, or in the rare case when the judge surmises such a wish from an examination of the forum's substantive law. As one critic suggested, it is as if Ehrenzweig were "allergic" to foreign law.[15] "In its practical effect ... [Ehrenz-

---

7. Id. at 45. The only exception Ehrenzweig recognizes to the above statement is for "cases involving interests of a foreign government qua government." Id.

8. Id. at 94–95.

9. Ehrenzweig, Nutshell, supra n.1, at 39, citing as example a rule invalidating usurious contracts regardless of whether they are valid at the place of contracting, performance, or domicile. In such cases, the domestic rule applies "[i]n the absence of constitutional restraint," id., and supersedes any "true" choice of law to the contrary.

10. Cases of self-limited statutes are rare. See Graham v. General U.S. Grant Post, 43 Ill.2d 1, 248 N.E.2d 657 (1969) (Illinois dram shop act does not apply to out-of-state injury). Interestingly, even in cases involving such statutes, Ehrenzweig does not rule out the applicability of the *lex fori* as the "residuary" law.

11. The simple fact is that legislatures ordinarily do not think about, and therefore do not provide for, the self-limiting effect of local *substantive* law. The self-limitation of local law is a *conflicts*-law function which Ehrenzweig does not reach because of his focus on the interpretation of local *substantive* law. See Kahn–Freund, General Prob-

lems of Private International Law, 143 Recueil des Cours 139, 246 (1974–III).

12. Ehrenzweig, Nutshell, supra n.1, at 46–47.

13. Currie's analysis considers the policy of the foreign law in the process of determining whether the case at hand presents a false or a true conflict or an unprovided for case, and applies foreign law in false conflicts in which the forum is disinterested. See supra § 2.9.

14. Thus, Ehrenzweig's unilateralism is introspective and ethnocentric. For the differences between Ehrenzweig's unilateralism and mainstream unilateralism, See S. Symeonides, An Outsider's View of the American Approach to Choice of Law 59–61 (1980).

15. See Kegel, Crisis, supra n.1 at 227, referring to "[Ehrenzweig's] allergy to the 'governing' foreign law." See also Evrigenis, Tendances Doctrinales Actuelles en Droit International Privé, 118 Recueil des Cours 313, 370–385 (1966); Evrigenis, Book Review 18 Rev. Hellénique 471 (1966). Ehrenzweig acknowledged that under his theory, the application of foreign law is the "exception from the basic rule calling for the application of the lex fori." Ehrenzweig,

weig's approach] is perhaps no more than a very considerable expansion of the French doctrine of the *vocation subsidiaire*[16] and the German doctrine of the *Verlegenheitsanwendung*[17] of the *lex fori,* [that is, the] application [of forum law] where for some reason no other law can be applied.... These doctrines are intended to fill gaps, to remove an exceptional 'embarrassment' (this is what the German word really means); Ehrenzweig elevated this counsel of despair to a rule of virtue...."[18]

A central theme in Ehrenzweig's approach is his oft-stated contention that traditional conflicts theory erroneously presupposed the existence of a "superlaw"[19] that preordained, through direction or restraint, binding choice-of-law rules. He correctly noted that in the United States there are few federal constitutional constraints and few federal treaties or statutory provisions touching upon conflicts problems and that, consequently, the (particular state) forum is the source of conflicts law. This is not a startling proposition: most commentators would agree that conflicts rules are local law, even those derived from national constitutional law or nationally adopted international treaties. The lack of a "superlaw" explains the lack of external compulsion to formulate particular conflicts rules but obscures, through the tendentious connotation of the label, that even the forum is not an island unto itself. The fact that local law is the source of conflicts rules does not mean that even when such rules are inapplicable to a case, the choice-of-law decision must be confined exclusively to examining the policies of the forum's substantive rules. This exceedingly narrow focus makes impossible the formulation of *new* choice-of-law rules capable of addressing the needs of the interstate or international system,–rules that include the traditional concerns for predictability, harmony, and justice in the individual case.[20] In fact, it could well make impossible the formulation of *any* choice-of-law rules.[21]

Treatise, supra n.1, at 314. But he insisted that this is so only "[a]nalytically not quantitatively." Id.

16. See H. Batiffol & P. Lagarde, Droit international privé, I, nos. 345 ff., (7th ed. 1981). Footnote in original, renumbered and expanded. The French rule has since been changed: Cass. 11 and 18 Oct. 1988, 78 Rev. crit. 368 (1989) (with annot. by Lequette, id. at 277).

17. Melchior, Grundlagen des deutschen Internationalen Privatrechts, Ch. 13, pp. 101 ff. (1932). Footnote in original, renumbered and expanded.

18. Kahn–Freund, General Problems of Private International Law, 143 Recueil des Cours 139, at 247 (1974–III). See Evrigenis, Book Review, supra n. 15, at 472 ("The preeminence of the *lex fori* is itself the postulate with which Ehrenzweig's system begins and on which it is based. It is virtually the *sum total* of his system." (Authors' translation, emphasis in the original)). See also Briggs, An Institutional Approach to

Conflict of Laws: "Law and Reason" versus Professor Ehrenzweig, 12 UCLA L. Rev. 29 (1964) and Ehrenzweig's rejoinder in 53 Cal. L. Rev. 535 (1965).

19. See A. Ehrenzweig, Private International Law 75–107, *et passim* (1967).

20. See D. Cavers, The Choice of Law Process 22 (1965); Westbrook, A Survey and Evaluation of Competing Choice-of-Law Methodologies: The Case for Eclecticism, 40 Mo. L. Rev. 406, 458 (1975); Hay, Flexibility versus Predictability and Uniformity in Choice of Law, 226 Recueil des Cours 281 (1991–I).

21. For example, in the statistically rare cases in which the forum's substantive rule is expressly inapplicable to multistate cases, a decision not to apply it to such cases does not yield a new choice-of-law rule but simply implements extant and expressed legislative intent. In the more frequent cases in which the forum's substantive rule is not expressly inapplicable to multistate cases,

If this is true, then the internal inconsistency in Ehrenzweig's approach would be apparent: on the one hand, this approach acknowledges– apparently for the time being only–the binding nature[22] of traditional, bilateral, "true" rules that point to foreign law; on the other hand, the approach itself is incapable of producing any new rules, unilateral or bilateral,[23] and thus tends to institutionalize the dominance of the *lex fori*.

Anticipating the dangers of forum shopping that his theory would generate, Ehrenzweig proposed a transformation of the negative doctrine of *forum non conveniens* into a positive test of *forum conveniens*, which would allow assertion of adjudicatory jurisdiction only when the forum has appropriate connections with the case–"proper law in a proper forum."[24] He was particularly critical of the unfairness of transient jurisdiction based on mere personal service.[25] However, he conceded that abolition of this and other similar jurisdictional bases was not likely to occur,[26] a prediction proved accurate by the Supreme Court's decision in *Burnham v. Superior Court*.[27] Decisions such as *Shaffer v. Heitner* and *World-Wide Volkswagen Corp. v. Woodson*, which purport to adopt the "minimum contacts" test for "*all* assertions of state court jurisdiction,"[28] may have had some effect in requiring a closer relationship between the cause of action and the forum exercising jurisdiction. The fact remains, however, that in most cases plaintiffs continue to be able to choose from among several possible forums. Thus, Ehrenzweig's dream of *lex propria in foro proprio*[29] is as remote today as it was during Ehrenzweig's time.[30]

the decision to apply or not to apply it to such cases has precedential value only for cases involving that same rule rather than for cases involving the same pattern of disputes. Finally, Ehrenzweig's all-too-frequent resort to the lex fori as the " 'residuary' rule, *as a matter of 'nonchoice,'* " see his summary supra at n. n.1, (emphasis added) clearly does not produce any new *choice-of-law* rules.

22. See supra n.4.

23. See supra n.21.

24. See Ehrenzweig, Private International Law, supra n.1, at 107–110.

25. See Ehrenzweig, From State Jurisdiction to Interstate Venue, 50 Or. L. Rev. 103 (1971); The Transient Rule of Personal Jurisdiction—The "Power" Myth and Forum Conveniens, 65 Yale L.J. 289 (1956).

26. A. Ehrenzweig, Private International Law, supra n.1, at 234; see A. Ehrenzweig & E. Jayme, 2 Private International Law 15–17, 21–44 *passim* (1973). See also Hay, International versus Interstate Conflicts Law in the United States, 35 RabelsZ 429, 431–33 (1971).

27. 495 U.S. 604, 110 S.Ct. 2105, 109 L.Ed.2d 631 (1990).

28. Shaffer v. Heitner, 433 U.S. 186, 212–14, 97 S.Ct. 2569, 2584–85, 53 L.Ed.2d 683 (1977), (emphasis added); World–Wide Volkswagen Corp. v. Woodson, 444 U.S. 286, 100 S.Ct. 559, 62 L.Ed.2d 490 (1980).

29. See 1 A. Ehrenzweig, Private International Law, supra n.1, at 107.

30. "I believe that practical considerations argue in favor of seeking to bridge the distance between the choice-of-law and jurisdictional inquiries.... [W]hen a suitor seeks to lodge a suit in a State with a substantial interest in seeing its own law applied to the transaction in question, we could wisely act to minimize conflicts, confusion, and uncertainty by adopting a liberal view of jurisdiction, unless considerations of fairness or efficiency strongly point in the opposite direction." Shaffer v. Heitner, 433 U.S. at 225–26, 97 S.Ct. at 2591 (Brennan, J., dissenting in part). For discussion see infra § 2.14 n.53. See also Allstate Ins. Co. v. Hague, 449 U.S. 302, 101 S.Ct. 633, 66 L.Ed.2d 521 (1981) (discussed extensively in Chapter 3).

In a book review written in 1963, Robert Leflar, another one of the chief protagonists of the conflicts revolution, wrote: "[T]ime is still young, the law is still growing, neither Ehrenzweig nor Currie's purports to know all the answers, and both of these scholars ... become part of the earth on which their successors will build."[31] Indeed they have.

C.   FUNCTIONAL ANALYSES

§ 2.11   Several modern American writers accept Currie's concept of a state's "interest" or "concern," but considerably broaden his analysis by advocating a weighing of these interests as a way of resolving cases of "true conflicts."

Among these writers are Professors Arthur T. von Mehren and Donald T. Trautman who developed a choice-of-law approach they call "functional analysis."[1] The fact that this approach was developed in the context of a casebook, coupled with the approach's subtlety and sophistication,[2] seriously impedes any attempt at summarization. It is fair to say, however, that the first four steps of functional analysis are methodologically, though not philosophically, similar to interest analysis and its identification of false conflicts and apparent conflicts.[3] The major differences between the two methods appear in the handling of true conflicts. Unlike interest analysis, functional analysis openly advocates policy weighing, guided by specific criteria.[4] The first criterion is the relevant strength of the policies of the involved states. In measuring the strength of the respective policies, the court is to consider the conviction with which a state adheres to a policy, the appropriateness of that state's rule to the effectuation of its underlying policy, and the relative significance to the states concerned of the vindication of their policies. For example, all other factors being equal, the court should prefer to satisfy an emerging rather than a regressing policy, or a policy underlying a

31. Leflar, Book Review, 16 Stan. L. Rev. 233, 239 (1963).

§ 2.11

1. A.T. von Mehren and D.T. Trautman, The Law of Multistate Problems 76, 102–105, 109–115, 178–210. (1965). See also von Mehren, Recent Trends in Choice-of-Law Methodology, 60 Cornell L.Q. 927 (1975).

2. W. Reese, M. Rosenberg & P. Hay, Conflict of Laws—Cases and Materials 492 (9th ed. 1990) ("The functional approach is not a sport for dullards. A serious question is whether it plumbs deeper than all but a few judges and lawyers are prepared to dig or follow. For those who can keep pace, the analysis is intellectual stimulation of a high order ... ").

3. For example, von Mehren and Trautman analogize those cases to the false-conflict situation in which "regulatory rules" do conflict but one jurisdiction appears to

be predominantly "concerned." A.T. von Mehren & D.T. Trautman, supra n.1, 342–75. However, no clear guidelines for the determination of a predominantly concerned jurisdiction are given. See Kay, Book Review, 18 J. Legal Ed. 341, 346–48 (1966) (concluding that there is no real difference between the "concerned jurisdiction" and Currie's "interested state" and generally finding little difference between the two approaches). See also McDougal, Comprehensive Interest Analysis Versus Reformulated Governmental Interest Analysis: An Appraisal in the Context of Choice-of-Law Problems Concerning Contributory and Comparative Negligence, 26 UCLA. L. Rev. 439 (1979); Gorman, Book Review, The Law of Multistate Problems, 115 U. Pa. L. Rev. 288 (1966); Kay, Testing the Modern Critics Against Moffatt Hancock's Choice of Law Theories, 73 Calif. L. Rev. 525 (1985).

4. See von Mehren & Trautman, supra n.1, at 376–406.

specific rule rather than a policy underlying a general principle. The court also should engage in a comparative evaluation of the asserted policies, judging their strength and merits not only in comparison with the policies of other concerned states, but also in comparison with the policies of all states sharing the same legal and cultural tradition. For cases that cannot be resolved through a rational choice among the various domestic or multistate policies, the court can select a commonly-held multistate policy, or construct a new multistate rule,[5] or, finally, apply the rule of the state that has the most effective control over the subject matter.

For those cases that remain unresolved after all these steps have been taken, functional analysis proposes certain other guidelines, such as applying the rule that best promotes multistate activity or interferes least with the parties' intentions.[6] Only when all other routes have been explored and found ineffectual do von Mehren and Trautman admit that the forum appropriately can apply its own law,[7] but on the condition that, all other factors being equal, the forum is a concerned state. A neutral forum, in contrast, should not apply its own law, but it legitimately can apply the rule of a concerned state that approximates most closely the forum's rule. It is, however, desirable that such a forum exploit its impartial position and choose solutions that promote multistate activity and uniformity of decisions.[8]

5. See von Mehren, Special Substantive Rules for Multistate Problems: Their Role and Significance in Contemporary Choice of Law Methodology, 88 Harv. L. Rev. 347 (1974). See also McDougal, The New Frontier in Choice of Law—Trans–State Laws: The Need Demonstrated in Theory and in the Context of Motor Vehicle Guest–Host Controversies, 53 Tulane L. Rev. 731 (1979) who would develop "trans-state" rules through "comprehensive interest analysis." For the suggested "national consensus law" of products liability in the Agent Orange litigation, see infra § 3.54 n.18.

6. von Mehren & Trautman, supra n.1, at 406–08.

7. It may be noted that logic indeed requires the application of the *lex fori* as a final resort, i.e. when all else fails. It does not follow from this, however, that—as a matter of policy—choice-of-law rules should be formulated only in exceptional cases: such a narrow approach will very likely bring about the contingency leading to the application of the *lex fori*. See also Zweigert, Some Reflections on the Sociological Dimensions of Private International Law or What is Justice in the Conflict of Laws, 44 U. Colo. L. Rev. 283, at 292 ff. (1973) who, for similar reasons (last resort), would also opt for the "better law." In practice, this may lead to the "better law" rather quickly. See infra § 2.13 nn.9–21.

8. In 1974, Professor von Mehren suggested that one can expediently resolve certain true conflicts through a compromise of the conflicting state policies, rather than a full vindication of the policies of the one state and a complete subordination of those of the other state. This compromise would take the form of a special substantive rule constructed ad hoc for the case at hand and derived from the laws of both or all states involved in the case. For example, one can resolve a true conflict between the strict liability law of one state and the law of another state that denies liability by constructing a special substantive rule that would allow the recovery of only half of plaintiff's actual damages, or of certain items only, such as medical expenses and loss of earnings. See von Mehren, Special Substantive Rules for Multistate Problems: Their Role and Significance in Contemporary Choice of Law Methodology, 88 Harv. L. Rev 298, 367–69 (1974). Similarly, in a situation in which one state has a strict liability rule and a ceiling on recovery and the other state has a negligence rule and unlimited recovery, the resulting conflict could be resolved by a special substantive rule that would allow the plaintiff to recover damages exceeding those imposed by the ceiling of the strict liability state if the plaintiff proves negligence, and below the ceiling if she does not prove negligence. See id. at 369–70.

In his early writings, Russell J. Weintraub proposed a "functional approach" that also advocated a weighing of interests, but identified with more specificity the relevant criteria.[9] For torts cases, these criteria included: (a) the advancement of clearly discernible trends in the law, such as the trend in tort law toward distribution of loss through liability insurance; (b) the prevention of unfair surprise to the defendant, a factor that is weakened by the presence of insurance; (c) the suppression of anachronistic or aberrational laws; and (d) consultation of the conflicts rules of the other interested states in order to determine whether they have, through functional analysis, declared their policies with regard to similar cases.[10] Weintraub also took the next step of distilling these criteria into two result-oriented rules-a plaintiff-favoring for non-false tort conflicts, and a "rule of validation" for contract conflicts.[11] Weintraub explained his plaintiff-favoring preference by saying that "recovery, with loss-distribution through the tortfeasor's liability insurance, represents the most pervasive aspect of tort developments in this coun-

For similar suggestions, see Twerski & Mayer, Toward a Pragmatic Solution of Choice-of-Law Problems—At the Interface of Substance and Procedure, 74 N.W.U. L. Rev. 781 (1979) (proposing, *inter alia*, the following: that a guest-statute conflict be resolved by allowing the suit but raising the standard of proof so that the guest-plaintiff can recover only if he proves ordinary negligence by "clear and convincing evidence," id. at 793; that a products liability conflict between a negligence and a strict liability rule be resolved by shifting the burden of proof to the defendant to show the absence of negligence, id. at 799; and that a statute of frauds conflict be resolved by allowing the promisee to recover if she can prove the existence of the contract by clear and convincing evidence, id. at 797. For other proposals to create substantive rules for multistate cases, see the writings of Juenger and McDougal, discussed infra § 2.12 nn.19–20.

For a judicial endorsement of the notion of special substantive rules for multistate cases, see In re Agent Orange Product Liability Litigation, 580 F.Supp. 690, 713 (E.D.N.Y.1984) (contemplating the creation of an "national consensus" substantive law for products liability).

The above suggestions resemble the substantive-law method of the Roman *praetor peregrinus*, see supra § 2.2. Today, they may sound anomalous, perhaps because in the meantime, as Trautman suggests, "[w]e have become so accustomed by tradition and theory to ideas of conflict, choice and selection." Trautman, The Relation Between American Choice of Law and Federal Common Law, 41 Law & Contemp. Prob. 105, 118 (1977). Yet, it may be worth asking whether it is a good idea, in a discipline devoted to resolving conflicts, to reject *a*

priori the notion of a compromise, of seeking a middle ground.

9. See R. Weintraub, Commentary on the Conflict of Laws 284 et seq. (3d ed. 1986).

10. See id. at 284–91. Ehrenzweig might have called these criteria "non-rules" as he did the rules of the Second Restatement, particularly its § 6, discussed below. See Ehrenzweig, A Counter–Revolution in Conflicts Law? From Beale to Cavers, 80 Harv. L. Rev. 377, 381 (1966). However, as noted below, the rules of the Second Restatement strike a balance between policy criteria (in § 6) and concrete connecting factors. The "weighing" approaches of von Mehren/Trautman and Weintraub in the main lack the concrete connecting factors, while the approaches of Currie and Ehrenzweig do no or little weighing but instead point to the *lex fori*. Even the "weighing approaches" often lead to the *lex fori*, precisely for lack of concrete connecting factors that would point to another law.

11. See R. Weintraub, Commentary, supra n.9, at 360, proposing that true conflicts and no-interest cases be resolved by applying the law that favors the plaintiff unless that law is "anachronistic or aberrational" or the state with that law "does not have sufficient contact with the defendant or the defendant's actual or intended course of conduct to make application of its law reasonable." For contract cases, Weintraub formulates a rule that heavily favors the validating law. See id. at 397–98. For another rule proposed by Weintraub for product liability conflicts, see Weintraub, Methods For Resolving Conflict-of-Laws Problems in Mass Tort Litigation, 1989 U. Ill. L. Rev. 129, 148 (1989).

try over the past several decades,"[12] and that "[i]t makes sense to have a choice-of-law rule in accord with widely shared and clearly discernible trends in the domestic laws whose conflicts we are trying to resolve."[13]

In the 2001 edition of his *Commentary*, Weintraub conceded that his earlier proposed tort rule "was really an attempt at 'better law' analysis,"[14] which was necessary at a time when tort laws were so drastically different from state to state, with some states holding on to anachronistic anti-recovery rules. With so many states having since moved and continuing to move in the opposite direction, says Weintraub, "[t]imes have changed."[15] Weintraub now proposes a new "consequences-based approach,"[16] that "chooses law with knowledge of the content of the laws of each of the [involved] states ... [and] seeks to minimize the consequences that any such state is likely to experience if its law is not applied."[17] According to this approach, the court should (1) identify the policies underlying the conflicting laws of the involved states; (2) determine whether the non-application of a state's law would cause that state "to experience consequences that it is its policy to avoid;"[18] and (3) ensure that "application of the law of a state that will experience consequences ... [is] fair to the parties in the light of their contacts with that state."[19] Weintraub acknowledges that his approach may not provide answers for cases that present either the true-conflict or the no-interest paradigms,[20] and suggests that "courts need default rules."[21] Among the default rules or rather approaches he proposes are comparative impairment and the better-law criterion. However, he emphatically states that the better-law criterion should only be used in non-false conflicts and that "the better law should be selected by an objective determination that the disfavored law is anachronistic or aberrational."[22]

One criticism leveled against the interest-weighing that Weintraub and other functional analysts advocated is that, to do it well, one must devote to it significant time and resources, and, even when both are available, there is little assurance of avoiding subjective assessments or producing predictable results. American state law is ordinarily found not

---

12. Weintraub, *Commentary*, supra n.9, at 359.

13. Id. Professor Leflar offers a similar defense for his better-law approach, infra § 2.13, namely, that courts prefer the better law anyway and that we might as well recognize this "fact." However, there may well be a difference between realistically recognizing a factual state of affairs, on the one hand, and elevating it to the status of a choice-of-law "consideration," theory, or rule, on the other.

14. R. Weintraub, Commentary on the Conflict of Laws, 356 (4th ed. 2001).

15. Id.

16. See id. at 347 ff.

17. Id. at 347.

18. Id. at 350.

19. Id. Weintraub apparently believes that this approach is different from comparative impairment. See id. at 355, where Weintraub states that "a rule of comparative impairment" can serve as a default rule for those non-false conflicts that his approach does not resolve. He does state that "[t]he Louisiana Conflicts Code ... is an attempt to codify a consequences-based approach." Id.

20. Weintraub questions the "no interest" or "unprovided for" labels and suggests that many of these conflicts can be resolved by "re-examin[ing] the tentative conclusion that neither state has a policy that it will advance by applying its law" Id. at 407.

21. Id. at 355.

22. Id. at 417.

in codes, as in civil-law countries, but rather in diverse statutes and, more often, in judicially established rules. Thus, an analysis of the policies underlying a state's law may point the examining court in different directions.[23] And, to the extent that policies and interests of several jurisdictions are to be examined and weighed, "not even a very ponderous Brandeis brief could marshal the relevant considerations."[24] These are serious objections, especially because American conflicts law is litigation-oriented.[25] The more optimistic view is that, although it is not easy, interest-weighing is not as difficult as is presented to be, at least in the purely interstate context.[26] In broad outline, the laws of the several states are remarkably similar, and the policies behind those laws are largely shared and thus presumptively familiar to the examining court. This familiarity enables the court, on comparing the points at which significant variations do occur, to identify the purpose or policy that the variation seems to serve and to assess the strength of that policy. This is not a search in legislative history but an observation based on common background. For the most part, the court is merely asked to think about why a rule exists and to consider whether that purpose should, or even can be given effect in the case at hand. The evaluation of policies behind conflicting laws is of course more difficult when there is no such shared legal background; this will often be true in the international context.

D. VALUE–ORIENTED APPROACHES

1. *In General*

§ 2.12 Despite their spirited opposition to the traditional theory in so many respects, Currie's[1] and Ehrenzweig,[2] and to a lesser extent

---

23. Cavers, Contemporary Conflicts Law in American Perspective, 131 Recueil des Cours 77, 145 (1970–III). See also Fisher v. Huck, 50 Or.App. 635, 624 P.2d 177 (1981). As one judge noted, in the context of Currie's interest analysis: "Intra-mural speculation on the policies of other states has obvious limitations because of restricted information and wisdom. It is difficult enough to interpret the statutes and decisional rules of one's own state." Tooker v. Lopez, 24 N.Y.2d 569, 597, 301 N.Y.S.2d 519, 543, 249 N.E.2d 394, 411 (1969) (Breitel, J., dissenting), emphasis added. Similarly: "it is one thing . . . to identify the social interests which substantive rules of law seek to further in internal situations and quite another to project these interests into situations with a foreign element." A. Anton, Private International Law 39 (1967). See also T. De Boer, Beyond Lex Loci Delicti 463–464 (1987).

24. B. Currie, Selected Essays on the Conflict of Laws 182 (1963). See also Juenger, Choice of Law in Interstate Torts, 118 U.Pa. L. Rev. 202, 215–217 (1969).

25. See Kahn–Freund, General Problems of Private International Law, 143 Recueil des Cours 139, at 399 ff. (1974–III);

Leflar, Choice–Influencing Considerations in Conflicts Law, 41 N.Y.U. L. Rev. 267, 282–304 (1966); Leflar, Conflicts Law: More on Choice–Influencing Considerations, 54 Cal. L. Rev. 1584, 1585 (1966); De Nova, Historical and Comparative Introduction to Conflict of Laws, 118 Recueil des Cours 443 at 605 (1966–II).

26. See supra § 2.9 n.52.

§ 2.12

1. Although Currie was a leader in the movement away from jurisdiction-selection and towards rule-selection, his own approach to rule-selection was guided by the notion of satisfying governmental interests rather than accomplishing particular substantive results. While it is true that by being tilted towards the *lex fori*, Currie's approach tends to favor plaintiffs as a class, it is rather unlikely that this favoritism was an *intended* aim of his approach. In fact, Currie specifically decried the better-law approach. See Currie, Selected Essays on the Conflict of Laws, 104–06, 154 n.82 (1963).

2. Ehrenzweig was more sympathetic to material-justice considerations. See Ehrenz-

Weintraub and von Mehren and Trautman,[3] remained within the confines of the classical view of private international law in one basic respect—they subscribed to the same core assumption that the function of conflicts law is to achieve "the *spatially* best solution"[4] ("conflicts justice") rather than "the *materially* best solution"[5] ("material justice"). The classical view is usually associated with Savigny, although both Story and later Beale had also espoused it. It proceeds from the basic premise that the function of conflicts law is simply to refer each multistate case to the *state* that has the "most appropriate" relationship for supplying the applicable law, rather than to directly search for the proper *law* or, much less, the proper *result*.[6] Despite differences on defining and especially measuring the "propriety" of such a relationship, the proponents of the classical view are unanimous in their belief that this propriety is to be defined in geographical or spatial terms rather than in terms of the content of the applicable law or the quality of the solution it produces.[7] Whether this solution is good or bad depends on that law's goodness or badness, and that is something that is beyond the control of conflicts law. After all, conflicts exist because different societies have arrived at different value judgments reflected in their respective laws as to how to resolve legal disputes. As long as multistate disputes are resolved by means of choosing the law of one state over the other, such a choice is bound to satisfy one society and one party and aggrieve another. This being so, the choice of the applicable law cannot afford to be motivated by whether it will produce a "good" or "just" resolution of the actual dispute.[8] Hence, so the argument goes, conflicts law cannot

weig, "False Conflicts" and the "Better Rule": Threat and Promise in Multistate Tort Law, 53 Va. L. Rev. 847, 853 (1967). Nevertheless, Ehrenzweig justified his *lex-fori* approach in terms that had nothing to do with the pursuit of material justice. Furthermore, his acquiescence to "true rules," most of which were value-neutral, was antithetical to the pursuit of material justice.

3. Weintraub's general approach and especially his plaintiff-favoring rule clearly exceeded the confines of the classical view of "conflicts justice" to the extent they advocate the pursuit of substantive considerations such as "the trend in tort law toward distribution of loss through liability insurance," or "the suppression of anachronistic or aberrational laws." See supra § 2.11, text accompanying n.10. Whether the same is true with regard to von Mehren and Trautman's approach is unclear insofar as their choice-criteria seem motivated by conflictual rather than substantive considerations.

4. Kegel, Paternal Home and Dream Home: Traditional Conflict of Laws and the American Reformers, 27 Am. J. Comp. L. 615, 616–17 (1979).

5. Id. See also Symeonides, Material Justice and Conflicts Justice in Choice of Law, in International Conflict of Laws for the Third Millennium: Essays in Honor of Friedrich K. Juenger, 125 (Borchers & Zekoll eds. 2000).

6. Indeed, the implicit if not explicit assumption of the classical school is that in the great majority of cases, the law of the proper state *is* the proper law. See Symeonides, supra n. 5, 126–27.

7. See Kegel, The Crisis of Conflict of Laws, 112 Recueil des Cours 91, at 184–85 (1964) ("[W]hat is considered the best law according to its content, that is, *substantively*, might be far from the best spatially.")

8. In Dean Griswold's words: "[T]o say that each state must seek the result which it regards as just ... is simply to deny the existence and purpose of the conflict of laws ... [N]ot only is this a denial of true justice, ... but also a denial of the law itself." Quoted in Cavers, The Choice of Law Process 22–23 (1965). In the words of an Aus-

expect to achieve "material justice," that is, the same type and quality of justice as is pursued in fully domestic situations, although it should strive to achieve "conflicts justice" by ensuring the application of the law of the proper state.[9]

Directly opposed to the "conflicts-justice" view is the "material-justice" view. It begins with the premise that multistate cases are not qualitatively different from fully domestic cases and that a judge's duty to resolve disputes *justly and fairly* does not disappear the moment the judge encounters a case with foreign elements. Resolving such disputes in a manner that is substantively fair and equitable to the litigants should be an objective of conflicts law as much as it is of internal law. Conflicts law should not be content with a different or lesser quality of justice but should aspire to attain "material or substantive justice." Thus, this view rejects the classical presumption that the law of the proper state is necessarily the proper law and instead directly scrutinizes the applicable law to determine whether it actually produces the "proper" *result*.[10] Again, opinions differ on defining the "propriety" of the result, but the various versions of this view agree that the propriety must be determined in material rather than in spatial terms.[11] This view is much older than is generally believed. Historical precedents include the Byzantine commentators' preference for the *philanthropoteron* result,[12] the Italian statutists' preference for the forum's *statuta favorabilia* over foreign *statuta odiosa*,[13] and Magister Aldricus's call for the application of the *potior et utilior* law.[14] Having remained in the periphery of choice-of-law thinking for centuries, this view acquired new, eloquent advocates during the 20th Century especially in the United States, in the writings of David F. Cavers,[15] George W. Stumberg,[16]

---

tralian judge, "the courts cannot compare justice according to differing laws in order to say what satisfied the ends of justice in some abstract sense." Oceanic Sun Line Shipping Co. Inc. v. Fay (1988) 165 CLR 197, at 238 (Brennan J.)

9. "[E]xcept perhaps in certain cases of 'false' or 'no' conflict, the standards of justice applied to fully domestic cases cannot be achieved in multistate cases." von Mehren, Choice of law and the Problem of Justice, 41 Law & Contemp. Prob. 27, 42 (1977).

10. Thus, substantive justice is fused with conflicts justice, and both become co-equal goals of the choice-of-law process. As Kegel put it, under this view, "[s]ubstantive law and conflicts law are therefore not opposed as under the traditional private international law; rather conflicts law is only a facet of substantive law.... [C]onflicts law disappears into the 'black hole' of substantive law." Kegel, *Paternal Home*, supra n.4, at 617.

11. It must be noted, however, that save perhaps for its most extreme versions, this

view was not intended to serve as a complete substitute for the classical view of conflicts justice, but rather as a general corrective of the classical view. The difference between the proponents of the two views lies in their perception regarding the need for such a corrective. The original classical view rejects the need for such a corrective in all but the rarest cases, precisely because it assumes that the application of the spatially proper law necessarily produces a proper result. The second view believes that this corrective is always needed, precisely because it rejects the above assumption and searches directly for the materially proper result.

12. See Maridakis, L'inaplicabilité du droit étranger à Byzance, 2 Mélanges Fredericq 79 (1965).

13. See 1 Lainé, Introduction au droit international privé, 146, 264 (1888).

14. See Code cisianus E.VIII. 218 § 46.

15. See infra text accompanying nn.23–34.

16. The first edition of George W. Stumberg's Principles of Conflict of Laws (1937)

Robert A. Leflar,[17] Russell J. Weintraub,[18] Friedrich K. Juenger,[19] and Luther M. McDougal,[20] as well as in Germany in the writings of Konrad Zweigert[21] and Wilhelm Wengler.[22]

David F. Cavers contributed a highly original essay,[23] at the height of the vested-rights/local law controversy, foreshadowing such subse-

advocated more emphasis on "social ends," much in contrast to the then traditional learning. See id. at p. 15, particularly n.39. The statement was repeated, unchanged, in the second edition (1951), at 17, but was dropped in the third (1963), perhaps because the development had by then begun to catch up with the views expressed.

17. See infra § 2.13.

18. See supra § 2.11.

19. See F. Juenger, Choice of Law and Multistate Justice, 145–73, 191–208 (1993). (For earlier works on this theme, see Juenger, Choice of Law in Interstate Torts, 118 U. Pa. L. Rev. 202, 205 (1969); Juenger, Leflar's Contributions to American Conflicts Law, 31 So. Car. L. Rev. 413 (1980); Juenger, Mass Disasters and the Conflict of Laws, 1989 U. Ill. L. Rev. 105, 126.) In this fascinating book, Juenger advocated what he called a "substantive-law" approach, a term intended to evoke the most ancient conflicts approach-that of the Roman *praetor peregrinus* (see supra § 2.2) who, in resolving disputes between Roman and non-Roman citizens, constructed ad hoc substantive rules derived from the laws of Rome, Greece, and other Mediterranean countries. Juenger traced the development and use of this approach from ancient Greece to Rome and through the middle ages to the 20th century, and then explored the advantages of this approach over both the bilateral and the unilateral choice-of-law methods. He proposed that, for each conflicts case, the court should draw from among the laws of involved states and construct a substantive rule that best accords with modern substantive-law trends and standards. For example, for products liability conflicts, Juenger proposed that, from among the laws of the states of conduct, injury, product acquisition, and domicile of the parties, the court should choose "[a]s to each issue . . . that rule of decision which most closely accords with modern standards of products liability." Id. at. For a review of Juenger's book, see Zekoll, A Review of "Choice of Law and Multistate Justice" in International Conflict of Laws for the Third Millennium: Essays in Honor of Friedrich K. Juenger, 9 (Borchers & Zekoll eds. 2000). See also Borchers, A Look Forward, A Look

Back: Juenger's First Major Conflicts Article, in id. at 3. For a critique, see Symeonides, Material Justice and Conflicts Justice, in id. at 125; Kegel, Paternal Home and Dream Home: Traditional Conflict of Laws and the American Reformers, 27 Am. J. Comp. L. 615 (1979); Kegel in F. Juenger, Zum Wandel des Internationalen Privatrechts 35 at 36 (113 Schriften der Juristischen Studiengesellschaft 1974) (criticizing Juenger's suggestion that, in determining the "better law," a court might consider such traditional connecting factors as nationality, domicile, situs, etc.: "Why only these? Why not look around the world at large to find the best rule? Why not also look to the past and into the future? After all, the best would be the best!"(Authors' translation)).

20. See McDougal, Towards the Application of the Best Rule of Law in Choice of Law Cases, 35 Mercer L. Rev. 483 (1984). McDougal takes the material-justice view beyond the confines of the conflictual or selectivist method by advocating a search for the "best" rule of law, which (unlike the "better law") assumes that courts are not limited to choosing from among the laws of the involved states, but rather they "can, and should, in many cases construct and apply a law specifically created for the resolution of choice of law cases." Id. at 483–84. McDougal describes the best rule of law as the "one that best promotes net aggregate long-term common interests," id. at 484, and gives two examples of such rules: for noneconomic loses, he proposes a rule that permits "complete recovery of all losses, pecuniary and nonpecuniary, and of all reasonable costs incurred in obtaining recovery, including reasonable attorneys' fees and litigation costs." id. at 533; For claims concerning punitive damages, he proposes a rule that imposes such damages "on individuals who engage in outrageous conduct and who are not adequately punished in the criminal process." Id.

21. See Zweigert, Some Reflections on the Sociological Dimensions of Private International Law or What is Justice in the Conflict of Laws, 44 U. Colo. L. Rev. (1973).

22. See Wengler, The General Principles of Private International Law, 104 Recueil des Cours 274 (1961–III).

23. Cavers, A Critique of the Choice-of-Law Problem, 47 Harv. L. Rev. 173 (1933) (discussed supra § 2.8).

quent formulations as those of Leflar and Cheatham & Reese.[24] In his own summary of his approach,[25] Cavers suggested (1) close analysis of the facts of the case, (2) comparison of the "proffered rule of law" with "the rule of the forum (or other competing jurisdiction)" with respect to the results they would entail, and (3) appraisal of the results "from the standpoint of justice between the litigating individuals or . . . broader considerations of social policy." The object is, he wrote, that "the choice . . . would not be the result of the automatic operation of a rule or principle of selection but of a search for a just decision in the principal case."[26] This approach (also characterized as "look-before-you-leap"[27]) was endorsed by some commentators[28] but was criticized by others. One author compared this and other "result-selective" approaches with a "discretionary system of equity"[29] that would turn the clock "back to the medieval beginnings of private international law."[30] These critical assessments equate Cavers's approach with the "better law" approach (discussed below) but are best reserved for the latter. Applied to Cavers, they are too harsh: they seize on some perhaps overgeneralized statements and overlook his cautious formulations elsewhere, particularly in his important book *The Choice of Law Process* in which he emphasized the need for choice-of-law "rules."[31] In 1972, Professor Cavers wrote an

24. See Cheatham & Reese, Choice of the Applicable Law, 52 Colum. L. Rev. 959 (1952).

25. See Cavers, supra n.23, at 192–193.

26. Id.

27. De Nova, Historical and Comparative Introduction to Conflict of Laws, 118 Recueil des Cours 443, 599 (1966–II).

28. See Hancock, Three Approaches to the Choice-of-Law Problem: the Classificatory, the Functional and the Result Selective, XXth Century Comparative and Conflicts Law—Legal Essays in Honor of Hessel E. Yntema 365, 372 ff. (1961).

29. A. Anton, Private International Law, 40 (1967).

30. Id. See also Neuhaus, Legal Certainty Versus Equity in the Conflict of Laws, 29 Law & Contemp. Prob. 795, 802 (1963) ("In a democratic and pluralist society, the standards for judgment cannot be purely personal or irrational; the judge must be guided by generally recognized standards capable of rational cognition. This is the essential difference between a democratic legal order and so-called Khadi justice which decides individual cases in accordance with the judge's sense of equity and without reliance on any objective standards.").

31. "We may have to accept the articulated *ad hoc* decision as an interim substitute [for the development of rules and prin-

ciples], but we should persevere in the search for rules or principles which would determine when the law of a state which served one purpose should be preferred to the law of another state which served a different purpose." D. Cavers, The Choice of Law Process 121 (1965). In this work he also proposed several principles of which those related to tort show a "territorialist bias" (as Cavers acknowledged, id., at 134–135) and drew the most comment. See, e.g., Baade, Counter–Revolution or Alliance for Progress?, 46 Tex. L. Rev. 141 (1947); Ehrenzweig, A Counter–Revolution in Conflicts Law? From Beale to Cavers, 80 Harv. L. Rev. 377, 394, 399–400 (1966); Symposium, The Value of Principled Preferences, 49 Tex. L. Rev. 236 (1971); von Mehren, von Mehren, Recent Trends in Choice-of-Law Methodology, 60 Cornell L.Q. 927, 954–58 (1975); Westbrook, A Survey and Evaluation of Competing Choice-of-Law Methodologies: The Case for Eclecticism, 40 Mo. L. Rev. 406, 423–26 (1975). For an extension of Cavers's application of the law of the state of injury in tort, see Twerski, Enlightened Territorialism and Professor Cavers, 9 Duq. L. Rev. 373 (1971).

It is also important to note that in formulating "principles of preference," Cavers assumes—in contrast to the more open-ended approaches of Leflar and others—that there are relatively few archetypal multistate situations to which they would apply. See Cavers, Contemporary Conflicts Law in American Perspective, Hague Academy, 131

addendum[32] to his 1933 article and further clarified the position adopted there and in his book. While he had indeed "sought an alternative to particularization" and thus advocated the "broad principles ... termed 'principles of preference,' "the approach was not intended to abandon the search for rules.[33] Rather, his main focus—among the relatively few archetypal situations ("law-fact patterns")—is on those involving "protective laws" with which the modern state surrounds the individual. Courts and legislators should address the question of "under what circumstances ... the more protective law [should be preferred].... Candor in identifying the circumstances ... would ... [it is believed] yield fewer departures from past decisions (as distinguished from their rationales) than one might suppose."[34]

2. The "Better Law" Approach

§ 2.13   Robert A. Leflar subscribed to the view that the First Restatement's rules should be replaced not by another set of rules but rather by a set of flexible "choice-influencing considerations" that should guide the court's choice of the applicable law. In two successive law review articles[1] he finalized a non-hierarchical list of five such considerations and provided thoughtful supporting rationale. His list is shorter than those of others[2] but also rather general: (1) predictability of results, (2) maintenance of interstate and international order, (3) simplification of the judicial task, (4) advancement of the forum's governmental interest, and (5) the application of the better rule of law. Leflar wrote that through reference to these considerations, "courts can replace with statements of real reasons the mechanical rules and circuitously devised approaches which have appeared in the language of conflicts opinions, too often as cover-ups for the real reason that underlay the decisions."[3] The first three considerations restate classical private international law goals, while the last two, each in a different way, point homeward.

Regarding the better-law criterion, Leflar was quick to stress that it was "only one of five, more important in some types of cases than in

---

Recueil des Cours 77, 152 (1970–III). See also Neuhaus, Savigny und die Rechtsprechung aus der Natur der Sache, 15 RabelsZ 364, 371 (1949).

32.   Cavers, Addendum 1972, in P. Picone & W. Wengler, Internationales Privatrecht 166 (1974), reprinted in 17 Harv. Int'l L. J. 651 (1976).

33.   "We will not ... fulfill the objectives of the conflict of laws unless we can provide rules ... under which the same cases will be decided the same way no matter where the suit is brought. ...[W]e [should] ... constantly hold up uniformity of result as a major objective...." D. Cavers, The Choice of Law Process, 22 (1965). See generally, Hay, Flexibility versus Predictability and Uniformity in Choice of Law, 226 Recueil des Cours 281 (1991–I).

34.   Id., passim.

§ 2.13

1.   See Leflar, Choice–Influencing Considerations in Conflicts Law, 41 N.Y.U. L. Rev. 367 (1966); Leflar, Conflicts of Law: More on Choice–Influencing Considerations, 54 Calif. L. Rev. 1584 (1966). See also Leflar, The Nature of Conflicts Law, 81 Colum. L. Rev. 1080 (1981).

2.   See Cheatham & Reese, Choice of the Applicable Law, 52 Colum. L. Rev. 959 (1952); Yntema, The Objectives of Private International Law, 35 Can. B. Rev. 721, 734–735 (1957).

3.   Leflar, Conflicts of Law: More on Choice–Influencing Considerations, 54 Calif. L. Rev. 1584, 1585 (1966).

others, almost controlling in some but irrelevant in others.''[4] Nevertheless, because Leflar did not assign a priority to any of his criteria,[5] and because, at least at the beginning, many courts paid lip service to the other four considerations (which are similar to considerations advanced by others, including § 6 of the Second Restatement), the better-law criterion is the most conspicuous of the five and the one for which Leflar is either criticized or praised. Most of the criticism comes from academic authors.[6] Judges generally are more receptive, perhaps understandably, and some are enthusiastic supporters.[7] Leflar's better-law approach is followed in Minnesota and Wisconsin with regard to tort and contract conflicts, and in New Hampshire, Rhode Island, and Leflar's home state of Arkansas with regard to tort conflicts only.[8] Thus, eight centuries after Magister Aldricus, the better-law approach has taken hold on American soil.

Although the better-law criterion is "only one of five," it can easily become the controlling criterion. Indeed, by not expressly assigning to it a residual role, Leflar allowed it to become the decisive criterion in all the close cases. At least in the early years, this is precisely how courts employed this criterion, while paying lip service to the other four.[9] It is one thing to use a result-oriented criterion as a tie breaker of last resort[10] and another thing to use it as a *co-equal* criterion. The latter use,

4. R. Leflar, L. McDougal & R. Felix, American Conflicts Law 300 (4th ed. 1986).

5. Id. at 279.

6. See, e.g., Cavers, The Value of Principled Preferences, 49 Tex. L. Rev. 211, 212–13, 214, 215 (1971); Baade, Counter–Revolution or Alliance for Progress?, 46 Tex. L. Rev. 141, 155 ff. (1947); 1 A. Ehrenzweig, Private International Law 97–98, 100–103 (1967); von Mehren, Recent Trends in Choice-of-Law Methodology, 60 Cornell L. Rev. 927, 952–953 (1975); S. Symeonides, The American Choice-of-Law Revolution in the Courts: Today and Tomorrow, 298 Recueil des Cours 1, 51–55, 109–116 (2003).

7. For warm praise by Justice Todd, the author of the majority opinion in Milkovich v. Saari, 295 Minn. 155, 203 N.W.2d 408 (1973), see Todd, A Judge's View, 31 S.C. L. Rev. 435 (1980). For support by academic authors, see Juenger, Leflar's Contributions to American Conflicts Law, 31 S. C. L. Rev. 413 (1980); Symposium in 52 Ark. L. Rev. 1 (1999) (containing articles by Watkins, Cox, Felix, McDougal, Simson, Weintraub and Whitten).

8. See infra § 2.25.

9. See infra nn. 14–21.

10. Any choice-of-law method will occasionally fail to resolve the conflict satisfactorily, and, when that happens, courts will make their own choices, and it hardly matters at that point whether they justify their

choice in terms of a *lex-fori* preference or the adoption of the better, more "progressive" law. See Zweigert, Some Reflections on the Sociological Dimensions of Private International Law or: What Is Justice in the Conflict of Laws?, 44 U. Colo. L. Rev. 283, 294 (1973) ("better law" as a "*residual rule*" (emphasis in the original)). As Zweigert noted in the context of cases in which the parties fail to invoke foreign law, "The judge applying foreign law is a dilettante, a beginner; he is timid. The judge applying the lex fori is a learned expert; he is a sovereign, superior. . . . On the whole the judicial process has a lower quality where the judge applies foreign law than where he applies [the] lex fori." Id. at 293. See also Shaffer v. Heitner, 433 U.S. 186, 225, 97 S.Ct. 2569, 2591, 53 L.Ed.2d 683 (1977), Brennan, J., dissenting in part: "Even when a court would apply the law of a different forum, as a general rule it will feel less knowledgeable and comfortable in interpretation, and less interested in fostering the policies of that foreign jurisdiction, than would the courts established by the State that provides the applicable law." For the context of this statement and for discussion see infra § 2.14 n.53. In the European context see Flessner, Interessenjurisprudenz im internationalen Privatrecht *passim* (1990) and Hay, Book Review, 39 Am. J. Comp. L. 437 (1991). Moreover, the use of the "better law" as a residual criterion even has the potential benefit of tempering

subconsciously but unavoidably, makes "better law" a first-choice criterion and threatens to displace other, more appropriate choice-considerations. "However much ... in practice the judge's choice of law may be influenced by his preference for the content of one law or another, it is inadvisable to elevate a fact of human weakness to a principle of legislative policy."[11] One should not be surprised to discover that "an approach that authorizes an *ad hoc*, unguided, and *ex post* choice of the 'better' law produces choices that reflect the subjective predilections of the judges who make the choices."[12] To the extent that judges tend to prefer domestic over foreign law, plaintiffs over defendants (foreign or domestic), or domestic over foreign litigants (plaintiffs or defendants), these preferences are bound to be reflected in the judges' decisions. The early cases from the five states that follow Leflar's approach exhibit all three of these tendencies to a higher than usual degree.[13] Although these tendencies are not parallel, they all stem from the same source–the judicial subjectivism that the better-law approach legitimizes.

For example, in the five states that follow Leflar's approach for tort conflicts, one encounters only five supreme court cases applying foreign law,[14] and only four cases finding the foreign law better than the forum's.[15] Three of the latter cases are among those that applied foreign

the normal forum preference with consideration of developing trends of the law with respect to the particular area in issue when there is no express legislative direction or prior case law.

11. Kahn–Freund, General Problems of Private International Law, 143 Recueil des Cours 139, at 466 (1974–III). See also Cavers, The Value of Principled Preferences, 49 Tex. L. Rev. 211, 215 (1971) (stating that the fact that courts will, in hard cases and when all else fails, choose what they view as the "better law" anyway is no reason to encourage them to do so in *all* cases).

12. S. Symeonides, The American Choice-of-Law Revolution in the Courts: Today and Tomorrow, 298 Recueil des Cours, 1, 110 (2003). See also Neuhaus, Legal Certainty Versus Equity in the Conflict of Laws, 29 Law & Contemp. Prob. 795, 802 (1963) ("In a democratic and pluralist society, ... the judge must be guided by generally recognized standards capable of rational cognition."); Maier, Coordination of Laws in a National Federal System: An Analysis of the Writings of Elliot Evans Cheatham, 26 Vand. L. Rev. 209, 256 (1973) (warning of the danger that the "better law" approach can become a substitute for analysis).

13. See Symeonides, supra n. 12 at 110–114.

14. See id. at 54–55, 110–111. The five cases are: Lichter v. Fritsch, 77 Wis.2d 178, 252 N.W.2d 360 (1977); Bigelow v. Halloran, 313 N.W.2d 10 (Minn. 1981); Schlem-

mer v. Fireman's Fund Ins. Co., 292 Ark. 344, 730 S.W.2d 217 (1987); Jepson v. General Cas. Co. of Wisconsin, 513 N.W.2d 467 (Minn. 1994); and Victoria v. Smythe, 703 A.2d 619 (R.I.1997). In addition, four workers' compensation cases applied non-forum law, thus bringing the total to nine cases applying non-forum law. See Hunker v. Royal Indem. Co., 57 Wis.2d 588, 204 N.W.2d 897 (1973); Busby v. Perini Corp., 110 R.I. 49, 290 A.2d 210 (1972); LaBounty v. American Ins. Co., 122 N.H. 738, 451 A.2d 161 (1982); Ferren v. General Motors Corp., Delco Battery Div., 137 N.H. 423, 628 A.2d 265 (1993). In all four of the latter cases, the employment relationship was centered in the non-forum state, which also had most of the other relevant contacts.

15. Three of those cases (*Lichter, Bigelow,* and *Schlemmer,* supra n. 14) applied foreign law. The fourth case, Maguire v. Exeter & Hampton Elec. Co., 114 N.H. 589, 325 A.2d 778 (1974), did not apply the "better" foreign law, perhaps because that law disfavored a forum defendant. In Clark v. Clark, 107 N.H. 351, 222 A.2d 205 (1966), a case that applied forum law, Chief Justice Kennison said: "If it is our own law that is obsolete or senseless (and it could be) we will try to apply the other state's law." At 355 and 209. J.H.C. Morris observed in reply: " 'And it could be': there's the rub. Could it be? Is there any case in which a court has said 'Our law on this point is a drag on the coat-tails of civilization; if our legislature won't repeal it, we

law, but in two of them that law favored a forum plaintiff,[16] while in the third case a legislative change before the trial had eliminated the difference between the foreign and forum law.[17] Of the two remaining cases that applied foreign law, in one case that law produced the same result as a forum statute that was inapplicable on technical grounds,[18] while in the other case the foreign state had most of the relevant contacts.[19]

The bias in favor of forum law is more visible in lower-court cases, many of which never reach the state supreme court. For example, Minnesota's intermediate court has applied a Minnesota rule after proclaiming it "better" than the conflicting foreign rule, even after the Minnesota legislature repealed the Minnesota rule and replaced it with a rule identical to the rejected foreign rule.[20] Sometimes, even higher courts fall in the same trap. For example, in *Keeton v. Hustler Magazine, Inc.*,[21] the New Hampshire Supreme Court held that New Hampshire's six-year statute of limitation was better than the shorter statutes of other states, even after the New Hampshire legislature had voted to shorten that statute.

By the turn of the 20th century, the extreme applications of the better-law criterion that characterized the 1970s and 1980s have become much less frequent. This change is probably related to the fact that most of the states that initially adopted Leflar's approach now combine it with

will give it the narrowest possible scope; whenever it conflicts with the law of another state concerned (however remotely), we will apply the other state's law'? I doubt it." Morris, Law and Reason Triumphant or: How Not to Review a Restatement. 21 Am. J. Comp. L. 322, 324 (1973).

16. See *Lichter*, supra n. 14 (applying foreign law and providing recovery to a forum plaintiff who would not recover under forum law); and *Bigelow*, supra n. 14 (applying Iowa law and allowing recovery for an *intentional* tort committed in Iowa against a resident of that state. The plaintiff worked in Minnesota and later moved her domicile to that state. Under Iowa, but not Minnesota, law, the plaintiff's action survived the death of the tortfeasor). For a lower-court case, see Boatwright v. Budak, 625 N.W.2d 483 (Minn.App.2001) (concluding that Iowa law was better than Minnesota's in that it provided recovery for a Minnesota domiciliary who was injured in an Iowa traffic accident while riding in a car owned by a national car rental company).

17. See *Schlemmer*, supra n. 14.

18. See Victoria v. Smythe, 703 A.2d 619 (R.I.1997).

19. In Jepson v. General Cas. Co. of Wisc., 513 N.W.2d 467 (Minn.1994), the court applied North Dakota law which disfavored a Minnesota plaintiff. However, ex-

cept for the plaintiff's domicile, all other pertinent factors and contacts pointed to North Dakota. The court found the better-law factor inapposite because the two states' laws were "neither better nor worse in an objective way, just different." 513 N.W.2d at 473.

20. See Wille v. Farm Bureau Mut. Ins. Co. 432 N.W.2d 784 (Minn. Ct. App. 1988) (holding that Minnesota's stacking rule was "better" than Indiana's anti-stacking rule, even though in the interim the Minnesota legislature repealed the Minnesota rule and replaced it with an anti-stacking rule identical to Indiana's). See also Meir v. Auto Owners Ins. Co., 1989 WL 14913 (Minn. App.1989) (*accord*). *But see* Stenzel v. State Farm Mut. Auto. Ins. Co. 379 N.W.2d 674 (Minn.App. 1986) (concluding that, *because* of its recent repeal, the same Minnesota rule could no longer be considered the better rule of law). In Jepson v. General Cas. Co. of Wisconsin, 513 N.W.2d 467 (Minn. 1994), the Minnesota Supreme Court disapproved of both *Wille* and *Stenzel*. See id. at 473: "We disagree with the views expressed in *Stenzel* and *Wille* . . . as to which is the better rule of law. From our present day vantage point, neither the law Minnesota had then, nor the law we have now, is clearly better."

21. 131 N.H. 6, 549 A.2d 1187 (1988).

other approaches and de-emphasize the better-law factor.[22] Recent cases tend to use "restrain and moderation" in employing the better-law criterion by: expressing misgivings on their ability to determine which law is better;[23] by stating that better law and forum law should not be seen as synonymous terms,[24] by employing the better-law criterion only as a tie-breaker,[25] or by blending the better-law approach with other modern approaches.[26] These developments are symptomatic of the increased eclecticism[27] and independence exhibited by many courts in employing the modern choice-of-law methodologies, but do not necessarily reduce the validity of the criticisms directed against the original version of Leflar's approach.

At the same time, these criticisms, and generally the excesses of the better-law approach, should not lead to the total expulsion of material-justice considerations from the choice-of-law process, provided of course that appropriate safeguards are put in place so as to avoid the dangers of

---

22. See infra n. 26.

23. See Jepson v. General Cas. Co. of Wisc., 513 N.W.2d 467 at 473 (Minn.1994) ("From our present day vantage point, neither the law Minnesota had then, nor the law we have now, is clearly better. Sometimes different laws are neither better nor worse in an objective way, just different. Because we do not find either stacking or anti-stacking to be a better rule in the sense Leflar intended, this consideration does not influence our choice of law."); State Farm Mut. Auto. Ins. Co. v. Gillette, 251 Wis.2d 561, 641 N.W.2d 662, 678 (2002) ("We cannot say that Manitoba law is anachronistic or fails to reflect modern trends.... While it is arguable that the Manitoba law barring noneconomic damages may not be a Wisconsin 'justice-serving rule,' the Manitoba law is founded on a rational basis and serves a discernible purpose."); Lommen v. The City of East Grand Forks, 522 N.W.2d 148, 152 (Minn.Ct.App. 1994) ("[N]either Minnesota's nor North Dakota's law is 'better' than the other ... neither ... is demonstrably antiquated or plainly unfair ... [they] simply differ."); Kenna v. So–Fro Fabrics, Inc., 18 F.3d 623 at 627 (8th Cir.1994) ("[W]e are not in a position to decide that either [state's law] is the better rule of law.").

24. *Jepson,* 513 N.W.2d at 473("If [it] were true [that] forum law would always be the better law ... [then] this step in our choice of law analysis would be meaningless."). See also Boatwright v. Budak, 625 N.W.2d 483 (Minn.App.2001) (concluding that non-forum law was better than forum law).

25. See Nesladek v. Ford Motor Co., 876 F.Supp. 1061 (D.Minn.1994) aff'd 46 F.3d 734 (8th Cir.1995), cert. denied 516 U.S.

814, 116 S.Ct. 67, 133 L.Ed.2d 28 (1995), stating that the better-law factor need not be considered when Minnesota's other choice-influencing factors "clearly dictate the application of one state's law." Id. at 1070. See also Ferren v. General Motors Corp., Delco Battery Div., 137 N.H. 423, 628 A.2d 265, 269 (1993); Lessard v. Clarke, 143 N.H. 555, 736 A.2d 1226 (N.H.1999); Nodak Mutual Ins. Co. v. American Fam. Mut. Ins. Co., 604 N.W.2d 91 (Minn.2000); Najarian v. National Amusements, Inc., 768 A.2d 1253 (R.I.2001).

26. See, e.g, Nodak Mut. Ins. Co. v. American Fam. Mut. Ins. Co., 604 N.W.2d 91, 94, 96 (Minn.2000) (describing the Minnesota approach as "the significant contacts test" and stating that "this court has not placed any emphasis on [the better-law] factor in nearly 20 years"); State Farm Mut. Auto. Ins. Co. v. Gillette, 251 Wis.2d 561, 641 N.W.2d 662 (2002) (prefacing its application of the five Leflar factors with a statement resurrected from a 30–year old precedent, to the effect that the primary choice-of-law rule in Wisconsin is that " 'the law of the forum should presumptively apply unless it becomes clear that nonforum contacts are of the greater significance.' " Id. at 676, quoting Hunker v. Royal Indem. Co., 57 Wis.2d 588, 599, 204 N.W.2d 897 (1973) (quoting Wilcox v. Wilcox, 26 Wis.2d 617, 634, 133 N.W.2d 408 (1965))); Cribb v. Augustyn, 696 A.2d 285 (R.I.1997), discussed infra § 2.19 nn 13–14; Najarian v. National Amusements, Inc., 768 A.2d 1253 (R.I.2001); Kenna v. So–Fro Fabrics, Inc., 18 F.3d 623 (8th Cir.1994) (decided under North Dakota conflicts law).

27. See infra §§ 2.19, 2.25; Symeonides, supra n. 12 at 95–96, 114–116.

ad hoc subjectivism. Such considerations have always been a part of the process, even in traditional private international law systems.[28] For example, virtually all private international law codifications contain result-oriented choice-of-law rules (*règles de conflit à coloration matérielle*), namely rules designed to accomplish certain substantive results that are considered a priori as desirable, such as: (1) favoring the formal or substantive validity of a juridical act, such as a testament, a marriage, or an ordinary contract; (2) favoring a certain status, such as the status of legitimacy or filiation, the status of a spouse, or even the dissolution of a status (divorce); or (3) favoring a particular party, such as a tort victim, a consumer, an employee, a maintenance obligee, or any other party whom the legal order considers weak or whose interests are considered worthy of protection. The first two objectives (favoring the validity of a juridical act or favoring a certain status) are accomplished by choice-of-law rules that authorize the court to apply whichever one of the laws of listed states validates the juridical act or confers the preferred status (*alternative-reference rules*).[29] The third objective (protecting a particular party) is accomplished through choice-of-law rules that: (a) provide alternative choices to the court as above; (b) allow the protected party, either before or after the events giving rise to the dispute, to choose the applicable law from among the laws of more than one state; or (c) protect that party from the adverse consequences of a potentially coerced or uninformed choice of law.[30]

The existence of so many result-oriented rules in traditional conflicts systems suggests that legislatures have always understood the need to temper the pursuit of "conflicts justice" with considerations of "material justice."[31] This in itself is not surprising. What might be surprising is that this phenomenon is now taken for granted and does not evoke the criticisms that have at times been directed against the better-law approach in the United States. One reason for this difference may be that because the better-law approach is intended for judicial application, that approach entails the unavoidable risk of judicial subjectivism.[32] In con-

28. For discussion and comparison of these rules, see S. Symeonides, Private International Law at the End of the 20th Century: Progress or Regress? 46–60 (1999); Vrellis, La justice "matérielle" dans une codification du droit international privé, in E Pluribus Unum, Liber Amicorum Georges Droz, 541 (1996).

29. See Symeonides, supra n. 28 at 49–56.

30. See id. at 56–60.

31. Cf. Symeonides, American Choice of Law at the Dawn of the 20th Century, 37 Willamette L. Rev. 1, 67 (2000) (suggesting that the fact that so many codified conflicts systems, which are typically perceived as the bastions of conflicts justice, saw it fit to enact so many choice-of-law rules specifically designed to accomplish a particular substantive result suggests either that this per-

ception is wrong or that the material-justice view has gained significant ground over the classical view; concluding that "this phenomenon suggests that the dilemma is no longer (and perhaps it never should have been) an "either or" choice between conflicts justice and material justice. Rather, it is a question of when, how, and how much the desideratum of material justice should temper the search for conflicts justice."

32. As Nygh points out: "one court's better law may be another's worse. It is only by reference to an ideology that a court can in some cases make a choice as to which is the better law; there needs to be a commitment in some cases to allowing the 'collective good' to prevail." P. E. Nygh, Conflict of Laws in Australia 29 (6th ed. 1995).

trast, this risk is avoided when result-selectivity is pursued by the legislature through carefully crafted choice-of-law rules where the desirable substantive result is defined through collective democratic processes.[33] Another reason might be that the better-law approach was advanced as an all-encompassing methodology to be employed in all cases, even if its proponent did not envision the better-law criterion to be the overriding choice-criterion, but rather one out of many. In contrast again, the legislative use of material-justice considerations is far less controversial because it remains exceptional and is employed only when there is general consensus on what the desired substantive result ought to be.

The above comparison may suggest that many of the differences between the American and the continental European approaches have more to do with the differences in the relative role of legislators and judges in their respective legal systems than with a genuine disagreement in fundamental policy. Indeed, it may not be too much of an oversimplification to say that much of what American approaches endeavor to do judicially, European systems endeavor to do legislatively.[34] However, the very use of different implements tends to magnify the real and apparent differences in implementation. American solutions appear more ad hoc, more subjective, more extreme, while European solutions appear more objective, consistent, and moderate. Yet the real differences are often differences in degree rather than in substance.[35]

V. THE SECOND RESTATEMENT

§ 2.14 Most approaches and analyses since the First Restatement, except perhaps Currie's, sought a formula for the application of foreign law in appropriate cases and "the right line between excess of rigidity ... and excess of flexibility."[1] The American Law Institute's Second Restatement drew on much of the thought of the period during which it was drafted (1952–1971) and attempted to provide as much of "the right line," the balance, as was possible in light of the development of the law at that time. Beyond *restating*, the work also aspired to be a guide for

---

33. See Symeonides, Material Justice and Conflicts Justice in Choice of Law, in International Conflict of Laws for the Third Millennium: Essays in Honor of Friedrich K. Juenger, 125, 139–40 (P. Borchers & J. Zekoll eds. 2000) (arguing that "there is an important qualitative difference between result-selectivism in legislation and result-selectivism in adjudication. In the former, the desirable result is determined in advance and *in abstracto* through the consensus mechanisms of the collective democratic processes. In the latter, the result is chosen *ex post facto* and *in concreto* and often by a single individual who, with the best of intentions, cannot easily avoid the dangers of subjectivism.")

34. See Symeonides, PIL supra n.28, at 77.

35. Id. Indeed, many of the ideas that were advocated in the United States during the second half of the 20th century also surfaced in Europe, usually in a more moderate form. This is not to say that the former caused the latter. After all, capable independent minds confronted with similar problems are likely to arrive at similar solutions even if they were to function in isolation.

§ 2.14

1. Kahn–Freund, General Problems of Private International Law, 143 Recueil des Cours 139, 468 (1974–III).

the future,[2] an aspect that clearly distinguishes it from the First Restatement as well as from Restatements in other fields of law.

Except with respect to relatively few areas for which it provides clear rules,[3] the Second Restatement's system is characterized by three principal features: the policies of Section 6, the concept of the "most significant relationship," and the lists of particularized connecting factors.

Section 6 is the cornerstone of the entire Restatement. It provides a list of general policy considerations that draws[4] on the considerations presented in a 1952 article by Professor Cheatham and the Restatement's Reporter, Professor Reese.[5] The list is prefaced by the statement that a court must first follow a statutory directive of the forum to the extent such directive is constitutional. In the absence of such a directive, the court is to consider the following factors in choosing the applicable law: (1) the needs of the interstate and international systems; (2) the relevant policies of the forum state; (3) the relevant policies of other interested states and their respective interests in having their law applied to the particular issue; (4) the protection of party expectations; (5) the basic policies underlying the particular field of law, (6) the objectives of certainty, predictability, and uniformity of result; and (7) the ease of determining and applying the law identified as applicable.

From a philosophical perspective, Section 6 is important in that it establishes the ideology of the Restatement in a way that distinguishes it from other rival modern theories such as Leflar's "better-law" approach or Currie's interest analysis. For example, the "better-law" criterion is noticeably absent[6] from the list of factors contained in § 6. Moreover, the list is broader and qualitatively different from the policies relied upon by Currie's, whose analysis disregards, de-emphasizes, or expressly rejects most of the § 6 factors other than the policies of the forum and the other involved state(s). The contrast between interest analysis and the Restatement is clearest in their varying degrees of sensitivity towards "the needs of the interstate and international systems" and the need for "uniformity of result." To Currie's ethnocentric attitude toward both of these goals,[7] the Restatement juxtaposes a universalistic perception of

---

2. See Reese, Choice of Law: Rules or Approach, 57 Cornell L. Rev. 315 (1972); Reese, The Present State of Choice of Law in the United States, in: International Law Association 1873–1973, The Present State of International law 361 (M. Bos, ed., 1973).

3. See Reese, supra n.2, at 368–369; Reese, Discussion of Major Areas of Choice of Law, 111 Recueil des Cours 315, 360 ff. (1964–I). The Restatement's rules are described infra nn.27 *et seq.*

4. Reese, Conflict of Laws and the Restatement, Second, 28 Law & Contemp. Prob. 679, 682 (1963).

5. Cheatham & Reese, Choice of the Applicable Law, 52 Colum. L. Rev. 959 (1952).

6. The original article by Cheatham & Reese, supra n.5, had contained two additional policies: the desirability of applying forum law unless there is a good reason for not doing so, and justice in the individual case. Reese reiterated the first policy in 1964 (supra n.3, "Discussion . . . ," at 342) and Ehrenzweig applauded it, supra § 2.10 n.9, at 400 n.101. The second policy comes close to a "better law," result-selective approach (supra n.5, at 980). Neither policy was ultimately adopted by the American Law Institute in the formulation of § 6.

7. See, e.g., B. Currie, Selected Essays on the Conflict of Laws 614 (1963) (specifically dismissing the view that a state should be guided in its choice-of-law decisions by

private international law reflected in the statement that "the most important function of choice-of-law rules is to make the interstate and international systems work well[,] ... to further harmonious relations between states and to facilitate commercial intercourse between them."[8] The contrast is hardly surprising, since, unlike interest analysis which was conceived from the perspective of the forum judge confined to the role of the "handmaiden"[9] of the forum legislature, the Restatement was drafted from the perspective of a neutral forum[10] under the auspices of the American Law Institute, a body that strives for national uniformity.

From a methodological viewpoint, Section 6 is important in that it establishes the test that should guide the application of almost all other sections of the Restatement, most of which incorporate § 6 by reference.[11] The test consists of multiple and diverse[12] factors that, by themselves, will not enable a court to make a choice because they are not listed in any order of priority and because they will often point in different directions in a given case.[13] Even so, these factors suggest that the Restatement's approach is not jurisdiction-selective[14] in the same sense as this was characteristic of the older practice. While the Restatement calls for the application of the law of the state with the "most significant relationship"—a term that evokes jurisdiction-selecting notions—and while the Restatement often designates that state through specific rules, most of these rules are presumptive or tentative (see infra) and can be displaced through a reference to § 6. At that point, the policy-analysis part of § 6 becomes critical and helps convert the process from one of jurisdiction-selection to one of rule-selection and leads to

the "needs of the interstate and international system").

8. Restatement Second, Conflict of Laws (Second) § 6 cmt. d (1971).

9. See Peterson, Weighing Contacts in Conflicts Cases: The Hand–Maiden Axiom, 9 Duquesne L. Rev. 436 (1971).

10. Reese, Discussion of Major Areas of Choice of Law, 111 Recueil des Cours 315, 357 ff. (1964–I); Reese, Conflict of Laws and the Restatement, Second, 28 Law & Contemp. Prob. 679, 692 (1963). Compare Currie's reaction to the latter passage in Currie, The Disinterested Third State, 28 Law & Contemp. Probs. 754, 765–766 (1963).

11. See, e.g., Restatement (Second) § 145 (torts):

"(1) [Tort liability to be determined according to the law of the state which] has the most significant relationship to the occurrence and the parties under the principles stated in § 6.

(2) Contacts to be taken into account in applying the principles of § 6.... include: ..."

12. The eclectic diversity of these factors provides a basis for the conclusion

reached by many that competing conflicts theories will, in the future, continue to co-exist and that there will not be one "true approach" to all conflict-of-law situations. See Batiffol, Le pluralisme des méthodes en droit international privé, 139 Recueil des Cours 75, 106 (1973–II); Cheatham, American Theories of Conflict of Laws, 58 Harv. L. Rev. 361, 392 (1945); Tooker v. Lopez, 24 N.Y.2d 569, 596, 301 N.Y.S.2d 519, 542, 249 N.E.2d 394, 411 (1969) (Breitel, J., dissenting) ("Certain it is that contacts theory or governmental interest theory ... all help to explain the several influences effective in reaching results, but no one of them is entitled to recognition as a universal touchstone, yesterday, today, or tomorrow;"); Neumeier v. Kuehner, 31 N.Y.2d 121, 130, 335 N.Y.S.2d 64, 71, 286 N.E.2d 454, 459 (1972) (Breitel, J., concurring) ("it is undesirable to lay down prematurely major premises based on shifting ideologies in the choice of law.").

13. Restatement, Second, § 6, cmt. (c), at 12.

14. But see Kay, Book Review, 18 J. Legal Ed. 341, 346 (1966).

blending the multilateral with the unilateral approaches.[15] Secondly, the factors of § 6, as well as the specific sections of the Restatement, are *issue*-oriented. Resolution of a particular issue is referred to the law of particular law state, not because of an *a priori* choice but rather as a result of the individualized policy analysis that § 6 requires. This emphasis on particular issues also means that different issues in a single case may be governed by different laws,[16] a splitting process known as *dépeçage*.

The ubiquitous "most-significant-relationship" formula is the Restatement's other fundamental concept. While § 6 enunciates the guiding principles of the choice-of-law process, the most-significant-relationship formula describes the *objective* of that process: to apply the law of the state that, with regard to the particular issue, has the most significant relationship with the parties and the dispute. This is not a new concept. Westlake in England referred to "the most real connection" as early as 1880,[17] and one can find references to similar concepts in some American cases in the 1940s and 1950s.[18] The similarity with Savigny's concept of the "seat" of a legal relationship is readily apparent,[19] except that in the Restatement, the "seat" is not necessarily that of the entire relationship but rather of operative issues. Even traditional European codes have used similar concepts,[20] as have more recent codifications and treaties,[21] regardless of whether this is the result of American influence. What is new in the Restatement is the elevation of the most-significant-

15. See S. Symeonides, Private International Law at the End of the 20th Century: Progress or Regress? 15 (1999) (concluding that "despite a Savignian-sounding exhortation to apply the law of the state of the 'most significant relationship,' and despite other elaborate appearances of a multilateral approach, the Restatement Second is ample enough to include a unilateral approach."); Peterson, American Private International Law, in Symeonides, supra, at 430–31 ("The presumptive rules of the Second Restatement are essentially multilateral, referring categories of disputes to those legal systems to which they bear the 'most significant relationship' . . . One of the central principles of § 6, however, under which [the] presumptions of such rules can be rebutted, is consideration of 'the relevant policies of the forum.' This invites a unilateral approach to choice of law, by defining the spatial reach of domestic law through interpretation of underlying policy.").

16. See, e.g., with reference to torts, Restatement, Second, Conflict of Laws § 145, cmnt. (d) (1971); with respect to contracts: id. § 188, cmt. (d), at 579. See also infra nn.49–51; Casper v. Cunard Line, Ltd., 560 F.Supp. 240 (E.D.Pa.1983).

17. J. Westlake, A Treatise on Private International Law § 201, at 237 (2d ed. 1880).

18. For contracts see: W.H. Barber Co. v. Hughes, 223 Ind. 570, 63 N.E.2d 417, 423 (1945); Chinchilla v. Foreign Tankship Corp., 195 Misc. 895, 91 N.Y.S.2d 213 (City Ct.1949), modified 197 Misc. 1058, 97 N.Y.S.2d 835 (Sup.Ct.1950), judgment affirmed 278 App.Div. 556, 102 N.Y.S.2d 438 (1951); Auten v. Auten, 308 N.Y. 155, 124 N.E.2d 99 (1954). For torts see, Lauritzen v. Larsen, 345 U.S. 571, 73 S.Ct. 921, 97 L.Ed. 1254 (1953); Noel v. Airponents, Inc., 169 F.Supp. 348 (D.N.J.1958).

19. See the last connecting factor listed in connection with torts, infra n.23, and, in contract (Restatement (Second) § 188(3)) providing in essence that, when a contract was negotiated and to be performed in the same state, that state's law will usually be applied (i.e., it is the "center"). See also § 146. For Savigny, see supra § 2.6 nn.10–13.

20. See, e.g. Article 25 of the Greek Civil Code of 1940, which provides that, in the absence of choice of law by the parties, contracts are to be governed by the law of which, "according to all the special circumstances, is the proper law of the contract."

21. See infra § 2.27.

relationship concept to a *pervasive* reference. Although this reference is inherently vague and thus uncertain (a criticism to be addressed below), the specific connecting factors the Restatement utilizes draw heavily on traditional learning, including the rules of the First Restatement. One contribution of the Second Restatement thus lies in the decision of its drafters *not* to abandon achievements of the past but to soften[22] the rigidity of the traditional approach by making the single connecting factor (e.g., place of injury) *one* among *several*[23] to be considered and by providing the concept of the "most-significant relationship" as a guiding principle. A corollary of the "most significant relationship" test is that the parties, by their own choice, should be able to give their relationship a center, that is, stipulate the applicable law. "Party autonomy," which dates at least to the sixteenth century European statutist conflicts theory[24] but was rejected by the First Restatement, was endorsed by the Second Restatement subject to some limitations,[25] and now finds nearly universal acceptance in the case law.[26]

In relatively few cases, the Restatement identifies *a priori* the state with the most significant relationship through black-letter rules. This is the case with most of the sections devoted to property and succession issues.[27] In cases involving land, the applicable law is almost invariably the "law that would be applied by the courts of the situs."[28] This is as close as the Restatement comes to prescribing black-letter choice-of-law rules.[29]

In other cases, the Restatement tentatively identifies the state of the most significant relationship through presumptive rules that instruct the

---

22. On the gradual "softening of concepts" in the history of conflicts theory see Kahn–Freund, General Problems of Private International Law, 143 Recueil des Cours 139, 406–09 (1974–III).

23. Connecting factors suggested for tort (§ 145) include: the place where the injury occurred; the place where the conduct causing the injury occurred; the domicile, nationality, residence, place of business, or place of incorporation of the parties, and the "place where the relationship, if any, between the parties is centered." Similarly for contract (§ 188), the connecting factors include: the place of negotiation, formation, or performance of the contract, the place where the object of the contract is located, and, again, the parties' domicile, nationality, residence, place of business or incorporation.

24. See F. Juenger, Choice of Law and Multistate Justice, 8, 10, 17, 33–41 (1993); Lipstein, The General Principles of Private International Law, 135 Recueil des Cours 96, 119–20 (1972–I); Kahn–Freund, supra n.22, at 407.

25. See Restatement, Second, § 187 (discussed infra ch. 18).

26. See infra §§ 18.1–18.12.

27. For succession to movables, see Restatement (Second) §§ 260–65; For inter-vivos transactions involving movables, see §§ 245–55. See also the unilateral choice-of-law rules contained in §§ 285 (divorce), 286 (nullity of marriage), and 289 (adoption).

28. For inter vivos transactions involving land, see Restatement (Second) §§ 223, 225–32. For succession to land, see §§ 236, 239–42. This phrase is often accompanied by the prediction that these courts "usually" will apply their own law. For a recent critique of these rules and the way in which they have been applied by courts, see Weintraub, "At Least, to Do No Harm": Does the Second Restatement of Conflicts Meet the Hippocratic Standard? 56 Md. L. Rev. 1284, 1307–1309 (1997).

29. These rules are subject to the traditional escape mechanisms of the generic type, such as *ordre public* and *renvoi*. For example, the above-quoted phrase regarding land is an explicit authorization for *renvoi*, which contains the potential for applying, in appropriate cases, a law other than that of the situs state.

judge to apply the law of a certain state, unless it appears that in the particular case another state has a "more significant" relationship. For example, all ten of the Restatement sections that designate the law governing various types of torts conclude with the following escape clause: "unless, with respect to the particular issue, some other state has a more significant relationship under the principles stated in section 6 to the occurrence and the parties, in which event the local law of the other state will be applied."[30] This clause is one of the most repeated phrases in the entire Restatement.[31] In some instances, the presumptive rules are even more equivocal and amount to no more than mere pointers in the direction of the presumptively applicable law. The pertinent sections provide that the state with the most significant relationship will "usually" be one particular state.[32]

Finally, in the remaining and most difficult cases, the Restatement does not even attempt to enunciate presumptive rules. It simply provides a non-exclusive, non-hierarchical list of the factual contacts or connecting factors that should be "taken into account" by the judge in choosing the applicable law. This choice is to be made "under the principles stated in § 6" by "taking into account" the above factual contacts "according to their relative importance with respect to the particular issue."[33] This language suggests that the policy part of this analysis should carry more weight than the evaluation of the factual contacts. Yet, courts have tended to do it the other way around by first focusing on the factual contacts listed in the pertinent Restatement section and then, if ever, on the policies of § 6. When the contacts of state A are more numerous than

30. See, e.g., Restatement, Second, § 152 which provides that, in an action for an invasion of privacy, the applicable law is the local law of the state where the invasion occurred, "unless, with respect to the particular issue, some other state has a more significant relationship."

31. See, e.g., Restatement, Second, §§ 146–51, 153–55, 175. In the area of contract conflicts, the "unless" clause appears in most of the sections devoted to particular contracts. See, e.g., §§ 189–93, 196.

32. For example, in the area of tort conflicts, eleven of the nineteen sections devoted to specific tort issues conclude with the adage that "[t]he applicable law will usually be the local law of the state where the injury occurred." See Restatement (Second) § 156 (tortious character of conduct), § 157 (standard of care), § 158 (interest entitled to legal protection), § 159 (duty owed to plaintiff), § 160 (legal cause), § 162 (specific conditions of liability), § 164 (contributory fault), § 165 (assumption of risk), § 166 (imputed negligence), and § 172 (joint torts); one section (§ 169) provides that for intrafamily immunity the applicable law "will usually be the local law of the state of the parties' domicil;" and only the

remaining seven sections are unaided by such a presumption. See §§ 161, 163, 168, 170–71, and 173–174.

In contract conflicts, Restatement, Second, § 188 provides that, subject to some exceptions, "[i]f the place of negotiating the contract and the place of performance are in the same state, the local law of this state will usually be applied." Similarly, § 198 provides that "[t]he capacity of a party to contract will usually be upheld if he has such capacity under the local law of the state of his domicil," while § 199 provides that contractual "[f]ormalities which meet the requirements of the place where the parties execute the contract will usually be acceptable." Similar language is found in many other sections of the Second Restatement.

33. See, e.g., Restatement, Second, §§ 145, 188. According to Borchers, courts rely on these general open-ended sections of the Restatement such as §§ 145, 188 and, especially § 6, much more frequently than on the specific sections that contain presumptive rules. See Borchers, Courts and the Second Conflicts Restatement: Some Observations and an Empirical Note, 56 Md. L. Rev. 1232, 1240–46 (1997).

those of state B, some courts assume that state A is the one that has the more significant relationship without testing that assumption under the principles of § 6. In contrast, when the factual contacts are evenly divided between the two states, courts look to the policies of § 6, but many courts pay lip service to most of the policies listed therein, and confine themselves to examining "the relative policies of the forum" and of "other interested states."[34] It seems that cases that follow the first practice differ little from cases that follow a "grouping of contacts" approach, while cases that follow the latter practice differ little from cases that follow a pure interest analysis.[35]

The Second Restatement drew severe criticism, both while it was still in preparation and upon its adoption by the American Law Institute. Currie's was critical, as was Ehrenzweig who spoke of its "non-rules,"[36] invoked "Law and Reason" against its adoption,[37] and pleaded for its withdrawal.[38] Cavers was more sympathetic. He was troubled, however, by the fact that although policy factors such as those stated in § 6 invariably call for a preference, the preference had not been stated in terms "both articulate and principled."[39] In Europe, the initial reaction was also critical.[40] One writer spoke of "legal impressionism,"[41] a term later also adopted by Nadelmann.[42] In contrast, J.H.C. Morris, chief editor of five editions of *Dicey's Conflict of Laws*, considered the Second

34. See See Symeonides, The Judicial Acceptance of the Second Conflicts Restatement: A Mixed Blessing, 56 Md. L. Rev. 1248, 1263 (1997).

35. See Juenger, Conflict of Laws: A Critique of Interest Analysis, 32 Am. J. Comp. L. 1, 21–22 (1984) (concluding that "many courts prefer a melange of the Second Restatement and interest analysis."). See also Kay, Theory into Practice: Choice of Law in the Courts, 34 Mercer L. Rev. 521, 572 (1984).

36. Ehrenzweig, A Counter–Revolution in Conflicts Law? From Beale to Cavers, 80 Harv. L. Rev. 377, 381 (1966).

37. See, e.g., Ehrenzweig, The Most Significant Relationship in the Conflict of Laws—Law and Reason versus the Restatement, Second, 28 Law & Contemp. Prob. 700 (1963); Ehrenzweig, Parental Immunity in the Conflict of Laws: Law and Reason versus the Restatement, 23 U. Chi. L. Rev. 474 (1956).

38. See Ehrenzweig, The Second Conflicts Restatement: A Last Appeal for its Withdrawal, 113 U. Pa. L. Rev. 123 (1965).

39. Cavers, Contemporary Conflicts Law in American Perspective, 131 Recueil des Cours 77, 145–46 (1970–III). See also Cavers, Re–Restating the Conflict of Laws: The Chapter on Contracts, XXth Century Comparative and Conflicts Law—Legal Essays in Honor of Hessel E. Yntema 349 (1961); Sedler, The Contract Provision in

the Restatement Second: An Analysis and a Critique, 72 Colum. L. Rev. 279 (1972); Leflar, The Torts Provisions in the Restatement (Second), 72 Colum. L. Rev. 267 (1972); von Mehren, Le Second "Restatement" of the Conflict of Laws, 101 Clunet 815 (1974); von Mehren, Recent Trends in Choice-of-Law Methodology, 60 Cornell L. Rev. 927 (1975); Weintraub, The Contracts Proposals of the Second Restatement of Conflict of Laws—A Critique, 46 Iowa L. Rev. 713 (1961).

40. See Audit, Le Second "Restatement" du Conflit de Lois aux Etats–Unis, Travaux du Comité Français: De Droit International Privé 29 (1977–79); Rodolfo de Nova, Il "Restatement, Second, Conflict of Laws," 10 Riv. Dir. Int'le Priv. Proces. 424 (1974); Vischer, Das Neue Restatement "Conflict of Laws," 38 Rabelsz 128 (1974); Nadelmann, Impressionism and Unification of Law: The EEC Draft Convention on the Law Applicable to Contractual and Non–Contractual Obligations, 24 Am. J. Comp. L. 1, 11 (1976).

41. Loussouarn, Cours général de droit international privé, 139 Recueil des Cours 269, 338, 342 (1973–II).

42. Nadelmann, Impressionism and Unification of Law: The EEC Draft Convention on the Law Applicable to Contractual and Non–Contractual Obligations, 24 Am. J. Comp. L. 1, 11, 12, 21 (1976).

Restatement "the most impressive, comprehensive and valuable work on the conflict of laws that has ever been produced in any country, in any language, at any time."[43]

At least initially, the Second Restatement's principal characteristic lay in the *approach* it provided. But the fact that the Restatement provided an approach rather than rules does not warrant its dismissal as being limited to "non-rules" or as being impressionistic. Earlier discussion pointed to the interrelationship of the underlying policies of § 6, of the most-significant-relationship concept, and of the specific connecting factors the Restatement provides to aid in the determination and localization of the latter: an approach designed to lead to rules through future development in the case law.[44] In some areas, it is possible to identify *typical* law-fact patterns early and to determine the respective place of the most significant relationship in advance,[45] subject, of course, to the continuing corrective function of § 6 and the policies identified there. In many areas, however, the case law must first grow before patterns become discernible, the application of the approach gains in consistency, and rules with precedent value emerge. In the latter type of case, this takes time and the judicial task is difficult.[46] The degree to which the courts have adopted the Second Restatement,[47] however, attests to their willingness to undertake the task of accommodating the concerns of policy and interest analysis suggested by the scholars and to develop new rules.

43. Morris, Law and Reason Triumphant or: How Not to Review a Restatement, 21 Am. J. Comp. L. 322, 330 (1973).

44. In discussing *Babcock v. Jackson*, Professor Reese noted that the decision "left open the most important question of all, namely whether one should seek to develop rules of choice of law or rather give the courts no guidance other than that they should consider a number of factors in arriving at their decisions. This basic question remains unanswered in the United States today. The uncertainty or ambiguity of *Babcock* is reflected in the Restatement ..." Reese, The Present State of Choice of Law in the United States, in: International Law Association 1873–1973, The Present State of International law 361 (M. Bos, ed., 1973) ("The Present State ... "), at 364–365. But also: "... the American Law Institute is clearly in favour of rules," id. at 366, and accomplishes this through the statement of rules in cases where the law is sufficiently developed to do so, through guidance in the form of presumptions, *passim,* and, one should add, through numerous and carefully drafted illustrations designed to show the application of a section to hypothetical but often typical case situations. See also Reese, Choice of Law: Rules or Approach, 57 Cornell L. Rev. 315, 334 (1972) (suggesting that the work of the courts will lead to

concrete rules for specific issues which will be satisfactory (and applicable) to the great majority of cases); Reese, Choice of Law in Torts and Contracts and Directions for the Future, 16 Colum. J. Trans. L. 1, 39–44 (1977); Reese, The Second Restatement of Conflict of Laws Revisited, 34 Mercer L. Rev. 501, 517 (1983); Bodenheimer, The Need for a Reorientation in American Conflicts Law, in: Internationales Recht und Wirtschaftsordnung, Festschrift für F. A. Mann 124, 141 (1977); Hay, Reflections on Conflicts Law Methodology, 32 Hastings L.J. 1644 (1981).

45. See the German Codification of choice of law for unjust enrichment of 1999: Art. 38, Int. Law to be Civil Code (EGBGB), Bundesgesetzblatt 1999, I, 1026. For discussion, see Hay, From Rule–Orientation to "Approach" in German Conflicts Law: The Effect of the 1986 and 1999 Codifications," 47 Am. J. Comp. L. 633, 643–44 (1999).

46. See Nadelmann, Impressionism and Unification of Law: The EEC Draft Convention on the Law Applicable to Contractual and Non–Contractual Obligations, 24 Am. J. Comp. L. 1, 11 (1976) ("The courts are very much left on their own."). But see supra n.44.

47. See infra § 2.23.

Difficulties do exist, however, in other respects. It is a judicial task of some magnitude to define the place of the most significant relationship in light of § 6 and of the multiple connecting factors, or to weigh factors for their "relative" significance.[48] Moreover, since the Restatement is issue-oriented, "relative significance" is to be determined "with respect to the *particular issue*."[49] The English approach, in contrast, seeks to identify a *single* "proper law." In contract cases, the "proper" law applies to *all* issues arising from the contract and therefore avoids a splitting of issues (*dépeçage*).[50] With *dépeçage* encouraged in the Restatement, law-fact patterns multiply rather than become reduced to archetypal situations as Cavers had envisioned.[51] Thus, the rules one can expect from the judicial application of the Restatement's approach will have to be fairly *narrow* and will depend on the parties, the nature of the case (e.g., intra-family litigation or commercial), and the area of the law involved.

Another difficulty lies in the fact that all Restatement illustrations are deliberately drafted from the perspective of a *neutral* forum.[52] Yet very few cases arise in a completely neutral forum. If the forum is not neutral, the forum-oriented elements in the policies of § 6 mentioned earlier may gain in relative importance. The specific geographic contacts enumerated in various Restatement sections (for instance, § 145 with respect to tort) may serve as a restrictive influence on a "homeward trending" court and lead to the adoption of a middle ground. However, if the forum is not neutral, then there is a danger that a policy in favor of furthering local governmental interests, which is mentioned in § 6, might result in a general preference for forum law.[53] If this danger

---

48. See Restatement, Second, §§ 145(2), 188(2), with respect to torts and contracts, respectively: "These contacts are to be evaluated according to their relative importance with respect to the particular issue."

49. Id. (emphasis added).

50. Morris, Law and Reason Triumphant or: How Not to Review a Restatement, 21 Am. J. Comp. L. 322, at 327 (1973). Also in favor of avoiding unnecessary *dépeçage*, Hay, supra n.45, at 647–48, in connection with the Restatement's provision on restitution which repeats the "relative importance" language of the other sections see: § 221(2). But see Reese, Dépeçage: A Common Phenomenon in Choice of Law, 73 Colum. L. Rev. 58, 59–60 (1973), who thinks that the development of narrow choice-of-law *rules*—in contrast to broad jurisdiction-selective references—necessarily requires the application of different laws to different issues in appropriate cases. Similarly, Wilde, *Dépeçage* in the Choice of Tort Law, 41 So. Cal. L. Rev. 329 (1968). In reviewing the Restatement, the Swiss scholar Professor Vischer also notes that the Restatement's emphasis on "par-

ticular issues" will increase the frequency of *dépeçage* but thought that this result might be tolerable in the American *domestic*-interstate-context because of the shared common law background. Vischer, Das neue Restatement "Conflict of Laws," 38 RabelsZ 128, 149 (1974).

51. See Cavers, Contemporary Conflicts Law in American Perspective, 131 Recueil des Cours 77, 152 (1970–III).

52. See supra n.10.

53. See, e.g., Justice Brennan's dissent in Shaffer v. Heitner, 433 U.S. 186, 224–25, 97 S.Ct. 2569, 2591, 53 L.Ed.2d 683 (1977). Brennan acknowledged that the "jurisdictional and choice-of-law inquiries are not the same" but pointed to Justice Black's dissent in Hanson v. Denckla, 357 U.S. 235, 258, 78 S.Ct. 1228, 1242, 2 L.Ed.2d 1283 (1958), who had noted that both inquiries "are often closely related and to a substantial degree depend upon similar considerations." As a matter of policy, Brennan said, "practical considerations argue in favor of seeking to bridge the distance between the choice-of-law and jurisdictional inquiries." Therefore, at least, "when a

materializes, then the Restatement's considerable and innovative achievement will be lost.

Lastly, the Restatement continues, by hypothesis, the litigation-oriented pattern of American conflicts approaches. In other words, it is self-defining through litigation. By providing an approach for the elaboration of rules often yet unknown rather than suggesting rules for judicial acceptance, it shares with most other approaches a lack of certainty and predictability for conflicts situations in which there has been no prior litigation.[54] "Most conflicts discussions concern court cases on torts and regulatory laws, yet most lawyers' work is directed to other matters. Law is applied to a far greater extent by lawyers in their offices than by courts."[55] Predictability is thus important whether or not litigation occurs. These problems do not result from the peculiar "American context"—the Common-law legal system and the need to resolve various state statutory conflicts—as some have suggested.[56] After all, statutory conflicts are much more common in civil-law countries.[57]. In these countries, settled judicial precedents fill the statutory gaps. In the United States, matters are more in flux and the filling of gaps is just

suitor seeks to lodge a suit in a State with a substantial interest in seeing its own law applied . . ., we could wisely act to minimize conflicts, confusion, and uncertainty by adopting a liberal view of jurisdiction, unless considerations of fairness or efficiency strongly point in the opposite direction." *Shaffer* concerned the exercise of jurisdiction by Delaware over out-of-state defendants, all present or former directors of a Delaware corporation, in a suit arising out of an alleged breach of their fiduciary duties as corporate officers. In this *narrow* context, Delaware might well be said to have a regulatory interest in the conduct of the internal affairs of a domestic corporation (Restatement (Second) § 309), justifying *both* the exercise for jurisdiction *and* the application of its law to the merits of the case. However, it does not follow–and the quoted language is overgeneral in this respect–that (a) jurisdiction follows applicable law as the result of a unilaterally declared "state interest" in the application of local law, nor (b) that local jurisdiction, without more, should automatically result in the application of the *lex fori*. When the choice of law results from the "most significant relationship" test, "minimum contacts" for jurisdiction will likely be present. The reverse obviously is not true. Thus, besides status cases (but see infra ch. 15), a merger of choice of law and jurisdiction is true only in cases of state exercise of *regulatory* power. In all other cases, the two *may*, but *need not,* coincide depending on the particular facts of the case. Any other approach, such as the one the quoted language suggests, would make "state interest" the most im-

portant criterion among the value goals and principles the Second Restatement provides and would frustrate its objective to aid in the elaboration of principled choice-of-law rules. The *jurisdictional* territorialism of Pennoyer v. Neff, 95 U.S. (5 Otto) 714, 24 L.Ed. 565 (1877), which *Shaffer* and subsequent decisions laid to rest, would be replaced by the new territorialism of the *lex fori*. For further discussion see infra § 3.20; Hay, The Interrelationship Between Jurisdiction and Choice of Law in U.S. Conflicts Law, 28 Int'l & Comp. L.Q. 161 (1979); Hay, Reflections on Conflicts Law Methodology, 32 Hastings L.J. 1644 (1981).

54. Kahn–Freund, supra n.22. at 246 and 339–340. In contract cases, the problem is alleviated somewhat by the parties' ability to stipulate the applicable law. Supra nn.24–26. For comparison with modern European law, see Hay, Flexibility versus Predictability and Uniformity in Choice of Law, 226 Recueil des Cours 281 (1991–I).

55. Cheatham, Review of Currie's Selected Essays, 62 Mich. L. Rev. 1475, 1477 (1964).

56. Kahn–Freund, supra n.22, at 246, 253 n.114, 339–340.

57. More recently, the question of constitutional-law constraints on choice of law has received increasing attention in some countries. See Müller-Freienfels, "Vorrang des Verfassungsrechts und Vorrang des Privatrechts," Beiträge zum Handels-und Wirtschaftsrecht–Festschrift für Rittner 425 (Löwisch et al., eds., 1991).

beginning. The break with the traditional system has left a void, considerable uncertainty, and a groping for new rules and precedents. The development of these new rules and precedents will take considerable time as will the resolution of the difficulties detailed above. The precise direction of the case law—in terms of the "coexistence"[58] of the various approaches and their value-goals—continues to remain unclear.

However, there is evidence that an accommodation is taking place: the developing case law under the Second Restatement reflects many of the concerns and incorporates many of the compatible techniques suggested by scholars over the last 40 years. Today, more than three decades after its official promulgation, the Restatement appears to dominate the American methodological landscape.[59] It is followed by a plurality of jurisdictions: 22 jurisdictions in tort conflicts, and 24 in contract conflicts.[60] The Restatement's proponents will probably interpret this high degree of judicial acceptance as a vindication of their position and a repudiation of the Restatement's critics, while the latter will probably interpret the dominance of the Restatement as a race down to the lowest common denominator. The truth could well be somewhere in the middle.[61]

VI.   THE JUDICIAL REVOLUTION

A.   THE CHRONOLOGY OF THE REVOLUTION IN TORTS AND CONTRACTS

1. *Introduction*

§ 2.15 It is generally believed that academic commentators have had a greater influence in the development of conflicts law than of any other branch of American law. Whether this is due to the perceived esoteric nature of the subject matter, the dearth of English doctrine during the formative period of American conflicts law, or the relatively infrequent occurrence of conflicts cases in general—which makes diffi-

---

58. See Hay, Reflections on Conflicts Law Methodology, 32 Hastings L.J. 1644 (1981).

59. See Symeonides, The Judicial Acceptance of the Second Conflicts Restatement: A Mixed Blessing, 56 Md. L. Rev. 1248, 1268–69 (1997).

60. For a list of these states, see infra § 2.23. For important caveats regarding the classification of states as following the Restatement Second, see infra § 2.19.

61. All three viewpoints are represented in the latest scholarly symposium devoted to the Restatement. See The Silver Anniversary of the Second Conflicts Restatement, 56 Md. L. Rev. 1193–1410 (1997) (containing articles by Borchers, Reynolds, Richman, Symeonides, Weintraub, and

Weinberg). In the meantime, the debate on whether to begin drafting a Third Restatement has already begun. See Symposium: Preparing for the Next Century–A New Restatement of Conflicts, 75 Ind. L. J. 399–686 (2000) (containing articles by Shreve, Juenger, Richman, Reynolds, Symeonides, and Weinberg, and comments by Borchers, Dane, Gottesman, Hill, Maier, Peterson, Posnak, Reimann, Reppy, Sedler, Silberman, Lowenfeld, Simson, Singer, Twerski, and Weintraub); Symposium: American Conflicts Law at the Dawn of the 21st Century, 37 Willamette L. Rev. 1–298 (containing articles by Symeonides, Juenger, Kay, von Mehren, Weinstein, and Wenitraub and commentaries by Cox, Nafziger, Sedler, Shreve, and Whitten).

cult the accumulation of judicial expertise on the subject—is beside the point. The fact remains that it is academic commentators like Story and later Beale who provided the theoretical underpinnings of the traditional choice-of-law system that lasted for more than a century. It is also academic commentators like Cook, Cavers, and Currie's who have pinpointed and articulated that system's deficiencies and have instigated dissension from it.

After having presented these academic dissents, it is now time to examine their impact on the "living law" of judicial decisions—to examine, in other words, to what extent and at what pace was the scholastic revolution transformed into a judicial revolution. A good way to do this is to focus on two typical and important traditional choice-of-law rules, the *lex loci delicti* and the *lex loci contractus*,[1] and to compare their judicial following before and since the scholastic revolution.

2. *The Erosion of the Lex Loci Delicti Rule*

§ 2.16 Although revolutions seem to erupt overnight, discerning eyes can see the harbingers long before the actual eruption. The same is true of the conflicts revolution, at least in retrospect. Conflicts casebooks are replete with cases in which courts created exceptions to, or openly manipulated, the *lex loci delicti* rule. Many of these cases spoke in language that was indicative of later developments. For example, *Levy v. Daniels' U–Drive Auto Renting Co.*,[1] and *Haumschild v. Continental Cas. Co.*[2] are cited as examples of manipulative characterization, which they were, but they were also harbingers of things to come in that both cases spoke of the policies or purposes of the substantive rules involved in the conflict. Similarly, *Grant v. McAuliffe*[3] and *Kilberg v. Northeast Airlines, Inc.*[4] are cited as examples of a misuse of the substance versus procedure dichotomy, which they were, but they were also examples of the courts' increasing impatience with the fortuitous way in which the *lex loci delicti* rule operated. Finally, although seemingly unrelated, *Lauritzen v. Larsen*[5] was a cue from the Supreme Court of the United States that reliance on multiple factors was not only acceptable but also more preferable than reliance on a single connecting factor for determining the law applicable to tort conflicts.

Be that as it may, for all practical purposes, in the area of tort conflicts, the revolution began in 1963 with the seminal New York case of *Babcock v. Jackson*,[6] which was the first case to openly abandon the

§ 2.15

1. At the same time, it should be pointed out that most other traditional choice-of-law rules have survived the conflicts revolution virtually unscathed.

§ 2.16

1. 108 Conn. 333, 143 A. 163 (1928).

2. 7 Wis.2d 130, 95 N.W.2d 814 (1959).

3. 41 Cal.2d 859, 264 P.2d 944 (1953).

4. 9 N.Y.2d 34, 172 N.E.2d 526, 211 N.Y.S.2d 133 (1961).

5. 345 U.S. 571, 73 S.Ct. 921, 97 L.Ed. 1254 (1953) (discussed infra § 17.63)

6. 12 N.Y.2d 473, 240 N.Y.S.2d 743, 191 N.E.2d 279 (N.Y. 1963), discussed infra § 17.29. Although earlier cases had laid the foundation, see, e.g., W.H. Barber Co. v. Hughes, 223 Ind. 570, 63 N.E.2d 417, 423 (Ind. 1945) (adopting a significant-contacts

traditional *lex loci delicti* rule. By 1977, half of the states had abandoned the rule, and by the turn of the century a total of 42 jurisdictions[7] had done so. The chronological order in which this occurred is shown in Chart 1 and Table 1 below, and documented in the accompanying text and footnotes. For purposes of comparison, Chart 2 shows the parallel erosion of the *lex loci contractus* rule, which is discussed later in this section.

Chart 1. The Erosion of the Lex Loci Delicti Rule

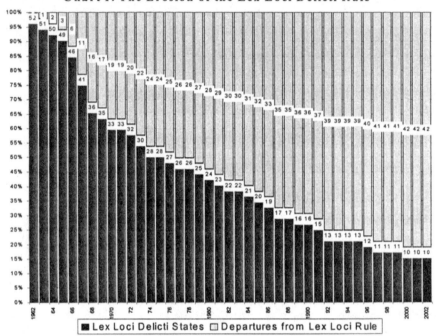

approach for contract conflicts); Auten v. Auten, 308 N.Y. 155, 124 N.E.2d 99, 101–03 (1954) (adopting a center-of-gravity approach to a contract conflict, but also examining the interests of the competing jurisdictions), *Babcock* is generally considered as marking the beginning of the revolution.

7. This number includes the District of Columbia and the Commonwealth of Puerto Rico. By 2001, the number of jurisdictions that have abandoned the *lex loci delicti* rule rose to 42. The last jurisdiction to do so is Montana. See Phillips v. General Motors Corp., 298 Mont. 438, 995 P.2d 1002 (2000).

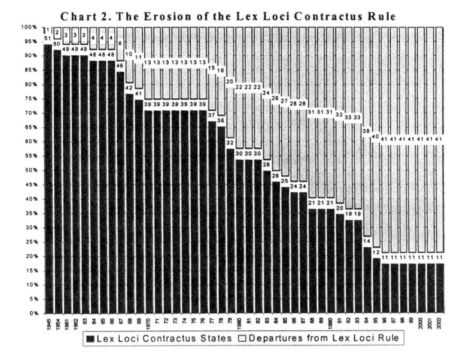

Chart 2. The Erosion of the Lex Loci Contractus Rule

TABLE 1. CHRONOLOGICAL TABLE OF DEPARTURES FROM THE *LEX LOCI DELICTI* RULE

Lex loci states		Departures from *lex loci* rule				
1962	**52**					
1963	51	1	New York			
1964	50	1	Pennsylvania			
1965	49	1	Wisconsin			
1966	46	3	Minnesota	New Hampshire	Puerto Rico	
1967	41	5	California	Dist. of Columbia	Kentucky	New Jersey / Oregon
1968	36	5	Alaska	Arizona	Iowa	Mississippi / Rhode Island
1969	35	1	Missouri			
1970	33	2	Illinois	Maine		
1971	33					
1972	32	1	North Dakota			
1973	30	2	Colorado	Louisiana		
1974	28	2	Oklahoma	Washington		
1975	28					
1976	27	1	Massachusetts			
1977	**26**	1	Arkansas			
1978	26					
1979	25	1	Texas			
1980	24	1	Florida			
1981	23	1	Hawaii			
1982	22	1	Michigan			
1983	22					
1984	21	1	Ohio			
1985	20	1	Idaho			
1986	19	1	Connecticut			
1987	17	2	Indiana	Nebraska		
1988	17					
1989	16	1	Utah			
1990	16					
1991	15	1	Delaware			
1992	13	2	South Dakota	Tennessee		
1993	13					
1994	13					
1995	13					
1996	12	1	Nevada			
1997	11	1	Vermont			
1998	11					
1999	11					
2000	10	1	Montana			
2001	10					
2002	10					
2003	**10**	**42**				

Alabama
Georgia
Kansas
Maryland
New Mexico
North Carolina
South Carolina
Virginia
West Virginia
Wyoming

As Table 1 indicates, most of the departures from the *lex loci delicti* rule, a total of 16, occurred in the 1960s, thus establishing that decade as the decade of the revolution. The period of 1967–69, during which the

Restatement was published in the form of Official Proposed Drafts, was particularly active. This may explain the fact that eight of the eleven jurisdictions that abandoned the traditional rule during that three-year period appeared to opt for the Second Restatement, although three of them later switched to another approach.[8] Besides these eight jurisdictions, the breakdown for the decade of 1960–69 was five jurisdictions opting for interest analysis,[9] two jurisdictions for Leflar's approach,[10] and one for a significant-contacts approach.[11]

During the 1970s, that is from 1970 to 1979, 11 other jurisdictions abandoned the *lex loci delicti* rule. The equipoise point was the year 1977, at which time as many jurisdictions (26) adhered to the *lex loci* rule as had abandoned it. The break-down among the states that abandoned the rule during this decade was six states (Illinois, Maine, Colorado, Oklahoma, Washington, and Texas) opting for the Second Restatement,[12] two states (Minnesota and Arkansas) opting for Leflar's approach,[13] two states (Louisiana and Massachusetts) for a mixed approach,[14] and one state (North Dakota) for a significant-contacts approach.[15]

8. These jurisdictions are listed below in chronological order followed by the pertinent case: *District of Columbia*: Myers v. Gaither, 232 A.2d 577, 583 (D.C.1967); *Kentucky*: Wessling v. Paris, 417 S.W.2d 259, 259–61 (Ky.1967); *Oregon*: Casey v. Manson Constr. & Eng'g Co., 247 Or. 274, 428 P.2d 898, 907 (1967); *Alaska*: Armstrong v. Armstrong, 441 P.2d 699, 701–03 (Alaska 1968); *Arizona*: Schwartz v. Schwartz, 103 Ariz. 562, 447 P.2d 254, 257 (1968); *Iowa*: Fuerste v. Bemis, 156 N.W.2d 831, 833 (Iowa 1968); *Mississippi*: Mitchell v. Craft, 211 So.2d 509, 515 (Miss.1968); *Missouri*: Kennedy v. Dixon, 439 S.W.2d 173, 184 (Mo.1969). Kentucky, Oregon, and the District of Columbia later switched to other approaches. See infra §§ 2.24–2.25.

9. These jurisdictions were New York, Pennsylvania, Wisconsin, California, and New Jersey. See Babcock v. Jackson, 12 N.Y.2d 473, 240 N.Y.S.2d 743, 191 N.E.2d 279 (1963); Griffith v. United Air Lines, Inc., 416 Pa. 1, 203 A.2d 796, 805 (1964); Wilcox v. Wilcox, 26 Wis.2d 617, 133 N.W.2d 408, 415 (1965); Reich v. Purcell, 67 Cal.2d 551, 63 Cal.Rptr. 31, 432 P.2d 727, 730–31 (1967); Mellk v. Sarahson, 49 N.J. 226, 229 A.2d 625, 629–30 (1967). Pennsylvania later switched to a combined approach that includes interest analysis as well as reliance on the Second Restatement and Professor Cavers's "principles of preference." See, e.g., Cipolla v. Shaposka, 439 Pa. 563, 267 A.2d 854, 856–57 (1970) (Cavers); Miller v. Gay, 323 Pa.Super. 466, 470 A.2d 1353, 1354–56 (1983) (interest analysis and Second Restatement). Wisconsin later

switched to Leflar's choice-influencing considerations. See, e.g., Heath v. Zellmer, 35 Wis.2d 578, 151 N.W.2d 664, 672 (1967); Lichter v. Fritsch, 77 Wis.2d 178, 252 N.W.2d 360, 363 (1977).

10. These jurisdictions were New Hampshire and Rhode Island. See Clark v. Clark, 107 N.H. 351, 222 A.2d 205, 210 (1966); Woodward v. Stewart, 104 R.I. 290, 243 A.2d 917, 923 (1968).

11. This jurisdiction was Puerto Rico. See Widow of Fornaris v. American Sur. Co., 93 P.R.R. 28, 46, 93 D.P.R. 29 (1966).

12. See Ingersoll v. Klein, 46 Ill.2d 42, 262 N.E.2d 593, 596 (Ill. 1970); Beaulieu v. Beaulieu, 265 A.2d 610, 616 (Me.1970); First Nat'l Bank v. Rostek, 182 Colo. 437, 514 P.2d 314, 320 (Colo. 1973); Brickner v. Gooden, 525 P.2d 632, 637 (Okla.1974); Johnson v. Spider Staging Corp., 87 Wn.2d 577, 555 P.2d 997, 1000 (1976); Werner v. Werner, 84 Wn.2d 360, 526 P.2d 370, 376 (1974); Gutierrez v. Collins, 583 S.W.2d 312, 318 (Tex.1979). For caveats regarding such classifications see infra § 2.19.

13. See Milkovich v. Saari, 295 Minn. 155, 203 N.W.2d 408, 413 (Minn. 1973); Wallis v. Mrs. Smith's Pie Co., 261 Ark. 622, 550 S.W.2d 453, 458–59 (1977).

14. See Jagers v. Royal Indem. Co., 276 So.2d 309, 311–13 (La.1973); Pevoski v. Pevoski, 371 Mass. 358, 358 N.E.2d 416, 418 (1976).

15. See Issendorf v. Olson, 194 N.W.2d 750, 755 (N.D.1972).

During the 1980s, nine jurisdictions abandoned the *lex loci* rule, of which six (Florida, Ohio, Idaho, Connecticut, Nebraska, and Utah) opted for the Second Restatement,[16] one (Indiana) opted for a significant-contacts approach,[17] another (Michigan) for the *lex fori* approach,[18] and another (Hawaii) for a mixed approach.[19]

Finally, from 1990 to 2000, six more states followed suit in abandoning the *lex loci rule*, and all but one of them (Nevada)[20] seem to have opted for the Second Restatement.[21] No other state has followed suit in the new century. Thus, by the end of 2003, a total of 42 jurisdictions had abandoned the *lex loci delicti* rule, while ten jurisdictions appeared to adhere to it. This corresponds to a ratio of 81 to 19%. From a population perspective, the ratio is 84.5 to 15.5%.[22] These jurisdictions are discussed later.

3. *The Erosion of the Lex Loci Contractus Rule*

§ 2.17 In contract conflicts, the first abandonment of the *lex loci contractus* rule occurred as early as 1945, in the Indiana case of *W.H. Barber Co. v. Hughes*[1] which employed "a method used by modern teachers of Conflict of Laws in rationalizing the results obtained by the courts in decided cases."[2] The method was no other than the "center of gravity"[3] approach, which was to be later popularized by the 1954 New York case of *Auten v. Auten*.[4] Although *Auten* is generally considered as

16. See Bishop v. Florida Specialty Paint Co., 389 So.2d 999, 1001 (Fla.1980); Morgan v. Biro Mfg. Co., 15 Ohio St.3d 339, 474 N.E.2d 286, 288 (1984); Johnson v. Pischke, 108 Idaho 397, 700 P.2d 19, 22 (1985); O'Connor v. O'Connor, 201 Conn. 632, 519 A.2d 13, 21–22 (1986); Crossley v. Pacific Employers Ins. Co., 198 Neb. 26, 251 N.W.2d 383, 386 (1977) (relying alternatively on the Second Restatement and the *lex loci delicti* with the same result); Harper v. Silva, 224 Neb. 645, 399 N.W.2d 826, 828 (1987) (interpreting *Crossley* as having adopted the Second Restatement); Forsman v. Forsman, 779 P.2d 218, 220 (Utah 1989).

17. See Hubbard Mfg. Co. v. Greeson, 515 N.E.2d 1071, 1073–74 (Ind.1987) (holding that "when the place of the tort is an insignificant contact," the court will turn to the Second Restatement, but stopping short of embracing the policy-analysis component of the Second Restatement or of abandoning the *lex loci rule* in general).

18. See Sexton v. Ryder Truck Rental, Inc., 413 Mich. 406, 320 N.W.2d 843, 857 (1982).

19. See Peters v. Peters, 63 Haw. 653, 634 P.2d 586, 593–94 (1981) (applying a blend of interest analysis and Leflar's choice-influencing considerations).

20. See Motenko v. MGM Dist., Inc., 112 Nev. 1038, 921 P.2d 933, 935 (1996)

(adopting a *lex fori* approach in tort cases unless "another State has an overwhelming interest").

21. These states were: *Delaware*: See Travelers Indem. Co. v. Lake, 594 A.2d 38, 47 (Del.1991); *South Dakota*: See Chambers v. Dakotah Charter, Inc., 488 N.W.2d 63, 67 (S.D.1992); *Tennessee*: See Hataway v. McKinley, 830 S.W.2d 53, 59 (Tenn.1992); *Vermont*: See Amiot v. Ames, 166 Vt. 288, 693 A.2d 675, 677 (1997); and *Montana*: See Phillips v. General Motors Corp., 298 Mont. 438, 995 P.2d 1002 (2000).

22. See Symeonides, The American Choice-of-Law Revolution in the Courts: Today and Tomorrow, 298 Recueil des Cours, 1, 70, 76 (2003).

§ 2.17

1. 223 Ind. 570, 63 N.E.2d 417, 423 (1945). For a discussion of this case, see Yonover, The Golden Anniversary of the Choice of Law Revolution: Indiana Fired the First Shot, 29 Ind. L. Rev. 1201 (1996).

2. Id. at 586, 63 N.E.2d at 423.

3. Id.

4. 308 N.Y. 155, 124 N.E.2d 99, 101 (1954).

marking the beginning of the revolution in contract conflicts, it had no following until the 1960s. Even then, dissension was slow to spread and it took three decades (until 1984) for one half of the states to abandon the *lex loci contractus* rule. By 2003, 41 jurisdictions[5] had done likewise. The chronological order in which they did so is shown in Chart 2 and Table 2 and is documented in the accompanying text and footnotes.

5. This number includes the District of Columbia and the Commonwealth of Puerto   Rico.

TABLE 2. CHRONOLOGICAL TABLE OF DEPARTURES FROM THE *LEX LOCI CONTRACTUS RULE*

Year	*Lex loci* states	Departures from *lex loci* rule				
1944	**52**					
1945	51	1	Indiana			
1954	50	1	New York			
1961	49	1	Puerto Rico			
1962	49					
1963	49					
1964	48	1	Oregon			
1965	48					
1966	48					
1967	46	2	California	Washington		
1968	42	4	Idaho	New Hampshire	Vermont	Wisconsin
1969	41	1	Dist. of Columbia			
1970	39	2	Arizona	Delaware		
1971	39					
1972	39					
1973	39					
1974	39					
1975	39					
1976	39					
1977	37	2	Iowa	Kentucky		
1978	36	1	Missouri			
1979	32	4	Arkansas	Colorado	Illinois	Minnesota
1980	30	2	Mississippi	New Jersey		
1981	30					
1982	30					
1983	28	2	Maine	Pennsylvania		
1984	26	2	Ohio	Texas		
1985	25	1	Massachusetts			
1986	24	1	North Dakota			
1987	24					
1988	21	3	Hawaii	North Carolina	W. Virginia	
1989	21					
1990	21					
1991	20	1	Oklahoma?			
1992	19	1	Louisiana			
1993	19					
1994	14	5	Connecticut	Montana	Nebraska	Nevada	S. Dakota
1995	12	2	Alaska	Michigan		
1996	11	1	Utah			
1997	11					
1998	11					
1999	11					
2000	11					
2001	11					
2002	11					
2003	**11**	**41**				

Alabama
Florida
Georgia
Kansas
Maryland
New Mexico
Rhode Island
South Carolina
Tennessee
Virginia
Wyoming

As both Chart 2 and Table 2 indicate, the revolution spread at a much slower and even pace in contracts than it did in torts. During the 1960s only nine jurisdictions abandoned the *lex loci contractus* rule, and seven of them did so in the 1967–69 period, which coincided with the ferment surrounding the publication of the Second Restatement. Four of those jurisdictions (Idaho, New Hampshire, Vermont, and Washington) adopted the Restatement,[6] two jurisdictions (Puerto Rico and Wisconsin) adopted a significant-contacts approach influenced by the Restatement,[7] and three jurisdictions (Oregon, California, and the District of Columbia) adopted interest analysis.[8]

During the 1970s, nine additional states abandoned the *lex loci contractus* rule, and all but two of them (Arkansas and Minnesota)[9] opted for the Second Restatement.[10]

The decisive decade was the 1980s during which eleven additional states abandoned the *lex loci contractus* rule, thus shifting the balance against it in 1985. These states split almost evenly between the Second Restatement[11] and a mixed approach that in most instances includes reliance on the Restatement.[12]

6. See Rungee v. Allied Van Lines, Inc., 92 Idaho 718, 449 P.2d 378, 382 (1968); Consolidated Mut. Ins. Co. v. Radio Foods Corp., 108 N.H. 494, 240 A.2d 47, 49 (1968); Pioneer Credit Corp. v. Carden, 127 Vt. 229, 245 A.2d 891, 894 (1968); Baffin Land Corp. v. Monticello Motor Inn, Inc., 70 Wn.2d 893, 425 P.2d 623, 627–28 (1967). In 1968, Vermont's reliance on the Second Restatement was only partial. *Pioneer Credit Corp.* relied in part on § 188 of the Second Restatement but did not actually apply it. However, later cases have assumed adoption of the Second Restatement. See, e.g., Amiot v. Ames, 166 Vt. 288, 693 A.2d 675, 677 (1997). Similarly, in 1967, Washington's approach looked more like a significant-contacts approach inspired by the Second Restatement. However, later cases have relied more directly on the Restatement.

7. See Maryland Cas. Co. v. San Juan Racing Ass'n, 83 D.P.R. 538, 83 D.P.R. 559 (1961); Green Giant Co. v. Tribunal Superior, 104 D.P.R. 489 (1975); Urhammer v. Olson, 39 Wis.2d 447, 159 N.W.2d 688, 689 (1968). Wisconsin later switched to Leflar's approach. See Haines v. Mid–Century Ins. Co., 47 Wis.2d 442, 177 N.W.2d 328, 333 (1970); Schlosser v. Allis–Chalmers Corp., 86 Wis.2d 226, 271 N.W.2d 879, 885–86 (1978).

8. See Lilienthal v. Kaufman, 239 Or. 1, 395 P.2d 543, 549 (1964); Travelers Ins. Co. v. Workmen's Compensation Appeals Bd., 68 Cal.2d 7, 64 Cal.Rptr. 440, 434 P.2d 992, 994 (Cal. 1967); McCrossin v. Hicks Chevrolet, Inc., 248 A.2d 917, 921 (D.C.1969). All three of these jurisdictions later switched to a combined approach that includes interest analysis. See infra § 2.25.

9. See Standard Leasing Corp. v. Schmidt Aviation, Inc., 264 Ark. 851, 576 S.W.2d 181, 184 (1979) (significant-contacts approach); Hague v. Allstate Ins. Co., 289 N.W.2d 43, 48–49 (Minn.1978) (Leflar's choice-influencing considerations).

10. These jurisdictions are listed below in chronological order. *Arizona*: See Burr v. Renewal Guar. Corp., 105 Ariz. 549, 468 P.2d 576, 577 (1970); *Delaware*: See Oliver B. Cannon & Son, Inc. v. Dorr–Oliver, Inc., 394 A.2d 1160, 1166 (Del.1978); *Iowa*: See Joseph L. Wilmotte & Co. v. Rosenman Bros., 258 N.W.2d 317, 327 (Iowa 1977); *Kentucky*: See Lewis v. American Family Ins. Group, 555 S.W.2d 579, 581–82 (Ky. 1977); *Missouri*: See National Starch & Chem. Corp. v. Newman, 577 S.W.2d 99, 102 (Mo.Ct.App.1978)(cited with approval in Fruin–Colnon Corp. v. Missouri Hwy. Transp. Comm'n, 736 S.W.2d 41 (Mo. 1987)); *Colorado*: See Wood Bros. Homes, Inc. v. Walker Adjustment Bureau, 198 Colo. 444, 601 P.2d 1369, 1372 (Colo. 1979); *Illinois*: See Champagnie v. W.E. O'Neil Constr. Co., 77 Ill.App.3d 136, 395 N.E.2d 990, 997 (1979).

11. In chronological order, the jurisdictions that abandoned the *lex loci contractus* rule in favor of the Second Restatement during this period were as follows: *Mississippi*: See Spragins v. Louise Plantation, Inc., 391 So.2d 97 (Miss.1980); Boardman v. United Servs. Auto. Ass'n, 470 So.2d 1024, 1032–33 (Miss.1985); *Maine*: See Baybutt Constr. Corp. v. Commercial Union Ins. Co., 455 A.2d 914, 918–19 (Me.1983); *Ohio*: See Gries Sports Enters. v. Modell, 15 Ohio St.3d 284, 473 N.E.2d 807, 810 (1984); *Texas*: See Duncan v. Cessna Aircraft Co., 665 S.W.2d 414, 421 (Tex.), judgment rev'd on other grounds sub nom. Smithson v. Cessna Aircraft Co., 665 S.W.2d 439, 445 (Tex. 1984);*West Virginia*: The West Virginia Supreme Court of Appeals has not adopted

12. See p. 78.

Finally, from 1990 to 1996, ten states abandoned the *lex loci contractus* rule, and all but three of them (Oklahoma,[13] Louisiana,[14] and Nevada)[15] opted for the Second Restatement.[16] No other state has followed suit since that time. Thus, by the end of 2003, a total of 41 jurisdictions had abandoned the *lex loci contractus* rule, while eleven continued to adhere to it. This corresponds to a ratio of 79 to 21% in terms of jurisdictions and an 80 to 20% in terms of population.[17] These jurisdictions are discussed later.

the Second Restatement for contracts in general but has drawn heavily from it in insurance contract conflicts. See Cannelton Indus., Inc. v. Aetna Cas. & Sur. Co. of America, 194 W.Va. 186, 460 S.E.2d 1 (1994); Adkins v. Sperry, 190 W.Va. 120, 437 S.E.2d 284 (1993); Clark v. Rockwell, 190 W.Va. 49, 435 S.E.2d 664 (W.Va.1993); Nadler v. Liberty Mut. Fire Ins. Co., 188 W.Va. 329, 424 S.E.2d 256 (1992); Lee v. Saliga, 179 W.Va. 762, 373 S.E.2d 345 (1988); see also New v. Tac & C Energy, Inc., 177 W.Va. 648, 355 S.E.2d 629 (1987) (applying § 196 of the Second Restatement to an employment contract).

12. In chronological order, the jurisdictions that abandoned the *lex loci contractus* rule in favor of a mixed approach during this period were as follows: *New Jersey*: See State Farm Mut. Auto. Ins. Co. v. Estate of Simmons, 84 N.J. 28, 417 A.2d 488, 493 (1980); *Pennsylvania*: See Guy v. Liederbach, 501 Pa. 47, 459 A.2d 744, 753 (1983); *Massachusetts*: See Bushkin Assocs., Inc. v. Raytheon Co., 393 Mass. 622, 473 N.E.2d 662, 668–69 (1985); *North Dakota*: See Apollo Sprinkler Co. v. Fire Sprinkler Suppliers & Design, Inc., 382 N.W.2d 386, 390 (N.D.1986); *North Carolina*: See Boudreau v. Baughman, 322 N.C. 331, 368 S.E.2d 849 (1988) (interpreting the phrase "appropriate relation" in the forum's version of U.C.C. art. 1–105 as being equivalent to the phrase "most significant relationship" as used in the Second Restatement); *Hawaii*: See Lewis v. Lewis, 69 Haw. 497, 748 P.2d 1362 (1988) (interpreting Peters v. Peters, 63 Haw. 653, 634 P.2d 586 (1981), a tort conflict, as having adopted a significant-relationship test with primary emphasis on the state with the "strongest interest").

13. See Bohannan v. Allstate Ins. Co., 820 P.2d 787, 797 (Okla.1991) (stating that the court would be willing to apply the law of a state other than that of the *locus contractus* upon a showing that such other state "has the most significant relationship with the subject matter and the parties"). Many commentators believe that Oklahoma should be listed as a *lex loci contractus*

state, however, because an Oklahoma statute, although often disregarded, compels adherence to that rule. See Symeonides, Choice of Law in the American Courts in 1994: A View "from the Trenches," 43 Am. J. Comp. L. 1, 3 n.6 (1995).

14. See La. Civ. Code Ann. arts. 3537– 3540 (West 1994) (enacted in 1992) (providing rules based on the notion that the applicable law should be the law of that state whose policies would be most seriously impaired if its law were not applied). For discussion of these articles by their drafter, see Symeonides, Louisiana Conflicts Law: Two "Surprises," 54 La. L. Rev.497, 522–27 (1994).

15. See Hermanson v. Hermanson, 110 Nev. 1400, 887 P.2d 1241 (1994) (a status case re-interpreting earlier contract conflicts as having adopted a "substantial relationship test").

16. In chronological order, these jurisdictions were: *Connecticut*: See Williams v. State Farm Mut. Auto. Ins. Co., 229 Conn. 359, 641 A.2d 783 (1994); *Montana*: See Casarotto v. Lombardi, 268 Mont. 369, 886 P.2d 931 (1994), judgment rev'd on other grounds 517 U.S. 681, 116 S.Ct. 1652, 134 L.Ed.2d 902 (1996); *Nebraska*: See Powell v. American Charter Fed. S. & L. Ass'n, 245 Neb. 551, 514 N.W.2d 326 (1994) (explicitly adopting the Second Restatement). An earlier case, Shull v. Dain, Kalman & Quail, Inc., 201 Neb. 260, 267 N.W.2d 517 (1978), had also applied the Second Restatement. Id. at 520–21; *South Dakota*: See Stockmen's Livestock Exch. v. Thompson, 520 N.W.2d 255 (S.D.1994); *Alaska*: See Palmer G. Lewis Co. v. ARCO Chem. Co., 904 P.2d 1221, 1227 (Alaska 1995) (interpreting Ehredt v. DeHavilland Aircraft Co. of Canada, Ltd., 705 P.2d 446 (Alaska 1985), a tort case, as having adopted the Second Restatement for contract conflicts as well); *Michigan*: See Chrysler Corp. v. Skyline Indus. Servs., Inc., 448 Mich. 113, 528 N.W.2d 698 (1995); *Utah*: See American Nat'l Fire Ins. Co. v. Farmers Ins. Exch., 927 P.2d 186 (Utah 1996).

17. See S. Symeonides The American Choice-of-Law Revolution in the Courts:

B. THE REVOLUTION AT THE BEGINNING OF THE 21st CENTURY

1. Introduction

§ 2.18 As the preceding sections have demonstrated, the great majority of American jurisdictions have abandoned the traditional theory in both tort and contract conflicts. Despite occasional difficulties, identifying these states and separating them from the traditional states is relatively easy. Thus, as the dawn of the 21st century, there is little doubt that the revolution that began in the 1960s has prevailed. However, as we have seen, the revolution has had several branches. It has produced not a single new regime, but multiple regimes. The abandonment of the traditional theory has led to the development of several alternative "modern" methodologies and combinations among them. This section attempts to identify the methodology followed in each of the fifty states of the United States, the District of Columbia, and the Commonwealth of Puerto Rico.[1] The three tables reproduced below show the various methodological camps in tort and contract conflicts and the jurisdictions that seemed to belong to each, at the end of 2003.

However, before relying on these tables, the reader must be forewarned that they can be misleading unless they are read together with the accompanying text and the caveats, provisos, and qualifications hereafter stated.

2. Caveats

§ 2.19 The first caveat is that classifying a state into a particular methodological camp is by no means an exact science.[1] Difficulties arise from a variety of sources, ranging from the total lack or dearth of authoritative precedent, to precedents that are either equivocal or exceedingly eclectic. For example, since 1937, the Supreme Court of Rhode Island has not had an opportunity to reconsider its adherence to the *lex*

Today and Tomorrow, 298 Recueil des Cours, 1, 75–76 (2003).

§ 2.18

1. For older classifications of jurisdictions according to conflicts methodology, see Borchers, The Choice-of-Law Revolution: An Empirical Study, 49 Wash. & Lee L. Rev. 357, 367–76 (1992); Kay, Theory into Practice, Choice of Law in the Courts, 34 Mercer L. Rev. 521, 591–92 (1983); Smith, Choice of Law in the United States, 38 Hastings L.J. 1041, 1172–74 (1987); Symeonides, Choice of Law in the American Courts in 2000: As the Century Turns , 42 Am. J. Comp. L. 1, 12–15 (2001). The classifications and the discussion here draws

from S. Symeonides, The American Choice-of-Law Revolution in the Courts: Today and Tomorrow, 298 Recueil des Cours, 1, 64–153 (2003).

§ 2.19

1. "[I]n drawing the 'methodological map' of American conflicts law, one cannot aspire to the precision expected in real cartography. Even the rough division into the 'modern' and the traditional camps would have to be understood as a soft, permeable, and constantly shifting line that is not valid for all purposes." S. Symeonides, W. Perdue & A. von Mehren, Conflict of Laws: American, Comparative, International, 283–84 (1998).

loci contractus rule.[2] Because the same court was among the first to abandon the *lex loci delicti* rule[3] and has since remained at the forefront of the conflicts revolution in tort conflicts, one is tempted to infer that this court will also abandon the *lex loci contractus* rule. Such an inference would be as plausible as the educated guesses federal courts make in diversity cases.[4]

Yet, even educated guesses are not entirely safe because there exist examples of states that have abandoned the traditional theory in torts but not in contracts or vice versa,[5] and at least in one of those states, Florida, this dichotomy is not accidental.[6] Even if one concludes that a particular state no longer belongs in the traditional camp, one still has to face the more difficult question of placing that state into one or another of the modern methodological camps. For example, it may be plausible to assume that Rhode Island will eventually adopt for contract conflicts the same better-law approach it adopted for tort conflicts, but such assumption would not be not entirely safe since, as will be explained later,[7] many states follow a different modern choice-of-law methodology for torts and contracts respectively.

Another example is Tennessee's position in contract conflicts. The supreme court of that state has not encountered a contract conflict since its 1992 abandonment of the traditional theory in tort conflicts.[8] One could plausibly infer that this court will also abandon the traditional theory in contract conflicts on the next available opportunity. One could further infer that, because the court's endorsement of the Second Restatement in tort conflicts was wholehearted, the court will likely adopt the Second Restatement for contract conflicts as well.[9] Nevertheless, it is better to err on the side of caution and to keep Tennessee in the traditional column for contract conflicts.

On the other hand, Illinois has been classified in the Second Restatement camp for contract conflicts despite the lack of supreme court precedent to that effect. The reason for being less cautious here is that for almost three decades, the Supreme Court of Illinois has not only followed consistently and wholeheartedly the Second Restatement for

---

2. See infra § 2.21 n.68.

3. See Woodward v. Stewart, 104 R.I. 290, 243 A.2d 917 (1968).

4. See, e.g., Judge Friendly's famous statement: "Our principal task ... is to determine what the New York courts would think the California courts would think on an issue about which neither court has thought." Nolan v. Transocean Air Lines, 276 F.2d 280, 281 (2d Cir.1960).

5. For example, West Virginia has abandoned the traditional theory in contracts but not in torts. See infra § 2.21. Along with Rhode Island, Florida and Tennessee have abandoned the traditional theory in torts but not in contracts. See id.

6. See Sturiano v. Brooks, 523 So.2d 1126 (Fla.1988) (reaffirming the *lex loci*

contractus rule and specifically refusing to extend to contract conflicts the "most significant relationship" formula earlier adopted for tort conflicts).

7. See infra § 2.20.

8. See Hataway v. McKinley, 830 S.W.2d 53, 59 (Tenn.1992).

9. Additional support for this inference may be garnered by one of the court's older decisions, Goodwin Brothers Leasing, Inc. v. H & B Inc., 597 S.W.2d 303 (Tenn.1980), which cited favorably §§ 6, 188, and 203 of the Second Restatement, id. at 308, although the decision was not based on the Restatement.

tort conflicts, but has also routinely left undisturbed lower court decisions that confidently applied the Restatement to contract conflicts.[10]

Another obstacle to an accurate classification is the exceeding eclecticism of the courts that have abandoned the traditional theory. As said elsewhere, "[F]ew cases rely exclusively on a single policy-based approach. Courts tend to be less interested in theoretical purity and more interested in reaching what they perceive to be the proper result. The majority of cases that have abandoned the traditional approach tend to use modern approaches interchangeably and often as a posteriori rationalizations for results reached on other grounds."[11] To some extent, this eclecticism is reflected by the separate column called "combined modern" which appears in Tables 3 through 5 below. However, that column is reserved only for those states that overtly, knowingly, and repeatedly combine more than one modern methodology. If instances of unknowing, latent, or occasional eclecticism were to be included in that column, it would absorb most other columns. As said elsewhere, "[i]f one had to define *the* dominant choice-of-law methodology in the United States today, it would have to be called *eclecticism*."[12] Nevertheless the cases of the occasional eclecticism are quite numerous. For example, in its latest decision on tort conflicts, the Rhode Island Supreme Court described its approach as follows:

> In this jurisdiction ... we follow ... the interest-weighing approach. In so doing, we ... determine ... the rights and liabilities of the parties 'in accordance with the law of the state that bears the most significant relationship to the event and the parties.' ... That approach has sometimes been referred to as a rule of 'choice-influencing considerations.'
>
> In applying the interest-weighing or choice-influencing considerations, we consider ... [Leflar's five choice-influencing considerations and the four factual contacts listed] in Restatement (Second) Conflict of Laws, § 145(2).[13]

---

10. See, e.g., Olsen v. Celano, 234 Ill. App.3d 1045, 600 N.E.2d 1257, 1260 (1992) (noting that the most-significant-contacts test applies to contract conflicts); Illinois Tool Works v. Sierracin Corp., 134 Ill. App.3d 63, 479 N.E.2d 1046, 1050 (1985) (applying the Second Restatement to a contract conflict); Champagnie v. W.E. O'Neil Constr. Co., 77 Ill.App.3d 136, 395 N.E.2d 990, 997 (1979); Society of Mount Carmel v. National Ben Franklin Ins. Co., 268 Ill. App.3d 655, 643 N.E.2d 1280, 1286 (1994), appeal after remand 291 Ill.App.3d 360, 682 N.E.2d 1180 (1997). For federal cases, see, e.g., Massachusetts Bay Ins. Co. v. Vic Koenig Leasing, Inc. 136 F.3d 1116, 1122 (7th Cir.1998).

11. Symeonides, Perdue & von Mehren, supra n.1, at 119.

12. Kozyris & Symeonides, Choice of Law in the American Courts in 1989: An Overview, 38 Am. J. Comp. L. 601, 602 (1990).

13. Cribb v. Augustyn, 696 A.2d 285, 288 (R.I.1997) (citations omitted). See also Najarian v. National Amusements, Inc., 768 A.2d 1253 (R.I.2001) (blending choice-influencing considerations with Second Restatement). For another recent example of eclecticism from Minnesota, see Nodak Mut. Ins. Co. v. American Family Mut. Ins. Co., 604 N.W.2d 91 (Minn.2000). *Nodak* described the Minnesota approach as "the significant contacts test," id. 94, 96, which, however, relies not on *contacts*, but on Leflar's five choice-influencing *factors*, which, as the court applied them, are not really five, but rather one–the "[a]dvancement of the forum's governmental interest." Id. at 94.

In other words, this court follows a blend of three or perhaps five different approaches: an "interest-weighing approach" (which is interest analysis but is itself combined with the very weighing of interest that Currie proscribed), the Second Restatement, and Leflar's choice-influencing considerations. But that is not all; the court further suggested that Rhode Island follows a common-domicile rule for tort conflicts (perhaps inspired by New York's *Neumeier* rules), at least when the common domicile is in Rhode Island and the parties have a pre-existing relationship.[14] Ordinarily, such a virtually boundless eclecticism would justify placing Rhode Island in the "combined modern" column. However, because it is unclear whether this decision is an aberration, it is safer to keep Rhode Island in the better-law column where it has been since 1968.

Another aspect of the eclecticism phenomenon is that certain courts' commitment to a particular methodology is half-hearted. This is particularly true with states that purport to follow the Second Restatement. For example, some cases use the Restatement solely as an escape from a traditional choice-of-law rule that coexists with the Restatement,[15] other cases use the Restatement as a camouflage for a "grouping-of-contacts" approach,[16] while other cases use it as a vehicle for merely restraining but not avoiding interest analysis.[17] One can find examples of such disparate treatment of the Restatement in the same jurisdiction.[18] Finally, some states prefer to use only the general, open-ended, and flexible sections of the Restatement, such as §§ 145, 187 and especially § 6, and

For a critique of *Nodak*, see Symeonides, Choice of Law in the American Courts in 2000: As the Century Turns, 49 Am. J. Comp. L. 1, 8–11, 21–22 (2001).

14. See *Cribb*, 696 A.2d at 288: "[I]n situations in which the [Restatement § 146] factors (a) [place of injury] and (b) [place of conduct] are the only ones pointing to the law of another state and factors c) [parties' domicile] and (d) [seat of their relationship] point strongly to applying Rhode Island law, the latter two factors trump the earlier two, and Rhode Island law is applied."

15. See, e.g., O'Connor v. O'Connor, 201 Conn. 632, 519 A.2d 13, 21 (1986) (adopting the Second Restatement "for those cases in which application of the doctrine of lex loci [delicti] would produce an arbitrary, irrational result"); Hubbard Mfg. Co. v. Greeson, 515 N.E.2d 1071, 1073 (Ind. 1987) (holding that, "when the place of the tort is an insignificant contact," the court will turn to the significant contacts–but not necessarily the policy analysis–of the Second Restatement).

16. See, e.g., Palmer G. Lewis Co. v. ARCO Chem. Co., 904 P.2d 1221 (Alaska 1995); Powell v. American Charter Fed. S. & L. Ass'n, 245 Neb. 551, 514 N.W.2d 326 (1994); Stockmen's Livestock Exch. v. Thompson, 520 N.W.2d 255 (S.D.1994) (per curiam); Selle v. Pierce, 494 N.W.2d 634 (S.D.1993); Hataway v. McKinley, 830 S.W.2d 53 (Tenn.1992); American Nat'l Fire Ins. Co. v. Farmers Ins. Exch., 927 P.2d 186 (Utah 1996); Forsman v. Forsman, 779 P.2d 218 (Utah 1989).

17. See, e.g., Williams v. State Farm Mut. Auto. Ins. Co., 229 Conn. 359, 641 A.2d 783 (1994); O'Connor v. O'Connor, 201 Conn. 632, 519 A.2d 13 (1986); Esser v. McIntyre, 169 Ill.2d 292, 661 N.E.2d 1138 (Ill. 1996); Nelson v. Hix, 122 Ill.2d 343, 522 N.E.2d 1214 (1988); Veasley v. CRST Int'l, Inc., 553 N.W.2d 896 (Iowa 1996); Chrysler Corp. v. Skyline Indus. Servs., Inc., 448 Mich. 113, 528 N.W.2d 698 (1995); Gilbert Spruance Co. v. Pennsylvania Mfrs. Ass'n Ins. Co., 134 N.J. 96, 629 A.2d 885 (1993).

18. Compare Stockmen's Livestock Exch. v. Thompson, 520 N.W.2d 255 (S.D. 1994), and Selle v. Pierce, 494 N.W.2d 634 (S.D.1993), both of which relied more on state contacts than on state interests, with Chambers v. Dakotah Charter, Inc., 488 N.W.2d 63 (S.D.1992), which relied more on state interests and less on state contacts.

avoid using the specific sections that contain mildly confining presumptive rules.[19]

The final obstacle to an accurate classification is the fact that sometimes supreme court precedents are equivocal or simply irreconcilable. For example, in contract conflicts, the precedents from North Carolina,[20] Oklahoma,[21] and West Virginia[22] are equivocal enough so as to be susceptible to different interpretations and thus to raise legitimate doubts as to whether these states properly belong in the Second Restatement column. Similar doubts exist regarding Arkansas' classification as a significant-contacts state because the precedents from that state are virtually irreconcilable.[23]

Even if the above difficulties and uncertainties were to be eliminated, one might have good reason to object to classifying states on the basis of the choice-of-law methodology because such classifications tend to inflate the importance of methodology in explaining or especially predicting court decisions. Reality is much different. As noted elsewhere, *"of all the factors that may affect the outcome of a conflicts case, the factor that is the most inconsequential is the choice-of-law methodology followed by the court."*[24] Indeed, methodology rarely drives judicial decisions. The opposite is closer to the truth. "[T]he result in the case often appears to have dictated the judge's choice of law approach at least as much as the approach itself generated the result."[25]

The above are only some of the examples of the difficulties and uncertainties encountered in any attempt to draw bright demarcation lines between the various methodological camps. In light of these uncertainties, one might wonder whether classifications such as the ones reproduced below are more harmful than helpful. This question admits different answers. The view adopted here is that, on balance, these classifications are helpful, at least as tentative indications of where a particular jurisdiction stands, *provided* that they are used with appropriate caution, keeping in mind the above caveats.

---

19. See Borchers, Courts and the Second Restatement: Some Observations and an Empirical Note, 56 Md. L. Rev. 1232 (1997).

20. See supra § 2.17 n.12.

21. See supra § 2.17 n.13.

22. See supra § 2.17 n.11.

23. For example in McMillen v. Winona National & Savings Bank, 279 Ark. 16, 648 S.W.2d 460, 462 (1983), and Standard Leasing Corp. v. Schmidt Aviation, Inc., 264 Ark. 851, 576 S.W.2d 181, 184 (1979), the Arkansas Supreme Court applied a significant-contacts approach. In Stacy v. St. Charles Custom Kitchens of Memphis, Inc., 284 Ark. 441, 683 S.W.2d 225, 227 (1985), however, the Court seems to have reverted to the *lex loci contractus* rule. Writing in 1987, one commentator classified Arkansas

as a First Restatement (*lex loci* contractus) state. See Smith, supra § 2.18, n.1, at 1053–55, 1172. In Threlkeld v. Worsham, 30 Ark.App. 251, 785 S.W.2d 249 (1990), a lower court applied the "better-law" approach to a sale contract. Id. at 252–53.

24. Symeonides, Choice of Law in the American Courts in 1994: A View "from the Trenches," 43 Am. J. Comp. L. 1, 2 (1995).

25. Sterk, The Marginal Relevance of Choice of Law Theory, 142 U. Pa. L. Rev. 949, 951 (1994); see also Sutherland v. Kennington Truck Serv., Ltd., 454 Mich. 274, 562 N.W.2d 466, 468 (1997) ("[I]n practice, all the modern approaches to conflicts of law are relatively uniform in the results they produce."); Sterk, supra, at 962 ("[C]itation to academic theory has served more as window dressing than as a dispositive factor in deciding choice of law cases.").

3. The Methodological Camps

2.20 Subject to the above caveats and qualifications, the three tables reproduced below show the choice-of-law methodologies followed in the fifty states, the District of Columbia and the Commonwealth of Puerto Rico. Table 3 is an alphabetical list by jurisdiction. Table 4 shows the various methodological camps in tort conflicts, while Table 5 does likewise with regard to contract conflicts.

TABLE 3. ALPHABETICAL LIST OF STATES AND CHOICE-OF-LAW METHODOLOGIES

State	Traditional	Signif. contacts	Restatement 2nd	Interest Analysis	Lex Fori	Better Law	Combined Modern
Alabama	T+C						
Alaska			T+C				
Arizona			T+C				
Arkansas		C				T	
California				T			C
Colorado			T+C				
Connecticut			T+ C?				
Delaware			T+C				
District of Columbia				T			C
Florida	C		T				
Georgia	T+C						
Hawaii							T+C
Idaho			T+C				
Illinois			T+C				
Indiana		T+C					
Iowa			T+C				
Kansas	T+C						
Kentucky			C		T		
Louisiana							T+C
Maine			T+C				
Maryland	T+C						
Massachusetts							T+C
Michigan			C		T		
Minnesota						T+C	
Mississippi			T+C				
Missouri			T+C				
Montana	T		C				
Nebraska			T+C				
Nevada		C			T		
New Hampshire			C			T	
New Jersey				T			C
New Mexico	T+C						
New York							T+C
No. Carolina	T	C					
North Dakota		T					C
Ohio			T+C				
Oklahoma			T+C?				
Oregon							T+C
Pennsylvania							T+C
Puerto Rico		T+C					
Rhode Island	C					T	
So. Carolina	T+C						
So. Dakota			T+C				
Tennessee	C		T				
Texas			T+C				
Utah			T+C				
Vermont			T+C				
Virginia	T+C						
Washington			T+C				
West Virginia	T		C				
Wisconsin						T+C	
Wyoming	T		C?				
TOTAL 52 / 52	Torts 11 Contracts 10	Torts 3 Contracts 5	Torts 21 Contracts 25	Torts 3 Contracts 0	Torts 3 Contracts 0	Torts 5 Contracts 2	Torts 6 Contracts 10

T = Torts   C = Contracts

TABLE 4. METHODOLOGICAL CAMPS IN TORT CONFLICTS

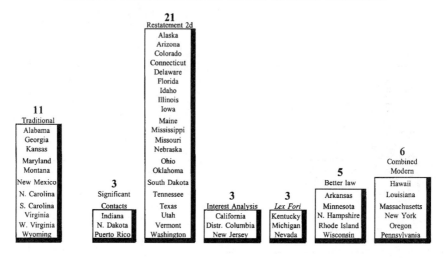

11 Traditional	3 Significant Contacts	21 Restatement 2d	3 Interest Analysis	3 Lex Fori	5 Better law	6 Combined Modern
Alabama		Alaska				Hawaii
Georgia		Arizona				Louisiana
Kansas		Colorado				Massachusetts
Maryland		Connecticut				New York
Montana		Delaware				Oregon
New Mexico		Florida				Pennsylvania
N. Carolina		Idaho				
S. Carolina		Illinois			Arkansas	
Virginia		Iowa	California	Kentucky	Minnesota	
W. Virginia	Indiana	Maine	Distr. Columbia	Michigan	N. Hampshire	
Wyoming	N. Dakota	Mississippi	New Jersey	Nevada	Rhode Island	
	Puerto Rico	Missouri			Wisconsin	
		Nebraska				
		Ohio				
		Oklahoma				
		South Dakota				
		Tennessee				
		Texas				
		Utah				
		Vermont				
		Washington				

TABLE 5. METHODOLOGICAL CAMPS IN CONTRACT CONFLICTS

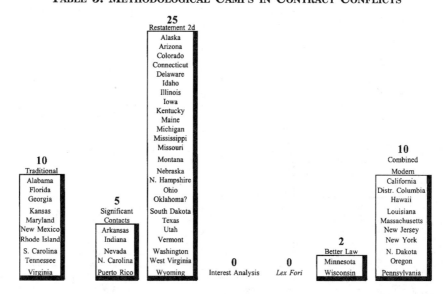

10 Traditional	5 Significant Contacts	25 Restatement 2d	0 Interest Analysis	0 Lex Fori	2 Better Law	10 Combined Modern
Alabama		Alaska				California
Florida		Arizona				Distr. Columbia
Georgia		Colorado				Hawaii
Kansas		Connecticut				Louisiana
Maryland		Delaware				Massachusetts
New Mexico		Idaho				New Jersey
Rhode Island		Illinois				New York
S. Carolina	Arkansas	Iowa				N. Dakota
Tennessee	Indiana	Kentucky			Minnesota	Oregon
Virginia	Nevada	Maine			Wisconsin	Pennsylvania
	N. Carolina	Michigan				
	Puerto Rico	Mississippi				
		Missouri				
		Montana				
		Nebraska				
		N. Hampshire				
		Ohio				
		Oklahoma?				
		South Dakota				
		Texas				
		Utah				
		Vermont				
		Washington				
		West Virginia				
		Wyoming				

4. Traditional States

§ 2.21 As the above tables indicate, 10 states continue to follow the traditional theory in tort conflicts and eleven states do so in contract conflicts. For the reader's convenience these states are shown again in Table 6.

TABLE 6. TRADITIONAL STATES

TORTS	CONTRACTS
Alabama	Alabama
	Florida
Georgia	Georgia
Kansas	Kansas
Maryland	Maryland
New Mexico	New Mexico
North Carolina	
	Rhode Island
South Carolina	South Carolina
	Tennessee
Virginia	Virginia
West Virginia	
Wyoming	Wyoming
Total 10	Total 11

As Table 6 indicates, the two columns are not identical. Florida, Rhode Island, and Tennessee have abandoned the traditional theory in tort conflicts but not in contract conflicts, while North Carolina, and West Virginia have done the reverse. In any event, it would be a mistake to assume that all the states listed in Table 6 are equally committed to the status quo or that they will remain so for the same length of time. Although predictions are risky, the following discussion of recent cases might be helpful to counsel contemplating litigation in these jurisdictions.

Tort Conflicts. Regarding tort conflicts, of the 10 states listed above in the traditional column, only Alabama has recently and categorically reaffirmed its adherence to the *lex loci delicti* rule.[1] The highest courts of Kansas,[2] Maryland,[3] Virginia,[4] and

§ 2.21

1. See Fitts v. Minnesota Mining & Manufacturing Co., 581 So.2d 819 (Ala. 1991); Powell v. Sappington, 495 So.2d 569 (Ala.1986); Norris v. Taylor, 460 So.2d 151 (Ala.1984); Holman v. McMullan Trucking, 684 So.2d 1309 (Ala.1996); Griffin v. Summit Specialties, Inc., 622 So.2d 1299 (Ala. 1993); Etheredge v. Genie Industries, Inc., 632 So.2d 1324 (Ala.1994). See also Fitzgerald v. Austin, 715 So.2d 795 (Ala.Civ.App. 1997); Ex parte Exxon Corporation, 725 So.2d 930 (Ala.1998).

2. See Ling v. Jan's Liquors, 237 Kan. 629, 703 P.2d 731 (1985). But see infra n. 6.

3. See Chambco v. Urban Masonry Corp., 338 Md. 417, 659 A.2d 297 (1995), on remand 106 Md.App. 788 (1995) (applying

the *lex loci delicti*, virtually without discussion). But see infra n.7.

4. The last time the Supreme Court of Virginia has had an opportunity to consider the question of abandoning the *lex loci delicti* rule was in 1979. In McMillan v. McMillan, 219 Va. 1127, 253 S.E.2d 662 (1979), the Court considered but rejected plaintiff's appeal to abandon the *lex loci* in favor of the Second Restatement because it is "susceptible to inconstancy" and tends to create "uncertainty and confusion" 253 S.E.2d at 664. Applying the interspousal immunity rule of the *lex loci delicti*, the Court refused to allow an action by a Virginia wife against her Virginia husband, which was allowed under Virginia law. The next time the Court encountered a tort conflict was in 1993, in Jones v. R.S. Jones

Wyoming[5] have applied the *lex loci delicti* rule in recent years, but their commitment to it does not appear to be as firm as Alabama's. For example, in recent years, in dealing with insurance conflicts, the Supreme Court of Kansas has been increasingly employing policy-analysis, although disguised in traditional *ordre public* jargon.[6] Similarly, although Maryland's highest court has applied the *lex loci* for generic tort conflicts as late as 1995, the court has, since the early 1980s, employed straight policy analysis in tort actions arising in the context of workers' compensation.[7] As explained below, the remaining five states are even more lukewarm in their commitment to the *lex loci* rule. They appear to retain the rule in name only, by evading it through transparent escape devices, such as the *ordre public*, or even "comity."

Boone v. Boone[8], a case decided by the South Carolina Supreme Court, is a typical example. *Boone* was an interspousal-immunity conflict in which two spouses domiciled in South Carolina, a state that allows interspousal tort suits, were involved in an accident in Georgia, a state that does not allow such suits. The court acknowledged its past adher-

---

and Assoc., Inc., 246 Va. 3, 431 S.E.2d 33 (1993) and Buchanan v. Doe, 246 Va. 67, 431 S.E.2d 289 (1993), decided on the same day. In both of these cases, however, none of the parties urged the Court to abandon the *lex loci delicti* rule, and the Court saw no reason to reconsider it. In *Jones*, the Court applied the *lex loci* which, however, was more favorable to the forum plaintiff than was the *lex fori*. In *Buchanan*, where the situation was the reverse, the Court found a way to apply the *lex fori* while professing adherence to the *lex loci* rule.

5. See Jack v. Enterprise Rent–A–Car Co. of Los Angeles, 899 P.2d 891 (Wyo. 1995). This was an action by a Wyoming resident against a California rental agency for injury sustained in a Wyoming traffic accident, caused by a car rented by defendant in California to a driver of unspecified domicile. Under California, but not Wyoming, law the rental company would be held liable. The court's choice-of-law discussion was confined to a few sentences: "It is thoroughly established as a general rule that the *lex loci delicti* . . . is the law that governs and is to be applied with respect to the substantive phases of torts. . . . The accident occurred in Wyoming. In addition, the [victims] resided in Wyoming, the negligent operation of the vehicle occurred in Wyoming, and the damages were sustained in Wyoming." *Jack*, 899 P.2d at 894–95.

6. See infra nn.54–55; Hartford Accident & Indemnity Co. v. American Red Ball Transit Co., 262 Kan. 570, 938 P.2d 1281 (1997), cert. denied 522 U.S. 951, 118 S.Ct. 372, 139 L.Ed.2d 290 (1997); Safeco Insurance Co. v. Allen, 262 Kan. 811, 941 P.2d 1365 (1997); St. Paul Surplus Lines v. In-

ternational Playtex, Inc., 245 Kan. 258, 777 P.2d 1259 (1989), cert. denied 493 U.S. 1036, 110 S.Ct. 758, 107 L.Ed.2d 774 (1990). In 2003, the Kansas Supreme Court decided not to review a decision of the intermediate court that provided a good opportunity for reconsidering the lex loci delicti rule. See Raskin v. Allison, 30 Kan. App.2d 1240, 57 P.3d 30 (2002), *review denied* Feb 05, 2003 (applying Mexican compensatory-damages law to a Babcock-pattern case arising out of a boating accident in Mexico involving only Kansas domiciliaries vacationing in Mexico).

7. See Hauch v. Connor, 295 Md. 120, 133, 453 A.2d 1207, 1214 (1983) (holding that the choice-of-law decision in these conflicts "turned on the determination of which jurisdiction had the greater interest"); Bishop v. Twiford, 317 Md. 170, 562 A.2d 1238, 1241 (1989)(holding that such conflicts are to be governed by the law of the "jurisdiction that has the greatest interest at stake."). See also Hutzell v. Boyer, 252 Md. 227, 249 A.2d 449 (1969). In each of these cases the court applied Maryland law and allowed a Maryland employee to recover tort damages against his Maryland employer, even though the worker's compensation statute of the state of the employment accident precluded such recovery. In Powell v. Erb, 349 Md. 791, 709 A.2d 1294 (1998), the court employed the same analysis and, once again, applied Maryland's pro-recovery law to an action arising out of an employment accident in Pennsylvania, despite a Maryland statute that seemed to require the application of Pennsylvania law.

8. 345 S.C. 8, 546 S.E.2d 191 (2001).

ence to the *lex loci delicti* rule,[9] which in this case would dictate the application of the Georgia immunity rule. However, the court noted with relief, "foreign law may not be given effect in this State if it is 'against good morals or natural justice.' "[10] The court opined that it would be "contrary to 'natural justice' "[11] to preclude one spouse from suing the other, as the Georgia rule did, and hence the court declined to apply it.

Although few people would quarrel with this result, the process by which the court arrived at it left much to be desired. For example, while the interspousal immunity rule may be outmoded and arguably ill-advised, it is far fetched to say that it is "against natural justice," or that it is so repugnant and "shocking" to the forum's sense of justice and fairness as to meet Cardozo's classic *ordre public* test[12]. Moreover, from a methodological perspective, one would expect that the court would at least pause to consider whether the *lex loci* rule was worth preserving before shortcutting to, and misapplying, an exception to the rule. It is one thing to adhere to a rule because it is rationally and functionally defensible, and another thing to adhere to a rule because it can be easily evaded. Had the court followed through with its own analysis of South Carolina policies in abandoning the immunity rule[13], the court could have easily concluded that those policies would be promoted by their application to this case (which involved South Carolina spouses) without offending Georgia's policies of protecting Georgia marriages or, more likely, Georgia insurers. In other words, this was a classic false conflict. The court could easily resolve it by applying the law of the common domicile (as other courts did in the vast majority of similar cases since *Haumschild*[14]) and without resorting to gimmicks that were necessary in the *Haumschild* days, but not today.

---

9. In an earlier case, Dawkins v. State, 306 S.C. 391, 412 S.E.2d 407 (1991), the same court refused to a apply the *ordre public* exception in an action brought against the State of South Carolina by a Georgia citizen who was injured in Georgia by a convict who escaped from a nearby South Carolina prison. The court applied Georgia law, which favored the State of South Carolina.

10. *Boone*, 546 S.E.2d at 193.

11. Id. at 194.

12. See Loucks v. Standard Oil Co. of New York, 224 N.Y. 99, 120 N.E. 198, 202 (1918) (asking whether the foreign law "shock[s] our sense of justice" or "menaces the public welfare" or "violate[s] some fundamental principle of justice, some prevalent conception of good morals, some deep-rooted tradition of the common weal").

13. See *Boone*, 546 S.E.2d at 194 ("It is the public policy of our State to provide married person with the same legal rights and remedies possessed by unmarried persons.").

14. Haumschild v. Continental Cas. Co., 7 Wis.2d 130, 95 N.W.2d 814 (1959) (characterizing interspousal-immunity as a family-law issue to be governed by the law of the spouses' domicile rather than the *lex loci*). Eight state supreme courts have used cases of this pattern as the opportunity to abandon the *lex loci delicti* rule. Six of those cases involved interspousal immunity. See Armstrong v. Armstrong, 441 P.2d 699 (Alaska 1968) (Alaska spouses, accident in Yukon territory); Schwartz v. Schwartz, 103 Ariz. 562, 447 P.2d 254 (1968) (New York spouses, Arizona accident); Pevoski v. Pevoski, 371 Mass. 358, 358 N.E.2d 416 (1976) (Massachusetts spouses, New York accident); and Forsman v. Forsman, 779 P.2d 218 (Utah 1989) (California spouses, Utah accident). Two cases involved intrafamily immunity. See Balts v. Balts, 273 Minn. 419, 142 N.W.2d 66 (1966) (Minnesota parent and child, Wisconsin accident); Jagers v. Royal Indem. Co., 276 So.2d 309 (La. 1973) (Louisiana parent and child, Mississippi accident).

Georgia's adherence to the traditional theory is subject to the usual escapes but also to a peculiar rule which forbids Georgia courts from applying the common law (as opposed to the statutory law) of another state.[15] This essentially means that the *lex loci delicti* and *lex loci contractus* rules are inapplicable whenever the locus of the tort or contract is in another state which has not enacted a statute on the matter. Even when these rules are applicable, however, Georgia courts tend to find a way to avoid them. For example, in a manner typical of courts that purport to like the traditional theory but not its results, the Supreme Court of Georgia has recently avoided the *lex loci delicti* rule by stretching the meaning of the traditional *ordre public* exception. The court held that a Virginia rule that did not impose strict liability on manufacturers was so "radically dissimilar"[16] to the Georgia strict-liability rule as to justify its rejection on public policy grounds. Observers who find it incongruous for a court to be conservative on conflicts law and liberal on substantive law may be tempted to conclude that a more pragmatic explanation for the Court's refusal to apply Virginia law was the fact that that law was unfavorable to a Georgia plaintiff who acquired the product in Georgia.[17]

New Mexico's highest court has recently acknowledged its past adherence to the *lex loci delicti* rule but did not in fact apply it.[18] "This rule is not utilized," said the court, "if such application would violate New Mexico public policy."[19] While this statement does not in itself entail a departure from the traditional theory, the court's use of the forum's public policy is essentially incompatible with that theory under which *ordre public* is supposed to function only defensively (i.e., as a means of preventing the application of an objectionable foreign law that is found applicable under the forum's choice-of-law rule). In this case, the court did not even examine the content of the law of the foreign *locus delicti*—which it defined as the place of the injury—and applied the law of the forum state, which was also the place of conduct, under a reasoning that approximates a modern policy analysis.[20] It should there-

---

15. See Trustees of Jesse Parker Williams Hospital v. Nisbet, 189 Ga. 807, 7 S.E.2d 737 (1940); Menendez v. Perishable Distributors, Inc.,254 Ga. 300, 329 S.E.2d 149 (1985); Avnet, Inc. v. Wyle Labs., Inc., 263 Ga. 615, 437 S.E.2d 302 (1993); Shorewood Packaging Corp. v. Commercial Union Ins. Co., 865 F.Supp. 1577 (N.D.Ga.1994); In re Tri–State Crematory Litigation, 215 F.R.D. 660 (N.D.Ga.2003).

16. Alexander v. General Motors Corporation, 267 Ga. 339, 478 S.E.2d 123, 124 (1996), on remand 224 Ga.App. 238, 481 S.E.2d 7 (1997).

17. *Alexander* was a products liability action arising out of a traffic accident in Virginia in which a Georgia motorist had been injured while driving a General Motors car he had purchased in Georgia. Finding the laws of the two states to be "radi-

cally dissimilar," 478 S.E.2d at 124, the Court held that "the rule of *lex loci delicti* should not be applied," id. at 123, because its application would be "antithetical" or "contrary" to "the public policy of [Georgia]." Id. at 124. For a critique, see Symeonides, Choice of Law in the American Courts in 1996: Tenth Annual Survey, 45 Am. J. Comp. L. 447, 453–55 (1997).

18. See Torres v. State, 119 N.M. 609, 894 P.2d 386 (1995).

19. *Torres*, 894 P.2d at 390.

20. In contrast to *Alexander*, supra n.16, the use of the public policy exception and the resulting application of the *lex fori* in *Torres* was not as self-serving because the forum state, which was also the place of conduct, had a law that was favorable to a foreign plaintiff and unfavorable to a forum

fore come as no surprise that lower courts have interpreted the above quoted phrase as meaning that "policy considerations may override the place-of-the-wrong rule."[21]

The Supreme Court of North Carolina also threatened "abjur[ing] the *lex loci commissi* rule" if "the governmental interests and public policy of our state would [so] require."[22] But since it found another way to avoid the application of the *lex loci*,[23] the court did not follow up on that threat. Since then the court has encountered two more tort conflicts. It applied the *lex loci* in the first one,[24] but not in the last one[25] preferring instead to resolve the conflict on the basis of "public policy considerations"[26] derived from the forum's workers' compensation statute.[27]

If recent decisions are any indication, West Virginia may be the state closest to abandoning the *lex loci* rule. In McKinney v. Fairchild International, Inc.,[28] the Supreme Court of that state, which in recent years had been increasingly relying on the Second Restatement for insurance conflicts,[29] came close to extending the Restatement to tort

defendant (the State itself). In this sense, *Torres* can be usefully contrasted with *Dawkins*, supra n.9, which involved the converse pattern (*lex fori*) unfavorable to forum defendant (the State) and favorable to foreign plaintiff, and foreign *lex loci* favorable to forum defendant (the State). In that case the court applied the *lex loci* showing no sympathy for the plaintiff's *ordre public* argument.

21. Estate of Gilmore, 124 N.M. 119, 946 P.2d 1130, 1135 (App.1997). Despite acknowledging that the Supreme Court "ha[d] not embraced the Restatement Second with respect to choice-of-law issues in either tort or contract," id. at 1136, this court relied heavily on the Second Restatement. It described New Mexico's approach as "reflecting a desire for the greater certainty presumably provided by more traditional approaches ... [but] tempered by recognition that important policy considerations cannot be ignored." Id. According to the court, this meant that "we begin with a strong presumption in favor of application of the place-of-the-wrong rule, but we will not close our eyes to compelling policy arguments for departure from the general rule in specific circumstances." Id.

22. Leonard v. Johns–Manville Sales Corp. 309 N.C. 91 at 96, 305 S.E.2d 528 at 531 (1983).

23. The Court concluded that the *locus* state had "[n]o law one way or another on this issue," *Leonard*, 309 N.C. at 96, 305 S.E.2d at 531. Consequently, said the Court, "the rule of *lex loci commissi* does not apply. Instead we hold that North Carolina law applies." Id.

24. See Boudreau v. Baughman, 322 N.C. 331, 368 S.E.2d 849 (1988).

25. See Braxton v. Anco Electric, Inc., 330 N.C. 124, 409 S.E.2d 914 (1991).

26. *Braxton*, 409 S.E.2d at 916.

27. The Court acknowledged the *lex loci* rule but noted that the same result would be obtained through a *renvoi* from the *lex loci* to the *lex fori*. See id. at 916–17. In Gbye v. Gbye, 130 N.C.App. 585, 503 S.E.2d 434 (1998), review denied 349 N.C. 357, 517 S.E.2d 893 (1998), North Carolina's intermediate court concluded that the Supreme Court's adherence to the *lex loci* rule was "steadfast" and "strong," 503 S.E.2d at 435, 436, and "decline[d] any request to carve out a more 'modern approach' to the rule's application." Id. at 436. The court applied the *lex loci*'s parental immunity rule to an action between two domiciliaries of the forum state.

28. 199 W.Va. 718, 487 S.E.2d 913 (1997).

29. See infra § 2.23 n.5. See also Oakes v. Oxygen Therapy Services, 178 W.Va. 543, 363 S.E.2d 130 (1987) (quoting in full §§ 145, 146 and 6 of the Second Restatement and determining the applicable law on a grouping-of-contacts basis); Vest v. St. Albans Psychiatric Hospital, Inc., 182 W.Va. 228, 387 S.E.2d 282 (1989) (acknowledging the *lex loci delicti* rule but eventually avoiding it through the use of the substance/procedure distinction). In Blais v. Allied Exterminating Company, 198 W.Va. 674, 482 S.E.2d 659 (1996), the court referred to the *lex loci delicti* as "the cornerstone of West

conflicts. In the end the Court applied the *lex fori* rather than the *lex loci* under both a traditional and a modern rationale.[30] In Mills v. Quality Supplier Trucking, Inc.,[31] the same court reiterated its earlier precedents according to which "the doctrine of lex loci delicti will not be invoked where 'the application of the law of a foreign state . . . contravenes the public policy of this State.' "[32] The Court held that Maryland's contributory-negligence rule contravened the public policy of West Virginia which had adopted the comparative-negligence rule. Finally, in Russell v. Bush & Burchett, Inc.,[33] the same court invoked a doctrine of deference–comity–not in order to defer to foreign law, but rather to reject it. *Russell* was a workers' compensation case arising out of an employment accident on the Kentucky end of a bridge connecting Kentucky and West Virginia. The injured employee was a Kentucky domiciliary, hired by defendant, a Kentucky employer, who in turn was hired through a public bidding by the West Virginia Division of Highways (DOH) to construct the bridge.

The question in *Russell* was whether the plaintiff employee was entitled to invoke the "deliberate intention" provision of the West Virginia workers' compensation statute, which deprives the employer of its statutory tort immunity.[34] The court held that "this question is not determined by the doctrine of *lex loci delicti*, but rather under the principles of comity."[35] The court explained that, although comity is often used as a shorthand term to explain why a court would defer to the laws of another state, the term comity was used here "in its meaning as a choice-of-law analytic approach that may lead to either applying *or* declining to apply the law of another jurisdiction."[36] The court further explained that comity rests on several principles, including the proverbial kitchen sink, and "most important[ly], the forum court['s] [right to] ask itself whether these [foreign-created] rights are compatible with its own public law and policy."[37] The court seized on this last "principle" and, without saying anything about the foreign law or any foreign-

---

Virginia's Conflict of Laws Doctrine," id. at 662, but in that case neither party had asked the court to abandon the rule and the case did not lend itself to such an undertaking. The case arose out of injury sustained in Virginia by Virginia residents, when their Virginia house was sprayed with excessive doses of an insecticide by the Virginia affiliate of defendant, a West Virginia exterminating company.

30. For a discussion of why this case should not be interpreted as an abandonment of the *lex loci* rule, see Symeonides, Choice of Law in the American Courts in 1997, 46 Am. J. Comp. L. 233, 248 (1998).

31. 203 W.Va. 621, 510 S.E.2d 280 (1998).

32. 510 S.E.2d at 282 (quoting Paul v. National Life, 177 W.Va. 427, 433, 352 S.E.2d 550 (1986)).

33. 210 W.Va. 699, 559 S.E.2d 36 (2001).

34. This provision allowed a tort action against an employer who "acted with a consciously, subjectively and deliberately formed intention" to cause injury to the employee. W.Va. Code § 23–4–2(c). The Kentucky workers' compensation statute apparently did not contain a similar provision. Following the *lex loci delicti* rule, the lower court held that the West Virginia statute was inapplicable, and granted a summary judgment for defendant.

35. *Russell*, 559 S.E.2d at 40.

36. Id. at n.4.

37. Id. at 40. Among the other principles were "legal harmony and uniformity among the co-equal states" and protection of the "rights and expectations of a party who has relied on foreign law." Id.

created right, concluded that West Virginia law should govern because West Virginia had "an *affirmative* public policy ... that all persons working on the ... bridge project would have all the benefits of West Virginia's workers' compensation law, including its 'deliberate intention' provisions."[38]

Again, few people would quarrel with the result. The court could have based this result on a simple factual finding that the plaintiff was a "covered employee" under West Virginia's workers' compensation statute.[39] Under these circumstances, the plaintiff should be entitled to the protection of that statute,[40] and regardless of comity, public policy, or contrary provision, if any, in the Kentucky workers' compensation statute. The court could have reached this result directly based on West Virginia's "affirmative public policy,"[41] without apologies and without the confused discussion of comity and vested rights, neither of which had anything to do with the case.

Contract Conflicts. Of the eleven states that adhere to the traditional method in contract conflicts, Alabama,[42] Florida,[43] Georgia,[44] Virginia[45] and Wyoming[46] seem more committed to the *lex loci contractus* rule than the remaining six states.

38. Id. at 40–41 (emphasis added).

39. The court did make such a finding when it stated that "the DOH required in its bidding process–and [the employer] contractually promised to the DOH in that process–that all ... bridge project workers would be covered by the West Virginia Workers' Compensation Act." Id. at 40.

40. " '[A]ll employees covered by the West Virginia Workers' Compensation Act ... are entitled to all benefits and privileges under the Act, including the right to file a direct deliberate intention cause of action... .' " Id. at 41 (quoting Bell v. Vecellio & Grogan, Inc., 197 W.Va. 138, 475 S.E.2d 138, 144 (1996)).

41. See text at n.38, supra.

42. See American Nonwovens, Inc. v. Non Wovens Engineering, S.R.L., 648 So.2d 565 (Ala.1994).

43. See Sturiano v. Brooks, 523 So.2d 1126 (Fla.1988) (reaffirming the *lex loci contractus* rule and specifically refusing to extend to contract conflicts the "most significant relationship" formula earlier adopted for tort conflicts).

44. See General Telephone Co. v. Trimm, 252 Ga. 95, 96, 311 S.E.2d 460, 462 (1984) (rejecting as "confusing" and "uncertain" the center-of-gravity approach and deciding to adhere to the *lex loci contractus* rule, "[u]ntil it becomes clear that a better rule exists."). But see Amica Mut. Ins. v. Bourgault, 263 Ga. 157, 429 S.E.2d 908 (1993) (relying on § 193 of the Second Re-

statement to interpret a Georgia insurance statute); Georgia's adherence to the *lex loci contractus* rule is subject to several exceptions. In addition to the exception described supra n.15, regarding non-statutory foreign law, Georgia courts do not apply the *lex loci contractus* rule when: (a) the contract is to be performed in a state other than the one in which it was made, see *Trimm*, 311 S.E.2d at 461; or (b) when the contract contains a valid choice-of-law clause. See Carr v. Kupfer, 250 Ga. 106, 296 S.E.2d 560 (1982). However, contracts made in Georgia and not containing a choice-of-law clause to the contrary are presumed to have been tacitly submitted by the parties to the law of Georgia. See General Electric Credit Corp. v. Home Indem. Co., 168 Ga.App. 344, 350, 309 S.E.2d 152 (1983).

45. See Buchanan v. Doe, 246 Va. 67, 431 S.E.2d 289 (1993); Erie Ins. Exchange v. Shapiro, 248 Va. 638, 450 S.E.2d 144 (1994); Lexie v. State Farm Mut. Auto. Ins. Co., 251 Va. 390, 469 S.E.2d 61 (1996), cert. denied 519 U.S. 981, 117 S.Ct. 433, 136 L.Ed.2d 331 (1996).

46. The Wyoming Supreme Court has vacillated between the *lex loci* and the Second Restatement. Cherry Creek Dodge, Inc. v. Carter, 733 P.2d 1024 (Wyo. 1987) cited the Restatement favorably but relied mostly on the "reasonable relationship" language of the forum's version of the U.C.C. Amoco Rocmount Co. v. The Anschutz Corp., 7 F.3d 909 (10th Cir. 1993), interpreted *Cherry Creek* as having adopted the Restate-

In 1984, the Georgia Supreme Court rejected as "confusing" and "uncertain" the Restatement (Second) approach and decided to retain the *lex loci contractus* rule "[u]ntil it becomes clear that a better rule exists."[47] Almost two decades later, in *Convergys Corporation v. Keener*,[48] the court restated its conviction that not such rule has emerged. The court stated that the modern approaches were "very complex"[49] and "[not] outcome determinative,"[50] and that the cases applying them "seem to turn on a court's interpretation of its own public policy considerations."[51] "Therefore," the court concluded, "until we are convinced that there is a better approach, Georgia will continue to adhere to the traditional conflicts of law rules."[52] It is unclear whether the court rejected the new approaches because they are too complex or because they are too flexible. The court's actual resolution of the conflict suggests that the court prefers even more flexibility but without any complexity. The court held that an Ohio choice-of-law clause was unenforceable because it conflicted with Georgia's public policy. Section 187(2) of the Second Restatement would allow the same result, but only after the court would answer affirmatively the following two questions (a) whether Georgia law would have been applicable in the absence of a choice-of-law clause, and (b) whether Georgia had a materially greater interest than Ohio. Apparently, the court was unwilling to be burdened with the complexity of these questions.

ment. In BHP Petroleum (Americas), Inc. v. Texaco Explor. & Prod., Inc., 1 P.3d 1253 (Wy. 2000), the Wyoming Supreme Court renounced the view that *Cherry Creek* had adopted the Second Restatement.

47. General Telephone Co. of Southeast v. Trimm, 252 Ga. 95, 311 S.E.2d 460, 462 (1984). But see Amica Mut. Ins. Co. v. Bourgault, 263 Ga. 157, 429 S.E.2d 908 (1993) (relying on Restatement (Second) § 193 to interpret a Georgia insurance statute).

48. 276 Ga. 808, 582 S.E.2d 84 (2003). Keener was domiciled and working in Ohio when he signed a non-compete agreement that contained an Ohio choice-of-law clause. After moving to Georgia to work for a competing employer, Keener filed an action in a Georgia federal court seeking a declaratory judgment that the non-compete agreement was unenforceable. The court found that the agreement violated Georgia's public policy and issued a nationwide injunction permanently enjoining the Ohio employer from enforcing it. See Keener v. Convergys Corp., 205 F.Supp.2d 1374 (S.D.Ga. 2002). On appeal, the Eleventh Circuit Court of Appeals certified to the Georgia Supreme Court the questions of whether Georgia would follow § 187(2) of the Restatement (Second), and whether in the case at hand Georgia would have a materially greater interest in applying its law. See Keener v. Convergys Corp.,

312 F.3d 1236 (11th Cir. 2002). The Supreme Court obliged with a categorical negative answer: "Because the Restatement (Second) Conflict of Laws has never been adopted in Georgia, and because we continue to refuse to enforce contractual rights which contravene the policy of Georgia, we answer in the negative." *Convergys*, 582 S.E.2d at 85. On remand, the Eleventh Circuit affirmed the District Court's injunction but reduced its territorial and temporal scope from nationwide to Georgia and only while Keener was domiciled in Georgia. See Keener v. Convergys Corporation, 342 F.3d 1264 (11th Cir.2003).

49. 582 S.E.2d at 87.

50. Id.

51. Id.

52. The complete statement is as follows:

[D]espite the adoption of some very complex rules in these jurisdictions, in actuality it does not appear that these rules are outcome determinative. Instead, the cases seem to turn on a court's interpretation of its own public policy considerations. Therefore, until we are convinced that there is a better approach, Georgia will continue to adhere to the traditional conflicts of law rules.

Id.

The highest courts of Kansas and Maryland have recently had an opportunity to abandon the *lex loci* rule, but the incentive to do so was diminished because both courts were able to evade the results of the rule. Significantly, however, both courts employed escape devices that, though couched in traditional jargon, suggest an increasing discomfort with traditional thinking.[53] The Kansas Supreme Court found it unnecessary to abandon the *lex loci* rule and "reserve[d] consideration of the Restatement's 'most significant relationship' test for a later day,"[54] because the traditional public policy exception—which the court employed offensively rather than defensively—enabled the court to avoid applying the *lex loci* so as to protect "[t]he interests of Kansas."[55]

Maryland's highest court has also used a similar notion of public policy and has spoken of state "interests" and "significant relations"[56] in avoiding the results of the *lex loci* rule, while professing adherence to it.[57] In its most recent decision on the subject, American Motorists Ins. Co. v. ARTRA Group, Inc.,[58] the court managed to avoid the *lex loci* rule by concluding, albeit erroneously,[59] that according to the conflicts law of

53. A similar discomfort can be observed at least in the intermediate courts of New Mexico and South Carolina. For New Mexico, see Reagan v. McGee Drilling Corp., 123 N.M. 68, 933 P.2d 867 (App. 1997), cert. denied 122 N.M. 808, 932 P.2d 498 (1997) (applying alternatively the public policy exception to the *lex loci* and the Second Restatement). But see Shope v. State Farm Ins. Co., 122 N.M. 398, 925 P.2d 515 (1996) (applying the *lex loci contractus* without discomfort or discussion). For South Carolina, see Sangamo Weston, Inc. v. National Surety Corp., 307 S.C. 143, 414 S.E.2d 127 (1992) (acknowledging that, "historically," the *lex loci contractus* rule had been followed in South Carolina) and noting that, with the record presently before it, the Court was "unable to address the question of whether South Carolina would adopt the more modern view of the [Second] Restatement" Id. at 147–48; Lister v. NationsBank, 329 S.C. 133, 494 S.E.2d 449 (App.1997) (applying alternatively the *lex loci* rule and the Second Restatement).

54. St. Paul Surplus Lines v. International Playtex, Inc., 245 Kan. 258, 777 P.2d 1259, 1267 (1989), cert. denied 493 U.S. 1036, 110 S.Ct. 758, 107 L.Ed.2d 774 (1990).

55. Id. ("The interest of Kansas exceeds [that of the other states].") See also Hartford Accident & Indemnity Co. v. American Red Ball Transit Co., 262 Kan. 570, 938 P.2d 1281 (1997) (accord), cert. denied 522 U.S. 951, 118 S.Ct. 372, 139 L.Ed.2d 290 (1997); Safeco Ins. Co. v. Allen, 262 Kan. 811, 941 P.2d 1365 (1997) (reaffirming both the *lex loci contractus* rule and the public policy exception enunciated in *St. Paul*) but

finding the exception inapplicable because the *lex loci* was "consistent with the stated policy of [Kansas law.]" Id. at 1372.

56. In Bethlehem Steel Corp. v. G.C. Zarnas & Co., Inc., 304 Md. 183, 498 A.2d 605 (1985), the court, using an expansive notion of public policy, refused to apply the law of Pennsylvania to a contract made in that state, and applied instead the law of Maryland. In an interesting footnote the court spoke of the two states' contacts and interests, and invoked a *renvoi* rationale. The court concluded that "Pennsylvania ha[d] no strong interest in having the contract provision enforced here . . . [because] had [this] suit . . . been brought in Pennsylvania, the Pennsylvania court would likely have decided the issue according to Maryland law [because of Maryland's 'significant contacts' with the case]." 498 A.2d at 609.

57. See also National Glass v. J.C. Penney, 336 Md. 606, 650 A.2d 246 (1994) (following § 187 of the Second Restatement in analyzing a choice-of-law clause); Kronovet v. Lipchin, 288 Md. 30, 415 A.2d 1096 (1980) (accord).

58. 338 Md. 560, 659 A.2d 1295 (1995) (action for declaratory judgment between an Illinois insurer and an Illinois insured on whether insurance policies issued in Illinois provided coverage for soil and groundwater contamination caused by the operation of the insured's paint-manufacturing factory located in Maryland).

59. Relying on the parties' representations, the Court assumed that under the Second Restatement which is followed in Illinois, an Illinois court would have applied

Illinois, the *locus contractus* state, "Maryland has the most significant relationship, or, at least, a substantial relationship with respect to the contract issue presented,"[60] and thus its law should apply under the *renvoi* doctrine. The court described its decision as "holding that Maryland's adherence to *lex loci contractus* must yield to a test such as Restatement (Second) Conflict of Laws § 188 when the place of contracting would apply Maryland law pursuant to that test,"[61] but insisted that this "is not a total jettisoning of *lex loci contractus*."[62] The court recognized that "[w]ith modern technology and modern business practices, the place of contracting becomes less certain and more arbitrary,"[63] and that " '[t]he lex loci contractus rule ... frequently elevates fortuitous and insignificant circumstances to crucial importance in establishing controlling law.' "[64] The court also said that its recent decisions invoking the *ordre public* exception and those adopting § 187 of the Restatement Second which "in effect, allow[s] the parties in their contract to select the jurisdiction with the most significant relationship,"[65] signified "some movement away from rigidly following the rule of *lex loci contractus*."[66] The court seemed to be satisfied that these two developments, coupled with the "limited *renvoi* exception" adopted in *ARTRA*, would suffice to preserve the *lex loci contractus* rule for the immediate future, but concluded as follows:

> *Lex loci contractus* is still the law in the majority of jurisdictions, although there is a significant modern erosion of the rule. If that erosion continues, however, this Court may, in the proper case, have

Maryland law because, although both the insurer and the insured were Illinois corporations and the insurance policies had been issued and delivered in Illinois, Maryland, as the state in which the insured risk was located, would have a more significant relationship to the dispute. Yet, slightly more than a month before *ARTRA* was decided, the Supreme Court of Illinois had held that an environmental insurance policy which, like the policy involved in *ARTRA*, was issued in Illinois to an Illinois insured by an insurer doing business in that state, was governed by Illinois law, even with regard to risks situated in other states. See Lapham–Hickey Steel Corp. v. Protection Mutual Ins. Co., 166 Ill.2d 520, 655 N.E.2d 842, 845 (1995).

60. *ARTRA*, 659 A.2d at 1304. The Court said that "in spite of the doctrine of *lex loci contractus*," Maryland courts should apply Maryland law to contracts made elsewhere when: "1) Maryland has the most significant relationship, or, at least, a substantial relationship with respect to the contract issue presented; and 2) The state where the contract was entered into ... would apply Maryland substantive law to the issue before the court." Id. This ex-

cerpt, as well as the rest of the opinion, suggests that the *renvoi* exception is to be employed only when the other state involved in the conflict employs a flexible approach, such as the Restatement Second's most-significant-relationship formula, and not when that state follows a mechanical rule such as the *lex loci solutionis* rule. What remains unclear is whether the determination that "Maryland has the most significant ... or, at least, a substantial relationship" is to be made independently by Maryland courts, or whether it is to be made under the precedents of the other involved state(s). For a case that seems to follow the former view, see The Rouse Co. v. Federal Ins. Co., 991 F.Supp. 460, 463 (D.Md.1998).

61. Id.

62. Id.

63. Id. at 1305.

64. Id. (quoting Cochran v. Ellsworth, 126 Cal.App.2d 429, 272 P.2d 904, 908 (1954)).

65. Id.

66. Id.

to reevaluate what the best choice-of-law rules ought to be to achieve simplicity, predictability, and uniformity.[67]

One would hope that when the Court realizes the inaccuracy of the first sentence in the above excerpt, the Court will follow up on the promise contained in the second sentence.

Finally, as noted earlier, Rhode Island and Tennessee belong to the traditional group only in name only. Indeed, as far as can be ascertained, the last time the Rhode Island Supreme Court applied the *lex loci contractus* rule was in 1937![68] In 1968, that court abandoned the *lex loci delicti* rule for tort conflicts.[69] Four years later, when the court encountered a contract conflict, the court held that the contract had been made in Rhode Island, that that state had "the most significant interest in th[e] matter,"[70] and that Rhode Island law was applicable "under whatever theory we follow."[71] The court also noted that, based on the record before it, the court "need not and do[es] not"[72] decide whether to adopt the modern approach it had earlier adopted for tort conflicts. This statement has been interpreted by some courts as an abandonment,[73] and by others as a reaffirmation[74] of the *lex loci contractus* rule. Because the Supreme Court of Rhode Island has yet to encounter a clear contract conflict, the Court has not had the opportunity to clarify this question. However, a 1992 decision,[75] in a case involving security interests—which could also be characterized as a contract case—leaves the impression that the days of the *lex loci contractus* are numbered if not over.[76]

Similar but less strong doubts might be voiced about Tennessee's classification as a *lex loci contractus* state. In 1975, the Supreme Court of Tennessee had expressly rejected an appeal to adopt "the dominant-contacts rule" for contract conflicts because of the rule's failure to produce uniformity.[77] However, in 1992, the same court adopted the Second Restatement's significant relationship approach for tort conflicts[78] and appeared unconcerned about the possibility that that approach may not be as conducive to certainty. Although the Court has yet to encounter a contract conflict since 1992, it would not be unreasonable

---

67. Id.

68. See Owens v. Hagenbeck–Wallace Shows Co., 58 R.I. 162, 192 A. 158 (1937).

69. See Woodward v. Stewart, 104 R.I. 290, 243 A.2d 917, 923 (1968).

70. A.C. Beals Co. v. Rhode Island Hospital, 110 R.I. 275, 286, 292 A.2d 865, 871 (1972).

71. Id at 287, 292 A.2d at 871.

72. Id.

73. See Everett/Charles Contact Products, Inc. v. Gentec, S.A.R.L., 692 F.Supp. 83, 89 (D.R.I.1988); Albany Ins. Co. v. Wisniewski, 579 F.Supp. 1004, 1013 (D.R.I. 1984); Roy v. Star Chopper Co., 442 F.Supp.

1010, 1015 (D.R.I.1977), aff'd 584 F.2d 1124 (1st Cir.1978).

74. See Soar v. National Football League Players' Ass'n, 550 F.2d 1287, 1290 (1st Cir.1977).

75. See Gordon v. Clifford Metal Sales Co., Inc. 602 A.2d 535 (R.I.1992).

76. *Gordon* is alternatively based on the "reasonable relation" language of the UCC § 1–105 and § 6 of the Second Restatement.

77. See Great American Ins. Co. v. Hartford Accident & Indem. Co., 519 S.W.2d 579, 580 (Tenn.1975).

78. See Hataway v. McKinley, 830 S.W.2d 53, 59 (Tenn.1992).

to expect that, when it does, the Court will abandon the *lex loci contractus* rule, perhaps in favor of the Second Restatement.

5. Significant–Contacts States

§ 2.22 As Tables 3 through 5 indicate, three jurisdictions (Indiana,[1] North Dakota,[2] and Puerto Rico)[3] follow a significant-contacts, "grouping of contacts" or "center of gravity" approach in tort conflicts, while five jurisdictions (Arkansas,[4] Indiana,[5] Nevada,[6] North Carolina[7] and Puerto Rico)[8] do so in contract conflicts. Historically, this approach had been the transitional point between the traditional theory and modern approaches, including the kindred approach of the Second Restatement. The difference with the Second Restatement is that courts following the significant-contacts approach do not engage in the in-depth policy analysis the Restatement requires nor are they bound by its presumptive rules, although they usually consider the same contacts as those listed in the Restatement. Indeed, these two features of the Restatement offer two different reasons for courts to choose the significant-contacts approach over the Restatement. While some courts feel more comfortable with contact counting and less comfortable with policy analysis, other courts prefer to avoid even the mild restraints contained in the Restatement's presumptive rules.

6. Second Restatement States

§ 2.23 Tables 3 through 5 make it clear that the Second Restatement is by far the most popular among the modern methodologies, being followed in 22 states in tort conflicts and 24 in contract conflicts. For the

§ 2.22

1. See Hubbard Mfg. Co., Inc. v. Greeson, 515 N.E.2d 1071 (Ind.1987) (holding that "when the place of the tort is an insignificant contact," the court will turn to the Restatement Second, but stopping short of embracing the policy-analysis component of the Restatement or of abandoning the *lex loci* rule in general). See also Simon v. United States, 805 N.E.2d 798 (Ind. 2004).

2. See Issendorf v. Olson, 194 N.W.2d 750, 755 (N.D.1972).

3. See Widow of Fornaris v. American Sur. Co., 93 P.R.R. 28, 46, 93 D.P.R. 29 (1966).

4. See Standard Leasing Corp. v. Schmidt Aviation, Inc., 264 Ark. 851, 576 S.W.2d 181 (1979); McMillen v. Winona National & Savings Bank, 279 Ark. 16, 648 S.W.2d 460 (1983). But see supra § 2.19 n.25.

5. See W.H. Barber Co. v. Hughes, 223 Ind. 570, 63 N.E.2d 417, 423 (Ind. 1945).

Among recent cases, see Dohm & Nelke v. Wilson Foods Corp., 531 N.E.2d 512, 513 (Ind.Ct.App.1988) (applying a significant-contacts approach); Barrow v. ATCO Mfg. Co., 524 N.E.2d 1313, 1314–15 (Ind.Ct.App. 1988) (following a significant-contacts approach, but also relying on the Second Restatement).

6. See Hermanson v. Hermanson, 110 Nev. 1400, 887 P.2d 1241 (1994).

7. The classification of North Carolina in this column may be questionable. It is based on Boudreau v. Baughman, 322 N.C. 331, 368 S.E.2d 849 (1988), which interpreted the phrase "appropriate relation" in the forum's version of U.C.C. § 1–105 as being equivalent to the phrase "most significant relationship."

8. See Maryland Cas. Co. v. San Juan Racing Ass'n, 83 P.R.R. 538, 83 D.P.R. 559 (1961); Green Giant Co. v. Tribunal Superior, 104 D.P.R. 489 (1975).

reader's convenience, another table showing only the Restatement states is reproduced below.

TABLE 7. SECOND RESTATEMENT STATES

TORTS	CONTRACTS
Alaska	Alaska
Arizona	Arizona
Colorado	Colorado
Connecticut	Connecticut
Delaware	Delaware
Florida	
Idaho	Idaho
Illinois	Illinois
Iowa	Iowa
	Kentucky
Maine	Maine
	Michigan
Mississippi	Mississippi
Missouri	Missouri
Montana	Montana
Nebraska	Nebraska
	New Hampshire
Ohio	Ohio
Oklahoma	Oklahoma?
South Dakota	South Dakota
Tennessee	
Texas	Texas
Utah	Utah
	Vermont
Washington	Washington
	West Virginia
Total 22	24

For all 22 states listed above as following the Restatement for tort conflicts there is express supreme court precedent to that effect.[1] The

---

§ 2.23

1. The cases that have adopted the Second Restatement for tort conflicts are reproduced below in alphabetical order by state. *Alaska*: Ehredt v. DeHavilland Aircraft Co. of Canada, Ltd., 705 P.2d 446, 453 (Alaska 1985) (relying exclusively on the Second Restatement); Armstrong v. Armstrong, 441 P.2d 699, 701–03 (Alaska 1968) (relying partly on the Second Restatement);

same is true with regard to 23[2] of the 24 states listed as following the Second Restatement for contract conflicts. The remaining state is Illinois which, for reasons explained earlier, can safely be classified as a Second Restatement state despite the lack of express high court precedent to

Arizona: Schwartz v. Schwartz, 103 Ariz. 562, 447 P.2d 254, 257 (1968); *Colorado*: First Nat'l Bank v. Rostek, 182 Colo. 437, 514 P.2d 314, 320 (1973); *Connecticut*: O'Connor v. O'Connor, 201 Conn. 632, 519 A.2d 13, 21–22 (1986); *Delaware*: Travelers Indem. Co. v. Lake, 594 A.2d 38, 47 (Del. 1991); *Florida*: Bishop v. Florida Specialty Paint Co., 389 So.2d 999, 1001 (Fla.1980); *Idaho*: Johnson v. Pischke, 108 Idaho 397, 700 P.2d 19, 22 (1985); *Illinois*: Ingersoll v. Klein, 46 Ill.2d 42, 262 N.E.2d 593, 596 (1970); *Iowa*: Fuerste v. Bemis, 156 N.W.2d 831, 833 (Iowa 1968); *Maine*: Beaulieu v. Beaulieu, 265 A.2d 610, 616 (Me.1970); see also Adams v. Buffalo Forge Co., 443 A.2d 932, 934 (Me.1982) (reiterating the court's adoption of the Second Restatement); Collins v. Trius, Inc., 663 A.2d 570 (Me.1995); *Mississippi*: Mitchell v. Craft, 211 So.2d 509, 515 (Miss.1968); *Missouri*: Kennedy v. Dixon, 439 S.W.2d 173, 184 (Mo.1969); *Montana:* Phillips v. General Motors Corp., 298 Mont. 438, 995 P.2d 1002 (2000)*; Nebraska*: Crossley v. Pacific Employers Ins. Co., 198 Neb. 26, 251 N.W.2d 383, 386 (1977) (relying alternatively on the Second Restatement and the *lex loci delicti* with the same result); Harper v. Silva, 224 Neb. 645, 399 N.W.2d 826, 828 (1987) (interpreting *Crossley* as having adopted the Second Restatement); *Ohio*: Morgan v. Biro Mfg. Co., 15 Ohio St.3d 339, 474 N.E.2d 286, 288 (Ohio 1984); *Oklahoma*: Brickner v. Gooden, 525 P.2d 632, 637 (Okla.1974); *South Dakota*: Chambers v. Dakotah Charter, Inc., 488 N.W.2d 63, 67 (S.D.1992); *Tennessee*: Hataway v. McKinley, 830 S.W.2d 53, 59 (Tenn.1992); *Texas*: Gutierrez v. Collins, 583 S.W.2d 312, 318 (Tex.1979); *Utah*: Forsman v. Forsman, 779 P.2d 218, 220 (Utah 1989); *Vermont*: Amiot v. Ames, 166 Vt. 288, 693 A.2d 675, 677 (Vt. 1997); *Washington*: Johnson v. Spider Staging Corp., 87 Wn.2d 577, 555 P.2d 997, 1000 (1976); Werner v. Werner, 84 Wn.2d 360, 526 P.2d 370, 376 (1974).

2. These states are listed below in alphabetical order: *Alaska*: See Palmer G. Lewis Co. v. ARCO Chem. Co., 904 P.2d 1221, 1227 (Alaska 1995) (interpreting Ehredt v. DeHavilland Aircraft Co. of Canada, Ltd., 705 P.2d 446 (Alaska 1985), a case involving a tort conflict, as having adopted the Second Restatement for contract conflicts as well); *Arizona*: Burr v. Renewal Guar. Corp., 105 Ariz. 549, 468 P.2d 576, 577 (1970); *Colorado*. Wood Bros. Homes,

Inc. v. Walker Adjustment Bureau, 198 Colo. 444, 601 P.2d 1369, 1372 (Colo. 1979) (en banc); *Connecticut*: Williams v. State Farm Mut. Auto. Ins. Co., 229 Conn. 359, 641 A.2d 783 (1994); *Delaware*: Oliver B. Cannon & Son, Inc. v. Dorr–Oliver, Inc., 394 A.2d 1160, 1166 (Del.1978) (relying in part on § 188 of the Second Restatement); *Idaho*: Rungee v. Allied Van Lines, Inc., 92 Idaho 718, 449 P.2d 378, 382 (1968); *Iowa*: Joseph L. Wilmotte & Co. v. Rosenman Bros., 258 N.W.2d 317, 327 (Iowa 1977); *Kentucky*: Lewis v. American Family Ins. Group, 555 S.W.2d 579, 581–82 (Ky.1977); *Maine*: Baybutt Constr. Corp. v. Commercial Union Ins. Co., 455 A.2d 914, 918–19 (Me.1983); *Michigan*: Chrysler Corp. v. Skyline Indus. Servs., Inc., 448 Mich. 113, 528 N.W.2d 698 (1995); *Mississippi*: Boardman v. United Servs. Auto. Ass'n, 470 So.2d 1024, 1032–33 (Miss.1985); Spragins v. Louise Plantation, Inc., 391 So.2d 97 (Miss. 1980); *Missouri*: Fruin–Colnon Corp. v. Missouri Hwy. Transportation Comm'n, 736 S.W.2d 41, 44 (Mo.1987); *Montana*: Casarotto v. Lombardi, 268 Mont. 369, 886 P.2d 931 (1994), judgment rev'd on other grounds, 517 U.S. 681, 116 S.Ct. 1652, 134 L.Ed.2d 902 (1996); *Nebraska*: Powell v. American Charter Fed. S. & L. Ass'n, 245 Neb. 551, 514 N.W.2d 326 (1994) (explicitly adopting the Second Restatement). An earlier case, Shull v. Dain, Kalman & Quail, Inc., 201 Neb. 260, 267 N.W.2d 517 (1978), had also applied the Second Restatement. Id. at 520–21; *New Hampshire*: Consolidated Mut. Ins. Co. v. Radio Foods Corp., 108 N.H. 494, 240 A.2d 47, 49 (1968); *Ohio*: Gries Sports Enters. v. Modell, 15 Ohio St.3d 284, 473 N.E.2d 807, 810 (1984); *South Dakota*: Stockmen's Livestock Exch. v. Thompson, 520 N.W.2d 255 (S.D.1994); *Texas*: Duncan v. Cessna Aircraft Co., 665 S.W.2d 414, 421 (Tex.), judgment rev'd on other grounds sub nom. Smithson v. Cessna Aircraft Co., 665 S.W.2d 439, 445 (Tex. 1984); *Utah*: American Nat'l Fire Ins. Co. v. Farmers Ins. Exch., 927 P.2d 186 (Utah 1996); *Washington*: Baffin Land Corp. v. Monticello Motor Inn, Inc., 70 Wn.2d 893, 425 P.2d 623, 627–28 (1967); *Vermont*: Pioneer Credit Corp. v. Carden, 127 Vt. 229, 245 A.2d 891, 894 (1968) (relying in part on § 188 of the Second Restatement but not actually applying it). Later cases have assumed adoption of the Second Restatement. See, e.g., Amiot v. Ames, 166 Vt. 288, 693 A.2d 675, 677 (1997).

that effect.[3] However, in two of these states (Oklahoma,[4] and West Virginia[5]), the available supreme court precedent is equivocal and thus the classification of these states in the Second Restatement column may be doubtful.

As Table 7 indicates, while most jurisdictions have adopted the Second Restatement for both tort and conflicts, a few jurisdictions have done so for only one or the other of these categories of conflicts. Thus two states (Florida and Tennessee) adopted the Restatement for tort conflicts only, while five states (Kentucky, Michigan, Montana, New Hampshire, and West Virginia) have done so for contract conflicts only. The reason for such divided loyalties is a deliberate choice in some instances[6] and lack of a good opportunity in other instances.[7]

In addition to the above states, many federal courts follow the Second Restatement in federal question cases.[8] Furthermore, on the

---

3. See supra § 2.19 n.10.

4. See supra § 2.17 n.13.

5. West Virginia's highest court has not adopted the Second Restatement for contracts in general but has drawn heavily from it in insurance contract conflicts. See Cannelton Indus., Inc. v. Aetna Cas. & Sur. Co. of America, 194 W.Va. 186, 460 S.E.2d 1 (1994); Adkins v. Sperry, 190 W.Va. 120, 437 S.E.2d 284 (1993); Clark v. Rockwell, 190 W.Va. 49, 435 S.E.2d 664 (1993); Nadler v. Liberty Mut. Fire Ins. Co., 188 W.Va. 329, 424 S.E.2d 256 (1992); Lee v. Saliga, 179 W.Va. 762, 373 S.E.2d 345 (1988); see also New v. Tac & C Energy, Inc., 177 W.Va. 648, 355 S.E.2d 629 (1987) (applying § 196 of the Second Restatement to an employment contract).

6. This is the case with Florida, Kentucky, Michigan, and New Hampshire. After adopting the Restatement (Second) for tort conflicts, Florida's highest court had several opportunities to do likewise for contract conflicts, but specifically refused to do so. See, e.g., Sturiano v. Brooks, 523 So.2d 1126, 1129 (Fla.1988). Kentucky at first abandoned the traditional theory in tort conflicts in favor of the Second Restatement, see Wessling v. Paris, 417 S.W.2d 259, 259–61 (Ky.1967), but one year later opted for the *lex fori* approach in another tort conflict, see Arnett v. Thompson, 433 S.W.2d 109, 113 (Ky.1968). Many years later, when that state's highest court encountered a contract conflict, the court found that its earlier adoption of the Restatement was appropriate for contract conflicts. Lewis v. American Family Ins. Group, 555 S.W.2d 579, 581–82 (Ky.1977). In Michigan, the reverse sequence was followed. In 1982, the Michigan Supreme Court first abandoned the traditional theory for tort conflicts in favor of the lex fori approach, see

Sexton v. Ryder Truck Rental, Inc., 413 Mich. 406, 320 N.W.2d 843, 857 (1982), and for many years it did not encounter a contract conflict. In 1995, when the Court encountered such a conflict in Chrysler Corp. v. Skyline Indus. Servs., Inc., 448 Mich. 113, 528 N.W.2d 698, 703 (1995), the court opted for the Second Restatement for contract conflicts, perhaps because by that time the novelty of the *lex fori* approach had worn off. The same sequence was followed in New Hampshire which adopted the better-law approach for tort conflicts in 1966 and the Second Restatement for contract conflicts in 1968. See Clark v. Clark, 107 N.H. 351, 222 A.2d 205, 210 (1966); Consolidated Mut. Ins. Co. v. Radio Foods Corp., 108 N.H. 494, 240 A.2d 47, 49 (1968).

7. For example, the Tennessee Supreme Court simply did not encounter a tort conflict in recent years (see supra § 2.19 nn.8–9) while the West Virginia Supreme Court did encounter such a conflict (see supra § 2.21 nn. 28–41) but arguably not of the kind that would necessitate an abandonment of the traditional theory.

8. See, e.g., American Home Assurance Co. v. L & L Marine Service, Inc., 153 F.3d 616 (8th Cir.1998) (admiralty jurisdiction); Bickel v. Korean Air Lines Co., 83 F.3d 127, 130–31 (6th Cir.) (arising under the Warsaw Convention), superseded on other grounds 96 F.3d 151 (6th Cir.1996); In re Lindsay, 59 F.3d 942, 948 (9th Cir.1995) (bankruptcy proceeding), cert. denied 516 U.S. 1074, 116 S.Ct. 778, 133 L.Ed.2d 730 (1996); Schoenberg v. Exportadora de Sal, 930 F.2d 777, 782 (9th Cir.1991), appeal after remand 19 F.3d 1309 (9th Cir. 1994), cert. denied 513 U.S. 1018, 115 S.Ct. 581, 130 L.Ed.2d 496 (1994) ("Federal common law follows the approach of the Restate-

issue of choice-of-law clauses, the Restatement is followed even in states that otherwise adhere to other approaches, including the traditional approach.[9]

In light of the above, it appears that more than three decades after its promulgation, the Restatement appears close to dominating the American methodological landscape. Once again, however, one should reiterate that this high numerical following does not necessarily entail a deep-seated commitment to, or intense loyalty toward, the Restatement.[10] In many cases it simply means that the Restatement offers the most convenient and also authoritative-sounding rationalization for results that the court would have reached under any other modern methodology.[11]

7. Interest Analysis and the Lex Fori Variant

§ 2.24 Tables 3 through 5, above, list only three jurisdictions (California,[1] the District of Columbia,[2] and New Jersey)[3] as following

ment (Second) of Conflict of Laws. . . ."); Edelmann v. Chase Manhattan Bank, N.A., 861 F.2d 1291, 1295 (1st Cir.1988) (case involving the Edge Act); Harris v. Polskie Linie Lotnicze, 820 F.2d 1000, 1003–04 (9th Cir.1987) (relying on the Restatement in a case arising under the Foreign Sovereign Immunities Act); Aaron Ferer & Sons v. Chase Manhattan Bank, N.A., 731 F.2d 112, 121 (2d Cir.1984); Corporacion Venezolana de Fomento v. Vintero Sales Corp., 629 F.2d 786, 795 (2d Cir.1980) (case arising under the Edge Act).

9. See, e.g., Cherry, Bekaert & Holland v. Brown, 582 So.2d 502, 507–08 (Ala.1991) (relying on Restatement, Second § 187, even though Alabama follows the traditional rules in both contract and tort conflicts); National Glass, Inc. v. J.C. Penney Props., Inc., 336 Md. 606, 650 A.2d 246, 248–51 (1994) (relying on § 187, even though Maryland follows the traditional rules in both contract and tort conflicts); Kronovet v. Lipchin, 288 Md. 30, 415 A.2d 1096, 1106 (Md. 1980) (same); SBKC Service Corp. v. 1111 Prospect Partners, L.P., 153 F.3d 728 (10th Cir.1998) (same with regard to Kansas); Nedlloyd Lines B.V. v. Superior Court, 3 Cal.4th 459, 11 Cal.Rptr.2d 330, 834 P.2d 1148, 1150–56 (Cal. 1992) (relying on § 187, even though in other conflicts California follows a combination of interest analysis with comparative impairment); North Bergen Rex Transport, Inc. v. Trailer Leasing Co., 158 N.J. 561, 568–69, 730 A.2d 843, 847–48 (1999) (same even though New Jersey generally follows interest analysis), Prows v. Pinpoint Retail Sys., Inc., 868 P.2d 809, 811 (Utah 1993) (relying on Restatement (Second) § 187 before Utah adopted the Restatement for other contractual issues).

10. See Symeonides, The Judicial Acceptance of the Second Conflicts Restatement:

A Mixed Blessing, 56 Md. L. Rev. 1248, 1261–63 (1997) (describing the various "gradations of commitment" to the Restatement and suggesting several other qualifications for such classifications).

11. Symeonides, supra n.10, attributes this high degree of judicial acceptance of the Second Restatement to the following reasons, not all of which are complimentary: (a) The Restatement provides the judge with virtually unlimited discretion; (b) The Restatement, as applied by judges, does not require hard thinking; (c) The Restatement is not ideologically "loaded;" (d) The Restatement is a complete "system;" (e) The Restatement carries the prestige of the American Law Institute; and (f) The Restatement has "momentum." See id. 1269–79. See also Borchers, Courts and the Second Conflicts Restatement: Some Observations and an Empirical Note, 56 Md. L. Rev. 1232, 1233–34, 1241–47 (1997) (demonstrating that many courts that profess adherence to the Restatement tend to follow its general, open-ended sections and to ignore its specific rule-like sections and suggesting that such use of the Restatement is "little more than a veil hiding judicial intuition," id. at 1233, and a camouflage for decisions reached on other grounds).

§ 2.24

1. See Reich v. Purcell, 67 Cal.2d 551, 63 Cal.Rptr. 31, 432 P.2d 727, 730–31 (1967).

2. See, e.g., Rong Yao Zhou v. Jennifer Mall Restaurant, Inc., 534 A.2d 1268, 1270 (D.C.App. 1987).

3. See Mellk v. Sarahson, 49 N.J. 226, 229 A.2d 625, 629–30 (1967).

interest analysis in tort conflicts[4] and none in contract conflicts.[5] In fact if one were to be completely literal, even those three jurisdictions should perhaps be listed elsewhere in that all three of them engage in the very weighing of state interests that Currie proscribed. Thus while New Jersey[6] and the District of Columbia[7] do so openly and unapologetically, California prefers to weigh not the interests themselves but rather the impairment that would result from subordinating them.[8] Thus, more than three decades after Currie's death, the strict judicial following of his theory appears close to extinction.

However, in the same manner that the high numerical following of the Second Restatement tends to inflate its importance in deciding actual cases, the low numerical following of interest analysis tends to undervalue the importance of that approach in influencing judicial decisions. In reality, interest analysis forms an integral part of virtually all states using a "combined modern" approach.[9] Moreover, interest analysis is often heavily employed by states that generally follow the Restatement. At least when the factual contacts are roughly evenly divided between the involved jurisdictions, court tend to abandon the Restatement and to resort to a disguised or undisguised interest analysis.[10] Finally, interest analysis provides ideological cover to the three states that follow the *lex fori* approach in tort conflicts–Kentucky[11] Michigan,[12] and Nevada.[13]

---

4. New York is not listed here because of its adherence to the *Neumeier* rules which in some instances may deviate significantly from interest analysis. See infra § 2.25 n.19. Similarly, with regard to contracts, New York is no longer an interest analysis state because it switched to a mixed approach since 1993. See infra § 2.25 n. 20.

5. Oregon, California, and the District of Columbia initially adopted interest analysis for contract conflicts. See Lilienthal v. Kaufman, 239 Or. 1, 395 P.2d 543, 549 (1964); Travelers Ins. Co. v. Workmen's Comp. Appeals Bd., 68 Cal.2d 7, 64 Cal. Rptr. 440, 434 P.2d 992, 994 (1967); and McCrossin v. Hicks Chevrolet, Inc., 248 A.2d 917, 921 (D.C.1969)). However, these jurisdictions eventually switched to a mixed approach. See infra § 2.25 nn. 9, 11, 17–18.

6. See, e.g., Eger v. E.I. Du Pont De-Nemours Co., 110 N.J. 133, 539 A.2d 1213 (1988).

7. See, e.g., Kaiser–Georgetown Comm. Health Plan, Inc. v. Stutsman, 491 A.2d 502 (D.C.App.1985); Stutsman v. Kaizer Found. Health Plan, 546 A.2d 367 (D.C.App.1988).

8. See Bernhard v. Harrah's Club, 16 Cal.3d 313, 546 P.2d 719, 128 Cal.Rptr. 215 (1976), cert. denied 429 U.S. 859, 97 S.Ct. 159, 50 L.Ed.2d 136 (1976); Offshore Rental Co. v. Continental Oil Co., 22 Cal.3d 157, 583 P.2d 721, 148 Cal.Rptr. 867 (1978) (following Baxter's comparative impairment theory discussed supra § 2.9 at nn.28–29).

9. See infra § 2.25.

10. See supra § 2.14 nn.34–35; Symeonides, The Judicial Acceptance of the Second Conflicts Restatement: A Mixed Blessing, 56 Md. L. Rev. 1248, 1262–63 (1997).

11. See Foster v. Leggett, 484 S.W.2d 827 (Ky.1972).

12. Sexton v. Ryder Truck Rental, Inc., 413 Mich. 406, 320 N.W.2d 843 (1982); Olmstead v. Anderson, 428 Mich. 1, 400 N.W.2d 292 (1987); Sutherland v. Kennington Truck Service, Ltd., 454 Mich. 274, 562 N.W.2d 466 (1997).

13. Motenko v. MGM Dist., Inc., 112 Nev. 1038, 921 P.2d 933, 935 (Nev. 1996) (adopting a *lex fori* approach in tort cases unless "another State has an overwhelming interest"); Northwest Pipe v. Eighth Judicial Dist. Court, 118 Nev. 133, 42 P.3d 244 (2002).

8. *Other Modern Approaches*

§ 2.25 Five states (Arkansas,[1] Minnesota,[2] New Hampshire,[3] Rhode Island[4] and Wisconsin)[5] follow Professor Leflar's choice-influencing-considerations in tort conflicts, and in two states (Minnesota[6] and Wisconsin)[7] do likewise in contract conflicts.

In tort conflicts, California follows interest analysis with the addendum of Baxter's comparative impairment theory.[8] However, in contract conflicts, at least those involving choice-of-law clauses, the California Supreme Court tends to rely heavily on the Second Restatement and to combine it with comparative impairment.[9] New Jersey[10] and the District of Columbia[11] combine interest analysis with the Second Restatement in contract conflicts, while Massachusetts[12] does likewise in both tort and contract conflicts. Hawaii follows a combination of interest analysis, the Second Restatement, and Leflar's choice-influencing considerations.[13] North Dakota follows the same combination in contract conflicts, but perhaps in different dosages.[14] Pennsylvania combines interest analysis and the Second Restatement but in tort conflicts it also draws from Cavers's principles of preference.[15] Louisiana has its own comprehensive codification which draws from the general American conflicts experience,

---

§ 2.25

1. See Wallis v. Mrs. Smith's Pie Co., 261 Ark. 622, 550 S.W.2d 453, 458–59 (1977).

2. See Milkovich v. Saari, 295 Minn. 155, 203 N.W.2d 408, 413 (1973).

3. See Clark v. Clark, 107 N.H. 351, 222 A.2d 205, 210 (1966).

4. See Woodward v. Stewart, 104 R.I. 290, 243 A.2d 917, 923 (1968).

5. See Heath v. Zellmer, 35 Wis.2d 578, 151 N.W.2d 664, 672 (1967).

6. See Hague v. Allstate Ins. Co., 289 N.W.2d 43, 48–49 (Minn.1978).

7. See Haines v. Mid–Century Ins. Co., 47 Wis.2d 442, 177 N.W.2d 328, 333 (1970); Schlosser v. Allis–Chalmers Corp., 86 Wis.2d 226, 271 N.W.2d 879, 885–86 (1978).

8. See. e.g. Bernhard v. Harrah's Club, 16 Cal.3d 313, 546 P.2d 719, 128 Cal.Rptr. 215, *cert. denied*, 429 U.S. 859, 97 S.Ct. 159, 50 L.Ed.2d 136 (1976); Offshore Rental Co. v. Continental Oil Co., 22 Cal.3d 157, 583 P.2d 721, 148 Cal.Rptr. 867 (1978).

9. See Nedlloyd Lines, B.V. v. Superior Court, 3 Cal.4th 459, 11 Cal.Rptr.2d 330, 834 P.2d 1148 (1992).

10. See Gilbert Spruance Co. v. Pennsylvania Mfrs. Ass'n Ins. Co., 134 N.J. 96, 629 A.2d 885 (1993).

11. See District of Columbia Ins. Guar. Ass'n v. Algernon Blair, Inc. 565 A.2d 564 (D.C.App.1989) (applying interest analysis but also relying on the Restatement Second); Owen v. Owen, 427 A.2d 933, 937 (D.C.1981) (mixed approach, described as a search for the "more substantial interest," but reduced to contact counting).

12. See Bushkin Associates, Inc. v. Raytheon Co., 393 Mass. 622, 473 N.E.2d 662 (1985) a contract conflict in which the court stated explicitly that, as it had previously done in tort conflicts, the court would not tie itself to any particular modern approach but would instead "feel free to draw from any of the various lists." The court drew from the Restatement Second and Leflar's lists, but applied them in a way that resembled interest analysis.

13. See Lewis v. Lewis, 69 Haw. 497, 748 P.2d 1362 (1988) contract conflict interpreting Peters v. Peters, 63 Haw. 653, 634 P.2d 586 (1981), a tort conflict, as having adopted a "significant relationship" test with primary emphasis on the state with the "strongest interest."

14. See American Family Mut. Ins. Co. v. Farmers Ins. Exchange, 504 N.W.2d 307 (N.D.1993); Starry v. Central Dakota Printing, Inc., 530 N.W.2d 323 (N.D.1995).

15. See, e.g., Cipolla v. Shaposka, 439 Pa. 563, 267 A.2d 854 (1970).

but also goes beyond that experience.[16] Oregon has followed the same
path and enacted a codification for contract conflicts.[17] However, in tort
conflicts, Oregon continues to combine interest analysis and the Second
Restatement, but "coupled with an almost irresistible forum presumption."[18] Finally, New York follows interest analysis combined with the
Neumeier rules in tort conflicts[19] and with a "significant contacts"
analysis in contract conflicts.[20]

VII. THE EVOLUTION OF PRINCIPLED RULES: A GOAL FOR THE FUTURE

§ 2.26   As the preceding discussion demonstrates, there is little
doubt that the conflicts revolution has *prevailed* over the traditional
theory. But to prevail is one thing and to *succeed* is another. The latter
cannot be judged by numbers alone. It can be judged by examining
whether the revolution has produced a new *system* to replace the old
one, and by how well the new system attends to the basic needs and
aspirations of the choice-of-law process, such as uniformity of result and
predictability of decisions. Judged in this light, the revolution did not
and could not have succeeded. To begin with, its most radical branch,
that of Brainerd Currie, subscribed to neither of the above goals[1] and
did not aspire to erect a new system.[2] Currie's analysis, as well as Ehrenzweig's, claimed particular insight into what courts really do[3] and

16. The Louisiana codification combines
elements from many modern American and
European approaches into a distinct identity. For discussion of this codification by its
drafter, see, *inter alia*, Symeonides, Private
International Law Codification in a Mixed
Jurisdiction: The Louisiana Experience, 57
RabelsZ 460 (1993); Symeonides, Les
grands problèmes de droit international
privé et la nouvelle codification de Louisiane, 81 Revue critique 223, 233–281
(1992); Symeonides, Louisiana's New Law
of Choice of Law for Tort Conflicts: An
Exegesis, 66 Tul. L. Rev. 677 (1992). For
judicial applications of the new codification,
see Symeonides, Louisiana Conflicts Law:
"Two Surprises," 53 La. L. Rev. 497 (1994).
For a demonstration as to how some well-
known cases might be resolved under the
codification, see Symeonides, Resolving Six
Celebrated Conflicts Cases Through Statutory Choice-of-Law Rules, 48 Mercer L. Rev.
837 (1997).

17. See O.R.S §§ 81–100 to 81–135, effective January 1, 2002, reproduced in 67
RabelsZ 748 (2003), and 3 Ybk. Int'l L. 405
(2001). For discussion, see Nafziger, Oregon's Project to Codify Choice-of-Law
Rules, 60 La. L. Rev. 1189 (2000); Nafziger,
Oregon's Conflicts Law Applicable to Contracts, 38 Willamette L. Rev. 397 (2002);
Symeonides, Codifying Choice of Law for

Contracts: The Oregon Experience, 67 RabelsZ 726 (2003).

18. Symeonides, Choice of Law in the
American Courts in 1994: A View "From
the Trenches," 43 Am. J. Comp. L. 1, 3 n.6
(1995) (quoting Professor Nafziger).

19. See Cooney v. Osgood Machinery,
Inc., 81 N.Y.2d 66, 595 N.Y.S.2d 919, 612
N.E.2d 277 (1993).

20. See In re Allstate Ins. Co. (Stolarz),
81 N.Y.2d 219, 597 N.Y.S.2d 904, 613
N.E.2d 936 (1993).

§ 2.26

1. See, e.g., B. Currie, Selected Essays
on the Conflict of Laws 614 (1963) (specifically dismissing the view that a state should
be guided in its choice-of-law decisions by
the "needs of the interstate and international system").

2. See Currie's denouncement of *all*
choice-of-law rules, supra § 2.14 n.7.

3. Ehrenzweig, for instance, pointed out
frequently that the formulation of his theory was the result of an examination of 10,-
000 judicial decisions. See, e.g., A. Ehrenzweig, Private International Law 88 (1967).
This point is also made by Hancock: "[i]t
enables [the judge] to decide relatively in-

undertook to provide a theoretical framework in justification of the practice. That "what courts were really doing" might not always be an appropriate solution, was not considered by Currie and Ehrenzweig. The "homeward" trend[4] became institutionalized in some courts with its consequence of law-selection through forum shopping, at a time when interstate and international contacts grew. More differentiated, weighing approaches–while highly sophisticated in some cases–imposed impracticable burdens on courts. Aspects of some of them, principally the "better law" approach, appeared simpler and thus seem to preserve the illusion of "analysis." In reality, however, such an approach would abandon the insights that the analytic approaches attempted to introduce and would either turn inward to the *lex fori,* or place undue emphasis on only *one* of the goals of conflicts law–justice in the individual case–at the expense of the integrity and stability of interstate and international conflicts law as a legal *system*, what Kegel calls "conflicts law justice."[5] The Second Restatement's more moderate approach, which expressly calls for consideration of the needs of the interstate and international system, cannot be accused of encouraging "home trending," but it too has failed to produce the necessary degree of predictabil-

frequent choice of law cases by the familiar process he uses every day in deciding domestic cases, that is, by considering the strength and significance of the policies of statutes and decisional rules. There is ample evidence that thoughtful judges have for many decades made the underlying policies of domestic rules (especially those of the forum) the real, motivating grounds of their decisions in choice cases. Under the traditional system it was not too difficult for a shrewd judge, having decided which domestic rule should control, to find a choice of law principle that would lead to that result." Hancock, Policy Controlled State Interest Analysis in Choice of Law, Measure of Damages, Torts Cases, 26 Int'l & Comp. L.Q. 799, 819 (1977).

4. The term was coined in 1932 by A. Nussbaum, Deutches Internationales Privatrecht 43. For brief discussion see P. Picone & W. Wengler, Internationales Privatrecht 306–07 (1974). Ehrenzweig, consistent with his rejection of a "superlaw" (supra § 2.10 n.19), preferred to speak of a "trend to stay at home." A. Ehrenzweig, Private International Law 104 (1967). See also supra § 2.14 n.53.

5. Kegel, Begriffs-und Interessenjurisprudenz im internationalen Privatrecht, in: Festschrift für Lewald 259, 270 ff. (1953); Kegel in F. Juenger, Zum Wandel des Internationalen Privatrechts 35, 44 (113 Schriften der Juristischen Studiengesellschaft 1974); Kegel & Schurig, Internationales Privatrecht 134 et seq., 145 (9th ed. 2004). A result of the American approach which intermingles considerations of substantive law policies with conflicts law is that "conflicts law disappears into the 'black hole' of substantive law." Kegel, Paternal Home and Dream Home: Traditional Conflict of Laws and the American Reformers, 27 Am. J. Comp. L. 615, 617 (1979). See also Hay, Reflections on Conflict-of—Laws Methodology, 32 Hastings L.J. 1644, 1659–62 (1981); Hay, Flexibility versus Predictability and Uniformity in Choice of Law, 226 Recueil des Cours 281 (1991–I). " . . . [F]ormulations of policies of various kinds of 'justice' are [not] necessarily helpful—except that one cannot be sufficiently emphatic in endorsing Kegel's rejection of 'substantive' as against 'private international law justice' as a guiding line for decisions in individual cases." Kahn–Freund, General Problems of Private International Law, 143 Recueil des Cours 139, at 466 (1974–III). In a case like *Babcock*, "[i]t may be 'just' or 'unjust' to [exempt the driver for liability under the Ontario guest statute] . . . , [b]ut the question is not whether it is just or not that the driver should be liable to the guest, the question is whether it is more just to apply the law of Ontario or that of New York. . . . [Judges may have preferences for one law over another but] it is inadvisable to elevate the fact of human weakness to a principle of legislative policy." Id. See also von Mehren, Choice of Law and the Problem of Justice, 41 Law & Contemp. Probs. 27 (1977). For a rejoinder, advocating choice of law solely on the basis of substantive law policies, see Morrison, Death of Conflicts, 29 Villanova L. Rev. 313 (1983–84).

ity in the two areas that formed the revolution's arena–tort and contract conflicts.

Indeed, all of the above approaches have succeeded in one respect but failed in another. They have succeeded in demonstrating the deficiencies of the rigid rules of the First Restatement and in persuading the great majority of courts to abandon them. But, to the extent these approaches aspired to do so, they failed to produce a new choice-of-law *system* with which to replace the old one. As the early New York experience shows,[6] courts have often produced *ad hoc* results and, in the process, have spent disproportionate effort on tasks that often are insoluble. "When any court embarks on a determination of the 'relevant policies of other interested states and the relative interests of those states in the determination of the particular issue' (*Restatement . . . § 6*), the endeavor, in many instances, is like skeet shooting with a bow and arrow: a direct hit is likely to be a rarity, if not pure luck."[7] As one observer put it, American conflicts law "has become a tale of a thousand-and-one-cases"[8] in which "each case is decided as if it were unique and of first impression."[9] Contradictory results in the case law, confusion, and also the "homeward trend" have been the resulting consequences.

While these consequences had been both predictable and understandable during the first years of the revolution, the question faced more than three decades later is whether this freewheeling experimentation, this "impressionisme juridique,"[10] or "judicial particularistic intuitionism"[11] has gone on a bit too long, and whether American conflicts law needs and is ripe for consolidation and standardization.[12] We believe

---

6. For the New York development from *Babcock* to *Neumeier* see infra §§ 17.29–17.30.

7. Fisher v. Huck, 50 Or.App. 635, 624 P.2d 177, 178 (1981), review granted 291 Or. 117, 631 P.2d 339 (1981). The case was settled and the appeal not pursued. See Nafziger & Dixon, Oregon's Choice-of-Law Process, 60 Or. L. Rev. 219 n.2 (1981).

8. Kozyris, Interest Analysis Facing its Critics, 46 Ohio St. L.J. 569, 578 (1985).

9. Id. at 580.

10. Loussouarn, Cours general de droit international privé, 139 Recueil des Cours 270, 338 (1973–II). See also Nadelmann, Impressionism and Unification of Law: The EEC Draft Convention on the Law Applicable to Contractual and Non–Contractual Obligations, 24 Am. J. Comp. L. 1 (1976).

11. Kozyris, supra n.8, at 580. See also id: "[A]ny system calling for open-ended and endless soul-searching on a case-by-case basis carries a high burden of persuasion. With centuries of experience and doctrinal elaboration behind us, we hardly need more lab testing and narrow findings. Rather, we need to make up our minds and

make some sense out of the chaos. . . . In my jurisprudential universe, fixed but revisable rules which lead to good results in the overwhelming majority of the cases, and which are supplemented by some general corrective principles to mitigate injustice in the remaining cases, are superior to, and incredibly more efficient than, a system in which each case is decided as if it were unique and of first impression."

12. See Reese, General Course on Private International Law, 150 Recueil des Cours 1, 61 *et passim* (1976–II). Reese argued that the conflicts experience since the revolution had "reached the stage where most areas of choice of law can be covered by general principles subject to imprecise exceptions. We should press on, however, beyond these principles to the development, as soon as our knowledge permits, of precise rules." Id. at 62; Rosenberg, Two Views on *Kell v. Henderson:* An Opinion for the New York Court of Appeals, 67 Colum. L. Rev. 459, 464 (1967) (arguing that the "unruly reasonableness" brought about by the abandonment of the "unreasonable rules" of the traditional theory, should be succeeded by a "principled reasonableness.") In his

that the answer must be an affirmative one. Courts need and are entitled to more guidance than the iconoclastic literature has provided.[13] In addition, the courts themselves must contribute to the evolution of new rules by avoiding excessively casuistic analyses and by articulating their decisions in a manner that can yield principled rules capable of serving as precedent in future cases. Conflicts law, in this respect, does not and should not differ from case law in general: once a problem has been analyzed and a rule articulated, the result should be a rule of precedent that may reasonably be expected to be followed in the future. Predictability in conflicts law is as important as it is in substantive law.[14] A reexamination of the policies and goals underlying choice-of-law rules has been necessary indeed. But, once undertaken, it should not have to be repeated in each new case that arises. Stability in conflicts law requires that this body of law, like any other, be governed by precedent and that the precedent be subject to change only to the extent that it has always been in our common law system.[15]

words, "[t]he problem is to escape both horns of the dilemma by avoiding both unreasonable rules and an unruly reasonableness that is destructive of many of the values of law." Id. at 464. See also D. Cavers, The Choice-of-Law Process 108–113, 121–23 (1965); Hay, Reflections on Conflict-of-Laws Methodology, 32 Hastings L.J. 1644, 1672 (1981); Kozyris, Interest Analysis Facing its Critics, 46 Ohio St. L. J. 569, 577–80 (1985); Reese, Choice of Law: Rules or Approach, 57 Cornell L. Rev. 315, 319 (1972); Rosenberg, The Comeback of Choice-of-Law Rules, 81 Colum. L. Rev. 946 (1981); Rosenberg, Comments on Reich v. Purcell, 15 U.C.L.A. L. Rev. 551, 644 (1968); Traynor, War and Peace in the Conflict of Laws, 25 Int'l & Comp. L.Q. 121, 127 (1976).

13. See also Kay, The Use of Comparative Impairment to Resolve True Conflicts, 68 Cal. L. Rev. 576, 610–17 (1980), who argues "for a return to basic principles, so that we may consolidate some of the competing approaches." Id. at 615. In her view, however, "the unifying element should be a preference for local law." Id. As she acknowledges in a different context elsewhere (id. at 610), the use of forum law in all cases presenting a "true conflict" does "not lack predictability ... but it undeniably lacks uniformity." Cf. Weintraub, Who's Afraid of Constitutional Limitations on Choice of Law?, 10 Hofstra L. Rev. 17, 35 (1981) ("We have not articulated a cogent, coherent, reasonably administrable conflicts methodology to whose banner all reasonable courts will rally."). See also Kay, A Defense of Currie's Governmental Interest Analysis, 215 Recueil des Cours 9 (1989–III).

14. With respect to Professor Kegel's concept of "conflicts justice," see supra n.5; Hay, Flexibility versus Predictability and Uniformity in Choice of Law, 226 Recueil des Cours 281 (1991–I); Hay, Reflections on Conflict-of-Laws Methodology, 32 Hastings L.J. 1644, 1659 (1981).

15. Cf. Ingber, The Interface of Myth and Practice, 34 Vand. L. Rev. 309, 315–18 (1981); L. Fuller, The Morality of Law 36 (1969). See also J.H.C. Morris, The Conflict of Laws 531 (3d ed. 1984):

"[N]one of the new American methods (except the choice-influencing factors of the Restatement Second) is suitable for adoption by English courts in international cases. We would do better to build on what is good in the traditional system, as the Restatement Second seeks to do, rather than to abolish that system altogether and start again. On the other hand, these methods have three lessons which we should do well to take to heart. The first is that choice of law rules should be flexible and should be flexibly applied. The second is that they should never be applied without some regard to the content of the foreign law referred to. The third is that we should be on the alert to identify and avoid the false conflicts, and not be afraid to decide such cases in accordance with the law that is common to both countries, rather than in accordance with traditional conflict rules."

Professor Hill in his comprehensive review of choice-of-law theory, and especially also of Professor Cavers's position, arrives at similar conclusions, certainly with respect to Morris' first and second points: Hill, The Judicial Function in Choice of

In some areas of the law—for instance, with respect to immovables (situs law)—the traditional rules have, for the most part, proved workable, and the Second Restatement and the courts have retained them, subject only to displacement in exceptional cases. When a court is asked to depart from a traditional rule, the court should consider the purposes and policies underlying the rule in order to determine whether to abandon or modify it. If the rule is to be changed, an initial step should be to determine from the purposes of the apparently conflicting rules whether they in fact present a true or a "false" conflict. The discussion in subsequent chapters contains a number of illustrations of situations presenting false conflicts.[16] By hypothesis, the conclusion that the case presents a false conflict warrants the application of forum law in cases in which the forum is one of the concerned states, or of the law of another concerned state when the forum is "disinterested."[17]

If the interests of the forum and the other state(s) or the purposes and policies underlying the conflicting rules do conflict, in the sense that both rules do claim application to the case, the forum must resolve the impasse. Easy solutions are the application of forum law, subject to constitutional limitations,[18] as Currie suggested, or a return to the traditional approach, perhaps in modified form, as exemplified by the New York Court of Appeal's decision in *Neumeier v. Kuehner*.[19] In the particular choice-of-law chapters in this volume, we advocate the elaboration of principled *rules* based upon the identification of policy objectives to be served in the particular area of the law. For torts, for instance, we emphasize the goals of spreading the risk of loss and of compensation for the injured party. In contracts, major policy objectives are: (a) "commercial security," which includes protection of the reliance interest of the parties (e.g., their expectation that they entered into a valid bargain) and of third parties; and (b) the freedom of parties with equal bargaining power to shape their own affairs, including their ability to stipulate the applicable law (party autonomy).[20] In these areas, and in others, the aim is to identify the goals and policies to be served by the applicable substantive law and to suggest choice-of-law rules that—in as objective a fashion as possible—will advance these goals and policies. The law selected in this fashion may or may not be the law of the forum or of

---

Law, 85 Colum. L. Rev. 1585 (1985). See also Hay, Flexibility versus Predictability and Uniformity in Choice of Law, 226 Recueil des Cours 281, 392–400 (1991–I).

16. See, e.g., Bing v. Halstead, 495 F.Supp. 517 (S.D.N.Y.1980) (discussed infra § 3.14 n.4).

17. It will be rare in practice that the forum is indeed neutral or disinterested. When it is, this may be the consequence of a deliberate choice by the parties, by means of a choice-of-court clause. See M/S Bremen v. Zapata Off–Shore Co., 407 U.S. 1, 92 S.Ct. 1907, 32 L.Ed.2d 513 (1972), mandate conformed 464 F.2d 1395 (5th Cir.1972). In such cases, the stipulation in favor of a

particular court will also often be accompanied by a choice-of-law clause. See Hoes of America, Inc. v. Hoes (Klaus–Gerd), 493 F.Supp. 1205 (C.D.Ill.1979). When the plaintiff unilaterally chooses a neutral (unconnected) forum, principles of forum non conveniens suggest that the court should dismiss the action in favor of, or order transfer to, the more convenient forum.

18. See infra §§ 3.20–3.35.

19. 31 N.Y.2d 121, 335 N.Y.S.2d 64, 286 N.E.2d 454 (1972), appeal after remand 43 A.D.2d 109, 349 N.Y.S.2d 866 (1973), discussed infra § 17.31.

20. See infra §§ 18.1–18.12.

a state that would also have been selected by the rules of the First Restatement. Such a result, however, is the *consequence* and not the *purpose* of the analysis. Instead, our aim is to suggest both approaches and rules that are principled and not *ad hoc* and may thereby become the basis for decisions that have precedential value. Courts and scholars may well differ with our particular suggestions as they assess the essential purposes and policies to be served by new choice of law rules. The point is that, while "we may have to accept the articulated *ad hoc* decision as an interim substitute, . . . we should persevere in the search for rules or principles which would determine when the law of one state which served one purpose should be preferred to the law of another state which served a different purpose."[21]

VIII.   CONFLICTS LAW REFORM IN OTHER COUNTRIES

§ 2.27   While American conflicts law was stumbling through a loud revolution, private international law in the rest of the world and especially in Europe was going through a quiet evolution[1] were the old rules

---

21.   D. Cavers, The Choice of Law Process 121 (1965); Rosenberg, The Comeback of Choice-of-Law Rules, 81 Colum. L. Rev. 946 (1981).

§ 2.27

1.   The reasons for which European PIL systems never—or never wholeheartedly—followed in the path of the American conflicts revolution, either in direction or in degree, are many and varied. With regard to continental Europe, the subject has been discussed authoritatively. See, e.g., Audit, A Continental Lawyer Looks at Contemporary American Choice-of-Law Principles, 27 Am. J. Comp. L. 589 (1979); Jayme, The American Conflicts Revolution and its Impact on European Private International Law, in Forty Years On: The Evolution of Postwar Private International Law in Europe, Centrum voor Buitenlands Recht en Internationaal Privaatrecht Universiteit van Amsterdam, 15 (1992); Kegel, Paternal Home and Dream Home: Traditional Conflict of Laws and the American Reformers, 27 Am. J. Comp. L. 615 (1979); Kropholler, & von Hein, From Approach to Rule–Orientation in American Tort Conflicts in Law and Justice in a Multistate World: Essays in Honor of Arthur T. von Mehren, 317 (Nafziger, & Symeonides, eds. 2002); Siehr, Ehrenzweigs lex-fori-Theorie und ihre Bedeutung für das amerikanische und deutsche Kollisionsrecht, 34 RabelsZ 583 (1970); Siehr, Domestic Relations in Europe: European Equivalents to American Evolutions, 30 Am. J. Comp. L. 37 (1982); Vischer, New Tendencies in European Conflict of Laws and the Influence of the US-Doctrine: A Short Survey, in Law and Justice in a Multistate World: Essays in Honor of Arthur T. von Mehren, 459 (Nafziger & Symeonides, eds. 2002); Vitta, The Impact in Europe of the American "Conflicts Revolution," 30 Am. J. Comp. L. 1 (1982). See also Symeonides, An Outsider's View of the American Approach to Choice of Law: Comparative Observations on Current American and Continental Conflicts Doctrine 159–374 (1980).

With regard to England, Professor Fentiman attributes this phenomenon to the lack of any perceptible influence by American legal realism and the fact that the American approaches have been perceived as being too closely associated with the peculiarities of American federalism and interstate conflicts. See Fentiman, English Private International Law, in S. Symeonides, Private International Law at the End of the 20th Century: Progress or Regress? at 169 (1999) ("[U]nlike their counterparts in the United States, English lawyers have never—or have never entirely—lost faith in the effectiveness and validity of traditional conceptions of legal reasoning. Certainly, English law never experienced the challenge (and response) to formalism represented by the American realist movement. . . . [I]f the American conflicts revolution is a realist revolution, it is striking how little English conflicts scholarship owes to both."). See also id. at 173–74. For other English perspectives, see Morris, supra n. 15; Fawcett, Cross–Fertilization in Private International Law, 53 Current Leg. Prob. 303 (2000);

where gradually repaired rather than abandoned. Partial codification of conflicts rules and settled judicial precedents provided the certainty and predictability in Europe that American law has lacked in its period of transition; this may explain in part the early European criticism of the new American approaches and experiments.[2] For a number of years, the European literature[3] has been replete with ideas for reform, some American-law inspired, others developed by drawing on comparative civil-law traditions. Judicial decisions began to depart from established patterns.[4] To the extent that some of these ideas for reform draw on American approaches which, in turn and as previously noted, had often resurrected much earlier European notions,[5] history is now coming full circle. So is the criticism of the new approaches now crossing the Atlantic in the opposite direction.[6] The noteworthy fact remains that the systems are drawing closer, and both are benefitting from increased communication and exchange of constructive criticism.

While this in itself is not surprising, what might be surprising is that this rapprochement has not been impeded, and it might have been facilitated, by the fact that many European countries have chosen to codify or recodify their conflicts law. Indeed, while conflicts law and legislation continue to be considered as inherently incompatible in the United States,[7] and while for awhile even Europeans expressed serious

Fawcett, Is American Governmental Interest Analysis the Solution to English Tort Choice of Law Problems? 31 Int'l & Comp. L.Q. 31 (1982).

2. See Kegel, supra n.1; Audit, supra n.1.

3. For an early survey see Juenger, Trends in European Conflicts Law, 60 Cornell L. Rev. 969 (1975). See also Siehr, supra n.1 at 591; Rehbinder, Zur Politisierung des internationalen Privatrechts, 1973 Juristenzeitung 151; Zweigert, Some Reflections on the Sociological Dimensions of Private International Law or: What Is Justice in the Conflict of Laws?, 44 U. Colo. L. Rev. 283, 292 (1973); Stegemann, Der Anknuepfungsgesichtspunkt der most significant relationship nach dem Restatement of the Laws, Second, Conflict of the Law 2nd im deutschen internationalen Deliktsrecht und Vertragsrecht (1995).

4. See Boys v. Chaplin, [1971] A.C. 356, 389 (H. L.), with Comment by Carter in 107 L.Q.R. 405 (1991) adopting a solution patterned after Babcock v. Jackson; Judgment of May 4, 1971, 31 Bverfg 58 (German Constitutional Court), applying constitutional-law principles to choice-of-law; Müller-Freienfels, Conflicts of Law and Constitutional Law, 45 Chicago L. Rev. 598 (1978). European courts at times also expressly relied on the American Restatement (Second): von Overbeck, Cours général de droit international privé, 176 Recueil des Cours 28 (1982–III).

5. See Lalive, Remarks, 90–2 Zeitschrift für Schweizerisches Recht 404, 407 (1971). See also Vitta, supra n. 1; Siehr, Domestic Relations in Europe: European Equivalents to American Evolutions, id. at 37; von Overbeck, supra n.4.

6. See Nadelmann, Impressionism and Unification of Law: The EEC Draft Convention on the Law Applicable to Contractual and Non–Contractual Obligations, 24 Am. J. Comp. L. 1, 11 (1976); and infra n.8.

7. For the scarcity of American conflicts legislation and "the persistent reluctance of American conflicts scholars to advocate legislative solutions," see Cavers, Legislative Choice of Law: Some European Examples, 44 So. Calif. L. Rev. 340, 359–60 (1971). For the reasons, see, e.g., Currie, Comments on Babcock v. Jackson, 63 Colum. L. Rev. 1233, at 1241 (1963) ("[N]ew efforts to find short cuts and syntheses should be sternly discouraged. We are beginning to recover from a long siege of intoxication resulting from overindulgence in generalities; for a while, at least, total abstinence should be enforced"); Reese, Statutes in Choice of Law, 35 Am. J. Comp. L. 395, 396 (1987) ("[n]o legislature, no matter how wise it may be, could envisage all of the almost endless possibilities."); Trautman, Reflections On Conflict-of-Laws Methodology, 32 Hastings L.J. 1612, 1621 (1981) ("[L]egislative direction is inherently incapable of capturing the nuance and sophistication neces-

misgivings on whether conflicts law is susceptible to codification,[8] those misgivings eventually gave way[9] to a fury of codification activity.[10]

Since the 1960s, more than twenty jurisdictions have codified or re-codified their conflicts law, in whole or in part, in the following chrono-

sary for just and satisfactory choice-of-law solutions"); Leflar, Choice-of-Law Statutes, 44 Tenn. L. Rev. 951 (1977); Sedler, Reflections on Conflict-of-Laws Methodology, 32 Hastings L.J. 1628, 1636 (1981). But see Peterson, New Openness to Statutory Choice of Law Solutions, 38 Am. J. Comp. L. 423, 423 ("We may be seeing a sea change in the attitudes of American conflicts scholars with respect to the use of statutes in solving conflicts problems."); Gottesman, Draining the Dismal Swamp: The Case for Federal Choice of Law Statutes, 80 Geo. L.J. 1 (1991); Kramer, On the Need for a Uniform Choice of Law Code, 89 Mich. L. Rev. 2134 (1991); Reese, Choice of Law: Rules or Approach? 57 Cornell L. Rev. 315 (1972); Symeonides, Exception Clauses in American Conflicts Law, 42 Am. J. Comp. L. 813, 817–18, 861–64 (1994).

8. See, e.g., Neuhaus, Empfiehlt sich eine Kodifizierung des internationalen Privatrechts?, 37 RabelsZ 453 (1973); O. Kahn–Freund, General Problems of Private International Law 80–84 (1976); Schwind, Problems of Codification of Private International Law, 17 Int'l & Comp. L.Q. 428, 431 (1968). On this side of the Atlantic, Nadelmann viewed codification efforts with concern and stated: "No worse time could be imagined for codification, be it for municipal purposes or for unification of the law on the regional or international level." Nadelmann, supra n.6, at 15. The debates on the desirability and feasibility of codifying conflicts law resembled the discussions in the United States during the preparation of the Second Restatement. They also resemble much earlier German discussion between Thibaut and Savigny, with Savigny arguing that " ... in our times a good code is not yet possible." Vom Beruf unsrer Zeit für Gesetzgebung und Rechtswissenschaft 49 (1814) (authors' translation).

9. Apparently, this is so even in England, the fountainhead of the common-law tradition. See, e.g., North, Problems of Codification in a Common Law System, 46 RabelsZ 490 (1982). Professor North who served as the Law Commissioner for England and Wales, assured his readers that "[c]odes are not monsters ... [and that] [e]ven if they are, they can be trained." Id. He then reported that "[t]here is now [in England] a steady and continuous programme of re-examination, reform and restatement in statutory form of ... [En-glish] rules of private international law," id. at 500, and predicted that "the next few years will witness a major transformation of English private international law from case law to reformed statute law," id. at 501, and that the end product would be "an 'English codification' or ... a necessary step in the process towards the production of a continental style of code." Id. In 1995, England enacted a statute on tort conflicts. See infra n.30. Two decades later, North observed that "[o]ne of the most marked changes of the 20th century has been the intrusion of statute into private international law, and area of the common law which was essentially created by judges." North, Private International Law: Change or Decay? 50 Int'l & Comp. L.Q. 477, 477 (2001). See also id. at 496 ("a most striking feature of the development of private international law over the last century has been that statute law has been the primary instrument of change.").

10. For a comprehensive review of codification efforts in several countries, see D. Fernández Arroyo, La codificación del derecho internacional privado en América Latina (1994); E. Vassilakakis, Orientations méthologiques dans les codifications récentes du droit international privé en Europe (1987); G. Parra Aranguren, Codificacion del derecho internacional privado en America (1998); Cavers, Legislative Choice of Law: Some European Examples, 44 So. Calif. L. Rev. 340 (1971); Ferrer–Correia, A., "Les problèmes de codification en droit international privé," 145 Recueil des Cours (1975); Jayme, Considerations historique et actuelles sur la codification du droit international privé, 177 Recueil des Cours 9, 51–85 (1982–IV); Rigaux, La méthode des conflits de lois dans les codifications et projets de codification de la dernière décennie, 74 Review critique de droit international privé 1 (1985); Rigaux, Codification of Private International Law: Pros and Cons, 60 La. L. Rev. 1321 (2000); von Overbeck, Les questions générales du droit international privé à la lumiere des codifications et projets récents, 176 Recueil des Cours 9 (1982–III); von Overbeck, De quelques règles générales de conflit de lois dans les codifications récentes, in Private Law in the International Arena–Liber Amicorum Kurt Siehr 545 (J. Basedow, e.o., eds. 2000)

logical order: the former Czechoslovakia (1964),[11] Poland (1965),[12] Portugal (1967),[13] Spain (1974),[14] the former East Germany (1975),[15] Hungary (1979),[16] Yugoslavia (1978 and 1983),[17] Austria (1979),[18]

11. See Act 97 of 1963 (effective April 1964) on Private International law and Procedure. For a French translation, see 54 Revue critique 614 (1965). For discussion, see Bystricky, Les traits généraux de la codification tchécoslovaque sur le droit international privé, 123 Recueil des Cours 409 (1968).

12. See Act of November 12, 1965, effective July 1, 1966, on Private International Law. For discussion, see Lasok, The Polish System of Private International Law, 15 Am. J. Comp. L. 330 (1967); Rajski, The New Polish Private International Law 1965, 15 Int'l & Comp. L.Q. 457 (1966); Pajor, Polish Private International Law, in S. Symeonides, Private International Law at the End of the 20th Century: Progress or Regress? 329 (1999).

13. See Portuguese Civil Code arts. 14–65 as revised in 1966. For a French trasnslation, see Asser Instituut, Les legislations de droit international privé 157 (1971) with an introductory note by Ferrer–Correia and Baptista–Machado; and 57 Rev. Critique 369 (1968). For discussion, see Garcia Velasco, Conception del derecho internacional privado en el nuevo codigo civil portuques (1971); Ferrer Correia, Les problèmes de codification en droit international privé, 145 Recueil des Cours, 55 (1975); Moura Ramos, Le droit international privé portugais, in S. Symeonides, supra n. 12, at 349. For an American perspective, see Cavers, supra n.7. For subsequent revisions, see Law no. 496/77, discussed in Moura Ramos, Portugal Droit de la famille Dispositions intéressant le droit international privé, 67 Revue critique, 598 (1978); Almeno de Sá, A revisão do Código Civil e a Constituição, 3 Revista de Direito e Economia 425 (1977); Baptista Machado, Lições de Direito Internacional Privado 404, 422–26 (2d ed. 1982). For the new codification of Macao, see 2 Ybk. Priv. Int'l L. 329 (2000). For discussion, see Marques Dos Santos, The New Private international Law Rules of Macao, 2 Ybk. Priv. Int'l L. 133 (2000); Moura Ramos, The Private International Law Rules of the New Special Administrative Region of Macau of the People's Republic of China, 60 La. L. Rev. 1281 (2000).

14. See Spanish Civil Code arts. 8–16 as revised in 1974. For the Spanish text and a German translation, see 39 RabelsZ 724 (1975). For a French translation, see 32 Ann. suisse dr. int'l 400 (1976). For discussion, see Carillo Salcedo, Le nouveau droit international privé espagnol, 32 Ann. suisse

dr. int'l 9 (1976); Hoffmann & Ortiz–Arce, Das neue spanische internationale Privatrecht, 39 RabelsZ 647 (1975).

15. See Act of 5 December 1975, translated into English and discussed in Juenger, The Conflicts Statute of the German Democratic Republic: An Introduction and Translation, 25 Am. J. Comp. L. 332 (1977).

16. See Law No. 13 of 1979 on Private International Law published in English in The Statutes of the Hungarian People's Republic (1982), with an introduction by Ferenc Mádl. For another English translation and discussion, see Gabor, A Socialist Approach to Codification of Private International Law in Hungary: Comments and Translation, 55 Tul. L. Rev. 63 (1980). See also Roman, Conflict of Laws Solutions in the Hungarian New Private International Law, 10 Int'l J. Leg. Inform. 169 (1982); Burián, Hungarian Private International Law, in S. Symeonides, supra n.12, at 263.

17. The Yugoslav codification was enacted in three installments in 1978, 1979, and 1983. For an English translation and an introductory note to the first two installments by Matic, see 27 Neth. Int'l L. Rev. 121 (1980). The third installment is reprinted in German in 49 RabelsZ 544 (1985) and, with comment by Firsching, in 3 IPRax 1 (1983). For discussion of the whole, see Sarcevic, The New Yugoslav Private International Law Act, 38 Am. J. Comp. L. 283 (1985); Stanivukovi_, Yugoslav Private International Law, in S. Symeonides, supra n.12, at 461.

For other Eastern European countries, see Mavi & Gabor, Harmonization of Private International Law in the Soviet Union and Eastern Europe: A Comparative Law Survey, 10 Review of Socialist Law 97 (1984); Jessel–Holst, Die Neuregelung des bulgarischen Internationalen Familienrechts im Familienkodex von 1985, 51 RabelsZ 35 (1987) (family conflicts law in Bulgaria).

18. See Federal Law of June 15, 1978 Bundesgesetzblatt 1729 (No. 109) (1978). For an English translation and discussion, see Palmer, The Austrian Codification of Conflicts Law, 28 Am. J. Comp. L. 197 (1980). See also, Manhardt, Die Kodifikation des osterreichischen internationalen Privatrechts (1978); Beitzke, Neues osterreichisches Kollisionsrecht, 43 RabelsZ 245 (1979).

Turkey (1982),[19] Peru (1984),[20] China (1985),[21] the Federal Republic of Germany (1986[22] and 1999[23]), Switzerland (1987),[24]

19. See Law No. 2675 of Nov. 22, 1982, on Private International Law and Procedure, reprinted in German, with comment by Krüger, in 2 IPRax 252 (1982). See also 46 RabelsZ 184 (1982). For discussion, see Uluocak, Réformes en droit international privé turk, 27 Annales de la Faculté de Droit d'Istanbul 211 (1980).

20. See Book X of the Peruvian Civil Code of 1984 (arts. 2046–2111). For Spanish text, see 129 Normas Legales, 128 (Oct. 1984). For an English translation and an introduction by Garro, see 25 I.L.M. 997 (1985). For an Argentine draft codification, see Dahl, 24 I.L.M. 269 (1985).

21. See Foreign Economic Contract Law of March 21, 1985. For discussion of this and other Acts, see Chen, Private International Law of the People's Republic of China: An Overview, 35 Am. J. Comp. L. 445 (1987); Junming, Choice of Law for Contracts in China: A Proposal for the Objectivization of Standards and Their Use in Conflicts of Law, 6 Ind. Int'l & Comp. L. Rev. 439 (1996); Zheng, Private International Law in the People's Republic of China: Principles and Procedures, 22 Tex. Int'l L.J. 231 (1987); Guojian, Contract in Chinese Private International Law, Int'l Com. L.Q. 648 (1989).

22. See Gesetz zur Neuregelung des IPR vom 25.7.1986, Bundesgesetzblatt I/1986, 1142. For an English translation with an introduction by G. Wegen, see 27 I.L.M. 1, 18 (1988). For commentary, see Basedow, Die Neuregelung des Internationalen Privat-und Prozeïrechts, Neue Juristische Wochenschrift, 2971 (1986); Böhmer, Das deutsche Gesetz zur Neuregelung des Internationalen Privatrechts von 1986, 50 RabelsZ 646 (1986); Jayme, Das neue IPR–Gesetz—Brennpunkte der Reform, in: IP-Rax—Praxis des Internationalen Privat-und Verfahrensrechts, 265 (1986); Lüderitz, Internationales Privatrecht im Übergang—Theoretische und praktische Aspekte der deutschen Reform, in Festschrift für Kegel II, 343 (1987); Sonnenberger, Le droit international privé allemand, in S. Symeonides, supra n.12, at 221; Wengler, Zur Technik der internationalprivatrechtlichen Rechtsanwendungsanweisungen des IPR-"Reform"gesetzes von 1986, 53 RabelsZ, 409 (1989); 10 Muenchener Kommentar-BGB/EGBGB (3d ed. 1998). See also the practical guide published by the Deutsches Anwaltsinstitut, Fachinstitut für Notare, Das neue IPR–Gesetz (1987). For the protracted history and the statute, see Siehr, Codification of Private International Law in

the Federal Republic of Germany, 31 Neth. Int'l L. Rev. 92 (1984); P. Dopffel, U. Drobnig & K. Siehr, Reform des deutschen internationalen Privatrechts (1980).

23. See Gesetz zum IPR für auïervertragliche Schuldverhältnisse und das Sachenrecht vom 21.5.1999, Bundesgesetzblatt 1999, I, 1026. For an English translation by Hay, see 47 Am. J. Comp. L. 650–52 (1999). For a French translation, see 88 Revue critique DIP 870 (1999). For discussion, see Hay, From Rule–Orientation to "Approach" in German Conflicts Law: The Effect of the 1986 and 1999 Codifications, 47 Am. J. Comp. L. 633 (1999); Reimann, Codifying Tort Conflicts: The 1999 German Legislation in Comparative Perspective, 60 La. L. Rev. 1297 (2000); Sonnenberger, La loi allemande du 21 mail 1999 sur le droit international privé des obligations non contractuelles et des biens, 88 Revue critique DIP 647 (1999).

24. Bundesgesetz über das Internationale Privatrecht (IPRG) vom 18. Dezember 1987–Loi féderale sur le droit international privé (LDIP) du 18 décembre 1987, 1988 BB I 5 (German, French and Italian text); For an English translation with an introduction by Symeonides, see 37 Am. J. Comp. L. 193 (1989). See also A. Bucher & P. Tschanz, Private International Law and Arbitration, Switzerland, Basic Documents, 1 (1996). For discussions in English, see Samuel, The New Swiss Private International Law Act, 37 Int'l and Comp. L.Q. 681 (1988); Siehr, Swiss Private International Law, in S. Symeonides, supra n.12, at 383; Vischer, Drafting National Legislation on Conflict of Laws: The Swiss Experience, 41 Law & Contemp. Prob. 31 (1977); Karrer, Arnold & Patocchi, Switzerland's Private International Law (2nd ed. 1994). For extensive Swiss commentary, see G. Broggini (ed.), Il nuovo diritto internazionale privato in Svizzera (1990); A. Bucher, Droit international privé suisse, vol. I.1 (1998), vol. I.2 (1995), vol. II (1992); F. Dessemontet (ed.), Le nouveau droit international privé suisse (1988); B. Dutoit, Commentaire de la loi fédérale du 18 décembre 1987 (1996); E. Geisinger & P. Patocchi, Code de droit international privé suisse annoté. La loi fédéral sur le droit international privé (1995); A. Heini, M. Keller, K. Siehr, F. Vischer & P. Volken, Kommentar zum Bundesgesetz über das Internationale Privatrecht (IPRG) vom 1. January 1989 (1993); H. Honsell, P.

Paraguay (1987),[25] Japan (1990),[26] Louisiana (1992),[27] Romania (1992),[28] Quebec (1994),[29] England (1995),[30] Italy (1995),[31] Vietnam (1995),[32] Tunisia (1998),[33] Venezuela (1998),[34] The Netherlands (2001),[35]

Vogt & A. Schnyder (eds.), Kommentar zum schweizerischen Privatrecht, Internationales Privatrecht (1996); M. Keller & K. Siehr, Einführung in die Eigenart des internationalen Privatrechts (3d ed. 1984); A. Schnyder, Das neue IPR–Gesetz (2d ed. 1990); I. Schwander, Einführung in das internationale Privatrecht. Allgemeiner Teil (2d ed. 1990), Besonders Teil (1998); F. Vischer & A. von Planta, Internationales Privatrecht (2d ed. 1982).

25. See Arts. 11–26 of the Civil Code of Paraguay as revised in 1987. For discussion, see Baus, Der neue Codigo Civil von Paraguay und seine Kollisionsnormen, 51 RabelsZ 440 (1987).

26. See Chin Kim, New Japanese Private International Law: The 1990 Horei, 40 Am. J. Comp. L. 1 (1992). See also Horei Application of Laws (General) Act No.10, as amended by 1986 No.84.

27. See Book IV of the Louisiana Civil Code, enacted into law by La. Act No. 923 of 1991, effective January 1, 1992. The text of the codification is published in 57 RabelsZ 508 (1993); 13 IPRax 56 (1993–1); and in 81 Revue critique DIP 223 (1992). For discussion of this codification by its drafter, see, *inter alia*, Symeonides, Private International Law Codification in a Mixed Jurisdiction: The Louisiana Experience, 57 RabelsZ 460 (1993); Symeonides, Les grands problèmes de droit international privé et la nouvelle codification de Louisiane, 81 Revue critique DIP 223 (1992); Symeonides, La Nuova Normativa della Louisiana sul DIP in Tema di Responsabilità Extracontrattuale, 29 Riv. dir. int'le priv. e proc. 43 (1993). For discussion of the judicial application of this codification, see Symeonides, Louisiana Conflicts Law: Two "Surprises," 54 La. L. Rev. 497 (1994); Borchers, Louisiana's Conflicts Codification: Some Empirical Observations Regarding Decisional Predictability, 60 La. L. Rev. 1061 (2000); Sedler, The Louisiana Codification and Tort Rules of Choice of Law, 60 La. L. Rev. 1331 (2000); Weintraub, Courts Flailing in the Waters of the Louisiana Conflicts Code: Not Waving but Drowning, 60 La. L. Rev. 1365 (2000).

28. See Lege cu privire la reglemontarca raporturilor de drept international privat, Monitorul Oficial 1.10. 1992 I Nr. 245, 1; German translation in RabelsZ 534 (1994); C_p_tn_, Das neue ruma_ische Internationale Privatrecht, RabelsZ 465 (1994).

29. See L.Q. 1991, ch. 64 (adopted in 1991, effective 1994) and composing Book

Ten of the Quebec Civil Code (arts. 3076– 3168). For discussion, see E. Groffier, La réforme du droit international privé québécois (1993); Castel, Commentaire sur certaines dispositions du Code civil du Québec se rapportant au droit international privé, Clunet 625 (1992); Glenn, Codification of Private International Law in Quebec, 60 RabelsZ 231 (1996); Groffier, La réforme du droit international privé québécois, 81 Revue critique 584 (1992); Prujiner, Canadian Private International Law, in S. Symeonides, *supra* n.12, at 127; Talpis & Castel, Le Code civil du Québec: Interprétation des règles du droit international privé, in La réforme du Code civil, 801 (1993).

30. See Private International Law (Miscellaneous Provisions) Act of 8 November 1995 (c 42) (codifying conflicts rules for torts). For discussion, see Morse, Torts in Private International Law: A New Statutory Framework, 45 Int'l & Comp. L.Q. 888 (1996); Reed, The Private International Law (Miscellaneous Provisions) Act 1995 and the Need for Escape Devices, 15 Civ. Just. Q. 305 (1996); Rodger, Ascertaining the Statutory Lex Loci Delicti: Certain Difficulties Under the Private International Law (Miscellaneous Provisions) Act 1995, 47 Int'l & Comp. L.Q. 205 (1998). The United Kingdom has also acceded to the Rome Convention on the law applicable to contractual obligations.

31. See Act No. 218 of 31 May 1995 (Riforma del sistema italiano di diritto internazionale privato). For Italian text, see Riv. dir. int'le priv. e proces. 905 (1995), with a commentary by several authors. For an English translation and an introduction by Giardina, see 35 I.L.M. 765 (1995). For commentary in English, see Ballarino & Bonomi, The Italian Statute on Private International Law, 2 Ybk. Priv. Int'l L. 99 (2000); Pocar & Honorati, Italian Private International Law, in S. Symeonides, supra n.12, at 279. For commentaries in other languages, see Boschiero, Appunti sulla riforma del sistema italiano di diritto internazionale privato (1996); F. Pocar, et al., Commentario del nuovo diritto internazionale privato (1996); S. Bariatti, et al. Riforma del sistema italiano di diritto internazionale privato (1996); Giardina, Les charactères généraux de la réform, 85 Revue critique 1 (1996); Ballarino, Personnes, famille, régimes matrimoniaux et successions dans la loi de réforme du d.i.p., 85 Revue critique 21 (1996); Pocar, Le droit des obligations

32.–35. See p. 116.

Russia (2002),[36] Estonia (2002),[37] and Oregon (2002).[38] Codification projects are under way in many other jurisdictions including Australia,[39] Belgium,[40] China,[41] Japan,[42] and Puerto Rico.[43]

During the same period, more than 30 international conventions have been concluded under the auspices of the Hague Conference on

dans le nouveau droit international privé italien, 85 Revue critique 41 (1996).

32. See Civil Code of the Socialist Republic of Vietnam of 1995, arts. 826–838. French translation by Que and Luong in 89 Revue critique DIP 298–304 (2000).

33. See Code of Private International Law (Law N. 98–97 of 27 November 1998), Official Journal of the Republic of Tunisia, 1 December p. 2332. French text in 88 Revue critique DIP 382–391 (1999).

34. Venezuela: See Act of 6 August, 1998 on Private International Law (Official Gazette No. 36.511) effective February 6, 1999. For an English translation, see 1 Ybk. Priv. Int'l L., 341 (1999); French translation, see 88 Revue critique DIP 392–401 (1999). For discussion, see Maekelt, Venezuelan Private International Law, in S. Symeonides, supra n.12, at 445; Parra–Aranguren, The Venezuelan Act of Private International Law of 1998, 1 Ybk. Priv. Int'l L., 103 (1999); Parra–Aranguren, Topics of Procedure in the Venezuelan 1998 Act of Private International Law, 60 La. L. Rev. 1241 (2000); Parra–Aranguren, La loi vénézuélienne de 1998 sur le droit international privé, 88 Revue critique DIP 3209 (1999).

35. See Act of 11 April 2001Regarding Conflict of Laws on Torts, Staatsblad 2001, 190, effective 1 June 2001. For English translation with an Introductory Note by P. Vlas, see Netherlands Int'l L. Rev. 221 (2003–2). For discussions of earlier drafts, see Boele–Woelki, Joustra, Steenhoff, Dutch Private International Law, in S. Symeonides, supra n.12, at 295; van Rooij & Polak, Private International Law in the Netherlands (1987; Vlas, Neue Entwicklungen im niederlaendischen IPR, insbesondere in der Rechtsprechung, IPRax 194 (1995).

36. See federal law n. 146 of 26 November 2001 enacting the third part of the Civil Code of the Russian Federation, Rossyiskaya Gazeta, n. 49 item 4553, 28/11/2001. The conflicts provisions comprise Title VI of Part Three, arts 1186–1224. For an English translation, see W. Butler, Civil Code of the Russian Federation, 437–450 (2002); P. Maggs, The Civil Code of the Russian Federation: Part 3, 37–50 (2002); 4 Ybk of Priv. Int'l L., 350–64 (2002). For a French translation with commentary by Bogdanova &

Litvinski, see 91 Revue critique DIP, 182–203 (2002). For discussion, see Lebedev, Muranov, Khodykin & Kabatova, New Russian Legislation on Private International Law, 4 Ybk. Priv. Int'l L. 117 (2002); Zvekov, The New Civil Code of the Russian Federation and Private International Law, 44 McGill L.J. 525 (1999).

37. See Private International Law Act of March 27, 2002, effective 1 July 2002 in The State Gazette, "Riigi Teataja" I 2002, 35, 217.

38. See O.R.S §§ 81–100 to 81–135, effective January 1, 2002, reproduced in 67 RabelsZ 748 (2003), and 3 Ybk. Int'l L. 405 (2001). For discussion, see Nafziger, Oregon's Conflicts Law Applicable to Contracts, 38 Willamette L. Rev. 397 (2002); Symeonides, Codifying Choice of Law for Contracts: The Oregon Experience, 67 RabelsZ 726 (2003).

39. See Nygh, Choice of Law in Torts in Australia, 2 Ybk. Priv. Int'l L. 55, 70–73 (2000).

40. See Eraw, Brief Description of the Draft Belgian Code pf Private International Law, 4 Ybk. Priv. Int'l L. 145 (2002).

41. See Chinese Society of Private International Law, Model Law of Private International Law of the People's Republic of China (6th Draft, 2002), 3 Ybk. Priv. Int'l L. 349 (2001).

42. See the drafts on contractual and non-contractual obligations reproduced in 39 Japanese Annual Int'l L. 185 (1996); 40 Japanese Annual Int'l L. 57 (1997).

43. See Academia Puertorriqueña de Jurisprudencia y Legislacion, Proyecto para la Codificación del Derecho internacional privado de Puerto Rico, (Symeonides & von Mehren, Rapporteurs, 1991). This project is now part of a comprehensive bill to revise the Puerto Rican Civil Code to be considered by the Puerto Rico legislature in 2004. For discussion of the *Projet*, see Symeonides, Revising Puerto Rico's Conflicts Law: A Preview, 28 Colum. J. Transn'l L. 413 (1990); Symeonides, Codifying Puerto Rico's Choice-of-Law for Contracts, in Law and Justice in a Multistate World: Essays in Honor of Arthur T. von Mehren, 419 (J. Nafziger & S. Symeonides eds. 2002).

Private International Law[44] and other international organizations, such as the Organization of American States.[45] In the European Union, the Brussels Convention of 1968 ("Brussels I")[46] has been replaced in 2002 by a Regulation ("Brussels II")[47] that is directly binding on member states, while the 1980 EEC Convention on the Law Applicable to Contractual Obligations ("Rome I"),[48] which is now in force in most of the original fifteen EU countries, will soon be complimented by a new Regulation ("Rome II"), which will codify the law applicable to non-contractual obligations arising from torts and acts other than torts. On July 22, 2003, the Commission of the European Communities submitted a "Proposal for a Regulation of the European Parliament and the Council on the Law Applicable to Non–Contractual Obligations,"[49] which

44. Since 1955, the Conference has produced 36 conventions, of which 25 are now in force. See Conférence de La Haye de Droit international privé, Recueil des conventions (1951–2003). See also the Conference's official web site at http://www.hcch.net/e.

45. See, e.g., the following Inter–American Conventions at the website of the Organization of American States at http://www.oas.org/juridico/english/treasub.html : Law Applicable to International Contracts (1994); Domicile of Natural Persons in Private International Law (1979); General Rules of Private International Law (1979); Conflicts of Laws Concerning Commercial Companies (1979); Conflict of Laws Concerning Checks (Jan. 1979); Conflict of Laws Concerning Checks (May 1979); Conflict of Laws concerning Bills of Exchange, Promisory Notes, and Invoices (1975); Personality and Capacity of Juridical Persons in Private International Law (1984). For discussion, see G. Parra-Aranguren, supra n.10; Maekelt, La Codificación Interamericana en Materia de Derecho Internaconal Privado en el Contexto Universal y Regional, in Libro Homenaje a Haroldo Valladao 157 (1997); Juenger, Contract Choice of Law in the Americas, 45 Am. J. Comp. L. 195 (1997).

46. In 1968, the then six member-states of the European Economic Community concluded the Brussels Convention on Jurisdiction and the Recognition and Enforcement of Judgments ("Brussels I"), which was the first multilateral attempt on the European continent to establish a comprehensive regime for jurisdiction and recognition of civil and commercial judgments rendered in the member states. For the text of the Convention, see [1990] O.J. C 189. In 1988, the convention was supplemented by a "parallel Convention" known as the "Lugano Convention" between the EU and the member states of the European Free Trade Associa-

tion (EFTA). See [1988] O.J. L 319, 9. The EFTA includes Austria, Finland, Iceland, Norway, Sweden, and Switzerland. In the meantime, Austria, Finland, and Sweden, have joined the EU.

47. See [2001] O.J. L.12/1, effective March 1, 2002.

48. 23 Official Journal of the European Communities No. L 266/1 (1980). See also Giuliano & Lagarde, Report to the Council, id. No. C 282/1 (1980). For discussion and further references, see Hay, Flexibility versus Predictability and Uniformity in Choice of Law, 226 Recueil des Cours 281 (1991–I). For a critical American appraisal, see Weintraub, How to Choose Law for Contracts and How Not To: The EEC Convention, 17 Tex. Int'l L.J. 155 (1982).

49. See COM(2003) 427 final, 2003/0168(COD), Brussels, 22.7.203. All references hereafter to "Rome II" are to this proposal. For discussion, see Symeonides, Tort Conflicts and Rome II: A View from Across, in Festschrift für Erik Jayme 935 (2004). For discussions of previous drafts, see Hamburg Group of Private International Law, Comments on the European Commission's Draft Proposal for a European Council Regulation on the Law Applicable to Non–Contractual Obligations (29/10/2002), 67 RabelsZ 1 (2003). For an earlier proposal by the Groupe européen de droit international privé, see, Proposal for a European Convention on the law applicable to non-contractual Obligations adopted at the Luxembourg meeting of 25–28 September 1998 at http://www.drt.ucl.ac.be/gedip/gedip-documents–8pe.html. For earlier discussions about the feasibility or desirability of this effort, see Sandrock, Die Europaeischen Gemeinschaften und die Privatrechte ihrer Mitgliedstaaten: Einheit oder Vielfalt?, Europaeisches Wirtschafts-u. Steuerrecht 1 (1994); Armbruester, Ein Schuldvertragsrecht fuer Europa? Bemer-

is scheduled for discussion by the European Parliament in the fall of 2004.

All of the above suggests that the prevailing American opinion that conflicts problems are insusceptible to statutory solutions is not espoused in many other parts of the world. In any event, regardless of one's opinion on the question of desirability or feasibility of conflicts legislation in the United States, there is no question that a great deal can be learned from a comparison of these codifications with the solutions developed by the case law in this country. To that end these codifications will be referred to throughout this book for purposes of comparison.

kungen zur Privatrechtsangleichung in der Europaeischen Union nach "Maastricht" und "Keck" 60 RabelsZ 72 (1996); von Bar, Vereinheitlichung und Angleichung von Deliktsrecht in der Euroaeischen Union, Zeitschrift fuer Rechtsvergleichung 221 (1994), Taupitz, Privatrechtsvereinheitlichung durch die EG: Sachrechts-oder Kollisionsrechtsvereinheitlichung?, Juristenzeitung 533 (1993). See also Struycken, Les conse-quences de l'intégration européenne sur le développement du droit international privé, 232 Recueil des Cours 257 (1992–I); Fallon, Les conflits de lois et de juridictions dans une éspace economique integre: L'experi-ence de la Communauté Européenne, 253 Recueil des Cours 9 (1995); Sonnenberger, Europarecht und Internationales Privatrecht, 95 Zeitschrift für Vergleichende Rechtswissenschaften 3 (1996).

Chapter 3

DETERMINING THE APPLICABLE LAW

Table of Sections

		Sections
I.	Introduction	3.1–3.2
II.	Pervasive Problems	3.13–3.19
	A. Characterization	3.3–3.12
	1. Introduction	3.3
	2. Subject Matter Characterization	3.4–3.5
	3. Connecting Factors	3.6–3.7
	4. Substance—Procedure Characterization	3.8–3.12
	a. In General	3.8
	b. Statutes of Limitation	3.9–3.12
	B. Renvoi	3.13–3.14
	C. Public Policy	3.15–3.16
	D. Public Policy—Penal and Governmental Claims	3.17–3.18
	E. Availability of Local Procedure and Remedy	3.19
III.	Problems of Federalism: Constitutional Limitations on Choice of Law	3.20–3.35
	A. Due Process and Full Faith and Credit: From Interest–Balancing to Minimum Contacts	3.20–3.30
	1. Introduction	3.20
	2. The Due Process Cases	3.21–3.23
	3. The Full Faith and Credit Cases	3.24–3.25
	4. Constitutional Limitations Analyzed	3.26–3.30
	a. Due Process	3.26–3.29
	b. Full Faith and Credit	3.30
	B. Privileges and Immunities, Equal Protection and Commerce	3.31
	1. Privileges and Immunities and Commerce	3.32–3.33
	2. Equal Protection	3.34
	3. Other Distinctions	3.35
IV.	Problems of Federalism: State Law in Federal Courts	3.36–3.48
	A. The Erie/Klaxon Doctrine: Policy Considerations	3.36
	B. Erie—Problems in Practice	3.37
	1. Byrd, Hanna and the Federal Rules	3.38–3.39
	2. Court–Closing Rules	3.40–3.41
	3. Interstate Forum Shopping	3.42
	a. Interpleader	3.43
	b. The 100–Mile Bulge Rule	3.44
	c. Supplemental Jurisdiction	3.45
	d. Federal Transfers	3.46
	C. Pervasive Erie/Klaxon Problems	3.26–3.48
	1. What Is "State Law"?	3.47
	2. Klaxon and Constitutional Limitations on Choice of Law	3.48

V. Problems of Federalism: Federal Common Law 3.49–3.55
    A. The Standard 3.49–3.50
    B. The Federal Interest 3.51–3.54
        1. Government Obligations 3.51
        2. Contractual Relations With the Government 3.52
        3. Tort–Related Issues 3.53
        4. Private Disputes Over Government–Created Rights 3.54
    C. When Is Federal Common Law Appropriate? 3.55
VI. International Treaties 3.56–3.60
    A. In General 3.56
    B. Multilateral Treaties 3.57
    C. Bilateral Treaties 3.58–3.59
    D. Conclusion 3.60

———————

I. INTRODUCTION

§ 3.1 Whenever state, and not federal,[1] law is applicable to a case, the choice-of-law rule determining which state's law is to be used, ordinarily[2] is a rule of the law of the forum. Even if federal law governs the cause of action, state law,[3] including state conflicts law,[4] may apply to the case as a result of a reference to, or incorporation of it by the federal law.

§ 3.2 In determining the applicable law, the court's analysis will include—expressly or by implication—a number of steps that are pervasive to the entire field of conflict of laws and to resolving its problems. An initial step involves the *characterization*[1] of the *subject matter* of the *case* or issues in the case (e.g., tort or contract, interspousal immunity as raising issues of tort or family law), the *issue,* and whether the question raises a problem of *procedure* or of *substantive* law. The inquiry will then seek to determine whether the issue to be resolved presents a true conflict or whether a "false conflict" exists with respect to the potential-

---

§ 3.1

1. For the applicability of federal law, see infra §§ 3.49, 3.56–3.60. See also infra Chapter 23.

2. Exceptions are choice-of-law rules contained in international conventions to which the United States is a party and which bind the states under the U.S. Constitution's Supremacy Clause and occasional provisions of federal law. See infra §§ 3.49, 3.56–3.60 and infra Chapter 23.

3. See United States v. Kimbell Foods, Inc., 440 U.S. 715, 99 S.Ct. 1448, 59 L.Ed.2d 711 (1979), on remand 600 F.2d 478 (5th Cir.1979) (state law standards adopted to determine the priority of federal liens stemming from federal lending programs).

4. Richards v. United States, 369 U.S. 1, 12–13, 82 S.Ct. 585, 592–93, 7 L.Ed.2d 492 (1962) (interpreting a provision of the Federal Tort Claims Act liability of the United States to be determined "in accordance with the law of the place where the act or omission occurred" to include the conflicts rules of that place). For an opinion cataloging the different approaches taken by courts in following *Richards*, see Gould Electronics Inc. v. United States, 220 F.3d 169 (3d Cir.2000).

§ 3.2

1. Continental terminology more frequently employs the term "qualification."

ly applicable foreign rule of law so as to make the use of local law appropriate.[2]

Assuming that the forum's choice-of-law rule[3] on the issue refers to the law of another state or country, the possibility exists that the latter's choice-of-law rules refer back to the forum or to yet a third state or country. The court of the forum must at this point decide whether to follow or otherwise consider this further reference, *renvoi,* or to ignore it and apply the local law to which its own, i.e. the forum's, choice-of-law rule initially referred.

The foreign law, to which the forum's choice-of-law rule refers, may occasionally differ substantially from that of the forum on the issue. When this difference is so fundamental as to offend the forum's notions of justice, the so-called *"public policy" exception* may lead to a refusal to apply the foreign law. Mere differences between the law of the forum and the foreign law are not enough to refuse application; in fact, if there were no differences, it would be likely that the case presents a "false conflict." One area, however, where a difference may be relevant, even though it does not violate the forum's public policy, concerns the rare case in which the forum lacks the judicial machinery or remedy[4] to apply the foreign law. The proper disposition of these types of cases raises difficult questions, for instance, whether it is more appropriate to dismiss the action without prejudice in anticipation of a proceeding elsewhere or whether there should be an adjudication on the merits by application of local law and local remedies to approximate the foreign result.

The sections immediately following address the pervasive problems of characterization, renvoi, public policy, and the availability of a local remedy. When the analysis indicates the application of a rule of the forum or of another jurisdiction, the further question may arise whether, on the facts of the particular case, the application of the law chosen is permissible in the context of our federal system. A portion of the chapter therefore explores the extent to which there are constitutional limitations on a state's choice of law. Such a limitation may be in the form of a prohibition, mainly for due-process reasons, to apply a particular rule of law or it may result from the displacement of state law by federal law. The latter, in turn, may result from the creation of "federal common law" or, when the action was brought in federal court, from a conflict between state and federal procedural law. These aspects of the displacement of state law by federal law involve the *Erie/Klaxon* doctrine[5] and are discussed in that context.

---

2. Supra § 2.6.

3. Choice-of-law rules with respect to specific areas of substantive law are discussed infra Chapters 13–23.

4. Slater v. Mexican National Railroad Co., 194 U.S. 120, 24 S.Ct. 581, 48 L.Ed.

900 (1904). For further discussion see infra § 3.19.

5. Erie Railroad Co. v. Tompkins, 304 U.S. 64, 58 S.Ct. 817, 82 L.Ed. 1188 (1938); Klaxon Co. v. Stentor Electric Manufacturing Co., 313 U.S. 487, 61 S.Ct. 1020, 85 L.Ed. 1477 (1941).

II. PERVASIVE PROBLEMS

A. CHARACTERIZATION

1. *Introduction*

§ **3.3** Legal thinking and analysis are a constant process of classification of facts to fit established categories. A simple example is determining whether a situation presents a tort or contract question. At each step in the problem-solving process it is necessary to ascertain the meaning of terms and rules to determine their application to the situation at hand. The same term may be used differently in different rules in one system and because conflict of laws problems involve more than one system of rules, the difficulty of characterization or classification is multiplied. The doctrinal context of any legal term includes the policy complex it is designed to implement in the system in which it is used.[1] In the conflict of laws, the problem of characterization essentially raises the question of whether the doctrinal context of the forum or of another system is going to be used to fix the meaning of a particular proposition.[2] Constant awareness of this problem is necessary in order to recognize the significant effect this process has upon the choice of law and the outcome of litigation.[3]

There has been a great deal of discussion of this problem[4] marked by much difference of opinion both in the United States and Europe.[5] Agreement is lacking even on nomenclature, with the terms "classifica-

---

§ 3.3

1. For instance, until this cause of action was abolished by statute, the "nature of the remedy for breach of promise to marry ... was contractual [in England]; in French law ... it is delictual." R. Graveson, Conflict of Laws 45 (7th ed. 1974). See also Huntington v. Attrill, [1893] A.C. 150 (P.C.): (judgment establishing defendant's liability not "penal" in nature and therefore entitled to recognition). The U.S. Supreme Court reached the same result in Huntington v. Attrill, 146 U.S. 657, 13 S.Ct. 224, 36 L.Ed. 1123 (1892). The case is discussed further infra § 3.17 n.7.

2. The discussion of characterization was introduced in this country by Lorenzen, The Theory of Qualifications and the Conflict of Laws, 20 Colum. L. Rev. 247 (1920). In England, characterization is usually traced to Leroux v. Brown, 138 Eng.R. 1119 (C.P.1852) in which a contract executed in France was held to be unenforceable because it violated the English Statute of Frauds which was characterized to be procedural and therefore applicable even to a foreign cause of action. The classification of a statute of limitations as procedural (affecting the remedy but not the right) dates

to Dupleix v. De Roven, 23 Eng. Rep. 950 (1705). See Ehrenzweig, Characterization in the Conflict of Laws: An Unwelcome Addition to American Doctrine, in: XXth Century Comparative and Conflicts Law—Legal Essays in Honor of Hessel E. Yntema 395 (1961).

3. "The tendency to assume that a word which appears in two or more legal rules, and so in connection with more than one purpose, has and should have precisely the same scope in all of them runs all through legal discussions. It has all the tenacity of original sin and must constantly be guarded against." Cook, The Logical and Legal Bases of Conflict of Laws, 159 (1942). See also Weintraub, The Impact of a Functional Analysis Upon the "Pervasive Problems" of the Conflict of Laws, 15 U.C.L.A. L. Rev. 817 (1968).

4. The classic treatment is Robertson, Characterization in the Conflict of Laws (1940).

5. Cook "Characterization" in the Conflict of Laws, 51 Yale L.J. 191 (1941); Cormack, Renvoi, Characterization and Preliminary Question in the Conflict of Laws, 14 So. Cal. L. Rev. 221 (1941); Lorenzen, The Qualification, Classification and Character-

tion," "qualification" and "characterization" being urged. Some concordance may be found on the proposition that the approach to the problem is divisible into three parts.[6] The first part deals with the determination of the general legal nature of the issue, for example, the determination of whether the court has before it a tort or contract question so that it may know whether to apply tort or contract conflict of laws rules or approaches. The second part concerns the definition and use of "connecting factors," a term employed to describe the word or words in a rule of reference which indicate the place whose law may be used to decide the issue. "Place of contracting," "place of wrong" and "domicile" are examples. Interest analysis and the most-significant-relationship approach of the Second Restatement also proceed from an initial identification of connecting factors. The third part relates to the extent of application: how much of the law to which reference is made should be applied? This aspect of characterization, in traditional doctrine, distinguishes between issues of "substantive" law and of "procedure": the forum will apply only the *foreign substantive law* but use its *own procedural law*.

The manner in which characterization should be approached has been very much disputed. The approaches have varied as to whether all or any of these matters are to be determined by the doctrinal context of the forum or of the other legal systems involved.[7] The first step, subject matter characterization, is controlled by practical necessity by the forum's legal system including its conflict-of-laws rules. The second part of the problem, identifying the significant connecting factors, is an integral portion of the conflict-of-laws doctrinal context to which the courts of the forum look for guidance in this kind of a case. As such, the significance of the connecting factors is subject to the policy of the forum reflected in its conflict-of-laws doctrine. The determination of the problem of the third step is more difficult and controversial. Here reliance on a rule of thumb is dangerous. Since one purpose of conflict-of-laws doctrine is to achieve some measure of uniformity of result without regard to the choice of forum, the law of the state under consideration in the third step should be viewed in its own policy context.[8] By such an approach the court may achieve the goal of maximum consistency

ization Problem in Conflict of Laws, 50 Yale L.J. 743 (1941); Falconbridge, Essays in the Conflict of Laws 50 et seq. (2d ed. 1954). For an extensive bibliography on characterization, see Kegel & Schurig, Internationales Privatrecht 325–27 (9th ed. 2004).

6. Compare Falconbridge, Conflict of Laws, Ch. 3 (2d ed. 1954) with Robertson, Characterization in the Conflict of Laws, 11 (1940) with Lorenzen, The Qualification, Classification and Characterization Problem in Conflict of Laws, 50 Yale L.J. 743 (1941). See also Graveson, supra n.1, at 43 et seq.

7. For summaries of the various views see Robertson, Characterization in the Con-

flict of Laws, Ch. II (1940); 1 Rabel, The Conflict of Laws, 52 (2d ed. 1958); Dicey & Morris, Conflict of Laws 33 et seq. (13th ed. 2000 by Collins).

8. See Cheatham, Problems and Methods in Conflict of Laws, Hague Academy, Recueil des Cours, 237, 334 (1960) ("Every rule of law and the terms of which it is made are to be interpreted and applied in the light of the policies which the rule is intended to advance and the terms to express. In conflict of laws, where several bodies of law may bear on the same occurrence, it is essential to keep in mind the guiding policies of the particular rule which we interpret and apply").

between the forum's conflict-of-laws policy and the policy of the state to which the forum has referred as applied to the case for decision.

2. Subject Matter Characterization

§ 3.4 Under traditional doctrine, particularly the approach of the First Restatement,[1] subject matter characterization was very important: once a case had been characterized as sounding in tort or contract, for example, predetermined choice-of-law rules would then refer to "the place of the injury" or "to the place of the making of the contract." Thus, characterization could affect the outcome of the litigation. At the same time, it provided a vehicle for courts to avoid undesirable results, by re-characterizing a case, to which then existing choice-of-law rules would have pointed. This practice may have achieved the best result in many cases but did not contribute to the elaboration of new principled choice-of-law rules.[2] The old "telegraph cases" are a good example. At that time, Arkansas law provided a tort remedy for mental anguish suffered as a result of negligence in the transmission or delivery of telegraph messages.[3] Thus, in cases in which the misdelivery occurred in the forum, the Arkansas court characterized the action as sounding in tort, applied the statute, and allowed recovery.[4] However, when the message was sent from Arkansas and misdelivered in a state which lacked a similar remedy, the Arkansas courts did not apply the "place of the injury" rule, which then prevailed in tort cases, but permitted a recovery under principles of breach of contract.[5] Similarly, in *Kilberg v. Northeast Airlines, Inc.*[6] the plaintiff sought to escape the low limit on wrongful death recoveries in effect in Massachusetts, where the plane had crashed, by seeking a recovery for breach of contract under New York law where the ticket had been purchased and the contract of

---

§ 3.4

1. See supra § 2.5.

2. Hancock, Three Approaches to the Choice–of–Law Problem: The Classificatory, the Functional, and the Result Selective, in: XXth Century Comparative and Conflicts Law—Legal Essays in Honor of Hessel E. Yntema 365, 369 (1961).

3. Ark. Stats. § 73–1813 (repealed 1957).

4. E.g., Western Union Telegraph Co. v. Chilton, 100 Ark. 296, 140 S.W. 26 (1911); Gentle v. Western Union Telegraph Co., 82 Ark. 96, 100 S.W. 742 (1907).

5. E.g., Western Union Telegraph Co. v. Flannagan, 113 Ark. 9, 167 S.W. 701 (1914); Western Union Telegraph Co. v. Griffin, 92 Ark. 219, 122 S.W. 489 (1909).

Also compare Irving Trust Co. v. Maryland Casualty Co., 83 F.2d 168 (2d Cir. 1936), cert. denied 299 U.S. 571, 57 S.Ct. 34, 81 L.Ed. 421 (1936) (fraudulent convey-

ance gives rise to an action in tort) with Marcus v. Kane, 18 F.2d 722 (2d Cir.1927) (fraudulent conveyance involves interests in land, to be governed by the law of the situs). Other leading examples of a change from the seemingly apparent tort characterization to something else include: Levy v. Daniels' U–Drive Auto Renting Co., 108 Conn. 333, 143 A. 163 (1929) (contract); Cortes v. Ryder Truck Rental, Inc., 220 Ill.App.3d 632, 581 N.E.2d 1 (1991), appeal dism'd, 143 Ill.2d 637, 587 N.E.2d 1013 (1992) (contract); Grant v. McAuliffe, 41 Cal.2d 859, 264 P.2d 944 (1953) (administration of estates); Haumschild v. Continental Casualty Co., 7 Wis.2d 130, 95 N.W.2d 814 (1959) (family law). But see Jack v. Enterprise Rent–A–Car Co. of Los Angeles, 899 P.2d 891 (Wyo. 1995) (Court does not follow the contract characterization of Levy and Cortes, supra, but stays with the tort characterization).

6. 9 N.Y.2d 34, 211 N.Y.S.2d 133, 172 N.E.2d 526 (1961).

carriage had been made. The *Kilberg* court rejected the suggested characterization but nonetheless applied New York law by characterizing the damage issue to be "procedural" (the third step in the characterization process) and, moreover, by considering the Massachusetts limit to violate New York's public policy.[7]

§ 3.5 Subject matter characterization continues to be the natural and necessary starting point for the analysis of any conflicts case. But the abandonment of rigid territorially-oriented rules of choice of law[1] will often shift the focus and make "labelling" less important. Thus, while the Restatement (Second) retains subject matter characterization,[2] it calls for the application, in most cases, of the law of the place with the "most significant relationship" to the "particular issue."[3] Similarly, interest analysis[4] focuses on the interest of the states concerned to have their respective law applied to the particular controversy. Thus, while the Pennsylvania court in *Griffith v. United Air Lines, Inc.*,[5] which involved a Colorado aircrash, accepted a "contract" characterization instead of one of "tort" and then applied the more favorable Pennsylvania law with respect to survival of actions, it is important to note that it did so because it considered Pennsylvania's policies and interests as more directly involved than those of Colorado. Since the Second Restatement employs the "most-significant-relationship" test both for contract (§ 188) and tort (§ 145) actions, the *Griffith* court might have come to Pennsylvania law just as easily with the Restatement's approach.

By focusing on issues, the new approach will help to avoid some of the mechanical results of the older law as well as the use of characterization as a "gimmick"[6] to get around undesirable results. In particular, it will eliminate some cases altogether when their intimate relationship with a particular jurisdiction discloses the existence of a "false conflict."[7]

---

7. The *Kilberg* decision is discussed further infra § 3.15 n.8 and § 17.9. For a more recent illustration see Chase Manhattan Bank v. CVE, Inc., 206 F.Supp.2d 900 (M.D.Tenn.2000).

§ 3.5

1. Supra §§ 2.4–2.5.

2. Restatement, Second, Conflict of Laws § 7, comment (b) (1971). See, e.g., Savage Arms, Inc. v. Western Auto Supply Co., 18 P.3d 49 (Alaska 2001)(treating question of a successor corporation's liability for a defective product manufactured by the predecessor corporation as a question of tort for choice-of-law purposes under the Second Restatement).

3. Id. § 6. See also id. § 145 (torts) and § 188 (contracts) and infra chs. 17–18.

4. Supra § 2.9.

5. 416 Pa. 1, 203 A.2d 796 (1964). See also Hughes v. Prudential Lines, Inc., 425 Pa.Super. 262, 624 A.2d 1063 (1993).

6. L. McDougal, R. Felix & R. Whitten, American Conflicts Law 404 (5th ed. 2001).

It has been suggested that the criticism of characterization as an "escape device" misapprehends its proper function: the "escape is merely from an incorrect rule; conversely no escape is necessary where the rule is properly formulated.... Critics of the conflict-'rule' method cannot seem to accept, or even to envisage that the concepts thus branded might express sound legal analysis rather than cover unavowable plots.... In [many] cases ... characterization achieved nothing but to place the issue where it belonged." Audit, A Continental Lawyer Looks at Contemporary American Choice–of–Law Principles, 27 Am.J.Comp.L. 589, 596 (1979). Characterization, this author concluded, therefore does not furnish an argument against "rules" in the conflict of laws but rather only against the rigid territorialism of the First Restatement. Id., at 595. For a response, see Juenger, Comments, id. 609, 611–12.

7. Supra § 2.9.

Nevertheless, in most cases subject matter characterization will be the necessary first step in the analysis: the problem area must be identified in order to see whether a conflict indeed exists; and, even if the case should present a false conflict but a foreign law is applicable to the issue, the applicable rule of decision must still be chosen on the basis of a characterization of the subject matter.

3. Connecting Factors

§ 3.6 The traditional case law employed specific connecting factors for the determination of the applicable law once the subject matter of the case had been characterized. Thus, the validity of a contract was to be determined by the place where it was made[1] and the law of the place of the injury[2] (and sometimes of the place of conduct[3]) governed a tort. This approach presented two principal problems. First, the connecting factor employed did not necessarily lead to a rational choice of law: thus, if A and B, both residents of X made a contract in Y, where they were casually present at the time, to be performed in Z, it makes little sense to select Y law to govern the contract's validity.

Second, the connecting factors chosen assumed an equivalence of the meaning of legal concepts which perhaps did not exist in fact. When, for instance, the forum's rule refers to the decedent's "domicile at death" for purposes of intestate succession to movables, does it or should it make a difference that the forum and the other jurisdiction have different conceptions as to where that domicile was?[4] Or, to return to a contract example, what if the place where the contract was "made," according to the standards of the forum, has a different rule which, if considered, would lead to the result that the contract was *not* made there? The underlying question here is whether forum law *alone* determines and then employs the appropriate connecting factor or whether the rules of the applicable foreign law are also relevant.

§ 3.7 It is suggested that the answer to the two problems inherent in the traditional approach should be that (1) a connecting factor should not be employed when it leads, mechanically, to an otherwise unrelated law, and (2) that the content of the foreign law selected is of some relevance. With respect to the latter, there is some difficulty with the suggestion inasmuch as consideration of the foreign law may lead to difficult cumulative use of rules or produce results which would not obtain in a purely domestic case.[1] At a minimum, however, consideration

---

§ 3.6

1. Infra § 18.14.

2. Infra § 17.2.

3. Infra § 17.5.

4. See In re Jones' Estate, 192 Iowa 78, 182 N.W. 227 (1921) (discussed infra § 4.36).

§ 3.7

1. See Marie v. Garrison, 13 Abb. N.Cas. 210 (N.Y.Super.1883), a case involving the substantive-procedural characterization of the Statute of Frauds of two states where cumulative characterization led to the application of neither statute, although both states would have barred the action if the contract had been a purely domestic contract. See infra § 3.8 n.4.

of the foreign rule within the context of the foreign law is of relevance in order to determine whether that law would have applied to a similar domestic case or whether, once again, the case presents a "false conflict."

In essence, the Second Restatement adopts the suggested approach when it provides for most cases[2] that the law of the place of the "most significant relationship" should be the applicable test. The emphasis on governmental policies in interest analysis likewise substitutes evaluation for predetermined mechanical rules. The switch from rigid and territorially-oriented rules to a more functional approach, however, also has its problems and dangers.[3] Especially when a court is inclined to favor forum law, the determination of what makes for the "most significant relationship" or what is a legitimate forum policy or interest[4] may rest on tenuous subjective factors: significance and interest may be in the eye of the beholder.[5] For this reason, some of the present authors have urged limitations on state choice-of-law rules and the development of new principled rules on the basis of the Restatement's approach.[6]

When the forum's connecting factors refer to the law of another jurisdiction, legal concepts encountered in the foreign law may differ from those of the forum. In such a case, and for the purpose of achieving uniformity in the decision-making process, "the meaning to be applied is that which prevails in the state whose local law governs the issue under the applicable choice-of-law rule."[7]

4. *Substance—Procedure Characterization*

a. *In General*

§ 3.8 When the forum's choice-of-law rule refers to the law of another jurisdiction, the question arises as to the extent of that reference: does it include both the foreign substantive and procedural law and, moreover, does it also include the foreign choice-of-law rules? Use of the foreign choice-of-law rule may entail further references—back to the

---

2. The Second Restatement preserves some specific choice-of-law rules. In addition to the traditional rules with respect to interests in land (situs law, § 223 et seq.) and intestate succession to movables (domicile at death, § 260), the Restatement contains isolated other rules selecting a specific jurisdiction: see, e.g., § 148 (fraud and misrepresentation) and § 192 (life insurance contracts).

3. See R. Weintraub, Commentary on the Conflict of Laws 55 et seq. (4th ed. 2001).

4. See Brilmayer, Legitimate Interests in Multistate Problems: As Between State and Federal Law, 79 Mich. L. Rev. 1315 (1981). For a critique of interest analysis see also Brilmayer, Interest Analysis and the Myth of Legislative Intent, 78 Mich. L.

Rev. 392 (1980). For additional literature see supra § 2.6 n.18.

5. See Allstate Insurance Co. v. Hague, 449 U.S. 302, 101 S.Ct. 633, 66 L.Ed.2d 521 (1981). This decision and the problem of constitutional limitations on choice of law are discussed infra § 3.23.

6. For limitations see infra § 3.23. For new rules see supra § 2.17 and infra §§ 17.31–17.36 (torts) and §§ 18.40–18.41 (contracts).

7. Restatement, Second, Conflict of Laws § 7, comment (c) (1971); Landmark Land Co., Inc. v. Sprague, 529 F.Supp. 971 (S.D.N.Y.1981), reversed 701 F.2d 1065 (2d Cir.1983).

forum or on to yet another foreign law (*renvoi*). This problem forms the subject of § 3.13; the present sections deal only with the use of foreign procedural law in addition to foreign substantive law.

The distinction between "substance" and "procedure" has medieval origins:[1] a court will apply foreign law only to the extent that it deals with the substance of the case, i.e., affects the outcome of the litigation,[2] but will rely on forum law to deal with the "procedural" aspects of the litigation.[3] The determination of whether a rule of law is one of substance or procedure is part of the third aspect of the process of characterization.

Traditional conflicts law contained a number of characterizations;[4] it often derived simply from an interpretation of whether a rule of law affected the "right" or the "remedy." Thus, the use of the term "voidable" in a Statute of Frauds originally resulted in a procedural characterization of the Statute, while a provision that an oral contract is "void" was considered to be substantive.[5] Modern American law predominantly characterizes the Statute of Frauds as substantive.[6]

The Second Restatement has abandoned the "substance"–"procedure" labels because they had led courts to "unthinking adherence to precedents regardless of what purposes were involved in the earlier classifications. Thus, for example, a decision classifying burden of proof as 'procedural' for local law purposes, such as in determining the constitutionality of a statute that retroactively shifted the burden,[7]

§ 3.8

1. See Ailes, Substance and Procedure in the Conflict of Laws, 39 Mich. L. Rev. 392, 396–401 (1941); Meijers, L'histoire des principes fondamentaux du droit international privé partir du Moyen Age, Hague Academy, 49 Recueil des Cours 547, 595 (III–1934). See also Risinger, "Substance" and "Procedure" Revisited With Some Afterthoughts on the Constitutional Problems of Irrebuttable Presumptions, 30 U.C.L.A. L. Rev. 189 (1982).

2. Cook, "Substance" and "Procedure" in the Conflict of Laws, 42 Yale L.J. 333, 344 (1933). See also Twerski & Mayer, Toward a Pragmatic Solution of Choice–of–Law Problems—At the Interface of Substance and Procedure, 74 N.W.L.Rev. 781, 784 (1979).

3. See, e.g., Witter v. Torbett, 604 F.Supp. 298 (W.D.Va.1984); Lincoln Nat. Life Ins. Co. v. NCR Corp., 603 F.Supp. 1393 (N.D.Ind.1984), affirmed 772 F.2d 315 (7th Cir.1985). Although related to the remedy, the allowance of prejudgment interest has been held to be governed by the law of the state whose law determines liability on the main claim. Entron, Inc. v. Affiliated FM Ins. Co., 749 F.2d 127 (2d Cir.1984).

4. See generally Restatement, Second, Conflict of Laws §§ 122 et seq. (1971). See

also infra Chapter 12 with respect to testimonial privilege.

5. Marie v. Garrison, 13 Abb.N.Cas. 210 (N.Y.Super.1883) (discussed supra § 3.7 n.1). This method of characterization of the Statute of Frauds derives from English law. McDougal, Felix & Whitten, American Conflicts Law 419 (5th ed. 2001).

6. See Restatement, Second, Conflict of Laws § 141 (1971). Massachusetts basically follows a substantive characterization but will adopt any connected law that will validate the transaction. Bushkin Associates, Inc. v. Raytheon Co., 393 Mass. 622, 473 N.E.2d 662 (1985). California applies its comparative impairment approach to the selection of the applicable Statute of Frauds. In Rosenthal v. Fonda, 862 F.2d 1398 (9th Cir.1988), this led to the selection of the New York statute (making the oral contract unenforceable) in factual circumstances where New York law probably would also have governed the contract itself.

7. See Levy v. Steiger, 233 Mass. 600, 124 N.E. 477 (1919).

might mistakenly be held controlling on the question whether burden of proof is 'procedural' for choice-of-law purposes. To avoid encouraging errors of that sort, the rules stated in this Chapter [of the Restatement (Second)] do not attempt to classify issues as 'procedural' or 'substantive.' Instead, they face directly the question whether the forum's rule should be applied.'"[8]

b.   *Statutes of Limitation*[1]

§ 3.9   Statutes of limitations illustrate both the traditional approach and the evolution of new concepts. Traditional conflicts law characterized statutes of limitation as procedural[2] because it is "the purpose of a statute of limitations . . . to protect both the parties and the local courts against the prosecution of stale claims."[3] The original version of the Second Restatement continued to provide for the application of the forum's statute.[4] Since the underlying rationale is that the forum's statute only affects the remedy,[5] the application of the forum's *longer limitation may encourage forum-shopping.*[6]

---

8. Restatement, Second, Conflict of Laws § 122, cmnt. (b) (1971).

§ 3.9

1. For extensive treatment see Grossman, Statutes of Limitation and the Conflict of Laws: Modern Analysis, 1980 Ariz. St. L.J. 1.

2. Grossman, supra n. 1, at 11 et seq.; Restatement of Conflict of Laws §§ 603, 604 (1934). Perhaps the earliest American decision adopting the procedural characterization is Pearsall v. Dwight, 2 Mass. 84 (1806). For modern cases see infra § 3.12 n. 7. But see infra § 13.12 at n.9.

In most foreign legal systems, time limitations are regarded as substantive. See, e.g., Canada: Tolofson v. Jensen, [1994] 3 S.C.R. 1022, 1071–72 (Can. 1994); England and Wales: Foreign Limitation Periods Act 1984, also adopted in Australia by New South Wales (New South Wales Choice of Law (Limitation Periods) Act 1993 No. 94) and by New Zealand (New Zealand Limitations Amendment Act 1996); European Community: Intergovernmental Convention (EC)—Rome Convention on the Law Applicable to Contractual Obligations, Act. 10 (1)(d), [1998] Official Journal C 27/34. The rule is the same in European national legal system (i.e., also with respect to claims other than in contract): See Rabel, 3 Conflict of Laws: A Comparative Study 511–12 (2d ed. 1964 by Bernstein). The United Nations (Vienna) Convention on the International Sale of Goods, entered into force for the United States on December 11,1994, avoids the characterization problem by providing an uniform rule in its Art. 8: claims covered

by the Convention, between parties in countries that are parties to the Convention are barred after four years.

3. Restatement, Second, Conflict of Laws § 142, cmnt. (d) (1971).

4. For the revision of the section, see infra at n.8.

The statement in the text assumes agreement on what constitutes a "statute of limitations." Many courts distinguish between statutes of "repose" (affecting liability and therefore "substantive" for conflicts purposes) and statutes of limitations' (barring the remedy and therefore "procedural"). See Thornton v. Cessna Aircraft Co., 886 F.2d 85 (4th Cir. 1989); Tanges v. Heidelberg North America, Inc., 93 N.Y.2d 48, 687 N.Y.S.2d 604, 710 N.E.2d 250 (1999). But see Baxter v. Sturm, Ruger & Co., 230 Conn. 335, 644 A.2d 1297 (1994); Etheridge v. Genie Industries, Inc., 632 So.2d 1324 (Ala. 1994) (statutes of repose are procedural).

5. See Restatement, Second, Conflict of Laws, § 143, cmnt. (c) (1971).

6. See Vick v. Cochran, 316 So.2d 242 (Miss.1975); Gordon v. Gordon, 118 N.H. 356, 387 A.2d 339 (1978); Hossler v. Barry, 403 A.2d 762 (Me.1979); Schreiber v. Allis–Chalmers Corp., 611 F.2d 790 (10th Cir. 1979); Steele v. G.D. Searle & Co., 428 F.Supp. 646 (S.D.Miss.1977); Culpepper v. Daniel Industries, Inc., 500 S.W.2d 958 (Tex.Civ.App.1973), error refused n.r.e.

In Sun Oil Co. v. Wortman, 486 U.S. 717, 108 S.Ct. 2117, 100 L.Ed.2d 743 (1988), the

The Uniform Conflict of Laws Limitations Act now adopts a qualified substantive characterization for statutes of limitations; as of June 2004, the Act was in force in only six states.[7] The Revisions of the Second Restatement envisioned, in the form proposed in 1986, the adoption of the "most significant relationship test" for the determination of the applicable statute of limitations. As ultimately adopted by the American Law Institute in 1988, the revision of § 142 of the Second Restatement does not go this far. While § 142, as revised, adheres to the practice of incorporating, by reference, the general principles of § 6, it then adopts a decided forum bias. It provides that, "in general, unless the exceptional circumstances of the case make such a result unreasonable," the forum's shorter statute of limitations applies. If the forum's statute is longer, it will also apply unless there is no significant forum interest and the state having a more significant relationship to the parties and the occurrence would bar the claim.[8] Apart from the continued forum bias of the provision, Section 142, as revised, also offers

U.S. Supreme Court held that statutes of limitation are by tradition procedural and that the forum did not violate the Due Process and Full Faith and Credit Clauses by applying its own longer statute of limitation to a claim governed by the substantive law of another jurisdiction. Justice Brennan, in concurrence, was troubled by the majority's reliance on tradition as justifying the forum in applying its own limitation. Rather than asking the "wrong question" whether a rule is substantive or procedural, 486 U.S. at 743, 108 S.Ct. at 2132–33, he suggested that careful analysis is required to determine whether application of forum law complied with the test announced in Phillips Petroleum Co. v. Shutts, 472 U.S. 797, 105 S.Ct. 2965, 86 L.Ed.2d 628 (1985), on remand 240 Kan. 764, 732 P.2d 1286 (1987), cert. denied 487 U.S. 1223, 108 S.Ct. 2883, 101 L.Ed.2d 918 (1988) (infra § 3.23). He concluded that the forum in *Wortman* had a sufficient procedural interest to justify application of its law. The danger with the majority's approach, as Justice Brennan noted, is that other longstanding procedural characterizations (e.g., with respect to remedies, burdens of proof and of production) or choice-of-law rules may be thought to be constitutional and not subject to review and examination only because they are "long established and still subsisting." 486 U.S. at 740, 108 S.Ct. at 2125, 2131. For an example of "statute-of-limitations shopping" through federal transfer, see Ferens v. John Deere Co., 494 U.S. 516, 110 S.Ct. 1274, 108 L.Ed.2d 443 (1990) (discussed infra § 3.46 nn.9–12).

7. See 12 U.L.A. 155 (1996). The states are Colorado, Minnesota, Montana, North Dakota, Oregon, and Washington. Arkansas repealed its earlier adoption. For an application, see Cropp v. Interstate Distributor Co., 129 Or.App. 510, 880 P.2d 464, review denied 320 Or. 407, 887 P.2d 791 (1994). In support of the Act: Cooper, Statutes of Limitation in Minnesota: The Problematic Return of the Substance–Procedure Distinction, 71 Minn. L. Rev. 363 (1986). Foreign legal systems generally follow a substantive characterization: supra n.2.

8. Restatement, Second, Conflict of Laws § 142 (1986 Revision, as approved 1988); for an application, see Cropp v. Interstate Distributor Co., 129 Or.App. 510 880 P.2d 464 (1994), review denied, 320 Or. 407, 887 P.2d 791 (1994); DeLoach v. Alfred, 192 Ariz. 28, 960 P.2d 628 (1998). See also, before the Revision, Drudge v. Overland Plazas Co., 531 F.Supp. 210 (S.D.Iowa 1981); Ashland Chemical Co. v. Provence, 129 Cal.App.3d 790, 181 Cal. Rptr. 340 (1982).

See also the 1992 revision of the provision "Governing Liberative Prescription" of the Louisiana Civil Code of 1870. The revision resembles the Restatement revision but displays a lesser forum bias, especially in cases when the forum has the shorter statute. The Restatement, Second revision results in the application of non-forum law in these cases only if there are "exceptional circumstances" which would make the application of forum law unreasonable. La. C. C. art. 3549 (1992). See Symeonides, Louisiana Conflicts Law: Two "Surprises", 54 La. L. Rev. 497, 530–48 (1994). In Marchesani v. Pellerin–Milnor Corp., 269 F.3d 481 (5th Cir. 2001), the court held that Art. 3549 does not distinguish between statutes of limitation and statutes of repose. Thus, al-

no guidance when, in the case of the proviso of subsection (2) (longer statute at the forum), more than one other jurisdiction has a more significant relationship to the parties and the occurrence than does the forum. At least for cases in which the forum has the longer statute and is not the state of the most significant relationship, the solution of the Uniform Law appears preferable: characterizing the limitation as substantive results in the application of the same law to the claim and to the limitation.[9]

§ **3.10** As noted, the traditional American (procedural) characterization of the Statute of Limitations may encourage forum-shopping. Two exceptions are designed to alleviate this problem. The first exception is a judicial creation: when the foreign limitation is intended to extinguish the right and not only to bar the remedy, it will be considered to be "substantive." While, in theory, this could be true of a limitation of a common law cause of action as well as of one limiting a statutory right, the courts invariably limit the substantive characterization to limitations of rights created by statute.[1] The limitation is considered to be "built in."[2] Common examples are limitations in Wrongful Death Acts[3] and Shareholder Liability Acts.[4]

though Tennessee substantive law applied, Tennessee's 10–year statute of repose for product liability claims did not bar suit by a Tennessee domiciliary against a Louisiana manufacturer for injuries sustained in Tennessee. In contrast, in Tanges v. Heidelberg of North America, 93 N.Y.2d 48, 710 N.E.2d 250 (1999), the court considered Connecticut's statute of repose to be substantive.

9. The comments to § 142 as revised, make clear that the rule of § 142 applies also to other timebars, such as laches.

§ 3.10

1. Restatement, Second, Conflict of Laws § 143, cmnt. (c) (1971). See Jackson v. National Semi–Conductor Data Checker/DTS, Inc., 660 F.Supp. 65 (S.D.Miss. 1986); Morris Plan Industrial Bank of New York v. Richards, 131 Conn. 671, 42 A.2d 147 (1945), The Harrisburg, 119 U.S. 199, 7 S.Ct. 140, 30 L.Ed. 358 (1886); Taylor v. Murray, 231 Ga. 852, 204 S.E.2d 747 (1974); Indon Industries, Inc. v. Charles S. Martin Distributing Co., Inc., 234 Ga. 845, 218 S.E.2d 562 (1975); Kalmich v. Bruno, 553 F.2d 549 (7th Cir.1977), cert. denied 434 U.S. 940, 98 S.Ct. 432, 54 L.Ed.2d 300 (1977); Istre v. Diamond M. Drilling Co., 226 So.2d 779 (La.App.1969), writ issued 254 La. 929, 228 So.2d 485 (1969), cert. abandoned 255 La. 1089, 234 So.2d 191 (1970); Maki v. George R. Cooke Co., 124 F.2d 663 (6th Cir.1942), cert. denied 316 U.S. 686, 62 S.Ct. 1274, 86 L.Ed. 1758; White v. Govatos, 40 Del. 349, 10 A.2d 524 (1939); Earnhardt v. Shattuck, 232 F.Supp. 845 (D.Vt.1964); Holdford v. Leonard, 355 F.Supp. 261 (W.D.Va.1973); Price v. Litton Systems, 784 F.2d 600 (5th Cir.1986), on remand 651 F.Supp. 706 (S.D.Miss.1986).

However, the presence of a limitation within the statute itself is not necessarily conclusive on the substantive nature of the limitation. See Lillegraven v. Tengs, 375 P.2d 139 (Alaska 1962); Baldwin v. Brown, 202 F.Supp. 49 (E.D.Mich.1962); Bournias v. Atlantic Maritime Co., 220 F.2d 152 (2d Cir.1955).

2. See Marine Construction & Design Co. v. Vessel Tim, 434 P.2d 683 (Alaska 1967); Schreiber v. Allis–Chalmers Corp., 448 F.Supp. 1079 (D.Kan.1978), reversed 611 F.2d 790 (10th Cir.1979).

3. The Harrisburg, 119 U.S. 199, 7 S.Ct. 140, 30 L.Ed. 358 (1886); Gantes v. Kason Corp., 145 N.J. 478, 679 A.2d 106 (1996); Bonti v. Ford Motor Co., 898 F.Supp. 391 (S.D.Miss.1995); State of Maryland v. Eis Automotive Corp., 145 F.Supp. 444 (D.Conn.1956); Pack v. Beech Aircraft Corp., 50 Del. 413, 132 A.2d 54 (1957); O'Neal v. National Cylinder Gas Co., 103 F.Supp. 720 (N.D.Ill.1952); Chiasson v. R. E. A. Express Co., 269 F.Supp. 685 (D.N.H. 1966); Smith v. Turner, 91 N.H. 198, 17 A.2d 87 (1940); Wilson v. Massengill, 124 F.2d 666 (6th Cir.1942), cert. denied 316 U.S. 686, 62 S.Ct. 1274, 86 L.Ed. 1758 (1942); Francis v. Herrin Transportation Co., 432 S.W.2d 710 (Tex.1968), appeal after remand 473 S.W.2d 664 (Tex.Civ.App. 1971); Click v. Thuron Industries, Inc., 475 S.W.2d 715 (Tex.1972); Penry v. Wm. Barr, Inc., 415 F.Supp. 126 (E.D.Tex.1976); Price v. Litton Systems, Inc., 784 F.2d 600 (5th Cir.1986), on remand 651 F.Supp. 706 (S.D.Miss.1986).

4. White v. Govatos, 40 Del. 349, 10 A.2d 524 (1939); Broderick v. Pardue, 102

A somewhat broader view of the exception inquires whether the foreign limitation is directed toward the right so specifically as to warrant saying that it qualified the right.[5] This test is wider than the "built-in" test in that the limitation qualifying the right can be found outside the statute creating it.[6]

S.W.2d 252 (Tex.Civ.App. 1937); Norman v. Baldwin, 152 Va. 800, 148 S.E. 831 (1929).

See also Davis v. Mills, 194 U.S. 451, 24 S.Ct. 692, 48 L.Ed. 1067 (1904) (holding that a statute of limitation specifically directed at corporate directors liability statute qualified the right of action under the statute and that a suit brought after expiration of the period was barred wherever the suit was commenced); Byron v. Great American Indemnity Co., 54 R.I. 405, 173 A. 546 (1934) (holding that a statutorily created right of action against an insurer to recover on a judgment against its insured was qualified by the limitation contained in the statute that created the right and which required that the cause of action against the insured must be commenced within one year after the cause of action accrued); State of California v. Copus, 158 Tex. 196, 309 S.W.2d 227 (1958), cert. denied 356 U.S. 967, 78 S.Ct. 1006, 2 L.Ed.2d 1074 (1958) (holding that the limitation contained in a California statute, which created an obligation for an adult son to reimburse the state for sums expended by the state in the care and maintenance of an indigent parent in a state institution, was a substantive limitation on the statutory right); Whitley v. Hartford Acc. and Indem. Co., 532 F.Supp. 190 (N.D.Tex.1981), affirmed 670 F.2d 183 (5th Cir.1982) (Pennsylvania No–Fault Motor Vehicle Insurance Act's statute of limitation law was deemed substantive and applied in Texas).

5. Davis v. Mills, 194 U.S. 451, 24 S.Ct. 692, 48 L.Ed. 1067 (1904); Sokolowski v. Flanzer, 769 F.2d 975 (4th Cir.1985); Nieman v. Press & Equipment Sales Co., 588 F.Supp. 650 (S.D.Ohio 1984); Lillegraven v. Tengs, 375 P.2d 139 (Alaska 1962); Thomas Iron Co. v. Ensign–Bickford Co., 131 Conn. 665, 42 A.2d 145 (1945); Kalmich v. Bruno, 553 F.2d 549 (7th Cir.1977), cert. denied 434 U.S. 940, 98 S.Ct. 432, 54 L.Ed.2d 300 (1977); O'Neal v. National Cylinder Gas Co., 103 F.Supp. 720 (N.D.Ill.1952); Maki v. George R. Cooke Co., 124 F.2d 663 (6th Cir.1942), cert. denied 316 U.S. 686, 62 S.Ct. 1274, 86 L.Ed. 1758 (1942); Myers v. Alvey–Ferguson Co., 331 F.2d 223 (6th Cir. 1964); Chandler v. Humphrey, 177 Wash.

402, 31 P.2d 1012 (1934); Bournias v. Atlantic Maritime Co., 220 F.2d 152 (2d Cir. 1955).

6. In this regard, Justice Holmes, in Davis v. Mills, 194 U.S. 451, 24 S.Ct. 692, 48 L.Ed. 1067 (1904), stated as follows: "The common case is where the statute creates a new liability and in the same section or in the same act limits the time within which it can be enforced, whether using words of condition or not. But the fact that the limitation is contained in the same section or in the same statute is material only as bearing on construction. It is merely a ground for saying that the limitation goes to the right created, and accompanies the obligation everywhere. The same conclusion would be reached if the limitation was in a different statute, provided it was directed to the newly created liability so specifically as to warrant saying that it qualified the right." 194 U.S. at 454, 24 S.Ct. at 693. See also Kalmich v. Bruno, 553 F.2d 549 (7th Cir.1977), cert. denied 434 U.S. 940, 98 S.Ct. 432, 54 L.Ed.2d 300 (1977); Maki v. George R. Cooke Co., 124 F.2d 663 (6th Cir.1942), cert. denied 316 U.S. 686, 62 S.Ct. 1274, 86 L.Ed. 1758 (1942). See also Gomez v. ITT Educational Services, 348 Ark. 69, 71 S.W.3d 542 (2002)(applying the law of the injury state and not the forum in a wrongful death case where the injury state's period was shorter under essentially the "built in" test).

Other variations include the "attributes" test and the "foreign-court" test. The former seeks to examine whether the foreign limitation pleaded by the party has "attributes" which resemble a limitation of the forum which, under forum law, would be substantive. See Restatement, Second, Conflict of Laws § 143, cmnt. (c) (1971); Wood & Selick, Inc. v. Compagnie Generale Transatlantique, 43 F.2d 941 (2d Cir.1930).

Under the "foreign-court" test, the forum seeks to determine how the foreign court would characterize its own limitation. Jackson v. Continental Southern Lines, Inc., 172 F.Supp. 809 (W.D.Ark.1959); Pack v. Beech Aircraft Corp., 50 Del. 413, 132 A.2d 54 (1957); Goodwin v. Townsend, 197 F.2d 970 (3d Cir.1952); Leonard v. Wharton, 268 F.Supp. 715 (D.Md.1967), appeal

§ 3.11 The second exception to the traditional rule also seeks to guard against the enforcement of stale claims and the potential danger of forum shopping. It takes the form of "borrowing statutes" enacted by most jurisdictions.[1] The typical "borrowing statute" provides that the cause of action will be barred in the forum if it is barred where it arose, accrued, or originated.[2] It usually borrows not only the foreign limitation

dismissed 396 F.2d 452 (4th Cir.1968), cert. denied 393 U.S. 1028, 89 S.Ct. 624, 21 L.Ed.2d 571 (1969); Marshall v. Geo. M. Brewster & Son, Inc., 37 N.J. 176, 180 A.2d 129 (1962); Buhl v. Biosearch Medical Products, Inc., 635 F.Supp. 956 (D.Mont.1985); Keys v. Pullman Co., 87 F.Supp. 763 (S.D.Tex.1949); Page v. Cameron Iron Works, Inc., 259 F.2d 420 (5th Cir.1958); Earnhardt v. Shattuck, 232 F.Supp. 845 (D.Vt.1964); Norman v. Baldwin, 152 Va. 800, 148 S.E. 831 (1929). The major problem with this inquiry lies in the fact that the foreign characterization may not have been made for conflicts law purposes. Supra § 3.8, n. 6. See also Justice O'Connor's partial concurrence in Sun Oil Co. v. Wortman, 486 U.S. 717, 743, 108 S.Ct. 2117, 2133, 100 L.Ed.2d 743 (1988) (after agreeing that Kansas could constitutionally apply its own longer statute of limitations to a claim to which it could not apply its substantive law, she noted that "different issues might have arisen if Texas, Oklahoma, or Louisiana regarded its own statute of limitations as substantive. Such issues, however, are not presented in this case, and they are appropriately left unresolved....").

§ 3.11

1. Ala. Code 1975 § 6–2–17; Alaska Stat. 09.10.220; Ariz. Rev. Stat. § 12–506; West's C.R.S.A. § 13–80–118; 10 Del. § 8121; Fla. Stat. Ann. § 95.10; Title 36 Hawaii Rev. Stat. § 657–9; Ill.—Smith-Hurd Ann. 735 ILCS 5/13–210; Burns Ann. Ind. Code Ann., § 34–11–4–2 (2003); Iowa Code Ann. § 614.7; Kan. Stats. Ann., Code of Civ. Proc. § 60–516 (reconstituted in 2002); Ky. Rev. Stat. § 413.320; Mass. General Laws Ann. c. 260, § 9; Miss. Code 1972, § 15–1–65 ; Vernon's Ann. Mo. Stat. § 516.190; Neb. Rev. Stat. § 25–215; Nev. Rev. Stat. 11.020; N.Y. Civ. Prac. L. & R. § 202; N.C. Gen. Stat. § 1–21; 12 Okla. Stat. Ann. §§ 104–108 (West); 42 Pa. Cons. Stat. Ann. § 5521; R.I. Gen. 1956, Laws § 9–1–18; Tenn. Code Ann. § 28–1–112; Utah Code Ann. 1953 § 78–12–45; Tex. Civ. Prac. & Rem. Code § 73.031 (Vernon Supp. 2002); Va. Code § 8.01–247; Wash. Rev. Code Ann. § 4.16.290; W.Va. Code 55–2–17; Wis. Stat. Ann. 893.07; Wyo. Stat. 1997 § 1–3–117. See Annot., Validity, Construction, and Application, in Nonstatutory

Personal Injury Actions, of State Statute Providing for Borrowing of Statute of Limitations of Another State, 41 ALR 4th 1025 (1985). For the new Texas statute, see George, Annual Survey of Texas Law: Conflict of Laws, 55 S.M.U. L.Rev. 1283 (2003)

2. An example of such a "borrowing statute" provides as follows:

"When a cause of action has arisen in a state or territory out of this state, or in a foreign country, and, by the laws thereof, an action thereon cannot be maintained by reason of the lapse of time, an action thereon shall not be maintained in this state." 735 ILCS 5/13–210 (1993).

Such a statute is a rule of exclusion which operates to bar action barred elsewhere; it will not "borrow" a foreign limitation which is longer than that of the forum. See Pucci v. Litwin, 828 F.Supp. 1285 (N.D.Ill.1993); Stavriotis v. Litwin, 710 F.Supp. 216 (N.D.Ill.1988); Hollins v. Yellow Freight System, Inc., 590 F.Supp. 1023 (N.D.Ill.1984); Kalmich v. Bruno, 404 F.Supp. 57, 68 (N.D.Ill.1975), reversed on other grounds 553 F.2d 549 (7th Cir.1977), cert. denied 434 U.S. 940, 98 S.Ct. 432, 54 L.Ed.2d 300 (1977). See also Christner v. Chicago, Rock Island & Pacific Railway Co., 228 Mo.App. 220, 64 S.W.2d 752 (1933); Moe v. Shaffer, 150 Minn. 114, 184 N.W. 785 (1921). See generally Vernon, Statutes of Limitation in the Conflict of Laws: Borrowing Statutes, 32 Rocky Mt.L.Rev. 287 (1960); Note, Legislation Governing the Applicability of Foreign Statutes of Limitation, 35 Colum.L.Rev. 762 (1935); Note, Statute of Limitation, 47 Va.L.Rev. 299 (1961).

A "non-claim" statute setting short periods after which claims may not be filed against an estate has been held not to be a statute of limitations within the meaning of a borrowing statute: Owens v. Estate of Saville, 409 S.W.2d 660 (Mo.1966); for a decision that an action may be brought under a nonresident motorist statute against the deceased motorist's foreign executor after the non-claim period has run at the decedent's domicile, see Brooks v. National Bank of Topeka, 251 F.2d 37 (8th Cir.1958), but see Uniform Probate Code § 3–803(a)(1).

but also foreign tolling provisions.[3] Consistent with the principles of the First Restatement, most jurisdictions held that the cause of action arises in the jurisdiction where the last act to give rise to liability occurred.[4]

The typical borrowing statute has an exception in favor of residents of the forum. This has been held not to violate the Privileges and Immunities Clause of Art. IV, § 2 of the U.S. Constitution: Canadian Northern Ry. Co. v. Eggen, 252 U.S. 553, 40 S.Ct. 402, 64 L.Ed. 713 (1920). But consider: See Flowers v. Carville, 310 F.3d 1118 (9th Cir. 2002), the court considered the typical exception to the borrowing of the limitation of the state where the claim arose in favor of a citizen of Nevada who has held the claim from the time it accrued. The Nevada exception did not expressly state that the plaintiff must have been a citizen at the time the claim accrued. The court considered the statute to be constitutional on this basis, thereby distinguishing it from Saenz v. Roe, 526 U.S. 489, 119 S.Ct. 1518, 143 L.Ed.2d 689 (1999), in which the United States Supreme Court held California legislation, limiting benefits to needy families during their first year of in-state residence, as violative of their 14th Amendment right to travel.

3. Nowotny v. L & B Contract Industries, Inc., 933 P.2d 452 (Wyo.1997); Duke v. Housen, 589 P.2d 334 (Wyo.1979), cert. denied 444 U.S. 863, 100 S.Ct. 132, 62 L.Ed.2d 86 (1979); Sierra Diesel Injection Service v. Burroughs Corp., Inc., 648 F.Supp. 1148 (D.Nev.1986); Devine v. Rook, 314 S.W.2d 932 (Mo.App.1958); Martin v. Julius Dierck Equipment Co., 43 N.Y.2d 583, 403 N.Y.S.2d 185, 374 N.E.2d 97 (1978); Lowell Wiper Supply Co. v. Helen Shop, Inc., 235 F.Supp. 640 (S.D.N.Y.1964); Alberding v. Brunzell, 601 F.2d 474 (9th Cir.1979); United States ex rel. Sabella v. Newsday, 315 F.Supp. 333 (E.D.N.Y.1970); American Surety Co. of New York v. Gainfort, 219 F.2d 111 (2d Cir.1955); Conner v. Spencer, 304 F.2d 485 (9th Cir.1962); Ester, Borrowing Statutes of Limitation and Conflicts of Laws, 15 U. Fla. L. Rev. 33, 57 (1962); A. Ehrenzweig, Conflict of Laws, 430–31 (1962); but see Ohio Rev.Code § 2305.20; Payne v. Kirchwehm, 141 Ohio St. 384, 48 N.E.2d 224 (1943), appeal dismissed 320 U.S. 706, 64 S.Ct. 71, 88 L.Ed. 413 (1943); Palmieri v. Ahart, 111 Ohio App. 195, 167 N.E.2d 353 (1960).

Tolling in federal court. 28 U.S.C. § 1367 (d) provides that, when a federal district court declines to exercise supplemental jurisdiction over a state-law based claim, "The period of limitation for [such] claim

...shall be tolled... for a period of 30 days after it is dismissed unless State law provides for a longer tolling period." Raygor v. Regents of the University of Minnesota, 534 U.S. 533, 122 S.Ct. 999, 152 L.Ed.2d 27 (2002), held that the section did not apply to "State law claims asserted against nonconsenting state defendants" when those claims "are dismissed on Eleventh Amendment grounds" (barring suits against states by citizens of other states). Jinks v. Richland County, 349 S.C. 298, 563 S.E.2d 104, 108 (2002), held the federal tolling provision to be unconstitutional because § 1367 (d) "extends the waiver of sovereign immunity of political subdivisions thereby interfering with the State's sovereignty in violation of the Tenth Amendment and the Necessary and Proper Clause," reversed 538 U.S. 456, 123 S.Ct. 1667, 155 L.Ed.2d 631 (2003).

4. Colhoun v. Greyhound Lines, Inc., 265 So.2d 18 (Fla.1972); Boudreau v. Baughman, 322 N.C. 331, 368 S.E.2d 849 (1988); Manos v. Trans World Airlines, Inc., 295 F.Supp. 1170 (N.D.Ill.1969), but see Klondike Helicopters, Limited v. Fairchild Hiller Corp., 334 F.Supp. 890 (N.D.Ill. 1971); Vick v. Cochran, 316 So.2d 242 (Miss.1975); Waldron v. Armstrong Rubber Co., 54 Mich.App. 154, 220 N.W.2d 738 (1974), reversed on other grounds 393 Mich. 760, 223 N.W.2d 295 (1974), on remand 64 Mich.App. 626, 236 N.W.2d 722 (1975); Parish v. B.F. Goodrich Co., 395 Mich. 271, 235 N.W.2d 570 (1975); Martin v. Julius Dierck Equipment Co., 43 N.Y.2d 583, 403 N.Y.S.2d 185, 374 N.E.2d 97 (1978); Chartener v. Kice, 270 F.Supp. 432 (E.D.N.Y.1967); Sack v. Low, 478 F.2d 360 (2d Cir.1973); Stell v. Firestone Tire & Rubber Co., 306 F.Supp. 17 (W.D.N.C. 1969); Mack Trucks Inc. v. Bendix–Westinghouse Automotive Air Brake Co., 372 F.2d 18 (3d Cir.1966), cert. denied 387 U.S. 930, 87 S.Ct. 2053, 18 L.Ed.2d 992 (1967); Gross v. McDonald, 354 F.Supp. 378 (E.D.Pa. 1973); Schenk v. Piper Aircraft Corp., 377 F.Supp. 477 (W.D.Pa.1974), affirmed 521 F.2d 1399 (3d Cir.1975); Duke v. Housen, 589 P.2d 334 (Wyo.1979), cert. denied 444 U.S. 863, 100 S.Ct. 132, 62 L.Ed.2d 86 (1979); Besser v. E.R. Squibb & Sons, 75 N.Y.2d 847, 552 N.Y.S.2d 923, 552 N.E.2d 171 (1990).

In contract cases a majority of the courts hold that a cause of action arises or accrues

With the advent of modern choice-of-law rules, it seems desirable to reevaluate the reference in borrowing statutes so as to align the applicable limitation with the applicable substantive law. If this is not done, the limitation of a jurisdiction may be chosen which has no substantial relationship to, or interest in the litigation and whose substantive law may therefore not be applicable.[5] Although a few jurisdictions have considered a change in the reference for the determination of the applicable limitation,[6] most continue to adhere to the traditional approach.

Despite the relative success of borrowing statutes in limiting forum-shopping opportunities, problems remain: several jurisdictions have never enacted such a statute, and the limited scope of some statutes render them inapplicable to many fact situations that commonly arise.[7] In

in the jurisdiction in which the contract was to be performed and where the breach occurred. See Ester, Borrowing Statutes of Limitation and Conflict of Laws, 15 U. Fla. L. Rev. 33, 50 (1962); Bank of Boston Intern. of Miami v. Arguello Tefel, 626 F.Supp. 314 (E.D.N.Y.1986); Aviation Credit Corp. v. Batchelor, 190 So.2d 8 (Fla.App. 1966); Brown v. Cosby, 433 F.Supp. 1331 (E.D.Pa.1977); Baker v. First National Bank of Denver, 603 P.2d 397 (Wyo.1979).

A few jurisdictions refer to the defendant's residence. See Iowa Code Ann. § 614.7; Ariz. Rev. Stat. § 12–506; Mass General Laws Ann. c. 260, § 9; Tenn. Code Ann. § 28–1–112. Others refer to the residence of all the parties: See 14 Me. Rev. Stat. Ann. § 866. These statutes have the advantage of preventing the tolling provisions of a state other than the defendant's residence from subjecting him to an unusually long limitation. See Alberding v. Brunzell, 601 F.2d 474 (9th Cir.1979).

5. For illustrations of the incongruity which can occur, see McDaniel v. Ritter, 556 So.2d 303 (Miss.1989); Vick v. Cochran, 316 So.2d 242 (Miss.1975); Richardson v. Watkins Brothers Memorial Chapels, Inc., 527 S.W.2d 19 (Mo.App.1975); Trzecki v. Gruenewald, 532 S.W.2d 209 (Mo.1976); McIndoo v. Burnett, 494 F.2d 1311 (8th Cir.1974) and Alberding v. Brunzell, 601 F.2d 474 (9th Cir.1979). For further discussion, see R. Weintraub, Commentary on the Conflict of Laws 65–66 (4th ed. 2001). Restatement, Second, Conflict of Laws § 142, comment b (1971, as revised 1988) now advocates repeal or amendment of borrowing statutes to conform with the new § 142, discussed supra § 3.9. See also Dymond v. National Broadcasting Co., Inc., 559 F.Supp. 734 (D.Del.1983); Scott v. First State Ins. Co., 155 Wis.2d 608, 456 N.W.2d 152 (1990). See Gomez, § 3.12 n.1 (Restate-

ment (Second) Revision not mentioned and considered).

6. See Klondike Helicopters, Limited v. Fairchild Hiller Corp., 334 F.Supp. 890 (N.D.Ill.1971); Parish v. B.F. Goodrich Co., 395 Mich. 271, 235 N.W.2d 570 (1975); Richardson v. Watkins Brothers Memorial Chapels, Inc., 527 S.W.2d 19 (Mo.App. 1975); Sack v. Low, 478 F.2d 360 (2d Cir. 1973); Arneil v. Ramsey, 550 F.2d 774 (2d Cir.1977); Thigpen v. Greyhound Lines, Inc., 11 Ohio App.2d 179, 229 N.E.2d 107 (1967); Rose v. K.K. Masutoku Toy Factory Co., 597 F.2d 215 (10th Cir.1979); Schenk v. Piper Aircraft Corp., 377 F.Supp. 477 (W.D.Pa.1974), affirmed 521 F.2d 1399 (3d Cir.1975); Braune v. Abbott Laboratories, 895 F.Supp. 530, 565–66 (E.D.N.Y.1995). But see *Besser*, supra n. 4.

7. See Schreiber v. Allis–Chalmers Corp., 448 F.Supp. 1079, 1093 (D.Kan. 1978), reversed 611 F.2d 790 (10th Cir. 1979). In *Schreiber*, the Federal District Court of Kansas was sitting as a Mississippi court under the *Van Dusen* rule after a transfer from Mississippi. Van Dusen v. Barrack, 376 U.S. 612, 84 S.Ct. 805, 11 L.Ed.2d 945 (1964). Although the Court was presented with a clear case of forum shopping, it was unable to apply the Mississippi "borrowing statute" due to its limited scope and the limited construction given it by the Mississippi courts. Miss. Code, § 15–1–65. The Mississippi "borrowing statute" applies only in favor of a non-resident defendant who comes to reside in Mississippi after the claim against him was barred by the jurisdiction where he previously resided. Accordingly, the Mississippi "borrowing statute," as interpreted, was inapplicable in *Schreiber* since the defendant corporation was qualified to do business in Mississippi at the time the cause of action arose and was, therefore, a resident of Mississippi, precluding the operation of the "borrowing

recognition of these difficulties, a few jurisdictions have reevaluated the traditional doctrine that statutes of limitation are procedural. These jurisdictions consider limitations to be part of the applicable law to be selected for the case at bar, i.e.—in traditional terminology—to be "substantive," the practical result of the borrowing statutes.[8]

§ 3.12   The seminal decision was *Heavner v. Uniroyal, Inc.*[1] The case involved a products liability action against the manufacturer of an allegedly defective truck tire and against the seller of a truck trailer equipped with the tire. The plaintiff, a resident of North Carolina, had purchased the truck equipped with the tire in North Carolina and the accident had occurred in that state. Despite potential jurisdiction over both defendants in North Carolina, no action was brought there. The New Jersey suit was brought more than three years after the accident and after the expiration of the applicable North Carolina statute of limitation. Under New Jersey's procedural characterization of limitations[2] and in the absence of a borrowing statute, the forum's limitation would have been applicable. However, the *Heavner* court held that (1) when the cause of action arises in another state, (2) the parties are all present and amenable to jurisdiction there, (3) New Jersey has no substantial interest in the matter, (4) the substantive law of the foreign state is to be applied, and (5) when its limitation period has expired at the time the suit is commenced, New Jersey will hold the suit barred. Although the holding was carefully limited, it was founded upon the general disfavor of the forum-shopping opportunities available under the common law rule, the essentially substantive impact of a statute of limitation of the forum on the parties involved, the comparative ease with which the forum can ascertain and apply a foreign limitation law, and upon New Jersey's lack of substantial interest in the matter.

Subsequent New Jersey decisions have tended to view *Heavner* as an exception to the common law rule that the law of the forum governs.[3] In *O'Keeffe v. Snyder*[4] the New Jersey Supreme Court held that *Heavner* does not apply unless all five preconditions, identified in *Heavner*, are

---

statute." 448 F.Supp. at 1093. See also infra § 3.48 for a discussion of constitutional implications.

8. For the new Uniform Conflict of Laws Limitation Act, see supra § 3.9 n.7. For the general substantive characterization in foreign legal systems, see supra § 3.9 n.2

§ 3.12

1. 63 N.J. 130, 305 A.2d 412 (1973). Although *Heavner* was to be the most authoritative pronouncement, earlier cases had purported to abandon the traditional rules in favor modern choice-of-law principles. See Gianni v. Fort Wayne Air Service, Inc., 342 F.2d 621 (7th Cir.1965); Horton v.

Jessie, 423 F.2d 722 (9th Cir.1970); Farrier v. May Department Stores Co., Inc., 357 F.Supp. 190 (D.D.C.1973). For a Restatement (Second) approach, see Gomez v. ITT Educational Services, Inc., 348 Ark. 69, 71 S.W.3d 542 (2002).

2. Marshall v. Geo. M. Brewster & Son, Inc., 37 N.J. 176, 180 A.2d 129 (1962).

3. 83 N.J. 478, 416 A.2d 862 (1980); Raskulinecz v. Raskulinecz, 141 N.J.Super. 148, 357 A.2d 330 (Law Div.1976). See also Busik v. Levine, 63 N.J. 351, 307 A.2d 571 (1973), appeal dismissed 414 U.S. 1106, 94 S.Ct. 831, 38 L.Ed.2d 733 (1973). See also infra n.6.

4. O'Keeffe v. Snyder, 83 N.J. 478, 416 A.2d 862 (1980).

met. More recently, decisions have stressed New Jersey's interest in the case as the reason for not applying *Heavner*.[5]

Other courts have refused to depart from the traditional procedural characterization of limitations, even when they have adopted modern approaches to the choice-of-law process in general.[6] Despite the general position of the Restatement, Second against retention of the "substantive"-"procedural" dichotomy and terminology,[7] it also retains, in the absence of a borrowing statute, both the common law rule (limitation of forum law) and its exception in cases in which the foreign limitation bars the right (e.g., is "built in" or "specific").[8] However, considering the force of the borrowing statutes in the great majority of states, the persuasiveness of the *Heavner* analysis, and the Restatement approach, the practical effect is to treat the limitations issue as substantive when effective by the law most significantly related and the persistence in the stated characterization of limitations issues as "procedural" rings rather hollow.[9]

---

5. In Warner v. Auberge Gray Rocks Inn, Ltee., 827 F.2d 938 (3d Cir.1987), the court held that the "narrow confines of *Heavner*" did not apply: since the plaintiff was a New Jersey domiciliary, New Jersey was an interested state and would therefore not apply the shorter statute of limitations of the Canadian place of injury but would apply the longer forum statute. The court noted that the then pending revision of § 142 of the Second Restatement, supra § 3.9, might ultimately bring about a more complete departure from the traditional rule. For a list of decisions adopting the modern view, see Restatement, Second, Conflict of Laws, 1986 Revisions, Reporter's Note to comment *e* (Supp., April 12, 1988). In New Jersey, the main emphasis seems to be a continued emphasis on the interest of the forum. See Gantes v. Kason Corp., 145 N.J. 478, 679 A.2d 106 (1996), (permitting a wrongful death action against a New Jersey manufacturer under New Jersey's statute of limitations). In that case, New Jersey had a "substantial interest in deterrence ... that is not outweighed by countervailing concerns over creating unnecessary and discriminatory burdens on domestic manufacturers or by fears of forum shopping and increased litigation in the courts of this state." *Heavner* was distinguished because in that case New Jersey's only contact was that it was the state of incorporation of the manufacturer. In *Gantes* the defective machine had been manufactured in New Jersey.

Decisions in other jurisdictions include: Perkins v. Clark Equipment Co., 823 F.2d 207 (8th Cir.1987); Warner v. Auberge Gray Rocks, Inn, Ltee, 827 F.2d 938 (3d Cir. 1987); Myers v. Cessna Aircraft Corp., 275 Or. 501, 553 P.2d 355 (1976) (forum law as a result of interest analysis); Air Products & Chemicals, Inc. v. Fairbanks Morse, Inc., 58 Wis.2d 193, 206 N.W.2d 414 (1973) (interest analysis leads to forum law, the same as a procedural characterization would).

6. See Hughes v. Prudential Lines, Inc., 425 Pa.Super. 262, 624 A.2d 1063 (1993); Alaska Airlines, Inc. v. Lockheed Aircraft Corp., 430 F.Supp. 134 (D.Alaska 1977); Stephens v. Household Finance Corp., 566 P.2d 1163 (Okl.1977). In Griffith v. United Air Lines, Inc., 416 Pa. 1, 203 A.2d 796 (1964), Pennsylvania had adopted interest analysis in torts. In Mack Trucks, Inc. v. Bendix–Westinghouse Automotive Air Brake Co., 372 F.2d 18, 21 (3d Cir.1966), cert. denied 387 U.S. 930, 87 S.Ct. 2053, 18 L.Ed.2d 992 (1967), the court held that *Griffith* extended only to substantive issues. See also Jagers v. Royal Indemnity Co., 276 So.2d 309 (La.1973) (interest analysis applied to intra-family immunity issue) and Wright v. Fireman's Fund Insurance Co., 522 F.2d 1376 (5th Cir.1975). *Mack Trucks* and *Wright* illustrate the problem faced by federal courts, sitting in diversity, in cases where the state courts have not yet indicated a change in the law with respect to a particular issue. See infra § 3.47. See also Jamison v. Cooper, 754 F.2d 1568 (11th Cir.1985) (Georgia forum—Georgia limitation). Similarly: Bailey v. Skipperliner Indus., 278 F.Supp. 945 (D.Ind.2003)

7. Quoted in part supra § 3.8 n.8.

8. Restatement, Second, Conflict of Laws §§ 142–43 (1971).

9. In a slightly different context see Gantes v. Kason Corp., 145 N.J. 478, 679 A.2d 106 (1996); DeLoach v. Alfred, 192 Ariz. 28, 960 P.2d 628 (1998).

B. RENVOI

§ 3.13 When the characterization of the subject matter and an examination of the choice-of-law rules and of the policies have disclosed the existence of a "true conflict"[1] to which, under forum law, the law of another jurisdiction is to be applied, the question arises: how much of the foreign law? The preceding section addresses one aspect of the problem: the forum applies the foreign substantive law, while issues characterized as "procedural" are governed by the law of the forum. A further question is whether the reference to the foreign law also encompasses the choice-of-law rules of that jurisdiction. Consideration of the foreign choice-of-law might disclose that the foreign jurisdiction—had the action been commenced there—would have referred to the forum (*remission*). Alternatively, the foreign conflicts rule might refer to yet another (third) jurisdiction (*transmission*). Both possibilities are collectively known as the problem of *renvoi*.

American law expressly provides for the consideration of foreign conflicts law (*renvoi*) in only a limited number of specific cases.[2] Early commentators[3] and most of the cases[4] rejected the more general use of renvoi. The reasons offered in the case law include that renvoi is (1) a

§ 3.13

1. See supra § 2.6.

2. See Restatement, Second, Conflict of Laws §§ 223 (validity and effect of a transfer of an interest in land), 245 (validity and effect of a transfer of an interest in a chattel), 260, 263 (succession to interests in movables); U.C.C. §§ 2–402 (rights of creditors against sold goods), 2A–105 (law applicable to leased goods covered by certificate of title), 4–102 (applicability of the Article on bank deposits and collections), 6–102 (bulk transfers) (repeal of Article 6 recommended); 8–106 (applicability of the Article on investment securities), 9–103 (perfection provisions of the Article on secured transactions); Richards v. United States, 369 U.S. 1, 12–13, 82 S.Ct. 585, 592–593, 7 L.Ed.2d 492 (1962): reference in the Federal Tort Claims Act to the law of the "place where the act or omission occurred" includes the whole law (including conflicts law) of that place. The decisions collected in the Reporter's Note to Restatement, Second, Conflict of Laws § 8 (1971) support, but are also limited to, the specific Restatement sections cited above. See generally von Mehren, The Renvoi and Its Relation to Various Approaches to the Choice–of–Law Problem, in: XXth Century Comparative and Conflicts Law–Legal Essays in Honor of Hessel E. Yntema 380 (1961); 1 Rabel, The Conflict of Laws 75 (2d ed. 1958); Falconbridge, Essays on the Conflict of Laws, chs. 6–10 (2d ed. 1954). For an opinion cataloging the different approaches taken by courts in following *Richards*, see Gould Electronics Inc. v. United States, 220 F.3d 169 (3d Cir.2000).

3. E.g., Lorenzen, The Renvoi Theory and the Application of Foreign Law, 10 Colum. L. Rev. 190 (1910).

4. From among the cases see Neto v. Thorner, 718 F.Supp. 1222 (S.D.N.Y.1989); Aurora National Bank v. Anderson, 132 Ill. App.2d 217, 268 N.E.2d 552 (1971); Maroon v. State, Department of Mental Health, 411 N.E.2d 404 (Ind.App.1980); Clark v. Clark, 107 N.H. 351, 222 A.2d 205 (1966); Lewandowski v. National Grange Mutual Insurance Co., 149 N.J.Super. 591, 374 A.2d 489 (Law Div.1977); In re Damato's Estate, 86 N.J.Super. 107, 206 A.2d 171 (App.Div. 1965); Wyatt v. Fulrath, 38 Misc.2d 1012, 239 N.Y.S.2d 486 (Sup. Spec. Term 1963), judgment affirmed 16 N.Y.2d 169, 264 N.Y.S.2d 233, 211 N.E.2d 637 (1965); Conklin v. Horner, 38 Wis.2d 468, 157 N.W.2d 579 (1968). See also Milkovich v. Saari, 295 Minn. 155, 203 N.W.2d 408 (1973). A number of courts refused to employ renvoi but noted that its use would not have resulted in the application of a different substantive law: Hawley v. Beech Aircraft Corp., 625 F.2d 991 (10th Cir.1980); Rutherford v. Gray Line, Inc., 615 F.2d 944 (2d Cir.1980); Patch v. Stanley Works (Stanley Chemical Co. Division), 448 F.2d 483 (2d Cir. 1971). One court approved the renvoi doctrine in a case concerning a conditional sales contract but noted that its use would not result in the application of a different substantive

manipulative device to explain the application of a different law,[5] that (2) the forum's conflicts rules should not be displaced by those of another jurisdiction,[6] and that (3) the "circular process" of renvoi would add to the confusion in choice of law.[7]

None of these objections is persuasive. The first two objections overlook one of the important objectives of conflicts law: to minimize the effect that litigation was commenced in this rather than in another forum and to achieve, to the greatest extent possible, uniformity of decisions.[8] The third objection—the circularity of renvoi—assumes that both jurisdictions' choice-of-law rules refer to each other and that a reference back to the forum would trigger the process anew. The answer is two-fold. Often, there will not be any circularity. Thus, in cases of transmission, it may well happen that A, the forum, refers to B, the latter to C, and C to itself.[9] In this situation the use of renvoi by A would assure that all three courts would reach the same result. Blind adherence by A to its own conflicts rules would produce a different result in A than in B and C. Circularity also does not happen if only A, but not B, employs renvoi. In this case, A refers to B, B refers to A and would not accept a reference back: A law applies.

Nevertheless, a mechanical use of renvoi by all concerned jurisdictions could theoretically produce the problem of circularity. In this case, however, it is suggested that the forum accept the reference to its own law, refer no further, and apply its own law. This is the practice of most jurisdictions that do employ renvoi.[10] This is good policy: the foreign conflicts rule itself discloses a disinterest to have its own substantive law

law: Davis v. P. R. Sales Co., 304 F.2d 831 (2d Cir.1962).

But see Nolan v. Borger, 95 O.L.A. 225, 203 N.E.2d 274 (Ohio Prob. Ct., Montgomery Co. 1963) (adopts the "foreign court theory" in a case involving the construction of an Ohio will devising Missouri realty); the "foreign court theory" is discussed further infra n.10.

5. E.g., Clark v. Clark, 107 N.H. 351, 222 A.2d 205 (1966).

6. See Conklin v. Horner, 38 Wis.2d 468, 157 N.W.2d 579 (1968).

7. In re Damato's Estate, 86 N.J.Super. 107, 206 A.2d 171 (App.Div.1965).

8. "Domestic courts referred abroad should not blind themselves to foreign rules of conflict of laws. They should instead, as a matter of course, look first to the 'whole law' of the other state, and undertake to dispose of the case as the foreign court would dispose of it; and if the foreign court would in its disposition apply some rule of conflict of laws the domestic court should do the same . . . [unless] it is clear that it does not lead to a definite and satisfactory disposition of the particular case." Griswold, Renvoi Revisited, 51 Harv. L. Rev. 1165, 1182 (1938).

9. Illustration: a French citizen dies domiciled in Germany, leaving personal property in the United States. In the case of intestate succession, the court of the situs would ordinarily apply the law of the decedent's domicile at death. Restatement, Second, Conflict of Laws § 260 (1971): Germany; German courts would apply the law of nationality: France; French law is the same. Cf. Harris v. Polskie Linie Lotnicze, 820 F.2d 1000 (9th Cir.1987) (discussed infra § 3.54 n.1); see also Estate of Wright, 637 A.2d 106 (Me. 1994) (Swiss renvoi to New York law considered and accepted in succession case).

10. See, e.g., *Austria:* Federal Statute on Conflict of Laws § 5(2), Bundesgesetzblatt 1978, No. 304; *France:* Cass. Civ. June 24, 1878, D.P. 79.1.56, S. 78.1.429 and Cass. Reg. February 22, 1882, S. 82.1.393 (Forgo case); *Germany:* Introductory Law to the Civil Code (EGBGB) Art. 4(1) (1986), and Kegel & Schurig, Internationales Privatrecht 393–94 (9th ed. 2004); *Japan:* X v. Y, [1994] H.J. (1493) 71 (S.Ct. of Japan), transl. in 18 Japanese Ann. Int'l L. 142 (1995); *Switzerland:* Federal Statute on Private International Law Art. 14 (1987). For the German provision see also Ebenroth & Eyles, Der Renvoi nach der Novellierung

applied, indeed it recognizes the significance of the forum's law for the particular case; the case therefore probably presents a "false conflict." This view was expressly adopted by the Court of Appeals of Maryland.[11] Furthermore, since uniformity in result would not otherwise be achieved in these circumstances, ease in the administration of justice is furthered by the application of forum law rather than by the use of foreign law.

§ 3.14 The Second Restatement in its § 8(2) and (3), now advocates the use of renvoi in two circumstances: "when the objective of the particular choice-of-law rule is that the forum reach the same result on the very facts involved as would the courts of another state ... subject to considerations of practicality and feasibility" and "when the state of

des deutschen Internationalen Privatrechts, 1989 IPRax 1. For comparative treatment see Bauer, Renvoi im internationalen Schuld-und Sachenrecht (1985). European law makes one exception: there is no renvoi in choice of law for contract. Rome Convention on the Law Applicable to Contractual Obligations Art. 15; Germany, EGBGB Art. 35 (1). In addition, the EU Commission's Proposal for a Regulation for the Law Applicable to Non–Contractual Obligations would also exclude renvoi in cases of tort injury without mandate, and unjust enrichment. Art. 20 COM (2003) 0427; *Japan:* X v. Y, [1994] H.J. (1493) 71 (S.Ct.) transl. in 18 Japanese Ann. Int'l L. 142 (1995).

English law developed the "foreign court theory" in Re Annesley, [1926] Ch. 692. The issue concerned the validity of a will, executed according to English requirements as to form, by an English woman who died in France. According to English law her domicile at death was France, but she had not acquired a domicile in France according to French law. Following the English conflicts rule to the "domicile at death," as defined by English law, the court proceeded to decide the case as if it were a French court. It found that a French court would refer to the law of the decedent's nationality (England) and, if the decedent was domiciled in France according to that law, would accept the reference and apply its own law. Thus, French law governed. As a result, some of the legacies abated which would not have been the result under English law. See, similarly, Re Ross, [1930] 1 Ch. 377, and Re Duke of Wellington, [1947] Ch. 506 in which the result differed only because the foreign law would not accept the renvoi. For discussion see Graveson, Conflict of Laws 65 et seq., particularly at 68–72 (7th ed. 1974). It is suggested that the "foreign court theory" unnecessarily complicates the use of renvoi and also defeats one of its objectives, the ease in the administration of justice. In *Annesley,* the application of French law did not further the interests of

the forum, uniformity of result could not be achieved under the circumstances, and ease in the administration of justice was not achieved when the English court, through the use of the "foreign court theory," chose to end the circularity at the point of the reference to French law rather than English law when French law invoked the English law of nationality. The simpler approach would have been to refer to France initially and to accept the reference back to England. In *Ross* and *Duke of Wellington,* the same result would have been achieved by following the simple approach to renvoi suggested above and in the text rather than the "foreign court theory." English law has increasingly declined to engage in renvoi. For tort cases, s. 9(5) of the Private International Law (Miscellaneous Provisions Act 1995) now excludes. See also Briggs, In Praise and Defense of *Renvoi,* 47 Int'l & Comp. L.Q. 877 (1998).

The "foreign court theory" was also used in Nolan v. Borger, 95 O.L.A. 225, 203 N.E.2d 274 (Ohio Prob.Ct., Montgomery Co. 1963) involving the testator's intent to make a class gift of realty located in Missouri: "the Court of the forum looks to the whole law of Missouri and in order to avoid the circular problem [of renvoi], it decides the case as if it were sitting in the 'choice of law' state, namely Missouri [and, under that law, Ohio law became applicable]." 203 N.E.2d at 278 (1963), emphasis added. Sitting as a Missouri court, of course, does not avoid the problem of circularity: it merely shifts the decision of when to cut off the process of circular references or of whether the court (here: the foreign jurisdiction) will accept the renvoi. The Ohio court could have achieved the same result through the use of the direct renvoi. Cf. Restatement, Second, Conflict of Laws § 240 (1971).

11. American Motorists Ins. Co. v. ARTRA Group, Inc., 338 Md. 560, 659 A.2d 1295 (1995). See also infra § 3.14 n.3.

the forum has no substantial relationship to the particular issue or the parties" and all other interested states would apply the same law. Both provisions emphasize the objective of uniformity of decision. The difference between the provisions perhaps lies in the supposition that, if the forum does have a substantial relationship to the issue or the parties, its interests or policies may outweigh the objective of uniformity of decision.[1] In fact, whenever the more modern decisions consider foreign conflicts law at all, it is usually for the purpose of identifying the interests of the forum in their relation to the interests of other concerned jurisdictions.[2] The use of renvoi principles as part of modern choice-of-law analysis thus in effect achieves uniformity of decision by identifying "false conflicts."[3]

§ 3.14

1. See Pfau v. Trent Aluminum Co., 55 N.J. 511, 526, 263 A.2d 129, 137 (1970) ("We see no reason for applying Connecticut's choice-of-law rule. To do so would frustrate the very goals of governmental-interest analysis. Connecticut's choice-of-law rule does not identify that state's interest in the matter. *Lex loci delicti* was born in an effort to achieve simplicity and uniformity, and does not relate to a state's interest in having its law applied to given issues in a tort case."). But see *infra* n.3.

2. Chance v. E. I. Du Pont De Nemours & Co., Inc., 371 F.Supp. 439, 446 (E.D.N.Y. 1974). See also Neal v. Butler Aviation International, Inc., 460 F.Supp. 98, 103 (E.D.N.Y.1978): in action by Texas minor children for the wrongful death of their fathers in Vietnam, New York which "has no governmental interest in the parties or their controversy would apply the Texas statutory choice-of-law [referring to the law of Vietnam]" to determine whether the children have an independent cause of action, with the statute of limitations tolled during their infancy.

3. In American Motorists Ins. Co. v. ARTRA Group, Inc., 338 Md. 560, 659 A.2d 1295 (1995), the court was not ready for "a total jettisoning of *lex loci contractus*," but reached a result consistent with the Second Restatement's most-significant-relationship approach by adopting, citing to the second edition of this treatise, a "limited *renvoi* exception ... when 1) Maryland has the most significant relationship, or, at least, a substantial relationship with respect to the contract issue presented; and 2) the state where the contract was entered into would not apply its own substantive law, but instead would apply Maryland substantive law ...". 338 Md. at 579, 659 A.2d at 1304.

See also Kramer, Return of the Renvoi, 66 N.Y.U. L. Rev. 979 (1991). For further comment on *ARTRA*, see S. Symeonides, W. Perdue & A. v. Mehren, Conflict of Laws: American Comparative, International–Cases and Materials 78–82 (2d ed. 2003). *ARTRA* was followed in Commercial Union Ins. Co. v. Porter Hayden Co., 116 Md.App. 605, 698 A.2d 1167 (1997).

See also United States v. Neal, 443 F.Supp. 1307, 1315 (D.Neb.1978) ("Nebraska's interest in having its guest statute apply outside its geographical boundaries must not be very strong in light of the Nebraska Supreme Court's continued adherence to the rule of *lex loci delicti*"); Tramontana v. S. A. Empresa De Viacao Aerea Rio Grandense, 350 F.2d 468, 475 (D.C.Cir.1965), cert. denied 383 U.S. 943, 86 S.Ct. 1195, 16 L.Ed.2d 206 (1966) (court applied Brazilian limits on wrongful death recovery for death of Maryland resident killed in a mid-air collision over Brazil, stating "if a Maryland court would not disregard Brazilian law for the benefit of one of its residents in a suit brought there, why should a court sitting in the District of Columbia do so at the expense of substantial and legitimate interests of Brazil?").

A chance to use renvoi either directly or as a means to identify a false conflict was missed in Haumschild v. Continental Casualty Co., 7 Wis.2d 130, 95 N.W.2d 814 (1959). In a suit arising out of a California accident, Wisconsin characterized the interspousal immunity issue as one of "family law" rather than "tort" and applied forum law as the law of the parties' domicile. Rather than substituting one label for another, the same result could have been achieved by following and accepting California's choice-of-law rule which referred to the law of domicile. For further analysis see

Besides the use of renvoi as part of interest analysis, few American courts have adopted the more extensive use of the doctrine as suggested by § 8 of the Second Restatement.[4] However, the specific direction for its use in a number of instances[5] and its more general use as part of interest analysis achieves the Restatement's objective in indirect ways. Nevertheless, even greater openness on the part of the courts to the content of the foreign jurisdiction's choice-of-law rules would be desirable, especially in cases of transmission. Uniformity of decision should remain a principal goal of conflicts law; it is not always served by an interest analysis in which local interests tend to dominate. Renvoi does aid in the identification of the extent of conflict and the presence of "false conflicts." Its role in achieving uniformity of decision in the case of true conflicts, however, remains largely unexplored, perhaps as a result of insufficient agreement on the relative importance of that goal.[6]

R. Weintraub, Commentary on the Conflict of Laws 88 et seq. (4th ed. 2001).

4. See Matter of Estate of Wright, 637 A.2d 106 (Me.1994) (testator died domiciled in Switzerland; Swiss law permits the choice of law of nationality; testator had chosen Maine law; Maine law applied).

There is another application of renvoi, as yet unexplored in American law: the "hidden renvoi" which has received attention principally in the German conflicts literature. For instance, one of the German choice-of-law rules for divorce is the law of the parties' nationality. In the case of a divorce action by two Americans, the search will not disclose an "American" divorce law. Instead, the applicable (substantive) divorce law is "hidden" in American jurisdictional rules: it is the lex fori of the court with divorce jurisdiction—the parties common (or separate) American domicile. See Hay, Die Anwendung US-amerikanischer jurisdiction-Regeln als Verweisungsnormen bei Scheidung von in Deutschland wohnhaften Amerikanern, 1988 IPRax 265; Hay, The American "Covenant Marriage" in the Conflict of Laws, 64 La.L. Rev. 43, (2004) (in the context of recognition and dissolution of covenant marriages in Europe). See also Kegel & Schurig, Internationales Privatrecht 411–14 (9th ed. 2004) with additional examples; Hanisch, Die "versteckte" Rückverweisung im internationalen Familienrecht, 1966 Neue Juristische Wochenschrift 2085; Kegel, Die Grenze von Qualifikation und Renvoi im internationalen Verjährungsrecht (1962).

If one objective is the ease of application of law, such a use of renvoi may also permit the forum to apply local law without, thereby, prejudicing the interests of the foreign jurisdiction. An American example is Bing v. Halstead, 495 F.Supp. 517 (S.D.N.Y.1980) which involved the sending of a letter by the defendant to the plaintiff, a New York domiciliary, at the latter's New York address; the letter was received in Costa Rica, the plaintiff's long-term residence, and there caused her mental anguish. Arizona and New York law provided for a cause of action; Costa Rica did not. The New York court could have allowed a recovery in one of three ways: apply Arizona law as the law of the place of conduct; apply New York law since there was no conflict as between Arizona and New York (in both instances disregarding Costa Rica as having no or little interest); or apply Arizona law on the ground that Costa Rican law provides that jurisdiction for tort claims lies at the place where the wrongful conduct or act took place. Ley Organica del Poder Judicial art. 184 (1977). The last suggestion derives the applicable law from the foreign law's jurisdictional provision (hidden renvoi). Instead, the New York court found that Arizona and New York had no interest, applied Costa Rican substantive law (as the law of the place of injury), and denied recovery.

5. Supra § 3.13 n.2.

6. The language of § 8(2) of Restatement, Second, Conflict of Laws (1971) itself is ambivalent on this point: "*when* the objective of the particular choice-of-law rule is that the forum reach the same result . . . ," emphasis added. See also Hay, supra § 2.6 n.21; Kramer, supra n.3; Briggs, In Defense and Praise of *Renvoi*, 47 Int'l & Comp. L.Q. 877 (1998).

C. PUBLIC POLICY[1]

§ 3.15   Under the traditional approach to choice of law, the forum's territorially-oriented rule might refer to a law, the application of which would be offensive to the public policy of the forum. In these circumstances, the forum might then refuse to entertain the foreign cause of action and, in effect, deny the plaintiff access to its courts. Judge Cardozo counseled against a parochial use of the public policy exception in his classic statement in *Loucks v. Standard Oil Co.*: courts should not close their doors, unless application of the foreign law "would violate some fundamental principle of justice, some prevalent conception of good morals, some deep-rooted tradition of the common weal."[2]

The public policy exception to the enforcement of rights based on foreign law is to be construed narrowly: fundamental policies of the forum must be offended; mere differences between the law of the forum and of the foreign jurisdiction are not enough,[3] nor may the denial of access to the local courts discriminate against a foreign cause of action which would be entertained if it had arisen locally.[4] In circumstances when the test is satisfied, for instance with respect to gambling claims,[5] the question arises whether the forum should dismiss or, in application

---

§ 3.15

1. For a brief discussion of the origin and history of the public-policy exception see H. Battifol & P. Lagarde, 1 Droit International Privé nos. 354–55 (7th ed. 1981). See generally, Lorenzen, Territoriality, Public Policy and the Conflict of Laws, 33 Yale L.J. 736 (1924); Paulsen & Sovern, Public Policy in the Conflict of Laws, 56 Colum. L. Rev. 969 (1956); Simson, The Public Policy Doctrine in Choice of Law: A Reconsideration of Older Themes, 1974 Wash.U.L.Q. 391. See also Comment, Choice of Law: A Fond Farewell to Comity and Public Policy, 74 Calif. L. Rev. 1447 (1986). See also Hay, On Comity, Reciprocity, and Public Policy in U.S. and German Judgment Recognition Practice, in: Basedow et al. (eds.), Liber Americorum Kurt Siehr 237 (2000).

Specific aspects of public policy are discussed in their substantive contexts below. See, e.g., infra § 18.5 with respect to usury and ch. 24 with respect to judgment recognition.

2. 224 N.Y. 99, 111, 120 N.E. 198, 202 (1918). An example of a restrictive use of the public policy exception in New York is Mertz v. Mertz, 271 N.Y. 466, 3 N.E.2d 597 (1936) which refused to entertain an interspousal tort claim arising out of a Connecticut automobile accident because of New York's then existing immunity rule. The decision was subsequently interpreted to have been "in reality . . . a *choice-of-law* decision . . . ," based on the predominance of New York's "contacts", with the parties in Intercontinental Hotels Corp. v. Golden, 15 N.Y.2d 9, 13, 254 N.Y.S.2d 527, 529, 203 N.E.2d 210, 212 (1964) (enforcing a Puerto

Rican gambling debt, returned to Cardozo's test in *Loucks,* perhaps even narrowed the exception: the foreign claim, to be denied enforcement locally, must be "inherently vicious, wicked, or immoral, and shocking to the prevailing moral sense.") See also Annot., 71 A.L.R.3d 178 (1976).

3. See Restatement, Second, Conflict of Laws § 90, cmnt. (c) (1971); Beach, Uniform Interstate Enforcement of Vested Rights, 27 Yale L.J. 656, 662 (1918). For the public policy defense in the context of the recognition of judgments, see infra §§ 24.20–.21, 24.44.

The scope of the exception is similarly limited in other conflicts systems: For *English* law, see R. Graveson, Conflict of Laws 165 et seq. (7th ed. 1974); *Austrian* Federal Statute on Conflict of Laws § 6, Bundesgesetzblatt 1978, No. 304; *German* Introductory Law to the Civil Code (EGBGB) Art. 6 and Kegel & Schurig, Internationales Privatrecht 525 et seq. (9th ed. 2004) with cases; *Swiss* Federal Statute on Conflict of Laws Private International Law Art. 17. In *France,* public policy appears to play a somewhat larger role: see Battifol & Lagarde, supra n. 1, at 358 et seq.

4. Hughes v. Fetter, 341 U.S. 609, 71 S.Ct. 980, 95 L.Ed. 1212 (1951).

5. Ciampittiello v. Campitello, 134 Conn. 51, 54 A.2d 669 (1947); Dorado Beach Hotel Corp. v. Jernigan, 202 So.2d 830 (Fla. App.1967), appeal dismissed 209 So.2d 669 (1968). But cf. Intercontinental Hotels Corp. v. Golden, 15 N.Y.2d 9, 254 N.Y.S.2d 527, 203 N.E.2d 210 (1964). Resorts Intern., Inc. v. Zonis, 577 F.Supp. 876 (N.D.Ill.1984)

of its own law, rule on the merits. Judge Cardozo, in *Loucks,* had assumed that the forum's choice would result in the application of the foreign law (Massachusetts' limitation on wrongful death recoveries, measured by the defendant's culpability) or in dismissal, but not the application of local law. The Second Restatement draws a fine distinction between refusal to entertain an action and the application, for public policy reasons, of forum law. As to the former, it states the narrow rule of *Loucks* and provides, on the authority of *Home Insurance Co. v. Dick,*[6] that the rule "does not justify striking down a defense good under the otherwise applicable law.... Such action involves more than a mere denial of access to the court. Rather, it is a preliminary step to the rendition of a judgment on the merits [which would be] a violation of due process if the State has no reasonable relationship to the transaction and the parties."[7] This, of course, is precisely what happened in *Pearson v. Northeast Airlines, Inc.*[8] in which the court applied the foreign law to the question of liability but refused application of the foreign damage limitation.

§ 3.16   *Pearson* and the language quoted from the Second Restatement, point toward the role of public policy in the context of modern conflicts theory. The forum with no relationship to the issues or the parties will either apply the foreign substantive law chosen by application of its conflicts rule or, when the foreign law is offensive to local public policy in the sense discussed, will dismiss the action.[1] In the interstate context, it should be rare that the law of one state is so offensive to another as to merit non-application under the public policy reservation.[2] On the other hand, in cases in which the forum does have a relationship to the issues or to the parties,[3] the forum may apply local

(enforcing New Jersey gambling claims would violate Illinois public policy; action dismissed).

6.   281 U.S. 397, 50 S.Ct. 338, 74 L.Ed. 926 (1930) (discussed infra § 3.21).

7.   Restatement, Second, Conflict of Laws § 90, comment (a) (1971). But see *Austrian* Federal Statute on Conflict of Laws § 6, Bundesgesetzblatt 1978, No. 304 ("A provision of the foreign law is not to be applied when its application would lead to a result which is incompatible with the basic values of the Austrian legal system. In its stead, if necessary, the comparable provision of Austrian law is to be applied") (Authors' translation). Similarly, see for *France:* Battifol & Lagarde, supra n.1, at 364.

8.   309 F.2d 553 (2d Cir.1962), cert. denied 372 U.S. 912, 83 S.Ct. 726, 9 L.Ed.2d 720 (1963) (construing Kilberg v. Northeast Airlines, Inc., 9 N.Y.2d 34, 211 N.Y.S.2d 133, 172 N.E.2d 526 (1961) to have refused the application of the Massachusetts wrongful death limitation on public policy and

procedural characterization grounds and considering the result to be constitutional). In Davenport v. Webb, 11 N.Y.2d 392, 230 N.Y.S.2d 17, 183 N.E.2d 902 (1962), the court retracted the "procedural" basis of its decision in *Kilberg*. That decision, in wrote, "express[ed] this State's strong public policy with respect to limitations in wrongful death actions." 183 N.E.2d at 904.

§ 3.16

1.   If the forum is as unrelated to the issues or the parties, as supposed in the text, dismissal will ordinarily be the consequence of a determination of forum non conveniens. For discussion of this (jurisdictional) doctrine, see infra §§ 11.9–11.13.

2.   See generally L. McDougal, R. Felix & R. Whitten, American Conflicts Law 331 (5th ed. 2001).

3.   For the question of how substantial the relationship has to be, see Allstate Insurance Co. v. Hague, 449 U.S. 302, 101 S.Ct. 633, 66 L.Ed.2d 521 (1981); Phillips Petroleum Co. v. Shutts, 472 U.S. 797, 105 S.Ct. 2965, 86 L.Ed.2d 628 (1985), and the cases discussion infra § 3.23.

law and, in so doing, may base its choice on considerations of local public policy.

A state will rarely have no relationship to the issues or to the parties. In the context of modern conflicts law, public policy will therefore rarely function as a defense against the use of an unacceptable rule of foreign law. Instead, considerations of public policy enter earlier in the analysis: as part of the choice-of-law process itself. This also appears clearly from two of the "choice-of-law principles" suggested by the Restatement, Second, in its § 6: "... (b) the relevant policies of the forum, (c) the relevant policies of other interested states and the relative interests of those states in the determination of the particular issue ..." Moreover, the Restatement's emphasis on an issue-by-issue approach in choice-of-law (*dépeçage*)[4] supports results such as that reached by the court in *Pearson*.[5]

D. PUBLIC POLICY—PENAL AND GOVERNMENTAL CLAIMS

§ 3.17   "The courts of no country execute the penal laws of another ..."[1] Although originally stated in the context of criminal law, the doctrine is much wider: it extends to foreign criminal law, punitive provisions of foreign private law,[2] and foreign governmental claims, for instance for taxes.[3] The doctrine derives from the principle of territorial

4. On dépeçage, see Weintraub, Commentary on the Conflict of Laws 94 et seq. (4th ed. 2001) and supra § 2.15 n.7.

5. Supra § 3.15 n.8.
Considerations of public policy will be part of the choice-of-law process under all of the modern approaches. They will be particularly evident when a court makes its determination on the basis of the better law approach, discussed supra at § 2.11. Thus, in reviewing Kell v. Henderson, 47 Misc.2d 992, 263 N.Y.S.2d 647 (1965), affirmed 26 A.D.2d 595, 270 N.Y.S.2d 552 (1966) and Professor Leflar's comments on that decision (54 Cal. L. Rev. 1584 (1966)), the Minnesota Supreme Court stated in Milkovich v. Saari, 295 Minn. 155, 203 N.W.2d 408 (1973): "[New York is concerned to] have these cases determined according to rules consistent with New York concepts of justice, or at least not inconsistent with them. That will be as true for nondomiciliary litigants as for domiciliaries. This interest will not manifest itself clearly if the out-of-state rule does not run contrary to some strong socio-legal policy of the forum, but it will become a major consideration if there is such a strong opposing local policy.... [T]his consideration leads to preference for what is regarded as the better rule of law, ... New York has such a preference, and ... it is a vigorous one.... [T]he combina-

tion of the last two items, governmental interest and better rule of law, called for the application of New York law." 203 N.W.2d at 414. For an egregious example of applying forum law to an unrelated claim (rather than dismissing the action), see Lilienthal v. Kaufman, 239 Or. 1, 395 P.2d 543 (1964) (discussed infra § 3.29 nn.3–5).

§ 3.17

1. The Antelope, 23 U.S. (10 Wheat.) 66, 123, 6 L.Ed. 268 (1825) (slave trade).

2. See Blaine v. Curtis, 59 Vt. 120, 7 A. 708 (1887) (triple interest declared to be penal); Adams v. Fitchburg Railroad Co., 67 Vt. 76, 30 A. 687 (1894) (wrongful death recovery according to degree of culpability); Raisor v. Chicago & Alton Railroad Co., 215 Ill. 47, 74 N.E. 69 (1904) (same); Bettys v. Milwaukee & St. Paul Railway Co., 37 Wis. 323 (1875) (double damages for injuries to livestock); Langdon v. New York, Lake Erie & Western Railroad Co., 58 Hun. 122, 11 N.Y.S. 514 (1st Dept.1890) (treble damages for rate discrimination). See Kutner, Judicial Identification of "Penal Laws" in the Conflict of Laws, 31 Okla. L. Rev. 590 (1978).

3. See, e.g., The Attorney General of Canada v. R.J. Reynolds Tobacco Holdings, Inc., 268 F.3d 103 (2nd Cir. 2001), cert.

sovereignty of public international law: "No principle of general law is more universally acknowledged, than the perfect equality of nations. . . . It results from this equality, that no one can rightfully impose a rule on another."[4] The rule, as applied by the forum to deny recovery on a foreign penal or governmental claim, is thus also an expression of the public policy of the forum.[5] And just as the traditional general public policy exception came to be narrowly defined, so did the objection to the enforcement of foreign penal and governmental claims.

In an early decision, the United States Supreme Court adopted a narrow definition of a "penal claim." *Huntington v. Attrill*[6] concerned the enforcement of a New York determination, under a New York statute, making corporate directors liable for all debts of the company upon failure to file a required report. The Court said: "The question whether a statute of one State, which in some aspects may be called penal, is a penal law in the international [i.e., conflicts] sense so that it cannot be enforced in the courts of another State, depends upon the question whether its purpose is to punish an offense against the public justice of the State, or to afford a private remedy to a person injured by the wrongful act."[7] The language quoted is said to be dictum because the Court was dealing with the recognition of a foreign judgment under the Full Faith and Credit Clause and not with an action on a claim.[8] In a later case in which the Court required recognition of a judgment enforcing a tax claim,[9] the Court stated "a cause of action on a judgment is different from that upon which the judgment was entered."[10] This

denied 537 U.S. 1000, 123 S.Ct. 513, 154 L.Ed.2d 394 (2002)(refusing to adjudicate a RICO action where underlying theory was based on last tax revenues to Canada); Philadelphia v. Cohen, 15 A.D.2d 464, 222 N.Y.S.2d 226 (1961), affirmed 11 N.Y.2d 401, 230 N.Y.S.2d 188, 184 N.E.2d 167 (1962), cert. denied 371 U.S. 934, 83 S.Ct. 306, 9 L.Ed.2d 270 (1962). See generally Leflar, Out–of–State Collection of State and Local Taxes, 20 Vand. L. Rev. 443 (1976).

4. The Antelope, 23 U.S. (10 Wheat.) 66, 122, 6 L.Ed. 268 (1825).

5. Cf. The Attorney General of Canada v. R.J. Reynolds Tobacco Holdings, Inc., 268 F.3d 103 (2d Cir. 2001), cert denied 537 U.S. 1000 123 S.Ct. 513, 154 L.Ed.2d 394 (2002), which held that the common-law revenue rule barred a RICO action by the Canadian government against various tobacco companies for an alleged conspiracy to smuggle cigarettes into Canada and thereby avoid paying Canadian taxes. The court held that absent a clear statement to the contrary, it would not construe RICO to override the revenue rule, and since the claim was for lost tax revenue, the rule was implicated. A lengthy dissent argued that the revenue rule is not implicated by Cana-

da bringing a RICO action because the revenue rule is limited in its operation to the enforcement of tax judgments or claims for taxes as such, not claims under the forum court's law in which taxes are an element of the damages. See also Terenzio v. Nelson, 107 N.J.Super. 223, 258 A.2d 20 (App.Div. 1969) and also infra n.7.

6. 146 U.S. 657, 13 S.Ct. 224, 36 L.Ed. 1123 (1892).

7. 146 U.S at 673–74, 13 S.Ct. at 230. The English Privy Council reached the same result in a case between the same parties and on the same facts: Huntington v. Attrill, [1893] A.C. 150. New York subsequently approved of the test in *Huntington* in Loucks v. Standard Oil Co., 224 N.Y. 99, 120 N.E. 198 (1918), in which Judge Cardozo articulated the classic test for the public policy exception, supra § 3.15 n.2.

8. See Restatement, Second, Conflict of Laws § 120, comment (d) (1971).

9. Milwaukee County v. M.E. White Co., 296 U.S. 268, 279, 56 S.Ct. 229, 235, 80 L.Ed. 220 (1935).

10. But cf. Wisconsin v. Pelican Insurance Co., 127 U.S. 265, 292, 8 S.Ct. 1370, 1377, 32 L.Ed. 239 (1888).

language, together with the *Erie/Klaxon* doctrine[11]—that there is no general federal common law or conflicts law—does require a differentiation among (1) foreign judgments based upon a penal or governmental claim, (2) foreign statutes establishing such claims, and (3) foreign penal or governmental claims that derive more directly from the common law, such as for exemplary or punitive damages. *Huntington* was recently cited with approval by the Supreme Court as authority for refusing to allow a state court to punish a defendant with punitive damages for out-of-state conduct.[12]

§ 3.18 A *judgment* of a sister state, based upon a penal claim within the U.S. Supreme Court's definition in *Huntington* or based upon a tax claim, is entitled to recognition under the Full Faith and Credit Clause.[1] The enforcement of a foreign penal *claim,* not reduced to a money judgment or entitled to recognition as part of a sister-state's "public act," remains within the province of the states. With respect to "penal" claims, the states generally follow the U.S. Supreme Court's definition in *Huntington,*[2] though they define penal narrowly "to confine it more strictly to the criminal law.[3] With respect to tax claims, most of the states now maintain reciprocal statutes for the collection of taxes.[4]

The situation is different in relation to foreign countries. Even though there are no treaties in force between the United States and other nations for the recognition of civil judgments,[5] foreign-country

11. Erie Railroad Co. v. Tompkins, 304 U.S. 64, 58 S.Ct. 817, 82 L.Ed. 1188 (1938); Klaxon Co. v. Stentor Electric Manufacturing Co., 313 U.S. 487, 61 S.Ct. 1020, 85 L.Ed. 1477 (1941). These cases are discussed in detail infra § 3.36.

12. State Farm Mutual Auto Ins. Co. v. Campbell, 538 U.S. 408, 123 S.Ct. 1513, 155 L.Ed.2d 585 (2003).

§ 3.18

1. See supra § 3.17 nn.7–10; Holbein v. Rigot, 245 So.2d 57 (Fla.1971), mandate conformed 247 So.2d 475 (Fla.App.1971) (recognition of judgment for punitive damages); Magnolia Petroleum Co. v. Hunt, 320 U.S. 430, 438, 64 S.Ct. 208, 213, 88 L.Ed. 149 (1943) ("We are aware of no exception [to the requirement of Full Faith and Credit] in the case of a money judgment in a civil suit" (dictum)). For discussion of the Full Faith and Credit Clause and modern case law, see infra Chapter 24.

2. Supra § 3.17 n.7.

3. See L. McDougal, R. Felix & R. Whitten, American Conflicts Law 163 (5th ed. 2001); Restatement, Second, Conflict of Laws § 89, cmnt. (a) (1971).

4. A large majority of states have enacted such statutes: CCH, State Tax Guide ¶ 7 (1997). Decisional law in New Mexico, New

Jersey, Nevada, and Wyoming also allows the collection of other states' taxes.

5. The only such treaty that had been proposed—the Convention for the Reciprocal Recognition and Enforcement of Judgments in Civil Matters between the United States and the United Kingdom—ultimately failed to be adopted because of British concerns about relatively high damage awards in the United States, especially in products liability cases. Even this convention excluded judgments for taxes and "to the extent that they are for punitive or multiple damages." See Art. 2(a) and (b) of the London (July 1976) draft, reproduced in Hay & Walker, The Proposed Recognition–of–Judgments Convention Between the United States and the United Kingdom, 11 Tex. Int'l L.J. 421, 452 (1976). For comment see id. at 424 n.21, 425–26. In 1992, the United States proposed that the Hague Conference on Private International Law consider drafting a worldwide convention on jurisdiction and the recognition of judgments. It also failed. See infra § 24.7.

The common provision in United States treaties of friendship, commerce and navigation that "nationals and companies of either Party shall be accorded national treatment with respect to access to courts of justice and to administrative tribunals and agencies within the territories of the

judgments are now ordinarily recognized and enforced on the same basis as sister-state judgments.[6] However, this recognition has not been extended to judgments for taxes, fines, or other penalties, although there may be no genuine basis for distinguishing some of these from other state judgments.[7] It follows that *claims,* based on foreign-country law and not reduced to judgment, similarly may not be enforced.[8] Bilateral tax treaties deal with the avoidance of double taxation or the exchange of information, but not with the enforcement of claims.[9]

E. AVAILABILITY OF LOCAL PROCEDURE AND REMEDY

§ **3.19** "A State will not exercise judicial jurisdiction if it cannot provide appropriate relief."[1] As the Restatement's Comment notes, this "rule ... is closely allied with the rules on forum non conveniens[2] ... and public policy...."[3] *Slater v. Mexican National Railroad*[4] is the leading authority on the subject. The plaintiffs had sued in Texas for injuries sustained by Slater in Mexico which subsequently resulted in his death. According to Mexican law, damages were to be paid in periodic installments which, similar to alimony and support, were modifiable upon a change in circumstances. There was no similar remedy at common law and it was thought that justice could not be done by giving a different kind of relief as a substitute. "To reduce a liability conditioned as this was to a lump sum would be to leave the whole matter to a mere guess."[5] The result, therefore, was dismissal.

Under modern analysis, cases like *Slater* can often be decided under forum law, either because it has the most significant relationship to the issues or the parties,[6] or because an alternative subject matter character-

other Party ... in pursuit and in defense of their rights" does not extend to the issues discussed in the text. The provision relates primarily to such issues as the posting of bond for security for costs, the right to proceed in *forma pauperis,* and the like. Treaty between the United States and Germany art. VI(1) and Protocol No. 6, 7 U.S.T. 1840; T.I.A.S. 3593; 273 U.N.T.S. 3 (entered into force July 14, 1956); Wilson, Access to Courts Provisions in United States Commercial Treaties, 47 Am. J. Int'l L. 20 (1953).

6. See infra Chapter 24.

7. See Scoles, Interstate and International Distinctions in Conflict of Laws, 54 Calif. L. Rev. 1599, 1605 (1966). To assure recognition of foreign-country judgments, a number of states have adopted the Uniform Foreign Money Judgments Recognition Act: infra § 24.36. The Act specifically excludes judgments for taxes, fines or other penalties: § 1(2).

8. See, e.g., The Attorney General of Canada v. R.J. Reynolds Tobacco Holdings,

Inc., 268 F.3d 103 (2d Cir. 2001), cert. denied 537 U.S. 1000, 123 S.Ct. 513, 154 L.Ed.2d 394 (2002); see supra § 3.17 n. 5.

9. See Kronauer, Information Given for Tax Purposes from Switzerland to Foreign Countries, 30 Tax L. Rev. 47 (1974). See also United States v. Harden, [1963] Can. Sup. Ct. 366, 41 Dom. L.R. 2d 721 (1963) (no enforcement in Canada of U.S. tax claim reduced to judgment).

§ 3.19

1. Restatement, Second, Conflict of Laws § 85 (1971).

2. Infra §§ 11.9–11.13.

3. Restatement, Second, Conflict of Laws § 95, cmnt. (b) (1971).

4. 194 U.S. 120, 24 S.Ct. 581, 48 L.Ed. 900 (1904).

5. 194 U.S. at 128, 24 S.Ct. at 584.

6. In Carter v. Tillery, 257 S.W.2d 465 (Tex.Civ.App.1953), error refused n.r.e., for instance, this could have been the solution

ization permits application of a law other than that of the place of the injury.[7] Even if alternatives of this kind do not exist, the dissimilarity exception and consequent dismissal of the cause of action should be used sparingly, unless there does exist a more convenient and appropriate forum within the United States. Sister-state remedies and procedures under foreign-country law[8] can usually be approximated by an American court;[9] instead of insisting on equivalence of remedies, as the *Slater* court had done, justice appears to be served better with an approximation of remedies than by a dismissal. This now also seems to be the view in Texas where the dissimilarity rule has been abandoned.[10]

III. PROBLEMS OF FEDERALISM: CONSTITUTIONAL LIMITATIONS ON CHOICE OF LAW

A. DUE PROCESS AND FULL FAITH AND CREDIT: FROM INTEREST–BALANCING TO CONTACTS

1. *Introduction*

§ 3.20 As a result of the way in which the U.S. Supreme Court has addressed issues of constitutional limitations to choice of law, due process and full faith and credit principles have often been intermingled. If construed broadly, either clause could address most choice-of-law limitation problems.[1] However, each clause speaks to essentially different considerations: The Due Process Clause addresses issues of the territorial reach of state power and the fairness to individuals in the exercise of

but was not (the court adhered to the dissimilarity rule): the parties, Texas residents, were injured on their return from New Mexico to Texas when they lost course and their private plane crashed in Mexico. *But see* Trailways, Inc. v. Clark, 794 S.W.2d 479, writ denied (Tex. Civ. App. 1990): Texas law applied to the liability of Mexican bus company for accident in Mexico on the basis of interest and most-significant-relationship analysis. See also <u>Hudson</u>, infra n. 7.

7. Hudson v. Continental Bus System, 317 S.W.2d 584 (Tex.Civ.App.1967). Accord: Garza v. Greyhound Lines, Inc., 418 S.W.2d 595 (Tex.Civ.App.1967) (personal injury action against commercial carrier characterized as arising out of the contract of carriage made in Texas).

8. Cf. In re Will of Heller–Baghero, 26 N.Y.2d 337, 310 N.Y.S.2d 313, 258 N.E.2d 717 (1970) (upholding surrogate's exercise of discretion in admitting will of non-domiciliary to original probate).

9. Cf. R. Weintraub, Commentary on the Conflict of Laws 79–81 (4th ed. 2001);

Hay, Unjust Enrichment in the Conflict of Laws: A Comparative View of German Law and the American Restatement 2d, 26 Am. J. Comp. L. 1, 35–40 (1978).

10. Gutierrez v. Collins, 583 S.W.2d 312 (Tex.1979). The "most significant relationship" test is now used exclusively in Texas. See also Total Oilfield Services, Inc. v. Garcia, 711 S.W.2d 237 (Tex.1986); Trailways, Inc. v. Clark, 794 S.W.2d 479 (Tex.App. 1990); see also supra n.6.

§ 3.20

1. Leflar, Constitutional Limits on Free Choice of Law, 28 L. & Contemp. Prob. 706, 711 (1963); Kirgis, The Roles of Due Process and Full Faith and Credit in Choice of Law, 62 Cornell L. Rev. 94, 95 (1976); Martin, Constitutional Limitations on Choice of Law, 61 Cornell L. Rev. 185, 186, 195 (1976); Martin, A Reply to Professor Kirgis, 62 Cornell L. Rev. 151 (1976); Hay, Full Faith and Credit and Federalism in Choice of Law, 34 Mercer L. Rev. 709 (1983); Hay, Judicial Jurisdiction and Choice of Law: Constitutional Limitations, 59 U. Colo. L. Rev. 9 (1988).

that power.[2] Full Faith and Credit, on the other hand, balances conflicting state interests by commanding that the states respect the sovereignty of sister states in a federal context.[3] When the forum applies its law so that it imposes a burden on a party that another law would not, it may deprive the party of life, liberty, or property.[4] By contrast, governmental interests of affected states in multistate transactions result in the desire of the forum to advance the policies of its law if it may do so consistent with Due Process. In these circumstances, if the forum applies its law and if this law differs from the law of the situs of the events or the domicile of the parties, the interests or policies of the other state or states may be frustrated. If the interests of the affected other state clearly outweigh the forum's interest, the question arises whether Full Faith and Credit may require that the forum defer and not apply its law.

In early decisions, the U.S. Supreme Court used Full Faith and Credit to impose on the forum the affirmative duty to apply the law of some other state to a particular case.[5] In so doing, the Court held that the interest of one state, as expressed in its statute, outweighed the interest of the forum state in applying its own law. Where the Court undertakes to weigh competing state interests it introduces an element into choice of law that goes far beyond the limitations of due process. When used in this manner to identify the controlling law, Full Faith and Credit imposes a positive constitutional requirement that the forum apply the law of a particular interested state. The clause in this sense, therefore, is not merely a negative limit preventing the use of forum law, but a positive prescription of law. The Supreme Court in these cases performed the task of balancing the conflicting state interests and chose the interest that would prevail.[6]

In modern times, however, the Supreme Court has abandoned the attempt to strike a balance between conflicting state interests[7] and has used the clause merely as a negative limitation on the application of forum law. When the Court uses Full Faith and Credit in this manner it clearly equates the effects of that clause with the limitations of due process.[8]

The following sections trace the development of the case law under both clauses and show that the one test of constitutional limitations of choice of law is whether the law to be applied has a sufficient relationship with the multi-state transaction in question to permit its application.

2. Kirgis, supra n.1, at 95; Hay, Full Faith and Credit . . . , supra n.1, at 717 et seq.

3. Kirgis, supra n.1 at 110; Hay, Full Faith and Credit..., supra n.1, passim; Martin, Personal Jurisdiction and Choice of Law, 78 Mich. L. Rev. 872, 881 (1980).

4. Leflar, supra n.1, at 711.

5. E.g., Bradford Electric Light Co. v. Clapper, 286 U.S. 145, 52 S.Ct. 571, 76 L.Ed. 1026 (1932) (discussed infra § 3.24 n.2); Leflar, supra n.1, at 711.

6. See infra § 3.24 n.4.

7. Infra § 3.24, at n.11 et seq.

8. Leflar, supra n.1, at 706; see the discussion infra § 3.24 n.10.

2. *The Due Process Cases*

§ **3.21** The leading older case relying on Due Process as a limitation on state choice of law is *Home Insurance Co. v. Dick.*[1] The plaintiff, Dick, brought suit in Texas against a Mexican insurance company and two New York companies that had reinsured the risk.[2] While the insured[3] was living in Mexico, the Mexican company issued him the policy to cover loss to a tug but only while in Mexican waters. The insurers defended the Texas suit on the grounds that it was brought more than one year after the loss and that a policy term, valid in Mexico, barred any action commenced after one year. The Texas court rejected the defense and instead applied Texas law that held invalid any claim limitation shorter than two years. The U.S. Supreme Court reversed, holding that the Texas court's rejection of the contract term, valid in Mexico, violated Due Process.[4] When Texas deprived the insurers of their defense, it imposed a liability that was extinguished where the contract was made, and thus took the defendants' property. The Court held that Texas could not validly affect the insurance in a case in which "nothing in any way relating to the policy sued on, or to the contracts of reinsurance, was done or required to be done in Texas."[5] The state was without power to affect "the rights of parties beyond its borders having no relation to anything done or to be done within them."[6]

The lasting importance of *Dick* is the Court's references to the forum's relationship to the issue.[7] Because of the absence of any signifi-

---

§ 3.21

1. 281 U.S. 397, 50 S.Ct. 338, 74 L.Ed. 926 (1930).

2. Jurisdiction was quasi-in-rem, based on garnishment of the defendant's Texas property. Assertion of jurisdiction in this manner is now precluded by the Court's decision in Rush v. Savchuk, 444 U.S. 320, 100 S.Ct. 571, 62 L.Ed.2d 516 (1980), on remand 290 N.W.2d 633 (1980). However, even if jurisdiction had been based on the defendants' business activity in Texas, application of Texas law to an unrelated claim could still raise constitutional questions. See Martin supra § 3.20, n.3. An example is John Hancock Mutual Life Insurance Co. v. Yates, 299 U.S. 178, 57 S.Ct. 129, 81 L.Ed. 106 (1936) in which Georgia had jurisdiction but was not permitted to apply its law to New York events and transactions. See infra § 3.28 n.4.

3. The policy was issued in Mexico to Bonner who assigned the policy to Dick. Dick's permanent residence was Texas, but he was living in Mexico at the time of the assignment. The policy had named Dick as a possible transferee of benefits. See Weintraub, Commentary on the Conflict of Laws 597–98 (4th ed. 2001). Subsequent histori-

cal research has revealed that Dick was a bona fide Texan, and that his journey to Mexico was quite brief. See Rensberger, Who Was Dick? Constitutional Limitations on State Choice of Law, 1998 Utah L. Rev. 37.

4. The case raised no Full Faith and Credit issues because the Clause applies only to sister states.

5. 281 U.S. at 408, 50 S.Ct. at 341.

6. Id. at 410, 50 S.Ct. at 342.

7. *Dick's* due process aspect relates largely to the state's absence of "power" over the defendant because of lack of a relationship *to the State.* Nevertheless, fairness *to the defendant* has been a major factor in the formulation of criteria for limitations on choice of law in the literature. Professor Martin observed correctly that " . . . differing treatment of contacts in the jurisdiction and choice-of-law cases turns things on their head. In the typical jurisdiction case, overreaching on the part of the forum state results at worst in inconvenience and greater expense for the defendant. In the typical conflicts case . . . if the plaintiff has chosen his forum wisely, the defendant will lose a case he would other-

cant connections between the forum and the cause of action,[8] the Supreme Court concluded that, "Texas was therefore without power to affect the terms of contracts so made."[9] The Due Process Clause's negative proscriptions were applied in *Dick:* the Constitution commands that when a state has no significant contact with the parties or the occurrence it *may not* apply its law to alter the rights or duties of the parties.[10]

In *Hartford Accident & Indemnity Co. v. Delta & Pine Land Co.,*[11] the Supreme Court broadened the scope of the due process limitation. Delta had entered into a contract with the Hartford company in Tennes-

---

wise have won, simply because the forum has asserted its legislative jurisdiction.... [F]rom the defendant's perspective, it seems irrational to say that due process requires minimum contacts ... merely to hale him into the forum's court while allowing more tenuous contacts to upset the very outcome of the case." Martin, Personal Jurisdiction and Choice of Law, 78 Mich. L. Rev. 872, 879–80 (1980).

Another case involving "minimum contacts" for choice-of-law purposes case is John Hancock Mutual Life Insurance Co. v. Yates, 299 U.S. 178, 57 S.Ct. 129, 81 L.Ed. 106 (1936) although the Court based its decision on Full Faith and Credit. *Yates* is discussed in the infra § 3.28.

Both the case law and the literature use "contacts" language to describe the test for valid judicial jurisdiction as well as to define when a state's law may be applied to a given issue. There is much reason to suggest (see Martin, supra this n.) that the test should be stricter for choice-of-law purposes than for jurisdiction. In order to differentiate more clearly, the authors herein use expressions such as "(substantial) (significant) relationship" or "(substantial) (significant) contacts" when the discussion concerns choice of law. At times, especially, in connection with case law analysis, simple or "minimum" contacts language may also be used which, however, must not obscure the fact that the *quality* of contacts required for choice of law and for jurisdiction may or need not be the same.

8. The plaintiff's domicile is not enough, without other contacts, to give a state jurisdiction over an absent defendant. See Home Insurance Co. v. Dick, 281 U.S. 397, 50 S.Ct. 338, 74 L.Ed. 926 (1930); Silberman, *Shaffer:* End of an Era, 53 N.Y.U. L. Rev. 33, 85 (1978).

9. 281 U.S. at 408, 50 S.Ct. at 341.

10. *Dick's* sufficient-relationship test explains the result of New York Life Insurance Co. v. Head, 234 U.S. 149, 34 S.Ct. 879, 58 L.Ed. 1259 (1914). In *Head* the

insured applied for insurance in Missouri with a New York insurer; the policy provided that it should be deemed to have been issued in New York and treated as a New York contract. Later, the insured transferred the policy to his daughter in New Mexico who obtained a loan there against the cash surrender value of the policy. The loan was not repaid. The Supreme Court held that Missouri could not force the company to pay the full policy amount when due rather than apply the reserve to discharge the loan as permitted by New York law. A subsequent case, New York Life Insurance Co. v. Dodge, 246 U.S. 357, 38 S.Ct. 337, 62 L.Ed. 772 (1918), indicates that the Court's stated reason for both cases was a reliance based on the "place of contracting" test. In both *Head* and *Dodge* the technical place of contracting was not Missouri, therefore Missouri could not alter the contracts. *Head* and *Dodge* differ, however, because in *Dodge* Missouri had a continuing contact with the transaction because the insured remained in that state. The Court finally allowed Missouri to apply its law in Mutual Life Insurance Co. of New York v. Liebing, 259 U.S. 209, 42 S.Ct. 467, 66 L.Ed. 900 (1922) where the substantial contacts of Missouri included the place of contracting. The outcome of *Head* and *Liebing* would be the same under a significant relationship test. Only *Dodge* would be decided differently. In *Dodge,* therefore, the Court imposed an unnecessary constitutional limit, thus demonstrating the danger of constitutionalized choice-of-law rules. The forum state in *Dodge,* although not the technical place of contracting, had sufficient contact with the transaction and sufficient interest in the parties to apply its law without violating Due Process or Full Faith and Credit. See also Hoopeston Canning Co. v. Cullen, 318 U.S. 313, 63 S.Ct. 602, 87 L.Ed. 777 (1943) (New York permitted to regulate out-of-state reciprocal insurance companies insuring New York risks even if contracts made out of state).

11. 292 U.S. 143, 54 S.Ct. 634, 78 L.Ed. 1178 (1934).

see to insure losses resulting from employee embezzlement. After an employee, who was working for Delta in Mississippi, had embezzled money, Delta sought to recover from the insurer in that state. Suit was brought after the expiration of the time limit for filing claims as established in the policy. The limitation was invalid in Mississippi but permitted in Tennessee. The U.S. Supreme Court reversed a judgment for the plaintiff on the grounds that imposition of liability by the forum, Mississippi, violated Due Process when such liability was barred by the law of Tennessee. Because of the exclusive force attributed to the place-of-making rule, the Court reasoned that Mississippi was powerless to alter vested rights created by another state, even though Mississippi had an interest in the transaction, and had several contacts with the events.[12] The Court would not adhere to *Delta & Pine* on similar facts today.[13]

§ 3.22   In *Watson v. Employers Liability Assurance Corp., Limited*,[1] and *Clay v. Sun Ins. Office, Limited*,[2] the Court held that a state with a significant relation to the transaction may apply its law. The Court no longer required some particular key factor, such as the place of contracting, but rather looked to the interests of the forum and the significance of its contacts with the transaction. In *Watson*, the Court allowed Louisiana to provide a direct action remedy against an insurance company for an injured party. The state statute did not require a preliminary finding of liability on the part of the insured. The defendants relied on policy terms, valid where the contract was made, that provided for no liability until the insured's liability was first established. The Supreme Court distinguished *Dick* and *Delta & Pine* as cases in which the forum had no contact with the transaction. In *Watson*, by contrast, the injury occurred in Louisiana, the forum and the plaintiff's domicile. The Court considered these contacts "enough to show Louisiana's legitimate interest in safeguarding the rights of persons injured there," so as to permit the application of Louisiana law.[3]

12. The employee had worked in the forum and thus the plaintiff as well as defendant had done business there. Application of Mississippi law would not have been unfair because by expressly insuring a risk there, the defendant could expect Mississippi law to apply. Cf. Allstate Insurance Co. v. Hague, 449 U.S. 302, 308 n. 11, 101 S.Ct. 633, 638 n. 11, 66 L.Ed.2d 521 (1981), rehearing denied 450 U.S. 971, 101 S.Ct. 1494, 67 L.Ed.2d 623 (1981) (discussed infra § 3.23). Because these facts would be considered significant, the due process limitation would not be followed today. See infra § 3.22 nn.1–2.

13. "That case . . . has scant relevance for today. It implied a choice-of-law analysis which, for all intents and purposes, gave an isolated event—the writing of the bond in Tennessee—controlling constitutional significance, even through there might be contacts with another state . . . which would make application of its law neither unfair

nor unexpected." Allstate Ins. Co. v. Hague, 449 U.S. 302, 308 n. 11, 101 S.Ct. 633, 638, 66 L.Ed.2d 521 (1981). This decision is discussed infra § 3.23.

§ 3.22

1.   348 U.S. 66, 75 S.Ct. 166, 99 L.Ed. 74 (1954).

2.   377 U.S. 179, 84 S.Ct. 1197, 12 L.Ed.2d 229 (1964).

3.   348 U.S. at 73, 75 S.Ct. at 170. The *Watson* court relied on several grounds. Its Due Process analysis found both sufficient physical contacts to legitimate the state's exercise of power and no unfairness in that exercise. The defendant's nationwide insurance coverage made it reasonable for it to expect liability in any state. Furthermore, the Court's Full Faith and Credit analysis also permitted the Louisiana action. The Court considered the conflicting state interests but held that the Constitution did not

In *Clay v. Sun Insurance Office, Limited,*[4] the Supreme Court also found sufficient contacts with the forum so that the application of its law did not violate due process. The defendant insurer issued a policy of world wide protection for personal property[5] to the plaintiff in Illinois. Shortly thereafter the insured moved to Florida where the loss was sustained two years later. Suit was filed more than one year after the loss which violated the limitation of action clause of the policy. That limitation was valid in Illinois, but not in Florida. The Supreme Court sustained the Florida forum's application of its own law, allowing the insured to recover, solely on the sufficiency of Florida contacts.[6]

§ 3.23   The U.S. Supreme Court's modern approach to due process limitations on choice of law begins with *Allstate Insurance Co. v. Hague.*[1] In *Hague,* the Court upheld Minnesota's application of forum law (which permitted "stacking" of uninsured motorist insurance benefits) to a claim arising from the accidental death of a Wisconsin resident in Wisconsin. The uninsured operator of the other vehicle was also a Wisconsin resident. Writing for the plurality, Justice Brennan—as he had in his partial dissent in *Shaffer*[2]—identified three "contacts" with

---

automatically compel deference to the other state when, as in this case, Louisiana's interest outweighed the interests of the other involved states.

4. 377 U.S. 179, 84 S.Ct. 1197, 12 L.Ed.2d 229 (1964).

5. Worldwide coverage should lead to a fair application of any law, because the company can reasonably expect losses and suits wherever it insures a risk. See also the quotation supra § 3.21 n.13.

6. By the time *Clay* was decided the Supreme Court had abandoned its attempts to balance competing state interests which had also been prevalent in the Full–Faith–and–Credit cases. See supra § 3.7 n.4. Instead, the Court decided *Clay* purely upon Due Process grounds. Even though the policy had been purchased with a lump sum payment (Sun Insurance Office Limited v. Clay, 265 F.2d 522, 524 (5th Cir.1959), a fact not mentioned by the Supreme Court), Florida's contacts were minimally sufficient for due process purposes.

§ 3.23

1. 449 U.S. 302, 308 n. 11, 101 S.Ct. 633, 638, 66 L.Ed.2d 521 (1981). The discussion of *Hague* is based in part on Hay, Reflections on Conflict of Laws Methodology, 32 Hastings L.J. 1644 (1981).

See also Kozyris, Reflections on *Allstate*—The Lessening of Due Process in Choice of Law, 14 U.C. Davis L. Rev. 889 (1981); Lowenfeld & Silberman, Choice of Law and the Supreme Court: A Dialogue Inspired by Allstate Insurance Co. v. Hague, 14 U.C. Davis L. Rev. 841 (1981).

The discussion that follows accepts the U.S. Supreme Court's several opinions in the case at face value and thus leaves aside the possibility, suggested by Professor Weintraub, that the state laws actually did not differ. As he showed, Minnesota interprets its minimum coverage statute as requiring stacking, while Wisconsin permitted the parties to an insurance contract to stipulate for or against it. The insurance contract in issue was ambiguous and, in keeping with ordinary principles of construction and case law elsewhere, might properly have been construed against the insurer so as not to exclude stacking. Weintraub, Who's Afraid of Constitutional Limitations on Choice of Law?, 10 Hofstra L. Rev. 17, 18 et seq. (1981). In addition to Professor Weintraub's contribution the symposium on Choice–of–Law Theory After Allstate Insurance Co. v. Hague, 10 Hofstra L. Rev. 1 (1981) also contains papers by Cavers, Davies, Leflar, Martin, Reese, Sedler, Silbermann, Twerski, von Mehren and Trautman. For extensive criticism see also Hill, Choice of Law and Jurisdiction in the Supreme Court, 81 Colum. L. Rev. 960 (1981); Hay, Refining Personal Jurisdiction in the United States, 35 Int'l & Comp. L.Q. 32, 57–58 (1985). For an overview see Hay, Judicial Jurisdiction and Choice of Law: Constitutional Limitations, 59 Colo. L. Rev. 9 (1988).

2. Shaffer v. Heitner, 433 U.S. 186, 223, 97 S.Ct. 2569, 2589, 53 L.Ed.2d 683 (1977). For comment see Hay, The Interrelation of Jurisdiction and Choice–of–Law in U.S. Conflicts Law, 28 Int'l & Comp. L.Q. 161, 173 (1979); Hill, supra n.1.

the case which, in the aggregate, satisfied the restated test "that for a State's substantive law to be selected in a constitutionally permissible manner, that State must have a significant contact or significant aggregation of contacts, creating state interests, such that choice of its law is neither arbitrary nor fundamentally unfair."[3] First, the fact that the decedent had worked in Minnesota on a commuting basis for 15 years and was thus a member of the Minnesota work force gave Minnesota an "interest." "While employment status may implicate a state interest less substantial than does resident status, that interest is nevertheless important. The State of employment has police power responsibilities towards the non-resident employee.... [S]uch employees use state services and amenities and may call upon state facilities in appropriate circumstances."[4] He summarized: "Employment status is not a sufficiently less important status than residence ... when combined with [the decedent's] daily commute ... and the other Minnesota contacts ..., to prohibit the choice-of-law result...."[5] It is no doubt true that one type of status is not necessarily less important than another: it depends for what purpose one asks the question. That employment status in Minnesota should give that state "police power responsibilities" and an interest in what happens between two Wisconsin residents in Wisconsin and in the insurance obligations entered into in Wisconsin is a jump in logic that is difficult to follow. It would be stretching it far already to apply this reasoning if the accident had occurred while the decedent was commuting to or from work in Minnesota: even that had not been the case.

The second contact—Allstate's business presence in Minnesota—is said to be important for the same reason that it was in *Clay.* In that case, the Court had said that one reason why Florida could apply its law to an out-of-state insurance contract was that the defendant company, licensed to do business in Florida, "must have ... known that it might be sued there."[6] The result may well have been right because "Florida [for regulatory reasons] had sufficient interest in the case to justify application of its law."[7] However, Florida's interest in *Clay* was a necessary conceptual link. Without it, it does not follow that amenability to suit should also result in the application of local law. A further important distinction of course is that, in *Clay,* the loss was incurred in Florida two years after the insured had moved there. This difference is not noted.

The third contact—plaintiff's move to Minnesota following the accident and appointment there as the estate's personal representative—is equally irrelevant. Surely both the subjective determination that "there is no suggestion that [the plaintiff] moved to Minnesota in anticipation of this litigation or for the purpose of finding a legal climate especially

3. 449 U.S. at 313, 101 S.Ct. at 640.

4. 449 U.S. at 314, 101 S.Ct. at 640–41.

5. 449 U.S. at 317, 101 S.Ct. at 642.

6. 377 U.S. at 182, 84 S.Ct. at 1199.

7. Reese, Limitations on the Extraterritorial Application of Law, 4 Dalhousie L.J. 589, 602 (1978).

hospitable to her claim"[8] and the conclusion that, moreover, Minnesota has an interest in the administration of a local estate and, with it, in a recovery by the personal representative[9] are bootstrap arguments. A post-accident change of domicile has never been enough[10]—because of the *potential* for forum shopping—and administration of a Minnesota estate occurred only because the plaintiff chose to pursue an alleged debtor of the decedent, the insurer, in Minnesota rather than elsewhere.[11]

In sum, the plurality opinion in *Hague* does not present an analytical framework. After posting a requirement of "significant" contacts (presumably for due process purposes), three contacts are addressed of which only the first is genuine and not contrived. Even that contact, the Minnesota-based employment relation of the decedent, unconnected as it

8.   449 U.S. at 319, 101 S.Ct. at 643.

9.   Id.

10.   "[T]he post-accident residence of the plaintiff-beneficiary is constitutionally irrelevant to the choice-of-law question." 449 U.S. at 337, 101 S.Ct. at 653 (Powell, J., dissenting). See also Reich v. Purcell, 67 Cal.2d 551, 63 Cal.Rptr. 31, 432 P.2d 727 (1967) ("Although plaintiffs now reside in California, their residence and domicile at the time of the accident are the relevant residence and domicile"); Perloff v. Symmes Hospital, 487 F.Supp. 426 (D.Mass.1980). See also R. Weintraub, Commentary on the Conflict of Laws 420 et seq. (4th ed. 2001). Miller v. Miller, 22 N.Y.2d 12, 290 N.Y.S.2d 734, 237 N.E.2d 877 (1968) (discussed infra § 17.29) is contrary. While that decision may be open to criticism on choice-of-law grounds, it is constitutionally defensible: the defendant had moved to the plaintiff's state after the accident so that the application of plaintiff's law (forum law) perhaps did not constitute unfair surprise. See also Comment, Legislative Jurisdiction, State Policies and Post–Occurrence Contacts in Allstate Insurance Co. v. Hague, 81 Colum. L. Rev. 1134 (1981); Hancock, The Effect of a Post–Occurrence Change of Domicile Upon a Choice of Law Determining the Validity of Other–Insurance Clauses in an Accident Policy, Studies in Modern Choice of Law 391, 420 (1984).

11.   Hague presents an interesting parallel to Rush v. Savchuk, 444 U.S. 320, 100 S.Ct. 571, 62 L.Ed.2d 516 (1980). If Borst, the uninsured motorist in Hague, had been insured by Allstate (State Farm) by a policy issued in Wisconsin (Indiana) and Hague's personal representative (Savchuk) had sued Borst (Rush) in Minnesota (Minnesota) after the occurrence in Wisconsin (Indiana),

by attaching the obligation of Allstate (State Farm), it seems clear that quasi-in-rem jurisdiction would not have existed in Minnesota because the forum was not significantly related to the litigation, i.e., the occurrence or the parties, and the "location" of the property i.e., the obligation, was not by itself sufficient. Additionally, in *Hague,* Mrs. Hague was appointed in Minnesota as ancillary personal representative of the nonresident decedent. Under Minnesota Statutes, § 524.3–201(a)(2), venue for appointment proceedings for a decedent "not domiciled in this state" is in a "county where property of the decedent was located at the time of his death." Subsection (d) of this same section provides that: "For the purpose of aiding determinations concerning the location of assets which may be relevant in cases involving non-domiciliaries, a debt, other than one evidenced by investment or commercial paper . . . is located where the debtor resides or, if the debtor is a person other than an individual, at the place where it has its principal office." Under the Minnesota statute, the debt due from Allstate to Hague was not, by itself, sufficient to support appointment of a personal representative even though a personal representative would have standing to sue on the debt. This would appear to emphasize Minnesota's interest as being limited to that as forum only. In view of these circumstances, it is difficult to justify either the Minnesota court's identification of the administration of the estate as an "interest" for purposes of governing substantive rights of the parties to the contract (289 N.W.2d 43, 47 (1978)) or the United States Supreme Court's apparent approval of that characterization (449 U.S. at 318, 101 S.Ct. at 643.

is with the occurrence, is too slim a reed on which to hang the choice-of-law decision.[12]

Justice Stevens's concurrence distinguishes between the full–faith–and–credit aspect of the case—infringement of Wisconsin's own state interests ("sovereignty")—and due process to the defendant. The two provisions indeed address different concerns.[13] It is troublesome, however, that he finds due process satisfied in that the expectations of the parties were not frustrated and there was no element of unfair surprise just because the decedent had paid three uninsured motorist premiums, covering his three vehicles, and because "stacking" is the more usual rule of substantive law in the United States. Thus, while the analytic framework is appropriate, the analysis particularizes too much with respect to the individual case and provides no test by which to determine the "significance" of the required contacts. Justice Powell's dissent, while accepting the plurality's basic test ("significance"), in contrast, finds significant contacts lacking: "The plurality's opinion is understandably vague in explaining how trebling the benefits to be paid to the estate of a nonresident employee furthers any substantial state interest relating to employment. Minnesota does not wish its workers to die in automobile accidents, but permitting stacking will not further this interest."[14]

The plurality of four and the single concurrence thus attempt to state a test. The plurality largely ignores its own test and fairly manufactures "contacts," while the single concurrence accepts a most minimal connection for the application of forum law. The 4–1–3 decision[15] is thus less than helpful in addressing our fragmentation.

In summary, the Court permits the application of the law of any state that is significantly related to the issue. The fact that another state has an interest, or that a different choice-of-law rule or theory would

---

12. "[While the decedent worked in Minnesota and the insurer had insured against losses in Minnesota], ... the fact remains that the accident actually took place in Wisconsin, that Minnesota therefore lacked any meaningful contact with the case, and that Wisconsin substantive law must therefore apply where it conflicts with that of Minnesota."

13. Apart from Wisconsin's "sovereignty," there is another aspect: "The Full Faith and Credit Clause is one of several provisions in the Federal Constitution designed to transform the several States from independent sovereignties into a single, unified Nation ... [T]he fact that a choice-of-law decision may be unsound as a matter of conflicts law does not necessarily implicate the federal concerns embodied in the Full Faith and Credit Clause." 449 U.S. at 322–24, 101 S.Ct. at 645–46 (Stevens, J., concurring). It is submitted that the conclusion does not follow from the basic principle. "It seems to me that disagreement as to which

of conflicting or competing state laws applies raises a federal question under the Full Faith and Credit Clause and that our hope for a better general legal system would be well severed by wider application of that clause." Jackson, The Supreme Court in the American System of Government 41 (1955).

14. 449 U.S. at 339, 101 S.Ct. at 654 (Powell, J., dissenting).

15. Justice Stewart did not participate in the decision of the case.

Minnesota had applied its law in accordance with the "better law" approach to choice of law. In Jepson v. General Cas. Co. of Wisconsin, 513 N.W.2d 467, 473 (Minn. 1994), the Minnesota Supreme Court said about that state's anti-stacking provision (since repealed): "From our present day vantage point, neither the law Minnesota had then, nor the law we have now, is clearly better. Sometimes different laws are neither better nor worse in an objective way, just different."

refer to the law of another state or would produce a fairer or better result is not a due process question. Due Process reduces to the single consideration: what constitutes sufficient connection with the transaction, so that application of forum law is permissible?[16]

The *Hague* test was applied in 1985 in *Phillips Petroleum Co. v. Shutts*,[17] a Kansas class action in which 97% of the members of the plaintiff class had no connection with the forum and in which 99% of the gas leases giving rise to their claims for interest on delayed royalty payments were located in states other than Kansas. The Kansas Supreme Court had upheld the application of Kansas law to all claims because "the law of the forum should be applied unless compelling reasons exist for applying a different law"[18] which, it thought, was not the case. Invoking the language in *Hague*,[19] the United States Supreme Court disagreed. It conceded that Kansas had a regulatory interest, given Phillips Petroleum's ownership of some of the leases and conduct of business there. Furthermore, by not opting out, the nonresident members of the plaintiff class could be said to have consented to Kansas jurisdiction. However, the "assumption of jurisdiction [may not be used] as an added weight in the scale when considering the permissible constitutional limits on choice of substantive law."[20] In view of "Kansas' lack of 'interest' in claims unrelated to that State, and the substantive conflict with jurisdictions such as Texas [the location of other leases and residence of some claimants], we conclude that an application of Kansas law to every claim in this case is sufficiently arbitrary and unfair as to exceed constitutional limits."[21] On remand, the Kansas trial court inter-

---

16. Occasionally, due process considerations may be implicated when the forum's choice-of-law rule refers to the law of a state that is "disinterested." See Day & Zimmermann, Inc. v. Challoner, 423 U.S. 3, 96 S.Ct. 167, 46 L.Ed.2d 3 (1975), discussed infra §§ 3.47–3.48.

In McCluney v. Joseph Schlitz Brewing Co., 649 F.2d 578 (8th Cir.1981), affirmed 454 U.S. 1071, 102 S.Ct. 624, 70 L.Ed.2d 607 (1981), the court held that the Missouri service letter statute could not constitutionally be applied to a contract made between Wisconsin residents and to be performed in Wisconsin, even though the employment relationship between the parties had originally been entered into in Missouri. Citing to *Hague,* the court held that the contract in issue was a Wisconsin contract and that the earlier contacts with Missouri were both too tenuous and also unrelated to the contract. The U.S. Supreme Court affirmed without opinion, Justice Stevens dissenting on other grounds.

See also In re Adoption of Baby Boy S, 22 Kan.App.2d 119, 912 P.2d 761, 766–67 (1996), cert. denied 519 U.S. 870, 117 S.Ct. 185, 136 L.Ed.2d 123 (1996). A child conceived in Ohio was born in Kansas when his unmarried mother moved there after terminating her relationship with the father. In a Kansas adoption proceeding, the court applied Kansas law to terminate the father's parental rights. The court stated, with respect to the objection that application of Kansas law would violate due process and permit unwed mothers to forum-shop: "in our mobile society, the place of conception of a child carries little weight. However, requiring an unwed father to make substantial efforts to remain in contact with an unwed mother and participate in the pregnancy and birth of the child, wherever it occurs, is not an unreasonable expectation."

17. 472 U.S. 797, 105 S.Ct. 2965, 86 L.Ed.2d 628 (1985).

18. Shutts v. Phillips Petroleum Co., 235 Kan. 195, 221–22, 679 P.2d 1159, 1181 (1984).

19. Supra n. 3.

20. 472 U.S. at 821, 105 S.Ct. at 2979.

21. Id.

See also Greenstein. Is the Proposed U.C.C. Choice of Law Provision Unconstitutional?, 73 Temple L. Rev. 1159 (2000), suggesting that the new § 1–301 may vio-

preted the laws of the other states in a fashion which produced results similar to those under Kansas law, and the Kansas Supreme Court agreed.[22] It also applied this interpretation in a parallel case, *Wortman v. Sun Oil Co.*,[23] and the U.S. Supreme Court affirmed: "[I]t is not enough that a state court misconstrue the law of another State. Rather, our cases make plain that the misconstruction must contradict law of the other State that is clearly established...."[24] A dissent by Justice O'Connor, joined by the Chief Justice, concluded that the majority's decision "discards important parts of our decision in *Shutts* ... and of the Full Faith and Credit Clause. Faced with the constitutional obligation to apply the substantive law of another State, a court that does not like that law apparently need take only two steps ... to avoid ... it. First, invent a legal theory so novel or strange that the other State has never had an opportunity to reject it; then, on the basis of nothing but unsupported speculation, 'predict' that the other State would adopt that theory if it had a chance."[25]

An interesting use, however, of due process principles as a territorial limit on state authority was employed by the Supreme Court in *State Farm Mutual Automobile Ins. Co. v. Campbell*.[26] *State Farm* involved a very large punitive damage award in a claim for bad faith failure to settle a claim on the part of an insurance company. The plaintiffs were awarded $1 million in compensatory damages and $145 million in punitive damages by the Utah state courts. The Supreme Court struck down the punitive damage award on due process grounds. Undoubtedly, the central holding of the case will prove to be the majority's admonition that few punitive damage awards that are in excess of a "single-digit" ratio to the compensatory damages will survive constitutional attack.[27] But part of the majority's concern as well was that the Utah judgment in effect amounted to an extraterritorial regulation of events having no

late Full Faith and Credit by permitting the parties to choose law having no relationship to the transaction in contravention of the interests of a state having a significant relationship to the transaction. The suggestion does not convince. New § 1–301, by its own terms, provides that parties may not stipulate away, in consumer contracts, from the mandatory rules in force at the consumer's residence or from the law of the contract formation. In all other transactions, mandatory rules of the forum or of an interested third state may be expected to be given effect by way of the traditional public policy (ordre public) exception.

But see Gerling Global Reinsurance Corp. of America v. Low, 296 F.3d 832 (9th Cir. 2002), rev'd on other grounds, 539 U.S. 396, 123 S.Ct. 2374, 156 L.Ed.2d 376 (2003). The U.S. Court of Appeals had upheld California's version of the Holocaust Victim Insurance Relief Act, see supra this n., distinguishing *Gallagher* on the ground that California's law only required informa-

tion to be filed by companies seeking to do business for the first time. The U.S. Supreme Court reversed on the ground that California's required inquiry into foreign governmental practices impermissibly intruded upon the federal (President's) exclusive power to conduct foreign affairs. See *infra* § 3.56.

22. 240 Kan. 764, 732 P.2d 1286 (1987), cert. denied 487 U.S. 1223, 108 S.Ct. 2883, 101 L.Ed.2d 918 (1988).

23. 241 Kan. 226, 755 P.2d 488 (1987), affirmed 486 U.S. 717, 108 S.Ct. 2117, 100 L.Ed.2d 743 (1988).

24. Sun Oil Co. v. Wortman, 486 U.S. 717, 730, 108 S.Ct. 2117, 2126, 100 L.Ed.2d 743 (1988).

25. Id. at 749, 108 S.Ct. at 2136.

26. 538 U.S. 408, 123 S.Ct. 1513, 155 L.Ed.2d 585 (2003).

27. Id. at 425, 123 S.Ct. at 1524.

meaningful connection to that state. The plaintiffs argued vigorously, and the jury apparently agreed, that the insurer should be punished not only for its actions towards the plaintiffs but for having perpetuated a "nationwide" scheme that injured similarly situated policyholders elsewhere.[28] In this regard, the Court also found the judgment to be infirm. "A State cannot punish a defendant for conduct that may be lawful where it occurred,"[29] observed the majority. Citing *Huntington v. Attrill*[30] for the proposition that laws can operate beyond a state's borders only through comity of other states the Court concluded that "as a general rule, a State [does not] have a legitimate concern in imposing punitive damages to punish a defendant for unlawful acts committed outside of the State's jurisdiction."[31] Probably the *State Farm* decision, despite the territoriality and comity language, will not be the harbinger of any wholesale revival of strict due process limitations on choice of law outside of the punitive damage arena. The case does, however, certainly signal the Court's continuing interest in ensuring that punitive damages are limited to their legitimate regulatory purposes.

3.   *The Full Faith and Credit Cases*

§ 3.24   As with Due Process, the Supreme Court at one time used the Full Faith and Credit Clause affirmatively to mandate choice of law in order to prevent the forum from denying a party a defense he would have under some other law. Analysis of the case law shows that this approach has been largely abandoned. However, full faith and credit analysis also applies to another situation. Thus, unconstitutionality may be claimed when the forum denies redress to a party because a claim arising under the law of another state is not recognized by the forum.

The major full faith and credit cases have involved worker compensation statutes. The issues concerned what state law should apply when the state where the employer and employee formed their relationship and the state of injury were not the same. As with Due Process, the early decisions enforced affirmative requirements mandating the choice of law. More recently, however, the Court requires only minimum contacts with the forum as a precondition for the application of its law. Thus, while the Court has often spoken in terms of governmental interests rather than fairness to individuals because of the nature of full faith and credit analysis,[1] the decisions parallel the development in due process analysis.

---

28.   Id. at 421, 123 S.Ct. at 1521.

29.   Id. at 421, 123 S.Ct. at 1522.

30.   146 U.S. 657, 13 S.Ct. 224, 36 L.Ed. 1123 (1892).

31.   538 U.S. at 421, 123 S.Ct. at 1522. The Ninth Circuit had reached the same result in White v. Ford Motor Co., 312 F.3d 998, 1014 (9th Cir.2002), opinion amended on denial of rehearing 335 F.3d 833 (9th Cir.2003): the jury may consider defendant's conduct in other states to arrive at a judgment as to its reprehensibility , but it may not "award enough money to deter conduct (or at least unlawful conduct) in other states." The White Court relied on BMW of North America v. Gore, 517 U.S. 559, 116 S.Ct. 1589, 134 L.Ed.2d 809 (1996), forecasting, 312 F.3d at 1017, that a state may not assess damages to change (deter) conduct in other states.

§ 3.24

1.   See supra § 3.20 nn.2–3.

The leading example for a mandated choice-of-law rule is *Bradford Electric Light Co., Inc. v. Clapper.*[2] The defendant had hired Clapper in Vermont to aid in the maintenance of its electrical power equipment. While on temporary duty in New Hampshire, Clapper was killed. The administratrix sued in New Hampshire, bringing an action in negligence. The Vermont worker compensation statute, however, purported to provide the exclusive remedy for any work-related injury occurring within or without Vermont. The U.S. Supreme Court held that New Hampshire could not entertain the negligence suit in contravention of the Vermont statute. The Court reasoned that statutes are "public acts" and that, therefore, New Hampshire could not deny the extraterritorial application of rights created under the Vermont statute because of the full faith and credit requirement. The Court recognized that a court might refuse to enforce a foreign cause of action if obnoxious to its policy but held that the Constitution prohibited the rejection of a valid defense based on a foreign statute. Additionally, the Court noted that New Hampshire, as the place of injury, had only a casual connection with the incident, whereas Vermont's interests were more involved and Vermont had most of the contacts—the employment contract was made there and both parties had been Vermont residents. Nevertheless, the Court did not stress the interests of the states and made no reference to the underlying policy of Vermont's worker compensation law—to compensate injuries while limiting employer's liability; instead, it concentrated on the need for New Hampshire to recognize the employer-employee relationship created by the Vermont statute.[3]

Three years after *Clapper,* the Court decided *Alaska Packers Association v. Industrial Accident Commission.*[4] In contrast to *Clapper,* which involved a conflict between a strict liability statute and a common law negligence recovery, *Alaska Packers* was concerned with two compensation statutes both of which provided exclusive recovery in lieu of any other remedy. The employer-employee relation was formed in California for work to be performed in Alaska. The employee, who was injured in Alaska, filed a claim with the California Accident Commission on his return to that state. His employer, the Alaska Packers Association, then sued to set aside the award. The Supreme Court held that California was entitled to apply its law despite the agreement of employer and employee that the compensation law of Alaska would apply to them, and despite the purported exclusivity of the Alaska statute. The Court first noted[5]

2. 286 U.S. 145, 52 S.Ct. 571, 76 L.Ed. 1026 (1932).

3. It has also been suggested that *Clapper* should be regarded as a case in which the Court, in the days before *Erie,* simply announced a rule of federal common law: "the Supreme Court . . . did not reverse the decision of the highest court of a state but rather superintended the choice of law process in an inferior federal court. . . ." Thus, "the case is more easily seen as an early indication of the Court's inclination toward

interest analysis." Allo, Book Review, 30 J. Leg. Ed. 612, 618 (1980).

4. 294 U.S. 532, 55 S.Ct. 518, 79 L.Ed. 1044 (1935).

5. The Court also dismissed a Due Process challenge to the California compensation award because a state has power to regulate in-state contracts for work to be performed out-of-state. The forum clearly had sufficient physical connections with both plaintiff and defendant to justify the

that Full Faith and Credit does not *always* require a state to look to the other state's law because the "absurd" result would be that each state's law would be enforceable only in the other state.[6] Rather, the Constitution compels deference to the foreign law only when the governmental interests of the other state outweigh the interests of the forum. The Court relegated to itself the ultimate duty of balancing the interests and of determining which were the weightier. In *Clapper,* New Hampshire had to defer to the more important interests of Vermont, especially because in so doing, no important interest of New Hampshire was infringed. The Court in *Alaska Packers,* however, found that a vital interest of California—the compensation of its domiciliaries under the terms of its statute—would be abridged if the Alaska law applied.

While the Court in *Alaska Packers* purported to balance state interests, it also relied on the "obnoxious" test developed in *Clapper.* The Court had recognized in *Clapper* that the forum could refuse to enforce sister state statutes if so doing would be obnoxious to domestic policy.[7] Thus, in *Alaska Packers* the Court took the California Supreme Court's holding as a declaration that Alaska's different statute was obnoxious to California; Full Faith and Credit was therefore not violated by the application of California law.

In *Pacific Employers Insurance Co. v. Industrial Accident Commission,*[8] the Court again mentioned the obnoxiousness test, as created in *Clapper* and used in *Alaska Packers;*[9] however, the weighing of governmental interests was in the forefront of the analysis. In *Pacific Employers,* the California Accident Commission again gave a recovery despite the conflicting compensation statute of Massachusetts. The injury occurred in California, unlike in *Alaska Packers,* thus the forum state was the state of injury and the sister state the place of the formation of the employment relationship, as in *Clapper.* Unlike in *Clapper,* however, the Supreme Court upheld the application of forum law. While the Court examined the conflicting interests of the states, it simply held that the Full Faith and Credit Clause did not require a state to ignore its policy to enforce another state's statute.[10]

exercise of power. Furthermore, because the employment relation was created in the forum, it was fair for forum law to apply.

6. 294 U.S. at 547, 55 S.Ct. at 523.

7. In this sense, *Clapper* paralleled Hughes v. Fetter decided later. The forum was required to defer to sister state law unless it violated domestic public policy— i.e. unless it was obnoxious. *Hughes* is discussed infra §§ 3.25, 3.40.

8. 306 U.S. 493, 59 S.Ct. 629, 83 L.Ed. 940 (1939).

9. The fact that Nevada's damage limitation would be "obnoxious" to California also justified denial of Full Faith and Credit in Nevada v. Hall, 440 U.S. 410, 99 S.Ct. 1182, 59 L.Ed.2d 416 (1979). See also Note,

Sovereign Immunity in Sister State Courts, 80 Colum. L. Rev. 1493, 1499–1502 (1980).

10. "Weighing" seemed to have disappeared with the Court's decision in Cardillo v. Liberty Mutual Insurance Co., 330 U.S. 469, 476, 67 S.Ct. 801, 805, 91 L.Ed. 1028 (1947) in which the Court said that the propriety of the application of District of Columbia law "depends upon some substantial connection between the District and the particular employee-employer relationship, a connection which is present in this case.... And as so applied the statute fully satisfies any constitutional questions of due process and full faith and credit." The two tests seemed to have merged: R. Weintraub, Commentary on the Conflict of Laws 623 et seq. (4th ed.2001).

The apparent "departure" from *Clapper* in *Pacific Employers* was expressly recognized in *Carroll v. Lanza.*[11] As in *Clapper,* the plaintiff sought a common law negligence recovery in the forum despite the exclusive worker compensation statute of the state where the employee lived and where the employment relationship was formed.[12] The Court held that *Pacific Employers* had recognized that Full Faith and Credit did not require application of a foreign statute that conflicts with the policy of the forum. The Court noted that the forum where the injury occurred had important interests relating to medical care and dependents to serve and to protect; notwithstanding the fact that this plaintiff had no special connection with Arkansas and imposed no burdens on her institutions, the Court held that "cases of this type"[13] could be adjudicated by the law of the forum.

Thus, *Carroll,* in effect if not word, overruled *Clapper.*[14] If the Court had followed the analysis of *Clapper,* Arkansas would have been required to defer to the law and policy of Missouri, unless that law was obnoxious to Arkansas or, at least, its policies were considered to have greater weight. The Court made no inquiry into the underlying policies of the statutes; it considered only the stated exclusivity of the forum statute and dispensed with the need that the latter specifically, or even by inference, considered the sister state's statute to be obnoxious to the policy of the forum. Furthermore, the opinion in *Carroll,* stating that the court was deciding "cases of this type," indicates that anytime that the forum is the place of injury,[15] that fact alone will provide sufficient contact to permit the application of local law despite contrary statutes in other states. *Carroll v. Lanza,* as interpreted, brings full faith and credit analysis into step with Due Process concepts.[16] The Court summarized the test in Richards v. United States:

11. 349 U.S. 408, 75 S.Ct. 804, 99 L.Ed. 1183 (1955).

12. The plaintiff, Carroll, sued Lanza, a general contractor in Arkansas. Carroll and his immediate employer lived in Missouri, but the injury had occurred in Arkansas. Missouri law barred common law recoveries from a general contractor; in Arkansas, the compensation law did not extend to general contractors who were considered third parties and thus liable to negligence suits.

13. Carroll v. Lanza, 349 U.S. 408, 413, 75 S.Ct. 804, 807, 99 L.Ed. 1183 (1955). In a limited sense, the Court returned to the "obnoxiousness" test in Nevada v. Hall, 440 U.S. 410, 99 S.Ct. 1182, 59 L.Ed.2d 416 (1979). However, since the accident had occurred in the California forum, the decision is also compatible with *Carroll.* However, the special circumstance that a State of the Union was a party prompted the Court, in its footnote 24, to consider and to reject the question whether "California's exercise of jurisdiction ... poses ... [a] substantial

threat to our constitutional system of cooperative federalism." This aspect is not present in the typical case between private litigants and the language quoted therefore does not detract from the conclusion reached with respect to *Carroll.* See infra § 3.31 n.3.

14. See Weintraub, supra n.10, at 624–25; but see id. at 629 n.207, 642 n.265.

15. It is important to note, however, that the place of injury in *Carroll* was not fortuitous since Arkansas was the state of Carroll's longterm employment. Nonetheless, Arkansas had little interest in the aftermath of the injury; arguably, Missouri had the stronger interests. For this reason, one commentator suggests that *Carroll* may exceed what should be constitutional limits. Posnak, Choice of Law: A Very–Curried Leflar Approach, 34 Mercer L. Rev. 731 (1983). See also Kramer, Rethinking Choice of Law, 90 Colum. L. Rev. 277 (1990).

16. See supra n.10.

Where more than one State has sufficiently substantial contact with the activity in question, the forum State, by analysis of the interests possessed by the States involved, could constitutionally apply to the decision of the case the law of one or another state having such interest in the multistate activity.[17]

By this analysis, the Supreme Court permits the states significantly related to the parties or the issue to adopt whatever choice of law provisions suit their needs. The only real Constitutional limitation is that the law chosen be the law of a state having some significant "contact" or relation with the transaction.[18]

§ 3.25 As noted initially, Full Faith and Credit issues are also involved when one state refuses to entertain an action based on the law of a sister state. In *Hughes v. Fetter*,[1] the Supreme Court held that Wisconsin could not dismiss a claim based on the Illinois wrongful death statute. All the parties were residents of Wisconsin, but the accident had occurred in Illinois. The Wisconsin Court interpreted its wrongful death statute, that gave relief only for accidents occurring within the state, as barring recovery. The Supreme Court held that Full Faith and Credit required the recognition of the Illinois statute as a "Public Act." The Court reasoned that because Wisconsin, by statute, gave recovery for wrongful death, such a claim, although based on the Illinois statute, could not be repugnant to Wisconsin public policy, especially because all

---

17. Richards v. United States, 369 U.S. 1, 15, 82 S.Ct. 585, 594, 7 L.Ed.2d 492 (1962).

18. One line of cases, so far not expressly overruled, still affirmatively imposes choice-of-law rules. Although these cases may not stand if the Court applied the analysis of *Carroll* and *Richards,* they remain a special category where perceived needs of national uniformity require a choice of law mandated by the Constitution. Cf. Pennsylvania v. New York, 407 U.S. 206, 92 S.Ct. 2075, 32 L.Ed.2d 693 (1972); Texas v. New Jersey, 379 U.S. 674, 85 S.Ct. 626, 13 L.Ed.2d 596 (1965). These are escheat cases and their result may also be put on jurisdictional grounds. Thus, it may be said that intangibles have their situs at the last known address of the creditor and are subject to escheat there, and that the forum applies local law to escheat of local assets.

Another line of cases involves fraternal benefit societies and is best represented by Order of United Commercial Travelers of America v. Wolfe, 331 U.S. 586, 67 S.Ct. 1355, 91 L.Ed. 1687 (1947). In these cases, the Supreme Court has held that various insurance benefits provided by the fraternal societies to their members may be governed only by the law of the home state of the

society. The Court found a need to keep the rights and duties of all members uniform no matter where they lived. See Weintraub, supra n.10, at 627 et seq. The society and its members are considered an undivided entity to be governed by the law that granted the society's charter. The fraternal benefit cases are unique and *Wolfe,* the most recent case, was decided in 1947. While the cases have not been overruled, their continued validity is doubtful, given the Court's unwillingness to constitutionalize choice of law. But cf. CTS Corp. v. Dynamics Corp. of America, 481 U.S. 69, 107 S.Ct. 1637, 95 L.Ed.2d 67 (1987); see also infra § 23.6 n.10.

§ 3.25

1. 341 U.S. 609, 71 S.Ct. 980, 95 L.Ed. 1212 (1951). Hughes v. Fetter is regarded by Weintraub to be an exceptional case: "A state's forum-closing rule should be immune from attack under the Full Faith and Credit Clause unless the state's interest in the application of that rule is outweighed by the national need for a uniform result under the public act, record, or judicial proceeding of another state." Weintraub, Commentary on the Conflict of Laws 680–81 (4th ed. 2001). See also id., at 635–37.

parties were Wisconsin residents and the possibility existed that no other court would have jurisdiction.[2]

In *Broderick v. Rosner*,[3] the Court required the recognition by New Jersey courts of a New York statute imposing assessments on the stockholders of an insolvent bank. The New Jersey court had raised "impossible" procedural barriers to protect its citizens from the assessment. The Supreme Court ruled that a state may not deny enforcement of claims based on sister state law through the guise of merely affecting the remedy.[4] Full Faith and Credit required deference to the regulatory laws of New York because New Jersey had no legitimate policy that would be impinged by the enforcement.

A more recent foray into full-faith-and-credit principles as applied indicates a generally deferential attitude towards state choice of law and the merger of due process and full-faith-and-credit principles signaled in the *Hague* case.[5] In *Franchise Tax Board of California v. Hyatt*,[6] the Supreme Court confronted a case in which a Nevada taxpayer sued in Nevada state court the California state tax agency claiming that the tax agency engaged in intentionally tortious activity in auditing the Nevada taxpayer. The Nevada state courts refused to give the tax agency the benefit of the full sovereign immunity that it enjoyed under California law and the Supreme Court held that the Nevada courts were under no obligation to do so under full-faith-and-credit principles. Citing and following the *Hague* plurality opinion,[7] the unanimous Court concluded that the action had more than sufficient connection with Nevada to allow for application of the forum state's law.

4. *Constitutional Limitations Analyzed*

a. *Due Process*

§ 3.26 The Supreme Court's elaboration, in *Shaffer*,[1] *Kulko*,[2] *World–Wide Volkswagen*[3] and *Rush*,[4] on the minimum-contacts test for

2. However, there is no reason to assume that jurisdiction could not have been exercised in Illinois under non-resident motorist legislation or that the Wisconsin court, under notions of forum non conveniens, could not have required the defendant to consent to jurisdiction in Illinois. For criticism see Weintraub, supra n.1, at 636.

3. 294 U.S. 629, 55 S.Ct. 589, 79 L.Ed. 1100 (1935).

4. See also the discussion supra § 3.22 n.4.

5. See supra § 3.23.

6. 538 U.S. 488, 123 S.Ct. 1683, 155 L.Ed.2d 702 (2003).

7. Id. at 495, 123 S.Ct. at 1688, 155 L.Ed.2d 702.

§ 3.26

1. Shaffer v. Heitner, 433 U.S. 186, 97 S.Ct. 2569, 53 L.Ed.2d 683 (1977) (discussed infra § 7.6).

2. Kulko v. Superior Court, 436 U.S. 84, 98 S.Ct. 1690, 56 L.Ed.2d 132 (1978) (discussed infra § 8.32 et. seq.).

3. World–Wide Volkswagen Corp. v. Woodson, 444 U.S. 286, 100 S.Ct. 559, 62 L.Ed.2d 490 (1980) (discussed infra § 8.31 et seq.) See also infra § 9.9.

4. Rush v. Savchuk, 444 U.S. 320, 100 S.Ct. 571, 62 L.Ed.2d 516 (1980), on remand 290 N.W.2d 633 (Minn.1980). Asahi Metal Industry Co., Ltd. v. Superior Court of California, 480 U.S. 102, 107 S.Ct. 1026, 94 L.Ed.2d 92 (1987), on remand 236 Cal. Rptr. 153, 734 P.2d 989 (1987) additionally focuses on "fairness" as an element seemingly separate from the minimum-contacts

state court jurisdiction, originally announced in *International Shoe*[5] holds important implications for choice of law. *Hague's*[6] reliance on a contacts concept for the permissible reach of applicable law presents some interesting puzzles.

The jurisdiction cases narrow the permissible bases for the exercise of judicial jurisdiction somewhat and thereby effectively eliminate some instances in which the choice of forum law would most likely violate constitutional limits. *Home Insurance Co. v. Dick*[7] showed that local law may *not* be applied when no significant relation to the forum exists. *Phillips Petroleum Co. v. Shutts*[8] restated *Dick* and also drew on *Hague:* Kansas, the forum, had to have "a 'significant contact or aggregation of contacts' to the claims asserted by each member of the plaintiff class, contacts 'creating state interests' in order to ensure that the choice of Kansas law is not arbitrary or unfair.... Given Kansas's lack of 'interest' in claims unrelated to that State, ... application of Kansas law to every claim in this case is sufficiently arbitrary and unfair as to exceed constitutional limits."[9]

Shutts, like *Dick,* was a case without *any* meaningful forum contacts. In *Hague,* the Court restates and reformulates the requirement of *Dick* that there be a significant relationship to the forum for forum law to apply, proceeds to find sufficient contacts,[10] but fails to provide guidance as to how to measure sufficient significance. In effect, the *Hague* decision seems to suggest that the Court will not involve itself in the choice-of-law process so long as the forum has the most minimal contacts that might support the application of the *lex fori*.

Hague perhaps overlooks that there is a need for tests for the determination of when a court may apply its law to adjudicate the parties' dispute just as there must be tests for the determination of judicial jurisdiction.[11] This results from the fact that many of the same concerns are present in jurisdiction and choice of law. In both instances, constitutional due process provides protection for the defendant: it

inquiry. It is suggested that this decision essentially rests on forum non conveniens grounds and does not add to general jurisdiction theory. It is discussed further infra § 9.9.

5. International Shoe Co. v. State of Washington, 326 U.S. 310, 66 S.Ct. 154, 90 L.Ed. 95 (1945).

6. Allstate Insurance Co. v. Hague, 449 U.S. 302, 101 S.Ct. 633, 66 L.Ed.2d 521 (1981). For discussion see supra § 3.23.

7. 281 U.S. 397, 50 S.Ct. 338, 74 L.Ed. 926 (1930).

8. 472 U.S. 797, 105 S.Ct. 2965, 86 L.Ed.2d 628 (1985), on remand 240 Kan. 764, 732 P.2d 1286 (1987), cert. denied 487 U.S. 1223, 108 S.Ct. 2883, 101 L.Ed.2d 918 (1988).

9. 472 U.S. at 821–22, 105 S.Ct. at 2979. For the aftermath of *Shutts* see supra § 3.23, following n.22.

10. But see the criticism offered supra § 3.23.

11. See Hay, The Interrelation of Jurisdiction and Choice of Law in U.S. Conflicts Law, 28 Int'l & Comp. L. Q. 161 (1979). See also Weintraub, supra § 3.23, n.1, at 33. However, Professor Weintraub does not believe that the decision is troublesome from a *constitutional* point of view. *Id., passim.* Professor Juenger went further: the Minnesota Supreme Court's decision, upheld in *Hague,* was—to him—a "superbly sensible decision." Juenger, Supreme Court Intervention in Jurisdiction and Choice of Law: A Dismal Prospect, 14 U. Cal. Davis L. Rev. 907, 917 (1981).

guards his "individual liberty interest"[12] in jurisdiction and proscribes the application of a law that is "arbitrary or unfair."[13] But, whatever its merits might be, *Hague* and its progeny establish that choice-of-law doctrine is largely a matter of state law, and that constitutional intervention will be rare.

§ 3.27 Fairness is obviously a flexible concept, but essentially it is measured by the facts and the parties' activities in relation to the forum state. It is unfair to exercise jurisdiction when the person has no contact with the state. Contact need not be physical, however. Fairness and the significance of contacts are also measured by purposeful activity directed to the forum[1] or by the type and quantum of benefits derived from the state seeking to exercise power. Separately, or in some combination, these factors make it reasonable for the defendant to anticipate being subjected to the state's adjudicatory power. Finally, if the cause of action of the plaintiff is related to the defendant's connection with the state, the exercise of jurisdiction over the defendant comports with traditional notions of fair play. On the other hand, a state may not subject a minimally related defendant to its jurisdiction on a cause of action that does not *"arise from"*[2] those contacts. Thus, Due Process requires for jurisdiction a *nexus* between the defendant, and the forum, and, if this connection be slight, also to the cause of action.[3]

This discussion is relevant to choice of law because application of the *lex fori* often follows jurisdiction.[4] Power to exercise jurisdiction, however, does not automatically give the state constitutional authority to apply forum law: while jurisdiction and choice of the *lex fori* will often coincide,

---

12. Insurance Corp. of Ireland, Ltd. v. Compagnie des Bauxites de Guinee, 456 U.S. 694, 702–03 n. 10, 102 S.Ct. 2099, 2104 n. 10, 72 L.Ed.2d 492 (1982).

13. Supra n.9.

§ 3.27

1. E.g. Hanson v. Denckla, 357 U.S. 235, 78 S.Ct. 1228, 2 L.Ed.2d 1283 (1958). Cf. Pearson v. Northeast Airlines, Inc., 309 F.2d 553 (2d Cir.1962) (en banc), cert. denied 372 U.S. 912, 83 S.Ct. 726, 9 L.Ed.2d 720 (1963). Whether the activity must be directed to the forum or whether, for instance in products liability, contacts brought about through the "stream of commerce" will suffice for judicial jurisdiction, is discussed further infra at §§ 9.9 in connection with Asahi Metal Industry Co., Ltd. v. Superior Court of California, 480 U.S. 102, 107 S.Ct. 1026, 94 L.Ed.2d 92 (1987).

2. See Helicopteros Nacionales de Colombia, S.A. v. Hall, 466 U.S. 408, 104 S.Ct. 1868, 80 L.Ed.2d 404 (1984), on remand 677 S.W.2d 19 (Tex.1984) (discussed infra § 9.9.)

3. Shaffer v. Heitner, 433 U.S. 186, 97 S.Ct. 2569, 53 L.Ed.2d 683 (1977).

4. Martin, Constitutional Limits on Choice of Law, 61 Cornell L. Rev. 185, 202–03 (1976).

The jurisdictional and choice-of-law inquiries are *related.* But, as the Court has stated often, they are *not the same.* The *Shutts* Court reemphasized the point: " . . . While a State may, for the reasons we have previously stated, assume jurisdiction over the claims of plaintiffs whose principal contacts are with other States, it may not use this assumption of jurisdiction as an added weight in the scale when considering the permissible jurisdictional limits on choice of substantive law.... The issue of personal jurisdiction . . . is entirely distinct from the question of constitutional limitations on choice of law . . ." 472 U.S. at 821, 105 S.Ct. at 2979. For additional discussion see Hay, Judicial Jurisdiction and Choice of Law: Constitutional Limitations, 59 Colo. L. Rev. 9 (1988). *Shutts* therefore may represent a slight limitation of the seemingly open-ended reach of *Hague.* Compare O'Connor, J., dissenting in Sun Oil Co. v. Wortman, 486 U.S. 717, 730, 108 S.Ct. 2117, 2126, 100 L.Ed.2d 743 (1988) (discussed supra § 3.23 n.26).

the "minimum contacts" for one do not always provide the necessary "significant contacts" for the other.[5] Jurisdiction and choice of law address two different questions. Jurisdiction considers whether it is *fair* to cause this defendant to travel to this state; choice of law asks the further question of whether the application of this substantive law which will determine the merits of the case is fair to *both* parties. Thus, for choice of law there must be a sufficient nexus *between the transaction* to be adjudicated *and the forum* as well as to the parties. Some examples serve to illustrate these distinctions.

§ 3.28   That the contacts needed for jurisdiction and for choice of law are not always identical is also demonstrated by some cases in which the plaintiff travels to the defendant's domicile to sue him at his home. Jurisdiction is readily established, but the propriety of applying the *lex fori* does not automatically follow. In *Young v. Masci*,[1] the plaintiff, a New Yorker, brought suit in New Jersey against a domiciliary of that state. Suit was based on a New York statute making automobile owners liable for injuries caused by others who used the car with permission. The defendant had given permission to a third party to drive the defendant's car to New York where the bailee struck and injured the plaintiff. The defendant asserted that New York could not constitutionally impose liability on a nonresident owner. The Supreme Court, in affirming judgment for the plaintiff, rejected this argument, holding that the New York statute could impose such liability because the defendant set in motion the acts that caused the injury. Stated in more current terminology, Young engaged in such purposeful activity directed towards New York that he could expect that state's law to apply to him.[2] Given the defendant's expectations that New York law might apply and the nexus of the law with the transaction, the application of New York law was not unfair so as to violate due process. *Young* concerned only the constitutionality of the New York statute, not whether New Jersey should apply it. The question was therefore not in issue whether New Jersey could have applied forum law to *protect* the local *defendant*. Since the transaction also had contacts with New Jersey (place of bailment, registration of automobile, point of origin of the trip, domicile of defendant), there was sufficient contact with New Jersey as well: in effect, the application of *either* law would have been constitutional.

The same issue, whether forum law may apply when all the significant contacts lie in the out-of-state plaintiff's home state, is raised more clearly by *Lilienthal v. Kaufman*.[3] In this case the defendant Kaufman, an Oregonian, went to California where he entered into an agreement

---

5. Hay, The Interrelation of Jurisdictional Choice of Law in U.S. Conflicts Law, 28 Int'l & Comp. L.Q. 161 (1979).

§ 3.28

1. 289 U.S. 253, 53 S.Ct. 599, 77 L.Ed. 1158 (1933).

2. Under modern jurisdictional analysis, these contacts would be sufficient to give

New York jurisdiction and often plaintiff would sue at home. On the facts of this case, if plaintiff had sued in New York, application of New York law also would have been constitutionally appropriate. Cf. Scheer v. Rockne Motors Corp., 68 F.2d 942 (2d Cir.1934).

3. 239 Or. 1, 395 P.2d 543 (1964).

with the plaintiff to enter a joint venture. Pursuant to the agreement and while still in California, Kaufman executed and delivered to Lilienthal two promissory notes representing his investment in the venture. When Lilienthal demanded payment of the notes, he discovered that Kaufman had been declared a spendthrift under an Oregon statute. Kaufman's guardian used his statutory power to avoid payment of the notes. Lilienthal sued in Oregon and sought application of California law as the law of the place where the transaction occurred, where the notes were executed and delivered. California would not recognize the disability of a spendthrift.[4] The Oregon court observed that the most significant relationship was with California but upheld the guardian's avoidance upon a finding that Oregon's public policy of protecting spendthrifts required application of Oregon law.

The nexus between the forum and the transaction was clearly missing in *Lilienthal*. The only connection to the forum was the *defendant's* domicile. Furthermore the application of the *lex fori* deprived the *plaintiff* of his legitimate expectation that the transaction with another who came into his state, made completely in his state, would be governed by his state's law. The plaintiff was not connected with the forum, nor did he engage in any purposeful activity or derive any benefit from the forum. Application of forum law to deny his claim was therefore unfair and thus should have been considered a violation of due process.[5]

§ 3.29 A choice-of-law analysis that uses the concepts of due process as applied to jurisdiction in order to determine when a state has the sufficiently "significant contacts" constitutionally to apply its law overlooks that jurisdictional and choice-of-law considerations, while similar, are not the same.[1] The connection of the state must be to the *defendant* to gain jurisdiction. The nexus of the state and the *transaction*

---

4. Had litigation occurred in California, a California court—using *any* of the approaches to choice-of-law—would surely have applied forum law. The defendant's *status* of a spendthrift under Oregon law would have been irrelevant for the determination of the *consequences* of such status in the forum. Cf. Estin v. Estin, 334 U.S. 541, 68 S.Ct. 1213, 92 L.Ed. 1561 (1948). Civil law countries arrive at like solutions: capacity is governed by a party's "personal law" (ordinarily the law of nationality) but the effectiveness of a person's acts, when done within the forum, is determined by forum law in the interest of commercial certainty. For France, see 2 Battifol & Lagarde, Droit international privé no. 491 (7th ed. 1983); for Germany, see Introductory Law to the Civil Code (EGBGB), as revised (supra § 2.18 n.6), arts. 7 and 12; Kegel & Schurig, Internationales Privatrecht 559–562 (9th ed. 2004); Hay, Internationales Privatrecht 180–82 (2d ed.2002).

5. At most, Oregon's public policy should have led the court not to entertain the action, leaving the plaintiff free to sue elsewhere. The decision on the merits unconstitutionally deprives him of his claim.

The *Lilienthal* court also referred to its earlier decision in Olshen v. Kaufman, 235 Or. 423, 385 P.2d 161 (1963), involving essentially identical facts except that the plaintiff was a resident of Oregon and the transaction had taken place in Oregon, in order to demonstrate Oregon's strong governmental interest. In adopting Currie's view that courts are instruments of state policy, the *Lilienthal* court extended the *Olshen* holding, required by Oregon law, to *Lilienthal,* a case with extra-state facts. A "restrained" interpretation of forum law, especially in view of the Constitutional problems noted above, might have avoided the *Lilienthal* result even under Currie's approach to choice of law.

§ 3.29

1. Supra § 3.27 n.4.

provides the necessary relation for the application of local law. Such a view of due process analysis can adequately deal with issues of fairness to the parties—plaintiffs *and* defendants; it can also test when a state's power is sufficient to adjudicate by application of the *lex fori*. However, a due process analysis cannot address problems of conflicting state interests: when may a state with significant relation to a transaction apply its law and disregard the contrary existing interests of a sister-state? In a few limited areas the Supreme Court has set the balance of conflicting state interests; but largely the need for respect for conflicting policies and interests must be perceived by the states themselves and is self-imposed. The following section explores what constitutional requirements, if any, may exist that would impose a duty on states to defer to countervailing interests of other states.

b.   Full Faith and Credit

§ 3.30   It was suggested earlier that due process in choice-of-law should require a higher quality of contacts than for jurisdiction.[1] However, this has not been the development of the case law. The task of balancing state interests and of preventing undue parochialism might then fall to the Full Faith and Credit Clause.

It might be urged that an ideal choice-of-law system should only permit the application of the law of a state that had a *significant* state interest in the transaction.[2] Superimposing a requirement of a significant or substantial state interest on the minimum "due process" requirements to find a constitutional choice of law thus expands the inquiry into the difficult area of inter-state relations. It is the purpose of the Full Faith and Credit clause to insure extraterritorial effect for the government acts of a state[3] and to provide a uniform nationwide rule where needed.[4] Thus, under an invigorated Full Faith and Credit

---

§ 3.30

1.   Cf. supra § 3.21 n.7. See infra n.2.

2.   Reese, Limitations on the Exterritorial Application of Law, 4 Dalhousie L.J. 589, 602 (1977).

In writing about judicial *jurisdiction* Professor Brilmayer states: "[A]n occurrence in the forum state of no relevance to a totally domestic cause of action is an unrelated contact, a purely jurisdictional allegation with no substantive purpose. If a fact is irrelevant in a purely domestic dispute, it does not suddenly become related to the controversy simply because there are multi-state elements." Brilmayer, How Contacts Count: Due Process Limitations on State Court Jurisdiction, 1980 Sup. Ct. Rev. 77, 82–83. Thus, "forum/litigation contacts do not automatically suffice to afford jurisdiction." Id. at 88. These ideas obviously lend themselves to application with respect to *choice of law.* Brilmayer, Legitimate Interests in Multistate Problems: As Between State and Federal Law, 79 Mich. L. Rev.

1315 (1981). The use of "significant"—interest language in the text (see also supra § 3.21 n.7) is intended to have a similar thrust. Ideally, perhaps, the law chosen should be that of the "most significantly related" state. To require this, however, would overlook competing interests of other states that are also of genuine importance. The use of "significant" or "substantial" is intended to take this into account. When state interests or policies conflict, more than a *minimal* relation should be required for the application of the *lex fori* (as distinguished from the exercise of judicial jurisdiction): the relation to the forum should be "significant," "substantial." For additional comment see Hay, Full Faith and Credit and Federalism in Choice of Law, 34 Mercer L. Rev. 709 (1983); Pielemeier, Why We Should Worry About Full Faith and Credit to Laws, 60 S. Cal. L. Rev. 1299 (1987).

3.   Primarily judgments: see infra Chapter 24.

4.   See Leflar, Constitutional Limits on Free Choice of Law, 20 L. & Contemp. Probs. 706, 725 (1963).

Clause, a state could not apply its law, even if it had the requisite "contact" (i.e. power plus fairness), if, in so doing it would impair a predominant interest of a sister state or violate a national interest.

In some areas the Supreme Court has provided for the concerns of national uniformity by creating "federal common law."[5] However, the court has left almost completely undefined any limits on the extraterritorial effect of state policy as embodied in a statute so long as a state has *power,* in due process terms, to apply its law. The Court now seems to have rejected a state interest approach, despite its once active balancing of interests to determine what law should apply.[6] The balancing of state interests is thus left to the states themselves. As the case law (discussed in specific subject matter chapters in this volume) shows, the states often strike the balance in their own favor. Further "constitutionalization" of choice of law, for instance through the creation of federal common law, is considered in Part V of this chapter.

B. PRIVILEGES AND IMMUNITIES, EQUAL PROTECTION AND COMMERCE

§ 3.31 Both the Privileges and Immunities[1] and Equal Protection[2] Clauses are designed to eliminate discriminatory classifications that

5. See infra § 3.49 et seq.

6. Nevada v. Hall, 440 U.S. 410, 99 S.Ct. 1182, 59 L.Ed.2d 416 (1979), presented the Court with a unique opportunity to balance state interests because the defendant was a State of the Union and interposed, as defenses to an action for injuries caused by an automobile owned by the state and driven by one of its employees, both its sovereign immunity and a Nevada statutory limitation on recoveries against the state. After rejecting the sovereign immunity defense, the Court noted that California had a substantial interest (protection of residents who are injured on its highways), an interest so substantial that it had waived its own immunity for like cases. Under these circumstances, California could well regard the Nevada limitation as "obnoxious" to its policy. The Court stated in its n.24: "California's exercise of *jurisdiction* in this case poses no substantial threat to our constitutional system of cooperative federalism. Suits involving traffic accidents outside of Nevada could hardly interfere with Nevada's capacity to fulfill its own sovereign responsibilities. We have no occasion, in this case, to consider whether different state policies, either of California or of Nevada, might require a different analysis or a different result." Emphasis added. The italics show how jurisdictional and choice-of-law considerations blended into each other. Full Faith and Credit considerations, to which the footnote was appended, were

seen in power (Due Process) terms. The interest analysis, moreover, emphasized California's interest, with only passing reference to Nevada's. The other state's interest may be expected to be even less important when the defendant is not a State of the Union but a private party. See supra § 3.24 n.13. See also Note, Sovereign Immunity in Sister-State Courts, 80 Colum. L. Rev. 1493, 1494–1502 (1980). That case was reaffirmed by Franchise Tax Board of California v. Hyatt, 538 U.S. 488, 123 S.Ct. 1683, 155 L.Ed.2d 702 (2003). See supra § 3.25.

See also Simmons v. Montana and Oregon, 206 Mont. 264, 670 P.2d 1372 (1983), declining to exercise jurisdiction over Oregon in a tort action arising from negligence in laboratory testing provided by Oregon as a regional medical service. Noting that *Hall* permitted the assertion of personal jurisdiction over a sister state, the Montana court declined to do so on the basis of comity in order to further, as the *Hall* Court had put it, "harmonious interstate relations." 440 U.S. at 426, 99 S.Ct. at 1191. The plaintiff was thus left to pursue his remedies in Oregon.

§ 3.31

1. U.S. Const., Art. IV, § 2. See U.S. Const., Amend. XIV, § 1; J. Nowak & R. Rotunda, Constitutional Law § 10.3 (6th ed. 2000) [hereinafter cited as: Constitutional Law].

2. U.S. Const. Amend. XIV, § 1.

have no legally justifiable (rational) basis. In some circumstances, the Commerce Clause also can have this effect. In the conflict-of-laws setting, the clauses come into play when a state applies a local rule in a case with multistate contacts in a fashion which discriminates against the out of state party because of nonresidence or noncitizenship or attempts to engage in invalid extraterritorial regulation.[3]

In order to form a unified nation and to treat all similarly situated persons equally, these constitutional clauses limit the state's power to classify according to citizenship or place of residence. Unlike Due Process or Full Faith and Credit, however, the Privileges and Immunities and Equal Protection clauses do not invalidate the forum's choice of its own law as opposed to the law of another state. These Clauses merely require the forum to have a law that applies equally to citizen and noncitizen alike.[4]

1. Privileges and Immunities and Commerce Clauses

§ **3.32** Often referred to as the comity clause, the Privileges and Immunities Clause provides that: "The Citizens of each State shall be entitled to all the Privileges and Immunities of Citizens in the several States."[1] Early decisions gave limited scope to the comity clause.[2] In *Corfield v. Coryell*, Justice Bushrod Washington confined the rights contained in the clause to those "which are in their nature, fundamental; which belong of right, to the citizens of all free governments; and which have at all times been enjoyed by the citizens of the several states which compose this Union."[3] Additionally, the guarantee of the clause is unavailable to corporations.[4]

---

3. For two comprehensive articles dealing with the Privileges and Immunities and Equal Protection clauses, see Currie & Schreter, Unconstitutional Discrimination in the Conflict of Laws: Privileges and Immunities, 69 Yale L.J. 1323 (1960) [hereinafter cited as Currie & Schreter I] and Currie & Schreter, Unconstitutional Discrimination in the Conflict of Laws: Equal Protection, 28 U. Chi. L. Rev. 1 (1960) [hereinafter cited as Currie & Schreter II]. See Toomer v. Witsell, 334 U.S. 385, 68 S.Ct. 1156, 92 L.Ed. 1460 (1948). See also Zobel v. Williams, 457 U.S. 55, 102 S.Ct. 2309, 72 L.Ed.2d 672 (1982); Varat, State Citizenship and Interstate Equality, 48 U. Chi. L. Rev. 487 (1981). For a decision striking down a statute as invalid on Commerce Clause grounds for engaging in impermissible extraterritorial regulation, see Healy v. The Beer Institute, 491 U.S. 324, 109 S.Ct. 2491, 105 L.Ed.2d 275 (1989).

4. The Equal Protection clause applies more broadly to "persons." See infra § 3.34 n.3.

§ 3.32

1. Supra § 3.31 n.1.

2. See, e.g., Conner v. Elliott, 59 U.S. (18 How.) 591, 15 L.Ed. 497 (1855); Ferry v. Spokane, Portland & Seattle Railway Co., 258 U.S. 314, 42 S.Ct. 358, 66 L.Ed. 635 (1922). See § 10.3 Constitutional Law, supra § 3.31 n.1, at 10.3.

3. 6 Fed.Cas. 546, 551–52 (No. 3230) (C.C.E.D. Pa. 1823).

4. Paul v. Virginia, 75 U.S. (8 Wall.) 168, 19 L.Ed. 357 (1869); Blake v. McClung, 172 U.S. 239, 19 S.Ct. 165, 43 L.Ed. 432 (1898). The reason for the exclusion of corporations is the historical power of a state

Later, however, the Clause was expanded to protect more than only "fundamental" rights.[5] The leading case, *Blake v. McClung*,[6] held that Tennessee could not give priority to its own citizens in the distribution of an insolvent firm's assets to the detriment of nonresidents. The Court in *Blake* noted, however, that the right of noncitizens to enjoy the Privileges and Immunities of citizens of the forum state is not absolute. Thus, the thrust of the comity clause is that any distinction based on citizenship must have a reasonable basis or fall as unconstitutional discrimination.[7] In some cases, preference for local residents may be justified. In *LaTourette v. McMaster*,[8] the Court upheld a South Carolina statute which required that all licensed insurance brokers reside in the state. The discrimination against nonresidents was upheld on two grounds. First, the Court emphasized that the distinguishing feature in the statute was residence, not citizenship. Because the Constitution, the Court said, bans only *citizenship* classifications, a statute drawn in terms of residency poses no problems. This reasoning is unpersuasive and no longer should be followed.[9] Second, the Court pointed to what now appears to be the only proper justification for the discriminatory aspects

to exclude foreign corporations completely. But see infra § 3.34 n.3 with respect to the Equal Protection Clause.

5. See, e.g., Chalker v. Birmingham & North Western R. Co., 249 U.S. 522, 39 S.Ct. 366, 63 L.Ed. 748 (1919); Travis v. Yale Towne Manufacturing Co., 252 U.S. 60, 40 S.Ct. 228, 64 L.Ed. 460 (1920). Currie & Schreter I, at 1339–40.

6. 172 U.S. 239, 19 S.Ct. 165, 43 L.Ed. 432 (1898).

7. Id.; Toomer v. Witsell, supra § 3.1, n.3, at 1337–39; McGrovney, Privileges or Immunities Clause, Fourteenth Amendment, 4 Iowa L. Bull. 219 (1918). Cf. Hague v. CIO, 307 U.S. 496, 511, 59 S.Ct. 954, 962, 83 L.Ed. 1423 (1939) (Roberts, J.).

8. 248 U.S. 465, 39 S.Ct. 160, 63 L.Ed. 362 (1919).

9. Currie v. Schreter I, at 1343–19, 1383. In Blake v. McClung, 172 U.S. 239, 19 S.Ct. 165, 43 L.Ed. 432 (1898) the court had rejected the notion that a statute discriminating in terms of "residence" automatically avoided the Constitutional demand of equal privileges and immunities to "citizens." The Court reasoned that by denying priority to "nonresidents," citizens of other states were consequently deprived of equal treatment. In *LaTourette* the Court reasoned that because a residence classification barred *both* citizens of other states *and* *nonresident* citizens of the forum state, no unconstitutional discrimination among *citizens* existed. This idea was followed in Douglas v. New York, N.H. & H.R. Co., 279 U.S. 377, 49 S.Ct. 355, 73 L.Ed. 747 (1929) and in Missouri ex rel. Southern Railway Co. v. Mayfield, 340 U.S. 1, 71 S.Ct. 1, 95 L.Ed. 3 (1950). Currie and Schreter call the residence/citizenship distinction "disingen-

uous and specious" (at 1344), and point out that in Travis v. Yale & Towne Manufacturing Co., 252 U.S. 60, 40 S.Ct. 228, 64 L.Ed. 460 (1920), the Court recognized that a residence classification had the "necessary effect" of also discriminating against citizens of other states. (Currie & Schreter I, at 1346). In fact, most residence-based classifications discriminate primarily against *citizens* of other states in favor of local *citizens*. (Id. at 1343–44). Furthermore, in the cases that relied on the residence/citizenship distinction, the discrimination in question was also justified by a legitimate reason. The true basis for the decisions may therefore be the validity of the underlying reason for the discrimination, not merely that the statute was based on residence. (Id. at 1346). Thus, in Toomer v. Witsell, 334 U.S. 385, 396, 68 S.Ct. 1156, 1162, 92 L.Ed. 1460 (1948), rehearing denied 335 U.S. 837, 69 S.Ct. 12, 93 L.Ed. 389 (1948), the Court stated that the Privileges and Immunities Clause "does bar discrimination against citizens of other states where there is no substantial reason for the discrimination beyond the mere fact that they are citizens of other states. But it does not preclude disparity of treatment in the many situations where there are perfectly valid independent reasons for it. Thus the inquiry in each case must be concerned with whether such reasons do exist and whether the degree of discrimination bears a close relation to them." Furthermore, in *Toomer* the Court specifically found that couching the statute in terms of residence could not remove it from the prescription of the Privileges and Immunities Clause. Id. at 397, 68 S.Ct. at 1162–63. See also Chalker v. Birmingham & North Western Railroad Co.,

of the statute: the discrimination had a rational basis.[10] The state's conceded authority and power to regulate insurance brokers could be effectuated more easily if all brokers were local residents. As in other areas of Constitutional review, the Court did not attempt to find that the regulation was wise or the best way to achieve a goal.[11]

The Privileges and Immunities Clause does not apply to corporations.[12] In some respects, however, the Commerce Clause can act as protector of out-of-state businesses against local laws that favor local businesses or place unreasonable burdens on their ability to do business

249 U.S. 522, 39 S.Ct. 366, 63 L.Ed. 748 (1919); Currie & Schreter I, at 1347. In Baldwin v. Fish & Game Commission of Montana, 436 U.S. 371, 98 S.Ct. 1852, 56 L.Ed.2d 354 (1978), Montana's regulation of elk-hunting imposing restrictions and higher fees on non-residents not unconstitutional under Privileges and Immunities and Equal Protection Clauses. Hicklin v. Orbeck, 437 U.S. 518, 98 S.Ct. 2482, 57 L.Ed.2d 397 (1978) (Alaska's preferential hiring of residents for work under state leases violative of Privileges and Immunities Clause).

Supreme Court of N.H. v. Piper, 470 U.S. 274, 105 S.Ct. 1272, 84 L.Ed.2d 205 (1985) invalidated the New Hampshire rule that limited admission to the Bar to residents of New Hampshire. The protections afforded citizens under the Privileges and Immunities Clause are at times very close to those considered protected by the Equal Protection Clause. See Zobel v. Williams, 457 U.S. 55, 102 S.Ct. 2309, 72 L.Ed.2d 672 (1982) which invalidated Alaska's natural resources income distribution scheme which measured dividends to citizens by length of residence within the state. The majority relied on the Equal Protection Clause while the concurring opinions rested on the Privileges and Immunities Clause. Noted 12 U.C.L.A.-Alaska L. Rev. 119 (1983). Modern state cases, however, continue to employ the residence-citizenship distinction, though apparently recognizing it analytical weakness. See Owens Corning v. Carter, 997 S.W.2d 560 (Tex.), cert. denied sub nom., Moore v. Owens–Corning, 528 U.S. 1005, 120 S.Ct. 500, 145 L.Ed.2d 386 (1999) (upholding statutes applying forum non conveniens and limitations borrowing provisions only to persons not "legal residents" of Texas).

10. In Conner v. Elliott, 59 U.S. (18 How.) 591, 15 L.Ed. 497 (1855), Louisiana validly restricted community property rights only to women married in or residing in the state. The purpose was to fulfill the expectations of those not connected with

Louisiana that common law property rights would attend their marriage. See Currie & Schreter I, supra § 3.31 n.3, at 1341. In Ferry v. Spokane, Portland & Seattle Railway Co., 258 U.S. 314, 42 S.Ct. 358, 66 L.Ed. 635 (1922), Oregon granted dower to nonresident widows only in the land which their husbands owned at death. Resident widows received dower in all lands which their husband had ever owned during life. The purpose was to protect the rights of local purchasers who might be unaware of the existence of a wife's dower claim if she did not reside in the state. See Currie & Schreter I, at 1344; 1346–47; 1383.

Several other cases, however, do not fit easily within this analysis and uphold discriminations without any justification. For example, in Chambers v. Baltimore & Ohio Railroad Co., 207 U.S. 142, 28 S.Ct. 34, 52 L.Ed. 143 (1907), an Ohio statute permitted recovery for wrongful death occurring outside Ohio only if the decedent were a resident of Ohio. The courts of Ohio were thus open to redress the death of Ohio citizens but the same court could give no aid to the representatives of citizens of other states, even if these decedents were killed by an Ohio defendant. See Currie, The Constitution and the "Transitory" Cause of Action, 73 Harv. L. Rev. 36, 58–59; Currie & Schreter I, supra § 3.31 n.3, at 1385; and 207 U.S. at 151, 157, 159–60, 28 S.Ct. at 36, 39–40 (McKenna, J., dissenting). The Court did not attempt to justify this discrimination by finding any legitimate state purpose. Rather, it held that the state made no classification among plaintiffs who represented the deceased; the statute, therefore, was not unconstitutional. The continued validity of the case has been questioned. Currie & Schreter I, at 1385. Chambers could possibly be justified on forum non conveniens since the residence of both parties and the situs of the accident were outside of Ohio.

11. See Constitutional Law, §§ 11.4, 14.1.

12. See infra § 23.6.

in state. Statutes that burden the internal affairs of foreign corporations may be invalid under the Commerce Clause.[13] Certain kinds of pricing statutes can also be invalidated on Commerce Clause grounds by having the practical effect of regulating prices in other states. For example in *Healy v. The Beer Institute*,[14] a statute that required sellers of beer in Connecticut to certify that the price was no higher than the sale price in border states was held to be unconstitutional because "the undeniable effect of controlling commercial activity occurring wholly outside the boundary of the State."[15]

§ 3.33   Several rules of state procedure that differentiate between citizens and noncitizens do not violate the Privileges and Immunities Clause. In *Chemung Canal Bank v. Lowery*,[1] a statute of limitations for actions to enforce judgments was held constitutional even though the statute was tolled for resident plaintiffs when the defendant was absent from the state, but the defendants' absence had no such effect for nonresident plaintiffs.[2] The difference was justified because the state had a good reason to toll the statute for local plaintiffs, but if the same benefit was extended to nonresidents, undesirable forum shopping could result. If the nonresident judgment creditor happened to find the defendant in the state, he could collect on a claim perhaps long extinguished in the state where the judgment arose. The nonresident would be using his status as a nonresident to gain an unfair advantage. The statute's distinction thus allows the state to protect local creditors whose claims are frustrated by debtors who flee the jurisdiction and, at the same time, to guard against recovery on stale claims held by out-of-state residents.[3]

The doctrine of forum non conveniens is another procedural device that may discriminate against noncitizens but is useful in preventing plaintiffs from utilizing liberal jurisdictional bases to gain an advantage

---

13. See, e.g., CTS Corp. v. Dynamics Corp. of America, 481 U.S. 69, 107 S.Ct. 1637, 95 L.Ed.2d 67 (1987) (invalidating Illinois anti-takeover statute that applied to foreign corporations where 10% or more of stock held by Illinois residents). See infra § 23.6.

14. 491 U.S. 324, 109 S.Ct. 2491, 105 L.Ed.2d 275 (1989).

15. Id. at 337, 109 S.Ct. 2491, 105 L.Ed.2d 275. However, not every effort to use a state's economic leverage has this effect. The Court upheld a Maine statute that endeavored to obtain what amounts to a "group discount" on prescription drugs for its residents against a similar challenge. See Pharmaceutical Research and Manufacturers of America v. Walsh, 538 U.S. 644, 123 S.Ct. 1855, 155 L.Ed.2d 889 (2003).

§ 3.33

1. 93 U.S. (3 Otto.) 72, 23 L.Ed. 806 (1876).

2. A similar situation is presented in Canadian Northern Railway Co. v. Eggen, 252 U.S. 553, 40 S.Ct. 402, 64 L.Ed. 713 (1920) where Minnesota's "borrowing" statute of limitations was upheld. Enforcing a shorter limitation on nonresidents whose own statute had run lessened the crowding of the forum's courts and prevented forum shopping. Currie & Schreter I, at 1389.

3. See also Watkins v. Conway, 385 U.S. 188, 87 S.Ct. 357, 17 L.Ed.2d 286 (1966). The Court's alternative grounds in *Lowery* seem to apply to causes of action not reduced to judgment. The absent debtor is obligated to pay at the creditor's residence. When he fails to pay, the debtor is in contempt of the law of the creditors domicile only and not the forum state's law. The forum is entitled to use the debtor's absence to toll only the limitations running in favor of its creditors. Additionally, the refusal to aid nonresident creditors works no hardship since the creditor can reduce the claim to judgment and thereafter keep the liability alive by revival of the judgment. Currie & Schreter I, at 1387–89.

over a defendant who is available in another more convenient forum (forum shopping).[4] The doctrine explains *Douglas v. New York, New Haven & Hartford Railroad Co.*[5] in which the Supreme Court upheld New York's dismissal of a Connecticut plaintiff's suit based on a foreign cause of action against a Connecticut defendant who did business in New York. The decision asserted that it is permissible to limit access to overcrowded local courts to those who paid for maintaining the courts.[6] A forum's obligation to hear cases, however, extends beyond granting access to its courts only to those who pay.[7] Rejecting a noncitizen's suit, when a similar action by a citizen would be heard, is justified only because the denial advances some permissible interest of the state.[8] Thus, in *Douglas,* New York had no interest in the dispute since all the contacts were outside the state.[9]

The narrow limits of cases like *Douglas* were forcefully stated in *Howlett v. Rose.*[10] In that case, the courts below had applied Florida law which extended sovereign immunity to state governmental entities in federal actions under § 1983. Justice Stevens wrote for an unanimous Court:

> The fact that a rule is denominated jurisdictional does not provide a court an excuse to avoid the obligation to enforce federal law.... It is settled that a court ... may not avoid its parallel obligation under the Full Faith and Credit Clause to entertain another State's cause of action by invocation of the term "jurisdiction" ... [or] evade the strictness of the Privileges and Immunities Clause.... [T]he same is true with respect to ... the Supremacy Clause.

2. *Equal Protection*

§ 3.34 The Equal Protection Clause of the Fourteenth Amendment commands each state not to "deny to any person within its jurisdiction the equal protection of the laws."[1] The Clause requires similar treatment for similarly situated persons, unless a classification differentiating among them relates to, and is designed to achieve, a legitimate governmental purpose.[2]

---

4. See generally Gulf Oil Corp. v. Gilbert, 330 U.S. 501, 67 S.Ct. 839, 91 L.Ed. 1055 (1947).

5. 279 U.S. 377, 49 S.Ct. 355, 73 L.Ed. 747 (1929). Currie & Schreter I, at 1379–80.

6. The decision also rested on the distinction between residence and citizenship. See supra § 3.32 n.9.

7. Cf. Hughes v. Fetter, 341 U.S. 609, 71 S.Ct. 980, 95 L.Ed. 1212 (1951); see also supra § 3.25 n.1. See generally Currie & Schreter I, at 1384.

8. Currie & Schreter I, at 1383.

9. Significant contacts for choice of law purposes are not in issue in this case; the case relates only to access to the courts.

10. 496 U.S. 356, 381–82, 110 S.Ct. 2430, 110 L.Ed.2d 332 (1990).

§ 3.34

1. U.S. Const. Amend. XIV, § 1.

2. See Constitutional Law, §§ 14.1, 14.2; Currie & Schreter II, at 5. The Equal Protection test is different when fundamental rights are involved. Then the state must show a compelling interest to justify the classification. Constitutional Law, §§ 14.1, 14.2.

The Equal Protection Clause applies to "persons" and thus encompasses corporations.[3] However, the clause is limited in application to those "within the jurisdiction" of the state. The major equal protection cases have dealt with corporations where the issue of presence "within the jurisdiction" was critical. In *Kentucky Finance Corp. v. Paramount Auto Exchange Corp.*,[4] plaintiff foreign corporation had brought an action in Wisconsin to replevy an automobile in defendant's wrongful possession. Wisconsin law provided that local claimants could require an officer of a foreign corporation to submit to pretrial examination in any county in Wisconsin, whereas nonresident natural persons could be examined only in the county where personal service was obtained, and Wisconsin residents could be examined only in their home county. The Court rejected the notion that the corporation was not present within the jurisdiction. By virtue of bringing suit in Wisconsin courts, the corporation went into the state and was, therefore, present for the purposes of that undertaking and was subject to examination only under the same conditions as nonresident individuals. Thus, any person invoking the protection of the courts must be granted Equal Protection.[5]

§ 3.35 Other procedural distinctions are equally invalid. For example, the Court has struck down provisions allowing a foreign corporation to be sued in any county, when the proper venue for local corporations or resident natural persons is in the county where they do business or reside,[1] and provisions permitting substituted service, without notice, in the case of foreign corporations when different provisions

IV. PROBLEMS OF FEDERALISM: STATE LAW IN FEDERAL COURTS

A. THE ERIE/KLAXON DOCTRINE: POLICY CONSIDERATIONS

§ 3.36 *Klaxon Co. v. Stentor Electric Manufacturing Co.*[1] held that a federal court sitting in diversity must apply the choice-of-law rules of

---

3. The Equal Protection clause applies to all "persons": citizens, aliens, and corporations. See Yick Wo v. Hopkins, 118 U.S. 356, 6 S.Ct. 1064, 30 L.Ed. 220 (1886). With respect to corporations see Pembina Consol. Silver Mining & Milling Co. v. Pennsylvania, 125 U.S. 181, 8 S.Ct. 737, 31 L.Ed. 650 (1888). But see Connecticut General Life Insurance Co. v. Johnson, 303 U.S. 77, 85, 58 S.Ct. 436, 440, 82 L.Ed. 673 (1938) (Black, J., dissenting); Wheeling Steel Corp. v. Glander, 337 U.S. 562, 579, 69 S.Ct. 1291, 1300, 93 L.Ed. 1544 (1949) (Douglas, J., dissenting). Equal protection also protects citizens from discrimination based on duration of residence unsupported by an independently valid state interest. See Zobel v. Williams, 457 U.S. 55, 102 S.Ct. 2309, 72 L.Ed.2d 672 (1982) (noted 12 U.C.L.A.-Alaska L. Rev. 119 (1983)).

4. 262 U.S. 544, 43 S.Ct. 636, 67 L.Ed. 1112 (1923); Currie & Schreter II, at 8–9. See the dissent of Brandeis and Holmes, 262 U.S. at 551–53, 43 S.Ct. at 639.

5. The earlier decision in Blake v. McClung, 172 U.S. 239, 19 S.Ct. 165, 43 L.Ed. 432 (1898) had still taken the position that the pursuit of a claim within the state did not constitute presence within the jurisdiction.

§ 3.35

1. Power Manufacturing Co. v. Saunders, 274 U.S. 490, 47 S.Ct. 678, 71 L.Ed. 1165 (1927).

§ 3.36

1. 313 U.S. 487, 61 S.Ct. 1020, 85 L.Ed. 1477 (1941). The Delaware federal court

the state in which it sits. The Supreme Court thus extended *Erie Railroad Co. v. Tompkins*[2] to encompass choice of law: "Otherwise, the accident of diversity of citizenship would constantly disturb equal administration of justice in coordinate state and federal courts sitting side by side."[3] This view recognizes conflict of laws as a part of state common law which identifies the rule of decision in state law; a federal court in diversity cases applies that rule of decision as a neutral forum in a manner that is consistent with the practice of the state in which it sits. Three decades later, in *Day & Zimmermann, Inc. v. Challoner*[4] the U.S. Supreme Court adhered to this view and required the federal court in Texas to apply the Texas place-of-tort rule referring to Cambodia despite the federal court's finding that Cambodia was a disinterested state and, moreover, that, in the appellate court's opinion,[5] Texas itself would not have applied the law of the place of the tort.

Notwithstanding the Supreme Court's unquestioning adherence, *Klaxon* seems neither constitutionally required nor necessarily to follow from *Erie* as a matter of policy.[6] In *Erie,* the policy of uniformity of

had applied New York law to the question whether interest was to be added to a jury verdict in favor of the plaintiff in an action for breach of a contract made in New York. The U.S. Supreme Court reversed: the Delaware federal court was not free to characterize the interest issue as substantive for itself, but should have determined how Delaware would characterize the issue and should then have followed that characterization.

Federal courts sitting in the District of Columbia are not required to follow the *Erie/Klaxon* doctrine but nevertheless do so analogously to promote uniformity and in deference to the District. When District law is silent, federal courts look to Maryland law. Gray v. American Express Co., 743 F.2d 10 (D.C.Cir.1984).

In federal question cases, federal common-law-choice of law rules apply. Corporacion Venezolana de Fomento v. Vintero Sales Corp., 629 F.2d 786 (2d Cir.1980), cert. denied 449 U.S. 1080, 101 S.Ct. 863, 66 L.Ed.2d 804 (1981). For an application see Aaron Ferer & Sons Ltd. v. Chase Manhattan Bank, 731 F.2d 112 (2d Cir.1984) (applying § 188 of the Second Restatement). It seems as yet undecided whether *Klaxon* requires reference to state law or whether federal choice-of-law rules apply when the court has both federal question and diversity jurisdiction: Trinh v. Citibank, N.A., 623 F.Supp. 1526 (E.D.Mich.1985), affirmed 850 F.2d 1164 (6th Cir.1988), cert. denied 496 U.S. 912, 110 S.Ct. 2602, 110 L.Ed.2d 282 (1990) (federal and state law pointed to same result).

2. 304 U.S. 64, 58 S.Ct. 817, 82 L.Ed. 1188 (1938). The plaintiff had been injured

by a projecting object on a railroad car on the railroad's right of way in Pennsylvania. He brought suit in New York federal court. The trial court refused to apply Pennsylvania common law (under which the plaintiff would have been considered a trespasser) and ruled that the question was one of "general law." The jury brought in a verdict of $30,000 and the Second Circuit affirmed. The U.S. Supreme Court reversed. See discussion following n.5 infra.

For purposes of diversity jurisdiction, the determination of a litigant's state citizenship is controlled by federal common law, not by the law of any state. Kantor v. Wellesley Galleries, Ltd., 704 F.2d 1088 (9th Cir.1983); Rodriguez Diaz v. Sierra Martinez, 665 F.Supp. 96 (D.Puerto Rico 1987), judgment vacated 853 F.2d 1027 (1st Cir.1988); Wilson By And Through Wilson v. Kimble, 573 F.Supp. 501 (D.Colo.1983) (minor retains father's domicile though living with estranged mother); state citizenship is equivalent of domicile: Crowley v. Glaze, 710 F.2d 676 (10th Cir.1983). For discussion of when a citizen of the United States who resides abroad is a citizen of a particular state for purposes of diversity jurisdiction, see 54 A.L.R.Fed. 422 (1981).

3. 313 U.S. at 496, 61 S.Ct. at 1021–22.

4. 423 U.S. 3, 96 S.Ct. 167, 46 L.Ed.2d 3 (1975).

5. Challoner v. Day & Zimmermann, Inc., 512 F.2d 77, 81, 84–85 (5th Cir.1975), cert. granted, judgment vacated 423 U.S. 3, 96 S.Ct. 167, 46 L.Ed.2d 3 (1975).

6. See Borchers, The Origins of Diversity Jurisdiction, The Rise of Legal Positiv-

decision between state and federal courts sitting in the same state was but one aspect. Indeed, had this been the only ground, the *Erie* decision could have rested, as did the concurrence of Justice Reed,[7] on the interpretation of the words "the laws of the several states" in the Judiciary Act of 1789[8] to include not only state statutory but also state decisional law. Instead, the majority chose to focus on the previous assumption by the federal courts that they had "power to declare rules of decision which Congress was confessedly without power to enact as statutes."[9] In the absence of congressional (federal) law-making power, the practice of declaring general rules of decision therefore " . . . invaded rights which in our opinion were reserved by the Constitution to the several states."[10] This led the Court to conclude that "there is no federal general common law,"[11] a statement which, even when uttered, was overbroad.[12]

Klaxon seems not to rest on the same constitutional prohibitions, despite the Court's statement to the contrary.[13] As a number of commentators have shown,[14] the ordering of the relations among the States of the Union is a uniquely *federal* function. The reach of state laws, albeit limited by the loose standards of the Due Process and Full Faith and Credit Clauses,[15] should no more be left to the unilateral determination by individual states than is the determination of their physical boundaries. Authority for federal lawmaking in conflicts law moreover need not be derived from principles of "federalism"[16] alone; it may also be based on the Full Faith and Credit Clause.[17]

ism, and a Brave New World for *Erie* and *Klaxon*, 72 Tex. L. Rev. 79 (1993) (*Klaxon* unwise and unnecessary).

7. 304 U.S. at 90–92, 58 S.Ct. at 828.

8. See § 34 of the Judiciary Act of 1789, 1 Stat. 92 (as amended: 28 U.S.C.A. § 1652).

9. 304 U.S. at 72, 58 S.Ct. at 819.

10. 304 U.S. at 80, 58 S.Ct. at 823.

11. 304 U.S. at 78, 58 S.Ct. at 822.

12. In Hinderlider v. La Plata River & Cherry Creek Ditch Co., 304 U.S. 92, 58 S.Ct. 803, 82 L.Ed. 1202 (1938), decided the same day as *Erie,* "federal common law" was used to apportion an interstate stream.

13. "We are of opinion that the prohibitions declared in *Erie* . . . against such independent determinations by the federal courts extends to the field of conflict of laws." 313 U.S. at 496, 61 S.Ct. at 1021. It is noteworthy that the *Erie* decision held that the federal court could not decide the issue of liability according to "general" law but had to apply state law and seemed to *assume* that the appropriate state law was that of Pennsylvania. There was no suggestion that the forum's (New York's) choice-

of-law rules would refer to Pennsylvania although this, no doubt, would have been the result under the First Restatement.

14. For a summary see Hay, Reflections on Conflict of Laws Methodology, 32 Hastings L.J. 1644, 1673 (1981). See also Pollak, In Praise of Friendly, 133 U. Pa. L. Rev. 39, 52 (1984).

15. Supra §§ 3.20–3.30.

16. In World–Wide Volkswagen Corp. v. Woodson, 444 U.S. 286, 293, 100 S.Ct. 559, 565, 62 L.Ed.2d 490 (1980), the Court relied on "principles of interstate federalism" in further refining its approach to state judicial jurisdiction. A corollary is Zschernig v. Miller, 389 U.S. 429, 88 S.Ct. 664, 19 L.Ed.2d 683 (1968) (Oregon's "Iron Curtain Statute" impermissibly invaded the federal foreign relations power). To put it differently, the ordering of the relationships between the Union (or its components) and foreign nations is a federal function.

17. 1 W. Crosskey, Politics and the Constitution in the History of the United States 541–57 (1953). See Nadelmann, Conflict of Laws: International and Interstate 213–14 (1972).

The policy basis for *Klaxon* also seems different from *Erie*. As in *Erie* the Court was concerned that there be uniformity of decision as between state and federal courts sitting in the same state: it opted for intrastate over interstate uniformity with respect to conflicts decisions by federal courts. The assumption of the Court has been that avoidance of intrastate forum shopping requires the application of *Erie* to conflicts law. However, to the extent that federal conflicts decisions are based on the existence of federal authority to order relations among the states— which, according to *Erie,* would not be the case with respect to substantive law—such decisions would *supersede* state conflicts law under the Supremacy Clause.[18] Under this view, the states would be required to apply the federal conflicts law in state court cases. Thus, both intrastate *and* interstate uniformity could be achieved by adopting a federal conflicts law. However, *Erie* was in fact a conflicts case and the Court's recent decision in *Challoner*[19] reaffirms its adherence to *Klaxon* in requiring federal courts to apply state choice of law in diversity cases. Meanwhile, *Allstate Insurance Co. v. Hague*[20] teaches that the Court will not interfere with the choice-of-law process in state courts except in those isolated cases where the absence of *any* significant state contact and interest of a state precludes the application of its local law on due process grounds.[21]

The interplay of *Erie* and *Klaxon* raises a number of practical problems, considered in subsequent sections. Part V explores the extent to which federal common law does exist and the possible future directions that its development may take.

B. *ERIE*—PROBLEMS IN PRACTICE

§ 3.37 The *Erie* doctrine requires the application of state law whenever the issue in question is "outcome determinative," that is: "does it significantly affect the result of litigation for a federal court to disregard a law of a State that would be controlling in an action upon the same claim by the same parties in a State court?"[1] As the Supreme Court eventually reformulated this test, federal courts may resort to federal common law only if application of federal common law will not

---

18. G. Gilmore, The Ages of American Law 21, 32–34, 95–98 (1977); Westen & Lehman, Is There Life for *Erie* after the Death of Diversity?, 78 Mich. L. Rev. 311, 370 n.176 (1980).

19. Day & Zimmermann, Inc. v. Challoner, 423 U.S. 3, 96 S.Ct. 167, 46 L.Ed.2d 3 (1975).

20. Supra § 3.23.

21. There has been growing criticism of *Klaxon,* especially also for the wholesale forum-shopping it encourages in tort, particularly mass tort cases. See Borchers, supra n.6; Symposium: Conflict of Laws and Complex Litigation Issues in Mass Tort Lit-

igation, 1989 U. Ill. L. Rev. 35 (with contributions by Juenger, Lowenfeld, and Weintraub). For a proposed legislative solution, see infra § 3.46 n.20. See also American Law Institute, Complex Litigation Project 6.01 (1994)(proposing federal choice-of-law rules for application in consolidated cases). For additional references, see Yonover, Ascertaining State Law: The Continuing *Erie* Dilemma, 38 DePaul L. Rev. 1 (1988) (see particularly n.217).

§ 3.37

1. Guaranty Trust Co. v. York, 326 U.S. 99, 109, 65 S.Ct. 1464, 1470, 89 L.Ed. 2079 (1945).

upset the "twin aims of the *Erie* rule: discouragement of forum-shopping and avoidance of inequitable administration of the laws."[2] Thus, the Supreme Court has required resort to state law when the claim was barred under state law,[3] when state law provided that contributory negligence be pleaded as an affirmative defense,[4] when state law provided that an action was not commenced, and the statute of limitations tolled, until the summons is actually served,[5] and when state law prescribed the standard for setting aside a verdict as excessive,[6] in addition to issues more directly relating to what may be regarded as substantive areas of the law.[7] The literal application of the "outcome determinative" test appeared to lead to an ever expanding coverage of issues by the *Erie* doctrine since it is difficult to imagine an issue that could not affect the outcome of litigation. Some limitation on the reach of *Erie* became inevitable in the administration of justice in the federal courts.

2. Hanna v. Plumer, 380 U.S. 460, 468, 85 S.Ct. 1136, 1142, 14 L.Ed.2d 8 (1965).

3. Id. See also Sun Oil Co. v. Wortman, 486 U.S. 717, 108 S.Ct. 2117, 100 L.Ed. 743 (1988) (the forum may constitutionally apply its longer statute of limitations to a foreign claim; a federal court sitting in diversity would have to do likewise). For criticism of *Wortman*, see supra § 3.9 n.6.

4. Palmer v. Hoffman, 318 U.S. 109, 63 S.Ct. 477, 87 L.Ed. 645 (1943).

5. Walker v. Armco Steel Corp., 446 U.S. 740, 100 S.Ct. 1978, 64 L.Ed.2d 659 (1980) (adhering to Ragan v. Merchants Transfer and Warehouse Co., 337 U.S. 530, 69 S.Ct. 1233, 93 L.Ed. 1520 (1949)). Further examples include: Woods v. Interstate Realty Co., 337 U.S. 535, 69 S.Ct. 1235, 93 L.Ed. 1524 (1949) (federal court closed, under state law, to plaintiff who failed to qualify to do business in the state; on court closing see infra); Cohen v. Beneficial Industrial Loan Corp., 337 U.S. 541, 69 S.Ct. 1221, 93 L.Ed. 1528 (1949) (state law with respect to posting security for costs in shareholder's derivative suit). With respect to whether an arbitration clause stays litigation compare Prima Paint Corp. v. Flood & Conklin Manufacturing Co., 388 U.S. 395, 87 S.Ct. 1801, 18 L.Ed.2d 1270 (1967) (federal standard if the contract is covered by the Federal Arbitration Act) with Bernhardt v. Polygraphic Co. of America, 350 U.S. 198, 76 S.Ct. 273, 100 L.Ed. 199 (1956) (state). See also Bullins v. City of Philadelphia, 516 F.Supp. 728 (E.D.Pa.1981) (state rule providing for award of prejudgment interest to plaintiffs in wrongful death suits for delay caused by defendants was "substantive" for diversity purposes).

The Statute of Frauds is substantive for *Erie* purposes and state law applies: Leh-

man v. Dow Jones & Co., Inc., 606 F.Supp. 1152 (S.D.N.Y.1985), affirmed in part, reversed in part 783 F.2d 285 (2d Cir.1986). The availability and amount of pre-judgment interest in a contract action is a substantive matter to which state law applies in diversity cases. See Webco Industries v. Thermatool Corp., 278 F.3d 1120 (10th Cir. 2002).

6. Gasperini v. Center for Humanities, Inc., 518 U.S. 415, 116 S.Ct. 2211, 135 L.Ed.2d 659 (1996) (application of the different federal standard might lead to substantial variations between verdicts in federal and state courts, thus implicating the twin aims of *Erie*). The decision is discussed infra § 3.39 n.24.

See also Servicios Comerciales Andinos, S.A. v. General Electric Del Caribe, Inc., 145 F.3d 463 (1st Cir.1998) (Puerto Rican rule on attorney's fees "substantive" for *Erie* purposes, but "procedural" for conflicts purposes, thus resulting in the application of the Puerto Rican rule by the federal court); Gil de Rebollo v. Miami Heat Associations, Inc., 137 F.3d 56 (1st Cir. 1998) (clash between federal and Puerto Rican Rules of Federal Procedure on whether attorney's fees are "costs"; federal rule prevailed).

7. The district court's application of the federal doctrine of *forum non conveniens* rather than Florida's rule did not address a matter of substance and did not transgress the *Erie* limitations. "The *forum non conveniens* doctrine is a rule of venue, not a rule of decision." Sibaja v. Dow Chemical Co., 757 F.2d 1215, 1219 (11th Cir.1985). See also Nolan v. Boeing Co., 919 F.2d 1058, 1068 n.11 (5th Cir.1990), cert. denied 499 U.S. 962, 111 S.Ct. 1587, 113 L.Ed.2d 651 (1991).

1. *Byrd, Hanna and the Federal Rules*

§ 3.38 *Byrd v. Blue Ridge Rural Electric Cooperative, Inc.*[1] and *Hanna v. Plumer*[2] marked the turning point in the expanding effect of the "outcome determinative" test and placed some practical limits on the *Erie* doctrine. In *Byrd* the defense was raised that the plaintiff was the defendant's statutory employee under the state worker compensation act and was therefore barred from bringing an action at law. The *Erie* issue was whether this question should be decided by the court, as provided by state law, or by the jury as provided by federal law. The Supreme Court reversed the appellate court's resort to state law and directed that federal law be followed. The Court concluded that although the "outcome" might be affected if the question were submitted to the jury, "there are affirmative countervailing considerations at work here. The federal system is an independent system for administering justice to litigants.... An essential characteristic of that system is the manner in which, in civil common-law actions, it distributes trial functions between judge and jury and, under the influence—if not the command—of the Seventh Amendment, assigns the decisions of disputed questions of fact to the jury."[3]

The exception to the "outcome determinative" test in the concept of "countervailing considerations" seemingly would permit the Court to balance state and federal interests in deciding to apply state or federal law to particular issues. This would be a broad expansion of the federal judicial function and could lead to the development of considerable federal common law.

However, such a view would greatly overstate the import of *Byrd*. First, the reference, in passing, to the Seventh Amendment has meanwhile been made more definite. The Court held in 1963 that the right to jury trial in federal courts, both in diversity and other actions, is a matter of federal law under the Seventh Amendment.[4] Second, if *Erie* rests on constitutional grounds, as is arguably the case, "countervailing considerations" are only appropriate with respect to those areas in which *Erie* expressed a *policy*, that is *after* the constitutional threshold requirement has been met that federal authority exists for federal rulemaking. Third, even within the limited confines in which "countervailing considerations" could lead to the adoption of federal standards, the Court has shown considerable restraint in expanding "federal law."[5]

§ 3.38

1. 356 U.S. 525, 78 S.Ct. 893, 2 L.Ed.2d 953 (1958).

2. 380 U.S. 460, 85 S.Ct. 1136, 14 L.Ed.2d 8 (1965).

3. 356 U.S. at 537, 78 S.Ct. at 900. See also Gasperini v. Center for Humanities, Inc., 518 U.S. 415, 116 S.Ct. 2211, 135 L.Ed.2d 659 (1996) (New York law requiring *appellate* courts to apply the state law

standard de novo to review a verdict for excessiveness does not bind the federal appellate court). For discussion, see infra § 3.39 n.24.

4. Simler v. Conner, 372 U.S. 221, 83 S.Ct. 609, 9 L.Ed.2d 691 (1963).

5. See, for instance, the discussion infra at § 3.49 et seq. with respect to "federal common law;" R. Weintraub, Commentary on the Conflict of Laws 583 (3d ed. 1986).

§ 3.39 *Hanna v. Plumer*[1] involved a difference between state law which required service upon an executor by actual delivery in hand and then-Rule 4(d)(1) (now Rule 4(e)(2)) of the Federal Rules of Civil Procedure which permits service at the defendant's dwelling by delivery to an adult residing therein. In *Hanna,* service effected by leaving the papers with the defendant-executor's wife was sustained under the Federal Rule. In sustaining the force of the Federal Rules of Procedure over the competing state law, the court concluded that "the adoption of Rule 4(d)(1) . . . neither exceeded the congressional mandate embodied in the Rules Enabling Act nor transgressed constitutional bounds, and that the Rule itself is therefore the standard against which the District Court should have measured the adequacy of service."[2] As one commentator noted, "where there is no relevant Federal Rule of Civil Procedure . . . the Rules of Decision Act[3] [governs]. Where the matter in issue is covered by a Federal Rule . . . the [Rules] Enabling Act . . . constitutes the relevant standard."[4] The latter Act, consistent with the constitutional underpinnings of *Erie,* permits the promulgation of Federal Rules of Civil Procedure provided that they do "not abridge, enlarge or modify any substantive right." The Court's statement, in *Hanna,* that "the *Erie* rule has never been invoked to void a Federal Rule"[5] should not therefore be read to suggest that a Federal Rule is never subject to scrutiny. Instead, the test to be met is the proviso in the Rules Enabling Act, as derived from *Erie.* At the same time, however, *Erie* addressed a situation where, as the Court perceived it at that time, federal lawmaking authority was lacking. In contrast, "the constitutional provision for a federal court system (augmented by the Necessary and Proper Clause) carries with it congressional power to make rules governing the practice and pleading in those courts, which in turn includes a power to regulate matters which, though falling within the uncertain area between substance and procedure, are rationally capable of classification as either."[6] In *Hanna* itself, application of the Federal Rule might deprive the defendant of a defense (improper service under state-law standards) but not "abridge, enlarge or modify any substantive right," within the language of the Rules Enabling Act. The Federal Rule instead related to the manner of proceeding in federal court. It was therefore valid and to be applied. The same applies to the Federal Rules of Evidence. They apply "generally to civil actions and proceedings" in federal courts and

---

But see occasional appellate court decisions such as Brown v. Pyle, 310 F.2d 95 (5th Cir.1962); Monarch Insurance Co. of Ohio v. Spach, 281 F.2d 401 (5th Cir.1960). See also Meador, State Law and the Federal Judicial Power, 49 Va. L. Rev. 1082 (1963); Vestal, Erie R.R. v. Tompkins: A Projection, 48 Iowa L. Rev. 248 (1963).

§ 3.39

1. 380 U.S. 460, 85 S.Ct. 1136, 14 L.Ed.2d 8 (1965).

2. 380 U.S. at 463, 85 S.Ct. at 1140.

3. Supra § 3.36 n.7.

4. Ely, The Irrepressible Myth of *Erie,* 87 Harv. L. Rev. 693, 698 (1974).

5. 380 U.S. at 470, 85 S.Ct. at 1143.

6. Id. at 472, 85 S.Ct. at 1144. See also Hargrave v. Oki Nursery, Inc., 646 F.2d 716 (2d Cir.1980).

before federal magistrates (Rule 1101(b)), although it is often more difficult in this area to determine whether the inconsistent rule of state law is one of "evidence" or of state substantive law.[7]

After *Hanna* it is unlikely that any direct clash between a Federal Rule of Civil Procedure and a state rule will be resolved in favor of the state rule.[8] The question of course remains *when* is there a "direct clash"? *Ragan v. Merchants Transfer & Warehouse Co.*[9] had held that Federal Rule 3, which provides that an action commences upon "the filing [of] a complaint with the court," does not toll the state statute of limitations when state law requires service of the summons as a condition for tolling. A number of subsequent decisions considered *Ragan* to have been overruled by *Hanna*.[10] The question came up again in 1980 and the U.S. Supreme Court, in *Walker v. Armco Steel Corp.*,[11] adhered to its previous decision in *Ragan*. The Court noted that it is the function

---

7. United States v. Silverman, 745 F.2d 1386 (11th Cir.1984) (federal court properly enforced subpoena for records of complaint against lawyer under Fed. Rules Crim. Proc., Rule 17(a) and Fed. Rules Evid., Rule 501; state law of confidentiality was not applicable). Federal Rules of Evidence, rather than state law, govern admissibility of evidence in diversity cases, including admissibility of evidence of insurance. Reed v. General Motors Corp., 773 F.2d 660 (5th Cir.1985). But see Legg v. Chopra, 286 F.3d 286 (6th Cir. 2002) (state statute requiring a medical expert to be licensed in the state or a contiguous state applies in a diversity case; no conflict with either Federal Rule of Evidence 601 or 702).

See Conway v. Chemical Leaman Tank Lines, Inc., 540 F.2d 837 (5th Cir.1976), appeal after remand 610 F.2d 360 (1980). In re Air Crash Disaster Near Chicago, Illinois on May 25, 1979, 526 F.Supp. 226 (N.D.Ill.1981) involved the question whether the admissibility of evidence as to the portion of decedent's past earnings which were subject to taxation as an indicator of the tax liability for future earnings had decedent lived was governed by federal or state law. Unable to characterize the issue as "procedural" or "substantive," the court concluded that, under *Erie* and *Hanna*, state law should be applied in order to avoid the "inequitable administration of the laws" as between federal and state courts. Some rules expressly refer to state law if a claim or defense under state law is at issue. See, e.g., Rules 302 (presumptions), 501 (testimonial privileges), 601 (witness competency). Compare Norfolk & Western Railway Co. v. Liepelt, 444 U.S. 490, 100 S.Ct. 755, 62 L.Ed.2d 689 (1980) (Federal Employers Liability Act is designed to create "uniformity throughout the Union," 444 U.S. at 493 n.5, 100 S.Ct.

at 757 n.5, and thus requires federal rule) with Gulf Offshore Co. v. Mobil Oil Corp., 453 U.S. 473, 101 S.Ct. 2870, 69 L.Ed.2d 784 (1981), on remand 628 S.W.2d 171 (Tex.App.1982), error refused n.r.e., cert. denied 459 U.S. 945, 103 S.Ct. 259, 74 L.Ed.2d 202 (1982) (Outer Continental Shelf Lands Act explicitly authorizes adoption of state law unless inconsistent with federal law, therefore " 'specifically rejected national uniformity' as a paramount goal," 453 U.S. at 487, 101 S.Ct. at 2880, and state law applied). See generally Wellborn, The Federal Rules of Evidence and the Application of State Law in the Federal Courts, 55 Tex. L. Rev. 371 (1977); Seidelson, The Federal Rules of Evidence: Rule 501, *Klaxon* and the Constitution, 5 Hofstra L. Rev. 21 (1976). See also Wm. T. Thompson Co. v. General Nutrition Corp., Inc., 671 F.2d 100 (3d Cir.1982): in federal antitrust litigation which also involved pendent claims under state antitrust law, federal common law of privileges—favoring admissibility—and not state-law accountant-client privilege applied. The court left open which rule would apply if the claims were tried separately.

8. R. Weintraub, Commentary on the Conflict of Laws 663 (4th ed. 2001).

9. 337 U.S. 530, 69 S.Ct. 1233, 93 L.Ed. 1520 (1949).

10. E.g., Smith v. Peters, 482 F.2d 799 (6th Cir.1973), cert. denied 415 U.S. 989, 94 S.Ct. 1587, 39 L.Ed.2d 886 (1974); Sylvestri v. Warner & Swasey Co., 398 F.2d 598 (2d Cir.1968). See also *Hanna*, 380 U.S. at 474–78, 85 S.Ct. at 1145–48 (Harlan, J., concurring).

11. 446 U.S. 740, 100 S.Ct. 1978, 64 L.Ed.2d 659 (1980).

of a statute of limitation to establish a "deadline after which the defendant may legitimately have peace of mind."[12] As such, the "service requirement [of the state statute was] an 'integral' part of the statute of limitations both in this case and in *Ragan*."[13] Rule 3, it held, was not "intended to toll a state statute of limitations, much less … to displace state tolling rules…. Rule 3 governs the date from which various timing requirements of the *federal* rules begin to run, but does not affect state statutes of limitation."[14] Through interpretation,[15] a direct clash was avoided. Since Rule 3 was found not to apply and since the state tolling provision was an integral part of the statute of limitation, the state rule applied.[16]

The *Erie* doctrine thus retains at least two central mysteries at its core. One is determining when a federal rule or statute actually conflicts with state law. The other is the vitality of *Byrd* as a guide for determining whether to apply state or federal law in cases in which no federal

12. Id. at 751, 100 S.Ct. at 1985.

13. Id. at 752, 100 S.Ct. at 1986.

14. Id. at 751, 100 S.Ct. at 1985. In Alonzo v. ACF Property Management, Inc., 643 F.2d 578 (9th Cir.1981), the question was whether the federal observation of Veterans' Day (a day on which the federal courts were closed) tolled California's statute of limitation when California observed the holiday on a different date. In application of *Ragan* and *Walker,* the court held that state law governed and remanded for a determination of whether the day in question constituted a "day appointed by the President" within the meaning of the California computation of time statute. If, however, the cause of action is founded on federal law, *Walker* has been held not to apply and the stop-on-filing rule apparently implied by Rule 3 governs. See West v. Conrail, 481 U.S. 35, 107 S.Ct. 1538, 95 L.Ed.2d 32 (1987). Federal Rule 3 (and the computation-of-time provisions in Rule 6) have been held to apply in federal actions even when the state statute of limitations must be borrowed. See Sain v. City of Bend, 309 F.3d 1134 (9th Cir. 2002)(section 1983 action).

15. See the Court's reference to the Note of the Advisory Committee on the Rules which had recognized the potential problem but had left open its resolution. 446 U.S. at 751 n.10, 100 S.Ct. at 1985 n.10. The balance of the opinion then addresses the *function* of Rule 3 and of state limitation and tolling provisions.

In Olympic Sports Products, Inc. v. Universal Athletic Sales Co., 760 F.2d 910 (9th Cir.1985), cert. denied 474 U.S. 1060, 106 S.Ct. 804, 88 L.Ed.2d 780 (1986), the question was whether Federal Rule 41(b) (discretionary) or Cal. Code Civ. Proc. § 583(b)

(mandatory) governs dismissal for failure to prosecute in a diversity suit. Following a *Hanna* analysis, the court concluded that enforcement of the federal rule would not transgress *Erie* policies. It acknowledged that a California Supreme Court decision had noted that some section 3(b) policies are the same as those underlying statutes of limitations but concluded that the California decisions do not clearly consider "section 583(b) a statute of limitation." 760 F.2d at 916. The distinction is a very fine one, especially in light of the U.S. Supreme Court's language in *Walker* (supra nn.11–14), which the court did not cite. Nonetheless, the decision seems correct if, as the court suggests at 915, the California rule, despite its wording, is discretionary in its application. In that event the conflict disappears and no reason exists why the federal rule should not be applied. If the rules were to differ, application of the federal rule would still be justified as a housekeeping rule applicable to the federal forum alone. See infra § 3.40 n.11.

16. *Ragan* had also suggested that Rule 3 might toll a statute of limitations when the action seeks to enforce a right under a federal statute. In *Walker,* the Court expressly left this question open. *Id.* at n.11. See also Hernas v. City of Hickory Hills, 507 F.Supp. 103 (N.D.Ill.1981): in a federal question case, plaintiffs also asserted pendent claims of common law replevin and negligence, and one defendant counterclaimed for slander. Since "matters of pleading are governed by the Federal Rules of Civil Procedure regardless of the source of the substantive law," id. at 105, the claimant did not have to meet the strict pleading requirements for slander under Illinois law.

statute or rule is applicable. The more recent Supreme Court cases offer no clear answer on either score.

While *Walker* and *Ragan* suggested a very narrow reading for federal statutes and rules, later cases take a much broader view of the scope of federal law. In *Stewart Organization, Inc. v. Ricoh*[17] the Court confronted a conflict between the federal policy of enforcing exclusive forum selection clauses, and the then-existing Alabama rule voiding such clauses on public policy grounds. While this case might seemed to have presented the classic "unguided" *Erie* question—because the federal rule was of common law origin[18]—the Court held that the Alabama rule actually conflicted with a federal statute, and that because the federal statute was valid Alabama state law must yield. The federal statute, however—Section 1404 of the Judiciary Code—says nothing explicitly about party forum choice. To the contrary, Section 1404(a) merely provides for venue transfer between federal courts to serve "the convenience of the parties" and "in the interest of justice...."[19] Despite the lack of explicit reference to party choice, the Court held that the statute's policy was broad enough to take account of private expressions of venue preference, meaning that the contrary state law must yield.

Nearly as striking in its zeal to interpret federal law broadly was *Burlington Northern Railroad Co. v. Woods.*[20] *Burlington*, another case concerning Alabama law, involved the application in federal court appeals of a state statute imposing a mandatory ten percent penalty in case in which a defendant took an appeal that resulted in an affirmance of the judgment. The Court held that the state statute must yield to Federal Rule of Appellate Procedure 38, which provides that "just damages" may be imposed on a party taking a frivolous appeal.[21] The Court held that Appellate Rule 38 was broad enough to displace the state statute.

Burlington and *Stewart* evince a much different approach to deciding what constitutes a "conflict" between a federal rule or statute and state law than that demonstrated by *Walker* and *Ragan*. In *Walker* and *Ragan* the Court seemed to take something like an "impossibility" approach. A federal statute or rule conflicted only if it were impossible to apply both it and the state rule. Because Federal Rule 3 could literally be applied without disrupting the state rule of tolling the statute of limitations on service of the complaint, no conflict existed and state law governed under the Rules of Decision Act. But no such explanation can take account of *Stewart* and *Burlington*. In both cases, both the state and federal rules could have co-existed peacefully. The Court could have said, for instance, in *Stewart* that the Alabama rule of voiding forum selection clauses held sway, but that Section 1404(a) applied to allow

17. 487 U.S. 22, 108 S.Ct. 2239, 101 L.Ed.2d 22 (1988).

18. See, e.g., The Bremen v. Zapata Offshore Co., 407 U.S. 1, 92 S.Ct. 1907, 32 L.Ed.2d 513 (1972).

19. 28 U.S.C.A. § 1404(a).

20. 480 U.S. 1, 107 S.Ct. 967, 94 L.Ed.2d 1 (1987).

21. Fed. R. App. Proc. 38.

venue transfer under the standards normally applied in the absence of a forum clause. The Court could have said in *Burlington* that the state affirmance penalty applied, and that discretionary penalties for a frivolous appeal could be applied as well—perhaps with an offset for the mandatory penalty imposed by state law. In both cases, however, the Court displaced state law entirely so that federal law could occupy the zone without any need to take account of state policies.

While this latter approach means that state law has a diminishing role to play in diversity cases, the *Stewart–Burlington* line of cases is probably the best predictor for most cases of how the Court will resolve such questions in the future. *Ragan*, decided very early in the life of the *Erie* doctrine, took an extremely narrow view of Rule 3—so narrow that many lower court cases before *Walker* concluded that *Ragan* was no longer good law.[22] *Walker's* reaffirmance of *Ragan* was a much a bow to *stare decisis* as it was to the validity of *Ragan's* methodology, and the "broad" view of federal policy seems to have captured large majorities of the Court in more recent times. The Supreme Court's later decision in *Semtek International Inc. v. Lockheed Martin Corp.*,[23] discussed extensively in the section below, somewhat in the mold of *Walker* and *Ragan*, took a very narrow (perhaps implausibly so) view of a Federal Rule. In *Semtek* the rule in question was Rule 41, dealing with the meaning of "with prejudice" in the context of a voluntary dismissal. The Court there held that "with prejudice" language in the rule only prevented refiling in the same court and had no preclusive effect in other courts. *Semtek*, though, appears to be a special case motivated by the Court's concern that a more literal reading of Rule 41 would have given it effect beyond the permissible bounds of the Rules Enabling Act. Absent, then, the sorts of concerns present in *Walker* and *Semtek* it seems likely that the Court will continue to give fairly broad interpretation to federal procedural laws.

As to the vitality of *Byrd* "balancing" approach, seemingly rejected by *Hanna's* articulation of the "twin aims" test,[24] the Court has also given mixed signals. The current source of the confusion is the Court's opinion in *Gasperini v. Center for Humanities, Inc.*[25] *Gasperini* involved a New York "tort reform" statute directing New York appellate courts (and, apparently by implication, trial courts) to set aside verdicts that "deviate[] materially from what would be reasonable compensation."[26] This standard was intentionally more searching than deferential "shocks

---

22. See also Freer, The State of *Erie* After *Gasperini*, 76 Tex. L. Rev. 1637, 1642 n.46 (1998).

23. 531 U.S. 497, 121 S.Ct. 1021, 149 L.Ed.2d 32 (2001).

24. See supra n.10.

25. 518 U.S. 415, 116 S.Ct. 2211, 135 L.Ed.2d 659 (1996).

26. N.Y. Civ. Prac. L. & R. § 5501(c). For discussions of the conflict between state

and federal law in *Gasperini*, see Freer, supra n.22, at 1639–41; Floyd, *Erie* Awry: A Comment on Gasperini v. Center for Humanities, Inc., 1997 B.Y.U. L. Rev. 267, 267–69; Perdue, The Sources and Scope of Federal Procedural Common Law: Some Reflections on *Erie* and *Gasperini*, 26 U. Kan. L. Rev. 751 (1998); Rowe, Not Bad for Government Work: Does Anyone Else Think the Supreme Court is Doing a Halfway Decent Job in Its *Erie–Hanna* Juris-

the conscience" standard applied by New York courts before the passage of the statute, and generally applied by federal courts as a matter of common law. Moreover, the statute provided for de novo review of trial court decisions, a marked departure for the usual "abuse of discretion" standard applied before statute in New York courts, and as a matter of common law in federal courts.[27] *Gasperini* partially resembled *Byrd* in that the relative role of judge and jury in federal court was implicated, and the *Gasperini* plaintiff (who lost a large verdict when the lower federal courts applied the New York statute) also invoked the spectre of the Seventh Amendment—in this case, though, its "reexamination" clause.[28]

In a dépeçage ruling, the Court held that the federal *trial* court must apply the state statute rather than the federal common-law standard, because failure to do so would lead to forum shopping, thus frustrating the "twin aims" that the Court articulated in *Hanna*.[29] But, citing for *Byrd* for the first time in decades,[30] the Court concluded that New York's statutory mandate of *de novo* appellate review of must give way to the federal rule of deferential, abuse-of-discretion review.[31] As commentators have noted, the Court's rationale for adhering to federal policy is somewhat unclear, just as it was in *Byrd*.[32] At some points the Court appears to be merely "influenced" by the Seventh Amendment, while in other points it appears to be saying that the result follows directly from the Seventh Amendment, making *Erie* and the Rules of Decision Act essentially irrelevant.[33]

Probably the fairest reading of *Gasperini* and the earlier cases under the Rules of Decision Act is that *Hanna* "twin aims" test holds sway in most circumstances. The open-ended *Byrd* balancing test is confined to certain limited circumstances, of which the only clearly identifiable one is the allocation of responsibility between judge and jury. In this circumstance, federal policy is strong and state law gives way even if displacing state law might encourage intrastate forum shopping.

2. *Court–Closing Rules*

§ 3.40 A number of cases involve state rules or policies closing the local courts to certain actions.[1] These rules give rise to two questions: when may a state constitutionally employ a forum-closing rule and, secondly, is such a rule or policy binding on federal courts sitting in the

---

prudence?, 73 Notre Dame L. Rev. 963 (1998).

27. See Floyd, supra n.25, at 268.

28. Freer, supra n.22, at 1657.

29. *Gasperini*, 518 U.S. at 428, 116 S.Ct. at 2220, 135 L.Ed.2d 659.

30. See Freer, supra n.22, at 1657 (*Gasperini* contains Supreme Court's first discussion of *Byrd* in 38 years).

31. 518 U.S. at 430, 116 S.Ct. at 2225, 135 L.Ed.2d 659.

32. Freer, supra n.22, at 1657.

33. Freer, supra n.22, at 1658.

§ 3.40

1. The present discussion only concerns suits on original causes of action. In the area of judgments, the Full Faith and Credit Clause mandates the recognition of a sister-state money judgment even if the underlying cause of action could not have been brought in the forum. Fauntleroy v. Lum, 210 U.S. 230, 28 S.Ct. 641, 52 L.Ed. 1039 (1908).

same state in application of the *Erie* doctrine. *Hughes v. Fetter*[2] addressed the first issue and held that Wisconsin could not close its courts to an action under the Illinois Wrongful Death Act in circumstances where the forum had no strong policy against such actions. The latter was evidenced by the fact that such actions could be brought for a death suffered in Wisconsin. The forum should of course be able to close its courts for reasons of *forum non conveniens*. This might be the case when the case involves either foreign parties or foreign facts. In *Hughes* all the parties were Wisconsin residents, while all of the facts related to Illinois. The Supreme Court concluded that the denial of a Wisconsin forum could not be considered an application of *forum non conveniens* and was based only on the foreign origin of the cause of action.[3]

Angel v. Bullington[4] addressed the question of forum-closing rules in federal courts sitting in diversity. The plaintiff had foreclosed on Virginia land upon the North Carolina buyer's default and sought to enforce a deficiency against the buyer in North Carolina. North Carolina state law provided that, in a case like this, the holder of notes secured by a deed of trust was not entitled to a deficiency judgment. On appeal, the North Carolina Supreme Court ordered dismissal on the basis of the statutory provision. The plaintiff did not seek review of the state court decision by the U.S. Supreme Court but, instead, brought a new action in the federal district court in North Carolina. The resulting judgment in plaintiff's favor was reversed by the U.S. Supreme Court on the ground that the constitutionality of North Carolina's forum-closing rule was res judicata because the plaintiff failed to seek further review of the state court decision so that the issue could no longer be reopened collaterally. The dissents by Justices Jackson, Reed, and Rutledge raised questions whether the North Carolina state court judgment was *on the merits* rather than simply addressing the *power* of the state courts to entertain the action. However, the controlling issue was whether the state could close its courts and constitutionally deny the plaintiff a forum. On that issue, the North Carolina court had been closed notwithstanding the plaintiff's constitutional protestations and, failing an appeal, that issue was concluded. The Supreme Court then addressed the second question of whether the application of *Erie* principles called for a parallel closing of the federal courts in the state. On this second issue the Court applied *Erie* and held that the federal court was also closed to the plaintiff because "a federal court in North Carolina [sitting in diversity] cannot give that which North Carolina has [constitutionally] withheld."[5]

The Rules of Decision Act provides for the application of state law by federal courts "as rules of decision in civil actions ... " except "where the Constitution or treaties of the United States or Acts of

---

2. 341 U.S. 609, 71 S.Ct. 980, 95 L.Ed. 1212 (1951). See also supra § 3.25.

3. See R. Weintraub, Commentary on the Conflict of Laws 681 (4th ed. 2001); Stein, *Erie* and Court Access, 100 Yale L.J. 1935 (1991).

4. 330 U.S. 183, 67 S.Ct. 657, 91 L.Ed. 832 (1947).

5. 330 U.S. at 192, 67 S.Ct. at 662.

Congress otherwise require or provide ... ,"[6] and the Judicial Code establishes that "district courts shall have original jurisdiction."[7] It can be argued that a forum-closing rule technically is not a "rule of decision," and the general grant of diversity jurisdiction could be regarded as sufficient basis for federal courts to ignore a state forum-closing rule. Such a view, however, would give too much weight to the technical difference between a forum-closing rule and a rule of substantive state law denying recovery which a federal court would be bound to follow under the Rules of Decision Act and, indeed, *Erie*.[8] The Supreme Court said as much in *Angel v. Bullington* when it noted that the North Carolina statute was "expressive of North Carolina policy. The essence of diversity jurisdiction is that a federal court enforces State law and State policy."[9] This statement suggests that federal courts must follow *all* state forum-closing rules.[10] However, such a reading would be too broad since not all state forum-closing rules express state policies that reach the federal court. A suggested test is that "state forum-closing rules that are rationally applicable only when trial is held in the state [court and do not go to substantive issues], should not be followed when the forum is shifted to a federal court sitting in the state. Forum non conveniens is one such solely forum-centered policy."[11] By contrast, North Carolina's forum-closing rule in *Angel v. Bullington* may be regarded to express a substantive policy, protective of North Carolina debtors; to the extent that it is constitutional, it should be applied by a federal court sitting in diversity.

Recent authorities, however, seem to give a larger role to federal common law than this would suggest. The doctrine of forum non conveniens, for instance, operates as a kind of door closing (or, in its absence, a door opening) doctrine. Nonetheless, the weight of authority is quite heavily on the side of applying the federal doctrine in diversity cases because it "is a rule of venue, not a rule of decision."[12]

The Supreme Court's decision in *Semtek International Inc. v. Lockheed Martin Corp.*[13] may indicate, however, increased scrutiny of Federal Rules of Civil Procedure. In *Semtek* the plaintiff filed a California state court action, which was removed to a California federal court on diversi-

---

6. 28 U.S.C.A. § 1652.

7. 28 U.S.C.A. § 1332(a)(1).

8. R. Weintraub, supra n.3, at 601–02. But cf. Hargrave v. Oki Nursery, Inc., 646 F.2d 716 (2d Cir.1980).

9. 330 U.S. at 191, 67 S.Ct. at 662.

10. See Marquez v. Hahnemann Medical College and Hospital, 435 F.Supp. 972, 973 (E.D.Pa.1976) (*Erie* precludes the "maintenance in the federal courts of suits to which the state [has] closed its doors," citing to Woods v. Interstate Realty Co., 337 U.S. 535, 69 S.Ct. 1235, 93 L.Ed. 1524 (1949)). For discussion of a case parallel to *Marquez* see infra § 3.41 n.2 et seq.

For non-access statutes for failure to qualify as a foreign corporation see § 23.7 infra.

11. R. Weintraub, supra n.3. See also supra § 3.39 n.15.

12. Sibaja v. Dow Chemical Corp., 757 F.2d 1215, 1219 (11th Cir.), cert. denied, 474 U.S. 948, 106 S.Ct. 347, 88 L.Ed.2d 294 (1985). See also Rivendell Forest Prods. Ltd. v. Canadian Pacific Ltd., 2 F.3d 990, 992 (10th Cir.1993) (Surveying authorities and concluding that cases and commentators are "virtually unanimous" in endorsing application of federal law).

13. 531 U.S. 497, 121 S.Ct. 1021, 149 L.Ed.2d 32 (2001).

ty grounds, alleging various business torts against the defendant. The defendant successfully moved to dismiss the action under California's two-year statute of limitations. The dismissal order purported to dismiss the plaintiff's claims " 'in their entirety on the merits and with prejudice.' "[14] Under California law, a statute of limitations dismissal generally would not preclude relitigation in another forum with a longer applicable statute. Although the plaintiff appealed the judgment of dismissal, however, it did not contest the purported "merits" dismissal by the district court. The Ninth Circuit eventually affirmed the judgment of dismissal.

The plaintiff then refiled the case in a Maryland state court. Maryland has a longer statute of limitations and no applicable borrowing statute. The Maryland trial court, however, dismissed the action on res judicata grounds, reasoning that the earlier federal judgment's effect was determined by federal law, and that since the district court had entered a "merits" dismissal that this precluded relitigation. Maryland's intermediate appellate court affirmed, its highest court declined to review the matter, and the United States Supreme Court then granted certiorari.

A unanimous Court began by rejecting the opposing contentions of the parties regarding the principles that should control. The plaintiff contended that under the old case of *Dupasseur v. Rochereau*[15] state law must control the effect of a federal court diversity judgment. The Court rejected this argument because *Dupasseur*'s holding rested upon the Conformity Act under which—before the passage of the Rules Enabling Act and the consequent adoption of the Federal Rules of Civil Procedure—federal courts followed state law in non-equity procedural matters.

On the other hand, the Court also rejected the defendant's contention that the effect of the district court's dismissal was controlled by Federal Rule of Civil Procedure 41(b). Rule 41(b) provides that except for dismissal on jurisdictional, venue or improper party joinder grounds, an involuntary dismissal "operates as an adjudication on the merits" unless the dismissing court otherwise specifies. In this case, not only had the dismissal not otherwise specified, it had expressly stated that the dismissal was a merits dismissal. The Court rejected the defendant's line of argument, however, as resting upon what it called a faulty, "unstated minor premise"[16] that all merits dismissals have claim preclusive effect. Rather, said the Court, such a dismissal under Rule 41(b) merely "relates to the dismissing court itself,"[17] i.e., it precludes refiling of the same action in the same court but not in other courts.

Interestingly, the Court's narrow reading of Rule 41(b) was clearly influenced by *Erie* and Rules Enabling Act concerns. If, said the Court, Rule 41(b) also precluded relitigation in other courts it "would arguably

14. Id. at 499, 121 S.Ct. at 1023.

15. 88 U.S. (21 Wall.) 130, 22 L.Ed. 588 (1875).

16. 531 U.S. at 501, 121 S.Ct. at 1025.

17. Id. at 505, 121 S.Ct. at 1027.

violate the jurisdictional limitation of the Rules Enabling Act.... "[18] In addition, according to the Court, such an interpretation of Rule 41(b) "would in many cases violate the federalism principle of *Erie* ... by engendering 'substantial variations [in outcomes] between state and federal litigation' "[19] and would thereby encourage intrastate forum shopping.

There are important implications to the Court's discussion. First, the Court's reference to the Rules Enabling Act indicates that it is clearly conscious of that Act as a limitation on the scope of the Federal Rules. In past cases, the Court has given only a nod to limitations on federal power to adopt procedural rules and statutes.[20] Second, and probably more surprisingly, the Court's discussion appears to view the "twin aims"—i.e., the avoidance of forum shopping and inequitable administration of the laws—of *Erie* as independently limiting the scope of Federal Rules of Civil Procedure. This appears to reject the proposition clearly advanced in *Hanna* that the "twin aims" test exists only as a limitation on federal court *common law* power to create procedural norms applicable in federal courts. Indeed *Hanna* expressly rejected as "fundament[ally] flaw[ed]" the contention that the likelihood of forum shopping could invalidate or limit the application of a Federal Rule of Civil Procedure in federal court.[21]

The ultimate resolution of this tension between *Semtek* and *Hanna* remains in doubt.[22] Notably, the *Semtek* court did not hold that Rule 41(b) was invalid nor did it do more than suggest that a broader reading of the rule would have been problematic. Indeed the Court advanced several practical justifications for its reading of the rule and purported to ground its reading both in precedent and in the text of the rule. Thus, *Semtek*'s discussion of the Rules Enabling Act and *Erie* is properly viewed as dictum. It does suggest, however, that the Court is open to *Erie*-based arguments for limiting the scope of the Federal Rules and that broad application of them may not always be appropriate.

§ 3.41 A different problem is involved when a rule of state law does not *close* the local forum but seeks to *restrict* litigation to a particular forum in the state. A number of decisions have held that a state rule providing that certain actions, for instance against municipali-

---

18.   531 U.S. at 503, 121 S.Ct. at 1025.

19.   531 U.S. at 504, 121 S.Ct. at 1026 (internal citations omitted).

20. See, e.g., Stewart Organization v. Ricoh, 487 U.S. 22, 108 S.Ct. 2239, 101 L.Ed.2d 22 (1988); Hanna v. Plumer, 380 U.S. 460, 472, 85 S.Ct. 1136, 1144, 14 L.Ed.2d 8 (1965) (Federal Rule is valid as long as it is "rationally capable" of being classified as procedural).

21. *Hanna*, 380 U.S. at 469, 85 S.Ct. at 1143, 14 L.Ed.2d 8.

22. Some commentary suggests that *Semtek* does signal the Court's willingness to treat the second sentence of the Rules Enabling Act as a significant limitation on the scope of Federal Rules of Civil Procedure. See Stephen Burbank, *Semtek*, Forum Shopping and Federal Common Law, 77 Notre Dame L. Rev. 1027 (2002) (concluding that *Semtek* was correctly decided); Note, Leading Cases, 115 Harv. L. Rev. 467, 467 (2001) ("the Court in Semtek correctly recognized that the importance of the jurisdictional limitation of the Rules Enabling Act").

ties, may only be brought in state court will not close the federal forum.[1] The problem has arisen in the context of state law provisions requiring a claimant to pursue the cause of action before a non-judicial hearing panel before proceeding with litigation. An example is *Edelson v. Soricelli*[2] which involved a Pennsylvania statutory requirement that plaintiffs in medical malpractice suits first take recourse to the state Arbitration Panels for Health Care before appealing (for a trial de novo) to the Pennsylvania state Court of Common Pleas. The federal trial court dismissed plaintiff's complaint on the basis of the statutory requirement and the Third Circuit affirmed. The case did not involve an attempt, by state law, to close the federal forum,[3] but rather the interposition of another forum before litigation in either state or federal courts. The majority opinion in the Third Circuit rejected the argument that the state rule was a procedural requirement which, under *Hanna*,[4] need not be followed in federal court because "federal plaintiffs seeking medical malpractice damages … may not have rights superior to state citizen plaintiffs…."[5] Plaintiff also argued, and the Third Circuit acknowledged, that with only nine of 2,466 claims having reached the arbitral hearing stage, the "ambitious state program has fallen woefully short of the promise."[6] However, the Court did not agree that "countervailing considerations," under *Byrd*,[7] existed to permit disregard of the state rule. Pennsylvania's strong state interest[8] dictated a narrow reading of *Byrd*.[9]

The majority's rejection of the procedural characterization excepted from *Erie* by *Hanna* is based primarily on the Supreme Court's interpretation of *Erie* as precluding "maintenance in the federal courts of suits to which the state has closed its doors."[10] The *Edelson* case of course did not involve a true forum-closing rule. Rather the rule shifted hearing functions to an arbitration panel. That panel had "powers of fact finding, subpoena and, … may determine liability and award damages.

---

§ 3.41

1. Markham v. City of Newport News, 292 F.2d 711 (4th Cir.1961); Baton Rouge Contracting Co. v. West Hatchie Drainage District, 279 F.Supp. 430 (N.D.Miss.1968). But see Zeidner v. Wulforst, 197 F.Supp. 23 (E.D.N.Y.1961).

2. 610 F.2d 131 (3d Cir.1979). In Mattos v. Thompson, 491 Pa. 385, 421 A.2d 190 (1980), the Pennsylvania Supreme Court subsequently overturned the Pennsylvania statute on state constitutional grounds. See also White v. Lavigne, 741 F.2d 229 (8th Cir.1984).

3. The trial court had dismissed the complaint without prejudice to file anew after completion of arbitration in accordance with the state requirement.

4. Hanna v. Plumer, 380 U.S. 460, 85 S.Ct. 1136, 14 L.Ed.2d 8 (1965) (discussed supra at § 3.39).

5. 610 F.2d at 134.

6. Id. at 136 ("[A] resounding flop.")

7. Byrd v. Blue Ridge Rural Electric Cooperative, Inc., 356 U.S. 525, 78 S.Ct. 893, 2 L.Ed.2d 953 (1958) (discussed supra § 3.38).

8. The Court noted that, contrary to *Byrd*, Pennsylvania had a strong state interest when it adopted the arbitration procedures: "It is the purpose of this act to make available professional liability insurance at a reasonable cost, and to establish a system through which a person … can obtain a prompt determination of his claim and the determination of fair and reasonable compensation." 40 P.S. § 1301.102.

9. 610 F.2d at 140.

10. Marquez v. Hahnemann Medical College and Hospital, 435 F.Supp. 972, 973 (E.D.Pa.1976) (citing to Woods v. Interstate Realty Co., 337 U.S. 535, 69 S.Ct. 1235, 93 L.Ed. 1524 (1949)).

In sum, … it functions as a judicial entity."[11] Its findings had the force of evidence in any de novo appeal. As the dissent pointed out, the fact that only two of 2,466 claims reached the Court of Common Pleas after arbitration shows that the Pennsylvania statute achieves what may have been its intended objective: to discourage parties from seeking a second trial. Judge Rosenn therefore concluded "that the panel is a surrogate for the state court."[12] Comparing *Woods v. Interstate Realty Co.*[13] with *Railway Co. v. Whitton's Administrator*,[14] the dissent argued that "a state may limit all right to recovery for a substantive cause of action … [but] having created a substantive right may not limit the forum for a right to recovery to only state courts."[15]

The problem presented by *Edelson* will continue to be important as states seek new ways for the efficient resolution of claims. They may take the form of changes in substantive law—for instance, from tort principles to "no-fault" systems[16]—and the (often concurrent) establishment of expert panels to speed up the settlement process. These are important state concerns and questions will arise again as to the extent to which the exercise of federal jurisdiction should or should not conform to state practice so long as the state rule has not altogether abolished a judicial remedy. However, even if the grant of diversity jurisdiction and the Supreme Court's language in *Railway Co. v. Whitton's Administrator*[17] were no obstacles to a displacement of initial federal jurisdiction, there are still important "countervailing" federal concerns. The *Edelson*

11. 610 F.2d at 143 (Rosenn, J., dissenting.)

12. Id. at 145; Esfeld v. Costa Crociere, S.p.A., 289 F.3d 1300 (11th Cir.2002) (federal law applies).

13. 337 U.S. 535, 69 S.Ct. 1235, 93 L.Ed. 1524 (1949).

14. 80 U.S. (13 Wall.) 270, 286, 20 L.Ed. 571 (1871) ("In all cases where a general right is thus conferred, it can be enforced in any Federal court within the State having jurisdiction of the parties. It cannot be withdrawn from the cognizance of such Federal court by any provisions of State legislation that it shall only be enforced in a State court.").

15. 610 F.2d at 145 (Rosenn, J. dissenting). See also Wheeler v. Shoemaker, 78 F.R.D. 218 (D.R.I.1978) (Rhode Island statute, similar to Pennsylvania's in *Edelson*, held not to oust federal court's jurisdiction). The Third Circuit adhered to *Edelson* in Hamilton v. Roth, 624 F.2d 1204 (3d Cir. 1980) (in the context of pendent jurisdiction rather than diversity). For the subsequent change in Pennsylvania state law see supra n.2.

Shoemaker, supra, was distinguished, and the medical-panel requirement upheld, in the following decisions: Feinstein v. Massa-

chusetts General Hospital, 643 F.2d 880, 885 n. 7 (1st Cir.1981) (collecting cases), Alisandrelli v. Kenwood, 724 F.Supp. 235 (S.D.N.Y.1989); Hines v. Elkhart General Hospital, 465 F.Supp. 421 (N.D.Ind.1979), affirmed 603 F.2d 646 (7th Cir.1979); DiAntonio v. Northampton–Accomack Memorial Hospital, 628 F.2d 287 (4th Cir.1980); Seoane v. Ortho Pharmaceuticals, Inc., 472 F.Supp. 468 (E.D.La.1979), affirmed 660 F.2d 146 (5th Cir.1981); Martin v. Choudhuri, 563 F.Supp. 207 (W.D.Wis. 1983). The *Edelson* result was also reached in Byrnes v. Kirby, 453 F.Supp. 1014 (D.Mass.1978) and in Davison v. Sinai Hospital of Baltimore, Inc., 462 F.Supp. 778 (D.Md.1978), affirmed 617 F.2d 361 (4th Cir.1980); Cf. Reichelderfer v. Illinois Central Gulf Railroad, 513 F.Supp. 189 (N.D.Miss.1981) (Tennessee statute governing Tennessee Medical Malpractice Review Board held to the procedural significance only to the state courts of Tennessee and therefore inapplicable in a diversity action in a federal court outside the state of Tennessee).

16. For discussion of choice of law with respect to no-fault legislation in the area of motor vehicle accident liability see infra § 17.42.

17. 80 U.S. (13 Wall.) 270, 286, 20 L.Ed. 571 (1871).

case did not involve consensual arbitration: the state rule made it mandatory. A right to jury trial is thus not only postponed to a second stage in the prosecution of a claim but also becomes more expensive because of the delay. These factors "... run contrary to the federal interest in allowing the full and fair litigation to be decided by the jury."[18] On the other hand, industrial accident litigation has been successfully transferred to the worker compensation administrative system which is the forerunner of many subsequent "no-fault" insurance (compensation) mechanisms. There seems to be no reason not to expect similar success in some other areas if appropriate legislation undertakes to modify the traditional tort system.[19]

3.　*Interstate Forum Shopping*

§ 3.42　The policy objective of *Erie* and *Klaxon* is intrastate decisional harmony. The price, especially of *Klaxon*,[1] is continued interstate divergence.[2] In some cases, the requirement that the federal court apply local law does not advance intrastate harmony, for instance because the state court would have lacked jurisdiction to entertain the action. These are: federal interpleader, cases in which the federal court has jurisdiction under the 100–mile "bulge" rule, and the cases of pendent jurisdiction. Some cases of federal transfer are also troublesome. The applicability of the *Erie/Klaxon* doctrine to these cases should therefore be reconsidered.

18. Edelson v. Soricelli, 610 F.2d 131, 148 (3d Cir.1979) (Rosenn, J., dissenting) (citing to Wheeler v. Shoemaker, 78 F.R.D. 218, 226 (D.R.I.1978)).

The constitutional concerns were addressed in Feinstein v. Massachusetts General Hospital, 643 F.2d 880 (1st Cir.1981) and in Davison v. Sinai Hospital of Baltimore, Inc., 462 F.Supp. 778, 781 (D.Md. 1978), affirmed 617 F.2d 361 (4th Cir.1980). In *Davison,* the claimants had argued that the fact that the arbitrator's findings were presumptively valid in a de novo trial violated the Seventh Amendment right to trial by jury. The trial court rejected the argument on the authority of Meeker v. Lehigh Valley Railroad Co., 236 U.S. 412, 35 S.Ct. 328, 59 L.Ed. 644 (1915) which held that a rule providing that a findings of the Interstate Commerce Commission are prima facie evidence in civil action does not violate the Seventh Amendment. The court also cited to a state decision reaching the same result under the state constitution: Attorney General v. Johnson, 282 Md. 274, 385 A.2d 57 (1978), appeal dismissed 439 U.S. 805, 99 S.Ct. 60, 58 L.Ed.2d 97 (1978). Cf. Simler v. Conner, 372 U.S. 221, 83 S.Ct.

609, 9 L.Ed.2d 691 (1963). Furthermore, the reference to *Meeker* presupposes that medical malpractice boards are administrative tribunals and not, in Judge Rosenn's words, judicial entities. Whether they are "administrative or judicial" will depend on the particular state statutory scheme, but there appears to be little doubt with respect to Pennsylvania's former statute in *Edelson.*

19. It is another question to what extent, as a matter of choice of law, one state should honor suit limitations adopted by another. See Bledsoe v. Crowley, 849 F.2d 639 (D.C.Cir.1988) (stay of local action pending plaintiff's compliance with Maryland's medical claim arbitration requirement).

§ 3.42

1. See text supra § 3.36, particularly nn.16–19.

2. See Borchers, The Origins of Diversity Jurisdiction, The Rise of Legal Positivism, and a Brave New World for *Erie* and *Klaxon*, 72 Tex. L. Rev. 79 (1993) (noting interstate disuniformity created by *Klaxon*).

a. Interpleader

§ 3.43 The Federal Interpleader Act[1] permits a stakeholder to interplead wherever any of the claimants reside and to require other claimants to pursue their claims or to protect their interests in that forum. The jurisdiction of state courts does not, of course, reach that far.[2]

Notwithstanding these jurisdictional differences, *Griffin v. McCoach*[3] extended the *Erie/Klaxon* principles to interpleader actions. Yet, use of the local law may result in the application of a law relatively unrelated to the case or to any of the other claimants. In these circumstances, in which the federal district court is really exercising nationwide rather than state-wide jurisdiction,[4] it seems preferable to allow the federal court to act as a neutral forum and fashion its own choice-of-law reference which would then result in the application either of the law most appropriately connected to the case or of a new substantive rule for these unique "federal" cases. Intrastate forum-shopping is not an issue in the absence of jurisdiction in the state courts.

Indeed, application of local state law in interpleader cases may increase interstate forum-shopping. While it is true that it is the stakeholder and not the claimant who initiates the action, the reality is that "the bill of interpleader will be filed as a reflex action in the judicial district in which the first claimant sues the stakeholder."[5] Freedom on the part of the federal court to depart from the *Erie/Klaxon* principles would lead to less forum-shopping and, at the same time, not affect or undercut these principles.[6]

---

§ 3.43

1. 28 U.S.C.A. § 1335.

2. But see the early suggestion by Justice Traynor that "It is doubtful whether today the United States Supreme Court would deny to a state court the interstate interpleader jurisdiction that federal courts may exercise." Atkinson v. Superior Court, 49 Cal.2d 338, 348, 316 P.2d 960, 966 (1957) cert. denied 357 U.S. 569, 78 S.Ct. 1381, 2 L.Ed.2d 1546 (1958). The Supreme Court's subsequent jurisdictional cases, particularly Shaffer v. Heitner, 433 U.S. 186, 97 S.Ct. 2569, 53 L.Ed.2d 683 (1977), do not answer this question directly.

3. 313 U.S. 498, 61 S.Ct. 1023, 85 L.Ed. 1481 (1941). For an application see Matter of Franklin, 709 F.Supp. 109, 111 n. 4 (E.D.Va.1989); see Aetna Life Ins. Co. v. Johnson, 206 F.Supp. 63, 66 (N.D.Ill.1962).

4. A similar problem exists when a federal bankruptcy court exercises jurisdiction over "related" claims derived from state law. For discussion see infra § 23.11 et seq.

5. R. Weintraub, Commentary on the Conflict of Laws 684 (4th ed. 2001). For more extensive discussion see id. at 683–85.

6. See A.L.I., Study of the Division of Jurisdiction Between State and Federal Courts 45 (1965); Freund, Federal State Relations in the Opinions of Judge Magruder, 72 Harv. L. Rev. 1204, 1211 (1959). See also Phillips Petroleum Co. v. Shutts, 472 U.S. 797, 105 S.Ct. 2965, 86 L.Ed.2d 628 (1985), on remand 240 Kan. 764, 732 P.2d 1286 (1987), cert. denied 487 U.S. 1223, 108 S.Ct. 2883, 101 L.Ed.2d 918 (1988) which held that, in a class action, the forum may not apply forum law to absent members of the plaintiff class who have no connection to the forum. The implications for the application of forum law to all aspects of an interpleader action are obvious. The answer may be that interpleader does not, or should not lie in a variety of cases (for instance, that it does not serve as an alternative to a bankruptcy proceeding) (cf. State Farm Fire & Cas. Co. v. Tashire, 386 U.S. 523, 87 S.Ct. 1199, 18 L.Ed.2d 270 (1967)) or that the federal court must make its own choice of the applicable state law in derogation of *Griffin,* supra n.3.

b. *The 100–Mile Bulge Rule*

§ 3.44 Rule 4(k)(1)(B) of the Federal Rules of Civil Procedure permits service on third-party defendants and specified additional third parties to a pending suit or counterclaim within a 100–mile radius of the place of suit, without regard to the territorial boundaries of the state in which the federal court sits. Thus, in certain metropolitan areas, "the federal court will be able to reach vast population centers outside the state … "[1] This situation is analogous to the interpleader problem discussed in the preceding section: the requirement that the federal court apply the law of the state in which it sits does not advance intrastate decisional harmony, as sought by *Erie* and *Klaxon,* because state courts could not have reached, and applied local law to, the additional foreign parties, while the dangers of interstate forum-shopping have been increased. Again, *Klaxon* should not apply in these cases, and the federal courts should be free to select the appropriate substantive state law.

c. *Supplemental Jurisdiction*

§ 3.45 Frequently, parties to a case properly in federal court will assert claims that do not independently invoke a basis of federal subject matter jurisdiction. The federal courts long recognized that they could entertain such nonfederal, nondiversity claims so long as they were so closely related to the jurisdiction-invoking claim as to be considered part of the same case or controversy as that claim. The leading explication of this power over "ancillary" or "pendent" claims was *United Mine Workers v. Gibbs.*[1] The doctrine is now codified under the rubric "supplemental jurisdiction."[2] Because claims invoking supplemental jurisdiction, by definition, do not invoke federal question jurisdiction, they are not governed by federal law. Under *Erie*, then, these claims are governed by state law, including state conflict of laws rules.

In some cases, federal statutes provide for out-of-state service.[3] In these cases, if such service results in personal jurisdiction for purposes of

---

§ 3.44

1. Vestal, Expanding the Jurisdictional Reach of the Federal Courts: The 1963 Change in Federal Rule 4, 38 N.Y.U. L. Rev. 1053, 1065 (1963).

§ 3.45

1. 383 U.S. 715, 726, 86 S.Ct. 1130, 1139, 16 L.Ed.2d 218 (1966). The Court held that claims were sufficiently related if they shared a "common nucleus of operative fact" so that one would normally expect them to be tried together. Id. at 725, 86 S.Ct. at 1138, 16 L.Ed.2d 218.

2. 28 U.S.C.A. § 1367. Section 1367(a) grants supplemental jurisdiction to the full extent of the Constitution, a limit explicated by Gibbs. Section 1367(b) withdraws supplemental jurisdiction over particular types of claims in diversity cases. See generally Freer, Compounding Confusion and Hampering Diversity: Life After Finley and the Supplemental Jurisdiction Statute, 40 Emory L.J. 445, 469–86 (1991). On supplemental jurisdiction, see Symeonides, A Reappraisal of the Supplemental Jurisdiction Statute—28 U.S.C.A. § 1367, 74 Ind. L.J. 1 (1998).

3. E.g., Investment Co. Act, 15 U.S.C.A. § 80a–43; Public Utility Holding Co. Act of 1935, 15 U.S.C.A. § 79y; Securities and Exchange Act of 1934, 15 U.S.C.A. § 78aa. See

the state law claim,[4] the federal court would again apply local state law in circumstances where a state court could not do so for lack of jurisdiction. As in the other areas noted above, there is therefore again potential for increased interstate forum shopping which would be alleviated by freeing the federal courts from the constraints of the *Klaxon* doctrine.

d. *Federal Transfers*

§ 3.46   Under § 1404(a) of the Judicial Code[1] a federal district may transfer a civil action to any other district where it might have been brought originally, if, in the interest of justice, this is indicated for the convenience of the parties and witnesses.[2] *Van Dusen v. Barrack*[3] held that in these circumstances the transferee court must apply the law of the transferor court: the transfer is to change the place of trial, for reasons of convenience, but not the applicable law.

There are, however, cases for which the rule should be less categorical. First, if a state court in the transferor court's state would not have had jurisdiction—for instance in interpleader or under the "bulge" rule (both discussed above)—, application of transferor law gives rise to the objections noted earlier.[4] Second, even if there were jurisdiction in the state courts of the transferor state, those courts might have dismissed for forum non conveniens. Again, forum shopping would be encouraged[5]

also 28 U.S.C.A. §§ 1471, 1472, 1473 (jurisdiction in bankruptcy) and Bankruptcy Rule 704, discussed infra § 23.12 n.3. See Comment, Pendent Personal Jurisdiction and Nationwide Service of Process, 64 N.Y.U. L. Rev. 113 (1989).

4. The authorities are divided on this point. For the proposition that there is personal jurisdiction over the pendent non-federal claim, see International Controls Corp. v. Vesco, 593 F.2d 166, 175 n. 5 (2d Cir.1979), cert. denied 442 U.S. 941, 99 S.Ct. 2884, 61 L.Ed.2d 311 (1979); Emerson v. Falcon Manufacturing, Inc., 333 F.Supp. 888 (S.D.Tex.1971). For the contrary view see Trussell v. United Underwriters, Limited, 236 F.Supp. 801 (D.Colo.1964). See also Cable News Network, Inc. v. American Broadcasting Companies, Inc., 528 F.Supp. 365 (N.D.Ga.1981) (under doctrine of pendent jurisdiction federal court may assert jurisdiction over a new party even if the claim against the new party does not involve a federal question).

§ 3.46

1. 28 U.S.C.A. § 1404(a).

2. See also 28 U.S.C.A. § 1407(a), dealing with transfers for consolidation of pretrial proceedings in multidistrict litigation.

3. 376 U.S. 612, 84 S.Ct. 805, 11 L.Ed.2d 945 (1964), on remand 236 F.Supp.

645 (E.D.Pa.1964). This section explores the application of the *Van Dusen* doctrine in diversity cases. For discussion of the question of whether it should also apply to transfers under §§ 1404(a) and 1407(a) of cases involving claims under federal law, see Marcus, Conflicts Among Circuits and Transfers Within the Federal Judicial System, 93 Yale L.J. 677 (1984).

4. A number of cases have held that a § 1404(a) transfer may be ordered in these circumstances and, although left open in *Van Dusen* (infra at n.6), the transferor's law might apply: e.g., Smith v. Peters, 482 F.2d 799, 802 (6th Cir.1973), cert. denied 415 U.S. 989, 94 S.Ct. 1587, 39 L.Ed.2d 886 (1974); Schreiber v. Allis–Chalmers Corp., 448 F.Supp. 1079 (D.Kan.1978), reversed 611 F.2d 790 (10th Cir.1979) (discussed infra § 3.48 n.6). See also Chancellor v. Lawrence, 501 F.Supp. 997 (N.D.Ill.1980) which sustained an objection to improper venue under 28 U.S.C.A. § 1391(b) but invited plaintiff to move for a transfer under § 1406 to the proper venue (Texas) where " ... all events having 'operative significance' ... [were] centered." The case is also discussed supra § 3.28 n.11.

5. See D. Currie, The Federal Courts and the American Law Institute, Part II, 36 U. Chi. L. Rev. 268, 310 (1969). See also

if the law of the transferor state is applied in these circumstances. *Van Dusen* had expressly left the *forum non conveniens* question open[6] but at least some trial courts applied transferor law in such a case.[7] Third, the application of the transferor state's law would seem to encourage forum shopping and thus to be inappropriate when the transfer was effected on motion by the *plaintiff.* Apart from open attempts to gain the benefit of the transferor state's law, there may be procedural reasons for a plaintiff to make such a motion: the defendant may have been improperly served so that, but for a transfer, the plaintiff faces dismissal in the forum or (perhaps also in combination with the foregoing) the statute of limitations has run in the transferee state.[8]

Without inquiring into the plaintiff's reasons (or, perhaps better: motives) for seeking the transfer, the U.S. Supreme Court adhered to the *Van Dusen* requirement (application of transferor law) in *Ferens v. John Deere Co.*[9] Pennsylvania plaintiffs brought a claim arising out of personal injuries suffered in Pennsylvania against the Delaware defendant with principal place of business in federal court in Mississippi where, unlike in Pennsylvania the statute of limitations had not yet run. Plaintiffs sought transfer to Pennsylvania where their action was dismissed by application of the Pennsylvania statute of limitations. The majority of the Supreme Court reversed. It noted that the transfer of venue, by the terms of the statute, is to turn on "convenience rather than the possibility of prejudice resulting from a change in the applicable law."[10] The Court acknowledged that the plaintiffs perhaps engaged in forum shopping. But they "had an opportunity for forum shopping in the state courts because both the Mississippi and Pennsylvania courts had jurisdiction and because they each would have applied a different statute of limitations. Diversity jurisdiction did not eliminate these forum shopping opportunities; instead, under *Erie,* the federal courts had to replicate

Schreiber v. Allis–Chalmers Corp., 448 F.Supp. 1079 (D.Kan.1978), reversed 611 F.2d 790 (10th Cir.1979) (discussed infra § 3.48 n.6).

6. 376 U.S. at 640, 84 S.Ct. at 821.

Another question is whether state or federal law governs *forum non conveniens* decisions in diversity cases. The Supreme Court has expressly left this question open. Piper Aircraft Co. v. Reyno, 454 U.S. 235, 102 S.Ct. 252, 262 n. 13, 70 L.Ed.2d 419 (1981), although lower courts have generally concluded that federal law applies. See supra § 3.40 n.12.

7. In re Air Crash Disaster at Boston, 399 F.Supp. 1106 (D.Mass.1975); In re Korean Air Lines Disaster of September 1, 1983, 664 F.Supp. 1478 (D.D.C.1986); In re EPIC Mortgage Insurance Litigation, 701 F.Supp. 1192 (D.Va.1988) affirmed in part, reversed in part 910 F.2d 118 (4th Cir. 1990). Cf. Jackson v. West Telemarketing

Corp. Outbound, 245 F.3d 518 (5th Cir. 2001), cert. denied 534 U.S. 972, 122 S.Ct. 394, 151 L.Ed.2d 299 (2001) (in case in which the district court did not specify statutory basis for the transfer but apparently made the transfer on the basis of the forum selection clause requiring that suit be brought in the transferee court, court applied choice-of-law rules of the transferee court).

8. Cf. Smith v. Peters, 482 F.2d 799 (6th Cir.1973), cert. denied 415 U.S. 989, 94 S.Ct. 1587, 39 L.Ed.2d 886 (1974); United States v. Berkowitz, 328 F.2d 358 (3d Cir. 1964), cert. denied 379 U.S. 821, 85 S.Ct. 42, 13 L.Ed.2d 32 (1964). See also Note, Choice of Law in Federal Court After Transfer of Venue, 63 Cornell L. Rev. 149, 154 (1977).

9. 494 U.S. 516, 110 S.Ct. 1274, 108 L.Ed.2d 443 (1990).

10. 494 U.S. at 528, 110 S.Ct. at 1282.

them."[11] The dissent by four Justices pointed to another aspect of the *Erie* policy: intrastate uniformity of decisions. "[O]ne must be blind to reality to say that it is the *Mississippi* federal court in which these plaintiffs have chosen to sue. That was merely a way station en route to suit in the *Pennsylvania* federal court. The plaintiffs were seeking to achieve exactly what *Klaxon* was designed to prevent: the use of a Pennsylvania federal court instead of a Pennsylvania state court in order to obtain application of a different substantive law."[12]

With respect to a fourth area of concern—where the transferor court lacked jurisdiction[13] or when there was improper venue—[14] courts do not regard *Van Dusen* as applicable. The law of the transferee court will apply to substantive, as well as choice-of-law[15] issues. With respect to the three areas mentioned earlier, it is suggested that the *Van Dusen* doctrine likewise should not bind the transferee court to the transferor's law.

Section 1407, enacted in 1968,[16] permits the consolidation, by means of transfer, in a single federal court of actions sharing common questions of fact. The consolidation is for the "convenience of the parties and witnesses" and has for its purpose the "just and efficient conduct" of the actions so consolidated. It is used frequently in mass tort litigation, such as airplane crashes. The multidistrict consolidation statute lacks choice-of-law provisions, and *Van Dusen* has therefore been thought to govern.[17]

11. Id. See also Jackson v. West Telemarketing Corp. Outbound, 245 F.3d 518 (5th Cir.2001), cert. denied 534 U.S. 972, 122 S.Ct. 394, 151 L.Ed.2d 299 (2001).

12. 494 U.S. at 535, 110 S.Ct. at 1286 (Scalia, J. dissenting). The majority, in stressing the "convenience" aspect of the transfer statute, was concerned with the systemic costs of litigation at an inconvenient place.

Intrastate uniformity was achieved In re TMI, 89 F.3d 1106 (3d Cir.1996), cert. denied 519 U.S. 1077, 117 S.Ct. 739, 136 L.Ed.2d 678, albeit as a result of statutory provisions. The Price–Anderson Amendments Act of 1988 provides that the "substantive rules of decision in [any public liability action] shall be derived from the § of the State in which the nuclear incident involved occurred." 42 U.S.C.A. § 2014(hh). For claims involving the Three Mile Island incident, Pennsylvania law, including its statute of limitations, therefore applied, even as to actions transferred from Mississippi which then had a longer statute.

13. Roofing & Sheet Metal Services, Inc. v. La Quinta Motor Inns, Inc., 689 F.2d 982 (11th Cir.1982).

14. Subacz v. Town Tower Motel Corp., 567 F.Supp. 1308 (N.D.Ind.1983).

15. Ellis v. Great Southwestern Corp., 646 F.2d 1099 (5th Cir.1981) (transfer pursuant to § 1406(a)); Houston Oil & Minerals Corp. v. SEEC, Inc., 616 F.Supp. 990 (W.D.La.1985).

16. Multidistrict Litigation Act of 1968, 82 Stat. 109, 28 U.S.C.A. § 1407.

17. See Atwood, The Choice–of–Law Dilemma in Mass Tort Litigation: Kicking Around *Erie*, *Klaxon*, and *Van Dusen*, 19 Conn. L. Rev. 9, 18 (1986) (collecting authorities).

In the typical transfer for consolidation of trial of claims arising from a commercial aircrash, the trial court may be applying different law to the claims of passengers in adjoining seats killed or injured under the same circumstances. For an example see In re Aircrash Disaster Near Chicago, Illinois, on May 25, 1979, 15 Avi. 18, 137, 500 F.Supp. 1044 (N.D.Ill.1980), reversed in part and affirmed in part 16 Avi. 17, 240, 644 F.2d 594 (7th Cir.1981), cert. denied 454 U.S. 878, 102 S.Ct. 358, 70 L.Ed.2d 187 (1981). These interstate air carrier cases perhaps call not only for a "federal" choice of law rule but also for "federal" substantive rules. "We have previously urged the enactment of a federal aviation disaster law which would make uniform the legal principles applicable in aviation disaster cases. It is unjust as well as ludicrous that such issues as the standard of liability (no-fault,

Again, forum shopping may be involved in the choice of the initial forum. There have therefore been calls for federal (common law or statutory) choice-of-law rules for these cases;[18] the American Law Institute, in its Complex Litigation Project[19] suggests such rules.

In a transfer between circuits, the transferee court does not apply the transferor's interpretation of federal law but applies its own circuit's view.[20] In this instance, the defendant may engage in forum shopping in seeking transfer.[21]

In several of the areas noted, the federal court should be free to make its own choice of the applicable state law. Even in the more typical transfer case, in which the transferor has jurisdiction and the transfer is effected on the defendant's motion, *Van Dusen* may paint with too broad a brush. The *Erie*-principles which underlie the decisions indeed call for the application of the transferor's law when the transfer only serves to provide a more convenient courtroom for trial. Short of amounting to forum non conveniens, however, the § 1404(a) transfer—" ... for the convenience of parties and witnesses, in the interest of justice ... "— may also involve a case where the action itself is more closely related to the transferee forum. By selecting the initial forum, the plaintiff has selected the law. This type of forum-shopping, however, does not differ from that generally available to plaintiffs when, in the interstate setting, multiple fora. have jurisdiction to entertain the action: it is not an *Erie* problem (that state substantive law be applied), but a *Klaxon* problem (that state conflicts law be applied).[22]

C. PERVASIVE ERIE/KLAXON PROBLEMS

1. What Is "State Law"?

§ 3.47 A majority of states adhere to the Uniform Certification of Questions of Law Act or its 1995 successor.[1] When such a procedure exists, federal courts have a mechanism to ascertain the applicable state

comparative negligence, contributory negligence), the measure of damages, whether ... damages for pain and suffering are recoverable ... , the applicable statute of limitations ... should vary from case to case arising out of the same disaster depending on the vagaries of the applicable state law." In re Air Crash Disaster Near Chicago, Illinois on May 25, 1979, 526 F.Supp. 226, 233 (N.D.Ill.1981). See Lowenfeld, Mass Torts and the Conflict of Laws: The Airline Disaster, 1989 U. Ill. L.Rev. 157.

18. See supra § 3.36 n.20.

19. Id.

20. In re Korean Air Lines Disaster of Sept. 1, 1983, 829 F.2d 1171 (D.C.Cir.1987), judgment affirmed 490 U.S. 122, 109 S.Ct.

1676, 104 L.Ed.2d 113 (1989); Marcus, Conflicts Among Circuits and Transfers Within the Federal Judicial System, 93 Yale L.J. 677, 686, 702, 721 (1984).

21. See Brilmayer & Lee, State Sovereignty and the Two Faces of Federalism: A Comparative Study of Federal Jurisdiction and the Conflict of Laws, 60 Notre Dame L. Rev. 833, 861 n.126 (1985).

22. For criticism of *Klaxon*, see supra § 3.36, especially n.20. For discussion of "federal common law," see infra § 3.49 et seq.

§ 3.47

1. 12 U.L.A. Supp. v.3, 5 (1998) (27 states and the District of Columbia and Puerto Rico follow the 1967 Act; four states follow its 1995 successor).

rule of decision. However, many states lack such a procedure. In many cases, a federal court must therefore rely upon state precedents to determine the rule that the state would use.[2] When the issue involves a question of state conflicts law, some areas of which are more in flux today than is substantive law, the danger is particularly great that it may apply a rule which the state courts might no longer follow.

In *Lester v. Aetna Life Insurance Co.*[3] the Fifth Circuit had dealt with an action on an insurance policy issued in Wisconsin by a Connecticut insurer for the benefit of a Louisiana citizen. The court refused to apply Louisiana's usual choice-of-law rule, referring to a contract's place of making, because, doing so, would lead to the application of the law of a state (Wisconsin) which had " *... no interest in the case,* no policy at stake."[4] Wisconsin had no interest, in the court's view, because the defendant was not a Wisconsin insurer; its protective policies were thus

---

2. State court precedents, however, may be lacking or may be unreliable. Thus, under Pennsylvania law, an opinion "joined by fewer than a majority of the justices of the ... Supreme Court is not binding or controlling precedent." Vargus v. Pitman Manufacturing Co., 675 F.2d 73, 74 (3d Cir. 1982). For the precedential value of intermediate appellate decisions in Pennsylvania and the persuasive force of state supreme court plurality opinions, see McGowan v. University of Scranton, 759 F.2d 287 (3d Cir.1985), appeal after remand 837 F.2d 1242 (1988). The Fifth Circuit regards intermediate state appellate court decisions as authoritative and binding on federal courts in the absence of evidence that the state supreme court disapproved such decisions. Birmingham Fire Ins. Co. of Pa. v. Winegardner and Hammons, Inc., 714 F.2d 548 (5th Cir.1983).

When a state is subdivided into two or more appellate districts the question arises to what appellate decisions a federal court should look in the absence of a state supreme court decision. Commercial Discount Corp. v. King, 552 F.Supp. 841 (N.D.Ill. 1982) held that appellate decisions of the district in which the federal court sits must be followed in preference to conflicting decisions from other appellate districts. Murry v. Sheahan, 991 F.Supp. 1052 (N.D.Ill.1998) takes a contrary view: Under Erie, a federal court "must apply the law that ultimately would be applied were the case to be litigated in the state courts." 568 F.Supp. at 539–40. The federal court thus should not look to its counterparts within the same district (encouraging inter-district intrastate forum-shopping) but should rather determine or, in the case of conflict within state appellate decisions, forecast how the state supreme court would decide the issue. It would seem that *Murry* states the correct

view of the *Erie* mandate. See Kula v. J.K. Schofield & Co., Inc., 668 F.Supp. 1126 (N.D.Ill.1987) and Connecticut Mut. Life Ins. Co. v. Wyman, 718 F.2d 63 (3d Cir. 1983) (in the absence of state supreme court decision, pronouncements of lower state courts are to be given proper regard but not conclusive effect); Klippel v. U–Haul Co. of Northeastern Michigan, 759 F.2d 1176, 1181 (4th Cir.1985) (disregard New York Appellate Division decisions if convinced that New York Court of Appeals would not follow them); Motor Club of America Ins. Co. v. Hanifi, 145 F.3d 170 (4th Cir.1998), cert. denied 525 U.S. 1001, 119 S.Ct. 509, 142 L.Ed.2d 423 (1998) (predicting what New York Court of Appeals would decide).

The state law to be applied is that in effect at the time of appeal and not as it existed at the time of trial. Awrey v. Progressive Cas. Ins. Co., 728 F.2d 352 (6th Cir.1984), cert. denied 474 U.S. 920, 106 S.Ct. 250, 88 L.Ed.2d 258 (1985). See also infra n.9.

In the Virgin Islands, as a result of Territorial statutory direction, the federal courts apply the Restatements of the Law in the absence of other statutory law. 1 V.I.C. § 4; Deary v. Evans, 570 F.Supp. 189 (D.V.I. 1983).

See Yonover, Ascertaining State Law: The Continuing *Erie* Dilemma, 38 DePaul L. Rev. 1 (1988).

3. 433 F.2d 884 (5th Cir.1970), cert. denied 402 U.S. 909, 91 S.Ct. 1382, 28 L.Ed.2d 650 (1971).

4. Quoted from the court's explanation of *Lester* in Challoner v. Day & Zimmermann, Inc., 512 F.2d 77, 80 (5th Cir.1975) (original emphasis).

inapplicable. At the same time, Louisiana did have a protective interest when a Louisiana insured was involved. Through interest analysis, the court thus identified a false conflict and applied the forum's (Louisiana's) substantive law.

The Fifth Circuit followed this approach in *Challoner v. Day & Zimmermann, Inc.*,[5] a personal injury case arising from the premature explosion of an artillery round in Cambodia. Again, the court found a false conflict: Cambodia was said to have no interest in the liability of an American manufacturer toward an American claimant, while both the defendant's place of principal business (Pennsylvania) and the states of the victims' domiciles (Wisconsin and Tennessee) did. All of the American states, including the forum and place of manufacture (Texas), were strict liability states. In the absence of a conflict among interested states, the court applied the local law of the forum, expressing the belief that Texas would do the same, notwithstanding its earlier adherence to the place of tort rule. The U.S. Supreme Court reversed.[6] In a brief per curiam opinion the Court simply quoted the operative language from *Klaxon* and added: "A federal court in a diversity case is not free to engraft onto those state rules exceptions or modifications which may commend themselves to the federal court but which have not commended themselves to the State in which the federal court sits."[7]

5. 512 F.2d 77 (5th Cir.1975), discussed further infra § 3.48, n.19.

6. Day & Zimmermann, Inc. v. Challoner, 423 U.S. 3, 96 S.Ct. 167, 46 L.Ed.2d 3 (1975).

7. 423 U.S. at 4, 96 S.Ct. at 168. The Fifth Circuit remanded to the trial court, 546 F.2d 26 (5th Cir.1977), in which the claim was settled after receipt of a deposition from a Cambodian lawyer that Cambodia, as the place of the tort, would apply the law of the place of manufacture (Texas). See R. Weintraub, Commentary on the Conflict of Laws 569 n.23 (2d ed. 1980) (reference not included in later editions). See also infra § 3.48 n.19.

See also Factors Etc., Inc. v. Pro Arts, Inc., 652 F.2d 278 (2d Cir.1981), cert. denied 456 U.S. 927, 102 S.Ct. 1973, 72 L.Ed.2d 442 (1982). The case involved the question whether the "right of publicity" constituted a descendible property right for the purpose of entitling a company holding an exclusive license from Elvis Presley to exploit commercially his name and likeness to seek an injunction against the distribution of a poster by another company after the singer's death. The Second Circuit reversed the decision by the federal district court in New York (496 F.Supp. 1090 (S.D.N.Y.1980)) and held that the right of publicity did not survive Mr. Presley's death under the law of Tennessee where Mr. Presley had lived and where the licen-

see company was incorporated. It based its decision on the prior determination of Tennessee law by the Sixth Circuit in Memphis Development Foundation v. Factors Etc., Inc., 616 F.2d 956 (6th Cir.1980), cert. denied 449 U.S. 953, 101 S.Ct. 358, 66 L.Ed.2d 217 (1980). The dissent in *Pro Arts* noted that "there was *no interpretation* of *any* Tennessee law by the Sixth Circuit, only a declaration of what that court thought would be a preferable general common law rule for that state." 652 F.2d at 284, Mansfield J., dissenting, original emphasis. In Rogers v. Grimaldi, 875 F.2d 994, 1002 & n.10 (2d Cir.1989), the court backed away from the "truncated approach" used in *Factors, Etc.* Instead, it adopted in the "two-step process," consisting of the "uncertain task of predicting what the *New York* [state] courts [i.e., the *state courts of the forum*] would predict the *Oregon* courts would rule as to the contours of a right of publicity under Oregon law." (emphasis added.). See also Jackson v. West Telemarketing Corp. Outbound, 245 F.3d 518 (5th Cir.2001), cert. denied 534 U.S. 972, 122 S.Ct. 394, 151 L.Ed.2d 299 (2001).

In Samuelson v. Susen, 576 F.2d 546, 551 (3d Cir.1978), the district court was said to be "warranted in prophesying that the Pennsylvania courts would apply Ohio law" since Ohio "has the more 'significant relationship' to the dispute ... [and since that] approach ... is also consistent with that of

It was noted earlier that the *Erie/Klaxon* doctrine promotes intrastate harmony at the price of continued interstate divergence in choice of law.[8] The effect of *Challoner* may be to endanger intrastate harmony as well: so long as federal courts may not anticipate changes in state conflicts law, " ... a party who would benefit from application of a standard, territorially-oriented choice-of-law rule reflected in the most recent pronouncement of the highest court of the state would do well to choose the federal district court as forum. Conversely, a party will have far greater chance of success in the state supreme court, if he wishes to argue that the conflicts rule formerly accepted in the state would produce an irrational and unjust result in the case and should be changed in accord with current trends elsewhere."[9]

A similar problem was involved in *McKenna v. Ortho Pharmaceutical Corp.*[10] in which *Erie* and *Klaxon* were followed but *interstate* forum-shopping resulted from the federal court's manipulation of the *foreign* law. The federal district court in Pennsylvania had correctly applied Pennsylvania's borrowing statute but was reversed by the Court of Appeals for its reading of the applicable Ohio statute of limitations. Against clear evidence that the Ohio statute commenced to run with the injury,[11] the majority held that Ohio would no longer adhere to this view in the future but would adopt the more widely used discovery-of-injury test. With the letter of *Klaxon* followed, in the sense that the federal court in Pennsylvania did refer to Ohio law as a Pennsylvania state court would have done, there is little room for challenge in the Supreme Court. Yet, depending on the way a Pennsylvania state court would have construed the Ohio statute, decisions like *McKenna* encourage *both* intrastate and interstate forum shopping.[12]

the Restatement 2d ... " See also In re Air Crash Disaster Near Chicago, Illinois on May 25, 1979, 526 F.Supp. 226, 231 (N.D.Ill.1981) in which the court had to deal with state court decisions which had subsequently been overruled (but in a different context) in order to divine what the state courts would now do: " ... having to rely upon overruled cases as evidence of how another court would likely rule on issues if they arose in a different posture strikes us as only slightly more reliable than predictions of the future arrived at by reading the entrails of sheep."

8. See supra § 3.36.

9. R. Weintraub, Commentary on the Conflict of Laws 672 (4th ed. 2001). For a (fortuitous) decision in a non-conflicts setting, in which intrastate harmony was restored, see Pierce v. Cook & Co., 518 F.2d 720 (10th Cir.1975), cert. denied 423 U.S. 1079, 96 S.Ct. 866, 47 L.Ed.2d 89 (1976): In *Pierce*, Tenth Circuit granted relief from its earlier judgment and remanded the case to the district court after the Oklahoma Supreme Court, in a case involving different plaintiffs but arising out of the same

occurrence, had announced a new rule of decision. The relief granted was based on Federal Rule 60(b)(6): "any other reason justifying relief." Other circuits have declined to follow *Pierce*: Biggins and DeWeerth v. Baldinger, 38 F.3d 1266 (2d Cir. 1994), cert. denied 513 U.S. 1001, 115 S.Ct. 512, 130 L.Ed.2d 419 (1994); McGeshick v. Choucair, 72 F.3d 62 (7th Cir.1995), cert. denied 517 U.S. 1212, 116 S.Ct. 1834, 134 L.Ed.2d 937 (1996); Norgaard v. DePuy Orthopaedics, Inc., 121 F.3d 1074 (7th Cir. 1997). "If Congress cannot tell a federal court to reopen a judgment to give the losing side the benefit of a change of law, neither may a state. Legitimate interests in finality also counsel against revision." *Norgaard*, 121 F.3d at 1078.

10. 622 F.2d 657 (3d Cir.), cert. denied 449 U.S. 976, 101 S.Ct. 387, 66 L.Ed.2d 237 (1980).

11. 622 F.2d at 669–72 (Higginbotham, J., dissenting).

12. See also Schreiber v. Allis–Chalmers Corp., 448 F.Supp. 1079 (D.Kan.1978), rev'd 611 F.2d 790 (10th Cir.1979), discussed infra § 3.48, n.6. See also Factors

2. *Klaxon and Constitutional Limitations on Choice of Law*

§ **3.48**   Sections 3.20–3.35 dealt with constitutional limits on choice of law. Both the U.S. Supreme Court's early decision in *Home Insurance Co. v. Dick*[1] and its decisions in *Allstate Insurance Co. v. Hague* and in *Phillips Petroleum Co. v. Shutts*[2] stated that a state may not apply its law when it has no significant contact with the transaction or occurrence. In *Dick* and *Shutts,* the Court found the application of forum law to be unconstitutional. In *Hague,* it did not. The standard, as formulated in *Hague,* is: "[F]or a State's substantive law to be selected in a constitutionally permissible manner, that State must have a significant contact or significant aggregation of contacts, creating state interests, such that choice of its law is neither arbitrary nor fundamentally unfair."[3]

If a state court, under the circumstances of a given case, may not apply local law, it would follow that a federal court sitting in diversity also may not do so. Conversely, it should be equally true that a state may not apply the law of *another* state when the latter has no "significant contact ... creating a state interest ... ,"[4] and that a federal court sitting in diversity again also may not do so. Both decisions of the Fifth Circuit, in *Lester* and *Challoner*,[5] in which the court refused to follow the state's choice-of-law rule, stopped short of asserting that the application of the state's rule would be unconstitutional. Rather, the court found a false conflict and applied local law because it believed that the state courts would no longer follow the previously announced choice-of-law rule when it referred to the law of a disinterested state.

In *Schreiber v. Allis–Chalmers Corp.*,[6] the Kansas plaintiff was injured in Kansas by a product manufactured by Allis–Chalmers, a Delaware company with its business headquarters in Wisconsin. After expiration of the Kansas statute of limitations but before expiration of the Mississippi statute, the plaintiff sued in the federal district court in Mississippi from which a § 1404(a) transfer to Kansas was effected. The federal district court in Kansas, as the transferee court, faced the question whether, under the doctrine of *Van Dusen*,[7] it was obligated to apply Mississippi law, particularly its statute of limitations.[8] The trial

---

Etc., Inc. v. Pro Arts, Inc., 652 F.2d 278 (2d Cir.1981), cert. denied 456 U.S. 927, 102 S.Ct. 1973, 72 L.Ed.2d 442 (1982).

§ 3.48

1.   281 U.S. 397, 50 S.Ct. 338, 74 L.Ed. 926 (1930) (discussed supra § 3.21).

2.   449 U.S. 302, 101 S.Ct. 633, 66 L.Ed.2d 521 (1981).

3.   Id. at 313, 101 S.Ct. at 640.

4.   Id.

5.   Supra § 3.47 nn.3–5. See also supra § 3.47 n.7.

6.   448 F.Supp. 1079 (D.Kan.1978), rev'd 611 F.2d 790 (10th Cir.1979) (critically noted by Grossman, Statutes of Limitations and the Conflict of Laws: Modern Analysis, 1980 Ariz. St. L.J. 1, 56–64 (1980); Martin, Statutes of Limitations and Rationality in the Conflict of Laws, 19 Washburn L.J. 405 (1980)).

7.   See supra § 3.46.

8.   "For choice-of-law issues concerning 'substantive' law, Mississippi uses a 'center of gravity' approach, in which governmental interest analysis plays a major role. For statutes of limitations, however, Mississippi

court refused to apply the Mississippi limitation, principally on the ground that the the defendant's contacts[9] with Mississippi were insufficient to allow the exercise of personal jurisdiction over a claim unrelated to the forum. It followed that, without jurisdiction in the transferor court, the *Van Dusen* doctrine did not bind the transferee. Since the decision rested on jurisdictional grounds, the remainder of the opinion is dictum. In it, the court did suggest, however, that "... the right-remedy and substance-procedure distinctions urged by plaintiff ... [even though of long standing, do] not compel the conclusion that their application cannot violate due process,"[10] and that due process would indeed be infringed if a state applied local law when it "... 'has no other contact with the parties or with the facts except that it is the forum.' "[11] Similarly, full-faith-and-credit principles dictated deference to the law and policies of a sister state (Kansas) when the forum had no contact or interest.[12] In sum, the court found that Mississippi lacked jurisdiction and that, even if it had jurisdiction, both due process and full-faith-and-credit principles precluded the application of Mississippi law, with the result that the Kansas transferee court was similarly precluded, i.e. freed from the mandate of *Van Dusen*.

The Tenth Circuit reversed.[13] With respect to jurisdiction in the Mississippi state or federal court, the Tenth Circuit pointed to *Perkins v. Benguet Consolidated Mining Co.*,[14] in which the U.S. Supreme Court had held that the state may exercise jurisdiction when the defendant had carried on "a continuous and systematic, but limited part of its general business" in the state. On the choice of law side, the court concluded that a Mississippi court would not depart from the traditional procedural characterization of the local six-year limitation,[15] that a Mississippi court would therefore be bound to apply that limitation, and that the Kansas transferee court would have to do likewise. It did not address the question whether the application of the Mississippi law, although characterized as "procedural," was constitutional.

In *Sun Oil Co. v. Wortman*,[16] the U.S. Supreme Court sanctioned a forum state's use of its own longer statute of limitations to entertain a claim to which it may not apply its substantive law. The majority arrived at its decision by adhering to a *procedural* characterization of statutes of limitation.[17] While *Wortman* involved the review of a state court decision,

had refused to abandon the traditional rule [that such a statute is 'procedural' and that local law therefore applies]." Grossman, supra n.6, at 59.

9. The defendant had maintained a manufacturing plant in Mississippi but the defective machinery had not been made there. Prior to 1973, moreover, its activities in the state consisted of sales and sales promotions. 611 F.2d at 793.

10. 448 F.Supp. at 1098.

11. Id. at 1097, quoting Weintraub, Due Process and Full Faith and Credit Limitations on a State's Choice of Law, 44 Iowa L. Rev. 449, 464 (1959).

12. 448 F.Supp. at 1098–1100.

13. Schreiber v. Allis-Chalmers Corp., 611 F.2d 790 (10th Cir.1979).

14. 342 U.S. 437, 448, 72 S.Ct. 413, 419, 96 L.Ed. 485 (1952).

15. 611 F.2d at 794.

16. 486 U.S. 717, 108 S.Ct. 2117, 100 L.Ed.2d 743 (1988). For criticism see supra § 3.9 n.6.

17. The Court declined to adopt the outcome-determinative (substantive) characterization of limitations which Guaranty Trust Co. of New York v. York, 326 U.S. 99, 65

the decision is of course also dispositive of the question raised in *Schreiber*. The Court held subsequently, in *Ferens v. John Deere Co.*,[18] that the transferee federal court, on transfer by the *plaintiff*, must apply the statute of limitations that the transferor court would have applied.

Challoner[19] presents a similar problem. In concluding that a false conflict existed and that the application of forum law was therefore permissible, the Fifth Circuit had first found that Cambodia had no interest in the case nor a policy at stake. However, there is, at least superficially, a difference between *Schreiber* and *Challoner*. In *Schreiber*, the Kansas transferee court had concluded that the transferor court could not constitutionally have applied the law of Mississippi where it sat because all of the relevant contacts lay with the Kansas forum. In the trial court's view only Kansas had the requisite contacts and interests. In *Challoner*, in contrast, the federal court disregarded the local choice-of-law rule—upon finding that Cambodia lacked an interest in the case— and, instead, opted for a conflicts methodology of its own which then led it to forum law. It is this independence in approach which the U.S. Supreme Court rejected in its reversal[20] and caused it to reiterate its adherence to *Klaxon*. As a consequence, it is uncertain whether federal courts, under *Klaxon*, may anticipate changes in the state approach to choice of law.[21] However, what if the Fifth Circuit had gone further in its analysis and had found that the Texas choice-of-law rule (place of tort) would lead to the law of a state lacking the contact necessary for a constitutionally permissible application of its law? What choice would it have been allowed to make then, and according to what standards? These questions were not before the Supreme Court in *Challoner;* they also were not addressed by the Tenth Circuit in *Schreiber*.

As a result of the intrastate parallelism required by *Klaxon*, the choice-of-law process in the federal courts thus raises the same questions as to constitutional limitations as does choice of law in state courts. Despite its shortcomings in formulation and, especially so far, in applica- tion, the *Hague* and *Shutts* decisions have reaffirmed the test for choice of law in state courts: significant contacts with the forum are required for the application of forum law. Logically, *Klaxon* should serve to carry

S.Ct. 1464, 89 L.Ed. 2079 (1945) had adopted for *Erie* purposes.

18. 494 U.S. 516, 110 S.Ct. 1274, 108 L.Ed.2d 443 (1990). See also supra § 3.46 n.12.

19. Challoner v. Day & Zimmermann, Inc., 512 F.2d 77 (5th Cir.1975), opinion vacated 423 U.S. 3, 96 S.Ct. 167, 46 L.Ed.2d 3 (1975), on remand 546 F.2d 26 (5th Cir. 1977).

20. See supra § 3.47 n.7.

21. In *Challoner*, the Fifth Circuit's false-conflicts analysis led to forum law, as it usually does (see supra §§ 2.6, 2.17),

while the then applicable state choice-of-law rule pointed to the place of injury (in this case, away from the forum). A state court might also have changed the approach. However, it may well have opted for the Restatement Second's "most-significant-re- lationship" approach. On the facts of *Chal- loner*, the actual result may not have been different. However, it is a matter of some importance what kind of (new) approach is to be adopted in a state for choice of law in general. The *Erie/Klaxon* policy leaves this task to the state courts.

this test over into diversity actions in federal courts. *Challoner,* which antedated *Hague,* leaves the question open.[22]

V. PROBLEMS OF FEDERALISM: FEDERAL COMMON LAW

A. THE STANDARD

§ 3.49 *Erie*[1] stands for the proposition that there "... is no such thing as valid *general* federal law, because the federal government is one of limited legislative powers. Accordingly, there is no such thing as valid *general* federal *common law,* because courts acting in a common law capacity possess only as much power as the legislature possesses. Hence, in fashioning common law, the federal courts ... may declare independent *federal* common law, provided they confine their lawmaking to areas in which Congress itself may legislate."[2] Thus, while *Erie* prevents federal courts from striking out on their own to create general, substantive common law rules, it does not prevent the creation of preemptive federal common law rules if federal interests are intense.

With respect to rules of procedure, it has been suggested that the Rules of Decision Act[3] precludes the adoption of common law rules of procedure.[4] However, the Act neither says so nor is it restricted to diversity cases.[5] The only fact lending support to this argument is the Act's enumeration which does not refer to "common law." That this omission is largely irrelevant has been ably demonstrated by others: the distinction between federal statutory and common law is one of source and emphasis, not of authority, as shown by the fact that Article III of the Constitution, containing language similar to the Rules of Decision Act, does encompass cases arising under federal common law.[6]

Both with respect to substantive law and to procedural rules, federal courts thus do have power to declare independent federal common law in

---

22. The scant lower court authority explicitly addressing the issue has found the constitutional limits applicable. See, e.g., United States Fire Ins. Co. v. Goodyear Tire & Rubber Co., 726 F.Supp. 740, 744 (D.Minn.1989).

§ 3.49

1. Erie RR Co. v. Tompkins, 304 U.S. 64, 58 S.Ct. 817, 82 L.Ed. 1188 (1938).

2. Westen & Lehman, Is There Life For *Erie* After the Death of Diversity? 78 Mich. L. Rev. 311, 338–39 (1980) (emphasis in original). Cf. Jay, Origins of Federal Common Law: Part One, 133 U. Pa. L. Rev. 1003 (1985); Merrill, The Common Law Powers of Federal Courts, 52 U. Chi. L. Rev. 1 (1985); Field, Sources of Law: The Scope of Federal Common Law, 99 Harv. L. Rev. 881 (1986).

3. 28 U.S.C.A. § 1652 ("The laws of the several states, except where the Constitution or treaties of the United States or Acts of Congress otherwise require or provide, shall be regarded as rules of decision in civil actions in the courts of the United States, in cases where they apply").

4. Ely, The Irrepressible Myth of *Erie,* 87 Harv. L. Rev. 693, 698, 717–18 (1974); Redish & Phillips, *Erie* and the Rules of Decision Act: In Search of the Appropriate Dilemma, 91 Harv. L. Rev. 356, 358, 360–61 (1977).

5. Westen & Lehman, supra n.2, at 366–69.

6. Westen & Lehman, supra n.2, at 369–70 (citing Illinois v. City of Milwaukee, 406 U.S. 91, 98–101, 92 S.Ct. 1385, 1390–91, 31 L.Ed.2d 712 (1972)); Note, The Federal Common Law, 82 Harv. L. Rev. 1512, 1513 n.13 (1969); Note, Federal Common Law and Article III: A Jurisdictional Approach to *Erie,* 74 Yale L.J. 325, 332–33 (1964).

areas in which there is federal legislative *authority*. In the "vindication of federal concerns the federal courts have, in general, the same creative function and the same range of remedial authority as do state courts in their different sphere of competence."[7]

§ 3.50 The *authority* for federal judicial law-making derives from:[1] (1) congressional legislation federalizing an area,[2] (2) from a constitutional allocation of power to federal courts or to another branch of the federal government,[3] (3) and from the authority to safeguard particularly

---

7. Hill, The Law–Making Power of the Federal Courts: Constitutional Preemption, 67 Colum. L. Rev. 1024, 1072–73 (1967). See also Texas v. Pankey, 441 F.2d 236 (10th Cir.1971); Friendly, In Praise of *Erie*—and of the New Federal Common Law, 39 N.Y.U. L. Rev. 383 (1964). But see Mishkin, Some Further Last Words on *Erie*, 87 Harv. L. Rev. 1682, 1684–85 (1974). For a more restrictive view see City of Milwaukee v. Illinois and Michigan, 451 U.S. 304, 101 S.Ct. 1784, 68 L.Ed.2d 114 (1981) (discussed infra § 3.54 n.17).

§ 3.50

1. Some of this material derives from Hay, Unification of Law in the United States: Uniform State Laws, Treaties and Judicially Declared Federal Common Law, in: J.N. Hazard & W.J. Wagner, Legal Thought in the United States of America Under Contemporary Pressures 261, 273–292 *passim,* particularly at 288–89 (1970). See also Trautman, The Relation Between American Conflicts Law and Federal Common Law, 41 Law & Contemp. Prob. 105 (Spring 1977).

2. See, e.g., with respect to labor law, Textile Workers Union v. Lincoln Mills, 353 U.S. 448, 456, 77 S.Ct. 912, 918, 1 L.Ed.2d 972 (1957) (The "substantive law to apply ... is federal law, which the courts must fashion from the policy of our national labor laws.").

3. E.g.: *Admiralty:* From the combination of Art. III, § 2 of the Constitution (defining the federal judicial power to extend to "admiralty and maritime jurisdiction") and Art. I, Sec. 8 (legislative power of Congress), the Supreme Court has drawn the conclusion that "Congress has paramount power to fix and determine the maritime law which shall prevail throughout the country" and that, "in the absence of some controlling statute the general maritime law as accepted by the federal courts constitutes part of our national law." Southern Pacific Co. v. Jensen, 244 U.S. 205, 215, 37 S.Ct. 524, 528, 61 L.Ed. 1086 (1917). See also Maru Shipping Co., Inc. v. Burmeister & Wain American Corp., 528 F.Supp. 210, 214 (S.D.N.Y.1981) (issues in the case re-

quired court "to apply a body of federal maritime law of torts and contracts. Where the federal law of the sea provides ... no clear precedent ... , [the court] may look to the prevailing law of the land as applied by the states." The court drew, inter alia, on the Restatement, Second, Torts and, for the measure of damages for breach of implied warranty, on the U.C.C.). See also Fireman's Fund American Insurance Co. v. Boston Harbor Marina, Inc., 285 F.Supp. 36 (D.Mass.1968), judgment vacated on other grounds 406 F.2d 917 (1st Cir.1969); Cohen v. Hathaway, 595 F.Supp. 579 (D.Mass. 1984) (suits in admiralty are governed by federal substantive and procedural law).

Cases to which a state is a party: Art. III, § 2 also confers original jurisdiction in suits between States of the Union and has led to the creation of federal common law. E.g., Cissna v. Tennessee, 246 U.S. 289, 38 S.Ct. 306, 62 L.Ed. 720 (1918) (boundary disputes); Texas v. New Jersey, 379 U.S. 674, 85 S.Ct. 626, 13 L.Ed.2d 596 (1965); Hinderlider v. La Plata River & Cherry Creek Ditch Co., 304 U.S. 92, 110, 58 S.Ct. 803, 811, 82 L.Ed. 1202 (1938), ("jurisdiction concerning rights in interstate streams is not different from those concerning boundaries. These have been recognized to present federal questions ... " to be decided by federal common law in the absence of statute. Thus, "a right claimed under 'federal common law,' in an area of federal preemption established not by Congress but by the Constitution, is a right arising 'under the Constitution' within the meaning of the Supremacy Clause...."). See also Texas v. Pankey, 441 F.2d 236, 240 (10th Cir.1971): federal question jurisdiction based on federal common law in an action in which Texas sought to enjoin New Mexico residents from polluting interstate river; Note, Sovereign Immunity in Sister–State Courts, 80 Colum. L. Rev. 1493, 1506–12 (1980) (suggesting federal choice-of-law rules for suits against states in sister state courts). See also Resolution Trust Corp. v. Schuster, 57 F.3d 1231 (3d Cir.1995), cert. dismissed 517 U.S. 1101, 116 S.Ct. 1292, 134 L.Ed.2d 468 (1996) (dealing with the question when

strong federal concerns, even in the absence of legislation, both by negative control of state law[4] and by affirmative rule making.[5] The power

Congressional enactment displaces state law and/or federal common law).

4. Federal statutory law of course preempts state law under the Supremacy Clause. Most questions in this area thus relate to the question whether the statute was *intended* to have a preemptive effect: cf. e.g., Campbell v. Hussey, 368 U.S. 297, 301, 82 S.Ct. 327, 329, 7 L.Ed.2d 299 (1961), rehearing denied 368 U.S. 1005, 82 S.Ct. 596, 7 L.Ed.2d 547 (1962) with Florida Lime & Avocado Growers, Inc. v. Paul, 373 U.S. 132, 83 S.Ct. 1210, 10 L.Ed.2d 248 (1963). In other cases, however, state law will be struck down, not because federal statutory law preempts it, but because it invades a federal domain. Thus, Zschernig v. Miller, 389 U.S. 429, 88 S.Ct. 664, 19 L.Ed.2d 683 (1968), rehearing denied 390 U.S. 974, 88 S.Ct. 1018, 19 L.Ed.2d 1196 (1968), invalidated Oregon's "iron-curtain statute," denying inheritance rights to certain aliens, as an impermissible intrusion into the federal foreign relations power. See also infra § 3.56. The many decisions under the Commerce Clause that resulted in the overturning of state statutes and regulations are classic examples. The issue, the U.S. Supreme Court wrote, is "uniformity versus locality.... More accurately, the question is whether the State interest is outweighed by a national interest in the unhampered operation of interstate commerce." California v. Zook, 336 U.S. at 728, 69 S.Ct. at 843 (1949).

The Cuban Liberty and Democratic Solidarity (Libertad) Act of 1996 [Helms–Burton Act], P.L. 104–114, 110 Stat. 785, reprinted in Note following 22 U.S.C.A. § 6021, amended the Cuban Democracy Act of 1992. P.L. 102–484, reprinted in Note following 22 U.S.C.A. § 6001. The new Act enables any United States National who owns property confiscated by Cuba to sue anyone who "traffics" in the property. "Traffics" includes purchasing. No United States court may decline to entertain such an action on the basis of the act of state doctrine. Id. § 302. If a financial institution such as the International Monetary Fund or the Inter–American Development Bank makes a loan to Cuba over United States opposition, the United States will withhold equal amounts in payments to that institution. Id. § 104. The European Union's Council of Ministers have adopted a regulation that authorizes E.U. companies sued under Helms–Burton to bring "clawback" suits against the European subsidiaries of companies that have used the act. Canada

has enacted legislation punishing Canadian companies, including subsidiaries of U.S. companies, that refuse to trade with Cuba in compliance with Helms–Burton. Thus far, the President, acting pursuant to his statutory authority, has regularly issued six-month suspensions of civil actions under the law.

5. Texas v. Pankey, 441 F.2d 236, 240 (10th Cir.1971) ("As the field of federal common law has been given necessary expansion into matters of federal concern and relationship (where no applicable federal statute exists, as there does not here), the ecological rights of a State in the improper impairment of them from outside the State's own territory, now would and should, we think, be held to be a matter having basis and standard in federal common law.... "). See also Note, Federal Common Law and Interstate Pollution, 85 Harv. L. Rev. 1439 (1972). In 1981, the Supreme Court held that, when there is federal legislation in the area, federal common law could not be used to impose more stringent standards. City of Milwaukee v. Illinois and Michigan, 451 U.S. 304, 101 S.Ct. 1784, 68 L.Ed.2d 114 (1981) (discussed further infra § 3.54 n.17). See also supra n.3.

See also Howard v. Lyons, 360 U.S. 593, 79 S.Ct. 1331, 3 L.Ed.2d 1454 (1959) and United States v. Gillock, 445 U.S. 360, 100 S.Ct. 1185, 1192 n.10, 63 L.Ed.2d 454 (1980) (federal officials' immunity from liability for libel derives from federal common law); Banco Nacional de Cuba v. Sabbatino, 376 U.S. 398, 84 S.Ct. 923, 11 L.Ed.2d 804 (1964), on remand 272 F.Supp. 836 (S.D.N.Y.1965), judgment affirmed 383 F.2d 166 (2d Cir.1967), cert. denied 390 U.S. 956, 88 S.Ct. 1038, 19 L.Ed.2d 1151 (1968), (adoption of the Act–of–State doctrine as a matter of federal common law, subsequently limited by federal statute: 79 Stat. 653, 22 U.S.C.A. § 2370(e)(2), with *Sabbatino* itself overturned in Banco Nacional de Cuba v. Farr, 383 F.2d 166 (2d Cir.1967)) cert. denied 390 U.S. 956, 88 S.Ct. 1038, 19 L.Ed.2d 1151 (1968); Kaiser Steel Corp. v. Mullins, 455 U.S. 72, 102 S.Ct. 851, 856, 70 L.Ed.2d 833 (1982) (in union's action to enforce collective bargaining agreement, in which jurisdiction was based on the Labor Management Relations Act and the Employment Retirement Income Security Act, and in which defendant raised illegality of the agreement under the antitrust laws, held that while "there is no statutory code of federal contract law, ... illegal promises

to declare federal common law, relating to matters of federal concern and based on the three sources identified above, exists in diversity cases as well as in federal-question cases.[6]

The existence of the power to declare federal common law does not mean, however, that it will be exercised in all cases or that, when exercised, the federal court will adopt a new federal standard as opposed to an adoption of state law as the federal standard.[7] Further, and while constitutionally *permissible,* the formulation of federal common law may not be *appropriate* in all cases lest *Erie*-policies[8]—that results in state and federal courts not differ materially—be frustrated. To define "appropriateness" is both difficult and elusive. In holding judicial lawmaking inappropriate in the *Wallis* case,[9] the Supreme Court addressed the question as follows: "[N]ormally the guiding principle is that a significant conflict between some federal policy or interest and the use of state law in the premises must first be specifically shown. It is by no means enough that, as we may assume, Congress could under the Constitution readily enact a complete code of law governing transactions in federal mineral leases among private parties. Whether latent federal power should be exercised to displace state law is primarily a decision for Congress. Even where there is related federal legislation in an area . . . 'Congress acts . . . against the background of the total *corpus juris* of the states . . . ' Hart & Wechsler, The Federal Courts and the Federal System 435 (1953). Because we find no significant threat to any identifiable federal policy or interest, we do not press on to consider other questions relevant to involving federal common law, such as the strength of the state interest in having its own rules govern, . . . the feasibility of creating a judicial substitute . . . and other similar factors." The following section explores the circumstances in which the presence of a federal interest appropriately calls for the formulation of federal common law.[10]

will not be enforced in cases controlled by the federal law.").

6. Miree v. DeKalb County, Georgia, 433 U.S. 25, 29, 97 S.Ct. 2490, 2493, 53 L.Ed.2d 557 (1977).

7. Compare United States v. Kimbell Foods, Inc., 440 U.S. 715, 99 S.Ct. 1448, 59 L.Ed.2d 711 (1979) and Wilson v. Omaha Indian Tribe, 442 U.S. 653, 99 S.Ct. 2529, 61 L.Ed.2d 153 (1979), cert. denied 449 U.S. 825, 101 S.Ct. 87, 66 L.Ed.2d 28 (1980) (state law adopted as the standard) with United States v. Little Lake Misere Land Co., Inc., 412 U.S. 580, 93 S.Ct. 2389, 37 L.Ed.2d 187 (1973) (federal standard): both cases arose under "federal law."

8. See Hanna v. Plumer, 380 U.S. 460, 85 S.Ct. 1136, 14 L.Ed.2d 8 (1965).

9. Wallis v. Pan American Petroleum Corp., 384 U.S. 63, 68–69, 86 S.Ct. 1301, 1304, 16 L.Ed.2d 369 (1966), on remand 366 F.2d 210 (5th Cir.1966). Quoting from Wallis, the Court reached the same conclusion in Miree v. DeKalb County, Georgia, 433 U.S. 25, 97 S.Ct. 2490, 53 L.Ed.2d 557 (1977) (discussed infra § 3.54 n.5).

10. For brief further mention of statutory construction (including gap filling) see infra § 3.54 n.17. The other area of judicial lawmaking—the exercise of negative control (supra n.4)—receives no further consideration.

B. THE FEDERAL INTEREST[1]

1. *Government Obligations*

§ 3.51 One of the clearest examples of the existence of a federal interest concerns the Government's liability for dealing in commercial paper. In an early case[2] the Supreme Court identified a federal policy, derived from an overall statutory scheme, in favor of protecting the Federal Deposit Insurance Corporation against the diversity of state laws with respect to liability. Less clear are cases in which the Government is the plaintiff and seeks to invoke the liability of a private defendant as, for instance, in the *Clearfield Trust* case[3] in which a bank had guaranteed a wrongfully endorsed Government check. Even in this case, however, the Supreme Court rejected the bank's defense which was valid under state law:

> The rights and duties of the United States on commercial paper which it issues are governed by federal rather than local law.... The authority to issue the check had its origins in the Constitution and the statutes of the United States and was in no way dependent on the laws of Pennsylvania ... The duties imposed on the United States ... have their roots in the same federal sources....
>
> The application of state law ... would subject the rights and duties of the United States to exceptional uncertainty. It would lead to great diversity in results by making the identical transactions subject to the vagaries of the laws of the several states. The desirability of a uniform rule is plain.[4]

The importance of this decision lies in the two criteria on which it relied, both of them observed in different form earlier. In order to fashion federal law, it is a first prerequisite that the particular legal problem lie generally within the area of federal competence; however, by itself this would not be enough to preempt equally valid state law. A

---

§ 3.51

1. See supra §§ 3.49 n.2 and 3.50 n.1. See also Chow, Limiting *Erie* in a New Age of International Law: Toward a Federal Common Law of International Choice of Law, 74 Iowa L. Rev. 165 (1988).

2. D'Oench, Duhme & Co. v. Federal Deposit Insurance Corp., 315 U.S. 447, 62 S.Ct. 676, 86 L.Ed. 956 (1942), An earlier case, Deitrick v. Greaney, 309 U.S. 190, 60 S.Ct. 480, 84 L.Ed. 694 (1940), had held that the banking acts were designed to set up a comprehensive system of law, i.e. preempt state law, with gaps to be filled by the federal judiciary. Murphy v. Federal Deposit Ins. Corp., 61 F.3d 34 (D.C.Cir. 1995), took the position that the financial Institutions Reform, Recovery, and Enforcement Act of 1989 (FIRREA) preempts the federal common law doctrine of *D'Oench*.

Motorcity of Jacksonville, Ltd. v. Southeast Bank, N.A., 83 F.3d 1317 (11th Cir.1996), upon reconsideration 120 F.3d 1140 (11th Cir.1997), cert. denied 523 U.S. 1093, 118 S.Ct. 1559, 140 L.Ed.2d 791 (1998) disagreed.

3. Clearfield Trust Co. v. United States, 318 U.S. 363, 63 S.Ct. 573, 87 L.Ed. 838 (1943).

4. 318 U.S. at 366–67, 63 S.Ct. at 575. See also National Metropolitan Bank v. United States, 323 U.S. 454, 65 S.Ct. 354, 89 L.Ed. 383 (1945), which involved 144 checks fraudulently issued and presented. Relying on *Clearfield* and older precedent, the Court held that the negligence of the Government did not insulate the bank from an action on its guarantee of the forged signatures.

second element must also be present which differs from that noted in decisions exercising negative control. In those cases, for instance in the field of interstate commerce, state law had to yield only when unreasonably burdensome; under the *Clearfield* rule, in contrast, preemption of state law in favor of federal decisional law requires the finding that a strong need exists for national uniformity. This approach, which runs through most of the case law analyzed below, permits differentiation but, at the same time, is also the source of additional difficulty. Thus, in litigation between two banks concerning their respective rights in U.S. commercial paper,[5] the Court held that state law determined the rights of private parties, while federal law would control the construction of the instrument or a determination of the rights of the United States. The dissenting justices thought, in contrast, that the federal law merchant which *Clearfield* had held applicable to transactions in U.S. commercial paper should govern all such transactions. As the decision stands, some rights in government paper are now governed by federal law while the laws of the several states govern other rights. Since authority for federal preemption existed in *Parnell* as much as in *Clearfield,* the retreat from *Clearfield* seems a result of the lack (in the Court's view) of a strong need for uniformity.[6]

Assuming that uniformity is indeed strongly needed with respect to a given problem, the question may arise whether an earlier federal rule should yield when state law subsequently becomes uniform. This question was before a lower court which was asked to depart from an earlier federal decisional rule and to apply state law on the ground that state law had become uniform with the universal adoption of the Uniform Commercial Code.[7] The court refused to do so, observing that a strong federal interest (protection of the federal treasury from liability) was still present and implying that even uniform state law should not be able to change federal liability. If generally followed,[8] this case would suggest a third criterion: the substantive content of the otherwise applicable state law. In most instances, however, it would seem that "the state commercial codes 'furnish convenient solutions in no way inconsistent with adequate protection of the federal interest....' We therefore decline to

---

5. Bank of America National Trust & Savings Association v. Parnell, 352 U.S. 29, 77 S.Ct. 119, 1 L.Ed.2d 93 (1956).

6. But see two cases in which the Court found (in contrast to *Parnell*) a strong federal policy and therefore declined to follow state law: Free v. Bland, 369 U.S. 663, 82 S.Ct. 1089, 8 L.Ed.2d 180 (1962); Yiatchos v. Yiatchos, 376 U.S. 306, 84 S.Ct. 742, 11 L.Ed.2d 724 (1964). In both cases the Supreme Court upheld the beneficiary designation in U.S. Savings Bonds against state law which would have defeated it, on the ground that free alienability of the bonds was necessary in light of the federal policy of promoting the sale of government bonds.

7. United States v. Bank of America National Trust & Savings Association, 288

F.Supp. 343 (N.D.Cal.1968), affirmed 438 F.2d 1213 (9th Cir.1971), cert. denied 404 U.S. 864, 92 S.Ct. 54, 30 L.Ed.2d 108 (1971). See also United States v. Cloverleaf Cold Storage Co., 286 F.Supp. 680 (N.D.Iowa 1968).

8. Most federal courts do follow the state version of the U.C.C. See, e.g., Woods–Tucker Leasing Corp. v. Hutcheson–Ingram Development Co., 30 U.C.C. Rep. Serv. 1505, 1511, 642 F.2d 744, 749 (5th Cir. 1981) (dictum); In re King–Porter Co., 446 F.2d 722, 732 (5th Cir.1971); United States v. Wegematic Corp., 360 F.2d 674 (2d Cir. 1966); Natus Corp. v. United States, 371 F.2d 450 (Ct.Cl.1967).

override intricate state laws of general applicability on which private creditors base their daily commercial transactions."[9]

The *Clearfield–Parnell* distinction thus involved a balancing of federal and state interests *both* for the purpose of determining whether there is a federal interest to treat the issue as one of federal law *and* whether, as a matter of content, a new federal rule should be formulated or state law adopted. The area of federal liens furnishes a good example. In a number of lower court decisions,[10] courts have applied a federal rule, while decisions of the U.S. Supreme Court,[11] culminating in *Kimbell*

9. United States v. Kimbell Foods, Inc., 440 U.S. 715, 729, 99 S.Ct. 1448, 1459, 59 L.Ed.2d 711 (1979) (quoting from United States v. Standard Oil Co., 332 U.S. 301, 309, 67 S.Ct. 1604, 1609, 91 L.Ed. 2067 (1947)).

It should be noted that *Kimbell Foods* involved government claims (lien priorities under lending programs of the Small Business Authority and Farmers Home Administration) as had *Clearfield*. The distinction which the Court seemed to draw between the two decisions may be that in *Clearfield*, national uniformity with respect to the rights and duties of the federal government was essential, while private interests, in *Kimbell Foods,* were paramount in those cases in which the government entered into *local* commercial transactions: "In structuring financial transactions, businessmen depend on state commercial law to provide the stability essential for reliable evaluation of the risks involved.... However subjecting federal contractual liens to the doctrines developed in the tax lien area could undermine that stability. Creditors who justifiably rely on state law to obtain superior liens would have their expectations thwarted whenever a federal contractual security interest suddenly appeared and took precedence. Because the ultimate consequences of altering settled commercial practices are so difficult to foresee, we hesitate to create new uncertainties, in the absence of careful legislative deliberation. Of course, formulating special rules to govern the priority of the federal *consensual* liens ... would be justified if necessary to vindicate important national interests. But neither the Government nor the Court of Appeals advanced any concrete reasons for rejecting well-established commercial rules which have proven workable over time." *Kimbell Foods,* 440 U.S. at 739–40, 99 S.Ct. at 1464–65 (emphasis added). See also United States v. Yazell, 382 U.S. 341, 86 S.Ct. 500, 15 L.Ed.2d 404 (1966) (discussed infra n.11).

10. United States v. Latrobe Construction Co., 246 F.2d 357 (8th Cir.1957), cert. denied 355 U.S. 890, 78 S.Ct. 262, 2

L.Ed.2d 189 (1957) (Government lien, recorded before any improvements or advances of money, is prior to miner's lien; priority is a matter of federal law because Government is involved); Ingraham v. Williams, 173 F.Supp. 1 (N.D.Cal.1959) (intervening Government lien cannot be defeated by merger of title with a subsequent lien when the Government lien is still valid under federal law); United States v. Sommerville, 324 F.2d 712 (3d Cir.1963), cert. denied 376 U.S. 909, 84 S.Ct. 663, 11 L.Ed.2d 608 (1964) (federal law determined liability of an auctioneer for conversion of property on which a federal lien had been perfected). See also Cassidy Commission Co. v. United States, 387 U.S. 875 (10th Cir. 1967); United States v. Carson, 372 F.2d 429 (6th Cir.1967). In United States v. Wells, 403 F.2d 596 (5th Cir.1968), the court applied federal law to loans of the Veterans Administration on the ground that this was necessary to assure uniform administration of the nationwide program. Accord: Branden v. Driver, 293 F.Supp. 871 (N.D.Cal.1968), affirmed 441 F.2d 1171 (9th Cir.1971) (federal policy concerning loan collections overrides state law barring sale of property to cover further deficiencies). The federal rule with respect to liens (first in time, first in right) was applied to a lien held by the Small Business Administration: Director of Revenue v. United States, 392 F.2d 307 (10th Cir.1968); Fred W. Beal, Inc. v. Allen, 287 F.Supp. 126 (D.Me.1968). But see Kimbell Foods, 440 U.S. 715, 99 S.Ct. 1448, 59 L.Ed.2d 711.

For the extent to which questions in condemnation actions are to be governed by federal law see United States v. 93.970 Acres of Land, 360 U.S. 328, 79 S.Ct. 1193, 3 L.Ed.2d 1275 (1959); United States v. Certain Property, 344 F.2d 142 (2d Cir. 1965); Higginson v. United States, 384 F.2d 504 (6th Cir.1967), cert. denied 390 U.S. 947, 88 S.Ct. 1034, 19 L.Ed.2d 1137 (1968).

11. In United States v. Brosnan, 363 U.S. 237, 80 S.Ct. 1108, 4 L.Ed.2d 1192 (1960), the Court held that state law ap-

Foods,[12] have increasingly looked to state law as the applicable standard. Merely because uniformity might be convenient, however, does not justify creation of a supreme federal rule, even one that borrows from state law. In *O'Melveny & Myers v. FDIC,*[13] a federal agency, acting as a receiver for a failed savings and loan, sued a law firm for malpractice. The Supreme Court held that state law must govern, even if application of state principles might produce varying results in similar cases brought in different fora. The crucial defect in the attempted invocation of federal law was the absence of any "significant conflict with an identifiable federal policy or interest."[14]

2. *Contractual Relations With the Government*

§ 3.52   Except with respect to contractual liens,[1] the courts have often held that state law is not applicable to contracts to which the federal government is a party and have resorted to "federal law" to provide uniform rules. These cases include leases entered into by the Government[2] and liquidated damage clauses in government

plied to the divestiture (including notice requirements) of a government lien in a foreclosure proceeding. The majority of the Court (5 Justices) explained its deference to state law on the ground that Congress, by using liens for its tax enforcement, had entered an area dominated by state law and that, without specific Congressional action, the Court should not use the judicial function to create a competing system of property rights in liens. The dissent by three Justices and the Chief Justice emphasized that three procedures exist under federal law to extinguish such a lien and that these should be the exclusive remedy in the light of the interests involved; at the very least, if state law were to be followed, notice to the Government should be required. In a subsequent decision, United States v. Buffalo Savings Bank, 371 U.S. 228, 229–230, 83 S.Ct. 314, 315, 9 L.Ed.2d 283 (1963) the Court expressly limited *Brosnan* as applying only to foreclosure proceedings and not to priorities. The federal doctrine of priority is based on the rule "first in time, first in right." United States v. City of New Britain, 347 U.S. 81, 74 S.Ct. 367, 98 L.Ed. 520 (1954). See generally Plumb, Federal Liens and Priorities—Agenda for the Next Decade, 77 Yale L.J. 228 (1967).

In *Kimbell Foods, supra* n.9, the Court finally drew a distinction between tax liens and contractual liens. See also United States v. Yazell, 382 U.S. 341, 86 S.Ct. 500, 15 L.Ed.2d 404 (1966): Texas law, providing for a wife's incapacity during coverture, determined liability under a small business loan which the government had negotiated on an individual contract basis with the

couple in question. The Eighth Circuit arguably erred when it looked "to federal regulations rather than state law for the rule of decision" when deciding whether the Farmers Home Administration retained a continuing security interest in collateral to whose sale it had consented. United States v. Missouri Farmers Assn., Inc., 764 F.2d 488 (8th Cir.1985), cert. denied 475 U.S. 1053, 1054, 106 S.Ct. 1281, 1282, 89 L.Ed.2d 588 (1986) (White, J., dissenting).

12. United States v. Kimbell Foods, Inc., 440 U.S. 715, 99 S.Ct. 1448, 59 L.Ed.2d 711 (1979). See also United States v. Fleet Bank (In re Calore Express Co.), 288 F.3d 22 (1st Cir. 2002) (applying U.C.C. as the federal common law to an issue involving setoff priority of a U.S. government claim; no need for independent federal rule); Morgan v. South Bend Community School Corp., 797 F.2d 471 (7th Cir.1986) (in a § 1983 civil rights claim state law, and not federal common law, governed question of who had authority to settle demoted plaintiff's case against school board).

13. 512 U.S. 79, 114 S.Ct. 2048, 129 L.Ed.2d 67 (1994).

14. Id. at 87, 114 S.Ct. at 2055, 129 L.Ed.2d 67.

§ 3.52

1. Supra § 3.51 nn.9, 11–12.

2. United States v. Allegheny County, 322 U.S. 174, 64 S.Ct. 908, 88 L.Ed. 1209 (1944) (interpretation of a federal lease governed by federal law); Girard Trust Co. v. United States, 149 F.2d 872 (3d Cir.1945)

contracts.[3] The basic view of these decisions is that the Government is a party to the action and drew up the contract pursuant to some federal authority. Because of the direct governmental relationship, the interest of the Government is assumed to be paramount over state interest. A different question arises when the Government is not a direct or primary party, for instance, when litigation involves subcontracts of parties working under a government contract.[4] In these cases, federal law might reach into private contracts if a sufficient federal interest exists. However, the Government's interest in these contract cases is usually only indirect and financial, and it is limited to the particular transaction as for instance when a subcontractor's recovery would increase the Government's cost under the main contract.[5] There is no need for uniformity; the position of the Government is no different in these cases from that of any private party. Consistently with this view, subleases between private parties often have been held not to be governed by federal law because no substantial federal interest could be identified.[6]

3.   Tort–Related Issues

§ **3.53**   In an early decision, the U.S. Supreme Court held that the Government's relation with persons in the armed services requires application of uniform federal law, for instances, in cases in which the government seeks to recover amounts expended for a soldier's hospitalization, his pay, and the loss of his services because of negligent injury by the defendant.[1] In the reverse situation, the Court has held that an

(general, that is: federal, law of landlord and tenant controls in Government leases); American Houses v. Schneider, 211 F.2d 881 (3d Cir.1954) (assignee of government lease subject to federal law because of the Government's security interest in the lease). See also United States v. Little Lake Misere Land Co., 412 U.S. 580, 93 S.Ct. 2389, 37 L.Ed.2d 187 (1973) (invalidating state statute purporting to affect federal government's interest in land); Conille v. Secretary of Housing and Urban Development, 840 F.2d 105 (1st Cir.1988) (lease with federal government subject to federal law).

3.   Priebe & Sons, Inc. v. United States, 332 U.S. 407, 68 S.Ct. 123, 92 L.Ed. 32 (1947); United States v. Le Roy Dyal Co., 186 F.2d 460 (3d Cir.1950), cert. denied 341 U.S. 926, 71 S.Ct. 797, 95 L.Ed. 1357 (1951). Another area for the applicability of federal law are claims of the United States under federal loan programs: United States v. Ellis, 714 F.2d 953 (9th Cir.1983).

4.   See Note, Choice of Law in Prime–Sub Government Contract Disputes, 48 Boston U. L. Rev. 613 (1968). For a decision upholding the parties' contractual choice of "Federal law of government contracts" in an action based on diversity jurisdiction see

NRM Corp. v. Hercules, Inc., 758 F.2d 676 (D.C.Cir.1985).

5.   See United States v. Taylor, 333 F.2d 633 (5th Cir.1964); American Pipe & Steel Corp. v. Firestone Tire & Rubber Co., 292 F.2d 640 (9th Cir.1961). See also National Union Fire Insurance Co. v. D & L Construction Co., 353 F.2d 169 (8th Cir.1965), cert. denied 384 U.S. 941, 86 S.Ct. 1462, 16 L.Ed.2d 539 (1966).

6.   Wallis v. Pan American Petroleum Corp., 384 U.S. 63, 86 S.Ct. 1301, 16 L.Ed.2d 369 (1966); for an excerpt from this decision see supra § 3.51 n.4.

§ 3.53

1.   United States v. Standard Oil Co., 332 U.S. 301, 67 S.Ct. 1604, 91 L.Ed. 2067 (1947). However, the Court refused to create a substantive rule in this case, noting that the field was "properly within Congress' control . . . concerning which it has seen fit to take no action." 332 U.S. at 316, 67 S.Ct. at 1612. Since state law could not apply, the defendant was not liable. As Justice Jackson noted in his dissent, however, "the law of torts has been developed almost exclusively by the judiciary . . . by common law methods." 332 U.S. at 318, 67 S.Ct. at

on-duty serviceman who is injured due to the negligence of government officials may not recover under the Federal Tort Claims Act[2] and that the ordinary rule, allowing the government to be impleaded as a third-party defendant for purposes of indemnity or contribution,[3] does not apply in circumstances when the original action is brought by a member of the armed services against a private defendant.[4]

In *Bowen v. United States*,[5] the Seventh Circuit held that state law determined whether a pilot's contributory negligence barred his action under the Federal Tort Claims Act. To arrive at its decision, the Court had to construe the meaning of the word "law" in the Act's reference to "the law of the place where the act or omission occurred." Specifically, the issue was whether *Richards v. United States*[6] applied, in which the Supreme Court had held that the Act's language referred to whole law of the state in which the act or omission occurred (including its conflicts law), or whether the federal standard announced in *Kohr v. Allegheny Airlines, Inc.*[7] governed. The latter decision had held that a federal standard governed claims for contribution and indemnity arising out of midair collisions because of the "prevailing federal interest in uniform air law regulation."[8] *Kohr* was distinguished since it had involved a third-party claim and did not arise under the Federal Tort Claims Act.[9] The Seventh Circuit noted that the U.S. Supreme Court had both been

---

1613. Congress has since created a statutory right of recovery. See 42 U.S.C.A. § 2651(a).

2. Feres v. United States, 340 U.S. 135, 71 S.Ct. 153, 95 L.Ed. 152 (1950).

3. United States v. Yellow Cab Co., 340 U.S. 543, 71 S.Ct. 399, 95 L.Ed. 523 (1951).

4. Stencel Aero Engineering Corp. v. United States, 431 U.S. 666, 97 S.Ct. 2054, 52 L.Ed.2d 665 (1977). *Feres* and *Stencel* were forcefully confirmed by United States v. Shearer, 473 U.S. 52, 105 S.Ct. 3039, 87 L.Ed.2d 38 (1985), on remand 772 F.2d 896 (3d Cir.1985) mainly because such suits would require civilian courts to second-guess military decisions. Government contractors, in turn, traditionally had available defenses against third party tort claims, derived from common law negligence principles or based on an agency relationship with the government so as to enable them to invoke its immunity. The latter defense often fails for lack of an actual agency relationship and the former as a result of modern (strict) products liability law. As a result, a federal common law "government contractor defense" is now recognized. Boyle v. United Technologies Corp., 487 U.S. 500, 108 S.Ct. 2510, 101 L.Ed.2d 442 (1988).

5. 570 F.2d 1311 (7th Cir.1978).

6. 369 U.S. 1, 82 S.Ct. 585, 7 L.Ed.2d 492 (1962).

7. 504 F.2d 400 (7th Cir.1974), cert. denied 421 U.S. 978, 95 S.Ct. 1980, 44 L.Ed.2d 470 (1975).

8. 504 F.2d at 403. The court derived the federal interest from Justice Jackson's language in Northwest Airlines v. Minnesota, 322 U.S. 292, 303, 64 S.Ct. 950, 956, 88 L.Ed. 1283 (1944), that "Air as an element in which to navigate is even more inevitably federalized by the commerce clause than is navigable water" and from the passage of the federal Aviation Act of 1958, 49 U.S.C.A. § 1301 in which "Congress expressed the view that the control of aviation should rest exclusively in the hands of the federal government." 504 F.2d at 404. See also Norfolk & Western Ry. Co. v. Liepelt, 444 U.S. 490, 100 S.Ct. 755, 62 L.Ed.2d 689 (1980) (admissibility of taxation of earnings governed is a rule of "federal common law" in cases arising under the Federal Employers' Liability Act because of Congressional intent, in enacting FELA to create uniformity throughout the nation and to provide compensation).

9. *Kohr* had previously been distinguished in Smith v. Cessna Aircraft Corp., 428 F.Supp. 1285 (N.D.Ill.1977) which held that the federal standard announced in *Kohr* did not apply in a case involving a single private plane on an intrastate flight.

unwilling to extend federal admiralty jurisdiction to aviation accidents[10] and had reiterated its interpretation of the Federal Tort Claims Act in *Miree*.[11] Accordingly, *Richards* rather than *Kohr* applied, and state law supplied the rule of decision with respect to the issue of contributory negligence. The Supreme Court's more recent decision in *O'Melveny & Myers v. FDIC*,[12] refusing to create a federal law of attorney malpractice in actions brought by federal receivers, serves as a clear reminder that state law must apply unless a clear conflict with federal policy can be identified.

4. *Private Disputes Over Government–Created Rights*

§ 3.54 Federally-created rights are often in issue in private litigation. In determining whether these rights are to be viewed under federal rather than state law, the courts display an even greater restraint in creating federal law. Resolution of the issue under state law is favored unless federal interest or policy clearly requires uniform results.[1] Thus, the competence of an insured under a national service life insurance policy to change his beneficiary was held to be a federal question,[2] but the power of a guardian to effect such a change was not.[3] Similarly, the question of whether an illegitimate child qualified under the Jones Act was said to be a federal question,[4] but whether the term "children" in the Copyright Renewal Statute included illegitimates was not.[5]

10. Executive Jet Aviation, Inc. v. City of Cleveland, 409 U.S. 249, 93 S.Ct. 493, 34 L.Ed.2d 454 (1972). See also supra § 3.46 n.9 (quoting from In re Air Crash Disaster Near Chicago, Illinois on May 25, 1979, 526 F.Supp. 226 (N.D.Ill.1981)).

11. Miree v. DeKalb County, Georgia, 433 U.S. 25, 97 S.Ct. 2490, 53 L.Ed.2d 557 (1977)(discussed infra § 3.54 n.6).

12. 512 U.S. 79, 114 S.Ct. 2048, 129 L.Ed.2d 67 (1994).

§ 3.54

1. See, e.g., The Black & Decker Disability Plan v. Nord, 538 U.S. 822, 123 S.Ct. 1965, 155 L.Ed.2d 1034 (2003) (noting that Congress expected that the courts would develop a federal common law under ERISA). When a federally created right of action has no accompanying statute of limitations, state law of limitations usually applies. See, e.g., Hardin v. Straub, 490 U.S. 536, 109 S.Ct. 1998, 104 L.Ed.2d 582 (1989) (limitation and tolling rules in federal civil rights actions borrowed from state law).

2. Dyke v. Dyke, 227 F.2d 461 (6th Cir. 1955), cert. denied 352 U.S. 850, 77 S.Ct. 70, 1 L.Ed.2d 61 (1956); Eureka Federal Sav. and Loan Ass'n v. Kidwell, 672 F.Supp. 436 (N.D.Cal.1987) (federal common law governs internal operations of savings and loan associations, including claims for

breach of fiduciary duties by officers, because of strong federal interest in their uniform treatment).

3. Roecker v. United States, 379 F.2d 400 (5th Cir.1967), cert. denied 389 U.S. 1005, 88 S.Ct. 563, 19 L.Ed.2d 600 (1967). *Dyke,* supra n.2 and *Roecker* can be reconciled on the basis that the former only decided the right of the insured to change the beneficiary under his own policy, while the latter touched upon the rights and duties of guardians which are normally governed by state law. To determine the issue in accordance with federal law would be burdensome to the guardian in *Roecker* by subjecting him to the different standards of different applicable laws; this burden was not counterbalanced by any strong federal interest.

4. In re Petition of Risdal & Anderson, Inc., 266 F.Supp. 157 (D.Mass.1967). See also Middleton v. Luckenbach Steamship Co., 70 F.2d 326 (2d Cir.1934), cert. denied 293 U.S. 577, 55 S.Ct. 89, 79 L.Ed. 674 (1934).

5. De Sylva v. Ballentine, 351 U.S. 570, 76 S.Ct. 974, 100 L.Ed. 1415 (1956). The rule in *DeSylva* may have been affected by subsequent decisions. See Levy v. Louisiana and Glona v. American Guarantee & Liability Insurance Co., 391 U.S. 68, 73, 88 S.Ct.

Some cases involve the issue whether a federal right should be created in the first place. Thus, in *Miree v. DeKalb County*[6] petitioners were survivors of deceased passengers and a victim of an airplane crash. They claimed as third-party beneficiaries under a government grant contract requiring the county to maintain land adjacent to the airport in a manner permitting normal operations. In fact, surrounding areas had been used as a garbage dump, attracting birds that were ingested into the plane's engines. The Supreme Court held that state and not federal law applied; its opinion drew heavily on *Clearfield Trust,*[7] *Parnell,*[8] and *Wallis.*[9] In contrast to *Clearfield Trust,* "petitioners' breach-of-contract claim against respondent will have no direct effect upon the United States or its Treasury.[10] ... The parallel between Parnell and [this case] is obvious. The question of whether petitioners may sue respondent does not require decision under federal common law since the litigation is among private parties and no substantial rights or duties of the United States hinge on its outcome."[11] Any federal interest—for instance, to advance federal aviation policy by promoting compliance with federal safety regulations—is " 'far too speculative, far too remote a possibility to justify the application of federal law to transactions essentially of local

1509, 1515, 20 L.Ed.2d 436, 441 (1968), which held that illegitimate children could recover for the wrongful death of their mother and that a mother could recover for the wrongful death of her illegitimate child. These decisions declared unconstitutional a long-standing interpretation of the Louisiana Wrongful Death Act which had restricted recoveries to legitimate children. Labine v. Vincent, 401 U.S. 532, 91 S.Ct. 1017, 28 L.Ed.2d 288 (1971), permitted Louisiana to differentiate in its inheritance laws. Weber v. Aetna Casualty & Surety Co., 406 U.S. 164, 92 S.Ct. 1400, 31 L.Ed.2d 768 (1972) and Gomez v. Perez, 409 U.S. 535, 93 S.Ct. 872, 35 L.Ed.2d 56 (1973) distinguished *Labine* on the ground that the statutes in question unconstitutionally disadvantages illegitimates (while, in *Labine,* the testator could have taken remedial action). However, Trimble v. Gordon, 430 U.S. 762, 97 S.Ct. 1459, 52 L.Ed.2d 31 (1977), which held that state intestacy laws could not discriminate between children on the basis of birth in or out of wedlock, casts doubt on the continued validity of *Labine.* But cf. Mathews v. Lucas, 427 U.S. 495, 96 S.Ct. 2755, 49 L.Ed.2d 651 (1976) permitting a presumption of dependency for legitimates but not for illegitimates for purposes of survivor's benefits. The rights of illegitimate children are discussed further infra § 16.3.

See also T. B. Harms Co. v. Eliscu 339 F.2d 823 (2d Cir.1964), cert. denied 381 U.S. 915, 85 S.Ct. 1534, 14 L.Ed.2d 435 (1965) (dispute over property rights in a copyright does not raise a federal question and no federal jurisdiction exists. The jurisdiction conferred by the copyright laws extends only to the causes of action created by the statute (such as for infringement or construction) but not to ancillary matters). See also Bartsch v. Metro–Goldwyn–Mayer Inc., 391 F.2d 150 (2d Cir.1968), cert. denied 393 U.S. 826, 89 S.Ct. 86, 21 L.Ed.2d 96 (1968); Factors Etc., Inc. v. Pro Arts, Inc., 496 F.Supp. 1090, 1097 (S.D.N.Y. 1980), reversed on other grounds 652 F.2d 278 (2d Cir.1981), cert. denied 456 U.S. 927, 102 S.Ct. 1973, 72 L.Ed.2d 442 (1982) (Copyright Act of 1976 not intended to preempt common-law right of publicity).

6. 433 U.S. 25, 97 S.Ct. 2490, 53 L.Ed.2d 557 (1977).

7. Clearfield Trust Co. v. United States, 318 U.S. 363, 63 S.Ct. 573, 87 L.Ed. 838 (1943); see also supra § 3.51.

8. Bank of America National Trust & Savings Association v. Parnell, 352 U.S. 29, 77 S.Ct. 119, 1 L.Ed.2d 93 (1956).

9. Wallis v. Pan American Petroleum Corp., 384 U.S. 63, 86 S.Ct. 1301, 16 L.Ed.2d 369 (1966).

10. 433 U.S. at 29, 97 S.Ct. at 2494.

11. Id. at 31, 97 S.Ct. at 2495. The Court continued: "On the other hand, nothing we say here forecloses the applicability of federal common law in interpreting the rights and duties of the United States under federal contracts."

concern.' "[12] In addition, and " 'apart from the highly abstract nature of [the federal] interest, there has been no showing that state law is not adequate to achieve it.' "[13]

In his instructive concurrence, Chief Justice Burger emphasized that *Clearfield Trust* does not preclude " ... the application of 'federal common law' to all matters involving only the rights of private citizens.... I am not prepared to foreclose ... the possibility that there may be situations where the rights and obligations of private parties are ... dependent on a specific exercise of congressional regulatory power.... "[14] In the event that this power has not been exercised by legislation, " 'the inevitable incompleteness presented by all legislation means that interstitial federal law making is a basic responsibility of the federal courts.' "[15]

Interstate pollution is another possible circumstance in which federal common law might be created as a means for essential arbitrating between different sovereigns. The Supreme Court so held in *Illinois v. City of Milwaukee*,[16] holding that a federal law of nuisance governed in a cross-border water pollution dispute. Federal common law (like state common law) only exists until displaced by a statutory or regulatory structure. Later, in *Illinois*, the Court held that the Federal Clean Water Act had overtaken the common law rule.[17] Given the broad, federal codification of environmental standards, there are few, if any, areas in which federal common law governs interstate pollution.

C. WHEN IS FEDERAL COMMON LAW APPROPRIATE?

§ 3.55   The cases make it clear that federal common law may form the basis for federal-question jurisdiction[1] as well as in diversity jurisdiction.[2] In the former, federal legislation may often be involved or exist in incomplete form; in diversity, the existence of federal legislative *authority,* while a prerequisite,[3] often will not have been exercised at all.

The principles and policies underlying *Erie* explain the restraint shown by federal courts in formulating rules of federal common law.[4]

---

12. Id. at 32, 97 S.Ct. at 2495 (quoting from *Parnell,* 352 U.S. at 33–34, 77 S.Ct. at 121).

13. Id. at 32, 97 S.Ct. at 2495 (quoting from *Wallis,* 384 U.S. at 71, 86 S.Ct. at 1305).

14. Id. at 34, 97 S.Ct. at 2496.

15. Id. at 35, 97 S.Ct. at 2496 (quoting from United States v. Little Lake Misere Land Co., 412 U.S. 580, 593, 93 S.Ct. 2389, 2397, 37 L.Ed.2d 187 (1973)). See also infra n.17.

16. 406 U.S. 91, 92 S.Ct. 1385, 31 L.Ed.2d 712 (1972).

17. City of Milwaukee v. Illinois, 451 U.S. 304, 101 S.Ct. 1784, 68 L.Ed.2d 114 (1981).

§ 3.55

1. See supra § 3.54 n.17.

2. See supra § 3.50 n.6 and § 3.54 n.13.

3. See supra § 3.49 n.7 and § 3.50 nn.1–6.

4. Cheatham distinguished "federal common law" from "federal courts' law," whereby the latter referred to rules only applicable in federal courts (such as procedural rules) rather than generally. Comments by Elliott Cheatham on the True National Common Law, 18 Am. U. L. Rev. 372, 374 (1969).

Given the fact that federal governmental interests are ordinarily not directly at stake in diversity cases, it follows that the restraint appears even greater in those cases. With this difference in mind, and proceeding from the basic formulation in *Wallis*,[5] the test that emerges for diversity cases may be stated in the following terms: State law will usually govern the particular matter in controversy before a federal court in a case based on diversity of citizenship, unless the matter is in an area in which there is federal lawmaking authority, and (1) there is significant conflict, which is specifically shown, between some legitimate federal policy or interest and the use of state law concerning the specific point in issue, and further (2) the federal court determines that there is an overriding necessity for uniformity which requires a uniform federal rule.[6]

A significant conflict must be specifically shown because a federal rule would not be appropriate if the question in issue has only minimal or collateral federal contacts.[7] This criterion thus serves as a threshold test which must be satisfied before the question is reached whether a local or a federal rule is desirable from a conflicts standpoint; this test therefore bears resemblance to a jurisdictional requirement. The federal interest in fact presents a federal question.[8] The federal question may then be resolved in two ways: through the continued use of local law or, if point 2 of the test obtains, through a federal rule which preempts state law and thereby provides uniformity. The necessity requirement of point 2 balances the federal and state interests; it consists of an inquiry into the degree of state interest, the degree of federal interest, and into the feasibility of creating a judicial substitute, including the ease of formulating a rule and an evaluation of the increased burden assumed by the court in administering the rule and its ramifications.[9]

5. Wallis v. Pan American Petroleum Corp., 384 U.S. 63, 86 S.Ct. 1301, 16 L.Ed.2d 369 (1966).

6. See the narrow view taken by the Fifth Circuit in Jackson v. Johns–Manville Sales Corp., 750 F.2d 1314 (5th Cir.1985).

7. See, e.g., O'Melveny & Myers v. FDIC, 512 U.S. 79, 114 S.Ct. 2048, 129 L.Ed.2d 67 (1994) (state tort rules must apply unless clear conflict with federal policy identified).

8. See also Sylvane v. Whelan, 506 F.Supp. 1355, 1360 (E.D.N.Y.1981) (in an action to abate nuisance of nude bathing near a national recreational area, held: the alleged nuisance presented no significant federal question as to warrant creation of federal common law and assertion of federal question jurisdiction). For another statement of a test for the formulation of federal common law see In re "Agent Orange" Product Liability Litigation, 506 F.Supp. 737 (E.D.N.Y.1979) (federal interest found, id. at 749), reversed 635 F.2d 987 (2d Cir. 1980) (accepting the test but finding that a "federal policy is not yet identifiable," id. at

995); in contrast, the dissent found that "the paramount interests of the United States are in the welfare of its veterans and their fair and uniform treatment." 635 F.2d at 998 (Feinberg, C.J., dissenting).

9. The test suggested in the foregoing section is broader than the identification of "zones" of federal law proposed by some commentators (e.g., Hill, supra § 3.49, n.7, at 1025) because the case law shows that the confines of these "zones" fluctuate. They are therefore not very helpful as tools of analysis. A more useful approach is suggested by the Note, The Federal Common Law, 82 Harv. L. Rev. 1512 (1969) which posits a presumption in favor of state law (except with respect to international relations, remedies, or in the case of Congressional authorization) and then inquires whether circumstances exist which would justify overriding the presumption, such as "the need ... for federal law to further federal policies or foster uniformity." Id., at 1531. This approach, while quite parallel to the one suggested in the text, perhaps overstates—through the idea of a presump-

VI. INTERNATIONAL TREATIES

A. IN GENERAL

§ 3.56 Rules of conflicts law are rules of the forum. In the United States, conflicts law is therefore primarily state law, subject to the general constraints of federal law noted earlier. This is true regardless of whether the particular case presents an interstate or an international conflicts problem. However, both the federal treaty-making power[1] and the general federal power over "foreign affairs" may place additional limits on state conflicts law or supersede it with rules of federal law. Thus, in *Zschernig v. Miller,*[2] the Supreme Court held that an Oregon succession statute which conditioned succession by foreign heirs upon a finding that foreign governmental practices, especially in East bloc countries, assured receipt and not confiscation of the assets by the heirs amounted to a political assessment of the foreign country's governmental system and thus constituted an impermissible intrusion into the exclusive power of the federal government to conduct the foreign relations of the United States. Similarly, the Court decided in *Banco Nacional de Cuba v. Sabbatino*[3] that a foreign "Act of State" was not reviewable by the courts but that the assessment of such a foreign governmental act as perhaps violative of international law was a federal executive function in its conduct of United States foreign affairs. More recently in *American Ins. Ass'n v. Garamendi,*[4] the Supreme Court extended the foreign affairs preemptive power to non-treaty executive branch pronouncements.

Decisions like *Zschernig* and *Garamendi* limit the scope and reach of state law; they ordinarily do not supply a conflicts rule or a uniform rule of substantive law to be followed by state courts or by federal courts sitting in diversity. For international conflicts cases such rules, few as

---

tion—the role of state law and therefore disapproves of the result in Clearfield Trust Co. v. United States, 318 U.S. 363, 63 S.Ct. 573, 87 L.Ed. 838 (1943), and in United States v. 93.970 Acres of Land, 360 U.S. 328, 79 S.Ct. 1193, 3 L.Ed.2d 1275 (1959) because the inconvenience to the Government under state law is the same as the inconvenience to individuals in that state under a federal rule. Under the test in the text, the existence of a federal interest and of a need for a uniform rule applicable to it are enough.

§ 3.56

1. U.S. Const. Art. VI, cl. 2. See generally Chow, Limiting *Erie* in a New Age of International Law: Toward a Federal Common Law of International Choice of Law, 74 Iowa L. Rev. 165 (1988).

2. 389 U.S. 429, 88 S.Ct. 664, 19 L.Ed.2d 683 (1968). See also El Al Israel Airlines Ltd. v. Tseng, 525 U.S. 155, 119 S.Ct. 662, 142 L.Ed.2d 576 (1999) (Warsaw Convention is the exclusive source of private remedies in tort, even if none is provided to address the particular wrong).

3. 376 U.S. 398, 84 S.Ct. 923, 11 L.Ed.2d 804 (1964), on remand 272 F.Supp. 836 (S.D.N.Y.1965), judgment affirmed 383 F.2d 166 (2d Cir.1967), cert. denied 390 U.S. 956, 88 S.Ct. 1038, 19 L.Ed.2d 1151 (1968), as modified by 22 U.S.C.A. § 2370(e)(2) ("Hickenlooper" amendment to Foreign Relations Act). For an application of the doctrine, in the context of unjust enrichment, see First National Bank of Boston (International) v. Banco Nacional de Cuba, 658 F.2d 895 (2d Cir.1981), cert. denied 459 U.S. 1091, 103 S.Ct. 579, 74 L.Ed.2d 939 (1982). See also Hill, Sovereign Immunity and the Act of State Doctrine: Theory and Policy in United States Law, 46 Rabels Zeitschrift 118 (1982).

4. 539 U.S. 396, 123 S.Ct. 2374, 156 L.Ed.2d 376 (2003).

they are,[5] derive mainly from treaties or other international agreements[6] between the United States and foreign countries. Since a self-executing treaty or treaty provision enjoys the same force as a federal statute[7] it therefore overrides all state law[8] as well as prior federal statutory law. In addition, the fact that the federal treaty power is broader than, i.e., is not restricted to, the federal government's enumerated legislative powers[9] allows treaties to become a vehicle for the introduction of uniform rules.

B. MULTILATERAL TREATIES

§ 3.57   In the past, the United States participated in relatively few multilateral treaties that would introduce uniform rules of law.[1] Thus, for instance, it did not become a member of such important agreements as the Geneva Convention regarding bills of exchange and checks or of the Geneva (1923, 1927) Conventions concerning arbitration clauses and

---

5. But see supra § 3.55 n.9 (para. 2).

6. In addition to treaties, entered into by the President with the advice and consent of the U.S. Senate, the President may also enter into "executive agreements" with other countries upon joint resolution of Congress, upon ratification by Congress, or in the exercise of his independent Presidential powers, e.g. as Commander–in–Chief of the armed forces. "Status of Forces Agreements" are an example; they typically provide for the division of jurisdiction between the United States and the host country over American personnel stationed there. For the effect of executive agreements see Restatement (Third), Foreign Relations Law of the United States § 303 (1987).

7. See supra n.2.

8. Santovincenzo v. Egan, 284 U.S. 30, 52 S.Ct. 81, 76 L.Ed. 151 (1931).

9. Missouri v. Holland, 252 U.S. 416, 40 S.Ct. 382, 64 L.Ed. 641 (1920). See Hay, Supranational Organizations and United States Constitutional Law, 6 Va. J. Int'l L. 195, 196 et seq. (1966). See generally Symposium, Could a Treaty Trump Supreme Court Supreme Court Jurisdictional Doctrine, 61 Alb. L.Rev. 1159 (1998) (contributions by Borchers, Cox, Maier, Strauss, Weintraub & Zekoll).

§ 3.57

1. The United States is a member of these multilateral conventions which affect private law or may have an effect on private law relationships: Status of Aliens (Inter–American), 46 Stat. 2753, 132 LNTS 301; Inter–American Automotive Traffic, 61

Stat. 1129; Road Traffic (Geneva, 1949), 3 UST 3008, 125 UNTS 22 and Protocol 3 UST 3052, 125 UNTS 94; International Air Transport (Warsaw Convention), 49 Stat. 3000, 137 LNTS 11; International Civil Aviation (Chicago), 61 Stat. 1180, 15 UNTS 295 and Protocol (Montreal, 1954), 8 UST 170, 320 UNTS 217; Rights in Aircraft, 4 UST 1830, 310 UNTS 151; Consular Convention (see also § 3.58 n.2 infra), 47 Stat. 1976, 155 LNTS 291; Copyright: Mexico, 1902, 35 Stat. 1934, Buenos Aires, 1910, 38 Stat. 1785, Geneva, 1952 (Universal Copyright), 6 UST 2731, 216 UNTS 132; Investment Disputes, 17 UST 1270, 575 UNTS 159; Industrial property: Inventions, patents, designs, models (Buenos Aires, 1910), 38 Stat. 1811, 155 LNTS 170, Inter–American Trademark Conventions (Buenos Aires, 1910), 39 Stat. 1675, (Santiago, 1923) 44 Stat. 2494, 33 LNTS 47, (Washington, 1929) 46 Stat. 2907, 124 LNTS 357; Paris Union, 38 Stat. 1645, Hague Revision, 47 Stat. 1789, London Revision, 53 Stat. 1749, Lisbon Revision, 13 UST 1, Stockholm Revision, 21 UST 1583, 24 UST 2140; Service of Documents (Hague), TIAS 6638; Legal Personality of Foreign Companies (Inter–American), 55 Stat. 1201, 161 UNTS 217; Uniformity of Powers of Attorney (Inter–American), 56 Stat. 1376, 161 UNTS 229; Shipowners' liability to seamen (ILO No. 55), 54 Stat. 1693; Safety of Life at Sea, 16 UST 185, 536 UNT 27. See also the Hague Conventions on the Service of Documents, infra § 12.7, on the Taking of Evidence Abroad, infra § 12.9, on the Abolition of Legalization Requirements, infra § 12.7, and on the Civil Aspects of International Child Abduction, infra § 15.45. See Pfund, United States Participation in International

the execution of arbitral awards. However, in 1970 it acceded to the 1958 New York Convention on arbitration.[2] Similarly, the United States did not adhere to unification conventions in the Western Hemisphere, for instance, the Codigo Bustamente or the Montevideo Conventions. However, in 1964 the United States did join the Hague Conference on Private International Law and the Rome Institute for the Unification of Private Law (UNIDROIT)[3] and since that time has ratified Hague conventions: on service of documents,[4] on obtaining evidence abroad,[5] on the abolition of legalization requirements,[6] and on Civil Aspects of International Child Abduction.[7]

In recent years, the United States has actively participated in efforts to achieve international unification of important areas of law. A number of these projects have been ratified and become domestic law, while action on others is pending. Thus, the Convention on the International Sale of Goods entered into force for the United States on January 1, 1988,[8] the 1973 "Washington" Convention Providing a Uniform Law on the Form of an International Will[9] was ratified in 1991, and the Hague Convention on the Law Applicable to Trusts and on Their Recognition[10] is before the Senate. The Inter–American Convention on International Commercial Arbitration was ratified in 1990.[11]

In other areas, the United States has so far adhered to its historically cautious approach. Thus, while it is a member of the 1924 Hague Rules Convention[12] and the 1910 Brussels Salvage Convention,[13]

Unification of Private Law, 19 Int'l Lawyer 505 (1985).

2. 21 UST 2517 (Dec. 29, 1970). See generally, Springer, The United Nations Convention on the Recognition and Enforcement of Foreign Arbitral Awards, 3 International Lawyer (1969). See also infra § 24.48.

3. 77 Stat. 775 (1963).

4. TIAS 6638. For analysis of the effect of the Convention on U.S. law see infra § 12.7.

5. TIAS 7444, infra § 12.9.

6. TIAS 10072, infra § 12.7

7. 19 I.L.M. 1545 (1980), infra § 15.45–46. See also 42 U.S.C.A. § 11601–11610 (1996); Slagenweit v. Slagenweit, 63 F.3d 719 (8th Cir.1995).

8. 52 Fed. Reg. 6262. For discussion of this Convention see infra § 18.24.

9. 12 I.L.M. 1298 (1973); 99th Cong., 2d sess., Senate, Treaty Doc. 99–29 (1986). See Nadelmann, The Formal Validity of Wills and the Washington Convention of 1973 Providing the Form of an International Will, 22 Am. J. Comp. L. 365 (1974) and response by Curtis, 23 id. 119 (1975); Kearney, Report of the U.S. Delegation, 9 Real Prop. Prob. & Tr. J. 202 (1974). As of 1991, the Convention was in force in Belgium,

five Canadian provinces (Alberta, Manitoba, Newfoundland, Ontario, Saskatchewan), Cyprus, Ecuador, Libya, Niger, Portugal, Yugoslavia, United Kingdom, and the United States.

10. 23 I.L.M. 1388 (1984). Canada, Italy, Luxembourg, the Netherlands, the United Kingdom, and the United States are signatories, Italy and the United Kingdom so far have ratified the Convention. See Gaillard & Trautman, Trusts in Non–Trust Countries: Conflict of Laws and the Hague Convention on Trusts, 35 Am. J. Comp. L. 307 (1987), with additional references; Hayton, Hague Convention on the Law Applicable to Trust and on Their Recognition, 36 Int'l & Comp. L.Q. 260 (1987).

11. Organization of American States, Treaty Series, no. 9, no. B–35; Parker School of Foreign and Comparative Law, 1 World Arbitration Reporter (1987). As of January 1, 2003, the following states were parties: Brazil, Chile, Colombia, Costa Rica, Cuba, Dominican Republic, Ecuador, El Salvador, Guatamala, Honduras, Mexico, Panama, Paraguay, Peru, United States, Uruguay, Venezuela.

12. International Convention for the Unification of Certain Rules Relating to Bills of Lading for the Carriage of Goods by Sea, 51 Stat. 233, 120 INTS 155. The U.N.

---

13. See p. 225.

it has not ratified either the 1957 or 1961 Brussels conventions on shipowner's liability[14] nor the 1968 Luggage Convention and the 1969 Protocol to the 1924 Rules Convention. As a result, maritime liability continues to be governed by domestic legislation[15] which limits liability to the vessel's post-accident[16] value or to $420 per ton of its "limitation tonnage," whichever is greater. Quite inconsistently, the United States has long adhered to the Warsaw Convention[17] which contains both uniform substantive rules and limitations of a carrier's liability to passengers and for goods. Indeed, dissatisfaction with that Convention's low liability limit led to its denunciation by the United States (subsequently withdrawn) and the acceptance, by air carriers, of the Montreal Agreement of 1966 (since amended)[18] which provides a higher limit for accidental death (125,000 francs) and more detailed notice provisions for "United States flights"[19] than do the Convention or the 1955 Hague Protocol (not ratified by the United States). Those limits were further effectively raised to about $146,000, by the Department of Transportation's new IATA Intercarrier Agreement which required domestic and international carriers to partially waive the convention limits.[20] In the judicial application of the Warsaw Convention, moreover, United States courts have frequently (in cases arising before the Montreal Agreement) held the Convention to be "inapplicable" on the basis of a restrictive view of the required notice to passengers,[21] and one state trial court once considered both the Convention's liability and jurisdiction provisions to

---

Convention on the Carriage of Goods by Sea Act of 1978 (the "Hamburg Rules") is the subject of a symposium in 27 Am. J. Comp. L. 353–419 (1979). See also Klemm, Forum Selection in Maritime Bills of Lading under COGSA, 12 Fordham Int'l L.J. 459–493 (1989). The text is reprinted, id. at 421. See also S. Mankabady, The Hamburg Rules of the Carriage of Goods by Sea (1978); Moore, The Hamburg Rules, 10 J. Mar. L. & Comm. 1 (1978). The United States has signed, but not yet ratified, the Convention.

13. 37 Stat. 1658.

14. For discussion see Mendelsohn, The Public Interest and Private International Maritime Law, 10 William & Mary L. Rev. 783 (1969). See also Note, Limitation of Shipowner's Liability—the Brussels Convention of 1957, 68 Yale L.J. 1676 (1959).

15. 49 Stat. 1479, 46 U.S.C.A. § 183(b). See Mendelsohn, supra n.14.

16. Place v. Norwich & New York Transportation Co., 118 U.S. 468, 6 S.Ct. 1150, 30 L.Ed. 134 (1886); Dyer v. National Steam Navigation Co., 118 U.S. 507, 6 S.Ct. 1174, 30 L.Ed. 153 (1886); Thommessen v. Whitwill, 118 U.S. 520, 6 S.Ct. 1172, 30 L.Ed. 156 (1886).

17. 49 Stat. 3000, 137 LNTS 11, for comprehensive comment see Lowenfeld & Mendelsohn, The United States and the Warsaw Convention, 80 Harv. L. Rev. 497

(1967). For additional discussion see infra § 17.44 n.6.

18. See 14 C.F.R. § 203.4(c) (1990). The modification currently in force is the 4th Protocol to the Agreement, reprinted in S. Exec. Rep. No. 105–20, 21–32 (1998). The Protocol entered into force in the United States on March 4, 1999.

19. Flights originating, terminating, or with an agreed stopping place in the United States are covered.

20. Note, Reforming the Liability Provisions of the Warsaw Convention: Does the IATA Intercarrier Agreement Eliminate the Need to Amend the Convention, 20 Fordham Int'l L.J. 1768, 1769 (1997) (discussing IATA agreement and current state of Warsaw Convention Law).

21. See especially Lisi v. Alitalia–Linee Aeree Italiane, 370 F.2d 508 (2d Cir.1966), affirmed 390 U.S. 455, 88 S.Ct. 1193, 20 L.Ed.2d 27 (1968). According to the Court, the ticket in *Lisi* contained Lilliputian print and therefore did not comply with the notice requirement of Art. 3(1)(3) of the Convention. The Court's test thus resembles the approach found with respect to domestic contract law, especially in the case of adhesion contracts, and—in the opinion of the dissent (370 F.2d 508, 515 (2d Cir. 1966))—is inappropriate for the construction of a treaty, indeed may amount to "unwarranted judicial treaty-making."

be unconstitutional.[22] In contrast, the United States Supreme Court held in 1999 that the Convention preempts state law remedies for injuries suffered between the times of embarkation and disembarkation, even when the Convention does not provide any redress.[23]

C. BILATERAL TREATIES[1]

§ 3.58　The United States maintains a great number of bilateral treaties, the most important of which are treaties of friendship, commerce (or: establishment) and navigation; consular conventions; and tax treaties.[2]

U.S. judicial treatment appears to have changed under the Rehnquist court. In Chan, et al. v. Korean Air Lines, Ltd., 490 U.S. 122, 109 S.Ct. 1676, 104 L.Ed.2d 113 (1989) (wrongful death actions arising out of the downing of KAL 007 by Soviet air forces for trespass over the Sakhalin islands airspace), the Court held that failure to provide adequate notice of Convention limitations did not eliminate the per-passenger limitations of the Convention; the Montreal Agreement did not impose sanctions for the use of less than 10pt typeface; and that nothing in Art. 3 (or elsewhere) of the Convention imposed sanctions for failure to notify passengers of Convention limitations. The only sanctions imposed were found in the second sentence of Art. 3(2) and those subjected carriers to unlimited liability if they failed to deliver a ticket to the passenger (more the case in *Lisi*).

22. Burdell v. Canadian Pacific Airlines, Civil No. 66L 10799, 8 Int'l Legal Mat. 83 (1969) (Circuit Court of Cook County, Ill.). For analysis and criticism see Hay, Comments on *Burdell Canadian Pacific Airlines* and the Constitutionality of the Warsaw Convention, 58 Ill. St. B.J. 26 (1969). But see People ex rel. Compagnie Nationale Air France v. Giliberto, 74 Ill.2d 90, 97, 383 N.E.2d 977, 979 (1978), cert. denied 441 U.S. 932, 99 S.Ct. 2052, 60 L.Ed.2d 660 (1979) (venue provision does not violate due process). See Schoedel, Maritime Liability: Issues for the New Congress, 11 Mar. Law 105 (1986); Willams, The American Maritime Law of Fire Damage to Cargo: An Auto–Da–Fe for a Few Heresies, 26 Wm. & Mary L. Rev. 569 (1985); Greenman, Limitation of Liability: A Critical Analysis of United States Law in an International Setting, 57 Tul. L. Rev. 1139 (1983).

23. El Al Israel Airlines, Ltd. v. Tsui Yuan Tseng, 525 U.S. 155, 119 S.Ct. 662, 142 L.Ed.2d 576, 1999 CJ C.A.R. 277 (1999).

§ 3.58

1. The only comprehensive treatment is by Bayitch, Conflicts Law in United States Treaties, 8 Miami L.Q. 501 (1954), 9 id. 9 (1954), 9 id. 125 (1955), also published in book form as No. 1 of the University of Chicago International Legal Studies Series (1955).

2. The United States presently maintains 85 consular conventions and some 160 tax treaties (not counting multilateral treaties), and an additional number of general commercial treaties. See U.S. Department of State, Treaties in Force. Some aspects of commercial treaties are discussed in the following. For discussion of tax treaties see: Estes, Tax Treaties, 14 Int'l Lawyer 508 (1980); Rosenbloom & Langbein, United States Tax Treaty Policy: An Overview, 19 Colum. J. of Transnat'l L. 359 (1981); Vogel, Double Tax Treaties and Their Interpretation, 4 Int'l Tax & Bus. Lawyer 1–85 (1986); Graetz & O'Hear, The "Original Intent" of U.S. International Taxation, 46 Duke L. J. 1021 (1997); Forst, The U.S. International Tax Treatment of Partnerships: A Policy–Based Approach, 14 Berk. J. Int'l Law 239 (1996); Kaye, European Tax Harmonization and the Implications for U.S. Tax Policy, 19 B.C. Int'l & Comp. L. Rev. 109 (1996); West, Foreign Law in U.S. International Taxation: the Search for Standards, 3 Fla. Tax Rev. 147 (1996); Doernburg, Overriding Tax Treaties: the U.S. Perspective, 9 Emory Int'l L. Rev. 71 (1995); Giunta & Shang, Ownership of Information in a Global Economy, 27 G.W. J. Int'l L. & Econ. 327 (1993); Clark, Transfer Pricing, Section 482, and International Tax Conflict: Getting Harmonized Income Allocation Measures from Multinational Cacophony, 42 Am. U. L. Rev. 1115 (1993); Mezrich, International Tax Issues of the U.S. Pharmaceutical Industry, 10 Akron Tax J. 127 (1993); Green, The Future of Source–Based Taxation of the Income of Multinational Enterprises, 79 Cornell L.

Bilateral commercial treaties customarily accord nationals and companies of one of the contracting parties a variety of substantive rights in the territory of the other, including for instance:[3] civil capacity, the right to do business (including the right to incorporate), access to courts[4] and to credit, the right to own personal (and sometimes, real) property, protection of industrial property rights, protection against discriminatory taxation, and equality with nationals with regard to social insurance. The standard of treatment specified in modern treaty practice[5] is increasingly that of national treatment. Because of differences among the states, national treatment of foreign companies in the United States is defined as equivalent to the treatment extended by the particular state to companies of other states of the Union.[6]

National treatment provisions will often afford uniform and more advantageous treatment of foreign nationals in the United States than would existing state law; examples are state provisions that, in the absence of a treaty, would require incorporators[7] and directors[8] of a company, or certified shorthand reporters, funeral directors, masseurs,

Rev. 18 (1993); Mogle, Competent Authority Procedure, 23 G.W. J. Int'l L. & Econ. 725 (1990); Wallis, Economics, Foreign Policy, and United States–Japanese Trade Disputes, 22 Cornell Int'l L. J. 381 (1989). See also Covington, Dispute Resolution Under Tax Treaties: Current and Proposed Methods, 24 Texas Int'l L.J. 367–388 (1989); Titlow, International Double Taxation and the United States, 46 Tax 135 (1968); Owens, United States Income Tax Treaties: Their Role in Relieving Double Taxation, 17 Rutgers L. Rev. 428 (1963). See also Moore, The Permanent Establishment Concept in Tax Treaties: Old Bottles for New Wine?, 6 Queens L.J. 482 (1981). For analysis of a consular convention, see Lay, The United States Soviet Consular Convention, 59 Am. J. Int'l L. 876 (1965). See generally Luke, Consular Law and Practice (2d ed. 1990). For brief discussion of the Agreements Between the United States and the People's Republic of China on Civil Air Transport, Textiles, Maritime Transport, and Consular Affairs (19 Int'l Legal Mat. 1105 [1980]; see Note, 22 Harv. Int'l L.J. 2000 (1981)).

3. For comprehensive treatment, see Wilson, U.S. Commercial Treaties and International Law (1960); Walker, Modern Treaties of Friendship, Commerce and Navigation, 42 Minn. L. Rev. 805 (1958); Walker, Provisions on Companies in United States Commercial Treaties, 50 Am. J. Int'l L. 373 (1956).

4. Including such related matters as the right to proceed in forma pauperis and exemption from (discriminatory) requirements for posting security for court costs. See, e.g., Treaty with Germany (1954), Pro-

tocol paras. 7 and 6, respectively, 7 U.S.T. 1839.

5. See Walker, supra n.3, 809 et seq.

6. E.g., Art. XXV(3) of the Treaty with Germany, supra n.4. In reverse, provisions in commercial treaties permitting foreign companies to employ managerial personnel of their choice have given rise to civil rights litigation in U.S. courts. See Note, Commercial Treaties and the American Civil Rights Laws: The Case of Japanese Employers, 31 Stanford L. Rev. 947 (1979). The Circuits have reached conflicting results: Spiess v. C. Itoh & Co. (America), Inc., 643 F.2d 353 (5th Cir.1981), order vacated 664 F.2d 480 (5th Cir.1981) (Title VII of the Civil Rights of 1964 does not supersede the U.S.-Japanese treaty); Avigliano v. Sumitomo Shoji America, Inc., 638 F.2d 552 (2d Cir.1981), vacated and remanded 457 U.S. 176, 102 S.Ct. 2374, 72 L.Ed.2d 765 (1982), appeal pending (treaty provision does not exempt wholly owned Japanese subsidiary from requirements of Title VII). See also MacNamara v. Korean Air Lines, 863 F.2d 1135 (3d Cir.1988), cert. denied 493 U.S. 944, 110 S.Ct. 349, 107 L.Ed.2d 337 (1989).

7. E.g., 15 Pennsylvania Statutes § 2852–201 (1958), repealed in 1966: 15 Pennsylvania Statutes § 1201 (1967).

8. E.g., former § 27 of New York's Business Corporation Law had a requirement that one director must be a citizen. The General Corporation Law was repealed in 1974 and replaced by the Business Corporation Law and the Not–for–Profit Corporation Law which no longer have such a requirement.

physical therapists, and animal technicians[9] to be United States citizens. While the Supreme Court has declared unconstitutional similar provisions—for instance state statutes prohibiting aliens from entering a state's classified civil service,[10] or practicing law,[11] or working as an engineer,[12] or receiving state educational benefits,[13] serving as a notary public[14]—its earlier decisions upheld state power to exclude aliens from its police forces[15] and state power to exclude certification as a public school teacher of an alien unless he or she has manifested an intention to apply for citizenship.[16] The Supreme Court has drawn a line between those occupations which the state may constitutionally restrict to United States citizens and those which it may not deny to resident aliens. Unfortunately the test to determine when an occupation falls on one side of the line or the other is not unwavering. The state has the power " 'to preserve the basic conceptions of a political community' [which power] applies, not only to the qualifications of voters, but also to persons holding state elective or important nonelective executive, legislative, and judicial positions, for officers who participate directly in the formulation, execution, or review of broad public policy functions that go to the heart of representative government.' "[17] Applying this test the Court has upheld the power of the state to prevent a Frenchman from teaching French in the public schools but denied the power of the state to prohibit a lawfully resident Frenchman from practicing law solely because of his alien status.[18] In light of these Supreme Court decisions, bilateral treaties protecting aliens still perform a useful and perhaps essential function.

National treatment is particularly important in the area of workers' compensation in which the law of most of the states, in the absence of an applicable treaty, still discriminates against non-resident alien dependents claiming compensation for accidental death.[19] The incongruous

---

9. See Ambach v. Norwick, 441 U.S. 68, 82 n.1, 99 S.Ct. 1589, 1597 n. 1, 60 L.Ed.2d 49 (1979) (Blackmun, J., dissenting).

10. Sugarman v. Dougall, 413 U.S. 634, 93 S.Ct. 2842, 37 L.Ed.2d 853 (1973).

11. Application of Griffiths, 413 U.S. 717, 93 S.Ct. 2851, 37 L.Ed.2d 910 (1973).

12. Examining Board v. Flores de Otero, 426 U.S. 572, 96 S.Ct. 2264, 49 L.Ed.2d 65 (1976).

13. Nyquist v. Mauclet, 432 U.S. 1, 97 S.Ct. 2120, 53 L.Ed.2d 63 (1977).

14. Bernal v. Fainter, 467 U.S. 216, 104 S.Ct. 2312, 81 L.Ed.2d 175 (1984).

15. Foley v. Connelie, 435 U.S. 291, 98 S.Ct. 1067, 55 L.Ed.2d 287 (1978); Cabell v. Chavez–Salido, 454 U.S. 432, 102 S.Ct. 735, 70 L.Ed.2d 677 (1982); Bernal v. Fainter, 467 U.S. 216, 104 S.Ct. 2312, 81 L.Ed.2d 175 (1984); Gregory v. Ashcroft, 501 U.S. 452, 111 S.Ct. 2395, 115 L.Ed.2d 410 (1991).

16. Ambach v. Norwick, 441 U.S. 68, 99 S.Ct. 1589, 60 L.Ed.2d 49 (1979).

17. Sugarman v. Dougall, 413 U.S. 634, 647, 93 S.Ct. 2842, 2850, 37 L.Ed.2d 853 (1973); Burdick v. Takushi, 504 U.S. 428, 433, 112 S.Ct. 2059, 119 L.Ed.2d 245 (1992).

18. Compare Ambach v. Norwick, 441 U.S. 68, 99 S.Ct. 1589, 60 L.Ed.2d 49 (1979) with Application of Griffiths, 413 U.S. 717, 93 S.Ct. 2851, 37 L.Ed.2d 910 (1973), on remand 165 Conn. 807, 309 A.2d 689 (1973); Gregory v. Ashcroft, 501 U.S. 452, 111 S.Ct. 2395, 115 L.Ed.2d 410 (1991); Bernal v. Fainter, 467 U.S. 216, 104 S.Ct. 2312, 81 L.Ed.2d 175 (1984).

19. E.g., West Virginia Code § 23–4–15a (This statute remains discriminatory in that while nonresident alien beneficiaries are entitled to the same benefits as U.S. citizens, the Commissioner in his discretion may make, and such beneficiaries shall be required to accept, commutation of such benefits and lump sum settlements and payments). Nonresident alien dependents are the subject of special statutory rules in all but nine states. Five states expressly

result of such legislation is that the resident alien worker can recover for injuries but that his non-resident dependents cannot recover fully for his death. Beginning with the 1923 commercial treaty with Germany, U.S. treaties contained provisions safeguarding the claims of treaty nationals "regardless of their alienage or residence outside of the territory where the injury occurred. . . . "[20] However, beginning with the 1949 treaty with Uruguay (never ratified) and continued in later treaties—for instance, with Ireland (1950), Greece (1951), Israel (1951), Germany (1954), Netherlands (1956)—the earlier language was changed and has become less clear. These treaties provide that "nationals of either Party shall be accorded national treatment in the application of laws and regulations within the territories of the other . . . "[21] relating to worker compensation. Some fear has been expressed that this change will permit states with discriminatory legislation to deny recovery to non-resident treaty aliens through restrictive interpretation of the language "*within the territories.*"[22]

§ 3.59　　In several important areas, U.S. treaties expressly refer to state law and therefore do not guarantee uniform and nondiscriminatory treatment. With respect to rights in real property,[1] for instance, modern treaties contain stipulations and limitations which typically include: (1) National treatment with respect to leasing real property for the purpose of engaging in commercial activity covered by the treaty and for residential purposes; (2) "Other rights in real property permitted by the applicable laws;"[2] and (3) national treatment with respect to acquisition (but not continued holding) of real and personal property by testate or intestate succession. If, as a result of state law limitations[3]—assuming

include nonresident aliens on equal terms with other dependents. Five states exclude them from benefits altogether. Larson's Worker Compensation Law, Vol. 5, § 63.51 (1998).

20. Art. II, 44 Stat. 2132, 2134. In Antosz v. State Compensation Commissioner, 130 W.Va. 260, 43 S.E.2d 397 (1947), the West Virginia law was held inapplicable in a case arising under the Treaty with Poland which contained language identical to that of the 1923 German Treaty.

21. Art. IV(1), Treaty with Germany, 7 U.S.T. 1839.

22. See also Larson's Worker Compensation Law, Vol. 5, § 63.52 (1998).

§ 3.59

1. National treatment usually applies to rights in *personal* property, tangible and intangible: e.g., Treaty with Germany, 7 U.S.T. 1839, Art. IX(2). See also the provisions protecting property interests against discriminatory measures and restrictions and stipulating the conditions for expropriation: id., Art. V.

2. Id., Art. IX(1)(b).

3. See e.g., Ill.—S.H.A. ch. 6, ¶ 2, restricting alien ownership of real property to six years and providing for forced sale proceedings thereafter. Several aspects of alien land legislation have been held to be unconstitutional: e.g., the California prohibition against land ownership by aliens ineligible for citizenship, by the U.S. Supreme Court: Oyama v. State of California, 332 U.S. 633, 68 S.Ct. 269, 92 L.Ed. 249 (1948), and California, Montana, and Oregon forfeiture and escheat provisions, by the respective state supreme courts: Sei Fujii v. State, 38 Cal.2d 718, 242 P.2d 617 (1952); Haruye Masaoka v. People, 39 Cal.2d 883, 245 P.2d 1062 (1952); State v. Oakland, 129 Mont. 347, 287 P.2d 39 (1955); Namba v. McCourt, 185 Or. 579, 204 P.2d 569 (1949).

An exception to the usual reference to state law (as in the German Treaty quoted in the text) is the 1847 Treaty with Colombia, 9 Stat. 881, providing (in Art. XII) for freedom to dispose of, and to succeed to personal and real property. Similarly, the 1853 Treaty with Argentina, 10 Stat. 1005, confers "reciprocal national treatment"

such limitations to be constitutional[4]—the alien is ineligible to continue to own property so acquired, he is entitled to a "reasonable"[5] or fixed[6] period within which to dispose of the property at its market value[7] or on a national treatment basis.[8] In keeping with these provisions, consular conventions[9] also contain reservations in favor of local law for the determination of whether a consul may take temporary charge of an intestate's estate, be appointed administrator of it, and receive distribution on behalf of non-resident heirs.[10]

Similarly, treaties generally contain savings clauses in favor of state law that restricts the exercise of state-licensed professions (e.g., law) to citizens.[11] Such state restrictions, however, are often unconstitutional.[12] Finally, U.S. commercial treaties do not usually deal with the recognition and enforcement of foreign judgments.[13] This area as well is left to domestic law, federal or state.

with respect to the acquisition and disposition of property "of every sort." The latter provision was successfully invoked by a British subject under the most-favored-nation clause of the 1899 Property Convention, 31 Stat. 1939, in Texas v. Fasken (unreported, Bayitch, supra § 3.58, n.1, at 9 id. 133 n.220), appeal dismissed 274 U.S. 724, 47 S.Ct. 762, 71 L.Ed. 1329 (1927). The Treaty with Germany, on which the discussion in the text is based, as well as other modern commercial treaties do not have a most-favored-nation clause which would bring the older exceptional treaties into operation.

4. See supra n.3.

Under modern constitutional law, state laws which discriminate against aliens by restricting their right to own real property may well be unconstitutional. While there is no U.S. Supreme Court case directly on point, the reasoning of many of the cases would not allow such discrimination by a state as opposed to the federal government. See generally Comment, Nonresident Alien Inheritance of Nebraska Land: 1854–1971, 4 Creighton L. Rev. 304 (1971); Note, Conflict Between Local and National Interests in Alien Landholding Restrictions, 16 U. Chi. L. Rev. 315 (1949); Sullivan, Alien Land Law: A Re-evaluation, 36 Temple L.Q. 15 (1962); Comment, The Demise of the "Iron Curtain" Statute, 18 Vill. L. Rev. 49 (1962). Cf. Zschernig v. Miller, 389 U.S. 429, 88 S.Ct. 664, 19 L.Ed.2d 683 (1968), rehearing denied 390 U.S. 974, 88 S.Ct. 1018, 19 L.Ed.2d 1196 (1968), supra § 3.56 (Oregon statute, which not only purported to look to reciprocity in inheritance cases— as part of a determination of whether Oregon's escheat power should be exercised— but also required a political evaluation of the likelihood of confiscation of the inheritance by the foreign government, invalidat-

ed as an infringement of the federal power over foreign relations).

5. E.g., Art. IX(4) of the 1956 Treaty with the Netherlands, 8 U.S.T. 2043, 285 UNTS 231.

6. E.g., Art. IX(3), Treaty with Germany, supra n.1 (5 years).

7. Supra n.5.

8. E.g., Art. IX(4), Treaty with Germany, supra n.1 (national treatment and most-favored-nation treatment with respect to disposition of property).

9. The United States participates in the 1928 multilateral (Inter–American) Consular Convention, 47 Stat. 1976, which, however, does not contain provisions on the administration of estates. For a limited survey see Dolan, Treaty Provisions Affecting Inheritance Rights in the Western Hemisphere, 2 Int'l Lawyer 77, 84–88 (1967).

10. For discussion of trends in U.S. consular conventions see supra § 3.58 n.1, and Dolan, supra n.9.

11. E.g., Treaty with Germany, Protocol, para. 8, 7 U.S.T. 1839. Bayitch, Conflict Laws in United States Treaties, 8 Miami L.Q. 501 (1954).

12. See supra § 3.58 nn.10–13.

13. Bayitch, supra n.11, at 26–28. See also Nadelmann, The Common Market Judgments Convention and a Hague Conference Recommendation: What Steps Next?, 82 Harv. L. Rev. 1282, 1288–91 (1969). The United States, however, recognizes that the necessities of international commerce justify a broader role for arbitration of such agreements than would be allowed for domestic agreements. See Scherk v. Alberto–Culver Co., 417 U.S. 506, 94

D. CONCLUSION

§ 3.60   Traditionally, the United States has been reluctant to employ the treaty power when the effect would be to displace private law shaped (often with substantial variations) by the states and when, moreover, the federation does not possess independent domestic law-making power. However, the ratification of the Convention on the International Sale of Goods[1] and United States participation in such Hague Conference projects as the Decedents' Estates and Trust Recognition Conventions[2] may signal greater readiness to join in unification endeavors with respect to international conflicts problems in the future.

S.Ct. 2449, 41 L.Ed.2d 270 (1974), (arbitration of international agreement allowed notwithstanding that party opposing arbitration claimed U.S. securities law violation); Mitsubishi Motors Corp. v. Soler Chrysler–Plymouth, Inc., 473 U.S. 614, 105 S.Ct. 3346, 87 L.Ed.2d 444 (1985)(antitrust claim covered by arbitration agreement). See generally Park, Judicial Supervision of Transnational Commercial Arbitration: The English Arbitration Act of 1979, 21 Harv. Int'l L.J. 87, 107–10 (1980); Note, International Arbitration—Extraterritorial Application of United States Securities Laws Denied, 16 Harv. Int'l L.J. 705 (1975).

§ 3.60

1.   See supra § 3.57 n.8.

2.   For example, 23 I.L.M. 1388 (1984); See also supra § 3.57 n.10.

Chapter 4

DOMICILE

Table of Sections

                                                                    Sections
I.   Introduction—The Use of the Domicile Concept in Conflict of
     Laws 4.1–4.3
II. Preliminary Matters Significant in Considering Domicile 4.4–4.10
     A. Findings, Evidence and Preclusion by Prior Litigation........ 4.4–4.7
     B. Law Determining or Characterizing Domicile............... 4.8–4.10
III. Domicile Compared and Defined 4.11–4.16
     A. Domicile Compared to Nationality—International Conflicts 4.11–4.12
     B. Domicile Compared to Residence, Habitual Residence and
         Other Persistent Relationships....................... 4.13–4.14
     C. Domicile Defined 4.15–4.16
IV. Traditional Requirements for the Acquisition of a Domicile of
     Choice 4.17–4.27
     A. In General 4.17
     B. Physical Presence....................................... 4.18–4.19
     C. Intent Necessary for Domicile........................... 4.20–4.27
         1. In General 4.20
         2. Domicile of a Person Having Multiple Homes......... 4.21–4.23
         3. Intent Distinguished From Motive 4.24
         4. Freedom to Exercise Choice 4.25–4.27
V.   Geographic Boundaries of Domicile......................... 4.28–4.29
VI. Domicile as Affected by Status 4.30–4.45
     A. Domicile of Aliens 4.30–4.32
     B. Domicile of Married Persons 4.33–4.35
     C. Derivative Domicile 4.36–4.44
         1. Domicile of Origin 4.36
         2. Domicile of Minor—General 4.37
         3. Children Born Out of Wedlock 4.38
         4. Adopted Children 4.39
         5. Separated Parents 4.40
         6. Death of Parent 4.41–4.42
         7. Emancipation 4.43
         8. Marriage of Minor 4.44
     D. Capacity to Acquire a Domicile........................... 4.45
VII. Analogous Relationships of Corporate Entities................... 4.46

I. INTRODUCTION—THE USE OF THE DOMICILE CONCEPT IN CONFLICT OF LAWS

§ 4.1 In many areas of conflict of laws there is a need to identify a personal and persistent relationship between an individual and a governmental unit or geographic area. The most persistent of these possible relationships in the Anglo–American common law is identified as domicile.[1] This is a continuing relationship for an indefinite period which relates the individual to a place we most often call "home."[2] Because domicile is an enduring and persistent relationship, it is often viewed as the most significant personal relationship an individual has to a place. The concept of domicile is used in many areas of choice of law; for example, the law has traditionally identified the state of the domicile as that state which has the greatest interest in the marital relationship and in the parent and child relationship.[3] In those instances, the concept of domicile centers around the idea of a family home, hence in family law matters there occur references to the matrimonial or marital domicile of parties.[4] In a somewhat like manner, the prevailing choice of law for determining the distribution of movable property at death is the law of the decedents' domicile. It is believed that in most instances the state in which the individual lives has the greatest interest in the succession of family property and is the state with whose laws concerning succession the decedent is likely to be most familiar.[5] In other areas of law, the courts or the legislatures have evolved rules designed to protect individuals in personal circumstances and the courts often look to the law of the domicile in these matters as the state with which an individual's life has the most significant continuing relationship.

§ 4.2 Domicile is also frequently used to identify those upon whom a governmental body bestows privileges and benefits that are not extend-

§ 4.1

1. For the origin of the concept of domicile, see Nygh, The Reception of Domicil into English Private International Law, 1 Tasmanian U. L. Rev. 555 (1961).

2. Restatement, Second, Conflict of Laws §§ 11, 12 (1971). A popular definition is "That is properly the domicile of a person where he has his true, fixed, permanent home and principal establishment, and to which, whenever he is absent, he has the intention of returning." Story, Conflict of Laws, § 41 (8th ed. 1883). This has been frequently cited by courts. See Holt v. Hendee, 248 Ill. 288, 93 N.E. 749 (1910); Salem Independent School District v. Kiel, 206 Iowa 967, 221 N.W. 519 (1928); Gilman v. Gilman, 52 Me. 165 (1863); Shapiro v. Marcus, 211 Md. 83, 124 A.2d 846 (1956); In re Ozias' Estate, 29 S.W.2d 240 (Mo.App. 1930); Hart v. Lindsey, 17 N.H. 235 (1845); Collins v. Yancey, 55 N.J.Super. 514, 151 A.2d 68 (Law Div.1959); Cadwalader v. Howell, 18 N.J.L. 138 (1840); Perrin v. Perrin, 140 Misc. 406, 250 N.Y.S. 588 (1931); Horne v. Horne, 31 N.C. 99 (1848); Richards v. Huff, 146 Okla. 108, 293 P. 1028 (1930). The accuracy of many of the different definitions is discussed in Jacobs, Law of Domicile §§ 58 et seq. (1887) and Dicey & Morris, Conflict of Laws 117–21 (13th ed. by Collins 2002). See Reese, Does Domicile Bear a Single Meaning?, 55 Colum. L. Rev. 589 (1955).

3. See, e.g., Restatement, Second, Conflict of Laws §§ 70, 258, 285 (1971); Stumberg, The Status of Children in the Conflict of Laws, 8 U. Chi. L. Rev. 42 (1940); Graveson, Conflict of Laws 188 (7th ed. 1974).

4. See Goodrich, Matrimonial Domicile, 27 Yale L.J. 49 (1917); Castel, Canadian Conflict of Laws 389 (4th ed. 1997).

5. See, e.g., Restatement, Second, Conflict of Laws §§ 260, 263, 265 (1971).

ed to those who have their home and allegiances elsewhere or those who are called upon for governmental support. On the national level, this reciprocal relationship between government and its more persistent residents is usually called citizenship. In the United States, persons are citizens "of the State wherein they reside."[1] In this context, the domicile concept is often relied upon to determine state citizenship for matters as tax consequences, voting privileges, educational benefits in state institutions, and access to health care institutions maintained by a political unit within a geographic area. In non-federal nations in which the central national government provides the substantive law, citizenship is used as a principal choice-of-law connection for personal law matters.

§ 4.3 An important area of the law concerns the citizen's obligation to respond to the orders of government through its judicial branch. Here, it is frequently assumed that the persistent domicile relationship confers privileges and benefits upon the citizen and the citizen in turn has the obligation to respond to the courts of the domiciliary state.[1] This suggests that in a system for the resolution of disputes there is a need for a place where every individual can be reached by judicial process whether physically present at that place or not.[2] In the United States this place of state citizenship is the domiciliary state.

In view of the governmental and social need for a person to be identified with a particular geographic area or governmental unit, it is clear that some concept that identifies a reasonably persistent relationship with a governmental unit or geographic area is a useful part of law. It is also apparent that because this need arises in so many different contexts and for so many different purposes, any concept used will necessarily have some flexibility and varying significance in different circumstances.[3] The variety of circumstances in the conflict of laws in

---

§ 4.2

1. U.S. Const. Amend. XIV. Citizenship is the equivalent of domicile for purposes of diversity of citizenship jurisdiction of the federal court. See, e.g., Dunlap by Wells v. Buchanan, 741 F.2d 165 (8th Cir.1984); Prakash v. American University, 727 F.2d 1174 (D.C.Cir.1984); Kantor v. Wellesley Galleries, Ltd., 704 F.2d 1088 (9th Cir. 1983); Simmons v. Skyway of Ocala, 592 F.Supp. 356 (S.D.Ga.1984).

§ 4.3

1. Milliken v. Meyer, 311 U.S. 457, 61 S.Ct. 339, 85 L.Ed. 278 (1940), Restatement, Second, Conflict of Laws §§ 29–31 (1971). Use of domicile as a basis of personal jurisdiction seems not to be affected by Shaffer v. Heitner, 433 U.S. 186, 97 S.Ct. 2569, 53 L.Ed.2d 683 (1977) and its progeny. See infra § 4.9 n.1.

2. Restatement, Second, Conflict of Laws § 11 (1971). Perhaps as apt a defini-

tion as any is that of Justice Holmes in Bergner & Engel Brewing Co. v. Dreyfus, 172 Mass. 154, 157, 51 N.E. 531, 532 (1898): "[W]hat the law means by domicile is the one technically pre-eminent headquarters, which as a result either of fact or of fiction every person is compelled to have in order that by aid of it certain rights and duties which have been attached to it by the law may be determined." See also Graveson, Conflict of Laws 185 (7th ed. 1974); Castel, Canadian Conflict of Laws 71 (2d ed. 1986).

3. "The matter of the determination of any person's domicile arises in different ways and is construed by the courts for a variety of different purposes.... Definitions given in regard to the method of ascertaining the domicile for one purpose are not always applicable in ascertaining the domicile for another purpose." In re Jones' Estate, 192 Iowa 78, 81–82, 182 N.W. 227, 229 (1921). See McDonald v. Hartford Trust

which it is used warns that the concept of domicile may vary in application between different areas of the law.

II. PRELIMINARY MATTERS SIGNIFICANT IN CONSIDERING DOMICILE

A. FINDINGS, EVIDENCE AND PRECLUSION BY PRIOR LITIGATION

§ 4.4 The use of domicile as a jurisdictional basis particularly illustrates a caution that needs to be borne in mind throughout the consideration of domicile. This is a recognition that the *procedures* by which domicile is found to exist may lead to a finding or an assumption of domicile in a state when common sense doubts the particular individual has, in fact, the persistent relationship usually envisioned as domicile. Divorce and tax litigation illustrate this problem. In divorce, for example, domicile is usually treated as a necessary element in the acquisition of judicial jurisdiction.[1]

Likewise, the imposition of death taxes on intangibles of a decedent is ordinarily assumed to be based upon the domicile of a decedent within that governmental unit at the time of the decedent's death.[2] Consequently, one of the preliminary findings of a court considering its authority to proceed in a divorce or tax proceeding may be to determine the domicile of the party or parties involved. Because this finding of domicile is dependent upon the evidence brought before the court and because our system of dispute resolution relies upon the parties to inform the court, it is possible that different findings of domicile with regard to a particular individual may occur as courts in different states pass on the elements of litigation involving the affairs of a single individual. Also, it is possible that because some cases will find more ready support in the facts than others, the coincidence of a finding of domicile with the usual factual assumptions of domicile will vary.[3] Further, human beings quite

Co., 104 Conn. 169, 132 A. 902 (1926); Smith v. Croom, 7 Fla. 81 (1857); Abington v. Inhabitants of North Bridgewater, 40 Mass. 170 (1839); Gladwin v. Power, 21 A.D.2d 665, 249 N.Y.S.2d 980. See also Cook, The Logical and Legal Bases of the Conflict of Laws 194 (1942); Reese, Does Domicile Bear a Single Meaning?, 55 Colum. L. Rev. 589 (1955); Ehrenzweig, Conflict of Laws 240 (1962). But see Weintraub, Commentary on the Conflict of Laws 44 (3d ed. 1986)(" ... the common-sense recognition that the meaning of 'domicile' must shift with the use to which it is put, is not enough to preserve it as a viable and useful tool for conflicts analysis...."); Klein, A Critical Analysis of New Jersey's Domicile–Driven Choice of Law Methodology, 17 Seton Hall L. Rev. 204 (1987).

§ 4.4

1. Restatement, Second, Conflict of Laws §§ 70, 71 (1971). See infra § 15.6.

2. See, e.g., In re Dorrance's Estate, 309 Pa. 151, 163 A. 303 (1932), cert. denied 287 U.S. 660, 53 S.Ct. 222, 77 L.Ed. 570 (1932); In re Dorrance's Estate, 115 N.J.Eq. 268, 170 A. 601 (1934), aff'd Dorrance v. Thayer–Martin, 13 N.J.Misc. 168, 176 A. 902 (1935), aff'd 116 N.J.L. 362, 184 A. 743 (1936), cert. denied 298 U.S. 678, 56 S.Ct. 949, 80 L.Ed. 1399 (1936).

3. Domicile is the basis of citizenship in diversity jurisdiction of the federal court. Stine v. Moore, 213 F.2d 446 (5th Cir.1954). Usually when a party asserts a change in domicile for purposes of diversity jurisdiction, the burden of proof of the change rests on the party asserting the change. Hendry

reasonably differ on the specific view of the fact-law patterns that constitute domicile for particular purposes. As a consequence, the use of the concept can result in conflicting determinations. While this is a disturbing possibility, and seemingly raises constitutional questions, the Supreme Court has generally viewed this as one of the inherent elements of our federal system.[4] If our procedural system worked perfectly at all levels, the Supreme Court would be expected to resolve these issues. However, since our legal system is a human institution, such perfection cannot be expected.

§ 4.5   The famous *Dorrance* litigation illustrates this peculiar procedural difficulty in the tax setting. The courts of Pennsylvania and New Jersey each found that the decedent Dorrance had been domiciled within their state, and hence the intangibles which he left were subject to taxation by the laws of each of these states.[1] The United States Supreme Court declined to review either decision with the result that Pennsylvania received some $14 million dollars in tax and New Jersey an approximately equal amount. Although hindsight suggests some possible tactical alternatives,[2] the specter remains that under our legal system it is possible to have the assessment of multiple taxes based upon domicile as a result of conflicting findings by two or more states. If, as has been assumed in the tax cases, domicile is the only constitutional basis employed by the states involved for the asserted death tax on intangibles,[3] it would appear that one of the taxes is unconstitutionally assessed

v. Masonite Corp., 455 F.2d 955 (5th Cir. 1972), cert. denied 409 U.S. 1023, 93 S.Ct. 464, 34 L.Ed.2d 315 (1972). That proof must be demonstrated by a preponderance of the evidence. Scoggins v. Pollock, 727 F.2d 1025 (11th Cir.1984). But cf. Katz v. Goodyear Tire & Rubber Co., 737 F.2d 238 (2d Cir.1984); Avins v. Hannum, 497 F.Supp. 930 (E.D.Pa.1980).

4. Worcester County Trust Co. v. Riley, 302 U.S. 292, 58 S.Ct. 185, 82 L.Ed. 268 (1937). Justice Stone said, in the course of his opinion, "Neither the Fourteenth Amendment nor the full faith and credit clause requires uniformity in the decisions of the courts of different states as to the place of domicile." 302 U.S. at 299, 58 S.Ct. at 188. See Note, Determination of Domicil For Inheritance Tax Purposes by an Original Action in the United States Supreme Court, 46 Yale L.J. 1235 (1937). See also Wilson v. Willard, 183 Ga.App. 204, 358 S.E.2d 859 (1987).

§ 4.5

1. Supra § 4.4 n.2. The case is discussed infra § 4.23. See Restatement, Second, Conflict of Laws § 13 (1971). See also Nelson v. Miller, 201 F.2d 277 (9th Cir.1952).

2. See Note, Final Determination of Domicile in the United States, 9 Ind. L.J. 586 (1934); Chafee, The Federal Interplead-

er Act of 1936, 45 Yale L.J. 1161, 1170 (1936); Tweed & Sargent, Death and Taxes are Certain—But What of Domicile, 53 Harv. L. Rev. 68 (1939); Knapp, Solution of Double Domicile Problems, 18 Taxes 289 (1940); Farage, Multiple Domicile and Multiple Inheritance Taxes—A Possible Solution, 9 Geo. Wash. L. Rev. 375 (1941); Marsh, Conflict of Laws and Estate Planning, 4 Tex. Inst. 80 (1959).

3. Domicile at death is not the sole constitutional basis for levying an estate or inheritance tax on intangible personalty. State Tax Commission of Utah v. Aldrich, 316 U.S. 174, 62 S.Ct. 1008, 86 L.Ed. 1358 (1942), on remand 102 Utah 233, 129 P.2d 887 (1942) held that Utah may impose a tax upon a transfer by death of shares of stock in a Utah corporation forming part of the estate of a decedent domiciled in New York. The Court said: "Another State which has extended benefits or protection, or which can demonstrate 'the practical fact of its power' or sovereignty as respects the shares ... may likewise constitutionally make its exaction." 316 U.S. at 181–82, 62 S.Ct. at 1012. See also Curry v. McCanless, 307 U.S. 357, 59 S.Ct. 900, 83 L.Ed. 1339 (1939). See Friedman, Practical Aspects of Multiple State Taxation of Intangibles of Non-Resident Decedents Since the Aldrich Case, 24

if the concept of a single domicile of an individual also has constitutional stature.

In a somewhat similar case,[4] Connecticut joined in a New York action with the understanding that it would be bound by the court's decision, thus avoiding the dilemma of the *Dorrance* situation. This is an effective result because both states are voluntarily in the same court subject to that court's jurisdiction. However, there is no assurance that all states would be willing to submit their causes to the courts of a competing state, especially where it appears that the other state may apply a slightly different view of domicile.

In *Worcester County Trust Co. v. Riley*,[5] an attempt was made to employ the federal interpleader act to join the officials of the rival claimant states. The Supreme Court, however, found that such a procedure violated the 11th Amendment because the state was being sued in federal court without its consent.[6] In that case, Justice Stone stated that "Neither the 14th Amendment nor the Full Faith and Credit Clause requires uniformity in the decisions of the courts of different states as to the place of domicile. . . ."[7]

In a later case, *Texas v. Florida*,[8] involving a highly unusual fact pattern, the Supreme Court entertained an original suit in the nature of a bill of interpleader and upheld the master's finding that the decedent had been domiciled in Massachusetts rather than in any of the other states involved. However, original jurisdiction, the Supreme Court noted, is limited to cases in which the claims of the states asserting to be the domicile of the decedent would exceed the value of the estate.[9]

The Howard Hughes estate has raised some questions as to the continued strength of both *Worcester County Trust Co. v. Riley* and

Notre Dame Law. 41 (1948); Guterman, Avoidance of Double Taxation of Estates and Trusts, 95 U. Pa. L. Rev. 701 (1947); Howard, State Jurisdiction to Tax Intangibles: A Twelve Year Cycle, 8 Mo. L. Rev. 155 (1943); Morton & Cotton, Limitations on State Jurisdiction to Levy Death Taxes, 5 Miami L.Q. 449 (1951); Note, How Far Will Multi–State Death Taxation Go?, 1 Vand. L. Rev. 93 (1947).

4. In re Trowbridge's Estate, 266 N.Y. 283, 194 N.E. 756 (1935).

5. 302 U.S. 292, 58 S.Ct. 185, 82 L.Ed. 268 (1937). See Note, Determination of Domicil for Inheritance Tax Purposes by an Original Action in the United States Supreme Court, 46 Yale L.J. 1235 (1937).

6. The Eleventh Amendment to the Constitution provides: "The Judicial power of the United States shall not be construed to extend to any suit in law or equity, commenced or prosecuted against one of the United States by Citizens of another State or by Citizens or Subjects of any Foreign State." Compare California Fran-

chise Tax Board v. Hyatt, 538 U.S. 488, 123 S.Ct. 1683, 155 L.Ed.2d 702 (2003) (state courts are not required by the Full Faith and Credit Clause to give effect to the sovereign immunity rules of another state); Nevada v. Hall, 440 U.S. 410, 99 S.Ct. 1182, 59 L.Ed.2d 416 (1979)(permitting suit for personal injuries in the courts of another state).

7. Worcester County Trust Co. v. Riley, 302 U.S. 292, 299, 58 S.Ct. 185, 188, 82 L.Ed. 268 (1937).

8. 306 U.S. 398, 59 S.Ct. 563, 83 L.Ed. 817 (1939). The case is noted in 6 U. Chi. L. Rev. 708 (1939); 12 So. Cal. L. Rev. 469 (1939); 25 Va. L. Rev. 967 (1939). Observe however, that because federal constitutional law determines the content of due process, the determination of domicile for jurisdictional purposes would seem to be a federal constitutional issue in many situations. See infra § 6.4.

9. See Commonwealth of Massachusetts v. Missouri, 308 U.S. 1, 60 S.Ct. 39, 84 L.Ed. 3 (1939).

Texas v. Florida. In *California v. Texas*[10] the Supreme Court first denied, per curiam, California's motion to file a bill of complaint in original jurisdiction. Although concurring, four Justices indicated their belief that interpleader would lie or that *Texas v. Florida* was wrongly decided. Subsequently, the Fifth Circuit Court of Appeals in *Lummis v. White*[11] concluded that statutory interpleader jurisdiction did exist to determine the domicile of the decedent on the bill filed by the personal representative beset by claims of both California and Texas. The Fifth Circuit held that the case did not involve a controversy between the states, rather only each state against the decedent's personal representative. Further, the court opined, interpleader was not barred by the Eleventh Amendment which precludes only suits to impose liability to be paid from public funds and does not bar suits in which any impact on the state is incident to the determination of another issue. The Supreme Court reversed, reaffirmed the *Worcester County* case, and agreed to exercise original jurisdiction to decide the matter.[12] Justice Powell, joined by two other Justices, dissented in a strong opinion, emphasizing that multiple taxation based on indivisible domicile is offensive to due process for which a remedy should exist.

§ **4.6** In an attempt to avoid the very difficult consequence of divergent findings of domicile, many states have enacted statutes that authorize interstate compromise of death taxes when there are conflicting claims of domicile.[1] In addition, in the absence of compromise of the competing tax claims, several states have provided for binding arbitration to determine the domicile of the decedent.[2] These approaches, of course, require voluntary submission of the issue by the states involved. This leaves open the disturbing possibility of conflicting findings of domicile in states that do not undertake voluntary submission as well as in non-tax areas of the law in which domicile is significant.

§ **4.7** The problem presented by inconsistent findings of domicile with regard to jurisdiction for divorce is a highly interesting one, though somewhat different from that involved in the tax cases. In the United States it has generally been assumed and some courts have held that the existence of the domicile of one party within the state is a constitutional requirement for jurisdiction in divorce.[1] If a state of the United States purports to render a divorce decree upon the assumption that domicile is required for jurisdiction and upon a finding that one of the parties was domiciled within the state that determination of domicile may well be conclusive in litigation elsewhere notwithstanding factual indications to

---

10. 437 U.S. 601, 98 S.Ct. 3107, 57 L.Ed.2d 464 (1978).

11. 629 F.2d 397 (5th Cir. 1980).

12. Cory v. White, 457 U.S. 85, 102 S.Ct. 2325, 72 L.Ed.2d 694 (1982).

§ 4.6

1. See Uniform Interstate Compromise of Death Taxes Act, 8A U.L.A. 535.

2. Id. at 521.

§ 4.7

1. See Williams v. North Carolina, 325 U.S. 226, 65 S.Ct. 1092, 89 L.Ed. 1577 (1945); Rice v. Rice, 336 U.S. 674, 69 S.Ct. 751, 93 L.Ed. 957 (1949); Alton v. Alton, 207 F.2d 667 (3d Cir.1953).

the contrary.[2] This prospect is sometimes difficult to accept, but appears necessary because our system of dispute resolution leaves to the litigants the protection of the interests of the public and of the state.

To illustrate, if a matter is inappropriately presented, or is litigated in a manner reflecting the self-interests of the litigants, the court's conclusion may be binding upon others, including the state, simply because the system provides no other alternatives.[3] This is the product of the doctrines of preclusion by prior litigation. When an issue of jurisdiction over the person has been litigated or the individuals involved have had their day in court, the need for a reasonable end to litigation requires that the parties no longer may raise the question of jurisdiction.[4] Once a party has an opportunity to litigate a disputed issue, that party should be bound by the results. This concept of res judicata clearly applies in proceedings between the same litigants and those in privity with them. Although there are some lingering doubts whether this also bars litigation by the state in its own interest,[5] the probabilities are that preclusion will be extended to the state because the state's interests are deemed to be protected by the adversary system and the parties. This issue is discussed at greater length in the treatment of dissolution of marriage and of judgments.[6]

B. LAW DETERMINING OR CHARACTERIZING DOMICILE

§ 4.8 In most conflict-of-laws cases, the issue of what law is used to define domicile is not raised because the concept is often assumed to carry the same meaning in all common law jurisdictions. However, there may be variations in definition or emphasis that could lead to different results. Normally, the forum determines domicile according to the definitions and standards of its own law.[1] This stance is assumed in most cases

2. Cook v. Cook, 342 U.S. 126, 72 S.Ct. 157, 96 L.Ed. 146 (1951); Johnson v. Muelberger, 340 U.S. 581, 71 S.Ct. 474, 95 L.Ed. 552 (1951); Coe v. Coe, 334 U.S. 378, 68 S.Ct. 1094, 92 L.Ed. 1451 (1948); Sherrer v. Sherrer, 334 U.S. 343, 68 S.Ct. 1087, 92 L.Ed. 1429 (1948); Davis v. Davis, 305 U.S. 32, 59 S.Ct. 3, 83 L.Ed. 26 (1938); Restatement, Second, Conflict of Laws § 73 (1971). See also Tolson v. Arden, 89 Wash.App. 21, 947 P.2d 1242 (1997) (California's determination that decedent died domiciled in California binding as a matter of full faith and credit on later Washington proceedings).

3. Cf. Williams v. North Carolina, 317 U.S. 287, 63 S.Ct. 207, 87 L.Ed. 279 (1942).

4. Treinies v. Sunshine Mining Co., 308 U.S. 66, 60 S.Ct. 44, 84 L.Ed. 85 (1939); Stoll v. Gottlieb, 305 U.S. 165, 59 S.Ct. 134, 83 L.Ed. 104 (1938); American Surety Co. v. Baldwin, 287 U.S. 156, 53 S.Ct. 98, 77 L.Ed. 231 (1932); Baldwin v. Iowa State Traveling

Men's Association, 283 U.S. 522, 51 S.Ct. 517, 75 L.Ed. 1244 (1931); Raynor v. Stockton Savings & Loan Bank, 165 Cal.App.2d 715, 332 P.2d 416 (1958); Cummiskey v. Cummiskey, 259 Minn. 427, 107 N.W.2d 864 (1961); John Simmons Co. v. Sloan, 104 N.J.L. 612, 142 A. 15 (1928); Restatement, Second, Conflict of Laws § 96 (1971).

5. Cf. Williams v. North Carolina, 325 U.S. 226, 65 S.Ct. 1092, 89 L.Ed. 1577 (1945). But cf. Durfee v. Duke, 375 U.S. 106, 84 S.Ct. 242, 11 L.Ed.2d 186 (1963).

6. See infra §§ 15.6–15.11 and § 24.2.

§ 4.8

1. Restatement, Second, Conflict of Laws § 13 (1971); Wilson v. Willard, 183 Ga.App. 204, 358 S.E.2d 859 (1987); Torlonia v. Torlonia, 108 Conn. 292, 142 A. 843 (1928); In re Bain's Estate, 104 Misc. 508, 172 N.Y.S. 604 (Surr. 1918); In re Annesley, [1926] 1 Ch. 692. Cf. Mississippi Band of

out of necessity, for if domicile is employed as a pointing or choosing element by the forum in its choice-of-law rule, the forum must determine this issue, in theory at least, before it can identify the law to which it points. Put differently, the forum's definition of domicile is an integral part of the forum's choice-of-law rule that relies upon that definition. Thus determination of domicile is usually a matter of primary characterization for the forum.

§ 4.9 The forum's reliance on its own definition of domicile is equally an element of its law when it is determining an issue of its jurisdiction or the benefits to be conferred upon its citizens and domiciliaries since no choice of law reference is there involved. However, because the Constitution of the United States restrains the states in their jurisdictional reach and in some relationships with their citizens and citizens of other states, the determination of domicile may become an issue controlled by federal, common or constitutional law. For example, due process probably precludes a state from using a strained definition of domicile to exercise judicial jurisdiction over one whom the federal courts would consider to have had inadequate contact with the state to be deemed domiciled therein. The possible elevation of the definition of domicile to a federal constitutional level is also illustrated by the full-faith-and-credit cases, particularly those involving divorce in which it has been assumed that domicile is a constitutional prerequisite for jurisdiction. In *Williams v. North Carolina (II)* Justice Frankfurter noted: "Since an appeal to the full faith and credit clause raises questions arising under the constitution of the United States, the proper criteria for ascertaining domicile, should these be in dispute, become matters for federal determination."[1] Federal law will of course determine rights guaranteed to citizens of states under the United States Constitution, for example, voting age.[2]

§ 4.10 Another exception to the forum's reliance on its own definition of domicile involves seeking the meaning of domicile as employed in the law of another state. Thus, as between states of the United States, when considering the enforcement of a foreign court judgment to which jurisdictional attack has been made involving domicile, the second forum would measure domicile by the first forum's law if the first forum's definition of domicile satisfied any applicable federal standard.[1] Likewise,

Choctaw Indians v. Holyfield, 490 U.S. 30, 109 S.Ct. 1597, 104 L.Ed.2d 29 (1989).

§ 4.9

1. 325 U.S. 226, 231 n.7, 65 S.Ct. 1092, 1095 n.7, 89 L.Ed. 1577 (1945). There appeared to be no dispute as to the definition of domicile in *Williams*.

2. Jolicoeur v. Mihaly, 5 Cal.3d 565, 96 Cal.Rptr. 697, 488 P.2d 1 (1971); Ownby v. Dies, 337 F.Supp. 38 (E.D.Tex.1971). See also Mississippi Band of Choctaw Indians v. Holyfield, 490 U.S. 30, 109 S.Ct. 1597, 104 L.Ed.2d 29 (1989) (Federal law determines domicile under Indian Child Welfare Act); Rodriguez–Diaz v. Sierra–Martinez, 853

F.2d 1027 (1st Cir.1988). A federal standard for domicile is applied by federal courts in determining diversity jurisdiction. See, e.g., Kantor v. Wellesley Galleries, Ltd., 704 F.2d 1088 (9th Cir.1983); Michelson v. Exxon Research & Engineering Co., 578 F.Supp. 289 (W.D.Pa.1984), aff'd 745 F.2d 47 (3d Cir.1984); Rodriguez Diaz v. Sierra Martinez, 665 F.Supp. 96 (D.P.R.1987), judgment vacated 853 F.2d 1027 (1st Cir. 1988). See also supra § 3.36 n.2.

§ 4.10

1. Compare Restatement, Second, Conflict of Laws § 13, cmnts. (b), (c) (1971).

after the forum has made a choice-of-law reference to a foreign state in considering an issue in which the foreign state's rule provides a benefit to its domiciliaries, but not to others, the forum would be expected to apply the law of the foreign state for that determination. This second characterization of domicile is the same process as that used to determine the content and meaning of a foreign conflict-of-law rule since the court is seeking to achieve the same result at the forum as would be achieved by a court of the other state in the particular case.[2] An example of this could occur if the issue of the validity of a will of land were raised in a non-situs forum and the situs had adopted § 2–506 of the Uniform Probate Code. That section provides: "A written will is valid if executed in compliance with §§ 2–502 or 2–503 or if its execution complies with the law at the time of execution of the place where the will is executed, or of the law of the place where at the time of execution or at the time of death the testator is domiciled, has a place of abode or is a national." On looking to this portion of the law of the situs of the land, the forum court would adopt the situs definition of domicile in the application of § 2–506 to sustain the validity of the disposition, were that an issue. This approach is essentially an application of the whole law of the state to which reference is made under the policy of achieving uniformity of result with the other state in the case before the court.[3]

III.   DOMICILE COMPARED AND DEFINED

A. DOMICILE COMPARED TO NATIONALITY— INTERNATIONAL CONFLICTS

§ 4.11   In deciding international conflict-of-laws issues many nations employ the concept of national citizenship to determine certain personal rights and obligations.[1] In most instances this use of nationality is parallel to the use of domicile with which American lawyers are familiar. However, in a federal state, like the United States, it seems highly unlikely that personal law questions, such as those in which

---

2. Restatement, Second, Conflict of Laws § 13, cmnt. (c) (1971).

3. Cf. Matter of Schneider's Estate, 198 Misc. 1017, 96 N.Y.S.2d 652 (Surr. Ct. 1950).

§ 4.11

1. See de Winter, Nationality or Domicile, Hague Acad. of Int'l L., 3 Recueil des Cours 349, 358 (1969) where it is estimated that in 1968 there were 1450 million people in countries adhering to the domicile principle and 1600 million people in countries adhering to the nationality principle. In addition, 350 million people lived in countries which applied the nationality principle to their subjects and the domicile principle to

foreigners residing within their boundaries. See also 1 Rabel, The Conflict of Laws 117 (2d ed. 1958) for discussion of the evolution of the principle of nationality and a list of countries following it. See also Kuhn, Private International Law, 71–75 (1937); Lorenzen, The Pan–American Code of Private International Law, 4 Tulane L. Rev. 499 (1930); Offerhaus, The Private International Law of the Netherlands, 30 Yale L.J. 109, 250 (1921). A comprehensive review of nationality versus domicile is Bucher, Staatsangehörigkeits—und Wohnsitzprinzip, 28 Schweizerisches Jahrbuch für internationales Recht—Annuaire suisse de droit international 76–160 (1972).

domicile is utilized, could be effectively resolved on the basis of national citizenship.[2]

This is particularly true in the United States where most personal law topics such as marriage, divorce, child custody and succession of property are state law matters because they are among those subjects reserved to the states of the United States for determination. In most situations, the concept of domicile attaches to a person more quickly and can be changed more rapidly than citizenship. National citizenship persists even after a change of domicile. Considering this, a country of mostly immigrants such as the United States, could be expected to rely heavily upon the concept of domicile in order to bring promptly within the ambit of its law most of those matters which relate to the personal affairs of its population.[3] This preference for application of the domicile concept, as compared with a nationality concept, is also supported by the usual social instincts of people "who are keen to become part of the community of the country where they have settled as soon as they possibly can."[4] In civil law countries there appears a trend toward increased use of the domicile concept or its near equivalent, habitual residence.[5] Against this background there seems little likelihood that the states of the United States will shift their reliance on domicile to citizenship.[6]

§ 4.12 It is equally probable that many other nations of the world will continue to employ the concept of citizenship rather than domicile in some choice-of-law matters relating to the personal affairs of individuals. When the question arises in a foreign court that relies upon nationality for a choice-of-law reference involving a citizen of the United States it becomes important to accommodate that reference to the federal system

2. See Graveson, Conflict of Laws 185 (7th ed. 1974).

3. See de Winter, supra n.1, at 405, 407, 412.

4. de Winter, supra n.1, at 407. See Graveson, supra n. 2, at 190.

5. Bucher, supra n.1, observes that in many cases the trend is away from nationality and toward using domicile or habitual residence. Examples cited by him are the following: with respect to a person's capacity to act, for instance, to enter into commercial contracts, commercial security requires a reference to the place of acting or the place of domicile rather than to nationality. In the case of stateless persons or those with multiple nationality, it is the failure of "nationality" as a connecting factor. In the case of a married couple with different nationalities the objective of equality of treatment is served by the substitution of domicile. With respect to the protection of minors it is the difficulty of using foreign law in local proceedings which requires the giving up of references to nationality. Finally, with respect to renvoi the

objective of uniformity of decision among legal systems is better served by a reference to a law other than that of nationality.

Bucher concludes that the reasons for giving up the nationality principle differ, but all are prompted by "practical necessity and a reference to domicile is best suited to fill the gap whenever a reference to nationality is inappropriate or does not yield results." Id. at 131–32. See also de Winter, supra n.1 at 405; Baty, The Interconnection of Nationality and Domicile, 13 Ill. L. Rev. 363 (1919). Rabel also indicated that the domicile concept may resume its earlier importance. 1 Rabel, The Conflict of Laws 171 (2d ed. 1958). For further discussion of the domicile and nationality question, see Kuhn, Private International Law, 63–66 (1937); 1 Rabel, The Conflict of Laws, Ch. 4 (2d ed. 1958). L. P_alsson, Rules, Problems and Trends in Family Conflict of Laws, Hague Acad. Int'l. L., 199 Recueil des Cours 313, 378 (1986–IV).

6. Canada shares similar considerations regarding the preference of domicile over nationality. See Castel, Canadian Conflict of Laws 76 (4th ed. 1997).

of the United States. This accommodation is assisted by two considerations. The first is the increasing reliance by other nations on the concept of habitual residence and other domicile-like references that describe a persistent and continuing relationship between an individual and a governmental unit such as a state of the United States.[1] This may assist the forum to recognize, within its own nationality concept, that there is perhaps a more direct reference to the pertinent governmental unit in which an individual lives. This, in turn, can be bolstered by recognition that a reference to the place of citizenship of a United States citizen would include the normal choice-of-law reference to a state of the United States. This latter is assisted by the definition of state citizenship in the United States Constitution[2] for citizens of the United States are citizens "of the state wherein they reside" and, in this context, residence means domicile. Consequently, a choice-of-law reference by a foreign court to "the law of the United States" relating to the personal affairs of an individual includes the reference to the citizenship of that person in the state of his domicile. An easy transition to the law of the domicile is supported by that reference.

This easy reference works well when the individual in question is domiciled within a state of the United States. However, United States citizenship is more persistent than domicile and may continue as to individuals who are resident and domiciled in another nation. In that instance it is possible that reference to the "law of the United States" would include the traditional renvoi to the law of the foreign country in which the individual is domiciled. Another possibility is that the domicile of a citizen of the United States will continue in the state of the United States in which that citizen resided immediately prior to departure from the United States. It is also possible that the domicile of such an individual would continue within the state of his former residence for some purposes, for example, succession, even though the individual had acquired a sufficiently permanent residence in a foreign country to justify recognition of a divorce obtained there. It is likely that an analysis of the policies involved in a particular issue would resolve this matter in nearly all instances under the usual choice-of-law method now employed by most of the states of the United States. On the other hand, the possibility remains that in the case of a United States citizen domiciled in a foreign country the reference to citizenship from a foreign court would in turn justify the reference to the actual foreign domicile of the subject under circumstances in which it appears that a court of the United States would make that same reference.[3]

§ 4.12

1. See Cavers, Habitual Residence: A Useful Concept?, 21 Am. U. L. Rev. 475 (1972); Nadelmann, Habitual Residence and Nationality Tests at The Hague: The 1968 Convention on Recognition of Divorces, 47 Tex. L. Rev. 766 (1969); Cavers, Contemporary Conflicts Law in American Perspective, Hague Acad. of Int'l. L., 3 Recueil des Cours 77, 257, 273 (1970). See also Graveson, Conflict of Laws 193 (7th ed. 1974).

2. U.S. Const. Amend. XIV.

3. Cf. Sadat v. Mertes, 464 F.Supp. 1311 (E.D.Wis.1979), aff'd 615 F.2d 1176 (7th Cir.1980); Pemberton v. Colonna, 290 F.2d 220 (3d Cir.1961); Vidal v. South Am. Securities Co., 276 Fed. 855 (2d Cir.1921); Kaiser v. Loomis, 391 F.2d 1007 (6th Cir.1968);

B. DOMICILE COMPARED TO RESIDENCE, HABITUAL RESIDENCE AND OTHER PERSISTENT RELATIONSHIPS

§ 4.13 Statutory references that require a territorial link similar to domicile usually employ terms such as residence, habitual residence, habitat, or similar words.[1] In many instances, these terms are construed by American courts to have the same meaning as domicile,[2] but in others

Maple Island Farm v. Bitterling, 196 F.2d 55 (8th Cir.1952), cert. denied 344 U.S. 832, 73 S.Ct. 40, 97 L.Ed. 648 (1952). Since civil law countries would presumably accept or apply renvoi, this approach should follow in the usual case. The approach should also be appropriate in the "hidden renvoi" cases when the choice of law is in the jurisdictional rule. For example, if United States citizens, formerly domiciled in Illinois, but presently domiciled in Germany were to seek a divorce in Germany, the German courts would apply the divorce law of the state of nationality. This would refer the forum to the United States and probably then to Illinois. Illinois does not have choice-of-law rules regarding divorce because the applicable law is built into the Illinois concept of jurisdiction: the court with jurisdiction applies its own law. The court of the domicile has jurisdiction. Therefore Germany substantive law is most appropriate even though the renvoi is "hidden" in the jurisdictional rule. See supra § 3.14 n.4; Hay, 8 IPRax 265 (1988). Where there is proof that a United States citizen was domiciled in a foreign country, federal jurisdiction based on diversity of citizenship did not exist as diversity jurisdiction assumes citizenship of different states of the United States. See Simmons v. Rosenberg, 572 F.Supp. 823 (E.D.N.Y.1983); Sadat v. Mertes, 615 F.2d 1176 (7th Cir.1980); Smith v. Carter, 545 F.2d 909 (5th Cir.), cert. denied 431 U.S. 955, 97 S.Ct. 2677, 53 L.Ed.2d 272 (1977).

§ 4.13

1. Restatement, Second, Conflict of Laws § 11, cmnt. (k) (1971). For detailed discussion see Reese & Green, That Elusive Word "Residence," 6 Vand. L. Rev. 561 (1953). See also Corson, Reform of Domicile Law for Transients, Temporary Residents and Multi-Based Persons, 16 Colum. J.L. & Soc. Prob. 327 (1981); McClean, The Meaning of Residence, 11 Int'l. & Cong. L.Q. 1153 (1962); Beale, Residence and Domicil, 4 Iowa L. Bull. 3 (1918). The problem also arises in contract terminology. See Wit v. Berman, 306 F.3d 1256 (2d Cir. 2002), cert. denied 538 U.S. 923, 123 S.Ct. 1574, 155

L.Ed.2d 313 (2003) (voters may have only one "residence" for voting purposes, even if voter maintains two different homes and lives in each a substantial portion of the year); Hobbs v. Fireman's Fund American Insurance Cos., 339 So.2d 28 (La.App.1976); Clarkson v. MFA Mutual Insurance Co., 413 S.W.2d 10 (Mo.App.1967); Barker v. Iowa Mutual Insurance Co., 241 N.C. 397, 85 S.E.2d 305 (1955); Central Manufacturers Mutual Insurance Co. v. Friedman, 213 Ark. 9, 209 S.W.2d 102 (1948).

2. See e.g. Northwestern National Casualty Co. v. Davis, 90 Cal.App.3d 782, 153 Cal.Rptr. 556 (1979). Residence for purposes of taxation means domicile. See Borland v. Boston, 132 Mass. 89 (1882); In re Gillmore's Estate, 101 N.J.Super. 77, 243 A.2d 263 (App.Div.1968); Denny v. Sumner County, 134 Tenn. 468, 184 S.W. 14 (1916); Talley v. Commonwealth, 127 Va. 516, 103 S.E. 612 (1920). See also as to elections: Elam v. Maggard, 165 Ky. 733, 178 S.W. 1065 (1915); Vanderpoel v. O'Hanlon, 53 Iowa 246, 5 N.W. 119 (1880); Isaacson v. Heffernan, 189 Misc. 16, 64 N.Y.S.2d 726 (1946); Jones v. Burkett, 346 P.2d 338 (Okl. 1959); In re Stabile, 348 Pa. 587, 36 A.2d 451 (1944); Gower v. Carter, 195 N.C. 697, 143 S.E. 513 (1928); Seibold v. Wahl, 164 Wis. 82, 159 N.W. 546 (1916). To the same effect, to found jurisdiction: Schlawig v. De Peyster, 83 Iowa 323, 49 N.W. 843 (1891); Hislop v. Taaffe, 141 App.Div. 40, 125 N.Y.S. 614 (2d Dept.1910). For divorce: see Hinds v. Hinds, 1 Iowa 36 (1855); Miller v. Miller, 67 Or. 359, 136 P. 15 (1913); Hanson v. Hanson, 78 N.H. 560, 103 A. 307 (1918); De Meli v. De Meli, 120 N.Y. 485, 24 N.E. 996 (1890); Nagy v. Nagy–Horvath, 273 S.C. 583, 257 S.E.2d 757 (1979); Tower v. Tower, 120 Vt. 213, 138 A.2d 602 (1958). In divorce cases actual residence for a defined period is often required in addition to domicile. See Wiseman v. Wiseman, 216 Tenn. 702, 393 S.W.2d 892 (1965); Sosna v. Iowa, 419 U.S. 393, 95 S.Ct. 553, 42 L.Ed.2d 532 (1975). For settlement under Social Welfare Laws: see Inhabitants of Whately v. Inhabitants of Hatfield, 196

it is clear that this is not the purport of the legislation.[3] In statutes relating to the jurisdiction of courts[4] or to voting rights[5] or tax consequences,[6] the term residence is usually interpreted as the equivalent of domicile. On the other hand, there are statutes which make it clear that some other contact or concept is intended. For example, § 2–506 of the Uniform Probate Code[7] provides in part that a written will is valid if its execution complies with the law of the place where at the time of execution or at the time of death the testator is "domiciled, has a place of abode, or is a national." In that context it is clear that "place of abode" would constitute an intended territorial link of a less persistent nature than "domicile." In light of the purpose of the statute to validate the expectations of testators, it is probable that "place of abode" would be satisfied by a residence of lesser duration than even an habitual residence. It very likely would be satisfied by the relationship that exists when a person maintains a winter home even though residence at the domicile is not abandoned. By contrast, some statutes, such as those relating to jurisdiction for divorce,[8] may speak in terms of the qualified individual being "a resident of the state for six months . . . next

Mass. 393, 82 N.E. 48 (1907); Ashland County v. Bayfield County, 244 Wis. 210, 12 N.W.2d 34 (1943); but see North Yarmouth v. West Gardiner, 58 Me. 207 (1870). Cf. Hughes v. Illinois Public Aid Commission, 2 Ill.2d 374, 118 N.E.2d 14 (1954). On attachment: see Haggart v. Morgan, 5 N.Y. 422 (1851). On statute of limitations: see Hallet v. Bassett, 100 Mass. 167 (1868); Dignam v. Shaff, 51 Wash. 412, 98 P. 1113 (1909); Trask v. Karrick, 94 Vt. 70, 108 A. 846 (1920). On schools: see Fangman v. Moyers, 90 Colo. 308, 8 P.2d 762 (1932); State ex rel. School–District Board v. Thayer, 74 Wis. 48, 41 N.W. 1014 (1889). For licensing, see Board of Medical Registration and Examination v. Turner, 241 Ind. 73, 168 N.E.2d 193 (1960). For guardianship: see In re Fox' Guardianship, 212 Or. 80, 318 P.2d 933 (1957). Cf. Willenbrock v. Rogers, 255 F.2d 236 (3d Cir.1958). For public employment: cf. Choike v. City of Detroit, 94 Mich. App. 703, 290 N.W.2d 58 (1980), For rent control: see Sarraf v. Szunics, 132 Misc.2d 97, 503 N.Y.S.2d 513 (City Civ. Ct. 1986).

3. See McGrath v. Kristensen, 340 U.S. 162, 175, 71 S.Ct. 224, 232, 95 L.Ed. 173 (1950); cf. United States v. Scott, 472 F.Supp. 1073 (N.D.Ill.1979), aff'd 618 F.2d 109 (7th Cir.) cert. denied 445 U.S. 962, 100 S.Ct. 1650, 64 L.Ed.2d 238 (1980); Application of Tang, 39 A.D.2d 357, 333 N.Y.S.2d 964 (1972), appeal dismissed 35 N.Y.2d 851, 363 N.Y.S.2d 88, 321 N.E.2d 879 (1974); Edmundson v. Miley Trailer Co., 211 N.W.2d 269 (Iowa 1973). Cf. also Lopez, The Law of Domicile with Greater Compensation Rules Toward Policy–Oriented Rules

for Choice of Law, 17 Calif. Western L. Rev. 26 (1980). See also Bastian v. Personnel Bd. of Chicago, 108 Ill.App.3d 672, 439 N.E.2d 142 (1982), judgment vacated 98 Ill.2d 277, 456 N.E.2d 27 (1983), on remand 123 Ill. App.3d 963, 463 N.E.2d 845 (1984).

4. E.g., Milliken v. Meyer, 311 U.S. 457, 61 S.Ct. 339, 85 L.Ed. 278 (1940); Calhoun v. Somogyi, 190 Ga.App. 502, 379 S.E.2d 595 (1989); Huffman v. Huffman, 232 Neb. 742, 441 N.W.2d 899 (1989), appeal after remand 236 Neb. 101 459 N.W.2d 215 (1990); Myrick v. Superior Court, 256 P.2d 348 (Cal.App.1953), aff'd 41 Cal.2d 519, 261 P.2d 255 (1953). Cf. Will of Brown, 132 Misc.2d 811, 505 N.Y.S.2d 334 (Surr. Ct. 1986). Dunlap by Wells v. Buchanan, 741 F.2d 165 (8th Cir.1984); Prakash v. American University, 727 F.2d 1174 (D.C.Cir. 1984); Kantor v. Wellesley Galleries, Ltd., 704 F.2d 1088 (9th Cir.1983); Simmons v. Skyway of Ocala, 592 F.Supp. 356 (S.D.Ga. 1984).

5. E.g., Worden v. Mercer County Board of Elections, 61 N.J. 325, 294 A.2d 233 (1972); Jolicoeur v. Mihaly, 5 Cal.3d 565, 96 Cal.Rptr. 697, 488 P.2d 1 (1971); Wilkins v. Bentley, 385 Mich. 670, 189 N.W.2d 423 (1971).

6. E.g., Citizens Bank & Trust Co. v. Glaser, 70 N.J. 72, 357 A.2d 753 (1976); Matter of Ward's Estate, 168 Mont. 396, 543 P.2d 382 (1975).

7. 8 U.L.A. 281.

8. E.g., Cal. Civ. Code § 4530; Fla. Stat. Ann. § 61.021.

preceding"[9] the time when the benefit is available. This would normally be construed to mean domicile plus some calendar period of actual residence to satisfy the requirements of the statute. These durational residence statutes are designed to limit the access to the court or the particular benefit to those persons who have a persistent relationship with the state of some long standing.[10] Likewise, the term "inhabitant" has been held to mean domiciliary in cases involving divorce or probate.[11] Under other statutes, it is possible that the term "resident" will simply mean those persons currently living within a geographic area, e.g., in a provision requiring snow removal from sidewalks by "occupants" of abutting property.[12] Here it is clear that the purpose of the statute does not involve any durational requirement and domicile is not contemplated.

§ 4.14 In recent years the term "habitual residence" has become the subject of frequent use in international matters and international conventions.[1] Although habitual residence has eluded definition even

9. Cal. Civ. Code § 4530.

10. See Sosna v. Iowa, 419 U.S. 393, 95 S.Ct. 553, 42 L.Ed.2d 532 (1975); Sturgis v. Washington, 368 F.Supp. 38 (W.D.Wash. 1973), aff'd 414 U.S. 1057, 94 S.Ct. 563, 38 L.Ed.2d 464 (1973); Vlandis v. Kline, 412 U.S. 441, 93 S.Ct. 2230, 37 L.Ed.2d 63 (1973); Starns v. Malkerson, 326 F.Supp. 234 (D.Minn.1970), aff'd 401 U.S. 985, 91 S.Ct. 1231, 28 L.Ed.2d 527 (1971); Thompson v. Board of Regents, 187 Neb. 252, 188 N.W.2d 840 (1971).

11. Burch v. Burch, 195 F.2d 799, 804 (3d Cir.1952) (divorce); Bechtel v. Bechtel, 101 Minn. 511, 112 N.W. 883, 883 (1907) (divorce); Ambrose v. Vandeford, 277 Ala. 66, 167 So.2d 149, 150 (1964) (probate). Cf. Unanue v. Unanue, 141 A.D.2d 31, 532 N.Y.S.2d 769 (1988).

12. Mass. Gen. Laws Ann. C. 85, § 5; Re Goddard, 33 Mass. 504 (1835); Mich. Comp. Laws Ann. § 5.18.2; Rich v. Rosenshine, 131 W.Va. 30, 45 S.E.2d 499 (1947). Cf. San Patricio Co. v. Nueces County Hosp. Dist., 721 S.W.2d 375 (Tex.App. 1986).

§ 4.14

1. Cavers, Habitual Residence: A Useful Concept?, 21 Am. U. L. Rev. 475 (1972); Nadelmann, Habitual Residence and Nationality Tests at The Hague: The 1968 Convention on Recognition of Divorces, 47 Tex. L. Rev. 766 (1969); Schwind, Der "gewöhnliche Aufenthalt" im IPR, 80 Festschrift Ferid 423 (1988); Graveson, Conflict of Laws 193 (7th ed. 1974); Castel, Canadian Conflict of Laws 100 (2d ed. 1986).

The Hague Convention on Conflicts Between the Law of Nationality and the Law

of Domicile (1955) utilizes the term as do the Hague Convention on Form of Wills (1961), Jurisdiction, Applicable Law and Recognition of Decrees Relating to Adoptions (1965), Recognition of Divorces and Legal Separation (1970), International Administration of the Estates of Deceased Persons (1973), Law Applicable to Maintenance Obligations (1973), Law Applicable to Matrimonial Property Regimes (1978), Celebration and Recognition of The Validity of Marriages (1978), Law Applicable to Agency (1978), Civil Aspects of International Child Abduction (1980), International Access to Justice (1980), Law Applicable to Succession to the Estates of Deceased Persons (1988). In each the term "habitual residence" is used in circumstances in which the usage appears to contemplate a concept substantially the equivalent of that assumed in the usage of "domicile" in the United States. Compare the use of domicile as a primary jurisdictional basis in the Common Market Recognition of Judgments Convention. Habitual residence was also used in the unsuccessful proposed United States–United Kingdom Judgments Recognition Treaty. See Hay & Walker, The Proposed Recognition–of–Judgments Convention Between the United States and the United Kingdom, 11 Tex. Int'l L.J. 421, 428 (1976). A comprehensive exploration of the use of habitual residence is found in Mann, Der "gewöhnliche Aufenthalt" im Internationalen Privatrecht, 1956 Juristenzeitung 466, reprinted in Mann's Beiträge zum internationalen Privatrecht 25–38 (1976). See also the extensive use of habitual residence in the Swiss Conflicts Statute (1987, effective 1989); Inter–American Convention on Domicile of Natural Persons in Private In-

more completely than domicile, it connotes actual residence plus some continuity and persistence even though it does not connote the intended permanence or emphasis on expressed intent often associated with domicile.[2] Definition of the term "habitual residence" has been resisted in the belief that courts will have more latitude to relate the facts of the particular case to the common sense purpose of the use of the term, an approach sometimes overlooked in the use of domicile.[3] Even without formal definition, the term habitual residence has come to have several accepted features in its use particularly in Europe and in The Hague Conventions. Domicile historically has been given varying dimensions in different applications and in different courts. Concepts such as the revival of domicile of origins derivative domicile of married women, the requirement of intent to remain permanently, which were part of the domicile concept in English law, but not accepted elsewhere, led to a distrust of the term in Europe. To avoid the distasteful problems of the English concept and the uncertainties of meaning and proof of subjective intent, more recent legislation in Europe, England and The Hague Conventions have employed the term habitual residence.[4]

Habitual residence, consistent with the purpose of its use, identifies the center of a person's personal and family life as disclosed by the facts of the individual's activities. As one's principal residence where one's personal life is centered, a person may have but one habitual residence.[5] It appears that in most circumstances habitual residence has the same essential meaning that is usually associated with one's home. It is this concept of home that is fairly close to the concept of domicile as it has developed in modern usage in the United States,[6] though with perhaps

---

ternational Law of 1979, 18 Int'l. Leg. Mats. 1234.

2. Cruse v. Chittum [1974] 2 All E. R. 940, noted in 53 Can. Bar Rev. 135 (1975).

3. See Cavers, Habitual Residence: A Useful Concept?, 21 Am. U. L. Rev. 475, 485 (1972).

4. See Swiss Federal Statute on Private International Law, 18 December 1987, Art. 20; Council of Europe, "Committee of Ministers Resolution (72) I, 18 January 1972, Rule 9", 20 Nederlands Tijdschrift voor International Recht, 213, 215 (1973) which provides:

"No. 9. In determining whether a residence is habitual, account is to be taken of the duration and the continuity of the residence as well as of other facts of a personal or professional nature which point to durable ties between a person and his residence."

Similarly, Angenieux v. Hakenberg, 13/73, [1973] E.C.R. 935, 952, the court stated that permanent residence defined as "the place where a person habitually resides" in Regulation 3, Council of Europe, must be understood as "the place in which

he has established the permanent centre of his interests and to which he returns on the intervals between his tours." See (Great Britain) Recognition of Divorces and Legal Separations Act 1971, sec. 3; Domicile and Matrimonial Proceeding Act 1973 § 5; Children Act 1974 § 24.

For Hague Conventions employing habitual residence as a controlling contact listed supra n.1. The Hague Convention on Child Abduction was ratified by the United States in 1988.

See also the thorough comparison in J.D. McClean, Recognition of Family Judgments in the Commonwealth, 28 et seq. (1983); L. P_alsson, Rules, Problems and Trends in Family Conflict of Law, 199 Recueil des Cours 313, 334 (1986–IV).

5. D.W.M. Waters, Explanatory Report, Convention on the Law Applicable to Succession to the Estate of Deceased Persons, Hague Conf. Int'l. L., 56 (1989); Cruse v. Chittum [1974] 2 All E.R. 940.

6. See Juenger, Recognition of Foreign Divorces, 20 Am. J. Comp. L. 1, 5 (1972); Scoles, Choice of Law in Family Property

less emphasis on the intention to remain and without the instantaneous change that can sometime characterize domicile in the strict sense.

For instance, in *Walton v. Walton*,[7] a United States federal court, applying the Hague Convention on the Civil Aspects of International Child Abduction, confronted the question of where a five-year-old child was habitually resident. At the relevant point in time, the child had lived for about 18 months in Australia with his parents. The parents disputed whether the stay was to have been one of indefinite duration—a question that would be critical in determining domicile. But, the court—noting that the term habitual residence is more flexible than domicile—concluded that the child was habitually resident in Australia because, even if the stay was not indefinite, it was much more than a "mere visit" and all had gone there with the intention of remaining for some significant period.[8] In another extensive opinion applying the same convention, another federal court, in the case of *Mozes v. Mozes*,[9] confronted a case in which the parents had agreed that the mother would relocate with their children from Israel to the United States for a period of just over a year, while the father stayed behind. At the end of the period, the mother sued in a California state court for divorce and custody of the children. The father then petitioned in a federal court for return of the children under the Hague Convention. The federal district court ruled that the habitual residence of the children had shifted to California, but the court of appeals reversed and remanded for further consideration. In an extensive opinion drawing on foreign decisions the court of appeals concluded that the lower court had given insufficient attention to the shared intentions of the parents, which had apparently contemplated a stay of limited duration. Although not completely ruling out the possibility, the court was clearly skeptical that a change in habitual residence could be accomplished in a case in which at least one parent clearly contemplated a stay of limited duration. The distinction between *Mozes* and *Walton* is fairly clear. *Walton* involved the longer stay, it had no clear ending point and both parents had relocated. Both decisions, however, evidence the fact-intensive nature of the inquiry.

This relatively flexible and fact-intensive approach is consistent with leading cases in other countries. For instance, in *C. v. S.*,[10] the opinion in the House of Lords offered the following explanation of the term:

> [T]here is a significant difference between a person ceasing to be habitually resident in country A, and his subsequently becoming habitually resident in country B. A person may cease to be habitually resident in country A in a single day if he or she leaves it with a settled intention not to return to it but to take up long-term residence in country B instead. Such a person cannot, however,

Transactions, 209 Recueil des Cours 9, 24 (1988–II).

7. 925 F.Supp. 453 (S.D.Miss.1996).

8. See also Feder v. Evans–Feder, 63 F.3d 217, 224 (3d Cir.1995)(intended stay

need not be indefinite, but must be long enough to "acclimate" a child).

9. 239 F.3d 1067 (9th Cir. 2001).

10. In re J., [1990] 2 A.C. 562, [1990] 3 W.L.R. 492; [1990] 2 All E.R. 961 (H.L. 1990)

become habitually resident in country B in a single day. An appreciable period of time and a settled intention will be necessary to enable him or her to become so. During that appreciable period of time the person will have ceased to be habitually resident in country A but not yet have become habitually resident in country B.

As this discussion shows, habitual residence does avoid some of the odder features of strict domicile, including the notion that a person's connection with a state switches instantly.[11] As a result, habitual residence is quite a bit like domicile, with perhaps a bit more common sense stirred into the mix.

C. DOMICILE DEFINED

§ 4.15   As the territorial link between an individual and a place, domicile has been variously defined, often by its function and by description, as well as by analogy to other concepts to which it is similar. Thus the Second Conflicts Restatement defines it, by function, as the place to which the law accords "significance because of the person's identification with that place.... Every person has a domicile at all times and at least for the same purpose, no person has more than one domicile at a time."[1] Thus the function of domicile as a "legal headquarters" by which all persons are allocated to governmental units for legal purposes is an important element of domicile. This definition has the long approved support of Justice Holmes's famous quotation that "... what the law means by domicile is the one technically pre-eminent headquarters, which as a result either of fact or fiction every person is compelled to have in order that by aid of it, certain rights and duties which have attached to it by the law may be determined."[2] This persistent, enduring relationship assumed by domicile is a valuable and perhaps necessary

---

11. See also Friedrich v. Friedrich, 983 F.2d 1396, 1401–02 (6th Cir.1993), appeal after remand 78 F.3d 1060 (6th Cir.1996) (some passage of time required before a new habitual residence is acquired; habitual residence does not switch suddenly in the fashion of domicile); In re Bates, No. CA 122–89, High Court of Justice, Family Div'l Ct., Royal Courts of Justice, United Kingdom (1989)("settled purpose" of remaining in a place for a considerable period is required for habitual residence, though intent to remain indefinitely is not necessary).

§ 4.15

1. Restatement, Second, Conflict of Laws § 11 (1971).

2. Bergner & Engel Brewing Co. v. Dreyfus, 172 Mass. 154, 157, 51 N.E. 531, 532 (1898). In considering the plaintiff's domicile for purposes of federal diversity jurisdiction, the court stated in Freeman v. Northwest Acceptance Corp., 754 F.2d 553, 555 (5th Cir.1985):

The definition of "domicile" has not changed from that set forth more than a century ago by the Supreme Court: "[a] residence at a particular place accompanied with positive or presumptive proof of an intention to remain there for an unlimited time." Mitchell v. United States, 88 U.S. (21 Wall.) 350, 352, 22 L.Ed. 584 (1874).

Residence in fact, and the intention of making the place of residence one's home, are essential elements of domicile. Words may be evidence of a man's intention to establish his domicile at a particular place of residence, but they cannot supply the fact of his domicile there. In such circumstances, the actual fact of residence and a real intention of remaining there, as disclosed by his entire course of conduct, are the controlling factors in ascertaining his domicile.

Stine v. Moore, 213 F.2d 446, 448 (5th Cir.1954).

concept in the reasonable allocation of benefits and burdens in a world of territorial governments and migratory populations.

In defining domicile by descriptive terms, most authorities consider domicile to be the place with which an individual has the closest personal association in the sense of "home."[3] The connotations of home are varied, but usually include the elements described in the Restatement: "Where a person dwells and which is the center of his domestic, social and civil life."[4] For the vast majority of people, who have but one "fixed, permanent home and principal establishment, and to which, whenever.... absent, ... [have] the intention of returning,"[5] these definitions hold true in all applications. Likewise in most applications, there is little tension between the descriptive and functional elements of the domicile concept. However, the law's functional need for an important persistent relationship between an individual and a territorial unit may vary with the purpose for which the relationship is deemed significant. Likewise, it may vary with the governmental unit involved, i.e., nation, state (province), county or other governmental subdivision. As a consequence, even within the United States, courts utilizing the concept of domicile for different purposes and as to different issues may emphasize different elements to such an extent as to raise the question whether there are not several kinds of domicile.[6]

§ 4.16   The long-standing debate whether domicile is a unitary concept or multifarious was raised in the consideration of the first Restatement by Walter Wheeler Cook, who stated: "There is no doubt that what you might call the core of the concept is the same in all these situations; but as you get out towards what I like to call the twilight zone of the subject, I don't believe the scope remains exactly the same for all purposes."[1] The debate was continued during the consideration of the Second Restatement by many, including Ehrenzweig[2] and Wein-

---

3. Brignoli v. Balch, Hardy & Scheinman, Inc., 696 F.Supp. 37 (S.D.N.Y.1988); Kirkpatrick v. Transtector Systems, 114 Idaho 559, 759 P.2d 65 (1988); Matter of Adoption of T.R.M., 525 N.E.2d 298 (Ind. 1988), cert. denied 490 U.S. 1069, 109 S.Ct. 2072, 104 L.Ed.2d 636 (1989); State Election Bd. v. Bayh, 521 N.E.2d 1313 (Ind. 1988); Wilson v. Butler, 513 So.2d 304 (La. App.1987).

4. Restatement, Second, Conflict of Laws § 12 (1971). Compare Swiss Federal Statute on Private International Law of Dec. 18, 1987, Art. 20(1) " ... a natural person ... (a) has his domicile in the state where he resides with the intention of settling there; (b) has his habitual residence in the state where he lives during a certain period of time, even if this period is of predetermined limited duration."

5. Story, Conflict of Laws § 41 (8th ed. 1883). See Reese, Does Domicile Bear a Single Meaning?, 55 Colum. L. Rev. 589

(1955). Cf. Inter–American Convention on Domicile of Natural Persons in Private International Law of 1979, 18 Int'l Leg. Mats. 1234. Carter, Domicil: The Case for Radical Reform in The United Kingdom, 36 Int'l & Comp. L.Q. 713 (1987).

6. See Anton, Private International Law 181 (1967); de Winter, Nationality or Domicile, Hague Acad. of Int'l L., 3 Recueil des Cours 349, 420, 423 (1969).

§ 4.16

1. 3 Proceedings of American Law Institute 227 (1925). See also Greenwood v. Hildebrand, 357 Pa.Super. 253, 515 A.2d 963 (1986), appeal denied 515 Pa. 594, 528 A.2d 602 (1987).

2. Ehrenzweig, Conflict of Laws 240 (1962).

traub.[3] Professor Weintraub has suggested that domicile has so many variants that its continued use as if it were a unitary concept is misleading. As a consequence, he urged that the law would be better off if the concept were abandoned and reliance placed rather upon an analysis of the policies underlying the rules and statutes of the interested states relevant to the issue before the court.[4]

The Second Restatement agrees with Professor Cook and concludes that the "core of domicile is everywhere the same. But in close cases, decision on a question of domicile may sometimes depend upon the purpose for which the domicile concept is used in the particular case."[5] This situation is one which requires the greatest sensitivity of lawyers and judges that they may take cognizance of the flexibility of the concept as they consider different cases.[6]

It is, however, doubtful that it is possible or feasible to attempt to abandon the concept of domicile. Certainly the careful analysis that most writers suggest and most courts now attempt will sensitize the courts and lawyers to the problems incident to the flexibility of the domicile concept and result in fewer occasions of mechanical misapplication of the doctrine. The concept of domicile serves a valuable function in many cases, and as Professor Cavers once stated: "When a series of decisions involving the same issue has registered what the deciding courts believed to be the appropriate degree of connection in such cases, they are very likely to place a label on it. This is an intellectual economy that is well-nigh essential to the operation of a system of case law."[7]

IV. TRADITIONAL REQUIREMENTS FOR THE ACQUISITION OF A DOMICILE OF CHOICE

A. IN GENERAL

§ 4.17 Most of the litigated problems in the area of domicile concern the acquisition of a domicile of choice and center about the quality of an individual's physical presence at the place of the alleged domicile and the nature of his intention or attitude of mind regarding

---

3. Weintraub, An Inquiry Into the Utility of "Domicile" as a Concept in Conflicts Analysis, 63 Mich. L. Rev. 961 (1965).

4. Weintraub, Commentary on the Conflict of Laws 42 (4th ed. 2001). See also Corr, Interest Analysis and Choice of Law: The Dubious Dominance of Domicile, 4 Utah L. Rev. 651 (1983).

5. Restatement, Second, Conflict of Laws § 11, cmnt. (*o*) (1971).

6. "The tendency to assume that a word which appears in two or more legal rules, and so in connection with more than one purpose, has and should have precisely the same scope in all of them, runs all through

legal discussions. It has all the tenacity of original sin and must constantly be guarded against." Cook, "Substance" and "Procedure" in the Conflict of Laws, 42 Yale L.J. 333, 337 (1933).

7. Cavers, Habitual Residence: A Useful Concept?, 21 Am. U. L. Rev. 475, 487 (1972). For reforming legislation in the Commonwealth and for English reform proposals see Dicey & Morris, Conflict of Laws 121 (13th ed. by Collins 2000). See id. at 284–85. (reform in England for jurisdictional purposes as a result of the Brussels Convention and Regulation).

that place. As noted before, the core of the concept of domicile relates to the place where a person makes his home.[1] The concept of home includes living at a place under circumstances indicative of the center of a person's domestic and social life. The courts agree that this involves both a physical presence at that place and the coincident intention to make a home there.[2] An element of this intention is not to have a home at some other place. This latter is significant because of the assumption that a person can have but one domicile for a particular purpose and also as an influential element of intent.[3] Courts usually concentrate upon the mental attitude and aspects of the physical presence regarding the allegedly new domicile as compared to those regarding the prior domicile, because the concept contemplates that a domicile once acquired continues until another is gained.[4] The vagaries of evidence and the variety of lifestyles preclude the assignment of any order in which presence and intention must occur, but the authorities agree that they must co-exist at some time in order that the relationship with a place necessary for domicile may occur.[5] Variations in living patterns account for more of the differences in results than does the domicile concept itself; but this is to be expected in an intimate relationship such as domicile so largely dependent on proof of subjective intent.

B. PHYSICAL PRESENCE

§ 4.18   The element of physical presence is essential to confirm the requisite attitude of mind contemplated by the concept of domicile. As a consequence, a person who is to acquire a domicile of choice at a place must actually be present at that place during the time in which the

---

§ 4.17

1. Greenwood v. Hildebrand, 357 Pa.Super. 253, 515 A.2d 963 (1986), appeal denied 515 Pa. 594, 528 A.2d 602 (1987); Shapiro v. State Tax Commission, 67 A.D.2d 191, 415 N.Y.S.2d 282 (1979), reversed 50 N.Y.2d 822, 430 N.Y.S.2d 33, 407 N.E.2d 1330 (1980); Restatement, Second, Conflict of Laws §§ 11, 12 (1971). See supra § 4.1 n.2.

2. See Texas v. Florida, 306 U.S. 398, 59 S.Ct. 563, 83 L.Ed. 817 (1939); Irvin v. Irvin, 182 Kan. 563, 322 P.2d 794 (1958); In re Toler's Estate, 325 S.W.2d 755 (Mo. 1959); In re Publicker's Estate, 385 Pa. 403, 123 A.2d 655 (1956); Lawson v. Morgan, 352 F.Supp. 282 (E.D.Pa.1973); Hollowell v. Hux, 229 F.Supp. 50 (E.D.N.C.1964). See also Restatement, Second, Conflict of Laws § 15 (1971); Jacobs, Law of Domicile § 125 (1887); Wharton, Conflict of Laws § 56 (3d ed. 1905); Dicey & Morris, Conflict of Laws 177 (13th ed. by Collins 2000).

3. Restatement, Second, Conflict of Laws § 18 (1971).

4. Willis v. Westin Hotel Co., 651 F.Supp. 598 (S.D.N.Y.1986); Korn v. Korn, 398 F.2d 689 (3d Cir.1968); Kaiser v. Loomis, 391 F.2d 1007 (6th Cir.1968); Klemp v. Franchise Tax Board, 45 Cal.App.3d 870, 119 Cal.Rptr. 821 (1975); Owego Community Consolidated School District No. 434 v. Goodrich, 28 Ill.App.2d 407, 171 N.E.2d 816 (1960); Howard v. Howard, 499 So.2d 222 (La.App.1986); Littlefield v. Brooks, 50 Me. 475 (1862); Borland v. Boston, 132 Mass. 89 (1882); State ex rel. Ramey v. Dayton, 77 Mo. 678 (1883); In re Ingersol's Estate, 128 Mont. 230, 272 P.2d 1003 (1954); Ayer v. Weeks, 65 N.H. 248, 18 A. 1108 (1889); Suglove v. Oklahoma Tax Commission, 605 P.2d 1315 (Okla.1979); Greenwood v. Hildebrand, 357 Pa.Super. 253, 515 A.2d 963 (1986), appeal denied 515 Pa. 594, 528 A.2d 602 (1987); Bell v. Kennedy, L.R. 1 H.L. (Sc.) 307 (1868). See Restatement, Second, Conflict of Laws § 19 (1971).

5. Restatement, Second, Conflict of Laws § 15 (1971). Cf. White v. All America Cable & Radio, Inc., 642 F.Supp. 69 (D.P.R. 1986).

intention to make it his home exists.[1] For most people intention is confirmed by a physical presence of considerable duration looking toward an indefinite period of time. However, in light of the function that domicile serves, i.e., to identify a settled relationship with a place for a particular legal purpose, it is sometimes necessary to make a determination when the physical presence has been very brief. Consequently, no particular length of time is necessary in order to satisfy the requirement of physical presence if that stay at a place verifies the intention to make it a home.[2]

For example, if an individual living in one state of the United States resigns employment in that state and accepts a position of contemplated continuous employment in another state, sells the family house in the former state and makes his way, together with his family, to a new house that is acquired at the place of the new employment, intending and anticipating to stay there, the courts would assume that the new domicile attaches immediately upon arriving at the new home.[3] In this respect, domicile may differ from habitual residence, which is usually thought not to switch immediately upon relocation.[4] These cases are exceptional, but courts must deal with whatever fact pattern is presented, even though that fact pattern may stretch the underlying assumptions of the doctrine. In some instances, however, benefits or privileges arising out of domicile may require a durational presence of some fixed period of time to satisfy requirements for the particular benefit.[5] In that instance, of course, the durational presence is a condition in addition to the acquisition of domicile.

§ 4.19 In the case of the individual who has clearly manifested an intention to change to a new home and center of social activities, the

§ 4.18

1. Talmadge's Administrator v. Talmadge, 66 Ala. 199 (1880); Sheehan v. Scott, 145 Cal. 684, 79 P. 350 (1905); Holt v. Hendee, 248 Ill. 288, 93 N.E. 749 (1911); Matter of Pingpank, 134 A.D.2d 263, 520 N.Y.S.2d 596 (1987); Carter v. Sommermeyer, 27 Wis. 665 (1871). See Restatement, Second, Conflict of Laws § 16 (1971). Hatcher v. Anders, 117 Ill.App.3d 236, 453 N.E.2d 74 (1983). But see Mitchell v. Mackey, 915 F.Supp. 388 (M.D.Ga. 1996)(referring to the requirement that the person actually set foot in the new domicile as a "needless formality").

2. Hawes v. Club Ecuestre El Comandante, 598 F.2d 698 (1st Cir.1979); Mon Chi Heung Au v. Lum, 360 F.Supp. 219 (D.Haw. 1973), reversed on other grounds 512 F.2d 430 (9th Cir.1975); Parsons v. Bangor, 61 Me. 457 (1873); Stockton v. Staples, 66 Me. 197 (1877); Winans v. Winans, 205 Mass. 388, 91 N.E. 394 (1910); Horne v. Horne, 31 N.C. (9 Ired.) 99 (1848); Bixby v. Bixby, 361 P.2d 1075 (Okla.1961); Price v. Price, 156

Pa. 617, 27 A. 291 (1893); Bradley v. Lowry, Speers, Eq. 1 (S.C. 1842). See Restatement, Second, Conflict of Laws § 16 (1971).

3. Nagy v. Nagy–Horvath, 273 S.C. 583, 257 S.E.2d 757 (1979); White v. Tennant, 31 W.Va. 790, 8 S.E. 596 (1888). See also Marks v. Marks, 75 Fed. 321 (C.C.D.Tenn. 1896); St. Onge v. McNeilus Truck & Mfg., 645 F.Supp. 280 (D.Minn.1986). Cf. Perito v. Perito, 756 P.2d 895 (Alaska 1988).

4. See supra § 4.17.

5. See, e.g., Sosna v. Iowa, 419 U.S. 393, 95 S.Ct. 553, 42 L.Ed.2d 532 (1975). Cf. Greenwood v. Hildebrand, 357 Pa.Super. 253, 515 A.2d 963 (1986), appeal denied 515 Pa. 594, 528 A.2d 602 (1987). See also Cromley, Home Is Where I Hang My Divorce Decree: A Critical Appraisal of Sosna v. Iowa, 12 Cal. Western L. Rev. 452 (1976); Le Clercq, Durational Residency Requirements for Public Office, 27 S.C. L. Rev. 847 (1976); Comment, Age and Durational Residency Requirements As Qualifications For Candidacy: A Violation of Equal Protection?, 1973 U. Ill. L.F. 161.

question sometimes arises why that person's domicile should not change as soon as the old is abandoned even though the individual has not yet arrived at the new. Although this has sometimes been suggested as a possibility,[1] it is contrary to the clear weight of authority, probably because physical presence is ordinarily the principal confirming evidence of the intention of the person.[2] On the other hand, if domicile is largely a matter of intent, then physical presence may be only an evidentiary requirement to confirm intent. If there is other evidence, equally conclusive of intent, it may well be appropriate for a court to dispense with the requirement of physical presence and accept the substituted evidence. Such a case may happen where married persons are involved and one spouse moves the family home with the full consent and cooperation of the other spouse and it becomes important to identify the time when the new domicile of either or both of the spouses was established. Such a case could occur with an employee of the military or transportation services who has arranged with his spouse to move the family home while he is away on an extended trip with the intent not to return to the former home but to join the spouse and family at the new home. There seems to be no real reason why the law should not recognize that the new home has become the center for the personal and social life of the individuals involved even though one member of the family may not yet have been there.

Such circumstances appeared in *Bangs v. The Inhabitants of Brewster* and the fact pattern of *McIntosh v. Maricopa County*.[3] The last case involved a serviceman who was denied a resident's tax exemption for the house in Arizona his wife had acquired and in which the family home had been set up at his request. Admittedly, these cases are exceptionally rare, but they are instructive as to the nature of the domicile concept.[4]

§ 4.19

1. White v. Tennant, 31 W.Va. 790, 8 S.E. 596 (1888) (dictum); Wharton, Conflict of Laws § 58 (3d ed. 1905). See also Mitchell v. Mackey, 915 F.Supp. 388 (M.D.Ga. 1996)(requirement that individual actually set foot in new domicile is a "needless formality").

2. Opposing the doctrine of acquisition of domicile in itinere, White v. All America Cable & Radio, Inc., 642 F.Supp. 69 (D.P.R. 1986); Talmadge's Administrator v. Talmadge, 66 Ala. 199 (1880); Smith v. Croom, 7 Fla. 81 (1857); Littlefield v. Brooks, 50 Me. 475 (1862); Harvard College v. Gore, 22 Mass. (5 Pick.) 370 (1827); Shaw v. Shaw, 98 Mass. 158 (1867); Borland v. Boston, 132 Mass. 89 (1882); Horne v. Horne, 31 N.C. (9 Ired.) 99 (1848); Price v. Price, 156 Pa. 617, 27 A. 291 (1893); Northwestern Mortgage & Security Co. v. Noel Construction Co., 71 N.D. 256, 300 N.W. 28 (1941); Jacobs, Law of Domicile §§ 127–30 (1887).

3. Bangs v. Inhabitants of Brewster, 111 Mass. 382 (1873); Anderson v. Anderson's Estate, 42 Vt. 350 (1869) (here the assent or direction was by the guardian of an insane man). Lea v. Lea, 18 N.J. 1, 112 A.2d 540 (1955)(discussed in 17 U. Pitt. L. Rev. 97 (1955)). But see McIntosh v. Maricopa County, 73 Ariz. 366, 241 P.2d 801 (1952); Hart v. Horn, 4 Kan. 232 (1867). Cf. Sheehan v. Scott, 145 Cal. 684, 79 P. 350 (1905); Bloomfield v. City of St. Petersburg Beach, Florida, 82 So.2d 364 (Fla.1955); Gray v. O'Banion, 23 Cal.App. 468, 138 P. 977 (1913). Application of Davy, 281 App.Div. 137, 120 N.Y.S.2d 450 (1952).

4. An interesting question has come up in determining a person's domicile when the house in which he lives is cut by the boundary line dividing two states or municipal units. See Time Magazine, p. 6 (Aug. 13, 1979). That the individual desires himself to be a resident of one place or the other, while significant evidence of his intent, may not establish his domicile there. Blaine v. Murphy, 265 Fed. 324 (D.C.Mass. 1920); State ex rel. Flaugher v. Rogers, 226 Ind. 32, 77 N.E.2d 594 (1948). See Beale,

Of course, even though a domicile might be vicariously acquired through the agency of a spouse where the intention is clear, neither spouse could change the other's domicile by moving the family and its possessions without the absent spouse's knowledge and consent.[5] In such an instance, the change of domicile would be effective only as to that person actually engaging in the move.

C. INTENT NECESSARY FOR DOMICILE

1. *In General*

§ 4.20   Coincident to physical presence in a place, one must intend to make it his home for at least some period of time.[1] This must be a presently held intention, an attitude of mind by which the individual regards the place as home.[2] A troublesome question has been how long a person must intend to make a home in a location. Formerly it was frequently stated that the intention must be to remain permanently,[3] but

The Progress of the Law 1919–1920, 34 Harv.L.Rev. 50, 51 (1920). But cf. Follweiler v. Lutz, 112 Pa. 107, 2 A. 721 (1886). Chancey v. State, 141 Ga. 54, 80 S.E. 287 (1913). See also Application of Davy, 281 App.Div. 137, 120 N.Y.S.2d 450 (3d Dept.1952). A statute may, of course, authorize such a choice. Ala.Code 1940, T. 17, §§ 18, 19. See Coudert, Some Considerations in the Law of Domicil, 36 Yale L.J. 949 (1927); Heilman, Domicil and Specific Intent, 35 W. Va. L. Q. Rev. 262 (1929). Some of the cases have concluded that the location of most of the habitable portion of the structure determines the occupant's domicile. See Danforth v. Nabors, 120 Ala. 430, 24 So. 891 (1898); Abington v. Inhabitants of North Bridgewater, 40 Mass. (23 Pick.) 170 (1839). If the division is more nearly equal, the domicile is in that part most closely associated with the business of living. Blaine v. Murphy, 265 Fed. 324 (D.Mass. 1920); Chenery v. Waltham, 62 Mass. (8 Cush.) 327 (1851); Judkins v. Reed, 48 Me. 386 (1860); East Montpelier v. City of Barre, 79 Vt. 542, 66 A. 100 (1906). Both these latter groups of cases would seem to support the view that the domicile of one residing on the boundary line is in that political division with "which he is most closely related." Restatement, Second, Conflict of Laws § 18, cmnt. (h) (1971). See also Gray v. O'Banion, 23 Cal.App. 468, 138 P. 977 (1913). Application of Davy, 281 App. Div. 137, 120 N.Y.S.2d 450 (1952).

5. See Scholes v. Murray Iron Works Co., 44 Iowa 190 (1876); Porterfield v. Augusta, 67 Me. 556 (1877). Cf. Berc v. Berc, 407 N.W.2d 131 (Minn.App.1987).

§ 4.20

1. McDonald v. Hartford Trust Co., 104 Conn. 169, 132 A. 902 (1926); Bloomfield v. City of St. Petersburg Beach, Florida, 82 So.2d 364 (Fla.1955); Restatement, Second, Conflict of Laws § 18 (1971).

2. Chicago & Northwestern Railway Co. v. Ohle, 117 U.S. 123, 6 S.Ct. 632, 29 L.Ed. 837 (1886); Talmadge's Administrator v. Talmadge, 66 Ala. 199 (1880); Williams v. Roxbury, 78 Mass. (12 Gray) 21 (1858); Otis v. Boston, 66 Mass. (12 Cush.) 44 (1853); Hall v. Hall, 25 Wis. 600 (1870). Cf. Jacobs, Law of Domicile § 177 (1887).

3. See Jacobs, Law of Domicile § 62 (1887). In Winans v. Winans, 205 Mass. 388, 91 N.E. 394 (1910) it was suggested that it was necessary to have "the intention to remain either permanently or for an indefinite time without any fixed or certain purpose to return to the former place of abode...." The emphasis on an absence of intent to return to a former abode appears as an important element in regarding the present abode as a "permanent home." See District of Columbia v. Murphy, 314 U.S. 441, 62 S.Ct. 303, 86 L.Ed. 329 (1941); Gilbert v. David, 235 U.S. 561, 35 S.Ct. 164, 59 L.Ed. 360 (1915); Williamson v. Osenton, 232 U.S. 619, 624, 34 S.Ct. 442, 443, 58 L.Ed. 758 (1914); Hardin v. McAvoy, 216 F.2d 399 (5th Cir.1954); Jones v. Jones, 136 A.2d 580 (D.C.Mun.App.1957); Irons v. Irons, 242 Ind. 504, 180 N.E.2d 105 (1962); Nevin v. Nevin, 88 R.I. 426, 149 A.2d 722 (1959); Denny v. Sumner County, 134 Tenn. 468, 184 S.W. 14 (1916). See Note, Domicil of Refugees, 42 Colum. L. Rev. 640 (1942); Loewensohn, The Law of Domicil As

it seems clear that it need not be more than an intention to remain for some indefinite future time.[4]

Because the concept of home and the attitude of mind regarding it involves an element of persistence and continuity, there is some difference of view in the cases in which the intention is to make a home at a place for a fixed period, as for example, during a fixed term of employment, public service, or education. More recent cases have concluded that it is sufficient if there is an intention to make the place one's home for the time being, even though the duration of the stay may have definite limitations.[5] The fact that it is easier to demonstrate satisfaction of the requirement if one's intent is to remain there permanently or for an indefinite period of time should not preclude the establishment of a home even though one knows that the home will continue at the place only for a fixed period of time. In these cases the abandonment of a former home is an important element in the proof of an intention to make a place a home for a fixed period. Modern lifestyles demand accommodation of the situation in which a person knows that he will be changing his home at some time in the future. An individual can regard a place as his settled abode and have all of the normal attitudes of mind toward that place as home even though he may anticipate a future change of home. If such an individual were not permitted to obtain a domicile, many persons would be deprived of civil rights or benefits dependent on domicile and would be disenfranchised to the detriment both of themselves and of the community in which they lived.[6]

Applied to Refugees, 52 Juridical Rev. 28 (1940).

4. See District of Columbia v. Murphy, 314 U.S. 441, 62 S.Ct. 303, 86 L.Ed. 329 (1941); Ennis v. Smith, 55 U.S. (14 How.) 400, 14 L.Ed. 472 (1852); Gates v. Commissioner Internal Revenue, 199 F.2d 291 (10th Cir.1952); Arbaugh v. District of Columbia, 85 U.S. App. D.C. 97, 176 F.2d 28 (1949); Perito v. Perito, 756 P.2d 895 (Alaska 1988); Hartford v. Champion, 58 Conn. 268, 20 A. 471 (1890); Winans v. Winans, 205 Mass. 388, 91 N.E. 394 (1910); Putnam v. Johnson, 10 Mass. 488 (1813); Stevens v. Larwill, 110 Mo.App. 140, 84 S.W. 113 (1904); Robbins v. Chamberlain, 297 N.Y. 108, 75 N.E.2d 617 (1947); Price v. Price, 156 Pa. 617, 27 A. 291 (1893).

5. See Restatement, Second, Conflict of Laws § 18 (1971); Elkins v. Moreno, 435 U.S. 647, 98 S.Ct. 1338, 55 L.Ed.2d 614 (1978), on remand sub nom. Moreno v. University of Maryland, 645 F.2d 217 (4th Cir. 1981); Newman v. Graham, 82 Idaho 90, 349 P.2d 716 (1960); Wilkins v. Bentley, 385 Mich. 670, 189 N.W.2d 423 (1971); cf. Kelm v. Carlson, 473 F.2d 1267 (6th Cir. 1973).

6. In recent years, there has been a great deal of litigation attacking or invali-

dating durational residence requirements for welfare, education, or medical benefits or voting privileges. These cases suggest that the durational requirements cannot be applied to preclude the change of domicile and the acquisition of domicile. The durational requirements must serve some other purpose, e.g., reasonable evidentiary considerations or qualifications for the particular benefit or to provide necessary time for administration of the particular benefit in question. Even though these cases rely upon differing constitutional theories, from them it may be argued that the concept of domicile cannot include a required intent regarding the duration of one's intended residence. See Shapiro v. Thompson, 394 U.S. 618, 89 S.Ct. 1322, 22 L.Ed.2d 600 (1969); Memorial Hospital v. Maricopa County, 415 U.S. 250, 94 S.Ct. 1076, 39 L.Ed.2d 306 (1974); Dunn v. Blumstein, 405 U.S. 330, 92 S.Ct. 995, 31 L.Ed.2d 274 (1972); Whatley v. Clark, 482 F.2d 1230 (5th Cir.1973), cert. denied 415 U.S. 934, 94 S.Ct. 1449, 39 L.Ed.2d 492 (1974). Cf. Ramey v. Rockefeller, 348 F.Supp. 780, 788 (E.D.N.Y.1972) ("the only constitutionally permissible test is one which focuses on the individual's present intention and does not require him to pledge allegiance for an indefinite future"); Kendrick v. Parker, 258

Consequently, if an individual has employment at a place for a fixed period and demonstrates an intent to make it a home—such as by moving his family to that place, buying or leasing a residence, and participating in community and civic activities—that individual should be considered to be domiciled in that place.[7] There are many persons in our society who fall into this fact pattern: teachers, ministers, students, elected officials, and project employees, for example. As a consequence, in this country at least, a domicile of choice may be acquired by persons for whom it is impossible to establish a lifelong home and it is sufficient that the intent be to make a given place a home here and now.[8]

2. *Domicile of a Person Having Multiple Homes*

§ 4.21　Although in law a person can have but one domicile, it is clear that many persons have more than one living place.[1] For most people, of course, there is but one true home in the sense of the principal center of one's family and one's social and personal life. In those cases, however, where a person has two dwellings located at different places and spends considerable time in each, difficult evidentiary questions arise as to which is the principal home to which the concept of domicile will attach. In most instances, the fact pattern will indicate that one place is simply a temporary residence for recreational or other limited purpose and the other is the principal home. An important factor is the domicile which the individual had before acquiring the second home. Since a domicile once acquired continues until displaced by a subsequent domicile of choice, the acquisition of a second residence will not disturb the pre-existing domicile unless there is clear and convincing evidence to the contrary.[2] Thus, the burden usually is on the person attempting to

Ga. 210, 367 S.E.2d 544 (1988). However, there is no constitutional requirement that a person be allowed to acquire two voting residences even if he maintains homes in each location and spends a considerable part of the year there. See Wit v. Berman, 306 F.3d 1256 (2d Cir. 2002), cert. denied 538 U.S. 923, 123 S.Ct. 1574, 155 L.Ed.2d 313 (2003).

7. This is the usual type of evidence of intent to make a place a home. Intent reflected in overt acts is most significant. Cf. Mellon National Bank & Trust Co. v. Commissioner of Corp. & Taxation, 327 Mass. 631, 100 N.E.2d 370 (1951); Gosschalk v. Gosschalk, 28 N.J. 73, 145 A.2d 327 (1958); Bixby v. Bixby, 361 P.2d 1075 (Okla.1961); Matter of Reighard's Estate, 381 Pa. 304, 113 A.2d 305 (1955).

8. See Gilman v. Gilman, 52 Me. 165 (1863); Putnam v. Johnson, 10 Mass. 488, 501 (1813); Klutts v. Jones, 21 N.M. 720, 158 P. 490 (1916). See also Dignam v. Shaff, 51 Wash. 412, 98 P. 1113 (1909). The student may have a domicile in the school town, if he in fact makes his home there,

even though he will go elsewhere when the course is completed. People v. Osborne, 170 Mich. 143, 135 N.W. 921 (1912).

§ 4.21

1. Restatement, Second, Conflict of Laws § 18, comment (e) (1971); Mellon National Bank & Trust Co. v. Commissioner of Corp. & Taxation, 327 Mass. 631, 100 N.E.2d 370 (1951). Citizens Bank and Trust Co. v. Glaser, 70 N.J. 72, 357 A.2d 753 (1976); cf. Rice v. United Mercantile Agencies, 395 Ill. 512, 70 N.E.2d 618 (1946).

2. Willis v. Westin Hotel Co., 651 F.Supp. 598 (S.D.N.Y.1986); Hofferbert v. City of Knoxville, 470 F.Supp. 1001 (E.D.Tenn.1979); Taylor v. Milam, 89 F.Supp. 880 (W.D.Ark.1950); Easterly v. Goodwin, 35 Conn. 279 (1868); Dennis v. State, 17 Fla. 389 (1879); Viking Dodge, Inc. v. Hoffman, 147 Ill.App.3d 203, 497 N.E.2d 1346 (1986); Culbertson v. Board of Commissioners of Floyd County, 52 Ind. 361 (1876); Greene v. Greene, 28 Mass. (11 Pick.) 410 (1831); Sears v. Boston, 42 Mass.

establish a new domicile to show an intention has developed to make the new home the principal one and by that process displace the previously existing domicile.[3]

§ 4.22 Important evidence will be reflected in the amount of time that is spent at each of the residences and the purpose for which the time is spent.[1] The relative value of the different homes is also often significant as most persons view their principal home as that which is the larger or more valuable or more consistent with the individual's social and economic position. The individual's relationship to the community in which each home is located and the extent of one's participation in the community affairs often evince the individual's attitude toward that dwelling place and is significant evidence for the identification of the principal home. In this regard the cases demonstrate that actions speak louder, and are more persuasive evidence, than words or declarations.[2] Formal declarations are ordinarily admissible as evidence of an individual's attitude toward a place. Instances of this include descriptions of an individual as having a permanent residence at a particular place or being of a particular community as described in wills or other serious and formal documents. Even more significant perhaps, in the mind of the trier of fact, are the informal or casual statements that a person makes spontaneously without consideration of the legal consequences of the statement. Statements in personal letters that illustrate an individual's attitude toward one of several residences may be persuasive evidence with regard to one's attitude of mind.

§ 4.23 In the famous *Dorrance* litigation it was developed by abundant evidence that until 1925 Dr. Dorrance's domicile was in New Jersey. However, in that year he acquired a new residence in Pennsylvania retaining all the while his prior New Jersey home. Much evidence concerning the family life centered about the new residence, its size, the amount of time spent there, and relationships to the community, was submitted supporting the establishment of the Pennsylvania residence as the principal home. The Pennsylvania Supreme Court found that the burden had been carried, and held that Pennsylvania was Dr. Dorrance's

---

(1 Metc.) 250 (1840); Dupuy v. Wurtz, 53 N.Y. 556 (1873); Matter of Estate of Gadway, 123 A.D.2d 83, 510 N.Y.S.2d 737 (1987). In re Obici's Estate, 373 Pa. 567, 97 A.2d 49 (1953); In re Lassin's Estate, 33 Wn.2d 163, 204 P.2d 1071 (1949). See also Auerbach v. Kinley, 594 F.Supp. 1503 (N.D.N.Y.1984), judgment reversed in part 765 F.2d 350 (2d Cir.1985).

3. See Kanz v. Wilson, 703 So.2d 1331 (La.App.1997) (decedent's vague plans to leave nursing home for retirement community in another state not sufficient to establish domicile in other state); Scoggins v. Pollock, 727 F.2d 1025 (11th Cir.1984); Hendry v. Masonite Corp., 455 F.2d 955 (5th Cir.1972), cert. denied 409 U.S. 1023, 93 S.Ct. 464, 34 L.Ed.2d 315 (1972); Stine v. Moore, 213 F.2d 446 (5th Cir.1954).

§ 4.22

1. See Slocum v. DeWitt, 374 So.2d 755 (La.App.1979), writ denied 375 So.2d 1182 (La.1979). See also Texas v. Florida, 306 U.S. 398, 59 S.Ct. 563, 83 L.Ed. 817 (1939); Restatement, Second, Conflict of Laws § 18 (1971).

2. See Matter of Brunner's Estate, 41 N.Y.2d 917, 394 N.Y.S.2d 621, 363 N.E.2d 346 (1977); Graveson, Conflict of Laws 206 (7th ed. 1974); Castel, Canadian Conflict of Laws 76 (2d ed. 1986). Cf. Choike v. City of Detroit, 94 Mich.App. 703, 290 N.W.2d 58 (1980), appeal denied 408 Mich. 892, 291 N.W.2d 358 (1980).

domicile.[1] On the other hand, the courts of New Jersey took more seriously the evidence reflected in formal declarations as indicating a continuing intention to retain the domicile in New Jersey.[2] These cases illustrate both the significance of acts and style of life reflecting intention as contrasted with formal declarations constituting evidence of intention, the former prevailing in Pennsylvania, and the latter in New Jersey. They also illustrate the great influence that our procedural system has in permitting conflicting findings of domicile when the same doctrine is being applied by different courts. As has been noted, it is not unusual that two fact-finding agencies, acting upon the same evidence, may reach different conclusions.[3]

3. *Intent Distinguished From Motive*

§ 4.24   In considering the evidentiary problems involved in the demonstration of the requisite intent for the acquisition of a domicile of choice, it is important to distinguish between intent and motive. Ordinarily the motive or reason which leads a person to establish a home in a given place does not affect the acquisition of a domicile there.[1] On the other hand, in some cases motive may evidence an attitude of mind significant to the acquisition of domicile. Motive is not important because it may be good or bad; it is significant only if it indicates an intent not to make the place a home, that is, whether the alleged intention with regard to the place as a home is genuine.[2] Except for this limitation,

§ 4.23

1. In re Dorrance's Estate, 309 Pa. 151, 161, 163 A. 303, 311 (1932), cert. denied 288 U.S. 617, 53 S.Ct. 507, 77 L.Ed. 990 (1933).

2. In re Dorrance's Estate, 115 N.J.Eq. 268, 170 A. 601 (1934), aff'd mem., Dorrance v. Thayer–Martin, 13 N.J.Misc. 168, 176 A. 902 (1935), cert. denied 298 U.S. 678, 56 S.Ct. 950, 80 L.Ed. 1399 (1936); In re Dorrance, 116 N.J.Eq. 204, 172 A. 503 (1934); Hill v. Martin, 296 U.S. 393, 56 S.Ct. 278, 80 L.Ed. 293 (1935). Charles A. Lindbergh had strong ties and homes in Connecticut and Hawaii that were somewhat similar to those in the *Dorrance* dispute. The two states compromised, with Connecticut receiving approximately 2/3 and Hawaii 1/3 of the state death taxes even though it appeared Lindbergh strongly favored Hawaii as his "domicile." N.Y. Times, May 1, 1977.

3. See supra § 4.5 n.5. Cf. Los Angeles Airways, Inc. v. Lummis, 603 S.W.2d 246 (Tex.Civ.App.1980), cert. denied 455 U.S. 988, 102 S.Ct. 1610, 71 L.Ed.2d 847 (1982).

§ 4.24

1. Williamson v. Osenton, 232 U.S. 619, 34 S.Ct. 442, 58 L.Ed. 758 (1914); Morris v. Gilmer, 129 U.S. 315, 9 S.Ct. 289, 32 L.Ed. 690 (1889); Milliken v. Tri–County Electric Co-op., Inc., 254 F.Supp. 302 (D.S.C.1966); Young v. Pollak, 85 Ala. 439, 5 So. 279 (1888); Moon v. Moon, 265 Ark. 310, 578 S.W.2d 203 (1979); Thayer v. Boston, 124 Mass. 132 (1878); McConnell v. Kelley, 138 Mass. 372 (1885); Miller's Estate v. Commissioner of Taxation, 240 Minn. 18, 59 N.W.2d 925 (1953); In re Newcomb's Estate, 192 N.Y. 238, 84 N.E. 950 (1908); Gasper v. Wales, 223 App.Div. 89, 227 N.Y.S. 421 (1928); Robbins v. Chamberlain, 297 N.Y. 108, 75 N.E.2d 617 (1947); Frame v. Thormann, 102 Wis. 653, 79 N.W. 39 (1899), aff'd 176 U.S. 350, 20 S.Ct. 446, 44 L.Ed. 500 (1900).

2. Morris v. Gilmer, 129 U.S. 315, 9 S.Ct. 289, 32 L.Ed. 690 (1889); Rodriguez–Diaz v. Sierra–Martinez, 853 F.2d 1027 (1st Cir.1988); Roorda v. Volkswagenwerk, A.G., 481 F.Supp. 868 (D.S.C.1979); Succession of Barnes, 490 So.2d 630 (La.App.1986); Plant v. Harrison, 36 Misc. 649, 74 N.Y.S. 411 (1902); Matter of Reighard's Estate, 381 Pa. 304, 113 A.2d 305 (1955). Cf. Willenbrock v. Rogers, 255 F.2d 236 (3d Cir.1958). See Restatement, Second, Conflict of Laws § 18, cmnt. (f) (1971).

purpose in moving to a new location is irrelevant whether because of climate, tax laws, school facilities or business opportunities, or even to secure a divorce or to support illegal activities. While these may be reasons for making a place a home, they nevertheless do not contradict that intention. Consequently, the motive inducing an alleged change of domicile is probably only significant to the trier of fact in determining whether there was only the appearance of a change made for the purpose of securing some personal advantage.[3] In this connection, it is important to reiterate that the controlling intention is to make a home rather than to intend to acquire a domicile in the legal sense. This distinction was illustrated in the *Dorrance* cases as the Pennsylvania court[4] concluded that while Dorrance intended to retain his legal domicile, particularly for tax purposes, in New Jersey, he still had the intention to make Pennsylvania his home and the headquarters of his personal life. Where other evidence is rather equally divided between two residences which are potential domiciles, formal declarations of intent may be sufficient to carry the proof of an intent to make one the principal home.[5]

4. Freedom to Exercise Choice

§ 4.25 Historically, the courts and writers have stated that a person may not acquire a domicile of choice at a place where he is sent or is kept under physical or legal compulsion.[1] The necessary intention for a domicile of choice, requires that the party be free to exercise choice in selecting the place where he makes his home. The courts, however, have been sensitive to the variable degrees of coercion, economic, social, or legal, upon a person's free exercise of choice, and have begun to develop substantial exceptions to the position as traditionally stated. Business necessity, family interests, and other considerations may weigh very heavily and often necessitate establishing oneself in a place when personal preference is to live elsewhere. Yet, as noted regarding persons who of necessity intend to stay in a particular locale only for a definite

---

3. See, e.g., White v. INS, 75 F.3d 213 (5th Cir.1996) (invalidating INS regulation purporting to define "domicile" as permanent legal status in the United States); Hawes v. Club Ecuestre El Comandante, 598 F.2d 698 (1st Cir.1979); Wells v. Wells, 230 Ala. 430, 161 So. 794 (1935); Bethune v. Bethune, 192 Ark. 811, 94 S.W.2d 1043 (1936); Warren v. Warren, 127 Cal.App. 231, 15 P.2d 556 (1932); People v. Harlow, 9 Cal.App.2d 643, 50 P.2d 1052 (1935); Mills v. Mills, 119 Conn. 612, 179 A. 5 (1935); Janssen v. Janssen, 269 Ill.App. 233 (1933); Reik v. Reik, 112 N.J.Eq. 234, 163 A. 907 (1933); Perlman v. Perlman, 113 N.J.Eq. 3, 165 A. 646 (1933); Newton v. Newton, 13 N.J.Misc. 613, 179 A. 621 (Ch. 1935); Di Brigida v. Di Brigida, 116 N.J.Eq. 208, 172 A. 505 (1934); Lefferts v. Lefferts, 263 N.Y. 131, 188 N.E. 279 (1933); Fischer v. Fischer, 254 N.Y. 463, 173 N.E. 680

(1930); Ward v. Ward, 115 W.Va. 429, 176 S.E. 708 (1934). Cf. DeYoung v. DeYoung, 27 Cal.2d 521, 165 P.2d 457 (1946). Cf. Illegal Residence and the Acquisition of a Domicile of Choice, 33 Int'l & Comp. L.Q. 885 (1984).

4. See supra § 4.23 n.1. Cf. Allen v. Greyhound Lines, Inc., 583 P.2d 613 (Utah 1978).

5. See Restatement, Second, Conflict of Laws § 20, cmnt. (c), Special Note on Evidence (1971).

§ 4.25

1. See 1 Beale, Conflict of Laws 154 (1935); Stumberg, Principles of Conflict of Laws 26 (3d ed. 1963); Restatement, Second, Conflict of Laws § 17 (1971).

period of time, it could not be seriously maintained that a domicile could not be acquired in a place where a person went because of economic advantages. The distinction comes in the situation in which the presence under physical compulsion is inconsistent with the intention to regard the place as home or its equivalent for the particular purpose for which the determination is being made. Because domicile is used for different qualifying purposes it may be that a person can acquire a sense of home even at a place where he is compelled to live for the particular purpose for which domicile is being used. As a consequence, the traditional position is probably now reduced to a strong presumption that a person may not acquire a domicile of choice where he is sent or kept under physical or legal compulsion. The military service personnel cases are instructive.

§ **4.26** Service personnel have frequently been precluded from obtaining a domicile at a place to which they are ordered to go and serve.[1] Because the military person is compelled to obey orders, that person cannot choose to live elsewhere and, as a consequence, does not appear to exercise the necessary choice. Consequently, the presumption is that the domicile held at time of entry into service continues.[2] However, it is clear that military personnel may be in service voluntarily, or they may develop a relationship and an attitude of mind regarding the place where they are living that is much the same as the attitude of any member of the local community. For example, just as other members of the community, military personnel may seek to vote, engage in civic or political activities, be subjected to local taxation, have social ties and relationships with the community, engage in business affairs, and have a home in the sense of a stable living place. They may register their automobiles and obtain local driver's licenses; they may even purchase burial lots, execute their wills and codicils and describe themselves of

§ 4.26

1. See Codagnone v. Perrin, 351 F.Supp. 1126 (D.R.I.1972); Prudential Insurance Co. v. Lewis, 306 F.Supp. 1177 (N.D.Ala.1969); Bowman v. DuBose, 267 F.Supp. 312 (D.S.C.1967); People ex rel. Budd v. Holden, 28 Cal. 123 (1865); Island v. Fireman's Fund Indemnity Co., 30 Cal.2d 541, 184 P.2d 153 (1947); Hawkins v. Winstead, 65 Idaho 12, 138 P.2d 972 (1943); Hampshire v. Hampshire, 70 Idaho 522, 223 P.2d 950 (1950); Harris v. Harris, 205 Iowa 108, 215 N.W. 661 (1927); Dicks v. Dicks, 177 Ga. 379, 170 S.E. 245 (1933); Burgan v. Burgan, 207 La. 1057, 22 So.2d 649 (1945); Shenton v. Abbott, 178 Md. 526, 15 A.2d 906 (1940); Mooar v. Harvey, 128 Mass. 219 (1880); Ames v. Duryea, 6 Lans. 155 (N.Y. 1871) aff'd mem. 61 N.Y. 609; Draper v. Draper, 107 Ohio App. 32, 151 N.E.2d 379 (1958); Zimmerman v. Zimmerman, 175 Or. 585, 155 P.2d 293 (1945); Wallace v. Wallace, 371 Pa. 404, 89 A.2d 769 (1952); Bank of Phoebus v. Byrum, 110 Va. 708, 67 S.E. 349

(1910); Sasse v. Sasse, 41 Wn.2d 363, 249 P.2d 380 (1952); Thomas v. Thomas, 58 Wn.2d 377, 363 P.2d 107 (1961); Adams v. Londeree, 139 W.Va. 748, 83 S.E.2d 127 (1954). Note 21 Neb. L. Rev. 326 (1942); Note, Domicile of Military Personnel, 31 N.C. L. Rev. 304 (1953); Note, Limitations on Domicile of Choice of Military, 31 Okla. L. Rev. 167 (1978); Note, Domicil and The Serviceman, 19 Aust. L.J. 180 (1945).

2. Ellis v. Southeast Construction Co., 260 F.2d 280 (8th Cir.1958); Willenbrock v. Rogers, 255 F.2d 236 (3d Cir.1958); Detroit Auto. Inter–Insurance Exchange v. Feys, 205 F.Supp. 42 (N.D.Cal.1962); Nora v. Nora, 494 So.2d 16 (Ala.1986); Ober v. Bounds, 528 So.2d 247 (La.App.1988). See Sanftner, The Serviceman's Legal Residence: Some Practical Suggestions, 26 JAG J. 87 (1971); Comment, The Determination of Domicile, 65 Military L.R. 133 (1974). Cf. Northwestern National Casualty Co. v. Davis, 90 Cal.App.3d 782, 153 Cal.Rptr. 556 (1979).

this place, and certainly they may participate in banking and credit transactions and notify their correspondents of a permanent address at the place where they are assigned duty. Likewise, if they are not considered a member of the local community, it means they will be precluded from participating in political activities and enjoying certain legal and civil rights unless they return to their prior domicile or conduct these activities by correspondence.

As a consequence of these circumstances, exceptions have developed. The first is by judicial construction that service persons qualify within the purpose of the particular statute, which may require "residence" or "domicile" or may apply only to "habitants," considering the particular circumstances of the case. This may be accomplished by finding a local domicile. For example, if military personnel arrange to live with their families off the base, and with family members are otherwise engaged in the usual community related activities, the court may well find that they are domiciled at that place.[3] While it may be difficult to meet the burden of proving the necessary attitude toward the place required for domicile, still it is possible that the circumstances would indicate the intention to consider the place where stationed as home.[4]

A second development is legislative recognition of an express statutory exception. Some states have provided that after a specified period of time, often one year, service personnel may be presumed to be a domiciliary of that state for a particular purpose.[5] Most of these statutes have centered upon service of process and litigation, more particularly on jurisdiction for divorce. Several states have simply removed the requirement of domicile for divorce jurisdiction of service personnel and have substituted a period of residence within the state.[6] Other cases involving uses of domicile for a particular purpose, for example, diversity of citizenship or voting rights, further indicate that the service personnel may acquire a domicile for a particular purpose at the place where stationed. In fact the United States Supreme Court has concluded that a state constitutional provision preventing servicemen from acquiring a voting residence in Texas is a violation of equal protection.[7] Considering

3. Cf. Deese v. Hundley, 232 F.Supp. 848 (W.D.S.C.1964); Kendrick v. Parker, 258 Ga. 210, 367 S.E.2d 544 (1988), Restatement, Second, Conflict of Laws § 17, comment (d) (1971).

4. See Codagnone v. Perrin, 351 F.Supp. 1126 (D.R.I.1972); Ferrara v. Ibach, 285 F.Supp. 1017 (D.S.C.1968). Cf. Strait v. Laird, 406 U.S. 341, 92 S.Ct. 1693, 32 L.Ed.2d 141 (1972), on remand 464 F.2d 205 (9th Cir.1972); Schlanger v. Seamans, 401 U.S. 487, 91 S.Ct. 995, 28 L.Ed.2d 251 (1971); Eisel v. Secretary of the Army, 477 F.2d 1251 (D.C.Cir.1973); Ober v. Bounds, 528 So.2d 247 (La.App.1988).

5. See, e.g., Fla. Stat. Ann. § 47.081; N.M. Stat. Ann. § 22-7-4; see also Continental Ins. Co. v. McKain, 820 F.Supp. 890, 895 (E.D.Pa.1993)(noting state laws creating a rebuttable presumption that service personnel retain their domicile at time of induction).

6. Lauterbach v. Lauterbach, 392 P.2d 24 (Alaska 1964); Conrad v. Conrad, 275 Ala. 202, 153 So.2d 635 (1963); Wheat v. Wheat, 229 Ark. 842, 318 S.W.2d 793 (1958); Wallace v. Wallace, 63 N.M. 414, 320 P.2d 1020 (1958); Wood v. Wood, 159 Tex. 350, 320 S.W.2d 807 (1959). See infra Chapter 15 where divorces based on these statutes and their recognition are discussed in detail.

7. Carrington v. Rash, 380 U.S. 89, 85 S.Ct. 775, 13 L.Ed.2d 675 (1965), on remand 389 S.W.2d 945 (Tex.1965).

these developments it appears that although there remains a presumption that service personnel retain the domicile held at the time of entering service, that presumption may be rebutted by clear and unequivocal evidence to sustain a change of domicile to a place where stationed.[8]

§ **4.27** A prisoner is the other classic case usually cited to support the traditional rule that a person cannot acquire a domicile while living at a place under legal or physical compulsion.[1] Although it is frequently stated that "[i]t is impossible for a person to acquire domicile in the jail in which he is incarcerated,"[2] the approach of the recent cases in developing exceptions to the traditional rule for the benefit of servicemen has been extended to prisoners.

> "We hold that a litigant will not be precluded from establishing a domicile within the state for purposes of federal diversity jurisdiction solely because his presence there initially resulted from circumstances beyond his control. We recognize the importance of considering physical or legal compulsion in determining whether domicile is gained or lost, but we limit the application of involuntary presence to its operation as a presumption ordinarily requiring more than unsubstantiated declarations to rebut...."

In *Stifel v. Hopkins*,[3] a federal inmate of a Pennsylvania prison brought a diversity action against his parents and former attorney who were citizens of Ohio where the plaintiff was domiciled before his conviction and incarceration. The court recognized that citizenship as used in the federal statutes providing diversity of citizenship jurisdiction meant domicile. However, the meaning of domicile was construed not to preclude the prisoner plaintiff from establishing a domicile for federal diversity purposes solely because his presence in the state where incarcerated had resulted from circumstances beyond his control. In reaching the conclusion that conviction and imprisonment did not destroy a citizen's right to invoke the diversity jurisdiction of the federal courts, the court relied heavily upon the belief that an absolute presumption

---

8. See Codagnone v. Perrin, 351 F.Supp. 1126 (D.R.I.1972); Ferrara v. Ibach, 285 F.Supp. 1017 (D.S.C.1968); Bowman v. Du-Bose, 267 F.Supp. 312 (D.S.C.1967); Groh v. Egan, 526 P.2d 863 (Alaska 1974). See also supra n.2.

§ 4.27

1. Denlinger v. Brennan, 87 F.3d 214, 216 (7th Cir.1996)(prisoner retains pre-incarceration domicile for diversity jurisdiction purposes); Cohen v. United States, 297 F.2d 760 (9th Cir.1962), cert. denied 369 U.S. 865, 82 S.Ct. 1029, 8 L.Ed.2d 84 (1962); Barton v. Barton, 74 Ga. 761 (1885); Topsham v. Lewiston, 74 Me. 236 (1882); People v. Cady, 143 N.Y. 100, 37 N.E. 673 (1894); Baltimore v. Chester, 53 Vt. 315 (1881). In the *Cady* case, 143 N.Y. 100, 106, 37 N.E. 673, 675 (1894), it was said: "The

Tombs is not a place of residence. It is not constructed or maintained for that purpose.... A person cannot ... go there as a prisoner and gain a residence there ... " See also Nobuo Hiramatsu v. Phillips, 50 F.Supp. 167 (S.D.Cal.1943). Cf. Marathon County v. Milwaukee County, 273 Wis. 541, 79 N.W.2d 233 (1956).

2. Restatement, Second, Conflict of Laws § 17, cmnt. (c) (1971). See Westbury Union Free School District v. Amityville Union Free School District, 106 Misc.2d 189, 431 N.Y.S.2d 641 (1980) (mother of child born in jail retained prior domicile so child need not be educated by district in which jail located).

3. 477 F.2d 1116 (6th Cir.1973), (noted, U. Tol. L. Rev. 334 (1974)).

would "raise the spector [sic] of unconstitutionality by approving the application of an irrebuttable presumption of fact to a particular class of citizens."[4] In an exceptionally detailed and thoughtful opinion, Judge McCree reviewed the cases involving the denial of a domicile of choice by a person under physical or legal compulsion and concluded that prisoners appeared to be the only persons who might never be able to escape the rule, even though others who were able to escape the rule were subject to compulsion similar to that experienced by prisoners. The court stated:

> "We believe that the prisoner, like the serviceman or the Cabinet official, should not be precluded from showing that he has developed the intention to be domiciled at the place to which he has been forced to remove. No good reason appears for applying a contrary per se rule to him by making the presumption that he has retained his former domicile an irrebuttable one . . . .[5]

> " . . . In making this essentially factual determination, the court should accord weight to appellant's declarations of intentions, but in the circumstances of this case the physical facts pertaining to appellant's incarceration and to the conduct of his personal affairs assume perhaps a greater than usual significance because the appellant's statements of intention cannot bear on the fact of his initial relocation in Pennsylvania. The court should consider factors such as the possibility of parole for the appellant,[6] the manner in which the appellant has ordered his personal and business transactions, and any other factors that are relevant to corroboration of appellant's statements. These factors must be weighed along with the policies and purposes underlying federal diversity jurisdiction to determine whether appellant has overcome the presumption that he has maintained his former domicile."[7]

This case seems accurately to reflect the current status of the law and has been approved by other courts as a test for diversity jurisdiction[8] and voter registration.[9] Though, the declaration made in more recent cases that it requires "truly exceptional circumstances" for a prisoner to acquire a new domicile of choice *seems* no less accurate.[10] This fact-intensive approach is also consistent with the developments involving members of monastic orders and indigents who are required to live in

---

4. *Stifel*, 477 F.2d at 1125. Cf. Carrington v. Rash, 380 U.S. 89, 85 S.Ct. 775, 13 L.Ed.2d 675 (1965).

5. *Stifel*, 477 F.2d at 1124.

6. Footnote by court: "The fact that he is serving a life sentence, of course, lends a great deal of credibility to his assertion that he will never return to Ohio." Id. at 1127 n.7.

7. Id. at 1126–27.

8. Jones v. Hadican, 552 F.2d 249 (8th Cir.1977), cert. denied 431 U.S. 941, 97 S.Ct. 2658, 53 L.Ed.2d 260 (1977). Cf.

McKenna v. McKenna, 282 Pa.Super. 45, 422 A.2d 668 (1980) (divorce).

9. Dane v. Board of Registrars, 374 Mass. 152, 371 N.E.2d 1358 (1978). See Note, Prisoner's Voting Rights in Massachusetts, 3 N. Eng. J. of Prison L. 251 (1976).

10. See Jones v. Hadican, 552 F.2d 249, 251 (8th Cir.1977); Waste Recovery Corp. v. Mahler, 566 F.Supp. 1466, 1468 (S.D.N.Y. 1983).

public institutions.[11] The refugee who is forced to flee on account of political or racial persecution also has been excepted from the traditional rule because the requisite intent may be established notwithstanding the person's status as a refugee or a fugitive.[12]

Considering all factors, the best approach is to retain the presumption that a person may not acquire a domicile of choice in a place where he is present under physical or legal compulsion. In most cases there will be no change of domicile, either because of a preference to retain the domicile existing at the beginning of the compulsion,[13] or because there is so little possibility that an individual can demonstrate the requisite mental attitude toward the place of confinement. A presumption operates to avoid excessive litigation and to give guidance to administrative application.

V. GEOGRAPHIC BOUNDARIES OF DOMICILE

§ 4.28 As we have seen, domicile describes a legal relationship between a person and a place or governmental entity. Consequently, it sometimes is important to determine the extent of the place or the geographic area which is involved. How definitely must an abode be fixed in a given spot to permit a domicile to be established? Because of its function in choice of law, domicile must be fixed in an area subject to one system of law.[1] The person must have a domicile in some governmental unit.[2] Perhaps for most purposes, this is as definitely as one's domicile need be located.[3] A domicile in a nation may be adequate for one purpose such as federal taxation, whereas a domicile within a state or province of a nation would be necessary for other purposes, such as diversity

11. See Krasnov v. Dinan, 465 F.2d 1298 (3d Cir.1972); Sealey v. United States, 7 F.Supp. 434 (E.D.Va.1934); Coulombre v. Board of Registrars of Voters, 3 Mass.App. Ct. 206, 326 N.E.2d 360 (1975); Sturgeon v. Korte, 34 Ohio St. 525 (1878); Restatement, Second, Conflict of Laws § 17, comment (e) (1971). Cf. Coppedge v. Clinton, 72 F.2d 531 (10th Cir.1934); Wolcott v. Holcomb, 97 Mich. 361, 56 N.W. 837 (1893). But cf. Clark v. Robinson, 88 Ill. 498 (1878).

12. See Ennis v. Smith, 55 U.S. (14 How.) 400, 14 L.Ed. 472 (1853); Roboz v. Kennedy, 219 F.Supp. 892 (D.D.C.1963); Jacoubovitch v. Jacoubovitch, 279 App.Div. 1027, 112 N.Y.S.2d 1 (1952); Taubenfeld v. Taubenfeld, 276 App.Div. 873, 93 N.Y.S.2d 757 (1949); Van Vliet v. Blatt, 51 Pa. D. & C. 182 (Pa.Com.Pl.1944); Graumann v. Treitel (1940) 2 All.E.R. 188 (K.B.); May v. May, 169 L.T. 42 (1943); Restatement, Second, Conflict of Laws § 17, comment (g) (1971). But cf. McGrath v. Kristensen, 340 U.S. 162, 71 S.Ct. 224, 95 L.Ed. 173 (1950); Note, Domicile of Refugees, 42 Colum. L. Rev. 640 (1942); Loewensohn, The Law of

Domicil As Applied to Refugees, 52 Juridical Rev. 28 (1940); Status of Refugees, 7 Mod. L. Rev. 235 (1944).

13. See Groh v. Egan, 526 P.2d 863 (Alaska 1974).

§ 4.28

1. Restatement, Second, Conflict of Laws § 11, cmnt. (g) (1971).

2. See Bell v. Kennedy, L.R. 1 H.L. (Sc.) 307 (1868); Udny v. Udny, L.R. 1 H.L. (Sc.) 441 (1869); Jacobs, Law of Domicile § 77 (1887).

3. "A man may be domiciled in a country without having a fixed habitation in some particular spot in that country." In re Craignish, [1892] 3 Ch. 180, 192. Cf. In re Patience, 29 Ch. Div. 976 (1885)(lack of a settled habitation was thought to be evidence that the person did not intend to reside permanently in England, even though he had not left the country for 22 years); see also Willis v. Westin Hotel Co., 651 F.Supp. 598 (S.D.N.Y.1986).

jurisdiction or most choice-of-law matters. An issue of venue or voting, however, may require definition of domicile within still another or more precise governmental subdivision. A domicile in a state would generally include a home located at a particular spot therein, but it is not necessary that it be fixed at any particular spot in the state in order that a person should have the rights and responsibilities of a domiciliary of that state,[4] such as suing in diversity[5] or obtaining a divorce.[6]

§ 4.29 A similar, though not identical, problem arises in connection with the domicile of people who make their homes in vehicles or mobile homes. The test for determining the domicile for these people is largely the same as for any other but the problem of evidencing the requisite intention is considerable. Proof of intent to establish a settled connection in a particular place would result in the acquisition of a domicile there.[1] If the person does not settle down and develop the homing attitude toward any one place, his domicile, rather than changing continually, remains in the place where he was last domiciled before his nomadic life began.[2]

VI. DOMICILE AS AFFECTED BY STATUS

A. DOMICILE OF ALIENS

§ 4.30 In the concept of domicile there are overtones of citizenship or national allegiance. Certainly the rationalization of some ways in which domicile is employed suggest the relationship of citizens to their government. As an illustration, the obligation to respond to the courts of a state in which one is domiciled, i.e., jurisdiction, often is explained as the obligation one holds toward the government which protects him.[1] Similarly, certain benefits conferred upon persons domiciled within a state suggest the act of a sovereign regarding its citizens.[2] Still, domicile primarily relates to those social relationships that link an individual to a place through the concept of home. Consequently, there is no overriding difficulty that precludes a person whose national allegiance or citizenship

4. See Matter of Eisenberg's Estate, 177 Misc. 655, 31 N.Y.S.2d 380 (1941); Hartman v. Hartman, 132 W.Va. 728, 53 S.E.2d 407 (1949). Cf. Cooper v. Beers, 143 Ill. 25, 33 N.E. 61 (1892).

5. Marks v. Marks, 75 Fed. 321 (C.C.D.Tenn.1896).

6. Winans v. Winans, 205 Mass. 388, 91 N.E. 394 (1910); King v. King, 74 N.J.Eq. 824, 71 A. 687 (Err. & App. 1908).

§ 4.29

1. Restatement Second, Conflict of Laws § 12, cmnt. (d) and § 16, cmnt. (c) (1971).

2. See Howard v. Skinner, 87 Md. 556, 40 A. 379 (1898); State ex rel. Wooters v. Dardenne, 131 La. 109, 59 So. 32 (1912). Cf. Willis v. Westin Hotel Co., 651 F.Supp. 598 (S.D.N.Y.1986); In re Bourne's Estate, 181

Misc. 238, 41 N.Y.S.2d 336 (1943), aff'd 267 App.Div. 876, 47 N.Y.S.2d 134 (1944), appeal denied 267 App.Div. 961, 48 N.Y.S.2d 439 (1944). But cf. Kyser v. Board of Elections, 36 Ohio St.2d 17, 303 N.E.2d 77 (1973), appeal dismissed 415 U.S. 970, 94 S.Ct. 1547, 39 L.Ed.2d 863 (1974).

§ 4.30

1. See, e.g., Milliken v. Meyer, 311 U.S. 457, 61 S.Ct. 339, 85 L.Ed. 278 (1940); New York ex rel. Cohn v. Graves, 300 U.S. 308, 57 S.Ct. 466, 81 L.Ed. 666 (1937); Lawrence v. State Tax Comm'n, 286 U.S. 276, 52 S.Ct. 556, 76 L.Ed. 1102 (1932).

2. Cf. Vlandis v. Kline, 412 U.S. 441, 93 S.Ct. 2230, 37 L.Ed.2d 63 (1973).

is in one nation from establishing domicile in another country.[3] Ready examples are immigrants or other aliens residing in the United States who meet the requirement of both physical presence and intention to remain for an indefinite period of time.[4]

On the other hand, the status that an individual enjoys regarding the government of a country in which he is living may have some relevance to the matter of domicile. For instance, the nature of one's visa or the fact that someone has or has not sought immigrant status may be relevant in deciding whether that person intends to make the place his home.[5] However, like motive, visa status is not itself controlling on the acquisition of domicile, at least for many purposes.[6] For example, whether one were to be viewed as a domiciliary to determine jurisdiction to sue him and obtain a personal judgment would seem to depend upon the usual circumstances of the acquisition of domicile, at least absent a specific treaty exception. For example, persons holding non-immigrant visas to the United States either as temporary workers or as students on long-term renewable visas, ought not be precluded from suing and being sued as domiciliaries in a state where they otherwise have the equivalent persistent relationship.[7] Even the possibility that an alien may be illegally in the country and deportable would not preclude that individual from forming an actual intention to make his home at the place where he lived. Some courts have taken the position that to deny an alien access to the courts, e.g., for divorce, solely on the basis of being an alien, or in a non-immigrant status would be a denial of due process and equal protection.[8] This is an instance in which reliance upon habitual residence as distinct from domicile may well avoid some of these technical issues relating to domicile.[9]

§ 4.31 The use of domicile or citizenship or of distinctions between these concepts for the purpose of qualifying for governmental benefits is complicated by other considerations relating to the legislative purpose in providing the particular benefit.[1] The states, for instance, may impose additional requirements to qualify for particular benefits such as education. If domicile is the only requirement, then the issue becomes whether the individual alien can acquire a domicile and with aliens this is a mixed question of state and federal law. Aliens in the United States

---

3. Mather v. Cunningham, 105 Me. 326, 74 A. 809 (1909); Harral v. Harral, 39 N.J.Eq. 279 (1884). See Castel Canadian Conflict of Laws 72 (2d ed. 1986); Hoyles, Domicile, 48 Can. L.J. 474 (1912).

4. Williams v. Williams, 328 F.Supp. 1380 (D.Vi.1971); Gosschalk v. Gosschalk, 28 N.J. 73, 145 A.2d 327 (1958).

5. Alves v. Alves, 262 A.2d 111 (D.C.App.1970).

6. See, e.g., White v. INS, 75 F.3d 213 (5th Cir.1996)(INS rule requiring legal status to acquire a U.S. domicile invalid as conflicting with ordinary use of term "domicile").

7. E.g., *White*, 75 F.3d at 215–16.

8. Williams v. Williams, 328 F.Supp. 1380 (D.V.I.1971). See also Abou–Issa v. Abou–Issa, 229 Ga. 77, 189 S.E.2d 443 (1972). Cf. Cabral v. State, 112 Cal.App.3d 1012, 169 Cal.Rptr. 604 (1980). See Pilkington, Illegal Residence and the Acquisition of a Domicile of Choice, 33 Int'l & Comp. L.Q. 885 (1984).

9. See supra § 4.14 n.2.

§ 4.31

1. See Weinberger v. Salfi, 422 U.S. 749, 95 S.Ct. 2457, 45 L.Ed.2d 522 (1975).

are subject in most circumstances to visa requirements. Many visas assume or require the identification of a permanent residence outside the United States and an intention to retain that residence. In such cases, it would seem that the individual could not acquire a domicile at least for federal purposes.[2] On the other hand, if the visa is not so restricted, then it would seem that the person could acquire a domicile within the state of residence.[3]

Some forms of non-immigrant visas in the United States do not require the identification of a foreign domicile and its continuation. In *Elkins v. Moreno*,[4] the Supreme Court recognized this distinction under federal law and then concluded that even though federal law permitted the aliens in question to enter the United States and acquire a domicile in the United States, there remained a state law question as to whether the persons could become domiciled in Maryland under Maryland law at least for the purpose of attending the University of Maryland as a resident-tuition student. The Maryland Court subsequently concluded that there was nothing inherent in the status of a non-immigration alien that precluded the requisite intent to obtain a Maryland domicile.[5] However, some forms of visas expire if the foreign citizen forms the intent to remain the United States indefinitely. Thus, in *Carlson v. Reed*,[6] the court held that the holder of a "TD" nonimmigrant visa could not qualify for in-state tuition in California because she lacked the legal capacity to acquire a domicile in that state.

§ 4.32 A similarly complicated question arises when the person whose domicile is in question has resided abroad as a member of a group to whom extraterritorial privileges are granted. Although probably now an obsolete arrangement, this situation has arisen in some countries in which by treaty arrangement it is provided that citizens of a favored nation may have certain privileges, such as immunity from suit in specified classes of cases in the local courts, and may sue and be sued in the consular courts established by their own nation. On principle, acquisition of a domicile in such a community should be governed by the same general rules that prevail elsewhere. The privileges afforded by treaty arrangement should not affect the determination of the question whether or not an individual in fact makes his home in a given place. Both the American cases and the English decisions hold that one can acquire a domicile in such extraterritorial communities under the settled

---

2. Carlson v. Reed, 249 F.3d 876 (9th Cir. 2001).

3. Cf. Seren v. Douglas, 30 Colo.App. 110, 489 P.2d 601 (1971); Smith v. Smith, [1962] 3 S.A. 930.

4. See, e.g., White v. INS, 75 F.3d 213 (5th Cir.1996)(INS regulation requiring permanent legal status to acquire a U.S. domicile is invalid as conflicting with ordinary use of term "domicile").

5. Elkins v. Moreno, 435 U.S. 647, 98 S.Ct. 1338, 55 L.Ed.2d 614 (1978).

6. Toll v. Moreno, 284 Md. 425, 397 A.2d 1009 (1979), remanded 441 U.S. 458, 99 S.Ct. 2044, 60 L.Ed.2d 354 (1979), on remand 480 F.Supp. 1116 (D.Md.1979) and 489 F.Supp. 658 (D.Md.1980), aff'd sub nom. Moreno v. University of Maryland, 645 F.2d 217 (4th Cir.1981). See also Alves v. Alves, 262 A.2d 111 (D.C.App.1970). Cf. Cabral v. State, 112 Cal.App.3d 1012, 169 Cal.Rptr. 604 (1980).

rules governing the acquisition of domicile generally.[1] It would appear that the acquisition of a domicile by members of international communities within the United States is within the limitations outlined in *Elkins v. Moreno*.[2]

B. DOMICILE OF MARRIED PERSONS

§ 4.33 The law relating to the domicile of married persons is cluttered by much of the ancient mythology that surrounded the husband-and-wife relationship in social and legal systems quite different from that which exists today. Under early common law the wife had a very limited legal personality,[1] and the wife's domicile was assigned by operation of law to that of her husband.[2] This rule no longer obtains in the United States, if in fact it ever really obtained. In the usual case, married persons live together and have identical intent with regard to making a place their mutual home. Each are competent to make a choice of domicile,[3] and this results in a common domicile, not by operation of

§ 4.32

1. See In re Young John Allen, 1 Am. J. Int. L. 1029 (U.S. Ct. for China, 1907); Mather v. Cunningham, 105 Me. 326, 74 A. 809 (1909); Casdagli v. Casdagli, [1919] A.C. 145. Dicey & Morris, Conflict of Laws 137 (13th ed. by Collins 2000); McIlwraith, Domicile in Egypt, 34 L.Q. Rev. 196 (1918); Dickinson, The Domicile of Persons Residing Abroad Under Consular Jurisdiction, 17 Mich. L. Rev. 437 (1919); Huberich, Domicile in Countries Granting Exterritorial Privileges to Foreigners, 24 L.Q. Rev. 440 (1908); Note, 32 Harv. L. Rev. 432 (1919); Note, 58 U. Pa. L. Rev. 543 (1910); Note, 17 Mich. L. Rev. 694 (1919); Note, 28 Yale L.J. 810 (1919).

2. Elkins v. Moreno, 435 U.S. 647, 98 S.Ct. 1338, 55 L.Ed.2d 614 (1978).

§ 4.33

1. 1 Blackstone's Commentaries * 442. This is the reason assigned in many decisions. See, e.g., Williamson v. Osenton, 232 U.S. 619, 34 S.Ct. 442, 58 L.Ed. 758 (1914); Jenness v. Jenness, 24 Ind. 355, 87 Am. Dec. 335 (1865); Harteau v. Harteau, 31 Mass. (14 Pick.) 181, 25 Am. Dec. 372 (1833); Dutcher v. Dutcher, 39 Wis. 651 (1876).

2. See Beale, The Domicil of a Married Woman, 2 So.L.Q. 93 (1917). See also Kennedy v. Kennedy, 87 Ill. 250 (1877); Parrett v. Palmer, 8 Ind.App. 356, 35 N.E. 713 (1893); Mason v. Homer, 105 Mass. 116 (1870); Hackettstown Bank v. Mitchell, 28 N.J.L. 516 (1860); In re Hartman's Estate, 70 N.J.Eq. 664, 62 A. 560 (1906); Dolphin v.

Robins, 7 H.L. Cas. 390 (1859); In re Mackenzie, [1911] 1 Ch. 578. But see Thompson v. Love, 42 Ohio St. 61 (1884). Cf. Farran, On Marrying an Alien Abroad, 1956 Scots. L.T., 117 (1956).

3. In Craig v. Craig, 365 So.2d 1298 (La.1978) the court held that equal protection under state constitution protected the wife in acquisition of a separate domicile without cause. The following cases recognize the ability of a wife to acquire a separate domicile in circumstances in which it need not appear that she had cause for divorce. Mas v. Perry, 489 F.2d 1396 (5th Cir.1974)(dictum); Napletana v. Hillsdale College, 385 F.2d 871 (6th Cir.1967); Oxley v. Oxley, 159 F.2d 10 (D.C.Cir.1946); Gallagher v. Philadelphia Transportation Co., 185 F.2d 543 (3d Cir.1950); Floyd v. Floyd, 95 N.J.Eq. 661, 124 A. 525 (Err. & App. 1923); Brown v. TranSouth Financial Corp., 897 F.Supp. 1398, 1402 n.4 (M.D.Ala.1995); Antonelli v. Antonelli, 16 N.J.Super. 439, 84 A.2d 753 (1951); Buchholz v. Buchholz, 63 Wash. 213, 115 P. 88 (1911); Chisholm v. Chisholm, 105 Fla. 402, 141 So. 302 (1932); Commonwealth v. Booth, 266 Mass. 80, 165 N.E. 29 (1929); Commonwealth v. Rutherfoord, 160 Va. 524, 169 S.E. 909 (1933); Miller v. Miller, 205 N.C. 753, 172 S.E. 493 (1934); In re Babcock's Estate, 64 S.D. 283, 266 N.W. 420 (1936); Matter of Trippodo's Estate, 161 Misc. 542, 292 N.Y.S. 296 (Surr. Ct. 1936); see also Cheever v. Wilson, 76 U.S. (9 Wall.) 108, 19 L.Ed. 604 (1869); Shute v. Sargent, 67 N.H. 305, 36 A. 282 (1893); In re Geiser's Will, 82 N.J.Eq. 311, 87 A. 628 (1913).

law for either but by choice. Because this is the usual situation, there is a presumption that married persons have the same domicile.[4] Some courts may describe this common domicile as a domicile by operation of law assigned to the wife.[5] Although the factual and legal results may be the same, it seems this is a misdescription and American courts do, when it is significant, clearly make the distinction that each spouse may acquire a domicile of choice.[6] Under these circumstances, it seems clear that there is no need, functionally or otherwise, to attribute the domicile of one spouse to the other.

§ 4.34   The harshness of the early common law rule first brought about departure from the rule in the area of divorce. A deserted wife would be substantially without remedy were she not able to acquire or maintain a domicile separate from that of her husband.[1] Although it was occasionally asserted that these cases were limited to divorce, many of the cases recognized the acquisition of an independent domicile for any purpose. As stated by Justice Holmes, "The change that is good as against her husband ought to be good as against all."[2] From that beginning, the more recent authorities in the United States, both case and statute, recognize that either spouse may acquire a separate domicile whenever that person in fact makes a home apart from the other spouse, regardless of motive or propriety of conduct.[3] In short, although

---

4. See Restatement, Second, Conflict of Laws § 21 (1971).

5. See supra n.2.

6. See, e.g., Williamson v. Osenton, 232 U.S. 619, 34 S.Ct. 442, 58 L.Ed. 758 (1914); Grable v. City of Detroit, 48 Mich.App. 368, 210 N.W.2d 379 (1973); Blair v. Blair, 199 Md. 9, 85 A.2d 442 (1952); Jones v. Jones, 402 N.W.2d 146 (Minn.App.1987); Gladwin v. Power, 21 A.D.2d 665, 249 N.Y.S.2d 980 (1st Dept.1964); Commonwealth v. Rutherfoord, 160 Va. 524, 169 S.E. 909 (1933); Knapp v. State Farm Ins., 584 F.Supp. 905 (E.D.La.1984).

§ 4.34

1. On retention of domicile see Burtis v. Burtis, 161 Mass. 508, 37 N.E. 740 (1894); Harteau v. Harteau, 31 Mass. (14 Pick.) 181 (1833). On acquisition of domicile see Cheever v. Wilson, 76 U.S. (9 Wall.) 108, 19 L.Ed. 604 (1869); Hanberry v. Hanberry, 29 Ala. 719 (1857); Chapman v. Chapman, 129 Ill. 386, 21 N.E. 806 (1889); Jenness v. Jenness, 24 Ind. 355, 87 Am. Dec. 335 (1865); Kline v. Kline, 57 Iowa 386, 10 N.W. 825 (1881); Stevens v. Allen, 139 La. 658, 71 So. 936 (1916); Stevens v. Larwill, 110 Mo.App. 140, 84 S.W. 113 (1904); Sworoski v. Sworoski, 75 N.H. 1, 70 A. 119 (1908); Colvin v. Reed, 55 Pa. 375 (1867); Ditson v. Ditson, 4 R.I. 87 (1856); Craven v. Craven, 27 Wis. 418 (1871).

2. Williamson v. Osenton, 232 U.S. 619, 626, 34 S.Ct. 442, 443, 58 L.Ed. 758 (1914). On this point, see Watertown v. Greaves, 112 Fed. 183 (1st Cir.1901); Gordon v. Yost, 140 Fed. 79 (C.C.N.D.W.Va. 1905); Fitch v. Huff, 218 Fed. 17 (4th Cir.1914); Shute v. Sargent, 67 N.H. 305, 36 A. 282 (1892); White v. Glover, 116 N.Y.S. 1059 (1909), aff'd 138 App.Div. 797, 123 N.Y.S. 482 (1910).

3. This was held to be required by state equal protection in Craig v. Craig, 365 So.2d 1298 (La.1978). See Restatement, Second, Conflict of Laws § 21 (1971); Moon v. Moon, 265 Ark. 310, 578 S.W.2d 203 (1979); Boardman v. Boardman, 135 Conn. 124, 62 A.2d 521 (1948); Grable v. City of Detroit, 48 Mich.App. 368, 210 N.W.2d 379 (1973); Small v. Small, 96 Misc.2d 469, 409 N.Y.S.2d 379 (1978); Van Rensselaer v. Van Rensselaer, 103 N.H. 23, 164 A.2d 244 (1960); Younger v. Gianotti, 176 Tenn. 139, 138 S.W.2d 448 (1940), noted in 21 Neb. L. Rev. 330 (1942), 16 Tenn. L. Rev. 746 (1941); Risch v. Risch, 395 S.W.2d 709 (Tex. Civ.App. 1965), appeal dismissed, cert. denied 386 U.S. 10, 87 S.Ct. 881, 17 L.Ed.2d 703 (1967). Compare Burkhardt v. Burkhardt, 38 Del. 492, 193 A. 924 (1937)(noted in 4 U. of Pitt. L. Rev. 54 (1937)) with Feuerstein v. Feuerstein, 37 Del. 414, 183 A. 705 (1936). See also Commonwealth v. Rutherfoord, 160 Va. 524, 169 S.E. 909 (1933); Tate v. Tate, 149 W.Va. 591, 142

the marital relationship may give rise to a presumption that both married persons are domiciled at the same place, that presumption obtains only until it is shown that one of them has acquired a separate domicile of choice by satisfying the usual requirements.[4] This is a consequence of the present legal position of married persons and may occur while the relations between the parties are wholly amicable. Any uncertainty in some states stems from the fact that their courts have had little occasion to reexamine earlier holdings because there is seldom occasion for a married person, either husband or wife, to assert a domicile different from that of the other spouse.

§ 4.35 Prior to 1974, this trend toward equal ability of married spouses to acquire a domicile of choice was largely limited to the American cases and England continued to struggle with the common law rule.[1] However, even in England and other commonwealth countries, the trend was clearly toward enlarging the power of the wife to gain the advantages of a separate domicile in several circumstances.[2] Effective in 1974 the United Kingdom, by legislation, gave married women full capacity to acquire a domicile of choice.[3]

C. DERIVATIVE DOMICILE

1. *Domicile of Origin*

§ 4.36 Consistent with the concept that each individual must have a domicile at all times, the law assigns a derivative domicile to some individuals because of their relationship to others. The initial example of

S.E.2d 751 (1965); Smith v. Smith, 4 Mackey 255, 15 D.C. 255 (1885); Kline v. Kline, 57 Iowa 386, 10 N.W. 825 (1881); Thompson v. Love, 42 Ohio St. 61 (1884); Buchholz v. Buchholz, 63 Wash. 213, 115 P. 88 (1911). See further Oxley v. Oxley, 159 F.2d 10 (D.C.Cir.1946); Antonelli v. Antonelli, 16 N.J.Super. 439, 84 A.2d 753 (App.Div.1951); Goodrich, Conflict of Laws Since the Restatement, 23 A.B.A.J. 119, 122 (1937); Note, 28 Harv. L. Rev. 196 (1914); Note, 20 Mich. L. Rev. 86 (1921).

The lack of ability of a wife to acquire a separate domicile whenever she desires at times has been asserted in a few cases. Patrick v. Bank of Tupelo, 169 Miss. 157, 152 So. 838 (1934); Suter v. Suter, 72 Miss. 345, 16 So. 673 (1895); Hood v. Hood, 93 Mass. (11 Allen) 196, 87 Am. Dec. 709 (1865). Cf. Hagle v. Leeder, 442 S.W.2d 908 (Tex.Civ.App.1969).

4. See Restatement, Second, Conflict of Laws § 21 (1971); McGrath v. Zander, 177 F.2d 649 (D.C.Cir.1949). Cf. State v. Jones, 202 Neb. 488, 275 N.W.2d 851 (1979). But cf. Bolles v. Bolles, 364 So.2d 813 (Fla.App. 1978); Gordon v. Gordon, 369 So.2d 421 (Fla.App.1979).

§ 4.35

1. See Dicey & Morris, Conflict of Laws 139–43 (13th ed. by Collins 2000); Graveson, *Boardman v. Boardman* through English Eyes, 23 Conn. B.J. 173 (1949); Graveson, Jurisdiction, Unity of Domicile and Choice of Law, 3 Int'l L.Q. 371 (1950).

2. See Dicey & Morris, supra n.1 at 134; Graveson, Conflict of Laws 214 (7th ed. 1974); J.-G. Castel, Canadian Conflict of Laws 85–87 (4th ed. 1997).

3. The Domicile and Matrimonial Proceeding Act 1973, § 1. See also Atkin, The Domicile Act of 1976, 7 N.Z. U. L. Rev. 286 (1977); Rafferty, Domicile—The Need for Reform, 7 Man. L.J. 203 (1977). See supra § 4.16 n.7. For a discussion of problems arising under the English Domicile & Matrimonial Proceedings Act as relating to the revival of a married woman's domicile of origin on termination of her domicile of dependency see Wade, Domicile: A Re–Examination, 32 Int'l & Comp. L.Q. 1 (1983). Cf. supra § 4.14.

this is the domicile of origin which one receives at birth.[1] Because it is assigned before the individual has the capacity to exercise any choice in the matter, the domicile of origin is that of the parent who properly has custody of the child at birth.[2] In most instances this will be the common domicile of the parents of legitimate children. Since the domicile of origin is the first assigned, that domicile will continue until a new domicile is acquired.[3] In the United States, the domicile of origin serves only the function of initiating the succession of domiciles that one may acquire during lifetime.[4] Under English law, however, a peculiar significance has been ascribed to the domicile of origin as distinguished from a domicile of choice: "Its character is more enduring, its hold stronger, and less easily shaken off."[5] By the same token, the domicile of origin was more easily regained after having been replaced by a domicile of choice when the domicile of choice was subsequently abandoned.[6] The English law viewed the domicile of origin as a standby which was held in abeyance during the continuation of a domicile of choice and then revived whenever a domicile of choice was abandoned.[7] In most instances, the domicile of origin revived when a person abandoned a domicile of choice intending to return to the domicile origin. In those circumstances, the English cases held that the domicile of origin attached immediately

§ 4.36

1. Squire v. Vazquez, 52 Ga.App. 712, 184 S.E. 629 (1936); In re Fox' Guardianship, 212 Or. 80, 318 P.2d 933 (1957); Udny v. Udny, L.R. 1 H.L. (Sc.) 441 (1869); Restatement, Second, Conflict of Laws § 14(1) (1971).

2. Questions relating to the domicile of minors are discussed infra § 4.37 n.1. See Restatement, Second, Conflict of Laws § 14(2) (1971).

3. Ennis v. Smith, 55 U.S. (14 How.) 400, 14 L.Ed. 472 (1852); White v. Brown, 29 Fed.Cas. 982 (1848); Harvard College v. Gore, 22 Mass. 370, 5 Pick. 370 (Mass. 1827); Price v. Price, 156 Pa. 617, 27 A. 291 (1893); Bell v. Kennedy, L.R. 1 H.L. (Sc.) 307 (1868); Matter of Packard's Estate, 223 App.Div. 491, 228 N.Y.S. 591 (1928), aff'd per curiam 251 N.Y. 543, 168 N.E. 420 (1929); cf. Sivalls v. United States, 205 F.2d 444 (5th Cir.1953), cert. denied 346 U.S. 898, 74 S.Ct. 222, 98 L.Ed. 399 (1953).

4. See Gregg v. Louisiana Power and Light Co., 626 F.2d 1315 (5th Cir.1980); Prettyman v. Conaway, 14 Del. 221, 32 A. 15 (Super. 1891); Gilman v. Gilman, 52 Me. 165 (1863); cf. Harvard College v. Gore, 22 Mass. (5 Pick.) 370 (1827); Suglove v. Oklahoma Tax Commission, 605 P.2d 1315 (Okla.1979); Somerville v. Somerville, 5 Ves. Jr. 750 (1801).

5. Lord Macnaghten in Winans v. Attorney General, [1904] A.C. 287, 290, 73 L.J.K.B. 613, 615. See Inland Revenue Commissioner v. Bullock, [1976] 3 All E.R. 353, [1976] 1 W.L.R. 1178 (Ct. App.), Noted, 40 Mod. L. Rev. 476 (1977). See also Dicey & Morris, Conflict of Laws 134 (13th ed. by Collins 2000); Graveson, Conflict of Laws 195 (7th ed. 1974); Jacobs, Law of Domicile, § 115 et seq. (1887). Cf. Hogue v. Hogue, 242 S.W.2d 673 (Tex.Civ.App.1951). See also Castel, Canadian Conflict of Laws 85–87 (4th ed. 1997).

6. See Graveson, Reform of the Law of Domicile, 70 L.Q.Rev. 492 (1954).

7. See Dicey & Morris, Conflict of Laws 116 (13th ed. by Collins 2000). See also Wade, Domicile: A Re–Examination, 32 Int'l & Comp. L.Q. 1, 20 (1983), supporting the doctrine of revival of the domicile of origin and stating:

Abandonment, being a process whereby a previously implemented choice is negated, has as a legal consequence revival of the domicile of origin. It should not be confused with the different process of acquisition of a domicile of choice, whereby a previously implemented choice or the domicile of origin is replaced. The process of abandonment is not relevant to the situation where a domicile of choice is lost by acquisition of another domicile of choice nor to that which arises upon termination of a domicile of dependence. The process of acquisition may be germane to this latter situation but, where it

upon abandonment of the old domicile without any requirement that the individual actually set foot upon English soil before the domicile of origin became effective.[8]

This exception to the usual requirement of simultaneous presence and intent applied only in the case of domicile of origin under the English cases and not to the acquisition of a new domicile of choice.[9] The English concept of the domicile of origin was sometimes attributed to the circumstances in early England where most of those persons who left England did so as adventurers intending to return.[10] Also, during the evolution of the doctrine, England was a country of emigrants, and a greater reach of its law was achieved by the revival of the domicile of origin. By contrast, the circumstances in the United States led to the rejection of the concept of revival of the domicile of origin by the American courts.[11] The United States has been a country of mostly immigrants in which the concept of the domicile of choice was employed to absorb rapidly many people born in other lands into a highly mobile population, many of whom frequently moved from state to state in the federal system. As a consequence, the English doctrine never gained a substantial foothold in the United States. Even in England, the mobility of modern society has fostered both criticism of the rule and recommendation for its change.[12]

2. *Domicile of Minor—General*

§ 4.37 As discussed above, a domicile of origin is assigned an individual at birth by operation of law. Infants, like everyone else, need

is not, the domicile of origin automatically revives.

8. Udny v. Udny, L.R. 1 H.L. (Sc.) 441 (1869); King v. Foxwell, 3 Ch. Div. 518 (1876); Bradford v. Young, 29 Ch. Div. 617 (1885); In re Marrett, 36 Ch. Div. 400 (1887); Harrison v. Harrison [1953] 1 W.L.R. 865. The acquired domicile must be actually given up, however; an unperformed resolve to abandon it is not sufficient. Goods of Raffenel, 3 SW. & Tr. 49 (1863).

9. See Graveson, Conflict of Laws 200, 206 (7th ed. 1974).

10. Cf. In re Jones' Estate, 192 Iowa 78, 182 N.W. 227 (1921).

11. First National Bank v. Balcom, 35 Conn. 351 (1868); In re Jones' Estate, 192 Iowa 78, 182 N.W. 227 (1921); Ness v. Commissioner of Corporations and Taxation, 279 Mass. 369, 181 N.E. 178 (1932); Alvord & Alvord v. Patenotre, 196 Misc. 524, 92 N.Y.S.2d 514 (1949); Plant v. Harrison, 36 Misc. 649, 74 N.Y.S. 411 (1902); Restatement, Second, Conflict of Laws § 19 (1971); Stumberg, Conflict of Laws 31 (3d ed. 1963). But cf. Hyder v. Hyder, 16 Tenn. App. 64, 66 S.W.2d 235 (1932); Minor, Conflict of Laws § 66 (1901); Story, Conflict of Laws §§ 47, 48 (8th ed. 1883). Most of the few receptive early American authorities

limited the doctrine to cases in which the question arose while the party was returning to the domicile of origin. Jacobs, Law of Domicile § 191 (1887). See Reed's Appeal, 71 Pa. 378 (1872); Allen v. Thomason, 30 Tenn. (11 Humph.) 536 (1850); Denny v. Sumner County, 134 Tenn. 468, 184 S.W. 14 (1916). See also Stein v. Fleischmann Co., 237 Fed. 679, 680 (S.D.N.Y.1916). This narrow application was supported by 1 Wharton, Conflict of Laws §§ 59, 60 (3d ed. 1905).

12. See Graveson, Reform of the Law of Domicile, 70 L.Q. Rev. 492 (1954). The New Zealand Domicile Act of 1976, § 11 abolishes the revival doctrine in that country. See also Atkin, The Domicile Act of 1976, 7 N.Z.U. L. Rev. 286 (1977); Rafferty, Domicile, The Need for Reform, 7 Man. L.J. 203 (1977). But cf. Wade, supra n.7. Carter, Domicil: The Case for Radical Reform in The United Kingdom, 36 Int'l & Comp. L.Q. 713 (1987).

Proposals for reform continue to circulate. See Home Truths of UK's Proposed Bill, South China Morning Post, p. 5 (Dec. 13, 1992) (reporting on UK proposal to abolish revival doctrine).

to have a domicile somewhere to fix civil rights and liabilities. The minor child obviously is incapable of choosing a permanent abode and the domicile of origin will continue until replaced by another domicile. Until the child gains the capacity to acquire a domicile of choice, a domicile by operation of law will be assigned. The infant is under a disability and normally the infant's parents are entitled to custody and are responsible for the child's education and support. Correspondingly, the domicile of the minor child is that of the parent with whom the child is properly living.[1] This is the mutual domicile of the parents if the parents live together.[2] If the parents are separated, it is the domicile of the parent with whom the child properly resides or in whose custody the child is properly placed, that is, the domicile of the proper custodial parent.[3]

It is probable that under the modern custodial statutes a child's domicile does not shift to that of the father if the parents live apart and

§ 4.37

1. Restatement, Second, Conflict of Laws § 22 (1971); Clark, Domestic Relations § 4.3 (1968). Compare Gregg v. Louisiana Power and Light Co., 626 F.2d 1315 (5th Cir.1980)(child born to migratory parents domiciled in state of birth even though parents' domicile unknown).

2. In the earlier cases, before the recognition of the concepts of joint parental custody rights and the legal independence of married women, the mutual parental domicile was stated to be that of the father's. E.g., Delaware, Lackawanna & Western Railroad Co. v. Petrowsky, 250 Fed. 554 (2d Cir.1918), cert. denied 247 U.S. 508, 38 S.Ct. 427, 62 L.Ed. 1241 (1918); Bjornquist v. Boston & Albany Railroad Co., 250 Fed. 929 (1st Cir.1918), cert. denied 248 U.S. 573, 39 S.Ct. 11, 63 L.Ed. 427 (1918); Metcalf v. Lowther's Executor, 56 Ala. 312 (1876); Allgood v. Williams, 92 Ala. 551, 8 So. 722 (1890); Modern Woodmen v. Hester, 66 Kan. 129, 71 P. 279 (1903); Trammell v. Kansas Compensation Board, 142 Kan. 329, 46 P.2d 867 (1935); Sudler v. Sudler, 121 Md. 46, 88 A. 26 (1913); Beckmann v. Beckmann, 358 Mo. 1029, 218 S.W.2d 566 (1949); White v. White, 77 N.H. 26, 86 A. 353 (1913); A v. M, 74 N.J.Super. 104, 180 A.2d 541 (Co. 1962); Kennedy v. Ryall, 67 N.Y. 379 (1876); In re Hall's Guardianship, 235 N.C. 697, 71 S.E.2d 140 (1952); Application of Lorenz, 194 Or. 355, 241 P.2d 142 (1952); In re Fox' Guardianship, 212 Or. 80, 318 P.2d 933 (1957); Alburger v. Alburger, 138 Pa.Super. 339, 10 A.2d 888 (1940); Allen v. Thomason, 30 Tenn. (11 Humph.) 536, 54 Am. Dec. 55 (1850). See also Taylor v. State Farm Mutual Auto. Insurance Co., 248 La. 246, 178 So.2d 238 (1965); Restatement, Second, Conflict of Laws § 22 (1971).

3. See Restatement, Second, Conflict of Laws § 22, cmnt. (d) (1971); Mims v. Mims, 635 A.2d 320, 322 (D.C.App.1993), appeal after remand 686 A.2d 1059 (D.C.App.1997) (citing Second Restatement); Oxley v. Oxley, 81 U.S. App. D.C. 346, 159 F.2d 10 (1946); Niccum v. Lawrence, 186 Kan. 223, 350 P.2d 133 (1960); Ross v. Pick, 199 Md. 341, 86 A.2d 463 (1952); State ex rel. Larson v. Larson, 190 Minn. 489, 252 N.W. 329 (1934); Beckmann v. Beckmann, 358 Mo. 1029, 218 S.W.2d 566 (1949); Application of Enke, 129 Mont. 353, 287 P.2d 19 (1955), cert. denied 350 U.S. 923, 76 S.Ct. 212, 100 L.Ed. 808 (1955); Goldsmith v. Salkey, 131 Tex. 139, 112 S.W.2d 165 (1938). Cf. B.R.T. v. Executive Director of Social Service, etc., 391 N.W.2d 594 (N.D.1986); Allen v. Allen, 200 Or. 678, 268 P.2d 358 (1954). But cf. Faulk v. Faulk, 255 Ala. 237, 51 So.2d 255 (1951). See also In Interest of Gray, 131 Ill.App.3d 401, 475 N.E.2d 1116 (1985); Custody of a Minor (No. 3), 392 Mass. 728, 468 N.E.2d 251 (1984); Linville v. Price, 572 F.Supp. 345 (S.D.W.V.1983) (minor domiciled with relative acting in loco parentis). Non-conflict insurance cases often involve a determination of the issue whether a child is covered as "resident" in the named insured's household. In these cases residence or domicile is construed consistently with the purpose of the insurance contract. In such a case, a child may be "resident" in the household of both parents even though the parents are separated. See Davis v. Maryland Casualty Co., 76 N.C.App. 102, 331 S.E.2d 744 (1985). Cf. Londre by Long v. Continental Western Ins. Co., 117 Wis.2d 54, 343 N.W.2d 128 (App. 1983).

the child properly continues to live with the child's mother.[4] Further, this equality of parental rights appears to enjoy constitutional protection.[5] The domicile of origin assigned by operation of law to an infant, i.e., the domicile of the custodial parent at the time of the infant's birth, continues until the domicile of the custodial parent is changed; in that event the infant's domicile follows that of the custodial parent.[6] The minor cannot, before reaching the age of majority, establish a separate domicile for himself.[7] This is the case, whether the minor leaves the parental home of his own volition,[8] or is taken away by another.[9] This also follows even when the child is turned over by the parents to others to care for, absent abandonment or the appointment of a guardian.[10]

4. E.g., Oregon Rev. Stat. § 109.030:

Equality in rights and responsibilities of parents. The rights and responsibilities of the parents, in the absence of misconduct, are equal, and the mother is as fully entitled to the custody and control of the children and their earnings as the father. In case of the father's death, the mother shall come into as full and complete control of the children and their estate as the father does in case of the mother's death.

See N.Y. Dom. Rel. L. § 81; Perotti v. Perotti, 78 Misc.2d 131, 355 N.Y.S.2d 68 (1974). See also Ziady v. Curley, 396 F.2d 873 (4th Cir.1968); Willmore v. Willmore, 273 Minn. 537, 143 N.W.2d 630 (1966), cert. denied 385 U.S. 898, 87 S.Ct. 202, 17 L.Ed.2d 130 (1966); see also Binchy, Reform of the Law Relating to Domicile of Children: A Proposed Statute, 11 Ottawa L. Rev. 279 (1979).

5. See Quilloin v. Walcott, 434 U.S. 246, 255, 98 S.Ct. 549, 554, 54 L.Ed.2d 511 (1978) in which it is stated:

"We have recognized on numerous occasions that the relationship between parent and child is constitutionally protected. See, e.g., Wisconsin v. Yoder, 406 U.S. 205, 231–233, 92 S.Ct. 1526, 1541–42, 32 L.Ed.2d 15 (1972); Stanley v. Illinois, [405 U.S. 645, 92 S.Ct. 1208,]; Meyer v. Nebraska, 262 U.S. 390, 399–401, 43 S.Ct. 625, 626–27, 67 L.Ed. 1042 (1923). 'It is cardinal with us that the custody, care and nurture of the child reside first in the parents, whose primary function and freedom include preparation for obligations the state can neither supply nor hinder.'' Prince v. Massachusetts, 321 U.S. 158, 166, 64 S.Ct. 438, 442, 88 L.Ed. 645 (1944). And it is now firmly established that "freedom of personal choice in matters of . . . family life is one of the liberties protected by the Due Process Clause of the Fourteenth Amendment." Cleveland Board of Education v. LaFleur, 414 U.S. 632, 639–40, 94 S.Ct. 791, 796, 39 L.Ed.2d 52 (1974).

See also JMS v. HA, 161 W.Va. 433, 242 S.E.2d 696 (1978); Hammack v. Wise, 158 W.Va. 343, 211 S.E.2d 118 (1975).

6. See Application of Lorenz, 194 Or. 355, 241 P.2d 142 (1952). Restatement, Second, Conflict of Laws § 22 (1971). Cf. Metcalf v. Lowther's Ex'r, 56 Ala. 312 (1876); Kennedy v. Ryall, 67 N.Y. 379 (1876); Story, Conflict of Laws § 46 (8th ed. 1883). If custody is awarded one parent, the child's domicile appears to follow that of the custodial parent, even though the child may be residing elsewhere. See Conley v. Conley, 324 Mass. 530, 87 N.E.2d 153 (1949); Heard v. Heard, 323 Mass. 357, 82 N.E.2d 219 (1948); Richter v. Harmon, 243 N.C. 373, 90 S.E.2d 744 (1956); Application of Habeck, 75 S.D. 535, 69 N.W.2d 353 (1955).

7. In re Henning's Estate, 128 Cal. 214, 60 P. 762 (1900); Van Matre v. Sankey, 148 Ill. 536, 36 N.E. 628 (1893); In re Benton, 92 Iowa 202, 60 N.W. 614 (1894); Modern Woodmen v. Hester, 66 Kan. 129, 71 P. 279 (1903); Succession of Vennard, 44 La. Ann. 1076, 11 So. 705 (1892); Sudler v. Sudler, 121 Md. 46, 88 A. 26 (1913); People ex rel. Brooklyn Children's Aid Society v. Hendrickson, 54 Misc. 337, 104 N.Y.S. 122 (1907), aff'd 125 App.Div. 256, 109 N.Y.S. 403 (1908).

8. Taylor v. State Farm Mutual Auto. Insurance Co., 248 La. 246, 178 So.2d 238 (1965); Bangor v. Readfield, 32 Me. 60 (1850); Town of South Burlington v. Cambridge, 77 Vt. 289, 59 A. 1013 (1905).

9. Clemens v. Kinsley, 72 Idaho 251, 239 P.2d 266 (1951); Oldtown v. Falmouth, 40 Me. 106 (1855); Ross v. Pick, 199 Md. 341, 86 A.2d 463 (1952); cf. Roberts v. Robben, 188 Kan. 217, 362 P.2d 29 (1961). But cf. In re Webb's Adoption, 65 Ariz. 176, 177 P.2d 222 (1947).

10. See State ex rel. Carlson v. Hedberg, 192 Minn. 193, 256 N.W. 91 (1934); Application of Habeck, 75 S.D. 535, 69 N.W.2d

3. Children Born Out of Wedlock

§ **4.38** Historically, the law assigned the domicile of the father to his legitimate children and the domicile of the mother to illegitimate children until a child was legitimated. The law, social relationships, and family status upon which these theories were based are changing rapidly. Today, a child born out of wedlock and not acknowledged by its father takes the domicile of its mother as its domicile of origin.[1] If the child is legitimized as to the father and lives with the father, its domicile will then become that of the father.[2] However, if the legitimized child continues to live with its mother, its derivative domicile would continue with its mother. Likewise a child born to a single parent, would continue to have the domicile of the custodial parent even after marriage of the single parent.[3]

It seems probable that the cases, viewed in the setting of the diversity of family lifestyles now existing, will support the view that the

353 (1955). See also Allgood v. Williams, 92 Ala. 551, 8 So. 722 (1890); Jenkins v. Clark, 71 Iowa 552, 32 N.W. 504 (1887); Modern Woodmen v. Hester, 66 Kan. 129, 71 P. 279 (1903); Matter of Guardianship of D.L.L. and C.L.L., 291 N.W.2d 278 (S.D.1980). Contra, Delaware Lackawanna & Western Railroad Co. v. Petrowsky, 250 Fed. 554 (2d Cir.1918), cert. denied 247 U.S. 508, 38 S.Ct. 427, 62 L.Ed. 1241 (1918). On the control of a ward's domicile by a guardian, see In re Eleanor A., 84 Cal.App.3d 184, 148 Cal.Rptr. 315 (1978); In re Pratt, 219 Minn. 414, 18 N.W.2d 147 (1945); First Trust & Deposit Co. v. Goodrich, 3 N.Y.2d 410, 165 N.Y.S.2d 510, 144 N.E.2d 396 (1957). Cf. In re Huck, 435 Pa. 325, 257 A.2d 522 (1969), cert. denied 397 U.S. 1040, 90 S.Ct. 1360, 25 L.Ed.2d 651 (1970); Paulsen & Best, Appointment of Guardian in Conflict of Laws, 45 Iowa L. Rev. 212 (1960).

In Dunlap by Wells v. Buchanan, 741 F.2d 165, 167 (8th Cir.1984) (eight year old in Texan home for retarded retained parents' domicile in Arkansas despite appointment of Texas guardian). In considering the child's domicile for purposes of diversity, the court stated:

These general principles do not require us to adopt an unbending rule that a child such as Darin can never, under any circumstances, have a domicile other than that of his parents. Indeed it is entirely possible that a child may be shown by the evidence to have adopted such a domicile. In Elliott v. Krear, 466 F.Supp. 444 (E.D.Va.1979), the minor plaintiff's divorced mother, who had legal custody of him, was domiciled in California. The court held that the minor was domiciled in Virginia, however, because his mother had left him in the actual custo-

dy of his Virginia grandparents, who cared for him and were paying for all of his support.

See also Spurgeon v. Mission State Bank, 151 F.2d 702 (8th Cir.1945), cert. denied, 327 U.S. 782, 66 S.Ct. 682, 90 L.Ed. 1009 (1946) (emancipated minor may acquire domicile of own choice).

The traditional rule was applied to preclude a minor citizen of the United States, the child of Mexican parents, from attending school tuition-free in the Texas district where he lived with his sister. Martinez v. Bynum, 461 U.S. 321, 103 S.Ct. 1838, 75 L.Ed.2d 879 (1983).

§ 4.38

1. See Danbury v. New Haven, 5 Conn. 584 (1825); Glansman v. Ledbetter, 190 Ind. 505, 130 N.E. 230 (1921); Kowalski v. Wojtkowski, 19 N.J. 247, 116 A.2d 6 (1955); Thayer v. Thayer, 187 N.C. 573, 122 S.E. 307 (1924); In re Estate of Moore, 68 Wn.2d 792, 415 P.2d 653 (1966); Restatement, Second, Conflict of Laws § 22, cmnt. (c) (1971). Cf. Krakow v. Department of Public Welfare, 326 Mass. 452, 95 N.E.2d 184 (1950).

2. Restatement, Second, Conflict of Laws § 22 (1971); In re Adoption of Minor, 191 Wash. 452, 71 P.2d 385 (1937).

3. Wheeler v. Hollis, 19 Tex. 522, 70 Am. Dec. 363 (1857); In re Beaumont [1893] 3 Ch. 490; Restatement, Second, Conflict of Laws § 22, cmnt. (b), (1971). See Hicks v. Fox, 81 Minn. 197, 83 N.W. 538 (1900). See also Clark, Domestic Relations § 4.3 (1968); Levitt, The Domicile of an Infant, 92 Cent. L.J. 264, 284 et seq. (1923).

derivative domicile of nearly any infant, assigned by operation of law, is the domicile of the child's proper custodial parent. As a consequence, there seems no reason to distinguish between legitimate or illegitimate, acknowledged or unacknowledged, natural or adopted children and the earlier distinctions may even be constitutionally suspect.[4]

4. Adopted Children

§ 4.39 An adopted child during minority takes the domicile of its adoptive parents in the same fashion as does a natural child.[1] The effect of adoption is to create by law a relationship identical to that of a natural, legitimate parent and child. After adoption, a minor's domicile will follow that of the adoptive, custodial parent and not that of the natural parent.[2]

5. Separated Parents

§ 4.40 The concept of a child's domicile as following that of the proper custodial parent finds major support in the cases involving the domicile of children whose parents are separated. The child's domicile when the parents are separated is usually with that parent who enjoys a superior claim to the child's custody.[1] In many instances the custodial parent will be awarded custody of the children by the court dealing with the marital status.[2] In many states statutes specifically provide that parents have equal authority and control over their children and are equally entitled to custody.[3] Under such statutes the domicile of the minor child should follow that of the parent with whom the child properly resides unless the other parent has a superior custody claim in

---

4. Cf. Trimble v. Gordon, 430 U.S. 762, 97 S.Ct. 1459, 52 L.Ed.2d 31 (1977). See Krause, Illegitimacy, Law and Social Policy 59 (1971); Krause, Equal Protection for the Illegitimate, 65 Mich. L. Rev. 477 (1967).

§ 4.39

1. Miller v. Bode, 80 Ind.App. 338, 139 N.E. 456 (1923); Waldoborough v. Friendship, 87 Me. 211, 32 A. 880 (1895); Washburn v. White, 140 Mass. 568, 5 N.E. 813 (1886); Commonwealth v. Teitelbaum, 160 Pa.Super. 286, 50 A.2d 713 (1947).

2. In re Johnson, 87 Iowa 130, 54 N.W. 69 (1894); Woodward v. Woodward, 87 Tenn. 644, 11 S.W. 892 (1889); Restatement, Second, Conflict of Laws § 22, cmnt. (g) (1971).

§ 4.40

1. See, e.g., Boardman v. Boardman, 135 Conn. 124, 62 A.2d 521 (1948). See also Willmore v. Willmore, 273 Minn. 537, 143 N.W.2d 630 (1966), cert. denied 385 U.S. 898, 87 S.Ct. 202, 17 L.Ed.2d 130 (1966).

2. Toledo Traction Co. v. Cameron, 137 Fed. 48 (6th Cir.1905); In re Hughes, 73 Ariz. 97, 237 P.2d 1009 (1951); Niccum v. Lawrence, 186 Kan. 223, 350 P.2d 133 (1960); Kruse v. Kruse, 150 Kan. 946, 96 P.2d 849 (1939); Ross v. Pick, 199 Md. 341, 86 A.2d 463 (1952); Durfee v. Durfee, 293 Mass. 472, 200 N.E. 395 (1936); Hicks v. Fox, 81 Minn. 197, 83 N.W. 538 (1900); Application of Enke, 129 Mont. 353, 287 P.2d 19 (1955), cert. denied 350 U.S. 923, 76 S.Ct. 212, 100 L.Ed. 808 (1955); Lorenz v. Royer, 194 Or. 355, 241 P.2d 142 (1952); Griffin v. Griffin, 95 Or. 78, 187 P. 598 (1920); Groves v. Barto, 109 Wash. 112, 186 P. 300 (1919). Cf. Murphy v. Murphy, 380 Mass. 454, 404 N.E.2d 69 (1980).

3. E.g., Cal. Civ. Code §§ 197–198; Ill.— S.H.A. ch. 68, § 16; Iowa Code Ann. § 668.1; Kan. Stat. Ann. § 59–3003; Miss. Code § 93–13–1; N.H. Rev. Stat. Ann. § 463:4; Or. Rev. Stat. § 109.030. See Clark, Domestic Relations § 584; Note, Custody and Control of Children, 5 Fordham L. Rev. 460 (1936).

law.[4] This would seem to be the result even without a statute conferring equal custody rights upon the parents if the children are in fact properly living and properly in the custody of one of the parents.[5] If there is a separation and the child lives with neither parent, absent an independent guardian the child's domicile would seem to follow that of the parent who can properly claim custody,[6] or if both are equally entitled, the child's domicile would continue where it was prior to the time when the family broke up. This latter result assumes that the historical presumption in favor of the father's power to determine domicile for minor children no longer exists. Rather, it recognizes that parental rights regarding custody and parental ability to establish domicile being equal, the doctrine of derivative domicile for the child simply breaks down in some cases involving separated parents.

6. Death of Parent

§ 4.41 When the proper custodial parent dies, it would seem that the domicile of the child would shift to the other parent if that parent were entitled to the child's custody. It may be that this shift would not occur until the child actually began to live with the surviving parent.[1] If the non-custodial parent were found to be unfit, then it would seem that the child's domicile could be changed only after the appointment of a guardian, which appointment would seem probable in that situation. Likewise, it seems that a non-custodial parent who had abandoned the child must forfeit recognition as a proper custodial parent, and the child's domicile remains where it was until changed by a guardian or by emancipation.

4. Oxley v. Oxley, 159 F.2d 10 (D.C.Cir. 1946); Kline v. Kline, 57 Iowa 386, 10 N.W. 825 (1881). See State ex rel. Larson v. Larson, 190 Minn. 489, 252 N.W. 329 (1934); Mills v. Howard, 228 S.W.2d 906 (Tex.Civ. App.1950); Goldsmith v. Salkey, 115 S.W.2d 778 (Tex.Civ.App.1937), aff'd 131 Tex. 139, 112 S.W.2d 165 (1938); Ex parte Halvey, 185 Misc. 52, 55 N.Y.S.2d 761 (1945), aff'd 269 App.Div. 1019, 59 N.Y.S.2d 396 (1945), aff'd 295 N.Y. 836, 66 N.E.2d 851 (1946); In re Sagan, 261 Pa.Super. 384, 396 A.2d 450 (1978); cf. Allen v. Allen, 200 Or. 678, 268 P.2d 358 (1954). See also Goodrich, Custody of Children in Divorce Suits, 7 Cornell L.Q. 1 (1921).

5. See Scott v. Furrow, 141 Conn. 113, 104 A.2d 224 (1954).

6. Cf. In re Webb's Adoption, 65 Ariz. 176, 177 P.2d 222 (1947); Restatement, Second, Conflict of Laws § 22, comment (d) (1971). Cf. Elliott v. Krear, 466 F.Supp. 444 (E.D.Va.1979) (child's domicile with relatives acting in loco parentis even though mother in another state had legal custody);

Linville v. Price, 572 F.Supp. 345 (S.D.W.Va.1983) (similar).

§ 4.41

1. Ziady v. Curley, 396 F.2d 873 (4th Cir.1968); Simonds v. Simonds, 154 F.2d 326 (App.D.C.1946); Clark v. Jelinek, 90 Idaho 592, 414 P.2d 892 (1966); In re Skinner's Guardianship, 230 Iowa 1016, 300 N.W. 1 (1941) (noted 21 Neb. L. Rev. 326 (1942)); 16 Tul. L. Rev. 285 (1942); Roberts v. Robben, 188 Kan. 217, 362 P.2d 29 (1961); Application of Vallimont, 182 Kan. 334, 321 P.2d 190 (1958); Peacock v. Bradshaw, 145 Tex. 68, 194 S.W.2d 551 (1946); Restatement, Second, Conflict of Laws § 22, cmnt. (b) (1971). See Chumos v. Chumos, 105 Kan. 374, 184 P. 736 (1919); In re Peterson's Guardianship, 119 Neb. 511, 229 N.W. 885 (1930); In re Thorne, 240 N.Y. 444, 148 N.E. 630 (1925). Cf. Matter of Jackson, 592 S.W.2d 320 (Mo.App.1979); In re Wagner's Petition, 381 Pa. 107, 112 A.2d 352 (1955). Cf. Wade, Domicile: A Re-Examination, 32 Int'l & Comp. L.Q. 1 (1983).

It is usually assumed that if both parents are dead, the domicile of the minor is that of the last surviving parent at the time of the latter's death.[2] This assumes that the child is not in the custody of a proper guardian.[3] Consequently, it would seem that the last domicile would continue until the child acquires another derivative domicile or may be treated as emancipated when effect may be given the child's own choice of a permanent abode.[4] If the child takes up residence with a natural or an appointed guardian the child will derive a domicile from the guardian.[5] The right of grandparents to succeed the father and mother as natural guardians of the child has been recognized in several decisions.[6] The grandparent, as a natural guardian, may change the child's domicile when the child actually resides with the grandparent. In this instance there is a surrogate custodial parent recognized by the law. This power has been extended beyond grandparents to other relatives with whom orphaned children live,[7] and appears to be consistent with the policy of relating the domicile of the child as closely as possible to the place where the child makes his home.

2. See Abrams v. Daffron, 155 Ga.App. 182, 270 S.E.2d 278 (1980); In re Guardianship of Kowalke, 232 Minn. 292, 46 N.W.2d 275 (1950); Restatement, Second, Conflict of Laws § 22, cmnt. (b) (1971). See also In re Henning's Estate, 128 Cal. 214, 60 P. 762 (1900); Van Matre v. Sankey, 148 Ill. 536, 36 N.E. 628 (1893); In re Benton, 92 Iowa 202, 60 N.W. 614 (1894); Jenkins v. Clark, 71 Iowa 552, 32 N.W. 504 (1887); Sudler v. Sudler, 121 Md. 46, 88 A. 26 (1913).

3. See Restatement, Second, Conflict of Laws § 22, cmnt. (h), (i) (1971).

4. See Louisville & Nashville RR. Co. v. Kimbrough, 115 Ky. 512, 74 S.W. 229 (1903).

5. Ex parte Fletcher, 225 Ala. 139, 142 So. 30 (1932); Noonan v. Wingate, 376 Ill. 244, 33 N.E.2d 467 (1941); Johnson v. Smith, 94 Ind.App. 619, 180 N.E. 188 (1932); In re Guardianship of Kowalke, 232 Minn. 292, 46 N.W.2d 275 (1950); In re Pratt, 219 Minn. 414, 18 N.W.2d 147 (1945); In re Hall's Guardianship, 235 N.C. 697, 71 S.E.2d 140 (1952); Cribbs v. Floyd, 188 S.C. 443, 199 S.E. 677 (1938).

6. Lamar v. Micou, 112 U.S. 452, 5 S.Ct. 221, 28 L.Ed. 751 (1884); Lamar v. Micou, 114 U.S. 218, 5 S.Ct. 857, 29 L.Ed. 94 (1885); Lehmer v. Hardy, 294 Fed. 407 (D.C.Cir.1923); Churchill v. Jackson, 132 Ga. 666, 64 S.E. 691 (1909); In re Guardianship of Lehr, 249 Iowa 625, 87 N.W.2d 909 (1958); In re Benton, 92 Iowa 202, 60 N.W. 614 (1894); Smith v. Young, 136 Mo. App. 65, 117 S.W. 628 (1909); In re Hall's

Guardianship, 235 N.C. 697, 71 S.E.2d 140 (1952); In re Huck, 435 Pa. 325, 257 A.2d 522 (1969), cert. denied 397 U.S. 1040, 90 S.Ct. 1360, 25 L.Ed.2d 651 (1970); State v. Prosser, 78 S.D. 35, 98 N.W.2d 329 (1959). Cf. Petition for Habeas Corpus for Donald Peter Fore, 151 N.E.2d 777 (Ohio App. 1958), reversed 168 Ohio St. 363, 155 N.E.2d 194 (1958); Dawson v. Dawson, 241 S.W.2d 725 (Mo.App.1951); Munson v. Johnston, 16 N.J. 31, 106 A.2d 1 (1954). See Spiro, Domicile of Minors Without Parents, 5 Int'l & Comp. L.Q. 196 (1956).

7. See Lehmer v. Hardy, 294 Fed. 407 (D.C.Cir.1923); Delaware, Lackawanna & Western RR. Co. v. Petrowsky, 250 Fed. 554 (2d Cir.1918), cert. denied 247 U.S. 508, 38 S.Ct. 427, 62 L.Ed. 1241 (1918); Loftin v. Carden, 203 Ala. 405, 83 So. 174 (1919); Hughes v. Industrial Commission, 69 Ariz. 193, 211 P.2d 463 (1949); Harlan v. Industrial Accident Commission, 194 Cal. 352, 228 P. 654 (1924); In re Lancey's Guardianship, 232 Iowa 191, 2 N.W.2d 787 (1942); Jensen v. Sorenson, 211 Iowa 354, 233 N.W. 717 (1930); State ex rel. Brown v. Hamilton, 202 Mo. 377, 100 S.W. 609 (1907). Contra, Bjornquist v. Boston & Albany Railroad Co., 250 Fed. 929 (1st Cir.1918), cert. denied 248 U.S. 573, 39 S.Ct. 11, 63 L.Ed. 427 (1918). See also Sudler v. Sudler, 121 Md. 46, 88 A. 26 (1913); Matter of Afflick's Estate, 10 D.C. (3 MacArth.) 95 (1877); Hiestand v. Kuns, 8 Blackf. 345 (Ind.1847); Munday v. Baldwin, 79 Ky. 121 (1880); Greene v. Willis, 47 R.I. 375, 133 A. 651 (1926). Cf. In re Estate of Moore, 68 Wash.2d 792, 415 P.2d 653 (1966).

§ 4.42 While a guardian of the estate or conservator may be appointed as custodian of property wherever the property of a minor may be situated, such a guardian of the estate or conservator has no control over the ward's domicile.[1] However, a properly appointed guardian of the person normally has custody and power to change the domicile of the ward, although the ward probably does not assume the guardian's domicile until he resides with the guardian.[2] There has been more uncertainty whether a guardian can change a ward's domicile only within the state of his appointment,[3] or in a proper case, move it to another state.[4] In every case of domicile by operation of law, the law confers upon one party the control of the domicile of another because of the lack of competence of the latter.[5] Reconciling this with the policy that the domicile should be the state to which the individual is most closely related, a guardian should be permitted to change the domicile of the ward to another state if not otherwise restricted by the law of his appointment. In most instances, it appears that if the shift of domicile is in the best interests of the child, and was not to achieve a purpose in conflict with the interests of the ward, the courts will find that the domicile has shifted and that the change of domicile is within the authority of the guardian.[6]

7. *Emancipation*

§ 4.43 There is considerable authority that after emancipation a minor who has attained the age of discretion may acquire a separate domicile.[1] The age of discretion may vary,[2] but it is significant to note

§ 4.42

1. See Lamar v. Micou, 112 U.S. 452, 5 S.Ct. 221, 28 L.Ed. 751 (1884); Lamar v. Micou, 114 U.S. 218, 5 S.Ct. 857, 29 L.Ed. 94 (1885); Lehmer v. Hardy, 294 Fed. 407 (D.C.Cir.1923).

2. Louisville v. Sherley's Guardian, 80 Ky. 71 (1882); Mills' Guardian v. Hopkinsville, 11 S.W. 776, 11 Ky. L. Rep. 164 (1889); In re Pratt, 219 Minn. 414, 18 N.W.2d 147 (1945); First Trust & Deposit Co. v. Goodrich, 3 N.Y.2d 410, 165 N.Y.S.2d 510, 144 N.E.2d 396 (1957); School Directors of Borough of West Chester v. James, 2 Watts & S. 568, 583, 37 Am. Dec. 525 (Pa.1841); Restatement, Second, Conflict of Laws § 22, cmnt. (h) (1971). But see La. S.A.-Civ. Code art. 39. Cf. In re Adoption of Johnson, 399 Pa. 624, 161 A.2d 358 (1960). See generally Paulson & Best, Appointment of Guardians in Conflict of Laws, 45 Iowa L. Rev. 212 (1960).

3. Lamar v. Micou, 112 U.S. 452, 5 S.Ct. 221, 28 L.Ed. 751 (1884); Louisville v. Sherley's Guardian, 80 Ky. 71 (1882); Kirkland v. Whately, 86 Mass. (4 Allen) 462 (1862). But see Woodward v. Woodward, 87 Tenn. 644, 11 S.W. 892 (1889).

4. Ricci v. Superior Court, 107 Cal.App. 395, 290 P. 517 (1930); In re Waite, 190 Iowa 182, 180 N.W. 159 (1920); In re Pratt, 219 Minn. 414, 18 N.W.2d 147 (1945); Wheeler v. Hollis, 19 Tex. 522, 70 Am. Dec. 363 (1857); In re Kiernan, 38 Misc. 394, 77 N.Y.S. 924 (Surr. 1902).

5. Restatement, Second, Conflict of Laws § 23, cmnt. (f) (1971).

6. Restatement, Second, Conflict of Laws § 22, cmnt. (h) (1971). See Note, The Power to Change the Domicile of Infants and of Persons Non Compos Mentis, 30 Colum. L. Rev. 703 (1930). See also Miller v. Nelson, 160 Fla. 410, 35 So.2d 288 (1948).

§ 4.43

1. Appelt v. Whitty, 286 F.2d 135 (7th Cir.1961); Spurgeon v. Mission State Bank, 151 F.2d 702 (8th Cir.1945), cert. denied 327 U.S. 782, 66 S.Ct. 682, 90 L.Ed. 1009 (1946); Hollowell v. Hux, 229 F.Supp. 50 (E.D.N.C.1964); Bjornquist v. Boston & Albany Railroad Co., 250 Fed. 929 (1st Cir. 1918), cert. denied 248 U.S. 573, 39 S.Ct. 11, 63 L.Ed. 427 (1918); Town of Milford v.

2. See p. 281.

that by statute in several states minors at the age of 14 or more may nominate their guardian and make other decisions which affect their lives.[3] By emancipation, the minor assumes to act on his own responsibility, freed from parental authority, control, and assistance.[4] A change of domicile by a child's parents after the child's emancipation has no effect on the child's domicile.[5] In such a situation, the law has simply recognized that the minor has attained an age which permits him to acquire a domicile of choice by virtue of his independent existence.

8. *Marriage of Minor*

§ 4.44 A fairly common situation in which a minor should be allowed to establish a separate domicile is when the minor contracts a valid marriage. If the law permits an individual to assume the marriage relationship with its duties and responsibilities regarding the family unit, it seems rather clear that a married minor should have capacity to acquire a domicile of choice. The marriage relationship authorized by the law is inconsistent with the continued control and direction by the minor's parents. In some states the problem is settled by statutes which provide that a minor becomes of age upon marriage,[1] and other authorities simply indicate that marriage emancipates a minor.[2]

D. CAPACITY TO ACQUIRE A DOMICILE

§ 4.45 The capacity to acquire a domicile of choice depends largely upon one's ability to form the necessary intent to make one's home in a particular place. A mentally incompetent person may be unable to make

Town of Greenwich, 126 Conn. 340, 11 A.2d 352 (1940); Russell v. State, 62 Neb. 512, 87 N.W. 344 (1901); Ex parte Olcott, 141 N.J.Eq. 8, 55 A.2d 820 (1947); Washington Township v. Beaver Tp., 3 Watts and Serg. 548 (Pa.1842); Sherburne v. Hartland, 37 Vt. 528 (1865); Bonneau v. Russell, 117 Vt. 134, 85 A.2d 569 (1952). See also Woolridge v. McKenna, 8 Fed. 650, 681 (C.C.W.D.Tenn. 1881); Lewis v. Missouri, Kansas & Texas Railway Co., 82 Kan. 351, 108 P. 95 (1910). But see Gulf, Colorado & Santa Fe Railway Co. v. Lemons, 109 Tex. 244, 206 S.W. 75 (1918). Cf., Delaware, Lackawanna & Western Railroad Co. v. Petrowsky, 250 Fed. 554 (2d Cir.1918), cert. denied 247 U.S. 508, 38 S.Ct. 427, 62 L.Ed. 1241 (1918); Hall v. Fall, 235 F.Supp. 631 (W.D.N.C.1964); Wiggins v. New York Life Insurance Co., 2 F.Supp. 365 (E.D.Ky. 1932).

2. See Inhabitants of Town of Camden v. Inhabitants of Town of Warren, 160 Me. 158, 200 A.2d 419 (1964); In re Sonnenberg, 256 Minn. 571, 99 N.W.2d 444 (1959).

3. See, e.g., Uniform Probate Code §§ 5–203, 5–206, 5–410.

4. For what constitutes emancipation, see Jacobs v. Jacobs, 130 Iowa 10, 104 N.W. 489 (1905); Clark, Domestic Relations 240 (1968). Cf. Northwestern National Casualty Co. v. Davis, 90 Cal.App.3d 782, 153 Cal. Rptr. 556 (1979).

5. Restatement, Second, Conflict of Laws § 22, cmnt. (f) (1971). Cf. Linville v. Price, 572 F.Supp. 345 (S.D.W.Va.1983).

§ 4.44

1. E.g., West's Ann. Cal. Civ. Code § 204; Official Code Ga. Ann. § 74–108; Iowa Code Ann. § 599.1; Or. Rev. Stat. 109.520; see 5 Vernier, American Family Law § 282 (1938).

2. Appelt v. Whitty, 286 F.2d 135 (7th Cir.1961); Commonwealth v. Graham, 157 Mass. 73, 31 N.E. 706 (1892); State ex rel. Scott v. Lowell, 78 Minn. 166, 80 N.W. 877 (1899); Cochran v. Cochran, 196 N.Y. 86, 89 N.E. 470 (1909). But see Wiggins v. New York Life Insurance Co., 2 F.Supp. 365 (E.D.Ky.1932).

that choice, and, if so, he is unable to acquire a domicile of choice and his existing domicile would continue.[1] However, the fact that an individual may be incapable of managing his affairs in other respects does not necessarily preclude him from acquiring a domicile of choice if he has that limited ability.[2] It appears that a person may choose his domicile even though a guardian of the person has been appointed for him, at least if the guardian concurs.[3] There is reason for this distinction that even though a person may not be capable of doing some acts, he may yet have a sufficient degree of comprehension to formulate the mental attitude necessary to make a reasonable choice of a place of residence, particularly considering that domicile may be determined for different purposes. For example, in making a contract, the obligor must exercise capacity to undertake a burden and responsibility running in favor of another. In changing domicile, the necessary intention relates to understanding the making of a home and the choice of where that home is to be maintained,[4] a choice which merely subjects the person to the operation of the legal system at the new domicile—a system that must be presumed to guard rights and privileges and to operate equally as regards all persons domiciled therein.[5]

If the individual has been incompetent since infancy, it would appear that his domicile would continue to attach to that of his custodial parent if he remains a member of that parent's family.[6] If an incompetent does not remain a member of the family of his custodial parent, his domicile would appear to remain where it was at the time of the separation from the custodial parent until a guardian is appointed who has authority to change the ward's domicile.[7] If a guardian is appointed for one lacking capacity to choose a place of residence, considerations similar to those relating to the control of an infant's domicile by a guardian are applicable. The guardian of the incompetent should be able

---

§ 4.45

1. Gosney v. Department of Public Welfare, 206 Neb. 137, 291 N.W.2d 708 (1980); In re Estate of Peck, 80 N.M. 290, 454 P.2d 772 (1969), cert. denied 396 U.S. 942, 90 S.Ct. 376, 24 L.Ed.2d 242 (1969); Restatement, Second, Conflict of Laws § 23 (1971); See Paulson & Best, Appointment of Guardians in Conflict of Laws, 45 Iowa L. Rev. 212 (1960); Note, Power to Change the Domicile of Infants and Persons Non Compos Mentis, 30 Colum. L. Rev. 703 (1930).

2. Foster v. Carlin, 200 F.2d 943 (4th Cir.1952); Culver's Appeal, 48 Conn. 165 (1880); Cadwalader v. Pyle, 95 Kan. 337, 148 P. 655 (1915); Talbot v. Chamberlain, 149 Mass. 57, 20 N.E. 305 (1889); Concord v. Rumney, 45 N.H. 423 (1864); Groseclose v. Rice, 366 P.2d 465 (Okla.1961); Restatement, Second, Conflict of Laws § 23 (1971). Cf. Coppedge v. Clinton, 72 F.2d 531 (10th Cir. 1934); District of Columbia v. Stackhouse, 239 F.2d 62 (D.C.Cir.1956).

3. In re Sherrill's Estate, 92 Ariz. 39, 373 P.2d 353 (1962); Culver's Appeal, 48 Conn. 165 (1880); Talbot v. Chamberlain, 149 Mass. 57, 20 N.E. 305 (1889); Matthews v. Matthews, 141 So.2d 799 (Fla.App.1962); Mowry v. Latham, 17 R.I. 480, 23 A. 13 (1891). Restatement, Second, Conflict of Laws § 23, cmnt. (f) (1971).

4. See Concord v. Rumney, 45 N.H. 423 (1864); Restatement, Second, Conflict of Laws § 23 (1971).

5. See Note, 3 Cal. L. Rev. 491 (1915).

6. Monroe v. Jackson, 55 Me. 55 (1867); Washington Township v. Beaver Township, 3 Watts & Serg. 548 (Pa.1842); Sharpe v. Crispen, L.R. 1 Prob. & Div. 610 (1869); Restatement, Second, Conflict of Laws § 23, cmnt. (c) (1971).

7. Gosney v. Department of Public Welfare, 206 Neb. 137, 291 N.W.2d 708 (1980); Restatement, Second, Conflict of Laws § 23, comment (c) (1971).

to change the domicile of the ward subject to the authority of the appointing court.[8]

VII. ANALOGOUS RELATIONSHIPS OF CORPORATE ENTITIES

§ 4.46 Occasionally, the relationship of a corporation to the state of incorporation is described as a corporate domicile.[1] This is a rather unfortunate term, and confuses the concepts of corporate activities with those of individuals.[2] Most of the functions which domicile serves with regard to individuals are inapplicable to corporations. Certainly the focus of the domicile concept on family life is foreign to the corporate structure and the business world. Although courts occasionally use the term domicile to describe the relationship which a corporation has to state, it is much preferable to use the "state of incorporation" or other terms such as the "place of its principal office" to describe relationships which are significant in the corporate world.

---

8. See Uniform Probate Code, §§ 5–209, 5–312; Restatement, Second, Conflict of Laws § 23, cmnt. (f) (1971). See Holyoke v. Haskins, 22 Mass. (5 Pick.) 20, 16 Am. Dec. 372 (1827); In re Sheldon's Estate, 354 Mo. 232, 189 S.W.2d 235 (1945); In re Curtiss, 199 N.Y. 36, 92 N.E. 396 (1910); Anderson v. Anderson's Estate, 42 Vt. 350, 1 Am. Rep. 334 (1869); see also Mowry v. Latham, 17 R.I. 480, 23 A. 13 (1891). Cf. Bennet v. Bennet, 212 Ga. 292, 92 S.E.2d 11 (1956). But cf. Couyoumjian v. Anspach, 360 Mich. 371, 103 N.W.2d 587 (1960).

These following cases appear to presume power by the guardian's appropriate action to alter the domicile of an incompetent. Coppedge v. Clinton, 72 F.2d 531 (10th Cir. 1934); Grier v. Estate of Grier, 252 Minn. 143, 89 N.W.2d 398 (1958); State ex rel. Raymond v. Lawrence, 86 Minn. 310, 90 N.W. 769 (1902); Matter of Kassler, 173 Misc. 856, 19 N.Y.S.2d 266 (1940); In re Robitaille, 78 Misc. 108, 138 N.Y.S. 391 (Surr. 1912). The following indicate the guardian lacks such power at least in absence of express authority from the appointing court. Foster v. Carlin, 200 F.2d 943 (4th Cir.1952); Chew v. Nicholson, 281 Fed. 400 (D.Del.1922); Hayward v. Hayward, 65 Ind.App. 440, 115 N.E. 966 (1917); Rothfeld v. Graves, 264 App.Div. 54, 34 N.Y.S.2d 895 (1942); Commonwealth v. Kernochan, 129 Va. 405, 106 S.E. 367 (1921). Cf. In re Phillips' Estate, 190 So.2d 15 (Fla.App. 1966).

§ 4.46

1. See, e.g., Ohio & Mississippi Railroad Co. v. Wheeler, 66 U.S. (1 Black) 286, 17 L.Ed. 130 (1861); Johnson & Johnson v. Picard, 282 F.2d 386 (6th Cir.1960); Gay v. Bessemer Properties Inc., 159 Fla. 729, 32 So.2d 587 (1947); Pittsburgh–Des Moines Steel Co. v. Incorporated Town of Clive, 249 Iowa 1346, 91 N.W.2d 602 (1958); Bergner & Engel Brewing Co. v. Dreyfus, 172 Mass. 154, 51 N.E. 531 (1898); State v. Riss & Co., 335 S.W.2d 118 (Mo.1960), appeal dismissed 364 U.S. 338, 81 S.Ct. 124, 5 L.Ed.2d 99 (1960); In re Roche's Estate, 16 N.J. 579, 109 A.2d 655 (1954); Douglass v. Phenix Insurance Co., 138 N.Y. 209, 33 N.E. 938 (1893); Sease v. Central Greyhound Lines, 306 N.Y. 284, 117 N.E.2d 899 (1954); Allegheny County v. Cleveland & Pittsburgh Railroad Co., 51 Pa. 228, 88 Am. Dec. 589 (1865); Beale, Foreign Corporations § 71 (1904). The English view is to the same effect although for certain purposes a distinction of residence determined by where the control and management are located is drawn. Cheshire & North, Private International Law 188 (10th ed. 1979). See generally Reese & Kaufman, The Law Governing Corporate Affairs: Choice of Law and the Impact of Full Faith and Credit, 58 Colum. L. Rev. 1118 (1958).

2. Restatement, Second, Conflict of Laws § 11, comment (f) (1971). See Cook, Logical and Legal Bases of the Conflict of Laws, 207 (1942); Stevens, Corporations § 13 (2d ed. 1949); Francis, Domicil of Corporations, 38 Yale L.J. 335 (1929); Note, 14 U. Det. L.J. 136 (1951). See also infra § 23.1.

Chapter 5

BASIC CONSIDERATIONS IN PERSONAL JURISDICTION

Table of Sections

		Sections
I.	Introduction	5.1
II.	The Development of American Jurisdiction	5.2–5.4
	A. 1789–1877: Developing Full Faith and Credit Standards	5.2
	B. 1878–1944: Developing Due Process Standards	5.3
	C. 1945–Present: The Minimum Contacts Test	5.4
III.	Traditional Jurisdictional Relationships	5.5–5.9
	A. In Rem Jurisdiction	5.5
	B. Quasi in Rem Jurisdiction	5.6
	C. Status Jurisdiction	5.7
	D. In Personam Jurisdiction	5.8
	E. Continuing Significance of Traditional Categories	5.9
IV.	New Jurisdictional Relationships	5.10–5.13
	A. Specific Jurisdiction	5.10–5.12
	1. Related Contacts: Distinguishing Specific from General Jurisdiction	5.10
	2. Purposeful Availment	5.11
	3. Reasonableness	5.12
	B. General Jurisdiction	5.13
V.	The Need for Statutory Authorization	
	A. State Courts	5.14
	B. Federal Courts	5.15
VI.	Other Jurisdictional Issues Compared	5.16–5.18
	A. Notice and Opportunity to be Heard	5.16
	B. Competence of the Court—Subject Matter Jurisdiction	5.17
	C. Venue	5.18
VII.	Challenging Jurisdiction	5.19–5.21
	A. Direct Attacks	5.19–5.22
	1. Federal Court—FRCP 12(b)	5.19
	2. State Court	5.20
	B. Collateral Attacks	5.21
	C. Limited Appearances	5.22
VIII.	Continuing Jurisdiction	5.23

I. INTRODUCTION

§ **5.1** In this chapter, and the six that follow, we examine the law of personal jurisdiction. We cannot, of course, give a treatment as detailed as if the entire book were devoted to the subject.[1] But Conflicts is a tri-partite discipline, and one of those parts is jurisdiction.[2] Thus our aim is to examine personal jurisdiction both of itself and how it relates to the discipline's other major topics: choice of law and judgment recognition.

Most legal systems recognize the requirement that the parties and the transaction have some connection with that legal system before an organ of that system—paradigmatically a court—can take action. In the United States, the courts of a state can affect legal interests when they bear a reasonable relationship to the parties and the transaction.[3] In other words, the authority of courts is territorially bounded. The law that describes those limitations is that of personal or territorial jurisdiction.

The study of two clauses of the Constitution dominates American jurisdictional law. The first, and older, is the Full Faith and Credit Clause, which was part of the original Constitution.[4] It demands that state courts give "Full Faith and Credit ... to the public Acts, Records, and judicial Proceedings of every other State."[5] Although that clause has always been interpreted as a strong command to American courts to give conclusive effect to each others' judicial decrees,[6] from the earliest days of the Republic jurisdictionally infirm decrees were exempted from its scope.[7] The second important clause is the Due Process Clause of the Fourteenth Amendment, which was added to the Constitution after the Civil War.[8] By no later than the early part of the 20th century, the United States Supreme Court had established the Due Process Clause as a direct restraint on personal jurisdiction.[9] Jurisdictional law, and to a lesser extent choice of law,[10] operate at the intersection of these two

§ 5.1

1. For a comprehensive treatment of American jurisdiction, see Casad, Jurisdiction in Civil Actions (2d ed. 1991).

2. Siegel, A Retrospective on Babcock v. Jackson: A Personal View, 56 Alb. L. Rev. 693, 693 (1993).

3. See, e.g., International Shoe Co. v. Washington, 326 U.S. 310, 66 S.Ct. 154, 90 L.Ed. 95 (1945); Restatement, Second, Conflict of Laws § 24 (1971); von Mehren & Trautman, Jurisdiction to Adjudicate: A Suggested Analysis, 79 Harv. L. Rev. 1121 (1966).

4. U.S. Const. art. IV.

5. Id.

6. E.g., Mills v. Duryee, 11 U.S. (7 Cranch) 481, 3 L.Ed. 411 (1813). The Clause mentions only "States," but its effect was extended by legislation to all United States courts. Act of May 26, 1790, ch. 11, 1 Stat. 122.

7. See, e.g., D'Arcy v. Ketchum, 52 U.S. (11 How.) 165, 13 L.Ed. 648 (1850); Elliott v. Peirsol, 26 U.S. (1 Pet.) 328, 7 L.Ed. 164

(1828); Hampton v. McConnel, 16 U.S. (3 Wheat.) 234, 235, 4 L.Ed. 378, 379 (1818).

8. Proclamation 13, 40th Cong., 2d Sess., 15 Stat. App.at 708 (1868)

9. See Riverside & Dan River Cotton Mills v. Menefee, 237 U.S. 189, 193, 35 S.Ct. 579, 580, 59 L.Ed. 910, 912 (1915). The operation of the Due Process Clause as a direct restraint on jurisdiction may date back as far as Pennoyer v. Neff, 95 U.S. (5 Otto) 714, 24 L.Ed. 565 (1878), but this is uncertain. Compare De La Montanya v. De La Montanya, 112 Cal. 101, 44 P. 345 (1896) (Due Process Clause restrains state courts); Smith v. Colloty, 69 N.J.L. 365, 55 A. 805 (1903) (same) with Sadler v. The Boston and Bolivia Rubber Co., 140 App. Div. 367, 125 N.Y.S. 405 (1910), aff'd 202 N.Y. 547, 95 N.E. 1139 (1911) (Due Process Clause does not directly restrain state courts); Jester v. Baltimore Steam Packet Co., 131 N.C. 54, 42 S.E. 447 (1902) (same).

10. See, e.g., Phillips Petroleum v. Shutts, 472 U.S. 797, 105 S.Ct. 2965, 86 L.Ed.2d 628 (1985); Allstate Ins. Co. v.

constitutional commands. Our aim in this chapter is to sketch the broad outlines of the jurisdictional categories created by the joint operation of these clauses.

II. THE DEVELOPMENT OF AMERICAN JURISDICTION

A. 1789–1877: DEVELOPING FULL FAITH AND CREDIT STANDARDS

§ 5.2 The Full Faith and Credit Clause was part of the original Constitution[1]—in fact, a similar clause was part of the Articles of Confederation.[2] Under the common law, foreign judgments had only "evidentiary" effect, meaning that a judgment debtor might resist enforcement even of a fully litigated foreign judgment.[3] One of the Supreme Court's earliest interpretations of the Clause's implementing statute held the full-faith-and-credit principle requires state courts to give conclusive—not just evidentiary—effect to sister state judgments.[4] Because that implementing legislation, passed nearly contemporaneously with the Constitution,[5] expanded the Clause's effect to all courts "within the United States," federal courts were under the same duty with regard to state judgments.[6]

But soon after adopting the conclusive-effect approach, the Supreme Court suggested that an exception might exist for judgments rendered in violation of the "eternal principle[] of justice" that jurisdiction may not be exercised "over persons not owing [the State] allegiance or not subjected to [its] jurisdiction by being found within [its] limits."[7] What began as a suggestion quickly turned to doctrine, as the Supreme Court sustained many collateral attacks by American courts on the grounds that the rendering court lacked jurisdiction.[8]

In this era, the Supreme Court drew its understanding of these "eternal" jurisdictional principles from international standards that found their expression both in the common law and civilian legal

---

Hague, 449 U.S. 302, 101 S.Ct. 633, 66 L.Ed.2d 521 (1981).

§ 5.2

1. U.S. Const. art. IV.

2. Jackson, The Full Faith and Credit Clause: The Lawyer's Clause of the Constitution, 45 Colum. L. Rev. 1, 3–4 (1945).

3. Whitten, The Constitutional Limitations on State–Court Jurisdiction: A Historical–Interpretative Reexamination of the Full Faith and Credit and Due Process Clauses (Part One), 14 Creighton L. Rev. 499, 509–10 (1981).

4. Mills v. Duryee, 11 U.S. (7 Cranch) 481, 3 L.Ed. 411 (1813).

5. Act of May 26, 1790, 1 Stat. 122.

6. Pennoyer v. Neff, 95 U.S. (5 Otto) 714, 732–33, 24 L.Ed. 565, 572 (1878).

7. The quote comes from Justice Johnson's dissent in *Mills*, 11 U.S. (7 Cranch) 481, 3 L.Ed. 411 (1813), but this is clearly what the Court referred to five years later when it stated that the availability of a collateral attack on a sister state judgment for lack of jurisdiction was a "question [that] is still open." Hampton v. M'Connel, 16 U.S. (3 Wheat.) 234, 235 n.1, 4 L.Ed. 378, 379 n.1 (1818).

8. See, e.g., Galpin v. Page, 85 U.S. (18 Wall.) 350, 21 L.Ed. 959 (1873); D'Arcy v. Ketchum, 52 U.S. (11 How.) 165, 13 L.Ed. 648 (1850); Elliott v. Peirsol, 26 U.S. (1 Pet.) 328, 7 L.Ed. 164 (1828).

systems. The most important synthesis of these principles appeared in Justice Story's *Commentaries on the Conflict of Laws*, the first edition of which appeared in 1834.[9] These common law standards were sufficiently well understood that the Supreme Court could confidently declare that any judgment rendered in violation of them could be resisted in a sister court as "mere abuse."[10] These principles—which we refer to as the common law of jurisdiction—divide the subject into two broad categories, in rem and in personam.[11] The former refers to jurisdiction over property and the latter jurisdiction over persons.[12]

In rem jurisdiction is founded upon the connection of the defendant's property (the res) to the forum, and any resulting judgment is necessarily limited in its effect to the property.[13] The basis for in rem jurisdiction, therefore, is the court's dominion and control over property. Usually, in this early era, this meant that the property had to be seized by the court prior to entry of a judgment,[14] although some courts dispensed with the rule of pre-judgment attachment.[15]

In personam jurisdiction is founded upon the connection of the defendant's person to the forum. Unlike in rem judgments, in personam judgments are not limited in effect to any property.[16] In personam jurisdiction could be established in one of several ways. The defendant could owe the state "allegiance"[17] (meaning citizenship or domicile in the forum), could be personally served while physically present within the forum,[18] could consent to jurisdiction or voluntarily appear without immediately raising his jurisdictional objection.[19] An 1870 Supreme Court case, *Cooper v. Reynolds*,[20] provides an apt summary of these common law principles:

> Jurisdiction of the person is obtained by the service of process, or by the voluntary appearance of the party in the progress of the cause.
>
> Jurisdiction [in rem] of the res is obtained by a seizure under process of the court, whereby it is held to abide such order as the court may make concerning it. The power to render the decree or judgment which the court may undertake to make in the particular

---

9. F. Juenger, Choice of Law and Multistate Justice 29–30 (1993) (discussing Story, Commentaries on the Conflict of Laws (1st ed. 1834)).

10. *D'Arcy*, 52 U.S. (11 How.) at 174, 13 L.Ed. at 652.

11. Restatement, Second, Conflict of Laws, ch. 3, topic 2, intro. note (1971).

12. See infra §§ 5.5–5.8 for a more complete discussion of these categories.

13. Restatement, Second, Conflict of Laws, ch. 3, topic 2, intro. note (1971).

14. Cooper v. Reynolds, 77 U.S. (10 Wall.) 308, 318, 19 L.Ed. 931, 932 (1870). See also Republic National Bank of Miami v. United States, 506 U.S. 80, 113 S.Ct. 554, 121 L.Ed.2d 474 (1992) (in rem jurisdiction

continues even if the trial court loses control over the res).

15. See, e.g., Quarl v. Abbott, 102 Ind. 233, 1 N.E. 476 (1885); Strom v. Montana Central Ry. Co., 81 Minn. 346, 84 N.W. 46 (1900); Rice, Stix & Co. v. Peteet, 66 Tex. 568, 1 S.W. 657 (1886).

16. Restatement, Second, Conflict of Laws, ch. 3, topic 2, intro. note (1971).

17. *Mills*, 11 U.S. (7 Cranch) at 486, 3 L.Ed. at 414 (Johnson, J, dissenting).

18. Barrell v. Benjamin, 15 Mass. 354, 358 (1819).

19. Black, A Treatise on the Law of Judgments § 908 (1st ed. 1891).

20. 77 U.S. (10 Wall.) 308, 316–17, 19 L.Ed. 931, 932 (1870).

cause, depends upon the nature and extent of the authority vested in it by law in regard to the subject-matter of the cause.

It is to be observed that in reference to jurisdiction of the person, the statutes of the States have provided for several kinds of service of original process short of actual service on the party to be brought before the court, and the nature and effect of this service, and the purpose which it answers, depend altogether upon the effect given to it by the statute. So also while the general rule in regard to jurisdiction in rem requires the actual seizure and possession of the res by the officer of the court, such jurisdiction may be acquired by acts which are of equivalent import, and which stand for and represent the dominion of the court over the thing, and in effect subject it to the control of the court.

It is important to note that although these common law principles employed under the Full Faith and Credit Clause were well-established, they operated as indirect restraints on jurisdiction. They became relevant at the judgment recognition stage, and then only when the judgment was presented to another court.[21] Therefore, states could—and routinely did—pass statutes expanding their jurisdictional reach beyond the boundaries of the common law.[22] Such statutes were in no sense "illegal" or unconstitutional. They allowed states maximal authority to proceed against a judgment debtor's in-state assets, but became ineffective if enforcement required presentation of the judgment to another court.[23]

B.   1878–1944: DEVELOPING DUE PROCESS STANDARDS

§ 5.3   The other constitutional provision with substantial relevance to jurisdiction is the Due Process Clause of the Fourteenth Amendment. Prior to the Fourteenth Amendment's adoption in 1868, many state constitutions contained Due Process or "law of the land" clauses. At least one state case invalidated an expansive jurisdictional statute on state constitutional grounds,[1] although the majority view among state

---

21. Indirect jurisdictional rules are those that become relevant only at the stage of judgment recognition. See, e.g., Brand, Enforcement of Judgments in the United States and Europe, 13 J.L. & Commerce 193, 202 (1994).

22. H.C. Black, A Treatise on the Law of Judgments § 902 (1st ed. 1891) (describing such statutes).

23. A good example is D'Arcy v. Ketchum, 52 U.S. (11 How.) 165, 13 L.Ed. 648 (1850), in which the judgment was rendered under New York's "joint debtors" statute, which allowed for entry of a judgment

against all debtors on a single note, even without personal service or appearance of all of the debtors. Although the resulting judgment surely was effective to levy against all New York property of the debtors, the Supreme Court held that it was entitled to no effect in a Louisiana federal court because it violated the common law standard that the Supreme Court employed in interpreting the Full Faith and Credit Clause. Id. at 774, 11 L.Ed. at 652.

§ 5.3

1. Beard v. Beard, 21 Ind. 321 (1863).

courts apparently was that the scope of state court jurisdiction was a matter of legislative control.[2]

The process of linking jurisdictional law to due process notions began with one of the most famous cases in jurisdictional law, *Pennoyer v. Neff*.[3] The precise holding of *Pennoyer* is quite narrow, however, and rests entirely upon the Full Faith and Credit Clause.[4] In *Pennoyer* an Oregon state court rendered the judgment in question, and the Supreme Court held that an Oregon *federal* court hearing a trespass action challenging the validity of the earlier state decree should not recognize it.[5] The reason, said the Court, was that the Oregon state and federal courts were courts of "a different sovereignty," and that the federal court was therefore under no obligation to honor a judgment that would not be entitled to faith and credit in another state's courts.[6] The Oregon state court judgment was infirm under the common law jurisdictional standard that had been developed in applying full-faith-and-credit principles. It was not an in personam judgment because the non-resident defendant had not been personally served in the state, had not voluntarily appeared, and had not consented to jurisdiction.[7] The judgment was not in rem because although the defendant owned land in Oregon, the state court had not attached—or otherwise controlled—the land before it rendered the judgment.[8]

Had the *Pennoyer* Court concluded its opinion with these observations, it would not be possible to view the case as anything more than a modest extension and exposition of the Full Faith and Credit Clause.[9] But Justice Field, writing for a majority of the Court, went on to issue a famous and much-debated dictum that still today influences American jurisdictional law:

2. See, e.g., Hiller v. Burlington M.R.R. Co., 70 N.Y. 223 (1877) (rejecting as "novel" the contention that due process principles limit state court jurisdiction); see generally Whitten, The Constitutional Limitations on State Court Jurisdiction: A Historical–Interpretative Reexamination of the Full Faith and Credit and Due Process Clauses (Part Two), 14 Creighton L. Rev. 735, 799 (1981), Transgrud, The Federal Common Law of Personal Jurisdiction, 57 Geo. Wash. L. Rev. 849, 877 (1989).

3. 95 U.S. (5 Otto) 714, 24 L.Ed. 565 (1878). Whether *Pennoyer* itself completed the interjection of the Due Process Clause into the Fourteenth Amendment is the subject of some debate. The majority position among commentators appears to be that it did so. See, e.g., Oakley, The Pitfalls of a "Hint and Run" History: A Critique of Professor Borchers's "Limited View "of Pennoyer v. Neff, 28 U.C. Davis L. Rev. 591 (1995); Whitten, The Constitutional Limitations on State Court Jurisdiction: A Historical–Interpretative Reexamination of the Full Faith and Credit and Due Process Clauses (Part One), 14 Creighton L. Rev.

451 (1981). For an argument that *Pennoyer* itself was not responsible for imposing the Due Process Clause as a direct restraint on state courts, see Borchers, *Pennoyer*'s Limited Legacy: A Reply to Professor Oakley, 29 U.C. Davis L. Rev. 115 (1995); Borchers, The Death of the Constitutional Law of Personal Jurisdiction: From *Pennoyer* to *Burnham* and Back Again, 24 U.C. Davis L. Rev. 19 (1990).

4. Abrams & Dimond, Toward a Constitutional Framework for the Control of State Court Jurisdiction, 69 Minn. L. Rev. 75, 78 (1984).

5. *Pennoyer*, 95 U.S. at 732, 24 L.Ed. at 572.

6. Id.

7. Id. at 733, 24 L.Ed. at 572.

8. Id. at 731, 24 L.Ed. at 571.

9. The Supreme Court before *Pennoyer* had faced some factually similar cases, but had decided them primarily on state law grounds. See, e.g., Galpin v. Page, 85 U.S. (18 Wall.) 350, 368–72, 21 L.Ed. 959, 964–65 (1873); Cooper v. Reynolds, 77 U.S. (10 Wall.) 308, 321, 19 L.Ed. 931, 933 (1870).

Since the adoption of the Fourteenth Amendment to the Federal Constitution, the validity of such judgments may be directly questioned, and their enforcement in the State resisted, on the ground that proceedings in a court of justice to determine the personal rights and obligations of parties over whom that court has no jurisdiction do not constitute due process of law. Whatever difficulty may be experienced in giving to those terms a definition which will embrace every permissible exertion of power affecting private rights, and exclude such as is forbidden, there can be no doubt of their meaning when applied to judicial proceedings. They then mean a course of legal proceedings according to those rules and principles which have been established in our systems of jurisprudence for the protection and enforcement of private rights. To give such proceedings any validity, there must be a tribunal competent by its constitution—that is, by the law of its creation—to pass upon the subject-matter of the suit; and, if that involves merely a determination of the personal liability of the defendant, he must be brought within its jurisdiction by service of process within the State, or his voluntary appearance.[10]

By the early part of the twentieth century, the Supreme Court had construed this *Pennoyer* dictum to mean that any state court exercise of jurisdiction over non-residents[11] violated the Due Process Clause if it did not fall within one of the common law jurisdictional categories.[12] For in rem jurisdiction this meant prejudgment dominion and control over the defendant's property; for in personam actions against non-residents this meant in-state service, voluntary appearance or consent. This post-*Pennoyer* scheme of jurisdiction differed significantly from the pre-*Pennoyer* scheme.[13] After *Pennoyer*'s dictum was ultimately interpreted to bind state courts to the common law of jurisdiction, the standards under the Full Faith and Credit and Due Process Clauses merged, resulting in direct constitutional regulation of state court jurisdiction. Thus, a state statute attempting to expand state court jurisdiction beyond the common law categories was unconstitutional and void for any purpose.[14] Under the prior regime, such statutes were enforceable in rendering state courts, although judgments founded upon them were not entitled to recognition in the courts of "any other government."[15]

---

10. 95 U.S. at 731, 24 L.Ed. at 571.

11. Some state courts even interpreted *Pennoyer* to apply to resident defendants as well. See, e.g., De La Montanya v. De La Montanya, 112 Cal. 101, 108–116, 44 P. 345, 346–48 (1896); Raher v. Raher, 150 Iowa 511, 529–30, 129 N.W. 494, 500–01 (1911). The Supreme Court eventually rejected this view, and held that domicile in a state is a sufficient basis for in personam jurisdiction. See Milliken v. Meyer, 311 U.S. 457, 61 S.Ct. 339, 85 L.Ed. 278 (1940).

12. Riverside & Dan River Cotton Mills v. Menefee, 237 U.S. 189, 35 S.Ct. 579, 59 L.Ed. 910 (1915); Dewey v. Des Moines, 173 U.S. 193, 19 S.Ct. 379, 43 L.Ed. 665 (1899).

13. See supra § 5.2.

14. See, e.g., Flexner v. Farson, 248 U.S. 289, 39 S.Ct. 97, 63 L.Ed. 250 (1919); *Menefee*, 237 U.S. 189, 35 S.Ct. 579, 59 L.Ed. 910 (1915).

15. See, e.g., Goldey v. Morning News, 156 U.S. 518, 521, 15 S.Ct. 559, 560, 39 L.Ed. 517, 518 (1895).

The *Pennoyer* jurisdictional bases were adequate to handle most problems of that era. Individuals were not as mobile as nowadays, and being found—or owning property—within a state was often a reliable indicator that it was fair for that state to take jurisdiction. Significant difficulties developed, however. One was how to treat corporations. Corporations, as artificial persons, lack a physical embodiment and thus are not generally subject to jurisdiction by means of in-state service, even through the president.[16] The inability to obtain in personam jurisdiction over corporations by means of in-state service gave rise to the possibility of grave injustices, particularly for consumers of their products who might be forced to pursue them in distant states.[17] To handle this problem, the Supreme Court expanded greatly upon the notion of a defendant "consenting" to jurisdiction. In several cases, the Court held that if a non-resident defendant was "doing business" in the forum state, this was a manifestation of "consent" to jurisdiction in the forum.[18]

Another difficulty was the inability of these common law categories to handle common fact patterns. One recurrent example was the nonresident automobile driver who became involved in an accident with a resident in the forum state, but left the forum state before he could be served with process.[19] State legislatures responded to this problem by passing statutes that allowed plaintiffs to serve a state official fictitiously appointed as the defendant's "agent" to receive process—often the secretary of state—who would then in turn transmit the summons and complaint by mail to the non-resident defendant.[20] The Supreme Court eventually upheld these legislative efforts in the famous case of *Hess v. Pawloski*.[21] *Hess*, like the corporate jurisdiction cases, also relied upon the notion of "consent," reasoning that driving within a state was a

---

16. See, e.g., Riverside & Dan River Cotton Mills v. Menefee, 237 U.S. 189, 35 S.Ct. 579, 59 L.Ed. 910 (1915); Conley v. Mathieson Alkali Works, 190 U.S. 406, 23 S.Ct. 728, 47 L.Ed. 1113 (1903); *Goldey*, 156 U.S. 518, 15 S.Ct. 559, 39 L.Ed. 517. Some states, however, allowed for jurisdiction over corporations if the president or another officer could be served in the state. See, e.g., Pope v. Terre Haute Car & Mfg. Co., 107 N.Y. 61, 13 N.E. 592 (1887); Jester v. Baltimore Steam Packet Co., 131 N.C. 54, 42 S.E. 447 (1902).

17. Cf. Lafayette Ins. Co. v. French, 59 U.S. (18 How.) 404, 15 L.Ed. 451 (1855) (insurance policyholder allowed to sue corporation in policyholder's home because corporation did substantial business in policyholder's home state).

18. See, e.g., Chipman, Ltd. v. Thomas B. Jeffrey Co., 251 U.S. 373, 40 S.Ct. 172, 64 L.Ed. 314 (1920); International Harvester Co. of Am. v. Kentucky, 234 U.S. 579, 34 S.Ct. 944, 58 L.Ed. 1479 (1914); Old Wayne Mut. Life Ass'n of Indianapolis v. McDonough, 204 U.S. 8, 27 S.Ct. 236, 51 L.Ed. 345 (1907); but see Flexner v. Farson, 248 U.S. 289, 39 S.Ct. 97, 63 L.Ed. 250 (1919). For contemporaneous discussions of this era of case law, see Burdick, Service as a Requirement of Due Process in Actions in Personam, 20 Mich. L. Rev. 422 (1922); Scott, Jurisdiction over Nonresidents Doing Business Within a State, 32 Harv. L. Rev. 871 (1919).

19. See, e.g., Kane v. New Jersey, 242 U.S. 160, 37 S.Ct. 30, 61 L.Ed. 222 (1916).

20. For a discussion of these statutes and this era of case law, see Scott, Jurisdiction over Non–Resident Motorists, 39 Harv. L. Rev. 563 (1926).

21. 274 U.S. 352, 47 S.Ct. 632, 71 L.Ed. 1091 (1927).

sufficient manifestation of consent to jurisdiction by the nonresident motorist.[22]

It is clear, of course, that the Court did not rely upon "consent" in the ordinary sense of voluntary assent. In fact, the Court's implied consent rationale was unconnected to any mental state of the defendant. It rested upon the justice and practical necessity of the circumstance.[23] But this stretching of the fabric of the common law bases of jurisdiction eventually became powerful evidence of the need for a fundamental realignment in jurisdictional jurisprudence.

C. 1945–PRESENT: THE MINIMUM CONTACTS TEST

§ 5.4 The fundamental realignment foretold by the decay of the *Pennoyer*-era common law bases of jurisdiction[1] came about in *International Shoe Co. v. Washington*.[2] The plaintiff in *International Shoe* was the State of Washington, which brought an action through a state administrative agency, and ultimately the state courts, to require the defendant—a Delaware corporation with its principal offices in Missouri—to make statutory payments to the state unemployment insurance fund.[3] The defendant, as its name would suggest, was in the business of selling shoes, and for the years in question employed about a dozen salesmen in Washington.[4] The defendant supplied the salesmen with single shoes as samples; orders were actually filled by the home office in Missouri.[5] Commissions for the years in question totaled over $31,000.[6]

The defendant objected to the Washington state courts' exercise of jurisdiction over it, claiming that its activities in the state were insufficient to bring it within the "implied consent" rubric. In fact, the company's rather bizarre method of filling orders apparently was a conscious effort to avoid jurisdiction under a line of cases holding that "mere solicitation" of orders within a state was insufficient to establish consent.[7] The Court, however, discarded the consent metaphor.[8] In its place it substituted the more flexible notion that a defendant is subject to jurisdiction if it has "certain minimum contacts" with the forum in order to "not offend 'traditional notions of fair play and substantial justice.' "[9]

---

22. Id. at 356–57, 47 S.Ct. at 633–34, 71 L.Ed. at 1094–95.

23. Dodd, Jurisdiction in Personal Actions, 23 Ill. L. Rev. 427, 436 (1929).

§ 5.4

1. See supra § 5.3.

2. 326 U.S. 310, 66 S.Ct. 154, 90 L.Ed. 95 (1945).

3. Id. at 311–12, 66 S.Ct. at 156, 90 L.Ed. at 99–100.

4. Id. at 313, 66 S.Ct. at 156–157, 90 L.Ed. at 100.

5. Id. at 313–14, 66 S.Ct. at 156–157, 90 L.Ed. at 100–101.

6. Id. at 313, 66 S.Ct. at 156–157, 90 L.Ed. at 100.

7. See Cameron & Johnson, Death of a Salesman? Forum Shopping and Outcome Determination Under *International Shoe*, 28 U.C. Davis L. Rev. 769, 800 (1995).

8. *International Shoe*, 326 U.S. at 316–18, 66 S.Ct. at 158–159, 90 L.Ed. at 101–103.

9. Id. at 316, 66 S.Ct. at 158, 90 L.Ed. at 101 (quoting Milliken v. Meyer, 311 U.S. 457, 463, 61 S.Ct. 339, 343, 85 L.Ed. 278 (1940)).

This "minimum contacts"/"fair play and substantial justice" test was more comprehensive than its implied consent predecessor, and a more deliberate effort to link jurisdiction directly to basic fairness. Fair play, said the Court, requires enough "contacts ... as to make it reasonable ... to require the corporation to defend the particular suit."[10] Reasonableness depends, at least in part, on an "estimate of the inconveniences."[11] As for minimum contacts, the Court gave two polar examples of that term. Minimum contacts might exist when the corporation engages in "continuous and systematic" activities in the forum.[12] At the other end of the spectrum, "single or occasional acts of the corporate agent" might be enough to constitute minimum contacts if related to the suit.[13] Under this new test, the Court had little difficulty concluding that the International Shoe Company was amenable to jurisdiction. Its large volume of Washington business met the "continuous and systematic" test, and the direct nexus between the suit and its in-state activities met the "related act" test.[14]

A great deal of judicial and academic ink has been spilled attempting to unpack the notion of what constitutes minimum contacts.[15] To be sure, the minimum contacts test has some undesirable features, and the whole enterprise of judicially-supervised jurisdictional law carries with it uncertainty.[16] But there is no doubt that the minimum contacts test was an improvement over what went before it, and this explains its durability as the basic test for much of American jurisdiction.

As the minimum contacts test now so dominates jurisdictional law, in later chapters we discuss specific applications of it. Before undertaking this task, however, it is worthwhile to review some of the primary doctrinal developments in the first half century of the minimum contacts era. One of the most significant breaks that *International Shoe* appeared to make with the past was the diminished reliance on state sovereignty as the primary determinant of jurisdiction.[17] The major *Pennoyer*-era bases of jurisdiction depended upon symbolic assertions of state authority. For in rem jurisdiction the symbolic assertion consisted of the bringing of the defendant's property within the court's control; for the unwilling, non-resident defendant, in personam jurisdiction was conferred by the powerful symbol of a governmental official physically delivering the summons within the state's borders. In more directly

10. Id. at 317, 66 S.Ct. at 158, 90 L.Ed. at 102.

11. Id.

12. Id. at 320, 66 S.Ct. at 160, 90 L.Ed. at 104.

13. Id. at 318, 66 S.Ct. at 159, 90 L.Ed. at 103.

14. Id. at 320, 66 S.Ct. at 160, 90 L.Ed. at 104.

15. See, e.g., Weintraub, A Map out of the Personal Jurisdiction Labyrinth, 28 U.C. Davis L. Rev. 531, 531–32 n.5 (1995) (approximately 2300 reported minimum

contacts decisions in four years beginning in 1990).

16. See generally Borchers, Comparing Personal Jurisdiction in the United States and the European Community: Lessons for American Reform, 40 Am. J. Comp. L. 121 (1992).

17. See Lewis, The Three Deaths of "State Sovereignty" and The Curse of Abstraction in the Jurisprudence of Personal Jurisdiction, 58 Notre Dame L. Rev. 699 (1983).

linking jurisdiction to fairness, *International Shoe* seemed to downplay sovereignty.[18]

In recent times the Supreme Court has, however, occasionally stated that constitutional limitations on jurisdiction exist to check state sovereignty. In *Hanson v. Denckla*,[19] for instance, the Court stated that the due process limitations on jurisdiction are "more than a guarantee of immunity from inconvenient or distant litigation. They are a consequence of the territorial limitations on the power of respective States."[20] In *World–Wide Volkswagen Corp. v. Woodson*,[21] the Court described as a "related ... function" of the minimum contacts test ensuring "that the States, through their courts, do not reach out beyond the limits imposed on them by their status as coequal sovereigns in a federal system."[22] But the Court disavowed this language less than two years later,[23] and in other cases has suggested that sovereignty itself provides no check on state authority beyond that of basic fairness to defendants.[24]

Some of the Supreme Court's uncertainty over whether sovereignty remains an independent limitation on state court jurisdiction may explain the Court's recent suggestion that the minimum contacts test is itself subject to an overarching "reasonableness" test.[25] *Asahi Metal Industry Co. v. Superior Court*[26] was one of the relatively few cases in which the Supreme Court has considered the application of the minimum contacts test to foreign national defendants. The specific question in *Asahi* was whether a Japanese valve manufacturer could be haled into a California court to indemnify a Taiwanese motorcycle tube manufacturer, in a products liability matter, based upon the ultimate sale of the injury-causing tire-valve assembly in the forum state. Although the Court divided evenly on the question of whether the forum state sale of the finished product constituted minimum contacts, the Justices unanimously agreed that jurisdiction was unconstitutional because it failed to meet a broader standard of reasonableness.[27] Perhaps *Asahi*'s overarching reasonableness test is limited in application to the unusual facts of that case—the international parties and the collateral nature of the indemnity dispute.[28] The Court's willingness, however, to add a new

18. *International Shoe*, 326 U.S. at 316, 66 S.Ct. at 158, 90 L.Ed. at 101.

19. 357 U.S. 235, 78 S.Ct. 1228, 2 L.Ed.2d 1283 (1958).

20. Id. at 251, 78 S.Ct. at 1238, 2 L.Ed.2d at 1296.

21. 444 U.S. 286, 100 S.Ct. 559, 62 L.Ed.2d 490 (1980).

22. Id. at 299, 100 S.Ct. at 568, 62 L.Ed.2d. at 502.

23. See Insurance Corp. of Ireland v. Compagnie des Bauxites de Guinee, 456 U.S. 694, 702 n.10, 102 S.Ct. 2099, 2104 n.10, 72 L.Ed.2d 492, 501 n.10 (1982).

24. See, e.g., Phillips Petroleum v. Shutts, 472 U.S. 797, 105 S.Ct. 2965, 86 L.Ed.2d 628 (1985); Calder v. Jones, 465 U.S. 783, 104 S.Ct. 1482, 79 L.Ed.2d 804

(1984); Keeton v. Hustler Magazine, Inc., 465 U.S. 770, 104 S.Ct. 1473, 79 L.Ed.2d 790 (1984).

25. See Hay, Flexibility versus Predictability and Uniformity in Choice of Law, 226 Recueil des Cours 285, 322 (1991).

26. 480 U.S. 102, 107 S.Ct. 1026, 94 L.Ed.2d 92 (1987).

27. Id. at 113–16, 107 S.Ct. at 1032–34, 94 L.Ed.2d at 105–07; id. at 116–21, 107 S.Ct. at 1034–37, 94 L.Ed.2d at 107–10 (Brennan, J., concurring and concurring in the judgment).

28. See Perschbacher, Minimum Contacts Reapplied: Mr. Justice Brennan Has It His Way in *Burger King Corp. v. Rudzewicz*, 1986 Ariz. St. L.J. 585, 589 n.27 (suggesting limited role for *Asahi*).

layer to the jurisdictional test reveals that fundamental questions remain unanswered as to the ultimate nature of the constitutional inquiry.

Despite persistent uncertainties as to its boundaries, the scope of application of the minimum contacts test has expanded substantially since its original conception in *International Shoe*. Some language in *International Shoe* suggested that the minimum contacts test applies only to corporations,[29] but the Supreme Court rejected that view and applied it to individual defendants as well.[30] The most dramatic expansion in the reign of the minimum contacts test, however, occurred when the Court, in *Shaffer v. Heitner*,[31] transmuted the test from one applicable only to in personam actions to in rem actions as well. The minimum contacts test, as we have seen, developed as the successor to the implied consent test, which rationalized in personam jurisdiction even in cases in which the *Pennoyer*-era bases could not comfortably allow for it. But in *Shaffer*, the Court actually used the test to limit one of the *Pennoyer*-era bases: in rem jurisdiction through pre-judgment control and dominion over property. Although this in rem practice had gone largely unquestioned,[32] the Court concluded that pre-judgment attachment of the defendant's property was not constitutionally sufficient for jurisdiction unless the defendant had minimum contacts with the forum state.[33] In so doing, the Supreme Court moved toward ending the practical significance of the distinction between in personam and in rem actions. The tale of American jurisdiction is thus one of continual judicial evolution, a process likely to continue apace.

III.   TRADITIONAL JURISDICTIONAL RELATIONSHIPS

A. IN REM JURISDICTION

§ 5.5   As discussed above,[1] the common law of jurisdiction divided the subject into two broad categories: in rem and in personam. The Supreme Court, in *Shaffer v. Heitner*,[2] partially collapsed the significance of this division by holding that the minimum contacts test—initially developed as a substitute for the old "implied consent" theory of in personam jurisdiction[3]—also acts as a constitutional check on in rem

---

29. See *International Shoe*, 326 U.S. at 316–17, 66 S.Ct. at 158, 90 L.Ed. at 101–102.

30. See Shaffer v. Heitner, 433 U.S. 186, 204 n.19, 97 S.Ct. 2569, 2579 n.19, 53 L.Ed.2d 683, 697 n.19 (1977). Four Justices suggested in Burnham v. Superior Court, 495 U.S. 604, 610 n.1, 110 S.Ct. 2105, 2110 n.1, 109 L.Ed.2d 631, 639 n.1 (1990) that the notion of "continuous and systematic" contacts might apply only to business entities, not to individual defendants.

31. 433 U.S. at 204 n.19, 97 S.Ct. at 2579 n.19, 53 L.Ed.2d at 697 n.19.

32. One prescient opinion by Judge Gibbons went some considerable distance towards anticipating *Shaffer*. See Jonnet v. Dollar Sav. Bank, 530 F.2d 1123, 1132, 1136–37 (3d Cir.1976).

33. *Shaffer*, 433 U.S. at 212, 97 S.Ct. at 2583, 53 L.Ed.2d at 703.

§ 5.5

1. See supra § 5.2.

2. 433 U.S. 186, 204 n.19, 97 S.Ct. 2569, 2579 n.19, 53 L.Ed.2d 683, 697 n.19 (1977).

3. See supra § 5.4.

jurisdiction. The distinctions between the traditional categories retain some practical significance, however.[4]

In rem jurisdiction is literally jurisdiction over property. Of course, this is a fiction, because determining interests in property quite obviously affects the persons who claim ownership.[5] Justice Holmes put it this way: "If the technical object of the suit is to establish a claim against some particular person, with a judgment which generally in theory, at least, binds his body, or to bar some individual claim or objection, so that only certain persons are entitled to be heard in defense, the action is in personam.... If, on the other hand, the object is to bar indifferently all who might be minded to make an objection of any sort against the right sought to be established, and if any one in the world has a right to be heard on the strength of alleging facts which, if true, show an inconsistent interest, the proceeding is in rem.... All proceedings, like all rights, are really against persons.... Personification and naming the res as defendant are mere symbols, not the essential matter. They are fictions, conveniently expressing the nature of the process and the result; nothing more."[6]

Justice Holmes's formulation captures the essence of what is commonly called "true" or "pure" in rem jurisdiction.[7] True in rem cases make the res, a piece of property, the "defendant," and purport to dispose of the rights of the "whole world" with regard to the property.[8] A proceeding to dispose of property in a decedent's estate is an example of such a proceeding; the decree vests rights in the parties that are good as against the whole world.[9] An in rem decree, however, affects *only* the property.[10] It does not preclude a party in a later in personam action from relitigating factual and legal issues identical to those resolved in the in rem action.[11]

Two prominent features of in rem jurisdiction have been undercut partially by developments in constitutional law, however. One development, mentioned at the beginning of this section, is the doctrine of *Shaffer*. In rem jurisdiction traditionally proceeded upon the in-state locus of the property, without regard to the connection—or lack thereof—between the forum and any of the potential claimants.[12] True in rem jurisdiction is probably less affected by *Shaffer* than are other exercises

4. See infra § 5.9.

5. Restatement, Second, Conflict of Laws, ch. 3, topic 2, intro. note (1971).

6. Tyler v. Judges of the Court of Registration, 175 Mass. 71, 76, 55 N.E. 812, 814 (1900). See generally Fraser, Actions in Rem, 34 Cornell L.Q. 29 (1948); Smit, The Enduring Utility of In Rem Rules: A Lasting Legacy of *Pennoyer v. Neff*, 43 Brooklyn L. Rev. 600 (1977).

7. See, e.g., Faber v. Althoff, 168 Ariz. 213, 217, 812 P.2d 1031, 1037 (App.1990); Perlstein v. Perlstein, 152 Conn. 152, 157, 204 A.2d 909, 911 (1964); Vickery v. Garret-son, 527 A.2d 293, 301 (D.C.App.1987); Lewis, The Three Deaths of "State Sovereignty" and the Curse of Abstraction in the Jurisprudence of Personal Jurisdiction, 699, 702 (1983).

8. Restatement, Second, Conflict of Laws, ch. 3, topic 2, intro. note (1971).

9. Id.

10. Id.

11. See, e.g., Combs v. Combs, 249 Ky. 155, 60 S.W.2d 368 (1933).

12. Restatement, Second, Conflict of Laws §§ 59–63 (1971).

of in rem jurisdiction, but it remains subject to *Shaffer*'s command nonetheless.[13] The other abolished feature of in rem jurisdiction is the fiction that the "law assumes that property is always in the possession of its owner ... and it proceeds upon the theory that its seizure will inform him [of] any proceedings authorized by law upon such seizure...."[14] As a result, many state statutes provided for in rem notice in a manner unlikely to actually inform, such as publication[15] or posting[16] of the summons. This fiction, however, was relegated to the realm of the unconstitutional by a series of Supreme Court decisions holding that in all actions—whether denominated in rem or in personam—notice to interested parties must be "reasonably calculated" to actually notify them of the proceeding.[17] Ordinarily this means notification by mail or personal service; notification by publication or posting is constitutionally sufficient only as a last resort for parties who cannot be located with reasonable effort.[18]

B. QUASI IN REM JURISDICTION

§ 5.6 Quasi in rem jurisdiction, as its name suggests, is jurisdiction that resembles in rem jurisdiction, but not in all of its particulars. Quasi in rem, like true in rem, jurisdiction is premised on the court's pre-judgment dominion and control over property.[1] Quasi in rem proceedings traditionally shared in rem's important jurisdictional characteristic that the locus of the property within the forum state was, by itself, sufficient to establish jurisdiction.[2] Unlike in rem judgments, however, quasi in rem judgments do not bind "the whole world." Rather, they determine only the interests of the named parties in the property.[3] In that latter sense, quasi in rem proceedings are like in personam proceedings.

Within the category of quasi in rem proceedings, one can detect a further division. On one side are more classical quasi in rem proceedings that most closely resemble true in rem proceedings. In this category, "the plaintiff asserts an interest in [the res], and seeks to have his interest established against the claim of a designated person or per-

---

13. *Shaffer*, 433 U.S. at 196, 97 S.Ct. at 2575, 53 L.Ed.2d at 692; cf. 433 U.S. at 216, 97 S.Ct. at 2586, 53 L.Ed.2d at 705 (Powell, J., concurring) (arguing for the retention of true in rem jurisdiction for immovable property).

14. Pennoyer v. Neff, 95 U.S. (5 Otto) 714, 727, 24 L.Ed. 565, 570 (1878).

15. E.g., id.

16. E.g., Walker v. City of Hutchison, 352 U.S. 112, 77 S.Ct. 200, 1 L.Ed.2d 178 (1956).

17. See Mullane v. Central Hanover Bank & Trust Co., 339 U.S. 306, 318, 70 S.Ct. 652, 659, 94 L.Ed. 865 (1950).

18. Mennonite Board of Missions v. Adams, 462 U.S. 791, 103 S.Ct. 2706, 77 L.Ed.2d 180 (1983) (notice by publication constitutionally inadequate).

§ 5.6

1. Pennoyer v. Neff, 95 U.S. (5 Otto) 714, 728, 24 L.Ed. 565, 570 (1878).

2. See, e.g., Harris v. Balk, 198 U.S. 215, 25 S.Ct. 625, 49 L.Ed. 1023 (1905) (situs of debtor within forum state sufficient for quasi in rem jurisdiction over creditor).

3. Restatement, Second, Conflict of Laws ch. 3, topic 2, intro. note (1971).

sons."[4] The Second Conflicts Restatement lists as an example of such a proceeding an action to foreclose a mortgage.[5] The reason is that the foreclosure action establishes the mortgagor's rights in the property as against the mortgagee, but not as against other parties who claim an interest in the property in some other manner—say, for instance, through an easement. These classical quasi in rem proceedings resemble true in rem proceedings in the important sense that the proceeding is really "about" the property, and any judgment is limited in its effect to the property.[6] But even these classical quasi in rem proceedings differ significantly from true in rem proceedings in that the former resolve only certain claims as they regard certain parties.

On the other side of this division within quasi in rem proceedings are those that more closely resemble in personam proceedings. These proceedings—which result in what is sometimes called "attachment jurisdiction"[7]—really have nothing to do with the property; rather, the property's presence within the forum state is an excuse to assert a personal claim against the property's owner.[8] The classic example is *Harris v. Balk*,[9] in which the Supreme Court held that a state court could assert quasi in rem jurisdiction based upon the "attachment" of the body of a debtor. The debtor was held to be "property" of the creditor, which allowed the plaintiff to assert a wholly-unrelated claim against the creditor solely because the debtor had sojourned to the forum state.[10] A more modern example is the New York Court of Appeals' *Seider v. Roth*[11] doctrine, which allowed a plaintiff in an accident case to assert quasi in rem jurisdiction over a tortfeasor wherever the tortfeasor's *insurer* had an office. The theory was that the insurance policy was property that had its situs wherever the insurance company had an office.[12]

It is easy to see that the attachment type of quasi in rem proceeding is little different from an in personam action, except that as long as the proceeding remains quasi in rem[13] the effect of the judgment is limited to the property. But the prospect for abuse is great. Especially in today's mobile world, the fact that a defendant owns unrelated property in the forum bears little relationship to the fairness of litigating there.

4. Restatement, Second, Conflict of Laws ch. 3, topic 2, intro. note (1971).

5. Restatement, Second, Conflict of Laws ch. 3, topic 2, intro. note (1971).

6. Restatement, Second, Conflict of Laws ch. 3, topic 2, intro. note (1971).

7. See, e.g., Polacke v. Superior Court, 170 Ariz. 217, 222, 823 P.2d 84, 85 (App. 1991); Restatement, Second, Judgments § 8, cmnt. a (1982).

8. Restatement, Second, Judgments § 8 (1982).

9. 198 U.S. 215, 25 S.Ct. 625, 49 L.Ed. 1023 (1905).

10. Id.

11. 17 N.Y.2d 111, 216 N.E.2d 312, 269 N.Y.S.2d 99 (1966).

12. Id. at 114, 216 N.E.2d at 315, 269 N.Y.S.2d at 102.

13. As voluntary appearance in a case is a basis for in personam jurisdiction. See supra § 5.3. To cure the problem of converting in rem matters to in personam matters, many states allow what is known as a "limited appearance," which allows a defendant to defend in the case, without converting the matter to an in personam matter. See infra § 5.20.

It was especially the attachment type of quasi in rem jurisdiction at which *Shaffer v. Heitner*[14] was directed. The state court proceedings in *Shaffer* were a good example of attachment jurisdiction. The litigation was against directors and officers of the Greyhound Corporation for their alleged mismanagement of the company, and jurisdiction in the Delaware state courts was premised on attachment of their stock holdings, to which state law gave a fictional situs in Delaware as the state of incorporation.[15] The *Shaffer* Court pointed out that the assigning of the stock's situs to Delaware was no guarantee of its fairness as a forum, and decreed that henceforth "all assertions of state court jurisdiction must be evaluated according to the [minimum contacts] standards set forth in *International Shoe* and its progeny."[16] *Shaffer*'s evident goal—by requiring the existence of minimum contacts between the defendant and the forum even in proceedings that are not in personam—was to curb the abuses that the attachment type of quasi in rem jurisdiction allowed. In fact, the two famous examples cited above—*Harris v. Balk* and *Seider v. Roth*—have been specifically rejected by the Supreme Court. *Harris* was laid to rest by a footnote in *Shaffer*[17] and *Seider* by the subsequent case of *Rush v. Savchuk*.[18]

C. STATUS JURISDICTION

§ 5.7 An important exception to the in rem/in personam dichotomy is status proceedings. Status proceedings are those involving the personal relationships of persons, most commonly divorce and custody matters—though not matters ancillary to these, such as support.[1] Status matters resemble in rem matters, although the "res" is the relationship, which is generally given a fictional location in the domicile of any party to the relationship. Thus, a court in the domicile of either party to a divorce generally has jurisdiction to dissolve the marriage.[2] Again, however, such a court may well not have jurisdiction to award support, which is an in personam matter and thus requires jurisdiction founded upon an acceptable in personam basis.[3]

The same is true of child custody and support matters. Custody matters are status matters, and a state in which the person is present or domiciled generally has jurisdiction to determine custody.[4] Support mat-

---

14. 433 U.S. 186, 97 S.Ct. 2569, 53 L.Ed.2d 683 (1977).

15. Id. at 192, 97 S.Ct. at 2573.

16. Id. at 212, 97 S.Ct. at 2584.

17. *Shaffer*, 433 U.S. at 212 n.39, 97 S.Ct. at 2584 n.39, 53 L.Ed.2d at 703 n.39.

18. 444 U.S. 320, 100 S.Ct. 571, 62 L.Ed.2d 516 (1980).

§ 5.7

1. Restatement, Second, Conflict of Laws §§ 69–79 (1971). See also infra § 15.4 for a discussion of divorce jurisdiction.

2. See, e.g., Williams v. North Carolina, 317 U.S. 287, 63 S.Ct. 207, 87 L.Ed. 279 (1942); Haddock v. Haddock, 201 U.S. 562, 26 S.Ct. 525, 50 L.Ed. 867 (1906) (domicile of innocent spouse basis for jurisdiction); Restatement, Second, Conflict of Laws § 71 (1971).

3. See, e.g., Estin v. Estin, 334 U.S. 541, 68 S.Ct. 1213, 92 L.Ed. 1561 (1948); Restatement, Second, Conflict of Laws § 77 (1971). See also infra § 15.27 for a discussion of "divisible" divorces.

4. Restatement, Second, Conflict of Laws § 79 (1971). The Uniform Child Custody Jurisdiction Act—in force in all 50 states and the District of Columbia—and its federal counterpart, the Parental Kidnap-

ters, however, are in personam, and require an acceptable in personam basis for jurisdiction.[5]

Status matters have existed as an exception to the usual jurisdictional structure at least since *Pennoyer v. Neff*.[6] Moreover, jurisdiction in status matters appears not to have been affected by *Shaffer v. Heitner*. Although *Shaffer* broadly stated that "all assertions" of state court jurisdiction are subject to the minimum contacts test,[7] in a footnote the Court said that its opinion should not be taken to "suggest that jurisdictional doctrines ... such as particularized rules governing of status ... are inconsistent with the standard of fairness."[8] Most have understood this to mean that status matters continue to operate within the traditional framework, independent of the need to demonstrate minimum contacts between the absent party and the forum state.[9]

D. IN PERSONAM JURISDICTION

§ 5.8 All proceedings that do not fall into one of the other categories—in rem, quasi in rem or status—are in personam. Several classical bases for in personam jurisdiction were recognized by the common law and generally continue in effect today.[1] They are in-state service of an individual defendant,[2] voluntary appearance[3] and consent[4]—as well as those based upon the "allegiance" of the defendant to the forum state—such as nationality, domicile and residence.[5] All of these bases are

ping Prevention Act, 28 U.S.C.A. § 1738A, deny jurisdiction to any state that is not the child's "home state" in order to avoid a parent unhappy with a child's current custody decree from obtaining jurisdiction in a new state by forcibly removing the child. See generally Note, Interstate Child Custody and the Parental Kidnapping Prevention Act, 45 Hastings L.J. 1329 (1994).

5. See, e.g., Burnham v. Superior Court, 495 U.S. 604, 110 S.Ct. 2105, 109 L.Ed.2d 631 (1990); Kulko v. Superior Court, 436 U.S. 84, 98 S.Ct. 1690, 56 L.Ed.2d 132 (1978).

6. 95 U.S. (5 Otto) 714, 733–34, 24 L.Ed. 565, 572–73 (1878).

7. 433 U.S. at 212, 97 S.Ct. at 2584.

8. Id. at 208 n.30, 97 S.Ct. at 2582 n.30, 53 L.Ed.2d at 700 n.30.

9. See generally Bodenheimer & Neely–Kvarme, 12, U.C. Davis L. Rev. 229 (1979); cf. Cox, Would That *Burnham* Had Not Come to be Done Insane! ... and Some Thoughts on Divorce Jurisdiction in a Minimum Contacts World, 58 Tenn. L. Rev 497 (1991).

§ 5.8

1. See, e.g., Burnham v. Superior Court, 495 U.S. 604, 110 S.Ct. 2105, 109 L.Ed.2d

631 (1990) (in personam jurisdiction based upon in-state service of the defendant).

2. See, e.g., *Burnham*, 495 U.S. 604, 110 S.Ct. 2105, 109 L.Ed.2d 631; Barrell v. Benjamin, 15 Mass. 354, 358 (1819); Restatement, Second, Conflict of Laws § 28 (1971).

3. See, e.g., Adam v. Saenger, 303 U.S. 59, 58 S.Ct. 454, 82 L.Ed. 649 (1938); York v. Texas, 137 U.S. 15, 11 S.Ct. 9, 34 L.Ed. 604 (1890); Restatement, Second, Conflict of Laws §§ 33–34 (1971).

4. See, e.g., Lafayette Ins. Co. v. French, 59 U.S. (18 How.) 404, 407, 15 L.Ed. 451, 452 (1855); Restatement, Second, Conflict of Laws § 32 (1971).

5. References to the notion of a defendant being subject to in personam jurisdiction can be found at least as far back as Mills v. Duryee, 11 U.S. (7 Cranch) 481, 486, 3 L.Ed. 411, 414 (1813) (Johnson, J., dissenting). Interestingly, however, the Second Restatement takes the position that these bases, such as residence and domicile, were not accepted at common law, requiring statutory authorization of them. See, e.g., Restatement, Second, Conflict of Laws § 29, comment c (1971). The question is probably of only historical interest, however, as every or nearly every state has legislation that authorizes in personam jurisdic-

apparently constitutionally acceptable.[6] Beyond this traditional list extends the expansive minimum contacts test,[7] to which we devote substantial attention in later chapters.

E.   CONTINUING SIGNIFICANCE OF TRADITIONAL CATEGORIES

§ 5.9   As discussed above,[1] *Shaffer v. Heitner*[2] eliminated a good deal of the practical significance of the traditional categories of jurisdiction. *Shaffer* involved an exercise of quasi in rem jurisdiction. In fact, it was the most tenuous kind of quasi in rem jurisdiction—so-called "attachment jurisdiction"[3]—because the seized property (the stock certificates) bore no relationship to the underlying dispute of whether the corporation had been managed properly. The Supreme Court held that a state's decision to treat the property as fictionally present in the forum could not itself confer jurisdiction. In order to satisfy the Constitution, jurisdiction of this kind had to be independently tested for fairness under the minimum contacts test.[4]

By holding that in rem, quasi in rem and in personam jurisdiction are all subject to the same constitutional test, *Shaffer* eliminated a good deal of quasi in rem jurisdiction's utility from the plaintiff's point of view. Quasi in rem jurisdiction—particularly the attachment variety in which the dispute and the seized property are unrelated—was useful to plaintiffs precisely because it authorized jurisdiction in many cases in which in personam jurisdiction could not be asserted.[5] By collapsing the constitutional test, *Shaffer* ensures that there will be fewer cases in which quasi in rem jurisdiction is available and in personam is not.

Shaffer did not, however, declare in rem and quasi in rem jurisdiction unconstitutional. In fact, *Shaffer* appears to affect primarily only the attachment type of quasi in rem proceedings. True in rem and classical quasi in rem proceedings both involve a direct relationship between the property and the litigation.[6] While both are subject to the

---

tion upon such a basis, and the exercise of such jurisdiction is clearly constitutional. See, e.g., Milliken v. Meyer, 311 U.S. 457, 61 S.Ct. 339, 85 L.Ed. 278 (1940) (domicile); Blackmer v. United States, 284 U.S. 421, 52 S.Ct. 252, 76 L.Ed. 375 (1932) (United States citizenship requires a citizen to obey a federal court subpoena even when living abroad).

6.   See, e.g., *Burnham*, 495 U.S. 604, 110 S.Ct. 2105, 109 L.Ed.2d 631 (plurality opinion concluding that traditional bases of jurisdiction are automatically constitutional).

7.   See supra § 5.3.

§ 5.9

1.   See supra § 5.6.

2.   433 U.S. 186, 97 S.Ct. 2569, 53 L.Ed.2d 683 (1977).

3.   See, e.g., Polacke v. Superior Court, 170 Ariz. 217, 222, 823 P.2d 84, 85 (App. 1991); Restatement, Second, Judgments § 8, cmnt. a (1982).

4.   Shaffer v. Heitner, 433 U.S. 186, 212, 97 S.Ct. 2569, 2584, 53 L.Ed.2d 683, 703 (1977).

5.   See, e.g., Harris v. Balk, 198 U.S. 215, 25 S.Ct. 625, 49 L.Ed. 1023 (1905) (debtor's presence in forum state can create quasi-in-rem jurisdiction); Seider v. Roth, 17 N.Y.2d 111, 216 N.E.2d 312, 269 N.Y.S.2d 99 (1966) (insurance company's prospective obligation to defend and indemnify is property subject to attachment).

6.   See supra §§ 5.5—5.6.

minimum contacts test under *Shaffer*, it is hard to imagine a circumstance in which the presence of the property in the forum would not satisfy the minimum contacts test because of the necessarily direct link between the property and the dispute. *Shaffer* therefore affects cases in which the property is unrelated to the dispute, and the Court quite properly recognized that the presence of unrelated property is no guarantee of jurisdictional fairness.[7] While *Shaffer*'s effect is clearly substantial, its ultimate impact on in rem proceedings is perhaps less than one might imagine.

While the distinction between in personam, quasi in rem and in rem jurisdiction is constitutionally irrelevant, it may not be so for state law purposes. Even if in personam jurisdiction is not available as a matter of state law, quasi in rem jurisdiction is a possibility—provided, of course, that the minimum contacts test is not offended. A leading example is the New York Court of Appeals' decision in *Banco Ambrosiano S.P.A. v. Artoc Bank & Trust Ltd.*,[8] which involved a commercial dispute between two banks over repayment of a loan. The plaintiff commenced the action by seizing the defendant's New York bank accounts. New York's fairly narrow in personam jurisdictional statute[9] would not have allowed for jurisdiction, but New York's other jurisdiction statute—which allows for jurisdiction "over persons, property and status as might have been exercised heretofore"[10]—was held by New York's high court to authorize quasi in rem jurisdiction.[11] Because the defendant bank maintained regular dealings in New York, the Court of Appeals concluded that the minimum contacts test was satisfied, and thus the plaintiff was able to successfully invoke quasi in rem jurisdiction even though in personam jurisdiction was unavailable.[12]

Another significant aspect to the traditional categories, even after *Shaffer*, is the unique treatment of status matters. As noted above, status matters (such as custody and divorce) were recognized by the common law as requiring different jurisdictional treatment.[13] Thus, as a general proposition, the presence or domicile of one party is usually sufficient to allow jurisdiction in such cases.[14] *Shaffer* noted the existence of these specialized status rules, and was careful to leave them largely in their traditional form.[15]

A fascinating use of *in rem* jurisdiction has originated under the Anticybersquatting Consumer Protection Act, ("ACPA"),[16] which took effect on November 29, 1999. "Cybersquatting" is the practice of registering Internet domain names that potentially infringe on another's

---

7. See supra § 5.6.

8. 62 N.Y.2d 65, 464 N.E.2d 432, 476 N.Y.S.2d 64 (1984).

9. N.Y. Civ. Prac. L. & . R. § 302.

10. N.Y. Civ. Prac. L. & R. § 301.

11. *Banco Ambrosiano*, 62 N.Y.2d at 71–72, 464 N.E.2d at 435, 476 N.Y.S.2d at 67.

12. Id.

13. See supra § 5.7.

14. See supra § 5.7.

15. See *Shaffer*, 433 U.S. at 208 n.30, 97 S.Ct. at 2582 n.30, 53 L.Ed. at 700 n.30.

16. 15 U.S.C.A. § 1125(d). For an overview, see Note, Masters of Their Domains: Trademark Holders Now Have New Ways to Control Their Marks in Cyberspace, 5 Roger Williams U.L. Rev. 563 (2000).

trademark.[17] Often, the person registering the domain name hopes to profit at the expense of the owner of the mark by either intercepting internet traffic intended for the owner's business or by selling the domain name to the mark's owner. The ACPA seeks to combat unfair practices of this sort.

15 U.S.C.A § 1125(d)(1)(A) ("Cyberpiracy prevention") gives a civil cause of action against a registrant who "has a bad faith intention to profit from that mark" and "registers, traffics in, or uses a domain name that"—with regard to so-called "famous marks"—"is identical or confusingly similar to or dilutive of that mark." Such a civil action allows for damages against the registrant as well as other remedies, including cancellation of the domain name registration. A major practical problem, however, is that domain name registration is done electronically and fairly often under aliases,[18] making it difficult to find such registrants, let alone to serve and obtain *in personam* jurisdiction over them.

Thus, as an alternative to *in personam* civil actions, the ACPA provides that "[t]he owner of a mark may file an *in rem* civil action against a domain name in the judicial district in which the domain name registrar, domain name registry, or other domain name authority . . . is located. . . ."[19] The remedies in such *in rem* actions "shall be limited to a court order for the forfeiture or cancellation of the domain name or the transfer of the domain name to the owner of the mark."[20] As a practical matter, however, this relief is often the best that the holder of the mark can expect, making an *in rem* proceeding the preferred vehicle for many mark owners.[21] *In rem* proceedings are permitted, however, only if the mark owner "is not able to obtain *in personam* jurisdiction over [the

---

17. See, e.g., Caesars World, Inc. v. Caesars–Palace.Com, 112 F.Supp.2d 502 (E.D.Va.2000). The *in rem* jurisdictional provisions have also been applied to claims both for infringement and dilution. See Harrods Ltd. v. Sixty Internet Domain Names, 302 F.3d 214 (4th Cir. 2002). However, other courts take the position that the transfer-of-domain remedy available under the statute's *in rem* provisions cannot be used to redress a dilution claim. *See* Porsche Cars North America v. Porsche. Net, 302 F.3d 248, 260–61 (4th Cir. 2002).

18. See Note, supra note 16, at 576, n. 87.

19. 15 U.S.C.A. § 1125(d)(2).

20. 15 U.S.C.A. § 1125(d)(2)(D)(i). Under the ACPA, *in rem* actions must be brought in the district in which the domain-name authority or the entity registering the domain is located because this is the "situs" of the domain name. The Second Circuit summarized as follows:

"the ACPA's basic *in rem* jurisdictional grant, contained in subsection (d)(2)(A), contemplates exclusively a judicial district within which the registrar or other

domain-name authority is located. A plaintiff must initiate an *in rem* action by filing a complaint in that judicial district and no other. Upon receiving proper written notification that the complaint has been filed, the domain-name authority must deposit with the court documentation 'sufficient to establish the court's control and authority regarding the disposition of . . . the domain name,' as required by subsection (d)(2)(D). This combination of filing and depositing rules encompasses the basic, mandatory procedure for bringing and maintaining an *in rem* action under the ACPA."

See Mattel Inc. v. Barbie–Club.Com, 310 F.3d 293, 306 (2d Cir. 2002).

Add to fn. 24 (in 2001 Pocket Part):

Also distinguishing *Shaffer* on these grounds and upholding the ACPA *in rem* provision is Porsche Cars North America v. Porsche.net, 302 F.3d 248, 259–60 (4th Cir. 2002).

21. See, e.g., Heathmount A.E. Corp. v. Technodome.Com, 106 F.Supp.2d 860, 863 (E.D.Va.2000).

registrant] or 'though due diligence was not able to find' the registrant.[22] Interestingly, this provision thus puts a 'reverse' incentive on the mark owner to show that the registrant does *not* have minimum contacts with the forum state."[23]

Of course, this raises questions regarding the constitutionality of this use of *in rem* jurisdiction, at least if the registrant does not (or cannot be show to) have minimum contacts with the forum state. The courts that have considered this issue thus far have rejected the constitutional challenge. One court to consider expressly the *Shaffer* problem limited the Supreme Court's contacts requirement to "*in rem* proceedings where the underlying cause of action is unrelated to property which is located in the forum state."[24] That court distinguished ACPA *in rem* actions from the derivative action involved in *Shaffer* because under the ACPA "the domain name ... is not only related to the cause of action but is its entire subject matter."[25]

There is some appeal to this line of argument, as *Shaffer* clearly was directed at *quasi in rem* proceedings in which the property is unrelated to the subject matter of the dispute.[26] To sustain this argument, however, *Shaffer's* broad language, however, must be read non-literally to support the constitutionality of the ACPA's *in rem* provisions, as *Shaffer's* conclusion that the minimum contacts test covers "all assertions of state court jurisdiction" would seem to be at odds with allowing "contactless" *in rem* jurisdiction.[27]

Nevertheless, the ACPA's *in rem* provisions are a fair and needed innovation and should be upheld. First, because of the limited nature of the relief available (cancelation or transfer of the mark), allowing jurisdiction based upon a lesser showing than that required for *in personam* actions seems eminently fair. The limited kind of *in rem* jurisdiction allowed here is a fair cry from the abusive uses of *quasi in rem* jurisdiction sanctioned in the pre-*Shaffer* era.[28] Second, because the ACPA is a federal statute allowing such actions in federal court, the relevant constitutional yardstick is the Due Process Clause of the Fifth Amendment, not the Fourteenth Amendment, that governs state-court jurisdiction. Because the Fifth Amendment generally has been interpreted to presumptively allow for jurisdiction as long as the affected party

22. 15 U.S.C.A. § 1125(d)(2)(A)(ii).

23. See, e.g., *Heathmount*, 106 F.Supp.2d at 862.

24. *See Caesars World*, 112 F.Supp.2d at 504. Also distinguishing *Shaffer* on these grounds and upholding the ACPA *in rem* provision is Porsche Cars North America v. Porsche.net, 302 F.3d 248, 259–60 (4th Cir. 2002).

25. *See Caesars World*, 112 F.Supp.2d at 504.

26. See supra § 5.7.

27. *Shaffer*, 433 U.S. at 212, 97 S.Ct. at 2585. Note, however, that the Supreme Court has already read this language non-

literally so as not to limit the availability of state-court *in personam* jurisdiction based upon in-state service of the summons. See infra § 6.2, discussing Burnham v. Superior Court, 495 U.S. 604, 110 S.Ct. 2105, 109 L.Ed.2d 631 (1990).

28. See, e.g., Harris v. Balk, 198 U.S. 215, 25 S.Ct. 625, 49 L.Ed. 1023 (1905) ("attachment" of the body of a debtor of the defendant allowed plaintiff to proceed in an essentially *in personam* action against the defendant in an inconvenient forum with which defendant had no meaningful connection).

has contacts with the United States considered as a whole, as opposed to with the forum *state* only as generally required under the fourteenth amendment,[29] many uses of the ACPA may be insulated from meaningful constitutional attack. Finally, the *Shaffer* court itself recognized that there might be a need for *in rem* jurisdiction based solely on "the presence of the defendant's property ... when no other forum is available to the plaintiff."[30] By restricting *in rem* proceedings to those cases in which *in personam* jurisdiction cannot be obtained, Congress appears to have brought the ACPA's provisions within this safe harbor.

IV. NEW JURISDICTIONAL RELATIONSHIPS

A. SPECIFIC JURISDICTION

1. *Related Contacts: Distinguishing Specific from General Jurisdiction*

§ 5.10 The minimum contacts test first articulated by the Supreme Court in *International Shoe Co. v. Washington*[1] has continued for over a half century as the most significant jurisdictional test in the United States. *International Shoe* did not, however, offer a comprehensive definition of what that term means; instead, it set forth broad categories. At one end of the spectrum, the Court stated that a corporate defendant could be subjected to jurisdiction in a state in which it carried on "continuous and systematic"[2] activities, even on "causes of action arising from dealings entirely distinct from those activities."[3] At the other end of the spectrum, the Court suggested that far less substantial activities might give rise to jurisdiction if the defendant's "obligations arise out of or are connected with the activities within the state...."[4]

It is generally accepted today that this language in *International Shoe* creates an important dichotomy between "specific" and "general" jurisdiction.[5] *International Shoe* clearly accorded more weight to contacts that "arise out of or are connected with" the dispute. In modern

---

29. See infra § 10.2.

30. *Shaffer*, 433 U.S. at 211 n.37, 97 S.Ct. at 2583 n.37.

§ 5.10

1. 326 U.S. 310, 66 S.Ct. 154, 90 L.Ed. 95 (1945).

2. Id. at 317, 66 S.Ct. at 158, 90 L.Ed. at 102.

3. Id. at 318, 66 S.Ct. at 159, 90 L.Ed. at 103.

4. Id. at 319, 66 S.Ct. at 159, 90 L.Ed. at 103.

5. The origination of this term appears to be von Mehren & Trautman, Jurisdiction to Adjudicate: A Suggested Analysis, 79 Harv. L. Rev. 1121, 1135–45 (1966). Similar dichotomies appear in the jurisdictional law of other legal systems, although the terms "general" and "specific" are in wide usage only in the United States. See generally M. Reimann, Conflict of Laws in Western Europe: A Guide Through the Jungle 75–77 (1995); Borchers, Comparing Personal Jurisdiction in the United States and the European Community: Lessons for American Reform, 40 Am. J. Comp. L. 121 (1992); Hay, Flexibility Versus Predictability and Uniformity in Choice of Law, 226 Recueil des Cours 285, 311–15 (1991); Juenger, Judicial Jurisdiction in the United States and in the European Communities, 82 Mich. L. Rev. 1195 (1984); Comment, Related Contacts and Personal Jurisdiction: The "But For" Test, 82 Calif. L. Rev. 1545, 1550 n.35 (1994).

parlance, these are "related" contacts, and where they suffice they give rise to "specific" jurisdiction.[6] The term "specific" jurisdiction is descriptive because it is jurisdiction that is specific to the dispute. Because of the requirement that the contacts be "related" to the dispute, those contacts may well suffice for jurisdiction in the lawsuit at hand, but may not in another lawsuit relating to the defendant's activities in another state.[7]

"General" jurisdiction is jurisdiction founded upon a basis independent of the nature of the dispute between the parties.[8] Again, this term is descriptive because the basis for jurisdiction is "general" in the sense that applies generally to the defendant; it depends not upon the character of the dispute between the parties. The common law bases of jurisdiction are predominantly general. In-state service of individual defendants, domicile, residence, nationality, express consent and voluntary appearance are all bases of jurisdiction that do not require a court to inquire into the defendant's activities within the forum and how they relate to the litigation.[9] *International Shoe* also clarified that general jurisdiction exists—perhaps only over corporations[10]—if the defendant has "continuous and systematic" contacts with the forum.[11]

The dichotomy between specific and general jurisdiction is not without its detractors. Some have proposed an approach that blends the two by giving more weight to related contacts, but not categorizing them strictly upon their status as related or unrelated.[12] Others make the more radical suggestion that general jurisdiction be abolished altogether.[13] Whatever the merits of these proposals, however, it is clear that a fairly sharp dichotomy between the two still expresses the view of the Supreme Court.[14]

---

6. Hay, supra n.5, at 316.

7. See Note, Specific Jurisdiction and the "Arise from or Relate to" Requirement . . . What Does it Mean?, 50 Wash. & Lee L. Rev. 1265, 1269–70 (1993).

8. One commentator calls this "dispute-blind" jurisdiction to denote its independence from the causes of action. See Twitchell, The Myth of General Jurisdiction, 101 Harv. L. Rev. 610, 612 (1988).

9. Hay, supra n.5, at 311–15.

10. Burnham v. Superior Court, 495 U.S. 604, 610 n.1, 110 S.Ct. 2105, 2110 n.1, 109 L.Ed.2d 631 (1990).

11. E.g., Perkins v. Benguet Consol. Mining Co., 342 U.S. 437, 72 S.Ct. 413, 96 L.Ed. 485 (1952).

12. See, e.g., Lewis, A Brave New World for Personal Jurisdiction: Flexible Tests Under Uniform Standards, 37 Vand. L. Rev. 1 (1984); Richman, Part I—Casad's Jurisdiction in Civil Actions, Part II—A Sliding Scale to Supplement the Distinction Between General and Specific Jurisdiction, 72 Cal. L. Rev. 1328, 1338 (1984). For cases

appearing to adopt such an approach, see Cornelison v. Chaney, 16 Cal.3d 143, 545 P.2d 264, 127 Cal.Rptr. 352 (1976); Presbyterian Univ. Hosp. v. Wilson, 337 Md. 541, 654 A.2d 1324 (1995); Camelback Ski Corp. v. Behning, 312 Md. 330, 539 A.2d 1107, cert. denied 488 U.S. 849, 109 S.Ct. 130, 102 L.Ed.2d 103 (1988). Some older state cases have rationalized extremely expansive jurisdictional assertions by deftly moving contacts from category to category. See, e.g., Buckeye Boiler v. Superior Court, 71 Cal.2d 893, 458 P.2d 57, 80 Cal.Rptr. 113 (1969); Bryant v. Finnish Nat'l Airlines, 15 N.Y.2d 426, 260 N.Y.S.2d 625, 208 N.E.2d 439 (1965) (interpreting New York's Civil Practice Law and Rules § 301).

13. See, e.g., Maier & McCoy, A Unifying Theory for Judicial Jurisdiction and Choice of Law, 39 Am. J. Comp. L. 249 (1991).

14. See, e.g., Burnham v. Superior Court, 495 U.S. 604, 624, 110 S.Ct. 2105, 2117, 109 L.Ed.2d 631 (1990); Helicopteros Nacionales de Colombia v. Hall, 466 U.S.

Determining whether specific jurisdiction exists in a particular case depends, then, upon two separate considerations. The first is whether the contacts are "related" to the dispute. The second, assuming that the contacts are so related, is whether the contacts are constitutionally sufficient. The first of these questions is the subject of this section.

Oddly enough, the Supreme Court has never addressed the question of what constitutes a related contact. In many of the cases that the Court has faced, the contacts have either been obviously related[15] or obviously unrelated to the dispute.[16] The closest that the Court has ever come to facing the issue was *Helicopteros Nacionales de Columbia v. Hall*,[17] which was a case brought in the Texas state courts by the estates of four Americans killed in a Peruvian helicopter crash against a Columbian transportation company. *Hall* presented a close question as to whether the contacts were related to the cause of action. They were not related in the most direct sense, because the defendant's Texas activities—purchasing helicopter parts, negotiating the transportation contract, and sending its pilots for training[18]—were not of central relevance to the questions of liability and damages. On the other hand, the defendant's Texas activities undoubtedly bore a causal nexus to the accident.[19] A majority of the Supreme Court concluded, however, that the plaintiffs had conceded in their brief that the contacts were *not* related, and therefore analyzed the case only under the general jurisdiction rubric, and held that the contacts were insufficient to meet the test for general jurisdiction.[20] Only Justice Brennan's lone dissent, which concluded that the plaintiffs' brief had not conceded the issue, reached the question and argued for a broad notion of relatedness.[21] Under Brennan's broad conception of related contacts, the defendant's Texas activities were sufficient for specific jurisdiction apparently because the dis-

408, 414, 104 S.Ct. 1868, 1872, 80 L.Ed.2d 404 (1984).

15. See, e.g., Burger King Corp. v. Rudzewicz, 471 U.S. 462, 105 S.Ct. 2174, 85 L.Ed.2d 528 (1985) (franchise agreement with forum state company sufficient for jurisdiction in a suit for damages for breach of that agreement); Keeton v. Hustler Magazine Inc., 465 U.S. 770, 104 S.Ct. 1473, 79 L.Ed.2d 790 (1984) (libel action for a cartoon in a magazine of which at least 10,000 copies were sold in the forum state).

16. See, e.g., Perkins v. Benguet Consol. Mining Co., 342 U.S. 437, 72 S.Ct. 413, 96 L.Ed. 485 (1952) (suit activities in the Philippines allowed in an Ohio state court because corporation had temporarily relocated its headquarters to the forum).

17. Hall v. Helicopteros Nacionales De Colombia, 638 S.W.2d 870, 871 (Tex.1982), rev'd 466 U.S. 408, 104 S.Ct. 1868, 80 L.Ed.2d 404 (1984). The Supreme Court also heard the case of Carnival Cruise

Lines, Inc. v. Shute, 499 U.S. 585, 111 S.Ct. 1522, 113 L.Ed.2d 622 (1991), in which the lower court (the Ninth Circuit) had ruled that the contacts were related and that jurisdiction was constitutionally sufficient. See Shute v. Carnival Cruise Lines, 897 F.2d 377 (9th Cir.1990), rev'd 499 U.S. 585, 111 S.Ct. 1522, 113 L.Ed.2d 622 (1991). However, the Supreme Court disposed of the case on the basis of the forum selection clause, without reaching any constitutional issues at all. 499 U.S. at 593, 111 S.Ct. at 1527, 113 L.Ed.2d at 631.

18. Hall v. Helicopteros Nacionales De Colombia, 638 S.W.2d 870, 871 (Tex.1982), rev'd 466 U.S. 408, 104 S.Ct. 1868, 80 L.Ed.2d 404 (1984).

19. Note, supra n.7, at 1274.

20. *Hall*, 466 U.S. at 415, 104 S.Ct. at 1872, 80 L.Ed.2d at 411.

21. Id. at 419, 104 S.Ct. at 1874, 80 L.Ed.2d at 414.

pute between the parties would not have occurred had it not been for the forum-related activities.[22]

The task of determining the difference between related and unrelated contacts has thus fallen to lower courts. Two major camps have been staked out.[23] The broader test is known as the "but for" test, and it resembles the approach advocated by Justice Brennan's dissent in *Hall*. The leading illustration of this test is the Ninth Circuit's opinion in *Shute v. Carnival Cruise Lines*.[24] In *Shute* the court allowed specific jurisdiction over a cruise line in a Washington court, despite the fact that the accident occurred while the plaintiff was on board a ship in coastal waters off of California. The defendant's Washington activities included advertising and soliciting of customers, which the Ninth Circuit held were related to the dispute because the accident would not have occurred "but for" the defendant's successful efforts to induce the Washington-domiciled plaintiff to take one of its cruises.[25] While *Shute* may well represent the most dramatic application of the test to date, the Ninth Circuit is not alone in adopting it.[26]

In the other camp are those courts applying what is variously called the "proximate cause"[27] or "substantive relevance"[28] test. While applications of this test are not always models of clarity, it is substantially more restrictive than the "but for" test.[29] Under this test, a "but for"

22. Id. at 420, 104 S.Ct. at 1875, 80 L.Ed.2d at 414.

23. For discussions of the competing tests, see Comment, supra n.5 and Note, supra n.7.

24. 897 F.2d 377 (9th Cir.1990), rev'd on other grounds 499 U.S. 585, 111 S.Ct. 1522, 113 L.Ed.2d 622 (1991).

25. *Shute*, 897 F.2d at 385.

26. See Note, supra n.7, at 1277–79 (discussing cases in the Fifth, Sixth, Seventh and Ninth Circuits), including Prejean v. Sonatrach, Inc., 652 F.2d 1260 (5th Cir. 1981), In–Flight Devices Corp. v. Van Dusen Air, Inc., 466 F.2d 220 (6th Cir.1972) and Deluxe Ice Cream Co. v. R.C.H. Tool Corp., 726 F.2d 1209. The other student commentary on this subject also lists the Sixth and Seventh Circuits as agreeing with the Ninth Circuit's "but for" test, but describes the Fifth Circuit's position as "unclear," pointing to a later case appearing to reject it. See Comment, supra n.5, at 1569 citing Aviles v. Kunkle, 978 F.2d 201 (5th Cir.1992) (per curiam). Subsequent caselaw in the First Circuit, however, has upheld jurisdiction on facts very similar to *Shute*. See Nowak v. Tak How Investments, Ltd., 94 F.3d 708 (1st Cir.1996), cert. denied 520 U.S. 1155, 117 S.Ct. 1333, 137 L.Ed.2d 493 (1997); see also Chew v. Dietrich, 143 F.3d 24 (2d Cir.1998), cert. denied 525 U.S. 948, 119 S.Ct. 373, 142 L.Ed.2d 308 (1998) (ap-

parently applying the "but for" test and suggesting that the First Circuit might not follow the "proximate cause" test that competes with the "but for" test); MGM Studios Inc. v. Grokster, Ltd., 243 F.Supp.2d 1073 (C.D. Cal. 2003) (following Ninth Circuit cases) .. At least some state courts follow the "but for" test as well. See, e.g., EMI Music Mexico S.A. v. Rodriguez, 97 S.W.3d 847 (Tex. App. 2003) (in fact applying a test indistinguishable from the "but for" test); Presbyterian Univ. Hosp. v. Wilson, 337 Md. 541, 654 A.2d 1324 (1995).

27. See, e.g., RAR, Inc. v. Turner Diesel, Ltd., 107 F.3d 1272 (7th Cir.1997); Pizarro v. Hoteles Concorde Int'l, 907 F.2d 1256, 1259 (1st Cir.1990); Interface Group–Massachusetts, LLC v. Rosen, 256 F.Supp.2d 103, 107 (D. Mass. 2003) (applying an "overlay" between the proximate cause and "but for" tests); Dagesse v. Plant Hotel N.V., 113 F.Supp.2d 211 (D.N.H. 2000) (merely booking a hotel room through an "800" telephone number in the forum does not constitute a related contact for purposes of a slip-and-fall case involving an accident at one of the defendant's hotels in a non-forum state).

28. This term was first proposed in Brilmayer, How Contacts Count: Due Process Limitations on State Court Jurisdiction, 1980 Sup. Ct. Rev. 77, 82.

29. Note, supra n.7, at 1282.

relationship between the contacts and the dispute is a necessary, but not sufficient, condition for finding related contacts—just as "but for" causation is a necessary, but not sufficient, condition for finding proximate causation in tort law.[30] The question, of course, is what beyond a factual causal link between the contacts and the dispute is essential to placing the contacts in the "related" category. Here the courts diverge somewhat, but the underlying theme is that the contacts must bear a direct relationship to the dispute.[31] Under perhaps the most restrictive formulation of this test, the contacts only count as related if they also comprise an element of proof in the case, that is, if they have "substantive relevance."[32] A case like *Shute* would clearly fail under this test, because the forum contacts were irrelevant to the substance of the dispute between the parties.[33] As might be expected from the lack of Supreme Court guidance, an approximately equal number of courts follow each test.[34]

Both tests suffer from some obvious deficiencies. The "but for" test, if taken to its logical extreme, allows for jurisdiction in cases in which it seems extremely unlikely that the Supreme Court would permit it.[35] This test also goes some distance toward collapsing the distinction between specific and general jurisdiction by treating contacts as related even if they bear only a remote relationship to the dispute.[36] On the other hand, the more restrictive test is more malleable, more likely to lead to litigation over the question of what counts as a related contact, and could lead to applications that deprive the plaintiff of a fair and reasonable forum.[37] Unless and until the Supreme Court intervenes, the lower courts appear likely to remain in equipoise on the question.

2. *Purposeful Availment*

§ 5.11 Assuming that the contacts are related to the claim, the next question is whether they are constitutionally sufficient. Their

---

30. Hence the analogy that some courts draw between the two. See, e.g., *Pizarro*, 907 F.2d at 1259.

31. See Note, supra n.7, at 1283; Comment, supra n.5, at 1569.

32. Brilmayer, Related Contacts and Personal Jurisdiction, 101 Harv. L. Rev. 1444, 1463 (1988).

33. See, e.g., *Pizarro*, 907 F.2d at 1259.

34. Note, supra n.7, at 1283 (placing the First, Second, and Eighth Circuits in this category, and citing, inter alia, Pizarro v. Hoteles Concorde International, 907 F.2d 1256 (1st Cir.1990), Gelfand v. Tanner Motor Tours, Ltd., 339 F.2d 317 (2d Cir.1964), and Morris v. Barkbuster, Inc., 923 F.2d 1277 (8th Cir.1991)). The other student commentary also puts the First and Eighth Circuits in this camp. Comment, supra n.5, at 1569. Subsequent cases

in the First Circuit put that court's position in some doubt, however. See Nowak v. Tak How Investments, Ltd., 94 F.3d 708 (1st Cir.1996), cert. denied 520 U.S. 1155, 117 S.Ct. 1333, 137 L.Ed.2d 493 (1997) (upholding jurisdiction on facts very similar to *Shute*). The Seventh Circuit also clearly rejects the "but for" test. See *RAR*, 107 F.3d at 1272 (in a contract case, contacts are related only if "bear on the substantive legal dispute between the parties or inform the court regarding the economic substance of the contract."). Some state courts have also rejected the "but for" test in favor of a more restrictive test. See, e.g., State ex rel. Circus Circus Reno v. Pope, 317 Ore. 151, 161, 854 P.2d 461, 466 (1993).

35. Comment, supra n.5, at 1572–73.

36. See Hay, supra n.5, at 318 (criticizing Ninth Circuit's *Shute* decision).

37. *Shute*, 897 F.2d at 385–86.

constitutional sufficiency turns ultimately upon an understanding of the minimum contacts test. Because the Supreme Court has decided more specific jurisdiction cases than any other variety, the Court's guidance here is more comprehensive than elsewhere. A consistent theme in the Supreme Court's jurisprudence is that the sine qua non of specific jurisdiction is the defendant's "purposeful availment" of the benefits and protections of the forum.[1]

The Supreme Court's first important post-*International Shoe* specific jurisdiction case was *McGee v. International Life Insurance Co.*[2] In *McGee* the plaintiff was a California beneficiary of a life insurance policy written by a Texas company. Although the Texas company had neither agents nor offices in California, it created a voluntary relationship with the state when it purchased the policy in a reinsurance agreement with the original insurer, and then successfully solicited the policyholder to renew under the original terms.[3] When the policyholder died, the company refused to pay benefits, claiming that the death was a suicide.[4] The beneficiary—the policyholder's mother—obtained a default judgment in a California court against the company under a state statute authorizing jurisdiction over out-of-state insurance companies who insured state resident. The Texas courts refused to give the judgment faith and credit, maintaining that the California courts lacked constitutional authority to enter the default, but the Supreme Court reversed—holding that the company had minimum contacts with California.[5]

McGee is commonly regarded as the high-water mark for the jurisdictional authority of states.[6] The Court was willing to assume for purposes of the decision that the insurance company had no contact with California other than the single policy. Indeed, the Court's opinion contains strikingly broad language that directly linked the notion of due process to fairness. The Court emphasized that developments in transportation made it easier for non-resident parties to defend, indicated that the "substantial connection" of the contract with California was itself sufficient to establish jurisdiction, and worried that not allowing for jurisdiction in such cases would effectively insulate non-resident insurers from liability on "small or moderate" claims.[7]

While *McGee* signalled an extensive reach for states, the Court's next jurisdictional decision—handed down only months later—seemed to signal a contraction. *Hanson v. Denckla*[8] involved fairly complicated two-

§ 5.11

1. See Maltz, Reflections on a Landmark: Shaffer v. Heitner viewed from a Distance, 1986 B.Y.U. L. Rev. 1043, 1059–60; Stewart, A New Litany of Personal Jurisdiction, 60 U. Colo. L. Rev. 5, 6 (1989).

2. 355 U.S. 220, 78 S.Ct. 199, 2 L.Ed.2d 223 (1957).

3. Id. at 221, 78 S.Ct. at 200, 2 L.Ed.2d at 224.

4. Id. at 222, 78 S.Ct. at 200, 2 L.Ed.2d at 225.

5. Id.

6. Weintraub, Due Process Limitations on the Personal Jurisdiction of State Courts: Time for Change, 63 Ore. L. Rev. 485, 527–28 (1984).

7. Id. at 223, 78 S.Ct. at 201, 2 L.Ed.2d at 226.

8. 357 U.S. 235, 78 S.Ct. 1228, 2 L.Ed.2d 1283 (1958).

state litigation over the validity of a large trust. By the time the case reached the Supreme Court, the case boiled down to the validity of a Florida state court decree purporting to invalidate the trust, and thereby deprive the settlor's two grandchildren of the trust assets in favor of their maternal aunts who had already received approximately $500,000 under the residuary clause of the settlor's will.[9] The Florida court's invalidation of the trust depended upon it having jurisdiction over the trustee, a Delaware company, and thus the case reduced to the question of whether the trustee had minimum contacts with Florida.

The Supreme Court held that it did not. When the trust was created, the settlor was a Pennsylvania domiciliary.[10] The trustee's only relationship to Florida was that the settlor of the trust eventually relocated to that state, and continued to carry out small bits of trust administration from her new home.[11] This, the Court held, was an insufficient affiliating circumstance to allow for in personam jurisdiction over the trustee. In distinguishing the case at hand from *McGee*, the *Hanson* Court set forth the so-called "purposeful availment" test:

> The unilateral activity of those who claim some relationship with a nonresident defendant cannot satisfy the requirement of contact with the forum State. As the application of that rule will vary with the quality and nature of the defendant's activities, but it is essential in each case that there be some act by which the defendant purposefully avails itself of the privilege of conducting activities within the forum State, thus invoking the benefits and protections of its laws.[12]

In retrospect, the distinction between *McGee* and *Hanson* seems fairly clear. To be sure, the cases have some similarities. Both involved large corporate defendants with isolated contacts with the forum state. The crucial difference was that the *McGee* defendant voluntarily created a relationship with the forum state for its benefit, while the *Hanson* defendant's relationship with the forum state was an accidental byproduct of the activities of others that it could not reasonably control. In the parlance of *Hanson*'s test: the *McGee* defendant "purposefully avail[ed] itself of the privilege of conducting activities within the forum State" while the *Hanson* defendant had not.

Hanson's odd facts, especially the obvious injustice that would have resulted had the Florida decree depriving the grandchildren of any portion their grandmother's assets not been invalidated, might make one wonder whether the purposeful availment test has broad applicability. Subsequent developments have confirmed, however, that the purposeful availment test is the most significant mechanism for resolving questions of specific jurisdiction.

---

9. Id. at 238, 78 S.Ct. at 1231, 2 L.Ed.2d at 1288.

10. Id. at 251, 78 S.Ct. at 1238, 2 L.Ed.2d at 1296.

11. Id.

12. Id. at 253, 78 S.Ct. at 1239, 2 L.Ed.2d at 1297.

In *Shaffer v. Heitner*,[13] the Supreme Court employed the purposeful availment test to deny jurisdiction to the Delaware courts over the directors and officers of a Delaware-incorporated company. Although *Shaffer* is best known for its holding that the minimum contacts test is the ultimate determinant of the constitutionality of both in personam and in rem assertions of jurisdiction, a secondary aspect of the case is its holding that the individual defendants did not have minimum contacts with the forum state. The Court concluded, perhaps dubiously,[14] that the individual defendants' decision to become affiliated with a Delaware company did not amount to a purposeful availment of that state's benefits and protections.[15] A more obvious application of the test occurred in *Kulko v. Superior Court*.[16] In that case, the Court concluded that a California court did not have jurisdiction in a child support matter against a New York father who had merely acquiesced in his childrens' decision to relocate to their mother's house in the forum state.[17]

But perhaps the most dramatic evidence of the hegemony of the purposeful availment test in the realm of specific jurisdiction is *World–Wide Volkswagen Corp. v. Woodson*.[18] *World–Wide* was a products liability action arising from a automobile crash in Oklahoma. The injured passengers sued four defendants, two of which took the jurisdictional question to the Supreme Court. The two defendants were the New York retailer and the New York–New Jersey–Connecticut distributor of the car; the plaintiffs were New Yorkers who were in the process of relocating to Arizona when their car was struck from behind on an Oklahoma highway. The plaintiffs contended, and the Oklahoma Supreme Court agreed, that the Oklahoma state courts had jurisdiction over the defendants because the use of their car in Oklahoma was foreseeable and that the defendants therefore derived a significant benefit from the forum state.[19] The Supreme Court held, however, that foreseeability of a product's use in a state is insufficient for jurisdiction.[20] Rather, said the Court, "the foreseeability that is critical to due process analysis ... is that the defendant's conduct and connection with the forum State are such that he should reasonably anticipate being haled into court there."[21]

The Court clearly tied the notion of a defendant being able to foresee being subject to jurisdiction to the *Hanson* purposeful availment test. If a defendant purposefully avails itself of the benefits of the forum, this gives it "clear notice that it is subject to suit there...."[22] A

---

13. 433 U.S. 186, 97 S.Ct. 2569, 53 L.Ed.2d 683 (1977).

14. See, e.g., Juenger, Supreme Court Intervention in Choice of Law: A Dismal Prospect, 14 U.C. Davis L. Rev. 907, 909, 914 (1981).

15. 433 U.S. at 213, 97 S.Ct. at 2584, 53 L.Ed.2d at 703.

16. 436 U.S. 84, 98 S.Ct. 1690, 56 L.Ed.2d 132 (1978).

17. Id.

18. 444 U.S. 286, 100 S.Ct. 559, 62 L.Ed.2d 490 (1980).

19. Id. at 289, 100 S.Ct. at 563, 62 L.Ed.2d at 496.

20. Id. at 296, 100 S.Ct. at 566, 62 L.Ed.2d at 500.

21. Id. at 297, 100 S.Ct. at 567, 62 L.Ed.2d at 501.

22. Id. Not all arguably foreseeable effects, however, constitute purposeful availment. For example, in general, merely "pas-

defendant who makes an intentional effort to affiliate itself with the forum state can then take steps to insure itself or reduce its exposure, and it is maintaining of "an element of predictability to the legal system"[23] that makes the purposeful availment test the constitutional benchmark in specific jurisdiction cases. On the facts of *World–Wide*, the Court concluded that the purposeful availment test was not satisfied because the defendants challenging jurisdiction had not sold the car in Oklahoma, rather it had only been used in that state. Thus, in the mold of *Hanson*, the connection between the defendants and the forum was only the result of the "unilateral activity" of parties beyond the defendants' control.[24]

The purposeful availment test has not, however, always been a mechanism for denying jurisdiction. In *Burger King Corp. v. Rudzewicz*,[25] the Supreme Court allowed the Florida state courts to take jurisdiction over individual defendants who operated, in their home state of Michigan, a fast-food franchise of a national chain. The fast-food franchisor was a Florida company that claimed that the defendants had breached various terms of their franchise agreement. The Supreme Court held that the defendants had minimum contacts with Florida, and that several facts demonstrated that they had purposefully availed themselves of the forum's benefits; indeed the Supreme Court described the existence of a "purposeful" connection with the forum as "the constitutional touchstone."[26] Analogizing the case to *McGee*, the Court held that the franchise contract had a "substantial connection" to the forum because of the Florida locus of the franchisor.[27] The Court emphasized the defendants' "voluntary acceptance" of the benefits of the relationship with the Florida company,[28] and also pointed to a provision in the contract selecting Florida's as the governing state law as further evidence that the defendants had made an intentional effort to benefit from their association with the forum state.[29]

sive" web activity–i.e., maintaining a web site that is accessible in the forum–will not be sufficient for jurisdiction. *See, e.g.,* Young v. New Haven Advocate, 315 F.3d 256 (4th Cir. 2002) (libel case), cert. denied 538 U.S. 1035, 123 S.Ct. 2092, 155 L.Ed.2d 1065 (2003); Pavlovich v. Superior Court, 29 Cal.4th 262, 127 Cal.Rptr.2d 329, 58 P.3d 2 (2002); Smith v. Basin Park Hotel, Inc., 178 F.Supp.2d 1225 (N.D. Okla. 2001) (maintaining a "passive" website in the forum not sufficient for jurisdiction); Dagesse v. Plant Hotel N.V., 113 F.Supp.2d 211 (D.N.H. 2000) (merely maintaining a web page which is accessible in the forum and through which reservations can be booked does not constitute continuous and systematic contacts); Desktop Technologies, Inc. v. Colorworks Reproduction and Design, Inc., 1999 WL 98572 (E.D. Pa.). The notion that a merely "passive" website should be insufficient to establish jurisdiction without any additional contacts traces to Zippo Mfg. Co. v. Zippo Dot Com, 952 F.Supp. 1119 (W.D. Pa. 1997). The usefulness of this supposed distinction between "passive" and "active" websites is probably fading, however, as essentially all commercial websites now have some "active" component to them.

23. Id.

24. Id.

25. 471 U.S. 462, 105 S.Ct. 2174, 85 L.Ed.2d 528 (1985).

26. Id. at 474, 105 S.Ct. at 2183, 85 L.Ed.2d at 541.

27. Id. at 479, 105 S.Ct. at 2185, 85 L.Ed.2d at 545.

28. Id.

29. Id. at 481, 105 S.Ct. at 2186, 85 L.Ed.2d at 546.

The purposeful availment test can generate marginal cases, in which application is difficult, as cases such as *Kulko* and *Shaffer* demonstrate. But the test remains the most durable thread in the Supreme Court's specific jurisdiction jurisprudence, and it can fairly be said that without a finding of a voluntary affiliation between the defendant and the forum, jurisdiction is a constitutional impossibility.

3. *Reasonableness*

§ 5.12 An important development in jurisdictional law is the notion that the minimum contacts test is subject to an overarching reasonableness standard. When the Supreme Court first articulated the minimum contacts test it seemed to view the existence of minimum contacts as a proxy for fair and reasonable assertions of jurisdiction.[1] In *Burger King Corp. v. Rudzewicz*,[2] however, the Court suggested that there might be circumstances in which the minimum contacts test is satisfied, yet the "minimum requirements inherent in the concept of 'fair play and substantial justice' ... defeat the reasonableness of jurisdiction even [though] the defendant has purposefully engaged in forum activities."

That suggestion bore fruit in *Asahi Metal Industry Co. v. Superior Court*.[3] *Asahi*, as discussed above, involved an indemnity dispute in a California state court between a Taiwanese motorcycle tube manufacturer and the Japanese manufacturer of the valve allegedly incorporated in the finished tire tube. The Court divided evenly on the question of whether the resale of the finished product in the forum state was sufficient to establish the existence of minimum contacts.[4] The entire Court, however, agreed that asserting jurisdiction over the Japanese valve manufacturer in the indemnity matter would be unconstitutional. The Court's unanimous conclusion was based upon the "reasonableness" dictum in *Burger King*.

Three factors persuaded the *Asahi* Court that asserting jurisdiction over the Japanese defendant would be unreasonable. First was the foreign nationality of the defendant. The Court emphasized the great distance between the defendant's headquarters in Japan and the California courthouse, as well as the "unique burdens placed upon one who must defend oneself in a foreign legal system."[5] Second was the collateral nature of the indemnity dispute. The Japanese valve manufacturer had not been sued directly by the plaintiff, and the question of whether the Japanese valve manufacturer would be required to indemnify the Taiwanese tube manufacturer depended almost entirely on events and transactions occurring in Asia.[6] Third, the settlement of the underlying

---

§ 5.12

1. International Shoe Co. v. Washington, 326 U.S. 310, 316, 66 S.Ct. 154, 158, 90 L.Ed. 95, 102 (1945).

2. 471 U.S. 462, 477–78, 105 S.Ct. 2174, 2185, 85 L.Ed.2d 528, 544 (1985).

3. 480 U.S. 102, 107 S.Ct. 1026, 94 L.Ed.2d 92 (1987).

4. See supra § 5.11.

5. *Asahi*, 480 U.S. at 114, 107 S.Ct. at 1033.

6. Id.

dispute between the tort plaintiff and the Taiwanese tube manufacturer left the state court without a forum-domiciled plaintiff, thereby diminishing the California state court's interest in hearing the matter.

Asahi was bound to spawn a fair amount of confusion. Whatever defects there might be in the minimum contacts test, lawyers and courts could take some comfort in the large volume of case law has developed on the subject, allowing them to reason from an ample body of precedent. *Asahi*, however, was the Court's first—and remains its only—effort to apply the more general notion of jurisdictional reasonableness. The Court offered no hint as to whether the factors it deployed were all necessary for the finding of unreasonableness, or whether some lesser showing could suffice. The Court's opinion also does not make clear whether the three factors are the only ones that could be relevant to a showing of unreasonableness, or whether other factors (presumably not present in *Asahi*) might defeat jurisdiction.

Lower courts have treated *Asahi* cautiously. Those cases that have denied jurisdiction under the reasonableness test have involved, for the most part, foreign defendants.[7] Lower courts applying *Asahi* have not, however, read it as granting jurisdictional immunity to foreign defendants.[8] Although generalizations are difficult, it appears that in cases

---

7. See, e.g., OMI Holdings, Inc. v. Royal Ins. Co. of Canada, 149 F.3d 1086 (10th Cir.1998) (jurisdiction over Canadian insurer unreasonable where insurer sold few or no policies in forum and only connection to forum was that insured was there involved in litigation); Core–Vent Corp. v. Nobel Industries, 11 F.3d 1482 (9th Cir.1993) (jurisdiction would not be reasonably asserted over Swedish defendants alleged to have libelled a local plaintiff's product); Amoco Egypt Oil Co. v. Leonis Navigation Co., 1 F.3d 848 (9th Cir.1993) (jurisdiction would not be reasonably asserted in Washington court over dispute between two foreign parties regarding boating collision); Teledyne, Inc. v. Kone Corp., 892 F.2d 1404 (9th Cir.1989) (jurisdiction would be unreasonable over a foreign state-owned industry); Guardian Royal Exch. Assurance v. English China Clays, 815 S.W.2d 223 (Tex.1991) (jurisdiction would be unreasonable in a collateral dispute involving an English insurer); Parry v. Ernst Home Center Corp., 779 P.2d 659 (Utah. 1989) (unreasonableness an alternative rationale for dismissal in a products liability case involving Japanese defendants).

In a slight extension of *Asahi*, most courts have applied the overarching reasonableness standard even in cases involving assertions of general jurisdiction, even though *Asahi* itself was a specific jurisdiction case. See, e.g., Amoco Egypt Oil Co. v. Leonis Navigation Co., 1 F.3d 848 (9th Cir.

1993); Dalton v. R & W Marine, Inc., 897 F.2d 1359 (5th Cir.1990); Bearry v. Beech Aircraft Corp., 818 F.2d 370 (5th Cir.1987); de Reyes v. Marine Mgmt. & Consulting, 586 So.2d 103 (La.1991); but see Crane v. Carr, 814 F.2d 758 (D.C.Cir.1987).

8. See, e.g., Vermeulen v. Renault, 985 F.2d 1534 (11th Cir.1993), cert. denied 508 U.S. 907, 113 S.Ct. 2334, 124 L.Ed.2d 246 (1993) (large volume of United States sales of cars manufactured by French defendant renders jurisdiction over defendant reasonable); Sinatra v. National Enquirer, 854 F.2d 1191 (9th Cir.1988) (jurisdiction reasonable in libel claim asserted by a local plaintiff against Swedish defendants who knowingly made false statements to the effect that the plaintiff had been a patient in their clinic); Benitez–Allende v. Alcan Aluminio do Brasil, 857 F.2d 26 (1st Cir.1988) (jurisdiction over Brazilian manufacturer of defective pressure cooker reasonable because of large volume of local sales); Theunissen v. Matthews, 935 F.2d 1454 (6th Cir. 1991), appeal after remand 992 F.2d 1217 (6th Cir.1993) (jurisdiction reasonable over a Canadian defendant living in close proximity to the forum); A. Uberti v. Leonardo, 181 Ariz. 565, 892 P.2d 1354 (1995), cert. denied 516 U.S. 906, 116 S.Ct. 273, 133 L.Ed.2d 194 (1995) (jurisdiction can be reasonably asserted over an Italian manufacturer of a gun manufactured for sale in the United States and causing injury in the forum state); Domtar, Inc. v. Niagara Fire

involving close questions regarding the application of the minimum contacts test, *Asahi* and the foreign status of the defendant can tip the balance toward a finding that jurisdiction would be unconstitutional. On the other hand, a relatively strong showing that the minimum contacts test has been satisfied will allow a court to take jurisdiction even if the defendant is a foreign national. Moreover, not all foreign defendants stand on the same footing. At least one court found that jurisdiction over a Canadian company would not be unreasonable because of its relatively close proximity to the forum and the similarity of Canada's legal system, while leaving open the possibility that a similarly situated Japanese defendant might have been able to defeat jurisdiction.[9]

B. GENERAL JURISDICTION

§ 5.13 As discussed above,[1] an important division in jurisdictional law exists between so-called "general" and "specific" jurisdiction. General jurisdictional bases are those that allow for jurisdiction without regard to the character of the dispute. By contrast, specific jurisdictional bases are dependent on the character of the dispute.[2] Many of the common law bases of jurisdiction, such as in-state service of an individual defendant, are "general" in the sense that they allow for jurisdiction independent of the character of the dispute.

When, in *International Shoe Co. v. Washington*,[3] the Supreme Court created the minimum contacts test it suggested that it had both a specific and a general component. Summarizing the existing case law, the *International Shoe* Court concluded that "there have been instances in which the continuous corporate operations within a state were thought so substantial and of such a nature as to justify suit against it on causes of action arising from dealings entirely distinct from those activities."[4] At the other end of the spectrum, the Court suggested that even "single or isolated" activities might subject a defendant to jurisdiction if those activities were "related" or gave rise to the cause of action.[5] Although, as noted above,[6] the concept of what activities are "related" to the claim is a difficult one, the Court's suggestion that even "unconnected" yet "continuous and systematic" activities could give rise to jurisdiction was a clear indication that the minimum contacts test does support some assertions of general jurisdiction.

Ins. Co., 533 N.W.2d 25 (Minn.1995), cert. denied 516 U.S. 1017, 116 S.Ct. 583, 133 L.Ed.2d 504 (1995) (jurisdiction can be reasonably asserted over a Canadian defendant that knowingly insured a risk located in the United States).

9. See Aristech Chemical Int'l Ltd. v. Acrylic Fabricators Ltd., 138 F.3d 624, 627–28 (6th Cir.1998).

§ 5.13

1. See supra § 5.10.

2. For this reason, one commentator proposes the terms "dispute-blind" and "dispute-specific" to refer to general and specific jurisdiction, respectively. See Twitchell, The Myth of General Jurisdiction, 101 Harv. L. Rev. 610, 612 (1988).

3. 326 U.S. 310, 66 S.Ct. 154, 90 L.Ed. 95 (1945).

4. Id. at 318, 66 S.Ct. at 159.

5. Id. at 317, 66 S.Ct. at 159.

6. See supra § 5.10.

That suggestion was confirmed in *Perkins v. Benguet Consolidated Mining Co.*[7] *Perkins* involved an action by a shareholder of a Philippine-based mining company, in which the plaintiff claimed that the corporation had failed to pay dividends and issue stock to which she was entitled. The case was brought in an Ohio state court, and none of the activities that formed the basis for the action were performed in Ohio. Despite the lack of a forum connection, the Court upheld jurisdiction, describing the Fourteenth Amendment test as "one of general fairness to the corporation."[8] Borrowing from what the Court described as the "realistic reasoning in *International Shoe Co. v. Washington*," the Court concluded that the "continuous and systematic corporate activities" of the defendant were enough to subject it to general jurisdiction.[9] Crucial to the Court's conclusion were that the corporate president essentially conducted the company's business from his Ohio home during the World War II period, and that the company performed crucial corporate business such as writing checks, maintaining employees and sending business correspondence.[10]

The full implications of *Perkins* were unclear when the case was decided, and remain so today. Although the case clearly holds that regular, substantial and systematic corporate contacts allow the forum to take general jurisdiction, the decision offers no hint as to whether a lesser, but still substantial, quantum of contacts will suffice. The decision may well also be limited to circumstances in which no reasonable alternative forum is available.[11] Also unclear was whether this notion of contacts-based general jurisdiction applied only to business associations, or could be extended to individuals as well.

The Supreme Court's only return visit to the matter of contacts-based general jurisdiction has been *Helicopteros Nacionales de Colombia v. Hall*.[12] *Helicopteros* involved a wrongful death action brought in the Texas state courts by four American (but non-Texas) citizens. The four had been killed in an accident in Peru while flying in a helicopter owned by a Colombian company, which was the party defendant in the case. The four plaintiffs were employees of a Texas-based joint venture that had contracted with the Colombian defendant for helicopter transportation to and from construction sites for a Peruvian oil pipeline.[13]

The Texas state courts found that they had jurisdiction over the Colombian helicopter company, and thus upheld a substantial verdict for the plaintiffs. The United States Supreme Court, however, treated the case as one involving only general jurisdiction, construing the plaintiffs' brief to concede that the contacts were unrelated to the claim. Treating

7. 342 U.S. 437, 72 S.Ct. 413, 96 L.Ed. 485 (1952).

8. Id. at 445, 72 S.Ct. at 418.

9. Id. at 446, 72 S.Ct. at 418.

10. Id. at 447–48, 72 S.Ct. at 419.

11. See, e.g., Weintraub, Commentary on the Conflict of Laws 146–47 (1971); von Mehren & Trautman, Jurisdiction to Adjudicate: A Suggested Analysis, 79 Harv. L. Rev. 1121, 1144 (1966); Waits, Values, Intuitions, and Opinion Writing: The Judicial Process and State Court Jurisdiction, 1983 U. Ill. L. Rev. 917, 940.

12. 466 U.S. 408, 104 S.Ct. 1868, 80 L.Ed.2d 404 (1984).

13. Id. at 409, 104 S.Ct. at 1870.

the contacts as unrelated to the claim, the Supreme Court found them insufficient to allow for jurisdiction.

The Colombian defendant had some contacts with Texas. The contract for helicopter transportation that led to the fatal accident had been negotiated with the Texas-based joint venture in Texas. The Colombian defendant purchased about 80% of its helicopters and spare parts from a Texas company, and sent prospective pilots to be trained in Texas and to ferry the helicopters back to South America.[14] The Court held, however, that these contacts were insufficient to sustain general jurisdiction. Relying heavily on a pre-*International Shoe* case,[15] the Court announced that "purchases and related trips, standing alone, are not a sufficient basis for a State's assertion of jurisdiction."[16]

There is, of course, a huge gulf between *Perkins* and *Helicopteros*. Each stands towards one end of a long spectrum of corporate affiliations with the state. Lacking much guidance from the Supreme Court, courts have been conservative in their approach.[17] In fact, cases finding jurisdiction solely on the basis of truly unrelated contacts are sufficiently rare that one commentator has concluded that the existence of such jurisdiction is essentially a "myth."[18] Whether or not it qualifies as a myth, it is certainly true that courts usually have been reluctant to allow for jurisdiction based solely upon unrelated contacts.[19] Those cases that have allowed general jurisdiction usually have involved facts fairly similar to

14. Id. at 411, 104 S.Ct. at 1870.

15. Id. at 417, 104 S.Ct. at 1874 (citing Rosenberg Bros. & Co. v. Curtis Brown Co., 260 U.S. 516, 43 S.Ct. 170, 67 L.Ed. 372 (1923)).

16. Id.

17. See Twitchell, supra n.2, at 637 (noting often conclusory lower court reasoning as to existence or non-existence of general jurisdiction).

18. See Twitchell, supra n.2, at 630 ("With the emergence of specific jurisdiction, the exercise of general jurisdiction has become rare.").

19. See, e.g., Wilson v. Blakey, 20 F.3d 644 (5th Cir.1994), cert. denied 513 U.S. 930, 115 S.Ct. 322, 130 L.Ed.2d 282 (1994) (modest amount of personal business in state insufficient to support general jurisdiction over individual); Amoco Egypt Oil Co. v. Leonis Navigation Co., 1 F.3d 848 (9th Cir.1993) (unrelated shipping activities insufficient to sustain general jurisdiction); Doe v. National Medical Services, 974 F.2d 143 (10th Cir.1992) (testing of several hundred drug samples from forum insufficient to sustain jurisdiction in a case not related to one of those samples); Morris v. Barkbuster, Inc., 923 F.2d 1277 (8th Cir.1991) (con-

tractual negotiations in forum insufficient to sustain general jurisdiction); Sandstrom v. ChemLawn Corp., 904 F.2d 83 (1st Cir. 1990) (appointment of in-state agent for service not enough to allow for jurisdiction); Dalton v. R & W Marine, Inc., 897 F.2d 1359 (5th Cir.1990) (substantial unrelated charter boat activities insufficient to allow for general jurisdiction); Bearry v. Beech Aircraft Corp., 818 F.2d 370 (5th Cir. 1987) (substantial volume of sales in state by aircraft manufacturer insufficient to sustain jurisdiction on claim on aircrash outside of state); Travelers Indemnity Co. v. Calvert Fire Ins. Co., 798 F.2d 826 (5th Cir.1986) (sale of modest number of insurance policies in forum insufficient to establish general jurisdiction); Camelback Ski Corp. v. Behning, 307 Md. 270, 513 A.2d 874 (1986) (ski resort that accepts substantial number of skiers from forum not subject to general jurisdiction). Some cases that purport to rest on general jurisdictional principles clearly involve some important, related contacts. See, e.g., Gator.com Corp. v. L.L. Bean, Inc., 341 F.3d 1072 (9th Cir. 2003), rehearing en banc granted by 366 F.3d 789 (9th Cir. 2004) (jurisdiction justified on retailer's substantial electronic commerce in the forum, but dispute arose out of "cease and desist" trademark letter sent to the plaintiff in the forum).

Perkins.[20] An important factor in whether a corporation or other business entity will be subjected to jurisdiction is a continuing physical presence in the forum, usually in the form of an office or employees.[21] Non-physical associations, such as sales, solicitations or advertising, are less likely to qualify as "continuous and systematic."[22] The cautious attitude exhibited by courts towards general jurisdiction has some benefits, for—as commentators have pointed out—allowing for general jurisdiction over corporate defendants based solely upon unrelated business contacts creates an incentive for forum shopping.[23]

Another difficult question is whether the notion of contacts-based general jurisdiction applies to individual defendants, and—if so—under what circumstances. The applicability, in any form, of the minimum contacts test to individual defendants was in some doubt until the Supreme Court in *Shaffer v. Heitner*[24] so extended it. *Shaffer*, however, found minimum contacts wanting, and was in any event a specific jurisdiction case. In *Burnham v. Superior Court*,[25] a four-vote plurality of the Court suggested in a footnote dictum that "it may be that [contacts-based general jurisdiction] applies *only* to corporations...." The need for contacts-based general jurisdiction over individual defendants is less pressing than for business associations, because general jurisdiction over the former is available in the domicile.[26] There are, however, occasional cases finding general jurisdiction over individuals in a forum other than their domicile, usually if the individual has very substantial business

20. See, e.g., de Reyes (Aguilera) v. Marine Mgmt. & Consulting, 586 So.2d 103 (La.1991) (maintaining an office in the forum in which some management decisions are made is sufficient for general jurisdiction); Ex Parte Newco Mfg. Co., 481 So.2d 867 (Ala.1985) (substantial sales revenue from forum sufficient to establish general jurisdiction); St. Louis–San Francisco Ry. v. Gitchoff, 68 Ill.2d 38, 369 N.E.2d 52 (1977) (sales office with seven employees in forum sufficient for general jurisdiction); Laufer v. Ostrow, 55 N.Y.2d 305, 434 N.E.2d 692, 449 N.Y.S.2d 456 (1982) (corporate activities sufficient such that defendant was "doing business" in New York within the meaning of long-arm statute). See also Twitchell, supra n.2, at 633 (general jurisdiction usually allowed at defendant's "home base").

21. See Twitchell, supra n.2, at 633–34.

22. See, e.g., Bearry v. Beech Aircraft Corp., 818 F.2d 370 (5th Cir. 1987) (substantial volume of sales in state by aircraft manufacturer insufficient to sustain jurisdiction on claim on aircrash outside of state); Travelers Indemnity Co. v. Calvert Fire Ins. Co., 798 F.2d 826 (5th Cir.1986) (sale of modest number of insurance policies in forum insufficient to establish general jurisdiction); Camelback Ski Corp. v. Behning, 307 Md. 270, 513 A.2d 874 (1986) (ski resort that accepts substantial number

of skiers from forum not subject to general jurisdiction). But see United Brotherhood of Carpenters & Joiners of Am., 688 So.2d 246 (Ala.), cert. denied 521 U.S. 1118, 117 S.Ct. 2509, 138 L.Ed.2d 1012 (1997) (.5% of due paying members of a union in forum state sufficient for general jurisdiction over union); Davenport Mach. & Foundry Co. v. Adolph Coors Co., 314 N.W.2d 432 (Iowa 1982) (substantial sales of beer in forum sufficient to allow for general jurisdiction); Dillon v. Numismatic Funding Corp., 291 N.C. 674, 231 S.E.2d 629 (1977) (two-year pattern of sales to forum domiciliaries sufficient to allow general jurisdiction).

23. See, e.g., Maier & McCoy, A Unifying Theory for Judicial Jurisdiction and Choice of Law, 39 Am. J. Comp. L. 249 (1991) (urging abolition of most general jurisdictional bases); Kozyris, Reflections on *Allstate*—The Lessening of Due Process in Choice of Law, 14 U.C. Davis L. Rev. 889, 894 (1981) (general "doing business" jurisdiction inappropriately encourages forum shopping).

24. 433 U.S. 186, 204 n.19, 97 S.Ct. 2569, 2579 n.19, 53 L.Ed.2d 683 (1977).

25. 495 U.S. 604, 610 n.1, 110 S.Ct. 2105, 2110 n.1, 109 L.Ed.2d 631 (1990).

26. See, e.g., Milliken v. Meyer, 311 U.S. 457, 61 S.Ct. 339, 85 L.Ed. 278 (1940).

connections with the forum.[27] Contacts-based general jurisdiction over individuals, while rare, ought probably not be categorically excluded as a possibility, especially in cases in which no sensible alternative forum exists.

V. THE NEED FOR STATUTORY AUTHORIZATION

A. STATE COURTS

§ 5.14 In the early days of the United States, state courts exercised jurisdiction according to the common law of jurisdiction. In the case of in personam jurisdiction, this usually meant in-state service or appearance of a defendant,[1] and for in rem jurisdiction, attachment of the defendant's in-state property.[2] Gradually, these common law principles were incorporated into the Constitution: first into the Full Faith and Credit Clause,[3] and then into the Due Process Clause.[4] The consequence of this co-extension of the common law and constitutional principles was that the question of state law authorization for jurisdiction arose fairly rarely, because affirmative state authority for jurisdiction was usually supplied by the common law.

From early on, states seeking to expand their jurisdictional reach beyond the common law boundaries employed statutory innovations. Some states passed statutes clearly at odds with the common law principles of jurisdiction.[5] But as it became gradually accepted that the Due Process Clause operated as a direct restraint on state court jurisdiction, states attempting to expand their reach turned to jurisdictional innovations at least nominally in accord with the common law. The most popular route to reform was the "implied consent" basis for jurisdiction. States passed statutes that treated certain in-state activities, such as

---

27. See, e.g., ABKCO Indus. v. Lennon, 52 A.D.2d 435, 384 N.Y.S.2d 781 (1976) (forum has general jurisdiction over famous musician based upon substantial but unrelated business contacts). Of course, the cases finding that there is no general jurisdiction over individuals are plentiful. See, e.g., Wilson v. Blakey, 20 F.3d 644 (5th Cir.1994), cert. denied 513 U.S. 930, 115 S.Ct. 322, 130 L.Ed.2d 282 (1994); Fields v. Ramada Inn, Inc., 816 F.Supp. 1033 (E.D.Pa.1993). The Restatement, Second, Conflict of Laws takes the position in § 35(3) that contacts-based general jurisdiction is available over individual defendants if such individuals are "doing business" in the forum and "this business is so continuous and substantial as to make it reasonable for the state to exercise such jurisdiction."

§ 5.14

1. See, e.g., Barrell v. Benjamin, 15 Mass. 354, 358 (1819).

2. See, e.g., Pennoyer v. Neff, 95 U.S. (5 Otto) 714, 728, 24 L.Ed. 565, 571 (1878).

3. See, e.g., Pennoyer v. Neff, 95 U.S. (5 Otto) 714, 733, 24 L.Ed. 565, 572 (1878); Mills v. Duryee, 11 U.S. (7 Cranch.) 481, 3 L.Ed. 411 (1813).

4. See, e.g., Riverside & Dan River Cotton Mills v. Menefee, 237 U.S. 189, 35 S.Ct. 579, 59 L.Ed. 910 (1915).

5. See, e.g., 2 Black, A Treatise on the Law of Judgments § 902 (1st ed. 1891) (describing statutes allowing in personam jurisdiction over defendants based upon personal service outside the state); Hiller v. The Burlington and Missouri R.R. Co., 70 N.Y. 223 (1877) (discussing and applying New York Code of Civil Procedure § 432 which allowed for jurisdiction over corporations based upon in-state service of a corporate officer). As statutes "in derogation of the common law," they were often construed narrowly. See, e.g., Galpin v. Page, 85 U.S. (18 Wall.) 350, 369, 21 L.Ed. 959, 964 (1873).

soliciting customers or driving a car, as manifesting "consent" to the appointment of a state official as the defendant's "agent" for service of process. As long as the in-state activity was sufficient to make the assertion of jurisdiction reasonable, the Supreme Court upheld these statutes if they required the state official to transmit the process in a manner reasonably calculated to actually notify the defendant of the proceedings.[6]

The explosion in jurisdictional statutes occurred after *International Shoe Co. v. Washington*[7] was decided. *International Shoe*'s considerably more permissive test meant that many jurisdictional assertions not permitted by the common law were now constitutional. But, lacking any affirmative authority under state common law to take advantage of these now-expanded jurisdictional horizons, states needed to pass statutes to effectively extend their jurisdictional reach in the manner permitted by *International Shoe*.[8] Beginning with Illinois in 1955, states began to pass comprehensive jurisdictional statutes known as "long-arm statutes."[9] The metaphor, of course, is one for the expanded state court jurisdictional reach, hence the "long arm" of the state.[10] The result of these comprehensive jurisdictional statutes, now in force in every state and the District of Columbia,[11] has been to make inquiry into a state court's jurisdiction a two-step process. The first step is to examine whether the state has affirmative authority to exercise jurisdiction, either as a result of the common law or its long arm statute. The second is to ascertain whether that proposed exercise of jurisdiction offends the Due Process Clause. As a result, modern jurisdictional decisions almost always begin by noting that each of these steps is a necessary component of the jurisdictional calculus.[12]

Long-arm statutes fall into two groups. Some, patterned after the Illinois statute, set forth certain distinct categories of jurisdiction.[13] New York's statute,[14] for instance, provides that its courts have specific jurisdiction, inter alia, if the defendant "transacts any business within the state," "commits a tortious act within the state," "commits a

---

6. See, e.g., Hess v. Pawloski, 274 U.S. 352, 47 S.Ct. 632, 71 L.Ed. 1091 (1927) (upholding a Massachusetts statute treating driving in the forum state as an appointment of the Secretary of State as the defendant's agent for service); but see Wuchter v. Pizzutti, 276 U.S. 13, 48 S.Ct. 259, 72 L.Ed. 446 (1928) (striking down a statute similar to the *Hess* statute because the statute did not require actual notification of the defendant).

7. 326 U.S. 310, 66 S.Ct. 154, 90 L.Ed. 95 (1945).

8. See, e.g., Restatement, Second, Conflict of Laws § 30, cmnt. b ("When the question has arisen, the courts have usually held themselves without authority under their local law to exercise jurisdiction on bases not recognized by the common law unless authorized to do so by statute.").

9. 1 Casad, Jurisdiction in Civil Actions 4–3 (2d ed. 1991).

10. See generally Juenger, American Jurisdiction: A Story of Comparative Neglect, 65 U. Colo. L. Rev. 1 (1993) (noting generally poor drafting of such statutes).

11. See Casad, supra n.9, at 4–3.

12. See, e.g., Thompson v. Chrysler Motors Corp., 755 F.2d 1162, 1166 (5th Cir. 1985); Institutional Food Marketing v. Golden State Strawberries, Inc., 747 F.2d 448, 452 (8th Cir.1984); Trump v. Eighth Judicial Dist. Court of Nevada, 109 Nev. 687, 857 P.2d 740 (1993); Kubik v. Letteri, 532 Pa. 10, 614 A.2d 1110 (1992).

13. See Casad, supra n.9, at 4–3.

14. N.Y. Civ. Prac. L. & R. § 302.

tortious act without the state causing injury to person or property within the state" and also engages in substantial New York or interstate business. Such a statute clearly calls for an independent analysis quite apart from the question of whether the state's assertion of jurisdiction would be constitutional.[15]

A second kind of long-arm statute is one in the mold of California's, which provides that the California state courts have jurisdiction "on any basis not inconsistent" with the Constitution.[16] Such a statute clearly calls for only a "one-step analysis"[17] of whether jurisdiction comports with the Supreme Court precedents. While statutes written like New York's are probably more common, a large number of them have been construed by state courts to "go to the limits of due process."[18] As a result, many states have statutes that appear to fall into the category with the Illinois and New York statutes, but are interpreted as if they were the California statute. Statutes that are written or interpreted like California's decrease predictability somewhat because they throw state court jurisdiction to the mercy of the shifting Supreme Court precedents. Disciplined adherence to a statute like New York's constricts a state's jurisdictional reach slightly, but probably pays dividends in clearer standards. Nevertheless, it is hard to fault states for adopting statutes like California's. A natural desire to make courts reasonably accessible undoubtedly contributes to the drafting of expansive statutes, even if such statutes come at a moderate cost of diminished predictability.

B. FEDERAL COURTS

§ 5.15   The federal courts, like their state counterparts, began by applying the common law of jurisdiction. Federal court adhered to common law jurisdictional principles, even if local practice had been altered by statute.[1] It is now well accepted that without a special federal statute or rule federal courts have only their traditional jurisdictional authority.[2] Thus, the general structure of the jurisdictional inquiry in federal court parallels that in state court: first, statutory or rule-based authorization must be established; second, the constitutional boundaries

---

15. See, e.g., Ingraham v. Carroll, 90 N.Y.2d 592, 687 N.E.2d 1293, 665 N.Y.S.2d 10 (1997); Longines–Wittnauer Watch Co. v. Barnes & Reinecke, Inc., 15 N.Y.2d 443, 209 N.E.2d 68, 261 N.Y.S.2d 8 (1965).

16. See Cal. Code Civ. Proc. § 410.10.

17. Casad, supra n.9, at 4–5.

18. See, e.g., Hall v. Helicopteros Nacionales De Colombia, 638 S.W.2d 870 (Tex. 1982), rev'd on other grounds 466 U.S. 408, 104 S.Ct. 1868, 80 L.Ed.2d 404 (1984); Certain–Teed Prods. v. Second Judicial District Court, 87 Nev. 18, 23, 479 P.2d 781, 784 (1971). See generally Casad, supra n.9, at 4–5.

§ 5.15

1. See, e.g., Goldey v. Morning News, 156 U.S. 518, 15 S.Ct. 559, 39 L.Ed. 517 (1895) (refusing to apply a New York statute allowing for in personam jurisdiction over a corporation based solely on the in-state service of a corporate officer).

2. See, e.g., Omni Capital Int'l v. Rudolf Wolff & Co., 484 U.S. 97, 108 S.Ct. 404, 98 L.Ed.2d 415 (1987); Robertson v. Railroad Labor Bd., 268 U.S. 619, 624, 45 S.Ct. 621, 623–24, 69 L.Ed. 1119 (1925).

must be examined.[3] Federal courts are not under any strict mandate to consider jurisdictional questions in any particular order, however. In cases that raise challenges both to subject matter and personal jurisdiction a federal court has discretion to dismiss the case on either ground.[4]

The major source of federal court authorization to take personal jurisdiction appears in Federal Rule of Civil Procedure 4(k). Federal Rule 4(k)(1)(A) provides that a defendant is subject to personal jurisdiction if he "could be subjected to the jurisdiction of a court of general jurisdiction in the state in which the district court is located...."[5] Thus, in most cases, federal courts have exactly the same jurisdictional reach as their home state's courts. They begin by examining their home state's long-arm statute, and then proceed to consider the same constitutional test that applies to state courts.[6]

Federal Rule 4(k)(1)(B) contains what is popularly known as the "100–mile bulge" rule. It provides that a party is subject to personal jurisdiction if "joined under Rule 14 or Rule 19 and is served at a place within a judicial district of the United States and not more than 100 miles from the place from which the summons issues."[7] Thus for parties who are either impleaded or subject to mandatory joinder, federal courts can exercise personal jurisdiction without regard to state lines as long as the summons is actually served within the United States and no more than 100 miles from the courthouse. In multistate metropolitan areas, this provision can bring several additional states within the court's reach with respect to ancillary parties.[8]

Federal Rule 4(k)(1)(C) recognizes the broad jurisdictional rules applicable in interpleader cases.[9] A federal statute allows a federal court to hear cases involving rival claimants of diverse citizenship, as long as the claimants are minimally diverse.[10] Assuming that the case qualifies under the interpleader statute, other federal statutes allow a federal court hearing the interpleader action to restrain other actions anywhere

---

3. The special questions relating to the constitutional boundaries of federal court jurisdiction are considered infra §§ 10.2.

4. See Ruhrgas AG v. Marathon Oil Co., 526 U.S. 574, 119 S.Ct. 1563, 143 L.Ed.2d 760 (1999).

5. F.R.C.P. 4(k)(1)(A).

6. In fact, because federal courts have diversity subject matter jurisdiction, see 28 U.S.C.A. § 1332, they seem to be an even more plentiful source of cases on principles of state court jurisdiction than are the state courts themselves. See, e.g., Core–Vent Corp. v. Nobel Indus., 11 F.3d 1482 (9th Cir.1993) (applying California statute); Teledyne, Inc. v. Kone Corp., 892 F.2d 1404 (9th Cir.1989) (applying California statute); Third Nat'l Bank in Nashville v. WEDGE Group, Inc., 882 F.2d 1087 (6th Cir.1989)

(applying Tennessee statute); Rittenhouse v. Mabry, 832 F.2d 1380 (5th Cir.1987) (applying Mississippi statute); Petroleum Helicopters, Inc. v. Avco Corp., 804 F.2d 1367 (5th Cir.1986) (applying Louisiana statute); Fields v. Ramada Inn, Inc., 816 F.Supp. 1033 (E.D.Pa.1993) (applying Pennsylvania statute).

7. F.R.C.P. 4(k)(1)(B).

8. See Carrington, Symposium on the Fiftieth Anniversary of the Federal Rules of Civil Procedure: Continuing Work on the Civil Rules: The Summons, 63 Notre Dame L. Rev. 733, 752 (1988); see infra § 10.4.

9. F.R.C.P. 4(k)(1)(C).

10. See, e.g., State Farm Fire & Cas. Co. v. Tashire, 386 U.S. 523, 87 S.Ct. 1199, 18 L.Ed.2d 270 (1967) (upholding constitutionality of minimal diversity provision).

in the United States,[11] and allows for venue in the home district of any claimant,[12] essentially creating nationwide personal jurisdiction. These broad jurisdictional statutes are designed to avoid having interpleader actions fail for want of personal jurisdiction over all competing claimants. Federal Rule 4(k)(1)(D) is a more general exposition of the principle that federal courts must follow specific jurisdictional legislation. In several circumstances, Congress has decided that broader personal jurisdiction is necessary than that usually conferred on federal courts by borrowing their home state's long-arm statutes.[13]

Federal Rule 4(k)(2) also provides for broader federal court personal jurisdiction in some circumstances. That rule allows for personal jurisdiction in a federal court to the maximum extent permitted by the Constitution if the claim is one "arising under federal law," and with respect to "any defendant who is not subject to the jurisdiction of the courts of general jurisdiction of any state."[14] This addition to the federal rules was a response to the Supreme Court's decision in *Omni Capital International v. Rudolf Wolff & Co.*[15] In *Omni*, the Supreme Court held that a Louisiana federal court did not have personal jurisdiction over a foreign defendant in an action under federal securities laws because the Louisiana long-arm statute would not permit a state court to so exercise its jurisdiction. Rule 4(k)(2) was the response to Justice Blackmun's invitation to draft a "narrowly tailored service of process provision" covering such cases.[16] Were a case to arise on *Omni*'s facts today, Rule 4(k)(2) would authorize a federal court to bypass its home state's long-arm statute, and instead extend jurisdiction to the constitutional maximum.

VI.   OTHER JURISDICTIONAL ISSUES COMPARED

A.   NOTICE AND OPPORTUNITY TO BE HEARD

§ 5.16   In the United States there are other preconditions to effective judicial action commonly termed "jurisdictional." One important requirement is that the defendant be given reasonable notice of the proceedings against him.[1] A right to reasonable notice as an independent jurisdictional requirement evolved fairly recently. The two primary common law jurisdictional bases—in-state service of the defendant for in personam matters and pre-judgment attachment for in rem matters—did not require independent notice rules. In-state personal service, aside from conferring jurisdiction, clearly has the effect of notifying the

---

11.   28 U.S.C.A. § 2361.

12.   28 U.S.C.A. § 1397.

13.   See, e.g., 7 U.S.C.A. §§ 13a–1, 13a–2(4), 18(d) (Commodities Exchange Act); 15 U.S.C.A. § 22 (Clayton Act); 28 U.S.C.A. § 2361 (interpleader actions); see infra § 10.2.

14.   F.R.C.P. 4(k)(2).

15.   484 U.S. 97, 108 S.Ct. 404, 98 L.Ed.2d 415 (1987).

16.   Id. at 111, 108 S.Ct. at 413.

§ 5.16

1.   See, e.g., Mullane v. Central Hanover Bank & Trust Co., 339 U.S. 306, 70 S.Ct. 652, 94 L.Ed. 865 (1950); see infra §§ 12.2–12.4.

defendant of the action's pendency. As for in rem matters, the common law employed the fiction that the "law assumes that property is always in the possession of its owner ... and it proceeds upon the theory that its seizure will inform him [of] any proceedings authorized by law upon such seizure...."[2] Thus, state statutes governing in rem matters usually required only a feigned effort at informing the defendant, such as publication of a notice in a local newspaper.[3]

A right to reasonable notice gradually separated itself from the common law jurisdictional bases, however. Before the Supreme Court's *International Shoe* decision in 1945, states attempted to expand their jurisdictional reach by passing statutes that treated certain in-state activities, such as driving a car, as evidencing "implied consent" to jurisdiction in that state's courts. The Supreme Court upheld these "non-resident motorist" statutes as long as they required some reasonable effort to inform the defendant of the action's pendency,[4] but struck them down if they did not.[5] These results could not be explained in terms of the defendant's affiliation with the forum state, because in each case it was the same. Rather, the Supreme Court saw a right to reasonable notice as independently protected by the Due Process Clause.

With the Supreme Court's decision in *Mullane v. Central Hanover Bank & Trust Co.*[6] personal jurisdiction and notice clearly separated. *Mullane* involved a statutory action in the New York state courts brought by the trustees of a commonly-managed trust account to confirm their accounting. Although the Supreme Court held that New York state courts had personal jurisdiction over the beneficiaries, the Court found the statutory scheme calling for notice by publication in a newspaper constitutionally lacking. Regardless of the technical characterization of the action as in rem or in personam, the Court held that due process requires "notice reasonably calculated under all the circumstances, to apprise the interested parties of the pendency of the action...."[7] The Court held that for parties whose addresses are known, the constitutional minimum is notice by regular mail. Publication may be employed only as a last resort for affected persons who cannot be located with reasonable effort.[8] Later decisions made clear that *Mullane*'s "reasonably calculated" test applies even in true in rem matters,[9] and that test remains today as the constitutional benchmark for sufficient notice.[10]

---

2. Pennoyer v. Neff, 95 U.S. (5 Otto) 714, 727, 24 L.Ed. 565, 570 (1878).

3. See id. at 720, 24 L.Ed. at 568.

4. See, e.g., Hess v. Pawloski, 274 U.S. 352, 47 S.Ct. 632, 71 L.Ed. 1091 (1927) (notice by mail required).

5. See, e.g., Wuchter v. Pizzutti, 276 U.S. 13, 48 S.Ct. 259, 72 L.Ed. 446 (1928) (statute struck down because it did not require Secretary of State to transmit summons and complaint to the defendant).

6. 339 U.S. 306, 70 S.Ct. 652, 94 L.Ed. 865 (1950).

7. Id. at 314, 70 S.Ct. at 657.

8. Id. at 317, 70 S.Ct. at 658.

9. See, e.g., Schroeder v. City of New York, 371 U.S. 208, 83 S.Ct. 279, 9 L.Ed.2d 255 (1962); Walker v. Hutchinson, 352 U.S. 112, 77 S.Ct. 200, 1 L.Ed.2d 178 (1956).

10. See, e.g., Tulsa Professional Collection Servs. v. Pope, 485 U.S. 478, 108 S.Ct. 1340, 99 L.Ed.2d 565 (1988) (notification by mail constitutionally required for known creditors of an estate before claims can be barred).

Court systems have their own rules for effecting notice. An attempt to give notice in a manner not authorized by the local service provisions is ineffective, even if the method would be constitutionally satisfactory.[11] The federal court service provisions are consolidated in Federal Rule 4. Most states have some portion of their Civil Procedure code or rules devoted to service rules.[12] As is the case with regard to personal jurisdiction, objections to notice may be waived either by express agreement[13] or a failure to timely raise the matter.[14]

B. COMPETENCE OF THE COURT—SUBJECT MATTER JURISDICTION

§ 5.17   Courts are, as discussed above,[1] limited in their territorial reach by principles of personal jurisdiction. Another set of principles, those of court competence—or subject matter jurisdiction, as it is often termed—divide the authority between courts sitting within the same territory. For instance, states often divide the authority between their courts by the amount in controversy.[2] These rules are jurisdictional in the sense that a court has no power to hear a case not falling within the scope of its statutory authority. But such rules clearly do not implicate a court's territorial reach, hence they are rules of competence or subject matter jurisdiction.[3]

The most important, and probably most litigated, principles of subject matter jurisdiction are those that divide authority between state and federal courts. Article III of the Constitution governs the structure of all federal courts, both the Supreme and the inferior. Article III contains nine different heads of jurisdiction that may be given to federal courts. The conventional view is that it is within the purview of Congress to grant as much or as little as it sees fit of these heads of jurisdiction to lower federal courts.[4] Accordingly, Congress has given to lower federal courts some, but not all, of the authority that the Constitution would allow.[5]

---

11. See, e.g., Umbenhauer v. Woog, 969 F.2d 25 (3d Cir.1992) (unsuccessful effort to serve by international mail).

12. See, e.g., N.Y. Civ. Prac. L. & R. §§ 307–16.

13. See, e.g., Fed. R. Civ. P. 4(d).

14. See, e.g., Fed. R. Civ. P. 12(h)(1).

§ 5.17

1. See supra §§ 5.4–5.14.

2. See, e.g., Cal. Code Civ. Proc. § 86(a)(1) (California municipal courts have jurisdiction over civil matters involving less than $25,000).

3. See, e.g., Yousafzai v. Hyundai Motor America, 22 Cal.App.4th 920, 922, 27 Cal. Rptr.2d 569, 570 (1994) (considering whether amount in dispute brought the matter

within municipal court's subject matter jurisdiction).

4. The conventional view is best illustrated by Bator, Congressional Power over the Jurisdiction of the Federal Courts, 27 Vill. L. Rev. 1030 (1982). It is challenged by several commentators who argue that some or all of these grounds of jurisdiction are mandatory. See, e.g., Amar, A Neo–Federalist View of Article III: Separating the Two Tiers of Federal Jurisdiction, 65 B.U. L. Rev. 205 (1985) (three of nine heads of jurisdiction, including "arising under" head, must be conferred either on lower federal courts or the Supreme Court).

5. The three most important grants of federal court subject matter jurisdiction are federal question jurisdiction, see 28 U.S.C.A. § 1331, diversity jurisdiction, see

Unlike the issues of personal jurisdiction and notice, which are waived if not contested at the case's outset, the issue of subject matter jurisdiction remains open on direct review of the case, even upon the court's own motion.[6] A judgment is vulnerable to a collateral attack for lack of subject matter jurisdiction to the extent that the rendering court would allow such an attack.[7] Generally, therefore, a default judgment remains vulnerable to a collateral attack on the grounds that the rendering court lacked subject matter jurisdiction,[8] but a contested judgment cannot be attacked collaterally.[9]

C. VENUE

§ 5.18 Rules of venue also act as preconditions to a court hearing a case. Important venue principles are associated with the common law doctrine of forum non conveniens and statutory venue transfer in the federal courts, but these are discussed elsewhere.[1] Venue is largely a creature of statute. Both state and federal courts have venue statutes that govern them. State venue statutes usually determine the county in which the matter must be pursued.[2] The federal venue statute governs the federal judicial district in which the action must be pursued.[3]

The general federal venue statute has undergone a series of confusing revisions in recent years.[4] The principal effect of the amendments, however, has been to substantially relax the statutory venue constraints, in many cases making the venue limitations co-extensive with those

28 U.S.C.A. § 1332, and admiralty jurisdiction, see 28 U.S.C.A. § 1333. The authority conferred upon federal courts falls short of the constitutional maximum in several obvious ways. The diversity grant of jurisdiction contains a substantial amount in controversy, see 28 U.S.C.A. § 1332(a), and has always been interpreted to require full diversity of the parties, see Strawbridge v. Curtiss, 7 U.S. (3 Cranch.) 267, 2 L.Ed. 435 (1806), while the Constitution would allow for minimal diversity of the parties. See State Farm Fire & Cas. Co. v. Tashire, 386 U.S. 523, 87 S.Ct. 1199, 18 L.Ed.2d 270 (1967). The federal question statute has conventionally been interpreted to require that the federal right appear on the face of well pleaded complaint, see, e.g., Louisville & Nashville Railroad v. Mottley, 211 U.S. 149, 29 S.Ct. 42, 53 L.Ed. 126 (1908), while the parallel constitutional language requires only that the case contain some federal ingredient. See, e.g., Osborn v. Bank of the United States, 22 U.S. (9 Wheat.) 738, 6 L.Ed. 204 (1824).

6. See, e.g., F.R.C.P. 12(h)(3) (subject matter jurisdiction may be raised "by suggestion of the parties or otherwise" at any time during the proceedings); Louisville & Nashville R.R. v. Mottley, 211 U.S. 149, 29 S.Ct. 42, 53 L.Ed. 126 (1908) (lack of district court subject matter jurisdiction raised by the Supreme Court on its own motion without any suggestion from the parties).

7. See, e.g., Aldrich v. Aldrich, 378 U.S. 540, 84 S.Ct. 1687, 12 L.Ed.2d 1020 (1964).

8. See, e.g., Practical Concepts, Inc. v. Republic of Bolivia, 811 F.2d 1543 (D.C.Cir. 1987); Golden v. National Finance Adjusters, 555 F.Supp. 42 (E.D.Mich.1982).

9. See, e.g., Durfee v. Duke, 375 U.S. 106, 84 S.Ct. 242, 11 L.Ed.2d 186 (1963); Chicot County Drainage Dist. v. Baxter State Bank, 308 U.S. 371, 60 S.Ct. 317, 84 L.Ed. 329 (1940).

§ 5.18

1. See infra §§ 11.7–11.16.

2. See, e.g., Cal. Code Civ. Proc. § 395; N.Y. Civ. Prac. L. & R. § 503.

3. 28 U.S.C.A. § 1391.

4. For a discussion of the 1988 and 1990 changes, see Oakley, Recent Statutory Changes in the Law of Federal Jurisdiction and Venue: The Judicial Improvements Acts of 1988 and 1990, 24 U.C. Davis L. Rev. 735 (1991).

imposed by principles of personal jurisdiction. As a general proposition, the federal venue statute allows the litigation to proceed in any district in which any defendant "resides"—usually interpreted to mean "domiciled"[5]—as long as all of the defendants have the same home state.[6] Venue is also allowed in "a judicial district in which a substantial part of the events or omissions giving rise to the claim occurred, or a substantial part of the property that is the subject of the action is situated."[7] This phrase was intended to be broader than earlier versions of the statute, in which venue turned upon where the cause of action "arose."[8] As a fallback if neither of the foregoing provisions allow for a venue, the statute allows for venue in diversity cases in "a judicial district in which the defendants are subject to personal jurisdiction at the time the action is commenced," and in other cases in "a judicial district in which any defendant may be found."[9] The latter phrase is extremely cryptic, but may mean a judicial district in which any defendant is subject to personal jurisdiction.[10]

Much of the operation of the federal venue statute turns upon where the defendant resides. Because corporations have no natural residence, the venue statute assigns one in any judicial district "in which it is subject to personal jurisdiction."[11] In multi-district states, the statute treats a corporation as resident in any district "within which it contacts would be sufficient to subject it to personal jurisdiction if that district were a separate State, and, if there is no such district, the corporation shall be deemed to reside in the district within which it has the most significant contacts."[12] As a consequence, corporations doing business throughout the country are often amenable to suit in a large number of federal judicial districts.

Some vestiges of the so-called "local action" doctrine also continue to persist as venue principle that restricts the adjudication of actions involving realty to the forum of its situs. The local action rule's roots in the United States are usually traced to the venerable case of *Livingston v. Jefferson*,[13] which held that a trespass action could only be brought in the venue in which the land was situated. However, the weight of authority today is that the local action rule, if it exists at all, applies only to actions in which the title to land or an interest therein is in question and then only in disputes that "necessitate surveys, tract history investigations, and other miscellany peculiar to the locality...."[14]

---

5. See, e.g., Manley v. Engram, 755 F.2d 1463, 1466 n.3 (11th Cir.1985).

6. 28 U.S.C.A. § 1391(a)(1), (b)(1).

7. 28 U.S.C.A. § 1391(a)(2), (b)(2).

8. See, e.g., Leroy v. Great Western United Corp., 443 U.S. 173, 99 S.Ct. 2710, 61 L.Ed.2d 464 (1979).

9. 28 U.S.C.A. § 1391(a)(3), (b)(3).

10. See, e.g., Milwaukee Concrete Studios, Limited v. Fjeld Mfg. Co., 8 F.3d 441 (7th Cir.1993).

11. 28 U.S.C.A. § 1391(c).

12. 28 U.S.C.A. § 1391(c).

13. 15 Fed.Cas. 660 (C.C.D. Va. 1811) (No. 8,411) (Marshall, J.)

14. Fisher v. Virginia Elec. & Power Co., 243 F. Supp. 2d 538 (E.D. Va. 2003). See infra § 7.7.

Objections to venue, like those founded on personal jurisdiction or notice, must be raised at the outset of the litigation, or they are waived.[15] Venue objections are not a basis for a successful collateral attack, even on a default judgment.[16] Thus, venue objections must be presented immediately to the judgment rendering court, or they are lost forever.

VII.   CHALLENGING JURISDICTION

A.   DIRECT ATTACKS

1.   *Federal Court—FRCP 12(b)*

§ 5.19   Federal Rule of Civil Procedure 12 governs the process by which the defendant may raise many preliminary objections to the plaintiff's action. Many of the preliminary objections specified in Federal Rule 12—specifically subsection (b)—are jurisdictional in nature.[1] Federal Rule 12(b)(2) allows a defendant to move to dismiss for lack of personal jurisdiction, 12(b)(3) for lack of venue, and 12(b)(5) for a insufficient "service of process."

Federal Rule 12 requires that a defendant's objection to venue, notice or personal jurisdiction be presented at the outset of the case. A defendant can challenge venue, notice or personal jurisdiction in one of two ways. First, and probably more commonly, the challenge can be presented in a motion to dismiss the action. If the motion, the response to the motion, and the accompanying affidavits show that there are no disputed material facts, the court can rule without taking live testimony.[2] However, if the motion, the response and the accompanying affidavits reveal disputed material facts, the court must eventually resolve the disputed factual matters through live testimony.[3] This testimony may either be heard before the trial, or—especially if the jurisdictional issue is intertwined with the merits of the case—with the trial of the case.[4] A defendant can also preserve an objection to venue, notice or personal jurisdiction by raising the matter as an affirmative defense in the answer to the complaint.[5] This route allows the defendant to later raise the matter by motion.

Objections to venue, notice and personal jurisdiction are extremely easy to waive in federal court. In most circumstances, the objection to venue, notice or personal jurisdiction must be presented in the defendant's first filing or it is lost forever. Federal Rule 12(g) allows a defendant to respond to the complaint with a motion that combines

---

15. F.R.C.P. 12(h)(1).

16. See, e.g., Hembree v. Tinnin, 807 F.Supp. 109 (D.Kan.1992).

§ 5.19

1. F.R.C.P. 12(b).

2. See Data Disc, Inc. v. Systems Tech. Assoc., 557 F.2d 1280 (9th Cir.1977) (plaintiff need only make a "prima facie" show-

ing of jurisdiction if challenge does not involve live testimony).

3. See, e.g., *Data Disc*, 557 F.2d at 1285 n.2 (court may take testimony on jurisdictional matters either at or before trial).

4. Id.

5. F.R.C.P. 12(d).

multiple grounds for dismissing the action.[6] Thus, for instance, a defendant could properly make a combined motion to dismiss the action for lack of personal jurisdiction[7] and to dismiss the complaint for failure to state a claim upon which relief can be granted.[8] But if the defendant first responded to the complaint with a motion to dismiss the complaint for failure to state a claim, and then in a subsequent motion attempted to dismiss the action for lack of venue, notice or personal jurisdiction, those latter objections would be held waived.[9] An amended complaint that raises new claims requires a defendant to renew the objection to jurisdiction; failure to do so can result in a waiver.[10]

A defendant who suffers an adverse ruling on the jurisdictional issue is usually then required to defend the case on the merits. The usual practice in federal court is that appeals are taken only from the final judgments of district courts.[11] This applies to rulings on personal jurisdiction, though a defendant obviously does not waive the jurisdictional objection by defending on the merits at the trial level, and waiting until the end of the case to appeal the adverse jurisdictional ruling.[12] In extraordinary cases, a defendant may be able to obtain interlocutory review of an adverse jurisdictional ruling through a certified interlocutory appeal or by writ of mandamus.[13]

A major exception to the rules on waiving jurisdictional objections is subject matter jurisdiction. Unlike notice, venue and personal jurisdiction, subject matter jurisdiction can never be waived on direct review.[14] In fact it need not be raised by the parties. Courts are under a duty to raise the issue on their own motion, and there are famous instances of cases being dismissed on the United States Supreme Court's own motion because the federal district court lacked subject matter jurisdiction.[15] At least one court has concluded that subject matter jurisdiction is so fundamental that a challenge to subject matter jurisdiction must be resolved before reaching the question of personal jurisdiction, even if a lack of personal jurisdiction provides a more straightforward route to dismissal, though the Supreme Court eventually reversed, holding that a court was free to address the issues in either order.[16] The theory behind the durability of objections to subject matter jurisdiction, in contrast to the relatively fragility of other jurisdictional objections, is that the former implicate structural limitations on the power of federal courts

6. F.R.C.P. 12(g).

7. F.R.C.P. 12(b)(2).

8. F.R.C.P. 12(b)(6).

9. F.R.C.P. 12(h)(2).

10. See, e.g., Preferred RX, Inc. v. American Prescription Plan, Inc., 46 F.3d 535 (6th Cir.1995).

11. See 28 U.S.C.A. § 1291.

12. See, e.g., Carteret Sav. Bank v. Shushan, 919 F.2d 225 (3d Cir.1990).

13. See, e.g., Donatelli v. National Hockey League, 893 F.2d 459 (1st Cir. 1990).

14. See F.R.C.P. 12(h)(3).

15. See, e.g., Louisville & Nashville R.R. v. Mottley, 211 U.S. 149, 29 S.Ct. 42, 53 L.Ed. 126 (1908).

16. See, e.g., Marathon Oil Co. v. Ruhrgas, 145 F.3d 211 (5th Cir.1998) (en banc) (decision by a 16–7 vote), rev'd 526 U.S. 574, 119 S.Ct. 1563, 143 L.Ed.2d 760 (1999).

and the federal government, while the latter are personal rights that may be waived.[17]

2. *State Courts*

§ 5.20 A large number of state courts follow the Federal Rules of Civil Procedure as a matter of state law, or have a very similar procedural apparatus.[1] In those states the procedure for challenging jurisdiction is the same as that in federal court.[2] Some states, often those whose procedural law is still heavily influenced by New York's 1850 Field Code,[3] require a defendant to make a special appearance to successfully object to notice, venue or personal jurisdiction.[4] The procedure for objecting to jurisdiction through a special appearance differs in some important respects from the federal procedure. First, a successful special appearance requires that it be the defendant's first appearance in the action, and that the defendant raise *only* jurisdictional objections.[5] Under federal practice, a defendant could make a combined motion to dismiss the action for failure to state a claim and for lack of personal jurisdiction.[6] In a state that still requires a special appearance, combining jurisdictional and non-jurisdictional objections waives the issue of jurisdiction.[7] Second, states that still demand a special appearance require a defendant who suffers an adverse trial court ruling on jurisdiction to seek immediate appellate review, usually by writ of mandamus.[8] Defending the action on the merits, and attempting to seek review of the jurisdictional ruling on an appeal from the final judgment, constitutes a waiver of the jurisdictional issue.[9]

17. See, e.g., Insurance Corp. of Ireland v. Compagnie des Bauxites de Guinee, 456 U.S. 694, 102 S.Ct. 2099, 72 L.Ed.2d 492 (1982).

§ 5.20

1. Oakley & Coon, The Federal Rules in State Courts: A Survey of State Court Systems of Civil Procedure, 61 Wash. L. Rev. 1367 (1986) (large number of states follow federal rules as a matter of state law).

2. In New York, for instance, which does not follow the Federal Rules as a matter of state law, the procedure for objecting to jurisdiction follows that in federal court, at least in the sense that jurisdictional objections can be combined with other objections. See N.Y. Civ. Prac. L. & R. § 3211(e).

3. California is the leading example. Oakley & Coon, supra n.1, at 1383 ("California remains committed to code pleading.").

4. See, e.g., Alioto Fish Co. v. Alioto, 27 Cal.App.4th 1669, 34 Cal.Rptr.2d 244 (1994) (special appearance necessary to challenge jurisdiction).

5. See, e.g., Stafford v. People ex rel. Dep't of Public Works, 144 Cal.App.2d 79, 300 P.2d 231 (1956) (combining jurisdictional and non-jurisdictional objections is a waiver of jurisdictional objections).

6. See F.R.C.P. 12(g).

7. See, e.g., *Stafford*, 144 Cal.App.2d 79, 300 P.2d 231.

8. See, e.g., Jardine v. Superior Court, 213 Cal. 301, 2 P.2d 756 (1931) (relief by writ of prohibition); Pacific and Southwest Annual Conference of the United Methodist Church v. Superior Court, 82 Cal.App.3d 72, 85, 147 Cal.Rptr. 44, 51 (1978) (relief by writ of mandate); Muller v. Reagh, 148 Cal. App.2d 157, 306 P.2d 593 (1957) (appellate relief must be devoted exclusively to seeking review of jurisdictional issue).

9. See, e.g., San Diego County Dep't of Social Services v. Delay, 199 Cal.App.3d 1031, 1038, 245 Cal.Rptr. 216, 220 (1988) (trial on the merits without seeking immediate review of jurisdictional objection constitutes a waiver of jurisdictional issue).

B. COLLATERAL ATTACKS

§ 5.21   A defendant wishing to challenge a forum's jurisdiction also has the option of making a collateral attack on the judgment. A collateral attack is distinguished from a direct attack in that the former involves a second proceeding challenging the validity of a previously rendered judgment.[1] The availability of this method of challenging a court's jurisdiction has been long recognized.[2]

A right of collateral attack for lack of jurisdiction is closely circumscribed by the Full Faith and Credit Clause.[3] In order to be vulnerable to collateral attack, the judgment rendered must generally be a default judgment.[4] If the judgment debtor appeared in the first proceeding, objections to personal jurisdiction and notice are waived by the appearance.[5] Even objections to subject matter jurisdiction, which are not cured by a defendant's appearance, generally may not be contested collaterally unless the judgment was taken by default.[6] Second, the question of jurisdiction must not have been litigated and decided by the judgment-rendering court. If, for instance, a defendant were to appear in a state court to object to jurisdiction, have the objection overruled, and then make no further appearance, the forum would allow a judgment to be taken against the defendant by default. However, unlike default judgments in actions in which the judgment debtor made no appearance of any kind, such a judgment would not be vulnerable to a collateral attack in another state.[7] A United States court cannot, without violating the Full Faith and Credit Clause, allow an attack on another court's judgment on a ground not permitted by the judgment-rendering court.[8] Because United States courts generally do not allow their own judgments to be impeached in a collateral proceeding, absent fraud or some other extraordinary circumstance, a court is required to treat as conclusive another American court's determination that it had jurisdiction.

§ 5.21

1. See, e.g., Restatement, Second, Conflict of Laws § 96 (1971) (describing circumstances in which a collateral attack is allowed).

2. See, e.g., Hampton v. McConnel, 16 U.S. (3 Wheat.) 234, 4 L.Ed. 378 (1818).

3. See, e.g., Restatement, Second, Conflict of Laws § 96 (1971) (Full Faith and Credit Clause does not allow an attack on a judgment on grounds that would not be allowed under the local law of the court rendering the judgment).

4. See, e.g., Pennoyer v. Neff, 95 U.S. (5 Otto) 714, 24 L.Ed. 565 (1878) (judgment debtor allowed to attack earlier rendered default judgment); Jackson v. FIE Corp., 302 F.3d 515 (5th Cir. 2002) (judgment debtor must be allowed to challenge for lack of personal jurisdiction a default judgment in which no appearance was made by the judgment debtor).

5. See, e.g., Practical Concepts, Inc. v. Republic of Bolivia, 811 F.2d 1543, 1546 (D.C.Cir.1987).

6. See, e.g., Durfee v. Duke, 375 U.S. 106, 84 S.Ct. 242, 11 L.Ed.2d 186 (1963) (collateral attack for lack of subject matter jurisdiction not allowed where earlier judgment was not taken by default); Chicot County Drainage Dist. v. Baxter State Bank, 308 U.S. 371, 60 S.Ct. 317, 84 L.Ed. 329 (1940) (same); Hodge v. Hodge, 621 F.2d 590, 592 (3d Cir.1980) (same).

7. See Baldwin v. Iowa State Traveling Men's Ass'n, 283 U.S. 522, 51 S.Ct. 517, 75 L.Ed. 1244 (1931); Restatement, Second, Conflict of Laws § 96, illus. 1 (1971).

8. Restatement, Second, Conflict of Laws § 97 (1971).

Foreign court determinations, while not covered by the Full Faith and Credit Clause, are also respected absent some showing of fundamental unfairness in the proceedings.[9] Collateral attacks, for lack of jurisdiction, on foreign court judgments are subject to a general standard of fairness.[10] United States courts considering whether to enforce a foreign court's default judgment insist that the defendant have been given notice and a fair opportunity to defend, and that the foreign court had jurisdiction on a basis acceptable in an American forum.[11] Because recognition of foreign court judgments, unlike their domestic counterparts, is not the subject of a constitutional command the application of these principles is more flexible and necessarily varies significantly from court to court.

Collateral attacks to jurisdiction are, by their very nature, a riskier strategy than direct attacks. This is because a defendant who incorrectly believes that the judgment-rendering court lacks jurisdiction loses his opportunity to contest the case on the merits if he waits until a collateral proceeding to challenge jurisdiction. A defendant with a defense on the merits of a case is better off directly attacking jurisdiction because, if the jurisdictional attack is ultimately unsuccessful, he can then proceed to litigate the action on the merits.

C. LIMITED APPEARANCES

§ 5.22   As discussed above,[1] the primary difference between in rem and in personam actions is that in the former the effect of the judgment is limited to the property brought under the court's control at the outset of the litigation. A defendant's appearance, however, is a traditional basis for in personam jurisdiction.[2] Thus, a defendant who wishes to assert an interest in the property that is the subject of an in rem action runs the risk of converting the action to an in personam proceeding.[3]

To solve this problem, many courts allow a limited appearance.[4] A limited appearance is one that allows a party claiming an interest in the

9. See Schiereck v. Schiereck, 14 Mass. App.Ct. 378, 439 N.E.2d 859 (1982) (German court's custody determination recognized); Laskosky v. Laskosky, 504 So.2d 726 (Miss.1987) (Canadian court's judgment of custody recognized); see also Restatement, Second, Conflict of Laws § 98 (1971).

10. See Panama Processes, S.A. v. Cities Service Co., 796 P.2d 276 (Okla.1990) (attack on Brazilian judgment allowed only if a showing of fraud or lack of jurisdiction).

11. See, e.g., Cherun v. Frishman, 236 F.Supp. 292 (D.D.C.1964) (jurisdiction of foreign court must comport with United States' standard of due process); Rotary Club of Tucson v. Chaprales Ramos de Pena, 160 Ariz. 362, 773 P.2d 467 (1989) (judgment not enforced because of lack of notice); Davidson & Co. v. Allen, 89 Nev. 126, 508 P.2d 6 (1973) (Canadian judgment not recognized because Canadian court's as-

sertion of jurisdiction incompatible with American notion of "minimum contacts"); see generally Restatement, Second, Conflict of Laws § 98, cmnt. d (1971).

§ 5.22

1. See supra § 5.5.

2. See supra § 5.8.

3. See, e.g., Carolina Power & Light Co. v. Uranex, 451 F.Supp. 1044 (N.D.Cal. 1977).

4. See, e.g., N.Y. Civ. Prac. L. & R. § 320(c); Abercrombie v. Davies, 35 Del.Ch. 354, 118 A.2d 358 (1955) (plaintiff who commences an in rem action cannot convert to an in personam matter without committing "constructive fraud" on the defendant; Myers v. Myers, 341 Ill.App. 406, 94 N.E.2d 100 (1950).

res to assert that interest without "appearing" in the action in the sense of subjecting himself to the court's in personam jurisdiction. The name is thus descriptive: It is an appearance for the limited purpose of litigating one's interests in the res. It differs from a special appearance, because a special appearance is one made for the sole purpose of objecting to jurisdiction. And a limited appearance quite obviously differs from a general appearance, because a general appearance subjects the defendant to the court's in personam jurisdiction.

Because the Supreme Court, in *Shaffer v. Heitner*,[5] unified the constitutional test governing in personam and in rem jurisdiction, the frequency with which parties make limited appearances has declined markedly. Both in personam and in rem jurisdiction now require a showing that the defendant has minimum contacts with the forum state.[6] There are, therefore, relatively few cases in which a court has in rem jurisdiction but would not have in personam jurisdiction.[7] Such cases arise occasionally, however,[8] and when they do a defendant can usually make a limited appearance to assure the that matter remains an in rem action.

VIII.   CONTINUING JURISDICTION

§ 5.23   Jurisdiction over a party, once acquired, continues throughout all subsequent proceeding which are part of that original litigation.[1] As Justice Holmes pointed out in the leading case, this is a practical rule which avoids the necessity of arrest of a defendant, or similar measures, during the action's pendency.[2] As a consequence, a defendant before the court on any jurisdictional basis remains subject to its jurisdiction as to all subsequent proceedings such as appeals, but not as to other proceedings that are not an essential concomitant of the original suit.[3] The concept also applies to the plaintiff who, having put the court's machinery into motion, submits himself to jurisdiction on counterclaims, cross actions, setoffs and the like.[4] This rule has also been extended occasion-

---

5.   433 U.S. 186, 97 S.Ct. 2569, 53 L.Ed.2d 683 (1977).

6.   Id. at 195, 97 S.Ct. at 2575.

7.   See supra § 5.9.

8.   See, e.g., Banco Ambrosiano, S.P.A. v. Artoc Bank & Trust Ltd., 62 N.Y.2d 65, 464 N.E.2d 432, 476 N.Y.S.2d 64 (1984).

§ 5.23

1.   See Republic National Bank of Miami v. United States, 506 U.S. 80, 113 S.Ct. 554, 121 L.Ed.2d 474 (1992) (in rem jurisdiction continues even if the trial court loses control over the res); Michigan Trust Co. v. Ferry, 228 U.S. 346, 33 S.Ct. 550, 57 L.Ed. 867 (1913); Rice v. Rice, 222 Ark. 639, 262 S.W.2d 270 (1953); Sampsell v. Superior Court, 32 Cal.2d 763, 197 P.2d 739 (1948);

Clemens v. Kinsley, 72 Idaho 251, 239 P.2d 266 (1951); Gowins v. Gowins, 466 So.2d 32 (La.1985); White v. Deal, 496 So.2d 1175 (La.App.1986); Bailey v. Bailey, 867 P.2d 1267 (Okla.1994).

2.   See *Michigan Trust Co.*, 228 U.S. at 353, 33 S.Ct. at 552.

3.   See, e.g., New York Life Ins. Co. v. Dunlevy, 241 U.S. 518, 36 S.Ct. 613, 60 L.Ed. 1140 (1916); Pettie v. Roberts, 214 Ga. 750, 107 S.E.2d 657 (1959).

4.   See, e.g., Adam v. Saenger, 303 U.S. 59, 67–68, 58 S.Ct. 454, 458, 82 L.Ed. 649 (1938); Frank's Casing Crew & Rental Tools, Inc. v. PMR Techs., Ltd., 292 F.3d 1363 (Fed. Cir. 2002); Collins v. McCook, 17 La.App. 415, 136 So. 204 (1931); Restatement, Second, Conflict of Laws § 34 (1971).

ally to cross-actions for contribution between joint tortfeasors, by allowing a defendant who has satisfied a judgment to proceed against co-parties simply by service upon their attorneys in the underlying action.[5] The same concept applies to in rem proceedings; wrongful removal of the res from the state during the action's pendency does not deprive the court of jurisdiction.[6]

The concept of continuing jurisdiction sees its most frequent use during family law litigation. Courts often assert continuing jurisdiction over support matters long after the immediate issues in the dispute, such as property division, are settled.[7] The prevailing common law view was that custody matters were subject to the rule of continuing jurisdiction, so that jurisdiction was not lost by wrongful removal of the child from the state.[8] The Uniform Child Custody Jurisdiction Act, and its federal counterpart, now vest jurisdiction in a single court called the child's "home" state. These developments are addressed in Chapter 15.

---

5. See, e.g., Ohlquist v. Nordstrom, 143 Misc. 502, 257 N.Y.S. 711 (Sup.Ct.1932), aff'd mem. 262 N.Y. 696, 188 N.E. 125 (1933).

6. See Restatement, Second, Conflict of Laws § 58 (1971).

7. See, e.g., Rice v. Rice, 222 Ark. 639, 262 S.W.2d 270 (1953); Reynolds v. Reynolds, 21 Cal.2d 580, 134 P.2d 251 (1943); Gowins v. Gowins, 466 So.2d 32 (La.1985).

8. See, e.g., Sampsell v. Superior Court, 32 Cal.2d 763, 197 P.2d 739 (1948); Clemens v. Kinsley, 72 Idaho 251, 239 P.2d 266 (1951); Hatch v. Hatch, 15 N.J.Misc. 461, 192 A. 241 (1937).

Chapter 6

GENERAL JURISDICTION

Table of Sections

		Sections
I.	Introduction	6.1
II.	"Satellite" Bases of Jurisdiction	6.2–6.6
	A. Transient Jurisdiction—The Rule of In–State Service	6.2
	B. Consent	6.3
	C. Residence, Domicile and Nationality	6.4
	D. Appearance	6.5
	E. Jurisdiction by Necessity	6.6
III.	Contacts–Based General Jurisdiction	6.7–6.9
	A. Distinguished from Specific Jurisdiction	6.7
	B. Application to Individual Defendants	6.8
	C. "Continuous and Systematic" Contacts	6.9

I. INTRODUCTION

§ 6.1 The term "general jurisdiction," as it is used in the United States, refers to assertions of territorial jurisdiction that do not depend upon the character of the dispute between the parties.[1] The term was invented in an enormously influential law review article[2] and is intended to be descriptive. Bases of "general" jurisdiction are so-called because they allow for jurisdiction generally, and without regard to the nature of the parties' dispute.[3] General jurisdiction is distinguished from its counterpart "specific" jurisdiction, which is jurisdiction specific to the character of the dispute.[4]

Similar dichotomies exist in other legal systems, but the terms "specific" and "general" jurisdiction are in wide use only in the United States.[5] One of the distinguishing features of American jurisdiction law

---

§ 6.1

1. See supra § 5.10.

2. See von Mehren & Trautman, Jurisdiction to Adjudicate: A Suggested Analysis, 79 Harv. L. Rev. 1121, 1135–45 (1966).

3. For this reason, one commentator calls this type of jurisdiction "dispute-blind." See Twitchell, The Myth of General

Jurisdiction, 101 Harv. L. Rev. 610, 612 (1988).

4. See Hay, Flexibility versus Predictability and Uniformity in Choice of Law, 226 Recueil des Cours 285, 311–15 (1991).

5. See generally M. Reimann, Conflict of Laws in Western Europe: A Guide Through the Jungle 75–77 (1995); Hay, supra n.4, at 311–15.

is its fairly generous conception of general jurisdiction. The Brussels Convention and related treaties now regulate jurisdiction in civil and commercial cases as between domiciliaries of Western European countries.[6] Those conventions tolerate some assertions of jurisdiction that would be termed "general" in the United States, but they tolerate them only in a limited fashion. For instance, under these conventions, jurisdiction is available in an individual defendant's domicile and a corporate defendant's "seat."[7] These bases are considerably more modest than their American counterparts. To be sure, other countries have developed some jurisdiction rules that extend well beyond what would be tolerated under the United States Supreme Court's precedents, but the international trend is away from such assertions of jurisdiction and towards more modest and predictable ones.[8] General jurisdiction in the United States, however, remains a vital part of the legal landscape.

American general jurisdiction—both its existence and its scope—is certain to remain controversial. It guarantees that in many cases the plaintiff will have more than one forum from which to choose. The multiplicity of available fora, coupled with choice-of-law rules that tilt strongly towards the application of forum law,[9] create enormous incentives for plaintiffs to forum shop. The relative ease of forum shopping in the United States contrasts with international forum shopping. In the latter situation, parties and counsel can encounter language, cultural and legal differences that are far greater disincentives to suing away from home than those faced by domestic plaintiffs.[10] The prevalence of American forum shopping has led some to call for the abolition of general jurisdiction,[11] but forum shopping has defenders who argue that is the only available and practical method by which counsel can protect clients—particularly tort plaintiffs—from unfair and unjust laws.[12] The widespread use of general jurisdiction in the United States has also led to some controversial antidotes, most notably the doctrine of forum non conveniens.[13] Whatever its future, general jurisdiction is an important fact of the present, and thus demands close attention.

6. See Reimann, supra n.5, at 66–67.

7. See Reimann, supra n.5, at 70; Borchers, Comparing Personal Jurisdiction in the United States and the European Community: Lessons for American Reform, 40 Am. J. Comp. L. 121, 135 (1992).

8. This is demonstrated both by the existence of international agreements limiting the use of the "exorbitant" jurisdictional bases, see Borchers, supra n.7, at 130, and by changing national laws limiting the scope of some of the more outrageous rules. See, e.g., Pearce, The Comity Doctrine as a Barrier to Judicial Jurisdiction: A U.S.–E.U. Comparison, 30 Stan. J. Int'l L. 525, 565 (1994).

9. See Borchers, The Choice–Of–Law Revolution: An Empirical Study, 49 Wash. & Lee L. Rev. 357 (1992).

10. Reimann, supra n.5, at 70.

11. Maier & McCoy, A Unifying Theory for Judicial Jurisdiction and Choice of Law, 39 Am. J. Comp. L. 249 (1991).

12. See Juenger, Eason–Weinmann Center for Comparative Law Colloquium: The Internationalization of Law and Legal Practice: Forum Shopping, Domestic and International, 63 Tul. L. Rev. 553 (1989).

13. See infra §§ 11.7—11.16. This doctrine is generally not employed in European countries, see Pearce, supra n.8, at 542–44, and in any event is extremely uncertain in its operation. Hay, Transient Jurisdiction, Especially Over International Defendants: A Critical Comment on *Burnham v. Superior Court of California*, 1990 U. Ill. L. Rev. 593.

II. "SATELLITE" BASES OF JURISDICTION

A. TRANSIENT JURISDICTION—THE RULE OF IN–STATE SERVICE

§ 6.2 Historically, judicial jurisdiction began with the concept of physical power asserted by arresting and physically bringing the defendant before the court. As presence was the most primitive and certain manner of exercising physical power, when it existed no question of the authority of the court could be raised. Eventually, the practice of physically arresting the defendant gave way to personal, in-hand service of the summons on the defendant while in the forum state.[1]

The rule that a defendant is subject to in personam jurisdiction based solely upon the in-state service of the summons is one of the most enduring in American jurisdictional jurisprudence. It fits well with Holmes' famous dictum that the "foundation of jurisdiction is physical power,"[2] and found clear expression in Justice Story's 1834 treatise.[3] Later scholarship criticized Story's handling of his sources,[4] but more recent work has proved the correctness of Story's assertion that the rule is one whose origins extend well back into the common law.[5] Early and famous state cases endorsed it,[6] and by the time the Supreme Court decided *Pennoyer v. Neff*,[7] it was sufficiently well entrenched that the Supreme Court referred to it as one of the foundations of the common law of jurisdiction.

Transient jurisdiction is truly a "general" basis of jurisdiction. Its existence is entirely independent of the nature of the dispute between the parties. It depends, instead, solely upon whether the summons was delivered to the defendant while he was physically present in the state. The defendant's stay in the state can be extremely brief and unrelated to any business purpose; in one famous case, transient jurisdiction was upheld on a defendant served in an airplane while flying over the forum state.[8]

The harshness of this rule has made it vulnerable to criticism.[9] The rule is disfavored internationally; when England acceded to the European Union's Brussels Convention transient jurisdiction was added to the

---

§ 6.2

1. International Shoe Co. v. Washington, 326 U.S. 310, 316, 66 S.Ct. 154, 158, 90 L.Ed. 95 (1945) ("But now that capias ad respondendum has given way to personal service of summons . . .").

2. McDonald v. Mabee, 243 U.S. 90, 91, 37 S.Ct. 343, 343, 61 L.Ed. 608, 609 (1917).

3. J. Story, A Treatise on the Conflict of Laws § 539 (1834).

4. A. Ehrenzweig, A Treatise on the Conflict of Laws § 71 (1962).

5. Weinstein, The Dutch Influence on the Conception of Judicial Jurisdiction in 19th Century America, 38 Am. J. Comp. L. 73 (1990).

6. See, e.g., Barrell v. Benjamin, 15 Mass. 354 (1819).

7. 95 U.S. (5 Otto) 714, 722, 24 L.Ed. 565, 568 (1878).

8. See Grace v. MacArthur, 170 F.Supp. 442 (E.D.Ark.1959).

9. See, e.g., Ehrenzweig, The Transient Rule of Personal Jurisdiction: The "Power" Myth and Forum Conveniens, 65 Yale L.J. 289 (1956).

list of "exorbitant" bases that the signatory nations agreed not to enforce against domiciliaries of other signatory nations.[10] After the Supreme Court's opinion in *Shaffer v. Heitner*,[11] there was a belief among many commentators[12] and some lower courts[13] that in-state service was no longer sufficient, by itself, to establish jurisdiction. The source of the belief was the Supreme Court's statement that "all assertions of state court jurisdiction must be evaluated according to the standards set forth in *International Shoe* and its progeny."[14] While *Shaffer* was a case addressing quasi in rem jurisdiction, the Court's statement seemed broad enough to cover the entirety of state court jurisdiction, including the rule of transient jurisdiction.

10. See Hay, Transient Jurisdiction, Especially Over International Defendants: Critical Comments on *Burnham v. Superior Court of California*, 1990 U. Ill. L. Rev. 593.

11. 433 U.S. 186, 97 S.Ct. 2569, 53 L.Ed.2d 683 (1977).

12. See, e.g., Fyr, *Shaffer v. Heitner*: The Supreme Court's Latest Last Words on State Court Jurisdiction, 26 Emory L.J. 739, 770 (1977); Vernon, State Court Jurisdiction: A Preliminary Inquiry into the Impact of *Shaffer v. Heitner*, 63 Iowa L. Rev. 997, 1021 (1977) (after Shaffer v. Heitner the availability of transient jurisdiction is "open to substantial doubt"); Jay, "Minimum Contacts" as a Unified Theory of Personal Jurisdiction: A Reappraisal, 59 N.C. L. Rev. 429, 474 (1981) ("We may assume that the Court will restrict 'tag' jurisdiction whenever the occasion presents itself."); Silberman, *Shaffer v. Heitner*: The End of an Era, 53 N.Y.U. L. Rev. 33 (1978); Weintraub, Due Process Limitations on the Personal Jurisdiction of State Courts: Time For a Change, 63 Or. L. Rev. 485, 492 (1984) ("The traditional basis for personal jurisdiction that is most vulnerable [after Shaffer v. Heitner] is service on the defendant while he is transiently present in the forum."); Lewis, A Brave New World for Personal Jurisdiction: Flexible Test Under Uniform Standards, 37 Vand. L. Rev. 1, 60–65 (1984); Sedler, Judicial Jurisdiction and Choice of Law in Interstate Accident Cases: The Implications of *Shaffer v. Heitner*, 1978 Wash. U.L.Q. 329, 332; Vernon, Single Factor Bases of In Personam Jurisdiction— Speculation of the Impact of Shaffer v. Heitner, 1978 Wash. U.L.Q. 273, 303 (availability of transient jurisdiction "doubtful" after Shaffer v. Heitner); Note, Survey of Developments in North Carolina Law, 1987—*Lockert v. Breedlove*: The North Carolina Supreme Court Rejects the Minimum Contacts Analysis Under the "Transient Rule" of Jurisdiction, 66 N.C.L. Rev. 1051, 1060 (1987) (criticizing the North Carolina Supreme Court for upholding the constitu-

tionality of tag jurisdiction); cf. Reese, *Shaffer v. Heitner*: Implications for the Doctrine of *Seider v. Roth*, 68 Iowa L. Rev. 1023, 1023 (1978) (it is "by no means clear" that Shaffer v. Heitner declares tag jurisdiction unconstitutional); Note, The Physical Presence Basis of Personal Jurisdiction Ten Years After *Shaffer v. Heitner*, 62 Notre Dame L. Rev. 713, 730 (1987) (tag jurisdiction serves the goal of providing the plaintiff with a forum); see also Ehrenzweig, supra n.9 (criticizing the fairness of tag jurisdiction). Writing in 1929 Professor Dodd questioned the validity of tag jurisdiction: "Not only is there thus reason to doubt the appropriateness in all cases of conducting litigation in a state which has no relation to the controversy except the fact that the defendant is temporarily present therein, there is also strong ground for arguing that it is often highly desirable and altogether appropriate to try a case in a state in which the defendant may not be present at all." See Dodd, Jurisdiction in Personal Actions, 23 Ill. L. Rev. 427, 438 (1929).

13. See, e.g., Nehemiah v. Athletic Congress of U.S.A., 765 F.2d 42 (3d Cir.1985) (tag jurisdiction is unconstitutional absent "minimum contacts" between the defendant and the forum); Harold M. Pitman Co. v. Typecraft Software, 626 F.Supp. 305 (N.D.Ill.1986) (same); Schreiber v. Allis–Chalmers Corp., 448 F.Supp. 1079 (D.Kan. 1978) (same); cf. Amusement Equip., Inc. v. Mordelt, 779 F.2d 264 (5th Cir.1985) (tag jurisdiction is constitutional); Driver v. Helms, 577 F.2d 147 (1st Cir.1978), cert. denied 439 U.S. 1114, 99 S.Ct. 1016, 59 L.Ed.2d 72 (1979) (same); Humphrey v. Langford, 246 Ga. 732, 273 S.E.2d 22 (1980) (same); In re Marriage of Pridemore, 146 Ill.App.3d 990, 100 Ill.Dec. 640, 497 N.E.2d 818 (1986) (same); Lockert v. Breedlove, 321 N.C. 66, 361 S.E.2d 581 (1987) (same).

14. *Shaffer*, 433 U.S. at 212, 97 S.Ct. at 2584, 53 L.Ed.2d at 703.

However, when the Supreme Court finally addressed the question of transient jurisdiction's vitality in *Burnham v. Superior Court*,[15] the Court reaffirmed it.[16] A four-vote plurality led by Justice Scalia limited *Shaffer*'s dictum to the context of quasi in rem jurisdiction, and held that the historical pedigree of transient jurisdiction was, by itself, sufficient to establish its constitutional validity.[17] A four-vote concurrence led by Justice Brennan rejected Scalia's methodology, but reasoned that the decision of the defendant to journey to the forum state established a constitutionally-sufficient connection with the forum state, and thus upheld jurisdiction.[18] And Justice Stevens, apparently persuaded by both rationales, concurred only in the judgment.[19]

While in-state service is correctly viewed as an important part of the foundation of the common law of jurisdiction, it usually was limited in its application to individual defendants. In *Goldey v. Morning News*[20] the Supreme Court held that in-state service of a corporation's president did not authorize a federal court to take in personam jurisdiction over the corporation. Interestingly, some states allowed for transient jurisdiction over corporations based upon in-state service of a corporate officer, and continued to do so for two decades after the Supreme Court's *Goldey* decision, suggesting that the relative role of the Supreme Court and the state courts in developing jurisdictional law remained unsettled for a substantial period after *Pennoyer*.[21] In any event, the Supreme Court ultimately decided that the state court attempts to take transient jurisdiction over corporations were unconstitutional,[22] and since that time application of the rule has been restricted to individual defendants.

B.   CONSENT

§ 6.3   As a basis for jurisdiction, consent has a long but uneven history. At one time, the case law divided rather sharply between the notions of "implied" and "express" consent to jurisdiction. Even well before *Pennoyer v. Neff*,[1] the Supreme Court mandated recognition of judgments founded upon the implicit consent to jurisdiction of corpora-

---

15. 495 U.S. 604, 110 S.Ct. 2105, 109 L.Ed.2d 631 (1990).

16. For discussions of *Burnham* and its implications, see Borchers, The Death of the Constitutional Law of Personal Jurisdiction: From *Pennoyer* to *Burnham* and Back Again, 24 U.C. Davis L. Rev. 19 (1990); Hay, supra n.10; see generally Symposium on *Burnham*: The Future of Personal Jurisdiction, 22 Rutgers L. Rev. 559 (1991).

17. 495 U.S. at 607, 110 S.Ct. at 2109, 109 L.Ed.2d at 637.

18. Id. at 628, 110 S.Ct. at 2119, 109 L.Ed.2d at 650.

19. Id. at 640, 110 S.Ct. at 2126, 109 L.Ed.2d at 658.

20. 156 U.S. 518, 15 S.Ct. 559, 39 L.Ed. 517 (1894).

21. See, e.g., Sadler v. The Boston and Bolivia Rubber Co., 202 N.Y. 547, 95 N.E. 1139 (N.Y. 1911); Pope v. Terre Haute Car Mfg. Co., 87 N.Y. 137 (1881); Hiller v. Burlington & Miss. R.R. Co., 70 N.Y. 223 (1877); Jester v. Baltimore Steam Packet Co., 131 N.C. 54, 42 S.E. 447 (N.C. 1902).

22. See Riverside & Dan River Cotton Mills v. Menefee, 237 U.S. 189, 35 S.Ct. 579, 59 L.Ed. 910 (1915).

§ 6.3

1. 95 U.S. (5 Otto) 714, 24 L.Ed. 565 (1878).

tions doing a substantial amount of business in the forum state.[2] Eventually, this notion was extended to individual defendants with non-business contacts in the forum.[3] While the Supreme Court ultimately replaced this "implied consent" concept with the "minimum contacts" metaphor that today dominates jurisdictional law,[4] a good deal of modern jurisdiction has its roots in these implied consent cases. Moreover, the old notion of implied consent lives on in some limited circumstances, as some courts have construed business licensing statutes—which require the appointment of an agent for service of process—as evidence of a business's "consent" to jurisdiction in the forum.[5]

While implied consent is mentioned only occasionally today as a basis for jurisdiction,[6] express consent remains an important method of obtaining general jurisdiction. Express differs from implied consent in that the former turns upon some actual assent by the defendant to the notion that he will be subjected to jurisdiction in the forum state. The seminal modern case affirming express consent as a basis for jurisdiction is *National Equipment Rental v. Szukhent*.[7] In that case, the Supreme Court held that a pre-printed clause in a farm equipment lease providing for jurisdiction in the New York courts was a sufficient basis for requiring the Michigan lessors to defend that case away from home. Although Justice Black complained in his dissent that the provision in the lease was no "real" evidence of assent to jurisdiction,[8] the majority viewed the defendants' objection to personal jurisdiction as a personal right that they had waived by voluntarily entering into the agreement.[9]

The trend appears to be toward more expansive use of consent as a basis for jurisdiction. The Supreme Court has upheld against due process challenges so-called cognovit or confession agreements, in which a debtor agrees to have a judgment taken against him immediately if he breaches the agreement.[10] The effect of such agreements is far more drastic than a simple jurisdictional agreement in which a defendant agrees to be amenable to suit in a particular forum. While such agreements clearly

---

2. See, e.g., Lafayette Ins. Co. v. French, 59 U.S. (18 How.) 404, 15 L.Ed. 451 (1855).

3. See, e.g., Hess v. Pawloski, 274 U.S. 352, 47 S.Ct. 632, 71 L.Ed. 1091 (1927).

4. See, e.g., International Shoe Co. v. Washington, 326 U.S. 310, 66 S.Ct. 154, 90 L.Ed. 95 (1945); see also supra §§ 5.4—5.8.

5. See, e.g., D.J. Nelson v. World Wide Lease, Inc., 110 Idaho 369, 716 P.2d 513 (1986).

6. See, e.g., Shaffer v. Heitner, 433 U.S. 186, 216, 97 S.Ct. 2569, 2586, 53 L.Ed.2d 683, 705 (1977) (discussing as significant Delaware's failure to enact a statute "implying" the consent of officers and directors to jurisdiction as a condition of accepting their positions).

7. 375 U.S. 311, 84 S.Ct. 411, 11 L.Ed.2d 354 (1964).

8. See *National Equip.*, 375 U.S. at 318, 84 S.Ct. at 416, 11 L.Ed.2d at 359.

9. See id. at 317, 84 S.Ct. at 415, 11 L.Ed.2d at 359. The Supreme Court later reaffirmed the notion that personal jurisdiction is a personal right that may be waived by a defendant. See Insurance Corp. of Ireland, Ltd. v. Compagnie des Bauxites de Guinee, 456 U.S. 694, 702 n.10, 102 S.Ct. 2099, 2105 n.10, 72 L.Ed.2d 492, 502 n.10 (1982).

10. See, e.g., D.H. Overmyer Co., Inc. v. Frick Co., 405 U.S. 174, 92 S.Ct. 775, 31 L.Ed.2d 124 (1972). The classic treatment of this subject is Hopson, Cognovit Judgments: An Ignored Problem of Due Process and Full Faith and Credit, 29 U. Chi. L. Rev. 111 (1961).

can be void for overreaching,[11] the Supreme Court has refused to lay down a blanket rule against them.[12]

A more frequently litigated question, which presents itself in all jurisdictional agreements, is whether inequality of bargaining power as between the litigants provides a sufficient basis for refusing to enforce an agreement to jurisdiction. The Supreme Court's *National Equipment Rental, Limited v. Szukhent* case, though involving a pre-printed provision, did not appear to pit parties of greatly unequal bargaining power against each other.[13] The Supreme Court's later case of *The Bremen v. Zapata Off–Shore Co.*[14] seemed to reinforce the notion that an effective consent to jurisdiction must involve parties of relatively equal bargaining strength and actual bargaining. While *The Bremen* is not precisely applicable, because it involved an agreement to derogate from the jurisdiction of a federal court,[15] and the Court was apparently announcing common law rules applicable in admiralty cases,[16] the Supreme Court's repeated references to the sophistication of both parties suggested that these factors were essential for an effective agreement.[17]

Later events have proved, however, that effective agreements are not limited to situations involving parties of similar bargaining power. In several recent cases, the Supreme Court has enforced arbitration agreements entered into by parties of sharply disparate bargaining power.[18] The arbitration cases provide only an analogy, however, because of federal legislation favoring enforcement of arbitration agreements.[19] In *Carnival Cruise Lines, Inc. v. Shute*[20] the Supreme Court upheld a clause requiring that all litigation between the parties be conducted in a Florida court. That the Court was willing to uphold the agreement, despite the fact that appeared only in small type on the back of cruise ship ticket, is a strong indication that the adhesive nature of jurisdictional agreements rarely, if ever, provides a reason for voiding them.[21] Generally, therefore,

---

11. See, e.g., Atlantic Fin. Fed. v. Bruno, 698 F.Supp. 568 (E.D. Pa. 1988); Pearson v. Friedman, 112 So.2d 894 (Fla.App. 1959).

12. See, e.g., Swarb v. Lennox, 405 U.S. 191, 92 S.Ct. 767, 31 L.Ed.2d 138 (1972); D.H. Overmyer, Inc. v. Frick Co., 405 U.S. 174, 188, 92 S.Ct. 775, 783, 31 L.Ed.2d 124 (1972); see also Fiore v. Oakwood Plaza Shopping Ctr., 78 N.Y.2d 572, 585 N.E.2d 364, 578 N.Y.S.2d 115 (1991) (full-faith-and-credit effect of confessed judgment must evaluated on a case-by-case basis).

13. See *National Equip. Rental, Limited v. Szukhent*, 375 U.S. at 318, 84 S.Ct. at 416, 11 L.Ed.2d at 359.

14. 407 U.S. 1, 92 S.Ct. 1907, 32 L.Ed.2d 513 (1972).

15. See infra § 11.2 for a fuller discussion of these issues.

16. See, e.g, Maier, The Three Faces of *Zapata*: Maritime Law, Federal Common Law, Federal Courts Law, 6 Vand. J. Transnat'l L. 387 (1973).

17. 407 U.S. at 12, 92 S.Ct. at 1914.

18. See, e.g., Gilmer v. Interstate/Johnson Lane Corp., 500 U.S. 20, 111 S.Ct. 1647, 114 L.Ed.2d 26 (1991).

19. See 9 U.S.C.A. § 1 et. seq. (Federal Arbitration Act); see also Allied–Bruce Terminix Co. v. Dobson, 513 U.S. 265, 115 S.Ct. 834, 130 L.Ed.2d 753 (1995), on remand 684 So.2d 102 (Ala. 1995) (Federal Arbitration Act applies to all cases in state or federal court in which the agreement has an effect on interstate commerce).

20. 499 U.S. 585, 593, 111 S.Ct. 1522, 1527, 113 L.Ed.2d 622, 632 (1991).

21. For a more comprehensive discussion of Carnival Cruise, see infra §§ 5.10, 6.7. Commentary on the case has been mostly critical. See, e.g., Borchers, Forum Selection Agreements in the Federal Courts

jurisdictional agreements are voidable only on well-established defenses of contract law, such as fraud or duress.[22]

C. RESIDENCE, DOMICILE AND NATIONALITY

§ 6.4 An interesting and important question is the circumstance under which a personal affiliation with a state will render a defendant subject to that state's general jurisdiction. The notion that a defendant is amenable to jurisdiction in his "home" is a familiar one internationally,[1] and one of some considerable durability in the United States. The reasons for its durability stem from the notion that it is not unfair to expect the defendant to mount a defense at home, and the predictability that flows from having at least one forum in which the defendant is certainly amenable to suit.

Domicile was a jurisdictional basis that courts generally recognized at common law,[2] though it did not have the universal acceptance of the rule of in-state service.[3] Its constitutional sufficiency remained somewhat in doubt until the Supreme Court decided *Milliken v. Meyer*.[4] In *Milliken*, however, the Court stated unequivocally that "[o]ne ... incident of domicile is amenability to suit within the state even during sojourns without the state...."[5] Although most cases involve a defendant who has the same domicile at all relevant times, jurisdiction has been sustained where the defendant was domiciled in the forum at the time of underlying events, but had changed domicile by the time suit was filed.[6]

After *Carnival Cruise*: A Proposal for Congressional Reform, 67 Wash. L. Rev. 55 (1992); Mullenix, Another Easy Case, Some More Bad Law, *Carnival Cruise Lines* and Contractual Personal Jurisdiction, 27 Tex. Int'l L.J. 323 (1992).

22. See, e.g., The Bremen v. Zapata Off–Shore Co., 407 U.S. 1, 12, 92 S.Ct. 1907, 1914, 32 L.Ed.2d 513 (1972); Sparling v. Hoffman Constr. Co., 864 F.2d 635 (9th Cir.1988); Farmland Indus., Inc. v. Frazier–Parrott Commodities, Inc., 806 F.2d 848 (8th Cir.1986); AVC Nederland B.V. v. Atrium Inv. Partnership, 740 F.2d 148 (2d Cir. 1984); Ritchie v. Carvel Corp., 714 F.Supp. 700 (S.D.N.Y.1989); Stephens v. Entre Computer Ctrs., Inc., 696 F.Supp. 636 (N.D.Ga.1988).

§ 6.4

1. See, e.g., M. Reimann, Conflict of Laws in Western Europe: A Guide Through the Jungle 75 (1995) ("As a basic rule in Europe, the courts in the defendant's home state ... have general jurisdiction ..."); Smit, Common and Civil Law Rules of In Personam Adjudicatory Authority: An Analysis of the Underlying Policies, 21 Int'l & Comp. L.Q. 335, 347 (1972).

2. See, e.g., Henderson v. Staniford, 105 Mass. 504 (1870); In re Hendrickson, 40 S.D. 211, 167 N.W. 172 (1918); Fernandez v. Casey, 77 Tex. 452, 14 S.W. 149 (1890).

3. See, e.g., De La Montanya v. De La Montanya, 112 Cal. 101, 108, 44 P. 345, 346–48 (Cal. 1896) (domicile is not a sufficient basis for jurisdiction unless accompanied by in-state service); Raher v. Raher, 150 Iowa 511, 529–30, 129 N.W. 494, 500–01 (1911) (same). The Second Restatement takes the position that domicile was not an accepted basis of jurisdiction at the common law. See Restatement, Second, Conflict of Laws § 29, comment c (1971).

4. 311 U.S. 457, 61 S.Ct. 339, 85 L.Ed. 278 (1940).

5. Id. at 463, 61 S.Ct. at 342–43.

6. See, e.g., Owens v. Superior Court, 52 Cal.2d 822, 345 P.2d 921 (1959); Geelhoed v. Jensen, 277 Md. 220, 352 A.2d 818 (1976) (residence at time of relevant event sufficient for in personam jurisdiction). The following cases support this rule: Allen v. Superior Court, 41 Cal.2d 306, 259 P.2d 905 (1953); Ogdon v. Gianakos, 415 Ill. 591, 114 N.E.2d 686 (1953) (criticized by Clouse v. Andonian, 189 F.Supp. 78 (N.D.Ind.1960)); Cooke v. Yarrington, 62 N.J. 123, 299 A.2d 400 (1973).

Domicile is a technical concept, and under some circumstances a person might retain a domicile in a state with which he no longer has a strong connection.[7] It has been argued that in such circumstances domicile does not provide a fair basis for exercising general jurisdiction.[8] The constitutional sufficiency of a purely technical domicile as a basis for *in personam* jurisdiction was perhaps cast into some doubt by the Supreme Court's statement in *Shaffer v. Heitner* that "all assertions of state court jurisdiction"[9] must satisfy the minimum contacts test.[10] In the ordinary case domicile represents a connection between the defendant and the forum stronger than that demanded by the minimum contacts test, but a purely technical domicile might not indicate such a strong affiliation. Probably, though, any doubts as to the constitutional sufficiency of even a technical domicile were removed by the Supreme Court's opinion in *Burnham v. Superior Court*. In *Burnham* the Court upheld the sufficiency of in-state service as a basis for *in personam* jurisdiction.[11] In so doing, a plurality of the Court limited *Shaffer*'s "all assertions" dictum to quasi in rem cases.[12] If *Burnham* is ultimately seen to limit *Shaffer*'s dictum to in rem and quasi in rem actions, this would remove whatever lingering doubt might remain about the sufficiency of even a technical domicile as a basis for in personam jurisdiction.

An analogous problem is the sufficiency of nationality as a basis for jurisdiction. The situation arises fairly infrequently in domestic cases, because a United States citizen is generally considered a "citizen" of the state in which he is domiciled, which collapses the question with that of the sufficiency of domicile as a basis for jurisdiction.[13] The question is more likely to arise when a judgment of the court of a foreign nation is presented to a United States court for recognition. In such cases, courts have usually held a defendant's nationality sufficient for a foreign court to exercise jurisdiction,[14] and the cases finding nationality an insufficient connection usually have involved special circumstances making the exercise of jurisdiction especially unfair.[15]

In one case, the United States Supreme Court specifically affirmed nationality as a sufficient basis for jurisdiction. In *Blackmer v. United States*,[16] a United States citizen domiciled in France was served by the United States consul with subpoenas commanding him to testify in

7. See supra § 4.15 (discussing the definition of domicile).

8. See Weintraub, Commentary on the Conflict of Laws 203 (4th ed. 2001); Vernon, Single Factor Bases of *In Personam* Jurisdiction—A Speculation on the Impact of Shaffer v. Heitner, 1978 Wash. U.L.Q. 273, 301; Comment, Minimum Contacts Analysis of *In Personam* Jurisdiction Over Individuals Based on Presence, 33 Ark. L. Rev. 159 (1979).

9. 433 U.S. at 212, 97 S.Ct. at 2584, 53 L.Ed.2d at 703.

10. See supra n.8.

11. See supra § 6.2.

12. *Burnham*, 495 U.S. at 607, 110 S.Ct. at 2109, 109 L.Ed.2d at 637.

13. See Restatement, Second, Conflict of Laws § 31, cmnt. b (1971).

14. See, e.g., Henderson v. Staniford, 105 Mass. 504 (1870); Hamill v. Talbott, 72 Mo.App. 22 (1897); Matter of Denick's Estate, 36 N.Y.S. 518 (N.Y.Sup.1895).

15. See, e.g., Grubel v. Nassauer, 210 N.Y. 149, 103 N.E. 1113 (1913) (defendant absent from forum for six years prior to entry of judgment by foreign court).

16. 284 U.S. 421, 52 S.Ct. 252, 76 L.Ed. 375 (1932).

proceedings before a federal court. The petitioner did not appear, was adjudged in contempt, and then resisted enforcement on the ground that the federal court lacked "judicial jurisdiction to render a personal judgment. . . ."[17] The Supreme Court rebuffed his attack on the statute allowing the extra-territorial service of the subpoenas, holding specifically that his American citizenship meant that he "continued to owe allegiance to the United States."[18]

A more difficult question is whether "mere" residence, as opposed to domicile or nationality, can be a sufficient connection for the exercise of general jurisdiction over an individual defendant. Residence is a slippery concept, and its meaning can range from very impermanent living arrangements to connections that approximate or equal domicile.[19] In fact, while the term "residence" is frequently used in statutes, it is often interpreted to mean "domicile."[20] The Second Restatement takes the position that a defendant's residence is sufficient for the exercise of general jurisdiction "unless the individual's relationship to the state is so attenuated as to make the exercise of such jurisdiction unreasonable."[21] The case law seems to bear out the Second Restatement rule. Courts have been willing to allow general jurisdiction based upon residence, at least where the residence is one of substantial duration.[22] Many international conventions now use the term "habitual residence" as a way of avoiding some of the technical niceties of domicile.[23] This term connotes quite a strong personal connection, and there would seem to be little doubt that a defendant is subject to general jurisdiction in a state in which he is habitually resident.[24]

D. APPEARANCE

§ 6.5 A defendant who voluntarily appears in an action, without timely objecting to jurisdiction, submits to the court's general, in person-

---

17. Id. at 436, 52 S.Ct. at 254, 76 L.Ed. at 382.

18. 284 U.S. at 436, 52 S.Ct. at 254, 76 L.Ed. at 382. The notion that "allegiance" is a sufficient basis for an exercise of state authority appears occasionally in cases discussing the power of states. See, e.g., Skiriotes v. Florida, 313 U.S. 69, 61 S.Ct. 924, 85 L.Ed. 1193 (1941) (upholding conviction of a Florida domiciliary in a Florida court for using a diving suit to collect sponges in waters outside of the territory of Florida).

19. See generally Green, That Elusive Word, "Residence," 6 Vand. L. Rev. 561 (1953).

20. See, e.g., Manley v. Engram, 755 F.2d 1463, 1466 n.3 (11th Cir.1985) (interpreting term "residence" in general venue statute to mean "domicile").

21. Restatement, Second, Conflict of Laws § 30 (1971).

22. See, e.g., Myrick v. Superior Court, 256 P.2d 348 (Cal.App.), aff'd 41 Cal.2d 519,

261 P.2d 255 (1953); Geelhoed v. Jensen, 277 Md. 220, 352 A.2d 818 (1976) (two-year residence). The rule of these cases is also approved in Ehrenzweig, Conflict of Laws § 28 (1962); Green, supra n.19; Dambach, Personal Jurisdiction: Some Current Problems and Modern Trends 198, 231 (1958); see also Allen v. Superior Court, 41 Cal.2d 306, 259 P.2d 905 (1953); Cooke v. Yarrington, 62 N.J. 123, 299 A.2d 400 (1973); see generally Camden Safe Deposit & Trust Co. v. Barbour, 66 N.J.L. 103, 48 A. 1008 (1901); but see State v. Heffernan, 142 Fla. 496, 195 So. 145 (1940).

23. See, e.g. Hague Convention on the Civil Aspects International Child Abduction, 19 I.L.M. 1501 (1980) (Article 4: "The Convention shall apply to any child who was habitually resident in a contracting state immediately before any breach of custody or access rights.")

24. See Cavers, "Habitual Residence": A Useful Concept?, 21 Am. U. L. Rev. 475 (1972).

am jurisdiction.[1] This is a long-standing rule based upon the notion that an objection to personal jurisdiction is a matter of personal right that a defendant is free to raise or not raise at his election.[2]

A potential practical problem with the rule is that it might discourage a defendant from making a direct attack to the forum's jurisdictional authority for fear of making an "appearance" in the case and thereby submitting to the court's jurisdiction. A defendant always has the option of not appearing, allowing the forum to enter a default judgment, and then collaterally attacking the judgment when the judgment creditor attempts to enforce it.[3] The collateral attack route is risky, however, because if the court overrules the jurisdictional objection, the Full Faith and Credit Clause will generally preclude the judgment debtor from relitigating the merits.[4]

To protect defendants from this unhappy dilemma, all American courts have in place some procedure by which a defendant can appear in a case to object to jurisdiction without making a general appearance that will subject the defendant to the court's in personam jurisdiction.[5] All such procedures share some common features. Generally, they require a defendant to lodge the jurisdictional objection at the very outset of the case, and they require that the defendant not seek any affirmative relief from the court.[6]

Federal Rule of Civil Procedure 12 provides the mechanism in federal court that allows a defendant to directly attack the court's personal jurisdiction without submitting to the court's in personam jurisdiction. The Federal Rules provide that if a defendant responds to the plaintiff's complaint with an answer, any objection to personal jurisdiction is waived unless included as a defense in the answer.[7] If the defendant chooses to respond to the complaint with one of the preanswer motions allowed for by Federal Rule 12, one component of that motion must be a motion to dismiss for lack of personal jurisdiction.[8] Thus, in federal court, a defendant who fails to include an objection to personal jurisdiction in the first document he files has, in all probability, appeared in the case and thereby waived any opportunity to successfully object to

---

§ 6.5

1. See, e.g., Sherrer v. Sherrer, 334 U.S. 343, 68 S.Ct. 1087, 92 L.Ed. 1429 (1948); Adam v. Saenger, 303 U.S. 59, 58 S.Ct. 454, 82 L.Ed. 649 (1938); Sugg v. Thornton, 132 U.S. 524, 10 S.Ct. 163, 33 L.Ed. 447 (1889); Securities and Exchange Comm'n v. Blazon Corp., 609 F.2d 960 (9th Cir.1979).

2. Insurance Corp. of Ireland v. Compagnie des Bauxites de Guinee, 456 U.S. 694, 102 S.Ct. 2099, 72 L.Ed.2d 492 (1982); Mills v. Duryee, 11 U.S. (7 Cranch) 481, 3 L.Ed. 411 (1813).

3. See, e.g., Pennoyer v. Neff, 95 U.S. (5 Otto) 714, 24 L.Ed. 565 (1878) (collateral attack to a judgment allowed).

4. 95 U.S. at 729, 731, 24 L.Ed. at 571.

5. 1 Casad, Jurisdiction in Civil Actions 3–43 (2d ed. 1991).

6. See Restatement, Second, Conflict of Laws § 33 (1971).

7. F.R.C.P. 12(h)(1). This rule is softened in one modest respect. If a defendant responds to the plaintiff's complaint with an answer that omits any objection to personal jurisdiction, but then amends the answer as a matter of course within 20 days, as allowed in Federal Rule of Civil Procedure 15(a), the jurisdictional objection is preserved. See F.R.C.P. 12(h)(1).

8. F.R.C.P. 12(g), 12(h)(1).

the court's in personam jurisdiction. An amended complaint raising new theories can trigger anew a defendant's obligation to object to jurisdiction.[9] A defendant who responds to a complaint with a counterclaim is usually held to have waived any objection to jurisdiction, unless the counterclaim is compulsory.[10]

States whose procedural laws are still heavily influenced by New York's 1848 Field Code are even stricter with regard to making a successful direct attack on the court's personal jurisdiction. States that still follow the strict Code rules on special appearances require, as do the Federal Rules, that the defendant raise the jurisdictional objection at the very outset of the case.[11] But, unlike the Federal Rules procedure,[12] Code states do not allow the jurisdictional objection to be combined with objections that go to the merits of the matter.[13] Thus, for instance, under federal procedure, a defendant could—without waiving the jurisdictional objection—make a combined motion to dismiss a case because the court lacks personal jurisdiction and that the statute of limitations bars the action.[14] In states that follow the strict Code practice, however, such a "combined" motion would operate to waive the jurisdictional objection, forcing the defendant to first present the jurisdictional objection.[15] States that follow the strict Code practice also generally hold that proceeding to trial is a waiver of objections to personal jurisdiction.[16] Therefore, in a Code state, a defendant whose jurisdictional objection is overruled by a trial court must attempt to seek appellate review immediately by way of extraordinary writ or forego appellate review of the issue.[17] In federal practice, by contrast, a defendant who timely objects to jurisdiction preserves the issue for appeal from the final judgment in the case.[18]

Interestingly, although all states apparently provide some reasonable mechanism allowing a defendant to make a direct attack on a court's personal jurisdiction, such procedures were not always universal

9. See, e.g., Preferred RX, Inc. v. American Prescription Plan, Inc., 46 F.3d 535 (6th Cir.1995).

10. See, e.g., Adam v. Saenger, 303 U.S. 59, 58 S.Ct. 454, 82 L.Ed. 649 (1938); Dragor Shipping Corp. v. Union Tank Car Co., 378 F.2d 241 (9th Cir.1967); D.J. Nelson v. World Wide Lease, Inc., 110 Idaho 369, 716 P.2d 513 (1986).

11. See, e.g., Engel v. Davenport, 194 Cal. 344, 228 P. 710 (1924).

12. See F.R.C.P. 12(g) (motion to dismiss for lack of personal jurisdiction may be combined with other motions).

13. See, e.g., Braden Copper Co. v. Industrial Accident Comm'n, 147 Cal.App.2d 205, 305 P.2d 222 (1956) (mere mention of alternative ground for relief other than jurisdictional dismissal does not waive jurisdictional objection).

14. See F.R.C.P. 12(g), 12(h)(1) (allowing "combined" motions under Federal Rule 12).

15. See, e.g., In re Marriage of McFadden, 380 N.W.2d 6, 7 (Iowa Ct.App.1985) (party waived challenge to personal jurisdiction by joining it with a request for relief on the merits of the case); Kotlisky v. Kotlisky, 195 Ill.App.3d 725, 731, 552 N.E.2d 1206, 1209 (1990) (party wishing to contest personal jurisdiction must limit the challenge to jurisdictional matters, as opposed to the substantive issues of the lawsuit).

16. See, e.g., Kotlisky v. Kotlisky, 195 Ill.App.3d 725, 731, 142 Ill.Dec. 465, 552 N.E.2d 1206, 1209 (1990) (citing Ill. Rev. Stat. ch. 110, par. 2—301(c): proceeding to trial after losing the jurisdictional objection generally waives the objection).

17. Id.

18. 2A Moore, Moore's Federal Practice ¶ 12.12 (2d ed. 1995).

nor are they constitutionally required. In *York v. Texas*,[19] the Supreme Court confronted a Texas statute treating even special appearances as general appearances and thus a waiver of a defendant's right to contest the court's personal jurisdiction. Although the defendant vigorously pressed the argument that the Hobson's choice presented by this rule was so unfair as to violate the Due Process Clause, the Supreme Court rejected this contention, holding that the defendant's right of collateral attack was constitutionally sufficient.[20]

Even a defendant who timely objects to jurisdiction can, in extraordinary cases, waive or be estopped from pursuing the objection. In *Insurance Corporation of Ireland, Ltd. v. Compagnie des Bauxites de Guinee*,[21] the defendant timely objected to a federal district court's personal jurisdiction, but then proceeded to defy several court orders to comply with plaintiff's discovery requests as to the defendant's contacts with the forum. Eventually, invoking Federal Rule 37, the district court entered an order finding that the defendant was subject to its personal jurisdiction, and the United States Supreme Court affirmed.[22] Specifically rejecting its earlier statements suggesting that constitutional limitations on personal jurisdiction implicate matters of "interstate federalism," the Court held that the "personal" nature of the right to object to personal jurisdiction means that the right can be waived, or that the defendant's conduct can estop him from successfully raising the issue.[23]

E. JURISDICTION BY NECESSITY

§ 6.6 Courts occasionally appear to take jurisdiction upon the necessity of the case. The boundaries of this necessity doctrine, and whether it really exists, are the subject of some considerable debate.[1] There seems to be agreement, however, that where it exists it does so

19. 137 U.S. 15, 11 S.Ct. 9, 34 L.Ed. 604 (1890).

20. Id. at 20, 11 S.Ct. at 10, 34 L.Ed. at 605.

21. 456 U.S. 694, 102 S.Ct. 2099, 72 L.Ed.2d 492 (1982).

22. Insurance Corp. of Ireland, Ltd., 456 U.S. at 709, 102 S.Ct. at 2108, 72 L.Ed.2d at 505.

23. Id. at 702 n.10, 102 S.Ct. at 2104 n.10, 72 L.Ed.2d at 501 n.10.

§ 6.6

1. See, e.g., Brilmayer, How Contacts Count: Due Process Limitations on State Court Jurisdiction, 1980 Sup.Ct.Rev. 77, 108–110 (attempting to rationalize "necessity" cases on a minimum contacts theory); Cameron & Johnson, Death of a Salesman? Forum Shopping and Outcome Determination under *International Shoe*, 28 U.C. Davis L. Rev. 769, 776 (1995) (referring to necessity as a "theoretical" possibility in taking jurisdiction); Fraser, Jurisdiction by Necessity—An Analysis of the *Mullane* Case, 100 U.Pa.L.Rev. 305 (1951) (Supreme Court's *Mullane* decision cannot be explained on either traditional in personam or in rem grounds); Redish & Beste, Personal Jurisdiction and the Global Resolution of Mass Tort Litigation: Defining the Constitutional Boundaries, 28 U.C. Davis L. Rev. 917, 936, 937 (1995) (*Mullane* represents a "jurisdiction by necessity" approach if one defines "necessity" broadly); von Mehren, Adjudicatory Jurisdiction: General Theories Compared and Evaluated, 63 B.U. L. Rev. 279, 322 (1983) (jurisdiction by necessity exists but is rare); Symposium, Jurisdiction, Justice, and Choice of Law for the Twenty–First Century: Case Four, 29 New Engl. L. Rev. 669, 685 n.15 (1995) (arguing against jurisdiction by necessity); Note, Jurisdiction by Necessity: Examining One Proposal for Unbarring the Doors of our Courts, 21 Vand. J. Transnat'l L. 401 (1988) (comprehensive examination of doctrine).

under circumstances in which no reasonable alternative forum exists, and the connection of the parties and events makes the chosen forum a fair one.[2]

The Supreme Court case that appears to rest most squarely on a necessity theory is *Mullane v. Central Hanover Bank & Trust Co.*[3] *Mullane* was a case in which the trustees of a collectively-managed trust fund were required by statute to bring an action in the nature of an accounting to establish the propriety of their management of the fund.[4] Their (at least nominally) adverse parties were the beneficiaries of the fund, in this case 113 persons.[5] While *Mullane* is best known for its holding that the state statutes providing only for publication of the summons did not give adequate notice,[6] the Court held—before reaching the notice issue—that the New York state courts had personal jurisdiction over the beneficiaries.[7] Although *Mullane* was decided five years after the Supreme Court's invention, in *International Shoe Co. v. Washington*,[8] of the "minimum contacts" test, *Mullane* made no effort to rationalize its result in terms of contacts. In fact, it would have been impossible to demonstrate that each of the 113 beneficiaries had minimum contacts with New York, as some were contingent beneficiaries[9] who might well have been non-residents of the forum state and completely unaware of their interest in the matter. Rather, the majority simply stated that the forum state's interest in the case "is so insistent and rooted in custom as to establish beyond doubt the right of its courts to determine the interests of all claimants, resident or nonresident . . . ."[10]

As one influential contemporary commentator pointed out, *Mullane* is difficult to square with any conventional understanding of either in personam or in rem jurisdiction.[11] He concluded, therefore, that *Mullane* was really a case of jurisdictional necessity[12] because of the practical difficulty and expense of pursuing the nonresident beneficiaries in their home states in several different lawsuits. While some have tried to rationalize *Mullane* on more traditional grounds,[13] the consensus appears to be that *Mullane*—at the very least—is a *sui generis* departure from conventional jurisdictional categories.[14]

Since *Mullane*, the Supreme Court has continued to drop hints that the plaintiff's inability to find another reasonable forum can be, in an appropriate case, a substantial factor in allowing a court to take jurisdic-

---

2. See supra n.1 for authorities discussing.

3. Mullane v. Central Hanover Bank & Trust Co., 339 U.S. 306, 70 S.Ct. 652, 94 L.Ed. 865 (1950). See also Fraser, supra n.1.

4. 339 U.S. at 308, 70 S.Ct. at 654, 94 L.Ed. at 870.

5. Id. at 309, 70 S.Ct. at 654, 94 L.Ed. at 870.

6. See supra § 5.16.

7. 339 U.S. at 310, 70 S.Ct. at 655, 94 L.Ed. at 871.

8. 326 U.S. 310, 66 S.Ct. 154, 90 L.Ed. 95 (1945).

9. 339 U.S. at 309, 70 S.Ct. at 654, 94 L.Ed. at 870.

10. Id. at 312, 70 S.Ct. at 656, 94 L.Ed. at 872.

11. Fraser, supra n.1, at 310–11.

12. Id. at 311.

13. E.g., Brilmayer, supra n.1.

14. See supra n.1.

tion. In *Shaffer v. Heitner*,[15] while subjecting in rem jurisdiction to the same test that limits in personam jurisdiction,[16] the Supreme Court stated in a footnote that presence of in-state property might, by itself, confer jurisdiction "when no other forum is available to the plaintiff."[17] In *Helicopteros Nacionales de Colombia v. Hall*,[18] the Court, while describing jurisdiction by necessity as a "potentially far-reaching modification of existing law," refused to rule out its application in all cases.[19] And more recently, in *Burger King Corp. v. Rudzewicz*,[20] the Supreme Court stated that "the plaintiff's interest in obtaining convenient and effective relief" is among the factors that "sometimes serve to establish the reasonableness of jurisdiction upon a lesser showing of minimum contacts than would otherwise be required."

With only cryptic guidance from the Supreme Court, it remains difficult to discern whether jurisdiction by necessity is an independent doctrine. It seems to be at least equally plausible that jurisdiction by necessity is not an independent doctrine, but rather that the plaintiff's inability to reasonably carry out the litigation in another forum is a factor in the overall "reasonableness" of asserting jurisdiction.[21] If it is an independent doctrine, it is one applied only sparingly, although at least one lower court case has made aggressive use of it in helping to consolidate a complicated products liability case in a single forum.[22]

III. CONTACTS–BASED GENERAL JURISDICTION

A. DISTINGUISHED FROM SPECIFIC JURISDICTION

§ 6.7 In practice, the most commonly employed kind of general jurisdiction is that allowed for by the minimum contacts test. In fact, the terms "general" and "specific" jurisdiction were invented in a law review article written as an effort to make sense of the development of the minimum contacts test.[1] *International Shoe Co. v. Washington*[2] itself indicated that the minimum contacts test has both a specific and a general component. The Court stated that a corporation may be amenable to jurisdiction in a state in which it carries on "continuous and

---

15. 433 U.S. 186, 97 S.Ct. 2569, 53 L.Ed.2d 683 (1977).

16. See supra §§ 5.4—5.6.

17. 433 U.S. at 211 n.37, 97 S.Ct. at 2583 n.37, 53 L.Ed.2d at 702 n.37.

18. 466 U.S. 408, 104 S.Ct. 1868, 80 L.Ed.2d 404 (1984).

19. Id. at 418 n.13, 104 S.Ct. at 1874 n.13, 80 L.Ed.2d at 414 n.13.

20. 471 U.S. 462, 477, 105 S.Ct. 2174, 2184, 85 L.Ed.2d 528, 543 (1985).

21. See, e.g., Asahi Metal Indus. Co. v. Superior Court, 480 U.S. 102, 107 S.Ct. 1026, 94 L.Ed.2d 92 (1987) (due process test

subject to an overall "reasonableness" evaluation).

22. See In re DES Cases, 789 F.Supp. 552 (E.D.N.Y.1992), appeal dismissed 7 F.3d 20 (2d Cir. 1993).

§ 6.7

1. von Mehren & Trautman, Jurisdiction to Adjudicate: A Suggested Analysis, 79 Harv. L. Rev. 1121 (1966).

2. 326 U.S. 310, 66 S.Ct. 154, 90 L.Ed. 95 (1945).

systematic"[3] activities, even on "causes of action arising from dealings entirely distinct from those activities."[4] The Court also held, however, that less substantial activities might give rise to jurisdiction if the corporation's "obligations arise out of or are connected with the activities within the state ..."[5]

International Shoe clearly draws, therefore, a distinction between contacts that are unrelated to the dispute and those that are related. In order for unrelated contacts to render the defendant amenable to jurisdiction, they must be "continuous and systematic." When this threshold is met, the defendant is amenable to general jurisdiction based upon its contacts with the state. Related contacts, however, can give rise to jurisdiction without passing the threshold of substantiality required for contacts-based general jurisdiction. In fact, even a single, purposeful contact with a state can give rise to jurisdiction if related to the cause of action.[6] Such related-contact jurisdiction is specific jurisdiction, because (unlike general jurisdiction) it is dependent upon the character of the dispute.

The significance of the dichotomy between related and unrelated contacts makes necessary the development of a test for distinguishing the two. In many cases, of course, it is obvious whether the contact is related or unrelated. Some contacts are obviously related to the cause of action, because they by themselves form the basis of the claim for relief.[7] Other contacts are obviously unrelated, because they lack even a tangential relationship to the parties' dispute.[8]

It is, of course, the more marginal cases that present the greatest difficulty. In a large number of circumstances, the contacts with the forum state do not form the basis of the claim for relief, yet neither are they wholly unrelated to the operative facts in the litigation.[9] Courts and commentators alike have wrestled with the appropriate treatment of contacts that lie in this hinterland between related and unrelated.

Unfortunately, no Supreme Court case has addressed the appropriate treatment of these marginal contacts. Twice it appeared that the Supreme Court would confront the question, but in each instance the Court disposed of the case on other grounds.

In *Helicopteros Nacionales de Colombia v. Hall*,[10] the Court confronted a case which had been brought in the Texas state courts by four

---

3. Id. at 317, 66 S.Ct. at 158, 90 L.Ed. at 102.

4. Id. at 318, 66 S.Ct. at 159, 90 L.Ed. at 103.

5. Id. at 319, 66 S.Ct. at 159, 90 L.Ed. at 103.

6. See, e.g., McGee v. International Life Ins. Co., 355 U.S. 220, 78 S.Ct. 199, 2 L.Ed.2d 223 (1957).

7. See, e.g., id. (sale of life insurance policy to forum domiciliary both basis for cause of action and basis for jurisdiction).

8. See, e.g., Perkins v. Benguet Consol. Mining Co., 342 U.S. 437, 72 S.Ct. 413, 96 L.Ed. 485 (1952) (activities of corporation in forum state sufficient to establish jurisdiction even though claim based entirely on out-of-state activities of corporation).

9. See, e.g., Shute v. Carnival Cruise Lines, Inc., 897 F.2d 377 (9th Cir.1990), rev'd on other grounds 499 U.S. 585, 111 S.Ct. 1522, 113 L.Ed.2d 622 (1991) (in-state advertising led to out-of-state injury to plaintiff).

10. 466 U.S. 408, 104 S.Ct. 1868, 80 L.Ed.2d 404 (1984).

American (but non-Texan) plaintiffs arising out of a South American helicopter crash. The primary connection between the defendant (a South American helicopter transportation provider) and Texas was that the defendant had purchased most of its fleet, and sent its pilots to be trained, in Texas.[11]

The facts of *Helicopteros* presented a good example of contacts that were neither obviously related nor unrelated. The defendant's contacts were not directly related to Texas because all of the events relevant to liability occurred in South America. Yet the defendant's contacts were not wholly unrelated, because both the purchases and the pilot training bore a causal relationship to the fatal accident.

The Court, however, concluded that the brief for the plaintiffs had conceded that the contacts were unrelated, treated the case as one raising only a question of general jurisdiction, and held that Texas's attempted assertion of jurisdiction was unconstitutional.[12] Only the lone dissenter, Justice Brennan, reached the issue of whether the contacts were related to the cause of action. He concluded that the contacts were sufficiently related to allow for specific jurisdiction, and reasoned that Texas's assertion of jurisdiction passed constitutional muster.[13]

More recently, in *Shute v. Carnival Cruise Lines*,[14] the Ninth Circuit employed perhaps the broadest notion of relatedness possible. The plaintiff was injured while on board a cruise ship in territorial waters of the coast of California. The Ninth Circuit held that a federal court in the state of Washington could assert specific jurisdiction over the cruise ship operator because the defendant's in-state activities of advertising and soliciting customers in the forum were a "but for" cause of her injuries.[15] The Supreme Court reviewed the case, but never reached the question of whether the court in Washington had in personam jurisdiction.[16] The Court concluded that an exclusive forum selection clause printed on the back of the plaintiff's ticket for passage required dismissal of the case in favor of the contractually-selected court.[17]

The vacuum in Supreme Court authority has produced a predictable division in lower court authority. As discussed extensively above,[18] two major tests have emerged. In one camp are the courts that apply, as did the Ninth Circuit in *Shute*,[19] a "but for" test of relatedness. Under this test, the defendant's contacts are related, and thus can give rise to specific jurisdiction, if they have a causal nexus with the events that

---

11. Id. at 411, 104 S.Ct. at 1870, 80 L.Ed.2d at 409.

12. Id. at 418, 104 S.Ct. at 1874, 80 L.Ed.2d at 413.

13. Id. at 419, 104 S.Ct. at 1874, 80 L.Ed.2d at 414. (Brennan, J., dissenting).

14. 897 F.2d 377 (9th Cir.1990), rev'd on other grounds 499 U.S. 585, 111 S.Ct. 1522, 113 L.Ed.2d 622 (1991).

15. Id. at 385.

16. Carnival Cruise Lines, Inc. v. Shute, 499 U.S. 585, 588, 111 S.Ct. 1522, 1524, 113 L.Ed.2d 622, 628 (1991).

17. See infra § 6.3 for a discussion of the case on this point.

18. See supra § 5.10.

19. Shute v. Carnival Cruise Lines, 897 F.2d 377 (9th Cir.1990).

underlie the litigation.[20] In the other camp are courts that endorse a substantially more modest notion of what qualifies as a related contact. These courts variously apply tests referred to as the "substantive relevance"[21] and the "proximate cause"[22] test. While there is perhaps some variation as between courts that reject the "but for" test and apply one of its competitors, the underlying theme of these decisions is that the "but for" test is so potentially broad as to collapse the distinction between specific and general jurisdiction.[23] These tests require that the contacts bear something more than a bare causal nexus to the dispute. In order for contacts to qualify as related under these tests, they must play some significant role in determining the dispute between the parties.[24] The mere fact that the contact ultimately led to other events that produced the dispute between the parties is not—under either the "proximate cause" or "substantive relevance" tests—sufficient to qualify it as related.

B. APPLICATION TO INDIVIDUAL DEFENDANTS

§ 6.8 When, in *International Shoe Co. v. Washington*,[1] the Supreme Court created the minimum contacts test, it spoke ambiguously as to whether the test was one applicable to corporations and other business entities only, or whether it applied as well to individual defendants. The Court in some passages seemed to refer to the test as a substitute for determining corporate "presence,"[2] implying that the Court viewed the existing, pre-*International Shoe* bases of jurisdiction as sufficient for individual defendants. In other portions of the opinion, however, the Court spoke generically of "defendants,"[3] implying that all defendants—including, of course, individual defendants—were covered by the new test.

It is now settled that the minimum contacts test applies to all defendants, including individual defendants. In *Shaffer v. Heitner*, the Supreme Court—considering whether various corporate officers and directors were amenable to jurisdiction in the state of incorporation on a

---

20. For cases other than *Shute* applying this test, see Prejean v. Sonatrach, Inc., 652 F.2d 1260 (5th Cir.1981); In–Flight Devices Corp. v. Van Dusen Air, Inc., 466 F.2d 220 (6th Cir.1972); Deluxe Ice Cream Co. v. R.C.H. Tool Corp., 726 F.2d 1209 (7th Cir. 1984); Presbyterian Univ. Hosp. v. Wilson, 337 Md. 541, 654 A.2d 1324 (1995). Many of the competing authorities are collected in Comment, Related Contacts and Personal Jurisdiction: The "But For" Test, 82 Calif. L. Rev. 1545 (1994) and Note, Specific Jurisdiction and the "Arise from or Relate to" Requirement . . . What Does it Mean?, 50 Wash. & Lee L. Rev. 1265 (1993).

21. From a famous law review article. See Brilmayer, How Contacts Count: Due Process Limitations on State Court Jurisdiction, 1980 Sup. Ct. Rev. 77, 82.

22. See, e.g., Pizarro v. Hoteles Concorde Int'l, 907 F.2d 1256, 1259 (1st Cir. 1990).

23. For criticism of the Ninth Circuit's *Shute* case on these grounds, see Hay, Flexibility Versus Predictability and Uniformity in Choice of Law, 226 Recueil des Cours 285, 311–15 (1991).

24. See supra § 5.10.

§ 6.8

1. 326 U.S. 310, 66 S.Ct. 154, 90 L.Ed. 95 (1945).

2. Id. at 316, 66 S.Ct. at 158, 90 L.Ed. at 101.

3. Id.

derivative claim of corporate mismanagement—stated that "the *International Shoe* court believed that the standard it was setting forth governed actions against natural persons as well as corporations, and we see no reason to disagree."[4] However, a plurality of the Supreme Court more recently suggested that contacts-based general jurisdiction may not apply to individual defendants. In footnote dictum in *Burnham v. Superior Court of California*, the opinion for four members of the Court stated that although they "express[ed] no views on these matters . . . it may be that whatever special rule exists permitting 'continuous and systematic' contacts . . . to support jurisdiction . . . applies *only* to corporations . . . ."[5]

As a pure dictum, and a qualified one at that, the *Burnham* footnote certainly ought not be interpreted as an authoritative pronouncement to the effect that contacts-based general jurisdiction over individual defendants is an impossibility. It does raise, however, important questions about the frequency with which such jurisdiction is asserted over individual defendants, and the fairness of such assertions. One reason to think that such jurisdiction ought be a rare occurrence is the availability of general jurisdiction in a defendant's domicile or residence.[6] Given that a defendant is amenable to jurisdiction in his home state, the case for allowing yet another forum (with no direct relationship to the dispute) to take jurisdiction is a weak one. However, there may be cases in which an individual defendant has a strong connection, such a business office, with a state other than his domicile, which would make assertions of general jurisdiction fair.[7] Even though rare, assertions of contacts-based general jurisdiction over individual defendants probably should not be ruled out in all cases.

C. "CONTINUOUS AND SYSTEMATIC" CONTACTS

§ **6.9** The most analytically difficult issue in general jurisdiction is the quantum of unrelated contacts needed to subject a defendant to in personam jurisdiction. In *International Shoe Co. v. Washington*,[1] the Court stated that "continuous and systematic" contacts would suffice, but in so stating left open important questions. One obvious one is the

4. Shaffer v. Heitner, 433 U.S. 186, 204 n.19, 97 S.Ct. 2569, 2579 n.19, 53 L.Ed.2d 683, 698 n.19 (1977).

5. 495 U.S. at 609 n.1, 110 S.Ct. at 2110 n.1, 109 L.Ed.2d at 639 n.1 (emphasis in original).

6. See supra § 5.13.

7. See, e.g., ABKCO Indus. v. Lennon, 52 A.D.2d 435, 384 N.Y.S.2d 781 (1976) (forum has general jurisdiction over famous musician based upon substantial but unrelated business contacts). Of course, the cases finding that there is no general jurisdiction over individuals are plentiful. See, e.g., Wilson v. Blakey, 20 F.3d 644 (5th Cir.1994); Madara v. Hall, 916 F.2d 1510

(11th Cir.1990), cert. denied 513 U.S. 930, 115 S.Ct. 322, 130 L.Ed.2d 282 (1994); Fields v. Ramada Inn, Inc., 816 F.Supp. 1033 (E.D.Pa.1993). The Restatement, Second, Conflict of Laws takes the position in § 35(3) that contacts-based general jurisdiction is available over individual defendants if such individuals are "doing business" in the forum and "this business is so continuous and substantial as to make it reasonable for the state to exercise such jurisdiction."

§ 6.9

1. 326 U.S. 310, 66 S.Ct. 154, 90 L.Ed. 95 (1945).

definition of those terms. The words themselves connote a substantial amount of activity carried out over some period of time, but they do not lend themselves to any bright-line test. Another question left open is whether the existence of continuous and systematic contacts is a necessary, or merely a sufficient, condition of exercising general jurisdiction. It has been argued that the existence of continuous and systematic contacts is a sufficient, but not necessary, condition,[2] but the Supreme Court's view appears to be that their existence is a sine qua non of general jurisdiction.[3]

The fact, then, that the existence of "continuous and systematic" contacts is essential to asserting general jurisdiction means that it is crucial to develop some test for evaluating the sufficiency of the contacts. Unfortunately, no clear test has developed and Supreme Court guidance is scant. Only two Supreme Court cases have considered whether a defendant's contacts were sufficient to allow for general jurisdiction.

Perkins v. Benguet Consolidated Mining Co.[4] centered on an action by a shareholder of a Philippine-based mining company against the company. The shareholder maintained that the company had failed to make dividend payments and stock issuances to which she was entitled. She brought the case in the Ohio state courts, and endeavored to obtain general jurisdiction, as none of the events in question had any relationship with the forum state. The company's contacts with Ohio included the company president's performance of essential company business from his Ohio home during the World War II period, including writing checks, maintaining employees and sending business correspondence.[5] Quoting *International Shoe*'s language regarding "continuous and systematic" contacts,[6] the Court held that the company was subject to in personam jurisdiction in the Ohio state courts.

Perkins was an unusual case. The procedural posture of the case was atypical as the Ohio state courts had concluded that they did not have jurisdiction,[7] apparently as a matter of state law, which would have deprived the Supreme Court of any appellate jurisdiction.[8] A majority of the Court concluded, however, that the Ohio Supreme Court's decision rested at least in part on its mistaken understanding of the minimum contacts test, and remanded the action, whereupon the Ohio Supreme Court reversed its position and held that the action could be maintained in its courts.[9] In any event, the Supreme Court came very close to

---

2. See, e.g., Helicopteros Nacionales de Colombia v. Hall, 466 U.S. 408, 419, 104 S.Ct. 1868, 1875, 80 L.Ed.2d 404, 414 (1984) (Brennan, J., dissenting).

3. Helicopteros Nacionales de Colombia, S.A. v. Hall, 466 U.S. 408, 104 S.Ct. 1868, 80 L.Ed.2d 404 (1984).

4. 342 U.S. 437, 72 S.Ct. 413, 96 L.Ed. 485 (1952).

5. Id. at 447–48, 72 S.Ct. at 419.

6. Id. at 446, 72 S.Ct. at 418.

7. Id. at 448, 72 S.Ct. at 419, 96 L.Ed. at 494.

8. Indeed, the dissent maintained the majority was issuing no more than an "advisory opinion." 342 U.S. at 449, 72 S.Ct. at 420, 96 L.Ed. at 494.

9. Perkins v. Benguet Consol. Min. Co., 158 Ohio St. 145, 107 N.E.2d 203 (1952) (Ohio decision on remand).

issuing an advisory decision, which might have weakened the opinion's precedential force considerably.

A second curious feature of *Perkins* was the matter of whether the lack of an alternative forum influenced the Court's conclusion that the Ohio state courts had jurisdiction. The majority opinion did not address the matter directly, but as some have noted the plaintiff might not have had a realistic opportunity for redress in another court.[10] In fact, one commentator maintains that *Perkins* is really an example of jurisdiction by necessity.[11] The full implications of *Perkins* thus remain unclear, but most courts have understood *Perkins* to allow for general jurisdiction over a corporation or other business entity in the state of its principal operations.[12]

At the other end of the spectrum from *Perkins* is the Supreme Court's only other case on contacts-based general jurisdiction, *Helicopteros Nacionales de Colombia v. Hall*.[13] *Helicopteros* involved a wrongful death action brought in the Texas state courts by four American (but non-Texan) citizens. They were killed in an accident in Peru while flying in a helicopter owned by the Colombian defendant. The four plaintiff were employees of a Texas-based joint venture that had contracted with the Colombian defendant for helicopter transport to and from construction sites in Peru.[14]

As discussed above,[15] *Helicopteros* might have been an opportunity for the Supreme Court to explain the difference between related and unrelated contacts. The defendant's contacts with the United States consisted primarily of the purchase of about four million dollars worth of helicopters and spare parts from a Texas company, and sending its pilots to Texas for training and to ferry the helicopters to South America.[16] These contacts bore a "but for" causal relationship to the accident, but probably no stronger connection. The Supreme Court concluded, however, that the plaintiffs' brief before the Supreme Court had conceded that jurisdiction could be sustained only on a theory of general jurisdiction, and thus proceeded to treat the case in this fashion. Proceeding from this premise, the Supreme Court held that the Texas courts lacked jurisdiction, because "purchases and related trips, standing alone, are not a sufficient basis for a State's assertion of jurisdiction."[17]

Perkins and *Helicopteros* provide some guidance at the margins. However, one can imagine a literally infinite number of factual permuta-

---

10. See, e.g., Weintraub, Commentary on the Conflict of Laws 146–47 (1971); von Mehren & Trautman, Jurisdiction to Adjudicate: A Suggested Analysis, 79 Harv. L. Rev. 1121, 1144 (1966). See also Note, Developments in the Law—State Court Jurisdiction, 73 Harv. L. Rev. 909, 932 (1960) (*Perkins* has limited significance).

11. See Waits, Values, Intuitions, and Opinion Writing: The Judicial Process and State Court Jurisdiction, 1983 U. Ill. L. Rev. 917, 940.

12. See, e.g., Seymour v. Parke, Davis & Co., 423 F.2d 584, 587 (1st Cir.1970); Witt v. Reynolds Metals Co., 240 Va. 452, 455, 397 S.E.2d 873, 875 (1990).

13. 466 U.S. 408, 104 S.Ct. 1868, 80 L.Ed.2d 404 (1984).

14. Id. at 409, 104 S.Ct. at 1870.

15. See supra § 6.7.

16. 466 U.S. at 411, 104 S.Ct. at 1870.

17. Id. at 417, 104 S.Ct. at 1874.

tions falling in between the two cases. For instance, *Helicopteros* holds that substantial unrelated purchases will not sustain jurisdiction, but will substantial unrelated sales? *Perkins* implies that general jurisdiction over a business will lie in the state in which the business has its principal offices, but what if it has a branch office in the forum? or a regional sales office? or a small office that merely relays information to other offices? What about businesses that take official steps to register with a state government? or appoint an agent for service of process? or obtain a license to do business in the state? Unfortunately, as one might expect with a lack of clear legislative standards or Supreme Court guidance, conflicting authority can be found on any of these points.

Consequently, generalizations are treacherous, but, with that warning in mind, here are a few. First, successful efforts to invoke contacts-based general jurisdiction are fairly rare. One commentator goes so far as to call the entire doctrine a "myth."[18] While this might be something of an overstatement, courts are somewhat reluctant to exercise jurisdiction based solely on unrelated contacts, often (one suspects) because some alternative forum seems intuitively to be a preferable site for the litigation.

Second, cases that do allow for general jurisdiction usually resemble the facts of *Perkins* in some important particulars. The most important particular is that the defendant have some continuing physical presence in the forum, usually in the form of offices or employees.[19] Third, purely non-physical affiliations with a state make it much more difficult for a plaintiff to successfully invoke general jurisdiction.[20] Courts are severely

---

18. Twitchell, The Myth of General Jurisdiction, 101 Harv. L. Rev. 610 (1988).

19. See, e.g., Behagen v. Amateur Basketball Ass'n of the United States of America, 744 F.2d 731 (10th Cir.1984) (international organization with office of United States member in forum state subject to jurisdiction under a *Perkins* rationale); de Reyes v. Marine Mgmt. & Consulting, Ltd., 586 So.2d 103 (La.1991) (maintaining an office in the forum in which some management decisions are made is sufficient for general jurisdiction); Ex Parte Newco Mfg. Co., 481 So.2d 867 (Ala.1985) (substantial sales revenue from forum sufficient to establish general jurisdiction); St. Louis–San Francisco Ry. v. Gitchoff, 68 Ill.2d 38, 11 Ill.Dec. 598, 369 N.E.2d 52 (1977) (sales office with seven employees in forum sufficient for general jurisdiction); Zivalich v. International Bhd. of Teamsters, 662 So.2d 62 (La.App.1995), writ denied 666 So.2d 292 (La. 1996) (maintaining union employees and organizers in a state is sufficient for general jurisdiction over the union); Laufer v. Ostrow, 55 N.Y.2d 305, 434 N.E.2d 692, 449 N.Y.S.2d 456 (1982) (corporate activities sufficient that defendant was "doing business" in New York within the meaning

of long-arm statute); but see Nichols v. G.D. Searle & Co., 991 F.2d 1195 (4th Cir.1993) (maintaining 20 employees in a state insufficient to establish general jurisdiction); Romann v. Geissenberger Mfg. Corp., 865 F.Supp. 255 (E.D.Pa.1994) (maintaining an office for an employee based in forum not sufficient for general jurisdiction); see generally Twitchell, supra n.18, at 633 (general jurisdiction usually allowed at defendant's "home base").

20. See, e.g., Wilson v. Blakey, 20 F.3d 644 (5th Cir.1994), cert. denied 513 U.S. 930, 115 S.Ct. 322, 130 L.Ed.2d 282 (1994) (modest amount of personal business in state insufficient to support general jurisdiction over individual); Villar v. Crowley Maritime Corp., 990 F.2d 1489 (5th Cir. 1993) (mere ownership of corporate subsidiary in forum insufficient to establish general jurisdiction); Amoco Egypt Oil Co. v. Leonis Navigation Co., 1 F.3d 848 (9th Cir. 1993) (unrelated shipping activities insufficient to sustain general jurisdiction); Doe v. National Medical Servs., 974 F.2d 143 (10th Cir.1992) (testing of several hundred drug samples from forum insufficient to sustain jurisdiction in a case not related to one of

divided as to whether substantial in-state sales,[21] registering to do business or appointing an in-state agent for service of process[22] suffice to allow a court to exercise general jurisdiction. Perhaps all that one can say on this is that counsel who attempts to bring a case on a theory of general jurisdiction in a forum in which the defendant has no obvious physical presence had best make alternative plans for pursuing the case elsewhere in the event that the forum concludes that it lacks jurisdiction. Finally, attempting to take general jurisdiction over an individual defendant in a forum in which the defendant is neither domiciled nor resident is an extraordinarily chancy proposition. Such attempted assertions of jurisdiction are sustained occasionally,[23] but counsel who at-

those samples); Morris v. Barkbuster, Inc., 923 F.2d 1277 (8th Cir.1991) (contractual negotiations in forum insufficient to sustain general jurisdiction); Sandstrom v. Chem-Lawn Corp., 904 F.2d 83 (1st Cir.1990) (appointment of in-state agent for service not enough to allow for jurisdiction); Dalton v. R & W Marine, Inc., 897 F.2d 1359 (5th Cir.1990) (substantial unrelated charter boat activities insufficient to allow for general jurisdiction); Bearry v. Beech Aircraft Corp., 818 F.2d 370 (5th Cir. 1987) (substantial volume of sales in state by aircraft manufacturer insufficient to sustain jurisdiction on claim on air crash outside of state); Travelers Indem. Co. v. Calvert Fire Ins. Co., 798 F.2d 826 (5th Cir.1986) (sale of modest number of insurance policies in forum insufficient to establish general jurisdiction); In re Ski Train Fire in Kaprun, Austria on November 11, 2000, 257 F.Supp.2d 717 (S.D.N.Y. 2003) (in-state sales insufficient to support potential finding of general jurisdiction); American Overseas Marine Corp. v. Patterson, 632 So.2d 1124 (Fla.App.1994) (occasional unloading of goods in forum state insufficient for general jurisdiction); National Indus. Sand Ass'n v. Gibson, 897 S.W.2d 769 (Tex.1995) (mailings by lobbying group to in-state members insufficient to establish general jurisdiction); Camelback Ski Corp. v. Behning, 307 Md. 270, 513 A.2d 874 (1986) (ski resort that accepts substantial number of skiers from forum not subject to general jurisdiction).

21. Compare Travelers Indem. Co. v. Calvert Fire Ins. Co., 798 F.2d 826 (5th Cir.1986) (sale of insurance policies in forum state insufficient to establish general jurisdiction); In re Ski Train Fire in Kaprun, Austria on November 11, 2000, 257 F.Supp.2d 717 (S.D.N.Y. 2003) (in-state sales insufficient to support potential finding of general jurisdiction); Stark Carpet Corp. v. M–Geough Robinson, Inc., 481 F.Supp. 499 (S.D.N.Y.1980) ("mere" solicitation of business in forum does not satisfy New York's long-arm statute); Camelback

Ski Corp. v. Behning, 307 Md. 270, 513 A.2d 874 (1986) (ski resort's acceptance of skiers from forum state insufficient to establish general jurisdiction); Boaz v. Boyle & Co., 40 Cal.App.4th 700, 46 Cal.Rptr.2d 888 (1995) (in-state sales insufficient to establish general jurisdiction); Thomason v. Chemical Bank, 234 Conn. 281, 661 A.2d 595 (1995) (general jurisdiction sustained because of large amount of forum-state solicitation of business by defendant); Mayo v. Tillman Aero, Inc., 640 So.2d 314 (La.App. 1994) (advertising and sales in state insufficient to establish general jurisdiction) with Bearry v. Beech Aircraft Corp., 818 F.2d 370 (5th Cir. 1987) (substantial volume of forum sales sufficient to establish general jurisdiction); Davenport Mach. & Foundry Co. v. Adolph Coors Co., 314 N.W.2d 432 (Iowa 1982) (in-state beer sales sufficient to establish general jurisdiction); Reed v. American Airlines, Inc., 197 Mont. 34, 640 P.2d 912 (1982) (jurisdiction over airline in forum based upon in-state sales and advertising even though only flights to and from forum were occasional charters); Dillon v. Numismatic Funding Corp., 291 N.C. 674, 231 S.E.2d 629 (1977) (two year pattern of sales to forum domiciliaries sufficient to allow general jurisdiction).

22. Compare Sandstrom v. ChemLawn Corp., 904 F.2d 83 (1st Cir.1990) (appointment of in-state agent for service of process insufficient to establish general jurisdiction) with Sondergard v. Miles, Inc., 985 F.2d 1389 (8th Cir.1993), cert. denied 510 U.S. 814, 114 S.Ct. 63, 126 L.Ed.2d 32 (1993) (appointment of agency for service of process is sufficient to establish general jurisdiction); Ytuarte v. Gruner & Jahr Printing and Pub. Co., 935 F.2d 971 (8th Cir.1991); D.J. Nelson v. World Wide Lease, Inc., 110 Idaho 369, 716 P.2d 513 (1986) (same).

23. See, e.g., ABKCO Indus. v. Lennon, 52 A.D.2d 435, 384 N.Y.S.2d 781 (1976) (forum has general jurisdiction over famous musician based upon substantial but unre-

tempts to proceed on such a theory again runs a substantial risk of committing malpractice if he has not planned for the possibility of a jurisdictional dismissal.

lated business contacts). Of course, the cases finding that there is no general jurisdiction over individuals are plentiful. See, e.g., Wilson v. Blakey, 20 F.3d 644 (5th Cir.1994), cert. denied 513 U.S. 930, 115 S.Ct. 322, 130 L.Ed.2d 282 (1994); Fields v. Ramada Inn, Inc., 816 F.Supp. 1033 (E.D.Pa.1993). The Restatement, Second, Conflict of Laws takes the position in § 35(3) that contacts-based general jurisdiction is available over individual defendants if such individuals are "doing business" in the forum and "this business is so continuous and substantial as to make it reasonable for the state to exercise such jurisdiction."

Chapter 7

SPECIFIC JURISDICTION
IN TORT CASES

Table of Sections

		Sections
I.	Introduction	7.1
II.	Personal Injuries	7.2–7.5
	A. Products Liability—The "Stream of Commerce" Test	7.2
	B. Intentional Torts	7.3
	C. Negligence	7.4
	D. Other Strict Liability	7.5
III.	Injuries to Property	7.6–7.8
	A. Personal Property	7.6
	B. Real Property	7.7
IV.	Injuries to Reputation	7.8–7.10
	A. Libel	7.8
	B. Slander	7.9
	C. Invasion of Privacy	7.10
V.	Economic Injuries	7.11–7.12
	A. Interference with Contract and Related Torts	7.11
	B. Fraud and Related Torts	7.12

I. INTRODUCTION

§ 7.1 The expansion of the jurisdiction of American courts has occurred, in large part, in tort cases. A plurality of the United States Supreme Court jurisdictional cases since *International Shoe Co. v. Washington*[1] has involved a tort of some kind.[2] In retrospect, this is an unsurprising development. Probably no area of substantive law has seen as much change over the last 50 years as has the law of torts. The double effect of expanding boundaries of tort liability[3] and in personam jurisdic-

---

§ 7.1

1. 326 U.S. 310, 66 S.Ct. 154, 90 L.Ed. 95 (1945).

2. See, e.g., Asahi Metal Indus. Co. v. Superior Court, 480 U.S. 102, 107 S.Ct. 1026, 94 L.Ed.2d 92 (1987) (products liability); Helicopteros Nacionales de Colombia, S.A. v. Hall, 466 U.S. 408, 104 S.Ct. 1868, 80 L.Ed.2d 404 (1984) (wrongful death); Calder v. Jones, 465 U.S. 783, 104 S.Ct.

1482, 79 L.Ed.2d 804 (1984) (libel); Keeton v. Hustler Magazine, 465 U.S. 770, 104 S.Ct. 1473, 79 L.Ed.2d 790 (1984) (libel); Rush v. Savchuk, 444 U.S. 320, 100 S.Ct. 571, 62 L.Ed.2d 516 (1980) (automobile accident); World–Wide Volkswagen Corp. v. Woodson, 444 U.S. 286, 100 S.Ct. 559, 62 L.Ed.2d 490 (1980) (automobile accident).

3. See, e.g., Greenman v. Yuba Power Prods., Inc., 59 Cal.2d 57, 27 Cal.Rptr. 697, 377 P.2d 897 (1963) (recovery in strict

tion was bound to produce factual and legal patterns unknown in any previous era.

Despite their novelty, tort jurisdictional problems are analytically no different than others. In order for a court to have jurisdiction, it must have statutory, rule or common law authorization to hear the case, and the assertion of jurisdiction must not offend the Constitution. The first step usually involves interpretation of a state long-arm statute.[4] In some instances, tort cases have presented difficult questions of statutory interpretation, prompting state courts to interpret their long-arm statutes broadly.[5] The second step involves interpretation of the constitutional boundaries as articulated by the Supreme Court. And, of course, this usually means an application of the "minimum contacts" test. Thus, our general exposition[6] of the minimum contacts test is highly relevant for analysis of tort problems. In this chapter we discuss the application of the test to more specific, and frequently litigated, tort problems.

II. PERSONAL INJURIES

A. PRODUCTS LIABILITY—THE "STREAM OF COMMERCE" TEST

§ 7.2 The broadening of the bases of liability for sellers of defective products[1] coincided temporally with the broadening of in personam jurisdiction.[2] Consequently, some of the most challenging jurisdictional issues have arisen in products cases.

Initially, the most important products cases were a pair of state court decisions. In *Gray v. American Radiator and Standard Sanitary Corp.*,[3] the Illinois Supreme Court considered whether to take jurisdiction over an Ohio manufacturer of water valves. The valve in question had been manufactured in Ohio, and then sold to another company in

---

products liability); Escola v. Coca Cola Bottling Co. of Fresno, 24 Cal.2d 453, 150 P.2d 436 (1944) (Traynor, J., concurring) (suggesting a theory of strict products liability); Henningsen v. Bloomfield Motors, Inc., 32 N.J. 358, 161 A.2d 69 (1960) (recovery for a defective product allowed on a implied warranty theory).

4. This is true even if the court hearing the case is a federal court. See F.R.C.P. 4(k). See also supra § 5.15.

5. See, e.g., Gray v. American Radiator and Standard Sanitary Corp., 22 Ill.2d 432, 176 N.E.2d 761 (1961) (interpreting the term "tortious act" to mean where the effects of a tort are felt).

6. See supra §§ 5.10–5.13.

1. See, e.g., Greenman v. Yuba Power Prods., Inc., 59 Cal.2d 57, 27 Cal.Rptr. 697, 377 P.2d 897 (1963) (recovery in strict products liability); Escola v. Coca Cola Bottling Co. of Fresno, 24 Cal.2d 453, 150 P.2d 436 (1944) (Traynor, J., concurring) (suggesting a theory of strict products liability); Henningsen v. Bloomfield Motors, Inc., 32 N.J. 358, 161 A.2d 69 (1960) (recovery for a defective product allowed on a implied warranty theory).

2. See, e.g., McGee v. International Life Ins. Co., 355 U.S. 220, 78 S.Ct. 199, 2 L.Ed.2d 223 (1957); International Shoe Co. v. Washington, 326 U.S. 310, 66 S.Ct. 154, 90 L.Ed. 95 (1945).

3. 22 Ill.2d 432, 176 N.E.2d 761 (1961).

Pennsylvania, where it was incorporated into a hot water heater and the entire assembly was eventually sold to an Illinois consumer.[4] After being sold in Illinois, the water heater exploded (apparently because of a defect in the valve) and caused injury to the Illinois consumer.

This fairly ordinary fact pattern forced the Illinois Supreme Court to deal with difficult issues in the application of the minimum contacts test. The Ohio valve manufacturer did not have Illinois contacts sufficient for general jurisdiction, thus requiring the Illinois Supreme Court to decide whether the sale of the assembly, by itself, could support jurisdiction. Relying heavily on the United State Supreme Court's decision in *McGee v. International Life Ins. Co.*,[5] the Illinois court concluded that the in-state resale of the valve was sufficient to allow jurisdiction over the valve manufacturer.[6] The court pointed to the benefit enjoyed by the manufacturer in serving the Illinois market, and argued that fairness demanded making the Illinois courts available for the redress of injuries inflicted on Illinois residents.[7] The court also pointed to pragmatic·considerations favoring jurisdiction in the injury state, such as easy access to the physical evidence and witnesses.[8]

Taking a similarly broad view of state court jurisdiction in products cases was the California Supreme Court in *Buckeye Boiler Co. v. Superior Court.*[9] Factually, *Buckeye Boiler* was similar to *Gray*. The plaintiff, a California resident, was injured in that state, while on the job, when a pressure tank apparently manufactured by the defendant exploded. Unlike *Gray*, however, it was not clear how the product in question actually arrived in the forum state. The defendant claimed to have no record of selling any tank to the plaintiff's employer, although it had made some sales to another California company, and the exploded tank was clearly marked as one of the defendant's.[10] Notwithstanding the sketchy record, the California Supreme Court held that the case should not be dismissed for lack of jurisdiction. Relying on *Gray*, the court held that the company's knowledge or reasonable expectation that its products would be sold in the forum state was sufficient to allow for jurisdiction.[11]

Gray and *Buckeye Boiler* were major pillars of what came to be known as the "stream of commerce" theory of jurisdiction.[12] The theory behind these cases was that jurisdiction ought to follow the stream of

---

4. Id. at 438, 176 N.E.2d at 764.

5. 355 U.S. 220, 78 S.Ct. 199, 2 L.Ed.2d 223 (1957).

6. 22 Ill.2d at 442, 176 N.E.2d at 765.

7. Id.

8. Id. at 443–44, 176 N.E.2d at 766–67.

9. 71 Cal.2d 893, 80 Cal.Rptr. 113, 458 P.2d 57 (1969).

10. Id. at 897, 458 P.2d at 61, 80 Cal. Rptr. at 117.

11. Id. at 902–03, 458 P.2d at 64–65, 80 Cal.Rptr. at 120–21.

12. This phrase appears in jurisdictional opinions as early as the 1960s, see, e.g., Haldeman–Homme Mfg. Co. v. Texacon Indus., 236 F.Supp. 99 (D.Minn.1964); A.R. Indus. v. Superior Court, 268 Cal.App.2d 328, 73 Cal.Rptr. 920 (1968), but appears not to have gained wide currency until the United States Supreme Court used it to describe *Gray*. See World–Wide Volkswagen Corp. v. Woodson, 444 U.S. 286, 298, 100 S.Ct. 559, 567, 62 L.Ed.2d 490 (1980).

commerce to any forum in which the defendant's product is marketed. Thus, if a product is sold or resold in the forum, and causes injury there, the theory of *Gray* and *Buckeye* would allow for jurisdiction. In fact, some cases of that era went even further, and held that mere use of the product in the forum—without an in-state sale—would allow for jurisdiction.[13]

The United States Supreme Court did not weigh in on the question of jurisdiction in products cases until it decided *World–Wide Volkswagen Corp. v. Woodson*.[14] *World–Wide* involved facts somewhat akin to *Gray* and *Buckeye Boiler*, but with important differences making it a less attractive case for jurisdiction. *World–Wide* arose from a automobile crash in Oklahoma. The injured passengers sued four defendants, two of which took the jurisdictional question to the Supreme Court. The two defendants were the New York retailer and the New York–New Jersey–Connecticut distributor of the car; the plaintiffs were New Yorkers who were in the process of relocating to Arizona when their car was struck from behind on an Oklahoma highway. The plaintiffs contended, and the Oklahoma Supreme Court agreed, that the Oklahoma state courts had jurisdiction over the defendants because—even though the car had been purchased in New York—its use in Oklahoma was foreseeable and that the defendants therefore derived a significant benefit from the Oklahoma market.[15] The United States Supreme Court held, however, that foreseeability of a product's use in a state is insufficient for jurisdiction.[16] Rather, said the Court, "the foreseeability that is critical to due process analysis . . . is that the defendant's conduct and connection with the forum State are such that he should reasonably anticipate being haled into court there."[17]

The major factual difference, then, between *World–Wide* and cases like *Gray* and *Buckeye Boiler* is that the former involved only use of the product in the forum, while the latter involved products sold or resold in the forum. The Supreme Court was clearly conscious of the stream of commerce test; in fact, it specifically attributed it to *Gray*. And, in attributing it to *Gray*, the Court seemed to approve of it, at least in the circumstance of a forum state sale or resale of the product. The Court reasoned that a state court may take jurisdiction "over a corporation that delivers its products into the stream of commerce with the expectation that they will be purchased by consumers in the forum State. Cf. *Gray v. American Radiator & Standard Sanitary Corp*. . . . ."[18] The Supreme Court's reference to *Gray* was a bit cryptic, particularly the use of the "cf." signal in the citation. But its reference to the stream of

13. See, e.g., Mann v. Frank Hrubetz and Co., Inc., 361 So.2d 1021 (Ala.1978); Phillips v. Anchor Hocking Glass Corp., 100 Ariz. 251, 413 P.2d 732 (1966). But see Hapner v. Rolf Brauchli, Inc., 404 Mich. 160, 273 N.W.2d 822 (1978).

14. 444 U.S. 286, 100 S.Ct. 559, 62 L.Ed.2d 490 (1980).

15. Id. at 289, 100 S.Ct. at 563, 62 L.Ed.2d at 496.

16. Id. at 296, 100 S.Ct. at 566, 62 L.Ed.2d at 500.

17. Id. at 297, 100 S.Ct. at 567, 62 L.Ed.2d at 501.

18. Id. at 298, 100 S.Ct. at 567.

commerce test, and its contrast between product use and purchase in the forum state, seemed to suggest mild approval of cases such as *Gray* and *Buckeye Boiler*.

Many courts in the wake of *World–Wide* continued to take an expansive view of jurisdiction in products cases. Several post-*World–Wide* cases allowed for jurisdiction upon a simple showing that the product in question was sold to the consumer-plaintiff in the forum state.[19] Most have followed *World–Wide*'s admonition that mere use of the product in the forum does not suffice for jurisdiction,[20] although a few decisions have continued to allow for jurisdiction based upon product use in the forum state sale if coupled with other special factors weighing heavily in favor of taking jurisdiction.[21]

The fact pattern after *World–Wide* that caused lower courts the most difficulty, however, was the *Gray* fact pattern, in which the product in question was a *component* in a larger assembly, and it was the larger assembly resold in the forum. Some courts, following *Gray*, allowed for jurisdiction based upon component resale.[22] Others, however, held that mere forum state resale of the product would not, by itself, support jurisdiction.[23] This split among lower courts was bound to provoke Supreme Court intervention.

The Supreme Court did eventually decide a component parts resale case, but its decision did little to clarify matters. *Asahi Metal Industry Co. v. Superior Court*[24] involved the question of whether a Japanese valve manufacturer could be haled into a California court to indemnify a Taiwanese motorcycle tube manufacturer based upon the ultimate sale of the injury-causing tire-valve assembly in the forum state. Factually, *Asahi* strongly resembled *Gray*. In both cases, the allegedly defective product was manufactured and sold outside the forum, but the finished assembly was sold to the consumer and caused injury in the forum state. Unfortunately, however, the Court divided evenly on the question of whether the forum state sale of the finished product constituted minimum contacts.

A four-vote plurality led by Justice O'Connor approved of those lower court cases that held that resale of the finished product in the forum was insufficient to support jurisdiction. O'Connor suggested a test

---

19. See, e.g., Petroleum Helicopters, Inc. v. Avco Corp., 804 F.2d 1367 (5th Cir. 1986); Thompson v. Chrysler Motors Corp., 755 F.2d 1162 (5th Cir.1985); Bean Dredging Corp. v. Dredge Tech., 744 F.2d 1081 (5th Cir.1984).

20. See, e.g., Fidelity and Casualty Co. of New York v. Philadelphia Resins Corp., 766 F.2d 440 (10th Cir.1985); LaRose v. Sponco Mfg. Inc., 712 F.Supp. 455 (D.N.J. 1989); Price & Sons v. Second Judicial Dist., 108 Nev. 387, 831 P.2d 600 (1992).

21. See, e.g., Hedrick v. Daiko Shoji Co., 715 F.2d 1355 (9th Cir.1983) (product only

used in forum, but large scale manufacture of the product allows for jurisdiction in the forum); Rostad v. On–Deck, Inc., 372 N.W.2d 717 (Minn.1985) (product causing injury only used in forum, but thousands of similar products sold in the forum).

22. See, e.g., *Bean Dredging*, 744 F.2d 1081.

23. See, e.g., Humble v. Toyota Motor Co., 727 F.2d 709 (8th Cir.1984) (manufacturer of car seat not subject to jurisdiction in state in which the car was sold).

24. 480 U.S. 102, 107 S.Ct. 1026, 94 L.Ed.2d 92 (1987).

that required resale of the product plus some "[a]dditional conduct" indicating a purposeful effort to serve the forum state market.[25] With regard to the additional conduct that might suffice to demonstrate the existence of minimum contacts, Justice O'Connor suggested a special design of the product to serve the forum state's market, advertising in the forum state, customer support channels, or maintaining a sales agent in the forum.[26] Four Justices, led by Justice Brennan, disagreed with Justice O'Connor's interpretation of the stream of commerce test. These justices endorsed those lower court cases that held that resale of a product in the forum state usually should suffice for jurisdiction.[27] Justice Brennan's opinion pointed to the *World–Wide*'s apparently approving references to *Gray* as evidence that no "additional conduct" need be shown.[28] Justice Stevens refused to endorse either position, leaving the Court in equipoise as between the Brennan and O'Connor interpretations of the stream of commerce test.

The Justices did, however, unanimously agree that jurisdiction was unconstitutional on *Asahi*'s facts because the California court's assertion of jurisdiction failed to meet a broader standard of reasonableness.[29] Three factors persuaded the *Asahi* Court that asserting jurisdiction over the Japanese defendant would be unreasonable. First was the foreign nationality of the defendant. The Court emphasized the great distance between the defendant's headquarters in Japan and the California courthouse, as well as the "unique burdens placed upon one who must defend oneself in a foreign legal system."[30] Second was the collateral nature of the indemnity dispute. The Japanese valve manufacturer had not been sued directly by the plaintiff, and the question of whether the Japanese valve manufacturer would be required to indemnify the Taiwanese tube manufacturer depended almost entirely on events and transactions occurring in Asia.[31] Third, the settlement of the underlying dispute between the tort plaintiff and the Taiwanese tube manufacturer left the state court without a forum-domiciled plaintiff, thereby diminishing the California state court's interest in hearing the matter.

Asahi was bound to spawn confusion, and it has. Those courts that have chosen between the Brennan and O'Connor interpretations of the stream of commerce have divided on the question.[32] Others have managed to reach a decision without specifically endorsing either view.[33]

25. Id. at 111, 107 S.Ct. at 1031.

26. Id.

27. See supra n.19.

28. *Asahi*, 480 U.S. at 116, 107 S.Ct. at 1034 (Brennan, J., concurring and concurring in the judgment).

29. Id. at 113–16, 107 S.Ct. at 1033–34; id. at 116–21, 107 S.Ct. at 1034–37 (Brennan, J., concurring and concurring in the judgment).

30. *Asahi*, 480 U.S. at 114, 107 S.Ct. at 1033.

31. Id.

32. See, e.g., Irving v. Owens–Corning Fiberglas Corp., 864 F.2d 383 (5th Cir.1989) (Brennan view); Parry v. Ernst Home Ctr. Corp., 779 P.2d 659 (Utah 1989) (O'Connor view); Four B Corp. v. Ueno Fine Chemicals Industry, Ltd., 241 F.Supp.2d 1258 (D. Kansas 2003) (applying O'Connor view).

33. See, e.g., Stanton v. St. Jude Medical, Inc., 340 F.3d 690 (8th Cir. 2003) (no jurisdiction over out-of-state manufacturer of a coating used in a heart valve implanted in the plaintiff's decedent in the forum state); Pennzoil Products Co. v. Colelli & Assoc., 149 F.3d 197 (3d Cir.1998) (jurisdic-

Lower courts have treated *Asahi*'s "reasonableness" rationale with caution. Many cases that have implicated *Asahi*'s reasonableness rationale have been products cases, and those cases that have denied jurisdiction under the reasonableness test have involved, for the most part, foreign defendants.[34] Lower courts applying *Asahi* have not, however, read it as granting jurisdictional immunity to foreign defendants.[35] Although generalizations are difficult, it appears that in cases involving close questions regarding the application of the minimum contacts test, the foreign status of the defendant can tip the balance toward finding

tion exists under either theory because of direct and foreseeable resale of product in the forum); Beverly Hills Fan Co. v. Royal Sovereign Corp., 21 F.3d 1558, 1566 (Fed. Cir.1994), cert. dismissed 512 U.S. 1273, 115 S.Ct. 18, 129 L.Ed.2d 917 (1994) (choice between views not necessary on facts of case); Benitez–Allende v. Alcan Aluminio do Brasil, S.A., 857 F.2d 26 (1st Cir.1988) (product specifically marketed for forum); A. Uberti and C. v. Leonardo, 181 Ariz. 565, 892 P.2d 1354 (Ariz. 1995), cert. denied 516 U.S. 906, 116 S.Ct. 273, 133 L.Ed.2d 194 (1995) (jurisdiction in forum because product specially designed for the forum); Kin Yon Lung Industrial Co., Ltd. v. Temple, 816 So.2d 663 (Fla. App. 2002) (plaintiff unable to demonstrate distribution in forum); Price and Sons v. Second Judicial District Ct., 108 Nev. 387, 831 P.2d 600 (1992) (mere use of product in state does not suffice under either Brennan or O'Connor view in *Asahi*); Dillaplain v. Lite Indus., Inc., 788 S.W.2d 530 (Mo.App.1990) ("conscious" effort to serve forum market suffices under either view).

34. See, e.g., Core–Vent Corp. v. Nobel Indus., 11 F.3d 1482 (9th Cir.1993) (jurisdiction would not be reasonably asserted over Swedish defendants alleged to have libelled a local plaintiff's product); Amoco Egypt Oil Co. v. Leonis Navigation Co., 1 F.3d 848 (9th Cir.1993) (jurisdiction would not be reasonably asserted in Washington court over dispute between two foreign parties regarding boating collision); Teledyne, Inc. v. Kone Corp., 892 F.2d 1404 (9th Cir.1989) (jurisdiction would be unreasonable over a foreign state-owned industry); Guardian Royal Exch. Assurance v. English China Clays, 815 S.W.2d 223 (Tex.1991) (jurisdiction would unreasonable in a collateral dispute involving and English insurer); Parry v. Ernst Home Ctr. Corp., 779 P.2d 659 (Utah. 1989) (unreasonableness an alternative rationale for dismissal in a products liability case involving Japanese defendants).

In a slight extension of *Asahi*, most courts have applied the overarching reasonableness standard even in cases involving

assertions of general jurisdiction, even though *Asahi* itself was a specific jurisdiction case. See, e.g., Amoco Egypt Oil Co. v. Leonis Navigation Co., 1 F.3d 848 (9th Cir. 1993); Dalton v. R & W Marine, Inc., 897 F.2d 1359 (5th Cir.1990); Bearry v. Beech Aircraft Corp., 818 F.2d 370 (5th Cir.1987); de Reyes v. Marine Mgmt. & Consulting, 586 So.2d 103 (La.1991); but see Crane v. Carr, 814 F.2d 758 (D.C.Cir.1987).

35. See, e.g., Vandelune v. 4B Elevator Components Unlimited, 148 F.3d 943 (8th Cir.1998) (forum-state sale of allegedly faulty safety device sufficient for jurisdiction where sale was through a regular distribution channel and part of a conscious effort to exploit a discrete, multistate market); Vermeulen v. Renault, 985 F.2d 1534 (11th Cir.1993), cert. denied 508 U.S. 907, 113 S.Ct. 2334, 124 L.Ed.2d 246 (1993) (large volume of United States sales of cars manufactured by French defendant render jurisdiction over defendant reasonable); Sinatra v. National Enquirer, 854 F.2d 1191 (9th Cir.1988) (jurisdiction reasonable libel claim asserted by a local plaintiff against Swedish defendants who knowing made false statements to the effect that the plaintiff had been a patient in their clinic); Benitez–Allende v. Alcan Aluminio do Brasil, 857 F.2d 26 (1st Cir.1988) (jurisdiction over Brazilian manufacturer of defective pressure cooker reasonable because of large volume of local sales); Theunissen v. Matthews, 935 F.2d 1454 (6th Cir.1991) (jurisdiction reasonable over a Canadian defendant living in close proximity to the forum); A. Uberti v. Leonardo, 181 Ariz. 565, 892 P.2d 1354 (Ariz. 1995), cert. denied 516 U.S. 906, 116 S.Ct. 273, 133 L.Ed.2d 194 (1995) (jurisdiction can be reasonably asserted over an Italian manufacturer of a gun manufactured for sale in the United States and causing injury in the forum state); Domtar, Inc. v. Niagara Fire Ins. Co., 533 N.W.2d 25 (Minn.1995), cert. denied 516 U.S. 1017, 116 S.Ct. 583, 133 L.Ed.2d 504 (1995) (jurisdiction can be reasonably asserted over a Canadian defendant that knowingly insured a risk located in the United States).

that jurisdiction is unconstitutional. On the other hand, a relatively strong showing that the minimum contacts test has been satisfied allows a court to take jurisdiction even if the defendant is a foreign national.

Thus, while many jurisdictional opinions have been issued in products cases, fundamental questions remain unresolved. It seems clear that the mere fact that the plaintiff is a resident of the forum state, and that the injury occurred there, will not suffice for jurisdiction. The more difficult problems lie with forum state sales. Regular, direct forum state sales, with all of the usual efforts to exploit the market, should suffice for jurisdiction.[36] But it remains unclear the circumstances under which more tangential connections, such as component resale in the forum, suffice for jurisdiction.

B. INTENTIONAL TORTS

§ 7.3 Classic intentional torts such as assault, battery and false imprisonment present interesting jurisdictional questions only occasionally. The very nature of these torts usually locates the actions and the consequences in one place. As a result, courts have had little difficulty asserting jurisdiction over a defendant if the tort took place in the forum, even if the defendant was there only casually.[1] If, however, the tort occurred outside the forum, the mere fact that the plaintiff is domiciled in the forum usually will not suffice.[2]

The most difficult problems with regard to jurisdiction occur with intentional torts that implicate interests other than bodily integrity. Torts such as fraud, libel, intentional infliction of emotional distress, trademark infringement, malicious prosecution and interference with contract are all more likely to bring about harmful consequences in states other than those in which the tortious actions occurred. Although below we treat some of these torts separately, they can be placed within a unified conceptual framework.

The most significant Supreme Court cases on intentional tort jurisdiction are *Calder v. Jones*[3] and *Keeton v. Hustler*.[4] *Calder* and *Keeton* were decided on the same day, and both involved allegedly defamatory publications. In *Calder* the plaintiff, a famous entertainer, brought suit in her home state of California. The defendants were a writer and an editor—each domiciled in Florida—for a national publication with a substantial circulation in every state, and its largest circulation in

36. See, e.g., *Pennzoil*, 149 F.3d 197 (direct efforts to deal with ultimate purchaser in forum state suffices for jurisdiction); see also authorities cited supra n.35.

§ 7.3

1. See, e.g., Cooper v. Molko, 512 F.Supp. 563 (N.D.Cal.1981) (out-of-state defendants subject to jurisdiction in forum by virtue of having committed a battery in the forum); Knight v. San Jacinto Club, Inc., 96 N.J.Super. 81, 232 A.2d 462 (1967) (juris-

diction allowed in a battery case over an out-of-state defendant where battery took place in the forum).

2. See, e.g., Panchal v. Ethen, 648 So.2d 245 (Fla.App.1994) (interpreting Florida long-arm statute to preclude jurisdiction).

3. 465 U.S. 783, 104 S.Ct. 1482, 79 L.Ed.2d 804 (1984).

4. 465 U.S. 770, 104 S.Ct. 1473, 79 L.Ed.2d 790 (1984).

California. In *Keeton* the plaintiff also claimed that she had been defamed by material appearing in a publication of national circulation. Unlike the *Calder* plaintiff, however, the *Keeton* plaintiff did not sue in her home state. Instead, she chose to sue in New Hampshire (home to monthly sales of about 10,000 copies of the defendant's publication) because of its long statute of limitations.[5]

In each case, the Supreme Court held that the exercise of jurisdiction was constitutional. Of the two cases, *Calder* speaks most directly to the problems of taking jurisdiction in an intentional tort case. The plaintiff in *Calder* alleged not only a libel theory, she also pleaded intentional infliction of emotional distress and invasion of privacy.[6] The defendants argued that as mere employees of the offending publication, their connection with California was too attenuated to require them to defend the case there. The Supreme Court disagreed, however, pointing out that the material published concerned a California citizen and that the injury was thus suffered there. The Court, in language with relevance for intentional torts generally, reasoned that "[j]urisdiction ... is therefore proper in California based on the 'effects' of [the defendants'] Florida conduct in California."[7] The Court also seemed to assert that the purposeful nature of intentional torts allows for jurisdiction in circumstances in which jurisdiction would not be allowed for an analogous non-intentional tort. The Court pointed out that the defendants "are not charged with mere untargeted negligence. Rather, their intentional, and allegedly tortious, actions were expressly aimed at California."[8]

Calder's companion case, *Keeton*, was in some respects a better, and in some respects a worse, case for jurisdiction. It was a better case in the sense that the defendant was the publisher of the offending magazine, and thus enjoyed a more direct economic benefit from sales in the forum than the writer and the editor in *Calder*. It was, however, a worse case in that the plaintiff had no connection to the forum other than having there filed the case, and thus (unlike *Calder*) one could not say that the allegedly tortious activity was "targeted" at the forum. Despite these differences, the Supreme Court unanimously agreed that the assertion of jurisdiction was constitutional. The defendants advanced several arguments against jurisdiction. The defendants pointed to the limited connection between the plaintiff and the forum, the fact that the plaintiff's choice of the New Hampshire courts was an obvious instance of forum shopping, and the potential free speech implications of subjecting a defendant to broad jurisdiction in libel cases. With regard to each argument, however, the Court pointed out the defendant had purposefully created its connection with the forum by "continuously and deliberately exploiting the New Hampshire market...."[9]

---

5. Id. at 772–73, 104 S.Ct. at 1477.

6. *Calder*, 465 U.S. at 784, 104 S.Ct. at 1484.

7. Id. at 789, 104 S.Ct. at 1484.

8. Id. at 789, 104 S.Ct. at 1487.

9. Keeton v. Hustler, 465 U.S. 770, 781, 104 S.Ct. 1473, 1481, 79 L.Ed.2d 790 (1984).

Taken together, *Calder* and *Keeton* suggest that long-arm jurisdiction in intentional torts is long indeed. Many lower courts have interpreted *Calder* as standing for the proposition that in intentional tort cases minimum contacts exist wherever the defendant's actions have a foreseeable effect. This so-called "effects test" appears to be a majority view among lower courts.[10] Some courts, however, have rejected the pure effects test, especially in cases in which the defendant's connection to the forum seems otherwise attenuated. Analogizing to *Asahi*, several courts have required some additional connection between the defendant and the forum other than the occurrence of tortious effects.[11]

10. See, e.g., Dole Food Co. v. Watts, 303 F.3d 1104 (9th Cir. 2002) (fraud directed to forum establishes personal jurisdiction); Carteret Sav. Bank v. Shushan, 954 F.2d 141 (3d Cir.1992) (jurisdiction will lie in plaintiff's home state based upon out-of-state fraudulent representations have a foreseeable effect in plaintiff's home state); Hugel v. McNell, 886 F.2d 1 (1st Cir.1989) (jurisdiction in plaintiff's home state in a defamation case based upon effects test), cert. denied 494 U.S. 1079, 110 S.Ct. 1808, 108 L.Ed.2d 939 (1990); WNS, Inc. v. Farrow, 884 F.2d 200 (5th Cir.1989) (jurisdiction in plaintiff's home state in a fraud case based upon effects test); Williams Elec. Co. v. Honeywell, Inc., 854 F.2d 389 (11th Cir. 1988) (applying effects test in an antitrust matter); Gehling v. St. George's Sch. of Medicine, Ltd., 773 F.2d 539 (3d Cir.1985) (jurisdiction over defendant in forum because principal effects of alleged fraud and intentional infliction of emotional distress felt in forum); Stevens v. Meaut, 264 F.Supp.2d 226 (E.D. Pa. 2003) (intentional misrepresentation directed to forum establishes minimum contacts); Ashton Park Apartments v. Lebor, 252 F.Supp.2d 539 (W.D. Ohio 2003) (fraudulent communications directed at forum suffice to establish minimum contacts); Integral Development Corp. v. Weissenbach, 99 Cal.App.4th 576, 122 Cal.Rptr.2d 24 (2002) (trade secret misappropriation; conduct directed to forum); Allerton v. State of Florida Dep't of Ins., 635 So.2d 36 (Fla.App.1994) (taking jurisdiction in a fraud case based essentially upon an "effects" theory); Rye v. Atlas Hotels, Inc., 30 Mass.App.Ct. 904, 566 N.E.2d 617 (1991) (fraudulent representation directed a forum-domiciled plaintiff sufficient to establish minimum contacts); Trump v. Eighth Judicial Court of the State of Nevada, 109 Nev. 687, 857 P.2d 740 (1993) (jurisdiction over defendant in forum state because principal effect of alleged interference with contractual relations felt in forum state); Lebel v. Everglades Marina, Inc., 115 N.J. 317, 558 A.2d 1252 (1989)

(jurisdiction in plaintiff's home state in a fraud case based upon effects test); Johnson v. Bradbury, 233 N.J.Super. 129, 558 A.2d 61 (1989) (jurisdiction in plaintiff's home state in a fraud case); Wolpert v. North Shore Univ. Hosp., 231 N.J.Super. 378, 555 A.2d 729 (1989) (jurisdiction in plaintiff's home state in a misrepresentation case). See also Price v. Socialist People's Libyan Arab Jamahiriya, 294 F.3d 82, 95 (D.C. Cir. 2002) (minimum contacts cannot exist in an intentional tort case simply because the plaintiffs are forum residents if all conduct took place outside the forum).

11. See, e.g., United States of America v. Swiss American Bank, Ltd., 274 F.3d 610 (1st Cir. 2001) (showing of forum effects goes only to purposeful availment and does not necessarily establish relatedness necessary for specific jurisdiction); Far West Capital, Inc. v. Towne, 46 F.3d 1071 (10th Cir.1995) (rejecting a pure effects test in a commercial fraud case); Reynolds v. International Amateur Athletic Fed'n, 23 F.3d 1110 (6th Cir.1994), cert. denied 513 U.S. 962, 115 S.Ct. 423, 130 L.Ed.2d 338 (1994) (rejecting pure effects test in interference with business relations case); Wallace v. Herron, 778 F.2d 391 (7th Cir.1985) (rejecting a pure effects test in a malicious prosecution action); Hoechst Celanese Corp. v. Nylon Eng'g Resins, Inc., 896 F.Supp. 1190 (M.D.Fla.1995) (rejecting pure effects test and discussing competing authorities); Bils v. Bils, 200 Ariz. 45, 22 P.3d 38 (2001) (rejecting pure effects test); Roquette Am., Inc. v. Gerber, 651 N.W.2d 896 (Iowa 2002) (same); Holden v. Holden, 374 Pa.Super. 184, 542 A.2d 557 (1988) (rejecting jurisdiction in plaintiff's home state in a tortious interference with contract case between two individual parties). See also Harris v. Trans Union LLC, 197 F.Supp.2d 200 (E.D. Pa. 2002) (no showing that conduct was aimed at forum); Pavolich v. Superior Court, 29 Cal.4th 262, 127 Cal.Rptr.2d 329, 58 P.3d 2 (2002) (fact that some plaintiffs were forum residents and thus there felt the effects of defendant's alleged misappropriation of a

A resolution of these competing authorities may be possible. *Calder* does clearly state that foreseeable effects in the forum in an intentional tort case satisfy the "purposeful availment" test, and thus demonstrate the existence of minimum contacts.[12] However, the separate "reasonableness" prong of the constitutional test, developed most clearly in *Asahi*,[13] ought apply in intentional tort cases, just as it does in non-intentional tort cases. If the defendant can show some special difficulty in mounting a defense in the forum, the reasonableness prong of the constitutional test can defeat jurisdiction even though the defendant's conduct had a foreseeable effect in the forum. In fact many of these opinions apparently rejecting the effects test point to factors relevant to a reasonableness inquiry.[14]

C. NEGLIGENCE

§ 7.4 The Supreme Court's products liability cases, *World–Wide Volkswagen Corp. v. Woodson*[1] and *Asahi Metal Industry Co. v. Superior Court*,[2] are instructive as to the reach of long-arm jurisdiction in negligence cases, as negligence is usually one of the alternative theories of liability pleaded in a products case.[3] Both *World–Wide* and *Asahi* emphasize the importance of the "purposeful availment"[4] test in the context of non-intentional torts. As both of those cases make clear, the defendant must make intentional efforts to take advantage of the forum's benefits. Merely passive activity, such as a consumer's use of the defendant's product in the state, will not suffice for jurisdiction.[5] But, more active conduct, such as selling the product within the forum, or providing forum-state product service and support, often can suffice for jurisdiction.[6]

trade secret was insufficient to establish minimum contacts).

12. Calder v. Jones, 465 U.S. 783, 789–90, 104 S.Ct. 1482, 1487, 79 L.Ed.2d 804 (1984).

13. See supra § 7.2.

14. See, e.g., *Far West Capital, Inc.*, 46 F.3d at 1080 (other forum preferable because more activities and evidence there located); *Reynolds*, 23 F.3d at 1110 (foreign defendant and harm suffered was diffused); *Wallace*, 778 F.2d at 395 (evidence located primarily out of forum).

§ 7.4

1. 444 U.S. 286, 100 S.Ct. 559, 62 L.Ed.2d 490 (1980).

2. 480 U.S. 102, 107 S.Ct. 1026, 94 L.Ed.2d 92 (1987).

3. See, e.g., Exxon Co., U.S.A. v. Sofec, Inc., 517 U.S. 830, 116 S.Ct. 1813, 135 L.Ed.2d 113 (1996) (suit alleged, inter alia, strict products liability and negligence in

connection with loss of plaintiff's oil tanker, which broke away from a mooring facility); Ferens v. John Deere Co., 494 U.S. 516, 110 S.Ct. 1274, 108 L.Ed.2d 443 (1990) (plaintiff, who lost a hand in a farming accident, brought a tort action against defendant sounding in both negligence and products liability).

4. World–Wide Volkswagen Corp. v. Woodson, 444 U.S. 286, 297, 100 S.Ct. 559, 567, 62 L.Ed.2d 490 (1980) (quoting Hanson v. Denckla, 357 U.S. 235, 253, 78 S.Ct. 1228, 1240, 2 L.Ed.2d 1283 (1958)); Asahi Metal Indus. Co. v. Superior Court, 480 U.S. 102, 110, 107 S.Ct. 1026, 1031, 94 L.Ed.2d 92 (1987) (quoting Hanson v. Denckla, 357 U.S. at 253, 78 S.Ct. at 1240).

5. See, e.g., *World–Wide Volkswagen Corp.*, 444 U.S. 286, 100 S.Ct. 559, 62 L.Ed.2d 490 (1980).

6. See, e.g., Buckeye Boiler Co. v. Superior Court, 71 Cal.2d 893, 80 Cal.Rptr. 113, 458 P.2d 57 (1969); Gray v. American Radi-

Of course, claims of negligence arise in countless factual contexts other than the manufacture and design of products. The general framework set forth by *World–Wide* and *Asahi*, however, is highly instructive in evaluating assertions of jurisdiction in other kinds of negligence actions. Thus, the mere fact that a defendant's negligent action is alleged to have caused effect or injury in the forum state does not, by itself, satisfy the minimum contacts test.[7] A fortiori, in cases in which the injury or principal effect of the alleged negligence takes place out of state, the mere fact that the plaintiff is a forum domiciliary does not satisfy the minimum contacts test.[8] Specific jurisdiction in a negligence case can be constitutionally established only through forum state conduct or effects, and some purposeful effort on the part of the defendant to affiliate with the state, such as through directly serving a commercial market in the state.[9] Without an element of a purposeful connection

ator & Standard Sanitary Corp., 22 Ill.2d 432, 176 N.E.2d 761 (1961).

7. See, e.g., Finkbiner v. Mullins, 532 A.2d 609 (Del.Super.Ct.1987) (alleged negligent entrustment in another state, causing injury in the forum, not sufficient for jurisdiction); Harris v. Shuttleworth & Ingersoll, P.C., 831 So.2d 706 (Fla. App. 2002) (mere fact that alleged injury in legal malpractice case was felt in forum insufficient); Thompson v. Doe, 596 So.2d 1178 (Fla.App.1992) (jurisdiction cannot be established in a suit against individual president of a company whose alleged negligence in providing security at a store located in the forum caused injury in the forum); Johnson v. Ortiz, 244 Ill.App.3d 384, 185 Ill.Dec. 274, 614 N.E.2d 408 (1993) (alleged negligent entrustment of a car out of state to a driver who causes injury in the forum does not suffice for jurisdiction); H.A.W. v. Manuel, 524 N.W.2d 10 (Minn.App.1994) (negligently allowing child to be placed in exchange program in forum state where he caused injury does not suffice for jurisdiction over foreign parents); Hansford v. District of Columbia, 84 Md.App. 301, 578 A.2d 844 (1990) (negligently allowing out-of-state prisoner to escape who then comes to forum and causes injury insufficient to allow for jurisdiction over entity managing prison); Budget Rent–A–Car v. Eighth Judicial Dist. Court of Nevada, 108 Nev. 483, 835 P.2d 17 (1992) (alleged negligent entrustment of a car out of state to a driver who causes injury in the forum does not suffice for jurisdiction); O'Guin v. Estate of Pikul, 153 Misc.2d 526, 581 N.Y.S.2d 976 (1991) (alleged negligent failure to warn forum resident of murder plot does not allow for jurisdiction over out-of-state defendant under New York's long-arm statute); Arguello v. Industrial Woodworking Mach. Co., 838 P.2d 1120 (Utah 1992) (fact that allegedly negligently de-

signed machine caused injury in forum not sufficient for jurisdiction);

8. See, e.g., Doering v. Copper Mountain, Inc., 259 F.3d 1202 (10th Cir. 2001) (plaintiffs injured at Colorado ski resort could not establish personal jurisdiction in their home state of New Jersey); Gehling v. St. George's Sch. of Medicine, 773 F.2d 539 (3d Cir.1985) (jurisdiction cannot be established on a claim of injury to forum-domiciled plaintiff where plaintiff was injured in an allegedly negligently supervised out-of-state foot race); Elliott v. Van Kleef, 830 So.2d 726 (Ala. 2002) (out-of-state attorney merely agreeing to act a local counsel in a case involving a forum domiciliary does not subject himself to personal jurisdiction in the forum) Brokemond v. Marshall Field & Co., 612 N.E.2d 143 (Ind.App.1993) (injury to forum domiciliary in out-of-state eating establishment does not suffice for jurisdiction); Drago v. The Home Ins. Co., 486 So.2d 940 (La.App.1986) (out-of-state injury at a hotel to forum plaintiff does not satisfy minimum contacts test); Rye v. Atlas Hotels, Inc., 30 Mass.App.Ct. 904, 566 N.E.2d 617 (1991) (injury in a out-of-state hotel to a forum-domiciled plaintiff not sufficient to satisfy minimum contacts test); Tercero v. Roman Catholic Diocese of Norwich, Connecticut, 132 N.M. 312, 48 P.3d 50 (2002) (injury to parishioner resident in the forum allegedly inflicted by priest originally assigned to out-of-state diocese insufficient to establish minimum contacts in the forum).

9. See, e.g., Pemberton v. OvaTech, Inc., 669 F.2d 533 (8th Cir.1982) (injury in forum state plus other efforts to serve forum state market suffice for jurisdiction); First Union Nat'l Bank v. Bankers Wholesale Mortg., LLC, 153 N.C.App. 248, 570 S.E.2d 217 (2002) (negligent misrepresentations injuring local plaintiff plus intentional ef-

between the defendant and the forum, *Asahi*, *World–Wide* and a host of lower court cases make clear that any attempted exercise of jurisdiction by a forum state court will cross the constitutional line.

D. OTHER STRICT LIABILITY

§ 7.5   The most common context for claims of "strict," "absolute" or "faultless" liability is that of products liability cases. As discussed extensively above,[1] the leading Supreme Court decisions on strict products liability are *World–Wide Volkswagen v. Woodson*[2] and *Asahi Metal Industry Co. v. Superior Court*.[3] Those cases require application of so-called "stream of commerce" test and all of its attendant difficulties.

Of course, products cases are not the only context in which strict liability claims arise. There are other circumstances in which strict liability may be imposed, including liability for trespassing animals,[4] fires started on adjoining land,[5] and "abnormally dangerous" or "ultrahazardous" activities.[6] The notion of strict liability dates back to the common law, and the theory of liability for abnormally dangerous activities dates at least back to the English case of *Rylands v. Fletcher*.[7] In *Rylands*, the defendants maintained a reservoir on their land that broke through and flooded the plaintiff's land. *Rylands* has eventually come to stand for the proposition that such "abnormal and inappropriate" activities result in the defendant's liability for injury caused, even if the defendant exercised reasonable care.[8] In more modern contexts, strict liability claims have been based upon activities such as nuclear power generation, rocket propulsion, stunt aircraft flying and crop dusting.[9]

Most of the time, these relevant events that form the basis for a claim of strict liability take place in the same state. In other words, usually the relevant actions and consequences are localized in one jurisdiction. Occasionally, an animal wanders across a state line and causes injury in a foreign jurisdiction,[10] or an abnormally dangerous activity causes damage in another state,[11] but such cases are obviously the exception. In those rare cases presenting difficult jurisdictional issues, the "purposeful availment" test that applies to most specific jurisdiction problems[12] ought hold sway here. Thus, the mere fact that an

---

forts to serve the forum-state market suffice for jurisdiction); Boissiere v. Nova Capital, LLC, 106 S.W.3d 897 (Tex. App. 2003) (same); Jacobsen v. Oliver, 201 F.Supp.2d 93 (D.D.C. 2002) (alleged legal malpractice where a significant portion of the representation took place in the forum establishes minimum contacts).

§ 7.5

1.   See supra § 7.2.

2.   444 U.S. 286, 100 S.Ct. 559, 62 L.Ed.2d 490 (1980).

3.   480 U.S. 102, 107 S.Ct. 1026, 94 L.Ed.2d 92 (1987).

4.   Keeton, Prosser and Keeton on the Law of Torts 538–43 (5th ed. 1984).

5.   Id. at 544–45.

6.   Id. at 545–59.

7.   3 H.L. 330 (1868).

8.   Keeton, supra n.4, at 545.

9.   Id. at 557–58.

10.   See, e.g., Bader v. Purdom, 841 F.2d 38 (2d Cir. 1988) (out-of-state plaintiff bitten by in-state dog).

11.   In re Tutu Wells Contamination Litigation, 846 F.Supp. 1243 (D.V.I.1993).

12.   See supra § 5.11.

abnormally dangerous activity causes injury in the forum state should not, in the normal case, suffice to show minimum contacts. Rather, constitutionally sufficient contacts require a forum-state injury coupled with the defendant's intentional efforts to avail itself of the forum's benefits, such as by serving forum state markets.[13]

III.   INJURIES TO PROPERTY

A. PERSONAL PROPERTY

§ 7.6 Torts against interests in personal property often occur, quite obviously, as incidents of personal injury cases. To take the mundane example of an automobile accident, an element of recovery for a plaintiff injured while driving his car would include damage to the car. In that sense, recovery for damage to personal property does not present any interesting jurisdictional issues. If there is jurisdiction over the personal injury matter there is also jurisdiction to recover to the damage for the property, and if jurisdiction is lacking for one, it is lacking for both.[1]

More interesting issues are presented, however, if the tort is one that compensates directly for invasions of personal property interests. The two most important of these are conversion and trespass to chattels.[2] Generally these are classified as intentional torts, because in for both torts the defendant must knowingly make some use that is adverse to the owner of the personalty.[3] The two differ only in the severity of the invasion, conversion representing the tort appropriate for the more severe interferences with the enjoyment of personalty.[4]

In multistate cases of conversion or trespass to chattels, the jurisdictional dispute usually reduces to a question of whether there is jurisdiction in the plaintiff's domicile. Under the usual principles of general jurisdiction, there is jurisdiction in the defendant's domicile or other state in which the defendant has continuous and systematic contacts.[5] The more difficult problems arise, however, in attempting to determine where specific jurisdiction will lie.

Here, as in most areas involving questions of specific jurisdiction, the purposeful availment test is the major determinant.[6] Under this test, a defendant is subject to jurisdiction in a forum with which the defen-

---

13. See, e.g., *In re Tutu Wells*, 846 F.Supp. 1243 (defendant had minimum contacts in a strict liability case because of forum-state injury coupled with service of forum market).

§ 7.6

1. See, e.g., World–Wide Volkswagen Corp. v. Woodson, 444 U.S. 286, 100 S.Ct.

559, 62 L.Ed.2d 490 (1980) (treating claims for injuries and property damage together).

2. Keeton, Prosser & Keeton on the Law of Torts 85, 88 (5th ed. 1984).

3. Id. at 85, 90.

4. Id. at 90.

5. See supra §§ 6.5, 6.7–6.9.

6. See supra § 5.11.

dant has intentionally created a connection, and that connection is related to the dispute.[7] Usually, the presence of the allegedly converted or injured property in the forum is sufficient for specific jurisdiction, because the property's presence in the forum demonstrates an intentional connection with the forum.[8] One can perhaps imagine exceptional cases in which the presence of the property would not suffice to establish jurisdiction. For instance, the fact that allegedly converted property is being stored in a warehouse in the forum while in transit to another state might not suffice to establish jurisdiction in some cases. But such cases, if they exist at all, are very rare.

The more difficult cases arise if the plaintiff brings suit in his home state, while the defendant and the property are elsewhere. Usually, the plaintiff will seek to establish jurisdiction based upon the indirect economic injury being inflicted in the forum because the defendant's use of the property elsewhere is depriving the plaintiff of expected use of it in the forum. Plaintiffs pressing this argument for jurisdiction have met with mixed success. Courts have usually held that the mere fact the plaintiff is domiciled in the forum, and thus suffering economic injury there, is not sufficient for jurisdiction.[9] Those cases that have allowed for jurisdiction in the plaintiff's home state have usually depended on some more direct effort on the part of the defendant to affiliate with the forum. Thus, for instance, if the defendant comes to the plaintiff's home state, takes control of the property there, and then returns to the defendant's home state with the property, courts have allowed for jurisdiction in the plaintiff's home because of the defendant's intentional, related activities in the forum.[10] Other kinds of intentional affiliations with the forum state may also suffice, for instance, if the plaintiff is enticed from his home state to the defendant's home, and there the property is wrested from the defendant's control.[11] Although the factual permutations are innumerable, the crucial determinant is—as it is in so many circumstances—whether the defendant's conduct fulfills the purposeful availment test.

B. REAL PROPERTY

§ 7.7 Injuries to real property usually take the form of a claim for trespass or nuisance. It seems clear that specific jurisdiction exists for

---

7. See supra § 5.11.

8. See, e.g., Leeco Steel Prods., Inc. v. Ferrostaal Metals Corp., 698 F.Supp. 724 (N.D.Ill.1988) (stating in dictum that jurisdiction would lie in forum where property is located); Associated Trade Dev., Inc. v. Condor Lines, Inc., 590 F.Supp. 525 (S.D.N.Y. 1984) (same); Heslinga v. Bollman, 482 N.W.2d 921 (Iowa 1992) (jurisdiction in state in which dominion and control is exercised over property); Gutierrez v. Deloitte & Touche, 100 S.W.3d 261 (Tex. App. 2002) (conversion pleaded as one of the theories; defendants had purposeful connection with the forum).

9. See, e.g., Cycles, Ltd. v. W.J. Digby, 889 F.2d 612 (5th Cir.1989); American Sav. Bank v. Cheshire Management Co., 693 F.Supp. 42 (S.D.N.Y.1988); Associated Trade Dev., Inc. v. Condor Lines, Inc., 590 F.Supp. 525 (S.D.N.Y.1984); Stark Carpet Corp. v. M–Geough Robinson, Inc., 481 F.Supp. 499 (S.D.N.Y.1980).

10. See, e.g., Cofield v. Randolph County Comm'n, 844 F.Supp. 1499 (M.D.Ala. 1994); Heslinga v. Bollman, 482 N.W.2d 921 (Iowa 1992).

11. See, e.g., Gilson v. The Republic of Ireland, 682 F.2d 1022 (D.C.Cir.1982).

such a claim in the state in which the real property is situated.[1] Except in perhaps the most bizarre and unusual of circumstances, the purposeful availment test would be satisfied by the defendant's tortious conduct. It is extremely hard to imagine a realistic case in which the defendant could tortiously cause some injury to realty without intentionally affiliating with the situs state.

A more difficult question is whether jurisdiction can ever exist anywhere outside the state in which the realty is located. That question depends upon the scope and continued vitality of the common law "local action rule." The most famous and colorful illustration of the local action rule was *Livingston v. Jefferson*,[2] an opinion written by Justice Marshall while riding circuit.[3] *Livingston* was a trespass claim brought by the owner of Louisiana realty against former President Jefferson. The case was brought in federal court in Virginia—Jefferson's home—and dismissed by the court on the strength of the local action rule, because Louisiana (then still a territory) was the situs of the property, and the case could be brought only there. On the facts of *Livingston* this worked a considerable hardship on the plaintiff. Because the trespass action was in personam, under the then-prevailing jurisdictional structure Jefferson could be subjected to jurisdiction in Louisiana only in the unlikely event he could be personally served while in the forum.[4] As long as Jefferson stayed out of Louisiana, no suit was possible.

The vitality and parameters of the local action rule are in some considerable doubt. Some courts take the position that the local action rule is jurisdictional,[5] while others treat it as only a matter of venue, and that a judgment entered in violation of the rule is thus not vulnerable to collateral attack.[6] More fundamental is the question of the types of actions to which the rule extends. Not every lawsuit with any connection to realty necessarily falls within the ambit of the rule. The Second Conflicts Restatement takes the position (in opposition to *Livingston*) that the local action rule does not bar one state from entertaining a trespass action involving land in a foreign state, assuming that there is in personam jurisdiction over the defendant.[7] While such cases are rare, the Second Restatement's position seems to accord with the trend of recent authority,[8] and would have the sensible effect of limiting the local

§ 7.7

1. 2 Casad, Jurisdiction in Civil Actions 7–71 (2d ed. 1991); Anderson v. Sonat Exploration Co., 523 So.2d 1024 (Miss.1988) (deceit regarding mineral rights in real property sufficient for jurisdiction over nonresident tortfeasor).

2. 15 Fed.Cas. 660 (C.C.D.Va.1811)(No. 8,411).

3. For an interesting historical account of this case, see Degnan, *Livingston v. Jefferson—A Freestanding Footnote*, 75 Calif. L. Rev. 115 (1987).

4. Degnan, supra n.3, at 122.

5. 1 Casad, supra n.1, at 1–21 to 1–23.

6. Id. See, e.g., Fisher v. Virginia Elec. & Power Co., 243 F.Supp.2d 538 (E.D. Va. 2003) (rule of venue).

7. Restatement, Second, Conflict of Laws § 87 (1971).

8. The Second Restatement cites a few cases, the most prominent of which is Reasor–Hill Corp. v. Harrison, 220 Ark. 521, 249 S.W.2d 994 (1952). Other authorities tolerate an action for injury to out-of-state land where it is combined with other

action rule to disputes about the title of realty.[9] Thus, jurisdiction in disputes regarding injuries to real property exists in the state that is the situs of the realty, and other states with which the defendant has a purposeful, related connection.

IV. INJURIES TO REPUTATION

A. LIBEL

§ 7.8   The substantive aspects of defamation law are closely limited by the First Amendment.[1] At one time, some courts believed that the First Amendment placed limits on state court jurisdiction in defamation cases beyond those imposed by the Due Process Clause.[2] Although, as discussed below, the Supreme Court has rejected the idea that the First Amendment limits state court jurisdiction in defamation cases, states are free to constrict their long-arm statutes in defamation matters, and several have done so.[3]

The jurisdictional test applied in libel cases is broad. The Supreme Court's pronouncements on the subject are a pair of unanimous opinions

claims. See, e.g., Raphael J. Musicus, Inc. v. Safeway Stores, Inc., 743 F.2d 503, 510 (7th Cir.1984) (trespass action combined with breach of contract and fraud claims); Coastal Mall, Inc. v. Askins, 265 S.C. 307, 217 S.E.2d 725, 727 (1975) (claim for injury to real property combined with breach of contract, the subject of the action).

9.   See Degnan, supra n.3, at 122. See also Fisher v. Virginia Elec. & Power Co., 243 F.Supp.2d 538, 550 (E.D. Va. 2003) (rule's rationale applicable only in cases that "necessitate surveys, tract history investigations, and other miscellany peculiar to the locality. . . .").

§ 7.8

1.   The Supreme Court has held that the First Amendment, operating through the Fourteenth Amendment, imposes limitations on liability-creating rules of state defamation law. See, e.g., New York Times Co. v. Sullivan, 376 U.S. 254, 84 S.Ct. 710, 11 L.Ed.2d 686 (1964) (no recovery by a public official for defamation unless the false statement was made with actual malice); Gertz v. Robert Welch, Inc., 418 U.S. 323, 94 S.Ct. 2997, 41 L.Ed.2d 789 (1974) (where a matter is of public concern, states may not impose liability for defamation of a private figure without requiring some showing of fault; also, no recovery of certain types of damages absent a showing of malice); Phila-

delphia Newspapers, Inc. v. Hepps, 475 U.S. 767, 106 S.Ct. 1558, 89 L.Ed.2d 783 (1986) (where a matter is of public concern, First Amendment requires a private figure plaintiff to prove the falsity of the statement, as well as fault, before recovering damages). Cf. Milkovich v. Lorain Journal Co., 497 U.S. 1, 110 S.Ct. 2695, 111 L.Ed.2d 1 (1990) (the First Amendment does not require an additional separate constitutional privilege for "opinion" which would limit the application of state defamation laws).

2.   See, e.g., New York Times Co. v. Connor, 365 F.2d 567 (5th Cir.1966) (First Amendment considerations surrounding the law of libel require a greater showing of contract to satisfy the due process clause than is necessary in asserting jurisdiction over other types of tortious activity); Buckley v. New York Times Co., 338 F.2d 470 (5th Cir.1964) (same).

3.   N.Y. Civ. Prac. L & R. § 302 (jurisdiction in defamation cases only if defendant domiciled in New York); Conn. Gen. Stat. § 52–59b (no personal jurisdiction over non-resident who commits a tortious act in-state if the tort is defamation of character); Ga. Code Ann. § 9–10–91 (same); Minn. Stat. § 543.19 (no personal jurisdiction over non-resident who commits an out-of-state act causing in-state injury if the cause of action lies in defamation or privacy).

issued the same day, *Calder v. Jones*[4] and *Keeton v. Hustler.*[5] In *Calder* the plaintiff was a famous entertainer domiciled in California who sued the writer and the editor of a story in a national publication regarding a story that stated that the plaintiff drank so heavily as to be unable to fulfill her professional obligations. The plaintiff brought suit in a California state court, and the Supreme Court held that the court could take jurisdiction over the writer and the editor of the story. Aside from the writing of the story, the individual defendants had little in the way of relevant contacts with California. Nevertheless, the Court held that the contacts sufficed. The Court emphasized that the defendants' "intentional, and allegedly tortious, actions were expressly aimed at California" because they produced an article "that they knew would have a devastating impact upon [the plaintiff]."[6] The Court also pointed out that the largest part of the plaintiff's injury would be felt in California—where she was domiciled and worked—and the publication that employed the defendants had its largest circulation in California.

Calder's companion case *Keeton* had some features that made it a more attractive case for jurisdiction, and some that made it less compelling. Nonetheless, the result was identical. *Keeton*, like *Calder*, was a case involving an allegedly libelous publication in a periodical of national circulation. Unlike *Calder*, in which the defendants objecting to jurisdiction were the individuals responsible for producing the allegedly libelous writing, *Keeton* involved the question of whether the publisher itself could be subjected to jurisdiction. Also unlike *Calder*, the *Keeton* plaintiff brought her case in New Hampshire, which was neither her domicile, nor was it a state with an overly large circulation of the publication. Moreover, the *Keeton* plaintiff's choice of New Hampshire was an obvious instance of forum shopping, as it had been chosen for its long statute of limitations, which made it the only state that would have entertained the case.[7] None of these concerns was sufficient to defeat jurisdiction, however. The Court adjudged the lack of the *plaintiff*'s contacts with the forum to be irrelevant to the jurisdictional calculus, as long as the *defendant*'s contacts were constitutionally sufficient.[8] As to the forum-shopping concerns, the Court ruled that this was a problem of choice of law to be resolved—if at all—by New Hampshire's conflicts doctrine.[9]

The message of *Calder* and *Keeton* has certainly not been lost on lower courts. Most plaintiffs, of course, prefer for reasons of convenience to sue in their home state. Under *Calder*'s reasoning, the plaintiff's domicile is the place in which the bulk of the injury is suffered. Thus, courts have generally approved of jurisdiction in the plaintiff's domicile.[10]

4. 465 U.S. 783, 104 S.Ct. 1482, 79 L.Ed.2d 804 (1984).

5. 465 U.S. 770, 104 S.Ct. 1473, 79 L.Ed.2d 790 (1984).

6. *Calder*, 465 U.S. at 790, 104 S.Ct. at 1487.

7. *Keeton*, 465 U.S. at 773, 104 S.Ct. at 1477.

8. Id. at 779, 104 S.Ct. at 1480–81.

9. Id. at 778, 104 S.Ct. at 1480.

10. See, e.g., Gordy v. The Daily News, 95 F.3d 829 (9th Cir.1996) (jurisdiction allowed on a libel claim in which the offending publication was sent to fewer than 20 forum-state subscribers of the defendant newspaper); Hugel v. McNell, 886 F.2d 1

Those cases in which the plaintiff has chosen to sue outside of his home state have require the plaintiff to show either that some substantial amount of the reputational injury actually occurred in the forum, or that the defendant had contacts with the forum sufficient to allow for general jurisdiction.[11] Those relatively unusual circumstances in which jurisdiction has been denied in the plaintiff's home state have involved cases in which the connection between the libelous publication and forum has been extraordinarily weak.[12] Difficult questions can arise in attempting to determine, in the case of a corporate plaintiff, which is its "home" state. Courts here have not applied any formalistic test. Rather, following *Calder*, courts have attempted to determine whether the plaintiff did, in fact, suffer some appreciable amount of the injury in the forum.[13]

The problem of libel over the Internet has generated an impressive volume of case law and commentary. In the most common fact scenario, the plaintiff brings an action in his or her home state against an out-of-state defendant who the plaintiff alleges has libeled the plaintiff on a website, in a mass email, on a bulletin board or though some other virtual medium. The defendant's contacts with the forum state consist entirely or mainly of the effects on the plaintiff's reputation in the forum state. While this fact scenario might seem to be the virtual parallel of *Calder* and *Keeton*, the cases are severely divided and a surprising number of lower courts have rejected jurisdiction on these facts.[14] Some

(1st Cir.1989), cert. denied 494 U.S. 1079, 110 S.Ct. 1808, 108 L.Ed.2d 939 (1990) (jurisdiction allowed in plaintiff's home state for article disseminated nationally by a Washington, D.C. newspaper); First American First, Inc. v. National Ass'n of Bank Women, 802 F.2d 1511 (4th Cir.1986) (plaintiff's place of business in forum coupled with some business dealings of the defendant in the forum sufficient for jurisdiction); Emerson v. Cole, 847 So.2d 606 (Fla. App. 2003) (statements made in a telephone interview to a publication circulated in the forum state); Burt v. The Board of Regents of the Univ. of Nebraska, 757 F.2d 242 (10th Cir.1985) (allegedly libelous letter sent to Colorado hospitals about Colorado-domiciled plaintiff sufficient to allow for jurisdiction in Colorado); Curtis Publishing Co. v. Cassel, 302 F.2d 132 (10th Cir.1962) (plaintiff's domicile was forum and substantial circulation of defendant's magazine in the forum).

11. See, e.g., Madara v. Hall, 916 F.2d 1510 (11th Cir.1990) (jurisdiction does not lie in Florida because plaintiff suffered no substantial injury to reputation in that state and defendant's occasional musical performances there were insufficient to establish general jurisdiction).

12. See, e.g., Noonan v. Winston Co., 135 F.3d 85 (1st Cir.1998) (circulation of only a few hundred of the offending publications in the forum state; publication written in French and clearly directed a French, not American, audience); Reynolds v. International Amateur Athletic Federation, 23 F.3d 1110 (6th Cir.1994), cert. denied 513 U.S. 962, 115 S.Ct. 423, 130 L.Ed.2d 338 (1994) (no jurisdiction in Ohio because allegedly defamatory statements did not concern activities in Ohio and defendant's reputation was as an international athlete); Salgado v. Les Nouvelles Esthetiques, 218 F.Supp.2d 203 (D.P.R. 2002) (20 magazines and two videos insufficient on a misappropriation of image theory).

13. See, e.g., Casualty Assurance Risk Ins. Brokerage Co. v. Dillon, 976 F.2d 596 (9th Cir.1992) (jurisdiction does not exist in corporate plaintiff's state of incorporation where no substantial amount of harm to reputation actually occurred in forum); Hicklin Engineering, Inc. v. Aidco, Inc., 959 F.2d 738 (8th Cir.1992) (jurisdiction does not lie in corporate plaintiff's principal place of business because no showing of a substantial amount of harm there suffered).

14. Holding no jurisdiction: Revell v. Lidov, 317 F.3d 467 (5th Cir. 2002); Young v. New Haven Advocate, 315 F.3d 256 (4th Cir. 2002), cert. denied 538 U.S. 1035, 123 S.Ct. 2092, 155 L.Ed.2d 1065 (2003); Medinah Mining, Inc. v. Amunategui, 237

of the cases rejecting jurisdiction have created what one might call a "local content" exception, which is that jurisdiction does not exist if the publication has primarily local content likely to be of little interest to readers in the forum.[15] Others have been influenced by cases from other substantive areas which have emphasized the "interactivity" of the virtual medium and largely rejected jurisdiction in cases involving so-called "passive" websites.[16] While these exceptions might be justified on policy grounds, they seem hard to square, in particular, with *Keeton*, in which the plaintiff was essentially unknown in the forum and in which the statements about her likely went mostly unnoticed by readers in the forum and in which any "interaction" besides publication of the statements was non-existent.[17]

B. SLANDER

§ 7.9 Libel's cousin, of course, is slander. And, as is well known, the primary difference between the two is that libel actions concern written or other "fixed" defamatory statements, while slander concerns oral and other impermanent communications.[1] These differences be-

F.Supp.2d 1132 (D. Nev. 2002); Hydro Engineering, Inc. v. Landa, Inc., 231 F.Supp.2d 1130 (D. Utah. 2002); Machulsky v. Hall, 210 F.Supp.2d 531 (D.N.J. 2002); Oasis Corp. v. Judd, 132 F.Supp.2d 612 (S.D. Ohio 2001); Lofton v. Turbine Design, Inc., 100 F.Supp.2d 404 (N.D. Miss. 2000); Barrett v. Catacombs Press, 44 F.Supp.2d 717 (E.D. Pa. 1999); Jewish Defense Org. v. Superior Court, 72 Cal.App.4th 1045, 85 Cal.Rptr.2d 611 (1999); Conseco, Inc. v. Hickerson, 698 N.E.2d 816 (Ind. App. 1998); Griffis v. Luban, 646 N.W.2d 527 (Minn. 2002), cert. denied 538 U.S. 906, 123 S.Ct. 1483, 155 L.Ed.2d 225 (2003); Northwest Airlines, Inc. v. Friday, 617 N.W.2d 590 (Minn. App. 2000); Melvin v. Doe, 49 Va. Cir. 257 (1999).

Holding that jurisdiction exists: Northwest Healthcare Alliance, Inc. v. Healthgrades.com, Inc, 50 Fed. Appx. 339 (9th Cir. 2002), cert. denied 538 U.S. 999, 123 S.Ct. 1909, 155 L.Ed.2d 826 (2003); Nicosia v. De Rooy, 72 F.Supp.2d 1093 (N.D. Cal. 1999); Bochan v. LaFontaine, 68 F.Supp.2d 692 (E.D. Va. 1999); Blumenthal v. Drudge, 992 F.Supp. 44 (D.D.C. 1998); TELCO Communications Group, Inc. v. An Apple a Day, 977 F.Supp. 404 (E.D. Va. 1997); Wagner v. Miskin, 660 N.W.2d 593 (2003), cert. denied ___ U.S. ___, 124 S.Ct. 1156, 157 L.Ed.2d 1050 (2004); Becker v. Hooshmand, 841 So.2d 561 (Fla. App. 2003).

15. See, e.g., Revell v. Lidov, 317 F.3d 467 (5th Cir. 2002); Young v. New Haven Advocate, 315 F.3d 256 (4th Cir. 2002),

cert. denied 538 U.S. 1035, 123 S.Ct. 2092, 155 L.Ed.2d 1065 (2003).

16. The leading case in this regard is Zippo Manufacturing Co. v. Zippo Dot Com, 952 F.Supp. 1119 (W.D. Pa. 1997). The following Internet libel cases all cite *Zippo*: Revell v. Lidov, 317 F.3d 467 (5th Cir. 2002); Northwest Healthcare Alliance, Inc. v. Healthgrades.com, Inc., 50 Fed. Appx. 339 (9th Cir. 2002), cert. denied 538 U.S. 999, 123 S.Ct. 1909, 155 L.Ed.2d 826 (2003); Machulsky v. Hall, 210 F.Supp.2d 531 (D.N.J. 2002); Medinah Mining v. Amunategui, 237 F.Supp.2d 1132 (D. Nev. 2002); Oasis Corp. v. Judd, 132 F.Supp.2d 612 (S.D. Ohio 2001); Lofton v. Turbine Design Inc., 100 F.Supp.2d 404 (N.D. Miss. 2000); Bochan v. LaFontaine, 68 F.Supp.2d 692 (E.D. Va. 1999); Barrett v. Catacombs Press, 44 F.Supp.2d 717 (E.D. Pa. 1999); Blumenthal v. Drudge, 992 F.Supp. 44 (D.D.C. 1998); TELCO Communications v. An Apple a Day, 977 F.Supp. 404 (E.D. Va. 1997). Jewish Defense Org. v. Superior Court, 72 Cal.App.4th 1045, 85 Cal.Rptr.2d 611 (1999); Wagner v. Miskin, 660 N.W.2d 593 (N.D. 2003), cert. denied ___ U.S. ___, 124 S.Ct. 1156, 157 L.Ed.2d 1050 (2004).

17. For commentary on these cases, see Borchers, Internet Libel: The Hazards of a Non–Rule Approach to Jurisdiction, 98 Nw. U. L. Rev. 473 (2004).

§ 7.9

1. Restatement, Second, Torts § 568 (1965).

tween the two torts often lead to some substantive differences, such as the kinds of damages that must be proved to sustain the tort and the sorts of statements considered to be defamatory "per se."[2] The differences between libel and slander also seem to lead to difference in their jurisdictional treatment.

Slander cases seem to present relatively fewer multistate cases. Unless republished by mass media, slanderous statements are more likely to be local, with the plaintiff, the defendant and the defamatory utterance all in close geographical proximity. Of course, not all slander cases involve a local plaintiff, defendant and utterance. One notable difference between libel and slander in the context of long-arm jurisdiction is that the plaintiff's domicile seems to be a less important connection in slander cases than in libel. As noted in the previous section,[3] one of the Supreme Court's leading libel, jurisdictional cases placed heavy emphasis on the fact that the forum was the plaintiff's domicile.[4] As a result, the Court concluded that the defendants knew that the statements would there have a "devastating impact" on the plaintiff.[5]

While the Supreme Court has not addressed the question of what constitutes minimum contacts in a slander case, the lower courts addressing it have placed somewhat less weight on the plaintiff's home than the Supreme Court has appeared to in libel cases. Pretty uniformly, lower courts have held that the fact that the plaintiff lives in the forum, and there suffered the injury, is not sufficient—by itself—to sustain jurisdiction.[6] In order to sustain jurisdiction in a slander case, some other connection with the forum—other than the fact that it is the plaintiff's home—is usually necessary to sustain jurisdiction. If the statement is made in the forum, or at least republished in the forum, and the forum is the plaintiff's domicile, that will often be sufficient to sustain jurisdiction.[7] Another possible connection that might be sufficient to sustain jurisdiction is if the slanderous statements concern activities of the plaintiff that took place in the forum.[8] All of this is a fairly logical extension of the purposeful availment[9] test that dominates specific jurisdictional analysis. As the Supreme Court has made clear on several occasions, the mere fact that the plaintiff suffers injury in the forum is not, by itself, sufficient to sustain jurisdiction.[10] Rather, some

---

2. Keeton, Prosser and Keeton on the Law of Torts 788–97 (5th ed. 1984).

3. See supra § 7.8.

4. See Calder v. Jones, 465 U.S. 783, 788–89, 104 S.Ct. 1482, 1486, 79 L.Ed.2d 804 (1984).

5. Id. at 789, 104 S.Ct. at 1487.

6. See, e.g., Cacdac v. Sweet, 761 F.Supp. 594 (S.D.Ind.1989); Kearney v. Todd L. Smith, P.A., 624 F.Supp. 1008 (S.D.N.Y.1985).

7. See, e.g., Cole v. Doe, 77 Mich.App. 138, 258 N.W.2d 165 (1977). See also Wyatt v. Kaplan, 686 F.2d 276 (5th Cir.1982)

(stating in dictum that publication or republication in the forum would be necessary for jurisdiction under the Texas long-arm statute).

8. Cf. Burt v. Board of Regents of the Univ. of Nebraska, 757 F.2d 242, 245 (10th Cir.1985) (Seth, J., dissenting) (arguing that such a connection should be necessary in libel cases).

9. See supra § 5.11.

10. See, e.g, Asahi Metal Indus. Co. v. Superior Court, 480 U.S. 102, 107 S.Ct. 1026, 94 L.Ed.2d 92 (1987); World–Wide Volkswagen Corp. v. Woodson, 444 U.S. 286, 100 S.Ct. 559, 62 L.Ed.2d 490 (1980).

intentional affiliation with the forum by the defendant is required. Applied in the context of the tort of slander, this means that the mere fact that the plaintiff feels the impact on his reputation in the forum is not a sufficient connection for jurisdiction. Some additional affiliation with the forum, such as making the statement in the forum, is necessary to establish jurisdiction over the defendant.

C. INVASION OF PRIVACY

§ 7.10 The tort of invasion of privacy is really a constellation of related torts, the specifics of which vary considerably from jurisdiction to jurisdiction. Usually categorized as "invasion of privacy" torts are those based upon publications placing one in a "false light," activities that invade one's physical seclusion, the private disclosure of public facts, and the misappropriation of one's likeness or name for commercial purposes.[1] Claims on these theories often accompany defamation claims. In fact, one of the leading Supreme Court cases on jurisdiction in libel actions, *Calder v. Jones*,[2] also involved a claim of "false light" privacy.[3] To the extent, then, that privacy tort actions are founded upon an offending publication, the analysis usually tracks closely that in defamation actions. Often the plaintiff is able to obtain jurisdiction in the plaintiff's home state if the publication reaches an audience in forum state, because the harm to the plaintiff is predictably centered in that state.[4] Those cases that have not allowed for jurisdiction in the plaintiff's home state have usually involved circumstances in which the defendant's connection to the forum is quite tangential.[5]

§ 7.10

1. Keeton, Prosser and Keeton on the Law of Torts 851–65 (5th ed. 1984).

2. 465 U.S. 783, 104 S.Ct. 1482, 79 L.Ed.2d 804 (1984).

3. Id. at 785, 104 S.Ct. at 1484.

4. See, e.g., First American First, Inc. v. National Ass'n of Bank Women, 802 F.2d 1511 (4th Cir.1986) (jurisdiction allowed in the state of plaintiff's principal place of business in a libel and false light privacy action); Brown v. American Broadcasting Co., 704 F.2d 1296 (4th Cir.1983) (videotaping the plaintiff in the plaintiff's home state and the forum sufficient for jurisdiction in a privacy action); Landrum v. The Board of Commissioners of Orleans Levee Dist., 758 F.Supp. 387 (E.D.La.1991) (jurisdiction in plaintiff's home state where defendant had transacted a substantial amount of business by mail and wire communications crossing state lines into forum state); Edwards v. The Pulitzer Publishing Co., 716 F.Supp. 438 (N.D.Cal.1989) (jurisdiction reasonable in plaintiff's home state where plaintiff received, in forum state, a phone call and

letter from non-resident defendant relating to the subject of the dispute); Mays v. Laurant Publishing, Ltd., 600 F.Supp. 29 (N.D.Ga.1984) (jurisdiction in plaintiff's home state where publication occurred in a magazine of national distribution, including significant distribution in the forum state); Pegler v. Sullivan, 6 Ariz.App. 338, 432 P.2d 593 (1967) (jurisdiction in plaintiff's home state where offending publication consisted of a nationally televised program); Pierce v. Serafin, 787 S.W.2d 705 (Ky.App. 1990) (jurisdiction in plaintiff's home state where allegedly invasive letter sent to another party in the forum state).

5. See, e.g., Salgado v. Les Nouvelles Esthetiques, 218 F.Supp.2d 203 (D.P.R. 2002) (20 magazines and two videos insufficient on a misappropriation of image theory); Dotzler v. Perot, 899 F.Supp. 416 (E.D.Mo.1995), affirmed 124 F.3d 207 (8th Cir. 1997), cert. denied 522 U.S. 1148, 118 S.Ct. 1167, 140 L.Ed.2d 177 (1998) (little suggestion that defendant was directly involved in the offending communication, case dismissed for lack of personal jurisdiction).

The so-called "intrusion" form of the tort of invasion of privacy does not necessarily involve the publication of an offending communication. The simple act of disrupting the plaintiff's solitude can, in some circumstances, be sufficient to create tort liability. This form of invasion of privacy much resembles classic intentional torts such as assault and battery.[6] Jurisdictional disputes in such cases are fairly rare, but where they arise, the analysis resembles that applicable to classic intentional torts. Jurisdiction in such cases is universally accepted in the state in which the invasion took place, which is also usually the plaintiff's domicile.[7]

V. ECONOMIC INJURIES

A. INTERFERENCE WITH CONTRACT AND RELATED TORTS

§ 7.11 A fair amount of commercial litigation involves allegations of invasions of economic interests. The vessels for attempting to recover under such a theory are various, but include the torts of intentional interference with contract, intentional interference with prospective economic advantage, conspiracy to breach a contract and a breach of the covenant of good faith and fair dealing.[1]

Despite the relative frequency with which such claims are raised, the Supreme Court has not decided a case directly involving any one of these torts. Two lines of Supreme Court cases are the most directly analogous. One is the intentional tort line of cases, illustrated by the two libel cases: *Calder v. Jones*[2] and *Keeton v. Hustler*.[3] As discussed extensively above,[4] each of these cases took a fairly expansive view, allowing for state court jurisdiction wherever the plaintiff felt a significant effect of the defendant's tortious conduct. This so-called "effects" test[5] was premised on the fact that (unlike negligence and strict liability cases) the defendant's conduct could not be said to be "untargeted."[6] The foreseeable effects of such intentional conduct was held sufficient to fulfill the "purposeful availment" test.[7]

---

6. See supra § 7.3.

7. See, e.g., Brown v. American Broadcasting Co., 704 F.2d 1296 (4th Cir.1983); Hrubec v. National R.R. Passenger Corp., 778 F.Supp. 1431 (N.D.Ill.1991), reversed in part 981 F.2d 962 (7th Cir. 1992).

§ 7.11

1. See, e.g., In re S & D Foods, Inc., 144 B.R. 121 (Bkrtcy.Colo.1992); In re Aero–Fastener, Inc., 177 B.R. 120 (Bkrtcy.Mass. 1994) (debtor's adversary proceeding against another party).

2. 465 U.S. 783, 104 S.Ct. 1482, 79 L.Ed.2d 804 (1984).

3. 465 U.S. 770, 104 S.Ct. 1473, 79 L.Ed.2d 790 (1984).

4. See supra §§ 7.3, 7.8.

5. See supra § 7.3.

6. *Calder*, 465 U.S. at 789, 104 S.Ct. at 1487.

7. Id. at 789–90, 104 S.Ct. at 1487.

The other line of cases that provides an important analogy for economic torts is the contract line of cases. As with the intentional tort cases, the Supreme Court has taken a fairly expansive view of specific jurisdiction in the contract context. In *McGee v. International Life Insurance Co.*[8] the Court allowed a policyholder to sue in her home state to collect on a life insurance policy written by an out-of-state company that did very little business in the forum state. In *Burger King Corp. v. Rudzewicz,*[9] the Court allowed a large franchisor to sue one of its franchisees in the franchisor's home state. In *Burger King*, the franchisee's only significant contact with the forum state was to enter into and breach the franchise agreement, thus causing an economic effect that was felt primarily in the forum state.[10] The Supreme Court's contract cases provide an important analogy because economic torts often accompany claims for breach of contract, and the usually commercial nature of the underlying arrangement between the parties means that the sorts of effects felt by the parties are the same.

In any event, the relatively broad view of jurisdiction taken by the Supreme Court in these two lines of cases suggests that jurisdiction in economic torts must be expansive. In fact, lower courts have taken a fairly broad view of jurisdiction in economic torts. Many lower courts have applied an effects test, allowing for jurisdiction in a state in which the defendant's conduct has a foreseeable and substantial effect.[11] Often, of course, the state in which the principal economic effects are felt is the plaintiff's home state, and—quite naturally—most plaintiffs prefer to litigate at home. The effects test, and the plaintiff preference that it entails, is not, however, absolute. Here, as in other contexts in which it is applied,[12] the effects test is tempered by a reasonableness principle. Thus, in some cases, courts have refused to allow the plaintiff to sue at home, especially where a great deal of the relevant evidence is located in another forum, and that thus requiring the defendant to litigate in the plaintiff's home would impose an unreasonable burden.[13] One court refers to this as the "focal point" test; unless the forum state is the focal point of the allegedly tortious activity, the requisite purposeful connection is lacking.[14]

---

8. 355 U.S. 220, 78 S.Ct. 199, 2 L.Ed.2d 223 (1957).

9. 471 U.S. 462, 105 S.Ct. 2174, 85 L.Ed.2d 528 (1985).

10. 471 U.S. at 479–80, 105 S.Ct. at 2186.

11. See, e.g., Jet Wine & Spirits, Inc. v. Bacardi Ltd., 298 F.3d 1 (1st Cir. 2002); Vishay Intertechnology, Inc. v. Delta Int'l Corp., 696 F.2d 1062 (4th Cir.1982); Taubler v. Giraud, 655 F.2d 991 (9th Cir.1981); Bounty–Full Entertainment, Inc. v. Forever Blue Entertainment Group, Inc., 923 F.Supp. 950 (S.D.Tex.1996); Vons Companies, Inc. v. Seabest Foods, Inc., 14 Cal.4th 434, 926 P.2d 1085, 58 Cal.Rptr.2d 899 (1996).

12. See supra § 7.3.

13. See, e.g., Machulsky v. Hall, 210 F.Supp.2d 531 (D.N.J. 2002) (transacting business with forum-resident plaintiffs over the Internet insufficient by itself to show purposeful availment); Pavlovich v. Superior Court, 29 Cal.4th 262, 127 Cal.Rptr.2d 329, 58 P.3d 2 (2002) (showing of some harm on forum-resident plaintiff insufficient in trade secret appropriation case); Beckman v. Thompson, 4 Cal.App.4th 481, 6 Cal.Rptr.2d 60 (1992).

14. See IMO Industries, Inc. v. Kiekert AG, 155 F.3d 254 (3d Cir.1998) (defendant had not "expressly aimed" its conduct at the forum, thus forum cannot "be said to be the focal point of the tortious activity.").

B. FRAUD AND RELATED TORTS

§ 7.12 Fraud, misrepresentation, deceit and similar causes of action are fairly frequent subjects of commercial litigation. As is the case for interference with contract and like torts discussed in the last section, no Supreme Court authority bears directly on the jurisdictional calculus for the fraud family of torts. As mentioned in the last section, the Supreme Court's intentional tort and contract cases provide a reasonably close analogy.[1] For the fraud family of torts, however, perhaps the closest Supreme Court analogy is *Travelers Health Ass'n v. Virginia*.[2] In *Travelers*, the Supreme Court held that a Virginia court could assert jurisdiction over an out-of-state company selling securities to Virginia citizens, for the purpose of requiring the company to comply with the state's "blue sky" law. As the Court noted, one of the purposes behind the law is to prevent fraud upon purchasers,[3] and the direct and purposeful efforts of the company to take advantage of the local market created sufficient ties with the state to allow it to assert its jurisdictional power.[4]

Although *Travelers* does not directly address fraud cases, it is suggestive of a fairly broad jurisdictional reach. If, as in *Travelers*, a state can assert its jurisdictional authority to prevent fraud upon its citizens by an out-of-state company, *a fortiori* it should be able to give its citizens a forum to redress frauds perpetrated upon them by nonresident defendants. A similar conclusion follows from application of the "effects" test that has gained currency in evaluating jurisdiction in intentional torts.[5] An intentional fraud perpetrated upon a forum domiciliary gives rise to precisely the sort of foreseeable, forum-centered harm that the Supreme Court found sufficient in *Calder v. Jones*[6] and *Keeton v. Hustler*[7] to allow for jurisdiction in libel cases.

By and large, the lower court cases considering jurisdiction in fraud cases bear out the approach suggested. Courts have usually allowed plaintiffs in intentional fraud cases to bring suit in the plaintiff's home state because the defendant's action of defrauding a forum resident fulfills the purposeful availment requirement for specific jurisdiction.[8]

§ 7.12

1. See supra § 7.11.

2. 339 U.S. 643, 70 S.Ct. 927, 94 L.Ed. 1154 (1950).

3. Id. at 644, 70 S.Ct. at 928.

4. Id. at 646, 70 S.Ct. at 930.

5. See supra § 7.3.

6. 465 U.S. 783, 104 S.Ct. 1482, 79 L.Ed.2d 804 (1984).

7. 465 U.S. 770, 104 S.Ct. 1473, 79 L.Ed.2d 790 (1984).

8. See, e.g., Dole Food Co. v. Watts, 303 F.3d 1104 (9th Cir. 2002) (fraudulent scheme directed towards plaintiff in forum state sufficient to establish jurisdiction un-der the "effects" test); Neal v. Janssen, 270 F.3d 328 (6th Cir. 2001); Rainbow Travel Serv. Inc. v. Hilton Hotels Corp., 896 F.2d 1233 (10th Cir.1990); Micromedia v. Automated Broadcast Controls, 799 F.2d 230 (5th Cir.1986); Bowling v. Founders Title Co., 773 F.2d 1175 (11th Cir.1985); Interlease Aviation Investors II (ALOHA) L.L.C. v. Vanguard Airlines, Inc., 262 F.Supp.2d 898 (N.D. Ill. 2003); Verizon Online Servs. v. Ralsky, 203 F.Supp.2d 601 (E.D. Va. 2002); OSI Indus. v. Carter, 834 So.2d 362 (Fla. App. 2003); Tart v. Prescott's Pharmacies, Inc., 118 N.C.App. 516, 456 S.E.2d 121 (1995).

Those relatively rare cases in which a fraud plaintiff has been denied a home forum have involved circumstances in which the defendant could demonstrate an absence of any substantial commercial benefit from the defendant's dealings in the forum.[9]

Unlike intentional fraud and misrepresentation, actions founded upon merely negligent misrepresentations may well warrant different jurisdictional treatment. In the context of non-intentional torts, the Supreme Court has consistently held that the mere fact that the injury was suffered in the forum does not suffice to establish jurisdiction.[10] A plaintiff in a negligent misrepresentation case cannot, therefore, obtain a local forum without showing some related, purposeful conduct by the defendant directed at the forum.[11]

9. See, e.g., Bond Leather Co., Inc. v. Q.T. Shoe Mfg. Co., Inc., 764 F.2d 928 (1st Cir.1985) (guarantor of a debt dismissed from a fraud case brought by a local plaintiff because of a lack of direct commercial benefit to the defendant from dealings in the forum state); LaVallee v. Parrot–Ice Drink Prods. of Am., Inc., 193 F.Supp.2d 296 (D. Mass. 2002) (jurisdiction would be unreasonable even though plaintiff was a forum resident).

10. See, e.g., Asahi Metal Indus. Co. v. Superior Court, 480 U.S. 102, 107 S.Ct. 1026, 94 L.Ed.2d 92 (1987); World–Wide Volkswagen Corp. v. Woodson, 444 U.S. 286, 100 S.Ct. 559, 62 L.Ed.2d 490 (1980).

11. See, e.g., M.P. Paul v. International Precious Metals Corp., 613 F.Supp. 174 (S.D.Miss.1985) (plaintiff not entitled to sue in home state on a negligent misrepresentation theory against an out-of-state defendant); but see Home Owners Funding Corp. of America v. Century Bank, 695 F.Supp. 1343 (D.Mass.1988) (negligent misrepresentation with effects in forum combined with purposeful actions directed at forum sufficient for personal jurisdiction).

Chapter 8

SPECIFIC JURISDICTION
IN CONTRACT CASES

Table of Sections

		Sections
I.	Introduction	8.1
II.	Insurance Contracts	8.2
III.	Franchise and Similar Contracts	8.3
IV.	Employment and Personal Service Contracts	8.4
V.	Purchase and Sale Contracts	8.5
VI.	Construction Contracts	8.6
VII.	Leases	8.7
VIII.	Carriage Contracts	8.8

I. INTRODUCTION

§ **8.1** Contract cases are subject to the same basic jurisdictional methodology as are other cases. Fundamentally, any assertion of jurisdiction by a state court requires statutory or common law authorization[1] and must not offend the Constitution. Federal courts, for the most part, have the same territorial reach as their state court counterparts,[2] and to the extent that jurisdictional considerations for federal courts diverge from state courts, that divergence is explored elsewhere.[3] As discussed elsewhere, the form and content of jurisdictional statutes vary considerably from state to state.[4] The most important constitutional test is the minimum contacts which has been developed extensively since its introduction in 1945.[5]

Jurisdiction in contract cases, as in other cases, is divisible into the categories of specific and general. As discussed extensively elsewhere,[6] general jurisdiction is usually premised on "continuous and systematic" contacts between the defendant and the forum so as to make the defendant amenable to jurisdiction without regard to the character of

---

§ 8.1

1. See supra § 5.14.

2. F.R.C.P. 4(k)(1)(A); see also supra § 5.15.

3. See infra §§ 10.2–10.12.

4. See supra § 5.14.

5. See International Shoe Co. v. Washington, 326 U.S. 310, 66 S.Ct. 154, 90 L.Ed. 95 (1945)

6. See supra § 5.13.

the dispute between the parties. Contract cases, of course, do not present any special problems for general jurisdiction analysis because the jurisdictional question is independent of the substantive theories asserted in the litigation.

Specific jurisdiction, however, turns upon the character of the dispute. Contract cases therefore present somewhat different jurisdictional problems in this context. The Supreme Court has decided two major cases on specific jurisdiction in contract matters. The first was *McGee v. International Life Ins. Co.*[7] In *McGee* the Court held that a California citizen, the beneficiary of a life insurance policy issued by a Texas company, could obtain jurisdiction over the defendant in the California courts.[8] The lawsuit was to collect the proceeds of the policy, which the company had refused to pay under a suicide exclusion.

McGee is regarded as the "high-water mark"[9] for jurisdictional jurisprudence, and with good reason. The only demonstrated contact between the defendant and the forum state was the single insurance policy sold to the beneficiary's deceased. The Court advanced several rationales for allowing jurisdiction, all suggestive of an extremely expansive reach for state courts. The Court noted that the relatively modest size of the claim might make it impossible for the plaintiff to effectively pursue the defendant at its home in Texas.[10] Modern travel, noted the Court, made it more practicable for defendants to effectively defend their interests in foreign courts.[11] And the Court also noted the special jurisdictional statute passed by California asserting jurisdiction over foreign insurance companies selling to in-state customers. Such a statute, said the Court, demonstrated California's "interest" in obtaining jurisdiction, and thus was a significant factor favoring the assertion of jurisdiction.[12]

The Supreme Court's other pronouncement on contract jurisdiction was issued almost three decades after *McGee*. In *Burger King Corp. v. Rudzewicz*[13] the plaintiff was a national fast food chain centered in Florida. When one of its Michigan-based franchisees fell behind on its franchise payments, the franchisor brought suit in a Florida court for breach of contract, trademark infringement, and related claims. As in *McGee*, the Court concluded that the lower court's assertion of jurisdiction was constitutional.

The Court noted that some confusion existed among lower courts as to the proper application of minimum contacts principles in contract cases.[14] The Court rejected any categorical rule, stating that "an individ-

7. 355 U.S. 220, 78 S.Ct. 199, 2 L.Ed.2d 223 (1957).

8. Id. at 223, 78 S.Ct. at 201, 2 L.Ed.2d 223.

9. Weintraub, A Map out of the Jurisdictional Labyrinth 28 U.C. Davis L. Rev. 531, 535 (1995).

10. 355 U.S. at 223, 78 S.Ct. at 201, 2 L.Ed.2d 223.

11. Id.

12. Id. at 224, 78 S.Ct. at 201, 2 L.Ed.2d 223.

13. 471 U.S. 462, 105 S.Ct. 2174, 85 L.Ed.2d 528 (1985).

14. Id. at 478, 105 S.Ct. at 2185, 85 L.Ed.2d 528.

ual's contract with an out-of-state party *alone* [cannot] automatically establish sufficient minimum contacts in the other party's home forum. . . ."[15] But, emphasized the Court, the measure of whether a defendant can be subject to specific jurisdiction in contract cases is whether the entire course of dealing, including "prior negotiations and contemplated future consequences,"[16] establish that "the defendant purposefully established minimum contacts with the forum."[17]

Applying the purposefulness test, the Court concluded that the Michigan franchisees had sufficiently connected themselves with Florida to allow for the assertion of jurisdiction. First, the contract entered into by the Michigan franchisees was one substantially connected with Florida because of the Florida base of operations of the franchisor.[18] The contract called for a 20–year franchise relationship that required "continuing and wide-ranging contacts" between the parties.[19] All payments to the franchisor were directed to the franchisor's Florida headquarters, and the contract documents themselves made clear that the franchisor conducted its operations from its Florida base.[20] As a result, important communications with the franchisor were directed to Florida, and important negotiating decisions were made by the franchisor in Florida.[21] Further, the Court stressed that the contract had included a choice-of-law clause selecting Florida law.[22] While not dispositive of the jurisdictional question, the Court thought the choice-of-law clause to be further evidence that the franchisee had purposefully connected itself with that state by entering into the franchise relationship. While upholding the exercise of jurisdiction, the Court was quick to point out that less significant and enduring contractual relationships might not merit the same treatment. The Court specifically distinguished the case before it from the circumstance of " 'out-of-state consumers [owing] on modest personal purchases.' "[23]

Consistent with the *Burger King* Court's refusal to lay down any categorical rules, the majority suggested that "reasonableness" plays a large role in the jurisdictional calculus. This reasonableness factor can either expand or retract a court's jurisdictional reach. The Court identified " 'the burden on the defendant,' " " 'the forum state's interest,' " "the plaintiff's interest," "the interstate system's interest in obtaining the most efficient resolution of controversies," and the "shared interest of the several states in furthering substantive social policies"[24] as all being relevant considerations. Moreover, "[t]hese considerations sometimes serve to establish the reasonableness of jurisdiction upon a lesser

---

15. Id.

16. Id. at 479, 105 S.Ct. at 2185, 85 L.Ed.2d 528.

17. Id.

18. Id.

19. Id. at 480, 105 S.Ct. at 2186, 85 L.Ed.2d 528.

20. Id.

21. Id.

22. Id. at 481, 105 S.Ct. at 2187, 85 L.Ed.2d 528.

23. Id. at 485, 105 S.Ct. at 2189, 85 L.Ed.2d 528 (quoting decision of the Court of Appeals below).

24. Id. at 476, 105 S.Ct. at 2184, 85 L.Ed.2d 528 (quoting World–Wide Volkswagen v. Woodson).

showing of minimum contacts than would otherwise be required.''[25] Conversely, ''minimum requirements inherent in the concept of 'fair play and substantial justice' may defeat the reasonableness of jurisdiction even if the defendant has engaged in forum activities.''[26] Shortly after *Burger King*, the Supreme Court turned this last suggestion from dictum to holding.[27]

Taken together, *McGee* and *Burger King* show that the critical factor in specific jurisdiction in contract cases is whether the defendant can be shown to have purposefully availed itself of the benefits and protections of the forum state. However, in light of the *Burger King* formulation, no single factor can be dispositive. The defendants in both *Burger King* and *McGee* were subject to jurisdiction largely because the Court was convinced that each had advantaged itself of the commercial benefits of the forum to an extent such that an assertion of jurisdiction would be fair.

The cases leave open important questions. *McGee* seemed to rely heavily on the relatively disadvantaged economic status of the plaintiff as a factor in asserting jurisdiction. In *Burger King*, however, the plaintiff was the economically stronger party, showing that the relative economic strength of the parties is not always determinative. *Burger King* does, however, contain a strong hint that jurisdiction over consumers, and perhaps other economically weaker parties, might not be so expansive. In sum, the Supreme Court's sporadic treatment of specific contract jurisdiction suggests that it falls within the same general framework as other jurisdictional questions. However, the infinite number of factual permutations in contractual arrangements requires a careful examination of the substantiality of the defendant's connection with the forum state.

II. INSURANCE CONTRACTS

§ 8.2 The grandfather of Supreme Court jurisdictional opinions in contract cases is *McGee v. International Life Ins. Co.*,[1] which is—of course—a case involving an insurance contract. In *McGee* the insured purchased a life insurance policy in California from an Arizona insurer. Four years after the policy was issued, the International Life Insurance Co.—a Texas company and ultimately the defendant in the case—bought out the Arizona insurer, and thereby assumed its insurance obligations. The International Life Insurance Co. then mailed to the insured—still a California domiciliary—a reinsurance agreement offering him insurance on the same terms as originally purchased from the Arizona company.[2]

---

25. Id.

26. Id. at 477, 105 S.Ct. at 2184, 85 L.Ed.2d 528.

27. Asahi Metal Indus. v. Superior Court, 480 U.S. 102, 113, 107 S.Ct. 1026, 1033, 94 L.Ed.2d 92 (1987).

§ 8.2

1. 355 U.S. 220, 78 S.Ct. 199, 2 L.Ed.2d 223 (1957).

2. Id. at 221, 78 S.Ct. at 200, 2 L.Ed.2d 223.

He agreed, and continued to pay the premiums until his death two years later. There was no showing that the International Life Insurance Co. insured any other California citizen.

After his death, the insured's mother—the beneficiary of the policy—sent proof of death to the International Life Insurance Co. at its Texas office. The company refused to pay, claiming that the insured's death was a suicide.[3] The insured's mother sued the International Life Insurance Co. in the California state courts. She obtained a default judgment against the company, and, unable to collect on it, presented it to the Texas courts. The Texas courts denied enforcement on the grounds that the California court had exceeded its jurisdictional reach.

The United States Supreme Court disagreed and held that the California court did not transgress its constitutional boundaries in assuming jurisdiction over the International Life Insurance Co. To support its conclusion that the minimum contacts test would allow for jurisdiction over the insurance company, the Supreme Court offered several rationales. First, the Court noted that the boundaries of in personam jurisdiction had expanded considerably in the previous decades. The Court saw this expansion as being responsive to the realities of "modern transportation and communications [which] have made it much less burdensome for a party sued to defend himself in a State where he engages in economic activity."[4]

Second, the Court pointed to what it termed California's "manifest interest in providing effective means of redress for its residents when their insurers refuse to pay claims."[5] Particularly for matters involving modest amounts of money—as in the *McGee* case—the Court was concerned that forcing the insured to sue the insurer in the latter's home state would "effect[ively] mak[e] the company judgment proof."[6]

Third, the Court thought that the relative convenience of litigation favored a California forum. The Court noted that the witnesses to the crucial factual issue in the case—whether the policyholder had committed suicide—were likely to be located in California. Although the Court believed that the insurance company would suffer some inconvenience in being forced to litigate away from home, it thought the burden to be "nothing which amounts to a denial of due process."[7]

A fourth, and more latent, rationale was one that anticipated the "purposeful availment" test announced only months later in *Hanson v. Denckla*.[8] While much of the Court's discussion in *McGee* was directed to the specific facts of that case, the Court did offer one general formulation of a rule applicable to contract matters. The Court stated that "[i]t is sufficient for purposes of due process that the suit [is] based on a

---

3. Id. at 222, 78 S.Ct. at 201, 2 L.Ed.2d 223.

4. Id. at 223, 78 S.Ct. at 201, 2 L.Ed.2d 223.

5. Id.

6. Id.

7. Id. at 224, 78 S.Ct. at 201, 2 L.Ed.2d 223.

8. 357 U.S. 235, 253, 78 S.Ct. 1228, 1239, 2 L.Ed.2d 1283.

contract with a substantial connection [to the forum] State."[9] The "substantial connection" test is, of course, not a mechanical formulation. But the most substantial connection of the contract to California was that the policyholder lived in California at all relevant times. *McGee* thus seemed to announce a general rule that a suit on a contract between parties of different states may be pursued in the aggrieved party's home state, at least if the aggrieved party lived in that state at the time of contracting. At the very least *McGee* made clear that in insurance contract cases the policyholder normally may sue the company in the state in which he was living at the time of policy purchase.

Of course, not all insurance disputes fit into the relatively simple pattern of *McGee*. A host of other factual permutations have presented difficult questions as to whether jurisdiction can be asserted. One frequently arising fact pattern occurs when the insurance policy covers a movable risk—such an automobile or the insured's life or health—and the loss arises in a state other than the policyholder's domicile. In a large number of cases courts have held that specific jurisdiction does not lie simply because the loss occurs in the forum, even if the policy promises to cover losses in any state.[10] The dominant rationale of cases considering this fact pattern has been that an insurance policy's promise to cover losses regardless of the place of the loss does not necessarily entail a purposeful connection between the insurer the state in which the loss occurs. Of course, the unavailability of specific jurisdiction in such cases does not foreclose general jurisdiction, and many large insurance compa-

9. *McGee*, 355 U.S. at 223, 78 S.Ct. at 201, 2 L.Ed.2d 223.

10. See, e.g., OMI Holdings, Inc. v. Royal Ins. Co. of Canada, 149 F.3d 1086 (10th Cir.1998) (provision promising coverage throughout United States not enough to confer jurisdiction in forum in which insurer has no other significant contacts; collecting cases from other jurisdictions); Davis v. American Family Mut. Ins. Co., 861 F.2d 1159 (9th Cir.1988) (third party tort victim's domicile in forum insufficient for jurisdiction in automobile insurance dispute); Hunt v. Erie Ins. Group, 728 F.2d 1244 (9th Cir.1984) (promise to provide coverage over losses in all 50 states insufficient to establish jurisdiction where only connection is that loss occurred in the forum); Sungard Data Systems, Inc. v. Central Parking Corp., 214 F.Supp.2d 879 (N.D. Ill. 2002) (merely delivering policy documents to forum state insufficient to establish jurisdiction where neither policyholder nor insurer had a place of business in the forum state); Batton v. Tennessee Farmers Mut. Ins. Co., 153 Ariz. 268, 736 P.2d 2 (1987) (policy provision covering losses in all 50 states insufficient for jurisdiction over insurer where only substantial connection is that loss occurred in forum); Benefit Ass'n Int'l, Inc. v. Superior Court, 46 Cal.App.4th 827, 54 Cal.Rptr.2d 165 (1996) (accident in forum insufficient for jurisdiction over the insurer); Great–West Life Assurance Co. v. Guarantee Co. of North America, 205 Cal. App.3d 199, 252 Cal.Rptr. 363 (1988) (loss in forum insufficient to establish jurisdiction over insurer in dispute over a general business liability policy); Strickland Ins. Group v. Shewmake, 642 So.2d 1159 (Fla. App.1994) (place of accident in forum insufficient to establish jurisdiction over insurer in automobile insurance dispute); Bookman v. KAH Incorporated, Inc., 614 So.2d 1180 (Fla.App.1993) (fact that insured relocated to forum and health insurance continued as required by federal law insufficient for jurisdiction over insurer); State of Missouri ex rel. Illinois Farmers Ins. Co. v. Koehr, 834 S.W.2d 233 (Mo.App.1992) (accident in forum insufficient to establish jurisdiction over insurer in automobile insurance dispute); Malaysia British Assurance v. El Paso Reyco, Inc., 830 S.W.2d 919 (Tex. 1992) (reinsurance agreement); but see Payne v. Motorists' Mut. Ins. Cos., 4 F.3d 452 (6th Cir.1993) (promise to cover in all 50 states enough contact to provide for jurisdiction in state of loss); State Farm Mutual Automobile Ins. Co. v. Tennessee Farmers Mutual Ins. Co., 645 N.W.2d 169 (Minn. App. 2002) (same).

nies are amenable to general jurisdiction in every state because of their pervasive business activities.[11]

Although a loss occurring in the forum does not by itself establish jurisdiction, a forum loss is relevant to the jurisdictional question. A forum loss, coupled with some other fact evidencing the insurer's purposeful connection with the forum, has been held sufficient to establish jurisdiction. For instance, if the policyholder is involved in litigation in the forum, and the insurer asserts its right to defend the policyholder, this has been held sufficient allow for jurisdiction over the insurer in subsequent disputes over the insurer's good faith in conducting the defense.[12]

Another common fact pattern has involved immovable risks in the forum state. In contrast to movable risks—for which the general rule is that a loss occurring in the forum is not sufficient for specific jurisdiction—a loss involving an immovable risk in the forum usually establishes jurisdiction. Often this arises when the policyholder is a large company with operations in several different states, and suffers a loss involving one of those operations. In such cases, courts have appropriately held that the insurer's decision to insure risks immovably located in the forum evidences a purposeful connection between the insurer and the forum, thus allowing the forum's courts to take jurisdiction.[13]

III. FRANCHISE AND SIMILAR CONTRACTS

§ 8.3 Franchise contracts are an important component of the modern economy. For a person wishing to go into business for himself, they present an attractive option. Entering into a franchise contract—or a similar arrangement—allows the business owner to obtain the benefit of a widely-recognized trademark, standardized products and business practices, and national and regional advertising campaigns. In exchange, the business owner must make substantial franchise payments, conform to the contractually specified business practices, and often lease or purchase business equipment and supplies exclusively from the franchisor. Because many franchisors have a great number of franchisees, the franchisee usually must sign a standard agreement. Of course, not every franchisor-franchisee relationship is blissful, and litigation sometimes ensues. In the event that the franchise agreement does not include an

---

11. See supra § 5.13.

12. See, e.g., American Home Assurance Co. v. Sport Maska, Inc., 808 F.Supp. 67 (D.Mass.1992). See also Payne v. Motorists' Mut. Ins. Cos., 4 F.3d 452 (6th Cir.1993) (insurer's failure to defend litigation in forum, coupled with "50 state coverage" clause, sufficient to make insurer amenable to jurisdiction on litigation concerning good faith of insurer's activities).

13. See, e.g., Commonwealth of Puerto Rico v. SS Zoe Colocotroni, 628 F.2d 652

(1st Cir.1980); St. Paul Surplus Lines Ins. Co. v. Cannelton Industries, Inc., 828 F.Supp. 498 (W.D.Mich.1993); Southeastern Express Systems v. Southern Guaranty Ins. Co., 34 Cal.App.4th 1, 40 Cal.Rptr.2d 216 (1995), cert. denied 516 U.S. 1044, 116 S.Ct. 703, 133 L.Ed.2d 659 (1996); A.I.U. Ins. Co. v. Superior Court, 177 Cal.App.3d 281, 222 Cal.Rptr. 880 (1986); Domtar, Inc. v. Niagara Fire Ins. Co., 533 N.W.2d 25 (Minn. 1995), cert. denied 516 U.S. 1017, 116 S.Ct. 583, 133 L.Ed.2d 504 (1995).

enforceable forum selection clause,[1] jurisdictional questions can arise. Generally the litigation falls into one of two patterns. One is that the franchisor sues the franchisee, and selects as a forum the franchisor's home state. The other is that the franchisee sues the franchisor, and selects as a forum the franchisee's home state.

Burger King Corp. v. Rudzewicz,[2] the Supreme Court's most recent and leading case on jurisdiction in contract cases, falls into the first pattern. In *Burger King*, the franchisees were Michigan residents, who contracted with a large fast food restaurant chain which had its principal offices in Florida.[3] The franchise agreement gave the franchisees access to all of the usual benefits of the franchise relationship, including advertising, a trademark license, standard products and business practices, and training, cost-control and inventory-control guidance. The contract was to last 20 years, and required the franchisees to make a substantial initial payment, as well as continuing payments over the duration of the contract. Most of the face-to-face dealings between the franchisee and franchisor were conducted through franchisor's Michigan district office, although some dealings were directly with the Florida office, and one of the franchisees attended training sessions there as well.[4]

Hard economic times hit the area in which the franchise was located, and the franchisees fell behind on their obligations. The franchisor then sued the franchisees for breach of contract and trademark infringement in a Florida federal court. The franchisees moved to dismiss for lack of jurisdiction, but the motion was denied by the federal district court. After the franchisees lost at trial, they appealed to the Eleventh Circuit which reversed on the jurisdictional issue, reasoning that the franchisee's contacts with Florida were too slight to allow for jurisdiction.[5]

The Supreme Court, however, reversed the Eleventh Circuit and reinstated the judgment of the district court. The Court was quick to point out that not every contractual relationship with an out-of-state party will establish jurisdiction there.[6] The Court instead indicated that the test for jurisdiction in contractual disputes must be flexible and focus on the course of the negotiations, the expected consequences of the relationship, the terms of the contract, and their actual course of dealing.

§ 8.3

1. Often form franchise agreements contain forum selection clauses. See, e.g., The Packaging Store, Inc. v. Leung, 917 P.2d 361 (Colo.App.1996). For a discussion of the enforceability of such clauses, see Note, Forum Selection Clauses in Contracts Governed by New Jersey Franchise Practices Act are Presumptively Invalid, 28 Seton Hall L. Rev. 213 (1997).

2. 471 U.S. 462, 105 S.Ct. 2174, 85 L.Ed.2d 528 (1985).

3. Id. at 463, 105 S.Ct. at 2174, 85 L.Ed.2d 528.

4. Id. at 465, 105 S.Ct. at 2178, 85 L.Ed.2d 528.

5. Id. at 468, 105 S.Ct. at 2181, 85 L.Ed.2d 528.

6. Id. at 478, 105 S.Ct. at 2185, 85 L.Ed.2d 528.

Looking at these factors, the Court concluded that the franchisees were properly haled before the Florida court. First, their affiliation with Florida was purposeful. Although the franchisees had only limited physical contacts with Florida, they "deliberately 'reached out beyond' Michigan and negotiated with a Florida corporation for the purchase of a franchise and the manifold benefits that would derive from affiliation with a nationwide corporation."[7] Thus, the failure to make the scheduled payments and continued use of the trademarks after the termination of the franchise foreseeably caused injury to the franchisor. Second, the actual course of dealing between the parties was, according to the Court, more than sufficient to put the franchisee on notice that the corporation's home was in Florida. Although some of the dealings were with the Michigan office, major problems had consistently required the intervention of the Florida headquarters, and the contractual documents themselves made clear that the corporation was headquartered in Florida. Third, the existence of a Florida choice-of-law clause in the contract was identified by the Supreme Court majority as further evidence of the franchisee's purposeful availment of the benefits and protections of Florida law.[8]

Nor did the Court find any of the countervailing reasons offered by the franchisee sufficient to reject jurisdiction. The Court did not find persuasive the suggestion that the franchisees would be unable to call Michigan-based witnesses in their defense, and suggested that such a concern could be more easily accommodated through a change-of-venue motion. Nor did the Court think that the asserted inequality in bargaining power should give the franchisees a jurisdictional defense. The contract was one of long duration, at least one of the franchisees was an experienced businessman, and the district court found that the franchisor had not made any material misrepresentations.[9]

Burger King stands as a strong endorsement for allowing jurisdiction over franchisees in the franchisor's home state. But, as is generally the case with Supreme Court jurisdictional opinions, *Burger King* does not announce any clear rule. The Court took pains to make clear that less intense contractual relationships, such as a consumer's purchase of goods from an out-of-state mail order company, would not necessarily create jurisdiction outside the consumer's home state.[10] It remains unsettled how far one must journey down the continuum of intensity of contractual relationships before crossing the constitutional line.

In the context of franchise relationships, however, lower courts have generally found that the contractual ties with the franchisor's home state are sufficient to allow for jurisdiction. Thus even if the franchise agreement is of shorter duration than *Burger King*'s, or involves less money, or is missing some of the elements of franchisor control, courts

---

7. Id. at 479–80, 105 S.Ct. at 2186, 85 L.Ed.2d 528.

8. Id. at 481, 105 S.Ct. at 2187, 85 L.Ed.2d 528.

9. Id. at 486, 105 S.Ct. at 2189, 85 L.Ed.2d 528.

10. Id. at 485, 105 S.Ct. at 2189, 85 L.Ed.2d 528.

have upheld jurisdiction in the franchisor's home state in suits against franchisees.[11] Of course, *Burger King*'s rationale would appear to apply in reverse. Although apparently rarer, suits by franchisees against franchisors in the franchisee's home state generally survive attempted jurisdictional dismissals.[12]

IV. EMPLOYMENT AND PERSONAL SERVICE CONTRACTS

§ 8.4   Most disputes over employment or personal service contracts are local. In the majority of cases, both parties are resident in the same state and the services are performed locally. However, with increasing societal mobility a great number of such contracts are not purely local and disputes relative to them present difficult jurisdictional issues.

None of the Supreme Court's modern jurisdictional cases concern employment or personal services contracts. Lower courts that have confronted such cases have been required to apply the Supreme Court contract jurisdiction cases by analogy.[1] Nevertheless, the cases in this area can be fit into a small number of recurring factual patterns.

One common fact pattern is an employee who leaves his home state to take a job with an out-of-state or foreign employer, has a dispute with the employer, and then returns to his old home to sue the employer. Here the cases are divided. A fair number of cases have allowed jurisdiction in this circumstance.[2] An approximately equal number, however, have refused to allow such suits to proceed in the employee's home state.[3] Though divided, the cases do not appear to be inconsistent.

---

11. See, e.g., Youn v. Track, Inc., 324 F.3d 409 (6th Cir. 2003) (distributorship); State Street Capital Corp. v. Dente, 855 F.Supp. 192 (S.D.Tex.1994) (3–year franchise agreement); Wiener King Systems, Inc. v. Brooks, 628 F.Supp. 843 (W.D.N.C. 1986) (10–year franchise agreement); Harrelson Rubber Co. v. Dixie Tire and Fuels, Inc., 62 N.C.App. 450, 302 S.E.2d 919 (1983) (20–year franchise agreement); Minuteman Press Int'l, Inc. v. Sparks, 782 S.W.2d 339 (Tex.App.1989) (total franchisee arrears less than $10,000.00).

12. See, e.g., Harrelson Rubber Co. v. Layne, 69 N.C.App. 577, 317 S.E.2d 737 (1984).

§ 8.4

1. It is interesting to contrast the relative lack of guidance in this area with the explicit guidance provided by the Brussels Convention to courts of member states of the European Union. The Brussels Convention, and the Lugano Convention, both give an express jurisdictional preference to employees, though in slightly different ways. See Beaumont, A United Kingdom Perspec-

tive on the Proposed Hague Judgments Convention, 24 Brooklyn J. Int'l L. 75, 93–94 (1998). The Brussels Regulation, Council Regulation (EC) No. 44/2001 of Dec. 22, 2000 on Jurisdiction and the Recognition of Judgments in Civil and Commercial Matters, O.J. L. 12/01, which has replaced the Convention for most cases filed on or after March 1, 2002, retains these provisions in substantially the same form as the Convention.

2. See, e.g., Runnels v. TMSI Contractors, Inc., 764 F.2d 417 (5th Cir.1985); Moreno v. Milk Train, Inc., 182 F.Supp.2d 590 (W.D. Tex. 2002); Shah v. Nu–Kote Int'l Inc., 898 F.Supp. 496 (E.D.Mich.1995), affirmed 106 F.3d 401 (6th Cir. 1997); Clark v. Moran Towing & Transp. Co., 738 F.Supp. 1023 (E.D.La.1990); Babineaux v. Southeastern Drilling Corp., 170 So.2d 518 (La.App.), review denied 172 So.2d 700 (La.), cert. denied 382 U.S. 16, 86 S.Ct. 67, 15 L.Ed.2d 12 (1965); Mabry v. Fuller–Shuwayer Co., Ltd., 50 N.C.App. 245, 273 S.E.2d 509 (1981).

3. See, e.g., Conti v. Pneumatic Prods. Corp., 977 F.2d 978 (6th Cir.1992); Freu-

Rather, the crucial inquiry is to determine which party took the initiative. If the employer took the initiative to recruit the employee away from his then-home (and later the forum) state, courts generally allow jurisdiction.[4] However, if the employer's participation was passive, or limited to mere advertising in the forum, then courts have generally not allowed for jurisdiction.[5] Here the courts attempt to apply the purposeful availment test that so dominates specific jurisdiction. While actively seeking out an employee constitutes an intentional connection with the forum, merely agreeing to hire an employee who is resident in the forum does not.

Another recurring fact pattern involves employees who, while employed by an out-of-state employer, continue to perform some or all of their duties at home, and then attempt to sue the employer in the employee's home state. Here it is easier for employees to maintain the suit at home. Generally, courts take the view that knowingly maintaining an employee who works in the forum is a sufficient indication of the employer's purposeful connection with the forum.[6] However, if allowing the employee to perform services at home is merely for the employee's convenience, then the evidence of a purposeful connection might be absent and jurisdiction may not be allowed.[7]

Although in most employer-employee suits the employee is the plaintiff, in some cases the parties are reversed. Usually such cases involve an employee's breach of a non-competition clause or similar restriction in the employment contract. Usually, of course, the employer-plaintiffs prefer to sue at home. Here again, however, the question of whether jurisdiction can be maintained turns on fairly narrow factual

densprung v. Offshore Tech. Services, 186 F.Supp.2d 716 (S.D. Tex. 2002); Farbman v. Esskay Mfg. Co., 676 F.Supp. 666 (W.D.N.C.1987); Hall v. National Basketball Ass'n, 651 F.Supp. 335 (D.Kan.1987); Speckine v. Stanwick Int'l Inc., 503 F.Supp. 1055 (W.D.Mich.1980); Cross v. Lightolier Inc., 395 N.W.2d 844 (Iowa 1986); Robert Half of Iowa, Inc. v. Citizens Bank of Newburg, 453 N.W.2d 236 (Iowa App.1990); Thibodeaux v. King–Wilkinson, Inc., 386 So.2d 189 (La.App.), review denied 392 So.2d 668 (La.1980). See also Hainey v. World Am Communications, Inc., 263 F.Supp.2d 338 (D.R.I. 2003) (consulting services contract).

4. See, e.g., *Runnels*, 764 F.2d 417 (active recruitment efforts in forum state, jurisdiction allowed); *Mabry*, 273 S.E.2d 509 (same); *Robert Half*, 453 N.W.2d 236 (same).

5. See, e.g., *Conti*, 977 F.2d 978 (mere hiring of national recruitment firm does not subject employer to jurisdiction in employee's home state); Flores v. A.C., Inc., 2003 WL 1566507 (W.D. Tex. 2003); *Speckine*, 503 F.Supp. 1055 (employee took the initia-

tive in seeking out employer, no jurisdiction allowed); *Cross*, 395 N.W.2d 844 (employer did little active recruitment in forum, no jurisdiction).

6. See, e.g., English & Smith v. Metzger, 901 F.2d 36 (4th Cir.1990); Shah v. Nu–Kote Int'l Inc., 898 F.Supp. 496 (E.D.Mich. 1995), affirmed 106 F.3d 401 (6th Cir. 1997); Raymond, Colesar, Glaspy & Huss, P.C. v. Allied Capital Corp., 761 F.Supp. 423 (E.D.Va.1991); Herbert v. Direct Wire and Cable, Inc., 694 F.Supp. 192 (E.D.Va. 1988); Berrigan v. Southeast Health Plan, Inc., 676 F.Supp. 1062 (D.Kan.1987). See also CSX Transp., Inc. v. Union Tank Car Co., 247 F.Supp.2d 833 (W.D. Mich. 2002) (inspection service contract).

7. Cf. Romann v. Geissenberger Mfg. Corp., 865 F.Supp. 255 (E.D.Pa.1994) (no jurisdiction in the home state of a travelling salesman where relatively small portion of sales activity conducted in his home state); Skillsoft Corp. v. Harcourt General Inc., 146 N.H. 305, 770 A.2d 1115 (2001) (plaintiff-employee not allowed to sue at home for declaratory judgment regarding trade secret dispute).

distinctions. Generally, employers have not been able to obtain jurisdiction over employees who perform all or most of their duties outside the forum.[8] However, if the employee performs some substantial portion of his duties in the forum and the theory of relief is related to the performance of those duties, then jurisdiction has been allowed.[9] Again, the division in the cases is the result of the purposeful availment test. An employee who merely works for an employer based out-of-state cannot rationally be considered to have purposefully directed his activities at the employer's home state. However, if the employee performs some of the relevant duties in the employer's home state, this is strong evidence of a purposeful connection.

V. PURCHASE AND SALE CONTRACTS

§ 8.5 Purchase and sale agreements that cross state or international lines are quite common. Even the most ordinary of such contracts might well involve a buyer and a seller located in different states. From this rather mundane setting a wealth of difficult jurisdictional questions spring.

No Supreme Court decision directly addresses jurisdiction in matters involving the breach of a purchase agreement. The most closely analogous case is *Burger King Corp. v. Rudzewicz*,[1] discussed above relative to franchise contracts.[2] In *Burger King* the Eleventh Circuit rejected jurisdiction, reasoning in part that allowing jurisdiction in that case could—by analogy—subject interstate purchasers of consumer goods to faraway forums.[3] The Supreme Court, while reversing the Eleventh Circuit, stated that it shared the lower court's "broader concerns."[4] Evidently the Supreme Court's passing reference indicates that a relatively small, "one shot" purchase contract calls for a significantly different analysis than the 20–year, multi-million dollar franchise agreement at issue in *Burger King*. However, just as with other kinds of contracts, purchase agreements come in an infinite variety of shapes and sizes and can require the drawing of some very fine jurisdictional lines.

Notwithstanding the need to make some fine distinctions, some clear decisional patterns have emerged. One common scenario is a seller, who has sold goods to an out-of-state purchaser, attempting to get jurisdiction over the purchaser in the seller's home state for a failure to pay for the goods, or some other alleged breach. Courts consistently rule that jurisdiction over the purchaser is unconstitutional if the purchaser's only connection with the forum state is the placing of an order with the

---

8. See, e.g., Riblet Prods. Corp. v. Nagy, 191 A.D.2d 626, 595 N.Y.S.2d 228 (App. Div. 1993); Colt Plumbing Co. v. Boisseau, 435 Pa.Super. 380, 645 A.2d 1350 (1994).

9. See, e.g., Ciena Corp. v. Jarrard, 203 F.3d 312 (4th Cir.2000); T.M. Hylwa v. Palka, 823 F.2d 310 (9th Cir.1987); Nordmark Presentations, Inc. v. Harman, 557 So.2d 649 (Fla.App.1990).

§ 8.5

1. 471 U.S. 462, 105 S.Ct. 2174, 85 L.Ed.2d 528 (1985).

2. See supra § 8.3.

3. 471 U.S. at 485, 105 S.Ct. at 2189, 85 L.Ed.2d 528

4. Id.

forum-based seller.[5] Because the requirement that a defendant "purpose-fully avail"[6] itself of the forum's benefits, courts are usually only willing to allow for jurisdiction over an out-of-state purchaser if the purchaser takes affirmative efforts relative to the forum—other than merely placing an order. Thus, courts will usually allow for jurisdiction over an out-of-state purchaser if the purchaser actively sought out the seller or otherwise clearly initiated the transaction.[7]

In the reverse case, in which the buyer sues the seller for an alleged breach of the agreement, the focus remains on the question of which party initiated the transaction. Thus, mere passive selling to an out-of-state buyer does not, by itself, subject the seller to jurisdiction in the buyer's home state.[8] On the other hand, if the seller actively solicited the business in the forum, courts are usually willing to assert jurisdiction.[9] In fact, one court applies a so-called "aggressor" test; jurisdiction lies over an out-of-state party only if it is the aggressor in the transaction.[10]

The "aggressor" test, or some similar inquiry into the transaction's initiation, has some attractive features. One is that it heeds *Burger King*'s dictum that a party should not routinely be haled to a distant forum simply because it contracts with an out-of-state concern. The test has some serious drawbacks, however. The inquiry into which party initiated the transaction is intensively factual and of potentially uncertain resolution. Suppose, for instance, that the seller advertises in a trade magazine that is circulated in the forum, and in response the

---

5. See, e.g., Vetrotex Certainteed Corp. v. Consolidated Fiber Glass Prods. Co., 75 F.3d 147 (3d Cir.1996); Bowman v. Curt G. Joa, Inc., 361 F.2d 706 (4th Cir.1966); M & G Polymers USA, LLC v. CNC Containers Corp., 190 F.Supp.2d 854 (S.D.W.V. 2002); Cellutech, Inc. v. Centennial Cellular Corp., 871 F.Supp. 46 (D.D.C.1994); Christus St. Joseph's Health Systems v. Witt Biomedial Corp., 805 So.2d 1050 (Fla. App. 2002); Servo Instruments, Inc. v. Fenway Machine Co., 92 Ill.App.3d 509, 47 Ill.Dec. 309, 415 N.E.2d 34 (1980); Woodfield Ford, Inc. v. Akins Ford Corp., 77 Ill.App.3d 343, 32 Ill.Dec. 750, 395 N.E.2d 1131 (1979); S.B. Schmidt Paper Co. v. A to Z Paper Co., 452 N.W.2d 485 (Minn.App.1990).

6. See Hanson v. Denckla, 357 U.S. 235, 253, 78 S.Ct. 1228, 1239, 2 L.Ed.2d 1283 (1958).

7. See, e.g., St. Jude Medical, Inc. v. Lifecare Int'l, Inc., 250 F.3d 587 (8th Cir. 2001); Aristech Chemical Int'l Ltd. v. Acrylic Fabricators Ltd., 138 F.3d 624 (6th Cir. 1998) (breaching buyer sought out seller in forum state and placed a substantial order for a specialized product); Madison Consulting Group v. State of South Carolina, 752 F.2d 1193 (7th Cir.1985); Rusty Eck Ford–Mercury Corp. of Leavenworth v. American Custom Coachworks, Ltd., 184 F.Supp.2d

1138 (D. Kan. 2002); Ward v. Formex, Inc., 27 Ill.App.3d 22, 325 N.E.2d 812 (1975); but see Mountaire Feeds, Inc. v. Agro Impex, S.A., 677 F.2d 651 (8th Cir.1982) (no jurisdiction over a foreign buyer who initiated the transaction because buyer had no physical presence in the forum).

8. See, e.g., Hall's Specialties, Inc. v. Schupbach, 758 F.2d 214 (7th Cir.1985); Andrews Univ. v. Robert Bell Industries, Ltd., 685 F.Supp. 1015 (W.D.Mich.1988); Amusement Equipment, Inc. v. Mordelt, 595 F.Supp. 125 (E.D.La.1984); Beldock v. Braun, 465 F.Supp. 466 (S.D.N.Y.1979); Budgget Industries, Inc. v. Faber Engineering, L.L.C., 2003 WL 21087138 (Tex. App. 2003).

9. See, e.g., Peanut Corp. of Am. v. Hollywood Brands, Inc., 696 F.2d 311 (4th Cir. 1982); Uni–Bond, Ltd. v. Schultz, 607 F.Supp. 1361 (E.D. Wis.1985) (sale in forum plus anticipated future consequences sufficient for jurisdiction); Bruns v. DeSoto Operating Co., 204 Cal.App.3d 876, 251 Cal. Rptr. 462 (1988).

10. See, e.g., TRWL v. Select Int'l, Inc., 527 N.W.2d 573, 576 (Minn.App.1995) (collecting Minnesota cases applying the "aggressor" test). See also St. Jude Medical, Inc. v. Lifecare Int'l, Inc., 250 F.3d 587 (8th Cir.2001).

buyer places an order for the delivery of goods to the buyer's place of business. It is not immediately apparent which party would be considered the "aggressor" in such a transaction. Indeed, in a transaction like the hypothetical one, in which neither side takes any extraordinary steps to bring about the relationship, it may well be that neither side is the initiator or the aggressor in the sense employed in the case law. If so, this leads to the odd result that each side would be required to go to a foreign court to enforce the agreement. Given the uncertainties inherent in the application of the minimum contacts test in this context, parties may be well advised to attempt to pretermit the jurisdictional dispute with a forum selection or arbitration clause.[11]

VI. CONSTRUCTION CONTRACTS

§ 8.6 Construction contracts present their own array of novel jurisdictional questions. Indeed, a single construction project—even a simple one—usually brings about several contractual relationships. The most obvious is the relationship between the owner of the project and the general contractor. However, general contractors often employ subcontractors, and payment and performance are frequently guaranteed by bonds, which are usually issued by insurance companies. Those bonds may also give rise to contractual recourse rights against the holders of the bonds.

Notwithstanding this constellation of contractual relationships, the jurisdictional decisions can be grouped into a finite number of categories. Most importantly, there is a nearly per se rule that jurisdiction is available in the state in which the construction project is situated. This rule appears to apply without regard to the specifics of the contractual arrangement.[1] This rule fits well with the purposeful availment aspect of the minimum contacts test. A party that stands to benefit from a contractual relationship involving a project located in the forum has intentionally taken commercial advantage of the forum market, thus rendering is fair that such a party should be subject to jurisdiction.

More difficult questions arise in cases in which the defendant is sued in a forum that is not home to the construction project. A defendant is, of course, subject to general jurisdiction at its home base and perhaps in other forums.[2] Assuming, however, that the theory is one of specific jurisdiction, bringing the defendant before a court in a state removed from the construction site is much more problematic. The mere fact that

---

11. See infra §§ 11.2–11.7.

§ 8.6

1. See, e.g., Culp & Evans v. White, 524 F.Supp. 81 (W.D.N.Y.1981) (defendant's guarantee of performance of project in forum subjects it to personal jurisdiction); G & H Constr. Co. v. Daniels Flooring Co., 173 Ga.App. 181, 325 S.E.2d 773 (1984) (contractor alleged to have breached con-

struction contract subject to jurisdiction in state in which the project was to have taken place); Aetna Cas. & Surety Co. v. Looney, 98 Ill.App.3d 1057, 54 Ill.Dec. 444, 424 N.E.2d 1347 (1981) (defendant's agreement to indemnify bond company on project in Illinois subjects defendant to jurisdiction of the Illinois courts).

2. See supra § 6.9.

the plaintiff sues in its home state is clearly insufficient, by itself, to establish jurisdiction.[3] This is consistent with the general notion that merely contracting with a party in another state is insufficient to establish specific jurisdiction in that other state.[4] However, other factors besides the party's location can tip the balance in favor of jurisdiction. For instance, if important work, such as engineering work, relative to the project is performed in the forum, courts have allowed jurisdiction.[5] In general, then, specific jurisdiction will exist in a state other than the project location only if there are other significant connections with the forum.

VII. LEASES

§ 8.7 Leases of either personal or real property come in a wide variety of shapes and sizes. In some circumstances they can be disguised security interests in the "leased" property.[1] In other circumstances, they are a small part of a more complicated contractual relationship. For instance, in *Burger King Corp. v. Rudzewicz*[2]—the Supreme Court's most important case on contract jurisdiction[3]—one part of the relationship between the parties was an equipment lease, although the relationship was primarily one of franchisor-franchisee. Given the complexity that such relationships often entail, forum selection clauses are often part of the bargain which usually pretermits any inquiry into the usual jurisdictional questions.[4]

However, a jurisdictional analysis is occasionally necessary in the context of leases, and some generalizations are possible. One generalization is that if the lease is either for real property, or personal property that is expected to have a fixed situs, jurisdiction is available in the state in which the property is situated.[5] This holds true whether the action is

3. See, e.g., Blue Ball Properties, Inc. v. McClain, 658 F.Supp. 1310 (D.Del.1987); Condos v. Sun State Painting, Inc., 450 N.E.2d 86 (Ind.App.1983).

4. Burger King Corp. v. Rudzewicz, 471 U.S. 462, 485, 105 S.Ct. 2174, 2185, 85 L.Ed.2d 528 (1985).

5. See, e.g., Republic Int'l Corp. v. Amco Engineers, Inc., 516 F.2d 161 (9th Cir.1975) (jurisdiction in forum because some personnel located in forum for several months and crucial engineering work performed in the forum). Cf. Hyatt Int'l Corp. v. Coco, 302 F.3d 707 (7th Cir. 2002) (defendant purposefully reached out to plaintiff in the forum state allowing for jurisdiction in the plaintiff's home state even though the disputed construction project was to have taken place in Italy).

§ 8.7

1. Cf. Note, Choice of Law in Distinguishing Leases from Security Interests Un-

der the Uniform Commercial Code, 75 Tex. L. Rev. 375 (1996).

2. 471 U.S. 462, 105 S.Ct. 2174, 85 L.Ed.2d 528 (1985).

3. See supra § 8.1.

4. See, e.g., LINC Finance Corp. v. Onwuteaka, 129 F.3d 917, 921 (7th Cir.1997).

5. See, e.g., Reynolds Publishers, Inc. v. Graphics Financial Group, Ltd., 938 F.Supp. 256 (D.N.J.1996) (lease of computer equipment situated in forum sufficient to establish minimum contacts in action brought against allegedly breaching lessor); Sunrise Industrial Joint Venture v. Ditric Optics, Inc., 873 F.Supp. 765 (E.D.N.Y. 1995) (breach by lessee's guarantor of lease payments on real property located in forum constitutes minimum contacts with the forum); Hoag v. Sweetwater Int'l, 857 F.Supp. 1420 (D.Nev.1994) (lessor's breach of lease for truck-mounted drilling equipment to be used in forum constitutes mini-

brought by or against the lessee.[6]

Jurisdiction outside the state in which the leased property is situated is more difficult, but not impossible, to establish. In *Burger King* all of the leased property was physically located in Michigan, but the Supreme Court nonetheless allowed jurisdiction in Florida because the franchisor-lessor had its principal offices there.[7] However, the duration and intensity of the contractual relationship in *Burger King* was a significant factor in allowing jurisdiction, and thus the case does not stand for a per se rule that jurisdiction is always available in the lessor's home state. However, some decisions have allowed for jurisdiction in the lessor's home state on a *Burger King* rationale, especially in the context of significant commercial relationships.[8] More often, however, specific jurisdiction is not allowed in forums other than the situs of the property, usually on the theory that the defendant's activities relative to the lease do not establish purposeful availment of the forum's benefits.[9]

VIII.　CARRIAGE CONTRACTS

§ 8.8　Contracts to transport goods or persons present some difficult jurisdictional problems. As is the case with most particular types of contracts, the Supreme Court has not directly addressed their jurisdictional implications. Factually, the closest Supreme Court case is *Helicopteros Nacionales de Columbia v. Hall*,[1] in which the plaintiffs' decedents were killed while being transported by helicopter in South America. Wrongful death litigation ensued in Texas. While it might well have been possible to characterize the *Helicopteros* claim as one for breach of contract of safe passage, the case apparently proceeded on tort theories,[2] and—in any event—the exclusive reliance by plaintiffs' counsel on general jurisdiction limits the case's relevance for specific jurisdiction.[3] The other modern Supreme Court jurisdictional case involving a transportation contract—*Carnival Cruise Lines v.*

mum contacts with the forum); La Salle National Bank of Chicago v. Akande, 235 Ill.App.3d 53, 175 Ill.Dec. 780, 600 N.E.2d 1238 (Ill.App.1992) (guarantee of lease payments on real property located in forum sufficient to establish jurisdiction over guarantor).

6.　See supra n.5.

7.　*Burger King*, 471 U.S. 462, 105 S.Ct. 2174, 85 L.Ed.2d 528.

8.　See, e.g., Kentucky Oaks Mall Co. v. Mitchell's Formal Wear, Inc., 53 Ohio St.3d 73, 559 N.E.2d 477 (1990), cert. denied 499 U.S. 975, 111 S.Ct. 1619, 113 L.Ed.2d 717 (1991) (lease of commercial equipment from an Ohio company enough to establish jurisdiction in Ohio even though equipment physically located in Kentucky).

9.　See, e.g., Far West Capital, Inc., Steamboat Development Co. v. Towne, 46

F.3d 1071 (10th Cir.1995) (negotiations in forum and residence of one party in forum not sufficient to establish minimum contacts in dispute over lease of mineral rights in real property located outside the forum); Northern Trust Co. v. Randolph C. Dillon, Inc., 558 F.Supp. 1118 (N.D.Ill.1983) (lessee's making of payments to company located in forum insufficient to establish personal jurisdiction); Pres–Kap, Inc. v. System One, Direct Access, Inc., 636 So.2d 1351 (Fla.App.1994) (same).

§ 8.8

1.　466 U.S. 408, 104 S.Ct. 1868, 80 L.Ed.2d 404 (1984).

2.　Id. at 412, 104 S.Ct. at 1871, 80 L.Ed.2d 404.

3.　Id. at 415–16, 104 S.Ct. at 1872, 80 L.Ed.2d 404.

Shute[4]—was resolved on the basis of the exclusive forum selection clause printed on the back of the ticket for passage, and thus is also of little relevance on this point.

With regard to interstate transportation contracts, several different for a present themselves as possibilities for assertions of specific jurisdiction. The states of destination and departure are obvious possibilities, as are states through which the goods or persons pass during transport. The state of departure generally may assert jurisdiction on the theory that contract has a very substantial connection there.[5] States along the route of passage, however, appear to be generally unable to assert jurisdiction, even if the goods or persons make an intermediate stop there.[6] Other states with less substantial connections, such as the domicile of the aggrieved party or the state in which the transaction was nominally completed, also generally may not assert jurisdiction without some other additional connection.[7]

The most difficult problems center on whether the destination state can assert jurisdiction. Especially in the admiralty context, there is significant case authority for the proposition that the destination state does not have jurisdiction if the transported goods never reach their destination.[8] In contrast, in cases in which goods have actually reached their destination, courts have generally upheld jurisdiction there.[9] While this is admittedly a narrow distinction, it does fit with the notion that jurisdiction is a matter of accepting burdens commensurate with the benefits of doing business in a state.[10] In cases in which the shipper actually reaches the forum state, there is actual commercial benefit. In cases in which the shipper falls short of the destination, the benefits rendered by the forum state remain largely hypothetical.

4. 499 U.S. 585 111 S.Ct. 1522, 113 L.Ed.2d 622 (1991).

5. See, e.g., Kingsley & Keith (Canada) Ltd. v. Mercer Int'l Corp., 291 Pa.Super. 96, 435 A.2d 585 (1981).

6. See, e.g., Global Servicios v. Toplis & Harding, Inc., 561 So.2d 674 (Fla.App. 1990).

7. See, e.g., Gelfand v. Tanner Motor Tours, Ltd., 339 F.2d 317 (2d Cir.1964) (forum lacks minimum contacts merely because plaintiffs were domiciled in forum and tickets were there purchased when all other significant connections were with other states).

8. See, e.g., United Rope Distribs., Inc. v. Seatriumph Marine Corp., 930 F.2d 532 (7th Cir.1991); Asarco, Inc. v. Glenara, 912 F.2d 784 (5th Cir.1990); Francosteel Corp. v. The M/V Charm, 825 F.Supp. 1074, 1080 (S.D.Ga.1993), affirmed 19 F.3d 624 (11th Cir. 1994) ("ever where the defendant is bound to transport the cargo to the specific destination, 'minimum contacts' are lacking where the cargo failed to reach the destination, absent additional factors").

9. See, e.g., Granite & Quartzite Centre Inc. v. M/S Virma, 374 F.Supp. 1124 (S.D.Ga.1974); Mackensworth v. American Trading Transp. Co., 367 F.Supp. 373 (E.D.Pa.1973) (opinion written in rhyme: "Ship's single visit to Pennsylvania port, subjects the owner to that state's federal court...").

10. International Shoe Co. v. Washington, 326 U.S. 310, 320, 66 S.Ct. 154, 160, 90 L.Ed. 95 (1945).

Chapter 9

SPECIFIC JURISDICTION IN STATUTORY CASES

Table of Sections

		Sections
I.	Introduction	9.1
II.	Environmental Harm	9.2
III.	Copyright and Trademark Infringement	9.3
IV.	Patent Infringement	9.4
V.	Employment–Related Statutory Obligations	9.5
VI.	Securities and Related Statutes	9.6
VII.	Private Antitrust and Other Unfair Trade Actions	9.7
VIII.	Anti–Fraud Statutes	9.8

I. INTRODUCTION

§ 9.1 This chapter might strike the reader as having an odd subject. However, having surveyed in the last two chapters specific jurisdiction in the two great, common-law categories of private obligations—torts and contracts, respectively—it is necessary to consider statutorily created obligations. Of course, given the myriad of statutorily imposed obligations prevalent in the United States—health, employment-related, environmental, economic, intellectual property and business—no general survey could exhaust them. Moreover, some of the federal statutes have special jurisdictional provisions, aspects of which discussed below.[1] Nevertheless, some useful general observations can be made about judicial jurisdiction in each of these categories.

In the modern era, the Supreme Court has at least three times considered the reach of specific jurisdiction theories in the context of statutory claims. The first, of course, was in *International Shoe Co. v. Washington*,[2] the case that originated the "minimum contacts" doctrine.[3] The asserted liability of the defendant in that case was for unpaid unemployment compensation contributions. The Court framed the issue rather specifically, stating that the question was whether the defendant

---

§ 9.1

1. See infra §§ 9.2, 9.5–9.7.

2. 326 U.S. 310, 66 S.Ct. 154, 90 L.Ed. 95 (1945).

3. See supra § 5.4.

"has by its activities in the State of Washington rendered itself amenable to proceedings in the courts of that state to recover unpaid contributions to the state unemployment compensation fund exacted by state statutes."[4] Thus, the Court was clearly conscious of the statutory nature of the underlying claim.

As is well known, the Supreme Court upheld jurisdiction. The Court concluded that the presence of about a dozen salesmen within the state during the years in which the contributions were sought was a sufficient connection to justify jurisdiction. The *International Shoe* rationale rested on a notion of exchange.[5] By reaping the commercial benefit of allowing its salesmen to operate within the state, the company had to accept the burden of litigating statutory obligations, at least relative to the activities of salesmen physically within the state. As the Court put it: "*to the extent* that a corporation exercises the privilege of conducting activities within a state, it enjoys the benefits and protections of the laws of that state."[6] Directly invoking the exchange concept, the Court said that "so far as those obligations arise out of or are connected with the activities within the state, a procedure which requires the corporation to respond to a suit brought to enforce them within the state can, in most cases, hardly be said to be undue."[7]

The exchange concept also justified jurisdiction in *Travelers Health Association v. Virginia*.[8] In that case, the State of Virginia, acting through one of its administrative agencies, brought an action to obtain a cease and desist order against the defendants under a state "Blue Sky Law" requiring the sellers of securities to obtain a permit before selling to Virginians.[9] The defendants were a mail order health insurance company and its treasurer; both were located in Nebraska.[10] The health insurer had about 800 Virginia members. However, unlike the International Shoe Company, the corporate defendant in *Travelers* did not use any paid agents within the forum state.[11] Rather, it relied upon its existing customers to recommend others; upon such recommendations solicitations were mailed from the Nebraska office to the prospective customers in Virginia.[12] Payments were accepted from the Virginia customers, and the corporate defendant had investigated many claims within the forum state.[13]

In upholding jurisdiction, the Court emphasized the substantiality of the relationships created. The insurance policies, noted the Court, were "systematically and widely delivered in Virginia" and "Virginia courts were available [to the company] in seeking to enforce obligations created

---

4. *International Shoe*, 326 U.S. at 311, 66 S.Ct. at 156.

5. See generally Lewis, A Brave New World for Personal Jurisdiction: Flexible Tests Under Uniform Standards, 37 Vand. L. Rev. 1 (1984).

6. *International Shoe*, 326 U.S. at 319, 66 S.Ct. at 160 (emphasis added).

7. Id.

8. 339 U.S. 643, 70 S.Ct. 927, 94 L.Ed. 1154 (1950).

9. Id. at 644–45, 70 S.Ct. at 928.

10. Id. at 645, 70 S.Ct. at 928.

11. Id. at 646, 70 S.Ct. at 929.

12. Id.

13. Id.

by the group of certificates."[14] The Court was concerned that not allowing jurisdiction would create an asymmetry. The company would have access to Virginia courts if it so chose, but customers would be forced to journey to Nebraska, making litigation uneconomical in small cases.[15] The majority thus concluded that the balance tipped toward allowing the suit to proceed.

While the balance tipped towards allowing jurisdiction in *International Shoe* and *Travelers*, the Court reached the opposite result in *Shaffer v. Heitner*.[16] While *Shaffer* is best known for its holding that the minimum contacts test applies whether the proceeding is in personam, quasi in rem or in rem,[17] the Court's holding required it to decide whether the minimum contacts test allowed for jurisdiction. In *Shaffer* the plaintiff was a stockholder in the Greyhound corporation and filed in the Delaware state courts a derivative action against 28 former and current corporate officers and directors.[18] The essence of the plaintiff's allegations was that the defendants had violated their fiduciary duty to the stockholders by engaging in conduct that resulted in a civil antitrust judgment and civil contempt fine being levied against the company.[19]

While the forum state was the company's state of incorporation—clearly a sufficient nexus for jurisdiction over the company[20]—the Court thought that connection too tenuous to allow for jurisdiction over the individual defendants. While the Court recognized that Delaware statutory and common law defined the relationship of the officers and directors to their corporation, the majority thought that connection too insubstantial to allow the state courts to assert jurisdiction over the individual defendants. While the plaintiff argued, and the Court recognized, that the individual defendants received substantial benefits from the officer and director positions,[21] the Court thought them insufficient to require the defendants to accept the burden of personally defending themselves in Delaware. While the Court apparently thought that Delaware could enact a special "implied consent" statute making clear that acceptance of jurisdiction was a condition of taking an officer or director position, without such a statute the obligation to personally defend was disproportionate to the benefit.[22]

While, as is generally true in the field of American jurisdiction, there is no mechanical test, the common theme with regard to statutory claims is that jurisdictional analysis requires a weighing of benefits and burdens. In general, such suits are against businesses or individuals acting in a professional capacity. Taken together, *International Shoe*, *Travelers* and *Shaffer* call upon courts to ensure that the benefit derived from the business connection with the forum is sufficient to make it reasonable to

---

14. Id. at 648, 70 S.Ct. at 928.

15. Id. at 648, 70 S.Ct. at 929.

16. 433 U.S. 186, 97 S.Ct. 2569, 53 L.Ed.2d 683 (1977).

17. See supra §§ 5.5–5.6 for a discussion of this aspect of *Shaffer*.

18. Id. at 189–90, 97 S.Ct. at 2572.

19. Id.

20. See supra § 6.9.

21. Id. at 214, 97 S.Ct. at 2585.

22. Id. at 216, 97 S.Ct. at 2586.

require the defendant to defend away from home. Although, as investigation of the specific areas show, the weighing of this balance varies from context to context, the general methodology remains reasonably constant.

II. ENVIRONMENTAL HARM

§ 9.2   The question of personal jurisdiction over cross-border polluters is one of growing practical importance. There is a growing and impressive body of federal environmental laws, including the National Environmental Protection Act ("NEPA"),[1] the Comprehensive Environmental Recovery, Clean-up and Liability Act ("CERLCA"),[2] the Resource Recovery and Compensation Act ("RCRA"),[3] various incarnations of the Clean Air and Clean Water Acts, along with an astonishing variety of state environmental laws and regulations.[4] In many cases these statutes impose private liability, and for out-of-state defendants the question of in personam jurisdiction can be critical.

For the most part, the question of whether a court—either state or federal—can reach an out-of-state defendant is judged by the usual two-step process. First, the court must determine whether the forum state's long-arm statute applies, and second the court must determine whether the defendant has forum state contacts that render the attempted assertion of jurisdiction constitutional.[5] At least one important environmental statute, CERLCA, contains a special jurisdictional provision which provides for "nationwide service of process."[6] However, that provision covers only actions in which the United States is a party, and thus apparently does not reach private actions.[7] We elsewhere consider the significance of such specialized federal long-arm provisions.[8] In any event, the general question of how to apply minimum contacts jurisprudence in cross-border environmental cases is one of some considerable import.

The grandfather of cross-border environmental cases is *Ohio v. Wyandotte Chemicals Corp.*[9] In that case, the State of Ohio petitioned the United States Supreme Court for leave to file an original bill alleging that the defendants—Michigan, Delaware and Canadian companies—were dumping mercury into Lake Erie tributaries. Ohio alleged that this

---

§ 9.2

1. 42 U.S.C.A. § 4332.

2. 42 U.S.C.A. §§ 9601–75.

3. 42 U.S.C.A. §§ 6901–921.

4. See, e.g., Markell, States as Innovators: It's Time for a New Look to Our "Laboratories of Democracy" in Our Approach to Environmental Regulation, 58 Alb. L. Rev. 347 (1996) (discussing state regulation).

5. See, e.g., Chatham Steel Corp. v. Sapp, 858 F.Supp. 1130 (N.D.Fla.1994) (Florida long arm statute's tort provision

reaches defendant's conduct; defendant has minimum contacts with forum state).

6. 42 U.S.C.A. § 9613(f).

7. See, e.g., Waste Management of Wisconsin, Inc. v. Uniroyal, 23 Envt'l L. Rep. 20114 (D.Wis.1992); Violet v. Picillo, 613 F.Supp. 1563 (D.R.I.1985) (CERLCA's liability provisions cannot be read to imply national contacts approach to jurisdiction in private disputes).

8. See infra § 10.3.

9. 401 U.S. 493, 91 S.Ct. 1005, 28 L.Ed.2d 256 (1971).

dumping was responsible in part for the massive damage to the lake and the ensuing economic and personal harm. The Supreme Court denied leave to file the original bill in large part because the Court was convinced that the Ohio courts would have long-arm jurisdiction over the alleged polluters.[10]

Wyandotte thus seems to endorse a strong rule of allowing for jurisdiction over out-of-state polluters if the forum in the situs of the contaminated location.[11] *Wyandotte*'s authority on this point was, however, seemingly weakened by the Supreme Court's subsequent "stream of commerce" cases involving products liability. For instance, in *World–Wide Volkswagen v. Woodson*[12] the Supreme Court rejected jurisdiction in the accident state over the out-of-state seller of a defective automobile. Although the *World–Wide* dissent urged an analogy between the economic "stream" that brought the car to the accident state and the stream that brought the pollutants to Ohio,[13] a majority of the Supreme Court was not persuaded. In the subsequent case of *Asahi Metal Industry Co. v. Superior Court*[14] the Court reiterated that transport of the injurious product to the forum by a third party does not entail a finding that the defendant has minimum contacts with the forum[15] thus apparently further increasing the disjunction between *Wyandotte* and the stream-of-commerce cases.

It might be possible to reconcile *Wyandotte* with *World–Wide* and *Asahi* on the ground that the *Wyandotte* defendants engaged in harmful conduct that was knowingly directed at the forum. Unlike the *World–Wide* and *Asahi* defendants, the *Wyandotte* defendants worked their harm on the forum without the intervention of any intermediary party. This reconciliation, however, while probably satisfactorily explaining the Supreme Court cases, would render environmental enforcement difficult in many cases. Under this approach, *Wyandotte* could account for "direct" harm cases in which the contaminants find their way to the forum without the actions of a third party, but would leave "indirect" harm cases to the *World–Wide* and *Asahi* requirement of a strong showing of purposeful direction toward the forum.

Fortunately, courts have largely refused to transplant the *World–Wide* and *Asahi* line of cases to the environmental context. Instead they have showed a strong preference for allowing jurisdiction over the polluting defendants in the contaminated state even if the defendant makes a plausible showing that it did not know that its contaminants were being transported to the forum state. For instance, in *Violet v.*

---

10. Id. at 500, 91 S.Ct. at 1010.

11. This strong rule is the one adopted by the European Court of Justice under Article 5(3) of the Brussels Convention. See Handelswerkng G.J. Bier B. V. v. Mines de Potasse D'Alsace S.A., (Case No. 21/76) 1976 E.C.R. 1735 (1977) (jurisdiction allowed in state of injury).

12. 444 U.S. 286, 100 S.Ct. 559, 62 L.Ed.2d 490 (1980).

13. Id. at 306, 100 S.Ct. at 568 (Brennan, J., dissenting).

14. 480 U.S. 102, 107 S.Ct. 1026, 94 L.Ed.2d 92 (1987).

15. See supra § 7.2.

Picillo[16] one of the defendants was Rutgers University, a state university located in New Jersey and having little contact with the forum state of Rhode Island. Rutgers contracted for one year with a New Jersey company to dispose of certain hazardous compounds, and even demanded that the contractor produce licenses showing that it was permitted to conduct such disposal operations in New Jersey.[17] Apparently unknown to the University, its waste was transported to Rhode Island, the forum state, where it contributed to an environmental hazard. Rejecting the *World–Wide–Asahi* analogy, the court held that it had jurisdiction over the University. The court emphasized the desirability of providing a single forum in which to resolve all of the relevant disputes and that the defendants would not be materially prejudiced by defending in Rhode Island.[18]

Similarly in *Branch Metal Processing, Inc. v. Boston Edison Co.*[19] the defendant was a Massachusetts utility that sold scrap light poles to another Massachusetts company. The poles were resold and eventually were ground down to scrap metal in the forum state of Rhode Island. The transformers within the fixtures allegedly contained dangerous chemicals and caused a hazard during the recycling process.[20] The court held that it had jurisdiction over the Massachusetts utility notwithstanding the fact that the utility probably could not have expected that its fixtures would cause harm in Rhode Island.

These cases are in no manner aberrational. Rather, courts appear to have a nearly universal preference for allowing jurisdiction over out-of-state polluters in the contaminated state.[21] While this rule of allowing for jurisdiction in the contaminated state might seem a doubtful application of the "minimum contacts" and "purposeful availment" jurisprudence that dominates specific jurisdiction, it has strong practical justifications. Environmental cases, unlike more ordinary torts, are almost inevitably complex, multi-party cases. Narrow jurisdictional rules would require the breaking of such cases into many parts, and would consequently waste judicial and litigant resources. Moreover, the difficult questions of scientific evidence would usually be resolved much more easily close the site of contamination, rather than in a remote location.

III. COPYRIGHT AND TRADEMARK INFRINGEMENT

§ 9.3 Cross-border copyright and trademark infringement is increasingly common in the modern economy. With the growing importance of information technology, a great deal of wealth depends upon protecting rights in intellectual property. With the nearly perfectly fluid

---

16. 613 F.Supp. 1563 (D.R.I.1985).

17. Id. at 1567.

18. Id. at 1571.

19. 952 F.Supp. 893 (D.R.I.1996).

20. Id. at 904.

21. See, e.g., Chatham Steel Corp. v. Sapp, 858 F.Supp. 1130 (N.D.Fla.1994); Ida-

ho v. The M.A. Hanna Co., 819 F.Supp. 1464 (D.Idaho.1993); Baltimore and Ohio Chicago Terminal RR. Co. v. Soo Line RR. Co., 646 F.Supp. 327 (N.D.Ill.1986); Allied Towing Corp. v. Great Eastern Petroleum Corp., 642 F.Supp. 1339 (E.D.Va.1986).

transmission of information now available, infringing activity can take place simultaneously throughout the world. As a consequence, more numerous and difficult jurisdictional problems are certain to present themselves.

Infringement litigation falls into one of two basic patterns. One pattern—probably the more common—is that the alleged infringee brings suit against the alleged infringer seeking relief, usually damages and an injunction against further infringing activity. The second pattern is that the alleged infringer—often prompted by a threatening communication from the alleged infringee—sues for a declaration of non-infringement. Usually, of course, the plaintiff prefers to sue at home, and the defendant prefers not to be sued in the plaintiff's home.

In the first pattern—the alleged infringee brings suit—courts have taken a fairly expansive view. Although the Supreme Court has never addressed jurisdiction in an infringement case, its defamation cases provide a fairly close analogy. In *Keeton v. Hustler Magazine, Inc.*[1] and *Calder v. Jones*[2] the Supreme Court allowed the defamation plaintiffs to bring suit in states where the defamatory material was distributed on the theory that the forum-state distribution amounted to purposeful availment of the state's benefits and protections.[3] The defamation plaintiffs stand in a position similar to the alleged infringee; both claim that distribution of information caused them injury.

Lower courts have generally taken the expansive approach suggested by *Keeton* and *Calder*. If, as is usually the case, the infringee sues at home, the infringer's intentional distribution of a substantial amount of the infringing product in the forum state is sufficient to establish jurisdiction.[4] It is not essential, however, that the infringee sue at home. The infringee can choose another forum as long as the infringer has intentionally distributed the infringing product in the forum.[5] There is

§ 9.3

1. 465 U.S. 770, 104 S.Ct. 1473, 79 L.Ed.2d 790 (1984).

2. 465 U.S. 783, 104 S.Ct. 1482, 79 L.Ed.2d 804 (1984).

3. See supra § 7.8.

4. See, e.g., Cable/Home Communication Corp. v. Network Prods., Inc., 902 F.2d 829 (11th Cir.1990) (broadcast of infringing television program in forum sufficient for jurisdiction); Stabilisierungsfonds Fur Wein v. Kaiser Stuhl Wine Distributors Pty. Ltd., 647 F.2d 200 (D.C.Cir.1981) (distribution of allegedly infringing wine product in forum sufficient for jurisdiction); Kohler Co. v. Kohler Int'l, Inc., 196 F.Supp.2d 690 (N.D. Ill. 2002); Rainy Day Books, Inc. v. Rainy Day Books & Café, L.L.C., 186 F.Supp.2d 1158 (D. Kan. 2001); Beistle Co. v. Party U.S.A., Inc., 914 F.Supp. 92 (M.D.Pa.1996) (distribution of allegedly infringing party products in forum sufficient for jurisdiction); Infodek, Inc. v. Meredith–Webb

Printing Co., 830 F.Supp. 614 (N.D.Ga. 1993) (distribution of infringing card decks in forum sufficient for jurisdiction); Johannsen v. Brown, 788 F.Supp. 465 (D.Or. 1992) (distribution of infringing poster in plaintiff's home state sufficient for jurisdiction); Store Decor Division of Jas Int'l, Inc. v. Stylex Worldwide Industries, Ltd., 767 F.Supp. 181 (N.D.Ill.1991) (distribution of allegedly infringing sculptures in forum sufficient for jurisdiction). See also ICEE Distributors, Inc. v. J & J Snack Foods Corp., 325 F.3d 586 (5th Cir. 2003) (breach of agreement to allow exclusive distribution of trademarked products in the forum is sufficient).

5. See, e.g., Linzer v. EMI Blackwood Music, Inc., 904 F.Supp. 207 (S.D.N.Y.1995) (plaintiffs New Jersey residents; jurisdiction proper in New York because infringing songs distributed in New York).

growing litigation over the question of whether simply making the product, or allegedly infringing image or document, available through a homepage on the Internet renders the alleged infringer amenable to jurisdiction in any forum in which the homepage can be viewed.[6] The growing consensus that merely "passive" depiction through the Internet is not enough to render the party amenable to jurisdiction.[7] Apparently "something more"[8] than mere passive, electronic depiction is required to demonstrate the needed purposeful connection between the defendant and the forum.

It is not sufficient for jurisdiction that the infringee is located in the forum if the infringing product is not there distributed. For instance, in *Mantello v. Hall*,[9] the plaintiff was a New York play director. The defendants produced and presented a play in Florida, which the plaintiff claimed illegally infringed on his common law copyright to a play that he directed in New York. While the defendant had some connections to New York—including viewing plays, meeting with members of the theater community and hiring New York actors[10]—the court held these insufficient for jurisdiction. The critical fact was that the play was presented only in Florida and never in the forum state of New York.[11] Without the critical connection of distribution of the infringing product in the forum, courts have denied specific jurisdiction.[12] Moreover, the distribution in the forum must be intentional, or at least foreseeable; unintentional and unforeseeable distribution of the infringing product in the forum will not suffice.[13]

When the parties are reversed, because the alleged infringer brings a declaratory relief action to attempt to establish non-infringement, the courts are considerably less solicitous of arguments for expansive juris-

---

6. See generally, Note, Personal Jurisdiction in Cyberspace: Teaching the Stream of Commerce Dog New Internet Tricks, 22 U. Dayton L. Rev. 331 (1997) (discussing CompuServe v. Patterson, 89 F.3d 1257 (6th Cir.1996)).

7. See, e.g., Carefirst of Maryland, Inc. v. Carefirst Pregnancy Centers, Inc., 334 F.3d 390 (4th Cir. 2003); Cybersell, Inc. v. Cybersell, Inc., 130 F.3d 414 (9th Cir.1997); Bensusan Restaurant Corp. v. King, 126 F.3d 25 (2d Cir.1997); Accuweather Inc. v. Total Weather, Inc., 223 F.Supp.2d 612 (M.D. Pa. 2002)

8. Id. at 48. See also System Designs, Inc. v. New Customware Co., Inc., 248 F.Supp.2d 1093 (C.D. Utah 2003) (web site and directing training classes to the forum created minimum contacts); Inconnu Lodge v. Commbine.com, LLC, 214 F.Supp.2d 1204 (C.D. Utah 2002) (applying the "something more" test); Pavlovich v. Superior Court, 29 Cal.4th 262, 58 P.3d 2, 127 Cal. Rptr.2d 329 (2002).

9. 947 F.Supp. 92 (S.D.N.Y.1996).

10. Id. at 97.

11. Id. at 98.

12. See, e.g., Milwaukee Concrete Studios, Ltd. v. Fjeld Mfg. Co., 8 F.3d 441 (7th Cir.1993) (interpretation of venue statute); Bellepointe, Inc. v. Kohl's Dep't Stores, Inc., 975 F.Supp. 562 (S.D.N.Y.1997) (merely obtaining a business license in forum is insufficient for jurisdiction in infringement action where products not distributed in the forum); BP Chemicals Ltd. v. Formosa Chemical & Fibre Corp., 229 F.3d 254 (3d Cir.2000) (specific jurisdiction does not exist in trade secret infringement case because all alleged infringement took place outside forum); Pavlovich v. Superior Court, 29 Cal.4th 262, 58 P.3d 2, 127 Cal. Rptr.2d 329 (2002) (showing of some harm on forum-resident plaintiff insufficient in trade secret appropriation case).

13. See, e.g., Rano v. Sipa Press, Inc., 987 F.2d 580 (9th Cir.1993) (no jurisdiction over defendants where distribution in forum was unforeseeable).

diction. A good example is *Publications International, Ltd. v. Simon & Schuster, Inc.*[14] In that case the alleged infringer was an Illinois company that authored a book intended to be an "unofficial" guide to a popular, national television program. The production company for the television program, whose activities were largely centered in California, claimed that the book illegally infringed on its copyright to the television program and related trademarks. After receiving a letter from the television producers claiming that the book infringed, the book authors brought a declaratory relief action in an Illinois federal court. The infringer-plaintiffs claimed that the broadcast in Illinois of the allegedly infringed-with television program was a sufficient connection for jurisdiction. The court rejected this argument, describing the television producer's contacts with Illinois as "quite limited."[15]

If the parties were reversed, and the television show were alleged to be the infringing product, jurisdiction would have been permitted in Illinois. Why, then, a different approach in declaratory relief actions? First, if jurisdiction were as broadly available to infringers as to infringees, the already considerable incentive to win the race to the courthouse would be increased dramatically. In the common circumstance of two nationally distributed products, the party winning the race to the courthouse would always be able to dictate forum choice. Second, it seems unfair charge a party with a duty to defend in a remote forum because it broadly distributed a product with which *the other* party is alleged to have infringed.

Of course, this is not to say that the infringee can never be compelled to defend the declaratory relief action in the infringer's chosen forum. For instance, a national computer on-line service provider obtained jurisdiction over an out-of-state software author in a declaratory relief action because of a specific contractual relationship between the two centering on licensing the software.[16] In another case, jurisdiction was allowed over the alleged infringee in the infringer's chosen forum, but largely because it appeared that the parties had made the forum the center of their United States relationship relative to the products.[17] But, mere distribution of the infringed-with product in the forum is generally not sufficient for jurisdiction over the infringee.[18]

IV. PATENT INFRINGEMENT

§ 9.4 One might justifiably expect the jurisdictional analysis for patent infringement claims to mirror that for copyright and trademark

14. 763 F.Supp. 309 (N.D.Ill.1991).

15. Id. at 311.

16. See CompuServe, Inc. v. Patterson, 89 F.3d 1257 (6th Cir.1996).

17. See Modern Computer Corp. v. Ma, 862 F.Supp. 938 (E.D.N.Y.1994).

18. See, e.g., Ham v. La Cienega Music Co., 4 F.3d 413 (5th Cir.1993) (distribution of infringed-with song in forum insufficient to establish jurisdiction over the infringee in a declaratory relief action seeking a declaration of non-infringement); Zumbro, Inc. v. Imagine Foods, Inc., 861 F.Supp. 773 (D.Minn.1994) (distribution of the infringed-with product in, and sending an infringement letter to, the forum not sufficient for jurisdiction over the infringee).

infringement. Fairly often, for instance, patent infringement claims are raised as companions to other kinds of infringement claims, notably trademarks. Although a case can be made for unification of the standards for all kinds of intellectual property, patent cases retain their own distinctive flavor. One reason for this is that although patent cases are venued in the various federal district courts in the first instance,[1] appellate jurisdiction is vested exclusively in the Federal Circuit.[2] While the Federal Circuit often employs a "courtesy rule" of deference to regional circuit procedural law, that has developed its own, independent approach to the personal jurisdiction inquiry in patent cases because jurisdiction is "so intimately involved in the substance of enforcement of the patent right."[3] As it turns out, the Federal Circuit's independent approach in patent cases differs somewhat from majority approach among the regional circuits in trademark and copyright cases.

As with other kinds of intellectual property litigation, patent claims fall largely into two basic patterns. One is cases in which the alleged infringee sues the infringer for damages and an injunction against further infringement. The other is cases in which the alleged infringer—fearing impending infringement litigation—sues for a declaration to establish either or both of non-infringement or invalidity of the patent.

In the first category, actions brought by alleged infringees, the approach taken by the Federal Circuit closely follows that taken by the regional circuits in copyright and trademark cases.[4] In general, substantial, foreseeable sales of the infringing product within the forum suffice to establish jurisdiction over the infringer.[5] Even mere offers to sell the allegedly infringing product within the forum state have been held sufficient to establish minimum contacts.[6] Beyond that, even unwanted, though foreseeable, sales in the forum establish a purposeful connection between the infringer and the forum.[7] An infringer can apparently avoid jurisdiction in a state in which the infringing product is sold only if the sales activity is unforeseeable or truly trivial.[8]

§ 9.4

1. 28 U.S.C.A. § 1400.

2. 28 U.S.C.A. § 1295.

3. See Viam Corp. v. Iowa Export–Import Trading Co., 84 F.3d 424, 428 (Fed.Cir. 1996); see also 3D Systems, Inc. v. Aarotech Laboratories, Inc., 160 F.3d 1373 (Fed.Cir. 1998) (applying federal circuit law to both patent and closely related state claims with regard to assertion of personal jurisdiction).

4. See supra § 9.3.

5. See, e.g., Beverly Hills Fan Co. v. Royal Sovereign Corp., 21 F.3d 1558 (Fed. Cir.1994), cert. dismissed 512 U.S. 1273, 115 S.Ct. 18, 129 L.Ed.2d 917 (1994) (jurisdiction established over Taiwanese manufacturer of ceiling fans and its American importer because evidence established that in excess of 50 allegedly infringing units were available for sale in the forum through

several retail outlets); Wayne Pigment Corp. v. Halox and Hammond Group, Inc., 220 F.Supp.2d 931 (E.D. Wis. 2002) (delivery of eight samples to forum plus solicitation within the forum sufficient to establish jurisdiction); International Truck and Engine Corp. v. Dawson Int'l Inc., 216 F.Supp.2d 754 (N.D. Ind. 2002) (sales and solicitation in forum sufficient to establish jurisdiction)

6. See, e.g., *3D Systems, Inc.*, 160 F.3d at 1373.

7. See, e.g., Horne v. Adolph Coors Co., 684 F.2d 255 (3d Cir.1982) (substantial sales of alleged infringer's beer products on the "bootleg" market in the forum is sufficient to establish jurisdiction).

8. See, e.g., Max Daetwyler Corp. v. R. Meyer, 762 F.2d 290 (3d Cir.1985) (sale through several intermediaries of three ink

In the second category, declaratory relief actions brought by alleged infringers, the Federal Circuit has taken a considerably more expansive view. In trademark and copyright cases of the same ilk, courts have been reluctant to allow jurisdiction over the infringee because the infringed-with product is sold in the forum. The Federal Circuit, however, has taken a much more symmetrical view of the matter, essentially treating infringers and infringees alike, and thus generally rewarding the party who wins the race to the courthouse. While the Federal Circuit has recognized that "[i]t may seem at first blush strange in a declaratory judgment action to apply the same standard" to infringer and infringee, such an approach is warranted because "the question of personal jurisdiction is not a function of wrongdoing."[9] While, under this view, the mere sending of infringement "warning letters" is not enough to establish jurisdiction,[10] the sending of such letters—even to the alleged infringer's counsel—is an important contact demonstrating a purposeful connection to the state.[11] As a practical matter, the sending of such warning letters coupled with any significant distribution of the infringed-with product in the forum state will generally suffice to establish jurisdiction over the infringee.[12]

wiping blades in forum insufficient to establish jurisdiction over a German proprietor); Med–Tec Iowa, Inc. v. Computerized Imaging Reference Systems, Inc., 223 F.Supp.2d 1034 (S.D. Iowa 2002) (single sale insufficient). See also Response Reward Systems, L.C. v. Meijer, Inc., 189 F.Supp.2d 1332 (M.D. Fla. 2002) (merely making internet coupons for the product available in the forum via the Internet insufficient to establish jurisdiction).

9. See *Viam*, 84 F.3d at 428.

10. See, e.g., Silent Drive, Inc. v. Strong Industries, Inc., 326 F.3d 1194 (Fed. Cir. 2003) (warning letters without substantial other contacts insufficient for jurisdiction); Red Wing Shoe Co. v. Hockerson–Halberstadt, Inc., 148 F.3d 1355 (Fed.Cir.1998) (sending of warning letters to the forum not sufficient for jurisdiction in declaratory relief action to establish non-infringement); Genetic Implant Systems, Inc. v. Core–Vent Corp., 123 F.3d 1455, 1457 (Fed.Cir.1997) (stating in dictum that "sending infringement letters, without more activity in the forum state, is not sufficient to satisfy the requirements of due process."); Versatile Plastics, Inc. v. Sknowbest! Inc., 247 F.Supp.2d 1098 (E.D. Wis. 2003); see also Kransco Mfg. v. Markwitz, 656 F.2d 1376 (9th Cir.1981) (sending warning letters coupled only with one visit by patent holder to a trade show in the forum insufficient to establish jurisdiction over the infringee).

11. See, e.g., Deprenyl Animal Health, Inc. v. University of Toronto Innovations

Foundation, 297 F.3d 1343 (Fed. Cir. 2002) (negotiations and related contacts in a forum are sufficient to establish jurisdiction over the infringee in the forum); Akro Corp. v. Luker, 45 F.3d 1541 (Fed. Cir.1995) (sending of several warning letter to the alleged infringer in the forum, as well as the infringer's patent counsel located in another state, critical in demonstrating the infringee's purposeful connection with the forum state).

12. See, e.g., Inamed Corp. v. Kuzmak, 249 F.3d 1356 (Fed.Cir.2001) (warning letter directed to the forum coupled with prior licensing agreements and negotiations with plaintiff in the forum sufficient to satisfy minimum contacts test); *Genetic Implant*, 123 F.3d at 1455 (warning letters directed to alleged infringer in the forum as well as infringer's customers in the forum in an effort to develop forum market for infringee sufficient to establish jurisdiction over the infringee); *Viam*, 84 F.3d at 424 (warning letters directed to forum plus a marketing agreement for competing product that included the forum state sufficient to establish jurisdiction over the infringee); *Akro*, 45 F.3d at 1541 (warning letters plus sale of competing product through a distributor and licensee of the patent establishes jurisdiction over the patent holder). See also Deprenyl Animal Health, Inc. v. The University of Toronto Innovations Foundation, 297 F.3d 1343 (Fed. Cir. 2002) (in declaratory action by licensee against patent holder to establish non-infringement and invalidity, licensee could establish that patent

While the Federal Circuit's approach has a certain analytical symmetry, it is worth considering whether its policy foundations will support it. In particular, emphasis on the sending of warning letters as a significant jurisdictional contact might discourage patent holders from attempting to informally resolve their disputes, a factor the court acknowledges by not allowing letters alone to suffice for jurisdiction.[13] If the sending of such communications, coupled with a pre-existing distribution scheme for the competing product, is sufficient to allow the infringer to sue at home, the patent holder who takes these informal steps does so at the risk of losing control over forum choice. Under the Federal Circuit's approach, patent holders may actually be better advised to sue for infringement lest they find themselves defending away from home.

V.   EMPLOYMENT–RELATED STATUTORY OBLIGATIONS

§ 9.5   The employer-employee relationship in the United States is defined and modified by a large number of statutory obligations. Prominent among them are workers' compensation, unemployment insurance and anti-discrimination laws. While the details and purposes of these laws vary considerably among themselves and from state to state, certain common features appear with regard to jurisdictional questions.

The most important case of this ilk is, of course, *International Shoe Co. v. Washington*.[1] The asserted liability of the defendant in that case was for unpaid, statutorily required unemployment compensation contributions.[2] The subject of the allegedly unpaid benefits were about a dozen salesmen who carried out their activities in the forum state of Washington. As is well known, the Supreme Court upheld jurisdiction. The Court concluded that presence of the salesmen within the state during the years in which the contributions were sought was a sufficient connection to justify jurisdiction.

International Shoe came fairly close to creating a *per se* rule that jurisdiction is constitutional if the employee is in the forum state and doing the employer's work when the obligation arises. In such cases the forum-state activities are clearly related to the cause of action. And, as long as the employee is in the forum state on the company's business—and not some frolic of the employee's—there can be little question that the connection with the forum state meets the requisite standard of

---

holder had minimum contacts with licensee's home state based upon intentional creation of the business relationship and other voluntary activities such as the negotiation of the agreement between the parties).

13. See, e.g., *Red Wing*, 148 F.3d at 1361 (not allowing jurisdiction solely based upon the sending of such warning letters

because to do so would be inconsistent with federal policy favoring settlement of disputes).

§ 9.5

1. 326 U.S. 310, 66 S.Ct. 154, 90 L.Ed. 95 (1945).

2. *International Shoe*, 326 U.S. at 311, 66 S.Ct. at 156.

purposefulness for specific jurisdiction.[3] Conversely, the absence of any forum-related activities prevents an assertion of jurisdiction simply on the grounds that the court chosen by the plaintiff is the one most convenient to him.[4]

As seems to be true for non-statutory employment-related claims,[5] the most difficult questions arise relative to an employee who leaves his domicile to perform job duties in an other state, a claim there arises, and then the employee returns to his old home and brings suit on the claim. As also appears to be true for non-statutory claims,[6] the determinant appears to be whether the employer actively recruited the employee. If the employer actively recruited the employee out of the old domicile, courts will usually allow jurisdiction in the employee's old home on the theory that the employer's conduct amounts to a purposeful availment of the forum's benefits.[7] On the other hand, passive relocation without the active participation of the employer does not generally give the employee the right to return to the old home and obtain jurisdiction for claims arising from employment activities in the state of relocation.[8]

One federal employment-related statute of considerable jurisdictional significance is the Employees Retirement Income Security Act of 1974 ("ERISA").[9] ERISA is a broad federal statute that regulates almost all aspects of employment benefit plans. It contains its own special jurisdictional provision that provides that any action brought under ERISA in federal court "may be brought in the district where the plan is administered, where the breach took place, or where a defendant resides or may be found, and process may be served in any other district where a defendant resides or may be found."[10] Despite its broad language, ERISA's special jurisdictional statute has been held not to be available to

---

3. See, e.g., DiStefano v. Carozzi North America, Inc., 286 F.3d 81 (2d Cir. 2001); Rice v. Nova Biomedical Corp., 763 F.Supp. 961 (N.D.Ill.1991) (claim of wrongful firing of employee who worked in forum state allows for jurisdiction over employer and supervising employee).

4. See, e.g., Dobbs v. Chevron U.S.A., Inc., 39 F.3d 1064 (10th Cir.1994) (workers' compensation claim could not be successfully asserted in forum where injuries occurred in other states and work connections to the forum were very minimal); Dunn v. A/S Em. Z. Svitzer, 885 F.Supp. 980 (S.D.Tex.1995) (no jurisdiction in forum for a workers' compensation claim where injury occurred in a foreign country and employers had no related contacts with the forum).

5. See supra § 8.4.

6. See supra § 8.4.

7. See, e.g., Desktop Technologies, Inc. v. Colorworks Reproduction and Design, Inc., 1999 WL 98572 (E.D. Pa.); Aetna Casualty and Surety Co. v. Crowther, Inc., 221

Ill.App.3d 275, 163 Ill.Dec. 679, 581 N.E.2d 833 (1991) (jurisdiction allowed in Illinois on workers' compensation claim where Illinois employees recruited out of that state and transported to another state where they were then injured); Christiansen v. Elwin G. Smith, Inc., 598 A.2d 176 (Me. 1991) (jurisdiction in Maine allowed on workers' compensation claim where employee recruited out of Maine to perform job duties in another state and there injured).

8. See, e.g., Pytlik v. Professional Resources, Ltd., 887 F.2d 1371 (10th Cir.1989) (claim of retaliatory firing for having filed a workers' compensation claim).

9. 29 U.S.C.A. § 1001 et. seq.

10. 29 U.S.C.A. § 1132(e). A similar provision, 29 U.S.C.A. § 1451(d), applies in the case of multiemployer plans. This latter provision, however, also provides for jurisdiction in any district in which the defendant "does business," in addition to the fora provides for by Section 1132(e).

actions for declaratory relief filed by employers and other plan fiduciaries.[11] Rather, it appears to be confined in application largely to cases in
which employees sue employers (or other plan fiduciaries) in disputes
about employee benefits.[12]

The ERISA jurisdictional statute is broad, though it does not allow
the plaintiff to file in any district simply on a whim. By its terms it
requires some connecting event with the forum, such as the administration of the plan or breach of the plan provisions.[13] The list of connecting
events is quite broad. For instance, alleged breaches of plan provisions
would likely take place in the employee's home, while plan administration would likely take place in the employer's home offices. Thus, while
the list of potential fora is not infinite,[14] in most cases ERISA gives the
aggrieved plan participant a choice of courts in which to proceed.

VI.   SECURITIES AND RELATED STATUTES

§ 9.6   Both state and federal governments have enacted a wide
variety of statutes and administrative rules to protect purchasers of
securities and other kinds of investments. The most important of these
federal statutes are the so-called '33 and '34 acts, which—in the broadest
terms—require certain disclosures of information and prevent fraud and
certain misrepresentations in connection with the sale of securities.
There are other important federal statutes such as the Commodities
Exchange Act. Many states have so-called "Blue Sky" laws that impose
parallel obligations under state law.

The Supreme Court three times has addressed personal jurisdiction
in such cases, once directly and twice obliquely. The direct reference
came in *Travelers Health Association v. Virginia*.[1] In that case a Virginia
state administrative agency sued for a cease and desist order against the
defendants under a state securities law requiring a permit before selling
to Virginians.[2] The defendants were a mail order health insurance
company and its treasurer; both were located in Nebraska.[3] The health
insurer had about 800 Virginia members. The defendant relied upon its

---

11. See, e.g., Gulf Life Ins. Co. v. Arnold, 809 F.2d 1520 (11th Cir.1987); see
also T.M. Hylwa, M.D., Inc. v. Palka, 823
F.2d 310 (9th Cir.1987) (noting question of
statute's applicability but finding it unnecessary to resolve it).

12. See supra n.11.

13. See, e.g., Wellmark, Inc. v. Deguara,
257 F.Supp.2d 1209 (S.D. Iowa 2003); United Food & Commercial Workers Int'l Union–Industry Pension Fund v. Spartan
Stores, Inc., Civ. No. 92–C–3345 (N.D. Ill.
1992) (jurisdiction and venue in district because defendant's predecessor-in-interest
there administered the plan).

14. See, e.g., Waeltz v. Delta Pilots Retirement Plan, Inc., 301 F.3d 804 (7th Cir.

2002) (presence of two witnesses in forum
insufficient); Hammond v. Hernstrom, Civ.
No. 80–2051 (N.D. Ill. 1980) (venue and
jurisdiction not proper because no allegation of breach or plan administration in the
district); see also Camp v. Guercio, 464
F.Supp. 343, 345–46 (W.D.Pa.1979) (ERISA
venue and jurisdiction provisions overridden by more specific provisions of § 94 of
National Bank Act limiting suit against national banks to place in which the bank is
"established.").

§ 9.6

1. 339 U.S. 643, 70 S.Ct. 927, 94 L.Ed.
1154 (1950).

2. Id. at 644–45, 70 S.Ct. at 928.

3. Id. at 645, 70 S.Ct. at 928.

existing customers to recommend others; upon such recommendations solicitations were mailed from the Nebraska office to the prospective customers in Virginia.[4] Payments were accepted from the Virginia customers, and the corporate defendant had investigated many claims within the forum state.[5]

In upholding jurisdiction, the Court emphasized the substantiality of the relationships created. The insurance policies, noted the Court, were "systematically and widely delivered in Virginia" and "Virginia courts were available [to the company] in seeking to enforce obligations created by the group of certificates."[6] The Court was concerned that not allowing jurisdiction would create an asymmetry. The company would have access to Virginia courts if it so chose, but customers would be forced to journey to Nebraska, making litigation uneconomical in small cases.[7] The majority thus concluded that the balance tipped toward allowing the suit to proceed.

The first oblique reference occurred in *Leroy v. Great Western United Corp.*[8] In *Leroy*, Idaho state officials attempted—under Idaho state law—to block a takeover of an Idaho company by a Texas corporation. Alleging that enforcement of the Idaho state law would be unconstitutional, the Texas company brought suit in a Texas federal court, naming the Idaho officials as defendants. While noting that normally personal jurisdiction must be decided before that of venue, the Supreme Court reversed the usual order, disposing of the case on venue grounds by holding that the general federal venue statute would not permit the action to proceed in the Texas federal court.[9] Part of the Supreme Court's desire to avoid the question of personal jurisdiction stemmed from the majority's belief that the attempted assertion of jurisdiction in *Leroy* presented a difficult constitutional question.[10]

The second oblique reference occurred in *Omni Capital International v. Rudolf Wolff & Co.*[11] In *Omni*, the plaintiffs brought a claim in a Louisiana federal court on a theory of an implied right of action under the Commodities Exchange Act. The principal defendants then attempted to implead the British parties who had handled the transactions on the London market, and those British parties then moved to dismiss for lack of personal jurisdiction. The Supreme Court held that the British parties had been properly dismissed. The Supreme Court concluded that—unlike some other securities statutes, which are discussed below—the stated theory under the Commodities Exchange Act made no provision for so-called "nationwide service of process."[12] Given that lack of a special federal long-arm statute, the Court held that the amenability of the British parties to personal jurisdiction must be determined in the

---

4. Id.

5. Id.

6. Id. at 648, 70 S.Ct. at 930.

7. Id. at 648, 70 S.Ct. at 929.

8. 443 U.S. 173, 99 S.Ct. 2710, 61 L.Ed.2d 464 (1979).

9. Id. at 180, 99 S.Ct. at 2715.

10. Id. at 181, 99 S.Ct. at 2715.

11. 484 U.S. 97, 108 S.Ct. 404, 98 L.Ed.2d 415 (1987).

12. Id. at 105, 108 S.Ct. at 410.

usual fashion—application of the forum state's (Louisiana's) long-arm statute. Because the Louisiana long-arm statute concededly did not reach the British parties, the Court held them properly dismissed.

Omni prompted an important amendment to the federal rules of civil procedure, which is considered in detail elsewhere.[13] That provision, Federal Rule of Civil Procedure 4(k)(2), states that defendants who—like the British parties in *Omni*—would not be subject to personal jurisdiction in any state may be haled into court on federal law theories as long as the exercise of jurisdiction comports with the Fifth Amendment.[14] The drafters of this rule apparently believed that jurisdiction in such cases would be available as long as the defendant has minimum contacts with the United States as a whole,[15] although the viability of the so-called "national contacts" approach remains undecided by the Supreme Court,[16] and we consider these theories elsewhere.[17] In an event, *Omni* makes clear that in areas, like securities law, that are dominated by federal statutes, it is important to be conscious of the possibility of federal legislation altering the usual reference to state long-arm statutes.

One such federal statute is commonly referred to as Section 27 of the '34 Act.[18] In a series of famous opinions, lower federal courts have generally construed Section 27—for claims under the '34 Act—to override the usual requirement that the defendant be subject to jurisdiction under the forum state's long-arm statute and have minimum contacts with the forum state.[19] Lower federal courts, for the most part, have construed Section 27 and the corresponding constitutional limits under the Fifth Amendment's Due Process Clause to require only that the defendant have minimum contacts with the United States as a whole, rather than any particular state,[20] although as noted above the Supreme Court has been non-committal on this point.

Even accounting for these complications, the most important jurisdictional determinant in securities matters is whether the defendant's conduct has created foreseeable forum-state effects. Direct selling of securities to forum-state customers, as in *Travelers*, clearly has foreseeable in-state effects, and for that reason gives rise to jurisdiction in suits related to those sales.[21] On the other hand, if the sales efforts and related

13. See supra § 10.3.

14. Fed. R. Civ. P. 4(k)(2).

15. See Official Comments to F.R.C.P. 4(k).

16. See, e.g., *Omni*, 484 U.S. at 103 n.5, 108 S.Ct. at 408 n.5.

17. See infra § 10.2.

18. 15 U.S.C.A. § 78aa.

19. See, e.g., Securities Investor Protection Corp. v. Vigman, 764 F.2d 1309 (9th Cir.1985); Fitzsimmons v. Barton, 589 F.2d 330 (7th Cir.1979); Bersch v. Drexel Firestone, 519 F.2d 974 (2d Cir.1975) (Friendly, J.); Leasco Data Processing Equip. Corp. v.

Maxwell, 468 F.2d 1326 (2d Cir.1972) (Friendly, J.).

20. See, e.g., Pinker v. Roche Holdings Ltd., 292 F.3d 361 (3d Cir. 2002); *Securities Investor*, 764 F.2d at 1315; In re Daimlerchrysler AG Securities Litigation, 247 F.Supp.2d 579 (D. Del. 2003) (applying national contacts standard but finding contacts lacking); Nelson v. Quimby Island Reclamation Dist., 491 F.Supp. 1364, 1378 (N.D.Cal.1980).

21. See also Lewis v. Fresne, 252 F.3d 352 (5th Cir.2001) (direct selling to forum-state resident gave rise to minimum contacts in claim under state securities act); Securities and Exchange Comm'n v. Stead-

conduct are directed at an out-of-forum audience, the fact that some of the securities fall into the hands of forum residents cannot by itself give rise to jurisdiction because, under these circumstances, one can hardly say that the defendant has made any purposeful direction of his activities to the forum.[22]

VII. PRIVATE ANTITRUST AND OTHER UNFAIR TRADE ACTIONS

§ 9.7　Antitrust actions, as with other types of specialized statutory actions, present their own set of special jurisdictional problems. One problem is that of undifferentiated harm. Given the integrated state of the national—indeed, the world—economy, an illegal restraint of trade in one location can have ripple effects in remote locations.[1] A second problem, present with antitrust theories arising under the principal federal statutes, is whether federal law authorizes a broader jurisdictional reach than the usual requirement of minimum contacts the forum state.

Taking the latter problem first, the weight of authority is now that Section 12 of the Clayton Act[2] authorizes so-called "nationwide" service of process in private, federal antitrust actions.[3] As a special, federal long-

---

man, 798 F.Supp. 733 (D.D.C.1991), affirmed in part, vacated in part on another point, 967 F.2d 636 (D.C.Cir.1992) (sale to in-state customers gave rise to obligation to register under state Blue Sky law and allows state officials to enforce in home state courts); *Leasco Data Processing*, 468 F.2d at 1340 (defendant's alleged misrepresentations foreseeably relied upon in the forum gives rise to jurisdiction); Escoto v. U.S. Lending Corp., 675 So.2d 741 (La.App.1996) (alleged misrepresentations made in securities sold in forum state via a "private placement memorandum" supports jurisdiction under state Blue Sky Law over both individual and corporate defendants); Gutierrez v. Deloitte & Touche, 100 S.W.3d 261 (Tex. App. 2002).

22. See, e.g., *Bersch*, 519 F.2d at 999–1000.

§ 9.7

1. See Hovenkamp, Personal Jurisdiction and Venue in Private Antitrust Actions in Federal Courts: A Policy Analysis, 67 Iowa L. Rev. 485, 487 (1982).

2. 15 U.S.C.A. § 22.

3. See Go–Video, Inc. v. Akai Elec. Co., 885 F.2d 1406 (9th Cir.1989); Crompton Corp. v. Clarion Corp., 221 F.Supp.2d 683 (M.D. La. 2002); In re Isostatic Graphite Antitrust Litig., 2002–2 Trade Cas. (CCH) P73,827 (E.D. Pa. 2002); Amtrol, Inc. v.

Vent–Rite Valve Corp., 646 F.Supp. 1168 (D.Mass.1986); see also Hovenkamp, supra note 1, at 501–03 (citing Black v. Acme Markets, Inc., 564 F.2d 681) (5th Cir.1977); Coats Co. v. Vulcan Equip. Co., 459 F.Supp. 654 (N.D.Ill.1978); Centronics Data Computer Corp. v. Mannesmann, A.G. 432 F.Supp. 659 (D.N.H.1977); Cryomedics, Inc. v. Spembly, Ltd., 397 F.Supp. 287 (D.Conn. 1975).

The D.C. Circuit has held that section 12 applies only if the "venue" clause of that statute is satisfied. See GTE New Media Serv., Inc. v. BellSouth Corp., 199 F.3d 1343 (D.C.Cir.2000). Section 12 reads as follows:

Any suit, action or proceeding under the antitrust laws against a corporation may be brought not only in the judicial district whereof it is an inhabitant, but also in any district wherein it may be found or transacts business; an all process in such cases may be served in the district of which it is an inhabitant, or wherever it maybe be found. 15 U.S.C.A. § 22.

The "venue" clause—i.e., everything preceding the semicolon—allows venue where the defendant is an "inhabitant" or may "be found or transacts business" in the judicial district. If the *GTE* reading is correct, then the practical reach of section 12 would be considerably diminished. Other courts, however, have held that the general

arm statute, Section 12 of the Clayton Act implicates only the Fifth Amendment's Due Process Clause, not the Fourteenth Amendment applicable to the states, and usually applicable indirectly to federal court through their borrowing of state long-arm statutes.[4] While we discuss elsewhere[5] the Fifth Amendment's limitations on jurisdiction, suffice it to say there is considerable authority for the proposition that jurisdiction under this constitutional standard can often be assumed on the basis of the defendant's aggregate contacts with the United States as a whole.[6]

Of course, this broader jurisdictional rule has no applicability to unfair trade claims not covered by its ambit, including—obviously—antitrust and similar claims brought under state statutes. Whatever, however, the relevant forum—whether it be the forum state or the nation as a whole—determining whether jurisdiction can be asserted requires an assessment of the contacts with that forum.[7] Here the closest analogy is the intentional tort cases. As discussed above, courts appear to have settled on an "effects" test for jurisdiction. As noted earlier in this section, however, antitrust injury involves potentially diffuse effects. Therefore, allowing jurisdiction wherever an alleged antitrust violation had an effect would be tantamount to allowing worldwide jurisdiction.[8] Instead of taking this expansive approach, courts have settled on a pragmatic limitation, not unlike the one used to judge whether a plaintiff has "standing" to bring an antitrust action, which is whether the plaintiff has suffered a more specialized injury beyond that suffered by the public at large.[9] Similarly, private antitrust and other unfair trade cases may be brought only in fora in which the effects are direct and

---

venue statute, 28 U.S.C.A. § 1391, may be used to establish venue. In particular, subsection (d)—which provides that "an alien may be sued in any district"—removes any venue limitation on foreign defendants and would give section 12's service-of-process provision its full effect. See, e.g., Go–Video, Inc. v. Akai Elec. Co., 885 F.2d 1406, 1413 (9th Cir.1989). On balance, the *Go-Video* interpretation seems preferable because the venue clause of section 12 is written in permissive terms ("any suit ... may be brought") and because the general venue statute has been amended several times since the adoption of section 12 and it contains no exception for antitrust cases. The *GTE* interpretation relies heavily on the fact that the service-of-process clause–i.e., everything after the semicolon–applies "in such cases," which that court interpreted to refer to the entirety of the venue clause. The "such cases" language, however, could well just refer to "proceedings under the antitrust laws against a corporation." This point is discussed by Dodge, Antitrust and the Draft Hague Judgments Convention, 32 Law & Policy in Int'l Bus. 363, 367–68 (2001).

4. See infra § 10.2.

5. See infra § 10.2.

6. Hovenkamp, supra n.1, at 503–05.

7. The Supreme Court has only once made mention of personal jurisdiction in antitrust cases, in Goldlawr, Inc. v. Heiman, 369 U.S. 463, 82 S.Ct. 913, 8 L.Ed.2d 39 (1962). That case, however, merely construed the venue transfer statute, as all appeared to concede that jurisdiction was improperly asserted in the plaintiff's chosen forum.

8. Hovenkamp, supra n.1, at 503–05.

9. Id.; see also In re Magnetic Audiotape Antitrust Litig., 334 F.3d 204 (2d Cir. 2003) (possible effects in the forum sufficient to allow for jurisdictional discovery); Massachusetts School of Law at Andover, Inc. v. American Bar Ass'n, 142 F.3d 26 (1st Cir. 1998) (no personal jurisdiction over out-of-state individual defendants alleged to have engaged in an antitrust conspiracy directed at plaintiff where individual defendants took no significant actions in forum and had no connection to forum other than alleged injury felt within forum); Crompton Corp. v. Clariant Corp., 221 F.Supp.2d 683 (M.D. La. 2002) (minimum contacts established).

palpable, as opposed to merely the diffuse "ripple" effects felt throughout the nation and world, and in fora which are not manifestly inconvenient to the defendant.[10] If these two conditions are met, jurisdiction is proper.

VIII.   ANTI–FRAUD STATUTES

§ 9.8 Supplementing common law fraud and misrepresentation torts—whose jurisdictional implications are elsewhere discussed[1]—a host of anti-fraud statutes have been enacted at the federal and state levels. The best known general, federal anti-fraud statute is the Racketeer Influenced and Corrupt Organizations Act,[2] popularly known as "RICO." State anti-fraud statutes vary considerably in scope and coverage, although consumer fraud statutes have been enacted in many states.[3]

RICO, in particular, has had the effect of federalizing a great deal of business fraud and commercial tort litigation, and its broad reaching implications have been the subject of extensive commentary[4] and Supreme Court decisions.[5] RICO contains its own service-of-process provision allowing service "on any person in any judicial district in which such person resides, is found, has an agent, or transacts his affairs."[6] Most courts have interpreted this provision to allow for "nationwide service of process," which is a standard considerably more relaxed than the usual constitutional requirement of minimum contacts with the forum state.[7] As usually interpreted, the special service provision in RICO means that the Fifth Amendment's Due Process Clause provides the relevant constitutional limitation, and the Fifth Amendment is

---

10. See, e.g., Guinness Import Co. v. Mark VII Distributors, Inc., 153 F.3d 607 (8th Cir.1998) (no jurisdiction in action arising under state statute limiting right of distributor termination where defendant sold distributed products in forum state but only through an intermediary and did not control geographical distribution of products).

§ 9.8

1. See supra § 7.12.

2. 18 U.S.C.A. §§ 1961–68.

3. See generally Annot., Scope and Exemptions of State Deceptive Trade and Consumer Protection Acts, 89 A.L.R. 3d 399.

4. See, e.g., Posner, Clarifying a "Pattern" of Confusion: A Multi-factor Approach to Civil Rico's Pattern Requirement, 86 Mich. L. Rev. 1745 (1988).

5. See, e.g., Klehr v. A. O. Smith Corp., 521 U.S. 179, 117 S.Ct. 1984, 138 L.Ed.2d 373 (1997).

6. 18 U.S.C.A. § 1965(d).

7. See, e.g., ESAB Group, Inc. v. Centricut, Inc., 126 F.3d 617 (4th Cir.1997), cert.

denied 523 U.S. 1048, 118 S.Ct. 1364, 140 L.Ed.2d 513 (1998); Republic of Panama v. BCCI Holdings, S.A., 119 F.3d 935 (11th Cir.1997). There is growing authority, however, that RICO does not provide for jurisdiction as expansively as some of the other "nationwide service" statutes. Two circuit decisions have now held that 18 U.S.C.A. § 1915(b) is the provision of RICO that governs service of a summons. Subdivision (b) provides that process may be served "in any judicial district", but only if "the ends of justice require that other parties residing in any other district be brought before the court . . . ." This provision is significant, because it limits RICO's nationwide assertions of personal jurisdiction to a sort of ancillary jurisdiction necessary for bringing in other parties where all the parties could not be united in a single forum under ordinary minimum contacts principles. Both the Second and Ninth Circuits have now settled on this more limited reading of RICO's service provisions. See PT United Can Co. v. Crown Cork & Seal Co., 138 F.3d 65 (2d Cir.1998); Butcher's Union Local No. 498 v. SDC Investment, Inc., 788 F.2d 535 (9th Cir.1986).

generally interpreted to require minimum contacts with the United States as a whole.[8]

RICO, however, is not the only significant anti-fraud statute, and state statutes of this ilk have generated their share of litigation. Absent a special federal service provision the usual minimum contacts requirement applies. Specific jurisdiction in this context generally requires that the defendant direct its conduct towards forum-state victims. Thus, for instance, with the application of consumer fraud statutes, engaging in allegedly deceptive advertising that foreseeably reaches forum-state consumers is sufficient to create minimum contacts between the defendant and the forum.[9] However, the mere fact that the plaintiff is a forum-state domiciliary is not sufficient to establish jurisdiction if the defendant's activities cannot be shown to have been purposefully directed to the forum.[10]

8. See supra authorities cited n.7; see also infra § 10.2.

9. See, e.g., Workgroup Technology Corp. v. MGM Grand Hotel LLC, 246 F.Supp.2d 102 (D. Mass. 2003) (out-of-state hotel could be held to answer in plaintiff's home state for claim under deceptive business statute arising from dispute about booking a convention); State of Iowa ex rel. Miller v. Moneda Corp., 571 N.W.2d 1 (Iowa 1997) (allegedly deceptive mailings sent to forum-state consumers sufficient basis for jurisdiction); State of Iowa ex rel. Miller v. Baxter Chrysler Plymouth, Inc., 456 N.W.2d 371 (Iowa 1990), cert. denied 498 U.S. 998, 111 S.Ct. 556, 112 L.Ed.2d 563 (1990) (allegedly deceptive advertisements placed in a newspaper with a significant forum-state circulation sufficient basis for jurisdiction); State of Minnesota by Humphrey v. Granite Gate Resorts, Inc., 568 N.W.2d 715 (Minn.App.1997), affirmed 576 N.W.2d 747 (Minn.1998) (placing of allegedly deceptive advertisement on Internet and known to reach forum-state residents sufficient for jurisdiction).

10. Cf. Smith v. Sands Hotel & Casino, 1997 WL 162156 (D.N.J.1997) (no showing of "prior solicitation" of plaintiff, therefore no jurisdiction over defendant).

Chapter 10

SPECIAL JURISDICTIONAL PROBLEMS

Table of Sections

		Sections
I.	Introduction	10.1
II.	Federal Court Personal Jurisdiction	10.2–10.8
	A. Fifth and Fourteenth Amendment Standards	10.2
	B. Federal Rule of Civil Procedure 4(k)	10.3–10.5
	1. Incorporation of State Long–Arm Statutes	10.3
	2. The "100–Mile Bulge Rule"	10.4
	3. Federal Rule 4(k)(2)	10.5
	C. Admiralty Jurisdiction	10.6
	D. Bankruptcy Cases	10.7
	E. Removed Cases	10.8
III.	Class Actions	10.9–10.10
	A. Jurisdiction over Defendants	10.9
	B. Jurisdiction over Plaintiffs	10.10–10.11
	1. Opt-out Classes	10.10
	2. Mandatory Classes	10.11
IV.	Special Problems of Jurisdiction over Business Associations	10.12–10.17
	A. Partnerships and Other Unincorporated Associations	10.12
	B. Domestic Corporations	10.13
	C. Foreign Corporations	10.14–10.15
	1. Historical Development	10.14
	2. Current Jurisdictional Theory	10.15
	D. Corporate Parent–Subsidiary Relationships	10.16
	E. Jurisdiction over Individuals for Corporate or Fiduciary Activities	10.17
V.	Pendent Personal Jurisdiction	10.18
VI.	Foreign States and Instrumentalities	10.19

I. INTRODUCTION

§ 10.1 In the previous four chapters we explored the usual array of jurisdictional problems as they apply to civil litigation in United States courts. Ordinarily, a civil plaintiff faces four hurdles related to jurisdiction: subject matter jurisdiction, venue, personal jurisdiction and the giving of notice. From the standpoint of the discipline of the conflict of laws, the most important and involved of these is personal jurisdiction. In the ordinary circumstance, obtaining personal jurisdiction over the defendant or defendants requires that for each defendant there be affirmative authority to take jurisdiction—usually supplied by a statute or court rule—and that the exercise of jurisdiction not offend the Constitution. The latter principle is usually satisfied by demonstrating that the defendant has "minimum contacts" with the forum state so that requiring the defendant to appear does not offend "traditional notions of fair play and substantial justice."[1]

While that apparently straightforward two-step inquiry presents plenty of difficulties on its own, modern litigation presents its own array of special problems, to which this chapter is devoted. Essentially, the special problems can be divided into three classes. First, there are special problems created by the nature of the court. Here we consider in detail the degree to which the usual requirements of state court jurisdiction—which are normally followed by federal courts[2]—can be modified for federal litigation. Second, there are special problems created by the nature of the parties, usually the defendant. For instance, fictitious persons—usually corporations—can create special problems, particularly their relations to other parties. Governmental defendants, particularly foreign defendants, also warrant special consideration. Third, there are special problems created by the nature of the litigation. While the usual principles of jurisdiction developed in cases with a relatively small number of parties on each side, new forms of aggregate litigation with thousands of parties on each side can present special challenges for courts.

II.   FEDERAL COURT PERSONAL JURISDICTION

A.   FIFTH AND FOURTEENTH AMENDMENT STANDARDS

§ 10.2   The Fourteenth Amendment's Due Process Clause limits state-court jurisdiction. Ordinarily, assertions of state-court jurisdiction require that there be a state statute or court rule that authorizes the exercise of jurisdiction[1] and that each defendant have minimum contacts with the forum state.[2] In the case of state courts, the Fourteenth Amendment's Due Process Clause is the relevant one, because that amendment applies to the states.

In federal court litigation, the same standards normally apply, though it is the Fifth—not the Fourteenth—Amendment that limits

---

§ 10.1

1. International Shoe Co. v. Washington, 326 U.S. 310, 316, 66 S.Ct. 154, 158, 90 L.Ed. 95 (1945).

2. See supra § 5.15.

§ 10.2

1. See, e.g., Cal. Code Civ. Proc. § 410.10; N.Y. Civ. Prac. L & R. §§ 301, 302.

2. See Shaffer v. Heitner, 433 U.S. 186, 97 S.Ct. 2569, 53 L.Ed.2d 683 (1977).

exercises of federal authority.[3] However, under the conventional interpretation of former Federal Rule of Civil Procedure 4(e),[4] now codified in Federal Rule of Civil Procedure 4(k)(1), federal courts normally have the same jurisdictional reach as their state court counterparts, even if the plaintiff's claim is founded on federal law.[5] Thus, even though the Fourteenth Amendment does not directly limit federal court authority, its strictures are usually applied indirectly to federal courts by virtue of Federal Rule of Civil Procedure 4(k)(1).

In several cases, however, federal statutes or rules relax the usual requirement that federal courts assert no more territorial reach than their state court counterparts. Often this relaxation is accomplished by statutes purporting to authorize "nationwide service of process."[6] Courts generally interpret this awkward circumlocution as authorizing jurisdiction for federal courts to the extent that the Fifth Amendment will permit it. The Federal Rules, specifically Rule 4(k)(2), also authorize a broader territorial reach for federal courts in cases raising federal law issues in which no state court would be able to assert jurisdiction.[7]

The existence of these statutes and rules allowing federal courts broader territorial reach leads directly to an unresolved constitutional question, which is the extent to which the Fifth Amendment's Due Process Clause sets territorial limits on assertions of jurisdiction. The Supreme Court has thrice brushed by the question of Fifth Amendment limitations on personal jurisdiction without ever resolving it. In *Stafford v. Briggs*,[8] the Court considered the applicability of Section 2 of the Mandamus and Venue Act of 1962[9] to damage actions against federal officials for actions in the official capacities. The expansive provisions of this statute purported to allow jurisdiction against all defendants in a district where any defendant resided, and provided for extra-territorial

---

3. See infra § 10.3.

4. See, e.g., Arrowsmith v. United Press Int'l, 320 F.2d 219, 221 (2d Cir.1963) (en banc) (Friendly, J.).

5. See, e.g., ESAB Group, Inc. v. Centricut, Inc., 126 F.3d 617, 622 (4th Cir.1997), cert. denied 523 U.S. 1048, 118 S.Ct. 1364, 140 L.Ed.2d 513 (1998) (citing 4 Wright & Miller, Federal Practice and Procedure § 1067.1 (Supp. 1997)).

6. See, e.g., 15 U.S.C.A. § 22 (authorizing service on Clayton Act defendants "wherever [defendant] may be found"); 18 U.S.C.A. § 1915(d) (RICO actions); 42 U.S.C.A. § 9613(P) (CERCLA actions); Bankr. R. 7004(f); 15 U.S.C.A. § 78aa (Section 27 of the 1934 Act); 29 U.S.C.A. § 1132(e)(2) (ERISA actions). There is growing authority, however, that RICO does not provide for jurisdiction as expansively as some of the other "nationwide service" statutes. Two circuit decisions have now held that 18 U.S.C.A. § 1915(b) is the provision of RICO that governs service of a summons. Subdivision (b) provides that

process may be served "in any judicial district", but only if "the ends of justice require that other parties residing in any other district be brought before the court. . . ." This provision is significant, because it limits RICO's nationwide assertions of personal jurisdiction to a sort of ancillary jurisdiction necessary for bringing in other parties where all the parties could not be united in a single forum under ordinary minimum contacts principles. Both the Second and Ninth Circuits have now settled on this more limited reading of RICO's service provisions. See PT United Can Co. v. Crown Cork & Seal Co., 138 F.3d 65 (2d Cir.1998); Butcher's Union Local No. 498 v. SDC Investment, Inc., 788 F.2d 535 (9th Cir.1986).

7. See infra § 10.5.

8. 444 U.S. 527, 100 S.Ct. 774, 63 L.Ed.2d 1 (1980).

9. 28 U.S.C.A. § 1391(e).

service by certified mail.[10] For defendants being sued in a federal district court in a state with which they had little or no contact, such an application of the statute would have raised a serious question as to its constitutionality.

A majority of the Supreme Court avoided the constitutional question by interpreting the statute narrowly to apply only to mandamus actions, not to damage actions. Construing the statute against the background of the legislative history, the majority concluded that damage actions ought be subject to the usual requirements of personal jurisdiction and venue, thus avoiding issue of whether defendants without any contacts could be required to answer in a distant federal court.[11]

The two *Stafford* dissenters—Justices Stewart and Brennan—construed the Act to cover damages actions, and thus were required to address whether the statute violated the Fifth Amendment. Their answer was that the statute was constitutional. Echoing the sovereignty analysis of *World–Wide Volkswagen v. Woodson*,[12] which had been decided only a few days earlier, the dissenters reasoned that the defendants' contacts with the United States as a whole were sufficient to satisfy the Fifth Amendment. Answering the defendants' argument, the dissenters said:

> The short answer to this argument is that due process requires only certain minimum contacts between the defendant and the sovereign that created the court. [citing *Shaffer v. Heitner* and *International Shoe Co. v. Washington*]. The issue is not whether it is unfair to require a defendant to assume the burden of litigating in an inconvenient forum, but rather whether the court of a particular sovereign has power to exercise jurisdiction over a named defendant. The cases before us involve suits against residents of the United States in courts of the United States. No due process problem exists.[13]

This suggestion, neither endorsed nor rejected by the *Stafford* majority, gave rise to the so-called "national contacts" theory. The Supreme Court's subsequent treatment of this theory has been equivocal. Twice since then, in cases involving foreign defendants, the Court has gone out of its way to point out that the national contacts theory was not before it and that it was taking no position on it.[14]

Lower courts have been in a predictable quandary ever since. Essentially three positions have been staked out. One extreme is the so-called "pure" national contacts test. This approach transplants the traditional minimum contacts test to the national level. If one treats the United States as one large state, as long as the defendant has minimum

---

10. See *Stafford*, 444 U.S. at 531, 100 S.Ct. at 778, 63 L.Ed.2d 1 (quoting service provisions of the Act).

11. Id. at 542, 100 S.Ct. 774, 63 L.Ed.2d 1.

12. 444 U.S. 286, 294, 100 S.Ct. 559, 566, 62 L.Ed.2d 490 (1980).

13. *Stafford*, 444 U.S. at 554, 100 S.Ct. at 789, 63 L.Ed.2d 1.

14. Omni Capital International, Ltd. v. Rudolf Wolff & Co., Ltd., 484 U.S. 97, 105 n.5, 108 S.Ct. 404, 409 n.5, 98 L.Ed.2d 415 (1987); Asahi Metal Indus. Co. v. Superior Court, 480 U.S. 102, 113 n.*, 107 S.Ct. 1026, 1032 n.*, 94 L.Ed.2d 92 (1987).

contacts with that one large state, then assertions of jurisdiction by any federal court are constitutional.[15] This approach exalts the "sovereignty" strand of the Supreme Court's jurisdictional jurisprudence, most clearly stated in *World–Wide Volkswagen*.[16] By treating the Fourteenth Amendment as, in part, a limitation of state sovereignty, the necessary implication is that the Fifth Amendment—addressed to the federal government, not states—must treat the federal government as a unitary sovereign. This essentially was the position of the *Stafford* dissenters.

At the other extreme is the suggestion that jurisdiction is not a question of sovereignty at all, but rather a question of fairness to defendants. At this pole, the Fifth and Fourteenth Amendment standards are identical.[17] This approach draws some support from the Supreme Court's post-*World–Wide Volkswagen* emphasis on litigant fairness and apparent rejection of state sovereignty as an independent limitation on jurisdictional authority. The most obvious Supreme Court rejection of the *World–Wide Volkswagen* sovereignty strand occurred in *Insurance Corp. of Ireland, Ltd. v. Compagnie des Bauxites de Guinee*.[18] In that case, decided less than two years after *World–Wide Volkswagen*, the Court held that there was no "independent" federalism aspect to the due process analysis, but rather any limitation on jurisdiction was a function of the defendant's individual liberty interest. Some courts have concluded that the *Bauxites* rejection of the *World–Wide Volkswagen* sovereignty analysis undercuts the pure national contacts approach.[19]

There is an emerging better, moderate view that rejects both polar positions. Under this moderate view, the existence of minimum contacts with the nation as a whole is prima facie sufficient for jurisdiction. The defendant, however, can defeat jurisdiction by showing that the choice of forum is sufficiently inconvenient that it will handicap the defendant's ability to mount a defense. A good example of this middle approach is *Republic of Panama v. BCCI Holdings*.[20] In that case, the court held that banks with extensive operations on the east coast of the United States could not avoid jurisdiction in a federal district court located in Florida. Although the banks lacked minimum contacts with Florida, the court concluded that their eastern operations suggested that "Florida is not significantly more inconvenient than other districts in this country" and

---

15. See, e.g., In re Magnetic Audiotape Antitrust Litig., Tex. Int'l Magnetics, 334 F.3d 204 (2d Cir. 2003); Medical Mut. of Ohio v. deSoto, 245 F.3d 561, 575 (6th Cir.2001); ISI International, Inc. v. Borden Ladner Gervais LLP, 256 F.3d 548 (7th Cir. 2001); United States Securities and Exchange Comm'n v. Carrillo, 115 F.3d 1540 (11th Cir.1997); Busch v. Buchman, Buchman & O'Brien, 11 F.3d 1255 (5th Cir. 1994); Go–Video, Inc. v. Akai Elec. Co., 885 F.2d 1406 (9th Cir.1989); Lisak v. Mercantile Bancorp., Inc., 834 F.2d 668 (7th Cir. 1987); Federal Trade Commission v. Jim Walter Corp., 651 F.2d 251 (5th Cir. Unit A 1981); United States v. International Broth-

erhood of Teamsters, 945 F.Supp. 609 (S.D.N.Y. 1996).

16. 444 U.S. at 291, 100 S.Ct. at 564.

17. See, e.g., Republic of Panama v. BCCI Holdings S.A., 119 F.3d 935, 942 (11th Cir.1997) (summarizing competing views).

18. 456 U.S. 694, 702 n.10, 102 S.Ct. 2099, 2105 n.10, 72 L.Ed.2d 492 (1982).

19. See, e.g., *BCCI Holdings*, 119 F.3d at 942; Busch v. Buchman & O'Brien, 11 F.3d 1255 (5th Cir. 1994).

20. 119 F.3d 935 (11th Cir.1997).

noted that the "defendants have presented no evidence that their ability to defend this lawsuit will be compromised significantly" by the choice of forum.[21] Not only is this middle position gaining acceptance in the courts,[22] it has the support of influential commentators.[23]

The advantages of this middle approach are several.[24] First, it is consistent with later Supreme Court decisions suggesting that constitutional limitations on jurisdiction are both a matter of evaluating contacts with the forum *and* of individual fairness to the defendant.[25] By treating these separately, this approach seems consistent with the Supreme Court's late-evolving two-step approach. Second, it gives the political branches of the federal government some flexibility to allow for nationwide enforcement of important federal laws. It is significant that Congress has enacted these broad jurisdictional statutes in areas where slavish adherence to the requirement of contacts with a particular state would be problematic. The federal interpleader statute,[26] for instance, would be ineffectual if the competing claimants could not be brought before a single forum for a determination as to their relative rights. Third, it avoids abusive exercises of nationwide jurisdiction. A Florida defendant could avoid a small claims action in Alaska by demonstrating his inability to effectively mount a defense to such a suit in a distant forum.[27] A pure national contacts approach would leave such parties to the mercy of venue transfer and forum non conveniens motions. Finally, this position has at least the tentative endorsement of the Advisory Committee that drafted the 1993 amendments to the Federal Rules of Civil Procedure. The Committee recognized the authority for the national contacts approach, but then went on to state that "[t]here also may be a further Fifth Amendment constraint in that a plaintiff's forum selection might be so inconvenient to a defendant that it would be a denial of 'fair play and substantial justice' required by the due process clause, even though the defendant had significant affiliating contacts with the United States."[28] While, of course, these notes are not binding authority, they are persuasive, and the fact that Supreme Court ultimately promul-

---

21. Id. at 948.

22. Medical Mut. of Ohio v. deSoto, 245 F.3d 561, 575 (6th Cir.2001) (Gilman, J., concurring); Pinker v. Roche Holdings, Ltd., 292 F.3d 361 (3d Cir. 2002) (citing *BCCI Holdings* for its national contacts analysis and assuming that a fairness analysis is also required).

23. Id. at 945 n.18 (citing Fullerton, Constitutional Limitations on Nationwide Personal Jurisdiction in Federal Courts, 79 Nw. U. L. Rev. 1 (1984); Lusardi, Nationwide Service of Process: Due Process Limitations on the Power of the Sovereign, 33 Vill. L. Rev. 1 (1988); Wright & Miller, Federal Practice and Procedure § 1067.1 (1987)); see also Sann, Personal Jurisdiction in Federal Question Suits: Towards a

Unified and Rational Theory for Personal Jurisdiction Over Non–Domiciliary and Alien Defendants, 16 Pac. L.J. 1 (1984).

24. For commentary discussing this position and describing it as the majority approach, see, e.g., Casad, Personal Jurisdiction in Federal Question Cases, 70 Tex. L. Rev. 1589, 1600 (1992).

25. See, e.g., Asahi Metal Indus. Co. v. Superior Court, 480 U.S. 102, 113, 107 S.Ct. 1026, 1033, 94 L.Ed.2d 92 (1987).

26. 28 U.S.C.A. § 1397.

27. Cf. *World–Wide*, 444 U.S. at 296, 100 S.Ct. at 566, 62 L.Ed.2d 490.

28. 1993 Advisory Committee Notes to F.R.C.P. 4(k).

gated the revisions suggested by the Committee is some indication that its views are plausible.

B. FEDERAL RULE OF CIVIL PROCEDURE 4(k)

1. *Incorporation of State Long–Arm Statutes*

§ 10.3   Federal courts generally have the same territorial reach as their state court counterparts. Thus, in most cases—regardless of the basis for federal subject matter jurisdiction—federal courts follow their home state's long-arm statute. The duty of federal courts to follow local jurisdictional law has been long settled in diversity cases.[1] In large part, this duty to follow local jurisdictional law was grounded upon a reading of former Federal Rule of Civil Procedure 4(e). That rule provided that "service [of process] . . . may be made under the circumstances and in the manner" provided for by state statute.[2] This "under the circumstances" language was generally thought to incorporate state long-arm statutes.[3]

One potential complication is long-arm statutes, such as California's,[4] that allow for all of the jurisdiction that the Constitution will permit. Such statutes, unlike the more definite and limited type exemplified by New York's,[5] could be interpreted to incorporate the potentially more flexible limitations of the Fifth Amendment's Due Process Clause, rather than the Fourteenth Amendment's, which is applicable to states.[6] Even with long-arm statutes of the California type, however, courts generally held that federal courts, without a special federal long-arm statute,[7] had no more reach than their state-court counterparts.[8] This conclusion, at least in diversity cases, found implicit support in the Supreme Court's decision in *Insurance Corporation of Ireland, Ltd. v. Compagnie des Bauxites de Guinee.*[9] In *Bauxites*, a diversity case commenced in a federal district court located in Pennsylvania, the Supreme Court discussed the applicability of jurisdictional principles essentially as if the case had been commenced in a state court.

While the applicability of local jurisdictional law in diversity cases seemed relatively settled, the question remained less clearly decided in federal question cases. Under former Federal Rule of Civil Procedure 4(e) the majority, though not unanimous, view among the federal courts

§ 10.3

1. See, e.g., Arrowsmith v. United Press Int'l, 320 F.2d 219 (2d Cir.1963) (en banc) (Friendly, J.).

2. F.R.C.P. 4(e) (version effective until 1993).

3. See, e.g., United Elec., Radio and Machine Workers v. 163 Pleasant Street Corp., 960 F.2d 1080 (1st Cir.1992), appeal after remand 987 F.2d 39 (1st Cir.1993); De-James v. Magnificence Carriers, Inc., 654 F.2d 280 (3d Cir.), cert. denied 454 U.S. 1085, 102 S.Ct. 642, 70 L.Ed.2d 620 (1981).

4. Cal. Code Civ. Proc. § 410.10.

5. N.Y. Civ. Prac. L. & R. § 302.

6. See supra § 10.2.

7. See supra § 10.2.

8. Wells Fargo & Co. v. Wells Fargo Express Co., 556 F.2d 406, 417–18 (9th Cir.1977); Edward J. Moriarty & Co. v. General Tire & Rubber Co., 289 F.Supp. 381 (S.D.Ohio 1967).

9. 456 U.S. 694, 102 S.Ct. 2099, 72 L.Ed.2d 492 (1982).

was that they were required to follow local jurisdictional law.[10] A minority position, however, was that in federal question suits in federal court there was no necessary requirement of minimum contacts with the forum state.[11] This latter position was based upon the theory that the long-arm statutes that reach to the constitutional limits ought to be construed to reach as far as constitutionally permissible. In the case of federal courts, that relevant limit is the Fifth Amendment's Due Process Clause, which—as noted above[12]—is *prima facie* fulfilled as long as the defendant's aggregate contacts with the nation are enough to satisfy the minimum contacts test.

This circuit split was effectively resolved by the Supreme Court's decision in *Omni Capital International v. Rudolf Wolff & Co.*[13] *Omni* involved an attempted impleader action against two English defendants in a federal district court in Louisiana. The underlying action was based upon a federal statute, the Commodities Exchange Act—a statute that does not have an applicable special service-of-process provision. Concluding that the Louisiana long-arm statute could not reach the English parties, the district court dismissed. A divided en banc court of the Fifth Circuit affirmed.[14] Nine judges concluded that the impossibility of reaching the English defendants under the Louisiana statute precluded litigating against them; six judges would have construed Federal Rule 4 to allow jurisdiction to the extent consistent with the Fifth Amendment.[15]

The Supreme Court unanimously sided with the district court and the Fifth Circuit majority. Construing the pre–1993 version of Federal Rule 4, the Court held that "under Rule 4(e), a federal court normally looks either to a federal statute or to the long arm statute of the State in which it sits...."[16] Authorization of a more extensive jurisdictional reach, concluded the majority, would require legislative action or an amendment to the Federal Rules.[17]

In part codifying *Omni*'s reading, and in part picking up on the Court's suggestion for amendment, Federal Rule 4 was amended in 1993. Rule 4(k) now provides in its relevant part that a defendant in a federal court is subject to jurisdiction if the defendant is one "who could be subjected to the jurisdiction of a court of general jurisdiction in the state in which the district court is located ... "[18] While the language of the new Rule 4(k) is clear enough, the advisory committee comments make

---

10. See Comment, Federal Question Jurisdiction: Must a Defendant Have Minimum Contacts with the State Whose Long–Arm Statute is Used to Serve Process?, 54 La. L. Rev. 407, 10 (1993) (reporting that the First, Third, Fifth, Ninth and Eleventh circuits took the position under former F.R.C.P. 4(e) that state long-arm statutes apply in federal question cases).

11. Id. (reporting that the Sixth and Seventh Circuits took the position that federal courts were not required to follow local jurisdictional law in federal suits).

12. See supra § 10.2.

13. 484 U.S. 97, 108 S.Ct. 404, 98 L.Ed.2d 415 (1987).

14. Point Landing, Inc. v. Omni Capital Int'l Ltd., 795 F.2d 415 (5th Cir.1986) (en banc).

15. Id. at 428 (Wisdom, J., concurring in part and dissenting in part).

16. *Omni Capital*, 484 U.S. at 105, 108 S.Ct. at 410, 98 L.Ed.2d 415.

17. Id.

18. F.R.C.P. 4(k)(1)(A).

plain that it is intended to carry forward the essence of the previous version as to the territorial reach of federal courts.[19] Thus, absent special federal long-arm legislation[20] or one of the special circumstances discussed below,[21] federal courts have the same territorial reach as their state court counterparts.

2.   *The "100–Mile Bulge Rule"*

§ 10.4   Federal Rule 4(k)(1)(B) provides that a defendant is subject to personal jurisdiction in a federal court if he is one "who is a party joined under Rule 14 or Rule 19 and is served at a place within a judicial district of the United States and not more than 100 miles from the place where the summons issues ... "[1] This somewhat odd provision has been part of the Federal Rules since 1963 when it was enacted as Rule 4(f).[2] Its relocation to Rule 4(k) effected no substantive change.[3]

The 100–mile bulge rule functions as a narrowly tailored federal long-arm statute. It applies only to assertions of jurisdiction over third-party defendants and parties who, under Rule 19, are needed for just adjudication. The fact that it might be desirable to add the missing party does not alone qualify under the narrow circumstances of the bulge rule.[4]

Early on in the life of the 100–mile bulge rule, there was some doubt as to whether it operated to extend the in personam jurisdiction of federal courts, or whether it merely gave authority for the service of the summons on ancillary parties within 100 miles of the courthouse.[5] The "no jurisdictional effect" view was eventually rejected, largely on the pragmatic ground that if the bulge rule "did no more than [authorize delivery of the summons] it would have accomplished little."[6] State service statutes invariably provide that process can be served outside the state over parties subject to the court's in personam jurisdiction, so a rule merely authorizing delivery of the summons to ancillary parties within 100 miles of the federal court would be meaningless.[7]

Thus, successful invocation of the 100–mile bulge rule requires three showings. First, the party served under the rule must be one that comes

---

19. 1993 Advisory Committee Notes to F.R.C.P. 4(k).

20. See supra § 10.2.

21. See infra §§ 10.4–10.6.

§ 10.4

1. F.R.C.P. 4(k)(1)(B).

2. 1963 Advisory Committee Notes to F.R.C.P. 4(f).

3. 1993 Advisory Committee Notes to F.R.C.P. 4(k).

4. See, e.g., Freiman v. Lazur, 925 F.Supp. 14 (D.D.C.1996) (rule does not allow for extended jurisdiction over joint tortfeasor in a claim against that joint tortfeasor by the main plaintiff); see also Temple v. Synthes Corp., 498 U.S. 5, 111 S.Ct. 315, 112 L.Ed.2d 263 (1990) (joint tortfeasors are merely permissive, not necessary, parties).

5. See, e.g., Karlsen v. Hanff, 278 F.Supp. 864 (S.D.N.Y.1967) (rule does not give any in personam jurisdiction beyond that permitted by forum state's long-arm statute), overruled by Coleman v. American Export Isbrandtsen Lines, 405 F.2d 250 (2d Cir.1968).

6. *Coleman*, 405 F.2d at 252 (Friendly, J.).

7. Id.

within its terms, i.e., a Rule 14 or 19 party. Merely permissive co-defendants, for instance, are not within the ambit of the bulge rule.[8]

Second, the physical act of service must take place within the "bulge" area. The usual formalities of service must be followed, of course. For corporate defendants—undoubtedly the most frequently served parties under the bulge rule—the summons and complaint usually must be delivered to "an officer, a managing or general agent, or any other agent authorized by law to receive service of process. . . . "[9] If such a person cannot be found to be served within 100 miles of the courthouse, the bulge rule cannot be successfully invoked.[10] The "bulge" area includes only areas within a judicial district; a federal courthouse close to, say, the Canadian border would not give the parties license to serve an ancillary party in Canadian territory.[11] As to the definition of the 100 miles, courts have nearly universally interpreted this to mean 100 "air miles"—or, colloquially, "as the crow flies"—rather than 100 driving miles.[12] Of course, its narrow geographical scope means that the bulge rule is of use only in multistate metropolitan areas such as Omaha, New York City and Washington, D.C.; it adds nothing to the jurisdiction of courts not situated within 100 miles of any state boundary.

Third, the defendant must have contacts that make the assertion of jurisdiction fair. Courts have split as to the area with which the defendant must have contacts. The view urged by Judge Friendly in his famous decision for the Second Circuit is that the defendant's minimum contacts with the "bulge" state—i.e., the state in which service is effected under the bulge rule—will support jurisdiction.[13] The competing view—followed by a larger number of courts—is that the defendant must have minimum contacts with the "bulge" area itself, not merely the bulge state taken as a whole.[14]

The practical difference between the views is relatively slight. One could imagine a circumstance in which an ancillary party has its headquarters in a state bordering the forum state but more than 100 miles from the federal forum, and relatively few business activities within the "bulge area." If, say, the corporate president were served within the bulge area, jurisdiction would lie under Judge Friendly's view because of

---

8. See supra n.4.

9. F.R.C.P. 4(h)(1).

10. See, e.g., Langsam–Borenstein Partnership v. NOC Enterprises, Inc., 137 F.R.D. 217 (E.D.Pa.1990); Drames v. Milgreva Compania Maritima, S.A., 571 F.Supp. 737 (E.D.Pa.1983).

11. F.R.C.P. 4(k)(1)(B).

12. See, e.g., Sprow v. Hartford Ins. Co., 594 F.2d 412 (5th Cir.1979); Langsam–Borenstein Partnership v. Krausz, 137 F.R.D. 217 (E.D.Pa.1990); Pillsbury Co. v. Delta Boat & Barge Rental, Inc., 72 F.R.D. 630 (E.D.La.1976); Pierce v. Globemaster Baltimore, Inc., 49 F.R.D. 63 (D.Md.1969).

13. *Coleman*, 405 F.2d at 252.

14. See, e.g., Quinones v. Pennsylvania General Ins. Co., 804 F.2d 1167 (10th Cir. 1986); Sprow v. Hartford Ins. Co., 594 F.2d 412 (5th Cir.1979); Cummins Engine Co. v. Hyundai MIPO Dockyard Co. (In re Rationis Enterprises, Inc.), 210 F.Supp.2d 421 (S.D.N.Y. 2002); Langsam–Borenstein Partnership v. NOC Enterprises, Inc., 137 F.R.D. 217 (E.D.Pa.1990); Associates Commercial Corp. v. Lincoln General Ins. Co., 702 F.Supp. 104 (W.D.Pa.1988); Pillsbury Co. v. Delta Boat & Barge Rental, Inc., 72 F.R.D. 630 (E.D.La.1976); McGonigle v. Penn–Central Transp. Co., 49 F.R.D. 58 (D.Md.1969).

the defendant's contacts with the bulge state, while jurisdiction would not lie under the competing, "bulge area" view because of the lack of contacts with the bulge area. One might also imagine a difference if the bulge area encompasses three or more states. Under the "bulge area" view, presumably the defendant's contacts anywhere in the bulge area (even in a state other than the service state) ought to count, while Judge Friendly's view would count only contacts with the state in which service was effected. But, cases in which choosing between the two views makes any practical difference are rare—if they exist at all—and the 100–mile bulge rule provides a modest addition to the in personam jurisdiction of federal courts.

3. *Federal Rule 4(k)(2)*

§ 10.5 A 1993 amendment to the Federal Rules of Civil Procedure provides that:

> If the exercise of jurisdiction is consistent with the Constitution and the laws of the United States, serving a summons or filing a waiver is also effective, with respect to claims arising under federal law, to establish jurisdiction over the person of any defendant who is not subject to the jurisdiction of the courts of general jurisdiction of any state.[1]

This rule responded to the Supreme Court's decision in *Omni Capital International, Ltd. v. Rudolf Wolff & Co.*[2] In *Omni*, a suit arising under a federal statute, the Supreme Court concluded that the inability of the forum state's long-arm statute to reach the parties challenging jurisdiction necessitated their dismissal.[3] The Court recognized, however, a certain anomaly in constraining the enforcement of federal laws to the reach of state long-arm statutes, but suggested that the appropriate response would be a legislative one.[4] Federal Rule 4(k)(2) was intended to be that response.[5]

Rule 4(k)(2) is limited in its application, however. First, it adds nothing to the jurisdiction of federal courts in cases in which there is a special federal long-arm statute, as in some securities, environmental, and other cases.[6] Where one of those statutes provides for so-called "nationwide"—or, more grandly, "worldwide"—service of process, courts have *prima facie* allowed jurisdiction as long as the defendant has minimum contacts with the United States, considered as a single forum.[7]

Second, Rule 4(k)(2) requires that there be no state court that could reach the defendant. Thus, Rule 4(k)(2) does not allow the plaintiff to

---

§ 10.5

1. Fed. R. Civ. P. 4(k)(2).

2. 484 U.S. 97, 108 S.Ct. 404, 98 L.Ed.2d 415 (1987)

3. See supra § 10.3.

4. *Omni*, 484 U.S. at 105, 108 S.Ct. at 410.

5. See 1993 Advisory Committee Notes to F.R.C.P. 4(k)(2).

6. 15 U.S.C.A. § 22 (service may be made on a Clayton Act defendant "wherever [defendant] may be found"); 18 U.S.C.A. § 1915(b), (d) (broad service provisions for RICO defendants); see supra § 10.2.

7. See supra § 10.2.

choose a federal court in a state in which the defendant has few or no contacts if the defendant has enough contacts with some other state that he would be subject to jurisdiction under the relevant statutory and constitutional principles.[8] This limitation makes a great deal of sense. Without such limitation, the Rule would essentially be a license to forum shop throughout the United States against defendants in federal cases, subject only to venue and transfer limitations.

Third, Rule 4(k)(2) applies to "claims arising under federal law...."[9] This language obviously includes cases that qualify for federal question subject matter jurisdiction[10] and excludes those that qualify for federal subject matter jurisdiction only on the basis of the diversity of citizenship of the parties.[11] There is growing authority, however, that Rule 4(k)(2) also includes within its scope admiralty claims. In *World Tanker Carriers Corp. v. M/V Ya Mawlaya*,[12] the Fifth Circuit concluded that expansive language of the Rule encompassed more than classic "federal question" suits, but also included admiralty cases because of their essentially federal character.[13] The *World Tanker* interpretation has been followed outside the Fifth Circuit with relatively little dissent.[14]

Where it applies, Rule 4(k)(2) has generally allowed plaintiffs to hale defendants before federal courts on the so-called "national contacts" theory, often subject to the defendant's ability to defeat jurisdiction by showing genuine and serious inconvenience in litigating in the chosen forum.[15] Rule 4(k)(2) has proved to be of the most utility to litigants who file in federal courts located in states, such as New York, with long-arm statutes that clearly stop short of the constitutional limits. In cases founded on federal law, in which most of the defendant's contacts are with a state such as New York, but the long-arm statute does not reach its activities, Rule 4(k)(2) has proved useful in circumventing those statutory restrictions.[16] In most other cases Rule 4(k)(2) has proved little

---

8. See, e.g., United States v. Swiss American Bank, 191 F.3d 30 (1st Cir.1999) (defendant must make prima facie showing of alternative forum to avoid Rule 4(k)(2)); American Telephone & Telegraph Co. v. Compagnie Bruxelles Lambert, 94 F.3d 586 (9th Cir.1996); Warn v. M/Y Maridome, 961 F.Supp. 1357 (S.D.Cal.1997), affirmed 169 F.3d 625 (9th Cir.1999), cert. denied 528 U.S. 874, 120 S.Ct. 179, 145 L.Ed.2d 151 (1999).

9. F.R.C.P. 4(k)(2).

10. 28 U.S.C.A. § 1331.

11. 28 U.S.C.A. § 1332; see also In re Telectronics Pacing Sys., Inc. Litig., 953 F.Supp. 909 (S.D.Ohio 1997) (Rule 4(k)(2) does not apply to claims arising solely under state law).

12. 99 F.3d 717 (5th Cir.1996).

13. Id. at 722.

14. See, e.g., West Africa Trading & Shipping Co. v. London Int'l Group, 968

F.Supp. 996 (D.N.J.1997) (Rule 4(k)(2) applies to admiralty cases); Western Equities, Ltd. v. Hanseatic, Ltd., 956 F.Supp. 1232 (D.Vi.1997) (same); but see Eskofot v. E.I. Du Pont De Nemours & Co., 872 F.Supp. 81 (S.D.N.Y.1995) (Rule 4(k)(2) limited to federal questions suits based upon 28 U.S.C.A. § 1331).

15. See, e.g., ISI International, Inc. v. Borden Ladner Gervais LLP, 256 F.3d 548 (7th Cir. 2001) (employing a "national contacts" approach); United States v. International Brotherhood of Teamsters, 945 F.Supp. 609 (S.D.N.Y. 1996) (same); Pyrenee, Ltd. v. Wocom Commodities, Ltd., 984 F.Supp. 1148 (N.D.Ill.1997); see also supra § 10.2 (discussing national contacts and competing theories).

16. See, e.g., Aerogroup Int'l, Inc. v. Marlboro Footworks, Ltd., 956 F.Supp. 427 (S.D.N.Y.1996); United States of America v. International Brotherhood of Teamsters, 945 F.Supp. 609 (S.D.N.Y.1996).

more than an alternative rationale for results that could have been reached either by application of the forum state's long-arm statute or a special federal jurisdictional statute.[17]

The party resisting jurisdiction under Rule 4(k)(2) has the burden with regard to the question of whether any other state would have jurisdiction. Thus it becomes that party's burden to point the court to some other state that might have jurisdiction so that the court can assess whether that state's long-arm statute and the Fourteenth Amendment test—i.e., "minimum contacts" with that state—is met. If the party resisting jurisdiction does not carry this burden, the court then proceeds to the question of whether the constitutional test mandated by Rule 4(k)(2)—i.e., the question of whether jurisdiction would comport with the Fifth Amendment—is met. That latter test usually involves the question of whether the party resisting jurisdiction has minimum contacts with the United States as a whole.[18]

C. ADMIRALTY JURISDICTION

§ 10.6 Admiralty law is a fascinating topic, a complete exposition of which can be found in any of the treatises on the subject.[1] A grant of subject matter jurisdiction in admiralty and maritime cases has been with federal courts since the early days of the Republic.[2] In contrast to the parallel grant of diversity jurisdiction to federal courts,[3] the admiralty grant of jurisdiction has always carried with it a power for federal courts to expound substantive, common law rules.[4] Always subject to the authority of Congress to pass admiralty statutes, federal courts (and state courts where they have jurisdiction) have applied a relatively uniform body of common law, derived principally from international practice and received most directly from the English courts.[5] Thus, the rule of *Erie Railroad Co. v. Tompkins*,[6] which requires diversity courts to adhere to state substantive law, has no application in admiralty cases.

---

17. See, e.g., *Pyrenee*, 984 F.Supp. at 1159–60.

18. See, e.g., Glencore Grain Rotterdam B.V. v. Shivnath Rai Harnarain Co., 284 F.3d 1114 (9th Cir. 2002); Base Metal Trading, Ltd. v. OJSC Novokuznetsky Aluminum Factory, 283 F.3d 208 (4th Cir. 2002), cert. denied 537 U.S. 822, 123 S.Ct. 101, 154 L.Ed.2d 30 (2002); ISI International, Inc. v. Borden Ladner Gervais LLP, 256 F.3d 548, 552 (7th Cir. 2001); Graduate Mgmt. Admission Council v. RVR Narasimha Raju, 241 F.Supp.2d 589 (E.D. Va. 2003).

§ 10.6

1. See, e.g., Schoenbaum, Admiralty and Maritime Law (3d ed. 2001); Gilmore & Black, The Law of Admiralty (2d ed. 1975).

2. 1 Schoenbaum, supra n.1, at 16–18.

3. See generally Borchers, The Historical Origins of Diversity Jurisdiction, the Rise of Legal Positivism, and a Brave New World for *Erie* and *Klaxon*, 72 Texas L. Rev. 79 (1993).

4. See Norfolk Shipbuilding & Drydock Corp. v. Garris, 532 U.S. 811, 121 S.Ct. 1927, 150 L.Ed.2d 34 (2001) (recognizing cause of action in admiralty for negligence causing death). 1 Schoenbaum, supra n.1, at 63–65.

5. 1 Schoenbaum, supra n.1, at 63–65.

6. 304 U.S. 64, 58 S.Ct. 817, 82 L.Ed. 1188 (1938); see supra §§ 3.36—3.48.

The current statute (which has changed little from that enacted with the First Judiciary Act) vests admiralty jurisdiction in federal courts as follows:

> [T]he district courts shall have original jurisdiction, exclusive of the courts of the States, of: (1) Any civil case of admiralty or maritime jurisdiction, saving to suitors in all cases all other remedies to which they are otherwise entitled. (2) Any prize brought into the United States and all proceedings for the condemnation of property taken as prize.[7]

Of course, the phrase "of admiralty or maritime jurisdiction" is not self-defining, and an elaborate body of law has developed around this phrase. An important concept is that admiralty jurisdiction extends to commercially-navigable interstate bodies of water, even if they are inland; fairly early on the Supreme Court rejected the English rule that limited admiralty jurisdiction to the oceans.[8]

If one assumes that the waterway in question is navigable, as that term is used in this context, difficult questions of subject matter jurisdiction can still arise in tort, contract and other cases. In tort cases, for instance, the rule once was that the dispute was an admiralty case if the injury was felt on a navigable body of water.[9] This rule was partially repudiated by the so-called Admiralty Extension Act,[10] which extended admiralty tort jurisdiction to injuries suffered on shore if caused by a ship.[11] Tort jurisdiction was later limited in a series of cases beginning with *Executive Jet Aviation, Inc. v. Cleveland*,[12] which rejected admiralty jurisdiction in a case in which an airplane crashed into a navigable lake. Admiralty jurisdiction will not lie, held the Court, unless the wrong bears "a significant relationship to traditional maritime activity."[13] As a result of *Executive Jet* and its progeny, admiralty tort jurisdiction will not lie unless the injury is felt on navigable water (or the shore under the circumstances set forth in Admiralty Extension Act), it has a "substantial relation" to traditional maritime activities, and the injury has a potential impact on maritime commerce.[14]

Admiralty contract jurisdiction is no simpler a matter. Unlike torts, contract jurisdiction depends relatively little on territory. As traditional-

---

7. 28 U.S.C.A. § 1333.

8. See The Propellor Genesee Chief v. Fitzhugh, 53 U.S. (12 How.) 443, 13 L.Ed. 1058 (1851); see also 1 Schoenbaum, supra n.1, at 65–66.

9. See, e.g., The Admiral Peoples, 295 U.S. 649, 55 S.Ct. 885, 79 L.Ed. 1633 (1935).

10. 46 U.S.C.A. § 740.

11. 1 Schoenbaum, supra n.1, at 78–79.

12. 409 U.S. 249, 93 S.Ct. 493, 34 L.Ed.2d 454 (1972).

13. Id. at 268, 93 S.Ct. at 504, 34 L.Ed.2d 454.

14. See Calhoun v. Yamaha Motor Corp., U.S.A., 216 F.3d 338 (3d Cir.2000), on remand from 516 U.S. 199, 116 S.Ct. 619, 133 L.Ed.2d 578 (1996) (holding that a collision between a jet-ski and an anchored pleasure boat in territorial state waters bore a sufficient nexus to traditional maritime activity so as to invoke admiralty jurisdiction); Gibbs v. Carnival Cruise Lines, 314 F.3d 125 (3d Cir. 2002) (injuries to a minor while participating in a cruise ship's child-care program while sailing in navigable waters gives rise to an admiralty case). 1 Schoenbaum, supra n.1, at 86.

ly defined, admiralty jurisdiction exists over a contract dispute if the "contract 'is one . . . that relates to a ship in its use as such, or to commerce or to navigation on navigable waters, or to transportation by sea or to maritime employment.' "[15] However, contracts that are only preliminary to navigation, such as one for ship construction, do not fall within admiralty jurisdiction.[16]

Assuming that the case is one within the admiralty subject matter, the federal jurisdictional statute[17]—which provides for original, "exclusive" jurisdiction in the federal courts—might lead one to the conclusion that state courts have no role to play. However, the so-called "saving to suitors" clause later in that provision has been interpreted to allow state courts concurrent jurisdiction in admiralty matters that can be brought *in personam*.[18] Thus, for example, a plaintiff who is the victim of a maritime tort is free to bring an *in personam* action against the tortfeasor in state court.[19]

While the uniform body of admiralty law largely governs admiralty matters, state law still has a significant role to play.[20] State law is often borrowed to fill in "gaps" in the existing structure of admiralty jurisprudence, although state law must yield to federal legislation enacted pursuant to Congress's power to regulate the area.[21] Moreover, state courts hearing admiralty matters are free to apply state procedural law that does not pose a threat to the uniformity of admiralty jurisprudence.[22]

As to the personal jurisdiction of admiralty courts, tradition plays a larger role than it does in other areas of the law. As to in personam admiralty actions—whether they be tort, contract or some other theory—the usual rules of personal jurisdiction apply. Because there is no special, federal service statute applicable to in personam admiralty cases,[23] federal courts in admiralty must apply the forum state's long-arm statute through Federal Rule of Civil Procedure 4(k)(1)(A).[24] Because application of the state's long-arm statute brings with it the same constitutional limitations applicable to state courts, federal courts in admiralty hearing in personam actions generally have personal jurisdiction over defendants if they have minimum contacts with the forum state.

15. 1 Schoenbaum, supra n.1, at 120 (quoting J.A.R., Inc. v. M/V Lady Lucille, 963 F.2d 96 (5th Cir.1992)).

16. See, e.g., People's Ferry Co. v. Beers, 61 U.S. (20 How.) 393, 15 L.Ed. 961 (1858).

17. 28 U.S.C.A. § 1333.

18. 1 Schoenbaum, supra n.1, at 160 (citing Leon v. Galceran, 78 U.S. (11 Wall.) 185, 191, 20 L.Ed. 74 (1871)).

19. See, e.g., Foster v. Destin Trading Corp., 700 So.2d 199 (La.1997).

20. 1 Schoenbaum, supra n.1, at 149–55.

21. 1 Schoenbaum, supra n.1, at 155–60.

22. American Dredging v. Miller, 510 U.S. 443, 114 S.Ct. 981, 127 L.Ed.2d 285 (1994) (state court hearing admiralty case not required to follow federal doctrine of forum non conveniens).

23. 1 Schoenbaum, supra n.1, at 68 (federal courts hearing in personam admiralty cases must acquire jurisdiction under the strictures of F.R.C.P. 4, which incorporates state long-arm statutes and the "minimum contacts" test by reference).

24. See supra § 10.5.

An important extension to the in personam jurisdiction of admiralty courts is Federal Rule of Civil Procedure 4(k)(2). As discussed above,[25] Rule 4(k)(2) allows in personam jurisdiction to the maximum extent permitted by the Constitution "with respect to claims arising under federal law, to establish jurisdiction over the person of any defendant who is not subject to the jurisdiction of the courts of general jurisdiction of any state."[26] The principal constitutional limitation on the territorial reach of federal courts is the Fifth Amendment's Due Process Clause. As also discussed above,[27] this Clause generally has been interpreted more flexibly than its counterpart in the Fourteenth Amendment.[28] Most federal courts that have considered the issue have construed the phrase "arising under federal law" in Rule 4(k)(2) to encompass admiralty actions, allowing for this extended jurisdiction in cases in which state long-arm statutes will not reach the in personam admiralty defendant.[29]

Tradition has much to say in the area of admiralty in rem jurisdiction. Two special admiralty rules of import here. The first is Supplemental Rule B.[30] One of the principal advantages for plaintiffs of proceeding in admiralty is the relatively easy availability of attachment for judgment security purposes. Rule B applies to actions that would otherwise be purely in personam.[31] In Rule B actions the plaintiff may establish jurisdiction by attaching or arresting the defendant's assets within the jurisdiction, often a ship, its cargo, or intangible assets.[32] Rule B attachment is available only if the plaintiff can allege on information and belief that "the defendant cannot be found within the district."[33] The "cannot be found" requirement is two-fold. The plaintiff must be able to allege either that the summons and complaint cannot be physically delivered to the defendant or an appropriate agent within the district[34] or the plaintiff must be able to allege that the defendant "cannot be found" in the sense that the defendant does not have jurisdictional contacts with the district.[35] Any judgment is limited to the property—as it is for all in

25. See supra § 10.5.

26. F.R.C.P. 4(k)(2).

27. See supra § 10.2.

28. See supra § 10.2.

29. See, e.g., World Tanker Carriers Corp. v. M/V Ya Mawlaya, 99 F.3d 717 (5th Cir.1996) (Rule 4(k)(2) applies to admiralty cases); West Africa Trading & Shipping Co. v. London Int'l Group, 968 F.Supp. 996 (D.N.J.1997) (same); Western Equities, Ltd. v. Hanseatic, Ltd., 956 F.Supp. 1232 (D.V.I. 1997) (same); but see Eskofot v. E.I. Du Pont De Nemours & Co., 872 F.Supp. 81 (S.D.N.Y.1995) (Rule 4(k)(2) limited to federal questions suits based upon 28 U.S.C.A. § 1331).

30. F.R.C.P. Supp. R. B.

31. F.R.C.P. Supp. R. B(1).

32. See, e.g., Winter Storm Shipping v. TPI, 310 F.3d 263 (2d Cir. 2002), cert. denied 539 U.S. 927, 123 S.Ct. 2578, 156 L.Ed.2d 605 (2003) (authorizing Rule B attachment of electronic fund transfers).

33. F.R.C.P. Supp. R. B(1).

34. See, e.g., Chilean Line, Inc. v. U.S., 344 F.2d 757 (2d Cir.1965) (defendant had agent within district, making Rule B unavailable to plaintiff); Seawind Compania, S.A. v. Crescent Line, Inc., 320 F.2d 580 (2d Cir.1963) (same).

35. See, e.g., Det Bergenske Dampskibsselskab v. Sabre Shipping Corp., 341 F.2d 50 (2d Cir.1965); Seawind Compania v. Crescent Line, Inc., 320 F.2d 580 (1963); VTT Vulcan Petroleum, S.A. v. Langham–Hill Petroleum, Inc., 684 F.Supp. 389 (S.D.N.Y.1988); Integrated Container Service, Inc. v. Starlines Container Shipping, Ltd., 476 F.Supp. 119 (E.D.N.Y.1979).

rem actions—unless some basis for in personam jurisdiction is established.[36]

The arguably more exotic sort of attachment is that available under Supplemental Rule C.[37] Rule C applies in cases in which the plaintiff has a maritime lien and the property is arrested for the purpose of foreclosing on the lien.[38] Maritime liens can arise in a wide variety of circumstances including torts on a vessel,[39] possessory liens,[40] claims for cargo damage,[41] repairmen's and materialmen's liens,[42] and ship mortgages.[43] Assuming that the admiralty plaintiff makes the requisite allegations, the arrest of the property within the district is a sufficient jurisdictional basis to allow the plaintiff to proceed against the property.[44] American admiralty law still adheres to the personification fiction, in which the property—often a vessel—is treated as the offending party, and the action is truly "against" the property.[45]

The Supreme Court's decision in *Shaffer v. Heitner*,[46] which apparently collapsed the constitutional tests for in personam and in rem jurisdiction into a single test requiring that the affected parties (and not merely the property) have minimum contacts with the forum,[47] led to immediate speculation that Rule B and Rule C attachment were in constitutional danger.[48] However, for a wide variety of reasons, *Shaffer* has done little to undercut the usefulness of Rule B and Rule C attachment. First, *Shaffer*'s rationale—while apparently broad—impacts primarily cases in which the property has no relationship to the underlying claim.[49] While some Rule B attachments might fit this description, Rule C attachments involve a very direct relationship between the claim and the property, meaning that the presence of the property in the forum is relevant under any jurisdictional test.[50] Second, courts have distinguished *Shaffer* on the ground that the mobile nature of most admiralty property, and the distinctive nature of admiralty law generally, creates a necessity for—and constitutional authorization of—property-based jurisdiction not present in most civil cases.[51] Third, the federal

36. 2 Schoenbaum, supra n.1, at 478–80.

37. F.R.C.P. Supp. R. C.

38. F.R.C.P. Supp. R. C(1)(a).

39. See, e.g., Seguros Banvenez, S.A. v. S/S Oliver Drescher, 761 F.2d 855 (2d Cir. 1985).

40. See, e.g., Riffe Petroleum Co. v. Cibro Sales Corp., 601 F.2d 1385 (10th Cir. 1979).

41. See, e.g., Wood v. The Wilmington, 48 Fed. 566 (D. Md. 1880).

42. See, e.g., Petersen Towing Corp. v. Capt. Abrams, Inc., 388 F.Supp. 1166 (S.D.N.Y.1975).

43. See, e.g., 46 U.S.C.A. § 911 et. seq. (Ship Mortgage Act).

44. See 2 Schoenbaum, supra n.1, at 516–26.

45. See 2 Schoenbaum, supra n.1, at 516.

46. 433 U.S. 186, 97 S.Ct. 2569, 53 L.Ed.2d 683 (1977).

47. See supra § 5.5–5.6.

48. For a good discussion concluding that *Shaffer* would actually have little effect on admiralty cases, see Bohmann, Applicability of *Shaffer* to Admiralty In Rem Jurisdiction, 53 Tul. L. Rev. 135 (1978).

49. See supra § 5.5—5.6.

50. See, e.g., Amoco Overseas Oil Co. v. Compagnie Nationale Algerienne de Navigation, 605 F.2d 648, 655 (2d Cir.1979); Engineering Equip. Co. v. S.S. Selene, 446 F.Supp. 706 (S.D.N.Y.1978).

51. See, e.g., Winter Storm Shipping v. TPI, 310 F.3d 263 (2d Cir. 2002), cert. denied 539 U.S. 927, 123 S.Ct. 2578, 156

nature of admiralty litigation implicates the Fifth, not the Fourteenth, Amendment and its more relaxed jurisdictional requirements.[52] As a result, courts have been generally deferential to admiralty's special character, and upheld its use of jurisdictional fictions, even though those fictions have largely fallen into disfavor in civil cases generally.

D. BANKRUPTCY CASES

§ **10.7** The power of the federal judiciary to determine bankruptcy matters has always been an important and complicated element of the power of federal courts. Through 1978, federal district courts acted as bankruptcy courts, but district courts generally referred such matters to bankruptcy referees over which the district court retained essentially plenary authority.[1] The 1978 amendments to the Bankruptcy Code, however, made considerable changes to this structure by establishing in each federal district a court known as "The United States Bankruptcy Court" for that district.[2] The judges of these courts, however, were not judges within the meaning of Article III of the United States Constitution, principally because they served 14–year, not life, terms and did not enjoy any constitutional protection against salary reduction.[3] The sweeping authority of bankruptcy courts eventually prompted, in the famous case of *Northern Pipeline Construction Co. v. Marathon Pipe Line Co.*,[4] a successful constitutional challenge to this structure on the grounds that such broad federal court authority could only be exercised by life-tenured judges. Eventually, Congress amended the Bankruptcy Code to make bankruptcy courts a "unit" of the District Courts, with bankruptcy courts hearing certain "core" bankruptcy matters.[5]

Even with the post-*Northern Pipeline* amendments to the Bankruptcy Code significant private litigation can and does take place in adversary bankruptcy actions. The bankruptcy long-arm provision is Bankruptcy Rule 7004. Rule 7004 is a moderately confusing amalgamation of provisions on personal jurisdiction and the method of service. As to methods of service, Rule 7004 incorporates by reference most of Federal Rule of Civil Procedure 4.[6] Bankruptcy Rule 7004 also adds extensive provisions for service by first-class mail[7] and publication.[8]

L.Ed.2d 605 (2003); *Amoco*, 605 F.2d at 655; Day v. Temple Drilling Co., 613 F.Supp. 194, 197 (S.D.Miss.1985); Trans–Asiatic Oil Ltd., S.A. v. Apex Oil Co., 604 F.Supp. 4, 5–7 (D.P.R.1983); Grand Bahama Petroleum Co. v. Canadian Transp. Agencies, Ltd., 450 F.Supp. 447, 453 (W.D.Wash.1978).

52. See, e.g., *Amoco*, 605 F.2d at 655; Engineering Equipment Co. v. S.S. Selene, 446 F.Supp. 706 (1978).

§ **10.7**

1. C. Wright, Law of Federal Courts 57 (5th ed. 1994)

2. Id.

3. See U.S. Const. art. III (federal judges serve during "Good Behaviour").

4. 458 U.S. 50, 102 S.Ct. 2858, 73 L.Ed.2d 598 (1982).

5. Wright, supra n.1, at 60.

6. Bankr. R. 7004(a).

7. Bankr. R. 7004(b).

8. Bankr. R. 7004(c).

Bankruptcy Rule 7004 also includes two provisions that apparently bear on personal jurisdiction. One is subdivision (d) which provides that "[t]he summons and complaint and all other process except a subpoena may be served anywhere in the United States."[9] Similar federal provisions for "nationwide" service have been interpreted to authorize personal jurisdiction the maximum extent consistent with the Fifth Amendment's Due Process Clause.[10] However, subdivision (f)—added December 1, 1996[11]—removes any doubt regarding the breadth of the territorial authority of bankruptcy courts. In its pertinent part, that subsection provides: "If the exercise of jurisdiction is consistent with the Constitution and laws of the United States, serving a summons . . . in accordance with this rule or the subdivisions of [Federal Rule 4] made applicable by these rules is effective to establish personal jurisdiction. . . ."[12]

This provision bears some similarity to Federal Rule 4(k)(2) which authorizes personal jurisdiction in some federal actions to the maximum extent consistent with the Constitution.[13] One interpretive question is whether Bankruptcy Rule 7004 carries with it an important limitation found in Federal Rule 4(k)(2). Federal Rule 4(k)(2) authorizes personal jurisdiction to the Fifth Amendment maximum only if the plaintiff can establish that the defendant could not be reached by any state long-arm provisions, which are made applicable to the federal courts through Federal Rule 4(k)(1)(A).[14] Bankruptcy Rule 7004(f), however, has no similar limitation. It simply provides for personal jurisdiction to the Fifth Amendment maximum in all cases "arising in or related to a case" under the Bankruptcy Code.[15] Moreover, while Bankruptcy Rule 7004 incorporates most of Federal Rule 4, it pointedly does not incorporate subdivision (k),[16] which is further evidence that the omission of the Federal Rule 4(k)(2) limitation is intentional. Not surprisingly, therefore, the courts have concluded that plaintiffs invoking Bankruptcy Rule 7004(f) are not required to show that the defendant could not be reached by a state long-arm provision.[17]

The consequence is that the reach of bankruptcy courts is perhaps the broadest that one can imagine. This broad reach fits with an understandable desire to provide a single forum to finally determine all matters related to the debtor.[18] The result, however, is that it is extremely difficult to defeat an assertion of personal jurisdiction in the bankruptcy context. Under the longstanding provision allowing "nationwide"

---

9. Bankr. R. 7004(d).

10. See supra § 10.2.

11. At least one court has applied Bankruptcy Rule 7004(f) to cases filed before December 1, 1996 on the theory that retroactive application of the rule would not be unfair. See In re Pintlar Corp., 133 F.3d 1141 (9th Cir.1998), cert. denied 524 U.S. 933, 118 S.Ct. 2334, 141 L.Ed.2d 706 (1998).

12. Bankr. R. 7004(f).

13. See supra § 10.5.

14. See F.R.C.P. 4(k); see supra § 10.5.

15. Bankr. R. 7004(f).

16. Bankr. R. 7004(a).

17. In re Pintlar Corp., 133 F.3d 1141 (9th Cir.1998), cert. denied 524 U.S. 933, 118 S.Ct. 2334, 141 L.Ed.2d 706 (1998).

18. See, e.g., In re Lockwood Corp., 216 B.R. 628 (D. Neb. 1997) (broad jurisdictional rules are designed to prevent fragmentation of bankruptcy matters).

service, and now in light of Bankruptcy Rule 7004(f)'s direct reference to the Constitution, federal courts have usually applied a pure "national contacts" approach, allowing jurisdiction as long as the defendant has minimum contacts with the United States as a whole.[19] While broad personal jurisdiction has much to commend it in this context, a flexible due process analysis should not preclude a court from taking cognizance of a genuine and serious inconvenience to the defendant.[20]

E. REMOVED CASES

§ 10.8 Removal jurisdiction has been an important component of federal court authority since the First Judiciary Act.[1] Essentially, removal jurisdiction is a device for partially equalizing the relative power of the plaintiff and the defendant to select as between state and federal court. In most cases in which the plaintiff sues the defendant in a state court, and the case could have been originally filed in a federal court, the defendant may take the case to the federal court embracing the state court by filing in the federal court a notice of removal attaching the state court pleadings.[2] While federal court removal jurisdiction is mostly co-extensive with federal court original subject matter jurisdiction, there are significant ways in which the two diverge. One important difference relates to diversity cases. If one or more of the defendants is being sued in his home state's state courts, the defendants have no right of removal even if the case could have been filed originally in federal court on diversity grounds.[3] This limitation makes a fair amount of sense if one accepts the ostensible rationale for diversity jurisdiction of protecting out-of-state defendants from the threat of parochialism by local courts. A defendant sued in his home state's state courts presumably ought have nothing to fear in this regard and thus has no right to remove the case to the more neutral federal forum.

Removal has some modest consequences for the territorial reach of federal courts. One is that removal overrides the general venue provisions applicable to federal courts.[4] As long as the defendant removes the case to the federal court that embraces the state court there can be no

---

19. See, e.g., The Celotex Corp. v. Rapid Am. Corp., 124 F.3d 619 (4th Cir.1997) (jurisdiction would've been available under Rule 7004(f) under a national contacts theory but issue was not raised below and District Court's failure to raise it was not plain error); Diamond Mortgage Corp. of Illinois v. Sugar, 913 F.2d 1233 (7th Cir.1990), cert. denied 498 U.S. 1089, 111 S.Ct. 968, 112 L.Ed.2d 1054 (1991) (jurisdiction allowed under old rule on a national contacts theory); Michaelesco v. Estate of Richard (In Re Michaelesco), Cytomedix Inc. v. Little Rock Foot, 287 B.R. 901 (N.D. Ill. 2002); 288 B.R. 646 (D. Conn. 2003); In re TJN, Inc., 207 B.R. 502 (Bankr.D.S.C.1996) (same).

20. See supra § 10.3 (endorsing the moderate approach taken by courts of presumptively allowing jurisdiction on a national contacts theory, but allowing the defendant to defeat an assertion of jurisdiction by showing that the chosen forum is genuinely and seriously inconvenient).

§ 10.8

1. Wright, Law of Federal Courts 223 (5th ed. 1994).

2. 28 U.S.C.A. § 1441(a).

3. 28 U.S.C.A. § 1441(b).

4. 28 U.S.C.A. § 1391 (general federal venue statute).

successful objection to venue.[5] Once the case is removed to federal court, however, the defendant is then free to move for discretionary transfer of venue under Section 1404(a).[6]

The defendant's decision to file a notice of removal does not waive his right to move to dismiss for lack of personal jurisdiction. The Federal Rules of Civil Procedure generally require that the defendant object to personal jurisdiction immediately, either in the answer to the complaint or in the first motion, lest any objection be waived.[7] It is settled that the mere filing of a notice of removal does not waive the defendant's right to seek dismissal on personal jurisdiction grounds.[8]

Assuming the case is properly removed to federal court there remains the question of whether the state or federal rules of personal jurisdiction apply. In most cases the two are co-extensive, because Federal Rule 4(k)(1)(A) generally directs federal courts to employ their home state's long-arm statute. However, there can be significant differences between state and federal standards. In, for instance, a case filed in state court and removed on diversity grounds, the "100–mile bulge rule"[9] or the expanded reach available to federal courts under Federal Rule 4(k)(2)[10] might well be significant additions to the reach of the court that would not have been available had the case remained in state court.

This question arose as early as the 1895 Supreme Court case of *Goldey v. Morning News.*[11] At that time the New York courts followed the so-called *Pope* rule[12] which allowed for in personam jurisdiction over a corporation if a corporate officer were served in the state, even if merely visiting the state for non-business purposes. The federal courts followed the more conventional rule that transient service on a corporate officer did not subject the corporation to personal jurisdiction unless the officer were in the state for business purposes.[13] *Goldey* was a case commenced in the New York state courts in which the officer had been served while in the state for pleasure, and the state courts had assumed jurisdiction under the *Pope* doctrine. The corporation removed the case to the federal courts on diversity grounds, and the Supreme Court held that it would follow the federal doctrine and not yield to the New York rule.[14]

5. See, e.g., PT United Can Co. v. Crown Cork & Seal Co., 138 F.3d 65 (2d Cir.1998).

6. 28 U.S.C.A. § 1404(a) (venue transfer may be made on motion to serve the interests of justice and the convenience of the parties and the witnesses).

7. F.R.C.P. 12(b),(g),(h).

8. See, e.g., Holzsager v. The Valley Hospital, 646 F.2d 792, 796 (2d Cir.1981).

9. See F.R.C.P. 4(k)(1)(B); see also supra § 10.4.

10. See supra § 10.5.

11. 156 U.S. 518, 15 S.Ct. 559, 39 L.Ed. 517.

12. See Pope v. Terre Haute Car and Mfg. Co., 87 N.Y. 137 (1882).

13. See, e.g., *Goldey*, 156 U.S. at 520, 15 S.Ct. at 560, 39 L.Ed. 517.

14. Id. at 526, 15 S.Ct. at 562, 39 L.Ed. 517.

Since *Goldey*, federal courts have apparently universally assumed that removed cases are to be treated for purposes of personal jurisdiction as if they had been originally filed in federal court.[15] This approach has more than a century of precedent to commend it and also make a great deal of practical sense. Removal is taken at the defendant's initiative. To the extent that a defendant wishes to benefit from the potentially narrower territorial reach of state courts, the defendant could simply leave the case in state court.

III. CLASS ACTIONS

A. JURISDICTION OVER DEFENDANTS

§ 10.9 Class actions remain are important and controversial type of litigation. Although the concept of unnamed parties being virtually represented by others in litigation has its roots in ancient equity practice,[1] the modern history of the class action dates to 1966 when the Supreme Court adopted a new version of Federal Rule of Civil Procedure 23.[2] Rule 23, which has been the subject of exhaustive commentary, requires that any class action involve parties too numerous for practical joinder, adequate representation of the unnamed parties by the named ones, common questions of law or fact among the parties, and claims or defenses of the representative parties that are typical of the class.[3] These seemingly modest requirements have spawned furious debates over, for instance, whether mass tort suits can be brought as a class action.[4]

In theory, class actions can be brought either by plaintiff classes or against defendant classes. Rule 23, for instance, speaks of a class that "may sue or be sued."[5] In practice, however, a huge majority of class actions are brought by plaintiff classes, and there is doubt as to whether Rule 23 even permits defendant classes in some circumstances.[6]

With regard to the question of personal jurisdiction over defendants in class actions, the Supreme Court has never spoken directly. The case that comes closest to addressing the question is *Mullane v. Central Hanover Bank & Trust Co.*[7] In *Mullane*, the action involved the beneficiaries of 113 trusts held in a common trust fund created under New

---

15. See, e.g., Lee v. Ohio Cas. Ins. Co., 445 F.Supp. 189 (D.Del.1978) (applying 100–mile bulge rule to a case removed to federal court on diversity grounds); Deloro Smelting & Ref. Co. v. Englehard Minerals & Chem. Corp., 313 F.Supp. 470 (D.N.J. 1970) (same).

§ 10.9

1. C. Wright, Law of Federal Courts 507 (5th ed. 1994).

2. Id.

3. F.R.C.P. 23(a).

4. See, e.g., Amchem Prods., Inc. v. Windsor, 521 U.S. 591, 117 S.Ct. 2231, 2242, 138 L.Ed.2d 689 (1997) (attempted certification of a "sprawling" class of asbestos victims stretches Federal Rule 23 too far).

5. F.R.C.P. 23(a).

6. See, e.g., Henson v. East Lincoln Township, 814 F.2d 410 (7th Cir.1987) (attempted class action against a defendant class under Rule 23(b)(2) for equitable relief not permitted by the rule).

7. 339 U.S. 306, 70 S.Ct. 652, 94 L.Ed. 865 (1950).

York state law.[8] This arrangement had various advantages, not the least of which were economies of scale and risk spreading. Under New York state law, the trustees were required to bring actions every three years to account for their management of the trust.[9] The beneficiaries of these trusts—many of them not specifically named—were in at least a nominal sense the defendants in these accounting actions. The only notice given of the proceeding was publication of a citation in a local newspaper.[10]

Three representatives of the beneficiaries objected to the method of notice as well as to the state court's jurisdiction over the out-of-state beneficiaries. *Mullane* is undoubtedly best remembered for its holding that the mere publication of the notice in a newspaper is insufficient to satisfy the demands of due process.[11] But it is noteworthy that in order to reach the notice issue, the Supreme Court was required to discuss and overrule the objection to personal jurisdiction. The Court made no effort to rationalize in terms of "contacts" its holding that the court had jurisdiction over the nonresident parties. Rather, the Court simply reasoned that New York's "interest ... in providing a means to close trusts that exist by grace of its laws and are administered under the supervision of its courts is so insistent and rooted in custom as to establish beyond doubt the rights of its courts to determine the interests of all claimants.... "[12]

The implications of *Mullane* are debatable and have been extensively debated. It might well hold that the usual requirement of an individual jurisdictional assessment for each defendant is to be relaxed in cases in which a strict evaluation of the contacts of each defendant would render the proceedings impossible or impracticable to maintain. In *Mullane*, the only alternative to allowing the New York courts jurisdiction over the nonresidents would have been to have required the trustee to pursue the nonresidents in separate actions in their home states. Such a requirement would have destroyed the economies of scale that made the common trusts attractive to the beneficiaries.

Mullane cannot, however, stand for the broad proposition that jurisdiction is allowed over nonresidents simply because their joinder would be convenient. In the later case of *World–Wide Volkswagen v. Woodson*,[13] for instance, two of the principal defendants were clearly subject to personal jurisdiction in the forum state.[14] The Court, however, held that jurisdiction could not be maintained over the out-of-state dealer and distributor of the allegedly defective car, "even if the state is the most convenient location for litigation."[15]

8. Id. at 307–10, 70 S.Ct. at 654–55, 94 L.Ed. 865.

9. Id. at 309, 70 S.Ct. at 655, 94 L.Ed. 865.

10. Id. at 310, 70 S.Ct. at 655, 94 L.Ed. 865.

11. See infra § 12.3.

12. 339 U.S. at 313, 70 S.Ct. at 656, 94 L.Ed. 865.

13. 444 U.S. 286, 100 S.Ct. 559, 62 L.Ed.2d 490 (1980).

14. Id. at 298 n.3, 100 S.Ct. at 562 n.3, 62 L.Ed.2d 490.

15. Id. at 294, 100 S.Ct. at 565, 62 L.Ed.2d 490.

The line between cases of impracticability like *Mullane* and mere inconvenience like *World-Wide* is not always clear. At least one adventurous district court has taken an expansive view of jurisdiction over manufacturers of an allegedly defective drug. In *In re DES Cases*,[16] the court considered jurisdiction over defendant drug manufacturers in a huge class action brought on behalf of persons injured when New York women took the drug. A major complication in such cases is that it is usually impossible to prove which defendant manufactured the particular pills taken by each plaintiff, causing New York (and many other states) to adopt a theory of "national market share" liability.[17] Under this theory, in cases in which it cannot be determined which brand of a drug was taken, a plaintiff recovers fractionally against all manufacturers in proportion to the share of the national market occupied by each. As the district court noted, however, this theory works well only in cases in which all (or essentially) all of the manufacturers can be joined in the action.[18] This difficulty caused the court to take jurisdiction over all defendants—even those that could demonstrate that they had never distributed their product in the forum state—on a necessity theory similar to that which seemed to underlie *Mullane*.[19]

Cases like *Mullane* and *In re DES* are exceptional, however. The ordinary rule is that jurisdiction over defendants is evaluated by the familiar two-step test requiring statutory authorization for jurisdiction and the existence of a constitutionally-sufficient connection with the forum. Whether the action is one brought against a purported defendant class,[20] or by a plaintiff class against defendants,[21] courts routinely assume that the jurisdictional inquiry is separate for each defendant. In class actions in which the complained-of conduct is not localized to the forum, the requirement that each defendant have minimum contacts with the forum is a significant practical obstacle to maintaining the action.[22]

B. JURISDICTION OVER PLAINTIFFS

1. *Opt-out Classes*

§ 10.10 Federal Rule of Civil Procedure 23 allows for certification of class actions under any one of three subparts of subdivision (b). Rule 23(b)(1) allows for certification of class actions in which there is a risk of

---

16. 789 F.Supp. 552 (E.D.N.Y.1992) (Weinstein, J.), appeal dismissed 7 F.3d 20 (2d Cir.1993).

17. See, e.g., Hymowitz v. Eli Lilly and Co., 73 N.Y.2d 487, 541 N.Y.S.2d 941, 539 N.E.2d 1069, cert. denied 493 U.S. 944, 110 S.Ct. 350, 107 L.Ed.2d 338 (1989).

18. *DES Cases*, 789 F.Supp. at 576.

19. Id. at 588.

20. See, e.g., Henson v. East Lincoln Township, 814 F.2d 410, 416 (7th Cir.1987) (requirement that each defendant have minimum contacts with the forum is a large practical obstacle to many purported defendant class actions).

21. See, e.g., Travis v. Anthes Imperial Ltd., 473 F.2d 515 (8th Cir.1973) (evaluating jurisdiction over each defendant separately in a plaintiffs' class action brought against multiple defendants); Gutierrez v. Givens, 989 F.Supp. 1033 (S.D.Cal.1997) (same).

22. See, e.g., *Henson*, 814 F.2d at 416.

"incompatible standards of conduct" being set on the party opposing the class, or if individual adjudications "would as a practical matter be dispositive of the interests of other members."[1] Rule 23(b)(2) provides for class certification in cases in which injunctive or declaratory relief would be appropriate.[2] Rule 23(b)(3) allows for certification if "the questions of law or fact common to the members predominate over any questions affecting only individual matters, and that a class action is superior to other available methods for the fair and efficient adjudication of the controversy."[3]

Not all class actions are created equal, at least with regard to notice and the ability of class members to elect not to remain in the class. Rule 23(c)(2) provides that for all class actions certified under (b)(3), each class member who can be identified with reasonable effort must receive "individual notice," and that the notice must inform the recipient that "the court will exclude the member from the class if the member so requests...."[4] No such requirement of opt-out, individual notice exists for (b)(1) and (b)(2) classes, though courts sometimes exercise their discretion to require such notice even outside the context of (b)(3).[5] Thus, (b)(3) class actions are generally described as "opt-out" classes, while (b)(1) and (b)(2) class actions are often described as "mandatory" class actions. State class action rules generally either follow the federal dichotomy exactly, or follow it approximately in making some class actions opt-out and others mandatory.[6]

For actions other than class actions, jurisdiction over plaintiffs is a trivial problem, as plaintiffs by choosing the court and filing an action there consent to jurisdiction for all purposes relative to the action.[7] Unnamed class members, however, make no such choice; the decision to file in a particular forum is the election of the representative class members. Unnamed class members stand to have the legal rights and duties affected by the disposition of the class action. If, for instance, the class were to go to trial and lose, that judgment would be res judicata to any individual claim of a class member. Class members might also have liability for costs and attorneys fees of the opposing parties, though the mechanics of collecting from individual class members make this a remote possibility.

The Supreme Court addressed the problem of jurisdiction over unnamed plaintiffs in opt-out classes in *Phillips Petroleum Co. v. Shutts*.[8] The dispute in *Shutts* concerned interest on back royalty payments to the owners of various natural gas wells located in Kansas,

§ 10.10

1. F.R.C.P. 23(b)(1).

2. F.R.C.P. 23(b)(2).

3. F.R.C.P. 23(b)(3).

4. F.R.C.P. 23(c)(2).

5. See, e.g., 3 Newberg & Conte, Newberg on Class Actions § 16.17 (3d ed. 1992).

6. See, e.g., N.Y. Civ. Prac. L. & R. §§ 903, 904.

7. See, e.g., Adam v. Saenger, 303 U.S. 59, 58 S.Ct. 454, 82 L.Ed. 649 (1938) (plaintiff who filed in an unconnected forum consented to jurisdiction over counterclaim against plaintiff).

8. 472 U.S. 797, 105 S.Ct. 2965, 86 L.Ed.2d 628 (1985).

Oklahoma, Texas and Louisiana.[9] Claiming that they were owed interest on these back royalty payments, various well owners brought a class action in the Kansas state courts under a rule equivalent to Federal Rule 23(b)(3). The average claim of a class member was about $100 and the class comprised about 33,000 potential members.[10] About 3,400 potential members opted out of the class, and the notice could not be delivered to about 1,500 more, leaving a class of 28,100 members.[11]

The defendant claimed that the state court lacked jurisdiction over those unnamed class members who did not have minimum contacts with Kansas. The defendant maintained that the failure to opt out of the class was not a sufficient indication of assent to jurisdiction; apparently, the defendant's proposed solution was that absent class members should have to "opt in" to a class in order to be included.[12] The Supreme Court rejected the defendant's contentions, holding that the failure to opt out was sufficient for an absent plaintiff. In so doing, the Court took care to distinguish defendants from plaintiffs, noting that "[t]he burdens placed by a State upon an absent class-action plaintiff are not of the same order or magnitude as those it places upon an absent defendant."[13] The worst fate that an absent plaintiff is likely to suffer is to lose the right to recover; in a case such as *Shutts*—where the average claim was $100— the Court concluded that this was an insufficiently large burden to require more than a right to opt out.[14] The notice, however, must be reasonable in order for the class action judgment to have binding effect on the absent plaintiffs.[15]

Shutts essentially disposes of jurisdictional problems relative to absent plaintiffs in opt-out classes. *Shutts* might, perhaps, be distinguished from an opt-out class action in which the individual claims are large, in contrast to the very small claims involved in that case.[16] Moreover, *Shutts* clearly does not resolve the question of jurisdiction over absent class members in mandatory class actions, the subject of the next section.

2. *Mandatory Classes*

§ 10.11 The Supreme Court's most important opinion on jurisdiction in class actions, *Phillips Petroleum Co. v. Shutts*,[1] addressed only jurisdiction in opt-out classes.[2] In fact, *Shutts* specifically reserved judg-

9. Id. at 800, 105 S.Ct. at 2968, 86 L.Ed.2d 628.

10. Id. at 801, 105 S.Ct. at 2968, 86 L.Ed.2d 628.

11. Id.

12. Id. at 805, 105 S.Ct. at 2971, 86 L.Ed.2d 628.

13. Id. at 808, 105 S.Ct. at 2972, 86 L.Ed.2d 628.

14. Id. at 809, 105 S.Ct. at 2973, 86 L.Ed.2d 628.

15. See State v. Homeside Lending, Inc., 826 A.2d 997 (Vt. 2003).

16. But see In re National Life Ins. Co., 247 F.Supp.2d 486 (D. Vt. 2002) (opt-out notice sufficient in claim involving tax consequences of $700,000 life insurance policy).

§ 10.11

1. 472 U.S. 797, 105 S.Ct. 2965, 86 L.Ed.2d 628 (1985).

2. See supra § 10.10.

ment as to the appropriate analysis in mandatory actions.[3]

As commentators have noted,[4] the considerations are potentially quite different in mandatory class actions. In opt-out class actions, the plaintiff who stands to be bound by the results of an adjudication in a distant forum has at least elected to do so by not returning the opt-out form and requesting exclusion. The plaintiff in the mandatory class action has no such option under Federal Rule 23.[5] Lower courts have been predictably split on the question. Some have held that *Shutts* does not limit the authority of courts to adjudicate class actions with nonresident plaintiffs as long as those mandatory class actions meet the requirements of either Rule 23(b)(2) or 23(b)(3).[6] Other courts have read *Shutts* more expansively to require an opt-out right for non-resident plaintiffs who lack minimum contacts with the forum and who stand to lose a substantial claim to money damages.[7]

The Supreme Court has twice appeared poised to resolve this division, but has each time refused to address the question. In *Ticor Title Insurance Co. v. Brown*,[8] the Court granted certiorari on the question, but then dismissed the writ, concluding that the class might not be mandatory under Rule 23. More recently, the Supreme Court granted certiorari on the question in *Adams v. Robertson*,[9] but again dismissed the writ, this time because the due process question had not been preserved for resolution before the state supreme court from which the writ was taken.

It thus remains to be seen how the Supreme Court will resolve the matter. While guarantees of procedural fairness are important to unnamed class plaintiffs, wholesale importation of the minimum contacts principles into this context will do little to assure such fairness. As the *Shutts* court noted, the burdens on class plaintiffs are orders of magnitude smaller than those imposed on nonresident defendants. True mandatory class actions lack an opt-out right precisely such actions cannot be fairly maintained if individual adjudications are allowed. Because the

---

3. *Shutts*, 472 U.S. at 811 n.3, 105 S.Ct. at 2974 n.3, 86 L.Ed.2d 628.

4. See, e.g., Mullenix, Class Actions, Personal Jurisdiction, and Plaintiffs' Due Process: Implications for Mass Tort Litigation, 28 U.C. Davis L. Rev. 871 (1995); Wood, Adjudicatory Jurisdiction and Class Actions, 62 Ind. L.J. 597 (1986–87); Note, The Due Process Right to Opt Out of Class Actions, 73 N.Y.U. L. Rev. 480 (1998); Note, Are Mandatory Class Actions Unconstitutional?, 72 Notre Dame L. Rev. 1627 (1997).

5. See F.R.C.P. 23(c)(2).

6. See Note, Due Process Right, supra n.4, at 494–95 (collecting cases and concluding that the Delaware courts have largely limited *Shutts* to its facts).

7. See Note, Due Process Right, supra n.4, at 496 (discussing New York cases, including Woodrow v. Colt Industries, Inc., 77 N.Y.2d 185, 565 N.Y.S.2d 755, 566

N.E.2d 1160 (N.Y. 1991), extending *Shutts* to class actions that seek money damages, even if those class actions would be mandatory under the applicable rules); see also Grimes v. Vitalink Communications Corp., 17 F.3d 1553 (3d Cir.1994), cert. denied 513 U.S. 986, 115 S.Ct. 480, 130 L.Ed.2d 393 (1994) (holding that in a class action certified as a mandatory class under Rule 23(b)(1) and 23(b)(2) only those plaintiffs with minimum contacts with the forum could be bound by the court-approved settlement; all plaintiffs found to have minimum contacts based upon their stock ownership and tender).

8. 511 U.S. 117, 114 S.Ct. 1359, 128 L.Ed.2d 33 (1994).

9. 520 U.S. 83, 117 S.Ct. 1028, 137 L.Ed.2d 203 (1997).

risk of unfairness transcends state lines—for instance, if a large number of class plaintiffs spread throughout the world are competing for a limited fund—full injection of the territoriality principles inherent in the minimum contacts analysis would be likely to dramatically affect the utility and fairness of such litigation. Rather than focusing on territoriality, a more sensible question to ask and answer is whether there is any palpable unfairness to the unnamed, nonresident plaintiffs in allowing the matter to proceed as a mandatory class action. If there is no such unfairness, then whether those nonresident plaintiffs have minimum contacts with the forum ought have little weight in the analysis.[10]

IV. SPECIAL PROBLEMS OF JURISDICTION OVER BUSINESS ASSOCIATIONS

A. PARTNERSHIPS AND OTHER UNINCORPORATED ASSOCIATIONS

§ 10.12 In the area of business associations, the jurisdictional reach of courts is very much affected by substantive law concepts. In some circumstances a partnership may be viewed solely as an association of individuals who must be proceeded against as individuals.[1] In other situations, for example that of the limited partnership, the general partners are viewed as having unlimited liability arising out of the partnership activities, but the limited partner has no liability beyond that represented by possible claims against the partnership assets.[2] This latter principle is because the limited partner status is a device to encourage investment in circumstances in which the risk to the limited partner is the capital investment only. Similarly, common law associations and joint ventures were viewed simply as a collection of individuals who, absent incorporation, could be proceeded against only as individuals.[3] As business practices and the needs of modern economy have developed in the United States, however, most states now permit suits against a partnership in its firm name, as do most states with regard to associations.[4] This ability to proceed against the partnership or association by a firm or trade name has led to the treatment of the partnership as an entity for some purposes but not for others.[5]

---

10. See, e.g., Redish & Beste, Personal Jurisdiction and Global Resolution of Mass Tort Litigation, 28 U.C. Davis L. Rev. 917 (1995).

§ 10.12

1. See Crane & Bromberg, Law of Partnership § 1 (1968).

2. See Crane & Bromberg, supra n.1, § 26; Reuschlein & Gregory, Agency and Partnership § 264 (2d ed. 1990).

3. See Crane & Bromberg, supra n.2, §§ 24, 29, 35; Restatement, Second, Judgments § 61 (1982). Ford, Unincorporated

Non Profit Associations (1959); Sturges, Unincorporated Associations as Parties, 33 Yale L.J. 383 (1924); Ostrom v. Greene, 161 N.Y. 353, 55 N.E. 919 (1900); Harry Martin v. Joseph Curran et al., 303 N.Y. 276, 101 N.E.2d 683 (1951); Mounteer v. Bayly, 86 A.D.2d 942, 448 N.Y.S.2d 582 (1982).

4. E.g., Cal. Code Civ. Proc. § 388; Colo. Rev. Stat. Ann. § 13–50–105; Vt. Stat. Ann. Tit. 12, § 814. See Restatement, Second, Judgments § 61 (1982).

5. See Reuschlein & Gregory, supra n.2, § 207.

In nearly all circumstances it can be stated that general partners are liable and subject to jurisdiction as if they were individuals in any situation in which an individual under the same circumstances, would be subject to jurisdiction.[6] For example, partners may be subjected to jurisdiction by their consent or that of an agent properly acting for them.[7] Because partnerships are formed primarily for the purpose of accomplishing business objectives, jurisdiction to enforce contract or tort liability arising out of economic activities follow the same patterns that have developed with regard to individuals.[8] Thus, if the partnership is doing business within a state which provides for suits against partnerships in the firm name, it seems clear that would be a proper basis for jurisdiction in the state courts over causes of action arising out of that economic activity under the same circumstances as would an individual who had participated in the activity and caused the liability to arise.[9] Issues regarding partnership jurisdiction arising out of activities of the partnership are dependent upon the law of agency, as each partner is an agent of the firm.[10] Within this framework the analogies to individuals are appropriate. This also explains the protection afforded the limited partner, for neither the partnership nor the general partners are agents for the purpose of imposing additional liability upon the limited partner.[11] There seems to be at least one exception to following the direct analogy to individuals. Since we are concerned about obligations arising out of partnership activities and the individual's activities with regard to the partnership, the mere service on a partner, even a general partner, while in the forum state for reasons unrelated to the partnership activities will not subject the partnership to jurisdiction within the state. This assumes, of course, that the partnership has not engaged in activities which would otherwise subject it to the jurisdiction of the state.[12]

6. Restatement, Second, Conflict of Laws § 40 (1971).

7. See Restatement, Second, Conflict of Laws § 32 (1971); see supra § 8.13.

8. See Morton v. Environmental Land Systems, Limited, 55 Ill.App.3d 369, 370 N.E.2d 1106 (1977).

9. Restatement, Second, Conflict of Laws § 40, comment (b) (1971). See Sugg v. Thornton, 132 U.S. 524, 10 S.Ct. 163, 33 L.Ed. 447 (1889); United Mine Workers v. Coronado Coal Co., 259 U.S. 344, 42 S.Ct. 570, 66 L.Ed. 975 (1922); Esteve Brothers & Co. v. Harrell, 272 Fed. 382 (5th Cir. 1921); Vespe Contracting Co. v. Anvan Corp., 433 F.Supp. 1226 (E.D.Pa.1977); Woodfin v. Curry, 228 Ala. 436, 153 So. 620 (1934); Lewis Manufacturing Co. v. Superior Court, 140 Cal.App.2d 245, 295 P.2d 145 (1956); Lucky Five Mining Co. v. H. & H. Mines, Inc., 75 Idaho 423, 273 P.2d 676 (1954). See also Crane & Bromberg, Law of Partnership § 62 (1968); Reuschlein & Gregory, Agency and Partnership § 207 (2d Cir. 1990); Kaplan, Suits Against Unincorporated Associations, 53 Mich. L. Rev. 945 (1955); Richardson, Creditor's Rights and the Partnership, 40 Ky. L.J. 243 (1952); Magruder and Foster, Jurisdiction Over Partnerships, 37 Harv. L. Rev. 793 (1924). Cf. Rosenblum v. Judson Engineering Corp., 99 N.H. 267, 109 A.2d 558 (1954). But cf. L.C. Jones Trucking Co. v. Superior Oil Co., 68 Wyo. 384, 234 P.2d 802 (1951); International Aerial Tramway Corp. v. Konrad Doppelmayr & Sohn et al., 70 Cal.2d 400, 74 Cal.Rptr. 908, 450 P.2d 284 (1969); C.T. Carden et al. v. Arkoma Associates, 494 U.S. 185, 110 S.Ct. 1015, 108 L.Ed.2d 157 (1990).

10. See Uniform Partnership Act § 9.

11. See Campbell, Partnership Obligations and Their Enforcement, 32 Chi. Kent L. Rev. 127 (1954).

12. Restatement, Second, Conflict of Laws § 40, cmnt. (b) (1971).

Jurisdictional concepts are reflected in the enforceability of the judgment which is obtained in such actions. If a plaintiff proceeds against the partnership in the firm name, but service of process or jurisdiction has not been obtained over all of the partners, a resulting judgment for the defendant is conclusive upon the plaintiff as to all partners because the plaintiff is fully within the jurisdiction of the court.[13] On the other hand, if the judgment is for the plaintiff and against the partnership, that judgment is binding on the partnership as an entity and is effective to bind partnership assets wherever located, and will bind the personal liability of the partners who are subject to personal jurisdiction in the litigation.[14] In addition, it appears that a judgment for the plaintiff against a partnership would also determine the partnership liability of the unjoined partners but would not establish any liability beyond the partnership obligation for which the absent partner would be liable as a general partner.[15] Of course the absent partner could, in a subsequent suit for enforcement, raise any defenses personal to him to which the agency of the partner would not extend.

If the partnership is not subject to suit in the firm name in the second state, the action to enforce the judgment would need to be brought against the partners individually, but the judgment against the firm would be recognized as conclusive of the liability of the partners to the extent of their interests in the firm property.[16] If a partnership is not subject to suit in the firm name in the state in which it is doing business, the problem is identical with that of acquiring jurisdiction over individuals. Only the individual partners over whom the court acquires jurisdiction are bound by the judgment.[17]

Analogous to the partnership circumstance is that involving joint obligors and their liabilities. Several states have statutes that provide that joint obligors on contract obligations may be sued by proceeding against the defendant served even though other defendants may or may not have been served and if a judgment is recovered, it may be enforced against the joint property of all and the separate property of the defendants who are served.[18] Other unincorporated associations raise problems similar to those of partnerships and in most instances analogous approaches prevail.[19]

13. See infra §§ 24.1–24.2.

14. Restatement, Second, Judgments § 60, cmnt. (a) (1982). See, e.g., Ariz. Rev. Stat. § 29–104; Pa. R. Civ. Proc. 423. See also Detrio v. United States, 264 F.2d 658 (5th Cir.1959); Dillard v. McKnight, 34 Cal.2d 209, 209 P.2d 387 (1949).

15. See International Shoe Co. v. Hawkinson, 73 N.D. 677, 18 N.W.2d 761 (1945); Crane & Bromberg, supra n.1, § 62; Restatement, Second, Judgments § 60 (1982).

16. Restatement, Second, Conflict of Laws § 40, cmnt. (d) (1971); Detrio v. United States, 264 F.2d 658 (5th Cir.1959); East

Denver Municipal Irrigation District v. Doherty, 293 Fed. 804 (S.D.N.Y.1923). Cf. Brown v. Globe Laboratories, Inc., 165 Neb. 138, 84 N.W.2d 151 (1957). See also infra § 24.1.

17. See Restatement, Second, Conflict of Laws § 40, comments (d), (e) (1971).

18. See Reuschlein & Gregory, supra n.9, § 207(c).

19. See Restatement, Second, Conflict of Laws § 40 (1971); Restatement, Second, Judgments § 61 (1982). See also Ostrom v. Greene, 161 N.Y. 353, 55 N.E. 919 (1900).

B. DOMESTIC CORPORATIONS

§ 10.13 A corporation that is organized and incorporated under the laws of a state has always been assumed to be subject to the jurisdiction of the courts of that state. In nearly all situations that continues to be the case.[1] However, because the jural relationships involved in corporations are complex, and the legal issues arising in litigation among the parties incident to those relationships are equally complex, there might be some circumstances in which this historically sound rule may not be applicable, or its application tempered by *forum non conveniens*.

At common law, service was made upon "such head officer of a corporation as secured knowledge of the process to the corporation."[2] Statutes, of course, may and do provide for service in other ways and such methods are valid if they reasonably give notice to the responsible corporate officials.[3] The reason for the traditional rule, that a corporation is subject to *in personam* jurisdiction in the state of its incorporation, is based upon the theory that the corporation is the creature of the state to whose laws it owes corporate existence.[4] It was once common to treat the domestic corporation as a domiciliary of the state of incorporation in an analogy to the domicile of an individual.[5] As a consequence, the Federal Judicial Code treats the corporation as a citizen of the state in which it is incorporated. However, recognizing the fact that the place of incorporation may have only a technical and formal relationship to the activities of the corporation, federal law also treats the corporation as being a citizen of the state in which it has its principal place of business.[6] In addition, the Federal Judicial Code was amended to provide that in a direct action against a liability insurer, the insurer corporation should be deemed to be a citizen of the state in which the insured is a citizen, as well as its states of incorporation and principal place of business.[7] State law has added to these complexities by statutes dealing with the pseudo foreign corporation, i.e., a corporation which,

---

§ 10.13

1. Restatement, Second, Conflict of Laws § 41 (1971); George, In Search of General Jurisdiction, 64 Tul. L. Rev. 1097 (1990); Twitchell, The Myth of General Jurisdiction, 101 Harv. L. Rev. 610, 633 n.111 (1988) (rule so well established that it is rarely challenged). See also Bane v. Netlink, Inc., 925 F.2d 637, 640 (3d Cir.1991) (foreign corporation registration in forum state sufficient for general jurisdiction).

2. Kansas City, Fort Scott & Memphis Railway Co. v. Daughtry, 138 U.S. 298, 305, 11 S.Ct. 306, 308, 34 L.Ed. 963 (1891).

3. E.g., St. Mary's Franco–American Petroleum Co. v. West Virginia, 203 U.S. 183, 27 S.Ct. 132, 51 L.Ed. 144 (1906); Clearwater Mercantile Co. v. Roberts, Johnson,

Rand Shoe Co., 51 Fla. 176, 40 So. 436 (1906); Nelson v. Chicago, Burlington & Quincy Railway Co., 225 Ill. 197, 80 N.E. 109 (1907); Town of Hinckley v. Kettle River Railroad Co., 70 Minn. 105, 72 N.W. 835 (1897); Straub v. Lyman Land & Investment Co., 30 S.D. 310, 138 N.W. 957 (1912), aff'd 31 S.D. 571, 141 N.W. 979 (1913). See also Pinney v. Providence Loan & Investment Co., 106 Wis. 396, 82 N.W. 308 (1900).

4. Cf. Bank of Augusta v. Earle, 38 U.S. (13 Pet.) 519, 10 L.Ed. 274 (1839).

5. See Henn & Alexander, Law of Corporations § 81 (3d ed. 1983).

6. 28 U.S.C.A. § 1332(c). C. Wright, Law of Federal Courts § 27 (5th ed. 1994). See also infra § 23.3.

7. 28 U.S.C.A. § 1332(c)(1).

while technically incorporated in another state, has such an extensive and ongoing relationship with the forum that the forum subjects it to legislation as if it were a domestic corporation.[8] Further, many corporations have been incorporated in several states. From the foregoing, it appears that the concept that a corporation is subject to suit in the state in which it was incorporated must be stated as essentially that, in most instances, a corporation can be sued in several places, one of which is the place of incorporation or places of incorporation. This deference to the place of incorporation has been reinforced by the doctrine of *forum non conveniens* and the internal affairs rule.[9]

Against this background of a choice of multiple state fora in which the corporation can be sued, we must add the federal courts. As a consequence, much may depend upon the nature or subject matter of the lawsuit. For example, the significance of federal law has developed extensively, particularly with regard to corporate activities involving securities under the Federal Securities Exchange Act of 1934.[10] Under federal substantive or procedural law, litigation begun in a state court, i.e., the state court of the state of incorporation, might be removed to the federal courts not only because of the diversity of citizenship if that were to exist, but also because of the possibility that a federal question arises under one of the areas of federal corporate law.[11] Further, a suit against a corporation may involve issues that are more appropriately tried at the principal place of business rather than at the place of incorporation and the doctrine of *forum non conveniens* may be applicable to lead the court in the state of incorporation to defer to the state that is more appropriately related to the litigation.[12]

C. FOREIGN CORPORATIONS

1. *Historical Development*

§ **10.14** Under the modern developments of jurisdiction in the United States, a foreign corporation is subject to jurisdiction *in personam* essentially to the same extent as is an individual under analogous circumstances.[1] However, because the foreign corporation cases have

---

8. See, e.g., Cal. Corp. Code § 2115. See also Halloran & Hammer, Sec. 2115 of the New Calif. General Corp. Law, 23 UCLA L. Rev. 1282 (1976). Oldham, California Regulates Pseudo–Foreign Corporations, 17 Santa Clara L. Rev. 85 (1977); Comment, Quasi–Foreign Corporations, 7 Pac. L.J. 673 (1976).

9. See, e.g., Gulf Oil Corp. v. Gilbert, 330 U.S. 501, 67 S.Ct. 839, 91 L.Ed. 1055 (1947); Koster v. (American) Lumbermens Mutual Casualty Co., 330 U.S. 518, 67 S.Ct. 828, 91 L.Ed. 1067 (1947); Henn & Alexander, Laws of Corporations § 356 (3d ed. 1983); Restatement, Second, Conflict of Laws § 84 (1971); Barrett, The Doctrine of Forum Non Conveniens, 35 Calif. L. Rev.

380 (1949); Reese & Kaufman, The Law Governing Corporate Affairs, 58 Colum. L. Rev. 1118 (1958).

10. 15 U.S.C.A. §§ 78a–78jj. See Securities and Exchange Commission v. National Securities, Inc., 393 U.S. 453, 89 S.Ct. 564, 21 L.Ed.2d 668 (1969). See also Henn & Alexander, supra n.5, § 353 (3d ed. 1983).

11. See Wright, supra n.6, § 38 (discussing grounds for removal).

12. See supra n.9.

§ 10.14

1. Travelers Health Association v. Virginia, 339 U.S. 643, 70 S.Ct. 927, 94 L.Ed. 1154 (1950); Restatement, Second, Conflict of Laws § 42 (1971).

been significant in the general development of jurisdictional doctrine and because there remain some situations in which jurisdiction over foreign corporations may be distinguishable from individuals, additional attention is given foreign corporations at this point.

Historically, under very early decisions, because a corporation was viewed as a creature of the state which created it and as having no legal existence outside the boundaries of that state, a corporation could not be sued outside the state which chartered it.[2] Notwithstanding this view of the corporate entity, early cases permitted property in another state belonging to the corporation to be attached even though personal jurisdiction could not be asserted against the corporation itself.[3] Such a limited concept of jurisdiction was inadequate to meet the demands of ever-increasing corporate activity. The consent doctrine first evolved to subject foreign corporations to suit in states other than that in which they were chartered. Cases soon permitted a corporation to consent to suit other than where it was organized, and since a state could refuse to allow a foreign corporation to do business within its borders, it could require its consent. Process could then be served to secure jurisdiction by requiring a corporation to appoint an agent to receive process within the state.[4] When the foreign corporation actually made such an appointment within the forum, the forum could render a valid judgment against it.[5] The scope of the consent given or required by the statute would determine whether the jurisdiction by appointment of an agent to receive process extended to all causes of action or only to those arising out of the business within the state.[6]

The consent doctrine, however, had conceptual difficulties, particularly where the consent was not given in fact, but was to be implied by reason of corporate activities within the state. The courts responded by holding that a corporation could not refuse to appoint an agent for the service of process and thereby escape liability under the statutes.[7] There was also uncertainty as to the extent of a state's power to exclude a foreign corporation from doing business within its boundaries when the

2. The famous dictum of Chief Justice Taney, in Bank of Augusta v. Earle, 38 U.S. (13 Pet.) 519, 588, 10 L.Ed. 274, 308 (1839) stated this theory: "It is very true that a corporation can have no legal existence out of the boundaries of the sovereignty by which it is created. . . . It must dwell in the place of its creation and cannot migrate to another sovereignty." See Henderson, The Position of Foreign Corporations in American Constitutional Law ch. 5 (1918). See also St. Clair v. Cox, 106 U.S. 350, 1 S.Ct. 354, 27 L.Ed. 222 (1882); Fead, Jurisdiction over Foreign Corporations, 24 Mich. L. Rev. 633 (1926).

3. See Bushel v. Commonwealth Insurance Co., 15 S & R 173 (Pa.1827); Henderson, supra n.2.

4. Lafayette Insurance Co. v. French, 59 U.S. (18 How.) 404, 15 L.Ed. 451 (1855); St.

Clair v. Cox, 106 U.S. 350, 1 S.Ct. 354, 27 L.Ed. 222 (1882); see Beale, Foreign Corporations § 264 (1904).

5. Pennsylvania Fire Insurance Co. of Philadelphia v. Gold Issue Mining & Milling Co., 243 U.S. 93, 37 S.Ct. 344, 61 L.Ed. 610 (1917).

6. *Pennsylvania Fire*, 243 U.S. 93, 37 S.Ct. 344, 61 L.Ed. 610; State ex rel. Aetna Insurance Co. v. Fowler, 196 Wis. 451, 220 N.W. 534 (1928); Bagdon v. Philadelphia & Reading Coal & Iron Co., 217 N.Y. 432, 111 N.E. 1075 (1916).

7. International Harvester Co. v. Commonwealth of Kentucky, 234 U.S. 579, 34 S.Ct. 944, 58 L.Ed. 1479 (1914); Henrietta Mining & Milling Co. v. Johnson, 173 U.S. 221, 19 S.Ct. 402, 43 L.Ed. 675 (1899).

foreign corporation was engaged only in interstate commerce; this was resolved to permit jurisdiction to entertain certain litigation within the corporation's consent.[8]

It soon became apparent, however, that consent was not only a fiction, but that the theory was not broad enough to cover all situations where a foreign corporation justifiably should be subject to suit. Some authorities avoided this difficulty with a consent doctrine by rationalizing that a corporation was present wherever the corporate enterprise was being carried on.[9] However, this concept of corporate presence was also a fiction and the analogy to individuals was incomplete. For example, if a corporation withdrew from a state in which it had been engaged in business it was commonly accepted that the state could provide for subsequent service of process upon the corporation for causes of action which arose within the forum before its withdrawal.[10] There is no easy analogy to jurisdiction over individuals based on the presence within the forum, for mere presence within the state of an agent of the corporation, or even a principal officer, is insignificant as a basis for jurisdiction.[11]

In the evolution of the present theory of jurisdiction over corporations, courts concentrated upon the actual activities of the corporations and of agents on their behalf. This attention to the activities led to a further development of the doing-business statutes which were quite commonly adopted in the United States. The attention given the economic activities of corporations led to the recognition of the currently accepted theories of jurisdiction over foreign corporations. The currently accepted doctrine of jurisdiction over foreign corporations and, indeed, jurisdiction over individuals, as well, was forecast by Judge Learned Hand in his opinions in *Smolik v. Philadelphia & Reading Coal & Iron Co.*,[12] and *Hutchinson v. Chase & Gilbert.*[13] As Professor Scott para-

---

8. International Harvester Co., 234 U.S. 579, 34 S.Ct. 944, 58 L.Ed. 1479.

9. See Cahill, Jurisdiction over Foreign Corporations and Individuals Who Carry On Business Within the Territory, 30 Harv. L. Rev. 676 (1917); Henderson, supra n.2, ch. 5. See also Philadelphia & Railroad Co. v. McKibbin, 243 U.S. 264, 37 S.Ct. 280, 61 L.Ed. 710 (1917); Rosenberg Brothers & Co. v. Curtis Brown Co., 260 U.S. 516, 43 S.Ct. 170, 67 L.Ed. 372 (1923); Bank of America v. Whitney Central National Bank, 261 U.S. 171, 43 S.Ct. 311, 67 L.Ed. 594 (1923).

10. Mutual Reserve Fund Life Association v. Phelps, 190 U.S. 147, 23 S.Ct. 707, 47 L.Ed. 987 (1903); Houston Fearless Corp. v. Teter, 318 F.2d 822 (10th Cir. 1963); Electrical Equipment Co. v. Hamm, 217 F.2d 656 (8th Cir.1954); Dansby v. North Carolina Mutual Life Insurance Co., 209 N.C. 127, 183 S.E. 521 (1936); Yoder v. Nu–Enamel Corp., 140 Neb. 585, 300 N.W. 840 (1941). See Fead, Jurisdiction over Foreign Corporations, 24 Mich. L. Rev. 633

(1926); Note, 26 Harv. L. Rev. 749 (1913); Restatement, Second, Conflict of Laws § 48 (1971). In State of Washington ex rel. Bond & Goodwin & Tucker v. Superior Court, 289 U.S. 361, 53 S.Ct. 624, 77 L.Ed. 1256 (1933), it was held that a judgment rendered after service upon the Secretary of State as provided for by state statute, with no notice of the action being actually forwarded to the corporation nor required by the statute, did not constitute a violation of due process to a corporation that had left the state but was being sued on a cause of action which had arisen out of transactions which had occurred in the state while the corporation was there doing business.

11. St. Clair v. Cox, 106 U.S. 350, 1 S.Ct. 354, 27 L.Ed. 222 (1882).

12. 222 Fed. 148 (S.D.N.Y.1915).

13. 45 F.2d 139 (2d Cir.1930). See also Bomze v. Nardis Sportswear, Inc., 165 F.2d 33 (2d Cir.1948) (later opinion by same judge).

phrased it: "If a foreign corporation voluntarily does business within the state, it is bound by reasonable regulations of that business imposed by the state, not because it is found there, not because it has consented to those regulations, but because it is reasonable and just to subject the corporation to those regulations as though it had consented."[14] This does not avoid the uncertainties of the doctrine, for it is very difficult to determine in advance what dealings will subject a foreign corporation to local suit, but it is at least focusing on the activities and the reasonableness of imposing on the corporation an obligation to respond to litigation in the state because of those activities.[15]

2. *Current Jurisdictional Theory*

§ 10.15 The "minimum contacts" test that so dominates the jurisdictional inquiry in the United States began as a fiction to rationalize the notion of corporate presence. In *International Shoe Co. v. Washington*,[1] the State of Washington sought to sue a foreign corporation which had not formally qualified to do business in Washington. Salesmen for the company exhibited samples, one shoe of a pair, and took orders from customers in Washington which became contracts only when accepted by the seller in Missouri. It was contended that the company did no business in Washington and could not be compelled to submit to the jurisdiction of the courts of the state. In rejecting this contention, the Court took the view that "Due process requires only that ... a defendant ... have certain minimum contacts with [the forum] such that the maintenance of the suit does not offend 'traditional notions of fair play and substantial justice.' "[2] The reasonableness test of due process depends upon the " ... quality and nature of the activity in relation to the fair and orderly administration of the laws which it was the purpose of the Due Process Clause to insure.... [T]o the extent that a corporation exercises the privilege of conducting activities within a state, it enjoys the benefits and protection of the laws of that state. The exercise of that privilege may give rise to obligations; and, so far as these obligations arise out of or are connected with the activities within the state, a procedure which requires the corporation to respond to a suit brought to enforce them can, in most instances, hardly be said to be undue ..."[3] Although this test does not give precise predictability as to the consequences of corporate actions, it does have the merit of recognizing reality and placing the emphasis upon the significance of the activity carried on by the corporation in relationship to the purpose for which the forum seeks to assert jurisdiction. From *International Shoe v. Washington* it

14. Scott, Jurisdiction over Nonresidents Doing Business Within a State, 32 Harv. L. Rev. 871, 883 (1919).

15. Cf. Hutchinson v. Chase & Gilbert, 45 F.2d 139, 141–42 (2d Cir.1930).

§ 10.15

1. 326 U.S. 310, 66 S.Ct. 154, 90 L.Ed. 95 (1945).

2. Id. at 316, 66 S.Ct. at 158, 90 L.Ed. 95.

3. Id. at 319, 66 S.Ct. at 160, 90 L.Ed. 95.

would appear that any liability creating conduct, economic or non-economic, which has a substantial relationship to the forum, should afford a basis for jurisdiction, at least as to activities arising out of that conduct.

International Shoe also recognized that a single act or occasional acts of corporate agents "because of their nature and quality and the circumstances of their commission, may be deemed to render the corporation liable to suit."[4] A single act was held adequate as a basis for personal jurisdiction against a corporation in *McGee v. International Life Insurance Co.*[5] In *McGee,* the defendant mailed an insurance certificate to an insured in California and was held subject to personal jurisdiction under the California statute for litigation arising out of that single insurance transaction. The Court stated that "It is sufficient for purposes of due process that the suit was based on a contract which had substantial connection with that state."[6] *International Shoe* and *McGee* set in motion the major expansion of state court jurisdiction that exists today.[7]

Since *International Shoe* and *McGee,* the Supreme Court has added some limiting qualifications in two significant cases. The first, *Hanson v. Denckla*, held that a Delaware trust company was not subject as trustee to personal jurisdiction of the Florida courts when no activities in Florida had been initiated by the defendant.[8] The Court concluded that the unilateral activities of others could not subject the corporation to suit, but that it "is essential in each case that there be some act by which the defendant purposefully avails itself of the privilege of conducting activities within the forum state, thus invoking the benefits and protections of its laws."[9] The *Hanson* case also highlighted the similarity between the factors significant in determining jurisdiction and those relating to *forum non conveniens.* While convenience to the defendant in defending the suit is an important factor, the "jurisdictional restrictions are more than a guarantee of immunity from inconvenient or distant

4. 326 U.S. at 318, 66 S.Ct. at 159, 90 L.Ed. 95. Early state cases distinguish between individuals and corporations in basing jurisdiction on doing an act within the state: Yocum v. Oklahoma Tire & Supply Co., 191 Ark. 1126, 89 S.W.2d 919 (1936); Wallace v. Smith, 238 App.Div. 599, 265 N.Y.S. 253 (1st Dept.1933); Clesas v. Hurley Machine Co., 52 R.I. 69, 157 A. 426 (1931). But see McLeod v. Birnbaum, 14 N.J.Misc. 485, 185 A. 667 (1936). The same jurisdictional tests are applicable to individuals and corporations. See Shaffer v. Heitner, 433 U.S. 186, 204, n.19, 97 S.Ct. 2569, 2579 n.19, 53 L.Ed.2d 683 (1977).

5. 355 U.S. 220, 78 S.Ct. 199, 2 L.Ed.2d 223 (1957) (noted 44 Iowa L. Rev. 427 (1959)). Cf. Kaye–Martin v. Brooks, 267 F.2d 394 (7th Cir.1959), cert. denied 361 U.S. 832, 80 S.Ct. 84, 4 L.Ed.2d 75 (1959).

6. 355 U.S. at 223, 78 S.Ct. at 201, 2 L.Ed.2d 223.

7. For detailed discussions of these developments, see Brilmayer, How Contacts Count: Due Process Limitations on State Court Jurisdiction, 1980 Sup. Ct. Rev. 77; Brilmayer, Related Contacts and Personal Jurisdiction, 101 Harv. L. Rev. 1444 (1988), with rejoinder by Twitchell, 101 Harv. L. Rev 1465 (1088); Hay, Refining Personal Jurisdiction in United States Conflicts Law, 35 Int'l & Comp. L.Q. 32 (1986).

8. Hanson v. Denckla, 357 U.S. 235, 78 S.Ct. 1228, 2 L.Ed.2d 1283 (1958).

9. 357 U.S. at 253, 78 S.Ct. at 1240, L.Ed.2d 1283. See also Rush v. Savchuk, 444 U.S. 320, 100 S.Ct. 571, 62 L.Ed.2d 516 (1980), on remand 290 N.W.2d 633 (Minn. 1980) (discussed supra at § 7.14).

litigation.... However minimal the burden of defending in a foreign tribunal, a defendant may not be called upon to do so unless he has had the 'minimum contacts' with that state that are a prerequisite to its exercise over him."[10]

The significance of these two factors, i.e., purposeful activities and minimum contacts of the defendant with the forum, were further highlighted in *World–Wide Volkswagen Corp. v. Woodson.*[11] In *World-Wide Volkswagen,* the court denied jurisdiction of Oklahoma over a New York wholesaler and retailer of automobiles in a products liability case when the wholesaler and retailer had neither done any business in Oklahoma, nor had any reason to anticipate the use of the automobile in Oklahoma. In discussing the foreseeability factor, the court noted that foreseeability was not the mere likelihood that a product would find its way into the forum, but "rather, it is that the defendant's conduct, and connection with the forum state, are such that he should reasonably anticipate being haled into court there.... The Due Process Clause, ... gives a degree of predictability to the legal system that allows potential defendants to structure their primary conduct with some minimum assurance as to where that conduct will and will not render them liable to suit."[12]

Although it was not clear for some time whether the *International Shoe* "minimum contacts" test even applied to individuals, the Supreme Court settled the question in a terse footnote holding that the test does indeed apply to individuals.[13] The present concepts of jurisdiction over corporations and over individuals rest on the same basis: reasonableness in the relationship of the suit and the activities or contacts of the parties with the forum.[14] The foreign corporation may be subjected to jurisdiction by reason of its consent or ownership of property within a state, or by reason of activities within or having an effect within a state. Jurisdiction seems appropriately founded on activities within a state of a tortious nature or activities without a state causing an injury within it. If the activities are of an economic nature, "to the extent that a corporation exercises the privileges of conducting activities within a state, it enjoys the benefits and protections of the laws of the state. The exercise of that privilege may give rise to obligations; and, so far as those obligations arise out of or connect with the activities within the state, a procedure that requires that corporation to respond to a suit to enforce them can, in most instances, hardly be said to be undue."[15] The cost of defending a

---

10. Hanson v. Denckla, 357 U.S. 235, 251, 78 S.Ct. 1228, 1238, 2 L.Ed.2d 1283.

11. 444 U.S. 286, 100 S.Ct. 559, 62 L.Ed.2d 490 (1980).

12. Id. at 297, 100 S.Ct. at 567, 62 L.Ed.2d 490 (1980)

13. Shaffer v. Heitner, 433 U.S. 186, 204 n.19, 97 S.Ct. 2569, 2579 n.19, 53 L.Ed.2d 683 (1977).

14. Restatement, Second, Conflict of Laws § 24 (1971). For the suggestion that fairness and convenience, rather than relational factors, should be the principal considerations in assessing the constitutionality of the exercise of jurisdiction see Weintraub, An Objective Basis for Rejecting Transient Jurisdiction, 22 Rutgers L.J. 611, 616 (1991). For a critical view of the suggestion see Hay, Flexibility Versus Predictability and Uniformity in Choice of Law, Hague Academy of International Law, 226 Recueil des Cours 281 (1991–I).

15. International Shoe Co. v. Washington, 326 U.S. 310, 319, 66 S.Ct. 154, 160, 90 L.Ed. 95 (1945).

lawsuit arising out of economic activities within a state is reasonably a part of the cost of engaging in that type of business.

For truly "foreign" (i.e., non-American) corporations the burdens of defending in an American forum may lead a court to conclude that exercising jurisdiction is unconstitutionally unreasonable. In *Helicopteros Nacionales de Colombia v. Hall*[16] the Supreme Court refused to allow an assertion of general jurisdiction over a helicopter transport company despite the corporations multi-million dollar purchases of helicopter parts and related services in the forum state of Texas. Later in *Asahi Metal Industry Co. v. Superior Court*,[17] the Supreme Court refused to extend stream-of-commerce jurisdiction over the Japanese manufacturer of an allegedly defective tire valve, despite the fact that the valve was allegedly purchased and caused injury in the forum state of California.

In sum, the tests for jurisdiction over individuals and corporations are essentially the same. However, the corporate status of the defendant is not wholly irrelevant to the inquiry, especially when the assertion of jurisdiction would impose burdens disproportionate to the business benefits that the defendant has derived from the forum state.

D. CORPORATE PARENT–SUBSIDIARY RELATIONSHIPS

§ 10.16   One situation unique to corporate activity is the relationship between parent corporation and subsidiary corporation. Probably the most frequently cited case on this question is the Supreme Court's 1925 decision in *Cannon Manufacturing Co. v. Cudahy Packing Co.*[1] *Cannon* involved an attempted assertion of jurisdiction in North Carolina over a Maine corporation. While the defendant corporation had few business connections itself with the forum state, it had a wholly-owned Alabama subsidiary which had an office in the forum. The Supreme Court affirmed the lower court's conclusion that the action against the defendant corporation should be dismissed for lack of jurisdiction. While noting that "the defendant dominates the Alabama [subsidiary] corporation, immediately and completely" the Court pointed out that "[t]he existence of the [subsidiary] as a distinct corporation is, however, in all respects observed."[2] The Court went on to discuss factors that are relevant to whether the "corporate veil" ought be pierced, and concluded that because the corporate form had not been abused, the subsidiary's business presence could not be attributed to the parent for jurisdictional purposes.

While *Cannon* is a singularly important case, its boundaries are not well defined. An obvious limitation on its precedential value is that the

---

16.   466 U.S. 408, 104 S.Ct. 1868, 80 L.Ed.2d 404 (1984).

17.   480 U.S. 102, 107 S.Ct. 1026, 94 L.Ed.2d 92 (1987).

§ 10.16

1.   267 U.S. 333, 45 S.Ct. 250, 69 L.Ed. 634 (1925).

2.   Id. at 335, 45 S.Ct. at 251, 69 L.Ed. 634.

opinion disclaimed any reliance on the Constitution.[3] While *Cannon* seems to articulate a prudential rule that a subsidiary's activities in the forum do not—assuming that corporate formalities are obeyed—give rise to general jurisdiction over the parent, it overstates the matter to say that a subsidiary's forum-state activities are irrelevant for constitutional purposes. For instance, in the stream-of-commerce context[4] the Supreme Court has held that the existence of regularized distribution channels that sweep a product into the state is a factor in determining whether the manufacturer has minimum contacts with the forum.[5] Whether the manufacturer establishes these channels through distributors, franchisees, subsidiaries or some other mechanism ought matter little in determining whether its connection with the forum is sufficiently purposeful to allow for jurisdiction.

A leading case on this issue is *Delagi v. Volkswagenwerk, A.G.,*[6] in which the New York Court of Appeals held that mere advertising in New York was not enough in itself to subject a German corporation to *in personam* jurisdiction within the state. In so holding it also concluded that the foreign corporation was not present in the state for *in personam* jurisdiction because of the activity of a wholly owned New Jersey corporation where the subsidiary's activities were not so completely subject to the control of the parent that the subsidiary is in fact merely a department of the parent. In *DeLagi* the court found that the only organization doing business in New York was a separate corporate entity organized and owned by American investors and that neither the German corporation nor its New Jersey subsidiary were actually transacting sufficient business in New York to confer personal jurisdiction. In general, the cases indicate that the courts may attribute the activities of a subsidiary to a parent to constitute business within the forum by the parent only where either the subsidiary has no independent existence in fact and is merely an instrumentality of the parent or where the subsidiary is being used as the agent of the parent corporation within the state so that the acts of the agent are the acts of the parent.[7] Absent this kind of economic identification of the parent and subsidiary, juris-

---

3. Id. at 336, 45 S.Ct. at 251, 69 L.Ed. 634 ("No question of the constitutional powers of the State, or the federal Government, is directly presented.").

4. See supra § 7.2.

5. See, e.g., Asahi Metal Indus. Co. v. Superior Court, 480 U.S. 102, 112, 107 S.Ct. 1026, 1032, 94 L.Ed.2d 92 (1987) (plurality opinion).

6. 29 N.Y.2d 426, 328 N.Y.S.2d 653, 278 N.E.2d 895 (1972); Alder, New York's Doing Business Test, 5 N.Y.U. J. Int'l & Pol. 575 (1972); Comment, 39 Brooklyn L. Rev. 229 (1972). See Wellborn, Subsidiary Corpo-

ration in New York, 22 Buffalo L. Rev. 681 (1973).

7. See Alder, supra n.6; Frummer v. Hilton Hotels Intern., Inc. (U.K. Ltd.), 19 N.Y.2d 533, 281 N.Y.S.2d 41, 227 N.E.2d 851 (1967), cert. denied 389 U.S. 923, 88 S.Ct. 241, 19 L.Ed.2d 266 discussed supra §§ 8.26–27; see also Comment, 39 Brooklyn L. Rev. 229 (1972); cf. Poyner v. Erma Werke Gmbh, 618 F.2d 1186 (6th Cir.1980), cert. denied 449 U.S. 841, 101 S.Ct. 121, 66 L.Ed.2d 49 (1980); Walker v. Newgent, 442 F.Supp. 38 (S.D.Tex.1977), aff'd 583 F.2d 163 (5th Cir.1978), cert. denied 441 U.S. 906, 99 S.Ct. 1994, 60 L.Ed.2d 374 (1979).

diction over a subsidiary or corporation does not provide jurisdiction over the parent corporation.[8]

Nor does jurisdiction over the parent confer jurisdiction over the subsidiary.[9] A certain amount of artificiality exists in distinguishing parents from subsidiary corporations,[10] and the decisions to conduct business by utilizing agents or intermediate merchants or subsidiaries seem to be based upon circumstances unrelated to whether or not the jurisdiction over the parent defendant should exist. In any event, as in the reverse situation, a subsidiary-parent relationship does not automatically confer jurisdiction, though its existence is clearly relevant in evaluating contacts.

E. JURISDICTION OVER INDIVIDUALS FOR CORPORATE OR FIDUCIARY ACTIVITIES

§ 10.17 In the 1960s, courts began to develop what eventually became known as the "corporate shield" or "fiduciary shield" jurisdictional doctrine.[1] Courts that apply the doctrine take the position that fiduciaries (usually corporate officers) cannot be subjected to jurisdiction in their individual capacity in a distant forum for activities undertaken in their fiduciary (usually corporate) capacity.[2]

Both the origins and constitutional status of the doctrine are controversial. The idea that the long arm ought not reach individuals discharging their fiduciary duties apparently began in the New York courts.[3] The

8. See Cannon Mfg. Co. v. Cudahy Packing Co, 267 U.S. 333, 45 S.Ct. 250, 69 L.Ed. 634 (1925); Harris Rutsky & Co. Insurance Services, Inc. v. Bell & Clements Ltd., 328 F.3d 1122, 1134–25 (9th Cir. 2003); Epps v. Stewart Info. Servs. Corp., 327 F.3d 642 (8th Cir. 2003); Poyner v. Lear Siegler, Inc., 542 F.2d 955 (6th Cir.1976), cert. denied 430 U.S. 969, 97 S.Ct. 1653, 52 L.Ed.2d 361 (1977); Velandra v. Regie Nationale des Usines Renault, 336 F.2d 292 (6th Cir. 1964); Miller v. Trans World Airlines, Inc., 302 F.Supp. 174 (E.D.Ky.1969); Porter v. LSB Industries, 192 A.D.2d 205, 600 N.Y.S.2d 867 (1993) (interpreting New York long-arm statute); Perlman v. Great States Life Insurance Co., 164 Colo. 493, 436 P.2d 124 (1968); Lit v. Storer Broadcasting Co., 217 Pa.Super. 186, 269 A.2d 393 (1970); Conn v. ITT Aetna Finance Co., 105 R.I. 397, 252 A.2d 184 (1969); see also Else v. Inflight Cinema International, Inc., 465 F.Supp. 1239 (W.D.Pa.1979); Oddi v. Mariner–Denver, Inc., 461 F.Supp. 306 (S.D.Ind. 1978); Murdock v. Volvo of America Corp., 403 F.Supp. 55 (N.D.Tex.1975); Superior Coal Co. v. Ruhrkohle, A.G., 83 F.R.D. 414 (E.D.Pa.1979). But see Anthem Ins. Cos. v. Tenet Healthcare Corp., 730 N.E.2d 1227 (Ind.2000) (extensive activities of separate subsidiary in forum sufficient for general jurisdiction over parent).

9. See Blount v. Peerless Chemicals (P.R.) Inc., 316 F.2d 695 (2d Cir.1963), cert. denied 375 U.S. 831, 84 S.Ct. 76, 11 L.Ed.2d 62; Pauley Petroleum, Inc. v. Continental Oil Co., 43 Del.Ch. 516, 239 A.2d 629 (1968).

10. See Sun First National Bank of Orlando v. Miller, 77 F.R.D. 430 (S.D.N.Y. 1978); DCA Food Industries, Inc. v. Hawthorn Mellody, Inc., 470 F.Supp. 574 (S.D.N.Y.1979); Hitt v. Nissan Motor Co., Ltd., 399 F.Supp. 838 (S.D.Fla.1975).

§ 10.17

1. For discussions of its origins, see Sponsler, Jurisdiction over the Corporate Agent: The Fiduciary Shield, 35 Wash. & Lee L. Rev. 349 (1978); Note, Personal Jurisdiction and the Corporate Employee: Minimum Contacts Meet the Fiduciary Shield, 38 Stan. L. Rev. 813 (1986).

2. See, e.g., Weller v. Cromwell Oil Co., 504 F.2d 927 (6th Cir.1974); Cincinnati Sub–Zero Prods. v. Augustine Medical, Inc., 800 F.Supp. 1549 (S.D.Ohio 1992).

3. See Note, supra n.1, at 820–21, 827 (citing and discussing Marine Midland Bank

New York Court of Appeals, however, when finally confronted with the question of whether the doctrine is part of New York law, firmly rejected the proposition, holding the doctrine neither compelled by the long-arm statute, nor the Constitution, nor fairness.[4] While the doctrine's birth (notwithstanding its later death) can perhaps be explained in New York as an interpretation of New York's long-arm statute (which stops well short of the constitutional limits on jurisdiction), the doctrine eventually found its way out of New York and into states with long-arm statutes that do not resemble New York's.[5] For states with long-arm statutes that reach to the constitutional limit, application of the doctrine would require it to be a due process limitation on jurisdiction.

The notion that the doctrine has constitutional status was laid to rest in the Supreme Court's decision in *Calder v. Jones*.[6] *Calder* involved a libel claim brought by a California resident (the actress Shirley Jones) in the California courts against a Florida-domiciled "reporter" and the article's editor, who jointly produced an allegedly libelous article about the plaintiff. The article was published by a nationally distributed tabloid (whose president was the editor-defendant) with a substantial circulation in California. If the fiduciary shield doctrine were a doctrine of constitutional law, *Calder* would have been an ideal case for invoking it, because the question before the Supreme Court was jurisdiction over the reporter and the editor individually, and each indisputably acted in his fiduciary capacity. In the course of holding that both were subject to jurisdiction in California, the Court dismissed any suggestion that they were immunized from jurisdiction with the statement that the defendants' "status as employees does not somehow insulate them from jurisdiction."[7]

Despite its clear rejection in *Calder*, the doctrine continues to survive in some courts as a sort of sub-constitutional, prudential limit on jurisdiction. While the doctrine clearly could be legitimate as a matter of statutory interpretation in a state with a relatively short long-arm,[8] even courts in states with maximalist long-arm statutes continue to describe the doctrine as an "equitable" limitation on jurisdiction.[9]

v. Miller, 664 F.2d 899 (2d Cir.1981); United States v. Montreal Trust Co., 358 F.2d 239 (2d Cir.), cert. denied 384 U.S. 919, 86 S.Ct. 1367, 16 L.Ed.2d 439 (1966); Soltex Polymer Corp. v. Fortex Indus., Inc., 590 F.Supp. 1453 (E.D.N.Y.1984)).

4. See Kreutter v. McFadden Oil Corp., 71 N.Y.2d 460, 522 N.E.2d 40, 527 N.Y.S.2d 195 (1988).

5. See Rice v. Nova Biomedical Corp., 38 F.3d 909, 912 (7th Cir.1994) (describing the early New York cases as "impaired precedent[s]" because of their basis on the New York statute and eventual rejection by the New York Court of Appeals); Note, supra n.1, at 820–21; see generally Sponsler, supra n.1.

6. 465 U.S. 783, 104 S.Ct. 1482, 79 L.Ed.2d 804 (1984).

7. *Calder*, 465 U.S. at 789–90, 104 S.Ct. at 1487, 79 L.Ed.2d 804.

8. See Note, supra n.1, at 820–21; ISI International, Inc. v. Borden Ladner Gervais LLP, 256 F.3d 548, 552–53 (7th Cir. 2001) (fiduciary shield doctrine exists only as a matter of state law in the nature of a venue rule); Black v. Bryant, 905 F.Supp. 1046 (M.D.Fla.1995) (applying doctrine as a matter of interpretation of the Florida long-arm statute).

9. See, e.g., Rice v. Nova Biomedical Corp., 38 F.3d 909, 914 (7th Cir.1994), cert. denied 514 U.S. 1111, 115 S.Ct. 1964, 131 L.Ed.2d 855 (1995); Caldwell–Baker Co. v.

Because of its uncertain basis, the doctrine is subject to an astonishing variety of exceptions, making it difficult to invoke even in forums that ostensibly recognize it. Courts have variously refused to invoke it when the individual defendant is alleged to have committed a tort,[10] when the individual defendant has derived some "personal benefit" from the activities,[11] when the corporation is merely a shell or the corporate form has been abused,[12] when the individual defendant has been physically present in the forum (even without in-forum service)[13] and when the defendant (or the defendant's lawyer) has been uncooperative in the discovery process regarding jurisdiction.[14]

In short, the fiduciary or corporate shield doctrine's existence—except as a matter of statutory interpretation in states with less-than-maximal long-arm statutes—is very doubtful. However, it does not follow from this that an individual defendant is subject to jurisdiction in every case in which the corporate defendant can be reached. The corporate defendant, because of extensive business contacts, may well be subject to general jurisdiction in many fora in which the individual defendant is beyond reach. Moreover, the separate "reasonableness" inquiry into jurisdiction[15] might defeat jurisdiction over an individual defendant, but allow it over a corporate defendant, if the individual defendant is genuinely disadvantaged by the choice of forum while the corporate defendant has the resources to mount an effective defense. To the extent that the corporate shield doctrine was invented to ensure a careful, separate inquiry into jurisdiction over individual defendants, the doctrine's purposes can be served by precise application of the minimum contacts test and the independent reasonableness limitation on jurisdiction.

V. PENDENT PERSONAL JURISDICTION

§ 10.18   The increasing number of statutes providing for so-called "nationwide service of process,"[1] as well as the addition of Federal Rule of Civil Procedure 4(k)(2),[2] have led to a jurisdictional conundrum often referred to as "pendent personal jurisdiction."[3] The conundrum presents

---

S. Ill. Railcar Co., 225 F.Supp.2d 1243 (D. Kan. 2002); Johns v. Rozet, 770 F.Supp. 11, 17 (D.D.C.1991) (doctrine not applied because corporation undercapitalized); American Directory Service Agency v. Beam, 131 F.R.D. 635, 641 (D.D.C.1990) (not applying doctrine because of bad conduct of defendant during discovery process).

10.   See, e.g., Elbeco Inc. v. Estrella de Plato Corp., 989 F.Supp. 669 (E.D.Pa.1997); Note, supra n.1, at 823.

11.   *Rice*, 38 F.3d at 912–13; Note, supra n.1, at 824.

12.   See Note, supra n.1, at 825.

13.   Note, supra n.1, at 826.

14.   See, e.g., *American Directory*, 131 F.R.D. 635.

15.   See supra § 5.12.

§ 10.18

1.   See supra § 10.2.

2.   For a discussion, see supra § 10.5.

3.   See, e.g., Mills, Pendent Jurisdiction and Extraterritorial Service Under the Federal Securities Laws, 70 Colum. L. Rev. 423 (1970); Note, Removing the Cloak of Personal Jurisdiction from Choice of Law Analysis: Pendent Jurisdiction and Nationwide Service of Process, 51 Fordham L. Rev. 127 (1982) (hereinafter Note, Removing the Cloak); Note, Pendent Personal Jurisdiction and Nationwide Service of Process, 64 N.Y.U. L. Rev. 113 (1989) (hereinafter

itself most often in cases in which the plaintiff pleads in federal court a federal claim—for example, one arising under the securities laws—and joins with it state law claims arising out of the same operative facts.[4] Even without diversity of citizenship, the state law claims fall within the federal court's pendent subject matter jurisdiction.[5] If personal jurisdiction on the, say, securities law claim were obtained under the special nationwide service provision, the question arises as to whether that statute can also be used to assert pendent personal jurisdiction over the defendant on the state law claims.[6]

Through the mid–1960s, courts generally rejected assertions of pendent personal jurisdiction.[7] Those courts that rejected it pointed out that the nationwide service statutes did not expressly authorize service on the state law theories, and refused to find any implication in favor of such assertions from the mere fact that federal court subject matter jurisdiction so extended. Courts also suggested that there might be constitutional problems in subjecting defendants to the application of state laws that would not otherwise reach them.[8]

Since then, however, pendent personal jurisdiction has earned nearly universal acceptance from the federal courts,[9] though some writers

Note, Nationwide Service). Courts occasionally refer to the notion as one of "ancillary personal jurisdiction," see, e.g., US Telecom, Inc. v. Hubert, 678 F.Supp. 1500, 1507 (D.Kan.1987), although true ancillary personal jurisdiction is a somewhat different notion which is discussed below in this section.

4. See F.R.C.P. 18 (plaintiff may join all claims in one complaint).

5. See 28 U.S.C.A. § 1367 (codifying doctrine of "supplemental jurisdiction"); United Mine Workers v. Gibbs, 383 U.S. 715, 86 S.Ct. 1130, 16 L.Ed.2d 218 (1966).

6. Though less common, applications of pendent personal jurisdiction can be asserted in cases in which a state long-arm statute reaches some, but not all, of the claims pleaded by the plaintiff, but all of the claims are within the court's constitutional reach. See, e.g., Val Leasing, Inc. v. Hutson, 674 F.Supp. 53, 56 (D.Mass.1987) (claims not within the reach of the Massachusetts long-arm statute allowed to "piggyback" on claims within the scope of the statute); cf. Rice v. Nova Biomedical Corp., 38 F.3d 909, 913 (7th Cir.1994), cert. denied 514 U.S. 1111, 115 S.Ct. 1964, 131 L.Ed.2d 855 (1995) (noting that the district court had asserted jurisdiction on such a theory and that defendants had not contested it and suggesting that the theory "should probably be viewed as an interpretation of Illinois' long-arm statute rather than as some free-standing federal common law doctrine.").

7. See Note, Removing the Cloak, supra n.3, at 129 n.8 & 138 (collecting cases); Note, Personal Jurisdiction and the Joinder of Claims in Federal Court, 64 Tex. L. Rev. 1463, 1471 (1986) (identifying 1963 as the date that judicial hostility to pendent personal jurisdiction abated).

8. See Note, Removing the Cloak, supra n.3, at 129 (noting choice-of-law issue).

9. See, e.g., United States v. Botefuhr, 309 F.3d 1263 (10th Cir. 2002) (noting broad acceptance among federal courts and approving its use in some circumstances); ESAB Group, Inc. v. Centricut, Inc., 126 F.3d 617 (4th Cir.1997), cert. denied 523 U.S. 1048, 118 S.Ct. 1364, 140 L.Ed.2d 513 (1998) (pendent personal jurisdiction allowed over state claims appended to a RICO claim); IUE AFL–CIO v. Herrmann, 9 F.3d 1049 (2d Cir.1993), cert. denied 513 U.S. 822, 115 S.Ct. 86, 130 L.Ed.2d 38 (1994) (pendent personal jurisdiction allowed over state claims appended to an ERISA claim); Oetiker v. Jurid Werke, GmbH, 556 F.2d 1 (D.C.Cir.1977) (pendent personal jurisdiction allowed over state claims in a patent case); see also Robert C. Casad, Personal Jurisdiction in Federal Question Cases, 70 Tex. L. Rev. 1589, 1607–08 (1992) (noting trend towards acceptance of pendent personal jurisdiction and that "[t]he constitutionality of the practice is seldom questioned"); Note, Removing the Cloak, supra n.3, at 129 ("the growing trend of authority holds that a federal court may so extend the reach of its non-federal personal jurisdic-

continue to express concern about its fairness and constitutionality.[10] Courts have employed a variety of theories to support the extension of their personal jurisdiction to the state claims. They variously invoke considerations of judicial economy, a lack of prejudice to the defendant (because the federal claims will go forward in any event), the broad wording of the service statutes (which often refer to "actions" under federal law) and analogies to the common law development of pendent subject matter jurisdiction.[11]

Although the Supreme Court has never resolved its status, pendent personal jurisdiction is a sensibly modest extension of the adjudicatory authority of federal courts. Because the defendant is amenable to jurisdiction on the federal claim, little harm is done to the defendant by allowing jurisdiction over pendent state law claims, and forcing the plaintiff to sever the state claims for litigation in another forum accomplishes little. There are, however, some substantial unresolved questions with regard to the doctrine's boundaries.

One is its applicability to state courts. In many instances, state courts have concurrent jurisdiction over federal claims that are subject to nationwide service statutes. The constitutional standard that applies to attempted state-court exercises of jurisdiction under these statutes is unsettled, though there are good reasons to apply the same standards to both state and federal courts.[12] Assuming the same constitutional standard applies to both state and federal courts hearing federal claims that include nationwide service provisions, the doctrine of pendent personal jurisdiction ought apply with equal force in the state forum. While, however, this is a question of some theoretical interest, its practical significance is limited. Because plaintiffs have may file any such federal claims in federal court,[13] and defendants may remove to federal court any such claim filed in state court,[14] these cases will be litigated in state court only in the unlikely event that both the plaintiff and the defendant think that the state forum is to their advantage.

A second unresolved question is to what extent the doctrine can extend constitutional limits on jurisdiction. In the paradigmatic case—the plaintiff pleads a federal claim in federal court and appends state law

---

tion"); Note, Nationwide Service, supra n.3, at 116 ("For the past twenty years, courts have universally allowed such exercises of 'pendent personal jurisdiction.' "); Note, supra n.7, at 1471–72 ("By the 1970s, all the circuit courts that had considered the issue found this extension of judicial power permissible."). "Pendent venue," however, is apparently not allowed by some courts, as venue difficulties can be easily cured by a transfer under 28 U.S.C.A. § 1406. See Cameron v. Thornburgh, 983 F.2d 253 (D.C.Cir.1993). At least one court has allowed pendent venue. See VMS/PCA Ltd. Partnership v. PCA Partners Ltd. Partnership, 727 F.Supp. 1167, 1174 (N.D.Ill.1989) (cited in Casad, supra, at 1610 n.106).

10. See Casad, supra n.9, at 1609 (discussing cautionary statements on the practice expressed by the Advisory Committee on the Federal Rules of Civil Procedure).

11. See supra authorities cited n.9.

12. See Casad, supra n.9, at 1597 ("the jurisdictional reach of state courts should be extended in federal question cases as well").

13. See 28 U.S.C.A. § 1331 (all federal question claims are with the District Court's original jurisdiction without regard to the amount in controversy).

14. See 28 U.S.C.A. § 1441.

claims—the constitutionality of pendent personal jurisdiction is largely free from doubt. The widespread assumption is that the constitutional test for federal court exercises of in personam jurisdiction is *prima facie* satisfied by showing that the defendant has minimum contacts with the United States as a whole.[15] Thus, if the terms of the nationwide service statute are satisfied relative to the federal claims, the constitutionality of asserting jurisdiction on the state claims seems relatively clear.

Not every case, however, fits exactly this mold. Even without a nationwide service statute, the results of the jurisdictional inquiry can vary from claim to claim. Although rarely, courts sometimes conclude that the minimum contacts test is satisfied as to some, but not all, of the plaintiff's claims against the defendant.[16] Here the courts are split, with some taking jurisdiction over all the claims,[17] and others taking jurisdiction over only those claims that independently satisfy the requirement of minimum contacts with the forum state.[18] The better approach is probably to take jurisdiction over all the claims as long as they have a strong factual relationship. If the claims are closely intertwined, severing some of them will probably lead to duplicative litigation. However, if the factual relationship among the claims is weak (as can occur if the parties are of diverse citizenship and loosely related claims are joined largely to convenience the plaintiff) then severing and dismissing the claims that would not independently satisfy the standards for in personam jurisdiction is desirable.

A third unresolved question is the applicability of the doctrine beyond the relatively innocuous setting of appending state claims against defendants already subject to jurisdiction on the federal claim. More aggressive uses of the doctrine might include asserting closely related state claims against defendants other than those sued on the federal law claims ("pendent party" jurisdiction) or the defendant's impleading of third parties on purely state law theories (ancillary jurisdiction). Any sort of supplemental personal jurisdiction that involves joinder of an additional party is more doubtful as a matter of fairness—because the affected party would not be forced to defend in the forum at all were it not for the exercise of supplemental jurisdiction—and encounters much more difficulty with existing precedent.

Of the two, pendent party personal jurisdiction seems the most problematic. The Federal Rules Advisory Committee made clear that, at least in the context of the amendments to the federal rules, pendent party personal jurisdiction was not contemplated.[19] Moreover, such an exercise of jurisdiction is difficult to square with *World–Wide Volks-*

---

15. See supra § 10.2.

16. See, e.g., Anderson v. Century Prods. Co., 943 F.Supp. 137 (D.N.H.1996) (minimum contacts test satisfied as to tort causes of action but not as to contract cause of action); Nelson v. R. Greenspan & Co., 613 F.Supp. 342 (D.Mo.1985) (same).

17. See, e.g., *Nelson*, 613 F.Supp. 342.

18. See, e.g., *Anderson*, 943 F.Supp. at 147.

19. See Casad, supra n.9, at 1610.

wagen v. Woodson[20] in which the Supreme Court evaluated jurisdiction over each defendant separately, and expressly stated that convenience and the availability of jurisdiction over other defendants in the forum could not support jurisdiction over parties without minimum contacts in the forum state.[21] A case can be made, perhaps, for pendent party personal jurisdiction in narrow circumstances,[22] but as a full-scale extension of adjudicatory authority it seems doubtful.

A better case can be made for true ancillary personal jurisdiction, in which the defendant attempts to bring in other parties needed for defensive purposes, usually by impleading them or asserting their indispensability in the underlying action. One modest tool in this regard is the so-called "100–mile bulge" rule which allows defendants to assert personal jurisdiction over ancillary parties as long as they can be served within 100 miles of the courthouse and have contacts within that 100 mile zone.[23] In multistate urban areas this rule has some usefulness, but in most circumstances it has none. The fairness considerations are stronger in favor of ancillary than pendent party personal jurisdiction, because the defendant denied ancillary service may otherwise be forced to battle on two fora: once defending the primary action and then again attempting to obtain contribution or indemnity. Perhaps because of these stronger fairness considerations, ancillary personal jurisdiction of this kind is allowed under the Brussels and Lugano Conventions, which regulate jurisdiction in Western Europe.[24]

Despite its stronger claim to fairness, ancillary personal jurisdiction appears to enjoy no stronger support in the cases than does pendent party personal jurisdiction. In *Omni Capital International v. Rudolf Wolff & Co.*,[25] the defendant on a federal claim arising under the Commodities Exchange Act attempted to implead a foreign party who did not have a sufficient connection with the forum to satisfy its long-arm statute. The Supreme Court held that this lack of connection, coupled with the absence of any nationwide service statute applicable to the third-party defendant, required dismissal. Were ancillary personal jurisdiction a viable doctrine, *Omni* would have been a good candidate for its application, because the dismissal of the third-party defendant undoubtedly forced the defendant to pursue its indemnity action in another forum. *Omni* can perhaps be distinguished on the grounds that the ancillary theory was not urged, but the Supreme Court's clear separation of the requirements for personal and subject matter jurisdiction[26] suggests strongly that the Supreme Court would not have been receptive. A general theory of ancillary personal jurisdiction also suffers

20. 444 U.S. 286, 100 S.Ct. 559, 62 L.Ed.2d 490 (1980).

21. Id. at 294, 100 S.Ct. at 566, 62 L.Ed.2d 490.

22. Casad, supra n.9, at 1610.

23. See supra § 10.4.

24. See Borchers, Comparing Personal Jurisdiction in the United States and the European Community: Lessons for American Reform, 40 Am. J. Comp. L. 121, 128–29 (1992).

25. 484 U.S. 97, 108 S.Ct. 404, 98 L.Ed.2d 415 (1987).

26. Id. at 103–04, 108 S.Ct. at 409, 98 L.Ed.2d 415.

from the weakness that because a limited kind of it is authorized by the 100–mile bulge rule a more general application is difficult to imply in the existing service statutes. Despite, however, these theoretical weaknesses, there may be instances in which non-application would result in extreme unfairness to the defendant and in which such an assertion of jurisdiction should be allowed.

A fourth unresolved question is the appropriate choice-of-law approach with respect to the pendent state claims. Commentators have noted the choice-of-law issue[27] and appropriately suggested that the *Klaxon* rule[28] has a much diminished claim to application in this context.[29] The policy justification for *Klaxon*—avoidance of intrastate forum shopping between state and federal court[30]—is of no relevance in cases in which the state claims could not be maintained independently in state court. Thus, in choosing the law applicable to state claims brought before the court on a theory of pendent personal jurisdiction, federal courts are well advised to avoid the strong forum bias of state court choice-of-law doctrine, and instead attempt to choose a law that does not do violence to the defendant's reasonable expectations. In resisting near automatic application of forum law federal courts can avoid any significant unfairness that might otherwise be worked by application of the doctrine of pendent personal jurisdiction.

As is the case with supplemental subject matter jurisdiction,[31] pendent and ancillary personal jurisdiction are discretionary doctrines. If the so-called "anchor claim"–the one over which the court unquestionably has jurisdiction–disappears the courts will usually dismiss the other claims.[32]

VI. FOREIGN STATES AND INSTRUMENTALITIES

§ 10.19   The concept of sovereign immunity continues to exercise a significant gravitational pull over litigation involving foreign governments and their instrumentalities. Since 1952, the executive branch of the federal government has followed the so-called "restrictive view" of sovereign immunity.[1] Under this view, a foreign government is immune from suit for sovereign or governmental activities, but liable as would be a private party for commercial activities.

This view is largely codified in the Foreign Sovereign Immunities Act ("FSIA").[2] The FSIA starts with a presumption that a foreign state

---

27.   See, e.g., Casad, supra n.9, at 1608; Note, Removing the Cloak, supra n.3, at 131, 161–66.

28.   See supra § 3.36 et. seq.

29.   See Note, Removing the Cloak, supra n.3, at 161–66.

30.   Klaxon Co. v. Stentor Elec. Mfg. Co., 313 U.S. 487, 61 S.Ct. 1020, 85 L.Ed. 1477 (1941).

31.   28 U.S.C.A. § 1367(c).

32.   United States v. Botefuhr, 309 F.3d 1263 (10th Cir. 2002).

§ 10.19

1.   See Republic of Argentina v. Weltover, 504 U.S. 607, 612–13, 112 S.Ct. 2160, 2165, 119 L.Ed.2d 394 (1992).

2.   28 U.S.C.A. §§ 1602–11.

and its instrumentalities are "immune from the jurisdiction of the courts of the United States and of the States."[3] The FSIA makes several exceptions from this blanket immunity, including if the foreign state has waived its immunity,[4] claims involving property expropriated in violation of international law and the property itself (or property exchanged for it) is in the United States,[5] and claims involving property acquired by the United States by succession or gift of real property in the United States.[6] Except in certain limited circumstances in wrongful death actions, the FSIA never lifts the immunity of a foreign state or instrumentality from liability for punitive damages.[7] The question of whether an entity is a "foreign instrumentality" within the meaning of the statute can be a close one. In *Dole Food Co. v. Patrickson*,[8] the Supreme Court concluded that two corporations in which Israel had formerly owned a majority of the shares were not foreign instrumentalities because, at the time of the underlying events, the companies had been privatized and any governmental ownership existed "in companies one or more corporate tiers above"[9] the corporate parties to the case.

The FSIA links personal and subject matter jurisdiction. Jurisdiction—both personal and subject matter—exists over a foreign state if the state is not immunized by the terms of the Act.[10]

For purposes of private litigation, the FSIA makes several important and interlocking exceptions from foreign state immunity. Most critically, foreign states and instrumentalities are not immune from suit on claims "in which the action is based upon a commercial activity carried on in the United States by the foreign state; or upon an act performed in the United States in connection with a commercial activity of the foreign state elsewhere; or upon an act outside the territory in connection with a commercial activity of the foreign state elsewhere and that act causes a direct effect in the United States."[11] The FSIA defines "commercial activity" as "a regular course of commercial conduct or a particular commercial transaction or act[;] [t]he commercial character of an activity shall be determined by reference to the nature of the . . . act, rather than by reference to its purpose."[12] The Act also defines "commercial activity carried on in the United States by a foreign state" as a "commercial activity carried on by such state and having substantial contact with the United States."[13]

The FSIA also has an alternative tort liability provision that requires that the "personal injury or death, or damage to or loss of

3. 28 U.S.C.A. § 1604.

4. 28 U.S.C.A. § 1605(a)(1).

5. 28 U.S.C.A. § 1605(a)(3).

6. 28 U.S.C.A. § 1605(a)(4).

7. 28 U.S.C.A. § 1606.

8. 538 U.S. 468, 123 S.Ct. 1655, 155 L.Ed.2d 643 (2003).

9. Id. at 475, 123 S.Ct. at 1660, 155 L.Ed.2d 643.

10. 28 U.S.C.A. § 1330; see also Verlinden B.V. v. Central Bank of Nigeria, 461 U.S. 480, 485 n.5, 103 S.Ct. 1962, 1967 n.5, 76 L.Ed.2d 81 (1983).

11. 28 U.S.C.A. § 1605(a)(2).

12. 28 U.S.C.A. § 1603(d).

13. 28 U.S.C.A. § 1603(e).

property, occur[] in the United States" under circumstances similar to the United States' own liability under the Federal Tort Claims Act.[14] The FSIA, as well, lifts immunity for certain arbitration agreements and in traditional circumstances for the enforcement of in rem maritime rights against vessels owned by foreign states.[15]

In broad terms, the FSIA sets forth two principal criteria for proceeding against a foreign state or instrumentality. First, the subject matter of the litigation must be appropriate. Usually this requires the plaintiff to show that the activities upon which the litigation is based are commercial, and that the allegedly wrongful activities do not, therefore, implicate any genuinely sovereign or governmental prerogatives. Second, the litigation must have a sufficient territorial nexus with the United States. The FSIA addresses this second requirement in a variety of ways. The definition of a commercial activity carried on within the United States requires that the activity have a "substantial contact with the United States."[16] In order for activities carried on outside the United States to fit within the "commercial activity" exception, the plaintiff must show that the act in question "cause[d] a direct effect in the United States."[17] The special tort provisions mentioned above only cover injuries felt in the United States.[18] The provisions for the enforcement of certain in rem maritime rights require the traditional arrest of the vessel while in the territory of the court.[19]

The line between commercial and non-commercial activities is well illustrated by two Supreme Court decisions. In *Republic of Argentina v. Weltover, Inc.*,[20] the plaintiffs were two Panamanian corporations and a Swiss bank who were creditors on commercial notes guaranteed by the Argentine government. The Argentine government, concluding that it lacked the current funds to honor the guarantees, refinanced the debts by issuing government bonds—called "Bonods"—to the creditors. The Bonods allowed the creditor to specify one of several places of repayment, including New York City (the option chosen by each of the plaintiffs). When the Bonods became due, Argentina unilaterally rescheduled payment to a later date. Refusing to accept the new schedule, the plaintiff-creditors demanded payments on the terms of the bonds, and when none were forthcoming brought suit under the FSIA against the Argentine government and its central bank.

Argentina asserted that it was immune because its actions were non-commercial. A unanimous Supreme Court, however, concluded that Argentina's actions fit within the commercial activity exception. The Court reasoned that by issuing the Bonods, the Argentine government acted "not as regulator of a market, but in the manner of a private

---

14. See 28 U.S.C.A. § 1605(5); cf. 28 U.S.C.A. § 2680(a) (discretionary function exception to Federal Tort Claims Act).

15. 28 U.S.C.A. § 1605(b), (c).

16. 28 U.S.C.A. § 1603(e).

17. 28 U.S.C.A. § 1605(a)(3).

18. 28 U.S.C.A. § 1605(a)(5).

19. 28 U.S.C.A. § 1605(b).

20. 504 U.S. 607, 112 S.Ct. 2160, 119 L.Ed.2d 394 (1992).

player within it. . . .''[21] While Argentina clearly issued the Bonods for reasons of domestic policy (to make foreign investment in Argentina more attractive), its purpose was irrelevant in light of the FSIA's injunction that the commercial character of an activity " 'shall be determined by [its] nature . . . rather than . . . its purpose.' ''[22]According to the Court, Argentina' actions were inherently commercial because it entered "the bond market in the manner of a private actor. . . .''[23]

Shortly after *Weltover*, the Supreme Court decided in *Saudi Arabia v. Nelson*[24] that the Saudi government's activities were not commercial and thus immunized. In *Nelson*, the principal plaintiff was an American recruited to work as a systems monitor in a hospital owned and operated by the Saudi government. The principal plaintiff alleged that after he repeatedly reported safety problems to hospital and government officials, he was summarily seized and held in a jail cell where he was " 'shackled, tortured and beat. . . .' ''[25] About a month later, at the request of a Senator, the principal plaintiff was released and allowed to return to the United States.

Upon returning, he and his wife filed an action against the Saudi government, its hospital and the recruiting agency, the latter two of which were alleged to be instrumentalities of the Saudi government.[26] In their complaint, the plaintiffs raised only tort claims, which the majority described as falling into three categories. One category was intentional theories brought by the principal plaintiff relating to his alleged mistreatment during the arrest and detention. A second category sounded in negligence for failure to warn the principal plaintiff of the dangers of his employment. A third was brought derivatively on behalf of the principal plaintiff's wife for loss of consortium and her distress.[27]

A majority of the Court concluded that, even taking plaintiffs' allegations at face value, no commercial activity was alleged as the basis for recovery. While the majority conceded that some of the alleged activities were commercial—the principal plaintiff's recruitment and the entry into an employment contract—those allegations were not the basis for the suit because "those facts alone entitle [the plaintiffs] to nothing under their theory of the case."[28] The basis for the suit, rather, was the arrest and detention, which the majority characterized as quintessentially governmental activities. Relying on *Weltover*'s holding that commercial activities are those in which private actors can engage, the *Nelson*

21. Id. at 614, 112 S.Ct. at 2166, 119 L.Ed.2d 394.

22. Id. at 612, 112 S.Ct. at 2165, 119 L.Ed.2d 394 (quoting 28 U.S.C.A. § 1603(d)).

23. Id. at 617, 112 S.Ct. at 2167, 119 L.Ed.2d 394.

24. 507 U.S. 349, 113 S.Ct. 1471, 123 L.Ed.2d 47 (1993).

25. Id. at 353, 113 S.Ct. at 1475, 123 L.Ed.2d 47 (quoting complaint). Certain torture claims are now allowed by the FSIA,

but only against states designated as "state sponsors of terrorism." 28 U.S.C.A. § 1605(a)(7)(A). See infra notes 51–55 and accompanying text.

26. Id. at 356, 113 S.Ct. at 1477, 123 L.Ed.2d 47.

27. Id. at 354, 113 S.Ct. at 1476, 123 L.Ed.2d 47.

28. Id. at 358, 113 S.Ct. at 1478, 123 L.Ed.2d 47.

majority distinguished the earlier case by stating that "a foreign state's exercise of the power of its police has long been understood for purposes of the restrictive theory as peculiarly sovereign in nature."[29]

In contrast to *Weltover*'s unanimity, *Nelson* divided sharply on the question of whether the actions were commercial. Two justices concluded that the complaint alleged commercial activities as its basis, but concurred in the result because the allegations lacked a sufficient territorial nexus with the United States.[30] Another justice, joined in part by two others, agreed with the majority that the intentional tort theories failed to allege commercial activities, but thought that the negligent misrepresentation theories could go forward[31]—analysis that the majority dismissed as a "semantic ploy" to convert intentional torts to negligence theories.[32] Another justice dissented entirely, and would have allowed all of the plaintiffs' theories to proceed.[33]

The divided *Nelson* Court shows that the question of whether foreign activities are commercial or non-commercial can be very close. Some activities, such as the operation of a state-run passenger airline, are clearly commercial. Others, such as traditional law enforcement activities, are clearly non-commercial. But, cases like *Nelson*, in which the two blend together, arise with some frequency. *Nelson* and *Weltover* demonstrate that the methodology is largely intuitive. The current test attempts to assign the activity to a category of a fairly high level of abstraction ("bond issuance" in *Weltover* and "law enforcement" in *Nelson*) and then determines whether that category sits mostly on the private, commercial side of the line or the public, governmental side.[34]

The question of a territorial nexus to the United States can be equally vexing. The commercial activity exception to the FSIA refers to a territorial nexus in at least two ways. In order for a commercial activity to be "carried out within the United States" it must have "substantial contact with the United States."[35] The commercial activity exception also reaches, however, activities carried out in the foreign country that "cause a direct effect in the United States."[36]

The "substantial contact" requirement of the former is generally assumed to require more than "minimum" contacts.[37] Moreover, the

29. Id. at 361, 113 S.Ct. at 1479, 123 L.Ed.2d 47.

30. Id. at 364, 113 S.Ct. at 1481, 123 L.Ed.2d 47 (White, J., concurring in the judgment).

31. Id. at 370, 113 S.Ct. at 1484, 123 L.Ed.2d 47 (Kennedy, J., concurring in part and dissenting in part).

32. Id. at 363, 113 S.Ct. at 1480, 123 L.Ed.2d 47.

33. Id. at 377, 113 S.Ct. at 1487, 123 L.Ed.2d 47 (Stevens, J., dissenting).

34. See, e.g., Jungquist v. Bin Khalifa al Nahyan, 115 F.3d 1020 (D.C.Cir.1997) (personal promise by governmental official to provide medical care for injured plaintiff is not an action taken in the official capacity of the governmental official).

35. 28 U.S.C.A. § 1603(e).

36. 28 U.S.C.A. § 1605(a)(3).

37. See, e.g., In re Minister Papandreou, 139 F.3d 247, 252 (D.C.Cir.1998) ("We have never decided precisely what 'substantial contact' amounts to in the FSIA context, though we have said that it requires more than the minimum contacts sufficient to satisfy due process in establishing jurisdiction....") (citing Maritime Int'l Nominees Establishment v. Guinea, 693 F.2d 1094 (D.C.Cir.1983)).

intuitive sense of "carrying on" activities within the United States would entail the occurrence of the liability-creating events within American borders. In *Nelson*, for instance, the two justices who concurred in the judgment did so because the bulk of the liability-creating events took place in Saudi Arabia, meaning that the activity in question did not take place in the United States.[38]

The longer reach comes from the latter clause, allowing jurisdiction for extra-American commercial activities that cause a "direct effect" in the United States. The long reach of the "direct effect" provision was demonstrated in *Weltover*. None of the *Weltover* plaintiffs were Americans; the only significant connection with the United States was that each plaintiff had designated New York City as the place of payment on the bonds. The Supreme Court concluded that the "direct effect" test was met because the payment that was required to be made in New York had not been made as a proximate and immediate result of the defendant's actions.[39] Moreover, the Supreme Court disclaimed any requirement of foreseeability or substantiality of the effect, beyond merely asserting that the effect must be more than de minimis.[40]

Weltover's generous interpretation of the "direct effect" test raises important questions. First, it apparently rejects more restrictive tests that had been applied by lower courts.[41] Second, it raises the question of whether there might be applications of the "direct effects" test that are unconstitutional as overstepping the due process boundaries of jurisdiction.[42] *Weltover* itself confronted the constitutional question, and addressed it first by questioning whether due process limits on jurisdiction even apply to foreign states in light the Clause's application only to "persons."[43] The Court dropped at least one hint that its answer to the question might be negative by citing the famous case of *South Carolina v. Katzenbach*,[44] which held that states are not "persons" for due process purposes.[45] The Court, however, avoided confronting this question by concluding that Argentina did, in fact, have minimum contacts by virtue

---

38. *Nelson*, 507 U.S. at 370, 113 S.Ct. at 1484, 123 L.Ed.2d 47 ("Neither the hospital's employment practices, nor its disciplinary procedures, had any apparent connection to this country.").

39. *Weltover*, 504 U.S. at 618, 112 S.Ct. at 2168, 119 L.Ed.2d 394.

40. See Hanil Bank v. Pt. Bank Negara Indonesia, 148 F.3d 127, 132 (2d Cir.1998) (discussing *Weltover*).

41. See, e.g., Antares Aircraft, L.P. v. Federal Republic of Nigeria, 999 F.2d 33 (2d Cir.1993), cert. denied 510 U.S. 1071, 114 S.Ct. 878, 127 L.Ed.2d 74 (1994) (in order for there to be a "direct effect" in the United States "legally significant" actions must take place in the United States); see also *Hanil Bank*, 148 F.3d at 133 (discussing the "legally significant acts" test in light of *Weltover*).

42. See generally Note, The Scattered Remains of Sovereign Immunity for Foreign States After Republic of Argentina v. Weltover, Inc.—Due Process Protection or Nothing, 27 Vand. J. Transnat'l L. 673 (1994) (arguing for application of due process limits to FSIA jurisdiction); Note, God Save the King: Unconstitutional Assertions of Personal Jurisdiction over Foreign States in U.S. Courts, 82 Va. L. Rev. 357 (1996) (discussing potentially unconstitutional applications of FSIA jurisdiction).

43. *Weltover*, 504 U.S. at 618, 112 S.Ct. at 2168, 119 L.Ed.2d 394.

44. 383 U.S. 301, 86 S.Ct. 803, 15 L.Ed.2d 769 (1966).

45. See *Hanil Bank*, 148 F.3d at 134 (discussing *Weltover*'s citation of *Katzenbach*).

of its purposeful availment of American financial markets in designating New York as one of the potential places of repayment.[46]

In many cases, it is unnecessary to decide whether due process limits apply to assertions of jurisdiction under the FSIA. First, the relevant geographical area for assertions of minimum contacts is almost surely the United States as a whole.[47] Considering United States contacts as a whole, it is probably the rare foreign sovereign or instrumentality that could avoid jurisdiction.[48] Second, courts are likely to follow the lead of *Weltover* in construing the minimum contacts and "direct effect" tests as coterminous and thus mooting the question of whether due process provides any additional limitation on jurisdiction.[49] However, one well-reasoned opinion from the District of Columbia Circuit, interpreting a different provision of the FSIA, has held that foreign states are not "persons" for due process purposes.[50]

Nevertheless, *Weltover* probably extends about as far as a court reasonably ought go in asserting jurisdiction under the commercial activities rubric. The dispute had relatively little to do with the United States, and parties should not be able to create FSIA jurisdiction simply by ensuring that some trivial event takes place within American boundaries.

One important exception to this structure under the FSIA is the Flatow Amendment allowing an action in which "money damages are sought against a foreign state for personal injury or death that was caused by an act of torture, extrajudicial killing, aircraft sabotage, hostage taking, or the provision of material support or resources . . . for such an act. . . ."[51] Unlike the commercial activities exception, the torture provisions do not require any nexus to the United States other than the nationality of the plaintiff, and thus could apply to torture of American citizens taking place entirely within a foreign state.[52] Because such claims would, in most circumstances, would not involve the defendant state having minimum contacts with the United States, the question of whether the due process limitations on personal jurisdiction protect foreign states can be squarely presented. At least one well-reasoned opinion has concluded that foreign states are not persons and thus not protected by due process principles.[53] There are, however,

46. *Weltover*, 504 U.S. at 619, 112 S.Ct. at 2168, 119 L.Ed.2d 394.

47. See, e.g., Theo. H. Davies & Co., Ltd. v. Republic of Marshall Islands, 174 F.3d 969 (9th Cir.1998) (assuming that due process limits jurisdiction over foreign states and considering whether foreign state has minimum contacts with the United States as a whole); Straub v. A P Green, Inc., 38 F.3d 448, 452 (9th Cir.1994); Meadows v. Dominican Republic, 817 F.2d 517, 523 (9th Cir.), cert. denied 484 U.S. 976, 108 S.Ct. 486, 98 L.Ed.2d 485 (1987).

48. See, e.g., *Theo H. Davies & Co.*, 174 F.3d 969 (Republic of Marshall Islands has

sufficient regular activities in the United States such as to subject it to jurisdiction).

49. See, e.g., *Hanil Bank*, 148 F.3d at 132–34 (concluding that the minimum contacts test is also met in a case in which the "direct effect" test is satisfied).

50. Price v. Socialist People's Libyan Arab Jamahiriya, 294 F.3d 82 (D.C. Cir. 2002).

51. 28 U.S.C.A. § 1605(a)(7).

52. See, e.g., *Price*, 294 F.3d 82.

53. Id.

legislative protections against such claims being extended beyond their reasonable reach. Torture claims may only be stated against foreign states if the state has been designated by the executive branch "as a state sponsor of terrorism."[54] Moreover, even a state so designated must be first given a "reasonable opportunity to arbitrate the claim in accordance with accepted international rules of arbitration. . . ."[55]

Although not itself jurisdictional, the choice-of-law question under the FSIA is closely intertwined. Because the FSIA does not itself contain any liability-creating rules, courts that proceed beyond the immunity question must confront the question of which law to apply. Courts are divided as to how to approach the conflicts question with some following the *Klaxon* rule and thus applying the choice-of-law methodology of the state in which they sit, and others applying an independent, federal choice-of-law approach.[56] In practice, the difference in approach may not be significant, because the courts applying an independent approach have borrowed from the Second Conflicts Restatement, an approach like that of most state courts.[57] But, as is true in other areas,[58] the *Klaxon* rule has little claim to application in an area of the law in which the need for uniformity is strong.[59] Federal courts should reserve for themselves the power to apply an independent approach to conflicts questions under the FSIA, especially if the state conflicts approach could lead to application of an unusual state rule that would defeat a foreign sovereign's legitimate and reasonable expectations.

54. 28 U.S.C.A. § 1605(a)(7)(A).

55. 28 U.S.C.A. § 1605(a)(7)(B)(i).

56. See Joel M. Overton, Will the Real FSIA Choice-of-Law Rule Please Stand Up?, 49 Wash. & Lee L. Rev. 1591 (1992) (discussing split among courts).

57. See, e.g., Schoenberg v. Exportadora de Sal, 930 F.2d 777, 782 (9th Cir.1991) (borrowing Second Conflicts Restatement as the independent federal approach).

58. See supra § 10.18.

59. Cf. American Insurance Ass'n v. Garamendi, 539 U.S. 396, 123 S.Ct. 2374, 156 L.Ed.2d 376 (2003) (California's Holocaust Victim Insurance Relief Act pre-empted by federal foreign affairs concerns); Zschernig v. Miller, 389 U.S. 429, 88 S.Ct. 664, 19 L.Ed.2d 683 (1968).

Chapter 11

LIMITATIONS ON JURISDICTION

Table of Sections

		Sections
I.	Introduction	11.1
II.	Contractual Limitations on Forum Selection	11.2–11.7
	A. Exclusive and Non–Exclusive Forum Clauses	11.2
	B. Enforceability in Federal Courts	11.3–11.4
	1. Non–Diversity Cases	11.3
	2. Diversity Cases	11.4
	C. Enforceability in State Courts	11.5
	D. Interpretation and Scope of Forum Clauses	11.6
	E. Judgment Recognition Issues	11.7
III.	Forum Non Conveniens	11.8–11.14
	A. Introduction	11.8
	B. Significant Factors in Application	11.8–11.13
	1. Preference for Chosen Forum	11.9
	2. Availability of Another Forum	11.10
	3. Other Factors	11.11
	4. Methods of Application	11.12
	5. State Practice	11.13
	C. Federal Transfers	11.14
IV.	Immunities From Service	11.15
V.	Other Federal Limitations on State Court Jurisdiction	11.16
VI.	Native American and Indian Country Limitations	11.17

I. INTRODUCTION

§ 11.1 The existence of personal and subject matter jurisdiction does not necessarily guarantee a plaintiff his chosen forum. A significant number of other factors may require that the case be litigated elsewhere. One important additional source of limitations on forum choice is venue statutes. The general federal statute,[1] though broadened by successive amendments,[2] can deprive a plaintiff of a federal forum that might otherwise be available. State venue statutes can similarly restrict litigation to certain counties within the state. For instance, a fairly common

---

§ 11.1

1. See 28 U.S.C.A. § 1391.

2. See, e.g., Oakley, Recent Statutory Changes in the Law of Federal Jurisdiction and Venue: The Judicial Improvements Acts of 1988 and 1990, 24 U.C. Davis L. Rev. 735 (1991).

restriction is that real property matters must be litigated in the county in which the real property is situated.[3]

Venue statutes, however, are just one source of the limitations upon forum choice that exist beyond the confines of jurisdictional rules. Contractual agreements between parties can expand or contract the available forums.[4] Discretionary doctrines, whether of the common law or statutory variety, often have the effect of shifting the ultimate situs of the litigation to a court other than the one in which it was filed.[5] In practical terms these additional limitations on forum choice can dramatically impact litigation.

II. CONTRACTUAL LIMITATIONS ON FORUM SELECTION

A. EXCLUSIVE AND NON–EXCLUSIVE FORUM CLAUSES

§ 11.2   Parties to commercial transactions frequently stipulate to the forum in which their potential[1] disputes are to be resolved. The parties may so stipulate because the chosen forum has particular expertise in the subject matter, for reasons of convenience or neutrality, or simply to minimize the risk of complicated and expensive litigation over the threshold question of jurisdiction.

In evaluating the effect of a private agreement between parties as to forum choice, a fundamental question is whether the agreement is exclusive or non-exclusive. An exclusive agreement is one that requires that the litigation be brought only in the chosen forum, to the exclusion of others.[2] A non-exclusive forum clause is one that allows the parties to litigate in the chosen forum, but does not purport to exclude them from litigating in some other forum that otherwise has jurisdiction. In civil law systems, exclusive forum agreements are often referred to as "derogation" clauses and non-exclusive forum agreements as "prorogation" clauses.[3]

The difference between the two is, of course, dramatic. Both types of clauses—if enforced—can have considerable commercial utility because they diminish the uncertainty of forum choice, and consequently the parties' incentive to litigate jurisdictional questions. Of the two, exclu-

---

3. See, e.g., N.Y. Civ. Prac. L. & R. § 507.

4. See infra § 11.2–11.6. Ex parte CTB, Inc., 782 So.2d 188 (Ala.2000) (clause stating that a party "consents to jurisdiction and venue" is not exclusive).

5. See infra §§ 11.7–11.16.

§ 11.2

1. Although infrequently done, the parties may also stipulate to a forum after the dispute has arisen. See, e.g., Zapata Marine Service v. O/Y Finnlines, Ltd., 571 F.2d 208 (5th Cir.1978) (post-dispute agreement upheld).

2. See, e.g., Borchers, Forum Selection Agreements in the Federal Courts After *Carnival Cruise*: A Proposal for Congressional Reform, 67 Wash. L. Rev. 55, 56 n.1 (1992).

3. See, e.g., Perillo, Selected Forum Agreements in Western Europe, 13 Am. J. Comp. L. 162, 162–65 (1964).

sive forum clauses are today probably the more common and useful, because—if enforced—they go the greatest distance towards providing certainty as to where any dispute will be litigated.

Given the greatly differing effect between the two types of clauses, one might expect that parties would draft agreements that clearly indicate which type of agreement was contemplated. Such has not been the case, however. With astonishing frequency, parties have drafted clumsy clauses that are unclear as to what effect is intended, leaving courts with difficult questions of interpretation.[4] Courts have a mild preference for interpreting ambiguous clauses as exclusive,[5] but there is

---

4. Compare K & V Scientific Co., Inc. v. Bayerische Motoren Werke Aktiengesellschaft (BMW), 314 F.3d 494 (10th Cir. 2002) (clause stating that "Jurisdiction for all and any disputes arising out of or in connection with this agreement is Munich" is non-exclusive); Hunt Wesson Foods, Inc. v. Supreme Oil Co., 817 F.2d 75 (9th Cir. 1987) (clause stating that the California state courts "shall have jurisdiction" is non-exclusive) and First National City Bank v. Nanz, Inc., 437 F.Supp. 184 (S.D.N.Y. 1975) ("Supreme Court of New York shall have jurisdiction of any dispute" is non-exclusive) with ASM Communications, Inc. v. Allen, 656 F.Supp. 838 (S.D.N.Y.1987) (clause stating that "jurisdiction and venue shall be in" the New York courts is exclusive); compare Keaty v. Freeport Indonesia, Inc., 503 F.2d 955 (5th Cir.1974) (clause stating that the "parties submit to the jurisdiction of the courts of New York" is non-exclusive) and Sall v. G.H. Miller & Co., 612 F.Supp. 1499 (D.Colo.1985) ("I specifically consent to and submit to the courts of the state of Illinois" is a non-exclusive agreement) and Walter E. Heller & Co. v. James Godbe Co., 601 F.Supp. 319 (N.D.Ill.1984) ("submit to the jurisdiction of" is a non-exclusive agreement) with Zions First Nat'l Bank v. Allen, 688 F.Supp. 1495 (D.Utah 1988) (clause stating that the parties "expressly submit[] to the jurisdiction of" is an exclusive agreement) and Furry v. First Nat'l Monetary Corp., 602 F.Supp. 6 (W.D.Okla.1984) ("submit to the jurisdiction of" is an exclusive agreement).

5. See Borchers, supra n.2, at 82.

Courts of other nations also generally prefer to interpret forum clauses as exclusive. Article 23 of EC Regulation No. 44/2001 on Jurisdiction and the Enforcement of Civil and Commercial Judgments, in force in the European Community as well as the "Parallel" (Lugano) Convention which extends the former to the six EFTA countries (Austria, Iceland, Finland, Norway, Sweden, and Switzerland) provide that

the jurisdiction of the chosen court "shall be exclusive ... ". [2001] Official Journal L 012/1. The ten new members of the European Union (as of May 2004) are also governed by this Regulation.

For *Germany:* see the German Supreme Court decision of 1969 in: Lindenmaier–Möhring, § 38 ZPO, No. 9/10: even a suit by German firm in New York does not confer jurisdiction on New York court for defendant's counterclaim when the contract stipulated for a German forum. See also German Supreme Court in: Lindenmaier–Möhring, § 38 ZPO No. 18 = LM 1973, 10–12, Bl. 492 (1972); 60 BGHZ 85 (1972). By like token, German courts have also refused to entertain actions brought in violation of a clause stipulating in favor of an exclusive foreign forum: 25 R.I.W. 495 (Ct. App. Hamburg 1979) (Soviet Union); 1973 MDR 1025 (Ct. App. Hamburg 1973) (Lebanon). See also German Supreme Court, in: 1971 MDR 376 (1971); 1971 NJW 325 (1970). See generally Katholnigg, Internationale Zuständigkeitsvereinbarungen nach neuem Recht, 1974 Betriebsberater 395.

For *Switzerland:* see Art. 5(1) of the Federal Law on Private International Law (1987, entered into force 1989): "Unless the contrary appears from the agreement, the chosen court shall have exclusive jurisdiction." (Authors' translation). Art. 5, para. 1 of the 1965 Hague Convention on the Choice of Court likewise provides that "Unless the parties have otherwise agreed only the chosen court or courts shall have jurisdiction." Recueil des Conventions de la Haye 96, 99 (1980 ed.). For Austria and Switzerland see also Jung, Gerichtsstandsvereinbarungen im deutsch-schweizerischen und deutsch-österreichischen Handelsverkehr, 27 Recht der Internationalen Wirtschaft 814 (1981).

Under § 4(3)(6) of the English Foreign Judgments Act of 1933 judgments obtained in violation of a choice-of-forum clause are not entitled to recognition.

little excuse for leaving such a fundamental matter to the vagaries of court interpretation. Other difficult questions of interpretation of clauses have been presented by awkward references to the intended forum or fora, leaving courts in a quandary as to whether the drafters intended to choose a state court, a federal court, or either one.[6]

As a manifestation of the notion that the defendant's consent was a good basis for in personam jurisdiction, non-exclusive forum agreements obtained favor fairly early on in American jurisprudence. The notion that this consent could be expressed in a contract between the parties before any litigation was contemplated found its clearest expression in the Supreme Court's opinion *National Equipment Rental v. Szukhent*.[7]

The acceptance of exclusive forum clauses was slower to come about and is a process still underway even today. Early on, American courts refused to honor exclusive forum clauses on the theory that they effected an illegal "ouster" of the court's jurisdiction.[8] As of 1950, one commentator could report that "[w]ith almost boring unanimity American courts have refused to enforce contractual provisions conferring exclusive jurisdiction on a court or courts of a particular sister state or foreign country."[9] Cracks in the ouster edifice appeared shortly thereafter, however.[10] With the Supreme Court's decision in *The Bremen v. Zapata*

For a summary of European approaches to choice-of-court clauses see Roman, Transnational Contracts in the Swiss Draft Statute and in the General European Context 9–31 (Library of Congress 1981); Geimer & Schütze, Internationale Urteilsanerkennung §§ 75, 76, 96, and especially 197 n.147 (1983/84) and Geimer & Schütze, Europäisches Zivilverfahrensrecht, Part II (2nd ed. 2004). Forum-selection clauses are often combined with choice-of-law clauses, for instance, to assure that the chosen court will apply its own law. To assure that neither party has an advantage, these clauses are at times drafted in the alternative, for instance: defendant's court and law. On such "floating clauses," see Rasmussen–Bonne, Alternative Rechts-und Forumswahlklauseln (1999).

6. Compare LFC Lessors, Inc. v. Pacific Sewer Maintenance Corp., 739 F.2d 4, 8 (1st Cir.1984) (clause pointing to "courts of the commonwealth of Massachusetts" interpreted to mean either state or federal courts in that state); Zimmerman Metals, Inc. v. United Eng'rs & Constructors, Inc., 720 F.Supp. 859 (D.Colo.1989) ("courts of Colorado" means both state and federal courts); Page Constr. Co. v. Perini Constr. Co., 712 F.Supp. 9 (D.R.I.1989) (reference to the "Massachusetts courts" means both state and federal courts; Brinderson–Newberg Joint Venture v. Pacific Erectors, Inc., 690 F.Supp. 891, 892 (C.D.Cal.1988) (clause stating that the "situs of any suit . . . shall

be the County of Orange, State of California" held to refer to both state and federal courts); International Inv. & Equine Consultants, Inc. v. Jebrock, 573 F.Supp. 592 (W.D.Pa.1983) (clause stating that the "exclusive venue shall be the State of Delaware" held to encompass both state and federal courts; City of N.Y. v. Pullman, Inc., 477 F.Supp. 438 (S.D.N.Y.1979) with In re Fireman's Fund Ins. Cos., 588 F.2d 93 (5th Cir.1979) (venue in the "County of Essex and State of New Jersey" held to refer only to state court).

7. 375 U.S. 311, 84 S.Ct. 411, 11 L.Ed.2d 354 (1964).

8. See, e.g., Nute v. Hamilton Mut. Ins. Co., 72 Mass. (6 Gray) 174 (1856); see also Home Insurance Co. v. Morse, 87 U.S. (20 Wall.) 445, 453, 22 L.Ed. 365 (1874) (refusing to honor a Wisconsin statute purporting to prevent insurance companies from removing a case to federal court on the grounds that "agreements in advance to oust the courts of the jurisdiction conferred are illegal and void").

9. Note, Agreements in Advance Conferring Exclusive Jurisdiction on Foreign Court, 10 La. L. Rev. 293, 293 (1950). For a more recent discussion of the history, see Gruson, Forum–Selection Clauses in International and Interstate Commercial Agreements, 1982 U. Ill. L. Rev. 133.

10. See, e.g., Cerro De Pasco Copper Corp. v. Knut Knutsen, O.A.S., 187 F.2d 990 (2d Cir.1951).

Off–Shore Co.[11]—an admiralty case upholding an exclusive forum clause in a commercial contract selecting an English court—widespread (though not universal) rejection of the ouster doctrine was underway. As discussed below, a large majority of American jurisdictions now enforce exclusive forum clauses under appropriate circumstances.

The relatively recent American acceptance of exclusive forum clauses brings national practice into line with most of international practice. The Brussels Regulation and Brussels and Lugano Conventions all allow for exclusive forum clauses in many circumstances,[12] and national laws in other parts of the world generally favor the concept.

B. ENFORCEABILITY IN FEDERAL COURTS

1. *Non–Diversity Cases*

§ 11.3 As discussed above,[1] federal courts—led by the United States Supreme Court—were hostile to exclusive forum clauses until the second half of the twentieth century. The theory behind this hostility was that such clauses illegally "ousted" the jurisdiction of the court.[2] Several factors combined to substantially overthrow the ouster doctrine. The passage in 1925 of the Federal Arbitration Act[3] helped to provide some momentum towards acceptance of exclusive forum clauses, because an arbitration clause—as a specialized kind of forum clause[4]—"ousts" the jurisdiction of courts just as surely as does a conventional forum clause. A pair of Second Circuit decisions in the early 1950s enforcing exclusive forum clauses also helped to influence other courts to reconsider strict application of the ouster doctrine.[5]

Without question, however, the principal instrument in the overthrow of the ouster doctrine was the Supreme Court's opinion in *The Bremen v. Zapata Off–Shore Co.*[6] *The Bremen* involved a contract between a Texas and a German company for the towing of the Texas

---

11. 407 U.S. 1, 92 S.Ct. 1907, 32 L.Ed.2d 513 (1972).

12. For the EU (except Denmark), see EC Council Reg. No. 44 (2001), [2001] O.J. 012/1, Art. 23(1). Special Rules apply to insurance, consumer contracts (Arts. 13, 17, 21), limiting the freedom of choice for the protection of the weaker party. For discussion of the Conventions, see Kegel & Schurig, Internationals Privatrecht 1070–77 (9th ed. 2004). See also Reimann, Conflict of Laws in Western Europe: A Guide Through the Jungle 76, 81 (1995).

§ 11.3

1. See supra § 11.2

2. See, e.g., Nute v. Hamilton Mut. Ins. Co., 72 Mass. (6 Gray) 174 (1856); see also Home Insurance Co. v. Morse, 87 U.S. (20 Wall.) 445, 453, 22 L.Ed. 365 (1874) (refusing to honor a Wisconsin statute purporting to prevent insurance companies from removing a case to federal court on the grounds that "agreements in advance to oust the courts of the jurisdiction conferred are illegal and void").

3. 9 U.S.C.A. §§ 1 et. seq.

4. See, e.g., Scherk v. Alberto–Culver Co., 417 U.S. 506, 94 S.Ct. 2449, 41 L.Ed.2d 270 (1974).

5. See Wm. H. Muller & Co. v. Swedish Am. Line Ltd., 224 F.2d 806 (2d Cir. 1955), cert. denied 350 U.S. 903, 76 S.Ct. 182, 100 L.Ed. 793 (1955); Cerro De Pasco Copper Corp. v. Knut Knutsen, O.A.S., 187 F.2d 990 (2d Cir.1951).

6. 407 U.S. 1, 92 S.Ct. 1907, 32 L.Ed.2d 513 (1972).

company's oil rig from the Gulf of Mexico to the Adriatic Sea.[7] Bad weather damaged the rig, and after it was towed to the safety of a Florida port, the Texas company sued the German towing company by proceeding in rem against the German company's tug, invoking the admiralty jurisdiction of the Florida court.[8] The towing contract included an exclusive forum clause stating that " '[a]ny dispute arising must be treated before the London Court of Justice,' "[9] and a parallel action had, in fact, been filed in an English court.[10]

The United States Supreme Court, rejecting the ouster doctrine, held that the clause was not per se unenforceable. A rule of per se refusal to enforce forum clauses would, reasoned the Court, "be a heavy hand indeed on the future development of international commercial dealings by Americans."[11] The Court noted that enforcement of exclusive forum clauses accorded "with ancient concepts of freedom of contract" and that exclusive forum clauses had received a qualified endorsement from the Second Restatement of Conflicts, promulgated just shortly before the opinion in *The Bremen*.[12]

The Court did not insist that every exclusive forum clause be enforced. An agreement affected by "fraud, undue influence, or over-weening bargaining power" would be voided.[13] In a more general sense, an agreement might be "unreasonable and unenforceable," or simply absurd, as for instance "an agreement between two Americans to resolve their essentially local disputes in a remote alien forum."[14] But nothing about the agreement at issue in *The Bremen* suggested that the Texas company could make the "strong showing" necessary to void the agreement. The contract was made between two sophisticated companies of approximately equal bargaining power, and there was every indication that all aspects of the contract, including the forum clause, had been "freely negotiated."[15] Moreover, the forum clause selected a neutral forum with an excellent reputation in admiralty matters.[16]

The Bremen while lending enormous impetus towards acceptance of exclusive forum clauses in federal court, left open important questions. *The Bremen* was an admiralty case and in a strict sense was precedent only in those matters. As commentators then noted, the question of whether the principle announced in *The Bremen* would extend to other federal actions, other than admiralty cases, was unsettled.[17] The question

---

7. Id. at 2, 92 S.Ct. at 1909, 32 L.Ed.2d 513.

8. Id. at 3–4, 92 S.Ct. at 1910, 32 L.Ed.2d 513.

9. Id. at 2, 92 S.Ct. at 1909, 32 L.Ed.2d 513.

10. Id. at 4 n.4, 92 S.Ct. at 1910 n.4, 32 L.Ed.2d 513.

11. Id. at 9, 92 S.Ct. at 1913, 32 L.Ed.2d 513.

12. Id. at 11, 92 S.Ct. at 1914, 32 L.Ed.2d 513.

13. Id. at 12, 15, 92 S.Ct. at 1914, 32 L.Ed.2d 513.

14. Id. at 16–17, 92 S.Ct. at 1916–17, 32 L.Ed.2d 513.

15. Id. at 17, 92 S.Ct. at 1917, 32 L.Ed.2d 513.

16. Id.

17. Maier, The Three Faces of *Zapata*: Maritime Law, Federal Common Law, Federal Courts Law, 6 Vand. J. Transnat'l L. 387 (1973).

of whether *The Bremen* applies if the federal court assumes jurisdiction on the basis of diversity is a difficult one discussed in the next section.[18] Most lower courts agree that if the basis of a federal court's subject matter jurisdiction is something other than diversity (usually federal question or admiralty jurisdiction) the principles announced in *The Bremen* apply.[19]

Even assuming, however, that *The Bremen* applies, difficult questions can remain. One, of course, is whether a party has made a showing that the forum clause was affected by fraud, duress, or one of the other standard contract defenses mentioned by the Supreme Court. Although courts often recite that a showing of fraud or duress renders a forum clause inoperative, in practice clauses are rarely denied enforcement on this ground. Further narrowing the scope of cases in which a clause might be denied enforcement on these grounds is that, in the context of arbitration clauses, the Supreme Court has held that the fraud or duress must be specific to the clause.[20] A mere allegation that the entire contract was infected by fraud or duress will not suffice. Lower courts have generally taken this tack with forum clauses by not allowing generalized suggestions of fraud or duress to defeat the enforcement.[21]

Another difficult question of application is when the chosen forum is so unreasonable as to negate the parties' choice. Federal courts have shown little sympathy for parties who agree to a forum and then argue that the choice is so unreasonably inconvenient that they should be relieved of the agreement. In general, federal courts find that even distant fora are sufficiently accessible to allow enforcement of the clause.[22] If the essential character of the forum changes between the time

---

18. See infra § 11.4.

19. See, e.g., AVC Nederland B.V. v. Atrium Inv. Partnership, 740 F.2d 148 (2d Cir.1984); Bense v. Interstate Battery Sys. of Am., 683 F.2d 718 (2d Cir.1982); Crown Beverage Co. v. Cerveceria Moctezuma, S.A., 663 F.2d 886 (9th Cir.1981); Ritchie v. Carvel Corp., 714 F.Supp. 700 (S.D.N.Y. 1989); but see Coastal Steel Corp. v. Tilghman Wheelabrator, Ltd., 709 F.2d 190 (3d Cir.1983)(refusing to decide issue because of similarity of state and federal standards).

20. See Scherk v. Alberto–Culver Co., 417 U.S. 506, 519 n.14, 94 S.Ct. 2449, 2457 n.14, 41 L.Ed.2d 270 (1974).

21. See, e.g., Sparling v. Hoffman Constr. Co., 864 F.2d 635 (9th Cir.1988) (arbitration agreement); Farmland Indus., Inc. v. Frazier–Parrott Commodities, Inc., 806 F.2d 848 (8th Cir.1986); AVC Nederland B.V. v. Atrium Inv. Partnership, 740 F.2d 148 (2d Cir.1984); Ritchie v. Carvel Corp., 714 F.Supp. 700 (S.D.N.Y.1989); Stephens v. Entre Computer Ctrs. Inc., 696 F.Supp. 636 (N.D.Ga.1988); see also Northwestern Nat'l Ins. Co. v. Donovan, 916 F.2d 372, 377 (7th Cir.1990) (party has a duty to

read agreement; ignorance of existence of forum clause no defense to its enforcement); Norwegian Cruise Line v. Clark, 841 So.2d 547 (Fla.App. 2003) (fact that consumer has only a short time to read the clause and decide whether to take the cruise does not foreclose enforcement); Info. Leasing Corp. v. Jaskot, 151 Ohio App.3d 546, 784 N.E.2d 1192 (2003) (clause enforced against out-of-state gas station owner with essentially no connection to the forum).

22. See, e.g., Forsythe v. Saudi Arabian Airlines, Corp., 885 F.2d 285 (5th Cir.1989) (Saudi administrative tribunal is an adequate alternative forum); Commerce Consultants Int'l, Inc. v. Vetrerie Riunite, S.p.A., 867 F.2d 697 (D.C.Cir.1989) (Italy is an adequate alternative forum); Sun World Lines, Ltd. v. March Shipping Corp., 801 F.2d 1066 (8th Cir.1986) (West Germany is a reasonable alternative forum); Pelleport Investors, Inc. v. Budco Quality Theatres, Inc., 741 F.2d 273 (9th Cir.1984) (California is a reasonable forum notwithstanding the fact that the witnesses are on the East Coast); Crown Beverage Co. v. Cerveceria

of the agreement and the litigation, however, courts have been much more likely to excuse a party from the obligation to litigate in the chosen forum. In federal litigation, this most commonly occurred when the parties, prior to the 1979 Iranian revolution, contracted to have cases heard in the Iranian courts.[23]

The most difficult and controversial matter in the wake of *The Bremen* has been its suggestion that inequality of bargaining power might be a defense to the enforcement of a forum clause. In *Carnival Cruise Lines, Inc v. Shute*,[24] however, the Supreme Court rejected the notion that uneven bargaining power, or the fact that the forum clause appears in a consumer form contract, necessarily defeats enforcement. At issue in *Carnival Cruise* was a forum clause printed on the back of a cruise ship ticket requiring any dispute between the passenger and the company to be litigated in Florida.[25] A passenger, resident in the State of

Moctezuma, S.A., 663 F.2d 886 (9th Cir. 1981) (Mexico is acceptable alternative forum); Republic Int'l Corp. v. Amco Eng'rs., Inc., 516 F.2d 161 (9th Cir.1975) (Uruguay is a reasonable alternative forum); Ernst v. Ernst, 722 F.Supp. 61 (S.D.N.Y.1989) (France is a reasonable alternative forum); Samson Plastic Conduit & Pipe Corp. v. Battenfeld Extrusionstechnik GMBH, 718 F.Supp. 886 (M.D.Ala.1989) (West Germany is a reasonable alternative forum); Damigos v. Flanders Compania Naviera, S.A.—Panama, 716 F.Supp. 104 (S.D.N.Y.1989) (Greece is an acceptable alternative forum); Tisdale v. Shell Oil Co., 723 F.Supp. 653 (M.D.Ala.1987) (Labor Commission of Saudi Arabia is a reasonable alternative forum); Ronar, Inc. v. Wallace, 649 F.Supp. 310 (S.D.N.Y.1986) (West Germany is an adequate alternative forum); The Warner & Swasey Co. v. Salvagnini Transferica S.p.A., 633 F.Supp. 1209 (W.D.N.Y.1986) (Italy is a reasonable alternative forum for a patent action); Santamauro v. Taito do Brasil Industria E Comercia Ltda., 587 F.Supp. 1312 (E.D.La.1984) (Brazil is a reasonable alternative forum); but see Karlberg European Tanspa v. JK–Josef Kratz Vertriebsgeselischaft MbH, 699 F.Supp. 669 (N.D.Ill.1988) (West Germany is an unreasonable forum because German courts will not as effectively enforce Sherman Act claims); Morse Electro Prods. Corp. v. S.S. Great Peace, 437 F.Supp. 474 (D.N.J.1977) (stating in dictum that Nationalist China is an unreasonable alternative forum); Copperweld Steel Co. v. Demag–Mannesmann–Boehler, 347 F.Supp. 53, 55 (W.D.Pa.1972) ("obvious impracticality of conducting litigation in Germany" renders forum agreement unenforceable).

23. See, e.g., McDonnell Douglas Corp. v. Islamic Republic of Iran, 758 F.2d 341 (8th Cir.1985) (unforeseeable changed circumstances in Iran make clause unenforceable because it would be impossible for McDonnell Douglas to litigate in that forum); Rockwell Int'l Sys. v. Citibank, 719 F.2d 583 (2d Cir.1983) (unforeseeable changed circumstances in Iran make clause unenforceable); Continental Grain Export Corp. v. Ministry of War–Etka Co., 603 F.Supp. 724 (S.D.N.Y.1984) (changed circumstances allow U.S. courts to exercise jurisdiction despite forum selection clause); but see National Iranian Oil Co. v. Ashland Oil, Inc., 817 F.2d 326 (5th Cir.1987) (no changed circumstances because clause entered into in 1979 and Islamic revolution was then foreseeable; however, practical effect of decision is to leave Iranian corporation without a remedy); see generally Stein, Jurisprudence and Jurists' Prudence: The Iranian Forum Clause Decisions of the Iran–U.S. Claims Tribunal, 78 Am. J. Int'l L. 1, 6 (1984); Note, Mandatory Forum Selection Clauses and Foreign Sovereign Immunity: Iran's Litigation Problems in United States Courts, McDonnell Douglas Corp. v. Islamic Republic of Iran, 12 Brooklyn J. Int'l L. 553, 574–76 (1986) (discussing issue); Note, Changed Circumstances and the Iranian Claims Arbitration: Application to Forum Selection Clauses and Frustration of Contract, 16 Geo. Wash. J. Int'l L. & Econ. 335 (1982); Comment, National Iranian Oil Co. v. Ashland Oil Co.: All Dressed up and Nowhere to Arbitrate, 63 N.Y.U. L. Rev. 1142 (1988) (criticizing *National Iranian*'s holding that the Iranian revolution was foreseeable at the time of contracting).

24. 499 U.S. 585, 111 S.Ct. 1522, 113 L.Ed.2d 622 (1991).

25. Id. at 587–88, 111 S.Ct. 1524, 113 L.Ed.2d 622.

Washington, slipped and was injured while aboard one of the company's ships and then attempted to bring an admiralty suit in a federal court located in her home state.[26]

The Supreme Court held that the forum clause deserved enforcement and that any litigation would have to be brought in Florida. On the question of whether the inequality of bargaining power and the form nature of the contract were sufficient to deny effect to the forum clause, the Court offered three rationales for allowing enforcement. First, the Court thought it unreasonable to impose a requirement of actual bargaining on a "routine" transaction such as the sale of a cruise ship ticket.[27] Second, because the company was at a risk of a multiplicity of suits in different fora as a result of the differing domiciles of its passengers, it had a special need to include such forum clauses in its agreements for passage.[28] Third, the Court thought it self-evident that the clauses, by reducing the company's cost of doing business, would benefit all passengers through lower fares.[29]

It is, of course, debatable whether the Supreme Court's rationales make sense. Certainly the harshness of the *Carnival Cruise* decision stands in sharp contrast to the Brussels and Lugano Conventions (and now Brussels Regulation), all of which have special jurisdictional rules that favor consumers.[30] Commentary on *Carnival Cruise* has been almost universally negative,[31] and it was temporarily overruled by statute, though that enactment has since been repealed, reinstating the decision.[32] In any event, *Carnival Cruise* demonstrates the dramatic shift that American jurisprudence has taken from almost universal hostility towards exclusive forum clauses to enthusiastic acceptance.[33]

---

26. Id. at 588, 111 S.Ct. 1522, 113 L.Ed.2d 622.

27. Id. at 593, 111 S.Ct. at 1527, 113 L.Ed.2d 622.

28. Id.

29. Id.

30. Borchers, Comparing Personal Jurisdiction in the United States and the European Community: Lessons for American Reform, 40 Am. J. Comp. L. 121, 135 (1992).

31. See, e.g., Borchers, Forum Selection Clauses in the Federal Courts After *Carnival Cruise*: A Proposal for Congressional Reform, 67 Wash. L. Rev. 55 (1992); Liesemer, *Carnival's* Got the Fun ... and the Forum: A New Look at Choice-of-Forum Clauses and Unconscionability Doctrine After Carnival Cruise Lines, Inc v. Shute, 53 U. Pitt. L. Rev. 1025 (1992); Mullenix, Another Easy Case, Some More Bad Law: *Carnival Cruise Lines* and Contractual Personal Jurisdiction, 27 Tex. Int'l L.J. 323 (1992); Richman, *Carnival Cruise Lines*: Forum Selection Clauses in Adhesion Contracts, 40 Am. J. Comp. L. 977 (1992); but see Solimine, Forum–Selection Clauses and

the Privatization of Procedure, 25 Cornell Int'l L.J. 51 (1992).

32. See P.L. 103–206, § 309 (1993) (repealing a 1992 enactment which had had the effect of overruling *Carnival Cruise*).

33. Clauses are still not enforceable, however, if the court finds their enforcement to be in conflict with a specific federal statute. In Richards v. Lloyd's of London, 107 F.3d 1422 (9th Cir.1997), cert. denied 525 U.S. 943, 119 S.Ct. 365, 142 L.Ed.2d 301 (1998) the panel held that a choice-of-law and choice-of-forum clause both pointing towards England were both void as conflicting with the anti-waiver provisions of the Securities Act of 1933, though the en banc court construed the statutes not to forbid such a choice. See 135 F.3d 1289 (9th Cir.1998) (en banc). Courts have shown an increasing preference for upholding such clauses. See, e.g., Allen v. Lloyd's of London, 94 F.3d 923 (4th Cir.1996); Bonny v. Society of Lloyd's, 3 F.3d 156 (7th Cir. 1993), cert. denied 510 U.S. 1113, 114 S.Ct. 1057, 127 L.Ed.2d 378 (1994); Roby v. Corporation of Lloyd's, 996 F.2d 1353 (2d Cir.

2. *Diversity Cases*

§ 11.4 As discussed in the last section, in federal cases in which the basis for jurisdiction is one other than the diversity of the parties, courts universally apply the principles of *The Bremen* and *Carnival Cruise* favoring enforcement of exclusive forum clauses. The situation is somewhat more complex, however, when the basis for federal subject matter jurisdiction is diversity of the parties. In diversity cases, federal courts are usually required to apply the same "substantive" law that would be applied by their state court counterparts, including the conflict of law principles applicable in state court.[1] In many federal diversity suits involving an exclusive forum clause, this presents no real difficulty, because the law of most states is in accord with the pro-enforcement philosophy of *The Bremen* and *Carnival Cruise*.[2] This is not always the case, however; some state courts continue to adhere to the "ouster" doctrine, and thus refuse to enforce exclusive forum clauses.[3] There is also the possibility of more subtle differences between state and federal law. A state court might, for instance, adopt the basic pro-enforcement philosophy of *The Bremen*, but refuse to follow *Carnival Cruise* on the grounds that it goes too far in allowing the enforcement of adhesive forum clauses.[4] A federal court sitting in diversity in a state in which the law on this subject differs materially from federal law faces the difficult choice of whether to follow state law or follow *The Bremen* and *Carnival Cruise*.

A partial answer to this question was provided by the Supreme Court's decision in *Stewart Organization, Inc. v. Ricoh Corp.*[5] *Stewart* was a diversity action filed in an Alabama federal court, and Alabama was, until recently, one of relatively few states to adhere to the ouster doctrine.[6] The agreement between the parties contained an exclusive forum clause selecting a court in Manhattan, which would include either a New York state court there located or the Federal District Court for the Southern District of New York.[7] Attempting to enforce the clause, the defendant sought to have the case transferred under the federal

---

1993), cert. denied 510 U.S. 945, 114 S.Ct. 385, 126 L.Ed.2d 333 (1993).

§ 11.4

1. See, e.g., Erie R.R. Co. v. Tompkins, 304 U.S. 64, 58 S.Ct. 817, 82 L.Ed. 1188 (1938); Klaxon Co. v. Stentor Electric Mfg. Co., 313 U.S. 487, 61 S.Ct. 1020, 85 L.Ed. 1477 (1941).

2. See infra § 11.5.

3. Until fairly recently, Alabama refused to enforce such clauses. See, e.g., Keelean v. Central Bank, 544 So.2d 153 (Ala.1989); Redwing Carriers, Inc. v. Foster, 382 So.2d 554, 556 (Ala.1980). However, the Alabama Supreme Court has now overruled these cases. See Professional Ins. Co. v. Suther-land, 700 So.2d 347 (Ala.1997). Some states prohibit by statute the enforcement of certain types of forum selection clauses, but such state laws too are overridden by § 1404. See, e.g., Kerobo v. Southwestern Clean Fuels Co., 285 F.3d 531 (6th Cir. 2002) (Michigan franchisee protection law).

4. Cf. Mechanics Laundry & Supply, Inc. v. Wilder Oil Co., 596 N.E.2d 248 (Ind. App.1992) (arguing for a state law rule that an exclusive forum clause be the subject of actual bargaining).

5. 487 U.S. 22, 108 S.Ct. 2239, 101 L.Ed.2d 22 (1988).

6. See supra n.3.

7. 487 U.S. at 24, 108 S.Ct. at 2241, 101 L.Ed.2d 22.

venue transfer statute[8] to the Southern District of New York, but the district court, however, denied the motion because it thought the Alabama ouster rule controlled.[9]

The Supreme Court held, however, that the district court erred in deferring to the Alabama policy. Because the question of whether to transfer the case to another federal district court was governed by a federal statute[10] the Court held that federal standards necessarily governed over state ones.[11] Because the fundamental question under the federal venue transfer statute is whether transfer will serve "the convenience of parties and witnesses, [and] the interests of justice,"[12] the parties' selection must be "a significant factor" weighing in favor of transferring the case.[13]

Stewart is, of course, only a partial answer to the question of whether federal or state standards will apply in diversity cases because the federal venue transfer statute allows for transfer only to other federal courts. If the forum clause points to a state court or the court of a foreign nation, the transfer statute has no application. In *Stewart*, three justices addressed the question of whether federal or state standards would apply in such a case, two arguing in favor of federal standards and one in favor of state law.[14] The split among the justices is reflective of a split among federal courts, which are approximately equally divided between applying state and federal law.[15] Application of federal law has, of course, the advantage of reducing the incentive for interstate forum shopping, although application of state law preserves

---

8. 28 U.S.C.A. § 1404(a).

9. 487 U.S. at 24, 108 S.Ct. at 2241, 101 L.Ed.2d 22.

10. 28 U.S.C.A. § 1404(a).

11. 487 U.S. at 31–32, 108 S.Ct. at 2245, 101 L.Ed.2d 22.

12. 28 U.S.C.A. § 1404(a).

13. 487 U.S. at 29, 108 S.Ct. at 2244, 101 L.Ed.2d 22. Some courts, however, has understood the "significant factor" language as being essentially a mandatory command to transfer a case involving a valid clause, even if the party resisting enforcement might be able to make a showing of material inconvenience in litigating in the transferee forum. P & S Business Machs., Inc. v. Canon USA, Inc., 331 F.3d 804 (11th Cir. 2003).

14. See 487 U.S. at 33 108 S.Ct. at 2245, 101 L.Ed.2d 22. (Kennedy, J., concurring joined by O'Connor) (stating that *The Bremen*'s "reasoning applies with much force to federal courts sitting in diversity"); id. at 33, 108 S.Ct. at 2246, 101 L.Ed.2d 22 (Scalia, J., dissenting) (state law must con-

trol because the question is essentially a substantive question of contract law).

15. See, e.g., Northwestern Nat'l Ins. v. Donovan, 916 F.2d 372, 374 (7th Cir.1990) (application of federal law "probably correct"); Jones v. Weibrecht, 901 F.2d 17, 19 (2d Cir.1990) (federal law); Alexander Proudfoot Co. World Headquarters v. Thayer, 877 F.2d 912 (11th Cir.1989) (state law); Manetti–Farrow, Inc. v. Gucci Am., Inc., 858 F.2d 509, 512 (9th Cir.1988) (federal law); Farmland Indus., Inc. v. Frazier–Parrott Commodities, Inc., 806 F.2d 848 (8th Cir.1986) (state law); General Eng'g Corp. v. Martin Marietta Alumina, Inc., 783 F.2d 352, 356 (3d Cir.1986) (state law); Ritchie v. Carvel Corp., 714 F.Supp. 700 (S.D.N.Y. 1989) (federal law); TUC Elecs., Inc. v. Eagle Telephonics, Inc., 698 F.Supp. 35 (D.Conn.1988) (federal law); Sterling Forest Assoc. v. Barnett–Range Corp., 673 F.Supp. 1394 (E.D.N.C.1987) (state law), rev'd on other grounds 840 F.2d 249 (4th Cir.1988). See also Conference on Jurisdiction, Justice, and Choice of Law for the Twenty–First Century, 29 New Engl. L. Rev. 517, 530–76 (seven of eight commentators taking the position that state law must govern).

uniformity of outcome as between a federal court and its home state's courts.

C. ENFORCEABILITY IN STATE COURTS

§ 11.5   Through the middle part of the twentieth century, state courts were every bit as hostile to exclusive forum clauses as were their federal court counterparts.[1] However, the Supreme Court's opinion in *The Bremen v. Zapata Off-Shore Co.*,[2] endorsing reasonable forum clauses, touched off an almost complete turnabout in state courts. Heavily influenced by *The Bremen* and other Supreme Court opinions in its wake, almost every state now allows for exclusive forum clauses under some circumstances.[3] In fact, it is difficult to find recent, viable state court authority endorsing the ouster doctrine.[4] A few states have older authorities—not yet squarely overruled—applying the ouster doctrine,[5] and a few have retained some vestige of the old doctrine in a very limited form.[6]

§ 11.5

1. See Note, Agreements in Advance Conferring Exclusive Jurisdiction on Foreign Court, 10 La. L. Rev. 293, 293 (1950).

2. 407 U.S. 1, 92 S.Ct. 1907, 32 L.Ed.2d 513 (1972).

3. See, e.g., Abadou v. Trad, 624 P.2d 287 (Alaska 1981); Societe Jean Nicolas et Fils v. Mousseux, 123 Ariz. 59, 597 P.2d 541 (1979); Bos Material Handling, Inc. v. Crown Controls Corp., 137 Cal.App.3d 99, 186 Cal.Rptr. 740 (1982); Funding Systems Leasing Corp. v. Diaz, 34 Conn.Supp. 99, 378 A.2d 108 (Conn.Com.Pl.1977); Elia Corp. v. Paul N. Howard Co., 391 A.2d 214 (Del.Super.1978); Manrique v. Fabbri, 493 So.2d 437 (Fla.1986); Brinson v. Martin, 220 Ga.App. 638, 469 S.E.2d 537 (1996); Prudential Resources Corp. v. Plunkett, 583 S.W.2d 97 (Ky.App.1979); Hauenstein & Bermeister, Inc. v. Met–Fab Indus. Inc., 320 N.W.2d 886 (Minn.1982); Electrical Prods. Consol. v. Bodell, 132 Mont. 243, 316 P.2d 788 (1957); Air Economy Corp. v. Aero–Flow Dynamics, 122 N.J.Super. 456, 300 A.2d 856 (App. Div. 1973); Export Ins. Co. v. Mitsui S.S. Co., 26 A.D.2d 436, 274 N.Y.S.2d 977 (N.Y.App.Div.1966); Perkins v. CCH Computax, Inc., 333 N.C. 140, 423 S.E.2d 780 (1992); Eads v. Woodmen of the World Life Ins. Society, 785 P.2d 328 (Okla. App. 1989); Reeves v. Chem Indus. Co., 262 Or. 95, 495 P.2d 729 (1972); Central Contracting Co. v. C.E. Youngdahl & Co., 418 Pa. 122, 209 A.2d 810 (1965); St. John's Episcopal Mission Ctr. v. South Carolina Dep't of Social Servs., 276 S.C. 507, 280 S.E.2d 207 (1981); Green v. Clinic Masters, Inc., 272 N.W.2d 813 (S.D. 1978); Exum v. Vantage Press, Inc., 17 Wn.App. 477, 563

P.2d 1314 (1977); State ex rel. Kuhn v. Luchsinger, 231 Wis. 533, 286 N.W. 72 (1939). For a discussion of the authorities in many states, see Annot., Validity of Contractual Provisions Limiting Place or Court in Which Action May be Brought, 31 A.L.R.4th 404.

4. An exception until recently was Alabama. See, e.g., White–Spunner Constr. v. Cliff, 588 So.2d 865 (Ala.1991). Alabama courts now, however, enforce reasonable forum clauses that derogate from their jurisdiction. See Professional Ins. Corp. v. Sutherland, 700 So.2d 347 (Ala.1997).

5. See, e.g., McCarty v. Herrick, 41 Idaho 529, 240 P. 192 (1925). See also Park, Bridging the Gap in Forum Selection: Harmonizing Arbitration and Court Selection, 8 Transnat'l L. & Contemp. Probs. 19, 24 n.29 (1998) (concluding that as of 1998 Idaho, Iowa, Maine, Montana and Texas do not generally enforce exclusive forum selection clauses, and that the situation is unclear in North Carolina and Georgia).

6. See, e.g., Accelerated Christian Educ., Inc. v. Oracle Corp., 925 S.W.2d 66 (Tex. App.1996) (limiting earlier case of Leonard v. Paxson, 654 S.W.2d 440 (Tex.1983) to cases in which the choice of a specific venue in Texas conflicts with the venue statute); Prows v. Pinpoint Retail Sys., 868 P.2d 809 (Utah 1993) (limiting earlier case of Petersen v. Ogden Union Ry. & Depot Co., 110 Utah 573, 175 P.2d 744 (1946) to circumstances in which choice of the specific venue in Utah conflicts with the venue statute). See also Park, supra n.5, at 24 n.29 (surveying state decisions).

Of course, simply because a state no longer adheres to the ouster doctrine does not mean that it is required to follow every detail of federal doctrine. Some state courts might be persuaded, for instance, that while the basic premises underlying the Supreme Court's decision in *The Bremen* are correct, its subsequent decision in *Carnival Cruise Lines v. Shute*,[7] endorsing the use of forum clauses in consumer contracts goes too far.[8] Efforts by state legislatures to protect consumers and other special classes are certainly not foreclosed.[9] In sum, while federal doctrine has been enormously persuasive to states, important distinctions between state and federal court practice are likely to continue and state innovation may well produce improvements to the law in this area.

D. INTERPRETATION AND SCOPE OF FORUM CLAUSES

§ 11.6 Forum clauses, particularly poorly drafted ones, can present some difficult questions of interpretation. One frequently arising question, discussed above,[1] is whether the clause is intended to be exclusive or non-exclusive. Parties who employ ambiguous constructions, such as that "jurisdiction shall be in" a given court,[2] invite litigation over the clause's meaning and run a significant risk that the clause will be interpreted in a manner not to their liking. Parties also invite trouble by drafting clauses that state that "the courts of" a given state or nation have jurisdiction.[3] Such clauses invite litigation over whether state courts, federal courts, or both, are contemplated, and in the case of a foreign court, failure to specify the court within the nation can lead to uncertainty.

These fundamental questions of interpretation are probably the most frequently litigated, but others arise as well. One is the question of what claims fall within the scope of the clause. Usually, of course, the forum clause is part of a larger agreement, and frequently such clauses

---

7. 499 U.S. 585, 111 S.Ct. 1522, 113 L.Ed.2d 622 (1991).

8. Cf. Wilder v. Absorption Corp., 107 S.W.3d 181 (Ky. 2003) (in arbitration case finding the alternative forum in the state of Washington to be unreasonably burdensome to a former employee in dispute with his former employer); Carnival Cruise Lines, Inc. v. Superior Court, 234 Cal. App.3d 1019, 286 Cal.Rptr. 323 (1991) (enforcement of a clause in a passenger ticket depends on whether the passengers had adequate notice of the clause); Mechanics Laundry & Supply, Inc. v. Wilder Oil Co., 596 N.E.2d 248 (Ind.App.1992) (arguing for a state law that an exclusive forum clause be the subject of actual bargaining).

9. See, e.g., Mont. Code Ann. § 27–5–14 (an agreement between parties to submit any future controversies to arbitration is not valid where a contract for consideration of $5,000 or less is at issue).

§ 11.6

1. See supra § 11.2.

2. See, e.g., Hunt Wesson Foods, Inc. v. Supreme Oil Co., 817 F.2d 75 (9th Cir.1987) (clause stating that California state courts "shall have jurisdiction"); Citro Florida, Inc. v. Citrovale, S.A., 760 F.2d 1231 (11th Cir.1985) (clause stating that "the place of jurisdiction is Sao Paulo, Brazil").

3. See, e.g., TUC Elecs., Inc. v. Eagle Telephonics, Inc., 698 F.Supp. 35, 39 (D.Conn.1988) (clause referring to "a court of original jurisdiction of the state of New York"); Spatz v. Nascone, 364 F.Supp. 967 (W.D.Pa.1973) (clause referring to "the courts of the commonwealth of Pennsylvania").

purport to govern all claims "related to" the contract or employ some similar construction. Usually courts have given clauses a transactional reading, meaning that all claims that are part of the same transaction are covered by the clause.[4] Occasionally, however, courts have found that transactionally related claims are not within the scope of the clause. Often when courts exclude transactionally related claims from the scope of the agreement the claims are statutory with some independent, quasi-public purpose, and the courts' decision to exclude the claims seem to stem as much from doubts about whether such claims are properly the subject of private agreement.[5] The Supreme Court's recent broad acceptance of arbitration of even antitrust and securities claims[6]—both formerly assumed not to be arbitrable subjects—should help to evaporate whatever differential treatment such claims have received in the context of interpretation of forum clauses.

Another interpretive question that arises in the context of forum clauses is what, if any, effect they have on non-parties to the agreement. Here the approaches of the courts diverge sharply. Some courts have held that non-parties to the forum clause (but parties to the litigation) have the same rights and duties as parties to the forum agreement.[7] Others have held that non-parties to the forum agreement are not bound by, and may not enforce, the agreement, unless some element of traditional contract law—such as third party beneficiary status—would confer those rights and duties.[8] Still others have refused to give any effect to

4. See, e.g., Mitsubishi Motors Corp. v. Soler Chrysler–Plymouth, Inc., 473 U.S. 614, 626–28, 105 S.Ct. 3346, 3353–55, 87 L.Ed.2d 444 (1985) (arbitration clause); Crescent Int'l, Inc. v. Avatar Communities, Inc., 857 F.2d 943 (3d Cir.1988); Bense v. Interstate Battery Sys., 683 F.2d 718 (2d Cir.1982); Knutson v. Rexair, Inc., 749 F.Supp. 214 (D.Minn.1990).

5. See, e.g., Seward v. Devine, 888 F.2d 957 (2d Cir.1989)(RICO claim); Crown Beverage Co. v. Cerveceria Moctezuma, S.A., 663 F.2d 886 (9th Cir.1981).

6. See, e.g., Mitsubishi Motors Corp. v. Soler Chrysler–Plymouth, Inc., 473 U.S. 614, 105 S.Ct. 3346, 87 L.Ed.2d 444 (1985); Rodriguez de Quijas v. Shearson/American Express, Inc., 490 U.S. 477, 109 S.Ct. 1917, 104 L.Ed.2d 526 (1989).

7. See, e.g., Brock v. Entre Computer Ctrs., Inc., 740 F.Supp. 428 (E.D.Tex.1990); Stephens v. Entre Computer Ctrs., Inc., 696 F.Supp. 636 (N.D.Ga.1988); Grossman v. Citrus Assoc. of the N.Y. Cotton Exch., Inc., 706 F.Supp. 221 (S.D.N.Y.1989).

8. See, e.g., Hays & Co. v. Merrill Lynch, Pierce, Fenner & Smith, Inc., 885 F.2d 1149 (3d Cir.1989) (bankruptcy-trustee plaintiff bound by forum selection clause because he stands in the shoes of the party to the agreement); Farmland Indus., Inc. v. Frazier–Parrott Commodities, Inc., 806 F.2d 848 (8th Cir.1986) (state law applied; non-parties to agreement cannot be bound); Moretti & Perlow Law Offices v. Aleet Assoc., 668 F.Supp. 103 (D.R.I.1987) (assignment of rights effective as to forum selection clause); Consolidated Bathurst, Ltd. v. Rederiaktiebolaget Gustaf Erikson, 645 F.Supp. 884 (S.D.Fla.1986) (third-party beneficiary enforcing contract including a forum selection clause is bound by the clause); Interpool, Ltd. v. Through Transp. Mut. Ins. Assoc., 635 F.Supp. 1503 (S.D.Fla. 1985) (arbitration agreement; third-party beneficiary is bound by the agreement); Lemme v. Wine of Japan Import, Inc., 631 F.Supp. 456 (E.D.N.Y.1986) (forum selection clause enforceable because it was expressly incorporated by reference); Thomas v. Price, 631 F.Supp. 114 (S.D.N.Y.1986); Crescent Corp. v. Proctor [sic] & Gamble Corp., 627 F.Supp. 745 (N.D.Ill.1986) (non-contracting party has the right to invoke forum selection clause after being drawn into the litigation); Clinton v. Janger, 583 F.Supp. 284 (N.D.Ill.1984) (third-party beneficiary may enforce a forum clause); Process and Storage Vessels, Inc. v. Tank Service, Inc., 541 F.Supp. 725 (D.Del.1982) (third-party beneficiary of an agreement seeking to enforce the agreement is bound

forum clauses that affect only a small fraction of the parties.[9] Of course, the clause must be part of the contractual relationship between the parties. A clause that is a material addition to the terms of a contract, and not accepted by the other party, does not have the mutual assent necessary for contractual formation, and thus is not enforceable.[10] Most difficulties related to the scope and interpretation of forum clauses can be avoided by careful drafting, although a certain amount of litigation over the meaning of contractual terms, including forum clauses, is inevitable.

The approach of binding only those parties who would be bound under traditional concepts of contract law is strongly supported by the Supreme Court's decision in Equal Employment Opportunity Commission v. Waffle House, Inc.[11] In that case, an employer had entered into a contract with one of its employees that required arbitration to resolve any disputes arising from the employment relationship. The Equal Employment Opportunity Commission (a federal agency) brought a civil action arising out of an employment dispute between the employee and the employer and the employer contended that the agency was limited to seeking relief in the arbitral forum. The Court rejected this contention. The majority reasoned that because the agency did not require the employee's consent to pursue the matter it in no respect stood in the shoes of the employee. Rather it was a distinct party with distinct legal rights and obligations. Thus, the arbitration clause could not bind the agency because "[i]t goes without saying that a contract cannot bind a nonparty."[12]

E. JUDGMENT RECOGNITION ISSUES

§ 11.7 A separate question is what effect will be given a judgment rendered in violation of an exclusive forum clause. Domestically, under the Full Faith and Credit Clause, it would seem that a court would be required to recognize a judgment rendered by another American court in violation of an exclusive forum clause as long as the rendering court had some constitutionally permissible basis for asserting jurisdiction.[1] With regard to judgments of foreign nations, the Uniform Foreign Money–Judgment Recognition Act would appear to leave it to the discretion of the judgment-recognizing court as to whether to give effect to a judgment of a foreign nation rendered in violation of an exclusive forum

by the forum clause); Richardson Eng'g Co. v. International Business Machs. Corp., 554 F.Supp. 467 (D.Vt.1981) (a non-party who novates a contract is bound by a forum selection agreement).

9. Snider v. Lone Star Art Trading Co., Inc., 659 F.Supp. 1249 (E.D.Mich.1987).

10. See, e.g., TRWL v. Select Int'l Inc., 527 N.W.2d 573 (Minn.App.1995).

11. 534 U.S. 279, 122 S.Ct. 754, 151 L.Ed.2d 755 (2002).

12. Id. at 294, 122 S.Ct. at 769, 151 L.Ed.2d 755. But see Net2phone, Inc. v. Superior Court, 109 Cal.App.4th 583, 135 Cal.Rptr.2d 149 (2003) (allowing enforcement against a "closely related" party as a matter of state contract law).

§ 11.7

1. Cf. Milliken v. Meyer, 311 U.S. 457, 61 S.Ct. 339, 85 L.Ed. 278 (1940) (mistake of law not grounds for refusal to enforce sister-state judgment).

clause.[2] The courts of other nations often will not give effect to judgments rendered in violation of exclusive forum clauses, making the Uniform Act's approach desirable.[3]

III. FORUM NON CONVENIENS

A. INTRODUCTION

§ 11.8 The previous discussion of jurisdiction showed that there are many limitations upon the existence of power in courts to exercise judicial jurisdiction. The earlier portion of this chapter was concerned with limitations arising from the parties' consensual agreement. However, there are several additional limitations that are imposed upon courts either internally or externally under which they are obligated to decline to exercise jurisdiction which may otherwise exist. Statutory limitations upon the particular court have previously been discussed, i.e., instances in which the state simply has chosen not to exercise its full constitutional power.[1] Further, even though a court may have jurisdiction over the parties to a lawsuit on a transitory cause of action, considerations of justice and convenience to all concerned may lead the court in its discretion to refuse to exercise its jurisdiction and to force the plaintiff to sue the defendant in a more appropriately available forum. This is the major doctrinal limitation on the exercise of jurisdiction which may otherwise exist and is known as the doctrine of *forum non conveniens.*[2] It

---

2. Uniform Foreign Money–Judgment Recognition Act § 4(b)(5) ("A foreign judgment need not be recognized if the proceeding in a foreign court was contrary to an agreement between the parties under which the dispute in question was to be settled. . . .").

3. See, e.g., German Supreme Court decision of 1969, in Lindenmaier–Möhring, § 39 ZPO, No. 9/10 (refusing recognition to a New York judgment rendered in violation of an exclusive forum clause selecting German courts; the German party did not waive the benefit of the stipulation by suing in New York).

§ 11.8

1. See supra § 5.14.

2. See Blair, The Doctrine of Forum Non Conveniens in Anglo–American Law, 29 Colum. L. Rev. 1 (1929); Hansell, The Proper Forum for Suits Against Foreign Corporations, 27 Colum. L. Rev. 12 (1927); Dainow, The Inappropriate Forum, 29 Ill. L. Rev. 867 (1935); Foster, Place of Trial in Civil Actions, 43 Harv. L. Rev. 1217 (1930); Barrett, The Doctrine of Forum Non Conveniens, 35 Calif. L. Rev. 380 (1947); Braucher, The Inconvenient Federal Forum, 60 Harv. L. Rev. 908 (1947); Restatement, Second, Conflict of Laws § 84 (1971).

See also Ehrenzweig, The Transient Rule of Personal Jurisdiction: The "Power" Myth and Forum Conveniens, 65 Yale L.J. 289 (1956); Currie, Jurisdiction over Alien Manufacturers, 18 Wayne L. Rev. 1585 (1972); Morley, Forum Non Conveniens, 68 Nw. U. L. Rev. 24 (1973); Yukins, The Convenient Forum Abroad, 20 Stan. L. Rev. 57 (1967); Inglis, Jurisdiction, Forum Conveniens and Choice of Law, 81 L.Q. Rev. 380 (1965); Pryles, Towards the Doctrine of Forum Conveniens, 52 Aust. L.J. 678 (1978); Smith, Conflict of Laws–Forum Non Conveniens, 52 Can. B. Rev. 315 (1974); Trachtman, Jurisdiction of State Courts—Forum Non–Conveniens—Foreign Torts—Comity, 84 A.J.I.L. 760 (1990); Freedman, Foreign Plaintiffs in Product Liability Actions: The Defense of Forum Non–Conveniens, Quorum Books (1988); Duque, The Second Circuit Review–1986–1987 Term: Civil Procedure: The Southern District Examines the Doctrine of Forum Non Conveniens: Carlenstolpe v. Merck & Co., Inc., 54 Brooklyn L. Rev. 379 (1988); Stewart, Forum Non–Conveniens: A Doctrine in Search of a Role, 74 Calif. L. Rev. 1259 (1986); Eilender, Forum Non–Conveniens and Comprehensive Hazardous Waste Coverage Suits, 90 Colum. L. Rev. 1066 (1990); see also Stein, *Erie* and Court Access, 100 Yale L.J. 1935 (1991).

is designed to avoid the hardship on the defendant and on the court that can result from undue forum shopping possible under accepted concepts of jurisdiction.[3]

A major portion of the concepts of due process discussed previously as constitutional limitations upon jurisdiction have involved the hardship and inconvenience to the defendant and the convenience of the forum as regards its relationship to the parties and to the case. Very similar factors are to be considered in the application of *forum non conveniens*. The relational factors of the forum to the parties and the transaction previously discussed were deemed to be so significant that in their absence the court could not constitutionally act. However, assuming that the required threshold of constitutional relationship is satisfied, there may still exist sufficient hardship in a particular case considering the convenience of all concerned, including the court, that the case should more appropriately be tried elsewhere. Thus, although the factors in *forum non conveniens* are closely related to the jurisdictional factors,

The doctrine was in early use in Scottish law. See Clements v. Macaulay, 4 Macpherson (Sess. Cas., 3d ser.) 583, 592 (1866), confirmed in Societe de Gaz de Paris v. Société Anonyme de Navigation "Les Armateurs Francais," [1926] Sess. Cas. (H.L.) 13, 20. The English House of Lords originally consistently declined to adopt the doctrine for England. The Atlantic Star, [1974] A.C. 436. In 1978 it permitted a stay, adopting the test of "what justice in the particular case demands." MacShannon v. Rockware Glass, Ltd., [1978] A.C. 795. The doctrine was finally accepted in English law in The Abidin Daver, [1984] A.C. 398, [1984] 1 All. E.R. 470. See also Spiliada Maritime Corp. v. Cansulex, Ltd., [1986] 3 All. E.R. 843. P.M. Canadian practice parallels the use of the doctrine in the United States. Castel, Canadian Conflict of Laws 221 et seq. (2d ed. 1986).

For a comprehensive comparative study of the doctrine of *forum non conveniens*, see Declining Jurisdiction in Private International Law: Reports to the XIVth Congress of the International Academy of Comparative Law (Fawcett, ed., 1995).

3. Gulf Oil Corp. v. Gilbert, 330 U.S. 501, 67 S.Ct. 839, 91 L.Ed. 1055 (1947); Koster v. Lumbermens Mut. Casualty Co., 330 U.S. 518, 67 S.Ct. 828, 91 L.Ed. 1067 (1947); Running v. Southwest Freight Lines, Inc., 227 Ark. 839, 303 S.W.2d 578 (1957); Price v. Atchison, Topeka & Santa Fe Ry. Co., 42 Cal.2d 577, 268 P.2d 457, 43 A.L.R.2d 756 (1954), cert. denied 348 U.S. 839, 75 S.Ct. 44, 99 L.Ed. 661 (1954); Winsor v. United Air Lines, Inc., 52 Del. 161, 154 A.2d 561 (1958); Hagen v. Viney, 124 Fla. 747, 169 So. 391 (1936); Whitney v. Madden, 400 Ill. 185, 79 N.E.2d 593 (1948),

cert. denied 335 U.S. 828, 69 S.Ct. 55, 93 L.Ed. 382 (1948); Stewart v. Litchenberg, 148 La. 195, 86 So. 734 (1920); Universal Adjustment Corp. v. Midland Bank, Ltd., 281 Mass. 303, 184 N.E. 152, 87 A.L.R. 1407 (1933); Johnson v. Chicago, Burlington & Quincy R.R. Co., 243 Minn. 58, 66 N.W.2d 763 (1954); Elliott v. Johnston, 365 Mo. 881, 292 S.W.2d 589 (1956); Jackson & Sons v. Lumbermen's Mut. Casualty Co., 86 N.H. 341, 168 A. 895 (1933); Gore v. United States Steel Corp., 15 N.J. 301, 104 A.2d 670, 48 A.L.R.2d 841 (1954), cert. denied 348 U.S. 861, 75 S.Ct. 84, 99 L.Ed. 678 (1954); Bata v. Bata, 304 N.Y. 51, 105 N.E.2d 623 (1952); Plum v. Tampax, Inc., 402 Pa. 616, 168 A.2d 315 (1961), cert. denied 368 U.S. 826, 82 S.Ct. 46, 7 L.Ed.2d 30 (1961); Disconto Gesellschaft v. Terlinden, 127 Wis. 651, 106 N.W. 821 (1906), aff'd 208 U.S. 570, 28 S.Ct. 337, 52 L.Ed. 625 (1908). Cf. Bourestom v. Bourestom, 231 Wis. 666, 285 N.W. 426 (1939). But cf. Loftus v. Lee, 308 S.W.2d 654 (Mo.1958); Lansverk v. Studebaker–Packard Corp., 54 Wn.2d 124, 338 P.2d 747 (1959). For extensive discussion see Dicey & Morris, Conflict of Laws 385–424. (13th ed. by Collins et al., 2000); Schuz, Controlling Forum–Shopping: The Impact of MacShannon v. Rockware Glass Ltd., 35 Int'l & Comp. L.Q. 374 (1986). For *Canada* see Castel, supra n.2. See also Verheul, The *Forum (Non) Conveniens* in English and Dutch Law and Under Some International Conventions, 35 Int'l & Comp. L.Q. 413 (1986). A comprehensive international comparative study is Declining Jurisdiction in Private International Law: Reports to the XIVth Congress of the International Academy of Comparative Law (Fawcett ed. 1995).

courts applying *forum non conveniens* compare the relative convenience of two or more available forums, each of which may well be authorized to exercise jurisdiction under constitutional doctrine. As a consequence, the doctrine of *forum non conveniens* has been viewed as one in which a court will exercise its discretion to remit the parties to trial in another available forum. This should not, however, be viewed as arbitrary discretion, for the doctrine has well-defined standards for the exercise of that discretion and constitutes a limitation, a limitation imposed upon the forum by its own law.[4]

The United States Supreme Court, in the leading case of *Gulf Oil Corp. v. Gilbert*,[5] stated the considerations underlying the doctrine of *forum non conveniens* as follows:

> If the combination and weight of factors requisite to given results are difficult to forecast or state, those to be considered are not difficult to name. An interest to be considered, and the one likely to be most pressed, is the private interest of the litigant. Important considerations are the relative ease of access to sources of proof; availability of compulsory process for attendance of unwilling, and the cost of obtaining attendance of willing, witnesses; possibility of view of premises, if view would be appropriate to the action; and all other practical problems that make trial of a case easy, expeditious and inexpensive. There may also be questions as to the enforceability of a judgment if one is obtained. The court will weigh relative advantages and obstacles to fair trial. It is often said that the plaintiff may not, by choice of an inconvenient forum, "vex," "harass," or "oppress" the defendant by inflicting upon him expense or trouble not necessary to his own right to pursue his remedy. But unless the balance is strongly in favor of the defendant, the plaintiff's choice of forum should rarely be disturbed.

> Factors of public interest also have place in applying the doctrine. Administrative difficulties follow for courts when litigation is piled up in congested centers instead of being handled at its origin. Jury duty is a burden that ought not to be imposed upon the people of a community which has no relation to the litigation. In cases which touch the affairs of many persons, there is reason for holding the trial in their view and reach rather than in remote parts of the country where they can learn of it by report only. There is a local interest in having localized controversies decided at home. There is an appropriateness, too, in having the trial of a diversity case in a forum that is at home with the state law that must govern the case, rather than having a court in some other forum untangle problems in conflict of laws, and in law foreign to itself.[6]

---

4. In federal practice, failure of the district court to make factual findings sufficient for a determination that it considered and evaluated all legally relevant factors may require reversal and remand. See

DeShane v. Deere & Co., 726 F.2d 443 (8th Cir.1984).

5. 330 U.S. 501, 67 S.Ct. 839, 91 L.Ed. 1055 (1947).

6. 330 U.S. at 508, 67 S.Ct. at 843, 91 L.Ed. 1055. The *Gilbert* analysis was reaf-

B. SIGNIFICANT FACTORS IN APPLICATION

1. *Preference for Chosen Forum*

§ 11.9 The tension between the plaintiff's efforts to reach the defendant and the defendant's efforts to avoid suit or, at least, to be required to respond only in a court to whose jurisdiction the defendant is reasonably subject, are initially resolved by the constitutional standard of due process. Once the plaintiff has satisfied this constitutional standard in the choice of available forums, this leads to strong policy reasons that the chosen forum should not disturb the plaintiff's choice unless there are exceptional reasons for it. As a consequence, there is a strong presumption that the forum is appropriate if constitutional jurisdictional standards are met. This presumption is frequently stated to the effect that the court hesitates to disturb the plaintiff's choice of forum and will not do so unless the balance of factors is strongly in favor of the defendant.[1]

In *Piper Aircraft Co. v. Reyno*,[2] the U.S. Supreme Court approved a "distinction between resident plaintiffs and foreign plaintiffs.... When the home forum has been chosen, it is reasonable to assume that this choice is convenient. When the plaintiff is foreign, however, this assumption is much less reasonable. Because the central purpose of any *forum non conveniens* inquiry is to ensure that the trial is convenient, a foreign plaintiff's choice deserves less deference."[3] The distinction thus drawn counteracts the attractiveness of American procedure and, in products

---

firmed in Piper Aircraft Co. v. Reyno, 454 U.S. 235, 102 S.Ct. 252, 70 L.Ed.2d 419 (1981). For applications compare In re Union Carbide Corp. Gas Plant Disaster at Bhopal, India, 809 F.2d 195 (2d Cir.1987), cert. denied 484 U.S. 871, 108 S.Ct. 199, 98 L.Ed.2d 150 (1987) with In re Air Crash Disaster Near New Orleans, La., 821 F.2d 1147 (5th Cir.1987), cert. granted and judgment vacated on other grounds 490 U.S. 1032, 109 S.Ct. 1928, 104 L.Ed.2d 400 (1989). See also Vargas v. M/V Mini Lama, 709 F.Supp. 117 (E.D.La.1989).

Gilbert has also significantly influenced state court practice. See, e.g., DeVries v. Bankers Life Co., 128 Ill.App.3d 647, 471 N.E.2d 230 (1984); Espinosa v. Norfolk & Western Ry. Co., 86 Ill.2d 111, 427 N.E.2d 111 (1981). For *intra* state application of the doctrine see Griffith v. Mitsubishi Aircraft Int'l, Inc., 136 Ill.2d 101, 554 N.E.2d 209 (1990) and Carlberg v. Chrysler Motors Corp., 199 Ill.App.3d 127, 556 N.E.2d 1284 (1990).

Dismissal for *forum non conveniens* by a federal court does not, however, preempt a state court from entertaining the claim, for instance when the state has an "open-courts" policy. Chick Kam Choo v. Exxon

Corp., 486 U.S. 140, 108 S.Ct. 1684, 100 L.Ed.2d 127 (1988). It has been suggested that the special federal interest in maritime law may justify the federal court in entering an order expressly precluding further inconsistent action by the state court. Id. at 149, 108 S.Ct. at 1691, 100 L.Ed.2d 127, and id. at 151, 108 S.Ct. at 1692, 100 L.Ed.2d 127 (White, J. concurring). But cf. American Dredging Co. v. Miller, 510 U.S. 443, 114 S.Ct. 981, 127 L.Ed.2d 285 (1994) (state court sitting in admiralty need not follow federal forum non conveniens rule).

§ 11.9

1. See Gulf Oil Corp. v. Gilbert, 330 U.S. 501, 67 S.Ct. 839, 91 L.Ed. 1055 (1947); Mobil Tankers Co. v. Mene Grande Oil Co., 363 F.2d 611 (3d Cir.1966), cert. denied 385 U.S. 945, 87 S.Ct. 318, 17 L.Ed.2d 225 (1966); Byrd v. Southern Ry. Co., 203 A.2d 37 (D.C.App.1964). See also Restatement, Second, Conflict of Laws § 84, cmnt. (c) (1971).

2. 454 U.S. 235, 102 S.Ct. 252, 70 L.Ed.2d 419 (1981).

3. Id. at 255–56, 102 S.Ct. at 266, 70 L.Ed.2d 419.

liability, of substantive American tort law for foreign litigants.[4] It is a corollary of this approach that differences between forum and foreign law should not defeat a dismissal for *forum non conveniens* which is otherwise indicated.[5] Dismissals for *forum non conveniens* in cases brought by foreign plaintiffs have been substantial in number in the wake of *Piper*.[6] One potential ambiguity in the distinction between "local" and "foreign" plaintiffs is whether a United States plaintiff domiciled in a judicial district other than the forum is treated as local for *forum non conveniens* purposes. There is now strong authority that all American plaintiffs are "local" for *forum non conveniens* purposes.[7]

2. Availability of Another Forum

§ 11.10 As earlier observed, the doctrine of *forum non conveniens* compares the convenience of the chosen forum to others that are available. As a consequence, it is necessary that there be another

---

4. "As a moth is drawn to the light, so is a litigant drawn to the United States." Smith Kline & French Lab., Ltd. v. Bloch, [1983] 2 All. E.R. 72, 74 (C.A. 1982, per Lord Denning, M.R.).

5. See, e.g., Murray v. British Broadcasting Corp., 81 F.3d 287 (2d Cir.1996) (unavailability of contingent fees in alternative forum does not preclude *forum non conveniens* dismissal even in the face of an argument that the litigation could not be financed in any other way); Coakes v. Arabian Am. Oil Co., 831 F.2d 572 (5th Cir. 1987) (no contingent-fee system in England at that time); Syndicate 420 at Lloyd's London v. Early Am. Ins. Co., 796 F.2d 821 (5th Cir.1986) (defenses not available under Louisiana law might be allowable in English proceeding); de Melo v. Lederle Lab., 801 F.2d 1058 (8th Cir.1986) (no punitive damages in Brazil); Jennings v. Boeing Co., 660 F.Supp. 796 (E.D.Pa.1987), order amended, reconsideration denied 677 F.Supp. 803 (E.D.Pa.1987), aff'd 838 F.2d 1206 (3d Cir.1988) (no punitive damages available in English or Scottish courts); Carlenstolpe v. Merck & Co., Inc., 638 F.Supp. 901 (S.D.N.Y.1986) (Swedish law less favorable to defendant drug company).

But see Holmes v. Syntex Lab., Inc., 156 Cal.App.3d 372, 202 Cal.Rptr. 773 (1984) (whether the alternative forum is "suitable"—discussed infra § 11.11—is to be determined with reference to the possibility that the applicable law in the alternative forum will be less favorable to the plaintiff). Reaching the same result, but doing so on the basis of interest analysis (which pointed to California law), see Corrigan v. Bjork Shiley Corp., 182 Cal.App.3d 166, 227 Cal.

Rptr. 247, cert. denied 479 U.S. 1049, 107 S.Ct. 921, 93 L.Ed.2d 973 (1987). See Comment, Considerations of Choice of Law in the Doctrine of Forum Non Conveniens, 74 Cal. L. Rev. 565 (1986). The question has not yet arisen whether a California federal court, sitting in diversity, should apply the view of *Piper* and of the federal cases or should consider the content of the applicable law in the alternative forum in accordance with *Holmes* and *Corrigan*. It is suggested that federal law should apply in analogy to the law applicable to forum selection clauses.

6. E.g., Scottish Air Int'l Inc. v. British Caledonian Group, 81 F.3d 1224 (2d Cir. 1996); Murray v. British Broadcasting Corp., 81 F.3d 287 (2d Cir.1996); In re Union Carbide Corp. Gas Plant Disaster at Bhopal, India in Dec., 1984, 809 F.2d 195 (2d Cir.1987), cert. denied 484 U.S. 871, 108 S.Ct. 199, 98 L.Ed.2d 150 (1987); Gonzalez v. Naviera Neptuno A.A., 832 F.2d 876 (5th Cir.1987); as well as the decisions cited in the preceding note. But see Peregrine Myanmar Ltd. v. Segal, 89 F.3d 41 (2d Cir.1996); In re Air Crash Disaster Near New Orleans, La. on July 9, 1982, 821 F.2d 1147 (5th Cir.1987), judgment vacated on other grounds, 490 U.S. 1032, 109 S.Ct. 1928, 104 L.Ed.2d 400 (1989), on remand 883 F.2d 17 (5th Cir.1989).

7. See, e.g., Wiwa v. Royal Dutch Petroleum Co., 226 F.3d 88, 102–03 (2d Cir. 2000), cert. denied 532 U.S. 941, 121 S.Ct. 1402, 149 L.Ed.2d 345 (2001); Guidi v. Inter–Continental Hotels Corp., 224 F.3d 142 (2d Cir.2000). See also Iragorri v. United Technologies Corp., 274 F.3d 65 (2d Cir. 2001).

available forum in which the plaintiff's action may be tried.[1] There is some difference in the cases as to whether the alternative forum must have been available at the time the plaintiff originally initiated the lawsuit, or whether the defendant's consent to the jurisdiction of a more convenient forum is adequate.[2] It would seem that the flexibility of the doctrine of *forum non conveniens,* which includes the considerations of matters arising in the trial after the acquisition of jurisdiction, should permit a court to consider another court conveniently available even if it were the result of compromise and was not previously available to the plaintiff without consent.[3] This result seems to be supported by the cases in which the parties are required, as a condition of dismissal, to waive the statute of limitations in the other available forum.[4] The otherwise available forum, of course, should be one in which the plaintiff can obtain a remedy which is substantially the same and is as reflective of justice as that available in the chosen forum.[5] Of course, if the chosen

§ 11.10

1. See, e.g., El–Fadl v. Central Bank of Jordan, 75 F.3d 668 (D.C.Cir.1996) (*forum non conveniens* dismissal inappropriate without a showing that the proposed alternative forum would have jurisdiction). But see Islamic Republic of Iran v. Pahlavi, 62 N.Y.2d 474, 478 N.Y.S.2d 597, 467 N.E.2d 245 (1984), cert. denied 469 U.S. 1108, 105 S.Ct. 783, 83 L.Ed.2d 778 (1985): availability of an alternative forum not an absolute precondition but only one of several factors. However, the case involved an action by a foreign government against its own nationals and therefore may not be precedent for actions brought by U.S. citizens or residents. See infra n.8 and Banco Ambrosiano, S.P.A. v. Artoc Bank & Trust, Ltd., 62 N.Y.2d 65, 73, 476 N.Y.S.2d 64, 68, 464 N.E.2d 432, 436 (1984).

2. See Schertenleib v. Traum, 589 F.2d 1156 (2d Cir.1978); Vargas v. A.H. Bull S.S. Co., 44 N.J.Super. 536, 131 A.2d 39 (1957), aff'd 25 N.J. 293, 135 A.2d 857 (1957), cert. denied 355 U.S. 958, 78 S.Ct. 545, 2 L.Ed.2d 534 (1958). Cf. Manu Int'l S.A. v. Avon Prod., Inc., 641 F.2d 62 (2d Cir.1981). But see Hill v. Upper Mississippi Towing Corp., 252 Minn. 165, 89 N.W.2d 654 (1958). Under the specific language of the Federal Transfer Statute, 28 U.S.C.A. § 1404(a) the defendant's consent to jurisdiction elsewhere is not alone sufficient to make that district one "where [the case] might have been brought" as specifically required by that section. Hoffman v. Blaski, 363 U.S. 335, 80 S.Ct. 1084, 4 L.Ed.2d 1254 (1960).

3. See R. Weintraub, Commentary on the Conflict of Laws 262 (4th ed. 2001).

4. See Air Prods. & Chem., Inc. v. Lummus Co., 252 A.2d 543 (Del.1969); Vargas v. A. H. Bull S.S. Co., 44 N.J.Super. 536, 131 A.2d 39 (1957), aff'd 25 N.J. 293, 135 A.2d 857 (1957), cert. denied 355 U.S. 958, 78 S.Ct. 545, 2 L.Ed.2d 534 (1958). For the view that the alternate forum need not have been available initially but may become available as a result of the defendant's consent, see Veba–Chemie A.G. v. M/V Getafix, 711 F.2d 1243, 1245–46 (5th Cir.1983); Perusahaan Umum Listrik Negara Pusat v. M/V Tel Aviv, 711 F.2d 1231, 1238 n.19 (5th Cir.1983).

5. See Piper Aircraft Co. v. Reyno, 454 U.S. 235, 102 S.Ct. 252, 70 L.Ed.2d 419 (1981). For a critical view of *Piper* see Note, Forum Non Conveniens in the Absence of An Alternative Forum, 86 Colum. L. Rev. 1000 (1986) (suggesting that the adequacy of the remedy should be an important criterion). See also Nemariam v. Federal Democratic Republic of Ethiopia, 315 F.3d 390 (D.C. Cir. 2003), cert. denied ___ U.S. ___, 124 S.Ct. 278, 157 L.Ed.2d 141 (2003) (foreign claims commission not an adequate alternative forum because it lacked the authority to pay claims to individual plaintiffs).

Unless litigation is already pending in another court (see paragraph immediately following), European courts will not dismiss for *forum non conveniens.* The doctrine is also not part of European Community law on the jurisdiction of courts in civil and commercial matters. See Kropholler, Europäisches Zivilprozessrecht anno. 20 preceding Art. 2 (7th ed. 2002). A recent exception is the EC Council Regulation No. 2201/2203, [2003] Official Journal L338/1, on Jurisdiction and Enforcement of Judgments in Matrimonial Matters and in Matters of Parental Responsibility. Its Art. 15 permits a court to transfer a child custody

forum is unable to grant appropriate relief, it will dismiss the suit.[6] Although this is in part a consideration of the public policy of a state in accepting a case,[7] it is clear that courts are more likely to consider dismissing a suit if there is another available forum in which the plaintiff could obtain more appropriate relief.[8]

3. Other Factors

§ 11.11 As Justice Jackson observed in *Gulf Oil Corp. v. Gilbert*, both the private interests of the parties and the public interests of the respective forums are involved in the doctrine.[1] One of the private factors relating to the parties is the domicile of the parties, the courts showing a great deal of hesitation to dismiss a suit brought by one of their own residents, or against a defendant resident in the forum, and in some instances the courts have suggested that *forum non conveniens* will be applied only where none of the parties involved in the litigation is a

matter to a court "better placed to hear the case." Such a transfer may be made upon application of a party, on the court's own motion, or even upon the request of another court with which the child has a "particular connection." Id., Art 15(2).

6. See Restatement, Second, Conflict of Laws § 85 (1971).

7. See supra, § 3.19; Slater v. Mexican Nat'l Ry. Co., 194 U.S. 120, 24 S.Ct. 581, 48 L.Ed. 900 (1904). Cf. Intercontinental Hotels Corp. v. Golden, 15 N.Y.2d 9, 254 N.Y.S.2d 527, 203 N.E.2d 210 (1964).

8. See Restatement, Second, Conflict of Laws § 85, cmnt. b (1971). See, e.g., Matson Navigation Co. v. Stal–Laval Turbin AB, 609 F.Supp. 579 (N.D.Cal.1985). In contrast, when the other forum lacks jurisdiction (e.g., in the case of one of several co-defendants) and the party in question declines to consent to jurisdiction there, dismissal for *forum non conveniens* is improper: Watson v. Merrell Dow Pharmaceuticals, Inc., 769 F.2d 354, 356–57 (6th Cir.1985); Liaw Su Teng v. Skaarup Shipping Corp., 743 F.2d 1140, 1147 (5th Cir.1984) (availability of alternate forum is "the essential predicate for dismissal"); Perusahaan Umum Listrik Negara Pusat v. M/V Tel Aviv, 711 F.2d 1231 (5th Cir.1983). For a contrary view, see supra n.1.

When litigation is already pending in a foreign forum, an American court may abstain from exercising jurisdiction and dismiss in favor of the foreign forum. Brinco Mining, Ltd. v. Federal Insurance Co., 552 F.Supp. 1233 (D.D.C.1982); Rolls Royce (Canada), Ltd. v. Cayman Airways, Ltd., 617 F.Supp. 17 (S.D.Fla.1985). In *England* as well, a court has "jurisdiction to stay an

action" in favor of proceedings pending abroad. The identity of the parties may make a difference. Thus, abstention may be denied and indeed the simultaneous prosecution of foreign litigation may be enjoined when the plaintiffs are U.S. citizens or residents and trial in the United States is merely inconvenient but not oppressive for the foreign defendant. American Home Assur. Co. v. Insurance Corp. of Ireland, 603 F.Supp. 636 (S.D.N.Y.1984). In *Germany*, in contrast, pendency of a foreign proceeding *requires* that the domestic proceeding be stayed. However, the foreign proceeding must satisfy certain preconditions, chief among them that the ultimate foreign judgment would be entitled to recognition in Germany and that the foreign proceeding does not constitute an onerous burden for a German party. Baumbach/Hartmann, Zivilprozessordnung § 261 annot. 4(B) [No. 7] (57th ed. 1999). In the *European Communities*, Art. 27 of the EC Regulation No. 44/2001 and Art. 21 of the Brussels and Lugano Conventions on Jurisdiction and the Enforcement of Civil and Commercial Judgments similarly mandate abstention by the second court. Except for the European Regulation and Conventions and bilateral treaties, *France* has traditionally been hostile to the defense of *lis pendens* seeking stay or dismissal; however that attitude seems to be moderating. Batiffol/Lagarde, 2 Droit International Prive no. 676 (7th ed. 1983).

§ 11.11

1. 330 U.S. 501, 508, 67 S.Ct. 839, 843, 91 L.Ed. 1055 (1947). See also Murty v. Aga Khan, 92 F.R.D. 478 (E.D.N.Y.1981).

resident of the forum.[2] More than in the constitutional standard, considerations relating to the trial are pointed out as being significant in *Gulf Oil,* including the access to sources of proof, the availability of witnesses and the like.[3] In practice, cases such as *Piper Aircraft Co. v. Reyno*[4] that involve both foreign plaintiffs and in which most or all of the liability-creating events occurred outside the United States are the most likely to be dismissed on forum non conveniens grounds.[5]

A factor that is significant to both the parties and the courts so far as ease of the trial is concerned, and hence relates to both private and public concerns, is the presence of choice-of-law questions to be considered by the court. If the forum is so unrelated to the transaction that it will be required to consider difficult questions of choice of law involving the law of another available forum, this is an appropriate factor to be considered in the application of *forum non conveniens.*[6]

2. See as to the plaintiff's domicile: Pollux Holding, Ltd. v. Chase Manhattan Bank, 329 F.3d 64 (2d Cir. 2003), cert. denied ___ U.S. ___, 124 S.Ct. 1145, 157 L.Ed.2d 1041 (2004) (less deference given to plaintiff's forum choice where plaintiff is foreign); Thomson v. Continental Ins. Co., 66 Cal.2d 738, 59 Cal.Rptr. 101, 427 P.2d 765 (1967); McDonnell–Douglas Corp. v. Lohn, 192 Colo. 200, 557 P.2d 373 (Colo. 1976). But see Alcoa S.S. Co., Inc. v. M/V Nordic Regent, 654 F.2d 147 (2d Cir.1980), cert. denied 449 U.S. 890, 101 S.Ct. 248, 66 L.Ed.2d 116 (1980); Rini v. New York Central R.R. Co., 429 Pa. 235, 240 A.2d 372 (1968); In re Marriage of Dunkley, 89 Wn.2d 777, 575 P.2d 1071 (1978). Domicile of the defendant: Cf. Silver v. Great Am. Ins. Co., 29 N.Y.2d 356, 328 N.Y.S.2d 398, 278 N.E.2d 619 (1972); Texas City Ref., Inc. v. Grand Bahama Petroleum Co., 347 A.2d 657 (Del.1975). Domicile of either party: See Seaboard Coast Line R.R. Co. v. Swain, 362 So.2d 17 (Fla.1978). Cf. Deupree v. Le, 402 A.2d 428 (D.C.App.1979). But cf., Piper Aircraft Co. v. Reyno, 454 U.S. 235, 102 S.Ct. 252, 70 L.Ed.2d 419 (1981); Pain v. United Technologies Corp., 637 F.2d 775 (D.C.Cir.1980), cert. denied 454 U.S. 1128, 102 S.Ct. 980, 71 L.Ed.2d 116 (1981). See generally Restatement, Second, Conflict of Laws § 84, cmnt. (f) (1971); Note, *Forum Non Conveniens and American Plaintiffs in the Federal Courts,* 47 U. Chi. L. Rev. 373 (1980); Note, *Forum Non Conveniens and Foreign Plaintiffs in the Federal Courts,* 69 Georgetown L.J. 1257 (1981).

3. See Rini v. New York Cent. R.R. Co., 429 Pa. 235, 240 A.2d 372 (1968); Wahl v. Pan Am. World Airways, Inc., 227 F.Supp. 839 (S.D.N.Y.1964). See also Da Costa Fonseca v. Frota Oceanica Brasileira, S.A., 67 A.D.2d 636, 412 N.Y.S.2d 145 (1979); Mergenthaler Linotype Co. v. Leonard

Storch Enters., Inc., 66 Ill.App.3d 789, 383 N.E.2d 1379 (1978). But see Wasche v. Wasche, 268 N.W.2d 721 (Minn.1978).

4. 454 U.S. 235, 102 S.Ct. 252, 70 L.Ed.2d 419 (1981).

5. See, e.g., Vasquez v. Bridgestone/Firestone, Inc., 325 F.3d 665 (5th Cir. 2003)(case properly dismissed where accident occurred in Mexico and plaintiffs were Mexican); Ford v. Brown, 319 F.3d 1302 (11th Cir. 2003).

6. See Gulf Oil Corp. v. Gilbert, 330 U.S. 501, 508, 67 S.Ct. 839, 843, 91 L.Ed. 1055 (1947); Irrigation and Indus. Dev. Corp. v. Indag S.A., 37 N.Y.2d 522, 375 N.Y.S.2d 296, 337 N.E.2d 749 (1975); Adkins v. Chicago, Rock Island & Pacific R.R. Co., 54 Ill.2d 511, 301 N.E.2d 729 (1973), cert. denied 424 U.S. 943, 96 S.Ct. 1411, 47 L.Ed.2d 349 (1976); Universal Adjustment Corp. v. Midland Bank, Ltd., 281 Mass. 303, 184 N.E. 152 (1933). Cf. Delaware, L & W R.R. v. Ashelman, 300 Pa. 291, 150 A. 475 (1930). But see Baade, Annual Survey of Texas Law–Conflict of Laws, 28 S.W.L.J. 166, 182 (1974). But cf. Van Dusen v. Barrack, 376 U.S. 612, 84 S.Ct. 805, 11 L.Ed.2d 945 (1964) (discussed infra § 11.14).

However, the U.S. Supreme Court has held that a plaintiff may not defeat a motion to dismiss on the ground of *forum non conveniens* merely by showing that the substantive law that would be applied in the alternative forum is less favorable to the plaintiff than that of the present forum. Piper Aircraft Co. v. Reyno, 454 U.S. 235, 102 S.Ct. 252, 70 L.Ed.2d 419 (1981). But see supra § 11.10 n.4.

The *forum non conveniens* doctrine is "designed in part to help courts avoid conducting complex exercises in comparative

The more directly public concerns that have been identified relate to the expense of litigation being imposed upon the forum,[7] the burden of jury duty and delays incident to crowded calendars.[8] The doctrine of *forum non conveniens* does not seem to be limited to any particular kind of case.[9] The early specific rule that a court would not entertain suits concerning the internal affairs of a foreign corporation has been largely absorbed in the broader *forum non conveniens* doctrine.[10] The doctrine is applied to both federal and non-federal causes of action in the absence of compulsory venue provisions.[11] While the outer limits of *forum non conveniens* are still subject to development, it seems clear that the doctrine, appropriately applied, is consistent with the constitutional guarantees of equal protection, privileges and immunities, and full faith and credit.[12] The doctrine could be used as an important check on the

law." *Piper Aircraft,* 454 U.S. at 251, 102 S.Ct. at 263, followed in the following decisions, inter alia: Sibaja v. Dow Chem. Co., 757 F.2d 1215, 1218–19 (11th Cir.1985)(Costa Rican law); Rolls Royce (Canada), Ltd. v. Cayman Airways, Ltd., 617 F.Supp. 17 (S.D.Fla.1985) (Canadian law); Zinsler v. Marriott Corp., 605 F.Supp. 1499 (D.Md.1985) (Austrian law). For a state court decision invoking this factor, see DeVries v. Bankers Life Co., 128 Ill.App.3d 647, 471 N.E.2d 230 (1984) (Iowa law).

For a good discussion of the relevance of, and weight to be given private and public interest factors, see Lubbe v. Cape PLC, [2001] 1 W.L.R. 1545 (H.L.) opting for the private interest because of plaintiffs' inability to receive legal aid to finance investigations and litigation expenses in the alternative forum (South Africa), which was the place of residence of all plaintiffs: motion to dismiss action in England denied.

7. See S.D. Sales Corp. v. Doltex Fabrics Corp., 92 N.J.Super. 586, 224 A.2d 345 (1966), affirmed 96 N.J.Super. 345, 233 A.2d 70 (App.Div.1967); Vaage v. Lewis, 29 A.D.2d 315, 288 N.Y.S.2d 521 (1968).

8. See Parsons v. Chesapeake & Ohio Ry. Co., 375 U.S. 71, 84 S.Ct. 185, 11 L.Ed.2d 137 (1963); Fender v. St. Louis Southwestern Ry. Co., 49 Ill.2d 1, 273 N.E.2d 353 (1971); Universal Adjustment Corp. v. Midland Bank, Ltd., 281 Mass. 303, 184 N.E. 152 (1933).

9. See, e.g., Bata v. Bata, 304 N.Y. 51, 105 N.E.2d 623 (1952).

10. Koster v. Lumbermens Mut. Casualty Co., 330 U.S. 518, 67 S.Ct. 828, 91 L.Ed. 1067 (1947); Note, *Forum Non Conveniens as a Substitute for the Internal Affairs Rule,* 58 Colum. L. Rev. 234 (1958).

11. See Missouri ex rel. Southern Ry. Co. v. Mayfield, 340 U.S. 1, 71 S.Ct. 1, 95 L.Ed. 3 (1950).

12. See Douglas v. New York, New Haven & H.R. Co., 279 U.S. 377, 49 S.Ct. 355, 73 L.Ed. 747 (1929); Hughes v. Fetter, 341 U.S. 609, 71 S.Ct. 980, 95 L.Ed. 1212 (1951); Currie, The Constitution and the "Transitory" Cause of Action, 73 Harv. L. Rev. 36 (1959). The *forum non conveniens* doctrine has been invoked as a basis for dismissal when all parties were Guatemalan entities and there were no witnesses, documents or other evidence in the American forum, even though there had been an express contractual choice of the latter. Banco Metropolitano v. Desarrollo de Autopistas, 616 F.Supp. 301 (S.D.N.Y.1985). The decision relied on Proyecfin de Venezuela v. Banco Indus., 760 F.2d 390 (2d Cir.1985). The latter decision, however, had merely confirmed that the *forum non conveniens* doctrine remains applicable even as to cases arising under the Foreign Sovereign Immunities Act and that the choice-of-forum clause in favor of alternative fora (including New York) was non-exclusive. The *Banco Metropolitano* court thus treated a choice-of-court clause analogously to choice-of-law stipulations which require a connection to the forum (§ 18.6 infra). When the parties consented, by stipulation, to the local forum's jurisdiction, they presumably did so for a reason (e.g., the expertise of New York courts) so that a decision like *Banco Metropolitano* substitutes the *court's* convenience for the inconvenience of the parties which they themselves had agreed to assume. When the parties are both foreign, it is no doubt true that they cannot compel a court to hear their case when this is inconvenient for the latter and when the foreign parties

exercise of jurisdiction based on fortuitous presence of the defendant within the state.

4. *Methods of Application*

§ 11.12   Once the court concludes that it should apply the doctrine of *forum non conveniens* and exercise its discretion not to entertain the case, it may exercise this discretion in a variety of ways. For example, it may dismiss the case outright[1] or it may dismiss on condition[2] or stipulation[3] that the defendant accept service in a more convenient forum. It is through the use of conditions and stipulations incident to dismissal that the state courts are able to effect the practical result of a transfer which is beyond their power.[4]

In addition to the accumulation of common law authorities there has been considerable statutory development that has reinforced the doctrine of *forum non conveniens*. For example, the Uniform Child Custody Jurisdiction Act spells out specific considerations which require the court to assure that it is an appropriate forum[5] and provides that should the court find that it is an inconvenient forum, it may "stay the proceedings upon . . . any . . . conditions which may be just and proper, including the condition that a moving party stipulate his consent and submission to the jurisdiction of the other forum."[6] This statute has been enacted in all of the American jurisdictions.[7] The Uniform Interstate and International Procedure Act also expressly authorizes the utilization of *forum non conveniens*.[8] Other states have followed this pattern of statutory develop-

---

have no due process claim to a right to be heard. However, it was in the interests of international commercial concerns that New York law now provides that courts may not dismiss for *forum non conveniens* in the face of a choice-of-court clause in favor of New York when the case involves obligations of $1 million in the aggregate and when New York law has also been chosen. N.Y. Gen. Oblig. Law § 5–1402. While there are no *Erie*-implications in the application of the *forum non conveniens* doctrine, supra § 3.37 n.5, decisions like *Banco Metropolitano* may lead to forum-shopping by encouraging a party to resort to the federal courts in New York in order to escape from a choice-of-court clause.

For the *forum non conveniens* doctrine in New York in cases not covered by § 5–1402 of the General Obligations law, supra this note, see N.Y. Civ. Prac. L. & R. § 327.

§ 11.12

1. See, e.g., Johnson v. Chicago, B & Q Ry. Co., 243 Minn. 58, 66 N.W.2d 763 (1954); Mergenthaler Linotype Co. v. Leonard Storch Enterprises, Inc., 66 Ill.App.3d 789, 383 N.E.2d 1379 (1978).

2. See, e.g., Alcoa S.S. Co. Inc. v. M/V Nordic Regent, 654 F.2d 147 (2d Cir.1980), cert. denied 449 U.S. 890, 101 S.Ct. 248, 66 L.Ed.2d 116 (1980) (submission to jurisdiction and guarantee of judgment); Wendel v. Hoffman, 259 App.Div. 732, 18 N.Y.S.2d 96 (1940); but cf. Hill v. Upper Miss. Towing Corp., 252 Minn. 165, 89 N.W.2d 654 (1958).

3. See Vargas v. A.H. Bull S.S. Co., 25 N.J. 293, 135 A.2d 857 (1957), cert. denied 355 U.S. 958, 78 S.Ct. 545, 2 L.Ed.2d 534 (1958); Da Costa Fonseca v. Frota Oceanica Brasileira, S.A., 67 A.D.2d 636, 412 N.Y.S.2d 145 (1979); Restatement, Second, Conflict of Laws § 84, cmnt. e (1971).

4. Compare 28 U.S.C.A. § 1404(a) discussed infra § 11.14. See Da Costa Fonseca v. Frota Oceanica Brasileira, S.A., 67 A.D.2d 636, 412 N.Y.S.2d 145 (1979).

5. U.C.C.J.A. § 3, 9 U.L.A. 143.

6. U.C.C.J.A. § 7, 9 U.L.A. 233.

7. 9 U.L.A. 115 (1988).

8. Uniform Interstate and International Procedure Act, § 1.05, 13 U.L.A. 377 (1986).

ment in jurisdiction statutes,[9] and in the Uniform Probate Code.[10]

5. State Practice

§ 11.13 The previous discussion, blending state and federal citations, demonstrates that state and federal court application of *forum non conveniens* is generally identical. However, one must always be alert for the unusual circumstance in which state and federal practice diverge. A dramatic example is the Texas Supreme Court's decision in *Dow Chemical Co. v. Alfaro*[1] that the doctrine could not be applied in personal injury and wrongful death actions because it conflicted with Texas's "open courts" statute. Although *Alfaro* was legislatively overruled three years later,[2] it stands as a reminder that state and federal doctrine are not necessarily co-extensive in all circumstances.[3]

There are several instances in which there are federal limitations on state application of *forum non conveniens*. For example, under the Federal Employers Liability Act, a state must observe the venue privilege granted by the federal statute.[4] However, the Court has recognized that the doctrine of *forum non conveniens* may be applied if the forum is seriously inappropriate.[5] Even so, in this latter case, it would seem that the application of the state doctrine of *forum non conveniens* to the federal cause of action would be reviewable by the federal courts and hence federal law would determine the applicable limits of *forum non conveniens* in such cases.

A related problem is presented in cases in which the state concludes that it need not open its doors to the particular action. One example of this is *Testa v. Katt*[6] in which the plaintiff in a Rhode Island state court sought to recover treble damages against the defendant for violation of the Federal Emergency Price Control Act. The Supreme Court required the state court to open its doors to these actions. The Court rejected the view that the action could be declined by the state on the grounds that it

---

9. See, e.g., Pa. Judicial Code § 5322(e), 42 Pa. Cons. Stat. Ann. § 5322(e).

10. See Uniform Probate Code §§ 3–202, 8 U.L.A. 238; 7–203, 8 U.L.A. 550. Cf. U.P.C. § 7–305, 8 U.L.A. 559.

§ 11.13

1. 786 S.W.2d 674 (Tex.1990).

2. See Tex. Civ. Prac. & Rem. Code § 71.051 (applicable only to cases filed after September 1, 1993). See generally Comment, Section 71.051 of the Texas Civil Practice & Remedies Code—The Texas Legislature's Response to *Alfaro: Forum non Conveniens* in Personal Injury and Wrongful Death Litigation, 46 Baylor L. Rev. 99 (1994).

3. See also Miller v. American Dredging Co., 595 So.2d 615 (La.1992) (Louisiana law

precludes application of *forum non conveniens* in maritime cases), aff'd 510 U.S. 443, 114 S.Ct. 981, 127 L.Ed.2d 285 (1994) (state courts in admiralty cases need not apply federal doctrine of *forum non conveniens* because it is not an essential part of admiralty jurisprudence).

4. Pope v. Atlantic Coast Line R.R. Co., 345 U.S. 379, 73 S.Ct. 749, 97 L.Ed. 1094 (1953); Miles v. Illinois Cent. R.R. Co., 315 U.S. 698, 62 S.Ct. 827, 86 L.Ed. 1129 (1942); Baltimore & Ohio R.R. Co. v. Kepner, 314 U.S. 44, 62 S.Ct. 6, 86 L.Ed. 28 (1941).

5. Missouri ex rel. Southern Ry. Co. v. Mayfield, 340 U.S. 1, 71 S.Ct. 1, 95 L.Ed. 3 (1950).

6. 330 U.S. 386, 67 S.Ct. 810, 91 L.Ed. 967 (1947), noted 14 U. of Chi. L. Rev. 287 (1947); 15 U. of Kan. City L. Rev. 52 (1947).

was because it was viewed as a penal action. In older cases, the public policy of a state has been urged on one ground or another as a basis for declining jurisdiction in somewhat similar situations.[7]

In a series of cases the Supreme Court has held that states could not deny access to their courts when to do so would violate a treaty or agreement with a foreign nation under the federal foreign relations power.[8] This result would follow from the Supremacy Clause of the United States Constitution.[9] However, a more extensive limitation is expressed when the Supreme Court states that "[n]o state can rewrite our foreign policy to conform to its own domestic policies"[10] and "in respect of our foreign relations generally, state lines disappear. As to such purposes the state of New York does not exist."[11] In *Zschernig v. Miller*[12] the Supreme Court struck down an Oregon "iron curtain" statute escheating property succeeding to nonresident aliens unless certain conditions were met because "... even in the absence of a treaty, a State's policy may disturb foreign relations ..."[13] The Oregon statute was characterized as an unconstitutional "intrusion by the State into the field of foreign affairs which the Constitution entrusts to the President and Congress."[14] The *Zschernig* case would seem to leave almost no room for validity of state[15] or local[16] laws that purport to intrude in foreign affairs. However, uncertainties have arisen from subsequent cases in which the Court has not forthrightly confirmed its position.[17]

7. See, e.g., Herzog v. Stern, 264 N.Y. 379, 191 N.E. 23, cert. denied 293 U.S. 597, 55 S.Ct. 112, 79 L.Ed. 690 (1934); Poling v. Poling, 116 W.Va. 187, 179 S.E. 604 (1935); Hudson v. Von Hamm, 85 Cal.App. 323, 259 P. 374 (1927); Colorado v. Harbeck, 232 N.Y. 71, 133 N.E. 357 (1921). See Goodrich, Public Policy in the Law of Conflicts, 36 W. Va. L.Q. 156 (1930); see supra §§ 3.17–3.18.

8. See Clark v. Allen, 331 U.S. 503, 67 S.Ct. 1431, 91 L.Ed. 1633 (1947); United States v. Pink, 315 U.S. 203, 62 S.Ct. 552, 86 L.Ed. 796 (1942); United States v. Belmont, 301 U.S. 324, 57 S.Ct. 758, 81 L.Ed. 1134 (1937). See also supra §§ 3.56–3.60.

9. U.S. Const. art. VI.

10. United States v. Pink, 315 U.S. 203, 233, 62 S.Ct. 552, 567, 86 L.Ed. 796 (1942).

11. United States v. Belmont, 301 U.S. 324, 331, 57 S.Ct. 758, 761, 81 L.Ed. 1134 (1937).

12. 389 U.S. 429, 88 S.Ct. 664, 19 L.Ed.2d 683 (1968). See Linde, A New Foreign–Relations Restraint on American States, 28 Zeitschrift für ausländisches öffentliches Recht und Völkerrecht 595 (1968). See also infra Chapter 20.

13. 389 U.S. at 441, 88 S.Ct. at 671, 19 L.Ed.2d 683.

14. Id. at 432, 88 S.Ct. at 666, 19 L.Ed.2d 683.

15. See, e.g., In re Kraemer's Estate, 276 Cal.App.2d 715, 81 Cal.Rptr. 287 (1969); Bethlehem Steel Corp. v. Board of Comm'rs, 276 Cal.App.2d 221, 80 Cal.Rptr. 800 (1969); Star–Kist Foods, Inc. v. County of Los Angeles, 42 Cal.3d 1, 227 Cal.Rptr. 391, 719 P.2d 987 (1986), cert. denied 480 U.S. 930, 107 S.Ct. 1565, 94 L.Ed.2d 758 (1987).

16. In recent years, various municipalities have enacted laws with obvious foreign relations motivations. See, e.g., Springfield Rare Coin Galleries, Inc. v. Johnson, 115 Ill.2d 221, 104 Ill.Dec. 743, 503 N.E.2d 300 (1986) (state and local laws singling out South Africa for unfavorable treatment are unconstitutional as conflicting with the federal government's exclusive foreign relations power). See generally Borchers & Dauer, Taming the New Breed of Nuclear Free Ordinances: Statutory and Constitutional Infirmities in Local Procurement Ordinances Blacklisting the Producers of Nuclear Weapons Components, 40 Hastings L.J. 87 (1988).

17. See Gorun v. Fall, 393 U.S. 398, 89 S.Ct. 678, 21 L.Ed.2d 628 (1969); Gorun v. Montana, 399 U.S. 901, 90 S.Ct. 2195, 26 L.Ed.2d 555 (1970); Goldstein v. Cox, 396 U.S. 471, 90 S.Ct. 671, 24 L.Ed.2d 663 (1970). The difficulties with Zschernig v. Miller and suggested appropriate tests for judicial action in this area are ably dis-

That the state courts are very seriously limited by the United States Constitution's allocation of the foreign relations power to the federal government is further demonstrated by the act of state doctrine which has been expressed as follows: "Every sovereign state is bound to respect the independence of every other sovereign state, and the courts of one country will not sit in judgment on the acts of the government of another, done within its own territory. Redress of grievances by reason of such acts must be obtained through the means open to be availed of by the sovereign powers as between themselves."[18]

In the famous *Sabbatino* case,[19] the Supreme Court applied the act of state doctrine and concluded that access to American courts could not be denied unless the United States was at war with the foreign government. The Court further held that the assets expropriated were located in Cuba, and that the courts of the United States would not examine the validity of a taking within its own territory by a foreign government which was recognized by this nation, in absence, at least, of express treaty, even if the taking otherwise violated international law. The Court emphasized that both state choice of law and jurisdiction must necessarily conform to the limits imposed by the federal government over issues of this kind: "However, we are constrained to make it clear that an issue concerned with a basic choice regarding the competence and function of the Judiciary and the National Executive in ordering our relationships with other members of the international community must be treated exclusively as an aspect of federal law."[20] Even though the considerations for applying the doctrine were modified by amendment to the Foreign Relations Act[21] after the *Sabbatino* case, the area remains one subject to

cussed in Maier, The Bases and Range of Federal Common Law in Private International Matters, 5 Vand. J. Trans. L. 133 (1971). See also Henkin, The Treaty Makers and the Law Makers: The Law of the Land and Foreign Relations, 107 U. Pa. L. Rev. 903 (1959); Hay, Unification of Law in the United States, in Legal Thought in United States Under Contemporary Pressures 281 (J. Hazard and W. Wagner eds., 1970).

18. Underhill v. Hernandez, 168 U.S. 250, 252, 18 S.Ct. 83, 84, 42 L.Ed. 456 (1897)(Fuller, J.). See Restatement, Third, Foreign Relations Law § 443 (1987).

19. Banco Nacional de Cuba v. Sabbatino, 376 U.S. 398, 84 S.Ct. 923, 11 L.Ed.2d 804 (1964).

20. 376 U.S. at 425, 84 S.Ct. at 939, 11 L.Ed.2d 804.

21. 22 U.S.C.A. § 2370(e)(2). See Hill, Sovereign Immunity and the Act of State Doctrine, 46 Rabels Zeitschrift 118 (1982). See also Herzog, La théorie l'Act of State dans le droit des Etats–Unis, 1982 Revue critique de droit international privé 617; Herzog, Conflict of Laws—1984 Survey of New York Law, 36 Syracuse L. Rev. 119, 165–66 (1985).

"The Act of State doctrine is a policy of judicial abstention from inquiry into the validity of an act by a foreign state within its own sovereignty.... It also differs from the Foreign Sovereign Immunities Act in that the Act of State doctrine may be invoked by private citizens whereas sovereign immunity may only be pleaded by the foreign state itself." Williams v. Curtiss–Wright Corp., 694 F.2d 300, 303 (3d Cir. 1982). See also Frolova v. Union of Soviet Socialist Republics, 558 F.Supp. 358 (N.D.Ill.1983), judgment affirmed 761 F.2d 370 (7th Cir.1985); Compania de Gas de Nuevo Laredo, S.A. v. Entex, Inc., 686 F.2d 322 (5th Cir.1982), cert. denied 460 U.S. 1041, 103 S.Ct. 1435, 75 L.Ed.2d 794 (1983); Allied Bank Int'l v. Banco Credito Agricola de Cartago, 757 F.2d 516 (2d Cir. 1985), cert. dismissed 473 U.S. 934, 106 S.Ct. 30, 87 L.Ed.2d 706 (1985)(holding act of state doctrine inapplicable with respect to Costa Rican decrees purporting to defer all payments on foreign debt, since situs of the debts in question was determined to be in the United States). See also Restatement,

federal control and the state courts do not have authority to develop nonconforming doctrine.

C. FEDERAL TRANSFERS

§ 11.14   One of the most important statutes relating to *forum non conveniens* is the federal venue transfer statute, 28 U.S.C.A. § 1404(a), which provides "for the convenience of parties and witnesses, in the interests of justice, a district court may transfer any civil action to any other district or division where it might have been brought."[1] This statute gives the federal courts a great deal of flexibility and provides for the alternative of transferring a case to another federal district court rather than dismissing the case. Although the statute is clearly a progressive step, it has engendered a great deal of litigation, particularly as regards the identification of the potential transferee courts. The language "where it might have been brought" has generated a great deal of controversy.[2] In one important case the Supreme Court held that the words authorizing transfer to any other district "where it might have been brought" referred only to the situation at the time the original suit was instituted and would not permit a transfer to a forum where the action could not originally have been commenced even though the defendant consented to the transfer.[3] This result has been criticized as unduly restrictive of transfers to convenient forums.[4]

The factors for determining whether a transfer should be made under the federal statute are essentially the same as those under the common law doctrine of *forum non conveniens*. However, a state finding of *forum non conveniens* is not *res judicata* on the question of a federal transfer because relevant factors such as docket status and place of trial relate to the particular court and not only to the state in which that court sits. As a consequence, in *Parsons v. The Chesapeake & Ohio Railroad Co.*, the Supreme Court stated "since different factual considerations may be involved in each court's determination, we hold that a prior state court dismissal on the ground of forum non conveniens can never serve to divest a federal district judge of the discretionary power

Third, Foreign Relations Law of the United States § 443, Reporters' Note 4 (1987)(suggesting that there should not be a search "for an imaginary situs for property that has no real situs, but [a determination] how the act of the foreign state in the particular circumstances fits within the reasons for the act of state doctrine and for the territorial limitation.").

§ 11.14

1. This provision was included in the 1948 revision of the Judicial Code and followed by a year the explicit common law development of *forum non conveniens* by the United States Supreme Court in Gulf Oil Corp. v. Gilbert, 330 U.S. 501, 67 S.Ct.

839, 91 L.Ed. 1055 (1947) and Koster v. Lumbermens Mut. Casualty Co., 330 U.S. 518, 67 S.Ct. 828, 91 L.Ed. 1067 (1947). See Braucher, The Inconvenient Federal Forum, 60 Harv. L. Rev. 908 (1947); Wright, Law of Federal Courts § 44 (5th ed. 1994). Some of the matters relating to federal transfers are treated in a different context supra § 3.46.

2. See Wright, Law of Federal Courts § 44 (5th ed. 1994).

3. Hoffman v. Blaski, 363 U.S. 335, 80 S.Ct. 1084, 4 L.Ed.2d 1254 (1960).

4. Masington, Venue in the Federal Courts—The Problem of the Inconvenient Forum, 15 U. Miami L. Rev. 237 (1961).

vested in him by Congress to rule upon a motion to transfer under § 1404(a)."[5] Notwithstanding the similarity of the factors involved, the Court has also concluded that § 1404(a) would permit a transfer on a lesser showing of inconvenience than would justify dismissal under *forum non conveniens*.[6] Section 1404(a) has largely replaced the common law doctrine of *forum non conveniens* at the federal level,[7] but § 1404(a) does not apply to international cases in which the alternative forum is outside of the United States. In those cases the common law doctrine continues to be effective and available for the federal courts.[8]

As was noted in *Gulf Oil Corp. v. Gilbert*,[9] the choice-of-law issues in a case are important factors in the application of *forum non conveniens*. Under the common law doctrine, the dismissal and trial in another forum may result in a different law being applied by the alternative forum. Under § 1404(a), however, the Supreme Court has ruled that the transferee court must apply the same law that the transferor court would apply. This results because the purpose of § 1404(a) was generally intended "on the basis of convenience and fairness, simply to authorize a change of courtrooms."[10] Observe that under this approach, a trial court

---

5. Parsons v. Chesapeake & Ohio Ry. Co., 375 U.S. 71, 84 S.Ct. 185, 11 L.Ed.2d 137 (1963).

6. Norwood v. Kirkpatrick, 349 U.S. 29, 75 S.Ct. 544, 99 L.Ed. 789 (1955). See also Central States, Southeast and Southwest Areas Pension Fund v. Brown, 587 F.Supp. 1067 (N.D.Ill.1984); Continental Ill. Nat. Bank & Trust Co. v. Stanley, 606 F.Supp. 558, 563 (N.D.Ill.1985). Thus, while a court will not disturb the plaintiff's choice of forum and will not dismiss for *forum non conveniens* unless strong factors support the defendant's motion (supra § 11.10), a lesser showing of inconvenience will support a transfer under § 1404(a). "[T]he choice of forum [by the plaintiff] is only one of the many factors to consider." Harris Trust & Sav. Bank v. SLT Warehouse Co., 605 F.Supp. 225, 227 (N.D.Ill.1985). See also infra nn.9–10. But see Exide Corp. v. Electro Servs., Inc., 596 F.Supp. 1404, 1406 (E.D.Pa.1984) asserting, despite earlier reference to *Norwood* (this note), that "plaintiff's choice of forum is 'a paramount consideration' and 'should not be lightly disturbed.' . . . " Transfer was nevertheless granted. It appears that *Harris Trust*, supra, more accurately states the approach when the issue is transfer and not dismissal for *forum non conveniens*. The existence of a *permissive* forum selection clause does not prevent the court from ordering a § 1404(a) transfer for the convenience of the parties. Leasing Serv. Corp. v. Patterson Enters., Ltd., 633 F.Supp. 282 (S.D.N.Y.1986); Morales v. Navieras de Puerto Rico, 713 F.Supp. 711 (S.D.N.Y. 1989) (followed *Patterson* and transferred

the action to the District of Puerto Rico pursuant to 28 U.S.C.A. § 1404); International Honeycomb Corp. v. Transtech Serv. Network, Inc., 742 F.Supp. 1011 (N.D.Ill. 1990); Piekarski v. Home Owners Sav. Bank, 743 F.Supp. 38 (D.D.C.1990).

7. See Quackenbush v. Allstate Ins. Co., 517 U.S. 706, 722, 116 S.Ct. 1712, 1724, 135 L.Ed.2d 1 (1996) (stating that § 1404(a) has "superseded" *forum non conveniens* in matters in which federal transfer is possible).

8. E.g., Piper Aircraft Co. v. Reyno, 454 U.S. 235, 102 S.Ct. 252, 70 L.Ed.2d 419 (1981); Prack v. Weissinger, 276 F.2d 446 (4th Cir.1960); Vanity Fair Mills, Inc. v. T. Eaton Co., 234 F.2d 633 (2d Cir.1956), cert. denied 352 U.S. 871, 77 S.Ct. 96, 1 L.Ed.2d 76 (1956); De Sairigne v. Gould, 83 F.Supp. 270 (S.D.N.Y.1949), affirmed mem. 177 F.2d 515 (2d Cir.1949), cert. denied 339 U.S. 912, 70 S.Ct. 571, 94 L.Ed. 1338 (1950). Penwest Dev. Corp. Ltd. v. Dow Chem. Co., 667 F.Supp. 436 (E.D.Mich. 1987).

9. 330 U.S. 501, 67 S.Ct. 839, 91 L.Ed. 1055 (1947).

10. Van Dusen v. Barrack, 376 U.S. 612, 84 S.Ct. 805, 11 L.Ed.2d 945 (1964). See also Currie, Change of Venue and the Conflict of Laws, 22 U. Chi. L. Rev. 405 (1955); Kaufman, Further Observations on Transfers Under Section 1404(a), 56 Colum. L. Rev. 1 (1956); Litman, Considerations of Choice of Law in the Doctrine of Forum Non Conveniens, 74 Calif. L. Rev. 565 (1986) (explaining California law).

trying cases transferred for consolidation of trial in complex litigation, such as that resulting from an air crash, may be trying the case as to some parties under one law, and as to other parties under another law. If this relates to measure of damages, or limitation on damages, the possibility exists of different recovery by different parties otherwise similarly situated in the same lawsuit. This may present a strong argument for the need for uniform conflict-of-laws rules in commercial air traffic cases, perhaps through federal law.[11]

The rule that the transferor law applies in § 1404 transfers has been extended even to circumstances in which the *plaintiff* seeks the transfer. In *Ferens v. John Deere Co.*,[12] the plaintiff filed a products liability action based upon an accident in Pennsylvania. The plaintiff, however, filed the case in Mississippi (which apparently had *in personam* jurisdiction because of the defendant's substantial, nationwide business activities) to take advantage of Mississippi's six-year statute of limitations, and the absence of any borrowing statute that would cover the case.[13] The plaintiff sought a transfer to Pennsylvania, which was granted. Because the transfer was a § 1404 transfer, designed only to effect a "change of courtrooms,"[14] the Supreme Court—dividing five to four—ruled that Mississippi law applied. This left the plaintiff with the best of both worlds: the local forum and the foreign law. While the dissent harshly criticized this result as absurd, the oddness of the result was largely a result of Mississippi's narrow borrowing statute and long statute of limitations—features of Mississippi law that have since changed.[15] The opposite result of applying transferee law would simply have the effect of preventing plaintiffs from requesting such transfers.

There are also three other federal venue transfer statutes. One, 28 U.S.C.A. § 1406, allows a federal district court to transfer the case to another federal court in the event that the transferor court lacks venue.[16] The statute allows the district court either to dismiss, or to transfer to another district court in which the case could have been brought, if a transfer serves "the interest of justice."[17] Usually, of course, the plaintiff prefers the transfer route because a dismissal may be fatal if the limitation period has expired in the interim, while a transfer avoids that problem. A similar statute is 28 U.S.C.A. § 1631, which allows dismissal or transfer in the event that there is a jurisdictional defect in the original filing. In contrast to transfers under § 1404, it is settled that a transfer under either § 1406 or § 1631 requires the application of the law that would have been applied by the transferee court.[18] Any other

---

11. These issues are discussed in greater detail supra § 3.36 n.20 and § 3.46 n.17.

12. 494 U.S. 516, 110 S.Ct. 1274, 108 L.Ed.2d 443 (1990).

13. Id. at 519–20, 110 S.Ct. at 1278, 108 L.Ed.2d 443.

14. Id. at 523, 110 S.Ct. at 1279, 108 L.Ed.2d 443 (quoting Van Dusen v. Barrack, 376 U.S. 612, 637, 84 S.Ct. 805, 819, 11 L.Ed.2d 945 (1964)).

15. See Miss. Code Ann. § 15–1–65 (action barred in another jurisdiction barred in Mississippi).

16. 28 U.S.C.A. § 1406(a).

17. Id.

18. See, e.g., Adam v. J.B. Hunt Transp., Inc., 130 F.3d 219, 230 (6th Cir. 1997); Schaeffer v. Village of Ossining, 58 F.3d 48, 50 (2d Cir.1995).

result would, of course, be unfair by allowing the plaintiff to law shop by filing in courts that obviously lacked jurisdiction or venue simply to obtain the benefit of the application of favorable choice-of-law rules.

The other transfer statute is 28 U.S.C.A. § 1407. Section 1407 allows the transfer, for pre-trial purposes only, of related cases filed in different federal district courts.[19] Usually this section has been employed in complicated mass disaster or mass tort cases. There is good authority that in § 1407 transfers the transferee court applies its own law.[20]

IV. IMMUNITIES FROM SERVICE

§ 11.15 International law has long provided for immunity for the representatives of foreign sovereigns such as ambassadors and ministers. Although in the United States this is probably a part of the federal law because of the authorization of the federal government to act in the area of foreign relations, state courts still observe (or by force of statute or treaty are required to observe) this immunity, and it provides a frequently enforced exception to state law jurisdiction.[1]

State law also recognizes, either by common law or statute, immunity from service of process on nonresidents who are in the state in response to the needs of litigation. This immunity seems not to be jurisdictional, but rather to be within the policy of the state to accord or to limit, since it seems clear that if the state finds it necessary or appropriate to assert its jurisdiction over a person under such circumstance in which they would otherwise normally be immune by virtue of this immunity, its action would be recognized elsewhere under the Full Faith and Credit Clause.[2] States also usually grant an immunity from service if the defendant is lured to the forum by trick or fraud.[3] However,

---

19. See Lexecon, Inc. v. Milberg, Weiss, Bershad, Hynes & Lerach, 523 U.S. 26, 118 S.Ct. 956, 140 L.Ed.2d 62 (1998) (transfer for pre-trial activities only).

20. E.g., In re Korean Air Lines Disaster of Sept. 1, 1983, 664 F.Supp. 1478 (D.D.C.1986) (R.B. Ginsburg, J.).

§ 11.15

1. See Restatement, Second, Conflict of Laws § 83 (1971); Restatement, Third, Foreign Relations Law § 467 et seq. (1987); Annot.: Supreme Court's Views on Foreign Sovereign Immunity Act, 102 L.Ed. 1093 (1990). See also the Foreign Sovereign Immunities Act, 28 U.S.C.A. § 1605 which bars state and federal jurisdiction unless one of its exceptions applies. See Gibbons v. Udaras na Gaeltachta, 549 F.Supp. 1094 (S.D.N.Y.1982) and Alberti v. Empresa Nicaraguense De La Carne, 705 F.2d 250 (7th Cir.1983) (commercial exception); Maritime International Nominees Establishment v. Republic of Guinea, 693 F.2d 1094 (D.C.Cir. 1982), cert. denied 464 U.S. 815, 104 S.Ct.

71, 78 L.Ed.2d 84 (1983) (implied waiver); Frolova v. Union of Soviet Socialist Republics, 558 F.Supp. 358 (N.D.Ill.1983), judgment affirmed 761 F.2d 370 (7th Cir.1985) (tort exception). The sending state can waive the immunity of its envoys. Arts. 31, 32, para. 4, Vienna Convention on Diplomatic Relations, 23 U.S.T. 3227, T.I.A.S. No. 7502, 500 U.N.T.S. 95. See Fernandez v. Fernandez, 208 Conn. 329, 545 A.2d 1036 (1988), cert. denied 493 U.S. 958, 110 S.Ct. 376, 107 L.Ed.2d 361 (1989). See supra § 10.19.

2. See Restatement, Second, Conflict of Laws § 83, cmnt. b (1971); Wangler v. Harvey, 41 N.J. 277, 196 A.2d 513 (1963); Santos v. Figueroa, 87 N.J.Super. 227, 208 A.2d 810 (1965). See also Keefe & Roscia, Immunity and Sentimentality, 32 Cornell L.Q. 471 (1947).

3. See, e.g., Wyman v. Newhouse, 93 F.2d 313 (2d Cir.1937) (false promise of romantic interlude if defendant would visit plaintiff); Terlizzi v. Brodie, 38 A.D.2d 762,

the fraud immunity is not without boundaries and generally requires a showing of true fraud in drawing the defendant into the forum. If, for example, the defendant is legitimately invited to the forum to attempt to settle a potential dispute, and the plaintiff fails to disclose the possibility that the defendant might be served with process, courts have held that the defendant is not immune from service.[4]

V. OTHER FEDERAL LIMITATIONS ON STATE COURT JURISDICTION

§ 11.16 As discussed in earlier chapters, the most significant limitation on state court jurisdiction is the Due Process Clause of the Fourteenth Amendment. The foreign relations power, discussed in the last section, may also operate to limit state court jurisdiction in some circumstances. Limitations upon the exercise of jurisdiction by a state court may, however, also arise from federal constitutional limitations other than due process and foreign relations. For example, the Supreme Court has at times required the dismissal of suits against interstate transportation companies which are deemed to burden interstate commerce out of proportion with any connection the forum has with the case.[1]

The Commerce Clause also continues to act as a significant independent limitation on state authority with regard to the taxation of businesses engaged in selling strictly by mail order. In *Quill Corp. v. North Dakota*,[2] the Supreme Court considered North Dakota's attempted imposition of a use tax on goods sold to state residents by an out-of-state mail order company. Although the company sold substantial amounts to North Dakota customers, it lacked any physical presence in the state in the form of offices or salespersons.[3] The company challenged the imposition of the tax on both due process and commerce clause grounds. A majority of the Court held that imposition of the use tax did not offend

329 N.Y.S.2d 589 (1972) (defendants lured to New York from New Jersey under the pretense that they had won free theater tickets).

4. See, e.g., Manitowoc Western Co. v. Montonen, 250 Wis.2d 452, 639 N.W.2d 726 (2002) (defendant drawn to forum for settlement negotiations not immune). However, some courts have taken a broader view of the fraud exception and granted immunity on these facts. See, e.g., K Mart Corp. v. Gen–Star Industries Co., 110 F.R.D. 310 (E.D. Mich. 1986); E/M Lubricants, Inc. v. Microfral, S. A. R. L., 91 F.R.D. 235 (N.D. Ill. 1981).

§ 11.16

1. Davis v. Farmers' Co-op. Equity Co., 262 U.S. 312, 43 S.Ct. 556, 67 L.Ed. 996 (1923); International Milling Co. v. Colum-bia Transportation Co., 292 U.S. 511, 54 S.Ct. 797, 78 L.Ed. 1396 (1934). Neither case, however, has been cited by any Supreme Court decision subsequent to *International Milling*'s mention in a dissenting opinion in Norwood v. Kirkpatrick, 349 U.S. 29, 75 S.Ct. 544, 99 L.Ed. 789 (1955). See generally Farrier, Suits Against Foreign Corporations as a Burden on Interstate Commerce, 17 Minn. L. Rev. 381 (1933); Restatement, Second, Conflict of Laws § 84, cmnt. (e) (1971). It seems likely that this doctrine will not be applied to other than transportation companies. See Trojan Eng'g Corp. v. Green Mountain Power Corp., 293 Mass. 377, 200 N.E. 117 (1936).

2. 504 U.S. 298, 112 S.Ct. 1904, 119 L.Ed.2d 91 (1992).

3. Id. at 301–02, 112 S.Ct. at 1907–08, 119 L.Ed.2d 91.

due process because the company had purposeful, related contacts with the state.[4] However, following earlier case law,[5] the Court held that imposition of the tax on a company whose sole connection with the state was mail order sales violated the Commerce Clause's command that there be a "substantial nexus" with the state.[6] While the Court pointed out that there is some similarity between the "minimum contacts" and "substantial nexus" tests, in the context of mail order selling they remain distinct.[7] At least in this context, the Court thought it important to maintain a "bright line rule" that would preserve a "safe harbor" for companies that conduct their business through the mail.

Despite the holding in *Quill Corp.*, however, it is clear that the due process and commerce clause inquiries have grown closer over time. In the ordinary circumstance, the Commerce Clause places no additional limitations on jurisdiction beyond those imposed by the Due Process Clause. However, in the context of state taxation of interstate business, the Commerce Clause remains an important independent limitation on state authority.

VI. NATIVE AMERICAN AND INDIAN COUNTRY LIMITATIONS

§ 11.17 In the United States, there are very significant limitations on the jurisdiction of state courts, and even federal courts, by reason of the United States Constitution, federal law and treaties relating to Native Americans and Indian Country. American Indian tribes (of which about 500 are federally recognized) and individuals in the lower 48 states own some 57 million acres of land, held in trust by the United States, on or near more than 300 Indian reservations.[1] This amounts to about 2 1/2% of all land in the United States and in the aggregate is comparable to the land area of Kansas. The Navajo reservation in Arizona, Utah, and New Mexico is by itself the size of West Virginia and is larger than eight states.

The geographic area affected by the special jurisdictional and substantive principles of Indian law is even larger than the above figures would indicate. For most purposes, exclusive Indian jurisdictional and substantive law applies not just on land owned by Indians but in "Indian country," which includes all lands within the exterior boundaries of Indian reservations.[2] Thus, land owned by non-Indians within reserva-

---

4. Id. at 308, 112 S.Ct. at 1911, 119 L.Ed.2d 91.

5. See, e.g., National Bellas Hess, Inc. v. Department of Revenue of Illinois, 386 U.S. 753, 87 S.Ct. 1389, 18 L.Ed.2d 505 (1967).

6. 504 U.S. at 313, 112 S.Ct. at 1913–14, 119 L.Ed.2d 91 (citing Complete Auto Transit, Inc. v. Brady, 430 U.S. 274, 97 S.Ct. 1076, 51 L.Ed.2d 326 (1977)).

7. Id. at 312, 112 S.Ct. at 1913, 119 L.Ed.2d 91.

§ 11.17

1. See Clark, State Court Recognition of Tribal Court Judgments: Securing the Blessings of Civilization, 23 Okla. City U. L. Rev. 353, 354 (1998); Getches, Rosenfelt & Wilkinson, Cases and Materials on Federal Indian Law 1–17 (1979).

2. For most purposes, analysis centers on "Indian country," which is defined by federal statute, 18 U.S.C.A. § 1151. Indian country, from which state law is normally

tion boundaries is Indian country and is subject to the limitations discussed below. Indian lands are especially important today because they contain vast mineral[3] and water resources[4] that are important to the nation's economy and energy policy. Further, Indian lands almost doubled in 1991 when Alaska Natives received more than 40 million acres to which they were entitled under the Alaska Native Claims Settlement Act of 1971.[5] There are more than 1.6 million Indians, about .75% of the nation's total population, approximately half of whom live on or near Indian reservations.[6] Many Indian reservations also include substantial non-Indian populations.[7]

The tribal court system is itself vast, and becoming more so with each passing year. In 1976, there were 117 tribes operating courts; those tribal courts then decided about 70,000 cases annually.[8] By 1998 there

excluded, includes all land within the exterior boundaries of federally-recognized Indian reservations. 18 U.S.C.A. § 1151(a). The congressional purpose was to treat all such land as one jurisdictional unit to avoid "an impractical pattern of checkerboard jurisdiction" that would require "law enforcement officers operating in the area ... to search tract books in order to determine" jurisdiction. Seymour v. Superintendent, 368 U.S. 351, 358, 82 S.Ct. 424, 428, 7 L.Ed.2d 346 (1962), on remand 59 Wn.2d 913, 369 P.2d 309 (1962). In addition to the exterior boundary provision, Indian country also includes all "dependent Indian communities," see United States v. Sandoval, 231 U.S. 28, 34 S.Ct. 1, 58 L.Ed. 107 (1913), and Indian allotments. 18 U.S.C.A. § 1151(b), (c). See generally Cohen, Handbook of Federal Indian Law ch.1D (1982). 18 U.S.C.A. § 1151 is a criminal statute but it applies to civil actions as well. DeCoteau v. District County Court, 420 U.S. 425 n.2, 95 S.Ct. 1082 n.2, 43 L.Ed.2d 300 (1975).

The establishment of Indian country as a separate jurisdiction area under tribal jurisdiction does not deny equal protection or otherwise violate constitutional limitations. The jurisdictional designation is not based on race but rather on the governmental status of Indian tribes. E.g., Fisher v. District Court, 424 U.S. 382, 96 S.Ct. 943, 47 L.Ed.2d 106 (1976). For Indian civil jurisdiction over non-Indians on Indian lands see Babbitt Ford, Inc. v. Navajo Indian Tribe, 710 F.2d 587 (9th Cir.1983), cert. denied 466 U.S. 926, 104 S.Ct. 1707, 80 L.Ed.2d 180 (1984); Duro v. Reina, 495 U.S. 676, 110 S.Ct. 2053, 109 L.Ed.2d 693 (1990), on remand 910 F.2d 673 (9th Cir. 1990) (an Indian tribe may not assert criminal jurisdiction over a non-member Indian); Cotton Petroleum Corp. v. New Mexico, 490 U.S. 163, 109 S.Ct. 1698, 104 L.Ed.2d 209 (1989) (the state (of New Mexico) may val-

idly impose severance taxes on the same on-reservation production of oil and gas by non-Indian lessees as is subject to the Tribe's own severance tax); Mississippi Band of Choctaw Indians v. Holyfield, 490 U.S. 30, 109 S.Ct. 1597, 104 L.Ed.2d 29 (1989) (twins were domiciled on the tribe's reservation within the meaning of the ICWA's exclusive tribal jurisdiction provision, and the chancery court was without jurisdiction to enter an adoption decree).

3. E.g., U.S. Federal Trade Comm'n, Staff Report on Mineral Leasing on Indian Lands 3–10 (1975); American Indian Policy Review Comm'n, Final Report, 338–39 (1977); Council of Energy Resources Tribes, Control and Reclamation of Surface Mining on Indian Lands (1979) (Report prepared for Office of Surface Mining, U.S. Department of Interior).

4. E.g., National Water Comm'n, Water Policies for the Future 473–83 (1973); Cohen, supra n.2, ch. 10.

5. 43 U.S.C.A. § 1601–28. For a news account see N.Y. Times, June 1, 1990, Sec. A, p. 1. See generally Lazurus & West, The Alaska Native Claims Settlement Act: A Flawed Victory, 40 Law & Contemp. Prob. 132 (1976). It has not been resolved whether such lands are Indian country. See supra n.2 Cohen, supra n.2, ch. 14A.

6. See generally Statistical Abstract of the United States Tables 19 & 44 (1990); Getches, et. al., supra n.1, at 7.

7. As a result of the General Allotment Act of 1887, 25 U.S.C.A. §§ 331–358 et seq., and other policies, some Indian lands were made available for homesteading by non-Indians. On some reservations, non-Indians outnumber Indians. E.g., Moe v. Confederated Salish and Kootenai Tribes, 425 U.S. 463, 96 S.Ct. 1634, 48 L.Ed.2d 96 (1976).

8. Clark, supra n.1, at 360–61.

were 170 tribal court systems, and as of the early 1990's the Navajo tribal courts alone handled in excess of 85,000 cases annually.[9]

The usually applicable state jurisdictional rules may be altered if American Indians are involved. Congress has broad power over Indian affairs under the Indian Commerce Clause[10] and has a special trust relationship toward Indian tribes.[11] Historically, Congress has implemented its powers and obligations by exempting Indians and tribal governments from the operation of state laws.[12] Thus, as a general matter, state law is normally preempted in Indian country, where federal and tribal laws govern.[13] For example, state legislative jurisdiction does not extend to Indian country so that Indian tribes and individuals are not subject to state taxes,[14] zoning requirements,[15] property laws,[16] and

9. Clark, supra n.1, at 361.

10. U.S. Const. art I, § 8, cl. 3 ("The Congress shall have Power ... to regulate Commerce ... with the Indian Tribes."). See generally Morton v. Mancari, 417 U.S. 535, 94 S.Ct. 2474, 41 L.Ed.2d 290 (1974); McClanahan v. State Tax Comm'n, 411 U.S. 164, 93 S.Ct. 1257, 36 L.Ed.2d 129 (1973).

11. See, e.g., Morton v. Mancari, 417 U.S. 535, 94 S.Ct. 2474, 41 L.Ed.2d 290 (1974); Seminole Nation v. United States, 316 U.S. 286, 62 S.Ct. 1049, 86 L.Ed. 1480 (1942); Cherokee Nation v. Georgia, 30 U.S. (5 Pet.) 1, 8 L.Ed. 25 (1831). See generally Chambers, Judicial Enforcement of the Federal Trust Responsibility to Indians, 27 Stan. L. Rev. 1213 (1975).

12. See, e.g., McClanahan v. State Tax Comm'n, 411 U.S. 164, 169, 93 S.Ct. 1257, 1260, 36 L.Ed.2d 129 (1973) (" '[T]he policy of leaving Indians free from state jurisdiction and control is deeply rooted in the Nation's history.' "); White Mountain Apache Tribe v. Bracker, 448 U.S. 136, 142, 100 S.Ct. 2578, 2583, 65 L.Ed.2d 665 (1980) ("The tradition of Indian sovereignty over the reservation and tribal members ... is reflected and encouraged in a number of congressional enactments demonstrating a firm federal policy of promoting tribal self-sufficiency and economic development."); Warren Trading Post Co. v. Arizona State Tax Comm'n, 380 U.S. 685, 690, 85 S.Ct. 1242, 1245, 14 L.Ed.2d 165 (1965) ("Congress has, since the creation of the Navajo Reservation nearly a century ago, left the Indians on it largely free to run the reservation and its affairs without state control ... "). See also Merrion v. Jicarilla Apache Tribe, 455 U.S. 130, 102 S.Ct. 894, 71 L.Ed.2d 21 (1982), appeal after remand 842 F.2d 1200 (10th Cir.1988) (upholding Indian tribe's power to impose an oil and gas severance tax on mining activities of lessees). Cf. Clinton, State Power Over Indian Reservations: A Critical Comment on Burg-

er Court Doctrine, 26 S.D.L. Rev. 434 (1981); Note, Sovereign Immunity—Indian Tribal Sovereignty—Tribes not Immune from Suits Arising from Off–Reservation Business Activity, 102 Harv. L. Rev. 556 (1988).

13. See, e.g., White Mountain Apache Tribe v. Bracker, 448 U.S. 136, 142–45, 100 S.Ct. 2578, 2583–84, 65 L.Ed.2d 665 (1980); Mescalero Apache Tribe v. New Mexico, 630 F.2d 724, 728–31 (10th Cir.1980), cert. granted and judgment vacated 450 U.S. 1036, 101 S.Ct. 1752, 68 L.Ed.2d 234 (1981), on remand reinstated 677 F.2d 55 (10th Cir.1982), affirmed 462 U.S. 324, 103 S.Ct. 2378, 76 L.Ed.2d 611 (1983). See generally Getches, et. al., supra n.1, at 295–99. Tribal law does not normally apply, however, to land owned in fee by non-Indians even if that land lies within the exterior boundaries of the reservation. In Atkinson Trading Co. v. Shirley, 532 U.S. 645, 121 S.Ct. 1825, 149 L.Ed.2d 889 (2001), the Supreme Court unanimously held that the Navajo tribe did not have the authority to require a non-Indian owner of a hotel located within the reservation's exterior boundaries to collect an 8% occupancy tax from guests. In so holding, the Court reaffirmed Montana v. United States, 450 U.S. 544, 101 S.Ct. 1245, 67 L.Ed.2d 493 (1981), which held normally a tribe's legislative competence does not extend to non-Indian fee land unless such the non-Indians enter into consensual relationships with the tribe or its members that contemplate such regulation or the conduct of the non-Indians is such that it threatens the political integrity, the economic security, or the health and welfare of the tribe. In *Atkinson Trading* the Court concluded that the hotel tax fell within neither of the *Montana* exceptions.

14. E.g., McClanahan v. State Tax Comm'n, 411 U.S. 164, 93 S.Ct. 1257, 36 L.Ed.2d 129 (1973) (state sales tax not ap-

15.–16. See page 513.

other regulatory laws.[17] The reverse is true outside of Indian country, where state law is normally not preempted and Indians are usually subject to state regulatory jurisdiction.[18]

State judicial jurisdiction in Indian country is also limited. As a result of a line of cases beginning with *Williams v. Lee*,[19] normally transitory causes of action, such as contract actions[20] and personal injury claims,[21] against Indians cannot be brought in state court if the cause of action arose in Indian country because affording a non-tribal forum would infringe on the tribe's authority over internal matters.[22] The state courts' jurisdiction in such circumstances is restricted and a state court

plicable to reservation Indian). But cf. Washington v. Confederated Tribes of Colville Indian Reservation, 447 U.S. 134, 100 S.Ct. 2069, 65 L.Ed.2d 10 (1980) (state sales tax not applicable to Indians in Indian country but Indian vendors required to collect state taxes on sales to non-Indians); California State Board of Equal. v. Chemehuevi Indian Tribe, 474 U.S. 9, 106 S.Ct. 289, 88 L.Ed.2d 9 (1985) (Indian vendors required to collect state tax on cigarettes sold to non-Indian purchasers even though statute did not expressly require tax be passed through to consumer).

15. E.g., Santa Rosa Band of Indians v. Kings County, 532 F.2d 655 (9th Cir.1975), cert. denied 429 U.S. 1038, 97 S.Ct. 731, 50 L.Ed.2d 748 (1977) (county zoning ordinance).

16. E.g., Minnesota v. United States, 305 U.S. 382, 59 S.Ct. 292, 83 L.Ed. 235 (1939) (state condemnation laws). See also O'Connell v. Hamm, 267 N.W.2d 839 (S.D. 1978).

17. Cf. South Dakota v. Bourland, 508 U.S. 679, 113 S.Ct. 2309, 124 L.Ed.2d 606 (1993)(Cheyenne River Sioux Indians lack the right to regulate fishing and hunting on certain tribal lands because treaty rights had been abrogated by subsequent federal statutes opening lands to the public for recreational purposes). See generally Cohen, supra n.2, ch. 5B; Note, *South Dakota v. Bourland:* The Court Replaces the Cavalry, 28 Loyola L. Rev. 675 (1995).

18. E.g., Mescalero Apache Tribe v. Jones, 411 U.S. 145, 93 S.Ct. 1267, 36 L.Ed.2d 114 (1973).

19. 358 U.S. 217, 79 S.Ct. 269, 3 L.Ed.2d 251 (1959).

20. E.g., Williams v. Lee, 358 U.S. 217, 79 S.Ct. 269, 3 L.Ed.2d 251 (1959); Kennerly v. District Court, 400 U.S. 423, 91 S.Ct. 480, 27 L.Ed.2d 507 (1971). Cf. O'Connell v. Hamm, 267 N.W.2d 839 (S.D.1978). Cf. Kiowa Tribe of Oklahoma v. Manufacturing Technologies, Inc., 523 U.S. 751, 118 S.Ct. 1700, 140 L.Ed.2d 981 (1998) (Indian tribe

has sovereign immunity from state court contract suit).

21. E.g., Strate v. A–1 Contractors, 520 U.S. 438, 117 S.Ct. 1404, 137 L.Ed.2d 661 (1997) (tribal court lacks jurisdiction in case involving auto collision between Indian and non-Indian on a federal easement). Schantz v. White Lightning, 502 F.2d 67 (8th Cir. 1974); Enriquez v. Superior Court, 115 Ariz. 342, 565 P.2d 522 (App.1977); Nelson v. Dubois, 232 N.W.2d 54 (N.D.1975).

22. E.g., Fisher v. District Court, 424 U.S. 382, 96 S.Ct. 943, 47 L.Ed.2d 106 (1976)(per curiam); Williams v. Lee, 358 U.S. 217, 223, 79 S.Ct. 269, 272, 3 L.Ed.2d 251 (1959) ("There can be no doubt that to allow the exercise of state jurisdiction ... would undermine the authority of the tribal courts over Reservation affairs and hence would infringe on the right of the Indians to govern themselves."). See Reynolds, Adjudication in Indian Country: The Confusing Parameters of State, Federal, and Tribal Jurisdiction, 38 Wm. & Mary L. Rev. 539 (1997); Govern, Jurisdiction: Conflicts of Law and the Indian Reservation, 8 Am. Ind. L. Rev. 361 (1980). Both tribal sovereign immunity and the jurisdiction of tribal courts can be waived, however. In C & L Enterprises, Inc. v. Citizen Band Potawatomi Indian Tribe of Oklahoma, 532 U.S. 411, 121 S.Ct. 1589, 149 L.Ed.2d 623 (2001), the plaintiff had been engaged by the defendant Indian tribe to do construction work on an off-reservation building. The contract included arbitration and choice-of-law clauses. When the tribe refused to pay on the contract the plaintiff demanded arbitration. The arbitrator made an award in favor of the plaintiff and then the plaintiff sought to confirm the award in an Oklahoma state court. The tribe appeared for the limited purpose of dismissing the confirmation action. The Supreme Court held that the clauses effected a waiver of the tribe's sovereign immunity and conferred jurisdiction on the Oklahoma state court to confirm the award.

cannot hear the case even if service of process is made on the defendant when outside of Indian country.[23]

This zone of tribal court jurisdiction is not unlimited, however. As a result of the *Williams* line of cases, "state courts typically refuse to adjudicate disputes involving Indians or reservation affairs only if the defendant is an Indian and if the transaction involves no substantial off-reservation contacts."[24] Thus, for instance, in *Strate v. A–1 Contractors*,[25] the Supreme Court held that tribal court jurisdiction was lacking in a personal injury case brought by the a non-Indian widow and her five Indian children against a non-Indian operator of a truck alleged to have negligently collided with the plaintiffs. The accident occurred on a federal highway right-of-way across the reservation, and the Court distinguished the on-reservation cases with the conclusion that the right-of-way was alienated, non-Indian land. In *Nevada v. Hicks*,[26] the Court held that there was a lack of both tribal judicial and legislative jurisdiction claim by an Indian against a state law enforcement official involving an allegedly illegal search of the Indian's on-reservation house. The search arose because the Indian was suspected of having illegally taken game off the reservation. The Court concluded that "tribal authority to regulate state officers in executing process related to the violation, off reservation, of state laws is not essential to tribal self-government or internal relations...."[27]

Indian plaintiffs also have access to state court in suits against non-Indians even if the action lacks substantial off-reservation contacts. This is the result of the a case that twice went to the Supreme Court. In *Three Affiliated Tribes v. Wold Engineering*[28] a tribe sued a non-Indian company on tort and contract theories for allegedly botched work done on the tribal water supply system. Despite the fact that the reverse case—for instance, the company suing the tribe for non-payment—would clearly have to be brought in tribal court, the Supreme Court allowed the tribe to elect state court. While the *Wold* reasoning creates an asymmetry and is somewhat perplexing,[29] it does have the effect of opening the door to concurrent state court jurisdiction in large categories of cases.

The policy in favor of self-government by Indian tribes is sufficiently strong that state courts lack jurisdiction over causes of action in Indian country even if the tribal court does not provide a remedy for the cause

---

23. E.g., Kennerly v. District Court, 400 U.S. 423, 91 S.Ct. 480, 27 L.Ed.2d 507 (1971); Annis v. Dewey County Bank, 335 F.Supp. 133 (D.S.D.1971); Gourneau v. Smith, 207 N.W.2d 256 (N.D.1973); Wyoming ex rel. Peterson v. District Court, 617 P.2d 1056 (Wyo.1980). See Canby, Civil Jurisdiction and the Indian Reservation, 1973 Utah L. Rev. 206, 221; Cohen, supra n.2, ch. 6B3.

24. Reynolds, supra n.20, at 547.

25. 520 U.S. 438, 117 S.Ct. 1404, 137 L.Ed.2d 661 (1997).

26. 533 U.S. 353, 121 S.Ct. 2304, 150 L.Ed.2d 398 (2001).

27. Id. at 364, 121 S.Ct. at 2312, 150 L.Ed.2d 398.

28. 476 U.S. 877, 106 S.Ct. 2305, 90 L.Ed.2d 881 (1986) (*Wold II*); 467 U.S. 138, 104 S.Ct. 2267, 81 L.Ed.2d 113 (1984) (*Wold I*).

29. Reynolds, supra n.20, at 550–54.

of action in question.[30] The reasoning is that the tribe should be able to decide how to resolve disputes, even to the point of affording no formal remedy at all. Federal courts sitting in diversity are subject to the same restraints on their jurisdiction as are their state court counterparts.[31] Moreover, federal courts must refrain from competing with tribal courts for civil cases. Regardless of the potential basis for federal subject matter jurisdiction, a tribal court system (including tribal appellate courts) must first be given the opportunity to determine whether it has subject matter jurisdiction before a federal court can litigate the matter,[32] unless Congress has strongly expressed a preference for another forum. In *El Paso Natural Gas Co. v. Neztsosie*,[33] the Supreme Court held that claims arising under the Price–Anderson Act, which expresses a strong preference for federal courts in cases related certain nuclear occurrences and expressly preempts other remedies, are not subject to the tribal exhaustion rule. The Court was, however, careful to limit the scope of its holding to only those federal questions subject to an express preference for a non-tribal forum; most issues of federal law—even those of preemption—remain subject to the requirement of tribal court exhaustion.

State courts have subject matter jurisdiction if the dispute in Indian country involves only non-Indians[34] or if the cause of action arises outside of Indian country.[35] In addition, state judicial jurisdiction applies on some Indian reservations pursuant to "Public Law 280,"[36] which extends state civil and criminal, but not regulatory, jurisdiction to specified reservations. However, states that exercised jurisdiction over claims arising on Indian reservations prior to the enactment of Public Law 280 cannot later disclaim that jurisdiction in an effort to shift such litigation to tribal courts.[37]

30. Enriquez v. Superior Court, 115 Ariz. 342, 565 P.2d 522 (App. 1977); Schantz v. White Lightning, 502 F.2d 67 (8th Cir.1974).

31. See Woods v. Interstate Realty Co., 337 U.S. 535, 538, 69 S.Ct. 1235, 93 L.Ed. 1524.

32. See, e.g., Iowa Mutual Ins. Co. v. LaPlante, 480 U.S. 9, 107 S.Ct. 971, 94 L.Ed.2d 10 (1987) (diversity case between an Indian and an insurance company over alleged bad faith refusal to settle a claim); National Farmers Union Ins. Cos. v. Crow Tribe, 471 U.S. 845, 105 S.Ct. 2447, 85 L.Ed.2d 818 (1985) (federal district court must abstain until tribal court has resolved its jurisdiction if possible basis for federal subject matter jurisdiction is federal question).

33. 526 U.S. 473, 119 S.Ct. 1430, 143 L.Ed.2d 635 (1999).

34. See *Strate*, 520 U.S. 438, 117 S.Ct. 1404, 137 L.Ed.2d 661. Cohen, supra n.2, ch. 6C.

35. DeCoteau v. District County Court, 420 U.S. 425, 95 S.Ct. 1082, 43 L.Ed.2d 300 (1975); Mescalero Apache Tribe v. Jones, 411 U.S. 145, 148–49, 93 S.Ct. 1267, 1270, 36 L.Ed.2d 114 (1973).

36. Act of Aug. 15, 1953, ch. 505, 67 Stat. 588 (codified as amended at 18 U.S.C.A. § 1162, 25 U.S.C.A. §§ 1321–26, 28 U.S.C.A. § 1360). See generally Goldberg, Public Law 280: The Limits of State Jurisdiction Over Reservation Indians, 22 U.C.L.A. L. Rev. 535 (1975); Bryan v. Itasca County, 426 U.S. 373, 96 S.Ct. 2102, 48 L.Ed.2d 710 (1976), on remand 303 Minn. 395, 246 N.W.2d 560 (1976).

37. See, e.g, *Wold II*, 476 U.S. 877, 106 S.Ct. 2305, 90 L.Ed.2d 881.

A state may not disclaim civil jurisdiction over an Indiana tribe's breach of contract and negligence suit nor condition its exercise of jurisdiction on the tribe's waiving of its common law sovereign immunity. Three Affiliated Tribes of Fort Berthold Reservation v. Wold Eng'g, P.C., 476 U.S. 877, 106 S.Ct. 2305, 90 L.Ed.2d 881 (1986), on remand 392 N.W.2d 87 (N.D.1986). For background on this case see Comment, 62 N.D.L. Rev. 559 (1986).

State courts may also be limited by Indian law principles even in those situations where the court has subject matter jurisdiction.[38] The authorities are divided on the question of whether, and how, state courts can make service of process on an Indian in Indian country.[39] If a valid judgment is obtained in a state court, the weight of authority is that execution of judgment may be had only through the tribal judicial system or other tribally approved procedure.[40] Cases involving adoption, guardianship, foster care placement and other issues relating to child custody are governed by the Indian Child Welfare Act of 1978.[41] Whether or not the child resides in Indian country, the Act requires that most such cases be transferred to tribal court or, if the tribal court declines to accept the case, that state judges apply a series of statutory preferences designed to see that Indian children are placed with Indian families.[42] The Act gives exclusive jurisdiction to tribal courts involving Indian children who are either resident or domiciled in a reservation, and the term "domicile" is given a uniform federal construction.[43] In *Mississippi Band of Choctaw Indians v. Holyfield*[44] the term "domicile" was given its ordinary construction, so that children take the domicile of their custodial parents at birth. As a consequence, matters involving the adoption of children born to Indian parents domiciled on a reservation are subject to the exclusive jurisdiction provisions of the Act.

As to the related question of the effect of tribal court judgments in state and federal courts, the law is somewhat unclear. It can be and has

---

38. See generally Cohen, supra n.2, chs. 2c, 6c.

39. Service in Indian country has been allowed. See, e.g., Bad Horse v. Bad Horse, 163 Mont. 445, 517 P.2d 893 (1974), cert. denied 419 U.S. 847, 95 S.Ct. 83, 42 L.Ed.2d 76 (1974); State Securities, Inc. v. Anderson, 84 N.M. 629, 506 P.2d 786 (1973); LeClair v. Powers, 632 P.2d 370 (Okla.1981). It has also been struck down. E.g., Francisco v. State, 113 Ariz. 427, 556 P.2d 1 (1976); United States v. Superior Court of Arizona, 144 Ariz. 265, 697 P.2d 658 (1985); Martin v. Denver Juvenile Court, 177 Colo. 261, 493 P.2d 1093 (1972); Service of Process allowed in Dixon v. Picopa Constr. Co., 160 Ariz. 251, 772 P.2d 1104 (1989) (treating the Indian lands as another state subject to long-arm statutes). See generally Canby, Civil Jurisdiction and the Indian Reservation, 1973 Utah L. Rev. 206, 225–27.

40. Joe v. Marcum, 621 F.2d 358 (10th Cir.1980) (garnishment); Annis v. Dewey County Bank, 335 F.Supp. 133 (D.S.D. 1971). But see Little Horn State Bank v. Stops, 170 Mont. 510, 555 P.2d 211 (1976), cert. denied 431 U.S. 924, 97 S.Ct. 2198, 53 L.Ed.2d 238 (1977). Cf. Shaffer v. Heitner, 433 U.S. 186, 97 S.Ct. 2569, 53 L.Ed.2d 683 (1977) (due process violated unless forum jurisdiction has minimum contacts with non-resident defendants in *rem* or *quasi in rem* action); Wildcatt v. Smith, 69 N.C.App. 1, 316 S.E.2d 870 (1984).

41. Indian Child Welfare Act of 1978, 25 U.S.C.A. §§ 1901–1963. See Matter of Appeal in Pima County, etc., 130 Ariz. 202, 635 P.2d 187 (App. 1981), cert. denied 455 U.S. 1007, 102 S.Ct. 1644, 71 L.Ed.2d 875 (1982). See also Guerrero, Indian Child Welfare Act of 1978: A Response to the Threat to Indian Culture Caused by Foster and Adoptive Placements of Indian Children, 7 Amer. Ind. L. Rev. 51 (1979). Trentadue & DeMontigny, The Indian Child Welfare Act of 1978: A Practitioner's Perspective, 62 N.D. L. Rev. 487 (1986); Lehmann, The Indian Child Welfare Act of 1978: Does it Apply to the Adoption of an Illegitimate Indian Child?, 38 Cath. U. L. Rev. 511 (1989); Tellinghuisen, The Indian Child Welfare Act of 1978: A Practical Guide with Limited Commentary, 34 S.D. L. Rev. 660 (1989); Recent Decisions, Mississippi Band of Choctaw Indians v. Holyfield, 28 Duquesne L. Rev. 589 (1990).

42. 25 U.S.C.A. § 1911.

43. Mississippi Band of Choctaw Indians v. Holyfield, 490 U.S. 30, 109 S.Ct. 1597, 104 L.Ed.2d 29 (1989).

44. Id.

been argued that tribal court judgments come within the general full-faith-and-credit command,[45] although some courts appear to treat tribal judgments under the comity principle generally applied to foreign country judgments.[46] However, some federal enactments now require that tribal court judgments be given full faith and credit in some circumstances or imply that they should be so treated,[47] and the emerging and better view is that tribal court judgments are to be given full faith and credit and are subject to collateral attack only on traditional grounds such as jurisdictional infirmity and fraud, subject perhaps to a reciprocity requirement.[48]

State criminal jurisdiction normally does not apply in Indian country, where a complex body of law provides for federal jurisdiction, tribal jurisdiction, or both.[49] In reservations subject to Public Law 280, however, state courts have criminal jurisdiction.[50]

45. Clark, supra n.1, at 367.

46. Clark, supra n.1, at 363.

47. Clark, supra n.1, at 367 (citing the Indian Child Welfare Act of 1978, 25 U.S.C.A. § 1911(d); Indian Claims Settlement Act of 1981, 25 U.S.C.A. § 1725(g); Defense of Marriage Act, 28 U.S.C.A. 1738C; the last of these purports to relieve Indian tribes of having to recognize same-sex marriages solemnized by states).

48. Clark, supra n.1, at 367. The author cites some statutory and case law examples of application of the full-faith-and-credit principles, though some courts have conditioned application of these principles upon a reciprocity requirement. See, e.g., id. at 369 (citing and discussing developments in Oklahoma and other states). Reciprocity is not part of interstate recognition practice and, indeed, is employed by only few states internationally. See infra § 24.36 n. 1. Such a requirement should have no place in the recognition of Indian-country courts.

49. See, e.g., Hagen v. Utah, 510 U.S. 399, 114 S.Ct. 958, 127 L.Ed.2d 252 (1994)(holding that petitioner not subject to tribal criminal jurisdiction because crime was actually committed outside the boundaries of the reservation). See generally Clinton, Criminal Jurisdiction over Indian Lands: A Journey Through a Jurisdictional Maze, 18 Ariz. L. Rev. 503 (1976); Cohen, supra n.2, ch. 6A; Adams, Order in the Courts: Resolution of Tribal/State Criminal Jurisdictional Disputes, 24 Tulsa L.J. 89 (1988); Wilson, Criminal Jurisdiction in Montana Indian Country, 47 Mont. L. Rev. 513 (1986); McGoldrick, Criminal Jurisdiction: Jurisdiction to Sentence and Convict for Lesser Induced Offenses Under Major Crimes Act: A Critical Assessment of the *Keeble* Legacy, 12 Am. Ind. L. Rev. 219 (1986); Note, Indian Reservation Status: "Pulling up the Nails" from the Uintah Indian Reservation Boundary, 28 Creighton L. Rev. 529 (1995).

50. See supra n.25.

Chapter 12

PROCEDURE

Table of Sections

		Sections
I.	Notice	12.2
	A. Method of Notice	12.3
	B. Opportunity to Be Heard	12.4
	C. Waiver of Notice	12.5
II.	Service Abroad of Documents	12.6–12.7
III.	Taking Evidence Abroad	12.8–12.9
IV.	Admissibility of Evidence: Testimonial Privilege	12.10–12.14
	A. Introduction	12.10
	B. Interstate Conflicts	12.11–12.12
	C. International Conflicts	12.13
	D. The Interstate and Convention Approaches Compared	12.14
V.	Proof of Foreign Law	12.15–12.19
	A. The Fact Approach to Foreign Law	
	1. Common Law Background	12.15
	2. Other Legal Systems	12.16
	B. State Statutes and Uniform Laws	12.17
	C. Federal Law	12.18
	D. When Proof Fails: Presumptions and Use of the Lex Fori	12.19

---

§ 12.1 Previous chapters dealt with the acquisition of judicial jurisdiction, including jurisdiction over out-of-state and extranational defendants. Jurisdiction, in a wider sense, also includes its proper exercise, principally in the form of proper notice in accordance with constitutional requirements of due process. The section immediately following addresses the notice requirement.

Litigation involving parties in foreign jurisdictions or issues that, according to the choice-of-law rules of the forum, require resolution under foreign law (sister-state or foreign-country law) raise further problems, many of them unique to international conflicts cases. Subsequent sections therefore address problems of service abroad of American documents, the taking of evidence abroad, and the ascertainment and proof of aspects of foreign law that become relevant in American litigation.

I. NOTICE

§ 12.2 Due process requires that a person, in addition to being properly subject to the jurisdiction of the court, have notice of the proceeding pending against him and an opportunity to be heard.[1] A judgment rendered by a court in contravention of these requirements is void where rendered, as violative of the Due Process Clause of the Fifth or Fourteenth Amendment, and consequently also not entitled to Full Faith and Credit in sister states. *A fortiori* a foreign judgment entered without proper notice to the American defendant will not be enforced in this country.[2]

A. METHOD OF NOTICE

§ 12.3 "The means employed must be such as one desirous of actually informing the absentee might reasonably adopt to accomplish it."[1] As a consequence, the means that must be employed to satisfy the due process requirement will vary with the circumstances. Thus, apart from personal service (even out of the jurisdiction),[2] notice left at the abode of a local domiciliary,[3] and notice by mail to a known address[4] are sufficient. On the other hand, notice by publication will not be sufficient if there is a known address[5] and may be required as an additional means of notifying the party when mailed notice does not reach him.[6]

§ 12.2

1. See generally Restatement, Second, Conflict of Laws § 25 (1971).

2. Julen v. Larson, 25 Cal.App.3d 325, 101 Cal.Rptr. 796 (1972)(also discussed infra § 12.7 n.4). See also infra §§ 24.11, 24.42. European Union law contains a strict requirement of proper service and notice. Art. 34, No. 20 EC Regulation 44/2001 precludes recognition of a judgment if the defendant was not "duly served ... in sufficient time ... to arrange for his defense." [2001] O.J. 012/1. Some national laws provide for fictitious means of service, such as the French practice of *remise au parquet* (service on an official, infra § 12.6 n.4). The requirement of a sufficient time "... to prepare [a] defense serves to require *actual* notice at some point, thus rendering national fictitious service provisions ineffectual in inter-European practice." Kropholler, Europäisches Zivilprozeßrecht, 336 (5th ed. 1996). A judgment on the basis of a cognovit clause would therefore not be entitled to recognition.

§ 12.3

1. Mullane v. Central Hanover Bank & Trust Co., 339 U.S. 306, 315, 70 S.Ct. 652, 657, 94 L.Ed. 865 (1950).

2. Allen v. Superior Court, 41 Cal.2d 306, 259 P.2d 905 (1953).

3. McDonald v. Mabee, 243 U.S. 90, 37 S.Ct. 343, 61 L.Ed. 608 (1917) (dictum).

4. See Mullane v. Central Hanover Bank & Trust Co., 339 U.S. 306, 318, 70 S.Ct. 652, 659, 94 L.Ed. 865 (1950). In some foreign legal systems, notice (and service) by mail are considered "sovereign acts". Therefore service may not be effected by mail abroad (instead treaty-mechanisms must be used, see infra § 12.6) and service by mail from abroad is impermissible. But see German Code of Civil Procedure (ZPO) § 175: if the foreign defendant has not named a local agent for receipt of documents, these may then be sent by mail and the act of posting with constitute the relevant and effective act, i.e. it will have taken place domestically and not extraterritorially. The disadvantage for the defendant is considerable: all time periods begin to run from the time of posting and while the mail is in transit.

5. Id. at 318, 70 S.Ct. at 659, 94 L.Ed. 865; Walker v. City of Hutchinson, 352 U.S. 112, 77 S.Ct. 200, 1 L.Ed.2d 178 (1956) (notice by publication in proceeding to determine compensation for condemned property held insufficient when landowner's name and address were known to the city and appeared on official records). Conversely, notice by publication is reasonable where

When the means employed for giving notice is reasonable, actual notice-receipt or knowledge of published notice-is ordinarily not required.[7] The Supreme Court's decision in *Wuchter v. Pizzutti*[8] invalidated a non-resident motorist statute providing for service on an official of the forum on the ground that the statute did not require the official to give notice to the absent defendant (although the latter had independent actual notice of the proceeding). The decision did not address whether compliance with a statutory requirement to give notice which failed to reach the party would violate due process. For the latter situation, the decision in *Hess v. Pawloski*,[9] upholding a non-resident motorist statute, remains unimpaired.[10] In addition, subsequent decisions cast doubt on the continued authority of *Wuchter*.[11]

Later cases make clear that the standard is still one of a reasonable effort to inform all parties with a significant stake in the outcome of the proceedings. Thus, for instance, the Supreme Court struck down a statute that allowed notification by publication of creditors of an estate where the creditors could have been easily identified and served by

---

the party's whereabouts are unknown. *Mullane*, 339 U.S. at 317, 70 S.Ct. at 658, 94 L.Ed. 865. See also Pierce v. Board of County Commissioners, 200 Kan. 74, 434 P.2d 858 (1967); Manley v. Nelson, 50 Haw. 484, 443 P.2d 155 (1968), appeal dismissed and cert. denied 394 U.S. 573, 89 S.Ct. 1299, 22 L.Ed.2d 555 (1969); Mennonite Board of Missions v. Adams, 462 U.S. 791, 103 S.Ct. 2706, 77 L.Ed.2d 180 (1983); Tulsa Professional Collection Services, Inc. v. Pope, 485 U.S. 478, 108 S.Ct. 1340, 99 L.Ed.2d 565 (1988), appeal after remand 808 P.2d 640 (Okl.1990).

6. Schmidt v. Schmidt, 291 Ala. 543, 283 So.2d 601 (1973) (Alabama Equity Rules held to comply with due process in providing for service by registered mail on out-of-state defendant and for further service by publication when the return receipt is not received within 15 days). See also Emery Transportation Co. v. Baker, 254 Iowa 744, 119 N.W.2d 272 (1963); R. Weintraub, Commentary on the Conflict of Laws 130 (4th ed. 2001).

7. See, e.g., Dusenbery v. United States, 534 U.S. 161, 122 S.Ct. 694, 151 L.Ed.2d 597 (2002)(certified mail constitutionally sufficient even though there was evidence that inmate-claimant never actually received the notice). In this vein: "The test under due process ... is not whether the absent spouse actually receives notice, but rather whether the method used was reasonably calculated to give actual notice." United States v. Smith, 398 F.2d 173, 177–78 (3d Cir.1968); Huling v. Kaw Valley Rail-

way and Improvement Co., 130 U.S. 559, 9 S.Ct. 603, 32 L.Ed. 1045 (1889) (acquisition of land for railroad right of way after notice by publication to non-resident landowner satisfies due process when landowner failed to designate an agent in the state). See also *Mullane*, 339 U.S. at 317, 70 S.Ct. at 658, 94 L.Ed. 865: " ... in the case of persons missing or unknown, employment of an indirect and even probably futile means of notification is all that the situation permits and creates no constitutional bar to a final decree foreclosing their rights;" General Motors Acceptance Corp. v. Thomas, 15 Ohio Misc. 267, 237 N.E.2d 427 (1968) receipt of notice signed by unauthorized third person, with no actual notice to defendant buyer, nevertheless permits entry of deficiency judgment over objection of failure to give notice because there had been "compliance with a prescribed procedure which in common experience results almost invariably in actual notice." For a decision upholding the service despite a false return by the sheriff, but in the absence of fraud or collusion on the part of the plaintiff, see Miedreich v. Lauenstein, 232 U.S. 236, 34 S.Ct. 309, 58 L.Ed. 584 (1914).

8. 276 U.S. 13, 48 S.Ct. 259, 72 L.Ed. 446 (1928).

9. 274 U.S. 352, 47 S.Ct. 632, 71 L.Ed. 1091 (1927).

10. See also Restatement, Second, Conflict of Laws § 25, cmnt. (e) (1971).

11. See infra § 12.5 and cases cited supra n.7.

mail.[12] Similarly, the Court has struck down statutes that allowed for notification of defendants in eviction proceedings to be notified simply by posting of the summons on the front door of the disputed premises[13] and to notify solely by publication parties likely to be affected by a foreclosure proceeding.[14]

B.   OPPORTUNITY TO BE HEARD

§ 12.4   The requirement of sufficient notice also includes that the notice adequately inform the party of the nature of the claim or proceeding[1] and that it be given in sufficient time to afford the defendant an adequate opportunity to defend.[2] The last requirement is now also reflected in several international instruments including the Brussels Regulation on Jurisdiction and Recognition and Enforcement of Judgments, which applies all members of the European Union,[3] except Denmark, the earlier proposal for a Convention between the United States and the United Kingdom on the Reciprocal Recognition of Judgments,[4] and the Hague Convention on the Service Abroad of Documents.[5]

12. See Tulsa Professional Collection Services, Inc. v. Pope, 485 U.S. 478, 108 S.Ct. 1340, 99 L.Ed.2d 565 (1988).

13. Greene v. Lindsey, 456 U.S. 444, 102 S.Ct. 1874, 72 L.Ed.2d 249 (1982).

14. Mennonite Bd. of Missions v. Adams, 462 U.S. 791, 103 S.Ct. 2706, 77 L.Ed.2d 180 (1983) (mortgagee denied due process by a state statute requiring only notice by publication and posting on the property prior to tax sale).

§ 12.4

1. Chapman v. Chapman, 284 App.Div. 504, 132 N.Y.S.2d 707 (1954), appeal denied 284 App.Div. 857, 134 N.Y.S.2d 173 (1954) (failure to give adequate notice of amendment of action for separation to one for divorce); Hewitt v. Hollahan, 56 N.J.Super. 372, 153 A.2d 371, 373–74 (App.Div.1959) (in action by welfare director to compel husband to support his wife, held that "no defendant should be required to go through 160 sections of a statute [plus supplements] to find out what he is charged with, especially when the 160 sections ... contain various and differing bases of liability.... Due process means more than mere notice to a person that he is a defendant—he is entitled to a complaint which informs him of the legal and factual basis of the charge which he is called upon to face"); In re Barger, 365 S.W.2d 89 (Mo.App.1963) (decree terminating rights of natural parents invalid for failure to give notice that award of permanent custody was contemplated); In re Estate of MacLean, 47 Wis.2d 396, 177 N.W.2d 874 (1970) (decree construing

will invalid for failure of sufficient notice to heirs); Julen v. Larson, 25 Cal.App.3d 325, 101 Cal.Rptr. 796 (1972) (discussed infra § 12.7 n.5).

2. Roller v. Holly, 176 U.S. 398, 20 S.Ct. 410, 44 L.Ed. 520 (1900).

3. Council Regulation (EC) No. 44/2001 on Jurisdiction and the Recognition of Judgments in Civil and Commercial Matters, [2001] O.J. L 012/1.

4. Art. 8(a) provided that recognition of a judgment is not required (upon defendant's motion to this effect) "where the defendant did not receive either actual notice of the proceeding in sufficient time to enable him to present his case or constructive notice substantially equivalent to that accepted by the law applicable in the court addressed." The Convention was never ratified. For analysis see Hay & Walker, The Proposed Recognition-of-Judgments Convention Between the United States and the United Kingdom, 11 Tex. Int'l L. J. 421, 442 (1976); Hay & Walker, "Projet d'une Convention anglo-américaine sur la reconnaissance des jugements et la Convention Communautaire," [1977] Cahiers de droit européen 1.

5. Art. 15 provides that judgment shall not be entered in a proceeding in which the defendant did not appear unless service was made in the manner provided and "the service or the delivery was effected in sufficient time to enable the defendant to defend." 20 U.S.T. 361; T.I.A.S. 6638; Recueil des Conventions de la Haye 76, 83 (1973 ed.)(discussed infra § 12.6).

C. WAIVER OF NOTICE

§ **12.5** In *Wuchter*,[1] the Supreme Court invalidated a state non-resident motorist statute providing for service on an absent defendant by service on a state official, but not requiring the latter to transmit notice to the defendant. The case is distinguishable from situations in which a party has waived notice of service by private agreement. This is typically the case in cognovit or confession-of-judgment clauses by which a party to a contract agrees that, in case of default, a particular person or "any attorney of record" may be appointed by the other party to accept service, enter an appearance and confess judgment on the former party's behalf.

The Supreme Court approved such an agreement in *National Equipment Rental, Limited v. Szukhent*,[2] a case in which the agent was not required to give notice but in fact had done so. The court noted that a different case "would be presented if ... [the agent] had not given prompt notice ... , for then the claim might well be made that [such] failure ... had operated to invalidate the agency."[3] The question of whether notice was or was not given or required to be given thus seemed to go more to the definition of the extent of the agency than to the question whether a party could waive the due-process protection of notice. Subsequent decisions of the Supreme Court have not addressed the due process standard directly but rather the voluntariness of cognovit clauses in adhesion-type stipulations,[4] while the Washington state court decision mentioned above[5] assumes that no due process problem existed. Waiver of notice, even if broadly phrased, should thus not automatically be considered as violative of due process, but be examined in the context of adhesion contracts. However, the Supreme Court's

§ **12.5**

1. Wuchter v. Pizzutti, 276 U.S. 13, 48 S.Ct. 259, 72 L.Ed. 446 (1928). The cases discussed in this section are also treated supra §§ 8.16, 8.19, 8.32.

2. 375 U.S. 311, 84 S.Ct. 411, 11 L.Ed.2d 354 (1964).

3. 375 U.S. at 318, 84 S.Ct. at 415, 11 L.Ed.2d 354.

4. D.H. Overmyer Co. v. Frick Co., 405 U.S. 174, 92 S.Ct. 775, 31 L.Ed.2d 124 (1972) ("due process rights to notice and hearing prior to ... judgment are subject to waiver," citing *National Equipment Rental*, and "this is not a case of unequal bargaining power or overreaching ... The facts of this case ... amply demonstrate that a cognovit provision may well serve a proper and useful purpose in the commercial world and at the same time not be vulnerable to constitutional attack"); Swarb v. Lennox, 405 U.S. 191, 201, 92 S.Ct. 767, 772, 31 L.Ed.2d 138 (1972), (*Overmyer* said not to be applicable "to contracts of adhesion, to

bargaining power disparity, and to the absence of anything received in return for a cognovit provision."). See also United States v. Local 1804–1, Int'l Longshoremen's Ass'n, AFL–CIO, 44 F.3d 1091, 1099 (2d Cir.1995) (citing *Overmyer* as support for the waiver of constitutional rights in civil cases where the waiver is "voluntary, knowing, and intelligent"), on remand 1996 WL 34153 (S.D.N.Y.1996); F.D.I.C. v. Aaronian, 93 F.3d 636 (9th Cir.1996) (holding that the burden to show absence of voluntariness, knowledge or intelligence falls upon the party challenging a cognovit clause). But see Jordan v. Fox, 20 F.3d 1250 (3d Cir.1994), on remand 1995 WL 141465 (E.D.Pa.1995) (holding that waiver by cognovit clause does not constitute waiver of the right to a hearing before or promptly after execution of the judgment where judgment is based upon the cognovit clause).

5. See supra n.4.

precedents in the area of contractual jurisdiction show that even severely unequal bargaining power alone will not invalidate private agreements of this kind.[6]

II.   SERVICE ABROAD OF DOCUMENTS[1]

§ 12.6   International litigation may frequently require the service of documents on parties in foreign jurisdictions. The older law (despite a 1954 Hague Convention on Civil Procedure to which the United States, moreover, was not a party)[2] showed significant national divergences and did not facilitate the conduct of international proceedings. Thus, few foreign countries permitted direct communication with their judicial officers or service of documents by consular officers of the issuing states but instead left the transmission of requests for service of documents and for other judicial assistance to diplomatic channels.[3] In addition, the practice of several civil law countries (originally among them Belgium, France, Greece, Italy, and the Netherlands) included *"notification au parquet"* (service on an absent foreign defendant by service on local authorities of the forum).[4] Combined with the exercise of "exorbitant" bases of jurisdiction,[5] for instance jurisdiction based solely on the nationality of the *plaintiff* (allowed for by the French civil code), the possibility existed in these states that default judgments could be entered against absent foreign defendants who had had no notice, could not have had notice, and may not have had any connection with the forum other than having dealt with one of its nationals. Even though such a judgment may not have been entitled to recognition elsewhere, for instance, in the United States,[6] it was of course valid where rendered and could be satisfied out of present or future assets there.[7] From the United States'

---

6.   See infra § 11.3.

§ 12.6

1.   For early commentary, see Hay, The United States and International Unification of Law: The Tenth Session of the Hague Conference, 1965 U. Ill. L. Forum 820, 853–60.

2.   Recueil des Conventions de la Haye 4 (1973 ed.)(reprinted in 1 Am. J. Comp. L. 282 (1962)).

3.   See Jones, International Judicial Assistance: Procedural Chaos and a Program for Reform, 62 Yale L.J. 515, 520–39 (1953).

4.   This practice differs from provisions in U.S. state law for service, for instance, on the secretary of state under non-resident motorist legislation or in actions arising out of business activity within the state, since the latter presuppose prior contact of the defendant with the state and may thus be seen as the proper exercise of state police or regulatory power or perhaps be explained as based on the defendant's implied consent to such service. See Hess v. Pawloski, 274 U.S. 352, 47 S.Ct. 632, 71 L.Ed. 1091 (1927);

Manley v. Nelson, 50 Haw. 484, 443 P.2d 155 (1968), appeal dismissed and cert. denied 394 U.S. 573, 89 S.Ct. 1299, 22 L.Ed.2d 555 (1969); Washington v. Superior Court, 289 U.S. 361, 53 S.Ct. 624, 77 L.Ed. 1256 (1933). In addition, service on a public official must be accompanied, at least in cases involving individual—non-corporate—defendants, by the forwarding of actual notice to the defendant by the public official. Wuchter v. Pizzutti, 276 U.S. 13, 48 S.Ct. 259, 72 L.Ed. 446 (1928). Both the factor of the defendant's prior connection with the forum and a requirement of actual notice to the defendant are lacking in *"notification au parquet."*

5.   See Weser, Bases of Judicial Jurisdiction in the Common Market Countries, 10 Am. J. Comp. L. 323, 324 (1961).

6.   See infra § 24.42.

7.   The Brussels Convention of the European Community and the (parallel) Lugano Convention abolish exorbitant jurisdictional rules with respect to domiciliary defendants

point of view, prior foreign law did not facilitate the service of documents abroad for purposes of litigation in this country and, if litigation took place abroad, exposed American defendants to substantial dangers and disadvantages.

United States practice, in turn, also gave insufficient assistance to foreign parties. Prior to 1964, the State Department did not consider the diplomatic channel to be the proper manner for the transmission of letters rogatory or other requests from foreign courts.[8] Early state court decisions at times refused assistance when foreign courts requested service on local parties[9] on grounds that the foreign court lacked jurisdiction and that local residents should not be subjected to suit in distant countries, thereby also often misconstruing the function of "service" in the foreign legal system.[10]

The 1964 amendments to the Judicial Code[11] remedied some of these deficiencies. Section 1781 authorizes the State Department to receive letters rogatory or other requests from foreign authorities, to transmit them to United States officers and courts, and to return them after execution. Section 1696 authorizes federal district courts to order service, upon any person residing within the district, of any document issued in connection with a proceeding before a foreign or international tribunal. The Hague Convention on the Taking of Evidence now appears in connection with Section 1781. The 1993 amendments to the Federal Rules of Civil Procedure make additional provisions for international service of documents. New Rule 4(f)—replacing Rule 4(i) of the 1963 version[12]—provides that service on individuals while outside the United States may be effected "by any internationally agreed means reasonably calculated to give notice, such as those means authorized by the Hague Convention...."[13] If a treaty is the *exclusive* means of international service—as the Hague Convention is for documents transmitted abroad to a signatory nation[14]—then the treaty service method is mandatory

but continue to permit their exercise with respect to defendants of non-member states. See infra § 24.38.

8. McCusker, Some United States Practices in International Judicial Assistance, 37 Dep't State Bull. 808, 810 (1957).

9. In re Romero, 56 Misc. 319, 107 N.Y.S. 621 (1907); In re Letters Rogatory Out of First Civil Court of City of Mexico, 261 Fed. 652 (S.D.N.Y.1919). But cf. De Villeneuve v. Morning Journal Association, 206 Fed. 70 (D.C.N.Y.1913). The continued authority of the decisions in *Romero* and *City of Mexico* was also questioned in In re Letters Rogatory from City of Haugesund, Norway, 497 F.2d 378 (9th Cir.1974) in light of the developments of state long-arm jurisdiction and 28 U.S.C.A. § 1696(a).

10. Foreign systems often do not consider service as an essential part in the exer-cise of jurisdiction but base jurisdiction on a variety of connecting factors (such as the defendant's domicile, the plaintiff's nationality, the presence of—even minimal—assets, and the like). As a result, "service" performs a notice function. For the importance of notice, see supra § 12.2 n.2. See also infra § 12.7 n.3.

11. P.L. 88–619, 78 Stat. 996, amending and adding sections to 28 U.S.C.A. See Smit, International Litigation Under the United States Code, 65 Colum. L. Rev. 1015 (1965).

12. See 1993 Advisory Committee Notes on Federal Rule of Civil Procedure 4(f).

13. F.R.C.P. 4(f)(1).

14. See Volkswagenwerk Aktiengesellschaft v. Schlunk, 486 U.S. 694, 108 S.Ct. 2104, 100 L.Ed.2d 722 (1988).

under Federal Rule 4(f).[15] In the absence of an applicable treaty, the rule allows for service in the manner allowed in the courts of general jurisdiction of the foreign country, or in the manner directed in response to a letter rogatory, as long as the means is reasonably calculated to give notice. The rule also allows for personal or certified mail service if not prohibited by the law of the country in which the service is being effected or service "by any other means not prohibited by international agreement as may be directed by the court." The rule is clearly intended to obviate the need for explicit statutory authorization for foreign service.

The 1993 version of Rule 4(f) only refers to service on individuals. However, Rule 4(h) now incorporates the provisions of Rule 4(f) for service on corporations and associations. The only means mentioned in Rule 4(f) but not available against corporations and associations is personal delivery. This is because it is impossible to "personally deliver" something to a fictitious person. This presents no obstacle to giving notice, however, because local service rules—including the federal rules—commonly provide for service by delivery to a managing agent or other important person in the association.

§ 12.7   The Hague Convention on Service Abroad of Judicial and Extrajudicial Documents in Civil and Commercial Matters[1] is of particular significance. It eliminates the practice of *"notification au parquet"*[2] and also deals effectively with the problem of default judgments noted earlier. Thus, Article 15 specifies that no default judgment shall be entered unless service was made in accordance with one of the methods prescribed by the receiving state for service in domestic actions against persons within its territory or unless the document was served in accordance with the Convention *and* was actually delivered to the defendant or his residence. The service provisions of the Convention, in

---

15. See 1993 Notes of Advisory Committee on F.R.C.P. 4(f).

§ 12.7

1. 20 U.S.T. 361; T.I.A.S. 6638 (appended to F.R.C.P. 4). Recueil des Conventions de la Haye 76 (1973 ed.). As of April 2004, the Convention is in force in: Antigua, Argentina, Bahamas, Barbados, Barbuda, Belarus, Belgium, Botswana, Bulgaria, Canada, China, Cyprus, Czech Republic, Denmark, Egypt, Estonia, Finland, France, Germany, Greece, Ireland, Israel, Italy, Japan, Korea, Kuwait, Latvia, Lithuania, Luxembourg, Malawi, Mexico, Netherlands, Norway, Pakistan, Portugal, Romania, Russian Federation, San Marino, Seychelles, Slovakia, Slovenia, Spain, Sri Lanka, Sweden, Switzerland, Turkey, Ukraine, United Kingdom (extended to Anguilla, Bermuda, British Virgin Islands, Cayman Islands, Central and Southern Line Islands, Falkland Islands and dependencies, Gibraltar, Guernsey, Hong Kong, Isle of

Man, Jersey, Montserrat, Pitcairn, St. Helena and dependencies, Turks and Caicos Islands), United States (extended to Guam, Puerto Rico, Northern Marianas and the Virgin Islands), and Venezuela. The United States has also adhered to the Hague Convention Abolishing the Requirement of Legalization for Foreign Public Documents which simplifies authentication of documents: T.I.A.S. 10072 (entered into force for the United States Oct. 15, 1981); see also infra § 24.35 n.8.

Within the European Union, except Denmark, EC Council Regulation No. 1348/2000, [2000] Official Journal L 160/37, adopts the Hague Convention to European Community needs and circumstances and provides for more simplified service of documents.

2. Art. 1 is ambiguous and subject to a different interpretation, but the interpretation stated in the text seems to have been accepted by the *parquet* states.

turn, provide, inter alia, for service by consular or diplomatic agents, by mail,[3] by judicial officers of the requested state, and by other methods permitted by the law of the requested state. These provisions, especially as they apply to default judgments, represent a change in international practice "in the direction of ... United States ... concepts of due

3. The courts are divided over the question whether Article 10(a) of the Convention permits *service* abroad by mail or whether service must be effected by use of the Convention's procedures and channels (e.g. transmission to the Central Authority of the state addressed). The latter view finds support in the different conceptions of the nature of "service" in legal systems (supra § 12.6 n.37) and in the use of the word "send" in Art. 10(a) as compared with "serve" in Art. 5 (concerning the function of the Central Authority). The wider views takes account of the facts that Art. 10, by its own terms, is intended to permit additional avenues for communication *and* permits states to restrict such additional avenues. It reads in part: "Provided the State of destination does not object, the present Convention shall not interfere with: (a) the freedom to send judicial documents, by postal channels, directly to persons abroad ... " Compare Ackermann v. Levine, 788 F.2d 830 (2d Cir.1986) (service by mail proper); Denlinger v. Chinadotcom Corporation, 110 Cal.App.4th 1396, 2 Cal.Rptr.3d 530 (2003)(service by mail allowed under Article 10) with Bankston v. Toyota Motor Corp., 889 F.2d 172 (8th Cir.1989); Nuovo Pignone v. Storman Asia M/V, 310 F.3d 374 (5th Cir. 2002)(service by mail not permitted because it would render Articles 2 through 7 meaningless). See also Arco Electronics v. Core Int'l, 794 F.Supp. 1144, 1147 (S.D.Fla.1992). Also, some courts have based their decisions not to permit service abroad by mail on their conclusion that the foreign country concerned would not have accepted an interpretation of Art. 10(a) as authorizing service by mail. See Gallagher v. Mazda Motor of America, 781 F.Supp. 1079 (E.D.Pa.1992) (service by mail into Japan improper).

German law does not permit service by mail, and Germany, as well as some other states, has made a reservation to Art. 10. German law also specifies that documents to be served in Germany be in German or accompanied by a German translation. Accordingly, service by mail of a German defendant has been held ineffective under the Convention. Richardson v. Volkswagenwerk, A.G., 552 F.Supp. 73 (W.D.Mo.1982). See Hartley v. Wheatherford Crane Co., 1986 WL 10643 (E.D.Pa.1986) (slip opn.);

Pochop v. Toyota Motor Co., Ltd., 111 F.R.D. 464 (S.D.Miss.1986). Representing minority view, see Precision Machine Works v. King, (N.D.Ill. 1986) (slip opn.). See also Harris v. Browning–Ferris Industries Chemical Services, Inc. et al., 100 F.R.D. 775 (D.La.1984)(process served by mail on German defendant also violated German language requirement; however, instead of granting defendant's motion to dismiss, court granted plaintiff an additional 30 days in which to serve defendant by means consistent with the Convention); Vorhees v. Fischer & Krecke, 697 F.2d 574 (4th Cir.1983); Anbe v. Kikuchi, 141 F.R.D. 498 (D.Hawai'i 1992); Chilean Nitrate Corp. v. M/V Hans Leonhardt, 810 F.Supp. 732 (E.D.La.1992). In the reverse situation, a New York federal court refused to recognize and enforce a German judgment, *inter alia,* for failure to comply with the Convention's provisions for service of process. The German court had sent the documents to the German Consulate General in New York which mailed them to the defendant by registered mail, return receipt requested. The court construed Art. 10 of the convention as not forbidding, without more, service by mail but found that service must still comply with local law, state or federal, under Art. 5. The method of service employed did not comply with New York law. Ackermann v. Levine, 610 F.Supp. 633 (S.D.N.Y.1985). On appeal this decision was affirmed in part and reversed in part. Art. 10(a) of the Convention permits service through "postal channels" in the absence of an objection by the signatory state. Since the United States had not made an objection, service by mail complied with the Convention, and the latter's provision superseded inconsistent state and prior federal law. Ackermann v. Levine, 788 F.2d 830 (2d Cir.1986). See also Aspinall's Club Ltd. v. Aryeh, 86 A.D.2d 428, 450 N.Y.S.2d 199 (1982) (service by federal marshall in accordance with Federal Rules of Civil Procedure is effective under the Convention despite more stringent requirements of New York law).

Within the European Union, Germany now accepts service by registered mail, subject also with respect to the language used. EC Regulation No. 1348/2000 supra n. 1 Art. 14. See Comments by Möller, [2003]

process."[4] This conclusion is now also supported by the case law; the decisions involve the adequacy of notice and interpret the Convention's provisions in the light of notions of due process.[5]

NJW 1571, and Schmidt, [2004] IPRax 13, 20.

4. Amram, 52 Dep't State Bull. 268 (1965).

5. Julen v. Larson, 25 Cal.App.3d 325, 101 Cal.Rptr. 796 (1972) affirmed a summary judgment for the defendant in plaintiff's action to enforce a Swiss default judgment. The court found that the documents served on defendant in California were written in German and not accompanied by a summary (in English) identifying the documents "as materials of legal significance." The court cited to West's Ann. Cal. Code of Civ. Proc. §§ 185 and 413.10(c) and to Art. 5 of the Hague Convention. Art. 5 requires a summary designed to give the "minimum information necessary for adequate notice." Id. at 329 and 799. The Convention specifies that the summary shall be in English, French, or the language of the serving state and that the latter may require translation into its language. The court concluded: "[W]e think the summary [but not necessarily the documents themselves] should normally be written in English, that is to say the language of the place of service." Id. at 330 and 800.

In Shoei Kako Co., Limited v. Superior Court, San Francisco, 33 Cal.App.3d 808, 109 Cal.Rptr. 402 (1973), the court faced the reverse situation, the adequacy of service on a Japanese corporation when documents had been transmitted by mail and were not written in Japanese. The court found that the documents had been received, as evidenced by an international mail receipt, that the service by mail complied with West's Ann. Cal. Code Civ. Proc. §§ 413.10 and 415.30, that Art. 5 (in conjunction with Art. 15(b)) of the Hague Convention permits service "by delivery to an addressee who accepts it voluntarily" unless such service is incompatible with the law of the State addressed. There was no evidence that Japanese law prohibits the transmission of documents by mail. Since the mode of service did not utilize transmission through a Central Authority under Art. 5, that provision's stipulation of English as an acceptable language did not apply. The court nevertheless upheld the service on the strength of expert testimony that all Japanese companies engaged in international trade employ English in their correspondence and on evidence that the company used English advertising materials. The court cited to language in *Julen*, supra, that "the process served must give defendant sufficient notice of the pending foreign proceedings to satisfy the require-

ments of due process of law," 25 Cal.App.3d at 327–328, 101 Cal.Rptr. at 797–798, and concluded: "The special appearance in these proceedings bespeaks that the purport of the documents was understood. Under these circumstances there was neither a lack of due process of law nor a violation of the letter or spirit of the treaty." 33 Cal. App.3d at 824, 109 Cal.Rptr. at 413. The court thus construed the "spirit" of the convention according to *American* notions of due process. Its reading of the "letter" of the Convention in effect extended the specification of English or French beyond Art. 5, thereby not according the foreign defendant the benefit of its own language (while *Julen* had provided that the summary should be in the language of the state where service was received), and severely restricted the value of a special appearance as a means for testing jurisdiction, including its proper exercise. The court took a different view when evidence was presented that Japan does not allow service by mail for litigation within its own courts. The court rather took the domestic law prohibitions service by private mail as conclusive evidence that Japan would not have assented to Article 10(a) had it believed the article to permit service by mail written within Japanese borders. Honda Motor Co. v. Superior Ct. of Santa Clara, 10 Cal.App.4th 1043, 12 Cal.Rptr.2d 861 (6th Dist. 1992).

In an extensive discussion of the Convention, the Third Circuit held that "the treaty . . . does not provide independent authorization for service of process in a foreign country. The treaty merely provides a mechanism by which a plaintiff authorized to serve process under the laws of its country can effect service that will give appropriate notice to the party being served and will not be objectionable to the country in which that party is served. . . . [W]e do not believe that the treaty in any way affects a state's chosen limits on the jurisdictional reach of its courts. If a state long-arm rule does not authorize service outside the United States, a litigant in that state would have no authority to invoke the methods of serving process provided in the treaty. . . . [T]he treaty merely serves as an adjunct to state long-arm rules, . . . it specifies a valid method of effecting service only if the state long-arm rule authorizes service abroad." DeJames v. Magnificence Carriers, Inc., 654 F.2d 280, 288–89 (3d Cir.1981), cert. denied 454 U.S. 1085, 102 S.Ct. 642, 70 L.Ed.2d 620 (1981). See also Narco Avionics v.

The courts were split on whether to pierce the corporate veil and to uphold service on the U.S. subsidiary as effective against the foreign parent on an alter-ego theory. In the event of piercing, only domestic service would be required, and the Hague Convention would be inapplicable.[6] *Schlunk v. Volkswagenwerk Aktiengesellschaft*[7] is representative of the decisions permitting piercing or assuming an agency relationship for purposes of service between the foreign parent and the local subsidiary. The court noted that the defendant German manufacturer (Volkswagen) did not question the existence of jurisdiction in Illinois to entertain the claim,[8] leaving as the only question whether service on its New Jersey subsidiary, Volkswagen of America, which did business in Illinois, subjected it to Illinois jurisdiction on an alter-ego theory. While the subsidiary had not been formally appointed as the defendant's agent for service, the court found that parent and subsidiary were so closely related, that the subsidiary was the defendant's "agent for service of process ... by operation of law."[9] The Supreme Court affirmed.[10] The Convention applies only when "there is occasion to transmit a judicial ... document for service abroad." It therefore did not apply when, under applicable state law, service was complete with service on the defendant's wholly owned subsidiary.[11] Justice Brennan, joined by Justices Marshall and Blackmun, expressed concern that a state-law definition of "service" might render use of the Convention optional rather than mandatory, but concurred in the judgment on the ground that the requirement of notice to the defendant had been satisfied.

Sportsman's Mkt., 792 F.Supp. 398 (E.D.Pa.1992).

6. Decisions *against* piercing include: Hamilton v. Volkswagenwerk A.G., No. 81–01–L (D.N.H. 1981), unreported, summarized in 28 Recht der Internationalen Wirtschaft 784, 791–92 (1982); Richardson v. Volkswagenwerk, A.G., 552 F.Supp. 73 (W.D.Mo.1982). *For* piercing: Ex parte Volkswagenwerk Aktiengesellschaft, 443 So.2d 880 (Ala.1983); Lamb v. Volkswagenwerk Aktiengesellschaft, 104 F.R.D. 95 (S.D.Fla.1985) (distinguishing *Richardson* on the ground that the *Richardson* plaintiff had failed to prove the extent to which the German defendant controlled the U.S. subsidiary).

7. 145 Ill.App.3d 594, 503 N.E.2d 1045 (1986), aff'd 486 U.S. 694, 108 S.Ct. 2104, 100 L.Ed.2d 722 (1988).

8. 503 N.E.2d at 1048, 1049. The court nonetheless proceeded to review on what basis Illinois could assert jurisdiction. The court conceded that the claim did not arise out of an Illinois contact, see id. at 1049, i.e. that there was no specific jurisdiction. In analyzing whether the German defendant was subject to Illinois' jurisdiction under the "doing business" provision of the Illinois long arm statute, the court focussed on the extent to which the defendant and its subsidiary were interrelated. It omitted the necessary further analytic step of determining whether the *subsidiary* had sufficient contacts with Illinois to permit the assertion of jurisdiction there. The court seems to have assumed that the subsidiary's appointment of an agent for service gave it a sufficient Illinois presence to subject it to jurisdiction there.

9. Id. at 1054. The court referred to the piercing doctrine but preferred a more general approach: "While courts in other jurisdictions have looked to whether a subsidiary is an alter-ego or mere department of its parent, Illinois courts have avoided such labels ... " Id. The language quoted in the text then followed, finding an agency "by operation of law" to exist.

10. 486 U.S. 694, 108 S.Ct. 2104, 100 L.Ed.2d 722 (1988) (noted 30 Harv. Int'l L.J. 277 (1989)). See also R. Griggs Group v. Filanto Spa, 920 F.Supp. 1100 (D.Nev. 1996) ("where service on a domestic agent of a foreign defendant is valid and complete, the Hague Convention has no further implications").

11. The defendant had not contested the propriety of Illinois law, permitting service on an agency theory or by means of piercing.

The 1993 revisions to the Federal Rules were made with *Schlunk* in mind. As noted above, the 1993 amendments added a new version of Rule 4(f) which specifically mentions the Hague Convention as a means of international service.[12] The 1993 amendments do not, however, alter the fundamental holding of *Schlunk*. If the lex fori allows for domestic service of documents, then the Hague Convention is an option but need not be followed; if the documents must be transmitted abroad to a signatory nation, then the Hague Convention is the exclusive means of service.[13]

A principal feature of the Convention for administrative purposes is the provision for the channeling of requests and the return (execution) of documents requested through a Central Authority in each contracting state: any "authority or judicial officer competent under the law of the [issuing] State" may transmit the documents directly to the Central Authority of the requested state, and the certificate of service will be returned directly to the former (Arts. 3 and 6). The Department of State is the "Central Authority" in the United States.

III. TAKING EVIDENCE ABROAD

§ 12.8 Judicial assistance for obtaining evidence from abroad for use in domestic litigation-traditionally by letters rogatory-is closely related to the service abroad of documents. In the United States, the State Department—exercising the function of a "Central Authority"—may receive letters rogatory from foreign sources for transmission domestically and from United States courts for transmission abroad.

Federal Rule 28(b) applies to the taking of depositions abroad. It provides that depositions may be taken abroad for use in a domestic proceeding (1) on notice before a person authorized to administer oaths under foreign or United States law, (2) before a person commissioned by the court, or (3) pursuant to a letter rogatory. Evidence obtained by means of a letter rogatory need not be excluded simply because it is not a verbatim record of the testimony. This provision is important because, in foreign practice, questions are often put by the judge who thereafter executes a narrative summary of the proceedings.

Foreign letters rogatory are executed in the United States pursuant to Section 1782 of the Judicial Code and Federal Rules 26 through 37. District courts have power to order persons residing or found in their territory to give testimony or to produce documents for use in a proceeding in a foreign or international tribunal, subject to the privilege against self-incrimination or other legal privilege.[1]

---

12. See supra § 12.6.

13. 1993 Advisory Committee Notes to F.R.C.P. 4(f).

§ 12.8

1. On testimonial privileges see infra § 12.10 et seq. In Petition of Avant Indus-

tries, Limited, Misc. No. M12–329, slip opinion (S.D.N.Y., Oct. 3, 1980), the court denied a motion seeking subpoenas compelling Avant Industries, through two of its agents, to appear for depositions for use by the movants in an Italian proceeding in circumstances where the Italian action had

However, there has been some dispute as to what constitutes a "tribunal" within the meaning of the statute. In the case of In re Letters Rogatory Issued by Director of Inspection of Government of India,[2] an Indian tax inspector presented letters rogatory to the district court seeking records of the Chase Manhattan Bank and an American company. These records were sought by the inspector in order to aid him in determining how much tax should be assessed against an Indian citizen. An ex parte order was entered which appointed a commissioner to take the letter rogatory and a subpoena duces tecum was issued to the company. The Indian citizen and the company moved to vacate the order and quash the subpoena; the motion was denied. The Second Circuit reversed. Looking to the legislative history of the statute, the court noted that the reference in committee reports to proceedings before foreign investigating magistrates was explained by a reference to investigations before French *juges d'instruction,* whose investigations had not been clearly within Section 1782 before the 1964 Amendments. Comparing the role of this official to that of the grand jury in Anglo–American law, the court pointed out that, while that official plays an active role in the investigation of cases, he does not have the same interest in obtaining a conviction as a prosecutor. In contrast, the Indian income tax officer had the sole responsibility for making and evaluating the government's case. Additionally, a tax assessor does not fit the American conception of the nature of a "tribunal." The Second Circuit therefore held that Section 1782 is "not so broad as to include all the plethora of administrators whose decisions affect private parties and who are not entitled to act arbitrarily, and one useful guideline is the absence of any degree of separation between the prosecutorial and adjudicative functions."[3]

In re Letters Rogatory from Tokyo District, Tokyo, Japan[4] suggested that the Indian tax assessor, in the case just discussed, could have obtained assistance by invoking the aid of Indian courts. In the Tokyo

been instituted by Avant and its agents and officers were available and ready to testify there. If, ultimately, the movants "cannot procure the discovery they seek in Italy, they should obtain letters rogatory from the Italian court directed to persons or documents found in this district." At this point in the foreign litigation, "this Court refuses to inject itself unnecessarily into this foreign proceeding." Given the presence and availability of the witnesses in Italy, "this Court would be abusing its discretion if it issued subpoenas compelling these individuals to testify in Italy."

2. 272 F.Supp. 758 (S.D.N.Y.1967), rev'd 385 F.1d 1017 (2d Cir.1967).

3. Id. at 1021. See also Fonseca v. Blumenthal, 620 F.2d 322 (2d Cir.1980) (The Superintendent of Exchange Control of Colombia acts in the government's interest-investigating and determining violations of law-and is therefore not a tribunal); In re Request for International Judicial Assistance from the Federative Republic of Brazil, 687 F.Supp. 880 (1988)(Brazilian police and tax authorities request for information denied because, by virtue of their "institutional interest in a particular result" and the lack of a court's exercise of an independent adjudicative function, they are not a tribunal).

4. 539 F.2d 1216 (9th Cir.1976). See also In re Letter of Request for Judicial Assistance from Tribunal Civil de Port-au-Prince, Republic of Haiti, 669 F.Supp. 403 (S.D.Fla.1987) (granting order requiring bank to produce financial records pertaining to a former Minister of Finance of Haiti who fled Haiti along with former President-for-Life Jean Claude Duvalier). See also Foden v. Gianoli Aldunate, 3 F.3d 54 (2d Cir.1993), cert. denied 510 U.S. 965, 114 S.Ct. 443, 126 L.Ed.2d 376 (1993) (competency proceedings are judicial for § 1782 purposes).

case, the letters requested immediate assistance in the taking of *in camera* depositions of certain persons for use in criminal investigations and possible future criminal trials in Japan arising out of a Lockheed scandal.[5] The U.S. District Court issued subpoenas duces tecum. The witnesses moved to quash them on the ground that the Tokyo District Court was not a "tribunal" because, under the circumstances, it was not acting as an adjudicatory body but pursuant to a request by the Tokyo prosecutor's office.[6] The motion was denied, but the court granted a stay of its orders. On appeal, the Ninth Circuit affirmed. It pointed out that the purpose of the 1964 Amendments was to broaden existing law and to permit extension of international assistance to bodies of a quasi-judicial or administrative nature. In addition, the court concluded that Congress intended for the district courts to have discretion to grant assistance to foreign investigating magistrates.[7]

American discovery procedures are generally available in aid of pending or imminent[8] litigation abroad.[9] As such, discovery in the United States may be an important alternative to suit in the United States

---

5. It was disclosed in 1976 that Lockheed Aircraft Corporation had paid millions in bribes and payoffs to foreign government officials to promote sales of airplanes. Because of one scandal involving Japanese politicians, the Japanese cancelled a $1.3 billion order for Lockheed antisubmarine aircraft. The New York Times Index 1976, at 867–68.

6. The witnesses had based their argument on In re Letters of Request to Examine Witnesses from Court of Queen's Bench for Manitoba, Canada, 59 F.R.D. 625 (N.D.Cal.1973), affirmed 488 F.2d 511 (9th Cir.1973). In that case the letters were sent by the Canadian court on behalf of three commissioners appointed to study a forestry and industrial project and to make a report to legislative or executive bodies. The district court held that § 1782 did not authorize courts to compel testimony on behalf of foreign governmental entities whose purpose is to carry out investigations unrelated to quasi-judicial or judicial controversies. In the court's view, the definition of "tribunal" requires that the body in question have the "power to make a binding adjudication of facts or law as related to the rights of litigants in concrete cases." 59 F.R.D. at 630. The Ninth Circuit, in the Tokyo case correctly considered this decision inapplicable to the question whether the district court should assist the Japanese prosecutor in the case at bar when the controversy apparently was judicial in nature.

7. See also In re Request for Assistance from Ministry of Legal Affairs of Trinidad

and Tobago, 848 F.2d 1151 (11th Cir.1988), cert. denied 488 U.S. 1005, 109 S.Ct. 784, 102 L.Ed.2d 776 (1989)(request by Attorney General and Minister of Legal Affairs of Trinidad and Tobago was request by "interested person," and purpose was the use of documents at a trial—"for use in a proceeding in a foreign tribunal"—and thus fulfilled both requirements of 28 U.S.C.A. § 1782(a)). But see In re Request for International Judicial Assistance from the Federative Republic of Brazil, 687 F.Supp. 880 (S.D.N.Y.1988)(where letters rogatory requesting information desired by the Brazilian equivalent of a prosecuting attorney are signed by a Brazilian judge, the letters will not be implemented unless there is a clear indication that they will not simply be automatically forwarded to the prosecuting official and that the judge who signed them will exercise an independent adjudicative function).

8. Other common law systems are more restrictive. Thus, Canadian law requires that a foreign action is pending and that the foreign court has ordered or requested discovery. Canada Evidence Act § 46; J.-G. Castel, Canadian Conflict of Laws 132–42 (4th ed. 1997).

9. See Malev Hungarian Airlines v. United Technologies International, Inc., 964 F.2d 97 (2d Cir.1992), cert. denied 506 U.S. 861, 113 S.Ct. 179, 121 L.Ed.2d 125 (1992); Application of Gianoli Aldunate, 3 F.3d 54 (2d Cir.1993), cert. denied 510 U.S. 965, 114 S.Ct. 443, 126 L.Ed.2d 376 (1993); Eco Swiss China Time Ltd. v. Timex Corp., 944 F.Supp. 134 (D.Conn.1996).

when it may be feared that the American court may dismiss for forum non conveniens in circumstances of scant contacts with the forum.

Despite reasonable certainty as to most of the questions that arise under Section 1782, there continues to be disagreement among American courts on some points. One is whether the information sought must be discoverable under foreign law were the discovery sought in the forum nation. The circuit courts are sharply divided on this question.[10] Another is whether the foreign proceeding must be actually "pending" in order to trigger the statutory requirement of assistance from U.S. courts. The better view is that while the foreign proceeding need not have been formally commenced, it must be "imminent—very likely to occur and very soon to occur."[11]

United States v. Reagan[12] presents the situation where the American court requests assistance from abroad. The defendant was convicted of voluntary manslaughter for a homicide which took place aboard an American ship while in a German harbor. He had been arrested by German authorities, but released after a German judge found that there was no probable cause that he had committed the crime. The U.S. district court had sent a request, in the form of letters rogatory, for the investigative files of the German authorities. The files were sent and made available to the U.S. Attorney's office. One of the defendant's contentions on appeal was that the trial judge's request was outside the jurisdiction of the court. The Sixth Circuit rejected this argument. It asserted that Section 1781 implicitly recognizes such a power in the district courts. The court also suggested that issuance of letters rogatory is in the inherent powers of all courts, and moreover, that such steps taken to obtain evidence from a foreign power in criminal cases is within a federal court's powers over cases and controversies under Articles III of the Constitution.

As a complement to Section 1782, the United States has negotiated a fair number Mutual Assistance Treaties with other governments.[13] In a major opinion, the Eleventh Circuit court of appeals held that the treaty between the United States and Canada did not require a pending case in Canada in order for the Canadian authorities to be able to obtain

---

10. See, e.g., Advanced Micro Devices, Inc. v. Intel Corp., 292 F.3d 664 (9th Cir. 2002), affirmed ___ U.S. ___, 124 S.Ct. 2466, ___ L.Ed.2d ___ (2004) (evidence need not be admissible in foreign proceeding); Euromepa, S.A. v. R. Esmerian, Inc., 154 F.3d 24 (2d Cir.1998)(no requirement of foreign discoverability); In re Application of Asta Medica, S.A., 981 F.2d 1 (1st Cir.1992)(foreign discoverability required); In re Request for Assistance from Ministry of Legal Affairs of Trinidad & Tobago, 848 F.2d 1151 (11th Cir.1988)(same).

11. *Advanced Micro Devices*, 292 F.3d at 667 (§ 1782 triggered by E.U. agency's anti-competition investigation; no requirement in amended statute that any proceed-

ing be "pending") General Universal Trading Corp. v. Morgan Guaranty Trust Co., 936 F.2d 702, 706 (2d Cir.1991).

12. 453 F.2d 165 (6th Cir.1971), cert. denied 406 U.S. 946, 92 S.Ct. 2049, 32 L.Ed.2d 334 (1972). See also B & L Drilling Electronics v. Totco, 87 F.R.D. 543 (W.D.Okla.1978) (granting motion for letters rogatory directed to Canadian authority requesting oral examination of persons knowing facts material to movant's defense in breach of contract and fraud action).

13. See, e.g., The Treaty Between the United States and Canada on Mutual Legal Assistance in Criminal Matters, Mar. 18, 1985, 24 I.L.M. 1092.

subpoenas.[14] Moreover, although the Eleventh Circuit generally adheres to the view that discovery under Section 1782 requires that the information would be discoverable in the requesting country,[15] that court held that the treaty contained no such requirement and thus allowed subpoenas to issue in aid of a Canadian investigation even though no charges had been filed and similar subpoenas would not issue in Canada.

§ 12.9 The Hague Convention on the Taking of Evidence Abroad in Civil or Commercial Matters, which entered into force in the United States on October 7, 1972,[1] substantially reflects and therefore does not materially change American law and practice. It provides—in a manner similar to the Service of Documents Convention[2]—for the designation of a "Central Authority" in each contracting state which receives and executes "Letters of Request" but also permits the taking of evidence by diplomatic or consular officers of the requesting state of nationals of that state[3] and of nationals of the host state or of a third state, in the latter cases, however, subject to the approval of the host state.[4] The Convention contains one restriction with respect to American requests: Article 23 provides that a contracting party may declare "that it will not execute Letters of Request for the purpose of obtaining pre-trial discovery of documents as known in Common Law countries."[5] A number of Convention countries have made reservations pursuant to Article 23. In all but one the reservation extends to pretrial discovery attempts that seek

14. In re Commissioner's Subpoenas, United States of America, 325 F.3d 1287 (11th Cir. 2003).

15. See supra n. 10.

§ 12.9

1. 23 U.S.T. 2555, T.I.A.S. 7444, U.N.T.S. 231. It appears appended to 28 U.S.C.A. § 1781. As of June 2004, the Convention is in force in: Argentina, Australia, Barbados, Belarus, Bulgaria, China, Cyprus, Czech Republic, Denmark, Estonia, Finland, France, Germany, Israel, Italy, Kuwait, Latvia, Lithuania, Luxembourg, Mexico, Monaco, Netherlands, Norway, Poland, Portugal, Romania, Russian Federation, Seychelles, Singapore, Slovakia, Slovenia, South Africa, Spain, Sri Lanka, Sweden, Switzerland, Ukraine, United Kingdom (extended to Anguilla, Cayman Islands, Falkland Islands and dependencies, Gibraltar, Guernsey, Hong Kong, Isle of Man, Jersey, and the Sovereign Base Areas of Akrotiri and Dhekelia on the Island of Cyprus), United States (extended to Guam, Puerto Rico, and the Virgin Islands), and Venezuela. United States Dept. of State, Treaties in Force (Jan. 1, 1990). A tax claim is not "a civil or commercial matter" within the meaning of Convention: Re Anders Jahre, [1986] 1 Lloyds Rep. 496 (Court of Appeal), and comment by Mann, 102 Law Q. Rev. 505 (1986).

As in the case of the Hague Service Convention (supra § 12.7 n.1), the European Union also adopted more far-reaching rules for the taking of evidence in a member state for use in proceedings pending in another. EC Regulation No. 1206/2001, [2001] Official Journal L 174/1.

2. Supra § 12.7.

3. This provision may be declared inapplicable by contracting states, by means of an express reservation, at the time of signature, ratification, or accession. Art. 33.

4. Arts. 15–16. The requirement of prior approval may be waived: Art. 16, par. 2. See Prescott & Alley, Effective Evidence–Taking Under the Hague Convention, 22 Int'l Lawyer 939 (1988).

5. Insertion of this provision had been proposed by the United Kingdom. Working Document No. 62, Conference de La Haye de droit international privé, 4 Actes et documents de la Onzième session 171 (1970). The reason for the provision is that the "procedure [for pretrial discovery] varies widely among the various States and is not even uniform in all Common Law jurisdictions. Accordingly, some States may be quite prepared to accept letters for this purpose while other States may refuse them. Article 23 provides the machinery for the exercise of this option." Report by Ph. W. Amram, id. at 204.

unspecified documents and do not sufficiently substantiate the request, i.e. represent fishing expeditions.[6] In effect, these reservations continue prior practice. Germany goes further: its Article 23 reservation extends to *all* pretrial discovery requests. Given the importance of pretrial discovery in U.S. civil litigation, the Convention is therefore of limited value to U.S. litigants in respect of evidence that must be obtained in Germany.

Another question arises when documents or other evidence are located abroad, but the defendant is subject to the jurisdiction of the forum court: does the Convention provide the exclusive or at least primary remedy or may discovery be ordered in application of the usual state or federal rules? Lower court decisions were divided; some viewed the Convention as providing the primary procedure,[7] while others held that it was inapplicable, and therefore did not displace discovery procedures of domestic law, whenever there was proper jurisdiction over the defendant.[8] The U.S. Supreme Court rejected both views in *Societe Nationale Industrielle Aerospatiale v. United States District Court for Southern District of Iowa*.[9] It held that the Convention is applicable both to third parties and to litigants subject to the U.S. court's jurisdiction. However, the Convention does not displace the procedural rules of the forum; rather, it provides a parallel, optional procedure for obtaining evidence located abroad. The Court did take note of the importance of foreign interests and admonished trial courts to "exercise special vigilance to protect foreign litigants from the danger that unnecessary, or

---

6. See also In re Westinghouse Uranium Contract, [1978] A.C. 547. In that case, English companies were alleged to have participated in an international cartel of uranium and Westinghouse sought to obtain evidence in England through the use of letters of request, implicating participation by Rio Tinto Zinc Corporation in the cartel. The House of Lords was concerned that Westinghouse was merely on a "fishing expedition." Lord Wilberforce commented that, pursuant to Article 23 of the Hague Convention, the United Kingdom had in fact made a declaration that it would not execute letters of request for the purpose of pre-trial discovery of documents. Id. at 608. However, by interpreting the letters of request as specifying a particular schedule of documents, while blue penciling the words "or relating thereto," the House of Lords did not reject the letters of request as constituting an impermissible attempt at discovery. Id. at 611–612. For a critical view of American pretrial discovery in relation to the Hague Convention, see Stadler, Der Schutz des Unternehmensgeheimnisses im deutschen und U.S.-amerikanischen Zivilprozess und Rechtshilfeverfahren (1989) and rejoinder by Hay, Book Review, 103 Zeitschrift für Zivilprozess 511 (1990). For comparative treatment, see Hay, Informationsbeschaffung über schriftliche Unterlagen und Augenscheinsobjekte im Zivilprozess, in: Schlosser (ed.), Die Informationsbeschaffung für den Zivilprozess 1–61 (Vol. 8 of Veröffentlichungen der wissenschaftlichen Vereinigung für Internationales Verfahrensrecht, 1996).

Within the European Union, Regulation No. 1206/2001, supra n.1, is less restrictive. Art. 1(2) excludes requests to obtain "evidence which is not intended for use in judicial proceedings, commenced or intended."

7. E.g., Pierburg GmbH & Co. KG v. Superior Court of Los Angeles County, 137 Cal.App.3d 238, 186 Cal.Rptr. 876 (1982). For a view suggesting that the Convention provides an *exclusive* procedure and for a review of the early case law, see Comment, 132 U. Pa. L. Rev. 1461 (1984). For the position that the Convention should be used as a matter of first resort, see Maier, Extraterritorial Discovery: Cooperation, Coercion and the Hague Evidence Convention, 19 Vand. J. Transnat'l L. 239 (1986).

8. E.g., Laker Airways Ltd. v. Pan American World Airways, 103 F.R.D. 42, 48 (D.D.C.1984).

9. 482 U.S. 522, 107 S.Ct. 2542, 96 L.Ed.2d 461 (1987).

unduly burdensome, discovery may place them in a disadvantageous position."[10] However, the majority did not accept the dissenters' view that there should be a general presumption favoring the use of the Convention[11] nor thought that the existence of a foreign "blocking statute"[12] forbidding the production of evidence, without more, called for the use of the Convention.[13] Despite language suggesting that trial courts in their discretion give favorable consideration to the use of the Convention, the majority gave no specific guidance.[14] However, Justice Blackmun's carefully considered partial concurrence and partial dissent has proved persuasive to some lower courts and some have exercised their discretion to require first use of the Convention.[15] For the most part,

10. Id. at 546, 107 S.Ct. at 2557.

11. Id. at 568, 107 S.Ct. at 2568 (Blackmun J., concurring in part and dissenting in part). For a discussion of the post-*Aérospatiale* case law see Patrick J. Borchers, The Incredible Shrinking Hague Evidence Convention, 38 Tex. Int'l L.J. 73 (2003). The New Jersey state courts have, however, endorsed the "first use" approach as a matter of state law in implementing the convention. See id. at 83–84 (citing, inter alia, Husa v. Laboratoires Servier SA, 326 N.J.Super. 150, 740 A.2d 1092 (App. Div. 1999)).

12. See infra § 24.38 n.6 and § 25.42.

13. "It is well-settled that such statutes do not deprive an American court of the power to order a party subject to its jurisdiction to produce evidence even though the act of production may violate that statute.... Nor can the enactment of such a statute ... require American courts to engraft a rule of first resort onto the Hague Convention, or otherwise to provide the nationals of such a country with a preferred status in our courts. It is clear that American courts are not required to adhere blindly to the directives of such a statute." 482 U.S. at 544 n.29, 107 S.Ct. at 2556 n.29. Quoting from the Restatement, Third, of the Foreign Relations Law of the United States, § 442, Reporters's Note 5, at 359 (1987), the Court then added a conciliatory note: " ' On the other hand, the degree of friction created by discovery requests ... and the differing perceptions of the acceptability of American-style discovery under national and international law, suggest some efforts to moderate the application abroad of U.S. procedural techniques, consistent with the overall principle of reasonableness in the exercise of jurisdiction.' " Id.

14. 482 U.S. at 568, 107 S.Ct. at 2568 (Blackmun, J., concurring in part and dissenting in part).

In England, the parties may seek discovery only after the pleadings have defined the issues. Additionally, an English court does not have the power to order discovery against third parties. When evidence is located both in the United States and in the United Kingdom, and the dispute is brought before an English court, a party may therefore be tempted to gain a procedural advantage by invoking American discovery procedures. In order to have the parties conform to English practice, the English Court of Appeal has held that parties may apply to foreign courts for discovery of evidence for use in English proceedings only after first referring the request to the English court. South Carolina Insurance Co. v. Assurantie Maatshappij "De Zeven Provincien" NV and Others, [1985] 2 All.E.R. 1046 (C.A.).

For U.S.-German practice, see Junker, Discovery im deutsch-amerikanischen Rechtsverkehr (1987) and Stadler and Hay, both supra n.7. On occasion, German courts will in fact order acts to be done extraterritorially (as distinguished from the production of documents *in-state,* such as was involved in *Aerospatiale*). Thus, the German Supreme Court ordered an Italian to undergo a blood test in Italy for use in a paternity suit. BGH in 1986 NJW 2371. For comparative treatment in common law and continental practice, see Hay, supra n.6.

15. See, e.g., Umana v. SCM S.p.A., 291 A.D.2d 446, 737 N.Y.S.2d 556 (2002); Hudson v. Hermann Pfauter GmbH & Co., 117 F.R.D. 33 (N.D.N.Y.1987). For a discussion of the post-*Aérospatiale* case law see Borchers, supra n. 11. The New Jersey courts have adopted Justice Blackmun's approach as a matter of state law. See id. at 83–84 (citing, inter alia, Husa v. Laboratoires Servier SA, 326 N.J.Super. 150, 740 A.2d 1092 (App. Div. 1999)). For a comparative view and suggestions for accommodation of differences among legal systems, see Gerber, Extraterritorial Discovery and the Conflict of Procedural Systems: Germany and the United States, 34 Am. J. Comp. L. 745

however, lower courts have refused to require first resort to the Convention under the Supreme Court's comity analysis.[16]

The 1993 amendment to Federal Rule of Civil Procedure 28 refers to the possibility of foreign depositions under an international agreement. Rule 28(b) now lists as a possibility foreign depositions "pursuant to any applicable treaty or convention."[17] The Advisory Committee notes state that the purpose of the amendment is "to make effective us of the Hague Convention ... and of any similar treaties that the United States may enter into in the future...."[18] The amendment does not, however, appear to work any change in the principles adopted by the Supreme Court in the *Societe Nationale* case.[19]

IV. ADMISSIBILITY OF EVIDENCE: TESTIMONIAL PRIVILEGE

A. INTRODUCTION

§ 12.10   As a general rule, the law of the place of trial governs the admissibility of evidence.[1] Evidentiary rules concern the remedy for the enforcement of a right or claim and, for reasons of efficiency and convenience, are governed by the law of the place where suit is brought,[2] while rules, defining the right or claim may be governed by that law or by the law of another state. However, there are situations where the public policy of the state of the otherwise applicable substantive law may be so strong or where the law of the latter may have such an important

(1986). For a critical view of *Aerospatiale* see Bermann, The Hague Evidence Convention in the Supreme Court: A Critique of the *Aerospatiale* Decision, 63 Tul. L. Rev. 525 (1989).

For special rules applicable in the European Union, see supra nn. 1, 6.

16.   See Born & Hoing, Comity and the Lower Courts: Post-*Aerospatiale* Applications of the Hague Evidence Convention, 24 Int'l Lawyer 393 (1990). *But see* Reinsurance Co. of America, Inc. v. Administratia Asigurarilor de Stat, 902 F.2d 1275 (7th Cir.1990), affirming trial court's denial of request for post-judgment interrogatories against an insurance company wholly owned by the Romanian government because Romanian law, without exception, forbade compliance and no treaty for the resolution of insurance disputes exists between the United States and Romania (as distinguished from the situation in United States v. First National Bank of Chicago, 699 F.2d 341 (7th Cir.1983)). The Court relied on § 40 of Restatement, Second, Foreign Relations Law of the United States (1965) and on § 442 of the Restatement, Third (1987).

For an analogous decision see In re Grand Jury Proceedings, Yanagihara Grand Jury, 709 F.Supp. 192 (C.D.Cal.1989) (order directing California resident to sign consent directive to Swiss banking authorities for access to bank records did not violate international comity).

17.   F.R.C.P. 28(b)(1).

18.   1993 Advisory Committee Notes to F.R.C.P. 28.

19.   Id.

§ 12.10

1.   Restatement, Second, Conflict of Laws § 138 (1971). See also A Critical Examination of Some Evidentiary Privileges: A Symposium, 56 N.W. L. Rev. 206, 229 (1961). For comparative treatment, see D. Coester–Waltjen, Internationales Beweisrecht (1983).

2.   See Reese & Leiwant, Testimonial Privileges and Conflict of Laws, 41 Law & Contemp. Prob. 85, 89 (1977); Sterk, Testimonial Privileges: An Analysis of Horizontal Choice of Law Problems, 61 Minn. L. Rev. 461 (1977). For comparative treatment see D. Coester–Waltjen, Internationales Beweisrecht (1983).

bearing on the result of the litigation so as to "outweigh the inconvenience imposed upon the courts of the forum by requiring the application of the law of the locus."[3] Situations where public policy may dictate the application of an evidentiary rule other than that of the forum should be distinguished from situations where a rule phrased in evidentiary terms may in fact be a rule of substance.[4] In either instance, a law other than that of the forum law will be applied, but in the former circumstance the decision to apply another law is based on policy considerations that do not relate to the character of the claim. A situation which may call for the application of an evidentiary rule other than that of the forum is that of a privilege against the disclosure of confidential information.[5]

B. INTERSTATE CONFLICTS

§ 12.11   The claim of a testimonial privilege may involve the interests of three different states: (1) the state whose law governs the underlying claim, (2) the state which has the most significant relationship to the communication about which testimony is sought, and (3) the forum state.[1] Problems of assessing when the parties in one state court can invoke the privileges of another are not frequently discussed and relevant case law is sparse. The Second Restatement distinguishes between (a) communications privileged in the forum but not privileged in the state with the most significant relation with the communication and (b) communications not privileged in the forum but privileged in the state with the most significant relation with the communication.[2]

For the first situation the Second Restatement provides that, even if a communication would be privileged under the local law of the forum, evidence that is not privileged under the local law of the state which has the most significant relationship with the communication should be admitted in the forum.[3] Reliance is placed on *Levy v. Mutual Life Insurance Co.,*[4] which involved an action to recover on a life insurance

3. Morgan, Choice of Law Governing Proof, 58 Harv. L. Rev. 153, 158 (1944).

4. See Willitt v. Purvis, 276 F.2d 129 (5th Cir.1960) (where a rule governing admissibility of evidence of a decedent's dislike of a plaintiff-spouse or child for the purpose of reducing damages in a wrongful death claim was stated to be, in actuality, a rule relating to the measure of damages and therefore substantive).

5. See Restatement, Second, Conflict of Laws §§ 138, 139 (1971).

§ 12.11

1. Reese & Leiwant, Testimonial Privileges and Conflict of Laws, 41 Law & Contemp. Probs. 85, 91 (1977).

2. Restatement, Second, Conflict of Laws § 139 (1971).

3. Restatement, Second, Conflict of Laws § 139(1) (1971); Reese & Leiwant, supra n.1, at 93. In Mitsui & Co. (U.S.A.) Inc. v. Puerto Rico Water Resources Authority, 79 F.R.D. 72 (D.Puerto Rico 1978), the federal court in Puerto Rico declined to apply the forum's accountant-client privilege to depositions to be taken in New York (where the privilege did not exist) on the ground that New York had the greater interest in the application of its law. For the law applicable to privileges in diversity cases see also infra n.7.

4. 56 N.Y.S.2d 32 (1945). But see Wexler v. Metropolitan Life Insurance Co., 38 N.Y.S.2d 889 (N.Y.City Ct.1942). This case involved an action to recover indemnity benefits provided for in a policy for life insurance contracted for in New Hampshire. There was no provision in New Hampshire law for a patient-physician privilege. The court stated: "I believe that the testimony of these physicians as to matters

policy of which the plaintiffs were beneficiaries. The defendant insurance company had refused payment and sought rescission of the policy on the ground that the assured, in her application, had misrepresented her physical condition. The contract had been concluded in Georgia. In permitting the insurance company to examine the Georgia physicians, the court stressed that the assured had waived the right to assert any privilege and that such a waiver was allowed under the laws of Georgia. The effect of the waiver was that the communication was not privileged under the local law of the state with the most significant relationship with the communication (Georgia). While the communication may have been privileged according to the rules of the New York forum, New York was not the state with the most significant relationship with the communication.[5]

For the second situation noted above, the Second Restatement provides for the admission of a communication when it is not privileged in the forum or, if privileged, was not intended to protect a communication outside the state.[6] A decision in which the forum denied effect to a foreign privilege is *Abety v. Abety*.[7] As noted earlier, the forum state's

privileged under the laws of New York may not be taken by deposition in New Hampshire for use in the trial in New York. The public policy of this state does not permit the use of such evidence. The admissibility of this evidence is determined by the law of the forum.... The prohibition of the New York statute is a rule as to evidence or procedure and does not enter into the contract of insurance. The interpretation of the contract does not at all depend upon it. The rule affects the remedy and not the contract. In such cases, the law of the forum, and not the place of the contract, must govern." Id. at 890.

5. In the view of the Restatement, Second, the admission of this evidence would not defeat the expectations of the parties since the law on which they most likely relied was that of the state of most significant relationship to the communication. However, comment (c) to § 139 continues: "If this state [of the most significant relationship with the communication] has not chosen to make certain evidence privileged, its interests obviously will not be infringed if this evidence is admitted by the forum." The drafters apparently did not consider it important that the deceased in *Levy* had waived an existing privilege. The drafters thus equated the availability of a waiver procedure, when correctly utilized, with the case where the state with the most significant relationship to the communication has not chosen to make certain evidence privileged: "Admission of this evidence ... will usually be in the best interests of the forum state since such admission will assist the forum in arriving at the true facts and thus

making a correct disposition of the case." Ibid. The Second Restatement qualifies this approach by allowing countervailing considerations of strong forum policy to suppress admission of evidence even if the communication is not privileged, in the state with the most significant relationship with the communication. Cf. *Wexler*, 38 N.Y.S.2d 889.

6. Restatement, Second, Conflict of Laws, § 139(2) (1971). But see Reese & Leiwant, supra n.1, at 96: ("By creating a privilege the state of trial has made clear that it places a higher value on preserving the confidentiality of local communications than it does on arriving at the truth. Failure to recognize a foreign privilege based on the same values as those prevailing in the forum would ignore the value of seeking to accommodate conflicting interests and thus be antithetical to the needs of a multistate system.")

The Second Restatement itself qualifies the rule by stating that there may be "some special reason why the forum policy favoring admission should not be given effect." § 139(2). Such a reason may be that the other state is the state of the most significant relationship. Id., comment (d).

7. 10 N.J.Super. 287, 77 A.2d 291 (1950) (medical records and information, privileged in New York, not privileged in the forum). See also People v. Allen, 336 Ill. App.3d 457, 784 N.E.2d 393 (2003) (privilege not to admit results of blood test given by state in which the test was administered not given effect in forum where forum was

interest in deciding cases correctly should usually be dispositive of the issue of which evidence will be admitted. On the other hand, there may be important factors why the foreign privilege should be honored and the Second Restatement lists several.[8]

also the location of the underlying events and residence of all parties); Sterling Fin. Mgmt., L.P. v. UBS PaineWebber, 336 Ill. App.3d 442, 782 N.E.2d 895 (2002) (forum rule of admissibility applied over privilege of state with most significant relationship to the communications); Anas v. Blecker, 141 F.R.D. 530 (M.D.Fla.1992) (court applied Florida choice of law rules to admit evidence which would have been privileged in the state where the evidence was generated).

For purposes of federal diversity jurisdiction privileges have been considered to be outcome-determinative and thus governed by state law: United Coal Cos. v. Powell Const. Co., 839 F.2d 958 (3d Cir.1988); Independent Petrochemical Corp. v. Aetna Casualty and Surety Co., 117 F.R.D. 292 (D.D.C.1987); Union Planters National Bank v. ABC Records, Inc., 82 F.R.D. 472 (W.D.Tenn.1979). In application of the *Erie/Klaxon* doctrine, supra §§ 3.36 et seq., the federal court should apply the law of the state in which it sits, including that state's conflicts law, to determine whether a privilege may be invoked. Newton v. National Broadcasting Co., Inc., 109 F.R.D. 522 (D.Nev.1985). However, in Mitsui & Co. (U.S.A.) Inc. v. Puerto Rico Water Resources Authority, 79 F.R.D. 72 (D.Puerto Rico 1978), the court did not apply forum law (granting a privilege) but the law of the deposition state, New York, which did not recognize the privilege. The court reached this result primarily on the basis of interest analysis. Id. at 76–78. Although contradicting an earlier statement that Puerto Rico's "grouping of contacts" approach would lead to the application of Puerto Rican law (id. at 77 n.6), the court also concluded that its result was consistent with "Puerto Rico's approach to ... conflict of laws problems" and that "to impose Puerto Rico's privilege law to this communication would constitute an unconstitutional exercise of legislative power" (id. at 79). The court's independent determination of the applicable state law relating to privilege is at variance with the U.S. Supreme Court's decision in Day & Zimmermann v. Challoner, 423 U.S. 3, 96 S.Ct. 167, 46 L.Ed.2d 3 (1975), on remand 546 F.2d 26 (5th Cir.1977). The constitutional basis for the decision is still in doubt. See Schreiber v. Allis–Chalmers Corp., 448 F.Supp. 1079 (D.Kan.1978), rev'd 611 F.2d

790 (10th Cir.1979). For discussion of the application of state law in federal courts generally see supra § 3.36 et seq. See also Note, Privilege in Federal Diversity Cases, 10 Nat. Res. J. 861 (1970); Note, The Federal Rules of Evidence: Rule 501, Klaxon and the Constitution, 5 Hofstra L. Rev. 21 (1976). In contrast, federal law applies in federal question cases even if pendent claims under state law are involved: Wm. T. Thompson Co. v. General Nutrition Corp., Inc., 671 F.2d 100 (3d Cir.1982).

In a federal criminal trial the availability of any privilege is "governed by the principles of the common law as they may be interpreted by the courts of the United States in the light of reason and experience." Federal Rule of Evidence 501. For an extensive discussion of the marital communications privilege see United States v. Byrd, 750 F.2d 585 (7th Cir.1984), holding that communications made during a permanent separation are not privileged. For further discussion of Rule 501 see also In re Production of Records to Grand Jury, 618 F.Supp. 440 (D.Mass.1985).

8. Restatement, Second, Conflict of Laws § 139 (1971), cmnt. (d) states: "Among the factors that the forum will consider in determining whether or not to admit evidence are (1) the number and nature of the contacts that the state of the forum has with the parties and with the transaction involved, (2) the relative materiality of the evidence that is sought to be excluded, (3) the kind of privilege involved and (4) fairness to the parties." Of these, the first factor also includes the reliance that parties may have placed on the existence of a privilege, and the third suggests that effect should be given to a similar, albeit not identical, privilege of the other jurisdiction. The last criterion, fairness to the parties, is undefined and vague. See also Cepeda v. Cohane, 233 F.Supp. 465, 470 (S.D.N.Y.1964): "[T]he general rule that the law of the place of trial governs must give way to a public policy of the place of deposition, when the place of deposition has enunciated a strong public policy in favor of creating a privilege." See also Samuelson v. Susen, 576 F.2d 546 (3d Cir.1978), affirming Pennsylvania federal district court's application of Ohio law (conferring a privilege) as the law of the state of the most significant relationship.

§ 12.12 The previous discussion concerned only the forum state and the state which has the most significant relationship to the communication about which testimony is sought. However, as mentioned initially, the claim of a testimonial privilege may involve three states: the forum and the states with the most significant relationship to the substantive claim and to the communication, respectively. No court, so far as is known, has made specific mention as to what interests a third state, whose law may govern the underlying claim, has in considering whether to afford recognition of a privilege.[1] Presumably a forum court will consider that state's interest in following the choice of law approach of the Second Restatement. An indication that it should do so is suggested by the provision of § 139(2) that "special reasons" may be considered why a forum policy favoring admission should not be given effect. Interests of a third state, whose law may govern the underlying claim, must be assessed by the forum state when the forum determines the number and nature of contacts that it has with the practice and the transaction involved. Similarly, where testimony is sought by deposition in a third state, the greater the interest of the deposition state is in the parties to a communication the greater should be the deference that should be accorded to a privilege provided by its law.[2]

In any event, it should be clear that while testimonial privileges may be considered rules of evidence they are not necessarily rules respecting only the remedy. Where contacts are diverse, policy considerations of interested states should be looked to for guidance.[3]

C. INTERNATIONAL CONFLICTS

§ 12.13 Where evidence of a communication is sought from a witness residing abroad, provisions of the Hague Convention on the Taking of Evidence Abroad in Civil or Commercial Matters may be applicable.[1] The Convention recognizes the use of letters of request, the

---

§ 12.12

1. In Price v. Howard Cty. Gen. Hosp., 950 F.Supp. 141 (D.Md.1996), amended 1997 WL 873830 (D.Md.1997), the court stated that any state law privileges and the interests they protect must be protected to the extent that those interests do not conflict with federal privilege law. The court did not restrict this protection to the state with the strongest connection to the communication; thus it presumably also embraces the state with the strongest connection to the claim. The court does not identify any particular types of interests. In any event, the protection accorded state interest is subordinate the federal privilege law.

2. See generally Reese & Leiwant, Testimonial Privileges and Conflict of Laws, 41 Law & Contemp. Probs. 85, 85 (1977).

3. See also Webster v. Sun Co., Inc., 790 F.2d 157 (D.C.Cir.1986) (common-law privilege for communications to legislature governed by law of District of Columbia where memorandum was prepared and published; District's interest was more substantial than other jurisdictions').

§ 12.13

1. Hague Convention on the Taking of Evidence Abroad in Civil or Commercial Matters, March 18, 1970, 23 U.S.T. 2555, T.I.A.S. No. 7444, 847 U.N.T.S. 231. Text also in 28 U.S.C.A. § 1781, Notes [hereinafter cited as Convention]. For background see also Report of the U.S. Delegation on the Evidence Convention, 8 I.L.M. 804 (1969); Born & Hoing, Comity and the Lower Courts: Post Aerospatiale Applications of the Hague Evidence Convention, 24 Int'l Law 393 (1990). See also supra § 12.9.

technique used in the civil law,[2] as the principal means of obtaining evidence abroad.[3] Under the provisions of the Convention a letter of request should specify, *inter alia,* whether there is any requirement that evidence is to be given on oath or affirmation,[4] and whether any special method or procedure is to be followed.[5] However, measures of compulsion appropriate in the state of execution will apply to the same extent as are provided by its internal law for the execution of orders issued by the authorities of its own country or of requests made by parties in internal proceedings.[6]

Article 11 of the Convention unconditionally entitles the witness to claim all the privileges available under the domestic law of the state of execution.[7] In addition, a witness may claim all the privileges available under the domestic law of the state of request if the privileges are set forth in the letter of request,[8] or are otherwise brought to the attention of the executing authority by the issuing authority.[9]

A related question is whether a party to a United States proceeding can successfully invoke his Fifth Amendment privilege against self incrimination because of a reasonable fear of foreign prosecution on the basis of his testimony. The Supreme Court's answer to this question is negative. In *United States v. Balsys,*[10] the defendant was a resident alien subpoenaed to testify as to his wartime activities between 1940 and 1944. The government suspected the defendant of having engaged in

---

2. Letters of request issue when a court of one country requests another country, acting through its own courts and by the methods of court procedure of that country, to take the testimony of a witness residing in that foreign country. See generally, Weeks, A Treatise on the Law of Depositions (1880), p. 148, § 128. See also Orlich v. Helm Brothers, Inc., 160 A.D.2d 135, 560 N.Y.S.2d 10 (1990).

3. See Convention, Art. 1. See also Amram, U.S. Ratification of the Hague Convention on the Taking of Evidence Abroad, 67 Am. J. Int'l L. 104, 105 (1973).

4. Convention, Art. 3(h).

5. Convention, Arts. 3(i), 9.

6. Convention, Art. 10. For example, if a court in the United States were the court requested to examine a witness and the witness refused to testify, the court could order the witness to testify and enforce that order through its contempt powers to the same extent as in a domestic proceeding.

7. For instance, if the United States were the State of execution of a letter of request issued by another country, a witness would be allowed to claim the privilege against self-incrimination under the Fifth Amendment to the U.S. Constitution.

8. See Convention, Art. 3. But see Appeal Enterprises Ltd. et al. v. First Nat'l Bank of Chicago, 10 D.L.R. (4th) 317 (1984)

(Ct. App. Ontario): letters rogatory issued by Chicago federal court requiring accountant to testify may be given effect in Canada even though accountants enjoy testimonial privilege in the state of issue.

9. See In re Westinghouse Uranium Contract [1978] A.C. 547: the House of Lords concluded that since a United States District Court had upheld and communicated to the House of Lords the right of an individual witness to claim the privilege against self-incrimination under the Fifth Amendment to the United States Constitution, the witness could not be compelled to give evidence in England. Production of certain documents in this case might have exposed the English companies to liability under Arts. 85, 189, and 192 of the European Economic Community Treaty. See also Dicey & Morris, Conflict of Laws 211–12 (13th ed. by Collins et al. 2000). Because most American courts do not consider the Convention to be the exclusive or even the primary avenue for the taking of evidence abroad, resort to discovery under the Federal Rules of Civil Procedure may conflict with testimonial privileges under foreign law and may possibly invite retaliatory or blocking measures. See supra § 12.9 nn.11 et seq.

10. 524 U.S. 666, 118 S.Ct. 2218, 141 L.Ed.2d 575 (1998).

Nazi persecution and having concealed this information on his application for an immigrant visa. When subpoenaed to testify he claimed the privilege against self-incrimination stating that he feared prosecution by Lithuania (his former home) and Israel if forced to answer. The Supreme Court, however, ordered the subpoena enforced and the objection overruled on the grounds that a foreign criminal proceeding is not a "criminal case" within the meaning of the Fifth Amendment.

D. THE INTERSTATE AND CONVENTION APPROACHES COMPARED

§ 12.14 In the interstate setting, a jurisdiction may be concerned with a privileged communication if it is the state whose law governs the underlying claim, if it is the state which has the most significant relationship to the communication about which testimony is sought, or if it is the forum state.[1] Analogously, a jurisdiction in the international setting may be concerned with a privileged communication for one or more of the following reasons. It may be the state of execution of a letter of request (E) it may be the state which has the most significant relationship with the communication (C); or it may be the forum state (F).[2] These shorthand designations are useful for a comparison of how privileged communications are handled in the interstate setting (following the Second Restatement's rules) and internationally (under the Convention).

The following situations may serve as illustrations: First, the forum state (F) recognizes a privilege not recognized in the state which has the most significant relationship with the communication (C). Under the rules of the Second Restatement, evidence of a communication that is not privileged under C's law will be admitted in F even though the communication would have been privileged in F.[3] Similarly, under the Convention, where F is a state court in the United States or a federal court sitting in diversity and where C is also the state of execution (E), a witness in C would not be able to claim a privilege recognized in F, unless F's privilege has been confirmed to C in the letter of request.[4] Thus, both the Second Restatement and the Convention obtain the same result for analogous cases. For the exceptional case that F should have a strong public policy against admission of the evidence, the Second

---

§ 12.14

1. See supra § 12.11 n.1.

2. The shorthand designations have their origins in Weinstein, Recognition in the United States of the Privileges of Another Jurisdiction, 56 Colum. L. Rev. 535 (1956).

3. F's recognition of the privilege and concomitant exclusion of the testimony could be justified on the public policy ground that confidential information should not be revealed to a greater extent than

determined by F to be fair. See Weinstein, supra n.2, at 544. On the other hand, "the state which has the most significant relationship with the communication has a substantial interest in determining whether evidence of the communication should be privileged." Restatement, Second, Conflict of Laws, § 139, cmnt. (d) (1971). This result also comports with the probable expectation of the parties. See Reese & Leiwant, Testimonial Privileges and Conflict of Laws, 41 Law & Contemp. Probs. 85, 93 (1977).

4. See Convention, Art. 3.

Restatement provides that the evidence would not be admitted.[5] The same result could be achieved under the Convention by confirming the privilege to the requested authority.[6]

Second, in the case where a privilege is not recognized in F but is recognized in C, the Second Restatement provides for the admission of the evidence in F unless there is some special reason why the forum policy should not be given effect.[7] In this situation the Convention provides that, since C is also the state of execution (E), the witness would have the right to invoke E's privilege.[8] Again, however, a different result might obtain and the communication not admitted into evidence under the Second Restatement if there exist strong countervailing considerations.[9] In an appropriate case it may well be that the international nature of the particular case or request is a sufficient countervailing consideration so as to outweigh the usual forum policy of non-recognition.[10]

Finally, a witness may wish to invoke a privilege provided by the law of a third state. The Convention provides that a Contracting State may specify, by declaration, that it will respect duties and privileges existing under the law of states other than the state of origin and the state of execution.[11] The United States has not made such a declaration, thus leaving open the status of "third state" privileges. Since it is the law of the state executing the letter which governs the methods and procedures of execution, unless the Convention provides otherwise,[12] the solution of this question rests with the court which executes a letter of request.

V. PROOF OF FOREIGN LAW[1]

A. THE FACT APPROACH TO FOREIGN LAW

1. *The Common Law Background*

§ 12.15 "Law," in a strict territorial sense, comprises only the legal norms (statutory and decisional) that have binding force in the

---

5. Restatement, Second, Conflict of Laws § 139(1) and cmnt. (c) (1971).

6. Convention, Art. 11(b).

7. Restatement, Second, Conflict of Laws § 139(2) (1971).

8. Convention, Art. 11(a).

9. Restatement, Second, Conflict of Laws § 139(2) (1971).

10. Cf. In re Westinghouse Uranium Contract, [1978] A.C. 547. In this case, after the letters of request had been transmitted to England pursuant to civil proceedings in the United States, the United States Department of Justice intervened in an attempt to use any evidence so obtained for purposes of a grand jury investigation. The English tribunal could have denied the request simply on the ground that the Hague

Convention contemplates transmittal of evidence only for civil cases and not for criminal investigation. The House of Lords, however, went further: to allow the evidence to be used for grand jury investigations into alleged violations of U.S. antitrust laws constitutes an infringement of United Kingdom sovereignty.

11. See Convention, Art. 11.

12. Convention, Art. 9.

§ 12.15

1. See generally Reynolds, What Happens When Parties Fail to Prove Foreign Law?, 48 Mercer L. Rev. 775 (1997); Sass, Foreign Law in Federal Courts, 29 Am. J. Comp. L. 97 (1981); Sprankling & Lanyi, Pleading and Proof of Foreign Law in

court's own territory. A court, in this view, can only apply its own law. Foreign "law" thus is not "law," but, in situations having a requisite foreign connection, as determined by local law, constitutes a "fact" like any other fact of the case.

In Anglo–American law, this view can be traced to a decision by Lord Mansfield in 1774;[2] it was adopted by Chief Justice Marshall in 1804.[3] It extended both to foreign-country law and to the law of sister states, with the result that courts would not take judicial notice of either.[4] It was still reflected in §§ 621–622 of the First Restatement which merely provided for a presumption of identity of another state's *common law* with the *common law* of the forum. As a consequence of the fact-approach to foreign law, a party relying on foreign law had to plead and prove it in accordance with the rules of evidence (including examination and cross-examination of witnesses[5]), the issue would be decided by the trier of fact, often the jury, and the resulting decision, as a factual determination, would not be reviewable on appeal:[6] "a ... burdensome, inconvenient ... [and] absurd method of ascertaining foreign law."[7]

The situation was alleviated in some states by judicial decisions extending judicial notice to sister state (but not to foreign country) law.[8] In a great many other cases, in which foreign law was in issue but insufficiently proved or not at all, courts engaged in a presumption of identity with forum law.[9] Logically, the presumption should be limited to

American Courts, 19 Stan. J. Int'l L. 3 (1983); Wing, Pleading and Proof of Foreign Law in American Courts, A Selected Annotated Bibliography, 19 Stan. J. Int'l L. 175 (1983); Merryman, Foreign Law as a Problem, 19 Stan. J. Int'l L. 151 (1983); Note, Failure to Prove Foreign Law in U.S. Courts, 5 Ariz. J. Int'l L. & Comp. L. 228 (1988); Schlesinger, A Recurrent Problem in Transnational Litigation: The Effect and Failure to Invoke and Prove the Applicable Foreign Law, 59 Cornell L. Rev. 1 (1973); Sass, Foreign Law in Civil Litigation: A Comparative Study, 16 Am. J. Comp. L. 332 (1968); Hay, Die Anwendung ausländischen Rechts im internationalen Privatrecht: Vereinigte Staaten von Amerika, in: 10 Materialien zum ausländischen und internationalen Privatrecht 102 (1968); Miller, Federal Rule 44.1 and the "Fact" Approach to Determining Foreign Law—Death Knell for a Die–Hard Doctrine, 65 Mich. L. Rev. 615 (1967); Currie, On the Displacement of the Law of the Forum, 58 Colum. L. Rev. 964 (1958). See also Jefferies, Recognition of Foreign Law by American Courts, 35 Cinn. L. Rev. 578 (1966); Hay, International versus Interstate Conflicts Law in the United States, 35 Rabels Zeitschrift 429, 445–47 (1971); Alexander, The Application and Avoidance of Foreign Law in the Law of Conflicts, 70 Nw. L. Rev. 602 (1975); Symposium on Proof of Foreign and Interna-

tional Law, 18 Va. J. Int'l L. 609–751 (1978).

2. Mostyn v. Fabrigas, [1775] 1 Cowp. 161, 174.

3. Church v. Hubbart, 6 U.S. (2 Cranch) 187, 236, 2 L.Ed. 249 (1804).

4. Cf. Cox v. Morrow, 14 Ark. 603, 610 (1854).

5. See J. Wigmore, Evidence §§ 564–66, 690 (3d ed. 1940).

6. In addition, a mistake in the determination of foreign law would be a mistake of fact, and not of law, and arguably could give rise to a claim for unjust enrichment. Cf. Restatement, Restitution § 46(c) (1937).

7. R. Cramton, D. Currie & H. Kay, Conflict of Laws—Cases, Comments, Questions 53 (4th ed. 1987).

8. See, e.g., Choate v. Ransom, 74 Nev. 100, 323 P.2d 700 (1958); Prudential Insurance Co. of America v. O'Grady, 97 Ariz. 9, 396 P.2d 246 (1964); National Transportation Co. v. J.E. Faltin Motor Transportation Co., 109 N.H. 446, 255 A.2d 606 (1969); White v. White, 94 Idaho 26, 480 P.2d 872 (1971) (dictum).

9. See Restatement, First, Conflict of Laws §§ 621–22 (1934). Older cases are collected in 75 A.L.R.2d 529 (1961). Cases

the common law of sister states, possibly extending as far as statutory law of sister states[10] and the law of foreign legal systems based on the common law.[11] Thus, many decisions refused to extend the presumption to the law of civil law systems,[12] but others extended the presumption to virtually all foreign law,[13] even to the point of assuming that California's community property law was the same as the law prevailing in China.[14] The approach of the last group of cases blends into, and becomes indistinguishable from, the application of forum law to cases with foreign elements for which the applicable foreign law was not pleaded or proved on the ground that the parties are presumed to have chosen the local law by acquiescence.[15] To the extent that the local law is unconnected with the transaction, a fact which may preclude its express choice by the parties,[16] this result is analytically incorrect although it does serve the practical and desirable purpose of avoiding the necessity to dismiss the plaintiff's action for failure to prove an essential fact (the foreign law) of

involving foreign-country law include: Adamsen v. Adamsen, 151 Conn. 172, 195 A.2d 418 (1963) (Norwegian child custody laws); San Rafael Compania Naviera, S.A. v. American Smelting and Refining Co., 327 F.2d 581 (9th Cir.1964) (Peruvian contract law); Schacht v. Schacht, 435 S.W.2d 197 (Tex.Civ.App.1968) (Mexican divorce law); Enterprises and Contracting Co. v. Plicoflex, Inc., 529 S.W.2d 805 (Tex.Civ.App. 1975) (adequacy of service under Lebanese law); Stein v. Siegel, 50 A.D.2d 916, 377 N.Y.S.2d 580 (1975) (Austrian tort law); Noble v. Noble, 26 Ariz.App. 89, 546 P.2d 358 (1976) (parties' rights, in divorce action, to real estate located in Denmark); Maple v. Maple, 566 P.2d 1229 (Utah 1977) (Thai marriage law); Tallant v. State of Texas, 658 S.W.2d 828 (Tex.App.1983) (Mexican family law); Belanger v. Keydril Co., 596 F.Supp. 823 (E.D.La.1984), decision affirmed 772 F.2d 902 (5th Cir.1985) (age discrimination claim arising from alleged wrongful discharge in Zaire governed by Louisiana law in the absence of a showing that Zaire law differed). A case involving sister-state law is Jacobsen v. Bunker, 699 P.2d 1208 (Utah 1985) (California law). See also Rogers v. Grimaldi, 875 F.2d 994, 1003 (2d Cir.1989) ("We believe that New York courts would, as a matter of substantive interpretation, presume that the unsettled common law of another state would resemble New York's but that they would examine the law of the other jurisdiction and that of other states, as well as their own, in making an ultimate determination as to the likely future content of the other jurisdiction's law.").

10. See Ethridge v. Sullivan, 245 S.W.2d 1015 (Tex.Civ.App.1951); Fowler v. Fowler, 96 N.H. 494, 79 A.2d 24 (1951); Riffe v. Magushi, 859 F.Supp. 220 (S.D.W.Va.1994).

11. 1700 Ocean Avenue Corp. v. GBR Associates, 354 F.2d 993 (9th Cir.1965) (Canadian law). Cf. Reisig v. Associated Jewish Charities, 182 Md. 432, 34 A.2d 842 (1943) (on the basis of statutory authorization, court took judicial notice of Palestinian law since it was based on the "Common Law of England").

12. See, e.g., Western Union Telegraph Co. v. Way, 83 Ala. 542, 4 So. 844 (1887) (German law).

13. See, e.g., Tortuguero Logging Operation, Limited v. Houston, 349 S.W.2d 315 (Tex.Civ.App.1961), error refused n.r.e. (Costa Rica) and the cases cited supra n.9.

14. Louknitsky v. Louknitsky, 123 Cal. App.2d 406, 266 P.2d 910 (1954).

15. See Beverly Hills National Bank and Trust Co. v. Compania De Navegacione Almirante S.A., Panama, 437 F.2d 301, 307 (9th Cir.1971), cert. denied 402 U.S. 996, 91 S.Ct. 2173, 29 L.Ed.2d 161 (1971); Vulcanized Rubber and Plastics Co. v. Scheckter, 400 Pa. 405, 162 A.2d 400, 403 n.2 (1960).

16. See infra §§ 18.8–18.12 for discussion of the limitation on choice of law by the parties. In general, however, these limitations have been applied only to invalidate the choice of an unconnected foreign law which was sought to displace otherwise applicable forum law. The underlying logic—that parties should generally not be permitted to displace an applicable law by the choice of an unconnected law—usually does not prevent the application of the (equally unconnected) law of the forum. See infra § 12.19 nn.5, 10.

the case.[17] Section 12.19 will return to the use of presumptions and the consequences of failure to establish the applicable foreign law.

Statutory changes in the United States have modified the common law rule in many states and most particularly in the federal courts, in many instances moving closer to the intermediate foreign practice which regards foreign law as law and calls for its ascertainment by the court with the assistance of the parties. Subsequent sections detail these changes.

2. Other Legal Systems

§ 12.16 English law,[1] with some exceptions,[2] also follows the fact approach, as does France, but in more limited form.[3] On the other hand, most continental states,[4] as well as the states of the Russian Federation (as successor to the USSR)[5] and Latin American countries[6] have long held the view that foreign law is "law." In some instances this results in the rule that the court must ascertain the foreign law *ex officio,* even without the help of the parties, in accordance with the Roman law maxim *"iura novit curia."*[7] In others, parties may have the obligation to give assistance to the court.[8]

---

17. Walton v. Arabian American Oil Co., 233 F.2d 541 (2d Cir.1956), cert. denied 352 U.S. 872, 77 S.Ct. 97, 1 L.Ed.2d 77 (1956) (discussed infra § 12.19 nn.11 et seq.).

§ 12.16

1. Dicey & Morris, The Conflict of Laws 221–32. (13th ed. by Collins et al. 2000); Schmitthoff, Die Anwendung ausländischen Rechts im internationalen Privatrecht: England, 10 Materialien zum ausländischen und internationalen Privatrecht 88 (1968).

2. E.g., with respect to the law of Scotland (regarded as law and subject to judicial notice): Lord Macmillan in Elliot v. Lord Joicey, [1935] A.C. 209, 236. By statute, English courts may address requests to Commonwealth countries for opinions on the law applicable to cases pending before the former. Schmitthoff, supra n.1, at 95.

3. See Battifol/Lagarde, Traité de droit international privé s. 324 (Vol. 1, 8th ed. 1993); Audit, Droit International Privé s. 251 (1991); I. Zatjay, Zur Stellung des ausländischen Rechts im französischen internationalen Privatrecht (1963); Zatjay, Die Anwendung ausländischen Rechts im internationalen Privatrecht: Frankreich,10 Materialien zum ausländischen und internationalen Privatrecht 15, 17 (1968).

4. Kegel, General Report: Die Ermittlung ausländischen Rechts, 10 Materialien zum ausländischen und internationalen Privatrecht 157, 163–64 (1968).

5. Id. at 163–64. See also Art. 1228, Draft Civil Code of the Russian Federation (Tent. Draft 1998).

6. Kegel, supra n.4, at 162; Samtleben, id. at 57 et seq. See also Art. 2 of the Protocol to the Treaty of Montevideo and Arts. 408–413 of the Codigo Bustamente.

7. See, e.g., §§ 3–4 of the *Austrian* Federal Statute on Private International Law, Bundesgesetzblatt 1978, No. 304; § 293 of the *German* Code of Civil Procedure (ZPO); Art. 14(1) of the *Italian* Statute on the Reform of Provisions Respecting Private International Law of 1995, Suppl. ord. n.68 alla Gazzetta Ufficiale no. 128, June 3, 1995; Art. 16 of the *Swiss* Federal Statute on Private International Law of 1987 (entered into force 1989), Bundesblatt 1988, I, 5; Kegel, supra n.4, at 159. In these countries, courts will usually seek the assistance (in the form of "opinions") of foreign law experts, especially of the Institutes of Foreign and Comparative Law at the universities. The cost of these opinions is charged to the parties as part of court costs. For a comparative review see M. Keller & K. Siehr, Allgemeine Lehren des internationalen Privatrechts 495 et seq. (1986). For commentary in the context of *German* law, with reference to U.S. practice, see Hay & Hampe, Nichtermittelbarkeit ausländischen Rechts und Forum Non Conveniens, Recht der Internationalen Wirtschaft 760 (1998). For Swiss law, see K. Siehr, Das Internationale Privatrecht der Schweiz (2002).

See also the European Convention on Information on Foreign Law, European Treaty Series No. 117 (1969), as of 1997 in force in: Austria, Belgium, Bulgaria, Costa Rica, Cyprus, Denmark, Estonia, Federal Repub-

---

8. See p. 547.

B. STATE STATUTES AND UNIFORM LAWS

§ 12.17 Most states have adopted statutes providing for mandatory judicial notice of foreign law.[1] In most[2] the rule also extends to foreign-country law. Especially with respect to the latter, however, "judicial notice" does not mean that the parties are freed from the task of assisting the court, for instance by providing[3] references[4] to foreign statutory or decisional law or by adducing expert testimony.[5]

lic of Germany, Finland, France, Greece, Great Britain, Hungary, Iceland, Italy, Liechtenstein, Lithuania, Luxembourg, Malta, Netherlands, Norway, Poland, Portugal, Rumania, Russian Federation, Slovakia, Spain, Sweden, Switzerland, Turkey, Ukrainia. Under the Convention, judicial authorities of contracting states may request information on the law and procedure of another contracting state by transmitting a request, containing a statement of the nature of the case and the details as to the information sought, to the designated national liaison office of the other contracting state.

8. Kegel, supra n.4, at 166 et seq.

§ 12.17

1. See, e.g., Arkansas: ACA § 16–40–14; California: Cal. Evid. Code § 452; Colorado: C.R.S.A.   § 13–25–106;   Connecticut: C.G.S.A. § 52–163(a); Delaware: D.R.E. Rule 202; Florida: West's F.S.A. § 90.202; Georgia: O.C.G.A. § 24–1–4; Hawaii: HRS Rules of Evid. Rule 202 § 626–1(b); Idaho: Idaho Rules of Civ. Pro., Rule 44(d); Illinois: 735 ILCS 5/8–1003; Indiana: I.C. § 34–3–2–1; Kansas: Rules of Evid., K.S.A. § 60–409; Louisiana: L.S.A. C.E. Art. 202; Maine: 16 M.R.S.A. § 402; Maryland: Md. Cts & Jud Pro. § 10–501; Massachusetts: M.G.L.A.233 § 70; Michigan: MRE 202; Minnesota: MSA § 599.04; Mississippi: Ms St § 13–1–149; Missouri: VAMS § 509.202; Montana: MCA T. 26, Ch.10, Mont. Rules of Evid., Rule 202; Nebraska: Neb. Rev. St. § 25–12, 101; Nevada: N.R.S. 47.140; New Hampshire: NH St. Rev. Rule 201; New Jersey: NJRE 201; New Mexico: SCRA 1986, Rule 1–044; New York: McKinney's Statutes § 352; North Carolina: NC St. § 8–4; North Dakota: NDCC 31–10–03; Ohio: Ohio Civ. R. Rule 44.1; Oklahoma: 12 Okla. St. Ann. § 2201; Oregon: Or. St. § 40.090; Pennsylvania: 42 Pa. C.S.A. § 5327; Rhode Island: Gen. Laws 1956, § 9–19–3; South Carolina: Code 1976 § 19–3–120; South Dakota: SDCL § 19–8–1; Tennessee: Rules of Evid., Rule 202; Texas: Rules of Civil Evidence, Rule 203; Vermont:

Rules Civ. Proc. Rule 44.1; Washington: RCWA § 5.24.010; West Virginia: WV ST. § 57–1–4; Wisconsin: W.S.A. § 902.02; Wyoming: Wyo. Stat. § 1–12–301.

2. See, e.g., California: West's Cal. Evid. Code § 452(f); Florida: West's F.S.A. § 90.202; Georgia: O.C.G.A. § 24–1–4; Hawaii: HI St. § 621–1, Rule 202(c)(5); Indiana: In. St. Trial P. Rule 44.1; Kansas: Rules of Evid., K.S.A. sec. 60–409; Louisiana: LA C.E. Art. 202; Maryland: Md. Cts. & Jud. Pro. § 10–501; Massachusetts: M.G.L.A. 233 § 70; Michigan: M.R.E. 202; Mississippi: Ms. St. sec. 13–1–149; Montana: MCA T. 26, Ch. 10, Mont. Rules of Evid., Rule 202; Nevada: N.R.S. 47.140; New Jersey: N.J.R.E. 201; New Mexico: SCRA 1986, Rule 1–044 ; New York: McKinney's Statutes sec. 352; North Carolina: N.C.G.S. sec. 8–4; Ohio: Civ. P. Rule 44.1; Oklahoma: 12 Okla. St. Ann. sec. 2201; Oregon: Or. St. § 40.090; Pennsylvania: 42 Pa. C.S.A. § 5327; Tennessee: Rules of Evid., Rule 202; Texas: Rules of Civil Evidence, Rule 203; Vermont: Rules Civ. Proc., Rule 44.1; West Virginia: WV St. § 57–1–4; Wyoming: W.S. 1977 § 1–12–301.

3. For example, Florida provides that judicial notice of foreign state or country law is mandatory only when the law is brought to the attention of the court by the party relying on it. Fla. Stat. Ann. § 90.203. But see Cunningham v. Brown, 51 N.C.App. 264, 276 S.E.2d 718 (1981), appeal after remand 62 N.C.App. 239, 302 S.E.2d 822 (1983), review denied 308 N.C. 675, 304 S.E.2d 754 (1983).

4. A general reference to the law of a foreign jurisdiction is typically not sufficient. In one case, for example, the court held that the relying party must "supply the court with a clear understanding" of the foreign law and provide authoritative sources. Ritcher v. Childers, 2 Conn.App. 315, 478 A.2d 613, 615 (1984).

5. In re Hua, Child of Baker, 62 Ohio St.2d 227, 405 N.E.2d 255 (1980) (expert

Roughly half the states adopted the Uniform Judicial Notice of Foreign Law Act,[6] originally proposed in 1936. The Act requires the forum to take judicial notice of sister state law, but not of foreign-country law. It provides in § 5 that foreign law shall be an issue *for the court,* but otherwise retains the common law requirement of pleading and proof, including observance of the rules of evidence.[7] In at least two states, Maryland[8] and New Jersey,[9] the Act was modified to provide for judicial notice of foreign country law as well. The New Jersey provision is the more far-reaching by providing for mandatory judicial notice if foreign law was pleaded and judicial notice requested.[10] In this regard, it resembles the earlier New York law.[11]

The Uniform Judicial Notice of Foreign Law Act was replaced in 1962 by the Uniform Interstate and International Procedure Act.[12] It requires that a party intending to rely on foreign law (without distinction between sister-state and foreign-country law) give notice in the pleadings or "other reasonable written notice" (§ 4.01), provides that the issue of foreign law is one for the court, "not jury" (§ 4.03), permits the court to "consider any relevant material or source, including testimony, whether or not submitted by a party or admissible under the rules

testimony establishing Vietnamese law). For nn.4–6 see also N.Y. Civ. Prac. L. & R. § 4511; Kans. R. Civ. Proc. § 60–409.

6. 9A Uniform Laws Annotated 553. The states include: Colorado, Delaware, Illinois, Kansas, Kentucky, Louisiana, Maine, Maryland, Minnesota, Missouri, Montana, Nebraska, New Jersey, New York, North Dakota, Ohio, Oklahoma, Pennsylvania, Rhode Island, South Carolina, South Dakota, Tennessee, Washington, Wisconsin, and Wyoming. 13 U.L.A. 496 (Master ed. 1980). The Act has now been replaced by the Uniform Interstate and International Procedure Act (infra n.12) for the states that have adopted the latter. Eleven other states have adopted provisions similar to § 4.03 of the Uniform Interstate and International Procedure Act that foreign law is to be determined by the court, not the jury, and that the determination is subject to review on appeal as a ruling of law. The Uniform Judicial Notice of Foreign Law Act takes the same approach in its § 3. See also Teitz, Transnational Litigation 228 (1996).

7. Thus, the "best evidence rule" may apply, with the result that foreign law may be proved by expert testimony only if the applicable statutory text is not available. See Groome v. Freyn Engineering Co., 374 Ill. 113, 28 N.E.2d 274 (1940) (Russian law); Demas v. Harvouros, 99 Pitt. L.J. 177 (1951); In re Demczuck's Estate, 8 Pa.D. & C.2d 462 (Pa.Orph.1957). While none of these older cases has been overruled, the issue does not appear to have arisen in more recent cases. In Greenberg v. Roth-

berg, 72 Ga.App. 882, 35 S.E.2d 485 (1945) the court ruled that a foreign city ordinance could neither be judicially noticed nor proved by testimony of an attorney claiming to be familiar with the ordinance.

8. See supra § 12.15 n.11. Md.Code Courts and Judicial Proceedings §§ 10–501 to 10–507 (1989) (in the case of foreign countries, limited to common law jurisdictions).

9. New Jersey Stat. Ann. §§ 2A:–82–27 to 2A:82–33 (1976).

10. See Sporn v. Celebrity, Inc., 129 N.J.Super. 449, 324 A.2d 71 (Law Div.1974) (Court need not notice foreign law if statutory preconditions not met); But see Public Service Coordinated Transport v. Marlo Trucking Co., 108 N.J.Super. 232, 260 A.2d 855 (App.Div.1970) (court may notice law of foreign state even without request by a party).

11. Supra n.6.

12. 13 U.L.A. 355 (1986). Among the states that adopted this Uniform Act: Ark. Code Ann. §§ 16–4–101 to 16–4–108 (1987); Cal. Evid. Code § 310 D.C. Code §§ 13–421 to 13–434 (1989); 735 ILCS 5/8–1007 (2004); Mass. General Laws Ann. c. 223A §§ 1–14; Mich. Comp. Laws Ann. §§ 600.1852, 600.2114a; 600.2118a (1981). Michigan, however, has only adopted §§ 2.04, 3.02, 4.01–4.03, 5.01–5.05. 42 Pa. Cons. Stat. Ann. §§ 5321–5329. The Act is also in force in the Virgin Islands, see 5

of evidence" (§ 4.02), and stipulates that the foregoing provisions do "not repeal or modify any other law of this state permitting another procedure for the determination of foreign law" (§ 4.04). The last provision thus serves to preserve more liberal provisions of state law, while the Act's own liberal provisions will supersede more restrictive Common Law and statutory approaches. The Act no longer contains a reference to "judicial notice," the meaning of which had been unclear in prior law (as being mandatory or discretionary, and in terms of any obligation of the parties, and its extent, to assist the court). Furthermore, the Act shifts the ascertainment of foreign law to the court, giving the latter a large measure of freedom in a manner akin to some Continental approaches, and makes the court's determination "subject to review on appeal as a ruling on a question of law" (§ 4.03).[13]

In 1977, however, the Uniform Interstate and International Procedure Act was withdrawn by the National Conference of Uniform Commissioners from recommendation for enactment because it was judged to obsolete. In particular, states that model the Federal Rules of Civil Procedure generally have an analog of Federal Rule 44.1.[14] However, state statutes based upon this Act or its 1936 predecessor remain on the books in many states.

C. FEDERAL LAW

§ 12.18 Federal Rule of Civil Procedure 44.1, which went into effect in 1966, is modeled after the Uniform Interstate and International

V.I.C. §§ 4901–4943. For Texas see infra n.13.

13. The following cases have dealt with Art. IV of the Uniform Act: American Aviation, Inc. v. Aviation Insurance Managers, Inc., 244 Ark. 829, 427 S.W.2d 544 (1968) (Arkansas law applied under Ark. Code Ann. § 27–2504 [§§ 4.01–4.03 of the Uniform Act] since neither party had given notice of intent to rely on Texas law nor pleaded it); Bridgeman v. Gateway Ford Truck Sales, 296 F.Supp. 233 (E.D.Ark. 1969), judgment amended 311 F.Supp. 695 (E.D.Ark.1970) (defendant's reference to Texas law in the answer held to be sufficient notice); Deposit Guaranty National Bank v. River Valley Co., 247 Ark. 226, 444 S.W.2d 880 (1969) (briefs on foreign law submitted at court's request satisfy reasonable notice requirement; statute's intent said to be to allow consideration of foreign law at any point in the litigation); Yarbrough v. Prentice Lee Tractor Co., 252 Ark. 349, 479 S.W.2d 549 (1972) (notice of intent to invoke foreign law need not be spelled out, but inference of applicability of foreign law from the complaint will suffice); see also Lubbock Production Credit Association v. Hubble, 599 P.2d 434 (Okl.App. 1979) (even though Texas law not pleaded nor special written notice given of intent to rely on Texas law, brief in support of motion was clearly based on it and notice was therefore sufficient). Decisions in which judicial notice was taken of foreign law include: Turkey Express, Inc. v. Skelton Motor Co., 246 Ark. 739, 439 S.W.2d 923 (1969); O'Neal v. Warmack, 250 Ark. 685, 466 S.W.2d 913 (1971); Turner v. Ford Motor Co., 81 Mich.App. 521, 265 N.W.2d 400 (1978) (defendant's citation to foreign law in brief in support of defendant's motion for accelerated judgment held to be adequate notice). Other than Arkansas, few states which have adopted the act have generated case law on these sections of the Uniform Act.

Texas Rule of Civil Evidence 203 appears generally to have been patterned after Federal Rule of Civil Procedure 44.1. In the words of one court, it is "a hybrid by which the presentation of the foreign law to the court resembles the presentment of evidence but which ultimately is decided as a question of law." AG Volkswagen v. The Honorable Rogelio Valdez, 897 S.W.2d 458, 461 (Tex.App.1995). For another application, see Gardner v. Best Western International, Inc., 929 S.W.2d 474 (Tex.App.1996).

14. See infra § 12.18.

Procedure Act and hence contains provisions substantially identical to the latter's §§ 4.01–4.03.[1] The following addresses separately the various problems raised by the Rule.

Notice Requirement. In at least one case, lack of reasonable notice did not cause the trial court to exclude material on foreign law, although very special circumstances obtained.[2] However, it may be inferred from appellate decisions (refusing to consider foreign law issues not properly raised at the trial level)[3] that proper ("reasonable", including timely) notice to invoke foreign law is necessary.[4]

Burden of Proof. Prior to Rule 44.1, a party relying on foreign law had to prove it by competent evidence. Rule 44.1 seemingly relaxes this requirement. Thus, to avoid the "potential drastic consequences" of a dismissal based on an inadequate record, one court granted plaintiff 30 days to supply evidence in rebuttal of defendant's expert testimony.[5]

§ 12.18

1. "A party who intends to raise an issue concerning the law of a foreign country shall give notice by pleadings or other reasonable written notice. The court, in determining foreign law, may consider any relevant material or source, including testimony, whether or not submitted by a party or admissible under the Federal Rules of Evidence. The court's determination shall be treated as a ruling on a question of law." 28 U.S.C.A. Rule 44.1, as amended (Supp. 1990). See generally Sass, Foreign Law in Federal Courts, 29 Am. J. Comp. L. 97 (1981).

Since the determination of foreign law is now a question of law, the presence of an issue of foreign law does not "obstruct the court's disposition of a motion for summary judgment." Galu v. Swissair: Swiss Air Transport Co., Ltd., 734 F.Supp. 129 (S.D.N.Y.1990), decision affirmed 923 F.2d 842 (2d Cir.1990); United States v. Panhandle Eastern Corp., 693 F.Supp. 88 (D.Del. 1988); Prudential Lines, Inc. v. General Tire Intern. Co., 440 F.Supp. 556 (S.D.N.Y. 1977) adhered to on reargument 448 F.Supp. 202 (1978); Fleischmann Distilling Corp. v. Distillers Co., Ltd., 395 F.Supp. 221 (S.D.N.Y.1975); Burnett v. Trans World Airlines, Inc., 368 F.Supp. 1152, 1156 (D.N.M.1973). See also Instituto Per Lo Sviluppo Economico Dell'Italia Meridionale v. Sperti Products, Inc., 323 F.Supp. 630 (S.D.N.Y.1971).

2. First National Bank of Arizona v. British Petroleum Co., 324 F.Supp. 1348 (S.D.N.Y.1971) (permission granted to raise issue of foreign law seven years after the beginning of the trial because the issue could not have been raised earlier without prejudicing a motion for summary judgment made before the adoption of Rule 44.1

in 1966); Thyssen Steel Co. et al. v. M/V Kavo Yerakas et al., 911 F.Supp. 263 (S.D. Tex., Houston Div. 1996) (foreign law permitted to be raised four years after suit was originally filed since there was no "unfair surprise").

3. Ruff v. St. Paul Mercury Insurance Co., 393 F.2d 500 (2d Cir.1968); cf. Putnam Resources v. Pateman, et al., 958 F.2d 448, 466 n.19. See also infra n.19. In Morse Electro Products Corp. v. S.S. Great Peace, 437 F.Supp. 474, 487–88 (D.N.J.1977) the court held that the failure of the parties to invoke Chinese law and, despite requests to do so, to submit supplemental pleadings amounted to an abandonment of rights and liabilities under that law which had been expressly stipulated in the bill of lading. The court proceeded to decide the case under principles of admiralty and state law.

4. DP Aviation et al. v. Smiths Industries Aerospace and Defense Systems Ltd., 268 F.3d 829 (9th Cir. 2001); Hidden Brook Air, Inc. v. Thabet Aviation International, Inc., et al., 241 F.Supp.2d 246 (S.D.N.Y. 2002). See also Whirlpool Fin. Corp. v. Seveaux, 96 F.3d 216 (7th Cir. 1996). Even though more liberal than earlier law, especially the Common Law, a rule requiring notice of intent to invoke foreign law in all cases may still be too restrictive. Thus, there may be cases in which foreign law should be applied *ex officio*. This may be true in custody cases, in which determination of the child's welfare may include the necessity of ascertaining the law of the jurisdiction of the foreign applicant seeking custody, or in status cases generally. A.A. Ehrenzweig, Private International Law (General Part) 182–83 (1967). See also infra n.8.

5. Allianz Versicherungs–Aktiengesellschaft v. Steamship Eskisehir, 334 F.Supp.

Other decisions suggest that the submission of the relevant statute alone may be sufficient evidence.[6] The taking of evidence abroad is now also facilitated by a Hague Convention on this problem which is in force in the United States.[7]

When the parties have not raised an issue of foreign law it is presumed that they agree that foreign law should not be considered.[8] In such a case, the general rule is that the court will apply the lex fori.[9]

Sources and Materials Used by the Court. Rule 44.1 expressly authorizes the use of sources and materials without regard to the usual

1225 (S.D.N.Y.1971), on reargument 353 F.Supp. 84 (1972).

6. First National City Bank v. Compania de Aguaceros, S.A., 398 F.2d 779 (5th Cir.1968); Bamberger v. Clark, 390 F.2d 485 (D.C.Cir.1968).

But see: Gates v. P.F. Collier, Inc., 256 F.Supp. 204 (D.Hawaii 1966), judgment affirmed 378 F.2d 888 (9th Cir.1967), cert. denied 389 U.S. 1038, 88 S.Ct. 774, 19 L.Ed.2d 827 (1968) (in a decision announced eight days after the entry into force of Rule 44.1, submission of a Japanese statute, without explanatory case law, was held insufficient to prove that Japanese law invalidated the contract); Usatorre v. The Victoria, 172 F.2d 434 (2d Cir.1949) (in a decision rendered prior to Rule 44.1, the burden of proof was not met by submission of a copy of the foreign statute and the introduction of uncontroverted expert testimony).

7. Convention on the Taking of Evidence Abroad in Civil or Commercial Matters, 23 U.S.T. 2555, 847 U.N.T.S. 231, TIAS 7444 (discussed supra § 12.9). For the European Union, see supra § 12.9 nn.1, 6, and 14.

8. See, e.g., Carey v. Bahama Cruise Lines, 864 F.2d 201 (1st Cir.1988); Nikimiha Securities Ltd. v. Trend Group, Ltd., 646 F.Supp. 1211 (E.D.Pa.1986); Howard Fuel v. Lloyd's Underwriters, 588 F.Supp. 1103 (S.D.N.Y.1984); Clarkson Co. Ltd. v. Shaheen, 660 F.2d 506 (2d Cir.1981), cert. denied 455 U.S. 990, 102 S.Ct. 1614, 71 L.Ed.2d 850 (1982); Geiger v. Keilani, 270 F.Supp. 761 (E.D.Mich.1967); Michael v. S.S. Thanasis, 311 F.Supp. 170 (N.D.Cal. 1970); Jetco Electronic Industries Inc. v. Gardiner, 325 F.Supp. 80 (S.D.Tex.1971); Kearney v. Savannah Foods & Industries, Inc., 350 F.Supp. 85 (S.D.Ga.1972); Walter v. Netherlands Mead N.V., 514 F.2d 1130 (3d Cir.1975), cert. denied 423 U.S. 869, 96 S.Ct. 133, 46 L.Ed.2d 99 (1975) (in the absence of any effort to prove foreign law, the court assumed that the law of the Netherlands Antilles was consistent with that of

the forum, citing to Leary v. Gledhill, infra § 12.19 nn.12, 16). In Gkiafis v. Steamship Yiosonas, 387 F.2d 460 (4th Cir.1967), the court stated that federal courts are not permitted to take judicial notice of foreign law. Accord: Amdur v. Zim Israel Navigation Co., 310 F.Supp. 1033 (S.D.N.Y.1969); Wachs v. Winter, 569 F.Supp. 1438 (E.D.N.Y.1983); Shonac Corp. v. AMKO Int'l, 763 F.Supp. 919 (S.D.Ohio 1991). Cf. Savannah Sugar Refining Corp. v. S.S. Hudson Deep, 288 F.Supp. 181 (S.D.N.Y.1968); see also Nikimiha Securities Ltd. v. Trend Group Ltd., 646 F.Supp. 1211 (E.D.Pa. 1986) (advisory committee notes to 44.1 indicate that court may apply foreign law even if not requested by parties but choosing not to do so); Vishipco Line v. Chase Manhattan Bank, N.A., 660 F.2d 854 (2d Cir.1981), cert. denied 459 U.S. 976, 103 S.Ct. 313, 74 L.Ed.2d 291 (1982). The strong stand against considering Rule 44.1 as permitting "judicial notice" reinforces the conclusion that notice to invoke foreign law is necessary. Supra nn.3–4. However, reversion to "judicial notice" language (not contained in Rule 44.1) is unfortunate since it may draw into question both the parties' obligation to assist the court in the ascertainment of foreign law and the problem of whether a court should raise the issue *ex officio*. The former is an appropriate requirement. However, refusal to entertain issues of foreign law *ex officio* may be unfortunate in some cases. See supra n.4.

9. Vishipco Line v. Chase Manhattan Bank, N.A., 660 F.2d 854 (2d Cir.1981) cert. denied 459 U.S. 976, 103 S.Ct. 313, 74 L.Ed.2d 291 (1982); Bartsch v. Metro–Goldwyn–Mayer, Inc., 270 F.Supp. 896 (S.D.N.Y.1967), on appeal 391 F.2d 150 (2d Cir.1968), cert. denied 393 U.S. 826, 89 S.Ct. 86, 21 L.Ed.2d 96 (1968). See A.A. Ehrenzweig, supra n.4, at 181; Restatement, Second, Conflict of Laws § 136, cmnt. (h), Rep. Note (1971). But see also infra § 12.19 nn.11, 12–15.

rules of evidence.[10] Thus, parties may tender expert testimony and affidavits by experts,[11] English language translations of foreign texts and foreign treatises,[12] even unauthenticated copies of foreign laws,[13] and the court may itself question expert witnesses and consider other material *ex officio*.[14]

Scope of Appellate Review. The Advisory Committee on Rules[15] noted that, since Rule 44.1 treats the determination of foreign law as a ruling on an issue of "law," appellate review should not be confined to the "clearly erroneous" standard of Rule 52(a). The Fifth Circuit adopted this view in 1968, holding that its review was not controlled by the trial court's determination nor by the expert testimony offered at the trial. It reversed the decision below, which had concluded that the foreign law was unclear and thus should not be applied, and instead interpreted the relevant Panamanian statute itself.[16] The District of Columbia Circuit and the Seventh Circuit take similarly wide views of their review functions,[17] while a decision by the Third Circuit merely acknowledged

---

10. See supra n.1. See also Martinez v. Dow Chem. Co., 219 F.Supp.2d 719 (E.D.La. 2002) (State Department country reports not excludable as hearsay, but admissible with regard to fairness of foreign judicial system).

11. See Films by Jove, Inc. v. Berov, 250 F. Supp. 2d 156 (E.D.N.Y. 2003); Galu v. Swissair: Swiss Air Transport Co., Ltd., 734 F.Supp. 129 (S.D.N.Y.1990), affirmed 923 F.2d 842 (2d Cir.1990); A/S Kreditt–Finans v. Cia Venetico De Navegacion S.A., 560 F.Supp. 705 (E.D.Pa.1983), aff'd 729 F.2d 1446 (3d Cir. 1984); Instituto Per Lo Sviluppo Economico Dell'Italia Meridionale v. Sperti Products, Inc., 323 F.Supp. 630 (S.D.N.Y.1971); Noto v. Cia Secula di Armanento, 310 F.Supp. 639 (S.D.N.Y.1970). A legal expert need not be admitted to practice in countries whose laws are at issue. Merican, Inc. v. Caterpillar Tractor Co., 596 F.Supp. 697 (E.D.Pa.1984); see also Gardner v. Best Western International Inc., 929 S.W.2d 474 (Tex.App.1996); Universe Sales Co. v. Silver Castle, Ltd., 182 F.3d 1036 (9th Cir. 1999); Tschira v. Willingham, 135 F.3d 1077 (6th Cir. 1998).

12. See Henry v. S/S Bermuda Star, 863 F.2d 1225 (5th Cir.1989); Markakis v. SS Volendam, 475 F.Supp. 29 (S.D.N.Y.1979); United States v. McClain, 545 F.2d 988 (5th Cir.1977); Ramsay v. Boeing Co., 432 F.2d 592 (5th Cir.1970).

13. Ramirez v. Autobuses Blancos Flecha Roja, S.A. De C.V., 486 F.2d 493 (5th Cir.1973) (Mexico); Haarhuis v. Kunnan Enterprises, Ltd. et al., 177 F.3d 1007 (D.C. Cir. 1999) (Taiwan).

14. See, e.g., United States v. One Lucite Ball Containing Lunar Material, 252 F. Supp. 2d 1367 (S.D. Fla. 2003) (court ap-

pointed own expert on Honduran law). See generally Peritz, Determination of Foreign Law Under Rule 44.1, 10 Tex. Int'l L.J. 67, 74 et seq. (1975); see also authorities cited supra § 12.15 n.1; 62 A.L.R. Fed. 521.

15. See 1968 Advisory Committee Notes, F.R.C.P. 44.1.

16. First National City Bank v. Compania de Aguaceros, S.A., 398 F.2d 779 (5th Cir.1968). In Ramsay v. Boeing, Co., 432 F.2d 592 (5th Cir.1970), the court affirmed the trial court's ruling with respect to Belgian law but only after undertaking its own analysis of the affidavits, expert testimony, and an authoritative treatise. See also Randall v. Arabian American Oil Co., 778 F.2d 1146 (5th Cir.1985); Perez & Compania, S.A. v. M/V Mexico I, 826 F.2d 1449 (5th Cir.1987). The fact that the trial court's determination is subject to review, however, does not relieve the party from presenting available or obtainable material at the trial court level. Banque Libanaise Pour Le Commerce v. Khreich, 915 F.2d 1000, 1006 (5th Cir.1990). See also In re Avantel, 343 F.3d 311 (5th Cir.2003).

17. Bamberger v. Clark, 390 F.2d 485 (D.C.Cir.1968) (court reversed trial court on the basis of its own interpretation of the relevant German statute after characterizing the foreign-law question as one of law). In Milena Ship Mgmt. Co. v. Newcomb, 804 F.Supp. 859 (E.D.La.1992), affirmed 995 F.2d 620 (5th Cir.1993), cert. denied 510 U.S. 1071, 114 S.Ct. 877, 127 L.Ed.2d 74 (1994), the court deferred to on administrative agency's interpretation of Yugoslav Law. The court stated that the "Lasting Legacy" of Bamberger is that "deference to the agency's interpretation of foreign law

the suggested wide standard but affirmed the trial court's determination without independent analysis.[18] As noted earlier, foreign law will not be considered on appeal unless the issue was raised at the trial level.[19]

D. WHEN PROOF FAILS: PRESUMPTIONS AND USE OF THE LEX FORI

§ 12.19 What law applies when no proof of foreign law was offered in a case displaying foreign-law factors, when foreign law was properly raised but the particular party failed to sustain the burden of proof, or—in a legal system providing for the ascertainment of foreign law *ex officio* the content of the foreign law cannot be determined?

In the first case, the forum will treat the case as one arising under local law and apply the latter:[1] "Since . . . the parties did not see fit to question the application of Pennsylvania law, we infer that this state was in fact the situs of most of the allegedly wrongful conduct and accordingly decide the issue . . . on the basis of our own law."[2] As noted earlier, the application of the lex fori on the basis of party acquiescence may be seen as a form of choice of law by the parties. Ordinarily, however, American law restricts party autonomy to the choice of a related law.[3] The application of the—potentially unrelated—lex fori in these cases, on the basis of party acquiescence, is therefore a departure. American courts thus seemingly apply different standards to the choice of the lex fori (and consequent displacement of foreign law) than holds true in the reverse case. This assumes, perhaps unrealistically in many cases, that the parties in fact made a *choice*. It is perhaps more probable, but leads to the same result, that the foreign element of the case was to them incidental. This accords with Lord Wright's dictum that, for English law to apply, a connection of the issue to England "is not, as a matter of principle, essential."[4]

can be appropriate". See also Kaho v. Ilchert, 765 F.2d 877, 881 (9th Cir.1985); Twohy v. First Nat'l Bank of Chicago, 758 F.2d 1185 (7th Cir.1985).

18. Mathey v. United States, 491 F.2d 481 (3d Cir.1974). This decision is not necessarily contrary to the cases cited supra nn.16–17, since the issue involved sister-state and not foreign-country law.

19. Supra n.3. Despite the implication in Bartsch v. Metro–Goldwyn–Mayer, Inc., 391 F.2d 150, 155 (2d Cir.1968), cert. denied 393 U.S. 826, 89 S.Ct. 86, 21 L.Ed.2d 96 (1968) that the appellate court could undertake an original and independent analysis of a foreign law issue suggested by the parties, the same court refused to do so in Ruff v. St. Paul Mercury Insurance Co., 393 F.2d 500 (2d Cir.1968) when no notice of the foreign law issue had been given in the trial court. See also Putnam Resources v. Pateman, 958 F.2d 448 (1st Cir.1992).

§ 12.19

1. Comment (h) to § 136, Restatement, Second, Conflict of Laws (1971). See, e.g., Torah Soft, Ltd. v. Drosnin, 224 F.Supp.2d 704, 712 (S.D.N.Y. 2002) ("It is well-established that in the absence of proof of foreign law, the law of the forum governs.")

2. Vulcanized Rubber and Plastics Co. v. Scheckter, 400 Pa. 405, 408 n.2, 162 A.2d 400, 403 n.2 (1960).

3. Restatement, Second, Conflict of Laws § 187(2) (1971). For criticism of the restrictive U.S. rule see Hay, International versus Interstate Conflicts Law in the United States, 35 Rabels Zeitschrift 429, 459 n.152 (1971).

4. Vita Food Products Inc. v. Unus Shipping Co., [1939] A.C. 277 (P.C.). This view (i.e., not implicit choice of forum law, but applicability of forum law absent invocation of another) treats choice-of-law rules

The problem is much more difficult when a foreign law issue was raised but the party failed to sustain its burden of proof. A fact-approach to foreign law would logically require that failure to sustain the burden of proof necessarily results in a non-suit, directed verdict or summary judgment, as the case may be.[5] The courts have tempered this harsh result through the use of a variety of presumptions: (1) that the foreign law is based on the common law and is thus the same as the common law of the forum,[6] (2) the foreign law is the same as forum law,[7] (3) the foreign law is based on generally recognized principles of law common to civilized nations,[8] or (4) that the parties acquiesced in the application of forum law in the alternative.[9]

The decisions in *Walton*[10] and *Leary*[11] show the difficulties. In *Walton*, the court rejected the plaintiff's argument that "rudimentary tort principles" were involved (allowing the application of the "identical" lex fori) because in "countries where the common law does not prevail [Saudi Arabia], our doctrines relative to negligence, and to a master's liability for his servant's acts, may well not exist or be vastly different."[12] The plaintiff's alternative reason for the application of the lex fori—that Saudi Arabia has no law or legal system and, in that sense, is "uncivilized"[13]—was also rejected for lack of proof to that effect.

not as mandatory, but as a means for the resolution of a claim. In this, it is consistent with the change from the vested-rights approach of the First Restatement to the "general principles of the Second Restatement" and with other contemporary approaches to choice-of-law. See supra ch. 2.

5. Walton v. Arabian American Oil Co., 233 F.2d 541 (2d Cir.1956), cert. denied 352 U.S. 872, 77 S.Ct. 97, 1 L.Ed.2d 77 (1956) (plaintiff's tort action for personal injuries dismissed for failure to prove Saudi Arabian law). See also Philp v. Macri, 261 F.2d 945 (9th Cir.1958). In Weiss v. Hunna, 312 F.2d 711, 717 n.3 (2d Cir.1963), cert. denied 374 U.S. 853, 83 S.Ct. 1920, 10 L.Ed.2d 1073 (1963) (discussing the hypothetical possibility that, in different circumstances, the case would have to be dismissed for failure to plead and prove Austrian law).

6. See Ohio Southern Express Co. v. Beeler, 110 Ga.App. 867, 140 S.E.2d 235 (1965); Copeland Planned Futures, Inc. v. Obenchain, 9 Wn.App. 32, 510 P.2d 654, 659 (1973) (presumption of identity of sister-state law); Argo Welded Products, Inc. v. J.T. Ryerson Steel & Sons, Inc., 528 F.Supp. 583, 588–89 (E.D.Pa.1981) (New Jersey law presumed to be the same as Pennsylvania's with respect to damages for loss of good will). See also supra § 12.15 n.11.

7. See the cases collected supra § 12.15 n.9 and Tiner v. State, 279 Ala. 126, 182

So.2d 859 (1966). See also supra § 12.15 n.14.

8. Compagnie Generale Transatlantique v. Rivers, 211 Fed. 294 (2d Cir.1914), cert. denied 232 U.S. 727, 34 S.Ct. 603, 58 L.Ed. 817 (1914); Arams v. Arams, 182 Misc. 328, 45 N.Y.S.2d 251 (1943); Tidewater Oil Co. v. Waller, 302 F.2d 638, 641 (10th Cir.1962) (in the absence of proof, the court refused to assume that Turkey had a workmen's compensation law similar to Oklahoma's but presumed that "Turkey recognizes the universal fundamental principle [of the duty to exercise due care] and that its courts ... will grant compensable redress for the unexcused violation of that duty").

9. See Leary v. Gledhill, 8 N.J. 260, 84 A.2d 725 (1951) and supra § 12.18 n.9 and § 12.19 nn.2–5.

10. Walton v. Arabian American Oil Co., 233 F.2d 541 (2d Cir.1956), cert. denied 352 U.S. 872, 77 S.Ct. 97, 1 L.Ed.2d 77 (1956).

11. Leary v. Gledhill, 8 N.J. 260, 84 A.2d 725 (1951) and supra § 12.18 n.9 and § 12.19 nn.2–5.

12. 233 F.2d at 545.

13. Plaintiff's argument was derived from Justice Holmes's statement that the place-of-tort rule does not apply "where a tort is committed in an uncivilized country." Slater v. Mexican National Railroad Co., 194 U.S. 120, 129, 24 S.Ct. 581, 584, 48 L.Ed. 900 (1904). See also American Ba-

Proceeding from a determination that the law of the place of tort applied, the court therefore dismissed plaintiff's action for failure to prove that law.[14]

In *Leary,* the New Jersey Supreme Court rejected the first presumption mentioned above because the issue related to French law. For the same reason it also rejected the use of the second presumption, but a lower court subsequently applied it in another case (involving Dutch law).[15] Nevertheless, the Court in *Leary* adopted and affirmed the lower court's position but based itself on the fourth presumption and not on the third as the trial court had done. *Leary* thus demonstrates some eagerness to avoid a harsh result which might result from the "lack of an applicable law" and a degree of judicial flexibility in achieving that goal. *Walton,* in this sense, reached an unfortunate result that today should be avoidable in most cases.[16] Both cases, however, demonstrate the difficulties inherent in an approach which engages in presumptions—largely fictions—to avoid harsh results and to do justice. A view advocated in England has equal value for American law: "[I]t is better to abandon the terminology of presumption, and simply to say that where foreign law is not proved, the court applies ... [local] law."[17] The Austrian law and the Swiss draft statute[18] now also provide for the application of forum law when the foreign law cannot be ascertained. In the United States, there is now also authority for the view that, when

nana Co. v. United Fruit Co., 213 U.S. 347, 355–56, 29 S.Ct. 511, 512, 53 L.Ed. 826 (1909); Cuba Railroad Co. v. Crosby, 222 U.S. 473, 478, 32 S.Ct. 132, 56 L.Ed. 274 (1912).

14. For a collection of cases where the court applied forum law under similar circumstances, usually on the basis of various presumptions, see R. Weintraub, Commentary on the Conflict of Law 111 n.265 (4th ed. 2001). Furthermore, as Weintraub correctly points out, a functional approach to choice of law may not have led to the application of Saudi Arabian law in the first place under the factual circumstances of the case: Walton, an Arkansas citizen, had been temporarily in Saudi Arabia where his automobile collided with defendant's truck, driven by defendant's employee. Defendant was a Delaware corporation, licensed to do business in the New York forum and also did substantial business in Saudi Arabia. Given the flexibility of modern choice-of-law rules, there will be only few case situations in which a court will feel compelled to apply a foreign law. These will often be cases involving foreign immovable property, security interests, and questions of status (but not the incidents of such status, see infra §§ 15.28 et seq.), as well as those cases, presumably, in which the case displays no connection whatever to the forum. See Restatement, Second, Conflict of Laws, cmnt. (b) (1971). Similarly, an English

court will insist on proof of foreign law (and not apply the lex fori) in a limited number of cases. Dicey & Morris, Conflict of Laws 232 (13th ed. by Collins et al. 2000)(citing R. v. Nagib, [1917] 1 K.B. 359 (dismissal of bigamy prosecution upon failure to prove preexisting marriage valid under foreign law)).

15. Somerville Container Sales v. General Metal Corp., 39 N.J.Super. 348, 120 A.2d 866 (App.Div.1956), modified 39 N.J.Super. 562, 121 A.2d 746 (1956). See also Mick v. American Dental Association, 49 N.J.Super. 262, 139 A.2d 570 (App.Div. 1958), certification denied 27 N.J. 74, 141 A.2d 318 (1958). Since neither Illinois nor German law had been pleaded or proved, the court felt justified in assuming that the applicable law was the same as the forum's. The court cited both to *Leary,* supra n.12, and to *Somerville,* supra this note, but did not make a distinction between the presumption of identity and an implied agreement or acquiesence that forum law should apply. See also C.I.T. Corp. v. Edwards, 418 P.2d 685 (Okla.1966).

16. See supra n.15. But see Kramer, Interest Analysis and the Presumption of Forum Law, 56 U. Chi. L. Rev. 1301 (1989).

17. Dicey & Morris, supra n.15, at 232.

18. Supra § 12.16 n.7, § 4(2) and Art. 15(3), respectively.

proof of foreign law fails, local law is the only law available and should be applied,[19] only excepting the special circumstances noted earlier.[20]

Finally, legal systems which provide for the determination of the applicable law by the court *ex officio* and also charge it with the task of determining the content of that law, face similar but not identical problems. Since the choice-of-law decision does not depend on an express invocation of foreign law by the parties, the question will regularly be whether party conduct during litigation (e.g., reliance on forum law) may be taken as an implied choice of law by the parties.[21]

All systems will require the parties to support the court in its task.[22] But, despite best efforts, it may prove impossible to ascertain the content of the applicable law. Solutions include: application of an analogous rule of law from the *same* legal system,[23] search for and application of a rule of law from a *related* legal system (such as of a French rule for a Belgian case),[24] the lex fori as the ultimate substitute.[25]

19. Cal. Evid. Code § 311(a) authorizes the application of California law when sister-state or foreign-country law cannot be determined if "the ends of justice require," subject to the limitation that it can do so "consistently ... with the Constitution of the United States and the Constitution of this State." See also Rymanowski v. Rymanowski, 105 R.I. 89, 249 A.2d 407 (1969); Pioneer Credit Corp. v. Carden, 127 Vt. 229, 245 A.2d 891 (1968); Stein v. Siegel, 50 A.D.2d 916, 377 N.Y.S.2d 580 (1975); Kem Manufacturing Corp. v. Howland, 121 R.I. 601, 401 A.2d 1284 (1979); Fishbein v. Guerra, 131 Vt. 493, 309 A.2d 922 (1973); United States v. Cardinal, 452 F.Supp. 542 (D.Vt.1978); Miller v. A.N. Webber, Inc., 484 N.W.2d 420 (Minn.App.1992); Keene Corp. v. Gardner, 837 S.W.2d 224 (Tex.App. 1992).

20. Supra n.15.

21. At this point, the conceptual problem noted with respect to American law does not arise because European law, for instance, provides for much broader party autonomy. See Art. 3 Rome Convention on the Law Applicable to Contractual Obligations. The conceptual problem does arise in the context of approaches that suggest that the lex fori applies unless application of another law is claimed, in essence a departure from the *ex officio*-principle. See Flessner, Interessenjurisprudenz im inter-

nationalen Privatrecht, in: Beiträge zum ausländischen und internationalen Privatrecht, Band 53, 113–29 (Tübingen 1990). This approach finds support, as a practical matter, in the general view that the *ex officio*-principle does not require the court to advise the parties of their options. They may therefore have the lex fori applied by default or by an assumed implied choice. For criticism see Hay & Hampe, Nichtermittelbarkeit ausländischen Rechts und Forum Non Conveniens, Recht der Internationalen Wirtschaft 760 (1998).

22. See Kegel & Schurig, Internationales Privatrecht 658 (9th ed. 2004).

23. E.g., Art. 14(2) *Italian* Statute of 1995.

24. See the German Reichsgericht (RG 163, 367); see also Art. 23(2) *Portuguese* Civil Code of 1965 (the law that is subsidiarily applicable).

25. E.g., § 4(2) *Austrian* Statute of 1978; § 5(2) *Hungarian* Decree–Law No. 13/1979; Art. 14(2) *Italian* Statute of 1995; Art. 7, para. 3, *Romanian* Statute No. 105 of Sept. 22, 1992 on Private International Law; Art. 1228(3) Draft Civil Code of the *Russian Federation* (Tent. Draft 1998); Art. 16(2) *Swiss* Statute of 1987; BGH NJW 1982, 1215 for Germany. For commentary see also Hay & Hampe, supra n.21, at 760.

Chapter 13

FORMING DOMESTIC RELATIONSHIPS

Table of Sections

Sections

I. Marriage and Other Forms of Domestic Relationships as a Problem in the Conflict of Laws 13.1–13.4
   A. Marriage as a Contract and a Status 13.1
   B. Marriage: Significant Policies 13.2
   C. Marriage as an Incidental Question 13.3
   D. Competing Approaches in Choice of Law: Domicile and Nationality 13.4
II. Law Governing Recognition of Marriage 13.5–13.19
   A. The Traditional Statement 13.5
   B. Requirements of Place of Celebration 13.6
   C. Prohibitions of the Domicile of the Parties 13.7–13.13
     1. Form and Capacity 13.7
     2. Substantive Prohibition 13.8
     3. Prohibitions Upon Remarriage After Divorce: Progressive Polygamy 13.9
     4. Miscegenation 13.10
     5. "Incestuous" Marriages 13.11
     6. Non-age—Consent of Parent 13.12
     7. Marriage Evasion Legislation 13.13
   D. Effect in Third State of Marriage Void by Law of Domicile 13.14
   E. Marriage of Parties With Different Domiciles 13.15
   F. The Covenant Marriage 13.16
III. Unusual Marriages, Same–Sex Marriages and Unions, Contractual Domestic Arrangements 13.17–13.23
   A. Unusual Marriages 13.17–13.19
   B. Same–Sex Marriages and Unions 13.20–13.22
   C. Other Partnerships 13.23

I. MARRIAGE AND OTHER FORMS OF DOMESTIC RELATIONSHIPS AS A PROBLEM IN THE CONFLICT OF LAWS

A. MARRIAGE AS A CONTRACT AND A STATUS

§ 13.1 It has been common to speak of marriage as a contract. The statutes of many of our states declare marriage to be a "civil contract."[1] Marriage is a consensual transaction; the element of mutual assent must be present. But it is clear that, traditionally, marriage is much more than a contract. Once the contract is executed, marriage becomes an enduring relationship. "When formed, this relation is no more a contract than 'fatherhood' or 'sonship' is a contract."[2] Once created, the marriage is subject to dissolution only through legal proceedings or the death of one of the spouses. This distinctive characteristic of permanence distinguishes the marriage status from a purely consensual transaction.[3]

Marriage is traditionally the most important of the domestic relations. The state, as well as the immediate parties, has an interest in it: marriage has been the traditional foundation of the family, and around the family many of our social institutions were built.

Today, there are additional forms of community between two people. The informal marriage of the common law ("common law marriage") is still a recognized form of marriage in several states. But what of cohabitation of persons, with or without contractual arrangements, their current or future rights to property, support, or even inheritance?

Same-sex relationships are recognized as traditional-type marriages in some countries (in the United States only in Massachusetts), as registered partnerships—with rights akin to marriage—in much of Europe, and, increasingly, as "civil unions" in the United States. Same-sex unions as well as heterosexual non-marriage arrangements all raise conflict-of-laws problems, in the main with respect to the recognition of the incidents of the arrangement. This chapter therefore does not focus on marriage alone, as in previous editions, but also considers other forms of domestic unions.

B. MARRIAGE: SIGNIFICANT POLICIES

§ 13.2 The policies reflected in the law concerning marriage are designed to respond to the need to assure full consent freely given in entering the relationship and the protection of those to whom this

---

§ 13.1

1. See, e.g., Iowa Code Ann. § 595.1; Mich. Comp. Laws Ann. § 551.2; N.Y. Dom. Rel. Law § 10. See also Jambrone v. David, 16 Ill.2d 32, 156 N.E.2d 569 (1959).

2. Ditson v. Ditson, 4 R.I. 87, 101 (1856). See Washington v. Washington, 486 S.W.2d 668 (Mo.App.1972). See also Dolan v. Dolan, 259 A.2d 32 (Me.1969). Cf. Wash-ington Statewide Organization of Stepparents v. Smith, 85 Wn.2d 564, 536 P.2d 1202 (1975); Nevarez v. Bailon, 287 S.W.2d 521 (Tex.Civ.App.1956).

3. See Engdahl, Proposal for a Benign Revolution in Marriage Law and Marriage Conflicts Law, 55 Iowa L. Rev. 56 (1969).

relationship has direct social significance, particularly the parties, their offspring and possible subsequent spouses.[1] The two strongest policies seem to be: (1) to assure complete individual freedom in the exchange of consents and (2) to sustain its validity once the relationship is assumed to have been freely created.[2]

The states most concerned with the furtherance of these policies are those where the consent is effectively given, where the parties were domiciled at that time or later, and where the incidents of this enduring relationship are to be enjoyed. Clearly several states may be differently involved and in each the relevant policies may have varying force.[3] In most instances, the state or nation best situated to regulate the consensual aspects is the state in which the marriage is celebrated, i.e., where the exchange of consents is given and manifested. Because the relationship is so personal and so concerned with social structure, the states in which the parties are domiciled at the time of the marriage and following have an appropriate interest in both consensual elements and the incidents of the marriage. This interest of the domiciliary state at time of celebration is sufficient in some cases to impose effective limitations on out of state marriages of its citizens. For example, the domiciliary state has an interest in assuring free consent, for example requirements of age and parental consent, but normally the desire to uphold a marriage results in validating the marriage by the law of the state of celebration. As between the states of domicile at time of marriage and the domicile of the couple after marriage, the latter seems more significantly concerned but the law of either would probably be applied to validate the marriage.[4]

§ 13.2

1. See Headen v. Pope & Talbot, Inc., 252 F.2d 739 (3d Cir.1958); Arcand v. Flemming, 185 F.Supp. 22 (D.Conn.1960).

2. See H. Clark, Law of Domestic Relations 66 (1968). In Matter of Estate of Murnion, 212 Mont. 107, 686 P.2d 893, 897 (1984) this policy is reflected in the assertion that the "presumption in favor of matrimony is one of the strongest known to the law and that every intendment of the law is in favor of matrimony, which presumes morality and not immorality, marriage and not concubinage, legitimacy and not bastardy."

3. See, e.g., Metropolitan Life Insurance Co. v. Manning, 568 F.2d 922 (2d Cir.1977); Headen v. Pope & Talbot, Inc., 252 F.2d 739 (3d Cir.1958); Wilkins v. Zelichowski, 43 N.J.Super. 598, 129 A.2d 459 (App.Div. 1957), reversed 26 N.J. 370, 140 A.2d 65 (1958); Matter of Peart's Estate, 277 App. Div. 61, 97 N.Y.S.2d 879 (1950). See also Fine, The Application of Issue–Analysis to Choice of Law Involving Family Law Matters in the United States, 26 Loyola L. Rev. 31, 295 (1980); Taintor, Marriage in the Conflict of Laws, 9 Vand. L. Rev. 607

(1956); Restatement, Second, Conflict of Laws ch. 11, Intro. note, p. 231 (1971). Cf. Ehrenzweig on Conflict of Laws §§ 138, 139 (1962). P.S.J. Smart, Interest Analysis and Marriage, 14 Anglo–Am. L. Rev. 225 (1985); R. Fentiman, Validity of Marriage and the Proper Law, 44 Camb. L.J. 256 (1985).

4. See Spiegel v. Rabinovitz, 121 F.3d 251 n. 2 (7th Cir. 1997) (although Illinois does not provide for common law marriage, a common law marriage, valid under the law of the couple's domicile at the time it was concluded, would be recognized in Illinois, even if the couple subsequently changed its domicile to Illinois); Yi Ning Ma v. Mei Fang Ma, 483 N.W.2d 732 (Minn. App.1992)(recognition of marriage valid under Chinese law despite subsequent change of domicile to Minnesota). A reference to another law in these circumstances may well be to the whole law of the other jurisdiction, i.e. including its conflicts law (renvoi). See supra §§ 3.13–3.14. Clearly this should be true if the validation policy could only be furthered in this manner. See Barrons v. United States, 191 F.2d 92 (9th Cir.1951); Comment, Renvoi Revisited, 51 Harv. L. Rev. 1165, 1199 (1938); Maddaugh, Validity of Marriage and the Conflict of

Most controversies involve the enjoyment of some incident of this persistent relationship and these may occur in several states in which the policy orientation to the aspects of the marriage may vary from close to remote.[5] However, in most cases the policy of validation, which is common to all states, will cause a state in which an enjoyment of an incident is claimed to refer to the domiciliary state or the state of celebration as being more significantly concerned. Because marriage is a continuing relationship, there is normally a need that its existence be subject to regulation by one law without occasion for repeated redetermination of the validity.[6] Human mobility ought not to jeopardize the reasonable expectations of those relying on an assumed family pattern. Consequently, the courts will usually look to a law deemed to be appropriately applicable to the parties at the time the relationship is begun.

The factors of time and the source of the attack on a marriage are also significant as a consequence of the reasonable expectations of those relying on an assumed marriage. For example, in *Wilkins v. Zelichowski*,[7] a young couple went from New Jersey to Indiana where the bride, age 16, could marry. Later, on attaining the age of 18, New Jersey granted the bride an annulment on the basis of the domicile's interest in protecting its young people. In *State v. Graves*,[8] on the other hand, the domiciliary court refused to convict parents of contributing to the delinquency of their children ages 13 and 15 by assisting the youngsters in going to another state to marry and return to the domicile. While in both these cases the validity of the marriage was raised soon after the celebration, the successful attack was an internal attack by one of the parties to the marriage so the policy of protecting the parties was dominant. That policy was also dominant in the second case in which the external attack by the State, a non-party, was rejected. One would have little doubt that in the *Graves* case an annulment would have been granted the teenage bride had it been sought shortly after the marriage.

In re May's Estate illustrates the same factors.[9] There, after some 32 years of an apparently successful marriage, a child of the marriage attempted to preclude her father from appointment as administrator of her mother's estate by attacking the marriage, valid in Connecticut

Laws: A Critique of the Present Anglo–American Position, 23 U. Toronto L.J. 117 (1973); Restatement, Second, Conflict of Laws § 283, cmnt. (m) (1971).

5. See Gibson v. Hughes, 192 F.Supp. 564 (S.D.N.Y.1961).

6. See, e.g., Henderson v. Henderson, 199 Md. 449, 87 A.2d 403 (1952). Often principles of preclusion will apply. See Hupp v. Hupp, 239 Va. 494, 391 S.E.2d 329 (1990) (Pennsylvania determination of validity of marriage and paternity under Pennsylvania law were res judicata and barred reexamination under Virginia law).

7. 26 N.J. 370, 140 A.2d 65 (1958).

8. 228 Ark. 378, 307 S.W.2d 545 (1957). See also State v. Austin, 160 W.Va. 337, 234 S.E.2d 657 (1977) in which charge of putative 22–year-old husband contributing to the delinquency of a minor by marrying his 15–year-old bride out of state was initiated by others than the bride. The court used the West Virginia marriage evasion act to apply West Virginia law under which there was no crime and the marriage was voidable, but valid until annulment. No annulment had occurred.

9. In re May's Estate, 305 N.Y. 486, 114 N.E.2d 4 (1953). See also Reese, Marriage in American Conflict of Laws, 26 Int'l & Comp. L.Q. 952, 960 (1977).

where celebrated, on the basis that the parties were uncle and niece (of half blood) and that the marriage was invalid as incestuous at the domicile in New York. The expectations of the parties of long duration were protected from the external attack.[10] Usually other relevant policies also lead to the result of sustaining the validity of an assumed marriage by such an appropriate law.[11] It is only where there is rather violent conflict between the enjoyment of an incident and the assumed social order where enjoyment is sought that an otherwise valid marriage will be denied recognition.[12]

As scholars in this area have pointed out, the courts could and should treat all questions simply as claims to incidents[13] but such has not been the course of the decisions. Rather, in both local law and conflicts litigation, the traditional approach has been to determine the existence of the relationship and to permit the disposition of other issues to follow. However, in recent choice-of-law cases, the courts have begun to recognize that the enjoyment of different incidents of marriage involves different policies.[14] Consequently, a uniform reference to a single state to resolve all choice-of-law questions involving marriage cannot be expected.

C. MARRIAGE AND OTHER RELATIONSHIPS AS AN INCIDENTAL QUESTION

§ 13.3   In the consideration of issues relating to marriage or other domestic relationships, courts and the legal profession tend to think of

10. See also In re Miller's Estate, 239 Mich. 455, 214 N.W. 428 (1927); In re Lenherr's Estate, 455 Pa. 225, 314 A.2d 255 (1974); Spradlin v. State Compensation Commissioner, 145 W.Va. 202, 113 S.E.2d 832 (1960). Cf. Perry v. Richardson, 336 F.Supp. 451 (E.D.Pa.1972). Contra: Catalano v. Catalano, 148 Conn. 288, 170 A.2d 726 (1961). But cf. Perez v. Finch, 320 F.Supp. 787 (E.D.Wash.1970). Fattibene v. Fattibene, 183 Conn. 433, 441 A.2d 3 (1981); Matter of Pecorino's Estate, 64 A.D.2d 711, 407 N.Y.S.2d 550 (1978), appeal denied 46 N.Y.2d 708, 414 N.Y.S.2d 1025, 386 N.E.2d 1337 (1979); cf. Jones v. International Tel. & Tel. Corp., 462 So.2d 1348 (La.App.1985), writ denied 466 So.2d 469 (La.1985).

11. See, e.g., Holland America Insurance Co. v. Rogers, 313 F.Supp. 314 (N.D.Cal.1970).

12. See Borchers, *Baker v. General Motors*: Implications for Interjurisdictional Recognition of Non–Traditional Marriages, 32 Creighton L. Rev. 147, 154–58 (1998) (surveying precedents). In agreement with the statement in the text, Koppelman, Same–Sex Marriage, Choice of Law, and Public Policy, 76 Tex. L. Rev. 921, 946 (1998).

13. See Baade, Marriage and Divorce in American Conflicts Law: Governmental In-

terests Analysis and the Restatement (Second), 72 Colum. L. Rev. 329 (1972); Engdahl, Proposal for a Benign Revolution in Marriage Law and Marriage Conflicts Law, 55 Iowa L. Rev. 56 (1969); Reese, Marriage in American Conflicts Law, 26 Int'l & Comp. L.Q. 952 (1977); Swan, A New Approach to Marriage and Divorce in the Conflict of Laws, 24 Toronto L.J. 17 (1974); Taintor, Marriage in the Conflict of Laws, 9 Vand. L. Rev. 607 (1956); R. Weintraub, Commentary on the Conflict of Laws 289–95 passim (4th ed. 2001). Cf. 2 A. Ehrenzweig & E. Jayme, Private International Law 39 (1973).

14. E.g., Metropolitan Life Insurance Co. v. Manning, 568 F.2d 922 (2d Cir.1977); Holland America Insurance Co. v. Rogers, 313 F.Supp. 314 (N.D.Cal.1970). Cf. Reese, Marriage in American Conflicts Law, 26 Int'l & Comp. L.Q. 952, 954 (1977); Seidelson & Bowler, Determination of Family Status in the Administration of Federal Acts: A Choice of Law Problem For Federal Agencies and Courts, 33 Geo. Wash. L. Rev. 863 (1965). See also Strasser, *Baker* and Some Recipes for Disaster: On DOMA, Covenant Marriages, and Full Faith and Credit Jurisprudence, 64 Brooklyn L. Rev, 307, 342 (1998).

the incidence of the relationship as attaching to its status in such a way that the bundle of incidents constitute the relationship. In view of this, the tendency in local law consideration is to approach issues in this area by determining whether the status exists of which the incidents are a part. Consequently, courts have frequently viewed status as a preliminary issue from which the determination of incidents will flow. Similarly, the significance of a person's status and its relevance arises in conflict-of-laws litigation almost exclusively concerning questions regarding the incidents of the relationship, such as succession or claim to property, or a claim for support, or a claim for damages in tort. In conflict of laws it seems necessary to consider the questions concerning each incident or its enjoyment as the significant issue which most, but not all of the time, will be controlled by the existence or nonexistence of the status. Because the principal issue in multistate litigation usually will concern property, support, or tort, the issues regarding the status arise only incidentally to the principal claim. This circumstance leads to the question whether a court seeking to resolve a matter of succession, for example, will apply forum law to decide whether the validity of the claimant's status or the laws of the jurisdiction where it was established. This conflict-of-laws problem has attracted considerable attention in the literature; it is the problem of the "incidental question."[1] In recent American cases, the consideration of issues involving such incidental questions, like those involving *renvoi*, are likely to be viewed as part of the choice-of-law policy analysis of separate issues without preconceived allocation to the law of the forum (lex fori) or the law otherwise applicable to the principal issues (lex causae). This seems to be the case whether the principal issues in litigation involve a claim based on local law or on the law of another state.[2] Like other issues, the dominant policies and significant relationships relevant to the particular issue including the purpose for which the determination of status is pertinent will guide the court in seeking a just result.[3]

§ 13.3

1. See A.E. Gotlieb, The Incidental Question Revisited, 26 Int'l & Comp. L.Q. 734 (1977) (collecting authorities and literature). See also Cavers, Contemporary Conflicts Law in American Perspective, 75 Recueil de Cours 140 (1970–III). Cf. Reese, Depecage: A Common Phenomenon in Choice of Law, 73 Colum. L. Rev. 58 (1973); R. Schuz, When is a Polygamous Marriage Not a Polygamous Marriage, 46 Mod. L. Rev. 653 (1983).

2. See Gotlieb, supra n.1, at 761. Cf. Metropolitan Life Insurance Co. v. Manning, 568 F.2d 922 (2d Cir.1977); Mills v. State Farm Mut. Auto. Ins. Co., 827 F.2d 1418 (10th Cir.1987); Stutsman v. Kaiser

Foundation Health Plan, 546 A.2d 367 (D.C.App.1988).

3. See Gotlieb, supra n.1, at 780:

The cases establish three points beyond any doubt: that actual conflicts can and do arise in the selection of rules to apply to incidental questions; that the overwhelming majority of cases, virtually all of them, deal with problems that relate in one form or another to personal status; and that, as Currie observed, "the determination of status is almost never the ultimate object of an action." [Currie, On Displacement of the Law of the Forum, 58 Colum. L. Rev. 964, 1022 (1958), Selected Essays on Conflict of Laws, 69 (1931)] ... These cases will involve prob-

D. COMPETING APPROACHES IN CHOICE OF LAW: DOMICILE AND NATIONALITY

§ 13.4 As observed in the discussion of the incidental question, the courts of the United States traditionally have applied a single choice-of-law reference to the place of celebration for the determination of issues relating to marriage. More recent departures from this tendency will be considered in subsequent discussion. Outside of the United States, however, most legal systems distinguish between formal and substantive validity of marriage.[1] Matters of form are referred to the law of the place of celebration, while the personal law determines substantive conditions.[2] The personal law used is that of the domicile in some nations and in others, that of the nationality or citizenship of the individual[3] although the validation policy also has substantial force.[4] Like the courts of the United States, the personal law often sustains a marriage valid

lems of interpretation, policy, consistency, uniformity, equity and fairness.... There seems little reason to doubt that judges in dealing with these complicated cases of conflicting laws, multiple relationships, so-called limping marriages and other similar conditions, will have so many facts and rules within their reach that they will tend to attain the solutions which they perceive to be fair, and find, somehow, the legal reasoning which will justify their conclusions. When we look at some of the methods or devices available to a judge—characterizing the main problem (as one of succession personal law, land, contract, etc.) with all its implications for the choice of applicable laws; applying *renvoi* either partially or completely or not applying it; engaging in "secondary" characterization of the selected foreign rules; classifying them as substantive or procedural or by subject matter, so as to obtain the desired connecting factor; interpreting or construing a foreign rule or decision or a domestic rule or decision; dealing with incidental questions directly; selecting, changing or developing an existing choice-of-law rule; discerning public policy imperatives or the public order of the forum—it becomes obvious that the courts have all the tools they need to make their way toward the decision which they consciously or unconsciously wish to reach. Cf. Mills v. State Farm Mutual Auto. Ins. Co., 827 F.2d 1418 (10th Cir.1987).

§ 13.4

1. 1 Rabel, The Conflict of Laws 224 (2d ed. 1958); Dicey & Morris, Conflict of Laws 651 (13th ed. 2000 by Collins); R. Graveson, Conflict of Laws, 251 (7th ed. 1974). See generally L. Pålsson, Marriage in Comparative Conflict of Laws: Substantive Condi-

tions (1981); Fentiman, Validity of Marriage and the Proper Law, 44 Camb. L.J. 256 (1985); Smart, Interest Analysis, False Conflicts and Essential Validity of Marriage, 14 Anglo–Am. L. Rev. 225 (1985). See Vervaecke v. Smith, [1983] 1 A.C. 145; Fentiman, The Validity of Marriage and the Proper Law, 44 Camb. L.J. 256 (1985).

2. See Swan, A New Approach to Marriage and Divorce in the Conflict of Laws, 24 U. Toronto L.J. 17 (1974). Maddaugh, Validity of Marriage and the Conflict of Laws: A Critique of the Present Anglo–American Position, 23 U. Toronto L.J. 117 (1973). The approach of validating a marriage by reference to the place of celebration appears to be gaining preference in private international law over the personal law of the parties. See Hague Convention on Celebration and Recognition of the Validity of Marriages (1976), 25 Am. J. Comp. L. 399, 400 (1977) which provides:

"Article 9. A marriage validly entered into under the law of the State of celebration or which subsequently becomes valid under that law shall be considered as such in all Contracting States, subject to the provisions of this Chapter."

See also Glenn, The 1976 Hague Conventions on Marriage and Matrimonial Property Regimes, 55 Can. B. Rev. 586 (1977); Fisher, The Australian Adoptions of The Hague Convention, 2 Queensland Inst. of Tech. L.J. 17 (1986); Gordon, Foreign Marriage, 18 Fam. L. 178 (1988).

3. 1 Rabel, supra n.1, at 224; 2 A. Ehrenzweig & E. Jayme, Private International Law 147 (1973); R. Graveson, Conflict of Laws 230 (7th ed. 1974).

4. See Dicey & Morris, Conflict of Laws 651 et seq. (13th ed. 2000 by Collins);

where performed.[5] In legal systems that now recognize same-sex registered partnerships or civil unions, the treatment of these closely tracks that of the traditional marriage,[6] including a presumption in favor of validity.[7]

II. LAW GOVERNING RECOGNITION OF MARRIAGE

A. THE TRADITIONAL STATEMENT

§ 13.5 The usual statement of the traditional doctrine in the United States on the validity of a marriage is that a marriage is valid everywhere if valid under the law of the state where the marriage takes place, except in rare instances.[1] The most prominent exceptions are those marriages involving polygamy and incest, i.e., the enjoyment of the incidents of which are positively prohibited by the local law.

Swan, A New Approach to Marriage and Divorce in the Conflict of Laws, 24 U. Toronto L.J. 17 (1974). See also A. Ehrenzweig & E. Jayme, supra n.3, at 148, 199; Hussain v. Hussain, (1982) 3 All. E.R. 369; Lawrence v. Lawrence (1985) 1 All. E.R. 506.

5. 1 Rabel, supra n.1, at 267.

6. See, e.g. Germany, Introductory Law to the Civil Code (EGBGB) Art. 17b (2002): in principle, the law of the state of registration govern validity and property rights arising from a registered partnership. If that law does not provide for such rights or for support, the general provisions (common law of nationality, last common habitual residence, etc.-see Art. 14) apply. Art. 17(b)(1). Substantive rights, however, are limited by the rights that German law provides for partnerships registered there. Art. 17(b)(4). The applicable German law is the Statute on Domestic Partnerships [Gesetz über Lebenspartnerschaften], BGBl. 2001, I, 266; as amended BGBl. 2001, I, 3513, effective January 1, 2002. For discussion and references, see J. Kropholler, BGB-Studienkommentar annos. 10–19 preceding § 1353 BGB (6th ed. 2003).

For same-sex *marriage*, see for *Belgium*: Fiorini, New Belgian Law on Same Sex Marriage and the PIL Implications, 52 Int'l & Comp. L. Q. 1039 (2003); for *Ontario*, *Canada*: Halpern v. Canada (Attorney General), [2003] O.J. No. 2268; for *The Netherlands*: Wasmuth, in: H. Krüger & H.-P. Mansel (eds.), Liber Amicorum Gerhard Kegel 237 (2002).

For a comparative overview of same-sex registered partnerships in Europe, see J. Basedow, K. Hopt, H. Kötz & P. Dopffel (eds.), Die Rechtsstellung gleichgeschlechtlicher Lebensgemeinschaften (=Vol. 70 Bei-

träge zum Ausländischen und Internationalen Privatrecht, 2000). See also infra § 13.20 et seq.

7. See, e.g., Germany, Art. 17(b)(3) EGBGB, supra n.6: if there exist partnerships between the same parties registered in more than one state, the last in time determines what rights arise under Art. 17 (b)(1).

§ 13.5

1. Restatement, Second, Conflict of Laws § 283(2) (1971); Reese, Marriage in American Conflict of Laws, 26 Int'l & Comp. L.Q. 952 (1977). See Renshaw v. Heckler, 787 F.2d 50 (2d Cir. 1986); Vandever v. Industrial Comm'n, 148 Ariz. 373, 714 P.2d 866, 869 (1985); Sohnlein v. Winchell, 230 Cal.App.2d 508, 41 Cal.Rptr. 145 (1964); In re Marriage of Fetters, 41 Colo. App. 281, 584 P.2d 104 (1978); Singh v. Singh, 213 Conn. 637, 569 A.2d 1112, 1118 (1990); Jay v. Jay, 212 A.2d 331 (D.C.App. 1965); Young v. Garcia, 172 So.2d 243 (Fla. App.1965); Bogen v. Bogen, 261 N.W.2d 606 (Minn.1977); McMorrow v. Schweiker, 561 F.Supp. 584, 590 (D.N.J. 182); In re Macklin's Estate, 82 Misc.2d 376, 371 N.Y.S.2d 238 (Surr.1975); Bronislawa K. v. Tadeusz K., 90 Misc.2d 183, 393 N.Y.S.2d 534 (Fam. Ct.1977); Estate of Crittenden, 29 Or.App. 189, 562 P.2d 609 (1977); Matter of Booker's Estate, 27 Or.App. 779, 557 P.2d 248 (1976); Zwerling v. Zwerling, 270 S.C. 685, 244 S.E.2d 311 (1978); State v. Austin, 160 W.Va. 337, 234 S.E.2d 657 (1977); Taylor v. Taylor, 160 W.Va. 124, 230 S.E.2d 924 (1976). Cf. In re Reed's Marriage, 226 N.W.2d 795 (Iowa 1975). Lopez v. Bonner, 439 P.2d 687 (Okla.1967). See also Mission Ins. Co. v. Industrial Commission, 114 Ariz. 170, 559 P.2d 1085 (App. 1976).

Very few marriages are alleged to exist unless the requirements of the state where entered into are satisfied, this being the law most immediately before the parties. Considering that the parties almost always satisfy the law of the place of celebration, the rule stated is the result of the combined force of the policy to assure free consent and the policy sustaining the validity of the marriage once assumed. Even if a marriage may not satisfy all the requirements of the place where celebrated, the validation policy may well lead to its being sustained if the state with the significant personal law contact would sustain it. For example, if the law of the state where the parties were both domiciled or where they first were domiciled as a married couple would sustain the marriage, other states subsequently becoming involved would likely uphold the marriage.[2]

Illustrative of this view is the approach of the court in the *Shippy* case[3] in Washington. In concluding that the place of celebration rule did not preclude a marriage being valid under the domicile of the parties when the issue arose as to whether a claimant was the deceased putative husband's surviving spouse, the court stated:[4]

"There are, however, exceptions to applying the traditional rule that the validity of a marriage is governed by the law of the state where the marriage was contracted. At this juncture we take note of the distinction between marriage as a status and the incidents of marriage. As stated in Restatement (Second) of Conflict of Laws, *Status*, ch. 11, at 231 (1971):

'[I]n law, a status can be viewed from two standpoints. It can be viewed as a relationship which continues as the parties move from state to state, or it can be viewed from the standpoint of the incidents that arise from it.' . . .

"Here, we deal with the incidents of the Shippy's marriage as it affects Washington, but must determine preliminarily the validity of the status. One of the exceptions to which we have referred is that a marriage should not necessarily be invalid in other states if it would be valid under the law of some other state having a substantial relation to the parties and the marriage. . . .

"Therefore, in light of this state's strong present interests, and to protect the expectations of James and Inge, we will . . . give validating effect to the California nunc pro tunc decree and validate Inge's otherwise void marriage. Consequently, as the 'surviving spouse' of James

---

2. See Restatement, Second, Conflict of Laws § 283, comment (i) (1971). See also

UNIFORM MARRIAGE AND DIVORCE ACT:

"Section 210 (Application). All marriages contracted . . . outside this state that were valid at the time of the contract or subsequently validated by the laws of the place in which they were contracted or by the domicile of the parties are valid in the state."

9A U.L.A. 147, 176–77 (1987); Reese, Marriage in American Conflict of Laws, 26 Int'l & Comp. L.Q. 952 (1977). Cf. Spalding v. Commissioner of Internal Revenue, 537 F.2d 666 (2d Cir.1976); Estate of Crittenden, 29 Or.App. 189, 562 P.2d 609 (1977).

3. In re Estate of Shippy, 37 Wn.App. 164, 678 P.2d 848 (1984); followed in State v. Rivera, 95 Wn.App. 961, 977 P.2d 1247 (Wash.App. 1999).

4. 678 P.2d at 850, 851, 852.

Shippy, Inge is entitled to be treated as such for all purposes in the administration and distribution of his estate.''

Only when a claimed incident of the marriage is sought to be enjoyed in a state where such enjoyment violates strong public policy will a marriage otherwise valid be denied effect.[5]

The converse of the validity rule cannot safely be assumed. While it may be said on abundant authority that the general American rule is that a marriage valid where entered into is valid everywhere,[6] it is doubtful that the rule may be phrased as one of the lex loci contractus.[7] It is desirable to analyze the problem further, however, especially in regard to the situations where a marriage, valid where contracted, is denied recognition at the domicile of the parties, or elsewhere.

B.　REQUIREMENTS OF PLACE OF CELEBRATION

§ 13.6　Under the usual view in the United States, first consideration in assessing the validity of a marriage is to determine compliance with the requirements of the law where the alleged marriage took place. If the parties comply with the rules of the place the marriage is celebrated, they usually will be recognized elsewhere as husband and wife, even in a state where stricter or different rules concerning formality are in force.[1] This is shown in the frequent recognition of foreign "common law" marriages in states that do not permit this informal method of entering the matrimonial status.[2]

5.　See Restatement, Second, Conflict of Laws § 284, comment (c) (1971). See also Rhodes v. McAfee, 224 Tenn. 495, 457 S.W.2d 522 (1970).

6.　See supra n.1.

7.　Cf. Morris Plan Co. v. Converse, 15 Cal.App.3d 399, 93 Cal.Rptr. 103 (1971); Rhodes v. McAfee, 224 Tenn. 495, 457 S.W.2d 522 (1970); Hager v. Hager, 3 Va. App. 415, 349 S.E.2d 908 (1986).

Nebraska, however, seems to have expressly adopted the converse. In Randall v. Randall, 216 Neb. 541, 345 N.W.2d 319 (1984) the court stated:

We have long held in this jurisdiction that the validity of a marriage is generally determined by the law of the place where it was contracted. Specifically, we have said in Abramson v. Abramson, 161 Neb. 782, 787, 74 N.W.2d 919, 924 (1956): 'The general rule is that the validity of a marriage is determined by the law of the place where it was contracted; if valid there it will be held valid everywhere, and conversely if invalid by the lex loci contractus, it will be invalid wherever the question may arise. See also Scott v. Scott, 153 Neb. 906, 46 N.W.2d 627 (1951); Forshay v. Johnston, 144 Neb. 525, 13 N.W.2d 873 (1944).

It appears to us that the rationale for this rule compels the result in this case. If indeed marriage is a contract, then it seems to follow that the validity of the contract should be determined by the law of the place where the contract is entered into, when entered into, and the validity should not be determined by hindsight.

§ 13.6

1.　Hallett v. Collins, 51 U.S. (10 How.) 174, 13 L.Ed. 376 (1850); In re Perez' Estate, 98 Cal.App.2d 121, 219 P.2d 35 (1950); Yi Ning Ma v. Mei Fang Ma, 483 N.W.2d 732 (Minn.App. 1992); Gallegos v. Wilkerson, 79 N.M. 549, 445 P.2d 970 (1968); In re Lenherr's Estate, 455 Pa. 225, 314 A.2d 255 (1974); Dalrymple v. Dalrymple, 2 Hagg. Cons. 54 (1811); Korf v. Korf, 38 Wis.2d 413, 157 N.W.2d 691 (1968). Cf. Ponina v. Leland, 85 Nev. 263, 454 P.2d 16 (1969).

2.　Bloch v. Bloch, 473 F.2d 1067 (3d Cir.1973); Spiel v. Rabinovitz, 121 F.3d 251 (7th Cir. 1997); Orr v. Bowen, 648 F.Supp. 1510 (D.Nev.1986); Old Republic Ins. Co. v. Christian, 389 F.Supp. 335 (E.D.Tenn. 1975); Cook v. Carolina Freight Carriers Corp., 299 F.Supp. 192 (D.Del.1969); Johnson v. Lincoln Square Properties, Inc., 571

On the other hand, if that law prescribes compliance with certain formalities to be essential, omission to meet those requirements may preclude the recognition of the marriage elsewhere. While invalidity in this latter case of noncompliance is often stated or assumed, the cases are inconclusive[3] on this issue because all but a few of those which hold marriages invalid under this view are instances in which the marriage also would appear to be invalid under the law or policy of the other interested states.[4] Consequently, it seems probable that a highly interest-

S.2d 541 (Fla.App. 1990); Metropolitan Life Insurance Co. v. Holding, 293 F.Supp. 854 (E.D.Va.1968); Parish v. Minvielle, 217 So.2d 684 (La.App.1969); Laccetti v. Laccetti, 245 Md. 97, 225 A.2d 266 (1967); Jennings v. Jennings, 20 Md.App. 369, 315 A.2d 816 (1974); Whitley v. Whitley, 778 S.W.2d 233 (Mo.App.1989); Pope v. Pope, 520 S.W.2d 634 (Mo.App.1975); Bourelle v. Soo–Crete, Inc., 165 Neb. 731, 87 N.W.2d 371 (1958); Clark v. Clark, 52 N.J.Eq. 650, 30 A. 81 (Ch.Div.1894); Gallegos v. Wilkerson, 79 N.M. 549, 445 P.2d 970 (1968); Hulis v. M. Foschi & Sons, 124 A.D.2d 643, 507 N.Y.S.2d 898 (1986); Matter of Estate of Jenkins, 133 Misc.2d 420, 506 N.Y.S.2d 1009 (Surr. 1986); Gordon v. Gordon, 27 Misc.2d 948, 211 N.Y.S.2d 265 (1960), motion denied 13 A.D.2d 710, 215 N.Y.S.2d 1020 (1961); Boykin v. State Industrial Accident Commission, 224 Or. 76, 355 P.2d 724 (1960); Matter of Estate of Foster, 180 W.Va. 250, 376 S.E.2d 144 (W.V.1988). Cf. Albina Engine and Machine Works v. O'Leary, 328 F.2d 877 (9th Cir.1964), cert. denied 379 U.S. 817, 85 S.Ct. 35, 13 L.Ed.2d 29 (1964); Gibson v. Hughes, 192 F.Supp. 564 (S.D.N.Y.1961); In re Trigg's Estate, 3 Ariz.App. 385, 414 P.2d 988 (1966), aff'd 102 Ariz. 140, 426 P.2d 637 (1967); In re Watts' Estate, 31 N.Y.2d 491, 341 N.Y.S.2d 609, 294 N.E.2d 195 (1973); Walker v. Hildenbrand, 243 Or. 117, 410 P.2d 244 (1966); Andrews v. Signal Auto Parts, Inc., 492 S.W.2d 222 (Tenn.1972); Peffley–Warner v. Bowen, 113 Wn.2d 243, 778 P.2d 1022 (1989). But cf. Metropolitan Life Insurance Co. v. Chase, 294 F.2d 500 (3d Cir.1961); Grant v. Superior Court, 27 Ariz.App. 427, 555 P.2d 895 (1976); Walker v. Yarbrough, 257 Ark. 300, 516 S.W.2d 390 (1974); Nevarez v. Bailon, 287 S.W.2d 521 (Tex.Civ.App.1956); Delaney v. Delaney, 35 Conn.Supp. 230, 405 A.2d 91 (1979); Enis v. State, 408 So.2d 486 (Miss.1981); George v. George, 389 So.2d 1389 (Miss.1980); Mott v. Duncan Petroleum Trans., 51 N.Y.2d 289, 434 N.Y.S.2d 155, 414 N.E.2d 657 (1980); Jim's Water Service v. Eayrs, 590 P.2d 1346 (Wyo.1979). Of particular interest is Bowers v. Wyoming State Treasurer ex rel. Workmen's Compensation Div., 593 P.2d 182 (Wyo.1979) in which a provision of the

Worker's Compensation Act which required a "marriage solemnized by a legal ceremony" was held unconstitutional as a denial of equal protection when applied to so restrict the traditional choice of law rule to refuse recognition of common law marriages valid in the state of inception. The court said there was no state purpose served by the choice-of-law rule requiring a ceremonial marriage. This conclusion however did not, in the court's view, in any way weaken Wyoming's requirement of a ceremony for domestic marriages.

See also n.4 infra.

3. Indicating statutes regulating manner by which marriages are solemnized are directory only, see Picarella v. Picarella, 20 Md.App. 499, 316 A.2d 826 (1974); People v. Benu, 87 Misc.2d 139, 385 N.Y.S.2d 222 (1976); Maxwell v. Maxwell, 51 Misc.2d 687, 273 N.Y.S.2d 728 (1966). Cf. In re Levie's Estate, 50 Cal.App.3d 572, 123 Cal.Rptr. 445 (1975); Schoenbrod v. Siegler, 20 N.Y.2d 403, 283 N.Y.S.2d 881, 230 N.E.2d 638 (1967); Hager v. Hager, 3 Va.App. 415, 349 S.E.2d 908 (1986); Dicey & Morris, Conflict of Laws 651 (13th ed. 2000 by Collins); Swan, A New Approach to Marriage and Divorce in the Conflict of Laws, 24 U. Toronto L.J. 17, 21 (1974).

4. Tatum v. Tatum, 241 F.2d 401 (9th Cir.1957); Gamez v. Industrial Commission, 114 Ariz. 179, 559 P.2d 1094 (1976); Smith v. Anderson, 821 So.2d 323 (Fla.App. 2002);In re Reed's Marriage, 226 N.W.2d 795 (Iowa 1975); Canale v. People, 177 Ill. 219, 52 N.E. 310 (1898); Jordan v. Missouri & Kansas Telephone Co., 136 Mo.App. 192, 116 S.W. 432 (1909); In re Hall, 61 App.Div. 266, 70 N.Y.S. 406 (1901); Herndon v. Herndon, 9 Misc.2d 1047, 174 N.Y.S.2d 568 (1957). Cf. Bobb v. Secretary, Dept. of Health, Education and Welfare, 312 F.Supp. 225 (S.D.N.Y.1970); Jambrone v. David, 16 Ill.2d 32, 156 N.E.2d 569 (1959); Walker v. Hildenbrand, 243 Or. 117, 410 P.2d 244 (1966). But cf. Cruickshank v. Cruickshank, 193 Misc. 366, 82 N.Y.S.2d 522 (1948); Kitzman v. Kitzman, 167 Wis. 308, 166 N.W. 789 (1918).

ed state, for instance, the common domicile of the parties, would validate a marriage it deems worthy although not satisfying the required formalities of the place entered into.[5] In validating the marriage of the forum's domiciliaries even though the law of the place of celebration has in some regard not been satisfied,[6] several cases have recognized the interest of the domiciliary state as being more significant than that of the state of celebration.[7] Few, however, have articulated this choice clearly[8] even though the policy considerations support such a conclusion. In some cases, particular requirements of the state of celebration are interpreted as merely directory. In the latter event, noncompliance does not invalidate the marriage, though it may subject the participants to minor forms of punishment.[9]

The common law marriage cases also seem instructive here as they frequently state that the law of the place of inception of the alleged marriage controls but is not satisfied in cases which appear particularly offensive to the forum court. The cases typically involve couples from a "ceremony only" state traveling into a "common law marriage" state for brief stays and then one claiming a valid marriage resulted. See, e.g., Grant v. Superior Court In and For Pima County, 27 Ariz.App. 427, 555 P.2d 895 (1976) (overnight in Texas hotel insufficient to establish marriage); Smith v. Anderson, 821 So.2d 323 (Fla.App. 2002) (traveling to Georgia twice a year did not satisfy common law marriage requirement under Georgia law for purposes of recognition in Florida); Goldin v. Goldin, 48 Md.App. 154, 426 A.2d 410 (1981) (ski weekend in Pennsylvania not sufficient evidence particularly when young children slept in same room with couple); Matter of Brack's Estate, 121 Mich.App. 585, 329 N.W.2d 432 (1982) (one night in Georgia motel enroute to Florida insufficient to establish common law marriage); Laikola v. Engineered Concrete, 277 N.W.2d 653 (Minn.1979) (three-week vacation in Montana insufficient to overcome claim of "second wife" by a subsequent ceremonial marriage); Hesington v. Hesington's Estate, 640 S.W.2d 824 (Mo.App.1982) (weekend in Oklahoma insufficient and contrary to Missouri public policy); Stein v. Stein, 641 S.W.2d 856 (Mo.App.1982) (elderly couple on bus through Pennsylvania); Matter of Lamb's Estate, 99 N.M. 157, 655 P.2d 1001 (1982) (tape recorded vows in New Mexico and overnight in Texas insufficient); In re Bivians' Estate, 98 N.M. 722, 652 P.2d 744 (App. 1982), cert. quashed 98 N.M. 762, 652 P.2d 1213 (1982) (occasional short trips to Texas and Colorado insufficient to sustain common law marriage by New Mexico residents). But cf. Braddock v. Taylor, 592 S.W.2d 40 (Tex.Civ.App.1979), error refused n.r.e.

5. See Restatement, Second, Conflict of Laws § 283 comment (1971). Cf. 2 A. Ehrenzweig & E. Jayme, Private Int'l Law 150 (1973); Baade, Marriage and Divorce in American Conflicts Law: Governmental–Interests Analysis and the Restatement (Second), 72 Colum. L. Rev. 329, 375 (1972).

6. See Restatement, Second, Conflict of Laws § 283, cmnt. (i) (1971).

7. See, e.g., Succession of Goss, 304 So.2d 704 (La.App.1974), writ denied 309 So.2d 339 (La.1975); Sullivan v. American Bridge Co., 115 Pa.Super. 536, 176 A. 24 (1935) noted 83 U. Pa. L. Rev. 801 (1935); Appelbaum v. Appelbaum, 9 Misc.2d 677, 168 N.Y.S.2d 970 (1957); Matter of Caeti's Will, 207 Misc. 353, 138 N.Y.S.2d 496 (Surr.1955); Bays v. Bays, 105 Misc. 492, 174 N.Y.S. 212 (1918); Ruding v. Smith, 2 Hagg. Cons. 371 (1821); Portwood v. Portwood, 109 S.W.2d 515 (Tex.Civ.App.1937).

8. See Anonymous v. Anonymous, 46 Del. 458, 85 A.2d 706 (1951); Succession of Hernandez, 46 La.Ann. 962, 15 So. 461 (1894); Wilkins v. Zelichowski, 26 N.J. 370, 140 A.2d 65 (1958); Wilcox v. Wilcox, 46 Hun. 32 (N.Y. 1887). Cf. Sirois v. Sirois, 94 N.H. 215, 50 A.2d 88 (1946); Capasso v. Colonna, 95 N.J.Eq. 35, 122 A. 378 (Ch.Div. 1923), affirmed 96 N.J.Eq. 385, 124 A. 760 (Err. & App.1924); In re Palmer's Estate, 192 Misc. 385, 79 N.Y.S.2d 404 (Sur.1948). See also Jaffey, The Essential Validity of Marriage in English Conflict of Laws, 41 Mod. L. Rev. 38 (1978); Reese, Marriage in American Conflict of Laws, 26 Int'l & Comp. L.Q. 952, 956 (1977). See generally L. Plsson, Marriage in Comparative Conflict of Laws: Substantive Conditions (1981).

9. Compare Teamsters Local 639 Employer's Pension Trust v. Johnson, 1992 WL 200075 (D.D.C. 1992) (a marriage contracted by underage parties is not void but only voidable and subject to the minor punishment of being open to direct attack),

An interesting application of the general rule is shown by a federal case involving marriage by correspondence. A man in Minnesota sent to the woman, who was living in Missouri, a written agreement in duplicate, signed by him, whereby the parties undertook to assume from that date henceforth the relation of husband and wife. The woman signed the papers and sent one copy back to the man. It was held that this acceptance constituted a valid marriage in Missouri and the woman could recover damages, as widow, in Minnesota, for wrongful death of the husband.[10] The validity of the marriage was treated as depending upon compliance with the laws of Missouri.[11]

The same principles are applicable to the question of the validity of a marriage by proxy. If such a marriage is permitted by the law of the place where performed, and it probably is permitted unless positive legislation forbids it, the marriage so contracted is valid elsewhere, at least so far as formal requirements are concerned.[12]

with Estate of Toutant, 247 Wis.2d 400, 633 N.W.2d 692 (App. 2001) (Texas marriage void for non-compliance with Wisconsin's six-month waiting period between divorce and remarriage). From among the older decision, see Dumaresly v. Fishly, 10 Ky. (3 A.K. Marsh) 368 (1821); Inhabitants of Hiram v. Pierce, 45 Me. 367, 71 Am.Dec. 555 (1858); Picarella v. Picarella, 20 Md.App. 499, 316 A.2d 826 (1974); People v. Benu, 87 Misc.2d 139, 385 N.Y.S.2d 222 (1976); Maxwell v. Maxwell, 51 Misc.2d 687, 273 N.Y.S.2d 728 (1966); Bays v. Bays, 105 Misc. 492, 174 N.Y.S. 212 (1918); Hilliard v. Hilliard, 24 Misc.2d 861, 209 N.Y.S.2d 132 (1960); Reaves v. Reaves, 15 Okla. 240, 82 P. 490 (1905); Portwood v. Portwood, 109 S.W.2d 515 (Tex.Civ.App.1937). Cf. De Potty v. De Potty, 226 Ark. 881, 295 S.W.2d 330 (1956); Estate of Crittenden, 29 Or. App. 189, 562 P.2d 609 (1977).

10. Great Northern Railroad Co. v. Johnson, 254 Fed. 683 (8th Cir.1918). See also Beale, Progress of the Law, 1918–1919, 33 Harv. L. Rev. 1, 13.

11. The court noted that Missouri did not require cohabitation for a common law marriage. This may imply that perhaps the court would have decided the other way had Missouri been a state which required cohabitation as well as consent for a common law marriage. However, it seems likely that under the force of the policy to sustain marriages that compliance with either state's requirements would have been adequate. See Restatement, Second, Conflict of Laws § 283, cmnt. (j) (1971). Cf. Peffley–Warner v. Bowen, 113 Wn.2d 243, 778 P.2d 1022 (1989).

12. Barrons v. United States, 191 F.2d 92 (9th Cir.1951); Ex parte Suzanna, 295 Fed. 713 (D.C.Mass.1924); United States ex rel. Aznar v. Commissioner of Immigration, 298 Fed. 103 (D.C.N.Y.1924) (noted 33 Yale L.J. 777 (1925)); United States ex rel. Modianos v. Tuttle, 12 F.2d 927 (D.C.La.1925); Silva v. Tillinghast, 36 F.2d 801 (D.C.Mass. 1929); Torres v. Torres, 144 N.J.Super. 540, 366 A.2d 713 (Ch.Div.1976); Fernandes v. Fernandes, 275 App.Div. 777, 87 N.Y.S.2d 707 (1949); In re Valente's Will, 18 Misc.2d 701, 188 N.Y.S.2d 732 (Surr. 1959); In re Marriage of Holemar, 27 Or.App. 613, 557 P.2d 38 (1976); Restatement, Second, Conflict of Laws § 283 (1971). See Cosulich Societa Triestina Di Navigazione v. Elting, 66 F.2d 534 (2d Cir.1933). See also Apt v. Apt, [1947] p. 127; Lorenzen, Marriage by Proxy and the Conflict of Laws, 32 Harv. L. Rev. 473 (1919); Stern, Marriage by Proxy in Mexico, 19 So. Cal. L. Rev. 109 (1945); A. Ehrenzweig, supra n.12, at 155; Dicey & Morris, Conflict of Laws 691 (13th ed. 2000 by Collins); R. Graveson, Conflict of Laws 256 (7th ed. 1974).

As a matter of amusing interest, a couple was allowed to marry by cell phone in Belgium in 2003. http://www.anano-va.com/news/story/sm_833785.html. However, their "marriage" still required registration. This was so because most Continental systems provide that a marriage can be concluded–domestically–only by compliance with (secular) civil law requirements. See, e.g., German Introductory Law to the Civil Code (EGBGB) Art. 13 (III) (1). A limited exception applies to foreign nationals who comply with their national law, have a ceremony performed by an authorized official of their home country, and comply with local domestic registration requirements. Id. (2). See Kegel & Schurig, Internatio-

Federal law provides that marriages celebrated in a foreign country in the presence of a consular officer of the United States, between persons who would be authorized to marry in the District of Columbia, shall be valid for all purposes.[13] In the meantime, a regulation of the U.S. Department of State forbids U.S. consular officers from celebrating marriages[14] but permits them to act as "official witnesses."[15] The present effect of the statutory provision is therefore in doubt.

Marriages performed on the high seas give rise to an interesting problem. Although it has been sometimes said that there is no law on the high seas,[16] yet for many purposes the nation whose flag the ship is flying has been held to have jurisdiction over the ship. Therefore it is not surprising to find that compliance with the law of the flag is required for a marriage to be validly contracted.[17] In the United States, there is no such thing as a flag of a particular state, the only flag being that of the United States. As a result, there must be a modification of the general rule. Since the one who exercises the greatest amount of control over the ship is her owner, and the state most closely connected with the owner is the state of its domicile, it has been held that the marriage to be valid must conform to the law of the owner's domicile.[18]

C. PROHIBITIONS OF THE DOMICILE OF THE PARTIES

1. Form and Capacity

§ 13.7 The usual statement that a marriage valid where entered into is valid everywhere makes no distinction between the form of the ceremony and the capacity of the parties to enter the marriage relation.[1]

nales Privatrecht 811 et seq. (9th ed. 2004).

13. 12 Stat. 79 (1860), 22 U.S.C.A. § 1172 (1979). See Parry, A Conflicts Myth: The American "Consular" Marriage, 67 Harv. L. Rev. 1187 (1954). For a comparative perspective, see Galanter & Krishnan, Personal Law and Human Rights in India and Israel, 34 Isr. L. Rev. 101, 123 (2000).

14. 22 C.F.R. § 52.1. See also 7 M. Whiteman, Digest of International Law 609 (1970).

15. 22 C.F.R. § 52.2(b).

The Hague Convention on Celebration and Recognition of the Validity of Marriages (1976) provides: "Article 9 ... A marriage celebrated by a diplomatic or consular official in accordance with his law shall similarly be considered valid in all Contracting States, provided that the celebration is not prohibited by the State of celebration." 25 Am. J. Comp. L. 399, 400 (1977).

16. See Norman v. Norman, 121 Cal. 620, 54 P. 143 (1899).

17. Restatement, Second, Conflict of Laws § 283, Reporter's Note (1971). See also A. Ehrenzweig, supra n.12, at 154; R. Graveson, Conflict of Laws 278 (7th ed. 1974).

18. Johnson v. Baker, 142 Or. 404, 20 P.2d 407 (1933); Fisher v. Fisher, 250 N.Y. 313, 165 N.E. 460 (1929) (noted 78 U. Pa. L. Rev. 109 (1929)); 38 Yale L.J. 1129 (1929); see Bolmer v. Edsall, 90 N.J.Eq. 299, 106 A. 646 (Ch.Div.1919). But cf. Norman v. Norman, 121 Cal. 620, 54 P. 143 (1898). Considering the problems of shared and corporate ownership, the feasibility of such an approach seems doubtful except as a rationale for validating a marriage.

§ 13.7

1. See Yarbrough v. United States, 341 F.2d 621 (Ct.Cl.1965). English law has distinguished between formal validity and essential validity and treats capacity and consanguinity as essential requirements to be governed by the law of the domicile. R. Graveson, Conflict of Laws 263 (7th ed. 1974); Dicey & Morris, Conflict of Laws 653 (13th ed. 2000 by Collins). See also D. Brad-

While abundant authority upholds the validity of marriages by this broad test, there is a substantial number of cases denying validity to a foreign marriage contracted by a party when he was forbidden to marry, or forbidden to enter the particular marriage in question, by the law of his domicile. Further consideration of these issues is undertaken in the differing situations in which various prohibitions may be relevant.

2. *Substantive Prohibition*

§ **13.8**   A man and woman, both domiciled in Michigan, wish to marry, but their marriage is forbidden by Michigan law. Can they, by crossing the state line into Indiana, where it may be assumed the marriage would be legal, enter into a marriage which will be good at their domicile or in a third state?

The question arises in cases involving several types of prohibition upon marriage. Chief among them are provisions forbidding remarriage after divorce, provisions against marriage of relatives within certain degrees, statutes establishing a certain age below which parties are declared incapable of marrying and, formerly, miscegenation statutes. Although conformity with the law where the marriage takes place is generally necessary,[1] the place where a man and a woman happen to be at the time of their marriage ceremony may not have a significant interest in their marriage. The marriage relation, both in its creation and in its termination, is a matter of importance to the state with which one is most intimately connected (i.e., ordinarily the domicile), as well as to the parties.

The law of the forum (technically the domicile of one of the spouses) generally applies to divorce.[2] What is the significance of the domiciliary law in the equally important matter of creating the status in the first place? The strong public policy for upholding the validity of marriage wherever possible may well sustain a marriage satisfying the common domicile of the parties even though it may not meet the requirements of the place of celebration. Should domiciliary law also strike down a marriage otherwise valid? If the union in question is one forbidden by the law of the domicile, there is a clash between the general policy of upholding the validity of marriage and that of sustaining the particular state's ideas of propriety and good morals. In most cases involving incidents of the marriage (for instance, succession rights), compliance with the law at the place of celebration results in a marriage the validity of which is universally recognized. If, however, the legislative prohibition

shaw, Capacity to Marry, 15 Anglo–Am. L. Rev. 12 (1986); Fentiman, The Validity of Marriage, 44 Camb. L.J. 256 (1985); Smart, Interest Analysis and Essential Validity of Marriage, 14 Anglo–Am. L. Rev. 225 (1985).

§ **13.8**

1. See McIlvain v. Scheibley, 109 Ky. 455, 59 S.W. 498 (1900); Blaisdell v. Bic-

kum, 139 Mass. 250, 1 N.E. 281 (1885); Schaffer v. Krestovnikow, 88 N.J.Eq. 192, 102 A. 246 (1917), affirmed 88 N.J.Eq. 523, 103 A. 913 (1918). But see City of Philadelphia v. Williamson, 10 Phila. 179 (Pa. 1873). See also supra § 13.6 n.3.

2. See infra §§ 15.4–15.5.

at the common domicile, at the time of the marriage or immediately following, is explicit in declaring the marriage void, or if the violation of the domiciliary notion of good morals as to the incident in question is flagrant, the attempted marriage may fail. If there is a matter of appropriate concern, such as polygamy, incest, or non-age, the courts of the common domicile may deny recognition of the marriage otherwise valid even though this is seldom done.[3]

It is the domicile of the parties immediately following the purported marriage that usually is most concerned with the validity of the marriage, as demonstrated by an interesting group of older cases. These hold that if a divorced person leaves the state and acquires a domicile elsewhere and then marries (the marriage being valid by the law of the new domicile) within the prohibited time, the marriage is nevertheless good.[4] It will be so recognized in the jurisdiction where the divorce was granted, even though it would have been declared void had the party remained domiciled there.[5] The selection of the state most significantly concerned with the marriage in question normally can only be determined whit respect to a particular issue in a specific case. Clearly it would most often be the state where the parties live as a family; but that state changes with increased mobility of people. With the advent of "no-fault" divorce laws and the concomitant disappearance of prohibitions against remarriage within certain time limitations, these decisions now only demonstrate the general principle but have lost their practical importance.

Refusal to recognize the validity of a foreign marriage may have unfortunate results. Even so, there is no absolute necessity to know at the instant of marriage which state's law will be applicable to all issues that may arise concerning it. As the continuing marriage relationship is undertaken and expectations develop, the state most significantly concerned and related would seem to be the intended family domicile of the parties,[6] in a mobile society, at the time it arises.

3. See Restatement, Second, Conflict of Laws § 283, comment (j) (1971); Note, 26 Harv. L. Rev. 536 (1913). See also Cunningham v. Cunningham, 206 N.Y. 341, 353, 99 N.E. 845, 850 (1912) (Werner, J., dissenting) ("But marriage, although initiated by contract, creates a status with manifold continuing rights, duties, and obligations. These ... must necessarily be subject to the law of the domicile, for otherwise the state would have no control over its subjects or citizens."). Cf. Beddow v. Beddow, 257 S.W.2d 45 (Ky.1952). Weber v. Weber, 200 Neb. 659, 265 N.W.2d 436, 440 (1978) (refusing to recognize a Dominican Republic bilateral divorce: "The state is impliedly a party to the marriage contract and has an interest in the continuance and dissolution of the marital relation.").

4. E.g., Garrett v. Chapman, 252 Or. 361, 449 P.2d 856 (1969); Fitzgerald v. Fitzgerald, 210 Wis. 543, 246 N.W. 680 (1933).

5. State v. Fenn, 47 Wash. 561, 92 P. 417 (1907); Pierce v. Pierce, 58 Wash. 622, 109 P. 45 (1910). See Inhabitants of West Cambridge v. Inhabitants of Lexington, 18 Mass. (1 Pick.) 506 (1823); People v. Steere, 184 Mich. 556, 151 N.W. 617 (1915); Scott v. Attorney General, L.R. 11 Prob.Div. 128 (1886). Reaching the same result, though the decision is not put expressly on this ground, is Webster v. Modern Woodmen of America, 192 Iowa 1376, 186 N.W. 659 (1922).

6. See Restatement, Second, Conflict of Laws § 283, cmnt. (c), (d), (j) (1971); Mpiliris v. Hellenic Lines, Ltd., 323 F.Supp. 865, 877 (S.D. Tex. 1969). See W. Cook, The Logical and Legal Bases of the Conflict of Laws, ch. XVII (1942); Taintor, What Law

3. *Prohibitions Upon Remarriage After Divorce: Progressive Polygamy*

§ 13.9 Statutes restricting further marriage of divorced persons once were common and took a variety of forms. For instance, they forbade the marriage of both innocent and guilty parties within a stated time after the rendition of the decree, imposed a prohibition upon the guilty party only, or left it to the court to impose or remove such restriction. Restrictions of this kind no longer exist today as all states have adopted some kind of "no-fault" divorce laws. To the extent that such restrictions continue to exist they raise the question whether the out-of-state marriage of a person subject to such a restriction will be recognized at home.[1]

Under the divorce practice in a declining number of jurisdictions, moreover, an absolute decree is not first entered, but merely an interlocutory order or decree nisi, which is made absolute at some later date.[2] Until this decree is made final, the parties are not divorced; a second marriage meanwhile is bigamous under the concept that the first one still exists.[3] Statutory provisions declaring divorced persons incapable of marrying until the expiration of the period in which an appeal may be taken from the divorce decree may be construed as making that decree conditional and thus preventing remarriage until such time had elapsed.[4]

Governs the Ceremony, Incidents and Status of Marriage, 19 Bost. U. L. Rev. 353, 375 (1939). See also Stinson, Law Applicable to Marriage, 16 U. Cinn. L. Rev. 81 (1942). Cf. Storke, The Incestuous Marriage, 36 U. Colo. L. Rev. 473 (1964); Strasser, For Whom Bell Tolls: On Subsequent Domiciles Refusing to Recognize Same–Sex Marriages, 66 U. Cin. L. Rev. 339, 350 & n. 57 (1998).

§ 13.9

1. These statutes may be subject to substantive constitutional limitations even in local non-conflict circumstances as violating the fundamental right to marry. Cf. Loving v. Commonwealth of Virginia, 388 U.S. 1, 87 S.Ct. 1817, 18 L.Ed.2d 1010 (1967); Zablocki v. Redhail, 434 U.S. 374, 98 S.Ct. 673, 54 L.Ed.2d 618 (1978); Chlystek v. Kane, 540 F.2d 171 (3d Cir.1976). See Foster, Marriage: A "Basic Civil Right of Man," 37 Ford. L. Rev. 51 (1968); Glendon, Marriage and the State: The Withering Away of Marriage, 62 Va. L. Rev. 663 (1976); Comment, A Constitutional Analysis of Pennsylvania's Restrictions Upon Marriage, 83 Dick. L. Rev. 71 (1978). The latter article notes that several states have recently repealed restrictions on remarriage to a paramour. For a collection of cases upholding as well as invalidating restrictions, see Developments in the Law: Constitutional

Constraints on Interstate Same–Sex Marriage Recognition, 116 Harv. L. Rev. 2028, 2039 (2003). See also Strasser, Unity, Sovereignty, and the Interstate recognition of Marriage, 102 W.Va. L. Rev. 393, 408 (1999).

2. Cal. Civ. Code §§ 4512, 4513 (1981); cf. Wis. Stat. Ann. 767.37, 765.03(2) (1981). See also H. Clark, Law of Domestic Relations § 13.8 (1968); R. Graveson, Conflict of Laws, 262 (7th ed. 1974).

3. Pettit v. Pettit, 105 App.Div. 312, 93 N.Y.S. 1001 (1905); Earle v. Earle, 141 App. Div. 611, 126 N.Y.S. 317 (1910); Warter v. Warter, L.R. 15 Prob. Div. 152 (1890). See Knoll v. Knoll, 104 Wash. 110, 176 P. 22 (1918); State v. Grengs, 253 Wis. 248, 33 N.W.2d 248 (1948). Cf. Scott v. Scott, 153 Neb. 906, 46 N.W.2d 627 (1951); Matter of Caeti's Will, 207 Misc. 353, 138 N.Y.S.2d 496 (Surr.1955); Sherman v. Sherman, 213 N.Y.S.2d 216 (1961). But cf. Matter of Peart's Estate, 277 App.Div. 61, 97 N.Y.S.2d 879 (1950); Randall v. Randall, 216 Neb. 541, 345 N.W.2d 319 (1984).

4. Accord, Eaton v. Eaton, 66 Neb. 676, 92 N.W. 995 (1902); McLennan v. McLennan, 31 Or. 480, 50 P. 802 (1897). It was suggested, though not decided, by the Wisconsin court, that this rule might

Upon the first question, recognition at home of the foreign marriage of a divorced person forbidden to remarry by his domiciliary law, the authorities are divided. Most cases have followed the usual view validating the marriage, i.e., a marriage valid where contracted is valid everywhere.[5] This view seems to be growing stronger as the statutory prohibitions on remarriage become less common either because of repeal or constitutional limitation.[6] However, a considerable number, mostly older cases, had taken the opposite view.[7] While the policy of validation seems most strong in regard to nearly all incidents, generalizations are difficult because the statutes restricting such marriages vary and this could significantly affect the results in particular cases. Thus, if the prohibition against marriage is applicable only to the guilty party in the divorce suit, it may be called penal, to be narrowly construed and not effective outside the state.[8] Or, in addition to the prohibition against this particu-

be applicable to a general prohibition upon remarriage within a year from the decree. Lanham v. Lanham, 136 Wis. 360, 117 N.W. 787 (1908). But see, In re Wood's Estate, 137 Cal. 129, 69 P. 900 (1902); Griswold v. Griswold, 23 Colo.App. 365, 129 P. 560 (1913); Matter of Peart's Estate, 277 App.Div. 61, 97 N.Y.S.2d 879 (1950); Willey v. Willey, 22 Wash. 115, 60 P. 145 (1900); State v. Fenn, 47 Wash. 561, 92 P. 417 (1907). See also In re Kelley's Estate, 210 Or. 226, 310 P.2d 328 (1957) in which after the death of the second husband, final order of divorce from the first husband was entered nunc pro tunc to a date prior to the marriage to the second husband. In re Estate of Shippy, 37 Wn.App. 164, 678 P.2d 848 (1984) (divorce nunc pro tunc to date prior to second husband's death).

5. Lembcke v. United States, 181 F.2d 703 (2d Cir.1950); Wheelock v. Freiwald, 66 F.2d 694 (8th Cir.1933); State v. Graves, 228 Ark. 378, 307 S.W.2d 545 (1957); Mohn v. Tingley, 191 Cal. 470, 217 P. 733 (1923); In re Winder's Estate, 98 Cal.App.2d 78, 219 P.2d 18 (1950); Loth v. Loth's Estate, 54 Colo. 200, 129 P. 827 (1913); Smallwood v. Bickers, 139 Ga.App. 720, 229 S.E.2d 525 (1976); Bituminous Casualty Corp. v. Wacht, 84 Ga.App. 602, 66 S.E.2d 757 (1951); Dudley v. Dudley, 151 Iowa 142, 130 N.W. 785 (1911); Farrell v. Farrell, 190 Iowa 919, 181 N.W. 12 (1921); Pickard v. Pickard, 241 Iowa 1307, 45 N.W.2d 269 (1950); Commonwealth v. Lane, 113 Mass. 458, 18 Am.Rep. 509 (1873); In re Estate of Kinkead, 239 Minn. 27, 57 N.W.2d 628 (1953); Citrynell v. Citrynell, 86 Misc.2d 60, 382 N.Y.S.2d 256 (1976); Van Voorhis v. Brintnall, 86 N.Y. 18, 40 Am.Rep. 505 (1881); Matter of Peart's Estate, 277 App. Div. 61, 97 N.Y.S.2d 879 (1950); Woodward

v. Blake, 38 N.D. 38, 164 N.W. 156 (1917); Stephenson v. Stephenson, 41 Tenn.App. 659, 298 S.W.2d 36 (1956); State v. Shattuck, 69 Vt. 403, 38 A. 81 (1897). Cf. Henderson v. Henderson, 199 Md. 449, 87 A.2d 403 (1952); Lieblein v. Charles Chips, Inc., 32 A.D.2d 1016, 301 N.Y.S.2d 743 (1969), affirmed 28 N.Y.2d 869, 322 N.Y.S.2d 258, 271 N.E.2d 234 (1971). See Loughran v. Loughran, 292 U.S. 216, 54 S.Ct. 684, 78 L.Ed. 1219 (1934). In Bannister v. Bannister, 181 Md. 177, 29 A.2d 287 (1942), the court held a marriage, before a divorce decree became final, valid in view of a statute passed by the state of the domicile where the divorce was granted empowering courts to make nunc pro tunc orders in certain cases where steps to make the decree final had not been taken. Noted 7 Md. L. Rev. 254 (1943).

6. See supra n.1.

7. Wilson v. Cook, 256 Ill. 460, 100 N.E. 222 (1912); Succession of Gabisso, 119 La. 704, 44 So. 438 (1907); In re Stull's Estate, 183 Pa. 625, 39 A. 16 (1898); Pennegar v. State, 87 Tenn. 244, 10 S.W. 305 (1888); Knoll v. Knoll, 104 Wash. 110, 176 P. 22 (1918); Lanham v. Lanham, 136 Wis. 360, 117 N.W. 787 (1908). Cf. Brown v. Sheridan, 83 Ga.App. 725, 64 S.E.2d 636 (1951); Matter of Rogers' Estate, 569 P.2d 536 (Okla.App. 1977).

8. Commonwealth v. Lane, 113 Mass. 458, 18 Am.Rep. 509 (1873); Van Voorhis v. Brintnall, 86 N.Y. 18, 40 Am.Rep. 505 (1881); Olsen v. Olsen, 27 Misc.2d 555, 209 N.Y.S.2d 503 (1960); Almodovar v. Almodovar, 55 Misc.2d 300, 284 N.Y.S.2d 910 (1967). See Restatement, Second, Conflict of Laws § 283, cmnt. (k) (1971). Cf. In re Sanders' Estate, 147 Cal.App.2d 450, 305 P.2d 655 (1957); Matter of Peart's Estate,

lar marriage there may be a statutory recognition of the "good where contracted, good everywhere" rule, which may be held to restrict the prohibition to marriages contracted within the prohibiting state.[9]

In this situation of declining strength of the invalidating policies, it should take an exceptional case for a court to refuse recognition of a valid foreign marriage of its domiciliaries even in face of a local prohibition. For example, in one of the few relatively recent cases invalidating such a foreign marriage,[10] an Oklahoma court denied a surviving spouse appointment as administrator of her second husband's estate when the decedent, after eleven days cohabitation, had initiated annulment proceedings on the grounds of the prohibition but was killed in an auto accident on the way to the hearing. All the events occurred before the six-month remarriage prohibition on the wife had expired which strengthened the invalidation policies of the forum while the internal attack after less than two weeks of cohabitation precluded any strength to the policies of recognizing family expectations or presumed contributions to the estate. The court precluded the surviving spouse from obtaining a windfall from a voidable marriage.

The issue on which the decision turns is not, it is believed, whether the statute prohibiting the marriage is an expression of the public policy of the state enacting the statute.[11] A policy against such marriages is surely shown by the legislative declaration prohibiting them.[12] But the policy thus expressed runs afoul, in these cases, of other policies which are well settled, whether expressed in positive terms by statute or not. One is the general policy upholding a marriage whenever possible. Others relate to the particular issue involved. To deny the marriage may relieve one from an obligation solemnly entered into; it may defeat family expectations of many years standing; it may illegitimize innocent children born of the union; the passage of time alone may make satisfaction of some of the policies improbable, while strengthening others. The controlling issue becomes whether the policy of prohibition, as expressed by the legislative body, is strong enough in regard to the particular issue before the court to prevail over the policies furthered by upholding the marriage.[13] If the statutory language is unmistakable, the

277 App.Div. 61, 97 N.Y.S.2d 879 (1950); Citrynell v. Citrynell, 86 Misc.2d 60, 382 N.Y.S.2d 256 (1976); Pennegar v. State, 87 Tenn. 244, 10 S.W. 305 (1888). See also Hartley, Bigamy in Conflict of Laws, 16 Int'l & Comp. L.Q. 680 (1967). Hartley, Recognition of American Marriages and Divorces in Canada, 17 Buffalo L. Rev. 71 (1967); Maddaugh, Validity of Marriage and the Conflict of Laws: A Critique of the Present Anglo–American Position, 23 U. Toronto L.J. 117 (1973).

9. Griswold v. Griswold, 23 Colo.App. 365, 129 P. 560 (1913).

10. Matter of Rogers' Estate, 569 P.2d 536 (Okla.App. 1977).

11. Cf. Matter of Donlay's Estate, 280 App.Div. 37, 111 N.Y.S.2d 253 (1952); Wright v. Kroeger, 219 Or. 102, 345 P.2d 809 (1959).

12. See the language of the court in Lanham v. Lanham, 136 Wis. 360, 117 N.W. 787 (1908).

13. See Matter of Peart's Estate, 277 App.Div. 61, 97 N.Y.S.2d 879 (1950); R. Weintraub, Commentary on the Conflict of Laws 293 (4th ed. 2001). Cf. Swan, A New Approach to Marriage and Divorce in Conflict of Laws, 24 U. Toronto L.J. 17, 41 (1974): "A domestic invalidating rule might not be applicable if . . . the circumstances of the marriage and the future conduct of the parties indicate that there may be no good

court may feel there is little it can do but follow it.[14] However, in most instances, the result in a particular case should, and will in large measure, depend upon which of the competing policies has a greater weight with the court.

An example of the policy analysis that is most appropriate is found in the *Lenherr* case[15] in which the Pennsylvania Supreme Court recognized a West Virginia marriage of Pennsylvania domiciliaries who had married in violation of a Pennsylvania paramour statute prohibiting marriage after divorce for adultery. The issue was whether, on the death of one of the parties, the surviving spouse of the questioned marriage, after nearly 40 years of married life, could claim a marital exemption against the Pennsylvania inheritance tax. The court stated:

> "In resolving that conflict, we must realize that the strength of the policy behind Section 169 depends to a significant degree upon the incident of marriage under consideration. For example, the legislature has determined that at least one incident of marriage—the legitimacy of the children—is not to be denied despite the prior adjudication of adultery. See, Act of June 17, 1971. Our task, therefore, is to balance on the one hand the policy behind Section

reason to invalidate the marriage." But cf. Maddaugh, Validity of Marriage and the Conflict of Laws: A Critique of the Present Anglo–American Position, 23 U. Toronto L.J. 117, 145 (1973) ("If the incident is not one that would be permitted to persons married under its own laws, then enjoyment should be denied by that state."). Compare Lawrence v. Lawrence, [1985] 3 W.L.R. 125, 2 All.E.R. 733(CA); [1985] 2 W.L.R. 86, 1 All.E.R. 506 (Fam.) (discussed in T. Downes, Recognition of Divorces and Capacity to Remarry, 35 Int'l & Comp. L.Q. 170 (1986) and Lipstein, Recognition of Divorces, Capacity to Marry, Preliminary Questions and Dépecage, 35 Int'l & Comp. L.Q. 178 (1986)).

14. See Wright v. Kroeger, 219 Or. 102, 345 P.2d 809 (1959). Cf. Laikola v. Engineered Concrete, 277 N.W.2d 653 (Minn. 1979); In re Ommang's Estate, 183 Minn. 92, 235 N.W. 529 (1931) (criticized in Note, 16 Minn. L. Rev. 172, 184 (1932)). The experience of Wisconsin with its statute prohibiting remarriage without prior court approval by one under obligation of a support order for minor children in the custody of another demonstrates the policy tensions in this area. See Korf v. Korf, 38 Wis.2d 413, 157 N.W.2d 691 (1968). In re Estate of Ferguson, 25 Wis.2d 75, 130 N.W.2d 300 (1964) so construed the statute as not to be given extraterritorial effect and not within the Wisconsin Marriage Evasion Act. Following that case, the legislature amended the statute to make it expressly applicable

to out of state marriages. In State v. Mueller, 44 Wis.2d 387, 171 N.W.2d 414 (1969), the defendant, after having been refused permission to marry by the Wisconsin court, went to Illinois and married in violation of the Wisconsin statute. His conviction was sustained under the Act and the Act viewed as a limitation on the actions of Wisconsin residents with criminal sanctions only. The marriage in the foreign state was not affected. In Zablocki v. Redhail, 434 U.S. 374, 98 S.Ct. 673, 54 L.Ed.2d 618 (1978) the statute was held unconstitutional as an infringement on the fundamental right of marriage in violation of the equal protection clause.

15. In re Lenherr's Estate, 455 Pa. 225, 314 A.2d 255 (1974). See Recent Development, 13 J. Fam. L. 871 (1974). See also Reese, Marriage in American Conflict of Laws, 26 Int'l & Comp. L.Q. 952, 965–66 (1977):

> "Development of choice of law principles in the area of marriage should be made in the light of the basic values involved. These are (a) the interest of a State in not having its domiciliaries contract marriages of which it disapproves; (b) the general policy favouring the validation of marriages, (c) protection of the expectations of the parties that their marriage is a valid one and (d) furtherance of the objectives of the statute, such as one dealing with succession or support, whose application is in question. Values (a) and

169, *as it relates to the marital exemption to the inheritance tax,* against the need for uniformity and predictability of result on the other."[16]

In declining "to apply Pennsylvania law to invalidate this marriage for this purpose,"[17] the court concluded that the policies behind the tax exemption, reasonable expectation of the parties and presumed contribution of the surviving spouse to the estate, would be furthered. Purposes of the marriage prohibition, deterrence of adultery and protection of the sensibilities of the aggrieved first spouse, could not be achieved.

4. *Miscegenation*

§ 13.10 In the unfortunate era of overt racial segregation, sharp policy conflicts arose in the United States as a result of violations of statutes against miscegenation. Persons of different races, domiciled in a state where their marriage was forbidden, traveled to a state where it was allowed, went through a marriage ceremony and returned to their domicile. Many older decisions from the Southern states declared such attempted unions void,[1] although such attitudes were not always limited to the South.[2] Refusal to recognize a marriage on such grounds of local public policy can no longer be sustained. Marriage restrictions based on race are invalid under the Constitution of the United States.[3] A fortiori, recognition of a valid foreign marriage could not be denied on such legally irrelevant grounds. Even before the development of constitutional compulsion, miscegenation policies had lost strength as inconsistent with a democratic society and such foreign marriages were recognized where the enjoyment of a particular incident did not involve permanent cohabitation.[4]

(c) are likely to vary with the issue and the facts of the case."

16. *Lenherr's Estate*, 314 A.2d at 258 (original emphasis).

17. Id. at 259. Cf. Bogen v. Bogen, 261 N.W.2d 606 (Minn.1977) in which in a dissolution proceeding by the wife after 14 1/2 years of marriage, the court sustained the marriage celebrated in Nebraska during a six-month restriction in Minnesota, the domicile, and then dissolved it with a property division that probably would not have been available if the marriage were invalid.

§ 13.10

1. State v. Tutty, 41 Fed. 753 (C.C.S.D.Ga.1890); Succession of Gabisso, 119 La. 704, 44 So. 438 (1907); State v. Kennedy, 76 N.C. 251, 22 Am.Rep. 683 (1877); State v. Bell, 66 Tenn. (7 Baxt.) 9 (1872); Kinney v. Commonwealth, 71 Va. (30 Grat.) 858, 32 Am.Rep. 690 (1878).

2. Compare Inhabitants of Medway v. Inhabitants of Needham, 16 Mass. 157, 8 Am. Dec. 131 (1819) with Wilbur's Estate v. Bingham, 8 Wash. 35, 35 P. 407 (1894); In

re Takahashi's Estate, 113 Mont. 490, 129 P.2d 217 (1942).

3. See Loving v. Virginia, 388 U.S. 1, 87 S.Ct. 1817, 18 L.Ed.2d 1010 (1967); United States v. Brittain, 319 F.Supp. 1058 (N.D.Ala.1970); Perez v. Lippold, 32 Cal.2d 711, 198 P.2d 17 (1948); Drinan, The Loving Decision and the Freedom to Marry, 29 Ohio St. L.J. 358 (1968); Weitzman, Legal Regulation of Marriage Tradition and Change, 62 Cal. L. Rev. 1169 (1974); Riley, Miscegenation Statutes, A Re–Evaluation of Their Constitutionality in Light of Changing Social and Political Conditions, 32 So. Cal. L. Rev. 28 (1958); Weinberger, A Reappraisal of the Constitutionality of Miscegenation Statutes, 42 Cornell L.Q. 208 (1957); Ehrenzweig, Miscegenation in the Conflict of Laws, 45 Cornell L.Q. 659 (1960); Taintor, Marriage in the Conflict of Laws, 9 Vand. L. Rev. 607, 627 (1956); H. Clark, Law of Domestic Relations § 2.13 (1968).

4. See, e.g., Whittington v. McCaskill, 65 Fla. 162, 61 So. 236 (1913); Miller v. Lucks, 203 Miss. 824, 36 So.2d 140 (1948).

5. *"Incestuous" Marriages*

§ 13.11   While prohibitions against incest are general, legislative policy differs in defining that degree of relationship within which an attempted marriage is regarded as incestuous. If the various statutes are to be taken as announcing that infringements thereof are "in violation of the Divine law,"[1] there certainly is a difference of legislative opinion as to what is divine. The policy conflict for the court is similar to that involving the earlier policy concerning remarriage after divorce. Does the local prohibition represent a policy so strong that the court at the domicile will declare the attempted marriage void, instead of applying the usual approach of validating the marriage?[2] Instances where a marriage good where contracted has been declared void at the domicile because of the relationship of the parties are in the minority.[3] Indeed, some of the states that used to refuse recognition to foreign marriages of their divorced citizens nevertheless upheld these marriages.[4] This appears to be the case because most of these statutes cover common ground, and variations are matters of degree and not substantial conflicts of policy.[5]

6. *Non–Age—Consent of Parent*

§ 13.12   Statutes generally establish a minimum age for marriage and frequently require consent by parents to the marriage of minors. Young people desiring to marry not infrequently seek to avoid the effect

---

§ 13.11

1. Per Lord Wensleydale in Brook v. Brook, 9 H.L. Cas, 193, 245 (1861).

2. See Bucca v. State, 43 N.J.Super. 315, 128 A.2d 506 (Ch.Div.1957); Mazzolini v. Mazzolini, 168 Ohio St. 357, 155 N.E.2d 206 (1958); Storke, The Incestuous Marriage—Relic of the Past, 36 Colo. L. Rev. 473 (1964).

3. Osoinach v. Watkins, 235 Ala. 564, 180 So. 577 (1938); Catalano v. Catalano, 148 Conn. 288, 170 A.2d 726 (1961); Bucca v. State, 43 N.J.Super. 315, 128 A.2d 506 (Ch.Div.1957); Johnson v. Johnson, 57 Wash. 89, 106 P. 500 (1910). See Incuria v. Incuria, 155 Misc. 755, 280 N.Y.S. 716 (Dom.Rel.Ct. 1935). But see In re Miller's Estate, 239 Mich. 455, 214 N.W. 428 (1927).

4. Compare People ex rel. Schutt v. Siems, 198 Ill.App. 342 (1916), concerned the marriage of cousins in Wisconsin. The man was from Minnesota, the woman from Illinois, by whose law cousins could not lawfully marry. Her "disability" did not prevent a valid marriage) with In re Mortenson's Estate, 83 Ariz. 87, 316 P.2d 1106 (1957) (marriage of first cousins invalid). See also Leszinske v. Poole, 110 N.M. 663,

798 P.2d 1049 (1990) (upholding uncle-niece marriage that was valid in celebration state but void in domiciliary state); In re Landolfi, 283 A.D.2d 497, 724 N.Y.S.2d 470 (N.Y.A.D. 2 Dept. 2001) (out-of-state common law marriage upheld even though the domiciliary state had abolished such marriage). See also Gonzales–Jimenez de Ruiz v. U.S., 231 F.Supp.2d 1187 (M.D.Fla. 2002); Smith v. Anderson, 821 So.2d 323 (Fla.App.2002); Mason v. Mason, 775 N.E.2d 706 (Ind.App. 2002).

5. The strength of the policies supporting unusual restrictions on marriage seem to be declining generally. See Glendon, Marriage and the State: The Withering Away of Marriage, 62 Va. L. Rev. 663 (1976). Cf. O'Neill v. Dent, 364 F.Supp. 565 (E.D.N.Y.1973). Johnson v. Rockefeller, 58 F.R.D. 42 (S.D.N.Y.1972). Israel v. Allen, 195 Colo. 263, 577 P.2d 762 (1978) held a statute prohibiting marriage between siblings unconstitutional when applied to parties so related by adoption indicating that there was insufficient state interest to prohibit such a marriage. See also Foster, Marriage: A "Basic Civil Right of Man," 37 Ford. L. Rev. 51 (1968); Note, Marriage and Divorce for the Devils Lake Indian Reservation, 47 N.D. L. Rev. 317 (1971).

of the particular restriction at their domicile by marriage in another jurisdiction. The question then again arises whether the marriage, valid where entered, will be valid at home. Generally the answer is in the affirmative,[1] although there is some dissent.[2]

In cases involving either age limitations or possible incest, the factors of time and whether the attack on the marriage is internal or external are very significant.[3] As noted earlier, if the marriage in question has continued for a long time and the attack is collateral, i.e., by someone other than a party, this greatly strengthens the validation policy to protect those relying on the marriage. By like token, policies restricting marriage because of affinity (e.g., between cousins[4]) or of non-age[5] recede.

In sum, the recognition of the marriage is to be expected in most cases because of the common policy of all states concerned validate the marriage and because differences in legislative policy reflected in the statutory age variations and other matters are usually slight.[6]

7. *Marriage Evasion Legislation*

§ 13.13 The Uniform Marriage Evasion Act addresses the concern of the home state about having its domiciliaries evade requirements of local law by marrying out of state. It was approved by the National Conference of Commissioners on Uniform Laws in 1943,[1] but has since

§ 13.12

1. Husband v. Pierce, 800 S.W.2d 661 (Tex.App.1990); State v. Graves, 228 Ark. 378, 307 S.W.2d 545 (1957); McDonald v. McDonald, 6 Cal.2d 457, 58 P.2d 163 (1936); Spencer v. People, 133 Colo. 196, 292 P.2d 971 (1956); Mangrum v. Mangrum, 310 Ky. 226, 220 S.W.2d 406 (1949); Levy v. Downing, 213 Mass. 334, 100 N.E. 638 (1913) (which turns largely on jurisdiction to annul); Reid v. Reid, 72 Misc. 214, 129 N.Y.S. 529 (1911); Hilliard v. Hilliard, 24 Misc.2d 861, 209 N.Y.S.2d 132 (1960); Courtright v. Courtright, 11 Dec.Rptr. 413 (Ohio Com. Pl. 1899). Cf. Duley v. Duley, 151 A.2d 255 (D.C.Mun.App.1959); In re Marriage of Fetters, 41 Colo.App. 281, 584 P.2d 104 (1978).

2. Wilkins v. Zelichowski, 26 N.J. 370, 140 A.2d 65 (1958); Cunningham v. Cunningham, 206 N.Y. 341, 99 N.E. 845 (1912); Ross v. Bryant, 90 Okla. 300, 217 P. 364 (1923); see Smith v. Smith, 84 Ga. 440, 11 S.E. 496 (1890). Cf. State in Interest of I., 68 N.J.Super. 598, 173 A.2d 457 (Juv. & Dom.Rel. 1961); Callow, Teenage Marriage, Misconduct and the Law, 53 A.B.A.J. 541 (1967).

3. See supra § 13.1.

4. See In re May's Estate, 305 N.Y. 486, 114 N.E.2d 4 (1953) (uncle-niece, noted 34

B.U.L. Rev. 82 (1954); Leszinske v. Poole, 110 N.M. 663, 798 P.2d 1049 (App. 1990) (uncle-niece: valid if valid under the law of celebration unless violative of the law of domicile, the law of nature, or the common consent of nations)

5. Compare Wilkins v. Zelichowski, 26 N.J. 370, 140 A.2d 65 (1958) with State v. Graves, 228 Ark. 378, 307 S.W.2d 545 (1957); See Uniform Marriage and Divorce Act, § 208, 9A U.L.A. 147, 170 (1987); 5 Fam. L.Q. 205, 216 (1971); Moore, Defenses Available in Annulment Actions, 7 J. Fam. L. 239 (1967); Note, The Uniform Marriage and Divorce Act–Marital Age Provisions, 57 Minn. L. Rev. 179 (1972).

6. Cf. Restatement, Second, Conflict of Laws § 283, cmnt. (j) (1971). See Turner, Marriage of Minors, 8 West.Aust.L. Rev. 319 (1968). Compare R. Graveson, Conflict of Laws 251, 272 (7th ed. 1974); 2 A. Ehrenzweig & E. Jayme, Private International Law 159 (1973); Dicey & Morris, Conflict of Laws 651 et seq. (13th ed. 2000 by Collins).

§ 13.13

1. It has been replaced by the Uniform Marriage and Divorce Act, § 210, which reflects the validation policy of supporting a marriage valid at the time of celebration or subsequently validated either by the law of

been withdrawn. It has been adopted in five states.[2] Eleven other states adopted portions of the act.[3] Legislation generally follows the first section of the Uniform Act which provided "that if any person residing and intending to continue to reside in this state who is disabled or prohibited from contracting marriage under the laws of this state shall go into another state or country and there contract a marriage prohibited and declared void by the laws of this state, such marriage shall be null and void for all purposes in this state...." As between two states that have enacted the whole Uniform Act, no substantive change is made in the usual conflicts treatment, for the prohibited marriage is ineffective where entered into as well as at the domicile.[4] But if a person goes from a Uniform–Act state to one without it, and then contracts a marriage prohibited by his other domiciliary law but allowed in the second state, the effect is to deny recognition of the marriage at the domicile. Under the statute, the domiciliary law will refuse recognition of marriage that could not have been entered into under its law.[5] Cases under the evasion statutes form the primary authority for the recognition of the domicile immediately after the marriage as having the power, although seldom exercised in the absence of statute, to deny recognition of an otherwise valid foreign marriage. The evasion statutes reflect a policy of declining strength and are inconsistent with the two primary policies in this area of assuring free consent and of upholding marriages otherwise valid.[6]

D. EFFECT IN THIRD STATE OF MARRIAGE VOID BY LAW OF DOMICILE

§ 13.14 Most cases discussed so far involve a marriage, forbidden by the law of the domicile, celebrated in a state where it is valid by local law, with its validity called into question at the domicile. As seen above, while the domiciliary law generally recognizes the validity of the relationship, it may refuse to do so in response to strong local policy. If the domicile refuses to recognize the parties as married, the question arises whether a court in another state should reach the same conclusion. In view of the very strong policy of validation, it is difficult to determine whether a domiciliary state would in fact hold *this* marriage invalid.[1]

the place of celebration or the domicile of the parties. 9A U.L.A. 147, 176–77 (1987).

2. These states are Illinois, Louisiana, Massachusetts, Vermont and Wisconsin. See 9A U.L.A. XXI (1957).

3. See Taintor, Marriage in The Conflict of Laws, 9 Vand. L. Rev. 607, 629 (1956); Storke, The Incestuous Marriage—Relic of the Past, 36 U. Colo. L. Rev. 473, 484 (1964).

4. In re Canon's Estate, 221 Wis. 322, 266 N.W. 918 (1936). But cf. Korf v. Korf, 38 Wis.2d 413, 157 N.W.2d 691 (1968); In re Estate of Campbell, 260 Wis. 625, 51 N.W.2d 709 (1952).

5. In re Mortenson's Estate, 83 Ariz. 87, 316 P.2d 1106 (1957); Meisenhelder v. Chicago & North Western Ry. Co., 170 Minn. 317, 213 N.W. 32 (1927), 26 Mich. L. Rev. 327 (1928); Ginkowski v. Ginkowski, 28 Wis.2d 530, 137 N.W.2d 403 (1965). Cf. Smith v. Smith, 99 N.H. 362, 111 A.2d 531 (1955); Korf v. Korf, 38 Wis.2d 413, 157 N.W.2d 691 (1968).

6. Cf. Uniform Marriage and Divorce Act § 210, 9A U.L.A. 147, 176–77 (1987); Restatement, Second, Conflict of Laws § 283 (1971).

§ 13.14

1. Restatement, Second, Conflict of Laws § 283, cmnt. (k) (1971).

Further, the relation the forum bears to the parties may make it, at the time the issue arises, the state most significantly concerned. For example, if after a brief residence in the state of their common domicile at the time of the marriage, a couple move, and makes its family home in a second state for many years, and the issue concerning their marriage arises in the second state in the context of a wrongful death claim brought by this estate, the forum would most likely validate the marriage by a reference to the place of celebration.[2] Such a result would be appropriate unless the *forum's* own policy is particularly violated, which seems highly unlikely. On analysis, uniformity of result with the domicile at the time of marriage or immediately thereafter is not always to be expected. The issue is rarely presented. However, a Wisconsin case involved this question. An Illinois woman, under prohibition to marry after divorce, went to Indiana with an Illinois man, where they married. By Illinois law the attempted marriage was void. The Wisconsin court held that the woman could not recover as a widow under the compensation act for the man's death.[3] The Illinois rule, by which the foreign marriage of a divorced party within the prohibited time is considered void, was followed in a Michigan case. After an Illinois man had been divorced, he and an Illinois woman went through a marriage ceremony in Michigan within the prohibited (waiting) time. When he left her, it was held that he could not be prosecuted in Michigan for desertion.[4]

These cases do not seem to have had significant following in other states or at home.[5] The policy of validation expressed in the Uniform Marriage and Divorce Act in favor of upholding the marriage seems preferable.[6]

E. MARRIAGE OF PARTIES WITH DIFFERENT DOMICILES

§ 13.15 So far the discussion has assumed that the significant conflict exists between the law of the place of celebration and that of the

2. Cf. Metropolitan Life Insurance Co. v. Manning, 568 F.2d 922 (2d Cir.1977); Seidelson & Bowler, Determination of Family Status in the Administration of Federal Acts: A Choice of Law Problem for Federal Agencies and Courts, 33 Geo. Wash. L. Rev. 863, 887 (1965); 2 A. Ehrenzweig & E. Jayme, Private Int'l Law 141 (1973). But cf. Baade, Marriage and Divorce in American Conflicts Law: Governmental Interests Analysis and the Restatement (Second), 72 Colum. L. Rev. 329, 377 (1972); Maddaugh, Validity of Marriage and the Conflict of Laws: A Critique of the Present Anglo–American Position, 23 U. Toronto L.J. 117(1973).

3. Hall v. Industrial Commission, 165 Wis. 364, 162 N.W. 312 (1917). It is to be noted that historically Wisconsin and Illinois were harsh on prohibited remarriage, that both had adopted the now obsolete Marriage Evasion Act, and that the Wisconsin law on remarriage outside the state after divorce was the same as that of Illi-

nois. Cf. Ehrenzweig, Miscegenation in The Conflict of Laws, 45 Cornell L.Q. 659, 665 (1960).

4. People v. Steere, 184 Mich. 556, 151 N.W. 617 (1915) (criticized in 13 Mich. L. Rev. 592 (1915)). The grounds for so holding are not clearly set out. See also Meisenhelder v. Chicago & North Western Railway, 170 Minn. 317, 213 N.W. 32 (1927).

5. In Owen v. Owen, 178 Wis. 609, 190 N.W. 363 (1922), the plaintiff, who sought annulment of his marriage, was a Wisconsin man who induced defendant to marry him in Michigan the day after she got her divorce in Illinois, where such remarriage was forbidden. The court refused annulment and held the marriage was valid. Cf. Boehm v. Rohlfs, 224 Iowa 226, 276 N.W. 105 (1937); In re Ommang's Estate, 183 Minn. 92, 235 N.W. 529 (1931). See also Ehrenzweig, Conflict of Laws 378 (1962).

6. Uniform Marriage and Divorce Act § 210, 9A U.L.A. 176 (1987); Ma v. Ma, 483 N.W.2d 732 (Minn.App. 1992).

state in which both parties were domiciled at the time of marriage or immediately thereafter. However, it has been suggested, primarily in English cases, that each of the parties to a marriage must have capacity to marry by the law of his or her separate domicile and, if the law of either prohibits the marriage, it is invalid.[1] While the concept of determining one's capacity by one's personal law leads to this conclusion, the significant relationship of the marriage to the state and its society seems disregarded in such a suggestion. A requirement of complying with the law of both domiciles, sometimes called the dual domicile rule, has been effectively criticized by Cheshire and North.[2] It seems not to have acceptance in the United States.[3] The American cases, like the English, in which the parties did not have a common domicile at the time of marriage, have in fact upheld the marriage or, if the marriage was invalidated, have had the additional contact of being the common domicile of the parties at the time or immediately following the marriage.[4] The approach taken in these cases is discussed in previous sections. No American case has been found invalidating an otherwise valid marriage in which the forum's only contact was as the domicile of but one party at the time of the marriage.[5]

On principle, it seems clear that to be sufficiently concerned with a marriage to declare it invalid under its local policy, a state should have

§ 13.15

1. See Dicey & Morris, Conflict of Laws 651 et seq. (13th ed. 2000 by Collins); R. Graveson, Conflict of Laws 263 (7th ed. 1974). Cf. Beale, Conflict of Laws § 132.5 (1935). See also Davis, Capacity to Contract a Polygamous Marriage, 5 Fed. L. Rev. 294 (1973); Jaffey, The Essential Validity of Marriage in the English Conflict of Laws, 41 Mod. L. Rev. 38 (1978); Note, Capacity to Contract a Polygamous Marriage, 36 Mod. L. Rev. 291 (1973); Note, Capacity for Polygamy, 32 Camb. L.J. 43 (1973).

2. Cheshire & North, Private International Law 721 et seq. (13th ed. 1999). See also Baty, Capacity and Form of Marriage in the Conflict of Laws, 26 Yale L.J. 444 (1917); Hartley, The Policy Basis of the English Conflict of Laws of Marriage, 35 Mod. L. Rev. 571 (1972).

3. The Cheshire–North position, supra n. 2, is discussed in Reed, Essential Validity of Marriage: The Application of Interest Analysis and Depecage to Anglo–American Choice of Law Rules, 20 N.Y.L.S. J. Int'l & Comp. L. 387 (2000). See Mpiliris v. Hellenic Lines, Limited, 323 F.Supp. 865 (S.D.Tex. 1969), affirmed 440 F.2d 1163 (5th Cir. 1971); Garrett v. Chapman, 252 Or. 361,

449 P.2d 856 (1969); Restatement, Second, Conflict of Laws § 283, cmnt. (i) (1971); L. McDougal III., R. Felix & R.Whitten, American Conflicts Law 715 (5th ed. 2001). But cf. Restatement of Conflict of Laws § 132 (1934).

4. See, e.g., Mpiliris v. Hellenic Lines, Limited, 323 F.Supp. 865 (S.D.Tex.1969), affirmed 440 F.2d 1163 (5th Cir.1971); Catalano v. Catalano, 148 Conn. 288, 170 A.2d 726 (1961); People ex rel. Schutt v. Siems, 198 Ill.App. 342 (1916); B___ aka L___ v. L___, 65 N.J.Super. 368, 168 A.2d 90 (Ch.Div.1961); Bucca v. State, 43 N.J.Super. 315, 128 A.2d 506 (Ch.Div.1957); Hilliard v. Hilliard, 24 Misc.2d 861, 209 N.Y.S.2d 132 (1960); State v. Ross, 76 N.C. 242, 22 Am. Rep. 678 (1877); Mazzolini v. Mazzolini, 168 Ohio St. 357, 155 N.E.2d 206 (1958); Garrett v. Chapman, 252 Or. 361, 449 P.2d 856 (1969); In re Kelley's Estate, 210 Or. 226, 310 P.2d 328 (1957). Cf. Barrons v. United States, 191 F.2d 92 (9th Cir.1951); Gibson v. Hughes, 192 F.Supp. 564 (S.D.N.Y.1961); In re May's Estate, 305 N.Y. 486, 114 N.E.2d 4 (1953); Owen v. Owen, 178 Wis. 609, 190 N.W. 363 (1922).

5. See also Restatement, Second, Conflict of Laws § 283, Reporter's Note (1971).

more substantial contact with the marriage than the domicile of one of the parties at the time of the marriage.[6] Because marriage is a social institution, it is the state in which the parties live as a family that has the most substantial interest. Living together as a family within a state seems necessary to give a state sufficient interest to impose upon the parties a requirement other than those already satisfied elsewhere.

Other forms of domestic relationships are the subject of §§ 13.20–13.23 infra.

F. THE COVENANT MARRIAGE

§ 13.16   As a reaction to easy dissolution of marriage in all states of the United States as a result of no-fault legislation, at times coupled with short waiting periods,[1] Louisiana pioneered the "covenant marriage" as a stricter, less readily dissolvable form of marriage. Covenant marriage legislation has since also been enacted in Arizona and Arkansas.[2]

A covenant marriage is an optional alternative form to the traditional marriage. It differs from the latter in that the parties sign a contract ("Declaration of Intent") in which they choose local law (e.g., Louisiana law), agree to submit to counseling, and–by having chosen Louisiana law (in the example)–to a one-year's waiting period for a no-fault dissolution.

The waiting period for no-fault dissolution is strikingly similar to European no-fault divorce law,[3] but exceeds that of some American jurisdictions (e.g., Nevada) and of divorce havens like Haiti and the Dominican Republic, the divorce decrees of which–if rendered in a consensual proceeding–will be recognized by some states in the United States.[4] The other aspects of the parties' contract ("Declaration of Intent"), in particular their choice of the covenant state's law, have no counterpart in non-covenant states or in European law.

There is no doubt that a covenant marriage will be recognized as valid in other jurisdictions in application of the *lex celebrationis*.[5] The

---

6. See Cheshire & North supra n.2; Restatement, Second, Conflict of Laws § 283 (1971).

§ 13.16

1. See infra at §§ 15.3, 15.7, 15.22–15.23.

2. La. R.S. 9:272 et seq.; Arizona Stats. Ann. 25–901 et seq.; Arkansas Code Ann. § 9–11–801 et seq.

For discussion, see Spaht, Louisiana's Covenant Marriage: Social Analysis and Legal Implications, 59 La. L. Rev. 63 (1998); Spaht & Symeonides, Covenant Marriage and the Law of Conflict of Laws, 32 Creighton L. Rev. 1085 (1999); Hay, The American "Covenant Marriage" in the Conflict of Laws, 64 La. L. Rev. 43 (2003), reprinted in

John Witte, Jr. and Michael Broyde (eds.), Covenant Marriage in Comparative Perspective ____ (2004).

3. See, e.g., for Denmark: Nielsen, Equality and Care in Danish Family Law and Law of Inheritance, in: Dahl et al. (eds.), Danish Law in European Perspective 176 (1996) (one year); France: Code civil Art. 237 (six years); Germany: Civil Code (BGB) § 1566 in conjunction with § 1565 (one year if consensual, three years if contested); Spain: Civil Code. Art. 86 (one year). For Finland, see Kangas, Family Law and Inheritance Law, in: Pöyhönen (ed.), An Introduction to Finnish Law 222 (2d. ed. 2002) (minimum six months' reconciliation period).

4. See infra §§ 15.20 n. 10, 15.22 n. 1.

more important question is whether a non-covenant state[6] will grant a divorce on local law grounds or defer to the chosen (covenant state's) law and its counseling and waiting requirements. If the question arises in a civil law country, the court may well apply covenant-state law if its choice-of-law rules for divorce refer to the parties' home law.[7] In the United States, in contrast, there are no choice-of-law rules for divorce. The applicable law typically follows jurisdiction, meaning: local law applies. Since the petitioner will have a close connection to the forum,[8] there is no reason to treat of him or her differently than other local petitioners whose marriage was contracted in-state or, for that matter, in a third state.[9] The somewhat curious result than is that the limitations on dissolution of a covenant-state marriage may be effective when dissolution is sought in a foreign country but not in a non-covenant state within the United States.[10]

III. UNUSUAL MARRIAGES, SAME–SEX MARRIAGES AND UNIONS, CONTRACTUAL DOMESTIC ARRANGEMENTS

A. UNUSUAL MARRIAGES

§ 13.17   The unitary concept of the recognition or nonrecognition of the marriage status as controlling all the incidents flowing from the status could lead to an all-or-nothing approach in the recognition of foreign marriages that are inconsistent with accepted views of marriage in the forum. Anglo–American law at one time supported such an approach and refused recognition to marriages that did not fit "marriage as understood in Christendom ... defined as the voluntary union for life of one man and one woman to the exclusion of all others."[1] English

---

5. Supra §§ 13.5–13.6.

6. The question does not arise if the forum is also a covenant-marriage state: it will either honor the parties' choice of the *lex celebrationis* or apply the possibly identical *lex fori*.

7. German law furnishes an illustration: the applicable law for divorce is (1) the law of the spouses' common citizenship, if one of them retains it; (2) the law of their common habitual residence or their last marital common habitual residence, if one of them retains it; (3) the law of the state to which the spouses have the closes connection. Art. 17 in conjunction with Art. 14(1), Introductory Law to the Civil Code (EGBGB). If the various references in Art. 14 do not lead to an applicable law, German law applies. Art. 17(1), 2d sentence.

8. For divorce jurisdiction, see infra §§ 15.6–15.7. The text addresses the *ex parte* or contested bilateral divorce. Local

law will apply as a matter of course in the consensual bilateral divorce (i.e., the court will refer to covenant-state law ex officio). See also infra § 15.9.

9. It has been suggested that non-observance of the limitations that flow from the parties' "Declaration of Intent" may give the respondent a remedy for breach of contract. Katherine Shaw Spaht, supra n. 3, 59 La. L. Rev. at 103. This, of course, does not address the question of the law applicable to the dissolution of the marriage.

10. For discussion of covenant marriages, especially in the context of dissolution sought in a non-covenant state, see Hay, supra n.2.

§ 13.17

1. Lord Penzance in Hyde v. Hyde, L.R. 1 Prob. & Div. 130, 133 (1866). Clearly the marriage need not be "Christian," however, if monogamous, and the validity of a Japa-

courts persisted in this view for a long time, while American courts took a more relaxed view of unusual or informal marriages quite early,[2] perhaps under the influence of the American frontier environment. The asserted rule that no recognition will be given to foreign marriages that are not monogamous unions of one man and one woman for life can no longer be accepted. Under the influence of cases and legislation involving particular incidents, both in England and in the United States, unusual marriages, valid under appropriate foreign law, are recognized as valid for particular purposes. Such limited recognition does not, however, involve a recognition of the right to exercise, in the forum, all the incidents usual to the marriage relation (especially, the right to cohabitation).

Although several of the restrictions on marriage, such as underage parties, have been litigated, the most difficulty has involved actual or potential polygamous marriages. Some of the difficulty is engendered by the fact that procedures available to Anglo–American courts are not designed to afford relief in situations in which marital rights and duties

nese marriage has been upheld early in England. Brinkley v. Attorney General, L.R. 15 Prob. Div. 76 (1890).

The *Hyde* case involved a Mormon marriage performed in Salt Lake City Utah Territory by Brigham Young, Governor. The husband was later excommunicated from the Mormon Church and the wife declared single and capable of remarriage in a proceeding in Utah where she had remained at all times. The husband returned to England and sought a divorce. The court dismissed the petition because in the court's view, the Utah marriage was potentially, though not actually, polygamous. However, it is pointed out in Bartholomew, Recognition of Polygamous Marriages in America, 13 Int'l & Comp. L.Q. 1022, 1031 (1964):

Our conclusion is, therefore, that at no time was the practice of polygamy lawful in the State of Deseret or the Territory or State of Utah. It is ironic that the marriage contracted by Hyde in Utah in 1853 should have stimulated Sir James Wilde to such rhetoric, for poor Mr. Hyde could no more have lawfully taken a second wife in Utah than he could have in England: all Sir James's rhetoric was therefore monumentally irrelevant.

The question that now arises is: what was the attitude of the American courts to those plural marriages which were in fact contracted in Utah by the Mormons. The answer seems to be that their attitude was exactly the same as the attitude of an English court would have been to an attempt to contract plural marriages in England: the second and subsequent marriages were regarded as invalid and,

certainly after 1862, bigamous. Since polygamy was not sanctioned by the law of Utah Mormon marriages were not potentially polygamous; they were as monogamous as any English marriage was. The first marriage that a man contracted was therefore regarded as a perfectly valid monogamous marriage: execration was saved for the plural marriage.

On present-day Mormon polygamous marriages in the United States—contracted and tolerated in Utah, Arizona, Idaho, Nevada, and Montana—, see Krause, Marriage for the New Millenium: Heterosexual, Same Sex—Or Not All?, 34 Fam.L.Q. 271, 289 (2000).

2. See supra n.1. In re Bethell, 38 Ch. Div. 220, 234 (1888). In this interesting case, an Englishman in Africa contracted a union with a woman of a native tribe according to its rites. He was domiciled in England, but no point was made of that, the case turning on the point whether this was a "marriage." The court said not, and held a child born to the parties was not legitimate. Compare the decision with the American decisions in Indian cases infra § 13.17, and the language of Judge Campbell in Kobogum v. Jackson Iron Co., 76 Mich. 498, 507, 43 N.W. 602, 605 (1889) ("While most civilized nations in our day very wisely discard polygamy . . . yet it is a recognized and valid institution among many nations, and in no way universally unlawful. We must either hold that there can be no valid Indian marriage, or must hold that all marriages are valid which by Indian usage are so regarded."). For the United States, see infra § 13.19.

are of a sort different from those familiar to the forum.[3] Formerly held social and religious views seemingly contributed to other difficulties. An example of the latter may be the refusal, on the part of English courts, to recognize foreign marriages which were potentially, though not actually, polygamous.[4] The rule that a marriage was invalid, even between one man and one woman, under law that permitted plural spouses, continued in England for nearly a century.[5] American courts, however, rejected only foreign marriages which were *actually* polygamous.[6] Although much of the more tolerant view now taken by the English courts is because of the Matrimonial Proceedings (Polygamous Marriages) Act of 1972, the recognition of unusual foreign marriages for the purpose of enforcing inoffensive incidents of those marriages had earlier foretold the change.[7]

3. See, e.g., Fateh Muhammad v. Sardav Begum Suna, 1956 S.C. 367. An early recognition of this involved the statute of 20 and 21 Vict. c. 85 (1858), which vested the jurisdiction of the ecclesiastical courts in "the Court for Divorce and Matrimonial Causes." In denying an application for restitution of conjugal rights to a party to a Mohammedan marriage, the court made the following remarks: "We must remember that the English ecclesiastical law is founded on the assumption that all the parties litigant are Christians.... " Ardasee Cursetjee v. Perozeboye, 10 Moore P.C. 375 (1856). See also Hyde v. Hyde, L.R. 1 Prob. & Div. 130 (1866). In Nachimson v. Nachimson, 1930 Prob. 217, 99 L.J.P. 104, 143 L.T.R. 254, the argument was made that an action for judicial separation between parties to a Russian marriage could not be maintained in an English court because the possibility of a Russian consent divorce prevented the marriage from falling within the traditional English definition of marriage as a voluntary union for life. The court, however, permitted the action and held that the manner of dissolution did not affect the validity of the marriage. Cf. Nevarez v. Bailon, 287 S.W.2d 521 (Tex.Civ.App.1956); Victor v. Victor, 177 Ariz. 231, 866 P.2d 899 (App. 1993) (court cannot force husband to grant wife a Jewish divorce because Jewish marital rights are not familiar to the forum and not germane to its civil, secular jurisdiction).

4. Hyde v. Hyde, L.R. 1 Prob. & Div. 130 (1866). See Fitzpatrick, Non–Christian Marriage, 2 J. Comp. Leg., N.S. 359 (1900); 8 J. Comp. Leg., N.S. 466 (1901). See also Cowen, A Note on Potentially Polygamous Marriages, 12 Int'l & Comp. L.Q. 1407 (1963); Cretney, Immigrants' Marriages, 118 New L.J. 777 (1968); Hoolahan, Potentially Polygamous Marriages, 110 Law J. 519 (1960); R. Schuz, When is a Polygamous Marriage Not a Polygamous Marriage, 46 Mod. L. Rev. 653 (1983).

5. See Earnshaw, Polygamy and Matrimonial Relief, 122 New L.J. 705 (1972); Poulter, *Hyde v. Hyde*—A Reappraisal, 25 Int'l & Comp. L.Q. 475 (1976).

6. See Bartholomew, Recognition of Polygamous Marriages in America, 13 Int'l & Comp. L.Q. 1022 (1964); 2 A. Ehrenzweig & E. Jayme, Private International Law 165 (1973).

7. See Dicey & Morris, Conflict of Laws 701 (13th ed. 2000 by Collins); R. Graveson, Conflict of Laws, 244 (7th ed. 1974); Hartley, Polygamy and Social Policy, 32 Mod. L. Rev. 155 (1969); Webb, Mutation of Polygamous Marriages, 16 Int'l & Comp. L.Q. 1152 (1967); Webb, Polygamy and the Eddying Winds, 14 Int'l & Comp. L.Q. (1965); RLW, When a Marriage Is Not a Marriage, 111 Sol. J. 900 (1967). The Matrimonial Proceedings (Polygamous Marriage) Act of 1972 was replaced by § 47 of the Matrimonial Causes Act of 1973, 27 Halsbury's Stat. of Eng. 763–64 (4th ed. 1987) which provides:

47. Matrimonial relief and declarations of validity in respect of polygamous marriages

(1) A court in England and Wales shall not be precluded from granting matrimonial relief or making a declaration concerning the validity of a marriage by reason only that the marriage in question was entered into under a law which permits polygamy.

(2) In this section "matrimonial relief" means—

(a) any decree under Part I of this Act;

(b) a financial provision order under section 27 above;

(c) an order under section 35 above altering a maintenance agreement;

(d) an order under any provision of this Act which confers a power exercisa-

A Court of Appeals decision recognized the right of inheritance of a "t'sip," or secondary wife of a Chinese merchant of Penang.[8] A prior potentially polygamous marriage was recognized to bar the husband from contracting another marriage in England[9] and to require another to maintain his abandoned wife and child.[10] Today the English view is to

ble in connection with, or in connection with proceedings for, such decree or order as is mentioned in paragraphs (a) to (c) above;

(dd) an order under Part III of the Matrimonial and Family Proceedings Act 1984;

(e) an order under Part I of the Domestic Proceedings and Magistrates' Courts Act 1978.

(3) In this section "a declaration concerning the validity of a marriage" means—

(a) a declaration that a marriage is valid or invalid; and

(b) any other declaration involving a determination as to the validity of a marriage;

being a declaration in a decree granted under section 45 above or a declaration made in the exercise by the High Court of its jurisdiction to grant declaratory relief in any proceedings notwithstanding that a declaration is the only substantive relief sought in those proceedings.

(4) This section has effect whether or not either party to the marriage in question has for the time being any spouse additional to the other party; and provision may be made by rules of court—

(a) for requiring notice of proceedings brought by virtue of this section to be served on any such other spouse; and

(b) for conferring on any such other spouse the right to be heard in any such proceedings, in such cases as may be prescribed by the rules.

The broad sweep of Section 47, which was Section 1 of the 1972 Act, seems clearly to permit any matrimonial relief even if the place of celebration permits polygamy, i.e., even if the marriage was potentially polygamous. However, Section 11 of the same Act, which was Section 4 of the 1972 Act, provides that a marriage is void on the grounds "(d) in the case of a polygamous marriage entered into outside England and Wales, that either party was at the time of the marriage domiciled in England and Wales.... For the purposes of paragraph (d) of this subsection a marriage may be polygamous although at its inception neither party has any spouse additional to the other."

Hussein v. Hussein, (1982) 3 All.E.R. 369, was an action for judicial separation brought by the wife who was domiciled in Pakistan at the time of her marriage in Pakistan to the husband who was domiciled in England. The law of Pakistan permitted the husband but not the wife to take another spouse. The husband defended on the assertion that the marriage was invalid under Section 11. The Court of Appeal, Ormrod L.J., concluded that the marriage was valid under Section 11 because each party was incapacitated by the law of their domicile from taking a second spouse. Rather clearly the Court recognized the policy force of Section 47 to overcome the "not very happily phrased" Section 11(d) in its reconciliation of these sections of the same original enactment. The alternative "would mean that all marriages contracted abroad by people domiciled in this country in accordance with the local law would be void if that law permitted polygamy in any form" (p. 372). The opinion resolves the ambiguity of the Act by clearly limiting this application of Section 11(d) to actually polygamous marriages. The court's resolution, including its reference to domiciliary law to validate a questioned marriage, supports the recognition of a foreign marriage as valid unless there is strong reason to the contrary. Cf. Fentiman, The Validity of Marriage and the Proper Law, 44 Camb. L.J. 256, 273 (1985). But cf. A. Briggs, Polygamous Marriages and English Domiciliaries, 32 Int'l & Comp. L.Q. 737 (1983). The Law Commissions of England and Scotland have recommended that the concept of potential polygamy be discarded and that no marriage be considered polygamous unless it is actually polygamous. Law Commission Working Paper No. 83; Scottish Law Commission Consultative Memorandum No. 56, discussed in Schuz, supra n.4 and Deech, Family Law, 1982 All. E.R. Annual Review 146.

8. Cheang Thye Phin In v. Tan Ah Loy, [1920] A.C. 369; Kam Chin Chun Ming v. Kam Hee Ho, 45 Haw. 521, 371 P.2d 379 (1962) (illegitimate children born of concubinage could inherit). But cf. In re Bethell, 38 Ch.Div. 220 (1888).

9. Baindail v. Baindail (1946) P. 122.

10. Iman Din v. National Assistance Board (1967) 2 Q.B. 213. Cf. Mohamed v. Knott (1969) 1 Q.B. 1.

recognize a foreign marriage as valid unless there is some strong reason to the contrary.[11]

§ 13.18 The issue of recognizing a matrimonial association other than a monogamous union for life so far has most frequently arisen in the United States with regard to the marriage among the American Indians. The issue usually arose in connection with the inheritance of property and frequently turned on the legitimacy of children, who claimed, or through whom claim was made to a property interest.

Marriage among the Indians varied with tribal custom and the social status of the parties. Spouses became husband and wife by living together, the cohabitation sometimes being preceded by a gift or payment by the groom to the bride's parents.[1] Divorce or termination of the marriage was equally simple. When the parties ceased to live together, the marriage was brought to an end.[2] Such "Indian custom" marriages and divorces continue to be recognized by many tribes today.[3] Although polygamy is now virtually extinct among Indians, the practice was common historically.[4]

Indians in Indian country are normally subject to tribal law, not state law, and the legal protection afforded tribal self-government is strongest in areas involving internal tribal matters such as marriage and divorce.[5] As a result, marriages and divorces involving Indians in Indian country will normally be respected by state and federal courts, either as a matter of choice of law[6] or by reason of full faith and credit.[7]

An almost unanimous line of decisions holds that marriages contracted between tribal members, according to the laws or customs of their tribe, are to be upheld, in the absence of a federal statute rendering such tribal laws and customs invalid.[8] This is not a recognition of the

---

11. Dicey & Morris, Conflict of Laws 651 et. seq. (13th ed. 2000 by Collins). Cf. Poulter, *Hyde v. Hyde*—A Reappraisal, 25 Int'l & Comp. L.Q. 475 (1976); Cretney, Immigrants' Marriages, 118 New L.J. 777 (1968). See also Nygle, The Case of the Polygamous Migrant, 6 Aust. L.J. 3 (1965).

§ 13.18

1. See P. Farb, Man's Rise to Civilization 67, 110 (1968). The gift or payment to the family or parties to the marriage is a custom that continues in many societies today, including in western cultures.

2. Id.

3. See e.g., Estate of Harold Humpy, 6 Ind. L. Rep. I–6 (Interior Bd. of Ind. App. 1979); Estate of Guo-ha, 6 Ind. L. Rep. I–23 (Interior Bd. of Ind. App. 1979). But see Smith v. Babbitt, 96 F.Supp.2d 907 (D. Minn. 2000) (children born of cohabitation are not "heirs" because Minnesota does not recognize Indian custom of marriage through cohabitation).

4. H. Driver, Indians of North America 230 (2d ed. 1969). On present-day polyga-

mous practices, see Krause, supra § 13.17 n.1.

5. See supra § 11.19.

6. See, e.g., Matter of Marriage of Red Fox, 23 Or.App. 393, 542 P.2d 918 (1975); F. Cohen, Handbook of Indian Law, ch. 6. § D3 (1981 ed.).

7. See 28 U.S.C.A. § 1738 (requiring full faith and credit to the "acts records and judicial proceedings" of "any State, Territory, or Possession of the United States"). Authorities are divided as to whether this includes Indian tribes. See Cohen, supra n.6.

8. Yakima Joe v. To–Is–Lap, 191 Fed. 516 (C.C.Or. 1910); Wall v. Williamson, 8 Ala. 48 (1845); Moore v. Wa-me-go, 72 Kan. 169, 83 P. 400 (1905); Kobogum v. Jackson Iron Co., 76 Mich. 498, 43 N.W. 602 (1889); La Framboise v. Day, 136 Minn. 239, 161 N.W. 529 (1917); People ex rel. La Forte v. Rubin, 98 N.Y.S. 787 (1905); Ortley v. Ross, 78 Neb. 339, 110 N.W. 982 (1907); Meagher v. Harjo, 72 Okl. 206, 179 P. 757 (1919);

informal agreement of parties to take each other as husband and wife known as a common law marriage, but a marriage according to the customs of the Indians.[9] Courts have likewise regarded as valid the marriage of a non-Indian, who, in Indian country and in accordance with tribal customs, has taken an Indian woman as his wife.[10] Where the tribal members are not residing in Indian country at the time of the alleged marriage, the customs of the tribe have been held inapplicable. The marriage was invalid, unless it complied with state law.[11] The same limitation has been applied to cohabitation of tribal and non-tribal parties which commenced outside Indian country.[12]

The question of the validity of the Indian custom of divorce by separation has been in issue in determining the legitimacy of offspring from a later cohabitation with another spouse. There is little doubt that such a divorce is recognized as valid when the separation took place in Indian country and when the marriage was contracted there.[13] Divorce in

Morgan v. McGhee, 24 Tenn. (5 Humph.) 13 (1844); First National Bank v. Sharpe, 12 Tex.Civ.App. 223, 33 S.W. 676 (1896); In re Wo-gin-up's Estate, 57 Utah 29, 192 P. 267 (1920); Connolly v. Woolrich, 3 Low. Can. L.J. 14 (1867). But see Roche v. Washington, 19 Ind. 53, 81 Am. Dec. 376 (1862). Cf. Uniform Marriage and Divorce Act § 206, 9A U.L.A. 107, 107 (1979) ("A marriage may be solemnized ... in accordance with any ... mode of solemnization recognized by any Indian Nation or Tribe or Native Group."); Barrett v. Barrett, 878 P.2d 1051, 1053 (Okla. 1994).

9. La Framboise v. Day, 136 Minn. 239, 161 N.W. 529 (1917); Buck v. Branson, 34 Okl. 807, 127 P. 436 (1912); Smith v. Babbitt, supra n. 3. Most tribes include provisions on marriage and divorce in their tribal codes. See Cohen, supra n.6. For discussion of the difference between common law and tribal custom marriages, including the addition of new license requirements, see In re Validation of Loretta Francisco, No. A–CV–15–88, http://www.tribal-institute.org/opinions/1989.NAAN.0000013.htm (S.Ct. of the Navajo Nation 1989)(validation of common-law marriage denied). For good discussion of Navajo marriage customs in the context of a choice-of-law decision (as between Arizona and Navajo law), see Apache v. Republic Nat'l Life Ins. Co. et al., 3 Nav. R. 250, http://www.tribal-institute.org/opin-ions/1982.NANN.0000050.htm (Dist. Ct. of the Navajo Nation, Dist. Window Rock, Ariz. 1982), at ¶ 23 et seq.

For examples of tribal marriage law (here: Navajo), see In the Matter of Documenting the Marriage: Ellen M. Slim and Tom Slim, Deceased, 3 Nav. Rep. 218, http://www.tribal-institute.org/opin-

ions/1982.NANN.0000060.htm (Dist. Ct. of the Navajo Nation, Crownpoint, NM. 1982)(traditional customary divorce replaced by Indian judicial divorce by 1940 statute, 9 NTC Se. 407; surviving spouse of customary marriage not recognized as such for failure of deceased spouse's dissolution of previous marriage by judicial decree); Validating the Marriage of Rose M. Garcia and Alfred Garcia, No. A–CV–02–84, http://www.tribal-institute.org/opinions/1985.NANN.0000004.htm, (Ct. App. of the Navajo Nation 1985)(Navajo and non-Navajo can contract marriage only by complying with applicable state or foreign law, 9 NTC § 2, validation of marriage contracted according to Navajo custom denied).

10. *La Frambois v. Day*, 136 Minn. 239, 161 N.W. 529; Johnson v. Johnson's Administrator, 30 Mo. 72, 77 Am.Dec. 598 (1860); Morgan v. McGhee, 24 Tenn. (5 Humph.) 13 (1844); Connolly v. Woolrich, 3 Low. Can. L.J. 14 (1867). But see Follansbee v. Wilbur, 14 Wash. 242, 44 P. 262 (1896).

11. Roche v. Washington, 19 Ind. 53, 81 Am.Dec. 376 (1862); State v. Ta-cha-na-tah, 64 N.C. 614 (1870). However, if state or federal laws permit marriage of tribal members living off the reservation by compliance with tribal custom, the marriage is valid and merits the same presumptions as any valid marriage. See Ponina v. Leland, 85 Nev. 263, 454 P.2d 16 (1969).

12. Banks v. Galbraith, 149 Mo. 529, 51 S.W. 105 (1899) holding that where an Indian woman, with her parents, left the tribe and went to Missouri, and was there sold to a white man with whom she lived, there was no Indian marriage but Missouri law controled.

13. Marris v. Sockey, 170 F.2d 599 (10th Cir.1948), cert. denied 336 U.S. 914,

this fashion is not recognized, however, when the parties do not reside in Indian country.[14]

§ 13.19 Instances in which American courts have been called upon to recognize other types of non-monogamous marriages are less common. One decision recognized the wife of a Muslim marriage to be entitled to compensation as a widow under the state's worker's compensation act.[1] The deceased had only one wife, but could lawfully have had four under Muslim law.[2] In another case, a California court considered the policy concerns relevant to the particular incident of the marriage at issue and divided the widow's share of an estate between the decedent's two surviving wives of a foreign polygamous marriage.[3] The court stated:

> The decision of the trial court was influenced by the rule of "public policy;" but that rule, it would seem, would apply only if decedent had attempted to cohabit with his two wives in California. Where only the question of descent of property is involved, "public policy" is not affected.... "Public policy" would not be affected by dividing the money equally between the two wives, particularly since there is no contest between them and they are the only interested parties.[4]

Thus, there is a difference between the circumstances under which a state will create a marriage relation for its domiciliaries and or recognize the existence of that status when contracted by parties domiciled elsewhere. Presumably no American state would permit a local domiciliary to contract a marriage with two persons at the same time.[5] However,

---

69 S.Ct. 605, 93 L.Ed. 1078 (1949); Wall v. Williamson, 8 Ala. 48 (1845); La Framboise v. Day, 136 Minn. 239, 161 N.W. 529 (1917); James v. Adams, 56 Okl. 450, 155 P. 1121 (1915). In Cyr v. Walker, 29 Okl. 281, 116 P. 931 (1911), the court went so far as to declare a divorce by tribal custom effective, though the man married a woman who was not a member of the tribe in Illinois. But see *In re Marriage of Slim,* supra n. 9: pure customary divorce (without formality abolished in Navajo law).

14. In re Wo-gin-up's Estate, 57 Utah 29, 192 P. 267 (1920); Connolly v. Woolrich, 3 Low. Can. L.J. 14 (1867). In this latter case the marriage was in the Indian country according to tribal custom and therefore good. The separation was after the husband (a white man) had brought the wife back to Lower Canada to live. The attempted divorce was invalid. Cf. Johnson v. Johnson's Administrator, 30 Mo. 72, 77 Am.Dec. 598 (1860) (white man abandoned woman prior to his return, and the divorce was held valid). Cf. Yakima Joe v. To–Is–Lap, 191 Fed. 516 (C.C.Or. 1910). But cf. Moore v. Wa-me-go, 72 Kan. 169, 83 P. 400 (1905).

§ 13.19

1. Royal v. Cudahy Packing Co., 195 Iowa 759, 190 N.W. 427 (1922). See Kapigian v. Der Minassian, 212 Mass. 412, 99 N.E. 264 (1912). In this case the marriage was between two Christians, domiciled in Turkey. The marriage ended when the wife became a Muslim and married another. The court recognized both the marriage and its termination. But in Ng Suey Hi v. Weedin, 21 F.2d 801 (9th Cir.1927), the child of a second wife of a polygamous marriage by an American citizen residing in China was held to be illegitimate and therefore denied entry to this country under immigration laws. See supra § 13.17 n.8.

2. See Polydore v. Prince, 19 Fed.Cas. 950, No. 11,257 (D.Me.1837) ("If a Turkish or Hindoo husband were traveling in this country with his wife, or temporarily resident here, we should, without hesitation, acknowledge the relation of husband and wife between them.").

3. In re Dalip Singh Bir's Estate, 83 Cal.App.2d 256, 188 P.2d 499 (1948).

4. 83 Cal.App.2d at 261, 188 P.2d at 502.

5. See Application of Sood, 208 Misc. 819, 142 N.Y.S.2d 591 (1955).

courts will, in appropriate cases and circumstances, recognize a foreign-created status between persons domiciled there at the time that does not conform to its requirements for their status. How far recognition can be given not only to the status, but to its incidents, is not clear.[6] It may be doubted whether a foreign visitor would be permitted to cohabit here with his four wives although even this is uncertain. Children of the union would probably be recognized as legitimate.[7] If the case involves succession to movables, the reference should be to the domiciliary law of the deceased and distribution made accordingly. Even a question concerning the devolution of real property or a claim by four spouses under worker's compensation legislation should be decided on the basis of recognition of the foreign marriage so that the reasonable expectations of family members under their personal law could be given the maximum effect possible under forum law.[8]

B. SAME–SEX MARRIAGES AND UNIONS

§ 13.20   A same-sex marriage can now be contracted in Belgium, Ontario (Canada), and The Netherlands.[1] In the United States, two early state court decisions, interpreting the respective state constitutions, concluded that limiting the institution of marriage to opposite-sex couples was an equal protection violation.[2] However, both decisions were

6. Restatement, Second, Conflict of Laws § 284 (1971).

7. Cf. Uniform Marriage and Divorce Act § 207(c), 9A U.L.A. 147, 168 (1987) ("'(c) Children born of a prohibited marriage are legitimate"); Trimble v. Gordon, 430 U.S. 762, 97 S.Ct. 1459, 52 L.Ed.2d 31 (1977). See also infra Chapter 16.

8. It is not uncommon for courts in the United States to recognize multiple spouses as the result of fraud or estoppel. See Uniform Marriage and Divorce Act § 209, 9A U.L.A. 147, 174 (1987); In re Ricci's Estate, 201 Cal.App.2d 146, 19 Cal.Rptr. 739 (1962); Sousa v. Freitas, 10 Cal.App.3d 660, 89 Cal.Rptr. 485 (1970). See also Engdahl, Proposal for a Benign Revolution in Marriage Law and Marriage Conflicts Law, 55 Iowa L. Rev. 56, 109 (1969); Reese, Marriage in American Conflict of Laws, 26 Int'l & Comp. L.Q. 952 (1977). Courts are more frequently applying concepts of the putative spouse to protect persons who enter an invalid marriage in good faith. The practical effect is that a non-spouse may share some of the incidents of a marriage. See Uniform Marriage and Divorce Act § 209, 9 U.L.A. 147, 174 (1987). Predictable choice-of-law resolutions have yet to be developed in this area, but the identification of the states having significant relationships to the issue involved seems to parallel those of recognized marriages in attempting to imple-

ment the reasonable expectations of all parties concerned. For a detailed analysis and sensitive discussion of the choice of law considerations see Fine, Choice of Law for Putative Spouses, 32 Int'l & Comp. L.Q. 708 (1983).

§ 13.20

1. Belgium: Fiorini, New Belgian Law on Same–Sex Marriage and PIL Implications, 52 Int'l & Comp. L. Q. 1039 (2003); Netherlands: Wasmuth, in: H. Krüger & H.-P. Mansel (eds.), Liber Amicorum Gerhard Kegel 237 (2002); Ontario: Halpern v. Canada (Attorney General), 2003 O.J. No. 2268 (common law definition of marriage offends the equality of same-sex couples under Sec. 15(1) of the Canadian Charter of Rights and Freedoms). See also Caswell, Moving Toward Same–Sex Marriage, 80 Can. Bar Rev. 810 (2001); Pickel, Judicial Analysis Frozen in Time: EGALE Canada, Inc. v. Canada (Attorney General), 65 Sak. L. Rev. 243 (2002).

2. See Baehr v. Lewin, 74 Haw. 530, 852 P.2d 44 (1993), reconsideration granted in part and mandate clarified 74 Haw. 650, 875 P.2d 225 (1993), on remand sub nom. Baehr v. Miike, 1996 WL 694235 (Haw.Cir. Ct. 1996); Brause v. Bureau of Vital Statistics, 1998 WL 88743 (Alaska Super. 1998). For the view of the U.N. Human Rights Committee, see infra § 13.22 n.1.

effectively overruled by statewide initiatives that amended the respective state constitutions.

Subsequently, the Vermont Supreme Court and the Massachusetts Supreme Judicial Court also held that the then current law, restricting marriage to heterosexual couples, was unconstitutional under their respective state constitution.[3] The Vermont court gave the state legislature the option to extend the institution of marriage to same-sex couples or to give them a parallel form in which to live their relationship. The Vermont Legislature chose the latter option, enacting a law that gives same-sex couples the right to enter into a "civil union" with substantially the same benefits enjoyed by traditional married persons. In Massachusetts, the state's highest court similarly struck down the state's marriage law on state constitutional law grounds. When the state legislature failed to act within the time set by the court, same-sex marriages became legal in Massachusetts in May 2004.[4] Some municipalities in other states, for instance San Francisco, albeit without legal authorization to do so, have also issued marriage licenses to same-sex couples. The San Francisco marriages were later voided by the California Supreme Court.

An early response to these developments on the federal level was the adoption of the "Defense of Marriage Act" (hereafter: DOMA).[5] Based on Congressional authority to define the effect of the full-faith-and-credit command of the Constitution, the statute does not define that command affirmatively—as did three prior statutes[6]–but limits it. A marriage, it declares, is the union between man and woman, and the states of the United States are therefore free *not* to accord recognition to other (i.e., same-sex) unions, even if valid where entered into. As of January 2004,

3. Baker v. Vermont, 170 Vt. 194, 744 A.2d 864 (1999); Goodridge et al. v. Department of Public Health, 440 Mass. 309, 798 N.E.2d 941 (2003).

4. 15 Vt. St. Ann. § 1201 et seq. (2003). For Massachusetts, see Goodridge v. Department of Public Health, 440 Mass. 309, 798 N.E.2d 941 (2003). The state's governor ordered that licenses be issued only to couples whose home states would recognize the Massachusetts marriage. Since no other state, to date, provides for same-sex marriages, the governor's action effectively limits the availability of a Massachusetts same-sex marriage to local domiciliaries. The constitutionality of this restriction has not yet been tested. See also Cal. Fam. Code § 299.2, effective Jan. 1, 2005, providing for civil issues and the recognition of civil unions entered into elsewhere.

In Europe, there is also a growing trend to introduce alternative forms for same-sex relationships. The "registered partnership" is the functional equivalent of Vermont's "civil union." Except for the designation as a "marriage," it confers on the civil-union partner the same benefits that a spouse

would enjoy. See, e.g., Germany: Gesetz über Lebenspartnerschaften (LPartG), BGBL 2001, I, 266, as amended BGBl 2001, I, 3513. See also infra § 13. Countries with partnership legislation include, in Europe: Denmark, Finland, France, Germany, Hungary, Iceland, Norway, Portugal, Sweden; in Canada: civil union (Quebec), registered partnership in British Columbia, Nova Scotia. For an earlier European overview, see J. Basedow et al. (eds.), Die Rechtsstellung gleichgeschlechtlicher Lebensgemeinschaften (= Vol 70, Beiträge zum ausländischen und internationalen Privatrecht, 2000). For a bibliography of foreign literature, see Kegel & Schurig, Internationales Privatrecht 886–87 (9th ed. 2004).

For the consequences of dissolution, see also infra at §§ 15.1 n.5, 15.26 nn.5–6, 15.30 n.8, 15.39 n.4.

5. 28 U.S.C.A. § 1738C.

6. 28 U.S.C.A. §§ 1738 (basic Full–Faith and Credit implementing statute) (see infra Chapter 24), 1738A (child custody decrees), 1738B (support decrees) (for the two latter, see Chapter 15).

37 states had passed statutes against the recognition of non-traditional unions.[7]

In a case of a Vermont civil union, a Connecticut court held that it did not have subject-matter jurisdiction to dissolve a Vermont civil-union: its jurisdiction extended only to "family matters."[8] Characterization (supra, chapter 3) provided a way not to address the issue. In contrast, a New York court recognized a party to a Vermont civil union as a spouse for purposes of New York's wrongful death statute; both plaintiff and the decedent had been New York domiciliaries before and after entering into the civil union. The court noted that New York lacks a statutory prohibition against recognition (it is a non-DOMA state), that it recognizes out-of-state common-law marriages although its law does not provide for them, and that recognition of Vermont civil unions therefore did not violate New York's public policy.[9]

Same-sex marriages, as noted, have become available in Massachusetts and abroad. More foreign countries no doubt will follow that trend. Similarly, there will most probably be efforts to introduce this form of domestic relationship in other states of the United States as well. If so, the constitutionality of state statutes under the DOMA and of that statute itself may be in issue: the Full–Faith-and-Credit Clause (Art. IV, Sec. I) authorizes Congress to prescribe the manner in which sister-state judgments are to be proved and to provide the "effect" they shall have. Does this include the power to define *which* judgments (assuming, for instance, that a civil union has been judicially recognized in the state of

7. For earlier literature, see Symposium, Interjurisdictional Marriage Recognition, 32 Creighton L. Rev. 1 (1998) (contributions by Coolidge, Hogue, Myers, Marcin, Solimine, Bailey, Graham–Siegenthaler, Borchers, Wardle, Duncan, Whitten, Holland, Rensberger, Strasser and one student author); Symposium, 16 Quinnipiac L. Rev. 1 (1996); Allen, Same–Sex Marriage: A Conflict of Laws Analysis for Oregon, 32 Williamette L. Rev. 619 (1996); Cox, Same–Sex Marriage and Choice-of-Law: If We Marry in Hawaii, Are We Still Married When We Return Home?, 1994 Wisc. L. Rev. 1033; Henson, Will Same–Sex Marriages be Recognized in Sister States: Full Faith and Credit and Due Process Limitations on States' Choice of Law Regarding the Incidents of Marriage Following Hawaii's *Baehr v. Lewis*, 32 U. Louisville J. Fam. L. 551 (1994); Hovermill, A Conflict of Laws and Morals: The Choice of Law Implications of Hawaii's Recognition of Same–Sex Marriages, 53 Md. L. Rev. 450 (1994); Kramer, Same–Sex Marriage, Conflict of Laws, and the Unconstitutional Public Policy Exception, 106 Yale L.J. 1965 (1997).

8. Rosengarten v. Downes, 71 Conn. App. 372, 802 A.2d 170 (2002), cert. for appeal granted 261 Conn. 936, 806 A.2d 1066 (2002).

In Burns v. Burns, 253 Ga.App. 600, 560 S.E.2d 47 (2002), Ga. cert. denied (2002), the court refused to recognize a Vermont civil union as equivalent to "marriage" in a case, in which a custody consent decree prohibited a parent from exercising child visitation rights while living with someone not a spouse or related by blood: Vermont itself distinguishes between "marriage" and "civil union," hence there was no reason to treat it as a marriage. Even if it were like a marriage, Georgia, by legislation, had opted to define "marriage" as restricted to the union between man and woman, referring also to the Defense of Marriage Act (DOMA), above. *But see* Salluco v. Alldredge, 17 Mass.L.Rep. 498 (Mass. Sup. 2004): after same-sex marriage became legal in Massachusetts (supra n. 4), the court exercised its "general equity jurisdiction" to dissolve a Vermont civil union between a Massachusetts and an Arkansas resident.

9. Langan v. St. Vincent's Hospital of New York, 196 Misc.2d 440, 765 N.Y.S.2d 411 (N.Y.Super. 2003).

its creation[10]) are entitled to recognition under the Clause? If so, how to resolve the conflict between §§ 1738 and 1738C (i.e., effects vs. subject matter): has § 1738 been amended?[11]

C. OTHER PARTNERSHIPS

§ 13.21 While same-sex marriage changes the traditional concept and definition of the institution of marriage, civil unions (Vermont-style) and European registered partnerships do not: they provide an equivalent, but different form of domestic relationship for same-sex parties. They are not an alternative form of marriage (like the covenant marriage) and are therefore not available to opposite-sex partners.[1]

Heterosexual couples, who choose to cohabit without marriage,[2] may of course structure their relationship, by contract, in much the same way as they would have, by law, as married spouses or registered same-sex partners. Prenuptial agreements are an example;[3] similar agreements can be concluded, of course, without a view toward marriage or in the course of a relationship. There are limits, however, usually designed to

---

10. The result may well be different when the out-of-state same-sex marriage or civil union has been created in a state providing for it, but has not been the subject of any judicial recognition, there or elsewhere. There is persuasive argument that—interstate—the Full Faith and Credit Clause is irrelevant to the question because it already permits exceptions to its command for unpalatable results. See Borchers, *Baker v. General Motors*: Implications for Interjurisdictional Recognition of Non–Traditional Marriages, 32 Creighton L. Rev. 147, 154–58 (1998). See also *Rosengarten*, supra n. 8. Obviously, international marriages or civil unions, not being subject to *any* Full Faith and Credit command, may have to yield to local standards. *But see* § 13.22 n.1 infra.

11. The recognition of foreign-country same-sex marriages or civil unions obviously is not affected by the interpretation of the (interstate) reach of the Full Faith and Credit command. Recognition may then depend on the particular state's public policy, legislatively (DOMA) or judicially expressed. It is an open question to what extent international standards do or should influence the answer: in 2003, the United Nations Human Rights Committee, established under Art. 28 of the International Covenant on Civil and Political Rights, found Australia, a member state, in violation of Art. 26 of the Charter by denying a pension to the same-sex partner of a deceased war veteran. See Murphy, UN Challenges Ruddock, Australian Financial Review (Nov. 4, 2003) at A5. The United States became a member of the Convention in 1992, subject to the "understanding"

that "distinctions on the basis of … sex … [are] permitted when … rationally related to a legitimate governmental purpose…".

§ 13.21

1. German law illustrates these points particularly well. Parties to a registered partnership enjoy virtually all the rights and assume all the responsibilities (e.g. for support) as spouses in a marriage have. In addition, they also enjoy rights conferred on spouses by law: the registered partner, for instance, succeeds to his or her deceased same-sex partner's rights as lessee (Civil Code § 563(1), 2d sentence), the cohabiting (unmarried) opposite-sex partner does not, but must secure new agreement from the lessor. This is a result that cohabitants obviously cannot change by contract between themselves (see text, next paragraph). For discussion and further illustration of the different legal consequences flowing from registered same-sex partnerships, on the one hand, and unmarried opposite cohabitation, see J. Kropholler, BGB—Studienkommentar annos. 10–19 before § 1353 (6th ed. 2003).

2. For thoughtful discussion of legal and social problems of marriage, same-sex unions, and unmarried cohabitation, see Krause, Marriage for the New Millennium: Heterosexual, Same Sex–Or Not at All?, 34 Fam. L.Q. 271 (2000).

3. See Uniform Premarital Agreement Act, in force in 26 states and the District of Columbia.

protect the weaker party: the Uniform Premarital Agreement Act protects against overreaching (Sec. 6(a)) and has a public interest (public policy) exception (Sec. 6(b). The German Supreme Court held prenuptial agreements about post-divorce support and matrimonial property to be unconstitutionally burdensome, thus expressing the same policy.[4]

In the case of cohabitation outside the recognized forms of marriage or civil union/registered partnership, these matters become issues of contract law and, with it, the applicable contract choice-of-law approach of the forum. This may or may not lead it to the law where the contract was concluded, but, assuming the sufficient nexus to the parties, make applicable the forum's limiting (protective) policies. Choice of law in contract is the subject of Chapter 18.

---

4. Decisions of Feb. 6 and March 29, 2001, [2001] FamRZ 343 and 985, respectively.

Chapter 14

MARITAL PROPERTY

Table of Sections

		Sections
I.	Preliminary Policy Observations	
	A. Introduction	14.1
	B. Common Law System	14.2
	C. Community or Marital Property System	14.3
	D. Matrimonial Property as Conflict of Laws Issues	14.4
II.	Immovables	
	A. Land Owned at Time of Marriage	14.5
	B. Land Acquired After Marriage	14.6
	C. Income From Immovables	14.7
III.	Movables	
	A. Movables Owned at Time of Marriage	14.8
	B. Movables Acquired Subsequent to Marriage	14.9
	C. Income from Movables	14.10
	D. Accrual Values: Insurance, Pensions, Etc.	14.11
IV.	Subsequent Intentional Property Transactions	14.12
V.	The Separate Property and Quasi Community Property Concepts	14.13
	A. Characterization of Separate Property	14.13
	B. Quasi–Community Property	14.14
VI.	Contractual Modification of the Marital Property Regime	14.15
VII.	Debts	14.16

I. PRELIMINARY POLICY OBSERVATIONS

A. INTRODUCTION

§ **14.1** Any society that considers the family an important social and economic unit affords significant protection to the family and its members. This protection takes different forms and appears in many areas of the law. As an example, protective policies are reflected in most areas of the law relating to domestic relations, property, succession of property, and creditors' claims against personal assets. In responding to the same local law policies of protecting the economic and social unit of the family, a particular state may use approaches that are effective immediately upon marriage during the life of the parties, such as dower, homestead, or community property; a state may emphasize limitations upon the ability to convey property; or a state may choose to rely on protections in the form of forced succession at death or on property settlements on termination of the marriage during lifetime. The policies incident to the mutual support obligations imposed upon family members are reflected in the concerns in marital property, as is the protection of the state from the burden of supporting indigent persons and from the threat of social instability resulting from the destruction of the family unit. In considering property issues, the protection of reasonable expectations and the recognition of the presumed contributions that family members make to the accumulation of assets, as well as economy in the transmission of property from generation to generation, are usually of significant weight.[1]

In the law relating to spousal property, the policies supportive of equality of the sexes and policies promoting justness and fairness among the family participants and beneficiaries of the assets accumulated by the family unit have particular influence on the courts, although this influence is often unarticulated. In opposition to the protection of family interests, there are the policies supportive of freedom of alienation or testation and those protective of third parties such as creditors, who by advancing credit to a member of the family unit may very well have contributed to the accumulation of the assets in question. Because the spouses are the primary members of the nuclear family, most of the legal interests and limitations center on these two parties. The questions to which our attention is directed in this chapter pertain to the property interests that each spouse acquires in the assets of the other at the time the marriage is entered into, or the assets acquired subsequently.[2] Although one cannot consider an isolated segment of the protective interests incident to the marriage completely separate from others and still do justice, the discussion will focus on the treatment of the *inter vivos* aspects of marital property in this chapter and postpone detailed consideration of interests or expectancies in succession on death to a later chapter.

B. COMMON LAW SYSTEM

§ 14.2 In nearly every legal system, marriage has had an important impact on the property rights of the husband and wife. Under the older common law rules, by complying with the requirements for a valid marriage, the husband became the owner of the wife's chattels, acquired

---

§ 14.1

1. See Scoles, Conflict of Laws and Non-barrable Interests in Administration of Decedents' Estates, 8 U. Fla. L. Rev. 151, 155 (1955). See also Younger, Marital Regimes: A Story of Compromise and Demoralization, Together With Criticism and Suggestions for Reform, 67 Cornell L.Q. 45 (1981); Deech, Family Law, 1982 All. E.R. Ann. Rev. 146, 158, Note, Marital Property Rights of Separately Domiciled Spouses, 22 J. Fam. L. 311 (1984); Oldham, Conflict of Laws and Marital Property Rights, 39 Baylor L. Rev. 1255 (1987); Finch, Choice-of-law and Property, 26 Stetson L. Rev. 257 (1996).

2. See Restatement, Second, Conflict of Laws §§ 233, 257 intro. note (1971). See also Marsh, Marital Property in Conflict of Laws 11 (1952); Schreter, "Quasi–Community Property" in the Conflict of Laws, 50 Cal. L. Rev. 206 (1962); Scoles, Choice of Law in Family Property Transactions, 209 Recueil des Cours 17 (1988–II).

an interest in her land, and was empowered to reduce to possession her choses in action. The wife, on the other hand, became immediately entitled to dower, which, in its inchoate form, was an effective limitation upon *inter vivos* disposition of land without consent. The common law has everywhere been changed to recognize substantially now the equal rights of the parties to the marriage.[1] Although the statutes vary in detail, they provide a general pattern of individual ownership, by each spouse of his or her own property, subject to a statutory forced succession share somewhat analogous to dower if the marriage terminates on death and to an equitable allocation of property in the event that the marriage terminates by *inter vivos* dissolution. This pattern, even though largely statutory, is what is that generally followed in more than 40 of the American states, loosely called the common law property states.

C. COMMUNITY OR MARITAL PROPERTY SYSTEM

§ 14.3 In several of the states of the United States, as well as in many other countries, the form of shared ownership by husband and wife known as marital, matrimonial or community property, has been in force for many years.[1] In general, under the marital property system,

§ 14.2

1. In part, this results from constitutional compulsion. See Reed v. Reed, 404 U.S. 71, 92 S.Ct. 251, 30 L.Ed.2d 225 (1971), mandate conformed 94 Idaho 542, 493 P.2d 701 (1972); Orr v. Orr, 440 U.S. 268, 99 S.Ct. 1102, 59 L.Ed.2d 306 (1979), on remand 374 So.2d 895 (Ala.Civ.App. 1979), writ denied 374 So.2d 898 (1979); Boan v. Watson, 281 S.C. 516, 316 S.E.2d 401 (1984). See Siegel, The Modernization of Marital Status Law: Adjudicating Wives' Rights to Earnings, 1860–1930, 82 Geo. L.J. 2127 (1994); Hedrick, Protection Against Spousal Disinheritance: A Critical Analysis of Tennessee's New Forced Share System, 28 U. Mem. L. Rev. 561 (1998); O'Connor, Marital Property Reform in Massachusetts: A Choice for the New Millennium, 34 New Eng. L. Rev. 261 (1999); Graham, The Uniform Marital Property Act: A Solution for Common Law Property Systems?, 48 S.D.L. Rev. 455 (2003).

§ 14.3

1. Eight states in territories acquired by the United States from Spain, Mexico and France have incorporated the community property concept into their property law: Arizona, California, Idaho, Louisiana, Nevada, New Mexico, Texas and Washington. In 1986, Wisconsin joined the group of community property states by adopting the Wisconsin Marital Property Act. See Taylor & Raabe, Wisconsin's Uniform Marital Property Act: Community Property Moves East, 12 Comm. Prop. J. 83 (1985). The Wiscon-

sin Act is based on the Uniform Marital Property Act (UMPA) promulgated by the National Conference of Commissioners on Uniform State Laws in 1983. 9A U.L.A. 21 (Supp. 1985). See Cantwell, The Uniform Marital Property Act: Origin and Intent, 68 Marq. L. Rev. 383 (1985); Reppy, The Uniform Marital Property Act: Some Suggested Revisions for a Basically Sound Act, 12 Comm. Prop. J. 163 (1985). Regarding the conflict-of-laws aspects of the Wisconsin Act, see Note, Migrating Couples and Wisconsin's Marital Property Act, 68 Marq. L. Rev. 488 (1985). See also Erlanger, From Common Law Property to Community Property: Wisconsin's Marital Property Act Four Years Later, 1990 Wis. L. Rev. 769 (1990). See generally Charmatz & Daggett, Comparative Studies in Community Property Law (1955, 1977); de Funiak & Vaughn, Principles of Community Property 55 (2d ed. 1971). See also Reppy & Samuel, Community Property in the United States (2d ed. 1982); McClanahan, Community Property Law in the United States (1982 and 1984 Supp.); Cross, Community Property: A Comparison of the Systems in Washington and Louisiana, 39 La. L. Rev. 479 (1979); Pedersen, Matrimonial Property Law in Denmark, 25 Mod. L. Rev. 137 (1965); Younger, Community Property, Women and the Law School Curriculum, 48 N.Y.U. L. Rev. 211 (1973); Note, Married Womens' Rights Under Matrimonial Regimes of Chile and Columbia, 7 Harv. Women's L.J. 221 (1984); 4 Int'l Ency. Comp. L. §§ 4–52 et.

each spouse owns an undivided one-half interest in all assets acquired by their labors during the marriage with management privileges resting in one or both parties to the marriage.[2] As the familiarity with the advantages of particular aspects of both the common law and the marital property systems becomes more general throughout the United States, individual states borrow from systems different from their own so that a particular state may have elements of both systems reflected in its law.

D. MATRIMONIAL PROPERTY AS CONFLICT OF LAWS ISSUES

§ 14.4   Conflict-of-laws questions arise concerning both property owned by the parties at the time of the marriage and that acquired subsequently. These questions may occur either during the marriage, for example, in actions concerning title or proceedings by creditors or on termination of the marriage by dissolution or death. Within the United States, a common fact pattern illustrates the potential questions. Assume a person domiciled in Maine, a common law property state, marries a resident of California, a community property state, in Maine where the couple thereafter lives as husband and wife, and each owns assets both in and out of their respective home states. What law will identify the rights each acquires in the property of the other by reason of the marriage? What law determines their rights in assets which are subsequently acquired while living in Maine? What if assets are moved from one state to another? Suppose, after some years in Maine, they move and change their domicile to Texas, a community property state, and then have further acquisitions or make other investments? What effect, if any, does the change make in property owned at the time of their removal; by what law are rights in further additions to their wealth to be determined?[1]

seq. (1985). Cantwell, Protecting Spousal Rights in a Domicile Change, 14 Community Prop. J. 72 (1988); Symeonides, In Search of New Choice of Law Solutions, 13 Comm. Prop. J. 11 (1986); Ratner, Community Property, Right of Survivorship, and Separate Property Contributions to Marital Assets: An Interplay, 41 Ariz. L. Rev. 993 (1999); Still, Marital Liability in Texas: Till Death, Divorce, or Bankruptcy do they Part, 44 Baylor L. Rev. 1 (1992).

2. At one time, some additional states had adopted community property systems for tax purposes but these are no longer in effect.

§ 14.4

1. On community property conflict of laws problems generally, see H. Marsh, Marital Property in the Conflict of Laws (1952); de Funiak & Vaughn, Principles of Community Property 212 (2d ed. 1971); 1 Rabel, The Conflict of Laws 353 (2d ed.

1958); 2 Beale, The Conflict of Laws §§ 237.1–238.2, 289.2 (1935); H. Daggett, The Community Property System in Louisiana (1931); R. Hendrickson, Interstate and International Estate Planning 55 (1968); Restatement, Second, Conflict of Laws §§ 233, 257 (1971); Davie, Matrimonial Property in English and American Conflict of Laws, 42 Int'l & Comp. L.Q. 855 (1993); Fehrman, Conflict of Laws: The Availability of Community Property to Satisfy a Judgment, 15 Comm. Prop. J. 28 (1988); Juenger, Marital Property and the Conflict of Laws: A Tale of Two Countries, 81 Col. L. Rev. 1061 (1981); Clausnitzer, Property Rights of Surviving Spouses and the Conflict of Laws, 18 J. Fam. L. 471 (1980); de Funiak, Conflict of Laws in the Community Property Field, 7 Ariz. L. Rev. 50 (1965); Deering, Separate and Community Property and the Conflict of Laws, 30 Rocky Mt. L. Rev. 127 (1958); Johanson, The Migrating Client: Estate Planning for the Couple

The marital property regime of a married couple may be governed by express contract between them.[2] If there is a valid, express contract, it can control the outcome of most marital property issues, either to modify the otherwise existing regime or to except from its operation particular assets or to substitute for a marital property regime, a regime of separate property. In absence of a contract, the law imposes or assumes a marital property regime of one of the two general types noted above, depending upon the state of the dominant interest.[3] In most instances, the state of dominant interest, as in other matters involving family and marital concerns, is the domicile of the parties. As will be observed in our discussion of the issues, matrimonial property litigation involve conflicts in time as well as conflicts of place or jurisdiction. This is because the marital property systems of the different states will accord

From a Community Property State, 9 Inst. Est. Planning 8–1 (1975); Leflar, From Community to Common Law State, 99 Trusts & Est. 882 (1960); Schreter, "Quasi–Community Property" in the Conflict of Laws, 50 Cal. L. Rev. 206 (1962); Brown, Conflict of Laws Between Community Property and Common Law States in Division of Marital–Property on Divorce, 12 Mercer L. Rev. 287 (1961); Note, Community Property in a Common Law Jurisdiction: A Seriously Neglected Area of the Law, 16 Washburn L.J. 77 (1976); Notes, 32 Calif. L. Rev. 152 (1944), 43 Harv. L. Rev. 1286 (1930), 38 N.D. L. Rev. 475 (1962). The complexity of the practical problems of migratory couples is exceptionally well illustrated in Halbach, Logan, Moore & Schwartz, Estate Planning for the Migratory Executive, 5 Real Prop. Prob. & Tr. J. 407 (1970); Lintner, Marital Property Rights and Conflict of Laws When Spouses Reside in Different States, 11 Comm. Prop. J. 283 (1984); Symeonides, In Search of New Choice-of-Law Solutions to Some Marital Property Problems of Migrant Spouses: A Response to Critics, 13 Comm. Prop. J. 11 (1986); Note, Marital Property Rights of Separately Domiciled Spouses and Conflicts of Laws, 22 J. Fam. L. 311 (1984); Sampson, Interstate Spouses, Interstate Property, and Divorce, 13 Tex. Tech. L. Rev. 1285 (1982); J. Oldham, Conflict of Laws and Marital Property Rights, 39 Baylor L. Rev. 1255 (1987); Spaht & Symeonides, Covenant Marriage and the Law of Conflicts of Laws, 32 Creighton L. Rev. 1085 (1999); Rigby, Matrimonial Regimes: Recent Developments, 60 La. L. Rev. 405 (2000).

As to international conflict of laws, see, e.g., J.-G. Castel, Canadian Conflict of Laws 489 et seq. (4th ed. 1997); McLeod, The Conflict of Laws 371 (1983) (Canada); Shava, Israeli Conflict of Laws Relating to Matrimonial Property—A Comparative Commentary, 31 Int'l & Comp. L.Q. 307 (1982); Thiele, The German Marital Property System: Conflict of Laws in a Dual–Nationality Marriage, 12 Cal. W. Int'l L.J. 78 (1982); Atkin, Matrimonial Property Going Overseas, 11 N.Z.U. L. Rev. 183 (1984); Rafferty, Matrimonial Property and the Conflict of Laws, 20 U.W. Ont. L. Rev. 177 (1982); Bruch, Symeonides & Weisberger, Conflict Rules for Marital Property, 35 Am. J. Comp. L. 255 (1987); Schoenblum, Choice of Law and Succession to Wealth: A Critical Analysis of the Ramifications of the Hague Convention on Succession to Decedents' Estates, 32 Va. J. Int'l L. 83 (1991); Estin, Families and Children in International Law: An Introduction, 12 Transnat'l & Contemp. Probs. 271 (2002).

2. de Funiak & Vaughn, Principles of Community Property 333 (2d ed. 1971). Cf. K. Siehr, Domestic Relations in Europe: European Equivalents to American Evaluations, 30 Am. J. Comp. L. 37, 51 (1982); McKnight, Annual Survey of Texas Law–Family Law, 35 S.W. L.J. 93, 98 (1981). See also Graham, The Uniform Premarital Agreement Act and Modern Social Policy: The Enforceability of Premarital Agreements Regulating the Ongoing Marriage, 28 Wake Forest L. Rev. 1037 (1993); Bix, Choice of Law and Marriage: A Proposal, 36 Fam. L.Q. 255 (2002); Younger, Antenuptial Agreements, 28 Wm. Mitchell L. Rev. 697 (2001). See also Buckley & Ribstein, Calling a Truce in the Marriage Wars, 2001 U. Ill. L. Rev. 561.

For examples of foreign approaches, see Germany, BGB (Civil Code) § 1408 et seq. and J. Kropholler, Studienkommentar—BGB anno. preceding § 1408 (6th ed. 2003); Switzerland, Federal Statute on Private International Law Arts. 52–56 (1987).

3. Cf. Burns, DeNichols v. Curlier Revisited, 14 Osgoode Hall L.J. 797 (1976).

different rights or interests in assets acquired before or during a marriage and while the parties are domiciled in a particular state having one or another of these systems.

Matrimonial property cases illustrate the need for a single reference under a concept of unity to approach the resolution of issues regarding spousal participation in property. Because of the practice of tracing the characterization of personal movable assets used to acquire land and the consequent reference to the domicile of the parties, the concept of scission, the so-called situs rule is largely irrelevant.[4] The recent widespread development of the rule of equitable allocation of all assets on divorce further demonstrates the anomaly of a different approach to allocation of assets to spouses when marriage is terminated by death and when it is terminated by divorce. All but a few of the states of the United States equitably allocate the property of the parties on divorce.[5] Incident to divorce, the courts unhesitatingly assume jurisdiction to make an equitable allocation of all assets between the parties wherever the property is located whether the assets are tangible, intangible or land.[6] Because of the assumption of domicile as a jurisdictional basis for divorce, this is tantamount to a choice-of-law reference to the domicile for the determination of rights in marital property. Most states apply a concept of marital property on dissolution during lifetime that allocates all assets acquired during the marriage in patterns similar to community property concepts, without regard to location of the assets. The reach of the forum in applying a single reference is unlimited, because of personal jurisdiction over the parties. Historically, Anglo–American courts have viewed the allocation of property to the surviving spouse when the marriage is terminated at death as limited by the jurisdiction over assets and later, surviving claimants not the parties to the marriage.[7] From the perspective of the spouse, this suggests he or she is treated differently when the marriage is terminated by death rather than divorce even though the policy considerations relating to the spouse's share are very similar.[8] Choice-of-law considerations should reflect these similar policies and the jurisdictional factors should be considered only an aspect of implementation of the choice-of-law rule. The spouse's share when the marriage is terminated on death is merely a post-mortem projection of the spouse's share during lifetime which is enforced on termination of

4. See infra § 14.6.

5. Forty-one states now undertake to make an equitable allocation of the parties property on lifetime dissolution of the marriage. See, e.g., 21 Fam. L.Q. 456 (1988).

6. See, e.g., Uniform Marriage & Divorce Act § 307; Scheible, Marital Property in Tennessee, 15 Memphis St. U.L. Rev. 475 (1985).

7. See infra §§ 20.2–20.4, 20.15–20.16.

8. As was stated in Sullivan v. Burkin, 390 Mass. 864, 460 N.E.2d 572, 577 (1984):

There have been significant changes since 1945 in public policy considerations bearing on the right of one spouse to treat his or her property as he or she wishes during marriage. The interests of one spouse in the property of the other have been substantially increased upon the dissolution of marriage by divorce.... It is neither equitable nor logical to extend to a divorced spouse greater rights in the assets of an inter vivos trust created and controlled by the other spouse than are extended to a spouse who remains married until the death of his or her spouse.

the marriage by divorce. These considerations call for a single reference, to the domicile on both occasions of termination of the marriage.[9]

The reference to "spouse" for purposes of property rights may not be limited to the traditional meaning of a living or surviving husband or wife, but may extend to a partner of another kind of domestic relationship. Thus, Vermont's "civil union" statute provides expressly that "spouse," as used in that state's law, includes the same-sex partner of a civil union.[10] Specific mention is made of property rights, including the right to hold property as tenants by the entireties, and the right to take by intestate succession.[11] Because Vermont is a common-law property state, the civil union legislation does not raise the question whether a party to such a union has a community-property interest in property located elsewhere. However, a claim to property outside Vermont, may arise as a result of a person's status as a spouse under Vermont law, in the case of intestacy or with respect to survivor's, insurance, or other such benefits. If such benefits are claimed under federal law, they will probably be denied because the Defense of Marriage Act (DOMA) expressly defines "spouse" as "only ... a person of the opposite sex."[12] States that have enacted legislation pursuant to DOMA may likewise deny benefits or property rights claimed under their law, while non-DOMA states may apply Vermont law as a matter of a regular choice-of-law analysis, subject to a review of the result's compatibility with the public policy of the forum.[13]

Interstate recognition of domestic partnerships, other than traditional marriage, and of the rights incident to them under the law where they were concluded, is as yet unsettled.[14] While the discussion in this chapter centers on traditional matrimonial property rights and questions, it is important to bear in mind that the same considerations may be applicable to other forms of domestic partnerships.

II. IMMOVABLES

A. LAND OWNED AT TIME OF MARRIAGE

§ **14.5** It seems appropriate at the outset to dispose of a matter, which essentially is a non-problem in the United States, generated by

---

9. See infra §§ 20.2, 20.15. Nova Scotia provides for equitable allocation of the married couple's assets on any dissolution of the marriage by reason of death, divorce, nullity or separation. A. Bisset–Johnson, "Whatever Happened to Exempt Property," An Overview of the Matrimonial Property Act of Nova Scotia, 9 Dalhousie L.J. 788 (1985). See also Scoles, Choice of Law in Family Property Transactions, 209 Recueil des Cours 17, 58, 81 (1988–II).

10. See also supra § 13.20 et seq.

11. 15 V.S.A. § 1204(e)(1) (2003).

12. 1 U.S.C.A .§ 7. See In re Goodale, 298 B.R. 886 (Bankr.W.D.Wash. 2003).

13. See Langan v. St. Vincent's Hospital of New York, 196 Misc.2d 440, 765 N.Y.S.2d 411 (2003), upholding the wrongful death claim, under New York law, of a New York domiciliary who had entered into a Vermont civil union with the decedent, another New York domiciliary. The result is consistent with 15 V.S.A. § 1204(e)(2) (2003), which expressly extends the right to claim in wrongful death, under Vermont law, to the survivor of a civil union.

14. See supra §§ 13.20–13.22, 15.1, 15.26, 15.30 n.1, 15.39 n.4.

over statement of the so-called situs rule in conflict of laws. It has generally been assumed in the United States that questions concerning the creation of interests in land are governed by the law of the place where the land is located. Under this view, the law of the situs would determine what, if any, interest one spouse has in the other's land as an incident to the marriage relation.[1] The law of the state where the land or immovable is situated will determine whether the particular issue, if one exists, will be controlled by the local law of the situs, or by reference to some other law, for example, the domicile of the parties.[2] Since no community property rights attach at the time of the marriage to existing assets, the issue with regard to immovables has only arisen as to common law property in the form of dower rights in land attaching at the time of marriage. In recent years all common law property states have moved away from dower and inchoate rights in land and have shifted to protected succession interests and protection against certain nonconsenting *inter vivos* transfers.[3] Real property homestead does continue to be a significant spousal protection interest in some states, but the relationship to the marital domicile and the practice of taking the family residence in some form of joint and survivor title has tended to minimize any conflicts litigation.[4] As a consequence, there is currently little occasion for a conflict-of-laws issue to arise involving land solely by virtue of marriage.

B.   LAND ACQUIRED AFTER MARRIAGE

§ 14.6   The significant conflict-of-laws issues relating to marital property rights in land arise incident to land acquired during marriage. The acquisition of land usually calls into operation an important practical limitation on the effect of the assumed situs reference: the tracing rule that marital rights in assets used to purchase land will be recognized in the land after purchase.

A New Mexico case provides a good illustration.[1] In that case the parties were married in Washington, D.C. at a time when the husband

---

§ 14.5

1. See, e.g., Millikin Trust Co. v. Jarvis, 34 Ill.App.2d 180, 180 N.E.2d 759 (1962); Nott v. Nott, 111 La. 1028, 36 So. 109 (1904); Newcomer v. Orem, 2 Md. 297, 56 Am.Dec. 717 (1852); Vertner v. Humphreys, 22 Miss. (14 Smedes & M.) 130 (1850); In re Majot's Estate, 199 N.Y. 29, 92 N.E. 402 (1910); Restatement, Second, Conflict of Laws § 233 (1971). Cf. Cayce v. Carter Oil Co., 618 F.2d 669 (10th Cir.1980); Nevins v. Nevins, 129 Cal.App.2d 150, 276 P.2d 655 (1954). See generally Hay, The Situs Rule in European and American Conflicts Law–Comparative Notes, in: Hay & Hoeflich (eds.), Property Law and Legal Education: Essays in Honor of John E. Cribbet 109 (1988).

2. Newcomer v. Orem, 2 Md. 297, 56 Am.Dec. 717 (1852); Vertner v. Humphreys,

22 Miss. (14 Smedes & M.) 130 (1850); Restatement, Second, Conflict of Laws § 233 (1971). The whole law of the situs is considered because a situs state may well recognize the greater interest of the domicile in marital affairs. Compare the discussion of the Texas situs reference to the domicile in Reeves v. Schulmeier, 303 F.2d 802 (5th Cir.1962). Cf. Leff v. Leff, 25 Cal. App.3d 630, 102 Cal.Rptr. 195 (1972).

3. See, e.g., Uniform Probate Code §§ 2–201, 2–202, 8 U.L.A. 74–81 (1983).

4. See Scoles, Conflict of Laws and Non-barrable Interests in Administration of Decedents' Estates, 8 U. Fla. L. Rev. 151, 154 (1955).

§ 14.6

1. Hughes v. Hughes, 91 N.M. 339, 573 P.2d 1194 (1978). See Comment, In–Migra-

was in military service. At the time of the marriage, the husband was domiciled in Iowa, a common law state, and the parties continued to consider Iowa as their marital domicile. After eleven years of marriage, the parties moved to New Mexico, a community property state. Prior to obtaining their domicile in New Mexico, the parties accumulated assets, largely as the result of the income of the husband. These assets were used to purchase or to make down payments on a ranch and some apartments in New Mexico at or about the time of the move to New Mexico. About a year after moving to New Mexico, the husband was ordered to combat duty, and was out of the country as a prisoner of war for some six years. The wife and the children maintained their residence in New Mexico and the wife managed and developed the New Mexico properties. Later, after the husband returned, the marriage between the parties was dissolved and the issue relating to the allocation of the assets arose incident to that dissolution. The court recognized that the marital property interests of the spouses was governed by the marital domicile in Iowa as to assets accumulated during that time, and upon moving these assets to New Mexico, that the rights in the New Mexico land purchased with those assets would continue to be recognized with the incidents that they had in Iowa. Thus the marital interest that attaches to movable assets acquired by the spouses according to the law of their domicile at the time of acquisition is recognized and traceable into real property located in another state in which those assets are invested. This has been the consistent result under the cases[2] although the earlier cases oversimplified the characterization of separate property under the common law system as being the substantial equivalent of separate property under the community property system.[3]

tion of Couples from Common Law Jurisdictions: Protecting the Wife at the Dissolution of the Marriage, 9 N.M. L. Rev. 113 (1979).

2. A leading older case is Brookman v. Durkee, 46 Wash. 578, 90 P. 914 (1907). See also Rau v. Rau, 6 Ariz.App. 362, 432 P.2d 910 (1967); In re Burrows' Estate, 136 Cal. 113, 68 P. 488 (1902); Ford v. Ford, 276 Cal.App.2d 9, 80 Cal.Rptr. 435 (1969); Ellington v. Harris, 127 Ga. 85, 56 S.E. 134 (1906); Hughes v. Hughes, 91 N.M. 339, 573 P.2d 1194 (1978); Restatement, Second, Conflict of Laws § 234, cmnt. (a) (1971). For discussion, see McCarren & Bean, Standards for Tracing Marital Property Back to Non–Marital Property, 17 Colo. Law. 853 (1988); Comment, Community Property and the Problem of Migration, 66 Wash. U.L.Q. 773 (1988); Cantwell, Protecting Spousal Rights in a Domicile Change, 14 Community Prop. J. 72 (1988); Chappell, A Uniform Resolution to the Problem a Migrating Spouse Encounters at Divorce and Death, 28 Idaho L. Rev. 993 (1992).

Cf. Brenholdt v. Brenholdt, 94 N.M. 489, 612 P.2d 1300 (1980); Huston v. Colonial Trust Co., 266 S.W.2d 231 (Tex.Civ.App. 1954), error refused n.r.e.; Toledo Society for Crippled Children v. Hickok, 252 S.W.2d 739 (Tex.Civ.App.1952), rev'd on other grounds 152 Tex. 578, 261 S.W.2d 692 (Tex. 1953), cert. denied 347 U.S. 936, 74 S.Ct. 631, 98 L.Ed. 1086 (1954). But cf. Millikin Trust Co. v. Jarvis, 34 Ill.App.2d 180, 180 N.E.2d 759 (1962).

The situation is further complicated when the parties are unmarried cohabitants. Reppy, Choice of Law Problems Arising when Unmarried Cohabitants Change Domicile, 55 SMU L. Rev. 273 (2002).

3. See Abel, Barry, Halsted & Marsh, Rights of a Surviving Spouse in Property Acquired by a Decedent While Domiciled Outside California, 47 Cal. L. Rev. 211 (1959); Sampson, Common Law Property in a Texas Divorce, 42 Tex. B.J. 131 (1979); Johanson, Community Property: Common Law Assets and the Migrant Client, (BNA 1971). Cf. Singleton v. St. Louis Union

The reason generally given for the tracing rule is that one's title to money, or other assets, is not lost by moving it across a state line and turning it into some other form of property. This usually is based on choice-of-law considerations that protect the reasonable expectation of the parties in their interests under the law of the state of their domicile. However, the leading California case[4] rested its decision on constitutional grounds that property rights vested under the prior marital domicile could not be altered simply by moving the assets into a community property state. The approach taken in this line of authority is consistent with the longstanding theories of equitable tracing to achieve justice and equity among the parties in interest. The same approach has been applied to land purchased in a common law jurisdiction with the separate or community funds of spouses domiciled in a community property state. If the separate funds are used, the land remains separate property of the spouse who provided the separate assets. If, however, the land is purchased by one of the spouses with community funds in that spouse's name only, the interest of the other spouse persists and enables that spouse to follow, by constructive trust principles, the community interest in the land acquired with community assets.

The leading American case involved a husband who wrongly took funds belonging to the community from Louisiana and invested them in Missouri land, taking title in his own name. The husband was compelled to hold the title in trust to protect the wife's interests.[5] However, as in any trust, third party rights may intervene between the time of the purchase by one spouse and the assertion of the other's interest.[6] This recognition of the tracing of community property rights into assets held in common law states is confirmed in the Uniform Disposition of Community Property at Death Act.[7] If the land in question is purchased

Trust Co., 191 S.W.2d 143 (Tex.Civ.App. 1945), error refused n.r.e.; Stewart & Orsinger, Fitting a Round Peg into a Square Hole: Section 3.63, Texas Family Code and the Marriage that Crosses State Lines, 13 St. Mary's L.J. 477, 495–96 (1982). In modern cases, the distinction between the concepts of separate property in common law and in community property systems is generally recognized. Cf. Cameron v. Cameron, 641 S.W.2d 210, 221 (Tex.1982).

4. In re Thornton's Estate, 1 Cal.2d 1, 33 P.2d 1 (1934). Cf. In re Kessler's Estate, 177 Ohio St. 136, 203 N.E.2d 221 (1964). But cf. People v. Bejarano, 145 Colo. 304, 358 P.2d 866 (1961); Bassett, Repealing Quasi–Community Property, 22 U.S.F. L. Rev. 463 (1988). But see Koehler v. Koehler, 182 Misc.2d 436, 697 N.Y.S.2d 478 (1999).

5. Depas v. Mayo, 11 Mo. 314, 49 Am. Dec. 88 (1848). See also Edwards v. Edwards, 108 Okla. 93, 233 P. 477 (1924). Even if the land were purchased with community funds in a "separate property"

state with the wife's consent the result should be the same. Note, 32 Calif. L. Rev. 182, 187 (1944). See also Palmer v. Palmer, 654 So.2d 1 (Miss.1995).

6. Thus that interest might be cut off by a sale to a bona fide purchaser. Cf. Neuner, Marital Property and the Conflict of Laws, 5 La. L. Rev. 167, 172 (1943); Bank of United States v. Lee, 38 U.S. (13 Pet.) 107, 10 L.Ed. 81 (1839); De Lane v. Moore, 55 U.S. (14 How.) 253, 14 L.Ed. 409 (1852); O'Neill v. Henderson, 15 Ark. 235, 60 Am. Dec. 568 (1854); Lezine v. Security Pacific Financial, 14 Cal.4th 56, 58 Cal.Rptr.2d 76, 925 P.2d 1002 (1996); In re Marriage of Lutz, 74 Wash.App. 356, 873 P.2d 566 (1994).

7. Uniform Disposition of Community Property Rights at Death Act § 1, 8A U.L.A. 124–127 (1983). Adopted in Alaska, Arkansas, Colorado, Connecticut, Hawaii, Kentucky, Michigan, Montana, New York, Oregon, Virginia, and Wyoming. Cf. Estate of Bach, 145 Misc.2d 945, 548 N.Y.S.2d 871 (Sur. 1989).

partially with separate property and partially with funds of the community, the question is complicated as a mathematical matter but the principle of tracing does not change, and the proportionate interests of the parties are recognized.[8]

C. INCOME FROM IMMOVABLES

§ 14.7   Another situation in which there may be an argument that the law of the situs of land may control the spouse's rights in marital property involves income from land outside the matrimonial domicile. Not only is there the general difference between the views of community property and common law property systems, but there is difference of view regarding income from separate property among the community property states themselves. For example, California provides that the rents, income and profits received by either spouse from separate assets are the separate property of the spouse whose property earned them. Texas, on the other hand, views income from separate property of the spouses as community property.[1] It seems clear that if the spouses are domiciled in a community property state and one of them were to purchase with community funds land located in a common law state, that the income from that land in the common law state would be viewed as community property under the usual tracing concepts.[2] If land in a common law state is acquired by one of a married couple with his or her separate property, and they later move to a community property state and the land is not sold, the question becomes more difficult as to the characterization of the income from that separate property after the domicile in the community property state has been acquired. If the matrimonial domicile is in a state which follows the view of California, it would seem that there is no conflict and that the income would belong to the spouse whose separate assets were producing the income.[3]

8. Cf. In re Gulstine's Estate, 166 Wash. 325, 6 P.2d 628 (1932).

§ 14.7

1. See de Funiak & Vaughn, Principles of Community Property, 160 (2d ed. 1971); Lay, Tax and Estate Planning for Community Property and the Migrant Client, 24 (1970); Johanson, The Migrating Client: Estate Planning for the Couple from a Community Property State, 9 Inst. Est. Planning 8–1, 8–17 (1975). See also McClanahan, Community Property Law in the United States, §§ 6:10–6:13 (1982); Ridgell v. Ridgell, 960 S.W.2d 144 (Tex.App. 1997).

2. Cf. Depas v. Mayo, 11 Mo. 314, 49 Am.Dec. 88 (1848); Bonati v. Welsch, 24 N.Y. 157 (1861); Fleck v. Fleck, 79 N.D. 561, 58 N.W.2d 765 (1953). But cf. re Hunter's Estate, 125 Mont. 315, 236 P.2d 94 (1951).

3. In re Pepper's Estate, 158 Cal. 619, 112 P. 62 (1910); Spreckels v. Spreckels, 116 Cal. 339, 48 P. 228 (1897); Lewis v. Johns, 24 Cal. 98, 85 Am. Dec. 49 (1864). Cf. Millikin Trust Co. v. Jarvis, 34 Ill. App.2d 180, 180 N.E.2d 759 (1962); In re Clark's Will, 59 N.M. 433, 285 P.2d 795 (1955). This result is usually reached only if the Spanish Law has been modified by statute. Commissioner of Internal Revenue v. Skaggs, 122 F.2d 721 (5th Cir.1941), cert. denied 315 U.S. 811, 62 S.Ct. 796, 86 L.Ed. 1210 (1942). The natural enhancement in value during coverture of separate property is not property acquired during the marriage that would cause it to fall into the community. See Conley v. Moe, 7 Wn.2d 355, 363, 110 P.2d 172, 175 (1941). The authorities are not in agreement on how royalties on oil leases from separate property should be treated. Marsh, Community Property and the Conflict of Laws: Problems of the Oil and Gas Investor and Operator, 13 Inst. Oil and Gas L. and Tax., 301, 307, 317 (1962).

On the other hand, if the domicile of the parties would characterize the income as community in this situation,[4] there is a conflict; considering, however, the policies incident to marital property interests, the situs rule would be designed for the protection of owners domiciled in the state of the situs, and the situs should defer to the more dominant interests of the state of the domicile of the parties. The income on receipt should be characterized as separate or community according to the marital domicile at the time that income is acquired.[5] Since this appears simply a matter of the acquisition of a movable, i.e., income, during the marriage, it seems not a matter which should be referred to the situs's control.[6]

III.   MOVABLES

A. MOVABLES OWNED AT TIME OF MARRIAGE

§ 14.8   In the United States there is not likely to be a question concerning marital rights in movables owned at the time of marriage because no state now provides for an immediate marital interest in the movable assets of the other spouse at the time of marriage. There are some non-barrable interests available to the surviving spouse of a decedent which cannot be defeated by certain conveyances or transfers during a lifetime, but it is clear that these interests are generally related to the law of the decedent's domicile under the characterization as succession problems.[1] Even though this now appears to be a non-problem in the United States, there are a substantial number of older cases that indicate that the matrimonial domicile of the couple will determine the interest that each spouse has in the movable property of the other owned at the time of the marriage.[2] The rule has been assumed more than

---

4. See, e.g., Frame v. Frame, 120 Tex. 61, 36 S.W.2d 152 (1931) (result compelled by Texas Constitution); Stewart v. Commissioner of Internal Revenue, 35 B.T.A. 406 (1937), affirmed 95 F.2d 821 (5th Cir.1938); C.C. Harmon, 1 T.C. 40 (1942), aff'd 139 F.2d 211 (10th Cir. 1943), rev'd on other grounds 323 U.S. 44, 65 S.Ct. 103, 89 L.Ed. 60 (1944). In all of these cases the land was situated in the community property state and the spouses were also domiciled in the community property state. Cf. Schreter, "Quasi Community Property" in the Conflict of Laws, 50 Cal. L. Rev. 206, 234 (1962).

5. The law of the situs of property has been held to control the marital nature of its income. Commissioner of Internal Revenue v. Skaggs, 122 F.2d 721 (5th Cir.1941), cert. denied 315 U.S. 811, 62 S.Ct. 796, 86 L.Ed. 1210 (1942); In re Clark's Will, 59 N.M. 433, 285 P.2d 795 (1955). But cf. Millikin Trust Co. v. Jarvis, 34 Ill.App.2d 180, 180 N.E.2d 759 (1962). In Johnson v.

Commissioner, 88 F.2d 952 (8th Cir.1937) a resident of a common law state was not permitted to split income because it came from community assets acquired in a community state.

6. See Restatement, Second, Conflict of Laws § 234, Reporter's Note (1971).

§ 14.8

1. See, e.g., Uniform Probate Code § 2–201; Restatement, Second, Conflict of Laws § 265 (1971).

2. Mason v. Fuller, 36 Conn. 160 (1869); Lyon v. Knott, 26 Miss. 548 (1853); Harrall v. Wallis, 37 N.J.Eq. 458 (1883), affirmed sub nom. Harral v. Harral, 39 N.J.Eq. 279, 51 Am. Rep. 17; Craycroff v. Morehead, 67 N.C. 422 (1872). See Harding, Matrimonial Domicile and Marital Rights in Movables, 30 Mich. L. Rev. 859 (1932); Stumberg, Marital Property and the Conflict of Laws, 11 Tex. L. Rev. 53 (1932).

explained, and may very well be the most convenient as regards the total interest in movable assets of the parties.[3] It is also supported by the policies of the states generally applicable in the marital property area. In most instances, the marital domicile will be the common domicile of the parties at the time of the marriage or that which they establish immediately after the marriage. The American cases are quite old and have generally utilized the domicile of the husband at the time of the marriage as the matrimonial domicile.[4]

This older statement of the rule does not accord with the present universal acceptance of equal property rights for men and women. In response to the recognition of equal property rights of the spouses, the American Law Institute has taken the position that marital rights of a spouse in the movables of the other should be determined by the law of the domicile of the owner at the time of the marriage.[5] The Hague Convention on Matrimonial Property (not in force for the United States) provides that if the spouses have not designated the applicable law, their matrimonial property regime is governed by the internal law of the state in which "both spouses establish their first habitual residence after marriage."[6] Although there is some potential doubt as to applicable the law be if the couple have not yet established a marital domicile, the convention considered this tolerable in order to localize the regime where the spouses did in fact establish an habitual residence.[7] This reference to the first common domicile seems a reasonable resolution of this issue and appears preferable because it would result in subjecting the parties to a uniformly single governing law and it could reasonably

---

3. See 1 Rabel, Conflict of Laws 356 (2d ed. 1958).

4. In addition to the authorities cited supra n.2, see Jaffrey v. McGough, 83 Ala. 202, 3 So. 594 (1888); Parrett v. Palmer, 8 Ind.App. 356, 35 N.E. 713 (1893); Townes v. Durbin, 60 Ky. (3 Metc.) 352, 77 Am. Dec. 176 (1861); Routh v. Routh, 9 Rob. (LA) 224, 41 Am. Dec. 326 (La.1844); Arendell v. Arendell, 10 La. Ann. 566 (1855); Mason v. Homer, 105 Mass. 116 (1870); Kneeland v. Ensley, 19 Tenn. (Meigs) 620, 33 Am. Dec. 168 (1839). But cf. McIntyre v. Chappell, 4 Tex. 187 (1849). See also Minor, Conflict of Laws § 81 (1901); M. Wolff, Private International Law § 337 (1945); Goodrich, Matrimonial Domicile, 27 Yale L.J. 49 (1917); Ehrenzweig on Conflict of Laws § 245 (1962).

5. Restatement, Second, Conflict of Laws § 257 (1971). See also Locke v. McPherson, 163 Mo. 493, 63 S.W. 726 (1901). Cf. Bartke, Community Property Law Reform in the United States and in Canada—A Comparison and Critique, 50 Tul. L. Rev. 213 (1976) (discussing the constitutional compulsion involved: "Classifications based upon sex ... are inherently suspect, and must therefore be subjected to

strict judicial scrutiny," citing Frontiero v. Richardson, 411 U.S. 677, 688, 93 S.Ct. 1764, 1771, 36 L.Ed.2d 583 (1973)); Barham, Community Property: Symposium on Equal Rights, Introduction: Equal Rights for Women Versus the Civil Code, 48 Tul. L. Rev. 560 (1974). See also McClanahan, Community Property Law in the United States, § 13:2 (1982); Note, Marital Property Rights of Separately Domiciled Spouses, 22 J. Fam. L. 311 (1984); Newman, Incorporating the Partnership Theory of Marriage into Elective–Share Law: The Approximation System of the Uniform Probate Code and the Deferred–Community–Property Alternative 49 Emory L.J. 487 (2000).

6. Hague Convention on the Law Applicable to Matrimonial Property Regimes, Art. IV (1976), reprinted in 25 Am. J. Comp. L. 394, 395 (1977).

7. Glenn, The 1976 Hague Conventions on Marriage and Matrimonial Property Regimes, 55 Can. B. Rev. 586, 598 (1977). See Philip, Hague Draft Convention on Matrimonial Property, 24 Am. J. Comp. L. 307 (1976); Estin, Families and Children in International Law: An Introduction, 12 Transnat'l L. & Contemp. Probs. 271, 273–77 (2002).

be assumed that the parties were by the act of marriage submitting themselves to the law of their first common domicile. Thus it would seem to accord with the reasonable expectations of the parties even absent their agreed choice of law.

B. MOVABLES ACQUIRED SUBSEQUENT TO MARRIAGE

§ 14.9   Consistent with the policies discussed above, the interests of a spouse in the movables acquired by the parties to the marriage subsequent to its celebration will in most instances be determined by the law of their common domicile that attaches following their marriage.[1] A subsequent change in the situs of the movables has no effect upon the

---

§ 14.9

1. See, e.g., Seizer v. Sessions, 132 Wn.2d 642, 940 P.2d 261 (1997). Blackwell v. Blackwell, 606 So.2d 1355 (La.App.1992); Reeves v. Schulmeier, 303 F.2d 802 (5th Cir.1962); Burton v. Burton, 23 Ariz.App. 159, 531 P.2d 204 (1975); Jizmejian v. Jizmejian, 16 Ariz.App. 270, 492 P.2d 1208 (1972); Kraemer v. Kraemer, 52 Cal. 302 (1877); Matter of Estate of Ashe, 114 Idaho 70, 753 P.2d 281 (App. 1988), affirmed 117 Idaho 266, 787 P.2d 252 (1990); Berle v. Berle, 97 Idaho 452, 546 P.2d 407 (1976); Newcomer v. Orem, 2 Md. 297, 56 Am. Dec. 717 (1852); Lyon v. Knott, 26 Miss. 548 (1853); Brenholdt v. Brenholdt, 94 N.M. 489, 612 P.2d 1300 (1980); In re Crichton's Estate, 20 N.Y.2d 124, 281 N.Y.S.2d 811, 228 N.E.2d 799 (1967); Davis v. Zimmerman, 67 Pa. 70 (1870); In re Marriage of Jacobs, 20 Wn.App. 272, 579 P.2d 1023 (1978); Restatement, Second, Conflict of Laws § 258 (1971). Cf. Ober v. Bounds, 528 So.2d 247 (La.App.1988); Stier v. Stier, 178 Cal.App.3d 42, 223 Cal.Rptr. 599 (1986); Sharp v. Sharp, 830 So.2d 328 (La.App. 2002), writ denied 839 So.2d 45 (La.2003); Peters v. Haley, 762 So.2d 695 (La.App. 2000), writ denied 766 So.2d 547 (La. 2000); Lytal v. Lytal, 818 So.2d 111 (La.App.2001); Mayhew v. Mayhew, 205 W.Va. 490, 519 S.E.2d 188 (1999); Campbell v. Campbell, 120 Idaho 394, 816 P.2d 350 (App.1991).

Choses in action, as well as tangible chattels are within the rules discussed. Dempster v. Stephen, 63 Ill.App. 126 (1896). Cf. Swope v. Mitchell, 324 So.2d 461 (La.App. 1975); Herrera v. Health & Social Services, 92 N.M. 331, 587 P.2d 1342 (App. 1978).

Claims for a personal tort have caused difficulty. George, Whose Injury? Whose Property? The Characterization of Personal Injury Settlements Upon Dissolution of Marriage in Community Property States, 32 Idaho L. Rev. 575 (1996); Reeves v. Schul-

meier, supra, applying laws of marital domicile. Cf. Williams v. Pope Manufacturing Co., 52 La. Ann. 1417, 27 So. 851 (1900), a claim for false imprisonment was held not to be "property acquired within the state" so as to make the community property rule of Louisiana applicable to it. Bruton v. Villoria, 138 Cal.App.2d 642, 292 P.2d 638 (1956); Choate v. Ransom, 74 Nev. 100, 323 P.2d 700 (1958); Jaeger v. Jaeger, 262 Wis. 14, 53 N.W.2d 740 (1952); Nelson v. American Employers' Insurance Co., 258 Wis. 252, 45 N.W.2d 681 (1951); Powers v. Powers, 105 Nev. 514, 779 P.2d 91 (1989). See also infra § 14.16 nn.19–20.

The matter becomes more complicated where the spouses voluntarily and without marital discord live apart, residing and working in different states. This was the situation the court in Keller v. Department of Revenue, 292 Or. 639, 642 P.2d 284 (1982) faced: Here, husband and wife lived and earned income in Washington and Oregon, respectively. The court held that, since Washington law did not tie a wife's community property rights to a Washington domicile, and since, due to the voluntary nature of the arrangement, the spouses could not be considered to be "living separate and apart" within the meaning of the Washington statute, the husband's Washington income was community property, and the wife's share thereof taxable to her under Oregon law.

Consider also Lane–Burslem v. Commissioner of Internal Revenue, 659 F.2d 209 (D.C.Cir.1981), holding that England had the most significant relationship with earnings of a Louisiana domiciliary married, living and working in England. Thus, plaintiff could not claim that one-half of her income was tax exempt as belonging to her English spouse under Louisiana's community property laws. See also Note, Marital Property Rights of Separately Domiciled Spouses, 22 J. Fam. L. 311 (1984).

interests of the spouses in existing assets.[2] The American decisions recognize that an existing interest acquired by one spouse in particular assets of another continues so far as those assets are concerned, even though the domicile of the spouses is subsequently changed to another state.[3] This result is supported both by the concepts of recognizing vested interests and reasonable expectations of the parties and the other policies incident to the area, and has, at least in California, been viewed as being required by constitutional doctrine.[4]

If the parties change their marital domicile by moving to another jurisdiction and there acquire property the issue, of course, arises as to marital rights in this newly acquired property. On the basis of the policies supporting the interest of the current domicile as the state of having the dominant interest in the determination of these issues, it would appear that the domicile at the time of acquisition will control unless for some reason the original domicile between the parties would continue to prevail. This latter qualification raises the issue regarding changes in marital property regime in the parties subsequent to marriage. The parties normally can enter an effective ante-nuptial agree-

2. See, e.g., Moore v. Ferrie, 14 Cal. App.4th 1472, 18 Cal.Rptr.2d 543 (1993); Burton v. Burton, 23 Ariz.App. 159, 531 P.2d 204 (1975); Rau v. Rau, 6 Ariz.App. 362, 432 P.2d 910 (1967); Hughes v. Hughes, 91 N.M. 339, 573 P.2d 1194 (1978); Restatement, Second, Conflict of Laws § 259 (1971). Cf. Dawson v. Capital Bank and Trust Co., 261 So.2d 727 (La.App.1972) (noted Note, 47 Tul. L. Rev. 888 (1973)). See also In re Marriage of Landry, 103 Wn.2d 807, 699 P.2d 214, 216 (1985); Mahmud v. Mahmud, 444 So.2d 774 (La.App. 1984); Gilbert v. Gilbert, 442 So.2d 1330 (La.App.1983), writ denied 445 So.2d 1231 (La.1984); In re Succession of Hubbard, 803 So.2d 1074 (La.App.2001); Hand v. Hand 834 So.2d 619 (La.App.2002), writ denied 842 So.2d 1103 (La.2003).

3. E.g., Moore v. Ferrie, 14 Cal.App.4th 1472, 18 Cal.Rptr.2d 543 (1993); Jaffrey v. McGough, 83 Ala. 202, 3 So. 594 (1888); Rau v. Rau, 6 Ariz.App. 362, 432 P.2d 910 (1967); Ladd v. Ladd, 265 Ark. 725, 580 S.W.2d 696 (1979); Quintana v. Ordono, 195 So.2d 577 (Fla.App.1967); Wallack v. Wallack, 211 Ga. 745, 88 S.E.2d 154 (1955); Lichtenberger v. Graham, 50 Ind. 288 (1875); Hughes v. Hughes, 91 N.M. 339, 573 P.2d 1194 (1978); In re Estate of Perry, 480 S.W.2d 893 (Mo.1972). Cf. Commonwealth v. Terjen, 197 Va. 596, 90 S.E.2d 801 (1956). See also Restatement, Second, Conflict of Laws § 259 (1971); Gilbert v. Gilbert, 442 So.2d 1330 (La.App.1983), writ denied 445 So.2d 1231 (La.1984); Pascoe v. Keuhnast, 642 S.W.2d 37 (Tex.App.1982), appeal dismissed 463 U.S. 1201, 103 S.Ct. 3528, 77 L.Ed.2d 1381 (1983); Howard v.

Howard, 499 So.2d 222 (La.App.1986); Estate of Hanau v. Hanau, 730 S.W.2d 663 (Tex.1987); In re Estate of Nicole Santos, 648 So.2d 277 (Fla.App.1995); Nahar v. Nahar, 656 So.2d 225 (Fla.App.1995); Blackwell v. Blackwell, 606 So.2d 1355 (La.App. 1992).

4. In re Thornton's Estate, 1 Cal.2d 1, 33 P.2d 1 (1934). See also Paley v. Bank of America National Trust & Savings Association, 159 Cal.App.2d 500, 324 P.2d 35 (1958). Subsequent legislation in California has been based on the control over succession by the decedent's domicile or on equitable property allocation on divorce. See Abel, Barry, Halsted and Marsh, Rights of a Surviving Spouse in Property Acquired by a Decedent While Domiciled Outside California, 47 Cal. L. Rev. 211 (1959); Schreter, "Quasi–Community Property" in the Conflict of Laws, 50 Cal. L. Rev. 206 (1962); In re Miller, 31 Cal.2d 191, 187 P.2d 722 (1947); In re Krey's Estate, 183 Cal.App.2d 312, 6 Cal.Rptr. 804 (1960). Addison v. Addison, 62 Cal.2d 558, 43 Cal.Rptr. 97, 399 P.2d 897 (1965); Fredericks v. Fredericks, 226 Cal.App.3d 875, 277 Cal.Rptr. 107 (1991). Federal law may override state law as to ownership of federal bonds. Free v. Bland, 368 U.S. 811, 82 S.Ct. 50, 7 L.Ed.2d 21 (1961), reversed 369 U.S. 663, 82 S.Ct. 1089, 8 L.Ed.2d 180 (1962), but federal law may not be used to defraud a spouse of community rights, Yiatchos v. Yiatchos, 376 U.S. 306, 84 S.Ct. 742, 11 L.Ed.2d 724 (1964); Roebling v. Office of Personnel Management, 788 F.2d 1544, 1548 (9th Cir. 1986).

ment applicable to acquisitions during their entire married life. In the early English case of *DeNicols v. Curlier*[5] the House of Lords concluded that, absent an express agreement, there was a tacit agreement between the parties incorporating the law of the state of their original marital domicile in France. Following this approach, the English court held that the tacit agreement based on French law continued during their lifetime to control assets subsequently acquired after moving to England.[6] Considering the mobility of the world population, there is great difficulty in implying such a persistent agreement from the law of the married couple's domicile at the time of marriage. As has been observed above, marital rights in property are imposed by the law as an incident of the state's interest in the marriage relationship and the protection of its domiciliaries. Because this dominant interest flows from an existing domicile within the state, applying the law of the current domicile to determine marital rights in assets initially acquired seems best designed to accommodate the interests of the parties and of the states involved.

Some legal systems retain the doctrine of immutability by which marital rights and movables are fixed by the law of the first marital domicile and continue notwithstanding the acquisition of a new domicile.[7] However, it is apparent that legal systems other than those of the Anglo–American countries are changing in this regard. For example, the Hague Convention on Matrimonial Property provides that the original habitual domicile or designated state may be replaced by a subsequent habitual residence in several circumstances.[8] Even though some uncertainty remains in the English cases, it appears that *DeNicols v. Curlier* will be limited to cases in which the parties have controlled their marital property regime by express contract.[9] As is observed in an able analysis, the immutability doctrine fails because its inflexibility ignores changed circumstances. On the other hand, full mutability, i.e., applying the law of the last domicile, tampers with vested rights. Partial mutability, i.e., to determine marital rights by the marital domicile at the time the issues arise except as to vested rights acquired under the law of a former domicile is an effective compromise.[10] Some U.S. jurisdictions by statute apply the law of the marital domicile at the time of divorce, even if the property was acquired by a party then domiciled in a different state.[11]

5. [1900] A.C. 21.

6. In re DeNicols, [1900] 2 Ch.Div. 410. See also Beaudoin v. Trudel, [1937] 1 D.L.R. 216.

7. Juenger, Marital Property and the Conflict of Laws: A Tale of Two Countries, 81 Col. L. Rev. 1061 (1981); Shava, Israeli Conflict of Laws, Matrimonial Property, 31 Int'l & Comp. L.Q. 307, 312 (1982); Palsson, Rules, Problems and Trends in Family Conflict of Laws 199 Recueil des Cours 313, 378 (1986–IV).

8. Hague Convention on the Law Applicable to Matrimonial Property Regimes, Arts. 4, 6, 7 (1976), reprinted in 25 Am. J. Comp. L. 394, 395–96 (1977).

9. Dicey & Morris, Conflict of Laws 1089 (13th ed. 2000 by Collins); Graveson, Conflict of Laws 360 (7th ed. 1974). As to Canadian authorities, see also McLeod, The Conflict of Laws 371–79 (1983); Comment, Choice of Laws—Matrimonial Regimes—Recognition in Ontario of Foreign Express or Implied Marriage Contract or Settlement, 60 Can. B. Rev. 180 (1982); Rafferty, Marital Property and the Conflict of Laws, 20 U.W. Ont. L. Rev. 177 (1982).

10. Burns, DeNicols v. Curlier Revisited, 14 Osgood Hall L.J. 797, 806 (1976).

11. See, e.g., Dawson–Austin v. Austin, 920 S.W.2d 776 (Tex.App.1996), rev'd 968 S.W.2d 319 (Tex.1998), rev'd on other grounds 968 S.W.2d 319 (Tex.1998).

In absence of a marriage settlement applicable to all acquisitions during marriage, the English law and the Canadian law seems substantially similar to the view taken by courts in the United States.[12] The cases in the United States are quite uniform in applying the law of the marital domicile at the time the property is acquired, but respect the continued existence of marital rights acquired during an earlier domicile elsewhere.[13] Even if there were a tacit contract between the parties it would seem that it could be limited by the laws of the place in which, subsequent acquisitions occurred and to which the parties subsequently moved.[14]

12. See, e.g., Dicey & Morris, supra n.9; Graveson, supra n.9, at 360; Re Heung Won Lee, 36 D.L.R.2d 177 (B.C. 1962). Cf. Waters, Matrimonial Property Entitlements and the Quebec Conflict of Laws, 22 McGill L.J. 315 (1976); Graffier, La Qualification du regime des biens des epoux en droit international privé québecois, 22 McGill L.J. 658 (1976). But contrast McKinney v. McKinney, [1980], 17 R.F.L.(2d) 308 (B.C.S.C.) with Woodward v. Woodward, [1981], 30 B.C.L.R. 351 (S.C.). Both involved the issue of the applicability of the British Columbia Family Relations Act in proceedings to divide marital property brought by the British Columbia wife against the husband residing in Alberta and Saskatchewan, respectively. In the former, but not in the latter case, the Act was held to apply, the distinction being that only in McKinney did the spouses maintain a common marital domicile in British Columbia prior to separation. *McKinney* was also distinguished in a British Columbia proceeding where the husband objected to the court's jurisdiction. Britten v. Britten, [1983], 50 B.C.L.R. 131 (S.C.). *Woodward* was followed in Jeske v. Jeske, [1982], 39 B.C.L.R. 396 (S.C.); Caldwell v. Simms, 1995 CarswellBC 197 (British Columbia Supreme Court, 1995).

With respect to the enforceability of antenuptial agreements, see Hansson v. Hansson, [1981], 26 B.C.L.R. 231 (S.C.), which utilized the courts' power under the British Columbia Act to vary the terms of an antenuptial agreement not in conformity with the provisions of the Act. See also Schaub v. Schaub, [1984], 51 B.C.L.R. 1 (S.C.); Albanese v. Albanese, 1997 CarswellBC 1588 (British Columbia Supreme Court, 1997).

13. Dawson–Austin v. Austin, 920 S.W.2d 776 (Tex.App.1996), reversed 968 S.W.2d 319 (Tex.1998); Breitenstine v. Breitenstine, 62 P.3d 587 (Wyo.2003); Hand v. Hand, 834 So.2d 619 (La.App.2002), writ denied 842 So.2d 1103 (La.2003); In re Popkin & Stern, 292 B.R. 910 (8th Cir.B.A.P.

2003, aff'd 85 Fed.Appx. 543 (8th Cir. 2004); Reeves v. Schulmeier, 303 F.2d 802 (5th Cir.1962); Boyd v. Curran, 166 F.Supp. 193 (S.D.N.Y.1958); Birmingham Waterworks Co. v. Hume, 121 Ala. 168, 25 So. 806 (1899); Burton v. Burton, 23 Ariz.App. 159, 531 P.2d 204 (1975); Rau v. Rau, 6 Ariz. App. 362, 432 P.2d 910 (1967); Rozan v. Rozan, 49 Cal.2d 322, 317 P.2d 11 (1957); Saul v. His Creditors, 5 Mart. (N.S.) 569, 16 Am. Dec. 212 (La.1827); Hicks v. Pope, 8 La. 554, 28 Am. Dec. 142 (1835); Cameron v. Rowland, 215 La. 177, 40 So.2d 1 (1948); Muus v. Muus, 29 Minn. 115, 12 N.W. 343 (1882); Hughes v. Hughes, 91 N.M. 339, 573 P.2d 1194 (1978); In re Majot's Estate, 199 N.Y. 29, 92 N.E. 402 (1910); McCollum v. Smith, 19 Tenn. (Meigs) 342, 33 Am. Dec. 147 (1838); Castro v. Illies, 22 Tex. 479, 73 Am. Dec. 277 (1858); Restatement, Second, Conflict of Laws § 259 (1971); Johanson, The Migrating Client: Estate Planning for the Couple from a Community Property State, 9 Inst. Est. Planning 8–1, 8–23 (1975). Cantwell, Protecting Spousal Rights in a Domicile Change, 14 Comm. Prop. J. 72 (1988); McCarven & Bean, Standards for Tracing Marital Property, 17 Colo. Lawyer 853 (1988); Comment, Community Property and Migration, 66 Wash. U. L.Q. 773 (1988). Cf. Schecter v. Superior Court, 49 Cal.2d 3, 314 P.2d 10 (1957); Choate v. Ransom, 74 Nev. 100, 323 P.2d 700 (1958); Jaeger v. Jaeger, 262 Wis. 14, 53 N.W.2d 740 (1952); Nelson v. American Employers' Insurance Co., 258 Wis. 252, 45 N.W.2d 681 (1951). But cf. Benj. H. McElhinney, Jr., 17 T.C. 7 (1951); Robinson v. Robinson, 778 So.2d 1105 (La.2001). See also cases cited supra § 14.9 n.1.

14. Saul v. His Creditors, 5 Mart. (N.S.) 569, 16 Am. Dec. 212 (La.1827). Cf. In re Miller, 31 Cal.2d 191, 187 P.2d 722 (1947); Addison v. Addison, 62 Cal.2d 558, 43 Cal. Rptr. 97, 399 P.2d 897 (1965); But see Ducharme v. Ducharme, 316 Ark. 482, 872 S.W.2d 392 (1994).

C. INCOME FROM MOVABLES

§ 14.10 The rule that the law of the current marital domicile controls movables at the time of acquisition should also apply, as suggested earlier,[1] to the income from separate property removed to a community property jurisdiction by spouses from a common law state. Although the new marital domicile cannot change the nature of ownership of acquisitions that occurred during a domicile elsewhere, it can reasonably govern its present domiciliaries by its marital property rule. Of course, if the domicile treats the income from the separate property as separate property of the owner's spouse, there is no conflict. This approach seems to be a reasonable accommodation of the interests of the states and parties concerned.[2] The state of the location of property has little concern for the marital rights and property acquired within its borders except for the protection of its revenue and of third parties. Those interests can adequately be served by its laws relating to taxation and transfers. Situs states, qua situs, will therefore ordinarily refer to the domicile.[3] In addition, it is convenient to have subsequent acquisitions governed by a single rule for ownership.

D. ACCRUAL VALUES: INSURANCE, PENSIONS, ETC.

§ 14.11 The recognition, in recent years, of community property rights in intangible assets such as insurance, pensions, and other contractual interests has greatly complicated the accounting involved in application of the approach here suggested. For the married couple, one of whom is employed by an interstate employer, rights in their earnings may present extremely complex calculations. First, the local law difficulties are great in determining what marital interests attach to rights in private or public pension plans, term or other life insurance, profit sharing plans, and annuities, any of which may have different ownership

§ 14.10

1. See supra text at § 14.7 n.1.

2. Compare In re Frees' Estate, 187 Cal. 150, 201 P. 112 (1921) and Lewis v. Johns, 24 Cal. 98, 85 Am.Dec. 49 (1864) with Oliver v. Robertson, 41 Tex. 422 (1874) and Stewart v. Commissioner, 95 F.2d 821 (5th Cir.1938). If the spouse has to contribute time and energy to produce the income from the separate property the courts more readily hold that such income is community property. See LeSourd, Community Property Status of Income From Business Involving Personal Services and Separate Capital, 22 Wash. L. Rev. 19 (1947); Note, The Enhanced Value of Separate Property Shall Be Deemed Community Property ... Jensen v. Jensen, 9 Thurgood Marshall L. Rev. 201 (1984). See also Marsh, Community Property and Conflict of Laws Problems of the Oil and Gas Investor and Operator, 13 Inst. Oil & Gas L. & Tax. 301 (1962); Schreter, "Quasi–Community Property" in

the Conflict of Laws, 50 Cal. L. Rev. 206 (1962); Rozan v. Rozan, 49 Cal.2d 322, 317 P.2d 11 (1957). Cf. Tirado v. Tirado, 357 S.W.2d 468 (Tex.Civ.App.1962) Wagoner v. Wagoner, 294 Ark. 82, 740 S.W.2d 915 (1987)(noted 42 Ark. L. Rev. 173 (1989)); See also Sevareid, Increase in Value of Separate Property in Pennsylvania: A Change in What Women Want? 68 Temp. L. Rev. 557 (1995).

3. See, e.g., Boyd v. Curran, 166 F.Supp. 193 (S.D.N.Y.1958); Hicks v. Pope, 8 La. 554, 28 Am. Dec. 142 (1835); Pearl v. Hansborough, 28 Tenn. (9 Humph.) 426 (1848); Edrington v. Mayfield, 5 Tex. 363 (1849). Cf. Reeves v. Schulmeier, 303 F.2d 802 (5th Cir.1962); Everson v. Everson, 264 Pa.Super. 563, 400 A.2d 887 (1979), modified and affirmed 494 Pa. 348, 431 A.2d 889 (1981). But cf. Benj. H. McElhinney, Jr., 17 T.C. 7 (1951).

or contract theories applicable.[1] Secondly, the marital rights of the spouses vary depending on the length of time they are domiciled in

§ 14.11

1. See, e.g., In re Marriage of Brown, 15 Cal.3d 838, 126 Cal.Rptr. 633, 544 P.2d 561 (1976); Cearley v. Cearley, 544 S.W.2d 661 (Tex.1976); Reppy, Community and Separate Interests in Pensions and Social Security Benefits After "Marriage of Brown" and ERISA, 25 U.C.L.A. L. Rev. 417 (1978). See also Comment, Community and Separate Property Interests in Proceeds: The Risk Payment Doctrine in State Courts and Its Federal Estate Life Insurance Tax Consequences, 52 Wash. L. Rev. 67 (1976); Pattiz, In a Divorce or Dissolution Who Gets the Pension Rights: Domestic Relations Law and Retirement Plans, 5 Pepperdine L. Rev. 191 (1978); Comment, Apportionment of Community Property Interests in Prospective Military Retirement Benefits upon Divorce, 9 St. Mary's L.J. 72 (1977); Comment, Community Property Aspects of Private Pension Plan Benefits in Louisiana, 26 Loyola L. Rev. 389 (1980); Note, Allard v. Frech, 20 St. Mary's L.J. 373 (1989); McCarty v. McCarty, 453 U.S. 210, 101 S.Ct. 2728, 69 L.Ed.2d 589 (1981); Mortenson v. Mortenson, 409 N.W.2d 20 (Minn. App.1987) (military pension); In re Marriage of Gallo, 752 P.2d 47 (Colo.1988); Wiist, Trust Income: Separate or Community Property? 51 Baylor L. Rev. 1149 (1999); In re Marriage of Branstetter, 508 N.W.2d 638 (Iowa 1993); In re Marriage of Duggan, 659 N.W.2d 556 (Iowa 2003); Potts v. Potts, 142 Md.App. 448, 790 A.2d 703 (2002).

An area that has recently commanded attention and seen increased litigation is that of professional degrees. See, e.g., Note, Equitable Interest in Enhanced Earning Capacity: The Treatment of a Professional Degree at Dissolution, 60 Wash. L. Rev. 431 (1985); Roadhouse, The Problem of the Professional Spouse: Should an Educational Degree Earned During Marriage Constitute Property in Arizona?, 24 Ariz. L. Rev. 763 (1982); Note, Drapek v. Drapek, 399 Mass. 240, 503 N.E.2d 946 (1987), 22 Suffolk U.L.R. 1277 (1988); Note, Professional Degrees Not Divisible Assets, 1988 Utah L. Rev. 216 (1988); Note, Professional Licenses as Marital Property, 73 Cornell L. Rev. 133 (1989); Note, A Professional Degree on Marital Property, 29 Ariz. L. Rev. 353 (1987); Bissett–Johnson & Newell, Professional Degrees in Marital Property, 15 Comm. Prop. J. 63 (1988); Gailov & McGill, The Equitable Distribution of Professional Degrees upon Divorce, 10 Campbell L. Rev. 69 (1987); Comment, Law and Equity and Professional Degrees, 9 Whittier L. Rev. 151 (1987); Berry, Limited Classification of

Human Capital as Marital Property, 11 J. Contemp. Legal Issues 881 (2001).

Other developing subjects of marital property disputes include copyrights and fertilized eggs. Ciolino, Why Copyrights are not Community Property, 60 La. L. Rev. 127, (1999); Nayo, Revisiting Worth: The Copyright as a Community Property Problem, 30 U.S.F.L. Rev. 153 (1995); Backe, Community Property and the Copyright Act: Rodrigue's Recognition of a Community Interest in Economic Benefits 61 La. L. Rev. 655 (2001); Ciolino, How Copyrights Became Community Property (Sort of): Through the Rodrigue v. Rodrigue Lookingglass, 47 Loy. L. Rev. 631 (2001); Lang, Rodrigue v. Rodrigue: The Fifth Circuit Holds that Copyright and Community Property Law Can Peacefully Coexist, 76 Tul. L. Rev. 541 (2001); Rodrigue v. Rodrigue, 218 F.3d 432 (5th Cir.2000), cert. denied 532 U.S. 905, 121 S.Ct. 1227, 149 L.Ed.2d 137 (2001); Roosevelt, The Newest Property: Reproductive Technologies and the Concept of Parenthood, 39 Santa Clara L. Rev. 79 (1998).

The 1981 U.S. Supreme Court decision in *McCarty*, supra this n., which held that federal law preempted state community property laws with respect to the division of military pensions accruing to one spouse, was the subject of much controversy. See, e.g., Note, The Federal Military Retirement System Preempts State Community Property Law at Divorce: McCarty v. McCarty, 1982 B.Y.U. L. Rev. 443. In 1983, Congress overturned this result by adoption of the Uniformed Services Former Spouses' Protection Act, pursuant to which state courts may treat military pensions as either separate or community property under the applicable state law. 10 U.S.C.A. § 1408(c)(1). See Schwartz & McClure, Division of Federal Pension Benefits, 11 Comm. Prop. J. 165 (1984); Note, Divisibility of Military Nondisability Retirement Pension Benefits Upon Marriage Dissolution: McCarty v. McCarty, The Uniformed Services Former Spouses' Protection Act, and Beyond, 22 J. Fam. L. 333 (1984); Pierre, The Divisibility of Military Retired Pay in Louisiana in Light of McCarty, Mansell, and the Uniformed Former Spouses Protection Act, 17 S.U.L. Rev. 149 (1990); In re Marriage of Walters, 220 Cal.App.3d 1062, 269 Cal.Rptr. 557 (1990). A detailed governmental interest analysis of *McCarty* as well as the subsequent congressional enactment permitting some application of state marital property law, 10 U.S.C.A. § 1408, is explored in Graham, State Marital Property Laws and Fed-

different jurisdictions and depending on possible choice-of-law clauses in the contracts.[2] The rights in pension and other fringe employment benefits probably are cumulative by reason of seniority with interest factors being compounded while the conflict-of-laws approach assumes discrete units of ownership based on time. This complexity may very well lead to a theory of equitable apportionment responsive to the court's view of fairness in light of all the variables.[3]

erally Created Benefits, 29 Wayne L. Rev. 1 (1982). From among the many decisions, cf., e.g., Forsman v. Forsman, 694 S.W.2d 112 (Tex.App.1985), error refused n.r.e; In re Marriage of Harmon, 184 Cal.App.3d 754, 217 Cal.Rptr. 329 (1985), cause transferred 230 Cal.Rptr. 129, 724 P.2d 1154 (1986); Casas v. Thompson, 42 Cal.3d 131, 228 Cal. Rptr. 33, 720 P.2d 921 (1986), cert. denied 479 U.S. 1012, 107 S.Ct. 659, 93 L.Ed.2d 713 (1986). As to federal preemption of state marital property and divorce law generally, see Reppy, Conflicts of Laws Problems in the Division of Marital Property, 1 Valuation and Distribution of Marital Property, § 10.03 (1985). See also Ober v. Bounds, 528 So.2d 247 (La.App.1988).

Federal law has become very significant in protecting spouses of annuitants under the amendments to the Employee Retirement Income Security Act (ERISA), 29 U.S.C.A. § 1001 et seq. by the Retirement Equity Act of 1984, 98 Stat. 1426 (1984) mandating provisions for spouses in qualified plans. Problems under English law are discussed in Masson, Pensions and Divorce, 15 Fam. L. 291 (1985). The Supreme Court has held that ERISA preempts attempted testamentary dispositions of pension benefits by non-participating spouses. See Boggs v. Boggs, 520 U.S. 833, 117 S.Ct. 1754, 138 L.Ed.2d 45 (1997).

2. See Parson v. United States, 460 F.2d 228 (5th Cir.1972); Aetna Life Insurance Co. v. Schmitt, 404 F.Supp. 189 (M.D.Fla. 1975); Allen v. Allen, 484 So.2d 269 (La. App.1986), writ denied 488 So.2d 199 (La. 1986), cert. denied 479 U.S. 850, 107 S.Ct. 178, 93 L.Ed.2d 114 (1986); Little v. Little, 513 So.2d 464 (La.App.1987); Trotter v. Trotter, 503 So.2d 1160 (La.App.1987); Matter of Marriage of Booker, 833 P.2d 734 (Colo.1992); Gaulding v. Gaulding, 503 S.W.2d 617 (Tex.Civ.App.1973); Pattiz, In a Divorce or Dissolution Who Gets the Pension Rights: Domestic Relations Law and Retirement Plans, 5 Pepperdine L. Rev. 191, 260 (1978). Cf. MFA Life Insurance Co. v. Kyle, 630 F.2d 322 (6th Cir.1980); Rose v. Rose, 483 So.2d 181 (La.App.1986); Anderson v. Anderson, 520 So.2d 1236 (La. App.1988), writ denied 521 So.2d 1187 (La.

1988); Dunham v. Dunham, 602 So.2d 1139 (La.App.1992)(reflecting statute that overturned Anderson); Taylor v. Taylor, 105 Nev. 384, 775 P.2d 703 (1989); Dewey v. Dewey, 745 S.W.2d 514 (Tex.App.1988), writ denied 766 S.W.2d 263 (1988); Johnson v. Johnson, 605 So.2d 1157 (La.App.1992); Woodward v. Woodward, 117 Ariz. 148, 571 P.2d 294 (App. 1977); Swope v. Mitchell, 324 So.2d 461 (La.App.1975); Otto v. Otto, 80 N.M. 331, 455 P.2d 642 (1969); Johanson, The Migrating Client: Estate Planning for the Couple from a Community Property State, 9 Inst. Est. Planning 8-1, 8–31 (1975). See Gilbert v. Gilbert, 442 So.2d 1330 (La.App.1983), writ denied 445 So.2d 1231 (La.1984), a dispute relating to one spouse's federal civil service disability retirement pension, holding that Georgia law applied to claim since the couple was domiciled there during entire term of employment, and moved to Louisiana only after that spouse's retirement. See also In re Marriage of Landry, 103 Wn.2d 807, 699 P.2d 214 (1985) (character of property— pension—determined by law of domicile at time of acquisition). In Nationwide Resources Corp. v. Massabni, 143 Ariz. 460, 694 P.2d 290 (App. 1984), the court considered a partnership interest to be personalty, holding that its classification depends on the law of the matrimonial domicile at the time of its acquisition.

3. Cf. Woodward v. Woodward, 117 Ariz. 148, 571 P.2d 294 (App.1977); Reppy, Community and Separate Interests in Pension and Social Security, 25 U.C.L.A. L. Rev. 417 (1978); Note, Common Law Concepts of Life Insurance in Community Property Jurisdictions: Recommendations for a Practical Approach, 18 Ariz. L. Rev. 182 (1976). Berry v. Berry, 647 S.W.2d 945 (Tex.1983); Note, Valuation of Retirement Benefits in the Omitted Property Case, 24 S. Tex. L.J. 895 (1983); Note, Disability Benefits as Marital Property, 24 J. Fam. L. 657 (1986); Comment, Interdisciplinary Analysis of Division of Pension Benefits, 37 Baylor L. Rev. 107 (1985), Zisblatt v. Zisblatt, 693 S.W.2d 944 (Tex.App.1985) (N.J. corporation held to be sole stockholder's alter ego

IV. SUBSEQUENT
INTENTIONAL PROPERTY TRANSACTIONS

§ 14.12   Although marital property rights, with which we are here concerned, are recognized as attaching and becoming fixed at the time of acquisition of the asset, those interests may be modified or varied by subsequent agreement or dealing by the parties. Most community property jurisdictions allow the parties to, by agreement, convey or give property away or change the nature of its ownership.[1] For example, a couple who own assets in California in which they have California community property rights, may place them in a joint and survivor form of ownership or one may make a gift to the other so that the donee holds the assets as separate property.[2] Clearly, if done within the authority of the law of the marital domicile, no conflicts problem is presented.[3] If, however, the parties take assets elsewhere and in another jurisdiction transfer or deal with them in a manner different from that allowed by the marital domicile, other considerations arise. Although it may be argued that the marital domicile, as the state of dominant interest, should control the capacity of its domiciliaries to modify their marital property regime, other policy forces merit attention.[4]

and part of Texas community); Barbo, Ablamis v. Roper: Preemption of the Non-employee Spouse's Community Property Rights in ERISA Pension Plans, 49 Wash. & Lee L. Rev. 1085 (1992); Strauss, Characterization for Purposes of Divorce: Retirement Pension Benefits vs. Disability Benefits, 11 J. Contemp. Legal Issues 234 (2000).

§ 14.12

1. See de Funiak & Vaughn, Principles of Community Property 333 (2d ed. 1971); Greene, Comparison of the Property Aspects of the Community Property and Common–Law Marital Property Systems and Their Relative Compatibility With the Current View of the Marriage Relationship and the Rights of Women, 13 Creighton L. Rev. 71 (1979).

2. See de Funiak & Vaughn, supra n.1, at 344.

3. An interesting example of the absence of a genuine conflicts issue in this regard is found in Ossorio v. Leon, 705 S.W.2d 219 (Tex.App.1985) in which a Mexican married couple deposited funds in a Texas bank account as joint tenants with the right of survivorship. By the law of Mexico, the domicile of the married couple, the account contract and the husband's will evinced the husband's effective gift of the funds should his wife survive him. The law of Texas would not have recognized this transfer as modifying the marital regime. In sustaining the wife's claim to the account

and denying that of the husband's heirs, the court stated: "The resolution of this matter will have no effect whatsoever on the State of Texas or any of its citizens. The bank no longer has an interest in the lawsuit. Whether the bank pays the money to the appellant or the appellees is of no consequence to the bank or to the State. Also, the Ossorios' justified expectations deserve to be protected. Thus, the Ossorios have established the State of Mexico has a more significant relationship to the issue of ownership than the State of Texas. We consequently hold, based on King v. Bruce [145 Tex. 647, 201 S.W.2d 803 (1947)] and Duncan v. Cessna, [665 S.W.2d 414 (Tex.1984)] that the gift made to appellant was valid under the laws of Mexico, and that the laws of Mexico should apply."

4. See King v. Bruce, 145 Tex. 647, 201 S.W.2d 803 (1947), cert. denied 332 U.S. 769, 68 S.Ct. 82, 92 L.Ed. 355 (1947), in which a Texas married couple transferred $5,800 in community funds from a Texas bank to a New York bank. The couple then went to New York, withdrew the money, in 4,000 silver dollars and $1,800 in cashiers checks, entered into a contract purporting to divide the money between them as their individual separate property and physically divided the silver dollars and cashier's checks so each had $2,900. Mrs. Bruce then returned to Texas with "her" $2,900 and deposited it in an account in her name

In a leading case, domiciliaries of Spain sent cash and securities to New York and placed the funds in joint and survivor accounts with New York financial institutions expressly subject to New York law. The husband died and, as the surviving joint tenant, the wife succeeded to these New York assets. The wife later disposed of the assets by her will, executed according to New York law, and the Spanish heirs of the husband obtained the appointment of an ancillary administrator of the husband who claimed one-half the property held in New York at the husband's death as matrimonial property not subject to disposition by the husband or wife. The New York Court of Appeals upheld the disposition by the New York joint accounts notwithstanding the contrary prohibitions of the Spanish law, stating:

But New York has the right to say as a matter of public policy whether it will apply its own rules to property in New York of foreigners who choose to place it here for custody or investment, and to honor or not the formal agreements or suggestions of such owners by which New York law would apply to the property they place here. (Cf. Decedent Estate Law, § 47; Personal Property Law, Consol. Laws, c. 41, § 12–a.)

It seems preferable that as to property which foreign owners are able to get here physically, and concerning which they request New York law to apply to their respective rights, when it actually gets here, that we should recognize their physical and legal submission of the property to our laws, even though under the laws of their own country a different method of fixing such rights would be pursued.

Thus we would at once honor their intentional resort to the protection of our laws and their recognition of the general stability of our Government which may well be deemed inter-related things.[5]

A similar approach had been taken earlier by the New York Court in *Hutchison v. Ross*[6] in which an *inter vivos* trust established in New York by a Quebec husband for benefit of his wife was sustained under New York law to which the trust instrument referred. In both cases there was an overt, well evidenced, intent held by both husband and wife[7] to deal

---

individually. A creditor who obtained a Texas judgment against the husband a week after the New York transactions was permitted to recover on his garnishment of Mrs. Bruce's individual Texas bank account. The court viewed the New York transaction as ineffective to destroy the community property character of the funds because the law of Texas as the matrimonial domicile controlled.

5. Wyatt v. Fulrath, 16 N.Y.2d 169, 264 N.Y.S.2d 233, 236, 211 N.E.2d 637, 639 (1965). Compare McCasland v. McCasland, 68 N.Y.2d 748, 506 N.Y.S.2d 329, 497 N.E.2d 696 (1986) in which a married couple, longtime New York residents, moved to Florida where they were later divorced. The Florida divorce decree incorporated a property settlement. Still later, the wife sought

equitable distribution of marital property in New York, including New York corporations formed and owned by the husband. The lower courts in New York denied jurisdiction on the theory that plaintiff's domicile in New York was the exclusive basis for the proceeding as a "matrimonial action." The Court of Appeals reversed, finding "in rem" over the assets sufficient to sustain the proceeding.

6. 262 N.Y. 381, 187 N.E. 65 (1933).

7. Compare In re Kann's Estate, 253 Cal.App.2d 212, 61 Cal.Rptr. 122 (1967) on adequacy of evidence. Cf. Sloan v. Jones, 192 Tenn. 400, 241 S.W.2d 506 (1951); but cf. King v. Bruce, 145 Tex. 647, 201 S.W.2d 803 (1947), cert. denied 332 U.S. 769, 68 S.Ct. 82, 92 L.Ed. 355 (1947).

with the property during their lifetime at its situs differently than was customary or permissible at their domicile. The express intention of the parties to the marriage in a planned transaction with their property at its situs in reliance on the law of the financial "marketplace" was held to override the law of their domicile designed to protect them. To do this in order to protect third parties relying on the "market" transactions would clearly be expected; to extend this to the primary parties involves a recognition of the freedom of individuals knowingly to waive domiciliary protections and intentionally to seek the financial sanctuary of a stable and reliable international center of wealth management.[8] The maintenance of that international financial center is a dominant interest of the forum when weighed against the limitations imposed by a state on extra-territorial transactions of its domiciliaries in a mobile world. The effect of subsequent intentional dealing with their property is not necessarily inconsistent with a recognition of the initial acquisition of marital property rights by the law of the marital domicile.[9]

V. THE SEPARATE PROPERTY AND QUASI–COMMUNITY PROPERTY CONCEPTS

A. CHARACTERIZATION OF SEPARATE PROPERTY

§ 14.13 There has been a major problem, frequently overlooked, caused in part by the lack of an available procedure at the forum to give effect to the protections implicit in marital property of a foreign jurisdiction and in part to the semantic assumption that "separate property" in a common law state is the same as "separate property" in a community property system. In the case of a couple moving from a community property system to a common law state, the spouses are treated as equal owners, for instance, tenants in common, of the assets subject to community property.[1] On death of one, the surviving spouse may retain his or her half of the assets and assert a forced share in the other half as the "property of the deceased," thus acquiring a windfall of more than the intended spousal protection under either system. In the converse case of a couple going from a common law state to a community state, the "separate property" of the acquiring spouse may be viewed as "separate property" in the community state and, on termination of the marriage by dissolution or death, the other spouse is unprovided for because there are no "community" assets to divide and no "forced share."[2] Thus, the

8. Cf. Intercontinental Planning, Ltd. v. Daystrom, Inc., 24 N.Y.2d 372, 300 N.Y.S.2d 817, 248 N.E.2d 576 (1969).

9. See In re Crichton's Estate, 20 N.Y.2d 124, 281 N.Y.S.2d 811, 228 N.E.2d 799 (1967). See also DeFrance v. DeFrance, 273 A.D.2d 468, 710 N.Y.S.2d 612 (2000). Cf. In re Estate of Clark, 21 N.Y.2d 478, 288 N.Y.S.2d 993, 236 N.E.2d 152 (1968); In re Marriage of Whelchel, 476 N.W.2d 104 (Iowa App.1991). See also Uniform Disposi-

tion of Community Property Rights at Death Act, § 8, 8 U.L.A. 133 (1983).

§ 14.13

1. See Lay, Tax and Estate Planning for Community Property and Migrant Clients, 62, 216 (1970); Leflar, From Community to Common Law State, 99 Tr. & Est. 882 (1960).

2. Cf. In re O'Connor's Estate, 218 Cal. 518, 23 P.2d 1031 (1933); Escrow Service

nonacquiring or surviving spouse fails to get the protection intended by either state. The policy of both states is frustrated.

That the problem of characterizing separate property can be very difficult is illustrated by the Texas situation. The Texas courts have held that "separate property" cannot be divided or allocated to the other spouse on divorce.[3] If a couple moves from a common law state where their assets have been acquired by the husband during a long marriage to Texas, and then get divorced, there is no "community property" to divide. If the separate property cannot be reached, the court "has no choice but to leave the wife with no means of support."[4] As has been pointed out in a perceptive analysis:

> "The problem is largely semantic: while both marital property systems employ a concept labeled 'separate property,' those words do not have the same meaning. . . .

> "It is true that 'common law separate property' assets or rights brought into Texas by a husband come with legal title vested in him. However, it follows logically that the property also must come to the state attached with whatever equitable claims the wife has under the statutes and case law of the common law jurisdiction. Thus, if the husband's separate property is subject to equitable division in the state of origin, it must be similarly subject to such treatment in Texas. Indeed, in the author's opinion, if the *property itself* is subject to periodic alimony in the original state, it should be identically treated here. This distinction between legal and equitable title is familiar to Texas courts. Often legal title is irrelevant; for example, although legal title to an item of community property is wholly vested in one spouse, the assertion of equitable community property rights in a divorce action and an award of the entire asset to the other spouse is in no way impeded.

Co. v. Cressler, 59 Wn.2d 38, 365 P.2d 760 (1961).

3. Eggemeyer v. Eggemeyer, 554 S.W.2d 137 (Tex.1977), appeal after remand 623 S.W.2d 462 (Tex.App.1981), involving real property. See Castleberry, Constitutional Limitations on the Division of Property upon Divorce, 10 St. Mary's L.J. 37 (1978); McKnight, Annual Survey of Texas Law–Family Law, 32 S.W.L.J. 109, 124 (1978); McKnight, Annual Survey of Texas Law–Family Law, 35 S.W.L.J. 93, 99, 134 (1981). The holding in *Eggemeyer* was upheld and applied to personalty in Cameron v. Cameron, 641 S.W.2d 210 (Tex.1982). See also Shanks v. Treadway, 110 S.W.3d 444, 448 (Tex. 2003). Harden & Lindsay–Smith, Beware Migrating Spouses, Texas Lacks a Quasi-community Property Probate Statute: It Could be a Long Cold Winter, 3 Tex. Wesleyan L. Rev. 91 (1996).

4. Muns v. Muns, 567 S.W.2d 563 (Tex. Civ.App.1978). However, while separate property cannot constitutionally be divested upon divorce in Texas, certain property will not be "regarded as" separate property pursuant to § 3.63 of the Texas Family Code if, although acquired in a common law state, it would have been considered community property had the acquiring spouse resided in Texas at that time. See Cameron v. Cameron, 641 S.W.2d 210 (Tex.1982), confirmed in Cook v. Cameron, 733 S.W.2d 137 (Tex. 1987), restated in Schlueter v. Schlueter, 975 S.W.2d 584, 587 (Tex. 1998). Spouses are also obligated to use separate funds for community expenses with no expectation of reimbursement from community funds, if financial circumstances render that necessary. Oliver v. Oliver, 741 S.W.2d 225 (Tex. App.1987)

"In sum, if *Eggemeyer* prohibits divestment of a spouse's 'separate personalty' upon divorce, the rule should only apply to property fitting the Texas definition of separate property, i.e., that acquired while single, or by gift, descent, or devise during marriage, or recovery for personal injuries. The problem of semantics is resolved when the appropriate definition of 'separate property' follows the property across state lines."[5]

This, in effect, is the approach adopted by the Supreme Court of Texas, which held that, upon divorce in Texas, common law marital property should not be regarded by Texas courts as "separate" property in the context of that state's community property law, but, if acquired during marriage (except by gift, devise or descent) should be divided in the same manner as community property, regardless of the spouses' domicile at acquisition.[6] A Texas statute now codifies the principle that property that would be community property under Texas law is so treated in a divorce proceeding between Texans, even if the property was acquired by a spouse then domiciled in another state.[7]

Fortunately, several courts have recognized this semantic difficulty and so doing "does no violence to either the statutes of Arizona, or Illinois, and carries out the basic law of both jurisdictions that a fair division of marital property be made at time of divorce."[8]

B. QUASI–COMMUNITY PROPERTY

§ 14.14   As earlier noted, spouses who migrate from common law states to community property states late in their life may fall into a gap

5. Sampson, Common Law Property in a Texas Divorce, 42 Tex. B.J. 131, 132, 133 (1979). See also Johanson, The Migrating Client, Estate Planning for the Couple from a Community Property State, 9 Inst. Est. Planning 8–1, 8–9 (1975). Cf. Vernon's Ann. Tex. Const. Art. XVI, § 15 (amended 1980); J. Oldham, Property Division in a Texas Divorce of a Migrant Spouse: Heads He Wins, Tails She Loses?, 19 Houston L. Rev. 1 (1981); Weisberger, Selected Conflict of Laws Issues in Wisconsin's Marital Prop. Act, 35 Am. J. Comp. L. 295 (1987).

6. Cameron v. Cameron, 641 S.W.2d 210, 220–21 (Tex.1982). See also Note, 14 St. Mary's L.J. 789 (1983); Note, Cameron v. Cameron, Divestiture of Separate Personalty on Divorce, 35 Baylor L. Rev. 168 (1983).

7. See Dawson–Austin v. Austin, 920 S.W.2d 776, 778 (Tex.App.1996) (summarizing law and citing Texas Family Code § 3.63(b)), rev'd on other grounds 968 S.W.2d 319 (Tex.1998).

8. Rau v. Rau, 6 Ariz.App. 362, 432 P.2d 910, 914 (1967). Similarly, Hughes v. Hughes, 91 N.M. 339, 573 P.2d 1194, 1201

(1978)("we hold that the characterization of this property as separate must be made under the applicable laws of the State of Iowa and therefore the property is subject to all the wife's incidents of ownership, claims, rights and legal relations provided in any and all of the laws of the State of Iowa that affect marital property."). See also Burton v. Burton, 23 Ariz.App. 159, 531 P.2d 204 (1975); Jizmejian v. Jizmejian, 16 Ariz.App. 270, 492 P.2d 1208 (1972); Lorenz–Auxier Financial Group, Inc. v. Bidewell, 160 Ariz. 218, 772 P.2d 41 (App. 1989); Berle v. Berle, 97 Idaho 452, 546 P.2d 407 (1976); Braddock v. Braddock, 91 Nev. 735, 542 P.2d 1060 (1975). Cf. Ladd v. Ladd, 265 Ark. 725, 580 S.W.2d 696 (1979); LeClert v. LeClert, 80 N.M. 235, 453 P.2d 755 (1969); Nelson v. Nelson, 61 Wn.2d 608, 379 P.2d 717 (1963); Adderson v. Adderson, 36 D.L.R. (4th) 631 (Alta. C.A. 1987); Vladi v. Vladi, 39 D.L.R. (4th) 563, 5 R.F.L.3d 337 (N.S.S.C. 1987); Pershadsingh v. Pershadsingh, 40 D.L.R. (4th) (Ont. H.L.S. 1987); In re Popkin & Stern, 292 B.R. 910 (8th Cir.B.A.P.2003), aff'd 85 Fed. Appx. 543 (8th Cir. 2004).

between the protection offered by each system. Spouses retiring to, say, California may have little or no community property as defined by California law, and community property states generally lack the protection against disinheritance of a forced or elective share.[1] The community property states—Arizona, California, Idaho, Louisiana, Nevada, New Mexico, Texas, Washington and Wisconsin—have taken various legislative steps to deal with the migratory couple problem, and those responses generally fall under the heading of "quasi-community property."

The problem can arise either on death or divorce. It can arise at death when the deceased spouse disinherits the surviving spouse, and the survivor has no claim to the deceased spouse's separate property and cannot invoke a forced or elective share. Some states—including California, Idaho, Louisiana and Washington—have addressed the problem at death by giving the surviving spouse community property rights in the deceased spouse's separate property if that separate property would have been community property under the forum state's law.[2]

The problem is probably more common on divorce. An in-migrating spouse with little separate property and little or no community property can be left destitute on divorce, even though that spouse would have been protected by equitable distribution under the regime of the state from which the couple migrated. For that reason, apparently all of the traditional community property states have extended quasi-community property rights on divorce.[3]

VI. CONTRACTUAL MODIFICATION OF THE MARITAL PROPERTY REGIME

§ 14.15 Both the community property and common law property states in the United States generally permit the matrimonial property regime between the parties to be controlled or substantially modified by either ante-nuptial or post-nuptial agreements.[1] The intentional and

§ 14.14

1. See Erlanger & Monday, The Surviving Spouse's Right to Quasi–Community Property: A Proposal Based on the Uniform Probate Code, 30 Idaho L. Rev. 671, 671–72 (1994).

2. See Erlanger & Monday, supra n.1, at 672 n.5 (citing Cal. Prob. Code §§ 66(a), 101, 102; Idaho Code §§ 15–2201, 15–2202; La. Civ. Code Ann. art. 3526; Wash. Rev. Code Ann. §§ 26.16.220, 26.16.230, 26.16.240). Louisiana does not use the term "quasi-community property, though the operation of its statute is similar." See Erlanger & Monday, supra n.1, at 672 n.5.

3. Erlanger & Monday, supra n.1, at 672 n.5; Comment, A Uniform Resolution to the Problem a Migrating Spouse Encounters at Divorce and Death, 28 Idaho L. Rev. 993, 1013–14 (1992). For classic treatments

of the problem, see Schrecter, "Quasi–Community Property" in the Conflict of Laws, 50 Calif. L. Rev. 206 (1962); Lay, Migrants from the Community Property States—Filling the Legislative Gap, 53 Cornell L. Rev. 832 (1968); Symeonides, Choice of Law Solutions to Property Problems, 13 Comm. Prop. J. No. 3, p. 11 (1986); Comment, The Surviving Spouse's Right to Quasi–Community Property: A Proposal Based on the Uniform Probate Code, 30 Idaho L. Rev. 671 (1994).

§ 14.15

1. See de Funiak & Vaughn, Principles of Community Property § 90 (2d ed. 1971); Cross, The Community Property Law in Washington, 49 Wash. L. Rev. 729 (1974); Uniform Probate Code § 2–204, 8 U.L.A. 82–84 (1983). See also Juenger, Marital

knowing consent or waiver of rights is respected in most situations, although after marriage there may be different requirements than before marriage. Cases involving the effect of contracts on marital property rights are not numerous in the American reports, due probably to the comparative infrequency of such transactions in this country.[2] On the basis of the same policies that are persuasive in recognizing the marital domicile's significance in considering marital property issues, that law normally would be most appropriate in the determination of contract questions relating to marital property. However, the relevance of a person's domicile may have a greater significance than the marital domicile for some issues, for instance, capacity to enter an ante-nuptial agreement. The appropriate policy analysis in resolving conflict-of-laws questions as to particular issues in these contracts that identifies the marital domicile or other significant law at the time of entering into the contract is probably not different from other contracts.[3] The contract controlling or modifying the marital regime, if valid by the appropriate law, will usually be held valid in other states and will govern the rights of the parties, unless for some reasons it stands prohibited by the law where it is sought to be enforced.[4]

Although it seems clear that the parties may either identify the law to govern their marital property regime[5] or may control the regime itself

Property and the Conflict of Laws: A Tale of Two Countries, 81 Col. L. Rev. 1061 (1981). See also McClanahan, Community Property Law in the United States, ch. 8 (1982 and 1984 Supp.); Henderson, Marital Agreements and the Rights of Creditors, 11 Comm. Prop. J. 105 (1984). See the Wisconsin Marital Property Act for an exhaustive provision dealing with recognition and permissible scope of marital property agreements. Wis. Stat. Ann. § 766.58. See also Whitmore v. Mitchell, 152 Ariz. 425, 733 P.2d 310 (App. 1987); Cladis v. Cladis, 512 So.2d 271 (Fla.App.1987); Uhrig v. Pulliam, 713 S.W.2d 649 (Tenn.1986); Quade v. Quade, 238 Mich.App. 222, 604 N.W.2d 778 (1999); Cary v. Cary, 937 S.W.2d 777 (Tenn. 1996).

2. See Sokolov, Marriage Contracts: Is There a Need, in Krauskopf, ed., Marital and Non–Marital Contracts, 13 (1979); P. Ashley, Oh Promise Me But Put it in Writing: Living Together Agreements, Without, Before, During and After Marriage, 22 (1978). Stork v. First National Bank of South Carolina, 281 S.C. 515, 316 S.E.2d 400 (1984); Hughes, Antenuptial Agreements, 19 Ind. L. Rev. 171 (1986); Note, Antenuptial Agreements in Ohio, 12 Ohio N.U. L. Rev. 153 (1985). Cf. Gustafson v. Jensen, 515 So.2d 1298 (Fla.App.1987); Lewis v. Lewis, 69 Hawaii 497, 748 P.2d 1362 (1988); DeLorean v. DeLorean, 211 N.J.Super. 432, 511 A.2d 1257 (Ch.Div. 1986); Vien Estate v. Vien Estate, 49 D.L.R.

(4th) 558 (Ont. 1987); Note, Marriage as Contract and Marriage as Partnership: The Future of Antenuptial Agreement Law, 116 Harv. L. Rev. 2075 (2003).

3. See infra Ch. 18. See Auten v. Auten, 308 N.Y. 155, 124 N.E.2d 99 (1954); Hutchison v. Ross, 262 N.Y. 381, 187 N.E. 65 (1933). In re Estate of Knippel, 7 Wis.2d 335, 96 N.W.2d 514 (1959). Cf. In re Weeks' Will, 294 N.Y. 516, 63 N.E.2d 85 (1945); Baffin Land Corp. v. Monticello Motor Inn, Inc., 70 Wn.2d 893, 425 P.2d 623 (1967). See also Stone, The Law Governing Rights in Property Under a Prenuptial Contract, According to the English and American Cases, 13 Bost. U. L. Rev. 219 (1933).

4. See Restatement, Second, Conflict of Laws § 258 (1971). See also Long v. Hess, 154 Ill. 482, 40 N.E. 335 (1895); Kleb v. Kleb, 70 N.J.Eq. 305, 62 A. 396 (1905), affirmed 71 N.J.Eq. 787, 65 A. 1118 (5) (1907); Castro v. Illies, 22 Tex. 479, 73 Am.Dec. 277 (1858); Fuss v. Fuss, 24 Wis. 256, 1 Am.Rep. 180 (1869). See also Morris, The Conflict of Laws 413–18 (3d ed. 1984); McLeod, The Conflict of Laws 371–79, 383–98 (1983); Rafferty, Marital Property and the Conflict of Laws, 20 U.W. Ont. L. Rev. 177 (1982).

5. See, e.g., The Hague Convention on the Law Applicable to Matrimonial Property Regimes, Art. 3, 6 (1976), 25 Am. J. Comp. L. 394, 395 (1977); Restatement,

by their contract, most of the cases fall within the latter category.[6] Consequently, the issue often is phrased in terms of the effect of the contract on assets located in a particular jurisdiction. Here, the situs has frequently applied its own law after recognizing the validity of the contract.[7] Because of the tracing rules, however, the source of funds is very important and as a consequence, the reference usually is viewed as involving movables.[8] Although there has been considerable litigation in the past as to whether an ante-nuptial contract was intended to cover both property owned by the parties at the time of the marriage and subsequent acquisitions of property,[9] it appears that this is simply an issue of interpretation, i.e., determining the intent of the parties from the language used and the circumstances surrounding their transaction.[10] There seems no doubt but what the contract may and normally would control the marital property regime between the parties.[11]

VII. DEBTS

§ 14.16 In community property states, the distinctions between separate and community assets leads to a somewhat parallel distinction as to what debts can be enforced against separate and community assets. In response to these issues, the courts have developed the concepts of separate debts and community debts.[1] The most ready example of a separate debt is one incurred by a spouse prior to marriage. Since the community is the "partnership" of the spouses that acquires community

Second, Conflict of Laws §§ 234, 258 (1971); K. Siehr, Domestic Relations in Europe: European Equivalents to American Evolutions, 30 Am. J. Comp. L. 37, 51 (1982).

6. See H. Marsh, Marital Property and the Conflict of Laws 218 (1952).

7. Id. Restatement, Second, Conflict of Laws §§ 234, 258 (1971). See also Heine v. Mechanics' & Traders' Insurance Co., 45 La. Ann. 770, 13 So. 1 (1893); Richardson v. De Giverville, 107 Mo. 422, 17 S.W. 974 (1891).

8. See supra text § 14.6 n.1.

9. Besse v. Pellochoux, 73 Ill. 285, 24 Am. Rep. 242 (1874); Long v. Hess, 154 Ill. 482, 40 N.E. 335 (1895); Castro v. Illies, 22 Tex. 479, 73 Am. Dec. 277 (1858); Fuss v. Fuss, 24 Wis. 256, 1 Am.Rep. 180 (1869).

10. Thus in Le Breton v. Miles, 8 Paige 261 (N.Y. 1840), the contract, though made in New York, was expressed in the French language, between persons who declared their intention to live in France. It provided for a form of marital property ownership well known to the French law. The court held that the contract was governed by the law of France. See Mueller v. Mueller, 127 Ala. 356, 28 So. 465 (1900). Kinross–Wright v. Kinross–Wright, 248 N.C. 1, 102 S.E.2d

469 (1958). See also McLeod v. Board, 30 Tex. 238, 94 Am.Dec. 301 (1867). Cf. Bradley v. Bradley, 725 S.W.2d 503 (Tex.App. 1987); Dewey v. Dewey, 745 S.W.2d 514 (Tex.App.1988); Winger v. Pianka, 831 S.W.2d 853 (Tex.App.1992).

11. Kleb v. Kleb, 70 N.J.Eq. 305, 62 A. 396 (1905), affirmed 71 N.J.Eq. 787, 65 A. 1118 (5) (Err. & App. 1907). See La.Civil Code art. 2332 (1981); Bilbe, Management of Community Assets, 39 La. L. Rev. 409, 436 (1979); Samuel, The Retroactivity Provisions of Louisiana's Equal Management Law: Interpretation and Constitutionality, 39 La. L. Rev. 347, 364, 400 (1979); cf. Pascal, Updating Louisiana's Community of Gains, 49 Tulane L. Rev. 555 (1975). See also Cross, Community Property: A Comparison of the Systems in Washington and Louisiana, 39 La. L. Rev. 479, 481, 484 (1979).

§ 14.16

1. See de Funiak & Vaughn, Principles of Community Property 378 (2d ed. 1971). See also McClanahan, Community Property Law in the United States, §§ 10:1–10:13; Note, Sharing Debts and Creditors and Debtors Under the Uniform Marital Property Act, 69 Minn. L. Rev. 111 (1984).

assets, the separate ante-nuptial debt of one spouse is appropriately payable from the spouse's separate property.[2] Also a debt incurred in the management of separate property would seem to be chargeable against the separate property of the spouse incurring the obligation.[3] It may even be arguable that that spouse's share of the community should be subject to the "separate" debt if the separate property is inadequate.[4] The attitude of the states is very diverse on the treatment of debts[5] and, historically, has been further complicated by the husband's management powers over the community. However, the trend toward equal management by both spouses[6] has extended the liability of the community assets and occasioned the presumption that debts by either party during the marriage are community debts.[7]

The "partnership" concept of marriage in community property states leads first to a characterization of the obligation in question, as either separate or community. This issue would seem to be an issue which should be determined by the circumstances surrounding the parties and the creditor at the time the transaction occurs since it involves identification of the entity liable for the obligation. Although the expectation of the creditor, as well as that of the spouses, is significant, the marital domicile has a strong interest in allocating liability between the spouses.[8] After the obligor, separate spouse or community, has been determined by the characterization of the obligation, the question arises as to the assets from which that obligation can be satisfied.[9] This involves an identification or second characterization of the manner in which assets are held, i.e., separate or community. As we have noted before, the rules of the marital domicile usually have been viewed as the most appropriate to determine this issue. On this two-step analysis, it would seem that consideration of the expectations of the creditor might lead to the selection of the governing rule from different states in resolving these two issues since the first seems more of a contract matter while the second more a property issue. This seems to have led to the conclusion in some early cases that the nature of the

---

2. See Wiggins v. Rush, 83 N.M. 133, 489 P.2d 641 (1971). But see Weiner v. Weiner,

3. See de Funiak & Vaughn, supra n.1, at 383.

4. Id. at 418. Cf. Pacific Gamble Robinson Co. v. Lapp, 95 Wn.2d 341, 622 P.2d 850 (1980).

5. de Funiak & Vaughn, supra n.1, at 384, 388.

6. See Bartke, Community Property Law Reform in the United States and in Canada—A Comparison and Critique, 50 Tul. L. Rev. 213 (1976); Barkam, Community Property: Symposium on Equal Rights, Introduction: Equal Rights for Women Versus the Civil Code, 48 Tul. L. Rev. 560 (1974); Samuel, the Retroactivity Provisions of Louisiana's Equal Management Law: In-

terpretation and Constitutionality, 39 La. L. Rev. 347 (1979); Cross, Community Property: A Comparison of the Louisiana, 39 La. L. Rev. 479 (1979); Dickerson, To Love, Honor, and (Oh!) Pay: Should Spouses be Forced to Pay Each Other's Debts? 78 B.U.L. Rev. 961 (1998); Alexander, Building "A Doll's House": A Feminist Analysis of Marital Debt Dischargeability in Bankruptcy, 48 Vill. L. Rev. 381 (2003).

7. See de Funiak & Vaughn, supra n.1, at 383.

8. See, e.g., Pacific States Cut Stone Co. v. Goble, 70 Wn.2d 907, 425 P.2d 631 (1967). Cf. Park Bank–West v. Mueller, 151 Wis.2d 476, 444 N.W.2d 754 (App.1989); Sprick v. Sprick, 25 S.W.3d 7 (Tex.App. 1999).

9. See H. Marsh, Marital Property in Conflict of Laws 142 (1952).

debt, as separate or community, was determined by the law governing the contract.[10] The semantic difficulty of separate and community discussed earlier[11] meant that if a spouse contracted a debt in a non-community state that it was viewed as chargeable only against that spouse's separate property even if it was in furtherance of the usual income producing activities of the couple domiciled in a community state.[12] That this semantic fallacy not only led to an illogical result but also frustrated the policy of both the concerned states was pointed out by a leading scholar[13] and subsequently recognized by the court which had been most influential in the earlier development.

In two cases, decided the same day, the Supreme Court of Washington held that the contract aspects of this matter were governed by the rule of the state most significantly related to the transaction[14] which seems to continue the two-step analysis. However, in *Pacific States Cut Stone Co. v. Goble*,[15] the court extended its analysis as to the property that could be reached and concluded that there was a false conflict since all of the property of the couple except property held separately by the wife could be reached for the general business obligation entered into by the husband in either of the states. Hence the general business debt incurred by the husband in Oregon could be asserted against community assets in Washington and the policy of both states advanced.[16] This recognition of the false conflict between the state of the transaction and the state of the marital domicile which was the situs of the property being pursued may indicate that the two-step analysis outlined above and confirmed by the Washington court is the choice of law of the state of the situs of the property. This could lead to the conclusion that in most cases the issue would be posed "whether assets in this state are subject to the debts acquired elsewhere under the circumstances of this case." This would seem to make the approach not very dissimilar from the traditional approach that the availability of particular assets to creditors is dependent upon the law that a situs court would apply.[17] In any event, the situs court should consider both the transactional policies and those relating to the marital property concepts when it is a community state and the marital domicile.[18] The strong presumption that any obligation entered into by a spouse after marriage is probably on behalf

10. Escrow Service Co. v. Cressler, 59 Wn.2d 38, 365 P.2d 760 (1961); Achilles v. Hoopes, 40 Wn.2d 664, 245 P.2d 1005 (1952); Clark v. Eltinge, 29 Wash. 215, 69 P. 736 (1902); La Selle v. Woolery, 11 Wash. 337, 39 P. 663 (1895), reversed on rehearing 14 Wash. 70, 44 P. 115 (1896). Cf. Sarbacher v. McNamara, 564 A.2d 701 (D.C.App.1989).

11. See text supra § 14.13 n.5.

12. E.g., La Selle v. Woolery, 14 Wash. 70, 44 P. 115 (1896).

13. H. Marsh, supra n.9, at 148.

14. Baffin Land Corp. v. Monticello Motor Inn, Inc., 70 Wn.2d 893, 425 P.2d 623 (1967); Pacific States Cut Stone Co. v. Goble, 70 Wn.2d 907, 425 P.2d 631 (1967).

15. 70 Wn.2d 907, 425 P.2d 631 (1967).

16. Accord Bainum v. Roundy, 21 Ariz. App. 534, 521 P.2d 633 (1974). Cf. Pacific Gamble Robinson Co. v. Lapp, 95 Wn.2d 341, 622 P.2d 850 (1980); In re LeSueur, 53 B.R. 414 (Bankr.Ariz.1985); In re Sweitzer, 111 B.R. 792 (Bankr.Wis.1990).

17. Cf. Everson v. Everson, 264 Pa.Super. 563, 400 A.2d 887 (1979) modified and affirmed 494 Pa. 348, 431 A.2d 889 (1981).

18. Cf. Neuner, Marital Property and the Conflict of Laws, 5 La. L. Rev. 167, 173 (1943).

of the community is likely to result in the availability of community property for payment. In a common law state, the liability of each "partner" for obligations properly entered into on behalf of the community partnership will probably subject any property owned by either party unless the community is viewed as a limited partnership.

Tort obligations incurred by the spouses probably will be approached in a similar fashion[19] although there the transactional circumstances are less significant than the extent to which the marital domicile will attach vicarious liability to the "community" as an entity. The situations in which a spouse acquires a cause of action against a third party seems appropriately considered in the same manner as the ownership of other assets.[20]

---

19. See, e.g., Wis. Stat. § 766.55(2)(cm); Curda–Derickson v. Derickson, 266 Wis.2d 453, 668 N.W.2d 736 (2003) (application in the context of spouse's obligation to make restitution for criminal conduct).

20. Cf. Reeves v. Schulmeier, 303 F.2d 802 (5th Cir.1962).

Chapter 15

DISSOLUTION OF DOMESTIC RELATIONSHIPS AND ITS CONSEQUENCES

Table of Sections

		Sections
I.	Interstate Recognition of Dissolution Decrees	15.1–15.14
	A. Introduction	15.1–15.5
	1. In General	15.1–15.3
	2. Domicile and Choice of Law	15.4–15.5
	B. Ex Parte Divorces	15.6–15.7
	1. Full Faith and Credit and the Domicile Requirement: The *Williams* Cases	15.6
	2. Domicile and Durational Residence Requirements	15.7
	C. Inter Partes Divorces	15.8–15.11
	D. The Effect of a Collateral Determination of Invalidity	15.12–15.13
	E. Conclusion and Outlook	15.14
II.	Annulment in the United States	15.15
III.	International Recognition of Dissolution Decrees	15.16–15.25
	A. Recognition of Foreign–Country Judicial Divorces in the United States	15.17–15.23
	B. Recognition of Foreign Non-judicial Divorces in the United States	15.24–15.25
	C. Recognition of U.S. Divorces Abroad	15.26
IV.	Incidents of Divorce Decrees: Support and Custody	15.27–15.43
	A. Divisible Divorce	15.27–15.29
	B. Support Obligations	15.30–15.37
	1. Establishing the Support Obligation by Judicial Decree	15.30
	2. Enforcement and Modification of Support Decrees	15.31
	a. Lump Sum Child Support and Claims for Additional Support	15.32–15.33
	b. Modification of Support Decrees	15.34
	c. Choice of Law for Modification	15.35
	d. Summary	15.36
	3. International Recognition	15.37–15.38
	C. Child Custody	15.39–15.43
	1. Obtaining Custody	15.39
	2. Interstate Recognition and Modification	15.40–15.42
	3. International Recognition and Modification	15.43

I. INTERSTATE RECOGNITION OF DISSOLUTION DECREES

A. INTRODUCTION

1. *In General*

§ 15.1 A marriage may be terminated by divorce, historically for reasons specifically enumerated by statute. These reasons, "grounds," were designed to permit a judicial determination that one of the parties was at "fault," that is, had committed a marital offense. Increasingly, however, legislatures adopted "no fault" divorce statutes. The "irretrievable breakdown" of a marriage or the "living apart" of the spouses for a specified period have become the exclusive ground in a number of states of the United States while, in a great many additional states, these grounds were added to the traditional grounds for divorce which focus on "fault." As a result, no states today retain divorce legislation based solely on fault.[1] The change from "fault" to "no fault" divorce law also signaled a change in terminology in many states from "divorce" to "dissolution of marriage."

Some states continue to provide for a "limited divorce," the divorce or separation from bed and board (divorce *a mensa et thoro*). These divorces may involve property settlements very much like those in a "full" divorce. Moreover, several states provide for the possibility of converting a limited divorce into a full divorce. Even if no such possibility exists, the living-apart which results from the limited divorce will subsequently furnish the grounds for a full divorce in no-fault states.[2]

Another formalized domestic relationship is the "civil union" between same-sex partners, as it now exists in Vermont and has been introduced for legislative consideration elsewhere.[3] Its dissolution and

---

§ 15.1

1. In states in which a "no fault" ground is additional to the traditional grounds, an allegation of fault remains an important route for petitioners. An allegation and proof of fault often will lead to a prompt divorce, while no-fault divorces frequently involve waiting periods or required attempts at conciliation.

The "covenant marriage", first introduced by Louisiana in 1997, is intended to give marriages greater stability through solemnity of form and greater difficulty of dissolution. The Louisiana model permits divorce only for specified grounds, such as adultery or commission of a felony, or—on no-fault basis—upon two years' separation. The law thus chooses a middle ground between fault-based and mere consensual and quick divorce. La.R.S. 9:307. Arizona and Alabama have meanwhile adopted similar legislation. Ariz. Stat. Ann. § 25–901 et seq.; A.C.A. § 9–11–801 et seq. Proposals are pending in other states. For a discussion of the choice-of-law issues raised by covenant marriages, see Spaht & Symeonides, Covenant Marriage and the Conflict of Laws, 32 Creighton L. Rev. 1085 (1999), and, critically, Hay, The American "Covenant Marriage" in the Conflict of Laws, 64 La.L.Rev. 43 (2003).

Same-sex couples may marry in Massachusetts. See supra § 13.20 n. 4. In other states civil-union legislation provides a way to establish formalized domestic relationships. See infra at n. 3.

2. For discussion see H.D. Krause & D.D. Meyer, Family Law in A Nutshell 353–356, 393–94 (4th ed. 2003).

3. 15 Vermont Stat. Ann. (V.S.A.) § 1201 et seq. (2003).

the consequences of dissolution follow the same rules that apply to divorce.[4] The extra-state effects of civil unions, including their attributes and the consequences of their dissolution, are as yet uncertain.[5] The discussion in this chapter therefore focuses primarily on the dissolution of traditional marriages and its consequences.

Non-formalized domestic relationships, i.e. cohabitation of heterosexual or same-sex couples, usually do not raise issues with respect to dissolution.[6] However, such relationships may raise questions with regard to support and division of property.[7]

§ 15.2   Annulment, which will be treated in more detail in a subsequent section, theoretically differs from divorce since it is a determination that a marriage never existed, thus does not "dissolve" a valid existing marriage. In practice, the distinction is sometimes blurred. This results from the fact that the substantive grounds for divorce and annulment sometimes overlap, for instance when a statute designates

4. See 15 V.S.A. §§ 1204(d), 1206 (2003). See supra § 13.20.

5. For discussion of the Defense of Marriage Act (DOMA), see supra § 13.19.

6. When heterosexual couples intend their (non-formalized) relationship to be tantamount to "marriage," some states will recognize this relationship as a "common law marriage." Such a marriage is subject to judicial dissolution. See Stringer v. Stringer, 689 So.2d 194 (Ala.Civ.App. 1997) (dictum); People v. Schmidt, 228 Mich.App. 463, 579 N.W.2d 431, 433 (1998) (referring to unpublished Alabama divorce decree of common-law marriage).

The "putative spouse" doctrine differs from the "common law marriage:" it does not treat cohabiting parties, who hold themselves out as married, as being married in fact, but—typically because common-law marriages are unknown in that jurisdiction—seeks to mitigate the effects of an attempted marriage gone awry, for instance, for defects as to form, or to protect the innocent party of a bigamous relationship. At issue will often be insurance benefits that the putative spouse claims. See Uniform Marriage and Divorce Act § 209, 9A U.L.A. 238 (1987); Huff v. Director, 40 F.3d 35 (3d Cir. 1994); Blakesley, The Putative Marriage Doctrine, 60 Tulane L. Rev. 1 (1985).

7. Marvin v. Marvin, 18 Cal.3d 660, 134 Cal.Rptr. 815, 557 P.2d 106 (1976), was the landmark decision holding that, even absent an express agreement, courts could fashion remedies to protect parties of a nonmarital relationship in their lawful expectations, for instance, by making rehabilitative awards grounded on an implied-in-fact con-

tract, unjust enrichment, and the like. On remand, the trial court in *Marvin* made such an award, 5 Fam. L. Rep. 3079, 3085 (1979), rev'd 122 Cal.App.3d 871, 176 Cal. Rptr. 555, 559 (1981) on a finding of "no damage, ... no unjust enrichment." See also Connell v. Francisco, 127 Wash.2d 339, 898 P.2d 831 (1995). For discussion of decisions upholding claims of cohabitants, see Bruch, Cohabitation in the Common Law Countries a Decade After *Marvin*: Settled In or Moving Ahead, 22 U.C. Davis L. Rev. 717 (1989). For a survey of state law concerning express agreements, see Gordon, The Necessity and Enforcement of Cohabitation Agreements: When Strings Will Attach and How to Prevent Them—A State Survey, 37 Brandeis L.J. 245 (1998).

Marvin, though expressed in gender-neutral language, is thought not to extend to same-sex couples. See Comment, The Illusory Rights of Marvin v. Marvin for the Same–Sex Couple versus the Preferable Canadian Alternative–M. v. H., 38 Cal. W. L. Rev. 547 (2002). Same-sex partners receive limited protection–short of a civil union, supra n. 3–as a result of state or municipal non-discrimination law concerning employment benefits. See, e.g., City of Atlanta v. Morgan, 268 Ga. 586, 492 S.E.2d 193 (1997) ("dependent," defined as someone who "relies on another for financial support" in City's benefits ordinance, includes an employee's domestic partner); Tyma et al. v. Montgomery County, Maryland, 369 Md. 497, 801 A.2d 148 (2002) (upholding county code's provision defining "immediate family" to include, for public employees, "the employee's domestic partner, if the partner is receiving County benefits;" same with respective to "relative;" with "domestic

bigamy as a ground for divorce rather than annulment,[1] that annulment serves to terminate violable, or possibly even void marriages, and that the declaration of nullity does not always operate *ab initio* but at times only as of the time of the decree.[2] In the last-mentioned case, annulment thus resembles divorce. Additionally, children of an annulled marriage are protected. Thus, despite the theoretical distinction between annulment and divorce, a *de facto* "marriage" did exist in many annulment cases and the manner of its "termination" therefore also raises important questions of jurisdiction and recognition.

§ 15.3 The change from fault to no-fault dissolution of marriage (and, today, of a civil union) is accompanied by a decreasing emphasis on the *public interest* in the supervision of the maintenance of domestic relationships and their termination. The primary focus shifts to the parties. Thus, when the propriety of a dissolution is at issue in a state other than the state of rendition, the case will often be viewed in due process terms, very much similar to those obtaining with respect to all civil litigation.[1] This development holds implications beyond substantive divorce law: traditional notions of what constitutes permissible jurisdiction to grant a divorce, of appropriate choice-of-law principles in divorce, and of the consequences of divorce (alimony, support, child custody) may be affected. These problems will be explored in subsequent sections.

2. *Domicile and Choice of Law*

§ 15.4 Most American courts have applied the substantive law of the forum in divorce actions[1] because of the historical assumption that the forum was acting as the state of the matrimonial domicile of the parties. The courts have continued to apply local law regardless of whether the marriage was originally celebrated in the forum, whether the forum was or now is the matrimonial domicile of the parties (where they last lived together as husband and wife), and whether the marital offense or the breakdown of the marriage had occurred there or else-

---

partner" defined as "a person of the same sex").

§ 15.2

1. See 750 Ill. Comp. Stat. § 5/401.

2. Uniform Marriage and Divorce Act § 208(3), 9A U.L.A. 147 (1987) adopted in Arizona, Colorado (in part), Illinois, Kentucky, Minnesota, Missouri, Montana and Washington.

§ 15.3

1. For an illustration of the public-interest orientation of the traditional case law, see the discussion of the *Williams* cases, infra § 15.6.

The effect of a same-sex civil union (and of its consequences and dissolution) in a

state other than the state of celebration is as yet unclear. For discussion of the Defense of Marriage Act, see supra § 13.19.

§ 15.4

1. See R. Weintraub, Commentary on the Conflict of Laws 296 (4th ed. 2001); Restatement, Second, Conflict of Laws § 285 (1971). See also Wasserman, Divorce and Domicile: Time to Sever the Knot, 34 Wm. & Mary L. Rev. 1 (1997).

In the case of "covenant marriages," the parties originally chose covenant-state law. Nonetheless, a later state with divorce jurisdiction, e.g., petitioner's (new) state of domicile may, and usually will apply its own, possibly more permissible law. See Hay, The American "Covenant Marriage" in the Conflict of Laws, 64 La.L.Rev. 43 (2003).

where.[2] With this identity of forum and applicable law, the principal conflicts issues involved the granting and recognition of interstate divorces are thus relate to the divorcing court's jurisdiction.[3] The application of local substantive law also means that the assertion of jurisdiction should therefore be based on an especially close nexus of the forum to the parties and their relationship.

Domicile within the state has traditionally furnished that close link to the divorcing court. So strong was the assumption that domicile was a requisite for divorce jurisdiction that the U.S. Supreme Court asserted (perhaps incorrectly) in 1945 that this requirement had not been questioned by any "court in the English-speaking world"[4] since the adoption of the Constitution. In the United States, the evolution of the domicile concept as furnishing the basis for divorce jurisdiction progressed from the state of the matrimonial domicile[5] to the (separate) domicile of the innocent spouse,[6] to the domicile of either spouse.[7] Despite this development from a single forum to multiple states with divorce jurisdiction, the domicile orientation has persisted to give the proceeding the resemblance of one *in rem*. The marriage, the status, has been viewed as having a situs (at the domicile of one of the parties) and the court at the situs has jurisdiction over the marriage, the res, for the purpose of dissolving it.[8]

§ 15.5 More recently, a number of states have enacted statutes authorizing the granting of a divorce to military personnel who have been stationed continuously (but not domiciled[1]) in the state for a specified period of time, usually a year.[2] Similarly, the Second Restate-

2. Alton v. Alton, 207 F.2d 667 (3d Cir. 1953)(Hastie, J., dissenting).

3. But see the discussion of the effect of a collateral determination of invalidity, infra § 15.12.

4. Williams v. North Carolina, 325 U.S. 226, 229, 65 S.Ct. 1092, 89 L.Ed. 1577 (1945). However, as Judge Hastie pointed out in Alton v. Alton, domicile as a jurisdictional requirement for divorce "is no ancient landmark of the common law. I do not know of any evidence that such a concept even existed in the jurisprudence of 18th century England or that it could even possibly have been a part of the conception of procedural due process at the time our Constitution was adopted." 207 F.2d 667, 681 (3d Cir.1953) (dissenting opinion).

5. See Atherton v. Atherton, 181 U.S. 155, 21 S.Ct. 544, 45 L.Ed. 794 (1901); Cavers, Contemporary Conflicts Law in American Perspective, Hague Academy, 131 Recueil des Cours 75, 252 ff. (1970–III).

6. Haddock v. Haddock, 201 U.S. 562, 26 S.Ct. 525, 50 L.Ed. 867 (1906); Beale, Haddock Revisited, 39 Harv. L. Rev. 417 (1926).

7. Williams v. North Carolina, 317 U.S. 287, 63 S.Ct. 207, 87 L.Ed. 279 (1942).

8. In *Williams I,* the Court stated that "the historical view that a proceeding for a divorce was a proceeding *in rem* ... was rejected by the Haddock case [supra n.6]" but emphasized that "such a suit [also] is not a mere *in personam* action." 317 U.S. 287, 297, 63 S.Ct. 207, 87 L.Ed. 279.

§ 15.5

1. Service personnel, except when living off the base and intending to make their home in the state (Ferrara v. Ibach, 285 F.Supp. 1017 (D.S.C.1968)), do not acquire a domicile at the place where they are stationed absent other evidence of intent to make a home in that state: Restatement, Second, Conflict of Laws § 17, cmnt. (d) (1971); Anno., 21 A.L.R.2d 1163 (1962); Thames, Domicile of Service Men, 34 Miss. L.J. 160 (1963); Nora v. Nora, 494 So.2d 16, 18 (Ala.1986); Gowins v. Gowins, 466 So.2d 32, 35 (La.1985); Newman v. Newman, 558 So.2d 821, 825 (Miss.1990); Blessley v. Blessley, 91 N.M. 513, 577 P.2d 62, 63–64 (1978). But see also supra § 4.26.

2. See Leflar, Conflict of Laws and Family Law, 14 Ark. L. Rev. 47 (1960). See also Green, Long & Murawski, Dissolution of Marriage § 4.04 (1986). The constitutionali-

ment has adopted the position that divorce jurisdiction may be based on close connecting factors other than domicile, such as long continued presence within the state,[3] and the divorce entitled to interstate recognition. New York has exercised jurisdiction on the basis that it was the state of the celebration of the marriage in circumstances where the parties were domiciled elsewhere at the time of suit.[4] However, dictum in the Supreme Court's 1975 decision in *Sosna v. Iowa* reiterates that " . . . this Court has often stated that 'judicial power to grant a divorce—jurisdiction strictly speaking—is founded on domicil.' "[5] As will be seen, the question of whether domicile is or is not necessary for divorce jurisdiction is of little importance today in *inter partes* divorces, that is, in divorce actions in which both parties participate. The question is of great importance, however, in the case of *ex parte* divorces and in the case of divorces obtained abroad.

Requiring a "substantial connection" to the forum (albeit not domicile) will ordinarily continue to ensure that the application of forum law also means the application of a significantly related law. Judge Hastie, in *Alton*,[6] had suggested that the focus be on the applicable law: application of the law most significantly related to the parties and the marriage would avoid substitution of forum standards for those of the "home state", however defined, and obviate the need for difficult jurisdictional determinations, such as in *Williams*.[7] This is, in fact, the practice of many civil-law jurisdictions.[8]

ty of these statutes has invariably been upheld by state courts: In re Marriage of Ways, 85 Wn.2d 693, 538 P.2d 1225 (1975) (upholding constitutionality of statute but dismissing action for plaintiff's failure to meet 90 days' durational residence requirement); Lauterbach v. Lauterbach, 392 P.2d 24 (Alaska 1964), followed in Perito v. Perito, 756 P.2d 895 (Alaska 1988); Wallace v. Wallace, 63 N.M. 414, 320 P.2d 1020 (1958); Wood v. Wood, 159 Tex. 350, 320 S.W.2d 807 (1959). See also Annot., Validity and Construction of Statutory Provisions Relating to Jurisdiction of Court for Purposes of Divorce for Servicemen, 73 A.L.R.3d 431 (1997). In Viernes v. District Court In and For Fourth Judicial District, 181 Colo. 284, 509 P.2d 306 (1973), the court regarded domicile to be a constitutional prerequisite for divorce jurisdiction which it regarded to require "significant contact" with Colorado. While the plaintiff had satisfied the servicemen's statute's 90-day residence requirement the court found that Colorado did not have "significant contact" with the marriage.

In England, Indyka v. Indyka, [1967] 3 W.L.R. 510 (H.L.) similarly signaled a departure from a domicile requirement in favor of jurisdiction based on the plaintiff's "real and substantial connection" to the forum. 2 Dicey & Morris, Conflict of Laws

769 et seq. (13th ed. by Collins 2000). *Indyka's* common law standard was abolished by the Family Law Act, 1986, which implements the Hague Convention: recognition of a foreign divorced based on the either party's habitual residence or domicile in or nationality of the state of rendition.

3. Restatement, Second, Conflict of Laws § 72 (1971); see also Reporter's Note, id., at pp. 221–22.

4. David–Zieseniss v. Zieseniss, 205 Misc. 836, 129 N.Y.S.2d 649 (1954). See also Carr v. Carr, 60 A.D.2d 63, 400 N.Y.S.2d 105 (2d Dep't 1977) (holding that the marital res follows the wife after she leaves her husband for reasons of cruelty and establishes subject matter jurisdiction in New York for purposes of reviewing the validity of the husband's subsequent foreign-country divorce and remarriage).

5. 419 U.S. 393, 407, 95 S.Ct. 553, 42 L.Ed.2d 532 (1975) (citing to *Williams II*). But see infra § 15.6 nn.6–7.

6. Alton v. Alton, 207 F.2d 667 (3d Cir.) (Hastie, J., dissenting).

7. Infra § 15.6.

8. See, e.g. Introductory Law to the German Civil Code (EGBGB) Art. 17 in connection with Art. 14: law of common

B.　EX PARTE DIVORCES

1.　*Full Faith and Credit and the Domicile Requirement: The Williams Cases*

§ 15.6　The early landmark cases of *Williams v. North Carolina* (I)[1] and (II)[2] arose from a prosecution for bigamous cohabitation of two North Carolina parties who, having left their respective North Carolina spouses, had obtained Nevada divorces, married each other in Nevada, and returned to North Carolina. In *Williams I,* the Supreme Court reversed the North Carolina decision which, in finding the defendants guilty of bigamy, had denied full faith and credit to the Nevada divorce. The Court held, and thereby overruled *Haddock,*[3] that the domicile of *one* spouse, *either* spouse, is a sufficient basis for divorce jurisdiction. The decision did not reach the question whether the defendants had in fact acquired a domicile in Nevada when seeking their divorces there. In *Williams II* the Supreme Court upheld the subsequent North Carolina decision finding that the parties had not acquired a Nevada domicile, that the *ex parte* Nevada decisions were therefore not entitled to recognition, and that the parties' attempted remarriage constituted bigamous cohabitation.[4]

The reach of the *Williams II* decision is not clear. To begin with, Nevada had based its jurisdiction on the domicile of the petitioners, rather than asserting jurisdiction on some other basis. Since the proceedings had been *ex parte,* the actual existence of jurisdiction (domicile) was thus open to question in a collateral proceeding in Nevada as well as in a

nationality, subsidiarily that of common (or last common) habitual residence, subsidiarily that of another close connection. In contrast, divorce *jurisdiction* is broader. It exists, inter alia, if the parties are habitually resident in the forum as well if only one is habitually resident unless, in the latter case, the decision would not be entitled to recognition in the home state (nationality) of one of the parties: German Code of Civil Procedure § 606a, para. 1, nos. 2, 4. In the European Union, except Denmark, there is divorce jurisdiction in the Member State, in which the spouses are "habitually resident," were last habitually resident and one of them still is, respondent is habitually resident (or if petitioner is, in the case of a consensual bilateral divorce), among other grounds, as well as in the member state of the spouses' common citizenship (or "domicile" in the case of English or Irish parties, with "domicile" given the common-law meaning of those countries). Art. 3, Council Regulation (EC) 2201/2003, [2003] Official Journal L 338. As does American law, European law thus requires a relationship of some sort to the forum for divorce jurisdic-

tion–even in the case of consensual bilateral divorce. In addition, and contrary to American law, but in keeping with Judge Hastie's suggestion in *Alton,* Europeans also apply "home law," however defined, to the substance of the divorce petition. Exceptions, leading to forum law, apply, inter alia, when "home law" does not permit divorce and the applicant is a forum resident. For brief summary, see Hay, supra § 15.1, n.1, at nn. 60–61.

§ 15.6

1.　317 U.S. 287, 63 S.Ct. 207, 87 L.Ed. 279 (1942).

2.　325 U.S. 226, 65 S.Ct. 1092, 89 L.Ed. 1577 (1945).

3.　Supra § 15.4 n.6.

4.　The Supreme Court decided on the same day that the absent spouse, just like the state of domicile as in *Williams,* may also collaterally attack the *ex parte* divorce. See Esenwein v. Commonwealth of Pennsylvania, 325 U.S. 279, 65 S.Ct. 1118, 89 L.Ed. 1608 (1945).

sister state.[5] The Supreme court's statement, in *Williams II*, that "judicial power to grant a divorce ... is founded on domicil"[6] therefore addressed a question not before it—such as whether North Carolina could constitutionally have withheld recognition if the basis of jurisdiction asserted by Nevada had only been the petitioners' six-weeks' residence. Even if taken together with the Court's decision in *Williams I*, the language quoted falls short of a *holding* that domicile is required for divorce jurisdiction. *Williams I* had held that a court could exercise divorce jurisdiction even though the forum state was not the matrimonial domicile of the parties and that domicile of one spouse was sufficient. *Williams I* did not address the question whether another nexus to the forum might also confer divorce jurisdiction, a question also not before the Court in *Williams II*. The Court's language in *Williams II*, quoted above and oft-repeated in subsequent case law, is therefore—strictly speaking—dictum.[7]

This view of the *Williams* decisions is further supported by the inconsistency in the Court's approach to the question of whether domicile is a federal constitutional concept for the purpose of interstate divorce jurisdiction. If domicile is the required constitutional basis, the Full Faith and Credit Clause would require recognition if there was domicile and other constitutional requirements—that is, those relating to notice and a competent court—were satisfied; denial of recognition would be justified only if no domicile existed; the domicile issue would thus be a *federal question* as part of the full-faith-and-credit requirement and, as such, subject to review by the Supreme Court. Justice Frankfurter recognized this question and wrote in a footnote to his opinion: "Since an appeal to the Full Faith and Credit Clause raises questions under the Constitution ... , the proper criteria for ascertaining domicil, should these be in dispute, become matters for federal determination."[8] Despite the different views of the Nevada and North Carolina courts on the question of petitioner's domicile in Nevada, the Court did not consider "the criteria ... [to] be in dispute," but concluded that " ... we cannot say that North Carolina was not entitled to draw the inference that

---

5. If the proceeding had been *inter partes,* jurisdictional issues which were or could have been litigated will ripen into *res judicata* and may not be reopened collaterally: Treinies v. Sunshine Mining Co., 308 U.S. 66, 60 S.Ct. 44, 84 L.Ed. 85 (1939); American Surety Co. v. Baldwin, 287 U.S. 156, 53 S.Ct. 98, 77 L.Ed. 231 (1932). See also infra § 15.9 n.1 et seq.

6. Williams v. North Carolina, 325 U.S. 226, 229, 65 S.Ct. 1092, 1095, 89 L.Ed. 1577 (1945).

7. The Court cited in support of its statement the earlier decisions in Bell v. Bell, 181 U.S. 175, 21 S.Ct. 551, 45 L.Ed. 804 (1901) and in Andrews v. Andrews, 188 U.S. 14, 23 S.Ct. 237, 47 L.Ed. 366 (1903).

Neither case supports the language in *Williams II*. In *Bell*, the Court equated a statutory requirement of one-year's *bona fide* residence with domicile but also found that the residence requirement had not been satisfied. Similarly, in *Andrews*, the South Dakota divorce in issue had been granted under a statute requiring domicile (as had Nevada's statute in *Williams)*, the Supreme Court's review resulted in the conclusion that the *asserted* bases for jurisdiction had not been satisfied and not in a decision that these bases were improper (residence) or exclusive (domicile).

8. 325 U.S. at 231 n.7, 65 S.Ct. at 1095 n.7.

petitioners never abandoned their domiciles in North Carolina. . . .''[9] The Court, in the absence of an allegation by the parties to the contrary, apparently viewed domicile as a unitary concept—a "historic notion common to all English-speaking courts"[10]—the factual components of which could properly be left to a jury determination. But, as the case itself demonstrated, the unitary concept of domicile, may lead to different results depending on a particular jury's evaluation of the facts. In the Court's view, however, "neither the Fourteenth Amendment nor the Full Faith and Credit Clause . . . requires uniformity in the decisions of the courts of different states as to the place of domicil. . . ."[11] Yet, if domicile is a constitutional requirement derived from due-process considerations, it does seem that a *federal* standard should prevail. In *Williams II* such a standard was not elaborated; at best, the Court adopted the North Carolina standard (or assumed that it was the same as any federal standard) as well as the North Carolina application of this standard; it found that the North Carolina jury had "fairly assessed . . . cogent evidence."[12]

As Justice Rutledge wrote in his dissent in *Williams II*, "domicile . . . combines the essentially contradictory element of permanence and instantaneous change. No legal conception, save possibly 'jurisdiction,' of which it is an elusive substratum, affords such possibilities for uncertain application."[13] Despite such uncertainty the majority required only that North Carolina accord "proper weight," "respect" and "great deference" to the Nevada determination.[14] It is submitted that such an approach would be proper if domicile were only a *permitted* basis for jurisdiction—similar to "doing business"—with the result that different minds could arrive at different evaluations of the facts. In contrast, if domicile is the constitutionally *required* basis for jurisdiction, the *constitutional standard* should not be left to differing definition by the various state courts. The *Williams II* decision is therefore inconclusive, a circumstance which may also explain why the practice of several states—with respect to service personnel, under long-arm statutes, or otherwise—seeks to establish *inter partes* jurisdiction in divorce cases. The jurisdictional pitfalls of the *ex parte* divorce are then avoided.

2. *Domicile and Durational Residence Requirements*

§ 15.7   The U.S. Supreme Court decision in *Sosna v. Iowa*[1] also did not clarify the problem. The issue was the constitutionality of Iowa's requirement of one-year's continuous residence, construed as equivalent to domicile, against the contention that the requirement unconstitution-

---

9. Id. at 237, 65 S.Ct. at 1098.

10. Id. at 234, 65 S.Ct. at 1097.

11. Id. at 231, 65 S.Ct. at 1095 (citing Worcester County Trust Co. v. Riley, 302 U.S. 292, 299, 58 S.Ct. 185, 188, 82 L.Ed. 268 (1937)).

12. Id. at 236, 65 S.Ct. at 1098.

13. Id. at 258, 65 S.Ct. at 1108.

14. Id. at 234, 65 S.Ct. at 1097.

§ 15.7

1. 419 U.S. 393, 95 S.Ct. 553, 42 L.Ed.2d 532 (1975).

ally impaired the right to travel. Noting that divorce often entails other questions, such as support and custody, the Supreme Court upheld the requirement and said: "With consequences of such moment riding on a divorce decree issued by its courts, Iowa may insist that one seeking to initiate such a proceeding have the modicum of attachment to the State required here."[2] The Court did not uphold the residence requirement as a substitute for domicile, because Iowa requires both,[3] but as an additional requirement, designed to assure that the State does not become "a divorce mill for unhappy spouses who have lived there as short a time as appellant."[4] This statement alone would have sufficed, but the Court continued: "Perhaps even more important, Iowa's interests extend beyond its borders and include the recognition of its divorce decrees by other States under the Full Faith and Credit Clause.... *For that purpose,* this Court has often stated that 'judicial power to grant a divorce—jurisdiction strictly speaking—is founded on domicil.' "[5] Domicile as a jurisdictional requirement was not before the Court, the *additional* requirement of a *durational* residence requirement was. Reference to domicile was relevant only insofar as a one-year residence requirement will make it more likely that another state will agree that the petitioner was in fact domiciled in Iowa at the time of the divorce. Domicile was thus only indirectly relevant and, since the case did not involve interstate recognition, the repetition of the *Williams* language was again dictum. Also troubling is the italicized portion of the last quotation, since it implies a difference between the tests for in-state and interstate validity of a divorce, a problem to which we return below.

Read narrowly, *Sosna* only upholds as reasonable the state's imposition of the additional *state* requirement of one-year's durational residence. This requirement is found, in one form or another, in 48 states, with the one-year requirement being the most common.[6] Nevertheless, whether dictum or not, both the majority and one of the dissents[7] (a total of eight Justices) *assumed* that domicile is a jurisdictional requirement but do not address the question whether some other criterion might not also establish a "nexus between person and place of such

---

2. 419 U.S. at 407, 95 S.Ct. at 561.

3. See Korsrud v. Korsrud, 242 Iowa 178, 45 N.W.2d 848 (1951).

4. 419 U.S. at 407, 95 S.Ct. at 561.

5. Id. (emphasis added). Cf. Kurland, The Supreme Court, The Due Process Clause and the In Personam Jurisdiction of State Court, 25 U. Chi. L. Rev. 569, 585 (1958) ("[W]ith the Full Faith and Credit Clause as an overriding principle ... a [jurisdictional] premise [that notions of state sovereignty limit a state's jurisdiction to cases where it had enforcement powers] only puts the question; it does not answer it. The real question becomes not whether a state could itself enforce a judgment, but rather under what circumstances the *na-*

tional power should be used to assist the extraterritorial enforcement of a state's judicial decrees.") (emphasis added).

6. 419 U.S. at 404–05, 95 S.Ct. at 559–60. The exceptions are Louisiana (La. Civ. Code Ann. art. 10) and Washington (Wash. Rev. Code Ann. § 26.09.010) which appear to require domicile only.

Vermont's civil-union legislation expressly refers to the residency requirements applicable to divorce: 15 V.S.A. § 1206 (2003). These provide that no application may be filed until after six months of residency and that no decree may issue until after one year's residency: 15 V.S.A. § 592 (2003).

7. Id. at 424–27, 95 S.Ct. at 569–71 (Marshall and Brennan, JJ., dissenting).

permanence as to control the creation of legal relations and responsibilities of the utmost significance."[8]

C. INTER PARTES DIVORCES

§ 15.8 In an *inter partes* divorce both spouses participate in the proceeding, even though the degree and quality of the "participation" may be very slight, as following discussion will show. The distinction between a divorce *inter partes* and one *ex parte* becomes especially important in two types of cases: when the validity of the divorce is attacked in a second forum for lack of jurisdiction of the court of rendition and when the divorce decree purports to deal with issues "incident" to the dissolution of the status itself, such as alimony, child support and child custody. In an *inter partes* divorce both the determination of jurisdiction of the divorcing court and the adjudication of "incidents" are conclusive under the general principles of preclusion[1] and are entitled to the same effect under the Full Faith and Credit Clause as they enjoy in the state of rendition.[2] In *ex parte* divorces, jurisdiction in the divorcing court remains subject to review in a second state a the discussion of the *Williams* cases[3] showed. An adjudication of "incidents" in an *ex parte* divorce likewise is not conclusive on a second court: this separation of determinations relating to the status itself and of the "incidents" of the status and its dissolution is known as the "divisible divorce" concept and is discussed in another section below. The subsection immediately following gives additional attention to the effect of a collateral decision of invalidity of a divorce in the original state of rendition as well as in other states.

8. Id. at 407, 95 S.Ct. at 561 (quoting from Williams v. North Carolina (II), 325 U.S. 226, 229, 65 S.Ct. 1092, 1094, 89 L.Ed. 1577 (1945)).

The Second Restatement advocates that courts should be able to exercise divorce jurisdiction on close connecting factors other than domicile supra § 15.5 n.3. Despite the Supreme Court's important decision in Shaffer v. Heitner, 433 U.S. 186, 208, 97 S.Ct. 2569, 53 L.Ed.2d 683 (1977) substantially affecting the entire law of jurisdiction, the matter continues to be in doubt. The Court stated in that decision "that jurisdiction over many types of actions which now are or might be brought *in rem* would not be affected by a holding that *any* assertion of state court jurisdiction must satisfy the *International Shoe* standard." (emphasis added). In footnote 30 on that page the Court further stated: "We do not suggest that jurisdictional doctrines other than those discussed in the text, such as the particularized rules governing adjudications of status, are inconsistent with the standard of fairness." See also Garfield, The Transitory Divorce Action: Jurisdiction in

the No–Fault Era, 58 Tex. L. Rev. 501, 546–47 (1980) (the domicile requirement as something approaching a constitutional requirement " . . . is out of step with the way people live today. . . . The most effective solution would be a Uniform Divorce Jurisdiction Act. . . ."). For England, see supra § 15.5 n.2.

§ 15.8

1. See infra Ch. 24.

2. The fact, discussed subsequently, that alimony, support, and custody decrees are ordinarily modifiable in the state of rendition does not detract from the statement in the text: under Full Faith and Credit, F–2 may do what F–1 may or will do, but no more. Uniforms laws, reinforced by additional federal implementing statutes to the Full Faith and Credit Clause, now provide particularized rules with respect to custody and support. See infra § 15.30 et seq.

3. Williams v. North Carolina, 325 U.S. 226, 65 S.Ct. 1092, 89 L.Ed. 1577 (1945); see supra § 15.6.

In an *inter partes* divorce, the decision of the court of rendition as to its jurisdiction is conclusive and not open to collateral attack, save to the extent that the state of rendition itself permits collateral attack and review. This follows from the Full Faith and Credit Clause and the pervasive policy of preclusion.

§ 15.9   In the early case of *Davis v. Davis*,[1] the Supreme Court required the District of Columbia to recognize a Virginia divorce in circumstances in which the wife had "appeared there and by plea put in issue [the husband's] allegation as to domicil, introduced evidence to show it false, took exceptions to the commissioner's report, and sought to have the [Virginia] court sustain them and uphold her plea. Plainly, the determination of the decree upon that point is effective for all purposes of this litigation."[2] In the leading case of *Sherrer v. Sherrer*,[3] the respondent in the Florida divorce proceeding had entered a general appearance and had filed an answer denying the allegations of the complaint, including the allegation as to jurisdictional facts, but had not further challenged them during the proceeding by cross-examination, by offering evidence in rebuttal, or, subsequently, by appealing the adverse ruling. In the companion case of *Coe v. Coe*,[4] the former wife attempted to attack collaterally the divorce granted *her*, on her cross-petition, in Nevada, by alleging lack of jurisdiction in the Nevada court. In both *Sherrer* and *Coe*, the Supreme Court required recognition of the divorce since the parties had been "given *full opportunity* to contest the jurisdictional issues,"[5] even though, unlike in *Davis*, they had not in fact contested these issues. The *Coe* decision is additionally supported by notions of estoppel—that the party who sought and obtained the divorce[6] or subsequently received and accepted benefits from a nondomiciliary divorce[7] may not collaterally seek to impeach the divorce, seek to have it held to be invalid, for alleged jurisdictional defects.

In *Cook v. Cook*,[8] the Supreme Court broadened the test of *Sherrer* and *Coe* and extended the conclusive effect of the prior proceeding on a subsequent collateral attack to a case in which the respondent was merely personally served within the rendering forum and therefore *could have* contested the jurisdictional facts, even though there had not been

§ 15.9

1.   305 U.S. 32, 59 S.Ct. 3, 83 L.Ed. 26 (1938).

2.   Id. at 40, 59 S.Ct. at 6.

3.   334 U.S. 343, 68 S.Ct. 1087, 92 L.Ed. 1429 (1948).

4.   334 U.S. 378, 68 S.Ct. 1094, 92 L.Ed. 1451 (1948).

5.   Id. at 384, 68 S.Ct. at 1096 (emphasis added).

6.   See Diehl v. United States, 438 F.2d 705 (5th Cir.1971), cert. denied 404 U.S. 830, 92 S.Ct. 67, 30 L.Ed.2d 59 (1971); Elliott v. Hardcastle, 271 Ark. 90, 607 S.W.2d 381 (1980); Clagett v. King, 308 A.2d 245 (D.C.App.1973); Scribner v. Scrib-

ner, 556 So.2d 350, 353 (Miss.1990). Contra Costa County ex rel. Petersen v. Petersen, 234 Neb. 418, 451 N.W.2d 390, 393 (1990); Restatement, Second, Conflict of Laws § 74 (1971). See also Clark, Estoppel Against Jurisdictional Attack on Decrees of Divorce, 70 Yale L.J. 45 (1960).

7.   See McCarthy v. McCarthy, 361 Mass. 359, 280 N.E.2d 151 (1972); Camacho v. Camacho, 617 So.2d 685 (Ala.Civ.App. 1992) (former wife estopped to contest jurisdiction to divorce where she benefited by remarriage).

8.   342 U.S. 126, 127–28, 72 S.Ct. 157, 159, 96 L.Ed. 146 (1951).

an appearance. The result of this line of cases—from *Davis* to *Cook*—is that informed consent to jurisdiction of the rendering court will suffice. This consent may be found in the respondent's opportunity—after proper service and notice *or* upon appearance—to contest the jurisdiction. Failure to do so precludes subsequent relitigation of the jurisdictional facts except to the extent that the forum of rendition so permits.[9]

§ 15.10   Despite the development just detailed, courts will draw the line at sham participation or in cases of patent unfairness to a party. As in all cases of issue preclusion, considerations of fairness affect the conclusive effect of prior litigation.[1] Thus, when one party has put in a sham appearance or was represented by counsel retained by the other party, the rule of *Cook* has not been followed.[2] Indeed, the decision of the Supreme Court in *Shaffer v. Heitner*[3] suggests that assertion of *in personam* jurisdiction without sufficient contacts may be unconstitutional.[4]

§ 15.11   No Supreme Court decision has addressed the question whether the state of the previous domicile may contest the validity of an out-of-state *inter partes* divorce, for instance in connection with a prosecution for bigamy. The *Williams* cases, in an *ex parte* context, furnish an example. The Supreme Court in *Williams II* had still asserted that " . . . those not parties to a litigation ought not be foreclosed by the interested actions of others; especially not a State which is concerned with the vindication of its own social policy and has no means . . . to protect the interest against the selfish action of those outside its borders."[1] Subsequent decisions, however, barred other third parties, such as a child[2] or the second spouse,[3] from attacking an *inter partes* divorce. At least as to these third parties, the broad sweep of the *Williams II* language has been restricted, and it may be expected that, despite the language

---

9.   See Ch. 24 for more detailed discussion of preclusion and of the Full–Faith-and-Credit requirement.

§ 15.10

1.   Supra § 15.9 n.9.

2.   Staedler v. Staedler, 6 N.J. 380, 78 A.2d 896 (1951); Day v. Day, 237 Md. 229, 205 A.2d 798 (1965) In re Marriage of Modnick, 33 Cal.3d 897, 191 Cal.Rptr. 629, 663 P.2d 187, 191–197 (1983); Jucker v. Jucker, 190 Conn. 674, 461 A.2d 1384, 1386–87 (1983); Lindsey v. Lindsey, 388 N.W.2d 713, 716 (Minn.1986); Lance v. Lance, 195 Mont. 176, 635 P.2d 571, 574–576 (1981); Clarke v. Clarke, 423 N.W.2d 818, 820–822 (S.D. 1988), appeal after remand 478 N.W.2d 834 (S.D.1991). The Reporter's Note to § 73, Restatement, Second, Conflict of Laws at p. 224 (1971) also considers it doubtful whether such minimal contacts or appearances satisfy constitutional requirements with respect to consent.

3.   Supra § 15.7 n.8.

4.   The Court's careful statement that its decision was not meant to address traditional bases for jurisdiction in status matters, among other areas, goes to the *in rem* nature of *ex parte* divorces, given the *in rem* nature of the *Shaffer* case itself. 433 U.S. 186, 214, 97 S.Ct. 2569, 2585, 53 L.Ed.2d 683 (1977). See also World–Wide Volkswagen Corp. v. Woodson, 444 U.S. 286, 100 S.Ct. 559, 62 L.Ed.2d 490 (1980).

§ 15.11

1.   Williams v. North Carolina II, 325 U.S. 226, 230, 65 S.Ct. 1092, 1095, 89 L.Ed. 1577 (1945).

2.   Johnson v. Muelberger, 340 U.S. 581, 71 S.Ct. 474, 95 L.Ed. 552 (1951); Goldsmith v. Goldsmith, 19 N.Y.2d 939, 281 N.Y.S.2d 344, 228 N.E.2d 400 (1967), cert. denied 389 U.S. 831, 88 S.Ct. 99, 19 L.Ed.2d 90 (1967).

3.   Cook v. Cook, 342 U.S. 126, 72 S.Ct. 157, 96 L.Ed. 146 (1951); Virgil v. Virgil, 55 Misc.2d 64, 284 N.Y.S.2d 568 (1967).

quoted, the same restriction applies to the original state of domicile when the out-of-state divorce was *inter partes,* that is, when the parties had the opportunity to protect and vindicate their own interests. The state's role as a "third party to a marriage," which the *Williams II* language seemed to identify, would then be restricted to the protection of the stay-at-home spouse against unilateral (*ex parte*) actions by the other in a distant forum. The view advocated here is also not affected by the provision of the Uniform Divorce Recognition Act[4] which establishes a presumption of domicile in the original state when the parties were domiciled there immediately before and after obtaining an out-of-state divorce. When both parties participated in the out-of-state divorce, full faith and credit attaches to the preclusive effect of the out-of-state decree, according to the *rendering forum's* standards of preclusion, and no legislation by the original home state, for instance in the form of the Uniform Divorce Recognition Act, can overcome this *constitutionally* mandated effect for itself or for the benefit of other third parties.

D. THE EFFECT OF A COLLATERAL DETERMINATION OF INVALIDITY

§ **15.12** There is still some uncertainty in the case law concerning the effect, in the original state of the rendition of a divorce, of a collateral determination of invalidity in another. Illustratively, must Nevada accord recognition to the North Carolina decision in *Williams,* above, or may it treat the Nevada divorce as valid *in Nevada?* It is obvious that uniformity of the effect of decisions and avoidance of "limping marriages" is desirable: "If there is one thing that the people are entitled to expect from their lawmakers, it is rules of law that will enable individuals to tell whether they are married and, if so, to whom."[1]

---

4. Uniform Divorce Recognition Act § 2(a), 9 U.L.A. 641, 661 (1979). See Comment, Statutory Presumptions of Domicile in Divorce: Full Faith and Credit and Due Process, 67 Colum. L. Rev. 1320 (1967). In refusing to recognize a Dominican Republic divorce in application of the Uniform Act, the Nebraska Supreme Court also said: "The state is impliedly a party to the marriage contract and has an interest in the continuance and dissolution of the marital relation." Weber v. Weber, 200 Neb. 659, 265 N.W.2d 436, 440 (1978). The same result was reached, on quite similar facts, in Slessinger v. Secretary of Health & Human Services, 835 F.2d 937, 940–43 (1st Cir. 1987 (construing Rhode Island law). See also Dobesh v. Dobesh, 216 Neb. 196, 342 N.W.2d 669, 671 (1984) (court, "state," may make orders for the distribution of property where the agreement between the parties is unconscionable); Robinson v. Robinson, 778 So.2d 1105, 1117 (La. 2001) (refusal to recognize North Carolina's distribution of marital property in view of

Louisiana's strong interest). See also infra § 15.20 nn.7, 9–10.

§ 15.12

1. Estin v. Estin, 334 U.S. 541, 553, 68 S.Ct. 1213, 1220, 92 L.Ed. 1561 (1948) (Jackson, J., dissenting). Similarly, in overruling *Haddock* and adopting the rule that divorce jurisdiction exists at the separate domicile of *each* spouse, Justice Douglas wrote for the majority in Williams v. North Carolina I, 317 U.S. 287, 299, 63 S.Ct. 207, 213, 87 L.Ed. 279 (1942): "But if one is lawfully divorced and remarried in Nevada and still married to the first spouse in North Carolina, an even more complicated and serious condition would be realized.... [A] man would have two wives, a wife two husbands. The reality of a sentence to prison proves that that is no mere play on words. Each would be a bigamist for living in one state with the only one with whom the other state would permit him lawfully to live."

Yet in *Colby v. Colby*, Nevada refused to recognize a Maryland decree holding a prior Nevada divorce decree invalid. The Nevada court reasoned that petitioner "does not ask us to merely accord full faith and credit to the Maryland decree. Instead, we are asked to give it greater credit and respect then the prior decree of our own State lawfully entered. Full faith and credit does not require, nor does it contemplate, such action from us."[2] Although the decision found some support in the literature,[3] it is not only unfortunate policy but also bad law. The full-faith-and-credit requirement is not relative: it requires the second state to give the same effect to a valid sister state decree as the decree enjoys there. In *Sutton v. Leib*,[4] decided ten years before *Colby*, the U.S. Supreme Court required Illinois to give full faith and credit to a New York decision annulling a Nevada marriage on the ground that a prior Nevada divorce was invalid and the party therefore had a spouse living at the time of the attempted remarriage. The New York Court of Appeals had noted that "it appears assumed that the [Nevada divorce] decree is valid and binding in the state where it is rendered."[5] In reversing and remanding the Illinois refusal to recognize the New York annulment, the Supreme Court addressed this point: "This leads us to hold the conclusion of the Court of Appeals . . . is incorrect under the facts of this case. The marriage ceremony performed . . . must be held invalid because [the party] then had a living [spouse]. The New York annulment held the marriage void."[6] The New York decree annulling the marriage " . . . is entitled to full faith throughout the Nation, *in Nevada as well as in Illinois*."[7]

The Nevada court in *Colby* distinguished *Sutton*. It asserted that "in holding that the Illinois federal court must give full faith and credit to the New York annulment decree (and stating, by dictum, that Nevada would have to do the same), *the Supreme Court did not indicate that . . . [the] Nevada divorce was not valid in Nevada*. That question was not presented for decision."[8] Yet it is difficult to see how, at least indirectly, the "question was not presented [or necessary] for [the] decision" since, as the Supreme Court noted, the annulment would be valid only if the divorce was not. The conclusion therefore must be that the sister state

---

2. 78 Nev. 150, 157, 369 P.2d 1019, 1023 (1962), cert. denied 371 U.S. 888, 83 S.Ct. 186, 9 L.Ed.2d 122 (1962). This rationale was adopted in Jensen v. Barnes, 33 Colo.App. 333, 519 P.2d 1223, 1224 (1974). See also Kessler v. Fauquier National Bank, 195 Va. 1095, 81 S.E.2d 440, cert. denied 348 U.S. 834, 75 S.Ct. 57, 99 L.Ed. 658 (1954). But see Southard v. Southard, 305 F.2d 730 (2d Cir.1962) (giving conclusive effect to Connecticut decision holding husband's prior Nevada divorce to be void).

3. See Foster, Recognition of Migratory Divorces: Rosenstiel v. Section 250, 43 N.Y.U. L. Rev. 429, 433 (1968); cf. Powell, And Repent at Leisure, 58 Harv. L. Rev. 930, 936 (1945).

4. 342 U.S. 402, 72 S.Ct. 398, 96 L.Ed. 448 (1952).

5. Sutton v. Leib, 188 F.2d 766, 768 (7th Cir.1951).

6. Sutton v. Leib, 342 U.S. 402, 409, 72 S.Ct. 398, 403, 96 L.Ed. 448 (1952).

7. Id. at 408, 72 S.Ct. at 402 (emphasis added). The Court cited specifically to Treinies v. Sunshine Mining Co., 308 U.S. 66, 60 S.Ct. 44, 84 L.Ed. 85 (1939). That decision is discussed infra §§ 24.2, 24.10.

8. Colby v. Colby, 78 Nev. 150, 157, 369 P.2d 1019, 1022–23 (1962) (emphasis in original).

decree—in *Colby,* the Maryland determination—is entitled to recognition everywhere, including in the original state of rendition, to the extent that it was rendered by a court with jurisdiction over the parties and the subject matter.[9] The recourse against a wrong decision lies in appeal. Unless appealed, the decision is entitled to the same preclusive effect as it enjoys in the state of rendition; collateral attack is precluded.[10] The fact that, as in *Colby,* an appeal or certiorari was sought but not granted, does not alter the result. States are not free to accord or withhold recognition on the policy grounds invoked in *Colby.*[11] "[T]he Full Faith and Credit Clause puts the Constitution behind a judgment instead of the too fluid, ill-defined concept of 'comity'."[12]

§ **15.13** The problem raised by the Nevada decision in *Colby* and addressed by the Supreme Court's decision in *Sutton v. Leib*—"who is married to whom"—must be distinguished from other issues which also arise from a collateral determination of the invalidity of a divorce but do

---

9. The Nevada court distinguished *Colby* in its decision in Farnham v. Farnham, 80 Nev. 180, 391 P.2d 26 (1964) in which it accorded recognition to an Arizona money judgment for alimony which had accrued under a Michigan divorce decree. The Michigan decree, in turn, had been entered after, and presumably in disregard of, a prior ex parte Nevada divorce. The Nevada court held that the Arizona court had jurisdiction over the parties, that Nevada could not "look behind a foreign money judgment" (citing to Fauntleroy v. Lum, 210 U.S. 230, 28 S.Ct. 641, 52 L.Ed. 1039 (1908), (discussed infra § 24.20), and that the Michigan judgment did "not purport to set aside the earlier Nevada . . . decree." In addition, the Nevada decree had been "silent on the question of alimony." Nevada as well as other courts thus were left free to decide alimony questions separately. "Colby has nothing whatever to do with divisible divorce doctrine." 391 P.2d at 27 (1964). The language quoted therefore does not support the view that "Nevada . . . partially withdrew from . . . [Colby] in Farnham . . ." See also Haws v. Haws, 96 Nev. 727, 615 P.2d 978, 980 (1980)(California judgment susceptible to collateral attack in Nevada to extent it may be attacked in Calif.). Leflar, McDougal & Felix, American Conflicts Law 243 n.8 (4th ed. 1986).

10. For additional discussion of the full-faith-and-credit requirement and the policy of preclusion see infra §§ 24.1–24.2.

11. See Baker v. General Motors Corp., 522 U.S. 222, 118 S.Ct. 657, 664, 139 L.Ed.2d 580 (1998) (Supreme Court interpretation of the Full Faith and Credit Clause "support[s] no roving 'public policy exception'"to the enforcement of sister-state judgments); see also Borchers, *Baker*

v. General Motors: Implications for Interjurisdictional Recognition of Non–Traditional Marriages, 32 Creighton L. Rev. 147, 173–79 (1998) (discussing *Baker*'s rejection of any public policy defense to the enforcement of judgments).

12. Williams v. North Carolina II, 325 U.S. 226, 228, 65 S.Ct. 1092, 1094, 89 L.Ed. 1577 (1945). The New Hampshire Supreme Court reached the right result in Braun v. Braun, 116 N.H. 714, 366 A.2d 484 (1976) but for the wrong reason. In that case, the husband filed for and obtained a Maryland divorce after the wife had obtained a divorce in New Hampshire. The wife had appeared to contest jurisdiction in Maryland and later litigated the merits of the case there. The New Hampshire court noted that all of the couple's property was located in Maryland and that the Maryland court had divided it equally. It then noted that the full-faith-and-credit requirement sets only minimum standards for recognition and that New Hampshire was therefore free to accord greater effect: the Court recognized the Maryland decree as a matter of "comity." As the discussion in the text suggests, the fact that both parties litigated Maryland's jurisdiction and the substantive issues in Maryland entitled the resulting decree to recognition in New Hampshire and elsewhere under the Full Faith and Credit Clause, even if it should have wrongly disregarded a prior New Hampshire determination. Recognition was required. Both the reference to comity and to the location of property are inapposite, the latter because it introduces notions of *forum conveniens* or choice-of-law ("most significant relationship") which are not relevant to the issues of whether jurisdiction was asserted within constitutional limits or of recognition.

not relate to the *status* of the parties. Thus, the conclusions reached above with respect to *Colby* would not preclude Nevada from according or denying inheritance rights to Nevada property to a Nevada divorcee despite a finding elsewhere that the Nevada divorce was invalid and the party therefore a "widow" rather than a "divorcee." So long as Nevada treats in-state and out-of-state parties equally it has the power to adopt whatever rules it pleases for intestate succession to local property, a question which has nothing to do with the determination of the status for *status purposes*.[1]

Similarly, there may be differences between the parties' *status* as married or divorced for tax purposes. Thus, the Second Circuit held in the leading case of *Estate of Borax v. Commissioner*[2] that payments made to a wife after a Mexican divorce and remarriage to another were properly deductible as alimony for federal income tax purposes despite a determination by a New York court, upon full litigation of the issues, that the Mexican divorce was invalid. Judge Friendly, citing to *Sutton v. Leib*, dissented on the ground that the New York "judgment not only is binding in New York but is entitled to recognition in every state, as indeed it would be if the challenged divorce had been granted by a sister state."[3] Nevertheless, the Second Circuit adhered to the view of the majority in *Borax* in its 1976 *Spalding* decision in which it allowed the marital deduction to the estate of the purported wife of a New York resident despite a New York determination that his Nevada divorce from his previous wife was invalid because California, the place of the decedent's domicile, had not declared the Nevada divorce and subsequent remarriage to be invalid.[4] The Court quoted Judge (now Justice) Marshall's language in *Borax* that "by depriving the determination of invalidity [of the divorce, the *status* decision] of any federal tax significance *the rule of validation* avoids a measure of unevenness and uncertainty: all those taxpayers who have obtained a divorce ... are treated the same, regardless of whether the spouse against whom the decree has been obtained is able to, and does, invoke the power of another jurisdiction to declare the divorce invalid."[5]

A few days later the Second Circuit upheld the Tax Court's decision denying the marital deduction to the second wife of a New York decedent whose prior Mexican divorce had been held invalid in New York (*Gold-*

---

1. See Weintraub, Commentary on the Conflict of Laws 304–05 (4th ed. 2001). See also Sutton v. Leib, 342 U.S. 402, 409, 72 S.Ct. 398, 403, 96 L.Ed. 448 (1952)("The determination that the New York adjudications must be given full faith and credit in Illinois, however, does not decide this controversy.... [A] question of *state law* remains. Does Illinois give the marriage ceremony of an annulled marriage sufficient vitality to release Leib, the respondent, from his obligation to pay alimony subse-quently due?")(emphasis added). For an international example see supra § 13.3 n.3.

2. 349 F.2d 666 (2d Cir.1965), cert. denied 383 U.S. 935, 86 S.Ct. 1064, 15 L.Ed.2d 852 (1966). See also Wondsel v. Commissioner, 350 F.2d 339 (2d Cir.1965).

3. 349 F.2d at 676 (2d Cir. 1965).

4. Estate of Spalding, 537 F.2d 666 (2d Cir.1976).

5. 349 F.2d at 670 (2d Cir. 1965)(emphasis added).

water).[6] The Court reconciled this decision with its decision in *Spalding,* above, by making the cases turn on whether the determination of the invalidity of the prior divorce had been made by the state of the *decedent's domicile* or by another state. The Seventh Circuit similarly deferred to the state of the *decedent's domicile* in deciding a marital deduction issue, in this case disallowing the deduction since a court of that state had previously held the foreign divorce invalid (*Steffke*).[7] The court referred to *Sutton,* but the facts leave it unclear whether *Sutton* would have applied if a state other than the state of the decedent's domicile had made the determination of invalidity or whether, in contrast, the case would then have been governed by the *Borax* "rule of validation." The *Borax* rule was expressly rejected by the Ninth Circuit in 1977 in *Lee v. Commissioner* which noted that "to provide a federal tax law of marriage would create greater confusion in divorce courts than now exists. Some individuals would be validly married for all purposes except federal taxes, and others validly married for federal tax purposes only."[8] However, the decision in this case is not as contrary to *Borax* and subsequent Second Circuit decisions as the quoted language would indicate. The case involved the ability of parties to file a joint federal income tax return at the time when they were California domiciliaries and in circumstances when California refused to recognize the validity of a prior Mexican divorce. It is therefore possible, on the facts, to reconcile *Lee* with *Goldwater* and *Steffke.*

The discussion of these cases illustrates the earlier conclusion that the *Sutton* rule with respect to the determination of a person's *status* and the recognition that the Full Faith and Credit Clause requires to be accorded that determination by other states need not necessarily carry over into areas which, strictly speaking, are not status questions. It becomes rather a question of tax policy, in the cases just reviewed, whether a "rule of validation" should be adopted for the protection of the second spouse *(Borax)*, whether the allowance of a marital deduction to a "surviving spouse," and the concomitant determination of whether someone qualifies as a "spouse" for *that purpose,* should be regarded as a question concerning the administration of estates and therefore be referred to the law and judicial action of the decedent's domiciliary state *(Spalding, Goldwater)*, or whether status has a *unitary* meaning and effect. These problems will be considered further in Section IV(A), below, which deals with the "divisible divorce" concept.

---

6. Estate of Goldwater, 539 F.2d 878 (2d Cir.1976), cert. denied sub nom. Lipkowitz v. Commissioner, 429 U.S. 1023, 97 S.Ct. 641, 50 L.Ed.2d 624 (1976). For discussion of the *Borax* and *Goldwater* decisions see also Note, The Haitian Vacation: The Applicability of Sham Doctrine to Year–End Divorces, 77 Mich. L. Rev. 1332, 1341–44 (1979).

7. Estate of Steffke, 538 F.2d 730 (7th Cir.1976), cert. denied sub nom. Wisconsin Valley Trust Co. v. Commissioner, 429 U.S. 1022, 97 S.Ct. 639, 50 L.Ed.2d 624 (1976).

8. 550 F.2d 1201 (9th Cir.1977). See also Felt v. Commissioner, T.C. Memo 1987–465 (U.S.Tax Ct.1987) (foreign divorce valid, even if doubtful under state law, until declared invalid by a court in application of the "rule of validation" of *Borax*).

E. CONCLUSION AND OUTLOOK

§ 15.14 *Ex parte* divorces are subject to collateral attack on jurisdictional grounds, absent estoppel. If jurisdiction for an *ex parte* divorce was based on traditional domicile of one party, supported by the evidence, the divorce is entitled to recognition. However, with no clear resolution of the question of whether domicile is constitutionally required as the basis for jurisdiction, the validity of *ex parte* divorces with a jurisdictional basis less substantive than domicile may often remain in doubt. In view of the declining state interest in marriage and the increasing focus on the parties and their litigation of the issues, it may well be that the Supreme Court would sustain a residential relationship to the divorcing forum of a reasonable duration as adequate to support the application of local law and policy, so long as the absent spouse received proper notice. Such a development is particularly likely in view of the adoption of no-fault dissolution of marriage. This development, which essentially recognizes dissolution by consent, will also reduce the incentive to seek an out-of-state *ex parte* divorce, especially since such a proceeding will leave other issues (support, custody) unresolved.[1] *Inter partes* divorces, rendered in the domiciliary state, will now be the rule; *ex parte* divorces will remain in the case of the deserting spouse. In the latter case, the abandoned spouse will ordinarily satisfy all local jurisdictional requirements except in circumstances of desertion shortly after a change of domicile, such as in *Sosna*.[2]

The rule of *Sherrer* and *Cook*[3] precludes collateral attack of an *inter partes* divorce. If consensual, as most *inter partes* divorces are, especially in a no-fault situation, it then becomes irrelevant whether the jurisdictional basis for the divorce was domicile, the residence standard of service personnel statutes,[4] or another criterion evidencing a close connection as envisioned by the Second Restatement.[5]

Durational residence requirements vary. To the extent that they are short or not invoked, *inter partes* divorces may in fact be granted by courts with little connection to the marriage, a development quite contrary to the rationale underlying the traditional concepts. The late Judge Hastie had therefore urged that any abandonment of domicile requirements or, stated differently, divorce on a purely consensual, *in personam* basis, be accompanied by the use of a law other than forum law.[6] This might be the law of the last matrimonial domicile or some other law more closely connected to the marriage than the forum.

§ 15.14

1. See the discussion of "divisible divorce," infra § 15.27, n.1 et seq.

2. Supra § 15.7 n.1 et seq.

3. Supra § 15.9 nn.3, 8.

4. Supra § 15.5 n.2.

5. Supra § 15.5 n.3.

6. Alton v. Alton, 207 F.2d 667 (3d Cir. 1953) (Hastie, J., dissenting). See also Restatement, Second, Conflict of Laws § 285, cmnt. (d) (1971); Baade, Marriage and Divorce in American Conflicts Law: Governmental–Interest Analysis and the Restatement (Second), 72 Colum. L. Rev. 329, 334 (1972); Garfield, The Transitory Divorce Action: Jurisdiction in the No–Fault Era, 58 Tex. L. Rev. 501, 535–39 (1980).

Differentiation between jurisdiction and applicable law in divorce is common in civil law countries and appropriate whenever divorce jurisdiction is based on essentially transient jurisdiction. With today's no-fault divorce and the decreasing incentive to shop for a more favorable substantive divorce law, Judge Hastie's suggestion is no longer so important as it once was in the U.S. interstate setting.[7] It is still relevant for international cases, to be considered subsequently.

II.   ANNULMENT IN THE UNITED STATES

§ 15.15   As noted in an introductory section,[1] divorce and annulment sometimes overlap because a particular ground may support an action for divorce in one state while serving as the basis for annulment in another, because annulment does not always operate *ab initio,* and because the decree may also give rise to support obligations. As a result, divorce and annulment are at times alternative modes for the termination of a "marriage" or a civil union.

There is uniform agreement that a state may annul a marriage in circumstances in which it has jurisdiction to grant a divorce. These include the domicile of both parties,[2] the domicile of one spouse,[3] and personal jurisdiction over both spouses.[4] Additionally, a majority of states and the Second Restatement support jurisdiction in the state of celebration of the marriage, provided that there is personal jurisdiction over the defendant.[5] Analytically, the last two jurisdictional bases are the

---

7.   The text suggests by implication that Judge Hastie's proposal should perhaps continue to be considered in circumstances where the divorce is not consensual and jurisdiction is based on connecting factors less than domicile. Since an *inter partes* divorce may also determine issues of alimony, support, custody and the like, it appears appropriate that a nondomiciliary forum should, at least with respect to those issues, apply a law more closely connected with those issues than its own.

Baade, supra n.6, at 340, takes the position that a "state that grants non-fault divorces to one spouse over the objections of the other should recognize all foreign ex parte divorces of its domiciliaries." As subsequent discussion with respect to the "divisible divorce" concept will show in further detail (infra at § 15.27, n.3), the foreign *ex parte* divorce only determines the *status* of the parties but does not adjudicate other issues such as support and custody. Baade's suggestion that the foreign ex parte divorce should be recognized without further inquiry, when essentially the same result could have been obtained at home, is thus not at variance with the distinction drawn in the preceding paragraph and is in accord with the basic position adopted in the text.

§ 15.15

1.   Supra § 15.2 nn.1–2. In Vermont, the rules for marriage annulment and divorce apply equally to civil unions: 15 V.S.A. §§ 1204(d), 1206.

2.   Sutton v. Leib, 342 U.S. 402, 72 S.Ct. 398, 96 L.Ed. 448 (1952). Compare Wrigley v. Wrigley, 99 Wis.2d 802, 300 N.W.2d 81 (1980).

3.   Shima v. Shima, 130 F.2d 809 (D.C.Cir.1942); Whealton v. Whealton, 67 Cal.2d 656, 63 Cal.Rptr. 291, 432 P.2d 979 (1967) (dictum); L.v.L., 414 A.2d 510 (Del. 1980) (applying Del.C. § 1504(a)); Manndorff v. Dax, 13 Conn.App. 282, 285, 535 A.2d 1324 (1998).

4.   Whealton v. Whealton, 67 Cal.2d 656, 63 Cal.Rptr. 291, 432 P.2d 979 (1967). The holding of this case follows, by analogy, from the *Sherrer* rule, supra § 15.9, n.3, and finds independent support in the choice-of-law rule in annulment which refers to a single (not necessarily forum) law, infra at § 15.16, n.1ff. Cf. Brawer v. Pinkins, 164 Misc.2d 1018, 626 N.Y.S.2d 674 (Sup. Ct. N.Y. 1995).

5.   Restatement, Second, Conflict of Laws § 76(b) (1971); see also Reporter's Note.

same; the difference lies in a possible change in the applicable law, to be discussed below. Whether other "close connecting factors" also make for annulment jurisdiction is as open a question as it is for divorce.[6] As in divorce, the extent of interstate recognition due to a sister state's annulment decree depends on the propriety of the exercise of jurisdiction by the rendering court.[7]

§ 15.16   There has long been considerable uncertainty as to the law applicable to annulment. This difficulty results from the fact that, conceptually, annulment addresses defects in the marriage existing at the time of celebration rather than the subsequent conduct of the parties. Consequently, and despite the overlap between annulment and divorce observed earlier, the law of the forum, even if the parties are now local domiciliaries, may be an inappropriate choice for the annulment of a marriage celebrated elsewhere. The modern view therefore favors the application of the law where the marriage was contracted.[1] This rule encompasses not only marriages celebrated according to traditional civil or religious proceedings[2] but also marriages by proxy[3] and common law marriages.[4]

The rule may appropriately be different if an annulment is sought for defects other than those recognized by the law of celebration. Thus, a

---

6. The Restatement, Second, supports this basis in § 76(b) by reference to the state whose law is to be applied in accordance with §§ 283(1), 286. The latter, in turn, specifies the law of the state of "most significant relationship." The Restatement, however, further requires that this state also have personal jurisdiction over the defendant which, again, makes this jurisdictional basis blend into those discussed supra nn.4 and 5. The question is unanswered whether a close connection of *one* spouse, short of domicile, makes for *ex parte* annulment jurisdiction.

7. Sutton v. Leib, 342 U.S. 402, 72 S.Ct. 398, 96 L.Ed. 448 (1952); Wrigley v. Wrigley, 99 Wis.2d 802, 300 N.W.2d 81 (1980).

§ 15.16

1. Whealton v. Whealton, 67 Cal.2d 656, 63 Cal.Rptr. 291, 432 P.2d 979 (1967); Brawer v. Pinkins, 164 Misc.2d 1018, 626 N.Y.S.2d 674 (1995). The Second Restatement reaches the same result by specifying the law which "determines the validity of the marriage." Restatement, Second, Conflict of Laws § 286 (1971). That law, in turn, is said to be *inter alia* the law of the state where the marriage was contracted. Id. § 283(2).

2. Annulment is at times but another aspect of the recognition (or nonrecognition) of a marriage. Thus, in an unusual case in New York, a husband's defense in a support action brought by his wife sought a

dismissal on the ground that the present marriage was void for bigamy because the wife had previously married another man in a Roman Catholic ceremony in Poland and never obtained a divorce. The court found that Poland does not recognize religious marriages, that such non-recognition does not offend New York public policy since several Western European countries also require civil ceremonies in addition to (optional) religious ceremonies for a valid marriage, that the status of a Western European country's marriage would be accepted by New York in accordance with the law of celebration, and that no reason therefore existed to apply different standards to Polish law and practice. The wife's prior religious marriage, in application of Polish law, therefore had not been validly contracted; consequently, her present marriage to the defendant was not bigamous and not void. Matter of Bronislawa K. v. Tadeusz K., 90 Misc.2d 183, 393 N.Y.S.2d 534 (1977); Hassan v. Hassan, 2001 WL 1329840 (2001).

3. In re Valente's Will, 18 Misc.2d 701, 188 N.Y.S.2d 732 (Sur. 1959); In re Blankenship, 133 B.R. 398 (Bankr. N.D. Ohio 1991); Farah v. Farah, 16 Va.App. 329, 429 S.E.2d 626, 629 (1993).

4. See Bloch v. Bloch, 473 F.2d 1067 (3d Cir.1973); In re Reed's Marriage, 226 N.W.2d 795 (Iowa 1975); Matter of Lamb's Estate, 99 N.M. 157, 655 P.2d 1001, 1002–1003 (1982); Matter of Estate of Foster, 180 W.Va. 250, 376 S.E.2d 144, 147–149 (1988).

marriage may presumably be annulled according to the law of the parties' domicile even if valid under the law of the state of celebration, for instance when the marriage was celebrated there in evasion of the domiciliary law. An example is the Uniform Marriage Evasion Act which, although withdrawn by the Commissioners on Uniform State Laws, continues to be in force in a few states.[5] A different choice of law may also be indicated when the annulment is not sought by one of the parties to the marriage but by a third party—a parent, a child, or an heir—all of which may make considerations relevant which are additional to, or different from, those under the law of celebration. These special cases, involving a strong interest or policy of a state other than the state of celebration, are recognized by the Second Restatement when it advocates a reference to the law of the state which has "the most significant relationship to the spouses and the marriage."[6]

The consequences of annulment, as in divorce, may also be determined by a law other than the law governing the annulment. In the simple case of an annulment in the state of celebration of the marriage and domicile of the parties, all issues will be governed by the law of the forum. On the other hand, if annulment is sought *ex parte* at the domicile of one of the parties, concepts akin to that of "divisible divorce"[7] may apply in order to protect an absent spouse in his or her property rights under the law of the state of celebration or another applicable law. The necessity for such splitting of the choice-of-law reference or of the status decision and the adjudication of the incidents of the status is readily apparent in those cases where an applicable law makes provisions for post-annulment support, when a property settlement must be made or custody of children be determined.

III. INTERNATIONAL RECOGNITION OF DISSOLUTION DECREES

A. RECOGNITION OF FOREIGN–COUNTRY JUDICIAL DIVORCES IN THE UNITED STATES

§ 15.17 The full-faith-and-credit requirement of United States domestic law does not apply to foreign decrees. Moreover, foreign legal

---

5. 9A U.L.A. XXI (1965); 750 Ill. Comp. Stat. 5/216 (1993). For similar legislation see Mass. Gen. Laws Ann. c. 207, § 10 (1981); 15 Vt. Stat. Ann. § 5 (1989); Wash. Rev. Code Ann. § 765.04; Wis. Stat. Ann. 765.04 (1981). See also Laikola v. Engineered Concrete, 277 N.W.2d 653, 655–58 (Minn.1979) ("cohabitation and holding out as husband and wife must be of sufficient duration in the common law state to create a public reputation of husband and wife"). Conversely, the section permits the forum to validate a marriage under its or a third state's law in appropriate cases even though the marriage may not have been valid, or be defective, in the state of celebration. See Bloch v. Bloch, 473 F.2d 1067 (3d Cir.1973);

Bowlin v. Bowlin, 55 N.C.App. 100, 285 S.E.2d 273 (1981). But cf. Vandever v. Industrial Commission, 148 Ariz. 373, 714 P.2d 866 (App.1985) (requiring a stay of some duration in validating state).

6. Restatement, Second, Conflict of Laws § 283(1) (1971). This section by its own terms refers more directly to cases involving the *validity* of a marriage rather than annulment. Nevertheless, § 286, particularly comment (a), which deals with annulment (in combination with § 76), incorporates § 283 by reference. See also supra n.2. For additional discussion see supra § 13.2.

7. Infra § 15.27 n.1 et seq.

systems, especially those of the civil law orbit, may not base jurisdiction for divorce on notions of domicile.[1] Similarly, they also may not apply the *law of the forum* but may find the applicable law by reference to the law of *nationality* of the parties or one of them.[2] Originally, there may not have been much difference between a reference to the domiciliary or national law since nationality usually coincided with domicile. In the highly mobile societies of modern Western Europe, this is no longer the case. Large numbers of people now live and work in countries other than the country of their nationality with which they nevertheless retain close ties and to which they frequently return. The reference to the substantive law of the country of nationality today thus serves to guard against the dangers of migratory divorces.[3] At the same, alternative references, such as under the new German statute, to the law of habitual residence, facilitate divorce in a state with which the parties have become closely connected.

The introduction of (same-sex) civil unions in many European countries,[4] may vary the rules for their dissolution from those applicable

§ 15.17

1. In the European Union—except Denmark, which opted out—Council Regulation (EC) 2201/2003 on Jurisdiction and Recognition of Judgments in Matrimonial Matters and in Matters of Parental Responsibility [2003] Official Journal L 338/1, provides for jurisdiction in the courts of the member state where both spouses are now habitually resident, were last habitually resident together and one spouse still is, where either spouse is habitually resident and both seek the divorce, or, in the case of an ex parte divorce, where the applicant is habitually resident, defined as having lived there for at least one year immediately preceding. A national (or in the case of the United Kingdom, a domiciliary) need is "habitually resident" if he or she has lived in the state for a minimum of six months. Art. 3. The provision thus seeks to identify, on the basis of various connecting factors, a state with a relationship to one or both of the parties sufficient to warrant the exercise of divorce jurisdiction. It is the *exclusive* basis for divorce jurisdiction when the respondent is either habitually resident or a national of a member state. Art. 6. Resulting judgments are entitled to recognition in all other member states. Art. 21 et seq.

When Art. 2 does not apply, national law continues to define divorce jurisdiction, but the ensuing decree will not be entitled to automatic recognition in other EU states. Under *German* law, for instance, a court has jurisdiction if at least one of the spous-

es is a German citizen or was a German citizen at the time of marriage, if both parties are habitually resident in Germany (same as under the Regulation), and, subject to an exception, if only one of them was so resident. See German Code of Civil Procedure (ZPO) § 606a. In the case of *England*, there is no divergence between national law and the Regulation: there is divorce jurisdiction if either party was "habitually resident" in England "throughout the period of one year." Domicile and Matrimonial Proceedings Act § 5(2) (1973).

2. For *Germany*, see Art. 17(I)(1) in combination with Art. 14(I) EGBGB, as revised (1986). Art. 14 provides alternative references, listed in order of priority, and proceeding from the law of the parties' common nationality, to the law of their common (or last joint) habitual residence, to a law chosen by the parties (subject to conditions), and so forth. See also Lüderitz, 1987 IPRax 74; Hay, 1989 IPRax 197. For *France*, see H. Batiffol & P. Lagarde, 2 Droit international privé 79 ff. (7th ed. 1981). Some legal systems claim exclusive divorce jurisdiction when both parties are nationals of the particular country. A reference to the law of nationality by another forum, even if now the domicile or habitual residence of the parties, then leads to the undesirable conclusion that the forum lacks jurisdiction. See comment by Samtleben, [1982] IPRax 119.

3. Judge Hastie made a similar suggestion for American law. See supra § 15.14 n.6.

to divorce. In Germany, for instance, a civil union is also dissolved by judicial decree, but the applicable law is the substantive law of the state where the union was registered.[5] A bilateral dissolution will be decreed on the basis of a mutual declaration by the parties to this effect after a year's waiting period has elapsed.[6] "Domicile," in the American sense is not required for a bilateral or an *ex parte* divorce. This circumstance has never prevented the recognition of European dissolutions of marriages (divorce). Nothing different should obtain the case of dissolution of civil unions. The impediment will rather lie in the impediment which the Defense of Marriage Act (DOMA)[7] represents to the recognition of the civil union (or, for that matter, to a same-sex marriage) in the first place and, as a logical result, of its "dissolution" and of the consequences of the latter, such as support and custody rights. It is with respect to the consequences of dissolution that the recognition problem is likely to arise.[8]

These differences in jurisdictional bases and applicable law pose some problems for the recognition of a foreign divorce (or dissolution of a foreign civil union) in the United States. To American courts, under traditional doctrines, the substantive law applied by the foreign court is not relevant.[9] Since an American court would have applied forum law in a local proceeding, it would accept a foreign court's use of its own law and, conversely, not be inclined to grant recognition to a foreign divorce just because the foreign court applied American substantive law.[10] For the American court the most important question will rather be whether the foreign court had jurisdiction. In the U.S. interstate setting, a jurisdictional inquiry is relevant only if the out-of-state divorce was *ex parte*;[11] under the principles of *Sherrer, Coe* and *Cook*[12] a collateral attack

---

4. See supra § 13.19.

5. See Introductory Law to the Civil Code (EGBGB) Art. 17b (1). For the law applicable to divorce, see supra n. 2.

6. Law on Registered Domestic Partnerships (Gesetz über die Eingetragene Lebenspartnerschaft–LPartG), as amended, Bundesgesetzblatt 2001, I, 3513, § 15(2) No. 1. An *ex parte* dissolution requires a three-year waiting period from the date that petitioner has notified his or her partner of the wish to discontinue the partnership.

7. See supra at § 13.19 and infra § 15.21 n.6.

8. See also infra at § 15.21 n.6.

9. But see Gould v. Gould, 235 N.Y. 14, 138 N.E. 490 (1923).

10. The American emphasis on jurisdiction and the application of local law to divorce may enable a foreign court to apply its own law by accepting the renvoi. See supra §§ 3.13–3.14. To illustrate: the foreign conflicts rule refers to the party's law

of nationality, in the case of an American presumably the law of his last American domicile. That law contains no choice-of-law provisions for divorce; rather, it is implicit that the American court would use its own substantive law if it had jurisdiction in the matter. The foreign court thus may inquire whether, under American law, it has jurisdiction and, if so, *derive* from its *jurisdiction* a reference to its own substantive law as the applicable law. Use of its own law will have no effect on the recognition of the decree in the United States, yet obviously be easier than a need to research and apply unfamiliar foreign (American) law. This "hidden renvoi" has been used in Austria, Germany, and Switzerland. See Hay, The American "Covenant Marriage" in the Conflict of Laws, 64 La. L. Rev. 43 (2003), with references.

11. Supra § 15.6 n.1 et seq.

12. Sherrer v. Sherrer, 334 U.S. 343, 68 S.Ct. 1087, 92 L.Ed. 1429 (1948); Coe v. Coe, 334 U.S. 378, 68 S.Ct. 1094, 92 L.Ed.

is precluded when the divorce was *inter partes.* The rationale for the result in *inter partes* cases—no collateral attack of the rendering court's jurisdiction—is that the parties had an opportunity to raise the jurisdictional defect in the original action, for instance lack of domicile (if domicile is indeed constitutionally required). If a party did not avail himself or herself of that opportunity or, having lost on the objection, failed to appeal, the policy of preclusion[13] requires that no second opportunity, in the form of a collateral attack, be extended.

In the international setting, the foreign rendering court's jurisdiction in an *ex parte* dissolution of marriage (or of a civil union) is as much open to review as it would be in an interstate case. Moreover, *any* recognition of a foreign judgment or decree depends on jurisdiction of the foreign court as tested by *United States* standards.[14] In the ordinary civil case other than dissolution of marriage, in which both parties participated, the actual basis on which jurisdiction was asserted by the foreign court is irrelevant because U.S. law permits the exercise of jurisdiction by the parties' consent.[15] The problem is more difficult with respect to dissolution of domestic relationships. In American states still requiring domicile for divorce jurisdiction (and, potentially, for the dissolution of a civil union) and especially if domicile should be considered to be a *constitutionally required* basis for such jurisdiction, consent alone may not be enough. *Sherrer, Coe,* and *Cook,* do allude to the informed consent of the parties in the *inter partes* divorce. However, this consent is, at most, consent to let a decision to an issue (jurisdiction) stand unappealed or not to exercise the opportunity to litigate it. The important point is that jurisdiction (domicile) *was* or *could have been* litigated in the original forum. In a civil law country, however, domicile may not be a basis for divorce jurisdiction.[16] Even in an *inter partes* setting there may therefore not be an opportunity to litigate the issue and to appeal an adverse ruling; as a consequence, a collateral attack would not be precluded. Theoretically, foreign dissolutions granted in civil-law countries in which the parties did not obtain a ruling on the fact of domicile (fact preclusion) would then be open to collateral attack on jurisdictional grounds. Plainly a more differentiated rule is needed. This may be achieved by considering three distinct types of cases.

§ 15.18   A first category of cases includes citizens of other nations who obtained a foreign dissolution that is subsequently in issue in the United States. In most of these cases, the divorce[1] will have been rendered in a country with a close connection to the parties in the

---

1451 (1948); Cook v. Cook, 342 U.S. 126, 72 S.Ct. 157, 96 L.Ed. 146 (1951). For discussion see supra § 15.9.

13.   Infra § 24.1 et seq.

14.   For detailed discussion see infra § 24.42.

15.   See supra § 6.3.

16.   "[M]ost countries do not even have a concept equivalent to our notion of domicile." Juenger, Recognition of Foreign Di-

vorces, 20 Am. J. Comp. L. 1, 19 (1972). But see supra n.2 and infra § 15.19 n.1.

§ 15.18

1.   The discussion in this section and through § 15.23 addresses existing law with respect to *divorce* decrees. Dissolution of civil unions theoretically presents no different problems. Its treatment, however, is uncertain at this time for reasons mentioned supra at § 15.17 nn.7–8.

Restatement sense[2] (their home state, or a state protective of the interests of the home state through application of the law of nationality). An American court, at a much later point in time—when one or both of the parties now find themselves in the United States—has no interest (of the kind North Carolina asserted in *Williams*) to invalidate the foreign divorce and to create a "limping marriage." In such a case, the divorce should be recognized if valid where rendered.[3]

§ 15.19   A second type of case involves U.S. citizens domiciled or resident abroad. If they were domiciled *in fact* in the country of the dissolution, a divorce decree will no doubt be recognized even though jurisdiction was asserted on other grounds, for instance because domiciliary jurisdiction may be unknown to the foreign system.[1] The case does not differ factually from an interstate divorce. The situation is different when the parties are only resident, but, for lack of intent to stay, not domiciled abroad, for instance in the case of American military personnel.[2] The situation is, technically, not analogous to divorces under service personnel statutes in the interstate setting since the lack of domicile *could* have been raised in the latter,[3] but often not in the foreign proceeding. Nevertheless, these divorces should also be accorded recognition: not only will the parties have a sufficiently close connection to the forum (closer, often, than to their technical domicile back in the United States) but the interest of the domiciliary state, if any, will have been safeguarded by the application of the latter's law by the rendering court. Considerations underlying traditional notions of divorce jurisdiction seek to assure that both the interests of the spouses be safeguarded and that possible concerns of the domiciliary state not be evaded. The foreign *inter partes* divorce in which domiciliary law[4] was applied satisfies these

---

2. Supra § 15.5 n.3.

3. See also Baade, Marriage and Divorce in American Conflicts Law: Governmental–Interest Analysis and the Restatement (Second), 72 Colum. L. Rev. 329, 347 (1972), citing to a decision of the Board of Immigration Appeals, In re B., 1 I & N Dec. 677, 679, 1943 WL 6356 (1943). It is a different case when foreign spouses *with domicile in the United States* obtain a divorce in their country of nationality. In many cases recognition of such divorces (jurisdiction on the basis of nationality) may be appropriate: see cases collected by Baade, at 349 n.119. In many others it may not be, especially when the foreign sojourn was brief and the U.S. domicile in reality has the closest connection to the parties and their marriage. Id. at 350. Such a case should therefore be treated as falling into the third category, infra § 15.20, or exceptionally (when the foreign law would not recognize an American divorce) be treated analogously to the case discussed infra § 15.24 n.9. Will of Brown, 132 Misc.2d 811, 505 N.Y.S.2d 334 (1986).

§ 15.19

1. See supra § 15.17 n.1. For earlier German cases see Baade, Marriage and Divorce in American Conflicts Law: Governmental Interest Analysis and the Restatement (Second), 72 Colum. L. Rev. 329, 345 n.98 (1972).

2. Baade's study indicates that such cases were relatively frequent at the time. Id. at 350.

3. The court in Lauterbach v. Lauterbach, 392 P.2d 24 (Alaska 1964), see supra § 15.5 n.2, asserted that domicile was not the sole jurisdictional ground but that other close connecting factors would also support divorce jurisdiction. This assertion, of course, does not dispose of the possibility that domicile may be *constitutionally* required. The parties became precluded from relitigating the constitutional question, if any, when they failed to litigate it and, upon an adverse decision, failed to appeal since an *opportunity* to litigate this question existed in the rendering forum.

4. Baade, supra n.1 at 350, reaches the same result by analogizing foreign divorces

objectives; such a divorce is not easy avenue for the dissolution of a marriage.

§ **15.20**   The third class of cases involves the *consensual* divorce of American domiciliaries who travel to a foreign forum for that particular purpose. In the past, such easy divorces could be obtained in Mexico where jurisdiction could be founded on the signing of the municipal register and a divorce obtained on *local law grounds* within a period as short as 24 hours. "It was a blatant example of 'forum shopping,' and it is difficult to imagine a more 'bogus' decree."[1] To an English court, such a procedure "does not accord with our notions of genuine divorce."[2] Nevertheless, the New York Court of Appeals recognized such a Mexican divorce in *Rosenstiel v. Rosenstiel*. It noted that lower New York courts had long recognized such divorces, largely as an escape valve for parties unable to obtain a local divorce under New York's divorce law which then recognized adultery as the sole ground for divorce. The Court formulated broadly: "The State or country of true domicile has the closest real public interest in a marriage but, where a New York spouse goes elsewhere to establish a synthetic domicile to meet technical acceptance of a matrimonial suit, our public interest is not affected differently by a formality of one day than by a formality of six weeks [as in Nevada]."[3] The resulting abandonment of domicile as the sole jurisdictional basis approaches the Restatement test of *in personam* divorce jurisdiction.[4] This view finds support in a subsequent New York lower court decision. It held the legislative attempt to supersede the *Rosenstiel* result (by presuming a New York domicile at the time of the foreign divorce if the parties had a New York domicile immediately before and after the divorce)[5] to have no effect on the recognition of Mexican

of servicemen to interstate cases. For the reason given at n.3 supra, this analogy is not valid because of the jurisdictional differences, except in cases discussed supra n.1. A better reason in favor of recognition is the invariable application of U.S. domiciliary law (via the nationality standard), thus assuring equivalence of grounds and preventing "easy" divorces thorough evasion of U.S. domiciliary law.

§ **15.20**

1.   Messina v. Smith, [1971] 3 W.L.R. 118, 137–138 (referring to Mountbatten v. Mountbatten, [1959] p. 43). A party to a sham marriage may be estopped to deny its validity when a declaration of invalidity is sought for ulterior motives. In Vervaeke v. Smith, [1982] 2 All. E.R. 144, the House of Lords refused to recognize the Belgian annulment of prostitute Vervaeke's earlier sham marriage to Smith which marriage Vervaeke sought to avoid so she could claim the substantial English estate of her employer Messina whom she married in Italy and who died at the wedding reception. This exceptional instance of the English

court's refusal to recognize the Belgian decree is discussed in Deech, Family Law, 1982 All. E.R. Annual Rev. 146; Jaffee, Recognition of Foreign Nullity Decrees, 32 Int'l & Comp. L.Q. 500 (1983); 40 Camb. L.J. 201 (1981).

2.   Indyka v. Indyka, [1969] 1 A.C. 33, 88 (Lord Pearce).

3.   16 N.Y.2d 64, 73, 262 N.Y.S.2d 86, 90, 209 N.E.2d 709, 712 (1965). For comment see D. Currie, Suitcase Divorce in the Conflict of Laws, 34 U. Chi. L. Rev. 26 (1966). Prior to *Rosenstiel*, Justice Traynor questioned whether contacts with a foreign country other than domicile might not also make for valid divorce jurisdiction. Scott v. Scott, 51 Cal.2d 249, 331 P.2d 641, 645 (1958) (Traynor, J., concurring). The court recognized a Mexican divorce after finding that the husband had been domiciled in Mexico.

4.   Supra § 15.5 n.3.

5.   N.Y. Dom. Rel. L. § 250. This provision was taken from the Uniform Recognition and Divorce Act, 9A U.L.A. 461 (Supp.

divorces since *Rosenstiel* had done away with domicile as a jurisdictional requirement.[6] Massachusetts and the Virgin Islands courts adopted the *Rosenstiel* result relatively early,[7] but several other states did not.[8] In 1971, Mexico adopted a six-months' residency requirement for foreigners seeking a divorce, thus ending the era of "quickie" divorces. However, Haiti and the Dominican Republic continue to provide them.

The introduction of no-fault dissolution of marriage in all states will now make the acceptance of *Rosenstiel*-type divorces easier for American courts called upon to extend recognition of such divorces. The availability of a no-fault divorce at the forum removes the public policy concerns with respect to different, "easier" grounds available in the foreign forum. The remaining jurisdictional differences, when thus not used to evade local substantive law, have not been considered to be an obstacle to the recognition of Mexican divorces in Connecticut and New Jersey[9] and of Haitian Dominican Republic divorces in Indiana, Massachusetts, New York, and Tennessee.[10]

§ 15.21 Taken by itself, the position announced in the language quoted from the *Rosenstiel* decision of course cannot alter any constitutional requirement of domicile or equivalent close connection to the divorcing forum, if such a requirement in fact exists. Since the losing

---

1965) (subsequently withdrawn: U.L.A. Master ed. 1981, at 75). See also Mayer v. Mayer, 66 N.C.App. 522, 311 S.E.2d 659 (1984), review denied 311 N.C. 760, 321 S.E.2d 140 (1984).

6. Kakarapis v. Kakarapis, 58 Misc.2d 515, 296 N.Y.S.2d 208 (1968). See also Lappert v. Lappert, 20 N.Y.2d 364, 283 N.Y.S.2d 26, 229 N.E.2d 599 (1967); Greschler v. Greschler, 51 N.Y.2d 368, 434 N.Y.S.2d 194, 414 N.E.2d 694 (1980) (recognizing Dominican Republic divorce in the absence of fraud).

7. McCarthy v. McCarthy, 361 Mass. 359, 280 N.E.2d 151 (1972); Perrin v. Perrin, 408 F.2d 107 (3d Cir.1969). For additional states and cases see infra nn.9–10.

8. See, e.g., Warrender v. Warrender, 79 N.J.Super. 114, 190 A.2d 684 (1963), affirmed per curiam 42 N.J. 287, 200 A.2d 123 (1964).

9. Yoder v. Yoder, 31 Conn.Supp. 345, 330 A.2d 825 (1974). However, the child support obligations created by the Mexican court were not recognized (possibly on the basis that such judgments are never final, although no such point is clearly stated). Kazin v. Kazin, 81 N.J. 85, 405 A.2d 360 (1979) (second husband who had helped his wife to obtain a Mexican divorce from her first husband is now estopped from attacking its validity); Raspa v. Raspa, 207 N.J.Super. 371, 504 A.2d 683 (1985); Bruneau v. Bruneau, 3 Conn.App. 453, 489 A.2d 1049 (1985).

10. Scherer v. Scherer, 405 N.E.2d 40 (Ind.App.1980) (recognition on the basis of estoppel); Poor v. Poor, 381 Mass. 392, 409 N.E.2d 758 (1980) (same); Hyde v. Hyde, 562 S.W.2d 194 (Tenn.1978). For Tennessee: see also Terrell v. Terrell, 578 S.W.2d 637 (Tenn.1979) (Haitian divorce valid because wife had submitted to jurisdiction there and claim for alimony barred in Tennessee because not asserted in the Haitian court). For New York see supra n.6. But see Weber v. Weber, 200 Neb. 659, 265 N.W.2d 436 (1978) (no recognition to Dominican Republic divorce under Uniform Divorce Recognition Act, generally denying recognition to foreign divorces when both parties are Nebraska domiciliaries at the time the action was commenced). The case is also noted supra § 15.11 n.4. See also the decisions cited infra § 15.22 n.1. McFarland v. McFarland, 70 N.Y.2d 916, 524 N.Y.S.2d 392, 519 N.E.2d 303 (1987) (found no basis that recognition of the Dominican Republic divorce judgment would do violence to some public policy of the state); Becker v. Becker, 143 Misc.2d 500, 541 N.Y.S.2d 699 (1989) (although the plaintiff may be entitled to recognition and enforcement of the provisions of the Dominican Republic divorce judgment, she is not entitled to conversion of the judgment to a New York State judgment); Rabbani v. Rabbani, 178 A.D.2d 637, 578 N.Y.S.2d 213 (1991) (separation agreement incorporated in Dominican Republic divorce decree recognized).

spouse, in a contested[1] *inter partes* divorce of the *Rosenstiel*-type often could not have litigated the domicile issue in the foreign forum,[2] the decision recognizing the divorce may therefore itself be open to constitutional attack on appeal.[3] However, in the absence of an appeal or upon denial of certiorari, the constitutional issues once again ripen into *res judicata* for purposes of recognition of the (now American) decision in other states of the Union.[4] Thus, as long as *one* state will recognize such a migratory divorce, means exist for its "domestication" and acceptance of other states under full-faith-and-credit principles,[5] even though recognition might have been denied in the latter states in an original proceeding seeking recognition.

Similar questions may arise with respect to other questions of status, confirmed or recognized by judgment in F–1 and now sought to be recognized in F–2 which would not have recognized the status (or, for that reason, entertained an action for its dissolution) as an original matter.[6]

§ 15.22 Easy foreign divorces have lost much of their significance—except when the reason is speed—with the reform of substantive American divorce law. The principle, however, that some states may recognize foreign *inter partes* divorces of American domiciliaries, even if

§ 15.21

1. If the foreign *inter partes* divorce was *consensual,* notions of estoppel would seem to preclude collateral attack. Accord: Scherer v. Scherer, supra § 15.20 n.10. Different considerations may apply when the foreign divorce was a sham, for instance for the purposes of enabling income earning spouses to escape the higher "married" tax rate in favor of the single rate. This problem is discussed in Note, The Haitian Vacation: The Applicability of Sham Doctrine to Year–End Divorces, 77 Mich. L. Rev. 1332 (1979).

2. Supra § 15.17 nn.14–16.

3. Estoppel may additionally bar review of the validity of a foreign divorce. Clagett v. King, 308 A.2d 245 (D.C.App.1973) (plaintiff estopped from asserting invalidity of his own prior Mexican divorce on jurisdictional grounds in order to obtain annulment of present marriage); Poor v. Poor, 381 Mass. 392, 409 N.E.2d 758 (1980) (husband estopped from challenging wife's Haitian divorce in which he had participated); Schlinder v. Schlinder, 107 Wis.2d 695, 321 N.W.2d 343 (1982) (the husband is estopped from questioning the validity of his Mexican divorce from his first wife, but the Mexican divorce procured from his second wife is invalid). Similarly: Estate of Warner, 687 S.W.2d 686 (Mo.App.1985). See also Restatement, Second, Conflict of Laws § 74 (1971). Strong policy considerations support the argument that, after voluntary submission to the foreign jurisdiction, the parties should be estopped or precluded from collaterally attacking the resulting decision.

4. Supra § 15.6 n.5 and § 15.12 nn.4–12.

5. How to "domesticate" a foreign divorce may occasionally present procedural problems. Thus, when a husband sought declaratory relief that his Mexican divorce from his previous wife was valid because he and his present wife were now "nervous" about the matter, a New York court dismissed the action for failure to state a "justiciable controversy requiring the intercession of this court." Einhorn v. Einhorn, (N.Y. Sup. Ct. Kings County, 1976, unreported).

6. See supra §§ 13.19, 15.1 nn.3–5, 15.17 nn.7–8 for same-sex marriages or civil unions. Under the Defense of Marriage Act (DOMA), 28 U.S.C.A. 1738C, a statute implementing (in this case, rather: defining) the Full Faith and Credit Clause, states need not grant full faith and credit to unions that are not between man and woman. What if the issue has already been adjudicated in F–1, as part of litigation on another claim (e.g., support or as for declaratory relief): Will DOMA trump the Full Faith and Credit Clause and not only its earlier general implementing statute, 28 U.S.C.A. § 1738. See also Hay, The American "Covenant Marriage" in the Conflict of Laws, 64 La. L. Rev. 43 (2003).

the rendering court's jurisdiction is not based on domicile but only on residence or even the mere appearance of the parties, continues to be important. For speed in shedding bonds, the "easy" divorce of former Mexican law has meanwhile been replaced by the even "easier" procedures available in Haiti and the Dominican Republic as part of "package tours" which include flight, weekend accommodation, and divorce, with arrangements available over the internet.[1]

The broad language of *Rosenstiel,* quoted above,[2] virtually disclaiming any interest on the part of the domiciliary state, would support the recognition even of these types of divorces. A better argument in favor of such recognition lies in the analogy of these cases to *Sherrer*[3] and the U.S. Supreme Court's policy of discouraging relitigation of marital issues when the parties made a mature choice and knowingly waived the protection available under U.S. law by participating in the foreign divorce. In addition, "the formal discouragement of forum shopping is inappropriate at a stage when a foreign divorce has already been granted and any forum shopping taken place. The paramount concern at this stage is to avoid the limping marriage."[4] This view would therefore distinguish between the assertion of *initial* divorce jurisdiction on the basis of insufficient contacts (and the resulting possibility of forum shopping) and recognition of divorces already procured. However, the suggestion—as well as the broad language in *Rosenstiel*—seem overgeneral. Recognition of such a divorce for the policy reasons stated may well be appropriate when the recognizing court is that of a third state. Whether the *domiciliary* state has as little interest as the *Rosenstiel* language suggests is open to question. In such a case, the result— recognition or denial—perhaps should turn on whether the domiciliary state has now adopted the no-fault approach to dissolution of marriage[5] *or* the rendering court applied the law of the domiciliary state. In both

---

§ 15.22

1. There are any number of law firm websites advertising such services. See also generally, http://www.usemb.gov.do/Consular/ACS/divorceDR.htm (Embassy of the United States of America to the Dominican Republic).

See supra § 15.20 n.10; Kraham v. Kraham, 73 Misc.2d 977, 342 N.Y.S.2d 943 (1973) (recognizing Haitian divorce); Kugler v. Haitian Tours, Inc., 120 N.J.Super. 260, 293 A.2d 706 (1972) (denying recognition to Haitian divorce); Slessinger v. Secretary of Health and Human Services, 835 F.2d 937 (1st Cir.1987) (Rhode Island permits a party to attack a foreign divorce—Dominican Republic in this case—for lack of domicile where principles of estoppel does not pose a bar). But see, for New Jersey, Kazin v. Kazin, 81 N.J. 85, 405 A.2d 360 (1979). The express adoption of "habitual residence" of one year in England, see supra § 15.9 n.7, does not appear to create problems: see the Supreme Court's assumption in Sosna v.

Iowa, 419 U.S. 393, 95 S.Ct. 553, 42 L.Ed.2d 532 (1975) (discussed supra § 15.7) that Iowa's one-year durational residence requirement would provide added support (presumption?) in a collateral proceeding for a determination that the party had in fact been domiciled in Iowa. In Kulko v. California Superior Court, 436 U.S. 84, 98 S.Ct. 1690, 56 L.Ed.2d 132 (1978), discussed infra § 15.31 n.2, the underlying Haitian divorce of the parties appears to have been considered valid by implication. See also supra text accompanying n.14.

2. Supra § 15.20 n.3.

3. Sherrer v. Sherrer, 334 U.S. 343, 68 S.Ct. 1097, 92 L.Ed. 1429 (1948); see supra § 15.9.

4. Hall, Cruse v. Chittum: Habitual Residence Judicially Explored, 24 Int'l & Comp. L.Q. 1, 5 (1975). See also supra § 15.20 n.13.

5. See Hyde v. Hyde, 562 S.W.2d 194 (Tenn.1978).

cases, home state interests would indeed not have been affected, except that local waiting periods would have been evaded. The fact that the foreign jurisdiction has a shorter waiting period, or none, and encourages the use of its courts as a divorce mill does not go to substantive interests[6] and should not be of concern to the recognizing court; the divorce should be recognized.[7]

 § **15.23** In the U.S. interstate setting it is not required that the parties appear personally before the court of the divorcing forum in order for the preclusive effect of the *Sherrer* doctrine[1] to apply. Instead, but on the conditions that the appearance was not fraudulently induced or that the essential element of knowing consent was not otherwise lacking,[2] the parties may appear by attorney and on the basis of depositions. In the international context, however, recognition has not been extended to mail-order divorces[3] and foreign *ex parte* divorces of American domiciliaries are problematic.[4] In these cases, ordinary principles find application—for the protection of the stay-at-home spouse—and the foreign court's jurisdiction must be found to have been based on the existence, in fact,[5] of domicile or its equivalent.[6] It should be noted, in conclusion, that judgments and decrees of Indian tribal courts in the United States are not considered to be foreign nation judgments and are thus entitled to full faith and credit in state courts.[7]

B. RECOGNITION OF FOREIGN NON–JUDICIAL DIVORCES IN THE UNITED STATES

 § **15.24** Under Islamic law, a husband of Muslim faith may divorce a wife by the issuance of a *talaq,* the triple repetition of words of divorce

6. Substantive concerns of the home state (e.g., in the maintenance of the marriage if possible) may be (minimally) affected where home-state law, but not the foreign law, requires conciliation attempts as a prerequisite to dissolution of the marriage.

7. See also Swisher, Foreign Migratory Divorces—A Reappraisal, 21 J. Fam. Law 9 (1982/83).

§ 15.23

1. Supra § 15.9.

2. See supra § 15.10 nn.1–2.

3. Rosenbaum v. Rosenbaum, 309 N.Y. 371, 130 N.E.2d 902 (1955).

4. *Ex parte* divorces of foreigners, domiciled abroad, should be treated in the same manner as the category of cases summarized supra § 15.18 nn.1–2. Cf. Carr v. Carr, 46 N.Y.2d 270, 413 N.Y.S.2d 305, 385 N.E.2d 1234 (1978) (discussed infra § 15.33 n.2).

5. The American court will have to undertake a *factual* determination because the

issue ordinarily could not have arisen in the foreign proceeding. See Scott v. Scott, 51 Cal.2d 249, 331 P.2d 641 (1958); In re Marriage of Stich, 169 Cal.App.3d 64, 214 Cal. Rptr. 919 (1985) (the court rejected defendant-husband's argument that his wife was estopped from challenging the validity of a Mexican divorce, since he barely met the time requirements for residency and returned to the U.S. immediately upon the receipt of his decree); Williams v. Williams, 1993 WL 331874 (Del. Fam. Ct. 1993) (denying recognition of Guatemalan divorce because the parties had not been domiciled there). But see supra § 15.19 n.1.

6. See the Restatement, Second, test of other close connection. See also supra § 15.5 n.3.

7. Cf. Matter of Adoption of Buehl (Duckhead v. Anderson), 87 Wash.2d 649, 555 P.2d 1334 (1976); Jim v. CIT Financial Services Corp., 87 N.M. 362, 533 P.2d 751 (1975); Teague v. Bad River Band of the Lake Superior Tribe of Chippewa Indians, 265 Wis.2d 64, 665 N.W.2d 899, 908 (2003). See also supra § 13.17.

before witnesses, while Judaism permits divorce by deliverance to the wife of a bill of divorcement, *get*.[1] In some Muslim countries,[2] divorce now requires a judicial decree. In many, however, the operative act is the *talaq* and any official participation, such as registration with a court, serves only evidentiary or similar purposes but does not alter the unilateral and private nature of the divorce. Similarly, the Rabbinical court exercises only a supervisory function to assure observance of proper procedures by the parties in the delivery and acceptance of the *get*. The question thus arises, albeit only infrequently, whether and under what circumstances such a private religious, or other non-judicial[3] divorce will be recognized in this country.

In the United States a religious non-judicial divorce obtained in the *United States forum* by a local resident will not be recognized.[4] In

§ 15.24

1. See Dicey & Morris, 2 Conflict of Laws 744–48 (13th ed. by Collins et al. 2000). On the *get*, see infra n.7.

2. See Anderson, Modern Trends in Islam: Legal Reform and Modernisation in the Middle East, 20 Int'l & Comp. L.Q. 1 (1971); Stone, The Recognition in England of Talaq Divorces, 14 Anglo–American L.Rev. 363 (1985). Under Pakistani law, notice of the *talaq* must be given to a public authority. Its effect is then suspended for 90 days and an Arbitration Council is established to attempt a reconciliation of the parties. The English House of Lords has held that such a *talaq* derives from a "judicial or other proceeding" within the meaning of the Recognition of Divorces and Legal Separations Act of 1971, entitling it to recognition in England: Quazi v. Quazi, [1980] A.C. 744. A bare *talaq* does not constitute a "proceeding" within the meaning of the act. See Chandhary v. Chandhary, [1985] Fam. 19 (C.A.). The Family Law Act 1986 also distinguishes, in § 46(1)(2), between divorces obtained "by means of proceedings" and all others, but also offers no definition of "proceedings". For comment see Pilkington, Transnational Non–Judicial Divorces Under the Family Act of 1986, 37 Int'l & Comp.L.Q. 131 (1988); Reed, Transnational Non–Judicial Divorces: A Comparative Analysis of Recognition Under English and U.S. Jurisprudence, 18 Loyola L.A. Int'l & Comp. L.Q. 311 (1996).

3. Other non-judicial divorces include those granted by legislative or executive bodies or, within the United States, reached by private agreement according to Indian tribal custom on Indian reservations. For an example of the former see Sorenson v. Sorenson, 122 Misc. 196, 202 N.Y.S. 620 (1924), affirmed 219 App.Div. 344, 220 N.Y.S. 242 (1927) (recognition of divorce granted by King of Denmark). Sherif v.

Sherif, 76 Misc.2d 905, 352 N.Y.S.2d 781 (1974) (Court recognized a divorce obtained in Egypt in accordance with Egyptian laws by Moslem Egyptian nationals). With respect to a divorce according to Indian tribal customs see Marris v. Sockey, 170 F.2d 599 (10th Cir.1948), cert. denied 336 U.S. 914, 69 S.Ct. 605, 93 L.Ed. 1078 (1949); Sanders v. Robinson, 864 F.2d 630 (9th Cir.1988), cert. denied 490 U.S. 1110, 109 S.Ct. 3165, 104 L.Ed.2d 1028 (1989) (a tribal court has jurisdiction over a marriage dissolution action between an Indian plaintiff and non-Indian defendant residing on the reservation). Non-judicial divorces—by unilateral act or by contract of the parties—are also possible under Chinese, Japanese and Korean law and under Soviet law prior to 1944. See K. Kleinrahm & H.-C. Partikel, Die Anerkennung ausländischer Entscheidungen in Ehesachen 145 et. seq. (2d ed. 1970).

In England the problem is more substantial than in the United States: "in 1971 it was estimated that about 150 remarriages ... each year followed an extrajudicial divorce; about one-half of these followed a *talaq*. ... The numbers are likely to be larger now than in 1971." The Law Commission, Working Paper No. 77, Family Law: Financial Relief After Foreign Divorce, ¶ 11 n.59 (1980).

4. See Shikoh v. Murff, 257 F.2d 306 (2d Cir.1958) (New York Islamic divorce, as evidenced by a declaration made in New York, by local resident from non-resident spouse invalid); Chertok v. Chertok, 208 App.Div. 161, 203 N.Y.S. 163 (1924) (New York rabbinical divorce invalid). In New York, this result follows primarily from a constitutional provision, infra n.9. However, although case law is sparse, the same result may be expected to be adopted elsewhere on the ground that local statutory provisions applicable to divorce are exclusive. To this effect:

England, a religious divorce obtained in England before 1974 by foreign domiciliaries, whose home law regarded the divorce as valid, would be recognized.[5] Subsequent to 1974, a divorce may be obtained in England only by decree of a court of civil jurisdiction.[6]

American courts do accord recognition to religious divorces obtained by foreign domiciliaries abroad and valid where obtained.[7] For instance,

Maklad v. Maklad, 2001 WL 51662 (2001) (refusing to recognize the validity of an Islamic rite divorce done in Connecticut by Connecticut domiciliaries). For extensive discussion of American law in this area, see Comment, United States Recognition of Foreign, Nonjudicial Divorces, 53 Minn. L. Rev. 612 (1969). But see Shapiro v. Shapiro, 110 Misc.2d 726, 442 N.Y.S.2d 928 (1981), discussed infra n.8. A close case is a divorce obtained by a U.S. domiciliary while in a foreign consulate located within the United States. A New Jersey court recognized such a divorce. See Chaudry v. Chaudry, 159 N.J.Super. 566, 388 A.2d 1000 (1978) (recognizing *talaq* performed at Pakistani consulate; divorced wife then living in Pakistan).

5. See Dicey & Morris, supra n.1, at 730–31 *et seq.*

The 1971 Recognition of Divorces and Legal Separations Act provides for the recognition of "overseas divorces," defined as divorces obtained "in any country outside the British Isles." A divorce by talaq, pronounced in England and confirmed in writing to Pakistani authorities in accordance with Pakistani law and thus effective there, was nonetheless not entitled to recognition in England since not (entirely) obtained by acts done "outside the British Isles." R. v. Home Secretary, ex parte Ghulam Fatima, [1985] 2 Q.B. 190. See Carter, Decisions of British Courts During 1984, 55 Brit. Yb. Int'l L. 347, 359 (1985).

6. Family Law Act 1986, § 44(1); Dicey & Morris, supra n.1, at 728.

The rule is similar elsewhere. E.g., in Germany, a marriage can only be dissolved by judicial decree. Art. 17, para 2, Introductory Law to the Civil Code (EGBGB), as amended, now so provides unequivocally. For the prerequisites of a judicial divorce, Art. 17, para. 1, refers to the law of the parties' nationality. However, public policy would prohibit the use of a judicially endorsed *talaq*. See P. Hay, Internationales Privatrecht 298–302 (2d ed. 2002). In contrast, the validity of a divorce obtained *abroad* is governed by the law applicable to the marriage (Art. 17 in connection with Art. 14 Introductory Law to the Civil Code, EGBGB), i.e. the law of common nationality, common (last) domicile or other close

connection. That law therefore determines the validity of a non-judicial divorce.

7. See Machransky v. Machransky, 31 Ohio App. 482, 166 N.E. 423 (1927) (Russian Rabbinical divorce). In Shapiro v. Shapiro, 110 Misc.2d 726, 442 N.Y.S.2d 928 (1981), modified as to counsel fees 88 A.D.2d 592, 449 N.Y.S.2d 806 (1982), the Rabbinical Court of Israel had ordered the husband in 1963 to perform the ritual acts of the *get*. He had fled Israel and took up residence in New York. After the Rabbinical Court of Tel Aviv had issued another order in 1979, the wife, a resident of Israel, sought enforcement in New York. The New York court noted that she would be entitled to a divorce under New York law, on the ground of abandonment, but also found that a civil divorce would not be recognized in Israel. "Under the principle of comity, [the court] recognize[d] the Israeli decree and will enforce the directives therein.... Defendant is ordered to schedule an appointment with the Rabbinical Council of America and he is to perform all the ritual acts of the 'get' ceremony in accordance with the directions of the Rabbinical Court."

The problem of securing a *get* is also important for Jewish couples resident in the United States since both orthodox and conservative Judaism require a religious divorce in addition to a civil divorce. When the parties have signed a marriage contract (*ketubah*) and it contains a provision requiring submission of marital disputes to a Jewish tribunal (*Beth Din*), the matter may be resolved under principles of contract law. Thus, the New York Court of Appeals held in Avitzur v. Avitzur, 58 N.Y.2d 108, 459 N.Y.S.2d 572, 446 N.E.2d 136 (1983), cert. denied 464 U.S. 817, 104 S.Ct. 76, 78 L.Ed.2d 88 (1983), that the *ketubah* was a contract and that the appropriate remedy was specific performance. The matter is more difficult when there is no *ketubah* to enforce but remarriage of a civilly divorced woman is impossible because of the husband's failure and refusal to obtain a *get*. In New York, Domestic Relations Law § 253 (McKinney 1986) addresses the problem by requiring the plaintiff in a divorce action to file, prior to final judgment, a verified statement that he or she has taken all steps to remove all barriers to the defendant's re-marriage. "Barriers" are defined to include "religious ... restraint[s]". Id. § 253(3). Such filing notwithstanding, a divorce shall not be entered if the clergyman who had solemnized the marriage files a verified statement that the plaintiff has not removed such barriers. Id. § 253(6). It has been argued that at least § 253(6) violates the First Amendment Establishment-of-Religion Clause because it involves both secular and religious authorities in the divorce process. Warmflash, The New York Approach to Enforcing Religious Marriage Contracts: From *Avitzur* to the *Get* Statute, 50 Brooklyn L. Rev. 229, 252 (1984). The article is a detailed treatment of the subject with comprehensive references to the literature and case law. See additionally, Barshay, The Implications of the Constitution's Religion Clauses on New York Family Law, 40 How.L.J. 205 (1996); Leichter, The Problem of Getting the "Get"—Impact of Jewish Divorce Law on Matrimonial Litigation, 16–6 Matrimonial Strategist 4 (1998). See also Chambers v. Chambers, 122 Misc.2d 671, 471 N.Y.S.2d 958 (1983) (holding that the application of the statute to a separation agreement contracted before its enactment would be an unconstitutional impairment of contract). The *Chambers* court also said, in dictum, that the application of the statute in uncontested divorces might violate the defendant's due process rights. Shapiro v. Shapiro, 168 A.D.2d 491, 562 N.Y.S.2d 733 (1990) (the Plaintiff's conclusory assertions that the *get* which the defendant attempted to obtain failed to satisfy the provisions of Domestic Relations Law § 253(3) were unsupported by any documentary proof); Friedenberg v. Friedenberg, 136 A.D.2d 593, 523 N.Y.S.2d 578 (1988) (in view of the fact that it was the husband who sought a judgment of divorce, the court deemed it reasonable to require a statement from him in compliance with Domestic Relations Law § 253(3) to remove any religious barriers to the wife's remarriage); Perl v. Perl, 126 A.D.2d 91, 512 N.Y.S.2d 372 (1987) (where either spouse has invoked the power of the state to effect a civil dissolution of a marriage, an oppressive misuse of the religious veto power by one of the spouses subjects the economic bargain which follows between them to review and potential revision). See further, for the interplay of civil and religious law and divorce recognition in New York, Golding v. Golding, 176 A.D.2d 20, 581 N.Y.S.2d 4 (1992) (separation agreement not enforced because signed by wife under threat of the *Get*); Tal v. Tal, 158 Misc.2d 703, 601 N.Y.S.2d 530 (N.Y.Sup.Ct.1993) (Israeli rabbinical divorce not recognized for lack of

personal jurisdiction, prior N.Y. rabbinical divorce not given weight because non-judicial). For additional case law, see 29 A.L.R.4th 746 (1981, with Sept. 1998 Supp.). For an overview see Broyde, The New York State Jewish Divorce Law, 30 Tradition: A Journal of Jewish Thought, 5–23 (summer 1995); see also Malnowitz and Broyde, The 1992 New York *Get* Law: An Exchange, 31 Tradition: A Journal of Jewish Thought, 23–41 (Spring 1997).

American courts differ on whether to assist a wife in obtaining a *get*. Compare Mayer–Kolker v. Kolker, 359 N.J.Super. 98, 819 A.2d 17 (2003), cert. denied 177 N.J. 495, 828 A.2d 922 (2003) (courts lack power to order the husband to cooperate in obtaining a *get*), with Kaplinsky v. Kaplinsky, 198 A.D.2d 212, 603 N.Y.S.2d 574 (1993) (affirming contempt sanctions against husband).

See also Nardi v. Segal, 90 Ill.App.2d 432, 433, 234 N.E.2d 805, 808 (1967) in which the court refused to enforce a claim of or child support arising out of an Israeli Rabbinical divorce on the ground that "matrimonial matters are solely governed by statute" and that the Uniform Foreign–Money Judgments Recognition Act, in force in Illinois, excludes "a judgment for support in matrimonial or family matters." While the court's decision is open to serious question, albeit based on Illinois precedents, the underlying assumption was that the Rabbinical divorce was valid and that only its incidents were not entitled to recognition.

A Canadian decision goes even further. In Schwebel v. Ungar, 42 D.L.R.2d 622 (1964), the parties had been Hungarian domiciliaries and been married there in accordance with Hungarian and Judaic law. While in an Italian refugee camp, the husband had divorced the wife by delivery of a *get,* a form of divorce recognized neither in Hungary nor in Italy. Subsequently, the parties settled in Israel. The wife remarried in Canada, where her second husband later sought a decree of nullity alleging that the wife's previous marriage had not been dissolved. The court upheld the divorce by *get* with reference to the wife's law of domicile *at the time of the remarriage,* finding that the divorce by *get* was valid in Israel. The reference to a law other than that of the place of divorce (Italy) or domicile at the time of divorce (Hungary) is highly unusual and was improper. See the criticism of Webb, Bigamy and Capacity to Marry, 14 Int'l & Comp. L.Q. 659 (1965). Such a reference may be proper under extraordinary circumstances, for instance in order to protect inheritance rights of issue of the second marriage or of the second spouse (a vali-

a New York court recognized a divorce obtained in Egypt, by Egyptians of Muslim faith, but seemingly domiciled in New York.[8] This decision is important in that it avoids limping marriages: if the court had invalidated the Egyptian divorce, the parties would have been regarded as divorced in Egypt but married in New York, while a divorce at their New York domicile would not have been entitled to recognition in Egypt for non-compliance with Islamic law. Such a result could then have been avoided only by two divorces, one civil and one religious.[9]

§ 15.25   The previous cases involved religious divorces of parties under their religious law when the original marriage had also been contracted abroad, presumably in conformance with the same religious law. It is another question whether a foreign religious divorce of a (civil) marriage originally contracted in the forum would also be entitled to recognition. Prior to the Family Law Act 1986, English courts have recognized a divorce by *talaq* of a marriage celebrated in England.[1] The question does not seem to have arisen in the United States.[2] However, at least in cases where the parties were domiciled in the country of the divorce and the divorce was valid there (presumably because obtained in compliance with the religious law of one of the parties), recognition should be extended. Such a divorce does not differ from other consensual divorces obtained at the foreign domicile of the parties. Whether recogni-

---

dation approach), or in a case in which the second spouse is the respondent (estoppel). None of these circumstances existed in the *Schwebel* case.

8. Sherif v. Sherif, 76 Misc.2d 905, 352 N.Y.S.2d 781 (1974). The court did not discuss the New York constitutional provision, which underlay the decision in *Shikoh* supra n.4, that divorces shall be granted only through judicial proceedings. N.Y. Const. Art. I, § 9(1). That prohibition thus seems limited to divorces obtained in *New York* but does not become a matter of such overriding public policy as to affect divorces obtained abroad. Also, while not clearly indicating whether or not the parties were indeed New York domiciliaries, the court cited to Gould v. Gould, 235 N.Y. 14, 138 N.E. 490 (1923) in which a French divorce of New York domiciliaries had been recognized. 352 N.Y.S.2d at 784 n.4.

9. It is interesting to note that until recently French law also made it burdensome to obtain a divorce for parties whose foreign religious personal law provided for special procedures. In the celebrated *Levi-çon* case, the Cour de Cassation held that French courts lacked jurisdiction in such circumstances thereby requiring parties to obtain their divorce abroad. For discussion of the case and recent changes see H. Batiffol & P. Lagarde, 2 Droit international privé, No. 448, at 89 et. seq. (7th ed. 1981). See also Matter of Bronislawa K. v. Tadeusz

K., 90 Misc.2d 183, 393 N.Y.S.2d 534 (1977) (discussed supra § 15.16 n.2).

§ 15.25

1. Russ v. Russ, [1964] P. 315. See also Qureshi v. Qureshi, [1971] 2 W.L.R. 518, [1972] Fam. 173 (discussed in Hartley, 34 Mod. L. Rev. 579 (1971)). Such a (bare) *talaq* is not a foreign "proceeding" and, in part, was obtained in England. Such a talaq today does not fall under the Savings Provision of the 1986 Act. See supra § 15.24. Similarly, a *get* written in England and delivered to the wife at a rabbinical court in Israel may effectively divorce the parties under Jewish law, but the divorce would not be entitled to recognition under the Family Law Act 1986. Berkovits v. Grinberg, [1995] Fam. 142, [1995] 1 All E.R. 681, [1995] 2 W.L.R. 553 (Fam.Div.). For a review of English law, see also Pilkington, Transnational Divorces under the Family Law Act of 1986, 37 Int'l Comp. L.Q. 131 (1988). With respect to the talaq, see Stone, The Recognition in England of Talaq Divorces, 14 Anglo–American L.Rev. 363. For *Australia*, see Z. v. Z., [1992] F.L.R. 291.

2. In one decision, the court advised the husband to "follow through" with the divorce proceeding then pending in the Rabbinical Court of Israel, perhaps justifying the assumption that a foreign religion divorce would be recognized. Zwerling v. Zwerling, 167 Misc.2d 782, 636 N.Y.S.2d 595 (1995).

tion should also be extended, as a matter of policy to a foreign religious *ex parte* divorce is open to serious question, even if valid abroad, when the moving party (ordinarily the husband) was not domiciled there.[3]

C. RECOGNITION OF U.S. DISSOLUTION DECREES ABROAD

§ 15.26 Other common law jurisdictions, such as Canada[1] and England, have also traditionally employed a jurisdictional approach which looks to domicile or another close connection to the forum.[2] An American divorce based on proper domiciliary jurisdiction would therefore be accorded recognition. With the adoption of the English Recognition of Foreign Divorces and Legal Separations Act (1971), in implementation of the Hague Convention on the same subject,[3] a foreign divorce will be recognized if based on any number of jurisdictional bases, among them the country of the parties' nationality or extended residence. The inclusion of residence as an acceptable jurisdictional basis is important in the light of the trend, however still limited and unclear, toward acceptance of this basis in American domestic law. In the important decision in *Cruse v. Chittum*,[4] the court accepted as sufficient for the recognition of a Mississippi divorce the rendering court's finding that the

---

3. An example is the case of a divorce by *talaq* when the wife is a domiciliary or resident of the Islamic country, the husband is not but appears—in person or by representative—for purposes of uttering the words of divorce. Since the wife ordinarily could not have obtained the divorce (see Ryan, 32 Can. B. Rev. 1027, at 1032, 1034 (1954)), her domicile would not confer divorce jurisdiction. Nor is the divorce truly *ex parte* in the American sense, since the only party who could initiate it, the husband, was not domiciled there. The divorce therefore resembles an *inter partes* (in personam) foreign divorce and may be recognized only in those jurisdictions which accept bilateral divorces generally. However, the husband-oriented nature of *talaq* distinguishes such a divorce from the usual *consensual inter partes* divorce and may suggest a different result.

§ 15.26

1. Canada: Divorce Act of 1985 § 3(1), R.S.C. 1985 (2d Supp.), c. 3 (continuous residence of one year within particular province). Australia: Matrimonial Causes Act, 1959–1966, § 95(2)–(3). For discussion and case law see Castel, Canadian Conflict of Laws ¶ 238, p. 372 (4th ed. 1997).

2. In England, the possibility of a wife's separate domicile was not recognized until relatively recent times, making it very difficult for the deserted wife to obtain a divorce when the husband had changed his domicile. The Recognition of Divorces and Legal Separations Act of 1971 as amended by the Domicile and Matrimonial Proceedings Act of 1973 now provides for divorce jurisdiction in England if either of the parties is domiciled in England or was there habitually resident (see supra § 15.17 n.1) throughout the period of one year.

3. Convention on the Recognition of Divorces and Legal Separations (1970), Hague Conference on Private International Law, Recueil des Conventions de la Haye 128 (1973).

4. [1974] 2 All E.R. 940. For discussion see Hall, *Cruse v. Chittum*: Habitual Residence Judicially Explored, 24 Int'l & Comp. L.Q. 1 (1975). See also Lawrence v. Lawrence, [1985] 3 W.L.R. 125, 2 All. E.R. 733 (C.A.): A Brazilian woman obtained a Nevada divorce and thereafter remarried in Nevada. In a later proceeding in England, the wife contested the validity of the remarriage on the ground that, since Brazil would not recognize the Nevada divorce, she lacked capacity to remarry. The Court of Appeal held, in effect, that under the Hague Convention and the particular implementing provision of the English Act, the recognition of the foreign divorce included the capacity of the divorced spouses to remarry. For discussion, see the contributions by Downes and Lipstein in 35 Int'l & Comp. L.Q. 170, 178 (1986).

petitioner had been a "bona fide resident" of the country for "more than one year" prior to suit. This approach does not differentiate between American divorces of Americans, Britons or third-country nationals.

With the adoption of same-sex marriage or civil union legislation in many European countries and two Canadian provinces[5] (with provision for the dissolution of such relationships on grounds and in a manner analogous to or identical with those applicable to divorce),[6] there appears to be no obstacle to the recognition, in those countries, of the dissolution of an American civil union that complies with American requirements.

IV.   INCIDENTS OF DIVORCE DECREES: SUPPORT AND CUSTODY

A.   DIVISIBLE DIVORCE

§ 15.27   The concept of the divisibility of the foreign (including sister-state) divorce appeared early in American case law.[1] Justice Douglas reiterated it in his concurring opinion in *Esenwein v. Commonwealth of Pennsylvania*,[2] and the U.S. Supreme Court adopted the concept in *Estin v. Estin*.[3] In that case, the Supreme Court upheld a New York court's decision that had upheld the continued validity of a judicially sanctioned New York separation agreement and the support obligation it established despite an intervening Nevada *ex parte* divorce decree and the contention that full faith and credit required recognition of the latter as superseding the agreement. The Court acknowledged that some might argue that "once a divorce is granted, the whole of the marriage relation is dissolved, leaving no roots or tendrils of any kind." However, two reasons required a contrary decision: first, while, consistent with the rule of *Williams I*,[4] Nevada as the domicile of the petitioner in the divorce proceeding had the power to change the marital status of the parties, New York as the domicile of the abandoned spouse had an interest in the livelihood and support of that spouse and therefore could provide that a judicially sanctioned support agreement survives the *ex parte* divorce. Secondly, moreover, the Court regarded the earlier New York support decree was a property interest which Nevada had no judicial power to affect: to do so would be an "attempt to exercise in personam jurisdiction over a person not before the court." Therefore, "the result in this situation is to make the divorce divisible—to give

5. See supra § 13.19.

6. See Germany, LPartG (supra § 15.17 n.6) § 15; for brief summary, see J. Kropholler, BGB–Studienkommentar annos. 10–19, particular annot. 19, preceding § 1353 (6th ed. 2003).

§ 15.27

1. See, e.g., Richardson v. Wilson, 16 Tenn. (8 Yer.) 67 (1835); Toncray v. Toncray, 123 Tenn. 476, 131 S.W. 977 (1910); Metzger v. Metzger, 32 Ohio App. 202, 167

N.E. 690 (1929)(noted 39 Yale L.J. 587 (1930)); Note, *Woods v. Woods:* The Missing Piece to Divisible Divorce in Arkansas, 39 Ark. L. Rev. 705 (1986).

2. 325 U.S. 279, 65 S.Ct. 1118, 89 L.Ed. 1608 (1945).

3. 334 U.S. 541, 68 S.Ct. 1213, 92 L.Ed. 1561 (1948).

4. Williams v. North Carolina, 317 U.S. 287, 63 S.Ct. 207, 87 L.Ed. 279 (1942).

effect to the Nevada decree insofar as it affects marital status and to make it ineffective on the issue of alimony." The second point of the decision and the conclusion are especially important because they show the reach of the divisible-divorce concept: even if no prior New York decree had existed, adjudication of property issues—other than those relating to property situated in the state of the rendition (in rem)—deals with the personal obligations of the parties, and therefore requires *in personam* jurisdiction. An *ex parte* divorce decree thus does not have an effect on such obligations whether or not previously reduced to judgment.

The *Estin* case involved an earlier support decree of the prior marital domicile of the parties. The case therefore did not answer directly (the first aspect of the decision, above) whether a claim for post-divorce alimony could also be brought in another state. The second point of the *Estin* opinion, and its reference to the due-process protection to which the absent spouse is entitled, signalled the limited answer the Court subsequently gave in *Vanderbilt v. Vanderbilt*.[5] In that case, the marital domicile had been California, the wife had moved to New York and the husband had subsequently obtained an *ex parte* Nevada divorce. The Court upheld a New York decision awarding alimony. However, the extension of *Estin* by *Vanderbilt* is limited by the fact that New York was the domicile of the wife at the time of the divorce and not a disinterested third state. For that reason, some have urged that a state, to which a party moved subsequently to the divorce, not be permitted to award post-divorce alimony lest alimony-shopping be encouraged.[6] However, to the extent that the divisible-divorce concept rests on due-process grounds, the second aspect of the *Estin* opinion noted above would not permit rights to be cut off in this fashion. The right to litigate the alimony or support question remains unaffected by the *ex parte* divorce.[7]

---

5. 354 U.S. 416, 77 S.Ct. 1360, 1 L.Ed.2d 1456 (1957). See also Newport v. Newport, 219 Va. 48, 245 S.E.2d 134 (1978).

6. R. Weintraub, Commentary on the Conflict of Laws 309 (4th ed. 2001).

7. The effect of the Supreme Court's decision in Shaffer v. Heitner, 433 U.S. 186, 97 S.Ct. 2569, 53 L.Ed.2d 683 (1977) on the particular situation represented by *Vanderbilt* is not clear. In *Vanderbilt,* the wife had proceeded against the former husband (who had obtained the *ex parte* Nevada divorce) in a quasi-in-rem proceeding in New York, sequestering his property there. Since the husband's only connection with New York consisted of the presence of property there—with no other grounds for personal jurisdiction over him—the nexus of forum-party-cause of action, which *Shaffer* requires, arguably was lacking. As Professor Vernon stated: "Prior to *Shaffer,* the spouse needing support was free to use the quasi in rem process to gain access to funds despite the absence of the other spouse from the forum state. The needy spouse could pick the forum in the sense of having the option of tracing the absent spouse's property or the absent spouse and bringing suit there. Applying *Shaffer* to support-alimony cases would limit what appears to have been the goal of the Court in the *Estin* line of cases—to protect the dependent spouse—in that such spouse would be denied the power to select the forum to determine property rights." Vernon, State–Court Jurisdiction: A Preliminary Inquiry into the Impact of *Shaffer v. Heitner*, 63 Iowa L. Rev. 997, 1017, (1978). The policy concerns clearly argue against the extension of *Shaffer* to the alimony-support cases. Whatever the ultimate resolution with respect to asset-based jurisdiction, however, *Shaffer* does not affect the divisible-divorce concept of *Estin* itself,—that personal rights and obligations of the absent spouse are not within the rendering court's jurisdiction in an *ex parte* divorce proceeding. On the contrary, the forum-party-cause of action nex-

Forum-shopping, on the other hand, may be prevented by the application of the law of the spouse's domicile at the time of the divorce in cases in which the forum is the state of the (different) post-divorce domicile or another third state.[8]

Foreign legal systems, where statutory rules on jurisdiction and choice of law are only exceptionally subject to further constitutional scrutiny,[9] clearly focus on the interests of the local (plaintiff) obligee in support matters and are therefore less concerned with forum shopping. European Union law provides for jurisdiction based on the plaintiff's connection to the forum,[10] German law retains asset-based jurisdiction as against non-EU ("Brussels I") defendants,[11] and German conflicts rules invoke German substantive law, as subsidiary law, when the otherwise applicable law contains no provision for support in favor of the local plaintiff-obligee.[12]

In the United States, Uniform Laws today essentially bring about similar results: uniform reciprocal support and custody legislation extend a state's jurisdictional reach, the proceeding becomes functionally *inter partes* and may thus obviate the due-process concern identified in *Estin*.

§ 15.28   The divisible-divorce concept stands for the proposition that the *ex parte* divorce does not affect personal claims to alimony and support.[1] However, does it follow that the domiciliary or other second

us required by *Shaffer* underlines that aspect of *Estin*. But see text following n.12. See also infra § 15.30 n.2 and § 15.31 n.2.

8. R. Weintraub, supra n.6. But see text immediately following.

9. Most foreign legal systems do not provide for constitutional review. In those that do, conflicts rules have seldom been struck down. For an example see BVerfGE 31, 58 NJW 1971, 1509 (German conflicts rule testing capacity to marry by parties' laws of nationality unconstitutional, because discriminatory, when effect would be to prevent remarriage by a party validly divorced under German law).

10. Council Regulation (EC) 44/2001, [2001] Official Journal L 012/1 ("Brussels I"), Art. 5 No.2.

11. See § 23 German Code of Civil Procedure (ZPO) in connection with Brussels I, supra n.10, Arts. 3, 4.

12. Introductory Law to the Civil Code (EGBGB) Art. 18(2).

§ 15.28

1. The *inter partes* divorce of course does affect these claims under the *res judicata* principles of Sherrer v. Sherrer, 334 U.S. 343, 68 S.Ct. 1087, 92 L.Ed. 1429 (1948); see supra § 15.9. For this reason it is advantageous for the petitioner to obtain personal jurisdiction over the absent spouse if that is possible. If the divorcing forum

was the marital domicile such jurisdiction will ordinarily exist. Jurisdiction has even been sustained at the last marital domicile in circumstances where the divorce had been obtained elsewhere (Scoggins v. Scoggins, 382 Pa.Super. 507, 555 A.2d 1314 (1989)) but a one time, not recent domicile at the forum is not enough. See Lieb v. Lieb, 53 A.D.2d 67, 385 N.Y.S.2d 569 (1976). In *Lieb* the court adopted the interpretation of "matrimonial domicile" as meaning "where the parties when last together made their home;" this definition also prevails in California, Idaho, Illinois, Kansas, Oklahoma, and Wisconsin. See also Muckle v. Superior Court, 102 Cal.App.4th 218, 125 Cal.Rptr.2d 303 (2002). In Levy v. Levy, 185 A.D.2d 15, 592 N.Y.S.2d 480 (1993) another New York intermediate appellate court criticized the *Lieb* case as too narrow in its interpretation of the New York long-arm statute. According to *Levy*, the fact that the forum state was at one time, for a substantial period, the domicile of the parties is enough to confer *in personam* jurisdiction over the defendant even if the most recent matrimonial domicile was elsewhere. See also Cato v. Cato, 27 Conn. App. 142, 605 A.2d 558 (1992), certification granted in part 222 Conn. 906, 608 A.2d 691 (1992) (jurisdiction exists where forum was last matrimonial domicile prior to separation).

state *must* grant such relief, for instance when it has no provision for post-divorce alimony? Some decisions have held that no special remedy need be provided.[2] It is preferable, however, to accord the claimant (the *ex parte* defendant in the divorce) such a remedy: the plaintiff in the *ex parte* divorce having chosen a forum in which post-divorce alimony is, or would have been available, should be subject to having this obligation enforced wherever the claimant (*ex parte* defendant) can secure personal jurisdiction.[3]

The *ex parte* divorce may have broader consequences, and affect legal interests beyond the status of the parties, when it is the law of the second state that is applicable to the issue or claim. Succession statutes which give inheritance right to a "surviving wife" are the simplest illustration. The *ex parte* divorce did effectively terminate the status of "wife" and a claim to inherit from the deceased forum spouse thus fails. The Supreme Court so held with respect to a wife's dower rights in *Simons v. Miami Beach First National Bank*.[4] The dower right was

Because of reciprocal support legislation, infra § 15.30 *et seq.*, obtaining jurisdiction by traditional means may be less important today. However, it bears remembering that long-arm statutes may also reach the absent spouse. An example is Bunker v. Bunker, 261 Ark. 851, 552 S.W.2d 641 (1977) in which long-arm jurisdiction was sustained over the absent spouse on the ground that the "personal indignities" of which petitioner complained had occurred in Arkansas. The court noted that petitioner sought to proceed *in personam* in order "to obtain personal judgments for alimony, child support, and attorney's fees." 55 S.W.2d at 642. The authority of the case is weakened by the fact that the forum was also the last matrimonial domicile of the parties. See also Warren v. Warren, 622 So.2d 864 (La. App. 1993) using long-arm statute to maintain jurisdiction over non-resident spouse in divorce proceeding).

All assertion of long-arm jurisdiction must of course satisfy the "minimum contacts" standard which the U.S. Supreme Court specifically reiterated in the support-jurisdiction context. See Kulko v. Superior Court, 436 U.S. 84, 98 S.Ct. 1690, 56 L.Ed.2d 132 (1978). Thus, a North Carolina decision was correct in holding that, although the wife had "negotiated" with her then husband's Georgia attorney by mail in order to acquire title to the parties' North Carolina property, she had not thereby "appeared" in the Georgia divorce proceeding. The Georgia court therefore did not have personal jurisdiction over her, her claims to alimony and child support were therefore not cut off but could be asserted in a subsequent North Carolina proceeding. Webber v. Webber, 32 N.C.App. 572, 232 S.E.2d 865 (1977). See also Conlon by Conlon v. Heck-

ler, 719 F.2d 788 (5th Cir.1983) (while the court at plaintiff's domicile had divorce jurisdiction, it had no jurisdiction for a declaration of paternity in the absence of personal jurisdiction over the putative father. Petitioner therefore could not claim social security benefits as deceased putative father's "child"). In Burnham v. Superior Court, 495 U.S. 604, 110 S.Ct. 2105, 109 L.Ed.2d 631 (1990), the Court confirmed the continued validity of jurisdiction based on transient service in a divorce action. On the effect of reciprocal support legislation, see infra §§ 15.30 *et seq.*

2. See Terrell v. Terrell, 578 S.W.2d 637 (Tenn.1979); Coleman v. Coleman, 361 Pa.Super. 446, 522 A.2d 1115 (1987).

3. One way to solve the problem (absent applicable reciprocal support legislation that provides a remedy), is not to tie the availability of support to the law of the divorcing state or to the forum, but to provide *alternative* references as a matter of *choice of law*. For an example, see German Introductory Law to the Civil Code (EGBGB Art. 18(2) (supra § 15.27 n.12)). This has not been the solution adopted by American case law.

4. 381 U.S. 81, 85 S.Ct. 1315, 14 L.Ed.2d 232 (1965). See also Burton v. Burton, 52 Tenn.App. 484, 376 S.W.2d 504 (1963)(wife's right to support cut off by *ex parte* divorce). This decision is the reverse of the *Estin* case, discussed supra § 15.27 n.3. Taken together, they support the statement in the text that the *ex parte* forum cannot affect personal rights of the absent spouse (*Estin*), that the forum with personal jurisdiction therefore remains free to determine the effect of the *ex parte* divorce on

inchoate and its maturing into a present right at the decedent's death was conditioned on the claimant's being his surviving "wife." A different question would be presented if, for instance, inheritance rights were to accrue to a former wife who was the "innocent" party in the divorce. In such a case, the *ex parte* divorce would affect the status of wife but could not bind her with respect to a finding of "fault." The existence of post-divorce claims, the "incidents" of divorce, are thus determined by the second state under the rules discussed above. These claims are state law issues, as the Supreme Court observed in a different context in *Sutton v. Leib*;[5] they are within the province of the *second* forum and are not subject to adjudication by the divorcing court in the *ex parte* proceeding. This concept also permits the petitioner in the *ex parte* proceeding to seek additional relief (for alimony) in a subsequent *in personam* proceeding.[6]

§ 15.29   In 1953, the Supreme Court extended the divisible-divorce concept, beyond property interests of the absent spouse, to include other issues not immediately connected with the status question, such as custody over minor children. In *May v. Anderson*,[1] the marital domicile was in Wisconsin before the wife left for Ohio, taking the children with her. The husband obtained an *ex parte* divorce in Wisconsin (with personal notice to the wife in Ohio) which purported to award him custody of the children. In Ohio proceedings in which the father sought to enforce the Wisconsin decree the Ohio courts considered the mother bound by, and themselves constrained to accord recognition to, the Wisconsin decree because the children had their technical domicile (derivative from their father) in Wisconsin at the time of the decree. The Supreme Court reversed. Writing for the majority, Justice Burton referred to *Estin* and stated that "rights far more precious to appellant than property rights will be cut off if she is to be bound by the Wisconsin award of custody." He therefore gave a negative answer to the question "whether a court of a state, where a mother is neither domiciled, resident nor present, may cut off her immediate right to the care, custody, management and companionship of her minor children without having jurisdiction over her in personam." Justice Frankfurter, in concurring, took a narrower view. His interpretation of the import of the majority opinion was that Ohio was not required to recognize the Wisconsin decree but was also not precluded from doing so. "For Ohio to give respect to the Wisconsin decree would not offend the Due Process Clause." However, given the express reference to *Estin* in the majority opinion and Justices Jackson's and Reed's dissent in which they also

---

personal claims, that is, to consider them to be cut off (*Simons* and *Burton*) or to survive the *ex parte* divorce (*Estin*). Similarly: Brady v. Brady, 151 W.Va. 900, 158 S.E.2d 359 (1967) (valid *ex parte* divorce terminates existing support order).

5.   342 U.S. 402, 72 S.Ct. 398, 96 L.Ed. 448 (1952); see also supra § 15.12 n.4.

6.   Blech v. Blech, 6 Ariz.App. 131, 430 P.2d 710 (1967); Portnoy v. Portnoy, 81 Nev. 235, 401 P.2d 249 (1965).

§ 15.29

1.   345 U.S. 528, 73 S.Ct. 840, 97 L.Ed. 1221 (1953). For further discussion see infra § 15.39 n.8.

considered the decision to rest on due-process grounds,[2] it seems clear that *May* did decide that the Wisconsin decree was invalid both in Wisconsin and elsewhere absent personal jurisdiction (including by long-arm statute, see below) over the absent parent. In these circumstances, the decree may not be accorded full faith and credit. Viewed in this way, a subsequent Kentucky decision, *Batchelor v. Fulcher*,[3] was right in disregarding an Indiana decree when there had not been personal jurisdiction over one parent, while a Maryland decision would then have been improper when it accorded full faith and credit to a custody decision of the state of the domicile of the children and one parent.[4] Although *May* had left open the question of the children's domicile at the time of the *ex parte* divorce, its emphasis of the due process rights of the absent parent—however questionable as a matter of policy—would make the domicile of the children irrelevant if still followed.

However, it seems clear that this view of *May* will no longer be followed today, a view now also reflected in the case law.[5] Instead, a custody decree entered in compliance with the Uniform Child Custody Jurisdiction Act will be enforced under the federal Parental Kidnapping Prevention Act.[6]

2. "The Court's decision holds that the state in which a child and one parent is domiciled and which is primarily concerned about its welfare cannot constitutionally adjudicate controversies as to his guardianship." Id. at 539.

There are repeated references in the case law and the literature to the Burton "plurality" opinion. See, e.g., Perry v. Ponder, 604 S.W.2d 306, 320 (Tex.Civ.App.1980); Comment, Developments in the Law—The Constitution and the Family, 93 Harv. L. Rev. 1157, 1248 (1980). The court in *Perry* suggests that the Frankfurter concurrence presents the opinion of the Court since it represents the narrowest ground on which the decision can rest. These suggestions overlook that Justice Frankfurter did not only concur "in the judgment," but concurred in the Burton opinion itself. The result in *May* would be altered by statute were the case to reoccur today. See Comment, supra, at 1248 and infra § 15.39.

3. 415 S.W.2d 828 (Ky.1967). Accord: Pasqualone v. Pasqualone, 63 Ohio St.2d 96, 406 N.E.2d 1121, 1127 (1980). See also Lewis v. Lewis, 471 S.W.2d 290 (Ky.1971). In Ohio, subsequent case law assumes the continued validity of *Pasqualone:* Engin v. Engin, 1984 WL 6053 (Ohio App. 10 Dist. 1984); In the Matter of Custody of Johnson, 1985 WL 8382 (Ohio App. 1985).

4. Miller v. Miller, 247 Md. 358, 231 A.2d 27 (1967). In Goldfarb v. Goldfarb, 246 Ga. 24, 268 S.E.2d 648 (1980), the court held that Georgia had jurisdiction to hear the mother's custody claim despite lack of personal jurisdiction over the father because of the close nexus of the "forum state to the subject of . . . child custody." Having found that a close nexus existed, the court concluded that it could not be "sidetracked by arguments founded in the Full Faith and Credit Clause." Apparently adopting Justice Frankfurter's analysis in *May,* text supra at n.2, the court wrote: "Those judgments dealing with the welfare of a child may be given peculiar scrutiny in each interested state, but they are not less valid within the boundaries of the state rendering them."

5. See D.A. State (In the Interest of W.A.), 63 P.3d 607, 614 (Utah 2002), cert. denied 538 U.S. 1035, 123 S.Ct. 2092, 155 L.Ed.2d 1065 (2003) ("the status exception [of *Shaffer v. Heitner*] of the plaintiff, in determining personal jurisdiction, extends to parental rights termination proceedings"); Tammie J.C. v. Robert T.R. (In re Thomas J.R.), 262 Wis.2d 217, 663 N.W.2d 734, 743 (2003) (personal jurisdiction not needed for a child custody proceeding).

6. See also 28 U.S.C.A. § 1738A; infra § 15.39 *et seq.*

B. SUPPORT OBLIGATIONS

1. *Establishing the Support Obligation by Judicial Decree*

§ 15.30 Support obligations—pre-and post-divorce child support and alimony, as well as separate maintenance[1]—are established in proceedings in which the court has personal jurisdiction over both parties. The continued availability of quasi-in-rem jurisdiction (attachment of the property of the absent spouse) for the adjudication of the support claim in an unrelated forum is in doubt as a result of the U.S. Supreme Court's decision in *Shaffer v. Heitner*.[2] For post-divorce obligations this

---

§ 15.30

1. With respect to the nature of the support obligation, see Orr v. Orr, 440 U.S. 268, 99 S.Ct. 1102, 59 L.Ed.2d 306 (1979) (statutory limitation of alimony to wives only is unconstitutional under equal protection) and the growing trend to include future rights, such as pension rights, in the alimony award, particularly in community and quasi-community states. See Bass, ERISA and the Treatment of Pensions etc. As Property Divisible in Divorce, 4 Fam. Law Rep. 4009 (1978), with references to the case law. See also Van Loan v. Van Loan, 116 Ariz. 272, 569 P.2d 214 (1977); Neal v. Neal, 116 Ariz. 590, 570 P.2d 758 (1977); In re Marriage of Furimsky, 122 Ariz. 385, 595 P.2d 177 (App. 1978), reversed on other grounds 122 Ariz. 430, 595 P.2d 662 (1979). In re Marriage of Thorlin, 155 Ariz. 357, 746 P.2d 929 (1987) (the court affirmed an award to the wife of a 42.9% interest in husband's military retirement pension); In re Marriage of Walters, 220 Cal.App.3d 1062, 269 Cal.Rptr. 557 (1990) (wife had community property interest in ex-husband's military retirement pension); In re Marriage of Branstetter, 508 N.W.2d 638 (Iowa 1993) (husband's pension subject to division in divorce proceeding); Potts v. Potts, 142 Md.App. 448, 790 A.2d 703 (Md. App. 2002) (awarding wife an interest in husband's pension).

Same-sex marriage or civil union legislation typically provides for post-dissolution support in appropriate cases, usually by express reference and by way of analogy to post-divorce support obligations. See, e.g., for Vermont, 15 V.S.A. §§ 1204(c), 1206; for Germany, LPartG, supra § 15.17 n.6, § 16. For interstate recognition and enforcement, see infra n. 8.

2. 433 U.S. 186, 97 S.Ct. 2569, 53 L.Ed.2d 683 (1977). See the discussion supra § 15.28 n.7. In many cases—desertion, for instance—long-arm statutes (matrimonial domicile, place of commission of the offense of non-support) or the uniform support legislation, infra nn.5, 7, may serve to establish *in personam* jurisdiction over the absent spouse; the property may then be

attached as security pending the decision on the merits. In Hurlbut v. Hurlbut, 101 Misc.2d 571, 421 N.Y.S.2d 509 (1979) the court found that it had personal jurisdiction over a French wife's action to recover a money judgment on sums allegedly due pursuant to a separation agreement embodied in a Mexican divorce decree because the marriage, the purchase of the marital residence, and the negotiation and execution of the separation agreement had all occurred in New York. In Pray v. Pray, 5 Fam. Law Rep. 2945 (D.C. Super. Ct. Fam. Div. 1979), the court found personal jurisdiction over Arabian American Oil Company on the basis of minimum contacts with the District of Columbia for the limited purpose of garnishment to enforce payment of support arrearages. In Bunker v. Bunker, 261 Ark. 851, 552 S.W.2d 641 (1977), the court sustained jurisdiction for divorce, alimony, child support and attorney's fees over nonresident husband on the ground that Arkansas was the last matrimonial domicile of the parties and where the defendant's alleged conduct created the cause of action for divorce, alimony and support. Both *Hurlbut* and *Bunker* present extreme fact situations but are arguably compatible with Kulko v. Superior Court, 436 U.S. 84, 98 S.Ct. 1690, 56 L.Ed.2d 132 (1978), since, in both cases, the defendant had prior contact with the jurisdiction and the cause of action was related to that contact. See also Rich v. Rich, 93 Misc.2d 409, 402 N.Y.S.2d 767 (1978), discussed infra § 15.33 n.2. But see Johansen v. Johansen, 305 N.W.2d 383 (S.D.1981) which held that a section of South Dakota's long-arm statute ("Failure to Support a Minor Child Residing in South Dakota," S.D.C.L. § 15–7–2(7)) conferred jurisdiction over petitioner's former husband who, after the parties' Minnesota divorce, had moved to Wyoming and had apparently never been in South Dakota. The decision seems inconsistent with *Kulko*. Similarly, In re Marriage of Highsmith, 130 Ill.App.3d 725, 86 Ill.Dec. 1, 474 N.E.2d 915 (1985) seems inconsistent with *Kulko* (see dissent by Stouder, J., id. at 917–18). The court assumed long-arm jurisdiction over a non-resident father for the commission of a

may be the *inter partes* divorce proceeding itself, as a result of which the issues become *res judicata* and entitled to full faith and credit under the principles of *Sherrer*,[3] subject to possible subsequent modification as to the extent of the obligation.[4] The obligation may also be established in a proceeding subsequent to the *ex parte* divorce in which jurisdiction is obtained over the absent party in the manner described in the preceding section.

The Uniform Reciprocal Enforcement of Support Act,[5] which was in force in some form in all states, provided additional procedures for the deserted spouse. It applied both to the enforcement of support orders and to original claims for support. Its procedures enabled the claimant to file in the local forum which forwarded the complaint to the state where the defendant is present. The court of the second state then exercised personal jurisdiction over the defendant and entered the appropriate support order. Particularly important was the Act's choice-of-law provision that the support obligation was to be determined according to the law of the state where the defendant was present at and during the time for which support is claimed.[6]

In 1992, the Uniform Interstate Family Support Act (UIFSA),[7] since amended, was approved by the National Conference of Commissioners of Uniform State Laws to supersede URESA. By now, it has been enacted by all states, while others retain aspects of URESA or (Arizona for limited purposes) enacted UIFSA without repealing URESA. It provides for exclusive continuing jurisdiction in the court that issued the support order so long as the obligor, obligee, or the child continues to reside in the state unless each party files a written consent to modification by the court of another state. For spousal support orders, the issuing court has exclusive continuing jurisdiction for the duration of the support obligation. Sec. 303 of UIFSA, however, contains an important change compared to URESA: when responding to a request to enforce another court's support order, the court shall apply the law of the forum to

---

tortious act (non-support) merely on the basis of his having sent the child to live in Illinois and by designating Illinois residents (grandparents) as her custodians. As in *Kulko,* an alternative remedy (URESA) was available.

3. 334 U.S. 343, 68 S.Ct. 1087, 92 L.Ed. 1429 (1948) supra § 15.9 n.3.

4. For subsequent modification, see infra subsection 2.

5. 9 U.L.A. 805 (1973) (1968 Revised Act) and 9 U.L.A. 885 (1973) (1958 Act).

6. For discussion see Note, Interstate Enforcement of Modifiable Alimony and Child Support Decrees, 54 Iowa L. Rev. 597 (1969) (1968 Act); Brockelbank & Infausto, Interstate Enforcement of Family Support (2d ed. 1971); Czapanskiy, Child Support and Visitation: Rethinking the Connections, 20 Rutgers L.J. 619 (1989).

The alternative to the choice of the "defendant's law" is the law of the obligee's habitual residence. The latter perhaps accords better with the obligee's needs and with forum interests. This approach has been adopted by some foreign legal systems. See, e.g., German Introductory Law to the Civil Code (EGBGB) Arts. 18(1), 18(2), in turn patterned after the Hague Convention on the Law Applicable to Maintenance Obligations. Due process concerns (for the defendant) may preclude such a plaintiff-contact dependent approach.

7. Unif. Interstate Family Support Act (amended 1996), 9 U.L.A. pt 1, 409 (Supp. 1998). For commentary, see Note, The Uniform Interstate Family Support Act: The New URESA, 20. U. Dayton L. Rev. 425 (1994); Legler, Coming Revolution in Child Support Policy: Implications of the 1996 Welfare Act, 30 Fam. L.Q. 519, 541, 555 (1996).

"determine the duty of support and the amount payable in accordance with the law and support guidelines of this State."[8] The enforcement of child support orders of sister states is now ensured through the "Full Faith and Credit for Child Support Orders Act" of 1994,[9] in which Congress exercised its powers under the "effect" provision of the Full Faith and Credit Clause: sister state support orders must be enforced and may not be modified unless the issuing state is no longer the residence of any contestant or of the child or the parties have filed a consent (i.e., a provision tracking UIFSA).

2. *Enforcement and Modification of Support Decrees*

§ 15.31 Support may be awarded to a spouse prior to and pending a divorce, or a separate maintenance obligation may be established. Upon the dissolution of a marriage, one spouse may be granted a property settlement or lump sum alimony or may be awarded continuing alimony for the future. Lump sum settlements between spouses are common, but lump sum settlements in lieu of child support are rare and indeed the two situations are quite different. A court can terminate the relationship of the spouses, while the parental relationship continues. Thus, while a final property settlement between the spouses may be appropriate and often desirable, it may be quite inappropriate in the case of child support and, if allowed to stand as a final settlement, can seriously prejudice subsequent needs of the child. The important question therefore arises whether a lump sum award for child support must be given full faith and credit and subsequent modification, i.e., a petition for additional support be denied.

Claims for alimony and child support (for instance for arrearage) which have been reduced to judgment are entitled to full faith and credit.[1] Past due amounts are rarely subject to modification in the state of rendition. However, most states provide for *prospective* modification.

---

8. While UIFSA, on its face, seems applicable to support orders that issue upon dissolution of a (same-sex) civil union, Section 303 may provide an avenue for states that have adopted DOMA (supra § 13.20, 15.17 n. 8) to deny recognition to such orders. Assuming that the order has been reduced to judgment in the state of rendition—for instance, for past-due amounts—, the interstate recognition of such a judgment seems mandated under the rule of Fauntleroy v. Lum, 210 U.S. 230, 28 S.Ct. 641, 52 L.Ed. 1039 (1908), discussed infra § 24.20.

In the European Union, the Regulation (EC) 44/2001 ("Rome I") provides for jurisdiction in the state of the support creditor's residence. Art. 5, No.2. The conflicts law of European countries may contain a number of possible references but, like Art. 18(2) of the German EGBGB, will use forum law (i.e. the claimant's law) as the default rule.

9. 108 Stat. 4063, 28 U.S.C.A. § 1738B.

§ 15.31

1. Barber v. Barber, 323 U.S. 77, 65 S.Ct. 137, 89 L.Ed. 82 (1944). See also Sistare v. Sistare, 218 U.S. 1, 30 S.Ct. 682, 54 L.Ed. 905 (1910); Lynde v. Lynde, 181 U.S. 183, 21 S.Ct. 555, 45 L.Ed. 810 (1901). For the recognition and enforcement of support decrees in the context of same-sex civil unions, see supra § 15.30 n.8. The same problem arises with respect to decrees for the equitable division of property upon dissolution of such a union which, in Vermont for instance, follows the rules applicable to divorce: 15 V.S.A. § 1204(d) (2003). Federal law now provides additional mechanisms for enforcement of child support: see the "Child Support Enforcement Amendments of 1984." 98 Stat. 1305. For enforcement in the international setting see infra § 15.36.

Two questions arise in this connection: (a) If the support award is modifiable where rendered, may modification also be sought, and decreed, in a second state where there is jurisdiction over the defendant?[2] (b) What law should govern modification, that of the sate of rendition or of the state where modification is sought? The following subsections address the questions raised in this and the preceding paragraph.

a. Lump Sum Child Support and Claims for Additional Support

§ 15.32 In *Yarborough v. Yarborough*[1] the Supreme Court required South Carolina to give full faith and credit to a Georgia lump-sum award for child support that purported to free the father from any future obligation. South Carolina was therefore precluded from awarding addi-

---

2. In Kulko v. California Superior Court, 436 U.S. 84, 98 S.Ct. 1690, 56 L.Ed.2d 132 (1978), the Supreme Court held, in application of its decision in Shaffer v. Heitner, 433 U.S. 186, 97 S.Ct. 2569, 53 L.Ed.2d 683 (1977) that California could not exercise jurisdiction over a non-resident defendant father for modification of a custody and support decree when the defendant did not have minimum contacts with California. *Kulko* was followed in Boyer v. Boyer, 73 Ill.2d 331, 22 Ill.Dec. 747, 383 N.E.2d 223 (1978). However, in Rich v. Rich, 93 Misc.2d 409, 402 N.Y.S.2d 767 (1978), the court invoked the U.S. Supreme Court's footnote 37 in Shaffer v. Heitner, 433 U.S. 186, 211, 97 S.Ct. 2569, 2584, 53 L.Ed.2d 683 (1977) in order to base jurisdiction for the enforcement of a support claim on the presence of property in New York when the defendant lived abroad and there was no other forum available to the plaintiff. It appears from the somewhat incomplete statement of the facts that plaintiff's claim arose from a Mexican decree: enforcement of a foreign judgment, if and when recognized, does not raise *Shaffer*-type jurisdictional issues inasmuch as that decision addressed original claims not reduced to judgment. The court's additional point that the defendant had availed itself of "the benefits of testate distribution in this State", even if it had merit, also addresses personal jurisdiction and does not furnish a "solid predicate for the exercise of *quasi in rem* jurisdiction." 93 Misc.2d at 415, 402 N.Y.S.2d at 770. But see Johansen v. Johansen, 305 N.W.2d 383 (S.D.1981), discussed supra § 15.30 n.2, and see Mandel-Mantello v. Treves, 103 Misc.2d 700, 426 N.Y.S.2d 929 (1980) (the court disagreed with the decision in Rich v. Rich inasmuch as it failed to address the issue of recognition of the Mexican divorce decree under CPLR 5301. It is only after the foreign country judgment has been shown to fulfill the statutory requisites set forth by the article on recognition of foreign country money judgments that the question of enforceability of the judgment against properties in that state can even be addressed).

Kulko has also been followed in New York in a case in which a decedent's first wife sought a declaration of invalidity of the decedent's *ex parte* Honduras divorce and subsequent Nevada remarriage in order to gain survivor's benefits. The court found that the second wife had no minimum contacts with New York and therefore dismissed for lack of jurisdiction. Carr v. Carr, 46 N.Y.2d 270, 413 N.Y.S.2d 305, 385 N.E.2d 1234 (1978).

There is continuing jurisdiction in the court which originally decreed the divorce and awarded support in a proceeding with jurisdiction over both parties to reach the now non-resident defendant for the purpose of enforcing or modifying the support order. See text, supra § 15.30, after n.8, on UIFSA. For prior law, to the same effect, see, e.g., Opperman v. Sullivan, In and For Bremer County, 330 N.W.2d 796 (Iowa 1983); Canty v. Canty, 392 Mass. 1004, 465 N.E.2d 770 (1984); Phillips v. Iowa Dist. Court for Johnson County, 380 N.W.2d 706 (Iowa 1986). Shinn v. Kreul, 311 S.C. 94, 427 S.E.2d 695 (S.C.App.1993) (forum entering original support order has continuing jurisdiction to modify even if neither party remains domiciled in the forum). But also see O'Donnell v. O'Donnell, 22 Mass.App. Ct. 936, 493 N.E.2d 889 (1986) (the fact that the plaintiff may seek relief in the court which originally granted the divorce and support decree does not bar her from seeking relief in another appropriate court).

§ 15.32

1. 290 U.S. 202, 54 S.Ct. 181, 78 L.Ed. 269 (1933).

tional support for educational and maintenance expenses for the minor child who was then living with her grandfather in South Carolina. Relying on *Sistare*,[2] the Court held that an unalterable support decree is entitled to full faith and credit; the father was entitled to rely on the finality of the Georgia decree; the imposition of additional obligations would therefore violate his due process rights. The decision is troublesome, "perfectly outrageous" in the opinion of one writer.[3] The parent-child relationship was viewed by the dissent and others to be a continuing relationship and the minor's later circumstances and the interest of South Carolina were not and could not be litigated.[4] In this respect, the nature of the case is substantially different from the ordinary transaction in which the rights of the parties can be settled once and for all.[5] Moreover, the minor had not been a party to the Georgia proceeding between her parents nor had a guardian *ad litem* been appointed for her; the Court dismissed an objection on this ground by pointing out that, as a minor, the child's domicile was that of her father until the divorce, giving the Georgia court "complete jurisdiction of the marriage status and, as an incident, power to finally determine the extent of the father's obligation. . . ." Notions of what quality of notice is required and when a child is entitled to separate representation in cases of potential conflict between its own and parental interests no doubt have undergone substantial evolution since *Yarborough*. On this basis alone, the Court might address at least this issue differently today. Despite this possibility, however, the point remains that—on the merits—the Court did not adequately address the continuing parent-child relationship, the differing needs of a maturing child, the interests of society, in the form of a second forum possibly being called upon to make provision for a needy child, as well as the related problem of abandoned children, in circumstances where the defendant *remained in the state of rendition.*

§ 15.33   On the other hand, complete rejection of *Yarborough* runs the danger of encouraging post-award forum-shopping if the second forum is free to judge the extent of the support obligation entirely by local law standards. For that reason, it is important to note that the Court did not rule out completely that subsequent modification might be possible in appropriate cases: "We need not consider whether South Carolina would have power to require the father, *if he were [now] domiciled there,* to make further provision for . . . support. . . ."[1] The

---

2. Sistare v. Sistare, 218 U.S. 1, 30 S.Ct. 682, 54 L.Ed. 905 (1910).

3. B. Currie, Full Faith and Credit, Chiefly to Judgments: A Role for Congress, 1964 Sup. Ct. Rev. 89, 118. The result of the *Yarborough* decision superficially resembles the provision of the Uniform Reciprocal Enforcement of Support Act, supra at § 15.30 nn.5–6, in that its focus—for the determination of the existence and the extent of a support obligation—is on the law of the state where the defendant is or was present at the relevant time. The two are distinguishable, however. The purpose of

UIFSA (and before it, URESA) is to prevent forum-shopping by the claimant, while *Yarborough* shields the obligor against all claims by denying any further obligation. But see infra § 15.33 nn.1, 3.

4. D. Currie, H. Kay & L. Kramer, Conflict of Laws 463 et seq. (6th ed. 2001).

5. Id.

§ 15.33

1. Yarborough v. Yarborough, 290 U.S. 202, 213, 54 S.Ct. 181, 185, 78 L.Ed. 269 (1933) (emphasis and bracketed language added).

California Supreme Court (Justice Traynor writing) seized on this language in *Elkind v. Byck*[2] and held that California could award additional support despite a prior Georgia lump-sum settlement when the father had subsequently moved to California. It also noted that the Uniform Reciprocal Enforcement of Support Act, in force also in Georgia, now permits the "state of the obligor's residence" to apply its law. While the Act cannot overcome the *Yarborough* decision to the extent that the latter rests on constitutional grounds, the Act does evidence recognition "that no state may freeze the obligations flowing from the continuing relation of parent and child." In the case of a change of domicile by the *obligor,* this holding is good policy and protects the interests of all parties as well as of the new state of domicile. In addition, the decision is consistent with *Yarborough* inasmuch as this contingency had been expressly left open. However, as a general proposition, the last-quoted language goes beyond *Yarborough* since it would apply equally to cases involving only a change of domicile by the minor *obligee.* The California court's position is good *policy* since, indeed, no state should be able to "freeze obligations flowing from the continuing relationship," but this is precisely the problem which *Yarborough* failed to address. Forum-shopping by the obligee should be discouraged when another law closely related to the obligor does provide relief. When the other forum attempts to freeze the obligation, the focus might then appropriately shift to the law most closely connected to the obligee.[3]

As a practical matter, the approach adopted in *Elkind* served to solve the *Yarborough* problem in most cases. Georgia appears to be the only state in which a lump-sum child support settlement may be awarded.[4] Cases like *Yarborough* will therefore arise only infrequently. Under UIFSA, however, modification may still be within the control of the original state of rendition. Supra § 15.30 *et seq.*

b. *Modification of Support Decrees*

§ 15.34 If the support decree is modifiable in the state of rendition, will a second forum, for instance the state of the obligor's or the obligee's new domicile, accord it recognition, and if appropriate, undertake a modification? The older case law required that the claim be final, either reduced to judgment or, as a claim, not subject to retroactive modification, before recognizing and enforcing it locally.[1] However, nei-

---

2. 68 Cal.2d 453, 67 Cal.Rptr. 404, 439 P.2d 316 (1968).

3. See supra § 15.30 n.6.

4. O.C.G.A. § 19–6–15 (2002); Esser v. Esser, 277 Ga. 97, 586 S.E.2d 627 (2003).

§ 15.34

1. See, e.g., Page v. Page, 189 Mass. 85, 75 N.E. 92 (1905); Levine v. Levine, 95 Or. 94, 187 P. 609 (1920). See also 2 J.H. Beale, Conflict of Laws 1392–1393 (1935). For modern cases adhering to this view,

see Maner v. Maner, 401 F.2d 616 (5th Cir. 1968); Catlett v. Catlett, 412 P.2d 942 (Okla.1966). Cf. Reysa v. Reysa, 521 S.W.2d 746 (Tex.Civ.App.1975); Dorey v. Dorey, 609 F.2d 1128 (5th Cir.1980), rehearing denied 613 F.2d 314 (1980) (held that *Maner* still accurately reflects Alabama law); McDougald v. Jenson, 596 F.Supp. 680 (N.D.Fla.1984) (Washington court did not give full faith and credit to a Florida custody decree, because custody decrees are always subject to modification "in

ther the policy of preclusion which underlies the Full Faith and Credit Clause,[2] nor the language of that constitutional provision,[3] admit of such an exception. As between the parties, the issue has been resolved by litigation in the first forum and the second forum should accord the same effect under its local law in order to preclude the obligor from escaping his obligation by flight. The Supreme Court did not provide direction. The clear practice of state courts was to recognize the foreign support order, when rendered by a court with competent jurisdiction, to give the parties an opportunity to litigate issues relative to modification, and then to issue a local decree of enforcement,[4] whether this is done on a theory of comity or under Full Faith and Credit. The early leading case was *Worthley v. Worthley*[5] in which the California Supreme Court enforced accrued arrearages under a New Jersey decree and established the obligation for future payments as a California decree. The Court noted that "there is no valid reason, in a case in which both parties are before the court, why California should refuse ... " to recognize the decree, especially since subsequent retroactive modification of past-due amounts or prospective modification of future installments would also be recognizable in California.[6] To hold otherwise would require extensive, expensive, and hence burdensome cross-country litigation. *Worthley* set the pattern for regular enforcement in other states.[7]

Under UIFSA,[8] the first court retains exclusive continuing jurisdiction so long as a party resides there. If this is not the case, or if the

the best interest" of the child); Wright v. Brown, 528 N.E.2d 824 (Ind.App. 2d Dist. 1988) (where the courts of the jurisdiction rendering the decree are empowered to cancel or modify the accrued arrearage, courts of a sister-state are at liberty to enforce payment of such arrears so long as the husband has not initiated proceedings to modify or cancel the arrears. See Griffin v. Griffin, 327 U.S. 220, 235, 66 S.Ct. 556, 563, 90 L.Ed. 635 (1946)).

2. Infra § 24.1.

3. See Justice Jackson's concurrence in *Barber* (discussed supra § 15.33 n.1).

4. Restatement, Second, Conflict of Laws § 109(2) (1971).

5. 44 Cal.2d 465, 283 P.2d 19 (1955).

6. If a change in the earlier award, i.e. modification, is sought, new notice must be given to the defendant. Griffin v. Griffin, 327 U.S. 220, 66 S.Ct. 556, 90 L.Ed. 635 (1946).

7. See Light v. Light, 12 Ill.2d 502, 147 N.E.2d 34 (1957); Johnson v. Johnson, 115 Ga.App. 749, 156 S.E.2d 186 (1967); Glickman v. Mesigh, 200 Colo. 320, 615 P.2d 23 (1980); Sanson v. Sanson, 466 N.E.2d 770

(Ind.App. 4th Dist. 1984); In re the Marriage of Whitley, 775 P.2d 95 (Colo.App. 1989) (since the California decree was docketed in the Colorado district court, and since Colorado was then the children's home state, the court was authorized to modify the decree in the best interests of the children according to the public policy of the state).

Under UIFSA, foreign modifiable decrees are entitled to the same weight as if entered by the forum. See, e.g.,(under URESA), Schoenfeld v. Marsh, 418 Pa.Super. 469, 614 A.2d 733 (1992) (Pennsylvania state court recognizes foreign decree under RURESA). See also Note, Stemming the Modification of Child–Support Orders by Responding Courts: A Proposal to Amend RURESA's Antisuppression Clause, 24 U.Mich.J.L.Ref. 405, 406 (1991) (listing states that have adopted RURESA).

8. Unif. Interstate Family Support Act (amended 1996), 9 U.L.A. pt 1, 409 (Supp. 1998). See Teseniar v. Teseniar, 74 P.3d 910, 914 (Alaska 2003) (continuing jurisdiction because mother and child still resided in Alaska); Linn v. Delaware Child Support Enforcement, 736 A.2d 954 (Del. 1999) (Minnesota lost continuing jurisdiction to

parties, in writing, agree to jurisdiction of another court, either the latter or a court with otherwise proper jurisdiction may proceed.

c. Choice of Law for Modification

§ 15.35 If the second forum undertakes to modify a sister state's decree or obligations due thereunder, what law should it apply? Justice Traynor indicated in *Worthley* that "either party may tender and litigate any plea for modification that could be presented to the courts of the state where the alimony or support decree was originally rendered."[1] This language therefore invokes the traditional full-faith-and-credit approach that whatever the first forum could or would do under its law, the second forum might also do.[2] In the *Worthley* case, the obligee had retained her New Jersey domicile but the obligor had become a California domiciliary. Under the Uniform Reciprocal Enforcement of Support Act,[3] a case like *Worthley* would have allowed the application of forum law, and not the law of the state of rendition, when the obligor subsequently became a domiciliary of the forum.[4]

Under UIFSA,[5] the choice-of-law focus shifts from the state of rendition to the forum where the first state's support order is in issue (e.g., for enforcement). Forum law[6] applies to the "duty of support and the amount payable." When no party nor the child continues to reside in the state of rendition, UIFSA provides no rule and the case law reviewed becomes relevant once again. It may be expected to shift, like UIFSA, to a forum orientation.

d. Summary

§ 15.36 Thus, while case law is not abundant, the following summarizes current approaches and permissible further extensions in the enforcement of modifiable foreign decrees:

> (i) When neither party continues to reside in the state of rendition, the second forum, under UIFSA, defers to F–1 (dismisses) or uses local law if so empowered by the parties to entertain the case (see supra). If the first forum entered *no* decree, presumably case law rules would apply. That it would continue to favor the obligor, seems doubtful.

modify support order when all parties, including the children, had left the state).

§ 15.35

1. Worthley v. Worthley, 44 Cal.2d 465, 474, 283 P.2d 19, 25 (1955).

2. See infra Ch. 24. Conversely, the forum need not entertain an action for modification when another forum is more convenient and has jurisdiction over both parties: Haynes v. Carr, 379 A.2d 1178 (D.C.App. 1977) (both parties resided in Maryland).

3. See also supra § 15.32 n.3 and § 15.30 nn.5–6.

4. For UIFSA, see infra § 15.36, text at (v).

5. Unif. Interstate Family Support Act (amended 1996), 9 U.L.A. pt 1, 409 (Supp. 1998); see supra § 15.30. The choice-of-law provisions are § 303, 604. See State v. Bromley, 987 P.2d 183, 190 (Alaska 1999) (discussing these provisions).

6. UIFSA, supra § 15.30 n.7, § 303.

(ii) Conversely, when the parties or at least the obligor continue to be domiciled in the state of rendition, the law of that state applies as a result of full-faith-and-credit considerations, including its rules preventing or permitting modification. This follows from *Yarborough* and, now by statute, from UIFSA § 303.

(iii) When the obligor now resides in the forum but the obligee has remained in the state of rendition, the *Worthley* court had assumed the applicability of the law of the state of rendition. *Yarborough* had left this question open[1] and the provisions of the Uniform Reciprocal Enforcement of Support Act and the Revised Act had referred to the obligor's domicile at the time the obligation arose.[2] The UIFSA changes the reference, in carefully limited language, to obligee's law.[3]

(iv) In all cases, it would seem that a private support agreement of the parties, including choice-of-law provisions contained in it and whether or not incorporated in a decree, may overcome the choice-of-law rule of URESA/RURESA or UIFSA.[4]

(v) A party entitled to support may proceed at common law in order to secure an order awarding, enforcing or modifying support *or* utilize the procedures available under UIFSA. The effect of utilizing first one and subsequently the other procedure on the earlier award under the respective first procedure is unclear. Since proceedings under UIFSA, despite the fact that they are carried on by mail, are *in personam* proceedings,[5] the first proceeding should be superseded under ordinary principles of preclusion.[6] However, the Montana Supreme Court held that a URESA order, which did not refer to a prior support award, did not modify it and did not bar the obligee from collecting arrearage under the support decree.[7] Under the new Full–Faith-and-Credit Statute,[8] first-state orders, obtained by a court exercising proper jurisdiction, are now entitled to recognition. The UIFSA,[9] where applicable, determines the modalities for modification.

§ 15.36

1. Supra at § 15.33 n.1.

2. See Mocher v. Rasmussen–Taxdal, 180 So.2d 488 (Fla.App.1965) (dictum).

3. Supra § 15.35 n.6.

4. Cf. Haag v. Barnes, 9 N.Y.2d 554, 216 N.Y.S.2d 65, 175 N.E.2d 441 (1961).

5. See supra § 15.30 nn.5–6.

6. See infra Ch. 24.

7. Campbell v. Jenne, 172 Mont. 219, 563 P.2d 574 (1977), cited with approval in In re Marriage of Petranek, 255 Mont. 458, 461, 843 P.2d 784 (1992). See also Illinois People ex rel. Winger v. Young, 78 Ill. App.3d 512, 33 Ill.Dec. 920, 397 N.E.2d 253 (1979) (responding court, under URESA, lacks authority to withhold child support payments until the custodial parent makes the child available for visitation). See Illinois Dept. of Public Aid v. Peterson, 156 Ill.App.3d 657, 108 Ill.Dec. 720, 509 N.E.2d 146 (1987). See also Annot., Construction and Effect of Provision of Uniform Reciprocal Enforcement of Support Act That No Support Order Shall Supersede or Nullify Any Other Order, 31 ALR 4th 347 (1984).

8. 28 U.S.C.A. § 1738B; see also supra § 15.30 n.9. See Hatamyar, Critical Applications and Proposals for Improvement of the Uniform Interstate Family Support Act and Full Faith and Credit for Child Support Orders Acts, 71 St.John's L. Rev. 1 (1997).

9. Unif. Interstate Family Support Act (amended 1996), 9 U.L.A. pt 1, 409 (Supp. 1998); see supra § 15.30.

3. *International Recognition*

§ 15.37 English courts recognize the divisible divorce concept in circumstances in which a previous American decree is subsequently in issue in litigation in England. Thus, the Court of Appeal has held that an *ex parte* Nevada divorce did not discharge a prior English maintenance order.[1] With respect to support, the obligation established by a foreign forum, e.g. an American court, must be a final determination.[2] Installments which are past due and no longer subject to modification may be severed from any modifiable part of the judgment and enforced.[3] In this respect English practice follows the older American approach, mentioned above.[4] In other countries, the 1973 Hague Convention on Recognition and Enforcement of Maintenance Orders may apply.[5] It provides for recognition of decrees rendered by a court or agency of the country of habitual residence of either obligor or obligee or of the country of common nationality. The 1956 New York Convention on establishing and enforcing support obligations[6] is designed to afford claimant legal and judicial assistance but it does not provide conflicts rules of its own. The German Foreign–Country Support Statute of 1986[7] was based on the New York Convention and was designed to mesh with support legislation in Anglo–American countries, particularly with the American Uniform Reciprocal Enforcement of Support Act.

In the United States, the First Restatement asserted that "no state will directly enforce a duty to support created by the law of another state [since] its enforcement is of no special interest to other states."[8] This parochial view overlooked the needs of children now living in the United

---

§ 15.37

1. Wood v. Wood, [1957] P.254.

2. See Harrop v. Harrop, [1920], 3 K.B. 386.

3. Re Macartney, [1921] 1 Ch. 522; Gutteridge, The International Enforcement of Maintenance Orders, 2 Int'l & Comp. L.Q. 155 (1948).

4. Supra § 15.34 n.1. For early discussion of the Canadian Model Uniform Reciprocal Enforcement of Maintenance Orders Act and of U.S.-Canadian reciprocal enforcement cooperation see Cavers, International Enforcement of Family Support, 81 Colum. L. Rev. 994, 1023–26 (1981).

5. U.K.T.S. 49 (1980); 21 Am. J. Comp. L. 156 (1973). The earlier (1958) Hague Convention on recognition and enforcement of support decrees, 539 U.N.T.S. 49 (1980), 21 Am. J. Comp. L. 156 (1973), remains in force as to ratifying states in cases in which the two states involved have not both adopted the 1973 convention.

6. As of 2003, United Nations Convention on the Recovery Abroad of Maintenance, 268 U.N.T.S. 44, is in force in: Algeria, Argentina, Australia, Austria, Barbados, Belarus, Belgium, Bolivia, Bosnia and Herzogovina, Brazil, Burkina Faso, Cambodia, Cape Verde, Central African Republic, Chile, China, Colombia, Croatia, Cuba, Cyprus, Czech Republic, Denmark, Dominican Republic, Ecuador, El Salvador, Estonia, Finland, France, Germany, Greece, Guatemala, Haiti, Holy See, Hungary, Ireland, Israel, Italy, Kazakhstan, Luxembourg, Macedonia, Mexico, Monaco, Morocco, Netherlands, New Zealand, Niger, Norway, Pakistan, Philippines, Poland, Portugal, Romania, Serbia and Montenegro, Slovakia, Slovenia, Spain, Sri Lanka, Suriname, Sweden, Switzerland, Tunisia, Turkey, United Kingdom, and Uruguay.

7. Gesetz zur Geltendmachung von Unterhaltsansprüchen im Verkehr mit ausländischen Staaten (Auslandsunterhaltsgesetz–AUG), 1986 Bundesgesetzblatt I, 2563. For detailed analysis, see Müller-Freienfels in: Festschrift für Kegel 389–432 (1987).

8. Restatement Conflict of Laws § 458, cmnt. (a) (1934).

States. Since then, the Second Restatement[9] and the case law[10] favored the recognition of foreign support decrees under principles of comity, even if still modifiable where rendered.[11] An example of a progressive decision is one rendered by a California District Court of Appeal which said, in reversing the trial court's dismissal of an action on an English decree: "The English decree being valid and subsisting, the appellant had the right to sue on that decree in the courts of this state. This does not mean, however, that she was entitled to have established as a money judgment the arrearages under the English decree. That decree, though established as a California judgment, could have no greater effect than it had in the jurisdiction of origin, England.... The judgment of the English court being subject to modification both prospectively and retroactively by the court that rendered it, ... the courts of this state are ... bound to afford respondent the opportunity to litigate the question of modification and to give him the same rights in that regard as he would have had in the English court."[12] In short, the court treated the English decree in the same manner as *Worthley*[13] had a sister-state decree.

In contrast, some cases still display a remarkably parochial approach. Thus, an Illinois court, relying on precedents dating to 1882, stated that "a foreign country, in matters of matrimony, may issue judgments or decrees which will be unenforceable in this country." It thought that the common law action of debt had been changed by adoption of the Uniform Foreign–Money Judgment Recognition Act which excludes judgments for "support in matrimonial and family matters," and therefore affirmed a dismissal of a claim for arrearage of child support.[14] The obligor in this case lived in Illinois, the plaintiff-obligee in Israel. Perhaps the court would have proceeded differently had an Illinois obligee sought to enforce a foreign support decree against a foreign obligor against the latter's Illinois property. A more extensive view of comity, providing some equality of treatment in both directions, seems a more desirable course. Such an approach would not be precluded by the Uniform Act which *mandates* the recognition of some foreign money judgments (and excludes support decrees from that mandate) but does not *preclude* more liberal recognition.

Although the United States has not adopted the U.N. Convention on the Recovery Abroad of Maintenance or the Hague Conventions on the Recognition and Enforcement of Decisions Relating to Maintenance Obligations, some states and foreign countries have worked out arrangements that are based on the "reciprocal" provision of the 1968 version of

9. Restatement, Second, Conflict of Laws §§ 92, 109 (1971).

10. A.A. Ehrenzweig & E. Jayme, 2 Private International Law 191, nn.85–86 (1973) (with references).

11. Restatement, Second, Conflict of Laws § 109, cmnt. (d) (1971).

12. Herczog v. Herczog, 186 Cal.App.2d 318, 323–24, 9 Cal.Rptr. 5, 9 (1960). Sanson v. Sanson, 466 N.E.2d 770 (Ind.App.1984)

(judgment for installment alimony entered in German divorce proceeding was enforceable in Indiana).

13. Worthley v. Worthley, 44 Cal.2d 465, 283 P.2d 19 (1955); supra § 15.36 n.5.

14. Nardi v. Segal, 90 Ill.App.2d 432, 234 N.E.2d 805 (1967). The case is also discussed briefly supra § 15.24 n.8.

the Uniform Reciprocal Enforcement of Support Act.[15] The 1986 German statute[16] for reciprocal enforcement was a direct response.

§ 15.38   When a foreign decree is recognized, the American court will also entertain claims for its modification.[1] A New York decision has gone further and entertained an action for modification even when the foreign decree was not modifiable under the law of the rendering court.[2] The court reasoned that, since recognition is extended only as a matter of comity and not under full faith and credit, it was free, perhaps even obliged in the case of a local obligee, to evaluate the needs of the parties and, if appropriate, to enter a modification. Another New York decision took the position that it would violate the public policy of the New York forum to allow a foreign decree to foreclose evaluation of the needs of New York obligees.[3] These decisions appear to be unduly restrictive. The policy of preclusion[4] which bars collateral attack when issues were fully and fairly litigated in the first forum apply equally in the interstate and international setting. The earlier criticism of *Yarborough* and the language of *Elkind*[5] concerned the problem of one state "freezing the obligations" which flow from the ongoing parental relationship in *child support* cases. The New York decision in *Goldberg,* however, concerned a separate maintenance agreement, entered into by the parties and subsequently incorporated in a foreign divorce decree. A court of competent jurisdiction can terminate the marital relationship and settle, with finality, the property rights of the spouses, as noted in the introductory section. There is therefore no reason why, unlike in child support cases (*Yarborough, Elkind*), the parties should not be precluded from collateral attack to the same extent that they would be in the forum of rendition.

C.   CHILD CUSTODY

1.   *Obtaining Custody*

§ 15.39   By practice in all states, custody decrees that do not altogether terminate the parental rights of one parent are always modifiable in order to take account of changed circumstances of the parents

---

15. See DeHart, URESA and Its Application to International Reciprocity, Int'l Leg. Practitioner, June 1984, at 45; DeHart, International Enforcement: Child Support and Child Custody (ABA Section on Family Law, 1986).

Again, the question arises—as yet unanswered—to what extent a participating American state will permit use of such a bilateral mechanism for the recognition and enforcement of European support orders in cases of civil unions.

16. Supra n.7.

§ 15.38

1. See Gutillo v. Gutillo, 30 A.D.2d 484, 294 N.Y.S.2d 438 (1968); Herczog v. Herc-

zog, 186 Cal.App.2d 318, 9 Cal.Rptr. 5 (1960). Kramer v. Kramer, 6 Conn.L.Rptr. 286 (Conn.Super.1992) (allowing modification of Israeli divorce decree to include support); Jesse v. Dep't of Revenue ex rel. Robinson, 711 So.2d 1179 (Fla.App. 1998) (dictum: Florida would have jurisdiction under URESA to modify German child support decree).

2. Goldberg v. Goldberg, 57 Misc.2d 224, 291 N.Y.S.2d 482 (1968), relying on N.Y. Fam. Ct. Act § 466(c).

3. See Brown v. Brown, 71 Misc.2d 11, 335 N.Y.S.2d 846 (1972).

4. See infra Ch. 24.

5. See supra § 15.32 nn.3–5 and § 15.33 nn.1–3.

and the child.[1] The universally stated basis for custody is the best interest of the child which may vary with the circumstances. In this sense, it may seem to be of small importance how the initial award of child custody came about, because an allegation of changed circumstances, even after the briefest lapse of time since the original decree,[2] would enable the losing parent to raise anew the issue of the *current* best interests of the child. However, the "clean hands doctrine" developed early by the case law, the rapid adoption by all of the states of the Uniform Child Custody Jurisdiction Act, and its successor, the Uniform Child Custody Jurisdiction and Enforcement Act (infra § 15.40 et seq.), as well as federal legislation[3] result in deference to the original custody award. Jurisdiction to award custody in the first instance therefore becomes the important question.

The traditional view was that only the courts of the child's domicile may award custody.[4] A more modern view was stated in *Sampsell v. Superior Court*,[5] subsequently adopted in § 79 of the Second Restate-

§ 15.39

1. See Kovacs v. Brewer, 356 U.S. 604, 78 S.Ct. 963, 2 L.Ed.2d 1008 (1958); Brokenleg v. Butts, 559 S.W.2d 853 (Tex. Civ.App.1977), cert. denied 442 U.S. 946, 99 S.Ct. 2894, 61 L.Ed.2d 318 (1979).

2. See Brengle v. Hurst, 408 S.W.2d 418 (Ky.1966) (modification three months after rendition of the first decree).

3. 28 U.S.C.A. § 1738A.

4. See, e.g., Brown v. Brown, 105 Ariz. 273, 463 P.2d 71 (1969). The Indian Child Welfare Act of 1978 vests exclusive jurisdiction over child custody proceedings involving an Indian child in the Indian tribe in whose reservation the child resides or is domiciled. 25 U.S.C.A. § 1911. In cases in which an Indian tribe has become subject to state jurisdiction, the Act provides a mechanism to reassume custody jurisdiction. 25 U.S.C.A. § 1919. Cf. in this connection the decision in Brokenleg v. Butts, 559 S.W.2d 853 (Tex.Civ.App.1977), cert. denied 442 U.S. 946, 99 S.Ct. 2894, 61 L.Ed.2d 318 (1979) in which the court found it to be in the best interests of the child that custody be awarded to the child's grandparents and she be kept in Texas rather than be returned to her mother and South Dakota's Rosebud Sioux Indiana Reservation. For a discussion of the extent of tribal sovereignty generally see the dissent of Justice Stevens, joined by Chief Justice Burger and Justice Rehnquist, in Merrion v. Jicarilla Apache Tribe, 455 U.S. 130, 102 S.Ct. 894, 913, 918–20, 71 L.Ed.2d 21 (1982). See also supra § 11.19 nn.29–30, and the further discussion infra § 15.45 n.11. Comment, Indian Child Welfare Act of 1978: Protecting Essential Tribal Interests, 60 Colo. L. Rev.

131 (1989); Pommersheim, Crucible of Sovereignty: Analyzing Issues of Tribal Jurisdiction, 31 Ariz. L. Rev. 329 (1989).

Custody questions may also arise upon the dissolution of a (same-sex) civil union or upon the death of one of the partners to such a union. The child may be the child of the (deceased) partner or a child jointly adopted by both. As to the latter: Vermont's civil-union statute broadly confers all attributes of marriage on civil unions (15 V.S.A. § 1204(a)) and specifically enumerates the rights of adoption (15 V.S.A. § 1204(e)(4)) and of custody (15 V.S.A. § 1204(d)); the comprehensive German law (supra § 15.17 n.6), in contrast, is silent with respect to these rights, thus leaving open whether parties to a registered partnership enjoy these rights by way of general analogy to the rights of married persons. When a right to *adopt* exists and is exercised, the resulting legal status should be recognized elsewhere: since, as a rule, any adult may adopt, the surrounding circumstance of a civil union should make no difference. See also infra chapter 16. *Custody*, in contrast, is subject to modification in a state that subsequently becomes the "home state" of the child (see infra § 15.42): states that have exercised their right under DOMA not to recognize same-sex unions may be unwilling to modify a custody decree in favor of the other, non-custodial partner of such a union, at least in circumstances where such a party is not the child's natural parent. The interstate and international recognition of decrees involving parties to same-sex unions is as yet unclear.

5. 32 Cal.2d 763, 197 P.2d 739 (1948).

ment. According to this view, concurrent jurisdiction exists in several states to deal with some aspects of custody. Thus, the state of the child's domicile has the power to give a (modifiable) decree awarding custody, the state of the child's physical presence could give temporary custody in an emergency, and the state where there is personal jurisdiction over both parents has the power to bind both parents by its decree. Conflicts among these states were to be avoided by appropriate respect for the decision of a prior forum, a notion which later found expression in the "clean hands" doctrine.[6] The problem with the *Sampsell* rule became evident in the case of interstate recognition when the second forum did not accord the desired deference and makes a contrary award to the locally resident parent.[7] One answer to this problem lay in assigning priorities among courts by self-restricting state legislation. Section 3 of the Uniform Child Custody Jurisdiction Act (UCCJA) undertook to do this.[8] It provided for primary jurisdiction in the home state of the child or the state that was the child's home state within six months before commencement of the action *and* a parent continued to live in that state. Subsequent subsections provided for cases in which the first two priorities were not applicable, in each case with a view to selecting a state which had a close relationship to the child or, for other reasons, was best qualified to evaluate the needs of the child. Section 14 granted exclusive power to modify a prior decree to the court that issued it, provided it continues to satisfy the jurisdictional provisions of the Act.

Both the *Sampsell* court's call for deference to a prior decree and the UCCJA's identification of a court with paramount jurisdiction raise the problem of the reach and meaning of the Supreme Court's decision in *May v. Anderson*.[9] As long as custody decrees were so drawn as to be modifiable in a second forum, however unfortunate that practice, the question of whether the first decree was invalid in the first state for lack of personal jurisdiction in application of *May* was primarily of importance in that state. The second state could either disregard the decree on jurisdictional grounds or modify for changed circumstances. With the UCCJA's definition of a primary "custody court," the jurisdiction of the first court to grant a decree, in constitutional terms, was again impor-

---

6. See A. Ehrenzweig, Conflict of Laws 293 et seq. (1962).

7. See Ratner, Legislative Resolution of the Interstate Child Custody Problem: A Reply to Professor Currie and a Proposed Uniform Act, 38 S. Cal. L. Rev. 183, 193 (1965).

8. 9 U.L.A. 143 (Master ed. 1988; 1991 pocket part p. 13): The Act is in force, with minor variations, in all states. Id., 1982 Supp. at 11. For analysis see Bodenheimer, The Uniform Child Custody Jurisdiction Act: A Legislative Remedy for Children Caught in the Conflict of Laws, 22 Vand. L. Rev. 1207 (1969); Bodenheimer, Progress Under the Uniform Child Custody Jurisdiction Act and Remaining Problems: Punitive

Decrees, Joint Custody, and Excessive Modifications, 65 Calif. L. Rev. 978 (1977); R. Weintraub, Commentary on the Conflict of Laws 328–31 (4th ed. 2001). For a discussion of the UCCJA's successor, see id. at 331–32.

9. 345 U.S. 528, 73 S.Ct. 840, 97 L.Ed. 1221 (1953). For earlier discussion of the decision, in the context of the divisible divorce concept, see supra § 15.30, n.1. The decision of the Ohio Supreme Court in Pasqualone v. Pasqualone, 63 Ohio St.2d 96, 406 N.E.2d 1121, 1125–27 (1980), analyzing *May* in the light of *Shaffer* and subsequent cases, reaches the same conclusion as the text at § 15.30. For the continued validity of *Pasqualone* see the discussion immediately following.

tant lest the objectives of the Act be defeated or easily circumvented. If *May* does stand for the proposition that custody is a personal right of each parent which may not be impaired without personal jurisdiction *and* should continue to be the Supreme Court's view, it would then follow that any primary "custody court" would have to have jurisdiction over *both* parents *in addition,* as the UCCJA provided for policy reasons, to being the court of the child's domicile (or another court having a close connection to the child).

The UCCJA has now been replaced, in 34 states (as of 2003), by the Uniform Child Custody Jurisdiction and Enforcement Act (infra § 15.41 et seq.).

2. *Interstate Recognition and Modification*

§ 15.40   If the requirements of *May* are not satisfied, and assuming that the Court were to adhere to that decision, a custody decree rendered in State X would not be entitled to recognition in State Y; indeed, a strict reading of *May* suggests that it *may not* be recognized in Y because recognition would be violative of the due-process rights of the absent parent in the X proceeding.

Even before adoption of the UCCJA and, now, the UCCJEA, as well as the Federal Parental Kidnapping Prevention Act,[1] the California Supreme Court had occasion to reexamine *Sampsell* in a case in which modification of an Idaho decree was sought in California on the occasion of the children's annual two-months' visit with their father, now a California resident.[2] A complicating factor was the father's allegation that the children had been mistreated by their stepfather in Alabama, where the stepfather and the child's mother were then living. The trial court dismissed, ordering the return of the children to their mother, and the father appealed. The California Court acknowledged the *Sampsell* rule of the jurisdiction of a court where a child is domiciled *or* present, in the latter case for temporary custody. However, it also addressed the question, left open in *Sampsell,* of when a court should defer to a foreign decree and when it should itself reexamine the custody award. Pointing to prior case law,[3] the court confirmed that, as a general principle, the parent entitled to custody under a prior decree can enforce that right unless there is an allegation and proof that this would endanger the health and safety of the child. Lest the exception result, as a practical matter, in an examination of all cases upon an allegation of mistreatment, the court suggested that the proper remedy lay in providing for the protection of the children pending an inquiry elsewhere (for in-

§ 15.40

1. 28 U.S.C.A. § 1738A(g).

Recognition and enforcement of custody decrees in the context of same-sex civil unions are as yet unclear and are not encompassed in the present treatment: see supra § 15.39 n.4.

2. Ferreira v. Ferreira, 9 Cal.3d 824, 109 Cal.Rptr. 80, 512 P.2d 304 (1973).

3. In re Kyle, 77 Cal.App.2d 634, 176 P.2d 96 (1947).

stance, in the child's present home state) and that a speedy examination by such a court elsewhere—with cooperation by the parents—could best be assured, not by a dismissal of the local petition, but by a stay of the local proceeding and the retention of jurisdiction until resolution elsewhere. Temporary custody was retained in the father pending a determination by the trial court in California of the danger of returning the child to the mother. The temporary order would be in effect pending the outcome of the Alabama litigation which the California court would then enforce by issuing its own writ.[4] The court expressly adopted the principle that "a parent with whom a child is visiting in another jurisdiction should not be permitted, *except in clearly compelling circumstances,* to use the occasion to seek to divest the other parent of a judicially decreed right of custody. To permit this would place a premium on the abuse of the right to visitation . . .".[5] This statement describes the "clean hands" doctrine[6] which subsequently found acceptance in a number of jurisdiction.[7]

§ 15.41   The Uniform Child Custody Jurisdiction Act and its successor, the Uniform Child Custody Jurisdiction and Enforcement Act, codify the "clean hands" doctrine in providing that jurisdiction to modify a decree remains exclusively in the court of rendition so long as it satisfies the Acts' jurisdictional provisions.[1] Section 3(a)(3) provides that mere presence of the child in the state is not enough unless it has been abandoned or an emergency exists.[2] That Act thus attempts to define a

4. The immediate outcome of the case was a reversal of the trial court's denial of the father's motion to transfer the case from San Francisco to Orange County where he lived.

5. 109 Cal.Rptr. 80, 512 P.2d at 316 (citing to Bergen v. Bergen, 439 F.2d 1008, 1015 (3d Cir.1971), emphasis added by the California court). See also Hedrick v. Hedrick, 571 P.2d 1217 (Okla.1977).

6. For a statement of the doctrine and citations to earlier case law see A.A. Ehrenzweig, Conflict of Laws 293 et seq. (1962). But as one commentator observed: " . . . it is not always clear which parent has 'dirty' or the 'dirtier' hands. For instance, under visitation arrangements a parent may legally have the child at his or her domicile, and a petition to a court in his or her state may be entirely in good faith. Conversely, a 'kidnapping' parent may have been pushed to his extreme by illegitimate interference with legal visitation or other partial custody rights. The proper legal remedy of course is a contempt of court proceeding against the interfering parent, rather than 'kidnapping.' This legal remedy, however—as it may have to enjoin very subtle behavior—often is inadequate, quite aside from possible jurisdictional problems." H. Krause, Family Law in A Nutshell 268–269 (1977). The California court's

solution of a stay of the local proceedings (and retention of jurisdiction combined, if necessary, with protective arrangements for the child) provides one solution. The Uniform Act, infra, now provides another.

7. See Commonwealth ex rel. Blank v. Rutledge, 234 Pa.Super. 339, 339 A.2d 71 (1975); In re Marriage of Saucido, 85 Wn.2d 653, 538 P.2d 1219 (1975) (both dismissals); cf. Petition of Giblin, 304 Minn. 510, 232 N.W.2d 214 (1975).

§ 15.41

1. Supra § 15.39 n.7. In Brown v. Brown, 104 Mich.App. 621, 305 N.W.2d 272 (1981), the court assumed jurisdiction to modify an Arizona custody decree when the child had been living in Michigan for seventeen months. In so doing it disregarded the "clean hands" provision of § 8 of the UCCJA (which, itself, contains the qualification: "Unless required in the interest of the child . . . ") on the ground that the provision should not be invoked to punish the parent at the expense of the child.

2. See also § 409 of the Uniform Marriage and Divorce Act. In E.P. v. District Court of Garfield County, 696 P.2d 254 (Colo.1985), the court held that Colorado had jurisdiction to provide temporary protective custody for children allegedly abused

single "court of custody." When such a court is in another state, the Act contemplates dismissal of the local action (in contrast to a stay as in *Ferreira,* above) and also preserves local jurisdiction in certain situations, for instance, when it is "in the best interests of the child because ... the child and his parents, or the child and *at least one contestant,* have a significant connection with this State ..." (Sec. 3(a)(2), emphasis added). The italicized language raises but does not answer the jurisdictional problem noted earlier in connection with *May*[3] in the relatively few cases in which custody is not contested and there is no personal jurisdiction over *both* parents.

§ 15.42 The UCCJA was adopted by all of the states. It has been replaced by 34 states (as of 2003), by the UCCJEA. However, the early case law under the original Act was uneven, especially with regard to the deference which courts should accord courts to the prior decision of another court, principally to those of the court of the original or present domicile of the child.[1]

A federal response was the passage of the Parental Kidnapping Prevention Act of 1980.[2] The Act requires "the appropriate authorities of every State [to] enforce according to its terms and [not to] modify except as provided in [the Act] any child custody determination made consistently with the provisions of this section by a court of another State." A custody decree is "consistent" with the Act if the rendering court had

---

while visiting father and his second wife in Colorado but under UCCJA, the issues concerning permanent modification of custody should be referred to the Wyoming court which had originally granted permanent custody to the Wyoming mother. This decision is noted 24 J. Fam. L. 338 (1986).

3. 345 U.S. 528, 73 S.Ct. 840, 97 L.Ed. 1221 (1953) (discussed supra § 15.29).

§ 15.42

1. See Turley v. Griffin, 508 S.W.2d 764 (Ky.1974) (declining to exercise jurisdiction to modify, despite prior Kentucky decree and present domicile of the father and presence of child in Kentucky, on the ground that the child now lived elsewhere and Kentucky court was therefore divested of jurisdiction; failure to apply Sec. 14 of the Act); Wheeler v. District Court In and For City & County of Denver, 186 Colo. 218, 526 P.2d 658 (1974) (Colorado court disregarded Illinois decree, although Illinois was the home state under Secs. 3 and 14, and considered jurisdiction to be in Colorado on the inexplicable ground that this was necessary to prevent "jurisdictional fishing with children as bait," 186 Colo. 218, 526 P.2d 658, 660); In re Marriage of Weinstein, 87 Ill.App.3d 101, 42 Ill.Dec. 243, 408 N.E.2d 952 (1980) (custody jurisdiction exercised on the basis of father's change of domicile and presence

of children when last marital domicile and children's home was in Montana). But see Petition of Giblin, 304 Minn. 510, 232 N.W.2d 214 (1975) (reversing trial court's disregard of Illinois decree and exercise of local jurisdiction to modify and directing trial court to proceed in light of Uniform Act); Vanneck v. Vanneck, 49 N.Y.2d 602, 427 N.Y.S.2d 735, 404 N.E.2d 1278, 1282 (1980) (where claim of sister state jurisdiction "is colorable, a New York court must heed the statutory command to defer adjudicating the dispute and communicate with the foreign court.") Further cases are collected in 96 A.L.R.3d 968 (1980). For an example of cooperative courts, see Alley v. Parker, 707 A.2d 77 (Me.1998) (Maine and California courts communicate with each other, Maine court dismisses for *forum non conveniens* when one party and the children were in California, a principal residence of the parties).

2. 28 U.S.C.A. § 1738A. For comment see Note, Judicial Wandering Through a Legislative Maze: Application of the Uniform Child Custody Jurisdiction Act and the Parental Kidnapping Prevention Act to Child Custody Determinations, 58 Mo. L. Rev. 427 (1993); Note, Interstate Child Custody and the Parental Kidnapping Prevention Act: The Continuing Search for a National Standard, 45 Hastings L.J. 1329 (1994).

jurisdiction under the law of its state and one of the following conditions were met: the state of the rendering court was the home state of the child at the time the proceedings were begun or had been the home state for six months prior to that date and the child is absent as a result of removal or retention; no other state has jurisdiction and the best interests of the child require the exercise of jurisdiction at the forum; the child is physically present and has been abandoned or an emergency exists. The Act also provides for continuing jurisdiction so long as the state remains the residence of the child *or* of any contestant. The Act also amended the Social Security Act to make available the Federal Parent Locator Service[3] and the Federal Fugitive Felon Act for cases of child-snatching involving interstate and international flight to avoid prosecution under applicable *state* felony statutes.[4]

The Parental Kidnapping Prevention Act implements the Full Faith and Credit Clause for those state custody decrees that meet the statute's jurisdictional standards. The Act does not "confer" jurisdiction[5] but provides for the recognition of decrees covered by it. Two of its provisions, however, will tend to limit the exercise of state court jurisdiction. They are the provision requiring courts to give contestants notice and an opportunity to be heard[6] and the prohibition against the exercise of custody jurisdiction during the pendency of a proceeding in another state.[7] However, differences between the Act and the UCCJA "can lead to contrary decisions regarding which proceeding won the race to the courthouse."[8] With respect to continuing jurisdiction, the UCCJA provides for such jurisdiction so long as one parent remains in the state and had contact with the child there.[9] The federal Act, in contrast, requires

3. 94 Stat. 3571–73 (amending 42 U.S.C.A. § 654).

4. 94 Stat. 3573 (amending 18 U.S.C.A. § 1073).

5. Siler v. Storey, 587 F.Supp. 986 (N.D.Tex.1984). For a decision showing the interplay between the UCCJA and the federal Act see Quenzer v. Quenzer, 653 P.2d 295 (Wyo.1982), cert. denied 460 U.S. 1041, 103 S.Ct. 1436, 75 L.Ed.2d 794 (1983); Note, 58 Mo. L. Rev. 427 (1993); and supra n.2.

6. 28 U.S.C.A. § 1738A(e).

7. 28 U.S.C.A. § 1738A(g). The UCCJA has a similar, albeit less strict provision. For an application see Jennings v. Jennings, 133 Ill.App.3d 753, 88 Ill.Dec. 806, 479 N.E.2d 419 (1985).

8. Coombs, Interstate Child Custody: Jurisdiction, Recognition, and Enforcement, 66 Minn. L. Rev. 713, 773 (1982). For an illustration see Templeton v. Witham, 595 F.Supp. 770 (S.D.Cal.1984). Erickson, The Parental Kidnapping Prevention Act: How Can Non–Marital Children Be Protected?, 18 Golden Gate L. Rev. 529–537 (1988); Schuetze, *Thompson v. Thompson*: The Ju-

risdictional Dilemma of Child Custody Cases Under the Parental Kidnapping Prevention Act, 16 Pepperdine L. Rev. 409–430 (1989); Wilson, The Parental Kidnapping Prevention Act: Is There an Enforcement Role for the Federal Courts?, 62 Wash. L. Rev. 841–862 (1987); Charlow, Jurisdictional Gerrymandering and the Parental Kidnapping Prevention Act, 25 Fam.L.Q. 299 (1991).

9. See Heartfield v. Heartfield, 749 F.2d 1138 (5th Cir.1985) (Texas has continuing jurisdiction over modification of visitation provisions of Texas decree when father was Texas resident and regardless of the residence of the mother and children); Kumar v. Superior Court, 32 Cal.3d 689, 696, 186 Cal.Rptr. 772, 652 P.2d 1003 (1982) (continuing jurisdiction exists until the child and all parties have moved away); In re Chapman, 466 N.E.2d 777 (Ind.App.1984) (where children were subject to the continuing jurisdiction of a different court, trial court had no jurisdiction to consider grandparents' petition for visitation rights); Barndt v. Barndt, 397 Pa.Super. 321, 580 A.2d 320 (1990) (the Courts of Pennsylva-

only that the state remains the residence of the child *or* of a contestant and thereby weakens the role of the child home state in the cases where only one parent continues to live in the forum state.

The federal Act does not confer custody jurisdiction on the federal courts; it is a statute mandating full faith and credit to *state* court decisions. A number of federal courts had assumed, however, that the Act gave rise to federal subject matter jurisdiction to permit a federal court to determine which of two competing state courts was entitled to assert custody jurisdiction "consistent with" the provisions of the federal Act.[10] In *Thompson v. Thompson*,[11] the U.S. Supreme Court held that the Act does not create an implied cause of action in federal court for such a determination. Compliance with the Act must therefore be tested in the usual fashion in which review of state court compliance with federal law is sought: by appeal within the state court system and, thereafter, by petition for certiorari to the U.S. Supreme Court.[12]

Tort suits[13] and damage actions under civil rights legislation[14] also provide relief in child custody cases. Federal law governs the child custody jurisdiction of Indian tribes.[15]

nia lacked subject matter jurisdiction in the initial proceeding modifying the North Dakota decree, giving custody of the children to their mother when mother and the children continued to reside in North Dakota); Atkins v. Atkins, 308 Ark. 1, 823 S.W.2d 816 (1992) (refusing recognition of earlier Louisiana decree because PKPA gave exclusive jurisdiction to Arkansas); Atkins v. Atkins, 623 So.2d 239 (La.App.1993) (deferring to Arkansas case of same name and agreeing that Arkansas had exclusive jurisdiction); Columb v. Columb, 161 Vt. 103, 633 A.2d 689 (1993) (Vermont does not have continuing jurisdiction where child has acquired a new "home state" under the UCCJA); Michalik v. Michalik, 172 Wis.2d 640, 494 N.W.2d 391 (1993) (Indiana had continuing jurisdiction under the UCCJA because one of the parties still resided there).

10. The widely differing views previously adopted by the Courts of Appeal are summarized in Evans v. Evans, 668 F.Supp. 639 (M.D.Tenn.1987).

11. 484 U.S. 174, 108 S.Ct. 513, 98 L.Ed.2d 512 (1988). For applications, see Canipe v. Canipe, 918 F.2d 955 (4th Cir. 1990); Cahill v. Kendall, 202 F.Supp.2d 1322 (S.D. Ala. 2002). For comment, see Weintraub, Commentary on the Conflict of Laws 344–345 (4th ed. 2001).

12. See also California v. Superior Court of California, 482 U.S. 400, 107 S.Ct. 2433, 96 L.Ed.2d 332 (1987): (the Extradition Act was held to prohibit the California Supreme Court from refusing extradition of father to Louisiana (where he had been charged with parental kidnapping) on the ground that Louisiana had failed to give full faith and credit to a California custody decision; it was for the Louisiana courts to

determine whether an offense had been committed which, in turn, required an inquiry, in Louisiana, of the effect to be given to the California decree).

13. See Lloyd v. Loeffler, 694 F.2d 489 (7th Cir.1982); Wasserman v. Wasserman, 671 F.2d 832 (4th Cir.1982), cert. denied 459 U.S. 1014, 103 S.Ct. 372, 74 L.Ed.2d 507 (1982). See Note, The Tort of Custodial Interference—Toward a More Complete Remedy to Parental Kidnapping, 1983 U. Ill. L. Rev. 229. See also Ankenbrandt v. Richards, 504 U.S. 689, 112 S.Ct. 2206, 119 L.Ed.2d 468 (1992) (recognizing domestic relations exception to diversity statute but refusing to apply it to intrafamilial torts).

14. See Hooks v. Hooks, 771 F.2d 935 (6th Cir.1985) (domestic relations exception to federal jurisdiction does not bar action under 24 U.S.C.A. § 1983 for damages for deprivation of child custody without due process); Stem v. Ahearn, 908 F.2d 1 (5th Cir.1990), cert. denied 498 U.S. 1069, 111 S.Ct. 788, 112 L.Ed.2d 850 (1991) (civil rights action by father in a child custody dispute, where the children's mother secured a temporary state court order certifying herself as the exclusive conservator of the child following charges of sexual abuse by the father. The case, however, was dismissed because the child protective services workers enjoy immunity from liability.); Norton v. Cobb, 744 F.Supp. 798 (N.D.Ohio 1990) (father's claim that false accusations of child abuse, which resulted in denial of visitation rights, state a constitutional vio-

15. See page 688.

For international cases, the 1980 Hague Convention on Civil Aspects of International Child Abduction[16] may be relevant. The Convention applies to children under 16 years of age and envisions the return of the child to the "home state" (or country) for custody proceedings. The

lation cognizable under the civil rights laws. Dismissed, however, based on pendent jurisdiction, and failure by father to state a constitutional deprivation).

15. The Indian Child Welfare Act of 1978, 92 Stat. 3069, 25 U.S.C.A. § 1901 contains provisions allocating jurisdiction between state courts and Indian tribes for "child custody proceeding[s]." This term "shall mean and *include* ... 'foster care placement' ... [and] 'termination of parental rights'...." § 1803(1), emphasis added. Despite the ambiguous use of the word "include," the Act has been construed to be restricted to foster care placement and termination of parental rights and not to extend to the award of custody to one or the other parent as a result of divorce. Malaterre v. Malaterre, 293 N.W.2d 139 (N.D. 1980). This interpretation is supported, in part by the Congressional finding (§ 1980(4)) that an "alarming high percentage of Indian families are broken up by the removal ... of their children ... and [their placement] in non-Indian foster homes ..." and by the stated purpose of Congress (§ 1902) to provide "minimum Federal standards for the removal of Indian children from their families ... and [their placement] in ... homes which will reflect the unique values of Indian culture...." Nevertheless, the Act is less than clear: if a divorce is granted between two Indians resident on the reservation or registered with the tribe, tribal jurisdiction (outside of this Act) exists and child custody will presumably be awarded to either parent or another member of the tribe. In the case of divorce of non-resident Indians or of a mixed marriage, jurisdiction may well lie in state courts and, if exercised (and not deferred to the tribe), may result in the award of custody to a non-Indian. In re Larch, 872 F.2d 66 (4th Cir.1989) (state court may award custody of an Indian child to a non-Indian parent as part of a divorce proceeding). This leads to the necessary assumption that the Act's purposes are, first, to keep the child with a *parent* (Indian or non-Indian) and only second to assure maintenance of the child's relation to the tribe in those cases in which the child is to be removed to a foster home or in which parental rights are to be terminated. For these cases, the Act provides for exclusive jurisdiction of the tribe if the child resides or is domiciled

within the reservation (§ 1911(a)), mandates a transfer of the cause from state court to the tribe, "in the absence of good cause to the contrary," when the Indian child is not so resident or domiciled (§ 1911(b)), and requires that federal, state, and tribal authorities give full faith and credit to Indian tribal custody proceedings "to the same extent that such entities give full faith and credit to the ... proceedings of any other entity" (§ 1911(d)). For discussion of the Act see also Hollinger, Beyond the Best Interests of the Tribe: The Indian Child Welfare Act and the Adoption of Indian Children, 66 U. Det. L. Rev. 451 (1989); Comment, Indian Child Welfare Act of 1978: Protecting Essential Tribal Interests, 66 Colo. L. Rev. 131 (1989); Matter of Appeal in Pima County, Etc., 130 Ariz. 202, 635 P.2d 187 (App.1981). For an application of § 1911(a), see Blandino v. Blandino, 52 Va.Cir. 572 (1999). See also Monsivais, A Glimmer of Hope: A Proposal to Keep the Indian Welfare Act of 1978 Intact, 22 Am. Indian L. Rev. 1 (1997). See also supra § 15.39 n. 4.

16. The Convention was ratified by the United States and entered into force on July 1, 1988. As of 2003, it has also been ratified by Argentina, Australia, Austria, Bahamas, Belize, Bermuda, Bosnia–Hercegovina, Burkina Faso, Canada, Cayman Islands, Chile, China, Columbia, Croatia, Cyprus, Czech Republic, Denmark, Ecuador, Falkland Islands, Finland, France, Germany, Greece, Honduras, Hungary, Ireland, Island, Israel, Italy, Luxembourg, Mauritius, Mexico, Monaco, Montserrat, Netherlands, Nevis, New Zealand, Norway, Panama, Poland, Portugal, Rumania, Simbabwe, Slovakia, Slovenia, Spain, St. Kitts, Sweden, Switzerland, Turkey, the United Kingdom and Venezuela. The International Child Abduction Remedies Act, 42 U.S.C. §§ 11601–10, implements the Convention. The Act, interim regulations, and a State Department analysis are also reproduced in 14 Fam. L. Rptr. 2057 (1988).

For a summary of the law and a comparison of domestic and international standards, see Blakesley, Comparativist Ruminations from the Bayou on Child Custody Jurisdiction: The UCCSA, the PKPA, and the Hague Convention on Child Abduction, 58 La. L. Rev. 449 (1998).

Convention does not require the violation of a prior decree but refers only, and vaguely, to a "wrongful" taking or retention under the law of the "home state." This reference presumably would incorporate the new federal act by reference. The deference to the "home state" does not apply, in the discretion of the court of the host state, when the child has been abroad for a year or more and has been integrated into a "new environment."[17]

The International Parental Kidnapping Act of 1993[18] makes it a crime to remove a child from the United States with intent to obstruct the exercise of parental rights. The latter is defined to include custody based on a court order or derived from a legally binding agreement between the parties.

3. *International Recognition and Modification*

§ 15.43　English[1] and continental[2] courts exercise custody jurisdiction on a wide range of jurisdictional bases, including nationality and

17. For application of the Convention in American courts, see Rydder v. Rydder, 49 F.3d 369 (8th Cir.1995) (child returned to Poland); Feder v. Evans–Feder, 63 F.3d 217 (3d Cir.1995) (defining "habitual residence"); Lops v. Lops, 140 F.3d 927 (11th Cir.1998) (children returned to Germany); Diorinou v. Mezitis, 132 F.Supp.2d 139 (S.D.N.Y.2000), affirmed and remanded 237 F.3d 133 (2d Cir. 2001)(according "full faith and credit" to Greek decision that child had not been unlawfully removed from New York, had been habitually resident in Greece at the time of the Greek decision, and ordering child's return to Greece). For application of the Convention in the United Kingdom, see Re: M., [1995] 1 F.L.R. 1021 (C.A. 1994).

Rights of access have been held not to be rights of custody enforceable under the Hague Convention. Croll v. Croll, 229 F.3d 133 (2d Cir. 2000), cert. denied 534 U.S. 949, 122 S.Ct. 342, 151 L.Ed.2d 258 (2001). Decisions abroad interpret *ne exeat* clauses as conferring "custody rights" within the meaning of the Convention: Silberman, The Hague Child Abduction Convention Turns Twenty: Gender Politics and Other Issues, 33 N.Y.U. J.Int'l L. & Pol. 221, 230 (2000). European Union law now expressly so provides: infra § 15.43 n.2.

Whether custody rights of a party to a same-sex union are cognizable under the Convention has not yet been adjudicated. See also supra § 15.39 n. 4.

18. 18 U.S.C.A. § 1204.

§ 15.43

1. Dicey & Morris, Conflict of Laws 808 (13th ed. by Collins 2000). With the Child Abduction and Custody Act of 1985, the United Kingdom gave effect to the "European Convention on Recognition and Enforcement of Decisions Concerning Custody of Children and on the Restoration of Custody of Children" as well as to the Hague Convention; see supra § 15.42 n.16. For discussion see Dicey & Morris, supra, at 808.

2. Kegel & Schurig, Internationales Privatrecht, 927–932 (9th ed. 2004); 2 A.A. Ehrenzweig & E. Jayme, Private International Law 247 ff. (1973). In the European Union, except Denmark, Council Regulation (EC) No. 2201/2003 on Jurisdiction and the Recognition and Enforcement of Judgments in Matrimonial Matters and in Matters of Parental Responsibility replacing earlier law as of March 2005, contains comprehensive provisions on child custody. The Regulation provides for general jurisdiction in questions relating to "parental responsibility" (defined broadly as relating to the child's person or property and confined to the child and its parents, Art. 2(6 and 7)) in the courts of the member state of the child's habitual residence (Art. 10). These courts retain jurisdiction ("continuing jurisdiction") when the child is lawfully removed to another member state and until it has acquired a new habitual residence there (Art. 11). Spouses may also confer jurisdiction by agreement on the divorce court and other "holders of parental responsibility" may similarly agree on a court ("prorogation of jurisdiction," Art. 12). Transfer to another court, on grounds similar to forum non conveniens, may be made in specified, limited cases (Art. 15). With the emphasis

presence of the child. The 1961 Hague Convention on the Protection of Minors[3] adopted the criterion of the child's habitual residence both for initial jurisdiction and for modification, but did not address the kidnapping problem.[4] American decrees are therefore subject to modification in Hague Convention states and many other civil law countries to the same extent as they are interstate, except that the reason invoked for modification will usually not concern the jurisdiction of the American rendering court but rather assert a perceived "change in circumstances," differences in the choice of law, or the public policy of the foreign forum. The result will be different in those countries, e.g. England,[5] that have adopted the 1980 Hague Convention on Civil Aspects of International Child Abduction.[6]

In the United States, custody decrees of other nations are also subject to modification, again on the familiar grounds of lack of original jurisdiction in the rendering court or a subsequent change of circumstances, subject to the requirements of the Hague Convention just mentioned.[7] Section 23 of the UCCJA applies to international situations but the various alternative (escape) grounds of jurisdiction it provides will enable a court to uphold local jurisdiction for modification when this seems desirable.[8] One may suppose that this will be true especially in

on the child's habitual residence, detailed provisions became necessary with respect to child abduction and its leading to the relitigation of the custody decision in a second state. Art. 21 provides that the courts of the state to which the child has been abducted lacks jurisdiction unless the child has resided there for at least one year after holder of the custodial right gained knowledge of its whereabouts and made no application for its return, and the child has settled in its new environment. Granting of access rights and the unlawful exercise of them (for instance, failure to return the child) are expressly covered by the jurisdiction and enforcement provisions. Arts. 45–47. Indeed, a certificate from the court of the child's habitual residence "shall be enforced in all other Member States without any special procedure being required" (Art. 47(1)).

3. Recueil des Conventions de la Haye 42 (1973). As of 2004, the Convention was in force in Austria, France, Germany, Italy, Latvia, Lithuania, Luxembourg, Netherlands, Poland, Portugal, Spain, Switzerland, and Turkey. A new Convention on the Protection of Minors, intended to replace the 1961 Convention, has been signed by: Australia, Austria, Belgium, Cyprus, Czech Republic, Denmark, Estonia, Finland, France, Germany, Greece, Ireland, Italy, Latvia, Luxembourg, Monaco, Morocco, the Netherlands, Poland, Portugal, Slovakia, Slovenia, Spain, Sweden, Switzerland, United Kingdom. See http://www.hcch.net/e/status/stat34e.html. As of 2004, only Australia,

the Czech Republic, Latvia, Monaco, Morocco, and Slovakia have ratified it. Additionally, Ecuador, Estonia, and Lithuania have acceded to it.

4. See Kropholler, Erste Erfahrungen mit dem Haager Minderjährigenschutzabkommen, 25 Neue Juristische Wochenschrift 371 (1972); Ehrenzweig & Jayme, supra n.2. The Convention, however, does provide for consultation and exchange of information between courts which may affect decisions to modify.

5. Supra n.1.

6. Supra § 15.42 n.16. See also the International Parental Kidnapping Crime Act, 18 U.S.C.A. § 1204.

7. Early cases are collected in Ehrenzweig & Jayme, supra n.2, at 251 n.59.

Recognition (and modification), in the United States, of custody decrees involving parties to a (same-sex) civil union are still open questions: see supra § 15.39 n. 4.

8. Ohio omitted § 23 when adopting the Act. Thus, the trial court was not required to recognize Scottish decree awarding child custody to former wife. Minton v. McManus, 9 Ohio App.3d 165, 458 N.E.2d 1292 (1983). Similarly: State ex rel. Rashid v. Drumm, 824 S.W.2d 497 (Mo.App.1992) (Missouri did not adopt § 23, therefore Saudi Arabia does not qualify as child's "home state"). Section 23 was also omitted by New Mexico and South Dakota. See also Horiba

those cases which involve a resident petitioner seeking to keep the child in the United States. A commendable, but isolated, effort to achieve international cooperation was the decision of a New Jersey court which conditioned permission to remove a child to France on petitioner's obtaining a French modification decree to the same effect.[9] Since both the UCCJA and the 1961 Hague Convention encourage and envision the exchange of information between courts, this practice may become more frequent in the future.[10]

In *Custody of a Minor (No. 3)*,[11] the Supreme Judicial Court of Massachusetts held that a child, properly living with his mother for over a year in Massachusetts, was domiciled there for purposes of custody jurisdiction, but that the Massachusetts Court would not, under the UCCJA, modify an Australian custody order entered pending the mother's appeal in Australia. The Australian order under which the father was granted custody was enforced and the parties relegated to the Australian courts for final resolution of the custody matter. The court stated: "We see no basis on this record for concluding that the Australian custody determination was not made in substantial conformity with G.L. c. 209B [UCCJA] or for concluding that the Australian court does

& Horiba, 151 Or.App. 489, 950 P.2d 340 (1997) (exercise of jurisdiction under UC-CJA in children's best interest; Japan not a "state" for purposes of the Act).

In Hovav v. Hovav, 312 Pa.Super. 305, 458 A.2d 972 (1983), the court deferred, on grounds of comity, to an Israeli decree based on religious law notions inasmuch as the guiding principle seeking to act in the best interest of the child had been respected. In Custody of a Minor (No. 3), 392 Mass. 728, 468 N.E.2d 251 (1984) (same; additionally, the court referred to the act's provision that local jurisdiction should not be exercised when an action is properly pending in another jurisdiction). See also Adkins v. Antapara, 850 S.W.2d 148 (Tenn. App.1992) (Panama is child's "home state" under § 23 of UCCJA). In contrast see Al-Fassi v. Al-Fassi, 433 So.2d 664 (Fla.App. 1983) (no recognition of Bahamian decree for failure to observe jurisdictional and hearing standards similar to the UCCJA) and Middleton v. Middleton, 227 Va. 82, 314 S.E.2d 362 (1984) (no recognition of English decree when jurisdiction had been obtained in England by parent spiriting child away from its domicile in the United States).

9. Levicky v. Levicky, 49 N.J.Super. 562, 140 A.2d 534 (1958); see also Commonwealth ex rel. Shoemaker v. Shoemaker, 211 Pa.Super. 188, 235 A.2d 455 (1967) (adjusting custody decree to take account of different school year calendar in Spain). In Tischendorf v. Tischendorf, 321 N.W.2d 405 (Minn.1982), cert. denied 460 U.S. 1037,

103 S.Ct. 1426, 75 L.Ed.2d 787 (1983), the court affirmed the trial court's denial of a motion for modification of a prior order providing for the child to visit his father in Germany for three weeks each summer. However, the court remanded the case to the trial court for inclusion of conditions in the decree: an increase in the irrevocable letter of credit required from the father as assurance for the child's return from $10,000 to a higher amount; for the father to provide roundtrip transportation for an adult to accompany the child to Germany; and for the father to obtain a German court order recognizing the exclusive jurisdiction of American courts for the determination of the child's custody and confirming the mother's right to custody, subject to the father's visitation rights. In In re Custody & Control, 120 F.Supp.2d 517 (D.V.I. 2000), the custody case was remanded to the Territorial Court of the Virgin Islands for the limited purpose of determining whether it was in the best interest of children for New Jersey state court to assume jurisdiction.

10. In the relations between the states of the United States and France informal agreement has been reached on the reciprocal enforcement of course orders with respect to custody and visitation rights in a fashion similar to the provisions of the UC-CJA: Records of the Conversations Held on September 8, 9, 10 and 11, 1981 in Paris Between American and French Experts (mimeo.).

11. 392 Mass. 728, 468 N.E.2d 251 (1984).

not now have jurisdiction under the jurisdictional prerequisites of G.L. c. 209B.... There is nothing in G.L. c. 209B that indicates that a Massachusetts court has discretion not to follow the mandates of § 2(d) and (3) or has the right to consider the substantive propriety of the underlying decision of the foreign court. If a Massachusetts court had the power to disregard a foreign judgment by considering the propriety of that judgment in a substantive, rather than a procedural, sense, the very purpose of the law would be undermined.... Our conclusion concerning the application of § 2(d) and (e) to bar interference with valid custody determinations of other jurisdictions in consistent with views expressed elsewhere under the Uniform Act."

In view of the divergent approaches that exist with respect to custody internationally, wide adoption of the 1980 Hague Convention on Civil Aspects of International Child Abduction will be a helpful further step toward cooperation among states.

Chapter 16

LEGITIMATION AND ADOPTION

Table of Sections

		Sections
I.	Legitimacy and Legitimation	16.1
	A. Status	16.1
	B. Inheritance Rights of Legitimate and Legitimated Children	16.2
	C. Inheritance Rights of Illegitimate Children	16.3
II.	Adoption	16.4
	A. Jurisdiction to Decree an Adoption	16.5
	B. Extrastate Consequences of Adoption	16.6
	C. International Adoptions	16.7–16.9

I. LEGITIMACY AND LEGITIMATION

A. STATUS

§ 16.1 Courts have historically treated legitimacy as a matter of status. The issue of legitimacy, however, is significant only as it relates to the incidents that result from the parent-child relationship. Nearly all cases in the United States involve inheritance. Consequently, while courts and writers talk in terms of status, the status has no separate significance[1] and legitimacy usually relates only to the resolution of succession problems. Because most inheritance cases involving legitimacy have concerned proof of paternity, this has led to a frequently assumed equivalence between parentage and legitimacy. With the extension of greater inheritance rights to children born out of wedlock, significant issues of legitimacy are becoming rare.

Legitimacy is that legal condition or quality attributable to the relationship enjoyed by those children born after a subsisting marriage of their parents. *Legitimation* is giving this legal characteristic to those natural children who were not so born.

The position of the illegitimate child at common law is well known. As Blackstone said: "The rights are very few, being only such as he can acquire, for he can inherit nothing, being looked upon as the son of

---

§ 16.1

1. But cf. Zepeda v. Zepeda, 41 Ill. App.2d 240, 190 N.E.2d 849 (1963), cert. denied 379 U.S. 945, 85 S.Ct. 444, 13 L.Ed.2d 545 (1964).

nobody, and sometimes called filius nullius, sometimes filius populi."[2] Subsequent marriage of the parents did not at common law render the child legitimate,[3] though the civil law rule took the contrary position. Important statutory changes have been made in the rights of the illegitimate child in the various states, both by allowing inheritance by children whose paternity the father has recognized in the required manner, and by legitimation of the offspring through subsequent marriage of the parents. Issues in particular cases may be resolved by one claiming as a child falling under the provisions of either type of statute.[4]

Whether a child at birth is legitimate is usually determined by the law of the domicile of the parent in question at the birth of the child.[5] Our primary concern is with questions arising in one state through an alleged legitimation subsequent to birth of an individual under the laws of another.

Legitimation may occur pursuant to several acts of the parent after birth. The subsequent marriage of the parents is recognized as such an act in all of the states of the United States;[6] however, in many states acknowledgment of paternity is also required. Acknowledgment without marriage is sufficient in some states although the necessary form of acknowledgment varies greatly. From such variations it becomes relevant to determine what state's law is significant in determining whether a child is to be treated as having the character of legitimacy.

The concept of legitimacy involves the family and allocation of family responsibilities and resources. As such, the domicile has a significant interest in the resolution of most of these problems. Where the parent and the child have been domiciled in a state from the time of the child's birth, legitimation of the child according to the law of that state[7]

---

2. Blackstone, Commentaries 459.

3. See White, Legitimation by Subsequent Marriage, 36 Law Q. Rev. 255 (1920); Guttman, Whither Legitimacy: An Investigation of the Choice of Law Rules to Determine the Status of Legitimacy, 14 Rutgers L. Rev. 764 (1960).

4. For a discussion of the Uniform Parentage Acts which shaped the state statutes see Glennon, Somebody's Child: Evaluating the Erosion of the Marital Presumption of Paternity, 102 W. Va. L. Rev. 547 (2000); Individual state statutes are analyzed in Haily, The Inheritance Rights of Illegitimate Children in Georgia: The Role of a Judicial Determination of Paternity, 16 Ga. L. Rev. 170 (1981). See also Silverman, Inheritance Rights of Non–Marital Children Under Michigan's 1993 Probate Code Changes, 1995 Det. C. L. Mich. St. U. L. Rev. 1123 (1995); For a detailed discussion of the American cases, see Krause, Illegitimacy: Law and Social Policy, *passim* (1971); Krause et al., Family Law—Cases, Comments, Questions 287 et seq. (5th ed. 2003); For a detailed discussion of American pater-

nity cases see Nolan, "Unwed Children" and Their Parents Before the United States Supreme Court from Levy to Michael H.: Unlikely Participants in Constitutional Jurisprudence, 28 Cap. L. Rev. 1 (1999).

5. Estate of Kajut, 22 Pa. D. & C.3d 123 (1981); Restatement, Second, Conflict of Laws § 287 (1971).

6. Schuster, Constitutional and Family Law Implications of the Sleeper and Troxel Cases: A Denouement for Oregon's Psychological Parent Statute, 36 Willamette L. Rev. 549, 693 n.80 (2000).

7. Estate of Baker, 105 Misc.2d 365, 432 N.Y.S.2d 78 (1980) (legitimate under English law). While the most frequent method of legitimation is by marriage of the parents subsequent to the child's birth, sometimes it is provided for by public recognition (see In re Marriage of Phillips, 274 Kan. 1049, 58 P.3d 680 (2002)), or by legislative fiat (McIlvaine v. AmSouth Bank, N.A., 581 So.2d 454, 37 A.L.R.5th 769 (1991)). A statute may make children legitimate even

will be recognized everywhere.[8] Conversely, if the acts relied upon for legitimation are insufficient by the law where both parties at all times are domiciled legitimacy probably does not result.[9] Still however, such a child might claim the right of inheritance without legitimation.[10]

The more troublesome questions have arisen when only one of the parties is domiciled in the state under whose law legitimation is claimed to have been accomplished. It now seems settled, however, that an act sufficient for legitimation by the law of the father's domicile legitimates the offspring.[11] Conversely, the law of the child's domicile should suffice to legitimate the child, particularly when the parent was acknowledged the child in a manner or form sufficient under that law. The underlying reason is that the status of legitimacy is to be preferred to that of illegitimacy and that no countervailing issues of fairness to the parent arise when the parent has done some affirmative act.[12]

With respect to artificial insemination, questions regarding legitimacy arise when the child is conceived from the sperm of a man other than

though the marriage of the parents is made void. See Hall v. Coleman, 242 Ga.App. 576, 530 S.E.2d 485 (2000). In re Wehr's Estate, 96 Mont. 245, 29 P.2d 836 (1934) permitted an illegitimate child to inherit local land because of legitimation through recognition although the act of recognition took place in Germany and before the passage of the local legitimacy statute upon which the inheritance was predicated. Note, however, that the question was one of inheritance only. Mata v. Moreno, 601 S.W.2d 58 (Tex. Civ.App.1980); Vance v. Vance, 286 Md. 490, 408 A.2d 728 (1979).

8. For American cases, see Wickware v. Session, 538 S.W.2d 466, 470 (Tex.Civ.App. 1976); Peirce v. Peirce, 379 Ill. 185, 39 N.E.2d 990 (1942); Milton v. Escue, 201 Md. 190, 93 A.2d 258 (1952); Howells v. Limbeck, 172 Ohio St. 297, 175 N.E.2d 517 (1961); In re McCausland's Estate, 213 Pa. 189, 62 A. 780 (1906); De Wolf v. Middleton, 18 R.I. 810, 26 A. 44 (1893), and 18 R.I. 810, 31 A. 271 (1895); In re Goodman's Trusts, 17 Ch.Div. 266 (1881); Restatement, Second, Conflict of Laws § 287 (1971). Cf. Adams v. Adams, 154 Mass. 290, 28 N.E. 260 (1891); Greenhow v. James' Executor, 80 Va. 636, 56 Am.Rep. 603 (1885); For an international case, see Shaw v. Gould, 3 H.L. 55 (1868) (England recognizing legitimacy established in Scotland).

9. But see In re Bassi's Estate, 234 Cal. App.2d 529, 44 Cal.Rptr. 541 (1965); In re Lund's Estate, 26 Cal.2d 472, 159 P.2d 643 (1945) (noted 33 Cal. L. Rev. 633 (1945); 59 Harv. L. Rev. 128 (1945)). These cases are discussed infra § 16.2.

10. See infra § 16.3.

11. Restatement, Second, Conflict of Laws § 287, cmnt. (f). Pfeifer v. Wright, 41 F.2d 464 (10th Cir. 1930), cert. denied 282 U.S. 896, 51 S.Ct. 181, 75 L.Ed. 789 (1931); 1 Rabel, Conflict of Laws 630 (2d ed. 1958); Stumberg, Conflict of Laws 333 (3d ed. 1963). Cf. Colpitt v. Cheatham, 267 P.2d 1003 (Okla.1954). For a far-reaching result see In re Bassi's Estate, 234 Cal.App.2d 529, 44 Cal.Rptr. 541 (1965)(discussed infra § 16.2).

12. Restatement, Second, Conflict of Laws § 287, cmnt. (g); In re Spano's Estate, 49 N.J. 263, 229 A.2d 645 (1967); Moretti's Estate, 16 Pa.D. & C. 715, 1932 WL 3752 (Pa. 1932). But see Lingen v. Lingen, 45 Ala. 410 (1871) (father's purposeful act to legitimate child in France not recognized for purposes of inheritance of Alabama land). Cf. Brown v. Finley, 157 Ala. 424, 47 So. 577 (1908). Irving v. Ford, 183 Mass. 448, 67 N.E. 366 (1903) (Virginia legislative act legitimating child when father was domiciled in Massachusetts not recognized for inheritance purposes). Matter of Estate of Del Valle, 126 Misc.2d 78, 481 N.Y.S.2d 232 (Sur. 1984); Davis by Lane v. Schweiker, 553 F.Supp. 158 (D.Md.1982).

Other legal systems as well tend to assimilate the position and rights of children "whose parents are not married" to an increasing extent to those of children of married parents, in some cases dropping any differentiation altogether. See, e.g., Germany, Act for the reform of the law pertaining to children [*Kindschaftsrechtreformgesetz*] Bundesgetzblatt 1947, I, 2942. Corresponding changes were made in the conflicts statute.

the woman's husband, also called heterologous artificial insemination.[13] Courts previously considered these children illegitimate.[14] However, many states have implemented statutes providing that children born through artificial insemination are the legitimate children of the woman who carries the child and her husband. These statutes laws often require that both the husband and wife consent to the process.[15]

B. INHERITANCE RIGHTS OF LEGITIMATE AND LEGITIMATED CHILDREN

§ 16.2   Questions with respect to the status of legitimacy usually arise in the context of inheritance claims. In the early case of *Olmsted v. Olmsted*,[1] the United States Supreme Court held that the Full Faith and Credit Clause does not require states to recognize a foreign status of legitimacy for purposes of inheritance of local land.[2] Inheritance rights are thus incidents of the status to be determined by local succession laws.[3] Despite this early technical distinction, it now seems established that "a state will give the same incidents to the status of legitimacy [whether by birth or subsequent legitimation[4]] created by a foreign law . . . that it gives to the status when created by its own law. . . ."[5]

---

13. McLaughlin & Bowser, Wiggins Wills & Administration of Estates in N.C. § 182.1 (4th ed. 2003). For more discussion regarding the equitable parent doctrine, see E.N.O. v. L.M.M., 429 Mass. 824, 711 N.E.2d 886 (1999).

14. Gursky v. Gursky, 39 Misc.2d 1083, 242 N.Y.S.2d 406 (1963).

15. In re Parentage of M.J., 203 Ill.2d 526, 787 N.E.2d 144 (2003). Although California began recognizing children conceived by heterologous artificial insemination as legitimate as early as 1968 (see People v. Sorensen, 68 Cal.2d 280, 284 n.2, 66 Cal. Rptr. 7, 437 P.2d 495, 498 n.2 (1968)), New York did not adopt this view until 1982, H. v. P., 90 A.D.2d 434, 457 N.Y.S.2d 488 (1982).

§ 16.2

1. 216 U.S. 386, 30 S.Ct. 292, 54 L.Ed. 530 (1910).

2. However, and in view of more recent case law and principles of comity, it is unlikely that a state may deny inheritance rights to children *legitimated* under local law so long as children *born* legitimate enjoy such rights. See the section immediately following concerning inheritance rights of illegitimate children. The continued authority of *Olmsted* is thus questionable, at least in cases in which the act of legitimation occurred at the common domicile of the parent and the child. See Estate of Luber, 109 Misc.2d 1065, 441 N.Y.S.2d 612 (1981).

3. In England, inheritance rights more closely follow the status of legitimacy. The latter in turn may be treated quite separately from the validity of the parent's marriage. Thus, in Hashmi v. Hashmi, [1972] Fam. 36, the court declared the children of the second marriage, celebrated in monogamous form in England, to be legitimate despite the existence of a prior Pakistani marriage since polygamous marriages are valid in Pakistan. At the same time, the court, in application of English law, granted a decree of nullity with respect to the second (English) marriage. With respect to inheritance rights, the early restrictive view of Birtwhistle v. Vardill, 7 Cl. & F. 895 (1840) has been substantially modified by statute. Dicey & Morris, The Conflict of Laws 857 et. seq. (13th ed. by Collins 2000). As a result of the Children Act 1989, illegitimacy is no longer relevant to parental consent to marriage or adoption.

4. Restatement, Second, Conflict of Laws § 287, cmnt. (b) (1971).

5. Id. § 288, cmnt. (b). The rule applies equally to succession to land and to personality. Kuchenig v. California Co., 410 F.2d 222 (5th Cir.1969), cert. denied 396 U.S. 887, 90 S.Ct. 176, 24 L.Ed.2d 162 (1969). Milton v. Escue, 201 Md. 190, 93 A.2d 258 (1952); Dayton v. Adkisson, 45 N.J.Eq. 603, 17 A. 964 (1889); Miller v. Miller, 91 N.Y. 315, 43 Am.Rep. 669 (1883); De Wolf v. Middleton, 18 R.I. 810, 26 A. 44 (1893), and 18 R.I. 810, 31 A. 271 (1895); Evans v.

Two important California decisions have taken a wide view in favor of legitimacy and accompanying inheritance rights. *In re Lund's Estate*[6] extended the rights of a pretermitted legitimated child to a child acknowledged by his father at times when neither the law of the child's or of the father's domicile would legitimate but which acknowledgments would have been sufficient in California where the father died domiciled. In *In re Bassi's Estate*[7] the court, following *Lund,* again found that legitimation was to be determined in accordance with California law, as the law of the decedent's domicile at death, regardless of whether the parent's acknowledgment was sufficient to create the status of legitimacy at the time or place where made: "there is nothing which precludes the application of the laws of succession of this state, as interpreted in the light of local statutes and policy governing the determination of legitimacy, so as to permit inheritance ...".[8] Thus, "the *factual status* between the father, the decedent, and [claimants] having once been established it followed the decedent to California. The [claimants] are entitled to inherit through their father, not only as heirs of his estate if he had died here, but also from their half-brother or other paternal relatives who do leave estate here."[9]

C. INHERITANCE RIGHTS OF ILLEGITIMATE CHILDREN

§ 16.3   At common law, an illegitimate child inherited from no one; by statute, however, most states granted inheritance rights to such a child with respect to its mother, but rarely as against the father.[1] A number of decisions by the Supreme Court have now substantially equalized the rights of illegitimate and legitimate(d) children.

In the companion cases of *Levy*[2] and *Glona,*[3] the Court permitted children born out of wedlock to sue in wrongful death for the loss of their mother and, likewise, for a mother to bring such an action for the loss of her child. A number of lower court decisions read *Levy* and *Glona* extensively "to require equality between marital and nonmarital chil-

Young, 201 Tenn. 368, 299 S.W.2d 218 (1957). See McNamara v. McNamara, 303 Ill. 191, 135 N.E. 410 (1922), cert. denied 260 U.S. 734, 43 S.Ct. 95, 67 L.Ed. 487 (1922)(noted 36 Harv. L. Rev. 83 (1922)). Cf. Howells v. Limbeck, 172 Ohio St. 297, 175 N.E.2d 517 (1961); Scott v. Key, 11 La.Ann. 232 (1856). Matter of Estate of Del Valle, 126 Misc.2d 78, 481 N.Y.S.2d 232 (Sur. 1984). But see In re Blanco's Estate, 117 Mich.App. 281, 323 N.W.2d 671 (1982) (Michigan law as law of situs of decedent's property and probable domicile of decedent controlled question of child's legitimacy).

6. 26 Cal.2d 472, 159 P.2d 643 (1945)(followed in Gonzales v. Harris, 514 F.Supp. 995 (E.D.Cal.1981)).

7. 234 Cal.App.2d 529, 44 Cal.Rptr. 541 (1965).

8. 234 Cal.App.2d at 553, 44 Cal.Rptr. at 555.

9. 234 Cal.App.2d at 550, 44 Cal.Rptr. at 553 (emphasis added). See also Allen v. Harvey, 568 S.W.2d 829 (Tenn.1978).

§ 16.3

1. Krause, Equal Protection for the Illegitimate, 65 Mich. L. Rev. 477, 478 (1967).

2. Levy v. Louisiana, 391 U.S. 68, 88 S.Ct. 1509, 20 L.Ed.2d 436 (1968).

3. Glona v. American Guarantee & Liability Ins. Co., 391 U.S. 73, 88 S.Ct. 1515, 20 L.Ed.2d 441 (1968).

dren in their legal relationship with their fathers,'"[4] as well as mothers including inheritance rights. The first Supreme Court decision on the subject, however, refused to extend inheritance rights of children to an illegitimate child who had been acknowledged by her father.[5] *Trimble v. Gordon*[6] seemingly reversed that position[7] when it struck down § 12 of the Illinois Probate Act which allowed illegitimate children to inherit by intestate succession only from their mothers. *Trimble* was subsequently narrowed by *Lalli v. Lalli*[8] which upheld a New York statute conditioning the illegitimate's right to inherit on a judicial determination of the decedent's paternity during his life time. However, the Equal Protection Clause requires that state law provides sufficient opportunity to prove paternity. The Court struck down Texas's one-year limitation[9] and Pennsylvania's six-year limitation[10] as too short.

State statutes and decisions differ widely on how paternity is to be established.[11] Given the narrow command of *Lalli* for the equal treatment of illegitimates, one solution to the problem therefore lies in the more extensive adoption of the Uniform Parentage Act.[12] Another solution is provided by § 2–109 of the Uniform Probate Code, also in force in

4. Krause, Child Support in America: The Legal Perspective 124 and 119 et seq. (1981).

5. Labine v. Vincent, 401 U.S. 532, 91 S.Ct. 1017, 28 L.Ed.2d 288 (1971).

6. 430 U.S. 762, 97 S.Ct. 1459, 52 L.Ed.2d 31 (1977). See also Reed v. Campbell, 476 U.S. 852, 106 S.Ct. 2234, 90 L.Ed.2d 858 (1986).

7. "To the extent that our analysis in this case differs from that in *Labine* (discussed supra n.5) the more recent analysis controls." 430 U.S. at 776, 97 S.Ct. at 1468.

8. 439 U.S. 259, 99 S.Ct. 518, 58 L.Ed.2d 503 (1978).

9. Mills v. Habluetzel, 456 U.S. 91, 102 S.Ct. 1549, 71 L.Ed.2d 770 (1982).

10. Clark v. Jeter, 486 U.S. 456, 108 S.Ct. 1910, 100 L.Ed.2d 465 (1988).

11. See Krause, supra n.4, at 136–37 n.59. See Lowell v. Kowalski, 380 Mass. 663, 405 N.E.2d 135 (1980) (judicial adjudication of paternity is one way of establishing the inheritance rights of an illegitimate, but not the only way: since it was stipulated that the father had on numerous occasions acknowledged the child as his, there was no justification for denying the right of the child to inherit as there was no chance of fraud). In Clark v. Jeter, 486 U.S. 456, 108 S.Ct. 1910, 100 L.Ed.2d 465 (1988), the Supreme Court held that a Pennsylvania law granting illegitimate children six years to establish the defendant's paternity did not provide an adequate opportunity to obtain support and therefore violated the

Equal Protection Clause. The 1984 federal child support amendments require states that wish to qualify under the federal program to enact 18–year statutes of limitation. P.L. 98–378, 98 Stat. 1305. In M.T.C. v. J.M.M., 60 Mass.App.Ct. 1106, 799 N.E.2d 606 (2003) the court denied the father's paternity claim because the father did not demonstrate the existence of a substantial parent-child relationship.

12. Currently, 19 states have adopted either the original See Unif. Parentage Act (2000) (prefatory note) and Unif. Parentage Act (1973) (prefatory note). Alabama, California, Colorado, Delaware, Hawaii, Illinois, Kansas, Minnesota, Missouri, Montana, Nevada, New Jersey, New Mexico, North Dakota, Ohio, Rhode Island, and Wyoming adopted the 1973 Act. Texas and Washington adopted the 2000 Act.

A number of foreign conflicts codifications or draft proposals now uniformly refer to the law of the child to determine its rights as against the parent(s). The 1997 German statute reforming the "law with respect to children" also replaced the relevant provisions of the Conflicts Statute. It drops all references to legitimacy and illegitimacy: paternity and the relationship between the child and each parent are governed by the law of the child's habitual residence, the unwed mother's claims against the father on account of the pregnancy are governed by the law of her habitual residence. Arts. 19, 21 EGBGB (Introductory Law to the Civil Code), as amended (1997).

only a minority of the states. Its subsection (b) provides that a person is the child of the father for purposes of intestate succession if the parents participated in a marriage ceremony before or after the child's birth (even if void), or if "paternity is established by an adjudication before the death of the father or is established thereafter by clear and convincing proof...." Until there is uniform law for the determination of paternity, *Lalli, Trimble,* and their progeny in combination, hold that—once paternity is established in conformity with the applicable state law—principles of equal protection require that an illegitimate child, like legitimate(d) children, may inherit from its father in the case of intestacy under the applicable succession law. *Lalli*, *Mills*, and *Clark* require state law to afford liberal opportunity to establish paternity.

A different question arises in the case of testate succession. Since the testator was free to provide or not to provide for any of his children, the testator's use of the words "children" or "issue" must therefore be construed as to include or to exclude children born out of wedlock. At least in the case in which the testator's paternity was established in his lifetime, the principles of *Lalli*[13] would seem to require an inclusive construction.[14] The same result should obtain when state law grants "children" a statutory share or a support allowance.

II. ADOPTION

§ 16.4   Adoption was unknown to the common law although well developed in Roman law and in other legal systems.[1] In the United States, adoption is accomplished by judicial or governmental proceeding; it is the process which creates the relation of parent and child between persons who are strangers in blood.[2] The conflict-of-laws issues involved relate, first, to the particular court's jurisdiction to grant an adoption and, second, to the effects (incidents) of the adoption in another forum. Choice-of-law issues are not involved in the adoption itself as the court applies the law of the forum.[3]

13. See supra text at n.8.

14. Cf. Restatement, Second, Conflict of Laws § 288, cmnt. (d) (1971). However, a number of decisions have interpreted references to "child," "heir," "issue" and the like in wills and trusts as including only legitimate children. H. Clark, The Law of Domestic Relations in the United States (2d ed. 1988). For criticism see H. Krause, Illegitimacy: Law and Social Policy 94 (1971).

§ 16.4

1. See 1 Rabel, Conflict of Laws 677 (2d ed. 1958); Huard, The Law of Adoption, Ancient and Modern, 9 Vand. L. Rev. 743 (1956). In England, no provision existed for adoption until 1926. Adoption of Children Act, 16 & 17 Geo. V, c. 29. The current adoption legislation is the Adoption Act of 1976, which was not implemented until January 1, 1988. B v. C 1996 S.L.T. 1370 1 Div (1996).

2. Occasionally, "adoption" may be used in a wider sense, for instance when a statutory provision refers to the "adoption" of an illegitimate child by his father. See McNamara v. McNamara, 303 Ill. 191, 135 N.E. 410 (1922), cert. denied 260 U.S. 734, 43 S.Ct. 95, 67 L.Ed. 487 (1922). Mace v. Webb, 614 P.2d 647 (1980). "Legitimation" is the more appropriate term in these circumstances.

3. Restatement, Second, Conflict of Laws § 289 (1971).

Forum law thus also determines who may adopt whom. Traditionally, the main differences in state substantive law had to do

A. JURISDICTION TO DECREE AN ADOPTION

§ 16.5   If all the parties concerned—the would-be adoptive parents, the child, and the natural parents or the child's guardian—are domiciled in the same state, no problems arise: the decree of adoption granted by a court of competent jurisdiction of that state is valid and will be recognized elsewhere.[1] When the parties have different domiciles, the question is more difficult. Because the child's best interests are paramount, foreign adoptions should not be made more difficult by the inability of the parties to find a court with proper jurisdiction. Adoption, safeguarded as it generally is by a court proceeding to protect the interests of the child, usually should result in a benefit to the child. At the child's domicile, then, there should be no objection on the point that the adoptive parents came from out of the state. Nor does the creation of the relation seem to cause danger to social institutions at the domicile of the parents, even if done outside the state. The only persons to be adversely affected are blood relations who otherwise might inherit property. Adoption at the domicile of the child, through voluntary acts of the adopting parents performed there, has been held valid both in the state of adoption[2] and elsewhere,[3] even where the adoptive parents had no domicile within the state. Decisions denying jurisdiction to grant an

with degrees of affinity and age (e.g., as to the latter, whether an adult may be adopted). More recently, the question has arisen whether same-sex couples or one party to a same-sex relationship may adopt (e.g., in the latter case, the child of the other). By focusing on the "best interests" of the child and on the statutory reference to "person," the Vermont Supreme Court– even before adoption of Vermont's civil-union legislation (supra § 13.20)–held that one party to a same-sex relationship may adopt the children of the other: Adoptions of B.L.V.B., and E.L.V.B., 160 Vt. 368, 628 A.2d 1271 (1993). Accord: In the Matter of Adoption of Two Children by H.N.R., 285 N.J.Super. 1, 666 A.2d 535 (1995); In re M.M.D. & B.H.M., 662 A.2d 837 (D.C.App. 1995). Vermont's civil-union law now expressly provides for the right to adopt: 15 V.S.A. § 1204(e)(4) (2003). For a statutory extension of a stepparent's standing to adopt to include other "individuals" who have the consent of the custodial parent, see Mont. Code Ann. § 42–4–302(2) (2003) (with express reference, in the "Official Comments," to the Vermont decision). For early discussion, see Starr, Adoption by Homosexuals: A Look at Differing State Court Opinions, 40 Ariz. L. Rev. 1497 (1998). For recent discussion, see Developments in the Law: II. Inching Down the Aisle: Differing Paths Toward the Legalization of Same–Sex

Marriage in the United States and Europe, 116 Harv.L.Rev. 2004, 2019–22 (2003).

§ 16.5

1.   See Kupec v. Cooper, 17 Fla.L.Weekly D470, 593 So.2d 1176 (Fla.Ct.App.1992); Fla. Jur 2d Family Law § 208 (updated in 2003); In re Petition to Adopt C.M.A., 557 N.W.2d 353 (Minn.App.1996); But see Doulgeris v. Bambacus, 203 Va. 670, 127 S.E.2d 145 (1962)(refusing recognition to a Greek adoption because the foreign judgment offended Virginia's public policy upon a finding that the adoption was intended to gain the domestic services of the child. While put on the basis that the adoption had not been in the best interest of the child, the result of the decision was to deny her inheritance rights from her adoptive brother).

2.   Appeal of Wolf, 13 A. 760 (Pa. 1888). See Ruth F. v. Robert B., 456 Pa.Super. 398, 690 A.2d 1171, 1185 (1997); Martinez v. Reed, 490 So.2d 303 (La.App.1986); In re Lynn M., 312 Md. 461, 540 A.2d 799 (1988).

3.   Van Matre v. Sankey, 148 Ill. 536, 36 N.E. 628 (1893); Succession of Caldwell, 114 La. 195, 38 So. 140 (1905); Fisher v. Browning, 107 Miss. 729, 66 So. 132 (1914); Zanzonico v. Neeld, 17 N.J. 490, 111 A.2d 772 (1955); Restatement, Second, Conflict of Laws § 78 (1971). Cf. In re Christoff's Estate, 411 Pa. 419, 192 A.2d 737 (1963).

adoption upon these facts[4] seem to be based upon interpretation of a particular statute, rather than upon any general principle of jurisdiction.

Can there be a valid adoption where the adopting parents are domiciled, assuming statutory procedure is followed, even though the child's domicile may be elsewhere? The affirmative answer given by the few authorities raising the question seems a desirable one.[5] It is the only answer that will make adoption possible in some cases, for the child cannot himself change his domicile, and his natural parents may be dead or may have abandoned him. In an adoption matter, the court is dealing with the future of a child and, as in custody cases, the best interests of the child are most significant. Consequently, if the domicile of either the child or the adoptive parent is in the forum, the court is likely to exercise its jurisdiction if to do so is in the best interests of the child.

In addition to the immediate parties—child and would-be adoptive parents—adoption also affects the natural parents, if living, or the child's guardian. Thus, in *Armstrong v. Manzo*[6] the Supreme Court set aside an adoption decree in favor of the child's mother and her new husband when the child's natural father, now divorced from the mother, had neither been notified by the proceeding nor consented to the adoption.[7]

4. Foster v. Waterman, 124 Mass. 592 (1878); Knight v. Gallaway, 42 Wash. 413, 85 P. 21 (1906); In re Sharon's Estate, 179 Cal. 447, 177 P. 283 (1918). See Annot., 33 A.L.R.3d 176 (1970). Cf. Matter of Adoption of Pollock, 293 Ark. 195, 736 S.W.2d 6 (1987)(holding birth of child in state alone not sufficient for jurisdiction).

5. Bartsch v. Bartsch, 636 N.W.2d 3 (2001); Matter of Adoption of J.L.H., 737 P.2d 915 (Okla.1987); Interest of M.L.K., 13 Kan.App.2d 251, 768 P.2d 316 (1989); Matter of Appeal of Pima, 118 Ariz. 437, 577 P.2d 723 (App.1977); In re Adoption of Baby Boy C., 31 Wn.App. 639, 644 P.2d 150 (1982); In re Adoption of MM aka NLM, 652 P.2d 974 (Wyo.1982); A. v. M., 74 N.J.Super. 104, 180 A.2d 541 (1962). Cf. In re Goodman's Adoption, 49 Del. 550, 121 A.2d 676 (1952); Klinger's Adoption, 5 Pa.D. & C.2d 767 (Pa.1956). But cf. 2 Beale, Conflict of Laws § 142.2 (1935) in which a contrary view was taken, i.e., that only the state of the child's domicile should have jurisdiction to permit adoption. This view is based upon the feeling that only the child's domicile will properly pay attention to the welfare of the child. Such a view ignores the public policy favoring adoption, the fact that the welfare of the child is generally best served by adoption, and finally, the fact that it may safely be assumed that since adoption is almost always a statutory proceeding under the scrutiny of a competent court that regard for the welfare of the

child will be a primary consideration in every instance.

The 1969 revised version of the Uniform Adoption Act, which was withdrawn from recommendation for enactment by the National Conference of Commissioners on Uniform State Laws in 1986, was replaced by the Uniform Adoption Act of 1994. Both versions take a position similar to that of the Restatement, Second. Section 4 of the 1969 Act and Section 3–101 of the 1994 Act both provide for jurisdiction in the state of the petitioner's or the child's residence or at the place where the agency is located that has control of the minor. Under the Uniform Adoption Act, adoption proceedings undertaken in a state that has proper jurisdiction under the Act will be recognized elsewhere in other states. Alaska, Arkansas, North Dakota, and Ohio adopted the 1969 Act but only Vermont has adopted the 1994 version. Unif. Adoption Act (1969); Unif. Adoption Act (1994). Oklahoma substantially adopted the 1953 version of the Act.

6. 380 U.S. 545, 85 S.Ct. 1187, 14 L.Ed.2d 62 (1965); Mayberry v. Flowers, 347 Ark. 476, 65 S.W.3d 418 (2002); Adoption of Hugh, 35 Mass.App.Ct. 346, 619 N.E.2d 979 (1993).

7. See also Stanley v. Illinois, 405 U.S. 645, 92 S.Ct. 1208, 31 L.Ed.2d 551 (1972)(unwed father has claim to custody upon mother's death with whom he had

In the interest of resolving disputes between adoptive and natural parents, states—either by statute[8] or court interpretation[9]—are applying

lived as against State of Illinois under whose law children of unwed fathers became wards of the state). However, in Quilloin v. Walcott, 434 U.S. 246, 98 S.Ct. 549, 54 L.Ed.2d 511 (1978), the Court retreated again when it upheld a Georgia statute under which an unwed father, who had not legitimated his child nor had lived in a home situation with the child, was not allowed to object to the child's adoption by the husband whom the mother had subsequently married. In Steven A. v. Rickie M. v. Kari S., 1 Cal.4th 816, 4 Cal.Rptr.2d 615, 823 P.2d 1216 (1992), the Court held that a California statutory provision creating a "presumed father" whose consent was required prior to adoption violated federal equal protection and due process rights because it could allow the mother to unilaterally preclude the biological father from becoming the presumed father.

Compare Lehr v. Robertson, 463 U.S. 248, 103 S.Ct. 2985, 77 L.Ed.2d 614 (1983)(following *Quilloin* when father had not established a relationship with the child) with Caban v. Mohammed, 441 U.S. 380, 99 S.Ct. 1760, 60 L.Ed.2d 297 (1979), on remand 47 N.Y.2d 880, 419 N.Y.S.2d 74, 392 N.E.2d 1257 (1979)(holding a New York statutory provision discriminating between father and mother to be unconstitutional when both were similarly situated). See also Adoption of a Child by R.K., 303 N.J.Super. 182, 696 A.2d 116 (1997)(New York Statute cannot violate fundamental parenting right; where clear and convincing evidence of father's failure to meet statutory requirements for developing relationship with his child is given, the court can deny parenting right); Raymond AA. v. Doe, 217 A.D.2d 757, 629 N.Y.S.2d 321 (1995): (unwed father's constitutional right to parent is limited; it maybe conditioned on a prompt showing of interest in custody—within the first six months—and a judicial determination of fitness also within the first six months). By statute, Oklahoma now also requires notice to an unwed father. 10 Okla. St. Ann. § 7505–4.1.

8. Ala. Code § 26–10A–21; Georgia, Ga. Code Ann. § 19–9–42(3); Montana, Mont. Code Ann. § 40–7–103(3); but see N.H. Rev. Stat. Ann. § 458–A:2(III); N.Y. Dom. Rel. Law § 75–c(3); see generally Hartfield, The Uniform Child Custody Jurisdiction Act and the Problem of Jurisdiction in Interstate Adoption: An Easy Fix?, 43 Okla. L. Rev. 621 (1990).

9. In re Marriage of Fontenot, 317 Mont. 298, 77 P.3d 206 (2003) (court had

jurisdiction over custody of parties' child under the UCCJEA in dissolution proceeding, where Montana was child's home state at the time wife filed petition, and, while child was absent from Montana at a later time, wife continued to live in Montana; Atchison v. Atchison, 256 Mich.App. 531, 664 N.W.2d 249 (2003) (applying the UCCJEA, court refused to accept jurisdiction of custody petition); but see Ruth v. Ruth, 158 N.C.App. 123, 579 S.E.2d 909 (2003) (show cause hearing against former wife for contempt of North Carolina order changing custody of children did not implicate UCCJEA); Adoption of Zachariah K., 6 Cal. App.4th 1025, 8 Cal.Rptr.2d 423 (1992) (proceeding to determine withdrawal of consent to adoption by birth parent is governed by the UCCJA); In re Adoption of Baby Girl B., 19 Kan.App.2d 283, 867 P.2d 1074 (1994) (applied UCCJA to adoption proceeding); DeBoer v. Schmidt, 442 Mich. 648, 502 N.W.2d 649 (1993) (applied UCCJA to adoption proceeding); Foster v. Stein, 183 Mich.App. 424, 454 N.W.2d 244 (1990); In re Adoption of a Child by T.W.C., 270 N.J.Super. 225, 636 A.2d 1083 (App. Div.1994) (applied the UCCJA to adoption proceedings); State ex rel. Torres v. Mason, 315 Or. 386, 848 P.2d 592 (1993) (en banc) (applied UCCJA to adoption proceeding); In re Adoption of B.E.W.G., 379 Pa.Super. 264, 549 A.2d 1286 (1988) (adoption proceedings are subject to UCCJA); Clark v. Gordon, 313 S.C. 240, 437 S.E.2d 144 (App.1993) (applied UCCJA to adoption proceeding); In re Termination of Parental Rights Over M.C.S., 504 N.W.2d 322 (S.D.1993) (UCCJA applies to parental termination proceedings); White v. Blake, 859 S.W.2d 551 (Tex. App.1993) (UCCJA does apply to a termination of parental rights proceeding); but see Williams v. Knott, 690 S.W.2d 605 (Tex. App.1985) (UCCJA does not apply to termination of parental rights proceeding); In re Termination of Parental Rights of Steven C., 169 Wis.2d 727, 486 N.W.2d 572 (App. 1992) (adoption proceedings are subject to UCCJA); but see Johnson v. Capps, 415 N.E.2d 108 (Ind.App.1981) (UCCJA does not apply to termination of parental rights proceeding).

But see also Williams v. Knott, 690 S.W.2d 605 (Tex.App.1985) (UCCJA does not apply to termination of parental rights proceeding); In re Termination of Parental Rights of Steven C., 169 Wis.2d 727, 486 N.W.2d 572 (App.1992) (adoption proceedings are subject to UCCJA); contra Johnson

the UCCJA or UCCJEA to establish jurisdiction in adoption proceedings. This produces a uniform method of determining jurisdiction and thus allows for decisions that will be recognized by all states.

B. EXTRASTATE CONSEQUENCES OF ADOPTION[1]

§ 16.6   An adoption decree entered by a court of competent jurisdiction will ordinarily be recognized everywhere.[2] The question of the decree's effect arises most often in the context of succession and is governed by the law applicable to the succession, i.e., in most cases the law of the decedent's domicile at death. In most cases, the decree will have the same effect as a local decree.[3]

The effect of an adoption is also in issue when the adopted child claims inheritance rights from its natural parents. Again, the issue will be decided by the applicable local succession law.[4] With respect to the

---

v. Capps, 415 N.E.2d 108 (Ind.App.1981) (UCCJA does not apply to termination of parental rights proceeding); Ward v. Ward, 272 Kan. 12, 30 P.3d 1001 (2001) (refusing to apply UCCJA to a guardianship proceeding); Amin v. Bakhaty, 812 So.2d 12 (La. App. 1st Cir. 2001), writ granted 794 So.2d 832 (La.2001), judgment aff'd 798 So.2d 75 (La.2001) (UCCJA does not apply to support matters).

§ 16.6

1. Emerging problems with respect to adoption by parties to same-sex marriages and civil unions are treated briefly supra at § 16.4 n.3 and infra at § 16.7 n.5.

2. See, e.g., Conley v. Walden, 171 Mont. 58, 555 P.2d 960 (1976). See also supra § 16.5 nn. 1–3. However, an early decision of the United States Supreme Court held that a state may recognize a sister state decree without giving the parties the same rights in the forum as they would have enjoyed under a local decree. Hood v. McGehee, 237 U.S. 611, 35 S.Ct. 718, 59 L.Ed. 1144 (1915). See also Slattery v. Hartford–Connecticut Trust Co., 115 Conn. 163, 161 A. 79 (1932): inheritance rights governed by the law of the place of adoption. But the forum should not treat a foreign adopted child differently from one adopted locally when the incidents of the relationship are substantially the same in both states. Restatement, Second, Conflict of Laws § 290 (1971). The attitude of the Court as reflected in Hughes v. Fetter, 341 U.S. 609, 71 S.Ct. 980, 95 L.Ed. 1212 (1951), discussed supra §§ 3.25, 3.40, suggests the probability that *Hood* would not be followed today. Estate of D'Angelo, 139 Misc.2d 5, 526 N.Y.S.2d 729 (1988), on reconsideration, 140 Misc.2d 522, 531 N.Y.S.2d 495 (1988); Cf. Matter of Male

Child Born July 15, 1985 to L.C., 221 Mont. 309, 718 P.2d 660 (1986); Lemley v. Barr, 176 W.Va. 378, 343 S.E.2d 101 (W.Va. 1986). The Interstate Compact on the Placement of Children supports this recognition. See Mont. Code Ann. § 41–4–101; Idaho Code § 32–1101. See also supra §§ 16.2–16.3 concerning inheritance rights of legitimated and illegitimate children. A permissible exception exists in the event that the foreign adoption violates local public policy. Restatement, Second, Conflict of Laws § 290, cmnt. (c) (1971). See, e.g., Tsilidis v. Pedakis, 132 So.2d 9 (Fla.App.1961) (adoption of adult by single person). Bonwich v. Bonwich, 699 P.2d 760 (Utah 1985), cert. denied 474 U.S. 848, 106 S.Ct. 142, 88 L.Ed.2d 117 (1985) (child custody); In re Estate of Hart, 165 Cal.App.3d 392, 209 Cal.Rptr. 272 (1984) (succession).

3. Matter of Estate of Chase, 127 A.D.2d 415, 515 N.Y.S.2d 348 (1987); In re Estate of Wagner, 50 Wn.App. 162, 748 P.2d 639 (1987); Restatement, Second, Conflict of Laws § 290, cmnt. (b). For exceptions see supra n.2.

4. See, e.g., Pazzi v. Taylor, 342 N.W.2d 481 (Iowa 1984) (law of decedent's domicile at death governs issue whether natural son, adopted by stepfather out-of-state, inherits); Warren v. Foster, 450 So.2d 786 (Miss. 1984) (law of decedent's domicile of death and situs of property—Mississippi—applicable and granting inheritance rights to natural son, although son was adopted in Tennessee, and under Tennessee law would be divested of any rights to inherit from natural parent); Matter of Avery's Estate, 176 N.J.Super. 469, 423 A.2d 994 (1980), cert. denied 85 N.J. 499, 427 A.2d 587 (1981) (law of decedent's domicile at death, not of

substantive issue, the courts are split: some view the adoption as effecting a complete substitution of the adoptive parents for the natural parents thus severing all links and ending all inheritance claims,[5] while others preserve the right to inherit from or through the natural parents.[6]

C. INTERNATIONAL ADOPTIONS[1]

§ 16.7 American law, to generalize, undertakes to serve the interests of the child by requiring the child or the adopter to have a special relation to the forum, that of domicile. Civil law jurisdictions, in contrast, usually open their adoption courts to all comers.[2] Because the relation between court and parties in civil law jurisdictions is so slight, the objective that the change in status reflect the best interests of the child is realized in those jurisdictions by a different approach to choice of law. The applicable law is not that of the forum, but the personal law of adopter or child.[3] Thus, the personal law of the adopter may govern the prerequisites of adoption, while the personal law of the child is applicable in some jurisdictions for the question of whose consent to adoption is necessary.[4] The same considerations apply to the recognition of foreign adoptions by "civil law" courts. A prerequisite to recognition is not only that the granting court was a court of competent jurisdiction but also that it applied the proper law.[5] The foreign adoption generally must

state of adoption, controlling as to right of natural child to inherit despite adoption).

5. See Shehady v. Richards, 83 N.M. 311, 491 P.2d 528 (1971) (on the ground that a contrary result would confer dual inheritance rights); In re Uihlein's Estate, 269 Wis. 170, 68 N.W.2d 816 (1955); Wailes v. Curators of Central College, 363 Mo. 932, 254 S.W.2d 645, 37 A.L.R.2d 326 (1953). See also Matter of Tapp's Estate, 569 S.W.2d 281 (Mo.App.1978); Cox v. Cox, 262 S.C. 8, 202 S.E.2d 6 (1974); In re Donnelly's Estates, 81 Wn.2d 430, 502 P.2d 1163 (1972).

6. Go International, Inc. v. Lewis, 601 S.W.2d 495 (Tex.Civ.App.1980); Prentice v. Parker, 376 So.2d 568 (La.App.1979); Massey v. Parker, 369 So.2d 1310 (La.1979); Meadow Gold Dairies v. Oliver, 535 P.2d 290 (Okla.1975); People ex rel. Bachleda v. Dean, 48 Ill.2d 16, 19, 268 N.E.2d 11 (1971). For discussion of the French approach, which distinguishes between full and limited adoption, see Krause, Creation of Relationships of Kinship, 4 Int'l Encyc. Comp. L. § 180 (1976).

§ 16.7

1. Some of the older material in this section is adapted from Hay, The United States and International Unification of Law: The Tenth Session of the Hague Conference, 1965 U. Ill. L. F. 820, 835–42.

2. Lipstein, Adoptions in Private International Law: Reflections on the Scope and the Limits of a Convention, 12 Int'l L. & Comp. L.Q. 835, 838 (1963); De Nova, Adoption in Comparative Private International Law, 104 Recueil des Cours 68, 75–112 (1961–III.). See also Krause, Creation of Relationships of Kinship, 4 Int'l Encyc. Comp. L. §§ 148–196 (1976). For a French perspective see Poisson–Drocourt, L'adoption international, 76 Revue critique de droit international privé 673 (1987). For a Spanish perspective, see Espluges, El "Nuevo" regimen juridicio de la adopcion internacional en EspaZa, 1 Rivista di diritto internazionale privato e processuale 33 (1997).

3. See, e.g., Germany, EGBGB (Introductory Law to the Civil Code) Arts. 22–23.

4. Lipstein, supra n.2, at 836. International cooperation may avoid many problems of enforcement. See, e.g., Adoption of Francesca M., 133 Misc.2d 152, 506 N.Y.S.2d 642 (Sur.1986).

5. When countries or states of the United States provide for same-sex marriage or a form of formalized partnership (e.g., civil union), they may or may not also provide for the partners' joint right to adopt, for one partner to adopt the child of the other, or for a partner to adopt a child to the same extent that a stranger may. The first is true

satisfy the personal law of the adopter with regard to aspects relating to the adopter and his or her qualifications and the personal law of the child with respect to requirements affecting the child.[6] As a result, American decrees of adoption may be entitled to recognition in these jurisdictions only if the requirements of the personal law of the adopter and of the child are met. Because the American court has considered only its own internal law, its decree involving either an adopter or a child who is not a national of the United States (and the latter is the rule in the cases under discussion) therefore may not be recognized in these jurisdictions, unless American substantive law contains the same or essentially similar requirements as the foreign personal law of the party.

Comparison of the substantive law of American jurisdictions with the result of an older survey of several foreign jurisdictions conducted by the United Nations Department of Economic and Social Affairs shows the existence of some significant differences:[7] from the point of view of recognition, both *conflicting* and indispensable *additional* requirements of the applicable law may prove to be obstacles. Some examples may suffice. Foreign jurisdictions require consent to the adoption by the child when it has reached a certain age, but differ as to what this age shall be; the range is from 10 to 21. In the United States, the age of consent to adoption is generally 12[8] or 14.[9] A child too young to be required to consent in an American jurisdiction may be old enough under his personal law. Furthermore, foreign jurisdictions vary greatly in requirements imposed on adopters: some require the child and the adopter to have the same nationality, almost all set a minimum age for adopters ranging from 18 to 50, many require an age differential from 10 to 30

---

in The Netherlands and in Vermont, the second in Denmark and The Netherlands. For Vermont, see 15 V.S.A. § 1204(e)(4) (2003). In Germany, domestic partnership law is silent on the matter, while traditional adoption law refers to married couples as well as to strangers. See BGB (Civil Code) § 1741. Adoption by same-sex couples jointly does not seem possible at present. See www.equalityforum.com/familyvalues-review.cfm (2003). To the extent that foreign-country adoptions (and, with them, their intrastate effects) are measured by forum standards, it may be expected that adoptions by same-sex couples, or a partner of such a relationship, will encounter divergent treatment elsewhere. For instance: "For a foreign adoption to be recognised in Ireland, it must comply with the definition of adoption in Irish law. This means that the rule that only married couples may jointly adopt will apply." See www.oasis.gov.ie/relationships/same_sex_relationships/adoption_and_same_sex_couples.html (2003). However, a single person may adopt.

6. De Nova, supra n.2, at 96; cf. A.P., Journal des Tribunaux 603 (1982), 10 Eur.

L. Dig. (Dec. 1982) (adoption by mother and stepfather, both Belgians at the time of adoption, was approved by the Belgium court notwithstanding the child was beyond the allowable age of adoption under the child's national law, Italy).

7. U.N. Dep't of Economic & Social Affairs, Comparative Analysis of Adoption Laws 21–25 (ST/SOA/30) (1956). Included in the study were Argentina, Bolivia, Canada (three Provinces used as representative), Denmark, France, Greece, Guatemala, Peru, Poland, Switzerland, United Kingdom, United States (four States used as representative), Uruguay, U.S.S.R., and (former) Yugoslavia. With respect to some of these, it is now also necessary to differentiate among adoptions by single persons, married couples, and parties to same-sex relationships. See supra n.5.

8. Ariz. Rev. Stat. § 8–106; Cal.Rules of Court, Rule 1464; Mass. General Laws Ann. ch. 210 § 2; 23 Pa.C.S.A. § 2711(a)(1).

9. Ala.Code § 26–10A–7; N.Y. Dom. Rel. Law § 111 (statute held unconstitutional on other grounds by In re Lily R., 283 A.D.2d 901, 724 N.Y.S.2d 231 (2001)).

years between child and adopter, some forbid adoptions on the basis of the single adopter's sex such as when a single male adopter seeks to adopt a single female, and some forbid adoptions by persons having other children and sometimes even invalidate adoptions upon the subsequent birth of a child to the adopter. Finally, there are differences with respect to the law applicable to the incidents of adoption.[10]

Some of the substantive differences between American and foreign adoption laws can be bridged by international treaties. For *bilateral* treaties between the United States and particular foreign countries a common provision assures that "nationals ... of either Party shall be accorded national treatment, within the territories of the other Party, with respect to acquiring property of all kinds of testate or intestate succession...."[11] Thus, in cases in which the foreign adoption as such is recognized, the incidents—particularly inheritance rights—that must be accorded to the parties concerned must be the same as those enjoyed by local parties.[12]

§ 16.8 A more comprehensive solution was attempted in the form of the 1965 *multilateral* Hague Convention on Jurisdiction, Applicable Law and Recognition of Decrees Relating to Adoptions.[1] A brief review shows why an instrument like this Convention did not alleviate the problems inherent in U.S.–foreign country adoptions.

The Convention was a "recognition and enforcement" convention: it established jurisdictional rules which, if satisfied, entitled a decree to recognition. But it neither mandated particular jurisdictional rules nor precluded the use of other jurisdictional bases. It applied to adoptions by one person or by spouses who were nationals or habitual residents of a contracting state, of a child who had never been married, was under 18 years of age, and was a national or a habitual resident of a contracting state. Stateless persons were deemed to have the nationality of the state of their habitual residence; and spouses satisfied the test of the Convention only when they had the same nationality or habitual residence. The

---

10. See Lipstein, supra n.2; Kennedy, Adoption in the Conflict of Law, 34 Can. B. Rev. 507 (1956).

11. Art. IX(3), Treaty of Friendship, Commerce and Navigation Between the United States and the Federal Republic of Germany, 7 U.S.T. 1840, T.I.A.S. 3593, 273 U.N.T.S. 3 (entered into force July 14, 1956).

12. In Corbett v. Stergios, 256 Iowa 12, 126 N.W.2d 342 (1964), the court had denied inheritance rights to a child adopted in Greece. The United States Supreme Court reversed, 381 U.S. 124, 85 S.Ct. 1364, 14 L.Ed.2d 260 (1965), on the basis of the U.S.-Greek Treaty of Friendship, Commerce and Navigation, 5 U.S.T. 1829, T.I.A.S. 3057 (entered into force Oct. 13, 1954). On remand, the Iowa Supreme Court granted the inheritance claim after finding that the differences between Greek and Iowa law did not offend Iowa public policy.

Corbett v. Stergios, 257 Iowa 1387, 137 N.W.2d 266 (1965). In view of the usual treaty language (see supra n. 11), the additional inquiry was improper.

§ 16.8

1. Hague Conference on Private International Law, Recueil des Conventions de La Haye 65 (1988 ed.). For additional discussion see Jenard, La dixième session de la Conférence de La Haye de droit international privé, 80 Journal des Tribunaux 65, 67–68 (1965). The Convention was in force in Austria, Switzerland, and the United Kingdom. Switzerland and the United Kingdom denounced the Convention in 2003. Since the convention contemplates relations between contracting states, the Swiss and British withdrawals in effect terminate the Convention.

Convention did not apply when adopters and child had the same nationality and habitual residence. The "authorities" of the adopters' state of habitual residence as well as those of the state of nationality had jurisdiction to grant adoptions; each contracting state was to designate the "authorities" that had power to grant or revoke adoptions. The granting authorities were to apply their own internal substantive law, but authorities whose jurisdiction was based on the adopters' habitual residence had to respect any prohibitions against adoption contained in the adopters' national law and expressly specified in a declaration by the state of nationality at the time of acceptance of the Convention. Prohibitions could be based on the fact that the adopter had children of his own, that there was only one adopter, the existence of a blood relationship between an adopter and the child, the previous adoption of the child by others, the requirement of a specified age differential between adopters and child, the ages of adopters and child, and on the fact that the child did not reside with the adopters. The granting authorities, furthermore, had to apply the child's national law with respect to the requirements of consent and consultation, except to the extent that they applied to the adopter, his family, or his spouse. In all cases, granting authorities were to act in the best interest of the child and to this end were to make thorough inquiries with respect to the adopters, the child, and the child's family. To ensure the widest possible notice, granting authorities were to give notice of the pending adoption to the state of the child's birth, nationality, and to any state which had jurisdiction to grant an adoption; in the case of annulment or revocation, notice had to be given to the granting state and to the states of the child's birth and nationality.

Adoptions, annulments, and revocations governed by the Convention and decreed by the proper authorities were to be recognized by all contracting states without further formality. In determining the jurisdiction of the decreeing authority, the enforcing state was bound by the former's findings of fact. Enforcement could be denied, however, when it would be manifestly contrary to the public policy of the forum.

The main objection, from the United States' point of view, was that the Convention would not ensure recognition of all American adoptions and that the selection between decrees entitled to recognition and those which are not was not based on compelling reason. Under the Convention, for instance, the child must never have been married; this is not generally provided in American statutes. Likewise, the Convention applied only to adoptions of children under 18, in contrast to the general position of American law that even adults may be adopted. The jurisdictional provisions illustrate the same point. If an American couple residing in the United States wished to adopt a child who was either a foreign national or resident, only United States courts had jurisdiction for purposes of the Convention; if a foreign couple with foreign residence wished to adopt a child who was an American citizen or resident, they would have to do so in their own country. Under American law, by contrast, American courts have jurisdiction in both cases; and, if the civil law notions of applicable law have been satisfied at least in result, a decree by a United States court would be recognized. The fact that the

Convention's provisions were not to be exclusive was small comfort for adoptions not falling under it, especially if the Convention provisions should, as a matter of practice, displace other approaches to adoption for states adhering to them. Furthermore, to return to the hypothetical, the Convention also did not protect foreign decrees in the United States to the same degree as existing law: If the country of the child's nationality or residence—in the first case described above—or the state of the adopters' nationality or residence—in the second case described above— or the state of the adopters' nationality or residence—in the second case—granted an adoption, United States courts would have to recognize it. But the Convention did not require recognition in the first case. The Convention's approach to jurisdiction, in short, was more restrictive than either the American or the Continental view.

In the modern context, and going beyond what seems sensible from the point of view of the United States, the Convention also falls far short of accommodating issues of adoption that arise in same-sex and unmarried heterosexual relationships.[2] All of these circumstances may explain the Convention's very limited initial following and its eventual demise (in 2003) as a result of the withdrawal by Switzerland and the United Kingdom.

§ 16.9   The Hague Conference completed the Convention on the Protection of Children and Cooperation in Respect of Intercountry Adoption in 1993.[1] As of April 2004, the Convention is in force in 42 nations.[2] The Convention governs intercountry adoptions between contracting states. The Convention requires contracting states to create a "Central Authority" responsible for making certain relevant determinations about the desirability of the adoption. If an adoption takes place in accord with the standards of the Convention, it requires that all contracting states recognize the adoption unless it is manifestly contrary to the public policy of the state asked to recognize it.

The Convention has a limited scope: it applies when the child is habitually resident in one contracting state and the adopting couple or person are habitually resident in another. It therefore does not address in-state adoptions that become an issue in another state nor adoptions involving a contracting and a non-contracting state. The state of origin determines whether the child can be adopted, the receiving state whether the adoptive parents are eligible and suitable to adopt (Arts. 4 and 5). The thrust of the Convention is to guard against international trafficking in children for the purpose of adoption. It does not provide solutions for most of the problems addressed above. The United States signed the Convention in 1994, but has not ratified it.

---

2. See supra § 16.7 n.5.

§ 16.9

1. Convention on Protection of Children and Cooperation in Respect of Intercountry Adoption, May 29, 1993, 32 I.L.M. 1139.

2. Albania, Andorra, Australia, Austria, Belarus, Bolivia, Brazil, Bulgaria, Burkina Faso, Canada, Chile, Colombia, Czech Republic, Costa Rica, Cyprus, Denmark, Ecuador, El Salvador, Finland, France, Germany, India, Israel, Italy, Latvia, Luxembourg, Mexico, Netherlands, Norway, Panama, Peru, Philippines, Poland, Romania, Slovakia, Spain, Sri Lanka, Sweden, Switzerland, United Kingdom, Uruguay, Venezuela.

Chapter 17

TORTS

Table of Sections

		Sections
I.	Introduction	17.1
II.	Choice–of–Law Approaches to Torts in General	17.1–17.76
	A. Traditional Approaches: The First Restatement's *Lex Loci*	
	Test	17.1–17.10
	1. The *Lex-Loci–Delicti* Rule	17.2–17.7
	2. Characterization	17.8–17.10
	B. Interest Analysis	17.11–17.20
	1. In General	17.11
	2. Interest Analysis and the *Lex-Fori* Variant in the	
	Courts	17.12–17.15
	a. False Conflicts	17.12
	b. True Conflicts	17.13
	c. Unprovided–For Cases	17.14
	d. The *Lex-Fori* Variant	17.15
	3. The "Comparative Impairment" Approach	17.16–17.20
	a. The California Version	17.16–17.19
	b. The Louisiana Version	17.20
	C. The "Better Law" Approach	17.21–17.23
	D. The Most–Significant–Relationship Test and the Second	
	Restatement	17.24–17.28
	1. Introduction	17.24–17.25
	2. The Case Law	17.26–17.28
	E. The New York Experience	17.29–17.32
	1. *Babcock* and Guest–Statute Conflicts	17.29
	2. From *Babcock* to *Neumeier*	17.30
	3. The *Neumeier* Rules	17.31
	4. Extending the *Neumeier* Rules to Other Loss–Distribu-	
	tion Conflicts: *Schultz* and *Cooney*	17.32
III.	From Rules to Approaches to Rules	17.33–17.50
	A. From Rules to Approaches	17.33–17.50
	1. Introduction	17.33
	2. Policy Analysis: A Synthesis	17.34
	3. Time for Rules?	17.35
	B. From Approaches to Rules	17.36–17.50
	1. The Distinction Between Loss–Distribution Rules and	
	Conduct–Regulation Rules	17.36–17.38
	a. The Origins and Meaning of the Distinction	17.36
	b. The Difficulties of the Distinction	17.37
	c. The Usefulness of the Distinction	17.38
	2. Loss–Distribution Conflicts	17.39–17.47
	a. Common–Domicile Cases	17.39
	b. Cases Analogous to Common–Domicile Cases	17.40
	(1) Domicile in states with same law	17.40

(2) Pre-existing relationship......................... 17.40
(3) Choice-of-law clauses 17.40
c. Split–Domicile Conflicts between the Laws of Two
    States.. 17.41
    (1) True Conflicts 17.42–17.44
        (a) Cases in which the conduct, the injury,
            and the tortfeasor's domicile are in a
            state whose law protects the tortfeasor..... 17.42
        (b) Cases in which the conduct, the injury,
            and the domicile of the victim are in a
            state whose law protects the victim 17.43
        (c) Cases in which the conduct and the tort-
            feasor's domicile are in a state whose
            law protects the tortfeasor, while the
            injury and the victim's domicile are in a
            state whose law protects the victim 17.44
    (2) No–Interest or Unprovided-for Cases 17.45
        (a) The Neumeier Pattern 17.45
        (b) The Hurtado Pattern....................... 17.45
        (c) Summary 17.45
d. Split–Domicile Conflicts Involving Three States 17.46
e. Summary and Rules................................. 17.47
3. Conduct–Regulation Conflicts 17.48–17.50
    a. Generic Conduct–Regulation Conflicts 17.48
    b. Summary and Rule 17.49
    c. Punitive–Damages Conflicts 17.50
        (1) The Pertinent Contacts and Typical Patterns
        (2) Three-or Two–Contact Patterns
        (3) Single–Contact Patterns
        (4) The Victim's Domicile or Nationality
        (5) Summary and Rule
IV. Particular Tort Problems 17.51–17.63
  A. Injury to Intangible Values 17.51
    1. Fraud and Misrepresentation 17.52
    2. Unfair Competition 17.53
    3. Alienation of Affections................................ 17.54
    4. Defamation and Invasion of Privacy 17.55
  B. Statutory Liability 17.56–17.62
    1. No–Fault Liability 17.56–17.58
      a. In General 17.56
      b. Law Governing the Tortfeasor's Liability.............. 17.57
      c. Coverage of the No–Fault Statutes 17.58
    2. Workers' Compensation 17.59
      a. Worker's Compensation Benefits 17.59
      b. Statutory Benefits and Tort Immunity 17.60
      c. Exclusivity With Regard to Subcontractors and
        Their Employees................................... 17.61
      d. Mutual Employment for Benefit of Two Employers..... 17.62
  C. Admiralty 17.63
V. Products Liability.....................................17.64–17.76
  A. In General 17.64
  B. Samples From the Case Law 17.65–17.73
    1. Common Denominators 17.65
      a. Recent Trends..................................... 17.65.
      b. Pertinent Contacts 17.66
      c. Typical Patterns 17.67
    2. Cases in Which Each State's Law Favors the Local
      Litigant (True Conflicts)............................... 17.68

　　　a.　Cases Applying the Pro–Defendant Law of a De-
　　　　　fendant–Affiliated State 17.69
　　　b.　Cases Applying the Pro–Recovery Law of a Vic-
　　　　　tim–Affiliated State 17.70
　　　　　(1)　Choice supported by three contacts 17.70
　　　　　(2)　Choice supported by two contacts................ 17.71
　　　　　(3)　Choice supported by one contact............17.72–17.74
　　3.　Cases in Which Each State's Law Favors a Litigant
　　　　Affiliated With the Other State........................ 17.75
　　　a.　Cases Applying the Pro–Recovery Law of a Defen-
　　　　　dant–Affiliated State 17.76
　　　b.　Cases Applying the Pro–Defendant Law of a Vic-
　　　　　tim–Affiliated State 17.77
　　　　　(1)　Choice supported by three contacts 17.77
　　　　　(2)　Choice supported by two contacts................ 17.78
　　　　　(3)　Choice supported by one contact................ 17.79
　C.　Choice-of-Law Rules 17.80–17.82
　　1.　Enacted Rules 17.80
　　2.　Proposed Rules 17.81
　　3.　Common Features and Differences 17.82
VI.　Territoriality and Personality in Tort Conflicts 17.83

I.　INTRODUCTION

§ 17.1　Chapter 2 surveyed the fundamental changes in theoretical approaches to choice of law that emerged during the second half of the twentieth century. These approaches have their principal origin in tort and contract cases.[1] Part I of this chapter presents these approaches in operation. Part II seeks to ascertain the extent to which, regardless of the approach the courts follow, the solutions they reach in recurring patterns of cases are sufficiently uniform to be susceptible of being recast into choice-of-law rules. Part III discusses some special but diverse categories of tort conflicts involving injury to intangible values and statutory liability. Finally, part IV focuses on products liability conflicts which, while being a species of tort conflicts, are nevertheless sufficiently distinct to require separate discussion.

With respect to Part I, the reader is reminded of the caveats stated in Chapter 2, regarding methodological classifications in general.[2] While a systematic treatment of the case law requires drawing distinctions and making classifications, it also runs the risk of overstating the differences. In reality, the lines tend to be much more fluid. Few courts are entirely

§ 17.1

1.　See Reese, Choice of Law in Torts and Contracts and Directions for the Future, 16 Colum. J. Trans. L. 1 (1977). Early decisions departing from the fixed rules of the First Restatement were in contract: W.H. Barber Co. v. Hughes, 223 Ind. 570, 63 N.E.2d 417, 423 (1945); Chinchilla v. Foreign Tankship Corp., 195 Misc. 895, 91 N.Y.S.2d 213 (N.Y.City Ct. 1949), modified 197 Misc. 1058, 97 N.Y.S.2d 835 (1950); Auten v. Auten, 308 N.Y. 155, 124 N.E.2d 99 (1954); in tort: Noel v. Airponents, Inc., 169 F.Supp. 348 (D.N.J.1958).

2.　See supra § 2.19.

consistent in approaching choice-of-law problems and few states adhere to a single approach in its pure form. Even decisions that purport to do so, often tend to draw on more than one approach or arrive at solutions explainable on several grounds and analyses. Writing in the 1980s, Robert Leflar spoke of the "current American eclecticism,"[3] and Willis Reese advised skepticism in reading choice-of-law decisions, especially those employing interest analysis: "at least on occasion, [courts] first determine upon the result they wish to reach and then more or less invent a purpose for the favored rule that would call for its application. . . . [C]hoice-of-law opinions are likely to be misleading unless . . . read . . . with skepticism, since the real reasons of the courts are likely to be omitted or submerged. . . . A clue to the courts' real motivation can be found in the fact that the great majority of the choice-of-law cases that have arisen in tort have resulted in the application of a local law rule favorable to the plaintiff."[4]

Empirical research for that period, confirmed the existence of these trends. A 1992 survey of approximately 800 reported tort choice-of-law decisions between 1960 and 1992 revealed several important decisional patterns. First, all of the major modern approaches to choice of law–the Second Restatement, interest analysis and Leflar's choice-influencing considerations–had a strong propensity to favor plaintiffs over defendants, local parties over out-of-staters, and forum over foreign law.[5] Second, for the most part, the performance of the modern approaches did not show statistically significant variations, thus confirming that the true modern approach is "eclectic."[6] Third, courts following modern approaches did perform differently than states still following the First Restatement in that the modern approaches all showed a statistically significant propensity to favor recovery, local litigants and forum law more often than the traditional approach.[7]

Research for the subsequent period confirms the continued—in fact increasing—eclecticism of choice-of-law decisions,[8] but also suggests that the pro-plaintiff, pro-recovery biases that characterized the use of modern approaches in the 1970s and 1980s appeared to have subsided. For example, a study of all the state supreme court decisions involving multistate torts in which the victim and the tortfeasor were domiciled in the same state and were involved in a tort that occurred in another state

---

3. R. Leflar, L. McDougal & R. Felix, American Conflicts Law 391–393 (4th ed. 1986). See also L. McDougal, R. Felix & R. Whitten, American Conflicts Law 479–80 (5th ed.2001); Reppy, Eclecticism in Choice of Law: Hybrid Method or Mishmash? 34 Mercer L. Rev. 645 (1983); Westbrook, A Survey and Evaluation of Competing Choice-of-Law Methodologies: The Case for Eclecticism, 40 Mo. L. Rev. 407 (1975).

4. Reese, Book Review, 33 Am. J. Comp. L. 332, 334, 335 (1985). See also Reese, Substantive Policies and Choice of Law, 2 Touro L. Rev. 1, 3 (1986).

5. Borchers, The Choice-of-Law Revolution: An Empirical Study, 49 Wash. & Lee L. Rev. 357, 370–74 (1992).

6. Id. at 377.

7. Id.

8. See S. Symeonides, W. Perdue & A. von Mehren, Conflict of Laws: American, Comparative, International, 299 (2d ed. 2003) ("eclecticism may well be *the* dominant choice-of-law methodology in the United States today"); S. Symeonides, The American Choice-of-Law Revolution in the Courts: Today and Tomorrow, 298 Recueil des Cours, 1, 94–96 (2003).

(common-domicile cases) reveals that the vast majority of those cases (and virtually all post–1980 cases) have applied the law of the common domicile, not only when it favored the plaintiff, but also when it favored the defendant.[9] Similarly, in split-domicile cases in which the conduct and the injury occurred in the home state of one of the parties, the majority of courts applied the law of that state, not only when it favored the plaintiff, but also when it favored the defendant.[10] Finally, 51% of product liability cases decided between 1900 and 2003 applied a law that favored the *defendant*.[11] Whether these new trends mean that the conflicts revolution has entered a consolidation phase or it has been met with a counter-revolution is a matter of interpretation. This is one of the question to be explored later in this chapter.

II. CHOICE–OF–LAW APPROACHES TO TORTS IN GENERAL

A. TRADITIONAL APPROACHES: THE FIRST RESTATEMENT'S *LEX LOCI* TEST

1. *The Lex–Loci–Delicti Rule*

§ 17.2   The territorialist approach based on the vested-rights theory,[1] was the cornerstone of the First Restatement, including its choice-of-law rules for torts,[2] which dominated American conflicts law during the first half of the 20th century. The place where the last event necessary to make the actor liable occurred was considered the place of the tort or *delict* and thus the source of the governing law: the law of the place of the wrong (*lex loci delicti commissi*).[3]

The place of the wrong is usually the place where the injury occurred because liability does not arise without an injury. In the substantial number of cases in which the wrongful conduct and the

---

9. See Symeonides, *The Revolution Today*, supra n.8, at 178–194.

10. See id. at 194–220.

11. See Symeonides, Choice of Law for Products Liability: The 1990s and Beyond, 1314–16 (2004). Although state courts applied a law that favored the plaintiff in 57% of the cases, the federal cases were more numerous and the federal courts applied a law that favored the defendant in 54% of the cases.

§ 17.2

1. See supra § 2.7. "The theory of the foreign suit is that although the act complained of was subject to no law having force in the forum, it gave rise to an obligation, an *obligatio* which, like other obligations follows the person, and may be enforced wherever the person may be found.

But as the only source of this obligation is the law of the place of the act, it follows that that law determines not merely the existence of the obligation, but equally determines the extent." Slater v. Mexican Nat'l R.R. Co., 194 U.S. 120, 126, 24 S.Ct. 581, 582, 48 L.Ed. 900 (1904) (Holmes, J.).

2. Restatement, Conflict of Laws § 377 (1934). The "place of the tort" is the subject of annotations in 133 A.L.R. 260 (1940); 77 A.L.R.2d 1266 (1961); 29 A.L.R. 603 (1970) 83 A.L.R.3d 338 (1978).

3. For a modern application of this rule, see Philip Morris Inc. v. Angeletti, 358 Md. 689, 752 A.2d 200 (2000) (putative class action involving nicotine addiction claims; holding that, under the First Conflicts Restatement's examples regarding "poison" injuries, the place of the tort was where the victims became addicted to nicotine, not where they ingested it).

injury occur in the same state, this rule works reasonably well. However, the mechanical application of the *lex loci* rule becomes troublesome when these contacts are not in the same state, or when another state also has a significant relationship either to the occurrence or the parties. For instance, when a court in the victim's home state is faced with damage limitations imposed by the place of the occurrence, the last event necessary to complete the cause of action is not necessarily the most significant factor.[4]

The importance of the "place of the last event" is well demonstrated by a leading older decision, *Alabama G. S. R. Co. v. Carroll.*[5] The Alabama plaintiff, a brakeman for the railroad, was injured in Mississippi when two train cars uncoupled during a run between the two states. The injury was attributed to a negligent inspection of the train by plaintiff's co-employees in Alabama, which failed to reveal the defective link that caused the uncoupling. The obstacle to plaintiff's recovery was the common law fellow-servant rule to which Mississippi continued to adhere. Alabama had an employer's liability statute that made employers liable for the injuries sustained by employees as a result of their co-employees' negligence. The court concluded that the place of the wrong was in Mississippi, and, since that state's rule did not vest the plaintiff with a right of recovery against his employer, the plaintiff had no such right in Alabama.[6] Despite Alabama's multiple connections with the parties and the case, the court held the Alabama statute inapplicable because the ostensibly critical last event did not occur there.[7] If, hypothetically, the negligent inspection had been in Mississippi and the uncoupling had occurred in Alabama, Carroll would have recovered. The fortuitous place of injury thus became all-important.[8]

---

4. See W. Cook, The Logical and Legal Bases of Conflict of Laws 317, 340 (1942)

5. 97 Ala. 126, 11 So. 803, 18 L.R.A. 433, 38 Am.St.R. 163 (1892).

6. "It is admitted, or at least it cannot be denied, that negligence of duty unproductive of damnifying results will not authorize or support a recovery. Up to the time the train passed out of Alabama, no injury had resulted. For all that occurred in Alabama, therefore, no cause of action whatever arose. The fact which created the right to sue, the injury without which confessedly no action would lie anywhere, transpired in the state of Mississippi. It was in that state, therefore, necessarily that the cause of action, if any, arose; and whether a cause of action arose or existed at all or not must in all reason be determined by the law which obtained at the time and place when and where the fact which is relied on to justify a recovery transpired." 97 Ala. at 134, 11 So. at 806.

7. The words "in Alabama" did not appear in § 2590 of the Alabama Code. The Alabama Employers' Liability Act was sub-

sequently amended to cover out-of-state injury if the contract of employment was made in Alabama. Ala. Code § 7540 (1928).

8. More than one hundred years later, an Alabama court faced a similar case, Fitzgerald v. Austin, 715 So.2d 795 (Ala. App. 1997), a case arising out of an Arkansas traffic accident in which an Alabama employee of an Alabama employer was injured while driving his employer's truck. The plaintiff's injuries were worsened by the fact that the truck did not have an operable seat belt. He sued his employer and his fellow servants who were responsible for installing the seat belt in Alabama. Under Arkansas law the defendants would be immune from liability. Under Alabama law it was arguable that the defendants would be liable. The plaintiff made all the arguments the plaintiff made in *Carroll*, and a few more. The court of appeals was unimpressed, but also felt powerless to consider carving an exception from the *lex loci delicti* rule because the Alabama Supreme Court had categorically reaffirmed that rule three times in the previous 15 years, most recently in 1991. See supra § 2.21 n.1.

§ 17.3 There are, however, situations in which the application of the law of the state of injury in cross-border torts (conduct in State X and injury in State Y) is reasonable–if the circumstances were such that the actor should have foreseen that its conduct in one state would produce injury in another state and if the latter state holds the actor liable for that conduct. Blasting cases, in which one deploys explosives in one state and causes injury in another, illustrate this point,[1] as do modern cases involving other cross-border torts.[2]

An interesting example of a reasonable application of the traditional approach is found in a Pennsylvania case in which the plaintiff alleged that he was bitten in New Jersey by a runaway dog that its owner kept in Pennsylvania.[3] New Jersey, but not Pennsylvania, would hold the owner liable regardless of fault. The court applied New Jersey law and held the owner liable. Because of the relative proximity between the owner's home and the place of the injury, the application of the law of the place of injury was reasonable.[4] The same cannot be said, however, about a case that applied the law of the state of injury in the converse situation in which the owner of animals was liable under the law of his home state but not under the law of the state of injury.[5]

§ 17.4 Vicarious liability cases present some of the several types of situations in which the place of the wrong may or may not govern.[1]

§ 17.3

1. Dallas v. Whitney, 118 W.Va. 106, 188 S.E. 766 (1936) (applying Ohio's liability without fault law to defendant's blasting in West Virginia that damaged plaintiff's plate glass in Ohio); Cameron v. Vandegriff, 53 Ark. 381, 13 S.W. 1092 (1890) (blasting in Indian territory–now Oklahoma–caused a rock to fall on plaintiff in Arkansas; Arkansas law applied). In Hunter v. Derby Foods, 110 F.2d 970 (2d Cir.1940), an action for wrongful death was brought in the federal district court in New York. The victim died in Ohio as a result of eating unwholesome canned meat he had purchased and eaten in Ohio. The defendant, a New York distributor, had secured the meat from one who had processed and canned it in South America. The defendant sold it to a wholesaler in Ohio, who in turn sold it to the grocer who sold it to the victim. An Ohio statute made it negligence per se to sell unwholesome food without disclosure of that fact to the buyer. The court held that the plaintiff would recover on a showing of a violation of the statute and need not prove lack of due care. See generally Annot. 133 A.L.R. 263 (1940).

2. See infra § 17.48 nn.24–39; S. Symeonides, The American Choice-of-Law Revolution in the Courts: Today and Tomorrow, 298 Recueil des Cours, 1, 221–230, 254–260 (2003).

3. Fischl v. Chubb, 30 Pa. D. & C. 40, 53 Montg. 116 (Pa. C.P. 1937) (relying on Comment to Restatement Conflict of Laws § 382(c)). In a modern dog-bite case, Bader by Bader v. Purdom, 841 F.2d 38 (2d Cir. 1988), the court permitted an impleader claim that was available under the law of the place of injury, Ontario, and imposed liability on New York residents for negligence in Ontario.

4. Had the plaintiff been bitten in a more distant state, a different result seems likely if an unfair, perhaps unconstitutional, result is to be avoided. See Reese & Flesch, Agency and Vicarious Liability in Conflicts of Law, 60 Colum. L. Rev. 764, 777 (1960).

5. Le Forest v. Tolman, 117 Mass. 109 (1875). For modern cases involving this pattern and reaching the opposite result, see Symeonides, supra n.2, 230–32, 248–254.

§ 17.4

1. Section 387 of the First Restatement provided that "[w]hen a person authorizes another to act for him in any state and the other does so act, whether he is liable for the tort of the other is determined by the law of the place of wrong." Comment (a) to this section gives the following explanation:

> In order that the law of the state of wrong may apply to create liability against the absentee defendant, he must

Judge Learned Hand's opinion in *Scheer v. Rockne Motors Corp.*[2] illustrates the application of this exception to the *lex loci delicti* rule. In *Scheer,* an employee of a New York defendant drove one of defendant's cars to Ontario where his negligent driving resulted in injury to the plaintiff (apparently also a New Yorker).[3] It was not established at trial whether the employee, a salesman who regularly used company cars in his New York–Pennsylvania territory, was authorized to take this excursion into Ontario. In the absence of such an authorization, the defendant would not be liable under New York law, but would be liable under Ontario law. The court reversed the trial court decision which had applied Ontario law. This exception to the *lex loci* rule can perhaps be explained by the desire to avoid unfair surprise to the defendant.[4]

The holding in *Scheer* purportedly distinguished the U.S. Supreme Court's decision in *Young v. Masci,*[5] which upheld the application of New York's owner-liability statute to a New Jersey defendant who had loaned his car to a friend without restriction. The friend took the car to New York where his negligent driving resulted in injury to the plaintiff. The Supreme Court rejected the defendant's argument that application of New York law, the *lex loci delicti,* by the New Jersey forum violated due process.[6] The Court reasoned that in light of the unrestricted permission given by the owner-defendant, there was no unfair surprise and no reason to make an exception to the *lex loci* rule. However, the distinction between the two decisions is not free from difficulty. As noted above, if a person sets off a blast of dynamite, or keeps a dog, either of which causes injury in another state, the actor may be held liable under the law of the second state.[7] Why should the result be different when the injury comes from the defendant's car and a person to whom the car is entrusted? Although the owner has not voluntarily submitted his car to the operation of the second state's law, he has voluntarily parted with it under circumstances that make the occurrence of the injury in the second state reasonably foreseeable. As between the owner and the victim, why should the latter bear the consequences of both disobedience of orders and negligence by the bailee?

in some way have submitted himself to the law of that state. It is sufficient if he has authorized or permitted another to act for him in the state in which the other's conduct occurs to where it takes effect. Thus, if A, in state X, authorizes B to act for him in state Y and B does so act, A is thereby subjected to the Y law." Rheinstein saw this rule as a "qualification for which no justification seems to exist within the conceptual framework of the Restatement." Rheinstein, The Place of Wrong: A Study in the Method of the Case Law, 19 Tul. L. Rev. 4, 14 (1944). But see infra n.4.

2. 68 F.2d 942 (2d Cir.1934).

3. "On the day in question he set out for Buffalo on an errand to Windsor, Ontario … He invited the plaintiff to go along …" Id. at 943.

4. See Siegmann v. Meyer, 100 F.2d 367 (2d Cir.1938), in which Judge Learned Hand held that a New York husband could not be held liable for his wife's tort in Florida under Florida law, when New York would not impose such a liability and the defendant himself had never been in Florida. The holding rests on due process grounds.

5. 289 U.S. 253, 53 S.Ct. 599, 77 L.Ed. 1158 (1933).

6. Chapter 3 details constitutional limitations on choice of law, particularly forum law.

7. Supra § 17.3 nn.1–3.

§ 17.5   The First Restatement allowed for other limited exceptions to the place of wrong rule in cases where the act occurred in one state and the injury in another. Thus, a person required by law to act in state X and whose action subsequently produces injury in state Y was exempted from liability under Y's law.[1] Similarly, one acting under a privilege conferred by state X would not be liable for results occurring in state Y.[2] Finally, the First Restatement provided that liability for injury by poisoning was governed by the place of poisoning and not by the law of the place where the harmful effect occurred.[3]

The *lex loci delicti* rule also presents problems in cases of loss of consortium where the place of the wrongful act differs from that where the loss is felt by the plaintiff. The place of the wrong could be either where the injured spouse has been harmed or the marital domicile where the complaining spouse suffers the absence of the injured spouse. Under the traditional rule, courts looked to the place of injury to the physically harmed spouse because that is where the last event necessary to create liability occurred.[4] The consortium action was viewed as derivative of the primary harm to the physically injured spouse.[5] Similarly, in an action for alienation of affections the place where the defendant's acts led the enticed spouse astray, rather than the marital domicile, was regarded as the place of the wrong.[6]

Dramshop act cases may also present two-state problems. If a defendant tavern keeper in a dramshop state serves an excess amount of liquor to a customer who then crosses a state line and causes an accident

---

§ 17.5

1. Restatement, First Conflict of Laws § 382(1) (1934).

2. Id. § 382(2).

3. Id. § 377, Note (Summary of Rules in Important Situations Determining Where a Tort is Committed) 1: "Except in the case of harm from poison, when a person sustains bodily harm, the place of the wrong is the place where the harmful force takes effect upon the body." Apparently, the only case on point is Moore v. Pywell, 29 App. D.C. 312, 9 L.R.A. (n.s.) 1078 (1907), which had engendered considerable confusion. The defendant, a District of Columbia druggist, negligently mixed a prescription in such a way that the deceased, a Maryland resident, died in Maryland after taking the drug there. Beale cited this case for the proposition that the court applied Maryland law because it was the place of the injury. See 2 Beale, The Conflict of Laws 1288 § 377.2 (1935). Weintraub, however, believes that the court applied forum law (place of acting). See Weintraub, Commentary on the Conflict of Laws, 347 (4th ed. 2001); see also Annot. 77 A.L.R.2d 1275 (1961). It is perhaps simpler to view the case as presenting a "false conflict": the issue was the availability of a wrongful

death action and both jurisdictions allowed such actions.

4. See Sestito v. Knop, 297 F.2d 33 (7th Cir.1961); Jordan v. States Marine Corp., 257 F.2d 232 (9th Cir.1958); McVickers v. Chesapeake & Ohio Ry. Co., 194 F.Supp. 848 (E.D.Mich.1961); Folk v. York–Shipley, Inc., 239 A.2d 236 (Del.1968); Conway v. Ogier, 115 Ohio App. 251, 184 N.E.2d 681 (1961). See generally Annot. 46 A.L.R.3d 880 (1972).

5. Even the Second Restatement considers the consortium action to be derivative. See Restatement, Second, Conflict of Laws § 154 (1971). However, the law that governs the suit of the physically injured spouse is that of the state of the most significant relationship, as determined by § 145. See Casey v. Manson Constr. Co., 247 Or. 274, 428 P.2d 898 (1967); Baedke v. John Morrell & Co. v. Pearson Services, Inc., 748 F.Supp. 700 (N.D.Iowa 1990).

6. See Marra v. Bushee, 447 F.2d 1282 (2d Cir.1971); Albert v. McGrath, 278 F.2d 16 (D.C.Cir.1960); Orr v. Sasseman, 239 F.2d 182 (5th Cir.1956). Cf. Gordon v. Parker, 83 F.Supp. 40, aff'd 178 F.2d 888 (1st Cir.1949) (similar result but court weighed interests). See also infra § 17.54.

in which the plaintiff is injured, is the place of the wrong the situs of the accident or where the liquor was sold to the driver? Courts frequently selected the law of the place of the accident.[7] A difficult problem arises when the forum has a dramshop act and is also the situs of the accident but intoxication occurred out-of-state. Even if the forum can exercise jurisdiction over the out-of-state defendant tavern consistent with current jurisdictional requirements, application of forum law may give rise to the same problem of "unfair surprise" as noted earlier in connection with the vicarious liability cases. The difficulty in fashioning a single rule results in part from the fact that dramshop legislation represents a form of business regulation, an allocation of enterprise risk, which must be balanced against the private interests of the parties.[8]

Even in cases in which wrongful conduct and injury are localized in the same state, the traditional *lex loci delicti* rule has led to questionable results. Most notable are the guest-statute and interspousal and intrafamily immunity cases. In guest-statute cases, the law of the place of the accident traditionally controlled despite the fact that the parties were both domiciled at the forum. As a result, the local plaintiff might be denied a recovery against the local defendant because the place of the accident had a guest statute that required a showing of more than ordinary negligence.[9] Use of the *lex loci delicti* in the interspousal and intrafamily immunity cases similarly could result in the application of foreign law by the forum to govern relationships between its domiciliaries.[10]

§ 17.6 Under the traditional theory, the law of the place of injury governed virtually all aspects of a cause of action in tort, such as the

---

7. See Graham v. General U.S. Grant Post No. 2665, 43 Ill.2d 1, 248 N.E.2d 657 (1969); Eldridge v. Don Beachcomber, Inc., 342 Ill.App. 151, 95 N.E.2d 512 (1950); Butler v. Wittland, 18 Ill.App.2d 578, 153 N.E.2d 106 (1958); Goodwin v. Young, 34 Mun. 252 (N.Y. S.Ct. 1884). But see Schmidt v. Driscoll Hotel, 249 Minn. 376, 82 N.W.2d 365 (1957), an early example of policy analysis; the case is discussed infra § 17.12.

8. In Bernhard v. Harrah's Club, 16 Cal.3d 313, 546 P.2d 719, 128 Cal.Rptr. 215 (1976), cert. denied 429 U.S. 859, 97 S.Ct. 159, 50 L.Ed.2d 136 (1976), forum law was applied under a "comparative impairment" test; unfair surprise was discounted because the Nevada defendant actively sought California patrons. The case is discussed infra § 17.19. Wimmer v. Koenigseder, 108 Ill.2d 435, 92 Ill.Dec. 233, 484 N.E.2d 1088 (1985) applied *Graham*, 43 Ill.2d 1, 248 N.E.2d 657, to a case where intoxication occurred out-of-state (no dramshop act) and injury occurred in Illinois: *Graham*, the court explained, holds that the Illinois act applies only when both sale and injury occur in Illinois.

9. See, e.g., Sharp v. Johnson, 248 Minn. 518, 80 N.W.2d 650 (1957); Loranger v. Nadeau, 215 Cal. 362, 10 P.2d 63 (1932); Fessenden v. Smith, 255 Iowa 1170, 124 N.W.2d 554 (1963); Pearson v. Erb, 82 N.W.2d 818 (N.D.1957). Kopp v. Rechtzigel, 273 Minn. 441, 141 N.W.2d 526 (1966) (abandoning place-of-wrong rule); Naphtali v. Lafazan, 8 A.D.2d 22, 186 N.Y.S.2d 1010 (1959). These cases have now all been overruled. For recent cases see infra § 17.39.

10. See, e.g., McMillan v. McMillan, 219 Va. 1127, 253 S.E.2d 662 (1979); Landers v. Landers, 153 Conn. 303, 216 A.2d 183 (1966), abrogated by statute, Conn. Gen. Stat.Ann. § 52–527d; Oshiek v. Oshiek, 244 S.C. 249, 136 S.E.2d 303 (1964) (overturned by statute); Lyons v. Lyons, 2 Ohio St.2d 243, 208 N.E.2d 533 (1965); Holder v. Holder, 384 P.2d 663 (Okla.1962); Robinson v. Gaines, 331 S.W.2d 653 (Mo.1960). See generally Annot. 92 A.L.R.3d 901, § 5 (1980). The last three cases have since been rejected. For recent cases, see infra §§ 17.7 n.8, 17.39 nn.9–10.

measure of damages;[1] the existence or nonexistence of a defense;[2] the availability of contribution or indemnity among tortfeasors;[3] the applicability of the *respondeat superior* rule;[4] the question of who owns or has an interest in the cause of action;[5] and whether a tort action survives the tortfeasor's death.[6] With regard to wrongful death, the traditional rule looked to the law of the place where the deceased suffered the fatal injury, rather than the place of death, to determine the existence of a cause of action[7] and the measure[8] and distribution of damages.[9]

§ 17.6

1. See Victor v. Sperry, 163 Cal.App.2d 518, 329 P.2d 728 (1958) (action between forum residents arising from car accident in Mexico; applying the more restrictive Mexican measure of damages because "the measure of damages is inseparably connected to the cause of action and cannot be severed therefrom." The case is discussed infra § 17.16. See also Hopkins v. Lockheed Aircraft Corp., 201 So.2d 743 (Fla.1967). Cf. Ryan v. Ford Motor Co., 334 F.Supp. 674 (E.D.Mich.1971) (place of tort governs question of prejudgment interest).

2. See Kemart Corp. v. Printing Arts Research Labs., Inc., 269 F.2d 375 (9th Cir.1959), cert. denied 361 U.S. 893, 80 S.Ct. 197, 4 L.Ed.2d 151 (1959) (defamatory privilege); Jones v. McKesson & Robbins, Inc., 237 F.Supp. 454 (D.N.D.1965) (probable cause as defense to malicious prosecution); Morisette v. Canadian Pacific Ry. Co., 76 Vt. 267, 56 A. 1102 (1904) (contributory negligence).

3. See Home Indem. Co. v. Poladian, 270 F.2d 156 (4th Cir.1959); Southwestern Greyhound Lines v. Crown Coach Co., 178 F.2d 628 (8th Cir.1949); LaChance v. Service Trucking Co., 215 F.Supp. 162 (D.Md. 1963); Bache v. Dixie–Ohio Express Co., 8 F.R.D. 159 (N.D.Ga.1948); Steger v. Egyud, 219 Md. 331, 149 A.2d 762 (1959); Builders Supply Co. v. McCabe, 366 Pa. 322, 77 A.2d 368 (1951); Charnock v. Taylor, 223 N.C. 360, 26 S.E.2d 911 (1943); Millsap v. Central Wisconsin Motor Transp. Co., 41 Ill. App.2d 1, 189 N.E.2d 793 (1963). See also Annot. 95 A.L.R.2d 1096 (1964). Contribution and indemnity, at least in states that have no such requirement, could also be treated as unjust enrichment problems under § 453 of the First Restatement: "When a person is alleged to have been unjustly enriched, the law of the place of enrichment determines whether he is under a duty to repay...." See Wade, Joint Tortfeasors and the Conflict of Laws, 6 Vand. L. Rev. 464, 474–76 (1953).

4. See, e.g., Knight v. Handley Motor Co., 198 A.2d 747 (D.C.App.1964).

5. See Texas & P R Co. v. Humble, 181 U.S. 57, 21 S.Ct. 526, 45 L.Ed. 747, (1901); Crown Coach v. Whitaker, 208 Ark. 535, 186 S.W.2d 940 (1945) (damages recovered by wife belong to marital community); Traglio v. Harris, 104 F.2d 439, 127 A.L.R. 803 (9th Cir. 1939), cert. denied 308 U.S. 629, 60 S.Ct. 125, 84 L.Ed. 524 (1939) (wife's claim not community property under law of place of the tort although the law of the marital domicile was otherwise); Roberson v. U Bar Ranch, Inc., 303 F.Supp. 730 (D.N.M.1968) (under law of place of injury wife can sue in own name without joinder of husband although marital domicile rule would bar her claim because of husband's contributory negligence): Cf. Maag v. Voykovich, 46 Wn.2d 302, 280 P.2d 680 (1955) (plaintiff cannot assert claim against marital community for injury received in noncommunity state). But see Reeves v. Schulmeier, 303 F.2d 802 (5th Cir.1962) (marital domicile determines nature of spouses' interest). Cf. Bruton v. Villoria, 138 Cal. App.2d 642, 292 P.2d 638 (1956) (same result through characterization of issue as property rather than tort).

6. See Orr v. Ahern, 107 Conn. 174, 139 A. 691 (1928) ("The power which gave the right could take it away"); Chubbuck v. Holloway, 182 Minn. 225, 234 N.W. 314 (1931), rev'd 182 Minn. 225, 234 N.W. 868 (1931); Allen v. Nessler, 247 Minn. 230, 76 N.W.2d 793 (1956); Burg v. Knox, 334 Mo. 329, 67 S.W.2d 96 (1933).

7. See, e.g., Pack v. Beech Aircraft Corp., 50 Del. 413, 132 A.2d 54 (1957); Wheeler v. Southwestern Greyhound Lines, 207 Ark. 601, 182 S.W.2d 214 (1944); Debbis v. Hertz Corp., 269 F.Supp. 671 (D.Md. 1967) (place of fatal injury governs [W. Virginia], although the conduct occurred in Virginia and the death in Maryland).

8. See, e.g., Hopkins v. Lockheed Aircraft Corp., 201 So.2d 743 (Fla.1967).

9. See, e.g., Komlos v. Compagnie Nationale Air France, 111 F.Supp. 393 (S.D.N.Y. 1952), rev'd 209 F.2d 436 (2d Cir.1953), cert. denied 348 U.S. 820, 75 S.Ct. 31, 99 L.Ed. 646 (1954).

§ 17.7 The traditional rule, although praised for its certainty and ease of application, created problems in cases involving claims for redress for nonphysical injuries. Locating the place of injury or the place of the last event necessary to raise liability was not always easy in cases of defamation,[1] invasion of privacy,[2] unfair competition,[3] and fraud.[4]

The *lex loci* rule, as the exclusive test for choice of law in tort, has been rejected by most states that have considered its application in recent years.[5] However, the rule continues to have adherents,[6] even with respect to guest-statute[7] and interspousal immunity cases,[8] the areas

§ 17.7

1. The rule of First Restatement § 377 looked to "where the defamatory statement is communicated." See, e.g., O'Reilly v. Curtis Publ'g Co., 31 F.Supp. 364 (D.Mass. 1940); Hartmann v. Time, Inc., 166 F.2d 127 (3d Cir.1947), cert. denied 334 U.S. 838, 68 S.Ct. 1495, 92 L.Ed. 1763 (1948); Sheldon–Claire Co. v. Judson Roberts Co., 88 F.Supp. 120 (S.D.N.Y.1949). However, even before the occurrence of significant changes in choice-of-law methodology, courts often employed a variety of approaches under the single publication rule and applied the law of the place of the defendant's act, the law of the plaintiff's domicile, and often forum law. Prosser, Interstate Publication, 51 Mich. L.Rev. 959, 971–78 (1953) discusses 10 possible approaches to the problem; Palmisano v. News Syndicate Co., 130 F.Supp. 17 (S.D.N.Y.1955), lists nine ways to deal with this question. See generally Annot. 58 A.L.R.2d 650 (1958). For further discussion see infra § 17.55.

2. See Sidis v. F–R Publ'g Corp., 113 F.2d 806 (2d Cir.1940), cert. denied 311 U.S. 711, 61 S.Ct. 393, 85 L.Ed. 462 (1940) (detailed magazine story about a "once" public figure); Gautier v. Pro–Football, Inc., 304 N.Y. 354, 107 N.E.2d 485 (1952) (New York privacy statute applied to television broadcast originating in Washington, D.C.); Donahue v. Warner Brothers Pictures, 194 F.2d 6 (10th Cir.1952) (Utah privacy statute governed local exhibition of film first displayed in California, where deceased had lived and where his heirs, the plaintiffs, reside).

3. See American Banana Co. v. United Fruit Co., 213 U.S. 347, 29 S.Ct. 511, 53 L.Ed. 826 (1909); Adam Hat Stores v. Lefco, 134 F.2d 101 (3d Cir.1943); Vanity Fair Mills, Inc. v. T. Eaton Co., 234 F.2d 633 (2d Cir.1956), cert. denied 352 U.S. 871, 77 S.Ct. 96, 1 L.Ed.2d 76 (1956) (the wrong takes place where the "passing off" occurs).

4. Restatement, First, Conflict of Laws § 377 n.4 (1934): "When a person sustains loss by fraud, the place of wrong is where the loss is sustained, not where fraudulent representations are made." For criticism of the rules of the First Restatement with respect to nonphysical injury, see L. McDougal, R. Felix & R. Whitten, American Conflicts Law 454–55 (5th ed.2001).

5. See supra § 2.16.

6. See supra § 2.21.

7. See, e.g., Cook v. Pryor, 251 Md. 41, 246 A.2d 271 (1968); Chewning v. Chewning, 20 N.C.App. 283, 201 S.E.2d 353 (1973); Hopkins v. Grubb, 160 W.Va. 71, 230 S.E.2d 470 (1977). In Tuggle v. Helms, 231 Ga.App. 899, 499 S.E.2d 365 (1998), the district court refused to apply Alabama's guest statute to a case arising out of an Alabama accident and involving only Georgia domiciliaries. The Court of Appeals reversed on other grounds without addressing the choice-of-law issue, but three of the court's seven members wrote separate opinions urging abandonment of the *lex loci* rule and the application of Georgia law under a modern policy analysis. But see Owen v. Owen, 444 N.W.2d 710 (S.D. 1989) (refusing on public policy grounds to apply Indiana's guest statute in a case arising from an Indiana accident involving South Dakota parties. South Dakota later abandoned the *lex loci* rule. See Chambers v. Dakotah Charter, Inc., 488 N.W.2d 63, 67 (S.D.1992)).

8. See, e.g., McMillan v. McMillan, 219 Va. 1127, 253 S.E.2d 662 (Va. 1979) (applying the interspousal immunity rule of the *lex loci* and barring an action between Virginia spouses which was allowed under Virginia law; rejecting plaintiff's appeal to abandon the *lex loci delicti* rule in favor of the Second Restatement because the latter is "susceptible to inconstancy" and tends to create "uncertainty and confusion," 253 S.E.2d at 664); Gbye v. Gbye, 130 N.C.App. 585, 503 S.E.2d 434, at 435, 436 (N.C.App. 1998), review denied 349 N.C. 357, 517

that have been the principal targets of criticism by modern theorists.[9] This loyalty to what now seems to be outdated territorialism is mainly justified by the certainty that the rule is supposed to provide.[10]

But this certainty may be elusive. Even when the state whose law governs under the *lex loci* rule has been ascertained, the forum court's problems may not be over. A case illustrating these problems is *Day & Zimmermann, Inc. v. Challoner*[11] in which the injury occurred in Cambodia. An American serviceman who was injured in that country by a prematurely exploding artillery shell brought a products liability action against the American manufacturer of the shells in federal district court in Texas. On the ground that Cambodia had no interest in a case that involved only American parties, the District Court refused to apply the *lex loci delicti* rule that was then followed in Texas. Instead, the trial court applied the Texas law of strict liability. The Court of Appeals affirmed, but the Supreme Court reversed and remanded. Because the *Erie-Klaxon* doctrine[12] requires the application of state substantive and

S.E.2d 893 (1998) (dismissing under Alabama's parental immunity rule an action that was allowed under North Carolina law in a case arising from an Alabama traffic accident involving the members of a North Carolina family); Algie v. Algie, 261 S.C. 103, 198 S.E.2d 529 (1973). But see Boone v. Boone, 345 S.C. 8, 546 S.E.2d 191 (S.C. 2001) (invoking the *ordre public* exception and refusing to apply Georgia's interspousal immunity rule which would bar a personal injury action between South Carolina spouses arising from a traffic accident in Georgia).

9. For a list of the *lex loci* states, see supra § 2.21. In 1994, the Supreme Court of Canada reverted to the *lex loci* rule in Gagnon v. Lucas and Tolofson v. Jensen, 3 S.C.R. 1022, 120 DLR 4th 289 (1994). Writing for the Court, Justice La Forest stated:

From the general principle that a state has exclusive jurisdiction within its own territories and that other states must under principles of comity respect the exercise of its jurisdiction within its own territory, it seems axiomatic to me that, at least as a general rule, the law to be applied in torts is the law of the place where the activity occurred, i.e., the *lex loci delicti*.... The rule has the advantage of certainty, ease of application and predictability. Moreover, it would seem to meet normal expectations. Ordinarily people expect their activities to be governed by the law of the place where they happen to be and expect that concomitant legal benefits and responsibilities will be defined accordingly. The government of that place is the only one with power to deal with these activities.... [A] multiplicity of competing exercises of state

power in respect of such activities must be avoided.

3 S.C.R. 1022, at 1049–52 (long passages omitted). Justice La Forest criticized the tendency of certain courts to apply the law of the parties' common domicile, a tendency that he attributed to the courts' dislike for the substantive laws of the *locus delicti*. Although these laws may appear to outsiders to be unwise, or unfavorable to plaintiffs, said the Justice, "one does not ordinarily ignore the law of the land in favour of those who visit.... [S]uch differences are a concomitant of the territoriality principle. While, no doubt ... the underlying principles of private international law are order and fairness, order comes first." Id. at 1058.

10. The allegiance to the *lex loci* has been explained by the Michigan Supreme Court: "That rule has been settled unanimously, understood thoroughly and thought to be as fair to all affected thereby as man might reasonably conceive unless of course, we are to make equity causes out of law actions.... [T]he quagmire of unanswered and perceivably unanswered questions arising out of the proposed new doctrine appears less attractive than our admittedly hard and fast—and occasionally unjust, it is true—rule that the law of the place of the wrong is applied when the forum is a Michigan court." Abendschein v. Farrell, 382 Mich. 510, 516, 170 N.W.2d 137, 139 (1969). See also Annot., 29 A.L.R.3d 603 (1970). For the new Michigan approach see infra § 17.15.

11. 423 U.S. 3, 96 S.Ct. 167, 46 L.Ed.2d 3 (1975). For criticism see supra §§ 3.47–3.48.

12. Supra §§ 3.47 et seq.

conflicts law in federal diversity actions, the remand contained the instruction to determine what law a Texas court would choose.[13] In these circumstances, if a Texas court were to apply the *lex loci delicti*, the federal court would encounter great difficulty in ascertaining the present and past law of a war-torn country such as Cambodia. The advantage of initial certainty would be lost as a result of the uncertainty about the content of the local law of the fortuitous place of the injury. In the case discussed, this result was avoided by a settlement after the plaintiff urged a use of renvoi[14] when it appeared from further evidence that a Cambodian court would have applied the Texas law of strict liability as the place of manufacture.[15]

2. *Characterization*

§ 17.8 Dissatisfaction with the rigidity of the *lex loci* rule has occasionally led to its avoidance, sometimes through resort to *renvoi*[1] or the public policy exception,[2] and more often through characterization.

13. But see 423 U.S. at 5, 96 S.Ct. at 168 (1975), Blackmun, J., concurring: "[A]s I read the Court's *per curiam* opinion, . . . the Court of Appeals is not foreclosed from concluding, if it finds it proper so to do under the circumstances of this case, that the Texas state courts themselves would apply the Texas rule of strict liability. If that proves to be the result, I would perceive no violation of any principle of *Klaxon* . . . . I make this observation to assure the Court of Appeals that, at least in my view, today's *per curiam* does not necessarily *compel* the determination that it is only the law of Cambodia that is applicable." (emphasis in original).

14. For discussion of renvoi see supra §§ 3.13–3.14.

15. See E. Scoles & R. Weintraub, 1978 Supplement to Cases and Materials on Conflict of Laws 150 (Note). For the decision of the Court of Appeals–remanding the case to the trial court and interpreting the Supreme Court's decision in accordance with the views of Justice Blackmun, supra n.13, see Challoner v. Day & Zimmermann, Inc., 546 F.2d 26 (5th Cir.1977).

§ 17.8

1. See supra §§ 3.13–3.14. For recent uses of renvoi, see, e.g., Braxton v. Anco Elec., Inc., 330 N.C. 124, 409 S.E.2d 914 (N.C. 1991) (applying the law of the state of employment rather than the law of the state of the accident because, inter alia, the latter state would have applied the law of the former state); American Motorists Ins. Co. v. ARTRA Group, Inc., 338 Md. 560, 659 A.2d 1295 (Md. 1995) (insurance con-

tract case applying the law of Maryland rather than the law of the state of the making of the contract because, arguably, the the latter state would have applied Maryland law).

2. See supra § 2.21 nn.16–30. For recent cases, see Mills v. Quality Supplier Trucking, Inc., 203 W.Va. 621, 510 S.E.2d 280 (1998) (using the public policy exception—which the court had earlier used to defeat the application of foreign guest statutes, intrafamily immunities, and charitable immunities—to defeat the application of Maryland's contributory-negligence rule which would have disadvantaged a West Virginia plaintiff); Alexander v. General Motors Corp., 267 Ga. 339, 478 S.E.2d 123, 124 (1996), on remand 224 Ga.App. 238, 481 S.E.2d 7 (1997) (avoiding the *lex loci delicti* rule by concluding that a Virginia rule that did not impose strict liability on manufacturers was so "radically dissimilar") to the Georgia strict-liability rule as to justify its rejection on public policy grounds. Virginia law was unfavorable to a Georgia plaintiff who had acquired the product in Georgia but was injured in Virginia; Torres v. State, 119 N.M. 609, 894 P.2d 386 (1995) (invoking the public policy exception and applying forum law without even examining the content of the law of the state of the injury); Owen v. Owen, 444 N.W.2d 710 (S.D.1989) (refusing on public policy grounds to apply Indiana's guest statute in an accident involving South Dakota domiciliaries, but also pointing out the forum's interests and Indiana's lack of interest); Boone v. Boone, 345 S.C. 8, 546 S.E.2d 191 (2001) (invoking the *ordre public* exception and refusing to apply Geor-

The latter, as described earlier,[3] may take the form of a characterization of the subject matter as something other than tort,[4] for instance contract, thus leading to the application of different choice-of-law rules. Characterization may also involve the classification of an issue as involving either substantive or procedural law. If characterized as procedural, the particular issue will be governed by forum law and not by the *lex loci*.

Subject matter characterization is well illustrated by an early Connecticut decision, *Levy v. Daniels' U–Drive Auto Renting Co.*[5] The defendant rented a car to X in Connecticut. While driving in Massachusetts, X negligently injured the plaintiff, a passenger in the car driven by X. The plaintiff urged the application of a Connecticut statute that held car lessors liable for damage caused by their lessees. Massachusetts, the place of the injury, did not provide for lessor liability; application of the *lex loci* would therefore have prevented recovery. The court held for the Connecticut plaintiff by characterizing the action as one in contract, not tort: since the Connecticut statute was part of the contract between the defendant and the lessee, the plaintiff could be regarded as an intended beneficiary and could maintain his claim against the lessor under contract choice-of-law rules. Despite early criticism of the decision,[6] the court reached the correct result through use of characterization as an escape device.[7] More modern policy-oriented approaches would resolve

gia's interspousal immunity rule which would bar a personal injury action between South Carolina spouses arising from a traffic accident in Georgia).

3. See supra §§ 3.4–3.5.

4. For example, although Maryland's highest court has applied the *lex loci delicti* for generic tort conflicts as late as 1995 (see Chambco v. Urban Masonry Corp., 338 Md. 417, 659 A.2d 297 (1995), applying the *lex loci delicti*, virtually without discussion), the court has, since the early 1980s, applied straight policy analysis to tort actions arising in the context of workers' compensation. See Hauch v. Connor, 295 Md. 120, 453 A.2d 1207 (1983) (holding that the choice-of-law decision in these conflicts "turned on the determination of which jurisdiction had the greater interest." Id. at 133, 453 A.2d at 1214); Bishop v. Twiford, 317 Md. 170, 562 A.2d 1238 (Md. 1989), (holding that such conflicts are to be governed by the law of the "jurisdiction that has the greatest interest at stake." Id. at 1241). In each of these cases the court applied Maryland law and allowed a Maryland employee to recover tort damages against his Maryland employer, even though the worker's compensation statute of the state of the employment accident precluded such recovery. In Powell v. Erb, 349 Md. 791, 709 A.2d 1294 (1998), the

court employed the same analysis and, once again, applied Maryland's pro-recovery law to an action arising out of an employment accident in Pennsylvania. The difference from the previous cases was that in *Powell* the accident had resulted in the employee's death. This difference would normally be insignificant except that Maryland has a statute that subjects wrongful death actions to the *lex loci delicti*. The *Powell* court held that since this statute "does not, by its terms, directly or explicitly, address wrongful death *in the workers' compensation context*," id. at 801, 709 A.2d at 1299 (emphasis added), the statute was inapplicable to the case at hand, thus freeing the court to follow a straight policy analysis.

5. 108 Conn. 333, 143 A. 163 (1928).

6. Note, 42 Harv. L. Rev. 433 (1929); Note, 27 Mich. L. Rev. 462 (1929).

7. See, e.g., Cortes v. Ryder Truck Rental, Inc., 220 Ill.App.3d 632, 581 N.E.2d 1 (1991), appeal dism'd, 143 Ill.2d 637, 167 Ill.Dec. 398, 587 N.E.2d 1013 (1992). The court applied the lessor liability statute of Wisconsin, where the rental agreement was executed, to hold the rental company liable for injuries, suffered in Indiana: "Although choice-of-law principles might indicate that ... Indiana law applied to the tort of negligence ... Ryder's liability was not based on negligence, directly or vicariously. Ryder's

the problem in a similar manner, albeit without resort to characterization.[8]

More recent uses of characterization may be seen as the harbingers of modern choice-of-law theories. Foreshadowing an outright break with the traditional rule, these decisions took advantage of the fact that the situations presented were "easy," thus providing a convenient vehicle for drawing the value of the *lex loci* rule into question. A leading case, *Haumschild v. Continental Casualty Co.*,[9] avoided resort to the *lex loci* by characterizing a wife's ability to sue her (then) husband for injuries resulting from an out-of-state car accident as presenting an issue of family law, to be governed by forum law as that of the marital domicile.[10] Application of the *lex loci*, and resort to renvoi, would have produced the same result since the choice-of-law rule of the state of the accident provided that the law applicable to intrafamily immunity was that of the familial domicile.[11] As in *Levy*, the result reached by characterization was appropriate under the circumstances. However, the domicile rule that emerged is not a satisfactory substitute for the *lex loci*[12] particularly when a third-party defendant seeks to implead the plaintiff's spouse for purposes of contribution.[13] In this situation, resort to the domiciliary law of the spouses, in circumstances where it provides immunity, may be unfair to the defendant or frustrate important policy concerns of the state of the accident. *Haumschild* thus offered only limited relief.[14] Again, modern choice-of-law theories reach sensible results without resort to characterization.

liability ... arose ... through its contractual relationship as lessor." The court identified the policy underlying the statute as assuring compensation to a person injured by the rented vehicle.

8. For recent cases involving the same or similar statutes, see S. Symeonides, The American Choice-of-Law Revolution in the Courts: Today and Tomorrow, 298 Recueil des Cours, 1, 246–47, 250–51, 259–60 (2003); Symeonides, Annual Choice-of-Law Surveys in 52 Am.J.Comp. L. __ (2004); 50 Am.J.Comp. L.1, 68–71 (2002); 47 Am. J. Comp. L. 327, 348–50 (1999); 44 Am. J. Comp. L. 181, 203–09 (1996); 42 Am. J. Comp. L. 599, 640–41 (1994).

9. 7 Wis.2d 130, 95 N.W.2d 814 (1959). The decision necessitated the overruling of several older cases, most notably Buckeye v. Buckeye, 203 Wis. 248, 234 N.W. 342 (1931), in which the application of the traditional rules had barred an action on similar facts.

10. See also Emery v. Emery, 45 Cal.2d 421, 289 P.2d 218 (1955), discussed infra § 17.16 n.5; Annot. 96 A.L.R.2d 973 (1964).

11. Supra n.9. Indeed, the concurrence rested on this ground: 7 Wis.2d at 145, 95 N.W.2d at 820 (Fairchild, J. concurring).

12. See S. Symeonides, W. Perdue & A. von Mehren, Conflict of Laws: American, Comparative, International 55 (1998) (suggesting that "the manipulation of characterization helped to produce good substantive results in [*Haumschild*], but it also helped to prolong the life of a bad choice-of-law rule, the *lex loci delicti*, while relieving those courts of responsibility for articulating why this rule should not apply in similar future cases.")

13. Initially, Wisconsin retained the *Haumschild* rule in this situation. See Haynie v. Hanson, 16 Wis.2d 299, 114 N.W.2d 443 (1962). However, by 1967, the court ejected the *lex loci* rule and applied a significant-contacts approach to this situation. Zelinger v. State Sand & Gravel Co., 38 Wis.2d 98, 156 N.W.2d 466 (1968). For the current approach to choice of law in tort in Wisconsin, see infra § 17.22.

14. While the *Haumschild* solution did not solve all problems and later gave way to a policy-interests-contacts approach, it proved to be influential in courts that continued to adhere to the *lex loci* rule. See Tucker v. Norfolk and Western Ry. Co., 403 F.Supp. 1372 (E.D.Mich.1975); Potter v. St. Louis–San Francisco Ry. Co., 622 F.2d 979 (8th Cir.1980); Olmstead v. Anderson, 428 Mich. 1, 400 N.W.2d 292 (1987).

§ 17.9 In *Kilberg v. Northeast Airlines, Inc.*,[1] the New York Court of Appeals used the substance-procedure characterization to avoid a wrongful death damage limitation of the state of the injury. The deceased, a New Yorker, was killed in Massachusetts on a flight originating in New York. The defendant, a Massachusetts corporation, invoked Massachusetts' $15,000 limitation for wrongful death damages. In holding for the plaintiff, the court listed public policy as one ground (because a New York constitutional provision prohibited damage limitations), but also characterized the measure of damages as a procedural issue to be governed by forum law.[2] Existing authority would have called for opposite conclusions on both the characterization and public policy grounds. However, application of the *lex loci* to this case, with its anachronistic damage limitation, seemed particularly intolerable in view of the fortuity of the place of the accident. The decision therefore appears to be an attempt to reach the "fair" result. However, concern for fairness to the local plaintiff does not address the question of fairness to the defendant to whom the decision denied a defense available under the *lex loci*. Characterization, once again, functioned as an escape device. The decision foreshadowed, but was not itself, a new approach to choice of law.[3] Application of modern choice-of-law theories (discussed below) to the *Kilberg* facts would make the substantive-procedural characterization unnecessary. Governmental interest analysis would lead to the application of forum law, as would the most-significant-relationship test.

§ 17.10 A third line of cases avoided the *lex loci delicti* by combining both subject matter and substance-procedure characterization. *Grant v. McAuliffe*[1] concerned the survival of an action after the tortfeasor's death. Under the law of Arizona (the place of the accident), the suit would have been barred, but California (the domicile of all of the parties) permitted actions against the estate of a tortfeasor. The California court

§ 17.9

1. 9 N.Y.2d 34, 211 N.Y.S.2d 133, 172 N.E.2d 526 (1961). See B. Currie, Selected Essays on the Conflicts of Law 690–710 (1963) (original citation: 1963 Duke L.J. 1). Comment, 28 U. Chi. L. Rev. 733 (1961).

2. The Court had rejected plaintiff's argument that the action was in contract, in the sense that the purchase of the ticket had created a contract for safe carriage. Since the appeal had been based and argued on this theory, the Court's holding actually results from its own definition of the issues. See 9 N.Y.2d at 42–51, 172 N.E.2d at 529–35, 211 N.Y.S.2d at 138–46 (concurrences of Fuld and Froessel, JJ.).

3. In Davenport v. Webb, 11 N.Y.2d 392, 230 N.Y.S.2d 17, 183 N.E.2d 902 (1962), the court retracted the "procedural" basis of the *Kilberg* decision. *Davenport* involved an action for the wrongful death of New Yorkers in a Maryland accident. The court refused to apply a New York statute that authorized pre-judgment interest, reasoning

that the *Kilberg* decision "must be held merely to express this State's strong public policy with respect to limitations in wrongful death actions."

Whether the rejection of part of the Massachusetts wrongful death statute violated Full Faith and Credit (as Judge Froessel noted in concurrence, in *Kilberg* 9 N.Y.2d at 50, 211 N.Y.S.2d at 146, 172 N.E.2d at 535) was answered in the negative in a later case concerning the same accident: Pearson v. Northeast Airlines, Inc., 309 F.2d 553 (2d Cir.1962) (en banc), cert. denied 372 U.S. 912, 83 S.Ct. 726, 9 L.Ed.2d 720 (1963). Both aspects of *Kilberg's* reasoning were rejected in Cherokee Labs., Inc. v. Rogers, 398 P.2d 520 (Okl.1965). For Full Faith and Credit as a limitation upon choice of law, see supra § 3.30.

§ 17.10

1. 41 Cal.2d 859, 264 P.2d 944, 42 A.L.R.2d 1162 (1953), also discussed infra § 17.16.

characterized the survival issue as procedural but also noted that the action concerned an estate under local administration and that forum law applied to claims against local "decedents' estates." An earlier New York case had decided the issue on the latter ground alone.[2] Modern choice-of-law theories would have reached the same result. As a consequence, the use of characterization as an "escape device" has now lost its earlier importance, except in jurisdictions that still adhere to the *lex loci* rule. In others, its use has become increasingly restricted and most now treat it as part of general policy analysis.[3]

B. INTEREST ANALYSIS

1. *In General*

§ 17.11 The leading proponent of interest analysis was the late Brainerd Currie. Because Currie's approach is discussed in detail in Chapter 2,[1] only a brief synopsis is necessary at this point. By focusing on governmental interests, Currie sought to advance the policies of the forum as embodied in its statutory or decisional law.[2] As a general rule, courts were to "look to the law of the forum as the source of the rule of decision."[3] Confronted with an assertion that foreign law governed, the forum was to look first to the policy underlying its own law; if "the relationship of the forum state to the case ... is such as to bring the case within the scope of the state's governmental concern," the forum would have an interest.[4] Currie believed that the foreign jurisdiction either would not have a substantial interest in most cases, or that the foreign interests would not be dissimilar from those of the forum. Most situations therefore present a "false conflict."[5] The false conflict notion, which has now received almost unanimous acceptance,[6] was not viewed by Currie as necessarily leading to forum law.[7] However, false conflicts usually do result in the application of forum law because courts often find it easier to identify local interests and, consequently, discount potential foreign interests.[8]

2. Herzog v. Stern, 264 N.Y. 379, 191 N.E. 23 (1934), cert. denied 293 U.S. 597, 55 S.Ct. 112, 79 L.Ed. 690 (1934).

3. See Restatement, Second, Conflict of Laws § 7, comment (b) (1971) with respect to subject matter characterization; but see infra § 17.25. With respect to the statute of limitations, the 1988 revision of § 142 of the Second Restatement also modifies but does not fully abandon the traditional procedural characterization see supra § 3.10. Cf. Heavner v. Uniroyal, Inc., 63 N.J. 130, 305 A.2d 412 (1973), and Pittston Co. v. Sedgwick James of New York, Inc., 971 F.Supp. 915 (D.N.J.1997) (limitation subject to interest analysis).

§ 17.11

1. See supra § 2.9.

2. B. Currie, Selected Essays on the Conflicts of Law 189 (1963).

3. Id. at 188.

4. Id.

5. On "false conflicts," see also supra § 2.9 and infra § 17.12.

6. Westbrook, A Survey and Evaluation of Competing Choice of Law Methodologies: The Case for Eclecticism, 40 Mo. L. Rev. 407, 422–23 (1975). But see Leflar, True "False Conflicts" et alia, 48 B.U. Rev. 164 (1968); Ehrenzweig, "False Conflicts" and "The Better Rule": Threat and Promise in Multistate Tort Law, 53 Va. L. Rev. 847 (1967).

7. B. Currie, supra n.2, at 189.

8. E.g., Miller v. Miller, 22 N.Y.2d 12, 290 N.Y.S.2d 734, 237 N.E.2d 877 (1968), motion denied 22 N.Y.2d 722, 292 N.Y.S.2d 107, 239 N.E.2d 204 (1968). Cf. Taylor v. Canady, 536 A.2d 93 (D.C.App.1988).

For situations in which both states have identifiable legitimate interests, thus presenting an "apparent conflict," Currie called for the reconsideration and "a more moderate and restrained interpretation of the policy or interests of one state or the other."[9] This would avoid the conflict, that is, again lead to a "false conflict." Thus, Currie's use of the "false conflict" terminology appears broader than when employed by others because it extends to cases that the court deems avoidable after a reconsideration of the policies of the involved states. If, upon reconsideration, "the conflict between the legitimate interests of the two states is unavoidable," forum law is to be applied.[10] Notwithstanding this process of considering the "social, economic, and administrative"[11] policies of the states involved, Currie stated that, in no instance is the court to "weigh" the competing interests in "true" or "unavoidable" conflict situations.[12]

Governmental interests, sometimes with a different label, are also part of several other modern conflicts theories.[13] Although the desire to effectuate the forum's policies is not the (stated) central thrust of these theories, their differences from Currie's formulation are often small in actual operation. Cavers' "principles of preference"[14] emphasize the necessity of looking to the socio-economic purposes of competing laws.[15] The functionalists, Weintraub[16] and von Mehren and Trautman,[17] also regard governmental interests as relevant to the choice-of-law process, but—unlike Currie—they openly admit and advocate a weighing of interests[18] over Currie's almost unqualified resort to forum law. Advancing the forum's governmental interests is also one of Leflar's choice-influencing considerations[19] and one of the Restatement Second's multiple choice-of-law criteria.[20] Finally, "evaluating the strength and perti-

---

9. See supra § 2.9 nn.17, 32.

10. Id.

11. B. Currie, supra n.2, at 357.

12. Id. Currie recognized that in rare situations a court might be "disinterested," in the sense that it is merely the forum for a case that involves only the interests of one or more foreign jurisdictions. Currie, The Disinterested Third State, 28 Law & Contemp. Prob. 754 (1963). See Reich v. Purcell, 67 Cal.2d 551, 63 Cal.Rptr. 31, 432 P.2d 727 (1967), discussed infra §§ 17.17–17.18. He suggested that in such cases, the court could (1) apply forum law if it is similar to one of the competing laws; or (2) construe one of the competing laws in a more restrained way (as above) in order to avoid the conflict between the two foreign laws; or (3) if the conflict was still unavoidable, apply forum law as such. In later years, Currie suggested that in the third situation, the court might candidly weigh the competing policies in a legislative fashion and decide the case on that basis. Currie, supra n.2, at 182. See also Sedler, The Governmental Interest Approach to Choice

of Law: An Analysis and Reformulation, 25 U.C.L.A. L. Rev. 181 (1977).

13. See Symeonides, American Choice of Law at the Dawn of the 20th Century, 37 Willamette L. Rev. 1, 26–28 (2000).

14. For discussion see supra §§ 2.8, 2.12 and infra §§ 17.39, 17.41–17.44.

15. D. Cavers, The Choice of Law Process 108 (1965).

16. Supra § 2.11.

17. Id.

18. R. Weintraub, Commentary on the Conflict of Laws 350 et seq., (4th ed. 2001); Weintraub, Comments on the Round-table Discussion of Choice of Law, 48 Mercer L. Rev. 871 (1997); A.T. von Mehren & D.T. Trautman, The Law of Multi–State Problems 376–78 (1965).

19. McDougal Felix & Whitlen, American Conflicts Law 357–72 (5th ed. 2001). For extensive discussion see supra § 2.13.

20. Restatement, Second, Conflict of Laws § 6(2)(b), (c) (1971). For discussion, see supra § 2.14.

nence of the relevant policies of all involved states"[21] is one of the judge's main tasks under the Louisiana conflicts codification.

The case law employing interest analysis presents a confusing picture. Imprecise and over-zealous citations to sundry authorities[22] often make it difficult to identify with certainty the theory upon which a case has been decided, if indeed the theories are fully distinguishable. This imprecision and hedging by the courts invites theorists to claim an important case as supporting their own thinking[23] and also leads to the application of different theories to successive cases. This "eclecticism" in the case law was noted earlier.[24] Conversely, some courts seem to go their own way, or purport to do so, without expressly relying on any particular academic theory. A good example is *Foster v. Leggett*,[25] a case discussed below,[26] which is classified by most casebooks, as well as by this book, as an interest-analysis case, even though the majority opinion contains no reference to Currie's writings or, for that matter, any academic commentary. This classification is correct in the sense that the court reached the precise result Currie advocated. At the same time, however, the court's heavy reliance on the forum's contacts and the absence of any discussion of policies suggests a contacts-based *lex-fori* approach that is potentially more parochial than Currie's.[27] Thus, as stated before,[28] classification of cases–no less than classification of states–in one or another methodological camp is both difficult and to some extent subjective. Just as the mere mention of "interests" and "policy" in a decision does not mean that the court subscribes to interest analysis, the failure to use these words does not necessarily mean a repudiation of that analysis. For these reasons, the review that follows exercises restraint in applying labels.

---

21. La. Civ. Code arts. 3515, 3519, 3537, 3542. For discussion by the drafter, see Symeonides, Louisiana's New Law of Choice of Law for Tort Conflicts: An Exegesis, 66 Tul. L. Rev. 677 (1992).

22. See, e.g., Mitchell v. Craft, 211 So.2d 509 (Miss.1968). In applying its comparative negligence law to a foreign accident involving local parties, the court cited and used Leflar's choice-influencing considerations and identified the forum as the place of the most significant relationship within the meaning of the Restatement Second. Later Mississippi cases understood the decision to adopt both the most substantial relationship test (Vick v. Cochran, 316 So.2d 242 (Miss.1975)) and interest analysis (Burns v. Burns, 321 So.2d 293 (Miss. 1975)). Today, Mississippi follows the Second Restatement but–as discussed in the text–that approach also focuses on interests and policies.

23. Babcock v. Jackson, 12 N.Y.2d 473, 240 N.Y.S.2d 743, 191 N.E.2d 279 (1963), is the best example. This is well illustrated in Comments on Babcock v. Jackson, 63 Colum. L. Rev. 1212 (1963), in which six scholars analyzed this landmark case and came to six different conclusions. *Babcock* is discussed infra at § 17.29.

24. Supra § 17.1 n.3; S. Symeonides, The American Choice-of-Law Revolution in the Courts: Today and Tomorrow, 298 Recueil des Cours, 1, 94–96 (2003); Cf. Juenger, Choice of Law in Interstate Torts, 118 U. Pa. L. Rev. 202, 204 (1969).

25. 484 S.W.2d 827 (Ky.1972).

26. See infra § 17.13.

27. See S. Symeonides, *The Revolution Today*, supra n.24, 103–105 (classifying Kentucky as a *lex-fori* state rather than as an interest-analysis state).

28. See supra §§ 2.19, 17.1.

2. *Interest Analysis and the Lex–Fori Variant in the Courts*

a. *False Conflicts*

§ 17.12   An early example of a governmental interest analysis is the decision in *Schmidt v. Driscoll Hotel*.[1] The Minnesota court refused to apply the *lex loci delicti* in the case of a Minnesota plaintiff who was injured in a Wisconsin accident caused by a driver who had become intoxicated at defendant's Minnesota bar. Minnesota had a dramshop act while Wisconsin did not. In rejecting the traditional rule, the court noted that application of that rule would defeat Minnesota's policies of subjecting barkeepers to liability and of compensating injured persons. Application of the traditional rule would also have defeated Wisconsin's "interest . . . in affording whatever remedies it deems proper for those injured there as the result of foreign violations of liquor laws."[2] In essence, the court therefore casts the facts in "false conflict" terms by attributing similar interests to both states. However, even if Wisconsin's interests were different, this case would still qualify as a false conflict based solely on Minnesota's interests. Since all parties were local and the dramshop Act violation occurred in Minnesota, one could easily conclude that only Minnesota had an interest in applying its law, whether that law was intended to regulate conduct or to compensate victims.[3]

Griffith v. United Air Lines, Inc.[4] illustrates an application of governmental interests analysis in a fashion more consistent with Currie's methodology. The plaintiff's decedent, a Pennsylvania domiciliary, had been killed in Colorado as a result of defendant's airplane crash during a flight between Philadelphia and Phoenix. Under Colorado law, which limited damages to earnings lost and expenses incurred between the time of injury and death, the plaintiff would recover virtually nothing, because the decedent died almost instantly upon the crash. Pennsylvania law, however, provided for recovery for the present value of the decedent's future earnings. Abandoning the *lex loci delicti* rule "in favor of a more flexible rule which permits analysis of the policies and interests underlying the particular issue before the court,"[5] the court held that forum law should govern. The court's discussion exemplifies the tendency to include all possible authorities and references,[6] but its analysis clearly demonstrates its concern to effectuate governmental interests.[7]

§ 17.12

1. 249 Minn. 376, 82 N.W.2d 365 (1957). For a decision using modern interest analysis on facts paralleling Schmidt v. Driscoll Hotel, Inc., see Rong Yao Zhou v. Jennifer Mall Rest., 534 A.2d 1268 (D.C.App.1987).

2. *Schmidt*, 249 Minn. at 380, 82 N.W.2d at 368.

3. See id. at 379, 368: "Here all parties involved were residents of Minnesota. Defendant was licensed under its laws and required to operate its establishment in compliance therewith. Its violation of the Minnesota [dramshop Act] occurred here. . . . By [applying this Act] . . . no greater burden is placed upon defendant than was intended by [the Act]."

4. 416 Pa. 1, 203 A.2d 796 (1964).

5. Id. at 21, 203 A.2d at 805.

6. The court referred to the leading case of *Babcock v. Jackson* (discussed infra § 17.29), the Second Restatement, and several commentators.

7. For later Pennsylvania cases, see McSwain v. McSwain, 420 Pa. 86, 215 A.2d 677 (1966) (intrafamily immunity rule of forum-domicile applied rather than place-of-wrong rule which permitted the suit); Kuchinic v. McCrory, 422 Pa. 620, 222 A.2d 897 (1966) (guest statute); Cipolla v. Shaposka, 439 Pa. 563, 267 A.2d 854 (1970), discussed infra at § 17.13 n.18. But see Madrin v. Wareham, 344 F.Supp. 166

The court discussed the policies underlying Colorado's limited recovery statute–prevention of speculative computation of expected earnings, protection of Colorado defendants from large verdicts–but aptly discounted them because the defendant was not a Colorado corporation and no Colorado court would be burdened with a computation.[8] Thus, Colorado had no continuing concern with the litigation other than the likelihood that some witnesses from Colorado would be called in Pennsylvania. In contrast, Pennsylvania was concerned for the decedent's estate and the well-being of local survivors.[9] Analysis of policies underlying the competing laws therefore revealed Colorado's "lack of interest"[10] and that "Pennsylvania's interest ... [was] great."[11] In this sense, *Griffith* presented a classic "false conflict."[12]

Interest analysis is thus useful for identifying false conflicts.[13] An initial focus on policies and interests permits a court to dispose of routine cases quickly. Such a focus will often show that the occurrence of the injury in a particular state does not implicate the policies embodied in that states laws. *Griffith*-type cases thus find all commentators who advocate the consideration of governmental interest, in agreement. The agreement dissipates when the facts yield a "true conflict," that is, a situation in which more than one state is legitimately interested in seeing its law applied.

b. True Conflicts

§ 17.13 Currie's favoritism for the *lex-fori* is demonstrated by some Kentucky cases that, though not expressly relying on his teachings, "appl[y] Kentucky substantive law whenever possible."[1] In *Wessling v.*

(W.D.Pa.1972) (most significant relationship).

8. Griffith v. United Air Lines, Inc., 416 Pa. 1 at 24, 203 A.2d at 807, (1964).

9. Id. at 24–25, 203 A.2d at 807.

10. Id. at 24, 203 A.2d at 807.

11. Id. at 24, 203 A.2d at 807.

12. Weintraub, in contrast, reads *Griffith* as weighing the potential interests. R. Weintraub, Commentary on the Conflict of Laws 385–86 (4th ed. 2001). However, mere discussion of potential interests does not necessarily mean that a court has weighed interests. In fact, such discussion is necessary as a first step in order to find the potential "false conflict." That Pennsylvania courts will weigh interests in "true conflicts" cases is evidenced in Cipolla v. Shaposka, 439 Pa. 563, 267 A.2d 854 (1970), discussed infra at § 17.13 n.18. Other courts, however, do admit to weighing, even in the "easier" *Griffith*-type case. See Fox v. Morrison Motor Freight, Inc., 25 Ohio St.2d 193, 267 N.E.2d 405 (1971), cert. denied 403 U.S. 931, 91 S.Ct. 2254, 29

L.Ed.2d 710 (1971) (limit on wrongful death recovery).

13. See, e.g., Reich v. Purcell, 67 Cal.2d 551, 63 Cal.Rptr. 31, 432 P.2d 727 (1967) (statutory limit on wrongful death recovery, disinterested third state), further discussed infra §§ 17.17–18; Gaither v. Myers, 404 F.2d 216 (D.C.Cir.1968) (local statute creating liability for injury resulting from owner's leaving keys in car and thief subsequently injuring plaintiff); Williams v. Rawlings Truck Line, Inc., 357 F.2d 581 (D.C.Cir.1965) (former owner of automobile estopped by New York law as only interested state to deny ownership for purposes of owner's liability); Fuerste v. Bemis, 156 N.W.2d 831 (Iowa 1968) (guest statute; although using most significant relationship test, court cites spurious conflict); Pfau v. Trent Aluminum Co., 55 N.J. 511, 263 A.2d 129 (1970) (guest statute; false conflict arises when parties' domiciles do not have guest statute but accident state does).

§ 17.13

1. Adam v. J.B. Hunt Transport, Inc., 130 F.3d 219, 231 (6th Cir.1997) (" 'Ken-

Paris,[2] the Kentucky Court of Appeals abandoned the *lex loci delicti* rule in favor of a most-significant-contacts approach influenced by a draft of the Second Restatement. The court applied Kentucky's pro-recovery law to a case arising out of an Indiana accident involving Kentucky parties. One year later, in *Arnett v. Thompson*,[3] the same court was faced with the converse pattern—a case arising from a Kentucky accident involving Ohio parties. Unlike Kentucky law, Ohio law barred the plaintiff's action, both because of her status as the driver's wife (interspousal-immunity rule) and because she was a "guest" in his automobile (guest-statute). The court abandoned the " 'most-significant-contacts' theory"[4] adopted in *Wessling*, apparently because that theory entailed a weighing of state interests and the concomitant possibility of applying non-forum law. "Upon further study and reflection,"[5] said the court:

> the court has decided that the conflicts question should not be determined on the basis of a weighing of interests, but simply on the basis of whether Kentucky has enough contacts to justify applying Kentucky law. Under that view if the accident occurs in Kentucky (as in the instant case) there is enough contact from that fact alone to justify applying Kentucky law.[6]

The court did not see any difficulty in reconciling this case with *Wessling*:

> The fact that we will apply Kentucky law where Kentucky people have an accident in Ohio or Indiana does not require that we apply Ohio or Indiana law where people of one of those states have an accident here, because the basis of the application is not a weighing of contacts but simply the existence of enough contacts with Kentucky to warrant applying our law.[7]

Thus, according to the Kentucky court, the occurrence of the accident in a given state is "enough" of a contact for applying forum law but not enough for applying non-forum law.[8] This point is made more explicit by *Foster v. Leggett*[9] in which the accident occurred in another state, Ohio, which was also the domicile of the defendant host-driver.[10]

tucky courts have apparently applied Kentucky substantive law whenever possible' ") quoting from Harris Corp. v. Comair, Inc. 712 F.2d 1069, 1071 (6th Cir.1983).

2. 417 S.W.2d 259 (Ky.1967).

3. 433 S.W.2d 109 (Ky.1968).

4. Id. at 112.

5. Id. at 113.

6. Id. The court's only reference to policies is a statement that "the policy of the law of this state is to allow recovery for injuries or death resulting from negligence." Id. at 114.

7. Id. at 113.

8. See also Adam v. J.B. Hunt Transport, Inc., 130 F.3d 219, 231 (6th Cir.1997) (stating that the "lesson" from Kentucky's

precedents is "clear" to the effect that when the accident occurs in Kentucky, "a Kentucky court ... 'should' apply Kentucky law.").

9. 484 S.W.2d 827 (Ky.1972). This case is extensively analyzed by four commentators (Reese, Sedler, Twerski and Weintraub) in: Symposium on *Foster v. Leggett*, 61 Ky.L.J. 368 (1972–73).

10. The defendant worked in Kentucky, maintained a room at the YMCA near his place of employment, and had his social relationships in that state, including his dating relationship with the deceased. Because of these Kentucky contacts, one could argue that this case was sufficiently analogous to the common-domicile pattern involved in *Wessling* as to justify the appli-

Kentucky was the domicile of the decedent guest-passenger and the state in which the trip originated and was to end. Ohio's guest-statute would bar the action, and thus would protect the Ohio driver and his insurer. Kentucky law would allow the action, and thus would protect the decedent's family. Thus, under the assumptions of interest analysis, both states would be interested in applying their laws. The court spoke of neither interests nor policies and, although it made a generic reference to "articles found in the Law Jurnals [sic], and articles by commentators,"[11] the court did not cite any of Currie's writings. However, the court did echo Currie's views in stating that the court's "primary responsibility is to follow its own substantive law"[12] and that "[t]he basic law is the law of the forum, which should not be displaced without valid reasons."[13] Whether such a valid reason existed in this case is not free from doubts, but the court did not appear to entertain any. In a fashion that—in mentality though not in language—resembles Currie's solution to true conflicts, the court concluded that, "if there are significant contacts—not necessarily the most significant contacts—with Kentucky, then Kentucky law should be applied."[14] The court acknowledged that its decisions in the three cases discussed here may justify the inference that "we have accepted the rule of 'most significant contacts' ... to apply to Kentucky residents involved in another state and the rule of 'enough contacts' for residents of other states involved in Kentucky."[15] Nevertheless, said the court, "[s]uch is not the holding or policy of this court."[16] While the court's interpretation of its holdings is entitled to respect, the court's failure to explain the absence of "valid reasons" for displacing forum law (other than reciting forum contacts) makes its analysis particularly vulnerable.[17]

Cipolla v. Shaposka[18] represents a different resolution of a case virtually identical to *Foster* under an approach that relies in part on interest analysis but also goes beyond it. As in *Foster*, the issue in *Cipolla* was the application of the guest statute of the accident state, Delaware, in an action brought by a Pennsylvania guest-passenger against his Delaware host-driver. Unlike the Kentucky court, however, the Pennsylvania court in *Cipolla* applied the Delaware guest-statute rather than the Pennsylvania common-law rule that would allow recov-

---

cation of Kentucky law on that basis. However, as explained in the text, this was not the basis of the court's decision.

11. 484 S.W.2d at 829.

12. Id.

13. Id. See also Harris Corp. v. Comair, Inc., 712 F.2d 1069 (6th Cir.1983); Blount v. Bartholomew, 714 F.Supp. 252 (E.D.Ky. 1988), aff'd 869 F.2d 1488 (6th Cir.1989).

14. 484 S.W.2d at 829.

15. Id.

16. Id.

17. See Reese, supra n.9, at 370. One author documents that, among 24 cases involving the *Foster* pattern (cases in which the conduct and the injury occur in the defendant's home state whose law protects the defendant), *Foster* is the only case that did *not* apply that state's law. See S. Symeonides, The American Choice-of-Law Revolution in the Courts: Today and Tomorrow, 298 Recueil des Cours, 1, 195–203 (2003).

18. 439 Pa. 563, 267 A.2d 854 (1970). The opinion is analyzed by eight commentators (Cavers, Ehrenzweig, Felix, Pelaez, Peterson, Sedler, Seidelson and Twerski) in: Symposium on *Cipolla v. Shaposka*, An Application of Interest Analysis, 9 Duquesne L. Rev. 360 (1971).

ery. The court found that Delaware's policies–protecting host-drivers and ensuring stability of insurance rates–were more pertinent because this case involved a Delaware host-driver and a car insured in Delaware. In the court's words, Delaware's contacts were "qualitatively greater than Pennsylvania's,"[19] and Delaware had "the greater interest in having its law applied."[20] Then, relying on Cavers's principles of preference,[21] the court explained: "It seems only fair to permit a defendant to rely on his home state's law when he is acting within that state.... Inhabitants of a state should not be put in jeopardy of liability exceeding that created by their state's law just because a visitor from a state offering higher protection decides to visit there."[22] Conversely, "[b]y entering the state ... the visitor has exposed himself to the risk of the territory and should not subject persons living there to a financial hazard that their law had not created."[23] Thus, to the extent it relied on interest analysis, the *Cipolla* court rejected both Currie's explicit proscription of weighing of state interests and his implicit preference for forum law or forum litigants. To the extent it relied on territorial contacts, the court suggested a new equilibrium between Currie's "personal-law principle"[24] and Beale's blind territorialism.[25] Whether this approach is called "principled territorialism,"[26] principled eclecticism, or a "mixed bag" approach, *Cipolla* offers a good example of how one can resolve a true conflict without automatically resorting to Currie's default position of applying forum law. The vast majority of cases reached the same result,[27] which has since been adopted by the *Neumeier* rules[28] and the Louisiana codification.[29]

19. 439 Pa. at 567, 267 A.2d at 856.

20. Id.

21. Discussed supra §§ 2.8, 2.12 and infra 17.39, 17.41–17.44.

22. 439 Pa. at 567, 267 A.2d at 856.

23. Id. (quoting D. Cavers, The Choice-of-Law Process 146–47 (1965)). For a case applying the "visitor's" law in a situation in which that law was not favorable to him, see Labree v. Major, 111 R.I. 657, 306 A.2d 808 (1973). However, in this case, the visitor was the defendant host-driver who was sued by his Massachusetts guest-passenger for injury arising from a Massachusetts accident. After weighing the interests of the two states, the court refused to apply the Massachusetts guest statute and applied instead Rhode Island's common-law which allowed recovery. The court stated: "We are required, in deciding this case, to weigh the interests of Massachusetts and Rhode Island.... Interest analysis, however, is not merely a determination of how a state may best protect its citizens as litigants. Rather, where the laws of two states with contacts in a case point to opposite results, interest analysis requires an assessment of the policy underlying each state's law. From such an assessment, a court can determine which result will advance the policy of one state without frustrating the result of the other." Id. at 668, 306 A.2d at 815. *Labree* is discussed further infra §§ 17.34 n.10, 17.45 nn.3–4.

24. See supra § 2.9 nn.14, 56, 58–59

25. See supra § 2.7.

26. S. Symeonides, W. Perdue & A. von Mehren, Conflict of Laws: American, Comparative, International 218, 224 (1998).

27. See Symeonides, *The Revolution Today*, supra n.17, at id.

28. Neumeier v. Kuehner, 31 N.Y.2d 121, 335 N.Y.S.2d 64, 286 N.E.2d 454 (1972), appeal after remand 43 A.D.2d 109, 349 N.Y.S.2d 866 (1973) discussed infra at § 17.31. The first part of *Neumeier* rule 2 provides that "[w]hen the driver's conduct occurred in the state of his domicile and that state does not cast him in liability for that conduct, he should not be held liable by reason of the fact that liability would be imposed upon him under the tort law of the state of the victim's domicile."

29. See La. Civ. Code art. 3544(2)(a) (discussed infra § 17.42 n.6: providing that when both the conduct and the injury occur

c. Unprovided–For Cases

§ 17.14 Interest analysis also encounters serious difficulties in that category of conflicts cases that Currie called "unprovided case[s],"[1] namely, cases in which none of the involved states has an interest in applying its law. The very use of the quoted term might be deemed as an admission on Currie's part that his prescription for such conflicts–applying the *lex fori*–was no solution at all.[2] In any event, very few cases seem to follow this prescription.[3] One of them is *Erwin v. Thomas*,[4] decided by the Oregon Supreme Court. The issue in *Erwin* was whether a Washington resident could recover for the loss of consortium of her husband, also a Washington resident, who had been injured in Washington as a result of the negligence of the Oregon defendant in operating a truck in Washington in the course of his Oregon employment. Oregon permitted the action, but Washington did not. The court concluded that Washington's defendant-protecting policy was not implicated in this case which did not involve a Washington defendant,[5] and that Oregon's plaintiff-protecting policy was not implicated in this case which did not involve an Oregon plaintiff.[6] Thus, said the court, "neither state has a vital interest in the outcome of this litigation" or, as Currie said,

in the defendant's home state, the law of that state applies).

§ 17.14

1. B. Currie, Selected Essays in the Conflict of Laws 152 (1963).

2. For a critique of this prescription, see supra § 2.9 nn.35–36. As in the forum preference cases noted above, the application of forum law in the "unprovided-for" case only substitutes an easy answer for genuine analysis. Twerski, *Neumeier v. Kuehner*: Where Are the Emperor's Clothes?, 1 Hofstra L. Rev. 104 (1973). Sedler suggests that Currie's unprovided-for cases be solved "by looking to the common policy of the involves states." Sedler, The Governmental Interest Approach to Choice of Law: An Analysis and A Reformulation, 25 U.C.L.A. L. Rev. 181, 235 (1977). He states (id. at 235 n.286) that this suggestion was followed in Labree v. Major, 111 R.I. 657, 306 A.2d 808 (1973). But see supra § 17.13 n.23 and infra §§ 17.34 n.10, 17.45 nn.3–4.

3. See S. Symeonides, The American Choice-of-Law Revolution in the Courts: Today and Tomorrow, 298 Recueil des Cours, 1, 209–220 (2003); For products liability cases, see Symeonides, Choice of Law for Products Liability: The 1990s and Beyond, 79 Tul. L. Rev. 1247, 1269–70, 1301–02, 1318–19 (2004).

4. 264 Or. 454, 506 P.2d 494 (1973).

5. The court also noted that Washington would not object to the application of Oregon law. See 264 Or. at 459, 506 P.2d at 496: "Washington has little concern whether other states require non-Washingtonians to respond to such claims. Washington policy cannot be offended if the court of another state affords rights to a Washington woman which Washington does not afford, so long as a Washington defendant is not required to respond. The state of Washington appears to have no material or urgent policy or interest which would be offended by applying Oregon law." In Fisher v. Huck, 50 Or.App. 635, 624 P.2d 177 (1981), the Oregon Court of Appeals questioned this analysis: "If the Erwin court ... is correct, it would seem to follow that a Washington court would permit a loss of consortium claim against a non-resident defendant. That conclusion seems highly unlikely and under the alternative analysis ... suggested [that such actions are simply against Washington's public policy regardless of the residence of the tortfeasor] that conclusion would not follow. By changing the semantics of the analysis only slightly, a different choice of law might result." 50 Or.App. at 639, 624 P.2d at 179.

6. See *Erwin*, 264 Or. at 459, 506 P.2d at 496: "it is stretching the imagination more than a trifle to conceive that the Oregon Legislature was concerned about the rights of all the nonresident married women in the nation whose husbands would be injured outside of the state of Oregon."

"neither state cares what happens."[7] In such a case, said the court, "an Oregon court does what comes naturally and applies Oregon law."[8]

In the years since *Erwin*, courts confronted with cases of the same pattern have been more broad-minded in identifying the forum state's interests. Even courts adhering to Currie's analysis have refused to accept his assumption that the forum state is interested in protecting its domiciliaries only but not out-of-staters similarly situated. For example in *Hurtado v. Superior Court*,[9] the California Supreme Court concluded that California was an interested state even though the application of its unlimited-compensatory-damages rule would benefit a Mexican plaintiff at the expense of a California defendant whose conduct in that state had caused the death of plaintiff's decedent.[10] Similarly, in *Kaiser-George-*

---

7. B. Currie, supra n.1, at 152.

8. *Erwin*, 264 Or. at 459–60, 506 P.2d at 496–97 (followed by quotation from Currie). For a critique of *Erwin* by Oregon's own intermediate court, see Fisher v. Huck, 50 Or.App. 635, 624 P.2d 177 (1981), which pointed out, inter alia, that had the action been brought in Washington and had the Washington court adopted the same approach as *Erwin*, the court would have to apply Washington law: "consistency ... [would obtain], but forum shopping would be encouraged." 50 Or.App. at 639, 624 P.2d at 179. In *Fisher* itself, the majority applied British Columbia law to a negligence action by a guest passenger against the host-driver for injuries incurred in British Columbia which permitted the action. The host was a British Columbia resident and the guest was en route to a new permanent job there. Oregon had no interest, being only the forum; British Columbia's policy was said to permit any guest, and not only local residents, to obtain compensation from negligent host-drivers; and the subsequent repeal of Oregon's guest statute showed no conflict in policy. The dissent would have applied Oregon's guest statute as it existed at the time of suit on the grounds that British Columbia law had no affirmative compensatory policy but simply did not protect negligent hosts, and that—with British Columbia law thus not particularly relevant—Oregon should apply its law, plaintiff having selected Oregon as the forum.

9. 11 Cal.3d 574, 114 Cal.Rptr. 106, 522 P.2d 666 (1974). *Hurtado* was a wrongful death action filed by Mexico domiciliaries for the death of their decedent in a California accident. The decedent was riding in a car owned and operated by a California domiciliary when it collided with a car owned and operated by another California domiciliary. Both cars were registered in California. Mexico, but not California, limit-

ed the amount of damages recoverable in wrongful death actions. Under Currie's assumptions, this could have been a no-interest case. By imposing limits on the amount of recoverable damages, Mexico had expressed an interest in "protect[ing] defendants from excessive financial burdens or exaggerated claims." 522 P.2d at 670. However, since neither of the defendants was a Mexican domiciliary, Mexico did not have an interest in protecting them. At the same time, Mexico did not have an interest in denying full recovery to its residents who were injured by non-Mexican defendants. Conversely, by not imposing a limit on the amount of recoverable damages, California had expressed an interest in protecting the victims of traffic accidents by ensuring full compensation to them. However, since neither the victim nor his survivors were California domiciliaries, California would not be interested on this ground.

10. This was so, said the court, because California's rule was motivated at least in part by a desire to deter conduct in that state. See id. at 671–72:

It is manifest that one of the primary purposes of a state in creating a cause of action ... is to deter the kind of conduct within its borders which wrongfully takes life ... [and] that a cause of action for wrongful death without any limitation as to the amount of recoverable damages strengthens the deterrent aspect of the civil sanction.... Therefore when the defendant is a resident of California and the tortious conduct giving rise to the wrongful death action occurs here, California's deterrent policy of full compensation is clearly advanced by application of its own law. This is precisely the situation in the case at bench. California has a decided interest in applying its own law to California defendants who allegedly caused wrongful death within its borders.

town Community Health Plan, Inc. v. Stutsman,[11] the District of Columbia Court of Appeals concluded that the District was interested in applying its unlimited-compensatory-damages rule–even though its application would benefit a Virginia plaintiff at the expense of a D.C. health care provider for a medical malpractice committed in defendant's Virginia hospital–because this rule reflected "a significant interest ... in holding [D.C.] corporations liable for the full extent of the negligence attributable to them."[12] Three years later, when the plaintiff's husband sued the same defendants for loss of consortium resulting from his wife's death, the same court concluded that Virginia was an interested state even though the application of that state's pro-defendant law would deny a Virginia plaintiff a remedy that the District's law allowed. The court thought that Virginia's denial of an action for loss of consortium was not intended to protect defendants or even hospitals operating in that state but rather was intended to "regulat[e] the legal rights of married couples domiciled in Virginia ... by giving a married woman the exclusive right to sue for damages for her personal injuries."[13] Finally, in *Ardoyno v. Kyzar*[14] a Louisiana court concluded that Louisiana was interested in applying its law even though that law would benefit a Mississippi defendant at the expense of a Louisiana plaintiff. Louisiana law denied an action for interference with contracts, while Mississippi law allowed such an action. The court assumed that the Louisiana rule was geared not towards protecting defendants as such but rather towards fostering competition with regard to employment contracts. Since the contract in question was entered into in Louisiana, that state was interested in applying its law even though a Louisiana plaintiff resisted, and a Mississippi defendant urged, the application of that law.

Thus, although all of the above four cases would qualify as unprovided-for cases under Currie's classificatory scheme, none of them was so classified by the courts that decided them because none of these courts subscribed to Currie's narrow conception of the forum's interests.[15] Although three of these cases applied forum law, that application was based on the existence, rather than the absence, of a forum interest.

For a similar conclusion in a case arising from the death of a Mexican domiciliary in an Arizona traffic accident, see Villaman v. Schee, 15 F.3d 1095, 1994 WL 6661 (9th Cir.1994) (unpublished opn.). The court concluded that Mexico had no interest in applying its limitations on the amount of recoverable damages for the benefit of a foreign defendant acting outside Mexico. The court also concluded, however, that "Arizona tort law is designed in part to deter negligent conduct within its borders; thus Arizona has a strong interest in the application of its laws allowing for full compensatory and punitive damages." 1994 WL 6661 at *4.

11. 491 A.2d 502 (D.C.1985).

12. Id. at 509. Another basis for the District's interest was thought to be the fact that the plaintiff, though a Virginia domiciliary, was employed in the District and had been referred to the Virginia hospital by her employer's HMO. The court concluded that "the District has an interest in protecting a member of its work force who contracts for health services with a District of Columbia corporation within this forum and then is injured by the negligence of that corporation's agents." Id. at 510.

13. 546 A.2d 367 at 374.

14. 426 F.Supp. 78 (E.D.La.1976).

15. For additional cases to the same effect, see Symeonides, supra n.3.

d. The Lex–Fori Variant

§ 17.15 As noted earlier, Currie's interest analysis was heavily biased in favor of the *lex fori* in both true conflicts and in unprovided-for cases.[1] The highest courts of Kentucky, Michigan, and Nevada have turned this bias into a doctrine or method. Their approach to tort conflicts, though influenced to some extent by interest analysis, is based on so blatant a presumption in favor of the *lex fori* as to justify this separate discussion.[2]

Kentucky's approach is illustrated by *Foster v. Leggett*, which was discussed supra.[3] According to this approach, "[t]he basic law is the law of the forum which should not be displaced without valid reasons,"[4] and such reasons are not present whenever the forum has "significant contacts–not necessarily the most significant contacts."[5] Michigan's approach is illustrated by *Sutherland v. Kennington Truck Service, Ltd.*,[6] although its development began earlier.[7] *Sutherland* arose out of a traffic accident in Michigan involving an Ohio plaintiff and an Ontario defendant. The plaintiff's action was timely under Michigan's three-year statute of limitation, but was barred by the statutes of both Ohio and Ontario which provided for a two-year limitation period.[8] The Michigan Supreme Court cited academic commentary to the effect that "each of the modern approaches tend to favor significantly the application of forum law"[9] and that "courts employing the new theories have a very strong preference for forum law that frequently causes them to manipulate the theories so that they end up applying forum law."[10] This preference, said the court, was "hardly surprising [because] the tendency toward forum law promotes judicial economy: judges and attorneys are experts in their state's law, but have to expend considerable time and

---

§ 17.15

1. See supra § 2.9 nn.37–42.

2. See S. Symeonides, The American Choice-of-Law Revolution in the Courts: Today and Tomorrow, 298 Recueil des Cours, 1, 91–93, 103–109 (2003) (classifying these three states in a *lex-fori* camp, separate from the interest analysis camp).

3. See supra § 17.13.

4. *Foster*, 484 S.W.2d at 829.

5. Id.

6. 454 Mich. 274, 562 N.W.2d 466 (Mich. 1997).

7. See Sexton v. Ryder Truck Rental, Inc., 413 Mich. 406, 320 N.W.2d 843 (Mich. 1982) (abandoning the *lex loci delicti* rule in favor of the *lex fori* approach). See also Olmstead v. Anderson, 428 Mich. 1, 400 N.W.2d 292 (Mich. 1987).

8. To its credit, the *Sutherland* court refused to resolve the conflict through the traditional mechanical characterization of statutes of limitations as procedural, which–in the absence of a borrowing statute–would have led to the application of the *lex fori*. Rather, the court decided to employ a full-fledged choice-of-law analysis that led to the same result.

9. *Sutherland*, 562 N.W.2d at 469 (citing Borchers, The Choice-of-Law Revolution: An Empirical Study, 49 Wash & Lee L. Rev. 357, 374–375 (1992)).

10. Id. at 469–70 (citing McDougal, The Real Legacy of *Babcock v. Jackson*: Lex Fori instead of Lex Loci Delicti and Now it's Time for a Real Choice-of-Law Revolution, 56 Alb. L. Rev. 795, 797 (1993)). See also *Sutherland*, 562 N.W.2d at 470, where the court opines that "only two distinct conflicts of law theories actually exist. One, followed by a distinct minority of states, mandates adherence to the *lex loci delicti* rule. The other, which bears different labels in different states, calls for courts to apply the law of the forum unless important policy considerations dictate otherwise."

resources to learn another state's law."[11] Turning "preference" into virtue, the court elevated this "tendency" into a choice-of-law method. According to this method, a Michigan court should apply Michigan law, unless a "rational reason"[12] exists to do otherwise. In determining whether such a rational reason exists, the court undertakes a two-step analysis. First, the court determines whether "any foreign state has an interest in having its law applied."[13] If not, the analysis ends and forum law applies. If a foreign state has an interest, then the court determine "if Michigan's interests mandate that Michigan law be applied, despite the foreign interests,"[14] in which case Michigan law again applies.

Applying this method, the court concluded that neither Ohio nor Ontario had an interest in applying their respective statutes of limitation, and thus "the *lex fori* presumption [was] not overcome, and [the court] need not evaluate Michigan's interests."[15] Ohio was not interested, said the court, because "a court could not apply Ohio law to this case without violating the defendants' due process rights."[16] The court did not explain why a defendant's due process rights are violated when a court applies a law that is favorable to him.[17] The court also concluded that Ontario was not interested in applying its two-year statute (even though that statute would protect the Ontario defendant) because, "according to Canadian and Ontario law, Ontario has an interest in having Michigan's statute of limitations applied in this case."[18] The basis for this statement was a recent decision of the Supreme Court of Canada[19] that had adopted the *lex loci delicti* rule for both substantive tort matters and for statutes of limitation. The *Sutherland* court did not explain why the *lex loci* rule, which the court had earlier discarded as

11. Id. at 470.

12. Id. at 471.

13. Id.

14. Id. Although the above sounds like a resurrection of Albert Ehrenzweig's approach, see supra § 2.10, that approach was intended to operate only in the absence of so-called "true" choice-of-law rules which, at least occasionally, would point to foreign law. See 1 Albert Ehrenzweig, Private International Law 75, 76, 89–90 (1967). Moreover, Ehrenzweig's approach contemplated a tightening-up of the jurisdictional rules so as to ensure that a court would not assume adjudicatory jurisdiction in the absence of a significant nexus with the case. See id. at 107–10. See also Ehrenzweig, A Proper Law in a Proper Forum: A "Restatement" of the "Lex Fori Approach," 18 Okla. L. Rev. 340 (1965). Needless to say, this development has yet to occur, in Michigan or elsewhere.

15. *Sutherland*, 562 N.W.2d at 473.

16. Id. at 472 (citing Allstate Ins. v. Hague, 449 U.S. 302, 101 S.Ct. 633, 66 L.Ed.2d 521 (1981), which is discussed supra § 3.23). Noting that "the only contact

that Ohio has with this litigation is that plaintiffs are Ohio residents," the court concluded that "the plaintiff's residence, with nothing more, is insufficient to support the choice of a state's law." 562 N.W.2d at 472.

17. The court would have been closer to the mark if it were to base Ohio's lack of interests on other grounds. For example, Ohio's shorter statute of limitation could have been designed to either protect Ohio defendants or protect Ohio courts from the burden of hearing stale claims. Since neither an Ohio defendant nor an Ohio court were involved in this case, one could conclude that Ohio was not interested in applying its shorter statute of limitation at the expense of an Ohio *plaintiff*.

18. Id. at 472. See also id. at 472–73: "[N]o Ontario court has expressed qualms about applying American law.... Ontario's courts have even applied American law when that law is detrimental to Canadian litigants."

19. Tolofson v. Jensen and Lucas v. Gagnon, 3 S.C.R. 1022, 120 DLR 4th 289 (1994) (discussed supra § 17.7 n.9.).

being mechanical and oblivious to state interests, became an accurate barometer of another state's "interest" in the modern sense of that word.[20]

In *Motenko v. MGM Dist., Inc.*,[21] the Supreme Court of Nevada used even starker terms in articulating that state's *lex fori* approach for tort conflicts. Under this approach, the *lex fori* governs, "unless another state has an *overwhelming* interest."[22] However, the court defined this test in terms of contacts rather than interests, by stating that another state has an overwhelming interest if it has two or more of the following contacts: "(a) it is the place where the conduct giving rise to the injury occurred; (b) it is the place where the injury is suffered; (c) [it is the place where the parties have their common] domicile, residence, nationality, place of incorporation, or place of business . . . ; (d) it is the place where the relationship, if any, between the parties is centered."[23] Applying this test, the court concluded that the *lex fori* governed because the other involved state, Massachusetts, had less than two of the above contacts.[24] *Motenko* was an action for loss of parental consortium brought by a Massachusetts domiciliary whose mother had been injured when she slipped on a loose tile in defendant's Nevada hotel. Massachusetts, but not Nevada, allowed the action. The *Motenko* result is consistent with

20. Nor did the court acknowledge that its reliance on a foreign choice-of-law rule essentially amounted to an adoption of the *renvoi* doctrine. Perhaps suspecting that *renvoi* does not mesh well with the *lex fori* approach, the court hastened to add: "[W]e in no way intend to breathe life into the doctrine of renvoi." *Sutherland*, 562 N.W.2d at 473 n.26. According to the court, *renvoi* occurs only when the forum "*applies* the entire law of th[e foreign] jurisdiction, including its choice of law rules." Id. (emphasis added). This was not the case here, said the court, "because we decline to apply any of Ontario's law . . . [and] look at Ontario's choice of law rules merely to determine Ontario's interests." Id.

21. 112 Nev. 1038, 921 P.2d 933 (1996). After acknowledging the shortcomings of the *lex loci delicti* rule, the court rejected plaintiff's plea to adopt the test of the Second Restatement because that test "suffers from two defects–lack of uniformity and lack of predictability." Id. at 935. Instead, the court adopted an approach that, in the court's view, "would harmonize Nevada's interest in stability in this area and the substantial relationship test." 921 P.2d at 935.

22. 921 P.2d at 935 (emphasis added).

23. Id.

24. Thus, upon closer examination, Nevada's *lex fori* presumption can be rebutted not upon a showing that the other state has an *interest*, much less an overwhelming one,

but rather upon a showing that Nevada has *contacts* that may or may not be overwhelming. This is so, not only because any two of the contacts on the *Motenko* list suffice to rebut the *lex fori* presumption, but also because the language describing these contacts is more flexible than, for example, the language used in a similar list found in § 145 of the Restatement (Second). For example, *Motenko* speaks of the "conduct giving rise to the injury" rather than of the "conduct causing the injury" as does the Restatement. More interestingly, *Motenko* speaks of "the place where the injury is *suffered*" rather than "the place where the injury occurred" as does the Restatement. Taking advantage of this phraseology, the court was able to conclude that the *Motenko* injury "has been suffered in [Massachusetts]," *Motenko*, 921 P.2d at 935, where the plaintiff lived, rather than in Nevada where the plaintiff's mother had been injured. Indeed, because of the nature of the injury involved in this case–loss of consortium–this conclusion was appropriate. More importantly, this may make it easier to rebut the *lex-fori* presumption in cases such as Haumschild v. Continental Cas. Co., 7 Wis.2d 130, 95 N.W.2d 814 (1959) (discussed supra § 17.8 nn.9–14) in which both parties are domiciled in the same non-forum state and the conflict in question involves an issue like intrafamily immunity or other similar issues of loss distribution.

the results reached by the majority of cases decided in other states[25] and would have been reached under any other choice-of-law approach: the victim's presence in Nevada was not fortuitous, the injury was caused by a defect in a Nevada *immovable*, the defendant was a Nevada corporation, and Nevada had a policy intended to protect that corporation. Thus, the court enunciated an approach that went far beyond the needs of the particular case. This became evident in the next case to reach the same court, *Northwest Pipe v. Eighth Judicial District Court.*[26]

Northwest Pipe arose out of a California traffic accident that caused the death of two Nevada domiciliaries and four California domiciliaries. Their survivors filed wrongful death actions in Nevada against the driver of the truck that caused the accident and his employer, both Oregon domiciliaries. The court rejected the defendants' argument that California law should govern, because they failed to rebut *Motenko*'s *lex fori* presumption. This was so because, in the court's opinion, California had only one of the non-forum contacts–the place of conduct. The court opined that the injury occurred in Nevada because this "was a wrongful death action in which the injury is to the survivors ... [and] *almost* all the survivors are Nevada residents"[27] and, "although the deaths occurred in California, the injury to the survivors occurred in Nevada."[28] Of course *not all* the survivors were Nevada residents. The survivors of the four California victims were California residents. For this reason, four of the court's seven members disagreed on this point, thus forming a majority for applying California law to the California plaintiffs' actions. Two members of the court dissented from the application of Nevada law to the Nevada victims as well. One of them observed that, under the court's approach, "it is unlikely that anything but Nevada law will ever apply."[29]

The three versions of the *lex fori* approach appear to differ in phraseology and nuance regarding the burden of rebutting the *lex fori* presumption. The Kentucky approach does not allow displacement of the *lex fori* if the forum state has "significant contacts—*not necessarily the most significant* contacts."[30] The Nevada approach speaks of "overwhelming interest," but actually contemplates contacts. The Michigan approach uses milder language ("rational reason"), but it is less permis-

---

25. See Symeonides, *The Revolution Today*, supra n. 2, at 195–203.

26. 118 Nev. 133, 42 P.3d 244 (2002).

27. Id. at 245–46 (emphasis added).

28. Id. at 246. Technically, with regard to the two Nevada victims, this was a semi-plausible argument if the actions were indeed only "wrongful death" actions. However, if as usual, these actions were accompanied by "survival actions" which seek recovery for the decedents' losses, then the court would have to concede that their injuries had occurred in California, thus leading to the application of California law.

29. Id. at 248 (Agosti, J. dissenting). See also id., stating that Nevada had "no relationship, significant or otherwise, to the occurrence of the accident," and that the application of Nevada law was "unreasonable" because "virtually every fact and circumstance giving rise to the causes of action, except the domicile of some of the plaintiffs, points to the application of California law."

30. *Foster*, 484 S.W.2d at 829 (emphasis added).

sive in actuality.[31] All three approaches, however, remain statistically, if not ideologically, attuned with Currie's approach in that they tend to produce the very results he advocated in the majority of cases—the application of the *lex fori*. In this sense they entail the risk of encouraging or legitimizing, especially in the lower courts, the very parochialism[32] that private international law has always fought to minimize.

3. The "Comparative Impairment" Approach

§ 17.16 The previous section showed the application of interest analysis in case law drawn from a number of jurisdictions and with respect to a number of issues in tort. The present section presents the evolution and application of this approach in two states, California and Louisiana, where it has been applied with consistency and further refinement.

a. The California Version

California's break from the traditional rule of the *lex loci delicti* did not come quickly or without examples of the harshness of the traditional rule. *Victor v. Sperry*[1] exemplifies the place-of-wrong rule and also illustrates why that rule has been rejected. The plaintiff, a California resident, had been injured in Mexico in a collision between a car driven by his California host and a car driven by another Californian and owned by a third Californian. Actions were brought against both drivers and the trial court found both of them negligent. The issue concerned the allowable measure of damages: the plaintiff had sought $40,000 and California law permitted unlimited recovery, but Mexican law (actually, the law of a Mexican state) allowed only two dollars for each lost workday and would thus limit the plaintiff to an award of $6,000. The court applied Mexican law to the plaintiff's action against his California host: "[S]ince the accident occurred in Mexico, plaintiffs' cause of action arose there and the character and measure of his damages are governed by the laws of Mexico. The measure of damages is inseparably connected

---

31. It has been suggested that "the *Sutherland* approach . . . can provide convenient rationalizations for judicial subjectivism, protectionism of forum litigants, or both, while giving the appearance of having an orderly system or 'method.'" Symeonides, Choice of Law in the American Courts in 1997, 46 Am. J. Comp. L. 233, 243 (1998). The author further suggests that "[r]ecent experience in Michigan's lower courts leads to the suspicion that a 'rational reason' for displacing Michigan law is more likely to be found when that law is unfavorable to a Michigan litigant, especially one of Michigan's big auto manufacturers." Id.

32. On the other hand, one member of the *Sutherland* court considered the court's

analysis to be too open to the *possibility* of applying foreign law. See *Sutherland*, 562 N.W.2d at 475 (Brickley, J., concurring in part and dissenting in part) ("[T]he majority's analysis requires Michigan courts to apply the law of another jurisdiction in certain cases. However, before a court can do this, it must first expressly refuse to apply the laws of this state. This refusal ignores and defeats the express will of the Legislature. Clearly, the courts of this state should avoid this outcome.").

§ 17.16

1. 163 Cal.App.2d 518, 329 P.2d 728 (1958).

to the cause of action and cannot be severed therefrom."[2] At the same time, however, the court rejected the plaintiff's contention that the Mexican law of strict liability regarding dangerous mechanisms applied to the owner of the second car, because liability without fault contravened the public policy of the California forum.[3]

In applying the *lex loci* rule, the court overlooked two prior state supreme court cases that had begun the trend of avoiding the rule whenever possible. Five years earlier, in *Grant v. McAuliffe*,[4] the court had characterized the survival of a cause of action as procedural, thus to be governed by forum law. Only three years earlier, in *Emery v. Emery*,[5] Justice Traynor had characterized the question of interspousal immunity in tort litigation as relating to capacity, and not to tort, thus to be governed by the law of the domicile which, in this case, was also the forum. However, application of *Grant* and *Emery* would not have resolved the problem presented by *Victor v. Sperry*. Both of the earlier cases had resulted in the application of California law to all issues. To have done so in *Victor* would not have aided the plaintiff, because the guest statute then in effect in California would have barred any recovery. The courts in *Grant* and *Emery* had not split the issues so that forum law applied to certain issues and foreign law to others.[6] These cases therefore would not have enabled the *Victor* court to afford the plaintiff a greater recovery.

§ 17.17 The place-of-wrong rule was finally abandoned in favor of interest analysis by Chief Justice Traynor in *Reich v. Purcell*,[1] a case in which the forum was, in the court's eyes, a "disinterested" third state.[2]

---

2. Id. at 524, 329 P.2d at 732

3. Id. at 526, 329 P.2d at 733. As Weintraub noted, the court overlooked that California law then in force imposed liability for injuries resulting from the negligence of any one using the automobile with the owner's permission. "[S]ince the driver of the other vehicle had been found to be negligent, the court reached a result, non-liability of the owner . . . , which was opposite the result that would have been reached under either Mexican or California law." R. Weintraub, Commentary on the Conflict of Laws 364 (4th ed. 2001). On the other hand, Mexico's $2–per-day limitation was held *not* to contravene California's public policy. *Victor*, 163 Cal.App.2d at 524.

4. 41 Cal.2d 859, 264 P.2d 944 (1953). The case is also discussed supra in § 17.10. See B. Currie, Selected Essays on the Conflicts of Law Ch. 3 (1963) (original citation: 10 Stan.L.Rev. 205 (1958)); Sedler, Characterization, Identification of the Problem Area, and the Policy–Centered Conflict of Laws: An Exercise in Judicial Method, 2 Rutgers Camd. L.J. 8, 49 (1970); Traynor, Is this Conflict Really Necessary?, 37 Tex. L.Rev. 657, 670 n.35 (1959). See also Tray-nor, Book Review, 1965 Duke L.J. 426, 431 in which he considers the case as presenting a "false conflict."

5. 45 Cal.2d 421, 289 P.2d 218 (1955).

6. In Kilberg v. Northeast Airlines, Inc., 9 N.Y.2d 34, 211 N.Y.S.2d 133, 172 N.E.2d 526 (1961) the Court of Appeals held that damage limitations were procedural and governed by forum law (which served to avoid the limitations of the situs), while other issues were left unaffected by this limited application of forum law. See also supra § 17.9.

§ 17.17

1. 67 Cal.2d 551, 63 Cal.Rptr. 31, 432 P.2d 727 (1967). See Comments on Reich v. Purcell, 15 U.C.L.A. L. Rev. 551 (1968) (comments by 12 Conflicts scholars (hereinafter *Comments*)).

2. *Reich*, 67 Cal.2d at 556, 63 Cal.Rptr. at 34, 432 P.2d at 730. B. Currie, The Disinterested Third State, 1959 Law & Contemp. Prob. 754. Currie believed that the disinterested forum was a very rare case. Id. at 765. He suggested that, when faced with this situation, a court could dismiss

Reich was a wrongful death action arising from a car collision in Missouri and involving a California defendant and the Reich family, which was in the process of moving its domicile from Ohio to California. Mrs. Reich and her son were killed in the accident. After completing the move,[3] Mr. Reich brought wrongful death actions seeking $55,000 in damages. Missouri limited wrongful death damages to $25,000, while California and Ohio allowed unlimited awards.[4]

In rejecting the *lex loci delicti* rule and holding Ohio law to be applicable, the court adopted an approach that made it unnecessary to resort to characterization: "The forum must search to find the proper law to apply based upon the interests of the litigants and the involved states."[5] Despite the reference to interest analysis,[6] however, the court offered little in the way of methodology. It provided no clear explanation of how interest analysis was to be employed: "As the forum we must consider all of the foreign and domestic elements and interests in this case to determine the rule applicable."[7] The analysis was based only on an identification of the possibly interested states and a general discussion of those states' interests. Beginning with a consideration of its own

the action on *forum non conveniens* grounds; avoid the conflict by construing the competing laws so as to find a false conflict; or, when a true conflict existed, to make the decision between competing laws. Finally, a court could "reasonably apply its own law," in a situation in which forum law and one of the other competing state's law coincide. Id. at 773, 780. However, he recognized that, if three different laws were presented, application of the law of the forum might not be justified and the forum could be left "to the free choice that amounts to the exercise of pure legislative judgment." Id. at 780.

3. In Huddy v. Fruehauf Corp., 953 F.2d 955 (5th Cir.1992), cert. denied 506 U.S. 828, 113 S.Ct. 89, 121 L.Ed.2d 52 (1992), a Texas resident, driving a truck from Texas to Georgia, was injured in an accident in Georgia. He sued the truck manufacturer in Texas. Four years later, the driver moved to New Jersey. The manufacturer had its principal place of business in Michigan. Texas, but not Michigan, recognized the doctrine of strict liability for defective products. The district court applied Michigan law to this issue, but the Fifth Circuit reversed. "The fact that [the question of whether the move affects choice of law] arises at all is testimony to the slow pace of justice in today's courts. ... To hold that Texas loses its interest in this case because [the driver] chose to move to another state during the litigation process would chain litigants to the state of residence at the time of the accident lest they lose the protection of the laws." Id. at 957.

4. Thus, unlike many of the other states in which the *lex loci* rule was abandoned in guest-statute cases, the California approach grew out of different tort issues, particularly the measure of damages. Guest-statute issues were considered by lower courts in California: Fuller v. Greenup, 267 Cal. App.2d 10, 72 Cal.Rptr. 531 (1968); Kelley v. Von Kuznick, 18 Cal.App.3d 805, 96 Cal. Rptr. 184 (1971). The California Supreme Court declared the statute unconstitutional on equal protection grounds in Brown v. Merlo, 8 Cal.3d 855, 106 Cal.Rptr. 388, 506 P.2d 212 (1973).

5. *Reich*, 67 Cal.2d at 553, 63 Cal.Rptr. at 33, 432 P.2d at 729. The Court cited *Grant*, and *Emery*, for the proposition that, "when application of the law of the place of the wrong would defeat the interests of the litigants and of the states concerned, we have not applied that law." Id. at 554, 63 Cal.Rptr. at 33, 432 P.2d at 729. Thus, by 1968 the Court read the earlier cases as illustrating some form of interest analysis.

6. But see Ehrenzweig: "The court has undertaken to fill the gap by adopting in language, though not in fact, the 'interest' teaching of Currie, and in fact, though not in language, the approaches of the New York Court of Appeals [Babcock v. Jackson et al. see infra] and of the Restatement, Second with their 'concerns' and 'significant relationships.' " Comment, supra n.1, at 573.

7. *Reich*, 67 Cal.2d at 555, 63 Cal.Rptr. at 34, 432 P.2d at 730. Cf. B. Currie, Selected Essays on the Conflicts of Law, 183–184 (1963).

status as the forum, the court concluded that it had no interest given the instant facts: the defendant's California domicile was irrelevant because California law did not protect the defendant, while the plaintiffs' post event move to California was said not to be controlling because "their residence and domicile at the time of the accident are the relevant domicile."[8]

Whether California as forum, the residence of the defendant at the time of the accident, and the current residence and domicile of the plaintiff, was disinterested is questionable.[9] At the very least, the fact that all parties were California residents would seem to justify the assertion of a local interest and hence the application of forum law under interest analysis. After discounting the forum's interest, the court looked to the applicable laws of Missouri and Ohio, in order to determine which state's policies would be furthered by the application of its law. The court discounted Missouri's interest because its damage limitation was understood to protect local defendants. As a result only Ohio was found to have an interest as the place of the plaintiff's domicile at the time of the decedent's death. In applying a "domicile at time of accident" rule[10] to secure a more substantial recovery for the plaintiffs, the court in

8. Id. at 34, 432 P.2d at 730. This approach is designed to avoid forum shopping which the court though would be encouraged if the new domicile were deemed an interested state. For other cases taking the same position, see Hall v. General Motors Corp., 229 Mich.App. 580, 582 N.W.2d 866 (1998) (discussed infra § 17.77 nn.8 ff.); Nesladek v. Ford Motor Co., 46 F.3d 734 (8th Cir.1995), cert. denied 516 U.S. 814, 116 S.Ct. 67, 133 L.Ed.2d 28 (1995) (discussed infra § 17.77 n.9). In Perloff v. Symmes Hospital, 487 F.Supp. 426 (D.Mass. 1980), a Massachusetts federal court, upon transfer from California, followed *Reich* and applied Massachusetts pro-defendant law to a case arising from a Massachusetts medical malpractice involving parties who, at the time of the malpractice, were domiciled in Massachusetts. Disregarding the plaintiff's post-injury change of domicile to California, the court found "no conflict of state interests which California law recognizes." Id. at 428. In Gore v. Northeast Airlines, Inc., 373 F.2d 717 (2d Cir.1967), a wrongful death action arising out of airplane crash in Massachusetts, the court concluded that the plaintiffs' post-accident change of domicile from New York to another state did not eliminate New York's interest in rejecting Massachusetts' $15,000 limitation on damages. In Miller v. Miller, 22 N.Y.2d 12, 290 N.Y.S.2d 734, 237 N.E.2d 877 (1968), motion denied 22 N.Y.2d 722, 292 N.Y.S.2d 107, 239 N.E.2d 204 (1968), the New York Court of Appeals applied the forum's no-limitation rule to a defendant who had moved from the accident state, Maine (which limited damages to $20,000), to New York before the institution of the suit but after the commission of the tort. Plaintiff's decedent was a New Yorker. The foregoing cases are distinguishable from Gordon v. Gordon, 118 N.H. 356, 387 A.2d 339 (1978), in which the court applied local law as that of the place of the accident in an interspousal immunity case and disregarded both the parties' pre-and post-accident domiciles (Massachusetts and Maine, respectively). See also supra § 3.23 n.10.

9. Professors Weintraub, Gorman, Scoles, Cheatham, and Horowitz all suggest that California was not disinterested. See Comments, supra n.1, at 561–62 567–68, 610–12, 631–32; Professor Cavers thought otherwise. Id. at 647 n.1. For other discussions of the effect of a post-event change of domicile, see, e.g., Hancock, The Effect of Post–Occurrence Change of Domicile, 7 Dalhousie L.J. 653 (1983); Note, Post Transaction or Occurrence Events in Conflict of Laws, 69 Colum. L. Rev. 843 (1969). See also § 7 of the 1978 Austrian federal law on conflicts of law: "A subsequent change in the circumstances relevant for a choice of law has no effect on completed transactions [fact situations]." 1978 Bundesgesetzblatt 1729.

10. Professor Kay sees this rule as necessary in the interest analysis scheme. *Comments* supra n.1, at 588 (citing B. Currie, Full Faith and Credit, Chiefly to Judgments: A Role for Congress, 1964 Sup. Ct. Rev. 89, 92–99).

effect reached the same result as if forum law had been applied: the absence of a damage limitation in both California and Ohio law in fact rendered the case a false conflict.[11] Although the court rejected the outright application of forum law, the opinion suggests at least the relevance of forum law: "A defendant cannot reasonably complain when compensatory damages are assessed in accordance with the law of his domicile and the plaintiffs receive no more than they would have had they been injured at home."[12]

§ 17.18 The decision in *Reich* left important questions unanswered. Chief among them were how courts should identify the interested states and their relevant policies and interests, and what courts should do when faced with a true conflict or an "unprovided for" case.[1] *Hurtado v. Superior Court*[2] shed some light on these questions. As in *Victor v. Sperry*,[3] *Hurtado* involved the applicability of a Mexican state limitation on compensatory damages. However, unlike *Victor*, *Hurtado* involved a California and a Mexican victim and his survivors. Citing *Reich* for the proposition that a damage limitation is serves to protect local defendants,[4] the court found the Mexican state not to have an interest because the defendant was a Californian.[5] The court—initially[6]— also did not seek to identify a California interest but proceeded to apply California law simply because Mexican state law was inapplicable. Thus, the court adopted a "forum preference"[7] approach in a situation that in the court's eyes appeared to exemplify the "unprovided for" case. As the discussion below shows, however, California had identifiable interests in *Hurtado,* and thus the decision cannot be considered conclusive on this point.[8] Moreover, one should not be quick to assume that a state's only interest in justice is its self-interest in and on behalf of its residents. Instead, a court should also be "interested" in doing justice to a foreign defendant as well as providing recovery to a foreign plaintiff when

---

11. This view is also consistent with one of Currie's solutions in the case of the disinterested third state. See Currie, supra n.2.

12. *Reich*, 67 Cal.2d at 556, 63 Cal.Rptr. at 35, 432 P.2d at 731.

§ 17.18

1. See Note, After *Hurtado* and *Bernhard:* Interest Analysis and the Search for a Consistent Theory for Choice of Law Cases, 29 Stan. L. Rev. 127, 130 (1976). The "unprovided for" situation is one where none of the potentially interested states has in fact a sufficient interest to see its law applied. See supra § 17.14.

2. 11 Cal.3d 574, 114 Cal.Rptr. 106, 522 P.2d 666 (1974).

3. 163 Cal.App.2d 518, 329 P.2d 728 (1958) (discussed supra § 17.16).

4. *Hurtado*, 11 Cal.3d at 581, 114 Cal. Rptr. at 110, 522 P.2d at 670.

5. This is not to say that Mexico was "disinterested" in the case: the welfare of its citizens certainly is a legitimate state interest. This "interest," however, was advanced by application of California law. Note, Choice of Measure of Damages in Wrongful Death, 63 Cal. L. Rev. 56, 58–60 n.15, 62–63 (1975).

6. Further inquiry into California's interests proved more revealing: See infra text at n.13.

7. Forum preference is inherent in Currie's conception of interest analysis. See B. Currie, Selected Essays on Conflicts of Laws 183 (1963); supra § 2.9 nn.37–42; Mihollin, The Forum Preference in Choice of Law: Some Notes in *Hurtado v. Superior Court*, 10 U.S.F. L. Rev. 625 (1976).

8. But see Weintraub, The Future of Choice of Law for Torts: What Principles Should be Preferred?, 41 Law & Contemp. Probs. 146, 153 (Spring 1977) (*Hurtado* the "best known of the no-interest cases").

appropriate, especially when the injury is an insured or enterprise risk. Currie himself stated that his analysis "[did] not imply the ruthless pursuit of self-interest by the states" and that "there is no need to exclude the possibility of rational altruism ... regardless of who the victim is."[9]

Beyond the problem of the "unprovided-for" case, the court also addressed the other question left open in *Reich,* how and when a court should consider foreign law:

> In short, generally speaking the forum will apply its own rule of decision unless a party litigant timely invokes the law of a foreign state. In such event he must demonstrate that the latter rule of decision will further the interest of the foreign state and therefore that it is an appropriate one for the forum to apply to the case before it [citing Currie].[10]

This might have concluded the decision. However, the court chose to respond also to the defendant's argument that California lacked any interest and that *Reich* required the application of Mexican state law.[11] The defendant had read *Reich* to say that only the plaintiffs' home state had an interest in the measure of damages and thus Mexican state law should govern this issue in the case at bar which involved Mexican plaintiffs. While stating that California had no interest in the compensation of the Mexican plaintiffs,[12] the court identified deterrence as a goal underlying California's unlimited damage rule and as a policy reason favoring the application of that rule to the conduct of a Californian within the state.[13] Consequently, *Reich* does not posit, as an invariable rule, that compensation for survivors is governed by the law of the plaintiff's domicile. Instead, the court's reading of *Reich* indicates that the forum's concern with conduct, and hence deterrence, provides a sufficient interest to justify the application of forum law. Since the concerns of the place of the wrong (compensation of local survivors and protection of local defendants), which are usually associated with wrongful death actions, were absent in *Hurtado,* the interest in deterrence came to the fore. The emphasis on the deterrence interest, combined

9. B. Currie, Selected Essays on the Conflict of Laws 185–86 (1963).

10. *Hurtado,* 11 Cal.3d at 581, 114 Cal. Rptr. at 110, 522 P.2d at 670. The first sentence of the language quoted in the text restates the general rule that foreign law must be invoked by the litigant who benefits from it. See F.R.Civ.Proc. 44.1 and supra § 12.18. In Continental law, where the court considers ex officio the choice-of-law question, the court must also evaluate the pertinent factors (e.g., for determining the closest connection in a contract conflict). There are occasional suggestions that the *lex fori* applies unless the parties invoke foreign law. See Flessner, Interessenjurisprudenz im internationalen Privatrecht (1990). Moreover, since the parties can choose the applicable law at the commencement of the action—including by contract—, the American and European practices are therefore quite parallel up to this point. However, the Continental practice differs widely with respect to the second sentence of the above quoted text—if a choice-of-law rule points to foreign law, and a party affected is unwilling to stipulate another law, that party need not demonstrate the appropriateness of the rule.

11. *Hurtado,* 11 Cal.3d at 582, 114 Cal. Rptr. at 111, 522 P.2d at 671.

12. But see text supra n.9.

13. *Hurtado,* 11 Cal.3d at 583, 114 Cal. Rptr. at 112, 522 P.2d at 672. But see Note, supra n.5, at 72–74.

with the lack of an interest on the part of the Mexican state, thus made *Hurtado* a "classic false conflicts" case.[14]

It is important to stress, however, that the discussion of California's interest in deterrence was not necessary for the decision of the case. Arguably, the discussion is dictum and proper analysis of *Hurtado* should focus primarily on the actual holding which excludes the deterrence interest.[15] While the court's expression of a forum preference seems to be at variance with the approach of other jurisdictions,[16] the actual result is in fact compatible with all approaches since in *Hurtado* the *lex fori* was also the *lex loci*. For example, the Second Restatement would lead to the application of the *lex loci* because no other state would have a "most significant relationship" than the *locus* state.[17] Even if, as suggested earlier, *Hurtado* is not really an "unprovided for" case, most states would have applied the law of the forum/locus state when that state has an interest in applying its law.[18]

§ 17.19 *Bernhard v. Harrah's Club*[1] involved a "true conflict." The case involved an action by a California resident for injuries sustained in California as a result of the negligent driving of other Californians who had become intoxicated at the defendant's gambling establishment in Nevada. California law imposed civil liability on tavern owners

---

14. Note, supra n.5, at 68. The deterrence factor was lacking in Jackson v. Koninklijke Luchtvaart Maatschappij N.V., 459 F.Supp. 953 (S.D.N.Y.1978) (on transfer from California) in which domiciliaries of New York, Pennsylvania, and Tennessee sought damages for injuries sustained in an air crash in Spain. Finding that California was uninterested, the court concluded that either the law of Spain or The Netherlands (the defendant's domicile) should govern because disregarding the laws of those countries, neither of which provided for punitive damages, would "impair significant interests of those states." Id. at 956. The court cited *Hurtado,* although the impairment language is also reminiscent of *Bernhard v. Harrah's Club.* See infra § 17.19 n.1.

15. The invocation of deterrence may also "fl[y] in the face of common sense" because defendants do not commit *negligent* acts against the background of compensatory (rather than punitive) damages. Rather, compensatory damage rules exist only for the purpose of providing compensation to injured plaintiffs or to protect defendants against excessive exposure. Reese, Book Review, 32 Am. J. Comp. L. 332, 334 (1985).

16. Neumeier v. Kuehner, 31 N.Y.2d 121, 335 N.Y.S.2d 64, 286 N.E.2d 454 (1972), appeal after remand 43 A.D.2d 109, 349 N.Y.S.2d 866 (1973) (discussed infra § 17.31).

17. Mihollin, supra n.7, at 630.

18. One author suggested that, when, as in *Hurtado*, both the conduct and the injury occur in the home state of one of the parties, most courts apply the law of that state, even if it is not the forum and even if that law does not favor the local domiciliary. See S. Symeonides, The American Choice-of-Law Revolution in the Courts: Today and Tomorrow, 298 Recueil des Cours, 1, 203–220 (2003) for citations and discussion.

§ 17.19

1. 16 Cal.3d 313, 319, 128 Cal.Rptr. 215, 218, 546 P.2d 719, 722 (1976), cert. denied 429 U.S. 859, 97 S.Ct. 159, 50 L.Ed.2d 136 (1976) ("[U]nlike Reich v. Purcell and Hurtado v. Superior Court where we were faced with 'false conflicts,' in the instant case for the first time since applying a governmental interest analysis as a choice of law doctrine in *Reich,* we are confronted with a 'true' conflicts case.") (citations omitted.) See Comment, After *Hurtado* and *Bernhard:* Interest Analysis and the Search for a Consistent Theory for Choice of Law Cases, 29 Stan. L. Rev. 127; Comment, 65 Cal. L. Rev. 290 (1977); Liew v. Official Receiver and Liquidator, 685 F.2d 1192 (9th Cir.1982) (the application of comparative-impairment analysis presupposes the existence of a true conflict); KL Group v. Case, Kay & Lynch, 829 F.2d 909 (9th Cir.1987).

under these circumstances,[2] while Nevada law did not. Underlying these differences was Nevada's concern to protect tavern owners from "ruinous liability"[3] and California's policy of protecting society from the acts of intoxicated individuals.[4] Drawing on the work of Professor Baxter[5] and an earlier contracts conflicts case,[6] the court employed a "comparative impairment" approach described as "seek[ing] to determine which state's interest would be more impaired if its policy were subordinated to the policy of the other state."[7] The court concluded that California's policy would suffer greater impairment than Nevada's. California's interest in protecting those injured by intoxicated persons was construed to include the imposition of liability on out-of-state taverns because accidents may occur as easily when a party becomes intoxicated out-of-state as when at home. Since the defendant Harrah's Club advertised in, and solicited customers from California, it had established a nexus with California and voluntarily subjected itself to the reach of California law. The court thought that Nevada's interests would not be impaired because the application of California law would affect only those—arguably few—Nevada taverns that solicited business in California.[8] In addition, the court found it persuasive that, although the Nevada Supreme Court had specifically refused to impose civil liability,[9] a Nevada statute imposed criminal liability on tavern owners for selling liquor to customers obviously intoxicated. However, unbeknown to the *Bernhard* court, this statute had been repealed three years before the *Bernhard* decision.[10]

The line of cases from *Reich* to *Hurtado* to *Bernhard* completed the break with traditional doctrine in California. The place of injury remains an important contact, but the focus of the inquiry has shifted to the effectuation of California interests, tempered in some cases by a weighing of interests in true conflicts in order to assess the degree of the "comparative impairment" that may be involved. Case law after *Bern-*

---

2. See Vesely v. Sager, 5 Cal.3d 153, 95 Cal.Rptr. 623, 486 P.2d 151 (1971), relying on Cal. Bus. & Prof. Code § 25602 (which making it a misdemeanor to sell liquor to an intoxicated person) to impose civil liability on the seller. In 1978, the California Legislature amended § 25602 and expressly abrogated *Vesely* and *Bernhard* on this point. See Cory v. Shierloh, 29 Cal.3d 430, 629 P.2d 8, 174 Cal.Rptr. 500 (1981).

3. *Bernhard*, 16 Cal.3d at 318, 128 Cal. Rptr. at 218, 546 P.2d at 722 (citing Hamm v. Carson City Nugget, Inc., 85 Nev. 99, 450 P.2d 358 (1969)).

4. Id. The policy was subsequently changed. See supra n.2.

5. Baxter, Choice of Law and the Federal System, 16 Stan. L. Rev. 1 (1963) (discussed supra § 2.9 n.28). See also Horowitz, The Law of Choice of Law in California, 21 U.C.L.A. L. Rev. 719 (1974).

6. People v. One 1953 Ford Victoria, 48 Cal.2d 595, 311 P.2d 480 (1957).

7. *Bernhard*, 16 Cal.3d at 320, 128 Cal. Rptr. at 219, 546 P.2d at 723.

8. In emphasizing the small "number" of taverns potentially liable under California law, the decision may invite a mere counting of "numbers" in the future. Furthermore, had Nevada been the forum, the "tally of the numbers" might have looked quite different. See also Reese, Book Review, 32 Am. J. Comp. L. 332, 335 (1985) for the suggestion that comparative impairment does not explain the decision, while the desire to compensate does.

9. See Hamm v. Carson City Nugget, Inc., 85 Nev. 99, 450 P.2d 358 (1969).

10. See 1973 Nev.Stats. ch. 604, § 8, at 1062 (repealing NRS § 202.100); Bell v. Alpha Tau Omega Fraternity, Eta Epsilon Chapter, 98 Nev. 109, 111, 642 P.2d 161, 162 (1982).

hard suggests that the search is not yet over.[11] Thus, in *Offshore Rental Co. v. Continental Oil Co.*,[12] the California Supreme Court applied Louisiana law, which prohibited an action by a California employer for the loss of the services of a key employee who was injured in Louisiana by defendant's employees. A California statute would allow the action, but the statute had not been applied squarely for several decades. The court concluded that California was not really committed to this statute, which was "archaic and isolated in the context of the federal union,"[13] and thus California's interest in applying its "unusual and outmoded statute [was] comparatively less strong."[14] The court also concluded that the Louisiana rule was in the "main stream," that Louisiana's interest in applying it was "stronger, [and] more current"[15] than California's corresponding interest, and that to apply California law "would strike at the essence of a compelling Louisiana law."[16] Thus, *Offshore* appeared to repudiate not only Currie's proscription of interest-weighing, but also Baxter's more subtle formulation that the court should only weigh the *effects* of the application or non-application of a state's law. Indeed, in a very real sense, *Offshore* engaged in a comparative evaluation of the conflicting *laws themselves*, thus coming perilously close to a better-law approach.[17]

b. *The Louisiana Version*

§ 17.20 The 1991 Louisiana Conflicts codification also employs comparative-impairment *terminology*. Article 3515 of the Louisiana Civil Code, which, like § 6 of the Second Restatement,[1] is the general and the

11. See Kanowitz, Comparative Impairment and Better Law: Grand Illusions in the Conflict of Laws, 30 Hastings L.J. 255 (1979), who advocates a return to pure governmental interest analysis. Professor Kay similarly believes that the question in all choice-of-law cases should not be "whose law is to be applied?," but rather: "under what circumstances is a departure from local [forum] law justified?" Kay, The Use of Comparative Impairment to Resolve True Conflicts: An Evaluation of the California Experience, 68 Cal. L. Rev. 577, 617 (1980). "Governmental interest analysis ... [accomplishes this] easily." Id. at 616. "The unifying element [to consolidate the competing approaches to choice of law] should be a preference for local law." Id. at 615. See also Kay, A Defense of Currie's Governmental Interest Analysis, 215 Recueil des cours 13 (1989–III).

12. 22 Cal.3d 157, 148 Cal.Rptr. 867, 583 P.2d 721 (1978). For another application of the "comparative impairment" approach in California see Cable v. Sahara Tahoe Corp., 93 Cal.App.3d 384, 155 Cal. Rptr. 770 (2d Dist. 1979).

13. *Offshore*, 583 P.2d at 726.

14. Id. at 728. In addition to relying on Baxter, the court relied on the writings of von Mehren and Trautman, Freund, and Leflar. See id. at 726.

15. Id. at 729.

16. Id. at 728.

17. S. Symeonides, The American Choice-of-Law Revolution in the Courts: Today and Tomorrow, 298 Recueil des Cours, 1, 103 (2003).

§ 17.20

1. The resemblance with the Restatement is even clearer in the Puerto Rico Draft Code, the residual article of which provides for the application of the law of the state with the "most significant connection to the parties and the dispute." Art. 45, Academia Puertorriqueña de Jurisprudencia y Legislacion, Proyecto para la Codificación del Derecho internacional privado de Puerto Rico, (Symeonides & von Mehren, Rapporteurs, 1991). The drafter explains the reasons for choosing this terminology in Symeonides, Revising Puerto Rico's Conflicts Law: A Preview, 28 Col. J. Trans'l L 401, 428–29 (1990).

residual article of the entire codification,[2] calls for the application of the law of the state "whose policies would be most seriously impaired if its law were not applied"[3] to the particular issue. The codification's drafter explains that the negative phrasing of the above article was intended to disassociate its approach from Currie's governmental interest analysis and other modern American approaches that "seem to perceive the choice-of-law problem as a problem of interstate competition rather than as a problem of interstate co-operation in conflict avoidance."[4] Although he acknowledges that this negative phraseology, as well as the use of the key-word "impaired," would evoke comparison with California's comparative impairment approach, he contends that the similarity is only phraseological.[5] He states that the codification "is based on the premise that the choice-of-law process should strive for ways to minimize the impairment of the interests of the involved states, rather than to maximize the interests of one state at the expense of the interests of the other states"[6] and that this is accomplished by "identifying the state which, in light of its relationship to the parties and the dispute and its

2. Article 3515 provides that, except as otherwise provided by the more specific articles of the codification, the applicable law shall be the law of "the state whose policies would be most seriously impaired if its law were not applied to that issue." That state is determined "by evaluating the strength and pertinence of the relevant policies of all involved states in the light of: (1) the relationship of each state to the parties and the dispute; and (2) the policies and needs of the interstate and international systems, including the policies of upholding the justified expectations of parties and of minimizing the adverse consequences that might follow from subjecting a party to the law of more than one state." La. Civ. Code, Art. 3515 (1991, effective Jan. 1, 1992). Similar phraseology is contained in articles 3519, 3537, and 3542 which are the residual articles for status, contract, and tort conflicts, respectively. For a discussion by the codification's drafter, see Symeonides, Private International Law Codification in a Mixed Jurisdiction: The Louisiana Experience, 57 RabelsZ, 460 (1993); Symeonides, Les grands problèmes de droit international privé et la nouvelle codification de Louisiane, 81 Revue critique 223 (1992); Symeonides, Louisiana's New Law of Choice of Law for Tort Conflicts: An Exegesis, 66 Tul. L. Rev. 677 (1992). For discussions by other authors, see infra n.10; Borchers, Louisiana's Conflicts Codification: Some Empirical Observations Regarding Decisional Predictability, 60 La. L. Rev. 1061 (2000); Jayme, Neue Kodifikation des Internationalen Privatrechts in Louisiana, 13 Praxis des Internationalen Privat-und Verfarensrechts (IPRax) 56 (1993–1). For discussion of cases decided under the new codification,

see Borchers, supra; the authors cited infra n. 10; Symeonides, Louisiana Conflicts Law: Two "Surprises," 54 La. L. Rev. 497 (1994). For discussion of how the codification would resolve some other well-known American cases, see Symeonides, Resolving Six Celebrated Conflicts Cases Through Statutory Choice-of-Law Rules, 48 Mercer L. Rev. 837 (1997).

3. La. Civ. Code art. 3515.

4. Symeonides, *Exegesis*, supra n.2 at 690.

5. See id. at 691–92:

The assumption that such a [terminological] resemblance entails an ideological or philosophical affinity [between the two approaches] should not be taken for granted, but should be tested through a careful examination of the specifics.... [S]uch an examination will reveal ... [that] the two approaches have much less in common than their acoustic resemblance might suggest. For example, the specific rules [of the Louisiana codification] deliberately steer away from the quantitative measurement of the impairment of state interests that is implicit, and sometimes even explicit, in Baxter's theory. Moreover, in designating the applicable law, these rules point to the law of a state other than the one to which Baxter would point.

See also id. at 708.

6. Id. at 690. The same statement is contained in the Reporter's Official Revision Comments. See La. Civ. Code Art. 3515 cmt. b.

policies rendered pertinent by that relationship, would bear the most serious legal, social, economic, and other *consequences* if its law were not applied to that issue."[7] Professor Weintraub has correctly concluded that this is a "consequences-based approach."[8]

For the purposes of this chapter, the importance of the Louisiana codification lies not so much in the general approach it enunciates in the above quoted residual article, but rather in the specific rules the codification provides for specific patterns of tort conflicts. These rules are discussed in some detail later because, although Louisiana's civilian heritage might suggest otherwise, these rules are drawn from, and may reflect, the American conflicts experience.[9] The general and residual article for tort conflicts is Article 3542, which provides that, except as otherwise provided in the more specific articles, tort conflicts are governed by the law of the state whose policies would be most seriously impaired if its law were not applied to the particular issue. That state is determined by evaluating the "strength and pertinence of the relevant policies" of the involved states in the light of: "(1) the pertinent contacts of each state to the parties and the events giving rise to the dispute, including the place of conduct and injury, the domicile, habitual residence, or place of business of the parties, and the state in which the relationship, if any, between the parties was centered; and (2) the policies referred to in Article 3515, as well as the policies of deterring wrongful conduct and of repairing the consequences of injurious acts."[10] The specific articles cover certain fact-law patterns in cases involving: "issues of conduct and safety" (Art. 3543); "issues of loss distribution and financial protection" (Art. 3544); certain products liability cases with enumerated Louisiana connections regardless of the type of issue involved (Art. 3545); and punitive damages in cases other than the above products cases (Art. 3546). Article 3547 provides an "escape" from

7. Id. (emphasis added).

8. See R. Weintraub, Commentary on the Conflict of Laws 355 (4th ed. 2001).

9. See Symeonides, Problems and Dilemmas in Codifying Choice of Law for Torts: The Louisiana Experience in a Comparative Perspective, 38 Am. J. Comp. L. 431, 443 (1990) (describing the codification as "a genuine product of the American conflicts experience"); Symeonides, *Codification in a Mixed Jurisdiction*, supra n.2 at 463 ("The raw material is mostly American, while the architecture and building technique bear unmistakable civilian imprints.").

10. La. Civ. Code Art. 3542. For a discussion of this and the other tort articles by their drafter, see Symeonides, supra n. 2; Symeonides, La nuova normativa della Louisiana sul diritto internazionale privato in tema di responsabilità extracontrattuale, 29 Riv. dir. int'le priv. e proc. 43 (1993). For discussion by other authors, see supra n. 2;

J–C. Cornu, Choice of Law in Tort: A Comparative Study of the Louisiana Draft on Delictual and Quasi–Delictual Obligations and the Swiss Statute on Private International Law (1989); Kozyris, Values and Methods in Choice of Law for Products Liability: A Comparative Comment on Statutory Solutions, 38 Am. J. Comp. L. 475 (1990); Kozyris, Conflicts Theory for Dummies: Après le Deluge, Where Are We on Producers Liability, 60 La. L. Rev. 1161 (2000); Perdue, A Reexamination of the Distinction between "Loss Allocating" and "Conduct–Regulating" Rules, 60 La. L. Rev. 1251 (2000); Sedler, The Louisiana Codification and Tort Rules of Choice of Law, 60 La. L. Rev. 1331 (2000); Weintraub, The Contributions of Symeonides and Kozyris in Making Choice of Law Predictable and Just: An Appreciation and Critique, 38 Am. J. Comp. L. 511 (1990); Weintraub, Courts Flailing in the Waters of the Louisiana Conflicts Code: Not Waving but Drowning, 60 La. L. Rev. 1365 (2000).

Articles 3543–3546; and, Article 3548 contains a special rule with regard to the domicile of some corporate tortfeasors. These articles are discussed later.[11]

C. THE "BETTER LAW" APPROACH

§ 17.21 The "better law," one of the five co-equal "choice influencing considerations" advanced by Leflar,[1] is defined in terms of the "superiority of one rule of law over another *in terms of socio-economic jurisprudential standards....*"[2] Application of the "better law," Leflar contends, tends to serve the ends of justice by putting the litigation in a "more impersonal, less subjective framework, rather than by choosing one or the other party."[3] Furthermore, he asserts that decision-making on this basis is the common practice of courts[4] and would also be more forthright by relieving courts from using such "manipulative devices" as characterization, definitions of domicile and residence, and renvoi.[5]

The approach is also reflected in the writings of other scholars,[6] but often with qualifications.[7] The choice-of-law principles of the Second Restatement omit the "better law" as a criterion.[8] Criticisms, often

---

11. See infra, §§ 17.39–17.50. One author who has studied the judicial application of these and the other articles of the codification during the decade since their enactment has reached some encouraging conclusions. Dean Patrick Borchers compared the affirmance rate in cases decided before and after the codification and found that the codification "has improved the affirmance rate, and by implication the predictability of decisions in conflicts cases." Borchers, supra n. 2, at 1068. See also id. (reporting that "the pre-codification . . . affirmance rate was 52.9%" and that "for post-codification decisions . . . the affirmance rate improved to 76.2%"). The author concludes that these results are "hopeful and suggestive that comprehensive conflicts codifications can produce significant benefits." Id. at 1062.

§ 17.21

1. Leflar, Choice Influencing Considerations in Conflicts Law, 41 N.Y.U. L. Rev. 267 (1966); Conflicts Law: More on Choice Influencing Considerations, 54 Cal. L. Rev. 1584 (1966). Leflar's approach is also discussed supra at § 2.13.

2. Leflar, supra n.1, N.Y.U. L. Rev. at 296; R. Leflar, L. McDougal & R. Felix, American Conflicts Law 297 (4th ed. 1986) (emphasis added). For the fifth edition (without Leflar), see L. McDougal, R. Felix & R. Whitten, American Conflicts Law 366 (5th ed. 2001).

3. Id.

4. Leflar, supra n.1, N.Y.U. L. Rev. at 302; McDougal Felix & Whitlen, American Conflicts Law 366 (5th ed. 2001). See also Hancock, Policy Controlled State Interest Analysis in Choice of Law, Measure of Damages, Torts Cases, 26 Int'l & Comp. L.Q. 799, 819–24 (1977).

5. McDougal Felix & Whitlen, American Conflicts Law 368 (5th ed. 2001).

6. See supra § 2.12.

7. See Cavers, Conflicts of Law Roundtable–The Value of Principled Preference, 49 Tex.L.Rev. 211, 215 (1971) ("I have recognized the influence of the better law in choice of law decisions not as a desideratum but as an inevitable psychological reaction in marginal cases, a tendency not to be encouraged but to be taken into account in explaining decisions."). But see Juenger, Choice of Law in Interstate Torts, 118 U. Pa. L.Rev. 202 (1969), who views the "better law" as a sufficient criterion by itself for the decision of choice-of-law cases. He refined his approach in his General Course on Private International Law, 193 Recueil des Cours 123–387 (1985–IV), in which he advocated "a selection process based on the qualitative evaluation of conflicting rules of decision." Id. at 321. For his criticism of interest analysis, see also Juenger, Choice of Law: How it Ought Not To Be, 48 Mercer L. Rev. 757 (1997).

8. See supra § 2.14 n.6.

severe, of the approach abound,[9] principally on the ground that the approach builds in a forum preference.[10] Leflar, in contrast, believed that courts would be more even-handed and apply foreign law when the local rule appears to be outmoded.[11] As subsequent discussion shows, the case law so far does not necessarily justify that confidence.

The "better law" approach has been followed in five states[12] in the following chronological order: New Hampshire,[13] Minnesota[14] Wisconsin,[15] Rhode Island,[16] and Arkansas.[17] However, by the turn of the century, most of these states tend to combine this approach with other approaches. This is especially true in Rhode Island[18] and Arkansas,[19] but, recently, also in Minnesota[20] and Wisconsin.[21]

9. See supra § 2.13 nn.6, 11–13.

10. See supra § 2.13.

11. McDougal Felix & Whitlen, American Conflicts Law 368 (5th ed. 2001).

12. It is interesting to note that virtually all cases initially adopting the better law approach have been tort or tort-related (wrongful death) actions. Even in Hague v. Allstate Ins. Co., 289 N.W.2d 43 (Minn. 1978), aff'd 449 U.S. 302, 101 S.Ct. 633, 66 L.Ed.2d 521 (1981), which involved the question of "stacking" insurance coverage, the court carefully noted that this was not an "ordinary contract case" but arose in the context of indemnity for a tort-type injury. For extensive discussion of *Hague* see supra § 3.23. See also Hime v. State Farm Fire & Cas. Co., 284 N.W.2d 829 (Minn.1979), cert. denied 444 U.S. 1032, 100 S.Ct. 703, 62 L.Ed.2d 668 (1980); Tillett v. J.I. Case Co., 580 F.Supp. 1276 (E.D.Wis. 1984), aff'd 756 F.2d 591 (7th Cir.1985).

13. In addition to the cases discussed infra, see Clark v. Clark, 107 N.H. 351, 222 A.2d 205 (1966); Taylor v. Bullock, 111 N.H. 214, 279 A.2d 585 (1971); Gagne v. Berry, 112 N.H. 125, 290 A.2d 624 (1972); Maguire v. Exeter and Hampton Elec. Co., 114 N.H. 589, 325 A.2d 778 (1974); Ferren v. General Motors Corp. Delco Battery Div., 137 N.H. 423, 628 A.2d 265 (1993); Benoit v. Test Systems, Inc. 694 A.2d 992, 142 N.H. 47 (1997); Lessard v. Clarke, 143 N.H. 555, 736 A.2d 1226 (1999).

14. In addition to the cases discussed infra, see Bigelow v. Halloran, 313 N.W.2d 10 (Minn.1981); Hague v. Allstate Ins. Co., 289 N.W.2d 43 (Minn.1978), aff'd 449 U.S. 302, 101 S.Ct. 633, 66 L.Ed.2d 521 (1981); Gimmestad v. Gimmestad, 451 N.W.2d 662 (Minn.Ct.App.1990); Lommen v. The City of East Grand Forks., 522 N.W.2d 148 (Minn. Ct.App.1994); Kenna v. So–Fro Fabrics, Inc., 18 F.3d 623 (8th Cir.1994); Nodak Mut. Ins. Co. v. American Fam. Mut. Ins. Co., 604 N.W.2d 91 (Minn. 2000).

15. In addition to the cases discussed infra, see Heath v. Zellmer, 35 Wis.2d 578, 151 N.W.2d 664 (1967); Zelinger v. State Sand & Gravel Co., 38 Wis.2d 98, 156 N.W.2d 466 (1968); Conklin v. Horner, 38 Wis.2d 468, 157 N.W.2d 579 (1968); Hunker v. Royal Indem. Co., 57 Wis.2d 588, 204 N.W.2d 897 (1973); Lichter v. Fritsch, 77 Wis.2d 178, 252 N.W.2d 360 (1977); Kuehn v. Childrens Hospital, Los Angeles, 119 F.3d 1296 (7th Cir.1997); State Farm Mut. Auto. Ins. Co. v. Gillette, 251 Wis.2d 561, 641 N.W.2d 662 (2002).

16. See Woodward v. Stewart, 104 R.I. 290, 243 A.2d 917 (1968); Victoria v. Smythe, 703 A.2d 619 (R.I.1997); Cribb v. Augustyn, 696 A.2d 285 (R.I.1997) (combination of better law, Second Restatement, and interest analysis); La Plante v. American Honda Motor Co., Inc., 27 F.3d 731 (1st Cir.1994); Tiernan v. Westext Transport, Inc., 295 F.Supp. 1256 (D.R.I.1969).

17. See Schlemmer v. Fireman's Fund Ins. Co., 292 Ark. 344, 730 S.W.2d 217 (1987); Threlkeld v. Worsham, 30 Ark.App. 251, 785 S.W.2d 249 (1990).

18. The approach of the Rhode Island supreme court is, by the court's own admission, highly eclectic. In Cribb v. Augustyn, 696 A.2d 285 (R.I.1997), the court described its approach as follows:

> In this jurisdiction ... we follow ... the interest-weighing approach. In so doing, we look at the particular case facts and determine therefrom the rights and liabilities of the parties "in accordance with the law of the state that bears the most significant relationship to the event and the parties." ... That approach has sometimes been referred to as a rule of "choice-influencing considerations."

In applying the interest-weighing or choice-influencing considerations, we consider ... [Leflar's five choice-influencing considerations and the four factual contacts listed] in Restatement (Second) Conflict of Laws, § 145(2).

19.–21. See p. 754.

The first decision to employ this approach was *Clark v. Clark*,[22] which presented the classic guest-statute conflict. A New Hampshire plaintiff sought the common law recovery offered by the New Hampshire forum against her New Hampshire spouse when the guest statute of the state of injury, Vermont, would have precluded recovery. The New Hampshire court rejected the traditional *lex loci delicti* rule and adopted an approach based on Leflar's "choice influencing considerations." Discarding three of Leflar's considerations as irrelevant,[23] the court focused on the advancement of the forum's governmental interest and particularly on the application of the better rule of law. The court concluded that the forum's common law recovery rule was superior to Vermont's restrictive guest statute. The court noted that guest statutes were a legislative response of the 1920s to problems that were no longer

Id. at 288 (citations omitted). See also Najarian v. National Amusements, Inc., 768 A.2d 1253 (R.I.2001) (blending choice-influencing considerations with Second Restatement); La Plante v. American Honda Motor Co., Inc., 27 F.3d 731 (1st Cir.1994) (decided under Rhode Island's conflict law; blending the better-law approach with interest analysis).

19. Arkansas decisions combine Leflar's approach with the Second Restatement. See Wallis v. Mrs. Smith's Pie Co., 261 Ark. 622, 550 S.W.2d 453 (1977); Williams v. Carr, 263 Ark. 326, 565 S.W.2d 400 (1978); Schlemmer v. Fireman's Fund Ins. Co., 292 Ark. 344, 730 S.W.2d 217 (1987). For criticism, see Hogue, Arkansas' New Choice of Law Rule for Interstate Torts, 1978 Wash. U.L.Q. 713.

20. See Nodak Mut. Ins. Co. v. American Fam. Mut. Ins. Co., 604 N.W.2d 91 (Minn. 2000). *Nodak* described the Minnesota approach as "the significant contacts test," id. 94, 96, which, however, relies not on contacts, but on Leflar's five choice-influencing factors, which–as the court applied them–are not really five, but rather one: the "[a]dvancement of the forum's governmental interest," id. at 94. Despite these statements, *Nodak* appears to adopt a presumptive *lex loci* rule. For a critique of *Nodak's* eclecticism, see Symeonides, Choice of Law in the American Courts in 2000: As the Century Turns, 49 Am. J. Comp. L. 1, 8–11, 21–22 (2001)

21. See State Farm Mut. Auto. Ins. Co. v. Gillette, 251 Wis.2d 561, 641 N.W.2d 662 (2002) (prefacing its application of the five Leflar factors with a statement resurrected from a 30–year old precedent, to the effect that the primary choice-of-law rule in Wisconsin is that "the law of the forum should presumptively apply unless it becomes clear

that nonforum contacts are of the greater significance." Id. at 676).

22. 107 N.H. 351, 222 A.2d 205 (1966).

23. Judge Kennison found that (1) predictability of results had no relevance "[e]xcept for the evils of forum shopping," 107 N.H. at 354, 222 A.2d at 208, because auto accidents "are not planned"; (2) maintenance of order among the states demands only "that a court apply the law of no state which does not have substantial connection with the total facts and with the particular issue being litigated." Id.; and (3) simplification of the judicial task presents no problem whenever a court applies its own law. Id. at 356, 222 A.2d at 208. This theme is echoed in other cases. See Milkovich v. Saari, 295 Minn. 155, 203 N.W.2d 408 (1973), discussed infra § 17.22. Predictability, however, does play a part even in accidental, unplanned events. As Professor Westbrook notes: "Even in the case of unplanned events, . . . a predictable choice-of-law rule helps a lawyer decide whether his client should sue or settle and where to sue. It reduces the time that must be devoted to legal research and writing briefs. Decisions must be made before suit is brought, during trial, and in deciding whether to appeal a trial court's decision. Uncertainty as to the applicable law can often cause problems which are as serious for those involved in tort litigation as the problems associated with planning commercial transactions. . . . [W]hen one attempts to devise a choice-of-law approach which will serve the interests of living, breathing human beings, it is important to place some emphasis on the factor of predictability." Westbrook, A Survey and Evaluation of Competing Choice-of-Law Methodologies: The Case for Eclecticism, 40 Mo. L. Rev. 407, 449–50 (1975) (citations omitted).

troublesome in the 1960s; that no states had recently enacted such statutes; and that states that had guest statutes had begun to construe them narrowly.[24] This line of reasoning shows how a court might intelligently assess the current strength of interests embodied in competing laws. When coupled with the forum's announced interest in providing relief in litigation between its own domiciliaries,[25] this assessment of the competing laws understandably led the court to apply forum law.

It is important to note that in choosing forum law as the better one, Chief Judge Kennison offered caveats for courts employing this approach. He stated that it was important that "a court apply the law of no state which does not have a substantial connection with the total facts and the particular issue being litigated."[26] This warning—which is suggestive of the Second Restatement's emphasis on contacts—serves to restrain courts from applying forum law, as the "better" law, to any case before them and thus preserves at least the possibility that foreign law might be the better law.[27] Furthermore, *Clark* also stands for the proposition that the better-law criterion is not alone determinative in all choice-of-law situations.[28] By including consideration of the forum's governmental interests, the *Clark* court left open the possibility that the

24. *Clark*, 107 N.H. at 356–57, 222 A.2d at 210.

25. Id. at 356, 222 A.2d at 209.

26. Id. at 354, 222 A.2d at 208. See also supra §§ 3.20–3.35 with respect to constitutional limitations on choice of law.

27. Id. at 355, 222 A.2d at 209. An example is Bigelow v. Halloran, 313 N.W.2d 10 (Minn.1981) in which the court admitted that Iowa's survival-of-action rule was "better" than Minnesota's opposite rule. However, in that case the application of Minnesota law would not have been justified under most other choice-of-law approaches. *Bigelow* involved an intentional tort committed in Iowa against a resident of that state by a Minnesota resident who later shot himself. In Maguire v. Exeter and Hampton Elec. Co., 114 N.H. 589, 325 A.2d 778 (1974), the forum recognized that its own law "lies in the backwater of the modern stream," but applied forum law based on governmental interests, Leflar's fourth choice influencing consideration. In Lichter v. Fritsch, 77 Wis.2d 178, 252 N.W.2d 360 (1977), the court found the foreign law not to be the better law but applied it anyway, based on choice influencing considerations. However, in doing so the court was able to provide recovery for a forum plaintiff, whereas local law would have barred the suit. See also Boatwright v. Budak, 625 N.W.2d 483 (Minn.App.2001) (holding that Iowa law was better than Minnesota's in that it provided recovery for a Minnesota domiciliary who was injured in

an Iowa traffic accident while riding in a car owned by a national car rental company). In Gagne v. Berry, 112 N.H. 125, 290 A.2d 624 (1972), the court applied the forum's common law rule, rather than Massachusetts' guest statute, in a case involving a Massachusetts guest and host, and a Vermont accident. See also Conklin v. Horner, 38 Wis.2d 468, 157 N.W.2d 579 (1968) and Milkovich v. Saari, 295 Minn. 155, 203 N.W.2d 408 (1973) (discussed infra § 17.22).

28. Recent cases seem to accept this proposition and use the better-law criterion as a tie-breaker. See, e.g., Nesladek v. Ford Motor Co., 876 F.Supp. 1061 (D.Minn. 1994), aff'd 46 F.3d 734 (8th Cir.1995), cert. denied 516 U.S. 814, 116 S.Ct. 67, 133 L.Ed.2d 28 (1995), stating that the better-law factor need not be considered when the other choice-influencing factors "clearly dictate the application of one state's law." Id. at 1070; Hughes v. Wal–Mart Stores, Inc., 250 F.3d 618, 621 (8th Cir. 2001) (decided under Arkansas conflict law; stating that the court "has been especially hesitant to pronounce the better law when other Leflar factors point decidedly towards the application of one state's law."); Ferren v. General Motors Corp. Delco Battery Div., 137 N.H. 423, 628 A.2d 265, 269 (1993); Lessard v. Clarke, 143 N.H. 555, 736 A.2d 1226 (1999); Najarian v. National Amusements, Inc., 768 A.2d 1253 (R.I.2001); Nodak Mut. Ins. Co. v. American Family Mut. Ins. Co., 604 N.W.2d 91 (Minn.2000).

forum may disregard its own arguably better law when other factors point to application of foreign law.[29] Conversely, the better foreign law might be ignored if local interests predominate.[30] In such cases, the decision is based essentially on the governmental interests of the forum and the better law question does not come into play.[31] *Clark* thus did not reach an unwarranted or unprincipled result. The Second Restatement or interest analysis alone would have reached a similar result.[32]

§ 17.22 The extreme to which the "better law" approach can be taken is evidenced by two guest-statute cases, *Conklin v. Horner*[1] and *Milkovich v. Saari.*[2] Both cases presented the reverse situation from that involved in *Clark* or the classic case of *Babcock v. Jackson.*[3] The parties were domiciled in a guest-statute state, while the accident occurred in the forum state which did not have such a statute and thus allowed recovery. Both courts chose forum law but, rather than basing their choice solely on the better-law criterion, they also invoked the forum's real or ostensible interests in applying its pro-recovery law. In *Conklin,* the forum's interests were said to be compensation for accident victims, protection of medical creditors, and the greater deterrent value of the common law standard of care. *Milkovich* noted the same concerns and found in addition that, as a "justice administering state,"[4] the forum was bound to do right by this plaintiff. Thus, rather than being false conflicts in which only the common-domicile states were interested in applying their laws, these became true conflicts in which the forum was also interested. Whether the forum's interests were equally strong as those of the common domicile is, of course, another question that most courts have answered in the negative. In fact, *Conklin* and *Milkovich* are the

---

29. Thus in Schneider v. Schneider, 110 N.H. 70, 260 A.2d 97 (1969), Massachusetts' interests in its interspousal immunity doctrine were held predominant when Massachusetts spouses were involved in a New Hampshire accident. New Hampshire did not have interspousal immunity. See also the cases cited supra n.28.

30. In Maguire v. Exeter & Hampton Elec. Co., supra n.27, this reasoning enabled the New Hampshire court to deny the survivors of a Maine decedent (killed while working for a New Hampshire defendant at New Hampshire job site) the benefit of Maine's unlimited wrongful death recovery. The court recognized the inferiority of the local damage limitation but concluded that the forum had sufficient interests to warrant application of local law.

31. See, e.g., Schwartz v. Consolidated Freightways Corp., 300 Minn. 487, 493, 221 N.W.2d 665, 669 (1974), appeal after remand 306 Minn. 564, 237 N.W.2d 385 (1975) ("[W]e hold that Minnesota's governmental interest in this case is sufficient to apply the Minnesota comparative negligence statute rather than the contributory negligence law of the State of Indiana so

that we need not decide the case under the better-law rule....")

32. See the *Babcock*-pattern cases discussed infra § 17.39; S. Symeonides, The American Choice-of-Law Revolution in the Courts: Today and Tomorrow, 298 Recueil des Cours, 1, 178–183 (2003).

§ 17.22

1. 38 Wis.2d 468, 157 N.W.2d 579 (1968), critically noted in Weintraub, Commentary on the Conflict of Laws 417–18 (4th ed. 2001).

2. 295 Minn. 155, 203 N.W.2d 408 (1973) (critically noted Comment, 58 Minn. L. Rev. 199 (1973)).

3. 12 N.Y.2d 473, 240 N.Y.S.2d 743, 191 N.E.2d 279 (1963) (discussed infra § 17.29.). For a recent New Hampshire case presenting the reverse *Babcock* pattern, see Lessard v. Clarke, 143 N.H. 555, 736 A.2d 1226 (1999) (applying the law of Ontario, the parties' common domicile, which provided for lower-recovery, rather than the law of New Hampshire, the accident state).

4. 295 Minn. at 170, 203 N.W.2d at 417.

only state supreme court decisions involving guest-statute conflicts of this pattern that did *not* apply the law of the parties' common domicile.[5]

Even when judged from the perspective of the better-law approach, these two cases seem to take the "better law" factor far beyond the extent *Clark* envisioned. In *Clark*, both parties were forum domiciliaries and the court was careful to note that sufficient contacts with both the parties and the occurrence were necessary:[6] better law was not simply to mean forum preference.[7] Both the *Conklin* and *Milkovich* courts ignored these caveats, apparently because they considered the foreign guest statute to be repugnant to their sense of justice and fairness.[8] If so, the use of the "better law" criterion became the functional equivalent of the traditional public policy exception to the application of foreign law.[9]

§ 17.23 However, the public policy exception has traditionally been narrowly construed. As best explained by Justice Cardozo, the exception allows a court to disregard otherwise applicable law only when that law "violate[s] some fundamental principle of justice, some prevalent conception of good morals, some deep rooted tradition of the common weal."[1] Use of this defensive *exception* as a choice-of-law *theory* has rightly been criticized as a "beguilingly easy [devise that] does not demand the hard thinking which careful formulation of narrower, more realistic, choice of law rules would require."[2] The traditional narrow construction of the exception, moreover, results from the acceptance of the view that courts should be required to articulate exactly why the foreign law is "pernicious and detestable."[3]

The "better law" approach—especially when the better-law criterion is the court's first rather than last resort[4]—provides far greater leeway

---

5. For documentation, see S. Symeonides, The American Choice-of-Law Revolution in the Courts: Today and Tomorrow, 298 Recueil des Cours, 1, 183–187 (2003). Even in cases involving the same pattern but issues other than guest statutes, the author identifies only two other cases that did *not* apply the law of the parties' common domicile. One of those cases (Arnett v. Thompson, 433 S.W.2d 109 (Ky. 1968), discussed supra § 17.13) was decided under Kentucky's *lex fori* approach, while the second case (Martineau v. Guertin, 170 Vt. 415, 751 A.2d 776 (2000)) was factually exceptional because, although the parties in were domiciled in the same state, they both resided in another state, and the accident occurred in a third state, the law of which was identical to the residence state.

6. See supra text accompanying § 17.21 nn.25–26.

7. See Jepson v. General Cas. Co. of Wisconsin, 513 N.W.2d 467, 473 (Minn. 1994): "If [it] were true [that] forum law would always be the better law ... [then] this step in our choice of law analysis would be meaningless."

8. Earlier Minnesota cases, while noting that the local common law rule was the better rule, did not resort to the doctrine because the facts permitted a satisfactory resolution on the basis of "significant contacts." Note, 58 Minn. L. Rev. 199, 201–02 n.17 (1973).

9. See generally Paulsen & Sovern, Public Policy in the Conflict of Laws, 56 Colum. L. Rev. 969 (1956). See also supra § 3.16.

§ 17.23

1. Loucks v. Standard Oil Co., 224 N.Y. 99, 111, 120 N.E. 198, 202 (1918). See also supra §§ 3.15–16.

2. See Paulsen & Sovern, Public Policy in the Conflict of Laws, 56 Colum. L. Rev. 969 (1956).

3. Goodrich, Foreign Facts and Local Fancies, 25 Va. L. Rev. 26, 33 (1938).

4. See supra § 2.13 at n.10. Unavoidably, there will be cases when analysis of competing interests, both public and private, will not provide clear answers. In such cases, courts will, and should, decide ac-

because a mere statement of the preference (or dislike) seems to suffice. This leeway combined with the selectivity with which this approach may be used—alone or mingled with interest analysis—can serve to disguise many other preferences or biases, either separately or in combination, such as a preference for forum law,[5] forum plaintiffs,[6] or forum defendants,[7] or a preference for recovery.[8] Evidence of these biases was conspicuous and plentiful in the cases decided under the better-law approach before the mid 1990s.[9] In later cases, these biases appear to be less pronounced, perhaps because, as noted earlier,[10] most of the states that initially adopted this approach have already begun to combine it with other approaches, and to de-emphasize the better-law factor. Indeed, in recent years, some courts have expressed misgivings on their

cording to what is deemed "better." Recognition of the fact that a "better law" criterion as a last resort has been and will be part of judicial practice does not warrant elevating this criterion into a first-line factor in choice-of-law methodology.

5. See supra § 2.13 nn. 14–21; S. Symeonides, The American Choice-of-Law Revolution in the Courts: Today and Tomorrow, 298 Recueil des Cours, 1, 110–112 (2003).

6. For example, as one author notes, "four of the five tort conflicts decided by the Rhode Island Supreme Court applied the law of the forum and granted recovery to a forum plaintiff." Symeonides, supra n. 5, at 112. He cites Woodward v. Stewart, 104 R.I. 290, 243 A.2d 917 (1968); Brown v. Church of the Holy Name of Jesus, 105 R.I. 322, 252 A.2d 176 (1969); Pardey v. Boulevard Billiard Club, 518 A.2d 1349 (R.I. 1986); and Cribb v. Augustin, 696 A.2d 285 (R.I. 1997). In the fifth case, Victoria v. Smythe, 703 A.2d 619 (R.I. 1997), the court applied non-forum law, but that law favored the forum plaintiff as much as the forum's law. See also La Plante v. American Honda Motor Co., Inc., 27 F.3d 731 (1st Cir. 1994) (decided under Rhode Island conflicts law; applying the forum's pro-recovery law to a products liability action in which the forum's only contact was the plaintiff's domicile). The author also notes that, "in two of the three cases in which the Minnesota Supreme Court applied foreign law (in both tort and contract conflicts), that law benefitted a forum plaintiff," Symeonides, supra at 112, and that "of the six tort conflicts decided by the New Hampshire Supreme Court, two cases applied forum law for the benefit of a forum plaintiff, three applied forum law for the benefit of a foreign plaintiff, and the sixth case applied forum law for the benefit of a forum defendant." Id. Finally, the author notes that, in the five states that follow Leflar's approach for tort conflicts, one finds only four supreme court

cases applying foreign law, "but—perhaps not coincidentally—in two of these cases that law favored a forum plaintiff." Symeonides, supra, at 111. (In the other two cases, the foreign law was, or became, the same as the forum's. See id.). See also Boatwright v. Budak, 625 N.W.2d 483 (Minn. App.2001) (holding that Iowa law was better than Minnesota's in that it provided recovery for a Minnesota plaintiff who was injured in an Iowa traffic accident while riding in a car owned by defendant, a national car rental company.)

7. See, e.g., Lommen v. The City of East Grand Forks, 522 N.W.2d 148 (Minn. Ct.App.1994). This case arose out of North Dakota accident caused by a Minnesota police officer who had pursued a stolen pickup truck at a high speed from Minnesota into North Dakota. The case ended in a collision with another vehicle in which plaintiff, an unsuspecting resident of North Dakota, was a passenger. She brought a personal injury action in Minnesota against the officer's employer, the City of East Grand Forks, Minnesota, but not North Dakota, provided immunity for the city. The court concluded that "overall the relevant considerations favor application of Minnesota law ... [because] Minnesota's ability to define the immunity of its officials should not vary according to the fortuitous facts of either the location of the accident or the citizenship of the injured party." Id. at 152. The court stated that "we do not prefer Minnesota law ... simply because Minnesota is the forum," id. at 151; that "North Dakota would not be offended by application of Minnesota law," id. at 151; and that "a North Dakota court, applying the Leflar methodology, would likely also choose Minnesota law." Id.

8. See supra n. 6.

9. For documentation, see Symeonides, supra n. 5, at 110–114.

10. See supra § 17.21 nn.18–21.

ability to determine which law is better,[11] or have tried to dispel the notion that better law and forum law are synonymous terms,[12] while other courts have employed the better-law criterion only as a tie-breaker,[13] or ignored it altogether.[14]

D. THE MOST–SIGNIFICANT–RELATIONSHIP TEST AND THE SECOND RESTATEMENT

1. *Introduction*

§ 17.24   The pervasive principle offered by the Second Restatement for choice of law also applies to torts: tort issues are to be determined by the law of the state that, with regard to the particular issue, has the "most significant relationship" to the occurrence and the parties.[1] The

11. See, e.g., Jepson v. General Cas. Co. of Wisconsin, 513 N.W.2d 467, 473 (Minn. 1994) ("Sometimes different laws are neither better nor worse in an objective way, just different. Because we do not find either stacking or anti-stacking to be a better rule in the sense Leflar intended, this consideration does not influence our choice of law."); Lommen v. The City of East Grand Forks, 522 N.W.2d 148, 152 (Minn.Ct.App. 1994) ("[N]either Minnesota's nor North Dakota's law is 'better' than the other ... neither ... is demonstrably antiquated or plainly unfair.... [They] simply differ."); Kenna v. So–Fro Fabrics, Inc., 18 F.3d 623, 627 (8th Cir. 1994) ("[W]e are not in a position to decide that either [state's law] is the better rule of law."); Lessard v. Clarke, 143 N.H. 555, 736 A.2d 1226, 1229 (1999) (expressing skepticism on whether "New Hampshire damages law is 'wiser, sounder, and better calculated to serve the total ends of justice,' ... than the competing law of Ontario."); Hughes v. Wal–Mart Stores, Inc., 250 F.3d 618, 621 (8th Cir. 2001) ("Courts often refrain from resolving a conflict of law question based on the better rule of law factor ... [because] laws do not necessarily lend themselves to being labeled either 'better' or 'worse.' ")

12. *Jepson*, 513 N.W.2d at 473 ("If [it] were true [that] forum law would always be the better law ... [then] this step in our choice of law analysis would be meaningless".) See also Boatwright v. Budak, 625 N.W.2d 483 (Minn. App. 2001) (holding that non-forum law was better than forum law).

13. See Nesladek v. Ford Motor Co., 876 F.Supp. 1061, 1070 (D. Minn. 1994) (stating that the better-law factor need not be considered when Minnesota's other choice-influencing factors "clearly dictate the application of one state's law."); Hughes v. Wal-Mart Stores, Inc., 250 F.3d 618, 621 (8th Cir. 2001) (stating that the court "has been

especially hesitant to pronounce the better law when other Leflar factors point decidedly towards the application of one state's law."); Ferren v. General Motors Corp. Delco Battery Div., 137 N.H. 423, 628 A.2d 265, 269 (1993); Nodak Mut. Ins. Co. v. American Family Mut. Ins. Co., 604 N.W.2d 91 (Minn. 2000); Lessard v. Clark, 143 N.H. 555, 736 A.2d 1226 (1999).

14. See Najarian v. National Amusements, Inc., 768 A.2d 1253 (R.I. 2001). In Nodak Mut. Ins. Co. v. American Family Mut. Ins. Co., 604 N.W.2d 91 (Minn.2000), the supreme court of Minnesota noted that "this court has not placed any emphasis on [the better-law] factor in nearly 20 years," id. at 96, prompting a lower Minnesota court to conclude that this factor "has been abandoned in recent years." Montpetit v. Allina Health System, Inc., 2000 WL 1486581 at *3 (Minn.App.2000). But see Boatwright v. Budak, 625 N.W.2d 483 (Minn.App.2001) (employing the better-law criterion and holding that non-forum law was better than forum law in that it provided recovery for a forum domiciliary against a national car rental company.)

§ 17.24

1. Restatement, Second, Conflict of Laws § 145(1) (1971) ("The General Principle"). For a more detailed discussion of the Restatement, see supra § 2.14. With respect to the Restatement's issue-orientation, see supra § 2.14 n.19. In assessing the Second Restatement, the Swiss scholar Professor Vischer arrived at the conclusion that its methodology represents a revival of statutist thinking (supra § 2.3). Unlike Continental approaches which seek to identify the "seat of the legal relationship" or the closest geographic connection, the Restatement is said to be concerned with the identification of state interests in the applica-

general principle is not explicitly defined; its elements, however, consist of the relevant contacts listed in § 145(2)[2] and the value goals set out in § 6.[3] The process is complicated by the fact that the Restatement assigns no particular weight or priority to the contacts of § 145 or to the principles of § 6. The analysis may therefore vary from issue to issue as well as from fact situation to fact situation containing identical issues.[4] Unlike its predecessor, the Second Restatement thus does not contain rules but an "approach."[5] However, the Second Restatement's approach provides a basis from which courts can create a body of specific rules covering specific situations.[6]

An examination of the principles of § 6 shows the substantial influence that the Second Restatement and other modern choice of law theories[7] have had on each other. Governmental interests analysis and a policy-oriented approach are suggested by § 6(2)(b) and (c), which require that the relevant policies of the forum and other interested states be considered. The list of principles encompass all of Leflar's choice-influencing considerations except that of the "better rule of law."[8] Finally, the Restatement provides no guidance or direction as to how a court should analyze "interests;" it thus accommodates aspects of the functionalist or interest-weighing approach.[9] At the same time, however, the Restatement maintains an important link with the past by retaining the place of the wrong as a relevant connecting factor.

§ 17.25 The general rule of § 145 (in combination with the principles of § 6) is particularized, and therefore provides more definite guidance, with respect to particular torts or individual tort issues. Thus § 146 provides that, in an action for personal injuries, "the local law of the state where the injury occurred determines the rights and liabilities

---

tion of local law or the scope and policy of a potentially applicable law, especially statutory law. Vischer, Das neue Restatement "Conflict of Laws," 38 Rabels Zeitschrift 128, 137–138 (1974). This assessment more accurately describes interest analysis than the Second Restatement. Interest analysis and policy determination do have their place in the Restatement's methodology. Its purpose, however, is to localize issues (see infra § 17.27 n.7), and, more importantly, through its "approach" to aid in the development of rules. See Reese, Choice of Law: Rules or Approach?, 57 Cornell L. Rev. 315 (1972); Reese, Choice of Law in Torts and Contracts and Directions for the Future, 16 Colum. J. Transnat'l L. 1, 16 (1977).

2. The contacts are (a) the place where the injury occurred, (b) the place where the conduct causing the injury occurred, (c) the domicil, residence, nationality, place of incorporation and place of business of the parties, and (d) the place where the relationship, if any, between the parties is centered. This list is not exclusive: Section 145(2) provides that "Contacts to be taken

into account ... include...." Thus, in any given case, contacts peculiar to the particular fact situation or issue may be considered.

3. See supra text at § 2.14 nn. 5–6.

4. See McDougal, Felix & Whitten, American Conflicts Law 337–38 (5th ed. 2001).

5. Reese, Choice of Law: Rules or Approach, 57 Cornell L. Rev. 315 (1972); see supra § 2.14.

6. See supra § 2.14 nn.44–47 *passim.*

7. Supra § 2.14.

8. Supra § 2.14 n.6.

9. The reasons include that substantive rules of law often were not established with the conflicts context in mind and that, even in the intrastate context, they may be designed to address varied needs and purposes. A choice-of-law rule of general applicability, therefore, cannot be abstracted from them but must be the result of policy analysis. See Restatement, Second, Conflict of Laws § 6, cmnts. (c), (e) (1971).

of the parties, unless, with respect to the particular issue, some other state has a more significant relationship under the principles of § 6 to the occurrence and the parties...." The same preference for the local law of the place of the injury is expressed with respect to the following issues: the tortious character of the conduct (§ 156), the standard of care (§ 157), the determination of whether an interest is entitled to legal protection (§ 158), the duty owed to the plaintiff (§ 159), causation (§ 160), conditions for liability (§ 162), contributory fault and assumption of risk (§§ 164, 165), imputed negligence (§ 166), and joint liability (§ 172). An exception is § 169 which refers questions of intra-family immunity to the local law of the parties' domicile. These sections on particular tort issues differ from § 146 (on personal injuries) in the emphasis they place on the law of the state of the injury. While § 146 makes primary reference to that law, the sections addressing particular tort issues refer first to § 145 (the general "most significant relationship" test) and, in a second subsection, particularize that the "applicable law will usually be the local law of the state where the injury occurred" (or, in § 169, the state of the parties' domicile).

For a number of other tort issues, the Restatement simply cross-references to the most-significant-relationship test of § 145, either because they are intimately related to the main claim or because they represent pervasive issues. Examples include: defenses (§ 161), duty or privilege to act (§ 163), survival of actions (§ 166), charitable immunity (§ 168), damages (§ 171), and contribution (§ 173). The Restatement extends this approach also to releases and covenants not to sue (§ 170) as well as to indemnity (§ 173), although, depending on the circumstances, a contract characterization may be more appropriate and, in some cases, would produce a different result.[1]

2. The Case Law

§ 17.26 *Kennedy v. Dixon*[1] illustrates the typical tort conflicts problem and its resolution by use of the "most significant relationship"

§ 17.25

1. Since the principal reference in the sections cited is to § 145, the result may often be expected to be the same as if § 188 had been applied: both specify the law of the state of the most significant relationship to the occurrence or contract, respectively, and to the parties. Occasionally, however, the result will differ depending on the characterization. In Bittner v. Little, 270 F.2d 286 (3d Cir. 1959), the plaintiff was injured in Virginia. He executed a release to one of the joint tortfeasors in New York, reserving his rights against the other. The reservation was valid in New York, but not in Virginia. The court applied the law of Virginia, as the place of the tort. Under the Restatement, § 146 (on personal injuries) would presumably also apply Virginia law to the tort, while § 170 refers to the most-

significant-relationship test of § 145 with respect to the release. It is possible, but perhaps not likely, that application of § 145 in these circumstances would result in the selection of a different law for the release than that applicable to the tort under § 146. In contrast, use of § 188, under a contract characterization, would insure appropriate consideration of the intent of the parties. The same concerns are applicable to the Restatement's tort characterization of contracts not to sue or to indemnify. See also McDougal, Felix & Whitten, American Conflicts Law 458 (5th ed. 2001). For additional discussion of particular torts, see infra § 17.51 et seq.

§ 17.26

1. 439 S.W.2d 173 (Mo.1969) (en banc). In alphabetical order by state, other cases that adopted the Restatement Second approach include: *Alaska:* Ehredt v. DeHavilland Aircraft Co. of Canada, Ltd., 705 P.2d 446, 453 (Alaska 1985) (relying exclusively on the Second Restatement); Armstrong v. Armstrong, 441 P.2d 699, 701–03 (Alaska 1968) (relying partly on the Second Restatement); *Arizona:* Schwartz v. Schwartz, 103 Ariz. 562, 447 P.2d 254 (1968) (interspousal immunity); Bryant v. Silverman, 146 Ariz. 41, 703 P.2d 1190 (1985); *Arkansas:* Williams v. State Farm Mut. Auto. Ins. Co., 737 F.2d 741 (8th Cir.1984), cert. denied 470 U.S. 1039, 105 S.Ct. 1414, 84 L.Ed.2d 800 (1985); but see Schlemmer v. Fireman's Fund Ins. Co., 292 Ark. 344, 730 S.W.2d 217 (1987); *Colorado:* First National Bank in Fort Collins v. Rostek, 182 Colo. 437, 514 P.2d 314 (1973) (guest statute) (discussed infra § 17.28); Conlin v. Hutcheon, 560 F.Supp. 934 (D.Colo.1983); Bolduc v. Bailey, 586 F.Supp. 896 (D.Colo.1984); Scheer v. Scheer, 881 P.2d 479 (Colo.App.1994); *Connecticut:* O'Connor v. O'Connor, 201 Conn. 632, 519 A.2d 13 (1986); Williams v. State Farm Mut. Auto. Ins. Co., 229 Conn. 359, 641 A.2d 783 (1994); *Delaware:* Travelers Indem. Co. v. Lake, 594 A.2d 38 (Del.1991); *District of Columbia:* Eli Lilly & Co. v. Home Ins. Co., 764 F.2d 876 (D.C.Cir.1985), conformed 794 F.2d 710 (D.C.Cir.1986), cert. denied 479 U.S. 1060, 107 S.Ct. 940, 93 L.Ed.2d 991 (1987); Pearce v. E.F. Hutton Group, Inc., 664 F.Supp. 1490 (D.D.C. 1987). Later cases have applied interest analysis. See, e.g., Rong Yao Zhou v. Jennifer Mall Rest., Inc., 534 A.2d 1268, 1270 (D.C.1987); *Florida:* Bishop v. Florida Specialty Paint Co., 389 So.2d 999, 1001 (Fla. 1980); Peoples Bank & Trust Co. v. Piper Aircraft Corp., 598 F.Supp. 377 (S.D.Fla. 1984); Foster v. United States, 768 F.2d 1278 (11th Cir.1985); Donaldson v. United States, 634 F.Supp. 735, 737 (S.D.Fla.1986); *Idaho:* Johnson v. Pischke, 108 Idaho 397, 700 P.2d 19, 22 (Idaho 1985); *Illinois:* Thera–Kinetics, Inc. v. Managed Home Recovery, Inc., 1997 WL 610305 (N.D.Ill. 1997); Pinorsky v. Pinorsky, 217 Ill.App.3d 165, 576 N.E.2d 1123, 160 Ill.Dec. 169 (1991); Ingersoll v. Klein, 46 Ill.2d 42, 262 N.E.2d 593 (1970) (wrongful death); Nelson v. Hix, 122 Ill.2d 343, 119 Ill.Dec. 355, 522 N.E.2d 1214 (1988), cert. denied 488 U.S. 925, 109 S.Ct. 309, 102 L.Ed.2d 328 (1988) (interspousal tort immunity); Mech v. Pullman Standard, 136 Ill.App.3d 939, 92 Ill. Dec. 45, 484 N.E.2d 776 (1984) (contribution and indemnity); Intamin, Inc. v. Figley–Wright Contractors, Inc., 605 F.Supp. 707 (N.D.Ill.1985) (same); Barry Gilberg, Ltd. v. Craftex Corp., Inc., 665 F.Supp. 585 (N.D.Ill.1987) (prima facie tort and unfair

competition claims); Kolentus v. Avco Corp., 798 F.2d 949 (7th Cir.1986), cert. denied 479 U.S. 1032, 107 S.Ct. 878, 93 L.Ed.2d 832 (1987); *Indiana:* Hubbard Mfg. Co. v. Greeson, 515 N.E.2d 1071, 1073–74 (Ind.1987) (holding that "when the place of the tort is an insignificant contact," the court will turn to the Second Restatement, but stopping short of embracing the policy-analysis component of the Restatement); Kolentus v. Avco Corp., 798 F.2d 949 (7th Cir.1986), cert. denied 479 U.S. 1032, 107 S.Ct. 878, 93 L.Ed.2d 832 (1987); *Iowa:* Veasley v. CRST Int'l, Inc., 553 N.W.2d 896 (Iowa 1996) (negligence); Fuerste v. Bemis, 156 N.W.2d 831 (Iowa 1968) (guest statute); *Maine:* Beaulieu v. Beaulieu, 265 A.2d 610 (Me.1970) (guest statute); Adams v. Buffalo Forge Co., 443 A.2d 932, 934 (Me.1982); Collins v. Trius, Inc., 663 A.2d 570 (Me. 1995); Mason v. Southern New England Conf. Ass'n, etc., 696 F.2d 135 (1st Cir. 1982); *Massachusetts:* Bushkin Assocs., Inc. v. Raytheon Co., 393 Mass. 622, 473 N.E.2d 662, 668 (1985). The Court declined "to tie Massachusetts conflicts law to any specific choice-of-law doctrine" but said that it would follow both the Second Restatement and Leflar's approach. A subsequent federal decision held, with express reference to *Bushkin,* that the "right of publicity" was governed by the law of the residence of the performers' exclusive licensee and not by the law of the performers' nationality. The analysis relied exclusively on the Second Restatement. Bi–Rite Enterps., Inc. v. Bruce Miner Co., Inc., 757 F.2d 440 (1st Cir.1985); *Mississippi:* Mitchell v. Craft, 211 So.2d 509, 515 (Miss.1968); O'Rourke v. Colonial Ins. Co. of CA, 624 So.2d 84 (Miss. 1993) (uninsured motorist benefits); Davis v. National Gypsum Co., 743 F.2d 1132 (5th Cir.1984); Price v. Litton Systems, Inc., 784 F.2d 600 (5th Cir.1986), on remand 651 F.Supp. 706 (S.D.Miss.1986); *Montana:* Phillips v. General Motors Corp., 298 Mont. 438, 995 P.2d 1002 (2000) (products liability); *Nebraska:* Harper v. Silva, 224 Neb. 645, 399 N.W.2d 826 (1987); *North Dakota:* Plante v. Columbia Paints, 494 N.W.2d 140 (N.D.1992) (products liability); Issendorf v. Olson, 194 N.W.2d 750 (N.D.1972) (contributory/comparative negligence); *Ohio:* Morgan v. Biro Mfg. Co., 15 Ohio St.3d 339, 474 N.E.2d 286, 288 (1984); Amon v. Grange Mut. Cas. Co., 112 Ohio App.3d 407, 678 N.E.2d 1002 (1996); Sholes v. Agency Rent-a-Car, Inc., 76 Ohio App.3d 349, 601 N.E.2d 634 (1991); Bowman v. Koch Transfer Co., 862 F.2d 1257 (6th Cir.1988); *Oklahoma:* Brickner v. Gooden, 525 P.2d 632 (Okl. 1974); *Oregon:* Casey v. Manson Constr. and Eng'g Co., 247 Or. 274, 428 P.2d 898

test. The fact pattern is the familiar one of *Babcock v. Jackson*.[2] In *Kennedy,* a St. Louis couple was accompanied on a trip to New York by a neighbor. On the return trip, an accident in Indiana resulted in the death of the driver and in injury to the neighbor, who brought suit against the driver's estate. Unlike the Missouri forum, Indiana, the state of the accident, had a guest statute that would have barred the plaintiff's claim. The decision adopted the "most significant relationship" test of the Second Restatement and addressed the problem of how that test is to be applied: "[W]e do not engage in the mere counting of the number of contacts but must evaluate them in order to determine what state has the most significant contacts."[3] The evaluation of the relevant contacts did not specifically refer to the principles of § 6, but is implicit in the analysis.[4] The court considered the Missouri contacts (domicile of the parties and center of their relationship to each other, origin and final destination of the trip), as well as Missouri's policy of protecting guests against negligent hosts. It concluded that forum law should govern the question of liability.

The same conclusion could have been reached by using interest analysis.[5] Indeed, since no Indiana parties were involved in the accident and since a guest statute is not intended to regulate the driver's conduct, Indiana would not have been an interested state: the case presented a "false conflict," a simple case under any modern choice-of-law theory. The Missouri court did not overlook this point when it stated that, in "hard" cases, the Second Restatement would prove less useful than in the *Kennedy v. Dixon* situation.[6]

(1967) (consortium), discussed infra at § 17.27. Later cases abandoned the Second Restatement in favor of a mixed approach that includes reliance on the Restatement. *Puerto Rico:* Leslie v. Construcciones Aeronauticas, 896 F.Supp. 243 (P.R. 1995); Jimenez v. American Airlines, Inc., 579 F.Supp. 631 (D.P.R.1983); for the Puerto Rican draft statute, see supra § 17.20 n.1. *South Dakota*: Chambers v. Dakotah Charter, Inc., 488 N.W.2d 63, 67 (S.D.1992); *Tennessee*: Hataway v. McKinley, 830 S.W.2d 53, 59 (Tenn.1992); *Texas:* Gutierrez v. Collins, 583 S.W.2d 312, 318 (Tex.1979); Robertson v. Estate of McKnight, 609 S.W.2d 534 (Tex.1980); Ritzmann v. Weekly World News, Inc., 614 F.Supp. 1336 (N.D.Tex. 1985) (defamation and invasion of privacy); Faloona v. Hustler Magazine, Inc., 799 F.2d 1000 (5th Cir.1986), cert. denied 479 U.S. 1088, 107 S.Ct. 1295, 94 L.Ed.2d 151 (1987); *Utah*: Forsman v. Forsman, 779 P.2d 218, 220 (Utah 1989); *Vermont*: Amiot v. Ames, 166 Vt. 288, 693 A.2d 675, 677 (1997); *Washington:* Williams v. State of Washington and State of Oregon, 76 Wash. App. 237, 885 P.2d 845 (1994) (wrongful death); Johnson v. Spider Staging Corp., 87

Wn.2d 577, 555 P.2d 997 (1976) (wrongful death); Werner v. Werner, 84 Wash.2d 360, 526 P.2d 370, 376 (1974); In re New England Fish Co., 749 F.2d 1277 (9th Cir.1984).

2. Discussed infra § 17.29.

3. *Kennedy*, 439 S.W.2d at 184.

4. See Haworth, The Mirror Image Conflicts Case: *Griggs v. Riley*, 1974 Wash. L.Q. 1, 6.

5. Comment, Changes in Tort Conflict of Laws in Missouri, 37 Mo. L. Rev. 268, 280 (1972). Cf. Johnson v. Spider Staging Corp., 87 Wn.2d 577, 555 P.2d 997 (1976).

6. *Kennedy*, 439 S.W.2d at 185. The court stated that, when the place of the "most significant relationship" cannot be determined, " ... the trial court should continue, as in the past, to apply the substantive law of the place of the tort." Id. For criticism of this view see Comment supra n.5, at 280; Haworth, supra n.4, at 7. However, the leading case of Neumeier v. Kuehner, 31 N.Y.2d 121, 335 N.Y.S.2d 64, 286 N.E.2d 454 (1972), appeal after remand 43 A.D.2d 109, 349 N.Y.S.2d 866 (1973) adopted this approach (see infra § 17.31).

Since *Kennedy*, many cases involving this pattern—situations in which the parties are domiciled in the same pro-recovery state and are involved in an accident in another state whose law limits or denies recovery—have not only been resolved in the same way through the application of the common-domicile law but have led to the abandonment of the *lex loci delicti* rule in favor of the Second Restatement.[7] A recent one among them is *Miller v. White*,[8] which applied Vermont law to an action between Vermont parties arising out of a single-car accident in Quebec.[9] The plaintiff would be entitled to a tort action under Vermont law, but not under Quebec law which confined the plaintiff to an administrative remedy and a much lower recovery. After discussing §§ 6 and 145 of the Second Restatement, the court emphasized the issue-by-issue feature of the Restatement's analysis and cited with approval the

Accord Restatement, Second, Conflict of Laws § 146. See also Reese, The Kentucky Approach to Choice of Law: A Critique, 61 Ky. L.J. 368 (1972–73) (discussing the "hard case" of Foster v. Leggett, 484 S.W.2d 827 (Ky.1972)). Unfortunately, imprecision in the court's language in *Kennedy* led to a troublesome decision in the Missouri Court of Appeals. In Griggs v. Riley, 489 S.W.2d 469 (Mo.App.1972), the court was faced with the reverse of *Kennedy*. The guest and host were Illinois domiciliaries and the accident occurred in Missouri. The situation was complicated by the existence of a second defendant, a Missouri resident who, under Missouri's contribution doctrine, could seek contribution from the host if he could be reached by the guest-plaintiff. The Illinois guest statute would have barred the suit against the host. Despite careful attention to the interaction between §§ 145 and 146, the court noted the "escape valve" language in *Kennedy* and the existence of two Missouri interests—compensation of those injured by negligence and protection of the Missouri defendants' right to contribution. The court held forum law to be applicable. Professor Reese, commenting on similar facts involved in Arnett v. Thompson, 433 S.W.2d 109 (Ky.1968), stated that it "seems reasonably clear" that the Second Restatement necessitated the opposite result. *Griggs* is critically noted in Haworth, supra n.4. Compare Byrn v. American Universal Ins. Co., 548 S.W.2d 186 (Mo.App.1977).

7. See infra § 17.39; S. Symeonides, The American Choice-of-Law Revolution in the Courts: Today and Tomorrow, 298 Recueil des Cours, 1, 178–183 (2003). For cases litigated in the common domicile, see O'Connor v. O'Connor, 201 Conn. 632, 519 A.2d 13 (1986) (applying Connecticut's pro-recovery law to action between Connecticut parties arising from traffic accident in Que-

bec, the law of which limited recovery); Travelers Indem. Co. v. Lake, 594 A.2d 38 (Del.1991) (applying Delaware's pro-recovery law to action between Delaware parties arising from traffic accident in Quebec, the law of which limited recovery). For cases litigated in the accident state, see Forsman v. Forsman, 779 P.2d 218 (Utah 1989) (applying California's pro-recovery law (non-immunity) to action between California spouses arising out of traffic accident in Utah, the law of which denied recovery (interspousal immunity)); Nelson v. Hix, 122 Ill.2d 343, 119 Ill.Dec. 355, 522 N.E.2d 1214 (1988), *cert. denied*, 488 U.S. 925, 109 S.Ct. 309, 102 L.Ed.2d 328 (1988) (applying Ontario's pro-recovery law (non-immunity) to action between Ontario spouses arising out of traffic accident in Illinois, the law of which (inter-spousal immunity) denied recovery).

8. 167 Vt. 45, 702 A.2d 392 (1997). The Supreme Court of Vermont adopted the Second Restatement in Amiot v. Ames, 166 Vt. 288, 693 A.2d 675 (1997), decided six months before *Miller*. However, *Miller* was the first case to actually *apply* the Restatement.

9. Plaintiff, defendant, and a group of friends drove from Vermont to Quebec, where the lower drinking age allowed them to drink legally. Shortly after leaving the bar and while still in Quebec, defendant drove off the road causing an accident in which plaintiff, a passenger in defendant's car, was injured. Another injured passenger sued the same defendant in federal court. See Griffith v. White, 929 F.Supp. 755 (D.Vt.1996). In contrast to *Miller*, the plaintiff in *Griffith* was not a domiciliary of Vermont but simply attended college in that state. Following the Restatement Second, the *Griffith* court held that Vermont law governed because Vermont had the

distinction between issues of conduct regulation and loss distribution.[10] The court characterized the pertinent issue in *Miller* as one that "raises competing policies that allocate post event losses"[11] and concluded that, with regard to such an issue, "the domicile of the parties is the most significant contact bearing on the determination of the relevant law."[12] Then the court examined the policies of the parties' common domicile, Vermont, in juxtaposition with the policies of the state of the accident, Quebec. Vermont's fault-based tort system, said the court, in addition to its compensatory function, "seek[s] to optimize the level of risky activity in society, reduce the occurrence and severity of injury-causing events, and provide relatively clear standards of conduct,"[13] while Quebec's no-fault system "seeks to expedite compensation to victims of automobile accidents, reduce the amount of tort litigation in Quebec courts, and guarantee relatively low automobile-insurance rates."[14] The court concluded that, in light of Vermont's contacts with the case, Vermont, had a "strong interest in applying its law,"[15] and that Quebec had " 'little interest in . . . the rights of action of an United States citizen against another United States citizen in an United States court.' "[16] The court also noted that most American cases involving the same pattern had been decided under the law of the common domicile,[17] and that "application of the law of the parties' domicile to this case would correspond with international norms and promote consistent treatment of accident victims across borders."[18] The court concluded that "the parties' residency

most significant relationship and the exclusive interest in applying its law.

10. See *Miller,* 702 A.2d at 394: ("If conflicting conduct-regulating laws are at issue, the law of the jurisdiction where the tort occurred will generally apply because that jurisdiction has the greatest interest in regulating behavior within its borders. But if competing 'postevent remedial rules' are at stake other factors are taken into consideration, chiefly the parties' domiciles." (quoting Cooney v. Osgood Mach., 81 N.Y.2d 66, 595 N.Y.S.2d 919, 612 N.E.2d 277, 280 (1993)). This distinction is discussed infra §§ 17.36–17.38.

11. *Miller,* 702 A.2d at 394.

12. Id. at 394–95.

13. Id. at 395.

14. Id.

15. Id. at 396. "The domicile of the plaintiff has a significant interest in assuring proper compensation to the victim because the 'social and economic repercussions of personal injury' will occur in plaintiff's domicile. . . . Vermont also has a significant interest in deterring risky behavior by domiciliaries who cross the northern border to take advantage of Quebec's lower drinking age, and generally has an interest in deterring negligent conduct by its licensed operators, wherever that

conduct may occur." Id. (citations omitted.)

16. Id. at 395 (internal quotations are from Reisch v. McGuigan, 745 F.Supp. 56, 61 (D.Mass.1990) and O'Connor v. O'Connor, 201 Conn. 632, 519 A.2d 13, 24 (1986)). The *Miller* court noted: "Pursuit of this claim will not raise insurance rates in Quebec nor hinder the administration of its courts. Quebec does not seek to deter negligent conduct by a fault-based determination of liability." Id. at 395–96. As further evidence of Quebec's "weak interest in this type of action," id. at 396, the court, using a *renvoi* syllogism, cited Quebec's recently enacted choice-of-law rules according to which tort actions involving parties domiciled in the same state are governed by the law of that state. See Quebec Civ. Code Art. 3126. The court took note of the Canadian Supreme Court's decision in Gagnon v. Lucas and Tolofson v. Jensen, 3 S.C.R. 1022, 120 DLR 4th 289 (1994), which had returned to the *lex loci delicti* rule. However, the *Miller* court took comfort in the comments of a Canadian commentator to the effect that *Gagnon/Tolofson* does not preempt Quebec conflicts law. See 702 A.2d at 396 n.3.

17. See *Miller,* 702 A.2d at 397 n.4.

18. Id. at 397.

and relationship in Vermont outweigh the other jurisdictional contacts with Quebec, and ... [hence] Vermont law applies"[19]

The law of the common domicile has also been applied under the Second Restatement to the not-so-false conflicts involved in the converse pattern in which the law of the common domicile is less favorable to recovery than the law of the accident state.[20] Among these cases, the latest is *Collins v. Trius, Inc.*,[21] in which the Supreme Judicial Court of Maine applied the law of the parties' common domicile, Canada, to a claim for pain and suffering arising out of a bus accident that occurred in Maine and involved exclusively Canadian parties.[22] The court noted that "[i]n applying the 'most significant contacts and relationship' test, it is necessary to isolate the issue, to identify the policies embraced in the laws in conflict, and finally to examine the contacts with the

19. Id. See also id. ("[T]he most important contacts for the issue before us are the domiciles of the parties and the place where the relationship between them is centered. Both parties are domiciled in Vermont. Their relationship as long-time friends is centered in Vermont, and the trip during which the accident occurred started and ended in Vermont."

In Matson by Kehoe v. Anctil, 979 F.Supp. 1031 (D.Vt.1997), none of the parties were domiciled in Vermont but they were involved in a traffic accident in that state. The plaintiff, a three-year-old child domiciled with her parents in Rhode Island, was seriously injured when the car in which she was riding, and which was driven by her father, rear-ended a car driven by the defendant, a Quebec domiciliary. In the ensuing personal injury action, defendant filed a third-party claim against plaintiff's parents seeking, *inter alia*, contribution for their fault in the plaintiff's injuries. Such contribution was available under Rhode Island law, but not under Vermont law. Relying on *Miller v. White*, supra n.8, the court began with the Restatement (Second)'s presumption that, in personal injury actions, the state with the most significant relationship "will usually be where the injury occurred." Id. at 1034. After examining the policies of § 6 in light of the factual contacts of § 145, the court concluded that "because both the conduct and the injury occurred in Vermont," id. at 1034, and neither Quebec nor Rhode Island had a more significant contact, Vermont had the most significant relationship and its law should govern. Said the court: "Vermont, as the site of the accident has a strong and obvious interest in 'regulating the conduct of persons within its territory and in providing redress for injuries that occurred there.' " Id., quoting Restatement (Second) § 145 cmnt. (d).

20. See Symeonides, *The Revolution Today*, supra n.7, at 183–194. Hataway v. McKinley, 830 S.W.2d 53 (Tenn.1992) (applying Tennessee's contributory negligence rule rather than Arkansas's comparative negligence rule to action between Tennessee parties arising out of scuba-diving accident in Arkansas); Chambers v. Dakotah Charter, Inc., 488 N.W.2d 63 (S.D.1992) (applying South Dakota's modified comparative negligence rule rather than Missouri's pure comparative negligence rule to action between South Dakota parties arising out of slip and fall accident on a South Dakota bus in Missouri); Ingersoll v. Klein, 46 Ill.2d 42, 262 N.E.2d 593 (1970) (applying Illinois damages law to a case arising from an Iowa accident involving Illinois parties); Issendorf v. Olson, 194 N.W.2d 750 (N.D. 1972) (applying North Dakota contributory negligence rule to a case arising from a Minnesota accident involving North Dakota parties); Johnson v. Pischke, 108 Idaho 397, 700 P.2d 19 (1985) (applying Saskatchewan worker's compensation immunity to a case arising from an Idaho accident involving Saskatchewan parties); Fuerste v. Bemis, 156 N.W.2d 831 (Iowa 1968) (applying Iowa guest statute to case arising from Wisconsin accident involving Iowa parties); Myers v. Langlois, 168 Vt. 432, 721 A.2d 129 (1998) (applying Quebec law and denying a tort action in a dispute between Quebec parties arising out of a Vermont accident).

21. 663 A.2d 570 (Me.1995).

22. The plaintiffs were Canadian residents traveling on a bus from New Brunswick to New York. The bus was owned by a Canadian corporation and was registered in Canada, and the passengers had purchased their tickets in Canada. Canadian law, but not Maine law, limited recovery for nonpecuniary losses.

respective jurisdictions to determine which jurisdiction has a superior interest in having its policy or law applied."[23] The court also noted that "[a]lthough Maine ha[d] a significant interest in regulating conduct on its highways,"[24] the issue at stake was "primarily 'loss-allocating' rather than 'conduct-regulating.' "[25] The court continued as follows:

> [O]ne incontestably valuable contribution of the choice-of-law revolution in the tort conflict field is the line of decisions applying common-domicile law ... The superiority of the common domicile as the source of law governing loss-distribution issues is evident. At its core is the notion of a social contract, whereby a resident assents to casting her lot with others in accepting burdens as well as benefits of identification with a particular community, and ceding to its lawmaking agencies the authority to make judgments striking the balance between her private substantive interests and competing ones of other members of the community.[26]

The court concluded that, in light of the parties' common domicile in Canada and its other contact with the case, "Canada has the most significant interest with respect to the issue of damages for non-pecuniary harm in this case."[27]

§ 17.27 *Casey v. Manson Construction & Engineering Co.*[1] demonstrates that the Second Restatement can be used effectively to resolve the "hard" cases in which the parties are domiciled in different states. The Oregon plaintiff sued for the loss of her husband's consortium when he was injured on the Washington jobsite of his Washington employer. Under the common law rule followed by Washington only a husband had such a cause of action, while no such restriction existed under Oregon law. The Oregon court applied the Washington rule. The court noted that the "most significant relationship" test did not provide an obvious answer to this situation: "Application of that rule to the facts of this case is fraught with difficulty."[2] The place of the accident was not fortuitous, since it was the jobsite and thus the situs of the employer-employee relationship. In addition, the parties were from different states. In terms of interests and contacts, the court found that Oregon's "chief concern [underlying its consortium statute] is that a wife's loss of her husband's society and affection should not go unnoticed."[3] The relevant Washington interest concerned the protection of defendants, particularly business employers, from liability in such situations.[4]

In the court's view, the place of the employer-employee relationship was of prime importance with respect to liability for the husband's

23. *Collins*, 663 A.2d at 573.

24. Id.

25. Id.

26. Id.

27. Id.

§ 17.27

1. 247 Or. 274, 428 P.2d 898 (1967) (critically noted in Tuchler, Oregon Conflicts: Toward an Analysis of Governmental Interests?, 48 Or. L. Rev. 45 (1968)).

2. *Casey*, 247 Or. at 288, 428 P.2d at 905.

3. Id. at 290, 906.

4. Id.

injuries. This view is reasonable because the claim arose from an enterprise risk for which insurance protection could be planned and negotiated.[5] The reference to Washington law also encompassed the plaintiff's action because the Restatement treats a consortium action derivatively: whether suit can be brought depends upon the state with the most significant relationship in the primary action, the husband's suit against the defendant.[6] The result therefore is reached by combining the choice-of-law *approach* of the Restatement, with regard to the husband-defendant relationship, with a *rule* with respect to the availability of a consortium action.[7]

§ **17.28** The Second Restatement was drafted during a period of transition from an inflexible territorialist approach to flexible policy-based approaches.[1] As its chief drafter Willis Reese acknowledged, it was

---

5. See also Wilson v. Faull, 27 N.J. 105, 141 A.2d 768 (1958).

6. Restatement, Second, Conflict of Laws Tentative Draft § 380a, cmnt. (a). This provision is currently found in Restatement, Second, Conflict of Laws § 158(1). Treating the wife's consortium action as derivative of the husband's primary action makes *Casey* analogous to cases like *Foster v. Legett* (discussed supra §§ 17.13, 17.15) in which the conduct, the injury and the tortfeasor's domicile are in a state whose law favors the tortfeasor. As noted by S. Symeonides, The American Choice-of-Law Revolution in the Courts: Today and Tomorrow, 298 Recueil des Cours, 1, 195–203 (2003), 23 of the 24 cases involving this pattern have applied the law of that state as *Casey* did. *Foster* was the only exception.

7. It has been suggested that, despite the foregoing analysis, the *Casey* court merely applied the *lex loci delicti*. See Comment, 48 Or. L. Rev. 45, 64 (1968). This view overlooks that geography remains an important factor in the approach of the Second Restatement which, like its predecessor, seeks to "localize" the tort. It differs from its predecessor by considering all relevant "geographies." Compare Twerski, Enlightened Territorialism and Professor Cavers—The Pennsylvania Method, 9 Duq. L. Rev. 373 (1971). See also supra § 17.24 n.1. It is also important to note that later Oregon cases have not read *Casey*'s rejection of forum preference and acceptance of the Second Restatement as precluding governmental interest analysis or other approaches to choice of law. In DeFoor v. Lematta, 249 Or. 116, 437 P.2d 107 (1968), an Oregon court injected interest analysis into its choice of law. The change in thinking did not affect the result, which would have been similar under the Second Restatement. Scoles, Oregon Conflicts: Three Cases, 49 Or. L. Rev. 273, 281 (1970). See

also Summers v. Interstate Tractor and Equip. Co., 466 F.2d 42, 48 (9th Cir.1972) (wrongful death damages) where, citing *Casey* and *DeFoor*, the court stated: "Oregon has rejected the place of wrong rule in favor of a standard which combines elements of the most significant contacts approach with those of the governmental interests approach."

Erwin v. Thomas, 264 Or. 454, 506 P.2d 494 (1973) (discussed supra § 17.14), presented the consortium issue again, but this time the factual pattern was almost the reverse of *Casey*. The plaintiff wife was a Washington resident whose husband was injured on the Washington worksite of the Oregon defendant-employer. On the basis of interests analysis the court found that neither state had a policy to be furthered through application of its law, that no conflict therefore existed, and that forum law should be applied. Unwilling to overrule *Casey* expressly, the court limited the most significant relationship test to cases presenting actual or true conflicts. See id. at 461–62, 506 P.2d at 497–98. In view of the court's treatment of the acts in *Erwin*, one may wonder if even the limited role that the court preserves for the Restatement will be of any significance. Only pure interest analysis could have led to the conclusion that *Erwin* did not present a true conflict. Thus, the *lex fori* might be applied in all but the most complicated of cases. Accord: Forsyth v. Cessna Aircraft Co., 520 F.2d 608, 612 (9th Cir.1975): "In the absence of a true conflict the lex fori applies." See also the critical analysis of *Erwin* by the Oregon Court of Appeals: Fisher v. Huck, 50 Or. App. 635, 624 P.2d 177 (1981) (discussed supra §§ 2.26 n.6, 17.14 nn.5,8).

§ **17.28**

1. Symeonides, The Need for a Third Conflicts Restatement (And a Proposal for

intended to be "a transitional work."[2] It was "written during a time of turmoil and crisis ... when rival theories were being fiercely debated, and when serious doubt was expressed about the practicality, and indeed the desirability, of having any rules at all."[3] Although Reese believed that "the formulation of rules should be as much an objective in choice of law as it is in other areas of law,"[4] Reese also knew that at that time tort and contract conflicts were not yet ripe for such rules.[5] This is why in these two areas the Second Restatement attempted no more than to "provide formulations that were ... broad enough to permit further development in the law."[6] Reese retained the firm hope, however, that in due time these formulations would permit the development of "more definite"[7] or "precise"[8] choice-of-law rules.

More than three decades after the Restatement's promulgation, it is appropriate to ask whether that time has come. The authors of this book subscribe to an affirmative answer, which they explain later in this chapter.[9] An early example of a judicial exploration of this question can be found in the decision of the Colorado Supreme Court's in *First National Bank in Fort Collins v. Rostek*.[10] A Colorado couple en route to Iowa was killed when the plane piloted by the husband crashed in South Dakota. The guardian of the wife's children brought a wrongful death action against the husband's estate. Application of the *lex loci delicti*, the Colorado choice-of-law rule at the time of the suit, would have left the plaintiff without a claim, because South Dakota's guest statute required proof of willful or wanton negligence by the pilot. Colorado did not have a guest statute. In holding for the plaintiff, the court adopted both specific rules and the "most significant relationship" test. The court endorsed the rejection of the *lex loci delicti*, but also questioned the efficacy of the modern theories, principally on the ground of lack of

Tort Conflicts), 75 Ind. L.J. 437, 443–44 (2000); Richman & Reynolds, Prologomenon to an Empirical Restatement of Conflicts, 75 Ind. L. J. 417, 417 (2000): ("Attempting to 'restate' the law of choice of law in 1971 was analogous to trying to write a history of World War II during the Battle of Stalingrad.")

2. Reese, The Second Restatement of Conflict of Laws Revisited, 34 Mercer L. Rev. 501, 519 (1983).

3. Id. at 518–19.

4. Reese, General Course on Private International Law, 150 Recueil des Cours, 1, at 61 (1976–II).

5. See Reese, supra n. 2, at 518.

6. Id. at 519

7. Id. at 518 (stating that torts and contract conflicts were not as yet susceptible to "hard and fast rules," but expressing the hope that "it will be possible to state more definite rules at some time in the future"). See also id. at 508.

8. Reese, General Course, supra n. 4, at 62 (arguing that the conflicts experience since the revolution had "reached the stage where most areas of choice of law can be covered by general principles subject to imprecise exceptions. We should press on, however, beyond these principles to the development, as soon as our knowledge permits, of precise rules.").

9. See infra §§ 17.34–35, 17.47, 17.49, 17.50. See also supra § 2.26.

10. 182 Colo. 437, 514 P.2d 314 (1973). See Nanda, A Positive but Uncertain Step Forward for Choice of Law Problem in Colorado: The *Rostek* Decision, 51 Den. L.J. 557 (1974); Walsh, Heads Lex Loci Delicti; Tails: Lex Loci Domicile—The Conflict of Laws Coin on Edge, 51 Den. L.J. 567 (1974); Comment, "Rules" v. "Approaches": Choosing a Choice of Law Rule for Colorado, 46 U. Colo. L. Rev. 107 (1974).

predictability.[11] The court therefore adopted two of the rules offered by Chief Judge Fuld of the New York Court of Appeals in *Neumeier v. Kuehner*.[12] One rule would apply the law of the parties' common domicile. The other offers a defendant the protection of the law of his domicile if the accident occurred there; but recovery is allowed if a plaintiff is injured in his state of domicile and if that state allows a guest to sue his host. On the facts, the first rule applied. For other situations the court regarded the Restatement's "most-significant-relationship" test as a starting point for the development of rules.[13] The result is choice-of-law adjudication that displays the certainty and predictability of rules wherever and whenever they can be fashioned, and an overriding principle of flexibility where rules are either in the process of developing or are impractical. By adopting the particular rules it did, Colorado took advantage of learning offered by other jurisdictions, principally New York.[14]

E. THE NEW YORK EXPERIENCE

1. *Babcock and Guest–Statute Conflicts*

§ 17.29 New York's break with tradition came with the well-known decision in *Babcock v. Jackson*.[1] The facts were compelling and contributed to making the break relatively easy. The parties, all New Yorkers and friends, were on a weekend trip to Ontario, Canada, when the defendant Jackson lost control of his car and struck a stone wall. The plaintiff Babcock, a guest in the car, was seriously injured. Upon return to New York, Babcock brought an action against her host-driver, alleging ordinary negligence. Ontario, unlike New York, had a guest statute[2] completely immunizing a host-driver against liability to an injured guest. Judge Fuld, writing for the majority, questioned whether New York should adhere to the *lex loci* rule which, in this case, would deny the plaintiff a remedy: "Shall the law of the place of the tort *invariably* govern the availability of relief for the tort or shall the

---

11. "All of the generally accepted approaches, however, suffer from a similar defect, namely, they are all 'approaches,' to be applied in a more or less *ad hoc* fashion, and containing indeterminate language with no concrete guidelines. Thus quite naturally, these approaches have exhibited a certain lack of both predictability of result and uniformity of application." *Rostek*, 514 P.2d at 318.

12. 31 N.Y.2d 121, 335 N.Y.S.2d 64, 286 N.E.2d 454 (1972) (discussed infra § 17.31).

13. *Rostek*, 514 P.2d at 320. See Reese, Choice of Law: Rules or Approach, 57 Cornell L. Rev. 315, 323–25 (1972).

14. See supra n.12.

§ 17.29

1. 12 N.Y.2d 473, 240 N.Y.S.2d 743, 191 N.E.2d 279 (1963), discussed in Comments on *Babcock v. Jackson*, 63 Colum. L. Rev. 1212 (1963) (comments by Cavers, Cheatham, Currie, Ehrenzweig, Leflar and Reese); Symposium on Conflict of Laws: Celebrating the 30th Anniversary of *Babcock v. Jackson*, 56 Alb. L. Rev. 693 (1993) (articles by Siegel, Weintraub, Juenger, Maier, Solimine, McDougall, Weinberg, Sedler, Borchers, Simson and Korn).

2. This guest statute has later amended to allow recovery in the event of gross negligence or willful misconduct. The Highway Amendment Act, 1966, Stat. Ont. 1966, c. 64 § 20.

applicable choice of law rule also reflect a consideration of other factors which are relevant to the purposes served by the enforcement or denial of the remedy?"[3]

Drawing on two non-guest-statute cases,[4] the court announced a new approach to tort choice-of-law problems that would focus on the "center of gravity" or "grouping of contacts." This approach demanded a "[c]omparison of the relative 'contacts' and 'interests' "[5] of the concerned jurisdictions. "Justice, fairness and 'the best practical result' may best be achieved by giving controlling effect of the law of the jurisdiction which, because of its relationship or contact with the occurrence of the parties, has the greatest concern with the specific issue raised in the litigation."[6] The approach would thus consider each legal issue separately.[7] In the particular case, New York was the home of both parties, the place where the trip began and was to end, and was the state where the automobile was registered and insured. Thus, New York was regarded as more intimately connected with the litigation than was Ontario. New York's interest in effectuating its compensation policy was therefore paramount. Conceding that the issue of care might be more appropriately adjudged by the *lex locus delicti,* Judge Fuld emphasized that "the rights and liabilities of the parties which stem from the guest-host relationship should remain constant and not vary and shift as the automobile proceeds from place to place."[8] These two factors seem to address dissimilar interests: "contacts and policy" look to post-accident considerations; but the "rights and duties of the parties" rest upon pre-accident considerations.[9]

The difficult question following *Babcock* was not how to apply it to various fact situations, but exactly what choice-of-law theory the court employed. Judge Fuld seemed content to call his approach a "center of gravity" or "grouping of contacts" doctrine. He regarded this approach as similar to the "most significant relationship" test of the Restatement, Second.[10] As a result of the court's failure to cast *Babcock* in the form of one of the modern theories, various commentators laid claim to *Babcock*.[11] However, the court's own framing of the issue[12] clearly follows the

---

3. 12 N.Y.2d at 477, 240 N.Y.S.2d at 746, 191 N.E.2d at 280–81 (emphasis in original).

4. Auten v. Auten, 308 N.Y. 155, 124 N.E.2d 99, 50 A.L.R.2d 246 (1954) (contracts); Kilberg v. Northeast Airlines, Inc., 9 N.Y.2d 34, 211 N.Y.S.2d 133, 172 N.E.2d 526 (1961) (limitation of damages).

5. *Babcock,* 12 N.Y.2d at 482, 240 N.Y.S.2d at 750, 191 N.E.2d at 284.

6. Id. at 481, 240 N.Y.S.2d at 749, 191 N.E.2d at 283.

7. Id. at 479, 240 N.Y.S.2d at 747, 191 N.E.2d at 281–82. This is also the Second Restatement's approach. See supra § 17.24 n.1.

8. Id. at 483, 240 N.Y.S.2d at 751, 191 N.E.2d at 285.

9. See Rosenberg, Two Views on *Kell v. Henderson,* 67 Colum. L. Rev. 459 (1967). The problems to which this two-sided approach can lead became evident in Dym v. Gordon, 16 N.Y.2d 120, 262 N.Y.S.2d 463, 209 N.E.2d 792 (1965) (discussed infra § 17.30).

10. *Babcock,* 12 N.Y.2d at 482, 240 N.Y.S.2d at 749, 191 N.E.2d at 283.

11. Comments on *Babcock v. Jackson,* 63 Colum. L. Rev. 1212 (1963) (Cavers, Cheatham, Currie, Ehrenzweig, Leflar and Reese). Brainerd Currie summed it up best: "Indeed the majority opinion contains items of comfort for almost every critic of the traditional system." Id. at 1234. See also Hancock, Some Choice of Law Problems Posed by Antique Statutes: Realism in

---

12. See p. 772.

Restatement's approach which requires consideration of the relevant contacts in the light of the principles of § 6. Thus, *Babcock,* like the Second Restatement, could not provide more than well-reasoned guidance for future cases. Unfortunately, the court's failure to do more resulted in a line of cases marked more by confusion than consistency.

2. *From Babcock to Neumeier*

§ 17.30 The problems inherent in the flexibility of *Babcock* became all too obvious in *Dym v. Gordon,*[1] where the court again confronted a situation of guest and host domiciliaries involved in an out-of-state accident. However, while the parties had known each other in New York, they had gone to Colorado separately and had attended summer school there. The accident had occurred on a short trip during their Colorado stay, and involved a third party in another car. On its face, the *Babcock* result seemed to control. Nevertheless, the court, speaking through Judge Breitel, found three significant factual differences that together led to an opposite result—the existence of another car and party (albeit from Kansas), the parties' temporary residence in Colorado, and the creation of the relationship in Colorado. Colorado's interest was found to be paramount: "Colorado has an interest in seeing that the negligent defendants' assets are not dissipated in order that the persons in the car of the blameless driver will not have their right to recovery diminished by the present suit."[2] The court analogized the guest-host relationship to other special relationships (husband-wife, employer-employee) where the place of the relationship had been found to be controlling; this enabled the court to distinguish *Babcock,* in which the place of the accident was "entirely fortuitous." The conclusion stemmed from the court's belief that the conduct of the parties was contingent upon the place of the relationship, and that their domicile or where the car was registered and insured were less relevant. That is, even if parties had different domiciles or the car had been registered elsewhere, the trip would have been made and the accident would have occurred.[3] The place of the accident thus acquired a significance not present in *Babcock.* In a sense, the common New York domicile of the parties became the fortuitous fact and New York's concern for the welfare of the parties and liability of insureds was not enough to outweigh the factual contacts with Colora-

---

Wisconsin and Rule Fetishism in New York, 27 Stan. L. Rev. 775, 727 (1975); Note, 22 Buff. L. Rev. 335, 337 (1974); Note, 25 Syracuse L. Rev. 1005, 1006 n.4 (1974). Id. at 1234.

12. See supra n.3 and accompanying text.

§ 17.30

1. 16 N.Y.2d 120, 262 N.Y.S.2d 463, 209 N.E.2d 792 (1965).

2. Id. at 124, 262 N.Y.S.2d at 466, 209 N.E.2d at 799. The court cited no authority

for this conclusion, a fact that illustrates the dangers of indiscriminate consideration of another state's policy. Weintraub, Commentary on the Conflict of Laws 398 n.214 (4th ed. 2001). Given the fact that the other car and party were from *Kansas,* the statement furthermore fails to explain the nature of *Colorado*'s interest. See also infra n.5.

3. See Tooker v. Lopez, 24 N.Y.2d 569, 593–94, 301 N.Y.S.2d 519, 540, 249 N.E.2d 394, 409 (1969) (Breitel, J., dissenting).

do.[4] Judge Fuld's dissent disapproved of the majority's use of the *Babcock* rationale. He saw no policy interest to be served by the application of Colorado's guest statute[5] and also questioned the importance that the majority attached to the fact that Colorado was the seat of the relationship. In his view, New York's interest in seeing its policy of compensation served was the only state interest involved.[6]

Dym v. Gordon probably misapplied *Babcock.*[7] It is not enough to isolate any issue, pick out some policy, and elevate one contact to a controlling position. Although the place of the tort was not as adventitious in *Dym* as it had been in *Babcock,* it still was not a relevant contact unless it was "of the kind that makes it reasonable for the state having that contact to desire to apply a policy underlying one of the state's rules.... "[8] Colorado's interests were unduly emphasized in this respect while New York's were insufficiently considered. Even the fact that Colorado was the seat of the relationship did not make that state a concerned jurisdiction.

In *Macey v. Rozbicki,*[9] the next case chronologically, the facts were more like *Babcock* and *Dym.* Again, both parties were New York domiciliaries, and the accident occurred in Ontario. The plaintiff had been staying at the defendant's Ontario summer home for a ten-day visit. On the seventh day, the plaintiff was injured during an intra-Ontario trip when the defendant's car collided with the car of a Canadian. Rather than engage in a discussion of the issues, the court merely counted contacts without discussion of the relevant policies and interests, found that the important ones were New York-related, and distinguished *Dym* on the facts. The concurrence rejected the majority's approach of counting contacts but accepted the result because only New York had an interest in seeing its policy served.[10]

---

4. *Dym,* 16 N.Y.2d at 126, 262 N.Y.S.2d at 468, 209 N.E.2d at 795–96.

5. Judge Fuld, citing Colorado authority, found the prime objective underlying the guest statute to be the protection of Colorado driver-defendants and their insurance carriers against fraudulent claims and law suits. Id. at 129, 262 N.Y.S.2d at 470, 209 N.E.2d at 797.

6. Id.

7. Weintraub, supra n.2, at 282. But see D. Cavers, The Choice of Law Process 295, 300–04 (1965).

8. Weintraub, Commentary on the Conflict of Laws 243 (1971). See id. at 282–83 (3d ed. 1986); id. 352–53 (4th ed. 2001).

9. 18 N.Y.2d 289, 274 N.Y.S.2d 591, 221 N.E.2d 380 (1966).

10. Citing to Currie, the concurrence employed interest analysis and also suggested that *Dym*'s seat-of-the relationship test

be discarded as irrelevant in interest analysis. 18 N.Y.2d at 296, 274 N.Y.S.2d at 596–97, 221 N.E.2d at 384 (Keating, J. concurring).

At the same time as the Court of Appeals was wrestling with the guest statute problem, lower courts also added to the corpus of guest statute law: Kell v. Henderson, 26 A.D.2d 595, 270 N.Y.S.2d 552 (3d Dept. 1966) (facts reverse from *Babcock,* i.e. Ontario parties and New York accident; New York law applied as a result of the place-of-wrong rule); Bray v. Cox, 39 A.D.2d 299, 333 N.Y.S.2d 783 (1972), motion denied 33 N.Y.2d 789, 350 N.Y.S.2d 653, 305 N.E.2d 775 (1973) (facts similar to Kell v. Henderson, supra; New York law applied through interest analysis). But see Arbuthnot v. Allbright, 35 A.D.2d 315, 316 N.Y.S.2d 391 (3d Dept.1970). See also Note 26 Vand. L. Rev. 340, 346 n.37 (1973). After *Neumeier v. Kuehner, infra,* only *Arbuthnot* can be said to be correct.

The Court of Appeals enjoyed more success in dealing with non-guest statute issues. In *Long v. Pan American World Airways, Inc.*[11] the court used a *Babcock* approach to avoid the application of a restrictive wrongful death statute. Plaintiffs represented the estates of Pennsylvania decedents who had been killed in an airplane explosion over Maryland. Although New York was a neutral forum, the court recognized the fortuitous nature of the Maryland situs of the accident and therefore refused to apply Maryland law which would have denied a recovery. The Pennsylvania contacts (the decedents' domiciles, the place of purchasing the tickets, and the place where the trip began and was to end) and the Pennsylvania interests (the protection of decedents' estates) led to the conclusion that Pennsylvania law should govern: "[There is] no suggestion in *Babcock* that its approach and principles were inapplicable to actions for wrongful death.... It would be highly incongruous and unreal to have the flexible principle of *Babcock* apply in a case where the victim of the tort is injured but not where he is killed."[12]

In *Miller v. Miller*,[13] the Court of Appeals faced a similar pattern as *Babcock*, except that, rather than denying recovery altogether, the accident state limited the amount of damages. Recognizing the lack of consistency in the *Babcock* line of cases, Judge Keating adopted the interest analysis approach used by the court in two earlier decedents' estates cases[14] and held in favor of the New York plaintiffs. Interest analysis displaced *Babcock* also in the next guest statute case, *Tooker v. Lopez*.[15] The guest and host were New York domiciliaries attending college in Michigan, where both were killed in an accident. A Michigan guest was also injured. Although *Dym* could be distinguished since the third party in *Tooker* was also a guest, the court admitted that "We cannot ... in candor rest our decision on this basis...."[16] Instead, the court rejected the contact counting of *Dym* and *Macey*,[17] discarded the seat of the relationship as a significant factor,[18] and held that only New York had an interest—to afford recovery for its domiciliaries. The result was predictable, but a more difficult question did not go unnoticed: what if the Michigan resident injured in this accident had sued in New York? The court indicated by dictum that, even in this situation, forum law

---

11. 16 N.Y.2d 337, 266 N.Y.S.2d 513, 213 N.E.2d 796 (1965).

12. Id. at 343, 266 N.Y.S.2d at 517–18, 213 N.E.2d at 799. See also MacKendrick v. Newport News Shipbuilding and Dry Dock Co., 59 Misc.2d 994, 302 N.Y.S.2d 124 (1969). Cf. Farber v. Smolack, 20 N.Y.2d 198, 282 N.Y.S.2d 248, 229 N.E.2d 36 (1967).

13. 22 N.Y.2d 12, 290 N.Y.S.2d 734, 237 N.E.2d 877 (1968), motion denied 22 N.Y.2d 722, 292 N.Y.S.2d 107, 239 N.E.2d 204 (1968). *Miller* was a wrongful death action arising from a Maine accident involving a New York victim and a New York defendant who at the time of the accident resided

in Maine. Maine, but not New York, limited wrongful death recovery to $20,000.

14. See In re Crichton's Estate, 20 N.Y.2d 124, 281 N.Y.S.2d 811, 228 N.E.2d 799 (1967); In re Estate of Clark, 21 N.Y.2d 478, 288 N.Y.S.2d 993, 236 N.E.2d 152 (1968).

15. 24 N.Y.2d 569, 301 N.Y.S.2d 519, 249 N.E.2d 394 (1969).

16. 24 N.Y.2d at 574, 301 N.Y.S.2d at 523, 249 N.E.2d at 397.

17. 24 N.Y.2d at 576–77, 301 N.Y.S.2d at 525–26, 249 N.E.2d at 398–99.

18. 24 N.Y.2d at 579 n.2, 301 N.Y.S.2d at 527 n.2, 249 N.E.2d at 400 n.2.

would be applied.[19] With *Tooker,* New York had now adopted a form of interest analysis.[20]

3. *The Neumeier Rules*

§ 17.31 In the last of the guest-statute line of cases, New York once more reversed field. Faced with the hypothetical that had troubled the concurring judges in *Tooker, Neumeier v. Kuehner*[1] announced a new mode of analysis. The question was what law governs when an Ontario plaintiff is injured in his own guest statute jurisdiction while riding as passenger of New York host-driver. Chief Judge Fuld resolved the question with the set of three narrowly drawn choice-of-law rules that he had proposed in his *Tooker* concurrence:

    1. When the guest-passenger and the host-driver are domiciled in the same state, and the car is registered there, the law of that state should control and determine the standard of care which the host owes to his guest.

    2. [(a)] When the driver's conduct occurred in the state of his domicile and that state does not cast him in liability for that conduct, he should not be held liable by reason of the fact that liability would be imposed upon him under the tort law of the state of the victim's domicile. [(b)] Conversely, when the guest was injured in the state of his own domicile and its law permits recovery, the driver who has come into that state should not—in the absence of special circumstances—be permitted to interpose the law of his state as a defense.

    3. In other situations, when the passenger and the driver are domiciled in different states, the rule is necessarily less categorical. Normally, the applicable rule of decision will be that of the state where the accident occurred but not if it can be shown that displacing the normally applicable rule will advance the relevant substantive law purposes without impairing the smooth workings of the multi-state system or producing great uncertainty for litigants.[2]

---

19. "Applying the choice of law rule which we have adopted, it is not an 'implicit consequence' that the Michigan passenger injured along with Miss Lopez should be denied recovery. Under the reasoning adopted here it is not at all clear that Michigan law would govern." Id. at 580, 301 N.Y.S.2d at 528, 249 N.E.2d at 400 (citation omitted).

20. Cramton, Currie & Kay, Conflict of Laws, Cases–Comments–Questions 239 (3d ed. 1981).

§ 17.31

1. 31 N.Y.2d 121, 335 N.Y.S.2d 64, 286 N.E.2d 454 (1972). See Symposium, *Neu-*

meier v. Kuehner: A Conflicts Conflict, 1 Hofstra L. Rev. 94 (1973).

2. 31 N.Y.2d at 128, 335 N.Y.S.2d at 70, 286 N.E.2d at 457–58. The *Neumeier* rules are further discussed infra §§ 17.31, 17.32, et passim. For a tabular presentation of the operation of the *Neumeier* rules and discussion of cases applying them, see Symeonides, Choice of Law in the American Courts in 1994: A View "From the Trenches," 43 Am. J. Comp. L. 1, 4–16 (1995); S. Symeonides, W. Perdue & A. von Mehren, Conflict of Laws: American, Comparative, International, 2745–48 (2d ed. 2003). For criticism, see Sedler, Interstate Accidents and the Unprovided For Case: Reflections on *Neumeier v. Kuehner*, 1 Hofstra L. Rev. 125 (1973); Sedler, Rules of Choice of Law Versus

On the facts of the case Rule 3 applied. This rule of course gives new vitality to the *lex loci delicti,* but allows displacement of that law upon showing that its non-application "Will advance the relevant substantive law purposes" of the other state, or states.[3] In *Neumeier* the court could find no New York "substantive law purposes" that would be advanced by displacement of Ontario law.[4] The court did not elaborate on how the proviso to Rule 3 should be used. In the absence of an explanation, it is possible that the court meant to maintain the methodology first announced in *Babcock.* More problematic is the source of these rules because they do not represent a distillation of the rationales and holdings contained in the *Babcock* line of cases.[5] On the other hand, only *Dym v. Gordon* would have been decided differently, that is by application of Rule 1.[6]

It is worth noting that *Neumeier* is the only guest statute case brought by a non-New York plaintiff. It is therefore distinguishable from its four predecessors. Moreover, Chief Judge Fuld's second and third rules might leave a New York plaintiff without a remedy in an out-of-state accident involving a foreign host.[7] On the other hand, in a case falling only under Rule 3, a forum plaintiff may have a better chance of

Choice-of-Law Rules: Judicial Method in Conflicts Torts Cases, 44 Tenn. L. Rev. 975, 987–94 (1977); Simson, The *Neumeier-Schultz* Rules: How Logical a "Next State in the Evolution of the Law" After *Babcock*?, 56 Alb. L. Rev. 913 (1993).

3. For cases involving two states, in addition to the state of injury, see infra § 17.46 nn.5–22.

4. Some commentators have argued that neither New York nor Ontario had any interest to be furthered on the factual circumstances of the case. Such a situation is "unprovided for" in the interest analysis method. Twerski, *Neumeier v. Kuehner*: Where are the Emperor's New Clothes?, 1 Hofstra L. Rev. 104 (1973); Sedler, supra n.2, at 125–130.

5. Rule 1 "codifies" the result in *Babcock, Macey* and *Tooker,* supra § 17.30, and as such may perhaps be said to be a rule of predetermined interest analysis. Twerski, supra n.4, at 118. The reverse situation, out-of-state parties injured in New York, never reached the Court of Appeals. Similarly, Rule 2 is wholly unsupported by a guest statute holding.

6. Twerski sees the rationale of the *Neumeier* rules and Judge Keating's reasoning in *Tooker* as mutually exclusive. He concludes that, although the *Tooker* facts would be governed by Rule 1 and thus the result would be undisturbed, the concern for territorial contacts and relationships ev-

idenced by the rules would demand in application of foreign law in *Tooker.* Twerski, supra n.4, at 117. The lower court guest statute rulings would also be overturned by use of Rule 1: Kell v. Henderson, 26 A.D.2d 595, 270 N.Y.S.2d 552 (3d Dept.1966), Bray v. Cox, 39 A.D.2d 299, 333 N.Y.S.2d 783 (4th Dept.1972), motion denied 33 N.Y.2d 789, 350 N.Y.S.2d 653, 305 N.E.2d 775 (1973). Miller v. Miller, 22 N.Y.2d 12, 290 N.Y.S.2d 734, 237 N.E.2d 877 (1968), motion denied 22 N.Y.2d 722, 292 N.Y.S.2d 107, 239 N.E.2d 204 (1968), which applied New York law to afford a New York plaintiff injured in Maine a more generous wrongful death recovery than Maine law provided, might have been decided otherwise under Rule 3, if the court were to treat the defendant as a Maine domiciliary. However, the defendant was a New York domiciliary before and after the accident, although at the time of the accident he was residing–permanently according to the dissent–in Maine. Even if the court were to treat the defendant as a Maine domiciliary, the court might view a forum plaintiff more favorably than the foreign plaintiff in *Neumeier.* See infra nn.7–8 and accompanying text.

7. See Pryor v. Swarner, 445 F.2d 1272 (2d Cir.1971) (pre-*Neumeier* case following Rule 3 as originally stated in Chief Judge Fuld's concurrence in *Tooker*). See also Cipolla v. Shaposka, 439 Pa. 563, 267 A.2d 854 (1970).

invoking the Rule's proviso, since "New York has a deep interest in protecting its own residents injured in a foreign state."[8]

4. Extending the Neumeier Rules to Other Loss–Distribution Conflicts: Schultz and Cooney

§ 17.32 For some time after *Neumeier* it was unclear whether the rules enunciated therein could or should be extended, directly or by analogy, to tort situations beyond guest statute cases, in New York[1] or in other jurisdictions.[2] The New York Court of Appeals resolved this uncertainty in *Schultz v. Boy Scouts of America, Inc.*[3] One part of *Schultz* involved a fact pattern that was the reverse of *Babcock*:[4] the plaintiffs and one of the defendants, the Boy Scouts, were domiciled in New Jersey,[5] which accorded that defendant charitable immunity, while the injury was deemed to have occurred in New York,[6] which did not accord such immunity. The court characterized the immunity rules as loss-

8. *Neumeier*, 31 N.Y.2d at 125, 335 N.Y.S.2d at 68, 286 N.E.2d at 456. Whether the rules result in unconstitutional discrimination against non-resident parties is a question. Judge Fuld thought not, but viewed it as "the result of the existence of disparate rules of law in jurisdictions that have diverse and important connections with the litigants and the litigated issue." 31 N.Y.2d at 126, 335 N.Y.S.2d at 68, 286 N.E.2d at 456. But see, Note, Unconstitutional Discrimination in Choice of Law, 77 Colum. L. Rev. 272, 289 n.88 (1977) (suggesting a violation of the Privileges and Immunities Clause in certain Rule 3 situations).

§ 17.32

1. See Rosenthal v. Warren, 475 F.2d 438 (2d Cir.1973), cert. denied 414 U.S. 856, 94 S.Ct. 159, 38 L.Ed.2d 106 (1973) (applying New York damages law to malpractice action filed by New York plaintiffs against Massachusetts doctor and hospital for injury arising out of Massachusetts medical procedure), criticized in Twerski, *Neumeier v. Kuehner*: Where are the Emperor's New Clothes?, 1 Hofstra L. Rev. 104, 124 n.53 (1973); Juodis v. Schule, 79 Misc.2d 955, 361 N.Y.S.2d 605 (1974) (applying Connecticut (situs) no-fault plan in suit involving New York parties); Walkes v. Walkes, 465 F.Supp. 638 (S.D.N.Y.1979) (applying New York law in wrongful death action filed by Florida plaintiff against New York defendant for death suffered in New York–*Neumeier* and interest analysis). Judge Weinstein has cautioned against unwarranted extension. Chance v. E.I. Du Pont De Nemours & Co., Inc., 371 F.Supp. 439, 444–45 (E.D.N.Y.1974). Reese, Choice of Law in Torts and Contracts and Directions for the Future, 16 Colum. J. Transnat'l L. 1, 16 (1977), regards these rules as

a good example for courts seeking to construct rules for different tort situations. The article also criticizes *Rosenthal*, supra. See id. at 10–11.

2. See First National Bank in Fort Collins v. Rostek, 182 Colo. 437, 514 P.2d 314 (1973) (discussed supra § 17.28 nn. 10 et seq.); adopting Rules 1 and 2 in toto, but using the "most significant relationship" test of the Second Restatement for other situations). But see Labree v. Major, 111 R.I. 657, 306 A.2d 808 (1973) (rejecting Rule 3).

3. 65 N.Y.2d 189, 491 N.Y.S.2d 90, 480 N.E.2d 679 (1985).

4. Babcock v. Jackson, 12 N.Y.2d 473, 240 N.Y.S.2d 743, 191 N.E.2d 279 (1963), on remand 40 Misc.2d 757, 243 N.Y.S.2d 715 (1963) (discussed supra § 17.29).

5. By the time of the trial, Boys Scouts had moved its domicile to Texas, the law of which denied charitable immunity. The court ignored the post-event change of domicile and treated Boy Scouts as a New Jersey domiciliary, noting that the change of domicile "provides New York with no greater interest in this action than it would have without the change." *Schultz*, 65 N.Y.2d at 194, 491 N.Y.S.2d 90, 480 N.E.2d 679. Thus, the court treated the problem as involving a choice between New York and New Jersey law.

6. Two counts alleged injuries sustained in New Jersey and were dismissed under New Jersey's charitable immunity law. The remaining two counts alleged injuries suffered in both New York and New Jersey. The latter fact sufficiently "implicate[d] New York's interests to require a resolution of the choice-of-law problem in the case." 480 N.E.2d at 683.

allocating rather than as conduct-regulating,[7] and concluded that the law of the state of the common domicile should be applied to this issue.[8] Thus, the court confirmed the applicability of the first *Neumeier* rule to cases of the reverse-*Babcock* pattern.

The second defendant, the Franciscan Brothers, had its domicile in Ohio.[9] Since the parties were domiciled in different states, *Neumeier* Rule 1 was inapplicable. Also inapplicable was Rule 2 because neither party was domiciled in a state whose law protected that party.[10] Thus, this plaintiffs claims against this defendant fell within the residual Rule 3, which calls for the application of the law of the "place of the accident,"[11] subject to a proviso contained in that rule. The Court chose to apply the proviso, displacing the law of the state of injury in favor of New Jersey law. It did so in the interests of treating both defendants alike and of applying to the plaintiff the principle, derived from the loss-allocation characterization of New Jersey law, that a party who accepts a state law's benefits must also accept its burdens.[12] The Court summarized previous New York case law as demonstrating that, in conflicts between loss-allocating rules, "the significant contacts are, almost exclusively, the parties' domiciles and the locus of the tort."[13]

From a methodological perspective, *Schultz* is important for several reasons. First, it confirmed the Court's commitment to adhering to the *Neumeier* rules even in difficult cases. Second, it reaffirmed and solidified the distinction first enunciated in *Babcock* between conduct-regulating rules and loss-distributing rules. The importance of this distinction both for New York and American conflicts law is discussed later.[14] Third, it expanded the scope of the *Neumeier* rules so as to make them applicable to conflicts between loss-distribution rules other than guest statutes.

---

7. "[L]oss-distributing rules ... [charitable immunity statutes as well as guest statutes] share the characteristic of being postevent remedial rules designed to allocate the burden of losses resulting from tortious conduct in which the jurisdiction of the parties' common domicile has the paramount interest.... [A]lthough it is conceivable that application of New York's law in this case would have some deterrent effect on future tortious conduct in this State, New York's deterrent interest is considerably less because none of the parties is a resident and the rule in conflict is loss-allocating rather than conduct-regulating." *Schultz,* 480 N.E.2d at 686.

8. Application of the law of the parties' common domicile "reduces forum-shopping opportunities because the same law will be applied by the common-domicile and locus jurisdictions ... , rebuts charges that the forum-locus is biased in favor of its own law ... , [furthers] mutuality and reciprocity [through] consistent application of the com-

mon-domicile law [regardless of which party is plaintiff or defendant and of where suit is brought, and thereby] produces a rule that is easy to apply and brings a modicum of predictability and certainty to an area of the law needing both." 480 N.E.2d at 687.

9. Ohio law denied charitable immunity in actions based on negligent hiring.

10. See *Neumeier* Rule 2, supra § 17.31.

11. *Neumeier* Rule 3, supra § 17.31.

12. "[A]pplication of the law of New Jersey ... would further that State's interest in enforcing the decision of its domiciliaries to accept the burdens as well as the benefits of that State's loss-distributing tort rules and its interest in promoting the continuation and expansion of defendant's charitable activities in that State." *Schultz,* 480 N.E.2d at 687.

13. Id. at 684.

14. See infra §§ 17.36–17.38.

The latter development, however, created some new technical problems arising from the fact that the *Neumeier* rules do not–because they need not–differentiate between the place of injurious conduct and the place of the resulting injury. Indeed, such differentiation was unnecessary because the *Neumeier* rules were devised for guest-statute conflicts in which the driver's conduct and the guest's injury coincide in the same state. Thus, when the first sentence of *Neumeier* Rule 2 [hereinafter "Rule 2a"] speaks of the "driver's conduct" it presupposes that any injury resulting from such conduct will also occur in the same state. Likewise, when the second sentence of the same rule [hereinafter "Rule 2b"] speaks of a "guest [being] injured in the state of his own domicile," it assumes that such an injury was the result of the host-driver's conduct, which also must have occurred in the same state.[15] These assumptions are both natural and logical. Traffic accident cases in which a driver's conduct in one state causes injury in another state are rare, even when the collision occurs *at* a state border.[16] However, after *Schultz* officially extended these rules to conflicts between loss-distribution rules other than guest statutes, the distinction between the place of conduct and the place of the resulting injury has acquired new significance for all those cases in which these two contacts do not coincide in the same state. Unfortunately, the *Schultz* court did not elaborate on this question because the answer would not have affected the outcome.[17]

15. Judge Weinstein's restatement of *Neumeier* Rule 2 in a non-guest-statute conflict uses the broader terms "defendant" (rather than host-driver) and "plaintiff" (rather than guest-passenger), but also makes clear that in non-guest statute conflicts only the conduct need be at the defendant's domicile and only the injury need be in the victim's domicile. See Hamilton v. Accu–Tek, 47 F.Supp.2d 330, 336 (E.D.N.Y. 1999) ("When the conduct occurs in the state of defendant's domicile, and he would not be liable under that state's laws, he should not be held liable under the tort law of the plaintiff's domicile. Conversely, when a plaintiff is injured in his own domicile, and the law of that state would permit him to recover, the defendant should not be allowed to interpose his own state's law").

16. In Judge Trucking Co., Inc. v. Cooper, 1994 WL 164519 (Del.Super.Ct.1994), the traffic accident occurred at the Delaware–Maryland border. After the impact, the involved vehicles ended up in Maryland, but there was a factual question as to whether the impact itself had occurred in Delaware. The court opined that "if the impact occurred in Delaware, then Delaware is the place where the negligent conduct *and the injury* took place." Id. at *3. (emphasis added). In Amiot v. Ames, 166 Vt. 288, 693 A.2d 675 (1997), a traffic accident in Quebec was claimed to have been caused by a Vermont driver's negligence in

Vermont. It was claimed that the driver had failed to deliver himself the insulin necessary to control his diabetes and that, as a result of that failure, he lost control of his car in Vermont and struck plaintiff's car, which was parked at the Canadian customs check point.

17. See S. Symeonides, W. Perdue & A. von Mehren, Conflict of Laws: American Comparative International, 269 (2d ed. 2003). *Schultz* involved tortious acts that had occurred in two states, New York and New Jersey, and had produced injuries in both of those states, but primarily in New Jersey. Rather than discussing the problem such a split between conduct and injury might present to the application of the *Neumeier* rules, the *Schultz* court designated one of the two states, New York, as the "locus of the tort," thus providing plaintiffs with a fighting chance to argue for the application of New York law. This designation, however, did not affect which of the *Neumeier* rules was applicable to the case or the outcome of the case. With regard to defendant Boy Scouts, a determination that the tort had occurred in New Jersey, rather than New York, would have made the case a false conflict that would be governed by the law of New Jersey because both parties were domiciled in that state. With regard to defendant Franciscan Brothers, a determination that the tort had occurred in New

However, this problem reappeared in *Cooney v. Osgood Machinery, Inc.*[18] This case arose out of an employment accident in Missouri in which Cooney, a domiciliary of that state, was injured by machinery owned by his Missouri employer, Mueller. The machinery was manufactured by Hill Acme and was sold in New York–through defendant Osgood Machinery, Inc., a New York sales agent–to a Buffalo company that sold it to Mueller ten years later. Cooney received workers' compensation benefits through his employer under Missouri law, and then brought a products liability action in New York against Osgood. Osgood third-partied Mueller and Hill Acme, seeking contribution. Only this third-party action was before the court in *Cooney.* Mueller would be liable for such contribution under New York law, but not under Missouri law which releases an employer who provides workers' compensation benefits from any tort claims by the employee or any third party.

The court reiterated the *Babcock-Schultz* distinction between conduct-regulating and loss-allocation rules, classified contribution rules into the latter category, and reaffirmed the applicability of the *Neumeier* rules to loss-allocating conflicts other than guest-statute conflicts. The court recognized that the first *Neumeier* rule was inapplicable because the disputants were domiciled in different states. But the court concluded that the case "presented a true conflict *in the mold of* Neumeier's second rule, where the local law of each litigant's domicile favors that party. Under that rule, the place of injury governs, which in this case means that contribution is barred."[19]

This statement would have been accurate if the dispute in *Cooney* concerned Mr. Cooney's initial products-liability action against Osgood *and if* the products liability law of Missouri was more favorable to Cooney than to Osgood. In such a case, Mr. Cooney could be analogized to the injured guest-passenger under Neumeier Rule 2b who is injured in his home state the law of which protects him, while Osgood could be analogized to the host-driver who acts in his home state whose law protects him. The resulting conflict then would not only be a true conflict between the laws of Missouri and New York, each of which would favor the local party, but also an internal conflict between Rules 2b and 2a, each of which would favor a different party.[20] However, one

Jersey again would have led to the application of New Jersey law under the third *Neumeier* rule, rather than under the escape from that rule, as had occurred in the actual case.

18. 81 N.Y.2d 66, 595 N.Y.S.2d 919, 612 N.E.2d 277 (1993), discussed in Symposium—*Cooney v. Osgood Machinery, Inc.*, 59 Brooklyn L.Rev. 1323 (1994) (articles by Sedler, Twerski, and Silberman); Conference on Jurisdiction, Justice, and Choice of Law for the twenty-First Century: Case Four, 29 New Eng.L.Rev. 669 (1995) (contributions by Borchers, Kramer, Maier, Silberman, Singer, Weintraub, and Cox).

19. *Cooney*, 612 N.E.2d 277 at 283 (emphasis added). The words "in the mold of" may signify the court's understanding that the case does not fall precisely within the scope of Rule 2, both because the conduct and the injury occurred in different states and because the dispute was one between joint-tortfeasors rather than between a victim and a tortfeasor. See infra nn.34–42, § 17.43 n.9. 21, § 17.44 nn.2–5.

20. See discussion infra at text accompanying nn.34–42, § 17.43 n.9. 21, § 17.44, and nn.2–5. Judging from the court's ultimate decision to apply Missouri law to the third-party action between Osgood and

should recall that the only action that was before the court in *Cooney* was Osgood's third-party action for contribution against Mueller. This reminder makes the case much more difficult in that it raises the following questions:

(a) Which party should be analogized to the injured guest-passenger under Rule 2b? Should it still be Cooney (who actually was not a party to the third-party action), Osgood (who was the complaining plaintiff in the third-party action), or Mueller (who had paid worker's compensation for injury he sustained in his home state whose law protects him)?

(b) Which party should be analogized to the defendant host-driver under Rule 2a? Should it still be Osgood who is the defendant in the products liability action but is a plaintiff in the third-party action and who acted in his home state whose law protects him; or should it be Mueller who is the actual defendant in the third-party action and who acted in his home state whose law protects him?

(c) Which injury is pertinent for purposes of the third-party action? Is it still Cooney's personal injury (which occurred in Missouri), Mueller's financial injury (which also occurred in Missouri), or Osgood's financial injury (having to pay compensation to Cooney) which occurred in New York?

(d) Which conduct is pertinent for the purposes of the third-party action? Is it Osgood's conduct in doing or not doing something with regard to the sale of the machinery in New York, or is it Mueller's conduct in modifying the machinery in Missouri? and

(e) In cases in which the conduct and injury occur in different states, is the place of conduct relevant for applying Neumeier Rule 2 or, for that matter, Rule 3?

The above are difficult questions that are susceptible to different answers. If nothing else, these questions suggest that, without further elaboration, the *Neumeier* rules may be ill-suited for cases in which the injurious conduct and the resulting injury occur in different states, or for cases in which the dispute is not between the injured victim and the tortfeasor but rather between joint tortfeasors.[21]

Mueller, one could surmise that the court might also have applied Missouri law to Cooney's underlying products liability action against Osgood. If so, this would mean that the court either considers the place of conduct to be irrelevant for Rule 2 purposes or that the court believes that Rule 2b trumps rule 2a.

21. The Louisiana codification avoids both of these pitfalls. Article 3544 (which, like the *Neumeier* rules, is applicable to conflicts between loss-distribution rules) differentiates between cases in which the conduct and the injury occurred in the same or in different states. Furthermore,

the article is confined to disputes "between a person injured by an offense or quasi-offense and the person who caused the injury." Disputes between joint tortfeasors, or between a tortfeasor and a person vicariously liable for his acts, are relegated to the flexible choice-of-law approach of Article 3542, the residual article. For the rationale for these two features by the Article's drafter, see Symeonides, Louisiana's New Law of Choice of Law for Tort Conflicts: An Exegesis, 66 Tul. L. Rev. 677, 715–731 (1992). For another case applying the *Neumeier* rules in a dispute between joint tortfeasors, see Gould Electronics Inc. v. United States,

The *Cooney* court must have recognized this deficiency because it proceeded to resolve the conflict under a full-fledged policy analysis, if not interest analysis.[22] After concluding that the interests of the two states were "irreconcilable,"[23] the court decided that on balance the law of Missouri should apply. The court explained that "this holding is consistent with the result reached historically, and reflects application of a neutral factor that favors neither the forum's law nor its domiciliaries.... [The] locus [*delicti*] tips the balance ... [because] ordinarily it is the place with which both parties have voluntarily associated themselves."[24] The problem was that, by the Court's own admission: Osgood "did nothing to affiliate itself with Missouri";[25] its sale activities were limited to New York and parts of Pennsylvania; the machine wound up in Missouri through no effort, or even knowledge, of Osgood; and consequently, Osgood "may not have reasonably anticipated becoming embroiled in litigation with a Missouri employer."[26] Once again, this recognition is a reminder that this case did not quite fit "in the mold" of *Neumeier* Rule 2, which was designed only for cases in which both parties associate themselves with the same state. Nevertheless, the court thought that the application of Missouri law could be supported by another, ostensibly independent, factor "that should, at times, play a role in choice of law: the protection of reasonable expectations."[27] The court reasoned that, although Osgood may not have reasonably anticipated the application of Missouri law, he also had no reasonable expectation that contribution would be available to it because, at the time of the sale, New York law did not provide for such contribution. By contrast, "[i]n view of the unambiguous [Missouri] statutory language barring third-party liability ... Mueller could hardly have expected to be haled before a New York court to respond in damages for an accident to a Missouri employee at the Missouri plant."[28] Thus, the court concluded

220 F.3d 169 (3d Cir.2000); cf. Caruolo v. John Crane, Inc., 226 F.3d 46 (2d Cir.2000) (joint and several liability).

22. The Court described its analysis as "evaluat[ing] the relative interests of jurisdictions with conflicting laws and, if neither can be accommodated *without substantially impairing* the other, finding some other sound basis for resolving the impasse." *Cooney*, 612 N.E.2d at 282 (emphasis added). The italicized phrase reminds the reader of a comparative impairment analysis. Certainly, it has nothing of the selfishness of Currie's original analysis.

23. *Cooney*, 612 N.E.2d at 283. "To the extent we allow contribution against Mueller, the policy underlying the Missouri workers' compensation scheme will be offended. Conversely, to the extent Osgood is required to pay more than its equitable share of a judgment, the policy underlying New York's contribution law is affronted. It is evident that one State's interest cannot be accommodated without sacrificing the other's, and thus an appropriate method for

choosing between the two must be found." Id.

24. Id. See also id. at 281–83 (referring to the *locus delicti*), the "traditional choice of law crucible," as an "appropriate ... 'tie breaker' because that is the only State with which both parties have purposefully associated themselves in a significant way ... [and because it] is a neutral factor, rebutting an inference that the forum state is merely protecting its own domiciliary or favoring its own law."

25. Id. at 283.

26. Id.

27. Id. at 283 (citing Restatement Second, Conflict of Laws § 6(2)(d)).

28. Id. at 284. In an important footnote, the court gave an additional reason as to why, on balance, the court was prepared to subordinate New York's interests in this case. The court observed that "New York law permitting contribution against an em-

that Missouri law should apply because "although the interests of the respective jurisdictions are irreconcilable, the accident occurred in Missouri, and unavailability of contribution would more closely comport with the reasonable expectations of both parties in conducting their business affairs."[29]

Although the Court could have ended the discussion at this point, the Court thought it necessary to address Osgood's contention that the application of Missouri law was offensive to New York's public policy. The court reiterated Cardozo's classic test for the *ordre public* exception[30] and eventually concluded that application of Missouri's contribution law was not repugnant to New York's public policy. The reaffirmation of Cardozo's test is a positive development, especially in light of the abuse that test had suffered in the hands of the same court in *Kilberg*.[31] The *ordre public* exception remains necessary for cases subject to the first *Neumeier* rule, or any other rule that does not contain a built-in escape clause. However, the fact that both the second and third *Neumeier* rules contain built-in escapes[32] that are capable of directly repelling an obnoxious foreign law obviates the need for an additional *ordre public* inquiry for cases disposed of under those rules.[33]

ployer is clearly a minority view.... A result that might impose New York law on the carefully structured workers' compensation schemes of other states–especially when the accident occurred there–is undesirable." Id. at n.2. (Indeed, in 1996, New York amended its law so as to make indemnification and contribution unavailable against the employer, except in cases of "grave injury" to the employee. See Omnibus Workers' Compensation Reform Act, L. 1996, ch. 635, § 90.) This footnote finds favor with proponents of many other choice-of-law theories, such as those of professors Weintraub, Leflar, or Juenger. Literally, the quoted statement reminds one of the reasoning of the California Supreme Court in Offshore Rental Co. v. Continental Oil Co., 22 Cal.3d 157, 148 Cal.Rptr. 867, 583 P.2d 721 (1978) (discussed supra § 17.19 nn.12–17) which exemplifies that state's version of comparative impairment. Although purporting to apply pure comparative impairment, *Offshore* also adopted significant elements from the writings of von Mehren and Trautman, Freund, and Leflar. *Offshore* found that California's pertinent rule was "isolated in the context of the laws of the federal union" *Offshore*, 583 P.2d at 726, while Louisiana's corresponding rule was "more prevalent," id., and more "main stream." Id. Based *in part* on that finding, the *Offshore* court decided to apply Louisiana law because the application of that law would impair California's interests less than the application of California law would impair Louisiana's interests. Professor Juenger thought that the above quoted

footnote from *Cooney* "holds forth the promise of a distinct improvement of New York conflicts law ... [in that] it relies on a teleological consideration ... , namely an assessment of the competing substantive rules' intrinsic quality." Juenger, *Babcock v. Jackson* Revisited: Judge Fuld's Contribution to American Conflicts Law, 56 Alb. L. Rev. 727, 741 n.121 (1993). His conclusion seems to be that such a "value judgment about competing ... rules" (id. 751 n.182) offers support for his proposed choice-of-law rule that calls for the application of the law that "most closely accords with modern tort law standards." Id. at 751.

29. *Cooney*, 612 N.E.2d at 284. By the same token, given the state of the law in 1958 when the machine was sold, Osgood could argue that mere sales agents could not have expected to be subject to strict liability for their involvement in the sale.

30. Loucks v. Standard Oil Co., 224 N.Y. 99, 120 N.E. 198 (1918).

31. See Kilberg v. Northeast Airlines, Inc., 9 N.Y.2d 34, 211 N.Y.S.2d 133, 172 N.E.2d 526 (1961) (discussed supra § 17.9.) The *Cooney* court did not even mention *Kilberg*.

32. Rule 2b contains a proviso allowing the showing or absence of "special circumstances," while Rule 3 is merely a presumptive rule.

33. *A fortiori*, this is true for cases handled under *ad hoc* free-wheeling analyses,

What the *Neumeier* rules are incapable of resolving is the internal conflict between themselves in cases in which the conduct and the injury occur in different states. One post-*Cooney* example suffices to illustrate the conflict between Rules 2a and 2b. *Bankers Trust Co. v. Lee Keeling & Associates, Inc.*,[34] involved conduct in Oklahoma by an Oklahoma defendant, that caused injury in New York to a New York plaintiff.[35] Oklahoma law favored the Oklahoma defendant, thus making applicable *Neumeier* Rule 2a, while New York law favored the plaintiff thus making applicable Rule 2b.[36] The court assumed that the only way to resolve the conflict between the two rules was by "determin[ing] the place *of the injury*,"[37] and that, under *Schultz*, that place is determined by finding "the place where the last event necessary to make the actor liable occurred."[38] Following this last-event rule, the court found that the injury had occurred in New York because the plaintiff's reliance on defendant's misrepresentation had taken place in that state and the resulting loss had been suffered there.[39] The court applied New York law under Rule 2b.[40] While the result is appropriate, the court's technical

such as interest analysis. As Brainerd Currie put it, interest analysis "summon[s] public policy from the reserves and place[s] it in the front lines where it belongs." B. Currie, Selected Essays on the Conflict of Laws 88 (1963). See also Phillips v. General Motors Corp., 298 Mont. 438, 995 P.2d 1002 (Mont. 2000) (concluding that, after the adoption of the Second Restatement, the *ordre public* exception became unnecessary and redundant because "[c]onsiderations of public policy are expressly subsumed within the most significant relationship approach.... [in that] [i]n order to determine which state has the more significant relationship, the public policies of all interested states must be considered.)" Id.

34. 20 F.3d 1092 (10th Cir.1994) (decided under New York conflicts law). Another case is Venturini v. Worldwide Marble & Granite Corp., 1995 WL 606281 (S.D.N.Y.1995), a case that was somewhat similar to *Cooney*. In *Venturini*, a New York company and a Michigan company filed third-party actions against a New Jersey employer for contribution and indemnification, in connection with an injury sustained in Michigan by a truck driver employed by the New Jersey company. Under New Jersey and Michigan law, an employer who provides worker's compensation benefits was immune from a claim for contribution by his joint tortfeasors. Under New York law contribution was available. The court concluded that under "the second *and* third Neumeier rules," 1995 WL 606281 at *3 (emphasis added), the law of Michigan applied to both actions and barred both the contribution and the indemnification claims. The court concluded that, for purposes of applying the *Neumei-*

er rules, the "place of wrong" is "'where the last event necessary to make the actor liable occurred.'" Id. The last event had occurred in Michigan where the truck driver was injured while unloading marble slabs that had been negligently loaded in New York.

35. The plaintiff, a New York banking corporation, agreed in that state to loan $105 million to a Texas oil producer. The loan was secured by the borrower's oil and gas reserves. In agreeing to provide the loan, plaintiff had relied on certain oil and gas reserve reports prepared in Oklahoma by defendant, an Oklahoma petroleum consultant company. After the borrower defaulted on the loan, the plaintiff discovered that the defendant's reports vastly had overstated the value of the borrower's oil and gas reserves. The plaintiff sued the defendant in federal district court in New York for negligence and negligent misrepresentation. The case was transferred to an Oklahoma federal court and, under *Van Dusen*, was decided under New York's choice-of-law rules.

36. The court recognized the tension between the *Neumeier* rules although it assumed that the tension was between Rules 2 and 3, rather than between Rules 2a and 2b. See *Bankers Trust*, 20 F.3d at 1097.

37. Id. (emphasis added).

38. Id. (quoting *Schultz*).

39. Id. at 1098.

40. Id. The court also noted the absence of any "special circumstances" which, under Rule 2b, may displace the *lex loci delicti* and the law of plaintiff's domicile. Id.

reading of *Schultz* is troublesome. Indeed, although several statements in *Schultz* may support the assumption that the "locus of the tort" is synonymous with the place of the injury, one should not take these statements literally. Furthermore, although the *Schultz* court did restate the last-event concept, the court also prefaced it with the qualifier "*[u]nder traditional rules.*"[41] There is no reason to assume that the *Schultz* court intended to resuscitate the traditional rules, especially since the court did not in fact *follow* the last-event rule.[42] In any event, this is one of the many technical problems resulting from the extension of the *Neumeier* rules to cross-border torts.

III. FROM RULES TO APPROACHES TO RULES

A. FROM RULES TO APPROACHES

1. *Introduction*

§ 17.33   Part II of this chapter, as well as Chapter 2, described the evolution of American conflicts law from the rigid territorial system of the First Restatement, to the choice-of-law revolution, to the new approaches that followed it. This Part attempts a synthesis of these approaches, and then explores whether the current state of the case law has produced, or is capable of producing, new choice-of-law rules for tort conflicts.

The First Restatement's rule for such conflicts, the *lex loci delicti*, proved too rigid and often arbitrary in its operation. This rigidity made necessary the utilization of all available escape devices: characterization, *ordre public*, the substance versus procedure dichotomy, and, occasionally, *renvoi*. Because of the frequent and widespread utilization of these escape devices, the Restatement was perceived as incapable of producing the legal certainty and predictability that its drafters had promised. In turn, this failure encouraged and nourished the revolution.

As it happens in many revolutions, the established system was demolished rather than repaired. The deficiencies of the Restatement's rules, coupled with the influence of American Legal Realism, which was the philosophical school of choice of most conflicts revolutionaries,[1] provoked an overreaction against *all* rules, which Brainerd Currie capsulized in his oft-quoted aphorism that "[w]e would be better off without choice-of-law rules."[2]

---

41. *Schultz*, 480 N.E.2d at 683 (emphasis added): "Under traditional rules, . . . when the defendant's negligent conduct occurs in one jurisdiction and the plaintiff's injuries are suffered in another, the place of the wrong is considered to be the place where the last event necessary to make the actor liable occurred."

42. *Schultz* treated New York as the "locus of the tort," even though New York was *not* the place of the "last event."

§ 17.33

1. For the influence of American legal realism on the American conflicts revolution, see Symeonides, An Outsider's View of The American Approach to Choice of Law 212–25, 229–34 (1980).

2. B. Currie, Selected Essays on the Conflict of Laws 180, 183 (1963).

One after the other, many courts gradually followed this trend. The majority of state courts of last resort discarded the *lex loci* rule as the *sole* basis for resolving tort conflicts and replaced it with flexible, perhaps too flexible, "approaches."[3] These approaches were largely inspired by the theories advanced by the revolution's intellectual leaders, most of whom were academic writers. However, in developing their approaches, most courts did not feel constrained to adopt a single theory or philosophical trend. Rather they merged academic approaches with each other or modified them by adding their own variations. As a result, the academic polyphony that characterized the scholastic revolution was succeeded by an even more conspicuous judicial polyphony. This explains why, as stated in the Introduction to this chapter, the lines tend to be fluid in the decided cases and why it is difficult to categorize states, or even individual decisions, as clearly following one or the other of the current methodologies.

While this polyphony is both necessary and enriching in periods of transition and experimentation, it can also be taxing on the resources of the lower courts. The bigger question is how long this transitional period should last. We shall return to this question later.[4] For now we shall attempt to suggest a synthesis of the existing trends for those courts that are not, for the time being, prepared to exit this transitional period.

2. *Policy Analysis: A Synthesis*

§ 17.34 When a court rejects the *lex loci delicti* rule and seeks another approach, its analysis should focus initially and primarily on considerations of policy.

a. *False Conflicts*

A first step is to determine, from the purposes of the two apparently conflicting rules, whether they conflict in fact. For instance, analysis may show, as in *Schmidt v. Driscoll Hotel*,[1] applying the pertinent rule of one state would promote that rule's purpose or policy, while applying the potentially competing rule of the other state would not. The latter may be the case when the second rule, by its terms or underlying policy, does not apply to multistate events or was not intended to regulate or benefit an out-of-state party. In these circumstances, there is *no real conflict of purpose*, and the appearance of a conflict of laws is simply *false or spurious*. Clearly then, one should apply only the rule whose purpose and policy would be furthered by its application, whether that be the rule of the forum or the other involved state. If, on the other hand, the purposes and policies of the two rules are the same, the forum should apply forum law.

---

3. See supra §§ 2.16, 2.22–2.25.

4. See infra § 17.35.

§ 17.34

1. 249 Minn. 376, 82 N.W.2d 365 (1957) (discussed supra § 17.12).

b. Conflicting Rules: Accommodation

When the legal rule of each state whose law is potentially applicable evidences a policy that would be furthered by the rule's application, the court must make a choice. Brainerd Currie's initial idea of automatically applying the law of the forum to every such conflict is neither a "choice" nor an acceptable solution. His later call for an enlightened and restrained reinterpretation of forum law comes closer to an acceptable formula, although it is difficult to distinguish it from other weighing approaches.[2] Be that as it may, it is worth to remember that, in deciding domestic cases, American courts have for generations engaged in identifying, evaluating, and–yes–weighing the policies and interests reflected in various state laws. Nothing makes it less appropriate for courts to do likewise in multistate cases–that is, weigh the conflicting state interests–provided they do so in an objective and forthright manner and explain the reasons for their conclusions.[3] A court's primary duty is to resolve the dispute between the parties but it should do so by *accommodating* rather than ignoring any conflicting state policies and interests. It should seek to apply the rule of the state whose interests are most appropriately furthered by the subordination of the interests of the other state. Section 6 of the Restatement (Second) identifies a number of pervasive choice-considerations, and its general tort provision (§ 145) lists those factors that appear most relevant for the determination of the state that has the most significant relationship to the occurrence and to the parties with respect to the particular issue.[4] Decisions like *Neumeier* and *Schultz*[5] attempt to reduce choice-considerations to new, but less rigid, rules.

c. Resolving the Impasse

Weighing of state interests, whether in the limited post-Currie way (such as suggested by the "comparative impairment" approach) or in the more far-reaching manner provided by the Second Restatement will not resolve all cases. In some cases, the conflicting state interests will be of equal strength and pertinence; in other cases it may be impossible to

---

2. See, e.g., von Mehren, Recent Trends in Choice-of-Law Methodology, 60 Cornell L. Rev. 927 (1975); Hancock, Some Choice of Law Problems Posed by Antique Statutes: Realism in Wisconsin and Rule Fetishism in New York, 27 Stan. L. Rev. 775 (1975); and Baxter, Choice of Law and the Federal System, 16 Stan. L. Rev. 1 (1963).

3. "[W]eighing of state interests is an appropriate, if not inevitable, means of resolving conflicts in any approach that acknowledges the existence of state interests. The question is not whether courts can or should weigh state interests, but rather how to weigh them, and how to resolve the resulting conflicts." S. Symeonides, The American Choice-of-Law Revolution in the

Courts: Today and Tomorrow, 298 Recueil des Cours, 1, 51 (2003).

4. In addition, the Second Restatement provides precise rules for some choice-of-law problems whenever there appeared, by tradition, to be relatively uniform agreement, for instance that situs law governs with respect to title to real property (§ 223). In tort, such definite rules are still lacking, although the Second Restatement attributes primary importance to the place of injury in the determination of the law applicable to personal injuries (§ 146) and for a number of other tort issues. See supra § 17.25.

5. See supra §§ 17.31–17.32.

determine the state that has the most significant relationship to the case. An impasse will then be present. In these circumstances, it is difficult to articulate a formula that is more concise than simply stating that the court should do justice between the parties.

Leflar suggests[6] that courts should apply the "better law" and, in so doing, take advantage of the choice-of-law setting to further the development of the law along desirable lines. Experience with cases decided under this approach shows, however, that courts will usually turn to forum law.[7] This may be appropriate, depending on the circumstances and the content of the law involved. However, the forum does not discharge its task to be "a justice administering state"[8] by an automatic, mechanical preference for its own law. Cavers's writings[9] suggest another approach that appears to be preferable.

In torts, a pervasive objective is to spread the risk, either by insurance or by imposition of the cost on the business or on the product. Thus, in situations in which an insured or enterprise risk is involved, the plaintiff should be entitled to the application of the more beneficial of the conflicting rules because the law is protective of the injured[10] and because the policy that favors the spreading of the risk will often be considered a superior policy by the states involved. The case law with respect to defamation and invasion of privacy,[11] and—to some extent—worker compensation[12] and products liability,[13] increasingly tends to select the "more favorable law." Several foreign systems also devised rules that permit alternative references in order to favor the plaintiff.[14]

6. Leflar, Choice Influencing Considerations in Conflicts Law, 41 N.Y.U. L. Rev. 267 (1966); Leflar, Conflicts Law: More on Choice–Influencing Considerations, 54 Cal. L. Rev. 1584 (1966).

7. See supra §§ 17.22–17.23 (also discussing other possible biases, such as favoring plaintiffs, or local litigants).

8. Milkovich v. Saari, 295 Minn. 155, 170, 203 N.W.2d 408, 417 (1973).

9. See supra § 2.12.

10. See Labree v. Major, 111 R.I. 657, 673, 306 A.2d 808, 818 (1973), allowing Massachusetts guests to recover from Rhode Island driver under Rhode Island ordinary negligence principles for injuries sustained in Massachusetts during a trip that began and was to end in Massachusetts, despite the Massachusetts rule restricting recovery to liability for gross negligence: "where a driver is from a state which allows a passenger to recover for ordinary negligence, the plaintiff should recover, no matter what the law of his residence or the place of the accident." The court expressly rejected the third *Neumeier* rule, supra § 17.31, as a variation of the traditional *lex loci* rule. See also R. Wein-

traub, Commentary on the Conflict of Laws 360 (3d ed. 1986), who advocated the application of the more favorable law, subject to exceptions, in "true conflicts" cases. For critical discussion of Weintraub's views see Seidelson, Interest Analysis: The Quest for Perfection and the Frailties of Man, 19 Duq. L. Rev. 207 (1981). For a refinement of Weintraub's position, see R. Weintraub, Commentary on the Conflict of Laws 346–57 (4th ed. 2001). For a codified example, see the 1999 German Codification on the law applicable to non-contractual obligations, Bundesgesetzblatt 1999, I, 1026, Article 40(4): "The injured person may bring his or her claim directly against the insurer of the person liable to provide compensation, if the law applicable to the tort or to the insurance contract so provides." For similar rules see infra n.14.

11. Infra § 17.55.

12. Infra § 17.59 et seq.

13. Infra § 17.64, et seq.

14. See e.g., the 1999 German Codification, supra n.10, Art. 40(1) ("Claims arising from tort are governed by the law of the state in which the person liable to provide compensation acted. The injured person

To resolve true conflicts in favor of recovery means that the resolution of the residual imbalance is left to the reform of the insurance system.[15] This is probably not far from what actually occurs now: the number of cases that fall into the final, residual category is very small indeed because most can be resolved by a policy analysis that identifies either the existence of a false conflict or of a genuine imbalance, and not an impasse, in the policies reflected in the rules that compete for application.

3. *Time for Rules?*

§ 17.35 It is believed that the above analysis can resolve most tort conflicts in a sound and rational manner. However, the question is whether this or any other similar analysis needs to be repeated for every single case, with all the attendant consequences on judicial resources,[1] or whether it should be reserved for those truly difficult cases for which the case law does not provide clear answers. Another way of asking this question is to inquire whether the experience accumulated since the beginning of the conflicts revolution now makes it possible to articulate new choice-of-law rules capable of rationally resolving most cases, while leaving the remaining cases to open ended ad hoc analyses, such as the one described in the preceding section. To ask this question is not to deny the revolution's contributions in renovating American conflicts law. In fact, one could argue that this is the best way to preserve the revolution's accomplishments. The fact that the revolution was necessitated by the deficiencies of the old rules should not mean that one should not aspire to develop new rules that are free from such deficiencies. With due respect to Currie's anti-rule sentiments,[2] "the formulation of rules should be as much an objective in choice of law as it is in other areas of law."[3] The pragmatic question is whether such rules are possible at the

---

may demand, however, that the law of the state where the result took effect be applied instead."); Swiss Federal Statute on Private International Law of Dec. 18, 1987, Art. 138 ("Claims resulting from injurious emissions emanating from an immovable are governed, at the choice of the injured party, by the law of the state in which the immovable is situated or by the law of the state in which the result [of such emission] occurred.") For a collection and discussion of such plaintiff-favoring rules, see S. Symeonides, Private International Law at the End of the 20th Century: Progress or Regress? 57–60 (1999). See also infra §§ 17.49, 17.76.

15. On choice-of-law problems with respect to no-fault insurance see infra § 17.56 et seq.

§ 17.35

1. See Kozyris, Interest Analysis Facing its Critics, 46 Ohio St. L.J. 569, 580 (1985)

("[A]ny system calling for open-ended and endless soul-searching on a case-by-case basis carries a high burden of persuasion. With centuries of experience and doctrinal elaboration behind us, we hardly need more lab testing and narrow findings. Rather, we need to make up our minds and make some sense out of the chaos.").

2. See supra § 17.33 n.2.

3. Reese, General Course on Private International Law, 150 Recueil des Cours 1, 61 (1976–II). To paraphrase Maurice Rosenberg, the "unruly reasonableness" brought about by the abandonment of the "unreasonable rules" of the traditional theory should be succeeded by a "principled reasonableness." Rosenberg, Two Views on *Kell v. Henderson*: An Opinion for the New York Court of Appeals, 67 Colum. L. Rev. 459, 464 (1967) ("The problem is to escape both horns of the dilemma by avoiding both unreasonable rules and an unruly reason-

present time–whether, in other words, the normal operation of *stare decisis* has produced, or is capable of producing, such rules. The *Neumeier* rules could be viewed as an example of such a development.[4] One of the questions explored below is whether, despite the deficiencies discussed earlier,[5] the *Neumeier* rules or similar rules are a positive development in American conflicts law. Another question is whether the case law in other states has also produced, or is capable of producing, similar or different rules.

To answer these questions, the discussion below divides the case law into fact-law patterns similar to the patterns contemplated by the *Neumeier* rules. The discussion compares the results reached by the case law with the solutions provided in the *Neumeier* rules, as well as those provided by two other rule-models: a statutory model, the Louisiana codification;[6] and an academic model, Professor Cavers's "principles of preference."[7] The discussion begins with the distinction between conduct-regulating and loss-distributing rules, which is the explicit or implicit basis of all three models.

B. FROM APPROACHES TO RULES

1. The Distinction between Conduct–Regulation Rules and Loss–Distribution Rules

a. The Origins and Meaning of the Distinction

§ 17.36 In its modern expression, the distinction between conduct-regulation rules, on the one hand and loss-allocation or loss-distribution, on the other, was first enunciated in *dicta* by the New York Court of Appeals in *Babcock*.[1] The court held that the New York host-driver was, under New York law, amenable to suit by his New York guest-passenger for injury received in Ontario despite the bar imposed on such suits by Ontario's guest-statute. However, the court also noted that it would have reached a different conclusion "had the issue related to the manner in which the defendant had been driving his car at the time of the accident . . . [or to] the defendant's exercise of due care."[2] In such a case, said the court, the state in which the conduct occurred "will usually have a predominant, if not exclusive, concern"[3] and that "it would be almost

---

ableness that is destructive of many of the values of law.").

4. However, these rules may have exceeded the confines of *stare decisis* to the extent they encompassed prescriptions for fact-patterns not yet adjudicated. For example, at the time the *Neumeier* rules were enunciated, the New York Court Appeals had not decided a case falling within the reverse-*Babcock* pattern (Rule 1) or any case falling within the scope of Rule 2. For criticism on this point, see Sedler, Interstate Accidents and the Unprovided-for Case: Reflections on *Neumeier v. Kuehner*, 1 Hofstra L. Rev. 125, 132–35 (1973).

5. See supra § 17.32.

6. See supra § 17.20.

7. See D. Cavers, The Choice of Law Process 139–80 (1965).

§ 17.36

1. Babcock v. Jackson, 12 N.Y.2d 473, 240 N.Y.S.2d 743, 191 N.E.2d 279 (1963) (discussed supra § 17.29).

2. *Babcock*, 12 N.Y.2d at 483, 240 N.Y.S.2d at 750, 191 N.E.2d at 284.

3. Id. "Where the defendant's exercise of due care in the operation of his automobile is in issue, the jurisdiction in which the

unthinkable to seek the applicable rule in the law of some other place.'"[4] In contrast, the issue actually involved in *Babcock* was

> not whether the defendant offended against a rule of the road prescribed by Ontario for motorists generally or whether he violated some standard of conduct imposed by that jurisdiction, but rather whether the plaintiff, because she was a guest in the defendant's automobile, is barred from recovering damages for a wrong concededly committed.[5]

With regard to such an issue, said the court, the state in which both parties were domiciled and their relationship was centered had "the dominant contacts and the superior claim for application of its law.'"[6]

The same court reiterated the above distinction in *Schultz*.[7] The court explained that in conflicts between "rules [that] involve the appropriate standards of conduct . . . , the law of the place of the tort 'will usually have a predominant, if not exclusive, concern' . . . because the locus jurisdiction's interests in protecting the reasonable expectations of the parties who relied on it to govern their primary conduct and in the admonitory effect that applying its law will have on similar conduct in the future assume critical importance.'"[8] Conversely, in conflicts between "rules [that] relate to allocating losses that result from admittedly tortious conduct, . . . rules such as those limiting damages in wrongful death actions, vicarious liability rules, or immunities from suit, considerations of the State's admonitory interest and party reliance are less important." In such conflicts, said the court, "[a]nalysis . . . favors the jurisdiction of common domicile because of its interests in enforcing the decision of both parties to accept both the benefits and the burdens of identifying with that jurisdiction and to submit themselves to its authority.'"[9] After concluding that both New Jersey's charitable-immunity rule and New York's no-immunity rule were loss-distribution rules, the court applied the law of the parties' common domicile, rather than the law of the place of the wrongful conduct.

Thus, with *Babcock* and then *Schultz*, the distinction between conduct-regulation rules and loss-distribution rules had taken roots in New York conflicts law. In *Padula v. Lilarn Props. Corp.*,[10] the New York Court of Appeals provided a more succinct definition of conduct-regulating and loss-distributing rules. It defined the former as those rules that "have the prophylactic effect of governing conduct to prevent injuries

---

allegedly wrongful conduct occurred will usually have a predominant, if not exclusive, concern. In such a case, it is appropriate to look to the law of the place of the tort so as to give effect to that jurisdiction's interest in regulating conduct within its borders, and it would be almost unthinkable to seek the applicable rule in the law of some other place."

4. *Babcock*, 12 N.Y.2d at 482–83, 191 N.E.2d at 279–80, 240 N.Y.S.2d at 750–51.

5. Id. at 483, 285, 750–51.

6. Id.

7. Schultz v. Boy Scouts of America, Inc., 65 N.Y.2d 189, 491 N.Y.S.2d 90, 480 N.E.2d 679 (1985) (discussed supra § 17.32).

8. *Schultz*, 65 N.Y.2d at 198, 491 N.Y.S.2d 90, 95–96, 480 N.E.2d 679, 684 (quoting *Babcock*).

9. Id.

10. 84 N.Y.2d 519, 620 N.Y.S.2d 310, 644 N.E.2d 1001 (1994).

from occurring"[11] and the latter as those rules that "prohibit, assign, or limit liability after the tort occurs."[12]

Since *Babcock*, the distinction has spread elsewhere. "While not every state has decided the issue, there are no states that have rejected [it]."[13] As two recent studies have demonstrated,[14] courts in many other states have adopted this distinction, explicitly or implicitly.[15] In 1991, Louisiana codified it, although it employed terminology intended to narrow down the category of conduct-regulating rules by referring to issues of "standards of conduct *and* safety."[16] The codification distinguishes between these issues and "issues of loss-distribution or financial protection,"[17] and provides different choice-of-law rules for each category. For the former category, the codification discounts the parties' domicile and focuses on the place or places of conduct and injury. For loss-distribution conflicts, the codification focuses on the parties' domicile, although it assigns a supporting role to the places of conduct and injury.

In the meantime, a parallel, but not identical, distinction has emerged elsewhere. For example, article 142(2) of the Swiss codification provides that, regardless of which law governs a tort case, "[r]ules of safety and conduct in force at the place of the act are [to be] taken into

11. Id. at 1002.

12. Id.

13. Cross, The Conduct–Regulating Exception in Modern United States Choice-of-Law, 36 Creighton L. Rev. 425, 441 (2003).

14. See Cross, supra n.13 (providing "overwhelming evidence" id. at 437; S. Symeonides, The American Choice-of-Law Revolution in the Courts: Today and Tomorrow, 298 Recueil des Cours, 1, 154 et seq. (2003).

15. See, e.g., Collins v. Trius, Inc., 663 A.2d 570 (Me.1995) (discussed supra § 17.26 nn.21–27); Miller v. White, 167 Vt. 45, 702 A.2d 392 (1997) (discussed supra § 17.26 nn.8–19); Myers v. Langlois, 168 Vt. 432, 721 A.2d 129 (1998); Schwartz v. Schwartz, 103 Ariz. 562, 447 P.2d 254 (1968); Woodward v. Stewart, 104 R.I. 290, 243 A.2d 917 (1968); Mellk v. Sarahson, 49 N.J. 226, 229 A.2d 625 (1967); Veasley v. CRST Int'l, Inc., 553 N.W.2d 896 (Iowa 1996); District of Columbia v. Coleman, 667 A.2d 811 (D.C.1995); Rong Yao Zhou v. Jennifer Mall Rest., 534 A.2d 1268 (D.C. 1987); Kuehn v. Childrens Hospital, Los Angeles, 119 F.3d 1296 (7th Cir. 1997); Matson by Kehoe v. Anctil, 979 F.Supp. 1031 (D.Vt.1997) (discussed supra § 17.26 n.19); Matson v. Anctil, 7 F.Supp.2d 423 (D.Vt.1998); Bauer v. Club Med Sales, Inc., 1996 WL 310076 (N.D.Cal.1996); Troxel v.

A.I duPont Inst., 431 Pa.Super. 464, 636 A.2d 1179 (1994); Moye v. Palma, 263 N.J.Super. 287, 622 A.2d 935 (1993); Dorr v. Briggs, 709 F.Supp. 1005 (D.Colo.1989); FCE Transp., Inc. v. Ajayem Lumber Midwest Corp., 1988 WL 48018 (Ohio App. 1988); Svege v. Mercedes Benz Credit Corp., 182 F.Supp.2d 226 (D.Conn. 2002); Ellis v. Barto, 82 Wn.App. 454, 918 P.2d 540 (1996), review denied 130 Wash.2d 1026, 930 P.2d 1229 (1997); Burney v. P V Holding Corp., 218 Mich.App. 167, 553 N.W.2d 657 (1996); Pittman v. Maldania, Inc., 2001 WL 1221704 (Del. Super.2001); Cropp v. Interstate Distrib. Co., 129 Or.App. 510, 880 P.2d 464 (1994) review denied, 320 Or. 407, 887 P.2d 791 (1994).

16. La. Civ. Code art. 3543 (reproduced infra § 17.49 n.1). This article provides that in conflicts involving these issues, the law of the place of conduct governs unless the injury occurred in another state that imposes a higher standard of conduct. In the latter case, the law of the state of injury governs, provided that the occurrence of the injury in that state was objectively foreseeable. For a similar provision, see art. 46 of the Puerto Rico Draft Code.

17. La. Civ. Code art. 3544 (discussed infra § 17.39–17.46, passim). For a similar provision, see art. 47 of the Puerto Rico Draft Code

consideration."[18] The Dutch,[19] Portuguese,[20] Hungarian,[21] and Tunisian[22] codifications contain similar provisions, as do the Hague conventions on traffic accidents and products liability,[23] and a proposed European Union Regulation ("Rome II").[24]

Implicit in these developments are certain assumptions about state interests and about how tort rules operate "in space." A state's policy of deterrence embodied in its conduct-regulating rules is implicated by all sub-standard conduct that occurs within its territory, regardless of whether the parties involved are domiciled in that state. Conversely, a state's loss-distribution policy may or may not extend to non-domiciliaries acting within its territory, but does extend to its domiciliaries even when they act outside that state. Put another way, conduct-regulating rules are territorially oriented, whereas loss-distribution rules are *usually* not territorially oriented.[25]

b.   *The Difficulties of the Distinction*

§ 17.37   While the above assumptions may or may not be questionable, what is questionable is the precision with which one can expect to classify conflicting tort rules into the one or the other of the above categories. Indeed, the line between conduct-regulating and loss-distributing rules is not always as clear as one would like.[1] Some tort rules such

18.   Swiss Federal Statute on Private International Law of December 18, 1987, Art. 142(2).

19.   See Act Regarding the Conflict of Laws on Torts of 11 April 2001, Staatsblad 2001, 190, art. 8 (the Act's other choice-of-law articles "shall not prevent the taking into account of traffic and other safety regulations, and other comparable regulations for the protection of persons or property in force at the place of the tort.")

20.   See Portuguese Civ. Code art. 45(3) (application of law of parties' common nationality or residence shall be "without prejudice to provisions of local state laws which must be applied to all persons without differentiation").

21.   See Hungarian Decree on Private International Law of 1979 § 33.1 (regardless of the law applicable to the tort, "[t]he law of the place of the tortious conduct shall determine whether the tortious conduct was realized by the violation of traffic or other security regulations.").

22.   See Tunisian Code of Private International Law of 1998, Art. 75 (regardless of the otherwise applicable law, "the rules of conduct and security in force at the place of the injurious event are taken into consideration." (Authors' translation).

23.   See Article 7 of the Hague Traffic Accidents Convention of 1971 ("Whatever may be the applicable law, in determining liability account shall be taken of rules relating to the control and safety of traffic which were in force at the place and time of the accident."); Article 9 of the Hague Convention on the Law Applicable to Products Liability of 1972 ("The application of Articles 4, 5 and 6 shall not preclude consideration being given to the rules of conduct and safety prevailing in the State where the product was introduced into the market.").

24.   See Proposal for a Regulation of the European Parliament and the Council on the Law Applicable to Non-contractual Obligations ("Rome II"), Art. 13 ("Whatever may be the applicable law, in determining liability account shall be taken of the rules of safety and conduct which were in force at the place and time of the event giving rise to the damage.").

25.   Symeonides, supra n.14, at 160.

§ 17.37

1.   See Symeonides, Choice of Law in the American Courts in 1994: A View "From the Trenches," 43 Am. J. Comp. L. 1, 17–18 (1995) (describing the difficulties encountered by New York courts); Symeonides, Louisiana's New Law of Choice of Law for Tort Conflicts: An Exegesis, 66 Tul. L. Rev. 677, 704–05 (1992) (acknowledging difficulties of this distinction under the Louisiana codification); Perdue, A Reexamination of the Distinction between "Loss Allocating" and "Conduct–Regulating" Rules, 60 La. L. Rev. 1251 (2000).

as "rules of the road"[2] and punitive-damages rules[3] are clearly conduct-regulating,[4] while some rules such as guest statutes[5] or intrafamily immunity rules are clearly loss-distributing.[6] However, there are many

2. Rules of the road are classic examples of conduct-regulating rules because they are designed to ensure the safety of the public by defining permissible and impermissible conduct and by imposing sanctions on violators. This category is not as small as most commentators assume. It includes not only speed limits and traffic-light rules, but also rules that prescribe the civil sanctions for violating traffic rules, including presumptions and inferences attached to the violation. For example, a rule providing that a person involved in a collision while driving intoxicated or while driving in excess of the speed limit is presumed negligent is primarily a conduct-regulating rule. Likewise, a rule providing that, in a rear-end vehicular collision, the driver of the rear car is presumed to be at fault is also primarily conduct-regulating. S. Symeonides, The American Choice-of-Law Revolution in the Courts: Today and Tomorrow, 298 Recueil des Cours, 1, 168 (2003).

3. As the word "punitive" suggests, the purpose of these rules is to punish the individual tortfeasor, as well as to deter other potential tortfeasors, rather than to compensate the victim who is, *ex hypothesi*, made whole through compensatory damages. To be sure, punitive damages also have a loss-allocation effect in the sense that they often involve large transfers of wealth from the defendant to the plaintiff side, but this is an effect of the punitive damage rule, not its purpose, which is to deter egregious conduct. Symeonides, id. 169. On the other hand, one could argue that, a state's decision not to impose punitive damages is motivated by loss-allocation factors, e.g., protecting an industry from potentially debilitating financial burdens. See Reppy, Codifying Interest Analysis in the Torts Chapter of a New Conflicts Restatement, 75 Ind. L. J. 591, 597 (2000). Reppy correctly concludes, however, that when two parties from a non-punitive damages state are involved in a tort in a state that imposes punitive damages, the punitive-damages rule of the latter state should govern because "the conduct-regulating rule here trumps the contrary loss-distributive rule," id., of the other state.

4. Other examples include rules that prescribe safety standards for work sites, buildings, and other premises. These rules are primarily conduct-regulating, although they may well have an impact on loss-allo-

cation. As Judge Posner noted in Spinozzi v. ITT Sheraton Corp., 174 F.3d 842 (7th Cir. 1999), a case involving safety standards in a foreign hotel, it would be both non-sensical and dangerous to impose on the hotel operator a duty to follow the safety standards in force in the home-states of the hotel guests. This would subject the operator "to a hundred different bodies of tort law," id. at 845, each imposing potentially inconsistent duties of care. "A resort might have a system of firewalls that under the law of some states or nations might be considered essential to safety and in others might be considered a safety hazard." Id.

5. See *Babcock*, supra § 17.36 at n.5; Cipolla v. Shaposka, 439 Pa. 563, 267 A.2d 854, 856 n.2 (1970) ("the fact that the accident occurred in Delaware is not a relevant contact because the Delaware [guest] statute does not set out a rule of the road."); Symeonides, supra n. 2, at 162 ("a guest statute is clearly loss-allocating but it has practically zero effect on the driver's conduct. A driver will not drive less carefully in a guest-statute state just because of the assurance that, if she is involved in an accident and she survives it, she will be immune from a suit by her guest-passengers.").

6. Other examples of rules that are primarily loss-distributive, even if they have a bearing on conduct, include: rules providing charitable immunity; rules imposing ceilings on the amount of damages or excluding certain types of damages, such as for pain and suffering; rules defining the beneficiaries of wrongful death actions, survival actions, and loss of consortium actions; the old rules providing that a tort action does not survive the tortfeasor's death; rules dealing with contribution or indemnification among joint tortfeasors; rules providing for no-fault automobile insurance, statutes of repose, which protect manufactures from suits filed after a designated number of years from the product's first use, corporate-successor liability or non-liability rules, and direct action statutes, namely statutes that allow the victim to directly sue the tortfeasor's insurer. Symeonides, *The Revolution Today*, supra n. 2, at 169–70. With regard to joint-tortfeasor rules, see Borchers, The Return of Territorialism to New York's Conflicts Law: *Padula v. Lilarn Properties Corp.*, 58 Alb. L. Rev. 775, 785 (1995) ("[p]arties, obviously, can do little to

tort rules that do not easily fit in either category, and some rules that appear to fit in *both* categories. In fact, at least one author has contended that "*most* tort rules"[7] belong to both categories, and that " 'the compensation and deterrence goals ascribed to the tort system cannot be separated.' "[8]

The case law offers several examples of rules in which courts ascribed to a rule such a dual function. For example, while most courts would agree that a rule that limits the amount of compensatory damages is purely loss-distributive, at least one court concluded that a rule that allows unlimited damages is at least in part conduct-regulating. In *Hurtado v. Superior Court*,[9] the California Supreme Court concluded that a California rule that did not limit the amount of wrongful-death damages was designed in large part to deter people from wrongfully killing other people.[10] It is of course conceivable that, over a long period of time, a rule that allows unlimited damages may affect the actor's conduct (by altering or reducing the level of the actor's activity), but only in cases of *non*-intentional torts in which the tortfeasor's activity does *not* endanger the actor's own safety.[11] However, it is difficult to accept the proposition that large damage awards have the effect of deterring wrongful deaths, especially in traffic-accident cases like *Hurtado* in which the tortfeasor's own safety is also at risk.[12] More importantly, leaving aside the actual impact on people's behavior, it is just as difficult to accept that the *purpose* of a rule that allows unlimited damages is to deter wrongful conduct as it is to accept that the *purpose*

choose their co-tortfeasors, and thus rules like this have, at most, minimal effect on conduct.").

7. Perdue, A Reexamination of the Distinction between 'Loss Allocating' and 'Conduct–Regulating' Rules, 60 La. L. Rev. 1251, 1252 (2000) (emphasis added).

8. Id. (quoting M. Trebilock, Incentive Issues in the Design of "No–Fault" Compensation Systems, 39 U. Toronto L. J. 19, 20 (1989)). Perdue argues that "[a]ll tort rules determine who will bear a loss and thus all are loss-allocating. In addition[,] ... most [of them] affect conduct ... [because] [l]oss-allocation creates incentives for those who must bear the loss to behave differently than they would if they did not bear the loss." Id. For a discussion of Perdue's arguments, see Symeonides, *The Revolution Today*, supra n. 2, at 161–72.

9. 11 Cal.3d 574, 114 Cal.Rptr. 106, 522 P.2d 666 (1974) (discussed supra §§ 17.14, 17.18).

10. For a critique of *Hurtado* on this point, "offer[ing] a long list of reasons why this conclusion is untenable," see Reppy, Eclecticism in Choice of Law: Hybrid Method or Mishmash? 34 Mercer L. Rev. 645, 669 (1983). For other cases reaching similar, though not as extreme conclusions, see Symeonides, *The Revolution Today*, supra n. 2, at 215–217.

11. Even in these cases however, this does not seem to be the reason for which a state decides not to limit the amount of damages. After all, unlimited damages are the norm. The lawmaker allows them because ordinarily the victim is entitled to recover her entire loss. On the other hand, limited damages are the exception. The lawmaker limits their amount, not because the victim is undeserving, but rather because, on balance, the lawmaker decides to reduce the financial burden on a particular class of tortfeasors. In both cases, the lawmaker's motives are loss-distributive rather than conduct-regulating.

12. For the same reason, one must reject the argument that the opposite of a guest statute (i.e., a common-law rule that allows the injured guest-passenger to sue the host-driver) is conduct regulating. In *Milkovich v. Saari*, 295 Minn. 155, 203 N.W.2d 408 (1973) (discussed supra § 17.22), the court came close to accepting such an argument but it did not base the holding on it. See 295 Minn. at 171 ("While there may be more deterrent effect in our common-law rule of liability as opposed to the guest statute requirement of gross negligence, [our] main governmental interest involved is that of any 'justice-administering state.' ").

of a rule that limits the amount of damages is to encourage or even condone wrongful conduct.[13]

This is not to deny that many tort rules have a dual *effect*, that is, they have a bearing on both conduct regulation and loss distribution. The *Schultz* pattern provides one example. In that case, both the majority and the dissenting opinions agreed that New Jersey's charitable immunity rule was a loss-distributing rule in that—like Ontario's guest statute in *Babcock*—its purpose was not to encourage or even condone negligent conduct by charitable corporations but rather to shield them from direct financial responsibility. On the other hand, the dissenting opinion argued strenuously that New York's charitable "nonimmunity" rule was conduct-regulating.[14] The argument is not entirely implausible, in that the non-immunity rule potentially has a dual effect: a loss-distributing effect to the extent the rule imposes financial responsibility on the actor and provides compensation to the victim, and a conduct-regulating effect to the extent the rule affects the actor's conduct by providing an additional incentive to act more carefully.

Dram shop acts provide another example of potentially dual-effect rules. A dram shop act has a conduct-regulating effect to the extent it makes it more likely that tavern owners will act more carefully and not serve apparently intoxicated patrons. However a dram shop act also has a loss-distributing effect to the extent it facilitates financial recovery for victims by making available to them an additional defendant, the tavern owner, and to place on the latter the economic loss of accidents caused by his drunk patrons. In contrast, a state's refusal to enact a dram shop act—or the enactment of an anti-dram shop act or a "social-host" act— has primarily a loss-distributing effect in that its purpose is to shield

---

13. The more probable purpose of a rule that limits the amount of compensatory damages is to reduce the financial burden on the class of people engaging in the particular conduct, be they drivers, surgeons, or manufacturers. The purpose is not to encourage substandard conduct, which may even harm the lawmakers themselves. Rather the purpose is to affix in advance the financial consequences of conduct that experience tells us will occur and will cause harm. The lawmaker simply recognizes that the conduct will, and should, occur (people will drive, surgeons will operate, manufacturers will produce), that some of this conduct will cause injury, and a decision must be made on which class of people will bear the loss, and how much of it. These loss-allocative decisions are value judgments lawmakers make every day. Symeonides, *The Revolution Today*, supra n.2, at 165.

14. See Schultz v. Boy Scouts of America, Inc., 65 N.Y.2d 189, 491 N.Y.S.2d 90 at 102, 480 N.E.2d 679 (Jason, J., dissenting),

arguing that the majority's characterization of this rule as loss-distributing was "obviously" erroneous. The majority responded rather summarily that "New York's rule holding charities liable for their tortious acts . . . is also a loss-allocating rule, just as New Jersey's charitable immunity statute is." Id. at 96 n.2. More than a decade later, a New Jersey court ignored *Schultz* and held that New York's non-immunity rule served a two-fold purpose of "both assur[ing] payment of any obligation to the person injured and giv[ing] warning that justice and the law demand the exercise of care." Butkera v. Hudson River Sloop "Clearwater," Inc., 300 N.J.Super. 550, 693 A.2d 520, 523 (1997). With such a dual characterization, the New Jersey court convinced itself that it could justify applying the New York rule against a New York charity whose conduct in New Jersey had injured a New Jersey resident there.

tavern owners or social hosts from financial responsibility, rather than to encourage them to act carelessly.[15]

Finally, another example of dual-effect rules is provided by a series of New York cases involving §§ 240–41 of New York's Labor Law, which impose upon the owner of an immovable absolute liability for injury caused by a defective scaffold to a construction worker working on the premises. Six cases decided by lower courts had characterized these provisions in three different ways[16] before the New York Court of Appeals had the opportunity to consider the matter in *Padula v. Lilarn Props. Corp.*[17] The court acknowledged that §§ 240–41 "embod[ied] both conduct-regulating and loss-allocating functions"[18] but concluded that the *primary* purpose of these rules was a conduct-regulating one.[19] Thus, the court provided a simple answer to a complex question: whenever a particular rule embodies both conduct-regulating and loss-distributing functions, the court is to focus on the rule's primary purpose and proceed accordingly.

15. Symeonides, *The Revolution Today*, supra n.2 at 166. According to this author, other examples of dual-effect rules include strict-liability rules, contributory-negligence rules, and "car-owner statutes," namely, statutes that impose vicarious liability on car owners for injuries caused by a driver using the car with the owner's consent.

16. The following cases classified § 240 as conduct-regulating: Zangiacomi v. Saunders, 714 F.Supp. 658 (S.D.N.Y.1989) (Connecticut accident, New York plaintiff, New York defendant—§ 240 not applied); Salsman v. Barden & Robeson Corp., 164 A.D.2d 481, 564 N.Y.S.2d 546 (3d Dep't 1990) (Massachusetts accident, Pennsylvania plaintiff, New York defendant: § 240 is "first and foremost [a] conduct regulating rule," although it has a certain "loss allocating aspect." This aspect "does not come into play until it has first been determined that the statute's conduct regulating rules have been violated."—§ 240 not applied). Thompson v. IBM Corp., 862 F.Supp. 79 (S.D.N.Y.1994) characterized § 240 as primarily a loss-distribution rule and applied it to a New York accident involving Massachusetts parties, *inter alia* "to avoid giving a competitive advantage to out-of-state contractors utilizing out-of-state workers." The following cases characterized § 240 as both conduct-regulating and loss-distributing: Calla v. Shulsky, 148 A.D.2d 60, 543 N.Y.S.2d 666 (1st Dept.1989) (Connecticut accident, New York plaintiff, New York defendant: "[T]he act of shifting financial responsibility often serves to regulate conduct by providing an inducement to exercise oversight in order to avoid the economic disincentive of vicarious liability."—§ 240 applied); Huston v. Hayden Bldg. Maint. Corp., 205 A.D.2d 68, 617 N.Y.S.2d 335 (2d

Dept.1994) (New Jersey accident, New York plaintiff, New York defendants: "[E]ven though [§ 240] serves a dual function at various times, our analysis should focus on which of those functions is applicable to the specific cause of action here."—§ 240 not applied.); Aviles v. The Port Authority of New York and New Jersey, 202 A.D.2d 45, 615 N.Y.S.2d 668 (1st Dept.1994) (New Jersey accident, New York plaintiff, defendant domiciled in New York and New Jersey—§ 240 not applied).

17. 84 N.Y.2d 519, 644 N.E.2d 1001, 620 N.Y.S.2d 310 (1994). In this case, a New York worker invoked §§ 240–41 in an action filed against a New York defendant for injuries the plaintiff had sustained in Massachusetts when he had fallen from a scaffold while working on a building owned by the defendant. For a discussion of this case and the distinction generally, see Borchers, The Return of Territorialism to New York's Conflicts Law: *Padula v. Lilarn Properties Corp.*, 58 Alb. L. Rev. 775 (1995).

18. *Padula*, 644 N.E.2d at 1003. The conduct-regulating function was "requiring worksites be made safe," id., while the loss-distributing function was the imposition of vicarious liability on the owner of the property for failure to provide a safe worksite. Id.

19. See id.: "We hold however, that sections 240 and 241 of the Labor Law are primarily conduct-regulating rules, requiring that adequate safety measures be instituted at the work site and should not be applied to the resolution of this tort dispute arising in Massachusetts." The court held these sections inapplicable to the Massachusetts accident.

While this answer is not profound, it is practical. It suggests that the difficulties in employing the above distinction are not insurmountable. Certainly, they are no more insurmountable than, for example, the difficulties of distinguishing between substance and procedure[20] or, in some close cases, even between contract and tort.[21] While this comparison may evoke the difficulties encountered in the characterization process under the traditional theory,[22] this similarity is only superficial. The traditional theory sought to ascribe labels to rules without regard to their underlying purpose. In contrast, the process of distinguishing between conduct-regulating and loss-distributing rules seeks to ascertain their true purposes and does so in a much more nuanced and focused manner. In other words, it asks the right questions and, more importantly, it is expected to provide reasons for the answers to which it arrives.[23]

c. *The Usefulness of the Distinction*

§ 17.38 Thus, despite the difficulties in its application, the distinction between conduct-regulating and loss-distributing rules provides a useful framework for resolving many tort conflicts. As Judge Weinstein observed, the distinction "serves as a proxy for the ultimate question of which state has the greater interest in having its law applied to the litigation at hand."[1] At least in a judicial choice of law,[2] this distinction focuses the parties' and the court's attention on the right questions and draws the lines along which the battle will be fought. It stands for the simple proposition that in conflicts between conduct-regulation rules, one should focus on the place or places of conduct and injury, whereas in conflicts between loss-distribution rules, one should also focus on the parties' connections, if any, with other states.[3] Put another way, this

---

20. See Borchers, supra n. 17, at 784 (1995) ("Many important and fundamental legal distinctions involve large areas of overlap. The distinction between substance and procedure is a good example.")

21. To paraphrase Professor Baxter, the process of distinguishing between the two categories "will sometimes be difficult, and reasonable disagreement may exist regarding the objectives of various internal rules. The process, however, is a familiar one rather than a unique concomitant of the choice analysis proposed." Baxter, Choice of Law in the Federal System, 16 Stan. L. Rev. 1, 12 n.28 (1963).

22. See supra §§ 3.4, 17.8–10.

23. Symeonides, *The Revolution Today,* supra n.2 at 170.

§ 17.38

1. Hamilton v. Accu–Tek, 47 F.Supp.2d 330, 337 (E.D.N.Y.1999).

2. Even when the distinction is codified, as in the case of the Louisiana codification, the distinction is not so rigid as to leave no

flexibility. To begin with, in many instances the codification's two articles (3543 and 3544) that provide for conduct-regulation and loss-distribution conflicts, respectively, lead to the same result, albeit for different reasons. See Symeonides, Louisiana's New Law of Choice of Law for Tort Conflicts: An Exegesis, 66 Tul. L. Rev. 677, 731–32 (1992). For those instances in which the two articles lead to a different result (such as a *Babcock*-type case in which an accident in one state involves a tortfeasor and a victim domiciled in another state), the court has flexibility from deviating from the legislatively prescribed result by utilizing the escapes the codification provides. See id. 733–34, 704–05 n.147

3. Surely, in hard cases or cases in which the distinction is unworkable, the lines may be adjusted or even stepped-over, but this does not mean that it is better to debate without lines. Precisely because this distinction is only "a proxy for the ultimate question," many commentators justifiably prefer to move these lines in a direction

distinction helps answer the primordial question of when to apply the *lex loci* and when not to, or, as *Babcock* put it, "[whether] the law of the place of the tort *invariably* [should] govern the availability of relief for the tort."[4] Although this is a very inelegant way of describing the judicial revolution in tort conflicts, this question encapsulates the courts' practical dilemmas in addressing those conflicts.

In turn, this is just another manifestation of the ancient dilemma between territoriality and personality.[5] The competition between these two grand principles is not a new phenomenon. Ignoring the lessons of history, Joseph Beale had pulled the pendulum all the way towards territoriality, and then Brainerd Currie pulled it almost all the way back towards personality. The cases decided since Currie's time suggest that neither he nor Beale was entirely wrong or entirely right.[6] Courts understand that, although contemporary states are still "territorially organized,"[7] their objectives are not exclusively territorial. They seek not only to "safeguard the health and safety of people and property within their bounds,"[8] but also to "prescribe modes of financial protection for those endangered."[9] When the objectives of one state clash with those of another, territoriality remains the starting point with regard to conduct regulation, and personality becomes the starting point with regard to loss allocation. The cases discussed below confirm this basic proposition.

2. *Loss–Distribution Conflicts*

a. *Common–Domicile Cases*

§ 17.39   One of the few uncontested gains of the American conflicts revolution in the arena of tort conflicts has been the increasing acceptance of the parties' domicile as the focal point around which to resolve, or at least debate, the conflicts between loss-distribution rules.[1]

---

that conforms to their conflicts philosophy. For example, Professor Reppy, who generally subscribes to this distinction, suggests that "if a court is unable to determine whether a tort rule is primarily conduct-regulating or primarily loss-distributive, the latter [should be] the default classification." Reppy, Codifying Interest Analysis in the Torts Chapter of a New Conflicts Restatement, 75 Ind. L. J. 591, 597 (2000). Professor Weintraub, who is skeptical of the whole distinction, proposes that the category of conduct-regulating rules "should be limited to rules intended to regulate conduct in the most immediate manner ... [such as] speed limits or right of way." R. Weintraub, Commentary on the Conflict of Laws 435 (4th ed. 2001). Professor Perdue, who argues that most tort rules are conduct-regulating, acknowledges that acceptance of her argument would lead to "a largely territorial choice of law rule for torts", a development which she welcomes because it is "consistent with the standard economic view of torts as primarily conduct-regulating." Perdue, A Reexamination of the Distinction between 'Loss Allocating' and 'Conduct–Regulating' Rules, 60 La. L. Rev. 1251, 1258 (2000).

4. *Babcock*, supra at § 17.29 n.3.

5. See Symeonides, Territoriality and Personality in Tort Conflicts, in Intercontinental Cooperation Through Private International Law: Essays in Memory of Peter Nygh, (T. Einhorn & K. Siehr, eds) 405 (2003).

6. See id.

7. D. Cavers, The Choice-of-Law Process 139 (1965).

8. Id.

9. Id.

§ 17.39

1. As one observer put it "there has been ... a universal perception ... that

When both the tortfeasor and the injured party are domiciled in the same state, opinions tend to converge on the proposition that that state has a better claim to apply its law than the state of conduct and/or injury.[2]

As noted earlier,[3] the vast majority (33 out of 42) of cases in which a court of last resort decided to abandon the *lex loci delicti* rule involved situations in which the parties were domiciled in the same state and were involved in an accident in another state. [4]All but one[5] of these cases applied the law of the common domicile.[6] Of these cases, 26 cases involved the *Babcock* pattern, that is, they were cases in which the law of the common-domicile state was more favorable to recovery than the law of the state of injury. All but one[7] of these cases applied the law of the common domicile in conflicts involving guest statutes;[8] inter-spousal[9] or

with respect to tort rules of the loss-distribution kind, the law of the parties' common home state has a much stronger claim to application than does the law of the locus." Korn, The Choice-of-Law Revolution: A Critique, 83 Colum. L. Rev. 772, 788–89 (1983).

2. "Under those circumstances, the locus jurisdiction has at best a minimal interest in determining the right of recovery or the extent of the remedy in an action by a foreign domiciliary for injuries resulting from the conduct of a codomiciliary that was tortious under the laws of both jurisdictions ... Analysis then favors the jurisdiction of common domicile because of its interest in enforcing the decisions of both parties to accept both the benefits and the burdens of identifying with that jurisdiction and to submit themselves to its authority." Schultz v. Boy Scouts of America, Inc., 65 N.Y.2d 189, 491 N.Y.S.2d 90, 96, 480 N.E.2d 679 (N.Y. 1985).

3. See supra § 17.26 nn.7–27.

4. For a tabular presentation and discussion of these cases, see Symeonides, Territoriality and Personality in Tort Conflicts, in Intercontinental Cooperation Through Private International Law: Essays in Memory of Peter Nygh, (T. Einhorn & K. Siehr, eds) 405 (2003).

5. The only case that applied the law of the place of the injury while abandoning general adherence to the *lex loci delicti* rule was Peters v. Peters, 63 Haw. 653, 634 P.2d 586 (1981). This case arose out of a Hawaii traffic accident in which a New York domiciliary was injured while riding in a rented car driven by her husband. Her suit against him and ultimately his insurer was barred by Hawaii's interspousal immunity law but not by New York's law. The court applied Hawaii law because the insurance policy which had been issued on the rental car in

Hawaii had been written in contemplation of Hawaii immunity law.

6. See cases cited infra nn.8–13. In addition, many cases decided during the *lex loci delicti* era but in deviation of that rule, such as Emery v. Emery, 45 Cal.2d 421, 289 P.2d 218, 223 (1955); Haumschild v. Continental Cas. Co. 95 N.W.2d 814, 7 Wis.2d 130 (1959) also involved this pattern and can be seen, at least in retrospect, as providing support for a common-domicile rule.

7. See Peters v. Peters, 63 Haw. 653, 634 P.2d 586 (1981) (discussed supra n.5).

8. In addition to *Babcock*, see Wilcox v. Wilcox, 26 Wis.2d 617, 133 N.W.2d 408 (1965) (Wisconsin parties, Nebraska accident and guest statute); Clark v. Clark, 107 N.H. 351, 222 A.2d 205 (1966) (discussed supra § 17.21 nn.22 et. seq., New Hampshire parties, Vermont accident and guest statute); Mellk v. Sarahson, 49 N.J. 226, 229 A.2d 625 (1967) (New Jersey parties, Ohio accident and guest statute); Wessling v. Paris, 417 S.W.2d 259 (Ky.1967) (discussed supra § 17.13) (Kentucky parties, Indiana accident and guest statute); Woodward v. Stewart, 104 R.I. 290, 243 A.2d 917 (1968) (Rhode Island parties, Massachusetts accident and guest statute); Kennedy v. Dixon, 439 S.W.2d 173 (Mo.1969) (discussed supra § 17.26 nn.1–6, Missouri parties, Indiana accident and guest statute); Beaulieu v. Beaulieu, 265 A.2d 610 (Me.1970) (Maine parties, Massachusetts accident and guest statute); First Nat'l Bank v. Rostek, 182 Colo. 437, 514 P.2d 314 (1973) (Colorado parties, South Dakota accident and guest statute); Bishop v. Florida Specialty Paint Co., 389 So.2d 999 (Fla.1980) (Florida parties, North Carolina accident and guest statute).

9. Armstrong v. Armstrong, 441 P.2d 699 (Alaska 1968) (Alaska spouses, accident

intrafamily[10] immunity; compensatory damages;[11] and other similar conflicts[12] between loss-distribution rules. In all but two of these cases, the common domicile was in the forum state.[13] The remaining seven cases also involved loss-distribution conflicts but presented the converse-*Babcock* pattern, that is, they were cases in which the law of the parties' common domicile was less favorable to recovery than the law of the state of the injury. Nevertheless, all seven cases applied the law of the common domicile.[14] In addition, the vast majority of cases decided after the particular court abandoned the traditional theory have also applied the law of the common domicile in both the *Babcock* pattern[15] and the

in Yukon territory); Schwartz v. Schwartz, 103 Ariz. 562, 447 P.2d 254, 257 (1968) (New York spouses, Arizona accident); Pevoski v. Pevoski, 371 Mass. 358, 358 N.E.2d 416 (1976) (Massachusetts spouses, New York accident); Forsman v. Forsman, 779 P.2d 218 (Utah 1989) (California spouses, Utah accident).

10. See Balts v. Balts, 142 N.W.2d 66, 273 Minn. 419 (1966) (Minnesota parent and child, Wisconsin accident); Jagers v. Royal Indem. Co., 276 So.2d 309 (La.1973) (Louisiana parent and child, Mississippi accident).

11. See Widow of Fornaris v. American Sur. Co., 93 P.R.R. 28, 93 D.P.R. 29 (1966) (Puerto Rico parties, accident in St. Thomas); Fox v. Morrison Motor Freight, 25 Ohio St.2d 193, 267 N.E.2d 405 (1971) (Ohio parties, Illinois traffic accident and limit on compensatory damages law); Brickner v. Gooden, 525 P.2d 632, 637 (Okla.1974) (Oklahoma parties, accident in Mexico); Gutierrez v. Collins, 583 S.W.2d 312 (Tex. 1979) (Texas parties, Mexico accident).

12. See Fabricius v. Horgen, 257 Iowa 268, 132 N.W.2d 410 (1965) (eligibility for wrongful death action, Iowa parties, Minnesota accident); Mitchell v. Craft, 211 So.2d 509, 515 (Miss.1968) (comparative negligence, Mississippi parties, Louisiana accident); Sexton v. Ryder Truck Rental, Inc., 413 Mich. 406, 320 N.W.2d 843 (1982) (vehicle owner's liability law, Michigan parties, Virginia accident); O'Connor v. O'Connor, 201 Conn. 632, 519 A.2d 13 (1986) (tort action vs. administrative remedy, Connecticut parties, Quebec accident); Travelers Indem. Co. v. Lake, 594 A.2d 38 (Del.1991) (tort action vs. administrative remedy, Delaware parties, Quebec accident and law limiting plaintiff to administrative remedy).

13. See Schwartz v. Schwartz, 103 Ariz. 562, 447 P.2d 254, 257 (1968); Forsman v. Forsman, 779 P.2d 218 (Utah 1989).

14. See Fuerste v. Bemis, 156 N.W.2d 831 (Iowa 1968) (Iowa parties and guest statute, accident in Wisconsin); Ingersoll v. Klein, 46 Ill.2d 42, 262 N.E.2d 593 (1970)

(Illinois parties and less favorable law on damages, accident in Iowa); Issendorf v. Olson, 194 N.W.2d 750 (N.D.1972) (North Dakota parties and contributory negligence rule, accident in Minnesota); Johnson v. Pischke, 108 Idaho 397, 700 P.2d 19 (1985) (Saskatchevan parties and worker's compensation immunity, accident in Idaho); Hubbard Mfg. Co. v. Greeson, 515 N.E.2d 1071 (Ind.1987) (Indiana parties and pro-manufacturer products liability law, injury in Illinois); Chambers v. Dakotah Charter, Inc., 488 N.W.2d 63 (S.D.1992) (South Dakota parties and contributory negligence rule, accident in Missouri); Hataway v. McKinley, 830 S.W.2d 53 (Tenn.1992) (Tennessee parties and contributory negligence rule, accident in Arkansas). In all but one of these cases (*Johnson v. Pischke*, supra), the common domicile was in the forum state.

15. See, e.g., Macey v. Rozbicki , 18 N.Y.2d 289, 274 N.Y.S.2d 591, 221 N.E.2d 380 (1966) (discussed supra § 17.30; applying New York's pro-plaintiff law to case arising from Ontario accident involving New York parties); Tooker v. Lopez, 24 N.Y.2d 569, 301 N.Y.S.2d 519, 249 N.E.2d 394 (1969) (discussed supra § 17.30; same in case arising from Michigan accident); Miller v. White, 167 Vt. 45, 702 A.2d 392 (1997) (discussed supra § 17.26 nn.8 et seq.; applying Vermont's pro-recovery law to a case arising out of Quebec accident involving Vermont parties); Nelson v. Hix, 122 Ill.2d 343, 119 Ill.Dec. 355, 522 N.E.2d 1214 (1988), cert. denied, 488 U.S. 925, 109 S.Ct. 309, 102 L.Ed.2d 328 (1988) (applying Ontario's non-immunity rule, rather than Illinois' inter-spousal immunity rule, to action between Ontario spouses arising out of Illinois traffic accident); Esser v. McIntyre, 169 Ill.2d 292, 214 Ill.Dec. 693, 661 N.E.2d 1138 (1996) (applying Illinois' pro-recovery law to action between Illinois parties arising out of injury sustained during the parties' common vacation in Mexico); Wendelken v. Superior Court, 137 Ariz. 455, 671 P.2d 896 (1983) (applying Arizona's pro-plaintiff compensatory damages law to case

converse pattern.[16] In one of these cases, the court said that "every American court that has considered th[is] question ... under a significant-contacts test has ruled that the law of the jurisdiction in which the parties are domiciled controls."[17]

The same is true of cases that have considered this question under another choice-of-law methodology. Indeed, while the above 32 cases relied on different choice-of-law theories and factors, the fact remains that they all applied the law of the parties' common domicile. As one recent study documents,[18] a total of 50 common-domicile cases have reached 34 state supreme courts with, and since, the abandonment of the *lex loci delicti* rule. Forty-four of these cases (or 88%) applied the law of the common domicile. Of the remaining six cases, two were factually exceptional,[19] one was overruled,[20] and the remaining three are old cases that are probably discredited.[21] Thus, looking at the actual results of these cases, one may accurately speak of the emergence of a common-domicile *rule*. In this sense, *Neumeier* Rule 1,[22] as well as the corresponding Louisiana rule[23] may be said to accurately reflect the contemporary practice in the rest of the United States.[24]

arising from accident in Mexico involving Arizona parties.); Cribb v. Augustyn, 696 A.2d 285 (R.I. 1997) (applying Rhode Island's pro-plaintiff statute of limitation in dispute between Rhode Island domiciliaries arising from incident in New Hampshire).

16. See, e.g., Collins v. Trius, Inc., 663 A.2d 570 (Me.1995) (discussed supra § 17.26 nn.21–27; applying Canadian law, which did not allow recovery for pain and suffering, to a case arising out of a Maine accident involving Canadian parties); Myers v. Langlois, 168 Vt. 432, 721 A.2d 129 (1998) (applying Quebec law and denying a tort action in a dispute between Quebec parties arising out of a Vermont accident); Lessard v. Clarke, 143 N.H. 555, 736 A.2d 1226 (1999) (applying the law of Ontario, the parties' common domicile, which provided for lower-recovery, rather than the law of New Hampshire, the accident state). See also, Schultz v. Boy Scouts of America, Inc., 65 N.Y.2d 189, 491 N.Y.S.2d 90, 480 N.E.2d 679 (1985) (discussed supra § 17.32, applying the charitable immunity rule of New Jersey, the state where the plaintiffs and one of the defendants were domiciled rather than the law of New York where the wrongful conduct occurred and which did not provide for charitable immunity).

17. Miller v. White, 167 Vt. 45, 702 A.2d 392, 394 n.4 (1997).

18. See S. Symeonides, The American Choice-of-Law Revolution in the Courts: Today and Tomorrow, 298 Recueil des Cours, 1, 178–191 (2003), from which this section draws.

19. The two cases are *Peters v. Peters*, described supra n.5, and *Martineau*, described supra § 17.22 n.5.

20. See *Dym v. Gordon* (discussed supra § 17.30).

21. Two of these cases, *Conklin*, and *Milkovich*, were decided under the better-law approach. See See Milkovich v. Saari, 295 Minn. 155, 203 N.W.2d 408 (1973), discussed supra § 17.22 (following a better-law approach and refusing to apply Ontario's guest statute in a suit by an Ontario guest-passenger against his Ontario host-driver arising out of a traffic accident in Minnesota, which did not have a guest statute); Conklin v. Horner, 38 Wis.2d 468, 157 N.W.2d 579 (1968) (discussed supra § 17.22). The third case, Arnett v. Thompson, 433 S.W.2d 109 (Ky.1968) (discussed supra § 17.13 n.3) was decided under Kentucky's *lex fori* approach. It applied Kentucky law to an action between Ohio spouses which would have been barred by both Ohio's interspousal immunity rule and Ohio's guest statute.

22. See supra § 17.31.

23. See La. Civ. Code art. 3544.

24. Professor Sedler believes that the common-domicile rule emerging from the cases is tied to the parties' affiliation with the forum state. According to Sedler, when the parties' common domicile is in the forum state, the courts apply that state's law regardless of whether it favors recovery. However, when the common domicile is in the non-forum state, the courts apply that

This rule encounters no criticism when applied to cases of the *Babcock* pattern which, after all, exemplifies the classic false conflict paradigm. Indeed the application of the law of the common domicile in these cases is universally acknowledged, even by skeptics, as the American conflicts revolution's "only unqualified success"[25] and its "most enduring contribution."[26] There is less agreement, however, for cases falling within the reverse-*Babcock* pattern. In these cases, the fact that the law of the state of injury favors recovery arguably generates a certain interest on the part of that state in deterring wrongful conduct within its territory and in ensuring recovery of medical costs resulting from the tort. This interest does not necessarily trump, but it does rival to some extent, the interest of the common-domicile state in denying or reducing recovery. Thus, the very presence of an interest, even a weak one, on the part of the injury-state prevents the easy classification of these conflicts into the classic false conflict paradigm. When these cases are litigated in the accident state, the temptation to apply forum law is stronger and, as *Milkovich* indicates, some courts may give in to this temptation.[27] However, as *Schultz*[28] illustrates, most cases decided after the early, pro-plaintiff phase of the revolution have reached the opposite result. By applying the law of the common domicile, even when that law did not favor recovery.[29] Both *Neumeier* Rule 1 and the Louisiana rule do likewise.[30]

In defending the application of this rule to cases of the reverse-*Babcock* pattern, the *Schultz* court spoke not only of the advantages of administrability, "predictability and certainty,"[31] and of discouraging forum shopping, but also about "rebut[ting] charges that the forum-locus is biased in favor of its own laws and in favor of rules permitting recovery."[32] The Court also based the rule on "concepts of mutuality and reciprocity."[33] Similarly, the Supreme Court of Maine spoke of "a social

state's law when it favors recovery, but are divided when it does not favor recovery. See Sedler, Choice of Law in Conflicts Torts Cases: A Third Restatement or Rules of Choice of Law?, 75 Ind. L. J. 615, 619–22 (2000). Professor Posnak endorses a common-domicile rule that is forum-and content-neutral but which would be only a presumptive rule. See Posnak,The Restatement (Second): Some Not so Fine Tuning for a Restatement (Third): A Very Well–Curried Leflar over Reese with Korn on the Side (or is it Cob?), 75 Ind. L. J. 561, 565 (2000).

25. Korn, The Choice-of-Law Revolution: A Critique, 83 Colum. L. Rev. 772, 788–89 (1983).

26. Id.

27. See supra *Milkovich, Conklin,* and *Arnett,* supra n.21.

28. See supra § 17.32.

29. See cases cited supra nn.14, 16.

30. *Neumeier* Rule 1 is reproduced supra § 17.31. The Louisiana rule is contained in Article 3544(1), which provides that the law of the common-domicile applies to "[i]ssues pertaining to loss distribution and financial protection ... as between a person injured by an offense or quasi-offense and the person who caused the injury...." However, unlike the *Neumeier* rule, the Louisiana rule is subject to escapes contained in articles 3547 ("exceptional cases") and 3548 ("corporate tortfeasors"). These articles authorize a judicial deviation from the common-domicile rule in appropriate cases. For the operation of these escape in cases like *Schultz,* see Symeonides, Resolving Six Celebrated Conflicts Cases Through Statutory Choice-of-Law Rules, 48 Mercer L. Rev. 837, 853–54 (1997).

31. Schultz v. Boy Scouts of America, Inc., 65 N.Y.2d 189, 491 N.Y.S.2d 90, 97–98, 480 N.E.2d 679 (1985)

32. Id.

33. Id.

contract notion whereby a resident assents to casting her lot with others in accepting burdens as well as benefits of identification with a particular community, and ceding to its lawmaking agencies the authority to make judgments striking the balance between her private substantive interests and competing ones of other members of the community."[34]

A "common-country" rule, for both of the above patterns, has emerged in the rest of the world. Indeed, the notion of applying the law of a country with which both parties are affiliated, either through domicile or nationality, appears prominently in recent private international law codifications and international conventions. This notion is implemented either through a common-domicile rule (as in the case of the Swiss[35] and Quebec[36] codifications, the Puerto Rican Draft Code,[37] and the Hague Convention on Products Liability[38]), or through an exception from the *lex loci* rule. The exception is phrased in terms of common habitual residence or common domicile (as in the proposed Rome II Regulation,[39] and the Dutch,[40] German,[41] Hungarian,[42] and Tunisian[43] codifications), or common nationality (as in the case of the Italian,[44] Polish,[45] Portuguese,[46] and Russian[47] codifications).[48] Other codi-

34. Collins v. Trius, Inc., 663 A.2d 570, 573 (Me.1995). *Collins* is discussed supra § 17.26 nn.21–27.

35. Article 133 of the Swiss Federal Law on Private International Law, Bundesblatt 1988, I, 5, which applies to torts in general, authorizes the application of the law of the parties' common habitual residence and only in the absence thereof the law of the state of conduct or injury. In the case of torts violating a preexisting legal relationship, the applicable law is that which governs that relationship. Special provisions apply to: *traffic accidents* (Art. 134, adopting the 1971 Hague Convention); *products liability* (Art. 135: defendant's place of business or residence or, at plaintiff's option, place of purchase unless product sold there without defendant's authorization; if foreign law is applicable, recovery is limited by Swiss law); *unfair competition* (Arts. 136–37: place where effect is felt); *emissions* (Art. 138: at plaintiff's option, place of conduct or of injury); *invasion of privacy through media* (Art. 139; at plaintiff's option, law of place of residence, defendant's place of business, or where the effect was felt); *direct action* (Art. 141: permitted under certain circumstances); *joint-tortfeasors* (Art. 140: independent determination of the applicable law).

36. See Quebec Civil Code, art. 3126 (adopted in 1991, effective 1994).

37. See Art. 47(a) of the Puerto Rican Draft Code of Private International Law.

38. See Article 5 of the 1972 Hague Convention on the Law Applicable to Products Liability (victim's habitual residence

and manufacturer's principal place of business).

39. See Commission of the European Communities, Proposal for a Regulation of the European Parliament and the Council on the Law Applicable to Non–Contractual Obligations, Art. 3(2), COM(2003) 427 final, 2003/0168(COD), Brussels, 22.7.203.

40. See Act of 11 April 2001 Regarding Conflict of Laws on Torts, Art. 3(3), Staatsblad 2001, 190, effective 1 June 2001 (law of the parties' common habitual residence or common seat displaces law of the place of conduct or injury).

41. See Article 40(2) of the 1999 German codification on the law applicable to non-contractual obligations, Bundesgesetzblatt 1999, I, 1026: ("If the person liable to provide compensation and the injured person had their habitual residence in the same state at the time the act took place, the law of that state shall be applied.") This is an exception to the lex loci rule of Art. 40(1), id.

42. See § 32(3) of Law No. 13 of 1979 on Private International Law (common-domicile law displaces *lex loci delicti*).

43. See Code of Private International Law (Law N. 98–97 of 27 November 1998), Art. 70(3), Official Journal of the Republic of Tunisia, 1 December p. 2332 (law of the parties' common habitual residence displaces law of the place of conduct or injury).

44. See Article 62 of Italian Act No. 218 of 31 May 1995 (Riforma del sistema italiano di diritto internazionale privato) (*lex*

45.–48. See p. 805.

fications contain exceptions which, though not explicitly phrased in common-domicile language, are very likely to be employed in common-domicile situations. This is the case, for example in the Austrian codification,[49] an English statute,[50] the Hague Traffic Accidents Convention,[51]

loci does not apply if parties are nationals *and* residents of the same state).

45. See Article 31(2) of Act of November 12, 1965, effective July 1, 1966, on Private International Law (if parties are domiciliaries *and* nationals of the same state, the law of that state applies to the exclusion of the *lex loci*).

46. After restating the *lex loci delicti* rule, Article 45 of the Portuguese Civil Code provides that if the tortfeasor and the victim have the same nationality or, failing that, the same habitual residence, and they "happen to be" in the state of the accident, the law of the common nationality or habitual residence applies, without prejudice to those provisions of the law of the accident state that "must be applied to all persons without differentiation."

47. See Civil Code of the Russian Federation art. 1219(2) (federal law n. 146 of 26 November 2001 enacting the third part of the Civil Code of the Russian Federation, Rossyiskaya Gazeta, n. 49 item 4553, 28/11/2001) (for torts committed "abroad," if parties are citizens or residents or juridical persons of the same country, that country's law displaces the law otherwise governing the tort.).

48. See also Chinese Society of Private International Law, Model Law of Private International Law of the People's Republic of China (6th Draft, 2002) art. 114, 3 Ybk. Priv. Int'l L. 349 (2001) (law of common nationality, domicile, or habitual residence displaces law of the place of conduct, injury, or closest connection). Isolated French decisions also look to the parties' common nationality: see 1973 Revue critique de droit internationale privé 89. But see Cass. Civ. D. 1963, Jur. 241. See also Gerber, Torts and Related Problem in the Australian Conflict of Laws 61 et seq. (1974); Edwards, Choice of Law in Delict: Rules or Approach?, 96 South African L.J. 48 (1979), advocating the application of the lex fori, except when a closer connection exists to another jurisdiction, for instance, on the basis of the domicile or nationality of the parties.

49. After restating the *lex loci delicti* rule, § 48 of the Austrian codification provides that "if the persons involved have a stronger connection to the law of one and the same other state, that law shall be determinative." § 48(1), 1978 Bundesgesetzblatt 1729, 1734.

50. See Private International Law (Miscellaneous Provisions) Act of 8 November 1995 (c 42). Section 11 of the Act provides that torts other than defamation are governed by "the law of the country in which the events constituting the tort or delict in question occur." Section 12 provides in part that the general rule of section 11 will be displaced "[i]f it appears, in all the circumstances, from a comparison of (a) the significance of the factors which connect a tort or delict with the country whose law would be the applicable law under the general rule; and (b) the significance of any factors connecting the tort or delict with another country, that it is substantially more appropriate for the applicable law for determining the issues arising in the case, or any of those issues, to be the law of the other country[.]" For a pre-Act case in which the common English domicile of the parties, among other factors, made England the country with "the most significant connection," see Boys v. Chaplin [1968] 2 W.L.R. 328, 331, aff'd [1969] 3 W.L.R. 322 (H.L.). See also Red Sea Ins. Co. v. Bouygues SA, [1994] 3 W.L.R. 926, (1994) 3 All E.R. 749 (P.C. 1994) (abandoning double actionability rule, then still in force in England and in the Hong Kong forum, in favor of the law of Saudi Arabia which had a more significant relationship).

51. Articles 4–6 of the 1971 Hague Convention on the Law Applicable to Traffic Accidents provide various exceptions to the *lex loci delicti* rule in favor of the law of the place of the car's registration, which in Europe usually coincides with the domicile of the owner. The first exception applies to single-car accidents and provides that the law of the state of registration displaces the *lex loci delicti* with regard to a victim who is a passenger if he habitually resides in a state other than the *locus delicti*, and with regard to a victim who is not a passenger if she habitually resides in the state of registration. The second exception applies to accidents involving two or more vehicles, and provides that the law of the state of registration displaces the *lex loci delicti* only if all the vehicles are registered in the same state. Art. 7 provides that "[w]hatever may be the applicable law, in determining liability account shall be taken of rules relating to the control and safety of traffic which were in force at the place and time of the accident."

and some other international conventions.[52] The above exceptions are not expressly confined to issues of loss distribution. However, they are more likely to be so confined in actual application because these codifications contain varying admonitions to the effect that, in applying another law, the court should "not prejudice" or should "take into consideration" the laws of conduct and safety prevailing at the place of conduct.[53] Thus, after decades of dominating the scene, the principle of territoriality was forced to cede important ground to the principle of personality, with regard to conflicts of the loss-distribution kind. However, as will be seen later, this concession is primarily confined to cases involving the common-domicile pattern.[54]

b. Cases Analogous to Common–Domicile Cases

(1) Domicile in states with same law

§ 17.40 Another pattern of cases that also qualify as false conflicts are cases in which the parties are domiciled in different states that adhere to the same or similar loss-distribution rules. For example, if, in a case like *Babcock*, the defendant was from New Jersey (rather than from New York) and if New Jersey (like New York), did not have a guest statute, there would be little argument that the resulting conflict would be as false as *Babcock* itself and that it should be resolved by allowing the action to proceed. Yet, under the *Neumeier* rules, this result can come about only in a roundabout way. Rule 1 is technically inapplicable

---

52. The 1969 Benelux Treaty Concerning a Uniform Law on Private International Law retains the *lex loci delicti* rule but provides that "if the consequences of a wrongful act belong to the legal sphere of a country other than the one where the act took place, the obligations which result therefrom shall be determined by the law of that other country." Article 14. The 1972 EEC Draft Convention on Contractual and Noncontractual Obligations (reproduced in 21 Am. J. Comp. L. 587 (1973)), which was eventually abandoned, provided a more elaborate exception to the *lex loci delicti* rule. Article 10 provided that "if, on the one hand, there is no significant link between the situation resulting from the event which has resulted in damage or injury and the country in which that event occurred and, on the other hand, the situation has a closer connection with another country, then the law of that other country shall apply." The article provided that such a connection must "normally be based on a connecting factor common to the victim and the author of the damage." This article was severely criticized for adopting the uncertainty of the Second Restatement and of the New York case law. See Jayme, 38 Rabels Z 583, 588 (1974). The Draft Convention was subsequently withdrawn and has been re-

placed by a convention ("Rome I") dealing only with contract conflicts (discussed infra § 18.40). For the proposed "Rome II" Regulation on Non–Contractual Obligations, see supra n. 39.

53. See, e.g., Art. 142(2) of Swiss Federal Law on Private International Law, Bundesblatt 1988, I, 5 ("Rules of safety and conduct in force at the place of the act are taken into consideration") regardless of the law applicable to the rest of the case; Art. 7 of Traffic Accidents Convention ("Whatever may be the applicable law, in determining liability account shall be taken of rules relating to the control and safety of traffic which were in force at the place and time of the accident."). See also Art. 45(3) of Portuguese Civil Code which provides that the application of the law of the parties' common-nationality or habitual residence shall be "without prejudice to provisions of local laws that must be applied to all persons without differentiation."

54. See Symeonides, Territoriality and Personality in Tort Conflicts, in Intercontinental Cooperation Through Private International Law: Essays in Memory of Peter Nygh, (T. Einhorn & K. Siehr, eds) 405 (2004).

because it requires that the parties be domiciled in "the *same* state"[1] for that state's law to apply. Thus, this case falls within the scope of Rule 3, which calls for the application of the law of the accident state, unless displacing that law would "advance the relative substantive law purposes"[2] of the other involved state, or states. Since in the cases discussed here, both other involved states–the parties's domiciles–have the same loss-distribution rule, there is little reason not to displace that *lex loci*.

Among the New York cases involving this pattern, one case ignored the *Neumeier* rules altogether and allowed recovery under the law of one party's domicile by "[a]pplying the so-called 'interest analysis' of *Babcock* and *Schultz*."[3] A second case recognized that *Neumeier* Rule 1 was "facially inapplicable,"[4] but concluded that the rationale underlying that rule militated in favor of the same result. The court reasoned that since the parties "have voluntarily aligned themselves with states that share a common perspective on this issue of law, neither can complain that this Court subjects them to the standard of care commensurate with the law of their respective domicile."[5] The court concluded that the application of the law of either party's domicile "fully comports with the policies served by the first *Neumeier* rule."[6] Finally, a third case followed the same reasoning and reached the same result through Rule 3.[7]

§ 17.40

1. See supra § 17.31 at n.2.

2. Id.

3. Reach v. Pearson, 860 F.Supp. 141, 143 (S.D.N.Y.1994). In *Reach*, the plaintiffs and defendants were domiciled in New Jersey and New York, respectively, and were involved in a traffic accident in Quebec. Quebec's no-fault law limited the amount of damages, whereas both New Jersey and New York provided for unlimited recovery. The court did not cite *Neumeier*, but quoted *Schultz*'s statement that "[t]he domicile of the parties ... becomes the more significant contact when the conflicting laws involve allocation of losses." Id. The court concluded that "New York's interests outweigh those of Quebec," id., because "the conflict relates to the allocation of losses rather than the governing standard of conduct ... , [t]he significant contact ... is the parties' domiciles ... , [and] Quebec, the locus jurisdiction, has the less significant interest in disputes between nonresidents." Id.

4. Diehl v. Ogorewac, 836 F.Supp. 88, 93 (E.D.N.Y.1993). In this case, a New York plaintiff was injured in a North Carolina accident while riding as a passenger in a car driven by a New Jersey defendant. Although all three states require passengers to wear seat belts, only North Carolina prohibited the admission into evidence of a plaintiff's failure to wear a seat belt. The court implicitly characterized the North Carolina rule as substantive and then concluded that the rule "does not regulate conduct since it does not purport to limit the scope of permissible conduct in North Carolina." Id. at 92. Rather, the court reasoned, "[t]he availability of a complete or partial defense to liability based upon the victim's use of a seat belt is a loss allocation rule[.]" Id. Thus, a conflict between this rule and the corresponding rules of the other two states was governed by the *Neumeier* rules which apply to conflicts between rules of loss distribution.

5. Id.

6. Id. The court also explained why the same result would follow under the escape provided in *Neumeier* Rule 3. See id. at 93–94.

7. See O'Connor v. U.S. Fencing Ass'n, 260 F.Supp.2d 545 (E.D.N.Y.2003). This case arose out of a fencing competition in California that resulted in injury to a New York amateur athlete who sued the competition's organizer, a Colorado-based corporation. New York and Colorado law, but not California law, allowed recovery. In holding for the plaintiff the court stated: "[T]he expectations of the parties could not be more clear. Both [parties] have 'chosen to identify themselves in the most concrete form possible, domicile, with jurisdiction[s] that have weighed the [pertinent] interests' ... and resolved the conflict in favor of recovery." Id. at 559 (quoting *Schultz*, 480 N.E.2d at 686).

Courts in other states reach similar results unaided or unimpeded by rules. For example, in *Bauer v. Club Med Sales, Inc.*,[8] which was decided under California's comparative impairment approach, the court used the common-domicile analogy, although the parties were domiciled in different states. *Bauer* arose out of an accident in an American-owned hotel in Mexico that caused the death of a California vacationer. The court applied Mexican law to the conduct-regulating issue of premises liability.[9] However, with regard to the amount of damages for the victim's wrongful death, the court took note of the parties' common affiliation with the United States, including defendant's status as an American corporation, and held that California's pro-recovery law should govern. The court found that "Mexico's only interest in having its damages limitation rules applied is to protect its resident defendants from excessive financial burdens. Since plaintiffs and the decedent are United States citizens and [defendant] is not a Mexico corporation, Mexico has no interest in having its damages rules apply."[10]

The Louisiana codification directly avoids the *lex loci* by providing that "[p]ersons domiciled in states whose law on the particular issue is substantially identical shall be treated as if domiciled in the same state."[11] This legal fiction, which is particularly useful in cases with multiple victims or defendants, enables a court to resolve these false conflicts by applying the law of the domicile of either party, unless the general escape of the codification dictates a different result. The American Law Institute has adopted a similar rule for mass tort cases.[12]

(2) Pre-existing Relationship

Another pattern that resembles the common-domicile pattern is present in situations in which the victim and the tortfeasor—whether or not they are domiciled in the same state—are parties to a pre-existing relationship that is centered in a state other than the state of injury. The

---

8. 1996 WL 310076 (N.D. Cal. 1996).

9. See id at *4 (recognizing "Mexico's sovereignty interest in enforcing its own construction standards within its borders.")

10. Id. at *6. The court rejected defendant's argument that the application of California would impair Mexico's interest in fostering tourism in Mexico: "While Mexico's tourism interest may be served by [defendant]'s presence there, [defendant], as a United States corporation, benefits from that presence. Neither Mexico's nor California's interest is served by limitations on damages for California citizens when a United States corporation is found negligent[.]"

11. La. Civ. Code art. 3544(1). In addition, in certain cases involving corporate tortfeasors, this common-domicile rule is subject to further expansion, or to contraction, through Article 3548 which provides

that a juridical person that is domiciled outside the forum state but transacts business in that state and incurs a tort obligation arising from such activity may be treated as a domiciliary of that state if such treatment is appropriate under the principles of Article 3542. For pertinent discussion, see Symeonides, Louisiana's New Law of Choice of Law for Tort Conflicts: An Exegesis, 66 Tul. L. Rev. 677, 759–63 (1992).

12. See American Law Institute, Complex Litigation: Statutory Recommendations and Analysis § 6.01(c)(2) and (3) (1994) ("Plaintiffs shall be considered as sharing a common habitual residence or primary place of business if they are located in states whose laws are not in material conflict.").

Swiss,[13] German,[14] and Dutch[15] codifications, as well as the Proposed Rome II Regulation[16] have adopted the notion that the law that governs the parties' pre-existing relationship displaces the law that would otherwise govern the tort.

In the United States, neither the literature[17] nor the case law have sufficiently explored this notion. However, the place in which the parties' relationship, if any, is centered is one of the contacts that courts consider under the Restatement (Second), or other modern approaches, in selecting the applicable law.[18] In some cases, like workers' compensation cases,[19] this contact carries significant weight.

(3) Choice-of-Law Clauses

A related question that also has not been systematically explored in the United States is the role of party autonomy in determining the law applicable to a tort. In other countries, there has been considerable hesitation to extend to torts the principle of party autonomy, which has been born and nourished in the law of contracts. The prevailing view has been that the parties may choose the applicable law only *after* the occurrence of the tort.[20] In keeping with this view, a provision of the

13. See Federal Law on Private International Law, Bundesblatt 1988, I, 5, codification, art. 133(3) ("when the tortious act constitutes a violation of a pre-existing legal relationship between the tortfeasor and the injured party, claims founded on this act are governed by the law applicable to that legal relationship.")

14. See Article 41(2)(1) of the 1999 of the law applicable to noncontractual obligations, Bundesgesetzblatt 1999, I, 1026 ("a special legal or factual relationship between the parties in connection with the obligation" may indicate a "substantially closer connection" to a state other the one whose law is designated as applicable by Articles 38–40, and in such a case, the law of the state of the closer connection applies.)

15. See Act of 11 April 2001Regarding Conflict of Laws on Torts, Art. 5, Staatsblad 2001, 190, effective 1 June 2001 (when the tort "is closely connected with an existing legal relationship" the law that governs that relationship displaces the otherwise applicable law).

16. See Commission of the European Communities, Proposal for a Regulation of the European Parliament and the Council on the Law Applicable to Non–Contractual Obligations, Art. 3(3), COM(2003) 427 final, 2003/0168(COD), Brussels, 22.7.203 (the otherwise applicable law is displaced by the law of a state that has a "manifestly closer connection" and such a connection "may be based ... on a pre-existing relationship between the parties, such as a contract that is

closely connected with the non-contractual obligation in question.")

17. Professor Cavers's Principles 4 and 5 provide that in such cases the law of the state where the relationship is centered applies, whether that state provides a higher (Principle 4) or lower (Principle 5) standard of financial protection for the victim than does the state of injury, and without mention of whether the former state is also the parties' domicile. See D. Cavers, The Choice of Law Process, 166, 177 (1965). However, the fact that Cavers confined his discussion of Principles 4 and 5 to cases in which the relationship in centered in the state of the parties' common domicile suggests that he intended these Principles to function as a common-domicile rule rather than to displace such a rule. Moreover, in discussing a case in which the parties are domiciled in the same pro-recovery state but do not have a pre-existing relationship, Cavers concludes that the law of the common domicile should govern because such a case would be a false conflict for which "there is no occasion to invoke [his] principle[s] since ... [they] do not come into play in false-conflict cases." Id. at 151.

18. See, e.g., Restatement (Second) § 145(2)(d) (1971).

19. See infra § 17.59 n.11.

20. But see Introductory Law to the Civil Code (EGBGB), Bundesgesetzblatt 1999, I, 1026, 1027. For comprehensive and

European Union's Rome II Regulation that would have allowed parties to agree on the law that would govern future torts between them was eventually changed to allow such agreements only if they are "entered into after the dispute arose."[21] However, there are indications that this view may be eroding. For example, one of the latest codifications, the Dutch, allows the parties to choose the law applicable to "any matter relating to a tort, delict or quasi delict" with virtually no restrictions, as long as the choice is "expressed or otherwise demonstrated with reasonable certainty."[22] Moreover, as noted earlier,[23] many foreign conflicts codifications provide that, if the tortfeasor and the injured party were parties to a preexisting relationship, then the law that governs that relationship will also govern their delictual rights and obligations arising from that relationship. If the relationship is based on a contract that contains a choice-of-law clause, that law will be the chosen law.

In the United States, both the Restatement (Second) and the only existing conflicts codifications—Louisiana's and Oregon's—confine party autonomy to *contractual* issues.[24] In the rest of the country, this question appears often in cases in which the parties to a tort were also parties to a contract that contains a choice-of-law clause.[25] The question then is whether—in addition to purely contractual claims—the clause also encompasses non-contractual claims,[26] including tort claims, arising from

comparative treatment of choice-of-law clauses in torts, see Hohloch, Das Deliktsstatut (1984); Dicey & Morris, The Conflict of Laws, 1487–97 (12th ed. 1993).

21. See, Commission of the European Communities, Proposal for a Regulation of the European Parliament and the Council on the Law Applicable to Non–Contractual Obligations, Art. 10(1), COM(2003) 427 final, 2003/0168(COD), Brussels, 22.7.203. See also Civil Code of the Russian Federation, Art. 1219(3) (federal law n. 146 of 26 November 2001 enacting the third part of the Civil Code of the Russian Federation, Rossyiskaya Gazeta, n. 49 item 4553, 28/11/2001).

22. See Art. 6 of Act of 11 April 2001Regarding Conflict of Laws on Torts, Staatsblad 2001, 190, effective 1 June 2001.

23. See supra nn.13–16

24. The pertinent section of the Restatement (Second), § 187, speaks of the law chosen by the parties "to govern their contractual rights." The same is true of the Louisiana and Oregon codifications. See La. Civ.Code art. 3540 ("conventional obligations"); O.R.S. 81.120 ("contractual rights and duties"). For discussion, see Symeonides, Codifying Choice of Law for Contracts: The Oregon Experience, 67 RabelsZ 726, 737 (2003).

25. For choice-of-court clauses, see Durdahl v. National Safety Assoc., Inc., 988 P.2d 525 (Wyo. 1999) (forum selection

clause governing "any and all claims involving this agreement" governed not only claims based on contract but also claims for promissory estoppel and fraudulent misrepresentation that necessarily implicated terms of distributorship contract); Bodzai v. Arctic Fjord, Inc., 990 P.2d 616 (Alaska 1999) (injured seaman's right to recover against his employer for unseaworthiness did not arise under the terms of his employment contract, and thus, the claim was not controlled by the contract's forum-selection clause; liability on that theory was not contractual in character, but derived from an absolute duty imposed by law). For foreign authorities, see Oberlandesgericht München, Wertpapier–Mitteilungen 602, 604 (1989); von Falkenhausen, Internationale Gerichtsstandsvereinbarungen und unerlaubte Handlung, Recht der Internationalen Wirtschaft, 420, 421–22 (1983).

26. For cases involving the question of whether the choice-of-law clause encompasses other non-contractual claims, see, e.g. Maddox v. American Airlines, Inc., 298 F.3d 694 (8th Cir.2002), cert. denied 537 U.S. 1192, 123 S.Ct. 1273, 154 L.Ed.2d 1026 (2003) (prejudgment interest); Krause v. Stroh Brewery Company, 240 F.Supp.2d 632 (E.D.Mich. 2002) (unjust enrichment and conversion). For attorney fees, see North Bergen Rex Transport v. Trailer Leasing Co., 158 N.J. 561, 730 A.2d 843 (1999) (attorney fees); Weatherby Assoc.,

the same relationship. Although arguably this is a matter of contractual *power*,[27] most American courts tend to view it as a matter of contractual *intent*, which in turn depends largely, but not exclusively, on the phrasing of the choice-of-law clause. Under this logic, a clause that explicitly encompasses "any and all disputes between the parties" is deemed to include tort claims, while a generic, less categorical clause is not.[28] At the same time, however, courts tend to scrutinize much more closely clauses

Inc. v. Ballack, 783 So.2d 1138 (Fla.App. 2001); Precision Tune Auto Care v. Radcliffe, 815 So.2d 708 (Fla. App. 2002); Walls v. Quick & Reilly, Inc., 824 So.2d 1016 (Fla. App. 2002); Dunkin' Donuts Inc. v. Guang Chyi Liu, 2002 WL 31375509 (E.D.Pa. 2002). For statutes of limitation, see Long v. Holland America Line Westours, Inc., 26 P.3d 430 (Alaska 2001); Nez v. Forney, 109 N.M. 161, 783 P.2d 471 (1989); Florida State Bd. of Admin. v. Eng'g & Envtl. Servs., Inc., 262 F.Supp.2d 1004 (D.Minn. 2003); Hemar Ins. Corp. v. Ryerson, 108 S.W.3d 90 (Mo.App.2003); Belleville Toyota, Inc. v. Toyota Motor Sales, U.S.A., Inc., 199 Ill.2d 325, 770 N.E.2d 177 (2002); Education Resources Institute v. Lipsky, 2002 WL 1463461 (Cal. App. 2002); Western Group Nurseries, Inc. v. Ergas, 211 F.Supp.2d 1362 (S.D.Fla. 2002); Shaw v. Rivers White Water Rafting Resort, 2002 WL 31748919 (E.D.Mich. 2002); Financial Bancorp, Inc. v. Pingree & Dahle, Inc., 880 P.2d 14 (Utah.Ct.App.1994); Hambrecht & Quist Venture Partners v. American Medical Int'l, Inc., 38 Cal.App.4th 1532, 46 Cal. Rptr.2d 33 (1995); Manion v. Roadway Package System, Inc., 938 F.Supp. 512 (C.D.Ill.1996); In re Western United Nurseries, Inc., 191 B.R. 820 (Bankr.D.Ariz. 1996); In re Fineberg, 202 B.R. 206 (Bankr. E.D.Pa.1996); Springfield Oil Services, Inc. v. Costello, 941 F.Supp. 45 (E.D.Pa. 1996).

27. See S. Symeonides, W. Perdue & A. von Mehren, Conflict of Laws: American, Comparative, International, 358–359 (2d ed. 2003((suggesting a distinction between "intended scope" and "permissible scope" of the choice-of-law clause).

28. For cases holding that the clause did not encompass contract-related tort claims between the same parties, see, e.g., Benchmark Elecs., Inc. v. J.M. Huber Corp., 343 F.3d 719 (5th Cir.2003), opinion modified on denial of rehearing 355 F.3d 356 (5th Cir.2003); Green Leaf Nursery v. E.I. DuPont De Nemours & Co., 341 F.3d 1292 (11th Cir.2003); Krock v. Lipsay, 97 F.3d 640 (2d Cir.1996);Valley Juice Ltd., Inc. v. Evian Waters of France, Inc., 87 F.3d 604 (2d Cir.1996); Caton v. Leach Corp., 896 F.2d 939, 942–43 (5th Cir.1990); Financial Trust Co. Inc. v. Citibank, N.A., 268

F.Supp.2d 561 (D.V.I. 2003); Gloucester Holding Corp. v. U.S. Tape and Sticky Products, LLC, 832 A.2d 116 (Del. Chan.2003); Owen J. Roberts School Dist. v. HTE, Inc., 2003 WL 735098 (E.D.Pa. 2003); Lewis Tree Service, Inc. v. Lucent Technologies Inc., 239 F.Supp.2d 322 (S.D.N.Y.,2002); Medline Industries Inc. v. Maersk Medical Ltd., 230 F.Supp.2d 857 (N.D.Ill.2002); MBI Acquisition Partners, L.P. v. Chronicle Publishing Co., 2001 WL 1478812 (W.D. Wis. 2001); Twinlab Corp. v. Paulson, 283 A.D.2d 570, 724 N.Y.S.2d 496 (2001); Florida Evergreen Foliage v. E.I. DuPont De Nemours & Co., 135 F.Supp.2d 1271 (S.D.Fla. 2001); Precision Screen Machines, Inc. v. Elexon, Inc., 1996 WL 495564 (N.D.Ill.1996); Union Oil Co. v. John Brown E. & C., No. 94 C 4424, 1994 WL 535108 (N.D.Ill. 1994); Shelley v. Trafalgar House Public Ltd. Co., 918 F.Supp. 515 (D.P.R.1996); Telemedia Partners Worldwide, Ltd. v. Hamelin Ltd., 1996 WL 41818 (S.D.N.Y.1996); Champlain Enterprises, Inc. v. United States, 945 F.Supp. 468 (N.D.N.Y.1996); Young v. W.S. Badcock Corp., 222 Ga.App. 218, 474 S.E.2d 87 (1996); Young v. Mobil Oil Corp., 85 Or. App. 64, 735 P.2d 654 (1987); Ezell v. Hayes Oilfield Const. Co., Inc. 693 F.2d 489 (5th Cir.1982), cert. denied, 464 U.S. 818, 104 S.Ct. 79, 78 L.Ed.2d 90 (1983).

For cases reaching the opposite conclusion, see Nedlloyd Lines B.V. v. Superior Court, 3 Cal.4th 459, 11 Cal.Rptr.2d 330, 834 P.2d 1148 (1992); Forrest v. Verizon Communications, Inc., 805 A.2d 1007 (D.C. 2002); Turtur v. Rothschild Registry Int'l Inc., 26 F.3d 304 (2d Cir.1994); Roby v. Corporation of Lloyd's, 996 F.2d 1353 (2d Cir. 1993); Wireless Distributors, Inc. v. Sprintcom, Inc., 2003 WL 22175607 (N.D.Ill. 2003); Birnberg v. Milk Street Residential Associates Ltd. P'ship, 2003 WL 151929 (N.D.Ill.2003); Twohy v. First Nat. Bank of Chicago, 758 F.2d 1185 (7th Cir. 1985); About.Com, Inc. v. Targetfirst, Inc., 2002 WL 826953 (S.D.N.Y. 2002).

For extensive discussion in *dicta*, see Kuehn v. Childrens Hospital, Los Angeles, 119 F.3d 1296, 1302 (7th Cir.1997) (Posner, J.).

that purport to encompass tort-like issues than do clauses confined to purely contractual issues.[29] Such a scrutiny is fully justified, especially in consumer contracts, standard-form contracts typically drafted by one party, or other contracts between parties with clearly unequal bargaining power.[30]

c. Split–Domicile Conflicts Between the Laws of Two States

§ 17.41 While common-domicile cases are more than likely to present the false conflict paradigm, split-domicile cases are more problematic. In interest analysis terminology, these cases are likely to present either the true conflict or the "no-interest" paradigms. The former paradigm is present when each state has a loss-distribution rule that protects its domiciliary, while the latter paradigm is present in the converse situation.

(1) True Conflicts

The discussion below begins with cases in which each party is domiciled in a state whose law protects its domiciliary. These cases are further subdivided into three patterns:

(a) cases in which both the conduct and the injury occur in the state of the tortfeasor's domicile;

(b) cases in which both the conduct and the injury occur in the state of the victim's domicile; and

(c) cases in which the tortfeasor's conduct occurs in the state of his domicile while the resulting injury occurs in the state of the victim's domicile.

---

29. See Symeonides, Perdue & von Mehren, supra n.27 at 360, 390; Symeonides, Choice of Law in the American Courts in 2002: Sixteenth Annual Survey, 51 Am. J.Comp.L.1, 67–68 (2003).

30. Sutton v. Hollywood Entertainment Corp., 181 F.Supp.2d 504 (D.Md. 2002), provides a good example of the potential abuse of choice-of-law clauses in consumer contracts. *Sutton* was a tort action for malicious prosecution and false imprisonment filed against a Maryland video store owner who had the plaintiff arrested for alleged shoplifting. Besides being innocent, the plaintiff was a customer/"member" of the defendant's video store, in that he had applied for and received a "membership" card allowing him to rent video discs. The membership agreement provided that "any dispute arising out of or relating *in anyway* to [plaintiff's] relationship with [defendant] shall be subject to final, non-appealable, binding arbitration. * * * Exclusive venue for any dispute resolution shall be in Portland, Oregon and Oregon law shall control for all purposes." Id. at 508 (emphasis added). Relying on the italicized language, the defendant moved to dismiss the action. The court denied the motion, after noting that the plaintiff's tort claims had "nothing whatsoever to do with the video rental contracts." Id. at 511. "It is logically untenable" said the court, "that the membership agreements were meant to cover ... accusations of theft. Taken to an extreme, Defendant's reading of the arbitration clause would require arbitration of claims such as a [defendant's] store ceiling falling in on customers, or a [defendant] store employee brutally attacking a customer ... who has signed a membership agreement." Id. at 512.

(a) Cases in which the conduct, the injury, and the tortfeasor's domicile are in a state whose law protects the tortfeasor

§ 17.42   *Foster v. Leggett*[1] and *Cipolla v. Shaposka*[2] are well-known illustrations of this pattern in that in both of them the accident (i.e., both the conduct and the injury) occurred in the state of the defendant's domicile which had a guest statute that protected the defendant and his insurer. *Foster* applied the law of the victim's domicile which was also the forum state, while *Cipolla* applied the law of the state of the accident which was also the defendant's domicile. As a recent study demonstrates, *Foster* is virtually alone among modern cases in applying the law of the victim's domicile in cases of this pattern.[3]

The first sentence of *Neumeier* Rule 2 (hereinafter Rule 2a) is "phrased in non-discretionary terms"[4] that require the same result as in *Cipolla*.[5] Both the Louisiana codification and Professor Cavers would reach the same result. The Louisiana rule, however, makes explicit what may be implicit in the *Neumeier* rule by providing that the law of the tortfeasor's domicile applies only if both his conduct and the resulting injury occurred in that state.[6] In addition, unlike the *Neumeier* rule, the Louisiana rule is subject to escapes.[7] Professor Cavers's Principle 2 provides that "[w]here the liability laws of the state in which the defendant acted and caused an injury set a lower standard of . . . financial protection than do the laws of the home state of the person suffering the injury, the laws of the state of conduct and injury should determine the standard of conduct or protection applicable to the case[.]"[8] In discussing the operation of this principle, Cavers used a variant of *Kilberg*,[9] in which a New York resident is killed in a Massachusetts traffic accident caused by a Massachusetts resident. Cavers thought that in such a case it would be appropriate to apply the

§ 17.42

1.   484 S.W.2d 827 (Ky.1972) (discussed supra § 17.13; applying Kentucky law rather than the Ohio guest statute and allowing an action by the survivor's of a Kentucky guest-passenger against an Ohio host-driver arising from an Ohio accident).

2.   439 Pa. 563, 267 A.2d 854 (1970) (discussed supra § 17.13; applying Delaware's guest-statute and thus denying recovery to a Pennsylvania plaintiff injured in Delaware while riding as a guest-passenger in the car owned and driven by a Delaware host-driver).

3.   See S. Symeonides, The American Choice-of-Law Revolution in the Courts: Today and Tomorrow, 298 Recueil des Cours, 1, 195–203 (2003), from which this section draws heavily. For a tabular presentation of the cases discussed here, see id. at 201.

4.   Barkanic v. General Admin. of Civil Aviation of the People's Republic of China, 923 F.2d 957, 962 n.5 (2d Cir.1991) (decided under New York conflicts law).

5.   Rule 2a provides as follows: "When the driver's conduct occurred in the state of

his domicile and that state does not cast him in liability for that conduct, he should not be held liable by reason of the fact that liability would be imposed upon him under the tort law of the state of the victim's domicile."

6.   La. Civ. Code art. 3544(2)(a) provides that "when both the injury and the conduct that caused it" occurred in the domicile of one party, the law of that state applies.

7.   See La. Civ. Code arts. 3547 ("exceptional cases"; described supra § 17.39 n.30) and 3548 ("corporate tortfeasors"; described supra § 17.40 n.11).

8.   D. Cavers, The Choice-of-Law Process 146 (1965). This Principle continues with an escape: "at least where the person injured was not so related to the person causing the injury that the question should be relegated to the law governing the relationship." Id.

9.   Kilberg v. Northeast Airlines, Inc., 9 N.Y.2d 34, 211 N.Y.S.2d 133, 172 N.E.2d 526 (1961) (discussed supra § 17.9).

Massachusetts damages limitation, because "[i]nhabitants of Massachusetts should not be put in jeopardy of liabilities exceeding those Massachusetts law creates simply because persons from states with higher standards of financial protection choose to visit there."[10]

New York courts have not encountered a guest-statute conflict that fits within this pattern. However, after *Schultz* extended the application of the *Neumeier* rules to other loss-distribution conflicts, state and federal courts in New York have adjudicated several cases involving this pattern and have resolved them consistently with Rule 2a.[11] Courts in other states have reached the same results in cases decided under the Second Restatement,[12] interest analysis,[13] comparative impairment,[14] the

---

10. Cavers, supra n.8 at 148–49. In addition, Cavers spoke approvingly of the court's decision in *Cipolla*, which he interpreted as following his Principle 2. See Cavers, *Cipolla* and Conflicts Justice, 9 Duq. L. Rev. 360, 362 n.8 (1971).

11. In addition to Cooney v. Osgood Mach., Inc., 81 N.Y.2d 66, 595 N.Y.S.2d 919, 612 N.E.2d 277 (1993) (discussed supra § 17.32), see Feldman v. Acapulco Princess Hotel, 137 Misc.2d 878, 520 N.Y.S.2d 477 (Sup. Ct. 1987) (personal injury action arising from a swimming pool accident at a Mexican resort hotel involving a New York plaintiff and a Mexican defendant, the owner of the hotel. Mexican law limited the amount of damages while New York law did not. The court applied Mexican law under Rule 2a); Barkanic v. General Admin. of Civil Aviation of the People's Republic of China, 923 F.2d 957 (2d Cir.1991) (decided under New York conflicts law; the court applied Chinese law to an action by the survivors of two American citizens who were killed in the crash in China of an airplane operated by defendant, an agency of the Chinese government. Unlike the law of the victims' domiciles, Chinese law drastically limited the amount of damages. Noting that Rule 2a is "phrased in non-discretionary terms, which unambiguously call for application of locus law," id. at 962 n.5, the court applied Chinese law under Rule 2a); Mascarella v. Brown, 813 F.Supp. 1015, (S.D.N.Y.1993) (wrongful death action resulting from a New York medical malpractice committed by a New York defendant against a North Carolina domiciliary. North Carolina law was more favorable to the victim than New York law. The court applied New York law under Rule 2a. The defendant third-partied a New Jersey corporation claiming contribution and indemnification for its part in the tort. Such contribution was permitted under New York law but was precluded under New Jersey law. The court applied New York law under Rule 2b); Pascente v. Pascente, 1993 WL

43502 (S.D.N.Y.1993) (Connecticut accident involving a Connecticut defendant and a New York victim—New York's contributory negligence law was more generous than was Connecticut's—the court characterized those laws as loss allocating and applied Connecticut's law under Rule 2a); Miller v. Bombardier, Inc., 872 F.Supp. 114 (S.D.N.Y. 1995) (personal injury and a loss of consortium actions filed by Connecticut spouses arising out of an injury suffered by the husband during a snowmobiling trip in Quebec that was organized by defendant, a Quebec corporation. Quebec law favored the defendant, while Connecticut law favored the plaintiffs. The court applied Quebec law under Rule 2a); Kranzler v. Austin, 189 Misc.2d 369, 732 N.Y.S.2d 328 (Sup.Ct. 2001) (applying New York's pro-defendant law to a case arising out of a New York traffic accident involving a New York defendant and a New Jersey plaintiff). See also Bankers Trust Co. v. Lee Keeling & Assoc., Inc., 20 F.3d 1092 (10th Cir.1994) (decided under New York conflicts law) and Venturini v. Worldwide Marble & Granite Corp., 1995 WL 606281 (S.D.N.Y.1995), both of which are discussed supra § 17.32 n.34. See also Bader v. Purdom, 841 F.2d 38 (2d Cir.1988) (action by a New York minor bitten by defendant's dog in Ontario. Defendants third-partied the minor's parents claiming contribution and indemnification for their negligent supervision of the child. Ontario law, but not New York law, permitted this claim. Apparently thinking of the main action, rather than the third-party claim for contribution, the court concluded that this case fell within the scope of Rule 3 and applied Ontario law. A concurring judge pointed out that, more properly, the case fell within the scope of Rule 2).

12. See, e.g., Casey v. Manson Constr. & Eng'g Co., 247 Or. 274, 428 P.2d 898 (1967), discussed supra § 17.27; McBride v. Whiting–Turner Contracting Co., 1993 WL 489487 (Del. Super. 1993) aff'd. 645 A.2d

13.–14. See p. 815.

lex-fori approach,[15] the better-law approach,[16] or a mixed approach.[17] These cases applied the pro-defendant law of the defendant-affiliated state–which was also the state of both the conduct and injury–rather than the pro-recovery law of the victim's domicile in disputes involving issues of compensatory damages,[18] loss of consortium,[19] workers' compensation immunity,[20] other immunities from suit, medical malpractice,[21] and contributory negligence defenses.[22]

568 (Del. 1994) (applying Maryland's law immunizing a Maryland employer from a tort suit brought by a Delaware worker injured in Maryland, while working for defendant's subcontractor.); Ricci v. Alternative Energy Inc., 211 F.3d 157 (1st Cir. 2000) (decided under Maine's conflicts law; applying Maine's pro-defendant law to a work-related accident in Maine that caused the death of Rhode Island worker); Marion Power Shovel Co. v. Hargis, 698 So.2d 1246 (Fla. App. 1997) (applying Florida's pro-defendant law to action of Illinois employee of Indiana subcontractor against Florida contractor arising out of Florida injury); Bowman v. Koch Transfer Co., 862 F.2d 1257 (6th Cir. 1988) (decided under Ohio conflict law; applying Illinois' limited-damages law to an action arising from an Illinois traffic accident involving an Illinois defendant and an Ohio victim; concluding that Illinois' interests in limiting the liability of its citizens for activity within that state was not counterbalanced by an equally strong Ohio interest since the children had left Ohio more than a year before their mother's death and had been living with their father in another state).

13. In addition to *Eger* and *Bledsoe*, discussed infra at text, see Amoroso v. Burdette Tomlin Mem'l Hosp., 901 F.Supp. 900 (D.N.J. 1995) (applying New Jersey's pro-defendant law to survival action filed against New Jersey hospital and building-owner by Pennsylvania domiciliary whose son died during a New Jersey surgery following an injury in the owner's premises).

14. See Tucci v. Club Mediterranee, S.A., 89 Cal.App.4th 180, 107 Cal.Rptr.2d 401 (2001) (discussed infra in text).

15. See Motenko v. MGM Dist., Inc., 112 Nev. 1038, 921 P.2d 933 (1996) (discussed supra § 17.15 nn.21–25; applying Nevada's pro-defendant law to an action for loss of parental consortium brought by a Massachusetts domiciliary whose mother had been injured when she slipped on a loose tile in defendant's Nevada hotel. Massachusetts, but not Nevada, allowed the action).

16. See, e.g., Benoit v. Test Systems, Inc., 142 N.H. 47, 694 A.2d 992 (1997) (applying New Hampshire's pro-defendant law, rather than Massachusetts' pro-plain-

tiff law, to action arising out of New Hampshire employment accident and filed by a Massachusetts employee against a New Hampshire employer who had borrowed plaintiff from his Massachusetts employer); Reed v. University of North Dakota, 543 N.W.2d 106 (Minn. App. 1996) (applying North Dakota pro-defendant immunity law, rather than Minnesota non-immunity law, and dismissing action against North Dakota state entity filed by Minnesota plaintiff for injury in North Dakota).

17. In addition to Cipolla v. Shaposka, 439 Pa. 563, 267 A.2d 854 (1970) (discussed supra § 17.13 n.18), see, e.g., Shuder v. McDonald's Corp., 859 F.2d 266 (3d Cir. 1988) (applying Virginia contributory-negligence law, rather than Pennsylvania comparative-negligence law, to an action filed against McDonald's by a Pennsylvania plaintiff who slipped and fell in the parking lot in one of defendant's Virginia restaurants); Blakesley v. Wolford, 789 F.2d 236 (3d Cir. 1986) (applying Texas pro-defendant medical consent and damages-limitation law to medical malpractice action filed by Pennsylvania domiciliary against Texas oral surgeon for surgery performed in Texas); Evans v. Valley Forge Convention Center, 1996 WL 468688 (E.D.Pa. 1996) (applying Pennsylvania's pro-defendant parental supervision law to action filed by New Jersey parents against Pennsylvania defendants arising out of Pennsylvania accident); Troxel v. A.I. duPont Institute, 431 Pa.Super. 464, 636 A.2d 1179 (1994) (discussed infra at nn.39–45).

18. See Bowman v. Koch Transfer Co., 862 F.2d 1257 (6th Cir.1988), supra n.12; Feldman v. Acapulco Princess Hotel, 137 Misc.2d 878, 520 N.Y.S.2d 477 (Sup. Ct. 1987), (supra n. 11; Barkanic v. General Admin. of Civil Aviation of the People's Republic of China, 923 F.2d 957 (2d Cir. 1991), supra n.11; Blakesley v. Wolford, 789 F.2d 236 (3d Cir. 1986), supra n.17.

19. See Motenko v. MGM Dist., Inc., 112 Nev. 1038, 921 P.2d 933 (1996), supra n.15; Miller v. Bombardier, Inc., 872 F.Supp. 114 (S.D.N.Y. 1995), supra n.11.

20. In addition to Eger v. E.I. Du Pont De Nemours Co., 110 N.J. 133, 539 A.2d 1213 (1988) (discussed infra nn.23–24) and

21.–22. See p. 816.

For example, in *Eger v. E.I. Du Pont De Nemours Co.*,[23] a case decided under interest analysis, a New Jersey court applied South Carolina's pro-defendant law, rather than New Jersey's pro-plaintiff law, to a New Jersey employee's action against a South Carolina employer arising out of an employment accident in South Carolina. South Carolina law immunized the South Carolina employer from a tort action, whereas New Jersey law provided a tort action for the employee and allowed his own employer, a New Jersey subcontractor, to recoup from the defendant the worker's compensation benefits paid to the employee. Nevertheless, the court concluded that New Jersey's interests in protecting its domiciliaries was "not strong enough to outweigh South Carolina's interest"[24] in immunizing employers operating in South Carolina from tort liability as a quid pro quo for requiring them to furnish workers' compensation coverage for their subcontractors' employees.

In *Tucci v. Club Mediterranee, S.A.*,[25] which was decided under California's comparative impairment, the court applied the pro-defendant law of the Dominican Republic to an action of a California domiciliary who was injured while working in the defendant's club in the Dominican Republic.[26] The court noted that California had an interest in adequately providing for employees hired in California, and in assuring that employers who solicited California employees were adequately insured through credit-worthy carriers regulated by California. However, the court found that the Dominican Republic also had an interest in making sure that employers in that country "face limited and predictable financial liability . . . and in . . . predictably defining the duties and liabilities of employers doing business within its border, all with the goal of encouraging business investment and development there."[27] The court concluded that the law of the Dominican Republic should govern because that country's interests would be more impaired if its law was not applied.

Likewise, in contrast to the much criticized New York case of *Rosenthal v. Warren*,[28] several medical malpractice cases applied the pro-

---

Tucci v. Club Mediterranee, S.A., 89 Cal. App.4th 180, 107 Cal.Rptr.2d 401 (2001) (discussed infra at nn. 25–27); see Benoit v. Test Systems, Inc., 142 N.H. 47, 694 A.2d 992 (1997) (described supra n.16); McBride v. Whiting–Turner Contracting Co., 1993 WL 489487 (Del. Super. 1993) aff'd. 645 A.2d 568 (Del. 1994), supra n.12; Ricci v. Alternative Energy Inc., 211 F.3d 157 (1st Cir. 2000), supra n.12; Marion Power Shovel Co. v. Hargis, 698 So.2d 1246 (Fla. App. 1997); supra n.12.

21. See infra nn. 29 et. seq.

22. See Shuder v. McDonald's Corp., 859 F.2d 266 (3d Cir.1988), supra n.17; Pascente v. Pascente, 1993 WL 43502 (S.D.N.Y.1993), supra n. 11.

23. 110 N.J. 133, 539 A.2d 1213 (1988).

24. Id. at 1218.

25. 89 Cal.App.4th 180, 107 Cal.Rptr.2d 401 (2001).

26. Under Dominican Republic law, the plaintiff would be confined to workers' compensation and Social Security benefits. Under California law, the plaintiff would be entitled to a tort action, because the employer had not procured workers' compensation insurance through a California carrier, as required by a California statute.

27. *Tucci*, 107 Cal.Rptr.2d at 408–09.

28. 475 F.2d 438 (2d Cir.1973), cert. denied 414 U.S. 856, 94 S.Ct. 159, 38 L.Ed.2d 106 (1973) (applying New York damages law to malpractice action filed by New York plaintiffs against Massachusetts

defendant law of the state in which the medical services were provided (which was also the provider's home state) rather than the pro-plaintiff law of the patient's home state.[29] For example, in *Bledsoe v. Crowley*,[30] a District of Columbia court refused to apply the forum's pro-plaintiff law to the action of a forum domiciliary arising from a medical procedure in Maryland. The court applied the pro-defendant law of Maryland, because Maryland was the "jurisdiction with the stronger interests."[31]A concurring judge would elevate this result to a general choice-of-law rule that would apply the law of the state in which the medical services are rendered. The judge reasoned that "patients are inherently on notice that journeying to new jurisdictions may expose them to [unfavorable]

doctor and hospital for injury arising out of Massachusetts medical procedure), criticized in Twerski, *Neumeier v. Kuehner*: Where are the Emperor's New Clothes?, 1 Hofstra L. Rev. 104, 124 n.53 (1973); Reese, Choice of Law in Torts and Contracts and Directions for the Future, 16 Colum. J. Transnat'l L. 1, 10–11 (1977).

29. In addition to the cases discussed in the text, see, e.g., Blakesley v. Wolford, 789 F.2d 236 (3d Cir. 1986) (applying Texas pro-defendant medical consent and damages-limitation law to medical malpractice action filed by Pennsylvania domiciliary against Texas oral surgeon for surgery performed in Texas); Mascarella v. Brown, 813 F.Supp. 1015 (S.D.N.Y.1993) (noted supra n.11). Courts tend to apply the law of the state in which the medical services are provided, regardless of whether that law favors the medical provider or the patient. See Symeonides, Choice of Law in the American Courts in 2003: Seventeenth Annual Survey, 52 Am. J. Comp. L. (2004). For example, four of the five cases decided in 2003 applied the law of that state. In two of those cases—Carter v. United States, 333 F.3d 791 (7th Cir. 2003), cert. denied ___ U.S. ___, 124 S.Ct. 1078, 157 L.Ed.2d 899 (2004), and Dugan v. Mobile Medical Testing Services, Inc., 265 Conn. 791, 830 A.2d 752 (2003)—that law favored the defendant, while in the other two—Jett v. Coletta, 2003 WL 22171862 (D.N.J.2003), and Vecchio v. Rye Brook Obstetrics–Gynecology, P.C., 2003 WL 22482046 (Conn.Super.2003)—that law favored the plaintiff. In the fifth case, Bucci v. Kaiser Permanente Found. Health Plan, 278 F.Supp.2d 34 (D.D.C. 2003), the court did not apply the law of the state in which the medical services were rendered, Virginia (which was also the plaintiff's domicile), because the plaintiff was employed in the District of Columbia and her choice of a medical care provider was controlled through a plan provided by her D.C. employer. The court rejected the defendant's argument of applying Virginia's $1 million cap on damages and held that the District's unlimited-damages law governed because of the District's strong interest in "protecting its workforce and promoting corporate accountability." Id. at 36. In so holding, the court followed Kaiser–Georgetown Community Health Plan, Inc. v. Stutsman, 491 A.2d 502 (D.C. 1985), which had also applied D.C. law in identical circumstances, because the plaintiff, though a Virginia resident, was "a member of D.C.'s workforce" and thus D.C. had an interest in protecting her. *Stutsman* also noted that the medical defendants, though operating in Virginia, were based in D.C. and concluded that this gave D.C. "a significant interest, reflected in the fact that it imposes no cap on liability for malpractice, in holding its corporations liable for the full extent of the negligence attributable to them." 491 A.2d at 509.

30. 849 F.2d 639 (D.C.Cir.1988).

31. Id. at 641. Maryland law required compulsory arbitration before a medical malpractice claim could be pursued judicially. Without resorting to arbitration, the plaintiff, a District of Columbia resident, filed his medical malpractice suit in the District. Employing interest analysis, the court held that Maryland law was applicable to the medical malpractice action, including Maryland's requirement for prior arbitration. The court specifically rejected plaintiff's argument that the arbitration requirement could not have extraterritorial effect, and remanded the case to the district court with instructions to stay proceedings until arbitration was conducted in Maryland. For a case decided under the traditional theory and reaching the opposite result, see Vest v. St. Albans Psychiatric Hospital, Inc., 182 W.Va. 228, 387 S.E.2d 282 (1989) (medical malpractice action by a West Virginia domiciliary arising from a medical procedure in a Virginia hospital; characterizing as procedural and refusing to apply a Virginia rule that required prior review of malpractice claims by a medical panel).

rules,"[32] that "[t]he maxim 'When in Rome do as Romans do' bespeaks the common sense view that it is the traveler who must adjust,"[33] and that doctors and health care providers should not have to differentiate among patients depending their state of origin.

In *Grover v. Isom*,[34] an Idaho court also applied the law of the state in which the medical services were provided, even though the defendant doctor was not domiciled in that state, Oregon, but rather in the patient's home state of Idaho.[35] The doctor maintained his clinic in Oregon and the case arose out of surgery he performed on plaintiff at that clinic. Following the Restatement Second, the Idaho court concluded that Oregon had the most significant relationship and its pro-defendant law should govern. The court noted that, in addition to the fact that the conduct and the injury occurred in Oregon, the plaintiff's presence in Oregon was "not fortuitous" because she "purposefully went to Oregon for the operation."[36] Moreover, because the doctor was licensed and practiced in Oregon, he "had every expectation that Oregon law would govern [his] business in Oregon,"[37] and Oregon had "an interest in making certain that oral surgeons practicing in Oregon are subject to Oregon laws and the Oregon standard of care."[38]

Finally, in *Troxel v. A.I. duPont Institute*,[39] a Pennsylvania court followed the same logic in a much closer case. The court applied the pro-defendant law of Delaware, the state in which a doctor treated a Pennsylvania patient, even though, in this unusual case, the plaintiff was not the patient but rather a friend of hers who contracted a contagious disease from the patient after the latter returned to her home in Pennsylvania.[40] The plaintiff sued the Delaware doctor for failing to inform the patient that she suffered from a contagious disease. The court noted Pennsylvania's interest in protecting its domiciliaries but concluded that this interest was "superseded by Delaware's interest in regulating the delivery of health care services in Delaware"[41] and in protecting defendants who acted in that state.[42] The court found that "the qualita-

---

32. *Bledsoe*, 849 F.2d at 647 (Williams, J., concurring).

33. Id.

34. 137 Idaho 770, 53 P.3d 821 (2002).

35. For other medical malpractice cases involving the common-domicile scenario, see Dugan v. Mobile Medical Test. Serv's, Inc., 265 Conn. 791, 830 A.2d 752 (2003) (applying New York's pro-defendant law to malpractice claim filed by a New York fireman domiciled in Connecticut against a Connecticut medical defendant arising from treatment in New York); Vecchio v. Rye Brook Obstetrics–Gynecology, P.C., 2003 WL 22482046 (Conn.Super.2003) (applying Connecticut's pro-plaintiff law to malpractice claim filed by a New York patient against a New York doctor and arising from treatment in Connecticut).

36. *Grover*, 53 P.3d at 824.

37. Id.

38. Id.

39. 431 Pa.Super. 464, 636 A.2d 1179 (1994), appeal denied 538 Pa. 648, 647 A.2d 903 (1994).

40. For this reason, one could argue that *Troxel* was a cross-border tort in which the conduct and the injury occurred in different states (Delaware and Pennsylvania, respectively). Cross-border torts are discussed infra at § 17.44.

41. *Troxel*, 636 A.2d at 1181.

42. See id. ("Insofar as the instant claim is focused upon [defendants] because of services rendered to a Pennsylvania resident in Delaware by a Delaware health care provider, the State of Delaware has the greater interest in the application of its law.... In treating [the patient] ... the

tive contacts of Delaware were greater and more significant than those of Pennsylvania,"[43] and reasoned that, when acting in Delaware, the defendant was "entitled to rely on the duties and protections provided by Delaware law."[44] The court concluded that any rule that would allow patients to carry with them the protective laws of their domiciles "when [they] travel . . . to Delaware to obtain medical care . . . would be wholly unreasonable, for it would require hospitals and physicians to be aware of and be bound by the laws of all states from which patients came to them for treatment."[45]

(b) Cases in which the conduct, the injury, and the domicile of the victim are in a state whose law protects the victim

§ 17.43 The second sentence of *Neumeier* Rule 2 (Rule 2b) addresses situations in which the conduct, the injury, and the injured person's domicile are in a state that provides a higher standard of protection for that person than does the law of the tortfeasor's domicile. Again, under interest analysis, these cases would be characterized as true conflicts. Rule 2b provides that the law of the victim's domicile applies, but this time an escape is available since that law applies "in the absence of special circumstances."[1] The Louisiana codification would reach the same result as Rule 2b. However, the Louisiana rule makes explicit what was implicit in the *Neumeier* rule by providing that both the conduct and the injury must have occurred in the state of the victim's domicile for that state's law to apply under that rule.[2] Furthermore, the Louisiana rule is confined to disputes between the victim and the tortfeasor and does not encompass disputes between or among tortfeasors.[3] Professor Cavers advocated the same result as *Neumeier* Rule 2b in his Principle 1. It provides that "[w]here the liability laws of

hospital was required to follow and abide by the laws of Delaware. As such, [defendants] were entitled to rely on the duties and protections provided by Delaware law.").

43. Id. at 1182.

44. Id. at 1181.

45. Id. The court failed to notice that, although the patient had traveled to Delaware for treatment, the actual plaintiff was not the patient, but rather her friend who did *not* in fact travel to Delaware. For a critique of *Troxel* on this point, see Symeonides, *The Revolution Today*, supra n.3, 225–227. In a subsequent case, the court allowed the plaintiff's action to proceed against the Pennsylvania doctor who had referred the patient to the Delaware hospital. See Troxel v. A.I. duPont Instit., 450 Pa.Super. 71, 675 A.2d 314 (1996), appeal denied 546 Pa. 668, 685 A.2d 547 (1996).

§ 17.43

1. Rule 2b provides as follows: "[W]hen the guest was injured in the state of his own domicile and its law permits recovery,

the driver who has come into that state should not—in the absence of special circumstances—be permitted to interpose the law of his state as a defense."

2. See La. Civ. Code art. 3544(2)(a). Cases in which only the injury occurred in the victim's domicile are also governed by that state's law, but only if that law is favorable to the victim and if the occurrence of the injury in that state was objectively foreseeable. See Art. 3544(2)(b) (discussed infra § 17.44 n.6). Cases in which only the conduct occurred in the victim's domicile are not subject to an a priori rule but are relegated to the flexible approach of Article 3542, the residual article.

3. See La. Civ. Code art. 3544, first sentence. Furthermore, this article is subject to two escapes contained in arts. 3547 ("exceptional cases"; described supra § 17.39 n.30) and 3548 ("corporate tortfeasors"; described supra § 17.40 n.11).

the state of injury set a higher standard of conduct or of financial protection against injury than do the laws of the state where the person causing the injury had acted or had his home, the laws of the state of injury should determine the standard and the protection applicable to the case[.]"[4] In explaining the rationale of this principle, Cavers used a variant of *Grant v. McAuliffe*[5] in which an Arizona domiciliary causes an accident in California that injures a California domiciliary. Cavers concluded that in such a case one should apply California's pro-plaintiff law rather than Arizona's pro-defendant law because California's "system of physical and financial protection would be impaired if a person who enters the territory of [that] state were not subject to its laws."[6] As for the defendant, said Cavers:

> [T]he fact that he would be held to a lower standard of care or of damages back in the state where he had his home ... or, indeed, the fact that he enjoyed an immunity there, all would ordinarily seem matters of little consequence to the state of the injury.... The defendant who is held to the higher standard is not an apt subject for judicial solicitude. He cannot fairly claim to enjoy whatever benefits a state may offer those who enter its bounds and at the same time claim exemption from the burdens.... Californians should not be put in jeopardy in California simply because an Arizonian ... had come into California from a state whose law provides a lower standard of financial protection than does California's.[7]

Cavers's arguments are compelling. This is why, as a recent study documents, the majority of courts that encountered cases of this pattern have reached the result described above, regardless of the choice-of-law methodology the courts followed.[8] This is true, not only of cases decided in New York where this result is dictated by *Neumeier* Rule 2b,[9] but also

---

4. D. Cavers, The Choice-of-Law Process 139 (1965). The Principle continues with an exception: "at least where the person injured was not so related to the person causing the injury that the question should be relegated to the law governing their relationship." Id.

5. 41 Cal.2d 859, 264 P.2d 944, 42 A.L.R.2d 1162 (1953) (discussed supra § 17.10).

6. D. Cavers, The Choice-of-Law Process 140 (1965).

7. Id. 140–142

8. See S. Symeonides, The American Choice-of-Law Revolution in the Courts: Today and Tomorrow, 298 Recueil des Cours, 1, 203–209 (2003), from which this section draws heavily. For a tabular presentation of the cases discussed here, see id. at 208.

9. In fact the New York cases are not exactly on point because they involve cross-border torts in which the tortfeasor's con-

duct had occurred in a state other than the one in which the victim was domiciled and suffered the injury. As explained earlier (supra § 17.32), these cases are more problematic in that they present the further conflict between Rule 2a and Rule 2b, with Rule 2a favoring the defendant and Rule 2b favoring the plaintiff. These cases do not seem to have recognized the latter conflict. See, e.g., Bankers Trust Co. v. Lee Keeling & Assoc., Inc., 20 F.3d 1092 (10th Cir.1994) (discussed supra § 17.32 n.34, decided under New York conflicts law; applying New York law to the malpractice action of a New York plaintiff injured in New York by the conduct of an Oklahoma defendant in Oklahoma); Bombardier Capital, Inc. v. Richfield Housing Center, Inc., 1994 WL 118294 (N.D.N.Y. 1994) (similar to *Bankers Trust*; applying Vermont law to an action brought by a Massachusetts/Vermont corporation against New York defendants for fraud in the inducement of a contract); Monroe v. Numed, Inc., 250 A.D.2d 20, 680 N.Y.S.2d

in other states. One subcategory of these cases involves situations in which a governmental entity that enjoys immunity from suit under the law of its home state engages in conduct in another state that does not accord such immunity, and causes injury there to a domiciliary of that state.

Nevada v. Hall[10] is the most well-known of these cases. In *Hall*, an employee of the University of Nevada, an entity that enjoyed sovereign immunity under Nevada law, drove to California on official university business and caused an accident there, injuring a California domiciliary. The California court refused to recognize Nevada's immunity, or Nevada's $25,000 limitation on damages. The court recognized Nevada's interest in protecting the financial well-being of Nevada entities, but found this interest to be much weaker than California's interest "in providing full protection to those who are injured on its highways through the negligence of both residents and non residents."[11] The court contrasted this case with *Bernhard v. Harrah's Club*[12] and concluded

707 (1998) (applying Florida law to a loss-of-consortium action arising out of the death of a Florida child whose death during surgery in Florida was attributed to a defective medical device manufactured in New York by a New York defendant; Florida, but not New York, allowed an action for loss of consortium); Caruolo v. A C & S, Inc., 1998 WL 730331 (S.D.N.Y.1998) (asbestosis case applying Rhode Island's pro-recovery law to a loss of consortium action by a Rhode Island plaintiff who was injured in that state; also applying New York law to an action by the same plaintiff against a New York defendant for injury sustained in New York); Kramer v. Showa Denko K.K., 929 F.Supp. 733 (S.D.N.Y.1996) (products-liability case discussed infra § 17.70 nn.1 ff.; erroneously applying the *Neumeier* rules to a punitive-damages conflict; awarding punitive damages under New York law to a New York victim injured in that state by a product manufactured in Japan by a Japanese corporation).

Another group of New York cases applied Rule 2b to disputes between joint tortfeasors (rather than between victims and tortfeasors) which, as seen in *Cooney* (supra § 17.32), do not easily fit within the mold of Rule 2b. See See, e.g., Glunt v. ABC Paving Co., Inc., 247 A.D.2d 871, 668 N.Y.S.2d 846 (1998) (*Cooney*-type case arising out of a New York traffic accident involving an Ohio victim, his Ohio employer, and a New York defendant; following *Neumeier* Rule 2 and applying New York law allowing the New York defendant to obtain indemnification from the Ohio defendant who would be immune from indemnification under Ohio law); Venturini v. Worldwide Marble & Granite Corp., 1995 WL 606281 (S.D.N.Y. 1995) (third-party actions for contribution

and indemnification filed by New York and Michigan companies against a New Jersey company arising out of injury sustained in Michigan by a truck driver employed by the New Jersey company; applying Michigan law under "the second *and* third Neumeier rules," id. at *3 (emphasis added), and denying contribution which would be available under New York law); Mascarella v. Brown, 813 F.Supp. 1015 (S.D.N.Y.1993) (third-party action by a New York defendant against a New Jersey corporation seeking contribution and indemnification for medical malpractice committed in New York by the New York defendant; applying New York law and allowing contribution which was not available under New Jersey law); Bader v. Purdom, 841 F.2d 38 (2d Cir.1988) (action by a New York minor bitten by defendant's dog in Ontario. Defendants third-partied the minor's parents claiming contribution and indemnification for their negligent supervision of the child. Such claim was permitted by Ontario law but not by New York law. Apparently thinking of the main action, rather than the third-party claim for contribution, the court concluded that this case fell within the scope of Rule 3 and applied Ontario substantive law. A concurring judge pointed out that, more properly, the case fell within the scope of Rule 2b).

10. 440 U.S. 410, 99 S.Ct. 1182, 59 L.Ed.2d 416 (1979).

11. Hall v. Nevada, 74 Cal.App.3d 280, 141 Cal.Rptr. 439, 442 (1977).

12. 16 Cal.3d 313, 128 Cal.Rptr. 215, 546 P.2d 719 (1976). *Bernhard* is discussed supra § 17.19.

that California had an even stronger interest in applying its law because, unlike *Bernhard* in which the defendant's conduct had occurred in Nevada, in *Hall* both "the State of Nevada's activities and the [victim's] injuries took place in California."[13] The court continued: "By thus utilizing the public highways within our state to conduct its business, Nevada should fully expect to be held accountable under California laws."[14] The United States Supreme Court upheld the constitutionality of the California court's decision after noting, *inter alia*, California's "substantial" interest in "providing full protection to those who are injured on its highways."[15]

Other courts have reached the same result in cases involving the issue of state immunity.[16] One sub-category of cases, that also reached the same result involve police car chases that began in one state and ended in another, causing injury in the latter state. In one of those cases,

13. *Hall*, 141 Cal.Rptr. at 442.

14. Id. See also id. ("Given the fact that Nevada has chosen to engage in governmental and business activity in this state, the necessary acquisition of additional insurance coverage to protect itself during such an activity is an entirely foreseeable and reasonable expense").

15. *Hall*, 440 U.S. at 423. In Franchise Tax Bd. of California v. Hyatt, 538 U.S. 488, 123 S.Ct. 1683, 155 L.Ed.2d 702, 71 USLW 4307 (2003), the shoe was on the other foot. A Nevada domiciliary sued a California state agency in Nevada claiming that he was injured in Nevada by the agency's intentional and negligent acts, some of which were committed in California and others in Nevada. The agency claimed immunity under California law. Relying on principles of comity, the Nevada Supreme Court ruled that the lower court should have declined to exercise its jurisdiction over the agency's negligent acts, because Nevada also accorded immunity for negligent acts that Nevada officials commit while exercising their official duties. On the other hand, since Nevada did not accord immunity for intentional torts of Nevada officials, the Nevada the court found no reason to accord such immunity for similar acts of California officials. In a unanimous opinion, the United States Supreme Court upheld the Nevada decision against a full faith and credit challenge, *inter alia*, because Nevada clearly had the requisite contacts to constitutionally apply its law (plaintiff's domicile, place of injury, and place of some of the conduct), and the Nevada Supreme Court "sensitively applied principles of comity with a healthy regard for California's sovereign status, relying on the contours of Nevada's own sovereign immunity from suit as a benchmark for its analysis." 123 S.Ct. at 1690. Thus, this was not a case

in which a state had exhibited a " 'policy of hostility to the public Acts' of a sister State." Id. (quoting Carroll v. Lanza, 349 U.S. 408, 413, 75 S.Ct. 804, 99 L.Ed. 1183 (1955)).

16. See Struebin v. Iowa, 322 N.W.2d 84 (Iowa 1982) (refusing to uphold Illinois' immunity and damages-limitation in a case arising from Iowa accident caused by Illinois's negligence in maintaining a bridge in Iowa. See id. at 87: "Iowa's interest in full compensation outweighs Illinois' interest in extending its statutory limitation to its Iowa torts."); Laconis v. Burlington County Bridge, 400 Pa.Super. 483, 583 A.2d 1218 (1990) (refusing to apply New Jersey immunity law to action filed against a New Jersey county by a Pennsylvania domiciliary who was injured on the Pennsylvania side of bridge connecting Pennsylvania to New Jersey and maintained by New Jersey county); Church v. Massey, 697 So.2d 407 (Miss. 1997) (refusing to apply Alabama's immunity law to action of Mississippi domiciliary arising from Mississippi accident caused by an Alabama state employee); Peterson v. Texas, 635 P.2d 241 (Colo. App. 1981) (Texas not immune from Colorado suit arising from Colorado tort injuring Colorado plaintiff); Wendt v. County of Osceola, 289 N.W.2d 67 (Minn. 1979) (refusing to recognize Iowa's immunity in action arising from Minnesota injury); Mianecki v. Second Judicial Dist. Court, 99 Nev. 93, 658 P.2d 422 (1983) (refusing to recognize Wisconsin's immunity in action arising from Nevada injury). But see Harris v. City of Memphis, 119 F.Supp.2d 893 (E.D.Ark. 2000) (invoking comity and applying Tennessee immunity law to Arkansas plaintiff's action against Tennessee city for failure to maintain adequate lighting on Arkansas side of bridge connecting Arkansas with Tennessee, which city had contractually agreed to maintain).

Biscoe v. Arlington County,[17] a policeman employed by defendant, a Virginia county, began chasing a suspected bank robber in that county. The chase continued into the District of Columbia where it ended in an accident injuring plaintiff, an unsuspecting bystander.[18] Under the law of Virginia, but not D.C., the Virginia county would be immune from liability. The court concluded that neither the Constitution's Full Faith and Credit clause nor principles of comity required the District to honor the county's immunity. The court held that, under choice-of-law principles, D.C. law governed because "the District's policies would be substantially more seriously thwarted by nonapplication of its law ... than would those of Virginia."[19] The court found that "Virginia's concern for the economic well-being of its counties ... [was] not an especially compelling one."[20] In contrast, the District's "interests in deterrence of potential tortfeasors and compensation of injured parties"[21] were "strongly implicated"[22] because the District was "the site of the most relevant conduct and all the injury,"[23] and the "defendants' acts created ... danger to District life and property."[24]

Other cases involving this pattern and similar facts reached the same result as *Biscoe*.[25] The only case that reached the opposite result is *Lommen v. The City of East Grand Forks*.[26] In this case, a Minnesota police officer began chasing a stolen car in Minnesota and continued into North Dakota where he collided with another car injuring its passenger, a North Dakota domiciliary.[27] In a brazen display of parochialism, the Minnesota court applied Minnesota immunity law under Leflar's choice-influencing considerations. The court completely discounted the plaintiff's argument that, when a North Dakota domiciliary is injured in North Dakota she has a valid expectation that the consequences of her injury will be determined under that state's law. Instead, the court found that the officer and his employer "had a substantial expectation of on-the-job tort immunity,"[28] which apparently they can carry with them on

---

17. 738 F.2d 1352 (D.C. Cir. 1984).

18. The victim, though a Maryland domiciliary, was working in the District of Columbia and the court treated him as a D.C. domiciliary, because of the "special and largely unique interest of the District in protecting persons who live in the surrounding suburbs and work in the District." Id. at 1361.

19. Id. at 1362.

20. Id. at 1361.

21. Id.

22. Id.

23. Id.

24. Id.

25. See, e.g., Skipper v. Prince George's County, 637 F.Supp. 638 (D.D.C. 1986) (police car chase from Maryland to District of Columbia, where the chased car injured D.C. resident–relying on *Biscoe* and applying D.C. law denying defendant the immunity Maryland law provided).

26. 522 N.W.2d 148 (Minn. App. 1994).

27. The victim sued both the officer and his employer, a Minnesota municipality. Under Minnesota law, both the officer and his employer were immune from liability, unless the officer's actions were "willful or malicious." Under North Dakota law, the officer would not be immune if his acts were "grossly negligent," and, regardless of the officer's immunity, his employer was not immune. Thus, to the extent it pertained to the police officer, this case fell within the pattern discussed here, because the officer acted within North Dakota. To the extent it pertained to the Minnesota employer, this case fell within the cross-border tort pattern discussed infra § 17.44, because the employer's acts or omissions occurred in Minnesota.

28. 522 N.W.2d at 150.

a high speed chase into other states. The court concluded that "overall the relevant considerations favor application of Minnesota law ... [because] Minnesota's ability to define the immunity of its officials should not vary according to the fortuitous facts of either the location of the accident or the citizenship of the injured party."[29] Apparently, the court did not realize that this argument could easily be turned around–the rights of an innocent North Dakota citizen, who is maimed in North Dakota, "should not vary according to the fortuitous facts of either ... the citizenship of the [maimer or his employer]." Indeed, whether it is the result of naivete or blind provincialism, Lommen cannot withstand the scrutiny of logic. It is discussed here for purposes of illustration, not emulation.

Fortunately, no other cases can be found that emulate the *Lommen* analysis, or the result, in situations involving this pattern.[30] To the contrary, as discussed later,[31] even cross-border tort cases in which the tortfeasor's conduct occurred outside the victim's home state and injured the victim in the latter state applied the pro-plaintiff law of that state. These cases suggest that, *a fortiori*, the same result is appropriate in intra-state torts in which the tortfeasor acts in the victim's home state and causes injury there.[32] To quote *Bledsoe* again, "[t]he maxim 'When in Rome do as Romans do' bespeaks the common sense view that it is the traveler who must adjust."[33]

(c) Cases in which the conduct and the tortfeasor's domicile are in a state whose law favors the tortfeasor, while the injury and the victim's domicile are in a state whose law protects the victim

§ 17.44 Far more problematic than the cases discussed above are split-domicile cases in which the tort is committed across state boundaries, with the conduct being in the tortfeasor's domicile and the resulting injury being at the victim's domicile. Products liability cases,[1] defamation cases, fraud cases, or any other cases involving a tort that can be committed from a distance can involve this pattern. When the state of the tortfeasor's domicile (which is also the place of his conduct) has a pro-defendant law, while the state of the victim's domicile (which is also the place of her injury) has a pro-recovery law, the resulting conflict is as true as they come. This conflict is more difficult than the conflicts involved in the patterns discussed above because here both the

---

29. Id. at 152.

30. In fact, the only other post-*lex loci* case that fits precisely within this pattern reached the opposite result. See Pelican Point Operations v. Carroll Childers Co., 807 So.2d 1171 (La. App. 2002), writ denied 816 So.2d 293 (La.2002) (applying Louisiana's pro-recovery law to a Louisiana plaintiff's action for injury caused to its Louisiana property by a Texas defendant who used self help in repossessing property in violation of Louisiana law).

31. See infra § 17.44.

32. See *Nevada v. Hall*, at text accompanying nn. 13–14 supra.

33. Bledsoe v. Crowley, 849 F.2d 639, 647 (D.C. Cir. 1988) (Williams, J., concurring).

§ 17.44

1. Products liability conflicts are discussed infra § 17.64 et seq.

personal contacts (domiciles) and the territorial contacts (conduct and injury) are evenly split, with a concomitant bearing on both state policies and party expectations.

As explained earlier,[2] the *Neumeier* rules were not designed for these conflicts because they were intended for guest-statute conflicts in which the conduct and the injury are bound to occur in the same state. However, because now these rules have been extended to cross-border torts, and because rules 2a and 2b are elliptically worded, an internal conflict arises between Rule 2a and Rule 2b. When a defendant acts in his home state, whose law protects him, and causes injury to the victim in her home state, whose law protects her, Rule 2a calls for the application of the law of the former state, while Rule 2b calls for the application the law of the latter state.[3] As seen earlier, even after *Schultz*, New York courts have failed to differentiate between conduct and injury. They continue to speak of the "locus of the tort" and, uncritically relying on dicta contained in *Schultz*, place this "locus" in the state "where the last event necessary to make the actor liable occurred"[4] namely, at the state of the injury.[5] This means that in cases of this pattern the place of conduct becomes irrelevant and, more importantly, that Rule 2b trumps Rule 2a, thus resulting in the application of the pro-recovery law of the state of injury, which is also the victim's domicile.

This result is not unpalatable, provided that certain safeguards are put in place to protect the defendant from the application of a law that he had no reason to anticipate. To that end, the Louisiana codification expressly subjects the application of the pro-recovery law of the victim's domicile to an objective foreseeability proviso.[6] Professor Cavers, who

---

2. See supra § 17.32.

3. See id. Similarly, if in the same case the injury occurs in third state, a conflict arises between Rule 2a and Rule 3. Rule 2a calls for the application of the law of the state of conduct while Rule 3 calls for the application of the law of the state "where the accident occurred" (meaning perhaps the place of injury) subject to the escape contained in that rule.

4. *Schultz*, 65 N.Y.2d at 195, 480 N.E.2d at 683, 491 N.Y.S.2d at 94.

5. See Bankers Trust Co. v. Lee Keeling & Assoc., Inc., 20 F.3d 1092 (10th Cir.1994) (discussed supra § 17.32 nn.34–40); Kramer v. Showa Denko K.K., 929 F.Supp. 733 (S.D.N.Y.1996) (discussed infra § 17.70 n.1). See also Hamilton v. Accu–Tek, 47 F.Supp.2d 330, 337 (E.D.N.Y.1999) ("In cases where the defendant's tortious conduct and the plaintiff's injury occur in different states 'the place of the wrong is considered to be the place where the last event necessary to make the actor liable occurred,'" quoting *Schultz* and citing Pes-

catore v. Pan American World Airways, Inc., 97 F.3d 1, 13 (2d Cir.1996); and Kush v. Abbott Lab., 655 N.Y.S.2d 520, 521, 238 A.D.2d 172 (1997)).

6. La. Civ. Code art. 3544(2)(b) provides that "when the injury and the conduct that caused it occurred in different states, ... the law of the state in which the injury occurred [applies], provided that (i) the injured person was domiciled in that state, (ii) the person who caused the injury should have foreseen its occurrence in that state, and (iii) the law of that state provided for a higher standard of financial protection for the injured person than did the law of the state in which the injurious conduct occurred." A similar defense is provided for products liability conflicts. See La. Civ. Code art. 3545(2) which provides that Louisiana products liability law shall not apply "if neither the product that caused the injury nor any of the defendant's products of the same type were made available in this state through ordinary commercial channels."

also advocates the same result subject to the same proviso, offers the following rationale for it:

> Th[e] system of physical and financial protection [of the state of injury] would be impaired ... if actions outside the state but having foreseeable effects within it were not also subject to its law.... [T]he fact that [the defendant] would be held to a lower standard of care or of damages back in the state where he ... [acted] or, indeed, the fact that he enjoyed an immunity there, all would ordinarily seem matters of little consequence to the state of the injury.... If he has not entered the state but has caused harm within it by his act outside it, then, save perhaps where the physical or legal consequences of his action were not foreseeable, it is equally fair to hold him to the standards of the state into which he sent whatever harmful agent, animal, object or message caused the injury.[7]

As a recent study documents, many courts have resolved these conflicts in the way suggested above by applying the pro-plaintiff law of the victim's home state and place of injury.[8] However, all of those cases involved situations in which the tortfeasor should have foreseen the occurrence of the injury in the victim's home state. For example in the products liability cases that applied the law of the pro-plaintiff law of the victim's home state,[9] the product had reached that state through ordi-

---

7. D. Cavers, The Choice-of-Law Process 140, 141 (1965).

8. See S. Symeonides, The American Choice-of-Law Revolution in the Courts: Today and Tomorrow, 298 Recueil des Cours, 1, 220–27 (2003), from which this section draws heavily. For a tabular presentation of the cases discussed here, see id. at 222.

9. These cases are discussed infra §§ 17.77–17.79; See, e.g., Eimers v. Honda Motor Co. Ltd, 785 F.Supp. 1204 (W.D.Pa. 1992) (applying New York's pro-plaintiff law to an action by a New York plaintiff injured in New York by a motorcycle acquired in that state and manufactured by a Japanese defendant in Japan); Savage Arms, Inc. v. Western Auto Supply Co., 18 P.3d 49 (Alaska 2001) (successor-liability conflict applying the pro-plaintiff law of Alaska, which was the victim's home state and injury, and the place of the product's acquisition); Tune v. Philip Morris Inc., 766 So.2d 350 (Fla. App. 2000) (applying Florida's pro-plaintiff law to an action filed against a tobacco manufacturer by a Florida domiciliary who was diagnosed with lung cancer in Florida after using tobacco products there and in New Jersey, his previous domicile); R–Square Inves. v. Teledyne Indus., Inc., 1997 WL 436245 (E.D. La. 1997) (applying Louisiana's pro-plaintiff law to an action of a Louisiana plaintiff injured in Louisiana by a product acquired in Minnesota and manufactured in Alabama by an Alabama manufacturer); Allstate Ins. Co. v. Wal–Mart, 2000 WL 388844 (E.D.La. 2000) (applying Louisiana's pro-plaintiff law to an action of a Louisiana plaintiff injured in Louisiana by a product acquired in Oklahoma and manufactured in Minnesota by a Minnesota manufacturer); In re Masonite Corp. Hardboard Siding Prod. Liab. Litig., 21 F.Supp.2d 593 (E.D.La. 1998) (noting Florida's strong interest in applying its law to protect its citizens from building materials that were sold and used in that state and could not withstand that state's extreme weather conditions); Hoover v. Recreation Equip. Corp., 792 F.Supp. 1484 (N.D.Ohio 1991) (applying Ohio's pro-plaintiff law to both products liability and successor liability claims by an Ohio resident injured in Ohio by a product manufactured in Indiana by an Indiana corporation which was acquired by another Indiana corporation). But see Poust v. Huntleigh HealthCare, 998 F.Supp. 478 (D.N.J. 1998) (applying New Jersey's pro-defendant compensatory damages law to products liability action filed against a New Jersey manufacturer by a Pennsylvania plaintiff who was injured by the product in Maryland).

nary commercial channels. Thus the defendant could not claim to be unfairly surprised by the application of that state's law.

Many other cases involving other cross-border torts,[10] including professional malpractice,[11] fraud and deceptive practices,[12] as well as more complex disputes between joint tortfeasors,[13] have also applied the pro-plaintiff law of the plaintiff's home state and place of injury.

One representative case is *Kuehn v. Childrens Hospital, Los Angeles*,[14] which was decided under Wisconsin's choice-influencing considerations. *Kuehn* was an action filed by the parents of a Wisconsin child who died in Wisconsin as a result of the negligence of a California hospital. The negligence consisted in improperly shipping to Wisconsin a

---

10. See, e.g., Monroe v. Numed Inc., 250 A.D.2d 20, 680 N.Y.S.2d 707 (3 Dept. 1998) (applying Florida's pro-plaintiff law to a loss-of-consortium action arising out of the death of a Florida child whose death during surgery in Florida was attributed to a defective medical device manufactured in New York by a New York defendant); Caruolo v. A C & S, Inc., 1998 WL 730331 (S.D.N.Y. 1998) (asbestosis case applying Rhode Island's pro-plaintiff law to a loss of consortium action by a Rhode Island plaintiff injured in Rhode Island); Brown v. Harper, 231 A.D.2d 483, 647 N.Y.S.2d 245 (1996) (applying New York's pro-plaintiff law to impose liability on a Pennsylvania dealer who sold a car to an uninsured driver who caused accident in New York injuring a New York domiciliary); Drinkall v. Used Car Rentals, Inc. 32 F.3d 329 (8th Cir. 1994) (applying Iowa's pro-plaintiff law to impose liability on Nebraska car rental company that rented a car in Nebraska to an unlicensed driver that caused an accident in Iowa injuring an Iowa domiciliary)

11. See, e.g., Bankers Trust Co. v. Lee Keeling & Assoc., Inc., 20 F.3d 1092 (10th Cir. 1994) (discussed § 17.32 nn.40; applying New York law to a case arising out of injury in New York sustained by a New York plaintiff and caused by the conduct of an Oklahoma defendant in Oklahoma); David B. Lilly Co., Inc. v. Fisher, 18 F.3d 1112 (3d Cir. 1994) (applying Delaware law to Delaware plaintiff's action for legal malpractice committed outside Delaware by out of state attorneys).

12. See Bombardier Capital, Inc. v. Richfield Hous. Ctr., Inc., 1994 WL 118294 (N.D.N.Y. 1994) (applying Vermont's pro-plaintiff law to an action brought by a Massachusetts/Vermont corporation against New York defendants for fraud in the inducement of a contract).

13. See, e.g., Glunt v. ABC Paving Co., Inc., 247 A.D.2d 871, 668 N.Y.S.2d 846 (4 Dept. 1998) (reverse *Cooney*-type case aris-

ing out of a New York traffic accident involving an Ohio victim, his Ohio employer, and a New York defendant; following *Neumeier* Rule 2 and applying New York law allowing the New York defendant to obtain indemnification from the Ohio defendant who would be immune from indemnification under Ohio law); Venturini v. Worldwide Marble & Granite Corp., 1995 WL 606281 (S.D.N.Y. 1995) (third-party actions for contribution and indemnification filed by New York company and Michigan company against a New Jersey company arising out of injury sustained in Michigan by a truck driver employed by the New Jersey company; applying Michigan law under "the second *and* third Neumeier rules," id. at *3 (emphasis added) and denying contribution, which would be available under New York law); Mascarella v. Brown, 813 F.Supp. 1015, (S.D.N.Y. 1993) (third-party action by a New York defendant against a New Jersey corporation seeking contribution and indemnification for medical malpractice committed in New York by the New York defendant; applying New York law and allowing contribution, which was not available under New Jersey law); Bader v. Purdom, 841 F.2d 38 (2d Cir. 1988) (action by a New York minor bitten by defendant's dog in Ontario. Defendants third-partied the minor's parents claiming contribution and indemnification for their negligent supervision of the child. Such claim was permitted by Ontario law, but not by New York law. Apparently thinking of the main action, rather than the third-party claim for contribution, the court concluded that this case fell within the scope of Rule 3 and applied Ontario law. A concurring judge pointed out that, more properly, the case fell within the scope of Rule 2b).

14. 119 F.3d 1296 (7th Cir. 1997).

package containing the child's bone marrow.[15] Under California law, the action did not survive the victim's death. Under Wisconsin law it did. The court applied Wisconsin law in an opinion authored by Judge Posner. The court took note of Wisconsin's interest "in obtaining for its residents the measure of relief that the state believes appropriate in tort cases."[16] However, the court also took care to explain why the California hospital should have foreseen the occurrence of the injury in Wisconsin, and thus the possibility of having to account under Wisconsin law–the hospital had shipped the package to Wisconsin based on a contractual arrangement with a Wisconsin hospital.[17] Furthermore, said the court, the only difference between California and Wisconsin law was "in the scope of liability for negligence, not in the standard of care. It [was] not as if California had required one method of packing and shipping bone marrow and Wisconsin another."[18]

In contrast, in *Troxel v. A.I. duPont Institute*,[19] a medical malpractice case, the foreseeability element was arguably tenuous, and this may have been part of the court's reason for reaching the opposite result. Another reason may have been that, unlike *Kuehn*, *Troxel* arose out of actual in-patient treatment and thus was a true action for medical malpractice. In *Troxel*, a Delaware hospital treated a Pennsylvania patient after referral from a Pennsylvania doctor. The patient returned to Pennsylvania and, unaware that she was suffering from a contagious disease, communicated that disease to her pregnant friend, the plaintiff, whose in utero child died as a result of the disease. The plaintiff sued the hospital for failure to inform its patient of the contagious nature of her disease and of the risk to pregnant women who might come into contact with her.

The Pennsylvania court recognized Pennsylvania's interest in protecting its citizens, but concluded that this interest was "superseded by Delaware's interest in regulating the delivery of health care services in Delaware"[20] and in protecting defendants who acted in that state.[21] The

15. Employees of the California hospital extracted bone marrow from the child and then shipped it via Federal Express to a Wisconsin hospital were it was to be reinserted into the child's bones. The marrow was improperly packaged and arrived in Wisconsin in unusable condition. This necessitated a second procedure which did not succeed in saving the child's life. This action was only for the negligence in improperly shipping the marrow and involved only a claim for the child's pre-death pain and suffering.

16. Id. at 1302.

17. See id.: "[D]efendant's failure to negotiate a choice of law provision when as in this case the defendant has a written contract with the potential plaintiff makes the claim that applying the law of another state would unsettle the defendant's legal obligations ring hollow."

18. Id. After examining the case under all five-choice influencing considerations, the court concluded that "[s]o strongly do the other considerations besides predictability favor Wisconsin law in this case that the application of that law was predictable–thus completing the sweep." Id. at 1303.

19. 431 Pa.Super. 464, 636 A.2d 1179 (1994), appeal denied 538 Pa. 648, 647 A.2d 903 (1994).

20. 636 A.2d at 1181.

21. See id.: "Insofar as the instant claim is focused upon [defendants] because of services rendered to a Pennsylvania resident in Delaware by a Delaware health care provider, the State of Delaware has the greater interest in the application of its law.... In treating [the patient] ... the hospital was required to follow and abide by the laws of Delaware. As such, [defendants]

court said that "the qualitative contacts of Delaware were greater and more significant than those of Pennsylvania,"[22] and that, when acting in Delaware, defendant was "entitled to rely on the duties and protections provided by Delaware law."[23] The court also stated that any rule that would allow patients to carry with them the protective law of their domicile "when [they] travel . . . to Delaware to obtain medical care . . . would be wholly unreasonable, for it would require hospitals and physicians to be aware of and be bound by the laws of all states from which patients came to them for treatment."[24]

This discussion of state interests simply confirms that these cases are veritable true conflicts, which in turn means that the two states' interests are more or less equally strong and pertinent. One element that can tip the scales in the one or the other direction is the actor's ability reasonably to foresee where the act will manifest its direct consequences. In *Kuehn*, it was beyond question that the California hospital should have foreseen that the consequences of its negligence in sending a package to Wisconsin would have been felt in Wisconsin.

Certainly, one could make the same argument in *Troxel*–the Delaware hospital doctors should have foreseen that, when they send an uncured and uniformed contagious patient back to her home in Pennsylvania, the consequences of that negligence would have been felt in Pennsylvania. The fact that the *Troxel* court did not accept this argument suggests that the court believed strongly that, from a systemic perspective, medical malpractice conflicts should be resolved invariably under the law of the place where the medical services are rendered, regardless of any other factors.[25] As seen earlier, cases like Bledsoe have adopted this very concept. However, there is a difference between cases like Bledsoe, in which a patient chooses to go to an out-of-state hospital for treatment, and cases like *Troxel* in which the victim has no relation with the hospital. In the latter cases, the court should look at the case from the perspective of the victim, who has never left her home state and has been injured there, and ask whether she deserves to rely on the protective law of her own state. Stated another way, foreseeability has two sides–that of the tortfeasor, and that of the victim. When, as in *Bledsoe*, both sides can foresee the eventuality of the injury occurring in the victim's home state, the foreseeability criterion may be less critical in resolving the conflict. But when, as in *Troxel*, only the tortfeasor is in a

---

were entitled to rely on the duties and protections provided by Delaware law."

22. Id. at 1182.

23. Id. at 1181.

24. Id. In a subsequent decision, the court allowed the plaintiff's action to proceed against the Pennsylvania doctor who had referred the patient to the Delaware hospital. See Troxel v. A.I. duPont Inst., 450 Pa.Super. 71, 675 A.2d 314 (1996), ap-

peal denied 546 Pa. 668, 685 A.2d 547 (1996).

25. See *Troxel*, 636 A.2d at 1181: "Pennsylvania law did not follow [the patient] when [she] traveled to Delaware to obtain medical care. Any other rule would be wholly unreasonable, for it would require hospitals and physicians to be aware of and be bound by the laws of all states from which patients came to them for treatment. This is not the law."

position to foresee this eventuality and the victim cannot, the scale tips against the tortfeasor, not the victim.[26]

(2) No–Interest or Unprovided-for Cases

§ 17.45 The converse of the cases discussed in the last three patterns are cases in which the conduct, the injury, and one party's domicile are in a state whose law protects the *other* party. One can subdivide these cases into two patterns: (a) cases in which the conduct and the injury occur in the domicile of the victim; and (b) cases in which they occur in the domicile of the tortfeasor.

a. The Neumeier Pattern

Neumeier v. Kuehner[1] and *Erwin v. Thomas*[2] are well know examples of the first pattern. In both cases the conduct and the injury occurred in the state of the victim's domicile and that state's law favored the foreign tortfeasor by denying recovery to the local victim. Under Currie's assumptions and terminology, these cases present the "unprovided-for" or "no-interest" paradigm because neither state has an interest in applying its law to protect the domiciliary of the other state. Under Currie's prescriptions, the law of the forum *qua* forum should govern these cases. As seen above, *Erwin* but not *Neumeier* followed those prescriptions.

Other cases reached the same *result* as *Erwin*, in the sense that they applied the pro-plaintiff law of the defendant's home state, but they did so for different reasons than *Erwin*. For example, in *Labree v. Major*,[3] a Rhode Island court applied Rhode Island's pro-plaintiff law not because Rhode Island was the forum, but rather because the court subscribed to the altruistic theorem that, when the defendant is from a recovery state, "the plaintiff should recover no matter what the law of his residence or the place of the accident."[4] In *Farrell v. Davis Enterprises, Inc.*,[5] a Pennsylvania court applied Pennsylvania's pro-plaintiff law, not because that state was the forum but rather because the court assumed that that law was in part designed to deter Pennsylvania tortfeasors, even when they acted outside Pennsylvania.[6] In *Kaiser-Georgetown Community*

---

26. Cf. P. Nygh, "The Reasonable Expectations of the Parties as a Guide to the Choice of Law in Contract and Tort," 251 *Recueil des Cours* 269, 296 (1995) ("The expectation of compensation is . . . reasonable and fundamental, as is the converse expectation that the liability be foreseeable").

§ 17.45

1. 31 N.Y.2d 121, 335 N.Y.S.2d 64, 286 N.E.2d 454 (1972) (discussed supra § 17.31).

2. 264 Or. 454, 506 P.2d 494 (1973) (discussed supra §§ 17.14, 17.27 n.7).

3. 111 R.I. 657, 306 A.2d 808 (1973) (discussed supra §§ 17.13 n.23, 17.34 n.10)

4. Id. at 818. *Labree* was a guest-statute conflict arising from a Massachusetts accident involving a Massachusetts guest-passenger and a Rhode Island host-driver. Massachusetts, but not Rhode Island, had a guest statute.

5. 1996 WL 21128 (E.D. Pa. 1996).

6. *Farrell* arose out of a New Jersey accident involving a New Jersey victim and two Pennsylvania joint tortfeasors. Pennsylvania's joint and several liability law was

Health Plan, Inc. v. Stutsman,[7] a District of Columbia court followed a similar logic and applied the District's unlimited-damages rule in part in order to hold D.C. defendants "liable for the full extent of the negligence attributable to them."[8]

In *Erny v. Estate of Merola*,[9] a New Jersey court followed a more circuitous route to the pro-plaintiff law of the *non-forum* state, New York. The case arose out of a three-car accident in New Jersey involving a New Jersey plaintiff and two New York defendants. The trial court found the two defendants 60% and 40% at fault, respectively. Under New York's joint and several liability statute, the plaintiff could recover 100% of her damages from either defendant, whereas under New Jersey law the plaintiff could recover only from the defendant who was 60% at fault (but who was insolvent). In dollar terms, this meant that the plaintiff would recover about $290,000 less under New Jersey law than under New York law.

The plaintiff argued that New York's pro-plaintiff law was intended "not only for the benefit of New York residents, but for out-of-state residents as well."[10] The intermediate court rejected the premise "that New York would welcome another state's imposition of full responsibility on its resident solely because New York law would permit it,"[11] and concluded that "[i]t would indeed be anomalous to apply foreign law solely to gain access to a deep pocket when local law denies that access."[12] The New Jersey Supreme Court reversed after managing to classify this as a false conflict in which New Jersey was uninterested and New York was interested in applying its law. The court found that New Jersey law was designed to protect certain defendants and to reduce the

---

more favorable to the plaintiff than was New Jersey's law.

7. 491 A.2d 502 (D.C. 1985).

8. Id. at 509. *Stutsman* was a medical malpractice action arising out of treatment in defendant's Virginia hospital and resulting in injury to a Virginia plaintiff. The defendant was a D.C. based corporation and Virginia, but not D.C., limited the amount of damages. The court concluded that the District had an interest in applying its unlimited-compensatory-damages rule, even though its application would benefit a Virginia plaintiff at the expense of a D.C. defendant because the D.C. rule reflected "a significant interest ... in holding [D.C.] corporations liable for the full extent of the negligence attributable to them." The court also based the District's interest on the fact that the plaintiff, though a Virginia domiciliary, was employed in the District and had been referred to the Virginia hospital by her employer's HMO. The court concluded that the District had an interest in "protecting a member of its work force who contracts for health services with a District of Columbia corporation within this forum

and then is injured by the negligence of that corporation's agents." Id. at 510. Three year's later, when the plaintiff's husband sued the same defendants for loss of consortium resulting from his wife's death in Stutsman v. Kaiser Foundation Health Plan, 546 A.2d 367 (D.C. App. 1988), the same court concluded that Virginia was interested in applying its pro-defendant law, even though that law denied a Virginia plaintiff a remedy that D.C. law allowed. The court thought that Virginia's denial of loss of consortium actions was not intended to protect defendants or hospitals operating in that state, but was instead designed to "regulat[e] the legal rights of married couples domiciled in Virginia ... by giving a married woman the exclusive right to sue for damages for her personal injuries." Id. at 374.

9. 171 N.J. 86, 792 A.2d 1208 (2002).

10. Erny v. Russo, 333 N.J.Super. 88, 754 A.2d 606, 614 (2000).

11. Id. at 615.

12. Id. at 614.

costs of car insurance. Since neither defendant was domiciled in New Jersey and neither drove a car insured there, New Jersey did not have an interest in applying its law. In contrast, said the court, "New York placed more value in protecting the innocent victim ... than reducing the cost of automobile insurance,"[13] and this policy was "aimed at protecting innocent victims of New York vehicle registrants, whether injured or harmed in New York or elsewhere,"[14] regardless of whether they were domiciled in or outside New York.[15] In addition, said the court, "the New York statute encourages its drivers to insure more adequately their vehicles and, inferentially, to drive with care."[16] Thus, the New York statute "expresses a weightier interest in both compensation and deterrence than does the New Jersey statute."[17] Hence, the court concluded, application of the New York statute in this case, which "involv[ed] only New York defendants whose cars are registered and insured in New York [would] further that governmental interest,"[18] while application of New Jersey law "would not further New Jersey's interest in reducing liability insurance rates."[19]

In concluding that New York had an interest in protecting non-New York victims injured outside New York, the New Jersey court in *Erny* relied on a 1970 federal district court case.[20] The court conveniently overlooked New York's authoritative decision in *Neumeier*,[21] which had held to the contrary in a similar case, and had quoted with approval a statement that New York law was "[not] intended to be manna for the entire world."[22]

Neumeier is by no means the only case to take this position and to apply the pro-defendant law of the accident state, which was also the plaintiff's domicile.[23] Other cases have also applied the same law, either

---

13. *Erny v. Estate of Merola*, 792 A.2d at 1218.

14. Id. at 1219.

15. Id. at 1220.

16. Id.

17. Id.

18. Id.

19. Id. at 1220–21. See also Butkera v. Hudson River Sloop "Clearwater," Inc., 300 N.J.Super. 550, 693 A.2d 520 (1997) (applying New York's non-immunity rule to the action of New Jersey plaintiffs injured in New Jersey by the acts of a New York charitable corporation that was immune under New Jersey law).

20. See Erny v. Estate of Merola 792 A.2d at 1219, relying on Johnson v. Hertz Corp., 315 F.Supp. 302, 304 (S.D.N.Y 1970).

21. 31 N.Y.2d 121, 335 N.Y.S.2d 64, 286 N.E.2d 454 (1972) (discussed supra § 17.31).

22. *Neumeier*, 286 N.E.2d. at 458–59 (quoting Willis Reese, Chief Judge Fuld and

Choice of Law, 71 Colum. L.Rev. 548 (1971)).

23. For other New York cases involving this pattern and reaching the same result under *Neumeier* Rule 3, see, e.g., Buglioli v. Enterprise Rent–A–Car, 811 F.Supp. 105 (E.D.N.Y. 1993), aff'd without op., 999 F.2d 536 (2d Cir. 1993) (applying New Jersey's pro-defendant law rather than New York's pro-plaintiff law to New Jersey plaintiff's action against New York car rental company that rented the car to a New Jersey driver who caused the New Jersey accident); Reale v. Herco, Inc., 183 A.D.2d 163, 589 N.Y.S.2d 502 (1992) (personal injury action by a New York minor injured in a Pennsylvania amusement park owned by defendant, a Pennsylvania corporation. Defendant fourth-partied minor's mother seeking contribution for her failure to supervise the child. Such contribution was allowed by Pennsylvania law but not by New York law. The court applied Pennsylvania law under Rule 3, and specifically rejected the mother's plea for applying New York law under the escape or under a pub-

by falling back to a *lex loci* rule, presumptive or otherwise, or by reading state interests differently.[24] For example, in *Waddoups v. Amalgamated Sugar Co.*,[25] which was decided under the Restatement (Second), the Utah Supreme Court concluded that because both the critical conduct and the resulting injury had occurred in Idaho and the plaintiffs' had their domiciles there, Idaho had the most significant relationship and its law should govern.[26] In *Miller v. Gay*,[27] a guest-statute conflict that was the converse of *Cipolla*,[28] the court concluded that neither state's relationship was more significant, and that reliance on state interests could not resolve the conflict. The court quoted *Cipolla*'s statement that defendants acting in their own state "should not be put in jeopardy of liability exceeding that created by their state's laws just because a visitor from a state offering higher protection decides to visit there."[29] The *Miller* court turned this statement around as follows: "Analogously, we conclude that inhabitants of a state (here Delaware) should not be accorded rights not given by their home states, just because a visitor from a state offering higher protection decides to visit there."[30]

Nodak Mutual Insurance Co. v. American Family Mutual Insurance Co.[31] illustrates that even cases decided under Minnesota's choice-influencing considerations may end up applying the pro-defendant law of the accident state in cases of this pattern. *Nodak* was an insurance subroga-

lic policy exception); LaForge v. Normandin, 158 A.D.2d 990, 551 N.Y.S.2d 142 (1990) (traffic accident in New York involving a Quebec plaintiff, two Quebec defendants, and four New York co-defendants. Under Quebec's no-fault law, the plaintiff could not recover damages from the Quebec defendants. The court held that the presence of the four New York co-defendants took the case outside the scope of Rule 1 and placed it under Rule 3. The court applied New York law even with regard to the Quebec defendants, reasoning that "New York's interest in protecting the contribution and apportionment rights of its domiciliaries is a significant interest, and we perceive no persuasive reason to displace the law of this State in the circumstances of this case."). For a case decided the opposite way under the exception of *Neumeier* Rule 3, see, Stevens v. Shields, 131 Misc.2d 145, 499 N.Y.S.2d 351 (Sup. Ct. 1986) (New York accident involving a New York victim and a Florida tortfeasor who was a minor. Under Florida law, but not New York law, the minor's parent would have been vicariously liable. The court invoked the exception to Rule 3 and applied Florida law, reasoning that Florida had a significant interest in the application of its law to its domiciliaries, and that the application of that state's law would not impair New York's interest in protecting its residents from liability because a New York defendant was not involved in the case).

24. See, e.g., Stutsman v. Kaiser Found. Health Plan, 546 A.2d 367 (D.C. 1988) (applying Virginia law to action for loss of consortium filed by a Virginia plaintiff for the death of his wife as a result of medical malpractice committed in Virginia by a District of Columbia health care provider. The District of Columbia, but not Virginia, allowed the action.)

25. 54 P.3d 1054 (Utah 2002).

26. *Waddoubs* was an action for wrongful termination and infliction of emotional distress. The plaintiffs, Idaho domiciliaries, were hired in Idaho for work in defendant's Idaho sugar processing plant. They were also fired in Idaho. The defendant had its headquarters in Utah, the law of which favored the plaintiffs, while the law of Idaho favored the defendant.

27. 323 Pa.Super. 466, 470 A.2d 1353 (1983).

28. See supra §§ 17.13 nn.18–30, 17.42. *Miller* arose out of a Delaware accident involving a Pennsylvania host-driver and a Delaware guest-passenger. Delaware, but not Pennsylvania, had a guest statute. The court applied the Delaware guest statute, barring the action.

29. See supra § 17.13 at n.22.

30. *Miller*, 470 A.2d at 1356.

31. 604 N.W.2d 91 (Minn. 2000) (also discussed supra § 17.23 n.14).

tion dispute arising from a North Dakota accident involving a North Dakota driver and a Minnesota driver.[32] North Dakota law favored the Minnesota insurer, while Minnesota law favored the North Dakota insurer. Predictably, each insurer invoked the law of the other state. The North Dakota insurer argued that Minnesota law should govern because Minnesota had a "strong interest in not allowing its insurers to recover no-fault benefits from out-of-state insurers"[33] when such benefits are not recoverable under Minnesota law so as to prevent those insurers from receiving "a windfall."[34] The court appropriately turned the argument around by pointing out that, if Minnesota law were applied then it would be the North Dakota insurer who would receive a windfall, because it would be able "to avoid paying ... money that it might otherwise have to pay"[35] under North Dakota law. In the end, the court applied the law of North Dakota, in part because, in the absence of special circumstances, "the state where the accident occurred has the strongest governmental interest."[36]

Finally, in *Boomsma v. Star Transport, Inc.*,[37] a Wisconsin court reached a similar result by applying Wisconsin's pro-defendant law, rather than Illinois' pro-plaintiff law, to a wrongful death action arising from a Wisconsin accident involving Wisconsin victims and an Illinois driver. The court acknowledged that Wisconsin's cap on wrongful death damages was not intended to protect foreign defendants,[38] but concluded that, on balance, Wisconsin law should govern because the plaintiffs failed to rebut the Second Restatement's *lex loci* presumption.[39] After noting that "plaintiffs had no 'justified expectation' that Illinois law would apply to their claims,"[40] the court observed: "[A]pplication of Illinois law ... would endorse a kind of lottery system for Wisconsin plaintiffs who are injured in Wisconsin. The 'winners' of the lottery would be those injured by states that do not cap wrongful death damages. The 'losers' would be those injured by fellow Wisconsinites, against whom recovery is limited."[41]

b.   The Hurtado Pattern

Hurtado v. Superior Court[42] is a well-known example of the second pattern described above. In that case the conduct, the injury, and the

---

32. The North Dakota driver was insured by a North Dakota insurer through a policy delivered in North Dakota, and the Minnesota driver was insured by a Minnesota insurer through a policy delivered in Minnesota. After paying no-fault benefits to its Minnesota insured, the Minnesota insurer sought to recoup those benefits from the North Dakota insurer. North Dakota, but not Minnesota, provided for such recoupment.

33.   604 N.W.2d at 95.

34.   Id.

35.   Id.

36.   Id. at 96.

37.   202 F. Supp.2d 869 (E.D.Wis. 2002).

38.   See id. at 878.

39.   The court also noted that the presence of a Wisconsin third-party defendants also militated in favor of Wisconsin law. See id.

40.   Id. at 879.

41.   Id.

42.   11 Cal.3d 574, 114 Cal.Rptr. 106, 522 P.2d 666 (1974) (discussed supra §§ 17.14, 17.18).

tortfeasor's domicile were in California, the law of which protected the foreign victim by allowing unlimited damages, while the victim was from a state that limited damages. Again, under Currie's assumptions and classifications, *Hurtado* would qualify as a no-interest case, insofar as each state's law favored the litigant domiciled in the other state. However, this classification is more questionable here because, unlike the *Neumeier* pattern in which the accident state denies recovery, here the accident state *favors recovery*. If the court interprets this law as motivated by a policy of deterrence, then the accident state becomes interested in applying its law in order to deter substandard conduct within its territory. Thus, a potential no-interest case becomes a false conflict. Right or wrong, this was precisely the conclusion of the California court in *Hurtado*.[43] Other courts have reached the same conclusion and the same result. For example, in *Villaman v. Schee*,[44] an Arizona court found that Arizona's unlimited-damages rule was partly designed to deter wrongful conduct and thus Arizona had an interest in applying it to an Arizona accident involving Arizona defendants and Mexican plaintiffs.[45] Similarly, in *Arcila v. Christopher Trucking*,[46] a Pennsylvania court applied Pennsylvania's pro-plaintiff compensatory damages law rather than New Jersey's pro-defendant law in an action filed by New Jersey plaintiffs against Pennsylvania defendants and arising out of a Pennsylvania accident. The court reasoned that the application of New Jersey law would not promote New Jersey's interest in protecting defendants, but would "impair Pennsylvania's interest . . . in deterring tortious conduct within its borders."[47] The court also noted that, since the defendants were Pennsylvania domiciliaries and had acted in Pennsylvania, they were "on notice–at least constructively–of Pennsylvania's law governing remedies for injuries caused by negligent conduct."[48]

c. Summary

The cases falling within the *Neumeier* and *Hurtado* patterns (a total of 17)[49] are not numerous enough to permit the drawing of categorical conclusions. Even so, it is worth noting that ten of these cases applied the law of the state in which both the conduct and the injury occurred and which had the additional contact of being the domicile of either the victim, as in *Neumeier*, or the tortfeasor as in *Hurtado*. In cases of the *Hurtado* pattern, the courts based the application of the pro-plaintiff law of the state of conduct and injury on the the questionable assumption that that law was intended to deter substandard conduct in that state. In

---

43. See supra § 17.14 n.10 § 17.18 at nn. 13–18. For a critique of *Hurtado* on this issue, see Reppy, Eclecticism in Choice of Law: Hybrid Method or Mishmash?, 34 Mercer L. Rev. 645, 699 (1983).

44. 15 F.3d 1095 (9th Cir. 1994).

45. Arizona law also provided for punitive damages, which are more clearly designed to deter wrongful conduct.

46. 195 F.Supp.2d 690 (E.D.Pa. 2002).

47. Id. at 694.

48. Id. at 695.

49. For a tabular presentation of these cases, see S. Symeonides, The American Choice-of-Law Revolution in the Courts: Today and Tomorrow, 298 Recueil des Cours, 1, 218 (2003), from which this section draws.

contrast, in cases of the *Neumeier* pattern, the courts seemed to base the application of the pro-defendant law of the state of conduct and injury, which was also the victim's domicile, on the assumption that the aggregation of these three contacts outweighs other considerations, such as state interests or party expectations.

These cases also do not seem to follow Currie's assumptions and prescriptions regarding the no-interest paradigm. For example, although according to Currie all 17 of these cases should have applied the law of the forum *qua* forum, only one case—*Erwin*—did so. Seven additional cases applied the law of the forum, but they did so because of the forum's additional contacts and affirmative interests, rather than in the absence of such interests. Similarly, the vast majority of these cases rejected Curie's personal-law principle, namely the notion that a state is interested in only protecting its domiciliaries but not similarly situated non-domiciliaries.[50] For example, 12 of the 17 cases applied a law that favored a foreign litigant at the expense of a forum litigant: five cases (*Neumeier, Stutsman, Miller, Nodak,* and *Buglioli*) applied a foreign law that favored a foreign defendant over a forum plaintiff; four cases (*Labree, Farrell, Keizer,* and *Erwin*) applied a forum law that favored a foreign plaintiff over a forum defendant; and three cases (*Hurtado, Villaman,* and *Arcila*) applied a forum law that favored a foreign plaintiff over a forum defendant.

Be that as it may, the question of which law should govern these cases is one that admits different answers. *Neumeier* Rule 3 as well as the Louisiana codification produce the same results as the majority of the above cases, while also providing the necessary flexibility for judicial deviation in appropriate cases.[51] The *Neumeier* rule calls for the application of the *lex loci delicti*, unless the application of another law "will advance the relevant substantive law purposes without impairing the smooth working of the multistate system or producing great uncertainty for litigants."[52] This exception is discussed later.[53] The Louisiana rule,

---

50. See supra § 2.9 nn. 14, 56, 58–59.

51. Professor Sedler concludes that the cases support a similar rule, which he formulates as follows: "When a plaintiff from a non-recovery state is involved in an accident with a defendant from a recovery state, and the accident occurs in the defendant's home state, recovery is allowed." Sedler, Choice of Law in Conflicts Torts Cases: A Third Restatement or Rules of Choice of Law?, 75 Ind. L. J. 615, 628 (2000). This formulation covers the cases of the *Hurtado* pattern. For cases of the *Neumeier* pattern, Sedler's rule is appropriately less categorical. It provides that "[w]hen the accident occurs in the plaintiff's home state, recovery will usually be allowed, but sometimes the courts apply the law of the plaintiff's home state denying recovery." Id. For similar rules, see Posnak, The Restatement (Second): Some Not so Fine Tuning

for a Restatement (Third): A Very Well–Curried Leflar over Reese with Korn on the Side (or is it Cob?), 75 Ind. L.J. 561, 565 (2000).

52. Neumeier Rule 3, supra § 17.31.

53. See infra § 17.46 nn. 3–22. In Gould Electronics Inc. v. United States, 220 F.3d 169 (3d Cir.2000), the court summarized the factors that New York courts consider in deciding whether to displace the law of the locus under *Neumeier* rule 3. According to this summary, displacement is more likely when one or more of the following factors are present: (1) when the parties' contacts with the locus state are a matter of fortuity rather than voluntary action; (2) when the tort does not occur in the domicile of either party; (3) when displacement will not encourage forum shopping nor create the appearance of favoring local litigants; (4)

which is phrased narrowly as to capture only cases in which both the conduct and the injury are in the home state of one of the parties,[54] is also accompanied by flexible escapes[55] that are more likely to be utilized in cases of the *Neumeier* pattern than the *Hurtado* pattern.[56]

d. *Split–Domicile Conflicts Involving Three States*

§ 17.46 *Neumeier* Rule 3 is so broad–and Rules 1 and 2 are so narrow–as to encompass many more cases than the no-interest cases discussed in the immediately preceding section. One can visualize the breadth of the rule by adding a third state in the mix, such as when parties domiciled in different states are involved in an accident in a third state.[1] Depending on the content of the laws of the involved states, such cases can present the false conflict, true conflict, or unprovided-for paradigms. Rather than attempting to sort out the many possibilities, Rule 3 returns to the *lex loci delicti* rule.[2] However, the latter rule is now phrased in non-categorical terms. It is no more than a presumptive rule and can be displaced upon a showing that such displacement "will advance the relevant substantive law purposes without impairing the smooth working of the multistate system or producing great uncertainty

when the parties are domiciled in states with similar laws; or (5) when the other state has a stronger interest than the locus state in applying its law.

54. See La. Civ. Code art. 3544(2)(a), which provides that split-domicile cases in which both the conduct and the injury occur in the home state of one party are governed by the law of that state. See also Puerto Rico Draft Code, art. 47(b)(1). Split-domicile *and* split-conduct-injury cases (other than those in which the injury occurred in the domicile of the victim whose law protects her) are not subjected to an *a priori* rule.

55. See La. Civ. Code art. 3547, which in "exceptional cases" authorizes a judicial deviation from Article 3544 (and other articles), if such deviation is appropriate under the general principles of the Louisiana conflicts codification. La. Civ. Code art. 3548 provides another escape with regard to corporate tortfeasors.

56. Yet, Duhon v. Union Pacific Resources Co., 43 F.3d 1011 (5th Cir. 1995), applied the escape in a case of the *Hurtado* pattern case. *Duhon* arose out of a Texas employment accident injuring a Louisiana worker who had been hired in Louisiana by a Texas subcontractor to work in Texas for a Texas general contractor. After receiving worker's compensation benefits through the subcontractor's carrier under Louisiana law, the worker sued the Texas general contractor in tort. Texas, but not Louisiana, allowed this action. Under La. Civ.

Code art. 3544(2)(a) (supra n.54), this case would be governed by Texas law because the conduct and the injury occurred in the defendant's home state. However, the court invoked the escape of Article 3547 and applied Louisiana's pro-defendant law after finding that Louisiana's policies would be more seriously impaired if its law were not applied to this issue. Although it confused contacts with interests, the court recognized the close interdependence between a rule that requires an employer to provide worker's compensation benefits and a rule that relieves that employer from tort liability. Because of this interdependence, allowing the worker to pick and choose would have resulted in an inappropriate *dépeçage*, which the court decided to avoid.

§ 17.46

1. For tables illustrating the many fact patterns that fall within the scope of Rule 3, see Symeonides, Choice of Law in the American Courts in 1994: A View "From the Trenches," 43 Am. J. Comp. L. 1, 5 (1995); S. Symeonides, W. Perdue & A. Von Mehren, Conflict of Laws: American, Comparative, International, 245–46 (2d ed. 2003).

2. In contrast, the Louisiana codification relegates all these cases to the flexible approach of article 3542 which calls for the application of the law of the state whose interests will be more impaired if its law were not applied.

for litigants."[3] This deliberately vague language can be a source of valuable flexibility in the judicial articulation of further exceptions from the *lex loci* rule.

In *Schultz v. Boy Scouts of America*,[4] the court invoked this exception and thus avoided the application of the pro-plaintiff law of the "locus of the tort" (New York) vis a vis the defendant Franciscan Brothers which was domiciled in Ohio. *Gilbert v. Seton Hall University*[5] involved a similar tri-state scenario and reached the same result. It involved a New Jersey defendant (Seton Hall) protected by New Jersey's charitable immunity rule, an injury in New York, a state that abolished charitable immunity, and a plaintiff who, although a student at defendant's New Jersey campus, was domiciled in Connecticut, which also abolished charitable immunity.[6] The court noted that the case fell within the scope of *Neumeier* Rule 3, but, barely mentioning Rule 3 again, the court proceeded to a full-fledged interest analysis concluding that New Jersey law should govern because New Jersey had a strong interest and New York had no interest in applying their respective laws. Despite the plaintiff's Connecticut domicile, the court treated the plaintiff's decision to attend college in New Jersey as equivalent to a choice of a domicile in New Jersey. This made the case functionally analogous to a common-domicile case, which *Neumeier* Rule 1 subjects to the law of the common domicile.[7] The plaintiff invoked *Cook v. Goodhue*,[8] a district court case that held that one rebuts the *lex loci* presumption of Rule 3 by showing that the non-application of the *lex loci* would advance the policies of *all* other involved states–not just one. The *Gilbert* court rejected the argu-

---

3. Neumeier Rule 3 (discussed supra § 17.31).

4. 65 N.Y.2d 189, 491 N.Y.S.2d 90, 480 N.E.2d 679 (1985) (discussed supra § 17.32).

5. 332 F.3d 105 (2d Cir. 2003).

6. The plaintiff was a member of a rugby team consisting of and organized by Seton Hall students. He sued Seton Hall for negligent supervision of a rugby game held in New York in which he suffered an injury that rendered him paraplegic

7. The court reasoned that the plaintiff "benefitted from the charitable immunity law of New Jersey by virtue of his voluntary decision to attend university in that state," Gilbert, 332 F.3d at 110. and hence "New Jersey ha[d] a strong interest in having him bear a related burden." Id. Conversely, "Connecticut's interest in according [plaintiff] the benefits of its charitable [non-]immunity policy is reduced because . . . he has avoided the policy's concomitant burden of paying the increased fees that a Connecticut institution, subject to negligence liability, must charge." Id.

8. 842 F.Supp. 1509 (N.D.N.Y.1994). *Cook* arose out of a New York traffic acci-

dent involving a Texas plaintiff and an Ontario defendant. The Ontario defendant invoked a provision of Ontario law that limited non-pecuniary damages to $240,000. Neither New York nor Texas imposed such a limitation. The court held that, under *Neumeier* Rule 3, New York law should govern unless the defendant demonstrated that he met the circumstances provided in the escape. Defendant argued that this burden is met if one demonstrates that displacing the *lex loci delicti* would promote the substantive policies of either of the other states involved in the conflict, and that since the application of Ontario's ceiling on recovery would promote the policies of that province in protecting its defendants, he had carried the burden of displacing the *lex loci*. "This is not so [said the court]. . . . There is no 'either' in the rule. Otherwise, it would be very easy for a party to demonstrate that the application of a particular state's law will advance the purposes of that law. . . . Defendant must show that the purposes of *all* relevant substantive laws will be advanced by application of Canada's limit. This requirement includes the laws of New York and Texas, as well as Canada." Id. at 1511 (emphasis added).

ment, stating that "[n]othing in *Schultz* evidences so numerical an approach,"[9] and pointing out that *Schultz* applied New Jersey's charitable immunity rule even though both other involved states, New York and Ohio, had a non-immunity rule.[10]

In *O'Connor v. U.S. Fencing Ass'n*[11] the home states of both parties (New York and California) allowed recovery, but the state of the accident did not. Thus, it was easier for the court to displace the *lex loci* rule, if only because, as noted earlier,[12] such a case is functionally analogous to *Babcock,* even though technically it falls within the scope of Rule 3.The court recognized the analogy and held that allowing recovery would be consistent with the parties' expectations since both parties had "chosen to identify themselves in the most concrete form possible, domicile, with jurisdiction[s] that have weighed the [pertinent] interests . . . and resolved the conflict in favor of recovery."[13]

In *Bodea v. Trans Nat Express, Inc.,*[14] the laws of the three states differed in all respects. The case arose out of a New York accident and involved an Ontario plaintiff and a Quebec defendant, driving in separate cars. The conflict involved the issue of damages for non-economic losses. Quebec did not allow such damages, Ontario allowed them but limited the amount, and New York allowed them without limits. Thus, the case fell within the scope of Rule 3. The defendant invoked the escape of Rule 3 and, apparently realizing that his chances of convincing the court to apply Quebec law were limited, made a more modest argument in favor of Ontario law. The court rejected the argument because it found "no reason why"[15] a Quebec resident "would expect that the laws of the Province of Ontario law to apply to an accident that occurred in New York."[16] The court noted that the analysis would differ

---

9. *Gilbert*, 332 F.3d at 112.

10. In a thoughtful dissent, Judge Sotomayor argued for certifying the question to the New York Court of Appeals to resolve the ambiguities that *Schultz* failed to resolve. Sotomayor noted that, although the majority opinion was a reasonable application of an interest-balancing approach as practiced in New York before the *Neumeier* rules, it was "not the only reasonable application" of New York's current conflicts law, particularly Rule 3 and its *lex loci* presumption. Id. (Sotomayor, J., dissenting). He argued that Rule 3 "seems to require something other than (and different from) general interest balancing," id. at 114,- which the *Neumeier* rules "were intended . . . to replace." Id. at 115. It requires that the policies "of all relevant states must be advanced before we can displace the *lex loci delicti*." Id. at 114. The test is "not which state among the three has the greatest interest in applying its law [but] rather . . . whether each state's interest would be advanced (or not hindered) by application of a law other than the lex loci delicti." Id. The

judge concluded that this case did not meet this test because "Connecticut's interests would be hindered by the application of New Jersey law." Id.

11. 260 F.Supp.2d 545 (E.D.N.Y. 2003).

12. See supra § 17.40, text accompanying nn.1–12.

13. *O'Connor,* 260 F.Supp.2d at 559, quoting *Schultz,* 480 N.E.2d at 686. For a similar case decided the same way, see Diehl v. Ogorewac, 836 F.Supp. 88 (E.D.N.Y.1993) (discussed supra § 17.40 n.4; New Jersey defendant (driver), New York plaintiff (passenger), North Carolina traffic accident; North Carolina law favorable to defendant, New Jersey and New York law favorable to plaintiff; following escape from Rule 3 and allowing recovery; analogized to common-domicile cases).

14. 286 A.D.2d 5, 731 N.Y.S.2d 113 (2001).

15. Id. at 118.

16. Id.

if Ontario and Quebec had the same law but, since they did not, "the situs of the accident (New York) 'is appropriate as a 'tie breaker' '"[17].

The use of the term "tie breaker" presupposes an actual tie (which should not be assumed a priori in all Rule 3 cases), and which may or may not have existed in *Bodea*. The fact is that Rule 3 resorts to the *lex loci* not as a tie breaker, but rather as the rule that was in place before *Babcock* and its progeny carved the exceptions articulated in *Neumeier* Rules 1 and 2. The only difference, and it is an important one, is that the *Neumeier* court recast the *lex loci* rule in a presumptive fashion, thus allowing its displacement upon a showing that such displacement "will advance the relevant substantive law purposes without impairing the smooth working of the multistate system or producing great uncertainty for litigants."[18] This deliberately vague language opens the door for the judicial articulation of further exceptions from the *lex loci* rule, but provides little guidance on the pertinent criteria for such exceptions.

In the three decades since *Neumeier*, the New York Court of Appeals has not provided these criteria. However, in *Gould Electronics Inc. v. United States*,[19] another court has summarized the circumstances under which New York courts displace the *lex loci* under *Neumeier* Rule 3. According to this summary, displacement is more likely when one or more of the following factors are present: (1) when the parties' contacts with the locus state are a matter of fortuity rather than voluntary action; (2) when the tort does not occur in the domicile of either party; (3) when displacement will not encourage forum shopping nor create the appearance of favoring local litigants; (4) when the parties are domiciled in states with similar laws; or (5) when the other state has a stronger interest than the locus state in applying its law.[20]

This summary is as good as any other. However, a review of the results of the cases suggests that, all other factors being equal, the *lex loci* is less likely to be displaced when it favors recovery than when it does not. Indeed, lower-court cases involving this tri-state pattern and decided after *Schultz* suggest a certain pro-recovery bent in that more cases have allowed recovery either by following the *lex loci* part of Rule 3,[21] or by utilizing the escape contained in that rule.[22] It remains to be

17. Id. The court also noted that "both plaintiffs and defendants have purposefully associated themselves with the laws of New York," id., and that their presence there was not fortuitous. The plaintiff traveled regularly through New York on his way to his apartment and job in Maryland, while the defendant, who was a truck-driver, drove frequently through New York.

18. Neumeier Rule 3, supra § 17.31

19. 220 F.3d 169 (3d Cir. 2000) (decided under New York conflicts law).

20. Id. at 187.

21. For cases following the *lex loci* part of Rule 3 and allowing recovery, see, e.g., Cook v. Goodhue, 842 F.Supp. 1509 (N.D.N.Y. 1994) (discussed supra § 17.46

n.8); McCann v. Somoza, 933 F.Supp. 362 (S.D.N.Y. 1996) (same result in a conflict among the no-fault statutes of three states, Connecticut (the accident state), New Jersey (the plaintiff's state), and New York (the defendant's state). The plaintiff could recover under the law of the first two, but not of the third state); Simons v. Marriott Corporation, 1993 WL 410457 (S.D.N.Y. 1993) (personal injury action by a New York plaintiff against a Texas hotel owner, arising out of plaintiff's "slip and fall" in that hotel); Weisberg v. Layne–New York Co., 132 A.D.2d 550, 517 N.Y.S.2d 304 (1987) (damages for the wrongful death of a New York domiciliary resulting from a New

22. See p. 841.

seen whether this trend will continue, or whether it will meet the approval of the New York Court of Appeals.

e. *Summary and Rules*

§ 17.47   The above discussion suggests that the case law on loss-distribution conflicts may be capable of producing some new, narrow choice-of-law rules. While disagreements about the precise content, and especially the wording, of these rules may well be inevitable, it appears that the following rules reflect the results reached by the majority of cases.[1]

> Rule 1 (*Common-Domicile Cases*). Cases in which the tortfeasor and the victim are domiciled in the same state are governed by the law of that state whether that law favors recovery (as in the *Babcock* pattern), or does not favor recovery (as in the reverse-*Babcock* pattern).[2]

> Rule 2. (*Analogous Cases*) Cases in which the tortfeasor and the victim are domiciled in different states which, however, adhere to substantially the same loss-distribution rules should be analogized to common-domicile cases and treated accordingly.

> Rule 3. (*Split-Domicile Cases*) Cases other than the above in which the tortfeasor and the victim are domiciled in different states which adhere to different loss-distribution rules are governed by the

Hampshire accident caused by a New Jersey defendant); Gleason v. Holman Contract Warehouse, Inc., 250 A.D.2d 339, 681 N.Y.S.2d 664 (3d Dept. 1998) (applying New Hampshire law and denying contribution between two foreign employers arising out of an injury in New Hampshire sustained by a New York employee).

22. See, e.g, Murphy v. Acme Mkts., 650 F.Supp. 51 (E.D.N.Y. 1986) (action by a New York plaintiff injured at a New Jersey job site owned by a Pennsylvania defendant, while working for a New York employer. New York's comparative negligence rule was more favorable to plaintiff than the New Jersey rule. The court applied New York law under the Rule 3 escape, reasoning that New York had an interest in protecting New York domiciliaries who are injured outside New York, while New Jersey had little interest in applying its loss-allocation rules when none of the parties were New Jersey domiciliaries); O'Connor v. U.S. Fencing Ass'n, 260 F.Supp.2d 545 (E.D.N.Y. 2003) (discussed supra nn.11–13); Diehl v. Ogorewac, 836 F.Supp. 88 (E.D.N.Y 1993) (discussed supra § 17.40 n.4); Armstead v. Nat'l R.R. Passenger Corp., 954 F.Supp. 111 (S.D.N.Y. 1997) (applying New York's pro-plaintiff comparative negligence law to action of New York plaintiff injured in Vir-

ginia on property belonging to a District of Columbia domiciliary, because of New York's "obvious interest in enforcing its determination that its own domiciliary whose own negligence is only partially responsible for her injuries should not go uncompensated." Id. at 112.Virginia had an all-or-nothing contributory negligence rule). One apparent exception from the above is Sheldon v. PHH Corp., 135 F.3d 848 (2d Cir. 1998), which, following the escape, applied New York law which denied recovery, rather than the *lex loci*, which allowed recovery. However, New York was both plaintiff's domicile and the defendant's principal place of business, and this made the case analogous to a common-domicile case. Moreover, this case was decided under Michigan conflicts law and considered New York's conflicts law only from the perspective of Michigan conflicts law.

§ 17.47

1. Since these rules are descriptive rather than prescriptive, they should be understood as allowing a different result in appropriate cases.

2. In cases of the latter pattern, the rule is "less categorical." See supra § 17.39, text accompanying 26–34.

law of that domiciliary state in which both the conduct and the injury occurred, whether that law favors recovery (as in *Hurtado*) or does not favor recovery (as in *Foster, Cipolla,* and *Neumeier*).[3]

Rule 4. (*Split-Domicile and Cross–Border Cases*) Cases other than the above in which only the injury occurred in the state of the victim's domicile are governed by the law of that state if that law protects the victim and if the occurrence of the injury in that state was objectively foreseeable.

Cases other than the above are not, at the present time, susceptible to an a priori choice-of-law rule. One option for such cases is to return to a presumptive *lex loci delicti* rule like *Neumeier* Rule 3. Another option is to adopt a presumptive pro-recovery rule that would give the court or the victim the right to choose between the laws of the place of the injurious conduct or the place of the resulting injury, subject to appropriate safeguards to be specified in the rule. Recent continental codifications have adopted such rules.[4] A third and perhaps preferable option might be to allow courts to experiment further without the restraints of any rule or presumption. In due time, such experimentation may propagate new rules capable of producing rational results in the majority of these cases.

3. *Conduct–Regulation Conflicts*

a. *Generic Conduct–Regulation Conflicts*

§ 17.48 As explained above, the *Neumeier* Rules are not intended to apply to conduct-regulating conflicts. The New York experience has not produced any rules for resolving such conflicts other than the *dicta* in *Babcock, Schultz,* and *Cooney* that these conflicts will almost invariably be resolved under the law of "the place of the tort." This affirms the premise that conduct-regulating rules are territorially oriented and suggests that, in conflicts between such rules, the domicile of the parties, or at least the victim, is a far less significant factor than it is in loss-distribution conflicts.[1]

---

3. This rule encompasses four sub-patterns: (a) cases in which the conduct and the injury occur in the state of the tortfeasor's domicile and in which that state's law favors the tortfeasor (see supra § 17.42); (b) cases in which the conduct and the injury occur in the state of the victim's domicile and in which that state's law protects the victim (see supra § 17.43); (c) cases in which the conduct and the injury occur in the state of the tortfeasor's domicile and in which that state's law protects the victim (supra § 17.45); and (d) cases in which the conduct and the injury occur in the state of the victim's domicile and in which that state's law protects the tortfeasor (id.). Whether the rule stated in the text

should be equally categorical in all four patterns may be debatable.

4. See supra § 17.34 n.14 and infra §§ 17.49, 17.80; For a collection and discussion of such plaintiff-favoring rules, see S. Symeonides, Private International Law at the End of the 20th Century: Progress or Regress? 57–60 (1999).

§ 17.48

1. This is not to say that domicile is an irrelevant contact. For example, if the violator of a conduct-regulating rule is a domiciliary of the enacting state, this state has an additional reason to insist on the rule's application. Similarly, if the victim of the violation is a domiciliary of the enacting

However, cases as old as *Carroll*[2] show that the "place of the tort" is not an unambiguous term. When conduct undertaken in one state produces injury in another state, either state may qualify as the place of the tort.[3] Rather than retreating to outmoded "last-event" notions, one should be prepared to accept the premise that when conduct and injury do not coincide in the same state, both of these contacts deserve equal consideration. Even with this caveat, however, conduct-regulation conflicts are less complicated than loss-distribution conflicts because of the diminished importance of domicile in conflicts of the former category. In fact, one can classify all conduct-regulating conflicts into two major patterns: (1) those in which the conduct and the injury occur in the same state; and (2) those in which the conduct and the injury occur in different states. Cases of pattern 2 can be further subdivided into cases in which the conduct-state prescribes: (a) the same; (b) a higher; or (c) a lower standard than the injury-state.

In cases falling within pattern 1, the law of the state of conduct and injury has the exclusive claim to apply its law. These are the cases for which the *Babcock* court said that "it would be almost unthinkable to seek the applicable rule in the law of some other place."[4] This is so even when both the tortfeasor and the victim are domiciled in such "other place." Cases confirming this elementary proposition are countless. They involve issues of premises' liability,[5] traffic safety,[6] work site safety,[7]

state, this state has an additional reason to insist on the rule's application. The point is, however, that a state has a general interest in enforcing its conduct-regulating rules even if neither the violator nor the victim resides in that state. For this reason, conduct-regulating conflicts should be analyzed and resolved by focusing more on the spatial aspects of the conduct and the injury, and less on the parties' domiciles. S. Symeonides, The American Choice-of-Law Revolution in the Courts: Today and Tomorrow, 298 Recueil des Cours, 1, 240 (2003).

2. Alabama Great Southern Ry. Co. v. Carroll, 97 Ala. 126, 11 So. 803, 18 L.R.A. 433, 38 Am.St.Rep. 163 (1892) (discussed supra § 17.2 n.5).

3. The definition of the "place of the tort" has also received extensive discussion in the European literature. The choice of the place of the tortious conduct focuses on the tortfeasor: he will be judged by the standards of the environment in which he acts. The place of injury (last event) is victim-oriented. She recovers for injuries caused by acts regarded as torts by her environment and not for that which does not constitute a tort locally. Kegel & Schurig Internationales Privatrecht 723 (9th ed. 2004). For discussion of the various party interests to be protected and served see also Stoll, Zweispurige Anknüpfung von Verschuldens-und Gefährdungshaftung im in-

ternationalen Deliktsrecht?, Konflikt und Ordnung, Festschrift für Ferid 397 (1978).

4. *Babcock*, 12 N.Y.2d at 483, 191 N.E.2d at 280, 240 N.Y.S.2d at 751. See also supra § 17.36 nn.3–4. See also Reese, Choice of Law in Torts and Contracts and Directions for the Future, 16 Colum. J. Transnat'l. L. 1, 13–14 (1977) (observing that with respect to the question whether the defendant's conduct was tortious, the "applicable law will, almost surely, be that of the state where the defendant acted if either (a) this law would [so] hold the conduct, or (b) the plaintiff's injury also occurred in the state.").

5. Najarian v. National Amusements, Inc., 768 A.2d 1253 (R.I. 2001); Kirschbaum v. WRGSB Assoc., 243 F.3d 145 (3rd Cir. 2001); Olson v. Empire Dist. Elec. Co., 14 S.W.3d 218 (Mo. App. 2000); Judge v. Pilot Oil Corp., 205 F.3d 335 (7th Cir. 2000); Garvin v. Hyatt Corp., 2000 WL 798640 (Mass. App. 2000); Wal–Mart Stores, Inc. v. Manning, 788 So.2d 116 (Ala. 2000); Ramey v. Wal–Mart, Inc. 967 F.Supp. 843 (E.D. Pa. 1997); Schechter v. Tauck Tours, Inc., 17 F.Supp.2d 255, (S.D.N.Y. 1998); Bauer v. Club Med Sales, Inc., 1996 WL 310076 (N.D. Cal. 1996); Spinozzi v. ITT Sheraton Corp., 174 F.3d 842 (7th Cir. 1999); Scheerer v. Hardee's Food Sys., Inc. 92 F.3d 702 (8th Cir. 1996); Scott v. Pilot Corp., 205 Wis.2d 738, 557 N.W.2d 257 (1996); Mc-

6.–7. See p. 844.

contributory negligence,[8] interference with contract,[9] and other issues.[10] All of these cases applied the law of a state in which both the conduct and the injury occurred, without considering the parties' domiciles. Conversely, some cases have held that the forum's conduct-regulating rule was inapplicable to an out-of-state accident involving exclusively forum domiciliaries.[11]

Govern v. Marriott Int'l, Inc. 1996 WL 470643 (E.D. La. 1996); Greco v. Grand Casinos of Mississippi, Inc. 1996 WL 617401 (E.D. La. 1996); Smith v. Florida Gulf Airlines, Inc., 1996 WL 156859 (E.D. La. 1996); Leane v. Joseph Entm't Group, Inc., 267 Ill.App.3d 1036, 642 N.E.2d 852 (1994); Barrett v. Foster Grant Co., Inc., 450 F.2d 1146 (1st Cir. 1971); Murphy v. Thornton, 746 So.2d 575 (Fla. App. 1999); DeMyrick v. Guest Quarters Suite Hotels, 944 F.Supp. 661 (N.D. Ill. 1996). See also Naghiu v. Inter–Continental Hotels Group, Inc., 165 F.R.D. 413 (D. Del. 1996) (holding that hotel's owner's liability for failure to provide safe conditions was governed by law of Zaire, where the hotel was located, but applying forum law because the evidence supplied by the parties regarding the content of Zaire law was inconclusive).

6. See Tkaczevski v. Ryder Truck Rental, Inc., 22 F.Supp.2d 169 (S.D.N.Y. 1998) (negligent parking of car that contributed to causing an accident); Ellis v. Barto, 82 Wash.App. 454, 918 P.2d 540 (1996), review den. 130 Wash.2d 1026, 930 P.2d 1229 (1997) (traffic rules); FCE Transp. Inc. v. Ajayem Lumber Midwest Corp., 1988 WL 48018 (Ohio App. 1988) (traffic rules).

7. See Augello v. 20166 Tenants Corp., 224 A.D.2d 73, 648 N.Y.S.2d 101 (1 Dept. 1996) (scaffolding law); Thompson v. International Bus. Mach., 862 F.Supp. 79 (S.D.N.Y. 1994) (scaffolding law).

8. See, e.g., District of Columbia v. Coleman, 667 A.2d 811 (D.C. 1995); Matson by Kehoe v. Anctil, 979 F.Supp. 1031 (D.Vt. 1997); Moye v. Palma, 263 N.J.Super. 287, 622 A.2d 935 (1993); Gray v. Busch Entm't Corp., 886 F.2d 14 (2d Cir. 1989); Kirby v. Lee, 1999 WL 562750 (E.D. Pa. 1999).

9. In Abogados v. AT & T, Inc., 223 F.3d 932 (9th Cir. 2000) (decided under California's comparative impairment approach), which involved an interference with a Mexican contract, the court found "nonsensical" the plaintiff's argument that "Mexico has no interest in regulating conduct that affects contracts made in Mexico." Id. at 935. Said the court: "[T]his case involves Mexico's determination of the scope of its substantive law: the point at which it will attach tort liability to conduct occurring within its borders. This decision

is designed both to protect potential defendants–including foreign defendants who might otherwise avoid doing business in Mexico–from liability for conduct that Mexico does not consider wrongful, and to limit plaintiffs from recovering even if such conduct damages them." Id. at 935–36. See also Bridas Corp. v. Unocal Corp., 16 S.W.3d 893 (Tex. App. 2000); EA Oil Serv., Inc. v. Mobil Explor. & Prod. Turkmenistan, Inc., 2000 WL 552406 (Tex. App. 2000) (decided under the Second Restatement; holding that Turkmenistan and Afghanistan had the most significant relationship because the interference occurred there and those countries had additional contacts and corresponding interests)

10. See, e.g., Richardson v. Michelin North America, Inc., 1998 WL 135804 (W.D.N.Y. 1998) (strict liability); BP Chem. Ltd. v. Formosa Chem. & Fibre Corp., 229 F.3d 254 (3d Cir. 2000) (misappropriation of trade secrets; holding that Taiwanese law should govern because Taiwan had the greatest interest in setting the standards for determining whether the trade information licensed in Taiwan and used there was protectable, and in determining whether the defendant acted tortiously in acquiring that information in Taiwan from another Taiwanese corporation); Baca v. New Prime, Inc., 763 N.E.2d 1014 (Ind. App. 2002) (applying Indiana's guest statute to an Indiana accident involving Missouri parties, in part because the statute was found to be conduct-regulating in that it "establish[ed] the standard of care owed by a driver to certain guests." Id. at 1019.

11. See Padula v. Lilarn Prop. Corp., 84 N.Y.2d 519, 620 N.Y.S.2d 310, 644 N.E.2d 1001 (1994), discussed supra § 17.37 nn. 17 ff; Huston v. Hayden Bldg. Maint. Corp., 205 A.D.2d 68, 617 N.Y.S.2d 335 (2 Dept. 1994); Salsman v. Barden & Robeson Corp., 164 A.D.2d 481, 564 N.Y.S.2d 546 (3 Dept. 1990); Zangiacomi v. Saunders, 714 F.Supp. 658 (S.D.N.Y. 1989); Clarke v. Sound Advice Live, Inc., 221 A.D.2d 227, 633 N.Y.S.2d 490 (1 Dept. 1995); Hardzynski v. ITT Hartford Ins. Co., 227 A.D.2d 449, 643 N.Y.S.2d 122 (2 Dept. 1996). See also Svege v. Mercedes Benz Credit Corp., 182 F.Supp.2d 226 (D.Conn. 2002) (holding that

The same is true of cases falling within pattern 2a, supra, namely cases in which the conduct and the injury occur in different states that adhere to the same standard of conduct. Again cases involving this pattern have consistently applied the law of the conduct state.[12] In policy terms, these cases are virtually indistinguishable from those falling within pattern 1 and both patterns present the false conflict paradigm.

The false conflict paradigm is also present in the cross-border torts falling within pattern 2b, supra, namely cases in which the tortfeasor's conduct violates the "higher" standard of the conduct-state but not the "lower" standard of the injury-state. *Schmidt v. Driscoll Hotel*,[13] and *Rong Yao Zhou v. Jennifer Mall Restaurant, Inc.*,[14] are two well-known dram shop act cases that exemplify this pattern. In both cases the conduct that was claimed to have caused the injury—the serving of the liquor to the intoxicated patron—occurred in a state that imposed civil liability for such conduct, while the resulting injury occurred in a state that did not impose such liability. Both cases properly applied the law of the conduct state,[15] as have other dram shop act cases,[16] but also cases involving car-owner liability statutes,[17] and other conduct-regulating

Connecticut's car owner's liability statute was conduct-regulating and thus was inapplicable to non-Connecticut owners and non-Connecticut accidents).

12. See, e.g., Pardey v. Boulevard Billiard Club, 518 A.2d 1349 (R.I.1986) (applying the Rhode Island dram shop act to an action by a Massachusetts plaintiff arising out of a Massachusetts accident caused by a driver who became intoxicated in defendant's Rhode Island tavern. Massachusetts had a dramshop act similar to Rhode Island's); Rutledge v. Rockwells of Bedford, Inc., 200 A.D.2d 36, 613 N.Y.S.2d 179 (1994) (applying New York's dramshop act to an action arising from a Connecticut accident caused by a driver who became intoxicated in defendant's New York tavern. Connecticut had a dramshop act similar to New York's); Platano v. Norm's Castle, Inc., 830 F.Supp. 796, 799 (S.D.N.Y. 1993) (same pattern same result on dramshop act liability, but awarding compensatory damages under Connecticut's more generous standards so as to better effectuate the deterrence policy embodied in New York's act); Elson v. Defren, 283 A.D.2d 109, 726 N.Y.S.2d 407 (2001) (vicarious liability of car owner); Boatwright v. Budak, 625 N.W.2d 483 (Minn. App. 2001) (same); Downing v. Abercrombie & Fitch, 265 F.3d 994 (9th Cir. 2001) (misappropriation of a person's picture and name).

13. 249 Minn. 376, 82 N.W.2d 365 (1957) (discussed supra § 17.12 n.1; applying Minnesota's dram shop act to impose civil liability on a Minnesota tavern owner whose intoxicated customer caused an accident in Wisconsin injuring plaintiff, also a

Minnesota resident. Wisconsin did not have a dram shop act).

14. 534 A.2d 1268 (D.C.App.1987) (applying the District of Columbia's dram shop act to impose civil liability on a D.C. tavern owner whose intoxicated customer caused an accident in Maryland. Maryland did not have a dramshop act).

15. In both cases the victim was also a domiciliary of the conduct state and thus the application of that state's law could have also been based on that state's compensatory interests. However, even in the absence of such an interest, the application of the law of the conduct state would be justified for reasons explained in the text.

16. See, e.g. Patton v. Carnrike, 510 F.Supp. 625 (N.D.N.Y. 1981) (involving the same pattern and reaching the same result as *Schmidt*).

17. These statutes impose on a car owner vicarious liability for injury caused by a driver while using the car with the owner's permission. Many cases applied the statute of the state in which the owner consented to the use of the car, even though the accident occurred in a state that did not have such a statute. See Veasley v. CRST Int'l, Inc., 553 N.W.2d 896 (Iowa 1996); Sexton v. Ryder Truck Rental, Inc., 413 Mich. 406, 320 N.W.2d 843 (1982); Farber v. Smolack, 20 N.Y.2d 198, 282 N.Y.S.2d 248, 229 N.E.2d 36 (1967); Burney v. PV Holding Corp., 218 Mich.App. 167, 553 N.W.2d 657 (1996); McKinney v. S & S Trucking, Inc., 885 F.Supp. 105 (D.N.J. 1995); Haggerty v. Cedeno, 279 N.J.Super.

rules,[18] as well as in federal cases applying the "headquarters doctrine."[19] Professor Cavers[20] had advocated the same result, which the Louisiana

607, 653 A.2d 1166 (A.D. 1995); Stathis v. National Car Rental Syst., 109 F.Supp.2d 55 (D.Mass. 2000). See also Gaither v. Myers, 404 F.2d 216 (D.C. 1968) (applying District of Columbia law to impose civil liability on a car owner whose car was stolen in the District of Columbia and was involved in a Maryland accident. The District of Columbia, but not Maryland, had a rule that required car owners to remove their keys from their vehicles when leaving them unattended.)

18. Pittman v. Maldania, Inc., 2001 WL 1221704 (Del. Super. 2001) is illustrative of conflicts involving other conduct-regulation rules. In this case, the defendant operated a water-ski rental office on the Delaware side of the Delaware/Maryland border. The state line runs exactly in front of the office door, so that one had to enter Delaware to rent the skis, but use them in Maryland. The laws of both states prohibited renting to persons below sixteen, but (unlike Maryland) Delaware additionally required the showing of a valid driver's license. After misrepresenting their ages, two Pennsylvania vacationers, ages 14 and 15, rented skis from defendant's Delaware office, and, while riding the skis in Maryland, collided with each other resulting in injury to the 14–year-old, the plaintiff. The plaintiff invoked Delaware law, while the defendant store-owner invoked Maryland law. Following the Second Restatement, the court held that Delaware law should govern, despite the presumption of Restatement § 146 in favor of the place of injury. The court found that: (1) this presumption was rebutted because the precise issue in this case was the defendant's conduct in renting the ski in Delaware to an underage person; (2) the Delaware statute reflected "a clear policy against renting jet skis to people who are unable to produce a valid driver's license"; (3) this policy was "part of a comprehensive statute on boating safety"; and (4) that such "statute regulating conduct should be enforced throughout the state." Id. at *4. The court also found that: (1) "Maryland ha[d] no conflicting policy"; (2) Delaware's law "[did] not interfere in any way with Maryland's regulation of water safety in its state," id.; and (3) the defendant, having acted in Delaware, could not complain about the application of Delaware law.

19. This doctrine was developed in cases decided under the Federal Tort Claims Act, which waives the sovereign immunity of the

United States for certain torts committed by its employees, but not for claims "arising in a foreign country." 28 U.S.C. § 2680(k). See Richards v. United States, 369 U.S. 1, 82 S.Ct. 585, 7 L.Ed.2d 492 (1962) (first enunciating the doctrine). Federal courts have created an exception to this non-waiver known as the "headquarters doctrine," which provides that if the particular act was planned in the United States, then the United States is not immune, even if the act was carried out in a foreign country and had its operative effects there. A series of cases applied this doctrine to acts that were planned in the United States, but executed in foreign countries.; Couzado v. United States, 105 F.3d 1389, 1394–96 (11th Cir. 1997); Sami v. United States, 617 F.2d 755, 761–63 (D.C.Cir. 1979); Donahue v. United States Dep't of Justice, 751 F.Supp. 45, 48–49 (S.D.N.Y. 1990); Glickman v. United States, 626 F.Supp. 171, 174 (S.D.N.Y. 1985); Alvarez–Machain v. United States, 331 F.3d 604 (9th Cir. 2003), cert. granted ___ U.S. ___, 124 S.Ct. 807, 157 L.Ed.2d 692 (2003), vacated 2004 WL 1563135 (9th Cir. 2004). For an analogous state case, see D'Agostino v. Johnson & Johnson, Inc., 133 N.J. 516, 628 A.2d 305 (1993) (applying New Jersey's corrupt practices statute to the retaliatory firing of a Swiss employee which had been orchestrated in New Jersey and carried out in Switzerland).

20. Cavers's third "principle of preference" provides that "[w]here the state in which a defendant acted has established special controls, including the sanction of civil liability, over conduct of the kind in which the defendant was engaged when he caused a foreseeable injury to the plaintiff in another state, the plaintiff ... should be accorded the benefit of the special standards of conduct and of financial protection in the state of the defendant's conduct, even though the state of injury had imposed no such controls or sanctions." D. Cavers, The Choice-of-Law Process 159 (1965). Cavers illustrated the application of this principle by discussing a dram shop act case, as well as a case in which the defendant engages in blasting operations in a state that imposes strict liability for such operations and causes injury in a state that follows a negligence rule. Cavers concludes that in both cases it is appropriate to apply the law of the place of conduct, so as to effectuate the deterrent and regulatory purposes of that law. When that law is violated by substandard conduct occurring within that

codification[21] has codified. This result is consistent with sound interest analysis, as well as party expectations. The application of the conduct-regulating rule of the conduct-state promotes that state's interest in policing conduct within its borders. The fact that the resulting injury occurs in another state does not diminish that interest,[22] nor does it generate an interest on the part of the latter state to apply its own law.[23] Moreover, there is nothing unfair in subjecting a tortfeasor to the law of the state in which he acted. Having violated the standards of that state, the tortfeasor should bear the consequences of such violation and should not be allowed to invoke the lower standards of another state.

This then leaves only the cross-border torts falling within pattern 2c, supra, namely cases in which the conduct in question does not violate the "lower" standards of the conduct-state but does violate the "higher" standards of the injury-state. In interest analysis terminology, these cases usually present the true conflict paradigm. The argument for applying the higher standard of the state of injury is stronger in cases involving intentional torts than in negligence cases. Indeed, not many people would question the right of a state to punish conduct that is intended to produce, and does produce, detrimental effects within its territory, even when that conduct takes place outside the state. As Justice Holmes stated almost a century ago, "[a]cts done outside the jurisdiction, but intended to produce and producing detrimental effects within it, justify a state in punishing the cause of the harm."[24] To this end, the United States Supreme Court has developed the so-called "effects doctrine," which could be described as a "reverse-headquarters" doctrine. In *Hartford Fire Ins. Co. v. California*,[25] the Court held that "the Sherman Act applies to foreign conduct that was meant to produce and did in fact produce some substantial effects in the United States."[26] The Court applied the Act to British insurance underwriters who, while in London, engaged in conduct designed to affect the California insurance market.

Several lower-court cases have applied the Sherman Act in the same fashion,[27] and one case, *United States v. Nippon Paper Industries*,[28] went as far as to uphold under the Act a criminal prosecution of a Japanese

---

state, such conduct "is just as bad when the victim is an outsider as an insider," id. at 160, regardless of whether the injury materializes within or without that state. Id. See also id. at 160–66.

21. See La. Civ. Code art. 3543(1) (reproduced infra § 17.49 n.1); Symeonides, Louisiana's New Law of Choice of Law for Tort Conflicts: An Exegesis, 66 Tul. L. Rev. 677, 705–710 (1992).

22. The effectiveness of the conduct-regulating rule of the conduct-state would be seriously impaired if exceptions to it were made for out-of-state injuries. See D. Cavers, The Choice-of-Law Process 160–166 (1965).

23. The fact that the injury-state allows a lower standard of conduct is irrelevant because that standard is designed to protect conduct within, not without, that state.

24. Strassheim v. Daily, 221 U.S. 280, 284, 31 S.Ct. 558, 55 L.Ed. 735 (1911).

25. 509 U.S. 764, 113 S.Ct. 2891, 125 L.Ed.2d 612 (1993).

26. Id. at 795–96.

27. See United States v. Aluminum Co. of America, 148 F.2d 416 (2d Cir. 1945); Filetech S.A. v. France Telecom S.A., 157 F.3d 922 (2d Cir. 1998) (accord). See also Restatement, Third, Foreign Relations § 402.

28. 109 F.3d 1 (1st Cir. 1997).

defendant for conduct in Japan (price-fixing) that was intended to and did produce detrimental effects in the United States. The court rejected defendant's argument that the presumption against extraterritoriality operates with greater force in the criminal arena than in civil litigation, and appeared unconcerned by the lack of precedent for criminal prosecution for wholly extraterritorial conduct.[29] The court was equally unsympathetic to defendant's comity argument. According to *Hartford Fire*, said the court, "comity concerns would operate to defeat the exercise of jurisdiction only in those few cases in which the law of the foreign sovereign required a defendant to act in a manner incompatible with the Sherman Act or in which full compliance with both statutory schemes was impossible."[30] Because in this case the defendant's conduct was illegal under both Japanese and American laws, there was "[no] concern about [defendant] being whipsawed between separate sovereigns."[31]

In cases involving negligent conduct, the argument for applying the higher standard of the state of injury may be less powerful psychologically, but it is still a fairly strong one, provided that the actor could have foreseen that his conduct in one state would produce injury in the other state. *Bernhard v. Harrah's Club*,[32] is a well-known example of such a case. *Bernhard* applied the law of California, the injury-state, and imposed civil liability on a Nevada tavern owner for conduct in Nevada for which Nevada law did not impose such liability. An important factor justifying the application of California law was that the defendant should have foreseen that its conduct in Nevada would produce harmful consequences in California. The geographic proximity of the defendant's operation to the California–Nevada border, the defendant's active solicitation of California patrons, and the composition of defendant's clientele made it foreseeable that tavern patrons might drive into California and cause an accident there. It is this foreseeability factor that tips the scales and makes the application of the law of the injury-state an appropriate solution to these otherwise difficult true conflicts.

29. See Id. at 6. The court also pointed out that there was sufficient precedent for applying a state's criminal statute to conduct occurring entirely outside the state's borders, as well as applying federal anti-drug statutes to wholly foreign conduct. See id.

30. Id. at 8.

31. Id. The court noted that if the government could prove its charges that the defendant had orchestrated a conspiracy to rig prices in the United States, the principle of comity should not shield the defendant from prosecution because, to do otherwise, "would create perverse incentives for those who would use nefarious means to influence markets in the United States, rewarding them for erecting as many territorial firewalls as possible between cause and effect." Id. A concurring judge examined whether the prosecution was reasonable under the standards prescribed by §§ 402 and 403 of the 1987 Restatement (Third) of the Foreign Relations Law of the United States and compatible with principles of international law. The judge answered in the affirmative because the United States was the specific target of the defendant's conduct and because Japan did not have sufficient incentives to prosecute that conduct.

32. 16 Cal.3d 313, 128 Cal.Rptr. 215, 546 P.2d 719 (1976) (discussed supra § 17.19).

Similarly, in *Hoeller v. Riverside Resort Hotel*,[33] a case similar to *Bernhard*[34] and decided under the Second Restatement, the Arizona court applied Arizona law and imposed civil liability a Nevada casino owner. The court compared Nevada's interest in "free[ing] tavern owners, and other alcohol purveyors such as casinos, from the cost and inconvenience of incurring either civil or criminal liability in the operation of their businesses"[35] with Arizona's "strong interest in providing an opportunity for its residents to recover full compensation from persons and businesses that contribute to automobile accidents on Arizona's highways ... [and] in holding tortfeasors responsible for their actions' foreseeable effects in Arizona."[36] The court also noted the casino's proximity to the Nevada/Arizona border and pointed out that the casino had gone to great lengths to attract Arizona clientele. Under these circumstances, the court reasoned, the casino should have known that "many of the patrons it seeks, many of those who sit at its tables and drink its [free] liquor, have come to the casino from Arizona and will return to Arizona ... in an intoxicated condition and ... may cause accidents that injure third persons in Arizona."[37]

Other dram shop act cases have reached the same result under similar circumstances.[38] One of these cases, *Blamey v. Brown*,[39] which was decided under Minnesota's better-law approach, was a closer case. The defendant, who operated a small tavern on the Wisconsin side of the Wisconsin/Minnesota border, did not advertise in Minnesota nor attempted to attract Minnesota customers. However, he occasionally sold liquor to Minnesota residents as in the present case in which he sold liquor to a Minnesota minor who drove back to Minnesota and caused an accident there injuring another Minnesota domiciliary. The court concluded that the bar's proximity to the border and the defendant's knowledge that some of his customers were Minnesotans allowed Minnesota courts to assume jurisdiction and to apply Minnesota's "better" law, which imposed liability on the bar owner.

---

33. 169 Ariz. 452, 820 P.2d 316 (App. 1991).

34. An Arizona domiciliary became intoxicated in the Nevada casino and on his return to Arizona caused an accident injuring plaintiff, another Arizona domiciliary

35. 820 P.2d at 320.

36. Id. The court also took note of the high number of accidents caused by drunk drivers (as well as the high number of drunk drivers arrested) in the particular Arizona county and surmised that many of these drivers "were given free alcohol at casinos in Nevada." Id. at 318.

37. Id. at 321.

38. See Zygmuntowicz v. Hospitality Invs., Inc., 828 F.Supp. 346 (E.D.Pa. 1993) (applying Pennsylvania's dramshop act against a New Jersey tavern owner for injury caused by one of his intoxicated patrons in Pennsylvania: "[T]he Defendant specifi-

cally targeted the Pennsylvania market and should, therefore, have expected and planned for possible suits under Pennsylvania law." Id. at 349); Sommers v. 13300 Brandon Corp., 712 F.Supp. 702 (N.D.Ill. 1989) (applying Indiana's dramshop act against an Illinois tavern owner for injury caused by one of his intoxicated patrons in Indiana); Carver v. Schafer, 647 S.W.2d 570 (Mo. App. 1983) (allowing unlimited recovery under Missouri law to the survivors of a Missouri domiciliary who was killed in a Missouri accident caused by a Missouri domiciliary who became intoxicated in defendant's Illinois tavern. Illinois law also imposed liability but limited the amount); City of Hastings v. River Falls Golf Club, 187 F.3d 640 (8th Cir. 1999). But see Estates of Braun v. Cactus Pete's, Inc., 108 Idaho 798, 702 P.2d 836 (1985).

39. 270 N.W.2d 884 (Minn. 1978), cert. denied 444 U.S. 1070, 100 S.Ct. 1013, 62 L.Ed.2d 751 (1980).

b. Summary and Rule

§ 17.49 The above review of the case law suggests that one can distill the solutions reached by cases involving conduct-regulation conflicts into a simple one-sentence rule: such conflicts are governed by the law of the state of conduct, except when the injury foreseeably occurs in another state that imposes a higher standard of conduct, in which case the law of the latter state governs.

A rule essentially producing this result has been adopted by most codifications enacted in the last decades of the 20th century. For example, the Louisiana[1] and Portuguese[2] codifications, as well as the Puerto Rican Draft Code[3] contain rules that are confined to conduct-regulation issues and which are virtually identical to the above rule.[4] Other codifications contain rules which, though not confined to conduct-regulation issues, resolve cross-border torts in the same way. The Dutch,[5] Swiss,[6]

§ 17.49

1. Article 3543 of the Louisiana codification provides as follows:

Issues pertaining to standards of conduct and safety are governed by the law of the state in which the conduct that caused the injury occurred, if the injury occurred in that state or in another state whose law did not provide for a higher standard of conduct.

In all other cases, those issues are governed by the law of the state in which the injury occurred, provided that the person whose conduct caused the injury should have foreseen its occurrence in that state.

A third paragraph provides an exception from the second paragraph and requires the application of the law of the forum state in those cases in which the conduct had been undertaken in that state "by a person who was domiciled in, or had another significant connection with, th[at] state." This "hometown justice" exception is criticized in Weintraub, The Contributions of Symeonides and Kozyris to Making Choice of Law Predictable and Just: An Appreciation and Critique, 38 Am. J. Comp. L. 511, 515–16 (1990). For a muted response, see Symeonides, Louisiana's New Law of Choice of Law for Tort Conflicts: An Exegesis, 66 Tul. L. Rev. 677, 713–14. (1992).

2. Paragraph 1 of Article 45 of the Portuguese Civil Code provides for the application of the law of the state of conduct or omission. Paragraph 2 provides that "[i]f the law of the state of injury holds the actor liable but the law of the state where he acted does not, the law of the former state applies, provided that the actor could foresee the occurrence of the injury in that

state." As an exception to the above, paragraph 3 provides for the application of the law of the parties' common-nationality or habitual residence, but "without prejudice to provisions of local laws that must be applied to all persons without differentiation."

3. See Art. 46 of the Puerto Rican Draft Code (providing that law of the conduct-state applies if the injury occurred there or in another state whose law did not provide for a higher standard of conduct; otherwise by the law of the injury-state "if that state's contacts with the defendant's actual or intended course of conduct were such as to make foreseeable the occurrence of the injury in that state.")

4. See also Professor Cavers's first "principle of preference" which provides in part that "[w]here the liability laws of the state of injury set a higher standard of conduct ... than do the laws of the state where the person who caused the injury has acted ... the laws of the place of injury shall determine the standard ... applicable to the case...." D. Cavers, The Choice-of-Law Process 139 (1965).

5. See Act of 11 April 2001 Regarding Conflict of Laws on Torts, Art. 3(2), Staatsblad 2001, 190 (law of place of "harmful impact" applies "unless the perpetrator could not reasonably have foreseen this.")

6. Article 133(2) of the Federal Law on Private International Law of 1987 provides that, in split-domicile cases, the law of the state of conduct applies, but if the injury foreseeably occurred in another state the law of the latter state applies. This provision applies only if the disputants are not

Quebec,[7] and Russian[8] codifications provide that in cross-border cases the law of the state of injury applies if its occurrence there was foreseeable, but do not explicitly condition such application on whether that law provides for a higher or for a lower standard than the state of conduct. The German,[9] Hungarian,[10] and Tunisian[11] codifications, and a Chinese Draft Code[12] provide for the application of the law of the state of conduct, but allow the application of the law of the state of injury at the request of the victim, without conditioning such application on foreseeability. Finally, the Italian[13] and Venezuelan[14] codifications and the proposed Rome II Regulation[15] do the reverse. They provide for the

parties to a pre-existing legal relationship that is governed by another law. Article 137 provides that claims resulting from injurious emissions emanating from an immovable are governed, at the choice of the injured party, by the law of the state in which the immovable is situated or by the law of the state in which the result of these emissions occurred. Even broader choices but subject to foreseeability provisos are given to the victim by articles 135 (products liability) and 139 (injury to rights of personality). Finally, Article 142(2) provides that, regardless of the law applicable to other issues, "[r]ules of safety and conduct in force at the place of the act are taken into consideration."

7.   Article 3126(1) of the Quebec Civil Code is similar Art. 133(2) of the Swiss statute described supra n.6.

8.   See Civil Code of the Russian Federation, Art. 1219(1) (federal law n. 146 of 26 November 2001, Rossyiskaya Gazeta, n. 49 item 4553, 28/11/2001).

9.   Article 40(1) of the 1999 German statute on the law applicable to non-contractual obligations, Bundesgesetzblatt 1999, I, 1026, provides: "Claims arising from tort are governed by the law of the state in which the person liable to provide compensation acted. The injured person may demand, however, that the law of the state where the result took effect be applied instead." The law applicable under Art. 40(1) is displaced by the law of the parties' common habitual residence according to Art. 40(2), and both laws may be refused application to the extent they "go substantially beyond that which is required for appropriate compensation . . . [or] obviously serve purposes other than the provision of appropriate compensation." Id. Art. 40(3). For a discussion of these provisions, see Hay, From Rule–Orientation to "Approach" in German Conflicts Law: The Effect of the 1986 and 1999 Codifications, 47 Am. J.Comp.L. 633 (2000).

10.   Section 32 of the Hungarian Decree on Private International Law of 1979 pro-

vides that in split-domicile cases, the law of the state of conduct applies, but "if it is preferable to the injured party," the law of the state of injury applies. It provides further that, if according to the law governing the tortious act or omission liability is conditioned on a finding of culpability, the existence of culpability can be determined by either the personal law of the tortfeasor or the law of the place of injury. Section 33 of the same statute provides for the application of "traffic or other security regulations" of the conduct state.

11.   See Code of Private International Law (Law N. 98–97 of 27 November 1998), Art. 70(2), Official Journal of the Republic of Tunisia, 1 December p. 2332 (injured party may choose between the laws of the place of conduct and the place of injury).

12.   See Chinese Society of Private International Law, Model Law of Private International Law of the People's Republic of China (6th Draft, 2002), art 112, 3 Ybk. Priv. Int'l L. 349 (2001) (court chooses between laws of place of conduct or injury, whichever is more favorable to the injured party).

13.   See paragraph 1 of Article 62 of Italian Act No. 218 of 31 May 1995 (Riforma del sistema italiano di diritto internazionale privato). In common-domicile situations, this paragraph is displaced by a common-domicile rule contained in paragraph 2 of the same article.

14.   Article 32 of Act of 6 August, 1998 on Private International Law (Official Gazette No. 36.511) effective February 6, 1999, provides for the application of the law of the state of injury unless the victim requests the application of the law of the state of conduct.

15.   The Rome II Regulation gives this option only for environmental torts. It provides that the applicable law is the law of the place of injury unless the injured party opts for the law of the place of conduct. See, Commission of the European Communities,

application of the law of the state of injury, but also allow the application of the law of the state of conduct if the victim so requests.

c. Punitive–Damages Conflicts[1]

§ 17.50 Rules imposing punitive damages are *par excellence* conduct-regulating rules in the "prophylactic" or deterrence sense described by the New York Court of Appeals.[2] The adjectives "punitive" and "exemplary," which are often used interchangeably, express the two purposes of punitive damages–punishment and deterrence. Punishment or retribution is individual but backward looking, in that it focuses on the individual wrongdoer and his or her specific misconduct. Deterrence or prevention is more general and forward looking, in that it focuses not only on the individual wrongdoer, but on others who might consider engaging in similar misconduct in the future. Thus, punitive damages differ in important respects from compensatory damages, the purpose of which is to compensate the victim, and hence are proportional to the victim's harm or loss.[3]

The fact that punitive damages are meant to *punish* the tortfeasor (in addition to deterring others) means: (a) that the stakes are much higher than in other conduct-regulation conflicts and thus a more cautious choice-of-law analysis is necessary;[4] and (b) that this analysis must include, as a very pertinent contact, the tortfeasor's domicile (or principal place of business or other similar affiliation). Conversely, the fact that punitive damages are designed to punish and deter tortfeasors rather than to compensate victims–who, *ex hypothesi*, are made whole through compensatory damages–means that the victim's domicile should, in principle, be irrelevant in punitive-damages conflicts.

Proposal for a Regulation of the European Parliament and the Council on the Law Applicable to Non–Contractual Obligations, Art. 7, COM (2003) 427 final, 2003/0168(COD), Brussels, 22.7.203.

§ 17.50

1. This section draws from Symeonides, Resolving Punitive–Damages Conflicts, 5 Ybk Priv. Int'l L. 1 (2004); S. Symeonides, The American Choice-of-Law Revolution in the Courts: Today and Tomorrow, 298 Recueil des Cours 1, 262–277 (2003).

2. Padula v. Lilarn Props. Corp., 84 N.Y.2d 519, 620 N.Y.S.2d 310, 644 N.E.2d 1001, 1002 (1994).

3. See State Farm Mut. Auto. Ins. Co. v. Campbell, 538 U.S. 408, 123 S.Ct. 1513, 1519, 155 L.Ed.2d 585 (2003) ("[C]ompensatory and punitive damages, although usually awarded at the same time by the same decisionmaker, serve different purposes.... Compensatory damages are intended to redress the concrete loss that the plaintiff has suffered by reason of the defendant's wrongful conduct.... By contrast, punitive damages serve a broader function; they are aimed at deterrence and retribution") (internal quotation marks omitted).

4. States, or at least litigants, tend to have strongly held views on the propriety and the permissible size of punitive damages awards. Compare, Fay v. Parker, 53 N.H. 342, 382 (1872) (characterizing punitive damages as "a monstrous heresy" and "an unsightly and unhealthy excrescence, deforming the symmetry of the body of law,") with Luther v. Shaw, 157 Wis. 234, 147 N.W. 18, 20 (1914) (characterizing punitive damages as "an outgrowth of the English love of liberty regulated by law" which "elevate[s] the jury as a responsible instrument of government, ... restrains the strong, influential, and unscrupulous, vindicates the right of the weak, and encourages recourse to, and confidence in, the courts of law by those wronged or oppressed by acts or practices not cognizable in, or not

(1) The Pertinent Contacts and Typical Patterns

If the above premises are correct, then one can conclude that pertinent contacts in these conflicts are: (1) the tortfeasor's domicile; (2) the place of the wrongful contact; and (3) the place of the resulting injury. A state that has one or more of these contacts will likely have an interest in applying its law, whether or not it imposes punitive damages. For example, the state of the conduct has the right to regulate (police, deter, punish, *or* protect) conduct within its borders. Similarly, the state in which this conduct produces its effects—the injury—has a right to determine what sanctions are appropriate for such conduct. Finally, the state of the defendant's domicile has the right to determine whether the sanction of punitive damages should be imposed on one of its domiciliaries. If the law of that state provides for punitive damages, the application of that law serves its underlying purpose of punishing that tortfeasor and deterring him and others from engaging in similar conduct in the future. Conversely, if that law prohibits punitive damages, then its application would serve its underlying purpose of protecting the tortfeasor from excessive financial exposure.

Putting factual contacts and substantive laws[5] in the mix produces the following eight typical patterns of potential or actual punitive-damages conflicts:

(a) cases in which all three of the above contacts are either in the same state or in different states, all of which impose punitive damages for the particular conduct (pattern 1);

(b) cases in which two of the above contacts are either in the same state or in two different states both of which impose punitive damages (patterns 2–4);

(c) cases in which only one of the above contacts is in a state that imposes punitive damages (patterns (5–7); and

(d) cases in which none of the above contacts are in a state that imposes punitive damages (pattern 8).[6]

As discussed below, American courts have awarded punitive damages in cases falling within each one of the above eight patterns. However, the majority of cases that awarded punitive damages fall within patterns 1–4. The thesis of this section is that the award of punitive damages is: (1) entirely appropriate in cases falling within

---

sufficiently punished, by the criminal law.").

5. With regard to punitive damages, the differences among the laws of the involved states are not as many as with other tort issues—they either impose or do not impose punitive damages for the conduct in question. To be sure, states that impose punitive damages may differ on the available or permissible amounts. For example, one state may limit the amount, either through an absolute cap, or in proportion to compensatory damages. These cases present a choice-of-law problem only if the claimant requests, and the court is prepared to award, an amount exceeding this limit. In practice one cannot find cases in which such differences have caused problems.

6. For a tabular presentation of these patterns, see Symeonides, Resolving Punitive–Damages Conflicts, 5 Ybk Priv. Int'l L. 1, 17 (2004).

patterns 1–4; (2) defensible in cases falling within patterns 5–7; and (3) inappropriate in cases falling within pattern 8. The balance of this section examines the cases of each pattern, in the above order.

(2) Three- or Two–Contact Patterns

Cases of the first pattern are the easy ones. In these cases, a state that has all three pertinent contacts (or three states each of which have a pertinent contact) imposes punitive damages. For example, a defendant acts in his home state and causes injury in that state to a domiciliary of another state. If the law of the former state imposes punitive damages for that conduct, that state has every interest in applying its law to punish that defendant and to deter other defendants from engaging in similar conduct in the future. Even if the victim's home state prohibits punitive damages, such a prohibition need not be heeded, because it is designed to protect tortfeasors acting or domiciled in that state, rather than to prevent victims domiciled there from recovering punitive damages. The same rationale should apply if the state that denies punitive damages is the forum state, whether or not it is also the victim's home state. In most cases, the forum's denial of punitive damages is designed to protect either forum defendants, or forum conduct, or both, and in this case the forum has neither of these contacts. Thus, the award of punitive damages under the law of the other state does not undermine the forum's policies. In the United States, this solution is widely accepted, even in states like Louisiana whose substantive law prohibits punitive damages in the vast majority of cases.[7] On the other hand, most civil law systems take exactly the opposite position, either through the *ordre public* exception, or through explicit blanket prohibitions against awarding punitive damages under any circumstances.[8] The same hostility towards punitive damages surfaces in recent efforts to draft a new convention on judgment recognition under the auspices of the Hague Conference of Private International Law.[9]

7. See La. Civ. Code art. 3546, which provides that punitive damages may be awarded if such damages are available under the law of a state or states that have any two or all of the following contacts: place of conduct, place of injury, or defendant's domicile. For discussion of the rationale of this article by its drafter, see Symeonides, Louisiana's New Law of Choice of Law for Tort Conflicts: An Exegesis, 66 Tul. L. Rev. 677, 735–49 (1992).

8. For example, Article 24 of the Proposed Rome II Regulation provides that the award of punitive damages "shall be contrary to Community public policy." Similarly, articles 135(2) and 137(2) of the Swiss codification provide that, in products liability and obstruction to competition cases governed by foreign law, "no damages may be awarded in Switzerland other than those

provided ... under Swiss law." See also article 40(3) of the EGBGB (Rev. 1999), which prohibits non-compensatory or "excessive" damages, and article 34 of the Hungarian codification of 1979, which provides somewhat more cryptically that Hungarian courts "shall not ... impose legal consequences not known to Hungarian law." For a critique of these provisions, see Symeonides, Resolving Punitive–Damages Conflicts, supra n.6, at 3–4, 31–33.

9. See Art. 33 of the Hague Preliminary Draft Convention on Jurisdiction and Recognition of Foreign Judgments in Civil and Commercial Matters of 30 October 1999 (providing that a foreign judgment that awards exemplary damages shall be recognized, but only to the extent that similar or comparable damages could have been awarded in the recognizing state).

In the next three patterns (2–4), a state with two relevant contacts (or two states, each of which have one relevant contact) imposes punitive damages, while a state with the third relevant contact does not. As the following discussion illustrates, the majority of American courts have awarded punitive damages in these cases.

In Pattern 2, the tortfeasor is domiciled in a state that imposes punitive damages, and, while in that state, engages in conduct that causes injury in another state that does not impose punitive damages.[10] This case presents the false conflict paradigm. The first state has an interest in applying its punitive-damages law so as to punish the tortfeasor who engaged in egregious conduct in that state, and to deter similarly situated potential tortfeasors. In contrast, the state of injury does not have an interest in applying its non-punitive damages law, because that law is designed to protect tortfeasors who are either domiciled in or have acted in that state, neither of which is the case here. Thus, the application of the law of the first state promotes the deterrence policies of that state, without impairing the defendant-protecting policies of the state of injury. Many cases involving this pattern have reached this precise result. One example is *In re Air Crash Disaster at Stapleton Int'l Airport, Denver*,[11] a case arising from the crash of a passenger plane in Colorado. In this case, Texas was both the airline's principal place of business and the place of the conduct most likely responsible for the crash. Texas, but not Colorado, provided for punitive damages in wrongful death actions. The court reiterated a principle articulated by the Seventh Circuit in *In re Air Crash Disaster Near Chicago, Illinois*,[12] and since followed in most air disaster cases to the effect that, "[b]ecause the place of injury is much more fortuitous than the place of misconduct or the principal place of business, its interest in and ability to control behavior by deterrence or punishment, or to protect defendants from liability is lower than that of the place of misconduct or the principal place of business."[13] The *Stapleton* court concluded that, since "Texas is both the site of the conduct to which an award of punitive damages could attach and defendants' principal place of business, . . . its relationship to this litigation is most significant,"[14] and its law should govern. The court acknowledged that Colorado might have an interest in regulating the conduct of corporations entering its territory to do business. However, the court concluded that this interest was "somewhat lessened when a foreign corporation attempts to shield itself from the more onerous laws of its home state by seeking refuge under Colorado law,"[15] and that "[t]he knowledge that the law of a

---

10. A functionally analogous variation of this pattern appears when the tortfeasor acts outside his home state, but in a state that also imposes punitive damage.

11. 720 F.Supp. 1445 (D.Colo. 1988).

12. 644 F.2d 594 (7th Cir.) cert. denied sub nom. 454 U.S. 878, 102 S.Ct. 358, 70 L.Ed.2d 187 (1981) (discussed infra n.43).

13. 720 F.Supp. at 1453.

14. Id.

15. Id.

corporation's principal place of business ... will be applied in the event of litigation is not likely to discourage corporations like [the defendant airline] from doing business in Colorado."[16]

Another example is *Jackson v. Travelers Ins. Co.*,[17] a case involving an action for bad faith insurance practices. In this case, the court held that Iowa's punitive-damages law applied to the insurer's conduct in that state,[18] even though the resulting injury to the Nebraska plaintiff had occurred in Nebraska, which did not allow such damages. The court found that Nebraska had no interest in protecting "all insurance companies nationwide regardless of whether they are Nebraska businesses,"[19] nor "in preventing punitive damages awards from other states to Nebraska citizens."[20] On the other hand, the court concluded that, because Iowa "was the location of the *cause* of the injuries[,] ... Iowa ha[d] a significant interest in using punitive damages to punish bad faith conduct that occurs in Iowa,"[21] and failure to apply Iowa law "would wholly frustrate Iowa's interest in deterring outrageous conduct."[22]

---

16. Id. For similar cases, see, e.g., Lewis–DeBoer v. Mooney Aircraft Corp., 728 F.Supp. 642 (D.Colo. 1990) (action by Colorado plaintiffs against the Texas manufacturer of a small airplane that crashed in Colorado, killing its Colorado passengers; Texas, but not Colorado, imposed punitive damages; after dismissing as fortuitous the occurrence of the injury in Colorado, the court concluded that, as the place of the defendant's conduct and principal place of business, Texas "ha[d] a greater policy interest in applying its laws and providing deterrence than Colorado ha[d] in preventing a windfall to its citizens." Id. at 645); Offshore Logistics, Inc. v. Bell Helicopter Textron, 1995 WL 555593 (E.D. La. 1995) (products liability case arising out of helicopter crash in Louisiana, which did not allow punitive damages; awarding punitive damages under the law of Texas, which was the place of the defendant's conduct and domicile).

For other product-liability cases involving this pattern and applying instead the non-punitive damages law of the state of injury, see Kemp v. Pfizer, Inc., 947 F.Supp. 1139 (E.D. Mich. 1996) and Rufer v. Abbott Labs., 118 Wash.App. 1080, 2003 WL 22430193 (2003). In *Kemp*, the product, a heart valve, was manufactured in California by a California corporation and caused the death of a Michigan patient in Michigan. The court acknowledged California's interest in applying its punitive damages law to "punish its corporate defendants and deter future misconduct," 947 F.Supp. at 1143, but concluded that, because the defendant was also doing business in Michigan, Michigan had an interest in extending to defendant the benefit of its defendant-protecting

law. The court resolved the dilemma under Michigan's *lex fori* approach and applied Michigan law.

17. 26 F.Supp.2d 1153 (S.D.Iowa 1998).

18. The insured was a nationwide company that did business in Iowa, and all of its decisions were made at the company's offices in Iowa.

19. 26 F.Supp.2d at 1162.

20. Id. at 1165.

21. Id. (emphasis added).

22. Id. at 1164. For a similar case, see Cunningham v. PFL Life Ins. Co., 42 F.Supp.2d 872 (N.D.Iowa 1999) (holding that Iowa punitive-damages law applied to action against an Iowa defendant who engaged in bad faith insurance practices in Iowa, causing injury to insureds domiciled in several states). For a slander case, see Ardoyno v. Kyzar, 426 F.Supp. 78 (E.D.La. 1976) (applying Mississippi law and allowing punitive damages in a slander action filed by a Louisiana plaintiff against a Mississippi defendant who made in Mississippi defamatory statements about plaintiff).

For a case involving the same pattern as *Jackson* and reaching the opposite result, see Northwestern Mut. Life Ins. Co. v. Wender, 940 F.Supp. 62 (S.D.N.Y. 1996). In this action for bad faith insurance practices filed by a New York insured against a Wisconsin insurer, the court applied New York law which did not allow punitive damages, because, although the defendant acted from Wisconsin and had its principal place of business there, it also did business in New York, and New York had an interest in protecting it.

In Pattern 3, a tortfeasor domiciled in a state that does not impose punitive damages, engages in conduct in another state that imposes such damages, and causes injury in the latter state.[23] This pattern presents a true conflict because both states have an interest in applying their laws. The first state has an interest in protecting its domiciliary tortfeasor from punitive damages, whereas the second state has an interest in deterring conduct in that state that causes injury there. On balance, the application of the law of the latter state is entirely justified. The fact that the defendant acted outside his home state weakens any argument that he relied on that state's law, while the fact that he acted in the other state destroys any argument of unfair surprise from the application of the latter state's law.

Cases involving this pattern have reached the result suggested above by allowing punitive-damages under the law of the state of conduct and injury. For example, in *Horowitz v. Schneider National, Inc.*,[24] the court applied Wyoming's punitive-damages law to an action arising from a Wyoming traffic accident, even though none of the parties were Wyoming domiciliaries. The court reiterated that "[t]he policy behind ... punitive damages is not compensation of the victim ... [but rather] deterrence through public condemnation,"[25] and found that Wyoming had a "paramount interest 'in the manner in which its highways are used and the care exercised by drivers.' "[26] Likewise, in *Isley v. Capuchin Province*,[27] an action for sexual abuse arising out of events in Wisconsin and filed against an out-of-state religious order, a Michigan court applied Wisconsin law, which imposed punitive damages. The court concluded that "Wisconsin's interest outweigh[ed] Michigan's interest,"[28] because Wisconsin had a "strong interest in protecting minors in Wisconsin from sexual abuse and in punishing those found guilty."[29]

In *Schoeberle v. United States*,[30] the court held that the law of Iowa, which was the place of both the pertinent conduct and the injury, should govern the question of punitive damages, even though the plaintiffs and

---

23. A functionally analogous variation of this pattern is when the injury occurs in a third state that also imposes punitive damages.

24. 708 F.Supp. 1573 (D.Wyo. 1989).

25. Id. In Wang v. Marziani, 885 F.Supp. 74 (S.D.N.Y. 1995), the court, after reiterating that "the imposition of punitive damages is a conduct-regulating rather than loss-allocating rule," id. at 77, held that Pennsylvania's punitive damages rule applied to a Pennsylvania traffic accident involving out-of-state parties, because Pennsylvania had an "overwhelming interest in regulating the conduct within its borders." Id. at 77–78. Similarly, in Villaman v. Schee, 15 F.3d 1095, 1994 WL 6661 (9th Cir. 1994), an Arizona court applied Arizona punitive-damages law to a wrongful death action filed by the estate of a Mexican domiciliary who was killed in an Arizona

accident caused by a non-Arizona defendant. The court found that "Arizona tort law is designed in part to deter negligent conduct within its borders," and thus Arizona had "a strong interest in the application of its laws allowing ... punitive damages." 1994 WL 6661 at *4.

26. Id. at 1577 (quoting Brown v. Riner, 500 P.2d 524, 526 (Wyo. 1972)).

27. 878 F.Supp. 1021 (E.D. Mich. 1995).

28. Id. at 1023.

29. Id. at 1024. See also Rice v. Nova Biomedical Corp., 38 F.3d 909 (7th Cir. 1994) (applying Illinois law to a defamation action filed against a Massachusetts defendant who defamed an Illinois plaintiff by statements made in Illinois; Illinois, but not Massachusetts, imposed punitive damages).

30. 2000 WL 1868130 (N.D.Ill. 2000).

some of the defendants were domiciled in Wisconsin, which did not allow such damages for the action in question. The court concluded that "Wisconsin's interest in protecting its resident corporate defendant ... from excessive liability [was] outweighed by Iowa's interest in applying its punitive damages law to conduct within its borders."[31] The court reasoned that, "[w]hen a balance between punishment and deterrence on the one hand and protection from excessive liability on the other must be struck, 'it is fitting that the state whose interests are more deeply affected should have its local law applied.' "[32] That state was Iowa, said the court, because, as the place of both the misconduct and the injury, "Iowa ha[d] an obvious interest ... in punish[ing] those responsible for [the] misconduct ... [and] in deterring such misconduct and occurrences in the future."[33]

In Pattern 4, a defendant domiciled in a state that imposes punitive damages engages in conduct in another state that does not impose such damages, and causes injury in the defendant's home state or in another state that also imposes punitive damages. *In re Air Crash Disaster at Washington D.C.*[34] involved this pattern. The defendant, a Florida-based airline, engaged in conduct in Virginia that caused its airplane to crash a few hundred yards into the District of Columbia. Both Florida and D.C., but not Virginia, imposed punitive damages. The court correctly applied D.C. law allowing punitive damages. It is true that, when the conduct occurs in a state that does not allow punitive damages, that state has a certain interest in applying its law to protect that conduct. However, the fact that the consequences of that conduct are felt in another state and are caused by a tortfeasor domiciled in a third state that also imposes punitive damages puts that interest in juxtaposition with the contrary interests of the latter two states. On balance, it is reasonable to conclude that the interest of the conduct state must give way.

(3) Single–Contact Patterns

Several cases have awarded punitive damages under the law of a state that had only one of the three relevant contacts, even though the

---

31. Id. at *14.

32. Id. at *13 (quoting In Re Air Crash Disaster Near Chicago, 644 F.2d 594, 613 (7th Cir. 1981)).

33. Id. In re Aircraft Accident at Little Rock, Arkansas, 231 F.Supp.2d 852 (E.D.Ark. 2002), aff'd 351 F.3d 874 (8th Cir.2003), reached the same result in a case arising from the crash-landing of an passenger plane in Little Rock, Arkansas, while en route from Texas. Arkansas law imposed unlimited punitive damages on an employer for the acts of its employees. Texas law capped the amount of punitive damages generally, and did not allow punitive damages against an employer who had not authorized or ratified the employee's wrongful

act. The court found that the critical conduct that caused the crash was pilot error, which occurred in Arkansas airspace. The court held that Arkansas law should govern the availability of punitive damages. The court acknowledged that Texas had an interest in shielding the defendant airline from punitive damages, but concluded that "Arkansas' interest in both punishing and deterring allegedly egregious conduct that occurs within its borders and which is harmful to its citizens is much stronger than Texas' interest in protecting its business from liability for acts committed outside Texas." Id. at 875.

34. 559 F.Supp. 333 (D.D.C 1983).

other two contacts were in a state or states that did not allow punitive damages. However, for every case that reached this result, there is at least one other case that reached the opposite result.

In Pattern 5, the defendant's home state imposes punitive damages and thus has an interest in punishing the defendant and deterring others from engaging in similar conduct in the future. However, both the defendant's conduct and the resulting injury occur in another state (or states) that does not impose punitive damages. In such a case, one could argue that the latter state has an interest in protecting, if not the defendant as such, at least the defendant's activity within its territory, which may be beneficial in other ways, such as by providing jobs for the local population. The resulting conflict is not an easy one, and this is why courts encountering such conflicts have reached different results. While most courts deny punitive damages,[35] a few courts have allowed them by applying the law of the defendant's domicile.[36]

35. See, e.g., In re Air Crash Disaster Near Chicago, 644 F.2d 594 (7th Cir. 1981), cert. denied 454 U.S. 878, 102 S.Ct. 358, 70 L.Ed.2d 187 (1981) (with regard to the plane's manufacturer); In re Aircrash Disaster Near Monroe, Michigan on January 9, 1997, 20 F.Supp.2d 1110 (E.D.Mich. 1998) (holding that actions arising out of Michigan crash of airplane operated by an airline headquartered in Kentucky, which allowed punitive damages, were governed by Michigan law, which did not allow such damages;) In re San Juan Dupont Plaza Hotel Fire Litigation, 745 F.Supp. 79 (D.P.R. 1990) (applying Puerto Rico law, which did not allow punitive damages, to actions arising out of Puerto Rico hotel fire and filed against non-Puerto Rico defendants domiciled in states that allowed punitive damages); George Lombard & Lomar, Inc. v. Economic Dev. Admin. of Puerto Rico, 1995 WL 447651, (S.D.N.Y. 1995) (applying Puerto Rico law and denying punitive damages for Puerto Rico conduct and injury).

36. Among the latter cases is Fanselow v. Rice, 213 F.Supp.2d 1077 (D.Neb. 2002), a traffic-accident case in which the state of injury had only a fortuitous connection with the defendants. Fanselow arose out of a two-car Nebraska collision that injured two Colorado domiciliaries riding in one of the cars. The defendants were the driver of the other car, a Texas domiciliary who moved to Oregon after the accident, and his employer, a Minnesota-based corporation. Of the four involved states, only Nebraska disallowed punitive damages. The court did not discuss the place of conduct, but one can assume that although the driver's conduct occurred in Nebraska, his employer's conduct or omission occurred in Minnesota. Focusing only on the domicile of the defendants, the court held that Minnesota law governed the plaintiffs' punitive damages claims against the employer, and Oregon law governed their claims against the driver. The court reasoned that the plaintiffs' home state did not have an interest in whether the defendants were subject to punitive damages. Thus, the only states concerned with punitive damages are those states "with whom defendants have contacts significant for choice of law purposes" (id. at 1084), i.e., Nebraska, Minnesota, and Oregon. The court found that Nebraska's policy of protecting defendants from punitive damages was not implicated in this case because the defendants' only connection with that state was the occurrence of the accident there. In contrast, the court reasoned, the case implicated the policies of both Minnesota and Oregon in punishing and deterring defendants, because the defendants were domiciled in those two states. Another case that also applied the punitive damages law of the defendant's principal place of business is Bryant v. Silverman, 146 Ariz. 41, 703 P.2d 1190 (1985), a case arising out of an airplane crash in Colorado, which prohibited punitive damages. However, in this case the court was influenced by the fact that the record did not reveal the place of the critical conduct (as between Arizona and Colorado), and that the victim was also an Arizona domiciliary. The court concluded that, "[s]ince this case involves an Arizona corporate defendant causing injury to an Arizona domiciliary, Arizona has the dominant interest in controlling [defendant's] conduct." Id. at 1196.

In Pattern 6, the state of conduct imposes punitive damages (and thus has an interest in punishing and deterring the particular conduct), while the defendant's domicile and the place of injury are in a state, or states, that do not impose punitive damages (and thus have an interest in protecting the defendant). This results in a true conflict between the laws of the state of conduct and the state of the defendant's domicile, with the state of injury simply playing a secondary role. As the cases discussed below indicate, one can find cases applying the law of any one of these three states.

For example, in *Long v. Sears Roebuck & Co.*,[37] a products liability case, the court applied the law of the place of wrongful conduct, which the court assumed to be the sale of a defective mower and a misrepresentation of its safety features. Both of these acts occurred in the District of Columbia,[38] which imposed punitive damages, while the injury occurred in Maryland, which did not allow such damages. The court applied D.C. law after concluding (a) that Maryland did not have an interest in applying its law because that law was not intended to protect foreign defendants; and (b) that the District of Columbia had an interest in deterring and punishing, through its punitive damages law, those defendants who engaged in reprehensible conduct in the District by selling unsafe products there and misrepresenting their safety features.

In contrast, in *Harlan Feeders, Inc. v. Grand Laboratories, Inc.*,[39] a product liability action arising from injury in Nebraska, the court applied Nebraska law, which prohibited punitive damages, rather than Iowa law, which allowed them. The product was manufactured in Iowa and was sold to the Nebraska plaintiff in Nebraska. Noting that "Nebraska has made a policy choice that punitive damages are inappropriate,"[40] the court equated that choice to a state "interest" and concluded that this interest was "not outweighed by Iowa's contrary interest in imposing punitive damages as a deterrent, at least not ... where the plaintiff is a resident of Nebraska, not Iowa, where the alleged injury occurred in Nebraska, not Iowa, as a result of use of a product manufactured by a South Dakota, not an Iowa, corporation, even when the corporation physically produced the product in Iowa."[41]

In *In re Air Crash Disaster at Sioux City, Iowa*,[42] a multiparty case involving wrongful death and survival actions arising from the crash of a passenger plane in Iowa, the pertinent contacts were scattered in several states. Correctly discounting the victims' domiciles, the court held that the punitive damages liability of the manufacturers of the plane and engines should be governed by the laws of the states of manufacture. The engine manufacturer had its principal place of business in New York, which allowed punitive damages, and had manufactured the engines in Ohio, which allowed such damages in survival actions, but not in

---

37. 877 F.Supp. 8 (D.D.C. 1995).

38. The mower had been manufactured in South Carolina, but neither party invoked that state's law.

39. 881 F.Supp. 1400 (N.D. Iowa 1995).

40. Id. at 1410.

41. Id.

42. 734 F.Supp. 1425 (N.D.Ill. 1990).

wrongful death actions. The plane manufacturer had its principal place of business in Missouri, the law of which is not given by the court, and manufactured the plane in California, which allowed punitive damage in survival actions but not in wrongful death actions.[43]

In Pattern 7, the state of the injury imposes punitive damages, but the state (or states) of the defendant's conduct and domicile prohibits such damages. Again, there is little doubt that this pattern presents the true conflict paradigm. The first state has an interest in deterring acts and punishing actors that cause injury within its territory, while the latter state has an interest in protecting its domiciliary actor from the heavy financial price of punitive damages.

From a constitutional perspective, the application of the law of the state of injury must satisfy the test that the Supreme Court enunciated in *BMW of North America, Inc. v. Gore*.[44] *Gore* held that a state's power to impose punitive damages for extraterritorial conduct is coextensive with that state's "interests in protecting its own consumers and its own economy."[45] Hence, the forum state of Alabama "d[id] not have the power ... to punish [defendant] for conduct that was lawful where it occurred and that had no impact on Alabama or its residents."[46] Thus, in assessing the amount of punitive damages, one should consider only the conduct that caused detrimental effects in the state of injury, and not the conduct that caused such effects in other states.[47]

From a choice-of-law perspective (and perhaps a constitutional perspective as well), the application of the punitive-damages law of the state

---

43. With regard to the third defendant, the airline, the court applied Illinois law, which did not allow punitive damages. Illinois was the airline's principal place of business and the place where the corporate decisions regarding the maintenance of the aircraft and the training of its flight crew were made.

In re Air Crash Disaster Near Chicago, 644 F.2d 594 (7th Cir. 1981), cert. denied 454 U.S. 878, 102 S.Ct. 358, 70 L.Ed.2d 187 (1981), a similar case arising out of a passenger plane crash in Illinois, involved actions against both the plane's manufacturer and the airline company. The manufacturer's home state, Missouri, allowed punitive damages, but the state of manufacture, California, did not. The airline's home state, New York, did not allow punitive damages, but the state in which it maintained the aircraft, Oklahoma, allowed such damages. Examining each conflict separately for each defendant, the court found a true conflict between the states that allowed and the states that prohibited punitive damages. The court broke the tie by applying the law of a third state, Illinois, which was the place of injury and which did not allow punitive damages. The court found that Illinois had

a "strong interest in having airlines fly in and out of the state, and ... in protecting [them] by disallowing punitive damages." 644 F.2d at 615–16. Similarly, in Freeman v. World Airways, Inc., 596 F.Supp. 841 (D.Mass. 1984), a case arising out of an airplane crash in Massachusetts, the court found that Massachusetts, which did not allow punitive damages, "ha[d] a significant interest in regulating conduct (deterrence or encouragement) of planes arriving at [its airports] during the winter." Id. at 847. The negligent conduct that caused the crash arguably occurred in other states that imposed punitive damages.

44. 517 U.S. 559, 116 S.Ct. 1589, 134 L.Ed.2d 809 (1996). See also State Farm Mut. Auto. Ins. Co. v. Campbell, 538 U.S. 408, 123 S.Ct. 1513, 155 L.Ed.2d 585 (2003).

45. *Gore*, 517 U.S. at 572.

46. Id. 572–73.

47. Such conduct may be considered, however, in assessing "the degree of reprehensibility of the defendant's conduct," id. at 574 n.21, which is one of the elements for determining whether to impose punitive damages.

of injury must satisfy one additional requirement–a showing that the occurrence of the injury in that state was objectively foreseeable. This requirement depends on the facts of the particular case but, for example, in products liability cases, it can be satisfied by showing that the product had been available in the state of injury through ordinary commercial channels.[48] One example is *Kramer v. Showa Denko K.K.,*[49] a products liability case that allowed punitive damages under the law of the state injury, New York (which was also the victim's domicile). Although the product had been manufactured by a Japanese defendant in Japan, which did not allow punitive damages, the product reached the New York market through ordinary commercial channels and the victim bought it and used it in that state. Thus, the imposition of the financial burden of punitive damages under New York law was a foreseeable and insurable risk that the manufacturer should expect to bear in exchange for deriving financial benefits from the New York market.[50]

On the other hand, some cases involving the same pattern have gone the other way. For example, in *Kelly v. Ford Motor Co.,*[51] another products liability case, the court refused to apply the punitive damages law of the state of injury, Pennsylvania, which was also the victim's domicile and the place where he had acquired the product. Instead, the court applied the law of Michigan, the manufacturer's home state and the place of manufacture, which prohibited punitive damages. The court acknowledged Pennsylvania's interests "in punishing defendants who injure its residents and ... in deterring them and others from engaging in similar conduct which poses a risk to Pennsylvania's citizens."[52] However, the court also found that Michigan had "a very strong interest"[53] in denying such damages, so as to ensure that "its domiciliary defendants are protected from excessive financial liability."[54] By insulating companies such as Ford, who conduct extensive business within its borders, said the court, "Michigan hopes to promote corporate migration into its economy ... [which] will enhance the economic climate and well being of the state of Michigan by generating revenues."[55]

---

48. For non-products cases awarding punitive damages under the law of the place of injury (and victim's domicile), see, e.g., Cooper v. American Express Co., 593 F.2d 612 (5th Cir. 1979) (awarding punitive damages under the law of the state of injury, even though the law of the defendant's domicile and place of conduct prohibited such damages); Ashland Oil, Inc. v. Miller Oil Purchasing Co., 678 F.2d 1293 (5th Cir. 1982) (awarding punitive damages under the law of the place of injury, even though such damages were prohibited by the state of the defendant's domicile and place of conduct). In both cases the foreseeability condition had been satisfied.

49. 929 F.Supp. 733 (S.D.N.Y. 1996).

50. For another example, see White v. Ford Motor Co., 312 F.3d 998 (9th Cir.

2002), opinion amended on denial of rehearing 335 F.3d 833 (9th Cir. 2003) (reducing as excessive, but otherwise allowing, a punitive damages award under Nevada law, in a products liability action filed against a car manufacturer by Nevada domiciliary for injury he suffered in Nevada. The car had been sold in Nevada through ordinary commercial channels.).

51. 933 F.Supp. 465 (E.D.Pa. 1996).

52. Id. at 470.

53. Id.

54. Id.

55. Id. For other cases reaching the same result, see Calhoun v. Yamaha Motor Corp., U.S.A., 216 F.3d 338 (3d Cir. 2000), cert. denied 531 U.S. 1037, 121 S.Ct. 627, 148 L.Ed.2d 536 (2000) (action by Pennsyl-

In re Air Crash Disaster at Washington D.C.,[56] was a more complex, multiparty case that encompassed both products and non-products actions, arising from the crash of an Air Florida plane in the District of Columbia, which allowed punitive damages. The products liability actions were filed against Boeing, a company that manufactured the plane in its home state of Washington, which prohibited punitive damages. The other actions were filed against the airline, a Florida-based company. The court rejected Boeing's argument that Washington law should govern, by pointing out that, while Washington had chosen to protect manufacturers at the expense of victims, "the sovereignty of other states prevents [Washington] from placing on the scales the rights of those injured elsewhere."[57] The court then focused on the actions against the airline, which was allegedly negligent in overseeing the de-icing of the plane before takeoff from the airport, which is located on the Virginia side of the Virginia–D.C. border. Virginia (unlike D.C.) prohibited punitive damages. The District of Columbia court found that, as between these two jurisdictions, D.C. had "the most significant relationship ... [because] the injurious effects of the [Virginia] conduct were predominantly felt in the District."[58]

(4) The Victim's Domicile or Nationality

In the last pattern (pattern 8) all three pertinent contacts are in a state or states that do not impose punitive damages for the conduct in question. In such a case, it is highly inappropriate to award punitive damages, even if, for example, the victim's home state imposes such damages, and even if that state is also the forum state. A case on point is *Phillips v. General Motors Corp.*,[59] in which the Montana Supreme Court awarded punitive damages to a Montana plaintiff under Montana law, even though Montana did not have any other pertinent contacts and the other involved states did not allow or limited such damages. *Phillips* was a products liability action filed against a Michigan manufacturer for injuries caused by one of its trucks that was manufactured in Michigan. The court reasoned that, because "punitive damages serve to punish and deter conduct deemed wrongful—in this case, placing a defective product into the stream of commerce which subsequently injured a Montana resident,"[60] Montana had a strong interest in "deterring future sales of

vania plaintiffs for injury they sustained in Puerto Rico while using a rented Japanese-made water craft–holding that plaintiffs' claims for punitive damages were governed by Puerto Rico law (which did not allow such damages) because "Puerto Rico's interest in regulating the activity that occurs in its territorial waters ... is more dominant." Id. at 348); Beals v. Sipca Securink Corp., 1994 WL 236018 (D.D.C. 1994) (refusing to apply the punitive damages law of the District of Columbia to action arising from injury there and filed against a Virginia defendant who manufactured the prod-uct in Virginia. Virginia law limited punitive damages); Selle v. Pierce, 494 N.W.2d 634 (S.D. 1993) (refusing to apply punitive damages law of place of injury and applying instead non-punitive damages law of state of conduct and defendant's domicile).

56. 559 F.Supp. 333 (D.D.C 1983).

57. Id. at 359.

58. Id. at 356.

59. 298 Mont. 438, 995 P.2d 1002 (2000).

60. Id. at 1012.

defective products in Montana and encouraging manufacturers to warn Montana residents about defects in their products as quickly and as thoroughly as possible."[61] However, the sale of the product took place not in Montana, but rather in North Carolina, which did not impose punitive damages. The purchaser was a North Carolina domiciliary who sold the truck to another North Carolina domiciliary, the victim, who later moved his domicile to Montana. The victim was killed not in Montana, but in Kansas (which limited punitive damages), while driving the car from Montana to North Carolina. Montana's interests in protecting its domiciliaries from harm was fully satisfied by applying Montana's compensatory damages law, which the court applied. Under the facts of this case, any additional interest Montana might have had in deterring conduct that injured Montana domiciliaries is far weaker than the contrary interests of Michigan in shielding from punitive damages Michigan manufacturers who manufacture products in Michigan.

Similar to *Phillips*, but more defensible, are certain cases decided under federal "antiterrorist" statutes, such as the Antiterrorist and Effective Death Penalty Act of 1996 (AEDPA).[62] This Act imposes punitive damages for death or personal injury of United States citizens who are victims of attacks sponsored or aided by states designated as sponsors of terrorism. Thus, the Act authorizes the award of punitive damages under the law of the victim's nationality, even when the conduct, the injury, and the defendant's domicile are all in another state that does not allow such damages. One such case is *Flatow v. Islamic Republic of Iran*,[63] which arose out of the death of an American student killed in a suicide bomb attack in the Gaza Strip. The court held that the AEDPA applied extraterritorially because Congress enacted it with the express purpose of "affect[ing] the conduct of terrorist states outside the United States, in order to promote the safety of United States citizens traveling overseas,"[64] and that this express purpose negated the usual

---

61. Id. For another case awarding punitive damages under the law of the plaintiff's domicile, see Thiele v. Northern Mut. Ins. Co., 36 F.Supp.2d 852 (E.D. Wis. 1999) (applying Wisconsin law as the better law in an action for bad faith insurance practices filed by a Wisconsin insured against a Michigan insurer who insured plaintiff's barn house in Michigan. Michigan did not allow punitive damages). For cases reaching the opposite result, see Gadzinski v. Chrysler Corp., 2001 WL 629336 (N.D.Ill. 2001) (applying Indiana law limiting punitive damages to an action by an Illinois plaintiff who purchased the defective product, a car, from an Indiana dealer and was injured in Indiana); Hernandez v. Aeronaves de Mexico, S.A., 583 F.Supp. 331 (N.D.Cal. 1984) (applying Mexican law and denying punitive damages in actions arising from the crash in Mexico of a Mexican airliner and resulting in death of California domiciliaries, but applying

California's more generous compensatory damages law); Tubos de Acero de Mexico, S.A. v. American Int'l Inv. Corp., Inc., 292 F.3d 471 (5th Cir. 2002) (holding that punitive damages were unavailable because the defendant was a Mexican corporation and the pertinent conduct and injury had occurred either in Mexico or in Louisiana, and neither jurisdiction allowed punitive damages).

62. 28 U.S.C. § 1605(a)(7). This Act lifts the sovereign immunity of foreign states designated by the U.S. State Department as sponsors of terrorism and provides a cause of action for U.S. citizens killed or injured by acts of terrorism sponsored or aided by these states.

63. 999 F.Supp. 1 (D.D.C. 1998).

64. Id. at 15 (citing legislative history).

presumption against extraterritoriality.[65] Another similar case is *Wagner v. Islamic Republic of Iran*,[66] which arose out of the death of a U.S. serviceman during the 1984 car-bombing of the U.S. embassy in Beirut, Lebanon. The court applied federal substantive law and awarded $12 million in compensatory damages and $300 million in punitive damages. Taking note of the September 11 attacks, the court said that "now, more than ever, . . . the acts of terrorists and their sponsors must be punished to the full extent to which civil damage awards might operate to suppress such activities in the future."[67]

The reason cases like *Wagner* are more defensible than *Phillips* is that, while the victim's Montana domicile in *Phillips* was no more than a coincidence, the victim's U.S. citizenship in *Wagner* was anything but a coincidence—the victim was a target of the attack *because* of his citizenship. Under these circumstances, the application of American punitive damages law is defensible.

(5) Summary and Rule

The preceding discussion provides a wide-ranging sample of tort cases involving punitive damages conflicts. These cases have been decided under a variety of modern choice-of-law methodologies, including the Restatement Second, interest analysis, and Leflar's choice-influencing considerations. However, as in many other tort conflicts, the use of one or another methodology does not appear to have had a perceptible bearing on the outcome of the cases. Consequently, it is unnecessary to dwell much on methodology and more fruitful to focus on the outcomes of cases.

As the above discussion indicates, American courts have awarded punitive damages in cases involving each of the first seven patterns defined above, namely cases in which the state that imposes punitive damages has all three, any two, or any one of the three pertinent contacts. If one were to compress these results into a *descriptive* choice-of-law rule, the rule would provide as follows: Subject to some exceptions, American courts award punitive damages if such damages are imposed by one or more of the following states: (1) the state of the defendant's domicile or principal place of business; (2) the state of the defendant's conduct; or (3) the state of the injury.[68] This rule does not include cases falling within Pattern 8 (the domicile cases) because these cases are both uncommon and extreme, but it does include the cases

---

65. Id. at 16. See also id. at 15 n. 7 (stating that such extraterritorial exception is consistent with international law, based on the principles of passive personality, protective, and universal). The court awarded $42 million in compensatory damages and $225 million in punitive damages.

66. 172 F.Supp.2d 128 (D.D.C. 2001).

67. Id. at 138.

68. If punitive damages are available only in the state of injury, the application of that state's punitive damages law is subject to the proviso that the occurrence of the injury in that state must have been objectively foreseeable. See text at nn. 48–50, supra.

falling within the three single-contact patterns (5–7) because these cases are more common and more defensible.

However, while being "defensible" is an acceptable attribute of *de facto* practice, it is not a sufficient attribute of a *prescriptive* rule, namely a rule that seeks to guide future practices. One who attempts to draft a prescriptive rule should aspire to a higher standard—a rule that has a solid foundation in judicial practice *and* takes a more evenhanded position towards these sharp conflicts. The view adopted here is that such a rule must be grounded on the cases falling within the two- or three-pattern cases, which are both more numerous and better-reasoned.

The Louisiana conflicts codification of 1991 has adopted this view,[69] as has the American Law Institute in drafting the Complex Litigation Project of 1994.[70] Although phrased differently,[71] the punitive damages rules of these two projects are based upon the three contacts discussed above: the place of conduct, the place of the defendant's domicile, and the place of injury. These rules provide that *punitive damages may be awarded if all three or any two of the above contacts are located in a state or states that allow such damages.* Thus, these rules steer a middle course between outright hostility and undue liberality toward punitive damages. For this reason, these rules can be challenged both from the left and from the right. The criticism from the left (mostly the American criticism) would be that the two-contact requirement is too restrictive. The criticism from the right (including perhaps from Europe) would be that these rules are not restrictive enough since, after all, they do not eradicate the "monstrous heresy"[72] of punitive damages. However, the role of conflicts law is not to eradicate heresies, but rather to define their proper spatial boundaries.

IV. PARTICULAR TORT PROBLEMS

§ 17.51 Parts I–III presented an overview of current choice-of-law methodology relating to torts in general. Part IV focuses on certain tort situations that present special problems, for instance because the loss incurred is an intangible value (as in alienation of affections and defamation), because the "place of the tort" may itself be non-territorial (torts on the high seas), or finally, because the subject matter is governed–in

69. See La. Civ. Code art. 3546, described supra n. 7.

70. See American Law Institute, Complex Litigation: Statutory Recommendations and Analysis § 6.06 (1994). For a discussion of this provision, see Juenger, The Complex Litigation Project's Tort Choice-of-Law Rules, 54 La. L. Rev. 907 (1994); Kozyris, The Conflicts Provisions of the ALI's Complex Litigation Project: A Glass Half Full? 54 La. L. Rev. 953 (1994); Nafziger, Choice of Law in Air Disaster Cases: Complex Litigation Rules and the Common Law, 54 La. L. Rev. 1001 (1994); Sedler, The Complex Litigation Project's Proposal for Federally–Mandated Choice of Law in Mass Torts Cases: Another Assault on State Sovereignty, 54 La. L. Rev. 1085 (1994); Symeonides, The ALI's Complex Litigation Project: Commencing the National Debate, 54 La. L. Rev. 843 (1994).

71. For a comparison of these two provisions, see S. Symeonides, W. Perdue & A. von Mehren, Conflict of Laws: American, Comparative, International, 282–83, 301–302 (1998).

72. Fay v. Parker, 53 N.H. 342, 382 (1872), supra n.4.

part or in whole–by similar but different statutory law. Examples of the last category are worker's compensation and conflicts between different no-fault compensation statutes for automobile accident victims, or between such a statute and a common-law liability approach. As the following discussion shows, the newer approaches to choice of law lend themselves equally well to the solution of some of these problems, while other problems may call for greater adherence to more fixed rules.

A. INJURY TO INTANGIBLE VALUES

Fraud and misrepresentation, defamation, unfair competition, and alienation of affection are typical cases in which the plaintiff is injured in an intangible value. The fact that intangibles do not have a specific physical situs, or have multiple such situses, suggests that the injury cannot be localized in a single place. This reduces the importance of the place of injury in these conflicts, without elevating the importance of the place of conduct, unless the primary policy goal is one of punishment.

1. Fraud and Misrepresentation

§ 17.52   In cases of fraud and misrepresentation, the choice of the applicable law is relatively easy. When the defendant's fraud or misrepresentation and the plaintiff's reliance occur in the same state, the choice-of-law question is easy.[1] When these events occur in different states, the applicable law is normally,[2] but not always,[3] the law of the state in which the plaintiff acted in reliance.

§ 17.52

1. Restatement, Second, Conflict of Laws § 148(1) (1971). See Texas Tunneling Co. v. Chattanooga, 204 F.Supp. 821 (E.D.Tenn.1962), aff'd in part, rev'd in part (not conflicts part), 329 F.2d 402 (6th Cir. 1964); Inacom Corp. v. Sears, Roebuck & Co., 254 F.3d 683, 688 (8th Cir. 2001) (defendant's conduct, and plaintiff's reliance and injury occurred in state of plaintiff's headquarters).

2. Subsection 2 of 148 of the Restatement lists several factors for determining the state of the "most significant relationship." They are (a) the place where the plaintiff relied, (b) where he received the representations, (c) where the defendant made the representations, (d) domicile, residence, nationality, and place of business of the parties, (e) where the tangible involved in the transaction was situated, and (f) where the plaintiff was to render performance under the contract which he was induced to conclude. Of these factors, (a), (b), and (d) through (f) focus either entirely or substantially on the interests of the plaintiff. To that extent they parallel subsection (1) of § 148, supra n.1. The place of the

defendant's conduct, which is also part of the test of subsection (1), thus is important mainly for factor (c). That factor is said to be analogous to the reference to the place of conduct of §§ 146–147 in the context of injuries to persons or tangible things. Id., comment (h). The case law also focuses mainly on the plaintiff and his interests. See General Dynamics Corp. v. Selb Mfg. Co., 481 F.2d 1204 (8th Cir.1973) cert. denied 414 U.S. 1162, 94 S.Ct. 926, 39 L.Ed.2d 116 (1974) (identification of place of harmful impact); St. Louis Union Trust Co. v. Merrill Lynch, et al., 412 F.Supp. 45 (E.D.Mo.1976), rev'd 562 F.2d 1040, 1054 n.20 (8th Cir.1977) cert. denied 435 U.S. 925, 98 S.Ct. 1490, 55 L.Ed.2d 519 (1978) (place of plaintiff's domicile, reliance, and injury); Wichita Fed. Sav. & Loan v. Landmark Group, Inc., 674 F.Supp. 321 (D.Kan. 1987); Palmer v. Beverly Enters., 823 F.2d 1105 (7th Cir.1987); Murphy v. Erwin–Wasey, Inc., 460 F.2d 661 (1st Cir.1972) (place of plaintiff's residence and reliance); Doody v. John Sexton & Co., 411 F.2d 1119 (1st Cir.1969) (plaintiff's domicile); Boulevard Airport v. Consolidated Vultee Aircraft Corp., 85 F.Supp. 876 (E.D.Pa.1949) (place

2. *Unfair Competition*[1]

§ 17.53 Compared to fraud and misrepresentation the matter is more difficult in the case of common law[2] torts for unfair competition

of plaintiff's business). Uncle Henry's Inc. v. Plaut Consulting Inc., 240 F.Supp.2d 63 (D.Me.2003) (plaintiff's domicile, reliance, and injury); Wadsworth, Inc. v. Schwarz–Nin, 951 F.Supp. 314, 322 (D.P.R. 1996) (misrepresentation and reliance); Continental Cas. v. Diversified Indus., 884 F.Supp. 937 (E.D.Pa.1995) (plaintiff's domicile, misrepresentation, and reliance); In re SmarTalk Teleservices Securities Litigation, 124 F.Supp.2d 505 (S.D.Ohio 2000) (same); Schiff v. Mazda Motor of America, Inc., 102 F.Supp.2d 891 (S.D.Ohio 2000) (same);Value House, Inc. v. MCI Telecomm. Corp., 917 F.Supp. 5 (D.D.C. 1996) (same). But see Autrey v. Chemtrust Indus. Corp., 362 F.Supp. 1085 (D.Del.1973) (place of loss or injury where four plaintiffs from different states suffered business losses in same state where fraudulent business representations were also made).

3. See, e.g., Cunningham v. PFL Life Ins. Co., 42 F.Supp.2d 872 (N.D.Iowa, 1999) (applying law of Iowa because defendant had its principal place of business there, a substantial portion of the fraudulent conduct occurred there, and Iowa had an interest in regulating the manner in which Iowa defendants did business); Grove v. Principal Mut. Life Ins. Co., 14 F.Supp.2d 1101 (S.D.Iowa, 1998) (same). See also Tingley Sys., Inc. v. CSC Consulting, Inc., 152 F.Supp.2d 95 (D.Mass.2001) (focusing on defendant's contacts); S.E.C. v. Infinity Group Co., 27 F.Supp.2d 559 (E.D.Pa.1998) (same).

§ 17.53

1. This section deals with the interstate aspects of unfair competition. A wide diversity of opinions has been expressed on unfair competition in the international context. The early case law referred to the place of conduct and consequently immunized a defendant from the application of American law, particularly federal antitrust law, when the conduct was lawful where done. American Banana Co. v. United Fruit Co., 213 U.S. 347, 29 S.Ct. 511, 53 L.Ed. 826 (1909); RCA Mfg. Co. v. Whiteman, 114 F.2d 86 (2d Cir.1940), cert. denied 311 U.S. 712, 61 S.Ct. 393, 85 L.Ed. 463 (1940). The decision in *American Banana* now has lost its authority. The *Banana* doctrine was limited by a 1927 decision that applied U.S. antitrust law to acts permitted under the law of the place where they were done, on the ground that the agreements intended

and effected a limitation of imports into the United States. Restatement, Third, Foreign Relations Law of the United States, §§ 415, 441 (1987). United States v. Sisal Sales Corp., 274 U.S. 268, 47 S.Ct. 592, 71 L.Ed. 1042 (1927). Subsequent decisions followed this trend and, in addition, no longer differentiated between American and foreign defendants. See United States v. National Lead Co., 63 F.Supp. 513 (S.D.N.Y.1945), aff'd 332 U.S. 319, 67 S.Ct. 1634, 91 L.Ed. 2077 (1947); Timken Roller Bearing Co. v. United States, 341 U.S. 593, 71 S.Ct. 971, 95 L.Ed. 1199 (1951). The application of U.S. antitrust law to conduct abroad was last restated in Hartford Fire Ins. Co. v. California, 509 U.S. 764, 113 S.Ct. 2891, 125 L.Ed.2d 612 (1993). Without weighing the interests of the States involved, the majority sees the problem of the extraterritorial application of U.S. law as one (a) of *jurisdiction to adjudicate* and (b) as one of congressional intent. In his partial dissent, Justice Scalia saw the problem as one of *jurisdiction to prescribe*, i.e., of choice of law. For a review, see Hay, 60 RabelsZ 303 (1996) (in German). Another view would presume the application of American law unless the connection with the United States is slight. For this position, see Weintraub, The Extraterritorial Application of Antitrust and Security Laws: An Inquiry into the Utility of the "Choice-of-Law" Approach, 70 Tex. L. Rev. 1799 (1992). Consolidated Gold Fields PLC v. Minorco, S.A. 871 F.2d 252 (2d Cir.) modified, 890 F.2d 569 (2d Cir.), cert. dismissed, 492 U.S. 939, 110 S.Ct. 29, 106 L.Ed.2d 639 (1989) is an example of a case in which it is arguable that the presumption in favor of application of United States public law should have been rebutted. For the view that the application of United States public law should be treated as other choice-of-law problems, and United States law applied only if the United States has the "most significant relationship" to the parties and the transaction, see Born, A Reappraisal of the Extraterritorial Reach of U.S. Law, 24 Law & Police in Int'l Business 1, 88 (1992). See also Reyes–Gaona v. North Carolina Growers Ass'n, Inc., 250 F.3d 861 (4th Cir.2001), cert. denied 534 U.S. 995, 122 S.Ct. 463, 151 L.Ed.2d 380 (2001) (federal age discrimination statute does not apply to foreign workers applying in foreign countries for U.S. jobs).

2. Common law unfair competition includes tortious interference with actual

when the defendant acts in one state and injures the plaintiff's business or deceives the public in another state. When the action arises in federal court sitting in diversity or when it is pendent to a federal claim, a preliminary question is whether federal or state law applies; most courts will apply state law.[3] State decisions continue to treat unfair competition claims as torts, and so does the Second Restatement.[4] However, the

and prospective contractual relationships, misappropriation, passing off, false advertising, disparagement, or injurious falsehood, and kinds of interference with economic relationships. See R. Callmann, 1 The Law of Unfair Competition, Trademarks and Monopolies § 2.15 (4th ed. 1981). See also Wells Fargo & Co. v. Wells Fargo Express Co., 358 F.Supp. 1065, 1084 (D.Nev.1973), vacated and remanded 556 F.2d 406 (9th Cir.1977). The rather inadequate common law remedies for false advertising have been replaced by § 43(a) of the Lanham Trade Mark Act of 1946, which prohibits false designations of origin and false descriptions. 15 U.S.C.A. §§ 1051–1127 (1976), particularly § 1125. Section 5 of the Federal Trade Commission Act (15 U.S.C.A. § 45(a)(1)) prohibits unfair methods of competition and unfair or deceptive acts or practices in or affecting commerce. Almost all states have enacted comparable statutes, some codifying or adding to the common law. See Ala. Code § 8–19–5 (1975); Alaska Stat. § 45.50.471; N.Y. Gen. Bus.Law § 349. See Alexander & Coil, The Impact of New State Unfair Trade Practices Acts on the Field of Unfair Competition, 67 Trademark Rep. 625, 630 (1977). However, a residual common law remains even in those states. Consequently, unfair competition claims can be brought in any state, but most of them are brought as added counts to allegations of federal trademark, copyright, or patent law violations.

3. Since claims based on state law are often brought pendent to a federal cause of action, two questions arise: whether federal law preempts the field and whether general federal law (federal common law) or state law applies to a claim not preempted. On the first question see Sears, Roebuck & Co. v. Stiffel Co., 376 U.S. 225, 84 S.Ct. 784, 11 L.Ed.2d 661 (1964), reh'g denied 376 U.S. 973, 84 S.Ct. 1131, 12 L.Ed.2d 87 (1964); Compco Corp. v. Day–Brite Lighting, Inc., 376 U.S. 234, 84 S.Ct. 779, 11 L.Ed.2d 669 (1964), reh'g denied 377 U.S. 913, 84 S.Ct. 1162, 12 L.Ed.2d 183 (1964); Goldstein v. California, 412 U.S. 546, 93 S.Ct. 2303, 37 L.Ed.2d 163 (1973); Kewanee Oil Co. v. Bicron Corp., 416 U.S. 470, 94 S.Ct. 1879,

40 L.Ed.2d 315 (1974); Bonito Boats, Inc. v. Thunder Craft Boats, Inc., 489 U.S. 141, 109 S.Ct. 971, 103 L.Ed.2d 118 (1989); Data General Corp. v. Digital Computer Controls, Inc., 357 A.2d 105 (Del.Ch.1975); Roy Export Co. v. Columbia Broad. Sys., Inc., 672 F.2d 1095 (2d Cir.1982). See also Dannay, The Sears–Compco Doctrine Today: Trademarks and Unfair Competition, 67 Trademark Rep. 132 (1977). With respect to preemption under the Copyright Act of 1976 see M. Nimmer, 1 Nimmer on Copyright § 1.01[B] (1997).

With respect to the applicable law—federal or state—see Pecheur Lozenge Co., Inc. v. National Candy Co., Inc., 315 U.S. 666, 62 S.Ct. 853, 86 L.Ed. 1103 (1942) (state law); Natural Footwear Ltd. v. Hart, Schaffner & Marx, 579 F.Supp. 543 (D.N.J.1983) (state law); Rohm and Haas Co. v. Adco Chemical Co., 689 F.2d 424 (3d Cir.1982); Midland–Ross Corp. v. Sunbeam Equip. Corp., 316 F.Supp. 171 (W.D.Pa.1970), aff'd 435 F.2d 159 (3d Cir.1970) (state law); Taussig v. Wellington Fund, Inc., 187 F.Supp. 179 (D.Del.1960), aff'd 313 F.2d 472 (3d Cir.1963), cert. denied 374 U.S. 806, 83 S.Ct. 1695 (2), 10 L.Ed.2d 1031 (1963) (universal principles); J. Kobak, Jr., Totem and Taboo: Growth of a Common Law of Unfair Competition in New York with Some Notes on the Effect of the Lanham Act of 1946, 17 N.Y.L.F. 941, 979 (1972); Zlinkoff, *Erie v. Tompkins:* In Relation to the Law of Trade–Marks and Unfair Competition, 42 Col. L. Rev. 955 (1942); Annot., 148 A.L.R. 139, 154–69 (1944); Note, 60 Harv. L. Rev. 1315, 1316–17 (1947); Comment, 70 Yale L.J. 406, 422–23 (1961).

4. There is a growing body of opinion that unfair competition claims should be treated separately because of the different value goals this area of the law addresses and protects. Callmann, What is Unfair Competition?, 28 Geo. L.J. 585, 588, 598–599, 604 (1940). The Restatement, Second, Law of Torts, retains in its coverage only the interference with actual or potential contractual relations. Other areas were considered to be related to trade regulation, labor disputes, or a separate law of unfair

presence of at least three interests or policies to be considered—regulation of conduct, protection of the injured party's business, and protection of the public—is reflected in a number of diverging approaches in the case law. The Second Restatement, while treating unfair competition as part of tort (§ 145), suggests that the most significant factor is not the place of injury, as in personal injury cases, but the place of the defendant's conduct.[5] A number of decisions undertake to apply the general most-significant-relationship test,[6] or apply forum law on the basis of governmental interest analysis.[7] These approaches treat too lightly the plaintiff's interest in not having his business impaired as well as the public's—most often identical with the plaintiff's own interest—in being protected against unfair competition and deceit. Except in circumstances in which the various connecting factors happen to coincide, protecting the plaintiff in his market and with respect to his customers or other competitors would seem better designed to advance the objectives of unfair competition law. A number of cases have therefore adopted the reference to the place where the claimant was injured in his business.[8]

competition and therefore excluded. The possibility of a separate Restatement for these areas was envisioned. Wade, Second Restatement of Torts Completed, 65 A.B.A.J. 366, 368 (1978); 4 Restatement (Second) of Torts, Intro. Note to Division Nine, 1–2 (1979). See also System Operations, Inc. v. Scientific Games Dev. Corp., 555 F.2d 1131, 1137 (3d Cir.1977) ("[I]t becomes our obligation to distill from those New Jersey choice-of-law principles a rule by which we can select the applicable body of product disparagement law.").

5. Restatement, Second, Conflict of Laws § 145, cmnt. (f) (1971). See T.G.I. Friday's Inc. v. International Rest. Group, Inc., 569 F.2d 895, 899 (5th Cir.1978); Data General Corp. v. Digital Computer Controls, Inc., 357 A.2d 105, 113 (Del.Ch.1975). Less clear are Texas decisions that focus on the law of the place where "the cause of action arose": General Adjustment Bureau, Inc. v. Fuess, 192 F.Supp. 542, 547 (S.D.Tex.1961); Oliver Gintel, Inc. v. Koslow's, Inc., 355 F.Supp. 236, 239 (N.D.Tex. 1973). See also American Heritage Life Ins. Co. v. Heritage Life Ins. Co., 494 F.2d 3, 15 n.3 (5th Cir.1974); Waples–Platter Cos. v. General Foods Corp., 439 F.Supp. 551 (N.D.Tex.1977) (claim implicitly treated as arising in Texas forum, perhaps because it was also plaintiff's place of business). See also Syntex Ophthalmics, Inc. v. Novicky, 745 F.2d 1423 (Fed.Cir.1984), cert. granted and judgment vacated on other grounds 470 U.S. 1047, 105 S.Ct. 1740, 84 L.Ed.2d 807 (1985) (stating that, in an action for misappropriation of proprietary information or trade secrets, Illinois courts would apply the law of the place where the wrong was committed or the benefit was obtained).

Syntex reaches the result urged in the main text at n.8. However, it is not necessarily a reliable statement of Illinois law because it relies on an Illinois decision dating to the *lex loci*-era of the First Restatement. See Smith v. Dravo Corp., 203 F.2d 369, 373 (7th Cir.1953). With the acceptance of the Second Restatement approach by Illinois, it is therefore not entirely certain whether Illinois will evaluate the interests at stake in the way suggested in the text and thereby arrive at the same result as the court in *Syntex*. The decision in Board of Trade of City of Chicago v. Dow Jones & Co., Inc., 108 Ill.App.3d 681, 439 N.E.2d 526 (1982), aff'd 98 Ill.2d 109, 456 N.E.2d 84 (1983) is also inconclusive. It concludes that "unfair competition is a tort" and that the law applicable to torts is determined on the basis of the most-significant-relationship test. However, the potentially unfair conduct involved in this suit for declaratory relief was to take place in Illinois, and the court's authority for the application of the Second Restatement test to the tort of unfair competition was Ingersoll v. Klein, 46 Ill.2d 42, 262 N.E.2d 593 (Ill.1970) (a wrongful death case).

6. See Honda Assoc., Inc. v. Nozawa Trading, Inc., 374 F.Supp. 886, 892 (S.D.N.Y.1974).

7. See Sims v. Mack Trucks, Inc., 444 F.Supp. 1277, 1281 (E.D.Pa.1978), rev'd on other grounds 608 F.2d 87 (3d Cir.1979), on remand 488 F.Supp. 592 (E.D.Pa.1980).

8. See Addressograph–Multigraph Corp. v. American Expansion Bolt & Mfg. Co., 124 F.2d 706 (7th Cir.1941), cert. denied 316 U.S. 682, 62 S.Ct. 1270, 86 L.Ed. 1755

Recent European codifications, like the Austrian,[9] Dutch,[10] Russian,[11] and Swiss codifications,[12] as well as the proposed Rome II Regulation,[13] employ a similar test.

3. *Alienation of Affections*

§ 17.54 In actions for alienation of affections[1] or for interference with a marriage, the focus is on the place of the defendant's conduct.[2] For example, the Restatement Second calls for the application of the law of the state in which the conduct principally occurred, unless, with respect to the particular issue, some other state has a more significant relationship.[3] The reason for preferring the defendant's place of conduct rather than the place of the spouses' domicile, if different, is said to be that the primary policy for allowing these causes of action is deterrence and punishment rather than payment of compensation.[4] The latest case

(1942); Vanity Fair Mills, Inc. v. T. Eaton Co., 234 F.2d 633 (2d Cir.1956), cert. denied 352 U.S. 871, 77 S.Ct. 96, 1 L.Ed.2d 76 (1956), reh'g denied 352 U.S. 913, 77 S.Ct. 144, 1 L.Ed.2d 120 (1956). Some of the cases cited in nn.5–7 supra also support this proposition. However, they do not represent clear authority because of the presence of other factors and the express reliance on a different methodology.

9. See Federal Statute of 15 June 1978 on Private International Law, 1978 Bundesgesetzblatt 1729, 1734, Art. 48.2 ("Damages and other claims arising from unfair competition shall be judged according to the law of the state where the market affected by the competition is located.").

10. See Act of 11 April 2001Regarding Conflict of Laws on Torts, Art. 4(1), Staatsblad 2001, 190, effective 1 June 2001 (applying law of the "State in whose territory the competitive action affects competitive relations." If the act was directed solely against a specific competitor, then the governing law is the law designated by the general choice-of-law rule for torts.).

11. See Civil Code of the Russian Federation, Art. 1222 (federal law n. 146 of 26 November 2001 enacting the third part of the Civil Code of the Russian Federation, Rossyiskaya Gazeta, n. 49 item 4553, 28/11/2001) (applying law of the "country whose market is affected by such competition" unless the "law or the essence of the obligation" point to another law).

12. See Federal Law on Private International Law of December 16, 1987 Bundesblatt 1988, I, 5, Arts. 136–137 (for unfair competition: law of the state where the effects of the unfair competition are felt or, if the act is designed to harm the business

of the injured party, the law of the place where the business is located; for obstructions to competition: law of the state where the injured party was harmed in its business interests; if foreign law is applicable, damages will be limited by the amount recoverable under Swiss law.)

13. See Commission of the European Communities, Proposal for a Regulation of the European Parliament and the Council on the Law Applicable to Non–Contractual Obligations, COM(2003) 427 final, 2003/0168(COD), Brussels, 22.7.203, Art. 5 (law of the country where competitive relations or the collective interests of consumers are or are likely to be directly and substantially affected. If act affects exclusively the interests of a specific competitor, then law of common domicile or closest connection applies.).

§ 17.54

1. "Heartbalm actions," such as for alienation have been abolished in a number of states, either by statute (heartbalm statutes) or case law. See, e.g., Ill. Rev. Stat., 1980, ch. 40, & 1901 et seq.; Fadgen v. Lenkner, 469 Pa. 272, 365 A.2d 147 (1976). See also Gaden v. Gaden, 29 N.Y.2d 80, 323 N.Y.S.2d 955, 272 N.E.2d 471 (A.D. 1971). However, Utah and a few other states still allow the action. See Williams v. Jeffs, 57 P.3d 232 (Utah App. 2002).

2. See, e.g., Marra v. Bushee, 317 F.Supp. 972 (D.Vt.1970), rev'd and remanded 447 F.2d 1282 (2d Cir.1971) for determination of where the defendant's conduct had principally occurred.

3. Restatement, Second, Conflict of Laws § 154 (1971).

4. See Greco v. Anderson, 615 S.W.2d 429 (Mo.App.1980) (Missouri forum applied

involving such an action stated that the reason for allowing the action is to protect the sanctity of marriages. However, contradicting the above logic, the court did not apply the law of the state in which the defendant acted, which allowed the action, and applied instead the law of the matrimonial domicile, which did not.[5]

4. *Defamation and Invasion of Privacy*

§ 17.55 In defamation and invasion of privacy, the rights of the victim—protection of reputation and the right to be let alone[1]—receive greater emphasis than do policies of deterrence or punishment. If the publication of the libel or slander or the invasion of privacy occurs in a single state, the distinction is usually[2] unnecessary: conduct and injury coincide.[3] The distinction becomes important, however, in cases of multistate publication. An initial question is whether the plaintiff has a single or multiple causes of action.[4] The majority of states has adopted the "single publication rule,"[5] but only a few states have adopted the Uniform Single Publication Act;[6] the latter, moreover, is silent as to

---

Massachusetts law where action for seduction by fraudulent promise to marry had been abolished, when most, but not all, of the acts had taken place in Massachusetts, plaintiff's domicile, and despite reaffirmation of the existence of such a cause of action in Missouri, defendant's domicile at some of the relevant times, Breece v. Jett, 556 S.W.2d 696 (Mo.App.1977)); Funderman v. Mickelson, 7 Fam. L. Rptr. 2419 (Iowa 1981) (finding "unmistakable trend away from alienation suits"); Seidelson, Interest Analysis: The Quest for Perfection and the Frailties of Man, 19 Duq. L. Rev. 207, 213, 225 (1981).

5. See Williams v. Jeffs, 57 P.3d 232 (Utah App. 2002) (applying Arizona law and dismissing an action for alienation of affections filed by an Arizona husband against Utah defendants arising from conduct that occurred in Utah. Utah, but not Arizona, allowed the action.) For critical discussion, see Symeonides, Choice of Law in the American Courts in 2002: Sixteenth Annual Survey, 51 Am.J.Comp.L.1, 24–25 (2003).

§ 17.55

1. Restatement, Second, Torts §§ 652A–I (1976).

2. Restatement, Second, Conflict of Laws § 149 (1971). In unusual circumstances, for instances when the defamation occurs aboard an airplane, a state other than the state of the overflight may have the most significant relationship to the tort. Id., comment (c).

3. Restatement, Second, Conflict of Laws § 149 (defamation) and § 152 (privacy) (1971). See Lawlor v. Gallagher Presi-

dents' Report, Inc., 394 F.Supp. 721 (S.D.N.Y.1975), remanded 538 F.2d 311 (2d Cir.1976); McSurely v. McClellan, 753 F.2d 88 (D.C.Cir.1985), cert. denied, 474 U.S. 1005(8), 106 S.Ct. 525(1), 88 L.Ed.2d 457 (1985). The law applicable to injurious falsehood is the same as for defamation. Id. § 151; see Kemart Corp. v. Printing Arts Research Labs., Inc., 269 F.2d 375 (9th Cir.1959), cert. denied 361 U.S. 893, 80 S.Ct. 197, 4 L.Ed.2d 151 (1959).

4. See O'Reilly v. Curtis Publ'g Co., 31 F.Supp. 364 (D.Mass.1940) (permitting an action for libel in Massachusetts and a separate action for the same libel in thirty-eight other states); Bibie v. T. D. Publ'g Corp., 252 F.Supp. 185 (N.D.Cal.1966); Peacock v. Retail Credit Co., 302 F.Supp. 418 (N.D.Ga. 1969), aff'd 429 F.2d 31 (5th Cir.1970), cert. denied 401 U.S. 938, 91 S.Ct. 927, 28 L.Ed.2d 217 (1971); Davis v. National Broad. Co., 320 F.Supp. 1070 (E.D.La.1970), aff'd 447 F.2d 981 (5th Cir.1971); Toanone v. Williams, 405 F.Supp. 36 (E.D.Pa.1975). The contrary view—limiting the plaintiff to a single cause of action—was adopted in the following decisions: Khaury v. Playboy Publ'ns, Inc., 430 F.Supp. 1342 (S.D.N.Y. 1977); Eliah v. Ucatan Corp., 433 F.Supp. 309 (W.D.N.Y.1977); Rinsley v. Brandt, 446 F.Supp. 850 (D.Kan.1977); Dixson v. Newsweek, Inc., 562 F.2d 626 (10th Cir.1977).

5. Restatement, Second, Torts § 577A, Reporter's Note (1977).

6. 14 Uniform Laws Ann. 375 (1990), in force in: Arizona, California, Idaho, Illinois, New Mexico, North Dakota, and Pennsylvania.

what law applies to the plaintiff's one cause of action. The case law contains numerous ideas for determining the applicable law.[7]

The Restatement Second provides that, in cases of multistate defamation, the governing law is that of the state of the most significant relationship. When the plaintiff is a natural person, that state is "usually" that person's domicile,[8] if the matter complained of was published in that state.[9] When the plaintiff is a corporation or other legal person, that state is usually the state of the principal place of business, provided again that the defamatory item was published in that state.[10] The

7. Five suggestions are contained in Dale Sys. v. General Teleradio, 105 F.Supp. 745 (S.D.N.Y.1952), and nine in Palmisano v. News Syndicate Co., 130 F.Supp. 17 (S.D.N.Y.1955). See also Note, Invasion of Privacy, 19 U. Pitt. L. Rev. 98 (1957).

8. Ehrenzweig, in contrast, urged that the law of the place of acting should apply to all intentional torts, including defamation. See Ehrenzweig, The Place of Acting in International Multistate Torts–Law and Reason versus the Restatement, 36 Minn. L. Rev. 1, 34 (1951); Ehrenzweig, Der Tatort im amerikanischen Kollisionsrecht der ausservertraglichen Schadenersatzansprüche, 1 Festschrift für Rabel 655, 682 et seq. (1954).

9. Restatement (Second) § 150(2) (1971). For cases following this subsection, see, e.g., Ruffin–Steinback v. dePasse, 267 F.3d 457 (6th Cir. 2001); Wells v. Liddy, 186 F.3d 505 (4th Cir. 1999), cert. denied 528 U.S. 1118, 120 S.Ct. 939, 145 L.Ed.2d 817 (2000); Williams v. U.S., 71 F.3d 502 (5th Cir. 1995); Hanley v. Tribune Publ'g Co., 527 F.2d 68, 69, 70 (9th Cir.1975); Motschenbacher v. R.J. Reynolds Tobacco Co., 498 F.2d 821 (9th Cir.1974); Moore v. Greene, 431 F.2d 584 (9th Cir.1970). See also Edwards v. Associated Press, 512 F.2d 258, 265 (5th Cir.1975); Miracle v. New Yorker Magazine, 190 F.Supp.2d 1192 (D.Haw., 2001); Abadian v. Lee, 117 F.Supp.2d 481 (D.Md.2000); Wilson v. Slatalla, 970 F.Supp. 405 (E.D.Pa. 1997); Bryks v. Canadian Broad. Corp., 928 F.Supp. 381 (S.D.N.Y.1996); Winn v. United Press Int'l, 938 F.Supp. 39 (D.D.C. 1996); Fornshill v. Ruddy, 891 F.Supp. 1062 (D.Md.1995); Xuncax v. Gramajo, 886 F.Supp. 162 (D.Mass.1995); Eliah v. Ucatan Corp., 433 F.Supp. 309 (W.D.N.Y.1977). See also Pearce v. E.F. Hutton Group, Inc., 664 F.Supp. 1490 (D.D.C.1987) (even though allegedly defamatory material was published in the District of Columbia, Missouri law applied as law of state of plaintiff's domicile and of the employment relationship giving rise to the publication).

For cases not applying the law of the plaintiff's domicile when it disfavored the plaintiff, see Gravina v. Brunswick Corp., 338 F.Supp. 1 (D.R.I.1972) (invasion of privacy, application of the law of the defendant's headquarters which was more favorable to the plaintiff); Negri v. Schering Corp., 333 F.Supp. 101 (S.D.N.Y.1971) (invasion of privacy, non-resident can recover under New York statute providing civil action for unauthorized commercial use of living person's picture); Ardoyno v. Kyzar, 426 F.Supp. 78 (E.D.La.1976) (application of Mississippi law—defendant's domicile—which allowed punitive damages when the law of the plaintiff's domicile—Louisiana—did not); Ritzmann v. Weekly World News, Inc., 614 F.Supp. 1336 (N.D.Tex.1985); Weyrich v. The New Republic, Inc., 235 F.3d 617 (D.C.Cir.2001); Wainwright's Vacations, LLC v. Pan American Airways Corp., 130 F.Supp.2d 712 (D.Md.2001).

The cases are divided on the law applicable to the "right of publicity." Factors Etc., Inc. v. Pro Arts, Inc., 652 F.2d 278 (2d Cir.1981), cert. denied 456 U.S. 927, 102 S.Ct. 1973, 72 L.Ed.2d 442 (1982), applied the law of the performer's domicile while Bi–Rite Enterps., Inc. v. Bruce Miner Co., Inc., 757 F.2d 440 (1st Cir.1985), applied the law of the residence of the performers' exclusive licensee. *Bi-Rite* rejected the application of the law of nationality or domicile as unworkable and noted that, in *Factors*, the place of domicile and exploitation of the rights coincided. See also Pielemeier, Constitutional Limitations on Choice of Law: The Special Case of Multistate Defamation, 133 U. Pa. L. Rev. 381 (1985).

10. Restatement, Second, § 150(3) (1971). For cases following this subsection, see, e.g., Hamilton Bank v. Kookmin Bank, 245 F.3d 82 (2d Cir.2001); Davidson v. Cao, 211 F.Supp.2d 264 (D.Mass. 2002); La Luna Enterp., Inc. v. CBS Corp., 74 F.Supp.2d 384 (S.D.N.Y.1999); Biospherics, Inc. v. Forbes, Inc., 989 F.Supp. 748 (D.Md.1997).

Restatement establishes the same presumptions in cases of multistate invasion of privacy.[11]

In the rest of the world, the Swiss codification and the proposed Rome II Regulation provide two contrasting choices. The Swiss codification gives plaintiffs a choice between or among the laws of the victim's habitual residence, or the place of injury (subject to a foreseeability proviso) and the defendant's habitual residence or principal place of business.[12] Rome II provides that the law of the forum displaces the otherwise applicable law[13] if the latter would be "contrary to the fundamental principles of the forum as regards freedom of expression and information."[14] This provision is drafted against the backdrop of a decision of the Court of Justice of the European Communities that held that the victim of a defamation may sue the publisher "either before the courts of the [EU] State where the publisher of the defamatory publication is established, which have jurisdiction to award damage for all the harm caused by the defamation, or before the courts of each [EU] State in which the publication was distributed and where the victim claims to have suffered injury to his reputation, which have jurisdiction to rule solely in respect of the harm caused in the [latter] State."[15] Finally, in an important decision, the High Court of Australia held that the law of Victoria would govern the action of a Victoria businessman who had been defamed by the publication in Victoria of material that had been downloaded there from the World Wide Web by subscribers to a business news service conducted by a New York publisher.[16] The plaintiff had limited his claims to the injury he suffered in Victoria and formally pledged not to sue outside Victoria.

B. STATUTORY LIABILITY

1. *No–Fault Liability*

a. *In General*

§ 17.56 Statutes that impose no-fault liability are common, not only in the area of mandatory automobile insurance,[1] but also in other

11. See Restatement (Second) § 153 (1971). For cases following this section, see, e.g.,Pearce v. E.F. Hutton Group, Inc., 664 F.Supp. 1490 (D.D.C. 1987); Faloona by Fredrickson v. Hustler Magazine, Inc., 799 F.2d 1000 (5th Cir. 1986); Dworkin v. Hustler Magazine, Inc., 668 F.Supp. 1408 (C.D.Cal. 1987), aff'd 867 F.2d 1188 (9th Cir.1989), cert. denied 493 U.S. 812, 110 S.Ct. 59, 107 L.Ed.2d 26 (1989); Page v. Something Weird Video, 908 F.Supp. 714 (C.D.Cal.1995) (same result under interest analysis).

12. See Swiss Federal Statute on Private International Law of December 18, 1987, Art. 139 (applicable to claims for injury to rights of personality through the media).

13. The otherwise applicable law can be the law of closest connection, or the parties'

common habitual residence, or the state of injury, in this order. See Commission of the European Communities, Proposal for a Regulation of the European Parliament and the Council on the Law Applicable to Non–Contractual Obligations, Art. 3, COM(2003) 427 final, 2003/0168(COD), Brussels, 22.7.203.

14. Rome II, Art. 6.

15. Fiona Shevill v. Press Alliance SA, Case C 68/93, [1995] ECR I—415, at § 33.

16. Dow Jones & Co. Inc. v. Gutnick, 210 CLR 575, 77 ALJR 255; 194 ALR 433; [2003].

§ 17.56

1. As an example see Michigan's Motor Vehicle Personal and Property Protection, MI.ST. 500.3101: (1) The owner or regis-

areas, such as products liability,[2] pollution law,[3] and medical malpractice.[4] Tort law and no-fault statutes effectuate different policies. Tort law seeks to deter negligence and to protect people from injury. If injury results and negligence is shown, the victim may claim compensation for all losses, economic and non-economic: the tortfeasor must restore what he took from the plaintiff.[5] No-fault statutes seek the efficient and equitable allocation of resources to victims of injury. The focus is not on deterrence but on the assumption that injury is an inevitable cost of automobile transportation, the provision of medical service, and the like. All drivers share the cost of automobile transportation by contributing to

trant of a motor vehicle required to be registered in this state shall maintain security for payment of benefits under personal protection insurance, property protection insurance, and residual liability insurance. Security shall only be required to be in effect during the period the motor vehicle is driven or moved upon a highway. Notwithstanding any other provision in this act, an insurer that has issued an automobile insurance policy on a motor vehicle that is not driven or moved upon a highway may allow the insured owner or registrant of the motor vehicle to delete a portion of the coverage under the policy and maintain the comprehensive coverage portion of the policy in effect.

Comparative Laws in other states: Ark.: A.C.A. §§ 23–89–202 to 23–89–208; Colo.: C.R.S.A. §§ 10–4–701 to 10–4–723; Conn.: C.G.S.A. § 38a–363 et seq.; D.C.: D.C.Code 1981, §§ 35–2101 to 35–2114; Fla.: Stat. Ann. §§ 627.730–627.741; Hawaii: HRS 431:10C–101 to 431:10C–121; Kan.: K.S.A. 40–3101 to 40–3121; Md.: Code 1957, art. 48A, §§ 538 to 547; Mass.: M.G.L.A. c. 90, §§ 34A, 34D, 34M, 34N, 34O; c. 175, § 113B; Minn.: M.S.A. §§ 65B.41 to 65B.71; N.J.: N.J.S.A. 39:6A–1 et seq.; N.Y.: Ins. Law §§ 5101–5109; N.D.: NDCC § 26.1–41–01 to 26.1–41–19; Ore.: O.R.S. § 743.800 et seq.; S.C.: Code 1976, § 38–77–10 et seq.; Utah: U.C.A. § 31A–22–309.

No-fault automobile insurance acts are considered to be constitutional, see Minnesota v. Cuypers, 559 N.W.2d 435 (Minn. App.1997). Mandatory insurance requirement of No–Fault Automobile Insurance Act does not violate federal or state constitutional rights to interstate or intrastate travel, since requirement merely regulates one mode of transportation, does not affect travel by bicycle, bus, train, or airplane, and is narrowly tailored to advance significant public interest of having insured drivers to compensate accident victims.

2. See Viscusi, Wading through the Muddle of Risk–Utility Analysis, 39 Am. U.L. Rev. 573 (1990). See also Malatesta v.

Mitsubishi Aircraft Int'l, 275 Ill.App.3d 370, 211 Ill.Dec. 710, 655 N.E.2d 1093 (1995) (common law claims of strict liability and negligence could form basis, under Connecticut law, for statutory product liability claim. Under Connecticut law, plaintiff may not plead common-law or statutory claims in addition to, or instead of, statutory products liability claim).

3. A very important field in the modern world is the area of pollution law. It is not discussed here broadly because the strict liability is–like in medical malpractice cases–mostly based on case law and not on statutes and therefore not within the coverage of this section. For further considerations see Heimert, Keeping Pigs out of Parlors: Using Nuisance Law to Affect the Location of Pollution, 27 Envtl. L. 403 (1997); Louka, Bringing Polluters before Transnational Courts: Why Industry Should Demand Strict and Unlimited Liability for the Transnational Movements of Hazardous and Radioactive Wastes, 22 Denv. J. Int'l L. & Pol'y 63 (1993); for pollution torts in general see Kanner, Review of Toxic Tort Litigation, C921 ALI–ABA 621(1994) 621; Babich, Understanding the New Era in Environmental Law, 41 S.C. L. Rev. 733(1990).

4. See Kozak, A Review of Federal Medical Malpractice Tort Reform Alternatives, 19 Seton Hall Legis. J. 599 (1995); Smith, Mental Health Malpractice in the 1990s, 28 Hous. L. Rev. 209 (1991). Regarding the special problem of awarding damages after international transportation disasters, see Lowenfeld, Science and Transportation: Accident Compensation in International Transportation, 63 J. Air L. & Com. 425, 425 (1997). See also the statutory liability of the seller of alcoholic beverages and a lessor in Illinois, 235 ILCS 5/6–21.

5. In the words of the California Supreme Court: requiring a wrongdoer to return the injured plaintiff to the status quo ante is simply a matter of "natural justice." Dillon v. Legg, 68 Cal.2d 728, 69 Cal.Rptr. 72, 441 P.2d 912, 914 (1968).

a common fund for the compensation of traffic victims. The actor's fault is no longer a precondition for recovery. In exchange, the victim recovers only the economic loss: tort claims, except when they exceed a specific threshold, are excluded.[6]

Choice-of-law problems may arise in a variety of situations: when tort-state parties are injured in a no-fault state and no-fault liability is imposed on the tort-state driver; when the reverse is the case;[7] when cars each occupied by parties from both types of states collide; or when different no-fault statutes are in issue.[8] In the last case, the first question is which no-fault act applies. There are different state approaches regarding application of no-fault automobile accident statutes. Some states make their own statutes applicable for every accident that occurred within the state, regardless of the domicile of the involved parties,[9] while others award statutory no-fault benefits on the basis of the law of the victim's and/or driver's residence.[10] Another approach is to

6. No-fault benefits and tort exemptions are thus reciprocally linked. But no-fault automobile liability statutes replace only traditional tort remedies arising from non-serious automobile accidents with a statutory scheme. For exemptions see Dougherty, What Constitutes Sufficiently Serious Personal Injury, Disability, Impairment, or the Like to Justify Recovery of Damages Outside of No-Fault Automobile Insurance Coverage, 33 A.L.R. 4th 767 (1981); Gajewski, Automobile Insurance Reform in New Jersey: Could a Pure No-Fault System Provide a Final Solution?, 25 Seton Hall L. Rev. 1219 (1995).

There have been several proposals to allow a choice between no-fault and fault-based car insurance, see O'Connell, A Draft Bill to Allow Choice Between No-Fault and Fault-Based Auto Insurance, (1990); O'Connell/Carroll/Horowitz/Abrahamse/Kaiser, The Costs of Consumer Choice for Auto Insurance in States Without No-Fault Insurance, 54 Md. L. Rev. 281 (1995). Such a possibility today exists in Pennsylvania, see 75 Pa. Cons. Stat. Ann. § 1705(a)(1).

7. See Miller v. Gay and Doucette, 323 Pa.Super. 466, 470 A.2d 1353 (1983) (inhabitants of a state should not be accorded rights not given them by their home state just because a visitor from a state offering higher protection decides to visit their state).

8. See Hooker v. Nationwide Mut. Ins. Co., 1997 WL 337623 (Ohio App. 1997) (unpublished). See generally Stenger, No-Fault Personal Injury Automobile Insurance: The Quebec and New York Experiences and a Proposal for California, 14 Hastings Int'l & Comp. L.Rev. 505, 509 (1991). On the special issue of whether the statute of repose in one state's product liability act is sub-

stantive or procedural, see White v. Marlin Firearms Co., 1996 WL 704378 (Conn.Super.1996) (procedural); Wayne v. Tennessee Valley Auth., 730 F.2d 392 (5th Cir.1984), cert. denied 469 U.S. 1159, 105 S.Ct. 908, 83 L.Ed.2d 922 (1985); Myers v. Hayes Int'l Corp., 701 F.Supp. 618 (M.D.Tenn.1988) (substantive).

9. See Cincinnati Ins. Co. v. Leeper, 1998 WL 123108 (Ohio App. 6 Dist.1998) (unpublished); Fitzgerald v. Austin, 715 So.2d 795 (Ala.Civ.App.1997), reh'g denied (Feb 06, 1998), cert. denied (May 22, 1998): There is no exception to lex loci delicti rule in workers' compensation cases; Commercial Union Ins. Co. v. Porter Hayden Co., 116 Md.App. 605, 698 A.2d 1167 (1997): Maryland had most significant relationship to liability insurance policies delivered in New York and was "principal location of the insured risk"; for a possible exception of that general rule see: Hooker v. Nationwide Mut. Ins. Co., 1997 WL 337623 (Ohio App.1997) (unpublished) (in an action for a personal injury, the local law of the state where the injury occurred determines the rights and liabilities of the parties, unless, with respect to the particular issue, some other state has a more significant relationship under the principles stated in [section] 6 to the occurrence and to the parties, in which event the local law of the other state will be applied).

10. See Miller v. White, 167 Vt. 45, 702 A.2d 392 (1997): Under "most significant relationship" test, Vermont law applied to driver's motion to dismiss passenger's action for personal injuries sustained in single vehicle accident that occurred in Quebec, Canada; driver and passenger were both domiciled in Vermont, accident occurred

apply the law of the state in which the insurance policy was issued and the vehicle was licensed and titled,[11] or to follow a general approach of searching for the law of the state with the most significant relationship.[12]

After finding the applicable law, the second important step is to determine whether and what the injured person can recover under that law. There are two basic approaches of the no-fault statutes regarding coverage: One provides benefits for every person injured in the enacting state, (regardless of domicile, place of vehicle registration, or place of issuance of any insurance police),[13] while the other awards no-fault

during a trip that started and was to end in Vermont, vehicle was registered in Vermont, parties' relationship as long-time friends was centered in Vermont, and Quebec had little interest in determining whether its Automobile Insurance Act precluded rights of action of United States citizen against another United States citizen in United States court; Vaughan v. Nationwide Mut. Ins. Co., 702 A.2d 198 (1997); State Farm Mut. Auto. Ins. Co. v. Boury, 289 Ill.App.3d 903, 682 N.E.2d 238 (1997) (Ohio law rather than Illinois law applied to issue of whether insured parents could recover underinsured motorist (UIM) benefits for loss of consortium under their five automobile policies after their child sustained debilitating brain damage and blindness in automobile accident in Illinois, where insureds lived in Ohio, policies were sold in Ohio, and child's injuries would be suffered and endured in Ohio). See also Restatement, Second, Conflict of Laws §§ 6, 145 (1971).

11. See Jepson v. General Cas. Co. of Wisconsin, 513 N.W.2d 467 (Minn. 1994) (North Dakota, rather than Minnesota law governed enforcement of anti-stacking provisions in automobile policy issued to cover vehicles licensed and titled in North Dakota, where rates were based on North Dakota experience and insured was injured in third state, although insured was Minnesota resident, purchased policy through Minnesota agency, and regularly used at least two of the covered vehicles in Minnesota); O'Connor v. O'Connor, 201 Conn. 632, 519 A.2d 13 (1986) (applying law of parties' common domicile and allowing a tort action that would not be allowed under the no-fault law of Quebec, where accident occurred); Marino v. New York Tel. Co., 944 F.2d 109 (2d Cir.1991) (New York statute setting forth procedures to be followed in disclaiming liability under liability policy delivered or issued for delivery in New York did not apply in an insurance dispute involving a policy which was not delivered or issued for delivery in New York, notwithstanding fact that parties stipulated to ap-

plication of New York law; this will usually also be the domiciliary state of the defendant); Olmstead v. Anderson, 428 Mich. 1, 400 N.W.2d 292 (1987) (where neither party to action arising out of automobile accident was citizen of state where accident occurred, that state had no interest in seeing its limitation of damage provision applied); Miller v. State Farm Mut. Auto. Ins. Co., 87 F.3d 822, 823, 825 (6th Cir.1996). In *Miller*, an Ohio federal district court held that, under Ohio's choice-of-law rules, Pennsylvania law applied because the instant case involved the interpretation of a contract executed in Pennsylvania by a Pennsylvania resident. This court affirmed, holding that this case sounded in contract and must be decided under Pennsylvania law. The true heart of the matter, i.e., whether to apply the "per person" or "per accident" limit stated in the policy, involved the interpretation of an insurance contract executed in Pennsylvania by a Pennsylvania resident with a company licensed to do business in Pennsylvania.

Problems also arise if the insured person moves to another state with a different no-fault statute after issuing of the policy. See New Jersey Mfgs. Ins. Co. v. MacVicar, 307 N.J.Super. 507, 704 A.2d 1343 (1998) (holding that after moving Pennsylvania had become principal location of risk, and thus Pennsylvania law applied).

12. See, e.g., Brown v. Brown, 1997 WL 754545 (Conn.Super.1997).

13. Some states differentiate in benefits to resident and nonresident beneficiaries. See, e.g., Miller v. White, 167 Vt. 45, 702 A.2d 392 (1997) (under Quebec's Automobile Insurance Act (Act), Quebec residents injured in automobile accidents are compensated by the Societe de l'Assurance du Quebec (Societe) on a no-fault basis, regardless of where the accident occurred. R.S.Q.1995 ch. A–25, Automobile Insurance Act § 7; nonresidents injured in a car accident while in Quebec may also recover under the Act, but only to the extent that they are "not responsible for the accident."); see general-

benefits only if the victim is a resident of the enacting state.[14] Especially in the second case, it is important to know whether the recovery under the applicable statute is exclusive, even if the requirements for payments in the special case are not met so that the non-resident victim will be precluded from claiming damages under tort law. The injured non-resident has usually not paid any money to the state's insurance fund so it is questionable whether he can recover instead of this under common law tort claims.[15] Another question is whether the victim may recover additional compensation if the tortfeasor is underinsured. The answer to this question depends on a proper interpretation of the underinsured motorists benefits provision of the applicable statute[16] and the victim's own insurance policy,[17] both of which presuppose an answer to the choice-of-law question of which state's law should govern such interpre-

ly Walsh, "A Stranger in the Promised Land?" The Non–Resident Accident Victim and the Quebec No–Fault Plan, 37 U. New Brunswick L.J. 173, 174–80 (1988) (summarizes different treatment of residents and nonresidents). In a system like Quebec's no-fault compensation is paid to victims by a government agency. See Stenger, No–Fault Personal Injury Automobile Insurance: The Quebec and New York Experiences and a Proposal for California, 14 Hastings Int'l & Comp. L. Rev. 505. Colorado law, § 10–4–707(1)(c), C.R.S. (1987 Repl.Vol. 4A) provides that this coverage shall apply to all accidental bodily injury arising out of accidents occurring within Colorado sustained by a passenger, who is neither the insured nor a relative, while occupying the described motor vehicle with the consent of the insured. See also Budget Rent–A–Car Corp. v. Martin, 855 P.2d 1377 (Colo.1993).

14. Contrary to the system in Quebec, see supra n.13, in which no-fault compensation is paid to victims by a government agency, no-fault insurance in New York for instance is purchased by individual motorists through private insurance companies. The New York's Comprehensive Motor Vehicle Insurance Reparations Act (the New York law) establishes that no-fault insurance is the type of personal injury auto insurance to be offered in the state. Thus, the New York State government does not actually provide insurance coverage as the Quebec government does. However, the State of New York closely regulates many aspects of the no-fault plan, including rates, rate increases, and medical fees charged for treating accident victims. The New York no-fault plan provides coverage for accidents, even if they occur outside New York State. The insured and the members of the insured's household are entitled to first party benefits for accidents occurring anywhere in the United States or Canada. The New York insurer has a lien on any recovery the insured may receive from a tort suit

in the jurisdiction where the accident occurred. See Stenger, No–Fault Personal Injury Automobile Insurance: The Quebec and New York Experiences and a Proposal for California, 14 Hastings Int'l & Comp. L. Rev. 505.

15. See Drake v. Gordon, 848 F.2d 701 (6th Cir.1988) (no-fault automobile scheme applied to nonresidents traveling on Michigan highways, regardless of duration of their stay; failure of out-of-state residents involved in accident to participate in the state security of payment system precluded their recovery under no-fault act, even though provisions of the Act denied them traditional common-law tort recovery).

16. See Kurent v. Farmers Ins. of Columbus, Inc., 62 Ohio St.3d 242, 581 N.E.2d 533 (1991) (when a no-fault state does not recognize claims against tortfeasors, the no-fault-state resident who is insured there does not get underinsured benefits from his own insurer). In Bouley v. Norwich, 222 Conn. 744, 610 A.2d 1245 (1992), and CNA Ins. Co. v. Colman, 222 Conn. 769, 610 A.2d 1257 (1992), the Connecticut Supreme Court ruled that an injured employee is not entitled to receive otherwise applicable underinsured motorist benefits from an automobile policy issued to his employer if the employee's injuries are otherwise compensable under the Workers' Compensation Act. In 1993, the Connecticut legislature, in response to these rulings, enacted Public Act 93–297 so that employees would be entitled to receive uninsured/underinsured motorist benefits under policies issued to their employers even if the employees are also entitled to receive workers' compensation benefits for the same injuries. Public Act 93–297 became effective for automobile accidents occurring on or after January 1, 1994. For accidents occurring before the victim could not be entitled to recovery.

17. See Assetta v. Safety Ins. Co., 43 Mass.App.Ct. 317, 318, 682 N.E.2d 931, 932

tation.[18] The cases are split between those that apply the law of the state of the accident[19] and those that apply the law of the state in which the insured purchased the insurance policy, which is usually the insured's home state and the place where the car is registered.[20]

b. Law Governing the Tortfeasor's Liability

§ 17.57 The territorial approach satisfies important policy concerns of the forum.[1] The states following this approach seek to expedite

(1997) (" 'The responsibility for construing language of an insurance contract is a question of law for the trial judge, and then for the reviewing court ... In interpreting insurance policies, 'we construe the words of the policy in their usual and ordinary sense,' ... and when appropriate, consider what an objectively reasonable insured, reading the relevant policy language would expect to be covered.' " Under Massachusetts law the victim of an underinsured or uninsured can get money if she "is legally entitled to recover from the owner or operator of the ... underinsured ... auto."); Dick v. Motorists Ins. Co., 103 Ohio App.3d 441, 659 N.E.2d 860, 863 (1995). Under Massachusetts law, "legally entitled to recover" has been construed to mean that the insured must show that the underinsured motorist is "at fault" or "negligent" and thus liable in a tort action; Noel v. Metropolitan Property & Liab. Ins. Co., 41 Mass. App.Ct. 593, 597, 672 N.E.2d 119 (1996). Other jurisdictions that have interpreted the phrase are in agreement with Massachusetts' construction. See Baker v. Continental Western Ins. Co., 748 F.Supp. 716, 722 (D.S.D.1990) (legally entitled to recover means that the insured must be able to establish fault on the part of the uninsured/underinsured motorist); Kalhar v. Transamerica Ins. Co., 129 Or.App. 38, 877 P.2d 656, 659 (1994) (same); Rose v. State Farm Mut. Auto. Ins. Co., 821 P.2d 1077, 1078–1079 (Okla.App.1991) (same); Sumwalt v. Allstate Ins. Co., 12 Ohio St.3d 294, 466 N.E.2d 544, 545 (1984) (same); A. Widiss, Uninsured and Underinsured Motorist Insurance, 7.1, 7.2, 34.1 (1995, 1997 Supp.).

18. While one law governs the interpretation of the insurance contract, there is no reason why the same law automatically will govern the disposition of all issues on this case. See Pevoski v. Pevoski, 371 Mass. 358, 360, 358 N.E.2d 416 (1976). The question is which state has the strongest interest (or most significant relationship) in the resolution of the particular issue presented. This can be the place of the accidents or the home state of the victim or the driver. See Aetna Cas. & Sur. Co. v. Thomas Holland, 1997 WL 736518 (Mass.Super.1997); Shope v. State Farm Ins. Co., 122 N.M. 398, 925 P.2d 515 (1996).

19. See, e.g., Kurent v. Farmers Ins. of Columbus, Inc., 62 Ohio St.3d 242, 581 N.E.2d 533 (1991) (when Ohio resident is injured in automobile accident in no-fault state, by resident of that state who is insured under that state's no-fault insurance laws, Ohio resident's legal right to recover from tortfeasor-motorist must be determined with reference to no-fault state's laws, and where no-fault state does not recognize claim against tortfeasor-motorist, Ohio insured is not entitled to collect uninsured motorist benefits from his own insurer); Williams v. State Farm Mut. Auto. Ins. Co., 229 Conn. 359, 641 A.2d 783 (1994); Mitchell v. State Farm Ins. Co., 315 Mont. 281, 68 P.3d 703 (2003); State Farm Mut. Auto. Ins. Co. v. Ballard, 132 N.M. 696, 54 P.3d 537 (2002); Crutchfield v. Landry, 778 So.2d 1249 (La. App. 2001).

20. See, e.g., State Farm Mutual Auto. Ins. Co. v. Gillette, 251 Wis.2d 561, 641 N.W.2d 662, 671 (2002); Travelers Indem. Co. v. Lake, 594 A.2d 38 (Del. 1991); O'Connor v. O'Connor, 201 Conn. 632, 519 A.2d 13 (1986); Thomas v. Hanmer, 109 A.D.2d 80, 489 N.Y.S.2d 802 (1985); Miller v. White, 167 Vt. 45, 702 A.2d 392 (1997); Ohayon v. Safeco Ins. Co. of Illinois, 91 Ohio St.3d 474, 747 N.E.2d 206 (2001); Cecere v. Aetna Ins. Co., 145 N.H. 660, 766 A.2d 696 (2001); Flaherty v. Allstate Ins. Co. 822 A.2d 1159 (Me.2003); Vaughan v. Nationwide Mut. Ins. Co., 702 A.2d 198 (D.C.App.1997); Montgomery v. Farmers Texas County Ins. Co., 786 So.2d 306 (La. App.2001); Zuviceh v. Nationwide Ins. Co. 786 So.2d 340 (La.App. 1st Cir. 2001), writ denied 801 So.2d 373 (La.2001); Southern Farm Bureau Cas. Ins. Co. v. Craven, 79 Ark.App. 423, 89 S.W.3d 369 (2002); Carr v. Isaacs, 2002 WL 553715 (Ohio App. 2002); Reidling v. Meacham, 148 Ohio App.3d 86, 772 N.E.2d 163 (2002); Dreisel v. Metro. Prop. & Cas. Ins. Co., 836 So.2d 347 (La. App. 2002), writ denied 840 So.2d 575 (La. 2003); Swartz v. McNabb, 830 So.2d 1093 (La. App. 2002), writ denied 836 So.2d 117 (La.2003).

§ 17.57

1. Engrafting no-fault liability on all out-of-state drivers may raise constitution-

compensation to victims of automobile accidents, reduce the amount of tort litigation in their courts, and guarantee relatively low automobile insurance rates.

This approach generally eliminates the right of an automobile accident victim to bring any personal injury claim in the state. A state's resident who is injured outside the state generally retains the right to recover damages under the law of the place of injury, and the insurer is subrogated to such rights to the extent the insurer has paid the victim's claim. Generally the insurer is also subrogated to the rights of a resident injured in the state by a nonresident, insofar as the insurer has compensated the resident. In such a case, the nonresident is liable to the insurer to the extent of his or her responsibility as determined by normal liability rules applicable in the state. Finally, the insurer is subrogated to the rights of a nonresident injured in the state by another nonresident to the extent of the benefits paid to the injured party.[2]

In other cases, especially when the plaintiff and the defendant do not have their domicile in the state of the the accident, the domiciliary state has a strong interest in applying its law to this case (domiciliary approach).[3] The domicile of the plaintiff has a significant interest in assuring proper compensation to the victim because the "social and economic repercussions of personal injury" will occur in plaintiff's domicile.[4] The domiciliary state of the defendant also has a significant interest in deterring risky behavior by domiciliaries who cross the border to take advantage of other states' law, and generally has an interest in deterring negligent conduct by its licensed operators, wherever that conduct may occur.

al problems; see Olmstead v. Anderson, 428 Mich. 1, 400 N.W.2d 292 (1987) (state with which defendant automobile driver had no contacts, other than fact that his insurer did business there, was constitutionally impermissible forum for action arising from automobile accident deaths of residents of that state).

2. Vermont, as example, has a traditional tort system of recovery for automobile accidents. Under this scheme, motor vehicle operators compensate third parties who have been injured by the operator's negligence. More often, insurance companies provide the compensation on behalf of their policyholders and the important relationship is between the insurance company and the policyholder, rather than the victim. Traditional tort systems tend to compensate victims at higher levels than no-fault systems and seek to optimize the level of risky activity in society, reduce the occurrence and severity of injury-causing events,

and provide relatively clear standards of conduct.

3. See Wilson v. League Gen. Ins. Co., 195 Mich.App. 705, 491 N.W.2d 642 (1992), appeal denied 442 Mich. 855, 498 N.W.2d 745 (1993) (owner of vehicle, who attended school in Texas and who was involved in accident in Tennessee, was precluded from recovering no-fault benefits for her injuries under automobile policy of her mother, a Michigan resident, even if she were a resident relative, where she neither registered nor insured vehicle in Michigan as required by statute; application of provision precluding coverage for owner or registrant of uninsured vehicle was not limited to automobiles driven on Michigan highways).

4. See Thomas v. Hanmer, 109 A.D.2d 80, 489 N.Y.S.2d 802, 805 (1985) (domicile of plaintiff has significant interest in guaranteeing adequate compensation to victim); O'Connor v. O'Connor, 201 Conn. 632, 519 A.2d 13 (1986); Miller v. White, 167 Vt. 45, 702 A.2d 392 (1997).

The needs of the international system also point to the law of the parties' domicile.[5] In the international sphere it is generally considered appropriate to apply the laws of the domiciliary state to tort claims that involve the residents of a single country, regardless of where the tort took place.[6] In these cases, strict application of the law of the place of the accident would result in preferential treatment of residents, who would reap the benefits of a traditional fault system outside of their home state, while simultaneously denying nonresidents the full benefits of the state's no-fault system for accidents within the state.[7] Conversely, application of the law of the parties' domicile to this case would correspond with international norms and promote consistent treatment of accident victims across borders.[8]

Many[9]—but by no means all[10]—of the cases decided in recent years applied the law of the insured's home state, which usually is also the place of the issuance of the insurance police and the car's registration. A number of reasons serve to explain why such importance is attached to the principal location of the insured risk. This location has an intimate bearing upon the risk's nature and extent and is a factor upon which the terms and conditions of the policy will frequently depend. For example, the cost of automobile liability or of collision insurance will probably be higher if the place where the automobile will be principally garaged during the term of the policy is an urban, as opposed to a rural, community. For these and other reasons, the location of the risk is a matter of intense concern to the parties to the insurance contract. And it can often be assumed that the parties, to the extent that they thought about the matter at all, would expect that the local law of the state where the risk is to be principally located would be applied to determine many of the issues arising under the contract. Likewise, the state where the insured risk will be principally located during the term of the policy has a natural interest in the determination of issues arising under the insurance contract. In the case of an automobile liability policy, the focus is on the location of the insured automobile, whose primary location is known to the parties at the time of entering into the contract.

b. *Coverage of the No–Fault Statutes*

§ 17.58 Some no-fault liability statutes are applicable to all accidents occurring within the enacting state, regardless of whether the injured party or the tortfeasor are insured in that state. On the other side, all limitations of coverage and exclusions are also applicable to

---

5. See Restatement, Second, Conflict of Laws § 6(2)(b) (1971).

6. See Gagnon v. Lucas and Tolofson, 3 S.C.R. 1022, 1060, 120 DLR 4th 289 (1994); Hague Convention on the Law Applicable to Traffic Accidents Art. 4(a), (b) (1961).

7. See Reach v. Pearson, 860 F.Supp. 141, 144 (S.D.N.Y.1994) (application of Quebec law would produce anomalous re-

sults); Reisch v. McGuigan, 745 F.Supp. 56 (1990) (same); O'Connor v. O'Connor, 201 Conn. 632, 519 A.2d 13 (1986) (same).

8. See Miller v. White, 167 Vt. 45, 702 A.2d 392 (1997).

9. See cases cited supra at § 17.56. n.20.

10. See cases cited supra at § 17.56. n.19.

claims arising from instate accidents.[1] These states deny nonresident transients their traditional tort remedies, even if barred from coverage under the statute.[2] But if the statute's requirements are fulfilled, a nonresident victim is entitled to benefits, even if he is insured outside the state.[3] Generally, nonresidents are required to buy insurance if they use a car in the state for a certain period of time[4] and, when they do, they are exempted from tort liability.[5] A few states allow restrictions of coverage in the insurance policy.[6]

A special problem is created by the so-called deemer statutes. These statutes provide a certain minimum insurance coverage to all victims of traffic accidents regardless of fault, and then give them the option (called "verbal option") of choosing full coverage or less than full coverage for certain non-economic losses. The verbal option prohibits suits for non-economic losses if the plaintiff's injury does not rise above a certain threshold (called "verbal threshold"). These statutes differ on how they treat nonresidents involved in an accident in the enacting state. Some statutes are applicable only to residents of the enacting state and exempt nonresidents,[7] while other statutes provide benefits to nonresidents who

§ 17.58

1. Overbaugh v. Strange, 254 Kan. 605, 867 P.2d 1016 (1994) (nonresident owner of motor vehicle operated on Kansas highway is subject to provisions of Kansas Automobile Injury Reparations Act).

2. See for Michigan Drake v. Gordon, 848 F.2d 701 (6th Cir. 1988).

3. Western Nat. Mut. Ins. Co. v. State Farm Ins. Co., 374 N.W.2d 441 (1985) (economic losses sustained by nonresident passenger in accident which occurred in Minnesota were compensable from insurer of Minnesota vehicle in which she was riding, rather than nonresident's out-of-state insurer licensed to do business in Minnesota, where no insured automobile owned by passenger was in state at time of accident); but see State Farm Mut. Auto. Ins. Co. v. Feldman, 359 N.W.2d 57 (Minn. App. 1984) (insurer licensed to do business in Minnesota must afford basic economic loss benefits on accident occurring in Minnesota even though insured is nonresident whose vehicle was not in Minnesota at time of accident).

4. The time limits vary widely; see as an example the 90 days limitation in Florida, West's F.S.A. § 627.733(2): Every nonresident owner or registrant of a motor vehicle which, whether operated or not, has been physically present within this state for more than 90 days during the preceding 365 days shall thereafter maintain security as defined by subsection (3) in effect continuously throughout the period such motor vehicle remains within this state. If the non-resident does not get insurance, he

does not get the benefits of the no-fault law after that time. See Epperson v. Dixie Ins. Co., 461 So.2d 172 (Fla.App.1984), review denied 471 So.2d 43 (Fla. 1985) (Georgia resident injured in insured Florida motor vehicle was barred from recovering personal injury protection benefits under Florida motor vehicle no-fault law from Florida owner's insurer because Georgia resident owned uninsured motor vehicle registered, licensed and garaged in Georgia but driven to work in Florida four or five days each week, so that uninsured vehicle was present in Florida more than 90 of the preceding 365 days).

5. Spence v. Hughes, 485 So.2d 903 (Fla. App. 1986); Johnson v. Liberty Mut. Ins. Co., 297 So.2d 858 (Fla.App.1974).

6. Lord v. Maryland Auto. Ins. Fund, 38 Md.App. 374, 381 A.2d 23 (1977): There is no legislative intent to bar any insurer from imposing a contractual territorial limitation that excludes nonresidents of the State. See Ohio Rev. Code 3937.18.

7. See Mont. Code Ann. § 61–6–303 ("The following vehicles and their drivers are exempt from the provisions of § 61–6–301 ... (9) a vehicle owned by a nonresident if it is currently registered in the owner's resident jurisdiction and he is in compliance with the motor vehicle liability insurance requirements, if any, of that jurisdiction"); 47 Okla. St. Ann. § 7–601(2) ("The nonresident owner of a motor vehicle not registered in this state may give proof of financial responsibility by providing proof of compliance with the financial

do not have no-fault coverage under the law of their home state.[8] At least one statute, that of New Jersey, provides that nonresidents involved in an accident in New Jersey are deemed to have selected the verbal option if they are insured by companies licensed to do business in that state.[9]

2. *Workers' Compensation*

a. *Workers' Compensation Benefits*

§ 17.59 Workers' Compensation statutes have now been adopted in every state.[1] They were designed to grant expedited—if not complete—compensation to workers injured while acting within the scope and course of their employment, without requiring them to prove employer fault.[2] In return for providing this compensation, the employer

responsibility laws of the state in which the vehicle is registered or by filing with the Department a certificate of an insurance company authorized to transact insurance in the state in which the vehicle is registered, or if such nonresident does not own a motor vehicle, then in the state in which the insured resides, provided such certificate otherwise conforms to the provisions of this article.'').

8. See Toter v. Knight, 278 Pa.Super. 547, 420 A.2d 676 (1980) (discussing Pennsylvania's No–Fault Act which provides that if the nonresident is domiciled in a state that provides for a no-fault plan for motor vehicle insurance, the nonresident is denied benefits available under the Pennsylvania Act and is remitted to benefits available under the plan of his home state, but if the nonresident is domiciled in state that does not provide for a no-fault plan then he is entitled to basic benefits provided under Pennsylvania's Act, 40 P.S. §§ 1009.110(c)(1), 1009.201).

9. This statute has been held constitutional against an equal protection challenge. See Whitaker v. DeVilla, 147 N.J. 341, 687 A.2d 738 (1997); see also Taylor v. Rorke, 279 N.J.Super. 63, 652 A.2d 207 (A.D.1995), certification denied 141 N.J. 99, 660 A.2d 1197; Taylor–Segan v. Rajagopal, 275 N.J.Super. 286, 645 A.2d 1272 (A.D. 1994); Adams v. Keystone Ins. Co., 264 N.J.Super. 367, 624 A.2d 1008 (A.D.1993); Dyszel v. Marks, 6 F.3d 116 (3d Cir.1993).

§ 17.59

1. The following federal statutes preempt state law in their respective areas: (1) the Federal Employees Compensation Act (5 U.S.C.A. § 8101); (2) the Federal Employers Liability Act for railroad employees (45 U.S.C.A. § 51); for an overview, see Beethe, Railroads Suing Injured Employees: Should the Federal Employers' Lia-

bility Act Allow Railroads to Recover from Injured Railroad Workers for Property Damages?, 65 UMKC L. Rev. 231 (1996)); (3) the Jones Act for Seamen (46 U.S.C.A. app. § 688, discussed infra § 17.63); and (2) the Longshore and Harbor Workers' Compensation Act (33 U.S.C.A. § 901). Double recovery is impermissible, see Sea–Land Ser. v. Workers' Comp., 41 Cal.App.4th 486, 42 Cal.Rptr.2d 865, 872, 878 (1995), review granted and opinion superseded, 45 Cal. Rptr.2d 644, 902 P.2d 1297 (1995), rev'd 14 Cal.4th 76, 58 Cal.Rptr.2d 190, 925 P.2d 1309 (1996).

2. See Haas, On Reintegrating Workers' Compensation and Employers' Liability, 21 Ga. L. Rev. 843, 846–48 (1987); Lambert, Comment, From Andrews to Woodson and Beyond: The Development of the Intentional Tort Exception to the Exclusive Remedy Provision–Rescuing North Carolina Workers from Treacherous Waters, 20 N.C. Cent. L.J. 164, 167 (1992); see also Jernigan, North Carolina Workers' Compensation § 1–2, at 3 (2d ed. 1995) (describing workers' compensation statutes as a trade-off between employers and employees whereby ''[o]ne gave up the right to common law damages in exchange for guaranteed, though limited, compensation [while] the other gave up liability in exchange for damages being limited to the employee's loss of earning capacity''); Skillern & Bolduan, Insurance Coverage for Employment–Related Claims: Real or Illusory?, SB96 ALI–ABA 87 (1997); Fisher, Royster v. Culp, Inc.: The North Carolina Supreme Court Takes a Stand Against Extending the Premises Exception to the ''Coming and Going'' Rule, 75 N.C. L. Rev. 2505 (1997); Maakestad & Helm, Promoting Workplace Safety and Health in the Post–Regulatory Era: A Primer on Non–OSHA Legal Incentives That Influence Employer Decisions To Control

benefitted from a statutory limit on employee recovery as well as receiving immunity from tort liability.[3] The various state statutes differ in many respects, such as: the kinds and levels of benefits they provide; the precise extent to which they exclude tort remedies against the principal employer, his employees, and related employers and their employees;[4] or allow a second recovery under a sister state's statute;[5] and

Occupational Hazards, 17 N. Ky. L.J. 9, 18 (1989). As to problems concerning workers' reproductive and genetic injuries and their exposure to toxins in the workplace see Macchiaroli Eggen, Toxic Reproductive and Genetic Hazards in the Workplace: Challenging the Myths of the Tort and Workers' Compensation Systems, 60 Fordham L. Rev. 843 (1992).

3. The workers' compensation statutes exclude actions by the injured employee against the employer, officers, directors, agents, servants or employees of the same employer seeking to recover damages in excess of amounts received or receivable from the employer under the workers' compensation statutes. See Cianci v. Nationwide Ins. Co., 659 A.2d 662 (R.I.1995). Generally, exclusivity provisions do not prohibit an action for intentional tortious conduct; see, e.g., Alabama Code §§ 25–5–14, 25–5–52; Alaska Stat. § 23.30.055; Ariz. Rev. Stat. § 23–1022; Cal. Labor Code § 3601; Raines v. Browning–Ferris Indus. of Ala., Inc., 638 So.2d 1334 (Ala.Civ.App.1993); But see Austin v. Ryan's Family Steakhouses, 668 So.2d 806 (Ala.Civ.App.1995) (holding that even if a co-employee was guilty of willful conduct, the plaintiff/employee could not recover from the employer outside the Workers' Compensation Act absent special circumstances); Adams Fruit Co., Inc. v. Barrett, 494 U.S. 638, 110 S.Ct. 1384, 108 L.Ed.2d 585 (1990) (exclusivity provisions in state workers' compensation laws do not bar migrant workers from bringing private action under Migrant and Seasonal Agricultural Worker Protection Act for intentional violations of the Act; see Migrant and Seasonal Agricultural Worker Protection Act, §§ 2 et seq., 504, 29 U.S.C.A. §§ 1801 et seq., § 1854). Furthermore the exclusivity provisions only apply to other remedies sought within the same state; see Dosanjh v. Bhatti, 85 Wash.App. 769, 934 P.2d 1210 (1997) (British Columbia's Workers' Compensation Act permits wrongful death action between co-workers covered by Act in foreign jurisdiction where accident occurred). For choice-of-law cases, see Russell v. Bush & Burchett, Inc., 210 W.Va. 699, 559 S.E.2d 36 (2001), cert. denied 537 U.S. 819, 123 S.Ct. 96, 154 L.Ed.2d 26 (2002); Rigdon v.

Pittsburgh Tank & Tower Co., Inc., 682 So.2d 1303 (La.App. 1996).

4. See supra n. 3, and infra § 17.61. The statutes differ on whether an employee of a subcontractor can sue the general contractor or his employees in tort, or whether an employee of the general contractor can sue the subcontractor. The immediate employer is usually granted such an immunity. Some statutes extend the workers' compensation obligation and corresponding tort immunity to an employer of an independent contractor with respect to the latter's employees and to a general contractor with respect to the employees of a subcontractor.

5. Second recovery is recognized for example under Alaska Statutes § 23.30.011(b). The Maryland Workmen's Compensation Act § 34:15–1 et seq. provides exclusive remedy in Maryland, but not in other jurisdictions, and hence award of compensation in Maryland for death of employee who was killed in that state, but who had been hired by contract of employment in New Jersey, did not bar subsequent award of compensation in New Jersey, upon which the Maryland award was credited, Hudson v. Kingston Contracting Co., 58 N.J.Super. 455, 156 A.2d 491 (1959). A different approach followed in New Jersey: A New Jersey resident who was employed as a truck driver in New York under contract of hiring which was made in New York, and who was injured in New York, was precluded from making claim under New Jersey Compensation Act, even if contract extended to work both in New York as well as New Jersey, where employee received compensation under the New York Workmen's Compensation Act, and hence made an "election" to proceed under the New York Act; Ritenour v. Creamery Service, 19 N.J.Misc. 82, 17 A.2d 283 (1941). See Brooks v. Eastern Airlines, Inc., 634 So.2d 809, 812 (Fla.App.1994) (holding that Florida statute providing that receipt of workers' compensation benefits under the laws of other state precluded additional benefits under Florida law was not limited to payments made in two or more states for coinciding terms of disability but also applied to a claimant who lawfully obtained benefits under the law of another state during an altogether separate interval of disability).

the way they handle possible tort claims by the employee against third parties,[6] or reimbursement claims by the employer against third parties.[7]

The most common choice-of-law questions arise when the employee is injured in a state other than the state of the employment contract or the employment relationship. When the employee is seeking only worker's compensation benefits, both the choice-of-law test and the constitutional-law test[8] are simple and appropriately lenient. Courts award such benefits under the law of: the state of injury,[9] the state where the contract of employment was concluded;[10] the state where the employment was principally located;[11] the state of the employer's place of

6. Most statutes permit independent tort actions against third parties at the same time. See, e.g., Ala. Code § 25–5–1. But see Colo. Stat. § 8–41–203 (requiring the injured employee to elect in writing between compensation under the Act or a tort remedy against the third party); Del. Workers Comp. Act, 19 Del.C. § 2363 (allowing employer to bring a tort action against the third party on the employee's behalf, if the latter fails to do so within a specified period from his injury); Hawaii, HRS § 386–8 (same); Ark. Code Ann. § 11–9–410 (allowing employer to join in an action by the employee against the third party and allocating recovery between the two plaintiffs); Ala. Code § 25–5–1 (providing for employer reimbursement from proceeds of tort action against third party); Fla. Stat. Ann. § 440.39 (same).

7. For example, such reimbursement is required under the laws of California, see Cal. Labor Code § 3852, Alabama, and Florida, see supra n.6, but not of Ohio. See Dailey v. Dallas Carriers Corp., 43 Cal. App.4th 720, 51 Cal.Rptr.2d 48, 51 (1996) (applying California law, which required third-party tortfeasors to reimburse employers for workers' compensation benefits, and holding that Ohio law, which disallowed reimbursement, was inconsistent with fundamental California policy); Knappenberger v. Bittner, 524 F.Supp. 777 (W.D.Pa.1981) (since no subrogation rights exist under Ohio workers' compensation law, it was not necessary to join workers' compensation insurer in a negligence action by an Ohio driver against a Pennsylvania driver arising out of an accident in Pennsylvania).

8. As noted in chapter 3, choice of law in the United States is subject to no constitutional restraint other than that the state of the applicable law must have a sufficient relationship to the issue and to the person, thing or occurrence as to make application of its law reasonable. The same is true in the area of workers' compensation. Under this standard, it seems permissible for a state to apply its workers compensation

statute if that state meets one or more of the following requirements: the employee was injured there; the employment was principally located there; the employer supervised the employee's activities from a place of business in the state; the state has the most significant relationship with respect to the employment contract to the issue of workers compensation; the parties have agreed in the contract of employment or otherwise that their rights would be governed by the workers compensation act of the state; or the state has some other reasonable relationship to the occurrence, the parties and the employment.

9. See Pacific Employers Ins. Co. v. Industrial Acc. Comm'n, 306 U.S. 493, 59 S.Ct. 629, 83 L.Ed. 940 (1939); Restatement, Second, Conflict of Laws § 181(a) (1971); L.R. Willson & Sons, Inc. v. PMA Group, 867 F.Supp. 335 (D.Md.1994), aff'd 62 F.3d 1415 (4th Cir.1995); Cleveland v. U.S. Printing Ink, Inc., 218 Conn. 181, 588 A.2d 194, 199 (1991); Powell v. Sappington, 495 So.2d 569, 571 (Ala.1986); Miller v. Hirschbach Motor Lines, Inc., 714 S.W.2d 652, 655 (Mo.App.1986); Dominion Caisson Corp. v. Clark, 614 A.2d 529 (D.C.App. 1992).

10. See Alaska Packers Ass'n v. Industrial Accident Comm'n, 294 U.S. 532, 55 S.Ct. 518, 79 L.Ed. 1044 (1935); Carrier Corp. v. Home Ins. Co., 43 Conn.Supp. 182, 648 A.2d 665, 666 (1994); Bolton v. Tulane Univ. of La., 692 So.2d 1113 (La.App.1997), writ denied 701 So.2d 982 (La.1997); Moore v. KLLM, Inc., 673 So.2d 1268 (La.App. 1996); D.L. Peoples Group, Inc. v. Hawley, 804 So.2d 561 (Fla. App. 2002) (holding that the employment contract was made in Florida, because the employer signed the contract there, and thus the employee who worked and was injured in Missouri was eligible for benefits under Florida law). But see, Burse v. American Int'l Airways, Inc., 262 Conn. 31, 808 A.2d 672 (2002) (requiring a "significant relationship" with the state of the contract).

11. See Restatement, Second, Conflict of Laws § 181(b) (1971); Pimental v.

business;[12] of the employee's home state;[13] the forum state, if the contract contained a choice-of-law clause to that effect;[14] or the state with the most significant relationship to the employment relationship or the accident.[15] It is generally held that workers' compensation benefits may be granted under the workers' compensation statute of a state of the United States, although the statute of a sister state also is applicable.[16]

b. Statutory Benefits and Tort Immunity

§ 17.60 However, the choice-of-law question, and to a lesser extent the constitutional question, is more difficult when the employee is seeking tort remedies—rather than, or in addition to—workers' compensation benefits, such as when the employee sues a general contractor or

Cherne Indus., 1996 WL 456373 (Conn.Super.1996); Carolina v. Romel Iron Works, 1994 WL 700424 (Conn.Super.1994); Way v. Sears, Roebuck, 1993 WL 540205 (Conn.Super.1993); Afflerbach et al. v. Furry, 1993 WL 465609 (Conn.Super.1993); Cleveland v. U.S. Printing Ink, Inc., et al., 218 Conn. 181, 588 A.2d 194 (1991); Burse v. American Int'l Airways, Inc., 262 Conn. 31, 808 A.2d 672 (2002); Pimental v. Cherne Indus., Inc., 46 Conn.App. 142, 698 A.2d 361 (1997), cert.denied 243 Conn. 922, 701 A.2d 343 (1997).

12. See Restatement, Second, Conflict of Laws § 181(c) (1971); Fliehler v. Uninsured Employers Fund, 310 Mont. 99, 48 P.3d 746 (2002) (holding that, although the employee worked outside Montana, his employment duties were "primarily controlled from Montana," and thus he was eligible for workers' compensation benefits under Montana law); Seubert Excavators, Inc. v. Anderson Logging Co., 126 Idaho 648, 889 P.2d 82 (1995); Frugard v. Pritchard, 112 N.C.App. 84, 434 S.E.2d 620 (1993); Malatesta v. Mitsubishi Aircraft Int'l, 275 Ill. App.3d 370, 211 Ill.Dec. 710, 655 N.E.2d 1093 (1995) (one of the factors considered).

13. See Cardillo v. Liberty Mut. Ins. Co., 330 U.S. 469, 67 S.Ct. 801, 91 L.Ed. 1028 (1947); Henriksen v. Younglove Const., 540 N.W.2d 254, 259 (Iowa 1995).

14. See Restatement, Second, Conflict of Laws § 181(e) (1971). However, most courts would not enforce choice-of-law clauses that exclude the application of the forum state's worker compensation law. See L.R. Willson & Sons, Inc. v. PMA Group, 867 F.Supp. 335 (D.Md.1994), aff'd 62 F.3d 1415 (4th Cir.1995); Rock v. Workmen's Comp. Appeal Bd., 92 Pa.Cmwlth. 491, 500 A.2d 183 (1985); Robert M. Neff v. W.C.A.B., 155 Pa.Cmwlth. 44, 624 A.2d 727 (1993); Miller v. Hirschbach Motor Lines, Inc., 714 S.W.2d 652, 655 (Mo.App.1986).

See also McIlvaine Trucking, Inc. v. Workers' Comp. Appeal Bd. (States), 570 Pa. 662, 810 A.2d 1280 (2002) (holding that an employee injured in Pennsylvania was eligible for benefits under Pennsylvania's workers' compensation system, despite a choice-of-law clause in the employment contract providing for the application of West Virginia law).

15. See Burse v. American Int'l Airways, Inc., 262 Conn. 31, 808 A.2d 672 (2002); Benoit v. Test Systems, Inc., 142 N.H. 47, 694 A.2d 992 (1997).

16. See Thomas v. Washington Gas Light, 448 U.S. 261, 100 S.Ct. 2647, 65 L.Ed.2d 757 (1980); Industrial Comm'n of Wis. v. McCartin, 330 U.S. 622, 67 S.Ct. 886, 91 L.Ed. 1140 (1947); Restatement, Second, Conflict of Laws § 182 (1971); Cleveland v. U.S. Printing Ink, Inc., 218 Conn. 181, 588 A.2d 194 (1991); L.R. Willson & Sons v. PMA Group, 867 F.Supp. 335 (D.Md.1994), aff'd 62 F.3d 1415 (4th Cir. 1995); Bryant v. Seward, 490 S.W.2d 497, 499 (Tenn.1973); Director, Office Workers' Comp., etc. v. National Van Lines, Inc., 613 F.2d 972, 981 (D.C.Cir.1979), cert. denied 448 U.S. 907, 100 S.Ct. 3049, 65 L.Ed.2d 1136 (1980); Roadway Exp., Inc. v. Warren, 163 Ga.App. 759, 295 S.E.2d 743, 746 (1982), cert. dismissed 464 U.S. 988, 104 S.Ct. 476, 78 L.Ed.2d 675 (1983); Brooks v. Eastern Airlines, Inc., 634 So.2d 809, 812 (Fla.App.1994); M & G Convoy, Inc. v. Mauk, 85 Md.App. 394, 584 A.2d 101, 105 (Md.Spec.App.1991), cert. denied 324 Md. 312, 596 A.2d 1078 (1991); Dailey v. Dallas Carriers Corp., 43 Cal.App.4th 720, 51 Cal. Rptr.2d 48, 51 (1996); M & G Convoy, Inc. v. Mauk, 85 Md.App. 394, 584 A.2d 101, 105 (Md.Spec.App.1991), cert. denied 324 Md. 312, 596 A.2d 1078 (1991). But see Brooks v. Eastern Airlines, Inc., 634 So.2d 809, 812 (Fla. App. 1994).

another employer who is immune from a tort action under the statutes of one but not all involved states.

From a constitutional perspective, a state that has any one of the contact listed above may apply its law to hold a defendant liable for tort, even though the defendant is declared immune from such liability by the worker's compensation statute of a sister state under which the plaintiff has obtained, or could obtain, an award against *another* person.[1] The same should be true even if the plaintiff *could* obtain, but has not obtained, an award against the defendant himself. It is uncertain whether a state may apply its local law to impose a tort liability on a defendant who is declared immune from such liability by the worker's compensation statute of a sister state under which the plaintiff has *already* obtained an award against the defendant. Although the Supreme Court has held that a state may grant supplemental workers' compensation benefits to a claimant who previously received similar benefits against the same person under the statute of a sister state,[2] it is doubtful that the Court will adopt the same solution for cases in which the claimant seeks recovery *in tort*. The award of supplemental workers' compensation benefits is not repugnant to the basic principle of workers' compensation, which is to impose absolute but limited liability upon the employer. In contrast, subjecting a party who already provided such benefits to further unlimited liability in tort would frustrate the workers' compensation policy of the state in which the award was rendered.[3]

Regarding choice of law, the Restatement (Second) provides that a defendant will be accorded immunity from tort liability if the defendant enjoys such immunity under the workers' compensation statute of a state that (1) requires the defendant to provide insurance against the particular risk and provides benefits for the plaintiff ; *and* (2) is also state of the injury, the principal location of the employment, the place from which the employer supervised the employee's activities, or has the most significant relationship to the contract of employment with respect to the issue of workers' compensation.[4] In practice, things do not work out as smoothly as the Restatement drafters envisioned, precisely because the contacts listed in (2) may be in different states that have conflicting workers' compensation statutes. Although the majority of cases seem to reach the result the Restatement contemplates by accord-

§ 17.60

1. Carroll v. Lanza, 349 U.S. 408, 75 S.Ct. 804, 99 L.Ed. 1183 (1955).

2. See Thomas v. Washington Gas Light, 448 U.S. 261, 100 S.Ct. 2647, 65 L.Ed.2d 757 (1980); Industrial Comm'n of Wisconsin v. McCartin, 330 U.S. 622, 67 S.Ct. 886, 91 L.Ed. 1140 (1947); Restatement, Second, Conflict of Laws § 182, cmnt. b (1971).

3. See Restatement, Second, Conflict of Laws § 183, cmnt. c (1971). A person declared immune from tort liability to an injured employee by an applicable workers'

compensation statute may nevertheless be liable for contribution or indemnity to a third person against whom a judgment in tort has been obtained. Whether he will be held liable is determined by the law selected by application of the rule of § 173. See Restatement, Second, Conflict of Laws § 184 cmt. c (1971).

4. See Restatement, Second, Conflict of Laws § 184(b) (1971). If the plaintiff already obtained an award, the defendant is entitled to immunity without having to show the connections listed in (2).

ing immunity to the defendant,[5] one also encounters cases that, for different reasons and in various circumstances, apply a law that does not accord such immunity.[6]

c. Exclusivity With Regard to Subcontractors and Their Employees

§ 17.61 In an employment relationship special problems of recovery can arise with regard to subcontractors and their employees. For example, if the subcontractor is injured, then the question arises whether the subcontractor is deemed to be an employee of the general employer under the applicable statute.[1] A more common question is whether the general contractor is deemed to be an employer of the subcontractor's employees, in which case the general contractor is required to provide coverage but is also immunized from tort liability under the applicable act.[2] Choice-of-law questions abound because many

5. See, e.g., Eger v. E.I. Du Pont De-Nemours Co., 110 N.J. 133, 539 A.2d 1213 (1988); Stuart v. Colorado Interstate Gas Co., 271 F.3d 1221 (10th Cir. 2001); Tucci v. Club Mediterranee, S.A., 89 Cal.App.4th 180, 107 Cal.Rptr.2d 401 (2001); Banks v. Virginia Elec. & Power Co., 205 F.3d 1332 (4th Cir. 2000), cert. denied 531 U.S. 815, 121 S.Ct. 50, 148 L.Ed.2d 19 (2000); Ricci v. Alternative Energy Inc., 211 F.3d 157 (1st Cir. 2000); Foshee v. Torch Operating Co., 763 So.2d 82 (La. App. 2000), writ denied 772 So.2d 658 (La.2000); Marion Power Shovel Co. v. Hargis, 698 So.2d 1246 (Fla. App. 1997); Littlefield v. Mobil Explor. & Prod., 988 F.Supp. 1403 (D.Utah 1996); Garcia v. American Airlines, Inc., 12 F.3d 308 (1st Cir. 1993); Duhon v. Union Pacific Res. Co., 43 F.3d 1011 (5th Cir. 1995); McBride v. Whiting–Turner Contr. Co., 1993 WL 489487 (Del. Super. 1993), aff'd. 645 A.2d 568 (Del. 1994); Farias v. Mattel, Inc., 153 Ariz. 113, 735 P.2d 143 (App. 1986).

6. See, e.g., Hughes Wood Products, Inc. v. Wagner, 18 S.W.3d 202 (Tex. 2000); Dominion Caisson Corp. v. Clark, 614 A.2d 529 (D.C.App. 1992); Braxton v. Anco Elec., Inc., 330 N.C. 124, 409 S.E.2d 914 (1991); Reid v. Hansen, 440 N.W.2d 598 (Iowa 1989); Connor v. Hauch, 50 Md.App. 217, 437 A.2d 661, 663 (1981), aff'd 295 Md. 120, 453 A.2d 1207 (1983); Powell v. Erb, 349 Md. 791, 709 A.2d 1294 (1998); Bishop v. Twiford, 317 Md. 170, 562 A.2d 1238 (1989); Kubasko v. Pfizer, Inc., 2000 WL 1211219 (Del.Super. 2000); Parra v. Larchmont Farms, Inc., 942 S.W.2d 6 (Tex. App. 1996); Osborn v. Kinnington, 787 S.W.2d 417 (Tex.App. 1990).

§ 17.61

1. See, e.g., Benner v. Wichman, 874 P.2d 949 (Alaska 1994) (Alaska act does not bar a tort action against a defendant who, under the relative nature of the work test, was a subcontractor, not an employee, of plaintiff's employer).

Consistent with the intent of the workers' compensation schemes to provide exclusive liability of employers, a general contractor should be protected from a subcontractor's claim for contribution for damages for injury sustained by a contractor's employee as result of subcontractor's negligence. Williams v. White Mountain Const. Co., 749 P.2d 423 (Colo. 1988).

2. See Cuffe v. Sanders Constr. Co., 748 P.2d 328 (Alaska 1988) (when a general contractor injures a subcontractor's employee by his own affirmative act of negligence, the general contractor remains liable without regard to the extent of his control over the subcontractor's work); Miller v. Northside Danzi Constr. Co., 629 P.2d 1389 (Alaska 1981) (a general contractor who, by operation of the contractor-under clause contained in Alaska Stats. § 23.30.045(a), has been required to pay workers' compensation benefits to the employee of an uninsured subcontractor is not an employer for purposes of tort immunity under this section, but he may set-off the amount of benefits paid to the subcontractor's employee). Statutorily authorized waiver of workers' compensation executed by subcontractor's employee does not relieve the general contractor of its obligation to provide coverage for the employee under statutory provision that deems the contractor to be the employer of the subcontractor's employees. See, e.g., Dominion Caisson Corp. v. Clark, 614 A.2d 529 (D.C.App. 1992) (the District's workers' compensation scheme does not extend statutory liability (and corresponding tort immunity) up the ladder of subcontrac-

of these cases involve at least two potential "employers" and contractual relationships, and often more than two states, each with different definitions and requirements. The Restatement (Second) provides the same choices in favor of tort immunity as described in the preceding section,[3] but does not answer the question of which state's definitions should prevail. The cases have not produced clear patterns.[4]

d. Mutual Employment for Benefit of Two Employers

§ 17.62   Where the employee is performing services for the mutual benefit of two employers at the time of the accident, such simultaneous employment should carry with it the statutory immunity afforded co-employees under the workers' compensation act. Before an employee may avail himself of such immunity, however, he must at minimum offer evidence sufficient to establish that such mutual employment in fact existed at the time of the accident for which the immunity is sought, and such evidence must be sufficient to establish the existence of an express or implied employment agreement between the parties.[1]

tors to the owner or general contractor; only the immediate employer is immune from tort liability); Goldsmith v. Allied Bldg. Components, Inc., 833 S.W.2d 378 (Ky.1992) (summary judgment is precluded when a genuine issue of material fact exists about the subcontractor's entitlement to the "up the ladder" defense so as to be entitled to invoke the exclusivity of workers' compensation remedies); Salyer v. Mason Technologies, Inc., 690 So.2d 1183 (Miss. 1997) (prime contractor was statutory employer of sub-subcontractor's employee, and thus, was immune from tort liability where sub-subcontractor provided compensation coverage to its employees pursuant to its contract with prime contractor); N.M. Stat. Ann. § 52–1–22 (a statutory-employer provision to make the general contractor liable for compensation benefits to subcontractor's employees also carries with it immunity from tort liability); Romero v. Shumate Constructors, Inc., 119 N.M. 58, 888 P.2d 940 (App.1994), rev'd on other grounds sub nom. Harger v. Structural Servs., 121 N.M. 657, 916 P.2d 1324 (1996); Boone v. Huntington & Guerry Elec. Co., 311 S.C. 550, 430 S.E.2d 507 (1993) (the statute's exclusivity provisions do not extend immunity to a subcontractor sued for negligence by the employee of the business owner, even though the statute makes the subcontractor a "statutory employee" of the owner for the purposes of workers' compensation liability).

3. See Restatement (Second) § 184, described supra § 17.60 at n.20.

4. See, e.g., Eger v. E.I. Du Pont De-Nemours Co., 110 N.J. 133, 539 A.2d 1213

(1988) (according immunity to general contractor under the law of the accident state); Stuart v. Colorado Interstate Gas Co., 271 F.3d 1221 (10th Cir. 2001) (same); Duhon v. Union Pacific Resources Co., 43 F.3d 1011 (5th Cir. 1995) (same); Braxton v. Anco Elec., Inc., 330 N.C. 124, 409 S.E.2d 914 (1991) (refusing to apply law of accident state which accorded immunity to other subcontractor); Dominion Caisson Corp. v. Clark, 614 A.2d 529 (D.C. 1992) (applying law of accident state which did not recognize the immunity of another subcontractor); Busby v. Perini Corp., 110 R.I. 49, 290 A.2d 210 (1972) (according immunity to general contractor under the law of the state in which both contractual relationships were centered); Banks v. Va. Elec. & Power Co., 205 F.3d 1332 (4th Cir. 2000), cert. denied 531 U.S. 815, 121 S.Ct. 50, 148 L.Ed.2d 19 (2000) (applying Virginia law and holding that a Delaware domiciliary employed in Maryland by a Maryland employer and injured in Virginia while working for a Virginia employer was a borrowed servant of the latter employer and thus was not entitled to a tort action); Foshee v. Torch Operating Co., 763 So.2d 82 (La. App. 2000), writ denied 772 So.2d 658 (La. 2000) (applying Texas law and holding that a Louisiana employee who was injured in Texas was the borrowed servant of a Texas employer and thus was not entitled to a tort action).

§ 17.62

1. Cuffe v. Sanders Constr. Co., 748 P.2d 328 (Alaska 1988).

C. ADMIRALTY[1]

§ 17.63 In the United States, contrary to some early case law, torts in navigable waters are now governed extensively by general (federal) maritime law.[2] However, when the tort is not one of a "maritime nature"[3] but is merely a tort that happens to have occurred in navigable waters, state law will usually be employed.[4] In selecting a state law under admiralty choice-of-law rules, federal courts use a most-significant-relationship approach.[5]

§ 17.63

1. For comprehensive discussion, see A.A. Ehrenzweig, Private International Law 196 et seq. (1967); Weintraub, Admiralty Choice-of-Law Rules for Damages, 28 J.Mar. L. & Com. 237 (1997); Symposium, Choice of Law and Admiralty, 7 Maritime Lawyer No. 2 (1982); Symeonides, Maritime Conflicts of Law From the Perspective of Modern Choice of Law Methodology, 7 Maritime Lawyer 223 (1982).

2. Moragne v. States Marine Lines, Inc., 398 U.S. 375, 90 S.Ct. 1772, 26 L.Ed.2d 339 (1970), on remand 446 F.2d 906 (5th Cir. 1971) ("Navigable waters of the United States," within the meaning of the federal Longshoremen's and Harbor Workers' Compensation Act, which limits coverage to injury occurring on such navigable waters, were held to include the high seas in a case in which injury and death occurred on the Atlantic Ocean 135 miles off the coast of the United States); Cove Tankers Corp. v. United Ship Repair, Inc., 528 F.Supp. 101 (S.D.N.Y.1981), aff'd 683 F.2d 38 (2d Cir. 1982). See also Wilder v. Placid Oil Co., 611 F.Supp. 841 (W.D.La.1985), aff'd 861 F.2d 1374 (5th Cir.1988) (discussion of what constitutes navigable waters for specific purpose of federal admiralty jurisdiction, finding Catahoula Lake, La., to be such a navigable water).

3. For the criteria for determining whether the tort is maritime, see Jerome B. Grubart, Inc. v. Great Lakes Dredge & Dock Co., 513 U.S. 527, 529–34, 115 S.Ct. 1043, 130 L.Ed.2d 1024 (1995).

4. Thomas v. United Air Lines, Inc., 24 N.Y.2d 714, 301 N.Y.S.2d 973, 249 N.E.2d 755 (1969), cert. denied 396 U.S. 991, 90 S.Ct. 484, 24 L.Ed.2d 453 (1969). See also Sea–Land Serv., Inc. v. Director, 540 F.2d 629 (3d Cir.1976); Oman v. Johns–Manville Corp., 764 F.2d 224 (4th Cir.1985), cert. denied 474 U.S. 970, 106 S.Ct. 351, 88 L.Ed.2d 319 (1985) (there is no admiralty jurisdiction over damage claims by land-based ship repair or construction workers for employment-related, asbestos-induced disease; for other attempts to bring asbestos litigation under federal law see supra § 3.54 n.18); Dierker v. Gypsum Transp., Ltd., 606 F.Supp. 566 (E.D.La.1985) (ship repairman not entitled to recover under federal law for mental anguish suffered when witnessing fatal crushing of fellow worker).

In wrongful death cases that occur on the high seas, but are not of a maritime nature (most obviously air crashes), the federal Death on the High Seas Act, 46 U.S.C. §§ 761–767 applies. See Zicherman v. Korean Air Lines Co., 516 U.S. 217, 116 S.Ct. 629, 133 L.Ed.2d 596 (1996). At least one circuit has recently interpreted the term "high seas" to exclude any water within the territorial waters of the United States, which now extend 24 nautical miles from shore. *See* In re Air Crash Off Long Island, New York, 209 F.3d 200 (2d Cir.2000). Air crashes resulting in death within territorial waters are thus governed by the applicable state law.

For cases involving conduct on internal navigable waters (e.g., serving of excessive liquor on a riverboat casino) and causing injury on land, see Horak v. Argosy Gaming Co., 648 N.W.2d 137 (Iowa 2002); Quinn v. St. Charles Gaming Co., Inc., 815 So.2d 963 (La. App. 2002) (writ denied 813 So.2d 412 (La. 2002); Young v. Players Lake Charles, L.L.C., 47 F.Supp.2d 832 (S.D. Tex. 1999). For a case involving the converse pattern, see Szollosy v. Hyatt Corp., 208 F.Supp.2d 205 (D. Conn. 2002) (product liability conflict arising from injury on navigable waters).

5. Calhoun v. Yamaha Motor Corp., U.S.A., 216 F.3d 338 (3d Cir.2000), on remand from 516 U.S. 199, 116 S.Ct. 619, 133 L.Ed.2d 578 (1996), cert. denied 531 U.S. 1037, 121 S.Ct. 627, 148 L.Ed.2d 536 (2000); Albany Ins. Co. v. Anh Thi Kieu, 927 F.2d 882, 891 (5th Cir.), cert. denied 502 U.S. 901, 112 S.Ct. 279, 116 L.Ed.2d 230 (1991).

When the case concerns injuries sustained by a "blue water seaman,"[6] the initial question is the applicability of the federal Jones Act.[7] The Act provides a remedy for "any seaman who shall suffer personal injury in the course of his employment." The Act clearly applies to American seamen[8] and American ships,[9] but taken in its "literal catholicity,"[10] the Act would also extend to foreign seamen injured on foreign vessels while in foreign waters. The case law, particularly the Supreme Court's *Lauritzen–Romero–Rhoditis*[11] trilogy, has restricted the Act's application to cases involving American seamen or having certain American contacts.

In *Lauritzen*, the Court enunciated a new methodology for determining whether the Jones Act applies to a maritime tort with foreign elements: rather than giving controlling significance to the place of the tort, one should engage in "ascertaining and valuing points of contact between the transaction and the states of governments whose competing laws are involved ... [and] weighing the significance of one or more connecting factors between the shipping transaction regulated and the national interest served by the assertion of authority."[12] The Court listed seven such connecting factors or contacts: 1) the place of wrongful act; 2) the law of the flag; 3) the allegiance or domicile of the injured; 4) the allegiance of the defendant shipowner; 5) the place of the contract; 6) the inaccessibility of the foreign forum; and 7) the law of the forum. Applying this test, the Court held that the Jones Act was inapplicable to an action brought by a Danish seaman for injuries he suffered aboard a Danish vessel in Cuban territorial waters. The plaintiff's only connection with the United States was that he had joined the ship in New York where he signed his employment contract. The contract itself, however, was written in Danish and contained a Danish choice-of-law clause.

The *Romero* case was similar to *Lauritzen*, except that the foreign seaman's injury had occurred while the foreign-flag ship was in American waters.[13] The Court dismissed the argument that the American locus

6. In 1982, the Jones Act was amended so as to prevent foreign "brown-water" seamen who are injured while working in oil exploration in foreign territorial waters from suing in the United States under *American* law, unless they establish that they have no remedy under the law of the country of their citizenship or residence or the foreign country in whose waters they suffered the injury. See 46 U.S.C. § 688(b)(1)-(2) as amended in 1982. Whether the amendment also purports to bar claims under *foreign* law is unclear. See Jackson v. North Bank Towing Corp., 213 F.3d 885 (5th Cir. 2000); Jackson v. North Bank Towing Corp., 742 So.2d 1 (La. App. 1999).

7. Act of June 5, 1920, Ch. 250, § 33, 41 Stat. 1007 (1920), codified as 46 U.S.C. § 688 as amended in 1982.

8. See infra n. 22.

9. See infra n. 21.

10. Lauritzen v. Larsen, 345 U.S. 571, 576, 73 S.Ct. 921, 97 L.Ed. 1254 (1953).

11. See Lauritzen v. Larsen, 345 U.S. 571, 73 S.Ct. 921, 97 L.Ed. 1254 (1953), Romero v. Int'l Terminal Operating Co., 358 U.S. 354, 79 S.Ct. 468, 3 L.Ed.2d 368 (1959), and Hellenic Lines Ltd. v. Rhoditis, 398 U.S. 306, 90 S.Ct. 1731, 26 L.Ed.2d 252 (1970).

12. *Lauritzen,* 345 U.S. at 582.

13. In addition, the plaintiff's action was brought not only under the Jones Act, but also under general maritime law. The Court correctly held that the criteria used to determine the applicability of the Jones Act should also be used to determine the applicability of the general maritime law. See *Romero,* 358 U.S. at 382. Another dif-

of the injury called for a different result than in *Lauritzen*. The Court reasoned that the plaintiff's recovery "should not depend on the wholly fortuitous circumstances of the place of injury,"[14] and that to subject ships to shifting standard of compensation "as the vessel passes the boundaries of territorial waters would be not only an onerous but also an unduly speculative burden, disruptive of international commerce and without basis in the expressed policies of this country."[15]

The *Rhoditis* case was identical to *Romero*, except that the shipowner, though a foreign national, was also a long-term permanent resident of the United States and had managed his shipping operations out of his offices in New York and New Orleans.[16] Thus, he had an American "base of operations," and this factor—which *Rhoditis* added to the seven *Lauritzen* factors—made the difference and justified the application of American law. The Court noted that the *Lauritzen* test was "not a mechanical one,"[17] and that the significance of the eight factors "must be considered in light of the national interest served by the assertion of Jones Act jurisdiction."[18]

The *Lauritzen* Court cautioned that the then seven (later eight) contacts are of variable importance depending on the circumstances of the particular case, and that three of them—the place of the wrongful act, the place of contract, and the inaccessibility of a foreign forum—are almost always unimportant.[19] One could say the same about at least three of the remaining four contacts. For example, unless one is prepared to encourage forum favoritism, the "law of the forum" should not be an independent choice-of-law factor; the allegiance of the shipowner is often diluted by incorporation in distant and uninterested countries; and the law of the flag is irrelevant when the flag is one of convenience.[20]

ference from *Lauritzen* was that the *Romero* plaintiff sued not only the Spanish shipowner but also three American corporations engaged in stevedoring and related operations aboard the ship.

14. *Romero*, 358 U.S. at 384.

15. Id. The Court held American law inapplicable to the plaintiff's action against the Spanish shipowner and affirmed the lower court's dismissal on grounds of forum non conveniens. The Court then ordered the continuance of the actions against the American defendants. For a critique of *Romero*, see Currie, The Silver Oar and All That: A Study of the Romero Case, 27 U.Chi.L.Rev. 1 (1959); Symeonides, supra n.1, 242 et seq.

16. The ship carried the Greek flag but the entire income of the ship was derived from voyages to or from American ports. The plaintiffs were Greek seamen who were injured aboard the ship while in the port of New Orleans.

17. *Rhoditis*, 398 U.S. at 308.

18. Id. at 309.

19. The place of wrongful act is "of limited application to shipboard torts, because of the varieties of legal authority over waters she may navigate," *Lauritzen*, 345 U.S. at 573–74; the place of the contract can be "fortuitous" and may lead to the undesirable phenomenon of different members of the crew being governed by a different law depending on where they had signed the contract, id. at 588; and the "inaccessibility of a foreign forum" is irrelevant to the choice-of-law inquiry, although it is relevant to the forum non conveniens inquiry. Id. at 589–90.

20. See Braekhus, Choice of Law Problems in International Shipping, 164 Recueil des cours 251, 278, 286–87 (1979). For cases dismissing this factor after determining that the flag was one of convenience, see Pandazopoulos v. Universal Cruise Line, Inc., 365 F.Supp. 208 (S.D.N.Y.1973); De Mateos v. Texaco Panama, Inc., 417 F.Supp. 411 (E.D.Pa.1976); Firipis v. The Margaritis, 181 F.Supp. 48 (E.D.Va.1960); Southern Cross S. S. Co. v. Firipis, 285 F.2d 651 (4th Cir. 1960).

Since the United States flag is not one of convenience, it seems clear that, when the injury occurs aboard an American-flag vessel, American law will almost certainly apply.[21] The same is true if the injured seaman is an American citizen or domiciliary, since American seamen were the intended primary beneficiaries of the Jones Act.[22] Finally, since *Rhoditis*, the "base of operations" has emerged as the most common, if not the most decisive, basis for applying American law, in the sense that, when the court finds that the shipowner has such a base in the United States, American law will govern, even if the other factors do not point to American law. This proposition is directly confirmed by the cases that found an American base of operations,[23] and indirectly by the cases that did not.[24]

21. See G. Gilmore & C. Black, The Law of Admiralty 477 (2d ed. 1975) ("American law will also be applied in actions brought on account of injuries suffered on American-flag ships, whether the plaintiffs are American or foreign, resident or non-resident, seamen, harborworkers, passengers, guests or, for that matter, pirates.") See also id. ("By taking out registry in this country, the shipowner consents in effect to the application of the law of the United States." Conversely, by taking out registry in a foreign country, American shipowners cannot avoid Jones Act liability. American courts "have pressed beyond the formalities of more or less nominal foreign registration to enforce against American shipowners the obligations which ... [American] law places upon them." Lauritzen, 345 U.S. at 587. For a case applying American law because the injury occurred on an American-flag vessel, see Zacaria v. Gulf King 35, Inc., 31 F.Supp.2d 560 (S.D.Tex.1999) (injury of Nicaraguan crewmember of United States-flagged shrimping vessel operating in Nicaraguan waters). But see Phillips v. Amoco Trinidad Oil Co., 632 F.2d 82 (9th Cir.1980) (American flag did not outweigh foreign contacts in case of drilling rig that operated at fixed location in foreign waters).

22. Lauritzen v. Larsen, 345 U.S. 571, 586, 73 S.Ct. 921, 97 L.Ed. 1254 (1953) (the United States "has a legitimate interest that its nationals and permanent inhabitants be not maimed or disabled from self-support."). For cases applying American law to actions of American seamen injured abroad, see, e.g., Neely v. Club Med Mgmt. Servs., Inc., 63 F.3d 166 (3d Cir.1995) (injury aboard foreign-registered and owned stationary vessel while in foreign waters); Coats v. Penrod Drilling Corp., 61 F.3d 1113 (5th Cir.1995) (injury and shipowner's base of operations were in United Arab Emirates); Nye v. A/S D/S Svendborg, 358 F.Supp. 145 (S.D.N.Y.1973), aff'd in part, rev'd in part, 501 F.2d 376 (2d Cir.1974), cert. denied, 420 U.S. 964, 95 S.Ct. 1356, 43 L.Ed.2d 442 (1975) (death aboard a Danish-flag ship within Spanish territorial waters); Farmer v. Standard Dredging Corp., 167 F.Supp. 381 (D.C.Del.1958) (injury during an employment exclusively within territorial waters of Venezuela); Powell v. McDermott Int'l, Inc., 588 So.2d 84 (La.1991) (injury off coast of West Africa aboard vessel registered and flagged in Panama, and owned by Panamanian corporation that was wholly owned by American corporation); Symonette Shipyards, Ltd. v. Clark, 365 F.2d 464 (5th Cir. 1966) (injury and death aboard Bahamian vessel on the high seas); McClure v. U. S. Lines Co., 368 F.2d 197 (4th Cir. 1966). See also Bartholomew v. Universe Tankships, Inc., 263 F.2d 437 (2d Cir.1959) (death of a seaman, who was a citizen of the West Indies but who was also a United States resident, aboard a Liberian vessel within United States waters). But see, Bilyk v. Vessel Nair, 754 F.2d 1541(9th Cir. 1985) (American law not applied to action brought by American citizen for injury suffered aboard foreign vessel on high seas when foreign country had all other contracts including a choice-of-law clause); Lockwood v. M/S Royal Viking Star, 663 F.Supp. 181 (C.D.Cal.1986) (American law not applied to action of American citizen suffered aboard foreign ship in foreign waters when foreign country had all other contacts including a choice-of-law clause).

23. See, e.g., Karvelis v. Constellation Lines SA, 608 F.Supp. 966 (S.D.N.Y.1985), aff'd 806 F.2d 49 (2d Cir.1986), cert. denied 481 U.S. 1015, 107 S.Ct. 1891, 95 L.Ed.2d 498 (1987) (while most of the *Lauritzen-Rhoditis* factors, as well as a choice-of-forum clause, all pointed to Greek law and courts, the defendants had "substantial contacts" in the United States since the ship was managed from New York, one of the co-defendants, a New York company, was its general agent, and New York accounts held the charterer's revenues.); Moncada v. Lemuria Shipping Corp., 491 F.2d 470 (2d Cir. 1974), cert. denied, 417

24. See p. 894.

U.S. 947, 94 S.Ct. 3072, 41 L.Ed.2d 667 (1974) (applying Jones Act to a dispute arising from the death of a Honduran seaman in Brazil; all of the defendant's stock was owned by Americans and the defendants also had a base of operations in the United States); Antypas v. Cia. Maritima San Basilio, S.A., 541 F.2d 307 (2d Cir.1976), cert. denied, 429 U.S. 1098, 97 S.Ct. 1116, 51 L.Ed.2d 545 (1977) (applying Jones Act and general maritime law to an action by a Greek seaman against a Panamanian corporation for injuries suffered aboard a Greek vessel on the high seas because "at least some of the stockholders of the shipowner . . . [were] American citizens"; the defendant operated the vessel through a joint venture with a New York-based and owned corporation that directly controlled the vessel; there were substantial advertisements in the American market, the earnings of the vessel were collected in New York, and the expenses of the vessel were paid from New York. Id. at 309–10); Mattes v. National Hellenic Am. Line, 427 F.Supp. 619 (S.D.N.Y.1977) (applying American law to an action of a Greek seaman against a Greek shipowner for injuries suffered aboard a Greek-flag vessel while in international waters, because of the vessel's "continuing and substantial business contacts with the United States," including that "most [of the vessel's] voyages either originated or terminated in the United States" carrying mostly American passengers and thus "deriv[ing] the better part of its substantial revenues from these American customers." Id. at 624–25); Fisher v. The Agios Nicolaos V, 628 F.2d 308 (5th Cir.1980), reh'g en banc denied, 636 F.2d 1107, cert. denied, 454 U.S. 816, 102 S.Ct. 92, 70 L.Ed.2d 84 (1981) (applying American law to action brought on behalf of survivors of a Greek seaman for fatal injuries suffered aboard a Greek-flag vessel within United States territorial waters, because the vessel's "entire business activity prior to the accident had been in the United States" and "its entire revenues therefore to be earned" were derived from American trade. 628 F.2d at 317–18); Southern Cross S.S. Co. v. Firipis, 285 F.2d 651 (4th Cir. 1960), cert. denied 365 U.S. 869, 81 S.Ct. 903, 5 L.Ed.2d 859 (1961) (Jones Act applied when vessel flew flag of Honduras, nominal owner was Liberian corporation, but 20% owned by Americans). See also Szumlicz v. Norwegian Am. Line, Inc., 698 F.2d 1192 (11th Cir. 1983); Sosa v. M/V Lago Izabal, 736 F.2d 1028, (5th Cir.1984); Public Adm'r v. Angela Compania Naviera, S.A., 592 F.2d 58 (2d Cir. 1979), cert. dismissed 443 U.S.

928, 100 S.Ct. 15, 61 L.Ed.2d 897 (1979); Cacho v. Prince of Fundy Cruises, Ltd., 722 A.2d 349 (Me. 1998); Williams v. Cruise Ships Catering, 299 F.Supp.2d 1273 (S.D.Fla. 2003); Henry v. Windjammer Barefoot Cruises, 851 So.2d 731 (Fla.App. 2003); Mihalopoulos v. Westwind Africa Line, Ltd., 511 So.2d 771 (La.App.1987); Allan v. Brown & Root, Inc., 491 F.Supp. 398 (S.D.Tex.1980); Gomez v. Karavias U.S.A., Inc., 401 F.Supp. 104 (S.D.N.Y. 1975); Pandazopoulos v. Universal Cruise Line, Inc., 365 F.Supp. 208 (S.D.N.Y.1973); Groves v. Universe Tankships, Inc., 308 F.Supp. 826 (S.D.N.Y.1970); Mpiliris v. Hellenic Lines, Ltd., 323 F.Supp. 865 (S.D.Tex. 1969); Tsakonites v. Transpacific Carriers Corp., 246 F.Supp. 634 (S.D.N.Y.1965); Pavlou v. Ocean Traders Marine Corp., 211 F.Supp. 320 (S.D.N.Y.1962); Firipis v. The Margaritis, 181 F.Supp. 48 (E.D.Va.1960).

24. See, e.g., Volyrakis v. M/V Isabelle, 668 F.2d 863, 864 (5th Cir.1982) (Jones Act inapplicable to action of Greek seaman injured aboard a Greek vessel in U.S. waters because the vessel was owned by a Panamanian corporation owned and managed by Greeks, the contract of employment selected Greece as the forum for disputes arising out of the employment relationship, and the Greek forum was not inaccessible; "That the injury occurred in United States waters is the sole factor in favor of applying United States law. That fact alone is not enough."). The additional fact that a New York corporation served as the vessel's American agent was also not enough since its president, holding an ownership interest, was also Greek and, in turn, represented a Liechtenstein corporation holding a 49% interest in the New York corporation); Pratt v. United Arab Shipping Co., 585 F.Supp. 1573 (E.D.La.1984) (vessel's periodic visits to U.S. insufficient to establish an American base of operations); See also Warn v. M/Y Maridome, 169 F.3d 625 (9th Cir. 1999), cert. denied 528 U.S. 874, 120 S.Ct. 179, 145 L.Ed.2d 151 (1999); Villar v. Crowley Mar. Corp., 782 F.2d 1478 (9th Cir. 1986); Morewitz v. Andros Compania Maritima, S. A., 614 F.2d 379 (4th Cir. 1980); Ioannidis/Riga v. M/V Sea Concert, 132 F.Supp.2d 847 (D.Or. 2001); Castillo v. Santa Fe Shipping Corp., 827 F.Supp. 1269 (S.D.Tex.1992); Jose v. M/V Fir Grove, 765 F.Supp. 1024 (D.Or.,1991); Flores v. Central Am. S.S. Agency Inc., 594 F.Supp. 735 (S.D.N.Y.1984); Cruz v. Maritime Co. of Philippines, 549 F.Supp. 285 (S.D.N.Y. 1982); Sfiridas v. Santa Cecelia Co. S.A., 358 F.Supp. 108 (E.D.Pa.1973).

Cases like *In re Complaint of Fantome, S.A.*,[25] illustrate that this factor too is susceptible to manipulation–some American shipowners go to great lengths to avoid having a base of operations in the United States in hopes of avoiding the application of American maritime law. In *Fantome*, the ship was entirely owned by an American family and was managed from the family's offices in Miami.[26] However, the shipowner meticulously created the facade of foreign "bases" of operation by keeping the ship away from American ports. Erroneously focusing on the ship rather than the shipowner, the district court found that there was no American base of operations because the ship's day-to-day operations and its repairs had taken place at the various locations in the Caribbean where she docked, and thus the ship "had numerous 'bases' of operations at the ports where it took on passengers, supplies and new crew members."[27] The Eleventh Circuit Court of Appeals reversed this finding as clearly erroneous and criticized the district court for placing "too much emphasis on the fact that the [ship] had never entered a United States port and too little emphasis on the extensive contacts between the United States and the shipowners."[28] Because of these latter contacts, the court concluded, the shipowner had an American base of operations which, together with other factors, justified the application of American law.[29]

The district court's decision in *Fantome* confirms Justice Harlan's view that many courts, at least lower courts, tend to be "mesmerized by contacts ... notwithstanding the purported eschewal of a mechanical application of the *Lauritzen* test."[30] Although in 1953 the *Lauritzen* test was a significant methodological step in the right direction, it was then, and it is now, prone to mechanical application.[31] In addition, the *Lauritzen-Rhoditis* factors, which were designed for personal injury or death cases, are ill-suited for other maritime tort conflicts.[32] The Supreme

25.   232 F. Supp.2d 1298 (S.D.Fla. 2002).

26.   The ship flew the flag of Equatorial Guinea and was owned by a Panamanian corporation that was in turn fully owned by an American family residing in Florida. The plaintiffs were the survivors of 31 foreign seamen who died when the ship sank on the high seas, while trying to outrun a category-five hurricane. The decision to outrun the hurricane was taken during a telephone conversation between the shipowner in the Miami office and the ship's captain.

27.   *Fantome*, 232 F.Supp.2d at 1307.

28.   Fantome S.A. v. Frederick, 2003 WL 215812 (11th Cir.2003) (quoted in Henry v. Windjammer Barefoot Cruises, 851 So.2d 731, 736 (Fla.App.2003)).

29.   These findings and conclusions helped a Florida state court reach the same result in another case involving the same shipowner and another one of his ships that also had never entered a United States

port. See Henry v. Windjammer Barefoot Cruises, supra n.28.

30.   Hellenic Lines v. Rhoditis, 398 U.S. 306, 318, 90 S.Ct. 1731, 26 L.Ed.2d 252 (1970) (Harlan J., dissenting).

31.   See, e.g., Koupetoris v. Konkar Intrepid Corp., 535 F.2d 1392 (2d Cir.1976); Manlugon v. A/S Facto, 419 F.Supp. 550 (S.D.N.Y.1976); In re Lidoriki Maritime Corp., 404 F.Supp. 1402 (E.D.Pa.1975); Damaskinos v. Societa Navigacion Interamericana, S.A., 255 F.Supp. 919 (S.D.N.Y.1966); Karakatsanis v. Conquestador Cia. Nav., S.A., 247 F.Supp. 423 (S.D.N.Y.1965); Shahid v. A/S J. Ludwig Mowinckels Rederi, 236 F.Supp. 751 (S.D.N.Y.1964); Lemonis v. Prudential–Grace Lines, 81 Misc.2d 614, 366 N.Y.S.2d 541 (1975).

32.   See, e.g., Sealord Marine Co., Ltd. v. American Bureau of Shipping, 220 F.Supp.2d 260 (S.D.N.Y. 2002) (suit against classification society); Carbotrade S.p.A. v. Bureau Veritas, 99 F.3d 86 (2d Cir. 1996)

Court has yet to revisit the matter and thus has not had the opportunity to take account of the progress that American conflicts law has made in the interim. One notable attempt to modernize the *Lauritzen* test can be seen in *Neely v. Club Med Management Services, Inc.*[33] In this case, the United States Court of Appeals for the Third Circuit proposed a two-step approach for determining whether American law would govern a maritime tort with foreign elements. The first step is to inquire on whether the American contacts are "substantial" enough to render American law potentially applicable. The court noted that the following contacts meet this threshold requirement: "injury to an American seaman or a seaman with American dependents, injury in American territory, American defendants, an American flagged ship, or a contractual choice of law clause specifying American law."[34] The second step is to determine whether the application of American law is "reasonable" by employing the test articulated for this purpose in § 403 of the Restatement (Third) of Foreign Relations Law.[35] Although opinions differ on this matter,[36] this new test would be an improvement over a mechanical application of the eight *Lauritzen-Rhoditis* contacts, which is so common among lower courts.

V. PRODUCTS LIABILITY[1]

A. IN GENERAL

§ 17.64   The last four decades of the 20th century saw the emergence of products liability law as a distinct body of law, at least partly independent from general tort and contract law from which it grew. In a life that parallels that of the American conflicts revolution, this new body of law was born in the 1960s, emancipated in the '70s, grew by

(same); Galapagos Corp. Turistica "Galatours", S.A. v. The Panama Canal Comm'n, 190 F.Supp.2d 900 (E.D. La. 2002) (suit by shipowner against Panama canal company). Claims arising from collisions on the high seas are usually governed by applicable provisions of the International Rules of the Road which the United States adopted in 1963 (33 U.S.C.A. §§ 1051–1094). When they are not applicable, the case law displays a distinct forum preference. Deslions v. La Compagnie Generale Transatlantique, 210 U.S. 95, 28 S.Ct. 664, 52 L.Ed. 973 (1908); Hess v. United States, 361 U.S. 314, 80 S.Ct. 341, 4 L.Ed.2d 305 (1960); The Belgenland, 114 U.S. 355, 5 S.Ct. 860, 29 L.Ed. 152 (1885); Puerto Rico v. SS Zoe Colocotroni, 456 F.Supp. 1327 (D.P.R.1978). In some cases, this may be the result of a preference for the application of the federal Death on the High Seas Act (46 U.S.C.A. §§ 761–768) which, in turn, applies only if American law governs the claim. See Noel v. Airponents, Inc., 169 F.Supp. 348 (D.N.J. 1958); Executive Jet Aviation, Inc. v. City of Cleveland, Ohio, 409 U.S. 249, 93 S.Ct. 493, 34 L.Ed.2d 454 (1972).

33.   63 F.3d 166 (3d Cir.1995). See also Symeonides, Maritime Conflicts, supra n.1, 242–64.

34.   *Neely*, 63 F.3d at 182.

35.   The court rejected reliance on the Second Conflicts Restatement because it "gives far too much general significance to the place of the wrongful act to constitute a satisfactory interpretation of *Lauritzen*." *Neely*, 63 F.3d at 183 n.15.

36.   For a critique of this test, see Weintraub, supra n.1 at 248–49.

§ 17.64

1.   This Part draws from Symeonides, Choice of Law for Products Liability: The 1990s and Beyond, 79 Tul. L. Rev. 1247 (2004), and Symeonides, The Choice of Law Revolution in the Courts: Today and Tomorrow, 298 Recueil des Cours 1, 278–356 (2003).

leaps and bounds in the '80s, and then began slowing down in the '90s.[2] Even during the slow periods, however, American courts face a much higher number of product liability cases than courts in the rest of the world[3] because, for a variety of reasons,[4] "Americans use their product liability law a lot while victims and courts elsewhere don't."[5] Naturally, the higher the number of product liability lawsuits, the higher the likelihood that many of them will have multistate elements, thus producing conflicts of laws. This is particularly true in the United States, which is essentially a single market, yet artificially segregated by state boundaries into multiple diverse products-liability regimes. Thus, for better or worse, American courts have had and continue to have the lion's share of product liability conflicts, and they have had to handle these conflicts with virtually no legislative guidance.[6]

Some of those conflicts arise out of "mass torts"[7] that involve injury to multiple persons, while others arise out of injury to a single person. Either way, however, these conflicts are inherently complex, for a variety of reasons.

First, although the prevalence of the term "products liability" tends to suggest that there is a well-defined category of "products" that are susceptible to uniform treatment, the reality is much different. For example, one can distinguish between products that are intended for use in one state, such as industrial or similar production-equipment, and

2. For the substantive development and numerical growth of American products liability law, see Zekoll, Liability for Defective Products and Services, in American Law in a Time of Global Interdependence: U.S. National Reports to the XVIth International Congress of Comparative Law, 121 (S. Symeonides & J. Reitz eds, 2002). The author reports that the number of personal-injury products liability filings in federal courts alone grew from 2,393 in 1975 to 32,856 in 1997 and then began to slow down to 26,886 in 1998, 18,781 in 1999, and 14,428 in 2000. See id. at 148–49. These numbers do not include filings in state courts where the numbers are lower. Id.

3. Professor Reimann reports that, on average, about 30,000 products liability actions (about one for every 90,000 inhabitants) are filed annually in the United States, whereas, for example, the European Commission reports "barely 100 court decisions ... in all the [EU] member states together," over a fifteen-year period." Reimann, Liability for Defective Products and Services: Emergence of a Worldwide Standard? General Report to the XVIth International Congress of Comparative Law, 57, 54 (Brisbane 2002).

4. For a discussion of the reasons, see Reimann, supra n.3 at 63–84; Zekoll, supra n.2 at 143–59.

5. Reimann, supra n. 3 at 53. See also id. at 57 ("products liability litigation in the United States is big business while it is of marginal importance in the rest of the world").

6. The only exception are the cases decided under the 1991 Louisiana conflicts codification, specifically La.Civ. Code Art. 3545. For a discussion of this article by its drafter, see Symeonides, Louisiana's New Law of Choice of Law for Tort Conflicts: An Exegesis, 66 Tul. L. Rev. 677, 749–759 (1992).

7. "Mass torts" involve injury to many victims as a result of a single act (e.g., the explosion at Bhopal, India) or of continuous acts (e.g., toxic or polluting emissions). "Mass torts" may occur at a predictable place (e.g., the gas plant at Bhopal) or at a fortuitous location (e.g., the site of an airplane crash). For choice-of-law discussion, see the symposium on "mass torts" (with contributions by Juenger, Lowenfeld, and Weintraub) in 1989 U. Ill. L. Rev. 35 et seq. See also American Law Institute, Complex Litigation: Statutory Recommendations and Analysis (1994) and Symposium discussing this Project in 54 La. L. Rev. 833 (1994) (articles by von Mehren, Trautman, Symeonides, Cooper, Juenger, Kalis, et al., Kozyris, Mullenix, Nafziger, Sedler, Seidelson, Shreve, and Wilkins).

products intended for use in more than one state, such as airplanes or other means of public transportation. In-between the two categories are consumer products, such as pharmaceuticals, appliances, foods, cosmetics, and personal vehicles that are used primarily but not exclusively in one state. While products in the last category are usually purchased directly by the user and eventual victim of the product, products in the first two categories are purchased by someone other than the victim and are usually not subject to the victim's control.

Second, products liability cases, whether they involve claims for injury caused *by* a product or for injury *to* the product,[8] tend to combine tort and contract-based theories of recovery (negligence, strict liability, or breach of warranty)[9] with all the attendant characterization problems that, at least in the older cases, tended to be decisive.[10]

8. See, e.g., Rocky Mountain Helicopters, Inc. v. Bell Helicopter Textron, Inc., 24 F.3d 125 (10th Cir.1994) (decided under Utah conflicts law; negligence and breach of warranty action for injury to a product caused by its defective design; applying Texas law under § 188 of the Second Restatement; Texas was the state of the manufacture of the product and the principal place of business of the defendant manufacturer).

9. See Kühne, Choice of Law in Products Liability, 60 Cal. L. Rev. 1, 2–4 (1972); Kozyris, Values and Methods in Choice of Law for Product Liability: A Comparative Comment on Statutory Solutions, 38 Am. J. Comp. L. 475 (1990); Herzog, Recent Developments in Products Liability in the United States, 38 Am. J. Comp. L. 539 (1990); L. McDougal, R. Felix & R. Whitten, American Conflicts Law 459–61 (5th ed.2001). See Martin v. Julius Dierck Equip. Co., 52 A.D.2d 463, 384 N.Y.S.2d 479, 482 (1976), aff'd 43 N.Y.2d 583, 403 N.Y.S.2d 185, 374 N.E.2d 97 (1978). See also Weintraub, A Proposed Choice-of-Law Standard for International Product Liability Disputes, 16 Brooklyn J. Int'l L. 225 (1990).

10. To the extent that the claim alleges the breach of an implied warranty—whether or not privity existed between plaintiff and defendant—a number of older cases applied the choice-of-law rules of the First Restatement. Thus, rather than seeking to identify the place of the most significant relationship for the transaction as a whole—which would result in a parallel approach for products liability and implied warranty cases—these decisions focus on the place of the making or of the performance of the contract. See Uppgren v. Executive Aviation Servs., Inc., 326 F.Supp. 709 (D.Md.1971); Tennessee Carolina Transp., Inc. v. Strick Corp., 16 N.C.App. 498, 192 S.E.2d 702 (1972), remanded 283 N.C. 423, 196 S.E.2d 711 (1973); Bohrer–Reagan

Corp. v. Modine Mfg. Co., 433 F.Supp. 578 (E.D.Pa.1977); Johnson v. Knight, 459 F.Supp. 962 (N.D.Miss.1978). Other cases have used U.C.C. § 1–105(1) as the basis for applying the law of the state of the injury on the ground that that state bears the required "appropriate relationship" to the claim. See Whitaker v. Harvell–Kilgore Corp., 418 F.2d 1010 (5th Cir.1969); Bilancia v. Gen. Motors Corp., 538 F.2d 621 (4th Cir.1976). Boudreau v. Baughman, 322 N.C. 331, 368 S.E.2d 849 (1988), reached the same result, but noted that the state of injury was also the place of the sale, distribution, delivery, and use of the product and thus had the most significant relationship with regard to the warranty claim. See also Premix–Marbletite Mfg. Corp. v. SKW Chems., Inc., 145 F.Supp.2d 1348 (S.D.Fla. 2001) (applying Florida law under UCC § 1.105(1) to an action by Florida buyer against Georgia seller of defective product purchased and used in Florida, because Florida had an appropriate relation to the transactions at issue, being the place of negotiation, purchase, and delivery of the product and the buyer's domicile and injury). Thornton v. Cessna Aircraft Co., 886 F.2d 85 (4th Cir.1989), applied the law of the accident state to plaintiff's tort claims and the law of the place of the product's acquisition (and also the victim's domicile) to his breach of warranty claims. See also R–Square Invs. Inc. v. Teledyne Indus., Inc., 1997 WL 436245 (E.D. La. 1997) (case involving a defective airplane engine that caused damage to the plane; employing contract analysis to claim for damage to the engine, and tort analysis to claim for damage to the plane; applying Minnesota law to the former and Louisiana law to the latter claim); Robinson v. American Marine Holdings, Inc., 2002 WL 873185 (E.D.La. 2002) (breach of warranty and redhibition action).

Third, the place of the injurious conduct, which in generic torts is an important connecting factor, may be quite "disconnecting" in products liability cases. This is because it is difficult to pinpoint the "place of conduct" in cases in which, for example, the product was designed in one state, tested in another, approved in another, and manufactured and assembled in yet another state.[11] Similarly, in certain categories of products, even the place of the injury may be difficult to pinpoint. This is so especially in cases of products with latent defects such as pharmaceuticals,[12] breast implants, asbestos or tobacco products[13] that the victims have used for long periods of time while residing in several states.

For better or for worse, state legislatures[14] have, for the most part,[15] refrained from providing solutions to products liability conflicts, thus

11. See, e.g., Patten v. General Motors Corp., 699 F.Supp. 1500 (W.D.Okla.1987) (involving a car designed in Michigan, manufactured in Ohio, and customized in Florida; concluding that "[b]ecause the conduct causing the injury occurred in so many different states, that factor is less important." Id. at 1505); Dorman v. Emerson Elec. Co., 23 F.3d 1354 (8th Cir.1994), cert. denied 513 U.S. 964, 115 S.Ct. 428, 130 L.Ed.2d 341 (1994) (involving a miter saw that was manufactured in Taiwan by a Taiwanese corporation under license from defendant, a Missouri corporation, which had designed and tested that line of products in Missouri); Crouch v. General Elec. Co., 699 F.Supp. 585 (S.D.Miss.1988) (involving helicopter engines designed and manufactured in Massachusetts and installed in helicopter in Connecticut; defendant had its principal place of business in New York, its headquarters in Connecticut, its engine manufacturing division's headquarters in Ohio, and its engine design and manufacturing division in Massachusetts); Rutherford v. Goodyear Tire & Rubber Co., 943 F.Supp. 789 (W.D.Ky.1996), aff'd 142 F.3d 436, (6th Cir.1998) (involving a car tire manufactured in Kansas by Goodyear, an Ohio corporation, purchased by Ford Motor Co., a Michigan corporation, and installed on a Ford car in Ford's Kentucky assembly plant). For the problem of testing products in a state "chosen because of its low liability laws," see Fawcett, Products Liability in Private International Law: A European Perspective, 238 Recueil des Cours 9, 127 (1993).

12. Braune v. Abbott Laboratories., 895 F.Supp. 530 (E.D.N.Y. 1995), is a typical example of peripatetic injury caused by a pharmaceutical product. In the 1950s, a drug known as DES and designed to prevent miscarriages was prescribed by doctors to pregnant women living in several states. The plaintiffs in Braune were among the daughters of those women, and had been exposed to DES during gestation in their mothers' wombs. As a result of that exposure, plaintiffs gradually developed various abnormalities in their reproductive organs, including infertility, miscarriages, and cervical cancer, which became evident when the plaintiffs reached child-bearing age. The plaintiffs, like their mothers, had lived in several states since the mothers had used the drug, thus raising difficult questions on when and where the injuries occurred. The court concluded that the injuries occurred in the states in which they were diagnosed. See also Millar–Mintz v. Abbott Labs., 268 Ill.App.3d 566, 645 N.E.2d 278 (1994) (applying Illinois' pro-plaintiff law to an action filed by a plaintiff whose mother had used DES in the 1940's while domiciled in Illinois. The plaintiff had lived in New York, California, and then in Illinois, where she was first advised of her infertility and its causal relation to her mother's use of DES).

13. See Tune v. Philip Morris, Inc., 766 So.2d 350 (Fla. App. 2000) (action against tobacco manufacturer brought by a plaintiff who used tobacco products for many years while domiciled in two states and who was diagnosed with lung cancer while domiciled in the second state); Philip Morris, Inc. v. Angeletti, 358 Md. 689, 752 A.2d 200 (2000) (class action against tobacco manufacturers by former and current Maryland domiciliaries who were addicted to tobacco products–decertifying class because it was unlikely that the "deleterious" effect of nicotine had taken effect upon the bodies of all plaintiffs in the same state).

14. For a federal attempt, see House Bill H.R. 3662, introduced in 1987, which proposed an amendment to Title 28 of the United States Code. The Bill provided in § 1659 that the law of the place of injury would govern all products liability actions in "any court of the United States which [are] brought by a citizen or subject of a

15. See p. 900.

leaving courts to their own devices. The next subdivision of this Part reviews the courts' performance over the last two decades, while the last subdivision discusses some choice-of-law rules that have been adopted or proposed for such conflicts.

B. SAMPLES FROM THE CASE LAW

1. *Common Denominators*

a. *Recent Trends*

§ 17.65 A review of products liability conflicts decided during the last two decades confirms the impression that this area of the law remains very much in a state of flux. The abandonment of the *lex loci delicti* rule in the majority of states has yet to produce a new rule or set of rules to take its place. Nor is it possible to discern an emerging general methodological or ideological trend or leaning. For example, although during the 1970s and early 1980s one might be tempted to conclude that courts tended to favor the victim, no such conclusion can be ventured for the case law of the late 1980s and the 1990s. If anything, cases decided during the latter period seem to tilt towards manufacturers rather than towards consumers. As a recent study documents, slightly more than half of the cases (51%) decided between 1990 and 2003 applied a law that favored the defendant.[1] Whether this is the outgrowth of the "tort reform" movement of the 1980s, or a series of conservative appointments to the federal bench during the same period, or a combination of these and other factors is unclear. What seems clear is that, at the beginning of the 21st century, products liability plaintiffs encounter more difficulties in recovering from manufacturers than in

foreign state against a United States citizen for injury that was sustained outside the United States and that relates to the manufacture, purchase, sale, or use of a product outside the United States." The purpose of the proposal was to discourage potential forum-shopping by foreign plaintiffs who might seek the advantages of American substantive and procedural law. Congress took no action on the bill. For an expression of the same policy concern in reverse (i.e., denying foreign remedies unknown to forum law and thus protecting forum defendants), see Art. 135(2) of the Swiss Statute, infra § 17.80 n.10.

15. For the Louisiana and Puerto Rico codifications, see infra § 17.80 n.1. See also the Model Uniform Product Liability Act, 44 Fed. Reg. 62714 (1979), which the U.S. Department of Commerce had offered for "voluntary adoption" by the states. The Act was designed to be comprehensive; its § 103(a) states that the Act "preempts existing law governing matters within its coverage, including the 'Uniform Commercial

Code' and similar laws; however, nothing in this Act shall prevent the recovery, under the 'Uniform Commercial Code' or similar laws, of direct or consequential economic losses." The Washington Products Liability statute is patterned after the Uniform Law but omits provisions for punitive damages. Wash. Rev. Code Ann. § 7.72.010 et seq. (1986 Pocket Part). The "tortious act" provision of Washington's long-arm statute confers jurisdiction under the products liability statute. See Hogan v. Johnson, 39 Wash.App. 96, 692 P.2d 198 (1984).

§ 17.65

1. See Symeonides, Choice of Law for Products Liability: The 1990s and Beyond, 79 Tul. L. Rev. 1247, 1314–16 (2004). Even when the forum state had a pro-plaintiff law, plaintiffs had a less than 50% chance of persuading the court to apply that law. In contrast, when the forum had a pro-defendant law, defendants had a 2:1 chance of persuading the court to apply that law. See id. at 1312.

previous decades. This is as true in multistate as in domestic products liability litigation.[2]

Similarly, recent cases do not support the anecdotal impression–which may have been justified in previous decades–that courts favor the law of the forum state. The aforementioned study documents that the cases that applied forum law in the above period outnumber the cases that applied foreign law by a relatively small margin (55 to 45%).[3] Moreover, in most of these cases, the forum state had additional contacts that could justify the application of its law, even if it was not the forum, and regardless of the choice-of-law theory the court followed.[4]

b. Pertinent Contacts

§ 17.66 One of the few common denominators that can be identified among recent cases is a list of factual contacts that courts usually take into account in identifying the concerned jurisdictions and in resolving products liability conflicts. These contacts are:

(1) the domicile, habitual residence, or "home state" of the party injured by the product (hereinafter referred to as plaintiff or "victim");[1]

(2) the place where the injury occurred;

(3) the place where the product was marketed (hereinafter referred to as the "place of acquisition");

(4) the place where the product was manufactured or designed; and

(5) the principal place of business of the manufacturer (hereinafter referred to as "defendant").[2]

The above list of contacts calls for explanation and qualification. First, the list should not lead to the inference that *all* of these contacts are taken into account in *all* cases. For example, cases decided under the *lex loci delicti* rule do not consider, and often do not mention, the other contacts. Second, as noted earlier, in some cases, one or more of these

---

2. According to Reimann, "American products liability law has become distinctly more cautious in the 1980s and 1990s.... [C]ourts have become significantly more conservative in practice. After favoring plaintiffs and pushing the boundaries of liability for decades, as of the 1980s, they began to protect defendants, refused to expand liability further, and in fact often retreated to earlier positions." Reimann, Liability for Defective Products and Services: Emergence of a Worldwide Standard? General Report to the XVIth Int'l Congress of Comp. L. at 52(Brisbane 2002).

3. See Symeonides, supra n.1, at 1317–20. State courts did apply forum law more frequently (67%) than federal courts (48%), but the federal cases were more numerous.

4. See id. at 1318. Nor did the courts favor the domiciliaries of the forum state (plaintiffs or defendants). In fact, only 40% of the cases applied a law that favored a local litigant. See id. at 1316–17.

§ 17.66

1. The term "victim" connotes a person physically injured by the product. In some cases, however (such as cases involving injury *to* the product), the plaintiff suffers only economic injury.

2. In some cases, parties other than the manufacturer, such as a distributor or seller of the product, may be defendants. Nevertheless, for reasons of simplicity, the term "defendant" is used hereinafter to denote the manufacturer, unless otherwise indicated.

contacts, such as the place of conduct or injury, may be located in more than one state. Third, each of the above contacts may be fortuitous in a given case, such as the place of injury in an airplane crash,[3] or the place of acquisition in the case of a product purchased by a tourist in a distant state.[4] Fourth, the above contacts are not necessarily of equal weight or pertinence. For example, the place of the product's acquisition is generally less pertinent when a party other than the victim acquired the product, or when the victim was not the original acquirer. Likewise, in today's world of multistate corporate mobility, the manufacturer's principal place of business is justifiably given less weight,[5] and in some cases—though not as many as one might expect—the defendant is not the manufacturer but rather the seller of the product. Finally, it has been argued that the place of manufacture should not be a pertinent contact.[6]

Despite the above qualifications, the above list of contacts remains a useful vehicle through which to catalogue and analyze products liability conflicts. The analysis, or at least the description of it, can be further facilitated by grouping these contacts into plaintiff-affiliating and defendant-affiliating contacts. Thus, the plaintiff's domicile and the place of injury are plaintiff-affiliating contacts, while the defendant's principal place of business and the place of the manufacture are defendant-affiliating contacts. The remaining contact, the place of the product's acquisition, is where, figuratively speaking, the two sides meet each other. However, at least when the product is acquired by the victim

---

3. See, e.g., In re Air Crash Disaster at Sioux City, Iowa, 734 F.Supp. 1425 (N.D.Ill. 1990) (discounting as fortuitous the occurrence of the injury in Iowa in a case involving a flight from Denver to Chicago).

4. See, e.g., Danielson v. National Supply Co., 670 N.W.2d 1 (Minn.App.2003) (involving a step-ladder that a Minnesota trailer-owner purchased while traveling through Texas).

5. See, e.g., In re Air Crash Disaster at Sioux City, Iowa, 734 F.Supp. 1425 (N.D.Ill. 1990) (noting that New York was General Electric's principal place of business only because the company's other holdings, unrelated to manufacture, were located in that state; discounting this contact for this reason); Crouch v. General Elec. Co., 699 F.Supp. 585 (S.D. Miss. 1988) (involving a defendant that had its principal place of business in New York, its headquarters in Connecticut, its engine manufacturing division's headquarters in Ohio, and its engine design and manufacturing division in Massachusetts).

6. See Kozyris, Values and Methods in Choice of Law for Product Liability: A Comparative Comment on Statutory Solutions, 38 Am. J. Comp. L. 475, 500 (1990) ("[T]he

mere making of a product, however defective, does not create the risk of causing harm.... Production is only a preparatory act which does not rise to the level of the wrongful conduct. The tort does not commence until the product is placed in a position to cause harm, i.e., is distributed to a potential user."); Rutherford v. Goodyear Tire & Rubber Co., 943 F.Supp. 789, 793 (W.D. Ky. 1996) ("Legal claims do not arise at the time or at the place of manufacture. They arise when an injury occurs. Thus, the place of injury, not the place of manufacture is the central focus of the cause of action."); Maly v. Genmar Indus., Inc., 1996 WL 28473 (N.D.Ill. 1996) (the court does not even mention the place of manufacture, apparently because of the court's conclusion that the critical conduct was "the placement of a defective product in the stream of commerce." id. at *2). In the European literature it is suggested that the reference be to the law of the place where the defective product was used or that "the place of the tort" be redefined not to mean the place of manufacture but the place where the danger of injury was created. See Stoll, Zweispurige Anknüpfung von Verschuldens- und Gefährdungshaftung im internationalen Privatrecht?, Festschrift für Ferid 397, 410 (1978).

rather than by a third party (as in the case of an airplane acquired by an airline company), this contact can be considered as a victim-affiliated contact and is treated as such in the discussion below.

c. *Typical Patterns*

§ 17.67   In the large majority of cases, the state whose law is applied has more than one, and often more than two, of the above five contacts.[1] When that state has contacts affiliated with both the victim and the defendant, the application of its law is not likely to be controversial.[2] The same is true of cases in which a state with victim-affiliating contacts has a law that is similar in policy or outcome to the law of a state with defendant-affiliating contacts. These "false conflicts" need not occupy us here.

Instead, the discussion below focuses on cases in which the law of a state with defendant-affiliating contacts differs in policy and outcome from the law of a state with victim-affiliating contacts. These differences can be grouped into two categories: (a) laws that, on the particular issue, favor the defendant (hereinafter "pro-manufacturer" laws); and (b) laws that, on the same issue, favor the victim (hereinafter "pro-recovery" or pro-plaintiff laws). Among the clearest and most common examples of the former category are statutes of repose that bar suits against manufacturers when filed after a specified number of years from the date the product was placed in the stream of commerce ("first use"), regardless of the time of the injury. Other examples are rules that limit compensatory damages, prohibit punitive damages, require showing of negligence as a condition of liability, or accord manufacturers special defenses such as

---

§ 17.67

1. According to Symeonides, Choice of Law for Products Liability: The 1990s and Beyond, 79 Tul. L. Rev. 1247, 1305–06 (2004), 85% of the cases decided between 1989 and 2003, applied the law of a state that had two or three of the above contacts. The majority of those cases (76%), applied the law of a state that had plaintiff-affiliating contacts (domicile, injury, and/or place of acquisition), but in 58% of those cases that state had a pro-defendant law.

2. For example, in Hubbard Mfg. Co., Inc. v. Greeson, 515 N.E.2d 1071 (Ind. 1987), the action was filed by Indiana plaintiffs against an Indiana manufacturer whose product caused the death of an Indiana worker in Illinois. After finding that the place of the tort was "insignificant to this suit," id. at 1073, the court concluded quickly that Indiana was the state of "the more significant relationship and contacts," since the product was manufactured there, both parties were from that state, and "the relationship between the deceased and the manufacturer was centered in

Indiana." Id. at 1074. See also Young v. Fulton Iron Works Co., 709 S.W.2d 927 (Mo.App.1986) (applying Missouri law to issue of successor liability in an action against a Missouri corporation filed by a Missouri resident injured in that state by a product manufactured in another state by defendant's predecessor corporation); Mahoney v. Ronnie's Road Service, 122 N.C.App. 150, 468 S.E.2d 279 (N.C.App. 1996), review denied 344 N.C. 438, 476 S.E.2d 118 (1996) (applying North Carolina's statute of repose to bar an action by an Arizona resident who was injured in North Carolina by a product manufactured in that state by a North Carolina domiciliary); Gadzinski v. Chrysler Corp., 2001 WL 629336 (N.D.Ill. 2001) (applying Indiana law to an action by an Illinois plaintiff who was injured in Indiana by a product he purchased from an Indiana dealer); Beals v. Sicpa Securink Corp., 1994 WL 236018 (D.D.C 1994) (applying Virginia's pro-defendant law to Virginia plaintiffs' actions against a Virginia manufacturer of ink that was manufactured in Virginia and caused injury in the District of Columbia).

"state of the art," etc. Among the clearest examples of pro-recovery laws are the absence of a statute of repose protecting manufacturers, and rules that impose punitive damages, strict liability or corporate liability on manufacturers.

The combination of pertinent contacts and product-liability laws produces two major typical patterns of product-liability conflicts, depending on the laws of the involved states and on whether each state has contacts affiliating it only with the plaintiff or only with the defendant. The first pattern encompasses cases in which all three plaintiff-affiliating contacts (domicile, injury, and acquisition) are located in a state or states that have pro-plaintiff laws, while both defendant-affiliating contacts (manufacture and manufacturer's principal place of business) are located in a state or states that have pro-defendant laws. The second pattern encompasses the converse cases in which all three plaintiff-affiliating contacts are located in a state or states that have pro-defendant laws, while both defendant-affiliating contacts are located in a state or states that have pro-plaintiff laws.[3]

Under the assumptions and terminology of interest-analysis, cases of the first pattern present the "true conflict" paradigm in which each state has an interest in applying its law, while cases of the second pattern present the "no-interest" or "unprovided for" paradigm in which neither state has an interest. This is because, under Currie's assumptions about state interests, particularly his "personal-law" principle, a state has an interest in applying its law, *inter alia*, when that law benefits that state's domiciliaries but not when it benefits out-of-staters, especially at the expense of local domiciliaries.[4]

Even if one subscribes to the notion of state interests, Currie's labels are problematic because they forejudge the answer to the basic question—whether in fact a state has an interest in applying its law to the particular case—a question that reasonable minds often answer differently. Indeed, as the following discussion demonstrates: most courts do not subscribe to Currie's assumptions; many courts do not employ his labels; and courts that employ these labels reach different conclusions regarding each state's interests than Currie would have reached. For example, some courts have concluded that certain cases that Currie would label as no-interest cases presented the false conflict scenario because one state did in fact have an interest in applying its law.[5] Nevertheless, the terms "true conflicts" and "no-interest" cases

---

3. A third in-between pattern encompasses all the remaining combinations, such as situations in which the three plaintiff-affiliating contacts (domicile, injury, and product acquisition) are located in different states the laws of which favor a different party.

4. See supra § 2.9 nn. 14, 56, 58–59.

5. See e.g., Gantes v. Kason Corp., 145 N.J. 478, 679 A.2d 106 (1996) (discussed infra § 17.76; concluding that, although

each party was affiliated with a state whose law favored the other party, this was not a no-interest case but rather a false conflict because one of the two states had an interest in applying its law); Jones v. SEPTA, 1993 WL 141646 (E.D. Pa. 1993) (discussed infra § 17.69 n. 9; concluding that, although each party was affiliated with a state whose law favored that party, this was not a true conflict but rather a false conflict

have prevailed in the literature and for this reason they are employed in the discussion below, although they are used in a descriptive rather than prescriptive sense. The discussion begins with those cases in which each state's law favors the local litigant (i.e., the potential "true conflicts"), and continues with cases in which each state's law favors the litigant affiliated with the other state (i.e., the potential "no-interest" cases).[6]

2. Cases in Which Each State's Law Favors the Local Litigant (True Conflicts)

§ 17.68 As said above, cases in which a state with the defendant-affiliating contacts (such as the state of the product's manufacture and/or the defendant's principal place of business) has a pro-defendant law, while a state with the victim-affiliating contacts has a pro-recovery law are likely to present the true conflict paradigm. As the cases below illustrate, the solutions to these conflicts are neither easy nor beyond question. Either state may apply its own law, depending in part on where the litigation takes place, as well as on many other variable factors.

a. Cases Applying the Pro–Defendant Law of a Defendant–Affiliated State

§ 17.69 Among these cases, *Kelly v. Ford Motor Co.*,[1] a diversity case decided under Pennsylvania conflicts law, presented the conflict in its starkest terms. The victim, a domiciliary of Pennsylvania was killed in that state by a car he acquired there. The defendant Ford, a Michigan-based corporation, had designed, tested, and manufactured the car in Michigan and sold it through a Pennsylvania dealer. Pennsylvania, but not Michigan, imposed punitive damages on the manufacturer. The court acknowledged Pennsylvania's interests "in punishing defendants who injure its residents and ... in deterring them and others from engaging in similar conduct which poses a risk to Pennsylvania's citizens."[2] However, the court found that Michigan had "a very strong interest"[3] in denying punitive damages to ensure that "its domiciliary defendants are

because one state's interest was attenuated).

6. These patterns are under inclusive in that they only cover cases in which the contacts affiliated with one party are situated either in the same state or in states whose laws favor the same party. Because the number of relevant contacts in product-liability conflicts is as high as five, many cases do not fit the above specification. One example is cases in which the three plaintiff-affiliating contacts (domicile, injury, and place of acquisition) are located in two or three different states and one of those states has a law that favors the plaintiff while the other favors the defendant. Considering that the same possibility exists

with regard to the two defendant-affiliating contacts, many more permutations are possible. Depending on the other factors, these permutations may present a true conflict with regard to one pair of states and a false, or no-interest conflict with regard to another pair of states. Nevertheless, for the sake of simplicity, the following discussion places all these "mixed" cases into the one or the other of the major patterns.

§ 17.69

1. 933 F.Supp. 465 (E.D.Pa.1996).

2. Id. at 470.

3. Id.

protected from excessive financial liability."[4] The court reasoned that "[b]y insulating companies such as Ford, who conduct extensive business within its borders, Michigan hopes to promote corporate migration into its economy ... [which] will enhance the economic climate and well being of the state of Michigan by generating revenues."[5] The court concluded that, if faced with such a conflict, the Pennsylvania Supreme Court would "adopt a test that focuses on either the place of the defendant's conduct or the defendant's ... principal place of business,"[6] both of which were situated in Michigan, rather than on the place of the victim's injury or domicile, both of which were situated in Pennsylvania, and "predicted" that the Pennsylvania court would "hold that Michigan's law prohibiting the award of punitive damages applies to the instant case."[7]

While this prediction has yet to materialize, *Kelly* remains noteworthy for resisting the temptation of favoring the local victim who is favored by local law.[8] Such resistance is easier in cases involving punitive damages (in which the defendant-affiliated contacts justifiably attract more attention) than in cases involving other issues, such as compensatory damages. Even so, cases involving issues other than punitive damages, such as issues of successor liability,[9] strict liability,[10] and statutes of

4. Id.

5. Id.

6. Id. at 469.

7. Id. at 470.

8. See also Gadzinski v. Chrysler Corp., 2001 WL 629336 (N.D.Ill. 2001) (refusing to award punitive damages under Illinois law to an Illinois plaintiff who was injured in Indiana by a product she purchased from an Indiana dealer. Indiana law did not allow punitive damages).

9. See, e.g., Jones v. SEPTA, 1993 WL 141646 (E.D. Pa. 1993). In this case, the defendant-affiliating contacts were situated in Nebraska, whose law favored the defendant, while the victim-affiliating contacts were split between two states. An Illinois resident was injured while working on an electrical wiring project in Pennsylvania, when his bucket truck came into contact with live electrical wires. He sued a Nebraska corporation that manufactured the truck in Nebraska, and its successor corporation, also a Nebraska corporation. The successor corporation would be liable under the law of Pennsylvania, but not Nebraska. Illinois law was not pleaded. The court noted that Pennsylvania's interest in compensating its citizens was not implicated because the plaintiff was not a Pennsylvania domiciliary, and that, for the same reason, its interest in ensuring adequate compensation for persons injured within its borders was "less pronounced." The court recognized that "Pennsylvania may have an interest in see-

ing that corporations whose products enter the stream of commerce and cause injury in the state not escape the liability that the state imposes on successor corporations, but again, when the injury has no other connection than that it occurred in Pennsylvania, Pennsylvania's interest is more remote than Nebraska's interest in determining the tort liability of its successor corporations." Id. at *7. The court concluded that "[o]n balance, ... Nebraska has a more significant relationship ... and a greater interest than does Pennsylvania." Id. at *8. Since both corporations were from Nebraska, and the acquisition agreement was made in that state, the successor corporation "may have a justified expectation that Nebraska law of successor non-liability ... will apply to it even when an injury for which its predecessor ... may have been liable occurred in another state." Id. at *6.

10. See, e.g., Beals v. Sicpa Securink Corp., 1994 WL 236018 (D.D.C.1994). In this case, the District of Columbia, which was the place of both the injury and the victims' employment, imposed strict liability and unlimited punitive damages for non-ultrahazardous activity, whereas Virginia, which was the place of manufacture and defendant's domicile, did not impose strict liability and limited punitive damages to $350,000. The product at issue was ink used to print currency. The plaintiffs, who were employees of the Bureau of Engraving and Printing in the District of Columbia, had been exposed to allegedly haz-

repose[11] have also reached the same result as *Kelly* and applied the pro-defendant law of a defendant-affiliated state rather than the pro-recovery law of a victim-affiliated state. However, in none of these cases did the latter state have all three of the victim-affiliating contacts that the forum state had in *Kelly*.[12]

b. Cases Applying the Pro–Recovery Law of a Victim–Affiliated State

§ 17.70 The above cases are outnumbered by cases of the same pattern that have reached the opposite result by applying the pro-plaintiff law of a state that had the plaintiff-affiliating contacts. These cases are discussed below, beginning with those in which the state with the pro-plaintiff law had all three plaintiff-affiliating contacts–the plaintiff's domicile and injury, and the place of the product's acquisition.

(1) Choice supported by three contacts

Kramer v. Showa Denko K.K.,[1] involved the issue of punitive damages and the same pattern as *Kelly*. The product, a medicinal drug, was purchased in New York by a domiciliary of that state who used it and suffered the injury also in that state. The product had been designed, tested, and manufactured in Japan by a Japanese corporation. New York, but not Japan, imposed punitive damages. The court erroneously assumed that the case was governed by the *Neumeier* rules,[2] and con-

---

ardous substances contained in this ink. The court recognized the District's interests "in protecting persons who work [there and] . . . in furthering its environmental policies through application of its tort laws," id. at *3, as well as Virginia's interest in regulating manufacturing activity within its borders and protecting manufacturers operating in that state. Id. at *4. Somehow, however, the court also assumed that Virginia's pro-defendant law reflected Virginia's interest in protecting the environment from hazardous substances. Id. at *3–4. Apparently because of this additional albeit fictional "interest," the court concluded that Virginia had greater interests and "more substantial contacts," id. at *3, than the District of Columbia.

11. In Mahoney v. Ronnie's Road Serv., 122 N.C.App. 150, 468 S.E.2d 279 (1996), review on additional issues denied, appeal dismissed by 344 N.C. 438, 476 S.E.2d 118 (1996) aff'd mem., 345 N.C. 631, 481 S.E.2d 85 (N.C.1997), the place of manufacture and the place of injury coincided in the forum state, North Carolina, which had a shorter statute of repose than the plaintiff's domicile, Arizona. Applying the forum's version of UCC § 1–105, which has been interpreted as being equivalent to the Second Restatement's most-significant-relationship formula, the court held that North Carolina's statute applied, thus barring the action, because "North Carolina, the site of manufacture, initial distribution, and injury, bears the 'most significant relationship to the transaction and the parties'." 468 S.E.2d at 282. See also Woessner v. Air Liquide Inc., 242 F.3d 469 (3d Cir.2001).

12. See cases cited supra nn.8–11. In In re Air Crash Disaster at Sioux City, Iowa, 734 F.Supp. 1425 (N.D.Ill.1990), the victim-affiliated contacts and the defendant-affiliated contacts were scattered in several states. The court rightly discounted the victim's domicile and held that the question of whether the two defendant manufacturers should be subject to punitive damages should be determined under the law of the place of design and manufacture of the product, rather than the law of the defendants' principal place of business, or the law of the place of the airplane crash.

§ 17.70

1. 929 F.Supp. 733 (S.D.N.Y.1996).

2. See supra § 17.31.

cluded that the second *Neumeier* rule "require[d]"[3] the application of New York law.

The court failed to notice that Rule 2 consists of two parts (Rules 2a and 2b) and that, as explained earlier, these two parts conflict with each other in split-domicile cross-border torts like *Kramer* in which the conduct and the injury occur in the tortfeasor's and the victim's home states, respectively.[4] Furthermore, the *Neumeier* rules were designed for conflicts between loss-distribution rules, not conduct-regulating rules, especially punitive-damages rules. In conflicts involving the latter rules, it is inappropriate to focus on the domicile of the victim who is ex hypothesi made whole through compensatory damages. Since punitive-damages rules are designed to punish the tortfeasor and deter similarly situated potential tortfeasors, proper analysis of punitive-damages conflicts should focus on the tortfeasor's home state, the place of conduct, and the place of injury.[5] In cases like *Kelly* and *Kramer*, only the last contact is in the state that seeks to punish and deter this conduct, while the first two contacts are in a state that does not espouse this policy of punishment, but rather seeks to spare the manufacturer from the financial burden of punitive damages. The resulting conflict is still a difficult one and the scales can be tipped either way. *Kelly* tilted towards the state of manufacture, while *Kramer* tilted towards the state of injury. *Kelly* gave policy reasons for the decision, while *Kramer* simply recited a rule that was both inapplicable and inconclusive. Nevertheless, the court's decision to apply New York is defensible. In addition to New York's two contacts, the fact that the product was sold there through ordinary commercial channels weakens any argument of unfair surprise on the part of the defendant. Foreign manufacturers who choose to market their products in the lucrative United States market are well aware of the possibility of punitive damages and are in a position to plan, insure, and price their products accordingly.

Cases involving issues other than punitive damages have also reached the same result as *Kramer* by applying the pro-recovery law of a state that had all three victim-affiliating contacts.[6] *Custom Products, Inc.*

---

3. *Kramer*, 929 F.Supp. at 741.

4. See supra §§ 17.32, 17.44. Rule 2a points to Japanese law because the defendant's conduct occurred in Japan and Japan did not impose punitive damages. Rule 2b points to New York law in that the victim was injured in her home state and that state's law permitted recovery of punitive damages.

5. See supra § 17.50.

6. See, e.g., Savage Arms, Inc. v. Western Auto Supply Co., 18 P.3d 49 (Alaska 2001) (successor-liability conflict resolved under the Second Restatement and applying the pro-recovery law of Alaska, which was the victim's domicile, place of injury, and the product's acquisition); Nelson v.

Sandoz Pharm. Corp., 288 F.3d 954 (7th Cir. 2002) (decided under New Jersey conflicts law; applying Indiana's pro-plaintiff discovery rule to Indiana plaintiff's action against New Jersey manufacturer for injury caused in Indiana by a product acquired there); Hoover v. Recreation Equip. Corp., 792 F.Supp. 1484 (N.D.Ohio 1991) (decided under the Second Restatement; applying Ohio law to both products liability and successor liability claims by an Ohio resident injured in that state by a slide manufactured in Indiana by an Indiana corporation that was acquired by another Indiana corporation; concluding that Ohio had both a closer relationship and a greater interest than did Indiana); Eimers v. Honda Motor Co., Ltd., 785 F.Supp. 1204 (W.D.Pa. 1992) (applying New York's pro-plaintiff law to an

v. Fluor Daniel Canada, Inc.,[7] is noteworthy because, although decided in a state that follows a *lex fori approach*, it did not apply the law of the forum which favored a local manufacturer. The case also illustrates the strategy that many manufacturers now employ in hopes of taking advantage of choice-of-law approaches that favor the *lex fori*. Rather than waiting to be sued for injuries their products caused, manufacturers strike first by filing actions for declaratory judgments in a favorable forum. In *Custom Products*, this forum was Kentucky, which "no doubt ... prefers the application of its own laws over those of another forum,"[8] and applies forum law whenever the forum has "significant contacts–not necessarily the most significant contacts."[9] In this case, those contacts were the product's manufacture and the manufacturer's principal place of business. The victim's domicile, place of injury, and the product's acquisition were all in Canada, the law of which favored the victim. Thus, under Currie's assumptions, this was a true conflict in that Kentucky would have an interest in applying its pro-manufacturer law to protect the Kentucky manufacturer, while Canada would have an interest in applying its pro-victim law to protect a Canadian victim injured in Canada. The court found that Canada had an "overwhelming interest,"[10] but rejected the manufacturer's arguments that Kentucky had any significant interest or even "significant contacts." The court noted that the Kentucky manufacturer, albeit being the nominal plaintiff, was not the "injured party"[11] and was "[f]or all practical purposes"[12] the defendant. The court found "no evidence that Kentucky's law was intended to shield [such] a party when they ... cause injury in [another] jurisdiction, and then seek to avoid paying damages,"[13] and concluded that "[t]he law of the forum cannot merely always follow the products of Kentucky corporations whenever they may cause injury in other jurisdictions."[14]

(2) Choice supported by two contacts

§ 17.71 When the state with the pro-plaintiff law has only two–rather than all three–plaintiff-affiliating contacts, its claim to apply its

action by a New York plaintiff injured in New York by a motorcycle acquired in that state and manufactured by a Japanese defendant in Japan); See also Tune v. Philip Morris, Inc., 766 So.2d 350 (Fla.App.2000) (applying Florida's pro-recovery law to an action filed against a tobacco manufacturer by a Florida domiciliary who was diagnosed with lung cancer in that state after using tobacco products in that state and in New Jersey, his previous domicile); In re Masonite Corp. Hardboard Siding Prod. Liab. Litig., 21 F.Supp.2d 593 (E.D.La. 1998) (decided under Florida's Second Restatement approach; noting Florida's strong interest in applying its law to protect its citizens from building materials that were sold and used in that state and which could not withstand that state's extreme weather conditions).

7. 262 F.Supp.2d 767 (W.D.Ky.2003).

8. Rutherford v. Goodyear Tire & Rubber Co., 943 F.Supp. 789, 789 (W.D. Ky. 1996).

9. Foster v. Leggett, 484 S.W.2d, 827, 829 (Ky. 1972).

10. *Custom Products*, 262 F.Supp.2d at 775.

11. Id. at 773.

12. Id. at 774.

13. *Custom Products*, 262 F.Supp.2d at 774. Noting that the Kentucky party "beat [the Canadian party] to the courthouse door," id., the court found that Kentucky had a "greater interest ... in deterring the type of lawsuit which might seek a choice of law advantage." Id.

14. Id. at 775.

law may be weaker, but not by much, at least when the product was commercially available in that state. Thus many cases applied the pro-plaintiff law of a state that was both the plaintiff's domicile and the place of injury, but not the place of the product's acquisition.[1] In *Smith v. DaimlerChrysler Corp.*,[2] which applied Delaware's
pro-plaintiff law to
a Delaware plaintiff's action against a Maryland dealer and a Michigan manufacturer arising out of an accident in Delaware, the court took note of the fact that the Maryland defendant, who was located "a few miles from the Delaware line,"[3] knowingly sold the product to a Delaware domiciliary, and "[could] not reasonably expect to be subject only to the laws of Maryland."[4] Similarly, as *Roll v. Tracor, Inc*
.[5] and *Johnson v.*
Ranch Steamboat Condominium Ass'n[6] indicate, the defendant's argu-
ments are not stronger in cases in which the state of injury is also the place of the product's acquisition, though not the plaintiff's domicile.

In *Roll*, the plaintiff, a New York serviceman, was injured at a military base in Nevada by countermeasure flares acquired by the base authorities in Nevada and manufactured by a Texas manufacturer in Texas. The laws of these states differed on the issue of corporate successor liability, with Nevada and New York laws favoring the plaintiff and Texas law favoring the defendant. The court characterized the successor-liability issue as one of tort law and specifically as one pertaining to loss-allocation rather than conduct-regulation. The court recognized that this was a true conflict between the law of Texas, and the laws of New York and Nevada. Texas had an interest in applying its rule of successor non-liability, because both the defendant and its predecessor corporation had their principal place of business in Texas. However, New York had an equal interest in applying its successor-liability rule so as to provide a remedy to its injured domiciliary, while Nevada had a parallel interest in applying its successor-liability rule so as to provide a remedy to a person injured within its borders.

The court noted that, under *Neumeier* rule 3, Nevada law presumptively governed, and concluded that the defendant did not rebut this presumption. The occurrence of the injury in Nevada was not fortuitous and generally Nevada's contacts were not insignificant. The plaintiff was

---

§ 17.71

1. These cases can be contrasted to cases such as *Normann, Denman, McKinnon, Egan,* and *Land* that applied the law of a state that had the same contacts and a *pro-defendant* law. These cases are discussed infra § 17.78.

2. 2002 WL 31814534 (Del.Super.2002)

3. Id. at *1.

4. Id.

5. 140 F.Supp.2d 1073 (D. Nev. 2001). This action, which was originally filed in New York and then transferred to Nevada, was decided under New York conflicts law.

6. 1999 WL 184068 (N.D.Ill. 1999). In *Johnson*, a Kansas domiciliary was injured in Colorado by a product acquired in Colorado and manufactured in Illinois. Colorado law favored the plaintiff, and Illinois law favored the defendant. Following the Second Restatement, the court acknowledged Illinois' interest in protecting Illinois corporations that manufacture products in that state, but concluded that Colorado's interest in protecting consumers injured in that state by products sold there was more compelling.

stationed in Nevada for some time and, more importantly, the defendant's products were used in Nevada's multiple military bases for many years, thus making foreseeable the occurrence of the injury in that state and the application of that state's law. The court reasoned: "It would be unreasonable for [defendant] to expect that Texas law would automatically shield it from successor liability in every state of the Union. It would be unjust to allow a corporation to escape liability and leave potential plaintiffs without a remedy by simply giving itself a reorganizational facelift, and at the same carry on the same business and manufacture the same product while using the same name, the same plant, and the same personnel."[7]

Finally, *Etheredge v. Genie Industries, Inc.*[8] and *Alexander v. General Motors Corp.*,[9] applied the pro-plaintiff law of a state that was both the plaintiff's domicile and the place of the product's acquisition, but not the place of injury. Ironically, both cases were decided in states following the *lex loci delicti* rule, and thus could not reach this result directly. *Etheredge* used the substance/procedure dichotomy as the reason for refusing to apply the pro-defendant statute of repose of the injury state and applied instead the statute of limitation of the forum state.[10] *Alexander* avoided the pro-defendant *lex loci delicti* by using the *ordre public* exception. A Georgia domiciliary, who purchased in Georgia a car manufactured by the defendant, was injured while driving the car in Virginia. Georgia, but not Virginia, imposed strict liability on manufacturers. Without considering the law of the state of manufacture, the court concluded that its choice was confined between the laws of Virginia and Georgia. The court invoked the *ordre public* exception as the ground for refusing to apply Virginia's negligence law and applied instead Georgia's strict-liability law. A dissenting judge in the court of appeals offered affirmative and more realistic reasons for applying Georgia law, by pointing out that Georgia had an interest in protecting Georgia consumers who acquire in Georgia products marketed in that state. Since the defendant had made the car available for sale in Georgia, that state's "policy of placing the burden on the manufacturer who markets a new product to take responsibility for injury to members of the consuming public for whose use and/or consumption the product is made"[11] was implicated in this case, even though the actual injury had fortuitously occurred in Virginia.

---

7. *Roll*, 104 F.Supp.2d at 1083.

8. 632 So.2d 1324 (Ala. 1994).

9. 267 Ga. 339, 478 S.E.2d 123 (1996).

10. In *Etheredge*, the plaintiff's domicile and place of acquisition were in Alabama, which had a statute of limitation favoring the plaintiff, while the place of injury was in North Carolina, which had a statute of repose favoring the defendant. The opinion does not disclose the place of the product's design and manufacture and the defen-

dant's principal place of business. Although Alabama is a *lex loci delicti* state, the Alabama Supreme Court refused to apply the statute of repose of the *locus* state because, in the court's opinion, that statute was procedural. The court applied instead Alabama's statute of limitation, permitting the action.

11. Alexander v. General Motors Corp., 219 Ga.App. 660, 466 S.E.2d 607, 613 (1995) (McMurray, J., dissenting).

(3) Choice supported by a single contact

§ 17.72 In general, very few states apply the pro-plaintiff law of a state that has only one plaintiff-affiliating contact. For example, only two cases can be found in which the court applied the pro-plaintiff law of a state whose only contact was that the product was purchased there— *Sanchez v. Brownsville Sports Ctr., Inc.*[1] and *Long v. Sears Roebuck & Co.*[2] However, in both of these cases, the parties did not plead the laws of the defendant-affiliated states, and confined their arguments between the pro-defendant law of a state that was the plaintiff's domicile and the place of injury, and the pro-plaintiff law of the state of the product's acquisition.[3]

In *Sanchez,* the product in question, an all-terrain vehicle (ATV), was manufactured by the Japanese defendant in Japan and was sold through a Texas dealer, and then resold second-hand to plaintiff in Mexico, nine years later.[4] The plaintiffs' child was killed while driving the vehicle in Mexico. The defendant argued for the application of Mexican law, which limited the amount of damages and favored the defendant in other respects, while the plaintiff invoked the law of Texas, which provided for strict liability and more generous compensatory damages. Following §§ 145 and 6 of the Restatement Second, the court held that Texas law should govern. The court noted that "Mexican law balances the need to provide relief to its citizens with the country's need to stimulate commerce by limiting the plaintiff's recovery."[5] The court implicitly concluded that Mexico's interests were weak as compared to Texas' interests resulting from the fact that Texas was the place where the particular product was first introduced into the stream of commerce. The court reasoned that, by adopting strict products liability laws, Texas had "expressed a clear interest in protecting its consumers and in regulating the quality of products in its stream of commerce."[6] Although the ATV eventually ended up in Mexico, the key factor is that the ATV

---

§ 17.72

1. 51 S.W.3d 643 (Tex. App. 2001).

2. 877 F.Supp. 8 (D.D.C. 1995).

3. For a case applying the pro-plaintiff law of a state whose only contact was the occurrence of the injury, see Martin v. Goodyear Tire & Rubber Co., 114 Wash. App. 823, 61 P.3d 1196 (2003). An Oregon domiciliary was killed in Washington when struck by metal ring that flew off a truck driven by another Oregon domiciliary unrelated to the victim. The ring was part of a wheel assembly that the truck driver purchased and installed on his truck in Oregon. Oregon's, but not Washington's, statute of repose barred the plaintiff's action against the manufacturer of the assembly. Noting that the Oregon statute was intended to protect Oregon defendants, the court concluded that "Washington's interest in protecting persons from injuries from defective

products within its borders outweighs Oregon's interest in protecting a [non-Oregon] manufacturer whose product arrives in Oregon through the stream of commerce and subsequently causes injury to a third party in another state." Id. at 1201

4. The particular ATV model was no longer distributed for sale in Texas but was distributed in Mexico. For the problem of "dumping products which are suspected of being, or have proved to be, unsafe in a State . . . which has been deliberately chosen because of its low liability laws," see Fawcett, Products Liability in Private International Law: A European Perspective, 238 Recueil des Cours 9, 126 (1993).

5. *Sanchez*, 51 S.W.3d at 670.

6. Id. at 669–70.

was originally placed in the stream of commerce in Texas, and thus Texas had "a strong interest in regulating the conduct of corporations that have business operations in the state."[7] The court noted that "[t]he expansive Texas system of tort liability for defective products serves as an incentive to encourage safer design and to induce corporations to control more carefully their manufacturing processes,"[8] and concluded that "this Texas interest would be furthered by the application of Texas law."[9]

Long v. Sears Roebuck & Co.,[10] involved the same pattern and reached the same result. However, the case also involved the issue of punitive damages and to that extent the outcome is more difficult to defend. In *Long*, the plaintiff was injured in his home state of Maryland by a lawn mower he bought from defendant in the District of Columbia. As in *Sanchez*, the defendant invoked the pro-defendant law of the state of injury, Maryland, but not the law of the state of manufacture, South Carolina. The court concluded that Maryland law, which limited non-economic damages and did not allow punitive damages, was not intended to protect foreign defendants who did not conduct business in Maryland nor engaged in conduct there. In contrast, said the court, the District of Columbia had an interest in deterring and punishing, through its unlimited compensatory and punitive damages, defendants who engage in reprehensible conduct in the District by selling unsafe products there and misrepresenting the product's safety features.

§ 17.73 A handful of cases applied the pro-recovery law of the state of the victim's domicile when that state did not have any other victim-affiliated contacts. Because in all but one[1] of these cases that state was also the forum state, one could ascribe protectionist motives to the courts that decided them. A closer examination, however, finds additional reasons justifying the results in all but two cases. For example, in *Huddy v. Fruehauf Corp.*[2] four of the five involved states (except for the defendant's principal place of business) all had a pro-plaintiff law.[3]

---

7. Id. at 670.

8. Id.

9. Id.

10. 877 F.Supp. 8 (D.D.C. 1995).

§ 17.73

1. In MacDonald v. General Motors Corp., 110 F.3d 337 (6th Cir.1997) (decided under Tennessee's conflicts law), the victim's domicile was not in the forum state. *MacDonald* was a wrongful death action arising from a Tennessee traffic accident caused by a brake defect in a van manufactured by GM in Michigan and sold in Kansas to the University of Kansas. The victim was a student from North Dakota who was a passenger in the van. Kansas, but not North Dakota, limited wrongful-death damages. Neither party argued for the application of Tennessee or Michigan law and the court found the contacts of those states to be inconsequential. The court concluded that, as the domicile of the victim and and the plaintiffs, "North Dakota has the most significant relationship to the measure of damages," id. at 344, that its pro-plaintiff law reflected "a strong interest in assuring that next of kin are fully compensated for the tortious death of its domiciliaries," id. at 345, and that "applying the Kansas statute would frustrate North Dakota's policy of fully compensating its domiciliaries for their injuries." Id. The court acknowledged that Kansas' ceiling on damages reflected an interest in protecting defendants from excessive jury verdicts, but concluded that this interest was not sufficiently compelling.

2. 953 F.2d 955 (5th Cir. 1992).

3. The plaintiff was a former Texas domiciliary who was injured in Georgia while driving a car purchased by his employer in

Similarly, in most of the other cases, the defendant did not plead the law of the state or states with the defendant-affiliating contacts. Thus, the court's choices were confined between the laws of the victim's home state, on the one hand and, on the other hand, a state that was the place of injury,[4] or the place of the products' acquisition,[5] or had both of the latter contacts.[6]

§ 17.74 In contrast to the above cases, *Phillips v. General Motors Corp.*[1] is difficult to defend.[2] *Phillips* was an action by the survivors of a

Tennessee. The defendant invoked the pro-defendant negligence law of its principal place of business, Michigan, but the product in question had been manufactured in Pennsylvania, the law of which favored the plaintiff, as did the law of all the other involved states. The court concluded that this was an insufficient reason to apply Michigan law and applied Texas' pro-plaintiff strict-liability law.

4. See La Plante v. American Honda Motor Co., Inc., 27 F.3d 731 (1st Cir.1994) (discussed infra § 17.74 n.2); Pollack v. Bridgestone/Firestone, Inc., 939 F.Supp. 151 (D.Conn.1996) (applying Connecticut's pro-plaintiff liability law to an injury suffered by a Connecticut domiciliary in an Ohio accident caused by a tire manufactured in Illinois by an Ohio corporation); Calhoun v. Yamaha Motor Corp., U.S.A., 216 F.3d 338 (3d Cir.2000), cert. denied 531 U.S. 1037, 121 S.Ct. 627, 148 L.Ed.2d 536 (2000) (decided under Pennsylvania conflicts law; applying Pennsylvania's pro-recovery law to issues of comparative negligence and compensatory damages to an action by Pennsylvania plaintiffs for injury sustained in Puerto Rico while using a rented Japanese-made water craft–also holding that plaintiffs' claims for punitive damages were governed by Puerto Rico law which does not allow such damages); Ford Motor Co. v. Aguiniga, 9 S.W.3d 252 (Tex. App. 1999) (applying Texas' unlimited compensatory damages law to an action by Texas domiciliaries arising from a Mexico accident involving a car acquired by plaintiffs in Louisiana and inspected in Texas. The defendants invoked Mexico's ceiling on damages, but did not invoke the law of the place of manufacture, apparently because that law did not impose such a ceiling.) See also Hensley v. United States, 728 F.Supp. 716 (S.D.Fla.1989) (Federal Tort Claims Act case decided under the "whole law" of New York as the place of the negligent omission, and applying the substantive law of Florida, as the state of "the greatest interest," to a crash of a small airplane in New Jersey caused in part by negligent omission of the air controllers in New York and killing its Florida passengers).

In Johnson v. Ford Motor Co., Inc., 2003 WL 22317425 (N.D.Ill.2003), the defendant pleaded the law of the state of manufacture, Kentucky, which by coincidence was also the state of injury. The plaintiffs were injured in Kentucky while returning from Florida to Illinois in a car they rented in Illinois. The court reasoned that, because of the fortuity of the accident's locale, the fact that Kentucky had two contacts with the case did not give it any greater interest in applying its law to issues of compensatory damages than the plaintiff's home state, which would bear the social consequences of non-recovery. "It cannot be reasonably inferred," said the court, "that Ford chose to manufacture in Kentucky to obtain the benefits of Kentucky tort laws." Id. at *3. The court held that Illinois' pro-recovery law would govern loss—distribution and Kentucky law should govern issues of conduct regulation—specifically whether plaintiffs' failure to wear seatbelts would reduce their recovery.

5. See, e.g., MacDonald v. General Motors Corp., 110 F.3d 337 (6th Cir.1997) (discussed supra n.1).

6. See, Danielson v. National Supply Co., 670 N.W.2d 1 (Minn.App.2003), the laws of both the state of injury (Arizona) and the state of acquisition (Texas) favored the defendant retailer, but their connections with the case were rather transient. The plaintiff, a Minnesota domiciliary, was injured during his Arizona vacation while using a step ladder that he bought for his motor home while driving through Texas. At issue was the timeliness of the plaintiff's action, which was barred by the statute's of limitation of Texas and Arizona but allowed by Minnesota's statute. The court held that the Minnesota statute should govern, either because it was procedural, or because Minnesota had a greater interest in providing a forum to its injured domiciliary than the other two states had in avoiding litigation of stale claims.

§ 17.74

1. 298 Mont. 438, 995 P.2d 1002 (2000).

2. La Plante v. American Honda Motor Co., Inc., 27 F.3d 731 (1st Cir.1994), a case

Montana family who perished in an accident in Kansas while on a trip from their home state of Montana to North Carolina, when their car exploded upon colliding with another car. The defendant General Motors, a Michigan-based corporation, manufactured the car in Michigan and sold it in North Carolina, where one of the victims purchased it while domiciled there. The defendant invoked the law of Kansas, which had a statute of repose that barred the action, allowed certain defenses not available to manufacturers elsewhere, and limited the amount of compensatory and punitive damages.[3] The plaintiffs invoked the law of Montana, which had no statute of repose, disallowed the manufacturer's defenses, and imposed no limits on compensatory or punitive damages. The court held that Montana had a more significant relationship and that its law should govern all issues of liability and damages. The court found that the purpose of Kansas' products liability law was "to regulate the sale of products in that state and to prevent injuries incurred by that state's residents due to defective products,"[4] and that this purpose "could not be implicated by the facts of this case as it involves neither a sale in Kansas nor an injury to a Kansas resident."[5] The court followed the same rationale even with regard to those rules of Kansas law that protected the manufacturer (such as its statute of repose or the state-of-the art defense) and concluded that these rules "were not enacted in order to grant a defense to a manufacturer when a non-Kansas resident is injured by a product not purchased in Kansas."[6] The court also concluded that Kansas' limitations on the amount of wrongful-death

decided under Rhode Island's better-law approach is equally indefensible. In this case, a Rhode Island domiciliary who was stationed in Colorado was injured in Colorado by a Honda all-terrain vehicle he acquired in that state. The vehicle had been designed and manufactured in Japan by a Japanese corporation. The defendant did not plead the law of Japan, but did plead the law of Colorado. Colorado, but not Rhode Island, limited compensatory damages to $250,000. The court assumed that the purpose of this limit was "to increase the affordability and availability of insurance by making the risk of insured entities more predictable ... [and] improve the predictability of risks faced by insurance companies." However, said the court, "[t]he concern of an insurance company is the risk associated with insuring each individual insured, not with denying an injured person damages that may be paid by another insurance company or person." Id. at 743. Consequently, the court concluded, there was "no reason why the Colorado legislature would be concerned with the affordability of insurance to a multinational Japanese corporation." Id. After noting that defendant sold its products in all fifty states, the court observed that "Colorado's damages law plays, at best, an insignificant role in setting [defendant's] insurance rates" and that defendant had not "ceased doing business in any state because of a failure by that state to limit the amount of damages a plaintiff may recover." Id. The court applied Rhode Island law.

3. The defendant also invoked the laws of North Carolina and Michigan, but did not adequately brief the court on the content of those laws.

4. *Phillips*, 995 P.2d at 1009.

5. Id.

6. Id. at 1009–10. The court disposed in a similar manner of defendant's argument regarding plaintiff's contributory negligence, which would have reduced plaintiff's recovery under Kansas law. While noting that the record contained no evidence of plaintiff's contributory negligence or where such negligence occurred, the court concluded that Kansas' comparative negligence rule was loss-allocating rather than conduct-regulating and that Kansas had "no interest in allocating responsibility for the injuries suffered by Montana residents and caused by a product purchased in North Carolina." Id. at 1010.

damages were intended "to alleviate a perceived crisis in the availability and affordability of liability insurance"[7] and, because no Kansas residents were involved in this case, Kansas had no interest in insisting on those limitations.

Finally, regarding punitive damages, the court focused more on the fact that Kansas law allowed such damages, rather than on the fact that it limited their amount, and concluded that Kansas did not have an interest in deterring the manufacturer because its conduct did not occur in Kansas. The conduct occurred in Michigan, where the car had been manufactured, and North Carolina, where the car had been introduced into the market, but the the defendant did not brief the court on the content of the laws of these states and thus the court's discussion was "somewhat general in nature."[8] In fact, North Carolina law was favorable to the defendant.[9] However, using a *renvoi*-type syllogism, the court concluded that North Carolina had no claim to apply its law because, under the *lex loci* rule followed in that state, a North Carolina court would have applied Kansas law. Thus, said the court, "any expectation General Motors had that the law of North Carolina would govern ... would not be justified."[10]

The court used a similar *renvoi* syllogism to discount Michigan's interest by relying on a similar case in which a Michigan court held that Michigan had "little interest in applying its law when its only contact with the dispute is the location of the manufacturer."[11] Even if Michigan had such an interest, the court reasoned, Michigan law should not be applied because its application "would tend to leave victims under compensated as states wishing to attract and hold manufacturing companies would raise the threshold of liability and reduce compensation."[12] This would allow a state with a high concentration of industry to "capture all of the benefits of a high threshold of liability and a low level of compensation ... by attract[ing] and retain[ing] manufacturing firms

---

7. Id.

8. Id. at 1010.

9. North Carolina requires proof of negligence in products liability actions and, more to the point, has a statute of repose that would bar the action. See Hall v. General Motors Corp., 229 Mich.App. 580, 582 N.W.2d 866 (1998) (discussed infra § 17.77 n.8 ff).

10. *Phillips*, 995 P.2d at 1013.

11. Id. at 1011, citing Farrell v. Ford Motor Co., 199 Mich.App. 81, 501 N.W.2d 567 (1993), appeal denied, 445 Mich. 863, 519 N.W.2d 158 (1994). *Farrell* is discussed infra § 17.77 n.8. While it is true that some Michigan cases have reached this result, see, e.g., Hall v. General Motors Corp., 229 Mich.App. 580, 582 N.W.2d 866 (1998) (discussed infra § 17.77 n.8 ff.; applying North Carolina's pro-manufacturer law, rather than Michigan's pro-plaintiff law, to a prod-

uct liability action filed by a North Carolina victim against General Motors which manufactured the car in Michigan, other cases reached the opposite result). See, e.g., Mahne v. Ford Motor Co., 900 F.2d 83 (6th. Cir. 1990), cert. denied, 498 U.S. 941, 111 S.Ct. 349, 112 L.Ed.2d 313 (1990) (discussed infra § 17.76 n. 26 ff.; applying Michigan's pro-plaintiff law, rather than Florida's pro-manufacturer law, to a products liability action of a Florida domiciliary who was injured in a Florida accident). Moreover, in the Michigan cases that did not apply Michigan law, Michigan law favored a foreign victim at the expense of a Michigan manufacturer. Thus, those cases did not present the converse and more difficult true-conflicts between the pro-plaintiff law of the plaintiff's home state and the pro-manufacturer law of the state of manufacture.

12. *Phillips*, 995 P.2d at 1011–12.

... within its borders while placing the costs of its legislative decision, in the form of less tort compensation, on the shoulders of nonresidents injured by its manufacturers' products."[13] This, said this court, "seems inherently unfair."[14]

Thus, after discounting the interests of the states of injury, conduct, and the defendant's home state, the court considered the interests of the victims' home state, Montana, the law of which favored the victims on liability, as well as compensatory and punitive damages. The court held that Montana's interests predominated in all respects. After noting that Montana adopted a strict liability standard "in order to afford 'maximum protection for consumers against dangerous defects in manufactured products with the focus on the condition of the product, and not on the manufacturer's conduct or knowledge,' "[15] the court stated that "the focus of Montana law is not only on the regulation of products sold in Montana, but also on providing the maximum protection and compensation to Montana residents."[16] The court reasoned that, because the victims in this case were Montana residents, the application of Montana's law of strict liability and full compensation "would further the purposes of Montana law by insuring that the costs to Montana residents due to injuries from defective products are fully borne by the responsible parties"[17] and would have "the salutary effect of deterring future sales of defective products in Montana and encouraging manufacturers to warn Montana residents about defects in their products as quickly and as thoroughly as possible."[18] The court reasoned that the application of Montana's punitive—damages law would serve the same policy of deterrence because "punitive damages serve to punish and deter conduct deemed wrongful—in this case, placing a defective product into the stream of commerce which subsequently injured a Montana resident."[19] Thus, the court concluded, Montana had a more significant relationship than Kansas and this displaced the *lex loci* presumption.

As said at the beginning, one is hard pressed to defend *Phillips*, at least to the extent it imposed punitive damages beyond the limits of Kansas law. On the other hand, the application of Montana law to liability and compensatory damages is more understandable–besides the equities of the case (a whole family perishing with only one minor child surviving), the five contacts were spread in four states, the occurrence of the injury in Kansas was fortuitous, and the product, though purchased in North Carolina, was commercially available throughout the United States, including Montana. Even so, it should be noted that most cases involving a pattern similar to *Phillips* did not apply the pro-plaintiff law of the victim's home state, but rather applied the pro-defendant law of

13. Id. at 1012.

14. Id.

15. Id. at 1012 (quoting Sternhagen v. Dow Co., 282 Mont. 168, 935 P.2d 1139, 1144 (1997)).

16. Id.

17. Id.

18. Id.

19. Id.

another state. However, in contrast to *Phillips,* that other state had *two* contacts–the place of injury and the place of the product's acquisition.[20]

3. Cases in Which Each State's Law Favors a Litigant Affiliated With the Other State

§ 17.75 As said above, in many cases, a state with defendant-affiliating contacts (such as the place of manufacture and/or the defendant's principal place of business) has a law that favors recovery against that defendant, while a state with victim-affiliating contacts (victim's domicile, place of injury, place of acquisition) has a law that denies recovery to that victim. According to Currie, these are the unprovided-for cases in which neither state is interested in applying its law and

20. For example, in LeJeune v. Bliss–Salem, Inc., 85 F.3d 1069 (3d Cir. 1996), a Pennsylvania court refused to apply the strict-liability law of the victim's home state of Pennsylvania, and applied instead the negligence law of Delaware, which was the place of the accident and the place of the product's acquisition. The court compared Pennsylvania's interest in "protect[ing] its citizens from defective products," id. at 1073, with Delaware's interest in "encouraging economic activity in the state . . . and lowering costs to consumers." Id. at 1072. The court concluded that, because most of the conduct had occurred in Delaware and the occurrence of the injury in that state was not fortuitous, Delaware's contacts were "qualitatively" more important and thus "Delaware ha[d] the greater interest in having its law applied." Id. Similarly, in Cianfrani v. Kalmar–AC Handling Systems, Inc., 1995 WL 563289 (D.N.J. 1995), a New Jersey court refused to apply the strict-liability law of Pennsylvania, the plaintiff's home state, and applied instead Delaware's negligence law to an action arising from an accident in plaintiff's Delaware employment site. The accident was caused by a defective fork lift leased by plaintiff's employer in Delaware. While recognizing Pennsylvania's interest in protecting its domiciliary plaintiff, the court held that, because this case involved a question of liability rather than damages, Delaware had a greater interest "in defining the circumstances under which people who do business in or ship goods to Delaware will be exposed to liability". Id. at *6. In Romani v. Cramer, Inc., 992 F.Supp. 74 (D.Mass. 1998), the victim was domiciled in Massachusetts, but was employed in Connecticut and was injured there while using a chair supplied by his employer. The chair had been manufactured by a Kansas corporation, apparently in Kansas, but neither party urged the application of Kansas law. Unlike Massachusetts, Connecticut had a statute of repose barring the plaintiff's action. The court found that the victim's domicile in Massachusetts did not give that state a sufficient interest to override "Connecticut's superior interest on all other fronts." Id. at 79. Connecticut's interest was superior because "Connecticut enacted its statute [of repose] to protect manufacturers from liability for products whose useful lives have expired . . . [and to] encourage[] manufacturers to freely sell products within its borders." Id. at 78. See also Allison v. ITE Imperial Corp., 928 F.2d 137 (5th Cir. 1991) (decided under Mississippi conflicts law; applying Tennessee's statute of repose, rather than Mississippi's statute of limitation, and barring the action of a Mississippi plaintiff for a Tennessee injury caused by a defective electrical circuit breaker sold and installed in Tennessee, but manufactured by a Pennsylvania-based defendant in Pennsylvania; the court did not describe Pennsylvania law); Tanges v. Heidelberg N. Am., Inc., 93 N.Y.2d 48, 687 N.Y.S.2d 604, 710 N.E.2d 250 (1999) (applying Connecticut's statute of repose barring an action brought by a New York domiciliary who was injured by a printing press while working for his employer in Connecticut); Calhoun v. Yamaha Motor Corp., U.S.A., 216 F.3d 338 (3d Cir. 2000), cert. denied 531 U.S. 1037, 121 S.Ct. 627, 148 L.Ed.2d 536 (2000) (action by Pennsylvania plaintiffs for injury sustained in Puerto Rico while using a rented Japanese-made watercraft; holding that plaintiffs' claims for punitive damages were governed by Puerto Rico law (which does not allow such damages) because "Puerto Rico's interest in regulating the activity that occurs in its territorial waters . . . is more dominant." Id. at 348); Schmidt v. Duo–Fast, Inc., 1995 WL 422681 (E.D. Pa. 1995) (applying New Jersey pro-defendant law to the claim of a Pennsylvania worker injured in a New Jersey construction accident caused by a tool

which should be resolved by resort to the law of the forum *qua forum*. As
the discussion below illustrates, many of these cases have in fact applied
the law of the forum, but not on this basis. Moreover, very few of these
cases have accepted Currie's assumption that a state that has a law that
disfavors the local litigant necessarily has no interest in applying it.[1] For
example, in cases that applied the pro-recovery law of a defendant-
affiliated state, the courts have done so on the basis of an affirmative
policy of deterring the manufacture of substandard products and were
unconcerned by the fact that the beneficiaries of such application would
be foreign victims.[2] Similarly, in cases that applied the pro-defendant law
of a victim-affiliated state, the courts have done so either on the basis of
a significant-contacts analysis that did not encompass consideration of
state interests,[3] or on the basis of an assumption that the pro-defendant
law of the victim's state was not confined to local defendants but was
rather intended to encompass foreign defendants as well.[4]

a. Cases Applying the Pro–Recovery Law of a Defendant–Affiliated State

§ 17.76 Among the cases that have applied the pro-recovery law of
a defendant-affiliated state, *Gantes v. Kason Corp.*[1] is the most representative. *Gantes* was an action brought by the survivors of a Georgia
woman killed in Georgia while working with a machine manufactured
thirteen years earlier in New Jersey, by a New Jersey-based corporation.
Georgia's ten-year statute of repose barred the action, which was timely
under New Jersey's two-year statute of limitations. Relying on a Georgia
case, the New Jersey court noted that the Georgia statute was designed
" 'to address problems generated by the open-ended liability of manufacturers so as to ... stabilize products liability underwriting.' "[2] Assuming
that the Georgia statute was "intended only to unburden Georgia courts

purchased from Pennsylvania but shipped
directly to New Jersey).

§ 17.75

1. Among these cases are In re Eli Lilly
& Co., Prozac Prod. Liab. Litig., 789
F.Supp. 1448, 1454 (S.D.Ind.1992) (action
by California residents injured in California
by a drug acquired and used in that state
against an Indiana manufacturer who manufactured the drug in Indiana; concluding
that "Indiana would have no interest in the
application of [its] more pro-plaintiff rule to
... cases in which plaintiffs have no connection to Indiana and the Indiana connections all involve the business of the defendant."); Rutherford v. Goodyear Tire &
Rubber Co., 943 F.Supp. 789 (W.D.Ky.
1996), aff'd 142 F.3d 436 (6th Cir.1998)
(discussed infra § 17.77 n.25 ff.); Mahne v.
Ford Motor Co., 900 F.2d 83 (6th. Cir.1990)
(discussed infra § 17.76 n.26 ff.); Dabbs v.

Silver Eagle Mfg. Co., 98 Or.App. 581, 779
P.2d 1104 (1989) (discussed infra § 17.76
n.27).

2. See, e.g., Gantes v. Kason Corp., 145
N.J. 478, 679 A.2d 106 (1996) (discussed
infra § 17.76 n.1 ff.).

3. See, e.g., Dorman v. Emerson Elec.
Co., 23 F.3d 1354 (8th Cir.1994), cert. denied 513 U.S. 964, 115 S.Ct. 428, 130
L.Ed.2d 341 (1994) (discussed infra § 17.77
n.1 ff.).

4. See, e.g., Hall v. General Motors
Corp., 229 Mich.App. 580, 582 N.W.2d 866
(1998) (discussed infra § 17.77 n.8 ff.).

§ 17.76

1. 145 N.J. 478, 679 A.2d 106 (1996).

2. Id. at 109 (quoting Chrysler Corp. v.
Batten, 264 Ga. 723, 450 S.E.2d 208, 212
(1994)).

and to shield Georgia manufacturers,"[3] the court concluded that Georgia had no interest in applying that statute, because the defendant was not a Georgia manufacturer, and Georgia courts were not involved in this case. Plaintiffs' Georgia domicile brought into play Georgia's general policy "of fair compensation for injured domiciliaries."[4] The Georgia statute subordinated that policy to the policy of protecting manufacturers, but only in those cases that involved Georgia manufacturers. Since the defendant in this case was not a Georgia manufacturer, Georgia had no real interest in applying its statute.[5]

In contrast, said the court, New Jersey had a "cognizable and substantial interest in deterrence that would be furthered by the application of its statute of limitations."[6] The court described the policies embodied in that statute which, as a result of the judicially-engrafted discovery rule, is permeated by "flexible, equitable considerations based on notions of fairness to the parties and the justice in allowing claims to be resolved on their merits."[7] The court also noted that the goal of tort law in general and products liability law in particular is "to encourage reasonable conduct, and, conversely, to discourage conduct that creates an unreasonable risk of injury to others."[8] Because the machine that caused the fatal injury had been "manufactured in, and placed into the stream of commerce from, [New Jersey],"[9] the court concluded, New Jersey had a "strong interest in encouraging the manufacture and distribution of safe products for the public and, conversely, in deterring the manufacture and distribution of unsafe products within the state."[10] The court rejected the lower court's conclusion that this interest in deterrence was outweighed by the possibility of unduly discouraging manufacturing in New Jersey.[11] Thus, by reading the forum's interests in a non-protectionist way, the court concluded that what might have been an unprovided-for case under Currie's analysis was in fact a false conflict in which only the forum was an interested state.

If *Kelly*[12] is noteworthy for favoring a foreign manufacturer at the expense of a local victim, *Gantes* is noteworthy for favoring a foreign victim at the expense of a local manufacturer. Of course, *Gantes* did so not for the sake of protecting the victim, but rather in pursuance of the forum's policy of deterring the manufacture of substandard products within its territory. While some commentators[13] and some courts,[14]

---

3. Id. at 114–15.

4. Id. at 115.

5. See also id. at 115 (concluding that the non-application of Georgia law "[would] not undermine Georgia's interest in compensating its injured residents because that interest is not actually implicated or compromised by allowing a products-liability action brought by Georgia residents to proceed against a non-Georgia manufacturer.").

6. Id. at 113.

7. Id. at 110.

8. Id. at 111.

9. Id.

10. Id. at 111–12.

11. See id. at 112. The court also dismissed the forum-shopping argument because, as shown by the defendant's contacts with the forum state, the plaintiff had legitimate reasons to sue there.

12. Kelly v. Ford Motor Co., 933 F.Supp. 465 (E.D.Pa.1996) (discussed supra § 17.69).

13. See, e.g., Kozyris, Values and Methods in Choice of Law for Product Liability: A Comparative Comment on Statutory Solutions, 38 Am. J. Comp. L. 475, 501 (1990)

14. See p. 921.

including the U.S. Supreme Court in dictum,[15] have questioned this policy, other courts have espoused it,[16] including courts sitting in the state with the defendant-affiliated contacts. For example, in *Mitchell v. Lone Star Ammunition, Inc.*,[17] the court concluded that Texas had a "substantial interest" in applying it pro-plaintiff law "as an incentive to encourage safer design and to induce corporations to control more carefully the manufacturing processes."[18] In *McLennan v. American Eurocopter Corp., Inc.*,[19] the court concluded that Texas had a strong interest in enforcing its strict product-liability law against manufacturers operating in that state, while noting that the application of that law did not impose an unexpected burden on a Texas-based manufacturer. In

(stating that: (1) "[the assumption] that imposing the stricter standards of the state of production to the-out-of-state distribution and harm may indirectly improve the in-state component as well … is … questionable in its logic of prohibiting what should be lawful to deter what is unlawful," (2) that "[a] purported 'moral' concern of the state of production about local activities which endanger people worldwide … is [also] not persuasive;" and (3) "Preferring the law of the state of production over those of distribution, harm and personal connections of the parties would be inconsistent with considerations both of allocating sovereign authority and of fairness to the parties.").

14. See, e.g., Hall v. General Motors Corp. 229 Mich.App. 580, 582 N.W.2d 866 (1998) (discussed infra § 17.77 n.8 ff.); Farrell v. Ford Motor Co., 199 Mich.App. 81, 501 N.W.2d 567 (1993), app. denied 445 Mich. 863, 519 N.W.2d 158 (1994) (discussed infra § 17.77 n.8.); Vestal v. Shiley Inc., 1997 WL 910373 (C.D.Cal.1997) (discussed infra § 17.77 n.8; noting California's interest in deterring California manufacturers from manufacturing defective products within its borders but concluding that that interest is adequately served by applying California law to the many actions filed by California plaintiffs).

15. In Piper Aircraft Co. v. Reyno, 454 U.S. 235, 260–61, 102 S.Ct. 252, 268, 70 L.Ed.2d 419 (1981), the Supreme Court, while holding that the dismissal of an action brought in Pennsylvania by Scottish plaintiffs on forum non conveniens grounds was not an abuse of discretion, discussed, but did not decide, whether the law of the place of manufacture, Pennsylvania, or the law of the plaintiffs' domicile and place of injury, Scotland, should apply. The Court stated that the incremental deterrence achieved by application of the law of the place of manufacture was not likely to be significant.

16. In addition to the cases discussed in the text, see, e.g., Lewis–DeBoer v. Mooney Aircraft Corp., 728 F.Supp. 642 (D.Colo. 1990), (concluding that Texas, as the place of the defendant's conduct and principal place of business, "ha[d] a greater policy interest in applying its laws and providing deterrence than Colorado ha[d] in preventing a windfall to its citizens." Id. at 645. Colorado was the victim's home state and place of injury.); In re Disaster at Detroit Metro. Airport on August 16, 1987, 750 F.Supp. 793 (E.D.Mich.1989) (applying California's pro-recovery strict-liability rule in order to effectuate California's policy of ensuring the manufacture of safe products within its borders).

17. 913 F.2d 242 (5th Cir. 1990).

18. Id. at 250. In *Mitchell*, the product was manufactured and sold in Texas by defendants who had their principal places of business in Maryland and California, respectively. The plaintiff were the survivors of Kentucky and New Mexico servicemen who were killed in North Carolina by defendants' defective munitions. North Carolina, but not Texas, had a statute of repose barring the plaintiffs' actions. The court concluded that North Carolina did not have an interest in applying its statute to protect foreign manufacturers and to deprive of a remedy persons injured in that state. In contrast, the court concluded that Texas had a substantial interest in encouraging the manufacture of safe products and that this interest was "particularly strong" in this case because "the defective product in question was manufactured and placed in the stream of commerce in the state of Texas." Id.

19. 245 F.3d 403 (5th Cir. 2001) (decided under Texas conflicts law and applying Texas pro-plaintiff law to an action of a Canadian domiciliary injured in Canada by a product manufactured by a Texas manufacturer in Texas).

DeGrasse v. Sensenich Corp.,[20] the court concluded that applying Pennsylvania law, which favored an Arkansas plaintiff at the expense of a Pennsylvania manufacturer, was in line with Pennsylvania's interests because "Pennsylvania's policy involves the attainment of broader objectives than simply ensuring full recovery for its domiciliary plaintiffs ... [such as] deterring the manufacture of defective products by, and assigning responsibility for such an activity to, Pennsylvania manufacturers."[21] Finally, in *Lacey v. Cessna Aircraft Co.,*[22] the court reiterated its earlier statement in *Reyno v. Piper Aircraft Co.*[23] that the application of Pennsylvania's strict liability law to a case involving a product that was manufactured in Pennsylvania and caused injury in British Columbia would "further Pennsylvania's interest in deterring the manufacture of defective products ... but would not impair British Columbia's interest in fostering industry within its borders."[24]

Even more numerous are the cases in which, without expressly articulating this policy, the courts allowed claims against a forum manufacturer that would have been barred by the statute of repose of the other, victim-affiliated, state. They did so either by characterizing the foreign statute as procedural,[25] or by concluding, as *Gantes* did, that the

---

20. 1989 WL 23775 (E.D.Pa. 1989).

21. Id. at *4. *DeGrasse* was a products-liability action filed by the survivors of two Arkansas passengers of a small airplane that crashed in Alabama. The defendant was a Pennsylvania corporation that manufactured the plane's propeller in Pennsylvania. The court dismissed as irrelevant the place of the injury and then focused on the laws of Arkansas and Pennsylvania, the first of which was more favorable to defendant. The court acknowledged that this could be an "unprovided-for" case in which Arkansas, the pro-defendant state, had no defendant to protect, while Pennsylvania, the pro-plaintiff state, had no plaintiff to protect. However, as noted in the text, the court refused to adopt such a narrow reading of state interests. The court concluded that the application of Pennsylvania law would not be unfair to a defendant domiciled and acting in that state. Analogizing this case to Cipolla v. Shaposka, 439 Pa. 563, 267 A.2d 854 (1970) (discussed supra §§ 17.13 n.18 ff., 17.42), the court said that "[j]ust as the defendant in Cipolla, a resident of defendant-protecting Delaware, was not subjected to liability exceeding that created by his home state law for conduct within that state merely because the victim came from a state offering higher protection to plaintiffs, neither should a defendant be afforded a bonus of the application of more favorable law regarding his allegedly tortious conduct in his home state merely because the plaintiff in the action happens to reside in a state where the law strikes a

balance which is generally less favorable to plaintiffs." DeGrasse, 1989 WL 23775 at *4.

22. 932 F.2d 170 (3d Cir. 1991).

23. 630 F.2d 149 (3d Cir. 1980).

24. *Lacey*, 932 F.2d at 188.

25. In Baxter v. Sturm, Ruger & Co., Inc., 230 Conn. 335, 644 A.2d 1297 (1994), a products liability action filed by an Oregon plaintiff against a Connecticut gun manufacturer for injury sustained in Oregon, the court concluded that *under Connecticut's* characterization standards, Oregon's statute of repose was procedural and thus would be inapplicable to an action filed in Connecticut. Thus the action was timely under Connecticut's statute of limitation. In Cosme v. Whitin Machine Works, Inc., 417 Mass. 643, 632 N.E.2d 832 (1994), it was Connecticut's statute of repose that was at issue. If applicable, that statute would have barred the plaintiff's action which was timely under Massachusetts' statute of limitation. The plaintiff, a Massachusetts domiciliary, had been injured in Connecticut while using machinery that the defendant, a Massachusetts corporation, had manufactured in Massachusetts and had delivered to plaintiff's employer in Connecticut. The court concluded that, despite the fact that Connecticut had characterized its statute of repose as procedural, statutes of repose are substantive, and thus a conflict involving such statutes is to be resolved under the same approach that the court follows for substantive issues. Apply-

foreign statute was not intended to protect forum manufacturers. Thus, in *Mahne v. Ford Motor Co.*,[26] the court concluded that Florida's statute of repose was intended to protect Florida manufacturers, not Michigan manufacturers such as the ones involved in this case. The latter "cannot argue that applying Michigan law would defeat their expectations," said the court, and "[t]hus, there is simply no reason to extend the benefits of the Florida statute of repose to the Michigan defendants."[27]

Similarly, other cases involving conflicts between the pro-victim law of a defendant-affiliated state and the pro-manufacturer law of a victim-affiliated state on issues such as strict liability,[28] punitive damages,[29]

ing Massachusetts' functional analysis but also relying on the Second Restatement, the court concluded that Massachusetts had a more significant relationship and a greater interest in having its law applied than did Connecticut. The court noted that Connecticut's characterization of its statute of repose as procedural indicated that that state had "a diminished expectation of having it apply in other jurisdictions as part of its substantive law." 417 Mass. at 649, 632 N.E.2d at 836.

26. 900 F.2d 83 (6th. Cir. 1990,)cert. denied, Ford Motor Co. v. Mahne, 498 U.S. 941, 111 S.Ct. 349, 112 L.Ed.2d 313 (1990).

27. *Mahne*, 900 F.2d at 88–89. See also Dabbs v. Silver Eagle Mfg. Co., 98 Or.App. 581, 779 P.2d 1104 (1989) review denied, 308 Or. 608, 784 P.2d 1101 (1989) (action of a Tennessee resident injured in Tennessee by a product acquired there and manufactured in Oregon by an Oregon-based defendant; concluding that Tennessee had no interest in applying its shorter statute of limitation barring the action, because no Tennessee defendant was involved in this case; applying Oregon's longer statute of limitation permitting the action); Marchesani v. Pellerin–Milnor Corp., 269 F.3d 481 (5th Cir. 2001) (decided under Louisiana conflicts law—applying Louisiana statute of limitations and allowing a products liability action that was barred by Tennessee's statute of repose—the action was brought against a Louisiana manufacturer by a Tennessee domiciliary who was injured in Tennessee by a product manufactured in Louisiana). In Davis v. Shiley, 75 Cal.Rptr.2d 826 (App. 1998), Oregon, the place of the victim's domicile and injury, had a statute of repose barring the action, whereas California, the state of manufacture and defendant's principal place of business, did not. The court allowed the action after finding the Oregon statute inapplicable because of Oregon's lack of interest in applying it to protect a foreign manufacturer at the expense of an Oregon domiciliary.

28. In Magnant v. Medtronic, Inc., 818 F.Supp. 204 (W.D.Mich.1993), the plaintiff, a Michigan domiciliary, sued a Minnesota corporation for injury sustained in Michigan as a result of a defect in a heart pacemaker designed and manufactured by the defendant and implanted in plaintiff in Minnesota. Minnesota, but not Michigan, imposed strict liability on manufacturers. In determining whether there was a good reason to displace Michigan's *lex fori* presumption, the court found that Minnesota had an interest in applying it pro-plaintiff law to Minnesota defendants "in order to provide them with certainty as to which law would apply and predictability of results." Id. at 207. The court also noted that the defendant "cannot complain that application of Minnesota law is unfair or contrary to its expectations." Id. As for Michigan's interests, the court reasoned, "[t]he interest in protecting citizens does not weigh in favor of Michigan law . . . because [plaintiff] would receive more rights under Minnesota law than under Michigan law." Id. Thus, the court concluded, "Minnesota's interests provide a sound reason for displacing Michigan law in this case." Id. See also In re Disaster at Detroit Metropolitan Airport on August 16, 1987, 750 F.Supp. 793 (E.D.Mich.1989) (multidistrict litigation case filed by residents of Michigan, Arizona, and Florida against Missouri manufacturer who manufactured in California a plane that crashed in Michigan; applying California's pro-recovery strict liability rule in order to effectuate California's policy of ensuring the manufacture of safe products within its borders); McLennan v. American Eurocopter Corp., Inc., 245 F.3d 403 (5th Cir.2001) (applying Texas strict-liability law to an action by a Canadian plaintiff who was injured in Canada by a helicopter manufactured in Texas by a Texas corporation).

29. See, e.g., Lewis–DeBoer v. Mooney Aircraft Corp., 728 F.Supp. 642, 645 (D.Colo.1990) (action by Colorado plaintiffs against the Texas manufacturer of a small airplane that crashed in Colorado killing its

successor liability,[30] and other issues[31] have also reached the same result by applying the law of the former state.

b. Cases Applying the Pro–Defendant Law of a Victim–Affiliated State

§ 17.77 The cases discussed in the preceding section are outnumbered by cases of the same pattern that reached the opposite result by applying the *pro-defendant* law of a state that had the plaintiff-affiliating contacts. These cases are discussed below, beginning with those in which the state with the pro-defendant law had all three plaintiff-affiliating contacts–the plaintiff's domicile and injury, and the place of the product's acquisition.

(1) Choice supported by three contacts

Dorman v. Emerson Electric Co.,[1] a case decided under the Second Restatement,[2] which establishes a presumption in favor of the place of

Colorado passengers; aside from punitive damages, which were permitted in Texas but not in Colorado, Texas law was generally more generous to the plaintiff with regard to compensatory damages and the burden of proof; after dismissing as fortuitous the occurrence of the injury in Colorado, the court concluded that Texas, as the place of the defendant's conduct and principal place of business, "ha[d] a greater policy interest in applying its laws and providing deterrence than Colorado has in preventing a windfall to its citizens." Id. at 645).

30. See, e.g., Standal v. Armstrong Cork Co., 356 N.W.2d 380 (Minn.App.1984) (applying pro-recovery Pennsylvania law to a claim of a Minnesota resident against Pennsylvania manufacturers); Ruiz v. Blentech Corp., 89 F.3d 320 (7th Cir.1996), cert. denied 519 U.S. 1077, 117 S.Ct. 737, 136 L.Ed.2d 677 (1997), 519 U.S. 1077, 117 S.Ct. 737, 136 L.Ed.2d 677 (1997) (holding that, under Illinois conflicts law, products-liability claims of an Illinois resident injured in Illinois by a product manufactured in California would be governed by Illinois law, while issues of successor liability would be governed by California's pro-recovery rule; eventually holding the latter rule inapplicable on the ground that California characterizes such rule as part of its products-liability law (rather than its corporate law)).

31. See, e.g., Torrington Co. v. Stutzman, 46 S.W.3d 829 (Tex. 2000) (applying Texas pro-plaintiff compensatory damages law to an action filed against a Texas-based corporation that manufactured a helicopter

in Texas; the place of injury and the victims' domiciles were in three different states); Champlain Enterp., Inc. v. United States, 945 F.Supp. 468 (N.D.N.Y. 1996) (action for recovery of pure economic loss filed by a New York plaintiff whose plane crashed in New York, against a Kansas defendant who manufactured the plane in Kansas; applying Kansas's pro-plaintiff law, but holding for defendant on the merits); Offshore Logistics, Inc. v. Bell Helicopter Textron, 1995 WL 555593 (E.D.La 1995) (applying Texas pro-plaintiff law to an action arising out of a Louisiana crash of a helicopter manufactured in Texas by a Texas defendant).

§ 17.77

1. 23 F.3d 1354 (8th Cir.1994), cert. denied 513 U.S. 964, 115 S.Ct. 428, 130 L.Ed.2d 341 (1994) (decided under Missouri conflicts law).

2. The Second Restatement applies its pervasive "most-significant relationship" test of § 145 to products liability, but in the case of personal injuries § 146 refers to "the state where the injury occurred" unless another state has a more significant relationship to the occurrence. For early cases applying the most-significant-relationship test, see Bowles v. Zimmer Mfg. Co., 277 F.2d 868, 76 A.L.R.2d 120 (7th Cir. 1960); Neville Chem. Co. v. Union Carbide Corp., 422 F.2d 1205 (3d Cir.1970), cert. denied 400 U.S. 826, 91 S.Ct. 51, 27 L.Ed.2d 55 (1970); Westerman v. Sears, Roebuck & Co., 577 F.2d 873, 879 (5th Cir.1978).

the injury,[3] is representative of this group of cases. The product, a miter saw, had been acquired by a domiciliary of British Columbia, Canada, and had caused injury to him in that province. That particular miter saw had been manufactured in Taiwan by a Taiwanese corporation under license from defendant, a Missouri corporation, which had designed and tested that line of products in Missouri.[4] Unlike Missouri, British Columbia did not impose strict liability on manufacturers. The court concluded that the plaintiff did not rebut the presumption established by § 146 of the Second Restatement in favor of the law of the place of injury, and thus the law of British Columbia governed. The plaintiff had argued that, because the saw had been designed in Missouri, that state had an interest in deterring substandard conduct within its territory. The court recognized the existence of this interest but found it insufficient to rebut the presumption.[5] The court enumerated the Canadian contacts and, without articulating any corresponding Canadian interests, concluded that "Canada's interests in and contacts with this case are at least as substantial as Missouri's."[6]

Considering the starting point of the court's analysis, the application of British Columbia law is not surprising. Indeed, if one begins with a presumptive *lex loci* rule and is thinking in terms of weighing factual contacts (rather than state interests in light of pertinent contacts), then there is nothing surprising in saying that in this case the presumption had not been rebutted by the forum's contacts which, although non-negligible, were less than overwhelming. However, there is more room for disagreement when the court purports to base the application of the

---

3. For other cases decided under a similar presumption, see Bain v. Honeywell Int'l, Inc., 257 F.Supp.2d 872 (E.D.Tex. 2002) (applying British Columbia's pro-defendant law to the action of an Australian residing in British Columbia and arising from an injury there); Walls v. General Motors, 906 F.2d 143 (5th Cir. 1990) (applying Oregon's statute of repose to bar action of Oregon plaintiff injured in Oregon by a car he acquired in that state); Walters v. Warren Eng'g Corp., 246 Ill.App.3d 1084, 617 N.E.2d 170 (Ill. App. 1993) (applying Kansas law to a Kansas plaintiff's action injured in Kansas by a machine partly manufactured in Illinois). For a case decided under Indiana's significant contacts approach, see In re Eli Lilly & Co. Prozac Prod. Liab. Litig., 789 F.Supp. 1448 (S.D.Ind. 1992) (action by California residents, injured in that state by a drug acquired and used there, against Indiana defendant who manufactured the drug in Indiana). For cases decided under article 3545 of the Louisiana codification (which requires the application of the law of the forum state if that state is also the victim's home state, place of injury, and place of acquisition), see Clark v. Favalora, 722

So.2d 82 (La. App. 1998), Orleans Parish Sch. Bd. v. United States Gypsum Co., 1993 WL 205091 (E.D.La. 1993), and Jefferson Parish Hosp. Dist. #2 v. W.R. Grace, 1992 WL 167263 (E.D.La. 1992). See also K.E. Pittman v. Kaizer Aluminum & Chem. Corp., 559 So.2d 879 (La. App. 1990) (same result under pre-codification law).

4. The miter saw had been purchased by a Canadian corporation that was affiliated with defendant and had been sold to a Canadian retailer without ever having entered the United States.

5. See *Dorman*, 23 F.3d at 1359. In Burleson v. Liggett Group Inc., 111 F.Supp.2d 825 (E.D.Tex. 2000), the plaintiffs did not articulate the interests of the state of manufacture in applying its pro-plaintiff law. The plaintiffs sued tobacco manufacturers seeking to recover damages caused by plaintiffs smoking of defendants' cigarettes. The action was specifically barred by a special Texas statute designed to protect tobacco manufacturers, and the court held that foreign manufacturers who distributed tobacco products in Texas fell within the protective scope of that statute.

6. *Dorman*, 23 F.3d at 1361.

pro-manufacturer law of the victim's home state on the ostensible interests of that state.[7]

One such case is *Hall v. General Motors Corp.*,[8] which held that the victim's home state was interested in barring his action against an out-of-state manufacturer who was not protected by the law of its home state. At the time of the injury, the plaintiff was domiciled in North Carolina[9] and was injured in that state by a car designed in Michigan[10]

---

7. For cases reaching the same result under Leflar's approach, see Hughes v. Wal–Mart Stores, Inc., 250 F.3d 618 (8th Cir. 2001); Nesladek v. Ford Motor Co., 46 F.3d 734 (8th Cir. 1995), cert. denied, 516 U.S. 814, 116 S.Ct. 67, 133 L.Ed.2d 28 (1995). In *Hughes*, the product was sold by an Arkansas defendant in Louisiana to the Louisiana plaintiffs, and caused the injury in Louisiana. The plaintiffs could recover against the defendant under Arkansas law, but not under Louisiana law. The court held that Louisiana law governed because only one of the five Leflar factors was dispositive—"maintenance of interstate and international order"—and this factor pointed to Louisiana, because that state had nearly all the significant contacts. Arkansas had no interest in applying its pro-plaintiff law against an Arkansas defendant when the plaintiff was not a resident of Arkansas and the injury did not occur there. Neither was the better-law factor dispositive, because Louisiana law was not particularly "archaic and unfair" and thus, said the court, "our subjective view of which law represents the more reasoned approach would not persuade us that Arkansas law should apply." 250 F.3d at 622. In *Nesladek*, which was decided under Minnesota's better-law approach, the court applied the pro-defendant statute of repose of Nebraska, which was the plaintiff's home state at the time of the injury, as well as the place of the injury and the product's acquisition.

8. 229 Mich.App. 580, 582 N.W.2d 866 (1998). For a virtually identical case involving the same pattern and another one of Michigan's "big three" manufacturers, see Farrell v. Ford Motor Co., 199 Mich.App. 81, 501 N.W.2d 567 (1993), app. denied, 445 Mich. 863, 519 N.W.2d 158 (1994). *Farrell* was a product liability/wrongful death action arising from a North Carolina accident in which a North Carolina domiciliary was killed by her1980 Ford station wagon. The action would be timely in Michigan, but would be barred by North Carolina's statute of repose. The court applied the North Carolina statute, after concluding that North Carolina had "an obvious and substantial interest in shielding Ford from open-ended products liability claims . . . and

[in] encourag[ing] manufacturers, such as Ford, to do business in North Carolina." 501 N.W.2d at 572. The court rejected the argument that this interest was "any less compelling solely by virtue of the fact that the defendant does not have a manufacturing plant located in the State of North Carolina." Id. On the other hand, the court concluded, "Michigan ha[d] little or no interest . . . in affording greater rights of tort recovery to a North Carolina resident than his own state affords him. . . . Michigan is merely the forum state and situs of defendant's headquarters. Such minimal interests are insufficient to justify the result oriented forum shopping which has been attempted." Id. at 572–73.

North Carolina's statute of repose was also applied in Vestal v. Shiley Inc., 1997 WL 910373 (C.D.Cal.1997), thus barring a product liability action by a North Carolina domiciliary against a California manufacturer of heart valves implanted in plaintiff during a North Carolina surgery. The court concluded that the application of California's statute of limitation which allowed the action "would impair North Carolina's effort to protect manufacturers who sell goods within its borders." Id. at *3. The court noted California's potential interest in deterring California manufacturers from manufacturing defective products within its borders, but concluded that that interest is adequately served by applying California law to the many actions filed by California plaintiffs. Id.

9. By the time of the filing of the action, the plaintiff had moved his domicile to Michigan. The court thought that it had to choose between the new and the old domiciles, and while acknowledging that the record did not reveal the plaintiff's motives for changing his domicile, the court decided to discount the change of domicile because of the potential for encouraging forum shopping. See *Hall*, 582 N.W.2d at 870. For another case that also discounted plaintiff's post-injury change of domicile to the forum state, see Nesladek v. Ford Motor Co., 46 F.3d 734 (8th Cir.1995), cert. denied 516 U.S. 814, 116 S.Ct. 67, 133 L.Ed.2d 28 (1995). In this case, plaintiff candidly ad-

10.   See p. 927.

by General Motors (GM), a corporation that has its headquarters and principal place of business in Michigan. The plaintiff's action was barred by North Carolina's statute of repose but would have been timely under Michigan's statute of limitation. The court acknowledged that Michigan's *lex fori* approach "most frequently favors using the forum's (Michigan's) law...."[11] Nonetheless, said the court, "Michigan courts ... use another state's law where the other state has a significant interest and Michigan has only a minimal interest in the matter."[12] The court concluded that this was such a case because North Carolina had "an obvious and substantial interest in shielding GM from open ended

mitted that Minnesota's pro-plaintiff law was part of the reason she had decided to move to Minnesota from Nebraska, after an accident in the latter state that caused the death of her son. Her action was barred by Nebraska's ten-year statute of repose but could have been maintained under Minnesota's "useful life" statute. The defendant Ford did business in Minnesota and a critical component of the car that had caused the Nebraska accident, the transmission gear-selection system, had been installed in the car in Ford's assembly plant in Minnesota. The court held that Nebraska's statute of repose applied, and dismissed the action under it. The court noted that "[b]ecause of the distinct presence of forum shopping in this case, we have good reason to believe that the balance of interests [and the other choice-influencing considerations] favor application of Nebraska law." 46 F.3d at 740. A dissenting judge accused the majority of "offer[ing] a sanction or punishment rather than an analysis as to choice of law." Id. at 741.

In Rice v. Dow Chemical Co., 124 Wn.2d 205, 875 P.2d 1213 (1994), the plaintiff was exposed to the product, a herbicide, while he was domiciled and working in Oregon but had moved his domicile to Washington before the injury had manifested itself. Thus, the plaintiff could not be accused of forum shopping. His action was timely under Washington's twelve-year statute of repose but would have been barred by Oregon's eight-year statute of repose. The court concluded that Oregon's statute applied because that state had a more significant relationship than did Washington, because: "The relationship between the parties occurred in Oregon, the injurious product was placed in the stream of commerce and sent to Oregon, at the time of the injurious contact Plaintiff lived in Oregon, and Plaintiff was exposed to the chemicals at work while employed in Oregon." 875 P.2d at 1218. After rejecting plaintiff's argument that the manifestation of the disease in Washington would make that state the

place of the injury, the court examined the respective interests of the two states and concluded that such an examination supported the application of Oregon law: "Oregon's interest ... in providing repose for manufacturers doing business in Oregon and whose products are used in Oregon," id. at 1219, was not extinguished by the plaintiff's subsequent move to Washington. Although Washington had an interest in protecting its residents, "residency in the forum state alone has not been considered a sufficient relationship to the action to warrant application of forum law." Id. The court reasoned that "[a]pplying Oregon law achieves a uniform result for injuries caused by products used in the state of Oregon and predictability for manufacturers whose products are used or consumed in Oregon." Id. Neither party offered evidence of the place of design, testing, or manufacture of the product, or of the defendant's principal place of business or state of incorporation. See id. 1218.

10. The car was manufactured in Ohio, but neither party urged the application of Ohio law.

11. *Hall*, 582 N.W.2d at 868.

12. Id. First, the court listed North Carolina's contacts *with the plaintiff* and, without explaining the relevance of those contacts to the issue at hand, proclaimed that North Carolina "obviously has a substantial interest in applying its law." See id. ("[P]laintiff lived in North Carolina, worked for a North Carolina employer, and was injured in North Carolina by a vehicle owned, registered, licensed, and insured in North Carolina, and plaintiff subsequently received medical treatment ... in North Carolina. North Carolina, *therefore*, obviously has a substantial interest in applying its law to this dispute.") (emphasis added). Eventually, the court concluded that North Carolina's interests did not depend on its contacts with the plaintiff, but rather on its contacts with the defendant.

products liability claims"[13] and that it was in that state's "economic interest to encourage GM to do business in its state."[14] The court also concluded that Michigan had "no interest in affording greater rights of tort recovery to a North Carolina resident than those afforded by North Carolina [and that] Michigan [was] *merely* the forum state and situs of defendant's headquarters."[15]

Of course, Michigan was not *merely* the forum state, and North Carolina's contacts with GM paled in comparison with Michigan's contacts. As a concurring judge noted, GM's relationship with North Carolina was "insignificant when compared to its enormous economic presence in Michigan and consequential effect on this state.... GM's headquarters and a significant part of its operations are located in Michigan."[16] Similarly, the court's statement that Michigan had no interest "in affording greater rights of tort recovery to a North Carolina resident than those afforded by North Carolina"[17] raises the corollary question of why North Carolina had an interest in affording a Michigan defendant greater protection than that afforded by Michigan. The court's answer that North Carolina was interested in encouraging GM to do business in that state may or may not be persuasive, if only because it creates the suspicion of favoritism for the forum litigant.[18]

This suspicion is dispelled somewhat by cases such as *Kemp v. Pfizer, Inc.*,[19] which applied Michigan's pro-defendant law for the benefit of a foreign manufacturer and at the expense of a forum victim. This was an action filed by the survivors of a Michigan domiciliary who died in Michigan as result of a malfunction of a heart valve implanted in him in a Michigan surgical procedure. The valve had been manufactured in California by defendant, a California corporation. California, but not Michigan, imposed punitive damages. The court acknowledged that, as the place of both the defendant's principal place of business and the product's manufacture, California had an interest in applying its law so as to "punish its corporate defendants and deter future misconduct."[20] However, the court concluded that, because the defendant was also doing business in Michigan, Michigan had an interest in extending to defendant the benefit of its defendant-protecting law. The court felt relieved

---

13. Id. at 869 (internal quotations omitted).

14. Id.

15. Id. (emphasis added)).

16. Id. at 870 (Matuzak, J., concurring).

17. Id. at 869.

18. See id. at 870–71 (Matuzak, J., concurring). After pointing out that because of defendant's enormous presence in Michigan, "applying this state's law should not defeat defendant's expectations," the judge questioned North Carolina's interest in applying its statute of repose: "Instead of protecting a North Carolina manufacturer,

the statute is being used to protect an out-of-state manufacturer for injuries sustained in North Carolina arising out of wrongs alleged to have been committed in Michigan or Ohio.... [T]here is no good reason to extend the benefits of the North Carolina statute of repose to defendant." See also the court's analysis of Florida's statute of repose in a virtually identical case, Mahne v. Ford Motor Co., 900 F.2d 83 (6th Cir. 1990), cert. denied 498 U.S. 941, 111 S.Ct. 349, 112 L.Ed.2d 313 (1990) (discussed supra § 17.76 n.26 ff).

19. 947 F.Supp. 1139 (E.D.Mich.1996).

20. Id. at 1143.

from having to engage in the "admittedly abstruse exercise"[21] of determining "which state's interest is greater"[22] because, under Michigan's *lex fori* approach, "where Michigan has a strong interest in applying its laws . . . , the Michigan courts would not displace its own laws in favor of the law of a foreign state."[23] Thus, the court dismissed the plaintiffs' claim for punitive damages.[24]

In *Rutherford v. Goodyear Tire & Rubber Co.*,[25] which was decided under Kentucky's *lex fori* approach, the court applied the pro-defendant law of Indiana, which was the plaintiff's home state and place of injury and, indirectly, the place of the product's acquisition. The product, a car tire, had been manufactured in Kansas by Goodyear, an Ohio corporation, and was purchased by Ford, a Michigan corporation, and mounted on a car in Ford's assembly plant in Kentucky. The car was sold to an Indiana motorist who, while driving in Indiana, collided with plaintiff's car. Indiana, but not Kentucky, had a statute of repose that barred the action. While acknowledging Kentucky's strong preference for the *lex fori*, the court concluded that in this case this preference was not warranted by the forum's contacts or interests and was outweighed by Indiana's "overwhelming interest."[26] The court reasoned that Kentucky's statute of limitation was "designed primarily to protect its own citizens or those injured within its boundaries . . . [and not to] regulat[e] products assembled within its boundaries."[27] The court opined that a certain "federalist concept," which the court did not define, "inherently limits the reach of any state's perceived interest to matters which occur within its boundaries or which impact its citizens."[28] The court rejected the plaintiff's plea to choose the law of the place where the product was manufactured or assembled, because such a choice would create practical difficulties in cases in which the design, testing, manufacture, and assembly take place in different states, and because: "Legal claims do not arise at the time or at the place of manufacture. They arise when an injury occurs. Thus, the place of injury, not the place of manufacture is the central focus of the cause of action."[29]

(2) *Choice supported by two contacts*

§ 17.78 In the cases discussed in the preceding section, the state with the pro-defendant law had all three victim-affiliated contacts.

---

21. Id.

22. Id.

23. Id.

24. In Harlan Feeders v. Grand Labs., Inc., 881 F.Supp. 1400 (N.D.Iowa 1995), the court refused to apply Iowa law, which imposed punitive damages, and applied Nebraska law, which did not allow such damages. The product was manufactured in Iowa and was sold to a Nebraska plaintiff in Nebraska and caused injury there. Said the court: "Nebraska has made a policy choice that punitive damages are inappropriate, and that interest is not outweighed by Iowa's contrary interest in imposing puni-

tive damages as a deterrent, at least not . . . where the plaintiff is a resident of Nebraska, not Iowa, where the alleged injury occurred in Nebraska, not Iowa, as a result of use of a product manufactured by a South Dakota, not an Iowa corporation, even when the corporation physically produced the product in Iowa." Id. at 1410.

25. 943 F.Supp. 789 (W.D. Ky. 1996).

26. Id. at 793.

27. Id. at 792.

28. Id.

29. Id. at 793.

Thus, under a mechanical significant-contacts or Second Restatement analysis, one could more easily conclude that that state had a more significant relationship than the state with the two defendant-affiliating contacts. Such conclusion may be more difficult in cases in which the first state has only two victim-affiliating contacts. Nevertheless, courts confronted with such cases have not acknowledged this difficulty. One example is *Denman v. Snapper Division*,[1] which was decided under the Restatement Second's *lex loci* presumption. In this case, a Mississippi domiciliary purchased in Mississippi a lawn mower that he lent to his son, who used it in North Carolina and was injured there.[2] The plaintiff's action in Mississippi was timely under that state's statute of limitation, but was barred by North Carolina's statute of repose. The court noted that under Mississippi conflicts law, "the law of the place of injury is presumed to apply unless another state has a more significant relationship."[3] The court concluded that the sale of the mower in Mississippi was "an insufficient basis for finding that Mississippi ha[d] a more significant relationship than North Carolina,"[4] and that "the fact that the mower entered the stream of commerce in Mississippi [did] not tip the balance in favor of applying Mississippi law."[5]

Like *Denman*, other cases involving this pattern have applied the pro-defendant law of a state that was only the victim's domicile and the place of injury (but not the place of acquisition), under the Restatement Second,[6] a significant-contacts approach,[7] or other approaches.[8] Also,

---

§ 17.78

1. 131 F.3d 546 (5th Cir. 1998), reh'g denied en banc, 137 F.3d 1353 (5th Cir. 1998).

2. The mower was manufactured in Georgia by defendant, a Georgia-based corporation, but neither party urged the application of Georgia law.

3. 131 F.3d at 550.

4. Id.

5. Id. For cases reaching the opposite conclusion on this point, see *Sanchez* and *Long*, discussed supra § 17.72.

6. See McKinnon v. F.H. Morgan & Co., Inc., 170 Vt. 422, 750 A.2d 1026 (2000). In this case, the plaintiff, a Quebec domiciliary, was injured in Quebec while riding a bicycle sold and serviced by the defendant in Vermont. The plaintiff invoked Vermont's pro-plaintiff law, but was apparently unprepared to rebut the presumption of Restatement Second § 146 in favor the place of injury, Quebec. The court applied the law of Quebec because, in addition to being the place of injury, Quebec was also the plaintiff's domicile and Vermont did not have more significant contacts.

7. For a case following such an approach, see Land v. Yamaha Motor Corp.,

U.S.A., 272 F.3d 514 (7th Cir. 2001) (decided under Indiana's significant-contacts approach). This case involved an action by an Indiana domiciliary injured in Indiana by a product manufactured in Japan by a Japanese manufacturer. The product was sold through a Kentucky dealer to an Indiana domiciliary who, many years later, sold it to another Indiana domiciliary. The court applied Indiana's statute of repose, barring the action, because Indiana's approach allows departure from the *lex loci delicti* only when the *locus delicti* has an "insignificant" relationship to the lawsuit. The court found that Indiana's relationship was not insignificant because Indiana was the place of the injury, the domicile of the victim and the product's owner, and the place where the product had been used for more than a decade. See also Crouch v. General Elec. Co., 699 F.Supp. 585 (S.D.Miss.1988) (applying North Carolina's statute of repose to bar an action filed by a North Carolina plaintiff who was injured in that state by a defective component of a helicopter manufactured in Massachusetts); Alves v. Siegel's Broadway Auto Parts, Inc., 710 F.Supp. 864 (D.Mass.1989) (action filed by the survivors of a Connecticut domiciliary who was killed in that state by a product manufactured by

8. See p. 931.

other cases have done the same by applying the statute or repose[9] or other pro-defendant law[10] of a state that was only the victim's domicile

a Wisconsin manufacturer in Wisconsin and sold by defendant, a Massachusetts corporation, to the victim's Massachusetts employer in Massachusetts; the seller impleaded the manufacturer for contribution and indemnification; applying Connecticut's statute of repose barring the action which was not barred by Massachusetts' statute of limitation, because Massachusetts did not have a more significant relationship with the case than did Connecticut).

8. See, e.g., Normann v. Johns–Manville Corp., 406 Pa.Super. 103, 593 A.2d 890 (1991), appeal denied 530 Pa. 645, 607 A.2d 255 (1992) (action by a Pennsylvania resident who was exposed to defendant's asbestos products while employed and domiciled in New York; New York, but not Pennsylvania, allowed defendant to assert the "state of the art" defense (defendant was an Ohio corporation but Ohio law was not described in the opinion); noting that New York would have an interest in making this defense available to foreign corporations doing business in New York; applying New York law because New York had a closer relationship and "by far a greater interest," 593 A.2d at 894, than Pennsylvania); See also Deemer v. Silk City Textile Machinery Co., 193 N.J.Super. 643, 475 A.2d 648 (1984), which is at least implicitly overruled by Gantes v. Kason Corp., 145 N.J. 478, 679 A.2d 106 (1996) (discussed supra § 17.76 nn. 1 ff.). In *Deemer*, the court applied the law of North Carolina, the place of injury and the victim's domicile, rather than the law of New Jersey, the place of manufacture. Unlike New Jersey, North Carolina had not adopted the doctrine of strict liability in products-liability cases. The court stated that whatever incidental benefits of deterrence might be gained by a liability judgment, "the principal aim of a product liability or other personal injury claim is fairly to compensate the injured party." 475 A.2d at 651. Other factors cited by the New Jersey court in its decision to apply North Carolina law were that the application of New Jersey law would deter the conduct of manufacturing operations in New Jersey and would cause an unreasonable increase in litigation which would unduly burden the New Jersey courts. In Egan v. Kaiser Aluminum & Chem. Corp., 677 So.2d 1027 (La.App.1996), writ denied 684 So.2d 930 (La.1996), the forum state, Louisiana, which was also the place of the victim's domicile and injury, prohibited punitive damages, while the state of manufacture, Ohio, allowed them. Applying the wrong conflicts law, the court decided to apply Louisiana substantive law, not because of

any concern for protecting the defendant, but rather in order to protect the forum's judicial system! Said the court, " 'Louisiana's interest lies in the protection of its judicial system, rather than domestic defendants, from what it might consider inherently speculative awards.' " 677 So.2d at 1038. This statement was taken from earlier Louisiana decisions, which had quoted even earlier Louisiana decisions, none of which however have explained why punitive damages awards are any more speculative than, say, awards for a deceased person's pain and suffering, or why the integrity of Louisiana's judicial system has not been tarnished by the fact that, since 1984, Louisiana substantive law imposes punitive damages in other categories of cases. See Symeonides, Choice of Law in the American Courts in 1996: Tenth Annual Survey, 45 Am. J. Comp. L. 447, 474 (1997).

9. See, e.g., Maly v. Genmar Indus., Inc., 1996 WL 28473 (N.D.Ill.1996). In this case the forum state, Illinois, which was also the victim's domicile and the place of the product's acquisition, had a statute of repose that barred the action, while the state of the accident, Wisconsin, did not have such a statute. The manufacturer was a Florida corporation but the court did not mention the place of manufacturing, apparently because of the court's conclusion that the critical conduct was "the placement of a defective product in the stream of commerce," id. at *2, which occurred in Illinois, where the victim had purchased the product. Confining its analysis to the policies of Illinois and Wisconsin, the court recognized quickly that they were contradictory. Illinois' policy was "pro business: to reduce the cost to manufacturers and distributors of doing business in Illinois by cutting legal costs caused by old strict liability lawsuits which are particularly difficult to defend due to loss of witnesses, poor record keeping, and changes in legal and technical standards on products." Id. at *2. Wisconsin's policy, on the other hand, "favors consumers over manufacturers, and apparently does not view proliferating products liability litigation a sufficient reason to deny consumers a cause of action in strict liability for injuries resulting from defective old products." Id. After examining the contacts of the two states, the court concluded that Illinois had the most significant relationship, because "[t]he conduct complained of happened in Illinois to an Illinois resident and the relationship of the parties occurred in Illinois." Id. Thus, the court concluded,

10. See p. 932.

and the place of the product's acquisition (but not the place of the injury). Finally, other cases have applied the statute of repose,[11] or other pro-defendant law[12] of a state that was only the place of the injury and the product's acquisition (but not the victim's domicile). For some reason, however, the latter cases failed to consider the place of manufacture and confined themselves to choosing between the law of the state of injury and acquisition, on the one hand, and the law of the victim's domicile on the other. Under these circumstances, the choice of the former law should not come as a surprise.

"[t]here is no reason to rank Illinois' pro-business tort policy as less significant than Wisconsin's pro-consumer policy." Id. See also Bonti v. Ford Motor Co., 898 F.Supp. 391 (S.D.Miss.1995), aff'd mem. 85 F.3d 625 (5th Cir.1996). This case arose out of a single-car accident in South Carolina that resulted in the death of plaintiff's husband, a North Carolina domiciliary. The car, a Ford Bronco, had been designed by Ford in Michigan, assembled in Kentucky, and sold to plaintiff in North Carolina. Five years after the accident and eight years after the purchase of the Bronco, the plaintiff sued Ford in Mississippi, which had no contacts with the case other than the fact that Ford was doing business in that state. The action was barred by North Carolina's statute of repose for products-liability actions and by South Carolina's three-year statute of limitation for wrongful death actions, but was timely under Mississippi law. Following the Second Restatement, the court concluded that North Carolina had the most significant relationship and applied North Carolina law, including that state's statute of repose which barred the action.

10. See, e.g., Garcia v. General Motors Corp., 195 Ariz. 510, 990 P.2d 1069 (App. 1999). In this case, the plaintiffs were Arizona domiciliaries and were involved in an accident in Idaho while riding in a car they rented in Arizona. The car was manufactured by a Michigan defendant in Michigan, but the parties did not plead Michigan law. Thus, the conflict was between the laws of Idaho, which did not allow evidence that the plaintiff was not wearing seatbelt, and Arizona, which permitted such evidence. The court held that Arizona had an interest "in encouraging its residents to wear seatbelts even outside its borders, as injuries resulting from not using seatbelts may well require medical care upon the residents' return to Arizona." Id. at 1078. The court also reasoned that it would be "incongruous

to allow Idaho's desire to 'fully' compensate nonresident Arizona plaintiffs to control in an Arizona court, when Arizona courts would permit the jury to consider whether to reduce the recovery of Arizona plaintiffs who fail to wear seatbelts." Id. In Thornton v. Sea Quest, Inc., 999 F.Supp. 1219 (N.D.Ind. 1998), the victim, an Indiana domiciliary, died in Arkansas as a result of a malfunction of scuba diving equipment that was manufactured in France and sold in Indiana by a California manufacturer and distributor. The issue was wrongful death recovery, and Arkansas law was more favorable to plaintiffs than Indiana law. Neither party pleaded French or California law. The court found that Indiana had a more significant relationship than Arkansas, as well as "a strong interest in preventing the sale of supposedly defective products within its borders." Id. at 1224.

11. See Romani v. Cramer, Inc., 992 F.Supp. 74 (D.Mass. 1998) (discussed supra § 17.74 n.20); Allison v. ITE Imperial Corp., 928 F.2d 137 (5th Cir. 1991); Tanges v. Heidelberg N. Am., Inc., 93 N.Y.2d 48, 687 N.Y.S.2d 604, 710 N.E.2d 250 (1999).

12. See, e.g., LeJeune v. Bliss–Salem, Inc., 85 F.3d 1069 (3d Cir. 1996) (strict-liability vs. negligence; discussed supra § 17.74 n.20); Cianfrani v. Kalmar–AC Handling Systems, Inc.,1995 WL 563289 (D.N.J. 1995) (same issues; discussed supra id.); Calhoun v. Yamaha Motor Corp., U.S.A., 216 F.3d 338 (3d Cir. 2000), cert. denied 531 U.S. 1037, 121 S.Ct. 627, 148 L.Ed.2d (2000) (punitive damages; discussed supra id.); Schmidt v. Duo–Fast, Inc., 1995 WL 422681 (E.D. Pa. 1995) (applying New Jersey pro-defendant law to the claim of a Pennsylvania worker injured in a New Jersey construction accident caused by a tool purchased from Pennsylvania but shipped directly to New Jersey).

(3) Choice supported by a single contact

§ 17.79 As noted earlier,[1] few cases apply the pro-plaintiff law of a state that has only one of the five pertinent contacts. Even fewer cases apply the *pro-defendant* law of a state that has only one contact. Besides cases decided under the traditional *lex loci delicti* rule,[2] one can find very few modern cases that apply the pro-defendant law of the state of injury.[3] However, one modern case applied the *lex loci* solely because of its neutrality towards all parties and substantive laws. In *Ness v. Ford Motor Co.*,[4] the court, after considering other options, concluded that

§ 17.79

1. See supra § 17.72.

2. In Fitts v. Minnesota Mining & Mfg. Co., 581 So.2d 819 (Ala.1991), the Supreme Court of Alabama applied the pro-defendant law of Florida to a products liability/wrongful death action arising out of the crash of a small airplane in Florida which resulted in the death of Alabama domiciliaries. The court did not mention the state of the manufacture of the airplane or of a suspect instrument (the stormscope) and much less the law of that state. Similarly, in Mullins v. M.G.D. Graphics Systems Group, 867 F.Supp. 1578 (N.D.Ga.1994), the entire choice-of-law discussion is exhausted in explaining why the *locus delicti* is in Georgia, where the injury occurred, rather than in the state of the injurious conduct. The case does not mention where the product was designed or manufactured or where the defendant had its principal place of business. It is only because of a passing reference to plaintiff's contention that New York law governed the action that the reader surmises that New York might have been involved in the case and that its law was more favorable to plaintiff than was Georgia's law. In Thornton v. Cessna Aircraft Co., 886 F.2d 85 (4th Cir.1989), a case arising from a small airplane crash and decided under the *lex loci* rule, the court concluded that "the occurrence of the crash in Tennessee is a significant contact sufficient to justify application of the Tennessee statute of repose." Id. at 89. That statute barred the action by the survivors of a South Carolina domiciliary who was killed in a Tennessee crash of his Cessna aircraft while en route from Ohio to South Carolina. Again, the court did not mention the place of manufacture or the manufacturer's principal place of business.

3. In Price v. Litton Systems, Inc., 784 F.2d 600 (5th Cir.1986), the Fifth Circuit upheld the district court's application of Alabama's pro-defendant law to products liability claims rising out of the crash of a helicopter in Alabama during a training mission from a base in Alabama. The allegedly defective equipment was designed in California and manufactured in Virginia by companies with their principal places of business in New York and Delaware. Texas and Iowa were the permanent domiciles of the two decedents involved. In applying Mississippi's Second Restatement "most significant relationship" test, the court found that the place of injury was a significant factor because it was not merely fortuitous that the helicopter crashed in Alabama since the flight was not scheduled to travel beyond the borders of that state. The court noted that, in addition to being the place of injury, Alabama, while not the permanent domicile of the decedents, was their place of residence at the time of the accident and was also the center of the parties' relationship. The court attached no significance to the deterrence interests of California (if a design defect were proven) or Virginia (if a manufacturing defect were proven). The compensatory interests of Texas and Iowa, the decedents' domiciles, were not considered substantial enough to warrant application of the law of those states rather than that of Alabama. In In re Disaster at Detroit Metropolitan Airport on August 16, 1987, 750 F.Supp. 793 (E.D.Mich.1989), the forum state, Michigan, was also the place of the injury, and its law did not allow punitive damages. California, the place of the airplane's manufacture also did not allow such damages, but Missouri, the manufacturer's principal place of business, did. The court concluded that a true conflict existed between California law, which sought to protect conduct in that state, and Missouri law, which sought to ensure responsible corporate decision-making by corporations having their principal place of business in that state. The court resolved the conflict by resorting to the law of the state of the injury, despite having earlier recognized that that state was uninterested.

4. 1993 WL 996164 (N.D. Ill. 1993) (unpublished). *Ness* was a products liability action filed by an Illinois resident who was injured in an Iowa single-car accident when the car in which he was riding as a passen-

"[s]ometimes an apparently arbitrary choice—like *lex loci delicti*—is a reasonable way of dealing with the problem of conflict of interest between states."[5] The court recognized that the state of the plaintiff's domicile had an "interest in seeing its citizens adequately compensated for their injuries,"[6] but also noted that the state of manufacture "has an interest in seeing that product-liability plaintiffs are not overcompensated, resulting in higher insurance premiums for Michigan manufacturers, higher costs, and lost jobs."[7] A rule calling for the application of the law of the state of manufacture, said the court, "would tend to leave victims uncompensated as states wishing to attract and hold manufacturing companies would raise the threshold of liability and reduce compensation."[8] Likewise, a rule applying the law of the victim's domicile "would permit a state with little manufacturing to endow its citizens with generous protection wherever they choose to travel without picking up any of the cost."[9] After also rejecting the notion of applying the law of the place of the product's acquisition (because products may be resold in other states and because product liability does not require privity), the court concluded that the "rule of *lex loci delicti* appears less objectionable once it is understood that there is no alternative that will yield a rational and fair result in all cases. . . ."[10]

C. CHOICE–OF–LAW RULES

§ 17.80   The inherent complexity of products liability conflicts as well as the courts' uneven performance in handling these conflicts raise the question of whether choice-of-law rules for these conflicts are desirable and, if so, whether they are feasible. This section provides the means for exploring these question by presenting some rules that have either been enacted or proposed for products liability conflicts in the last two decades.

1. *Enacted Rules*

In the United States, the only statutory rule is found in the 1992 Louisiana Conflicts Codification.[1] That rule provides that, subject to a

---

ger rolled over. The car was manufactured by Ford in Michigan and was registered and garaged in Illinois. At the time of the accident, it was driven by another Illinois resident in a trip that began and was to end in Illinois.

   5.   Id. at *2.

   6.   Id.

   7.   Id.

   8.   Id.

   9.   Id.

   10.   Id. at *3. For an identical holding in another products liability action, see Walters v. Maren Engineering Corp., 246 Ill. App.3d 1084, 617 N.E.2d 170 (1st Dist.,

1993) (applying Kansas law to a Kansas injury caused by a product manufactured in part in Illinois).

§ 17.80

   1.   See La. Civ. Code art. 3545:

Delictual and quasi-delictual liability for injury caused by a product, as well as damages, whether compensatory, special, or punitive, are governed by the law of this state: (1) when the injury was sustained in this state by a person domiciled or residing in this state; or (2) when the product was manufactured, produced, or acquired in this state and caused injury either in this state or in another state to a person domiciled in this state.

foreseeability/commercial unavailability exception,[2] the law of the forum state governs cases in which: 1) the injury was sustained in that state by a domiciliary or resident of that state; or 2) the product was manufactured, produced, or acquired in that state and victim was a domiciliary of that state or the injury occurred there. Cases in which the forum state lacks the above combinations of contacts are relegated to other rules that require an issue-by-issue analysis that, more likely than not, will lead to the application of non-forum law.[3]

In the rest of the world, the first set of choice-of-law rules for products liability was adopted in 1973 with the Hague Convention on the Law Applicable to Products Liability,[4] which is now in force in ten European countries.[5] The Convention provides that the law of the state of the victim's habitual residence applies, if that state is also: (a) the defendant's principal place of business; or (b) the place where the product was acquired by the victim.[6] If these conditions are not met, then the law of the state of injury applies, if that state is also: (a) the victim's habitual residence; or (b) the defendant's principal place of business; or (c) the place where the product was acquired by the victim.[7] When none of the above conditions are met, the victim is given a choice between the law of the state of injury and the law of state of the

The preceding paragraph does not apply if neither the product that caused the injury nor any of the defendant's products of the same type were made available in this state through ordinary commercial channels.

All cases not disposed of by the preceding paragraphs are governed by the other Articles of this Title.

For an explanation of the rationale of this article by its drafter, including the reasons for using a unilateralist technique, see Symeonides, Louisiana's New Law of Choice of Law for Tort Conflicts: An Exegesis, 66 Tul. L. Rev. 677, 749–59 (1992). For a critique, see Kozyris, Values and Methods in Choice of Law For Products Liability: A Comparative Comment on Statutory Solutions, 38 Am. J. Comp. L. 475 (1990); Weintraub, The Contributions of Symeonides and Kozyris to Making Choice of Law Predictable and Just: An Appreciation and Critique, 38 Am. J. Comp. L. 511 (1990). For cases applying this article, see Symeonides, Louisiana Conflicts Law: Two "Surprises," 54 La. L. Rev. 497 (1994). An almost identical rule is found in Article 48 of the Puerto Rican Draft Code. For discussion of that rule by its drafter, see Symeonides, Problems and Dilemmas in Codifying Choice of Law for Torts: The Louisiana Experience in Comparative Perspective, 38 Am. J. Comp. L. 431 (1990). For a critique, see Kozyris, supra.

2. See second paragraph of La. Civ. Code art. 3545, supra n.1. Article 3545 is also subject to a general escape provided in Article 3547 and available in all tort conflicts.

3. See the third paragraph of La. Civ. Code Art. 3545, supra n.1.

4. 11 Int'l Legal Materials 1283 (Nov. 1972). For comment on the Convention see Reese, 25 Vand. L. Rev. 29 (1972).

5. These countries are Croatia, Finland, FYROM, France, Luxembourg, Netherlands, Norway, Slovenia, Spain, and Serbia–Montenegro. See Conférence de La Haye de droit international privé, Recueil des conventions (1951–96).

6. See Convention art. 5 (the applicable law shall be the internal law of the State of the habitual residence of the person directly suffering damage, if that State is also: (a) the principal place of business of the person claimed to be liable, or (b) the place where the product was acquired by the person directly suffering damage).

7. Id. art. 4 (the applicable law shall be the internal law of the State of the place of injury, if that State is also: (a) the place of the habitual residence of the person directly suffering damage, or (b) the principal place of business of the person claimed to be liable, or (c) the place where the product was acquired by the person directly suffering damage).

defendant's principal place of business.[8] Finally, the Convention, like the Louisiana rule, provides that the defendant may prevent the application of the law of the place of injury or of the victim's habitual residence by proving that he could not reasonably have foreseen that the product that caused the injury or his products of the same type would be made available in those states through commercial channels.[9]

Both the Louisiana rule and the Convention adopt a territorial contact-counting approach. Unlike the Louisiana rule, however, the Convention allows the plaintiff to choose between the law of the defendant's principal place of business, and the law of the place of injury, but only in the event that the plaintiff's habitual residence, the defendant's principal place of business, and the place where the product was acquired are each in different jurisdictions. The territorial contact approach used in these two systems, by requiring at least two contacts to coincide in one jurisdiction before that jurisdiction's law becomes applicable, protects a defendant's expectations as to what law may govern his liability.

More recent national codifications have adopted a more direct pro-plaintiff approach. For example, the Swiss and Italian codifications allow the victim to choose between the laws of: (1) the state of the defendant's principal place of business or, in the absence thereof, his habitual residence; or (2) the state in which the product was acquired, "unless the defendant proves that the product has been marketed in that state without his consent."[10] The Quebec codification gives the victim the same choices but without the above quoted proviso.[11] The Russian codification adds a third choice—the victim's habitual residence or principal place of activity (subject to the same proviso),[12] while the Tunisian codification adds a fourth choice—the place of injury (without

---

8. Id. art. 6 (Where neither of the laws designated in Articles 4 and 5 applies, the applicable law shall be the internal law of the State of the principal place of business of the person claimed to be liable, unless the claimant bases his claim upon the internal law of the State of the place of injury.).

9. Id. art. 7 (Neither the law of the State of the place of injury nor the law of the State of the habitual residence of the person directly suffering damage shall be applicable ... if the person claimed to be liable establishes that he could not reasonably have foreseen that the product or his own products of the same type would be made available in that State through commercial channels.).

10. Article 135 of the Swiss Federal Statute on Private International Law, Bundesblatt 1988, I, 5, provides in part: "(1) Claims based on a defect in, or a defective description of, a product are governed, at the choice of the injured party: (a) By the

law of the state in which the tortfeasor has his principal place of business or, in absence thereof, his habitual residence; or (b) By the law of the state in which the product was acquired unless, the tortfeasor proves that the product has been marketed in that state without his consent." Article 63 of the Italian codification is substantially identical to the above, except that it speaks of the state in which the manufacturer has its "domicile or its head-office."

11. See Quebec Civil Code art. 3128.

12. See Civil Code of the Russian Federation, Art. 1221 (federal law n. 146 of 26 November 2001 enacting the third part of the Civil Code of the Russian Federation, Rossyiskaya Gazeta, n. 49 item 4553, 28/11/2001). This article also provides that, if the victim does not take advantage of these choices, the applicable law shall be determined under the general article for tort conflicts.

the proviso).[13] Finally, the proposed Rome II Regulation adopts a simpler rule that calls for the application of the law of the victim's habitual residence, but "[w]ithout prejudice to Article 3(2) and (3)."[14] The quoted phrase means that, in appropriate cases, a court may apply: (a) the law of the parties' common habitual residence; or (b) the law of a country that has a "manifestly closer connection" than the country or countries of either or both parties' residence.[15]

2. *Proposed Rules*

§ 17.81   Several academic commentators in the United States have also proposed rules for products liability conflicts.[1] First among them was Professor Cavers who proposed a rule that would allow the plaintiff to choose from among the laws of: (a) the place of the product's production or approval; (b) the place of the plaintiff's habitual residence if that place coincides with either the place of injury or the place where the plaintiff had acquired the product; or (c) the place of acquisition if that place is also the place of injury. However, the defendant may prevent the application of the laws of the states specified in (b) and (c) by showing that "he could not reasonably have foreseen the presence in th[ose] State[s] of his product which caused harm to the claimant or his property."[2]

Another rule proposed by Professor Kozyris[3] would also give the victim the choice of the law of the state of injury, if that state is also the

---

13. See Code of Private International Law (Law N. 98–97 of 27 November 1998), Art. 72, Official Journal of the Republic of Tunisia, 1 December p. 2332.

14. See COM(2003) 427 final, 2003/0168(COD), Brussels, 22.7.203, Article 4. This article also provides an exception if the defendant can show that the product was marketed in the victim's home country without the defendant's consent, in which case the law of the defendant's habitual residence governs.

15. For a discussion of this provision from the American perspective, see Symeonides, Tort Conflicts and Rome II: A View from Across, in Festschrift für Erik Jayme 935, 949–50 (2004).

§ 17.81

1. In addition to the rules discussed in the text, see F.Juenger, Choice of Law and Multistate Justice, 197 (1993); McConnell, A Choice-of-Law Approach to Products—Liability Reform, in New Directions In Liability Law (W. Olson ed. 1988).

2. See Cavers, The Proper Law of Producer's Liability, 26 Int'l & Comp. L.Q. 703, 728–29 (1977):

(a) Where a person claims compensation from the producer of a defective product for harm it caused to the claimant or his property, the claimant should be entitled to the protection of the liability laws of the State where the defective product was produced (or where its defective design was approved).

(b) If, however, the claimant considers the liability laws of that State (i) less protective than the laws of the claimant's habitual residence where either he had acquired the product or it had caused harm or (ii) less protective than the laws of the State where the claimant had acquired the product and it had caused harm, then the claimant should be entitled to base his claim on whichever of those two States' liability laws would be applicable to his case.

(c) The claimant, however, should not be entitled to base his claim on the laws of one of the States specified in the preceding paragraph if the producer establishes that he could not reasonably have foreseen the presence in that State of his product which caused harm to the claimant or his property.

3. See Kozyris, Values and Methods in Choice of Law for Products Liability: A Comparative Comment on Statutory Solu-

victim's habitual residence, and if the defendant's products were available in that state through commercial channels. If that choice is not available or is not exercised, Kozyris would apply the law of the state of the actual delivery of the product to the original acquirer. However, if the state of the actual delivery of the product is not also the state of its intended use, then the law of the latter state applies, provided that the supplier is so informed by the acquirer prior to delivery. Also, if the nature of the product is such that its intended use would obviously and substantially extend to more than one state, the law of a state of such intended use where the injury occurred applies or, in its absence, the law of the state of the victim's habitual residence.

Professor Weintraub proposes a simpler rule:[4] apply the law of the injured person's habitual residence, "whether this law is more or less favorable to the injured person than the law of other countries that have contacts with the defendant and the product."[5] This rule is subject to two exceptions. The first exception is the standard commercial unavailability proviso.[6] The second exception provides for the application of the pro-victim law of a country in which the defendant "has acted,"[7] if it is "desirable to punish and deter the defendant's outrageous conduct."[8]

Finally, the most recent proposal comes from Professor Symeonides.[9] His proposed rule differentiates between liability and damages. For

tions, 38 Am. J. Comp. L. 475, 492–93 (1990):

> (1) General Rule: Product liability actions against manufacturers for personal injury and death, including claims for compensatory and punitive damages, are governed by the local law of the state of the actual delivery of the product to the original acquirer.
>
> (2) Exceptions: (a) If the state of the actual delivery of the product is not also the state of its intended use, then the local law of the latter state will be applied provided that the manufacturer or authorized supplier is so informed by the acquirer prior to delivery.
>
> (b) If the nature of the product is such that its intended use would obviously and substantially extend to more than one state, the local law of a state of such intended use where the harm occurred will be applied or, in its absence, the local law of the state where victim habitually resided at the time of the harm.
>
> (c) Notwithstanding the preceding provisions, [where the victim had no direct or indirect transactional or other relational connection with the defendant], a claimant may, instead, choose to base his claim on the law of the state where the harm occurred if it coincides with the victim's habitual residence and if, at the time of harm the same products

of the same defendant were available there through commercial channels.

For a later iteration, see Kozyris, Conflicts Theory for Dummies: Après le Deluge, Where Are We on Producers Liability? 60 La. L. Rev. 1161, 1173–83 (2000).

4. For an earlier, much complex rule, see R. Weintraub, Commentary on the Conflict of Laws (1991 Supplement to 3d ed. 1986) 74–75. This rule distinguished between liability and compensatory damages, on the one hand, and punitive damages, on the other. The rule allowed the plaintiff to choose the applicable law under certain circumstances, but, if the plaintiff did not exercise those choices, the rule gave the defendant similar choices.

5. R. Weintraub, Commentary on the Conflict of Laws 424 (4th ed. 2001).

6. See id. (The defendant can avoid the application of the pro-victim law of victim's habitual residence by proving that the defendant could not reasonably have foreseen that the product or the defendant's products of the same type would be available there through ordinary commercial channels.).

7. Id. at 425.

8. Id.

9. See Symeonides, Choice of Law for Products Liability: The 1990s and Beyond,

liability, the rule gives to the injured person the right to choose the law of a state that has any two of the following contacts: (a) place of injury; (b) domicile or habitual residence of the injured party; (c) the place in which the product was made; or (d) the place in which the product was delivered to the first acquirer and final user.[10] If the injured party fails to make a choice (e.g., because the required combination of contacts is lacking or is unfavorable, or because the defendant successfully invokes the commercial unavailability defense), the defendant may choose the law of a state that has any *three* of the above contacts. If neither party makes a choice, the court will choose the law governing liability under the court's general approach for tort conflicts. Following the same approach, the court will also choose the law governing compensatory or punitive damages.[11]

3. Common Features and Differences

§ 17.82 *a. Pertinent Contacts.* Of the twelve rules discussed above, only six retain the place of injury as a connecting factor.[1] Moreover, only one of these rules allows the application of the law of the state of injury when that state has no other contacts.[2] Nine of the twelve rules use the victim's domicile or habitual residence as a connecting factor,[3] and four of those rules allow the application of that state's law even if that state

79 Tul. L. Rev. 1247, 1332 (2004). The proposed rule provides as follows:

1. *Liability.* a. Liability for injury caused by a product is determined, at the choice of the injured party, by the law of a state that has any two of the following contacts: (a) the place of injury; (b) the domicile or habitual residence of the injured party; (c) the place in which the product was made; or (d) the place in which the product was delivered to the first acquirer and final user.

The injured party's choice shall be disregarded upon proof that neither the product that caused the injury nor the defendant's products of the same type were available in the chosen state through ordinary commercial channels.

b. If the injured party fails to make a choice under 1(a), the defendant may choose the law of a state that has any three of the contacts listed in 1(a).

c. Cases not disposed of under 1(a) or 1(b) are governed by the law chosen by the court under . . . [the general rules or approach for tort conflicts].

2. *Damages.* If the defendant is liable under 1, the injured party's right to compensatory or punitive damages and the amount of such damages shall be determined by the court under the law chosen under the general rules or approach for tort conflicts.

For an earlier proposal by the same author, see Symeonides, The Need for a Third Conflicts Restatement (And a Proposal for Tort Conflicts), 75 Ind. L. J. 437, 450–51, 472–74 (2000).

10. The injured person's choice is subject to the standard commercial unavailability proviso. See the second paragraph of Rule 1a, supra n. 9.

11. In so doing, the court will guard against the possibility of an inappropriate *dépeçage.* See Symeonides, Tul. L. Rev. supra n. 9 at 1341.

§ 17.82

1. The six rules are those of Louisiana, Hague, Tunisia, Cavers, Kozyris, and Symeonides. Rome II may also lead to the application of the law of the place of injury, if that place has a "manifestly closer connection" than the country of the otherwise applicable law.

2. The Tunisian rule allows the victim to opt for the application of the law of the state of injury. The Hague Convention provides the same choice, but only if the other involved states do not have more than one contact.

3. The Swiss, Italian, and Quebec rules do not employ this factor.

has no other contacts.[4] Seven rules use the defendant's principal place of business or similar affiliation as a connecting factor,[5] and all but one of them[6] allow the application of the law of that state even in the absence of other contacts. Four rules use the place of manufacture as a pertinent contact,[7] and two of them allow the application of that state's law even in the absence of other contacts.[8] Finally, ten of the twelve rules employ a new connecting factor, the place in which the product was acquired,[9] and five of those rules allow the plaintiff to choose the law of that state even if it does not have any other contacts.[10]

b. Commercial Unavailability Exception. All but one[11] of the twelve rules contain an exception that prevents the application of the law of a state with plaintiff-affiliating contacts (domicile, injury, or product acquisition) upon a showing that the product or the defendant's products of the same type were not available in that state through ordinary commercial channels. This exception protects the defendant from unfair surprise by preventing the application of a law that the defendant had no reason to anticipate. In practice, this exception is rarely invoked and even more rarely applied.[12]

c. Party Choice. Nine of the twelve rules give the victim the option of choosing the applicable law,[13] although they differ on the circumstances under which the option can be exercised. For example, the majority of these rules allow the victim to choose the law of a state that has only one contact, three rules require the concurrence of two contacts,[14] and one rule (Hague) allows a victim choice only if none of the involved states has more than one contact. Finally, one of these rules (Symeonides) also gives a narrower and residual choice to the defendant under certain circumstances.

---

4. These rules are those of the Tunisian and Russian codifications (at the choice of the victim), the Rome II Regulation, and Weintraub's rule.

5. The Swiss, Italian, Quebec, Russian, and Tunisian rules allow the plaintiff to choose the law of the defendant's principal place of business or similar affiliation. The Hague Convention allows the same choice, but only if the other involved states do not have more than one contact. In Rome II, this contact becomes relevant only if the victim is domiciled in the country of the defendant's principal place of business.

6. The only exception is Rome II. See supra § 17.80 at nn. 14–15.

7. The four rules are those of Louisiana, Cavers, Weintraub (place of acting), and Symeonides.

8. Cavers gives plaintiffs the option of choosing the law of the state of production or approval. Weintraub applies the place of acting "when it is desirable to punish or deter the defendant's outrageous conduct." See supra § 17.81 at n.8.

9. Only Rome II and Weintraub do not employ this factor.

10. The five rules are those of the Swiss, Italian, Quebec, Russian, and Tunisian codifications. Professor Kozyris would also apply that law if the victim does not choose the law of a state that is both the victim's domicile and also the place of injury.

11. The only exception is Article 3128 of the Quebec Civil Code.

12. See Symeonides, Choice of Law for Products Liability: The 1990s and Beyond, 79 Tul. L. Rev. 1247, 1321 (2004) (stating that the exception has not been invoked in any of the American cases decided between 1989 and 2003).

13. The Louisiana codification, Rome II, and Weintraub's rule do not provide this choice. However, in an earlier proposal, Weintraub provided such a choice to both victims and defendants. See supra § 17.81 n.4.

14. This is the case with the rules of Cavers, Kozyris, and Symeonides.

The rules of the Swiss, Italian, Quebec, Russian, and Tunisian codifications, which give plaintiffs a virtually unfettered choice, are likely to produce one-sided results that many observers will find objectionable. In contrast, the rules that restrict the plaintiff's choices by requiring concurrence of more than one contact need not produce one sided results, or in any event, results that are too different than the results that the courts would otherwise reach. For example, one author contends that his proposed rule (which gives plaintiffs more choices than it gives to defendants) would actually reduce slightly the pro-plaintiff results American courts reached in the cases decided between 1989 and 2003.[15] Be that as it may, and despite its apparent unilateral outlook, the notion of giving parties the option of choosing the applicable law has some distinct practical advantages. It is a cost-saving tool that helps conserve judicial resources by relieving courts from the burdens and risks of a laborious and often inconsistent judicial determination and evaluation of state policies and interests. It also helps foster predictability. If the parties know beforehand what the applicable law will be, they are more likely to make an intelligent decision as to whether to litigate.

    d. Other Features. All the above rules are "jurisdiction-selecting" rather than content-oriented. However, to the extent they allow a party to choose the applicable law, these rules ensure that the content of the competing laws will be taken into account whenever that party is allowed to exercise that choice. Also, unlike the traditional rules, some of the rules discussed here require that, for a state to be selected as the one whose law applies, that state must have more than one of the pertinent contacts,[16] thus making less likely the application of the law of a state that has only a fortuitous connection. In most of these rules, these contacts must be affiliated with both the plaintiff and the defendant.[17] Most of the above rules do not require an issue-by-issue choice, and thus they avoid the complexities and potential dangers of *depeçage*.[18] Finally, although, as noted above, most of these rules are or appear to be biased in favor of plaintiffs, most of them are phrased in forum-neutral terms.[19]

15. See Symeonides, Choice of Law for Products Liability: The 1990s and Beyond, 79 Tul. L. Rev. 1247, 1341–48 (2004) (showing a 4% reduction (from 54% to 50%) in the number of cases that applied a pro-plaintiff law).

16. This is the case with the Louisiana, Hague, Cavers, Kozyris, and Symeonides rules.

17. To some extent, this is true even under those rules that allow the application of the law of a state that has only one plaintiff-affiliating contact, but subject that application to the commercial unavailability proviso.

18. The Symeonides rule differentiates between liability and damages and thus creates the possibility of *depeçage*. However, the rule gives the court both discretion and admonition to avoid an inappropriate *dépe-*

çage. The Weintraub rule also creates the possibility of *dépeçage*, which, however, is also avoidable for the same reasons.

19. The two possible exceptions are the Swiss and Louisiana codifications. Article 135(2) of the Swiss codification provides that when a products liability case is governed by foreign law, the court may not award damages "other than" (French version), or "beyond" (German version), those provided for under Swiss law. The French version may work as a prohibition of punitive damages which are not allowed under Swiss substantive law. The German version may work as fixing a ceiling on compensatory damages to the maximum amount permitted by Swiss law. Article 3545 of the Louisiana codification is phrased as a unilateral rule specifying the condition for applying forum law but not foreign law. It has

VI.   TERRITORIALITY AND PERSONALITY
IN TORT CONFLICTS

§ 17.83   From the beginning of its history, private international law approached the task of delineating the operation of state and national laws by posing questions such as the following: (1) do laws attach to a territory, or to the citizens or domiciliaries of that territory (territoriality versus personality)? (2) does a law operate only within the enacting state's territory, or beyond that territory as well (territoriality versus extraterritoriality)? and (3) does the application of a state's law within its territory necessarily exclude the application of the laws of other states? These questions usually are compressed into two competing basic principles–territoriality and personality of the laws–although it would be more accurate to speak of territoriality versus non-territoriality. Either way, the core question is when should the application of a state's law depend on territorial factors, and when should it depend on other, including personal, factors?[1]

Through the centuries, various systems have provided different answers to the above question, with the pendulum swinging from territoriality to personality and vice versa, but without one principle completely dislodging the other. For example, in the days of the Roman Empire, the principle of personality was the dominant, but not exclusive, principle, whereas in the days of the Italian statutists, the two principles coexisted, with personality embodied in "personal" statutes and territoriality embodied in "real" statutes.[2] With the emergence of modern nation-states and Jean Bodin's 16th century seminal works on territorial sovereignty,[3] territoriality began to gain ground, a trend that Huber expressed in two of his famous axioms in the 17th century.[4] In the United States, Joseph Story gave his own strong endorsement to territoriality in the 19th century,[5] and Joseph Beale elevated it to a commanding position in the 20th century. Beale believed that, "by its very nature law must apply to everything and must exclusively apply to everything within the boundary of its jurisdiction."[6] Thus, under Beale's scheme, a state's law should

---

been criticized for this reason. See Kozyris, Values and Methods in Choice of Law For Products Liability: A Comparative Comment on Statutory Solutions, 38 Am. J. Comp. L. 475, 509 (1990). However, this unilaterality is only apparent because Article 3545 is complemented by bilateral rules contained in articles 3542–46 of the same codification which determine when foreign law applies. See Symeonides, Problems and Dilemmas in Codifying Choice of Law for Torts: The Louisiana Experience in a Comparative Perspective, 38 Am. J. Comp. L. 431, 464–69 (1990).

§ 17.83

1.   For an in depth discussion of these questions, see Symeonides, Territoriality

and Personality in Tort Conflicts, in Intercontinental Cooperation Through Private International Law: Essays in Memory of Peter Nygh, (T. Einhorn & K. Siehr, eds) 405 (2004).

2.   See supra § 2.3.

3.   J. Bodin, Six livres de la république (1576).

4.   See supra § 2.5.

5.   See supra § 2.7.

6.   1 Beale, Conflict of Laws 46 (1935).

govern all torts occurring, contracts made, and property located within its territory.[7]

The American conflicts revolution was a rebellion against many, if not all, aspects of Beale's system; but the revolution was primarily a rebellion against the *lex loci delicti* rule and its underlying holistic assumption that all of torts law operates territorially. However, as *Babcock*[8] framed it, the revolution's goal was not to banish the *lex loci* rule altogether, but rather to determine whether "the law of the place of the tort [should] *invariably* govern the availability of relief for the tort."[9] This goal was far from being iconoclastic.

Following New York's lead in *Babcock*, 41 other jurisdictions have abandoned the *lex loci rule* as the inexorable rule for all tort conflicts.[10] As this chapter illustrates, these jurisdictions now rely on multiple contacts, factors, and policies, all of which are antithetical to the single-mindedness of the *lex loci* rule. Most of the new factors, such as the parties' domicile and their pre-existing relationship, are non-territorial. This is true not only of the center-of-gravity and significant-contacts approaches, but also of the Restatement (Second), interest analysis, the better law, and other contemporary approaches. Thus, in terms of choice-of-law *methodology*, the above developments amounted to a true revolution. One of the effects of this revolution is that territoriality is no longer the exclusive operating principle in tort conflicts. In fact, at least in theory, this principle has all but disappeared.

Nevertheless, when one looks at the *results* that the new multifaceted flexible approaches have produced since the *Babcock* days, one realizes that territoriality has not lost as much ground as it is commonly assumed. For example, (1) aside from loss-distribution conflicts of the common-domicile pattern, cases involving many other patterns have reached the same results as the *lex loci* rule would have produced: they applied the law of a state of injury, even if that state had additional contacts and even if the rationale for applying that law was partly based on those additional contacts or other factors; and (2) in some other categories of cases, the courts applied the law of the place of conduct

---

7. Even in Beale's doctrine, however, territoriality was not the exclusive principle, inasmuch as it was subject to exceptions, many of which were grounded on the vested rights theory. In Beale's words, "[t]he law of a state prevails throughout its boundaries and, *generally speaking*, not outside them." 1 Beale, Conflict of Laws 308 (1935). The question was which cases qualified for such exceptions, and for Beale and his Restatement the answer was "not many." Indeed, Beale's system allowed for much fewer "personal" exceptions than most continental systems, which had adopted the personality principle for most matters of capacity, personal status, and succession at death. Even in the 1930s, Beale's position was odd for a country like the United States that purported to be "one

nation, indivisible," notwithstanding the internal boundaries. With the advent of new means of transportation and communication and the increased mobility of people, state boundaries became even less important, and Beale's insistence on territoriality as the dominant principle made even less sense than before. This is why, during the second half of the 20th century, the exceptions to territoriality have grown exponentially.

8. Babcock v. Jackson, 12 N.Y.2d 473, 240 N.Y.S.2d 743, 191 N.E.2d 279 (1963) (discussed supra § 17.29).

9. Id. at 280–81.

10. See supra §§ 2.16, 17.39.

(rather than the place of injury) and thus produced a different result than the American version of the *lex loci* rule would produce. However, because the place of conduct is a territorial rather than a personal contact, these cases remain in the territorialist column.

Thus, in terms of the results of actual cases (rather than in terms of underlying rationale or methodology), territoriality has lost relatively little ground as a result of the American choice-of-law revolution.[11] The basic distinction *Babcock* enunciated between conduct-regulating and loss-distributing rules helps delineate this ground and the contemporary position of territoriality in resolving tort conflicts. Specifically:

(1) Territoriality has lost significant ground to the personality principle in conflicts between loss-distribution rules. However, the ground lost is confined to one category of cases—cases in which both the tortfeasor and the victim are domiciled or have significant affiliations with the same state (common-domicile cases), and are involved in a tort that occurred in another state or states.[12] In these cases, the courts have almost unanimously applied the law of the parties' common domicile. Thus, one can say that the principle of personality reigns supreme in loss-distribution conflicts of the common-domicile pattern.

(2) Conversely, territoriality continues to reign supreme in conflicts between conduct-regulating rules. In these conflicts, the courts disregard the parties' domiciles and focus on the two territorial contacts—the place of conduct and the place of injury. When both of these contacts are in the same state, the courts invariably apply the law of that state.[13] When these contacts are in different states, the courts choose one of those states, as explained above.[14] When they choose the law of the place of conduct, the result deviates from the *lex loci* rule as applied in the United States, but it is still a territorial result.

(3) This leaves the middle ground, namely, loss-distribution conflicts of the split-domicile pattern. This is the arena in which territoriality and personality continue to challenge each other. Al-

---

11. This statement is limited to tort conflicts. In contracts conflicts, the principle of territoriality lost more ground than in tort conflicts, when courts abandoned the *lex loci contractus* rule and began choosing the applicable law on the basis of multiple factors, many of which are non-territorial. Territoriality's biggest loss came with the wider recognition and expansive utilization of the principle of party autonomy. This principle is non-territorial in a dual sense: (a) it focuses on the individual parties and makes their volition the supreme principle; and (b) it allows the parties to choose the governing law—including an a-national, non-territorial law—independently from territorial connections. The extension of party autonomy to areas beyond contracts, such as successions and matrimonial prop-

erty, is also another dramatic example of the retreat of territoriality. See S. Symeonides, Private International Law at the End of the 20th Century: Progress or Regress?, 38–40, 48, 56–60 (1999). A less dramatic example is the gradual reduction of the scope of the situs rule for immovables. See S. Symeonides, Exploring the 'Dismal Swamp': The Revision of Louisiana's Conflicts Law on Successions, 47 La. L. Rev. 1029, 1043, 1052–54, 1075–76, 1090–92 (1987).

12. See supra § 17.39.

13. See supra § 17.48 nn. 4–12. For punitive damages conflicts, see § 17.49.

14. See supra § 17.48 nn. 13–39.

though the courts that have abandoned the *lex loci* rule consider both the personal and the territorial contacts, the majority of courts end up applying the law of the state that has the territorial contacts (even if that state also has a personal contact), rather than the state that has only a personal contact.[15] In that sense, one can say that, at least for now, territoriality continues to carry the day in these middle conflicts.

If one assumes that the goal of the American choice-of-law revolution was to banish territoriality from tort conflicts, one would have to conclude that the revolution has scored only a partial victory. However, as noted earlier, such an assumption would be incorrect. The revolution's goals were neither as deliberate nor as narrow. The chief goal was to free American choice-of-law from the shackles of a mechanical rule that inexorably required the application of the law of a state that had a single contact—which happened to be territorial—regardless of any other contacts or factors, and regardless of the issue involved in the conflict or the content of the conflicting laws. Judged in this light, the revolution has succeeded in demolishing not only this particular rule, but also the system that gave birth to it. Along the way, the revolution has brought about a new accommodation or equilibrium between territoriality and personality.

This equilibrium can form the basis for the next step in the evolution of American conflicts law, which, as argued earlier,[16] should lead to the formulation of new, issue-directed, content-sensitive, flexible and evolutionary choice-of-law rules based on the accumulated experience of American courts.

15. See supra §§ 17.41–17.46

16. See supra §§ 2.26, 17.35, 17.47, 17.49.

Chapter 18

CONTRACTS

Table of Sections

		Sections
I.	Choice of Law by the Parties (Party Autonomy)	18.1–18.12
	A. General Principles	18.1–18.2
	B. Limitations on Party Autonomy	18.3–18.7
	1. Questions of Interpretation and Construction	18.3
	2. Validity and Public Policy	18.4–18.5
	a. Public Policy Limitation in General	18.4
	b. Public Policy in Specific Contexts	18.5
	3. The Requirement of a "Substantial Relationship"	
	a. In General	18.6
	b. Satisfaction of the Requirement: Connecting Factors	18.7
	C. Second Restatement, § 187	18.8
	1. Connection with Chosen Law	18.9
	2. Public Policy Limitation	18.10
	3. Validation	18.11
	D. Section 1–105 of the Uniform Commercial Code	18.12
II.	Choice of Law in the Absence of Choice-of-Law Agreement	18.13
	A. The Classic Approach	18.14–18.15
	B. Modern Approaches	18.16–18.21
	1. Overview	18.16
	2. The Case Law: Issue Identification (Characterization) and Connecting Factors	18.17–18.20
	3. The Choice-of-Law Approaches in the Courts: Summary	18.21
III.	Contract Choice-of-Law by Subject Matter	18.22
	A. Contracts by Subject Matter	18.23–18.36
	1. Interests in Land	18.23
	2. Sales of Chattels	18.24–18.25
	a. Interstate Transactions	18.24–18.25
	i. Restatement and U.C.C.	18.24
	ii. Case Law	18.25
	b. International Transactions	18.25
	3. Insurance Contracts	18.26
	4. Suretyship	18.27
	5. Contracts for the Repayment of Money Lent	18.28
	6. Rendition of Services	18.29–18.31
	7. Agency	18.32–18.36
	8. Other Contracts	18.37
	B. Contract Issues	18.37
IV.	Choice-of-Law Alternatives	18.40–18.41
V.	Unjust Enrichment	18.42–18.48
	A. Introduction	18.42–18.43
	1. In General	18.42

    2. Case Categories 18.43
  B. Choice-of-Law Alternatives............................ 18.44–18.48
    1. Preexisting (Contractual) Relationships.................. 18.44
    2. Voluntary Bestowal of Benefits 18.45
    3. Claims Related to Tort 18.46
    4. Equitable Remedies.................................... 18.47
    5. Extent and Nature of Relief 18.48

I. CHOICE OF LAW BY THE PARTIES
(PARTY AUTONOMY)

A. GENERAL PRINCIPLES

§ 18.1   Parties enter into contracts with the intent and expectation to mutually bind themselves. Thus, as a general proposition, one can accept the statement that "in contracts, . . . there is but one basic policy, namely protection of the expectations of the parties,"[1] and that "predictability in choice-of-law decisions is an important value in contracts."[2] Such predictability is served, and party expectations are protected, by giving effect to the parties' own choice of the applicable law (*party autonomy*).[3]

The principle of party autonomy is "almost as ancient as conflicts law itself."[4] Indeed, it seems that party autonomy was recognized, albeit

---

§ 18.1

1. Reese, Choice of Law in Torts and Contracts and Directions for the Future, 16 Colum. J. Transnat'l L. 1, 21 (1977). See also Trautman, Some Notes on the Theory of Choice of Law Clauses, 35 Mercer L. Rev. 535 (1984); Note, Effectiveness of Choice-of-Law Clauses in Contract Conflicts of Law: Party Autonomy or Objective Determination?, 82 Colum. L. Rev. 1659 (1982).

2. Reese, supra n.1, at 17.

3. See Chief Justice Marshall's statement in Wayman v. Southard, 23 U.S. (10 Wheat.) 1, 48, 6 L.Ed. 253 (1825) (referring to a principle of "universal law . . . that, in every forum, a contract is governed by the law with a view to which it was made"); DeSantis v. Wackenhut Corp., 793 S.W.2d 670, 677 (Tex.1990) denied 498 U.S. 1048, 111 S.Ct. 755, 112 L.Ed.2d 775 (1991) ("This principle derives from the most basic policy of contract law, which is the protection of the justified expectations of the parties."); Fricke v. Isbrandtsen Co., Inc., 151 F.Supp. 465, 467 (S.D.N.Y.1957); Restatement, Second, Conflict of Laws § 187, comment (e) (1971); Gruson, Governing Law Clauses in Commercial Agreements—New York's Approach, 18 Colum. J. Transnat'l L. 323 (1980) (with extensive review of the case law); James, Effects of the Autonomy of the Parties on Conflicts of Law, 36 Chi. Kent. L. Rev. 34, (1959); Rheinstein, Book Review, 15 U. Chi. L. Rev. 478, 484 (1948). Parties will often wish to have their contractual relations governed by a single and uniform law. Lauritzen v. Larsen, 345 U.S. 571, 588, 73 S.Ct. 921, 931, 97 L.Ed. 1254 (1953); Clarkson v. Finance Co. of America at Baltimore, 328 F.2d 404 (4th Cir.1964); Siegelman v. Cunard White Star Ltd., 221 F.2d 189, 195 (2d Cir.1955). Such a need will be especially prominent when a contract is to be performed in several different places. For example, in *Lauritzen*, a Danish sailor was hired in New York to sail to Cuba and other countries. Familiarity with a particular state's legal system may also motivate a stipulation of the applicable law by the parties. National Sur. Corp. v. Inland Properties, Inc., 286 F.Supp. 173, 189 (E.D.Ark.1968). Finally, the judicial task becomes easier when the court honors the stipulation of the parties. *Siegelman*, 221 F.2d 189.

4. S. Symeonides, W. Perdue & A. von Mehren, Conflict of Laws: American, Comparative, International 338 (2d ed. 2003).

indirectly, by what may be regarded as the earliest known conflicts rule. A decree issued in Hellenistic Egypt in 120–118 B.C. provided that contracts written in the Egyptian language were subject to the jurisdiction of the Egyptian courts, which applied Egyptian law, whereas contracts written in Greek were subject to the jurisdiction of the Greek courts, which applied Greek law. Thus, by choosing the language of their contract, the parties could directly choose the forum and indirectly the applicable law.[5] In the middle ages, the French commentator Dumoulin (1500–1566) resurrected and championed party autonomy,[6] which has since been a gravamen of continental conflicts doctrine and practice. American transactional and judicial practice also recognized this principle as early as 1825.[7]

Party autonomy means that the parties are free to select the law governing their contract, albeit subject to certain limitations to be discussed later. The parties will usually do so by means of an express choice-of-law clause in their written contract. In the United States, it is rare that the stipulation will be an oral term in an oral contract,[8] and proof of an oral stipulation with respect to a written contract may be prevented by the parol evidence rule, if it applies.[9] Many recent codifications[10] and international conventions[11] including the Rome

---

5. See F. Juenger, Choice of Law and Multistate Justice 7–8 (1993).

6. See id. at 16–17; supra § 2.4 n.2.

7. See Wayman v. Southard, 23 U.S. (10 Wheat.) 1, 48, 6 L.Ed. 253 (1825); Pritchard v. Norton, 106 U.S. 124, 1 S.Ct. 102, 27 L.Ed. 104 (1882).

8. Nakhleh v. Chemical Construction Corp., 359 F.Supp. 357 (S.D.N.Y.1973).

9. Reese, supra n.1, at 22 n.65 (citing to Restatement, Second, Contracts § 239 (1981)). The parol evidence rule would not be a bar in cases governed by the Vienna Sales Convention. See infra n.12.

10. The two American codifications both allow an implied choice of law. The Louisiana codification provides for such a choice if the circumstances indicate that the parties have "clearly relied upon" the law of a certain state. La.Civ.Code Art. 3540 id. cmt. (e). The 2001 Oregon codification allows for a choice "clearly demonstrated from the terms of the contract," but requires an "express and conspicuous choice" for standard-form contracts drafted primarily by one party. See O.R.S. § 81.120(2). The 1991 Puerto Rico Draft Code provides (Art. 34) that the choice must be express or "must be demonstrated from the provisions of the contract or from the conduct of the parties." Among foreign codifications, the Austrian, Quebec, and Russian codifications allow for an implied choice of law by the parties. See Austrian Federal Law of June 15, § 35(1) 1978 Bundesgesetzblatt 1729

(No. 109) (1978); Quebec Civ. Code Art 3111; Russian Civ. Code Art. 1210(2), federal law n. 146 of 26 November 2001 enacting the third part of the Civil Code of the Russian Federation, Rossyiskaya Gazeta, n. 49 item 4553, 28/11/2001.

11. Art. 5 of the 1978 Hague Convention on the Law Applicable to Agency also envisions a choice that can be inferred "with reasonable certainty from the terms of the agreement . . . and the circumstances of the case . . . " Hague Conference on Private International Law, I Actes et documents de la Treizième session 42 (1978). This language was substituted for the requirement, in an earlier draft, that, absent an express choice, the "choice . . . must arise by necessary implication from the provisions of the contract and the surrounding circumstances" which was considered to be too restrictive. Hay & Müller-Freienfels, Agency in the Conflict of Laws, 27 Am. J. Comp. L. 1, 39 n.197 (1979). Article 7(1) of the 1985 Hague Convention for the Law Applicable to the International Sales of Goods provides that the choice must be express or "must be demonstrated from the terms of the contract and the conduct of the parties, viewed in their entirety." Finally, the 1994 International Convention on the Law Applicable to International Contracts (33 I.L.M. 732 (1994)) provides (Art. 7) that, in the absence of an express agreement, the choice of law "must be evident from the parties's behavior and from the

Convention,[12] allow oral stipulations as to the applicable law, or infer agreement from the parties' conduct or the circumstances of the case. The UN Convention on Contracts for the International Sale of Goods (commonly known as the: "Vienna Sales Convention"), which is in force for the United States,[13] provides—for cases to which it applies—that the parties may vary the applicable law (Art. 6), and that the contract (Art. 11) or its modification (Art. 29) do not require written form. Oral choice-of-law clauses, even in the context of a written contract therefore are permissible under the Convention, although, for practical purposes, rather unlikely. The Restatement Second also allows for an oral or an implied choice but distinguishes the latter from a hypothetical choice by providing that it "does not suffice to demonstrate that the parties, if they had thought about the matter, would have wished to have the law of a particular state applied."[14] As a practical matter, however, the injunction against resort to the parties' hypothetical intention adds little inasmuch as the Second Restatement's principal choice-of-law reference to the place of the "most significant relationship" includes many of the same factors, including party expectations, as would a hypothetical party intent.[15]

Ordinarily, the parties' choice will be taken to encompass only the substantive law of the chosen state, and not its conflicts law.[16] Similarly, the choice will not extend to foreign procedural law.[17] It is still an open

clauses of the contract considered as a whole."

12. The 1980 Convention on the Law Applicable to Contractual Obligations of the European Communities (now known, and hereafter referred to, as the "Rome Convention") provides in Art. 3(1) that "[t]he choice [of law] must be expressed or demonstrated with reasonable certainty by the terms of the contract or the circumstance of the case.") The current consolidated text of the Convention can be found at http://europa.eu.int/eur-lex/pri/en/oj/ dat/1998/c_027/ c_0271980126en00340053.pdf The Convention is now in force in the member states of the European Union, which is in the process of converting the Convention into a Regulation that will be directly binding on member states Countries. See Commission of the European Communities, Green Paper on the Conversion of the Rome Convention of 1980 on the Law Applicable to Contractual Obligations into a Community Instrument and its Modernisation (Brussels, 14.1.2003, COM(2002) 654 final), at http://europa.eu.int/eur-lex/en/ com/gpr/2002/com2002_0654en01.pdf

13. 15 U.S.C.A. Appendix. For further discussion see infra § 18.25.

14. Restatement, Second, Conflict of Laws § 187, cmnt. (a) (1971).

15. Restatement, Second Conflict of Laws § 188, cmnt. (b) (1971).

16. Restatement, Second, Conflict of Laws § 187, cmnt. (h) (1971). McGill v. Hill, 31 Wn.App. 542, 644 P.2d 680 (1982). Under the U.C.C., however, the parties' choice in matters governed by §§ 2–402, 4–102, 6–102, 8–106, and 9–103 is effective only "to the extent permitted by the law (including the conflict of laws rules) ... specified" by these sections: § 1–105(2). See also U.C.C. §§ 2A–105, 2A–106 (discussed infra § 18.37 n.3.) The general rule of the Restatement as well as the exceptions under the U.C.C. are designed to provide certainty and, in the case of the U.C.C., also to protect third party expectations (e.g., with respect to security interests). The conflicts rules of the law chosen by the parties are also excluded according to English law. Amin Rasheed Shipping Corp. v. Kuwait Ins. Co., [1983] 3 W.L.R. 241, 246 (H.L.). For comment see Mann, 33 Int'l & Comp. L.Q. 193 (1984) and Spiro, 33 Int'l & Comp. L.Q. at 199. The rule is the same in other legal systems, even if they would otherwise apply foreign conflicts law (*renvoi*, supra § 3.13): the law chosen by the parties is the *substantive* law of the particular legal system and excludes conflicts and procedural law. See e.g., Rome Convention, supra n.12, Art. 15.

17. With regard to statutes of limitation in particular, see Long v. Holland America Line Westours, Inc., 26 P.3d 430 (Alaska

question in some American jurisdictions whether the parties may stipulate the law applicable in *tort*, although the emerging trend is towards allowing such stipulations.[18]

There is insufficient authority to conclude that a choice-of-*court* clause incorporates a choice of the selected forum's law,[19] although the

2001); Belleville Toyota, Inc. v. Toyota Motor Sales, U.S.A., Inc. 199 Ill.2d 325, 770 N.E.2d 177 (2002); Education Resources Institute v. Lipsky, 2002 WL 1463461 (Cal. App. 2002); Western Group Nurseries, Inc. v. Ergas, 211 F.Supp.2d 1362 (S.D.Fla. 2002); Shaw v. Rivers White Water Rafting Resort, 2002 WL 31748919 (E.D.Mich. 2002); Financial Bancorp. Inc. v. Pingree & Dahle, Inc., 880 P.2d 14 (Utah App.1994); Federal Deposit Ins. Corp. v. Petersen, 770 F.2d 141, 142–43 (10th Cir.1985); Hambrecht & Quist Venture Partners v. American Medical Int'l, Inc., 38 Cal.App.4th 1532, 46 Cal.Rptr.2d 33 (1995); Manion v. Roadway Package System, Inc., 938 F.Supp. 512 (C.D.Ill.1996); In re Western United Nurseries, Inc. v. Estate of Adams, 191 B.R. 820 (Bankr.D.Ariz.1996); In re Fineberg, 202 B.R. 206 (Bankr.E.D.Pa.1996); Springfield Oil Services, Inc. v. Costello, 941 F.Supp. 45 (E.D.Pa. 1996); Nez v. Forney, 109 N.M. 161, 783 P.2d 471 (1989); Florida State Bd. of Admin. v. Law Eng'g & Envt'e. Servs., Inc., 262 F.Supp.2d 1004 (D.Minn.2003); Hemar Ins. Corp. v. Ryerson, 108 S.W.3d 90 (Mo.App.2003); Belleville Toyota, Inc. v. Toyota Motor Sales, U.S.A., Inc. 199 Ill.2d 325, 770 N.E.2d 177 (2002); Education Resources Institute v. Lipsky, 2002 WL 1463461 (Cal. App. 2002); Western Group Nurseries, Inc. v. Ergas, 211 F.Supp.2d 1362 (S.D.Fla. 2002). These decisions are based on the traditional (American) *procedural* characterization of statutes of limitations. Most foreign legal systems, in contrast, characterize them as substantive (supra § 3.9), as does the 1988 Uniform Limitations Act (id.).

18. This question is explored supra § 17.40 nn. 20–30. See also the annual choice-of-law surveys by Symeonides in 51 Am.J.Comp.L. 1, 67–68 (2003); 50 Am. J.Comp.L. 1, 38–40 (2002); 48 Am. J.Comp.L. 143, 160–61 (2000); 43 Am. J.Comp.L. 1, 63–67 (1995). For recent cases holding that the clause did *not* encompass contract-related tort claims, see, e.g. Benchmark Elecs., Inc. v. J.M. Huber Corp., 343 F.3d 719 (5th Cir.2003), opinion modified on denial of rehearing 355 F.3d 356 (5th Cir.2003); Green Leaf Nursery v. E.I. DuPont De Nemours & Co., 341 F.3d 1292 (11th Cir.2003), cert. denied __ U.S. __, 124 S.Ct. 2094, 158 L.Ed.2d 723 (2004); Financial Trust Co. Inc. v. Citibank, N.A.,

268 F.Supp.2d 561 (D.V.I. 2003); Gloucester Holding Corp. v. U.S. Tape and Sticky Products, LLC, 832 A.2d 116 (Del.Ch.2003); Owen J. Roberts School Dist. v. HTE, Inc., 2003 WL 735098 (E.D.Pa.2003); Sutton v. Hollywood Entertainment Corp., 181 F.Supp.2d 504 (D.Md. 2002); Thomas v. Fidelity Brokerage Services, Inc. 977 F.Supp. 791 (W.D. La. 1997); Krock v. Lipsay, 97 F.3d 640 (2d Cir. 1996); Valley Juice Ltd., Inc. v. Evian Waters of France, Inc., 87 F.3d 604 (2d Cir. 1996); Precision Screen Machines, Inc. v. Elexon, Inc., 1996 WL 495564 (N.D. Ill. 1996); Shelley v. Trafalgar House Public Ltd. Co., 918 F.Supp. 515 (D.P.R. 1996); Telemedia Partners Worldwide, Ltd. v. Hamelin Ltd., 1996 WL 41818 (S.D.N.Y. 1996); Chaplain Enterprises, Inc. v. United States, 945 F.Supp. 468 (N.D.N.Y. 1996); Young v. W.S. Badcock Corp., 222 Ga.App. 218, 474 S.E.2d 87 (1996). For cases reaching the opposite conclusion, see Wireless Distributors, Inc. v. Sprintcom, Inc., 2003 WL 22175607 (N.D.Ill. 2003); Birnberg v. Milk Street Residential Associated Ltd. P'ship, 2003 WL 151929 (N.D.Ill. 2003). Compare Kuehn v. Childrens Hospital, Los Angeles, 119 F.3d 1296, 1302 (7th Cir.1997) (Posner, J.) (reviewing authority and concluding that cases purporting not to allow tort choice-of-law stipulations can be distinguished as merely construing the stipulation not to cover tort claims); Lloyd v. Loeffler, 694 F.2d 489 (7th Cir.1982); Twohy v. First Nat. Bank of Chicago, 758 F.2d 1185 (7th Cir.1985) (choice of law governing tort upheld); Nedlloyd Lines B.V. v. Superior Court, 3 Cal.4th 459, 11 Cal. Rptr.2d 330, 834 P.2d 1148 (1992) (construing provision to include tort claim) with Ezell v. Hayes Oilfield Const. Co., Inc. 693 F.2d 489 (5th Cir.1982), cert. denied, 464 U.S. 818, 104 S.Ct. 79, 78 L.Ed.2d 90 (1983) (stipulation ineffective). See also Barrow v. ATCO Mfg. Co., 524 N.E.2d 1313 (Ind.App. 1988). Continental legal systems permit such a choice. For German law, see Introductory Law to the Civil Code (EGBGB) Art. 42, Bundesgesetzblatt 1999, I, 1026, 1027.

19. But see Lummus Co. v. Commonwealth Oil Refining Co., 280 F.2d 915, 91 A.L.R.2d 912 (1st Cir. 1960), cert. denied 364 U.S. 911, 81 S.Ct. 274, 5 L.Ed.2d 225 (1960) (stipulation for arbitration in New

lex-fori orientation of some modern choice-of-law theories may in practice bring about this result and the presence of other factors in the contract may lead a court to conclude that the parties made an implied choice of law.[20] In contrast, many civil law countries assume, following the maxim *"qui eligit iudicem, eligit ius,"* that a choice-of-forum clause also implies a choice of forum law.[21] Conversely, a choice-of-law clause does not, without more, operate as a selection of the foreign forum for jurisdictional purposes.[22] However, the Supreme Court has held that a choice-of-law clause is evidence of purposeful availment of the selected state's benefits and protections.[23]

Finally, American case law is rather inconclusive on the problem of "floating" clauses, namely agreements that provide for alternative fora and/or alternative applicable laws.[24] For example, a clause may provide for the jurisdiction of a court at the future plaintiff's (or defendant's) domicile or place of business and may stipulate for the application of

York "indicates choice of law"); Kress Corp. v. Edw. C. Levy Co., 102 Ill.App.3d 264, 58 Ill.Dec. 561, 430 N.E.2d 593, 595 (1981) (parties' conduct and express agreement to arbitrate in Illinois implies choice of Illinois state law, and not federal law, as it applies to arbitration); Compagnie d'Armament Maritime S.A. v. Compagnie Tunisienne de Navigation S.A., [1970] 3 W.L.R. 389 (H.L.) (reputable presumption that forum-selection clause is also intended to choose forum law).

20. See Chinchilla v. Foreign Tankship Corp., 195 Misc. 895, 91 N.Y.S.2d 213 (1949), modified on other grounds and aff'd 197 Misc. 1058, 97 N.Y.S.2d 835 (1950), aff'd 278 App.Div. 556, 102 N.Y.S.2d 438 (1951); Restatement, Second, Conflict of Laws § 187, cmnt. (a) (1971). See also Coastal States Gas Corp. v. Atlantic Tankers Ltd., 546 F.2d 15, 17 (2d Cir.1976) (" ... the law of New York governs this dispute. The charter party was drafted and executed in New York and the arbitration is to take place in New York"). However, this statement is less authoritative than it first appears because clause 55 of the charter party, as reproduced at 546 F.2d at 16 n.2, had provided for "arbitration in the City of New York, pursuant to the laws relating to arbitration there in force...." It is a matter of interpretation, not addressed by the court, whether the phrase "laws relating to arbitration" is limited to procedural rules or also extends to New York substantive law.

21. Article 3 of the Rome Convention, supra n.12, accepts a choice of the applicable law that appears with sufficient certainty from the circumstances. A forum selection clause traditionally has been regarded to be such a circumstance. See Kegel &

Schurig, Internationales Privatrecht 658 (9th ed. 2004).

22. See Algemene Bank Nederland, M.V. v. Mattox, 611 F.Supp. 144 (N.D.Ga. 1985); Dent–Air, Inc. v. Beech Mountain Air Service, 332 N.W.2d 904 (Minn. 1983)(choice-of-law clause does not confer jurisdiction in the absence of minimum contacts with the forum).

23. Burger King Corp. v. Rudzewicz, 471 U.S. 462, 482, 105 S.Ct. 2174, 2187, 85 L.Ed.2d 528 (1985): "[N]othing in our cases ... suggests that a choice-of-law provision should be ignored in considering whether a defendant has 'purposefully invoked the benefits and protection of a State's laws' for jurisdictional purposes. Although such a provision standing alone would be insufficient to confer jurisdiction, we believe that, when combined with the 20–year interdependent relationship [the defendant] established with Burger King's Miami headquarters, it reinforced his deliberate affiliation with the forum State and the reasonable foreseeability of possible litigation there." (emphasis in original). See also SD Leasing, Inc. v. Al Spain and Associates, Inc., 277 Ark. 178, 640 S.W.2d 451 (1982).

24. Because of the uncertainty about the (future) applicable law, such "floating" clauses were controversial in England. See, e.g., Musgrave v. HCA Mideast, Ltd., 856 F.2d 690 (4th Cir.1988). As a result of the Rome Convention, supra n.12, they should now be valid in all member states, including England. See Hay, Flexibility versus Predictability and Uniformity in Choice of Law, 226 Recueil des Cours 1991–I, 309 n.100 (1991). For comprehensive treatment, see Rasmussen–Bonne, Alternative Rechts-und Forumswahlklauseln (1989).

that state's law. Clauses like these (also known as "service or suit" (SOS) clauses) are common in some insurance contracts. Through these clauses, the insurer agrees in advance to submit to the jurisdiction of a court to be chosen by the insured, and also agrees that all disputes arising under the contract "shall be determined in accordance with the law and practice of such Court."[25] The question raised by a clause such as the one quoted is whether it constitutes a choice-of-law clause (in addition to being a choice-of-forum clause).[26] The majority of cases that have considered this question have concluded that these clauses are *not* choice-of-law clauses, or, if they are, then they encompass the "whole law" of the forum state, including its conflicts law.[27]

§ 18.2 Historically, party autonomy has support in American case law dating back well into the nineteenth century.[1] However, the drafters of the first Restatement, perhaps because of their view that party autonomy amounted to a license for private legislation, concluded that this principle was not sufficiently established to be included in the Restatement. The criticism was that party autonomy promotes certainty over other social policies, and that it enables the parties to evade the public policy of the state whose law would otherwise govern the contract.[2] However the criticism was misplaced because it assumed a rule of

---

25. Burlington Northern R.R. Co. v. Allianz Underwriters Ins. Co., 1994 WL 637011 at *2 (Del Super. 1994), appeal refused 653 A.2d 304 (Del.Supr.1994).

26. On whether such clauses are genuine choice-of-forum clauses, see Cannelton Industries, Inc. v. Aetna Cas. & Sur. Co., 460 S.E.2d 1 (W.Va. 1994); Price v. Brown Group, Inc., 206 A.D.2d 195, 619 N.Y.S.2d 414, 1994 WL 642419 (N.Y.A.D. 4 Dept. 1994) appeal denied 1995 WL 121748 (N.Y.A.D. 4 Dept. 1995).

27. See, e.g., Norfolk Southern Corp. v. California Union Ins. Co., 859 So.2d 167 (La.App. 1 Cir.2003); Liggett Group Inc. v. Affiliated FM Ins. Co., 788 A.2d 134 (Del.Super.2001); Burlington Northern R.R. Co. v. Allianz Underwriters Ins. Co., 1994 WL 637011 (Del. Super. 1994), appeal refused 653 A.2d 304 (Del.Supr.1994); North American Philips Corp. v. Aetna Cas. and Sur. Co., 1994 WL 555399 (Del.Super.1994); Carrier Corp. v. Home Ins. Co., 43 Conn. Supp. 182, 648 A.2d 665, (1994); Hoechst Celanese Corp. v. National Union Fire Ins. Co. of Pittsburgh, Pa., C.A. No. 89C–09–035 (Del. Super.1994); W.R. Grace & Co. v. Hartford Accident and Indemnity Co., 407 Mass. 572, 555 N.E.2d 214 (1990); Chesapeake Utilities Corp. v. American Home Ass. Co., 704 F.Supp. 551 (D. Del. 1989); Monsanto Co. v. Aetna Cas. & Sur. Co., Del. Super., C.A. No. 88C–01–118, (Jan. 19, 1991); Sequa Corp. v. Aetna Cas. & Sur. Co., C.A. No. 89C–04–001, (July 13, 1990); Inner–City Products Corp. v. Insurance Co.

of North America, 1993 WL 18948 (D. Del. 1993); Singer v. Lexington Ins. Co., 658 F.Supp. 341 (N.D.Tex.1986). For discussion of these and other cases, see Symeonides, Choice of Law in the American Courts in 1994: A View from the Trenches, 43 Am. J.Comp.L., 1, 67–72 (1995).

§ 18.2

1. The earliest relevant cases based their choice of law decisions upon the implied intent of the parties. Pritchard v. Norton, 106 U.S. 124, 1 S.Ct. 102, 27 L.Ed. 104 (1882); Wayman v. Southard, 23 U.S. (10 Wheat.) 1, 48, 6 L.Ed.253 (1825); Thompson v. Ketcham, 8 Johns. 189, 193, 5 Am.Dec. 332 (N.Y.1811); Andrews v. Pond, 38 U.S. (13 Pet.) 65, 78, 10 L.Ed. 61 (1839); J. Story, Commentaries on the Conflicts of Laws § 293(b) (2d ed. 1841). Early cases recognizing an express stipulation of law by the parties include Dolan v. Mutual Reserve Fund Life Ass'n, 173 Mass. 197, 53 N.E. 398 (1899); Griesemer v. Mutual Life Ins. Co. of New York, 10 Wash. 202, 38 P. 1031 (1894); Fonseca v. Cunard Steamship Co., 153 Mass. 553, 27 N.E. 665 (1891); Scott v. Perlee, 39 Ohio St. 63 (1883); Kellogg v. Miller, 13 Fed. 198 (C.C.D.Neb.1881); Arnold v. Potter, 22 Iowa 194 (1867). For the ancient origins of party autonomy, see F.K. Juenger, Choice of Law and Multistate Justice 17 (1993).

2. E. Gerli and Co., Inc. v. Cunard S.S. Co., 48 F.2d 115, 117 (2d Cir.1931); Siegelman v. Cunard White Star Ltd., 221 F.2d

party autonomy without any limitation.[3] In fact, and as the subsequent discussion details, party autonomy is not so unrestricted in American law. For example, ordinarily, the chosen law must bear some relationship to the parties or the transaction,[4] although many recent codifications[5] and international

189, 201 (2d Cir.1955) (Frank J., dissenting); 2 Beale, Treatise on the Conflicts of Laws § 332.2 (1935); cf. Note, Comments on Tentative Draft No. 6 of the Restatement, Second, 76 Harv. L. Rev. 1524, 1526 (1963); Weinberger, Party Autonomy and Choice of Law: The *Restatement, Second,* Interest Analysis and the Search for a Methodological Synthesis, 4 Hofstra L. Rev. 605, 618–23 (1976). Beale attacked party autonomy because "at their will ... [parties] can free themselves from the power of the law which would otherwise apply to their acts." 2 Beale, supra, § 332.2 at 1080. As a result, the First Restatement omitted any reference to party autonomy. For a history of the debate between the old proponents and opponents of party autonomy, see Yntema, Contract and Conflict of Laws: "Autonomy" in the Choice of Law in the United States, 1 N.Y.L.F. 46 (1955).

3. W. Cook, Logical and Legal Bases of the Conflicts of Law 392 (1942).

4. See Restatement (Second) Conflict of Laws § 187(2)(a) (1971) (discussed infra § 18.9); DeSantis v. Wackenhut Corp., 793 S.W.2d 670, 677 (Tex.1990), cert. denied 498 U.S. 1048, 111 S.Ct. 755, 112 L.Ed.2d 775 (1991) (the parties "cannot require that their contract be governed by the law of a jurisdiction which has no relation whatever to them or their agreement.") In some countries, a distinction is made between the choice of forum law and non forum law. England, it is said that "connection with English law is not, as a matter of principle, essential." Vita Food Products Inc. v. Unus Shipping Co. Ltd., [1939] A.C. 277 (P.C., per Lord Wright). Dicey & Morris, The Conflict of Laws 1214 (12th ed. 1993) also point out that, as a practical matter, the parties can also opt in favor of English law by not pleading foreign law, citing to Suisse Atlantique Societe d'Armament Maritime S.A. v. N.V. Rotterdamsch Kolen Centrale, [1967] 1 A.C. 361. The latter would also be true in American law. Whether Lord Wright's dictum would also apply in reverse, that is, require no connection of the transaction with the chosen law if the latter is that of a foreign country, is by no means clear. See Dicey & Morris, supra, at 1206, citing to two Australian decisions requiring a connection at n.19. Furthermore, Section 5(1) of the Supply of Goods Act of 1893 (replaced by the Sale of Goods Act 1979) when

these would otherwise be applicable. See Graveson, Conflicts of Laws 401, 443–44 (7th ed. 1974). In civil law countries, courts must ordinarily determine the applicable law *ex officio*. Local law applies only subsidiarily when the content of the otherwise applicable foreign law cannot be determined. See, e.g., § 4(2) of the Austrian Federal Statute on Private International Law, BGB1, 1978, No. 304. In France, the parties are free to stipulate the applicable law, and the New Code of Civil Procedure also extends this freedom to international arbitration agreements: Delaume, International Arbitration under French Law, 37 Arbitration J. 38, 41 (1982). The Inter–American Convention on the Law Applicable to International Contracts, 33 I.L.M. 732 (1994), provides for party autonomy subject to a public policy exception. For party autonomy in international agency see Marschall von Bieberstein, Limitation of Party Autonomy in Private International Law by Rules of Jus Cogens in Laws Protecting Agents and Distributors, Proc. Columbia Law School Symposium on International Contracts 93 (1981). The Law Concerning Commercial Contracts in Foreign Trade of the People's Republic of China (effective July 1, 1985) permits the contractual choice of law (Art. 5) and provides that in the absence of such a choice the law with the closest connection to the transaction shall be applied. There are no express limitations on the freedom to select the applicable law, but Art. 4 appears to make an exception in favor of local (Chinese) mandatory rules and notions of public and socioeconomic policy. For brief comment see Hug, 1985 IPRax 242.

5. See Austrian Federal Statute on Private International Law of 1978, § 35, BGB1, 1978, No. 304; German Introductory Law to the Civil Code (EGBGB) as Amended in 1986, Art. 27; Peruvian Civ. Code, Art. 2095 (1985); Quebec Civ. Code, Art. 3111; Russian Civ. Code, Art. 1210, federal law n. 146 of 26 November 2001, Rossyiskaya Gazeta, n. 49 item 4553, 28/11/2001; Swiss Federal Statute on Private International Law, Art. 116, Bundesblatt 1988, I, 5;, Art. 7; Tunisian Code of Private International Law (Law N. 98–97 of 27 November 1998), Art. 62, Official Journal of the Republic of Tunisia, 1 December p. 2332; Venezuelan Act of 6 August, 1998 on Private

conventions,[6] and the latest revision of the U.C.C.,[7] have eliminated or eased this requirement while policing party autonomy through other means. More importantly, the parties' choice of law may not override certain important policies of the forum or of the state whose law would otherwise be applicable,[8] and in some type of contracts, such as consumer or employment contracts, the parties' choice is subject to further specific restrictions.[9] Within these or similar limits, party autonomy is now recognized in virtually all western legal systems.[10] In the United States, this principle finds its formal expression in the all-important § 187 of the Second Restatement,[11] and § 1–105 of the Uniform Commercial Code,[12] both of which are discussed later.

International Law, Art. 29 (Official Gazette No. 36.511) effective February 6, 1999. For the Louisiana and Oregon codifications, see La.Civ.Code Art. 3540 cmnt. (f); O.R.S. § 81.120. Section § 5–1401 of New York's General Obligations Law contains a unilateral rule that, with regard to certain contracts, invites the choice of New York law, "whether or not such contract ... bears a reasonable relation to [New York]."

6. See, e.g., Rome Convention, Art. 3; Inter–American Convention (1994), Art. 7; Hague Convention on the Law Applicable to the International Sales of Goods (1985).

7. Article 1–105 of the Uniform Commercial Code requires a "reasonable relation" with the state whose law the parties have chosen. However, the latest revision of this Article retains this requirement only for consumer contracts. See U.C.C. § 1–301(e)(1) (2001 Revision). For other contracts, the revision specifically provides that choice-of-law agreements are "effective, whether or not the transaction bears a relation to the State or country designated" in the agreement. U.C.C. § 1–301(c). (2001 Revision). The only geographical limitation is that in contracts that do not have a relation with a foreign jurisdiction ("domestic transaction"), the parties may only choose the law of a state of the United States. See id.

8. See Restatement (Second) Conflict of Laws § 187(2)(b) (1971) (discussed infra § 18.10).

9. Many recent codifications either prohibit choice-of-law clauses in consumer or employment contracts (e.g. Swiss statute Art. 120(2)), or provide that such clauses may not deprive the consumer or employee of the protection provided by the mandatory rules of a state (usually the consumer's or employee's home state) that has certain enumerated connections. See Rome Convention, Arts 5–6; Austrian statute, §§ 41, 44; German law, Arts. 29–30; Swiss statute Art. 121(3) (limiting the choices in employment contracts); Puerto Rico Draft Code, Arts. 41–43 (consumer, employment and insurance contracts; discussed in Symeonides,

Codifying Choice of Law for Contracts: The Puerto Rico Projet, in Law and Justice in a Multistate World: Essays in Honor of Arthur T. von Mehren, 419, 433–34 (J. Nafziger, & S. Symeonides, eds., 2002); Oregon codification, O.R.S. § 81.105(2) (prohibiting choice-of-law clauses in certain Oregon consumer contacts). The 2001 revision of the U.C.C. contains similar limitations with regard to consumer contracts. See U.C.C. § 1–301(e) (2001 Revision). For other American statutes prohibiting or restricting party autonomy in certain contracts, see Symeonides, American Choice of Law at the Dawn of the 21st Century, 37 Willamette L. Rev. 1, 29–32 (2000).

10. See Weintraub, Functional Developments in Choice of Law for Contracts, 187 Recueil des Cours 239, 271 (1984) (observing that party autonomy is "perhaps the most widely accepted private international rule of our time.").

11. This section is discussed infra § 18.8 et seq. For cases adopting this section, see, e.g., Valley Juice Ltd., Inc. v. Evian Waters of France, Inc., 87 F.3d 604 (2d Cir. 1996); Nursing Home Consultants v. Quantum Health Services, Inc., 926 F.Supp. 835 (E.D.Ark.1996), aff'd 112 F.3d 513 (8th Cir.1997); Reynolds Publishers, Inc. v. Graphics Financial Group, Ltd., 938 F.Supp. 256 (D.N.J.1996); Allen v. Lloyd's of London, 94 F.3d 923 (4th Cir.1996), on remand 975 F.Supp. 802 (D.Va.1997); Bi–Rite Enterprises, Inc. v. Bruce Miner Co., 757 F.2d 440 (1st Cir.1985); Hughes Associates, Inc. v. Printed Circuit Corp., 631 F.Supp. 851 (N.D.Ala.1986); Satellite Financial Planning Corp. v. First Nat. Bank of Wilmington, 633 F.Supp. 386 (D.Del. 1986); Emhart Indus., Inc. v. Duracell Intern. Inc., 665 F.Supp. 549 (M.D.Tenn. 1987); Barry Gilberg, Ltd. v. Craftex Corp., Inc., 665 F.Supp. 585 (N.D.Ill.1987). Moreover, cases often assume that the Restatement provision does not represent a departure from prior law by citing pre-Restatement case law along with § 187. See Southern Int'l Sales Co., Inc. v. Potter &

---

12. See p. 955.

A preliminary question, and a difficult one, is which law will determine the existence and validity of the choice-of-law agreement with regard to issues such as capacity, form, formation, and defects such as error or duress. The three options are the *lex fori*, the chosen law, and the law that would normally govern the contract in the absence of a choice-of-law agreement (*lex causae*).[13] The Second Restatement employs the first two options: it assigns to the *lex fori* issues of misrepresentation, duress, undue influence, or mistake,[14] and to the chosen law all other issues of formation and validity, including capacity and form.[15] Both options offer the advantage of practicality and judicial economy. In addition, if pressed, one can defend the *lex fori* option by arguing that, to the extent that a choice-of-law agreement displaces some of the forum's choice-of-law rules, the forum should be free to determine under its own substantive standards whether such an agreement exists before allowing

12. See p. 955.Brumfield Division of AMF Incorporated and AMF Inc., 410 F.Supp. 1339, 1341–42 (S.D.N.Y.1976). Some courts, however, still refuse to follow § 187 and hold to the view that agreements as to the applicable law are suspect. See Convergys Corp. v. Keener, 276 Ga. 808, 582 S.E.2d 84 (2003).

12. Code comments, formally adopted by several states, often take the position that U.C.C. § 1–105 reflects prior law. See Cal. Comm. Code, § 1105; 6 Del. Code, § 1–105; Fla. Stat. Ann., § 671.1–105; Ill. 810 ILCS 5/1–105; Iowa Code Ann. ch. 35, § 554.1105; Mass. General Laws Ann. c. 106, § 1–105; Mich. Comp. Laws Ann. § 440.1105; Minn. Stat. Ann. § 336.1–105; N.J. Stat. Ann. 12A:1–105; N.Y. Uniform Com. Code (Consol. Laws) § 1–105; Code of South Carolina § 36–1–105; Code of Virginia, § 8.1–105; Wash. Code Ann. 62A.1–105.

The following states do not specify in comments that prior law is followed, but list in the judicial decisions section following the statute, cases that pre-date adoption of the UCC: Mississippi: Code 1972, § 75–1–105; Montana: Vernon's Ann.Mont.Stat. 400.1–105; Pennsylvania: 13 Pa. Cons.Stat. Ann. § 1105; Tennessee: Tenn.Code Ann. § 47–1–105; West Virginia: Code, § 46–1–105. The following states specify that courts will have to decide (UCC doesn't reflect prior law): Alabama: Code 1975, § 7–1–105; Kansas: Kans.Stat.Ann. § 84–1–105; Maine: 11 Maine Rev.Stat.Ann. § 1–105. The following specify that prior law is specifically overturned by the UCC's adoption: North Carolina: N.C. Gen.Stat. § 25–1–105; Oklahoma: 12A Okla.Stat.Ann. § 1–105. All other states officially adopt the UCC com-

ments, which refer to a few cases that pre-date the UCC.

13. See S. Symeonides, W. Perdue & A. von Mehren, Conflict of Laws: American, Comparative, International, 344 (2d ed. 2003).

14. See (Second), Conflict of Laws § 187, cmnt. b. ("[A] choice-of-law provision, like any other contractual provision, will not be given effect if the consent of one of the parties to its inclusion in the contract was obtained by improper means, such as ... duress, or undue influence, or by mistake. Whether such consent was in fact obtained by improper means ... will be determined by the forum in accordance with its own legal principles.") For a case relying on this comment, see Dunes Hospitality L.L.C. v. Country Kitchen Int'l, Inc., 623 N.W.2d 484 (S.D. 2001). However, in this case, the *lex fori* was also the *lex causae*.

15. See id. § 198 cmt. a (capacity "determined by the law chosen by the parties, *if they have made an effective choice.*"; § 199 cmt. a (same as to form), § 200 cmt. a (same for validity for issues other than capacity and form). See also Swiss codification art. 116(2), which provides that "the choice of law is governed by the chosen law." The Restatement follows the third option to the extent it assigns to the *lex causae* the question of whether the subject of the choice-of-law agreement is—or is not—one that the parties "could have resolved by an explicit provision in their agreement." See id. § 187, cmt. c. The answer to this question determines whether the enforceability of the choice-of-law agreement will be determine under § 187(1), which imposes no limitations, or rather § 187(2), which imposes public policy limitations.

such a displacement.[16] On the other hand, the option of applying the chosen law may entail some serious "bootstrapping" that can be avoided only by employing the policing mechanism of § 187(2)(b).[17] The third option—applying the law that would govern the contract in the absence of a choice-of-law agreement (*lex causae*)—avoids the bootstrapping problem, but also undercuts much of the convenience that efficiency that make choice-of-law clauses attractive to courts and litigants. The Rome Convention and most recent codifications follow this option.[18]

B. LIMITATIONS ON PARTY AUTONOMY

1. *Questions of Interpretation and Construction*

§ 18.3 When the parties choose a law solely for the purpose of construing or interpreting the items of their contract, their choice is not restricted.[1] The reason is that the choice-of-law clause is merely a shorthand expression for a more detailed definition of the rights and obligations of the parties.[2] An example is *Hellenic Lines, Ltd. v. Embassy of Pakistan*[3] in which the contract for the shipment of goods from Pakistan to the United States on a Greek vessel had selected English law to govern the interpretation and construction of the agreement. In a suit for delay in delivery, the U.S. court applied English law to the issue of the consignee's contractual duty to "discharge continuously" although this led to a result contrary to American law. Despite the fact that England lacked any significant contact with the cases, the application of English law was proper because the parties, rather than stipulate En-

---

16. See e.g. Siegelman v. Cunard White Star Ltd., 221 F.2d 189 (2d Cir.1955); Ehrenzweig, Adhesion Contracts in the Conflict of Laws, 53 Colum. L. Rev. 1072 (1953).

17. Section 187(2)(b) of the Second Restatement, discussed infra § 18.10, provides that the choice-of-law agreement will be disregarded if "application of the law of the chosen state would be contrary to a fundamental policy of a state which has a materially greater interest than the chosen state in the determination of the particular issue and which, under the rule of section 188, would be the state of the applicable law in the absence of an effective choice of law by the parties."

18. See, e.g., Rome Convention, Art. 3(4)); EGBGB, Art. 27(4); Louisiana Codification, Arts. 3537–3540); Oregon codification, §§ 81.110–81.115); Puerto Rico Draft Code, Arts. 34–35. In general, European doctrine assumes the existence of *two* contracts—the choice-of-law contract and the principal contract. As a result, the need for compliance with requirements as to form or other issues affecting validity may need to be reviewed separately.

§ 18.3

1. See Restatement, Second, Conflict of Laws § 187(1) (1971); Trilogy Development Group, Inc. v. Teknowledge Corp., 1996 WL 527325 (Del.Super.1996); Fort Howard Cup Corp. v. Quality Kitchen Corp., 1992 WL 207276 (Del.Super.); Falcon Tankers, Inc. v. Litton Systems, Inc., 300 A.2d 231 (Del.Super.1972); Hellenic Lines, Ltd. v. Embassy of Pakistan, 307 F.Supp. 947 (S.D.N.Y. 1969), aff'd in part, reversed in part 467 F.2d 1150 (2d Cir.1972); People v. Globe & Rutgers Fire Ins. Co., 96 Cal.App.2d 571, 216 P.2d 64 (1950); Duskin v. Pennsylvania–Central Airlines Corp., 167 F.2d 727 (6th Cir.1948), cert. denied 335 U.S. 829, 69 S.Ct. 56, 93 L.Ed. 382 (1948); Boole v. Union Marine Ins. Co. Ltd., 52 Cal.App. 207, 198 P. 416 (1921); International Paper Co. v. Midvale–Heppenstall Co., 63 Pa.D. & C.2d 627 (1973). See generally Annot., 60 A.L.R.2d at 471.

2. Restatement, Second, Conflict of Laws § 187, cmnt. (c) (1971).

3. 307 F.Supp. 947 (S.D.N.Y.1969), aff'd in part, reversed in part 467 F.2d 1150 (2d Cir.1972).

glish law, could have incorporated a provision in the contract defining the consignee's duties in language adopting the English meaning of "discharge continuously."

2. *Validity and Public Policy*

a. *Public Policy Limitation in General*

§ 18.4 Although most legal systems recognize the principle of party autonomy, they also agree on the need for some limitations, be they geographical, substantive, or both.[1] The geographical limitations are discussed elsewhere.[2] This section discusses substantive limitations, primarily those that come under the rubric of *public policy*. Since each state's public policy limits party autonomy in fully domestic contracts, it would be incongruous to leave multistate contracts completely unregulated. However, the fact that the limitations to party autonomy vary from one state to another raises an important preliminary question: *which state's* limitations will be used as the standard for policing party autonomy in multistate contracts, namely, which state's law will perform the role of the *lex limitatis*? The second question, discussed later, is which precise threshold, or what gradation of public policy, should be used in policing party autonomy in multistate contracts.

(1) Which State's Public Policy?

Regarding the first question, the three candidates for the role of the *lex limitatis* are: the *lex fori*, the chosen law, and the law that would be applicable in the absence of choice of law by the parties (hereafter referred to as *lex causae*).[3] Of course, in rare cases, these three laws, or any two of them, may coincide in the same state. The following discussion focuses on cases in which they do not.

The option of policing party autonomy through the chosen law is circular and should be eliminated for this reason. This leaves two

§ 18.4

1. See DeSantis v. Wackenhut Corp., 793 S.W.2d 670, 677 (Tex.1990), cert. denied 498 U.S. 1048, 111 S.Ct. 755, 112 L.Ed.2d 775 (1991) ("[T]he parties' freedom to choose what jurisdiction's law will apply to their agreement cannot be unlimited."); Restatement, Second, Conflict of Laws § 187(2)(b) (1971); Martino v. Cottman Transmission Systems, Inc., 218 Mich.App. 54, 60, 554 N.W.2d 17, 21 (1996); Kubis & Perszyk Associates, Inc. v. Sun Microsystems, 146 N.J. 176, 680 A.2d 618 (1996); Param Petroleum Corp. v. Commerce & Industry Ins. Co., 296 N.J.Super. 164, 686 A.2d 377 (1997); Wright–Moore Corp. v. Ricoh Corp., 908 F.2d 128, 132 (7th Cir. 1990); Haisten v. Grass Valley Medical Reimbursement Fund, Ltd., 784 F.2d 1392 (9th Cir.1986); B. M. Heede, Inc. v. West India Machinery & Supply Co., 272 F.Supp.

236, 241 (S.D.N.Y.1967); May v. Mulligan, 36 F.Supp. 596, 599 (W.D.Mich.1939), aff'd 117 F.2d 259 (6th Cir.1940), cert. denied 312 U.S. 691, 61 S.Ct. 622, 85 L.Ed. 1127 (1941); Turner v. Aldens, Inc., 179 N.J.Super. 596, 433 A.2d 439, 442, 443 (App.Div. 1981);. See also Carpinello, Testing the Limits of Choice of Law Clauses: Franchise Contracts as a Case Study, 74 Marq. L. Rev. 57 (1990); Hill, The Judicial Function in Choice of Law, 85 Colum. L. Rev., 1585, 1627 (1985).

2. See supra § 18.2 nn. 4–7; infra §§ 18.6, 18.9

3. For a discussion of these and additional options, see S. Symeonides, W. Perdue & A. von Mehren, Conflict of Laws: American, Comparative, International 345–46 (2d ed. 2003).

options: (1) the *lex fori*; and (2) the *lex causae*. The *lex fori* is relevant because party autonomy operates only to the extent the *lex fori* permits. The *lex causae* is relevant because, when party autonomy operates, it displaces the *lex causae*. If the application of the chosen law exceeds the public policy limits of *both* the *lex fori* and the *lex causae* (or if the two laws coincide in the same state), then the chosen law will not be applied. The difficulty arises when the two laws do not coincide in the same state and the chosen law violates the public policy limits of: (a) the *lex fori* but not the *lex causae*; or (b) the *lex causae* but not the *lex fori*.

The prevailing and better view is that the choice-of-law clause should be upheld in the first case and not upheld in the second case.[4] This means that the *lex limitatis* is the *lex causae* rather than the law of the forum *qua* forum. The majority of modern systems, including the Second Restatement[5] and the latest revision of the UCC,[6] adopt this view. In contrast to recent cases,[7] some of the older cases carelessly

4. The Puerto Rican Draft Code (Art. 35) takes the unique position that the chosen law is not to be applied if it violates restrictions on party autonomy imposed by *both* the *lex fori* and the *lex causae*. For the rationale of this provision, see Symeonides, Codifying Choice of Law for Contracts: The Puerto Rico Projet, in Law and Justice in a Multistate World: Essays in Honor of Arthur T. von Mehren, 419, 422–24 (J. Nafziger, & S. Symeonides, eds. 2002) ("even when the parties' choice exceeds the restrictions imposed by the *lex causae*, the choice should not be disregarded unless it be for reasons that the *lex fori* itself regards as serious enough for disregarding party autonomy in analogous fully domestic cases." Id. at 424).

5. See Restatement, Second, Conflict of Laws § 187(2)(b) (1971) (discussed infra this section and § 18.10; the application of the chosen law may not contravene the fundamental policy of the state whose law would be applicable under § 188 in the absence of an effective choice of law by the parties). However, § 187(2)(b) imposes an additional requirement–that the above state be one that "has a materially greater interest than the chosen state in the determination of the particular issue."

6. See U.C.C. § 1–301(f) (law that would govern "in the absence of [choice-of-law] agreement") (discussed infra).

7. See, e.g., DeSantis v. Wackenhut Corp., 793 S.W.2d 670, 677 (Tex.1990), cert. denied 498 U.S. 1048, 111 S.Ct. 755, 112 L.Ed.2d 775 (1991) (chosen law may not "thwart or offend the public policy of the state the law of which ought otherwise to apply."); Nedlloyd Lines B.V. v. Superior Court, 3 Cal.4th 459, 11 Cal.Rptr.2d 330, 834 P.2d 1148, 1152 n. 6. (1992) ("[In] a

case in which California is the forum, and the parties have chosen the law of another state, but the law of yet a third state, rather than California's, would apply absent the parties' choice … a California court will look to the fundamental policy of *the third state* in determining whether to enforce the parties' choice of law." (Emphasis added); Long v. Holland American Line Westours, Inc., 26 P.3d 430 (Alaska 2001) (invalidating Washington choice-of-law clause because that state's allowance of a clause shortening the limitation period would violate the fundamental policy of Alaska, the law of which would be applicable in the absence of a contrary choice-of-law clause). See also Ticknor v. Choice Hotels Int'l, Inc., 265 F.3d 931 (9th Cir. 2001)(invalidating choice-of-law clause under fundamental policy of *lex causae*, which was also the *lex fori*); J.S. Alberici Construction Co., Inc. v. Mid–West Conveyor Co., Inc., 750 A.2d 518 (Del.2000) (same); Roberts v. Energy Devt. Corp., 235 F.3d 935 (5th Cir. 2000); Application Group, Inc. v. Hunter Group, Inc.,61 Cal.App.4th 881, 72 Cal.Rptr.2d 73 (1998); Param Petroleum Corp. v. Commerce & Industry Ins. Co., 296 N.J.Super. 164, 686 A.2d 377 (1997); Blalock v. Perfect Subscription Co., 458 F.Supp. 123 (S.D.Ala.1978), aff'd 599 F.2d 743 (5th Cir.1979); Business Incentives Co., Inc. v. Sony Corp. of America, 397 F.Supp. 63 (S.D.N.Y.1975); Boyer v. Piper, Jaffray & Hopwood, Inc., 391 F.Supp. 471 (D.S.D. 1975); McQuillan v. "Italia" Societa Per Aziono Di Navigazione, 386 F.Supp. 462 (S.D.N.Y.1974), aff'd 516 F.2d 896 (2d Cir. 1975); MGM Grand Hotel, Inc. v. Imperial Glass Co., 65 F.R.D. 624 (D.Nev.1974) rev'd on other grounds 533 F.2d 486 (9th Cir. 1976), cert. denied 429 U.S. 887, 97 S.Ct.

examine whether the chosen law contravenes the public policy of the *lex fori* without explaining whether the *lex fori* also would have been the *lex causae*.[8]

To be sure, under the traditional *ordre public* exception, the public policy of the forum *qua* forum is always the last shield against the application of a repugnant foreign law, whether that law is chosen by the parties or through the forum's choice-of-law rules. Theoretically, this shield remains available to courts following the modern approaches, but according to Cardozo's classic test, it should only be employed in exceptional cases in which the applicable foreign law is "shocking" to the forum's sense of justice and fairness.[9] The Second Restatement recognizes this difference, at least as one of degree, between the roles of the traditional *ordre public* exception one the one hand, and the public policy exception in limiting party autonomy, on the other.[10]

239, 50 L.Ed.2d 168 (1976); O'Brien v. Shearson Hayden Stone, Inc., 90 Wn.2d 680, 586 P.2d 830 (1978), opinion supplemented 93 Wn.2d 51, 605 P.2d 779 (1980); Nasco, Inc. v. Gimbert, 239 Ga. 675, 238 S.E.2d 368 (1977); Gamer v. duPont Glore Forgan, Inc., 65 Cal.App.3d 280, 135 Cal. Rptr. 230 (1976); Reger v. National Ass'n of Bedding Manufacturers Group Ins. Trust Fund, 83 Misc.2d 527, 372 N.Y.S.2d 97 (1975); Lauritzen v. Larsen, 345 U.S. 571, 588–89, 73 S.Ct. 921, 931–32, 97 L.Ed. 1254 (1953) (Danish law applied according to the stipulation in a contract, entered into in New York between Danish employer and Danish seaman injured in Cuba and seeking to recovery under the Jones Act); Connecticut General Life Ins. Co. v. Boseman, 84 F.2d 701, 705 (5th Cir.1936), aff'd 301 U.S. 196, 57 S.Ct. 686, 81 L.Ed. 1036 (1937); Citizens National Bank v. Waugh, 78 F.2d 325, 327 (4th Cir.1935); Oceanic Steam Navigation Co. v. Corcoran, 9 F.2d 724, 733 (2d Cir.1925) (Hough, J., dissenting); Fricke v. Isbrandtsen Co., Inc., 151 F.Supp. 465, 468 (S.D.N.Y.1957). See The Miguel di Larrinaga, 217 Fed. 678 (S.D.N.Y.1914); Coats v. Chicago, Rock Island & Pacific Railway Co., 239 Ill. 154, 87 N.E. 929 (1909).

8. See Oceanic Steam Navigation Co. v. Corcoran, 9 F.2d 724, 733 (2d Cir.1925) (Hough, J., dissenting); F.A. Straus & Co., Inc. v. Canadian Pacific Railway Co., 254 N.Y. 407, 173 N.E. 564 (1930); Delta Bag Co. v. Frederick Leyland & Co., 173 Ill.App. 38 (1912). See May v. Mulligan, 36 F.Supp. 596 (W.D.Mich.1939), aff'd 117 F.2d 259 (6th Cir.1940), cert. denied 312 U.S. 691, 61 S.Ct. 622, 85 L.Ed. 1127 (1941); Compania De Inversiones Internacionales v. Industrial Mortgage Bank of Finland, 269 N.Y. 22, 198 N.E. 617 (1935), opinion amended 269 N.Y. 602, 199 N.E. 691 (1935); B.M. Heede Inc. v. West India Machinery and Supply Co.,

272 F.Supp. 236, 241 (S.D.N.Y.1967). The decision in Wyatt v. Fulrath, 16 N.Y.2d 169, 264 N.Y.S.2d 233, 211 N.E.2d 637 (1965) (discussed supra § 14.22) is an example. A Spanish couple had contracted with a New York bank to deposit money. The parties, who had never visited New York, stipulated for the application of the New York law of survivorship. The court upheld the choice upon the husband's death and disregarded the strong Spanish policy that would have limited the widow to one half the community property. The dissent argued that because New York lacked any interest in the transaction the court should defer to the policy of the only interested jurisdiction, Spain. 16 N.Y.2d at 176, 264 N.Y.S.2d at 238, 211 N.E.2d at 641 (Desmond, C.J., dissenting). However, New York—as an important international financial center—has an interest in providing a stable and predictable environment for transactions of foreigners. Thus, the real question should have been not whether the parties can rearrange the property relations between themselves but whether they can thereby affect the rights of third parties, for instance, and cut off the *legitime* of children under Spanish law.

9. See Loucks v. Standard Oil Co. of New York, 224 N.Y. 99, 120 N.E. 198, 201–02 (1918) (the foreign law must "offend our sense of justice or menaces the public welfare," or "violate some fundamental principle of justice, some prevalent conception of good morals, some deep-rooted tradition of the common weal," or "shock our sense of justice").

10. See Restatement, Second, Conflict of Laws § 187 cmnt. (g) (Noting that "[t]o be 'fundamental' within the meaning of [§ 187], a policy need not be as strong as

The Rome Convention employs a complex, multilayer system of policing party autonomy in favor of: (1) the law of the forum *qua* forum, (2) the *lex causae*, and (3) a state that may or may not be the state of the *lex causae*. With regard to (1), Article 16 of the Convention restates the traditional *ordre public* exception, which comes into play only when the application of the foreign law is "manifestly incompatible" with the forum's public policy,[11] while Article 7(2) reiterates that nothing in the Convention "shall restrict the application of the rules of the law of the forum in a situation where they are mandatory irrespective of the law otherwise applicable to the contract."[12] With regard to (2), Articles 5 and 6 of the Convention provide that a choice-of-law agreement may not deprive a consumer or an employee of the protection provided by the "mandatory rules" of the countries whose law would otherwise govern the consumer or employment contract, respectively. Finally, with regard to all other contracts, Article 3(3) of the Convention provides that, when "all the other elements relevant to the situation at the time of the choice are connected with one country only,"[13] a choice-of-law agreement may not prejudice the application of the "mandatory rules"[14] of that country. While a country that has "all" these elements most likely will be the state of the *lex causae*, the reverse is not true. Thus, a country that has significant connections may qualify as the state of the *lex causae* under the Convention but, unless that country has "all" the connections, its law may not be invoked to invalidate the parties' choice of another law. The gap can be filled by resort to Article 7(1) which allows the court to "give effect" to the "mandatory rules" of another country with which the situation has a "close connection."[15]

(2) Which Level of Public Policy?

After identifying the state whose law defines the limits of party autonomy (*lex limitatis*), the next question is to establish the threshold that the parties' choice of another law must exceed before being held unenforceable. If any difference between the *lex limitatis/causae* and the chosen law would defeat the parties's choice, then party autonomy would become a specious gift. As one court said, "[t]he result would be that

would be required to justify the forum in refusing to entertain suit upon a foreign cause of action under the rule of § 90," which enunciates the traditional ordre public test.). Unfortunately, the latest revision of the U.C.C. conflates the two concepts by stating that Cardozo's definition of public policy provides "a helpful touchstone" in determining whether the policy is "fundamental" under revised § 1–301. See § 1–301 cmnt. 6 (2001 Revision).

11. Rome Convention Art. 16 (the otherwise applicable law "may by refused only if [its] application is manifestly incompatible with the public policy ('ordre public') of the forum.")

12. Rome Convention Art. 7(2).

13. Rome Convention, Art. 3(3). See also the identical provision in Art. 27(3) of the German codification and a similar provision in Art. 1210(5) of the Russian Civil Code.

14. The concept of mandatory rules is discussed infra at nn. 25–35.

15. Rome Convention Article 7(1). However, this provision is not in effect in all countries that are parties to the Convention, such as Germany and the United Kingdom. The country contemplated by Art. 7(1) may be either the country of the *lex causae* or a third country.

parties would have the right to choose the application of another state's law only when that state's law is identical to [the *lex causae*]. Such an approach would be ridiculous."[16] Thus, there is a general consensus on the need for a higher public-policy threshold for multistate contracts than for fully domestic contracts. Predictably, however, the various systems differ in defining this threshold.

For example, the Second Restatement seems to set one of the highest thresholds when it provides in § 187(2)(b) that, before invalidating a choice-of-law clause, the court must be satisfied that: (a) the chosen law is contrary to a "fundamental policy" of the state of the *lex causae*; and (b) that that state has a "materially greater interest than the chosen state in the determination of the particular issue."[17] The 2001 Revision of the U.C.C. eliminates the second hurdle—it invalidates the choice only if it violates a "fundamental" policy of a state "whose law would govern in the absence of agreement."[18] Other codifications take the same position.[19] In contrast, the Rome Convention seems to pose a low threshold when it provides that the chosen law may not "prejudice the application of rules ... which cannot be derogated from by contract" ("mandatory rules").[20] However, as noted above, it is only "where all the other elements relevant to the situation ... are connected with one country only"[21] that the mandatory rules of that country may invalidate the parties' choice. Thus, ultimately the Rome Convention may be more liberal than the Restatement toward party autonomy. On the other hand, unlike the Restatement, the Convention exempts issues of contractual capacity and form from the scope of party autonomy and, through special provisions, protects consumers and employees from the consequences of an adverse choice of law.[22] Similarly, the Swiss codification, which appears to be the most deferential to party autonomy,[23] specifically prohibits choice-of-law clauses in consumer contracts and severely restricts them in employment contracts.[24]

(3) Public Policy and "Mandatory Rules"

As the above discussion indicates, European conflicts law (as well as the Inter–American Convention) distinguishes between *mandatory* rules of law and potentially applicable rules of law that violate *public policy*. Because, as noted below, the proposed revision of the U.C.C. also employs the concept of mandatory rules, it might be useful to briefly

16. Cherokee Pump & Equipment, Inc. v. Aurora Pump, 38 F.3d 246, 252 (5th Cir.1994).

17. Restatement, Second, Conflict of Laws § 187(2)(b) (1971).

18. UCC § 1–301(f).

19. See, e.g., La.Stat. Ann., Art. 3540, Or.Rev.Stat. § 81.125.

20. Rome Convention, Art. 3(3). As noted earlier, article 16 of the Convention contains the classic *ordre public* reservation in favor of *forum* law as such by providing that the application of foreign law may be refused only if it is "manifestly incompatible" with the public policy of the forum.

21. Rome Convention, Art. 3(3).

22. See Rome Convention, Arts. 5–6.

23. See Swiss statute, Arts. 116, 15.

24. See id., Arts. 120–21. For similar protections for consumers, see UCC § 1–301(e) (2001 Revision); Or.Rev. Code, § 81.115; Puerto Rico Draft Code, Art. 41.

describe the European version. The Rome Convention provides two definitions of mandatory rules: (a) rules that "cannot be derogated from by contract;"[25] and (b) rules that "must be applied whatever the law applicable to the contract."[26] The first are mandatory rules of *contract* law, and they may not be evaded by the contractual choice of another law.[27] The latter are mandatory in the *conflicts* sense, and they may be evaded by neither a contractual choice of law nor a judicial choice of law.[28]

Despite these and other differences, both types of mandatory rules embody public policy concerns and thus resemble other rules of public policy. However, there are two important differences. The first difference is one of degree and applies only to the first type of mandatory rules described above. A rule from which the parties cannot derogate by contrary agreement may or *may not* reflect the high threshold of public policy that triggers the application of either the *ordre public* exception under Article 16, or the similar mechanism of Article 7(2) of the Convention.[29] The second difference applies to both types of mandatory rules described above and pertains to the mode and time they operate as contrasted with the traditional *ordre public* exception. A *mandatory* rule of law operates assertively and preempts the choice-of-law process altogether. There is no question about what law governs: the mandatory rule does. An example may be the consumer protection rule imposing interest ceilings in installment contracts. In contrast, the *ordre public* exception operates defensively and comes into play after the operation of the choice-of-law process–in the present context through the parties' choice-of-law stipulation. If the process leads to a rule of law that offends the forum's public policy, the rule is held inapplicable.

Until recently, the concept of mandatory rules was not widely known in American case law. However, the 2001 revision of U.C.C. § 1–105 employs the concept of mandatory rules, albeit without using the specific term in the text, but with full acknowledgment of its origin in the Rome Convention.[30] The proposed new version of U.C.C. § 1–105, now § 1–301, provides that, in a consumer contract, the law chosen by

---

25. Rome Convention, Art. 3(3).

26. Id. Art. 7(1)(2). The Court of Justice of the European Communities has defined these rules as those "provisions compliance with which has been deemed to be so crucial for the protection of the political, social or economic order in the Member State concerned as to require compliance therewith by all persons present on the national territory of that Member State and all legal relationships within that State." Cases C–369/96, C–374/6 (rendered 23.11.1999) (*Arblade* case).

27. See id. Arts. 3(3) (general party autonomy article); 5(2) (consumer contracts); 6(1) (employment contracts).

28. Id., Arts. 7, 9(6).

29. A decision of the Paris Court of Appeals provides an example. See Cour d' Appel, Paris, Decision 22.3.1990, D. 1990, Somm. p. 176. The court noted that a French rule that prohibits an employee from waiving his or her rights to lay-off pay, or from agreeing to a shorter notice of termination, reflected a strong *internal* French public policy. The court concluded, however, that this rule did not qualify as a mandatory rule for purposes of Article 7(2) (or, a fortiori, a rule of *ordre public* under Article 16). Hence, an employee who had validly agreed to the application of non-French law could not automatically avail himself of the protection of this rule.

30. U.C.C. § 1–301, cmnt. 6 (2001 Revision).

the parties "may not deprive the consumer of the protection of any rule of law ... which both is protective of consumers and may not be varied by agreement"[31] of the consumer's home state or a state in which the consumer made the contract and took delivery of the goods.[32] For contracts not involving a consumer, the U.C.C. provides that a choice-of-law agreement will be disregarded if it violates a "fundamental"[33] policy of a state whose law would govern in the absence of the agreement. The accompanying Comments seem to conflate the two concepts by considering the operation of the mandatory rules an example of the fundamental policy exception.[34] However, the same comments separate the two concepts by stating that a rule may qualify as "mandatory" if "it must be applied ... without regard to otherwise-applicable choice of law rules ... and without regard to whether the designated law is otherwise offensive."[35] Moreover, the text of the revised section keeps the two concepts separate because the "mandatory rules" exception is contained only in the provision that applies to consumer contracts[36] and the "fundamental policy" exception is contained only in the provision that is applicable to other contracts,[37] without a cross-reference between the two provisions.

(4) "Fundamental Policy"

To state that only a "fundamental" policy may defeat party autonomy is easier to accept but difficult to define. The Second Restatement avoids such a definition,[38] but it does provide a few examples of rules that embody such a policy (statutes that make certain contracts illegal, and statutes intended to protect one party from "the oppressive use of

---

31. Id., § 1–301(e)(2).

32. The accompanying Comments explain that "[not all] rules that cannot be changed by agreement ... are, for that reason alone, mandatory rules. Otherwise, contractual choice of law ... would be illusory and redundant; the parties would be able to accomplish by choice of law no more than can be accomplished under Section 1–302, which allows variation of otherwise applicable rules by agreement." U.C.C. § 1–301, cmnt. 6 (2001 Revision).

33. Id., § 1–301(f).

34. See id. § 1–301, cmnt. 6 ("Application of the designated law may be contrary to a fundamental policy of the State or country whose law would otherwise govern *either* (I) because the substance of the designated law violates a fundamental principle of justice of that State or country or (ii) because it differs from a rule of that State or country that is 'mandatory' in that it must be applied in the courts of that State or country without regard to otherwise-applicable choice of law rules of that State or country and without regard to whether the

designated law is otherwise offensive." (emphasis added).

35. Id.

36. Id. § 1–301(e).

37. Id.§ 1–301(g).

38. The 2001 Oregon codification provides that a policy is fundamental "only if the policy reflects objectives or gives effect to essential public or societal institutions beyond the allocation of rights and obligations of parties to a contract at issue." O.R.S. § 81.125(2). The codification also provides that the chosen law does not apply "to the extent that its application would: (a) Require a party to perform an act prohibited by the law of the state where the act is to be performed under the contract; [or] (b) Prohibit a party from performing an act required by the law of the state where it is to be performed under the contract[.]" § 81.125(1). For the background and rationale of these provisions, see Symeonides, Codifying Choice of Law for Contracts: The Oregon Experience, 67 RabelsZ, 726, 739–42 (2003).

superior bargaining power,"[39] such as statutes protecting insureds against insurers), as well as examples of rule that do not embody such a policy (statutes of frauds, rules "tending to become obsolete," and "general rules of contract law, such as those concerned with the need for consideration).[40] As noted earlier, the Restatement also states that, to be fundamental in the sense of § 187(2)(b), a policy need not be as strong as the policy that justifies a refusal to apply foreign law under the traditional *ordre public* exception.[41]

Many cases reiterate the point that the forum will not disregard the choice-of-law clause simply because the chosen law differs in some respects from the *lex causae* or the *lex fori*,[42] but will do so only when the difference rises to a high level of public policy. Many cases, especially older ones, stop with a finding that the clause violates public policy and do not undertake to evaluate the strength of that policy.[43] More recent cases undertake to determine which public policies are "strong"[44] or, in the Restatement's words, "fundamental"[45] enough to justify overriding

---

39. Restatement Second, § 187 cmnt. g.

40. Id.

41. Id.

42. See, e.g., B.M. Heede, Inc. v. West India Machinery and Supply Co., 272 F.Supp. 236 (S.D.N.Y.1967); Naylor v. Conroy, 46 N.J.Super. 387, 134 A.2d 785 (App. Div.1957); A. S. Rampell, Inc. v. Hyster Co., 3 N.Y.2d 369, 165 N.Y.S.2d 475, 144 N.E.2d 371 (1957); Mittenthal v. Mascagni, 183 Mass. 19, 66 N.E. 425, 426 (1903); Swann v. Swann, 21 Fed. 299 (C.C.E.D.Ark.1884). See also Reese, Power of Parties to Choose Law Governing Their Contract, 1960 Proc. Am. Soc. Int'l Law 49, 54; Restatement, Second, Conflict of Laws § 187, cmnt. (g) (1971).

Differences between forum law and the chosen law and public policy concerns may only become apparent at the time of suit when the party invokes doctrines of forum law that are unknown or dissimilar to those of the chosen law. In a decision, in which several separate opinions undertake extensive analysis of the party autonomy problem, the California Supreme Court held a choice-of-law clause in favor of the law of Hong Kong to be valid and applicable to claims for breach of implied covenants of good faith and fair dealing and for violation of fiduciary duties. Nedlloyd Lines B.V. v. Superior Court, 3 Cal.4th 459, 11 Cal. Rptr.2d 330, 834 P.2d 1148 (1992).

43. E.g., Govett American Endeavor Fund Ltd. v. Trueger, 112 F.3d 1017 (9th Cir.1997); The Kensington, 183 U.S. 263, 269, 22 S.Ct. 102, 104, 46 L.Ed. 190 (1902); Johnston v. Commercial Travelers Mut. Accident Ass'n, 242 S.C. 387, 131 S.E.2d 91,

95 (1963); Dunlop Tire & Rubber Corp. v. Ryan, 171 Neb. 820, 108 N.W.2d 84, 88 (1961); Carl Hagenback and Great Wallace Show Co. v. Randall, 75 Ind.App. 417, 126 N.E. 501, 502–503 (1920); Mutual Life Ins. Co. v. Mullen, 107 Md. 457, 69 A. 385, 387 (1908); Keatley v. Travelers' Ins. Co., 187 Pa. 197, 40 A. 808 (1898). See also May v. Mulligan, 36 F.Supp. 596 (W.D.Mich.1939), aff'd 117 F.2d 259 (6th Cir.1940), cert. denied 312 U.S. 691, 61 S.Ct. 622, 85 L.Ed. 1127 (1941); Davis v. Jointless Fire Brick Co., 300 Fed. 1, 4 (9th Cir.1924).

44. Superfos Investments Ltd. v. First-Miss Fertilizer, 809 F.Supp. 450 (1992); Martino v. Cottman Transmission Systems, Inc., 218 Mich.App. 54, 60, 554 N.W.2d 17, 21 (1996); Kubis & Perszyk Associates, Inc. v. Sun Microsystems, 146 N.J. 176, 680 A.2d 618 (1996); Param Petroleum Corp. v. Commerce and Industry Ins. Co., 296 N.J.Super. 164, 686 A.2d 377 (1997); Ward v. Nationwide Mut. Automobile Ins. Co., 328 Md. 240, 247, 614 A.2d 85, 88 (Md. 1992); Kramer v. Bally's Park Place, Inc. 311 Md. 387, 390, 535 A.2d 466, 467 (Md. 1988); Lazard Freres & Co. v. Protective Life Ins. Co., 108 F.3d 1531, 1538 (2d Cir. 1997), cert. denied 522 U.S. 864, 118 S.Ct. 169, 139 L.Ed.2d 112 (1997); National Sur. Corp. v. Inland Properties, Inc., 286 F.Supp. 173, 188 (E.D.Ark.1968), aff'd 416 F.2d 457 (8th Cir.1969); Ury v. Jewelers Acceptance Corp., 227 Cal.App.2d 11, 38 Cal.Rptr. 376, 382 (1964); Bethlehem Steel Corp. v. G.C. Zarnas & Co., 304 Md. 183, 498 A.2d 605 (1985).

45. Thera–Kinetics, Inc. v. Managed Home Recovery, Inc., 1997 WL 610305 (N.D.Ill.1997); B.M. Heede, Inc. v. West In-

the parties' choice. Some courts measure the importance of a public policy by whether it is embodied in a statute or merely a common law rule,[46] while others indicate that a contract must be "immoral,"[47] "inherently vicious, wicked or immoral,"[48] "abhorrent to public policy,"[49] or "offensive to justice or public welfare"[50] before voiding a stipulation of law.[51] These various tests of course afford little guidance to parties who need to predict whether or not their contemplated stipulation will be upheld.

Some decisions provide more specific guidelines. A statutory prohibition of certain types of contracts, such as gambling or usurious loans, may not represent a strong public policy if it admits of many exceptions.[52] The Kentucky Court of Appeals has held that Kentucky's usury

dia Machinery and Supply Co., 272 F.Supp. 236, 241 (S.D.N.Y.1967); Winer Motors, Inc. v. Jaguar Rover Triumph, Inc., 208 N.J.Super. 666, 506 A.2d 817 (App.Div.1986). In Machado–Miller v. Mersereau & Shannon, LLP., 180 Or.App. 586, 43 P.3d 1207 (2002), an Oregon court had to determine whether California's policy against non-compete agreements was fundamental under § 187(2)(b) of the Second Restatement so as to defeat an Oregon choice-of-law clause in an Oregon employment contract. The court expressed serious misgivings about the facility and exactness of such a determination:

> To announce that a policy or a right is 'fundamental' is to announce a conclusion and not a premise, and the reasoning that leads to the conclusion is almost always obscure, hopelessly subjective, or expressed in verbal formulations that are of little help.... Further, whether a particular interest is deemed 'fundamental' under such indeterminate formulations depends on the level of generality at which the Court chooses to identify it. To the extent the interest is described at a high level of generality, it is likely to be 'fundamental,' and vice versa. Further, every piece of legislation, even the most apparently trivial, implements and therefore indicates the presence of some larger policy, which, in turn, serves an even larger one. A speed limit is not itself a fundamental policy statement, but its purpose is to promote highway safety, which is one way to protect the health, welfare and safety of citizens, which is, of course, one of the most fundamental of all public policies.

43 P.3d at 1211. Eventually, the court concluded that California's policy was fundamental "in the dictionary sense [of] 'basic, underlying and primary,' " id. at 1212, because it was contained in a statute phrased "at a high level of generality," id., and clearly stating a policy of prohibiting non-

compete agreements in order to maximize competition and minimize restraints on trade. The statute provided that "every contract by which anyone is restrained from engaging in a lawful profession, trade, or business of any kind is to that extent void." California Business and Professional Code § 16600.

46. See Wright–Moore Corp. v. Ricoh Corp., 908 F.2d 128 (7th Cir.1990); Davis v. Jointless Fire Brick Co., 300 Fed. 1, 4 (9th Cir.1924); Forney Industries, Inc. v. Andre, 246 F.Supp. 333, 334 (D.N.D.1965); May v. Mulligan, 36 F.Supp. 596 (W.D.Mich.1939), aff'd 117 F.2d 259 (6th Cir.1940), cert. denied 312 U.S. 691, 61 S.Ct. 622, 85 L.Ed. 1127 (1941).

47. Fonseca v. Cunard Steamship Co., Ltd., 153 Mass. 553, 27 N.E. 665, 667 (1891); Benton v. Safe Deposit Bank of Pottsville, P.A., 255 N.Y. 260, 174 N.E. 648 (1931).

48. Intercontinental Hotels Corp. v. Golden, 15 N.Y.2d 9, 254 N.Y.S.2d 527, 203 N.E.2d 210, 212 (1964).

49. Naylor v. Conroy, 46 N.J.Super. 387, 134 A.2d 785, 787 (App.Div.1957).

50. Intercontinental Hotels Corp. v. Golden, 15 N.Y.2d 9, 254 N.Y.S.2d 527, 203 N.E.2d 210, 212 (1964) (quoting Loucks v. Standard Oil Co., 224 N.Y. 99, 110, 120 N.E. 198, 201 (1918)) ("offend[s] our sense of justice or menace[s] the public welfare").

51. In Lehman Bros. Commercial Corp. v. Minmetals Int'l Non–Ferrous Metals Trading Co., 179 F.Supp.2d 118 (S.D.N.Y. 2000), the court held that a contract that was illegal under the law of the place of performance (here: China) was unenforceable in New York even if valid under the law chosen by the parties.

52. See Fine v. Property Damage Appraisers, Inc., 393 F.Supp. 1304, 1308, 1310 (E.D.La.1975) (covenant not to compete);

law is not "distinctive" enough to prevent enforcement of interstate contracts exceeding the Kentucky usury rate.[53] The implication is that an insignificant or technical divergence from a statute does not raise a strong public policy objection. A New York decision suggests that courts should not override a choice-of-law stipulation unless the legislature specifies that the statute applies to conflict-of-law situations.[54] In contrast, the penal nature of a statute presumably indicates that the legislature felt strongly about enforcement of the policy.[55]

b. Public Policy in Specific Contexts

§ 18.5 *Adhesion Contracts.* Some courts and commentators regard any contract drafted unilaterally and imposed upon a party by an economically stronger one as adhesive,[1] while others do so only when the contract contains unfair or unconscionable terms.[2] The Second Restatement adopts the first view but would not, for that reason alone, void a choice-of-law clause:[3] the chosen law will be ignored only if its application would be to the detriment of the weaker party.[4] In general, simple

Intercontinental Hotels Corp. v. Golden, 15 N.Y.2d 9, 254 N.Y.S.2d 527, 203 N.E.2d 210, 213 (1964) (gambling law contains exceptions such as offtrack betting, bingo, lotteries and horseracing); Ury v. Jewelers Acceptance Corp., 227 Cal.App.2d 11, 38 Cal. Rptr. 376, 382–83 (1964) (usury law exempts some institutions).

53. Big Four Mills, Ltd. v. Commercial Credit Co., Inc., 307 Ky. 612, 211 S.W.2d 831, 836 (1948).

54. Reger v. National Ass'n of Bedding Manufacturers Group Ins. Trust Fund, 83 Misc.2d 527, 372 N.Y.S.2d 97, 116 (1975).

55. MGM Grand Hotel, Inc. v. Imperial Glass Co., 65 F.R.D. 624, 632 (D.Nev.1974), reversed on other grounds 533 F.2d 486 (9th Cir.1976), cert. denied 429 U.S. 887, 97 S.Ct. 239, 50 L.Ed.2d 168 (1976); Govett American Endeavor Fund Ltd. v. Trueger, 112 F.3d 1017, 1022 (9th Cir.1997) (parties cannot avoid application of RICO by selection of the law of Jersey).

§ 18.5

1. Milanovich v. Costa Crociere, 954 F.2d 763 (D.C.Cir.1992); Boase v. Lee Rubber & Tire Corp., 437 F.2d 527, 530 (3d Cir.1970); Siegelman v. Cunard White Star Ltd., 221 F.2d 189, 204–06 (2d Cir.1955) (Frank, J., dissenting); McQuillan v. "Italia" Societa Per Azione Di Navigazione, 386 F.Supp. 462, 467 Fn. 11 (S.D.N.Y. 1974), aff'd 516 F.2d 896 (2d Cir.1975); Fricke v. Isbrandtsen Co., Inc., 151 F.Supp. 465, 467–68 (S.D.N.Y.1957); Gamer v. duPont Glore Forgan, Inc. 65 Cal.App.3d 280, 285–87, 135 Cal.Rptr. 230 (1976); Ury v. Jewel-

ers Acceptance Corp., 227 Cal.App.2d 11, 38 Cal.Rptr. 376, 381–83 (1964); Buraczynski v. Eyring, 919 S.W.2d 314 (Tenn.1996); Klos v. Polskie Linie Lotnicze, 133 F.3d 164 (2d Cir. 1997); Aviall, Inc. v. Ryder System, Inc., 913 F.Supp. 826 (S.D.N.Y. 1996), aff'd 110 F.3d 892 (2d Cir.1997); Rakoff, Contracts of Adhesion: An Essay in Reconstruction, 96 Harv.L.Rev. 1173, 1177 (1983); Ehrenzweig, Adhesion Contracts in the Conflicts of Laws, 53 Colum. L. Rev. 1072, 1075 (1953). On general conditions in form contracts, see H. Otto, Allgemeine Geschäftsbedingungen und Internationales Privatrecht (1984).

2. Chase Commercial Corp. v. Owen, 32 Mass.App.Ct. 248, 588 N.E.2d 705 (Mass. App.Ct. 1992); Reimonenq v. Foti, 72 F.3d 472 (5th Cir.1996); Hoy v. Sears, Roebuck & Co., 861 F.Supp. 881 (N.D.Cal.1994); Business Incentives Co., Inc. v. Sony Corp. of America, 397 F.Supp. 63, 67–69 (S.D.N.Y. 1975); Fairfield Lease Corp. v. Pratt, 6 Conn.Cir. 537, 278 A.2d 154, 155–56 (1971); Nordstrom & Ramerman, The Uniform Commercial Code and the Choice of Law, 1969 Duke L. J. 623, 630–31. See Boase v. Lee Rubber & Tire Corp., 437 F.2d 527, 530 (3d Cir.1970); Anderson v. First Commodity Corp. of Boston, 618 F.Supp. 262, 266–267 (W.D.Wis.1985).

3. Restatement, Second, Conflict of Laws § 187, cmmt. (b) (1971).

4. Restatement, Second, Conflict of Laws § 187, cmmt. (e) (1971). Cavers, "The Choice of Law Process" 195 (1965) ("Choice of Law clauses in adhesion contracts should

inequality of bargaining power and a lack of negotiation do not of themselves void a choice-of-law provision.[5]

Insurance Contracts. One of the most common examples of adhesion contracts are those for insurance. For this reason, state statutes tend to regulate in great detail insurance contracts; many statutes mandate their application to contracts that have certain enumerated connections with the enacting state;[6] and some statutes expressly prohibit choice-of-law or choice-of-forum clauses. For example, an Oregon statute provides that, for an insurance policy "delivered or issued for delivery in this state," any "condition, stipulation or agreement requiring such policy to be construed according to the laws of any other state or country ... shall be invalid."[7]

With two exceptions, the reported cases do not permit the insurer to stipulate away from the law of the insured's domicile lest protective rules of law of the latter be avoided.[8] However, such a stipulation will be honored, for instance in favor of the insurer's home state, if the chosen

be honored unless they would subject a party to oppressive or otherwise unfair conditions or requirements"). See also Boase v. Lee Rubber & Tire Corp., 437 F.2d 527 (3d Cir.1970) (one-year limit on bringing suit); Siegelman v. Cunard White Star Ltd., 221 F.2d 189 (2d Cir.1955) (exculpatory clause); Fricke v. Isbrandtsen Co., Inc., 151 F.Supp. 465 (S.D.N.Y.1957) (one-year limit on bringing suit); F.A. Straus & Co. v. Canadian Pacific R. Co., 254 N.Y. 407, 173 N.E. 564 (1930) (exculpatory clause). See also M/S Bremen v. Zapata Off–Shore Co., 407 U.S. 1, 92 S.Ct. 1907, 32 L.Ed.2d 513 (1972) (enforcement of choice-of-court clause in favor of English court results in application of English law which, in turn, would honor contract's exculpatory clause).

U.C.C. § 2A–106(1) restricts the parties' choice in a consumer lease to the law of the place of the lessee's residence at the time of the lease or within thirty days thereafter. See infra § 18.37 n.3.

5. See Burbank v. Ford Motor Co., 703 F.2d 865, 866–867 (5th Cir. 1983); Sall v. G.H. Miller Co., 612 F.Supp. 1499, 1505 (D.Colo.1985); Sullivan v. Savin Business Machines Corp., 560 F.Supp. 938, 939 (S.D.N.Y.1983); Bos Material Handling v. Crown Controls Corp., 137 Cal.App.3d 99, 186 Cal.Rptr. 740, 745 (1982); Meyer v. State Farm Fire and Cas. Co., 85 Md.App. 83, 582 A.2d 275, 278 (1990); Nguyen v. Lewis/Boyle, Inc., 899 F.Supp. 58, 58, 61 (D.R.I.1995).

6. For example, a Texas statute provides that "[a]ny contract of insurance payable to any citizen or inhabitant of this State by any insurance company ... doing

business within this State shall be ... governed by [the laws of this State] notwithstanding such ... contract ... may provide that the contract was executed and the premiums ... should be payable without this State." Tex.Ins.Code Ann. § 21.42. A North Carolina statute provides that "[a]ll contracts of insurance on property, lives, or interests in this State shall be deemed to be made therein, and all contracts of insurance the applications for which are taken within the State shall be deemed to be made within this State and are subject to the laws thereof." N.C.Gen.Stat. § 58–3–1. See also Wis.Stat. § 632.09 ("Every insurance against loss or destruction of or damage to property in this state ... is governed by the law of this state."; Min.Stat. § 60A.08(4) ("All contracts of insurance on property, lives, or interests in this state, shall be deemed to be made in this state."); Colo. Rev.Stat. § 10–4–711; Fla.Stat. § 627.727; Okla.Stat. tit. 36 § 3636; La.Rev.Stat. §§ 22:611, 22:655, 22:1406(D).

7. Or.Rev.Stat. §§ 742.001, 742.018. See also Tex.Ins.Code Ann. § 21.42.

8. Param Petroleum Corp. v. Commerce and Industry Ins. Co., 296 N.J.Super. 164, 686 A.2d 377 (N.J.Super.Ct.App.Div.1997); Nelson v. Aetna Life Ins. Co., 359 F.Supp. 271, 290–92 (W.D.Mo. 1973); Johnston v. Commercial Travelers Mut. Acc. Ass'n of America, 242 S.C. 387, 131 S.E.2d 91, 93, 95 (1963). But see Burge v. Mid–Continent Cas. Co., 123 N.M. 1, 933 P.2d 210 (N.M. 1996) (holding that where policy provides foreign choice of law, and both parties consent, foreign law applies). Note that it is indeterminate from this case whether for-

law affords the insured greater protection.[9] State regulatory interests thus largely displace party autonomy (in the sense discussed in § 18.4 with respect to "mandatory rules") and result in the application of the more favorable law. A second exception applies to group insurance. When an employer or an organization enters into a group insurance contract for its employees or members who may live in different states, both the insurer and the insureds have a legitimate interest in establishing uniform liability.[10] A stipulation in favor of the insurer's law is therefore reasonable, especially since the greater leverage possessed by the group bargaining agent also distinguishes this kind of contract from the typical adhesion contract.[11]

Usury. Most courts do not regard an interstate contract to borrow money at a higher rate than allowed by the borrower's home state as a violation of fundamental public policy.[12] The Second Restatement differentiates between small or technical differences and gross variations in interest rates, with the result that stipulations involving the latter would

eign law is more beneficial than NM law (state law of insured).

9. Haisten v. Grass Valley Medical Reimbursement Fund, Ltd., 784 F.2d 1392 (9th Cir.1986); State Farm Mut. Auto. Ins. Co. v. Baker, 14 Kan.App.2d 641, 797 P.2d 168 (1990); Nederland Life Ins. Co. v. Meinert, 127 Fed. 651 (C.C.A.Ind.1904), reversed 199 U.S. 171, 26 S.Ct. 15, 50 L.Ed. 139 (1905); Jones v. New York Life Ins. Co., 32 Okl. 339, 122 P. 702, 705 (1912); Missouri State Life Ins. Co. v. Lovelace, 1 Ga. App. 446, 58 S.E. 93, 99 (1907).

10. Reger v. National Ass'n of Bedding Manufacturers Group Ins. Trust Fund, 83 Misc.2d 527, 372 N.Y.S.2d 97, 114–15 (1975); Davis v. Humble Oil & Refining Co., 283 So.2d 783 (La.App.1973); Restatement, Second, Conflict of Laws § 192, cmnt. (h) (1971).

11. Reger v. National Ass'n of Bedding Manufacturers Group Ins. Trust Fund, 83 Misc.2d 527, 372 N.Y.S.2d 97, 114–15 (1975); Davis v. Humble Oil & Refining Co., 283 So.2d 783 (La.App.1973); Kahn v. Great–West Life Assurance Co., 61 Misc.2d 918, 307 N.Y.S.2d 238, 243 (1970). See generally cases cited in Annot., 53 A.L.R.3d 1095 (1973). But see Nelson v. Aetna Life Ins. Co., 359 F.Supp. 271, 290–92 (W.D.Mo. 1973).

12. Seeman v. Philadelphia Warehouse Co., 274 U.S. 403, 47 S.Ct. 626, 71 L.Ed. 1123 (1927); National Sur. Corp. v. Inland Properties, Inc., 286 F.Supp. 173 (E.D.Ark. 1968), aff'd 416 F.2d 457 (8th Cir.1969); Clarkson v. Finance Co., of America, 328 F.2d 404 (4th Cir.1964); Gamer v. duPont Glore Forgan, Inc., 65 Cal.App.3d 280, 135 Cal.Rptr. 230 (1976); Ury v. Jewelers Ac-

ceptance Corp., 227 Cal.App.2d 11, 38 Cal. Rptr. 376 (1964); Big Four Mills, Ltd. v. Commercial Credit Co., 307 Ky. 612, 211 S.W.2d 831 (1948). See also Morgan Walton Properties, Inc. v. International City Bank & Trust Co., 404 So.2d 1059 (Fla.1981) (notes executed and payable in Louisiana and secured by mortgages on Florida real property and providing for interest which would be usurious under Florida but not under Louisiana law are enforceable in Florida when transaction had a reasonable relation to Louisiana and either the express or the constructive intent of the parties was that Louisiana law should govern). But see Woods–Tucker Leasing Corp. v. Hutcheson–Ingram Development Co., 626 F.2d 401 (5th Cir.1980) (bankruptcy court applied state choice-of-law rules to usury question, found that "most-significant contacts" test pointed to forum law (law of the borrower's state which invalidated the stipulated rate of interest) despite contractual choice of validating law). On petition for rehearing, the court vacated and withdrew this opinion and aff'd the decision below. 642 F.2d 744 (1981). See also Admiral Ins. Co. v. Brinkcraft Development, Ltd., 921 F.2d 591 (5th Cir.1991) (following *Woods-Tucker*). The case is discussed infra § 23.14. In Whitaker v. Spiegel, Inc., 95 Wn.2d 661, 623 P.2d 1147 (1981), opinion amended 95 Wn.2d 661, 637 P.2d 235 (1981) (applying the Washington usury law, despite a choice-of-law clause stipulating Illinois law, on the basis of a Washington statute making Washington law applicable to all loans made to Washington residents. The case arose in the context of mail order installment purchases). For consumer protection in small loan transactions see also infra

be voided as violative of public policy.[13] Despite the criticism of this approach on the ground and that even minor differences in interest rates can have a significant economic impact,[14] the distinction seems reasonable. Most state usury laws are subject to a number of exceptions,[15] suggesting that no hard and fast lines should be drawn.

Protection of Employees. Statutes limiting the power of employers to bind their employees to covenants not to compete, by contrast, do represent a fundamental policy and provide far fewer exceptions than do usury statutes.[16] Courts almost always strike down or modify such covenants if they violate the law of the employee's home state, despite stipulations in the employment contract for a different law, on the ground that employees need protection against the superior bargaining position of employers.[17]

§ 18.28 infra. See also Bice Const. Co., Inc. v. CIT Corp. of South, Inc., 700 F.2d 465 (8th Cir.1983).

13. Restatement, Second, Conflict of Laws § 203 (1971). An example is O'Brien v. Shearson Hayden Stone, Inc., 90 Wn.2d 680, 586 P.2d 830 (1978), opinion supplemented 93 Wn.2d 51, 605 P.2d 779 (1980) in which the borrower's state allowed a maximum of 12% interest and the contract called for 25%. See Trautman, Some Notes on the Theory of Choice of Law Clauses, 35 Mercer L.Rev. 535, 551 (1984).

14. Sedler, The Contracts Provisions of the Restatement (2d): An Analysis and Critique, 72 Colum. L. Rev. 279, 316–19 (1972).

15. Ury v. Jewelers Acceptance Corp., 227 Cal.App.2d 11, 38 Cal.Rptr. 376 (1964).

16. See Fine v. Property Damage Appraisers, Inc., 393 F.Supp. 1304, 1310 (E.D.La.1975). This case has been questioned but not overruled by Simpson v. Kelly Services, Inc., 339 So.2d 490, 495 (La.App.1976), which states that only employer-employee situations are subject to the non-complete protection afforded by Louisiana, and not other situations that courts interpret (such as franchise situations taking place in *Fine*). See also Forney Industries, Inc. v. Andre, 246 F.Supp. 333, 334 (D.N.D.1965); Dresser Industries, Inc. v. Sandvick, 732 F.2d 783 (10th Cir.1984); DeSantis v. Wackenhut Corp., 793 S.W.2d 670 (Tex.1990), cert. denied 498 U.S. 1048, 111 S.Ct. 755, 112 L.Ed.2d 775 (1991). Rules protective of employees are classic examples of "mandatory rules," as the term is used in European conflicts law. Thus, the Rome Convention and some national codifications discussed earlier, take a negative stance toward choice-of-law clauses that purport to deprive employees of the protec-

tion of these rules. See supra § 18.4 at text accompanying nn. 22–24.

17. Blalock v. Perfect Subscription Co., 458 F.Supp. 123 (S.D.Ala.1978), aff'd 599 F.2d 743 (5th Cir.1979); Fine v. Property Damage Appraisers, Inc., 393 F.Supp. 1304 (E.D.La.1975); Boyer v. Piper, Jaffray & Hopwood, Inc., 391 F.Supp. 471 (D.S.D. 1975); Forney Industries, Inc. v. Andre, 246 F.Supp. 333 (D.N.D.1965); DeSantis v. Wackenhut Corp., 793 S.W.2d 670 (Tex. 1990), cert. denied, 498 U.S. 1048, 111 S.Ct. 755, 112 L.Ed.2d 775 (1991); Nasco, Inc. v. Gimbert, 239 Ga. 675, 238 S.E.2d 368 (1977); Frame v. Merrill Lynch, Pierce, Fenner & Smith Inc., 20 Cal.App.3d 668, 97 Cal.Rptr. 811 (1971). In Curtis 1000, Inc. v. Suess, 24 F.3d 941 (7th Cir. 1994), the differences between the chosen law of Delaware and the law of the employee's home and employment state of Illinois were "too slight to induce an Illinois court to take the rather drastic step of invalidating a consensual choice of law clause." Id. at 948. Nevertheless, the court affirmed the lower court opinion that disregarded the choice of Delaware law, because Delaware's sole connection as the state of the employer's incorporation was insufficient to sustain the choice. See id. ("Businesses incorporate in Delaware to take advantage of that state's corporation law, and its judicial expertise concerning corporate governance, rather than to conduct business there.")

Related to protection of employees are two decisions involving statutes to protect persons of similar status. In MGM Grand Hotel, Inc. v. Imperial Glass Co., 65 F.R.D. 624 (D.Nev.1974), reversed on other grounds 533 F.2d 486 (9th Cir.1976), cert. denied 429 U.S. 887, 97 S.Ct. 239, 50 L.Ed.2d 168 (1976), a Nevada statute required contractors to be licensed in Nevada to insure their solvency and thus protect subcontractors, materialmen and the gener-

The more difficult cases are those in which the employee resigns his employment in her home state and moves to another state to work for a competing employer there. If the first employment contract contains a non-compete covenant that is enforceable under the law of the first but not the second employment state, the result is a true conflict between the pro-employer law of the first state and the pro-employee law of the second state. A choice-of-law clause in the first contract stipulating for the law of the first state will make the case even closer, but, if litigation takes place in the second state, the clause will probably not be honored.[18] One case presenting this conflict is *Application Group, Inc. v. Hunter Group, Inc.*,[19] in which the employee did not even move her domicile to the second employment state. The employee was a Maryland domiciliary who, after resigning her job with a Maryland employer, began working for a competing California employer from her home in Maryland ("tele-commuting"). In the ensuing litigation in California, the court held that the non-compete clause contained in the Maryland contract was unenforceable in California after finding that California met all three prongs for disregarding the Maryland choice-of-law clause under § 187(2) of the Second Restatement, to wit: (1) California law would be applicable to this issue in the absence of the choice-of-law clause; (2) California had a materially greater interest in applying its law to this issue; and (3) enforcement of the non-compete clause would be contrary to a fundamental policy of California.

The court noted that, although Maryland had all the contacts relevant to the employment contract (which was not at issue), California had the contact that was most relevant with regard to the particular issue—the enforceability of the non-compete covenant in California. As to this issue, said the court, "the subject matter of the contract" was the employee's "subsequent employment which was, in this case, employment by a competitor who is 'located' in California."[20] Thus, to the extent that the covenant purported to restrict competition in California, California had the *most* pertinent contact which brought into play California's interest in protecting competing California employers and "business opportunities in California."[21] The court concluded that California had a strong interest in protecting both the employee and the second (California) employer. With regard to the employee, California had "a strong interest in protecting the freedom of movement of persons whom California-based employers ... wish to employ ... , regardless of

al public. The court found that this statute involved a fundamental public policy as contemplated by the Restatement, Second and therefore disregarded the California choice of law clause in the contract. In Southern Int'l Sales Co., Inc. v. Potter & Brumfield Division of AMF Incorporated, 410 F.Supp. 1339 (S.D.N.Y. 1976), a Puerto Rican statute prohibiting franchisors from imposing contract terms allowing franchise termination without cause was held to represent a fundamental public policy. The court's analysis indicated that such terms in franchise contracts were adhesive because of the franchisor's strong bargaining position.

18. For critical discussion of such cases, see Symeonides, Choice of Law in the American Courts in 2002: Sixteenth Annual Survey, 51 Am. J. Comp. L. 1, 64 (2003).

19. 61 Cal.App.4th 881, 72 Cal.Rptr.2d 73 (Cal.App.1998).

20. Id. at 87.

21. Id. at 88.

the person's state of residence."[22] With regard to the second employer, California had a "public policy which ensures that California employers will be able to compete effectively for the most talented, skilled employees in their industries, wherever they may reside,"[23] and thus California had an "interest in protecting its employers and their employees from anti-competitive conduct by out-of-state employers ... who would interfere with or restrict these freedoms."[24]

In *Keener v. Convergy's Corp.*,[25] Ohio was the first employer's state and the employee's first domicile, while Georgia was the second employer's state and employee's new domicile. The Georgia federal court refused to enforce the Ohio choice-of-law clause and non-compete covenant because the latter was contrary to the free-competition policy embedded in Georgia's constitution. The court acknowledged that "[t]his may wind up encouraging non-Georgia employees to 'flee to Georgia' to shed their [non-compete covenants]."[26] However, analogizing to "quickie divorces," the court said, "[t]he aches and pains of federalism ... have long formed part of the American legal fabric."[27]

These aches are even more serious when the case provokes litigation in both employment states. *Advanced Bionics Corp. v. Medtronic, Inc.*,[28] involved this scenario, with Minnesota and California being the first and second employment states, respectively. The first employer was a Minnesota corporation that hired a Minnesota domiciliary for work in Minnesota. The contract contained a Minnesota choice-of-law clause, as well as a non-compete covenant that was valid under Minnesota law. The employee resigned his job with the Minnesota employer and was hired by a competing California employer for work in California. The latter employer filed in California an action seeking a declaration that the non-compete covenant was unenforceable in California. In the meantime, the Minnesota employer filed an action for an injunction in Minnesota

---

22. Id. at 85.

23. Id.

24. Id. This reading of California interests drew a sharp rebuke from a California judge who dissented in a similar case in which the employee did move to California: "Relocating to California is not a chance to walk away from valid contractual obligations, claiming California policy as a protective shield. We are not a political safe zone vis-à-vis our sister states, such that the mere act of setting foot on California soil somehow releases a person from the legal duties our sister states recognize." Advanced Bionics Corp. v. Medtronic, Inc., 29 Cal.4th 697, 128 Cal.Rptr.2d 172, 59 P.3d 231 (2002), Brown, J., dissenting. See also id. (speaking of California's "political imperialism, absorbing every state into the California legal ethos").

25. 205 F.Supp.2d 1374 (S.D.Ga. 2002), aff'd in part, rev'd in part 342 F.3d 1264 (11th Cir.2003).

26. Id. at 1379.

27. Id. On appeal the Eleventh Circuit Court of Appeals certified to the Georgia Supreme Court the question of whether Georgia would follow § 187(2) of the Second Restatement and whether in this case Georgia would have a materially greater interest to apply its law. See Keener v. Convergys Corp., 312 F.3d 1236 (11th Cir. 2002). The latter court reaffirmed its refusal to adopt the Restatement as well as its refusal to enforce non-compete agreements. See Convergys Corp. v. Keener, 276 Ga. 808, 582 S.E.2d 84 (2003). The Eleventh Circuit affirmed the District Court opinion. See 342 F.3d 1264, 2003 WL 21983010 (11th Cir.2003)

28. 29 Cal.4th 697, 128 Cal.Rptr.2d 172, 59 P.3d 231 (2002).

enjoining the employee from violating the non-compete covenant. The lower courts in both states rendered conflicting judgments in favor of their respective employers[29] before the California Supreme Court set aside the California judgment. The latter court acknowledged that California had a "strong interest" in protecting the freedom of new California domiciliaries to seek employment in California, and that a California court "might reasonably conclude" that the Minnesota non-compete and choice-of-law clauses were "void in this state."[30] However, the court specifically refused to base its decision regarding the propriety of an antisuit injunction on choice-of-law factors and instead based it on principles of judicial restraint and comity.[31]

Protection of Franchisees. Statutes regulating franchises or distributorships are another example of statutes that restrict party autonomy in the interest of protecting the presumed weak party—the franchisee or distributee. Typically, these statutes prohibit waivers of their provisions, either directly or through the contractual choice of another state's law. Most of these statutes limit the scope of their operation to franchises or distributorships operating within the enacting state. Thus, when a contract purports, through a choice of another state's law, to opt out of such a statute, the only question the courts needs to answer is whether the contract falls within the reach of the statute.[32] Since more often than not the statute expressly delineates its territorial reach, the answer to

29. See Advanced Bionics Corp. v. Medtronic, Inc., 105 Cal.Rptr.2d 265 (Cal.App. 2001), review granted and opinion superseded 108 Cal.Rptr.2d 595, 25 P.3d 1078 (2001); Medtronic, Inc. v. Advanced Bionics Corp., 630 N.W.2d 438 (Minn.App. 2001).

30. 128 Cal.Rptr.2d at 179, 59 P.3d 231.

31. See id. (noting that these principles required "that we exercise our power to enjoin parties in a foreign court sparingly."). Holeman v. National Business Institute, 94 S.W.3d 91 (Tex.App.2002), involved a similar scenario as *Advanced Bionics,* except that the contract contained an exclusive choice-of-forum clause (in addition to a choice-of-law clause). A Georgia-based employer hired plaintiff for work in Texas and included in the contract a non-compete covenant, a Georgia choice-of-law clause, and a choice-of-forum clause mandating litigation in Georgia. After the employee began working for a competing Texas employer, the employee sued his former employer in Texas seeking a declaratory judgment that the covenant was unenforceable. Relying on the choice-of-forum clause, the trial court granted defendant's motion to dismiss, and the appellate court affirmed. The plaintiff argued, *inter alia,* that under Texas precedent, a Texas court would not enforce the non-compete covenant and that the choice-of-forum clause was a sinister device to circumvent Texas law. The court rejected all of plaintiff's arguments, stating that en-forcement of the choice-of-forum clause did not necessarily mean that a Georgia court would not apply Texas law and that, in any event, because of recent changes in Texas law, it was unclear whether Texas would find the non-compete covenant unenforceable.

32. For the converse phenomenon, see Fred Briggs Distr. Co., Inc. v. California Cooler, Inc. 2 F.3d 1156 (Table) (9th Cir. 1993) (disregarding a contractual choice of California franchise law because the case did not fall within the intended territorial reach of the California statute); Cromeens, Holloman, Sibert, Inc. v. AB Volvo, 349 F.3d 376 (7th Cir. 2003) (disregarding a contractual choice of Illinois franchise statute because the case did not fall within the statute's intended reach); Gravquick A/S v. Trimble Navigation Int'l. Ltd., 323 F.3d 1219 (9th Cir. 2003) (acknowledging that California's Dealers Act was intended for the protection of California dealers but honoring contractual choice of California Act in a contract between a foreign dealer and a California manufacturer); Compare Liberty Sales Assoc., Inc. v. Dow Corning Corp., 816 F.Supp. 1004 (D.N.J. 1993) (upholding the contractual choice of Michigan law because the plaintiff did not fall within the scope of the New Jersey Franchise Practices Act which would have invalidated such a choice).

this question usually is easy. For example, franchise statutes usually are applicable by their terms to franchisees domiciled in and/or franchises located in the enacting state. When the case at hand has both of these contacts with the enacting state and litigation occurs in that state, the application of that statute is virtually inevitable, notwithstanding a contrary choice-of-law clause. Cases so holding are abundant.[33] In fact, such clauses are likely to be disregarded even if the statute in question does not expressly prohibit them.[34]

When litigation occurs in the franchisor's state, the courts of that state tend to be less deferential to the protective statutes of the franchisee's state and more receptive to a contractual choice of the forum's law.[35] *Modern Computer Systems v. Modern Banking Systems,*[36] is representative of these cases. In a contract for a Minnesota franchise, the Minnesota franchisee and the Nebraska franchisor had chosen the law of Nebraska which had not enacted a franchisee-protecting statute. In contrast, Minnesota had a statute that accorded Minnesota franchisees more protection than traditional common law, and prohibited waiver of this protection, although the statute did not specifically prohibit the choice of another state's law. Assisted by Minnesota's Attorney General who appeared as *amicus curiae*, the plaintiff/franchisee argued that the application of Nebraska common law would frustrate the "fundamental policies" embodied in the Minnesota Franchise Act. At first, the court agreed and remanded the case to the district court, after finding that Minnesota, being the place of the performance of the contract and the plaintiff's domicile and incorporation, had the most significant relationship with the contract and thus would be the state of the *lex causae*. One year later, however, when the case again reached the court of appeals, the court reached the opposite conclusion and upheld the parties' choice

---

33. See Symeonides, Choice of Law in the American Courts in 1994: A View From the Trenches, 43 Am.J.Comp.L. 1, 61–63 (1994). For later cases, see, e.g., Power & Telephone Supply Co., Inc. v. Harmonic, Inc., 268 F.Supp.2d 981 (W.D.Tenn.2003) (invalidating under a Tennessee distributorship statute a California choice-of-law clause contained in a contract between a Tennessee distributor and a California manufacturer); Beatty Caribbean, Inc. v. Viskase Sales Corp., 241 F.Supp.2d 123 (D.P.R.2003) (invalidating under the Puerto Rico Dealers' statute an Illinois choice-of-law clause contained in a distributorship agreement between a Puerto Rico distributor and an Illinois manufacturer); Stawski Distributing Co., Inc. v. Browary Zywiec S.A., 349 F.3d 1023 (7th Cir., 2003), cert. denied ___ U.S. ___, 124 S.Ct. 2069, 158 L.Ed.2d 620 (2004); Healy v. Carlson Travel Network Associates, Inc., 227 F.Supp.2d 1080 (D.Minn.2002); Ticknor v. Choice Hotels Int'l, Inc., 265 F.3d 931 (9th Cir. 2001),

cert. denied 534 U.S. 1133, 122 S.Ct. 1075, 151 L.Ed.2d 977 (2002).

34. See Symeonides, supra n.33, at 55 ff.; Instructional Systems, Inc. v. Computer Curriculum Corp., 130 N.J. 324, 614 A.2d 124 (N.J. 1992); Wright–Moore Corp. v. Ricoh Corp., 908 F.2d 128 (7th Cir. 1990).

35. See S. Symeonides, W. Perdue & A. von Mehren, Conflict of Laws: American, Comparative, International 334–36 (1998). See JRT, Inc. v. TCBY Systems, Inc., 52 F.3d 734 (8th Cir. 1995) (decided under Arkansas conflicts law; franchise agreement for a Michigan franchise; contractual choice of Arkansas law upheld because Michigan anti-waiver statute "did not specifically target choice of law provisions," id. at 739, and because "even if ... Michigan has the greatest interest, ... no fundamental Michigan policy is at stake.... Fundamental state policies involve systemic problems affecting a class of contracts, not specific contract performance problems." Id.).

36. 858 F.2d 1339 (8th Cir. 1988) (decided under Nebraska conflicts law).

of Nebraska law. Noting that this was not an adhesion contract and that the territorial and personal contacts were divided almost evenly between the two states, the court held that the choice of the law of either state was reasonable and that Minnesota's policies were not sufficiently strong to override such a choice.[37] Shortly thereafter, Minnesota amended its Franchise Act, to expressly prohibit waiver of its provisions through "any condition, stipulation or provision, *including any choice of law provision.*"[38]

Formalities. Most modern cases involving formalities involve Statute of Frauds questions.[39] The case law ordinarily does not consider formalities to involve fundamental public policies. While formalities or prohibitions do evidence a protective concern, oppressive unfairness is unlikely to occur as a result of the selection of one state's law (and its formalities) over that of another.[40]

3. The Requirement of a "Substantial Relationship"

a. In General

§ 18.6 The case law generally favors for the enforcement of choice-of-law clauses that the chosen law bear a relationship of some significance to the transaction.[1] In addition to some unlikely concerns, for

37. See Modern Computer Systems v. Modern Banking Systems, 871 F.2d 734 (8th Cir. 1989).

38. Minn. Stat. § 80C.21 (1989) (emphasis added).

39. See Finnish Fur Sales Co., Ltd. v. Juliette Shulof Furs, Inc., 770 F.Supp. 139 (S.D.N.Y.1991); Paribas Properties, Inc. v. Benson, 146 A.D.2d 522, 536 N.Y.S.2d 1007 (1989); Nakhleh v. Chemical Construction Corp., 359 F.Supp. 357 (S.D.N.Y.1973) (oral contract selecting Saudi Arabian law); Swanson v. United–Greenfield Corp., 239 F.Supp. 299 (D.Conn.1965); A. S. Rampell, Inc. v. Hyster Co., 3 N.Y.2d 369, 165 N.Y.S.2d 475, 144 N.E.2d 371 (1957). Older cases deal with other formalities, such as the validity of contracts made on Sunday. See, e.g., Cameron v. Gunstock Acres, Inc., 370 Mass. 378, 348 N.E.2d 791 (1976).

40. But see Freedman v. Chemical Construction Corp., 43 N.Y.2d 260, 401 N.Y.S.2d 176, 372 N.E.2d 12 (1977) (refusal to honor choice of Saudi Arabian law to govern statute-of-frauds question). European law appears to be contrary. Art. 9 of the Rome Convention contains alternative (validating) rules for the issue of formal validity. One of them refers to the law "which governs under this Convention" which includes (Art. 3(4) in connection with Art. 8(I)) the law chosen by the parties, apparently without allowing rejection on public policy grounds.

With respect to capacity, the general American rule is that the applicable law is not that of a person's domicile but rather the general law governing the contract. Teas v. Kimball, 257 F.2d 817, 823 (5th Cir.1958). See generally, Annot. 18 A.L.R. 1516 (1922); 71 A.L.R. 744 (1931). But see Lilienthal v. Kaufman, 239 Or. 1, 395 P.2d 543 (1964), (discussed infra § 18.20 and supra § 3.29.).

§ 18.6

1. Armstrong v. Accrediting Council for Cont. Educ. & Trng, Inc., 980 F.Supp. 53 (D.D.C.1997), aff'd 168 F.3d 1362 (D.C.Cir. 1999), amended 177 F.3d 1036 (D.C.Cir. 1999) ("substantial nexus to this transaction"); Crawford v. Seattle, Renton & Southern Railway Co., 86 Wash. 628, 150 P. 1155, 1157 (1915) (a "real and not a mere fictitious, connection"), Consolidated Jewelers, Inc. v. Standard Financial Corp., 325 F.2d 31, 34 (6th Cir.1963) (share a "vital element"); Owens v. Hagenbeck–Wallace Shows Co., 58 R.I. 162, 192 A. 158, 163–64 (1937) ("real relation"); County Asphalt, Inc. v. Lewis Welding & Engineering Corp., 323 F.Supp. 1300, 1303 (S.D.N.Y.1970),aff'd 444 F.2d 372 (2d Cir.1971), cert. denied 404 U.S. 939, 92 S.Ct. 272, 30 L.Ed.2d 252 (1971) (share "significant events"); William Whitman Co. v. Universal Oil Products Co., 125 F.Supp. 137, 148 (D.Del.1954) (have a "material connection"); Seeman v. Phila-

instance that the absence of such a limitation might result in the selection of an exotic or bizarre law,[2] the principal reason for the limitation is that the choice of an unconnected law might extend party autonomy to essentially local transactions.[3] In such a case, the parties could evade the otherwise applicable local law[4] and thereby render state laws regarding contract validity meaningless.

Critics of the limitation on validation regard it as overbroad. They would require only that party autonomy be limited to transactions of an interstate or international character and, beyond that, would rely on the public policy exception to curb abuses.[5] Indeed, a variant of that view appears in the 2001 Revisions to Article 1 of the U.C.C., which, in contracts not involving a consumer,[6] would allow a choice-of-law clause

delphia Warehouse Co., 274 U.S. 403, 47 S.Ct. 626, 71 L.Ed. 1123 (1927) (have a "normal relation"); National Sur. Corp. v. Inland Properties, Inc., 286 F.Supp. 173, 190 (E.D.Ark.1968), aff'd 416 F.2d 457 (8th Cir.1969) (have a reasonable relationship or substantial connection); Stevenson v. Lima Locomotive Works, 180 Tenn. 137, 172 S.W.2d 812, 814–15 (1943) (a "real or substantial connection").

Cases refusing to enforce a choice-of-law clause on the *sole* ground that the chosen state lacked a substantial relationship are rare, but they do exist. See Sentinel Industrial Contracting Corp. v. Kimmins Industrial Service Corp., 743 So.2d 954 (Miss. 1999) (refusing to enforce a Texas choice-of-law clause in a contract providing for the dismantlement of an Exxon ammonia plant located in Mississippi and for its shipment and reassembly in Pakistan contained a choice of Texas law); Curtis 1000, Inc. v. Youngblade, 878 F.Supp. 1224 (N.D. Iowa 1995) (anti-competition clause in an Iowa employment contract that contained a choice of Delaware law—chosen law not applied because Delaware had no substantial relationship to contract and because the chosen law would be repugnant to a fundamental policy of Iowa); CCR Data Systems, Inc. v. Panasonic Communications & Systems Co., 1995 WL 54380 (D. N.H. 1995) (choice-of-law clause not upheld because chosen state had no relationship with the contract or the parties); Cable Tel Services, Inc. v. Overland Contracting, Inc., 154 N.C.App. 639, 574 S.E.2d 31 (2002); Robinson v. Robinson, 778 So.2d 1105 (La. 2001) (one spouse's brief residence in a state insufficient connection for a choice-of-law clause pointing to that state in a contract regarding the division of marital property—even though the Louisiana codification does not require the presence of such a connection).

2. See Yntema, Contract and Conflict of Laws: "Autonomy" in the choice of Law in the United States, 1 N.Y.L.F. 46, 60 (1955). However, parties do not indulge their whimsy in selecting a law. In addition, given the nature of international commerce, courts will at times have to deal with wholly unfamiliar laws even if a connection is required. See Tuchler, Boundaries to Party Autonomy in the Uniform Commercial Code: A Radical View, 11 St. Louis L.J. 180, 189–90 (1967). An example is Nakhleh v. Chemical Construction Corp., 359 F.Supp. 357 (S.D.N.Y.1973) (Saudi Arabia).

3. See, e.g., New England Mut. Life Ins. Co. v. Olin, 114 F.2d 131, 136 (7th Cir. 1940), cert. denied 312 U.S. 686, 61 S.Ct. 612, 85 L.Ed. 1123 (1941); Great Southern Life Ins. Co. v. Burwell, 12 F.2d 244–245 (5th Cir.1926), cert. denied 271 U.S. 683, 46 S.Ct. 633, 70 L.Ed. 1150 (1926); National Sur. Corp. v. Inland Properties, Inc., 286 F.Supp. 173 (E.D.Ark.1968), aff'd 416 F.2d 457 (8th Cir.1969); Dunlop Tire & Rubber Corp. v. Ryan, 171 Neb. 820, 108 N.W.2d 84, 88 (1961); Dolan v. Mutual Reserve Fund Life Ass'n, 173 Mass. 197, 53 N.E. 398, 399 (1899).

4. See, e.g., Clarkson v. Finance Co. of America at Baltimore, 328 F.2d 404, 407 (4th Cir.1964); Consolidated Jewelers, Inc. v. Standard Financial Corp., 325 F.2d 31, 34 (6th Cir.1963); United Divers Supply Co. v. Commercial Credit Co., 289 Fed. 316, 319 (5th Cir.1923); Shotwell v. Dairymen's League Cooperative Ass'n, Inc., 22 N.J.Misc. 171, 174, 37 A.2d 420, 422 (1944); Owens v. Hagenbeck–Wallace Shows Co., 58 R.I. 162, 192 A. 158, 164 (1937).

5. Ehrenzweig, Conflict of Laws 469 (1962); 2 Rabel, The Conflict of Laws: A Comparative Study, 357 (1947); Rheinstein, Book Review, 15 U. Chi. L. Rev. 478, 487–88 (1948); Tuchler, supra n.2, at 189–90.

6. For consumer contracts, U.C.C. § 1–301(e) (2001 Revision) requires that the

to operate "whether or not the transaction bears a relation to the State [or Country] designated."[7] On balance, the requirement that the chosen law be connected to the transaction is defensible if applied liberally and practically. Its complete absence might permit parties to avoid the common, but not fundamental, rules of contract law of both of their states solely because the interstate nature of their contract permits the choice of a third law. This is recognized by the Second Restatement and is discussed below.

As noted earlier,[8] in other legal systems, the modern trend is toward even greater liberality. Both the Rome Convention and the Inter-American Convention permit party autonomy, subject to the limitations discussed earlier (consumer and employment contracts, mandatory rules of the forum and of third states, public policy), and do not require "internationality."[9] For the rare case that foreign law is chosen for a local transaction, the Rome Convention (Art. 3(3)) provides that the stipulation is limited by the mandatory rule of the place of the transaction (whether or not it is the forum).

A 1984 New York statute directs that contractual stipulations providing for the application of New York law be given effect even if there are no substantial contacts with New York, provided that the contract involves a transaction in excess of $250,000, does not involve a consumer contract or one for personal services, and does not contravene the specific limitations of the U.C.C.[10] The same statute provides that if contracts containing such a clause and having a transaction value of one million dollars or more also provide for New York jurisdiction, New York courts must accept jurisdiction and may not dismiss for forum non conveniens.[11] The legislative policy objective was to enhance the importance of New York as an international commercial center, while affording parties the opportunity to select a sophisticated body of commercial law and a judicial system with substantial experience.[12]

---

chosen state bear a "reasonable relation" to the transaction. This provision further restricts party autonomy by providing that the choice-of-law clause may not deprive the consumer of the protection of rules that "may not be varied by agreement" of the consumer's home state or of a state in which the consumer made the contract and took delivery of the goods.

7. U.C.C. § 1–301(c) (2001 Revision). U.C.C. § 1–301(c) (1) and (2) differentiate between "domestic" (i.e., inter-U.S. transactions) and "international" transactions, respectively. Neither provision requires that a relation between the transaction and the state whose law stipulated in the clause, but U.C.C. § 1–301(c)(1) requires that the chosen state be a state of the United States.

8. See supra § 18.2 nn. 4–7.

9. See Rome Convention, Art. 3; Inter-American Convention, Art. 7.

10. For the U.C.C. limitations see supra §§ 18.2 n.7, 18.4 nn. 30–37.

11. N.Y. General Obligations Law §§ 5–1401, 5–1402. See also U.C.C. § 4A–507 (wholesale wire funds transfer may select law regardless of connection).

12. 1984 McKinney's Sess. Law News A–689–A–690 (Memorandum of Legislative Representative of the City of New York). See also Herzog, Conflict of Laws: 1984 Survey of New York Law, 36 Syracuse L. Rev. 131–33, 154 (1985).

b. *Satisfaction of the Requirement: Connecting Factors*

§ 18.7 The requirement of a connection to the chosen law is not satisfied in cases in which the domicile of the parties, the place of contract formation, and the place of performance all coincide, and some other state's law is chosen. These facts virtually exhaust all important elements of the transaction and no other state may therefore usually be selected by the parties.[1] It is similarly clear, by contrast, that the parties may select the law of the state that is the domicile of one of them and either the place of formation or of performance.[2] This is the most common case and holds true for the selection of a single applicable law as well as for "floating clauses." The more difficult situations are those in which these elements occur singly.

Place of Contract Formation. An older choice-of-law rule in contract referred to the place of contract formation.[3] This rule implies, *a fortiori,* that an election of that law by the parties would also be proper. However, this factor appears to be the weakest basis for party autonomy: such a contact is easy to manipulate and may result in an "interstate contract," that is a contract that becomes valid by virtue of the interstate factor although it would be defective in any state with a more real connection.[4]

Place of Performance. The contract's place of performance bears a more important relationship to the transaction than that of contract formation but, like the latter place, this too may be difficult to define. When a seller in Ohio manufactures a product pursuant to the buyer's order and brings it to New York and there installs it, where was the contract performed?[5] In view of this difficulty, it seems that the selection of any state in which the contract is to be performed at least in part will satisfy the requirement of a connection.[6]

§ 18.7

1. Crawford v. Seattle, Renton & Southern Railway Co., 86 Wash. 628, 150 P. 1155, 1157 (1915). But see Wyatt v. Fulrath, 16 N.Y.2d 169, 264 N.Y.S.2d 233, 211 N.E.2d 637 (1965) (discussed supra § 18.4 n.8).

2. E.g. Seeman v. Philadelphia Warehouse Co., 274 U.S. 403, 408, 47 S.Ct. 626, 627, 71 L.Ed. 1123 (1927); County Asphalt, Inc. v. Lewis Welding & Engineering Corp., 323 F.Supp. 1300, 1303 (S.D.N.Y.1970), aff'd 444 F.2d 372 (2d Cir.1971), cert. denied 404 U.S. 939, 92 S.Ct. 272, 30 L.Ed.2d 252 (1971); National Sur. Corp. v. Inland Properties, Inc., 286 F.Supp. 173, 189 (E.D.Ark.1968), aff'd 416 F.2d 457 (8th Cir. 1969); Mell v. Goodbody & Co., 10 Ill. App.3d 809, 295 N.E.2d 97, 99 (1973). See Annot., Validity and Effect of Stipulation in Contract to Effect That it Shall be Governed by Law of Particular State Which is Neither Place Where Contract is Made nor Place Where it is to be Performed, 16 A.L.R. 4th 967 (1982).

3. McBride v. Minstar, Inc., 283 N.J.Super. 471, 662 A.2d 592 (1994); Gordon v.

Clifford Metal Sales Co., 602 A.2d 535 (1992). See 2 J. Beale, Treatise on the Conflict of Laws § 332.4 (1935).

4. Prebble, Choice of Law to Determine the Validity and Effect of Contracts, 58 Cornell L. Rev. 433, 441 (1973). Another drawback of this connecting factor is that the "place of making" may be difficult to define in the case of a contract negotiated or signed in different places by different people. See 2 Beale, supra n.3, 1044–76.

5. County Asphalt, Inc. v. Lewis Welding & Engineering Corp., 323 F.Supp. 1300 (S.D.N.Y.1970) (Ohio law). Similarly, when a borrower sends money to a lender to repay money sent by the latter, it seems artificial to assume that there is only one place of performance. See, e.g., JRT, Inc. v. TCBY Systems, Inc., 52 F.3d 734 (8th Cir. 1995). Rocky Mountain Helicopters, Inc. v. Bell Helicopter Textron, Inc., 24 F.3d 125 (10th Cir.1994); Ury v. Jewelers Acceptance Corp., 227 Cal.App.2d 11, 38 Cal.Rptr. 376 (1964).

6. See Brink's Ltd. v. South African Airways, 93 F.3d 1022 (2d Cir. 1996), cert.

Domicile. The need to resort to a party's domicile as the state providing the applicable law is demonstrated by situations such as the one involved in *LaBeach v. Beatrice Foods Co.*[7] An employment contract was executed in England and performed in Nigeria by an employee, a resident of New York, of a Delaware corporation that had its principal place of business in Illinois. The New York court enforced the Illinois choice-of-law clause. Even when the interstate contacts are less diverse, courts will usually enforce a stipulation in favor of the law of one party's domicile.[8]

The State of Incorporation, Corporate Headquarters, Branches. The state of incorporation is usually considered to have too indirect a connection with the transaction to support the choice of its law.[9] The same is true of the state in which a corporate party maintains an office

denied 519 U.S. 1116, 117 S.Ct. 959, 136 L.Ed.2d 845 (1997); Duskin v. Pennsylvania–Central Airlines Corp., 167 F.2d 727 (6th Cir.1948), cert. denied 335 U.S. 829, 69 S.Ct. 56, 93 L.Ed. 382 (1948).

7. 461 F.Supp. 152 (S.D.N.Y.1978). The Rome Convention, in a situation like *La Beach*, would accept the stipulation of the domiciliary law but require additionally the application of protective mandatory rules of law in force in the state when the employee habitually performs the contract of employment. Rome Convention art. 6(2)(a).

8. See Advani Enterprises, Inc. v. Underwriters at Lloyds, 140 F.3d 157 (2d Cir. 1998); Sybron Transition Corp. v. Security Ins. Co. of Hartford, 107 F.3d 1250 (7th Cir.1997); Midwest Manufacturing Holding v. Donnelly Corp., 975 F.Supp. 1061 (N.D.Ill.1997); Craig v. Bemis Co., Inc., 517 F.2d 677 (5th Cir.1975); Boyer v. Piper, Jaffray & Hopwood, Inc., 391 F.Supp. 471 (D.S.D.1975); Reger v. National Ass'n of Bedding Manufacturers Group Ins. Trust Fund, 83 Misc.2d 527, 372 N.Y.S.2d 97 (1975). See also Business Incentives Co., Inc. v. Sony Corp., 397 F.Supp. 63 (S.D.N.Y. 1975); MGM Grand Hotel, Inc. v. Imperial Glass Co., 65 F.R.D. 624 (D.Nev.1974) reversed on other grounds 533 F.2d 486 (9th Cir.1976), cert. denied 429 U.S. 887, 97 S.Ct. 239, 50 L.Ed.2d 168 (1976).

Similarly, the selection of borrower's home state's law will be upheld. Kellogg v. Miller, 13 Fed. 198 (C.C.D.Nev.1881); Lanier v. Union Mortgage, Banking & Trust Co., 64 Ark. 39, 40 S.W. 466 (1897); Arnold v. Potter, 22 Iowa 194 (1867). An even stronger connection exists if the chosen domiciliary law is also that of the place where

the collateral is located. Consolidated Jewelers, Inc. v. Standard Financial Corp., 325 F.2d 31 (6th Cir.1963); Old Colony Trust Co. v. Penrose Industries Corp., 280 F.Supp. 698 (E.D.Pa.1968), aff'd 398 F.2d 310 (3d Cir.1968); Lanier v. Union Mortgage, Banking & Trust Co., 64 Ark. 39, 40 S.W. 466 (1897). The location of the collateral also justifies the selection of the law of the lender's home state. Consolidated Jewelers, Inc. v. Standard Financial Corp., 325 F.2d 31 (6th Cir.1963); Old Colony Trust Co. v. Penrose Industries Corp., 280 F.Supp. 698 (E.D.Pa.1968), aff'd 398 F.2d 310 (3d Cir.1968). See also U.C.C. § 2A–106; see generally supra § 18.5 n.4.

9. See, e.g. Brierley v. Commercial Credit Co., 43 F.2d 724 (D.C.Pa.1929), aff'd 43 F.2d 730 (3d Cir.1930), cert. denied 282 U.S. 897, 51 S.Ct. 182, 75 L.Ed. 790 (1931); United Divers Supply Co. v. Commercial Credit Co., 289 Fed. 316 (5th Cir.1923); Manufacturers Finance Co. v. B. L. Johnson & Co., 15 Tenn.App. 236 (1931); Stoddard v. Thomas, 60 Pa.Super. 177 (1915). However, some cases have found the a party's incorporation in a give state satisfied the "substantial relationship" or at least the "reasonable basis" requirement of Restatement Second § 187(2)(a). See Ciena Corp. v. Jarrard, 203 F.3d 312 (4th Cir.2000) (choice of Delaware law to govern validity of a non-competition clause upheld as having a sufficient connection to Delaware because plaintiff-employer's state of incorporation is Delaware); Nedlloyd Lines B.V. v. Superior Court, 3 Cal.4th 459, 11 Cal. Rptr.2d 330, 834 P.2d 1148 (1992); Hambrecht & Quist Venture Partners v. American Medical Int'l, Inc., 38 Cal.App.4th 1532, 46 Cal.Rptr.2d 33 (1995).

but which is not its principal place of business and has no other connection with the transaction.[10] When a corporation has its headquarters in one state, and branches or permanent agents in another, transactions between the latter and local residents of the second state have been treated as intrastate transactions not permitting a choice of law of another state such as that of the corporate headquarters.[11] By contrast, if the corporation does not maintain an office or an agent in the state which is the domicile of the other party, the parties will usually be able to stipulate the law of the corporation's principal place of business.[12] The case law does not articulate clearly the reasons underlying the various distinctions. The principal concern seems to be that, if a corporation could select the law of any state in which it maintains an office, a large corporation would then have an almost unlimited choice and render the requirement of a relationship to the transaction meaningless. But, as the movement towards liberalization of party autonomy continues it is likely that courts will validate choice based upon weaker connections.[13]

C. SECOND RESTATEMENT, § 187

§ 18.8 The Restatement Second restates the principle of party autonomy in § 187.[1] This important section "is followed by more Ameri-

10. See Duplan Corp. v. W.B. Davis Hosiery Mills, Inc. 442 F.Supp. 86 (S.D.N.Y. 1977); H.B. Fuller Co. v. Hagen, 363 F.Supp. 1325 (W.D.N.Y.1973); Joy v. Heidrick & Struggles, Inc., 93 Misc.2d 818, 403 N.Y.S.2d 613 (1977).

11. See New England Mut. Life Ins. Co. of Boston, Massachusetts v. Olin, 114 F.2d 131 (7th Cir.1940), cert. denied 312 U.S. 686, 61 S.Ct. 612, 85 L.Ed. 1123 (1941); Great Southern Life Ins. Co. v. Burwell, 12 F.2d 244 (5th Cir.1926), cert. denied 271 U.S. 683, 46 S.Ct. 633, 70 L.Ed. 1150 (1926); Albro v. Manhattan Life Ins. Co., 119 Fed. 629 (C.C.D.Mass.1902), aff'd 127 Fed. 281 (C.C.A.Mass.1904), cert. denied 194 U.S. 633, 24 S.Ct. 857, 48 L.Ed. 1159 (1904); Dolan v. Mutual Reserve Fund Life Ass'n, 173 Mass. 197, 53 N.E. 398 (1899); Locknane v. United States Savings and Loan Co., 103 Ky. 265, 44 S.W. 977 (1898).

12. See Tohato, Inc. v. Pinewild Management, Inc., 128 N.C.App. 386, 496 S.E.2d 800 (1998); Tschira v. Willingham, 135 F.3d 1077 (6th Cir.1998); Stromberg Metal Works, Inc. v. Press Mechanical, Inc., 77 F.3d 928 (7th Cir.1996); Albritton v. General Finance Corp., 204 F.2d 125 (5th Cir.1953); LaBeach v. Beatrice Foods Co., 461 F.Supp. 152 (S.D.N.Y.1978); Securities Investment Co. v. Finance Acceptance Corp., 474 S.W.2d 261 (Tex.Civ.App.1971), error refused n.r.e.; Ury v. Jewelers Acceptance Corp., 227 Cal.App.2d 11, 38 Cal. Rptr. 376 (1964); Big Four Mills Ltd. v.

Commercial Credit Co., Inc., 307 Ky. 612, 211 S.W.2d 831 (1948). See also Consolidated Jewelers, Inc. v. Standard Financial Corp., 325 F.2d 31 (6th Cir.1963); Dupree v. Virgil R. Coss Mortgage Co., 167 Ark. 18, 267 S.W. 586 (1924).

13. See, e.g., Nedlloyd Lines B.V. v. Superior Court, 3 Cal.4th 459, 11 Cal.Rptr.2d 330, 834 P.2d 1148 (1992).

§ 18.8

1. Restatement (Second), Conflict of Laws § 187 (1971) provides as follows:

(1) The law of the state chosen by the parties to govern their contractual rights and duties will be applied if the particular issue is one which the parties could have resolved by an explicit provision in their agreement directed to that issue.

(2) The law of the state chosen by the parties to govern their contractual rights and duties will be applied even if the particular issue is one which the parties could not have resolved by an explicit provision in their agreement directed to that issue, unless either

(a) the chosen state has no substantial relationship to the parties or the transaction and there is no other reasonable basis for the parties' choice, or

(b) application of the law of the chosen state would be contrary to a fundamen-

can courts than any other provision of the Restatement (Second), including some courts that otherwise follow the traditional theory."[2] In this sense, § 187 "appears to be a nearly universal principle in the United States."[3] For the most part, § 187 restated the previous case law discussed in the preceding sections, but it also departed from it in other respects noted below.

1. Connection with Chosen Law

§ 18.9 Subsection 1 of § 187 provides that, for issues that the parties "could have resolved by an explicit provision in their agreement,"[1] the parties' choice of law is not subject to any geographical or substantive limitations.[2]

Subsection 2 of § 187 provides that, for all other issues, the parties' choice of law will be honored if it meets the requirements specified in that provision. The first requirement is that the state of the chosen law must have a "substantial relationship to the parties of the transaction," as discussed earlier.[3] This requirement has not, as suggested,[4] resulted in a stricter test than the "reasonable" relationship test of the earlier

tal policy of a state which has a materially greater interest than the chosen state in the determination of the particular issue and which, under the rule of section 188, would be the state of the applicable law in the absence of an effective choice of law by the parties.

(3) In the absence of a contrary indication of intention, the reference is to the local law of the state of the chosen law.

2. S. Symeonides, W. Perdue & A. von Mehren, Conflict of Laws: American, Comparative, International 338 (2d ed. 2003).

3. Borchers, Choice of Law in American Courts in 1992: Observations and Reflections, 42 Am. J. Comp. L. 125, 136 (1994).

§ 18.9

1. Restatement (Second), Conflict of Laws § 187(2) (1971). Comment c states that "[w]hether the parties could have determined an issue by explicit agreement ... is to be determined by the local law of the state selected by application of the rule of § 188," namely the state whose law would govern in the absence of a choice-of-law clause. For a case following this comment, see Armstrong Business Services, Inc. v. H & R Block, 96 S.W.3d 867 (Mo.App. 2002). For a case applying the law of the forum *qua* forum, see Swanson v. Image Bank, Inc., 202 Ariz. 226, 43 P.3d 174 (2002), reversed on other grounds by case discussed in next note.

2. See supra § 18.3 discussing issues of interpretation and construction. For a recent case involving § 187(1), see Swanson v. Image Bank, Inc., 206 Ariz. 264, 77 P.3d

439 (2003). The issue in *Swanson* was whether the parties could waive the application of an Arizona statute that imposed treble damages on an employer who wrongfully withholds an employee's wages. The employee was an executive domiciled in Arizona, who entered into an employment contract with a Texas-based employer. The contract did not address the above issue, but it contained a Texas choice-of-law clause, and Texas law did not impose treble damages. The intermediate court found that, under Arizona law, the parties could not waive in advance an employee's right to treble damages, and thus whether they could do so through a choice of another state's law depended on whether the clause was enforceable under subsection 2 of Second Restatement § 187. Employing that subsection, the court held that, to the extent the clause amounted to an indirect waiver of the employee's rights, the clause was unenforceable as violative of a fundamental policy of Arizona. The Arizona Supreme Court reversed. Noting that the Arizona statute did not contain any language precluding an employee from waiving the right to treble damages and did not make the award of such damages mandatory for courts, the court concluded that this issue was one that the parties could resolve by agreement, either directly or indirectly through the choice of another state's law. Thus, the choice-of-law clause fell within the scope of § 187(1) and it should be upheld without subjecting it to the scrutiny of § 187(2).

3. See supra §§ 18.6, 18.7.

4. Weinberger, Party Autonomy and Choice-of-Law: The Restatement (Second),

cases.[5] The criticism, advanced in the context of the section, that the test amounts to mere contact-counting and should be replaced by a functional analysis of the conflicting laws and interests of the involved states,[6] in reality goes to the heart of party autonomy in general rather than to § 187: the simplicity and convenience of party autonomy—usually sustaining the validity of a contract provision—would be lost if the courts had to undertake a functional analysis of statutory purposes and state interests in every case. In the context of the Second Restatement, more specifically, party autonomy is an alternative choice-of-law method to a functional approach, such as that provided by Section 188, discussed later in this Chapter.[7]

Departing from previous case law, § 187(2) also permits the choice of an unrelated law if the parties have a "reasonable basis" for their choice.[8] The parties' interest in selecting an unrelated law may be that the chosen law is particularly well developed[9] or that they have greater familiarity with the chosen law,[10] or for other reasons.[11] This alternative test has received mixed support in the case law thus far.[12] The new

Interest Analysis, and the Search for Methodological Synthesis, 4 Hofstra L. Rev. 605, 615–16 (1976); Gruson, Governing Law Clauses in Commercial Agreements–New York's Approach, 18 Colum. J. Transnat'l L. 323 (1980) (with extensive review of the case law).

5. Gamer v. duPont Glore Forgan, Inc., 65 Cal.App.3d 280, 290, 135 Cal.Rptr. 230 (1976); Reger v. National Ass'n of Bedding Manufacturers Group Ins. Trust Fund, 83 Misc.2d 527, 539–40, 372 N.Y.S.2d 97 (1975).

6. Weinberger, supra n.2, at 612–13, 626.

7. A revision of comment (i) to § 187 of the Restatement, Second, Conflict of Laws (1986 Revisions) now makes it clear that the parties may elect to have different laws govern different issues of their contract. For an application see Kronovet v. Lipchin, 288 Md. 30, 415 A.2d 1096 (1980).

8. It is interesting to note that the test of a "reasonable basis" serves to broaden the scope of party autonomy in American law, while this and other tests now emerge in Europe to restrict the parties in their choice which, for instance in Germany, had heretofore been considered to be unlimited. See supra § 18.2 n.4.

9. In Radioactive, J.V. v. Manson, 153 F.Supp.2d 462 (S.D.N.Y. 2001), a case involving a music recording contract, the court noted that the chosen state of New York had sufficient contacts with the contract, and that, even in the absence of such

contacts, the choice of New York law would have been reasonable in light of the fact that New York courts "have significant experience with music industry contracts." Id. at 471.

10. Restatement, Second, Conflict of Laws § 187, cmnt. (f) (1971).

11. In Prows v. Pinpoint Retail Systems, Inc., 868 P.2d 809 (Utah, 1993), the court acknowledged that, although the chosen state of New York had no contacts with the contract or the parties, the contractual choice of New York law could be upheld under the other "reasonable basis" proviso of § 187(2)(a). The reasonable basis was enabling one of the parties, a Canadian corporation doing business in several American states, to rely on the law of a single American state and to plan accordingly. However, the court held that that proviso does not apply "when all the contacts are located in a single state and when as a consequence, there is only one interested state." Id. at 811. (quoting from Restatement Second § 187 cmt. d.). After listing Utah's numerous contacts, the court concluded that "Utah is the only state with an interest in the action," id., and that New York had no interest. From there, the court concluded that it was "not bound by New York law." Id.

12. No support: WOCO v. Benjamin Franklin Corp., 20 UCC Rep.Serv. 1015 (D.N.H.1976), aff'd 562 F.2d 1339 (1st Cir. 1977); American Freehold Land & Mortgage Co. v. Jefferson, 69 Miss., 770, 12 So. 464 (1892). But see Wyatt v. Fulrath, 16

Revision of the Uniform Commercial Code, which, as noted earlier,[13] no longer requires a connection with the chosen law in non-consumer contracts, has rendered even more innocuous the Restatement's requirement for a "reasonable basis."

2. Public Policy Limitation

§ 18.10 The most important limitation to party autonomy under the Restatement is the public policy limitation stated in § 187(2)(b). However, as noted earlier:[1] (1) the state whose public policy may defeat the parties' choice of law is not the state forum state *qua* forum, but rather the state whose law would, under § 188, govern the particular issue if the parties had not made an effective choice (*lex causae*); (2) the state of the *lex causae* must have a "materially greater" interest in the application of its law than the chosen state; and (3) only a "fundamental" policy of the *lex causae* may defeat the parties' choice.[2] Additionally, comment (g) states that, the more contacts the transaction has with the chosen state, the stronger the public policy of the state of the *lex causae* must be to overcome the stipulation. Conversely, a "weaker" policy of the *lex causae* state may overcome the stipulation in the face of fewer contacts with the chosen state. It is in this context that the criticism of contact-counting[3] has some merit. Recognition of the Second Restatement terminology which would require the contacts to be "significant," rather than numerous, would alleviate this problem.

3. Validation

§ 18.11 The policy of giving effect to the parties' intent to have a binding contract and the general policy of contract validation come into conflict when the law that the parties have chosen would invalidate the *whole* contract. In such a case, the civil law approach is to give effect to the choice and, if this be the result, invalidate the contract.[1] The

N.Y.2d 169, 264 N.Y.S.2d 233, 211 N.E.2d 637 (1965); M/S Bremen v. Zapata Off-Shore Co., 407 U.S. 1, 92 S.Ct. 1907, 32 L.Ed.2d 513 (1972) (choice of neutral forum and resulting choice of neutral law adequate basis for upholding clause).

While the courts will generally sustain a contract against the charge of usury if the contract is valid under the chosen law of a connected state (supra § 18.5, nn.9–12), the parties will not be permitted to gain an additional advantage by stipulating an *unrelated* law. Restatement, Second, Conflict of Laws § 203, comment (e) (1971). The "reasonable basis" for the choice must therefore relate to the kinds of concerns mentioned in the text. This will often be the case in shipping contracts. See supra n.2 and *The Bremen*.

13. See supra § 18.2 n.7.

§ 18.10

1. See supra § 18.4

2. For cases following § 187(2), see, e.g., DeSantis v. Wackenhut Corp., 793 S.W.2d 670, cert. denied, 498 U.S. 1048, 111 S.Ct. 755, 112 L.Ed.2d 775 (1991); Nedlloyd Lines B.V. v. Superior Court, 3 Cal.4th 459, 11 Cal.Rptr.2d 330, 834 P.2d 1148 (1992); cases cited supra § 18.4 n.7.

3. Weinberger, Party Autonomy and Choice-of-Law: The Restatement (Second), Interest Analysis, and the Search for Methodological Synthesis, 4 Hofstra L.Rev. 605, 631 (1976).

§ 18.11

1. For France, see Cass. in 1967 Revue critique de droit international privé 334; for Germany, BGH in 1969 Neue Juristische Wochenschrift 1760, 1761; OLG München

rationale is that "grounds for invalidity often protect one of the parties and he, who chooses a law, chooses its protection."[2] Invalidity of the contract effectuates the parties' choice and serves to uphold party autonomy. However, assuming that the parties bargained deliberately and in good faith, this result hardly comports with their intention to create a contract and their expectation that it will be valid. For this reason, the Second Restatement suggests that the choice of an invalidating law be treated as a mutual mistake and therefore disregarded.[3] The usual choice-of-law rules, for instance § 188, then determine the applicable law. However, a number of American decisions have taken the opposite position and have invalidated the contract.[4]

When the law chosen by the parties invalidates *only a part* of the contract, the parties' expectations of having a binding contract are satisfied. Consequently, in the absence of special circumstances, there is little reason to allow one party to pick the favorable and discard the unfavorable provisions of the chosen law. The Second Restatement does not support this type of private eclecticism, and most cases have expressly rejected it.[5]

D.   SECTION 1–105 OF THE UNIFORM COMMERCIAL CODE

§ 18.12   *The Present Law.* Section 1–105(1) of the Uniform Commercial Code (U.C.C.) provides that " ... when a transaction bears a reasonable relationship to this state and also to another state or nation the parties may agree that the law of either this state or of such other state or nation shall govern their rights and duties...."[1] There is a split

---

in 1990 Praxis des Internationalen Privat- und Verfahrensrechts 320.

2. Kegel & Schurig, Internationales Privatrecht 657 (9th ed. 2004).

3. Restatement, Second, Conflict of Laws § 187, cmnt. (e) and Reporter's Note (1971).

4. See Moyer v. Citicorp Homeowners, Inc., 799 F.2d 1445 (11th Cir.1986); George Foreman Associates, Ltd. v. Foreman, 389 F.Supp. 1308, 1311, 1314 (N.D.Cal.1974), aff'd 517 F.2d 354, 356 (9th Cir.1975); Pisacane v. Italia Societa Per Azioni Di Navigazione, 219 F.Supp. 424 (S.D.N.Y.1963); Fairfield Lease Corp. v. Pratt, 6 Conn.Cir. 537, 278 A.2d 154 (1971); General Electric Credit Corp. v. Beyerlein, 55 Misc.2d 724, 286 N.Y.S.2d 351 (1967), aff'd 30 A.D.2d 762, 292 N.Y.S.2d 32 (1968). Cf. S.E.C. v. Elmas Trading Corp., 683 F.Supp. 743 (D.Nev.1987), aff'd without op., 865 F.2d 265 (9th Cir.1988). But see Mamlin v. Susan Thomas, Inc. 490 S.W.2d 634 (Tex.Civ. App.1973); Crawford v. Seattle, Renton & Southern Railway Co., 86 Wash. 628, 150 P. 1155 (1915).

5. See, e.g., Boatland, Inc. v. Brunswick Corp., 558 F.2d 818 (6th Cir.1977) (invalidating under the chosen law a clause dealing with the termination of a dealership agreement); Hardy v. Monsanto Enviro–Chem Systems, Inc., 414 Mich. 29, 323 N.W.2d 270 (1982) (applying the chosen law to invalidate an indemnity clause); Stoot v. Fluor Drilling Services, Inc., 851 F.2d 1514 (5th Cir.1988) (accord); General Elec. Credit Corp. v. Beyerlein, 55 Misc.2d 724, 286 N.Y.S.2d 351 (1967), aff'd, 30 A.D.2d 762, 292 N.Y.S.2d 32 (1968) (applying the chosen law to invalidate a clause that cut off defenses against an assignee). But see Kipin Indus. v. Van Deilen Int'l, Inc., 182 F.3d 490 (6th Cir.1999) (disregarding the chosen law "to the extent" it invalidated a part of the contract).

§ 18.12

1. In United Counties Trust Co. v. Mac Lum, Inc., 643 F.2d 1140 (5th Cir.1981), rehearing denied 647 F.2d 1123 (5th Cir. 1981) the choice of New York law in a sale-leaseback agreement was ineffective under

of authority and opinion concerning the question whether the section adopts and restates the common law[2] or whether it modifies and departs from it,[3] except for purposes of gap-filling. The division of opinion results from a number of interpretative problems presented by the provision.

A literal reading of the section would require that, to be effective, a choice-of-law clause bear a reasonable relationship *both* to the chosen state *and* to the forum. As a result, party autonomy would be precluded if the forum is a disinterested state.[4] Alternatively, this apparent gap can be attributed to inartful draftsmanship[5] and disregarded. Supporting this view is the fact that the U.C.C. purports to cover all cases within its subject matter; no purpose, apart from *jurisdictional* notions of forum non conveniens, would be served by requiring the forum to have a reasonable relationship to the contract. In addition, the section clearly endorses party autonomy, a policy that would be frustrated if a choice-of-

U.C.C. § 1–105 when the agreement and the parties had no relation to New York. The law of the Georgia forum also was not applicable under U.C.C. § 1–105 for lack of an "appropriate relation" when the parties where incorporated in Kentucky and New Jersey, respectively, the agreement was negotiated and executed at their home offices, and when the only contact with Georgia was the location of the restaurant that was the subject of the agreement. The situs rule of U.C.C. § 9–102 also did not apply because the agreement was not a secured transaction. In cases in which the U.C.C. specifies the applicable law, a choice of a contrary law is effective only to the extent permitted by that law, including its conflicts law. U.C.C. § 1–105(2). The affected sections are: 2–402, 4–102, 6–102, 8–106, 9–103. U.C.C. § 2A–106 now limits choice of law clauses in consumer leases. In contrast, no limit applies to wholesale wire fund transfers: U.C.C. § 4A–507(b). See also Art. 7 of the Hague Convention on the Law Applicable to Contracts for the International Sale of Goods, infra § 18.25 n.13.

With respect to the "reasonable relationship" requirement, see also Siemens Medical Systems, Inc. v. Nuclear Cardiology Systems, Inc., 945 F.Supp. 1421 (D.Colo.1996); Carefree Vacations, Inc. v. Brunner, 615 F.Supp. 211 (W.D.Tenn.1985); Lectric's & Inc. v. Power Controls, Inc., 1995 WL 809558 (Mass.Super.1995); Arcata Graphics Co. v. Heidelberg Harris, Inc., 874 S.W.2d 15 (Tenn.Ct.App.1993). See generally Note, We're all in the Same Boat: Carnival Cruise Lines, Inc. v. Shute, 18 Brook.J.Int'l.L. 597 (1992); Viva Zapata: Toward a Rational System of Forum Selection Clause Enforcement in Diversity Cases, 66 N.Y.U.L.Rev. 422 (1991); Federal Arbitration Right, Choice-of-Law Clauses and State Rules and Procedure, 22 Sw.U.L.Rev. 159 (1992);

Grossman, Choice of Law in Interstate Livestock Sales: Nonuniform Warranty Provisions Under the U.C.C., 30 S.D. L. Rev. 214, 234–67 (1985).

2. Jett Racing & Sales, Inc. v. Transamerica Commercial Finance Corp., 892 F.Supp. 161 (1995); Mell v. Goodbody & Co., 10 Ill.App.3d 809, 295 N.E.2d 97, 99 (1973); Reporters' comments accompanying Ill.S.H.A. ch. 26, ¶ 1–105; Minn. Stat. Ann., § 336.1–105; S.C. Code 1976, § 361–105; West's Rev. Code Wash. Ann. 62A. 1–105; 1 Gilmore, Secured Interests in Personal Property § 10.8 at p. 316 (1965).

3. Reporters' comments to Cal. Commercial Code § 1105; Fla. Stat. Ann. § 671.1–105; Kansas Stat. Ann. § 84–1–105; N.Y. McKinney's Consol. Laws Book 62½, Part 1, § 1–105, annot. at p. 18; Wis. Stat. Ann. § 401.105. See Nordstrom, Choice of Law and the U.C.C., 24 Ohio St. L.J. 364, 370–72 (1963).

4. Prebble, Choice of Law to Determine the Validity and Effect of Contracts, 56 Cornell L. Rev. 433, 523–36 (1973); Tuchler, Boundaries to Party Autonomy in the Uniform Commercial Code: A Radical View, 11 St. Louis L.J. 180, 190–96 (1967). Prebble considers this to be a gap in the provision, to be filled by the common law.

Section 1–105(1) provides further that "failing such agreement [by the parties] this Act applies to transactions bearing an appropriate relation to this state." The Section leaves open what law applies in circumstances when the parties have not designated the applicable law and the transaction does *not* bear an "appropriate relation" to the forum. See also supra n.1.

5. Nordstrom & Ramerman, The Uniform Commercial Code and Choice of Law, 1969 Duke L.J. 623, 629.

law clause were to fail in circumstances when the forum is both disinterested and lacks a common law rule of party autonomy.[6]

Unlike the common law and the Second Restatement, U.C.C. § 1–105 does not expressly distinguish between stipulations of law for the purpose of interpretation and construction of the contract and those for the determination of the contract's validity. Again, if read literally, § 1–105 would restrict the parties to the selection of a reasonably related law for both purposes. The cases are divided.[7] However, since the parties are always free to incorporate expressly rules of interpretation from unconnected jurisdictions or of their own making, it seems pointless to prevent them from stipulating to such a jurisdiction for purposes of an incorporation by reference. The official comments to the U.C.C. are in accord with this conclusion.[8]

Section 1–105 also lacks a specific reference to a public policy limitation on party autonomy. While the widespread adoption of the U.C.C. will make most stipulations of the applicable law unnecessary or irrelevant in the U.S.,[9] differences with respect to policy still do occasionally arise,[10] especially also because interpretations of code provisions vary among the states. In addition, and despite the adoption of the Convention on the Recognition and Enforcement of Foreign Arbitral Awards whose relevant provision is patterned after § 1–105,[11] strong policy differences will continue to play an important role in international commercial transactions. However, because in the U.S. public policy exceptions are rare, the role is not a dominant one. However, application is infrequent.

At least one court has read the traditional public policy limitation into § 1–105.[12] The general code policies of good faith, commercial reasonableness and fairness in the Code's Article 1,[13]

6. Id.

7. Fuller Co. v. Compagnie Des Bauxites De Guinee, 421 F.Supp. 938 (W.D.Pa.1976) (requiring reasonable relationship for interpretation and construction) supporting *Fuller*: Nova Ribbon Products, Inc. v. Lincoln Ribbon, Inc., 1992 WL 392614 (E.D.Pa.); I.S. Joseph Co., Inc. v. Toufic Aris & Fils, 54 A.D.2d 665, 388 N.Y.S.2d 1 (1976) (not requiring connection); Falcon Tankers, Inc. v. Litton Systems, Inc., 300 A.2d 231 (Del.Super.1972) (not requiring connection).

8. "But an agreement as to choice of law may sometimes take effect as a shorthand expression of the intent of the parties as to matters governed by their agreement, even though the transaction has no significant contact with the jurisdiction chosen." U.C.C. Official Code comment 1.

9. E.g., Baker v. Gotz, 387 F.Supp. 1381, 1387 (D.Del.1975), aff'd 523 F.2d 1050 (3d Cir.1975); American Air Filter Co.,

Inc. v. McNichol, 361 F.Supp. 908, 911 (E.D.Pa.1973).

10. See Boudreau v. Baughman, 322 N.C. 331, 368 S.E.2d 849 (1988); Delhomme Industries, Inc. v. Houston Beechcraft, Inc., 669 F.2d 1049 (5th Cir.1982); Jones & McKnight Corp. v. Birdsboro Corp., 320 F.Supp. 39, 8 U.C.C. Rep.Serv. 307, 311 n.3 (N.D.Ill.1970); United States Leasing Corp. v. Keiler, 290 So.2d 427, 431 (La.App.1974); Mell v. Goodbody & Co., 10 Ill.App.3d 809, 295 N.E.2d 97, 100 (1973); Fairfield Lease Corp. v. Pratt, 6 Conn.Cir. 537, 278 A.2d 154 (1971).

11. Enacted July 31, 1970, 9 U.S.C.A. §§ 201–208; Testimony of Ambassador Richard D. Kearney that § 1–105 was used to draft this statute, as *quoted in* Fuller Co. v. Compagnie Des Bauxites De Guinee, 421 F.Supp. 938, 941 (W.D.Pa.1976).

12. Mell v. Goodbody & Co., 10 Ill. App.3d 809, 295 N.E.2d 97, 100 (1973).

13. Tuchler, supra n.4, at 195.

as well as the unconscionability provision of § 2–302(1), lend support to this result.[14]

Despite the interpretative difficulties reviewed above, § 1–105 has in practice turned out to be similar in scope to party autonomy at common law and under the Second Restatement. Several recent decisions have therefore intermingled § 1–105 and older common law cases[15] or equated § 1–105 with § 187 of the Second Restatement.[16]

The Proposed Law. In 2001, the National Council of Commissioners on Uniform State Laws and the American Law Institute adopted a proposed revised version of Article 1 of the U.C.C.[17] In this version, Section 1–105 is replaced by proposed Section 1–301. Like its predecessor, the new version applies only to contracts that are otherwise within the scope of the U.C.C., but, unlike its predecessor, it differentiates between contracts involving a consumer and other contracts ("business to business" transactions). The new version restricts party autonomy with regard to the former contracts and expands it with regard to the latter contracts.

For consumer contracts, Section 1–301 provides that the choice of law is not effective unless the chosen law bears a "reasonable relation"[18] to the transaction. Moreover, in a fashion similar to the Rome Convention, the section provides that, even when such a relation exists, the application of the chosen law may not deprive the consumer of the protection of those rules of law that are both "protective of consumers and may not be varied by agreement"[19] ("mandatory rules") of the state in which the consumer principally resides,[20] or, in certain sales contracts, the state of delivery.[21]

---

14. Fairfield Lease Corp. v. Pratt, 6 Conn.Cir. 537, 278 A.2d 154 (1971); R. Weintraub, Commentary on the Conflict of Law, 457 (4th ed. 2001); Prebble, supra n.4, at 534–35.

15. E.g., Marine Midland Bank v. United Missouri Bank, 223 A.D.2d 119, 643 N.Y.S.2d 528 (1996); Trilogy Development Group, Inc. v. Teknowledge Corp., 1996 WL 527325 (Del.Super.1996); I.S. Joseph Co., Inc. v. Toufic Aris & Fils, 54 A.D.2d 665, 388 N.Y.S.2d 1 (1976); Mell v. Goodbody & Co., 10 Ill.App.3d 809, 295 N.E.2d 97, 100 (1973).

16. Marine Midland Bank v. United Missouri Bank, 223 A.D.2d 119, 643 N.Y.S.2d 528 (1996); Greenray Industries, Inc. v. Charleswater Products, Inc., 1990 WL 26887 (D.Mass.); Gamer v. duPont Glore Forgan, Inc., 65 Cal.App.3d 280, 135 Cal.Rptr. 230 (1976); Reger v. National Ass'n of Bedding Manufacturers Group Ins. Trust Fund, 83 Misc.2d 527, 372 N.Y.S.2d 97 (1975); Morris v. Watsco, 385 Mass. 672, 433 N.E.2d 886 (1982); Prebble, supra n.4, at 533; Price v. ITT Corp., 651 F.Supp. 706 (S.D.Miss.1986); In re Merritt Dredging Co., Inc., 839 F.2d 203, 206–07 (4th Cir.

1988), cert. denied 487 U.S. 1236, 108 S.Ct. 2904, 101 L.Ed.2d 936 (1988).

17. As of the time of this writing (April 2004), the new version has not been adopted in any state.

18. U.C.C. § 1–301(e)(1) (2001 Revision).

19. U.C.C. § 1–301(e)(2) (2001 Revision). The concept of "mandatory rules" is discussed supra § 18.4.

20. U.C.C. § 1–301(e)(2)(A) (2001 Revision).

21. U.C.C. § 1–301(e)(2)(B) (2001 Revision) provides that, if the transaction is a sale of goods and the consumer both made the contract and took delivery of the goods in a state other than that of her principal residence, then the protection described in the text encompasses only the mandatory rules of the former state (i.e. not the residence state). This provision, which is influenced in part by Article 5 of the Rome Convention, "enables a seller of goods engaging in face-to-face transactions to ascertain the consumer protection rules to which those sales are subject, without the necessi-

In contracts not involving a consumer, Section 1–301 allows the parties to choose the applicable law (for matters of both construction and validity), even if the choice is that of a state that bears no relation to the transaction.[22] The only requirement is that, if the transaction does not bear a reasonable relation with a country other than the United States ("domestic" transaction), the chosen law must be that of a State of the United States.[23]

The proposed section also contains a general public policy reservation, which, however, does not apply to consumer contracts, apparently on the assumption that consumers are adequately protected through the mandatory rules described above.[24] As in the Second Restatement, the public policy reservation becomes operative only if the application of the chosen law conflicts with a "fundamental" policy of the state whose law would govern in the absence of a valid choice-of-law agreement.[25] The latter state is determined through the choice-of-law rules of the forum state.[26]

Finally, in the absence of an effective choice-of-law agreement, in both consumer and non-consumer contracts, the applicable law is the law selected through the choice-of-law rules of the forum state.[27] This is a welcome departure from Section 1–105(1), which authorized the forum to apply its own substantive law if the transaction bore "an appropriate relation" to the forum state.

II. CHOICE OF LAW IN THE ABSENCE OF CHOICE-OF–LAW AGREEMENT

§ 18.13   Choice of law in contract, in the absence of a valid stipulation of the applicable law by the parties, is even more difficult than in tort. The fact that the parties have deliberately struck a bargain gives rise to far greater expectations than in tort where "expectations" are at most on the level of not being unfairly surprised by the application of a particular law. The protection of party expectations in contract requires a high degree of predictability as to the applicable law. In recognition of these concerns, the older law, ultimately embodied in the First Restatement, had developed a few simple and straightforward rules. "These rules did not work well in practice. Primarily, this was

ty of determining the principal residence of each buyer." Id. cmnt. 3.

22. U.C.C. § 1–301(c) (2001 Revision).

23. See U.C.C. § 1–301(a) (distinguishing between "domestic" and "international" transactions) and § 1–301(c)(1) and (2) (2001 Revision). For international transactions, there is no limitation, and under § 1–302, the parties may even choose anational rules, such as those promulgated by intergovernmental organizations like UNCITRAL or Unidroit. See, § 1–301 cmnt. 2, § 1–302 cmnt. 2 (2001 Revision).

24. For the relation between "mandatory rules" and rules of public policy, see supra § 18.4.

25. U.C.C. § 1–301(f) (2001 Revision).

26. U.C.C. § 1–301(d), (f) (2001 Revision).

27. U.C.C. § 1–301(d) (2001 Revision). However, the application of the law thus chosen by the court may not deprive the consumer of the protection of the mandatory rules of the consumer's home state or of the state of sale and delivery as described supra. See id. cmnt. 3.

because they did not take proper account of the objectives of choice of law and of the policies of the local law rules involved. This may also have been because of the broad scope of their mechanical application."[1]

Contractual relationships arise in a great variety of settings, from the sale of goods, to employment contracts, to insurance. They may be single contracts, standard form contracts, they may have particular effects on third parties. The after-effects of contractual relationships may involve problems of unjust enrichment and restitution. Rules of broad application cannot do justice to the various interests and expectations involved. The Second Restatement therefore suggests an "approach," supplemented by a number of specific rules for particular contracts.

The "approach" of § 188 has its own uncertainties because it also claims wide applicability and provides little guidance as to the relative weight of the criteria suggested which would aid in the development of concrete rules which, in turn, are necessary in order to achieve the goal of predictability. Indeed, the parallelism between the "approach" of § 188 with respect to contract and of § 145 (torts)[2] may give insufficient attention to the different concerns with respect to choice-of-law in contract where party interests and expectations, as well as predictability of result, are foremost factors.[3]

The following first reviews the classic approach to choice of law in this area and then turns to the modern approaches. Other sections review contracts by subject matter and summarize the current state of the case law with respect to each of them. A concluding part takes a comparative view and suggests further alternatives. A separate part addresses problems of unjust enrichment.

A. THE CLASSIC APPROACH

§ 18.14 The classical approach to contractual conflicts remains important because several states still follow it[1] and for understanding subsequent developments. *Milliken v. Pratt*[2] adopted the law of the place

---

§ 18.13

1. Reese, Choice of Law in Torts and Contracts and Directions for the Future, 16 Colum. J. Transnat'l L. 1, 40 (1977). See generally Reese, American Choice of Law, 30 Am. J. Comp. L. 135 (1982); Blom, Choice of Law Methods in the Private International Law of Contract, 17 Can. Yb. Int'l L. 206 (1979) and 18 Can. Yb. Int'l L. 161 (1980).

2. Prebble, Choice of Law to Determine the Validity and Effects of Contracts: A Comparison of English and American Approaches to the Conflict of Laws, 58 Cornell L. Rev. 433, 456 (1973).

3. See also infra § 18.22 n.3.

§ 18.14

1. According to Symeonides, The American Choice-of-Law Revolution in the Courts: Today and Tomorrow, 298 Recueil des Cours 1, 75–77, 83–88 (2003), eleven states have yet to abandon the traditional approach in contract conflicts. These states are Alabama, Florida, Georgia, Kansas, Maryland, New Mexico, Rhode Island, South Carolina, Tennessee, Virginia, and Wyoming. However, as the author documents, only the first three states as well as Georgia have recently and clearly reaffirmed their commitment to that approach. For citations, see infra § 18.21 nn. 3–13.

2. 125 Mass. 374 (1878).

of contracting in order to uphold the validity of a married woman's contract that would have been invalid, for lack of capacity, under the law of her domicile. The court noted that "it is more just, as well as more convenient, to have regard to the law of the place of the contract ... than to require ... [the contracting parties] at their peril to know the domicil of those with whom they deal, and to ascertain the law of that domicil, however remote...."[3] The U.S. Supreme Court[4] applied a different reference—to the law of the place of performance—in *Pritchard v. Norton*.[5] However, it apparently did so for the underlying purpose of validating the contract, thereby protecting the expectations of the parties. Defendants had executed an indemnity bond in New York in favor of plaintiff's decedent who had become a surety on an appeal bond in Louisiana. Under New York law, applied by the circuit court, the indemnity agreement was unenforceable for lack of consideration. Under Louisiana law the indemnity contract would have been enforceable without present consideration. Instead of simply applying the law of the place of contracting, the court considered it more important to follow "the principle that in every forum a contract is governed by the law with a view to which it is made."[6] The Court therefore chose Louisiana law and upheld the contract. The quoted passages show the Court's concern with protecting the expectations of the parties by the use of a validating choice-of-law approach.

The territorial orientation of the First Restatement resulted in the adoption of the reference to the law of the place of contracting[7] on the assumption that this is the place where the rights of the parties "vest." The intention of the parties, whether expressed in a choice-of-law clause or inferred from their conduct or from the purpose of the contract, as in *Pritchard v. Norton*, plays no role: to allow parties to stipulate the applicable law would grant them legislative powers;[8] to "make the law of the place of performance govern the act of contracting is an attempt to give that law extraterritorial effect."[9] Section 333 of the First Restatement therefore endorsed the result of *Milliken v. Pratt*: "The law of the place of contracting determines the capacity to enter into a contract."

---

3. Id. at 382. Interesting additional and perhaps controlling factors were that Mrs. Pratt had executed the guaranty for her husband's debts in the state of her domicile, Massachusetts, and that the decision was rendered there. The Massachusetts court nevertheless treated the transaction as a Maine contract because it was in the latter state that the plaintiff acted on the guaranty by shipping goods to her husband and extending him credit (acceptance of an offer for a unilateral contract). The result, furthermore, did not offend Massachusetts public policy because in the meantime Massachusetts law had been changed to remove the incapacity of married women.

4. The decision preceded the adoption of the *Erie/Klaxon* doctrine (supra § 3.36 et seq.) according to which a federal court sitting in diversity must apply the substantive and conflicts law of the state in which it sits.

5. 106 U.S. 124, 1 S.Ct. 102, 27 L.Ed. 104 (1882).

6. 106 U.S. at 136, 1 S.Ct. at 112.

7. Restatement, First, Conflict of Laws § 332 (1934).

8. 2 J. Beale, A Treatise on the Conflict of Laws § 332.2 (1935).

9. Beale, What Law Governs the Validity of a Contract?, 23 Harv. L. Rev. 260, 267 (1909); Beale, supra n.8, § 332.3.

While the First Restatement referred to the place of contracting for questions of validity, it provided that questions concerning performance, including breach of excuse for non-performance, be governed by the place of performance.[10] However, comment (b) to § 358 provided that the law of the place of performance "is not applicable to the point where the substantial obligation of the parties is materially altered."[11] In practice, the supposed advantage of the place-of-contract rule,[12] itself the subject of severe criticism,[13] is therefore greatly impaired: " ... in application the boundaries of this doctrine are not easy to find."[14] Moreover, " ... any contract question can be related, on one or another sense, to the subject of performance"[15] and special problems arise in the case of the modern commercial contract with several places of performance.

§ 18.15   The early decision in *Emery v. Burbank*[1] accepted that, in principle,[2] the reference is to the law of contracting but recognized the need for exceptions. The case involved an oral promise, given in Maine, by a Massachusetts decedent to bequeath her entire estate to the Maine plaintiff if the latter would come to Massachusetts and care for her. The promise was unenforceable under the Massachusetts Statute of Frauds. A reference to the place of performance (rejected by the court because of its acceptance of the general principle of the law of contracting) or a procedural characterization of the Massachusetts Statute of Frauds would have led to the application of Massachusetts law. A procedural characterization, however, would not protect the property of Massachusetts residents situated in Maine, and a substantive characterization

---

10. For an application see Louis–Dreyfus v. Paterson Steamships, 43 F.2d 824 (2d Cir.1930); Texas Commerce Bank Nat. Ass'n v. Interpol '80 Ltd., Partnership, 703 S.W.2d 765 (Tex.App.1985). The distinction can be traced to Bartolus and his commentary on the Corpus Juris: Stein, Bartolus, the Conflict of Laws and the Roman Law, in: Multum non multa—Festschrift für Kurt Lipstein 251, 256 (P. Feuerstein & C. Parry eds. 1980).

11. Similarly Restatement, Conflict of Laws § 332 (1934).

12. See J. Beale, supra n.8, §§ 332.3–332.4.

13. " ... [M]echanistic type of thinking ... ": Hancock, Three Approaches to the Choice of Law Problem: The Classificatory, the Functional, and the Result–Selective, in: XXth Century Comparative and Conflicts Law, Legal Essays in Honor of Hessel E. Yntema 365, 366 (1961). See also Shapira, "Grasp all, Lose all": On Restraint and Moderation in the Reformulation of Choice of Law Policy, 77 Colum. L. Rev. 248, 250 (1977).

The rigidity of the First Restatement's approach was heightened by the fact that the "place of contracting" was determined on the basis of the substantive rules of contract law of the forum. See Restatement, Conflict of Laws § 311 et seq. (1934). The reason for applying the law of contracting, viz. that a binding obligation was vested there, is thus circular since the localization of that place results from a prior choice of law: see Cook, "Contracts" and the Conflict of Laws, 31 Ill. L. Rev. 143, 158–163 (1936). Cook, furthermore, showed that the vested rights theory does not necessarily protect foreign law-created rights unless the conflicts rules of the foreign forum were considered as well. Section 7(b) of the First Restatement, however, rejected the renvoi. Therefore " ... the right ... enforced by the forum ... would necessarily be a 'home-created' and not a 'foreign-created' right." Cook, The Logical and Legal Bases of the Conflict of Laws, 33 Yale L.J. 457, 469 (1924).

14. Louis–Dreyfus v. Paterson Steamships, 43 F.2d 824, 826 (2d Cir.1930).

15. Nussbaum, Conflict Theories of Contracts: Cases versus Restatement, 51 Yale L.J. 893, 918 (1942).

§ 18.15

1. 163 Mass. 326, 39 N.E. 1026 (1895).

2. Id. at 327, 39 N.E. at 1026.

would not have drawn in a contract made in Maine. In a decision that foreshadowed more modern policy analyses, Justice Holmes found that the local Statute of Frauds embodied " ... a fundamental policy.... If the policy of Massachusetts makes void an oral contract of this sort made within the State, the same policy forbids that Massachusetts testators should be sued here upon such contracts without written evidence, *wherever they are made.*"[3] The desired result thus already stated, a rule in keeping with accepted principles had to be formulated: "In our view, the statute whatever it expresses, implies a rule for procedure broad enough to cover this case. It is not necessary to decide exactly how broad the rule may be.... The rule extends, at least, to contracts by Massachusetts testators."[4]

The three "classic" decisions, including the notion of validation which was an important consideration in *Pritchard v. Norton,* summarize well the *rules* available for choice of law in contract as well as the exceptions (*Emery v. Burbank*) that local policy concerns may dictate. They reappear, as elements, in all of the more modern, more differentiated *approaches* to choice of law in contract which will be reviewed next. The modern approaches, however, permit greater attention to the type of contract involved; a subsequent section therefore relates the previous analysis to specific contracts.

B. MODERN APPROACHES

1. *Overview*

§ 18.16 Forum-oriented approaches to choice of law, principally Brainerd Currie's governmental interest approach, would affect the outcome of *Milliken v. Pratt*[1] and *Pritchard v. Norton,* but not of *Emery v. Burbank.* Other approaches that generally favor forum law recognize the different concerns of choice-of-law in contract and the need to uphold party expectations. Thus, one of Ehrenzweig's few "true rules" is the

---

3. Id. at 328, 39 N.E. at 1027 (emphasis added).

4. Id. at 329, 39 N.E. 1026. The same result could have been achieved more simply by different subject matter characterization: law of succession (governed by the decedent's domicile) rather than contract. See infra § 18.19. Justice Holmes recognized this possibility (loc. cit. supra) but did not rely on it because a reference to the law of domicile at death would leave the validity of the contract uncertain until that time. See also Bernkrant v. Fowler, 55 Cal.2d 588, 12 Cal.Rptr. 266, 360 P.2d 906 (1961), in which the court also assessed the contract's validity as of the time of making, in circumstances where a subsequent change of domicile to California (the domicile at death) would have made the contract invalid under the latter's law. Both decisions thus opt for certainty as of the time of making, although the ultimate results differed.

§ 18.16

1. Currie, Married Women's Contracts, 25 U. Chi. L. Rev. 227, 261 (1958) reprinted in Selected Essays 77 (1963) ("The sensible and clearly constitutional thing for any court to do, confronted with a true conflict of interests, is to apply its own law."). Later adherents to Currie's teachings are more sympathetic to interest-weighing. Nevertheless, the guidelines they provide offer little practical help to the courts. See, e.g., Sedler, The Governmental Interest Approach to Choice-of-Law: An Analysis and a Reformulation, 25 U.C.L.A. L. Rev. 181, 221–222 (1977) (advocating the use of local law when the forum has a "real interest" that would thereby be furthered "significantly.")

validation principle (*lex validitatis*): " ... courts of all countries and ages ... have tended to uphold the parties' validating intent and have thus held valid bargain contracts valid under *any* 'proper law.'[2] Cavers's "principles of preference,"[3] Leflar's "choice-influencing considerations"[4] and the Second Restatement[5] likewise reach results consistent with *Milliken v. Pratt*. Reese concludes, with justification, that in contracts, the courts "pay heed to the fact that the basic policy ... is the protection of justified expectations ... [and hence tend] to apply a law that will uphold the contract provided the parties are not of widely disparate bargaining power and the state of the validating law has substantial contacts with the transaction."[6]

The general tendency to apply the validating law provides a helpful starting point when the validity of a contract is in issue. Several problems, however, remain. (1) Since contracts relate to diverse subject matters, the contractual aspect of the transaction may appear less significant than other issues: problems of characterization may arise. (2) If a contract's validity is in issue, what factors provide the sufficient connection to a law to allow its application as the validating law? Similarly, what is the "proper law" when the case raises issues *other* than the validity of the contract?

2. The Case Law: Issue Identification (Characterization) and Connecting Factors

Contracts With Family–Law Aspects

§ 18.17 *Auten v. Auten*[1] was an early departure from the rigid rules of the First Restatement. In a suit for support payments due under a separation agreement, the New York trial court had decided that, under New York law, an earlier suit in England had in effect repudiated the support agreement between the parties to the law suit. The Court of Appeals reversed: the applicable law is neither that of the place of making or performance of the contract, but rather that of the center of gravity of the contract and the relationship.[2] Judge Fuld adduced as reasons that the place with the greatest interest in the problem should

---

2. A. A. Ehrenzweig, A Treatise on the Conflict of Laws 458 (1962) (original emphasis). See also Ehrenzweig, The Statute of Frauds in the Conflict of Laws: The Basic Rule of Validation, 59 Colum. L. Rev. 874, 992 (1959).

3. See D.F. Cavers, The Choice of Law Process 181 et seq. (1965).

4. See L. McDougal, R. Felix & R. Whitten, American Conflicts Law 523 (5th ed. 2001); Coyne, Contracts, Conflicts and Choice–Influencing Considerations, 1969 U. Ill. L. Forum 323, 343–44.

5. Restatement, Second, Conflict of Laws, Reporter's Note to § 194 (p. 619) (1971). See also id. § 188(2).

6. Reese, American Trends in Private International Law: Academic and Judicial Manipulation of Choice of Law Rules in Tort Cases, 33 Vand. L. Rev. 717, 737 (1980).

§ 18.17

1. 308 N.Y. 155, 124 N.E.2d 99 (1954).

2. See also Gillan v. Gillan, 236 Pa.Super. 147, 345 A.2d 742 (1975) (reaching a similar result by application of Restatement, Second, Conflict of Laws § 188(2) (1971)).

have paramount control, and that applying the law of the center of gravity would effectuate the probable intent of the parties and would enable courts to consider the best practical result.[3] Thus, the "better law approach," governmental-interest analysis, and party autonomy are all intermingled. The governmental interest of England to have its law applied, as well as the notion that a reference to that law would achieve the best result, find no apparent support in the opinion since the court made no reference to the content of that law. The further statement that, even under the traditional approach, English law would have been applicable as that of the place of performance[4] is not free from difficulty because it fails to address the question whether the relevant issue is the effect of the English suit or the continued effectiveness of the separation agreement.[5]

§ 18.18   An alternative approach[1] would have been to inquire into the *purpose* of the agreement between the parties.[2] The agreement concerned the separation of the spouses and the continued support of the wife. At issue are problems of *family law*,[3] also noted in passing by the court: the parties substituted their agreement " ... for the duties and responsibilities of support that would otherwise attach by English law."[4] As in the case of antenuptial agreement,[5] the "center of gravity" with

---

3. 308 N.Y. at 161, 124 N.E.2d at 102.

4. 308 N.Y. at 162–63, 124 N.E.2d at 103.

5. Reese, Chief Judge Fuld and Choice of Law, 71 Colum. L. Rev. 548, 550 (1971) (noting that the decision had the salutary effect of abolishing the old distinction between validity and performance for choice of law purposes. The court, however, had made express reference to the distinction and only achieves the merger by its failure to identify carefully the particular question in issue).

§ 18.18

1. The suggested inquiry into the *purpose of an agreement* recurs throughout the subsequent analysis and is discussed in greater detail infra §§ 18.21, 18.40.

2. New York decisions emphasizing the purpose of the contract are: Flammia v. Mite Corp., 401 F.Supp. 1121, 1126 (E.D.N.Y.1975), aff'd 553 F.2d 93 (2d Cir. 1977). Cf. Southern Int'l Sales Co. v. Potter & Brumfield Division of AMF Inc., 410 F.Supp. 1339, 1342 (S.D.N.Y.1976). Compare Pritchard v. Norton, 106 U.S. 124, 1 S.Ct. 102, 27 L.Ed. 104 (1882) (discussed supra § 18.14 n.4). The Louisiana codification specifically requires consideration of "the nature, type, and purpose of the contract." La.Civ. Code Art. 3537. See also id. cmnt (g) ("[T]he nature, type, and purpose of the contract may provide useful pointers for assessing the relative importance of the factual contacts and the relative pertinence

of multistate considerations. For example, in a contract with family-law aspects (e.g., child support agreement), the domicile of the parties would normally be more important than any of the [other] contacts ... , and the policy of 'facilitating and promoting multistate commercial intercourse ... would be far less relevant ... '").

3. Sedler, Characterization, Identification of the Problem Area, And the Policy–Centered Conflict of Laws: An Exercise in Judicial Method, 2 Rutgers Camden L.J. 8, 88 (1970).

4. Auten v. Auten, 308 N.Y. 155, 162, 124 N.E.2d 99, 102 (1954). It is important to note, however, that—*in the absence* of an agreement, as in *Auten*—current American law would not focus on the (last) matrimonial domicile or the residence of the obligee but on the "laws of any state where the obligor was present during the period for which support is sought." Uniform Reciprocal Enforcement of Support Act § 7. European law is contrary. Under the Brussels Convention there is judicial jurisdiction in the state of the obligee's habitual residence (Art. 5(2)) and under some national conflicts laws, the law applicable to maintenance claim will also be primarily that of the obligee's residence. See, e.g., German Introduction Law to the Civil Code (EGBGB) art. 18.

5. Cf. In re Estate of Knippel, 7 Wis.2d 335, 344, 96 N.W.2d 514, 519–19 (1959); Osborn v. Osborn, 10 Ohio Misc. 171, 176–

respect to domestic-relations issues may be found at the (last) matrimonial domicile of the parties, especially if, as in *Auten,* the obligee remained there. Thus, while the suggested approach would lead to the same result as that reached by the court, the focus on the *purpose* of the agreement discloses both its intimate relationship to domestic relations issues and, if viewed solely in contract terms, the objective to provide for the separate maintenance of the wife in *England.* Both the family relationship and the support to be provided by the English spouse in England clearly suggest that England is the place of the most significant relationship, the center of gravity. The suggested approach would avoid some unnecessary and indiscriminate contact counting and the invocation of an undisclosed, sometimes perhaps also insubstantial governmental interest, and subjective judgments about the "best result."

Another well-known decision, *Haag v. Barnes,*[6] raises similar problems. The agreement between the Illinois defendant and the New York plaintiff provided for the support of the parties' illegitimate child and provided that the contract "in all respects be interpreted, construed and governed by the laws of the State of Illinois."[7] Plaintiff sued in New York for support, maintaining that the contract did not constitute a bar in view of a provision of New York law that such an agreement "made by the mother ... shall be binding only when the court shall have determined that adequate provision has been made." The Court of Appeals affirmed the decision below which had upheld the contract under Illinois law. The Court treated the choice-of-law clause as but one factor. In addition, the Court pointed to the facts that the contract recited that the parties were Illinois residents, that the child was born in Illinois, that the contract was made in Illinois with the assistance of Illinois lawyers, and that the payments had been made from Illinois. These facts made Illinois the center of gravity and, given the level of support provided, New York public policy was not offended. Criticism of the decision—as presenting "an indiscriminate listing of contacts without regard for their relevance"[8]—abounds. Indeed, whenever contacts are used only as such, without discussion of their relevance and weight, the temptation to manufacture contacts will be great. In *Haag,* for instance, virtually all contacts support only one relevant fact, the father's Illinois residence. That fact is largely irrelevant, as are the child's place of birth, the place from which payments were made, or where the contract happened to have been concluded. The relevant issues—and the conflict—are the father's freedom to contract (including his choice of the applicable law)and the mother's and New York's concern for the welfare of a child

77, 226 N.E.2d 814, 818 (1966), aff'd 18 Ohio St.2d 144, 248 N.E.2d 191 (1969). But see Frey v. Estate of Sargent, 533 S.W.2d 142, 144 (Tex.Civ.App.1976) (place of performance).

6. 9 N.Y.2d 554, 216 N.Y.S.2d 65, 175 N.E.2d 441, 87 A.L.R.2d 1301 (1961).

7. Id. at 558, 216 N.Y.S.2d at 67, 175 N.E.2d at 442.

8. Reese, Chief Judge Fuld and Choice of Law, 71 Colum. L. Rev. 548, 552 (1971). See also R. Weintraub, Commentary on the Conflict of Laws 464 (4th 2001) (assuming that *Haag* involved an actual conflict, "to suggest that the lawyer-manufactured contacts ... would control, is to exalt a rigid formalism above New York's interest in the welfare of the child and the mother.").

resident in New York. All things being equal, principles of party autonomy alone should have resulted in the application of the chosen law. The facts showed the requisite connection with Illinois; a particular number of contacts or weight is not required.[9] However, the court chose to go beyond the stipulation. In that light, or in the event that the agreement had *not* contained a choice of law, or that the clause had been ineffective for whatever reason, a search for the *purpose* of the contract might again have supplied a more satisfactory answer, albeit possibly different in result. The purpose, the object of the contract was to provide for the child, to substitute a private agreement for the legal obligation which otherwise attaches to the father-child relationship. The principal residence of the child (New York) might then have appropriately been chosen to supply the applicable law,[10] while today the obligation might have been governed, in keeping with URESA or RURESA, by the law of the obligor's residence (Illinois).[11] The point is that, in *Haag* as in *Auten,* the family-law aspects and, with them, the purpose of the *particular contract* were largely ignored. The results reached, even if identical with those that the suggested approach would have produced, are therefore based on analyses that afford little guidance for the future.[12]

Contracts With Succession–Law Aspects

§ 18.19 The suggested focus on the *purpose* of the contract is apparent in contracts with succession-law aspects, typically contracts to make a will. The early decision in *Emery v. Burbank*, discussed above,[1] departed from the place-of-contract rule in order to protect the local testator. In *Rubin v. Irving Trust Co.*,[2] the court noted that "a contract to make or to refrain from altering a will amounts for all practical purposes to a testamentary disposition,"[3] and that, in deciding such a case, one is "not to be guided by the same considerations as ... in determining the applicability of our statute of frauds to the ordinary or commercial contract."[4] The court applied the law of New York, the

---

9. See supra at §§ 18.6–18.10.

10. See, e.g., Black v. Walker, 295 N.J.Super. 244, 684 A.2d 1011 (1996) (law and child's domicile applied).

11. Supra n.4.

12. Similar problems arose in cases concerning the liability of community property for the separate debt of one of the spouses. Baffin Land Corp. v. Monticello Motor Inn, Inc., 70 Wn.2d 893, 425 P.2d 623 (1967) also assessed contacts but overlooked the opportunity for an easier solution by identifying a false conflict. See Weintraub, supra n.8, at 380–81. Pacific States Cut Stone Co. v. Goble, 70 Wn.2d 907, 425 P.2d 631 (1967) recognized the false conflict and avoided the indiscriminate contact counting. Potlatch No. 1 Federal Credit Union v. Kennedy, 76 Wn.2d 806, 459 P.2d 32 (1969) presented a true conflict and therefore re-

quired analysis. Despite the reference to other factors, such as the expectations of the parties, the court adopts a view focusing on the *nature* of the problem, akin to the suggested inquiry into the *purpose* of the contract: "our system of community property is intricately tied to our system of *family law.*" 76 Wn.2d 806, 812, 459 P.2d 32, 36 (1969) (emphasis added). The court applied the law of the matrimonial domicile, Washington. The decision was followed in Johnson v. Spider Staging Corp., 87 Wn.2d 577, 582, 555 P.2d 997, 1001 (1976).

§ 18.19

1. 163 Mass. 326, 39 N.E. 1026 (1895) (discussed supra § 18.15).

2. 305 N.Y. 288, 113 N.E.2d 424 (1953).

3. Id. at 298, 113 N.E.2d at 427.

4. Id. at 300, 113 N.E.2d at 428.

decedent's last domicile and the place of administration.[5] Similarly, the decision in *In re Bulova's Will*,[6] noted that "the mere fact that an instrument is a contract does not mean that the conflicts rules are those associated with contract but rather, may be and would most likely be those associated with the jural relations directly affected by provisions of the agreement." The court applied Swiss law, as that of the situs, to determine the widow's ability to renounce the decedent's will and to claim an interest in his real property.

The California decision in *Bernkrant v. Fowler*[7] at first appears to take a different approach. The California court enforced an oral promise, valid in Nevada where it was made, to forgive the balance of a debt by testamentary disposition. The agreement had been concluded when both parties were Nevada residents; however, by the time of his death, the decedent had become a domiciliary of California which would not enforce such an agreement. The court applied Nevada law in order to protect the expectations of the parties: "Unless they could rely on their own law, they would have to look to the laws of all of the jurisdictions to which . . . [the testator] might move regardless of where he was domiciled when the contract was made."[8] Unlike *Emery v. Burbank, Rubin,* and *In re Bulova's Will*,[9] the California Court thus adopted a reference that did not focus on the succession aspect of the case which, as in *Emery* and *Rubin,* would have led to the decedent's domiciliary law. The cases are nevertheless compatible: in the three cases mentioned, the purpose of the contract was to effect a testamentary disposition, while in *Bernkrant*

5. The decision also contains center-of-gravity language, for instance that the contacts with Florida had been minimal.

6. 14 A.D.2d 249, 255, 220 N.Y.S.2d 541, 547 (1961), appeal denied 11 N.Y.2d 641, 225 N.Y.S.2d 1025, 180 N.E.2d 894 (1962).

7. 55 Cal.2d 588, 12 Cal.Rptr. 266, 360 P.2d 906 (1961).

8. Id. at 596, 12 Cal.Rptr. at 270, 360 P.2d at 910. Most commentators applauded the *Bernkrant* result, albeit for different reasons. Currie found the decision fully compatible with governmental-interest analysis: the application of Nevada law was the result of a reexamination of forum policy "with a view to a more moderate and restrained interpretation." Currie, The Disinterested Third State, 28 Law & Contemp. Prob. 754, 757 (1963). This view finds some support in the court's statement that "there is thus no conflict between the law of California and the law of Nevada." 55 Cal.2d at 596, 12 Cal.Rptr. at 270, 360 P.2d at 910. Cavers saw in *Bernkrant* support for the territorial starting point of his principles of preference. Cavers, Oral Contracts To Provide By Will and the Choice-of-Law Process—Some Notes on *Bernkrant,* in: Perspectives of Law, Essays for Austin Wakeman Scott 38, 49, 57 (1964). Leflar supported the decision both on grounds of

foreseeability of result for the parties and on better-law grounds because of the "tendency to regard statutes of frauds as relics from another century." Leflar, Choice–Influencing Considerations in Conflicts Law, 41 N.Y.U. L. Rev. 267, 230 (1966). Ehrenzweig regarded the decision as an example of the validation principle at work: Choice of Law in California—A "Prestatement," 21 U.C.L.A. L. Rev. 781, 784, 790 (1974). The decision, moreover, comports with the First Restatement (place of making) and with § 188(3) of the Restatement, Second, Conflict of Laws (1971) (place of making and of contemplated performance), particularly also because the court's emphasis of party expectations parallels the principle expressed in § 6(2)(d). See Reese, Dépeçage: A Common Phenomenon in Choice of Law, 73 Colum. L. Rev. 58, 62–63 (1973). As the text indicates, the decision is also compatible with the suggested approach which focuses on the purpose of the contract.

9. Emery v. Burbank, 163 Mass. 326, 39 N.E. 1026 (1895) (discussed supra § 18.15); Rubin v. Irving Trust Co., 305 N.Y. 288, 113 N.E.2d 424 (1953) (discussed supra n.2). In re Bulova's Will, 14 A.D.2d 249, 220 N.Y.S.2d 541 (1961) (discussed supra n.6).

the contract had a commercial purpose to be effected, in part, by a testamentary disposition: "the contract ... involved the refinancing of obligations arising from the sale of Nevada land and secured by interests therein."[10] The transaction was "an ordinary business arrangement ... with the addition of a contingent provision for forgiving the debt by will if the decedent should 'lost his gamble.' "[11] The different purpose of the contract—commercial transaction rather than testamentary gift—should indeed require reference to that law which will protect the parties in their expectations.[12]

Governmental Interest Analysis

§ 18.20 The previous discussion sought to identify the *purpose* or the relevant *issue* of a contract in order to determine the law which should most appropriately be applied, i.e. a process of analysis resembling characterization. The objective was the identification of an appropriately applied law. In contrast, governmental interest analysis, when applied to contract rather than to tort,[1] may de-emphasize the objectives of predictability and protection of party expectations and therefore be inappropriate. An example of an inappropriate sacrifice of party expectations is *Lilienthal v. Kaufman*.[2] The California plaintiff had advanced money to the Oregon defendant in connection with a joint venture of the parties and had received promissory notes therefor. The notes had been executed and delivered in California; the check in repayment of the notes and for profits from the joint venture was dishonored for insufficient

10. 55 Cal.2d at 595, 12 Cal.Rptr. at 270, 360 P.2d at 910.

11. Sedler, Characterization, Identification of the Problem Area, and the Policy–Centered Conflict of Laws—An Exercise in Judicial Method, 2 Rutgers—Camden L.J. 8, 93 (1970).

12. Another area in which characterization or, more accurately, proper identification of the issue, may affect the result may also be noted at this point. Under the 1962 version of § 9–103 of the U.C.C. a credit sale involving a security interest raised the difficult question whether § 1–105 or § 9–103 governed issues not directly related to the security interest. According to one view, the special provisions of §§ 9–102 and 9–103 governed whenever the contract contained a security interest. 2 G. Gilmore, Security Interests in Personal Property 1278–1280 (1965). Skinner v. Tober Foreign Motors, Inc., 345 Mass. 429, 187 N.E.2d 669 (1963) involved in oral modification of an installment term, valid under forum law, but not under Connecticut law which had not yet adopted the U.C.C. The question was whether repossession by the seller, in violation of the modification, entitled the purchaser to damages. The court properly focused on the particular issue, applied a contract characterization and held that the

modification valid under the applicable Massachusetts law: "the issue ... involves the duties of the parties under the primary obligation; neither party contests the validity or perfection of the security interest." 345 Mass. at 432–33, 187 N.E.2d at 671. See also Associates Discount Corp. v. Palmer, 47 N.J. 183, 219 A.2d 858 (1966). The 1972 version of Article 9 now makes it clear that "choice-of-law issues arising between the debtor and the secured creditor are governed by the general Code conflicts provision in 1–105(1)." Id. at 472. See also Petit, Choice of law Under Article Nine of the U.C.C., 7 Loyola U.L.J. 641 (1976). While the 1972 version provided the proper approach, the problem remains relevant for international transactions. The 1998 version of Article 9 would appear not to alter this result.

§ 18.20

1. See Griffith v. United Air Lines, Inc., 416 Pa. 1, 203 A.2d 796 (1964) (the forum, as the place of contracting and of the decedent's last domicile, ignored Colorado's damage limitation in a suit for damages following an airplane crash but applied Pennsylvania law.).

2. 239 Or. 1, 395 P.2d 543 (1964).

funds; plaintiff sued in Oregon for the unpaid balance and was met with the defense that the defendant had previously been declared a spendthrift and that his guardian had declared the obligations void. The Oregon Supreme Court acknowledged that California was the state of the most significant relationship because the transaction had been entered into there and because the notes were executed and payable in California—and that the "validation principle" also pointed to the application of California law. Nevertheless, since "courts are instruments of state policy,"[3] the public policy concern of Oregon to guard against the dissipation of a spendthrift's assets for the protection of his family—required that overriding importance be attached to that policy and the consequent application of Oregon law.[4]

The *Lilienthal* court thus did not even undertake the task of interpreting forum policy with restraint and moderation as had *Bernkrant* which then applied the other state's law,[5] but rather elevated its oddball local policy to be the only and decisive consideration.[6] Since California, had it been the forum, surely would have applied its law, the danger of forum-shopping is obvious.[7] The decision hardly favors "the facilitation of interstate business transactions"[8] and fails to protect the "justified expectations" of the parties.[9] One commentator went further: "Application of this Oregon law clearly disappointed the plaintiff's expectations and on the particular facts may have been unconstitutional."[10]

3. Id. at 16, 395 P.2d at 549.

4. The court also referred to the prior decision in Olshen v. Kaufman, 235 Or. 423, 385 P.2d 161 (1963) which had involved the same spendthrift. That case involved a purely intrastate (Oregon) transaction and therefore did not involve a conflict or the different party expectations as in *Lilienthal*. The rule of decision applicable to an intrastate situation is not, without more, necessarily appropriate, or the same, for an interstate conflicts case.

5. Bernkrant v. Fowler, 55 Cal.2d 588, 12 Cal.Rptr. 266, 360 P.2d 906 (1961).

6. See 239 Or. at 25, 395 P.2d at 553 (Goodwin, J., dissenting) ("[T]he policy of both states ... in favor of enforcing contracts, has been lost sight of. The majority view ... strikes me as a step backward toward the balkanization of the law of contracts").

7. L. McDougal, R. Felix & R. Whitten, American Conflicts Law 526 n.28 (5th ed. 2001); R. Weintraub, Commentary on the Conflict of Laws 467 (4th ed. 2001).

8. Kay, Book Review, 18 J. Legal Ed. 341, 345 (1966). See also Restatement, Second, Conflict of Laws § 6(2)(d) (1971)("the needs of the interstate and international systems" in connection with § 188(2)).

9. Restatement, Second, Conflict of Laws § 6(2)(d) (1971). Section 188, which incorporates § 6 by reference, particularizes further by listing the place of contracting, the place of negotiation, the place of performance, the location of the subject matter (in *Lilienthal*, the joint venture of the parties), and the places of residence and business of the parties. Of these, only the last are not in California for both parties. Subsection (3) provides further that, "if the place of negotiating and the place of performance are in the same state," that state's law applies. See also id. §§ 195 (law of the place where money is to be repaid) and 198 (capacity to make a contract determined by § 188 except that capacity will be *upheld if given under the law of domicile*). As the italicized language shows, the Restatement opts in favor of capacity if it exists either under the law of the contract or under the law of the party's domicile.

10. Reese, Limitations on the Extraterritorial Application of Law, 4 Dalhousie L.J. 589, 598–99 (1978); Hay, Flexibility versus Predictability and Uniformity in Choice of Law, Hague Academy, 228 Recueil des Cours 281, 380 (1991–I). But see Weinberg, On Departing from Forum Law, 35 Mercer L. Rev. 595, 605 (1984); Kramer, Rethinking Choice of Law, 90 Colum. L. Rev. 277, 233 (1990).

Subsequent Oregon decisions have considerably weakened the authority of *Lilienthal* by adopting a restrained interpretation of the forum's policy and by according greater weight to the law of the place of the most significant relationship.[11] In 2001, Oregon enacted a choice-of-law codification for contracts, the pertinent section of which has overruled *Lilienthal*.[12] Indeed, virtually none of the existing statutory choice-of-law rules would have allowed the result the *Lilienthal* court reached under interest analysis.[13]

11. Citizens First Bank v. Intercontinental Express, Inc. 77 Or.App. 655, 713 P.2d 1097 (1986). In Casey v. Manson Construction & Engineering Co., 247 Or. 274, 428 P.2d 898 (1967), a suit for loss of consortium, the court inexplicably overlooked *Lilienthal* when it said: "The view has been expressed, *though not, so far as we are aware, by any court,* that if both the forum state and the foreign state have legitimate interests in the application of their laws the court should apply the law of the forum.... [W]e are warned by highly regarded authority that '[s]tate chauvinism and interstate retaliation are dangers to be avoided' ... " 247 Or. at 293–94, 428 P.2d at 907 (emphasis added). In Kubeck v. Consolidated Underwriters, 267 Or. 548, 555, 517 P.2d 1039, 1042 (1974) the court rewrote history when it cited *Lilienthal* for the proposition that "this court has elected [not to] permit the fraudulent party to achieve his purposes...." Citizens First Bank v. Intercontinental Express, Inc., 77 Or.App. 655, 713 P.2d 1097 (1986); Manz v. Continental American Life Ins. Co., 117 Or.App. 78, 843 P.2d 480 (1992), modified on reconsideration by 119 Or.App. 31, 849 P.2d 549 (1993), and review denied by 317 Or. 162, 856 P.2d 317 (1993); Young v. Mobil Oil Corp., 85 Or.App. 64, 735 P.2d 654 (1987); Sims Snowboards, Inc. v. Kelly, 863 F.2d 643 (9th Cir.1988). On interest analysis generally, see also Weintraub, Functional Developments in Choice of Law for Contracts, Hague Academy, 187 Recueil des cours 243 (1984–IV). Louisiana has adopted a modified comparative impairment approach to choice of law in contract: La.Civ. Code, Prelim. Title, ch. 3, art. 37 (1991).

12. See O.R.S. § 81.112, which provides in part as follows:

(1) A party has the capacity to enter into a contract if the party has that capacity under the law of the state in which the party resides or the law applicable to this issue under [other sections of this Act].

(2) A party that lacks capacity to enter into a contract under the law of the state in which the party resides may assert that incapacity against a party that knew

or should have known of the incapacity at the time the parties entered into the contract....

Under the codification's other provisions, California law would be applicable to the issue involved in *Lilienthal*. See Symeonides, Codifying Choice of Law for Contracts: The Oregon Experience, 67 RabelsZ, 726, 734–36 (2003). However, this would not be the end of the case, because the *Lilienthal* scenario would trigger consideration of subsection (2) of the above quoted provision, under which, in the same scenario, the defendant could not have prevailed. See id. at 735. See also Symeonides, Resolving Six Celebrated Conflicts Cases Through Statutory Choice-of-Law Rules, 48 Mercer Law Review 837, 858–64 (1997) (discussing *Lilienthal* under article 3539 of the Louisiana codification, which was the model for the Oregon provision); Symeonides, Codifying Choice of Law for Contracts: The Puerto Rico Projet, in Law and Justice in a Multistate World: Essays in Honor of Arthur T. von Mehren, 419, 430–32 (J. Nafziger, & S. Symeonides, eds. 2002) (discussing art. 39 of the Puerto Rico Draft Code).

13. In many foreign legal systems capacity is often determined by reference to the party's law of nationality (or habitual residence) but, if the transaction took place in the forum and the party has capacity under that law, forum law will validate the transaction. See for France: Arrt. Lizardi, D. P. 1861, 1, 305 (Cass.); Germany: EGBGB art. 12. The rule thus protects *local* transactions, as California would have ruled if the *Lilienthal* litigation had arisen there. Less clear, but said to be the rule at least in Germany, is whether the forum would also protect the foreign market (as Oregon should have done in *Lilienthal*) by applying the validating rules of capacity of the latter to its own national who had acted there: Kegel & Schurig, Internationales Privatrecht 561 (9th ed. 2004). For England, see R. H. Graveson, Conflict of Laws 402–03 (7th ed. 1974). For statutory rules, see, e.g., Benelux Treaty Art. 2: "[A] person declared incapable by his law may not invoke his incapacity against one who, in a legal act,

Lilienthal presents a conflict between a state's protective policies and concerns and the contractual expectations of the parties. In contract, state concerns have generally not risen to the level of an overriding "public policy," except in subject matter over which a state exercises regulatory power, such as in insurance or workmen's compensation. Thus, the parties' stipulation of a validating law in contracts otherwise usurious under forum law has generally been honored.[14] The result should be the same in the absence of an express choice of law in furtherance of the predominant objectives of the protection of party interests, predictability, and, consequently, commercial security. Absent state regulation of the subject matter, as mentioned, governmental-interest analysis therefore should have no place in choice of law in contract. With respect to the *Lilienthal*-type of situation, this approach is recognized by § 198 of the Second Restatement, in its alternative reference to the law applicable to the contract (§ 188) or to the party's domiciliary law whenever the latter provides *for* contractual capacity.[15]

3. *The Choice-of-Law Approaches in the Courts: Summary*

§ 18.21 A 1981 survey of over 300 decisions showed that the majority of the states still largely adhered to the rules of the First Restatement.[1] By 1996 the list had shrunk to eleven states and there it remains as of 2004.[2] These states are: Alabama,[3] Florida,[4]

has in good faith and in conformity with the law of the place of the act considered him to be capable;" Rome Convention Art. 11 (as well as German codif. Art. 12): "In a contract concluded between persons who are in the same country, a natural person who would have capacity under the law of that country may invoke his incapacity resulting from another law only if the other party to the contract was aware of this incapacity at the time of the conclusion of the contract or was not aware thereof as a result of negligence;" Quebec Civ.Code Art. 3086: "A party to a juridical act who is incapable under the law of the country of his domicile may not invoke his incapacity if he was capable under the law of the country in which the other party was domiciled when the act was executed in that country, unless the other party was or should have been aware of the incapacity."

14. Supra § 18.5, nn. 12–15.

15. See supra n.9.

§ 18.21

1. See Weitnauer, Der Vertragsschwerpunkt (Vol. 105, Arbeiten zur Rechtsvergleichung, 1981). See also Symeonides, The American Choice-of-Law Revolution in the Courts: Today and Tomorrow, 298 Recueil des Cours 1, 70–75 (2003) (showing that, in 1981, 30 jurisdictions adhered to the tradi-

tional approach in contracts. This number fell to 25 in 1985.

2. See S. Symeonides, *The Revolution Today*, supra n.1 at id.

3. See American Nonwovens, Inc. v. Non Wovens Engineering, S.R.L, 648 So.2d 565 (Ala. 1994); Cherry, Bekaert & Holland v. Brown, 582 So.2d 502 (Ala.1991); Pines v. Warnaco, Inc., 706 F.2d 1173 (11th Cir. 1983). See Ideal Structures Corp. v. Levine Huntsville Development Corp., 396 F.2d 917, 921–26 (5th Cir.1968), reversing 251 F.Supp. 3, 7–8 (N.D.Ala.1966) which had followed the most-significant-relationship test; Harrison v. Insurance Co. of North America, 294 Ala. 387, 318 So.2d 253 (1975).

4. See Sturiano v. Brooks, 523 So.2d 1126 (Fla. 1988) (reaffirming the *lex loci contractus* rule and specifically refusing to extend to contract conflicts the "most significant relationship" formula earlier adopted for tort conflicts); Celotex Corp. v. AIU Ins. Co., 152 B.R. 652 (Bkrtcy.M.D.Fla. 1993); Starkenstein v. Merrill Lynch, Pierce, Fenner & Smith, Inc., 572 F.Supp. 189 (M.D.Fla.1983) (formation and obligations governed by law of place of making, matters concerning performance governed by law of latter); Boat Town U.S.A. Inc. v. Mercury Marine Division, 364 So.2d 15, 18 (Fla.App.1978).

Georgia,[5] Kansas,[6] Maryland,[7] New Mexico,[8] Rhode Island,[9] South Carolina,[10] Tennessee,[11] Virginia,[12] and Wyoming.[13]

5. See Convergys Corp. v. Keener, 276 Ga. 808, 582 S.E.2d 84 (2003) (refusing to adopt Second Restatement § 187); General Telephone Co. v. Trimm, 252 Ga. 95, 311 S.E.2d 460 (1984) (rejecting as "confusing" and "uncertain" the center-of-gravity approach and deciding to adhere to the *lex loci contractus* rule "[u]ntil it becomes clear that a better rule exists." Id. at 462.) But see Amica Mut. Ins. Co. v. Bourgault, 263 Ga. 157, 429 S.E.2d 908 (1993) (relying on Second Restatement § 193 to interpret a Georgia insurance statute). Georgia's adherence to the *lex loci contractus* rule is subject to several exceptions. Georgia courts do not apply this rule when: (a) the contract is to be performed in a state other than the state in which it was made, see Trimm, 252 Ga. 95, 311 S.E.2d 460 at 461; or (b) when the contract contains a valid choice-of-law clause. See Carr v. Kupfer, 250 Ga. 106, 296 S.E.2d 560 (1982). However, contracts made in Georgia and not containing a choice-of-law clause to the contrary are presumed to have been tacitly submitted by the parties to the law of Georgia. See General Electric Credit Corp. v. Home Indem. Co., 168 Ga. App. 344, 309 S.E.2d 152 (1983); Boardman Petroleum, Inc. v. Federated Mut. Ins. Co., 926 F.Supp. 1566 (S.D. Ga. 1995). For other recent cases, see Morgan v. Mar–Bel, Inc., 614 F.Supp. 438, 441 (N.D.Ga.1985) (dictum); Residential Industrial Loan Co. v. Brown, 559 F.2d 438, 440 (5th Cir.1977); Shorewood Packaging Corp. v. Commercial Union Ins. Co., 865 F.Supp. 1577 (N.D.Ga. 1994).

6. See St. Paul Surplus Lines v. International Playtex, Inc., 245 Kan. 258, 777 P.2d 1259, 1267 (1989) ("reserve[ing] consideration of the Restatement's 'most significant relationship' test for a later day," because the traditional public policy exception—which the court employed offensively rather than defensively—enabled the court to avoid applying the *lex loci* so as to protect "[t]he interests of Kansas."); Safeco Ins. Co. v. Allen, 262 Kan. 811, 941 P.2d 1365 (1997) (reaffirming both the *lex loci contractus* rule and the public policy exception enunciated in *St. Paul*, but finding the exception inapplicable because the *lex loci* was "consistent with the stated policy of [Kansas law.]" Id. at 1372.

7. See American Motorists Ins. Co. v. ARTRA Group, Inc., 338 Md. 560, 659 A.2d 1295 (1995) (adopting *renvoi* exception to *lex loci* rule and holding that Maryland's adherence to this rule "must yield to a test such as Restatement (Second) Conflict of Laws § 188 when the place of contracting would apply Maryland law pursuant to that

test." Id. at 1304); Bethlehem Steel Co. v. G.C. Zarnas & Co., Inc., 304 Md. 183, 498 A.2d 605 (1984) (employing both *renvoi* and *ordre public* exceptions); National Glass v. J.C. Penney, 336 Md. 606, 650 A.2d 246 (1994) (following Restatement Second § 187 in analyzing a choice-of-law clause); Kronovet v. Lipchin, 288 Md. 30, 415 A.2d 1096 (1980) (accord).

8. See Reagan v. McGee Drilling Corp., 123 N.M. 68, 933 P.2d 867 (1997), cert. denied (applying alternatively the public policy exception to the *lex loci* and the Second Restatement). But see Shope v. State Farm Ins. Co., 122 N.M. 398, 925 P.2d 515 (1996) (applying the *lex loci contractus* without discussion); State Farm Mut. Ins. Co. v. Conyers, 109 N.M. 243, 784 P.2d 986 (1989); In re Bennett, 51 B.R. 619 (Bkrtcy.N.M.1984) (place of contracting and injury, not place of residence, suffering of economic loss, or of location of bankruptcy estate); Sandoval v. Valdez, 91 N.M. 705, 580 P.2d 131, 133 (N.M. App.1978); Pound v. Insurance Co. of North America, 439 F.2d 1059 (10th Cir.1971).

9. The supreme court of Rhode Island has not had the opportunity to reconsider the *lex loci contractus* rule since the 1968 abandonment of the *lex loci delicti* rule. See Woodward v. Stewart, 104 R.I. 290, 243 A.2d 917, 923 (1968). Four years later, when the court encountered a contract conflict, the court found that the contract had been made in Rhode Island, that this state had "the most significant interest in th[e] matter," and that Rhode Island law should govern "under whatever theory we follow." A.C. Beals Co. v. Rhode Island Hospital, 110 R.I. 275, 292 A.2d 865, 871 (1972). A 1992 case involving security interests—which could also be characterized as a contract case—leaves the impression that the days of the *lex loci contractus* are numbered, if not over. See Gordon v. Clifford Metal Sales Co., Inc. 602 A.2d 535 (R.I. 1992). *Gordon* is alternatively based on the "reasonable relation" language of the UCC § 1–105 and Restatement Second § 6.

10. See Sangamo Weston, Inc. v. National Sur. Corp., 307 S.C. 143, 414 S.E.2d 127 (1992) (acknowledging that, "historically," the *lex loci contractus rule* had been followed in South Carolina and noting that, with the record presently before it, the court was "unable to address the question of whether South Carolina would adopt the more modern view of the [Second] Restatement" Id. at 147–48; Lister v. NationsBank,

11–3. See p. 1002.

The remaining 39 states plus the District of Columbia and the Commonwealth of Puerto Rico have adopted one of the modern flexible approaches, with the majority of them (24 states) following the Second Restatement.[14] Four states and Puerto Rico follow a significant contacts

329 S.C. 133, 494 S.E.2d 449 (1997) rehearing denied (applying alternatively the *lex loci* rule and the Second Restatement).

11. Tennessee's classification as a *lex loci contractus* state is doubtful. In 1975, the Supreme Court of Tennessee expressly rejected an appeal to adopt "the dominant-contacts rule" for contract conflicts because of the rule's failure to produce uniformity. Great American Ins. Co. v. Hartford Accident & Indemn. Co., 519 S.W.2d 579 at 580 (Tenn. 1975). However, in 1992, the same court adopted the Second Restatement's approach for tort conflicts and appeared unconcerned about the possibility that this approach may not be as conducive to certainty. See Hataway v. McKinley, 830 S.W.2d 53 (Tenn. 1992). Although the court has yet to encounter a contract conflict since 1992, it would not be unreasonable to expect that, when it does, the court will abandon the *lex loci contractus* rule, perhaps in favor of the Second Restatement. For lower court cases, see Central States Southeast and Southwest Areas Pension Fund v. Kraftco, Inc., 589 F.Supp. 1061 (M.D.Tenn.1984), judgment reversed on other grounds 799 F.2d 1098 (6th Cir.1986), cert. denied 479 U.S. 1086, 107 S.Ct. 1291, 94 L.Ed.2d 147 (1987) (absent expression of contrary intent by the parties, law of the place of making applies); Missouri Portland Cement Co. v. J.A. Jones Construction Co., 323 F.Supp. 242 (M.D.Tenn.1970), aff'd 438 F.2d 3 (6th Cir.1971) (place of contracting and performance in the same state); Great American Ins. Co. v. Hartford Accident & Indemnity Co., 519 S.W.2d 579 (Tenn. 1975). Cf. Boatland, Inc. v. Brunswick Corp., 558 F.2d 818 (6th Cir.1977) (place of contracting, center of gravity, choice-of-law clause); Lovett v. Wal–Mart Stores, 1993 WL 38001 (Tenn.App.). But see Agricultural Services Ass'n, Inc. v. Ferry–Morse Seed Co., Inc., 551 F.2d 1057 (6th Cir.1977) (Restatement 2d)

12. See Buchanan v. Doe, 246 Va. 67, 431 S.E.2d 289 (Va. 1993); Erie Ins. Exchange v. Shapiro, 248 Va. 638, 450 S.E.2d 144 (1994); Lexie v. State Farm Mut. Auto. Ins. Co., 251 Va. 390, 469 S.E.2d 61 (1996); Witter v. Torbett, 604 F.Supp. 298 (W.D.Va. 1984); Occidental Fire and Cas. Co. of North Carolina v. Bankers and Shippers Ins. Co. of New York, 564 F.Supp. 1501 (W.D.Va.1983) (contract formation governed by law of place of making; performance governed by law of place of performance); Brand Distributors, Inc. v. Insurance Co. of North America, 400 F.Supp. 1085 (E.D.Va.1974) (reversed on other grounds 532 F.2d 352 (4th Cir.1976)); Equitable Trust Co. v. Bratwursthaus Management Corp., 514 F.2d 565 (4th Cir.1975); Combined Properties v. American Mfrs. Mut. Ins. Co., 986 F.2d 1412 (4th Cir.1993); St. Paul Fire & Marine Ins. Co. v. Jacobson, 826 F.Supp. 155 (E.D.Va.1993), aff'd 48 F.3d 778 (4th Cir.1995).

13. The Wyoming Supreme Court has vacillated between the *lex loci* and the Second Restatement. Cherry Creek Dodge Inc. v. Carter, 733 P.2d 1024 (Wyo. 1987) cited the Restatement favorably but relied mostly on the "reasonable relationship" language of the forum's version of the U.C.C. Amoco Rocmount Co. v. The Anschutz Corp., 7 F.3d 909 (10th Cir. 1993), interpreted *Cherry Creek* as having adopted the Restatement. BHP Petroleum (Americas), Inc. v. Texaco Exploration and Production, Inc., 1 P.3d 1253 (Wy. 2000) renounced the view that *Cherry Creek* had adopted the Second Restatement.

14. *Alaska:* Palmer G. Lewis Co. v. ARCO Chem. Co., 904 P.2d 1221 (Alaska 1995) (interpreting Ehredt v. DeHavilland Aircraft Co. of Canada, Ltd., 705 P.2d 446 (Alaska 1985), a case involving a tort conflict, as having adopted the Second Restatement for contract conflicts as well)*; Arizona:* See Taylor v. Security National Bank, 20 Ariz.App. 504, 514 P.2d 257 (1973); Burr v. Renewal Guar. Corp., 105 Ariz. 549, 468 P.2d 576 (1970); *Colorado*: Power Motive Corp. v. Mannesmann Demag Corp., 617 F.Supp. 1048 (D.Colo.1985); Wood Bros. Homes, Inc. v. Walker Adjustment Bureau, 198 Colo. 444, 601 P.2d 1369 (1979); Siemens Medical Systems, Inc. v. Nuclear Cardiology Systems, Inc., 945 F.Supp. 1421 (D.Colo.1996); *Connecticut*: Williams v. State Farm Mut. Auto. Ins. Co., 229 Conn. 359, 641 A.2d 783 (1994); Giorgio v. Nukem, Inc., 31 Conn.App. 169, 624 A.2d 896 (1993); *Delaware*: Travelers Indemnity Co. v. Lake, 594 A.2d 38 (1991); *Idaho:* Rungee v. Allied Van Lines, Inc., 92 Idaho 718, 449 P.2d 378 (1968); Industrial Indem. Ins. Co. v. United States, 757 F.2d 982 (9th Cir.

approach;[15] two states follow Leflar's better law approach;[16] and nine states and the District of Columbia follow a combination of modern approaches.[17] It is important to emphasize, however, that any such

1985); Unigard Ins. Group v. Royal Globe Ins. Co., 100 Idaho 123, 594 P.2d 633, 636 (1979); *Illinois*: Bridge Prods., Inc. v. Quantum Chem. Corp., 1990 WL 19968 (N.D. Ill.); *Iowa*: Joseph L. Wilmotte & Co. v. Rosenman Bros., 258 N.W.2d 317 (Iowa 1977); *Kentucky:* Lewis v. American Family Ins. Group, 555 S.W.2d 579 (Ky. 1977); Prudential Resources Corp. v. Plunkett, 583 S.W.2d 97, 100 (Ky.App.1979); *Maine* : Baybutt Constr. Corp. v. Commercial Union Ins. Co., 455 A.2d 914 (Me. 1983); *Michigan*: Chrysler Corp. v. Skyline Industrial Services, Inc., 448 Mich. 113, 528 N.W.2d 698 (1995) (opting for the flexible policy analysis of the Restatement Second); *Mississippi:* FMC Finance Corp. v. Reed, 592 F.2d 238, 241 (5th Cir.1979); Bunge Corp. v. Biglane, 418 F.Supp. 1159 (S.D.Miss. 1976) ("appropriate relationship" under U.C.C.); *Missouri:* Bernstein v. Fidelity Union Life Ins. Co., 449 F.Supp. 327 (E.D.Mo. 1978). See Nelson v. Aetna Life Ins. Co., 359 F.Supp. 271 (W.D.Mo.1973); Citizens & Southern National Bank v. Bruce, 420 F.Supp. 795 (E.D.Mo.1976), aff'd 562 F.2d 590 (8th Cir.1977) ("Where the contract is made, performed, and where the transaction thereunder occurred."); O'Donnell v. St. Luke's Episcopal Presbyterian Hospitals, 800 F.2d 739 (8th Cir.1986); *Montana*: Casarotto v. Lombardi, 268 Mont. 369, 886 P.2d 931 (1994), cert. granted, judgment vacated on other grounds 515 U.S. 1129, 115 S.Ct. 2552, 132 L.Ed.2d 807 (1995); *Nebraska*: Powell v. American Charter Federal Sav. & Loan Assn., 245 Neb. 551, 514 N.W.2d 326 (1994); *New Hampshire*: Green Mountain Ins. Co. v. George, 138 N.H. 10, 634 A.2d 1011 (1993); Glowski v. Allstate Ins. Co., 134 N.H. 196, 589 A.2d 593 (1991); *Ohio:* Gries Sports Enters. v. Modell, 15 Ohio St.3d 284, 473 N.E.2d 807, 810 (1984); *Oklahoma*: Bohannan v. Allstate Ins. Co., 820 P.2d 787, 797 (Okla.1991); Roby v. Bailey, 856 P.2d 1013 (Okla.App.1993); *South Dakota*: Stockmen's Livestock Exchange v. Thompson, 520 N.W.2d 255 (S.D.1994); *Texas*: DeSantis v. Wackenhut Corp., 793 S.W.2d 670 (Tex.1990), cert. denied 498 U.S. 1048, 111 S.Ct. 755, 112 L.Ed.2d 775 (1991); Minnesota Mining and Manufacturing Co. v. Nishika, Ltd., 953 S.W.2d 733 (Tex.1997); Perez v. Alcoa Fujikura, Ltd., 969 F.Supp. 991 (W.D.Tex.1997); *Utah:* Prows v. Pinpoint Retail Systems, Inc. 868 P.2d 809 (Utah 1993); American National Fire Ins. Co. v. Farmers Ins. Exchange, 927 P.2d 186 (Utah 1996); Shearson Lehman Bros. v. M & L Investments, 10 F.3d 1510

(10th Cir.1993); *Vermont*: E.B. & A.C. Whiting Co. v. The Hartford Fire Ins. Co., 838 F.Supp. 863 (D.Vt.1993); *Washington*: Rutter v. BX of Tri–Cities, Inc., 60 Wn.App. 743, 806 P.2d 1266 (1991); *West Virginia*: Adkins v. Sperry, 190 W.Va. 120, 437 S.E.2d 284 (1993); Clark v. Rockwell, 190 W.Va. 49, 435 S.E.2d 664 (1993); Nadler v. Liberty Mut. Fire Ins. Co., 188 W.Va. 329, 424 S.E.2d 256 (1992).

15. These states are Arkansas, Indiana, Nevada, and North Carolina. See W.H. Barber Co. v. Hughes, 223 Ind. 570, 63 N.E.2d 417 (1945). See also Dohm & Nelke v. Wilson Foods Corp., 531 N.E.2d 512 (Ind. App. 1988); Barrow v. ATCO Mfg. Co., 524 N.E.2d 1313 (Ind. App. 1988); Hermanson v. Hermanson, 110 Nev. 1400, 887 P.2d 1241 (1994); Boudreau v. Baughman, 322 N.C. 331, 368 S.E.2d 849 (1988) (interpreted the phrase "appropriate relation" in the forum's version of U.C.C. art. 1–105 as being equivalent to the phrase "most significant relationship." Id. at 855). For Puerto Rico, see Maryland Cas. Co. v. San Juan Racing Ass'n, 83 D.P.R. 559 (1961); Green Giant Co. v. Tribunal Superior, 104 P.R. Dec. 489 (1975). After many years of employing a policy-based approach, New York has partly reverted to the center of gravity approach in contract conflicts. See In re Allstate Ins. Co. v. Stolarz, 81 N.Y.2d 219, 597 N.Y.S.2d 904, 613 N.E.2d 936 (1993).

16. These two states are Minnesota and Wisconsin. See Hime v. State Farm Fire & Cas. Co., 284 N.W.2d 829 (Minn. 1979); Hague v. Allstate Ins. Co., 289 N.W.2d 43 (Minn. 1978), aff'd 449 U.S. 302, 101 S.Ct. 633, 66 L.Ed.2d 521 (1981); Jepson v. General Cas. Co. of Wisconsin, 513 N.W.2d 467 (Minn. 1994); Nodak Mut. Ins. Co. v. American Family Mut. Ins. Co., 604 N.W.2d 91 (Minn. 2000); See Haines v. Mid–Century Ins. Co., 47 Wis.2d 442, 177 N.W.2d 328 (1970); Schlosser v. Allis–Chalmers Corp., 86 Wis.2d 226, 271 N.W.2d 879 (1978).

17. *New Jersey*, the *District of Columbia*, *Massachusetts*, and *Pennsylvania* combine interest analysis with the Second Restatement. See Gilbert Spruance Co. v. Pennsylvania Mfgrs. Ass'n Ins. Co., 134 N.J. 96, 629 A.2d 885 (1993); District of Columbia Ins. Guaranty Ass'n v. Algernon Blair, Inc. 565 A.2d 564 (D.C. App. 1989) (applying interest analysis but also relying on the Restatement Second); Owen v. Owen, 427 A.2d 933, 937 (D.C. 1981)

categorization is dangerous since the decisions in some states still seem uncertain as to the preferred approach, while others rather indiscriminately use all of the approaches.[18]

Another reason why the above tabulations must be used with care is that conflicts problems in contract of course arise in different contexts. A fixed reference point, in the manner of the First Restatement, may therefore be appropriate for the protection of party expectations in one case, while a more flexible center-of-gravity approach may be warranted in another. It was suggested earlier that a more useful method of analysis would focus on the *purpose* of the contract which, once identified, may aid in the development of particularized rules for specific contract issues, especially those not touching upon validity. An example, relating to insurance contracts, may serve to illustrate: Possible reference points are the place of contracting, the place where payment of the proceeds is to be made, or the location of the insured object at the time of loss. Both the case law under the First Restatement and § 193 of the Second Restatement apply the law of the principal location of the insured risk: the " ... purpose [of the parties] was to fix in advance their rights and liabilities in the event of an accident ... rather than to

(mixed approach, described as a search for the "more substantial interest," but reduced to contact counting); Bushkin Associates, Inc. v. Raytheon Co., 393 Mass. 622, 473 N.E.2d 662 (1985) (a contract case stating that, as it had previously done in tort conflicts, the court would not tie itself to any particular modern approach but would instead "feel free to draw from any of the various lists." The court drew from the Second Restatement and Leflar's lists, but applied them in a way that resembled interest analysis.); In re Danz' Estate, 444 Pa. 411, 283 A.2d 282 (1971) (German law as place of contracting and performance and thus is the applicable law under either Restatement); Goulding v. Sands, 237 F.Supp. 577 (W.D.Pa.1965), aff'd 355 F.2d 230 (3d Cir.1966) (governmental interest analysis leads to forum law); Azriel v. Frigitemp Corp., 397 F.Supp. 871 (E.D.Pa.1975) (center of gravity); Melville v. American Home Assurance Co., 443 F.Supp. 1064 (E.D.Pa. 1977), reversed 584 F.2d 1306 (3d Cir.1978) (Second Restatement), and Complaint of Bankers Trust Co. 752 F.2d 874 (3d Cir. 1984) (leading to the law of India) relying also on Griffith v. United Air Lines, Inc., 416 Pa. 1, 203 A.2d 796 (1964) (Second Restatement and governmental interest analysis). *New York* combines interest analysis with the center of gravity approach. See Matter of Allstate Ins. Co. (Stolarz), 81 N.Y.2d 219, 597 N.Y.S.2d 904, 613 N.E.2d 936 (1993), (discussed in Borchers, New York Choice of Law: Weaving the Tangled Strands, 57 Alb. L. Rev. 93, 104–11 (1993));

Philips Credit Corp. v. Regent Health Group, Inc., 953 F.Supp. 482 (S.D.N.Y. 1997) (Second Restatement and interest analysis). *Hawaii* and *North Dakota* follow a combination of interest analysis, the Second Restatement, and Leflar's choice-influencing considerations. See Lewis v. Lewis, 69 Haw. 497, 748 P.2d 1362 (1988) (contract conflict interpreting Peters v. Peters, 63 Haw. 653, 634 P.2d 586 (1981), a tort conflict, as having adopted a "significant relationship" test with primary emphasis on the state with the "strongest interest"); American Family Mut. Ins. Co. v. Farmers Ins. Exchange, 504 N.W.2d 307 (N.D. 1993); Starry v. Central Dakota Printing, Inc., 530 N.W.2d 323 (N.D. 1995). *Louisiana* and *Oregon* have their own comprehensive codifications. See La. Civ. Code, arts. 3537–3541, discussed in Symeonides, Private International Law Codification in a Mixed Jurisdiction: The Louisiana Experience, 57 RabelsZ 460, 495 et seq. (1993); O.R.S. §§ 81.100–81.135, discussed in Nafziger, Oregon's Conflicts Law Applicable to Contracts, 3 Ybk Priv. Int'l L. 391(2001); Symeonides, Codifying Choice of Law for Contracts: The Oregon Experience, 67 RabelsZ 726 (2003).

18. See Symeonides, The American Choice-of-Law Revolution in the Courts: Today and Tomorrow, 298 Recueil des Cours 1, 89–96 (2003) (prefacing similar classifications with caveats arising from the dearth of recent precedents in some states, and the frequency of equivocal or eclectic precedents in other states).

leave them dependent on the fortuitous circumstances of the place of the accident."[19] The Second Restatement, already contains a number of particularized rules; they are discussed below. For areas for which such rules have not yet been developed, its flexible approach in § 188 affords the opportunity to do so on the basis of teleological analysis of the contract issues involved.[20]

III. CONTRACT CHOICE–OF–LAW BY SUBJECT MATTER

§ 18.22 Section 188 of the Second Restatement, refers to the general principles of § 6, and, in subsection (2), lists as relevant connecting factors: the place of contracting, the place of negotiation, the place of performance, the location of the subject matter, and the domicile, residence, place of incorporation or place of business of the parties.

Subsection (3) provides an exception to the co-equal factors in subsection (2): whenever the place of negotiation and the place of performance are in the same state, the local law of that state applies. The reason for the exception is said to be that "[a] state having these contacts will usually be the state that has the greatest interest in the determination of issues arising under the contract."[1] The qualification "usually" recognizes that another state may have a greater interest in having its law applied: " ... the extent of a state's interest ... will depend upon the purpose sought to be achieved by that rule."[2] The purpose *of the rule,* while often an appropriate factor, may differ from the purpose of the *contract* which was the suggested focus of the analysis in the preceding section. To be sure, the connecting factors of subsection (2) permit such a focus, and the particularized rule of subsection (3) may do so as well. However, the emphasis on governmental interests may

19. Breen v. Aetna Cas. & Sur. Co., 153 Conn. 633, 639, 220 A.2d 254, 257 (1966). For decisions applying § 193 of Restatement II see: Lewis v. American Family Ins. Group, 555 S.W.2d 579, 582 (Ky.1977); American Home Assurance Co. v. American Employers Ins. Co., 384 F.Supp. 3, 6 (E.D.Pa.1974). See also Peterson v. Warren, 31 Wis.2d 547, 558, 143 N.W.2d 560, 564–65 (1966) (reference to Restatement, Second, of Conflict of Laws, Tentative Draft No. 6, § 346i). *Texas:* Most significant relationship in insurance contract is where insured's principal place of business and bulk of insured's operations and apparent focus of risk covered is located. Atlantic Mut. Ins. Co. v. Truck Ins. Exchange, 797 F.2d 1288 (5th Cir.1986).

20. The Inter–American Convention on the Law Applicable to International Contracts, 33 I.L.M. 732 (1994) (not yet in force) combines in its Art. 9 and 10 a "closed links" approach and the desire to achieve the appropriate result in each case

when the parties have not selected the applicable law. For a description of this convention see Juenger, The Inter–American Convention of the Law Applicable to International Contract Some Highlights and comparisons, 42 Am. J. Comp. L. 381 (1994). The Rome Convention in the European Union provides a more certain reference with its "characteristic performance" test. See infra § 18.22 n.3.

§ 18.22

1. Restatement, Second, Conflict of Laws § 188, cmnt. (f) (1971).

2. Id. The passage quoted cross-references to comment (c), in which the following example, among others, is given: "[A] state may have little interest in the application of a rule designed to protect a party against the unfair use of superior bargaining power if the contract is to be performed in another state which is the domicil of the person seeking the rule's protection."

lead to different results depending on the case and, in such circumstances, may be an inappropriate focus for choice of law in contract, as discussed earlier.[3]

Sections 189 through 199 provide particular rules for a number of situations.[4] The provisions, for instance those relating to agency, are treated in other contexts in the Restatement but are incorporated here. The following discussion in the main adopts the arrangement of the Restatement.

A. CONTRACTS BY SUBJECT MATTER

1. *Interests in Land*

§ 18.23 Contracts for the transfer of an interest in land (§ 189) differ from the transfer itself,[1] just as contractual duties arising from a transfer (§ 190) may, but need not affect the title. The usual rule that the transfer itself or questions relating to title are governed by the law of the situs[2] therefore need not apply. Thus, for instance, the capacity to make the contract may be determined by the law of the parties' common domicile[3] and covenants in a deed imposing personal obligations result-

---

3. European law also seeks to identify and apply the most closely connected law but employs a method that is perhaps less amorphous than the Restatement's. With exceptions (for instance, with respect to consumer and employment contracts), the applicable law is the law of the state of the habitual residence of the party who is to effect the "characteristic performance" (Rome Convention Art. 4). The payment of money, in this context, is *not* the characteristic performance: the counter performance is (the sale of goods, the rendition of services, etc.). Art. 4, para. 5 provides an escape clause for cases in which the characteristic performance cannot be determined or in which the contract is more closely connected with another state and law. Despite the escape clause, the Rome Convention may provide greater predictability than does the Restatement's *approach*. At the same time, it has been criticized as favoring the stronger party. For a review and comparison (with further references), see Hay, Flexibility versus Predictability and Uniformity in Choice of Law, Hague Academy, 226 Recueil des cours 281, 358–385 (1991–I).

4. In addition, § 202(2) provides that a contract will be denied enforcement (as distinguished from being declared invalid) when its performance would be illegal under the law of the place of performance. As the comments point out, no party expectations exist if the illegality were known, and, if unknown, could not be honored in this instance since neither a court in the state of performance nor in another can order illegal acts or award damages for the omission of illegal acts or award damages for the omission of illegal acts: Comment (e), at pp. 647–48. See infra also § 18.39.

§ 18.23

1. Restatement, Second, Conflict of Laws §§ 189, 191, cmnt. (a) (1971). See also infra Chapter 19.

2. Id. §§ 223 (validity and effect of conveyance), 224 (construction of instrument of conveyance), 226 (transfer by operation of law), 227 (acquisition by adverse possession), 228 (effect of mortgage), 229 (foreclosure), 230 (liens), 231–32 (power created by operation of law), 233–34 (effect of marriage), 235 (equitable interests), 236 (intestate succession), 238 (adoption as affecting succession), 239 (validity and effect of will), 241–42 (interests of surviving spouse), and 243 (escheat). The Oregon codification creates a "presumptive rule" that "Contracts involving the occupancy of real property, the land use of the property or the recording of interests in the real property are governed by the law of the state where the property is situated." O.R.S. § 81.135(2)(a), discussed in Nafziger, Oregon's Conflicts Law Applicable to Contracts, 3 Ybk. Priv. Int'l Law 391, 410 (2001).

3. Restatement, Second Conflict of Laws, § 189, cmnt. (d), illus. 2, 3 (1971).

ing in liability for damages upon breach,[4] may be governed by a law more significantly related to the particular issue than that of the situs. Such a law will be determined by the general principles of § 188 in conjunction with § 6. Nevertheless, the nature of the transaction is such that a focus on the *purpose* of the contract will often, even usually, lead to situs law as well.[5] Accordingly, §§ 189 and 190 adopt this reference in the absence of a contrary stipulation by the parties or of exceptional circumstances of the kind discussed.[6]

"Equitable conversion," whereby a contractual or testamentary direction to sell land prior to distribution of the proceeds may "convert" land into personal property, may bring into play choice-of-law rules applicable to movable rather than to immovable property. Since the underlying issue still relates to the disposition of the land, § 225 properly refers the question whether an equitable conversion has taken place to the law of the situs.[7]

2. *Sales of Chattels*

a. *Interstate Transactions*

i. *Restatement and U.C.C.*

§ 18.24   Both the Second Restatement, in § 191, and the Uniform Commercial Code, in § 1–105(1) in combination with § 2–401, deal with the sale of chattels. The Restatement provides, subject to the usual exception in favor of an express choice by the parties or a more significantly related law, that the law of the place should be applied "where under the items of the contract the seller is to deliver the chattel." U.C.C. § 1–105(1) provides for the application of forum law whenever the transaction bears an "appropriate relation" to the forum. Only a minority of states construe the reference to an "appropriate relation" so extensively as to permit the application of local law on the basis of only minimal contacts.[1] Instead, the trend is to equate "appropriate relation" with the "most significant relationship" of the Restate-

---

4. Restatement, Second, Conflict of Laws, § 190, cmnt. (a) (1971).

5. The approach of the Second Restatement is furthermore justified by the fact that the lines between contractual and title related claims are often fluid. Thus, a contract for the sale of land may, upon breach, result in a (contractual) claim for damages or in a title-related action to enforce the equitable title through an action for specific performance or, in reverse, to remove the cloud on the title by means of a quiet title action. See Harrison v. Rice, 89 Nev. 180, 510 P.2d 633, 635 (1973), appeal after remand 92 Nev. 645, 555 P.2d 1325 (1976). For an application of § 189, see also Traylor v. Grafton, 273 Md. 649, 332 A.2d 651, 659 (1975).

6. Texas Commerce Bank Nat. Ass'n v. Interpol '80 Ltd. Partnership, 703 S.W.2d 765 (Tex.App.1985).

7. See also Restatement, Second, Conflict of Laws § 278, cmmt. (e) (1971) (validity of trusts of land and equitable conversion).

§ 18.24

1. See Whitaker v. Harvell–Kilgore Corp., 418 F.2d 1010, 1016 (5th Cir.1969); Michael Schiavone & Sons, Inc. v. Securalloy Co., 312 F.Supp. 801, 803 n.1 (D.Conn. 1970). See also Warden, What Constitutes "Appropriate Relation to Forum", ISA Am. Jur.2d Commercial Code § 13 (1976), April 1997 Com.Supp.

ment.[2] Recent draft revisions of this Section would make this latter approach the explicitly preferred one by directing courts, in the absence of an effective choice-of-law clause, to apply their usual conflicts approach.[3]

The difference in approach thus lies in the particularization of a choice-of-law rule (place of delivery) by the Restatement, to be displaced only by a different rule of a more significantly related law, and the direct application of the most significantly related law by the U.C.C. However, given the almost universal adoption of the U.C.C., the substantive law applied will be the same in interstate transactions. This will not be so when particular Code provisions have been modified by some states or have been subject to different judicial construction or when the transaction is international in nature. In the last case, the U.C.C. § 1–105(1) may point to a law other than that of the forum, and § 191 of the Second Restatement, may again find application. Its reference to the place where "the seller is to deliver" may then be particularized by judicial adoption of the definition of U.C.C. § 2–401 that this is the place where the seller "completes his performance with reference to the physical delivery" of the goods.

ii. Case Law

A large number of the cases concerns damage claims[4] for breach of implied warranty. When these are decided on contract principles, rather than in tort[5] or as an independent claim,[6] the courts seldom cite to § 191 of the Second Restatement, but rather apply center-of-gravity notions.[7]

---

2. E.g., General Instrument Corp. v. Pennsylvania Pressed Metals, Inc., 366 F.Supp. 139, 146 (M.D.Pa.1973), aff'd 506 F.2d 1051 (3d Cir.1974); Petroleo Brasileiro, S.A. v. Ameropan Oil Corp., 372 F.Supp. 503, 508 n.23 (E.D.N.Y.1974); Larsen v. A.C. Carpenter, Inc., 620 F.Supp. 1084, 2 U.C.C.Rep. Serv.2d 433 (E.D.N.Y.1985), aff'd 800 F.2d 1128 (2d Cir.1986); American Electric Power Co., Inc. v. Westinghouse Electric Corp., 418 F.Supp. 435, 455 n.36 (S.D.N.Y.1976); Bunge Corp. v. Biglane, 418 F.Supp. 1159, 1163 (S.D.Miss.1976); In re Merritt Dredging Co., Inc., 839 F.2d 203 (4th Cir.1988), cert. denied 487 U.S. 1236, 108 S.Ct. 2904, 101 L.Ed.2d 936 (1988); Golden Rule Ins. Co. v. Hopkins, 788 F.Supp. 295 (S.D.Miss.1991). For the influx of interest analysis see Griffith v. United Air Lines, Inc., 416 Pa. 1, 21 n.17, 203 A.2d 796, 805 n.17 (1964) (§ 1–105 "permits analysis of the policies of interests underlying the particular issue before the court."); Golden Plains Feedlot, Inc. v. Great Western Sugar Co., 588 F.Supp. 985, 990 (D.S.D. 1984); In re Dakota Country Store Foods, Inc., 107 B.R. 977 (Bkrtcy.S.D.1989).

3. U.C.C. § 1–301(d) (2001 Revision).

4. For actions involving the purchase price see Boat Town U.S.A. Inc. v. Mercury Marine Division, 364 So.2d 15, 18 (Fla.App. 1978); Rhodes v. Superior Investigative Services, Inc., 437 F.Supp. 1012, 1016 n.2 (E.D.Pa.1977). In both cases the courts did not apply U.C.C. § 1–105 but the common law of the place of contracting and of performance. See also Larsen v. A.C. Carpenter, Inc., 620 F.Supp. 1084, 2 U.C.C.Rep. Serv.2d 433 (E.D.N.Y.1985), aff'd 800 F.2d 1128 (2d Cir.1986); Hercules & Co., Ltd. v. Shama Restaurant Corp., 566 A.2d 31 (D.C.Ct.App.1989).

5. Martin v. Julius Dierck Equipment Co., 52 A.D.2d 463, 466, 384 N.Y.S.2d 479, 482 (1976), aff'd 43 N.Y.2d 583, 403 N.Y.S.2d 185, 374 N.E.2d 97 (1978).

6. Sperry Rand Corp. v. Industrial Supply Corp., 337 F.2d 363, 368 (5th Cir.1964); Volkswagen of America, Inc. v. Young, 272 Md. 201, 220, 321 A.2d 737, 747 (1974).

7. E.g., Bowles v. Zimmer Manufacturing Co., 277 F.2d 868, 873 (7th Cir.1960); Neville Chemical Co. v. Union Carbide Corp., 422 F.2d 1205, 1211 (3d Cir.1970), cert. denied 400 U.S. 826, 91 S.Ct. 51, 27 L.Ed.2d 55 (1970); Continental–Wirt Electronics Corp. v. Sprague Electric Co., 329 F.Supp. 959, 963 (E.D.Pa.1971); Triangle

On their facts, most decisions would have been the same if the reference had been to the place of performance;[8] in both respects, they are therefore compatible with the Restatement provision.

The approaches of the Second Restatement and of the U.C.C. are more nearly identical with respect to the construction of a contract. While Second Restatement § 191 provides a reference to the place of delivery for the "validity of a contract [for the sale of goods] and the rights created thereby," § 204 provides, for all contracts, that a contract should be construed under the law generally applicable under § 188 (the place of the most significant relationship). The case law again largely ignores the Second Restatement provisions and refers questions of construction either to the contract's "center of gravity"[9] or the law of the place of making,[10] whereby the two often coincide on the facts of a given case.[11]

b. *International Transactions*

§ 18.25 The United Nations Convention on Contracts for the International Sale of Goods (also known as the "Vienna Convention") entered into force for the United States on January 1, 1988.[1] The

Underwriters, Inc. v. Honeywell, Inc., 457 F.Supp. 765, 768 (E.D.N.Y.1978), modified on other grounds 604 F.2d 737 (2d Cir. 1979), aff'd after remand 651 F.2d 132 (2d Cir.1981); Westerman v. Sears, Roebuck & Co., 577 F.2d 873, 879 (5th Cir.1978).

8. See Ionics, Inc. v. Elmwood Sensors, Inc., 896 F.Supp. 66 (D.Mass.1995), aff'd and remanded 110 F.3d 184 (1st Cir.1997); Sperry Rand v. Industrial Supply Corp., 337 F.2d 363, 369 (5th Cir.1964); Binkley Co. v. Teledyne Mid–America Corp., 333 F.Supp. 1183, 1185 (E.D.Mo.1971), aff'd 460 F.2d 276 (8th Cir.1972).

9. See Sanders v. Doe, 831 F.Supp. 886 (S.D.Ga.1993); Cosmopolitan Equities, Inc. v. Pacific Seafarers, Inc., 41 Misc.2d 772, 772, 246 N.Y.S.2d 412, 413 (1963). But see Bushkin Associates, Inc. v. Raytheon Co., 393 Mass. 622, 473 N.E.2d 662 (1985); Travenol Laboratories, Inc. v. Zotal, Ltd., 394 Mass. 95, 474 N.E.2d 1070, 1073 (1985) (both expressly adopting § 191 of the Second Restatement for the resolution of conflicts problems involving contracts).

10. See International Harvester Credit Corp. v. Ricks, 16 N.C.App. 491, 192 S.E.2d 707 (1972); Illinois Tool Works v. Sierracin Corp., 134 Ill.App.3d 63, 89 Ill.Dec. 40, 479 N.E.2d 1046 (1985) (California law applies as place where last act giving contract validity occurred; applicability of California law was factor in dismissal in Illinois for forum non conveniens).

11. McLouth Steel Corp. v. Jewell Coal & Coke Co., 570 F.2d 594, 601 (6th Cir.

1978), cert. dismissed 439 U.S. 801, 99 S.Ct. 43, 58 L.Ed.2d 94 (1978) (construing a requirements contract for coal according to the law of the place of making (Michigan) which was also the place of performance, thus arguably the contract's center of gravity). For further comparative treatment see Lorenz, Der Bereicherungsausgleich im deutschen internationalen Privatrecht und in rechtsvergleichender Sicht, Festschrift für Konrad Zweigert 199 (Bernstein, Drobnig, & Kötz, eds., 1981); for socialist countries, see Knapp, Die ungerechtsfertigte Bereicherung in den Rechten der europäischen sozialistischen Länder, supra, at 465.

§ 18.25

1. 52 Fed. Reg. 6262 (1987) 1987 WL 128849 (F.R.); 15 U.S.C.A.App. (2004). As of January 2004, the Convention is now in force, in addition to the United States, Argentina, Australia, Austria, Belarus, Belgium, Bosnia/Herzegovina, Bulgaria, Burundi, Canada, Chile, China, Colombia, Croatia, Cuba, Czech Republic, Denmark, Ecuador, Egypt, Estonia, Finland, France, Georgia, Germany, Greece, Guinea, Honduras, Hungary, Iceland, Iraq, Italy, Kyrgystan , Latvia, Lesotho, Lithuania, Luxembourg, Mauritania, Mexico, Moldova, Mongolia, Netherlands, New Zealand, Norway, Peru, Poland, Romania, Russian Federation, Singapore, Slovakia, Slovenia, Spain, St. Vincent & Grenadines, Sweden, Switzerland, Syrian Arab Republic, Uganda, Ukraine, Uruguay, Uzbekistan, Yugo-

Convention applies if the parties to the contract (1) have their places of business in different countries that have ratified the Convention, or (2) if the choice-of-law rules of the forum refer to the law of a contracting state.[2] Because of the second of these, parties who stipulate the application of a contracting state's law but do not wish to be subject to the Convention must *expressly* exclude the Convention's application.[3] The United States, Singapore, Slovakia, Czech Republic, and China ratified the Convention subject to a reservation (permitted by Article 95 of the Convention) that *excludes* the Convention's application as a result of a choice-of-law reference (No. 2 above). In these adopting states, the Convention will be applied *only* when the parties have businesses in different contracting states. The German ratification excludes application of the Convention by choice-of-law reference when the state to which the reference leads has made such an exclusion. Since the practice of states will therefore differ as to the applicability of the Convention, an express contractual stipulation in this regard is thus desirable.

The Convention's application, as stated, depends on the location of the parties' business, not upon their nationality. Thus, a contract between the French-based subsidiary or branch of an American corporation and an American-based corporation, perhaps even with its own parent, will be covered, but a contract between the American-based subsidiary or branch of a French-based enterprise and another American company will not be covered. It is also important to note that corporate separateness is not required: when a party has more than one place of business, the location of the one most closely connected with the transaction is determinative.

Part II of the Convention deals with the formation of contracts covered by it, i.e. offer and acceptance, while Part III deals with the rights and obligations of sellers and buyers, e.g. questions of modifica-

slavia, and Zambia. For commentary, see v. Caemmerer/Schlechtriem, Kommentar zum Einheitlichen UN–Kaufrecht (2d ed. (1995) (English translation and update by Schlechtriem, 1998); Schlechtriem et al. (eds.), Kommentar zum Einheitlichen Kaufrecht (3d ed. 2000); Lookofsky, Understanding the CISG in the U.S.A.: A Compact Guide to the 1980 United Nations Convention on Contracts for the International Sale of Goods (1995); Lookofsky, The 1980 United Nations Convention on Contracts for the International Sale of Goods, in: Blanpain, International Encyclopaedia of Laws—Contracts 1–156 (1993); Magnus, Die allgemeinen Grundsätze im UN–Kaufrecht, 59 Rabels Zeitschrift 467–94 (1995); Center for Comparative and Foreign Law Studies, UNILEX, International Case Law and Bibliography on the UN Convention on Contracts for the International Sale of Goods, Irvington-on-Hudson (N.Y.): Transnational Juris Publications (1995).

2. See for all possibilities of the Convention's application Pünder, Das einheitliche UN–Kaufrecht–Anwendung kraft kollisionsrechtlicher Verweisung nach Art. 1 Abs. 1 Lit.b UN–Kaufrecht, 1990 IPRax 869; Neumayer, Offene Fragen zur Anwendung des Abkommens der Vereinten Nationen über den internationalen Warenkauf, 1994 RIW 99; Siehr, Der internationale Anwendungsbereich des UN–Kaufrechts, 52 Rabelsz 587 (1988).

3. This result thus differs from the ordinary rule in American conflicts law that the stipulation of a state's law extends only to that state's "local law," and does not include that state's choice of law rules. Restatement, Second, Conflict of Laws § 187(3) (1971). By ratifying the Convention, contracting states have made it–as it were–their "local law for international cases:" hence there is a need to specify such a state's "local law for intrastate cases," if this is what the parties intend.

tion, breach or termination, damages, and ancillary duties.[4] The Convention provides parties with a ready-made framework for their international sale contracts, obviating the need to agree on a particular country's law (with perhaps insufficient knowledge of its content) or, absent such agreement, to have matters determined by choice-of-law rules which might be in flux.[5]

The 1964 Hague Convention Relating to a Uniform Law on the International Sale of Goods was adopted by nine countries.[6] For three of them (Germany, Italy and the Netherlands), it has been superseded by the Vienna Convention.

3. Insurance Contracts

§ 18.26   It is common knowledge that the insurance industry is highly regulated. What is less widely known is how deeply state statutory regulation extends into the field of conflict of laws. As noted earlier,[1] many state statutes mandate their application to insurance contracts that have certain enumerated contacts with the enacting state. In some of these statutes the enumerated contacts are significant. For example, in cases involving coverage for environmental contamination, some statutes mandate their application to cases in which the contaminated site is located in the enacting state.[2] In other statutes, the enumerated contacts

---

4. The Convention *excludes* consumer contracts as well as sales of stocks, other investment securities, and negotiable instruments. Unlike U.C.C. § 2–105, however, it does not define "goods" for purposes of showing what is *included*.

5. For analysis see J. Honnold, Uniform Law for International Sales Under the 1980 United Nations Convention (1982); Symposium, International Sale of Goods, 27 Am. J. Comp. L. 223–323 (1979); Bianca & Bonnell, eds., Commentary on the International Sales Law (1987). See also Winship, A Bibliography of Commentaries on the United Nations International Sales Convention, 21 Int'l Lawyer 585 (1987).

6. The Convention's text is reproduced at 13 Am. J. Comp. L. 453 (1964). The member states are Belgium, Gambia, Germany, Israel, Italy, Luxembourg, Netherlands, San Marino, and the United Kingdom. For commentary and criticism see Honnold, The Hague Convention of 1964, 1965 Law & Contemp. Prob. 327; Nadelmann, The Uniform Law of the International Sale of Goods: A Conflict of Laws Imbroglio, 74 Yale L.J. 448 (1964). Article 1 of the Convention provides substantive rules of law whenever (1) the contract provides for carriage of goods from one state to another, or (2) the offer and acceptance were made in different states, or (3) delivery is to take place in a state other than the

state in which the contract was concluded. An important feature, critically noted by Nadelmann is the provision of Art. II which excludes reference to ordinary principles of conflicts law. As a result, a contract for the sale of goods between American and Canadian parties could be subject to the rules of the Convention if litigation arose in a contracting state. The relatively low number of ratifications led to the elaboration of the Vienna Convention which is discussed above.

§ 18.26

1. See supra § 18.5. nn. 6–7.

2. For example, and Oregon statute provides that "Oregon law shall be applied in all cases where the contaminated property to which the action relates is located within the State of Oregon." Or.Rev.Stat. § 465.480(2)(a). The statute also provides that nothing in it "shall be interpreted to modify common law rules governing choice of law determinations for sites located outside the State of Oregon." Id. Thus, the statute preserves the possibility of applying Oregon law to non-Oregon sites as well. See also Mich.Comp.Laws § 324.1804 ("The law to be applied ... , including what constitutes 'pollution' is the law of this state, excluding choice of law rules."); Colo.Rev. Stat. §§ 13–1.5–104; Wis.Stat. § 299.33(4).

can be tenuous. For example, a Nevada statute mandates its application to: "1. *All* insurers authorized to transact insurance in this state; 2. *All* insurers having policyholders resident in this state; [and] 3. *All* insurers against whom a claim under an insurance contract may arise in this state."[3] As noted earlier, many of these statutes expressly prohibit choice-of-law clauses.[4] Statutes like the above are typical examples unilateral choice-of-law rules that delineate a priori the scope of application of the *lex fori* and essentially preempt a judicial choice-of-law analysis for all those cases that fall within their scope.[5] Consequently, one is well advised to search for such statutes before choosing a forum or searching for case law.

The most numerous among insurance conflicts are those involving automobile insurance. The majority of these cases involve the issue of uninsured or underinsured motorist (UM or UIM) coverage in actions brought by the insureds against their own insurers. The typical pattern is one in which a person who, in his or her home state purchased a policy insuring a car registered and garaged in that state, is involved in an accident in another state caused by an uninsured or underinsured motorist. A conflict results when the two states have different limits of or requirements for UM coverage, or take different positions on the validity of anti-stacking or setoff clauses contained in the policy. Like other insurance conflicts, these conflicts tend to depend heavily on local statutes, such as the ones described above. More common than the above are statutes that require the application of the law of the forum state if: (a) the insurance policy was delivered, or issued for delivery, in that state; or (b) the insured automobile is principally garaged there; or (c) the accident occurred there.

When the forum does not have such a statute, or when the court finds the statute inapplicable, the court resolves the conflict under the forum's judicial choice-of-law approach. Besides the few states that continue to follow the *lex loci contractus*, the majority of states follow approaches based on §§ 193 or 188 of the Second Restatement, or other similar flexible approaches. Regardless of the approach, however, most recent cases exhibit a trend away from applying the law of the place of

---

3. Nev.Rev.Stat. § 696B.020 (emphasis added). Similar statutes exist in other states. For example, a Texas statute provides that "[a]ny contract of insurance payable to any citizen or inhabitant of this State by any insurance company ... doing business within this State shall be ... governed by [the laws of this State] notwithstanding such ... contract ... may provide that the contract was executed and the premiums ... should be payable without this State." Tex.Ins.Code Ann. § 21.42. A North Carolina statute provides that "[a]ll contracts of insurance on property, lives, or interests in this State shall be deemed to be made therein, and all contracts of insurance the applications for which are taken within

the State shall be deemed to be made within this State and are subject to the laws thereof." N.C.Gen.Stat. § 58–3–1.

4. For example, an Oregon statute provides that, for an insurance policy "delivered or issued for delivery in this state," any "condition, stipulation or agreement requiring such policy to be construed according to the laws of any other state or country ... shall be invalid." Or.Rev.Stat. §§ 742.001, 742.018. See also Tex.Ins.Code Ann. § 21.42.

5. See Symeonides, American Choice of Law at the Dawn of the 21st Century, 37 Willamette L. Rev. 1, 28–32, 40–41 (2000).

the accident as such, perhaps because most of them employ a contract choice-of-law analysis. Most recent cases apply the law of the state where the insured automobile is principally garaged, which usually is also the state in which the insured is domiciled and/or the policy has been delivered,[6] but one still finds cases that continue to apply the law of the accident state.[7]

The Second Restatement in §§ 192 and 193, as well as the case law, distinguish between life and casualty insurance contract. With respect to life insurance contracts, section 192 provides that, in the absence of a contrary choice-of-law agreement, the applicable law is the law of the state in which the insured was domiciled at the time the policy was applied for, unless another state has a more significant relationship.[8] This rule is consistent with the case law, both before and after the Restatement,[9] and has its origin in the concern to protect insureds against adhesion contracts, a concern that is further reflected in their limited ability to select the applicable law by stipulation.[10]

6. See, e.g., State Farm Mut. Auto. Ins. Co. v. Gillette, 251 Wis.2d 561, 641 N.W.2d 662 (2002); Ohayon v. Safeco Ins. Co., 91 Ohio St.3d 474, 747 N.E.2d 206 (2001); Cecere v. Aetna Ins. Co., 145 N.H. 660, 766 A.2d 696 (2001); Fortune Ins. Co. v. Owens, 351 N.C. 424, 526 S.E.2d 463 (2000); Ryals v. State Farm Mut. Ins. Co., 134 Idaho 302, 1 P.3d 803 (2000); Great West Cas. Co. v. Hovaldt, 603 N.W.2d 198 (S.D.1999); U.S. Fidelity & Guar. Co. v. Preston, 26 S.W.3d 145 (Ky.2000); In re Allstate Ins. Co. (Stolarz), 81 N.Y.2d 219, 597 N.Y.S.2d 904, 613 N.E.2d 936 (1993) (discussed in Borchers, Choice of Law in the American Courts in 1992: Observations and Reflections, 42 Am. J. Comp. L. 124 (1994)); Flaherty v. Allstate Ins. Co., 822 A.2d 1159 (Me.2003). For discussion of these and other cases, see Symeonides, Choice of Law in the American Courts in 2002: Sixteenth Annual Survey, 51 Am.J.Comp.L. 1, 70–73 (2003); Symeonides, Choice of Law in the American Courts in 2001: Fifteenth Annual Survey, 50 Am. J. Comp. L. 1, 46–56 (2002).

7. See, e.g., Mitchell v. State Farm Ins. Co., 315 Mont. 281, 68 P.3d 703 (2003); State Farm Mut. Auto. Ins. Co. v. Ballard, 132 N.M. 696, 54 P.3d 537 (2002); Nodak Mut. Ins. Co. v. American Family Mut. Ins. Co., 604 N.W.2d 91 (Mn.2000); Csulik v. Nationwide Mut. Ins. Co., 88 Ohio St.3d 17, 723 N.E.2d 90 (2000); Williams v. State Farm Mut. Auto. Ins. Co., 229 Conn. 359, 641 A.2d 783 (1994).

8. A European Community Directive (No. 88/357, O.J. 1988, L172) requires member states to adopt detailed conflicts rules with respect to all types of insurance other than life insurance. The Directive focuses on the habitual residence of the insured and the location of the insured risk,

and has provisions, with limitations depending on the type of transaction (standard form insurance or special "large scale" hazard insurance), on contractual choice of law. See Fricke, Die Neuregelung des IPR der Versicherungsverträge im EGVVG durch das Gesetz zur Durchfhhrung versicherungsrechtlicher Richtlinien des Rates der Europäischen Gemeinschaften, 1990 IPRax 361; Dörner, Internationales Versicherungsvertragsrecht (1997).

9. See, e.g., Mayo v. Hartford Life Ins. Co., 354 F.3d 400 (5th Cir. 2004) (question of whether beneficiary had an insurable interest in the decedent's life determined by decedent's domicile); Zogg v. Penn Mut. Life Ins. Co., 276 F.2d 861, 863–64 (2d Cir.1960); Strubbe v. Sonnenschein, 299 F.2d 185, 97 A.L.R.2d 1386 (2d Cir. 1962); Barton v. National Life Assurance Co. of Canada, 91 Misc.2d 951, 398 N.Y.S.2d 941 (1977), reversed on other grounds 98 Misc.2d 300, 413 N.Y.S.2d 807 (1978); Brown v. Inter–Ocean Ins. Co., 438 F.Supp. 951 (N.D.Ga.1977); Strassberg v. New England Mut. Life Ins. Co., 575 F.2d 1262 (9th Cir.1978) (interest analysis).

10. See supra § 18.5. In the case of group life insurance provided by an employer, comment (h) to § 192 notes that " ... rights against the insurer are usually governed by the law which governs the master policy. This is so because it is desirable that each individual insured should enjoy the same privileges and protection." In addition, and in contrast to individual insurance policies, the insured under a group insurance contract may not need the same protection against adhesion contracts, given the employer's bargaining power. Reger v.

With regard to casualty insurance, § 193 of the Second Restatement calls for the application of the law of the state in which the parties understood was to be the "principal location" of the insured risk, unless, again, another state has a more significant relationship. This section too has significant following in the case law, but, when the insured risk is located in more than one state, the following is not universal. Indeed, especially in cases involving coverage for environmental contamination, courts are divided as to whether to apply a single law to all risks or instead apply the the law of each state to the risk situated in that state.[11] Some cases follow the first option—known as the "uniform-contract-interpretation" approach and usually based on § 188 of the Restatement—which focuses on the insurance contract and aspires to apply the law of a single state, even when the contract covers multiple risks situated in different states.[12] This approach usually leads to the application of the law of a state that is either the place of the making of the

National Ass'n of Bedding Manufacturers Group Ins. Trust Fund, 83 Misc.2d 527, 372 N.Y.S.2d 97 (1975). See also Oakley v. National Western Life Ins. Co., 294 F.Supp. 504 (S.D.N.Y.1968); Perkins v. Philadelphia Life Ins. Co., 586 F.Supp. 296 (W.D.Mo. 1984), aff'd 755 F.2d 632 (8th Cir.1985) (group life insurance contract governed by law of corporate insured's place of business and not by individual (employee's) residence). But see Nelson v. Aetna Life Ins. Co., 359 F.Supp. 271 (W.D.Mo.1973); Krauss v. Manhattan Life Ins. Co. of New York, 643 F.2d 98 (2d Cir.1981) (holding that, even though the master group life insurance policy was issued and delivered in New York, the suit was governed by the law of Illinois, the domicile of the insured and of the beneficiary and the location of the insured's employer).

11. For a discussion of these two options and the cases following them, see the annual choice-of-law surveys by Symeonides in 42 Am. J. Comp. L. 599, 645–49 (1994); 43 Am.J.Comp.L. 1, 75, 80–82 (1995); 44 Am.J.Comp.L. 181, 230–32 (1996); 45 Am. J.Comp.L. 447, 491–92 (1998); 47 Am. J.Comp.L. 327, 360–71 (1999).

12. See, e.g., Maryland Cas. Co. v. Continental Cas. Co., 332 F.3d 145 (2d Cir. 2003) (decided under New York conflicts law; critically noted in Symeonides, Choice of Law in the American Courts in 2003: Seventeenth Annual Survey, 52 Am. J.Comp. L. __ (2004); Lapham–Hickey Steel Corp. v. Protection Mut. Ins. Co., 166 Ill.2d 520, 655 N.E.2d 842, 845 (1995); Emerson Electric Co. v. Aetna Cas. & Sur. Co., 319 Ill.App.3d 218, 743 N.E.2d 629 (2001); Household International, Inc. v. Liberty Mut. Ins. Co., 321 Ill.App.3d 859, 749 N.E.2d 1 (2001); Asbestos Removal Corp. v. Guaranty Nat. Ins. Co., 48 F.3d 1215 (4th Cir. 1995) (Virginia conflicts law); Bituminous Cas. Corp. v. St. Clair Lime Co., 69 F.3d 547 (10th Cir. 1995) (Oklahoma conflicts law); Sequa Corp. v. Aetna Cas. & Sur. Co., 1995 WL 465192 (Del. Super. 1995); Aetna Cas. & Sur. Co. v. Dow Chemical Co., 883 F.Supp. 1101 (E.D.Mich.1995); Employers Ins. of Wausau v. Duplan Corp., 899 F.Supp. 1112 (S.D.N.Y. 1995); CPC Int'l, Inc. v. Aerojet–General Corp., 825 F.Supp. 795 (W.D.Mich.1993); Board of Regents of Univ. of Minn. v. Royal Ins. Co., 503 N.W.2d 486 (Minn.App.1993); Commercial Union Ins. Co. v. Porter Hayden Co., 97 Md.App. 442, 630 A.2d 261 (1993); Gould, Inc. v. Continental Cas. Co, 822 F.Supp. 1172 (E.D.Pa., 1993); Westinghouse Electric Corp. v Liberty Mut. Ins. Co, 233 N.J.Super. 463, 559 A.2d 435, (1989), Lumbermens Mut. Cas. Co. v. Connecticut Bank and Trust Co., 806 F.2d 411, 415 (2d Cir. 1986); Eli Lilly & Co. v. Home Ins. Co., 764 F.2d 876, 246 U.S.App.D.C. 243 (1985); Vigen Constr. Co. v. Millers Nat. Ins. Co., 436 N.W.2d 254 (N.D.1989); Eli Lilly & Co. v. Home Ins. Co., 764 F.2d 876 (D.C.Cir.1985). Questions of construction of the insurance contract are frequently referred to the law of the place of contracting: e.g., Brand Distributors, Inc. v. Insurance Co. of North America, 400 F.Supp. 1085 (E.D.Va.1974), reversed on other grounds 532 F.2d 352 (4th Cir.1976); Mission Ins. Co. v. Nethers, 119 Ariz. 405, 581 P.2d 250 (1978). See also Whiteside v. New Castle Mut. Ins., Co., 595 F.Supp. 1096 (D.Del.1984); McClaney v. Utility Equipment Leasing Corp., 560 F.Supp. 1265 (N.D.N.Y. 1983); Interface Flooring Systems, Inc. v. Aetna Cas. & Sur. Co., 261 Conn. 601, 804 A.2d 201 (2001) (law of tender of defense governed by place of insured risk). But see Snow v. Admiral Ins. Co., 612 F.Supp. 206, 209–10 (W.D.Ark. 1985).

contract or has other significant connections with the *contract* and the parties but not necessarily the location of the risk. More numerous are the cases that follow the second option—called "site-specific approach" and based on § 193—which abandons the goal of applying a single law to the whole contract and focuses instead on the interests of the state or states where the insured risks are located. The applicable law is usually the law of that state or states (the site-states), unless another state has a more significant relationship with regard to the particular issue.[13]

A slightly different problem from that involving multistate risks appears in situations in which the principal location of the insured risk[14] —or in life insurance policies the domicile of the insured—[15]changes between the time the policy was issued and the insured risk material-ized. While the application of a new law may affect the insurer's liability, for instance because the new law prohibits short time limitations or contains more stringent requirements for notices of default, the regula-tory interest of the new state justifies the change so long as it may exercise such regulatory power within the limits of due process.[16]

13. See, e.g., Reichhold Chemicals, Inc. v. Hartford Acc. & Indem. Co., 252 Conn. 774, 750 A.2d 1051 (Conn. 2000); Pfizer, Inc. v. Employers Ins. of Wausau, 154 N.J. 187, 712 A.2d 634 (1998); Unisys Corp. v. Ins. Co. of North America, 154 N.J. 217, 712 A.2d 649 (1998); HM Holdings, Inc. v. Aetna Cas. & Sur. Co., 154 N.J. 208, 712 A.2d 645 (1998); Reichhold Chemicals, Inc. v. Hartford Accident & Indemnity Co., 243 Conn. 401, 703 A.2d 1132 (1997); Gilbert Spruance Co. v. Pennsylvania Manufactur-er's Ass'n Ins. Co., 134 N.J. 96, 629 A.2d 885 (1993); Union Carbide Corp. v. Aetna Cas. & Sur. Co., 212 Conn. 311, 562 A.2d 15 (1989); Consolidated Mut. Ins. Co. v. Radio Foods Corp., 108 N.H. 494, 240 A.2d 47 (1968); Boardman Petroleum, Inc. v. Feder-ated Mut. Ins. Co., 135 F.3d 750 (11th Cir. 1998); NL Industries, Inc. v. Commercial Union Ins. Co., 154 F.3d 155 (3d Cir. 1998) (New Jersey conflicts law); LaFarge Corp. v. Travelers Indemnity Co., 118 F.3d 1511 (11th Cir. 1997) (Florida conflicts law); Mil-lipore Corp. v. Travelers Indemnity Co., 115 F.3d 21 (1st Cir. 1997) (Massachusetts con-flicts law); General Ceramics Inc. v. Fire-men's Fund Ins. Co., 66 F.3d 647 (3rd Cir. 1995); CPC International, Inc. v. North-brook Excess & Surplus Ins. Co., 46 F.3d 1211 (1st Cir. 1995) (Rhode Island conflicts law); Byers v. Auto–Owners Ins. Co., 119 S.W.3d 659 (Mo.App.2003); Param Petro-leum Corp. v. Commerce & Industry Ins. Co., 296 N.J.Super. 164, 686 A.2d 377 (1997); Hartford Acc. & Indem. Co. v. Dana Corp., 690 N.E.2d 285 (Ind.App. 1998); Al-bert Trostel & Sons Co. v. Employers Ins. of Wausau, 216 Wis.2d 382, 576 N.W.2d 88 (1998); Commercial Union Ins. Co. v. Port Hayden Co., 116 Md.App. 605, 698 A.2d

1167 (1997); Permacel v. American Ins. Co., 299 N.J.Super. 400, 691 A.2d 383 (1997); W.C. Richards Co., Inc. Hartford Indemnity Co., 682 N.E.2d 220 (Ill. App. 1997); and J. Josephson, Inc. v. Crum & Forster Ins. Co., 293 N.J.Super. 170, 679 A.2d 1206 (1996); Morton Int'l, Inc. v. Aetna Cas. & Sur. Co., 106 Ohio App.3d 653, 666 N.E.2d 1163 (1995); CXY Chemicals U.S.A. v. Gerling Global General Ins. Co., 991 F.Supp. 770 (E.D.La. 1998); Wysong & Miles Co. v. Em-ployers of Wausau, 4 F.Supp.2d 421 (M.D.N.C. 1998); EDO Corp. v. Newark Ins. Co., 1997 WL 76575 (D. Conn. 1997); In re Combustion, Inc., 960 F.Supp. 1056, 1062 (W.D.La. 1997); Green Mountain Power Corp. v. Certain Underwriters at Lloyd's London, 1995 WL 433597 (D. Vt. 1995); E.B. & A.C. Whiting Co. v. Hartford Fire Ins. Co., 838 F.Supp. 863 (D.Vt., 1993); Jones Truck Lines v. Transport Ins. Co., 1989 WL 49517 (E.D. Pa. 1989).

14. Clay v. Sun Ins. Office, Ltd., 377 U.S. 179, 84 S.Ct. 1197, 12 L.Ed.2d 229 (1964); Restatement, Second, Conflict of Laws § 193, cmnt. (d) (1971).

15. Restatement, Second, Conflict of Laws § 192, cmnt. (d) (1971). Phillips v. South Carolina Ins. Co., 607 F.Supp. 593 (M.D.Ga.1985) (when insured moved from South Carolina to Georgia and insurer al-lowed coverage to continue, policy became subject to Georgia law and insurer was re-quired to make available optional no-fault coverage as provided by Georgia statute).

16. Clay v. Sun Ins. Office, Ltd., 377 U.S. 179, 84 S.Ct. 1197, 12 L.Ed.2d 229 (1964). Compare Home Ins. Co. v. Dick, 281 U.S. 397, 50 S.Ct. 338, 74 L.Ed. 926 (1930).

Finally, another controversial issue in recent litigation is whether an insurer should cover punitive damages assessed against the insured.[17] As of 2003, 25 states allowed the insurability of punitive damages, nine states allowed it only in cases of vicarious liability, eight states prohibited it, and the remaining states had not taken a definitive stance.[18] Here, the conflicting policies are (a) ascertaining and protecting the justified expectations of the insured and the insurer, and (b) deterring the type of misconduct that evokes punitive damages by not allowing the insured to pass on the pain of punitive damages to the insurer. A common strategy in these cases is the use of declaratory judgment actions, either offensively or defensively. Many of these case involve the familiar race to the most hospitable forum, with the insurer bringing such an action in one state and the insured in another Again, the basic choice-of-law options are: (a) to focus on the insurance contract; or (b) to focus on the place where the risk was located and materialized. Although the courts remain divided between these two options, it seems that the forum's own position on the issue of the insurability of punitive damages weighs heavily in choosing between these two options.[19]

4. Suretyship

§ 18.27 Section 194 of the Second Restatement provides for the application of the law governing the principal (underlying) obligation to contracts of suretyship or guaranty. This is so because the contracts are intimately related in terms of subject matter, usually will have been concluded at or near the same time, and because uniformity with respect to the rights and liabilities of the parties is desirable.[1] The case law, in the main,[2] follows this approach;[3] decisions applying a different law may

---

17. For discussion of recent conflicts cases, see the annual choice-of-law surveys by Symeonides in 50 Am.J.Comp.L. 1, 56–57 (2002); 43 Am.J.Comp.L. 1, 75–80 (1995); 42 Am.J.Comp.L. 599, 649–50 (1994); 38 Am.J.Comp.L. 601, 621–23 (1990).

18. See J. Stein, Personal Injury Damages, § 4:37 (3d ed. 2003).

19. For representative cases, see Fluke Corp. v. Hartford Accident & Ind. Co., 145 Wash.2d 137, 34 P.3d 809 (2001); Hartford Accident & Ind. Co. v. American Red Ball Transit Co., Inc., 262 Kan. 570, 938 P.2d 1281 (1997); St. Paul Surplus Lines v. International Playtex, Inc., 245 Kan. 258, 777 P.2d 1259 (1989), cert. denied, 493 U.S. 1036, 110 S.Ct. 758, 107 L.Ed.2d 774 (1990), Zurich Ins. Co. v. Shearson Lehman Hutton, Inc., 84 N.Y.2d 309, 618 N.Y.S.2d 609, 642 N.E.2d 1065 (1994); Meijer, Inc. v. General Star Indem. Co., 826 F.Supp. 241 (W.D.Mich.1993); United States Gypsum Co. v. Admiral Ins. Co., 268 Ill.App.3d 598, 643 N.E.2d 1226 (1994); Stonewall Surplus

Lines Ins. Co. v. Johnson Controls, Inc., 14 Cal.App.4th 637, 17 Cal.Rptr.2d 713 (1993); American Home Assur. v. Safeway Steel Prod., 743 S.W.2d 693 (Tex. App. Austin 1987); Johnson Controls, Inc. v. American Motorists Inc., 719 F.Supp. 1459 (E.D. Wis. 1989); Alcolac Inc. v. St. Paul Fire & Marine Ins. Co., 716 F.Supp. 1541 (D. Md. 1989);

§ 18.27

1. Restatement, Second, Conflict of Laws § 194, cmnt. (b) (1971). The comment also refers to the "accessory," "subsidiary" nature of the contract of surety.

2. Some decisions focus on the law of the place of contracting if the same as place of performance. See, e.g., In re Leonard Bagley, 6 B.R. 387 (Bkrtcy.N.D.Ga.1980); Paul Revere Protective Life Ins. Co. v. Sigfried Weis and Robert F. Weis, 535 F.Supp. 379 (E.D.Pa.1981); General Telephone Co. of the Southeast v. Trimm, 706 F.2d 1117 (11th Cir.1983); Travelers Indemnity Co. v.

---

3. See p. 1017.

do so because of the common domicile or place of business of the parties[4] or because of the governmental interests of the forum.[5]

5. Contracts for the Repayment of Money Lent

§ 18.28   A part of the literature favors the application of the law of the debtor to afford him protection against the presumably economically stronger lender,[1] and legislation in a number of states provides protection for the consumer in small loan transactions, especially against

3. See p. 1017.Allied–Signal, Inc., 718 F.Supp. 1252 (D.Md.1989); Safeco Ins. Co. of America v. Criterion Investment Corp., 732 F.Supp. 834 (E.D.Tenn.1989).

3. E.g., L & A Contracting v. Southern Concrete Services, 17 F.3d 106, 109 (5th Cir.1994)(§§ 194 and 188 approach); Phoenix Arbor Plaza, Ltd. v. Jerry L. Dauderman, 163 Ariz. 27, 785 P.2d 1215 (1989) (application of § 194 but place of contracting was the same); District of Columbia Ins. Guaranty Ass'n v. Algernon Blair, Inc., 565 A.2d 564 (1989)(§ 194 approach in combination with place of contracting); Adams v. Agnew, 860 F.2d 1093, 1096 (C.A.D.C. 1988); Marshall Contractors, Inc. v. Peerless Ins. Co., 827 F.Supp. 91, 94 (D.R.I. 1993); General Electric Co. v. Keyser, 166 W.Va. 456, 275 S.E.2d 289 (1981)(§§ 194 and 188 approach); New England Merchants Nat. Bank v. Rosenfield, 679 F.2d 467, 471 (5th Cir.1982), cert. denied 459 U.S. 1173, 103 S.Ct. 819, 74 L.Ed.2d 1017 (1983).

4. See, e.g., Chase Manhattan Bank v. Greenbriar, 835 S.W.2d 720 (1992)(place of business/domicile as one important point among others); Amerco Marketing Co. of Memphis, Inc. v. Myers, 494 F.2d 904 (6th Cir.1974). See also Siata Int'l U.S.A. Inc. v. Insurance Co. of North America, 362 F.Supp. 1355 (E.D.Pa.1973), reversed and remanded 498 F.2d 817 (3d Cir.1974), inter alia, because the trial court had failed to consider a choice-of-law clause.

5. See Carey v. Bahama Cruise Lines, 864 F.2d 201 (1st Cir.1988)(importance of state interest); Ashland Chemical Co. v. Ross C. Provence, 129 Cal.App.3d 790, 181 Cal.Rptr. 340 (1982)(intended application of the statute of limitation); Van Vonno v. The Hertz Corp., 120 Wn.2d 416, 841 P.2d 1244 (1992); Potlatch No. 1 Federal Credit Union v. Kennedy, 76 Wn.2d 806, 459 P.2d 32 (1969); Granite Equipment Leasing Corp. v. Hutton, 84 Wn.2d 320, 525 P.2d 223 (1974). In *Granite Equipment,* the main obligation concerned a lease of equipment by a New York company to an Oregon motel. The

guaranty had been given in Washington to the New York company which maintained an office there by representatives of an Arizona company. When sued upon the guaranty, the Arizona company defended on the ground that its representatives had acted ultra vires. The Washington court applied neither the law of the main obligation—presumably Oregon's—nor that of the New York creditor. Rather, Washington's interest in the conduct of business transactions in Washington called for the application of the lex fori. The case, on its facts, thus resembles Lilienthal v. Kaufman, 239 Or. 1, 395 P.2d 543 (1964) (discussed supra § 18.20) if the latter had involved litigation in California.

§ 18.28

1. See R. Weintraub, Commentary on Conflict of Laws 481 et seq. (4th ed. 2001); Western, Usury in the Conflict of Laws: The Doctrine of the Lex Debitoris, 55 Cal. L. Rev. 123 (1967). See also Currier v. Tuck, 112 N.H. 10, 287 A.2d 625 (1972); A.L. Schwartz, Construction and Effect of UCC Art. 9, Dealing with Secured Transactions, Sales of Accounts, Contract Rights, and Chattel Paper, § 36, 30 A.L.R.3d 9 (1970); Annot., Conflict of Laws, 16 Am. Jur.2d § 87 (1979). New articles concerning this issue (but not generally favoring the law of the debtor): Letsou, The Political Economy of Consumer Credit Regulation, 44 Emory L.J. 587 (1995); Guenin, Choice of Law in Usury, 109 Banking L.J. 71 (1992). See also Greenwood Trust Co. v. Commonwealth of Massachusetts and Attorney General of the Commonwealth of Massachusetts, 776 F.Supp. 21 (D.Mass. 1991), rev'd. on other grounds 971 F.2d 818 (1st Cir.1992).

Application of the law of the place of the federally insured lender under federal banking law as exception to the general application of debtors law: first case Marquette National Bank of Minneapolis v. First of Omaha Service Corp. et al. State of Minnesota v. First of Omaha Service Corp. et al.,

usurious interest rates.[2] Small loan statutes apart, the case law tends to apply, in accordance with § 195 of the Second Restatement, the law of the place where the promissory note is payable.[3] This will ordinarily coincide with the law of contracting and the location of the lender.[4] Additionally, the "validation principle" serves to uphold contracts that may be usurious under forum law but not where made or to be performed.[5] Other than in the area of insurance, the debtor's law— except in the context of small (consumer) loans—yields to interests of interstate commerce and credit transactions.

439 U.S. 299, 99 S.Ct. 540, 58 L.Ed.2d 534 (1978). In 1980 extension of the protection in Congress, see 12 U.S.C.A. § 1831(d).

2. Statutory protections for small loan lenders (mostly consumers): Georgia O.C.G.A. § 7.4; Miss. Code Ann. §§ 75–67–101, 75–67–127, 75–67–205; New Hampshire RSA 399–A:3, A:4; N.M. Stat.Ann. § 58–15; N.Y. Bank. L. § 352, 353; N.D.Cent. Code § 13–03.1–15.1; Ohio Rev. Code §§ 1321.01, 1321.02; 19 R.I. Gen.Laws § 14.2; Cal.Const. Art. 15, § 1, Cal.Fin. Code § 21200, Cal.Bus. & Prof. Code § 10242, Cal.Civ.Code § 1916; S.C. Code Ann. § 34–29–140; S.D. Cod. Laws § 54–6–22; Alabama Code § 5–18–2, s. 8–8; Alaska Stat. § 45.45; Ark.Stat.Ann. § 4–57; Colo. Code §§ 5–3–104, 5–13–103; Conn.Gen.Stat. § 37–4; D.C.Code § 28–3301; Haw. Rev. Stat. § 478; Fla.Stat.Ann. § 687.01; Idaho Code § 28–42.201; Illinois 815 ILCS 205/4, 205 ILCS 670/1; Kan. Stat. Ann. § 16a–2–401; Iowa Code Annot. § 535; Kent. Rev. Stat. § 360; Mich.C.L.Ann. § 438; Minn. Stat.Ann. § 334; Mont. Code Ann. § 32–5–302; N.J.Stat.Ann. § 31.1; N.C.Gen.Stat. §§ 14–391, 24–8, 53–178; Ind.Code Ann. § 28–7–5–28, IC 24–4.5–3–104; W.Va.Code § 46A–3–105.

3. For an early decision see W.H. Barber Co. v. Hughes, 223 Ind. 570, 63 N.E.2d 417 (1945). See also Residential Industrial Loan Co. v. Brown, 559 F.2d 438 (5th Cir. 1977); Birger v. Tuner, 104 Misc.2d 63, 427 N.Y.S.2d 904 (1980).

4. See American Training Service, Inc. v. Commerce Union Bank, 415 F.Supp. 1101, 1104 (M.D.Tenn.1976), aff'd 612 F.2d 580 (6th Cir.1979); Tuition Plan, Inc. v. Zicari, 70 Misc.2d 918, 335 N.Y.S.2d 95 (1972); Suitt Construction Co., Inc. v. Seaman's Bank for Savings, 30 N.C.App. 155, 226 S.E.2d 408 (1976); Pacific Gamble Robinson Co. v. Lapp, 95 Wn.2d 341, 622 P.2d 850 (1980). But see: HIMC Investment Co. v. Siciliano, 103 N.J.Super. 27, 246 A.2d 502 (Law Div.1968) (borrower's law). Sec-

ond Restatement § 195 approach: Becker v. Marketing & Research Consultants, Inc., 526 F.Supp. 166, 169, 170 (D.Colo.1981); Hardaway Constructors v. Conesco Industries, 583 F.Supp. 617, 622 (D.N.J.1983); Finance America Corp. v. Moyler, 494 A.2d 926, 929, 930 (D.C.App.1985); Nelson v. Nationwide Mortg. Corp., 659 F.Supp. 611, 616 (D.D.C. 1987); Philips Credit Corp. v. Regent Health Group, Inc., 953 F.Supp. 482, 501 (S.D.N.Y.1997); Gainer Bank, N.A. v. Jenkins, 284 Ill.App.3d 500, 219 Ill.Dec. 809, 672 N.E.2d 317, 319 (1996); Bowmer v. Dettelbach, 109 Ohio App.3d 680, 672 N.E.2d 1081, 1082, 1085, 1086 (1996).

5. North American Bank, Ltd. v. Schulman, 123 Misc.2d 516, 474 N.Y.S.2d 383, (1984) (personal loan for $8,500 to an individual stipulated for the application of the law of Israel where lender's principal place of business was located; under Israeli law stipulated interest rate of 18 1/4% was valid; the New York ceiling was 16%; choice of Israeli law held unenforceable). It may now bear special emphasis, as the main text already suggests, that the more liberal view of usury statutes which, combined with validation principles, was designed to afford protection to the lender will now yield to the needs for consumer protection. See supra § 18.5 nn.1–5, 12–15; Restatement, Second, Conflict of Laws § 203 (1971); Key Bank of Alaska v. Myllie Jo Donnels, 106 Nev. 49, 787 P.2d 382 (1990); Industrial Development Bank of Israel Ltd. v. Jules Bier and Natanel Bier, 149 Misc.2d 797, 565 N.Y.S.2d 980 (1991), aff'd 182 A.D.2d 570, 582 N.Y.S.2d 429 (1992); Greenwood Trust Co. v. Commonwealth of Massachusetts and Attorney General of the Commonwealth of Massachusetts, 776 F.Supp. 21 (D.Mass. 1991), rev'd on other grounds 971 F.2d 818 (1st Cir.1992); In re McCorhill Publishing, Inc. v. Greater New York Savings Bank, 86 B.R. 783, 793 (Bkrtcy.S.D.N.Y.1988); In re Richard L. Giantvalley and Antoinette H. Giantvalley, 14 B.R. 457, 458 (Bkrtcy. D.Nev.1981). But see supra n.2.

6. *Rendition of Services*[1]

§ 18.29 The broad provision of § 196 of the Second Restatement, which calls for the application of the law of the state "where the contract requires that the services, or a major portion of the services, be rendered," is intended to apply to contracts with servants, independent contractors and agents and with persons exercising a public profession, as lawyers, doctors, brokers, commission agents and factors.[2] This statement is overbroad because special provisions apply to contracts of transportation (§ 197) and to agency (§§ 291–293) which are reviewed separately below. In addition, the section, by attempting to deal in such comprehensive fashion with disparate types of service contracts, cannot deal effectively with areas in which there are regulatory concerns, principally in the area of brokerage contracts.

A few decisions refer specifically to the place where the service is to be performed.[3] Most decisions invoke other reasons in order to reach the applicable law, for instance that the chosen law is that of the place of contracting or that of the contract's center of gravity. With few excep-

---

§ 18.29

1. Problems of agency are addressed separately infra §§ 18.32–18.36.

2. Restatement, Second, Conflict of Laws § 196, cmnt. (a) (1971). The Rome Convention similarly provides for the application of the law of the state where the services are to be rendered (Art. 6(2)(a))— While the parties may stipulate a different law, employee cannot be deprived thereby of protective mandatory rules of the otherwise applicable law. Section 10(2)(b) of the Oregon codification of contractual conflicts law creates a "presumptive rule" that "Contracts for personal services are governed by the law of the state where the services are to be primarily performed pursuant to the contract." See Nafziger, Oregon's Conflicts Law Applicable to Contracts, 3 Ybk. Priv. Int'l L. 391, 410 (2001).

3. Maxus Exploration Co. v. Moran Bros., Inc., 817 S.W.2d 50, 53 (Tex.1991); Zimmerman v. Board of Publications of Christian Reformed Church, Inc., 598 F.Supp. 1002 (D.Colo.1984); Fox–Greenwald Sheet Metal Co. v. Markowitz Brothers, Inc., 147 U.S.App.D.C. 14, 452 F.2d 1346 (1971), particularly at 452 F.2d 1346, 1355 nn.46–48; Menendez v. Saks and Co., 485 F.2d 1355, 1365–66 (2d Cir.1973), reversed 425 U.S. 682, 96 S.Ct. 1854, 48 L.Ed.2d 301 (1976); Citizens & Southern National Bank v. Bruce, 420 F.Supp. 795 (N.D.Ill.1970); Nasco, Inc. v. Gimbert, 239 Ga. 675, 238 S.E.2d 368 (1977); S & S Chopper Service, Inc. v. Scripter, 59 Ohio App.2d 311, 394 N.E.2d 1011 (1977); Wood Brothers Homes, Inc. v. Walker Adjustment Bureau, 198 Colo. 444, 601 P.2d 1369 (1979). As examples for the § 196 approach see Jump v. Goldenhersh, 619 F.2d 11, 13 (8th. Cir.1980); American Triticale, Inc. v. Nytco Services, Inc., 664 F.2d 1136, 1142 (9th Cir.1981); Barnes Group, Inc. v. Harper, 653 F.2d 175 (5th Cir., Unit B 1981); Zimmerman v. Board of Public. of Christian Reformed Church, 598 F.Supp. 1002, 1007 (D.Colo.1984); Schulke Radio Productions, Ltd. v. Midwestern Broadcasting Co., 6 Ohio St.3d 436, 453 N.E.2d 683 (1983); Ferrofluidics v. Advanced Vacuum Components, 968 F.2d 1463, 1468 (1st Cir.1992); Aiello v. United Air Lines, Inc., 818 F.2d 1196, 1198 (5th Cir.1987); Pruitt v. Levi Strauss & Co., 932 F.2d 458, 461 (5th. Cir.1991); Macurdy v. Sikov & Love, P.A., 894 F.2d 818, 822 (6th Cir.1990); Gateway Western Ry. v. Morrison Metalweld Process Corp., 46 F.3d 860, 864 (8th Cir.1995); Sequa Corp. v. Lititech, Inc., 780 F.Supp. 1349, 1351 (D.Colo.1992); Baedke v. John Morrell & Co., 748 F.Supp. 700, 707 (N.D.Iowa, 1990); Maine Surgical Supply v. Intermedics Orthopedics, 756 F.Supp. 597, 601 (D.Me.1991); Garcia v. American Airlines, Inc., 12 F.3d 308 (1st Cir.1993); New Mexico Federation of Labor v. City of Clovis, New Mexico, 735 F.Supp. 999 (D.N.M. 1990); Farris (Gary L. and Pamela K.) v. ITT Cannon, A Division of ITT Corp., 834 F.Supp. 1260 (D.Colo.1993); Perez v. Alcoa Fujikura, Ltd., 969 F.Supp. 991 (W.D.Tex. 1997); Mertz v. Pharmacists Mut. Ins. Co., 261 Neb. 704, 625 N.W.2d 197 (Neb. 2001) (citing § 196 of the Second Restatement).

tions,[4] the cases are nevertheless compatible with the Second Restatement's approach because the state selected was also that where performance was due.[5]

The reference to the law of the place of performance is more difficult when performance is due at more than one place, or when for some reason that place is fortuitous. Thus, in *Ketcham v. Hall Syndicate, Inc.*,[6] the court referred to the law of the publisher's place of business (which was also the place of contracting), rather than to the place where the

---

4. E.g., Wells v. 10–X Manufacturing Co., 609 F.2d 248 (6th Cir.1979) (place of contracting); Perlmuter Printing Co. v. Strome, Inc., 436 F.Supp. 409 (N.D.Ohio 1976) (place of contracting); Liberty Mut. Ins. Co. v. Triangle Industries, Inc., 182 W.Va. 580, 390 S.E.2d 562, 566 (1990); Nunez v. Hunter Fan Co., 920 F.Supp. 716, 717, 719–721 (S.D.Tex.1996); Salazar v. Coastal Corp., 928 S.W.2d 162, 167 (Tex. App.1996); Schlosser v. Allis–Chalmers Corp., 86 Wis.2d 226, 271 N.W.2d 879 (1978) ("better law" approach resulted in the application of the law of the place of offer). See also Richland Development Co. v. Staples, 295 F.2d 122 (5th Cir.1961) (application of Missouri law because brokerage contract was concluded in an airplane over Missouri).

5. *Employment Contracts:* See, e.g., Ferrofluidics Corp. v. Advanced Vacuum Components, Inc., 968 F.2d 1463 (1st Cir.1992) (New Hampshire as the place with the "most significant contacts" to the contract at the time the deal was closed was also the place of anticipated performance); Aiello v. United Air Lines, Inc., 818 F.2d 1196 (5th Cir.1987) (under the most significant relationship approach Texas Law was held to be applicable, also the place of anticipated performance); Pruitt v. Levi Strauss & Co., 932 F.2d 458 (5th Cir.1991)(Texas Law as the law of the place of performance and the applicable law under the most significant relationship approach, as well); Macurdy v. Sikov & Love, P.A., 894 F.2d 818 (6th Cir. 1990)(Second Restatement §§ 188, 196 the applicable law would be that of Pennsylvania); Gateway Western Railway Co. v. Morrison Metalweld Process Corp., 46 F.3d 860 (8th Cir.1995)(court held that Missouri had the most significant relationship to the case, particularly since it was in that state that the repairs were to be made); Sequa Corp. v. Lititech, Inc., 780 F.Supp. 1349 (D.Colo.1992)(the court said that, since most of the services under the contract were to be performed in Colorado, it had the most significant relationship to the contract); Farris v. ITT Cannon, 834 F.Supp. 1260 (D.Colo.1993)(Washington law controlled the issues raised because it was the

state with the most significant relationship to those common-law claims and the employee performed his services there); Baedke v. John Morrell & Co. v. Pearson Services, Inc., 748 F.Supp. 700 (N.D.Iowa 1990)(applying the forum's "most significant relationship" test, the court held that South Dakota law would apply, which was also the place of performance); Maine Surgical Supply v. Intermedics Orthopedics, 756 F.Supp. 597, 601 (D.Me. 1991)(concerning a distribution contract the court held that the law of Maine, as the state with the most significant contacts with the alleged contract between the parties, applied, the defendant delivered the medical supplies there and the plaintiff rendered a major portion of its services as a distributor in Maine); Crabtree v. Academy Life Ins. Co., 878 F.Supp. 727, 730 (E.D.Pa. 1995)(after analysis of the contacts of an attorney-client relationship with various states the court favored the application of the law of Pennsylvania, where the attorney had its principal place of business and where the contract was negotiated, made, and performed); Medtronic, Inc. v. Advanced Bionics Corp., 630 N.W.2d 438 (Minn. App. 2001) (Minnesota law on the enforceability of non-competition clauses governs where a Minnesota employee left his Minnesota employer to work in California); DeSantis v. Wackenhut Corp., 793 S.W.2d 670, 679 (Tex.1990), cert. denied 498 U.S. 1048, 111 S.Ct. 755, 112 L.Ed.2d 775 (1991)(court applied Texas law because Texas had the most significant relationship to the transaction and the place of performance of the personal service was Texas); Maxus Exploration v. Moran Bros., 817 S.W.2d 50, 53, 54, 57 (Tex.1991)(a drilling contract has its most significant relationship to Kansas, also the place of performance). Section 196 is a very popular rule, even with courts that do not as a matter of course follow the Second Restatement. See Borchers, Choice of Law in the American Courts in 1992: Observations and Reflections, 42 Am.J.Comp. L. 125 (1994).

6. 37 Misc.2d 693, 236 N.Y.S.2d 206 (1962), aff'd 19 A.D.2d 611, 242 N.Y.S.2d 182 (1963).

author of the cartoon strip "Dennis the Menace" created the strip, because the latter changed with the author's travels and thus was fortuitous. Likewise, in *Structural Dynamics Research Corp. v. Engineering Mechanics Research Corp.*,[7] the defendants were obligated to refrain from competing with their former employer and from disclosing confidential information to third parties in all markets in which the former employer did business. There were thus several "places of performance;" the court selected the law of the place of contract formation, buttressed by the facts that this was also the place where the defendants had acquired the information and which furnished the validating law.[8]

§ 18.30 Transportation contracts as noted earlier, are addressed by § 197 of the Second Restatement.[1] The section selects the place of dispatch or departure, and, in the case of round trips, the place of the initial departure.[2] The rationale is that that state usually has the greatest interest in the contract, will usually be the state whose law the parties may expect to apply, and that the rule will further certainty and predictability, all because " ... there can be no absolute certainty at the time of departure that the passenger or the goods will reach ... " the state of destination.[3] The case law reflects this approach, however mainly in situations in which the place of departure was also the place of contract formation.[4]

---

7. 401 F.Supp. 1102 (E.D.Mich.1975).

8. It is particularly noteworthy that the court did not apply the law of the forum which was the home of the defendants. Under that law, the contractual stipulations would have been invalid. See also Rutas Aereas Nacionales S.A. v. Robinson, 339 F.2d 265 (5th Cir.1964), modified with respect to damages 340 F.2d 614 (1965) (application of the law of Venezuela in a suit by an airline pilot because Venezuela was the place of contract formation, the business seat of the employer, and because the employment contract contained some references to Venezuelan law). In terms of § 196 of the Second Restatement, this case illustrates well when a more significant relationship to another law displaces the law of at least one of the places of performance which was also the forum. One court, however, applied § 188 to determine the applicable law in a case where performance was due in many places. National Starch and Chemical Corp. v. Newman, 577 S.W.2d 99 (Mo.App.1978).

Compare the solution of the Rome Convention: when these is more than one place of performance, the law of the country applies in which the place of business is located through which the employee was hired (Art. 6(2)(b)), unless "the contract is more closely connected with another country." The proviso also applies to the rule of subsection (a). See supra n.2.

§ 18.30

1. As noted in comment (a) to § 197, the section applies primarily to contract-based claims for damage to goods in interstate or international commerce will ordinarily be governed by federal law or treaty. See also Stillman v. Nickel Odeon, S.A., 608 F.Supp. 1050 (S.D.N.Y.1985) (discussed § 18.21 n.5).

2. Id. But see Rungee v. Allied Van Lines, Inc., 92 Idaho 718, 449 P.2d 378 (1968) (referred to the law of the state of destination for the question whether the plaintiff was entitled to attorney's fees after recovering insurance benefits from a carrier.) This led to forum law. The same result could have been achieved by a procedural characterization of the issue.

3. Restatement, Second, Conflict of Laws § 197, cmnt. (b) (1971). But see *Rungee* in which the court concluded that " ... the law of the state of destination will generally have a more significant relationship to the issue of proper settlement of damage claims. That is the state from which the insured will conduct his efforts to settle his claim. The insured would be unlikely to sue the carrier in the state of his abandoned residence." Id. at 723, 449 P.2d at 383. These considerations more properly address jurisdiction and the convenient forum.

4. Caruso v. Italian Line, 184 F.Supp. 862 (S.D.N.Y.1960). See also Fricke v. Is-

§ 18.31 While the Second Restatement thus differentiates between transportation contracts and those for other services rendered, it undertakes no distinction with respect to brokerage, an area in which a state may often be expected to have regulatory concerns. Thus, in *Intercontinental Planning, Ltd. v. Daystrom, Inc.*[1] a New York broker sought to enforce a claim for compensation against a New Jersey defendant for whom it had found another New Jersey company to acquire. Negotiations had taken place both in New York and New Jersey. The contract had been signed in New Jersey and did not satisfy New York's Statute of Frauds. The court did not seek to identify the contract's center of gravity or the place where the service was to be rendered but, instead, focused on the regulatory purpose of New York's form requirement:[2] "It is common knowledge that New York is a national and international center for the purpose of sale of businesses and interests therein. We conclude therefore that the Legislature ... intended to protect not only its own residents, but also those who come into New York and take advantage of our position as an international clearing house.... Our brokers and finders need only ensure that their agreements for compensation comply with the Statute of Frauds."[3] The court also stressed several New York contacts (advertisement in the *Wall Street Journal*, first agreement on the finder's fee in New York) and that New Jersey could not have an interest in having its law applied when doing so would render its residents liable in circumstances where the forum would not impose liability. The latter assertion leading to the conclusion that the case in fact presents a false conflict may misinterpret the purpose of New Jersey law which well might be designed to impose liability for benefits received.[4] Both the false conflicts analysis and the reference to New York

brandtsen Co., 151 F.Supp. 465 (S.D.N.Y. 1957) and Mulvihill v. Furness, Withy & Co., 136 F.Supp. 201 (S.D.N.Y.1955). In both cases the court ignored an express choice-of-law clause, for instance in *Mulvihill* because "this contract was made in New York for a voyage commencing in New York." 131 F.Supp. at 206. Whether a choice-of-law clause would be disregarded this easily today is doubtful. See supra §§ 18.2 et seq.

The Rome Convention also adopts a provision designed to combine predictability and the use of a closely connected law. It departs from the normal reference to the "characteristic performance" and instead selects the law of the carrier's principal place of business at the time of contract formation if that state is also the place of loading on discharge on the principal place of business of the consignor (Art. 4(4)). In cases, in which connecting factors do not coincide in this fashion the general closest connection test of subsection (1) applies.

§ 18.31

1. 24 N.Y.2d 372, 300 N.Y.S.2d 817, 248 N.E.2d 576 (1969).

2. See also Pallavicini v. International Telephone & Telegraph Corp., 41 A.D.2d 66, 341 N.Y.S.2d 281 (1973), aff'd 34 N.Y.2d 913, 359 N.Y.S.2d 290, 316 N.E.2d 722 (1974).

3. 24 N.Y.2d at 383–84, 300 N.Y.S.2d at 826–27, 248 N.E.2d at 582–83. See also Comment, New York's Choice-of-Law Quandary: A Conflict in Interest Analysis, 40 Brooklyn L. Rev. 726, 757–68 (1974).

4. In keeping with the subsequently adopted § 196 of the Second Restatement, the court also stated that "the services for which plaintiff claims compensation where substantially rendered in New York." 24 N.Y.2d at 384, 300 N.Y.S.2d at 827, 248 N.E.2d at 583. On the facts, however, negotiations took place in both states, the contract was executed in New Jersey, and the latter was also the location of the acquired company. See also Restatement, Second,

contacts attempt to square the result with traditional approaches to choice of law. Nevertheless, the regulatory concern seems paramount.[5]

7. Agency[1]

§ 18.32   Two of the three relationships that arise from agency are treated by the Second Restatement. Section 291 provides that the relationship of principal and agent (the internal relationship) is governed by the place of the most significant relationship, with cross-reference to §§ 187–188. The external relationship that between principal and third party is also to be governed by the law of the most significant relationship (§ 292), except that the local law of the agent's place of acting will validate his act if the principal had authorized him to act in that state or had led the third party to believe that the agent had authority.[2] No provision is made for the agent's contract with the third party and the rights and liabilities arising from it for them *inter se.* Consequently, and essentially no different from § 291, these questions are left to the general provisions of §§ 187–188.

§ 18.33   With respect to the *internal relationship,* the case law has employed all conceivable choice-of-law rules. They range from the place where the contractual relationship was created (place of execution),[1] to

Conflict of Laws § 199(2) (1971): ("Formalities which meet the requirements of the place where the parties execute the contract will usually be acceptable."). Comment (c), notes that this may not be so when " . . . rules embody strong policies, [such] as statutes regulating the form of contracts to make a will or designed for the protection of a particular class . . . " but concludes that "in any event" invalidity will no result if " . . . the requirements of the states involved differ only in matters of detail."

5. Skandia America Reinsurance Corp. v. Schenck, 441 F.Supp. 715, 723 (S.D.N.Y. 1977). In contrast the decision in Index Fund, Inc. v. Insurance Co. of North America, 580 F.2d 1158, 1162 (2d Cir.1978), cert. denied 440 U.S. 912, 99 S.Ct. 1226, 59 L.Ed.2d 461 (1979) considers *Intercontinental Planning* to combine the grouping-of-contacts and governmental-interest approaches. See also Gibbs–Brower Intern. v. Kirchheimer Bros. Co., 611 F.Supp. 122 (N.D.Ill.1985). Compare Denny v. American Tobacco Co., 308 F.Supp. 219 (N.D.Cal. 1970) (California court applied New York law to suit by California broker for finder's fee against New York defendant on the basis of the protective purpose of New York law) with Havenfield Corp. v. H & R Block, Inc., 509 F.2d 1263 (8th Cir.1975), cert. denied 421 U.S. 999, 95 S.Ct. 2395, 44 L.Ed.2d 665 (1975) (New York plaintiff, application of the validating law of Ohio on the basis of § 188 of the Second Restate-

ment). See also the subsection on agency, immediately following.

§ 18.32

1. For comprehensive and comparative discussion see Hay & Müller-Freienfels, Agency in the Conflict of Laws and the 1978 Hague Convention, 27 Am. J. Comp. L. 1 (1979) on which this section is based. Permission to use this material is gratefully acknowledged.

2. Restatement, Second, Conflict of Laws § 293(2) (1971) similarly contains a validating provision: ratification is to be effective if it would be so either under the law of the most significant relationship or under the law where the agent dealt with the third person. The Oregon codification creates a "presumptive rule" that "Agency contracts are governed by the law of the state where the agency's duties are to be primarily performed." See O.R.S. § 81.135(2)(e), (discussed in Nafziger, Oregon's Conflicts Law Applicable to Contracts, 3 Ybk. Priv. Int'l L. 391, 410 (2001)).

§ 18.33

1. Bank of America, National Trust & Savings Ass'n v. Horowytz, 104 N.J.Super. 35, 40, 248 A.2d 446, 449 (1968); Yoerg v. Northern New Jersey Mortgage Associates, 44 N.J.Super. 286, 130 A.2d 392 (1957); Louis Schlesinger Co. v. Kresge Foundation, 260 F.Supp. 763 (D.N.J.1966), vacated on

the place where the agency was to be performed,[2] and to the relationship's "center of gravity."[3] However, while several decisions do articulate their holding in terms of the "center of gravity," the practical result is usually the application of the *lex fori*.[4]

Two cases serve as illustrations: In *Warner v. Kressly*,[5] the plaintiff was licensed as a broker in the forum state (Washington) as well as in Oregon and Idaho. The defendant seller was an Idaho resident and the land was located both in Idaho and in British Columbia, Canada. Negotiations with a potential buyer were held in Idaho, a sales agreement was prepared by an Idaho attorney, and the escrow money was to be held in that state. The defendant denied liability for the brokerage commission with respect to the property in British Columbia because the plaintiff was not licensed there and local law bars unlicensed brokers from collecting commissions. The Washington court considered Idaho to be the state with the "most significant relationship" to the transaction and, applying Idaho law, allowed the recovery. The decision is, of course, but weak precedent for the Second Restatement, rule, since most other approaches—except that of the First Restatement—would have reached the same result. Since the British Columbia rule serves to protect local owners against unlicensed brokers, some would view it as a "self-limited" rule,[6] inapplicable—at least by its purpose, albeit not in language—to situations not involving local owners. In the same vein and for the same reason, British Columbia may be said not to have an "interest" in the application of its law; and, as between Washington and Idaho, the case was a false conflict.[7] Indeed, even if British Columbia had had an "interest," the rules (and "interests") of Washington and Idaho (to

other grounds 388 F.2d 208 (3d Cir.1968), cert. denied 391 U.S. 934, 88 S.Ct. 1847, 20 L.Ed.2d 854 (1968);. Complaint of Bankers Trust Co., 752 F.2d 874 (3d Cir.1984).

2. Matarese v. Calise, 111 R.I. 551, 561–2, 305 A.2d 112, 118 (1973); Davis v. Jouganatos, 81 Nev. 333, 402 P.2d 985 (1965); Wonderlic Agency, Inc. v. Acceleration Corp., 624 F.Supp. 801, 804 (N.D.Ill.1985).

3. Southern Intern. Sales Co. v. Potter & Brumfield Division of AMF Inc., 410 F.Supp. 1339 (N.D.N.Y.1976); Japan Petroleum Co. (Nigeria) Ltd. v. Ashland Oil, Inc., 456 F.Supp. 831, 840 (D.Del.1978); McMorrow v. Rodman Ford Sales, Inc., 462 F.Supp. 947 (D.Mass.1979). The "center of gravity" is often found to be at the forum. See, e.g., Leisure Group, Inc. v. Edwin F. Armstrong & Co., 404 F.2d 610 (8th Cir. 1968) (per curiam) affirming Edwin F. Armstrong & Co. v. Ben Pearson, Inc., 294 F.Supp. 163 (E.D.Ark.1967); Ames v. Ideal Cement Co., 37 Misc.2d 883, 235 N.Y.S.2d 622 (1962); Feinberg v. Automobile Banking Corp., 353 F.Supp. 508 (E.D.Pa.1973) (only contact with Pennsylvania was that the principal was domiciled there); Tyrone v. Kelley, 21 Cal.App.3d 817, 99 Cal.Rptr.

290 (1971) aff'd 9 Cal.3d 1, 106 Cal.Rptr. 761, 507 P.2d 65 (1973). In Snider Brothers Inc. v. Heft, 271 Md. 409, 317 A.2d 848 (1974), the court applied the lex fori without mention of the choice-of-law problem.

4. Supra n.3. See also William B. Tanner Co., Inc. v. WIOO, Inc., 528 F.2d 262 (3d Cir.1975); P.S. & E., Inc. v. Selastomer Detroit, Inc., 470 F.2d 125 (7th Cir.1972); Seneca Falls Machine Co. v. McBeth, 368 F.2d 915 (3d Cir.1966).

5. 9 Wn.App. 358, 512 P.2d 1116 (1973).

6. On "self-limited" choice-of-law rules, see De Nova, An Australian Case on the Application of Spatially Conditioned Internal Rules, 22 Rev. Hell. 25 (1969); Kelly, Localising Rules in the Conflict of Laws (1974); Sedler, Functionally–Restrictive Rules in American Conflicts Law, 50 So. Cal. L. Rev. 27 (1976); Lipstein, Inherent Limitations in Statutes and the Conflict of Laws, 26 Int'l & Comp. L.Q. 884 (1977); Hay, Comments on "Self–Limited Rules of Law" in American Conflicts Methodology, 30 Am. J. Comp. L. 129 (Supp. 1982).

7. The broker had complied with the licensing requirements of both states.

compensate brokers, to uphold contractual obligations, to estop him who has gained a benefit) might well have been stronger: a priori in Currie's analysis and similarly in those approaches which "weigh interests."[8] Only complete disregard of interest-analysis would require a choice between the approaches of the two Restatements. Even a choice of the First Restatement might have led to Idaho as the place where the agent was both authorized to act and did act.[9] Perhaps the only atypical aspect of the *Warner* decision therefore is that, while purporting to follow modern analysis and approaches, it disregards the false conflict and applies sister-state law.

Similarly, the express reference to New Jersey as the "center of gravity" in the decision of the Second Circuit in *Weston Funding Corp. v. Lafayette Towers, Inc.*[10] was not really relevant to the decision. The court had rejected the plaintiff's contention that New York law should govern (and a commission be allowed) in a case where the agent had secured a New Jersey bank commitment to finance a New Jersey construction project of the New Jersey defendant. Like *Warner,* this case seemingly contradicts the general trend to the *lex fori,* even when the rationale invoked is that of the "center of gravity." Furthermore, adoption of New Jersey law as that of the "center of gravity" resulted in a denial of the claim since the plaintiff was not licensed there; in other words, in contrast to *Warner,* there existed a true conflict. However, the real issue was whether the plaintiff could bring the action at all because a prior suit in New Jersey had proved unsuccessful: the issue thus concerned the preclusive effect of the prior New Jersey litigation. As the Second Circuit stated: "the choice of New Jersey law is res judicata between the parties since it actually was litigated and decided."[11] It was the New Jersey decision which conformed to the trend to the *lex fori,* while the Second Circuit's opinion with respect to the proper location of the center of gravity in New Jersey, rather than in the New York forum, was dictum.

At least numerically, decisions with a lex-fori orientation therefore predominate. This is true even when the asserted basis for the choice is the "center of gravity." The few cases focusing on the place of execution or performance also seem to do so in order to reach the lex fori.[12] In large measure this is the result of the fact that all cases, except, one,[13] involved brokers and claims relating to their commissions or the (wrongful)

8. See, e.g., Baxter's "comparative impairment" test, developed in Choice of Law and the Federal System, 16 Stan. L. Rev. 1 (1963) (as adopted in Bernhard v. Harrah's Club, 16 Cal.3d 313, 128 Cal.Rptr. 215, 546 P.2d 719 (1976), cert. denied 429 U.S. 859, 97 S.Ct. 159, 50 L.Ed.2d 136 (1976).).

9. A differentiated view of the transactions involved conceivably might have resulted in the application of British Columbia law to the transaction involving British Columbia land. However, the First Restatement did not favor *dépeçage* and all other

factors—contract formation, place of acting—were connected with Idaho.

10. 550 F.2d 710 (2d Cir.1977).

11. Id. at 715.

12. Supra nn.1–3.

13. In Award Incentives, Inc. v. Van Rooyen, 263 F.2d 173 (3d Cir.1959), a contract containing a restrictive covenant was executed in New York where much of the agent's work was done. Not surprisingly, the court held that New York law governed the validity of the restrictive covenant.

termination of their agency. Brokerage relationships are necessarily more localized than other agencies; several of the relevant factors, such as place of business of either party, place of executing, and place of performance will often coincide. Additionally, brokerage is uniquely subject to state regulation which reinforces any general predisposition for a choice of the lex fori. Caution thus requires the conclusion that the proper choice-of-law for the internal relationship in agency remains unsettled in American law.

§ **18.34**   With respect to the *external relationship*, the case law is scant. Among other reasons, this is no doubt a result of the fact that, within the U.S., substantive agency law is quite uniform. It is therefore rarely necessary to make choice-of-law decisions concerning issues of actual or apparent authority or on whether a relationship has been created by the agent between a third party and an undisclosed principal. In the interstate setting, there is therefore usually also no need to allocate issues to the law governing the main contract or to the law of the place of the agent's action. International cases are rare but may be expected to gain in importance.

Two decisions should be noted. In *Shasta Livestock Auction Yard, Inc. v. Bill Evans Cattle Management Corp.*,[1] an Idaho agent bought cattle from a California third party for delivery to his undisclosed Arizona principal's Idaho feedlot. The agent typified the modern agent who is in business for himself and acts on behalf of himself as well as for a number of principals. He conducted business on a "float," that is, selling to principals at less than the purchase price from the third party, plus commission in order to attract more business from principals as a result of lower prices and financing new transactions with third parties with incoming funds from consummations. In this case, his draft to the third party came in when there were insufficient funds to cover it, although the (lower) payment from the principal had been received and deposited. The third party sought recovery from the principal. California law releases a principal who has paid his agent before receiving notice of the third party's election to hold him responsible, while § 208 of the Second Restatement of Agency which the Idaho court adopted does not so release him. The Idaho court applied § 292 of the Second Restatement, and held that California law applied as the state with the most significant relationship. An interest analysis disclosed no relevant Idaho policy since any rule regarding the effect of payment by an undisclosed principal to a third party would be designed to protect either of them, yet neither was an Idaho resident in this case. Conversely, California was said to be interested because the third party resided there and would have expected the application of California law. Finally, the contract had been formed in California and was performed there by the third party (California as a place of acting). The court said nothing about the law applicable to the agent's authority to bind his principal in the first place. However, since it identified Idaho as the state where the internal

§ **18.34**
1.   375 F.Supp. 1027 (D.Idaho 1974).

relationship was formed,[2] California law necessarily governed the issue of authority[3].

§ 18.35 *Dorothy K. Winston & Co. v. Town Heights Development, Inc.*[1] presented a mixed internal-external relationship problem in which the plaintiff, through an agent, had been retained as a real estate broker for the Florida defendant's Florida land and now sought to recover the commission. The broker was not licensed in Florida. Viewed as an *internal*-relationship problem (plaintiff as defendant's agent), the place of contracting and the place of performance were both Florida (although the broker was not restricted to Florida alone in seeking buyers) and Florida law should have been applied, especially since the ultimate buyer was a Florida resident and Florida may be said to have had a regulatory interest. Viewed as an *external*-relationship problem (plaintiff as third party and defendant as the employing agent's principal), the case would require determination both of the place of the agent's acting *and* the capacity of the unlicensed defendant to enter into the main contract.[2] The District of Columbia court engaged in none of these considerations;

---

2. Id. at 1032.

3. Reese would refer the issue of whether a contractual relationship was created between the third party and the *undisclosed* principal to the law applicable to the main contract. Reese, Agency in the Conflict of Laws, in: XXth Century Comparative and Conflicts Law Legal Essays in Honor of Hessel E. Yntema 409, 417 (1960). The Second Restatement, includes undisclosed agency in its comprehensive rule which looks primarily to the place of acting. Restatement, Second, Conflict of Laws § 292, cmnt. (a) (1971). Under either approach, California law would have applied to the case under discussion.

It is interesting to speculate, however, whether California could have been said to be the place of the external relationship and whether its law should have determined the agent's authority if the substantive laws involved had been reversed, i.e., if liability had existed under California but not under Idaho law. Under the Restatement provision, such a change in facts would then require the further determination whether the Arizona principal had the necessary "close relationship" to California to be bound by and liable for the agent's acts. For this question, it might have been relevant that the undisclosed principal had done between 50% and 75% of its buying from the agent and that the latter had done between 60% and 75% of its business with the principal. It would therefore have been reasonable to conclude that the agent had been generally authorized to act for the principal. In the Restatement's view, such general authorization suffices to bind the principal in accordance with the law of the place

where the agent dealt with the third party, even if the principal himself had no relationship with that state. Restatement, Second, Conflict of Laws § 292, cmmt. (d), illus. 3 (1971). California law again would have been applicable. The situation may have been different only under yet another variation of the actual facts, viz. if either of the litigants had been an Idaho resident and the other a resident of California. In these circumstances, the policies and interests of the two states, and especially of the Idaho forum, to which § 6 of the Second Restatement refers, would have been relevant. The place of the agent's action (California), which in other circumstances would have made California law applicable to the external relationship, might then have been displaced for choice-of-law purposes by the law of the forum, depending on the state of the substantive law in the respective states (liability or release from liability). Similarly, and again as a result of interest analysis, California law might have been applied if, on the same facts, California had been the forum. Thus, while the outcome of the case in issue, as well as of the first hypothetical variation of the facts, are in accordance with the main provision of the Restatement, Second, this may only have been the case because the forum was "disinterested." A connection of the forum with the parties might have produced different and far less predictable results.

§ 18.35

1. 376 F.Supp. 1214 (D.D.C.1974).

2. Restatement, Second, Conflict of Laws § 292, cmmt. (f) (1971).

instead hinting at a comparative impairment approach,[3] it applied forum law and granted a recovery. Since the plaintiff was to seek investors or buyers in many states, the court concluded that the place of his acting was in many jurisdictions; the fact that the eventual buyer was Floridian was said to be fortuitous. Florida's interest, as evidenced by its licensing requirement, was thus discontinued. While perhaps correct in ultimate result, the decision is analytically unsatisfying. Like much of the case law reviewed in this Section as well as in connection with the internal relationship, the decision paints with a broad brush and is not concerned with close analysis of the various relationships and the possibly different laws applicable to them. In the interstate context, such fuzziness may be of little practical importance because substantive agency law displays few differences among the states except in the regulatory area. In the few cases in which differences are important, most decisions, except in *Winston,* have dealt adequately with the problem. Nevertheless, clearer rules are needed, especially for international cases which may be expected to become more frequent. So far, only the Second Restatement, undertakes to provide a systematic approach, but the flexibility it provides does require more supporting decisions than presently available to permit a clear statement of American law.

§ **18.36** For international agency contracts, the 1978 Hague Conference has produced a Convention. The United States participated in the drafting but has not ratified the Convention.[1] The Convention, now in force in France, Argentina, Portugal and the Netherlands, provides that the law of the state of the agent's business establishment or habitual residence governs the internal relationship with two exceptions. First, if the agent is to act primarily in the state of the principal's business establishment or, if he has none, habitual residence, the latter's law governs. This exception uses one criterion which also appears in American case law: the agent's place of acting.[2] Second, if the principal *or* the agent has more than one business establishment with which the agency relationship is most closely connected. This formation adopts, for its area of applicability, the modern approach of the "center of gravity."[3]

---

3. 376 F.Supp. at 1219.

§ 18.36

1. Official English and French texts in Hague Conference on Private International Law, I Actes et documents de la Treizième Session 42–47 (1978); English text also in 26 Am. J. Comp. L. 438 (1978). See also Marschall von Bieberstein, Limitation of Party Autonomy in Private International Law by Rules of Jus Cogens in Laws Protecting Agents and Distributors, Proc. Columbia Law School Symposium on International Contracts 93 (1981).

2. For another view favoring the law of the state where the parties "intended the agent to act" (as providing greater protection to third parties than do other references) see Steding, Die Anknüpfung der

Vollmacht im internationalen Privatrecht, 86 Zeitschrift für vergleicüende Rechtswissenschaft 25, 43–46 (1987).

3. "The initial focus on the agent's principal place of business is appropriate, first, because it is the law indicated by the connecting factor most closely connected with the party who performs the obligation characteristic of the agreement; secondly, because the agent's principal place of business is more likely to coincide with the place where he acts than is the principal's principal place of business; and thirdly, because this solution seems to do justice to the pivotal role of the agent, at the centre of the complex of relationships arising in an agency situation. As a connecting factor, the agent's principal place of business has the advantage of being clear and readily

It remains to be seen, however—especially against the background of U.S. case law—to what extent the criterion of the "closest connection," in so far as it is part of the Convention, will result in a body of case law which identifies relevant factors and resists the temptation of a *lex-fori* orientation.

For the external relationship the Convention combines, as a starting point, the agent's place of business and his place of acting. Article 11 provides that, as between the principal and the third person, "the existence and extent of the agent's authority and the effects of the agent's exercise or purported exercise of his authority shall be governed by the internal law of the State where the agent had his business establishment at the time of the relevant acts." The second paragraph, however, modifies this basic rule in important respects. It specifies the law of the *place of acting* in substitution for the place of the agent's business establishment, whenever: (a) the principal has his business establishment or habitual residence in that state and the agent acted in his name (disclosed agency); (b) the third party has his place of business or habitual residence in that state; (c) the agent acted at an exchange or auction; (d) the agent has no place of business. When "a party," i.e. any one of them, has more than one place of business, the third paragraph specifies the one "most closely connected" with "the relevant acts of the agent." In combination, the rules of the second and third paragraphs of Article 11 come very close to the principles of U.S. conflicts law and meet the concern that the third party be sufficiently protected. In international practice, alternative (b) may become particularly significant. Even when the agent does not enter into the transaction at the third party's place of business, the place-of-acting provisions will often come into place, for example, when a professional agent, with several places of business, deals with the third party from a branch office or from none of them. As a result, the practical importance of the manner in which the main rule weighs the respective interests (the agent's place of business, with no relationship to the third party or to the transaction) should not be over-estimated when viewed by itself. In many cases, the additional factors of the supplementary provisions of the second and third paragraphs of Article 11 will also be applicable, although for practical purposes this need not always lead to a different result in the end.

Article 15 is also of considerable importance for external relationships. It extends the application of the choice-of-law rules discussed to "the relationship between the agent and the third party arising from the fact that the agent has acted in the exercise of his authority, has exceeded his authority, or has acted without authority." In this respect, Article 15 accords with the modern American approach of the Second Restatement. However, Article 15 goes beyond the external relationship itself. It concerns the agent-third party relationship when, for lack of authority, no contractual relationship between principal and third party

ascertainable." Karsten, Report on the Preliminary Draft Convention, Prel. Doc. No. 5, at 14 (1976).

resulted from the "agent's" action. In fact a third type of relationship is involved, and the question rises whether its inclusion in an agency convention is appropriate. In some cases, the applicable law may well be the same as that which governs the external relationship. In the American view, for instance, this would ordinarily be the case when questions of unjust enrichment are involved to which, in the main, the law governing the underlying claim applies.[4] In other cases, sounding more directly in tort or contract (between third party and "agent"), other choice-of-law principles may be applicable. For these reasons, some might argue that it would have been preferable not to include aspects of the third party-agent relationship in the Convention, but to leave them for a more general convention on contractual and non-contractual obligations. The objection loses much of its force, however, in view of the flexible choice-of-law rules adopted by the Convention, primarily in Article 11.

8. *Other Contracts*

§ 18.37 The case law is insufficient to indicate definite rules or trends with respect to a number of other contracts, and the Second Restatement, also provides no or little guidance. The following therefore addresses these contracts only briefly.

Leases. A number of decisions apply the law of contracting,[1] while others refer to the location of the object of the lease. The latter would be the situs of the immovable property leased[2] or the principal or intended location of movable property.[3]

---

4. Restatement, Second, Conflict of Laws § 221 (1971); see infra §§ 18.42–18.48.

§ 18.37

1. E.g. Terkel v. Hearth Rooms, Inc., 410 F.Supp. 1160 (W.D.Pa.1976); Bank of Indiana, National Ass'n v. Holyfield, 476 F.Supp. 104 (S.D.Miss.1979) (also situs of movable property); United States Leasing Corp. v. Keiler, 290 So.2d 427 (La.App. 1974); Nytco Leasing, Inc. v. Dan–Cleve Corp., 31 N.C.App. 634, 230 S.E.2d 559 (1976), review denied 292 N.C. 265, 233 S.E.2d 393 (1977). Conventions of 1987 & 1988 as well as commentary in 51 RabelsZ #4 (1987).

2. Plum Tree, Inc. v. N.K. Winston Corp., 351 F.Supp. 80 (S.D.N.Y.1972). Some courts also considered the place of negotiation, execution and performance of the lease but these places coincided with the situs of the immovable property. See, e.g., Consolidated Sun Ray, Inc. v. Oppenstein, 335 F.2d 801, 803 (8th Cir.1964); Humble Oil & Refining Co. v. DeLoache, 297 F.Supp. 647, 651 (D.S.C.1969); Whitehorn v. Dickerson, 419 S.W.2d 713 (Mo.App.

1967). In Segal v. Greater Valley Terminal Corp., 83 N.J.Super. 120, 199 A.2d 48 (App. Div.1964), the plaintiff tried to argue that rights under a lease are *in personam* and therefore governed by the law of the place of contracting and performance. The court rejected the argument, considered the rights as *in rem* and applied the law of the situs.

3. Cf. Graham v. Wilkins, 145 Conn. 34, 40, 138 A.2d 705, 708 (1958); Bank of Indiana, National Ass'n v. Holyfield, 476 F.Supp. 104 (S.D.Miss.1979) (also the place of contracting). In the United States, a new Article 2A has been added to the Uniform Commercial Code to deal with the leasing of personal property. § 2A–106 deals with choice of law and choice of court clauses in consumer leases: the choice of the applicable law is unenforceable unless it is the law of the state where the lessee resides or will reside within 30 days of the effective date of the lease or where the leased goods are to be used; the jurisdiction chosen by a forum selection clause must be one which would also have had jurisdiction in the absence of the clause. The limitations of § 2A–106 do

Joint Ventures. In this area, at least two decisions considered the purpose of the joint venture as primarily relevant and applied the law of the place where the venture was to operate.[4]

Releases, Discharge, Accord and Satisfaction. Depending on whether a release or other settlement of a claim relates to tort or to contract, the Second Restatement, provides different approaches to choice of law. Section 170 provides for the application of the law applicable to the tort under § 145 for the determination of whether an instrument is a release or a covenant not to sue and of whether the instrument affects the liability of other joint tortfeasors. The effect of an agreement to discharge a contractual obligation, for instance an accord or satisfaction, is to be determined, according to § 212(2), by the law bearing the most-significant-relationship (§ 188) to the discharge. The apparent parallelism between the provisions—in both cases, reference to the law of the place of the most significant relationship—is misleading. If the applicable law for a discharge of a contractual obligation is to be determined independently, the result could be the application of " ... one state's law to the accord and satisfaction contract and another state's law to the underlying contract.... The anomaly presented by such an approach is aptly illustrated in this case, in which plaintiff might seek to apply California law to invalidate the purported contract of accord and satisfaction and Georgia law to validate the underlying contract."[5] The parallelism which the Second Restatement, seeks to achieve will be obtained when the effect of a release is determined according to the law selected for the tort, as envisioned by § 170,[6] and when the effect of a discharge

not apply to leases that are not consumer leases. Id., Official Comment. "Consumer leases" are defined in § 2A–103(1)(e) as those in which the lessee takes goods primarily for personal, family, or household purposes and for which payment does not exceed $25,000. See also § 2A–105, dealing with the territorial application of Article 2A to goods covered by a certificate of title.

Internationally, the Rome Institute for the Unification of Private Law has produced a Draft Convention on International Financial Leasing. The Convention is now in force in France, Italy and Nigeria (May 1st 1995). See Revue de Droit Uniforme 145 (1996). See Note, International Equipment Leasing: The UNIDROIT Draft Convention, 22 Colum. J. Trans. L. 333 (1984); Basedow, Leistungsstörungen in internationalen Leasingverträgen, 34 Recht der Internationalen Wirtschaft 1 (1988). There are currently no proposals for choice-of-law conventions in this area.

4. Teas v. Kimball, 257 F.2d 817, 823–24 (5th Cir.1958); Flammia v. Mite Corp., 401 F.Supp. 1121, 1126 (E.D.N.Y.1975), aff'd 553 F.2d 93 (2d Cir.1977). But see Ideal Structures Corp. v. Levine Huntsville Development Corp., 396 F.2d 917, 921–26 (5th Cir.1968) (application of the law of the

place of contracting), which the court regarded as being the applicable state (Alabama) choice-of-law rule, thereby reversing 251 F.Supp. 3, 7–8 (N.D.Ala.1966) (which had applied the most-significant-relationship test). Transatlantic Cement, Inc. v. Lambert Freres, 462 F.Supp. 363, 364–65 (S.D.N.Y.1978) (employing the "center of gravity" theory and applied the law of France, which was the residence of the defendants and the place of negotiation and agreement).

5. Eldon Industries, Inc. v. Paradies & Co., 397 F.Supp. 535, 539 (N.D.Ga.1975). The court applied the law applicable to the underlying contract.

6. Dworak v. Olson Construction Co., 191 Colo. 161, 551 P.2d 198, 200 (1976) (covenant not to sue); Weddington v. Jackson, 331 F.Supp. 1271 (E.D.Pa.1971). In McCluskey v. Rob San Services, Inc., 443 F.Supp. 65 (S.D.Ohio 1977), the court applied the law selected for the tort to determine the effect of the release, but also considered the release as a contract and applied the choice of law rules for contracts to determine the applicable law for the construction and interpretation of the release. Id. at 68–71.

is related to the underlying contract and determined by the *same* law selected for it.[7]

Checks and Notes. The obligations of an endorser of a draft or note and of a drawer of a draft, are determined by the local law of the state in which he delivered (i.e. dated) the instrument.[8]

Funds transfers. In addition to payment by check or credit card, electronic funds transfers are increasingly common. Some point-of-sale transactions and consumer payments are governed by the federal Electronic Fund Transfer Act, otherwise by the new Article 4A of the Uniform Commercial Code. Its § 4A–407 designates the law of the receiving bank's location as the applicable law for the rights and obligations between render and bank and the location of the beneficiary bank as between it and the beneficiary as well as for the issue when payment is make by means of a funds transfer by the originator. A device of the applicable law by the parties is expressly permitted, and there is no requirement that the law selected bear a reasonable relationship to the funds transfer. § 4A–507 (b). Subsection c is of great importance and wide applicability: it permits, again without a requirement of a reasonable relationship, a selection of the applicable law by and for the funds transfer *system*, thus also potentially affecting parties (e.g., intermediary banks) not in privity with each other. A most-significant-relationship rule applies to a potential conflict between inconsistent choices of the applicable laws by funds transfer systems by virtue of § 4A–507(d).

For international funds transfer, in 1992 the U.N. Commission on International Trade Law adopted a Model Law on International Credit Transfers.[9]

In Manos v. Trans World Airlines, Inc., 295 F.Supp. 1166 (N.D.Ill.1968) the court concluded that Illinois would not adhere to the place-of-execution rule and applied the law of the domicile of the survivors and next of kin to releases executed in a case arising out of an air crash in Rome, Italy. The court noted in passing that California and the District of Columbia were " ... the two possible jurisdictions whose law would apply ... " but left it unclear whether this was so because of the interest of those jurisdictions to have their law applied to the *releases* or whether these laws would also govern the underlying tort claim. Id. at 1167. See also Rutherford v. Gray Line, Inc., 615 F.2d 944, 947–48 (2d Cir.1980) (Pennsylvania law applies, as the law of the state with the "superior interest" to a release executed in Pennsylvania by a Pennsylvania plaintiff with respect to a Pennsylvania estate's claim for relief).

7. Supra n.5; Adams Laboratories, Inc. v. Jacobs Engineering Co., 486 F.Supp. 383, 388–90 (N.D.Ill.1980); A–T–O, Inc. v. Strat-

ton & Co., Inc., 486 F.Supp. 1323 (N.D.Ga. 1980).

8. Restatement, Second, Conflict of Law § 215(1) (1971). Cf. Citizens First Bank v. Intercontinental Express, Inc., 77 Or.App. 655, 713 P.2d 1097 (1986) (drawer's refusal to honor check treated as breach of contract, to be decided under contract choice-of-law principles rather than under § 215. The court noted, in dictum, that (a) § 215 is a specific application of the most significant relationship test of § 188 and (b) would lead to the same result in this case: application of Oregon law).

9. See Bergsen, A Payment Law for the World: UNCITRAL Model Law in International Credit Transfers, in Payment Systems of the World (Effros, ed., 1994); see also Felsenfeld, The Compatibility of the UNCITRAL Model Law on International Credit Transfers with Article 4C of the U.C.C., 60 Fordham L. Rev. 53 (1992).

Assignments. The Second Restatement distinguishes between the assignability of a contract right (§ 208) and the effects of an assignment (§§ 209–211). The former is governed by the law of the place of the most significant relationship to the contract and the parties, while the latter[10] are to be governed by the law most significantly related to the particular issue or by the rule of § 208.[11] These rules are in substantial agreement with the case law.[12]

Options. As in the case of contracts of accord and satisfaction, discussed earlier, a choice-of-law rule for options could focus either on the option contract as an independent agreement or relate the option to the principal contract which it contemplates and refer to the law which would be applicable to the latter. In many cases, the law of the ultimate contract may be the most appropriate reference, for it is there that the parties' business relationship will enter into effect.[13] This should be so particularly when the option concerns a contract for the purchase of immovable property, in which case the reference should be to the law of the situs.[14]

---

10. These are: the rights as between assignor and assignee, including capacity, formalities, substantial validity, existence of warranties, and the like (§ 209); the effect of payment or other performance to the assignor or assignee on the obligor (§ 210); and successive assignments (§ 211). See also infra § 19.29.

11. Section 210, provides for the discharge of the obligor if payment or performance would have this effect under the law selected by application of either § 208 or § 209. Section 211, supra n.8, refers to § 209 if the successive assignments are either governed by the same or by identical laws, to § 208 in other cases, and, exceptionally, to the law of the place where the books evidencing the account are kept in cases of assignments of accounts receivable of a business enterprise.

12. See Reporter's Notes to §§ 208–11, Restatement, Second, Conflict of Laws (1971). For § 208, see also Fox–Greenwald Sheet Metal Co. v. Markowitz Brothers, Inc., 452 F.2d 1346, 1355 (D.C.Cir.1971) (effectiveness of a contractual prohibition against assignments governed by the law applicable to the underlying construction contract which, in turn, was determined by the law of Maryland in application of § 196 because the contract required " ... performance of substantial size and duration" there). But see Freedom Finance Co., Inc. v. New Jersey Bell Telephone Co., 123 N.J.Su-

per. 255, 258, 302 A.2d 184, 186 (1973), aff'd 126 N.J.Super. 375, 314 A.2d 614 (App.Div.1974) (interest analysis). For § 209, see also Ivor B. Clark Co. v. Hogan, 296 F.Supp. 398, 403 (1968), modified 296 F.Supp. 407 (1969); American Optical Co. v. Curtiss, 56 F.R.D. 26 (S.D.N.Y.1971); DeAngelis v. Scott, 337 F.Supp. 1021 (W.D.Pa. 1972); Miller v. Wells Fargo Bank Int'l Corp., 406 F.Supp. 452, 481–82 (S.D.N.Y. 1975), aff'd 540 F.2d 548 (2d Cir.1976). Some courts apply the law of the place of assignment, see Diaz v. Southeastern Drilling Co. of Argentina, S.A., 324 F.Supp. 1, 4 (N.D.Tex.1969), aff'd 449 F.2d 258 (5th Cir. 1971); Tannerfors v. American Fidelity Fire Ins. Co., 397 F.Supp. 141, 156 (D.N.J.1975), aff'd 535 F.2d 1247 (3d Cir.1976) and justify the application by citing to § 209. See Travelers Ins. Co. v. Fields, 451 F.2d 1292, 1298 (6th Cir.1971), cert. denied 406 U.S. 919, 92 S.Ct. 1772, 32 L.Ed.2d 118 (1972).

13. Cf. supra n.4.

14. In an action for specific performance of an option, the court in Cummings v. Bullock, 367 F.2d 182 (9th Cir.1966) the court applied the law of the situs of real property. But see Clayman v. Goodman Properties, Inc., 518 F.2d 1026 (D.C.Cir. 1973) in which the court applied the law of the parties' common domicile (District of Columbia) to an option with respect to Maryland real property.

B. CONTRACT ISSUES

§ 18.38 The Second Restatement, as well as the case law, deals separately with a number of contract issues, either in order to provide a reference to a validating law (such as in the case of capacity[1]) or in order to assure their proper treatment in the context of the total contract. Thus, section 140 of the Second Restatement provides for the application of the general contract choice-of-law provisions (§§ 187–188) to the question whether a contract is integrated in a writing. On its face, § 140 could lead to the application of a different law to this issue than that which applies to other issues, such as validity. It is therefore important to read this section in light of comment c to § 140 that the issue of integration " ... should be determined by the law which governs the contract [itself]." Since this issue may " ... substantially affect the obligations of the parties under the contract,"[2] it is appropriate " ... that the rule as to integrated contract is part of the substantive law of contracts and ... not a rule of evidence"[3] and thus governed by the law applicable to the contract rather than—as a result of a procedural characterization—by the *lex fori*.

The issue of whether a contract must be in writing, or evidenced by a writing by the party to be charged, in short whether the Statute of Frauds has been satisfied, has sometimes turned on the language of the statute. Thus, in the early case of *Marie v. Garrison*,[4] the court applied neither the foreign statute nor that of the forum, because it regarded the former's language ("no action shall be brought") to be "procedural" and its own ("void") to be "substantive." Similarly, the forum's statute has been applied when it provided that "no action shall be brought" and was therefore considered to be "procedural."[5] Two sections of the Second Restatement, (§§ 141 and 199) now provide for the application of the general contract choice-of-law rules (§§ 187–188), in effect regarding the issue to be substantive.[6] In addition, and in order to protect the expecta-

---

§ 18.38

1. See supra § 18.20 nn. 9–13 and accompanying text.

2. Restatement, Second, Conflict of Laws § 140, comment (c) (1971).

3. Id., Reporter's Note and cases cited there. See also Burns Brothers Plumbers, Inc. v. Groves Ventures Co., 22 Ohio Misc. 154, 412 F.2d 202, 206 (6th Cir.1969); United States v. Hastings Motor Truck Co., 460 F.2d 1159, 1161 (8th Cir.1972); Bird v. Computer Technology, Inc., 364 F.Supp. 1336, 1343 (S.D.N.Y.1973).

4. 13 Abb. N. Cas. 210 (N.Y.Super.1883). However there was some indication that the promise may not have been covered by the foreign (Missouri) statute. Id. at 279–81.

5. See, e.g., Arsham v. Banci, 511 F.2d 1108, 1114 (6th Cir.1975) (court applied foreign state statute of frauds because it contained the word "void" and thus was substantive); Brown v. Valentine, 240

F.Supp. 539 (W.D.Va.1965); Perlmuter Printing Co. v. Strome, Inc., 436 F.Supp. 409, 413 (N.D.Ohio 1976); Tenna Manufacturing Co. v. Columbia Union National Bank and Trust Co., 484 F.Supp. 1214, 1219 (W.D.Mo.1980) (forum state's statute of fraud was procedural and also forum state had the greatest interest in applying its statute); Talmudical Academy of Baltimore v. Harris, 238 So.2d 161, 162 (Fla. App.1970).

6. Restatement, Second, Conflict of Laws § 141, cmnt. (b) (1971). The courts have applied various choice-of-law approaches to determine the applicable statute of frauds. See Paulson v. Shapiro, 490 F.2d 1 (7th Cir.1973) (place of contract and place of performance); Denny v. American Tobacco Co., 308 F.Supp. 219, 222–23 (N.D.Cal.1970) (center of gravity and interest analysis); O'Keeffe v. Bry, 456 F.Supp. 822, 827 (S.D.N.Y.1978) (interest analysis); Ehrman v. Cook Electric Co., 468 F.Supp. 98, 100–101 (N.D.Ill.1979) (most significant contacts).

tion of the parties,[7] "formalities which meet the requirements of the place where the parties execute the contract will usually be acceptable."[8] The same protection of party expectations can be achieved by according substantial weight to the place of the validating law in the determination of the place of the most significant relationship.[9]

§ 18.39   Most other contract issues, according to the provisions of the Second Restatement, are also governed by the general most-significant-relationship rule of § 188. They include misrepresentation and undue influence (§ 201), illegality (§ 202), usury (§ 203),[1] the nature and extent of the contractual obligations (§ 205), and the measure of recovery (§ 207). One exception is § 202(2), which provides for primary reference to the law of the place of performance in circumstances where performance is illegal there. Another exception is § 2–318 of the Uniform Commercial Code, which expressly precludes the seller from excluding or limiting (for instance, by stipulation to another law) its provision for third party beneficiaries of express or implied warranties.

Unlike the case of the Statute of Frauds, discussed above, in which application of the most-significant-relationship test will lead to the law applicable to the contract or to a law validating it, application of this test to these other issues may or may not lead to the law of the contract. Thus, with respect to misrepresentation or undue influence, party expectations cannot be satisfied for both parties and therefore recede in importance, while state policy concerns may be strongly felt. State interests are also important with respect to illegality, as recognized by § 202(2). Application of a law other than that applicable to the contract generally may therefore be warranted. It is also true that party expectations play only a limited role with respect to the "nature and extent of contractual obligations" covered by § 205 because these are typically problems of omission in the contract so that a law must be selected for the purpose of gap-filling.[2] This fact, however, does not necessarily justify a new and independent search for the law most significantly related to this problem. The same is true of § 207, with respect to which

---

7. Restatement, Second, Conflict of Laws § 199, cmnt. (c) (1971).

8. Id. § 199(2). See also Ehrenzweig, The Statute of Frauds in the Conflict of Laws, 59 Colum. L. Rev. 874, 876 (1959); Bernkrant v. Fowler, 55 Cal.2d 588, 595, 12 Cal.Rptr. 266, 269–70, 360 P.2d 906, 909–10 (1961); Bushkin Associates, Inc. v. Raytheon Co., 393 Mass. 622, 473 N.E.2d 662 (1985); Compagnie De Reassurance d'Ile de France v. New England Reinsurance Corp., 57 F.3d 56 (1st Cir.1995), cert. denied 516 U.S. 1009, 116 S.Ct. 564, 133 L.Ed.2d 490 (1995).

9. Restatement, Second, Conflict of Laws § 141, cmnt. (g) (1971). Denny v. American Tobacco Co., 308 F.Supp. 219, 223 (N.D.Cal.1970). See also Kossick v. United Fruit Co., 365 U.S. 731, 741, 81

S.Ct. 886, 893, 6 L.Ed.2d 56 (1961), rehearing denied 366 U.S. 941, 81 S.Ct. 1657, 6 L.Ed.2d 852 (1961) (application of maritime law rather than state law because the fact that " . . . we are dealing here with a contract . . . , voluntarily undertaken, . . . creates some presumption in favor of applying that law tending toward the validation of the alleged contract"). In Paulson v. Shapiro, 490 F.2d 1, 8 (7th Cir.1973), the court did not apply the forum state statute of fraud which would have invalidated the contract, because the justified expectation of the parties would have been defeated.

§ 18.39

1. See supra §§ 18.5 nn. 12–15, 18.28.

2. See Restatement, Second, Conflict of Laws § 205, cmnt. (c) (1971).

it has also been noted that, since the parties probably gave no thought to the measure of damages in the event of breach, their expectations will not be disappointed by the application of the law of one or the other state.[3] Both sections, without significantly advancing other interests, such as strongly felt policies of the forum, thus unnecessarily encourage the splitting (dépeçage) of contract issues. Isolating issues makes sense with respect to such problems as illegality, misrepresentation, and details of performance.[4] Mandatory rules of law may also override the otherwise applicable law.[5] Beyond these areas which call for special attention and treatment, the choice-of-law process is served far better by a reference to a single law most significantly related to the contract as a whole than to undertake such an analysis for a number of issues independently.[6] This is recognized in the Second Restatement, when it is noted that " … most issues … will usually be governed by a single law" and that only "on occasion … an approach directed to the particular issue … will provide a more helpful basis for decision."[7] However, since the general provision of § 188 does permit adjustment for the occasional atypical problem, the inclusion of a number of issues

3. Id., Restatement, Second, Conflict of Laws § 207, cmnt. (c) (1971). See Morris v. Watsco, 385 Mass. 672, 433 N.E.2d 886, 888 (1982) (in a case involving prejudgment interest " … it has been our practice to measure the damages recoverable for breach of contract according to foreign law where [that] law governs the contract").

4. Restatement, Second, Conflict of Laws § 206 (1971). The applicable law for such details of performance as manner, time or method is that of the place of performance. This rule provides certainty, comports with the probable expectations of the parties, and allows for the effectuation of the policies and concerns of the state of performance.

5. See supra, following n.1, with respect to U.C.C. § 2–318. Section 205 of the Second Restatement is also said to apply to moratorium statutes. Comment (f). These statutes express a state policy for the protection of debtors and, like U.C.C. § 2–318, may be regarded as mandatory and not subject to the usual choice-of-law approach of the § 188 of the Second Restatement.

6. Section 205 is a good example. While intended to be helpful for gapfilling (see discussion supra § 18.22 n.2), the section also purports to deal with sufficiency of performance, excuse for non-performance, moratorium statutes and impossibility and frustration (comment (f)) as well as with breach (comment (g)). Moratorium statutes aside (see supra n.5), these issues can all be related to the general law applicable to the contract, especially since the particular facts surrounding it permit for the selection of the most significantly related law under

§ 188, such as, place of performance or common domicile or place of business, any one of which would be appropriate for the resolution of the problems mentioned. Courts have, in determining choice of law, split contract issues. The law of the place of contracting governed matters concerning the making of the contract, Charles L. Bowman & Co. v. Erwin, 468 F.2d 1293 (5th Cir.1972); Brand Distributors, Inc. v. Insurance Co. of North America, 400 F.Supp. 1085 (E.D.Va.1974), reversed and remanded 532 F.2d 352 (4th Cir.1976), and the law of the place of performance governed concerning the performance of the contract, Equitable Trust Co. v. Bratwursthaus Management Corp., 514 F.2d 565 (4th Cir.1975), including anticipatory breach, William B. Tanner Co., Inc. v. WIOO, Inc., 528 F.2d 262 (3d Cir.1975), and breach, Peebles v. Murray, 411 F.Supp. 1174 (D.Kan.1976). Some courts, however, have adopted the most significant relationship approach in determining the applicable law for questions of breach. In Rhodes v. Superior Investigative Services, Inc., 437 F.Supp. 1012 (E.D.Pa.1977) the court determined the applicable law by analyzing the contacts of the place of contracting and the place of performance. See also Hutchins v. Bethel Methodist Home, 370 F.Supp. 954 (S.D.N.Y. 1974); Ingrassia v. Shell Oil Co., 394 F.Supp. 875 (S.D.N.Y.1975).

7. Restatement, Second, Conflict of Laws, Chapter 8, Topic 1, Title C: Introductory Note, at p. 631 (1971). See Morris v. Watsco, 385 Mass. 672, 433 N.E.2d 886 (1982).

not usually requiring special treatment in a separate title overstates the problem and encourages unnecessary dépeçage.

IV. CHOICE–OF–LAW ALTERNATIVES

§ 18.40   For states that have abandoned the certain rules of the First Restatement or now seek a substitute, the governmental-interest approach offers one alternative, albeit one that is often inward looking and tends to dispense with analysis. The Second Restatement offers a few particularized rules; its principal approach, however, calls for the application of the law of the place with the most significant relationship to the transaction and to the parties. The case law has particularized the approach with respect to some contracts, as reviewed in the preceding section. In a number of areas, however, the approach has not yet resulted in the evolution of particularized rules and, as discussed in the section immediately preceding, may even contribute to an unnecessary splitting of issues.

The 1980 Convention on the Law Applicable to Contractual Obligations of the European Communities ("Rome Convention")[1] adopts a test similar to that of the Second Restatement—referring to the law of the country with which the contract is "most closely connected"—but also provides a number of rebuttable presumptions for the determination of that law[2] and, in addition, contains special rules for consumer and employment contracts.[3] The most interesting of the presumptions is the

§ 18.40

1. For comment see Giuliano & Lagarde, Report to the Council, id. No. C282/1 (1980); Bennett in 17 C.M.L. Rev. 269 (1980); Delaume, The European Convention on the Law Applicable to Contractual Obligations: Why A Convention?, 22 Va. J. Int'l L. 105 (1971); Juenger, Parteiautonomie und objektive Anknüpfung im EG-Übereinkommen zum Internationalen Vertragsrecht, 46 Rabels Zeitschrift 57 (1982); Hay, Flexibility versus Certainty and Uniformity in Choice of Law, 226 Recueil des Cours 281 (1991–I). For other international conventions see supra § 18.24.

2. For an interesting analysis see Jaffey, The English Proper Law Doctrine and the EEC Convention, 33 Int'l & Comp. L.Q. 531 (1984). See also Williams, The EEC Convention on the Law Applicable to Contractual Obligations, 35 Int'l & Comp. L.Q. 1 (1986). In addition to the presumption discussed immediately following in the text, these are: situs law for contracts concerning immovables (see also supra § 18.23 n.5) and, for contracts for the carriage of goods, the law of the place of the carrier's principal place of business if this is also the place of loading, destination, or the consignor's principal place of business. Art. 5 (supra

§ 18.24). A contract's validity is determined by the law that would be applicable if the contract were valid (Art. 8); formal requirements are satisfied by reference either to the law applicable to the contract or to the law of execution (Art. 9). Art. 9 does not apply to contracts concerning immovables (situs law, supra Art. 4) or to consumer contracts (infra n.3).

3. The Convention's Art. 7 introduces a novel idea: when applying the law of a country according to the rules of the Convention, a court may give effect to the mandatory rules of the law of another country with which the transaction has a close connection if, under the law of that country, its mandatory rule is intended to have priority. This provision has engendered lively discussion in the literature: see Lando, New American Choice-of-Law Principles and the European Conflict of Laws of Contracts, 30 Am. J. Comp. L. 19 (1982); Discussion, Basle Symposium on the Law Governing Contractual Obligations, 33 Schriftenreihe des Instituts für Internationales Recht und Internationale Beziehungen, Juristische Fakultät, Universität Basel (1983); Coester, Die Berücksichtigung fremden zwingenden Rechts neben dem Vertragsstatut, 82 ZVglRWiss. 1 (1983); Hay, supra n.1 (with

one that equates the "closest connection" with the place where the "characteristic" service or performance is to be rendered.[4] The doctrine originated in Switzerland, which has also long been a proponent of the "closest connection" test,[5] and, at first glance, appears attractively simple. Its basic premise is that the payment of money is *not* characteristic of a contract, but that this is true of the counter performance. This leads to a focus on the party selling the goods, performing the service, and so forth. Even in the case of loans, one of the money transactions may be said to be more characteristic than the other: the repayment with interest. Nevertheless, the doctrine may have defects.[6] In installment contracts, the debtor's obligation may be subject to regulatory legislation and therefore be the more "characteristic" aspect of the transaction; the monetary aspect of a pawnshop transaction typically is the more important; reciprocal performances not involving money are difficult to accommodate in this system. As a practical result, the general determination of what constitutes the "characteristic obligation" without regard to the circumstances of the particular contract of the parties may lead to the application of the law of the economically " . . . stronger party: employers, banks, insurance companies, the closed professions."[7]

That the "stronger party" is often favored by the application of his home law is said to be a fact of life, especially since the stronger party probably could have imposed his law by a contractual choice-of-law clause.[8] The reading is, however, that the parties did not stipulate a law; it is therefore problematic to base a choice of law on what the parties would have done if they had thought about it. In addition, this orienta-

---

further references). Consumer contracts (Art. 5): law of the consumer's habitual residence. Employment contracts (Art. 6): the law of the place of habitual employment, the law of the place where the office hiring the employee is situated, or the most closely connected law. With respect to both kinds of contracts, the parties may not, by stipulating the applicable law, avoid mandatory rules of the otherwise applicable law. See also Sec. 27(2)(b) of the English Unfair Contract Term Act of 1977; von Marschall, The New German Law on Standard Contract Terms, 3 Lloyd's Mar. & Com. L.Q. 278 (1979).

4. Article 4 specifies further that this is the state where the party who is to carry out the characteristic performance had his habitual residence at the time of contract formation; or where that party had his principal establishment at that time if the performance is in pursuance of a contract concluded in the course of a business; or where that party had his subsidiary establishment if the performance is to be rendered by the latter. For discussion, in the context of an earlier draft, see d'Oliveira, "Characteristic Obligation" in the Draft EEC Obligation Convention, 25 Am. J. Comp. L. 303 (1977).

Article 1211 of the new Civil Code of the Russian Federation (federal law n. 146 of 26 November 2001, Rossyiskaya Gazeta, n. 49 item 4553, 28/11/2001) basically adopts Art. 4 of the Rome Convention but, in its third paragraph, particularizes for nineteen different types of contracts who is the party rendering the characteristic performance (e.g., the donor, the carrier, the lender, the bank in the case of a bank deposit). Para. 4 additionally specifies the state of the closest connection for a number of other transactions (e.g., for partnership contracts, the state in which the partnership's activity is carried out).

5. See BGE 60, II, 294 (1934). See Schnitzer, Handbuch des internationalen Privatrechts I, 52 and II, 639 (4th ed. 1957–58).

6. See d'Oliveira, supra n.4 (excellent summary of American and continental criticism).

7. D'Oliveira, supra n.4, at 327. But see supra n.3 with respect to employment contracts.

8. See also Martiny, in EGBGB–Münchener Kommentar Art. 28 annots. 35–36 (3d ed. 1998).

tion overlooks the growing concern for the "weaker party," especially in consumer contracts as reflected both in American and continental legislation. In some measure, this concern also leads to the application of the more "favorable" law, for instance in products liability,[9] and to the "better law" approach generally.

§ 18.41   Another proposal[1] proceeds from the doctrine of the characteristic obligation, and like it disregards the mere payment of money–because not characteristic–in the typical sale contract. The proposal refines the doctrine by focusing on the characteristic *purpose* of contracts so as to allow some individual consideration of the interests of the parties. Subject to a number of exceptions, this approach permits some categorization of contracts and, with it, introduces a measure of predictability.[2] American case law, when tested against this proposal frequently achieves similar results,[3] albeit not in any systematic fashion.[4]

9. Supra § 17.41.

§ 18.41

1. Weitnauer, Der Vertragsschwerpunkt (vol. 105, Arbeiten zur Rechtsvergleischung), at 106 n.452 (1981).

2. " . . . [A]ccount is taken only of interests in the application of a system of law *as such,* independently of the content of individual rules; there is (aside from narrow cases of party autonomy) no 'raisin theory' which would recognize a party's interest to apply only rules that are favorable to it, not those that are unfavorable. . . . One gets into the devil's kitchen by renouncing-in the already complex field of [Private International Law]-clear easily recognizable and easily manageable conflicts rules; the dissolution of conflicts law by the American reformers offers here the best demonstrative lesson." Kegel, Paternal Home and Dream Home: Traditional Conflict of Laws and the American Reformers, 27 Am. J. Comp. L. 615, 621–22 (1979).

3. Weitnauer, supra n.1, at 209. The proposal contains the following choice-of-law rules (American solutions in parentheses):

Contracts of Sale: place of delivery unless that state is not the place of business of either party; in the latter case: place of business of the seller. See also Restatement, Second Conflict of Laws § 191 (1971). *Exceptions:* situs law for the sale of immovables. See also Restatement, Second, Conflict of Laws § 189 (1971).

Employment Contracts: place of employment. See supra § 18.29 nn.3–5, except that the law of the place of the employer's business establishment should govern if there is more than one place of employment.

Rendition of Services: place of performance. See supra § 18.29 n.2.

Transportation Contracts: place of destination in the case of shipping contracts, otherwise the place of business of the dispatching party. Cf. supra § 18.30.

Publishing Contracts: place of publisher. Cf. supra § 18.29 n.6.

Agency: place of acting. Cf. supra §§ 18.32–18.35.

Brokerage: place of acting. But see supra § 18.31.

Life Insurance: habitual residence of the insured. See supra § 18.26.

Casualty Insurance: principal location of the insured risk. See supra § 18.26.

Leases: situs law for immovables, principal location for movables. See supra § 18.37.

Surety: habitual residence of surety. But see supra § 18.27.

Assignments: law applicable to the underlying obligation. Cf. supra § 18.37.

4. With respect to *commercial arbitration,* the Restatement, Second, Conflict of Laws provides in § 218, comment (b) that the applicable law is determined by reference to § 187 (party autonomy) or, failing an effective stipulation by the parties, to § 188 (place of the most significant relationship to the arbitration agreement or to the parties). The reference to § 188 may or may not accord with modern European practice, exemplified by the provisions of the New Code of Civil Procedure of France, which leaves the arbitrator free to decide "according to the rules which he deems appropriate," taking into account trade usage. See Delaume, International Arbitration under French Law, 37 Arbitration J. 37, 41

V. UNJUST ENRICHMENT[1]

A. INTRODUCTION

1. In General

§ 18.42 In contract, value restitution is awarded for "performances rendered in actual or supposed conformity with contractual obligations," in tort, "damage remedies can [now] be ignored and quasi-contract used as to any kind of legal wrong from which gains are realized," and, in a third group of cases, this remedy will lie generally when "the defendant has received something that should have gone to the plaintiff."[2] In addition, remedies lie for a significant number of equitable wrongs.

Restitution for equitable wrongs is achieved in part through the law of trusts and in part through the law of restitution proper. However, the fact that some cases are governed by trust principles does not change the fact that the issue still concerns unjustifiable enrichment. For choice-of-law purposes the question therefore is whether the restitutionary remedy shall be governed by, say, the underlying trust relationship (if any) or by another law. Chief among the equitable remedies growing out of the

---

(1982) with further references to the 1961 European Convention, the Rules of the International Chamber of Commerce, and the UNCITRAL Rules. See also G. Delaume, Transnational Contracts *passim* (rev. ed. 1980). On the use of *lex mercatoria* in international arbitration, see Lowenfeld, Lex Mercatoria: An Arbitrator's view, 6 Arbitration Int'l 133 (1990). For a call for a reexamination of choice of law in international commerce, see Baxter, International Business and Choice of law, 36 Int'l & Comp. L.Q. 92 (1987).

§ 18.42

1. For comprehensive analysis of German law prior to codification, see Schlechtriem, Bereicherungsansprüche im internationalen Privatrecht, in: von Caemmerer, ed., Vorschläge und Gutachten zur Reform des deutschen internationalen Privatrechts der ausservertraglichen Schuldverhältnisse 30 (1983). See now Art. 38 of the Introductory Law to the Civil Code (EGBGB), Bundesgesetzblatt 1999, I, 1026:

Article 38. *Unjust Enrichment.* (1) Claims for unjust enrichment for benefits received are governed by the law applicable to the legal relationship with respect to which the benefits were conferred.

(2) Claims for unjust enrichment based on an interference with a legally protected right are governed by the law of the state in which the interference occurred.

(3) All other claims for unjust enrichment are governed by the law of the state where the enrichment occurred.

Art. 42 EGBGB permits the parties to choose the applicable law after the events giving to the non-contractual obligation (including unjust enrichment) have occurred. For comment, see Hay, From Rule–Orientation to "Approach" in German Conflicts Law, 45 Am. J. Comp. L. 501 (1999). See also Art. 1223 of the Civil Code of the Russian Federation (federal law n. 146 of 26 November 2001, Rossyiskaya Gazeta, n. 49 item 4553, 28/11/2001) (providing that unjust enrichment is governed by the law of the country in which the enrichment occurred, but also allowing the parties to stipulate to the application of the lex fori; if the enrichment arose in connection with an existing or proposed legal relation, the law of the country in which that relationship was, or could be, based governs). For comparative treatment see Hay, Unjust Enrichment in the Conflict of Laws: A Comparative View of German Law and the American Restatement 2d, 26 Am.J.Comp.L. 1–49 (1977) (on which portions of this section are based). Permission to use this material is gratefully acknowledged. See also Bennett, Choice of Law Rules in Claims of Unjust Enrichment, 39 Int'l & Comp.L.Q. 136 (1990).

2. J. Dawson, Unjust Enrichment 23–24 (1951).

trust concept is the constructive trust, which permits restoration to a trust of assets wrongfully acquired with trust property and the tracing of assets to persons who are not trustees, that is, with respect to whom no trust or other fiduciary relationship existed. Beginning with an 1877 New York decision[3] that applied the constructive trust to stolen goods, the constructive trust has become a generalized and independent remedy, not necessarily based on an underlying trust relationship. Thus, even if unjust enrichment problems should ordinarily be governed by the law of the underlying relationship, some aspects of the constructive trust will require additional consideration. The equitable lien, aspects of subrogation, and equitable accounting raise similar problems and are discussed separately below.

2. Case Categories

§ 18.43   The first group of cases concerns claims arising from a preexisting contractual relationship, either actual or intended, such as: (a) when the contract has not come about (e.g., because of mistake), has become frustrated, impossible or illegal, or has been rescinded; (b) a quasi-contractual remedy in favor of the plaintiff who has breached after part performance and is unable to recover *ex contractu,* for instance because the prerequisites for "substantial performance" have not been met; (c) problems of contractual subrogation; (d) claims against third-party beneficiaries (upon failure of consideration in, or for set-offs arising from the main contract); and (e) claims for refunds for overpayment or multiple payment of a debt also belong in this category.

A second group, closely related to the first, concerns the voluntary bestowal of a benefit. In American law there is no general claim for *negotiorum gestio,*[1] not even for the payment of a money debt of another,[2] but in certain cases expenses incurred for the purchase of necessities for another may be recovered.[3] Despite the similarity of these claims to the express contractual relationships, actual or intended, involved in the first group of cases, it remains to be seen whether their choice-of-law aspects may not nevertheless require different treatment.

The third general group consists of unjust enrichment claims related in some way to tort. They include some aspects of workers' compensation claims, contribution among joint tortfeasors and subrogation with respect to tort claims.

The conversion of property raises a difficult question of classification. If seen as an aspect of tort, choice-of-law rules that focus on the

---

3.   Newton v. Porter, 69 N.Y. 133 (1877).

§ 18.43

1.   See the classic study by Dawson, Negotiorum Gestio: The Altruistic Intermeddler, 74 Harv. L. Rev. 817 (Pt. 1) and 1073 (Pt. 2) (1961). See also Dawson, The Self–Serving Intermeddler, 87 Harv. L. Rev. 1409 (1974); Wade, Restitution for Benefits Conferred Without Request, 19 Vand. L. Rev. 1183 (1966).

2.   Dawson, Unjust Enrichment 141 (1951).

3.   Restatement of Restitution §§ 113–115 (1937); Perillo, Restitution in a Contractual Context, 73 Columbia L. Rev. 1208, 1214 (1973). More cautiously, Dawson, supra n.2, at 140.

place of acting or of enrichment may be appropriate; alternatively, the relevant focus may be on the property aspect and then lead to the law of the transfer. Special difficulties arise for American law from the plaintiff's right of election "to waive the tort and sue in contract,"[4] that is to hold the tortfeasor to an implied contract. It remains to be seen whether this latter possibility justifies analogizing these cases to those in contract or whether the tort or property aspect (which will often coincide)[5] should furnish the principal focus. That the resolution of this question is of great practical, and not only academic, interest is shown by the consequences which attach to the choice, for instance with respect to the selection of an appropriate statute of limitations.

Equitable wrongs—the constructive trust and other equitable remedies mentioned briefly above—present similar difficulties of classification since some grow out of preexisting relationship while others do not. All of the foregoing may therefore be dealt with as part of a fourth category of "special" or "mixed" situations.

Much of the above suggests, implicitly, that the proper identification of the kind of unjust enrichment claim ("shift of assets")[6] involved will lead to the identification of the appropriate single law for its resolution of the conflict-of-laws. This may, but need not, be true. Thus it may be open to question whether a single law should govern the quasi-contractual claims of both parties with respect to their respective performances, which may be localized quite differently, and secondly, how the problem of differing standards for compensation should be resolved (e.g. as part of the quasi-contractual claim or by the lex fori as part of "procedure" rather than substance).

B. CHOICE–OF–LAW ALTERNATIVES

1. *Preexisting (Contractual) Relationships*

§ 18.44 The First Restatement adopted the general rule of applying the law of the place where the benefit was conferred.[1] As scholarly criticism has rightly pointed out, the rule left unclear whether the reference was to the place of acting or the place of enrichment.[2] In addition, the rule seemed unsatisfactory for those cases in which there was a preexisting relationship between the parties because the law so chosen might have but the most casual connection with that relation-

---

4. Restatement of Contracts § 72(2) (1932). Cf. Restatement, Second, Contracts § 69 (1981). For the emergence of a similar doctrine under the (civil) law of Quebec see Haanappel, La relation entre les responsabilités civiles contractuelle et délictuelle: L'arrt *Wabaso* en droit québécois et en droit comparé, 34 Revue internationale de droit comparé 103 (1982).

5. Zweigert & Müller-Gindullis, Quasi–Contracts, International Encyclopedia of Comparative Law, ch. 30, at 30–36 (1974).

6. See Zweigert & Müller-Gindullis, supra n.5 at 30–32; Perillo, supra n.3, at 1226 n.111.

§ 18.44

1. Restatement of Conflict of Laws § 453 (1934).

2. Cohen, Quasi–Contract and the Conflict of Laws, 31 L.A. Bar Bull. 71, 77 (1956).

ship.[3] For these reasons, and keeping with its general approach to choice-of-law, § 221 of the Second Restatement advocates the reference to the "local law" of the state that has the "most significant relationship" to the issue, defined in addition to other factors and contacts as the place "where a relationship between the parties was centered, provided that the receipt of enrichment was substantially related to the relationship." Comment (d) explains that this "relationship will usually be one of contract, agency, trust or tort." Furthermore: "When the enrichment was received in the course of the performance of a contract between the parties, the law selected by application of the rules of §§ 187–188 will presumably govern one party's rights in restitution against the other. The applicable law will be that chosen by the parties if they have made an effective choice under the circumstances stated in § 187."

Portions of this rule, especially when read against the background of the Restatement comment quoted above, bear a superficial resemblance to the English reference to the "proper law of the [underlying] contract,"[4] to Article 222 of the Codigo Bustamante,[5] and to the German reference to the law of the underlying legal relationship.[6]

The Second Restatement rule, however, is more complex than it first appears. The Comment generalizes it to relationships beyond contract, excludes the foreign conflicts law from its reference (and with it the possibility of *renvoi*), and in contract cases would honor the parties' choice of law as contained in the main contract. Some of these aspects require separate consideration. As a starting point however, the basic rule should be reviewed which essentially defines the *lex causae* as the law of the underlying (contractual) relationship in cases growing out of contracts.[7]

In an early criticism of the Second Restatement rule, Ehrenzweig proposed the application of the lex fori to restitutive claims[8] and showed that, in a number of cases, courts had in fact applied the lex fori.[9]

3. Morris, The Choice of Law Clause in Statutes, 62 L.Q. Rev. 170 (1946).

4. Dicey & Morris, The Conflict of Laws 1471, 1474–75 (12th ed. 1993 by Collins).

5. See Parra–Aranguren, Las Obligaciones extra-contractueles en derecho internacional privado, Revista de la Facultad de Derecho, Universidad Catolica Andres Bello, Ano Lectivo 1974–1975, 9 at 62 et seq. (Caracas 1975).

6. OLG Hamm RIW 1991, 155. See now Art. 38(1) Introductory Law to the Civil Code (EGBGB), Bundesgesetzblatt 1999, I, 1026 (1998).

7. 1 See Phoenix Canada Oil Co. Ltd. v. Texaco Inc., 560 F.Supp. 1372 (D.Del.1983).

8. Ehrenzweig, Restitution in the Conflict of Laws: Law and Reason Versus the Restatement Second, 36 N.Y.U. L. Rev. 1298 (1961). His criticism was directed against § 354k of the 6th Tentative Draft.

That provision, in contrast to the more differentiated final provision of § 221, distinguished only between unjust enrichment derived from a preexisting relation (equals law of that relationship) and unrelated enrichment (equals law of the place where benefit or enrichment was received).

9. Id. at 1306 (with cases). Other and also subsequent cases also often apply the *lex fori*: Beverly Hills National Bank and Trust Co. v. Compania De Navegacione Almirante S.A., Panama, 437 F.2d 301, 307 (9th Cir.1971), cert. denied 402 U.S. 996, 91 S.Ct. 2173, 29 L.Ed.2d 161 (1971) ("There is no choice of law problem. Both parties assume that California substantive law governs the constructive trust claim, or at least that state law simply follows general equitable principles"); Bank of America v. Saville, 416 F.2d 265, 267 n.1 (7th Cir.1969), cert. denied 396 U.S. 1038, 90 S.Ct. 685, 24

However, virtually all of his criticism of the Second Restatement rule drew on examples from the law of torts or trusts, or dealt with the voluntary bestowal of benefits. The pre-existing contractual relationship

L.Ed.2d 682 (1970) ("The parties appear to have treated California law as controlling substantive issues."); Bond v. Oak Manufacturing Co., 293 F.2d 752 (3d Cir.1961) (trial court assumed that Illinois law applied to a claim for quantum meruit arising from work performed under a contract which was unenforceable under the Statute of Frauds); Vulcanized Rubber and Plastics Co. v. Scheckter, 400 Pa. 405, 162 A.2d 400, 403 n.2 (1960) ("Since ... the parties did not see fit to question the application of Pennsylvania law, we infer that this state was in fact the situs of most of the allegedly wrongful conduct and accordingly decide the issue of fiduciary responsibility on the basis of our own law"); Curles v. Curles, 136 F.Supp. 916 (D.D.C.1955), aff'd 241 F.2d 448 (D.C.Cir.1957) (in an action between divorced couple concerning Virginia land, the court stated that the rule that a nonpaying cotenant holds his share as a trustee does not apply when the advancement is for a "wife or child or to any person for whom the purchaser is under an obligation to provide,") but did not discuss whether the existence of such an obligation is governed by the law of the situs—Virginia—or by the place of common residence—District of Columbia.

These cases, as well as those cited by Ehrenzweig, do not necessarily support the conclusion that the court chose the lex fori. Instead, in some cases the court apparently failed to see the choice-of-law problem and in others the parties' failure to plead the applicability of another law necessary under American law lead to the use of the lex fori.

On the other hand, there are several decisions in which the courts made a choice after deliberate analysis (governmental-interest test or most-significant-relationship test) with some of these decisions leading to a law other than the lex fori. See Kohr v. Allegheny Airlines, Inc., 504 F.2d 400 (7th Cir.1974), cert. denied 421 U.S. 978, 95 S.Ct. 1980, 44 L.Ed.2d 470 (1975) (federal common law of contribution and indemnity–comparative negligence standard–governs midair collisions rather than any law to which the forum's state conflicts law might refer); Denny v. American Tobacco Co., 308 F.Supp. 219 (N.D.Cal.1970) (California court applied New York law, after a governmental interest analysis, to a claim for a "finder's fee" for information leading to the acquisition of a subsidiary corporation); Bank of America v. Saville (supra this note) (Indiana court applied California law

because the "parties appear to have treated [it] as controlling substantive issues"); Quintana v. Ordono, 195 So.2d 577 (Fla. App.1967) (Cuban law applied to part of the claim dealing with property acquired in Cuba).

Decisions that apply the *lex fori*, but do so after substantial analysis, include: Kantlehner v. United States, 279 F.Supp. 122 (E.D.N.Y.1967) (New York law applied to contribution and indemnity claims arising from a Maryland plane crash under New York's most-significant-relationship test for which the decedent's New York residence was a major factor); Columbia Nastri & Carta Carbone S/p/A. v. Columbia Ribbon & Carbon Manufacturing Co., 367 F.2d 308, 311 (2d Cir.1966) (constructive trust for trademarks found to exist under New York law because most of the contacts had centered in New York); Maryland v. Capital Airlines, Inc., 280 F.Supp. 648 (S.D.N.Y. 1964) (New York law applied to claims for contribution and indemnity arising from a Maryland plane crash because Maryland's contacts with the occurrence are insufficient to show an interest in the outcome of the contribution claim and because New York was the place of the plane's sale); Van Rensselaer v. General Motors Corp., 223 F.Supp. 323 (E.D.Mich.1962), aff'd 324 F.2d 354 (6th Cir.1963), cert. denied 377 U.S. 959, 84 S.Ct. 1640, 12 L.Ed.2d 502 (1964), (Michigan law applied, under First Restatement test, to claim for compensation for use of an unsolicited business idea because Michigan was the place where the benefit was conferred and where the unjust enrichment occurred); Gibbs–Brower Intern. v. Kirchheimer Bros. Co., 611 F.Supp. 122 (N.D.Ill.1985) (most-significant-relationship test; lex fori applied to a quantum meruit claim in circumstances where the only link to another jurisdiction was plaintiff's incorporation there, although it maintained its general offices in yet a third state). See also Dews v. Halliburton Industries, Inc., 288 Ark. 532, 708 S.W.2d 67 (1986) (although the contract was entered into in Louisiana, Arkansas law applied when all acts upon which the finding of unjust enrichment was based had occurred in Arkansas. Although the court cited no authority, the decision, on the facts of the case, is consistent with the Second Restatement because Arkansas was the state of the most significant relationship both with respect to the underlying contract and to the occurrences giving rise to the claim.)

(actual or intended) received only passing mention: "Only on one condition will the court refrain from applying its own law, namely, where either party has properly relied on the application of another law."[10] That, of course, is precisely the point in an analysis which seeks to group case situations, rather than attempts the probably impossible task of formulating a "general rule," and which the Second Restatement seeks to achieve in § 221(1)(a). Thus, when restitution is sought for mistake in contract formation, upon rescission of the contract, or because of frustration or impossibility, at least one and possibly both parties have relied on the application of a given law or, at a minimum, had certain expectations as to the governing law. Under these circumstances, the general reference to the lex fori seems quite inappropriate.

Even apart from any expectations of the parties, a *general* reference to the lex fori is also inappropriate because it ignores other well-established choice-influencing considerations of modern American conflicts law. Occasionally even governmental interests may become relevant.[11] Thus again the more flexible approach of the Second Restatement will serve these objectives better than does a general reference to the lex fori.

A last possible objection to the Second Restatement rule, namely that restitution claims ordinarily will concern only one side of the transaction and thus should perhaps be governed by a law directly related to that claim and not by the law applying to the contract as a whole, seems equally unfounded. A "center of gravity" approach already takes account of performance and counter-performance, among other factors, to establish the "center." And just as the "center" thus established is not redefined in actions *on the contract,* for instance on the basis of which party happens to be n breach, no additional reason appears to justify redefining it for actions seeking *restitution* which arise out of the *same relationship.* The test of a contract's "center of gravity," or of the place of its "most significant relationship," amounts to an objective weighing of all surrounding circumstances and considerations in order to further and protect the interests of the parties in cases in which an express party stipulation is lacking or invalid.

2. *Voluntary Bestowal of Benefits*

§ 18.45 A voluntary bestowal of benefits may occur in the case of the payment of the debts of another and in involuntary bailment. In these cases, the Second Restatement would again, and appropriately so,

---

10. Ehrenzweig, supra n.8, at 1307.

11. Public policy concerns may occasionally remove quasi-contractual as well as contractual claims from the application of normal choice-of-law rules altogether. See Menendez v. Saks and Co., 485 F.2d 1355, 1369–70 (2d Cir.1973) (act-of-state doctrine applies to quasi-contractual claims), reversed on other grounds sub nom. See also Alfred Dunhill of London, Inc. v. Republic of Cuba, et al., 425 U.S. 682, 96 S.Ct. 1854, 48 L.Ed.2d 301 (1976). Public policy concerns are contained, in some measure, although admittedly not comprehensively, in the various components that constitute the "most significant relationship."

refer to the law of that relationship.[1] The situation is less clear when enrichment occurs without any previous relationship between the parties. Theoretically, these cases include all remaining forms of unjust enrichment and are often so treated in the literature[2] and in the Second Restatement.[3] However in view of the structure of the Second Restatement's provision (which lists several connecting factors in amplification of the general reference to the law of the "most significant relationship"), it seems more appropriate to separate the case situations into those involving the voluntary bestowal of a benefit, those in some way related to tort, and those arising from equitable wrongs. This division may allow closer scrutiny of the Second Restatement's provisions. The present section deals with the first of these subdivisions.

As a result of the absence of a general doctrine of *negotiorum gestio* in American law,[4] virtually the only other cases falling into this category are: the provision of necessities to another (in fact, a particular form of the payment of a obligation of another), third party donee situations not resulting from a third party beneficiary contract,[5] and improvements made by one upon land while in lawful possession of it, which improvements now inure to the benefit of another. All other illustrations given in the comments to the Second Restatement in some way relate to tort and accordingly will be treated subsequently.

Applied to improvements upon land, the Second Restatement test leads to the law of the situs.[6] Interestingly enough however, in a hypothetical case given in Illustration 9 to the Second Restatement section, preference is given to the law of the place where the benefit was received rather than to the law where the thing (an automobile) was when the benefit was bestowed. The reason for the difference seems to

---

§ 18.45

1. Restatement, Second, Conflict of Laws § 221, illus. 8 (1971).

2. See authorities cited supra § 18.43 n.5.

3. Restatement, Second, Conflict of Laws § 221, cmnt. (d) (1971).

4. Restatement of Restitution § 112 (1937). See Bloomgarden v. Coyer, 479 F.2d 201, 211 (D.C.Cir.1973). Exceptionally, claims may exist for compensation for performance of another's duty to supply necessities, of another's duty to the public, or for the preservation of another's life, health or property. The Restatement of Restitution § 117(2) also envisions the protection of another's credit but only in the setting of the payment of a negotiable instrument. This rule was adopted by §§ 171–77 of the Uniform Negotiable Instruments Law and has now been codified in § 3–603(2) of the Uniform Commercial Code. See also Dawson, Unjust Enrichment 127–29, 137–44 (1951).

English law, similarly, does not compensate the officious intermeddler, but Jewish (Talmudic) law does (not for expenses, but to the extent of the benefit bestowed). Webber, Observations on Some Cases of Unjust Enrichment in Jewish Law, 2 Dine Israel xxv (1970).

5. See, e.g., Restatement, Second, Conflict of Laws § 221, illus. 13 (1971) (executor of an estate pays a sum of money to X according to the provisions of a revoked will. A subsequent (and valid) will is then discovered which leaves nothing to X. In a case where the decedent died domiciled in State A, X was a resident of A but temporarily in B at the time of the mistaken payment, and A is the state of administration, A is the state of the most-significant relationship; its law determines whether the estate, through the executor, may recover the payment). In substantive law such a claim will ordinarily lie. See Restatement of Restitution § 19 & illus. 3, 6 (1937).

6. Restatement, Second, Conflict of Laws § 221, illus. 14 (1971).

be that "the location of land provides a more important contact than the location of a chattel."[7] As a general proposition, this statement may be acceptable. Moreover, the Second Restatement provision itself adopts the reference to the situs law as the primary rule for all things, land and chattel, by providing for its displacement only in such cases when the location of the thing (i.e. necessarily of a chattel) "was [not] substantially related to the enrichment." Nevertheless it remains unclear what quantity and quality of other factors destroy the substantiality and in what order of importance the other connecting factors must then be weighed in order to determine another applicable law.

It is apparent that the discharge of another's debt (whether or not a remedy exists under local substantive law) is not covered in a specific or predictable manner, since the resulting enrichment may be connected with any number of jurisdictions (place of acting, domicile of parties, etc.). In order to avoid *dépeçage,* the proper reference should be to the law of the debt. To be sure, that law will coincide with one of the connecting factors of § 221(2), but the point to be emphasized is that the focus should be on the law of the debt rather than on the satisfaction of one or several of the (other) flexible connecting factors for the reasons stated earlier.

The third party donee situation (not based on a preexisting third-party-beneficiary contract) similarly is left to the provisions of § 221(2). An illustration provided by the Comments[8] identifies as the place of the most significant relationship the place to which the underlying relationship also happened to be related. However, slight changes in the facts of the hypothetical (for instance, that X, or even X and the executor, are domiciled in State B) might lead to a different result. Since many of these situations will arise because of a (mistaken) supposition that an actual obligation existed, the equating of actual and supposed obligations and the referral of claims with respect to both to the law of the underlying "obligation" seems preferable to the less certain *Restatement* rule.

3. *Claims Related to Tort*

§ 18.46 A number of restitutive claims relate in some way to tort, that is, do not arise from a preexisting contractual relationship, even though a relationship may have existed between the parties. The latter is often true, for instance, in cases involving indemnity or contribution between tortfeasors, especially in a field like worker's compensation. Even when there is no preexisting relationship, such as in cases of conversion, the problem may be complicated further in American law because of the injured party's right "to waive the tort and sue in contract." Should the applicable *lex causae* therefore be that of the legal relationship, should the plaintiff—in a conversion case—have the option

---

7. Restatement, Second, Conflict of   **8.** Supra n.5.
Laws 221, cmnt. (d) (1971).

between the contractual *lex causae* or one focusing on other connecting factors, and should trespass therefore stand alone and require yet another definition of the *lex causae* applicable to restitutive claims arising from it?

It is in this area that the approach suggested by the Second Restatement creates difficulties in its application to concrete problems. Thus a conversion case[1] is subsumed under the heading of "the place where the relationship of the parties was centered" (where an implied-in-fact contract or other legal relationship was formed) because any wider reading of the term "relationship" would result in the tautology that the center is where the center is, while a case of misdirected delivery of goods and their use by a third party[2] is not treated as an election of a contract but, presumably, as a tort to which the law of the place where the benefit or enrichment was received is applied. The latter results is also suggested for compensation for the unauthorized use of land (trespass), a much clearer case of tort.[3] On the particular facts of the hypothetical cases, the suggested result are persuasive; nevertheless, it remains unclear what precise elements are decisive in determining the place of the most significant relationship when factual circumstances are different. The case law, similarly, has not provided further guidance thus far,[4] except in a few cases involving co-debtors in worker's compensation cases.[5] Yet the need for clearer rules is evident, especially because certain cases of tort may, in American law, be resolved by recourse to constructive trust notions, as discussed below. Since notions of "equitable interests" in the title to property are lacking in other legal systems, uniformity of result for essentially similar cases, regardless of remedy sought or awarded, should therefore be an important objective.

§ 18.46

1. Restatement, Second, Conflict of Laws § 221, illus. 6 (1971) ("A converts B's logs in state X and takes them to state Y, where he makes them into boxes. A is domiciled n X and B is domiciled in Y. B follows and demands the boxes and they are given to him. On these facts, X is presumably the state of most significant relationship to the question whether A can recover from B the amount by which he has increased the value of the lumber by making it into boxes").

2. Restatement, Second, Conflict of Laws § 221, illus. 10 (1971) ("A, who is under contract to supply goods to B in state X, delivers them in X to C, who is domiciled in state Y, in the mistaken belief that C is B's agent. On these facts, X is presumably the state of most significant relationship to the question whether A can recover from C the value of the goods").

3. Restatement, Second, Conflict of Laws § 221, illus. 12 (1971). In a case like this, of course, virtually all possible connecting factors will coincide: the situs, the place of acting, the place of enrichment, etc.

4. See Van Rensselaer v. General Motors Corp., 223 F.Supp. 323 (E.D.Mich. 1962), aff'd 324 F.2d 354 (6th Cir.1963), cert. denied 377 U.S. 959, 84 S.Ct. 1640, 12 L.Ed.2d 502 (1964) (Michigan federal court follows §§ 323 and 452 of the First Restatement and applies Michigan law to the question whether plaintiff could recover for the use of unsolicited business ideas sent to the defendant corporation after hearing defendant's president say in California that "GM would welcome suggestions from car conscious Californians" Michigan was the place where the benefit was conferred and where any unjust enrichment occurred); Official Airlines Schedule Information Service, Inc. v. Eastern Air Lines, Inc., 333 F.2d 672 (5th Cir.1964).

5. See Elston v. Industrial Lift Truck Co., 420 Pa. 97, 216 A.2d 318 (1966) and Wilson v. Faull, 27 N.J. 105, 141 A.2d 768 (1958). See also Pennington, Workmen's Compensation: Subrogation, Employer's Liability for Contribution, and Conflict of Las, 4 Forum 51 (1968); Note, Workmen's Compensation and the Conflict of Laws in New York, 53 Cornell L. Rev. 151 (1967).

Just as the underlying preexisting relationship (contractual or more general) seems a desirable concrete application in cases where such a relationship existed (even by supposition), a *general* reference to the "shift of assets" (bringing into play other connecting factors) seems a more appropriate way of dealing with case situations where such a shift cannot be related to a preexisting relationship of some kind. That the order of the subsidiary connecting factors which are relevant to the "shift of assets" must then be rearranged would seem to be a necessary consequence.

4. *Equitable Remedies*

§ 18.47 Contract and tort remedies are legal remedies; even quasi-contract is said to be a legal remedy "in form [although] equitable to the core."[1] In addition, equity jurisprudence provides additional remedies[2] which, like other equitable remedies (for instance the injunction), are available when the remedy at law is inadequate and sometimes afford an alternative avenue for relief (for instance in the form of an equitable lien in place of a damage action *ex contractu*). Thus an equitable lien has the effect of encumbering the property of the other who has been enriched (very much like a mortgage), in this manner conferring a property interest. A constructive trust may be impressed upon converted property or upon assets resulting from commingling, with the result that the recipient of the enrichment now holds the property in trust for the party incurring the loss; the latter again now has a property interest in the assets, very much the same as if he had been designated the beneficiary of an express trust.[3] The resulting trust inures to the benefit of the transferor of property to another (who now becomes trustee, with legal title, for the benefit of the former) in cases where the original purpose of the transfer has not been or cannot be effectuated. All of these remedies will give the injured party a property interest, as distinguished from return of the specific asset (for instance by replevin), or compensation in damages, neither of which may be possible, for instance (in the first case) when property has been commingled or the asset of another has been enriched or (in the second case) because of the insolvency of the debtor. In addition, the injured party may be able to seek an equitable accounting or trade his property into its product or to a third party. In the United States, with the exception of Louisiana, equitable remedies are fairly uniform. Except for some analogs, they are unknown to the civil law.

As the brief survey of equitable actions showed, the matter is essentially one of *remedy,* rather than one of different *substantive*

---

§ 18.47

1. Herrmann v. Gleason, 126 F.2d 936, 939 (6th Cir.1942).

2. Dawson Equitable Restitution 10 et. seq. Ames, Lectures on Legal History 149 et seq. (1913).

3. Bogert & Bogert, Handbook on the Law of Trusts 287 et seq. (5th ed. 1973). See also Dawson, Indirect Enrichment, Ius Privatum Gentium, Festschrift für Rheinstein, II, 789, 799 (1969).

liability. Thus, these remedies may apply to the same kinds of case situations, those arising from an underlying relationship as well as to those arising independently. In order that the difference in origin and nature of the remedy not distort the substantive results with respect to the claim reached by different legal systems, the applicable law should be the same.

Thus, equitable remedies, particularly the constructive trust, may be appropriate (when the remedy at law is inadequate) for claims arising from a preexisting relationship, such as for overpayment,[4] for funds improperly withheld[5] and for losses sustained (and concomitant enrichment of another) resulting from the breach of a fiduciary duty.[6] The resulting trust, similarly, may be used if a voluntary transfer has not achieved its purpose.[7] Except for the circumstance that the remedy at law is inadequate, the claims in the foregoing fact situations are the same as those discussed above. If the principal question thus is whether a claim for unjust enrichment exists at all, the answer must again be found in the law of the underlying relationship as the applicable *lex causae.* The Second Restatement, by implication, takes the same view.[8]

When there is no underlying relationship, such as in cases of conversion, including commingling[9] or unauthorized disposition, the *lex causae* must again be the law applicable to the "shift in assets" (as previously discussed) in order to determine whether the injured party

---

4. Grand Trunk Western Railroad Co. v. Chicago and Western Indiana Railroad Co., 131 F.2d 215 (7th Cir.1942).

5. Beverly Hills National Bank and Trust Co. v. Compania De Navegacione Almirante S.A., Panama, 437 F.2d 301 (9th Cir.1971), cert. denied 402 U.S. 996, 91 S.Ct. 2173, 29 L.Ed.2d 161 (1971) (in a suit in admiralty to recover charter hire due owner of vessel, trial court held that the defendant bank held proceeds of letters of credit, payable against prepaid bills of lading, as constructive trustee for the plaintiff owner; Court of Appeals upheld trial court's jurisdiction over equitable constructive trust claim, but reversed on the merits).

6. Vulcanized Rubber & Plastics Co. v. Scheckter, 400 Pa. 405, 162 A.2d 400 (1960) (court refused to impress a constructive trust in favor of a corporate purchasing syndicate on corporate shares purchased by a group with inside information which had caused a price rise in the shares because plaintiff syndicate, inter alia, was not pursuing a "corporate purpose"). See also supra n.8; Bank of America v. Saville, 416 F.2d 265 (7th Cir.1969), cert. denied 396 U.S. 1038, 90 S.Ct. 685, 24 L.Ed.2d 682 (1970) (constructive trust impressed on gift of stock worth approximately $57,000 by decedent to defendant while decedent, shortly before death, had become a ward

(conservatee) under the defendant's appointment as conservator of decedent's person).

7. Curles v. Curles, 136 F.Supp. 916 (D.D.C.1955), aff'd 241 F.2d 448 (D.C.Cir. 1957); see supra § 18.44 n.8.

8. See Restatement, Second, Conflict of Laws § 221, Introductory Note at p. 727, cmnt. (d) at p. 730, and illus. 6 (1971); see supra § 18.46 n.1 (a conversion case formulated in terms of whether the converter may recover compensation for the value added to the converted chattels, but which supports just as readily the choice of law suggested there for the injured party's action to impress a constructive trust on the assets in a case in which the converter had attained legal title). In addition, equitable accounting must necessarily also be governed by the law of the underlying relationship.

9. Cases of equitable liens will often be properly referable to the law of the situs since they represent property interests. On the other hand, they often serve as remedies (as discussed in the text) for claims arising from a preexisting (contractual or other) relationship (e.g. a building contract) and their proper *lex causae* should, in such cases, again be the law of the underlying relationship.

has a claim for unjust enrichment, for the satisfaction of which he may impress a constructive trust on the assets in the hands of the converter or may trace the assets to a third party.

5. *Extent and Nature of Relief*

§ 18.48   The preceding section signaled a difference between the claim for relief for unjust enrichment and the specific remedies available in legal systems. Two points require brief discussion.

Ehrenzweig's criticism of the Second Restatement approach[1] included the latter's suggestion that, in a case where F–1 requires compensation for the value of the asset converted, while F–2 provides for restitution of all benefits (including profits gained by resale),[2] the applicable law might be F–1, F–2, or depending on circumstances even F–3. This criticism is also not persuasive. If the objective of the *lex causae* reference is to permit for correction of the unjustifiable "shift of assets," it seems necessary that the same law determine that such a shift has occurred and in what manner, and to what extent, it is to be corrected. The introduction in this area of substance-procedure classification resulting in the application of the lex fori, in the foregoing example, to the extent of the correction of the shift may over-or under-compensate and again encourage forum-shopping. The balance between the parties, which the corrective restitutionary remedies seek to reestablish, must necessarily be struck by the lex causae.[3]

The answer is different when the remedy provided by the *lex causae* is unknown to the *lex fori* or, for that matter, when the reverse is true, for instance in common law-civil law conflict cases involving equitable remedies. In such cases, the foreign forum need not, indeed cannot, award a remedy unknown to its legal system,[4] while an American forum is put to the choice of restricting the relief to that available under the foreign *lex causae* or to give an equitable remedy against local assets.

§ 18.48

1. See supra § 18.43 n.7.

2. Compare Germany, BGB §§ 816, para. 1 and 818, para. 1.

3. By implication, the Second Restatement also supports this view by, as far as possible, seeking the identification of a single law [see cmnt c to § 221] by reference to the law of the "most significant relationship" (§ 221) and including in the scope of the Section not only "a person's right to recover" but also "the amount by which the other has been unjustly enriched" (Introductory Note to § 221 at p. 726). See also Kegel & Schurig, Internationales Privatrecht 618 (8th ed. 2000).

4. For the U.S., see L. McDougal, R. Felix & R. Whitten, American Conflicts Law 166–67 (5th ed. 2001) (with references). In addition to saying that a court does not have to fashion a remedy otherwise unknown to its legal system, the refusal of the recognition of a foreign judgment on grounds of difference in remedies (an area in which this problem typically arises) often contains an (unstated) objection on grounds of the ordre public. See Slater v. Mexican National Railroad Co., 194 U.S. 120, 24 S.Ct. 581, 48 L.Ed. 900 (1904); Rothstein v. Rothstein, 272 App.Div. 26, 68 N.Y.S.2d 305 (1947), aff'd 297 N.Y. 705, 77 N.E.2d 13 (1947); Carter v. Tillery, 257 S.W.2d 465 (Tex.Civ.App.1953), error refused n.r.e.; Flaiz v. Moore, 353 S.W.2d 74, 77 (Tex.Civ. App.1962), reversed 359 S.W.2d 872 (Tex. 1962); Ramirez v. Autobuses Blancos Flecha Roja, S.A. De C.V., 486 F.2d 493 (5th Cir.1973); Hayner v. Weinberger, 382 F.Supp. 762 (E.D.N.Y.1974).

It may at first seem attractive to permit the forum to grant the best available remedy, especially when the remedy will operate against local assets (e.g. the impressing of a constructive trust) and when, by hypothesis, the remedy at law is for some reason thought to be inadequate. Again, however, in so doing, the forum substitutes its own corrective mechanism (which, beyond "mechanism," goes to the quality of the relief) for that of the *lex causae* and, if the relief provided by the latter is thought to be inadequate, will therefore necessarily overcompensate. That the foreign forum in the reverse case (the example given first) will under-compensate results from the difference in the legal systems, rather than from choice. When a choice is possible, the nature and extent of the corrective relief is thus best left to the *lex causae*.

Chapter 19

PROPERTY

Table of Sections

			Sections
I.	Interests in Land		19.1–19.10
	A.	Introduction	19.1
	B.	The Situs Rule	19.2
	C.	Contract and Conveyance Distinctions	19.3
		1. Policy Analysis—Capacity	19.3
	D.	Particular Issues	19.4–19.5
		1. Conveyances: Effect and Construction	19.4
		2. Covenants	19.5
	E.	Equitable Interests	19.6–19.8
		1. Generally	19.6
		2. Equitable Servitudes	19.7
		3. Equitable Remedies	19.8
	F.	Encumbrances	19.9–19.10
II.	Tangible Movables		19.11–19.26
	A.	Policy Considerations	19.11
	B.	Chattel Transfers	19.12–19.15
		1. Contract and Property Issues	19.12
		2. Situs and Market Policies	19.13
		3. Prescription	19.14
		4. Removal of a Chattel	19.15
	C.	Chattel Security	19.16–19.26
		1. Introduction	19.16
		2. The Uniform Commercial Code	19.17–19.25
		a. Introduction	19.17
		b. Documents, Instruments, and Ordinary Goods	19.18
		c. Goods Covered by a Certificate of Title	19.19
		d. Accounts, General Intangibles and Mobile Goods	19.20–19.21
		e. Chattel Paper	19.22
		f. Minerals	19.23
		g. Uncertificated Securities	19.24
		h. Renvoi	19.25
		3. Treaties	19.26
III.	Intangibles		19.27–19.32
	A.	Introduction	19.27
	B.	Assignability of Intangibles	19.28
	C.	Assignment of Intangibles	19.29–19.31
		1. Introduction	19.29
		2. Assignments for the Benefit of Creditors	19.30
		3. Commercial Assignments	19.31
	D.	Corporate Stock	19.32

I. INTERESTS IN LAND

A. INTRODUCTION

§ 19.1 Conflict-of-laws rules concerning property[1] have undergone relatively little change in recent years, especially when compared to the substantial changes to the approaches to torts and contracts. Much of the substantive law of property in Anglo–American common law countries is rooted in the law of England where land law developed to an early maturity because realty was the focus of wealth, social status and family power. Many of the factors that bring divergence to choice of law in our modern world were not yet significant. Intangible wealth, international business travel and transactions and wealth migration had not yet developed and the law of torts, contracts, and business associations had yet to become complicated. These elements of law and society contribute to the development of substantive law variations and coincidentally to conflict of laws. In part, the absence of change in choice of law concerning property is due to the attraction of simplicity and stability in the property area. It is also because the traditional rules have been more responsive to relevant policies and purposes of both local substantive law and choice-of-law concerns. This does not mean there has been no recent movement in choice-of-law doctrines involving property. Rather, it is that the stress on the traditional views in property is less because they are more nearly consistent with policy forces in the area and any perceived injustice is less dramatic than in torts and contracts. Perhaps there is also another reason: the law in this area is less public and more within the restricted knowledge of the legal profession. The legal profession seems not often moved to genuine reform in any property area.

Land has always been recognized as unique; no two parcels are exactly alike. Likewise, our society, historically rooted in an agrarian economy reinforced by concepts of territorial sovereignty, has always placed a high emotional and protective value on land, identifying it with the security of the person, family, and home. It is thus not surprising that the law of the situs of land was early viewed as having the overwhelming if not exclusive claim to govern issues relating to land. The traditional view has been that the choice-of-law reference by a nonsitus court on nearly all issues was to the law of the situs and the normal expectation was that the situs would apply its own law.[2] Howev-

---

§ 19.1

1. This chapter will treat general matters relating to choice-of-law issues concerning property interests in both land and movables. The chapter will give principal attention to inter vivos transactions involving property interests. Succession of property at death, both testate and intestate, trusts, powers of appointment and the ad-

ministration of decedent's estates, are treated subsequently. Matrimonial property concerns are discussed in Chapter 14. For comparative treatment, with emphasis on German law, see Staudinger/Stoll, Internationales Sachenrecht (12th ed. 1985).

2. See, e.g., Story, Conflict of Laws, § 424 (3d ed. 1846); Goodrich, Two States and Real Estate, 89 Univ. Pa. L. Rev. 417

er, as our economy has come to be based upon credit and intangible evidences of wealth in which land is often regarded as like any other investment, competing policies have emerged that call for different considerations. Thus, changes are occurring that prune back the sometimes overstated situs rule to the policies which support it.[3]

The primary policy that supports the application of the law of the situs can be identified as the public concern with the manner in which land is used, occupied or developed.[4] Land use control is an important interest of the situs and its law seems an appropriate standard for that use. A second important concern is the state's interest in regularity of title to its land.[5] The Supreme Court has reaffirmed the primacy of the situs state in title matters.[6] This interest reflects concern over the optimum economic development and security of the market, so third parties who rely on the public record, or the land's physical features, use or occupation, should be able to look to the situs law for guidance in these matters. It is also significant that possessory interests are most easily determined and enforced at the place where the land is located. Nonsitus states have neither the interest nor the ability to serve conveniently the expectations of the public and of particular parties in this regard. Finally the situs state is interested in the public fisc and protection of its revenue system as it relates to land or to its transfer. Beyond these three broad concerns of the state in which land is located, there is less of a basis for the application of situs law other than lawyer convenience. Consequently, as particular issues relating to land are considered, it is important to appraise the purposes served by the rules that are potentially applicable to the particular issue in light of these three situs policies. If one or more of these three policies are not significantly furthered, other considerations may prevail.[7]

(1941); Dicey & Morris, Conflict of Laws 958 (13th ed. by Collins 2000). The venerable standing of the situs rule is evidenced in Stein, Bartolus, The Conflict of Laws and the Roman Law, in Multum non multa-Festschrift für Kurt Lipstein 251, 257 (P. Feuerstein & C. Parry, eds. 1980).

3. See, e.g., Mazza v. Mazza, 475 F.2d 385, 388 (D.C.Cir.1973). Cf. Fagone v. Fagone, 508 So.2d 644 (La.App.1987).

4. See R. Weintraub, An Inquiry Into the Utility of "Situs" as a Concept in Conflicts Analysis, 52 Corn. L.Q. 1 (1966); Hancock, In the Parish of St. Mary le Bow, in the Ward of Cheap, 16 Stan. L. Rev. 561, 571 (1964); Sedler, Moffatt Hancock & Conflict of Laws, 37 U. Toronto L.J. 62 (1987); Morris, Intestate Succession to Land and the Conflict of Laws, 85 L.Q. Rev. 339 (1969); Hay, The Situs Rule in European and American Conflicts, in Hay & Hoeflich, eds., Property Law and Legal Education— Essays in Honor of John E. Cribbet 109 (1988); Note, Modernizing the Situs Rule, 65 Tex. L. Rev. 585 (1987).

5. See Mazza v. Mazza, 475 F.2d 385, 391 (D.C.Cir.1973) where Judge McGowan stated:

"Although we do not attempt to resolve our choice of law problem simply by casting it within the mold of one or another of the traditional conflicts categories, it is still appropriate to determine whether the principals and policies which forged those rules are applicable to our situation. Concerns with the stability of use of, and marketability of title to, land were bases of the traditional conflicts rule that the law of the situs governs questions of succession to land...."

See also Restatement, Second, Conflict of Laws § 223 (1971).

6. See Baker v. General Motors Corp., 522 U.S. 222, 118 S.Ct. 657, 139 L.Ed.2d 580 (1998) (dictum).

7. See supra n.4; Hancock, Studies in Modern Choice of Law, chs. 10, 11, 12 (1984); Reese, Book Review, 9 Dalhousie L.J. 181 (1984); Note, Modernizing The Situs Rule, 65 Tex. L. Rev. 585 (1987).

B. THE SITUS RULE

§ 19.2 Historically, for many purposes interests in immovables, and interests in movables, have been subjected to different choice-of-law rules. As a consequence, property interests are characterized, for resolving conflict-of-laws issues, as either movables or immovables. The term immovables refers to interests in land and may generally be considered the equivalent of real property, but also included within this term are certain interests related to land, such as leaseholds which in other fields of the law may be viewed as personal property.[1] Whether an interest in a tangible thing is to be treated as a movable or an immovable for most purposes depends upon the law of the state in which the thing is located.[2]

In dealing with inter vivos transfers of an interest in land, the traditional rule continues to receive general recognition and is stated: the validity and effect of a conveyance of an interest in land and the nature of the interest which is transferred are determined by the law which would be applied by the courts of the situs, and those courts almost invariably apply their own law.[3] With little doubt, this statement of the usual approach is accurate in determining the formal validity of an

---

§ 19.2

1. Duncan v. Lawson, 41 Ch.D. 394 (1889); Restatement, Second, Conflict of Laws §§ 7, 222 (1971). Cf. In re Newark Shoe Stores, Inc., 2 F.Supp. 384 (D.Md. 1933); Checkers, Simon & Rosner v. Lurie Corp., 864 F.2d 1338 (7th Cir.1988). The range of things subject to this classification is demonstrated in Yiannopoulos, Movables and Immovables in Louisiana and Comparative Law, 22 La. L. Rev. 517 (1962). See, e.g., Denney v. Teel, 688 P.2d 803 (Okla. 1984) (holding that with respect to royalties from oil leases, royalties reduced to possession are to be distinguished from unaccrued royalties, the latter being interests in unpossessed oil in the ground and therefore to be classified as real estate; thus, the law of the situs of the land concerned was held to apply to issues of enforceability of oral contract granting royalties).

2. Restatement, Second, Conflict of Laws, Intro., ch. 9, top. 2 (1971); Dicey & Morris, Conflict of Laws 923–24 (13th ed. by Collins 2000). Cf. Sterling v. Blackwelder, 302 F.Supp. 1125 (E.D.Va.1968), affirmed 414 F.2d 1362 (4th Cir.1969); Echols v. Wells, 508 S.W.2d 118 (Tex.Civ.App. 1973), rev'd 510 S.W.2d 916 (Tex.1974). Instances have been found were a state has treated movable things within its jurisdiction as immovables. McCollum v. Smith, 19 Tenn. (Meigs) 342, 33 Am.Dec. 147 (1839). But they have lost their character of "immovables" by removal. Minor v. Cardwell, 37 Mo. 350, 90 Am.Dec. 390 (1866). Cf. In

re Estate of Tutules, 204 Cal.App.2d 481, 22 Cal.Rptr. 427 (1962). See also duPont v. Southern Nat. Bank of Houston, Texas, 575 F.Supp. 849 (S.D.Tex.1983), affirmed in part, vacated in part 771 F.2d 874 (5th Cir.1985), cert. denied 475 U.S. 1085, 106 S.Ct. 1467, 89 L.Ed.2d 723 (1986) (cooperative apartment located in New York, that state's law governs issue of whether the shares of a cooperative apartment corporation are classified as personalty or realty); In re WPMK Corp., 59 B.R. 991 (D.Haw. 1986) (situs determined measure of damages for breach in sale of time shares in real property).

3. Nebraska v. Iowa, 406 U.S. 117, 92 S.Ct. 1379, 31 L.Ed.2d 733 (1972); In re Lindsay, 59 F.3d 942, 948 (9th Cir.1995), cert. denied 516 U.S. 1074, 116 S.Ct. 778, 133 L.Ed.2d 730 (1996); Kuchenig v. California Co., 410 F.2d 222 (5th Cir.1969), cert. denied 396 U.S. 887, 90 S.Ct. 176, 24 L.Ed.2d 162 (1969); Restatement, Second, Conflict of Laws § 223 (1971). For traditional statements of the rule see, e.g., Story, Conflict of Laws § 429 (8th ed. 1883); McGoon v. Scales, 76 U.S. (9 Wall.) 23, 27, 19 L.Ed. 545, 546 (1869) ("It is a principle too firmly established to admit of dispute at this day, that to the law of the state in which the land is situated must we look for the rules which govern its descent, alienation, and transfer, and for the effect and construction of conveyances."). See also Thomson v. Kyle, 39 Fla. 582, 23 So. 12

instrument purporting to create or transfer an interest in land.[4] That the reference from a nonsitus forum to the situs is to the whole law of the situs is illustrated by statutes in many states that provide alternative references to validate a conveyance of local land as to form if the instrument complies with either the law of the state where the land is located, or the law of the place where the deed is executed.[5] Therefore, it is appropriate to say that a foreign court will apply whatever law would be applied by the situs to resolve the controversy relating to formal validity. This would include such issues as what constitutes delivery of a deed[6] and a determination of the nature of the interests transferred.[7] Even as to formalities however, such as writing, seal, witnesses, and acknowledgment, there may he difficulties in, always looking to the situs. Consider the requirement in some states that spouses joining in a conveyance must be separately examined as to their intentional joining in the transaction. These statutes are not simply formalities to assure perpetuation of necessary evidence to the transfer but rather are designed to protect against possible coercion or overreaching of one spouse by another. As a consequence, this may be a concern for the marital domicile in determining the relationship between the parties rather than a matter of significant concern to the situs.[8]

(1897); Worcester North Savings Institution v. Somerville Milling Co., 101 N.H. 307, 141 A.2d 885 (1958). For an analysis of the way the rule has been applied see Cook, Immovables and the Law of the Situs, 52 Harv. L. Rev. 1246 (1939); Goodrich, Two States and Real Estate, 89 U. Pa. L. Rev. 417 (1941); Ehrenzweig on Conflict of Laws § 231 et seq. (1962). For criticism of the traditional rule see Note, Modernizing the Situs Rule for Real Property Conflicts, 65 Tex. L. Rev. 585 (1987); Hay, The Situs Rule in European and American Conflicts Law—Comparative Notes, in: Hay & Hoeflich, eds., Property Law and Legal Education—Essays in Honor of John E. Cribbet 109 (1988); Scoles, Choice of Law in Family Property Transactions, 209 Recueil des Cours 13 (1988–II).

4. United States v. Crosby, 11 U.S. (7 Cranch) 115, 3 L.Ed. 287 (1812); Clark v. Graham, 19 U.S. (6 Wheat.) 577, 5 L.Ed. 334 (1821); Jaramillo v. McLoy, 263 F.Supp. 870 (D.Colo.1967); Otis v. Gregory, 111 Ind. 504, 13 N.E. 39 (1887); Pilcher v. Paulk, 228 So.2d 663 (La.App.1969); In re Strauss' Estate, 75 Misc.2d 454, 347 N.Y.S.2d 840 (1973); Roberson v. Queen, 87 Tenn. 445, 11 S.W. 38 (1889) (privy examination of party before specified officer); Rustad v. Rustad, 61 Wn.2d 176, 377 P.2d 414 (1963); Shattuck v. Bates, 92 Wis. 633, 66 N.W. 706 (1896). See also Gross Income Tax Division v. Bartlett, 228 Ind. 505, 93 N.E.2d 174 (1950).

5. See supra §§ 3.13–3.14; Lorenzen, The Validity of Wills, Deeds and Contracts as Regards Form in the Conflict of Laws, 20 Yale L.J. 427, 433 (1911); see also Restatement, Second, of Conflict of Laws § 223 (1971); Sewall v. Haymaker, 127 U.S. 719, 8 S.Ct. 1348, 32 L.Ed. 299 (1888); Jackson v. Hudspeth, 208 Ark. 55, 184 S.W.2d 906 (1945); Cole v. Steinlauf, 144 Conn. 629, 136 A.2d 744 (1957); Garrick v. Chamberlain, 97 Ill. 620 (1880); Stinson v. Geer, 42 Kan. 520, 22 P. 586 (1889); Green v. Gross, 12 Neb. 117, 10 N.W. 459 (1881). Most states have similar statutes with regard to wills devising land, see Lorenzen, supra at 432; Rees, American Wills Statutes: I, 46 Va. L. Rev. 613 (1960).

6. Freeland v. Charnley, 80 Ind. 132 (1881). Cf. F.P.P. Enterprises v. United States, 646 F.Supp. 713 (D.Neb.1986), aff'd 830 F.2d 114 (8th Cir.1987).

7. McGoon v. Scales, 76 U.S. (9 Wall.) 23, 19 L.Ed. 545 (1869); Sterling v. Blackwelder, 302 F.Supp. 1125 (E.D.Va.1968), affirmed 414 F.2d 1362 (4th Cir.1969); Jones v. Jones, 293 Ala. 39, 299 So.2d 729 (1974); Robards v. Marley, 80 Ind. 185 (1881); Pilcher v. Paulk, 228 So.2d 663 (La.App.1969); Bronson v. St. Croix Lumber Co., 44 Minn. 348, 46 N.W. 570 (1890); In re Strauss' Estate, 75 Misc.2d 454, 347 N.Y.S.2d 840 (1973); see also Hartsfield v. Lescher, 721 F.Supp. 1052 (E.D.Ark.1989). Cf. Jacobs v. Jacobs, 82 Or.App. 333, 728 P.2d 89 (1986).

8. See R. Weintraub, Commentary on the Conflict of Laws 542 (4th ed. 2001) (criticizing Smith v. Ingram, 130 N.C. 100,

C. CONTRACT AND CONVEYANCE DISTINCTIONS

1. Policy Analysis—Capacity

§ 19.3 Capacity to convey an interest in land has traditionally been governed, not by the law of the place where the instrument was executed or the domicile of the parties, but rather by the law of the situs.[1] Historically, this application of the usual view was most frequently made in transfers of land involving married women at a time when women lacked full contractual capacity. There may still be some limitations involving transfers by spouses, for example, one spouse may be restricted in becoming a surety for the other. In the situation in which a spouse joins in making a promissory note in one state, and gives as security for payment of the note a mortgage on land in another state, spousal capacity by the law of the first state but not by the law of the second state can raise this question. Under that situation, the court may well hold the promissory note valid as a personal obligation, but the mortgage invalid under the law of the situs.[2]

Since an early time, the courts used the distinction between contract and conveyance to enforce arms-length transactions. For example, the Massachusetts high court recognized a North Carolina contract to convey as valid, although made between parties who, in Massachusetts, could not have made such an agreement, thus recognizing a distinction between capacity to make a contract the subject matter of which was foreign land, and capacity to transfer the land itself.[3] In another case, the New Hampshire high court considered the application of a New Hampshire statute providing that a married woman's mortgage of her land as surety for her husband's debts should not be binding. The court interpreted the statute as applying only to mortgages of local land by married women within the state, and the foreclosure of a married

40 S.E. 984 (1902)), see also Gray v. Gray, 189 So.2d 735 (La.App.1966), writ denied 249 La. 766, 191 So.2d 142 (La. 1966); Hall v. Tucker, 414 S.W.2d 766 (Tex.Civ.App. 1967); see supra §§ 14.5–14.6.

§ 19.3

1. Post v. First National Bank of Springfield, 138 Ill. 559, 28 N.E. 978 (1891); Swank v. Hufnagle, 111 Ind. 453, 12 N.E. 303 (1887); Cochran v. Benton, 126 Ind. 58, 25 N.E. 870 (1890); Johnston v. Gawtry, 11 Mo.App. 322 (1882); Sell v. Miller, 11 Ohio St. 331 (1860); Linton v. Moorhead, 209 Pa. 646, 59 A. 264 (1904). But see In re Morris, 30 F.3d 1578 (7th Cir.1994) (law of state of incorporation governs corporate capacity to convey land); Kelly v. Davis, 28 La.Ann. 773 (1876).

2. Swank v. Hufnagle, 111 Ind. 453, 12 N.E. 303 (1887); Wood v. Wheeler, 111 N.C. 231, 16 S.E. 418 (1892).

3. Polson v. Stewart, 167 Mass. 211, 45 N.E. 737 (1897). Justice Holmes, speaking for the court, said:

"It is true that the laws of other states cannot render valid conveyances of property within our borders which our laws say are void, for the plain reason that we have exclusive power over the res. . . . But the same reason establishes that the lex rei sitae cannot control personal covenants not purporting to be conveyances, between persons outside the jurisdiction, though concerning a thing within it."

Cf. Jaramillo v. McLoy, 263 F.Supp. 870 (D.Colo.1967); Smith v. Ingram, 132 N.C. 959, 44 S.E. 643 (1903). But cf. Batman v. Cameron, 413 F.2d 999 (5th Cir.1969); Gray v. Gray, 189 So.2d 735 (La.App.1966), writ denied 249 La. 766, 191 So.2d 142 (1966).

woman's mortgage on New Hampshire land was permitted, where the bond and mortgage had been executed in Massachusetts at her domicile, by whose law the mortgagor was not incompetent.[4]

In this way the situs may conclude that because law restricting capacity is designed to protect persons, such protection is appropriately the concern of the individual's domicile and the domicile law should be applied rather than that of the situs. Where the facts are reversed, i.e., the law of the state most appropriately related to the note declares one party incompetent but the situs of the land empowers the spouse to make any conveyance, many cases have nevertheless given the creditor some relief. For example, some of the older cases concluded that the obligation should be a charge on the land[5] or that the mortgage could stand as security for the valid debt of the other spouse even though the owner was not personally liable on the note.[6] However, there have been cases in which the situs court concludes that if there was no valid obligation for which the mortgage could stand as security the mortgage could not be enforced.[7] In view of the validating policy regarding negotiated consensual transactions, and the progressively restricted area in which an individual can be considered incompetent or incapacitated, it seems that most instruments should be held valid if supported either by the situs or the domicile of the party in question.[8]

The capacity of a person to accept or hold an interest in land is likewise usually governed by the law of the situs.[9] But here the capacity of the transferee is usually related to the status of persons who can hold or use land and consequently is more related to situs interests. Still however, the basic policy issue is quite similar, that is whether the restrictive policy of the situs is so significantly related to use or third party reliance that it should be applied to the circumstances in question.[10]

4. Proctor v. Frost, 89 N.H. 304, 197 A. 813 (1938). Cf. Barber v. Barber, 51 Cal.2d 244, 331 P.2d 628 (1958); Smith v. Ingram, 132 N.C. 959, 44 S.E. 643 (1903); Phelps v. Decker, 10 Mass. 267 (1813). But cf. Kyle v. Kyle, 128 So.2d 427 (Fla.App.1961).

5. Frierson v. Williams, 57 Miss. 451 (1879); Shacklett v. Polk, 51 Miss. 378 (1875). See also Johnston v. Gawtry, 11 Mo.App. 322 (1882), affirmed 83 Mo. 339 (1884).

6. Thomson v. Kyle, 39 Fla. 582, 23 So. 12, 63 Am.St.Rep. 193 (1897); Post v. First National Bank of Springfield, 138 Ill. 559, 28 N.E. 978 (1891) (wife does not appear to have been a party to the note); Cochran v. Benton, 126 Ind. 58, 25 N.E. 870 (1890). But cf. Evans v. Beaver, 50 Ohio St. 190, 33 N.E. 643 (1893).

7. Burr v. Beckler, 264 Ill. 230, 106 N.E. 206 (1914).

8. Cf. In re Morris, 30 F.3d 1578 (7th Cir.1994) (transaction valid because corporation had capacity to convey under law of state of incorporation); Formant v. Bell, 250 A.2d 565 (D.C.App.1969); Hill v. Hill, 262 A.2d 661 (Del.Ch.1970), affirmed 269 A.2d 212 (Del.1970); Orland Properties, Inc. v. Broderick, 94 N.J.Super. 307, 228 A.2d 95 (1967); Cole v. Lee, 435 S.W.2d 283 (Tex. Civ.App.1968); Union Savings Bank v. De-Marco, 105 R.I. 592, 254 A.2d 81 (1969); Savannah Bank & Trust Co. v. Shuman, 250 S.C. 344, 157 S.E.2d 864 (1967).

9. Losson v. Blodgett, 1 Cal.App.2d 13, 36 P.2d 147 (1934). See also Restatement, Second, Conflict of Laws § 223 (1971).

10. Cf. Restatement, Second, Conflict of Laws § 223, cmnt. (d) (1971); Hartsfield v. Lescher, 721 F.Supp. 1052 (E.D.Ark.1989).

The cases in which courts have relied on the distinction between contracts and conveyances to avoid the situs rule seem appropriately considered as forerunners of the application of a policy interest analysis in land cases. Many multi-faceted real estate transactions do not fit easily into the categorization assumed by the situs rule. Typical of this situation are cases in which the parties are dealing in a business center in one state and land in another state is involved as security or otherwise. For example, in a case involving the possible application of District of Columbia limitations on unlicensed lenders, the court concluded that the law of the situs should be applied, not because it was the location of the land but because of the commercial policy validating the transaction. As the court stated:

> "Here we have a real estate transaction, involving a note, a security instrument, and a sizeable sum of money, challenged as to its validity because of a moneylending regulatory statute in the District of Columbia, where some of the activities in connection with the loan unquestionably took place.... [W]here there is a choice of jurisdictions, the preferable course is to select the law of the jurisdiction which would sustain the transaction, and here this is Maryland. This rule contributes to the certainty of commercial transactions, one of the prime objects of all commercial law.

> "We think, however, that no one point is conclusive on Maryland law applying, neither the situs of the property, the execution of all the documents in Maryland, nor the fact that Maryland law would sustain the transaction and District of Columbia law invalidate it; we must therefore apply the principles, and weigh and balance the two jurisdictions' contacts with the transaction in the manner set forth in the Restatement.... In accordance with these principles, weighing the factors that point respectively to Maryland or to the District of Columbia, as a source of law governing the transaction, we think that, on balance, the most weighty factors favor Maryland law."[11]

The contract and conveyance distinction has also been used to support enforcement of the contract to convey in a nonsitus forum.[12] In many cases involving real estate transactions the choice-of-law contacts center on the situs so that the law of the situs would be applicable under any approach.[13] Likewise a court may respond to what it views as a mandatory statute of the forum that calls for an application of the forum law

---

11. In re Parkwood, Inc., 461 F.2d 158, 171 (D.C.Cir.1971). See also Tuthill Finance v. Cartaya, 133 A.D.2d 343, 519 N.Y.S.2d 243 (1987), appeal dismissed 73 N.Y.2d 918, 539 N.Y.S.2d 301, 536 N.E.2d 630 (1989). Cf. Taggart & Taggart Seed, Inc. v. First Tenn. Bk. etc., 684 F.Supp. 230 (E.D.Ark. 1988), aff'd 881 F.2d 1080 (8th Cir.1989).

12. See, e.g., Hill v. Hill, 262 A.2d 661 (Del.Ch.1970), aff'd 269 A.2d 212 (Del.

1970); Matarese v. Calise, 111 R.I. 551, 305 A.2d 112 (1973); Estabrook v. Wise, 506 S.W.2d 248 (Tex.Civ.App.1974), appeal dismissed on settlement 519 S.W.2d 632 (Tex. 1974).

13. See, e.g., Cameron v. Gunstock Acres, Inc., 370 Mass. 378, 348 N.E.2d 791 (1976); Sparks v. Green, 259 Or. 93, 485 P.2d 400 (1971); In re Bellamah Community Devel., 107 B.R. 337 (Bankr.D.N.M. 1989).

as the situs.[14] However, even in doing so the court may reach a result more consistent with contract policies than would otherwise be applicable.[15]

A similar distinction between torts and conveyances occurs in cases involving fraudulent conveyances. For example, the law of the situs of the land ordinarily will determine whether a conveyance may be attacked by the grantor's creditors to enable those creditors to reach the land in the hands of the grantee.[16] The situs will also usually determine the rights of the creditor and the protection afforded by exemptions to the debtor in instances in which the creditor's claim is sought to be paid out of the debtor's land.[17] In this situation, situs law is determining the rights of third parties much as they do with regard to the parties who are entitled to the protection of the recording acts.[18] However, it would seem that the tort action against the grantor for a fraudulent conveyance by a creditor could be viewed by the forum as a matter distinct from the situs of the land. The choice-of-law reference in that instance would then follow the policy analysis appropriate for torts.[19] While purporting to make such an analysis, the New York Court of Appeals in a surprising decision[20] held that the measure of damages for fraudulent conveyance of Puerto Rico land is governed by the law of Puerto Rico as the most interested state, even though the debtor and the creditor were in New York and it appeared that the transfer to relatives by exercise of a power of attorney was directed from New York and the impact of the concealment of assets occurred in New York.[21]

D. PARTICULAR ISSUES

1. *Conveyances: Effect and Construction*

§ 19.4 Although the relevance of situs law to determine the effect of an instrument of conveyance as to the nature of the interest created

14. See Equilease Corp. v. Belk Hotel Corp., 42 N.C.App. 436, 256 S.E.2d 836 (1979), review denied 298 N.C. 568, 261 S.E.2d 121 (1979). Cf. Xanadu of Cocoa Beach v. Zetley, 822 F.2d 982 (11th Cir. 1987), cert. denied 484 U.S. 1043, 108 S.Ct. 777, 98 L.Ed.2d 863 (1988).

15. Savannah Bank & Trust Co. v. Shuman, 250 S.C. 344, 157 S.E.2d 864 (1967).

16. See Sylvester v. Sylvester, 723 P.2d 1253 (Alaska 1986); Moore v. Church, 70 Iowa 208, 30 N.W. 855 (1886); Manton v. J.F. Seiberling & Co., 107 Iowa 534, 78 N.W. 194 (1899). Cf. Irving Trust Co. v. Maryland Casualty Co., 83 F.2d 168 (2d Cir.1936), cert. denied 299 U.S. 571, 57 S.Ct. 34, 81 L.Ed. 421 (1936); F.P.P. Enterprises v. United States, 646 F.Supp. 713 (D.Neb.1986), aff'd 830 F.2d 114 (8th Cir. 1987).

17. McGoon v. Scales, 76 U.S. (9 Wall.) 23, 19 L.Ed. 545 (1869); Brine v. Hartford

Fire Insurance Co., 96 U.S. 627, 24 L.Ed. 858 (1877); Hughes v. Winkleman, 243 Mo. 81, 147 S.W. 994 (1912); Whipple v. Fowler, 41 Neb. 675, 60 N.W. 15 (1894); Harrison v. Harrison, 8 Ch.App. 342 (1873).

18. See Jaramillo v. McLoy, 263 F.Supp. 870 (D.Colo.1967).

19. Cf. Werner v. Werner, 84 Wn.2d 360, 526 P.2d 370 (1974).

20. James v. Powell, 19 N.Y.2d 249, 279 N.Y.S.2d 10, 225 N.E.2d 741 (1967).

21. Cf. Irving Trust Co. v. Maryland Casualty Co., 83 F.2d 168 (2d Cir.1936), cert. denied 299 U.S. 571, 57 S.Ct. 34, 81 L.Ed. 421 (1936); R. Weintraub, Commentary on the Conflict of Laws 544 (4th ed. 2001); Comment, Choice of Law in Fraudulent Conveyance, 67 Colum. L. Rev. 1313 (1967); Ehrenzweig & Westen, Fraudulent Conveyances in the Conflict of Laws: Easy Cases May Make Bad Law, 66 Mich. L. Rev. 1679, 1688 (1968).

seems clearly necessary[1] to protect third parties who rely on the title, it is not so clear that the law of the situs should always govern construction of a conveyance. It is desirable, to promote the security of land titles, that the precise interest conveyed by an instrument be ascertainable, as much as possible, from the face of the instrument. This being so, it would seem that if, by the situs law a phrase in a conveyance has a certain meaning, regardless of the intent of the grantor, or a phrase is presumed to have a particular meaning in the absence of a contrary provision, an instrument containing that phrase should be given the same effect. Under this approach, the meaning prevailing at the place of execution or at the domicile of the grantor would not be controlling.[2] However, conveyances are the result of arms length negotiated commercial transactions may well be distinguished in some situations from gratuitous transactions such as trusts. In an ordinary commercial transaction that language in a deed results from the bilateral considerations of the parties. Not only is it accepted by the parties, it may have been insisted upon by the grantee before being accepted. As between the original parties, their most likely intended meaning should be applied without regard to the law of the situs. The deed as a memorial of the negotiated transaction enjoys all the protection against unilateral modification such as that reflected in the statute of frauds. On the other hand, in a unilateral gratuitous transfer, the grantor's intent is deemed to be the primary consideration and these transactions usually involve questions relating to family property dispositions drawn to meet the donor's view of particular family needs. In cases involving gratuitous transfers, the law at the grantor's domicile has been applied in some instances because it is most likely the grantor would have expected the terms and to have the meaning which prevailed at that place.[3] These cases usually involve the immediate donee and not third parties. As to third parties, the need for a more convenient and predictable rule is clear. Perhaps as to third parties in the commercial cases, because the line between interpretation and construction is not clearly defined, uniformity of result should prevail and the uniform standard should be the law which would be applied by the situs. It is important to recognize that the situs should be expected to apply its own law on issues relating to the title of land, but that those issues which relate to family circumstances in gratuitous dispositions may be referred to the donor's domicile as they would by an explicit direction in the instrument.

§ 19.4

1. See, e.g., McGoon v. Scales, 76 U.S. (9 Wall.) 23, 19 L.Ed. 545 (1869); Cole v. Steinlauf, 144 Conn. 629, 136 A.2d 744 (1957); Bronson v. St. Croix Lumber Co., 44 Minn. 348, 46 N.W. 570 (1890); Note, 72 Harv. L. Rev. 1154, 1156 (1959); Restatement, Second, Conflict of Laws § 223 (1971).

2. Restatement, Second, Conflict of Laws § 224, cmnt. (b) (1971).

3. Restatement, Second, Conflict of Laws § 224, cmnts. (c), (d) (1971). See, e.g., Higinbotham v. Manchester, 113 Conn. 62, 154 A. 242 (1931); Moore v. Livingston, 148 Ind.App. 275, 265 N.E.2d 251 (1970); Gibson v. Boynton, 112 Kan. 173, 210 P. 648 (1922); Keith v. Eaton, 58 Kan. 732, 51 P. 271 (1897); Rose v. Rambo, 120 Miss. 305, 82 So. 149 (1919) (noted 31 Yale L.J. 438 (1922)). Cf. Juden v. Southeast Missouri Telephone Co., 361 Mo. 513, 235 S.W.2d 360 (1950).

2. *Covenants*

§ 19.5   Considering interests in land and the obligations of contract as involving distinct issues is also possible in determining the law relating to covenants of title. Should a distinction be drawn between a covenant that runs with the land like that of quiet enjoyment, and the covenant of seisin, which usually does not run with the land? There are reasons why issues concerning covenants that run with the land should be referred to the situs of the land. While not technically a part of the operative words of the grant, covenants are made only in connection with it, and are ancillary to it.[1] "They cannot be separated from the land, and transferred without it, but they go with the land as being annexed to estate."[2] Documents are recorded at the situs of the land and the rules of that jurisdiction commonly form the basis of opinions on the title. Deeds need to follow a form prescribed by the law of the situs to transfer title; it is impractical to have the covenant contained in the same instrument governed by a different rule. Consequently a nonsitus court should look to the law of the situs for resolution of the question whether a covenant runs with the land and issues relating to those covenants that do. A covenant against encumbrances, for instance, may be treated as broken when made and purely personal, or considered as running with the land and giving a claim for substantial damage when the encumbrance is removed, even though the land be then held by a remote grantee. This seems appropriate for the law of the situs to determine.[3] There is considerable authority for the view that the local law of the situs governs covenants which run with the land.[4] The principle finds application in several situations: Whether the covenant is to be implied from the terms of the grant is governed by the law of the situs;[5] so too, its effect as an estoppel against a grantor;[6] and what is necessary to constitute a breach of the covenant.[7]

It seems doubtful that a distinction should be made between those covenants for title that run with the land and those which are called

---

§ 19.5

1. Restatement, Second, Conflict of Laws § 190 (1971).

2. Dalton v. Taliaferro, 101 Ill.App. 592, 596 (1902) (quoting Kent).

3. Riley v. Burroughs, 41 Neb. 296, 59 N.W. 929 (1894); Platner v. Vincent, 187 Cal. 443, 202 P. 655 (1921) (covenant of quiet enjoyment). See Heilman, Conflict of Laws Treatment of Interpretation and Construction of Deeds in Reference to Covenants, 29 Mich. L. Rev. 277, 304 (1931); McDougal, Felix & Whitten, American Conflicts Law 585 (5th ed. 2001).

4. See, e.g., Fisher v. Virginia Electric & Power Co., 258 F. Supp. 2d 445 (E.D. Va. 2003) (covenant of quiet enjoyment); Crane v. Blackman, 126 Ill.App. 631 (1906); Lyndon Lumber Co. v. Sawyer, 135 Wis. 525,

116 N.W. 255 (1908). See also Ellis v. Abbott, 69 Or. 234, 138 P. 488 (1914).

5. Platner v. Vincent, 187 Cal. 443, 202 P. 655 (1921); Dalton v. Taliaferro, 101 Ill.App. 592 (1902); Fisher v. Parry, 68 Ind. 465 (1879). But see Worley v. Hineman, 6 Ind.App. 240, 33 N.E. 260 (1893). See Newsom v. Langford, 174 S.W. 1036 (Tex.Civ. App.1915), affirmed 220 S.W. 544 (Tex. Com.App.1920); cf. Restatement, Second, Conflict of Laws § 190 (1971).

6. Beauchamp v. Bertig, 90 Ark. 351, 119 S.W. 75 (1909); Smith v. Ingram, 132 N.C. 959, 44 S.E. 643 (1903).

7. Succession of Cassidy, 40 La.Ann. 827, 5 So. 292 (1888). See Newsom v. Langford, 174 S.W. 1036 (Tex.Civ.App.1915); Kling v. Sejour, 4 La.Ann. 128 (1849) (governed by the law of the situs because the covenant is a contract performable there).

purely personal. Some courts have made this distinction, holding that whether a covenant of seisin shall be implied is to be determined by the proper law of the contract not that of the situs.[8] If this is the view of the situs, a nonsitus forum should appropriately follow the reference. However, whether the situs court and more particularly a nonsitus forum should view a covenant as separated from a conveyance which gives it existence is doubtful.[9]

The distinction between covenants that are personal and those which are called "real" is an exceedingly technical one, which has been much criticized, and one that some courts have repudiated. It seems preferable to refer all questions regarding the so-called personal covenants, such as that of seisin, as well as those of other covenants for title, to the law that would be applied by the situs.[10]

E. EQUITABLE INTERESTS

1. *Generally*

§ 19.6 The various ways in which equitable interests in land are recognized call for separate treatment. The general approach that the law of the situs will determine the creation of interests in land applies to equitable as well as legal interests. This follows from the same considerations of convenience and control upon which the general rule as to legal interest is recognized. The law of the situs, for example, determines whether, as a result of certain transactions, a trust in land is created, even though under such circumstances the law of the forum would not have created a trust.[1] In this situation, the trust may be viewed as an extraordinary remedy imposed on the land and as such is only available at the situs. A trust so created by the courts or the law of the situs is recognized elsewhere.[2] If none is created, none will be recognized.[3]

---

8. Bethell v. Bethell, 54 Ind. 428, 23 Am.Rep. 650 (1876); Craig v. Donovan, 63 Ind. 513 (1878); Jackson v. Green, 112 Ind. 341, 14 N.E. 89 (1887).

9. A covenant wholly collateral to the grant should be distinguished, such as an agreement not to engage in competition with the grantor for a limited time. Such an agreement is controlled by the law appropriate to the contract. Robinson v. Suburban Brick Co., 127 Fed. 804 (4th Cir.1904).

10. Alcorn v. Epler, 206 Ill.App. 140 (1917); Crane v. Blackman, 126 Ill.App. 631 (1906); Segal v. Greater Valley Terminal Corp., 83 N.J.Super. 120, 199 A.2d 48 (1964); Lyndon Lumber Co. v. Sawyer, 135 Wis. 525, 116 N.W. 255 (1908). See 9 Calif. L. Rev. 234 (1921); 10 Calif. L. Rev. 174 (1922) (discussing Platner v. Vincent, 187 Cal. 443, 202 P. 655 (1921)). Cf. Restatement, Second, Conflict of Laws § 190 (1971); McDougal, Felix & Whitten, Ameri-

can Conflicts Law 585 (5th ed. 2001); Note, 38 Tulane L. Rev. 726 (1964).

§ 19.6

1. Detailed consideration of trust issues appears infra Chapter 21. Acker v. Priest, 92 Iowa 610, 61 N.W. 235 (1894); Knox v. Jones, 47 N.Y. 389 (1872).

2. See Restatement, Second, Conflict of Laws § 278 (1971). See also Seaman v. Cook, 14 Ill. 501 (1853); Depas v. Mayo, 11 Mo. 314, 49 Am.Dec. 88 (1848); Hawley & King v. James, 7 Paige 213, 32 Am.Dec. 623 (N.Y. 1838); Watkins v. Watkins, 160 Tenn. 1, 22 S.W.2d 1 (1929). Cf. Welch v. Trustees of Robert A. Welch Foundation, 465 S.W.2d 195 (Tex.Civ.App.1971).

3. Hartsfield v. Lescher, 721 F.Supp. 1052 (E.D.Ark.1989); F.P.P. Enterprises v. United States, 646 F.Supp. 713 (D.Neb. 1986), aff'd 830 F.2d 114 (8th Cir.1987); Perin v. McMicken's Heirs, 15 La.Ann. 154

However, the extraordinary remedy of constructive trust is the imposition of a personal obligation on the titleholder to reconvey would be enforceable where the obligor is subject to personal jurisdiction.[4] The local law of the situs also usually governs matters relating to the administration of a trust in land,[5] although if land is simply acquired as an investment by a trustee the situs has substantially less significance.[6]

2. Equitable Servitudes

§ 19.7 The preference for the application of the law of the situs extends to most issues involving equitable servitudes. It is possible that an equitable servitude may involve land on both sides of a state line, as in an interstate real estate development subject to mutual covenants involving building or use restrictions. However, most of the issues involve land located in a single state and are occasioned by attempted enforcement of the covenant by contract action elsewhere. Since most equitable servitudes arise out of covenants and contracts, it is possible to view them as obligations separate from the land itself.[1] Even so, because equitable servitudes relate to use and enjoyment of land, it appears that the situs must protect or enforce the rights arising out of equitable servitudes. If the situs would not enforce an equitable servitude, a person should not be permitted by proceeding in one state to limit the use of the land in another.[2] This seems consistent with the view that private titles to land or islands occurring in a river which forms the boundary between two states are to be determined by the law of the state in which the land or islands are found. The law of one state cannot extend title of its owners into the other state as land is added beyond the state line.[3] If enforcement is to occur at a nonsitus forum by application of a law different from that of the situs, it would seem that that enforcement would have to be based upon express contracts between the parties or their privies and would not extend to third parties relying

(1860); Levy v. Levy, 33 N.Y. 97 (1865); Penfield v. Tower, 1 N.D. 216, 46 N.W. 413 (1890); Purdon v. Pavey, 26 Can. 412 (1896); Parkhurst v. Roy, 7 Ont.App. 614, 618 (1882). Cf. Sarrica v. Sarrica, 41 A.D.2d 613, 340 N.Y.S.2d 568 (1973).

4. Cf. supra §§ 10.1, 10.2 and infra §§ 19.8, 24.10.

5. Beale v. Beale, 807 So.2d 797 (Fla. App. 2002) (availability of constructive trust as a remedy to enforce alleged oral promise to put realty in trust is governed by situs law); Beardsley v. Hall, 291 Mass. 411, 197 N.E. 35 (1935); Restatement, Second, Conflict of Laws §§ 276, 279 (1971). Cf. Hartsfield v. Lescher, 721 F.Supp. 1052 (E.D.Ark.1989).

6. See Central Standard Life Insurance Co. v. Gardner, 17 Ill.2d 220, 161 N.E.2d 278 (1959).

§ 19.7

1. See Reno, The Enforcement of Equitable Servitudes in Land: Part II, 28 Va. L. Rev. 1067 (1942); Clark, The Assignability of Easements, Profits and Equitable Restrictions, 38 Yale L.J. 139 (1928); Simpson, Fifty Years of American Equity, 50 Harv. L. Rev. 171, 215 (1936).

2. See Caldwell v. Gore, 175 La. 501, 143 So. 387 (1932).

3. Nebraska v. Iowa, 406 U.S. 117, 92 S.Ct. 1379, 31 L.Ed.2d 733 (1972); see also Baker v. General Motors Corp., 522 U.S. 222, 118 S.Ct. 657, 139 L.Ed.2d 580 (1998) (stating in dictum that land title determinations must be made by the situs state).

upon the record with regard to equitable interests in the land itself.[4]

3. Equitable Remedies

§ 19.8 As discussed above, courts sometimes draw distinctions between interests in real property created by a transaction between the parties and personal obligations arising out of those transactions in which foreign land was the subject matter. An analogous situation exists regarding equitable remedies. An old English case illustrates.[1] The plaintiff was a debtor of the defendant. The latter, in England, refused plaintiff's offers of payment and requests for an account, and by such procrastination evidently "lulled him into security." In the meantime the defendant brought suit against the plaintiff in the Island of St. Christopher, secured a judgment against him, and had the plaintiff's land there sold in satisfaction, buying it himself at a sum that was but a small part of its value. All of this was done without the plaintiff's knowledge. After discovery of the facts, the plaintiff sought relief in an equity court in England. In this proceeding he could not ask the English court to enforce a constructive trust created by the law of the situs, because, so far as it appeared, all that the defendant did in St. Christopher was in accordance with the law there prevailing. Hence it is assumed that by the law of the situs there was no trust existing in the land. But a court, having a defendant before it, may in a proper case order him to convey foreign land, if the decree can be complied with at the forum.[2] In the English case, the court, in reparation for the wrong committed by the defendant, ordered the defendant to reconvey to the plaintiff in England, subject to the payment of the defendant's claim.

The American cases are in accord. For example, in *Matarese v. Calise*,[3] the Supreme Court of Rhode Island considered a situation in which the plaintiff, an Italian citizen, arranged with the defendant, an

---

4. Cf. Graham v. Hamilton County, 224 Tenn. 82, 450 S.W.2d 571 (1969).

§ 19.8

1. Lord Cranstown v. Johnston, 3 Ves. Jr. 170 (1796). For treatment of the enforcement of decrees concerning land see infra § 24.10.

2. See, e.g., Massie v. Watts, 10 U.S. (6 Cranch) 148, 3 L.Ed. 181 (1810); Penn v. Lord Baltimore, 1 Ves. 444 (1750). See also supra §§ 10.3–10.5, Amey v. Colebrook Guaranty Savings Bank, 92 F.2d 62 (2d Cir.1937), cert. denied 302 U.S. 750, 58 S.Ct. 271, 82 L.Ed. 580 (1937); Lyle Cashion Co. v. McKendrick, 227 Miss. 894, 87 So.2d 289 (1956); Barbour, The Extra-Territorial Effect of the Equitable Decree, 17 Mich. L. Rev. 527 (1919); Currie, Full Faith and Credit to Foreign Land Decrees, 21 U. Chi. L. Rev. 620 (1954); Reese, Full Faith and Credit to Foreign Equity Decrees, 42

Iowa L. Rev. 183 (1957). On general enforcement of equity decrees and decrees relating to land, see infra §§ 24.9, 24.10.

3. 111 R.I. 551, 305 A.2d 112 (1973). Cf. Belsky v. Belsky, 324 So.2d 111 (Fla.App. 1975), cert. denied 336 So.2d 1180 (Fla. 1976); Bianchi v. Scott, 363 So.2d 289 (Miss.1978); Trivette's Estate v. Trivette, 564 S.W.2d 672 (Tenn.App.1977). The cases making disposition of foreign land on divorce are numerous. See, e.g., Williams v. Williams, 390 A.2d 4 (D.C.App.1978); Strang v. Strang, 258 Ark. 139, 523 S.W.2d 887 (1975); Parkey v. Baker, 254 Ark. 283, 492 S.W.2d 891 (1973); Schaheen v. Schaheen, 17 Mich.App. 147, 169 N.W.2d 117 (1969); Estabrook v. Wise, 506 S.W.2d 248 (Tex.Civ.App.1974), dismissed on settlement 519 S.W.2d 632 (Tex.1974); Farley v. Farley, 19 Utah 2d 301, 431 P.2d 133 (1967). Cf. Owen v. Stewart, 111 N.H. 350, 283 A.2d 492 (1971); Kindler v. Kindler, 60 A.D.2d 753, 400 N.Y.S.2d 605 (1977).

American citizen, to negotiate the purchase of Italian land from the owner who lived in the United States. The defendant made the purchase and took title in his own name, making payment with the plaintiff's funds. The defendant then told the plaintiff that the land was available only at seven times the original price. Upon discovery of this, the Italian citizen sued the defendant in Rhode Island, and the Rhode Island court, in this shade of *Massie v. Watts*,[4] ordered the defendant because of his fraud to convey the land to the plaintiff. The court characterized the matter as a contract action for performance in the United States. The remedy of constructive trust created a personal obligation enforceable in Rhode Island and the court found no need to refer to the law of Italy.[5] Similar relief has been afforded for breach of contract, even where by the law of the situs the plaintiff had no interest in the land as such.[6] In these cases, redress is being given for the personal wrong; the plaintiff is making no direct claim to the land, except as the nonsitus forum is able to effect a remedy.[7]

A third party to whom a fraudulent conveyance has been made ordinarily will be protected by the situs law absent knowledge of the wrongful conveyance.[8] However, if the third party's acceptance of the conveyance was tortious, the third party may be compelled to reconvey for the benefit of the injured person, even though by the situs law the conveyance may have given an indefeasible title. For example, in *Irving Trust Co. v. Maryland Casualty Co.*,[9] a corporation on the verge of insolvency transferred to certain creditors in New York property which included land in other states. The corporation subsequently became bankrupt, and in a suit in the federal district court in New York the trustee sought to compel the transferees (over whom the court had personal jurisdiction) to reconvey the land on the ground that a New York statute made the conveyance and acceptance of the title illegal under the circumstances. The Second Circuit held that if a violation of

---

4. 10 U.S. (6 Cranch) 148, 3 L.Ed. 181 (1810).

5. Cf. Walton v. The Arabian American Oil Co., 233 F.2d 541 (2d Cir.1956), cert. denied 352 U.S. 872, 77 S.Ct. 97, 1 L.Ed.2d 77 (1956). But see Christensen v. Christensen, 121 R.I. 272, 397 A.2d 900 (1979).

6. See Ex parte Pollard, Mont. & C. 239 (1840); Scott v. Nesbitt, 14 Ves. 438 (1808). See also Hodge v. Hodge, 621 F.2d 590 (3d Cir.1980); Bethell v. Bethell, 92 Ind. 318 (1884); Thompson v. Nesheim, 280 Minn. 407, 159 N.W.2d 910 (1968); Silver Surprize, Inc. v. Sunshine Mining Co., 74 Wn.2d 519, 445 P.2d 334 (1968). Cf. Donaldson v. Greenwood, 40 Wn.2d 238, 242 P.2d 1038 (1952).

7. "That such a power was exercised by the earlier chancellors no one will deny; that the interest in land called a constructive trust is a result, not a cause, of this

exercise of jurisdiction, is clear; and there is no reason for assuming that this ancient power has departed out of chancery, or that the chancellor cannot still exercise his prerogative, though the redress asked is for a purely personal wrong." Beale, Equitable Interests in Foreign Property, 20 Harv. L. Rev. 382, 386 (1907). For equitable remedies in connection with unjust enrichment see also supra § 18.47.

8. Cf. United States v. 5208 Los Franciscos Way, 252 F. Supp. 2d 1060 (E.D. Cal. 2003) (situs law determines whether a conveyance was fraudulent).

9. 83 F.2d 168 (2d Cir.1936), cert. denied 299 U.S. 571, 57 S.Ct. 34, 81 L.Ed. 421 (1936) (noted 50 Harv. L. Rev. 129 (1936); 4 U. Chi. L. Rev. 135 (1936)). Cf. Mallory Associates, Inc. v. Barving Realty Co., 300 N.Y. 297, 90 N.E.2d 468 (1949). But cf. James v. Powell, 19 N.Y.2d 249, 279 N.Y.S.2d 10, 225 N.E.2d 741 (1967).

the statute could be proven the defendants could be compelled to reconvey not only the land in New York, but also the land in other states by whose law the defendants had secured good title. The acceptance of the title being a tort, "[a]ny court" said Judge Learned Hand, "may compel the tortfeasor specifically to restore the property, whatever the law of the situs."[10]

The decree of a nonsitus court having personal jurisdiction over the parties is entitled to full faith and credit at the situs. Although the United States Supreme Court cases have been in some confusion,[11] it is believed that the doctrine of preclusion by prior litigation prevails over any contrary policy of the situs. In *Durfee v. Duke*,[12] the Supreme Court had the opportunity to review the competing policies of preclusion and prerogatives of the situs under the Constitution. In *Durfee* the Court concluded:

> "... From these decisions there emerges the general rule that a judgment is entitled to full faith and credit—even as to questions of jurisdiction—when the second court's inquiry discloses that those questions have been fully and fairly litigated and finally decided in the court which rendered the original judgment...."[13]

The cases in the state courts are in accord.[14]

---

10. 83 F.2d at 172. Cf. Widmer v. Wood, 243 Ark. 457, 420 S.W.2d 828 (1967).

11. See Fall v. Eastin, 215 U.S. 1, 30 S.Ct. 3, 54 L.Ed. 65 (1909). See also Baker v. General Motors Corp., 522 U.S. 222, 118 S.Ct. 657, 139 L.Ed.2d 580 (1998) (in dictum distinguishing between land title and personal obligations).

12. 375 U.S. 106, 84 S.Ct. 242, 11 L.Ed.2d 186 (1963).

13. 375 U.S. at 111, 84 S.Ct. at 245.

14. Day v. Wiswall, 11 Ariz.App. 306, 464 P.2d 626 (1970); Simpson v. Simpson, 267 A.2d 891 (Del.Super.1970); Swain v. Swain, 339 So.2d 453 (La.App.1976); Zorick v. Jones, 193 So.2d 420 (Miss.1966); Cuevas v. Cuevas, 191 So.2d 843 (Miss.1966); Pierrakos v. Pierrakos, 148 N.J.Super. 574, 372 A.2d 1331 (1977); Woodruffe v. DeMola, 146 N.J.Super. 51, 368 A.2d 967 (1976); Higginbotham v. Higginbotham, 92 N.J.Super. 18, 222 A.2d 120 (1966); Courtney v. Courtney, 40 N.C.App. 291, 253 S.E.2d 2 (1979); Small v. Carey, 269 Or. 35, 522 P.2d 1202 (1974). Cf. Simon v. Simon, 478 F.Supp. 548 (E.D.Pa.1979), affirmed 614 F.2d 771 (3d Cir.1979); Lea v. Dudley, 20 N.C.App. 702, 202 S.E.2d 799 (1974), appeal after remand 28 N.C.App. 281, 220 S.E.2d 828 (1976); Whitmer v. Whitmer, 243 Pa.Super. 462, 365 A.2d 1316 (1976), cert. denied 434 U.S. 822, 98 S.Ct. 67, 54 L.Ed.2d 79 (1977). But cf. McLam v. McLam, 85 N.M. 196, 510 P.2d 914 (1973). See also Dickerson v. Scott, 476 So.2d 524 (La.App.1985); Schmidt v. de Lottman, 428 So.2d 1056 (La.App.1983), writ denied 435 So.2d 432 (La.1983). But see Succession of Miller v. Moss, 479 So.2d 1035 (La.App. 1985), writ denied 484 So.2d 135 (La.1986) (holding that New Mexico district court, which rejected an holographic will for probate because of formal deficiencies under New Mexico law, the apparent domicile, was without power to render judgment as to rights in Louisiana real property, since law of situs governs acquisition, disposition and devolution of realty; thus, the will, valid by Louisiana law, was admitted to probate as to Louisiana land). See also Kirstein v. Kirstein, 64 N.C.App. 191, 306 S.E.2d 552 (1983) (holding that a judgment by Kentucky divorce court which did not order conveyance, but purported to award to husband the entire title to certain North Carolina realty held by husband and wife as tenants by the entireties was not entitled to full faith and credit, but wife was entitled to one-half); Christensen v. Christensen, 121 R.I. 272, 397 A.2d 900 (1979) (vacating order of Rhode Island Family Court purporting to impose lien on husband's New Hampshire real property, as operating directly on real estate and affecting title, rather than indirectly through personal jurisdiction of court over parties, and thus beyond court's jurisdiction).

F. ENCUMBRANCES

§ 19.9   Whether a credit transaction creates an interest which is foreclosable in land or other security interest in land is determined by the law that would be applied by the courts at the situs.[1] This approach has obtained even though the validity and the effect of the obligation which the encumbrance secures may be determined by the appropriate law relating to the contract. The law of the situs, which provides security to a creditor, which enables the creditor to proceed against the land, or which serves to inhibit a transfer of the land to persons relying on the record, seems appropriately related to the use and control of land by the situs. This application of situs law results under both the traditional choice-of-law view and under more modern approaches.[2] Under this approach such matters as the formal validity of a mortgage[3] and the capacity of the mortgagor[4] are determined by the law of the situs, although the situs may refer to other law to validate and sustain the commercial transaction.[5]

The nature of the interest in the land, which the secured creditor acquires, is determined by the law of the situs[6] and that also applies to foreclosure proceedings[7] as well as the right to redeem the land after foreclosure.[8] Except for the possibility of foreclosure by deed away from the situs, these latter issues relate closely to remedies and procedures normally available only at the situs. Whether a transaction creates a lien and the effect of a lien on the land is also referred to the situs; for example, a mechanic's lien has been allowed by the law of the situs to a

---

§ 19.9

1. Restatement, Second, Conflict of Laws § 228 (1971). Cf. Hartsfield v. Lescher, 721 F.Supp. 1052 (E.D.Ark.1989).

2. See supra § 19.3. See also In re Parkwood, Inc., 461 F.2d 158 (D.C.Cir.1971); In re Wolman, 314 F.Supp. 703 (D.Md.1970); Sterling v. Blackwelder, 302 F.Supp. 1125 (E.D.Va.1968), affirmed 414 F.2d 1362 (4th Cir.1969); Jaramillo v. McLoy, 263 F.Supp. 870 (D.C.Colo.1967); Jones v. Jones, 293 Ala. 39, 299 So.2d 729 (1974). Cf. Your Construction Center, Inc. v. Dominion Mortgage and Realty Trust, 402 F.Supp. 757 (S.D.Fla.1975); Savannah Bank & Trust Co. v. Shuman, 250 S.C. 344, 157 S.E.2d 864 (1967).

3. Restatement, Second, Conflict of Laws § 228 (1971); In re Wolman, 314 F.Supp. 703 (D.Md.1970); Alropa Corp. v. Bloom, 311 Mass. 442, 42 N.E.2d 269 (1942). See generally Currie & Lieberman, Purchase Money Mortgages and State Lines: A Study in Conflict–of–Laws Method, 1960 Duke L.J. 1, 42 (1960).

4. Thomson v. Kyle, 39 Fla. 582, 23 So. 12 (1897); Swank v. Hufnagle, 111 Ind. 453,

12 N.E. 303 (1887). Cf. Proctor v. Frost, 89 N.H. 304, 197 A. 813 (1938).

5. See, e.g., Proctor v. Frost, 89 N.H. 304, 197 A. 813 (1938); Union Savings Bank v. DeMarco, 105 R.I. 592, 254 A.2d 81 (1969); cf. Your Construction Center, Inc. v. Dominion Mortgage and Realty Trust, 402 F.Supp. 757 (S.D.Fla.1975).

6. Sterling v. Blackwelder, 302 F.Supp. 1125 (E.D.Va.1968), aff'd 414 F.2d 1362 (4th Cir.1969); In re Kellogg, 113 Fed. 120 (W.D.N.Y.1902), affirmed 121 Fed. 333 (1903); Danner & Co. v. Brewer & Co., 69 Ala. 191 (1881).

7. Harbor Funding Corp. v. Kavanagh, 666 A.2d 498 (Me.1995); Ricks v. Goodrich, 3 La.Ann. 212 (1848); Worcester North Savings Institution v. Somerville Milling Co., 101 N.H. 307, 141 A.2d 885 (1958); Elliott v. Wood, 45 N.Y. 71 (1871); Restatement, Second, Conflict of Laws § 229 (1971).

8. Resolution Trust Corp. v. Atchity, 259 Kan. 584, 913 P.2d 162 (1996) (deficiency judgment); Hughes v. Winkleman, 243 Mo. 81, 147 S.W. 994 (1912).

provider who has furnished materials to, or performed labor upon, real property within the state, although the agreement for the materials or labor was made elsewhere.[9] When a mortgage secures a debt negotiated in a state other than that of the situs, the law of the state most appropriately related to the particular issue may well determine the validity of the obligation and the enforceability of the contract as distinguished from any possible security in the land.[10] Also, whether the grantee of mortgaged premises has assumed the obligation to pay the debt is determined not by the law of the situs but by the law most appropriately related to the transaction as a contract matter.[11] That law may of course refer to the situs.[12] The same law determines the contractual effect of an assumption of the obligation.[13] The assignment of the contract is governed by the law applicable as a contractual matter[14] but the law of the situs determines whether the assignment is in a form proper to give the assignee the right to preclude an enforcement of the encumbrance.[15]

§ **19.10** Issues relating to deficiencies after foreclosure have raised many concerns in this area of choice of law. Although the deficiency issues are essentially matters of contract in which the security is inadequate to discharge the balance due, the relationship between this liability and the security has been important, particularly as it relates to residential sales.[1] In the event of a deficiency remaining after foreclosure and sale, where both note and mortgage are governed by the same law and suit is brought in another state for the deficiency, the existence and the extent of the right to recover are determined by the law of the situs and that appropriate to the contract. Recovery would not be limited by provisions of the internal law of the forum prohibiting deficiency judg-

---

9. Nuclear Corp. of America v. Hale, 355 F.Supp. 193 (N.D.Tex.1973), affirmed 479 F.2d 1045 (5th Cir.1973); Thurman v. Kyle, 71 Ga. 628 (1884); United States Investment Co. v. Phelps & Bigelow Windmill Co., 54 Kan. 144, 37 P. 982 (1894); Pullis Brothers Iron Co. v. Parish of Natchitoches, 51 La. Ann. 1377, 26 So. 402 (1899); Campbell v. Coon, 149 N.Y. 556, 44 N.E. 300 (1896). Cf. In re Wolman, 314 F.Supp. 703 (D.Md.1970); Albert and Harlow, Inc. v. Great Northern Oil Co., 283 Minn. 246, 167 N.W.2d 500 (1969); Allied Thermal Corp. v. James Talcott Inc., 3 N.Y.2d 302, 165 N.Y.S.2d 91, 144 N.E.2d 66 (1957).

10. Cooper v. Cherokee Village Development Co., 236 Ark. 37, 364 S.W.2d 158 (1963); Hall v. Hoff, 295 Pa. 276, 145 A. 301 (1929). See Fahs v. Martin, 224 F.2d 387 (5th Cir.1955). Cf. Union Savings Bank v. DeMarco, 105 R.I. 592, 254 A.2d 81 (1969); Cook v. Frazier, 765 S.W.2d 546 (Tex.App. 1989).

11. Liljedahl v. Glassgow, 190 Iowa 827, 180 N.W. 870 (1921).

12. See Schewe v. Bentsen, 424 F.2d 60 (5th Cir.1970). See supra § 18.23.

13. Wood v. Johnson, 117 Minn. 267, 135 N.W. 746 (1912). See Note, 25 Mich. L. Rev. 905 (1927).

14. See Restatement, Second, Conflict of Laws § 190 (1971).

15. Restatement, Second, Conflict of Laws § 228 (1971); President, etc., of City of Natchez v. Minor, 17 Miss. (9 Smedes & M.) 544, 48 Am.Dec. 727 (1848).

§ 19.10

1. See Currier v. Tuck, 112 N.H. 10, 287 A.2d 625 (1972); Bullington v. Mize, 25 Utah 2d 173, 478 P.2d 500 (1970). Cf. Equilease Corp. v. Belk Hotel Corp., 42 N.C.App. 436, 256 S.E.2d 836 (1979), review denied 298 N.C. 568, 261 S.E.2d 121 (1979). But cf. Industrial Credit Co. v. J.A.D. Construction Corp., 29 A.D.2d 952, 289 N.Y.S.2d 243 (1968).

ments[2] or restricting recovery to the difference between the debt and the true value of the land, rather than the amount realized on the sale.[3] Where the note is executed in one state and the land mortgaged lies in another, and the provisions of these states regarding deficiency judgments differ, the cases have not been uniform. One approach which unifies the applicable law is indicated by the holding that the contract is governed by the law intended by the parties, and that they must have intended it to be governed by the law of the situs of the land.[4] If the law applicable to the contract limits the recovery to the amount realized from the land, there would seem to be no basis for recovery of a deficiency anywhere, irrespective of the law of the situs, unless the law of the place of contracting is interpreted as intended to protect only holders of land situated within that state.[5] A more difficult problem

2. Catchpole v. Narramore, 102 Ariz. 248, 428 P.2d 105 (1967); Colodny v. Krause, 141 Ga.App. 134, 232 S.E.2d 597 (1977), cert. denied 434 U.S. 892, 98 S.Ct. 267, 54 L.Ed.2d 177 (1977); Goodman v. Nadler, 113 Ga.App. 493, 148 S.E.2d 480 (1966); Cooper v. Atlantic Federal Savings & Loan Association of Fort Lauderdale, 249 Md. 228, 239 A.2d 89 (1968); McGirl v. Brewer, 132 Or. 422, 432, 280 P. 508 (1929). Cf. Baker v. First National Bank of Denver, 603 P.2d 397 (Wyo.1979). But cf. Bullington v. Angel, 220 N.C. 18, 16 S.E.2d 411 (1941), aff'd on other grounds Angel v. Bullington, 330 U.S. 183, 67 S.Ct. 657, 91 L.Ed. 832 (1947); Maxwell v. Ricks, 294 Fed. 255 (9th Cir.1923).

3. Resolution Trust Corp. v. Atchity, 259 Kan. 584, 913 P.2d 162 (1996) (applying local law of situs which does not evaluate adequacy of consideration); Belmont v. Cornen, 48 Conn. 338 (1880); Provident Savings Bank & Trust Co. v. Steinmetz, 270 N.Y. 129, 200 N.E. 669 (1936); Bullington v. Mize, 25 Utah 2d 173, 478 P.2d 500 (1970). Similarly, moratorium statutes have been held not to prevent recovery in connection with mortgages on land in other states. Connecticut Mutual Life Insurance Co. of Hartford v. Hansell, 194 Minn. 41, 259 N.W. 390 (1935); Harris v. Metropolitan Casualty Insurance Co. of New York, 156 Misc. 692, 282 N.Y.S. 449 (1935) (noted 36 Colum. L. Rev. 487 (1936)). See also Bailey & Rice, The Extraterritorial Effect of the New York Mortgage Moratorium, 20 Cornell L.Q. 315 (1935); Note, 40 Colum. L. Rev. 867 (1940).

4. Resolution Trust Corp. v. Atchity, 259 Kan. 584, 913 P.2d 162 (1996); Stumpf v. Hallahan, 101 App.Div. 383, 91 N.Y.S. 1062 (1905), aff'd 185 N.Y. 550, 77 N.E. 1196 (1906). Cf. California Fed. Sav. & Loan Ass'n v. Bell, 6 Hawaii App. 597, 735 P.2d 499 (1987).

5. Cf. Reconstruction Finance Corp. v. Mercury Realty Co., 97 F.Supp. 491 (E.D.Mich.1951); Provident Savings Bank & Trust Co. v. Steinmetz, 270 N.Y. 129, 200 N.E. 669 (1936); Harris v. Metropolitan Casualty Insurance Co. of New York, 156 Misc. 692, 282 N.Y.S. 449 (1935) (noted 36 Colum. L. Rev. 487 (1936)); Baum v. Birchall, 150 Pa. 164, 24 A. 620 (1892); Bullington v. Mize, 25 Utah 2d 173, 478 P.2d 500 (1970). See also First Commerce Realty Investors v. K–F Land Co., 617 S.W.2d 806 (Tex.Civ.App.1981) (applying the Louisiana Deficiency Judgment Act to prevent a deficiency judgment with respect to a foreclosure sale of Texas real property). *First Commerce* was based on the following factors: the secured party's principal place of business was in Louisiana, the underlying loan was negotiated and to be performed there, all documents were executed in Louisiana, the promissory note and related guaranty provided for the applicability of Louisiana law, and the deed of trust explicitly referred to the underlying transaction as being subject to Louisiana law. The court rejected lender's argument that this issue should be determined by Texas law because of the compliance with Texas statutory procedures for foreclosure sales, holding that the issue related to the enforcement of the underlying note and guaranty and thus was governed by the law selected by the parties: "It is difficult to conceive of other steps that could have been taken by the parties to imprint this transaction with Louisiana law.... [T]he parties clearly bargained in the most specific terms for the application of Louisiana law. We see no reason to frustrate such intention so clearly expressed." 617 S.W.2d at 809. But cf. Gelpi v. Burke, 364 So.2d 1064 (La.App.1978) (refusing to apply Louisiana deficiency judgment statute to foreclosure sale of Texas land); see Neton, Annual Survey of Texas Law—Conflict

arises where the law of the situs restricts or denies it. In some states a mortgagee may recover the entire amount of the note, disregarding requirement of the law of the situs that the security first be exhausted.[6] On the basis of this it may very well appear that the mortgagee should likewise be able to disregard a law of the situs which completely confines his recovery to the security. This would be consistent with the view that deficiencies are based upon the contractual obligation between the parties and do not relate to interests in the security of the land itself.[7] There is, however, a qualification that if the availability of foreclosure at the situs is conditioned upon deficiency limitations regarding purchase money mortgages, or residential sale, the mortgagee may well be held to have submitted the disposition of the entire claim to the jurisdiction of the courts of the situs, so that the foreclosure judgment precludes further action.[8]

II. TANGIBLE MOVABLES

A. POLICY CONSIDERATIONS

§ 19.11 In most instances, the policy considerations of convenience, control, and protection of justified expectations described in the discussion of immovables require that the creation of interests in chattels should be of particular interest to, and subject to the law of, the place in which the chattel is located. Situs law is likely to be most appropriately concerned with goods within the confines of the state. Unlike land, however, chattels are movable and have no permanent situs. Consequently, different jurisdictions can have similar and successive concerns about chattels. This requires the identification of the interest of a situs state at a particular time.[1]

While the prevailing view of choice-of-law doctrine relating to chattels is about what these considerations indicate, variation occurs and examination of statutes and other authorities is necessary. Variation from the situs reference is most frequently occasioned by the relationship that chattel transfer problems have to contractual undertakings. This relationship tends to confuse characterization of property and contract issues as well as to make the intention of the parties highly significant.[2]

of Laws, 36 Sw. L.J. 397, 414–15 (1982). See also Comment, Application of California's Antideficiency Statutes in Conflict of Laws Contexts, 73 Calif. L. Rev. 1332 (1985).

6. Hall v. Hoff, 295 Pa. 276, 145 A. 301 (1929). Express choice-of-law clauses may be effective in this situation. Cf. Taggart & Taggart Seed, Inc. v. First Tenn. Bk. etc., 684 F.Supp. 230 (E.D.Ark.1988), aff'd 881 F.2d 1080 (8th Cir.1989).

7. This is the position of Restatement, Second, Conflict of Laws § 229, comnt. (e) (1971). Cf. Ferdie Sievers and Lake Tahoe Land Co., Inc. v. Diversified Mortgage In-

vestors, 95 Nev. 811, 603 P.2d 270 (1979); Key Bank of Alaska v. Donnels, 106 Nev. 49, 787 P.2d 382 (1990).

8. Cf. Battle v. Battjes, 274 Mich. 267, 264 N.W. 367 (1936); Id., 282 Mich. 696, 276 N.W. 874 (1937) (noted 35 Mich. L. Rev. 327 (1936)); Angel v. Bullington, 330 U.S. 183, 67 S.Ct. 657, 91 L.Ed. 832 (1947).

§ 19.11

1. See, e.g., Dobbins v. Martin Buick Co., 216 Ark. 861, 227 S.W.2d 620 (1950); Holt Motors, Inc. v. Casto, 136 W.Va. 284, 67 S.E.2d 432 (1951).

The interest of the situs may be overridden by other considerations as well. For example, the parties may agree upon the applicable law. In other situations, the law applied may be that of the owner's domicile. This latter has been the case in the creation of the interests in movables by operation of matrimonial property law.[3] Also, the devolution of personal movable estate on death is generally determined by the rules prevailing at the owner's domicile.[4] In each of these instances, the result can be explained on the analysis that the law of the situs in fact governs, because of its physical control, but the situs courts apply the rule of the domicile because it is convenient to treat uniformly all assets of the married couple or of a decedent's estate, so that the assets are treated as a unit no matter how scattered.

The medieval maxim that movables follow the person of the owner, "mobilia sequuntur personam" is occasionally used to support the domicile rule in the cases just mentioned. If the maxim is taken to express a rule of law, it seems broad enough to include a choice-of-law rule for the voluntary inter vivos transfer of personal property.[5] At the time the maxim originated, it probably stated a fact.[6] Articles of personal estate were few and of such nature that they could be, and no doubt often were, carried by the owner. Since travel was uncommon, the actual location of both the property and the owner was generally at the owner's domicile. No elaboration is needed to show that these assumed circumstances have long since passed into oblivion. Obviously, the statement that personal property has no locality of its own has been untrue for years, for movables do not in fact follow the person.[7]

Historically, it appears that the maxim was never intended to apply to the kinds of transfers with which we are here concerned. The early writers employing it had in mind the development of a convenient rule for the transfer of entire estates by operation of law or by general assignment. In illustrations of the operation of the maxim there is almost no instance of its application to transfers of individual chattels.[8]

---

2. Cf. In re Bulova's Will, 14 A.D.2d 249, 220 N.Y.S.2d 541 (1961), appeal denied 11 N.Y.2d 641, 225 N.Y.S.2d 1025, 180 N.E.2d 894 (1962); Pioneer Credit Corp. v. Morency, 122 Vt. 463, 177 A.2d 368 (1962). With respect to contract issues see supra Chapter 18, particularly §§ 18.24–18.25.

3. See supra §§ 14.18–14.19.

4. See infra §§ 20.3, 20.9.

5. See Story, Conflict of Laws §§ 379, 380, 390 (8th ed. 1883).

6. Wharton, Conflict of Laws § 297 (3d ed. 1905).

7. Lees v. Harding, Whitman & Co., 68 N.J.Eq. 622, 625, 60 A. 352, 353 (1905)

("That personal property has no situs seems rather a metaphysical position rather than a practical and legal truth."); Ames Iron Works v. Warren, 76 Ind. 512, 40 Am. Rep. 258 (1881) ("The fiction does, it must be owned, produce strange incongruities, and lead to almost grotesque results."). See also Schmidt v. Perkins, 74 N.J.L. 785, 67 A. 77 (1907).

8. See Von Bar, Private International Law 489–490 (Gillespie's trans. 1892); Kuhn, Private International Law 235 (1937). See also Ehrenzweig on Conflict of Laws 617 (1962); Lalive, The Transfer of Chattels in the Conflict of Laws 44 (1955); Zaphiriou, The Transfer of Chattels in Private International Law 39 (1956).

Although Story approved a reference to the owner's domicile for transfers inter vivos,[9] this view was vigorously disputed.[10] Although the domicile connection has enjoyed a revival for some purposes under the 2001 version of Article 9 of the Uniform Commercial Code,[11] the common law preference is for the situs. Present day conditions call for a choice-of-law reflective of the particular issues involved. Most of the time this is the law of the situs of tangible chattels at the time of the transaction.[12] When the chattel is normally delivered as a part of the transaction, the situs rule seldom raises problems for it is clearly the focal point of the transaction. When the transaction looks toward future delivery and the location of the chattel bears no significant relationship to the transaction until delivery, intention of the parties becomes very important. An analysis of the interests of the parties and of the states involved calls for an approach similar to that taken in the area of contracts, i.e., absent an effective agreement by the parties, the proper law is that local rule most significantly related to the issues presented by the particular facts.[13]

In the United States, state enactment of the Uniform Commercial Code has imposed statutory choice-of-law rules on transactions falling within its scope. The Uniform Commercial Code's coverage of commercial transactions makes distinctions between gratuitous transfers and commercial transfers quite significant.[14] In addition, the status of persons as original or third parties, as professionals or as nonprofessionals acting in the distribution and chattel financing system, and the time at which they enter into a transaction are important factors in predicting results. Because planning financial and business transactions often requires a high degree of certainty and predictability and because third parties often must rely on the effect of such transactions, the conflict-of-laws approach in commercial transactions has evolved toward rather specific rules justified by the policy analysis suggested above. The rules provided by the Uniform Commercial Code attempt to allocate risks in such a way as to enhance maximum predictability. Consequently, while the original parties usually may control choice-of-law issues among themselves, the impact of that choice upon the right and duties of other

---

9. Story, Conflict of Laws, § 379 (8th ed. 1883).

10. Wharton, Conflict of Laws, § 297 (3d ed. 1905).

11. U.C.C. § 9–301(1) (2001 version) (issues related to perfection of a security interest presumptively governed by law of debtor's location).

12. See Green v. Van Buskirk, 72 U.S. (5 Wall.) 307, 18 L.Ed. 599 (1866), and 74 U.S. (7 Wall.) 139, 19 L.Ed. 109 (1868); Lurie v. Blackwell, 2002 Wy. 110, 51 P.3d 846 (2002); Restatement, Second, Conflict of Laws § 244 (1971). Some of the older cases reflect Story's view. See, e.g., Whitney v. Dodge, 105 Cal. 192, 38 P. 636 (1894); Edgerly v. Bush, 81 N.Y. 199, 203 (1880);

Farmers' & Mechanics' National Bank v. Loftus, 133 Pa. 97, 19 A. 347 (1890).

13. See Restatement, Second, Conflict of Laws § 244 (1971). Cheshire & North, Private International Law 786 (11th ed. 1987); Cavers, The Conditional Sellers Remedies and the Choice of Law Process—Some Notes on Shanahan, 35 N.Y.U. L. Rev. 1126 (1960). Cf. Lalive, The Transfer of Chattels in the Conflict of Laws 74 (1955); Zaphirion, The Transfer of Chattels in Private International Law 31 (1956). For contracts see supra Chapter 18.

14. Gratuitous transfers in trust and at death are discussed infra, Chapters 20 and 21.

parties will significantly depend on the circumstances surrounding each subsequent transaction and the extent of the other parties' knowledge.[15]

B. CHATTEL TRANSFERS

1. *Contract and Property Issues*

§ 19.12 The Uniform Commercial Code does not deal with all the issues incident to chattel transfers. To provide both historical background to the Code and an indication of the law absent statutory direction, choice-of-law developments will first be discussed generally with the impact of the Uniform Commercial Code reserved to consideration of personal property security interests.

In nearly every dispute concerning non-gratuitous transfers of chattels, there are issues with elements of both contract and property law. For example, the parties may agree to buy and sell an article to be manufactured in the future by the seller. Prior to manufacture, this agreement creates no property interest, for the article bargained for is not in existence. At that point, the agreement is an executory contract and is governed by the rules relating to contracts. Even in sales of existing chattels, contractual aspects of the transaction may be separated from property questions. Thus, if the sale of an article is lawful where the transaction occurs, validation policies may permit suit to be maintained on a note subsequently given for the purchase price in a state where the sale of the goods would have been unlawful.[1] The relationship between contract and title aspects in a sale of movables is so close, that the Uniform Commercial Code has largely made the distinction obsolete in areas covered by the Code. However, analysis of the policies relevant to the particular issue raised supports the distinction in some personal property cases as it does in transactions regarding land.[2] The contract issues regarding a chattel would normally be determined by the law appropriate to them, though the effect of the agreement in creating or transferring an interest in movable property would be determined by the law appropriate to the property issues. Capacity to make a contract, though it concerns a movable elsewhere, is governed by the proper law relating to the contract issue,[3] while the capacity to transfer an interest

---

15. See Carlson v. Tandy Computer Leasing, 803 F.2d 391 (8th Cir.1986); Moyer v. Citicorp Homeowners, Inc., 799 F.2d 1445 (11th Cir.1986); In re Novack, 88 B.R. 353 (N.D.Okla. 1988).

§ 19.12

1. Atlantic Phosphate Co. v. Ely, 82 Ga. 438, 9 S.E. 170 (1889). See also the obsolete liquor prohibition cases. Sortwell v. Hughes, 22 Fed. Cas. 801 (C.C.D.N.H. 1852); Brockway v. Maloney, 102 Mass. 308 (1869); Bollinger v. Wilson, 76 Minn. 262, 79 N.W. 109 (1899). This distinction was not universally made. Some of the statutes expressly or by interpretation covered the contract for the sale as well as the sale itself. Brown v. Wieland, 116 Iowa 711, 89 N.W. 17 (1902).

2. Cf. Susi v. Belle Acton Stables, Inc., 360 F.2d 704 (2d Cir.1966), on remand 261 F.Supp. 219 (S.D.N.Y.1966); Alpert v. Thomas, 643 F.Supp. 1406 (D.Vt.1986); Lloyd v. Classic Motor Coaches, Inc., 388 F.Supp. 785 (N.D.Ohio 1974); Schultz v. Tecumseh Products, 310 F.2d 426 (6th Cir. 1962); Frericks v. General Motors Corp., 278 Md. 304, 363 A.2d 460 (1976).

3. See Restatement, Second, Conflict of Laws, Intro., ch. 9, Topic 3 (1971). Cf. Dunavant Enterprises, Inc. v. Ford, 294 So.2d

in the article is determined by the law applicable to the chattel transaction, normally that of the situs of the chattel at the time of the transfer.[4]

2. *Situs and Market Policies*

§ 19.13 In many cases, where the choice of law concerning a chattel interest is in question, the proper law of the contract, the parties' domicile, and the chattel's location may all point to the same applicable law. Even if the litigation concerning the rights of parties takes place elsewhere, the court in applying the foreign rule may depend on any one or all three of these contacts as the basis for its decisions. Also the substantive rules of each state may be the same, particularly with the harmonization produced by the Uniform Commercial Code. Decisions in such cases simply identify false conflicts and do not assist in resolving policy conflicts of states with different contacts or policies.[1]

An early English case is more clear.[2] Lumber was shipped from Russia to England in a Prussian vessel for an English buyer. After the ship wrecked in route, the goods were sold in Norway by the master of the ship under circumstances which gave the purchaser good title according to the law of Norway, though not according to English law. In a dispute between the original English buyer and the Norwegian purchaser, it was decided that the law of Norway must govern. The view was taken that "if personal property is disposed of in a manner binding according to the law of the country where it is, that disposition is binding everywhere."[3] American authority also supports this view, that a transfer of an interest in tangible personalty, effective by the law of the situs of the property at the time, is usually valid.[4] An interest thus

---

788 (Miss.1974); Phillips v. Englehart, 437 S.W.2d 158 (Mo.App.1968); Doppke v. American Bank & Trust Co., 402 S.W.2d 317 (Tex.Civ.App. 1966). But cf. GMAC v. Robinson, 263 A.2d 302 (Del.Super.1970); Equilease Corp. v. Belk Hotel Corp., 42 N.C.App. 436, 256 S.E.2d 836 (1979), review denied 298 N.C. 568, 261 S.E.2d 121 (1979).

4. Dalton v. Murphy, 30 Miss. 59 (1855); Farmers' & Mechanics' National Bank v. Loftus, 133 Pa. 97, 19 A. 347 (1890). Cf. Alexander v. Ling–Temco–Vought, Inc., 406 S.W.2d 919 (Tex.Civ.App.1966).

§ 19.13
1. See Shanahan v. George B. Landers Construction Co., 266 F.2d 400 (1st Cir. 1959); Nichols v. Mase, 94 N.Y. 160 (1883). Cf. Johnston Jewels, Limited v. Leonard, 156 Conn. 75, 239 A.2d 500 (1968); Continental Oil Co. v. Lane Wood & Co., 443 S.W.2d 698 (Tex.1969). Myers v. Columbus Sales Pavilion, Inc., 575 F.Supp. 805, 807 (D.Neb.1983), affirmed 723 F.2d 37 (8th Cir.1983) (finding the disposition of the case did not depend upon choice-of-law

analysis between two fora because "the law of Nebraska and Iowa is identical with respect to the passage of title to the [chattel]."). Cf. In re Novack, 88 B.R. 353 (N.D.Okla. 1988).

2. Cammell v. Sewell, 5 Hem. & M. 728 (1860).

3. 5 Hurl. & N. at 744 (1960). See Dicey & Morris, Conflict of Laws 963 (13th ed. by Collins 2000); Graveson, Conflict of Laws, 456 (7th ed. 1974). See also Alcock v. Smith (1892) 1 Ch. 238; Embiricos v. Anglo–Austrian Bank (1905) 1 K.B. 677.

4. E.g., Four Star Aviation, Inc. v. United States, 409 F.2d 292 (5th Cir.1969); Royal Baking Powder Co. v. Hessey, 76 F.2d 645 (4th Cir.1935), cert. denied sub.nom. Lowendahl v. Hessey, 296 U.S. 595, 56 S.Ct. 110, 80 L.Ed. 421 (1935); Mercantile Financial Corp. v. Sea Work Marine Services, Inc., 403 F.Supp. 979 (E.D.La.1975); McRae v. Bandy, 270 Ala. 12, 115 So.2d 479 (1959); Dobbins v. Martin Buick Co., 216 Ark. 861, 227 S.W.2d 620 (1950); GMAC v. Robinson, 263 A.2d 302 (Del.Super.1970); Mackey v.

created at the situs will be recognized in another state to which the article is subsequently taken, even though by the law of the second jurisdiction no title would have been acquired by the transaction.[5]

In the case of competing transfers to purchasers without notice, the policy of validation may be neutralized since it may equally be applicable to both transactions.[6] In that instance, the force of market policies at the situs seems to prevail.

Such an early case is *Green v. Van Buskirk*[7] in which the law of the domicile and that of the situs differed. There, the New York owner of certain safes located in Chicago executed and delivered in New York a mortgage upon them to another New Yorker. Before the mortgage was recorded or possession taken by the mortgagee, the chattels were attached in Illinois by a creditor of the mortgagor, also a New York citizen, and were later sold in that proceeding in Illinois. By Illinois law, the attaching creditor prevailed; by New York law, the mortgagee's right was superior. In subsequent litigation between the creditor and mortgagee in New York it was held that the Illinois law governed, the court taking the view that New York must give full faith and credit to the sale under the attachment proceedings in Illinois.[8] The result in such cases supports the view that the law of the situs is applicable to determine interests in the transfer of the chattel. This reference to the law of the situs "has the merit of adopting the law of the jurisdiction which has the actual control of the goods and the merit of certainty."[9]

Although the early cases seemed somewhat arbitrary in the application of the situs rule and often gave little explanation for its application,[10] it is clear that the circumstances of the parties are very significant. For example, where the owner left a diamond with a broker in New York with a memorandum reserving title, and the broker took the diamond to New Jersey and pledged it with a defendant without notice,

Pettyjohn, 6 Kan.App. 57, 49 P. 636 (1897); Frericks v. General Motors Corp., 278 Md. 304, 363 A.2d 460 (1976); Ames v. McCamber, 124 Mass. 85 (1878); J.C. Equipment, Inc. v. Sky Aviation, 498 S.W.2d 73 (Mo. App.1973); Emery v. Clough, 63 N.H. 552, 4 A. 796 (1886); Lees v. Harding, Whitman & Co., 68 N.J.Eq. 622, 60 A. 352 (1905); Zendman v. Harry Winston, Inc., 305 N.Y. 180, 111 N.E.2d 871 (1953); Alexander v. Ling–Temco–Vought, Inc., 406 S.W.2d 919 (Tex. Civ.App.1966); Restatement, Second, Conflict of Laws § 244 (1971). Cf. Bank of Lexington v. Jack Adams Aircraft Sales, 570 F.2d 1220 (5th Cir.1978); Fouke v. Fleming, 13 Md. 392 (1859).

5. Rabun v. Rabun, 15 La.Ann. 471 (1860); Sleeper v. Pennsylvania Railroad Co., 100 Pa. 259, 45 Am.Rep. 380 (1882).

6. Cf. Ehrenzweig, Treatise on Conflict of Laws 621 (1962).

7. 72 U.S. (5 Wall.) 307, 18 L.Ed. 599 (1866); Id., 74 U.S. (7 Wall.) 139, 19 L.Ed. 109 (1868). See also Guillander v. Howell, 35 N.Y. 657 (1866); Dalton v. Murphy, 30 Miss. 59 (1855).

8. See also Ames Iron Works v. Warren, 76 Ind. 512, 40 Am. Rep. 258 (1881); Clark v. Tarbell, 58 N.H. 88 (1877); Schmidt v. Perkins, 74 N.J.L. 785, 67 A. 77 (1907); Keller v. Paine, 107 N.Y. 83, 13 N.E. 635 (1887).

9. Lees v. Harding, Whitman & Co., 68 N.J.Eq. 622, 629, 60 A. 352, 355 (1905). Cf. Carlson v. Tandy Computer Leasing, 803 F.2d 391 (8th Cir.1986); Olivier v. Townes, 2 Mart., N.S., 93 (La. 1824).

10. Weinstein v. Freyer, 93 Ala. 257, 9 So. 285 (1891); Public Parks Amusement Co. v. Embree–McLean Carriage Co., 64 Ark. 29, 40 S.W. 582 (1897); Marvin Safe Co. v. Norton, 48 N.J.L. 410, 7 A. 418 (1886); Lees v. Harding, Whitman & Co., 68 N.J.Eq. 622, 60 A. 352 (1905).

the New Jersey court applied the New York law that a factor in possession could pass good title rather than the harsher view of New Jersey. In this situation, the factor obtained, by the first transaction, sufficient title and power to give his pledgee prior rights.[11] In this latter case, the transaction was one that contemplated resale and in which it would seem that commercial policy shifted the risk to the person using a factor as a means of transacting business. The original owner should have anticipated exposure of his title to third parties under these circumstances. A similar case is *Zendman v. Harry Winston, Inc.*,[12] in which a New York jeweler sent a diamond to a New Jersey dealer for display with a document retaining title. After a month's display, the New Jersey dealer sold the ring to a third party without notice at an auction. When the New York jeweler sued the purchaser to recover the stone in the New York courts, the court applied the law of New Jersey to protect the purchaser at the time of the second transaction. Here, both the market policies to protect purchasers at the auction, and the policy of imposing the risk upon the professional who had knowingly invested the dealer with apparent authority to sell were given effect.

3. *Prescription*

§ **19.14** Another instance in which the location of the chattel is highly significant in determining the applicable law relates to the acquisition or transfer of an interest by adverse possession or prescription. When a chattel is held in a single state for a time and in a manner sufficient for the holder to gain title to it by adverse possession under the law of that state, the title so acquired will be recognized elsewhere, even in a state whose internal law would require a longer period of adverse holding.[1] When a chattel is held adversely in two or more states successively, if the law of the state in which it is subsequently held would tack periods of prior holding to satisfy its requirements for the prescriptive period necessary for the new title, that title will be recognized in other states.[2] This simply recognizes that once title has been effectively transferred by the law of the situs, that title will be recognized elsewhere.

An emerging source of choice-of-law problems in this area relates to conflicting claims of title to stolen art objects. The dispute usually arises as between the rightful owner of the art at the time of the conversion

---

11. Dougherty Co. v. Krimke, 105 N.J.L. 470, 144 A. 617 (1929) (noted 17 Geo. L.J. 255 (1929); 38 Yale L.J. 988 (1929)). This rule is now codified by U.C.C. § 2–403.

12. 305 N.Y. 180, 111 N.E.2d 871 (1953). Cf. Lalive, The Transfer of Chattels in Conflict of Laws 185 (1955).

§ 19.14

1. Restatement, Second, Conflict of Laws § 246 (1971); Shelby v. Guy, 24 U.S.

(11 Wheat.) 361, 6 L.Ed. 495 (1826); Brown v. Brown, 5 Ala. 508 (1843); Waters v. Barton, 41 Tenn. (1 Cold.) 450 (1860).

2. Restatement, Second, Conflict of Laws § 246, cmnt. (b) (1971). See Wolff, Private International Law 530 (2d ed. 1950); Zaphiriou, The Transfer of Chattels in Private International Law 116 (1956).

and a good faith purchaser for value of the item. For the most part, the issue in dispute is the operation of a statute of limitations that might bar the original owner's efforts to replevy the object. While the limitations periods vary somewhat, the most significant questions are often those of accrual and tolling. In broad strokes, some states toll the running of the statute only if the original owner searches diligently for the stolen art object,[3] while others do not start the clock until the original owner makes a demand for the object's return and the demand is refused.[4] These differing rules express differing policy preferences: the "diligent search" rule is more solicitous of good faith purchasers and the "demand and refusal rule" more favorable to original owners; each has potentially different implications for art institutions and the public.[5]

The choice-of-law issues here can be challenging.[6] In many cases, the transaction can be connected with many different states and nations. The art might have been stolen in France by a United States citizen domiciled in Wisconsin and sold through a New York gallery to a Californian—to say nothing of the various intermediate exchanges that might have taken place. Essentially, courts have taken three different approaches. Some have applied forum law on the theory that the issue is a procedural one of the statute of limitations.[7] Others treat the question as one of title to moveable property and will validate the passage of title if the law of the state of the situs of the passage of title would so validate the transaction.[8] Still others question as one of a conflict of tort laws— essentially conversion—and usually apply the Second Restatement's most-significant-relationship theory.[9] It seems unlikely that the questions posed will fade in significance any time soon. Attempts to gain support for ratification of a convention on this point seem to be flagging[10] and some cases present such wrenching and emotional issues that convergence on the conflicts issues seems a ways off yet.

4. *Removal of a Chattel*

§ 19.15 Participation by the owner in circumstances leading to a claim by a third party has always been significant in resolution of issues

3. See, e.g., O'Keeffe v. Snyder, 83 N.J. 478, 416 A.2d 862 (N.J. 1980).

4. See, e.g., Solomon R. Guggenheim Foundation v. Lubell, 77 N.Y.2d 311, 567 N.Y.S.2d 623, 569 N.E.2d 426 (N.Y. 1991).

5. See Patricia Y. Reyhan, A Chaotic Palette: Conflict of Laws in Litigation Between Original Owners and Good Faith Purchasers of Stolen Art, 50 Duke L.J. 955, 1027–34 (2001).

6. See Symeonides, On the Side of the Angels: Choice of Law and Stolen Cultural Property, in: Private Law in the International Arena—Liber Amicorum Kurt Siehr 649–64 (J. Basedow, et. al., eds. 2000).

7. See Reyhan, supra n.5, at 1008–12 (citing O'Keeffe v. Snyder, 83 N.J. 478, 416 A.2d 862 (1980) as an example of this approach and criticizing this solution as sim-

plistic and unresponsive to the competing policy concerns).

8. See Reyhan, supra n.5, at 1012–18 (citing Winkworth v. Christie, Manson & Woods, Ltd., [1980] 1 Ch. 496 as a leading example of this approach).

9. See Reyhan, supra n.5, at 1018–22 (citing Charash v. Oberlin College, 14 F.3d 291 (6th Cir.1994) as an example of this approach).

10. See Stephanie Cuba, Note, Stop the Clock: The Case to Suspend the Statute of Limitations on Claims for Nazi–Looted Art, 17 Cardozo Arts & Ent LJ 447, 489 (1999)(noting that as of 1999 the Unidroit Convention on the International Return of Stolen or Illegally Exported Cultural Objects, June 24, 1995, 34 I.L.M. 1322, 1331 had been ratified by only Paraguay, Lithuania and China).

concerning the transfer of interests in chattels. In the conflict-of-laws setting, the consent of the owner to the removal of a chattel to another state has been important, but its significance has been explained on various grounds. Even so, it is now well settled that the law of the state of the new location is applicable to resolve issues regarding the effect of transactions concerning the chattel after its removal to a state even without the consent of the owner.[1] This seems to be an application of the more general rule that the law of the situs of the chattel at the significant time is most relevant. Under the common law rule that prevailed in the absence of statute, all states of the United States recognized the owner's interest previously acquired when he had neither knowledge of nor had consented to the chattel's removal to another state.[2] Mere moving of the chattel to another state does not affect existing interests.[3] On the other hand, if the removal to a state is with the owner's consent or knowledge, actual or imputed, the courts will usually require compliance with local recording statutes to protect the owner's interests from subsequent dealings within the state. Although the owner's consent or knowledge, and action after knowledge of the removal of the chattel to another state, are significant, this significance has been variously explained. Early rationalizations based on jurisdictional concepts[4] have been abandoned. Cases refusing attachment of property brought into a state by force or fraud[5] are not indicative of lack of power in the second state, but rather are recognized as being instances in which the situs state declines to exercise an existing power.[6] Even the early cases in which property was returned to the owner's domicile, whose courts then recognized his original title, are best explained on other than jurisdictional concepts.[7] The considerations most often ad-

§ 19.15

1. Restatement, Second, Conflict of Laws § 245 (1971).

2. The American cases and statutes previous to the Uniform Commercial Code are ably analyzed in Vernon, Recorded Chattel Security Interests in the Conflict of Laws, 47 Iowa L. Rev. 346 (1962). See also Comment, 47 Cal. L. Rev. 543 (1959); Note, 70 Yale L.J. 995 (1961).

3. Restatement, Second, Conflict of Laws § 247 (1971); National Trailer Convoy Co. v. Mount Vernon Bank and Trust Co., 420 P.2d 889 (Okla.1966).

4. See Note, 24 Harv. L. Rev. 567 (1911); Beale, Jurisdiction over Title of Absent Owner in a Chattel, 40 Harv. L. Rev. 805 (1927).

5. Powell v. McKee, 4 La.Ann. 108 (1849); Deyo v. Jennison, 92 Mass. (10 Allen) 410 (1865); Sea–Gate Tire & Rubber Co. v. Moseley, 161 Okl. 256, 18 P.2d 276 (1933); Timmons v. Garrison, 23 Tenn. (4

Humph.) 148 (1843); Houghton v. May, 22 Ont. L.R. 434, 23 Ont. L.R. 252 (1911). In all these cases the removal was made or caused by the creditor who was precluded from taking advantage of his own wrong. The result is the same where there is no removal to another state, if the creditor's seizure is a wrongful act. Ilsley v. Nichols, 29 Mass. (12 Pick.) 270, 22 Am. Dec. 425 (1831).

6. See McRae v. Bandy, 270 Ala. 12, 115 So.2d 479 (1959); Dobbins v. Martin Buick Co., 216 Ark. 861, 227 S.W.2d 620 (1950); Note, The Power of a State to Affect Title in a Chattel Atypically Removed to It, 47 Colum. L. Rev. 767, 785 (1947). Cf. Restatement, Second, Conflict of Laws § 56 (1971). But cf. Leflar, Constitutional Jurisdiction over Tangible Chattels, 2 Mo. L. Rev. 171 (1937).

7. See Edgerly v. Bush, 81 N.Y. 199 (1880); Wylie v. Speyer, 62 How.Prac. 107 (N.Y.1881). In both cases the court said

vanced for the recognition of the owner's interests, where the owner neither knew or consented, are: "(1) That it achieves a superior social and commercial result; (2) that it is consistent with traditional property concepts, i.e., the analogy to the thief and mere possessor; (3) that as between competing parties, the local buyer is the 'less' innocent . . . ."[8] All of these explanations recognize the determination of the issue by the situs under its policies. That the situs may and, under modern practice, will, more often apply its own law is reflected in the widely adopted Uniform Commercial Code which "applies to transactions bearing an appropriate relation to this state."[9] The Code tends to protect the non-commercial purchaser who purchases for his own use[10] or one who purchases from a dealer entrusted with the goods by the owner.[11] The Code has specific provisions applicable to security interests in goods taken, to another state requiring subsequent recording which generally reflect the pattern of the common law rule.[12] The policy of the situs to protect those consumers who purchase in the course of trade seems likely to be reflected in future developments of the law by statute or decision.[13]

C.   CHATTEL SECURITY

1. *Introduction*

§ 19.16   The credit economy of our modern society frequently requires that a lender, secured by an interest in a chattel, place possession of the chattel in the hands either of a merchant for resale or of a consumer purchaser. In these situations, the claim of the lender is represented only by unattached documents or prior rights established by operation of law involving forms of public notice. Because of these commercial facts of life, most of the problems of conflict of laws relating to chattels involve a secured creditor of a debtor who has, by design or otherwise, permitted competing claims by third persons to arise in the property.

In the conflict-of-laws setting, the typical situation is one in which the secured creditor records his security interest in the state where the goods are sold and delivered, but the debtor, after taking possession of the chattel, removes it to another state, and in the second state purports

---

that the lex domicilii governed, not mentioning the significance of removal without the owner's consent. See also Todd v. Armour, 19 Sc.L.R. 656, 659 (1882). Cf. Ehrenzweig, Treatise on Conflict of Laws § 235 (1962); Turnbull v. Cole, 70 Colo. 364, 201 P. 887 (1921); Judy v. Evans, 109 Ill.App. 154 (1903); Willys Overland Co. v. Evans, 104 Kan. 632, 180 P. 235 (1919).

8. Vernon, Recorded Chattel Securities in the Conflict of Laws, 47 Iowa L. Rev. 346, 362 (1962). Cf. B & G Budget Plan of Portland v. Young, 368 F.2d 731 (9th Cir. 1966).

9. U.C.C. § 1–105.

10. U.C.C. § 9–307 (1972 version).

11. U.C.C. § 2–103. Cf. Zendman v. Harry Winston, Inc., 305 N.Y. 180, 111 N.E.2d 871 (1953).

12. U.C.C. § 9–103 (1972 version).

13. See Vernon, Recorded Chattel Securities in the Conflict of Laws, 47 Iowa L. Rev. 346 (1962). Cf. Ehrenzweig on Conflict of Laws § 238 (1962); Budget Plan, Inc. v. Sterling A. Orr, 334 Mass. 599, 137 N.E.2d 918 (1956).

to sell or to borrow against the security of the goods. The subsequently informed original secured creditor, having not recorded his interest in the second state, finds himself in conflict with the subsequent purchaser or creditor who has perfected his claim under the law of the second state. Since possession frequently continues in the debtor, this tableau may be repeated to involve others with similar claims. It is a difficult question to determine which of two or more innocent parties bears the risk in such a situation when the debtor absconds or fails. On the one hand, there is the commercial policy of encouraging the extension of credit in order to facilitate the productive and distributive system, and on the other, to protect those who deal with the possessor of chattels without knowledge of prior claims. As we have seen, the common law in the United States generally recognized the rights which arose out of a transaction according to the law of the situs of the property at the time of that transaction.

Although the law had a varying history in the United States, the situs most frequently recognized that the rights of the first secured creditor perfected in the state where the property was then located, would be recognized subsequently in other states. This result generally followed if, at least, a secured creditor had not consented or otherwise been involved in the removal of the property to the second state, and if, on discovery, acted within a reasonable time to perfect his interest in the second state. This placed the risk of dealing with a person not known to be a debtor upon the members of the public and the credit system in the second state. Even one who was extremely cautious in surveying for a possible prior claim could be caught in the web of the prior interests, though acting in the best of faith.

2. The Uniform Commercial Code

a. Introduction

§ 19.17 In addressing these multistate problems, the Uniform Commercial Code undertook to consolidate the law relating to secured transactions in Article 9 of the Code, and to accompany this by repeal of existing conditional sales and chattel mortgage laws. In dealing with the multistate transactions, the Code draws distinctions regarding the nature of the collateral, and whether the parties were professionals or consumers in the chattel distribution and credit system. In those situations in which there is no practical way of protecting both the secured parties and third persons, the Code undertakes to specify exact periods during which the risk would be identified and located, and what steps need be taken to continue or to acquire protection in a secured transaction. By this approach, maximum effect is given to prediction and certainty, even though the result at times might seem harsh, or at least not what some might otherwise prefer.[1]

---

§ 19.17

1. See Coogan, Hogan & Vagts, Secured Transactions Under the Uniform Commer-cial Code, § 3A.06, pp. 212.12, 212.38 (1973). This chapter originally appeared as

The Code was first promulgated in 1952 and Pennsylvania enacted this early version in 1953. During the first 20 years of experience with the Code, several legislative variations and divided judicial constructions impaired the uniformity of Article 9. In light of this experience, Article 9 was substantially revised in 1972.[2]

In 1998, a completely revamped version of Article 9 was approved by both the American Law Institute and the National Conference of Commissioners on Uniform State Laws.[3] The official text carries a delayed effective date of July 1, 2001.[4] This 2001 version of Article 9 makes drastic changes to the choice-of-law provisions found in Section 9–103 of the 1972 version.[5] Although all 50 states enacted the 2001 version as of July 1, 2001 or shortly thereafter, a significant number of cases and interests continue to implicate the earlier version and thus the 1972 and 2001 versions are likely to be of practical relevance for some time, and thus both will be discussed. Consequently, when faced with a current problem, care must be taken to note the particular statutory form that is involved in the relevant states of the United States and in cases being read as possible authority.

The order of the 1972 version of Section 9–103 will be followed discussing the choice-of-law problems in this area. Because the Uniform Commercial Code includes intangibles within the scope of secured transactions under Article 9, some discussion of these matters is included at this point. As we concentrate on the issues arising under the 1972 version of Section 9–103, it should be borne in mind that choice-of-law issues not specifically covered under Article 9 may, if they fall under the Uniform Commercial Code, be covered by other provisions of the Code relating to choice of law such as the general provision in Section 1–105. If they are not covered by the Uniform Commercial Code, then the common law or other statutory provision in a particular state will prevail. For example, Section 1–105 permits the original parties to a security transaction to agree to a choice-of-law clause as to issues between them concerning validity and default, but the 1972 version of Section 9–103 governs rights of third parties without regard to the choice of law in the original transaction, a result continued in the 2001 version.[6]

Coogan, The New U.C.C. Article 9, 86 Harv. L. Rev. 477 (1973).

2. See White & Summers, The Uniform Commercial Code § 1 (2d ed. 1980).

3. McLaughlin & Cohen, The Impending Changes to Article 9, N.Y.L.J., p.3 (Dec. 9, 1998).

4. Id.

5. See 9 U.C.C. §§ 9–301—9–308 (2001 version); see also Borchers, Choice of Law Relative to Security Interests and Other Liens in International Bankruptcy 46 Am. J. Comp. L. Supp. 165 (1998) (discussing then-proposed version of Article 9).

6. See Coogan, Hogan & Vagts, supra n.1, § 3A.06. Considerable uncertainty developed under the 1962 Code regarding conflict of laws regarding chattel security because of the broad coverage of § 9–102, Policy and Scope of Article, reflected in the words "so far as concerns any personal property and fixtures within the jurisdiction of this state." See R. Weintraub, Commentary on the Conflict of Laws, § 8.31 (3d ed. 1986). These words were deleted in 1972 from § 9–102 which has the effect of referring all choice-of-law problems involving security interests to § 1–105 that are not specifically covered in § 9–103. See Review Committee Reasons for 1972 Change, 1972

In treating issues relating to different forms of collateral, the 1972 version of the Uniform Commercial Code breaks multistate transactions into those that relate to (1) documents, instruments and ordinary goods, (2) goods covered by certificate of title, (3) accounts, general intangibles, and mobile goods, (4) chattel paper, (5) minerals, and (6) uncertificated securities. Some of these distinctions carry forward to the 2001 version.

b. Documents, Instruments, and Ordinary Goods

§ 19.18 *1972 Version:* Included in subsection (b) of Section 9–103(1)[1] is the basic situs rule of Article 9 relating to ordinary nonmobile goods, i.e., other than those covered by a certificate of title[2] and those which are of the type normally used in more than one jurisdiction,[3] such as vehicles, construction equipment and shipping containers. Minerals[4] and uncertificated securities[5] are also excluded but possessory security interests in chattel paper[6] are subject to the rules of subsection 1. However, few of the problems dealt with in Section 9–103(1) are likely to occur when possessory security interests are involved.

Under Section 9–103(1), issues relating to the perfection of a security interest in collateral "are governed by the law of the jurisdiction where the collateral is when the last event occurs" on which is based an assertion concerning the perfection or nonperfection of a security interest. This formulation of the older rule, i.e., situs of the chattel at the time of the transaction, has engendered considerable debate and involves some uncertainties in its application.[7]

Amendments to Article 9 § 103 (1972). Cf. Matter of Williams, 608 F.2d 1015 (5th Cir. 1979). For some of the problems of chattel financing involving Louisiana under prior law, see In re Merritt Dredging Co., 839 F.2d 203 (4th Cir.1988), cert. denied Compliance Marine, Inc. v. Campbell, 487 U.S. 1236, 108 S.Ct. 2904, 101 L.Ed.2d 936 (1988); In re Hoover, 447 F.2d 195 (5th Cir.1971); Graves Motors, Inc. v. Docar Sales, Inc., 414 F.Supp. 717 (E.D.La.1976); Jones v. Bradford, 353 So.2d 1348 (La.App. 1977); Figuero v. Figuero, 303 So.2d 801 (La.App.1974). For choice-of-law clauses under the Code see supra § 18.12. For a situation in which the U.C.C. is viewed as inapplicable and applying the law of the forum as most significantly related because of the continuing relationship of the parties, see Alpert v. Thomas, 643 F.Supp. 1406 (D.Vt. 1986). Cf. supra § 18.24.

The 2001 choice-of-law provisions "determine the law governing perfection, the effect of perfection, and the priority of a security interest in collateral," which would appear to cover all third-party effects. U.C.C. § 9–301 (2001 version). Section 9–301 (2001 version) makes an exception only for specialized rules governing certain collateral, and thus would seem to insulate

issues of perfection from more general choice-of-law principles, including party autonomy.

§ 19.18

1. U.C.C. § 9–103 (1972 version).

2. U.C.C. § 9–103(2) (1972 version).

3. U.C.C. § 9–103(3) (1972 version).

4. U.C.C. § 9–103(5) (1972 version).

5. U.C.C. § 9–103(6) (1972 version).

6. U.C.C. § 9–103(4) (1972 version).

7. See, e.g., Kripke, The "Last Event" Test For Perfection of Security Interests Under Art. 9 of the Uniform Commercial Code, 50 N.Y.U. L. Rev. 47 (1975); Coogan, The New U.C.C. Article 9, 86 Harv. L. Rev. 477, 537 (1973); Murray, Choice of Law and Article 9: Situs or Sense?, 9 Hofstra L. Rev. 39, 72 (1980); R. Weintraub, Commentary on the Conflict of Laws 574–75 (4th ed. 2001); Juenger, Nonpossessory Security Interests in American Conflicts Law, 26 Am. J. Comp. L. 145, 166 (1978 Supp.); Coogan, Article 9—An Agenda for the Next Decade, 87 Yale L.J. 1012, 1051 (1978). But see In re Legel Braswell Government Securities Corp., 695 F.2d 506 (11th Cir.1983) (be-

There was some dissent from the choice-of-law reference to the situs,[8] but most criticism arose because the last event may be any of several occurrences which are necessary to perfect the security interest. Thus, the debtor must sign a written security agreement, the creditor must give value, the debtor must acquire rights in the collateral,[9] and unless perfection is automatic, the creditor perfect either by taking possession of the collateral, or more commonly, filing notice of his security interest.[10] These events need not occur in any particular order so that the location of the collateral at the time when the last occurs may be difficult to predict if the goods are moved from one state to another at crucial times.[11] For example, if Repair Service Co. in State X buys on credit a machine tool from Seller in State X for expected use at Repair Service's shop, in State X and Repair Service takes delivery in X and all requirements except filing have previously occurred, the security interest is perfected if filing occurs while the goods are in X. This is a reasonably controlled situation and Seller may protect itself against most foreseeable problems by prompt filing or by withholding delivery until after filing so it can be sure that all events have occurred while the goods are in State X. However, suppose that when filing is the last event, Repair Service has an unexpected need for the machine tool at its shop in State Y and immediately after taking delivery diverts its truck to Y so that at the time Seller files in X, the goods are in Y, not in X. The security interest is not perfected in Y and Y's law will apply and Y most likely would recognize a sale to a third party in Y or the security interest of another creditor perfected in Y before Seller files in Y. Of course, if the goods, or any part of them, remained in X at the time of filing, its law would apply to those goods in X.[12]

Suppose however in, the situation just discussed, that Seller and Repair Service understand the goods are going to be taken to another state for use there. In that event Section 9–103(1)(c) provides an exception to the last event rule to direct that the law of the state of the understood destination will govern perfection and its effect for 30 days after delivery to the debtor. A filing in State Y would be effective by State Y law for thirty days and thereafter if the goods do in fact reach State Y within the 30 days. However, if the goods were diverted to a third state or attached in a third state before reaching State Y, Y's law is effective to protect Seller only for the 30 day period and thereafter the

cause sale of certificate occurred in New York and certificate was located in New York when the security interest was perfected, the purchaser's status as a bona fide purchaser for value was governed by the New York Uniform Commercial Code).

8. See Murray, Choice of Law and Article 9: Situs or Sense?, 9 Hofstra L. Rev. 39, 83 (1980); R. Weintraub, Commentary on the Conflict of Laws 582–84 (4th ed. 2001); Coogan, The New U.C.C. Article 9, 86 Harv. L. Rev. 477, 555 (1973); Henson, Handbook on Secured Transactions Under the Uniform Commercial Code 220 (1973).

9. U.C.C. § 9–203(1) (1972 version).

10. U.C.C. §§ 9–302, 9–304, 9–306 (1972 version).

11. See White & Summers, The Uniform Commercial Code (2d ed. 1980).

12. Cf. In re Duplan Corp., 455 F.Supp. 926 (S.D.N.Y.1978); Interstate Tire Co. v. United States, 12 U.C.C Rep.Serv. 948 (D.Ariz.1973); In re Dennis Mitchell Industries, Inc., 419 F.2d 349 (3d Cir.1969).

situs rule of Section 9–103(1)(b) would govern. This thirty day grace period is effective only for purchase money security interests[13] and has limited utility.[14]

These provisions of the Uniform Commercial Code fairly well detail the means for protecting parties by structuring initial multistate secured transactions. The concept of perfecting the security interest instructs the parties when and where to file and the initial risks are generally rather easily identified even though the reasonableness of the situs reference continues to be questioned by some.[15] However, most problems occur after the security interest has been initially perfected and the goods are subsequently removed to another state where additional interests or claims to it are created. For example, continuing the hypothetical discussed above, suppose that Seller has properly perfected his security interest at the place where the goods were originally kept but subsequently Repair Service moves the good to another state and sells or creates another security interest in the machine tool. This situation is covered in Section 9–103(1)(d) and the policy of the Uniform Commercial Code is clear. The Seller has four months in which to comply with any requirements of the state of the new location to perfect his security interest there and, if he does so, the interest continues to be perfected thereafter. The policy of protecting the existing security interest prevails for a reasonable time over third party purchasers who might otherwise rely on the absence of local recording to advance credit or buy the goods.[16] The four-month rule requires the original creditor to keep reasonably informed of the location of the collateral and also permits those who are dealing with property kept locally to rely on the uncontested appearance of ownership in the debtor of goods which have been within the state for four months. The sharply defined shift in the risk enables parties to structure their transactions to afford themselves predictable protection.[17]

If the original secured creditor does not file within the four months after the collateral is brought into the state of the new location, the 1972 version of Article 9 provides that the security interest "becomes unperfected" and is unperfected as against a "purchaser after removal." Thus, the otherwise viable security interest must be filed at the new location within the four months to claim any priority as a secured interest. If it is so filed, that perfection relates back to the removal from the state of original perfection. If it is filed in the new location after the four months have expired, its effect dates from that filing and does not relate back to

---

13. U.C.C. § 9–107 (1972 version).

14. See White & Summers, supra n.11, at 969. Cf. Joint Holdings and Trading Co., Limited v. First Union National Bank, 50 Cal.App.3d 159, 123 Cal.Rptr. 519 (1975).

15. See White & Summers, supra n.11, at 964; R. Weintraub, Commentary on the Conflict of Laws 582–84 (4th ed. 2001).

16. Note that the definition of purchaser does not include a lien creditor or trustee in bankruptcy. White & Summers, supra n.11, at 976.

17. Cf. Utah Farm Production Credit Association v. Dinner, 302 F.Supp. 897 (D.C.Colo.1969); Farmers State Bank v. Production Credit Ass'n, 243 Kan. 87, 755 P.2d 518 (1988).

removal. This provision[18] is an explicit change by the 1972 revision to settle a conflict under the 1962 Code between the view that the former security interest had a four month priority which expired at the end of four months[19] and the view adopted in the new provision that the four months is simply a period of grace for filing.[20] Some courts have been influenced by the 1972 revision to reach a similar result when construing the earlier provisions of the 1962 Code.[21]

2001 Version: The 2001 version (with an effective date of July 1, 2001 in the official text)[22] of Article 9 makes some major changes in philosophy. Rather than the situs nexus that dominates the 1972 version, the 2001 version places considerably more emphasis on the personal connection of the debtor.[23] Moreover, the choice-of-law provisions in the 2001 version clearly cover not only perfection, but "the effect of perfection or non-perfection, and the priority of a security interest in collateral" as well, a formulation intentionally broader than the 1972 version's references to "the effect of perfection or non-perfection."[24] But, by referring to perfection and priority, the 2001 version also intentionally leaves other issues (most obviously questions of attachment, validity and characterization) to the more general principles of Section 1–105.[25]

The general rule is stated in Section 9–301(1): "[W]hile a debtor is located in a jurisdiction the local law of that jurisdiction governs perfection, the effect of perfection or non-perfection and the priority of a security interest in collateral."[26] Thus, as a general rule, under the 2001 version a creditor should file a financing statement in the jurisdiction that is the debtor's "location."

Of course, this places a large premium on determining where the debtor is "located" for Code purposes, and Section 9–307 defines that important term. Under Section 9–307, individual debtors are located "at the individual's residence."[27] A non-individual debtor "having only one place of business is located at its place of business."[28] A non-individual debtor having multiple places of business "is located at its chief execu-

---

18. U.C.C. § 9–103(1)(d) (1972 version).

19. See, e.g., American State Bank v. White, 217 Kan. 78, 535 P.2d 424 (1975); United States v. Burnette–Carter Co., 575 F.2d 587 (6th Cir.1978), cert. denied 439 U.S. 996, 99 S.Ct. 596, 58 L.Ed.2d 669 (1978).

20. See U.C.C. § 9–103, cmnt. 7 (1978); White & Summers, supra n.11, at 971. See also Willier & Hart Bender's U.C.C. Service, U.C.C. Reporter–Digest § 9–103, A–37, A–42 (1981).

21. See, e.g., United States v. Squires, 378 F.Supp. 798 (S.D.Iowa 1974); Massey–Ferguson Credit Corp. v. Wells Motor Co., Inc., 374 So.2d 319 (Ala.1979). See, e.g., Paccar Financial Corp. v. J.L. Healy Construction Co., 561 F.Supp. 342 (D.S.D. 1983); International Harvester Credit Corp.

v. Pefley, 458 N.E.2d 257, 37 UCC Rep. Serv. 907 (Ind.App.1983).

22. U.C.C. § 9–702 (2001 version).

23. See McLaughlin & Cohen, The Impending Changes in Article 9, N.Y.L.J., p.3 (Dec. 9, 1998); Borchers, Choice of Law Relative to Security Interests and Other Liens in International Bankruptcies, 46 Am. J. Comp. L. 165 (Supp.1998).

24. U.C.C. § 9–301 (2001 version); U.C.C. § 9–301, cmnt. 2 (2001 version).

25. U.C.C. § 9–301, cmnt. 2 (2001 version).

26. U.C.C. § 9–301(1) (2001 version).

27. 9 U.C.C. § 9–307(b)(1) (2001 version).

28. 9 U.C.C. § 9–307(b)(2) (2001 version).

tive office."[29] However, if these rules give the debtor a "location" outside the United States, and not in a country that requires the existence of security interests to be "publicly available as a condition or result of the security interest's obtaining priority over the rights of a lien creditor," then the Code gives the debtor a "location" in the District of Columbia. Though wildly fictional, the policy objective of "locating" such debtors in the District of Columbia is quite clear. If the debtor's residence or place of business is in a country that allows for security interests to be created in ways that cannot be ascertained by third parties—such as through title retention agreements[30]—a creditor must file a financing statement with the clerk in the District of Columbia in order to protect its rights as against third parties within the United States.

The Code contains other provisions for further determining a debtor's location. For "registered organization[s]"—most obviously corporations—the Code places their location in "the State" under whose law the organization is registered.[31] Because the "place of business" location contained in the preceding subsections is expressly made subject to these latter provisions, this "place of registration" rule must control over the place of business location. Thus, a corporation organized under Delaware law but with its exclusive or chief offices in, say, New York would be "located" in Delaware for Code purposes. Federal corporations and banks are subject to specialized rules that generally place their location in the state designated by federal law or by the organization if so authorized.[32] This "location" continues even if the organization's status as such has lapsed.[33] The United States is located in the District of Columbia, bank branches are generally located in the state in which they are licensed, and foreign air carriers are located in the state they have designated to receive service of process.[34]

Note that the rules locating registered organizations only apply if the organization is registered in a "State."[35] Thus, for instance, a corporation organized under the laws of Panama but with its chief executive office in Florida would not qualify as a registered organization under subsection (e), and thus would have to be located under the preceding subsections, which would place it in the state of its chief executive office—here Florida.

This leads to some odd permutations. Suppose a corporation is incorporated under the laws of country I and has its chief executive office, or sole place of business, in country B. If country I and country B both require public availability of security interests, the Code locates the corporation in country B, because the corporation is not incorporated under the law of a "State." This is a bit odd, because it is a reversal of the domestic situation, which would choose the place of incorporation.

---

29. U.C.C. § 9–307(b)(3) (2001 version).

30. Borchers, supra n.23, at 183–84.

31. U.C.C. § 9–307(e) (2001 version).

32. U.C.C. § 9–307(f) (2001 version).

33. U.C.C. § 9–307(g) (2001 version).

34. U.C.C. § 9–307(h), (i), (j) (2001 version).

35. U.C.C. § 9–307(e) (2001 version).

Consider other variations. If country I requires public availability and country B does not, then the Code locates the corporation in the District of Columbia. This is because, again, the corporation—lacking incorporation in a State (i.e., one of the United States)—must be treated under the preceding subsections. These subsections are willing to locate a debtor in the nation of its chief executive office or exclusive place of business, but only if the law of that country requires public availability of security interests. Under these facts the law does not, so the location reverts to the District of Columbia. If one supposes the reverse case, however—country I does not require public availability but country B does—then the debtor is located in country B, because the Code looks to the state of the chief executive office or sole place of business for all but U.S. corporations and is willing to so locate a debtor as long as the law calls for public availability. Suffice it to say that these rules are far from intuitive and in close cases a back-up filing in the District of Columbia may prove to be inexpensive malpractice insurance.

Moreover, the law of the debtor's location does not govern perfection and priority issues of all security interests. For possessory security interests—i.e., security interests that are perfected by creditor possession—the law of the state in which the collateral is located governs questions of perfection and priority.[36] Questions of perfection and priority in fixtures (i.e., personalty affixed to realty) and timber to be cut are governed by the situs state's law.[37]

The situs state's law also governs *some issues* relative to non-possessory security interests in "negotiable documents, goods, instruments, money, or tangible chattel paper...."[38] For security interests in collateral falling into these stated categories, the issue of perfection (i.e., the state in which to file) remains subject to the general debtor-location nexus, but questions of priority and the effect of perfection are governed by the situs nexus.[39] The comments make clear that the drafters intentionally separated questions of perfection and priority in this context, because to do otherwise would be to allow non-situs states to determine the priority of other kinds of liens (for example, execution liens) on the property.[40]

Of course, these new provisions raise the same problems of the continuity of perfection in cases in which the debtor or the collateral changes location—the latter being relevant for those security interests for which the situs nexus is still the relevant one. For security interests governed by the debtor-location nexus, if the debtor changes location the creditor generally has four months to file a financing statement in the debtor's new location.[41] Transfer of the collateral to a debtor located in a new jurisdiction gives the secured party a full year to file in the new

---

36. U.C.C. § 9–301(1) (2001 version).

37. U.C.C. § 9–301(3)(A), (C); U.C.C. § 9–301, cmnt. 5 (2001 version).

38. U.C.C. § 9–301(3) (2001 version).

39. U.C.C. § 9–301(3) (2001 version); U.C.C. § 9–301, cmnt. 7.

40. U.C.C. § 9–301, cmnt. 7.

41. U.C.C. § 9–316(a)(2) (2001 version); U.C.C. § 9–301, cmnt. 6 (2001 version).

jurisdiction.[42] Security interests that require the filing of a financing statement for perfection and are not subject to the debtor-location nexus generally also receive the benefit of the four-month period to file a financing statement in the new state.[43] "Gaps" in perfection are treated harshly, as the security interest "becomes unperfected and is deemed never to have been perfected as against a previous or subsequent purchaser of the collateral for value."[44]

c. *Goods Covered by a Certificate of Title*

§ 19.19 It has long been the theory and hope that most mobile goods, such as vehicles, would be covered by certificates of title issued by the state of registration, the transfer of which was necessary to affect the title of the goods and that all ownership and security interests would appear on the face of the certificate.[1] This is the theory behind Uniform Commercial Code Section 9–103(2).[2] Progress proved to be slow. First, the 1962 Uniform Commercial Code contained serious ambiguities that resulted in different constructions in different states,[3] particularly as to scope of coverage of the statutes both as to circumstances and nature of the goods, such as, boats, trailers, etc. Secondly, states were slow in adopting statutes making title certificates the mandatory and exclusive means of perfecting security interests. It was not until 1978 that Oklahoma adopted such a statute[4] so that all states now have them. The 1972 revision of Article 9 attempted to remove the ambiguities of the 1962 Code so interstate differences should be reduced along with the number of problems in, this area. Even so, the remaining variations among the states[5] and Canadian provinces[6] provide continuing potential for choice-of-law problems.

One of the major problems under the 1962 Code related to the protection to be given a purchaser relying on a clean local certificate of title. The problem was particularly acute for the nonprofessional consumer purchaser who bought an automobile with a clean local certificate from a local dealer, a buyer who had no genuine opportunity for self-protection. The 1972 revision deals with this problem by protecting such a purchaser "who is not in the business of selling goods of that kind to the extent that he gives value and receives delivery of the goods after issuance of the certificate and without knowledge of the security inter-

42. U.C.C. § 9–316(a)(3) (2001 version).

43. U.C.C. § 9–316(f)(2) (2001 version).

44. U.C.C. § 9–316(b) (2001 version).

§ 19.19

1. White & Summers, The Uniform Commercial Code 976 (2d ed, 1980).

2. Uniform Commercial Code § 9–103(2) (1972 version).

3. See R. Weintraub, Commentary on the Conflict of Laws 566 (4th ed. 2001); White & Summers, supra n.1, at 977.

4. 12A Okla. Stat. Ann. § 9–302(3), (4); 47 Okla. Stat. Ann. § 23.3 (1978).

5. See Meyers, Multi–State Motor Vehicle Transactions Under the U.C.C.: An Update, 30 Okla. L. Rev. 834, 892 (1977).

6. See IAC, Limited v. Princeton Porsche–Audi, 75 N.J. 379, 382 A.2d 1125 (1978); Associates Realty Credit Limited v. Brune, 89 Wn.2d 6, 568 P.2d 787 (1977).

est."[7] The certificate in such a case must neither show the security interest or indicate the possibility of undisclosed security interests. With the consumer buyer protected in this fashion, the remaining conflicts are among professionals who can protect themselves or take the known risks as they see fit in situations where there could possibly be two outstanding certificates of title.

The statute reduces the risks by providing that perfection of the security interest is governed by the law of the state "issuing the certificate" until four months after the removal of the goods from "that jurisdiction" and thereafter until the goods are registered elsewhere or the certificate surrendered.[8] After expiration of that time, the goods are no longer covered by that certificate. Since obtaining a new title certificate and transfer will require registration and usually surrender of the existing certificate, dual certificates should be a rarity. The practical operation of these provisions means that the original secured creditor has four months to locate the collateral and to take steps to protect himself by notifying the motor vehicle registration office of the state where the collateral is located, repossessing the collateral or taking other steps to restrain the debtor in possession from obtaining a clean title. Otherwise, after the four months have expired, the previous secured creditor is put at risk to the possibility of a clean local certificate being issued as the result of mistake or fraud, for the new clean certificate will take priority under the local law as the only viable certificate of title.[9]

Treatment under the 2001 version is perhaps the most straightforward. Section 9–303 provides that the local law "of the jurisdiction under whose certificate of title the goods are covered" covers all perfection and priority issues.[10] That local law governs until the certificate becomes ineffective under the issuing jurisdiction's law or the goods become covered under a certificate of title from another jurisdiction.[11] This issuing-jurisdiction nexus applies without regard to any other connection of the goods or the debtor to the issuing jurisdiction.[12] Sometimes non-uniform certificate of title statutes may differ from the U.C.C. on questions such as the period that a creditor has to refile in order to continue perfection of the security interest. In such cases, uniformity would counsel in favor of resolving the conflict in favor of the U.C.C. provision.[13]

d. Accounts, General Intangibles and Mobile Goods

§ 19.20 The most significant choice-of-law changes made by the 1972 version of Article 9 of the Uniform Commercial Code appear in

---

7. U.C.C. § 9–103(2)(d) (1972 version).

8. R. Weintraub, Commentary on the Conflict of Laws 580–82 (4th ed. 2001). Cf. In re Stults, 65 B.R. 652 (W.D.Mich. 1986); Community Credit Co. v. Gillham, 191 Neb. 198, 214 N.W.2d 384 (1974). But cf. Phil Phillips Ford, Inc. v. St. Paul Fire & Marine Insurance Co., 465 S.W.2d 933 (Tex.1971).

9. See White & Summers, supra n.1, at 979.

10. U.C.C. § 9–303(b) (2001 version).

11. U.C.C. § 9–303(b) (2001 version).

12. U.C.C. § 9–303(c) (2001 version).

13. See, e.g., In re Sorsby v. WFS Fin., Inc., 210 W.Va. 708, 559 S.E.2d 45 (W.V. 2001) (conflict between three-month period granted under non-uniform West Virginia enactment and four months granted under U.C.C. resolved in favor of U.C.C. rule).

Section 9–103(3) dealing with accounts, general intangibles and mobile goods not covered by certificates of title.[1] The 1962 Code referred issues concerning perfection and effect of security interests in accounts and contract rights to the state where the records were kept concerning the accounts or receivables,[2] while issues regarding general intangibles and mobile goods were referred to the location of the debtor's "chief place of business."[3] The difficult distinctions between accounts and contract rights on one hand and general intangibles on the other led to considerable confusion and double filing.[4] In addition, the place of record keeping by computer or accounting services had little relationship to credit investigations which centered on the debtor's location.[5] To avoid these difficulties, the 1972 revision deleted the confusing reference to contract rights and consolidated accounts and general intangibles, treating them together with uncertificated mobile goods by referring to the jurisdiction in which the debtor is located.

The section covers any account (other than those relating to minerals), and general intangibles (other than uncertificated securities). The mobile chattels that are covered "are of a type normally used in more than one jurisdiction, such as motor vehicles, trailers, ... construction machinery ... and the like, if the goods are equipment or are inventory leased or held for lease by the debtor to others, and are not covered by a certificate of title...."[6] Mobile equipment need not actually be used in more than one jurisdiction but only consist of the type normally so used,[7] but must be either equipment or inventory[8] that the debtor leases or holds for lease.

The principal purpose of the law in this area is to identify where financing statements should be filed to "allow subsequent creditors of the debtor-assignor to determine the true status of his affairs."[9] As the drafters suggest, this place should be one which creditors normally associate with the debtor and should be predictable with maximum certainty.[10] Since mobile goods may not stay long in one place and intangibles have no physical location, the situs rule fails as a reference to accommodate the purposes of the law.[11] The reference in Section 9–

---

§ 19.20

1. Uniform Commercial Code § 9–103(3) (1972 version).

2. U.C.C. § 9–103(1) (1962 version).

3. U.C.C. § 9–103(2) (1962 version). Cf. In re Dobbins, 371 F.Supp. 141 (D.Kan. 1973). See In re J.A. Thompson & Son, Inc., 665 F.2d 941 (9th Cir.1982) (applying the "chief place of business" test).

4. See R. Weintraub, Commentary on the Conflict of Laws 566 (4th ed. 2001); Gilmore, Security Interests in Personal Property § 12.5 (1965).

5. See White & Summers, The Uniform Commercial Code 988 (2d ed. 1980).

6. U.C.C. § 9–103(3) (1972 version).

7. U.C.C. § 9–103, cmnt. 5(b) (1972 version; comments 1978). See In re Dennis Mitchell Industries, Inc., 419 F.2d 349 (3d Cir.1969).

8. U.C.C. § 9–109 (1972 version).

9. U.C.C. § 9–103, cmnt. 5(a) (1972 version; cmnts. 1978).

10. U.C.C. § 9–103, cmnt. 5(a) (1972 version; cmnts. 1978).

11. Id.; White & Summers, supra n.5, at 987. See General Electric Credit Corp. v. Western Crane & Rigging Co., 184 Neb. 212, 166 N.W.2d 409 (1969). Cf. Susi v.

103(3) is to the law, including the conflict-of-laws rules,[12] of the "jurisdiction in which the debtor is located." The debtor's location is defined as (1) his place of business if he has but one, (2) as his chief executive office if he has more than one place of business and (3) otherwise as his residence. The definition of the debtor's location is designed to assure that the reference is to the place from which the debtor mainly manages the business operation related to the collateral;[13] the place where the availability of credit information about the debtor would be centered. Of course, chief executive offices and residences can be and are moved frequently. To accommodate this problem, the Code uses the four-month rule, contained in subsection one, and provides that a security interest becomes unperfected four months after a change of the debtor's location to another jurisdiction unless unperfected in the new jurisdiction.[14] Absent refiling in the new jurisdiction, the security interest is deemed to have been, unperfected as against a purchaser after the change.[15]

As discussed extensively above,[16] the 2001 version of Article 9 focuses heavily on the debtor-location nexus.[17] The default rule under the 2001 version is that the local law of the debtor's location governs perfection and priority issues.[18] As also discussed extensively above,[19] the debtor's location is determined by carefully drawn rules that generally "locate" individual debtors at their residence, unincorporated businesses at their chief executive office or sole place of business, and corporations and other registered entities at their place of registration.[20] A good deal of what was covered by Section 9–103(3) of the 1972 version will be subject to this general debtor-location nexus provided for in the 2001 version. A relocation of a debtor obviously leads to a change in the applicable law for security interests governed by the debtor-location nexus, though the 2001 version continues the principle of generally allowing four months for the creditor to refile.[21] Transfer of the collateral to a new debtor with a different location (as commonly happens with business reorganizations, mergers and the like) gives the creditor a full year to refile.[22]

Important categories of security interests, however, are subject to the situs nexus (in whole or in part) under the 2001 version. For

Belle Acton Stables, Inc., 360 F.2d 704 (2d Cir.1966), on remand 261 F.Supp. 219 (S.D.N.Y.1966).

12. See, e.g., In re Iroquois Energy Mgmt., LLC, 284 B.R. 28 (Bankr. W.D.N.Y. 2002).

13. U.C.C. § 9–103, cmnt. 5(c) (1972 version; cmnts. 1978); Bramble Transportation, Inc. v. Sam Senter Sales, Inc., 294 A.2d 104 (Del.1972).

14. U.C.C. § 9–103(3)(e) (1972 version).

15. Although the issue involves some uncertainty, the language of § 9–103(3)(e) (1972 version) would seem to indicate that, absent refiling within four months, a purchaser after the change during the four

months would prevail but a lien creditor or trustee in bankruptcy would not. Cf. White & Summers, supra n.5, at 989.

16. See supra § 19.18.

17. 9 U.C.C. § 9–301(1) (2001 version).

18. 9 U.C.C. § 9–301(1) (2001 version).

19. See supra § 19.18.

20. U.C.C. § 9–307 (2001 version).

21. U.C.C. § 9–301, cmnt. 6 (2001 version); U.C.C. § 9–316(a)(2001 version); U.C.C. § 9–316, cmnt. 2, ex. 1 (2001 version).

22. U.C.C. § 9–316(a)(3) (2001 version); U.C.C. § 9–316, cmnt. 2, ex. 4 (2001 version).

possessory security interests, the situs law determines perfection and priority issues.[23] Perfection and priority issues relative to security interests in fixtures and timber are also governed by the situs nexus.[24]

The 2001 version also provides that the local law of the situs determines *priority* issues if the collateral consists of "negotiable documents, goods, instruments, money, or tangible chattel paper...."[25] "Goods" is a particularly important category, as it is defined to include "all things movable when a security interest attaches," though it does not include "accounts, chattel paper, commercial tort claims, deposit accounts, documents, general intangibles, instruments, investment property, letter-of-credit rights, money, or oil, gas, or other minerals before extraction."[26] Questions of *perfection* (i.e., where to file), however, remain subject to the general debtor-location nexus.[27] This "bifurcated" approach is designed to allow creditors to file in the debtor's location (a location less likely to change than the collateral's situs), while respecting the authority of situs states to set the relative *priorities* of U.C.C. and non-U.C.C. (for example, judicial execution) liens.[28]

A separate section in the 2001 version applies to deposit accounts in banks. That provision—Section 9–304—provides that "[t]he local law of a bank's jurisdiction" governs perfection and priority issues regarding security interests in deposit accounts held at the bank.[29] The bank's jurisdiction is the jurisdiction expressly provided for in the account or agreed to between the bank and the customer-debtor, if there is one, and otherwise is the jurisdiction of the bank's office that maintains or services the account.[30] In the unlikely event that none of these rules produces a jurisdiction in which to place the bank, the bank's jurisdiction is situated in the state in which its chief executive offices are located.[31]

§ 19.21 International considerations are reflected in two provisions of Section 9–103(3) that modify the usual place of filing and choice-of-law reference. If the debtor is located outside the United States, the reference is to the law of the jurisdiction in the United States where the debtor has its major executive office in this country. Further if the debtor is located outside of both the United States and Canada and the collateral consists of accounts or general intangibles for money, the security interest can be perfected by notification of the account debtor.[1] Another exception is made when the debtor is a foreign air carrier under

---

23. U.C.C. § 9–301(2) (2001 version).

24. U.C.C. § 9–301(3) (2001 version); U.C.C. § 9–301, cmnt. 5, 6 (2001 version).

25. U.C.C. § 9–301(3) (2001 version).

26. U.C.C. § 9–102(a)(44) (2001 version).

27. U.C.C. § 9–301(1), (3) (2001 version); U.C.C. § 9–301, cmnt. 7 (2001 version).

28. U.C.C. § 9–301(1), (3) (2001 version); U.C.C. § 9–301, cmnt. 7 (2001 version).

29. U.C.C. § 9–304 (2001 version).

30. U.C.C. § 9–304(3), (4) (2001 version).

31. U.C.C. § 9–304(5) (2001 version).

§ 19.21

1. U.C.C. § 9–103(3)(c) (1972 version).

the Federal Aviation Act of 1958, in which event the reference is to the location of the designated agent for service of process.[2]

Although aircraft are included in the definition of mobile goods under Section 9–103(3)(a), it should be noted that the Federal Aviation Act[3] provides for recording with the Secretary of Transportation, any conveyance or instrument affecting title to any civil aircraft of the United States and that such instrument shall not be valid until so recorded.[4] However, the Federal Act also provides that the validity of any instrument to be recorded under it "shall be governed by the laws of the state ... in which such instrument is delivered, irrespective of the location or place of delivery of the property which is the subject of such instrument."[5] These confusing provisions raise difficult issues of federal preemption in which the state courts have more frequently found the Federal Act preemptive[6] than have federal courts.[7] The issue of federal preemption also exists regarding ships,[8] motor vehicles of more than 1000 pounds,[9] copyrights[10] and patents.[11]

In many situations involving these special kinds of mobile goods and intangibles, the practical course is to satisfy the recording requirements of both state and federal law.[12] In a related matter, the Supreme Court has indicated that even in an area of admitted federal preemption, security interests obtained by the Small Business Administration and the Farmer's Home Administration, the federal courts should look to state law for content and analogies of the federal common law, particularly to the Uniform Commercial Code.[13]

The 2001 version of Article 9 makes a considerable effort to address international concerns. As discussed extensively above,[14] the default rule under the 2001 version is to choose the local law of the debtor's location.[15] The debtor's location is determined by carefully drawn rules

2. U.C.C. § 9–103(3)(d) (1972 version).

3. 49 U.S.C.A. § 1403(a).

4. 49 U.S.C.A. § 1403(c).

5. 49 U.S.C.A. § 120.

6. E.g., Dowell v. Beech Acceptance Corp., 3 Cal.3d 544, 91 Cal.Rptr. 1, 476 P.2d 401 (1970), cert. denied 404 U.S. 823, 92 S.Ct. 45, 30 L.Ed.2d 50 (1971); O'Neill v. Barnett Bank, 360 So.2d 150 (Fla.App. 1978).

7. E.g., Sanders v. M.D. Aircraft Sales, Inc., 575 F.2d 1086 (3d Cir.1978); Haynes v. General Electric Credit Corp., 432 F.Supp. 763 (W.D.Va.1977), affirmed 582 F.2d 869 (4th Cir.1978). Industrial National Bank v. Butler Aviation International, Inc., 370 F.Supp. 1012 (E.D.N.Y.1974).

8. Federal Ship Mortgage Act, 46 U.S.C.A. § 951 et seq. (1976). See generally McDonnell, The Scope of Article 9, in Coogan, Hogan & Vagts, Secured Transactions Under the U.C.C., § 5A.10 (1979).

9. 49 U.S.C.A. § 14301.

10. The Copyright Act, 17 U.S.C.A. §§ 101, 301. See Note, Transfers of Copyrights for Security Under the New Copyright Act, 88 Yale L.J. 125 (1978).

11. The Patent Act, 35 U.S.C.A. § 1 et seq.

12. For an extensive discussion of the federal preemption issue in these areas, see McDonnell, The Scope of Article 9, Ch. 5A, Coogan, Hogan & Vagts, Secured Transactions Under the U.C.C., § 5A.10 (1979). See also supra §§ 3.49–3.50.

13. United States v. Kimbell Foods, Inc., 440 U.S. 715, 99 S.Ct. 1448, 59 L.Ed.2d 711 (1979), on remand 600 F.2d 478 (5th Cir.1979). See also United States v. Burlington Industries, 600 F.2d 517 (5th Cir.1979). See supra § 3.51 nn.6–8 and infra § 23.14 nn.11–14.

14. See supra § 19.18.

15. U.C.C. § 9–301(1) (2001 version).

that generally "locate" individual debtors at their residence, unincorporated businesses at their chief executive office or sole place of business, and corporations and other registered entities at their place of registration.[16] However, the 2001 version resists "locating" debtors in countries that do not make the existence of security interests publicly available. If the debtor would be so located, the Code assigns the debtor a "location" in the District of Columbia in an admirable effort to allow third parties to protect themselves through commercially reasonable efforts.[17] In close cases involving foreign debtors, secured parties are well advised to make an additional filing in the District of Columbia.

e. Chattel Paper

§ 19.22 Chattel paper and security interests in it are hybrids having characteristics of both tangibles and intangibles.[1] As a consequence, security interests in chattel paper[2] are treated differently under the 1972 version of Section 9–103(4)[3] depending on the manner in which the security interests are perfected. If the interest is perfected by taking possession of the chattel paper, the reference is to the location of the paper at the time possession is obtained, i.e., the chattel rule of Section 9–103(1). On the other hand, if the security interest is perfected by filing, i.e., is a nonpossessory security interest, the collateral is treated as an intangible and the location of the debtor controls under Section 9–103(3). Under this approach, it is possible to have competing perfected security interests, one by possession and one by filing. Ordinarily the first to perfect prevails, but, if the creditor who perfects the security interest by possession can demonstrate that possession was taken only after giving new value for the paper in the ordinary course of business and without knowledge of the existing security interest, the possessory creditor can prevail even if his security interest was perfected after the non-possessory creditor's security interest.[4]

Under the 2001 version, the situs connection generally determines the applicable law with regard to questions of priority. The local law of the state in which "negotiable documents, goods, instruments, money, or tangible chattel paper is located governs" priority issues.[5] Questions of perfection (i.e., where to file) remain subject to the general debtor-location nexus.[6] This bifurcated approach is designed to preserve the authority of situs states to set priorities as between U.C.C. and non-

---

16. U.C.C. § 9–307 (2001 version).

17. U.C.C. § 9–307(c) (2001 version).

§ 19.22

1. Murray, Choice of Laws and Multi Sale Transactions Under Article 9, Ch. 5B in Coogan, Hogan & Vagts, Secured Transactions under U.C.C. § 5B.–06[6] (1980).

2. Uniform Commercial Code § 9–105 (1972 version).

3. Uniform Commercial Code § 9–103(4) (1972 version).

4. U.C.C. § 9–308 (1972 version). See White & Summers, The Uniform Commercial Code 990 (2d ed. 1980).

5. U.C.C. § 9–301(3) (2001 version).

6. U.C.C. § 9–301(1), (3) (2001 version); U.C.C. § 9–301, cmnt. 7 (2001 version).

U.C.C. liens, while maintaining the general preference under the 2001 version for filing in the debtor's location.[7]

Questions of both priority and perfection for possessory security interests of all kinds are governed by the local law of the situs of the collateral.[8] The situs nexus here poses no risk to the creditor while he remains in possession of the collateral.

f. Minerals

§ 19.23 Another group of hybrid property interests are those in minerals and oil and gas in place which attach on extraction, such as, the participating interest or royalty in an oil lease. These interests may be transferred, divided, or encumbered by many persons in, many different situations. Since the purpose of the choice-of-law rules in this area is to identify a place for filing financing statements that is convenient and appropriate for the parties and the public, a special rule is provided in Section 9–103(5)[1] that relates neither to the location of the paper nor the parties but rather refers to the location of the wellhead or minehead.[2] This reference has the advantage of certainty and acceptance in the oil and gas industry growing out of an historically more direct relationship between owners and these interests in land.[3] It provides the prospective creditor with both a single record to search and a single place to file which can easily be determined[4] without regard to the various accounts or parties involved. These considerations are rational reasons for the reference to the wellhead by location rather than reaching this result by simply characterizing such ownership interests as "land" for all purposes.

The 2001 version of the Code continues this nexus. Section 9–301(6) provides that "[t]he local of the jurisdiction in which the wellhead or minehead is located governs the perfection, effect of perfection or non-perfection, and the priority of a security interest in as-extracted collateral."[5] Essentially the same rule governs, as another provision makes clear that "[t]he local law of the jurisdiction in which timber is to be cut" governs perfection and priority issues.[6] Post-extraction resources, however, are defined as "goods"[7] and thus treated under the more general rules that point to the situs of the goods.[8]

g. Uncertificated Securities and Other Investment Property

7. U.C.C. § 9–301(1), (3) (2001 version); U.C.C. § 9–301, cmnt. 7 (2001 version).

8. U.C.C. § 9–301(2) (2001 version).

§ 19.23

1. Uniform Commercial Code § 9–103(5) (1972 version).

2. See Coogan, Hogan & Vagts, Secured Transactions Under the Uniform Commercial Code, § 3A.06[6] (1973).

3. See U.C.C. § 11–103, cmnt. 8 (1978).

4. White & Summers, The Uniform Commercial Code, 991 (2d ed. 1980).

5. U.C.C. § 9–301(6) (2001 version).

6. U.C.C. § 9–301(5) (2001 version).

7. U.C.C. § 9–102(a)(45) (2001 version)

8. U.C.C. § 9–301(3) (2001 version).

§ **19.24** In 1977, Article 8 of the Uniform Commercial Code, dealing with investment securities was substantially revised. Incident to those changes in Article 8, Section 9–103(6)[1] was added to Article 9. An uncertificated security is a share or other participation in property or an enterprise of the issuer or an obligation of the issuer which is not represented by an instrument but which share is registered on the issuer's books, is one of a class or series of interests in the issuer, and is of a type commonly dealt with in securities markets.[2] Consistent with the choice of law reference to the law of the jurisdiction, in which the issuer is organized as to rights and obligations of the issuer with respect to securities under Article 8,[3] Section 9–103(6) refers to the same law to govern the perfection, and effect of perfection or nonperfection of a security interest in uncertificated securities.

The 2001 version makes a comprehensive effort to deal with security interests in investment property, which includes certificated and uncertificated securities, securities accounts, and commodities contracts and accounts.[4] The debtor's location[5] provides the nexus if the security interest is perfected by filing or by the automatic perfection rules.[6]

If the method of perfection is otherwise, the situs nexus generally governs. For certificated securities, the governing law as to perfection and priority is determined by the situs of the certificate.[7] For uncertificated securities, the issuer's jurisdiction—as set forth under U.C.C. Section 8–110(d)—provides the nexus. For securities accounts, the governing law as to perfection and priority is determined by the securities intermediary's jurisdiction under U.C.C. Section 8–110(e).[8] Section 8–110(e) generally places the securities intermediary in the jurisdiction set forth in the agreement between the parties, and failing such an agreement generally points to the jurisdiction in which the office handling the account is located.[9] In the case of commodities accounts and contracts, the commodity intermediary's jurisdiction provides the nexus.[10] A commodity intermediary's jurisdiction is determined by a set of rules much like those for securities intermediaries (and for banks holding deposit accounts[11]); those rules generally respect express agreements or designations, but failing some such express statement favor the jurisdiction in which the office handling the account is located.[12]

h. Renvoi

§ **19.25** In each of the subsections of Section 9–103, reference is directed to the law of a particular jurisdiction, including its conflict of

---

§ 19.24

1. Uniform Commercial Code § 9–103(6) (1972 version amended 1978).

2. U.C.C. § 8–102(1)(b).

3. U.C.C. § 8–106.

4. U.C.C. § 9–102(a)(45) (2001 version).

5. See supra § 19.18 for a discussion of the rules determining a debtor's location under § U.C.C. 9–307 (2001 version).

6. U.C.C. § 9–305(c) (2001 version).

7. U.C.C. § 9–305(a)(1) (2001 version).

8. U.C.C. § 9–305(a)(2) (2001 version).

9. U.C.C. § 8–110(e) (2001 version).

10. U.C.C. § 9–305(a)(4) (2001 version).

11. See supra § 19.20.

12. U.C.C. § 9–305(b) (2001 version).

laws rules. This is a form of statutory renvoi[1] that appears to have been included to assure uniformity of treatment between the forum, the state to which it is referred by its choice of law and any other state whose law would be applied by the state chosen by the forum. If all states involved have the same rule, for instance, the 1972 version of the U.C.C., there is no difficulty. If however, different versions exist, as for example, the 1962 Code's reference to the place accounts are kept and the 1972 Revision's reference to the location of the debtor, some confusion is possible. However, the purpose of the choice-of-law reference is to achieve uniformity with the chosen rule of the other state. In this setting, that may mean that the older rule might be applied if the forum had the revision and the state to which reference is made had the 1962 rule. Still the goal of uniformity probably would be achieved, even if the practical result is to lead the cautious creditor to file in both states, for that is what should be done when the law is in a state of flux. Hence the parenthetical inclusion of conflict of laws rules may remind the legal advisor of the creditor of the need for double filing. If the circumstances are reversed, the forum with the older rule may be able ultimately to apply the newer rule but in any event it will be achieving the desired conformity during the period of transition.

Renvoi is not an issue under the 2001 version of Article 9, as its choice-of-law provisions consistently and explicitly refer to "the local law" of the connected jurisdiction.[2] The comments make clear that this is an intentional effort to avoid renvoi issues that arise under the 1972 version.[3]

3. *Treaties*

§ 19.26 The United States has not become party to the Hague Convention on the Law Applicable to International Sales of Goods[1] or to that governing transfer of title on sale.[2] The first of these conventions applies to the contractual aspects of the sale and risks between the

§ 19.25

1. See Restatement, Second, Conflict of Laws § 222, cmnt. (e) (1971); supra §§ 3.13–3.14; cf. In Matter of Kokomo Times Publishing & Printing Co., 301 F.Supp. 529 (S.D.Ind.1968).

2. See U.C.C. §§ 9–301—9–307 (2001 version).

3. See U.C.C. § 9–301, cmnt. 3, example 1 (2001 version).

§ 19.26

1. See Seventh Hague Conference on Private International Law, 1 Am. J. Comp. L. 275 (1952).

2. Eighth Hague Conference on Private International Law, Draft Convention on the Law Governing the Transfer of Title in International Sales of Goods, 5 Am. J. Comp. L. 650 (1956). Neither has the United States become a party to the Draft Convention on the Jurisdiction of the Selected Forum in the Case of International Sale of Goods, 5 Am. J. Comp. L. 653 (1956), or the Convention Relating to a Uniform Law on the International Sales of Goods or its annexed Uniform Law on the International Sale of Goods, 3 Am. Soc. Int'l L., Int'l Leg. Mats. 855 (1964). Article II of the Uniform Law excludes rules of private international law, a provision which has caused considerable comment. See Nadelmann, The Uniform Law on the International Sale of Goods: A Conflict of Laws Imbroglio, 74 Yale L.J. 449 (1965); Tunc, A Reply to

original parties and excludes the matter with which we are concerned, i.e., the effects of the sale as respects all persons other than the parties.[3] The convention on the transfer of title uses an approach similar to the 1972 version of Article 9 of the Uniform Commercial Code and refers to the place where goods are located at the time a claim or interest comes into existence.[4] A better-received effort by the United Nations Commission on International Trade Law was the U.N. Convention on Contracts for the International Sale of Goods, approved by a conference of sixty-two states in 1980, and in force in the United States since 1988. Although Article 4(b) of the U.N. convention states that it is not concerned with the effect of the contract on the property, Article 42 does refer to the place where goods are to be resold for the determination of certain third party claims.[5]

An international system of recording, recognizing, and enforcing rights in aircraft is established by the Convention on the International Recognition of Rights in Aircraft to which the United States is a party.[6] This treaty controls over the law of an individual state of the United States.[7] The parties to the treaty undertake to recognize rights of property in aircraft including mortgages and similar rights which accord with the law of the nation, a party to the treaty, in which the aircraft was registered and the right recorded. The ranking of successive recordings is determined by the law of the state of registration at the time of recording.[8] Following the pattern of other certification of title systems, the convention requires all recorded rights to appear on the same record and the address of the record must be shown on the aircraft's certificate of registration. The rights of third parties are determined by the place of recording. The only exception to the priority of record appears to be claims for salvage or preservation of the aircraft by the law of the state where salvage occurs. The treaty details methods of foreclosure and

Professor Nadelmann: The Uniform Law on the International Sale of Goods, 74 Yale L.J. 1409 (1965). See also supra § 18.24 n.2. As to decisions of European courts relating to the effect of a change of situs of encumbered movables, see Schilling, Some European Decisions on Non–Possessory Security Rights in Private International Law, 34 Int'l & Comp. L.Q. 87 (1985).

3. Article 5.

4. See, e.g., Article 3 (transfer of title as to persons other than parties to the contract is governed by internal law of the country where the goods were located at the time when a claim was made concerning them).

5. See Honnold, U.N. Convention on Contracts for the International Sale of Goods 1980, 5 World Trade L. 265 (1981); Honnold, Overview, 27 Am. J. Comp. L. 223–26 (1979); Convention on International Sales, 19 Int'l Leg. Mats. 668, 671 (1980); D. Perratt, The Vienna Convention 1980, 1

Int'l. Contr. L. & Fin. Rev. 577 (1980). See also supra § 18.24 n.2.

6. The Convention on the International Recognition of Rights in Aircraft, entered into force for the United States on September 17, 1953, 4 U.S.T. 186630; TIAS 2847; 310 U.N.T.S. 151. The United States Ship Mortgage Act deals with ship mortgages, both domestic and foreign. For an analysis of the requirements under 46 U.S.C.A. § 951 for recognition of a foreign ship mortgage, see Morgan Guaranty Trust Co. v. Hellenic Lines Ltd., 621 F.Supp. 198 (S.D.N.Y.1985). See also A/S Kreditt–Finans v. Cia Venetico de Navegacion S.A. of Panama, 560 F.Supp. 705 (E.D.Pa.1983), affirmed 729 F.2d 1446 (3d Cir. 1984).

7. See, e.g., Triad Int'l Maintenance Corp. v. Guernsey Air Leasing, Ltd., 178 F. Supp. 2d 547 (M.D.N.C. 2001).

8. See *Triad Int'l Maintenance Corp.,* 178 F. Supp. 2d at 553.

protects the purchaser on foreclosure if the sale procedure complies with its provisions. This treaty replaces the provisions of otherwise applicable Uniform Commercial Code provisions.[9]

III. INTANGIBLES

A. INTRODUCTION

§ 19.27 The determination of the relevant law in the transfer of intangibles presents a different question from that of land and tangible chattels. It is easy to see that both land and chattels are located, and have their "situs," in a given state. It is also apparent that the law of that state may be significant as to what may be done with either land or chattels and the method of doing it. But, if a person has a claim against another arising out of contract or otherwise, and wishes to transfer this claim to a third person or to encumber it to secure a loan, there is little to suggest an analogy to the situs concerns incident to transfers of tangibles. It is obvious that this intangible claim has no actual location, but rather the concerns relate to the people involved and notice to the public so third parties may not be misled. Even so, the cases have for different purposes occasionally attributed a situs to intangibles.

Most, though not all, intangibles arise out of consensual transactions, i.e., contracts, and the transfer is usually a consensual transaction, i.e., assignment. However, the value of the intangible and its transfer and use for security purposes is often viewed as a property question, and when the intangible is chattelized in a document, the analogies to property predominate.

The analysis of this mixed problem of contract and property considerations is perhaps aided if the development of the rules of the law concerning the assignment of choses in action be kept in mind. Early common law doctrine considered the personal relation of obligor and obligee to be a vital part of the obligation, which could not be changed.[1] Assignment therefore was not allowed under that concept. But, it came to be recognized that the assignor could give the assignee a power of attorney to collect money, and the latter could keep what was recovered. Later, this was recognized as a transfer of property interests in contract rights. Equity courts protected the assignee for value, and the law courts subsequently recognized and applied the rules first developed in chancery for the transfer of interests in intangibles.

B. ASSIGNABILITY OF INTANGIBLE

§ 19.28 In considering the law that should apply to the assignment of an intangible, it is perhaps helpful to note first the nature of the

---

9. See U.C.C. § 9–103, comment 5(f) (1972 version; 1978 comments).

§ 19.27

1. A scholarly discussion of the traditional common law governing assignments is found in Corbin on Contracts § 856 (1951).

interest, the intangible, that is the subject of the purported assignment. For example, if the intangible is an interest in a trust, or wages arising out of employment, it would seem necessary to look first to the trust instrument, or the employment relationship, and their governing law, to determine whether the intangible is subject to being assigned to another. The issue of assignability of an intangible would seem to be most closely related to the original transaction out of which the obligation arose and hence should be determined by the law most significantly related to that original transaction and the parties to it, with respect to the issue of assignability. For example, whether an interest under a trust is subject to being assigned should be determined by the law of the state most significantly related to the trust as regards assignability,[1] and if the intangible is a contractual right, assignability would be determined by the law of the state that is most significantly related to the contract and the parties with regard to that issue of assignability.[2] Preference to the original transaction from which the intangible arose seems desirable because the assignability issue revolves around a consideration as to whether the obligation of the obligor is so personal that it cannot be discharged by performance to anyone other than the originally named obligee. This issue relates to the original parties to the original transaction rather than to the parties to the assignment itself. However, it is also clear that because a nonassignable intangible is an exception to the norm the expectations of the assignor and assignee that the interest is assignable should be protected unless the interests and policies relating to the original transaction demand that the interest be viewed as nonassignable.[3]

Assignability is not normally a problem with commercial paper. In dealing with a commercial intangible the analogous question is usually whether the interest is only assignable or whether it is also negotiable. The usual view in the United States is that the place of payment of commercial paper determines whether or not it is negotiable.[4] The reference to the place of payment for determining issues of negotiability with regard to commercial paper seems appropriate in that, after issuance, the parties to the paper have one principal thing in mind, that is,

---

§ 19.28

1. See, e.g., Hardy v. Hardy, 164 Cal. App.2d 77, 330 P.2d 278 (1958), 181 Cal. App.2d 317, 5 Cal.Rptr. 110 (1960). Cf. In re Freeman, 489 F.2d 431 (9th Cir.1973); Schrader v. Smith, 10 Misc.2d 475, 169 N.Y.S.2d 797 (1958); Caddie Homes, Inc. v. Falic, 211 Pa.Super. 333, 235 A.2d 437 (1967); 11 U.S.C.A. § 522(6).

2. Restatement, Second, Conflict of Laws § 208 (1971). See, e.g., Fox–Greenwald Sheet Metal Co. v. Markowitz Brothers, Inc., 452 F.2d 1346 (D.C.Cir.1971); Newspaper Readers Service, Inc. v. Canonsburg Pottery Co., 146 F.2d 963 (3d Cir. 1945); Wetherell Brothers Co. v. United States Steel Co., 105 F.Supp. 81 (D.Mass. 1952), affirmed 200 F.2d 761 (1st Cir.1952); Detroit Greyhound Employees Federal Credit Union v. Aetna Life Insurance Co., 7 Mich.App. 430, 151 N.W.2d 852 (1967), rev'd on other grounds 381 Mich. 683, 167 N.W.2d 274 (1969).

3. Cf. Downs v. The American Mutual Liability Insurance Co., 19 A.D.2d 376, 243 N.Y.S.2d 640 (1963), aff'd 14 N.Y.2d 266, 251 N.Y.S.2d 19, 200 N.E.2d 204 (1964).

4. See Restatement, Second, Conflict of Laws § 214 (1971). Cf. Lorenzen, The Conflict of Laws Relating to Bills and Notes 128 (1919); Stumberg, Commercial Paper and the Conflict of Laws, 6 Vand. L. Rev. 489 (1953).

payment at maturity at the place of payment, where presentment needs to be made. The policy of the law relating to commercial paper favors the protection of third parties taking an instrument in the usual course of business wherever it is transferred. This policy to further circulation and protect purchasers who take the paper on its face would seem to indicate that as against the maker and primary parties on the paper, there is little reason not to hold an instrument negotiable if it has that character by either the place of making, the place of payment, or the place of transfer. This would mean that third parties would be protected by any law under which they reasonably take the paper for value without notice of a defect and which law would validate the transfer.[5] Although the Uniform Commercial Code does not contain a specific choice-of-law rule for determining negotiability of commercial paper, many cases have historically relied upon the presumption that the parties intended that the law of the place of payment should govern.[6]

C. ASSIGNMENT OF INTANGIBLES

1. Introduction

§ 19.29 As noted above, when the law began to recognize the rights under a contract as transferable choses in action,[1] it became clear that the assignment of an intangible represented a transaction independent of the original transaction. Consequently, although the law most significantly related to the original transaction on the issue of assignability determines whether it could be assigned, the issues relating to the assignment itself, such as its validity, are subject to the law appropriately applicable to the assignment as a separate transaction. The assignment itself is a consensual agreement between the assignor and the assignee and as a separate consensual agreement its validity should be viewed as an ordinary contract issue in which the choice of law is subject to the party's control.[2] Absent a choice of law by the parties, an assignment's validity should be determined by the law most closely related to the assignment.[3] However, the parties to the assignment could

5. Cf. Uniform Commercial Code § 3–202; Restatement, Second, Conflict of Laws § 216 (1971).

6. See, e.g., Youngstown Sheet & Tube Co. v. Westcott, 147 F.Supp. 829 (W.D.Okla. 1957); McCornick & Co. v. Tolmie Brothers, 46 Idaho 544, 269 P. 96 (1928). It is arguable that this presumption of intention should be viewed as an agreement to have the law of the place of payment govern under Uniform Commercial Code § 1–105.

§ 19.29

1. Corbin on Contracts § 856 (1951).

2. Cf. Uniform Commercial Code § 1–105.

3. Dekorwin v. First National Bank of Chicago, 318 F.2d 176 (7th Cir.1963), cert.

denied 375 U.S. 922, 84 S.Ct. 266, 11 L.Ed.2d 165 (1963); Franklin Life Insurance Co. v. Falkingham, 229 F.2d 300 (7th Cir.1956); Callwood v. Virgin Islands National Bank, 221 F.2d 770 (3d Cir.1955); Dix v. Pineda, 205 F.2d 957 (9th Cir.1953); New England Mutual Life Insurance Co. v. Spence, 104 F.2d 665 (2d Cir.1939); Russell v. Grigsby, 168 Fed. 577 (6th Cir.1909); Appeal of Colburn, 74 Conn. 463, 51 A. 139 (1902); Glover v. Wells, 140 Ill. 102, 29 N.E. 680 (1892); Barbin v. Moore, 85 N.H. 362, 159 A. 409 (1932); Spencer v. Myers, 150 N.Y. 269, 44 N.E. 942 (1896); Restatement, Second, Conflict of Laws § 209 (1971). Cf. Tannerfors v. American Fidelity Fire Insurance Co., 535 F.2d 1247 (3d Cir.1976); American Optical Co. v. Curtiss, 56 F.R.D. 26 (S.D.N.Y.1971); Witt v. Realist, Inc., 18

not themselves control all of the rights that might arise with regard to subsequent parties who may acquire an interest in the transaction.[4]

2. Assignments for the Benefit of Creditors

§ 19.30 The practical importance of the rules governing general assignments for the benefit of creditors has disappeared in consequence of the federal bankruptcy act.[1] However, voluntary arrangements to secure creditors continue to be important, and range from the usual credit securing arrangements normally incident to any solvent business, to those credit arrangements which, under pressure of worried creditors, more nearly approach the earlier general assignment. The influence of the 1972 version of the Uniform Commercial Code Section 9–103, is significant in this area as most of the intangibles assigned will be receivables covered by those provisions.[2] As we have seen, the perfection of security interests in ordinary chattels under the Uniform Commercial Code is governed by the law of the jurisdiction where the collateral is located when the security interest is perfected.[3] On the other hand, the perfection of security interests in accounts, general intangibles and mobile goods under the 1972 version of the U.C.C. is governed by the law of the jurisdiction in which the debtor is located[4] which is the debtor's place of business if he has one, his chief executive office if the debtor has more than one place of business, and otherwise at the debtor's residence.[5] This approach seems consistent with the earlier authorities regarding general assignments for the benefit of creditors, both as to chattels[6] or intangibles[7] even though the earlier cases often preferred the debtor's domicile. Conceding that there is need for a single reference,

Wis.2d 282, 118 N.W.2d 85 (1962). See also supra § 18.38 nn.8–10, on assignment of contract rights. See also Boston Safe Deposit and Trust Co. v. Paris, 15 Mass.App.Ct. 686, 447 N.E.2d 1268, 1271 (1983) ("It is not doubted that Massachusetts law governs Paris's right to assign or otherwise deal with his interest in the trust, as the Commonwealth had the most significant relation to this subject."); RCA Corp. v. Tucker, 696 F.Supp. 845 (E.D.N.Y.1988) (issue of whether a conveyance is fraudulent as to a creditor is a tort issue calling for a tort choice-of-law approach rather than property law approach).

4. See Restatement, Second, Conflict of Laws § 209 (1971).

§ 19.30

1. 11 U.S.C.A. § 101 et seq. See infra § 23.11.

2. U.C.C. § 9–103(3) (1972 version). See, e.g., In re Iroquois Energy Mgmt., LLC, 284 B.R. 28 (Bankr. W.D.N.Y. 2002).

3. See U.C.C. § 9–103(1) (1972 version); see supra § 19.18.

4. U.C.C. § 9–103(3) (1972 version).

5. U.C.C. § 9–103(3)(d) (1972 version).

6. Livermore v. Jenckes, 62 U.S. (21 How.) 126, 16 L.Ed. 55 (1858); First National Bank of Rockville v. Walker, 61 Conn. 154, 23 A. 696 (1891); Train v. Kendall, 137 Mass. 366 (1884); J.M. Atherton Co. v. Ives, 20 Fed. 894 (D.Ky.1884); Judd v. J.W. Forsinger Co., 117 N.J.L. 35, 186 A. 525 (1936). Cf. Restatement, Second, Conflict of Laws § 250 (1971). But see Woodward v. Brooks, 128 Ill. 222, 227, 20 N.E. 685, 687 (1889).

7. Caskie v. Webster, 5 Fed. Cas. 271, No. 2,500 (E.D.Pa. 1851); Egbert v. Baker, 58 Conn. 319, 20 A. 466 (1890); Birdseye v. Baker, 82 Ga. 142, 7 S.E. 863 (1888); Howard National Bank v. King, 10 Abb.N.C. 346 (N.Y. 1881). The reason assigned was frequently that the claims have a situs at the assignor's domicile. See In re Dalpay, 41 Minn. 532, 43 N.W. 564 (1889). Contra: Kimball v. Plant, 14 La. 10 (1839); Zipcey v. Thompson, 67 Mass. (1 Gray) 243 (1854); Martin v. L. Potter & Co., 34 Vt. 87 (1861).

such as to the location of the debtor, as regards both tangibles and intangibles in the case of the general assignment for benefit of creditors, the jurisdictional reach of effective state law to deal with insolvencies is unclear. In view of the approach taken by the Uniform Commercial Code and the jurisdictional concepts that seem to prevail, it appears that state insolvency proceedings will likely be limited to concepts of jurisdiction based upon assets within the states, i.e., situs as to tangibles, and the residence or location of the debtor as regards intangibles.[8] Any attempt by a state under its procedure to prefer resident creditors over creditors of another state seems clearly invalid as a denial of equal protection.[9]

As discussed extensively above,[10] under the 2001 version of the Uniform Commercial Code the debtor-location nexus generally determines the applicable local law with regard to intangibles. Certain kinds of "intangibles," however, such as tangible chattel paper, are subject to the situs nexus.[11] In any event, it seems unlikely that the 2001 version of the Uniform Commercial Code, which makes the debtor's location the default nexus,[12] will disturb the common law preference for the debtor-location nexus in this area.

3. Commercial Assignments

§ 19.31 Although the parties to an assignment may control the applicable law as between themselves, the most difficult issues with regard to assignments relate to subsequent assignments or claims by third parties. Consequently, the significant issues relate to providing a predictable place for assignees to file a financing statement where subsequent parties can make a search to inform themselves regarding the debtor's assets. This calls for rules which are more nearly fixed and of certain predictability. This is the purpose of the Uniform Commercial Code; as most assignments will be commercial assignments, the rights of third parties are, in the United States, probably going to be controlled by the commercial practice reflected in the Uniform Commercial Code. Under the 1972 version of the Uniform Commercial Code, the perfection of a security interest in documents of title, negotiable instruments, or certified securities, is treated in the same fashion as for ordinary goods and must comply with the law of the state in which the collateral is when the last event occurs that perfects the security interest.[1] Accounts, general intangibles and chattel paper are linked together with mobile

8. See, e.g., In re Iroquois Energy Mgmt., LLC, 284 B.R. 28 (W.D.N.Y. 2002). Cf. Nadelmann, The National Bankruptcy Act and the Conflict of Laws, 59 Harv. L. Rev. 1025, 1046 (1946); Nadelmann, Legal Treatment of Foreign and Domestic Creditors, 11 Law & Contemp. Prob. 696 (1946). See infra §§ 23.10, 23.12–23.15.

9. Blake v. McClung, 172 U.S. 239, 19 S.Ct. 165, 43 L.Ed. 432 (1898). However, the extent of debtor's exemptions from creditors may be viewed as determined by the state of the domicile of the debtor as

being the state of the dominant interest. See In re Pederson, 105 B.R. 622 (D.Colo. 1989).

10. See supra §§ 19.18, 19.20.

11. See supra § 19.22.

12. U.C.C. § 9–301(1) (2001 version); see also supra § 19.18.

§ 19.31

1. U.C.C. § 9–103(1); see supra § 19.18.

goods and perfection of the security interest is governed by the law of the jurisdiction in which the debtor is located.[2] The 2001 version of the Uniform Commercial Code,[3] as a default rule chooses the debtor's location as the nexus for determining the applicable law,[4] but chooses the situs nexus for important categories of collateral, including most tangibles as well as collateral subject to a certificate of title.[5]

If the subject matter of the transaction is commercial paper, such as a negotiable instrument or a negotiable document of title, additional considerations need to be raised. Transactions dealing with commercial paper are usually outright transactions for value, and if commercial paper is used for collateral, the security interest is usually enforced by possession rather than a non-possessory claim of the nature which would be treated under Article 9. As a consequence, nearly all transactions involving negotiable paper are viewed differently than assignments of other intangibles. While the paper on which the obligation of a negotiable instrument is written may be viewed, only as evidence of the chose in action in which the holder has property, the paper is treated in the commercial world and by the law as having a much greater significance. The law relating to bills and notes developed under the law merchant; early common law rules about the nonassignability of choses in action played a small part in their history. They pass from hand to hand by indorsement and delivery; are subjects of larceny; are subject to attachment and may be levied upon in execution; in other words, they are treated as tangible property, i.e., the interests are chattelized in the instrument itself.[6] The conclusion from these considerations is that the transfer of such an instrument is to be governed by the law regulating the transfer of tangibles, the law of the situs of the instrument at the time of the transfer.[7] This is consistent with the purpose of commercial law and the Uniform Commercial Code, that the paper carry its story on its face so that it may be accepted or rejected without delay in the marketplace where it is found at the time of the transfer. This is particularly significant when the rights of parties subsequent to the original transaction such as holders or endorsers are involved. The ordinary method of transfer of negotiable instrument is by endorsement and delivery and necessarily involves dealing with the instrument itself. Even if the transfer is by assignment, the assignment will in practically all cases be coupled with delivery of the instrument. So the same approach is taken whether the question is considered one of assignment, negotiation, or a transfer of tangible property. Under the approach of the 1972 version of the Uniform Commercial Code, should the assignment purportedly take place elsewhere than where the instrument is located, and the rules of the two jurisdictions be different, the rule of the situs

---

2. U.C.C. § 9–103(3), (4); see supra §§ 19.20–19.21. Cf. United Bank Limited v. Cosmic International, Inc., 542 F.2d 868 (2d Cir.1976).

3. See supra § 19.18.

4. U.C.C. § 9–301(1) (2001 version).

5. U.C.C. § 9–301(3), (4) (2001 version); U.C.C. § 9–303 (2001 version).

6. Cf U.C.C. §§ 3–202, 9–106.

7. Cf. U.C.C. § 9–103(1); Restatement, Second, Conflict of Laws §§ 216, 244 (1971).

should prevail.[8] The 2001 version of the Uniform Commercial Code also chooses the situs nexus for possessory security interests.[9]

D. CORPORATE STOCK

§ 19.32   A share of stock in a corporation is a chose in action or intangible of a peculiar kind. The stock of the corporation represents the rights and duties of its stockholders and each share represents its fraction of all of the rights of ownership as well as the duties incident to ownership.[1] The share is generally represented by a certificate, which, by mercantile custom, is an instrument of value that is significant in the transfer of interests in the corporation.[2] So far as the dealings of the parties are to effect a change of relationship with the corporation, the law of the place of incorporation governs.[3] But the whole law of the state of incorporation is relevant and nearly all states provide that the transfer of the certificate transfers the ownership of the share itself.[4] When this is the law of the place of incorporation, then the law of the place where the certificate is located at the time of transfer will govern.[5] By the same reasoning, the same steps necessary to perfect the assignment of shares as against the corporation or attaching creditors of the assignor are governed by the whole law of the state in which the company is incorporated[6] and all of the American states except Delaware require attachment of the certificate.[7]

As between the assignor and assignee, the effect of an assignment as a contract[8] or the transfer of the certificate will be governed by the law

---

8. United States v. Guaranty Trust Co., 293 U.S. 340, 55 S.Ct. 221, 79 L.Ed. 415 (1934); Clanton v. Barnes, 50 Ala. 260 (1874); Brook v. Van Nest, 58 N.J.L. 162, 33 A. 382 (1895); Koechlin v. Kestenbaum Brothers (1927), 1 K.B. 889; Embiricos v. Anglo–Austrian Bank (1905), 1 K.B. 677. Cf. United States v. Arnhold & S. Bleichroeder, Inc., 96 F.Supp. 240 (S.D.N.Y.1951); Everett v. Vendryes, 19 N.Y. 436 (1859); Farmers' & Mechanics' National Bank v. Loftus, 133 Pa. 97, 19 A. 347 (1890); Restatement, Second, Conflict of Laws § 216 (1971). For further discussion, see Lorenzen, The Conflict of Laws Relating to Bills and Notes 134 (1919); Falconbridge, Conflict of Laws 294 (1947); Goodrich, Conflict Niceties and Commercial Necessities, 1952 Wis. L. Rev. 199; Rheinstein, Conflict of Laws in the Unif. Comm. Code, 16 Law & Contemp. Prob. 114 (1951); Stumberg, Commercial Paper and the Conflict of Laws, 6 Vand. L. Rev. 489 (1953).

9. U.C.C. § 9–301(2) (2001 version).

§ 19.32

1. U.C.C. § 8–102. See infra §§ 23.1–23.2.

2. See U.C.C. § 8–313.

3. Restatement, Second, Conflict of Laws § 303 (1971). Egan v. McNamara, 467 A.2d 733, 741 (D.C.App.1983) (law of corporation's domicile controls for purposes of determining who owns corporate stock).

4. See U.C.C. §§ 8–106, 8–313; Oliner v. Canadian Pacific Railway Co., 27 N.Y.2d 988, 318 N.Y.S.2d 745, 267 N.E.2d 480 (1970).

5. Petri v. Rhein, 162 F.Supp. 834 (N.D.Ill.1957), affirmed 257 F.2d 268 (7th Cir.1958); Mills v. Jacobs, 333 Pa. 231, 4 A.2d 152 (1939).

6. See Black v. J.W. Zacharie & Co., 44 U.S. (3 How.) 483, 11 L.Ed. 690 (1845); Shaw v. Goebel Brewing Co., 202 Fed. 408 (6th Cir.1913).

7. See U.C.C. §§ 8–313, 9–103(1) (1972 version). Cf. Bartlett v. General Motors Corp., 36 Del.Ch. 131, 127 A.2d 470 (1956); Brainard v. Canaday, 49 Del. 182, 112 A.2d 862 (1955); 8 Del. Code Ann. 16q.

8. Cf. Union National Bank v. Hartwell, 84 Ala. 379, 4 So. 156 (1888).

most closely connected to their transaction. In most instances the choice-of-law reference follows the Uniform Commercial Code pattern, and the effect is to sustain the validity of the transaction freely entered[9] which reflects the broad commercial policy present in this area of the law. Since the issues under the Uniform Commercial Code will be treated similarly in all concerned states, there frequently will be false conflicts involving these issues.

9. See Morson v. Second National Bank, 306 Mass. 588, 29 N.E.2d 19 (1940); Christy, The Transfer of Stock § 66 (4th ed. 1967). See also Henn, Law of Corporations 330 (2d ed. 1970); Lattin, The Law of Corporations 520 (2d ed. 1971).

Chapter 20

SUCCESSION

Table of Sections

		Sections
I.	Introduction	20.1
II.	Intestate Succession	20.2–20.4
	A. Immovables—Land	20.2
	B. Movables	20.3–20.4
III.	Testamentary Succession	20.5–20.14
	A. Introduction	20.5
	B. Wills of Immovables—Land	20.6–20.8
	1. Formal Validity	20.6
	2. Validity—Testamentary Trusts	20.7
	3. Construction	20.8
	C. Wills of Movables	20.9–20.14
	1. Validity	20.9
	2. Restrictions on Charitable Gifts	20.10
	3. Revocation	20.11–20.12
	a. By Instrument or Physical Act	20.11
	b. By Operation of Law	20.12
	4. Construction	20.13
	5. Validity—Testamentary Trusts	20.14
IV.	Family Protection—Forced Shares—Election	20.15–20.16
	A. Forced Shares	20.15
	B. Election	20.16
V.	International Wills	20.17
VI.	Devises to Aliens—Iron Curtain Statutes	20.18

I. INTRODUCTION

§ 20.1 In all legal systems recognizing private property, some provision is made for the transfer of assets from one generation to another. Within proper bounds this is a stabilizing force, socially and economically, to which great personal value is attached. Anticipating the extension of protection and ambition for family members and lifetime objectives affords very significant satisfactions for most human beings. In the Anglo–American system of law, this has resulted in a well recognized policy to validate and to give effect to the intention of owners and their intended dispositions of assets. Only in limited circumstances, for example, protection of creditors, family or the public fisc, do conflicting policies outweigh this policy of supporting intended dispositions.

Even intestate succession is assumed to rest on the unexpressed but presumed intent of the deceased owner. These policies underlying intergenerational transfers of property have significance in choice of law and difficult questions in succession arise out of the friction among historically crystallized presumptions of intent, current assumptions of presumed intent and broader public concerns. The discernible trend is toward increasing accommodation of the owner's intention when it is perceived.

II.　INTESTATE SUCCESSION

A.　IMMOVABLES—LAND

§ 20.2　Early English law and the early English social and economic structure placed great emphasis upon the succession to land. In the evolution of concepts of succession in early English law, almost no thought was given to multiple jurisdiction matters since the owner's center of family life and domicile coincided with the location of the land with which the owner's social and economic status and feudal obligations were associated. As a consequence of this historical pattern and the slowness with which reform in the property area follows social change, there is much antiquity in the conflict of laws regarding succession to land that makes little sense in the modern day world.

A modern illustrative situation may be posed in the circumstance in which a domiciliary of Michigan dies leaving real and personal property in Michigan and a farm in Ohio, with the usual stock of animals, supplies and implements upon it; further, the decedent leaves a mercantile business in Wisconsin, a vacation condominium in Mexico, an interest in a real estate development syndicate in Europe and shares of stock in several corporations chartered in many different states or countries. Management questions regarding the condominium are resolved by telephone or mail and investments are shifted and changed with frequently by telephone and via the internet. The owner of such an estate may very well look upon these different ventures as merely investments of particular assets in his estate and will consider his estate and its economic well-being as a unit without regard to where the parts are located. But different states of the United States and different nations of the world may well provide the rules which determine the devolution of parts of such an estate.

Consider first the situation in which the owner dies without having made a will. The traditional rule in the United States as to the descent of the land has been simple; land passes in accordance with the whole law prevailing at the place where the land is located. In a frequently cited case at the turn of the century, the Supreme Court of the United States pronounced in dictum: "It is a doctrine firmly established that the law of a state in which the land is situated controls and governs . . . its passage in case of intestacy."[1] Under this approach, the situs of the land will determine the identity of the takers and the size of the share of each of them in the land, without regard to the place where the decedent owner died domiciled, or where his family may be located.[2] In addition to the normal situation of identifying the intestate successors of land, the law of the situs has been applied to determine whether one may inherit local land from another for whose death he is criminally responsible.[3] In identifying the takers, the situs may look to law of other jurisdiction; for example, in the situation in which an adopted child is a potential successor, the law of the situs will ordinarily recognize the claim of a child validly adopted elsewhere to inherit the land.[4]

Important concerns of the state where land is located occur as to the use to which land is put and its effect on the economy. Equally significant concerns exist as to issues relating to the public fisc, including escheat, as well as the protection of third parties who rely upon the public records of the state where land is located. However, few of these concerns are present in the area of succession. It seems clear that the law of the situs has come to be so routinely applied in succession cases that its reach is overbroad and often defeats the superior interests or

§ 20.2

1. Clarke v. Clarke, 178 U.S. 186, 20 S.Ct. 873, 44 L.Ed. 1028 (1900). See Boman v. Gibbs, 443 S.W.2d 267 (Tex.Civ.App. 1969); Restatement, Second, Conflict of Laws § 236 (1971).

2. Succession of King, 201 So.2d 335 (La.App.1967); In re Kirkby's Estate, 57 Misc.2d 982, 293 N.Y.S.2d 1008 (1968) Matter of Fray, 721 P.2d 1054 (Wyo.1986); Matter of Silverman, 15 B.R. 843, 847 (Bankr. S.D.N.Y.1981) (the law of the state in which the property is located governs the disposition of intestate property). The Hague Convention on The Law Applicable to Succession to the Estates of Deceased Persons, 28 I.L.M. 146 (1989) has not been ratified by the U.S.

3. Harrison v. Moncravie, 264 Fed. 776 (8th Cir.1920), dismissed 255 U.S. 562, 41 S.Ct. 374, 65 L.Ed. 787 (1921). See Beale, Progress of the Law, 1919–1920: The Conflict of Laws, 34 Harv. L. Rev. 50, 61 (1920).

4. See, e.g., Kuchenig v. California Co., 410 F.2d 222 (5th Cir.1969), cert. denied 396 U.S. 887, 90 S.Ct. 176, 24 L.Ed.2d 162 (1969); Glanding v. Industrial Trust Co., 29 Del.Ch. 517, 46 A.2d 881 (1946); McLaughlin v. People, 403 Ill. 493, 87 N.E.2d 637 (1949); Greaves v. Fogel, 12 N.J.Super. 5, 78 A.2d 719 (1951). See also Restatement, Second, Conflict of Laws § 238, cmnt. (b) (1971). But cf. Fisher v. Browning, 107 Miss. 729, 66 So. 132 (1914). In the past there has also been considerable litigation of claims of children born out of wedlock.

These cases rarely refused inheritance rights in local land to one born out of wedlock but subsequently legitimated by the subsequent marriage of the parents. Birtwhistle v. Vardill, 7 Cl. & F. 895 (1840). Cf. In re Bruington's Estate, 160 Misc. 34, 289 N.Y.S. 725 (1936). Nearly all states of the United States recognized a foreign legitimation so by the whole law of the situs, the foreign legitimated child usually takes. See, e.g., Niles v. Niles, 35 Del.Ch. 106, 111 A.2d 697 (1955); In re Dauenhauer's Estate, 167 Mont. 83, 535 P.2d 1005 (1975); In re Spano's Estate, 49 N.J. 263, 229 A.2d 645 (1967); Howells v. Limbeck, 172 Ohio St. 297, 175 N.E.2d 517 (1961); Restatement, Second, Conflict of Laws § 237, cmnt. (b) (1971). But cf. In re Vincent's Estate, 189 Misc. 489, 71 N.Y.S.2d 165 (1947); In re Duquesne's Estate, 29 Utah 2d 94, 505 P.2d 779 (1973).

The situs may allow an illegitimate child to inherit local land and impose requirements concerning the recognition of the offspring by the parent. Van Horn v. Van Horn, 107 Iowa 247, 77 N.W. 846 (1899); Moen v. Moen, 16 S.D. 210, 92 N.W. 13 (1902).

The United States Supreme Court has held it unconstitutional for a state to discriminate against children born out of wedlock. Trimble v. Gordon, 430 U.S. 762, 97 S.Ct. 1459, 52 L.Ed.2d 31 (1977). As a consequence, variations in local law regarding treatment of illegitimate children have disappeared. See supra Chapter 16.

policy concerns of nonsitus states.[5] An example is the often cited case of *Clarke v. Clarke*.[6] In that Mr. and Mrs. Clarke lived in South Carolina where Mrs. Clarke died owning considerable real and personal property in South Carolina, and also land in Connecticut. Her will directed that her estate be equally divided among her husband and her children, share and share alike, and that the shares of her children be held in trust until they were of age. Upon probate of Mrs. Clarke's will in South Carolina, her husband brought suit to construe the will, and the South Carolina court held that the will worked an equitable conversion of the assets in Mrs. Clarke's estate so that the entire estate would be treated as if it were personal property and distributed accordingly. One of Mrs. Clarke's two children, a five-month old daughter, died about three months after Mrs. Clarke's death. Subsequently, Mr. Clarke, as administrator of the estate of this deceased child, administering the child's estate in Connecticut, brought suit in Connecticut for determination of his distributive share in the deceased child's estate and that of the surviving child. Under the Connecticut law, real property descended to the surviving child, whereas by the law of South Carolina both real and personal property passed equally to the father and to the surviving child, i.e., as sister of the decedent. Mr. Clarke, father of the infant decedent, argued that the earlier South Carolina litigation in the mother's estate had worked an equitable conversion of the Connecticut land and hence that it should be treated as personal property to give him rights in the infant's estate under the law of South Carolina.

In rejecting that argument and concluding that the Connecticut land devolved upon the surviving sister of the infant decedent, the court stated that the situs of land controlled, and that Connecticut had exclusive jurisdiction over the land within its borders. As a consequence, the South Carolina court was without jurisdiction over the Connecticut land and the South Carolina judgment therefore was not conclusive as to the rights in Connecticut land. The court further reasoned that the parties were not the same in Connecticut as in South Carolina, because the South Carolina guardian ad litem of the surviving daughter had no authority regarding the Connecticut land.

The case is an example of how the assumptions of the situs reference seem to so overwhelm a court that it does not look to the real issues. In this way, situs is somewhat of a security blanket to courts in conflict of laws cases because of its simplicity and seeming permanence. In the *Clarke* case, there seems first of all, a gross misunderstanding involving equitable conversion. Usually equitable conversion is a concept used for determining appropriate distribution in the estate of a decedent whose will or other instrument purports to convert his property. The doctrine does not control the subsequent disposition of property by one of that decedent's recipients. Consequently, it appears that most of the opinion in *Clarke* is only dictum. It would be nearly impossible to have

---

5. See policy discussion supra § 19.1.

6. Clarke v. Clarke, 178 U.S. 186, 20 S.Ct. 873, 44 L.Ed. 1028 (1900).

equitable conversion in an estate of a five-month old infant. Even so, the court's finding of inadequate representation of the infant in the South Carolina litigation overrides any holding as to preclusion by prior litigation. The fact that there was litigation in the mother's estate as to the share the infant took would not seem to preclude litigation in the infant's estate as to the intestate share her sister and father would receive from the infant's estate. If the concept of equitable conversion is limited as is suggested above, then the result in *Clarke* is the same that would be expected to be reached in an ordinary case in which there was no prior litigation, i.e., simply a case of intestate succession of land owned by an infant in which under the traditional conflicts rule, the law of the situs would govern.

Further, should the issue of prior litigation appropriately arise in a case between the same parties, it is submitted that the court should enforce the prior litigation as in *Durfee v. Duke.*[7] Consequently, even though all the court says in *Clarke v. Clark* about full faith and credit seems to be dictum, it also seems to be wrong.[8] This is poor support for what is supposed to be a leading case in the United States and it is submitted that reliance on *Clarke* is misplaced.

In a case in which the situs state's concerns about land use, public fisc or public record are not involved, it would seem that the concerns of the domicile of the decedent as the center of family life ought to determine what shares members of the decedent's family take in assets located in other jurisdictions. In light of this, the appropriateness of using the local law of the situs to determine the appropriate shares, the intestate shares among the members of the family in intestate litigation, seems outmoded.[9] Nevertheless, the situs rule for realty matters contin-

7. 375 U.S. 106, 84 S.Ct. 242, 11 L.Ed.2d 186 (1963).

8. See supra § 19.8. As is observed in the earlier discussion, the Supreme Court concluded "[w]hile this Court has not before had occasion to consider the application of the rule of *Davis, Stoel, Treinies,* and *Sherrer* in a case involving real property, we can discern no reason why the rule should not be fully applicable." 375 U.S. 106, 115, 84 S.Ct. 242, 247, 11 L.Ed.2d 186 (1963).

9. See R. Weintraub, Commentary on the Conflict of Laws § 8.7 (4th ed. 2001); Morris, Intestate Succession to Land and the Conflict of Laws, 85 L.Q. Rev. 339 (1969); Hancock, Equitable Conversion and the Land Taboo in Conflict of Laws, 17 Stan. L. Rev. 1095, 1115 (1965); Baxter, Choice of Law and the Federal System, 16 Stan. L. Rev. 1, 16 (1963); R.A. Sedler, Mofatt Hancock and Conflict of Laws, 37 U. Toronto L.J. 62 (1987). Cf. U.P.C §§ 2–201, 4–401. See also G. Miller, International Aspects of Intestate Succession, 1988 Conv. & Prop. L. 30 (1988); Note, Conflicts of Law

and Succession, Interest Analysis as an Alternative, 59 Tul. L. Rev. 389 (1984). In most civil law countries, perhaps in most countries of the world, the unity concept prevails. This concept calls for the application of the same law of succession to all assets in contrast to the scission approach that distinguishes between movables and immovables with regard to many issues in the common law states. With the recognition that choice of law rules should depend on the particular issue, it is to be expected that the situs rule will be further restricted. See Grahl–Madsen, Conflict Between the Principle of Unitary Succession and the System of Scission, 28 Int'l & Comp. L.Q. 598 (1979); Symeonides, Succession and Marital Property, 35 Am. J. Comp. L. 259, 264 (1987); Symeonides, Revising Louisiana's Conflicts Law in Succession, 47 La. L. Rev. 1029, 1093 (1987). See also Swedish Ministry of Justice, Report of Family Law Reform Commission, Summary p. 264 (Sou. 1987: 18); Swiss Federal Statute on Private International Law of Dec. 18, 1987, Art. 90–92.

ues to exert a powerful hold on American courts.[10] The Supreme Court's recent repetition of the doctrine that the situs state has exclusive authority over realty conveyances for full-faith-and credit purposes suggests that the situs rule is likely to remain vital.[11]

B. MOVABLES

§ 20.3 The owner of assets usually considers his accumulated wealth as a unit, i.e., as his estate wherever it is located. Presumably he would prefer, even in the absence of an adequately stated intention, that it descend as a unit to his family. While this presumption of intention has had little effect on the intestate succession to land, it appears to be an important reason for the choice-of-law doctrine in succession to movables. Not only is it assumed that the owner of movables would prefer those assets to pass as a unitary estate subject to a single law, but presumably also the owner would prefer that single law to be the law with which normally he would be most familiar—that of his domicile. Although domicile is, admittedly, sometimes a rather tenuous relationship to a state, most often it is an available single reference that accords with the reasonable expectations of the family. On this basis, unless changed by statute, it is well settled that movable property, wherever situated, will be distributed as provided by the whole law in force at the place where the decedent was domiciled at the time of his death.[1] The physical control of the situs may occasion separate administrations in cases where property is left in several states but the devolution of the assets remaining after liquidation will follow the law of the domicile.

---

10. See, e.g., Estate of Lampert, by Thurston v. Estate of Lampert by Stauffer, 896 P.2d 214, 219 (Alaska 1995) (applying situs law to determine effect of attempted conveyance).

11. Baker v. General Motors Corp., 522 U.S. 222, 118 S.Ct. 657, 139 L.Ed.2d 580 (1998) ("one State's judgment cannot automatically transfer title to land in another state," citing Fall v. Eastin, 215 U.S. 1, 30 S.Ct. 3, 54 L.Ed. 65 (1909)).

§ 20.3

1. Ennis v. Smith, 55 U.S. (14 How.) 400, 14 L.Ed. 472 (1852); Pyles v. Russell, 36 S.W.3d 365 (Ky.2000) (law of state of decedent's last domicile governs question of intestate inheritance of personal property by decedent's grandchildren who had been adopted as decedent's children); Nora v. Nora, 494 So.2d 16 (Ala.1986); Hewitt v. Cox, 55 Ark. 225, 15 S.W. 1026 (1891), rehearing by 55 Ark. 225, 17 S.W. 873 (1891); Estate of Apple, 66 Cal. 432, 6 P. 7 (1885); Lawrence v. Kitteridge, 21 Conn. 577, 56 Am.Dec. 385 (1852); Squire v. Vazquez, 52 Ga.App. 215, 183 S.E. 127 (1935); Barthel v. Johnston, 92 Idaho 94,

437 P.2d 366 (1968); Russell v. Madden, 95 Ill. 485 (1880); Caruso v. Caruso, 106 N.J.Eq. 130, 148 A. 882 (1930) (noted 42 Harv.L.Rev. 827 (1929)); In re Sherman's Estate, 76 Misc.2d 551, 351 N.Y.S.2d 570 (1974); In re Paroth's Estate, 72 Misc.2d 499, 340 N.Y.S.2d 433 (1971); Howard v. Reynolds, 30 Ohio St.2d 214, 283 N.E.2d 629 (1972); French v. Short, 207 Va. 548, 151 S.E.2d 354 (1966); White v. Tennant, 31 W.Va. 790, 8 S.E. 596 (1888). See W. Breslauer, The Private International Law of Succession in England, America and Germany 39 (1937); Restatement, Second, Conflict of Laws § 260 (1971). Cf. In re Estate of Perry, 480 S.W.2d 893 (Mo.1972); In re Kirkby's Estate, 57 Misc.2d 982, 293 N.Y.S.2d 1008 (1968); Gilbert v. Gilbert, 442 So.2d 1330 (La.App.1983), writ denied 445 So.2d 1231 (La.1984). See also Southeast Bank, N.A. v. Lawrence, 66 N.Y.2d 910, 498 N.Y.S.2d 775, 489 N.E.2d 744 (1985) (holding that, for choice-of-law purposes, rights of publicity constitute personalty and that, consequently, law of decedent's domicile governs issue who possesses a descendible, enforceable right of publicity).

Justice Holmes stated the proposition: "If this fund had passed by intestate succession, it would be recognized that by the traditions of our law the property is regarded as a universitas, the succession to which is incident to the persona of the deceased. As the states where property is situated, if governed by the common law, generally recognize the law of the domicile as determining the succession, it may be said that, in a practical sense at least, the law of the domicile is needed to establish the inheritance."[2] Sometimes this common law rule is codified.[3]

The law of the decedent's last domicile has been applied to determine whether an adopted child shares in the estate.[4] The same approach has been used to determine whether a child born out of wedlock, who has been acknowledged though not legitimated may share and what type of acknowledgment is necessary,[5] though the constitutional protection of out-of-wedlock children has rendered this latter issue moot.[6]

The same law will determine the share, if any, of kindred of the half-blood[7] and, likewise, the effect of a separation agreement between spouses upon the claim of a survivor in the personal estate of the deceased spouse.[8]

Damages collected under a death-by-wrongful-act statute for the killing of the decedent are usually distributed as provided for by the statute under which recovery is had.[9] This is because such damages are not treated, under the usual type of statute, as a part of the decedent's estate. They are given to the beneficiaries by the statute, and do not come through inheritance from the decedent. If under a particular statute the damages recovered are treated as if they were part of the decedent's estate, they will be distributed according to the domiciliary law, like other personal property.[10]

2. Bullen v. Wisconsin, 240 U.S. 625, 631, 36 S.Ct. 473, 474, 60 L.Ed. 830 (1916).

3. See Cal. Civ. Code § 946; 755 Ill. Comp. Stat. Ann. 5/2–1 (referring to "resident decedent").

4. Cook v. Todd's Estate, 249 Iowa 1274, 90 N.W.2d 23 (1958); Anderson v. French, 77 N.H. 509, 93 A. 1042 (1915). Cf. Slattery v. Hartford–Connecticut Trust Co., 115 Conn. 163, 161 A. 79 (1932).

5. In re Jones' Estate, 192 Iowa 78, 182 N.W. 227 (1921); Holmes v. Adams, 110 Me. 167, 85 A. 492 (1912); In re Sherman's Estate, 76 Misc.2d 551, 351 N.Y.S.2d 570 (1974). As to acknowledgment, see In re Forney's Estate, 43 Nev. 227, 184 P. 206 (1919) (noted 29 Yale L.J. 573 (1920)). Cf. In re Stacy's Estate, 131 Vt. 130, 300 A.2d 556 (1973).

6. See supra § 20.2 n.4.

7. Lawrence v. Kitteridge, 21 Conn. 577, 56 Am.Dec. 385 (1852).

8. Caruth v. Caruth, 128 Iowa 121, 103 N.W. 103 (1905). See Knapp v. Knapp, 95 Mich. 474, 55 N.W. 353 (1893).

9. In re Coe's Estate, 130 Iowa 307, 106 N.W. 743 (1906); State ex rel. Ralston v. Blain, 189 Kan. 575, 370 P.2d 415 (1962); In re Petrasek's Estate, 191 Misc. 9, 79 N.Y.S.2d 561 (1948). Cf. Gall v. Robertson, 10 Wis.2d 594, 103 N.W.2d 903 (1960). However, the law of the domicile may be relevant to identify distributees and parties with standing. Pennsylvania R. Co. v. Levine, 263 Fed. 557 (2d Cir.1920). Cf. Hartley v. Hartley, 71 Kan. 691, 81 P. 505 (1905); Ross v. Eaton, 90 N.H. 271, 6 A.2d 762 (1939); Di Medio v. Port Norris Express Co., 71 N.J.Super. 190, 176 A.2d 550 (1961); In re Sherman's Estate, 76 Misc.2d 551, 351 N.Y.S.2d 570 (1974); Matter of Dimirsky's Estate, 201 Misc. 118, 108 N.Y.S.2d 849 (1951).

10. Hartley v. Hartley, 71 Kan. 691, 81 P. 505 (1905).

§ 20.4   The reasons for the generally accepted rule that refers to the decedent's domicile in succession to movables is not often well articulated. To say it rests upon the rule that movables follow the person of the owner obviously does no more than state the result in different language, whether in English or as the maxim *"mobilia sequuntur personam."* Another explanation is "[i]f there are movables in a foreign country, the law of the domicile is given an extraterritorial effect by the courts of that country, and in a just and proper sense the succession is said to take place by force of, and to be governed by, the law of the domicile."[1] One may, with due respect, question these analyses. It is difficult to see how the law of Michigan, in our initial hypothetical, could project into Ohio and control the disposition of property there without the accommodation of this result by Ohio law. The physical power of the situs would seem to permit it to regulate the devolution of assets within it. The assets are in fact in Ohio, and Ohio may deal with them as it pleases, subject only to constitutional restrictions.

By reason of physical control, the disposition of a decedent's property is subject to the law of the situs of the property. However, if the decedent has died domiciled in another state, the conflict-of-laws doctrine of the situs looks to the rules for devolution of movables prevailing at the domicile, and not the local statute on the subject.[2] Thus, this conflict-of-laws rule is a part of the law of the situs of the property, unless modified by statute. The real reason for the choice-of-law reference seems to be one of convenience. The desirability of having a person's estate treated as a unit under a commonly recognized law, no matter how widely the items may be scattered, is a paramount consideration.[3] When an intangible is not represented by a document it has no particular situs and the reference by the forum would be directly to the domicile.[4]

This choice-of-law rule may be modified by statute. A few states have in the past provided that all personalty within the state, upon the death of the owner, is to be distributed in accordance with the local rule without reference to the law of the owner's domicile, and one of our states still so provides.[5] The escheat cases also support the theory that the situs has ultimate control. If a person leaves chattels in a state other than his domicile and there is no one entitled to the estate as next of kin, the property often goes as bona vacantia, not to the state of the

---

§ 20.4

1. Frothingham v. Shaw, 175 Mass. 59, 55 N.E. 623 (1899).

2. In re Barton's Estate, 196 Cal. 508, 238 P. 681 (1925); Howard v. Reynolds, 30 Ohio St.2d 214, 283 N.E.2d 629 (1972).

3. See Griswold, Renvoi Revisited, 51 Harv. L. Rev. 1165, 1194 (1938); Briggs, The Dual Relationship of the Rules of Conflict of Laws in the Succession Field, 15 Miss. L.J. 77 (1943); Scoles, Choice of Law in Family Transactions, 209 Recueil des

cours 17 (1988–II). Cf. Robbins v. National Bank of Georgia, 241 Ga. 538, 246 S.E.2d 660 (1978).

4. See Restatement, Second, Conflict of Laws § 260, cmnt. (a) (1971).

5. Miss. Code § 91–1–1; Partee v. Kortrecht, 54 Miss. 66 (1876); Richardson v. Neblett, 122 Miss. 723, 84 So. 695 (1920); Ewing v. Warren, 144 Miss. 233, 109 So. 601 (1926).

decedent's domicile, but to the state where the property is located.[6] But the situs may, even in these cases, refer to the owner's domicile as is done in descent.[7] In abandoned property cases involving intangibles, the United States Supreme Court has concluded[8] that the state of the last known address of the owner of the intangibles is the only state having jurisdiction to escheat. This is a reference to the assumed domicile of the owner which reinforces the domicile reference in a situation where competing claims are difficult to base on "situs."

Another instance which seems to show the control of the law of the situs is *Lynch v. Paraguay*[9] in which the decedent died domiciled in Paraguay leaving personal estate in England. The legislature in Paraguay sought, by a statute passed after the decedent's death, to declare his will invalid and to declare that his property should go to the Paraguayan government. The English court disregarded that legislation and looked to the requirements of the domiciliary law at the date of the death of the decedent. The choice of law rule of the situs applies the rule of the domicile as to the passing of personalty as the presumed preference of the owner at the time of his death.

III. TESTAMENTARY SUCCESSION

A. INTRODUCTION

§ 20.5 From the analogy to the rules governing inheritance of land by intestate succession and from the near universal doctrine throughout Anglo–American conflict of laws that refers questions concerning immovables to the law of the situs, one would expect testamentary disposition of land is to be governed by the law of the state where the land is situated.[1] This is the rule, and it has generally been applied to the

6. In re Estate of Rapoport, 317 Mich. 291, 26 N.W.2d 777 (1947); State by Van Riper v. American Sugar Refining Co., 20 N.J. 286, 119 A.2d 767 (1956); In re Barnett's Trusts (1902) 1 Ch. 847; Restatement, Second, Conflict of Laws § 266 (1971). See In re Forney's Estate, 43 Nev. 227, 184 P. 206 (1919); In re Menschefrend's Estate, 283 App.Div. 463, 128 N.Y.S.2d 738 (1954). Cf. In re Matous' Estate, 53 Misc.2d 255, 278 N.Y.S.2d 70 (1967). But cf. In re Utassi's Will, 15 N.Y.2d 436, 261 N.Y.S.2d 4, 209 N.E.2d 65 (1965) (applying the law of USSR under which the government of the then-USSR as a public corporation took as heir rather than as a sovereign taking by escheat); In the Matter of Khotim, 41 N.Y.2d 845, 393 N.Y.S.2d 702, 362 N.E.2d 253 (1977) (accord with *Utassi*).

7. In re Nolan's Estate, 135 Cal.App.2d 16, 286 P.2d 899 (1955). Cf. In re Utassi's Will, 15 N.Y.2d 436, 261 N.Y.S.2d 4, 209 N.E.2d 65 (1965); In re Lyons' Estate, 175 Wash. 115, 26 P.2d 615 (1933).

8. Delaware v. New York, 507 U.S. 490, 113 S.Ct. 1550, 123 L.Ed.2d 211 (1993) (State of incorporation of intermediary holding unclaimed securities has jurisdiction to escheat); Western Union Tel. Co. v. Pennsylvania, 368 U.S. 71, 82 S.Ct. 199, 7 L.Ed.2d 139 (1961); Texas v. New Jersey, 379 U.S. 674, 85 S.Ct. 626, 13 L.Ed.2d 596 (1965). In 1974, Congress acted to give the state in a "money order, traveler's check or similar instrument was purchased" priority to escheat or take custody of the sum payable on such instrument. 12 U.S.C.A. § 2503.

9. L.R. 2 P. & D. 268 (1871) (followed In Re Aganoor's Trusts, 64 L.J.Ch. 521 (1895)).

§ 20.5

1. Graveson, Conflict of Laws 520 (7th ed. 1974).

various questions which may arise in connection with a will devising land.[2] In cases involving testate succession, however, the intent of the testator, actual or presumed, has greater force than in cases of intestacy. Consequently, this factor often leads the situs to refer to the local law of some other state for resolution of a particular issue.[3] In many cases, the capacity of a testator to devise land will be viewed as controlled by the law of the situs and the situs may apply its own law and not that of the domicile, particularly if the effect is to validate a transfer.[4] On the other hand, there seems no reason why the situs should not, in an appropriate case, sustain the capacity of the testator by the law of his domicile.[5] The impact of the unitary concept of succession is seen in the restrictions on testation designed to protect those members of the testator's household that the custom of society indicates should be provided for before he considers gifts to strangers. While the situs may apply its own law to effect this "charity begins at home" protection,[6] it could well refer to the law of the owner's domicile as more significantly interested to identify the recipients.[7]

B. WILLS OF IMMOVABLES—LAND

1. Formal Validity

§ 20.6   The question of the form in which the will must be executed to pass land is determined by the whole law of the situs since the will operates as a conveyance or transfer. The situs has applied its local law in numerous cases[1] but this has been the source of inconvenience

---

2. See Restatement, Second, Conflict of Laws § 239 (1971); N.Y. E.P.T.L. §§ 3–5.1(b)(1), 5–3.3. See also Matter of Anderson's Estate, 571 P.2d 880 (Okla. App. 1977).

3. Wilcoxen v. United States, 310 F.Supp. 1006 (D.Kan. 1969). Cf. Estate of Taylor, 480 Pa. 488, 391 A.2d 991 (1978).

4. E.g., Carpenter v. Bell, 96 Tenn. 294, 34 S.W. 209 (1896).

5. Cf. Polson v. Stewart, 167 Mass. 211, 45 N.E. 737 (1897); Proctor v. Frost, 89 N.H. 304, 197 A. 813 (1938); A. Ehrenzweig, A Treatise on the Conflict of Laws 661 (1962).

6. Spence v. Spence, 239 Ala. 480, 195 So. 717 (1940); Ehler v. Ehler, 214 Iowa 789, 243 N.W. 591 (1932); Succession of Simms, 250 La. 177, 195 So.2d 114 (1965), cert. denied Kitchen v. Reese, 389 U.S. 850, 88 S.Ct. 47, 19 L.Ed.2d 120 (1967); Alexander v. Alexander, 357 So.2d 1260 (La.App. 1978); Banks v. Junk, 264 So.2d 387, 69 A.L.R.3d 1070 (Miss. 1972); Pfau v. Moseley, 9 Ohio St.2d 13, 38, 222 N.E.2d 639 (1966); Grigg's Estate, 54 D. & C. 25 (Pa. 1945). See also Price v. Johnson, 78 N.M. 123, 428 P.2d 978 (1967), appeal upon remand 79 N.M. 629, 447 P.2d 509 (1968). Cf. In re Plazza's Estate, 34 Colo.App. 296, 526

P.2d 155 (1974); Schalk v. Dickinson, 89 S.D. 263, 232 N.W.2d 140 (1975).

7. Cf. In re Dalip Singh Bir's Estate, 83 Cal.App.2d 256, 188 P.2d 499 (1948) (movables); In re Plazza's Estate, 34 Colo.App. 296, 526 P.2d 155 (1974) (allowance); Brooks v. Carson, 166 Kan. 194, 200 P.2d 280 (1948) (election); Succession of Goss, 304 So.2d 704 (La.App.1974), writ refused 309 So.2d 339 (La.1975), cert. denied Goss v. Zuckswert, 423 U.S. 869, 96 S.Ct. 133, 46 L.Ed.2d 99 (1975) (legitime); In re Estate of Clark, 21 N.Y.2d 478, 288 N.Y.S.2d 993, 236 N.E.2d 152 (1968) (movables); In re Will of Halpern, 48 A.D.2d 776, 368 N.Y.S.2d 845 (1975), aff'd without opn. In re Estate of Dewey, 39 N.Y.2d 1050, 387 N.Y.S.2d 426, 355 N.E.2d 386 (1976) (charity); Matter of Blankenship's Estate, 571 P.2d 874 (Okl. App. 1977) (allowance). But see Estate of Pericles, 266 Ill.App.3d 1096, 204 Ill.Dec. 51, 641 N.E.2d 10 (1994) (forum's more generous forced-share rule not applied to out-of-state realty).

§ 20.6

1. In re Georg's Estate, 298 F.Supp. 741 (D.V.I. 1969); Robertson v. Pickrell, 109 U.S. 608, 3 S.Ct. 407, 27 L.Ed. 1049 (1883);

because of the difficulty in making a will devising land in several states conform to the varying requirements in each.[2] The inconvenience is greater than an inter vivos transfer because land scattered in several states can be deeded by separate instruments, while the will is generally but a single instrument. The result has been statutory modification of the traditional rule in most states. The general effect of the statutes is to allow a devise of land to be executed in the form prescribed by the law of another state, usually the place of execution.[3] The evolution of these statutes over a century of experience is reflected in the Uniform Probate Code which provides:

> "A written will is valid if executed in compliance with Section 2–502 or 2–503, or if its execution complies with the law at the time of execution of the place where the will is executed, or of the law of the place where at the time of execution or at the time of death the testator is domiciled, has a place of abode or is a national."[4]

Under these validating statutes a third state as forum would apply whatever local law such a situs reference identified.[5]

The effect of these validating references "has made it practically impossible for a will to be formally invalid so far as the conflict of laws is concerned."[6] These validating references are also found in the Hague Convention of 1961 which in addition to the validating references for execution has a series of additional rules designed to provide maximum validity to wills which are executed away from the situs or domicile of

---

Calloway v. Doe ex dem. Joyes, 1 Blackf. 372 (Ind.1825); Lynch v. Miller, 54 Iowa 516, 6 N.W. 740 (1880); Succession of Hasling, 114 La. 293, 38 So. 174 (1905); Keith v. Johnson, 97 Mo. 223, 10 S.W. 597 (1889); Lapham v. Olney, 5 R.I. 413 (1858); First Christian Church of Guthrie, Kentucky v. Moneypenny, 59 Tenn.App. 229, 439 S.W.2d 620 (1968); French v. Short, 207 Va. 548, 151 S.E.2d 354 (1966); Matter of Reed's Estate, 233 Kan. 531, 664 P.2d 824 (1983), cert. denied 464 U.S. 978, 104 S.Ct. 417, 78 L.Ed.2d 354 (1983), aff'd 236 Kan. 514, 693 P.2d 1156 (1985) (under the common law, courts of states where real property is located have jurisdiction to probate a will devising the property and to determine the sufficiency of the form of the will).

2. Cf. Scott on Trusts § 589 (4th ed. 1987).

3. Irwin's Appeal from Probate, 33 Conn. 128 (1865); Lyon v. Ogden, 85 Me. 374, 27 A. 258 (1893); Lindsay v. Wilson, 103 Md. 252, 63 A. 566 (1906). See Rabel, The Form of Wills, 6 Vand. L. Rev. 533 (1953); Lorenzen, The Validity of Wills, Deeds, and Contracts as Regards Form in the Conflict of Laws, 20 Yale L.J. 427 (1911). Cf. In re Wilson's Will, 60 Misc.2d 290, 302 N.Y.S.2d 910 (1969).

4. U.P.C. § 2–506. This provision is identical to former (pre–1990 version) § 2–506 and is based upon and supersedes Section 7 of the Model Execution of Wills Act (1940) and is similar to the Uniform Wills Act, Foreign Executed (1910) which the model act superseded. Nearly all states of the United States have statutes similar at least in part to these provisions, see Reese, American Wills Statutes, 46 Va. L. Rev. 613, 856, at 905–06 (1960); Scoles & Rheinstein, Conflict Avoidance and Succession Planning, 21 L. & Contemp. Prob. 499, 502 (1956). The Uniform Probate Code provision is nearly identical to the earlier English legislation in the Wills Act 1963, § 1. The present English act evolved from the earlier Lord Kingsdown's Act, Wills Act, 1861, 24 & 25 Vict. Chap. 114. The Canadian provinces have similar legislation. See Falconbridge, Conflict of Laws 546 (2d ed. 1954). See also Estate of Grossen v. Vincent, 657 P.2d 1345 (Utah 1983) (language of U.P.C. § 2–506 was not intended only to validate wills made by decedent in another state or country).

5. Restatement, Second, Conflict of Laws § 239 (1971).

6. Note, The Wills Act, 1963, 13 Int'l & Comp. L.Q. 684, 691 (1964).

the decedent.[7]

The revocation of a will, so far as it devises land, is usually treated under the familiar situs rule.[8] If there is a statute in the forum or at the situs such as the Uniform Probate Code or one of the acts patterned after Lord Kingsdown's Act, the answer may be uncertain. Although the Hague Convention, English Wills Act of 1963, and some American statutes expressly include provisions dealing with revocation as well as execution[9] most of the acts expressly deal with questions of execution but omit any reference to revocation. These latter acts raise the issue whether a "revocation" is to be treated as an "execution." The statutes reflect an intent to validate the testator's intention and would clearly apply to revocation by a subsequent will or codicil. Consequently, it would seem that they should also operate to validate the intended revocation of a will if sustained by the law of a place where it occurred or the domicile or other law to which the statutes refer.[10]

The situs law has been applied to determine whether a will devising land is revoked by marriage or divorce or by subsequent birth of a child to the testator.[11] Also it has been applied to resolve the effect of a subsequent birth of a child in modifying a devise of land.[12] Because these forms of revocation involve matters of primary concern to the domicile, the situs may, and should, appropriately consider the effect of such events at the domicile.[13] Whether a sale by a testator of land devised operates as an ademption of the devise is in similar fashion held to be governed by the whole law of the situs.[14]

The rule that the law of the situs governs the disposition of immovables by will is applied in many other instances. That law determines whether land acquired after the execution of the will may pass

---

7. Hague Convention on the Formal Validity of Wills (1961), 9 Am. J. Comp. L. 705 (1960); Graveson, The Ninth Hague Conference of Private International Law, 10 Int'l & Comp. L.Q. 18, 21–25 (1961).

8. Trotter v. Van Pelt, 144 Fla. 517, 198 So. 215 (1940); Cornell v. Burr, 32 S.D. 1, 141 N.W. 1081 (1913).

9. See, e.g., N.Y. E.P.T.L. § 3–5.1.

10. Cf. Bayley v. Bailey, 59 Mass. (5 Cush.) 245 (1849); In re Traversi's Estate, 189 Misc. 251, 64 N.Y.S.2d 453 (1946) (nature of assets not specified); Matter of Garver's Estate, 135 N.J.Super. 578, 343 A.2d 817 (1975) (personal property). But see In re Barrie's Estate, 240 Iowa 431, 35 N.W.2d 658 (1949); In re Alberti [1955] 3 All. Eng. 730 (Prob.).

11. Ware v. Wisner, 50 Fed. 310 (C.C.D.Iowa 1883); Ensley v. Hodgson, 212 Ala. 526, 103 So. 465 (1925); Matter of Wimbush's Estate, 41 Colo.App. 289, 587 P.2d 796 (1978); Sternberg v. St. Louis Union Trust Co., 394 Ill. 452, 68 N.E.2d 892

(1946); Cox v. Harrison, 535 S.W.2d 78 (Ky. 1975); Succession of Austin, 527 So.2d 483 (La.App.1988), writ denied 532 So.2d 135 (La.1988).

12. Hanson v. Hoffman, 150 Kan. 121, 91 P.2d 31 (1939); Van Wickle v. Van Wickle, 59 N.J.Eq. 317, 44 A. 877 (1899); Rhode Island Hospital Trust Co. v. Hail, 47 R.I. 64, 129 A. 832 (1925).

13. In re Gailey's Will, 169 Wis. 444, 171 N.W. 945 (1919). Cf. In re Garver's Estate, 135 N.J.Super. 578, 343 A.2d 817 (1975); In re Traversi's Estate, 189 Misc. 251, 64 N.Y.S.2d 453 (1946); Hancock, Conceptual Devices for Avoiding the Land Taboo in Conflict of Laws: The Disadvantages of Disingenuousness, 20 Stan. L. Rev. 1, 2 (1967); Restatement, Second, Conflict of Laws § 239, cmnt. (i) (1971). But cf. In re Lans' Estate, 29 Misc.2d 758, 210 N.Y.S.2d 611 (1960).

14. Phillips v. Phillips, 213 Ala. 27, 104 So. 234 (1925) (noted 3 Wis. L. Rev. 380 (1926)).

under its terms,[15] the nature of the title conveyed;[16] whether the devise is in addition to or in lieu of dower[17] and the validity of a devise.[18] As to the last point, it must be noted that although there may be no inhibition by the law of the situs, the charter of a corporate devisee may prevent it from acquiring the property in question.[19] Chattels real, if characterized as immovables, are subject to the rules governing the devise of land.[20]

Even though the will has been admitted to probate as valid in the state of the testator's domicile, some state cases have concluded that this may not require its admission, without contest, to probate in another state where real estate is located, under the full faith and credit provision of the Constitution,[21] in absence of preclusion by prior litigation *inter partes.* However, the trend is to treat the will as a single dispositive instrument conclusively established at the domicile and given effect elsewhere.[22] The development of full faith and credit enforcement of preclusion by prior litigation also appears to predict that the usual doctrines of preclusion apply to probate of wills of land.[23]

2. *Validity—Testamentary Trusts*

§ 20.7   The traditional situs rule has also been applied to determine the validity of a trust in real property created by will.[1] This seems,

15. Frazier v. Boggs, 37 Fla. 307, 20 So. 245 (1896); Lindsay v. Wilson, 103 Md. 252, 63 A. 566 (1906); Wynne v. Wynne, 23 Miss. 251, 57 Am. Dec. 139 (1852); Applegate v. Smith, 31 Mo. 166 (1860).

16. West v. Fitz, 109 Ill. 425 (1884); Pratt v. Douglas, 38 N.J.Eq. 516 (1884).

17. Staigg v. Atkinson, 144 Mass. 564, 12 N.E. 354 (1887). But cf. Brooks v. Carson, 166 Kan. 194, 200 P.2d 280 (1948); Jarel v. Moon's Succession, 190 So. 867 (La.App.1939); Colvin v. Hutchison, 338 Mo. 576, 92 S.W.2d 667 (1936).

18. United States v. Fox, 94 U.S. (4 Otto) 315, 24 L.Ed. 192 (1876); Hobson v. Hale, 95 N.Y. 588 (1884); Ford v. Ford, 70 Wis. 19, 33 N.W. 188 (1887), 72 Wis. 621, 40 N.W. 502 (1888); Lewis v. Doerle, 28 O.R. 412 (1897). Cf. In re Jovanopoulos' Will, 51 Misc.2d 995, 274 N.Y.S.2d 249 (1966), aff'd 28 A.D.2d 1089, 285 N.Y.S.2d 581 (1967), aff'd 23 N.Y.2d 773, 297 N.Y.S.2d 139, 244 N.E.2d 708 (1968).

19. Starkweather v. American Bible Society, 72 Ill. 50, 22 Am.Rep. 133 (1874). Cf. White v. Howard, 38 Conn. 342 (1871).

20. Humble Oil & Refining Co. v. Copeland, 398 F.2d 364 (4th Cir.1968); Succession of Simms, 250 La. 177, 195 So.2d 114 (1965), cert. denied Kitchen v. Reese, 389 U.S. 850, 88 S.Ct. 47, 19 L.Ed.2d 120 (1967); Toledo Society for Crippled Children

v. Hickok, 152 Tex. 578, 261 S.W.2d 692 (1953), cert. denied 347 U.S. 936, 74 S.Ct. 631, 98 L.Ed. 1086 (1954); Peplin v. Bruyere, [1900] 2 Ch. 504; De Fogassieras v. Duport, 11 L.R.Ir. 123 (1881).

21. Selle v. Rapp, 143 Ark. 192, 220 S.W. 662 (1920); Guidry v. Hardy, 254 So.2d 675 (La.App.1971), writ refused 260 La. 454, 256 So.2d 441 (1972); Cornell v. Burr, 32 S.D. 1, 141 N.W. 1081 (1913); Matter of Estate of Reed, 768 P.2d 566 (Wyo.1989); Matter of Estate of Reed, 233 Kan. 531, 664 P.2d 824 (document which lacks the essential requirements of a valid will not admitted to probate, notwithstanding fact that a court in another state had seen fit to declare the instrument a valid will under that state's law).

22. Cf. U.P.C. §§ 2–506; see supra n.4.

23. See Durfee v. Duke, 375 U.S. 106, 84 S.Ct. 242, 11 L.Ed.2d 186 (1963); See also supra § 20.2 n.8. On preclusion by prior litigation see infra Chapter 24.

§ 20.7

1. Jones v. Habersham, 107 U.S. 174, 2 S.Ct. 336, 27 L.Ed. 401 (1883); Ford v. Ford, 80 Mich. 42, 44 N.W. 1057 (1890); Fischer v. Stuart, 104 N.J.L. 78, 138 A. 873 (1927) (noted 26 Mich. L. Rev. 438 (1928)); Mount v. Tuttle, 183 N.Y. 358, 76 N.E. 873 (1906) (noted 19 Harv. L. Rev. 457 (1906)); In re Strauss' Estate, 75 Misc.2d 454, 347

however, no reason to expect that a situs court would not validate a testator's intent and sustain a trust if the law of a reasonably related state would do so.[2] Suppose the will directs a sale of the lands in a testamentary trust under circumstances such that the doctrine of equitable conversion applies, by which land will be treated as a movable. If the situs applies the conversion doctrine, the subject matter of the devise may be considered a movable and the situs refer the validity of the disposition to domiciliary law.[3] The state of the situs of land is not then primarily concerned, for the property held in trust is not the local land but the proceeds of the sale.[4] Characterization should be recognized as a means of carrying forward the intention of its owner and not applied mechanically. The older cases held that if the will directs investments in land in another state, it is treated as making a devise of realty the validity of which will be determined by the law of the latter state.[5] These cases raise difficult questions in the administration of trusts. Clearly a trust once valid should not have its validity jeopardized or its applicable law changed solely by reason of investments which the trustee is authorized to make.[6] The better view recognizes the doctrine of equitable conversion as a means of validating a trust but not invalidating it. This is consistent with honoring the settlor's intent while avoiding irrelevant limitations on the trustee's investment authority.

N.Y.S.2d 840 (1973); Lewis v. Doerle, 28 O.R. 412 (1897). In re Piercy, [1895] 1 Ch. 83, apparently contra, is discussed in Beale, Equitable Interests in Foreign Property, 20 Harv. L. Rev. 382 (1907). See the more extensive treatment of trusts infra Chapter 21.

2. See, e.g., Merchants' Loan & Trust Co. v. Northern Trust Co., 250 Ill. 86, 95 N.E. 59 (1911). See also infra § 21.2.

3. See McGuire v. Andre, 259 Ala. 109, 65 So.2d 185 (1953); McCaughna v. Bilhorn, 10 Cal.App.2d 674, 52 P.2d 1025 (1935), noted, 24 Calif. L. Rev. 605 (1936), 49 Harv. L. Rev. 994 (1936), 50 Harv. L. Rev. 1119, 1152 (1937); Duckwall v. Lease, 106 Ind. App. 664, 20 N.E.2d 204 (1939); Moore v. Livingston, 148 Ind.App. 275, 265 N.E.2d 251 (1970); Penfield v. Tower, 1 N.D. 216, 46 N.W. 413 (1890); Chamberlain v. Chamberlain, 43 N.Y. 424 (1871); Hope v. Brewer, 136 N.Y. 126, 32 N.E. 558 (1892). If under the characterization made according to the law of the situs, no conversion occurs, the local situs law applies. See Appeal of Clarke, 70 Conn. 483, 40 A. 111 (1898), affirmed Clarke v. Clarke, 178 U.S. 186, 20 S.Ct. 873, 44 L.Ed. 1028 (1900); Toledo Society for Crippled Children v. Hickok, 152 Tex. 578, 261 S.W.2d 692 (1953), cert. denied 347 U.S. 936, 74 S.Ct. 631, 98 L.Ed.

1086 (1954). See also In re Berchtold (1923) 1 Ch. 192; In re Burke, 22 Sask. 142, 1 D.L.R. 318 (1927) (noted 41 Harv. L. Rev. 795 (1928)). Cf. In re Duval's Estate, 133 Vt. 197, 332 A.2d 802 (1975). But cf. Humble Oil & Refining Co. v. Copeland, 398 F.2d 364 (4th Cir.1968).

4. But see, (Lowe v. Plainfield Trust Co., 216 App.Div. 72, 215 N.Y.S. 50 (1926)). Cf. Toledo Society for Crippled Children v. Hickok, 152 Tex. 578, 261 S.W.2d 692 (1953), cert. denied 347 U.S. 936, 74 S.Ct. 631, 98 L.Ed. 1086 (1954).

5. Ford v. Ford, 70 Wis. 19, 33 N.W. 188 (1887), 72 Wis. 621, 40 N.W. 502 (1888); cf. Mount v. Tuttle, 183 N.Y. 358, 76 N.E. 873 (1906); but cf. United States Trust Co. v. Wood, 146 App.Div. 751, 131 N.Y.S. 427 (1911), affirmed 205 N.Y. 564, 98 N.E. 1118 (1912) (bequest of personalty in New York to be invested in land in Montana, invalid by law of both New York and Montana but valid by law of domicile of testator, held valid). Compare Ford v. Ford, 80 Mich. 42, 44 N.W. 1057 (1890); West Virginia Pulp & Paper Co. v. Miller, 176 Fed. 284 (4th Cir. 1909), cert. denied 220 U.S. 619, 31 S.Ct. 722, 55 L.Ed. 612 (1911). Cf. Norris v. Loyd, 183 Iowa 1056, 168 N.W. 557 (1918).

6. See infra § 21.2.

3. *Construction*

§ 20.8   The process of construction of a will, or of any written instrument, covers such variation of circumstances and gradations of intent that it defies specific definition. This makes it difficult to distinguish construction from the process of interpretation into which it shades. The emphasis of interpretation is factual, i.e., what do the words in a will reflect in the way of an intended resolution of the issue, or what did the testator in fact have in mind when he used the particular language found in his will.[1] On this question any relevant evidence should be considered by the court as an aid to determine the testator's attitude of mind. As to this process, legal doctrine has little application except for determining relevance and screening the self-serving offerings of the litigants.[2]

If the testator spells out the meaning and effect of the will's provisions, this of course controls. From this it seems clear that if the testator were to incorporate by reference the law of a particular state to be used to construe the provisions of the will, such a reference would be effective.[3] This is the position taken in the Section 2–703 Uniform Probate Code[4] which provides:

> The meaning and legal effect of a governing instrument is determined by the local law of the state selected in the governing instrument unless the application of that law is contrary to the provisions relating to the elective share described in Part 2, the provisions relating to exempt property and allowances described in Part 4, or any other public policy of this State otherwise applicable to the disposition.

When there is no choice-of-law clause in the will, and all available evidence of the testator's actual intention still leaves the issue unresolved, the legal process faces a difficult choice. The problem then is whether so little direction has been given by the testator that his attempted disposition should fail and the property be deemed to pass by the rules of intestacy, or whether the skeletal scheme provided by the testator should be filled out by presuming or ascribing intent. The policy of giving effect to the testator's intention usually requires that the latter alternative be taken. This process of completing or presuming the intention of the testator as to matters over which he could have exercised testamentary direction is called construction.[5] The presumptions that are applied in such instances range from ones of slight strength on the ill-defined border between interpretation and construc-

§ 20.8

1.   Note, Choice of Law Rules for Construction and Interpretation of Written Instruments, 72 Harv. L. Rev. 1154 (1959); Restatement, Second, Conflict of laws § 240, cmnt. (c) (1971). Cf. 2 A. Corbin, Corbin on Contracts § 534 (1950).

2.   Cf. 3 A. Corbin, Corbin on Contracts §§ 536, 537 (1950).

3.   See Restatement, Second, Conflict of Laws § 240, cmnt. (e) (1971); In re Quin's Estate, 77 Misc.2d 1077, 354 N.Y.S.2d 561 (1974).

4.   See also U.P.C. § 2–602 (pre–1990 version); N.Y. E.P.T.L § 3–5.1(h).

5.   T. Atkinson, Handbook of the Law of Wills § 146 (2d ed. 1953); Restatement, Second, Conflict of Laws §§ 240, 264, cmnt. (d) (1971).

tion, to those which, for practical purposes, override uncertain or unacceptable expressions of intention on the equally indistinct border between the rules of construction and the rules of law.[6] The cases reveal little judicial awareness of the gradations between what the testator would have preferred, what the court believes he should have preferred, or what the court deems will result from the circumstances. What is revealed, however, is that the construction process is used to accommodate the practical results the court considers it prefers or is compelled by authority to reach. In most cases, choice-of-law doctrines have little to do with selecting the result, but are often offered as a rationalization for it.

In much of what is called construction, choice-of-law doctrine should have little or no impact. As long as the process is directed at filling in details of the testamentary scheme along the guidelines provided in the will, the emphasis remains factual.[7] The legal frame of reference within which the testator planned his disposition is a significant fact whether it be that of the forum or a nonforum state. When the process shifts away from the factual and the presumptions to be applied override nonexplicit expressions of intention, the usual choice of law analysis should apply.

More specific suggestions may be offered concerning choice of law in construction of wills of land. In litigation among the beneficiaries of a decedent's estate, the matter can be approached as substantially a factual determination in which the circumstance of the testator, his family, and the law of his domicile at the execution of the will, are relevant considerations by the court in reaching a solution consistent with the reasonable expectations of the parties. In this instance, the law of the domicile of the testator at the time of execution is relevant as that most likely to have been a frame of reference for terminology and for planning the disposition of the estate.[8] While this seems little more than considering law as a relevant fact, it is often considered a choice-of-law rule.[9] Particularly would this likely be the legal frame of reference where

---

6. See T. Atkinson, supra n.5, § 146, at 814.

7. Choice of Laws Rules for Construction and Interpretation of Written Instruments Note, 72 Harv. L. Rev. 1154, 1161 (1959).

8. See Liberty Nat. Bank & Trust v. United States, 867 F.2d 302 (6th Cir.1989); Greenwood v. Page, 138 F.2d 921 (D.C.Cir. 1943). Fidelity & Columbia Trust Co. v. Lucas, 66 F.2d 116 (6th Cir.1933); In re Quin's Estate, 77 Misc.2d 1077, 354 N.Y.S.2d 561 (1974). Cf. Fishman v. Keating, 542 S.W.2d 314 (Mo.App.1976); Toledo Trust Co. v. Santa Barbara Foundation, 32 Ohio St.3d 141, 512 N.E.2d 664 (1987), cert. denied 485 U.S. 916, 108 S.Ct. 1089, 99 L.Ed.2d 250 (1988). But cf. In re Tonetti's Will, 53 Misc.2d 501, 279 N.Y.S.2d 299 (1967). See also Halbach, The Use of Powers of Appointment in Estate Planning, 45 Iowa L. Rev. 691, 716 (1960). Admittedly

the frame of reference of his draftsman might be more relevant but one of our incontrovertible fictions is to ascribe the language of a will to the testator. Cf. Lincoln v. Aldrich, 149 Mass. 368, 21 N.E. 671 (1889); In re Dialogue's Will, 159 Misc. 18, 287 N.Y.S. 237 (1936). White v. United States, 511 F.Supp. 570 (S.D.Ind.1981), aff'd 680 F.2d 1156 (7th Cir.1982) (law of the domicile of the testator at the time of death applies to interpreting a will for all purposes).

9. See Guerard v. Guerard, 73 Ga. 506 (1884); Keith v. Eaton, 58 Kan. 732, 51 P. 271 (1897); Houghton v. Hughes, 108 Me. 233, 79 A. 909 (1911); Ford v. Ford, 70 Wis. 19, 33 N.W. 188 (1887). See also Ford v. Ford, 80 Mich. 42, 44 N.W. 1057 (1890); Bolling v. Bolling, 88 Va. 524, 14 S.E. 67 (1891). Cf. Higinbotham v. Manchester, 113 Conn. 62, 154 A. 242 (1931); Staigg v. Atkinson, 144 Mass. 564, 12 N.E. 354 (1887);

land in more than one state passes by a single will.[10]

When litigation involves third parties, such as purchasers or mortgagees, then possible reliance upon the will as a recorded muniment of title becomes significant. If the issue involves a matter relating to the title or the extent of an interest transferred by a beneficiary, the interest of the situs in protecting those relying on the title record would seem to make the situs the appropriate reference.[11] A matter relating to the extent or nature of the interest passing by the will would likely involve a presumption that would prevail in absence of contrary intent expressed in the instrument itself. This type of issue appropriately falls under the usual choice-of-law reference to the whole law of the situs by a nonsitus forum or to the local law of the situs by the situs forum.[12]

Under this approach, the area of application of choice-of-law doctrine is limited to that part of the construction spectrum that deals essentially with rules of strongly presumed intent rather than actual intention. The difficulty of predicting results under such an approach is manifest. It is submitted, however, that there is presently no clear doctrinal solution available,[13] that the courts use the constructional process as a vehicle for decisions reached for reasons other than doctrine, and that the suggested approach is more nearly in accord with policy and practice than arbitrary references based solely on a characterization of the asset as movable or immovable.

C. WILLS OF MOVABLES

1. *Validity*

§ 20.9 When a person dies leaving movable property in one or more states, and leaves a will directing its disposition, the law of the state of the decedent's domicile at the time of death is of primary importance in deciding questions about the will.[1] This is the same

Martin v. Eslick, 229 Miss. 234, 90 So.2d 635 (1956), modified 229 Miss. 234, 92 So.2d 244 (1957); Zombro v. Moffett, 329 Mo. 137, 44 S.W.2d 149 (1931). Cf. Scoles, Apportionment of Federal Estate Taxes and Conflict of Laws, 55 Colum. L. Rev. 261, 270 (1955).

10. Cf. Restatement, Second, Conflict of Laws § 240, cmnt. (f) (1971). But cf. McCartney v. Osburn, 118 Ill. 403, 9 N.E. 210 (1886); In re Good's Will, 304 N.Y. 110, 106 N.E.2d 36 (1952).

11. Cf. Hening, Is the Construction of Wills Devising Real Estate Governed By the Rules of Construction of the Domicil of the Testator or the Rules of the Situs of the Property (pts. 1–2), 41 Am. L. Reg. N.S. 623, 718 (1902); Goodrich, Two States and Real Estate, 89 U. Pa. L. Rev. 417 (1941). See Peet v. Peet, 229 Ill. 341, 82 N.E. 376 (1907); Babb v. Rand, 345 A.2d 496 (Me. 1975); Jennings v. Jennings, 21 Ohio St. 56

(1871). See also In re Osborn's Estate, 151 Misc. 52, 270 N.Y.S. 616 (1934) (to determine whether general legacies in the will of a New York domiciliary were a charge on lands in New Jersey, the New York surrogate directed that the issue be tried in the courts of New Jersey). Cf. Humble Oil & Refining Co. v. Copeland, 398 F.2d 364 (4th Cir.1968).

12. Cf. Blood v. Poindexter, 534 N.E.2d 768 (Ind.Tax 1989); Matter of Estate of Allen, 237 Mont. 114, 772 P.2d 297 (1989); In re Good's Will, 304 N.Y. 110, 106 N.E.2d 36 (1952); Woolums v. Simonsen, 214 Kan. 722, 522 P.2d 1321 (1974).

13. See Restatement, Second, Conflict of Laws § 240, cmnt. (f) (1971).

§ 20.9

1. Restatement, Second, Conflict of Laws § 263 (1971). See, e.g., Reif v. Reif, 86 Ohio App.3d 804, 621 N.E.2d 1279 (1993);

approach taken in the devolution of personal estate by intestate succession, although there is greater room for the effective operation of intent in will cases. While the situs state could probably determine the devolution of the property,[2] the law of the domicile is recognized by the choice-of-law rule of the situs of the property. The reason for the recognition, as in the case of intestate succession, rests on the presumed intention or preference of the testator for the application of the law of his domicile. This is on the assumption that the domicile represents the legal system with which he is most familiar. The early purpose of the choice of law rule seems clearly to have been to validate and sustain the wills of strangers to the situs forum. New York's high court once put it this way:

> "The general principle that a disposition of personal property, valid at the domicile of the owner, is valid everywhere, is one of universal application. It had its origin in that international comity which was one of the first fruits of civilization, and in this age, when business intercourse and the process of accumulating property take but little notice of boundary lines, the practical wisdom and justice of the rule is more apparent than ever."[3]

In general, the domicile rule has worked as a validating reference because most cases arise at the situs in the process of administration and the forum will normally sustain the disposition if it satisfies either the local law or that of the domicile. Seldom has the law of the domicile at death been applied to invalidate a disposition by will.[4] Among the states of the United States, there are few invalidating differences in the law of the different states. What rare historical differences there have been in the formal requirements for wills have largely been removed by the adoption of uniform statutes regulating execution and by statutes recognizing the validity of wills executed elsewhere. Under the common law conflict-of-laws rule, if a will is sufficient by the law of the decedent's domicile at the time of his death, it is recognized as valid elsewhere even though it did not comply with the requirements of the domicile at the time the testator executed it.[5] However, the common law rule does not validate a will in the converse situation. Statutes in most of the American states, as in England and Canada, now validate a will which conforms to the requirement of the law of the place of execution or of the domiciliary law of the testator at the time of execution or at the time of death.[6] With the validating force of these statutes and the domicile rule,

In re Roberts' Estate, 509 P.2d 495 (Okla. App. 1972). Matter of Estate of Rivas, 233 Kan. 898, 666 P.2d 691 (1983); Carr v. Kupfer, 250 Ga. 106, 296 S.E.2d 560 (1982).

2. Cf. e.g., In re Estate of Hatcher, 439 So.2d 977 (Fla.App.1983); Frick v. Pennsylvania, 268 U.S. 473, 45 S.Ct. 603, 69 L.Ed. 1058 (1925).

3. Dammert v. Osborn, 140 N.Y. 30, 41, 35 N.E. 407, 409 (1893).

4. See Yiannopoulos, Wills of Movables in American International Conflicts Law: A

Critique of the Domiciliary "Rule," 46 Calif. L. Rev. 185, 197 (1958); In re Dehn's Will, 75 Misc.2d 85, 347 N.Y.S.2d 821 (1973); French v. Short, 207 Va. 548, 151 S.E.2d 354 (1966).

5. E.g., Blackwell v. Grant, 46 Ga.App. 241, 167 S.E. 333 (1933); In re Beaumont's Estate, 216 Pa. 350, 65 A. 799 (1907).

6. See Lorenzen, The Validity of Wills, Deeds and Contracts as Regards Form in the Conflict of Laws, 20 Yale L.J. 427 (1911); Rabel, The Form of Wills, 6 Vand.

nearly all results reached in the cases are consistent with achieving the maximum possible effect to the testator's plan of disposition. In the construction cases, the domicile at the time of execution is important. Although the traditional statement of the rule often overlooks the intention implementing effect of the domiciliary reference, the courts quite consciously attempt to accommodate this policy in deciding cases.

Specific applications of the general rule referring to the law of the domicile are many. The capacity of the property owner to make a will is sustained by the law of the domicile at death.[7] In actual contests of testamentary capacity, however, the issue will likely be tried as any local case in the forum on the assumption that the same test or testamentary capacity is common to all of the states.[8] The law of the domicile, as the family home, is usually also most pertinent in considering restrictions on testation for the protection of the family,[9] although any state in which property belonging to a decedent is situated probably may place restrictions upon the power to dispose of that property.[10] The law of the domicile has been found controlling in nearly all cases involving the forced share of a surviving spouse. In most instances, the family protection policy has resulted in either the domicile applying its own law[11] or

L. Rev. 533 (1953). Supra § 20.6 n.4. But see Matter of Estate of Campbell, 673 P.2d 645 (Wyo.1983) (issue whether bequest to beneficiaries voided by fact that they witnessed execution of codicil governed by law of state of execution).

7. Buresh v. First National Bank, 10 Or.App. 463, 500 P.2d 1063 (1972); Cameron v. Watson, 40 Miss. 191 (1866); Matter of Stewart's Will, 11 Paige 398 (N.Y.Ch. 1845). See generally Bozeman, The Conflict of Laws Relating to Wills, Probate Decrees and Estates, 49 A.B.A.J. 670 (1963).

8. Warner v. Warner, 14 Ark.App. 257, 687 S.W.2d 856 (1985) (proof of valid execution of will, including applicability of presumption of exertion of undue influence, governed not by law of state of execution, but by forum law).

9. American Bible Soc. v. Healy, 153 Mass. 197, 26 N.E. 404 (1891); Chamberlain v. Chamberlain, 43 N.Y. 424 (1871); In re Crichton's Estate, 20 N.Y.2d 124, 281 N.Y.S.2d 811, 228 N.E.2d 799 (1967); Crichton v. Succession of Crichton, 232 So.2d 109 (La.App.1970), writ refused 256 La. 274, 236 So.2d 39 (La. 1970), cert. denied Crichton v. McGehee, 400 U.S. 919, 91 S.Ct. 172, 27 L.Ed.2d 159 (1970); Buresh v. First National Bank, 10 Or.App. 463, 500 P.2d 1063 (1972); Memphis State University v. Agee, 566 S.W.2d 283 (Tenn.App.1977). Cf. Dreyfus v. First National Bank of Chicago, 424 F.2d 1171 (7th Cir.1970), cert. denied 400 U.S. 832, 91 S.Ct. 64, 27 L.Ed.2d 63 (1970); In re Estate of Clark, 21 N.Y.2d 478, 288 N.Y.S.2d 993, 236 N.E.2d 152 (1968); In re

Rougeron's Estate, 17 N.Y.2d 264, 270 N.Y.S.2d 578, 217 N.E.2d 639 (1966), cert. denied 385 U.S. 899, 87 S.Ct. 204, 17 L.Ed.2d 131 (1966). But cf. Estate of Renard, 100 Misc.2d 347, 417 N.Y.S.2d 155 (1979); N.Y. E.P.T.L. § 5–1.1–A(c)(7); Amend, The Surviving Spouse and the Est., Powers & Trusts Law, 33 Brooklyn L. Rev. 530 (1967). In re Ross, [1930] 1 Ch. 377 (power of an English testatrix domiciled in Italy to disinherit her son was held governed by the law of England, since under the law of Italy such matters were determined by the law of the nationality; noted 43 Harv.L.Rev.). See Scoles, Choice of Law in Family Property Transactions, 209 Recueil des Cours 17 (1988–II).

10. In re Lathrop's Estate, 165 Cal. 243, 131 P. 752 (1913). In determining whether a testator has bequeathed to charity a greater portion of his estate than the local statute permits, the courts consider the entire estate, wherever situated. Matter of Dwyer's Estate, 159 Cal. 680, 115 P. 242 (1911); Decker v. Vreeland, 220 N.Y. 326, 115 N.E. 989 (1917); Paschal v. Acklin, 27 Tex. 173 (1863). Where a gift of property is valid by the law of the domicile but invalid by that of the situs, a court of the domicile may in distributing other assets reduce the share of those who benefited by the invalidity by the amount which they received as a result thereof. Whalley v. Lawrence's Estate, 93 Vt. 424, 108 A. 387 (1919).

11. In re Binkow's Estate, 120 So.2d 15 (Fla.App.1960); Griley v. Griley, 43 So.2d 350 (Fla.1949); Henderson v. Usher, 125

the nondomicile situs of movables applying the law of the domicile favorably to the spouse.[12] In the few cases in which the nondomicile situs law appeared more favorable to the spouse than the domicile, with rare exceptions,[13] the forum applied the law of the domicile even though unfavorable to the surviving spouse.[14] In the area of interim family or spouse's allowances during the administrative probate process, the family protection policies often override the presumed intention of the testator, and the law of the forum, favorable to the surviving spouse, is frequently applied as a procedural or administrative matter.[15] In the absence of statute, the relevant law is that of the domicile at death, not that at the time of execution of the will.[16]

2. Restrictions on Charitable Gifts

§ 20.10 The policy of validating the intended disposition is also reflected in cases involving the restriction in statutes limiting the proportion of the estate which one may leave to charitable purposes.[1] Suppose a testator, dying domiciled in a state having no restriction, leaves all his personalty to a charitable society in another state where such a statute is in force. Such gifts are generally held valid on the theory that the statutes are restrictions on testamentary capacity, and thus inapplicable to nonresident testators.[2] As already indicated,[3] howev-

Fla. 709, 170 So. 846 (1936); In re Weiss' Will, 64 N.Y.S.2d 331 (1946). Cf. Murphy v. Murphy, 125 Fla. 855, 170 So. 856 (1936); Succession of Goss, 304 So.2d 704 (La.App. 1974), writ denied 309 So.2d 339 (La.1975), cert. denied 423 U.S. 869, 96 S.Ct. 133, 46 L.Ed.2d 99 (1975). Cf. Johnson v. LaGrange State Bank, 50 Ill.App.3d 830, 365 N.E.2d 1056 (1977), affirmed in part, reversed on other grounds 73 Ill.2d 342, 22 Ill.Dec. 709, 383 N.E.2d 185 (1978). But cf. Rose v. St. Louis Union Trust Co., 43 Ill.2d 312, 253 N.E.2d 417 (1969). See also supra n.8.

12. Cf. Roberts v. Chase, 25 Tenn.App. 636, 166 S.W.2d 641 (1942). The Hague Convention on The Law Applicable To Succession To The Estates of Deceased Persons (1988) generally applies the law of the habitual residence, substantially equivalent to domicile, and limits effective choice of law by the decedent to either the habitual residence or nationality. See infra § 20.16.

13. In re Gould's Estate, 140 N.E.2d 793 (Ohio Prob.1956), affirmed 140 N.E.2d 801 (Ohio App. 1956). Cf. In re Smith's Estate, 182 Misc. 711, 48 N.Y.S.2d 631 (1944) (express choice-of-law clause in the will given effect).

14. In re Kimmel's Estate, 193 Minn. 233, 258 N.W. 304 (1935). Cf. In re O'Connor's Estate, 218 Cal. 518, 23 P.2d 1031 (1933); Caruso v. Caruso, 106 N.J.Eq. 130, 148 A. 882 (1930); In re Bulova's Will, 14 A.D.2d 249, 220 N.Y.S.2d 541 (1961); In re

Gallagher's Estate, 10 Misc.2d 422, 169 N.Y.S.2d 271 (1957), affirmed 7 A.D.2d 1029, 184 N.Y.S.2d 782 (1959); Lane v. St. Louis Union Trust Co., 356 Mo. 76, 201 S.W.2d 288 (1947); In re McCombs' Estate, 80 N.E.2d 573 (Ohio Prob.1948). But cf. A. Ehrenzweig, A Treatise on the Conflict of Laws 676 (1962).

15. The family allowance cases must be distinguished from the forced share or dower cases in view of the common attitude that the family allowance is an incident and cost of administration rather than a substantive disposition of the decedent's estate. The significant policies vary greatly. See Scoles, Conflict of Laws and Nonbarrable Interests in Administration of Decedents' Estates, 8 U. Fla. L. Rev. 151, 172 (1955); see also infra Chapter 22.

16. Cf. In re Groos, [1915] 1 Ch. L.J. 572 (noted 28 Harv. L. Rev. 809 (1915)).

§ 20.10

1. See, e.g., Dreyfus v. First National Bank of Chicago, 424 F.2d 1171 (7th Cir. 1970), cert. denied 400 U.S. 832, 91 S.Ct. 64, 27 L.Ed.2d 63 (1970); Memphis State University v. Agee, 566 S.W.2d 283 (Tenn. App.1977).

2. Crum v. Bliss, 47 Conn. 592 (1880); Fellows v. Miner, 119 Mass. 541 (1876); American Bible Soc. v. Healy, 153 Mass.

er, such control is not necessarily confined to the state in which the testator is domiciled and a few courts have applied their own statutes to invalidate gifts by nonresident testators of local property.[4]

3. Revocation

a. By Instrument or Physical Act

§ 20.11 If a testator, having made a will disposing of personalty, decides to revoke it, this testamentary act is equally significant as an expression of intention as is that of execution. Traditionally, the courts have followed the rule, usually applied in other situations regarding testamentary disposition of personal property, that the law of the domicile should determine the effectiveness of the revocation.[1] In the case of a formally executed instrument of revocation, the usual approach sustaining the testator's intended disposition should clearly apply. Many forms of revocation, however, are provided and the different policies served by each should not be overlooked.

An intricate problem may arise, for example, when a testator has changed his domicile between the time of an alleged informal revocation and the time of his death, and the law of the two states differs on the question of revocation. Assume, for instance, that the decedent having made a will while domiciled in Michigan, revokes it by drawing a line through the signature, and assume further that this is sufficient revocation by Michigan law. Then the decedent moved to New York and died domiciled there, and assume that by New York law such a cancellation is not sufficient revocation and that the will is by New York law otherwise valid. For a second instance, assume the same facts but the converse rules of law in the two states; that by Michigan law cancellation was not sufficient revocation, but by New York law it is sufficient. Does the decedent in either case die testate or intestate?

The traditional attitude has been to determine this case, like the more formal one, by the law of the domicile at death.[2] It is submitted that the same concern for the testator's intention as was earlier shown in sustaining validly executed wills should apply here. Consequently, if there is a statute purporting to refer questions of execution to the domicile at the time of execution or to the place of execution, the

197, 26 N.E. 404 (1891); Dammert v. Osborn, 140 N.Y. 30, 35 N.E. 407 (1893); Mayor, & c., of Caterbury v. Wyburn, [1895] App.Cas. 89. But cf. Kerr v. Dougherty, 79 N.Y. 327 (1880).

3. Supra § 20.9 n.10.

4. In re Lathrop's Estate, 165 Cal. 243, 131 P. 752 (1913); cf. In re Layton's Estate, 217 Cal. 451, 19 P.2d 793 (1933).

§ 20.11

1. Rabe v. McAllister, 177 Md. 97, 8 A.2d 922 (1939); Mills v. Fogal, 4 Edw. Ch.

559 (N.Y.1844) (effect of birth of child as revocation); Bloomer v. Bloomer, 2 Bradf. Surr. 339 (N.Y.1853) (same). See generally Note, 64 U. Pa. L. Rev. 218 (1915).

2. Restatement, Second, Conflict of Laws § 263, cmnt. (i) (1971); Bozeman, Conflict of Laws Relating to Wills, Probate Decrees and Estates, 49 A.B.A.J. 670, 671 (1963).

intentional, albeit informal, revocation should receive the same treatment.[3] Revocation by act of destruction should likewise be validated if valid by the place it occurred or by the testator's domicile at that time.[4]

b. By Operation of Law

§ 20.12 Revocation by operation of law is not as simple because the pertinent policies vary greatly. This is emphasized by the problem of revocation of bequests by reason of divorce.[1] In determining an appropriate property settlement on divorce, the parties and the courts will naturally consider the law of the state of the current domicile as the background for their conclusions.[2] A statute of that state revoking a testamentary provision in favor of the former spouse is a guard against an unintended double portion. Upon a subsequent change of domicile prior to death, for a court to apply a governing law other than the domicile at time of the divorce may permit a double portion contrary to the expectation of all parties to the divorce, and, in the words of the New Jersey court, "would work an injustice by frustrating the clear expectations of the testator."[3] In the case of revocation by reason of marriage or subsequent birth of a child, the inappropriateness of the last domicile is not so apparent, because revocation operates as a family protection device in which the domiciliary state at death normally has the dominant interest.[4] Particularly would this be true if the births of different children were subject to varying laws. In such a case, the need for uniformity would call for a single reference, and the last domicile would probably be the most appropriate choice absent other indicia of intent. In such a highly unusual situation, a court could well be expected to consider the significant policies and to reach a solution by appropriate construction of a foreign execution or revocation statute. Most courts, however, in the few cases which have arisen, have quite rigidly applied the law of the last domicile in such matters.[5]

3. See In re Traversi's Estate, 189 Misc. 251, 64 N.Y.S.2d 453 (1946); Scoles & Rheinstein, Conflict Avoidance in Succession Planning, 21 Law & Contemp. Prob. 499, 505 (1956). Cf. supra § 20.9.

4. See supra § 20.6 n.10.

§ 20.12

1. See, e.g., U.P.C. § 2–804; In re Patterson's Estate, 64 Cal.App. 643, 222 P. 374 (1923).

2. This is because both jurisdiction for divorce and governing law are within the province of the law of the state of the plaintiff's domicile at the time of the action, i.e., local law. See Torlonia v. Torlonia, 108 Conn. 292, 142 A. 843 (1928); Stewart v. Stewart, 32 Idaho 180, 180 P. 165 (1919); Rose v. Rose, 132 Minn. 340, 156 N.W. 664 (1916); Matter of Garver's Estate, 135 N.J.Super. 578, 343 A.2d 817 (1975). See supra Chapter 15.

3. In re Garver's Estate, 135 N.J.Super. 578, 343 A.2d 817, 819 (1975). See also In re Patterson's Estate, 64 Cal.App. 643, 222 P. 374 (1923). Cf. Irwin's Appeal from Probate, 33 Conn. 128 (1865); In re Hollister's Estate, 18 N.Y.2d 281, 274 N.Y.S.2d 585, 221 N.E.2d 376 (1966); Moultrie v. Hunt, 23 N.Y. 394 (1861); In re Cutler's Will, 114 Misc. 203, 186 N.Y.S. 271 (1921). But see In re Traversi's Estate, 189 Misc. 251, 64 N.Y.S.2d 453 (1946).

4. Cf. American Bible Soc. v. Healy, 153 Mass. 197, 26 N.E. 404 (1891); Scoles, Conflict of Laws and Nonbarrable Interests in Administration of Decedents' Estates, 8 U. Fla. L. Rev. 151 (1955). But see Matter of Wimbush's Estate, 41 Colo.App. 289, 587 P.2d 796 (1978).

5. In re Patterson's Estate, 64 Cal.App. 643, 222 P. 374 (1923); Matter of Wimbush's Estate, 41 Colo.App. 289, 587 P.2d

In the second hypothetical case set out above, where the act done did not amount to a revocation by the law of the domicile when done, but did by the law of the domicile of the testator at death, it has been held that the will was revoked.[6]

4. *Construction*

§ 20.13   In the disposition of movable assets under an admittedly valid will, numerous questions of construction can arise. A typical kind of case is presented if a testator makes a bequest of the income of certain property for life to a person domiciled in another state, with a gift over to the life beneficiary's "heirs at law" or "next of kin." Is the determination of this class of takers to be made by the law of the testator's domicile or that of the domicile of the life beneficiary? As has been noted earlier in discussing constructions of wills of land,[1] the processes of interpretation and construction cover a wide range of problems and imperceptibly shade into each other. Construction, however, is primarily concerned with the giving effect to the testator's disposition in an instance in which his intention is unclear or unexpressed. Because the courts are attempting to give effect to his intention the testator may choose the law by which his will is to be construed.[2] If the testator furnishes no express direction, his intention, implied or assumed, still furnishes a guide to choice of law as to a will of movables.[3] On the

796 (Colo.App. 1978); In re Culley's Will, 182 Misc. 998, 48 N.Y.S.2d 216 (1944); Matter of Coburn's Will, 9 Misc. 437, 30 N.Y.S. 383 (1894); In re Smith's Estate, 55 Wyo. 181, 97 P.2d 677 (1940). But cf. In re Martin, Pac. 211 (1900); Note, 34 Harv. L. Rev. 768 (1921).

6. Matter of Coburn's Will, 9 Misc. 437, 30 N.Y.S. 383 (1894). In Matter of White's Will, 112 Misc. 433, 183 N.Y.S. 129 (1920), 6 Cornell L.Q. 212 (1920), the testator had moved to the second state before the alleged revocation (his marriage) took place. See Westerman v. Schwab, 43 Sc.L.R. 161 (1905), accord in result but evidently on the theory that the governing law is the domicile at the time of marriage. Cf. Senac's Succession, 2 Rob. 258 (La. 1842); In re Hollister's Estate, 18 N.Y.2d 281, 274 N.Y.S.2d 585, 221 N.E.2d 376 (1966).

§ 20.13

1. See supra § 20.8 n.1.

2. In re Taylor's Estate, 5 Ariz.App. 144, 424 P.2d 186 (1967); In re Estate of Sewart, 342 Mich. 491, 70 N.W.2d 732 (1955); In re Cook's Estate, 204 Misc. 704, 123 N.Y.S.2d 568 (1953), affirmed 283 App. Div. 1047, 131 N.Y.S.2d 882 (1954); Risher v. American Surety Co., 227 Wis. 104, 277 N.W. 160 (1938). Several states authorize testamentary choice of law by statute, e.g.,

Ill. Rev. Stat. c. 110 1/2, § 7–6; N.Y. Est., Powers & Trusts Law § 3–5.1(h). See generally Yiannopoulos, Wills of Movables in American International Conflicts Law: A Critique of the Domiciliary "Rule," 46 Calif. L. Rev. 185, 248 (1958); A. Ehrenzweig, A Treatise on the Conflict of Laws § 249 (1962). Cf. In re Dow's Estate, 81 Misc.2d 506, 366 N.Y.S.2d 831 (1975), modified and affirmed Will of Dow, 55 A.D.2d 323, 390 N.Y.S.2d 721 (1977); Frey v. Estate of Sargent, 533 S.W.2d 142 (Tex.Civ.App.1976), writ refused, n.r.e. But cf. In re Estate of Clark, 21 N.Y.2d 478, 288 N.Y.S.2d 993, 236 N.E.2d 152 (1968) (testator does not have control over mandatory provisions for spouse at the domicile).

3. See Harrison v. Nixon, 34 U.S. (9 Pet.) 483, 503, 9 L.Ed. 201 (1835) ("The language of wills is not of universal interpretation, having the same precise import in all countries, and under all circumstances. They are supposed to speak the sense of the testator, according to the received laws or usages of the country where he is domiciled, by a sort of tacit reference, unless there is something in the language which repels or controls such a conclusion. In regard to personalty in an especial manner, the law of the place of the testator's domicile governs in the distribution thereof, and will govern in the interpretation of

assumption that the testator is most familiar with the law of his domicile, it is assumed, when no contrary indication appears, that the testator would prefer to have the law of his domicile used as the legal frame of reference for his will.[4] The reference to the domicile has even been applied where the testator executed the will abroad in a foreign language.[5] Where the domicile of the testator was in one state when the will was executed, and in another at the time of his death, on the presumption that he was using language with which he was then familiar, the view is taken that the will should be construed according to the law of the former state.[6]

The law of the decedent's domicile likewise has been applied to resolve other analogous issues, as, for instance, whether a bequest is

wills thereof, unless it is manifest that the testator had the laws of some other country in his own view").

4. Harrison v. Nixon, 34 U.S. (9 Pet.) 483, 9 L.Ed. 201 (1835); Houghton v. Hughes, 108 Me. 233, 79 A. 909 (1911); Harding v. Schapiro, 120 Md. 541, 87 A. 951 (1913); Lincoln v. Aldrich, 149 Mass. 368, 21 N.E. 671 (1889); Second Bank–State Street Trust Co. v. Weston, 342 Mass. 630, 174 N.E.2d 763 (1961); In re Riesenberg's Estate Geerdts v. Riesenberg, 116 Mo.App. 308, 90 S.W. 1170 (1905); Rosenbaum v. Garrett, 57 N.J.Eq. 186, 41 A. 252 (1898); In re Battell's Will, 286 N.Y. 97, 35 N.E.2d 913 (1941); In re Fabbri's Will, 2 N.Y.2d 236, 159 N.Y.S.2d 184, 140 N.E.2d 269 (1957); Crandell v. Barker, 8 N.D. 263, 78 N.W. 347 (1898); In re Carter's Estate, 20 D. & C. 91 (O.C. Pa. 1933); Rhode Island Hospital Trust Co. v. Votolato, 102 R.I. 467, 231 A.2d 491 (1967); Skinner v. Brunsen, 69 R.I. 159, 32 A.2d 263 (1943); In re Ferguson's Will, [1902] 2 Ch.D. 483, 71 L.J. Ch. 360. See also In re Winslow's Estate, 138 Misc. 672, 247 N.Y.S. 506 (1930) (noted 31 Colum. L. Rev. 886 (1931) the testator and the beneficiary had different domiciles, and the statute of the testator's domicile defining "next of kin" had been changed between the time of his death and that of the life tenant); Teller v. Kaufman, 426 F.2d 128 (8th Cir.1970); Cosby v. Shackelford, 408 F.2d 1144 (10th Cir.1969); Santoli v. Louisville Trust Co., 550 S.W.2d 182 (Ky. App.1977); Boston Safe Deposit & Trust Co. v. Fleming, 361 Mass. 172, 279 N.E.2d 342 (1972), appeal dismissed 409 U.S. 813, 93 S.Ct. 46, 34 L.Ed.2d 69 (1972). The adoption cases may well represent an oversimplification of the intent of the testator. Cf. In re Trusts Created by Agreement With Harrington, 311 Minn. 403, 250 N.W.2d 163 (1977); In re Coe's Estate, 42 N.J. 485, 201 A.2d 571 (1964). Cf. also In re Pennington's Trust, 421 Pa. 334, 219 A.2d 353 (1966); In

re Duval's Estate, 133 Vt. 197, 332 A.2d 802 (1975). See also supra § 20.8. Estate of Buckley, 677 S.W.2d 946 (Mo.App.1984) (for purposes of construction of will and testator's intent, law of domicile at execution governs).

5. Caulfield v. Sullivan, 85 N.Y. 153 (1881); In re Kadjar's Estate, 200 Misc. 268, 102 N.Y.S.2d 113 (1950), affirmed 279 App. Div. 1008, 113 N.Y.S.2d 245 (1952). Cf. Restatement, Second, Conflict of Laws § 263 (1971). There is a difference of opinion as to whether, after the court at the domicile has construed a will devising land, other courts should follow the interpretation. For following the domiciliary construction, see White v. Keller, 68 Fed. 796 (5th Cir.1895); Ford v. Ford, 80 Mich. 42, 44 N.W. 1057 (1890). But see Appeal of Clarke, 70 Conn. 195, 39 A. 155 (1898), affirmed sub nom. Clarke v. Clarke, 178 U.S. 186, 20 S.Ct. 873, 44 L.Ed. 1028 (1900); McCartney v. Osburn, 118 Ill. 403, 9 N.E. 210 (1886).

6. Comer v. Comer, 195 Ga. 79, 23 S.E.2d 420 (1942); In re Pleasonton's Estate, 45 N.J.Super. 154, 131 A.2d 795 (App. Div.1957); In re Flagler's Will, 4 Misc.2d 705, 158 N.Y.S.2d 941 (1957); In re Gallagher's Estate, 10 Misc.2d 422, 169 N.Y.S.2d 271 (1957), affirmed 7 A.D.2d 1029, 184 N.Y.S.2d 782 (1959); Atkinson v. Staigg, 13 R.I. 725 (1882). See Holmes v. Holmes, 1 Russ. & M. 660 (1830). See also Johns Hopkins University v. Uhrig, 145 Md. 114, 125 A. 606 (1924) (under a local statute); Note, 23 Mich. L. Rev. 385, 386 (1925). Cf. Geier v. Mercantile–Safe Deposit & Trust Co., 273 Md. 102, 328 A.2d 311 (1974); First National Bank v. Shawmut Bank of Boston, 378 Mass. 137, 389 N.E.2d 1002 (1979); Royce v. Denby's Estate, 117 N.H. 893, 379 A.2d 1256 (1977); In re Childs' Estate, 63 Misc.2d 470, 312 N.Y.S.2d 390 (1970); Seeley v. Bedillion, 23 Ohio Misc. 4, 51 O.O.2d 128, 260 N.E.2d 639 (1969). Cf. N.Y.

absolute or upon trust.[7] So also, as to whether an active or a passive trust has been created;[8] whether a legacy lapses by reason of the prior death of the legatee;[9] and as to what passes under a residuary clause of a will.[10] The process of construction, as interpretation, has the objective of giving effect to the testator's intent. This primary consideration leads the courts first to explore all means of determining the testator's actual intent and, failing that, to ascribe to the testator an intent which it is reasonably anticipated he would have preferred, had he considered the matter. In this, choice of law has little significance except when the court passes those questions which the testator could have controlled and is concerned with those in which the result depends upon rules of law and not intent. In these situations, the usual choice of law rules apply.

IV. FAMILY PROTECTION—FORCED SHARES—ELECTION

A. FORCED SHARES

§ 20.14   Some family members, particularly spouses, are given the right to a force share of the estate notwithstanding the decedent's will. The choice-of-law problems for determining the forced share will first be discussed and then the problems incident to inconsistent elections in different jurisdictions will be explored. In the United States, the spouse is the only person generally provided a forced share although children are afforded this protection in Louisiana. In the community property states, spouses are primarily protected by marital property interests in assets which attach during lifetime.

The law of the decedent's domicile at death will generally determine the right of a surviving spouse to a statutory forced share out of the personal assets of the decedent.[1] We have earlier noted instances of this[2] and also the frequent application of the law of the situs as regards land

E.P.T.L. § 3–5.1(d); Scott, The Law of Trusts § 589, p. 247 (4th ed. 1989).

7. McCurdy v. McCallum, 186 Mass. 464, 72 N.E. 75 (1904).

8. Rosenbaum v. Garrett, 57 N.J.Eq. 186, 41 A. 252 (1898).

9. Lowndes v. Cooch, 87 Md. 478, 39 A. 1045 (1898); Persson v. Dukes, 280 Md. 194, 372 A.2d 240 (1977).

10. Proctor v. Clark, 154 Mass. 45, 27 N.E. 673 (1891).

§ 20.14

1. See Bullen v. Wisconsin, 240 U.S. 625, 36 S.Ct. 473, 60 L.Ed. 830 (1916); In re Randolph's Estate, 175 Kan. 685, 266 P.2d 315 (1954); Cohn v. Heymann, 544 So.2d 1242 (La.App.1989), writ denied 548 So.2d 1233 (La.1989). Cf. Matter of Estate of Lingscheit, 387 N.W.2d 738 (S.D.1986);

Matter of Estate of Reilly, 137 Misc.2d 780, 522 N.Y.S.2d 809 (1987); Re Collins, Royal Bk. etc. v. Kroogh, [1986] 1 All. E.R. 611. Widow's and family allowance claims follow an irregular pattern. See Veile v. Koch, 27 Ill. 129 (1862); Shannon v. White, 109 Mass. 146 (1872); Jones v. Layne, 144 N.C. 600, 57 S.E. 372 (1907); Restatement, Second, Conflict of Laws § 260 (1971). Cf. Scoles, Conflict of Laws and Nonbarrable Interests In Administration of Decedents' Estates, 8 Fla. L. Rev. 151, 172 (1955). See also Lotz v. Atamaniuk, 172 W.Va. 116, 304 S.E.2d 20 (1983) (domicile of testatrix at death governed issue whether estranged husband, living in adultery at time of her death, was precluded from renouncing will and electing to claim intestate share of estate).

2. See supra § 20.9 n.8.

subject to a forced share[3] and some exceptions to the situs rule.[4]

The policy recognizing the appropriate interest of the domicile in the interspousal rights in the estate is reflected in *Estate of Clark*.[5] In *Clark* the New York Court of Appeals held that the domicile's policies of spousal protection overrode the New York statute which provided that a nondomiciliary testator could choose to have testamentary dispositions construed and regulated by the laws of New York.[6] By distinguishing between statutes which restrict a decedent's testamentary power and those which provide for implementing the testator's intention, the Court of Appeals held that the New York statute permitting the testator to choose the law governing the disposition in his will did not encompass the ability to preclude the right accorded a spouse to elect to take in opposition to the will and concluded:

> "[W]e reject the notion that New York ought to impose upon its sister states its own views as to the adequacy of a surviving spouse's share.
>
> "In sum, Virginia's overwhelming interest in the protection of surviving spouses domiciled there demands that we apply its law to give the widow in this case the right of election provided for her under that law."[7]

The continuing standing of the *Clark* case in New York may be subject to some question as the New York statute was subsequently amended and the court in the *Renard*[8] case gave effect to a will containing a choice-of-law clause referring to New York to override a child's claim of legitime under French law. In *Renard,* the claim by an adult adopted son, an American citizen with dual French citizenship but domiciled in California, was asserted against New York assets in the estate of his mother, an American citizen formerly domiciled in New York for 30 years but recently retired to France. Considering the circumstance of child's claim in the *Renard* case in light of subsequent New York legislation, the *Renard* case may well be sufficiently distinguishable from the *Clark* case as not substantially to impair *Clark* as a precedent in matters spouse elections.[9]

---

3. Supra § 20.5 n.6 and § 20.6 n.11. See also Estate of Pericles, 266 Ill.App.3d 1096, 641 N.E.2d 10 (1994) (situs law applied to determine forced share in out-of-state realty).

4. See supra § 20.6 n.13.

5. In re Estate of Clark, 21 N.Y.2d 478, 288 N.Y.S.2d 993, 236 N.E.2d 152 (1968).

6. N.Y. E.P.T.L. § 3–5.1(h).

7. In re Estate of Clark, 21 N.Y.2d 478, 488, 288 N.Y.S.2d 993, 999, 236 N.E.2d 152, 158 (1968).

8. In re Estate of Renard, 108 Misc.2d 31, 437 N.Y.S.2d 860 (1981), aff'd 85 A.D.2d 501, 447 N.Y.S.2d 573 (1981), aff'd 56 N.Y.2d 973, 453 N.Y.S.2d 625, 439 N.E.2d

341 (1982). See N.Y. E.P.T.L. § 5–1.1(d)(7), (8) as amended 1986 (quoted infra n.14); Symeonides, Revising Louisiana's Conflicts Law on Successions, 47 La. L. Rev. 1029, 1093 (1987).

9. See, e.g., Matter of Rhoades, 160 Misc.2d 262, 607 N.Y.S.2d 893 (1994) (noting but not resolving *Clark/Renard* conflict). In 1986, the New York statute on the spouse's elective share was amended to provide that "the decedent's estate shall include all property of the decedent, wherever situated." 11 N.Y. EPTL § 5–1.1(d) (8) (1986). By appropriately asserting that New York, as the decedent's domicile, can base the New York surviving spouse's share on all the assets of the deceased wherever lo-

The limitation of the testator's choice-of-law autonomy is also reflected in the Hague Convention on the Law Applicable to Decedent's Estates which permits a testamentary choice of law reference to control forced share only when to the State where the deceased was a national or habitual resident at the time of his death.[10] Some bilateral treaties have been construed to allow choice-of-law provisions that override foreign forced-share statutes that would otherwise be applicable.[11]

The distinction made in the *Clark* case and application of the law of the domicile is reflected in statutory trends.[12] The strength of the interest of the domicile on the issue of spousal protection would not seem to be different in the situation in which the nonresident decedent had invested in forum land. For example, it seems unlikely that New York would have more concern for the spouse of an investor who buys New York land than of one who buys New York stocks and bonds.[13]

It needs to be recognized that different methods of family protection are employed in different states and countries. While the primary protection for surviving spouses in common law states of the United States is the elective or forced share discussed in this section, marital property or community property rights may be the method in other states or nations.[14] In addition, legislation providing for support or maintenance allowances from the decedent's estate offer significant family protection as well, and constitute the major protection for children in the United States. In the United States, these support allowances are generally considered and treated as administrative matters.[15] In lieu of the fixed forced share approach, common in U.S., English law

cated, the legislature has impliedly recognized the appropriateness of other states doing likewise. Further, reconciling this amendment with the previously existing provisions of the statute suggests an amendment by implication rather than attempted invidious discrimination against non-residents. But cf. Hendrickson, Choice of Law Directions for Disposing of Assets Situated Elsewhere than the Domicile of Their Owner—The Refractions of *Renard*, 18 Real Prop. Prob. and Tr.J. 407 (1983); Midonick & Ordover, Spousal Claims after *Renard*, 123 Trusts & Estates 14 (June 1984). See also Herzog, 1982 Survey of New York Law, Conflict of Laws, 34 Syracuse L. Rev. 113, 150–54 (1983).

10. Art. 5, Hague Convention on the Law Applicable to Succession to the Estates of Deceased Persons, 1988, 28 I.L.M. 146 (1989).

11. See, e.g., Estate of Wright, 637 A.2d 106 (Me.1994) (construing U.S.—Switzerland treaty to allow Swiss domiciled U.S. citizen to choose Maine law and thus avoid Swiss legitime; citing with approval In re: Schneider's Estate, 198 Misc. 1017, 96 N.Y.S.2d 652 (1950) and In re Estate of

Prince, 49 Misc.2d 219, 267 N.Y.S.2d 138 (1964)).

12. Cf. U.P.C. §§ 2–202, 2–703; Cal. Prob. Code § 120; Or. Rev. Stat. § 114.105. This direction of choice of law is further reflected in the extension of the forced share in a decedent's estate to include inter vivos transfers in which the decedent retains an interest or power of revocation and the inclusion of all assets in a divorce property settlement. In both instances the location of assets is disregarded and the law of the domicile is the controlling concern. Cf. e.g., Sullivan v. Burkin, 390 Mass. 864, 460 N.E.2d 572 (1984) ("It is neither equitable nor logical to extend to a divorced spouse greater rights in the assets of an inter vivos trust created and controlled by the other spouse than are extended to a spouse who remains married until the death of his or her spouse").

13. But cf. Toledo Society for Crippled Children v. Hickok, 152 Tex. 578, 261 S.W.2d 692 (1953), cert. denied 347 U.S. 936, 74 S.Ct. 631, 98 L.Ed. 1086 (1954).

14. See supra ch. 14.

15. See infra § 22.22.

uses the concept of maintenance and need to provide protection to spouses, children, and other dependents.[16] In addition to the surviving spouse's needs and resources, the English statute calls for more generous provision, reasonable in all the circumstances, for a husband or wife to be made from the decedent's estate as the court in its discretion determines.[17]

Although the circumstances differ, the basic concepts, calling for protection of the spouses and other family members on dissolution of the marriage by either divorce or death, are analogous and reflect social policies reflective of presumed contribution, probable needs for support, and concepts of family fairness, all policies centering on the family, and its maintenance as a social and economic unit. In the conflict-of-laws setting, these policies strongly suggest the predominant relationship to and concern of the state of the decedent's domicile, the usual center of family life. This choice-of-law reference to the domicile is explicit in the Uniform Probate Code provision for the surviving spouse's elective share.[18]

B. ELECTION

§ 20.15　Treatment of the general doctrine of election, as it pertains to wills, is beyond the scope of this discussion.[1] Some serious conflict-of-laws questions concerning elections arise, however, particularly with regard to the surviving spouse's forced share. Whether a testator's provision for a spouse is to be taken as being in lieu of dower or other statutory claim is a question of construction of the will and statute to be resolved as are other construction issues.[2]

The doctrine of election is designed to carry out the testator's intention and to achieve justice and fairness among his beneficiaries by avoiding "double portions" occasioned by the fortuitous location of assets. To accomplish this, a single dispositive standard is needed and the courts have placed emphasis upon the domicile of the decedent in

---

16. Inheritance provision for Family and Dependents Act 1975, §§ 1, 3.

17. Id., §§ 1, 2, 3; Prime, Family Provision—The Spouse's Application, 16 Fam. L. 95 (1986); Miller, Provision for a Surviving Spouse, 102 L.Q. Rev. 445 (1986); Miller, Family Provision on Death, 39 Int'l & Comp. L.Q. 261 (1990).

18. U.P.C. § 2–202. See also N.Y. E.P.T.L. § 5–1.1–A(c)(6), (7), as amended in 1986, which provides:

(7) The right of election granted by this section is not available to the spouse of a decedent who was not domiciled in this state at the time of death, unless such decedent elects, under paragraph (h) of 3–5.1, to have the disposition of his property situated in this state governed by the laws of this state.

(8) The decedent's estate shall include all property of the decedent, wherever situated.

§ 20.15

1. See Note, 23 Harv. L. Rev. 138 (1909); Note, 32 Harv. L. Rev. 288 (1919).

2. See supra §§ 20.8, 20.13; W. Breslauer, Private International Law of Succession In England, America and Germany 151–155 (1937). See also Heilman, Interpretation and Construction of Wills of Immovables in Conflict of Laws Cases Involving "Election," 25 Ill. L. Rev. 778 (1931); Scoles, Conflict of Laws and Elections in Administration of Decedent's Estates, 30 Ind. L.J. 293 (1955); In re Florey's Estate, 212 Neb. 665, 325 N.W.2d 643 (1982).

resolving inconsistent election problems relating to both movables and immovables.

If an election must be and is made at the domicile, the person so making the election cannot claim under the will at the domicile, and also claim under the statute in ancillary administration at the situs of the property.[3] This rule has been applied in cases in which the property in the other state was land; not on ground that the domiciliary state necessarily controlled the foreign land, but because the choice having been made, the person so making it was bound thereby.[4] The election often must be made at the domicile in the first instance.[5]

On the other hand, if an election is made or benefits accepted under the will in ancillary administration, this may not preclude a contrary election at the domicile.[6] However, the ancillary administration is not ignored but its distribution is set off against the domicile share.[7] This seems appropriate as these elective rights usually concern controversies among family members and the domicile is most significantly interested in their resolution.

A similar approach has occurred in election cases involving partial invalidity of the will. In a Pennsylvania case[8] involving this problem, in which the will of a testator domiciled in Pennsylvania was ineffective as to land in New Jersey, the person who was entitled to take the land under the law of the latter state was required to elect between relin-

3. Security Trust Co. v. Hanby, 32 Del. Ch. 70, 79 A.2d 807 (1951); Brooks v. Carson, 166 Kan. 194, 200 P.2d 280 (1948); Martin v. Battey, 87 Kan. 582, 125 P. 88 (1912); Jarel v. Moon's Succession, 190 So. 867 (La.App.1939); Russell v. Shapleigh, 275 Mass. 15, 175 N.E. 100 (1931); Wilson v. Cox, 49 Miss. 538 (1873). Cf. Colvin v. Hutchison, 338 Mo. 576, 92 S.W.2d 667 (1936); Huston v. Colonial Trust Co., 266 S.W.2d 231 (Tex.Civ.App.1954). Cf. Pfau v. Moseley, 9 Ohio St.2d 13, 222 N.E.2d 639 (1966).

4. In re Estate of Washburn, 32 Minn. 336, 20 N.W. 324 (1884); Lindsley v. Patterson, 177 S.W. 826 (Mo.1915). Cf. Bish v. Bish, 181 Md. 621, 31 A.2d 348 (1943). See Van Dyke's Appeal, 60 Pa. 481 (1869). But see Rannels v. Rowe, 166 Fed. 425 (8th Cir.1908); McGinness v. Chambers, 156 Tenn. 404, 1 S.W.2d 1015 (1928).

5. Slaughter v. Garland, 40 Miss. 172 (1866); Wilson v. Cox, 49 Miss. 538 (1873); Lindsley v. Patterson, 177 S.W. 826 (Mo. 1915). Cf. In re Patmore's Estate, 141 Cal. App.2d 416, 296 P.2d 863 (1956). That the renunciation, under the local statute, must also be made in the state where the land lies, see Apperson v. Bolton, 29 Ark. 418 (1874); In re Owsley's Estate, 122 Minn. 190, 142 N.W. 129 (1913); McGinness v.

Chambers, 156 Tenn. 404, 1 S.W.2d 1015 (1928). But see Scoles, Conflicts of Laws and Elections in Administration of Decedents' Estates, 30 Ind. L.J. 295, 298 (1955).

6. Gibson v. Gibson, 292 Fed. 657 (D.C.Cir.1923); Russell v. Shapleigh, 275 Mass. 15, 175 N.E. 100 (1931); In re Cummings' Estate, 153 Pa. 397, 25 A. 1125 (1893); Van Dyke's Appeal, 60 Pa. 481 (1869); Whalley v. Lawrence's Estate, 93 Vt. 424, 108 A. 387 (1919). Cf. In re Estate of Patmore, 141 Cal.App.2d 416, 296 P.2d 863 (1956).

7. Griley v. Griley, 43 So.2d 350 (Fla. 1949); Murphy v. Murphy, 125 Fla. 855, 170 So. 856 (1936); Van Dyke's Appeal, 60 Pa. 481 (1869).

8. Van Dyke's Appeal, 60 Pa. 481 (1869). Compare McGehee v. McGehee, 152 Md. 661, 136 A. 905 (1927) (noted 28 Colum. L. Rev. 252 (1928)); McGehee v. McGehee, 189 N.C. 558, 127 S.E. 684 (1925). The *McGehee* cases reached opposite results on whether a widow who had taken her intestate share of personalty at the domicile, South Carolina, where the will was invalid, could claim legacies in full from lands in Maryland and North Carolina, where the will was valid. See also Whalley v. Lawrence's Estate, 93 Vt. 424, 108 A. 387 (1919).

quishing the land and relinquishing the personalty left her under the will to the extent necessary to compensate the devisee under the will for the loss of the land. In some cases, however, the fortuitous location of assets may not give the domicile the control to make ultimate adjustment of the interests of the parties by means of final distribution.[9] In such a case, it seems that the policy of giving maximum effect to the intention of the testator requires such control to be exercised by any court in position by reason of available assets to do so.[10] The problem of election in conflict of laws is less a problem of choice of law and more a question of equity and fairness in spite of differing laws.

V. INTERNATIONAL WILLS

§ 20.16 In the United States, the formal validity of wills executed outside the forum state, whether executed in a sister state or in another country, are subject to the choice-of-law approaches which have been discussed. In an effort to provide greater assurance of the validity of wills executed either in the United States or in other countries, the United States served as host for the Diplomatic Conference on Wills in 1973. This conference resulted in the Washington Convention of 1973 providing the form of an international will.[1] The International Wills Convention is not only of interest because of the provisions for execution of international wills but also because it is an instance of recent increased United States participation in efforts to reach international accord on issues arising in conflict of laws. The discussions leading to the Convention on International Wills began in 1960 under the aegis of the governing council of Unidroit, the International Institute for the Unification of Private Law. The active involvement of the United States began in 1966 and culminated in the conference in 1973.[2] The United States Senate consented to ratification of the Convention in 1991.

The 1973 Convention obligates the parties to make the Uniform Law annexed to it a part of their local law and also carries a recommendation that the parties establish systems for the safekeeping and discovery of international wills. The Convention and the Uniform Law deal

---

9. See In re Estate of Patmore, 141 Cal. App.2d 416, 296 P.2d 863 (1956).

10. See McGehee v. McGehee, 152 Md. 661, 136 A. 905 (1927). Cf. Pearce v. Pearce, 281 Ill. 194, 118 N.E. 84 (1917).

§ 20.16

1. See U.P.C., Art. 2, Part 10, Prefatory Note, at 243.

2. See generally Johnson, Wills, Trusts, and Estates, 29 U.Rich.L.Rev. 1175, 1990 (1995); Pfund, United States Participation in International Unification of Private Law, 19 Int'l Lawyer 505 (1985); Amram, Present Status of International Law Respecting Wills and Administration of Estates, 8 Real

Prop., Prob. & Tr.J. 617 (1973); Fratcher, The Uniform Probate Code and the International Will, 66 Mich. L. Rev. 469 (1968); Wellman, Recent Unidroit Drafts on the International Will, 6 Int'l Lawyer 205 (1973); Wellman, Proposed International Convention Concerning Wills, 8 Real Prop., Prob & Tr.J. 622 (1973); Nadelmann, The Formal Validity of Wills and the Washington Convention 1973, Providing the Form of an International Will, 22 Am. J. Comp. L. 365 (1974); Note, International Will, 6 B.U. Int'l L.J. 317 (1988); Kearney, The International Wills Convention, 18 Int'l Law. 613 (1984); M. Brandon, UK Accession to the Wills Conventions, 32 Int'l & Comp. L.Q. 742 (1983).

only with the formal validity of wills and do not contain provisions relating to revocation or construction of wills or administration of decedent's estates. The provisions call for an extremely formal will execution so that the procedure will command international respect as being safe against imposition and mistake. The provisions for international wills under the Convention and Uniform Law are supplementary to existing rules regarding wills and do not preempt or exclude those other standards of testamentary validity.

In outline, the Uniform Law provides that a will shall be valid as regards form regardless of the place where it was made, the location or nature of the assets, or the nationality, domicile or residence of the testator if it complies with the provision of the uniform act.[3] The will must be written, attested by two witnesses and a person authorized to execute international wills.[4] A distinguishing feature of the international will is the certificate attached by the authorized person supervising the execution certifying to the satisfaction of the requirements for the valid execution.[5] This certificate, absent evidence to the contrary, is conclusive of the formal validity of the instrument as a will.[6] It is hoped that each state in the United States will establish a registry at a central location at which authorized persons may register information regarding international wills so that the wills may be identified and information provided for determining their location.[7]

Within the United States persons authorized to supervise the execution of international wills are attorneys admitted to practice law before the courts of the state.[8] Although the scope of the Convention and the Uniform Act is limited to formal validity, the general adoption of the Convention and Uniform Act by countries of the world would provide important security and guidance for those many testators who are concerned about the effectiveness of a will executed in a country other than their own, or of the effectiveness of a will executed in the country of their citizenship as to assets located elsewhere.

Subsequent to the International Wills Convention, the United States took an active part in the formulation of two Hague conventions on choice of law of great importance to those involved with international estates. The first was the 1984 Hague Convention on The Law Applicable to Trusts[9] and the second was the 1988 Hague Convention on The Law Applicable to Succession to the Estates of Deceased Persons.[10] The

3. Uniform Law on the Form of an International Will, Art. 1 (1973); U.P.C. § 2–1002.

4. See U.P.C. §§ 2–1003, 2–1004.

5. U.P.C. § 2–1005.

6. U.P.C. § 2–1006.

7. See Brandon, U.K. Accession to the Convention on the Establishment of a Scheme of Registration of Wills and on the Convention providing a Uniform Law on the Form of an International Will, 32 Int'l & Comp. L.Q. 742 (1983).

8. U.P.C. § 2–1009.

9. The Hague Convention on The Law Applicable To Trusts and on Their Recognition, Oct. 20, 1984 (discussed infra § 21.3).

10. 28 I.L.M. 146 (1989). See H. van Loon, The Hague Convention on The Law Applicable to Succession to The Estates of Deceased Persons, 1989 Hague Yearbook of Int'l L. 48; Scoles, Planning for The Multinational Estate, 3 Prob. & Prop. No. 3, 58 (1989). The Convention on Succession was

latter convention on succession provides choice-of-law directions on substantive issues in multinational decedent's estates in accordance with three basic objectives. First, it accommodates reasonable planning control by the testator; second, it provides the law of one nation to control substantive rights in the estate and third, the law of the nation in which the testator's personal life is centered, his home, applies to their estate. The Unites States has not yet ratified either Hague Convention.

Articles 3, 5, 6, and 7 form the heart of the succession convention; the most important are 5 and 6. Under Article 5, the estate owner can designate either the law of his habitual residence, i.e. his domicile, or the law of his nationality to govern the *whole* of his estate. In addition, Article 6 permits the testator to designate any law to govern the disposition of *particular* assets so long as this does not prejudice the mandatory rules, i.e. forced shares, of the nation whose law is otherwise applicable to his estate. Thus, the testator can choose the law applicable to any particular assets in his estate, but cannot avoid the forced shares of his habitual residence or nationality, whichever is applicable.

Article 7 provides that except as permitted by Article 6, the law designated by the testator (Art. 5), or applicable in absence of designation (Art. 3), governs the *whole* probate estate *wherever* the assets are located as to *substantive* issues. The convention does *not* reach nonprobate assets nor administration of the estate.

Article 3 determines which law governs absent testamentary direction. First, the nation of his citizenship, if the decedent was habitually resident there. Second, the nation of the decedent's habitual resident, *his home,* governs, if the testator has been resident there for more than five years. In the exceptional case in which the decedent was manifestly more closely related to the place of his nationality, the law of his nationality would apply. Third, if a less than five years resident, the law of the nationality applies unless the decedent was more closely connected to another state, as for example a recent immigrant.

VI. DEVISES TO ALIENS

§ 20.17 From time to time in the United States there have been ate statutes or common law restrictions placed on dispositions to aliens.[1] Although resident friendly aliens probably cannot constitutionally be precluded from ownership of property,[2] there are occasional state statutes that preclude nonresident aliens from the ownership of land[3] or

signed by Switzerland in 1989 and Argentina in 1990.

§ 20.17

1. See R. Powell, The Law of Real Property ¶ 101 (1991); A. Scott, The Law of Trusts § 117.2 (4th ed. 1987).

2. Cf. e.g., Hampton v. Mow Sun Wong, 426 U.S. 88, 96 S.Ct. 1895, 48 L.Ed.2d 495 (1976); Examining Board of Engineers, Architects and Surveyors v. Flores de Otero, 426 U.S. 572, 96 S.Ct. 2264, 49 L.Ed.2d 65 (1976).

3. See for example, Miss. Code, § 89–1–23; Neb. Rev. Stat. §§ 76–402, 76–403, 76–404, 76–405; see also Morrison, Limitations on Alien Investment in American Real Estate, 60 Minn. L. Rev. 621 (1976); Comment, Nonresident Alien Inheritance of Ne-

require that it be disposed of in a limited time.[4] These restrictions on real property are situs limitations and have been applied only by the situs courts.[5]

State law restrictions are frequently superseded by rights under treaties with particular nations,[6] but some of the treaties have been construed not to apply to dispositions of personal property.[7] Consequently, there are several states which have statutes limiting such dispositions by domiciliaries of the forum to aliens who are citizens and residents in nations whose laws would not reciprocally permit dispositions to United States citizens or would preclude the use and enjoyment of the bequest by the recipient.[8] During the period of international competition and tension following World War II, the statutes had some popularity and were used with some frequency to preclude dispositions to citizens of the former "Communist Bloc" nations of eastern Europe. In *Zschernig v. Miller*,[9] the Supreme Court appeared to strike down these so-called iron curtain statutes as an unconstitutional interference with the exclusive federal power over foreign relations. *Zschernig*, and the fall of the Soviet empire, have rendered his particular problem one of little practical import.

braska Land: 1854–1971, 4 Creighton L. Rev. 304 (1971).

4. Iowa Code Ann. § 567.3; Ky. Rev. Stat. §§ 381–290, 381–300; 60 Okla. Stat. Ann. § 123 (five-year limitation).

5. See, e.g., Shames v. Nebraska, 323 F.Supp. 1321 (D.Neb.1971), affirmed without oph. 408 U.S. 901, 92 S.Ct. 2478, 33 L.Ed.2d 321 (1972). Cf. Levc v. Connors, 171 Mont. 1, 555 P.2d 750 (1976), cert. denied 431 U.S. 973, 97 S.Ct. 2939, 53 L.Ed.2d 1071 (1977).

6. E.g., Corbett v. Stergios, 381 U.S. 124, 85 S.Ct. 1364, 14 L.Ed.2d 260 (1965);

Consul General of Yugoslavia v. Pennsylvania, 375 U.S. 395, 84 S.Ct. 452, 11 L.Ed.2d 411 (1964). See also supra § 3.59.

7. See, e.g., Clark v. Allen, 331 U.S. 503, 67 S.Ct. 1431, 91 L.Ed. 1633 (1947); Kolovrat v. Oregon, 366 U.S. 187, 81 S.Ct. 922, 6 L.Ed.2d 218 (1961).

8. 60 Okla. Stat. Ann. § 121; Wyo. Stat. § 34–15–101.

9. Zschernig v. Miller, 389 U.S. 429, 88 S.Ct. 664, 19 L.Ed.2d 683 (1968) (noted 21 Vand. L. Rev. 502 (1968)).

Chapter 21

TRUSTS AND POWERS
OF APPOINTMENT

Table of Sections

		Sections
I.	Trusts	21.1–21.7
	A. Introduction	21.1
	B. Validity	21.2–21.3
	1. Testamentary Trusts	21.2
	2. Inter Vivos Trusts	21.3
	C. Administration of Trusts	21.4–21.7
	1. Introduction	21.4
	2. Qualification of Foreign Trustees	21.5
	3. Administrative Issues	21.6
	4. Change in Place of Administration	21.7
II.	Powers of Appointment	21.8–21.13
	A. Introduction	21.8
	B. Validity of a Power	21.9
	C. Nature and Scope of a Power	21.10
	D. Exercise of Powers	21.11–21.13
	1. Generally	21.11
	2. Rule Against Perpetuities	21.12
	3. Exercise by Residuary Clause	21.13

I. TRUSTS

A. INTRODUCTION

§ 21.1 In the conflict of laws concerning trusts, the policy in favor of giving effect to the settlor's intention is exceptionally strong, as it is in non-conflict trust cases. Perhaps it is even stronger than the policy supporting party autonomy in contracts because of the shared policies of giving effect to the dispositive provisions of the owner of property. Translated to the choice-of-law problem, this policy of giving effect to the settlor's intention tends to sustain the settlor's disposition whenever possible. Exceedingly strong contrary local policy is necessary to overcome this preference toward validating the disposition in trust. This overriding and normally controlling consideration should be kept in mind as particular questions and trusts are approached. Questions here dealt with concerning trusts involve, first, the law by which the validity of the trust is assessed both as to form and substance; and second, the law applicable to questions pertaining to administration of the trust, assuming it is validly created. It is convenient also to separate testamentary and *inter vivos* settlements, and to bear in mind the distinction between movable and immovable assets.

B. VALIDITY

1. Testamentary Trusts

§ 21.2   The validity of a testamentary trust of land falls within the traditional reference to the situs and usually is determined by the law which would be applied by the courts of the situs.[1] The formal validity is dependent upon the validity of the will which creates the testamentary trust. While the traditional reference is to the location of the land, the situs of the immovable, almost all states in the United States have some version of Lord Kingsdown's Act.[2] These statutes generally sustain wills that are executed in accordance with the law of the place of execution or of the domicile of the deceased at the time of execution or at the time of death and, in the United States, have been patterned after the Uniform Wills Act and the Uniform Probate Code.[3] Under these statutes it is clear that the courts at the situs of land would not apply their local law to defeat testation, but in most instances would refer to the law which would sustain the will under these statutes.[4] If the question arises as to the formal validity of a testamentary trust of personal property, the validity of such a disposition is usually stated to be governed by the well-recognized reference to the testator's domicile at the time of death.[5]

§ 21.2

1. See Restatement, Second, Conflict of Laws § 278 (1971). Detailed treatment of conflict-of-laws problems may be found in the scholarly work, A. Scott & W. Fratcher, The Law of Trusts (4th ed. 1989). See also supra § 20.7. See also Report, Legal Problems in Controlling Devolution of Property Under Multi–State Trusts and Relevant Varying Situs Rules of Multiple Jurisdictions, 18 Real Prop. Prob. & Tr.J. 331 (1983).

2. The Wills Act, 1861, 24 & 25 Vict., Chap. 114. See Wills Act, 1963, Chap. 44 which provides that a will shall be treated as properly executed if it conforms to the internal law of the place of execution, or the domicile or habitual residence of the testator at the time of execution or at death, or of the state of which he was a national at time of execution or at death, or if it conforms to the law of the place where land is located. See also supra § 20.6.

3. See Uniform Probate Code § 2–506 which provides: "A written will is valid if executed in compliance with §§ 2–502 or 2–503 or if its execution complies with the law at the time of execution of the place where the will is executed, or of the law of the place where at the time of execution or at the time of death the testator is domiciled, has a place of abode, or is a national." Scott, supra n.1 § 650.

4. Cf. Restatement, Second, Conflict of Laws § 278, cmnt. (d) (1971). But cf. id. § 239(2).

5. Restatement, Second, Conflict of Laws §§ 263, 269 (1971); Handley v. Palmer, 91 Fed. 948 (W.D.Pa. 1899); Whitney v. Dodge, 105 Cal. 192, 38 P. 636 (1894); Taormina v. Taormina Corp., 35 Del.Ch. 17, 109 A.2d 400 (1954); Hussey v. Sargent, 116 Ky. 53, 75 S.W. 211 (1903); Rosenbaum v. Garrett, 57 N.J.Eq. 186, 41 A. 252 (1898); English v. McIntyre, 29 App.Div. 439, 51 N.Y.S. 697 (1898); Merritt v. Corties, 71 Hun. 612, 24 N.Y.S. 561 (1893); In re Roberts' Estate, 509 P.2d 495 (Okla.App.1972); Canterbury v. Wyburn, [1895] App. Cas. 89. Cf. Matter of Khotim, 41 N.Y.2d 845, 393 N.Y.S.2d 702, 362 N.E.2d 253 (1977). See also supra § 20.9.

However, again it must be noted that the validation statutes after the pattern of the Lord Kingsdown Act provide an easy renvoi to sustain the will validly executed elsewhere.[6]

When the issue relates to the intrinsic or substantive validity of the trust, the intention of the settlor becomes significant to sustain the trust. In the situation involving trusts of land, reference has been to the law of the situs and most of the courts have tended to apply the local law of the situs. However, several escape mechanisms such as a functional analysis of the statutory purpose involved,[7] of concepts of equitable conversion,[8] or a combination of these approaches in recognition of gifts to foreign trustees use[9] have been used to escape from a restrictive rule of the situs to sustain the trust.[10] In this regard a distinction should be drawn between a trust which is designed to hold a particular piece of land for the benefit of beneficiaries related to the land and the case in which land is held by the trustee simply as an investment. In the latter case, the reference to the situs of the land would seem inappropriate, even under the historical rule. When an issue of the validity of a trust of movables is raised separately from the issue of the validity of the will itself, the intention of the settlor is more directly recognized to sustain the trust.[11] Since the underlying policy of trust law is to carry out the intention of the testator, unless opposed by strong public policy, the courts will assume that the testator intended that the trust should be governed by the law that would sustain it. For example, where a trust is to be administered in a state other than that of the domicile, but by domiciliary law would be invalid from the outset under a rule that administration of such a trust would violate the policy of the domicile, if those objections do not prevail at the place of administration, the courts of the domicile will ordinarily hold the trust valid.[12] This policy of validating the intended disposition was also applied in a leading New York case where a Rhode Island testator created a trust to be administered in New York, which was valid by Rhode Island law but violated the New York rule against perpetuities, the New York court upheld the trust

6. See Scott, supra n.1, § 589. See also Rabel, The Form of Wills, 6 Vand. L. Rev. 533 (1953); Lorenzen, The Validity of Wills, Deeds, and Contracts as Regards Form in the Conflict of Laws, 20 Yale L.J. 427 (1911).

7. See, e.g., Ford v. Ford, 80 Mich. 42, 44 N.W. 1057 (1890). Cf. Kirkbride v. Hickok, 155 Ohio St. 293, 98 N.E.2d 815 (1951). But cf. Toledo Society for Crippled Children v. Hickok, 152 Tex. 578, 261 S.W.2d 692 (1953), cert. denied 347 U.S. 936, 74 S.Ct. 631, 98 L.Ed. 1086 (1954).

8. Cf. Moore v. Livingston, 148 Ind.App. 275, 265 N.E.2d 251 (1970); Despard v. Churchill, 53 N.Y. 192 (1873); Scott, supra n.1; R. Weintraub, Commentary on the Conflict of Laws 520–23 (4th ed. 2001).

9. See, e.g., Chamberlain v. Chamberlain, 43 N.Y. 424 (1871); Hope v. Brewer,

136 N.Y. 126, 32 N.E. 558 (1892); Scott, supra n.1., § 651.

10. For a comprehensive discussion see Hancock, In The Parish of St. Mary le Bow, in the Ward of Cheap, 16 Stan. L. Rev. 561, 576 (1964).

11. See In re Chappell's Estate, 124 Wash. 128, 213 P. 684 (1923); Restatement, Second, Conflict of Laws § 269 (1971); Scott, supra n.1, §§ 598, 600, 652. Cf. In re Henderson's Will, 40 N.J.Super. 297, 123 A.2d 78 (Ch.Div.1956).

12. Vansant v. Roberts, 3 Md. 119 (1852); Hope v. Brewer, 136 N.Y. 126, 32 N.E. 558 (1892). Cf. Hancock, In the Parish of St. Mary le Bow, in the Ward of Cheap, 16 Stan. L. Rev. 561 (1964). But cf. American Bible Society v. Pendleton, 7 W.Va. 79 (1873).

stating that the trust was governed by the law of the testator's domicile.[13] Of course, this recognition of the importance or the significance of the testator's intention also supports specific expressions of intention identifying the preferred applicable law.[14]

2. Inter Vivos Trusts

§ 21.3 The creation of a trust inter vivos is essentially a transfer of interests in property whether the assets are movable or immovable. In the case of land, the conveyance is viewed generally as any other gratuitous conveyance of land and validity is measured by the whole law of the situs.[1] This reference includes the common deed validation statutes, similar to the Lord Kingdown's Acts discussed above, which provide that a deed formally valid at the place of execution is valid as to land in the forum.[2] Substantive issues of validity are also viewed as governed by the law of the situs,[3] except for a few thoughtful cases looking at the particular issue and finding that the situs has no interest in the particular issue.[4] In the case of inter vivos transfers of movables, such as chattels or negotiable certificated securities, the law of the situs of the property has been very significant in sustaining the validity of a disposition.[5] A transfer in trust valid at the place where those movables were located would likely be viewed as valid everywhere.[6] As a consequence of

13. Cross v. United States Trust Co., 131 N.Y. 330, 30 N.E. 125 (1892); cf. Shannon v. Irving Trust Co., 246 App.Div. 280, 285 N.Y.S. 478 (1936), affirmed 275 N.Y. 95, 9 N.E.2d 792 (1937) (noted 84 U. Pa. L. Rev. 901 (1936)); Ministers & Missionaries, Benefit Board v. McKay, 64 Misc.2d 231, 315 N.Y.S.2d 549 (1970). But cf. In re Crum, 98 Misc. 160, 164 N.Y.S. 149 (1916).

14. See, e.g., Flaherty v. Flaherty, 138 N.H. 337, 638 A.2d 1254 (1994)(clause selecting Massachusetts law honored); In re Dumaine, 135 N.H. 103, 600 A.2d 127 (1991) (provision in trust selecting New Hampshire law given effect); cf. National Shawmut Bank v. Cumming, 325 Mass. 457, 91 N.E.2d 337 (1950); Amerige v. Attorney General, 324 Mass. 648, 88 N.E.2d 126 (1949); Howard Savings Institution v. Baronych, 8 N.J.Super. 599, 73 A.2d 853 (Ch.Div.1950); Scott, supra n.1, § 591; Wallace, Choice of Law for Trusts in Australia and U.S., 36 Int'l & Comp. L.Q. 454 (1987).

§ 21.3

1. See Restatement, Second, Conflict of Laws § 278 (1971); F.P.P. Enterprises v. United States, 646 F.Supp. 713 (D.Neb. 1986), affirmed 830 F.2d 114 (8th Cir.1987); First Nat'l Bank in Mitchell v. Daggett, 242 Neb. 734, 497 N.W.2d 358 (1993).

2. See, e.g., Cal. Civ. Code § 1189; Mich. Comp. Laws Ann. § 565.11.

3. See, e.g., Pond v. Porter, 141 Conn. 56, 104 A.2d 228 (1954); Amerige v. Attorney General, 324 Mass. 648, 88 N.E.2d 126 (1949); Peabody v. Kent, 153 App.Div. 286, 138 N.Y.S. 32 (1912), aff'd 213 N.Y. 154, 107 N.E. 51 (1914); A Scott & W. Fratcher, The Law of Trusts § 652 (1989).

4. Cf. West Virginia Pulp & Paper Co. v. Miller, 176 Fed. 284 (4th Cir.1909), cert. denied 220 U.S. 619, 31 S.Ct. 722, 55 L.Ed. 612 (1911); Ford v. Ford, 80 Mich. 42, 44 N.W. 1057 (1890). See Hancock, Conceptual Devices for Avoiding the Land Taboo in Conflict of Laws: The Disadvantages of Disingenuousness, 20 Stan. L. Rev. 1 (1967); Restatement, Second, Conflict of Laws § 278, comnt. (d) (1971); Rudow v. Fogel, 12 Mass.App.Ct. 430, 426 N.E.2d 155 (1981), holding the situs of the real property at issue not determinative of whether an oral agreement to hold land for benefit of a minor served to impose a constructive trust. Where property was located in Massachusetts, but all concerned were domiciled in New York, held that under Massachusetts' "functional approach" weighing significance of contacts and policies of states involved, New York law applies. Id. at 158–60. See also supra § 19.8.

5. See supra § 19.13. See also infra n.17.

6. See Scott, supra n.3, § 597. Cf. Warner v. Florida Bank & Trust Co., 160 F.2d

this, a settlor may normally take movable assets to a state where the proposed trust would be valid and establish the trust, to be administered there without much risk that it could be successfully attacked by reason of the law of another state.[7] In addition, unless a particular policy to the contrary is exceptionally strong, the law of the situs will also give effect to the policy of sustaining the intended disposition.[8] Because intent is such a significant factor in trust cases, a settlor's designation of governing law will be viewed as controlling.[9]

If no governing law is especially indicated, the validity of an inter vivos trust of movables is usually sustained by the law of any state having a reasonable relationship to it.[10] Although the choice-of-law rule so stated is very flexible, there is substantial unanimity among those who have reviewed the cases,[11] and this likewise is substantially the

766 (5th Cir.1947); Rose v. St. Louis Union Trust Co., 43 Ill.2d 312, 253 N.E.2d 417 (1969).

7. See Restatement, Second, Conflict of Laws § 270 (1971); National Shawmut Bank v. Cumming, 325 Mass. 457, 91 N.E.2d 337 (1950). Of course, the trust may be attacked under the law of the state where created, see, e.g., Johnson v. La Grange State Bank, 50 Ill.App.3d 830, 8 Ill.Dec. 670, 365 N.E.2d 1056 (1977), reversed on other grounds 73 Ill.2d 342, 22 Ill.Dec. 709, 383 N.E.2d 185 (1978); Rose v. St. Louis Union Trust Co., 43 Ill.2d 312, 253 N.E.2d 417 (1969).

8. See Restatement, Second, Conflict of Laws § 270, cmnt. (c)(1) (1971); Scott, supra n.3, § 600.

9. See, e.g., Dunkley v. Peoples Bank & Trust Co., 728 F.Supp. 547 (W.D.Ark.1989); Russell v. Wachovia Bank, N.A., 353 S.C. 208, 578 S.E.2d 329 (2003)(choice-of-law clause in inter vivos trust honored); Wright v. Rains, 106 S.W.3d 678 (Tenn. App. 2003)(same); Wilmington Trust Co. v. Wilmington Trust Co., 26 Del.Ch. 397, 24 A.2d 309 (1942); In re Pratt's Trust, 5 A.D.2d 501, 172 N.Y.S.2d 965 (1958), affirmed 8 N.Y.2d 855, 203 N.Y.S.2d 906, 168 N.E.2d 709 (1960). A. Scott, The Law of Trusts § 598 (3d ed. 1967, Supp. 1981). Cf. on construction issues, Town of Lee v. Town of Lincoln, 351 A.2d 554 (Me.1976); In re Pennington's Trust, 421 Pa. 334, 219 A.2d 353 (1966). See also United States Trust Co. v. Bohart, 197 Conn. 34, 495 A.2d 1034 (1985); Annan v. Wilmington Trust Co., 559 A.2d 1289 (Del.Sup.1989); Skolnik v. Rose, 55 N.Y.2d 964, 449 N.Y.S.2d 182, 434 N.E.2d 251 (1982).

10. See, e.g., Glaeske v. Shaw, 261 Wis.2d 549, 661 N.W.2d 420 (App.

2003)(Wisconsin law chosen to validate trust because it had the most significant relationship even though settlor was a Florida resident); Nahar v. Nahar, 656 So.2d 225 (Fla. App. 1995) (deferring to Dutch judgment applying Dutch law to a trust settled by Dutch subject); J.P. Morgan Delaware v. Henley–Paradis, 1993 WL 6866 (Del.Ch. 1993) (decedent's domicile and location of trust assets); Shannon v. Irving Trust Co., 275 N.Y. 95, 9 N.E.2d 792 (1937); Appeal of Fowler, 125 Pa. 388, 17 A. 431 (1889). Cf. Ford v. Newman, 64 Ill. App.3d 528, 21 Ill.Dec. 283, 381 N.E.2d 392 (1978), aff'd 77 Ill.2d 335, 33 Ill.Dec. 150, 396 N.E.2d 539 (1979) (construction issues where no choice-of-law clause); New England Merchants National Bank v. Mahoney, 356 Mass. 654, 255 N.E.2d 592 (1970).

11. W. Land, Trusts in the Conflict of Laws (1940); A. Ehrenzweig, A Treatise on Conflict of Laws § 244 (1962); G. Stumberg, Conflict of Laws 391–97 (3d ed. 1963); Cavers, Trusts Inter Vivos and the Conflict of Laws, 44 Harv. L. Rev. 161 (1930); Note, Trusts of Personal Property and the Conflict of Laws, 19 Colum. L. Rev. 486 (1919); Dean, Conflict Avoidance in Inter vivos Trusts of Movables, 21 Law & Contemp. Prob. 483 (1956); Ester & Scoles, Estate Planning and Conflict of Laws, 24 Ohio St. L.J. 270 (1963); Leflar, Estates and Trusts Conflict of Laws Problems, 37 Tr. Bull. 44 (No. 9, May, 1958); Scoles, Conflict of Laws in Estate Planning, 9 Fla. U. L. Rev. 398 (1956); Scott, What Law Governs Trusts?, 99 Tr. & Est. 186 (1960); Trowbridge, Conflict of Laws: Trustor's Right to Designate Controlling Law, 36 A.B.A.J. 913 (1950). Cf. Beale, Equitable Interests in Foreign Property, 20 Harv. L. Rev. 382 (1907); Beale, Living Trusts of Movables in the Conflict of Laws, 45 Harv. L. Rev. 969 (1932).

position of the American Law Institute.[12] This is clearly the import of the cases.[13] Two New York cases are illustrative. In *Hutchison v. Ross*,[14] through a transaction centered in New York, a settlor domiciled in Quebec created a trust of securities located in New York, with a New York trust company as trustee. The trust was invalid by law of the domicile, but valid by the law of New York. The New York court upheld the trust, emphasizing the fact that New York was the situs of the securities transferred to the New York trustee and that it was inferable that the settlor had intended the law of New York to govern. In a later case,[15] a New Jersey domiciliary, through a New York transaction, established a trust of securities then in New York with a New York trust

12. Restatement, Second, Conflict of Laws § 270 (1971). Superficially, in absence of an expressed intent by the settlor, the Restatement, Second would apply the law of the state with the closest connection concerning the issue in question. Little distinction in application seems possible however. The possibly significant connecting factors are indicated in the Restatement's view of the state having the closest connection. Id. § 270, comment (c):

  c. When law not designated by the settlor to govern validity of the trust. When the settlor does not designate a state whose local law is to govern the validity of the trust, or when the designation will not be given effect because the state has no substantial relation to the trust, the trust will be valid if valid under the local law of the state with which, as to the matter at issue, the trust has its most significant relationship under the principles stated in § 6.

  Of the states having relationships with the trust, much the most important insofar as the validity of the trust is concerned is the state, if any, where the settlor manifested an intention that the trust should be administered. On the question whether a settlor has manifested an intention that the trust shall be administered in a state other than that of his domicile, see § 267, Comment c.

  If the settlor has not manifested an intention that the trust should be administered in a particular state, the trust will be upheld if valid under the local law of the state which, as to the matter at issue, has the most significant relationship to the trust under the principles stated in § 6. Contacts which will be considered in determining the state of most significant relationship may include the state where the trust instrument was executed and delivered; the state where the trust assets were then located; the state of the domicile of the settlor at that time; and the state of the domicile of the beneficiaries.

A trust may also be valid, however, if valid under the local law of a state to which the trust has a substantial relation, even though it is not the state of the most significant relationship.

13. See Stetson v. Morgan Guaranty Trust Co., 22 Conn.Supp. 158, 164 A.2d 239 (1960); In re McCampbell's Trust, 36 Misc.2d 108, 232 N.Y.S.2d 522 (1962); In re Nicol's Trust, 3 Misc.2d 898, 148 N.Y.S.2d 854 (1956); In re Griswold's Trust, 99 N.Y.S.2d 420 (1950). Cf. Boyd v. Curran, 166 F.Supp. 193 (S.D.N.Y.1958). In Van Grutten v. Digby, 31 Beav. 561 (1862), an English woman, entitled to property under an English trust, married a Frenchman in France. A marriage settlement was executed which was invalid by French law, but which by English law was valid. The court decided that its effect on the English trust was to be determined by English law. See Viditz v. O'Hagan 2 Ch. 569 (1899). In Appeal of Fowler, 125 Pa. 388, 17 A. 431 (1889), the court only needed to decide that a Pennsylvania statute did not affect an Illinois settlement by reason of the fact that the trustee was a Pennsylvania corporation.

14. 262 N.Y. 381, 187 N.E. 65 (1933) (noted 33 Colum. L. Rev. 1151 (1933); 47 Harv. L. Rev. 350 (1933); 32 Mich. L. Rev. 696 (1934)).

15. Shannon v. Irving Trust Co., 246 App.Div. 280, 285 N.Y.S. 478 (1936), affirmed 275 N.Y. 95, 9 N.E.2d 792 (1937), noted, 84 U. Pa. L. Rev. 901 (1936). In a case difficult to explain, In re Bauer's Trust, 14 N.Y.2d 272, 251 N.Y.S.2d 23, 200 N.E.2d 207 (1964), the New York Court of Appeals held that New York's outmoded two-lives rule against perpetuities invalidated the exercise of a power of appointment under an inter vivos trust centered in New York but exercised by the will of the donor-donee valid at the English domicile of some 37 years. Cf. Guaranty Trust Co. v. Stevens, 28 N.J. 243, 146 A.2d 97 (1958).

company, but provided that the trust should be governed by the law of New Jersey. Under New Jersey law, the trust was valid, but under the law of New York it was not. Again, the court upheld the trust, applying the law of New Jersey, not as the law of the settlor's domicile but as the law intended by the settlor.

The pattern of conflicts litigation in trust is further reflected by another illustrative case, *Lewis v. Hanson*.[16] In *Lewis*, the settlor, while a resident of Pennsylvania, executed a trust agreement and delivered certain securities to a trust company in Delaware. The trustee was directed to administer the trust and pay the income to the settlor and then to distribute the property as the settlor should appoint by will. In holding that the circumstances indicated that the settlor intended to have the trust administered and governed according to the law of Delaware, the court stated: "In ... deciding what law is applicable to determine its validity, the most important facts to be considered are the intention of the creator of the trust, the domicile of the trustee, and the place in which the trust is administered."[17] These cases are considered typical and support an alternative choice-of-law reference to the law of any state substantially related to the transaction which will validate the inter vivos trust of movables.[18] As trusts have been a development in the common law countries, their recognition and enforcement in civil law countries has been uncertain. With increasing investment in foreign

---

16. 36 Del.Ch. 235, 128 A.2d 819 (1957), affirmed 357 U.S. 235, 78 S.Ct. 1228, 2 L.Ed.2d 1283 (1958).

17. Lewis v. Hanson, 36 Del.Ch. 235, 245, 128 A.2d 819, 826 (1957). See also Johnson v. La Grange State Bank, 73 Ill.2d 342, 22 Ill.Dec. 709, 383 N.E.2d 185 (1978). The settlor probably does not have complete autonomy in the matter of selecting the governing law; the law chosen should have some reasonable connection with the trust transaction. The ease of selecting a trustee and the place of administration make this a nominal requirement. See City Bank Farmers Trust Co. v. Cheek, 202 Misc. 303, 110 N.Y.S.2d 434 (Sup. 1952); In re Griswold's Trust, 99 N.Y.S.2d 420 (1950); Shannon v. Irving Trust Co., 275 N.Y. 95, 9 N.E.2d 792 (1937). Scoles, Choice of Law in Family Property Transactions, 209 Recueil des Cours. 17 (1988–II). Cf. King v. King, 218 Ga. 534, 129 S.E.2d 147 (1962). See also 871, in re Agostini's Estate, 311 Pa.Super. 233, 457 A.2d 861 (1983). Here, the court was faced with the issue whether the purchase by decedent of certificates of deposit as "trustee" for certain named "beneficiaries" was a tentative trust or a completed gift. At the time of the purchase, decedent was domiciled in Florida. However, all parties to the proceeding were domiciled in Pennsylvania. Also, all of the estate's assets were located and admin-

istered there. Under these circumstances, the court, in applying a "governmental interest analysis"/"most significant contacts or relationships" test held that Pennsylvania law governs, as no interest of Florida in applying its rules relating to trusts was evident. See also Matter of Moore, 129 Misc.2d 639, 493 N.Y.S.2d 924, 926 (1985) (applicable law in determining validity of trust determined by donor's intent, which can be derived from transfer of securities to New York corporate trustee). But see Neto v. Thorner, 718 F.Supp. 1222 (S.D.N.Y. 1989); Sanchez v. Sanchez De Davila, 547 So.2d 943 (Fla.App.1989), review denied 554 So.2d 1168 (Fla.1989).

18. After an exhaustive survey of the decisions, Professor Cavers concluded: "It is submitted, therefore, that (1) an express declaration of intention as to the law desired by the settlor to govern his trust may properly be respected where the state whose law is so designated has a substantial connection with the transaction. (2) Where there is no such express declaration, the court should examine the facts of the transaction and the circumstances surrounding it in an effort to ascertain and effectuate any intent which is inferable therefrom. (3) In a wholly colorless transaction, the law of the place of administration of the trust should be applied." Cavers, Trusts Inter Vivos and the Conflict of Laws, 44 Harv. L. Rev. 161, 195 (1930).

assets and their inclusion in trusts the concerns over international enforcement of trusts has increased. The Hague Convention on The Law Applicable to Trusts and on Their Recognition addresses these concerns.[19] The Trust Convention, which has not been ratified by the United States, reflects the choice-of-law approach common in the United States. It provides that the trust shall be governed by the law chosen by the settlor[20] and, in the absence of settlor's direction, the trust is governed by the law with which it is most closely connected.[21] The governing law is applicable to issues of validity, construction, effect, and administration of the trust[22] but different law may be applicable to severable aspects of the trust such as administration.[23]

C. ADMINISTRATION OF TRUSTS

1. *Introduction*

§ 21.4 In considering issues concerning trusts, the courts often distinguish between issues that go to the substance of the interests in the trust and questions that concern the administration of the trust or those procedures available for reviewing the management of the trust assets. In some ways this distinction follows the substance/procedure distinction followed in other areas.[1] Here, as in the substance/procedure dichotomy, it is sometimes difficult to distinguish an issue of substance from an issue of administration. The law relating to administration of trusts varies from state to state and trusts are administered in many different ways because of the individual circumstances of the trust, the parties, and the nature of the assets. For example, while most land trusts are administered where the land is located, it is possible for a trustee to purchase an interest in land as an investment in a state other

19. Hague Conference on Private International Law, Fifteenth Session, October 20, 1984. As of 1997, the Convention had been ratified by Australia, Canada, Italy, Malta, the Netherlands and the United Kingdom. See Hansmann & Mattei, The Functions of Trust Law: A comparative Legal and Economic Analysis, 73 N.Y.U. L. Rev. 434, 436 n.4 (1998). As of 2003 there have been no subsequent ratifications. Up-to-date information can be found on the Hague Conference's Web site at http://www.hcch.net. For a comparative assessment of the utility of trusts as a legal instrument, see id. For a discussion of the Convention and related conflicts problems, see Gaillard & Trautman, Trusts in Non–Trust Countries: Conflict of Laws and the Hague Convention on Trusts, 35 Am.J. Comp. L. 357 (1997).

20. Hague Convention on the Law Applicable to Trusts and on Their Recognition, October 20, 1984, art. 6.

21. Id., art. 7, E. Gaillard and D. Trautman, Trusts in Non–Trust Countries, The Hague Trust Convention, 35 Am. J. Comp. L. 307 (1987). D. Trautman & E. Gaillard, The Hague Convention Adopts A Convention for Trusts, 124 Trusts & Estates No. 2, 23 (Feb. 1985) (reprinting text of the convention).

22. Id., art. 8. See Hayton, Hague Convention on the Law Applicable To Trusts and on Their Recognition, 36 Int'l & Comp. L.Q. 260 (1987).

23. Id., art. 9. See A. Lavine & Paola Forging The Bonds of Trust, Financial Planning, 29 (Jan. 1988); P. Pfund, C. Grimes & M. Shea, New Vistas for International Planning, 123 Trusts and Estates 8 (Nov. 1984).

§ 21.4

1. See supra § 3.8. Cf. Restatement, Second, Conflict of Laws § 268(2) (1971).

than where the trust generally is administered.[2] Likewise, if a trust is created by will, the probate courts in some states still retain jurisdiction and supervision over the trust as an extension of the probate of the decedent's estate. As a result, significant issues relating to the nature of beneficiaries' interests may be brought into court under the guise of an administrative matter. On the other hand, an inter vivos trust in which the beneficiaries approve informal accounts by the trustee may never get into court for judicial supervision. In those cases, the judicial supervision is simply an alternative remedy available in the event that informal procedures break down. The trend, reflected in the Uniform Probate Code,[3] is toward less continuous court supervision and more toward treating trust litigation like litigation in any other areas, that is, resorting to the courts only when differences cannot be resolved or rights protected by nonjudicial methods.

2. *Qualification of Foreign Trustees*

§ 21.5 A preliminary and troublesome matter concerns the requirements for a trustee to qualify in the state in which the trust is to be administered. Although individuals who may be nonresidents of the forum where the trust is administered, because of constitutional restraints, probably cannot be precluded from serving as trustee solely by virtue of their nonresidence, the case is not so clear with regard to corporate trustees.[1] Corporations incorporated other than at the place of administration usually are required to qualify to do business or to qualify as trustee within the state of administration.[2] Although the active administration of a trust, in the sense that the administration is

---

2. See, e.g., Pitts v. First Union Nat'l Bank, 262 F.Supp.2d 593 (D. Md. 2003) (applying Pennsylvania law to an action challenging administration of a trust where the trust had been set up by a will probated in Pennsylvania and where the trust had been administered in that state since its creation).

3. See Uniform Probate Code Article 7, Part 1, General Comment. U.P.C. § 7–201(b) provides:

> (b) Neither registration of a trust nor a proceeding under this section result in continuing supervisory proceedings. The management and distribution of a trust estate, submission of accounts and reports to beneficiaries, payment of trustee's fees and other obligations of a trust, acceptance and change of trusteeship, and other aspects of the administration of a trust shall proceed expeditiously consistent with the terms of the trust, free of judicial intervention and without order, approval or other action of any court, subject to the jurisdiction of the court as invoked by interested parties or as otherwise exercised as provided by law.

Cf. Restatement, Second, Conflict of Laws §§ 267, 276 (1971). But cf. Rousseau v. United States Trust Co., 422 F.Supp. 447 (S.D.N.Y.1976).

§ 21.5

1. See, e.g., Shirk v. City of La Fayette, 52 Fed. 857 (D. Ind. 1892); Johnston v. State, 212 Ind. 375, 8 N.E.2d 590 (1937); A. Scott & W. Fratcher, The Law of Trusts §§ 558, 559 (4th ed. 1989). Cf. American Trust Co., Inc. v. South Carolina State Board, 381 F.Supp. 313 (D.S.C.1974). See also Succession of Batton v. Prince, 384 So.2d 506 (La.App.1980) (upholding appointment of out-of-state individual trustee). Matter of Estate of White, 133 Misc.2d 971, 509 N.Y.S.2d 252 (1986); Munford v. Maclellan, 258 Ga. 679, 373 S.E.2d 368 (1988).

2. The statutes are collected and discussed in Scott, supra n.1., § 558. Cf. Holladay v. Fidelity National Bank of Baton Rouge, 312 So.2d 883 (La.App.1975); Restatement, Second, Conflict of Laws § 267 (1971).

maintained in an office of the trustee, seems appropriately to be subject to the rules relating to doing business or prior qualification as trustee, there is considerable uncertainty as to what constitutes an act for which the state may reasonably require qualification to perform. For example, if a decedent dies domiciled in one state and leaves the residue of his estate to a trustee in another state in a trust to be administered in a second state, must the named trustee qualify at the domicile in order simply to receive and receipt for the assets in the decedent's estate? This issue is clouded by a number of statutes reflecting provincial protectionism favoring local trust companies.[3] The trend in the more enlightened jurisdictions, however, is toward permitting a foreign corporate trustee to receive distribution from a local estate,[4] or otherwise to acquire property in the state without local qualification; qualification being required only when the corporation maintains the principal place of administration of a trust within a state.[5]

3. *Administrative Issues*

§ 21.6 Aside from these preliminary questions in the initiation of trust administration, many difficult questions may arise subsequently during the administration of the trust.[1] For example, most of the matters of administration involve the powers of the trustee, such as the power to sell or lease or mortgage and the exercise of discretionary powers. The trustee's right to compensation and the right of indemnity for incurring appropriate expenses are also important questions. The propriety of investments is one of those matters which is usually controlled by the law governing the administration of the trust, and yet it illustrates how blurred is the line between substantive rights and matters of administration for the interests of the income and principal beneficiaries can be substantially affected by the trustee's investment policy. Conversely, the

3. See Matter of Smith's Estate, 2 Misc.2d 755, 153 N.Y.S.2d 110 (1956):

"The intendment of the Statute ... is to prevent competition ... by trust companies of states other than according reciprocal provisions...."

Cf. Nev. Rev. Stat. 662.245 (1971) (requiring a foreign trustee to associate as cofiduciary a banking corporation whose principal place of business is in this state).

4. See In re Farnsworth's Estate, 109 N.H. 15, 241 A.2d 204 (1968); Matter of Estate of Westpfal, 140 Misc.2d 487, 531 N.Y.S.2d 81 (1988); Risher v. American Surety Co., 227 Wis. 104, 277 N.W. 160 (1938). But see In re Lowe's Estate, 155 Kan. 679, 127 P.2d 512 (1942).

5. See U.P.C. § 7–105 which provides:

A foreign corporate trustee is required to qualify as a foreign corporation doing business in this state if it maintains the principal place of administration of any trust within the state. A foreign co-trustee is not required to qualify in this state solely because its co-trustee maintains the principal place of administration in this state. Unless otherwise doing business in this state, local qualification by a foreign trustee, corporate or individual, is not required in order for the trustee to receive distribution from a local estate or to hold, invest in, manage or acquire property located in this state, or maintain litigation. Nothing in this section affects a determination of what other acts require qualification as doing business in this state.

Cf. U.P.C. § 3–913.

§ 21.6

1. A. Scott & W. Fratcher, The Law of Trusts §§ 604–624 (4th ed. 1989).

settlor's provision for the income beneficiary may well control the pattern of investment which the trustee may pursue. Matters of administration are generally said to be governed by the law of the place where the trust is to be administered.[2] In most cases of a testamentary trust of movables the place of administration typically will be the domicile of the testator, as that is where his estate will be settled.[3] However, at least with regard to movables, the trust may be administered elsewhere if the testator indicates such an intention.[4] For example, such an intention is probably indicated where the testator dies domiciled in a state devising the residue of his estate to pour over into an existing inter vivos trust in a second state. It seems rather clear that the policies supporting testamentary additions to inter vivos trusts[5] support a finding that a testator would intend that the testamentary addition to the trust be administered in the other state subject to the same law as the existing inter vivos trust.

In the case of an inter vivos trust, if the instrument creating the trust contains provisions whereby the settlor expressly or impliedly indicates an intention that a trust be administered at a particular place, that intention will be honored.[6] However, in inter vivos trusts the question seldom arises because the settlor will ordinarily transfer the assets to the trustee at the place where the trust is to be administered and the trust will there be created. If a question does arise at the place of administration, it usually will concern whether it is appropriate for the court to entertain a complaint concerning an issue of administration, i.e., question of jurisdiction or forum non conveniens. If the matter

2. Restatement, Second, Conflict of Laws §§ 271, 172 (1971). This view has prevailed for a considerable time. See Beale, Equitable Interests in Foreign Property, 20 Harv. L. Rev. 382, 395 (1907). Cf. Hartsfield v. Lescher, 721 F.Supp. 1052 (E.D.Ark. 1989).

3. Farmers' and Mechanics' Savings Bank v. Brewer, 27 Conn. 600 (1858); Rosenbaum v. Garrett, 57 N.J.Eq. 186, 41 A. 252 (1898); Lozier v. Lozier, 99 Ohio St. 254, 124 N.E. 167 (1919). See Swetland v. Swetland, 105 N.J.Eq. 608, 149 A. 50 (1930).

4. See Campbell v. Albers, 313 Ill.App. 152, 39 N.E.2d 672 (1942); Amerige v. Attorney General, 324 Mass. 648, 88 N.E.2d 126 (1949); Smith v. Mercantile Trust Co., 199 Md. 264, 86 A.2d 504 (1952); In re Farnsworth's Estate, 109 N.H. 15, 241 A.2d 204 (1968); In re Carter's Estate, 6 N.J. 426, 78 A.2d 904 (1951); Matter of Tabbagh's Estate, 167 Misc. 156, 3 N.Y.S.2d 542 (1938); Application of City Bank Farmers Trust Co., 9 Misc.2d 183, 166 N.Y.S.2d 772 (1957); Risher v. American Surety Co., 227 Wis. 104, 277 N.W. 160 (1938). Cf. National City Bank v. Beebe, 131 N.Y.S.2d 67 (1954). For instance, in the case of a gift to a charity to be administered in a foreign state, if the gift is valid, a provision as to carrying out directions as to accumulation will be settled by the rule of the state where the gift is to be administered. Parkhurst v. Roy, 7 Ont. App. 614 (1881). Cf. Hope v. Brewer, 136 N.Y. 126, 32 N.E. 558 (1892). See, e.g., Conn. Gen. Stat. Ann. § 45–170(c) (testator may elect to have Connecticut law govern administration and disposition of his estate).

5. See, e.g., U.P.C. § 2–511; Uniform Testamentary Additions to Trusts Act § 1. See also In re Clark's Estate, 495 F.2d 102 (D.C.Cir.1973); In re York's Estate, 95 N.H. 435, 65 A.2d 282 (1949); Scott, supra n.1, § 609.

6. Restatement, Second, Conflict of Laws § 272 (1971); Scott supra n.1, §§ 610, 611; Robertson v. Hert's Administrators, 312 Ky. 405, 227 S.W.2d 899 (1950); Spicer v. New York Life Insurance Co., 237 Mo. App. 725, 167 S.W.2d 457 (1942); Haase v. Title Guarantee & Trust Co., 269 App.Div. 319, 55 N.Y.S.2d 428 (1945); Cocke v. Duke University, 260 N.C. 1, 131 S.E.2d 909 (1963); In re Holdeen's Trust, 58 D. & C.2d 602 (Pa. 1972).

comes before a court other than at the place of administration, a choice-of-law reference will be made to the place of administration. If no intention is expressed in the instrument, the place where the trust is to be administered would in general be that place with which it has the most substantial connection, that is, the place where the management of the trust assets is centered by the trustee.[7]

4. *Change in Place of Administration*

§ 21.7 An interesting case raising the possibility of a change in the law governing administrative matters arose in Delaware.[1] A New York donor set up a trust in New York. By the terms of the settlement, the adult beneficiaries were authorized to change the trustee. This was done and a Delaware trust company was appointed, following which the assets of the trust were transferred to Delaware. The question subsequently came up in an accounting regarding a deed of appointment. The court said that the transfer of the trust from a New York trustee to a Delaware trustee made the Delaware law applicable to the issue before it. Such a transfer of administration to a trustee in another state, for example where the beneficiaries reside, reflects both the flexibility of the trust device and the choice-of-law doctrines relating to it.[2]

---

7. This is the view reflected in Note, Trusts of Personal Property and the Conflicts of Law, 19 Colum. L. Rev. 486 (1919) ("In order to determine where the administration of the trust is located, consideration is given to the provisions of the instrument, the residence of the trustees, the residence of the beneficiaries, the location of the property, the place where the business of the trust is to be carried on"). See Restatement, Second, Conflict of Laws § 273, cmnt. (d) (1971); Scott, supra n.1, § 612; Swabenland, The Conflict of Laws in Administration of Express Trusts of Personal Property, 45 Yale L.J. 438 (1936). See also People v. First National Bank, 364 Ill. 262, 4 N.E.2d 378 (1936); Greenough v. Osgood, 235 Mass. 235, 126 N.E. 461 (1920); Curtis v. Curtis, 185 App.Div. 391, 173 N.Y.S. 103 (1918); Lozier v. Lozier, 99 Ohio St. 254, 124 N.E. 167 (1919). See First National Bank of Paterson v. National Broadway Bank, 156 N.Y. 459, 51 N.E. 398 (1898) (New York rule not applicable to trust created by Connecticut settlor for Connecticut beneficiaries, though trust fund was in stock of New York corporation). See, e.g., Boston Safe Deposit and Trust Co. v. Paris, 15 Mass.App.Ct. 686, 447 N.E.2d 1268, 1271 (1983) (Massachusetts law governs where assets held, trust administered, and trustee and original testatrix domiciled in Mass., while beneficiary's creditor located in Switzerland and certain only indirectly related documents contained governing law clause in favor of Swiss law; location of

property to be given greater weight than any other factor). Cf. Russell v. Wachovia Bank, N.A., 353 S.C. 208, 578 S.E.2d 329 (2003) (choice-of-law clause in inter vivos trust honored); Wright v. Rains, 106 S.W.3d 678 (Tenn. App. 2003) (same).

§ 21.7

1. Wilmington Trust Co. v. Wilmington Trust Co., 26 Del.Ch. 397, 24 A.2d 309 (1942) (noted 30 Geo. L.J. 788 (1942)).

2. Such transfers are not uncommon. See, e.g., Wilmington Trust Co. v. Sloane, 30 Del.Ch. 103, 54 A.2d 544 (1947); Martin v. Haycock, 22 N.J. 1, 123 A.2d 223 (1956); In re Henderson's Will, 40 N.J.Super. 297, 123 A.2d 78 (Ch.Div.1956); In re Smart's Trust, 15 Misc.2d 906, 181 N.Y.S.2d 647 (1958); Matter of Flexner's Trust, 7 Misc.2d 621, 166 N.Y.S.2d 469 (1957); In re Seale's Marriage Settlement, [1961] Ch. 574 (noted 77 L.Q. Rev. 473 (1961)). See also Restatement, Second, Conflict of Laws § 271, cmnt. g, § 272, cmnt. (e) (1971); A. Scott & W. Fratcher, The Law of Trusts §§ 614, 615 (§ 3, 1989); Hendrickson, Change of Situs of a Trust (pts. 1–9), 118 Tr. & Est. No. 1 at 18, No. 2 at 109, No. 3 at 26, No. 4 at 36, No. 5 at 49, No. 6 at 38, No. 7 at 33, No. 8 at 35, No. 9 at 51 (1979). Cf. Mills v. City of Philadelphia, 52 N.J.Super. 52, 144 A.2d 728 (1958); National City Bank v. Beebe, 131 N.Y.S.2d 67 (1954), aff'd 285 App.Div. 874, 139 N.Y.S.2d 238 (1955); Curtis v. Cur-

It seems clear that when a change of governing law occurs after the trust creation, by reason of a move either by court order[3] or consistent with the settlor's intention, the change should apply prospectively upon the trustee's administrative obligations and should not validate an administrative violation of the trust which had previously occurred under the earlier applicable law. Whether a change of the place of administration also changes the applicable substantive trust law is an issue which depends upon the intention of the settlor as to the interests which are given to the beneficiaries and to the nature of the particular issue which is raised.[4]

II. POWERS OF APPOINTMENT

A. INTRODUCTION

§ 21.8 Powers of appointment raise many interesting questions in conflict of laws. For a typical fact situation, assume a donor, domiciled in New York, transfers property by will or inter vivos trust to a trustee for a beneficiary-donee for life and after the donee's death to such persons as the donee shall appoint by will and, in default of an appointment, to named takers. Each of these parties, the donor, the trustee, the donee of the power, such person as the donee may designate, i.e., the appointee, and the takers in default may be domiciled in different states. The orthodox theory of the transfer of property by exercise of a power of appointment is that it is the donor's property which passes, that the donee is "merely the instrument by whom the original testator designates the beneficiary, and the appointee takes under the original will and not from the donee of the power."[1] This theory of relating the

---

tis, 185 App.Div. 391, 173 N.Y.S. 103 (1918). But cf. W. Land, Trusts in the Conflict of Laws 124 (1940).

Statutory developments are reflected in the U.P.C. § 7–305 which provides:

A trustee is under a continuing duty to administer the trust at a place appropriate to the purposes of the trust and to its sound, efficient management. If the principal place of administration becomes inappropriate for any reason, the Court may enter any order furthering efficient administration and the interests of beneficiaries, including, if appropriate, release of registration, removal of the trustee and appointment of a trustee in another state. Trust provisions relating to the place of administration and to changes in the place of administration or of trustee control unless compliance would be contrary to efficient administration or the purposes of the trust. Views of adult beneficiaries shall be given weight in determining the suitability of the trustee and the place of administration.

3. E.g., In re Henderson's Will, 40 N.J.Super. 297, 123 A.2d 78 (1956).

4. One law review commentator has stated: "The broad doctrine ... that a subsequent shift [in the operative factors] may operate to bring about a change in the governing law, would seem to be a logical holding." Note, Trust of Personalty and the Conflict of Laws, 89 U. Pa. L. Rev. 360, 366 (1941).

§ 21.8

1. Cotting v. De Sartiges, 17 R.I. 668, 671, 24 A. 530 (1892). See A. Scott & W. Fratcher, The Law of Trusts §§ 629–642, 661–664 (4th ed. 1989); Simes & Smith, Future Interests § 871 (2d ed. 1975 Supp.); Casner, Estate Planning—Powers of Appointment, 64 Harv. L. Rev. 185 (1950); Halbach, The Use of Powers of Appointment in Estate Planning, 45 Iowa L. Rev. 691 (1960); Note, 38 Harv. L. Rev. 661 (1925); Note, Choice of Law Governing Powers of Appointment Over Personality, 50 Colum. L. Rev. 239 (1950).

appointment back to the transaction by which the donor created the power, is constantly at variance with the modern recognition of the beneficial nature of general powers to the donee. The traditional theory of relation-back has not proved a meaningful basis for solution of local property questions nor for those in conflict of laws.[2] A consideration of the underlying policies is necessary to an appreciation of the results in most cases.

The local law policies and consequently the conflict of laws policies, vary depending upon whether the assets subject to the power are movables or immovables, whether the power is general or special, whether the donee of the power was also donor, whether the power was created or exercisable by will or deed, as well as the nature of the particular issue which is raised.

B. VALIDITY OF A POWER

§ 21.9 Initially, it is important to separate issues relating to the creation of the power from those involving its exercise. The creation of the power usually involves the unilateral act of the donor whose intention is of primary consideration. The validity of a power of appointment, therefore, is essentially an issue relating to the transaction creating the power, and validity is generally determined by the law which is applied to that transaction. For example, the law by which is assessed the validity of an inter vivos or testamentary trust of movables will be applied to determine both the validity of the trust and any power of appointment, general or special, created in the trust instrument.[1] Since the validity of the trust and the power of appointment both involve the donor's intent, recent cases have given the same weight to the donor's selection of governing law as is given to the settlor's expression of intention in trust cases.[2] If a power of appointment is not included in a trust, validity is normally resolved in the same manner as in the gratuitous creation of other interests in property. This means that the

2. See 5 American Law of Property 467 (1952) where it is stated:

> "Where a power of appointment is present in a situation calling for an application of the rules of conflict of laws the temptation to resort to the 'relation back' doctrine is obvious; but there is no reason to suppose that the doctrine will be any more meaningful in that field than elsewhere. Undoubtedly the law of powers of appointment and the considerations on which that law is based are significant in conflict of laws; but the 'relation back' doctrine, never a reason for the law of powers, is neither an adequate nor an accurate exposition of it."

See also Simes, supra n.1, § 911. Cf. In re Estate of Grady, 79 Wn.2d 41, 483 P.2d 114 (1971).

§ 21.9

1. Boston Safe Deposit & Trust Co. v. Prindle, 290 Mass. 577, 195 N.E. 793 (1935); Restatement, Second, Conflict of Laws § 269, comnt. (k), § 170 comnt. (f), § 278 (1971). See Matter of Moore, 129 Misc.2d 639, 493 N.Y.S.2d 924 (1985).

2. See, e.g., Lewis v. Hanson, 36 Del.Ch. 235, 128 A.2d 819 (1957), affirmed 357 U.S. 235, 78 S.Ct. 1228, 2 L.Ed.2d 1283 (1958); Amerige v. Attorney General, 324 Mass. 648, 88 N.E.2d 126 (1949); New England Merchants National Bank of Boston v. Mahoney, 356 Mass. 654, 255 N.E.2d 592 (1970). See also supra §§ 21.2–21.3. Roberts v. Northern Trust Co., 550 F.Supp. 729 (N.D.Ill.1982).

law of the situs of land determines the validity of a power in the land created by an inter vivos instrument or by a will.[3] In the unlikely case of a power of appointment over movables not created by a trust, except as otherwise intended by the donor, the situs would probably likewise control nontrust powers created by inter vivos transactions, while the domicile of the testator is the usual guide in powers of appointment created by will.[4]

C.   NATURE AND SCOPE OF A POWER

§ 21.10   Questions of construction of a power of appointment, for example whether it is general or special, or if special, its scope, are issues concerning the donor's intent. As such, their resolution calls for the approach, previously discussed, of interpretation and construction of the instrument creating the power.[1] For example, if the circumstances indicate the donor's intention regarding the nature of the power, there is no conflicts question raised.[2] If it is necessary to resort to construction of the instrument creating the power and it was created by will, absent choice-of-law directions, the law of the donor's domicile is significant.[3] On the other hand, if created inter vivos, the location of the property subject to the transaction is likely to be most significant.[4]

A rather common occurrence that calls for further analysis is when a donor gives the donee a general power of appointment and subsequently the donee reduces the power by release or disclaimer[5] from a general to a special power or from a presently exercisable power to a testamentary power. In such a situation, the question of whether the power is releasable would seem a matter going to the nature of the original power and therefore should be referred to the law applicable to the trust or transaction by which the power was created. However, the scope or nature of the resulting reduced power should be viewed as a question concerning the construction of the transaction by which the donee reduced the power,[6] for the donor intended the donee to have a free hand in dealing with the power.[7] This analysis suggests the conclusion that

---

3. See Durand & Herterich, Conflict of Laws and the Exercise of Powers of Appointment, 42 Cornell L.Q. 185, 190 (1957); Ester & Scoles, Estate Planning and Conflict of Laws, 24 Ohio St. L.J. 270, 273 (1963).

4. Cf. Restatement, Second, Conflict of Laws §§ 255, 256, 269 (1971).

§ 21.10

1. See supra §§ 19.4, 20.8, 20.13. Cf. Estate of Stober, 108 Cal.App.3d 591, 166 Cal.Rptr. 628 (1980).

2. See In re Fuller's Will, 72 N.Y.S.2d 498 (1947).

3. See supra § 20.13.

4. See supra § 21.3.

5. E.g., U.P.C. § 2–801; N.Y. E.P.T.L. § 10–9.2.

6. Cf. N.Y. E.P.T.L. § 3–5.1(g); Guaranty Trust Co. v. Stevens, 28 N.J. 243, 146 A.2d 97 (1958).

7. See Beals v. State Street Bank & Trust Co., 367 Mass. 318, 326 N.E.2d 896 (1975); In re Estate of Davis, 100 Misc.2d 498, 419 N.Y.S.2d 827 (1979). Cf. People v. Cooke, 150 Colo. 52, 370 P.2d 896 (1962); Dollar Savings & Trust Co. v. First National Bank, 32 Ohio Misc. 81, 285 N.E.2d 768 (1972); A. Scott & W. Flatcher, The Law of Trusts §§ 631, 635 (4th ed. 1989). But cf. Schneider v. Laffoon, 4 Ohio St.2d 89, 212 N.E.2d 801 (1965).

whether the donee has affected a release of a releasable power would seem analogous, for choice-of-law purposes, to an exercise of a power, and the court should refer to the law most favorable to sustaining the intended release, by alternative reference either to the law applicable to the trust or that applicable to the release transaction.

D.   EXERCISE OF POWERS

1. *Generally*

§ 21.11   The relevant choice of law in issues involving the sufficiency of an alleged exercise of a power of appointment is a more complex and frequent question than that involving creation. The exercise of a power involves the significance of acts of both the donor and donee. The intent of both is relevant, as is the nature of the power involved. If the donor of the power states explicitly the manner in which it is to be exercised, compliance with the donor's terms would seem to be sufficient.[1] The common case, however, is that in which the donee is authorized to appoint by will or by deed and the donor suggests no further detail.

The courts usually hold that the power, special or general, to appoint an interest in land either by will or inter vivos can be exercised only by an instrument which is valid and effective for that purpose according to the law of the situs[2] including any reference the situs might make to the donee's domicile.[3] Under this view, the issue as to whether a power over land has been exercised by a general devise which does not mention the power, is determined by the whole law of the state where the land is located.[4]

The choice of law relevant to the validity and effect of an exercise of a power of appointment in movables is not as well settled. While there has been some tendency to refer all questions to the donor's domicile,[5]

§ 21.11

1. Thus in the leading case of Sewall v. Wilmer, 132 Mass. 131 (1882), an appointment was authorized by a last will and testament, "or by any writing purporting to be her last will and testament," etc. See also Olivet v. Whitworth, 82 Md. 258, 33 A. 723 (1896). A frequent provision in inter vivos trusts calls for appointment in writing signed by the donee and delivered to the trustee. Cf. Simes & Smith, Future Interests § 972 (2d ed. 1975).

2. Blount v. Walker, 134 U.S. 607, 10 S.Ct. 606, 33 L.Ed. 1036 (1890); Security Trust & Safe Deposit Co. v. Ward, 10 Del. Ch. 408, 93 A. 385 (1915); Ligget v. Fidelity & Columbia Trust Co., 274 Ky. 387, 118 S.W.2d 720 (1938); Matter of Estate of Allen, 237 Mont. 114, 772 P.2d 297 (1989). Cf. Russell v. Joys, 227 Mass. 263, 116 N.E. 549

(1917); W. Land, Trusts in the Conflict of Laws 34–36 (1940).

3. See supra § 20.6; Restatement, Second, Conflict of Laws § 282 (1971).

4. Art Students' League v. Hinkley, 31 F.2d 469 (D.Md.1929), affirmed 37 F.2d 225 (4th Cir.1930); In re Kelly's Will, 174 Misc. 80, 20 N.Y.S.2d 6 (Surr. 1940).

5. Pitman v. Pitman, 314 Mass. 465, 50 N.E.2d 69 (1943); David v. Atlantic County Society for Prevention of Cruelty to Animals, 129 N.J.Eq. 501, 19 A.2d 896 (1941); Toledo Trust Co. v. Santa Barbara Foundation, 32 Ohio St.3d 141, 512 N.E.2d 664 (1987); Adams v. D'Hauteville, 72 R.I. 325, 51 A.2d 92 (1947). For a discussion of the variations of the traditional rule, see Durand & Herterich, Conflicts of Laws and the Exercise of Powers of Appointment, 42 Cornell L.Q. 185 (1957); Mulford, The Conflict of Laws and Powers of Appointment, 87 U.

more recent cases support an approach more in keeping with the nature of the particular power and the issue involved.[6] It should be kept in mind that a general power, presently exercisable, is a beneficial interest in property nearly the equivalent of ownership. A general testamentary power is also beneficial to the donee even though he can dispose of it only at death, he may do so then to the same extent as owned property. In all general powers, the object of the donor's bounty is the donee. On the other hand, a special power, whether exercisable by will or deed, is so limited that it usually is non-beneficial and the object of the donor's bounty is not the donee but those to whom he may appoint. In general powers, it would seem that the intent of the donee and the law of his domicile as an incident thereto should have a greater weight in choice-of-law than in the case of special powers.[7] In the latter case, the law applicable to the transaction creating the power has greater significance. Again, bearing in mind that if a general power is reduced to a special power by the unilateral act of the donee, the significance of the donee's intention and contacts remain dominant since the donor intended that the donee deal with the property as his own.[8]

The question of capacity of a donee seldom arises in the United States, and when it does there seems no reason why the maximum validation of the intention of the donor and donee should not be effected to sustain capacity by either the law applicable to the transaction by which the donor created the power, or that of the donee's domicile.[9] While might be argued that a general power of appointment is so tantamount to property that the donee must have capacity by his own domicile, the intention of both parties seems to favor sustaining an appointment if possible.[10]

Although authority is scant,[11] the issue of the formal validity of an instrument exercising the power seems more clearly to fall within the

Pa. L. Rev. 403 (1939); Fridman, Choice of Law Governing the Testamentary Exercise of Powers of Appointment Over Movables, 9 Int'l & Comp. L.Q. 1 (1960). Cf. In re Nicholas' Will, 50 Misc.2d 76, 269 N.Y.S.2d 623 (1966). See Roberts v. Northern Trust Co., 550 F.Supp. 729 (N.D.Ill.1982) (law of donor's domicile generally controls questions about donee's exercise of power of appointment; however, express choice of law will be honored).

6. See A. Scott & W. Fratcher, The Law of Trusts § 639 (1989). Matter of Moore, 129 Misc.2d 639, 493 N.Y.S.2d 924 (1985) (donor's intent governs; thus, New York law applied notwithstanding donor's Connecticut domicile, where securities transferred to New York corporate trustee, signatures of trust agreement acknowledged in New York and reference in indenture to New York provisions governing trustees' commissions).

7. Cf. In re Estate of Grady, 79 Wn.2d 41, 483 P.2d 114 (1971); N.Y. E.P.T.L. § 3–5.1(g) (pointing to law of decedent's domicile at death in most cases).

8. Cf. supra § 21.10 n.7.

9. See Restatement, Second, Conflict of Laws § 274 cmnt. (c) (1971); A. Ehrenzweig, A Treatise on Conflict of Laws 670 (1962). Cf. Guaranty Trust Co. v. Stevens, 28 N.J. 243, 146 A.2d 97 (1958).

10. Fridman, Choice of Law Governing the Testamentary Exercise of Powers of Appointment Over Movables, 9 Int'l & Comp. L.Q. 1 (1960).

11. See Matter of Stewart, 11 Paige 398 (N.Y.Ch.1845); In re Lewal's Settlement Trusts, 2 Ch. 391 (1981); Restatement, Second, Conflict of Laws, § 274 (1971). Cf. In re Sloan's Estate, 7 Cal.App.2d 319, 46 P.2d 1007 (1935); Matter of Marsland's Estate, 142 Misc. 230, 254 N.Y.S. 293 (Surr. 1931).

alternative reference to sustain the exercise of the power.[12] The courts do not appear to have considered the distinction between special and general powers in this regard to be significant.[13] Certainly as to property subject to a general power of appointment the wide discretion in the donee suggests that the donor must have intended an effective exercise by any law reasonably validating it.[14]

The questions of substantial validity that have arisen concerning the exercise of a power of appointment have usually been referred to the law which otherwise governs the transaction by which the power was created.[15] In some cases, this is explained on the relation-back theory, or as an incident to the donor's intention. The more recent cases, however, have emphasized the significance of the donor's intent in creating the trust and power of appointment. The exercise of the power is usually sustained. Illustrative is *In re Pratt's Trust*[16] in which a resident of Nevada created an inter vivos trust of movables in New York, appointed a New York trustee, and retained a general testamentary power to appoint the corpus. The settlor subsequently became a Florida domiciliary and died a few days after executing a will which exercised the power partially in favor of charities. Under the law of Florida, a bequest to a charity in a will executed so shortly before the testator's death was invalid, while in New York such bequests were unaffected by statute. On the question of distribution of trust corpus in New York, the New York court held that an express choice-of-law clause, which provided that the trust should be governed by New York law, applied both to the trust and the exercise of the power of appointment. As a consequence, the will constituted a valid appointment of the corpus having a situs in New York. The argument for separating the trust questions from the problem of testamentary exercise of the power was specifically urged, but both New York appellate courts treated the testamentary exercise of the power as being controlled by the law governing the trust in general. This case is one of several tending to

12. Sewall v. Wilmer, 132 Mass. 131 (1882); Guaranty Trust Co. v. Stevens, 28 N.J. 243, 146 A.2d 97 (1958); Halbach, The Use of Powers of Appointment, 45 Iowa L. Rev. 691, 716 (1960). Cf. Ward v. Stanard, 82 App.Div. 386, 81 N.Y.S. 906 (1903); Adger v. Kirk, 116 S.C. 298, 108 S.E. 97 (1921).

13. Cf. N.Y. E.P.T.L. § 3–5.1(g).

14. See Guaranty Trust Co. v. Stevens, 28 N.J. 243, 146 A.2d 97 (1958); cf. Boston Safe Deposit & Trust Co. v. Painter, 322 Mass. 362, 77 N.E.2d 409 (1948).

15. See Wilmington Trust Co. v. Wilmington Trust Co., 21 Del.Ch. 188, 186 A. 903 (1936) (noted 37 Colum. L. Rev. 125, 25 Geo. L.J. 464, 50 Harv. L. Rev. 1157 (1937)); Ligget v. Fidelity & Columbia Trust Co., 274 Ky. 387, 118 S.W.2d 720 (1938); Bundy v. United States Trust Co., 257 Mass. 72, 153 N.E. 337 (1926); Greenough v. Osgood, 235 Mass. 235, 126 N.E. 461 (1920); David v. Atlantic County Soci-

ety for Prevention of Cruelty to Animals, 129 N.J.Eq. 501, 19 A.2d 896 (1941); Matter of Harriman's Estate, 124 Misc. 320, 208 N.Y.S. 672 (Surr. 1924), affirmed 217 App. Div. 733, 216 N.Y.S. 842 (1926); McCreary's Estate, 29 D. & C. 93 (Pa. 1937), affirmed 328 Pa. 513, 196 A. 25 (1938). See also Mulford, The Conflict of Laws and Powers of Appointment, 87 U. Pa. L. Rev. 403 (1939). Cf. Galard v. Winans, 111 Md. 434, 74 A. 626 (1909); Fidelity Union Trust Co. v. Caldwell, 137 N.J.Eq. 362, 44 A.2d 842 (1945); In re Bauer's Trust, 13 A.D.2d 369, 216 N.Y.S.2d 920 (1961). In *Bauer* the court invalidated the appointment under the New York rule against perpetuities even though the donee was domiciled in England where the appointment in trust was to be administered. See infra § 21.12 n.1.

16. 5 A.D.2d 501, 172 N.Y.S.2d 965 (1958), aff'd 8 N.Y.2d 855, 203 N.Y.S.2d 906, 168 N.E.2d 709 (1960).

identify the validity of an exercise of the power of appointment with the validity of the trust by which the power was created, and to permit the law designated by the settlor donor to be controlling if that law has some reasonable connection with the trust and power of appointment.[17]

2. *Rule Against Perpetuities*

§ 21.12 A significant number of cases have raised questions of essential validity of the exercise of a power of appointment under the rule against perpetuities. *In re Bauer's Trust*[1] involved the exercise of a general testamentary power of appointment retained by the donor—donee over a trust created and established in New York while the settlor was domiciled there. Later, the donor moved her domicile to England where she resided for 37 years before her death. She left a will appointing her property to two nieces for life with the remainder to English charities. The appointment was valid in England but violated the archaic New York two lives rule which had been repealed before trial. The court rather mechanically applied the law governing the original trust and refused to validate the exercise by the English law, thereby holding that the appointment failed. Dissenting Judges Dye and Fuld argued that the exercise of the beneficial general power should be sustained as a clearly intended disposition by the owner, valid under her personal law. The case received considerable critical comment[2] and seemed inconsistent with a developing trend to validate intended dispositions as against the rule against perpetuities by any reasonably applicable law.[3] Shortly thereafter the New York legislature enacted a statutory choice-of-law rule effectively overruling *Bauer* and providing that the validity of the exercise of such a retained power would be determined by the donee's domicile.[4]

---

17. Accord, Lewis v. Hanson, 36 Del.Ch. 235, 128 A.2d 819 (1957), affirmed 357 U.S. 235, 78 S.Ct. 1228, 2 L.Ed.2d 1283 (1958); Wilmington Trust Co. v. Wilmington Trust Co., 26 Del.Ch. 397, 24 A.2d 309 (1942); First–Central Trust Co. v. Claflin, 73 N.E.2d 388 (Ohio C.P. 1947). See also Morgan Guaranty Trust Co. v. Huntington, 149 Conn. 331, 179 A.2d 604 (1962); Wilmington Trust Co. v. Sloane, 30 Del.Ch. 103, 54 A.2d 544 (1947); In re Von Gontard's Trust, 36 Misc.2d 529, 233 N.Y.S.2d 30 (Sup. 1962); In re Barton, 348 Pa. 279, 35 A.2d 266 (1944); Restatement, Second, Conflict of Laws § 274 (1971); Matter of Moore, 129 Misc.2d 639, 493 N.Y.S.2d 924 (1985); Will of Brown, 120 Misc.2d 799, 466 N.Y.S.2d 988 (1983).

§ 21.12

1. 14 N.Y.2d 272, 251 N.Y.S.2d 23, 200 N.E.2d 207 (1964).

2. E.g., Recent Decision, 29 Albany L. Rev. 115 (1965); Recent Decision, 31 Brooklyn L. Rev. 145 (1964); Recent Develop-

ment, 65 Colum. L. Rev. 348 (1965); Note, 50 Cornell L.Q. 513 (1965); Note, 10 N.Y.L. Forum 402 (1964); Comment, 40 N.Y.U. L. Rev. 793 (1965).

3. See Wilmington Trust Co. v. Wilmington Trust Co., 26 Del.Ch. 397, 24 A.2d 309 (1942). See also Shannon v. Irving Trust Co., 275 N.Y. 95, 9 N.E.2d 792 (1937). Cf. In re Chappell's Estate, 124 Wash. 128, 213 P. 684 (1923).

4. See N.Y. E.P.T.L. § 3–5.1(g). See also Matter of Renard, 100 Misc.2d 347, 417 N.Y.S.2d 155 (1979), affirmed 71 A.D.2d 554, 418 N.Y.S.2d 553 (1979), motion for leave to appeal denied 48 N.Y.2d 609, 424 N.Y.S.2d 1027, 400 N.E.2d 1351 (1979). See also Hendrickson, Choice–of–Law Directions for Disposing of Assets Situated Elsewhere than the Domicile of Their Owner—The Refractions of *Renard*, 18 Real Prop.Prob. & Tr.J. 407, 413–15 (1983).

A similar case came before the New York Court of Appeals seven years later.[5] In that case the donor created an inter vivos trust in New York for her son for life, then to her grandson, E.C., for life, with remainders as E.C. should appoint by will and, in default, to his distributees as in intestacy. The grandson domiciled in California, appointed in a trust that violated the rule against perpetuities but which under the California perpetuities *cy pres* statute would be reformed to terminate within the period of the rule against perpetuities and hence be valid. The beneficiaries and the takers in default litigated in California and the California court reformed the grandson's appointment in trust to validate it under the rule against perpetuities. The trust beneficiaries then sought payment from the New York trustee, asserting full faith and credit to the California decree, even though the New York trustee was not a party in California.[6] The New York court recognized the appointment as valid under the law of the donee's domicile, California. Although the *Acheson* case is distinguishable from *Bauer* because of the full-faith-and-credit issue, the emphasis on the law of the donee's domicile clearly validates the exercise. As pointed out by an eminent scholar discussing the case: "Is there really any discernible policy of New York which would invalidate the trust created by the donee if it is valid under the law of his domicile? . . . . Probably in most cases the donor has no real intention in the matter; but is it not reasonable to believe that he would prefer the law of the donee's domicile, if that would validate the disposition of the appointed property? . . . "[7]

From this it can be concluded that the donee's appointment should be valid if valid under the law of either the donor's domicile or the donee's domicile. There is only slight variation in the policy of the states regarding the rule against perpetuities. The shared policies of validating the intended disposition of both the donor and the donee should prevail over the slight policy variation in the detail of the states' rules against perpetuities. In the unlikely event that the appointment would violate a strong public policy of the donor's domicile, the disposition may be held invalid to permit the court supervising the trust administration to refuse to allow the donor's trustees to distribute to the donee's appointees. This rarely would be the case.

The complete abolition of the perpetuities rule in some states may present interesting conflicts problems. The widespread assumption appears to be that the placing of the situs of trust assets in a jurisdiction without a perpetuities rule will allow for perpetual trusts.[8] However, it seems quite possible that counts in other states with a strong connection—such as the settlor's domicile—might view the application of some

---

5. Acheson v. Dowell, (In re Morgan Guaranty Trust Co.), 28 N.Y.2d 155, 320 N.Y.S.2d 905, 269 N.E.2d 571 (1971), cert. denied Dowell v. Acheson, 404 U.S. 826, 92 S.Ct. 58, 30 L.Ed.2d 55 (1971).

6. Cf. Hanson v. Denckla, 357 U.S. 235, 78 S.Ct. 1228, 2 L.Ed.2d 1283 (1958).

7. A. Scott & W. Fratcher, The Law of Trusts § 635 (4th ed. 1989).

8. See, e.g., ABA Section of Real Property, Probate and Trust Law, Forum Shopping for Dynasty Trusts? Where do we send our Clients and Their Money? (1997)

perpetuities rule as one of mandatory application and thus overriding the usual choice-of-law reference.

3. *Exercise by Residuary Clause*

§ 21.13 The question most frequently litigated in the United States has been that of the proper law to determine whether the power has been effectively exercised. The donor of the power, for instance, leaves property in trust for the donee for life with remainder over to such person as the donee by last will shall appoint. The donee dies leaving a will in which he makes a residuary bequest of his estate but does not mention the power of appointment. The laws of the domiciles of the donor and donee of the power differ as to whether this is an effective exercise of the power of appointment. There is strong reason for saying that the answer to the question should be determined by the law of the domicile of the donee of the power. Whether the donee exercises the option is for the donee to determine, not the donor. And where the intention is not clearly expressed, but must be found by implication, or fixed by construction, the law most closely connected to this construction should be that with regard to which the will exercising the power was written, i.e., the donee testator's domicile. There is considerable support for the view that the question of the intent of the donee to exercise the power and the extent to which he intended to exercise it, are referred to the law in light of which his will is to be construed, normally, in absence of a choice-of-law clause[1] his domicile.[2] This is the view of the American Law Institute.[3] The greater number of cases, however, purport to refer the question to the law applicable to the transaction creating the trust but in so doing, most sustain the appointment.[4] Some nevertheless, have

§ 21.13

1. Cf. Russell v. Wachovia Bank, N.A., 353 S.C. 208, 578 S.E.2d 329 (2003)(choice-of-law clause in inter vivos trust honored); Wright v. Rains, 106 S.W.3d 678 (Tenn. App. 2003)(same); First National Bank of Chicago v. Ettlinger, 465 F.2d 343 (7th Cir. 1972). Matter of Moore, 129 Misc.2d 639, 493 N.Y.S.2d 924 (1985) (donor's intent, not donor's or donee's domicile governs).

2. Morgan Guaranty Trust Co. v. Huntington, 149 Conn. 331, 179 A.2d 604 (1962). Cf. United States v. Merchants National Bank, 261 F.2d 570 (5th Cir.1958); First National Bank of Arizona v. First National Bank of Birmingham, 348 So.2d 1041 (Ala. 1977); Guaranty Trust Co. v. Stevens, 28 N.J. 243, 146 A.2d 97 (1958); In re Flagler's Will, 4 Misc.2d 705, 158 N.Y.S.2d 941 (Surr. 1957); In re Huntington's Estate, 10 Misc.2d 932, 170 N.Y.S.2d 452 (Surr. 1957); Toledo Trust Co. v. Santa Barbara Foundation, 32 Ohio St.3d 141, 512 N.E.2d 664 (1987); Cleveland Trust Co. v. Shuman, 39 Ohio Misc. 136, 317 N.E.2d 256 (1974); In re McMullin's Estate, 490 Pa. 502, 417 A.2d 152 (1980). White v. United States, 680 F.2d 1156 (7th Cir.1982).

3. Restatement, Second, Conflict of Laws § 275 (1971).

4. Wilmington Trust Co. v. Wilmington Trust Co., 21 Del.Ch. 188, 186 A. 903 (1936); Lane v. Lane, 20 Del. 368, 55 A. 184 (1903); Galard v. Winans, 111 Md. 434, 74 A. 626 (1909); Sewall v. Wilmer, 132 Mass. 131 (1882); Tudor v. Vail, 195 Mass. 18, 80 N.E. 590 (1907); In re New York Life Insurance & Trust Co., 209 N.Y. 585, 103 N.E. 315 (1913); In re Bankers Trust Co., 9 Misc.2d 927, 169 N.Y.S.2d 698 (1957); In re McCampbell's Trust, 36 Misc.2d 108, 232 N.Y.S.2d 522 (1962); Bingham's Appeal, 64 Pa. 345, 27 L.I. 92 (1870); Harlow v. Duryea, 42 R.I. 234, 107 A. 98 (1919); Rhode Island Hospital Trust Co. v. Dunnell, 34 R.I. 394, 83 A. 858 (1912); Mulford, The Conflict of Laws and Powers of Appointment, 87 U. Pa. L. Rev. 403 (1939).

invalidated the exercise by the law governing the creation of the power.[5]

5. See, e.g., In re Erdman's Estate, 264 Cal.App.2d 335, 70 Cal.Rptr. 774 (1968); Bussing v. Hough, 237 Iowa 194, 21 N.W.2d 587 (1946). Farnum v. Pennsylvania Co. for Insurance, 87 N.J.Eq. 108, 99 A. 145 (1916), affirmed 87 N.J.Eq. 652, 101 A. 1053 (1917); In re Kelly's Will, 161 Misc. 255, 291 N.Y.S. 860 (1936), noted 50 Harv. L. Rev. 1119, 1155 (1937); Matter of Campbell's Estate, 138 Misc. 800, 248 N.Y.S. 344 (Surr. 1930); Cotting v. De Sartiges, 17 R.I. 668, 24 A. 530 (1892).

Chapter 22

PROBATE AND ADMINISTRATION OF ESTATES

Table of Sections

		Sections
I.	Probate	22.1–22.4
	A. Introduction	22.1
	B. Probate of Will of Movables	22.2
	C. Recognition of Foreign Probate	22.3
	D. Probate of Will of Immovables—Land	22.4
II.	Administration of Estates	22.5–22.22
	A. Introduction	22.5
	B. Place and Necessity of Administration	22.6–22.13
	1. Domicile	22.6
	2. Situs of Tangible Assets	22.7
	3. Chattels Temporarily Present Within a State	22.8
	4. Chattels Brought Into a State After Owner's Death	22.9
	5. Intangibles	22.10
	6. Commercial Paper	22.11
	7. Corporate Stock	22.12
	8. Life Insurance	22.13
	C. Powers of Personal Representative Outside Appointing State	22.14–22.20
	1. Power to Sue	22.14
	2. Other Acts	22.15
	3. Payment to a Foreign Representative	22.16
	4. Transfer of Claim by Personal Representative	22.17
	5. Suits Arising Out of Administration	22.18
	6. Actions Against Foreign Representatives	22.19
	7. Privity Between Foreign Representatives	22.20
	D. Creditors' Claims—Proof and Payment	22.21
	E. Spousal and Family Allowances	22.22
III.	Accounting and Distribution	22.23
IV.	Guardians and Conservators	22.24–22.26
	A. In General	22.24
	B. Conservators	22.25
	C. Guardians of the Person	22.26

I. PROBATE

A. INTRODUCTION

§ 22.1 The term "probate" is used in three different ways in the United States. The first two relate to the will. As applied to wills, "probate" means the proof or establishment, before the appropriate tribunal, that the document produced is a valid last will of the deceased. It also has the related or subsidiary meaning of the certification of such court that the will was executed by a competent testator in the manner prescribed by law.[1] It is also common to see reference to "probating an estate" or "avoiding probate." In this third context, "probate" refers to the entire process of administering a decedent's estate, often without distinction as to whether the decedent was testate or intestate. The context in which the term is used will identify the particular meaning the user has in mind.

The principal place of probate of the will and administration of a decedent's estate is normally in the state where the decedent was domiciled at death. That is where the family and property interests center and usually where those most concerned with the decedent's estate are located. Many advantages result, in the usual case, from first probating the will at the domicile and that is the custom and practice in absence of contrary controlling considerations.

B. PROBATE OF WILL OF MOVABLES

§ 22.2 The domiciliary probate of the will is nearly always very significant as to the movable assets in the estate. The preference for probate of the will of movables at the domicile is reflected in the common assumption that an ancillary court may decline probate until there has been probate at the domicile, unless good reason is otherwise shown.[1] Occasionally it has been suggested that this is a jurisdictional requirement with respect to wills of movables.[2] It seems clear, however, that there is jurisdiction to admit a will to probate, or to refuse it, wherever personal estate belonging to the decedent is located.[3] In a case in which there is no occasion for probate at the domicile, there seems to be no

§ 22.1

1. T. Atkinson on Wills 480 (2d ed. 1953).

§ 22.2

1. Vangrack, Axelson & Williamowsky, P.C. v. Estate of Abbasi, 261 F. Supp. 2d 352, 355 (D. Md. 2003); Valentine v. Elliott (In Re Estate of Delaney), 819 A.2d 968 (D.C. App. 2003), cert. denied __ U.S. __, 124 S.Ct. 1075, 157 L.Ed.2d 896 (2004); Stein v. Welch, 78 Wash.App. 251, 896 P.2d 740 (1995); Davis v. Upson, 230 Ill. 327, 82 N.E. 824 (1907) (noted 2 Ill. L. Rev. 605 (1908)); In re Corning's Will, 159 Mich. 474, 124 N.W. 514 (1910); Rackemann v. Taylor, 204 Mass. 394, 90 N.E. 552 (1910); In re Holden's Estate, 110 Vt. 60, 1 A.2d 721 (1938). Cf. Svoboda v. Svoboda, 61 Tenn. App. 444, 454 S.W.2d 722 (1969); Wagner v. Estate of Duncan, 546 S.W.2d 859 (Tex.Civ. App.1977).

2. Pratt v. Douglas, 38 N.J.Eq. 516 (Err. & A.1884); Ives v. Salisbury's Heirs, 56 Vt. 565 (1883).

3. Montgomery v. National Savings & Trust Co., 356 F.2d 806 (D.C.Cir.1966); Gordon v. Holly Woods Acres, Inc., 328 F.2d 253 (6th Cir.1964); In re Clark's Estate, 148

reason why adjudication elsewhere should be conditioned upon the prior probate of the will at the decedent's domicile, though the court of the situs of the property will very probably determine the validity of the will under the domiciliary law.[4] The question is not so much one of power as the convenient allocation of judicial business and the domicile is usually the more appropriate forum for initial probate. This policy of giving priority to the probate at the domicile is reflected in several sections of the Uniform Probate Code which require the court in ancillary jurisdiction to defer to the prior determination of domicile of the decedent and to give priority to the appointment of the domiciliary personal representative.[5]

C. RECOGNITION OF FOREIGN PROBATE

§ 22.3 A will admitted to probate as a valid will at the domicile of the decedent should be conclusively recognized as valid in all other states where the decedent left movables, and this is the general view of the authorities.[1] While this result is perhaps not required by the Constitution except as to parties to the first litigation, as some cases suggest,[2] the policies of unitary succession and preclusion by prior litigation support this as the preferred view.[3] In this connection, the distinction should be noted between informal probate (ex parte or common form) and formal probate after appropriate notice (solemn form) or participation of the

Cal. 108, 82 P. 760 (1905); Thompson v. Parnell, 81 Kan. 119, 105 P. 502 (1909); Morrison v. Hass, 229 Mass. 514, 118 N.E. 893 (1918); Gordon's Will, 50 N.J.Eq. 397, 26 A. 268 (1893); In re Heinz' Will, 50 Misc.2d 1072, 272 N.Y.S.2d 394 (Surr. 1966); Hesler v. Snyder, 422 P.2d 432 (Okla.1967); Restatement, Second, Conflict of Laws § 314 (1971). See Ughetta, Practical Problems in Administering Revocable Trusts and Pour–Over Wills Involving More Than One Jurisdiction, 113 Tr. & Est. 200 (1974); B. Laudy, B. Hunter & F. Woodbridge, Transnational Probate, 19 U. Miami Inter. Am. L. Rev. 285 (1988); In re Estate of Hatcher, 439 So.2d 977 (Fla.App.1983). Cf. Crosson v. Conlee, 745 F.2d 896 (4th Cir. 1984), cert. denied 470 U.S. 1054, 105 S.Ct. 1759, 84 L.Ed.2d 822; Ford v. Pace, 672 S.W.2d 219 (Tenn.App.1984) (where all property of decedent located in Ohio no jurisdiction of Tennessee court to determine heirship).

4. See supra § 20.9.

5. See, e.g., Uniform Probate Code (U.P.C.) §§ 3–202, 3–307.

§ 22.3

1. Maxfield v. Terry, 885 S.W.2d 216 (Tex.Civ.App. 1994); Goodman v. Winter, 64 Ala. 410, 38 Am.Rep. 13 (1879); Evans-

ville Ice & Cold–Storage Co. v. Winsor, 148 Ind. 682, 48 N.E. 592 (1897) (same); Succession of Gaines, 45 La.Ann. 1237, 14 So. 233 (1893); State ex rel. Ruef v. District Court, 34 Mont. 96, 85 P. 866 (1906); Matter of Horton's Will, 217 N.Y. 363, 111 N.E. 1066 (1916); McEwan v. Brown, 176 N.C. 249, 97 S.E. 20 (1918); Tripp v. Tripp, 240 S.C. 334, 126 S.E.2d 9 (1962), cert. denied 371 U.S. 888, 83 S.Ct. 187, 9 L.Ed.2d 123 (1962); Martin v. Stovall, 103 Tenn. 1, 52 S.W. 296 (1899); Jones v. Jones, 301 S.W.2d 310 (Tex.Civ.App.1957); Ives v. Salisbury's Heirs, 56 Vt. 565 (1883). Cf. DiMauro v. Pavia, 492 F.Supp. 1051 (D.Conn.1979), affirmed 614 F.2d 1286 (2d Cir.1979); State ex rel. Attorney General v. Wright, 194 Ark. 652, 109 S.W.2d 123 (1937); Kurtz v. Kurtz' Estate, 169 Md. 554, 182 A. 456 (1936). But cf. Schweitzer v. Bean, 154 Ark. 228, 242 S.W. 63 (1922); Shimshak v. Cox, 166 La. 102, 116 So. 714 (1928); Matter of Estate of Reed, 768 P.2d 566 (Wyo.1989).

2. E.g., Evansville Ice & Cold–Storage Co. v. Winsor, 148 Ind. 682, 48 N.E. 592 (1897); Ives v. Salisbury's Heirs, 56 Vt. 565 (1883). Cf. In re Rettig's Estate, 8 Ohio Misc. 38, 216 N.E.2d 924 (Ohio Prob.1964).

3. See Scoles, Interstate Preclusion by Prior Litigation, 74 Nw.U.L. Rev. 742 (1979). See also infra ch. 24.

parties. The limited recognition elsewhere given to informal probate rests upon the policy of unitary succession.[4] Where, however, there is appropriate notice or participation by the parties, as among the courts of the United States, one contest of a will should be adequate. In most instances, the domicile is the most appropriate forum for this single contest. Otherwise, repeated litigation permits the fortuitous location of assets and the nature of our federal system to be used for unwarranted personal advantage. Consequently, when it appears that a paper has been admitted to probate at the domicile as the valid testamentary disposition of the decedent's property, other states will naturally accept that probate as final. The situs of the property is interested in determining what the domiciliary state declares is the appropriate disposition of the decedent's goods. When the will is declared a valid will, that question is answered.

Full faith and credit must no doubt be given to the domiciliary probate of the will and the proceedings thereunder as to the assets in domiciliary state when those assets become involved in litigation elsewhere.[5] This assumes adequate notice even for an effective judgment in rem.[6] If the decree is an informal decree in rem, it will be limited as the result of the inadequacy of notice.[7] On the other hand, if there is adequate service or participation in the litigation, the preclusive policies of res judicata and full faith and credit go further.[8] For example, a finding that the decedent was domiciled in one state should preclude subsequent litigation on that jurisdictional fact[9] except as to the parties not participating in the first litigation.[10]

Although there has been some uncertainty about full faith and credit to decrees in probate, the United States Supreme Court cases indicate that there is no exception to the Full Faith and Credit Clause or the policies of preclusion by prior litigation for probate decrees. Where there is previous litigation, *inter partes,* either at the domicile or elsewhere, it is preclusive. The same considerations of jurisdictional relationship and adequate notice apply here as elsewhere.[11] Consequently, par-

4. Cf. Estate of Theodoropoulos, 93 Misc.2d 551, 402 N.Y.S.2d 927 (Surr. 1978); In re Gyfteas' Estate, 59 Misc.2d 977, 300 N.Y.S.2d 913 (1968); Bowen v. Johnson, 5 R.I. 112, 73 Am.Dec. 49 (1858); Olney v. Angell, 5 R.I. 198, 73 Am.Dec. 62 (1858).

5. Tilt v. Kelsey, 207 U.S. 43, 28 S.Ct. 1, 52 L.Ed. 95 (1907); Restatement, Second, Conflict of Laws § 317 (1971). Cf. In re Williams' Estate, 71 Misc.2d 243, 335 N.Y.S.2d 950 (Surr. 1972).

6. Cf. Mullane v. Central Hanover Bank & Trust Co., 339 U.S. 306, 70 S.Ct. 652, 94 L.Ed. 865 (1950).

7. See supra § 5.16.

8. See Treinies v. Sunshine Mining Co., 308 U.S. 66, 60 S.Ct. 44, 84 L.Ed. 85 (1939).

9. Estate of Rubert, 139 N.H. 273, 651 A.2d 937 (1994); Loewenthal v. Mandell,

125 Fla. 685, 170 So. 169 (1936); Torrey v. Bruner, 60 Fla. 365, 53 So. 337 (1910); Dalrymple v. Gamble, 68 Md. 523, 13 A. 156 (1888). See Willetts' Appeal, 50 Conn. 330 (1882); In re Fischer's Estate, 118 N.J.Eq. 599, 180 A. 633 (1935). In re Gifford's Will, 279 N.Y. 470, 18 N.E.2d 663 (1939).

10. Riley v. New York Trust Co., 315 U.S. 343, 62 S.Ct. 608, 86 L.Ed. 885 (1942); Tilt v. Kelsey, 207 U.S. 43, 28 S.Ct. 1, 52 L.Ed. 95 (1907); Overby v. Gordon, 177 U.S. 214, 20 S.Ct. 603, 44 L.Ed. 741 (1900); Voss v. Shalala, 32 F.3d 1269 (8th Cir.1994), cert. denied 513 U.S. 1168, 115 S.Ct. 1138, 130 L.Ed.2d 1099 (1995).

11. Restatement, Second, Judgments § 30 (1982).

ties to a formal probate of a will are bound either by res judicata or by claim preclusion[12] as to personal property by litigation resolving the choice of law reference to the domicile and the content of the domiciliary law. They may also be bound by issue preclusion as to land since the validity of the will as an issue has been previously litigated. The policies of preclusion by prior litigation are the same whatever the subject matter of the litigation.[13] One litigation is enough. Likewise, prior probate of a will in a state not the domicile of a decedent will be conclusive as to the disposition of property in that state.[14] But without contest or participation in the litigation it will not control elsewhere the question of validity of the will.[15] The converse proposition would be equally true. The denial of probate elsewhere than at the domicile of the testator will govern as to its effect upon property in the state denying probate, but it will not, in the absence of litigation, affect the question of validity of the will when it arises elsewhere.[16] Participants in a contest in the first state, however, may be precluded from further litigating the same questions on principles of preclusion by prior litigation.[17]

D. PROBATE OF WILL OF IMMOVABLES—LAND

§ 22.4 Some additional factors must be considered when the assets of a decedent include immovables located at a state other than at the domicile. The situs control over muniments of title requires that its law be followed. Consequently, probate of a will of land is required or excused as the situs statutes provide. The statutes of most states require some form of probate or registration in nearly all instances[1] although title to land may occasionally be established for practical purposes without probate.

The significance at the situs of probate as a valid will in another state is uncertain. The probate, even at the domicile, absent statute[2] or

---

12. For detailed analysis of the terms claim preclusion and issue preclusion, see A. Vestal, Res Judicata/Preclusion 13, 43, 189 (1969); Restatement, Second, Judgments § 17 (1982). See also infra § 24.1.

13. E.g., Durfee v. Duke, 375 U.S. 106, 84 S.Ct. 242, 11 L.Ed.2d 186 (1963); Treinies v. Sunshine Mining Co., 308 U.S. 66, 60 S.Ct. 44, 84 L.Ed. 85 (1939); Tilt v. Kelsey, 207 U.S. 43, 28 S.Ct. 1, 52 L.Ed. 95 (1907).

14. Overby v. Gordon, 177 U.S. 214, 20 S.Ct. 603, 44 L.Ed. 741 (1900); Jones v. Jones, 107 Ill.App. 464 (1903); Newcomb v. Newcomb, 108 Ky. 582, 57 S.W. 2 (1900); Walton v. Hall's Estate, 66 Vt. 455, 29 A. 803 (1894). Cf. Matter of Reed's Estate, 233 Kan. 531, 664 P.2d 824 (1983), cert. denied 464 U.S. 978, 104 S.Ct. 417, 78 L.Ed.2d 354 (1983), aff'd 236 Kan. 514, 693 P.2d 1156 (1985) (conclusive as to disposition of property in situs state, but not necessarily in domiciliary state).

15. Marr v. Hendrix, 952 S.W.2d 693 (Ky.1997) (undue influence issue not precluded because not earlier litigated); In re Clark's Estate, 148 Cal. 108, 82 P. 760 (1905); In re Longshore's Will, 188 Iowa 743, 176 N.W. 902 (1920); Scripps v. Durfee, 131 Mich. 265, 90 N.W. 1061 (1902). But see Ives v. Salisbury's Heirs, 56 Vt. 565 (1883).

16. But see In re Barney's Will, 94 N.J.Eq. 392, 120 A. 513 (1923) (noted 33 Yale L.J. 103 (1923)).

17. Treinies v. Sunshine Mining Co., 308 U.S. 66, 60 S.Ct. 44, 84 L.Ed. 85 (1939).

§ 22.4

1. Thompson v. Parnell, 81 Kan. 119, 105 P. 502 (1909). Cf. St. Charles Land Trust v. St. Amant, 253 La. 243, 217 So.2d 385 (1968).

2. See, e.g., U.P.C. § 3–408 (requiring notice and opportunity to contest "to all interested persons....").

preclusion *inter partes*[3] does not necessarily establish that the will validly passes land elsewhere.[4] The effect of the will to convey land normally is determined by the situs, but the admission of the will to probate at the domicile included finding of due execution and testamentary capacity. The situs would seem to have no greater interest in capacity than the domicile. Consequently, it would seem that the domiciliary probate should prevail in the absence of a peculiar additional requirement at the situs or a claim by a non-participating beneficiary. This view was taken in the early Massachusetts case of *Crippen v. Dexter*[5] but not widely adopted by the courts.[6] Most of the decisions that take the broad position that foreign probate does not establish validity or preclude contest at the situs of land[7] were decided before the development of preclusion policies by the more recent cases. The policies reflected in *Crippen v. Dexter* favoring a single standard for a decedent's will have been given effect by statutes providing that local effect be given to the probate of a will elsewhere.[8] A typical provision of these statutes provides:

> **§ 3–408.** A final order of a court of another state determining testacy, the validity or construction of a will, made in a proceeding involving notice to and an opportunity for contest by all interested persons must be accepted as determinative by the courts of this state if it concludes, or is based upon, a finding that the decedent was domiciled at his death in the state where the order was made.[9]

The trend of enactments of this type of statute will assist in removing much of the provincialism that is characteristic of the law of succession.[10] There seems to be no reason for distinguishing probate decrees or probate decrees affecting land from other forms of litigation in which the policies of preclusion by prior litigation bar redetermination of issues

---

3. Cf. supra § 22.3 n.13.

4. Keith v. Johnson, 97 Mo. 223, 10 S.W. 597 (1889); Matter of Estate of Reed, 768 P.2d 566 (Wyo.1989).

5. 79 Mass. 330 (1859).

6. See, e.g., Bowen v. Johnson, 5 R.I. 112, 73 Am.Dec. 49 (1858); Holland v. Jackson, 121 Tex. 1, 37 S.W.2d 726 (1931).

7. Robertson v. Pickrell, 109 U.S. 608, 3 S.Ct. 407, 27 L.Ed. 1049 (1883); Clarke v. Clarke, 178 U.S. 186, 20 S.Ct. 873, 44 L.Ed. 1028 (1900); Craig v. Carrigo, 353 Ark. 761, 121 S.W.3d 154 (2003); Selle v. Rapp, 143 Ark. 192, 220 S.W. 662 (1920); Keith v. Johnson, 97 Mo. 223, 10 S.W. 597 (1889); State ex rel. Ruef v. District Court, 34 Mont. 96, 85 P. 866 (1906); Cornell v. Burr, et al. In re Kimberly's Estate, 32 S.D. 1, 141 N.W. 1081 (1913). Cf. Second National Bank v. Thomson, 455 S.W.2d 51 (Ky.1970) (trustee and beneficiaries did not appear). Many of these cases rest on the exclusive jurisdictional concepts that were reflected in Clarke v. Clarke, 178 U.S. 186, 20 S.Ct. 873, 44 L.Ed. 1028 (1900) which seems questionable precedent on any issue involv-

ing preclusion by prior litigation. See supra § 20.2 n.6.

8. See, e.g., U.P.C. § 3–408; Atkinson, The Uniform Ancillary Administration and Probate Acts, 67 Harv. L. Rev. 619 (1954). For cases showing the application of such statutes see Carter v. Davis, 275 Ala. 250, 154 So.2d 9 (1963); Appeal of Murdoch, 81 Conn. 681, 72 A. 290 (1909); Torrey v. Bruner, 60 Fla. 365, 53 So. 337 (1910); Pratt v. Hawley, 297 Ill. 244, 130 N.E. 793 (1921); In re Longshore's Will, 188 Iowa 743, 176 N.W. 902 (1920); Roach v. Jurchak, 182 Md. 646, 35 A.2d 817 (1944); Keith v. Johnson, 97 Mo. 223, 10 S.W. 597 (1889); Ives v. Salisbury's Heirs, 56 Vt. 565 (1883); Simpson v. Cornish, 196 Wis. 125, 218 N.W. 193 (1928). But see In re Barrie's Estate, 240 Iowa 431, 35 N.W.2d 658 (1949), cert. denied 338 U.S. 815, 70 S.Ct. 55, 94 L.Ed. 493 (1949).

9. U.P.C. § 3–408.

10. See T. Atkinson on Wills 487 (2d ed. 1953); Rees, American Wills Statutes (pt. 2), 46 Va. L. Rev. 856, 905 (1960).

previously litigated. Land, however, retains a special character for full-faith-and-credit purposes. The Supreme Court's decision in *Baker v. General Motors*[11] seems to reaffirm the idea that the situs state need not honor a decree from a non-situs state affecting title to realty. Thus, eliminating parochialism in probate of realty matters will depend upon enlightened cooperation by sister-state courts.[12]

II. ADMINISTRATION OF ESTATES

A. INTRODUCTION

§ 22.5 Legal problems presented in the administration of a decedent's estate raise a variety of questions of law that occupy the legal profession. The questions are not simplified when the deceased, instead of leaving property in only one state, leaves an estate scattered about among several states, a common situation in the United States. A further complication is introduced into the law governing administration of decedent's estates by the history of the subject. In England, the jurisdiction to administer the personal estates of decedents was for many years vested in the ecclesiastic courts.[1] The ecclesiastic courts were subject to their own peculiar rules limiting the authority of the court of the ordinary and fixing the dividing line between the authority of the court of the Bishop and that of the Archbishop. These precedents as to jurisdiction based upon the division of affairs among the ecclesiastical courts have had an influence in the United States even though they were questionable authority in this country. In this country also, for many years, the probate courts were viewed as courts of limited jurisdiction somewhat apart from the courts of general jurisdiction. As a consequence, administration proceedings have often been viewed as of a local nature and slightly inferior to regular judicial proceedings. This attitude sometimes carries over to conflict-of-laws issues.

B. PLACE AND NECESSITY OF ADMINISTRATION

1. *Domicile*

§ 22.6 The principal question in a multistate estate often is to identify the state that has jurisdiction for administration. Administration at the last domicile of the deceased is usually preferable and, unless a statute requires it, the presence within the state of assets owned by the decedent is not a prerequisite to the appointment of an administrator at the domicile.[1] As has already been shown, the state of the domicile

---

11. 522 U.S. 222, 118 S.Ct. 657, 665, 139 L.Ed.2d 580 (1998).

12. Cf. Marr v. Hendrix, 952 S.W.2d 693 (Ky.1997) (refusing to give effect to a Florida decision to admit a will to probate insofar as Kentucky land is concerned).

§ 22.6

1. See Buchanan & Myers, The Administration of Intangibles in View of First National Bank v. Maine, 48 Harv. L. Rev. 911 (1935).

§ 22.6

1. Stein v. Welch, 78 Wash.App. 251, 896 P.2d 740 (1995); Watson v. Collins'

probably will determine the validity of a will of personalty.[2] Generally, too, the balance of the estate in the ancillary state after administration will be remitted to the domiciliary state for distribution.[3] But this need not be done and administration at the state of the domicile would seem a useless proceeding if there is nothing for the representative in that state to do.[4] However, if unitary administration is possible by the domiciliary personal representative, then the domiciliary personal representative should be appointed and that personal representative should proceed to collect assets elsewhere for administration at the domicile.[5]

2. Situs of Tangible Assets

§ 22.7 It is generally assumed that there may be administration wherever the decedent left movable property, regardless of the owner's domicile.[1] The same is true of land if, under statutory regulations at the situs, it is subject to administration.[2] However, the ancillary court may refuse administration until a principal administrator is appointed at the

Administrator, 37 Ala. 587 (1861); Matter of Jackson's Estate, 48 Ill.App.3d 1035, 6 Ill.Dec. 972, 363 N.E.2d 919 (1977); Holburn v. Pfanmiller's Administrator, 114 Ky. 831, 71 S.W. 940 (1903); Connors v. Cunard Steamship Co., 204 Mass. 310, 90 N.E. 601 (1910); Restatement, Second, Conflict of Laws §§ 314, 315 (1971). See also In re Estate of Elson, 120 Ill.App.3d 649, 76 Ill. Dec. 237, 458 N.E.2d 637 (1983).

2. See supra § 20.9; see also Reif v. Reif, 86 Ohio App.3d 804, 621 N.E.2d 1279 (1993).

3. See Restatement, Second, Conflict of Laws § 364 (1971). See also U.P.C. § 3–816.

4. See U.P.C. § 3–816. Cf. Morris v. Garmon, 291 Ark. 67, 722 S.W.2d 571 (1987), cert. denied 484 U.S. 816, 108 S.Ct. 69, 98 L.Ed.2d 33 (1987); Matter of Estate of Phelan, 235 Mont. 257, 766 P.2d 876 (1988).

5. Cf. In re Massaglia's Estate, 38 Cal. App.3d 767, 113 Cal.Rptr. 751 (1974); D. Currie, The Multiple Personality of the Dead: Executors, Administrators, and the Conflict of Laws, 33 U. Chi. L. Rev. 429, 432 (1966). In some jurisdictions, there may be a requirement that the personal representative also must be a resident. Succession of Ringen, 521 So.2d 587 (La.App. 1988). But see Owens v. Ford, 451 So.2d 796 (Ala.1984) (motive or purpose in establishing in-state domicile is irrelevant).

§ 22.7

1. Montgomery v. National Savings & Trust Co., 356 F.2d 806 (D.C.Cir.1966); In

re Glassford's Estate, 114 Cal.App.2d 181, 249 P.2d 908 (1952); In re Shultz' Estate, 180 Kan. 444, 304 P.2d 539 (1956); Barrett v. Barrett's Administrator, 170 Ky. 91, 185 S.W. 499 (1916); Riley v. Moseley, 44 Miss. 37 (1870); Spencer v. Wolf, 49 Neb. 8, 67 N.W. 858 (1896); Hesler v. Snyder, 422 P.2d 432 (Okla.1967); Restatement, Second, Conflict of Laws §§ 314, 315 (1971). Appointment of an ancillary administrator has been denied, however, even where there were local assets, when there were no local creditors and the appointment was unnecessary for the complete and proper distribution of the estate. In re Washburn's Estate, 45 Minn. 242, 47 N.W. 790 (1891). Cf. In re Williams' Estate, 130 Iowa 558, 107 N.W. 608 (1906). See generally Stimson, Conflict of Laws and The Administration of Decedents' Personal Property, 46 Va. L. Rev. 1345 (1960). See also Comment, The Need for Reform in Multistate Estate Administration, 55 Tex. L. Rev. 303 (1977). Cf. Walsh, Non–Resident Personal Representatives and the Register of Wills, 36 Pa.B.A.Q. 267 (1965). Matter of Pingpank, 134 A.D.2d 263, 520 N.Y.S.2d 596 (1987); Matter of Estate of Gadway, 123 A.D.2d 83, 510 N.Y.S.2d 737 (1987); Gordon v. Gordon, 110 A.D.2d 623, 487 N.Y.S.2d 574 (1985); Will of Nelson, 125 Misc.2d 451, 475 N.Y.S.2d 194 (1984); Estate of Pettit v. Levine, 657 S.W.2d 636 (Mo.App.1983).

2. Sprayberry v. Culberson, 32 Ga. 299 (1861); Matter of Estate of Reed, 768 P.2d 566 (Wyo.1989); Restatement, Second, Conflict of Laws §§ 314, 315 (1971); see supra §§ 6.2–6.4.

domicile and primary administration undertaken there.[3] Whatever the theory of succession to ownership when an owner dies, the state where the asset is located has historically exercised the power to determine whether local administration of an asset is required or may be avoided. As has been said elsewhere, the state of the situs may provide that the property may be distributed according to its own local rule of distribution, without reference to the domiciliary rules on the subject.[4] Even if domiciliary rules are looked to in determining distribution, the state of the situs may desire to tax the succession to the property; it may insist that the property be subject to claims of the decedent's creditors who prove their claims there before it is distributed to his legatees or next of kin. Unless a statute makes a specific requirement, even a trifling amount of property is sufficient on which to found a local administration.[5] As a part of local administration, the appointment of a personal representative is subject to the rules of a place of administration.[6]

It should be observed, however, that the mere location of assets at an inconvenient forum may not provide an appropriate place for administration of the estate in some cases. *Shaffer v. Heitner*[7] has suggested that a forum cannot exercise jurisdiction against a living owner solely by reason of the presence of assets. While it is possible to extend this reasoning to probate, it seems more likely that the situs of assets will continue to be viewed as adequate to support administration of those assets since the proceedings relate directly to the assets upon which jurisdiction is based. Still, *Shaffer* supports the trend toward unitary administration at the domicile.

3. Chattels Temporarily Present Within a State

§ 22.8 Jurisdiction for administration of tangible property does not present many difficulties if the property is kept within the state with some degree of permanence. The property is there, it belongs there, and the power of the situs state is clear. Suppose, however, that the property is but temporarily in the state at the time of the death of the owner, or is even in the process of transit through the state at that time. For example, a Massachusetts citizen who owns a collection of pictures may put them in an automobile and start for New York to exhibit them. While in Rhode Island on the way, our Massachusetts resident may very well meet with an accident and die. Do the car and pictures have a situs for administration in Rhode Island? Authority is not abundant, but there is support for the view that under such circumstances jurisdiction will not be exercised.[1] Certainly the policies favoring a unitary administra-

---

3. Cf. U.P.C. §§ 1–303, 3–307, 3–309.

4. See supra § 20.3; see also Marr v. Hendrix, 952 S.W.2d 693 (Ky.1997).

5. Cox v. Kansas City, 86 Kan. 298, 120 P. 553 (1912). See Lenn v. Riche, 331 Mass. 104, 117 N.E.2d 129 (1954); Power v. Plummer, 93 N.H. 37, 35 A.2d 230 (1943); In re Plybon, 157 W.Va. 366, 201 S.E.2d 315 (1973).

6. Cf. Restatement, Second, Conflict of Laws §§ 315, 316 (1971).

7. 433 U.S. 186, 97 S.Ct. 2569, 53 L.Ed.2d 683 (1977).

§ 22.8

1. Windbourne v. Eastern Air Lines, 479 F.Supp. 1130 (E.D.N.Y.1979); In re Chadwick's Estate, 309 So.2d 587 (Fla.App.

tion at the domicile and the considerations of convenience and economy to those otherwise interested in the estate suggest that it is important to avoid multiple administrations at such fortuitous places. However, it would seem that since a state has control of all property within its borders, the state in which the property happens to be situated would have power to administer it.[2] However, considerations of convenience would make it desirable in most cases for the state of temporary location to decline jurisdiction in favor of the state in which the chattel is ordinarily kept.

4. *Chattels Brought Into a State After Owner's Death*

§ 22.9 Another matter which causes some theoretical difficulty regards property brought into a state after the death of the owner. Can the courts of a state assume jurisdiction to administer such property? Jurisdiction to administer property brought into the state after the death of the owner is often asserted when no administration has previously been concerned with the property.[1] The important thing is that the property be cared for, accounted for, available to pay claims and the balance finally distributed. If the property is thus handled, and no rights of persons in the first state are prejudiced by reason of the administration in the second forum, this procedure does no harm.[2] Such a situation frequently exists when a domiciliary personal representative collects assets located elsewhere by informal means for administration at the domicile.[3] If there is no administrator appointed in the first state, the administration in the second state may serve to prevent waste or

1975); Christy v. Vest, 36 Iowa 285 (1873); Restatement, Second, Conflict of Laws § 318 (1971). Cf. Shelby v. Creighton, 65 Neb. 485, 91 N.W. 369 (1902). Estate of Boda, 124 Misc.2d 464, 476 N.Y.S.2d 476 (1984) (temporary presence of jewelry after auto accident not sufficient to establish jurisdiction to grant unlimited letters of administration for purposes of pursuing wrongful death action).

2. Power v. Plummer, 93 N.H. 37, 35 A.2d 230 (1943). Note that Shaffer v. Heitner, 433 U.S. 186, 97 S.Ct. 2569, 53 L.Ed.2d 683 (1977) could be extended to this situation by analogy and require that administration be declined.

§ 22.9

1. Neal v. Boykin, 132 Ga. 400, 64 S.E. 480 (1909); Matter of Allen's Estate, 239 N.W.2d 163 (Iowa 1976); Stearns v. Wright, 51 N.H. 600 (1872) (claim against debtor was involved); Appeal of Ela, 68 N.H. 35, 38 A. 501 (1894) (administrator was precluded from setting up the invalidity of the decree he had obtained as a defense to the failure to account for property he had brought in);

Morefield v. Harris, 126 N.C. 626, 36 S.E. 125 (1900) (same); Green v. Rugely, 23 Tex. 539 (1859); Restatement, Second, Conflict of Laws § 320 (1971). Cf. Matter of Estate of Widmeyer, 741 S.W.2d 758 (Mo.App. 1987); In re De Camillis' Estate, 66 Misc.2d 882, 322 N.Y.S.2d 551 (Surr. 1971). But see Embry v. Millar, 8 Ky. (1 A.K. Marsh) 300, 10 Am. Dec. 732 (Ky. 1818).

2. See Matter of Accounting of Hughes, 95 N.Y. 55 (1884) for an excellent discussion. In that case sending back the property to Pennsylvania, from whence it had come, would only have resulted in double commissions for the representatives.

3. See Alford, Collecting a Decedent's Assets Without Ancillary Administration, 18 S.W.L.J. 329, 331 n.9 (1964) (reporting incident in which the foreign domiciliary personal representative who wrote Judge Brockenbrough Lamb inquiring how movable property located in Virginia might be removed to the domicile; the judge responded: "Send a moving van."). Cf. In re Estate of Purnell, 482 So.2d 438 (Fla.App.1986).

conversion of the property.[4] But the property cannot be made the subject of administration in the second state if it was brought there by the administrator appointed in the first state for sale[5] or other purpose.[6] The personal representative in the state where an asset was originally subjected to administration has the right to possession and is its owner so far as third parties are concerned. Those rights will be recognized elsewhere.[7] If the property administered in the second state was taken wrongfully from a foreign administrator, the right of the custodian or administrator in the second state is subordinate to the right of the foreign administrator.[8]

It is important to distinguish from this prior issue the treatment of a debt as "assets" so that there may be administration and collection of that debt where the debtor has come into the state after the death of the creditor.[9] The debt obviously has no physical location anywhere, being intangible, and the thing to be accomplished is to make the debtor pay. He may be reached with legal process at his new place of abode; there is no certainty of being able to reach him elsewhere. Assuming the debtor can reasonably be sued there, the debt is properly enough regarded as having situs for administration in the state into which the debtor has come.

5. *Intangibles*

§ 22.10 The term "situs" of intangibles for purposes of administration is often used by the courts and writers. The reference to situs in such a connection states a legal conclusion rather than a physical fact for an intangible has no physical location. The conclusion usually referred to by a court identifying the situs of intangibles for administrative purposes is to identify a place at which it is reasonable to collect and administer the intangible.[1]

The simplest case is that of the ordinary chose in action, not evidenced by a document which can be treated as representing the claim

---

4. Emphasized in Neal v. Boykin, 132 Ga. 400, 64 S.E. 480 (1909). See Kaltsas v. Kaltsas, 22 Mass.App.Ct. 689, 497 N.E.2d 26 (1986), review denied 398 Mass. 1105, 499 N.E.2d 298 (1986).

5. Crescent City Ice Co. v. Stafford, 6 F.Cas. 804 (D.La.1877).

6. Matter of McCabe, 84 App.Div. 145, 82 N.Y.S. 180 (1903), affirmed 177 N.Y. 584, 69 N.E. 1126 (1904); Estate of Schley, 11 Phila. 139 (Pa. 1876); Restatement, Second, Conflict of Laws § 320 (1971).

7. See infra § 22.18. See also Estate of Pettit v. Levine, 657 S.W.2d 636 (Mo.App. 1983) (removal of decedent's securities from Florida after Florida court had acquired and exercised jurisdiction for administration did not serve to divest jurisdiction;

under these circumstances, Missouri court without jurisdiction to administer those securities).

8. Restatement, Second, Conflict of Laws § 320 (1971).

9. Although the early cases permitted a suit to collect a claim wherever the debtor could be located, see Pinney v. McGregory, 102 Mass. 186 (1869); Stearns v. Wright, 51 N.H. 600 (1872), considerations of forum non conveniens or constitutional limitation may preclude the suit where the forum is unrelated to the cause of action.

§ 22.10

1. See generally, Hopkins, Conflict of Laws in Administration of Decedents' Intangibles (pts. 1 and 2), 28 Iowa L. Rev. 422, 613 (1943).

itself. The statement is often made that a simple contract or other claim constitutes assets where the debtor resides; administration may be founded upon the claim and collection made there.[2] That does not, however, mean that the claim can be administered only in that state and not elsewhere. The debtor may be sued elsewhere than at his domicile, by a person appointed representative at the place where suit is brought.[3] The domicile of the debtor is enough on which to found jurisdiction because the debtor may be sued at his domicile, while the maintenance of a suit elsewhere will depend upon the jurisdictional circumstance relating to the forum.[4] The administration of commercial accounts receivable would seem to depart from this approach. On the analogy to the security assignments under the Uniform Commercial Code, it would appear that commercial accounts receivable should be administered at the place of business or residence of the person to whom the receivable is owed.[5]

Where the claim is one for death by wrongful act, the decisions are in some conflict. The difficulty presented by such a case under the common form of death statute is that a new action is created, the benefits of which accrue, not to the estate of the deceased, but to certain named beneficiaries. If the recovery for wrongful death under the statute is not available to the estate as assets, then the named beneficiaries or the personal representative, as trustee for the beneficiaries, only may sue.[6] In this latter case, the personal representative, as trustee, should not have to qualify locally to sue.[7] If the action for wrongful death of the

2. Cooper v. Beers, 143 Ill. 25, 33 N.E. 61 (1892); In re Hoffman's Estate, 6 Ill. App.3d 438, 286 N.E.2d 103 (1972); DiMauro v. Pavia, 492 F.Supp. 1051 (D.Conn. 1979), aff'd 614 F.2d 1286 (2d Cir.1979); Robbins v. National Bank of Georgia, 241 Ga. 538, 246 S.E.2d 660 (1978); Emery v. Hildreth, 68 Mass. (2 Gray) 228 (1854); Pinney v. McGregory, 102 Mass. 186 (1869) (though debtor comes there subsequent to death of decedent); In re Edwards' Estate, 87 Misc.2d 337, 385 N.Y.S.2d 253 (Surr. 1976); Hesler v. Snyder, 422 P.2d 432 (Okla.1967); Sayre's Executors v. Helme's Executors, 61 Pa. 299 (1869). While an ordinary debt is an asset at the domicile of the debtor, debts of the United States are assets at the domicile of the creditor since the United States is "present" in all states. United States v. Borcherling, 185 U.S. 223, 22 S.Ct. 607, 46 L.Ed. 884 (1902); Diehl v. United States, 438 F.2d 705 (5th Cir.1971), cert. denied 404 U.S. 830, 92 S.Ct. 67, 30 L.Ed.2d 59 (1971).

3. Saunders v. Weston, 74 Me. 85 (1882); Riley v. Moseley, 44 Miss. 37 (1870); Fox v. Carr, 16 Hun 434 (N.Y. 1879); see Restatement, Second, Conflict of Laws § 314(b), cmnt. (k) (1971).

4. There is old English authority, based on the rules governing ecclesiastical courts

to the effect that a judgment debt was an asset where recorded, Anonymous, 8 Mod. 244 (1724) (not a conflict-of-laws question, but one of division between the prerogative court and the court of the ordinary). However, the early American cases treated the judgment debt like that of the ordinary chose in action and as constituting assets at the domicile of the debtor. Miller v. Hoover, 121 Mo.App. 568, 97 S.W. 210 (1906); Swancy v. Scott, 28 Tenn. (9 Humph.) 327 (1848). See V-1 Oil Co. v. Ranck, 767 P.2d 612 (Wyo.1989).

5. Cf. U.C.C. § 9–103 (1972 version); see supra §§ 19.20–19.21. This approach will centralize the administration of the accounts receivable even though actual collection may necessitate suit elsewhere.

6. See, e.g., Komlos v. Compagnie Nationale Air France, 209 F.2d 436 (2d Cir.1953); Elliott v. Day, 218 F.Supp. 90 (D.Or.1962); Gross v. Hocker, 243 Iowa 291, 51 N.W.2d 466 (1952); Howard v. Pulver, 329 Mich. 415, 45 N.W.2d 530 (1951); Ghilain v. Couture, 84 N.H. 48, 146 A. 395 (1929).

7. Cf. infra § 22.14. See Windbourne v. Eastern Air Lines, 479 F.Supp. 1130 (E.D.N.Y.1979) in which it was noted that a wrongful death action, being for the spouse

decedent is an asset of the estate, it is sufficient to warrant the appointment of a personal representative. There is authority allowing the appointment of an administrator and prosecution of the suit at the domicile of the defendant[8] or where he is otherwise subject to suit[9] including the place where the injury occurred.[10]

The theory that there are assets for purposes of administration wherever a contract debtor of a decedent can be sued has led to an interesting situation under liability insurance policies. The right of indemnity of a decedent against an insurance company has generally been held to be sufficient assets on which to base appointment of an ancillary personal representative of the decedent where the insurance carrier is subject to suit.[11] This is essentially an alternative means of

and dependents does not require local qualification but suit to recover for pain and suffering belonging to the estate requires local ancillary letters. However, an action under the Warsaw Convention is a federal cause of action and a foreign representative can sue without local qualification even though capacity to sue in federal courts is usually determined by the law of the state in which the court sits.

8. Hartford & New Haven Railroad Co. v. Andrews, 36 Conn. 213 (1869); Missouri Pacific Railway Co. v. Lewis, 24 Neb. 848, 40 N.W. 401 (1888). But see Jeffersonville Railway Co. v. Swayne's Administrator, 26 Ind. 477 (1866); Perry v. St. Joseph & Western Railroad Co., 29 Kan. 420 (1883).

9. State ex rel. Chicago, Burlington & Quincy Railroad Co. v. Probate Court, 149 Minn. 464, 184 N.W. 43 (1921); In re Lowham's Estate, 30 Utah 436, 85 P. 445 (1906); McKenzie v. K.S.N. Co., 79 N.M. 314, 442 P.2d 804 (1968); Fickeisen v. Wheeling Electrical Co., 67 W.Va. 335, 67 S.E. 788 (1910); Restatement, Second, Conflict of Laws § 314 (1971). But see Ziemer v. Crucible Steel Co., 99 App.Div. 169, 90 N.Y.S. 962 (1904); In re Yarbrough's Estate, 126 Wash. 85, 216 P. 889 (1923), aff'd 126 Wash. 85, 222 P. 902 (1924).

10. Texair Flyers, Inc. v. District Court, 180 Colo. 432, 506 P.2d 367 (1973); Missouri Pacific Railway Co. v. Bradley, 51 Neb. 596, 71 N.W. 283 (1897); Jordan v. Chicago & Northwestern Railway Co., 125 Wis. 581, 104 N.W. 803 (1905). But see, Tri–State Loan & Trust Co. v. Lake Shore & Michigan Southern Railway Co., 76 Ind. App. 141, 131 N.E. 523 (1921) (noted 20 Mich. L. Rev. 369 (1922)).

11. See e.g., Hamilton v. Blackman, 915 P.2d 1210, 1216 (Alaska 1996); Campbell v. Davis, 274 Ala. 187, 145 So.2d 725 (1962) (noted 15 Ala. L. Rev. 220 (1962)); Price v. Sommermeyer, 195 Colo. 285, 577 P.2d 752 (1978), on remand 41 Colo.App. 147, 584

P.2d 1220 (1978); In re Klipple's Estate, 101 So.2d 924 (Fla.App.1958); Berry v. Smith, 85 Ga.App. 710, 70 S.E.2d 62 (1952); Furst v. Brady, 375 Ill. 425, 31 N.E.2d 606 (1940) (noted 8 U. Chi. L. Rev. 769 (1941); 27 Va. L. Rev. 953 (1941)); Gordon v. Shea, 300 Mass. 95, 14 N.E.2d 105 (1938) (noted, 23 Minn. L. Rev. 221 (1939)); In re Kandlbinder's Estate, 183 Neb. 178, 159 N.W.2d 199 (1968); Matter of Riggle's Estate, 11 N.Y.2d 73, 226 N.Y.S.2d 416, 181 N.E.2d 436 (1962); In re Edmundson, 273 N.C. 92, 159 S.E.2d 509 (1968). Cf. In re Estate of Fagin, 246 Iowa 496, 66 N.W.2d 920 (1954) (noted 41 Iowa L. Rev. 144 (1955)); Power v. Plummer, 93 N.H. 37, 35 A.2d 230 (1943); Kimbell v. Smith, 64 N.M. 374, 328 P.2d 942 (1958); In re Vilas' Estate, 166 Or. 115, 110 P.2d 940 (1941); Davis v. Cayton, 214 S.W.2d 801 (Tex.Civ.App.1948). In re Breese's Estate, 51 Wn.2d 302, 317 P.2d 1055 (1957). The Colorado historical development in this area is interesting. In Wheat v. Fidelity & Casualty Co., 128 Colo. 236, 261 P.2d 493 (1953), noted 26 Rocky Mtn. L. Rev. 93 (1953), the court held the claim was assets at the decedent's domicile. Van Trump's Estate v. National Insurance Underwriters, 517 P.2d 856 (Colo.App.1973) distinguished *Wheat* and held Colorado would appoint an ancillary administrator on the basis of the decedent's liability insurance where insurer did business in the state and Colorado residents were killed in a Colorado air crash. In Price v. Sommermeyer, supra, the court overruled *Wheat* and held the policy indemnity supported local administration where accident occurred in Colorado but neither plaintiffs nor defendant's decedent were Colorado residents but the insurance carrier was authorized to do business in Colorado. The court quoted the *Kandlbinder* case supra. "Piercing the form to the realities of this situation, the insurance company should be required to respond in [the] forum where its contracted risk reaches and where it does business."

obtaining effective jurisdiction over a claim against a nonresident deceased motorist—or other tortfeasor—at a forum convenient to the plaintiff.[12] Some cases and statutes, however, have relegated jurisdiction to administer such a claim to the decedent's domicile, on the theory that that is the more appropriate forum.[13] Following *Shaffer v. Heitner*,[14] the Supreme Court held in *Rush v. Savchuk*[15] that a defendant could not be sued where the only contact with the forum was the availability of the defendant's liability insurer. In *Rush* the forum was found to have no other relationship to the defendant and could not constitutionally entertain the case. It seems probable that this concern for the relationship of the defendant to the forum will preclude appointment of a personal representative and such a suit when the only defendant contact with the

12. See, e.g., Service Lines, Inc. v. Mitchell, 419 S.W.2d 525 (Ky.1967); Matter of Owens' Estate, 89 N.M. 420, 553 P.2d 700 (1976); In re Molzen's Will, 72 Misc.2d 46, 338 N.Y.S.2d 189 (Surr. 1972); In re George's Estate, 20 Ohio App.2d 87, 252 N.E.2d 176 (1969). Cf. In re Allen's Estate, 64 Misc.2d 920, 316 N.Y.S.2d 352 (Surr. 1970).

13. See In re Rogers' Estate, 164 Kan. 492, 190 P.2d 857 (1948); In re Roche's Estate, 16 N.J. 579, 109 A.2d 655 (1954). Cf. *Wheat*, 128 Colo. 236, 261 P.2d 493; Olson v. Preferred Automobile Insurance Co., 259 Mich. 612, 244 N.W. 178 (1932); Ill. Ann. Stat., ch. 110 1/2, ¶ 5–2. U.P.C. § 3–201 is an attempted codification of this area and provides:

Section 3–201. [Venue for First and Subsequent Estate Proceedings; Location of Property.]

(a) Venue for the first informal or formal testacy or appointment proceedings after a decedent's death is:

(1) in the [county] where the decedent had his domicile at the time of his death; or

(2) if the decedent was not domiciled in this state, [in any county] where property of the decedent was located at the time of his death.

. . .

(d) For the purpose of aiding determinations concerning location of assets which may be relevant in cases involving non-domiciliaries, a debt, other than one evidenced by investment or commercial paper or other instrument in favor of a non-domiciliary, is located where the debtor resides or, if the debtor is a person other than an individual, at the place where it has its principal office. Commercial paper, investment paper and other instruments are located where the instrument is. An interest in property held in trust is located where the trustee may be sued.

The close relationship between considering the rights under a liability insurance as assets for the appointment of an ancillary personal representative and the ability to sue a foreign personal representative when his decedent was subject to jurisdiction is demonstrated by the Kansas experience. *In re Rogers' Estate* denied the appointment of an ancillary administrator on basis of liability insurance in 1948. Later, Rogers was overruled by In re Preston's Estate, 193 Kan. 145, 392 P.2d 922 (1964). This was followed by Kan. Stat. Ann. 59–805 (1980) which limited jurisdiction to the decedent's domicile or location of the policy. The statute precludes a Kansas resident from getting the appointment of an ancillary administrator to effect recovery against the insurance company. See Kent v. Chase, 1 Kan.App.2d 251, 563 P.2d 1103 (1977). However, meanwhile the long-arm jurisdictional statute was enacted basing jurisdiction on commission of a tortious act within the State and in Barr v. MacHarg, 203 Kan. 612, 455 P.2d 516 (1969) the Kansas court held the foreign personal representative of a Michigan motorist could be sued in Kansas under the long-arm statute. The court relied on Hayden v. Wheeler, 33 Ill.2d 110, 210 N.E.2d 495 (1965).

This resolution of the problem may illustrate the natural progression in legal development that justice is better served by direct jurisdiction over the decedent's foreign domiciliary personal representative than the near fiction of the liability insurance being "Assets" but not "really assets" since it is only available to the third party beneficiary of the insurance. See Nichols v. Marshall, 491 F.2d 177 (10th Cir.1974).

14. 433 U.S. 186, 97 S.Ct. 2569, 53 L.Ed.2d 683 (1977).

15. 444 U.S. 320, 100 S.Ct. 571, 62 L.Ed.2d 516 (1980).

forum is the availability of the third party insurer. Although these cases might be though to cast some doubt on the constitutionality of appointing a personal representative based on a cause of action in tort or in contract arising out of the decedent's activities within the forum, the decedent's forum-related activities should distinguish *Rush*.[16]

6. Commercial Paper

§ 22.11 The law relating to commercial specialties early developed around the concept of the bond represented by the certificate. If the obligation owned by the decedent is a chose in action represented by a bond, it will be treated as assets at the place where the bond certificate is located at the death of the owner.[1] "The debt is where the bond is, being upon a specialty, but debt upon contract follows the person of the debtor; and this difference has often been agreed" is language from an early English case.[2] While the concept of the sealed instrument as the obligation and not merely the evidence thereof has been modified in some regards in more recent times, the notion of treating the paper as the property accords with modern commercial usage and continues to be justified on that basis.[3]

Modern commercial usage and law treat other commercial paper such as promissory notes in the same way, i.e., as assets where they are located at the time of the owner's death. Negotiable paper is treated in the commercial world as property, the rules governing its transfer follow the rules governing transfer of ordinary chattels and in some respects go even further in protecting transferees. Commercial paper may be the subject of larceny, of suits in replevin, may be attached and levied upon in execution, is "goods, wares and merchandise" within the statute of

---

16. See Moore v. Montes, 22 Ariz.App. 562, 529 P.2d 716 (1974) in which the court found sufficient jurisdictional nexus to justify appointment of an administrator to collect on claims arising when a Mexican decedent was driving the plaintiff's auto in Mexico when the accident occurred. The plaintiff sought recovery under a clause providing for coverage of others driving the car with her permission. The plaintiff's residence was in Arizona where the insurance was purchased. The court explained in its opinion that "The real party in interest here is not so much the estate of the decedent . . . as it is the insurance carrier which is liable to exonerate a claim against [the decedent's] estate as a result of its policy of insurance companies covering him as a permissive driver of the car involved in the accident." 529 P.2d at 718. This was the view taken 20 years ago in In re Estate of Fagin, 246 Iowa 496, 66 N.W.2d 920 (1954) and the Arizona court considered it "very timely today." Id. at 719. As the Iowa Court

stated: "In ultimate effect appellant is not the real party in interest. The real party is the insurance company." 66 N.W.2d at 924. Cf. Bankemper v. Boone County Aviation, Inc., 435 S.W.2d 58 (Ky.1968).

§ 22.11

1. Barclift v. Treece, 77 Ala. 528 (1884); In re De Lano's Estate, 181 Kan. 729, 315 P.2d 611 (1957); Matter of Caperonis' Estate, 95 Misc.2d 690, 408 N.Y.S.2d 231 (Surr. 1978); Beers v. Shannon, 73 N.Y. 292 (1878); Grant v. Rogers, 94 N.C. 755, 761 (1886). Cf. Flanagan v. Marvel, 94 F.Supp. 145 (D.Minn.1950), appeal dismissed 189 F.2d 966 (8th Cir.1951); Dominion National Bank v. Jones, 202 Va. 502, 118 S.E.2d 672 (1961). But see Dial v. Gary, 14 S.C. 573, 37 Am. Rep. 737 (1881); Cooper v. Beers, 143 Ill. 25, 33 N.E. 61 (1892).

2. Byron v. Byron, Cro. Eliz. 472 (1596) (cited in Beers v. Shannon, 73 N.Y. 292 (1878)).

3. See supra §§ 19.17–19.24.

frauds. It passes freely and frequently from hand to hand and elaborate rules have evolved for the protection of transferees.[4] In a commercial sense commercial papers are more like tangible chattels than choses in action. It would therefore seem for the purposes of the law in matters of administration, they should be treated like tangible chattels and the same rules applied.[5] This view finds support in the United States Supreme Court which has held that the state in which assets, consisting largely of promissory notes, were located was the proper place for their administration, denying the contention that those negotiable instruments should have been administered at the decedent's domicile.[6] This view has persisted and is followed by state courts and is consistent with modern legislation.[7]

The decisions regarding collection of negotiable instruments that are part of a decedent's estate are generally consistent with the mercantile theory of treating instruments as property. Thus payment by the maker to the domiciliary representative who holds the negotiable instrument is a valid defense to an action brought against the maker by an ancillary administrator at the maker's domicile.[8] And the maker cannot be required to pay one administrator when the note is in possession of another.[9] Payment to an ancillary administrator in the possession of a note has likewise been held to be a valid quittance.[10] Again, if negotiable paper in the hands of the domiciliary representative is endorsed by him, the transferee may sue the maker elsewhere in his own name.[11] While this result may be and sometimes is explained on the broader ground with the power of the domiciliary representative effectively to transfer the decedent's choses in action, it accords with the mercantile theory and the Restatement has applied the rule to transfers by ancillary administrators as well.[12]

4. Cf. U.C.C. §§ 3–104, 3–202, 3–301 et seq.

5. See Williams v. Zachary, 463 P.2d 343 (Okla.App.1969); Rosemont Enterprises, Inc. v. Lummis, 596 S.W.2d 916 (Tex. Civ.App.1980); Hopkins, Conflict of Laws in Administration of Decedents' Intangibles (pts. 1 and 2), 28 Iowa L. Rev. 422, 613 (1943); Restatement, Second, Conflict of Laws § 326 (1971).

6. Iowa v. Slimmer Jr., 248 U.S. 115, 39 S.Ct. 33, 63 L.Ed. 158 (1918).

7. See, e.g., Toner v. Conqueror Trust Co., 131 Kan. 651, 293 P. 745 (1930); In re Lang's Estate, 301 Pa. 429, 152 A. 570 (1930); *Williams*, 463 P.2d 343. Rosemont Enterprises, Inc. v. Lummis, 596 S.W.2d 916 (Tex.Civ.App.1980); Uniform Probate Code § 3–201; see supra § 12.10 n.13.

8. McNamara v. McNamara, 62 Ga. 200 (1879); Thorman v. Broderick, 52 La. Ann. 1298, 27 So. 735 (1900); Goodlett v. Anderson, 75 Tenn. (7 Lea) 286 (1881).

9. Smith v. Normart, 51 Ariz. 134, 75 P.2d 38 (1938).

10. Riley v. Moseley, 44 Miss. 37 (1870); Young v. O'Neal, 35 Tenn. (3 Sneed) 55 (1855); Restatement, Second, Conflict of Laws § 326 (1971).

11. Campbell v. Brown, 64 Iowa 425, 20 N.W. 745 (1884); Rand v. Hubbard, 45 Mass. (4 Metc.) 252 (1842); General Conference, Association of Seventh–Day Adventists v. Michigan Sanitarium & Benevolent Association, 166 Mich. 504, 132 N.W. 94 (1911); Owen v. Moody, 29 Miss. 79 (1855); Grignon v. Shope, 100 Or. 611, 197 P. 317, 198 P. 520 (1921). Cf. Cordoba v. Wiswall, 7 Ariz.App. 144, 436 P.2d 922 (1968). But see Stearns v. Burnham, 5 Me. (5 Greenl.) 261, 17 Am.Dec. 228 (1828); McCarty v. Hall, 13 Mo. 480 (1850). See also Hensley v. Rich, 191 Ind. 294, 132 N.E. 632 (1921).

12. Restatement, Second, Conflict of Laws § 326 (1971).

On a bearer instrument, the representative can sue in his own name in a state other than that of his appointment.[13] And, if a statute of the forum authorizes suit by a foreign representative, he may sue on an instrument payable to the order of the deceased.[14] A full acceptance of the mercantile theory would permit a foreign representative to sue its maker. On the other hand, payment to the representative at the debtor's domicile does not constitute a legal discharge against the domiciliary representative who holds the note.[15] Nor is payment to a domiciliary representative who does not hold the note a legal discharge as against an ancillary representative who does.[16] There is much support in language as well as in result for the mercantile theory.[17]

If a negotiable bill of lading or warehouse receipt has been given for a chattel, and by the law governing the transaction, possession of the chattel may thereafter be delivered only to one in possession of the document, it would seem, in accordance with the views just expressed, that the deceased owner's interest should be administered at the place where the document is located, rather than at the place where the chattel happens to be.[18]

7. *Corporate Stock*

§ **22.12** In determining where shares of stock are assets for purpose of administration, there are at least three possibilities: First, the domicile of the owner of the stock; second, the place of incorporation; third, the place where the certificates are kept at the time of the owner's decease, which generally will be at his domicile. The presence of a local transfer office is another possibility, seldom, however, put forth as an independent ground.

In the few cases which have treated shares of stock as assets at the domicile of the owner,[1] disregarding the location of the certificate, little explanation has been offered aside from the incorrect and misleading statement that the situs of personal property is at the domicile of the

---

13. Knapp v. Lee, 42 Mich. 41, 3 N.W. 244 (1879); Sanford v. McCreedy, 28 Wis. 103 (1871). Cf. Williams v. Zachary, 463 P.2d 343 (Okla.App.1969).

14. Eells v. Holder, 12 Fed. 668 (D. Kan. 1880).

15. Amsden v. Danielson, 19 R.I. 533, 535, 35 A. 70 (1896). See St. John v. Hodges, 68 Tenn. 334, 9 Baxt. 334 (1878). In McIlvoy v. Alsop, 45 Miss. 365 (1871), the court said, if the domiciliary representative refused to give up the note, the court should take precautions to protect the debtor in defending a suit by the assignee. Cf. Bull v. Fuller, 78 Iowa 20, 42 N.W. 572 (1889).

16. Young v. O'Neal, 35 Tenn. (3 Sneed) 55 (1855).

17. Eells v. Holder, 12 Fed. 668 (D.Kan. 1880); McNamara v. McNamara, 62 Ga. 200 (1879); Ames v. Citizens' National Bank, 105 Kan. 83, 181 P. 564 (1919); Owen v. Moody, 29 Miss. 79 (1855); St. John v. Hodges, 68 Tenn. (9 Baxt.) 334 (1878); Goodlett v. Anderson, 75 Tenn. (7 Lea) 286 (1881). But see Hensley v. Rich, 191 Ind. 294, 132 N.E. 632 (1921).

18. Restatement, Second, Conflict of Laws § 323 (1971).

§ 22.12

1. Miller's Estate v. Executrix of Miller's Estate, 90 Kan. 819, 136 P. 255 (1913) (noted 1 Va. L. Rev. 553 (1914)). See also Russell v. Hooker, 67 Conn. 24, 34 A. 711 (1895).

owner. This approach, however, could be a recognition of a unitary concept of administration with the domicile being the most convenient and appropriate forum.[2]

The older view seems to have been to treat the stock as assets at the place of incorporation.[3] This view attached little importance to the presence of the certificate, because as an early California decision stated: "A certificate of stock is, after all, only the evidence of certain contract rights against a corporation . . . it is the evidence of a right to property in this state. . . ."[4]

The commercial practice of treating the stock certificate as property has been a growing one in recent years and has found increasing recognition in decisions and statutes. Striking instances of this are the Uniform Stock Transfer Act and its successor, the Uniform Commercial Code, the provisions of which are now adopted in all of the states of the United States.[5] In commenting on the first of these statutes it was stated: "The effect of this act is to make the certificates of stock to the fullest extent possible representative of the shares and this is in accordance with mercantile usage."[6]

Prior to statutes such as these it was held that, where the domiciliary representative having possession of the certificates transfers them, the transferee may have the stock transferred to his name on the books of the corporation.[7] Modern authority gives increasingly greater emphasis to the presence of the certificate as a basis for administration.[8] Granting that the ultimate control of the transfer of shares of stock is in the state of incorporation, its adoption of the Uniform Commercial Code indicates that a transfer of the shareholder's interest would be ineffec-

---

2. Cf. Brooks v. Titusville Trust Co., 328 Mass. 472, 104 N.E.2d 437 (1952); In re Wilson's Estate, 127 N.Y.S.2d 772 (Surr. 1953); Dominion National Bank v. Jones, 202 Va. 502, 118 S.E.2d 672 (1961).

3. Grayson v. Robertson, 122 Ala. 330, 25 So. 229 (1899); Murphy v. Crouse, 135 Cal. 14, 66 P. 971 (1901); Kennedy v. Hodges, 215 Mass. 112, 102 N.E. 432 (1913); Richardson v. Busch, 198 Mo. 174, 95 S.W. 894 (1906); Gamble v. Dawson, 67 Wash. 72, 120 P. 1060 (1912). Cf. Albuquerque National Bank v. Citizens National Bank, 212 F.2d 943 (5th Cir.1954); London, Paris & American Bank v. Aronstein, 117 Fed. 601 (9th Cir.1902), cert. denied 187 U.S. 641, 23 S.Ct. 841, 47 L.Ed. 345 (1902). In the latter case, the decedent had been domiciled in California, and the corporation, though a foreign corporation, was compelled by law to have a transfer office in the state. See also Note, Suits Contesting Ownership of Corporate Stock, 25 Harv. L. Rev. 719 (1912).

4. Murphy v. Crouse, 135 Cal. 14, 66 P. 971 (1901). See also Richardson v. Busch, 198 Mo. 174, 95 S.W. 894 (1906).

5. U.C.C. §§ 8–102, 8–105, 8–313–8–317. These acts make transfer of the certificate, rather than transfer on the books of the company, the determining factor. See U.L.A.-U.C.C. p. xliii.

6. C. Terry, Uniform State Laws 341 (1920).

7. Brown v. San Francisco Gas Light Co., 58 Cal. 426 (1881); Luce v. Manchester & Lawrence Railroad, 63 N.H. 588, 589, 3 A. 618 (1886); Middlebrook v. Merchants' Bank of New York, 42 N.Y. (3 Key.) 135 (1866). Cf. In re Cape May & Delaware Bay Navigation Co., 51 N.J.L. 78, 16 A. 191 (1888).

8. Norrie v. Kansas City Southern Railway Co., 7 F.2d 158 (S.D.N.Y.1925), affirmed Norrie v. Lohman, 16 F.2d 355 (2d Cir.1926); Cordoba v. Wiswall, 7 Ariz.App. 144, 436 P.2d 922 (1968); Lohman v. Kansas City Southern Railway Co., 326 Mo. 819, 33 S.W.2d 112 (1930); Lockwood v. United States Steel Corp., 209 N.Y. 375, 103 N.E. 697 (1913); Nichols' Estate, 24 D. & C.2d 247 (Pa. 1961).

tive even though ordered by the court of the place of incorporation unless the court had control over the certificate.[9] A transfer ordered by a court having jurisdiction over the certificate would be recognized as valid at the place of incorporation.[10] Corporate stock should therefore be regarded as an asset and administered, as provided by the whole law of the state of incorporation, at the place where the certificate is located rather than in the state of incorporation.[11]

Where the shareholder's interest is not represented by a negotiable certificate, the mercantile theory seems inapplicable, and the administration would appear to be appropriate at the place of incorporation where the stock transfer books are kept[12] unless shares are transferred by the domiciliary personal representative to a third party.[13]

8. *Life Insurance*

§ 22.13 There is some uncertainty as to whether a life insurance claim payable to the personal representative or the estate of the insured is to be treated like a simple contract debt or like one represented by a certificate. There is some limited authority for treating a claim as assets at the domicile of the company regardless of the presence of the policy in a foreign state, the domicile of the insured.[1] Jurisdiction for administration and suit against the company may be had in a state where a local personal representative has the policy and where the company is subject to suit.[2] It has also been held that an action should not be maintained against the company at its domicile, if suit had been commenced previously at the domicile of the insured by the administrator who had the policy in his possession.[3] But a suit previously begun by a representative

---

9. The analogy to attachment and levy on shares is particularly apt. See U.C.C. § 8–317, Official Comment:

"In dealing with certificated securities the instrument itself is the vital thing, and therefore a valid levy cannot be made unless all possibility of the security's wrongfully finding its way into a transferee's hands has been removed. This can be accomplished only when the security is in the possession of a public officer, the issuer, or an independent third party. A debtor who has been enjoined can still transfer the security in contempt of court. See Overlock v. Jerome–Portland Copper Mining Co., 29 Ariz. 560, 243 P. 400 (1926)."

10. Cf. Direction Der Disconto–Gesellschaft v. United States Steel Corp., 267 U.S. 22, 45 S.Ct. 207, 69 L.Ed. 495 (1925). Certificates of a New Jersey corporation, endorsed in blank, were seized in accordance with English law in London, where they had been held by their German owners. Since by the law of New Jersey ownership of the shares depended on ownership of the certificates, and ownership of the certificates is determined by the law of their

situs, held that the person who under British law acquired title to the certificates as a result of the seizure had acquired title to the shares.

11. See Restatement, Second, Conflict of Laws § 324 (1971).

12. Restatement, Second, Conflict of Laws § 325 (1971).

13. See infra § 22.17; Restatement, Second, Conflict of Laws § 333 (1971).

§ 22.13

1. Re Miller, 5 Dem. 381 (N.Y.1887).

2. New England Mutual Life Insurance Co. v. Woodworth, 111 U.S. 138, 4 S.Ct. 364, 28 L.Ed. 379 (1884); New York Life Insurance Co. v. Smith, 67 Fed. 694 (9th Cir.1895); Rice v. Metropolitan Life Insurance Co., 152 Ark. 498, 238 S.W. 772 (1922). See also New York Life Insurance Co. v. Public Trustee, 2 Ch. 101 (Ct. App. 1924).

3. Cf. Sulz v. Mutual Reserve Fund Life Association, 145 N.Y. 563, 40 N.E. 242 (1895). The decision was put upon the

at the decedent's domicile who did not hold the policy has been held to be no bar to an action by an ancillary representative who did hold it.[4] Further, it has been held that the policy is assets at the place where it is kept.[5] Perhaps no categorical statement can be made. While there is some tendency to treat the written evidence of the contract, that is the policy, as significant in determining its situs for administration, payment to or suit by a personal representative, particularly the domiciliary representative, appointed in a state where the insurer is subject to suit, should prevail.

C. POWERS OF PERSONAL REPRESENTATIVE OUTSIDE APPOINTING STATE

1. *Power to Sue*

§ 22.14   The personal representative's power to sue, to collect claims, to take possession of property, and to do other acts in the course of administration in states other than the state of appointment, raise many questions of conflict of laws.[1] The inappropriate resolution of these questions can place a greatly increased burden of cost and inconvenience on the parties interested in the administration of an estate and the succession of its assets. There are few areas of the law that have been plagued to a greater extent by the lack of thoughtful consideration of policy, a lack of thought encouraged by jurisprudential myth and persistent provincialism.

It has long been assumed without support by any reasonable policy[2] that an administrator or executor cannot maintain an action on a claim of the deceased in a state other than the state of appointment.[3] This has

ground that the foreign court had first taken jurisdiction, not upon the ground that the foreign plaintiff held the policy.

4.   Merrill v. New England Mutual Life Insurance Co., 103 Mass. 245, 4 Am.Rep. 548 (1869). But in Steele v. Connecticut General Life Insurance Co., 31 App.Div. 389, 52 N.Y.S. 373 (1898), affirmed 160 N.Y. 703, 57 N.E. 1125 (1899) a voluntary payment to the representative at the domicile of the company was held no bar to a suit previously begun by the domiciliary representative. The policy had been pledged with the company in the lifetime of the insured. Cf. infra § 22.16; Restatement, Second, Conflict of Laws § 327 (1971).

5.   Johnston v. Smith, 25 Hun. 171 (N.Y. 1881).

§ 22.14

1.   See generally, B. McDowell, Foreign Personal Representatives (1957); A. Ehrenzweig on Conflict of Laws § 14, 44 (1962). See also Alford, Collecting a Decedent's Assets Without Ancillary Administration, 18 S.W.L.J. 329 (1964); Note, The

Extraterritorial Authority of Executors and Administrators to Sue and Collect Assets, 52 Iowa L. Rev. 290 (1966). See also Pryles, Wills, Probate and Administration Across State Frontiers, 58 Law Inst. J. 102 (1984) (Australia).

2.   See D. Currie, The Multiple Personality of the Dead: Executors, Administrators and the Conflict of Laws, 33 U. Chi. L. Rev. 429, 433 (1966).

3.   Johnson v. Powers, 139 U.S. 156, 11 S.Ct. 525, 35 L.Ed. 112 (1891); Ricard v. Birch, 529 F.2d 214 (4th Cir.1975); Eells v. Holder, 12 Fed. 668 (D.Kan. 1880); Noel v. St. Johnsbury Trucking Co., 147 F.Supp. 432 (D.Conn.1956); Hobart v. Connecticut Turnpike Co., 15 Conn. 145 (1842); Succession of Blalack, 209 So.2d 531 (La.App. 1968); Miller v. Hoover, 121 Mo.App. 568, 97 S.W. 210 (1906); Cannon v. Cannon, 228 N.C. 211, 45 S.E.2d 34 (1947); Sayre's Executors v. Helme's Executors, 61 Pa. 299 (1869); Mansfield v. McFarland, 202 Pa. 173, 51 A. 763 (1902); Gogan v. Jones, 197 Tenn. 436, 273 S.W.2d 700 (1954); Wilcox v.

led to inexplicable holdings such as that if a foreign administrator recovered a judgment, which judgment was satisfied, an action by a subsequently appointed local administrator was not barred.[4] Also a representative appointed in another state has been precluded from bringing a bill to revive a suit begun by the decedent during life,[5] and from dismissing a suit begun by the deceased.[6] Whether this view rests on formal considerations only[7] or on other considerations is discussed subsequently. Although many reasonably conclude that this traditional view is unconstitutional as a refusal, contrary to full faith and credit, to recognize the judicial proceedings by which the foreign personal representative has been appointed,[8] it has received tenacious support by some courts. This restrictive attitude has serious disadvantages in operation, for it makes more difficult, cumbersome and expensive the winding up of affairs of a person whose interests are scattered across state lines. Where the estate is not a large one, the burden is especially great.

The reasons usually given for denying the power to sue are that local creditors may be prejudiced and that the foreign personal representative is a creature of the law of another state whose power evaporates at the boundary of the state of appointment. This overlooks the trust relationship that underlies the position of personal representative. What the personal representative does is for the benefit of others, creditors or beneficiaries of the state, and the personal representative must account for any receipt or disbursement wherever made before discharge, as would a trustee. Creditors can file claims against the personal representative and the personal representative cannot discriminate on the basis of residence. Further, concerned creditors can obtain local administration. At bottom, convenience to local creditors is the only reason and

District Court, 2 Utah 2d 227, 272 P.2d 157 (1954); Tourton v. Flower, 3 P.Wms. 369 (1735). But see Note, The Statutory Successor, the Receiver and the Executor in Conflict of Laws, 44 Colum. L. Rev. 549 (1944); Goodwin v. Jones, 3 Mass. 514, 3 Am.Dec. 173 (1807) (referring to an interesting compact of 1648 allowing suit among the New England colonies).

4. Pond v. Makepeace, 43 Mass. (2 Metc.) 114 (1840). Cf. Assessors of Everett v. Albert N. Parlin House, Inc., 331 Mass. 359, 118 N.E.2d 861 (1954). But cf. Canfield v. Scripps, 15 Cal.App.2d 642, 59 P.2d 1040 (1936), certiorari denied 300 U.S. 658, 57 S.Ct. 431, 81 L.Ed. 867 (1937) holding that where a California administrator sued in Washington and, no objection having been raised to the suit, judgment was rendered on the merits for the defendant, the judgment was res judicata in a subsequent suit in California; Farmers & Merchants Trust Co. v. Madeira, 261 Cal.App.2d 503, 68 Cal. Rptr. 184 (1968).

5. Barclift v. Treece, 77 Ala. 528 (1884); Greer v. Ferguson, 56 Ark. 324, 19 S.W. 966 (1892); Goodwin v. Jones, 3 Mass. 514, 3

Am.Dec. 173 (1807); State ex rel. Mercantile National Bank v. Rooney, 402 S.W.2d 354 (Mo.1966); Eikel v. Burton, 530 S.W.2d 907 (Tex.Civ.App.1975). But cf. Eikel v. Bristow Corp., 529 S.W.2d 795 (Tex.Civ. App.1975). Capacity to sue in federal courts, at least in diversity cases, has been held to be governed by state law. See Davis v. Piper Aircraft Corp., 615 F.2d 606 (4th Cir.1980); Fennell v. Monongahela Power Co., 350 F.2d 867 (4th Cir.1965); Weinstein v. Medical Center Hospital, 358 F.Supp. 297 (D.Vt.1972).

6. Warren v. Eddy, 32 Barb. 664, 13 Abb. Prac. 28 (N.Y. 1861). Cf. Ricard v. Birch, 529 F.2d 214 (4th Cir.1975); Johnson v. Wachovia Bank & Trust Co., 22 N.C.App. 8, 205 S.E.2d 353 (1974).

7. It has been held in Michigan that the foreign representative may sue if he obtains local letters of administration before trial of the action. Gray v. Franks, 86 Mich. 382, 49 N.W. 130 (1891). See also Hodges v. Kimball, 91 Fed. 845 (4th Cir.1899); Leahy v. Haworth, 141 Fed. 850 (8th Cir.1905).

8. See D. Currie, supra n.2, at 433.

that element of convenience is a high price to pay for frustrating prompt settlement of multi-state estates when those creditors have not protected themselves by local appointment. The result in many cases is to permit the defendant to escape liability by reason of the confusion incident to a multistate case.[9]

That the reasons advanced for denying standing to sue are largely fictional is reflected in the many cases that permit a foreign personal representative to sue for wrongful death without local qualification because the recovery does not constitute assets of the estate available to creditors.[10] The suit is by the personal representative as trustee for the statutory beneficiaries. As a result of the hardships incident to the traditional denial of standing to sue, numerous statutes have been enacted allowing foreign personal representatives to sue locally, under such conditions as the legislature sees fit to impose. Another type of statute makes it possible for the foreign personal representative to secure local appointment without elaborate proceedings.[11] The force of these statutes, reinforced by statutory reform efforts such as the Uniform Probate Code, have essentially reversed this traditional rule in the United States.[12] It would appear that a foreign personal representative may, with regard to most of the issues that arise in administration, pursue a debtor of the estate in an appropriate forum outside of the state of the personal representative's appointment.[13]

Even though the Uniform Probate Code does not provide for a completely unitary administration, it makes significant strides in that direction within the framework of our federal system. Practical control by the domiciliary personal representative is promoted by giving the

---

9. Leonard v. Wharton, 268 F.Supp. 715 (D.Md.1967), appeal dismissed 396 F.2d 452 (4th Cir.1968), cert. denied 393 U.S. 1028, 89 S.Ct. 624, 21 L.Ed.2d 571 (1969). Cf. De Garza v. Chetister, 62 Ohio App.2d 149, 405 N.E.2d 331 (1978). But cf. Tomczak v. Erie Insurance Exchange, 268 F.Supp. 185 (W.D.Pa.1967).

10. Windbourne v. Eastern Air Lines, 479 F.Supp. 1130 (E.D.N.Y.1979); Weissfeld v. Herman Miller, 293 F.Supp. 995 (W.D.Mich.1968); Lumb v. Cooper, 266 A.2d 196 (Del. 1970). See supra § 22.10 nn.6, 7. Cf. Young v. Pattridge, 40 F.R.D. 376 (N.D.Miss. 1966). But cf. Weinstein v. Medical Center Hospital, 358 F.Supp. 297 (D.Vt. 1972); Merchants Distributors, Inc. v. Hutchinson, 16 N.C.App. 655, 193 S.E.2d 436 (1972). See also Blusy v. Rugh, 476 N.E.2d 874 (Ind.App.1985). But see Burcl v. North Carolina Baptist Hosp., Inc., 306 N.C. 214, 293 S.E.2d 85 (1982) (foreign personal representative must qualify to bring wrongful death action).

11. See Woerner, The American Law of Administration § 163 (3d ed. 1923); Comment, Conflict of Laws—Torts—Proper Party Plaintiff on Wrongful Death Actions, 54 Mich. L. Rev. 821 (1956).

12. Cf. B. McDowell, Foreign Personal Representatives 77 (1957); Note, The Statutory Successor, the Receiver and the Executor in Conflict of Laws, 44 Colum. L. Rev. 549 (1944); Moore, Estate Administration and the Conflict of Laws, 35 Va. L. Rev. 316 (1949); U.P.C. §§ 3–703, 4–205.

13. Cf. Restatement, Second, Conflict of Laws § 354 (1971); D. Currie, The Multiple Personality of the Dead: Executors, Administrators, and the Conflict of Laws, 33 U. Chi. L. Rev. 429 (1966); Lerner, The Need for Reform in Multistate Estate Administration, 55 Tex. L. Rev. 303 (1977); Note, The Amenability to Suit of Foreign Executors and Administrators, 56 Colum. L. Rev. 915 (1956). See Vangrack, Axelson & Williamowsky, P.C. v. Estate of Abbasi, 261 F.Supp.2d 352, 358 (D. Md. 2003); Biglan v. Biglan, 330 Pa.Super. 512, 479 A.2d 1021 (1984). See also McDonnell, Harris & Cantwell, The Final Gamble: Ancillary Administration Proceedings Under the Uniform Probate Code and in Non–U.P.C. Jurisdictions, 6 Prob. L.J. 211 (1985).

domiciliary personal representative priority for appointment in ancillary administration,[14] and by permitting the domiciliary personal representative to collect assets upon affidavit if there is no local administration.[15] The domiciliary personal representative may exercise all powers including the power to sue[16] within the ancillary state by filing copies of the domiciliary letters there and any bond he has posted.[17] The filing or receiving payment in an ancillary state constitutes consent to the jurisdiction of the ancillary court for proceedings related to the estate[18] and the original appointment gave that consent to the jurisdiction of the domiciliary court.[19] The domiciliary personal representative is given the same standing to sue or be sued as the decedent had immediately prior to his death.[20] As a consequence, the domiciliary personal representative can administer ancillary assets and those local persons concerned about the estate administration can secure either local or domiciliary review of the representative's acts relating to the ancillary assets.

2. Other Acts

§ 22.15   As is evident from the preceding discussion of the Uniform Probate Code, the statutory development in the United States tends to give substantially complete authority to the domiciliary personal representative to act elsewhere if the domiciliary letters are filed in the state where action is taken. Aside from this statutory development, the law is still in the process of development and uncertainties still exist when the question involved is not that of the foreign representative's capacity to sue, but the power to do other acts affecting matters in a state other than that of appointment. The question generally arises in connection with the authority of the domiciliary personal representative to pursue efforts to achieve unitary administration. It may also arise with regard to an ancillary representative whose acts purport to affect matters outside the state of his appointment.[1]

To put the matter concretely: Assume that a decedent dies domiciled in Michigan and an administrator is appointed in that state. Three situations are typical: Assume D has a boat left in an Indiana boatyard for repair. May the Michigan administrator go into Indiana and get the boat, if it is possible to do so without court help? Is the operator of the boatyard safe in turning over the boat to the Michigan administrator? And if the Michigan administrator gets the boat must he account for it in Michigan or in Indiana? Secondly, assume that the decedent had a debtor who lived in Indiana, may the Michigan personal representative collect the claim from the debtor and is the debtor protected from

---

14. U.P.C. § 3–203(g).

15. U.P.C. § 4–201.

16. U.P.C. § 4–204.

17. U.P.C. § 4–205.

18. U.P.C. § 4–301.

19. U.P.C. § 3–602.

20. U.P.C. § 3–703(c).

§ 22.15

1. Note that in Wilkins v. Ellett, 108 U.S. 256, 2 S.Ct. 641, 27 L.Ed. 718 (1883) involving voluntary payment by a debtor, payment was made to an administrator appointed in a state not the domicile of the decedent.

further liability if he voluntarily pays the Michigan administrator? And finally, if the debtor refuses to pay, may the Michigan administrator assign the claim to a stranger so that the stranger may sue the debtor, and if the latter pays a judgment secured against him, will he be exempt from further liability?

The answer to these questions will be influenced by the conception held of the nature of the interest that comes to the domiciliary representative. One view is that the domiciliary representative, whether executor or administrator, succeeds to the decedent's "title" to all personal estate, no matter where located, at least until that title is displaced by an appointment of an ancillary representative at the situs of the property. Even when he cannot maintain an action in another state, "the objection does not raise any defect of the administrator's title in the property, but upon his personal incapacity to sue as administrator except in the jurisdiction which appointed him."[2] "Letters granted by the courts of the domicile of the testator or the intestate by operation of law vest in the executor or administrator the entire personal estate of the testator or intestate, wherever situated. . . ."[3] Language to the same effect is found in many cases.[4]

"Title," of course, is not a tangible thing but a legal concept denoting the existence of certain powers and privileges which courts recognize as exercisable by a person with regard to a particular object. If the domiciliary representative has "title" to all of the decedent's personalty, he rather clearly could do all of the things that were hypothesized above. How does the domiciliary representative come to be vested with "title" to foreign movable property? One suggestion is that the personal estate is considered to be located at the decedent's domicile.[5] This is an incorrect assumption of the outdated and outworn maxim "mobilia sequuntur personam." Another explanation is the controlling effect of the principle that the succession to the personal estate of a deceased person is governed by the law of the state of his domicile at death.[6] Since the domiciliary rules of distribution govern, and also determine whether a will which provides for distribution is valid, the argument follows that the domiciliary representative is clothed with title to all property. While this argument reflects a policy favoring unitary succession and unified administration to avoid unnecessary expense and litigation, the conclusion as to administration seems not to result from the rules as to succession. Ordinarily distribution is made according to domiciliary rules and ordinarily a balance remaining after ancillary administration is

2. Wilkins v. Ellett, 108 U.S. 256, 2 S.Ct. 641, 27 L.Ed. 718 (1883). But cf. In re Washburn's Estate, 45 Minn. 242, 47 N.W. 790 (1891)(Gray, J.).

3. In re Cape May & Delaware Bay Navigation Co., 51 N.J.L. 78, 16 A. 191 (1888).

4. Murphy v. Crouse, 135 Cal. 14, 66 P. 971 (1901); In re Williams' Estate, 130 Iowa 558, 107 N.W. 608 (1906); Adams v. Batcheldor, 173 Mass. 258, 53 N.E. 824 (1899);

In re Washburn's Estate, 45 Minn. 242, 47 N.W. 790 (1891); Klein v. French, 57 Miss. 662 (1880); Luce v. Manchester & Lawson Railroad, 63 N.H. 588, 589, 3 A. 618 (1886); Valentine v. Duke, 128 Wash. 128, 222 P. 494 (1924).

5. In re Washburn's Estate, 45 Minn. 242, 47 N.W. 790 (1891).

6. Petersen v. Chemical Bank, 32 N.Y. 21, 88 Am.Dec. 298 (1865).

remitted to the principal administrator for distribution. But the first rule, based on the convenience of treating the estate as a whole, may be changed by statute and a state may have all local property distributed according to local statute as is occasionally done[7] Whether distribution will be made locally or the balance after ancillary administration remitted to the domicile of the decedent is generally viewed as a question of convenience and expediency.

It seems apparent that property left in a state at the death of an owner is subject to that state's control, no matter where the domicile of the owner happened to be. Appointment of a representative at that domicile cannot make him the owner of that property unless the law of the situs does so. Judicial language expressing this idea is plentiful. "It is a principle of almost universal jurisprudence, recognized in England, as well as in the American courts, with scarcely an exception, that the title of an executor or administrator does not extend beyond the territory of the government which grants it."[8] "Nor can it invest the administrator with title to any movable property, except to such as may be found within its limits."[9] The state where the property is located may be concerned with it in several ways. It may be concerned with taxing the succession or assuring that the property shall be subject to creditor's claims.[10] Also, the state may claim the property as bona vacantia, if there is no next of kin. Finally the state may, though as noted it seldom does, insist that it be distributed according to its own rules, regardless of the domicile of the decedent. However, these state concerns are limited and often are not adverse to domiciliary administration. If assumption of control over local assets by the domiciliary representative does not, in a given instance, interfere with any of these interests, there seems to be no reason for not permitting the domiciliary representative to act. It is convenient to handle the estate as a whole; it saves expense and time in settling the decedent's affairs, the rights of creditors cannot be prejudiced[11] and the only purpose of local administration would be the technical assertion of local power.[12]

There is authority recognizing the propriety of the domiciliary representative taking possession of foreign assets when possible, and even some stating his obligation to do so.[13] Also, the domiciliary personal

---

7. See supra § 20.5.

8. Swancy v. Scott, 28 Tenn. (9 Humph.) 327 (1848).

9. Dial v. Gary, 14 S.C. 573, 37 Am.Rep. 737 (1881). See also Grayson v. Robertson, 122 Ala. 330, 25 So. 229 (1899); McCord v. Thompson, 92 Ind. 565 (1884); Brown v. Smith, 101 Me. 545, 64 A. 915 (1906); Young v. O'Neal, 35 Tenn. (3 Sneed) 55 (1855).

10. See Gross v. Hocker Jr., 243 Iowa 291, 51 N.W.2d 466 (1952); Scoles, Conflict of Laws and Creditors' Rights in Decedents' Estates, 42 Iowa L. Rev. 341 (1957).

11. See infra § 22.21; D. Currie, The Multiple Personality of the Dead: Executors, Administrators and the Conflict of Laws, 33 U. Chi. L. Rev. 429, 433 (1966).

12. See In re Washburn's Estate, 45 Minn. 242, 47 N.W. 790 (1891).

13. In re Ortiz's Estate, 86 Cal. 306, 24 P. 1034 (1890); In re Washburn's Estate, 45 Minn. 242, 47 N.W. 790 (1891); Klein v. French, 57 Miss. 662 (1880); Shultz v. Pulver, 3 Paige Ch. 182 (N.Y. 1832), affirmed 11 Wend. 361 (N.Y.1833). See B. McDowell, Foreign Personal Representatives 144 (1957). Cf. In re Massaglia's Estate, 38 Cal. App.3d 767, 113 Cal.Rptr. 751 (1974); In re

representative has been permitted to exercise a power given in the will relating to local land.[14] If the personal representative does secure such assets, he must account for them.[15] All states share the policy of prompt collection of assets and the application of those assets to the purposes for which administration is undertaken in order to affect a prompt distribution to the successors of the property. Any validly appointed personal representative should be permitted to sue, especially where it is plain no injustice can result.[16]

3. *Payment to a Foreign Representative*

§ 22.16　The effect of a voluntary payment by a debtor to a domiciliary representative outside the state of the latter's appointment has raised some questions in light of the historical view that a personal representative's authority was limited to the state of appointment. Cases involving collection of negotiable paper by a representative presents a separate problem. The situation in which payment is made to a representative holding the instrument has been considered above[1] and the position taken that the holder may properly be regarded as the owner of the obligation. Even apart from the negotiable paper cases, however, the majority view of courts in the United States is that a voluntary payment to the domiciliary representative who has not qualified in the state where the debtor pays him is a valid discharge of the debtor, at least in the absence of local creditors and a local ancillary representative.[2] If the domiciliary representative is deemed to have "title" the result is consistent with that fiction, but the same immunity from further payment by

Shinn's Estate, 166 Pa. 121, 30 A. 1026, 1030 (1895). But see Cabanne v. Skinker, 56 Mo. 357 (1874). Cf. Campbell v. Tousey, 7 Cow. 64 (N.Y.1827); New York Breweries Co. v. Attorney General (1898) 1 Q.B. 205; Fugate v. Moore, 86 Va. 1045, 11 S.E. 1063 (1890). The Uniform Probate Code provides in § 3–704:

"A personal representative shall proceed expeditiously with the settlement and distribution of a decedent's estate and, except as otherwise specified or ordered in regard to a supervised personal representative, do so without adjudication, order, or direction of the Court, but he may invoke the jurisdiction of the Court, in proceedings authorized by this Code, to resolve questions concerning the estate or its administration."

14. See, e.g., Oglevie v. Stasser, 1 Kan. App.2d 315, 564 P.2d 563 (1977); Matter of Meister's Estate, 71 Wis.2d 581, 239 N.W.2d 52 (1976). See also Restatement, Second, Conflict of Laws § 338 (1971).

15. McPike v. McPike, 111 Mo. 216, 20 S.W. 12 (1892); Parsons v. Lyman, 20 N.Y. 103 (1859). See infra § 22.24.

16. Cf. Anderson v. Louisville & Nashville Railroad Co., 210 Fed. 689 (6th Cir. 1914); Windbourne v. Eastern Air Lines, 479 F.Supp. 1130 (E.D.N.Y.1979).

§ 22.16

1. See supra § 22.11.

2. Wilkins v. Ellett, 76 U.S. (9 Wall.) 740, 19 L.Ed. 586 (1869); Id., 108 U.S. 256, 2 S.Ct. 641, 27 L.Ed. 718 (1883); Selleck v. Rusco, 46 Conn. 370 (1878); In re Williams' Estate, 130 Iowa 558, 107 N.W. 608 (1906); Dexter v. Berge, 76 Minn. 216, 78 N.W. 1111 (1899); Carr v. Prudential Life Insurance Co., 27 N.Y.S.2d 349 (1940); Gray's Estate, 116 Pa. 256, 11 A. 66, 70 (1887). Contra, Ferguson v. Morris, 67 Ala. 389 (1880); Richardson v. Neblett, 122 Miss. 723, 84 So. 695 (1920); Vaughn v. Barret, 5 Vt. 333, 26 Am.Dec. 306 (1833). See Alford, Collecting a Decedent's Assets Without Ancillary Administration, 18 S.W.L.J. 329 (1964); Fizzell, Payment of Debt to Foreign Representatives or Heirs, 21 U. Mo. Bulletin, Law Series, No. 18 (1920); 1 Woerner, The American Law of Administration § 161 (3d ed. 1923).

the debtor has been given where the debtor has paid a foreign ancillary administrator.[3] The title theory seems refuted when the debtor makes payment to the foreign representative without knowing an ancillary representative has been appointed in the state, for substantial authority holds that payment in such a case relieves the debtor of further liability.[4] This approach relieves the debtor from ascertaining at his peril whether a local representative has been appointed and speeds the collection of assets.[5]

The result of the decisions, it is submitted, does not require any reference to title of the chose in action as an explanation. It is convenient, but not to be compelled, to have local administration everywhere there is a debtor. If money has been received by a properly appointed representative of the estate, that representative must account for it and it will be administered in the orderly manner that the law governing administration is designed to insure. To make the debtor pay twice merely in the interest of double administration is neither just nor necessary, and will only delay administration and increase its already heavy cost. A few cases raise uncertainties where there are local creditors[6] or the money is not distributed as local law directs.[7] Local creditors cannot be prejudiced if reasonably diligent.[8] Under the view of the American Law Institute, knowledge of the appointment of a local administrator is the sole determining factor.[9] In addition to the cases, most states have statutes recognizing the voluntary payment or delivery of chattels to a foreign representative.[10]

A voluntary payment by a foreign debtor to an administrator in the state of appointment will discharge the debtor, since in most instances

---

3. Wilkins v. Ellett, 108 U.S. 256, 2 S.Ct. 641, 27 L.Ed. 718 (1883); Morrison v. Berkshire Loan & Trust Co., 229 Mass. 519, 118 N.E. 895 (1918). But see Wolfe v. Bank of Anderson, 123 S.C. 208, 116 S.E. 451 (1923) (noted 37 Harv. L. Rev. 264 (1923)).

4. Ames v. Citizens' National Bank, 105 Kan. 83, 181 P. 564 (1919) (representative to whom payment was made held negotiable instruments); Compton's Administrator v. Borderland Coal Co., 179 Ky. 695, 201 S.W. 20 (1918); Maas v. German Savings Bank, 176 N.Y. 377, 68 N.E. 658 (1903). See Note, Conflict of Laws: Voluntary Surrender of Assets on Local Jurisdiction to Domiciliary Administrator, 4 Cal. L. Rev. 496 (1916); Restatement, Second, Conflict of Laws § 329 (1971).

5. Cf. U.P.C. § 4–202.

6. See Goodman v. First National Bank, 218 Ky. 229, 291 S.W. 54 (1927); Wolfe v. Bank of Anderson, 123 S.C. 208, 209, 116 S.E. 451 (1923). But the Maryland court has declared: "The validity of the payment does not in our opinion depend in any manner upon the fact of the non-existence of debts against the deceased in this state."

Citizens' National Bank v. Sharp, 53 Md. 521 (1880). Where the debtor is forced to pay twice, he should be able to recover the amount paid to the foreign ancillary administrator. Restatement, Second, Conflict of Laws § 329, comnt. (b) (1971).

7. See Richardson v. Neblett, 122 Miss. 723, 84 So. 695 (1920) (applying Mississippi's minority rule that domiciliary law does not apply to substantive issues of succession).

8. See infra § 22.21; Scoles, Conflict of Laws and Creditors' Rights in Decedents' Estates, 42 Iowa L. Rev. 341 (1957).

9. Restatement, Second, Conflict of Laws § 329 (1971). See Hopkins, Conflict of Laws in Administration of Decedents' Intangibles, 28 Iowa L. Rev. 422, 435 (1943).

10. See, e.g., U.P.C. § 4–201; Alford, Collecting a Decedent's Assets Without Ancillary Administration, 18 S.W.L.J. 329 (1964); Note, The Extraterritorial Authority of Executors and Administrators to Sue and Collect Assets, 52 Iowa L. Rev. 290 (1966); B. McDowell, Foreign Personal Representatives 163 (1957). Cf. In re Wipfler, 45 F.Supp. 171 (D.Mass.1942).

the debtor, by coming into the forum would be subjected to local suit by the administrator.[11] The approaches which have been stated with reference to the collection and payment of debts are, of course, equally applicable to the collection and delivery of chattels.[12] The common policy shared by the different states in these cases supports the position that a process which reasonably carries out the purposes of administration with the minimum expense and least amount of inconvenience should be supported.

4.   *Transfer of Claim by Personal Representative*

§ 22.17   In treating the powers of personal representatives, it is important to consider the effect of an assignment of a claim by an administrator or executor where the assignee is seeking to sue the debtor in a state where the representative has not qualified. Many of the decided cases involve the transfer of negotiable paper by the representative and a suit by the transferee.[1] There is no difficulty involved in allowing suit by the transferee if the mercantile theory of negotiable paper is accepted. The representative who holds the instrument holds the property and may dispose of it in the course of administration as he would dispose of any other personal estate of the decedent in his possession. The transferee's title should be recognized everywhere. Nor should it make a difference that the note is secured by a mortgage on foreign land. A representative appointed in one state cannot, perhaps, exercise control over land situated in another state in absence of statute, but if he may effectively transfer the note, the interest in the security should follow.[2]

There is authority recognizing the rights elsewhere of the assignee based upon the domiciliary representative's ownership of the decedent's movables whether the claim against the debtor was evidenced by a negotiable instrument or not.[3] But since the assignor could not have

11. Restatement, Second, Conflict of Laws § 327 (1971).

12. Restatement, Second, Conflict of Laws § 322 (1971).

§ 22.17

1. See, e.g., General Conference Association of Seventh–Day Adventists v. Michigan Sanitarium & Benevolent Association, 166 Mich. 504, 132 N.W. 94 (1911); Andrews v. Carr, 26 Miss. 577 (1853); Gove v. Gove, 64 N.H. 503, 15 A. 121, 122 (1888); Mackay v. St. Mary's Church, 15 R.I. 121, 23 A. 108 (1885); Munson v. Exchange National Bank, 19 Wash. 125, 52 P. 1011 (1898). In Luce v. Manchester & Lawson Railroad, 63 N.H. 588, 3 A. 618 (1886) there was involved a transfer of stock by the representative who had the certificates. See B. McDowell, Foreign Personal Representatives 63 (1957). See also Michigan Trust Co. v. Chaffee, 73 N.D. 86, 11 N.W.2d 108 (1943).

2. Restatement, Second, Conflict of Laws § 340 (1971).

3. See supra § 22.16 n.3; Petersen v. Chemical Bank, 32 N.Y. 21, 88 Am. Dec. 298 (1865); In re Cape May & Delaware Bay Navigation Co., 51 N.J.L. 78, 16 A. 191 (1888) (same); Camp v. Simon, 23 Utah 56, 63 P. 332 (1900); Valentine v. Duke, 128 Wash. 128, 222 P. 494 (1924). Contra, Stearns v. Burnham, 5 Me. 261, 5 Greenl. 261, 17 Am.Dec. 228 (1828) (promissory note); Brown, Jr. v. Smith, 101 Me. 545, 64 A. 915 (1906) (note secured by mortgage on local land); Reynolds v. McMullen, 55 Mich. 568, 22 N.W. 41 (1885) (mortgage on Michigan land, and foreign representative acting without court authorization); McCarty v. Hall, 13 Mo. 480 (1850) (promissory note); Heyward v. Williams, 57 S.C. 235, 35 S.E. 503 (1900). See Buchanan & Myers, The Administration of Intangibles in View of

sued outside his state of appointment these rights may be enforced only in states that permit suits to be brought in the name of the real party in interest[4] or the purchaser is otherwise protected by statutes such as the Uniform Probate Code.[5] Recovery by the assignee has been denied in cases in which an ancillary administrator has been appointed in the forum prior to the time of the assignment, and a similar restriction has been adopted by the Restatement.[6] As a further limitation it has been suggested that the assignment is effective only as to a debtor who resides in the state where the representative had qualified at the time the assignment was made,[7] but in the absence of local appointment this restriction seems likely not to be given effect.

Aside from the negotiable instrument cases, there is some theoretical difficulty in explaining how the domiciliary representative acting under authority of the appointing forum can exert legal control over the claim against a foreign debtor. Even so, the practical desirability of the rule in facilitating the collection of assets of an estate in a simple and prompt manner is supported by the policy favoring convenient administration.[8] The proceeds of the assignment are received by the representative for purposes of administration so the same considerations apply as in a voluntary payment by the debtor to the foreign representative[9] and administration is accomplished without delay or injury to anyone.

5. Suits Arising Out of Administration

§ 22.18 It has already been observed that, historically, a personal representative of a deceased person may not, in the absence of permissive forum law, sue in the courts of another state on a claim of the decedent.[1] Suppose, however, that the representative, in handling the affairs of the estate, has sold goods to a debtor who is now available for suit only in another state. Must the representative qualify in that state before he can sue on the debtor's agreement to pay? This claim does not run to the decedent, obviously, since it came into existence after the decedent's death. And the "estate" is neither an individual nor a corporation. The new claim runs to the representative as an individual, though acquired in the course of the business as administrator and must be accounted for when collected. In this situation, the law treats the personal representative as owner of the estate as to third parties, and the personal representative's suit in the foreign state as an individual asserting an obligation running directly to him. He may then sue[2] or be

First National Bank v. Maine, 48 Harv. L. Rev. 911, 924 (1935).

4. Restatement, Second, Conflict of Laws § 333, cmnt. (c) (1971).

5. See, e.g., U.P.C. § 3–714.

6. DuVal v. Marshall, 30 Ark. 230 (1875); Murphy v. Crouse, 135 Cal. 14, 66 P. 971 (1901); Restatement, Second, Conflict of Laws § 333(3) (1971).

7. Elmer v. Hall, 148 Pa. 345, 23 A. 971 (1892).

8. See B. McDowell, supra n.1, at 66.

9. See supra § 22.16.

§ 22.18

1. See supra § 22.14. Most states permit the suit by statute.

2. Kruskal v. United States, 178 F.2d 738 (2d Cir.1950); Turner v. Alton Banking

sued[3] upon such an agreement in another state. The representative to whom such claim runs, or his assignee, is the only proper person to enforce it.[4]

If a personal representative has taken a note from a debtor in payment for goods sold by the representative, the debtor must pay this administrator or his transferee. A payment to another representative at the domicile of the debtor is no discharge[5] and the representative as payee of such note could transfer it to a third party.[6]

The same analysis is applicable where the representative has reduced an asset to possession or a claim belonging to a decedent has been reduced to judgment. The judgment represents a new cause of action which never belonged to the decedent but arose in the course of the administration[7] and the representative, out of whose transaction it arose may sue upon it wherever jurisdiction can be asserted over the debtor "and the addition of his title in the declaration is a mere description which is rejected as surplusage."[8] This result is supported by many decisions.[9] By the same token, an administrator *de bonis non* may sue his predecessor in a foreign state for the balance found to be due by the appointing court.[10]

& Trust Co., 166 F.2d 305 (8th Cir.1948); Morse v. King, 73 N.J.L. 548, 63 A. 986 (1906); Restatement, Second, Conflict of Laws § 355 (1971); B. McDowell, Foreign Personal Representatives 38 (1957).

3. Crowe v. Di Manno, 225 F.2d 652 (1st Cir.1955); Cramer v. Phoenix Mutual Life Insurance Co., 91 F.2d 141 (8th Cir.1937), cert. denied 302 U.S. 739, 58 S.Ct. 141, 82 L.Ed. 571 (1937); Johnston v. Wallis, 112 N.Y. 230, 19 N.E. 653 (1889); Dahlberg v. Brown, 198 S.C. 1, 16 S.E.2d 284 (1941); Lang v. Lang, 17 Utah 2d 10, 403 P.2d 655 (1965); Restatement, Second, Conflict of Laws § 359 (1971).

4. See De Paris v. Wilmington Trust Co., 30 Del. 178, 7 Boyce 178, 104 A. 691 (1918); Kruskal v. United States, 178 F.2d 738 (2d Cir.1950); Eikel v. Bristow Corp., 529 S.W.2d 795 (Tex.Civ.App.1975).

5. McCord v. Thompson, 92 Ind. 565 (1884).

6. Mackay v. St. Mary's Church, 15 R.I. 121, 23 A. 108 (1885). Cf. *Eikel*, 529 S.W.2d 795.

7. "The debt was merged in the judgment which belonged to the administrator personally, subject to the duty to account to the estate of the decedent in the state of the latter's domicile. He holds the legal title, subject only to his trust as administrator." Hare v. O'Brien, 233 Pa. 330, 82 A. 475 (1912). See Turner v. Alton Banking & Trust Co., 166 F.2d 305 (8th Cir.1948);

Farmers & Merchants Trust Co. v. Madeira, 261 Cal.App.2d 503, 68 Cal.Rptr. 184 (1968); Wiel v. Curtis, Mallet–Prevost, Colt and Mosle, 66 Misc.2d 466, 321 N.Y.S.2d 250 (1970), affirmed 36 A.D.2d 1027, 322 N.Y.S.2d 628 (1971), affirmed 30 N.Y.2d 500, 329 N.Y.S.2d 818, 280 N.E.2d 649 (1972).

8. Moore v. Kraft, 179 Fed. 685 (7th Cir.1910). Cf. Kenney v. Kenney, 314 F.2d 268 (D.C.Cir.1963); Boone v. Wachovia Bank & Trust Co., 163 F.2d 809 (D.C.Cir. 1947).

9. *Moore*, 179 Fed. 685 (7th Cir.1910); McCraw v. Simpson, 208 Ark. 471, 187 S.W.2d 536 (1945); Lewis v. Adams, 70 Cal. 403, 11 P. 833 (1886); Talmage v. Chapel, 16 Mass. 71 (1819); Miller v. Hoover, 121 Mo.App. 568, 97 S.W. 210 (1906); Hare v. O'Brien, 233 Pa. 330, 82 A. 475 (1912). See also Restatement, Second, Conflict of Laws § 355 (1971). But see Morefield v. Harris, 126 N.C. 626, 36 S.E. 125 (1900). On notice requirements see Karpo v. Deitsch, 196 So.2d 180 (Fla.App.1967); Tapley v. Proctor, 150 Ga.App. 337, 258 S.E.2d 25 (1979).

10. Moore v. Fields, 42 Pa. 467 (1862). Cf. Gurley v. Lindsley, 459 F.2d 268 (5th Cir.1972), mandate withdrawn 466 F.2d 498 (5th Cir.1972); Kaltsas v. Kaltsas, 22 Mass. App.Ct. 689, 497 N.E.2d 26 (1986), review denied 398 Mass. 1105, 499 N.E.2d 298 (1986).

The principle that the administrator or executor may bring actions outside the state of appointment on claims or possession of assets asserted as the result of his administration is applied in other situations. If the personal representative is asserting a claim running to himself, he may sue as any other person may sue, even though the claim is acquired while acting as representative; of course the representative must account to the appointing court for anything received. Thus, when the legal title to property has vested in him under the law of the state of his appointment, he may sue for its recovery in another state.[11] Also the representative may execute a power of sale contained in a mortgage[12] or sell real estate in a foreign state as donee of a power in trust conferred by the will.[13] The authority as trustee has "no necessary relation to the office of executor and might with equal propriety have been conferred upon any others not named as executors."[14] One who under the civil law is the universal successor of the personal and real estate of the decedent may sue in a foreign state as owner.[15]

6. Actions Against Foreign Representatives

§ 22.19 Historically, the view was taken that an executor or administrator, appointed in one state, was not subject to suit in his representative capacity in the courts of another state under the laws of which the administrator was not appointed or otherwise authorized to act as a local representative.[1] The foreign representative is viewed as an officer of the court which appoints him, and is subject to the control of that court and usually is not interfered with by the courts of other states. Furthermore, so far as obligations incurred by the decedent are concerned, the representative's duty is only to pay them out of the property of the decedent which comes to his possession, and in the manner directed by law. The arguments in support of the traditional rule suggested that if the personal representative were made personally liable to suit other than in the state of appointment, he would be made liable on the obligation of another; if a judgment directed that he pay from the estate of the decedent in his possession, it would amount to an assumption by the forum of control over property in the course of

11. Patchen & Patchen v. Wilson, 4 Hill 57 (N.Y.1842); Hill v. Barton, 194 Mo.App. 325, 188 S.W. 1105 (1916).

12. Doolittle v. Lewis, 7 Johns. Ch. 45, 11 Am.Dec. 389 (N.Y. 1823); Thurber v. Carpenter, 18 R.I. 782, 31 A. 5 (1895); Hayes v. Frey, 54 Wis. 503, 11 N.W. 695 (1882).

13. Bacharach v. Spriggs, 173 Ark. 250, 292 S.W. 150 (1927); Green v. Alden, 92 Me. 177, 42 A. 358 (1898); Restatement, Second, Conflict of Laws §§ 338, 341 (1971).

14. Green v. Alden, 92 Me. 177, 42 A. 358 (1898).

15. Vanquelin v. Bouard, 15 C.B., N.S., 341 (1863).

§ 22.19

1. Vaughan v. Northup, 40 U.S. (15 Pet.) 1, 5, 10 L.Ed. 639 (1841); Jefferson v. Beall, 117 Ala. 436, 23 So. 44 (1898); Greer v. Ferguson, 56 Ark. 324, 19 S.W. 966 (1892); Hedenberg v. Hedenberg, 46 Conn. 30, 33 Am. Rep. 10 (1878); Judy v. Kelley, 11 Ill. 211, 50 Am.Dec. 455 (1849); Campbell v. Sheldon, 30 Mass. (13 Pick.) 8 (1832).

administration in the courts of another state. Finally, it was reasoned that the representative's status "exists only by force of the official character, and so cannot pass beyond the jurisdiction which grants it...."[2] The early historical restriction on suits against foreign representatives had few exceptions. For example, even a suit against a decedent in his lifetime usually could not be revived against the personal representative. Upon the decedent's death, personal jurisdiction over the decedent was considered lost.[3] Even a voluntary appearance by the representative in a suit brought in a state other than that of the appointment did not under the traditional view confer jurisdictions in matters affecting the estate.[4] In an ordinary personal action, consent by personal appearance confers jurisdiction, but the argument ran that the representative could not enlarge his authority by assumption.[5]

The present trend of authorities, however, clearly cuts through the fictions that were offered as limitations and now suits against foreign personal representatives are permitted in most cases. In all but a few states,[6] the traditional rule has been eroded away by statutory exceptions or the overruling of prior decisions. For example, the revival of pending suits against a nonresident who dies, by substitution of the foreign personal representative, is most frequently permitted.[7] In a leading case in New York, *Rosenfeld v. Hotel Corp. of America*,[8] a defendant died while a stockholders' derivative suit was pending. On motion of the plaintiffs, the trial court substituted as defendant the decedent's Massachusetts executors. The foreign executors asserted that personal jurisdiction could not constitutionally be imposed on them solely by reason of decedent's business activity in New York. The New York Court of Appeals held that the foreign personal representatives were properly subject to personal jurisdiction when their decedent had been subject to the jurisdiction of the court. In overruling prior New York cases to the contrary, the court relied on the cases under the nonresident motorist

2. Jefferson v. Beall, 117 Ala. 436, 23 So. 44 (1898).

3. Greer v. Ferguson, 56 Ark. 324, 19 S.W. 966 (1892); Judy v. Kelley, 11 Ill. 211, 50 Am.Dec. 455 (1849); Brown v. Fletcher's Estate, 146 Mich. 401, 109 N.W. 686 (1906).

4. Burrowes v. Goodman, 50 F.2d 92 (2d Cir.1931), cert. denied 284 U.S. 650, 52 S.Ct. 30, 76 L.Ed. 551 (1931); Greer v. Ferguson, 56 Ark. 324, 19 S.W. 966 (1892); Judy v. Kelley, 11 Ill. 211, 50 Am.Dec. 455 (1849). But see Newark Savings Institution v. Jones' Executors, 35 N.J.Eq. 406 (1882). Cf. Canfield v. Scripps, 15 Cal.App.2d 642, 59 P.2d 1040 (1936).

5. Jefferson v. Beall, 117 Ala. 436, 23 So. 44 (1898) ("Consent cannot give such jurisdiction, or extend the limited authority of the administrator to extraterritorial acts resulting in judgments against the estate.").

6. Cf. Palmer v. L. E. Leach Co., Inc., 60 F.R.D. 602 (D.Vt.1973); State ex rel. Mercantile National Bank v. Rooney, 402 S.W.2d 354 (Mo.1966). Even in these few states there would probably be jurisdiction to appoint an ancillary administrator who could be sued in most cases. See supra § 22.10. Cf. Price v. Sommermeyer, 195 Colo. 285, 577 P.2d 752 (1978), on remand 41 Colo.App. 147, 584 P.2d 1220 (1978); In re Kandlbinder's Estate, 183 Neb. 178, 159 N.W.2d 199 (1968); Matter of Owens' Estate, 89 N.M. 420, 553 P.2d 700 (1976); In re Edmundson, 273 N.C. 92, 159 S.E.2d 509 (1968).

7. Kibbey v. Mercer, 11 Ohio App.2d 51, 228 N.E.2d 337 (1967); Avery v. Bender, 126 Vt. 342, 230 A.2d 786 (1967); National Bank of Washington v. Equity Investors, 81 Wn.2d 886, 506 P.2d 20 (1973).

8. 20 N.Y.2d 25, 281 N.Y.S.2d 308, 228 N.E.2d 374 (1967).

statutes[9] and the Second Circuit's previous application of the New York long-arm statute to the foreign executor of a decedent who died prior to suit being filed.[10]

The nonresident motorist and the long-arm statutes both generally provide for jurisdiction against the foreign personal representative of a decedent by reason of acts of the decedent.[11] Nearly all jurisdictions have such statutes and the application of both to foreign personal representatives has been sustained with near unanimity.[12]

This statutory extension of suits against foreign personal representatives has led to a reconsideration of the possible reasons limiting such suits. An illustrative case is *Saporita v. Litner* in Massachusetts[13] in which jurisdiction over a Connecticut executor was sustained by reason of contractual arrangements and services received by the decedent in Massachusetts. The executor was served in hand in Massachusetts and the court did not rely on subsequent service under the long-arm statute. As a consequence, the court's holding that the foreign personal representative may constitutionally be sued where the decedent could have been subject to jurisdiction is a common law decision demonstrating that there is no policy reason for the former view that a foreign personal representative could not be sued outside the appointing state. As the court stated:

> Had the plaintiff commenced the action against the testator when he was living, the court would have had personal jurisdiction over him.... That he died before the action was commenced and his executor was appointed by a Connecticut court does not alter the court's jurisdiction since the defendant executor was served in hand in Massachusetts....

9. E.g., Hayden v. Wheeler, 33 Ill.2d 110, 210 N.E.2d 495 (1965). See supra § 8.24. See also Cox v. Crow, 336 F.Supp. 761 (N.D.Tex.1972).

10. United States v. Montreal Trust Co., 358 F.2d 239 (2d Cir.1966), cert. denied 384 U.S. 919, 86 S.Ct. 1366, 16 L.Ed.2d 440 (1966). See also Texair Flyers v. District Court, 180 Colo. 432, 506 P.2d 367 (1973).

11. E.g., V.H. v. Estate of Birnbaum, 543 N.W.2d 649 (Minn.1996); HRO v. Greenwich Catholic Elementary School Sys., 202 Conn. 609, 614, 522 A.2d 785 (1987); Tolson v. Hodge, 411 F.2d 123 (4th Cir.1969); In re Estate of Muscillo, 139 A.D.2d 429, 527 N.Y.S.2d 20 (1988). But see Crosson v. Conlee, 745 F.2d 896 (4th Cir. 1984), cert. denied 470 U.S. 1054, 105 S.Ct. 1759, 84 L.Ed.2d 822 (1985) (suit on contract claim against Florida-appointed executor of decedent who had operated business in Virginia; held, since all assets located in Florida, site of probate proceedings, court

would be unable to afford appropriate relief and should have declined jurisdiction).

12. E.g., Eubank Heights Apartments, Limited v. Lebow, 615 F.2d 571 (1st Cir. 1980); Worthley v. Rockville Leasecar, Inc., 328 F.Supp. 185 (D.Md. 1971); Barr v. Mac-Harg, 203 Kan. 612, 455 P.2d 516 (1969). Since the personal representative is subject to suit at the place where the accident occurred, that state's statute of limitations is not tolled. See, e.g., Rivera v. Taylor, 61 Ill.2d 406, 336 N.E.2d 481 (1975); Hossler v. Barry, 403 A.2d 762 (Me.1979); Broadfoot v. Everett, 270 N.C. 429, 154 S.E.2d 522 (1967). But see Tabas v. Crosby, 444 A.2d 250 (Del.Ch.1982) (Delaware "corporate directors' implied consent to service of process" statute could not be used to serve process on deceased nonresident director and suit could not be maintained against his personal representative).

13. Saporita v. Litner, 371 Mass. 607, 358 N.E.2d 809 (1976).

Having determined that the court had personal jurisdiction over the defendant as executor under the testator's will, we fail to perceive any sound reason why the general rule granting immunity to foreign executors should shield the defendant from suit in Massachusetts, where the parties lived and worked, where they made the contract, where they intended the contract to be performed, and where the plaintiff carried out her part of the agreement. The defendant has not shown how the exercise of jurisdiction here will unduly interfere with the jurisdiction of the Connecticut probate court or impose any inequitable burden on the defendant. . . . We perceive none.[14]

While the recent developments under long-arm statutes afford the most direct and practical authority for suits against foreign personal representatives, it is significant to note that such litigation has long been entertained in many areas either by reason of statute or common law decisions. For example, it has already been noted,[15] that the traditional limitation against suit does not apply where the representative is being sued upon a claim which arose, not against the decedent but against the representative. For instance, if an administrator, in the course of handling the affairs of the decedent, makes a contract, he may be sued upon that contract wherever he is properly served with process.[16] It is his contract, even though he may be entitled to reimbursement from the estate for expenditures thereupon, for the decedent obviously cannot incur new obligations and the "estate" has no legal identity other than the personal representative.

The immunity of an executor or administrator to suit outside the state where appointed has been further reduced in other situations. Perhaps the strongest case for allowing the representative to be sued is where he takes property that is part of the estate and goes into another state and wastes it or is about to convert it to his own use. In this instance, equity has long granted relief "to any person whose interest is thereby jeopardized, on the ground that, where a trust fund is in danger of being wasted or misapplied, the court of chancery, on the application of those interested, will intervene to protect the fund from loss."[17] This doctrine has been recognized and applied in a number of cases in various circumstances,[18] and is said to be necessary to prevent a failure of

14. Saporita v. Litner, 371 Mass. 607, 358 N.E.2d 809, 815 (1976). Cf. Gandolfo v. Alford, 31 Conn.Supp. 417, 333 A.2d 65 (1975). See also Mitsui Mfrs. Bank v. Tucker, 152 Cal.App.3d 428, 199 Cal.Rptr. 517 (1984) (California bank could bring suit against Arizona administratrix of decedent who had had substantial contacts with California and who, if alive, would have been subject to personal jurisdiction in California).

15. See supra § 22.18.

16. See e.g., Johnston v. Wallis, 112 N.Y. 230, 19 N.E. 653 (1889); Restatement, Second, Conflict of Laws § 358 (1971).

17. 1 Woerner, The American Law of Administration § 164 (3d ed. 1923). See Falke v. Terry, 32 Colo. 85, 75 P. 425 (1903).

18. See Clopton v. Booker, 27 Ark. 482 (1872); Falke v. Terry, 32 Colo. 85, 75 P. 425 (1903); Gribbel v. Henderson, 151 Fla. 712, 10 So.2d 734 (1942), aff'd on rehearing 153 Fla. 397, 14 So.2d 809 (1943); McAndrews v. Krause, 245 Minn. 85, 71 N.W.2d 153 (1955); Cutrer v. State of Tennessee ex rel. Leggett, 98 Miss. 841, 54 So. 434 (1911), (noted 11 Colum. L. Rev. 563 (1911)), 24 Harv. L. Rev. 664 (1911); Bergmann v. Lord, 194 N.Y. 70, 86 N.E. 828

justice.[19] Since an administrator is subject to the jurisdiction of the court which appointed him until he is finally discharged, his absence from the state will not preclude that court from rendering against him a decree entitled to full faith and credit in other states.[20] It is conceivable that the intervention of a foreign court will not always be necessary to prevent a failure of justice. Yet the immediate remedy of an equity decree seems clearly a more convenient and effective means of protecting the interests of the estate, and since the administrator's liability will be determined by the foreign court in accordance with the law of the state of his appointment,[21] he is subjected to no unfair standard.

Other cases allow an action to be brought against a foreign representative when he has assets of the estate in his possession in the state where the action is brought.[22] This is not necessarily on the ground of the representative's misconduct, for taking property of the estate to another state may be proper for its conservation, or in disposing of it most advantageously. Some courts allow the foreign representative to be sued wherever he may be personally served.[23]

Policy reasons support permitting suits against the foreign personal representative. When a decedent has acted or caused acts within a state other than his domicile sufficient to subject himself to the jurisdiction of its courts, there seems no reason why his personal representative charged with winding up the decedent's affairs should not equally be required to litigate there, whether by a substitution or original suit. Death does not alter the needs nor the power of the state in such cases. As he can be sued as the result of his personal act, so should his consent or waiver bind the foreign representative to the jurisdiction of the court. Respectable authority supports this conclusion,[24] in addition to those

(1909); Graham v. Graham, 452 Pa. 404, 305 A.2d 48 (1973). Cf. Restatement, Second, Conflict of Laws § 358(b) (1971).

19. Johnson v. Jackson, 56 Ga. 326, 21 Am.Rep. 285 (1876); Kaltsas v. Kaltsas, 22 Mass.App.Ct. 689, 497 N.E.2d 26 (1986), review denied 398 Mass. 1105, 499 N.E.2d 298 (1986); Cutrer v. Tennessee ex rel. Leggett, 98 Miss. 841, 54 So. 434 (1911). See Helme v. Buckelew, 229 N.Y. 363, 128 N.E. 216 (1920).

20. Michigan Trust Co. v. Ferry, 228 U.S. 346, 33 S.Ct. 550, 57 L.Ed. 867 (1913); Fitzsimmons v. Johnson, 90 Tenn. 416, 17 S.W. 100 (1891); Restatement, Second, Conflict of Laws § 359 (1971). See supra § 5.8. Cf. DiMauro v. Pavia, 492 F.Supp. 1051 (D.Conn.1979), aff'd 614 F.2d 1286 (2d Cir. 1979); Krimsky v. Lombardi, 78 Misc.2d 685, 357 N.Y.S.2d 671 (1974), affirmed 51 A.D.2d 600, 377 N.Y.S.2d 785 (1976).

21. Johnson v. Jackson, 56 Ga. 326, 21 Am.Rep. 285 (1876); Manion's Administrators v. Titsworth, 57 Ky. (18 B. Mon.) 582 (1857).

22. Oney v. Ferguson, 41 W.Va. 568, 23 S.E. 710 (1895); Fugate v. Moore, 86 Va. 1045, 11 S.E. 1063 (1890). Cf. Kaltsas v. Kaltsas, 22 Mass.App.Ct. 689, 497 N.E.2d 26 (1986).

23. Keiningham v. Keiningham's Executor, 139 Ky. 666, 71 S.W. 497, 24 Ky. Law Rep. 1330 (1903); Laughlin v. Solomon, 180 Pa. 177, 36 A. 704 (1897) (subject to the qualification, "unless it trenches unduly on the jurisdiction of another court already attached, or would expose parties subject to such jurisdiction to inequitable burdens.").

24. Lawrence v. Nelson, 143 U.S. 215, 12 S.Ct. 440, 36 L.Ed. 130 (1892); Benker v. Meyer, 154 Fed. 290 (C.C.A.Neb.1907); Newark Savings Institution v. Jones' Executors, 35 N.J.Eq. 406 (1882); Brown v. Brown, 35 Minn. 191, 28 N.W. 238 (1886); Netting v. Strickland, 18 Ohio CCR 136 (1899); Lieuallen v. Young, 115 Okla. 153, 241 P. 342 (1925); Giampalo v. Taylor, 335 Pa. 121, 6 A.2d 499 (1939). Cf. Shaw v. Stutchman, 105 Nev. 128, 771 P.2d 156 (1989). See also A. Ehrenzweig, Treatise on Conflict of Laws § 23 (1962).

early nonresident motorist cases which proceeded on the consent theory.[25]

The Uniform Probate Code resolves many of these statutory issues when they arise between enacting states. For example, a personal representative consents to the jurisdiction of the appointing court in any matter relating to the estate.[26] Likewise, receiving property or other acts within another state make the personal representative subject to suit there.[27] This gives convenient access to the courts by those interested in the estate. The domiciliary representative is given the same standing to sue or be sued in any state as the decedent had immediately prior to death[28] and jurisdiction over the personal representative based on acts of the decedent is provided.[29] Finally, judgments against one personal representative are binding on other personal representatives.[30]

Enforcement of a judgment obtained against a personal representative may not in fact raise any real problem. In many instances the real defendant is an insurance company[31] and the estate's general assets are not in fact involved. If the assets of the estate are involved, local ancillary assets may be available or the judgment may be presented as a claim at the domicile. The state of the domicile can determine the force of its policies in the matter "whenever the plaintiffs seek to satisfy their claims out of assets of the decedent's estate within the jurisdiction ... "[32] The adoption of long-arm statutes that provide for suits against foreign personal representatives also suggests that a state that permits such suits would not decline recognition of a judgment based on a similar statute. As was stated by the First Circuit Court of Appeals in enforcing such a judgment:

> In *Saporita* [supra] a Massachusetts creditor succeeded in obtaining a judgment in Massachusetts against an executor of a Connecticut estate. We cannot think that Massachusetts would decline to take the reciprocal view, and refuse to recognize a Texas judgment against a Massachusetts executor. It is true that the plaintiff *Saporita* obtained service in hand on the foreign executor in Massachusetts, whereas defendant here received only substituted service by mail, but we do not think that is a significant difference. If the

25. Cf. B. McDowell, Foreign Personal Representatives 95 (1957).

26. U.P.C. § 3–602. See generally Vestal, Multi–State Estates Under the Uniform Probate Code, 9 Creighton L. Rev. 529 (1976); Comment, The Need for Reform in Multistate Estate Administration, 55 Tex. L. Rev. 303 (1977).

27. U.P.C. § 4–301.

28. U.P.C. § 3–703(c).

29. U.P.C. § 4–302.

30. U.P.C. § 4–401.

31. See, e.g., Propst v. Fisher, 313 F.2d 248 (6th Cir.1963); see supra § 22.10. Cf. In

re Estate of Muscillo, 139 A.D.2d 429, 527 N.Y.S.2d 20 (1988).

32. Propst v. Fisher, 313 F.2d 248, 250 (6th Cir.1963). See also Leighton v. Roper, 300 N.Y. 434, 91 N.E.2d 876 (1950). Cf. Michigan Trust Co. v. Ferry, 228 U.S. 346, 33 S.Ct. 550, 57 L.Ed. 867 (1913); Peare v. Griggs, 8 N.Y.2d 44, 201 N.Y.S.2d 326, 167 N.E.2d 734 (1960). But cf. Restatement, Second, Conflict of Laws § 356 (1971); York v. Bank of Commerce & Trust Co., 19 Tenn. App. 594, 93 S.W.2d 333 (1936).

Texas long-arm would have reached the decedent, we do not believe it withered on his death.[33]

Effective resolution of a matter *inter partes* may make litigation away from the place of appointment more appropriate. It is usually better that such litigation be in control of the domiciliary representative, who normally has a protective interest in the estate, than an ancillary one appointed on the petition of the plaintiff. Hardships upon defendant foreign personal representatives may reasonably be alleviated by application of the doctrine of forum non conveniens. In short, there seems no reason why a personal representative should not be sued under essentially the same circumstances that any non-resident person or entity could be sued or whenever the decedent was subject to the jurisdiction on the cause of action in litigation.

7. *Privity Between Foreign Representatives*

§ **22.20** Rather than attempting to sue a foreign personal representative, as discussed in the previous section, suppose the foreign suit was brought against a representative who had qualified in the state in which the suit was brought. This representative may have been another individual, or, as commonly occurs, the representative appointed at the domicile may also have qualified as representative in the foreign state. Suppose judgment on the claim in the foreign state was rendered against the representative, but not paid. Now the claimant seeks to collect locally. Shall he proceed upon his original claim or can he rely upon his foreign adjudication of the matter as conclusive of the obligation?

The historically limited view of a personal representative's standing together with the in rem concept of estate administration has created uncertainties regarding the effect of prior litigation. Numerically, most of the cases have required the plaintiff to present and prove his original claim and the judgment against the foreign representative has been denied local effect.[1] Illustrating the traditional view, the Maine court stated in *Nash v. Benari:*[2]

> Where administrations of the estates of the same intestate are granted to different persons in different states, they are so far deemed independent of each other, that a judgment obtained against one will furnish no right of action against the other, to affect assets received by the latter in virtue of his own administration; for in

33. Eubank Heights Apartments, Limited v. Lebow, 615 F.2d 571, 573 (1st Cir. 1980), Cf. V–1 Oil Co. v. Ranck, 767 P.2d 612 (Wyo.1989).

§ 22.20

1. Stacy v. Thrasher, 47 U.S. (6 How.) 44, 12 L.Ed. 337 (1848); Johnson v. Powers, 139 U.S. 156, 11 S.Ct. 525, 35 L.Ed. 112 (1891); Johnson v. McKinnon, 129 Ala. 223, 29 So. 696 (1901); Richards v. Blaisdell, 12 Cal.App. 101, 106 P. 732 (1909) (noted 23 Harv. L. Rev. 565 (1910)); Strauss v. Phillips, 189 Ill. 9, 59 N.E. 560 (1901); Cresswell v. Slack, 68 Iowa 110, 26 N.W. 42 (1885); Nash v. Benari, 117 Me. 491, 105 A. 107 (1918); Braithwaite v. Harvel, 14 Mont. 208, 36 P. 38 (1894); State v. Fulton, 49 S.W. 297 (Tenn.Ch.App.1898). See also Restatement, Second, Conflict of Laws § 356 (1971).

2. 117 Me. 491, 105 A. 107 (1918).

contemplation of law there is no privity between him and the other administrator.... [T]he fact that one and the same person is administrator in both states does not alter the doctrine.... The two administrations are entirely unrestricted by each other....[3]

This attitude usually was not changed by the fact that the judgment was rendered in an action begun against the debtor in his lifetime, and continued, after his death, against the representative appointed where the action has been pending.[4] While most of the cases are quite old, some indirect support continues for the view they represent.[5]

That the historical view makes for inconvenience is apparent. It compels a creditor to select the particular administration where there are sufficient assets to pay in full all claims presented there, or to be prepared to establish repeatedly the facts upon which he bases his claim as many times as he has to prove it in order to collect. Contrary to basic concepts of justice, one trial does not end the litigation. It is submitted that this traditional view is based on theories of sovereignty having little place in the mobile society of a federal nation like the United States.[6]

Courts have applied this restrictive view to a judgment in the domiciliary state against a domiciliary administrator as against an ancillary administrator in another state,[7] to a judgment in another state against an ancillary administrator as against the domiciliary representative,[8] and to a judgment against an administrator with the will annexed as against the domiciliary administrator.[9] The concept that the representative of the decedent in one state is not in privity with the representative appointed in another is demonstrated in other situations as well. Thus, a judgment against an ancillary administrator in an action brought by him in one state did not preclude the administrator in another state from suing upon the claim.[10] The fact, however, that the

3. 117 Me. 491, 105 A. at 108 (1918).

4. Brown v. Fletcher's Estate, 146 Mich. 401, 109 N.W. 686 (1906), affirmed 210 U.S. 82, 28 S.Ct. 702, 52 L.Ed. 966 (1908). But see Creighton v. Murphy, Neal & Co., 8 Neb. 349, 1 N.W. 138 (1879).

5. Cf. Leonard v. Wharton, 268 F.Supp. 715 (D.Md.1967), appeal dismissed 396 F.2d 452 (4th Cir.1968), cert. denied, 393 U.S. 1028, 89 S.Ct. 624, 21 L.Ed.2d 571 (1969) (local statute of limitations barred action); In re Rettig's Estate, 8 Ohio Misc. 38, 216 N.E.2d 924 (Ohio Prob.1964) (local non-claim barred action).

6. See Stacy v. Thrasher, 47 U.S. (6 How.) 44, 12 L.Ed. 337 (1848) ("The different administrators deriving authority, as such, from different sovereignties are independent of each other and acquire rights over different assets, except as the residuums of ancillary administrations may by transmission to the primary administration become assets thereof"); see also McCord v. Thompson, 92 Ind. 565 (1884).

7. Cresswell v. Slack, 68 Iowa 110, 26 N.W. 42 (1885); Nash v. Benari, 117 Me. 491, 105 A. 107 (1918).

8. Stacy v. Thrasher, 47 U.S. (6 How.) 44, 12 L.Ed. 337 (1848); Braithwaite v. Harvel, 14 Mont. 208, 36 P. 38 (1894). Cf. First National Bank of Brush, Colorado v. Blessing, 231 Mo.App. 288, 98 S.W.2d 149 (1936) (recovery of judgment against ancillary administration held no bar to proof of same claim against domiciliary executor).

9. Brown v. Fletcher's Estate, 146 Mich. 401, 109 N.W. 686 (1906), affirmed 210 U.S. 82, 28 S.Ct. 702, 52 L.Ed. 966 (1908). Cf. Restatement, Second, Conflict of Laws § 353 (1971).

10. Ingersoll v. Coram, 211 U.S. 335, 29 S.Ct. 92, 53 L.Ed. 208 (1908) (noted 9 Colum. L. Rev. 248 (1909)). See also Aspden v. Nixon, 45 U.S. (4 How.) 467, 11 L.Ed. 1059 (1846).

prosecution of the claim is barred by the statute of limitations or non-claim in one state where there has been administration of decedent's property traditionally would not preclude an action upon the claim in another where the statute has not run,[11] but of course, under the borrowing concept, an ancillary state may bar a claim if it is barred at the domicile.[12]

A distinction making for a significant exception has been drawn in the case of a judgment secured against a foreign executor, a distinction having its origin in the source of title. "The executor's interest in the testator's estate is what the testator gives him. That of an administrator is only that which the law of his appointment enjoins."[13] Because of this difference, it has been held that there is privity between executors of the same decedent. Thus, where the same person was executor in two states, a judgment rendered against him in the court of primary administration was conclusive in the courts where the administration was ancillary.[14] Since the question is the effect that must be given in one state in the United States to a judgment of the court in another, the United States Supreme Court has the final authority upon it as an application of the Full Faith and Credit Clause of the Constitution. In *Hill v. Tucker*[15] the rule was laid down that there was privity between the executors of the same decedent and that a judgment against one in one state was prima facie controlling in an action against another in a different state. In the later case of *Carpenter v. Strange*[16] the Supreme Court held that a judgment in a state court against an executrix, at the domicile of the testator, was conclusive against the executrix in another state, where letters testamentary were later taken out, in a suit between the same parties for the same purpose. These early cases recognized that the need for ending litigation in administration was as great as elsewhere. In a subsequent case, however, it was held that there was no denial of full faith and credit when Michigan refused effect, as against the Michigan

---

11. Borer v. Chapman, 119 U.S. 587, 7 S.Ct. 342, 30 L.Ed. 532 (1887); Leonard v. Wharton, 268 F.Supp. 715 (D.Md.1967); appeal dismissed 396 F.2d 452 (4th Cir.1968), cert. denied 393 U.S. 1028, 89 S.Ct. 624, 21 L.Ed.2d 571 (1969); Wilson v. Hartford Fire Insurance Co., 164 Fed. 817 (8th Cir.1908); In re Rettig's Estate, 8 Ohio Misc. 38, 216 N.E.2d 924 (Ohio Prob.1964). Cf. Wilson's Estate v. National Bank of Commerce, 364 So.2d 1117 (Miss.1978). See supra §§ 3.9–3.12.

12. See, e.g., U.P.C. § 3–803(a).

13. Hill v. Tucker, 54 U.S. (13 How.) 458, 14 L.Ed. 223 (1851). See the discussion in Helme v. Buckelew, 229 N.Y. 363, 128 N.E. 216 (1920).

14. Owsley v. Central Trust Co., 196 Fed. 412 (S.D.N.Y.1912); Garland's Administrator v. Garland's Administrator, 84 Va. 181, 4 S.E. 334 (1887); Restatement, Second, Conflict of Laws § 353 (1971). See Carpenter v. Strange, 141 U.S. 87, 11 S.Ct. 960, 35 L.Ed. 640 (1891). In Louisiana it has been held that a judgment against an executor may be enforced against him in another state in which he has been appointed executor, Turley v. Dreyfus, 33 La.Ann. 885 (1881); and in two cases an executor was allowed to be sued personally on a judgment rendered against him in another state. Latine v. Clements, 3 Ga. 426 (1847); White v. Archbill, 34 Tenn. (2 Sneed) 588 (1855).

15. 54 U.S. (13 How.) 458, 14 L.Ed. 223 (1851). See Hopper v. Hopper, 125 N.Y. 400, 26 N.E. 457 (1891).

16. 141 U.S. 87, 11 S.Ct. 960, 35 L.Ed. 640 (1891). Cf. Holt, Extension of Non-Resident Motorist Statutes to Non-Resident Personal Representatives, 101 U. Pa. L. Rev. 223 (1952).

domiciliary executor, to a judgment against the administrator c.t.a. of the same decedent in another state.[17]

It would be convenient and just to have one adjudication of a matter settle it, but no more so with executors than administrators. Under statutes in most states, the common law distinction between executors and administrators has long largely been abandoned.[18] "Naming one as executor does not make him one, but gives him the right to become such by complying with the conditions of the statute."[19] "And, though an executor receives his power by the will of the testator, ... the validity of his acts in that capacity depend wholly on the probation of the will ... within the limits of that jurisdiction in which he claims the power to act."[20] The authority of both the executor and administrator would seem to be limited by the appointing state in just the same way, and the same seems equally true of the liabilities imposed. The alleged distinction between the cases in which one person is qualified as executor in both states and that in which a judgment against an administrator c.t.a. is sought to be forced against an executor does not rest upon any satisfactory reason.[21] The view favoring privity as in the earlier cases of *Hill and Carpenter*[22] is to be preferred.

The development of jurisdictional concepts under long-arm statutes[23] is a recognition of the changed circumstances in our society brought about by easy mobility. Sixty or more years ago, a defendant, with personal impunity might choose to stay out of litigation in a state in which he owned property involved in a contract or a tort action. Today, one cannot safely assume such freedom from risk beyond the assets there located. The situation is no different in the administration of estates. The domiciliary representative should, in most cases, be party to suits elsewhere and cannot safely avoid doing so. The statutory trend in permitting suits against personal representatives demonstrates a similar development in the personal representative cases as[24] has occurred in jurisdiction generally. From this it can be expected that once jurisdiction is established over a foreign personal representative that the resulting judgment will be enforced.[25]

The more recent development in the policy of terminating litigation under the concepts of res judicata and preclusion by prior litigation have been reflected in some estate administration cases. Rather clearly, decrees reviewing or approving accounts of fiduciaries are conclusive else-

17. Brown v. Fletcher's Estate, 210 U.S. 82, 28 S.Ct. 702, 52 L.Ed. 966 (1908).

18. 1 Woerner, The American Law of Administration § 172 (3d ed. 1923).

19. In re Birkholz's Estate, 197 N.W. 896 (Iowa 1924). Almost identical language is found in Stagg v. Green, 47 Mo. 500 (1871).

20. Hobart v. Connecticut Turnpike Co., 15 Conn. 145, 147 (1842).

21. See Note, 10 Colum. L. Rev. 248 (1910).

22. See supra nn.15–16.

23. See supra § 5.14.

24. See A. Ehrenzweig on Conflict of Laws §§ 23, 64 (1962). See also supra § 22.19.

25. See Eubank Heights Apartments, Limited v. Lebow, 615 F.2d 571 (1st Cir. 1980). Cf. Saporita v. Litner, 371 Mass. 607, 358 N.E.2d 809 (1976); V–1 Oil Co. v. Ranck, 767 P.2d 612 (Wyo.1989).

where.[26] The Supreme Court has precluded parties by prior litigation in a probate court even though substantive issues were involved, without concern over the status of the personal representatives.[27] Further, in *Durfee v. Duke*,[28] the Supreme Court indicated that the policy of preclusion by prior litigation was relevant in any kind of case and there applied it to in rem jurisdiction over land. In *Peare v. Griggs*, the New York Court of Appeals put it more directly and held that a New York administratrix who had litigated the negligence of her intestate in Virginia "had her full day in court in Virginia in a representative capacity ... and was properly barred from relitigating the same issues...."[29] Just as the Supreme Court makes no distinction between litigation based on in rem or in personam jurisdiction, the concepts of preclusion by prior litigation should be applicable in the administration of decedent's estates as well. This recognition of real parties in interest and the ordinary policies of preclusion would make litigation in multi-state estates less expensive and the outcome more predictable.[30]

Under the policies of preclusion by prior litigation, it may make a difference who is plaintiff and what result is reached in the first case. Suppose a creditor presents a claim against the estate and it is disallowed, judgment being entered against the claimant. That claimant should be barred from prosecuting the same claim against the representative in another state. It is submitted that the cases involving a judicial rejection of the claim of a creditor are distinguishable from that of an allowance of the claim; additional reasons exist for giving rejection in

---

26. A judgment against the personal representative for breach of duty has long been given full faith and credit. See Michigan Trust Co. v. Ferry, 228 U.S. 346, 33 S.Ct. 550, 57 L.Ed. 867 (1913). See also DiMauro v. Pavia, 492 F.Supp. 1051 (D.Conn.1979), affirmed 614 F.2d 1286 (2d Cir.1979); Krimsky v. Lombardi, 78 Misc.2d 685, 357 N.Y.S.2d 671 (Sup. Ct. 1974), aff'd 51 A.D.2d 600, 377 N.Y.S.2d 785 (1976).

27. Treinies v. Sunshine Mining Co., 308 U.S. 66, 60 S.Ct. 44, 84 L.Ed. 85 (1939). Cf. Riley v. New York Trust Co., 315 U.S. 343, 62 S.Ct. 608, 86 L.Ed. 885 (1942).

28. 375 U.S. 106, 84 S.Ct. 242, 11 L.Ed.2d 186 (1963). See supra § 8.4. Cf. Underwriters National Assurance Co. v. North Carolina Life and Accident etc., 455 U.S. 691, 102 S.Ct. 1357, 71 L.Ed.2d 558 (1982); Morris v. Jones, 329 U.S. 545, 67 S.Ct. 451, 91 L.Ed. 488 (1947).

29. Peare v. Griggs, 8 N.Y.2d 44, 201 N.Y.S.2d 326, 167 N.E.2d 734, 736 (1960). See also Benker v. Meyer, 154 Fed. 290 (C.C.A.Neb.1907); Owsley v. Central Trust Co., 196 Fed. 412 (S.D.N.Y.1912); McCord v. Smith, 43 So.2d 704 (Fla.1949); Latine v. Clements, 3 Ga. (3 Kelly) 426, 430 (1847);

In re Fischer's Estate. 118 N.J.Eq. 599, 180 A. 633 (1935); Valley National Bank v. Siebrand, 74 Ariz. 54, 243 P.2d 771 (1952); In re Buss' Estate, 71 S.D. 529, 26 N.W.2d 700 (1947). For a criticism of the privity concept in the general area of decedent's and debtor's estates, see Note, The Statutory Successor, the Receiver, and the Executor in Conflict of Laws, 44 Colum. L. Rev. 549 (1944). On the problem see also generally Hopkins, Conflict of Laws in Administration of Decedents' Intangibles (pt. 1), 28 Iowa L. Rev. 422 (1943); Hopkins, The Extraterritorial Effect of Probate Decrees, 53 Yale L.J. 221 (1944). Note, Full Faith and Credit to Judgments Against Estate Representatives, 48 Iowa L. Rev. 93 (1962). For statutory development see Uniform Probate Code § 4–401 which provides: "An adjudication rendered in any jurisdiction in favor of or against any personal representative of the estate is as binding on the local personal representative as if he were a party to the adjudication."

30. However, merely because the same person is the representative of multiple estates does not put the *estates* in privity. See, e.g., Jaramillo v. Burkhart, 999 F.2d 1241 (8th Cir.1993).

this situation conclusive effect in other states. While this distinction has not been discussed by the courts, it would nevertheless seem valid. In any quasi in rem action for the application of property to the payment of a debt, the court's jurisdiction over the defendant is limited by the property attached.[31] However, the plaintiff is personally in court and is subject to no restriction. This is illustrated by the well accepted principle that credit for the first recovery must be allowed in any subsequent suit. And it is consistent with the doctrine of submission to the jurisdiction of a court by one seeking its assistance in his behalf.[32] Consequently, since a judgment against a creditor is one in which personal jurisdiction over the losing party exists, it should be treated as conclusive of his cause of action in any subsequent suit. So far as the creditor is concerned, there is no defect possible by reason of any conceptualistic privity.[33] If a payment of a claim is made by any personal representative, it is discharged. The rejection of a claim on the merits should bar the creditor since, like payment, it goes to the existence of his claim and any personal representative should have the benefit of it. The policies affording the creditor a reasonable opportunity to obtain enforcement of his claim are satisfied; he has had his day in court and there seems no reason why he should be given another.[34]

This approach of binding the creditor by a rejection of his claim in the courts of another state rests, of course, upon a decision on the merits. If the claim were disallowed by the courts at the domicile, or elsewhere, because it was filed too late, or a local statute of limitations has run against it, the claim would not be barred on this theory of res judicata.[35] A bar in such a case would rest upon other considerations of policy. Likewise excluded from this particular argument are cases in which the prior disallowance is of a nonjudicial nature, such as a rejection by the personal representative which has not received court approval to give it the character of a judgment.[36]

Whenever, under general principles of common law, recovery of a judgment merges or so affects the original cause of action that no suit can thereafter be maintained on the latter,[37] recovery of a judgment by

---

31. Restatement, Second, Judgments §§ 8, 9, 30 (1980); cf. Shaffer v. Heitner, 433 U.S. 186, 97 S.Ct. 2569, 53 L.Ed.2d 683 (1977); Harris v. Balk, 198 U.S. 215, 25 S.Ct. 625, 49 L.Ed. 1023 (1905). See also Ward v. Boyce, 152 N.Y. 191, 46 N.E. 180 (1897); Scoles, Conflict of Laws and Creditors' Rights in Decedents' Estates, 42 Iowa L. Rev. 341 (1957).

32. Adam v. Saenger, 303 U.S. 59, 58 S.Ct. 454, 82 L.Ed. 649 (1938).

33. Cf. Grasser v. Blakkolb, 12 Wash. App. 529, 530 P.2d 684 (1975). But cf. Ingersoll v. Coram, 211 U.S. 335, 29 S.Ct. 92, 53 L.Ed. 208 (1908).

34. Goodall v. Marshall, 14 N.H. 161 (1843). Cf. Gunn v. Giraudo, 48 Cal.App.2d 622, 120 P.2d 177 (1941); Taylor v. Barron, 35 N.H. 484 (1857) (no litigation on merits); Groome v. Leatherwood, 240 N.C. 573, 83 S.E.2d 536 (1954); Appleton's Estate, 81 D. & C. 85, 67 Montg. Co. L. Rep. 181 (Pa. 1951). See also Sanborn v. Perry, 86 Wis. 361, 56 N.W. 337 (1893); Restatement, Second, Conflict of Laws § 357 (1971).

35. Cowden v. Jacobson, 165 Mass. 240, 43 N.E. 98 (1896); Buckingham Hotel Co. v. Kimberly, 138 Miss. 445, 103 So. 213 (1925). See also infra §§ 24.24–24.26.

36. E.g., Taylor v. Barron, 35 N.H. 484 (1857).

37. See infra §§ 24.1–24.2.

either an executor or an administrator has prevented suit on the original claim by another executor or administrator.[38]

D. CREDITORS' CLAIMS—PROOF AND PAYMENT

§ 22.21 As a general rule, all creditors, foreign as well as local, are permitted to prove their claims in any state in which an estate administration is conducted.[1] Each state in which proceedings are held determines in accordance with its own internal law the time allowed for proving claims[2] and the manner of proving them.[3] These limitations and procedures apply equally to both resident and non-resident creditors.[4] Most questions of priority in the payment of claims, in both the domiciliary and ancillary jurisdictions, are usually assumed to be determined by the law of the forum.[5] In the absence of proof that they have received something abroad, foreign creditors are allowed, according to the rule generally followed, to come in on the same basis as local creditors of the same class.[6] In a few cases it has been held that they may not do so in an

38. Lewis v. Adams, 70 Cal. 403, 11 P. 833 (1886); Restatement, Second, Conflict of Laws § 352 (1971).

§ 22.21

1. Restatement, Second, Conflict of Laws § 342 (1971).

2. Propst v. Fisher, 313 F.2d 248 (6th Cir.1963); Restatement, Second, Conflict of Laws § 345 (1971). A claim barred by the statute of limitations or non-claim of the domicile often may be proved in ancillary proceedings if not barred by the statute of the latter state. Borer v. Chapman, 119 U.S. 587, 7 S.Ct. 342, 30 L.Ed. 532 (1887); Owsley v. Bowden, 161 Ga. 884, 132 S.E. 70 (1926); Owens v. Saville's Estate, 409 S.W.2d 660 (Mo.1966). Cf. Estate of Wilson v. National Bank of Commerce, 364 So.2d 1117 (Miss.1978). And a claim barred by the statute of the forum may not be proved, although the period allowed by the domiciliary law has not elapsed. Leach v. Leach, 238 Mass. 100, 130 N.E. 262 (1921). Cf. Slater v. Stoffel, 313 F.2d 175 (7th Cir. 1963), cert. denied 375 U.S. 818, 84 S.Ct. 54, 11 L.Ed.2d 53 (1963); Oates v. Morningside College, 217 Iowa 1059, 252 N.W. 783 (1934) (noted 20 Iowa L. Rev. 690 (1935)). There has been some movement toward barring claims in ancillary administration that are previously barred at the decedent's domicile. See, e.g., Wimpfheimer v. Goldsmith, 298 A.2d 778 (Del.Ch.1972); U.P.C. § 3–803(a). Tulsa Professional Collection Services, Inc. v. Pope, 485 U.S. 478, 108 S.Ct. 1340, 99 L.Ed.2d 565 (1988), appeal after remand 808 P.2d 640 (Okla.1990) applied Mullane v. Central Hanover Bank & Trust Co., 339 U.S. 306, 70 S.Ct. 652, 94 L.Ed. 865 (1950) to require notice other than by publication to sustain a two month non-claim period as against known or reasonably ascertainable creditors.

3. Restatement, Second, Conflict of Laws § 346 (1971). See also Duehay v. Acacia Mutual Life Insurance Co., 105 F.2d 768 (D.C.Cir.1939); In re Hirsch's Estate, 146 Ohio St. 393, 66 N.E.2d 636 (1946).

4. Messenger v. Rutherford, 80 Ill. App.2d 25, 225 N.E.2d 94 (1967); Continental Coffee Co. v. Clark's Estate, 84 Nev. 208, 438 P.2d 818 (1968); Gardner Hotel Supply v. Clark's Estate, 83 Nev. 388, 432 P.2d 495 (1967).

5. Smith v. Union Bank of Georgetown, 30 U.S. (5 Pet.) 518, 8 L.Ed. 212 (1831); 1 Woerner, The American Law of Administration § 166 (3d ed. 1923); Restatement, Second, Conflict of Laws § 344 (1971). One state of the United States may not, however, give to its own citizens a preference not accorded to citizens of other states. Blake v. McClung, 172 U.S. 239, 19 S.Ct. 165, 43 L.Ed. 432 (1898). The actual results as to exemptions and priorities vary but forum law predominates. See Scoles, Conflict of Laws and Creditors' Rights in Decedents' Estates, 42 Iowa L. Rev. 341, 354 (1957).

6. McKee v. Dodd, 152 Cal. 637, 93 P. 854 (1908); McCord v. Smith, 43 So.2d 704 (Fla.1949); Miner v. Austin, 45 Iowa 221 (1876); In re McDougald's Estate, 272 App. Div. 176, 70 N.Y.S.2d 200 (3d Dept.1947); Tyler v. Thompson, 44 Tex. 497, 23 Am. Rep. 600 (1876); In re Hanreddy's Estate, 176 Wis. 570, 186 N.W. 744 (1922). Cf. Pirkle v. Cassity, 104 F.Supp. 318 (E.D.Tex.

ancillary administration but this seems to be on a theory of forum non conveniens.[7] An ancillary administrator may be authorized to sell land to pay debts proved in the state of ancillary administration, notwithstanding the personal estate at the domicile has not been exhausted.[8] Payment by any personal representative, of course, discharges the claim as to all.[9]

Suppose the decedent left insufficient property to pay all his debts. Since the administration is a separate affair in each state, should the court disregard as irrelevant whatever may be the general situation and order payment of distribution as though the problems of the local administration were the only ones to consider? The authorities show a disposition to regard the estate as a whole in order to do justice to creditors, even though otherwise courts often treat each administration as separate.[10] Distribution will not be ordered at the place of ancillary administration, where it is shown that there are unpaid creditors at the domicile and insufficient assets to pay them.[11] Where a creditor has received a dividend from the ancillary administration, this will be counted before he can share in a payment at the place of domiciliary administration, there being insufficient funds to pay all in full.[12] Local land has been ordered sold, even where there were no local debts, in order that the fund could be transmitted to the place of principal administration, where the funds were insufficient to pay creditors.[13]

A leading case holds that, where the estate is insolvent, "the several courts administering the affairs of the deceased, each being apprised of that situation, must no longer consider the assets within their respective controls as separate and distinct funds for distribution to the creditors within such jurisdiction, but as one entire fund, in which all creditors of the deceased having just claims of equal standing shall share pro rata."[14]

1952); Restatement, Second, Conflict of Laws § 342 (1971).

7. See Wedemann v. United States Trust Co., 258 N.Y. 315, 179 N.E. 712 (1932). Cf. V–1 Oil Co. v. Ranck, 767 P.2d 612 (Wyo.1989).

8. Rosenthal v. Renick, 44 Ill. 202 (1867); Cowden v. Jacobson, 165 Mass. 240, 43 N.E. 98 (1896); Lawrence's Appeal, 49 Conn. 411 (1881).

9. Schneller v. Vance, 8 La. 506 (1835); In re Cohen's Estate, 149 Misc. 765, 269 N.Y.S. 235 (Surr. 1933). Cf. Blondell v. Blondell, 157 Md. 15, 145 A. 184 (1929); In re Estate of Diederichs, 255 Wis. 221, 38 N.W.2d 489 (1949).

10. See discussion in Dawes v. Head, 20 Mass. (3 Pick.) 128 (1825); U.P.C. § 3–815. But see Owsley v. Bowden, 161 Ga. 884, 132 S.E. 70 (1926).

11. In re Gable's Estate, 79 Iowa 178, 44 N.W. 352 (1890); In re Branholt's Estate, 9 Mich.App. 504, 157 N.W.2d 488 (1968); Restatement, Second, Conflict of Laws § 348 (1971); Nadelmann, Insolvent Decedents' Estates, 49 Mich. L. Rev. 1129 (1951). Cf. Suydam v. Suydam, 404 F.2d 1332 (D.C.Cir.1968).

12. Ramsey v. Ramsey, 196 Ill. 179, 63 N.E. 618 (1902). But a creditor who has received full payment in the ancillary jurisdiction cannot be compelled by the court of the domicile of the decedent to refund a part of what he has received. Schneller v. Vance, 8 La. 506, 28 Am.Dec. 140 (1835).

13. Dow v. Lillie, 26 N.D. 512, 144 N.W. 1082 (1914).

14. In re Hanreddy's Estate, 176 Wis. 570, 186 N.W. 744, 746 (1922). See Sackett, Chapman, Brown & Cross v. Osgood, 149 F.2d 825 (D.C.Cir.1945); Hilliard v. Colclazier, 122 Colo. 60, 220 P.2d 353 (1950); In re Winter's Estate, 136 N.J.Eq. 112, 40 A.2d 648 (1945); In re Van Bokkelen's Estate, 282 N.Y. 687, 26 N.E.2d 814 (1940); In re Hirsch's Estate, 146 Ohio St. 393, 66 N.E.2d 636 (1946); In re Maxwell's Estate, 55 Montg. Co. L.R. 154 (Pa. 1939); See also Estate of Radu, 35 Ohio App.2d 187, 301

Although local assets were sufficient to pay local creditors in full, they were allowed only such proportion of their claims as the total assets bore to the total liabilities. Another court, however, which adopted the same rule, has held that until local creditors have received the entire share of their claims to which they are entitled, foreign creditors may be denied participation in local assets.[15] The solutions of some of the questions presented involve serious practical difficulties,[16] but the efforts to treat all creditors equally is not only to be commended, but is probably required by the Constitution.[17]

E. SPOUSAL AND FAMILY ALLOWANCES

§ 22.22 Statutes frequently make provision for payments out of the property of a decedent as an allowance to the surviving spouse or spouse and minor children, not by way of a distributive share of the estate, but in addition to it. The purpose is to provide for support during administration in the emergency created by the loss of the decedent. The general conditions governing the granting or withholding of the allowance need not concern us here,[1] but usually the award is viewed as governed by the law of the decedent's domicile and granted in administration there.[2] Should family allowance be ordered at the place of ancillary administration of a decedent's estate in some circumstances? When the surviving spouse as well as the decedent is a nonresident, an allowance has often been denied in ancillary administration,[3] the idea

N.E.2d 263, 266 (1973). Other instances of treating the estate as a whole may be found where no question of insolvency is presented. Thus, in paying legacies, legatees were compelled to account for what they had received upon intestate distribution in California property. Whalley v. Lawrence's Estate, 93 Vt. 424, 108 A. 387 (1919). Cf. Tod v. Mitchell, 228 Mass. 541, 117 N.E. 899 (1917). But cf. In re Estate of Gibbs, 73 Wyo. 425, 280 P.2d 556 (1955).

15. In re Estate of Brauns, 276 Mich. 598, 268 N.W. 890 (1936).

16. See 1 Woerner, The American Law of Administration § 167 (3d ed. 1923).

17. See Blake v. McClung, 172 U.S. 239, 19 S.Ct. 165, 43 L.Ed. 432 (1898). The liquidation, reorganization or rehabilitation of insurance carriers has occasioned analogous multi-state problems in state receivership proceedings. However, the states were more prompt in dealing with multi-state insurers than administration of multi-state estates of decedents. For example, widespread enactment of the Uniform Insurers Liquidation Act (1939), 13 U.L.A. [Master ed.] 429, has provided extensive cooperation among the states that has the effect of centralizing proceedings at the insurer's home office even where ancillary adminis-

tration is appropriate. See G. C. Murphy Co. v. Reserve Ins. Co., 54 N.Y.2d 69, 444 N.Y.S.2d 592, 429 N.E.2d 111 (1981). See also Underwriters National Assurance v. North Carolina Life & Accident etc., 455 U.S. 691, 102 S.Ct. 1357, 71 L.Ed.2d 558 (1982); Morris v. Jones, 329 U.S. 545, 67 S.Ct. 451, 91 L.Ed. 488 (1947); Cheatham, The Statutory Successors, The Receiver and Executor in Conflict of Laws, 44 Col. L. Rev. 549 (1944).

§ 22.22

1. For general discussion see 1 Woerner, The American Law of Administration § 89 (3d ed. 1923). See also Scoles, Conflict of Laws and Nonbarrable Interests in Administration of Decedents' Estates, 8 Fla. U. L. Rev. 151, 172 (1955); Scoles, Choice of Law in Family Property Transactions, 209 Recueil des Cours, 17 (1988–II).

2. In re Plazza's Estate, 34 Colo.App. 296, 526 P.2d 155 (1974); Matter of Nikiporez's Estate, 19 Wn.App. 231, 574 P.2d 1204 (1978); Cf. Moore v. Moore, 430 S.W.2d 247 (Tex.Civ.App.1968). See generally U.P.C. § 2–403 (model law with a $10,000 family exemption).

3. Lyons v. Egan, 107 Colo. 32, 108 P.2d 873 (1940); Smith v. Howard, 86 Me. 203,

being that this is a matter of local regulation for the domicile to determine. In some instances, the spouse has been permitted, at the ancillary administration, the allowance which was payable under the domiciliary law.[4] In a few cases in which the widow was a resident, though the husband was a nonresident who had wrongfully abandoned her, it was held that the widow was entitled to an allowance out of local property,[5] a result seemingly in accordance with the purpose of the statute in providing for support. But a nonresident spouse has usually been denied a local allowance, on the ground that the statute was not applicable to nonresidents.[6] This latter view can often frustrate the family protection policies of both states as a result of fortuitous location of assets. To avoid this, several states have granted allowances to nonresident claimants of nonresident decedents.[7] It would seem that the domiciliary law should determine the award and it should be payable from the ancillary assets to the extent those at the domicile are inadequate.[8] At least the minimum award of either the domicile or the ancillary state should be made in ancillary administration if it is in control of the assets from which such an award may be made.

III. ACCOUNTING AND DISTRIBUTION

§ **22.23** The ancillary representative is obliged to account to the court that appointed the representative.[1] If, in accordance with the order of that court, the representative transmits the balance remaining to the domiciliary representative, his responsibility as ancillary representative ceases.[2] Nor does the accountability in the state of ancillary administration extend to assets received by a person as principal administrator in the state of the domicile.[3] To this extent administration of the estate in each state is an independent matter resulting from the reasonable

29 A. 1008 (1894); In re Metcalf's Estate, 93 Mont. 542, 19 P.2d 905 (1933).

4. See In re Plazza's Estate, 34 Colo. App. 296, 526 P.2d 155 (1974); Smith v. Howard, 86 Me. 203, 29 A. 1008 (1894); Simpson v. Cureton, 97 N.C. 112, 2 S.E. 668 (1887). But see Smith v. Smith, 174 Ill. 52, 50 N.E. 1083 (1898) (not recoverable when not allowed by local law); Gaskins v. Gaskins, 311 Ky. 59, 223 S.W.2d 374 (1949); In re Schram's Estate, 132 Neb. 268, 271 N.W. 694 (1937).

5. See Wright v. Roberts, 116 Ga. 194, 42 S.E. 369 (1902); Jones v. Layne, 144 N.C. 600, 57 S.E. 372 (1907); Hyder v. Hyder, 16 Tenn.App. 64, 66 S.W.2d 235 (1932).

6. See In re Beauchamp's Estate, 23 Del.Ch. 377, 2 A.2d 900 (Orph. 1938); In re Zimmerman's Estate, 195 Minn. 38, 261 N.W. 467 (1935); Jaeglin v. Moakley, 236 Mo.App. 254, 151 S.W.2d 524 (1941); Krumenacker v. Andis, 38 N.D. 500, 165 N.W. 524 (1917) (noted 18 Colum. L. Rev. 494 (1918), 2 Minn. L. Rev. 390 (1918)).

7. In re Foreman's Estate, 16 Cal. App.2d 96, 60 P.2d 310 (1936); In re McCombs' Estate, 52 O.L.A. 353, 80 N.E.2d 573 (Ohio Prob.1948); In re Pugh's Estate, 22 Wn.2d 83, 154 P.2d 308 (1944).

8. See In re Plazza's Estate, 34 Colo. App. 296, 526 P.2d 155 (1974).

§ 22.23

1. Lawton v. National Surety Co., 248 Mass. 440, 143 N.E. 333 (1924); Groome v. Leatherwood, 240 N.C. 573, 83 S.E.2d 536 (1954); In re Crawford, 68 Ohio St. 58, 67 N.E. 156 (1903); Restatement, Second, Conflict of Laws § 362 (1971).

2. Emery v. Batchelder, 132 Mass. 452 (1882).

3. See Ware v. Ware, 302 Ky. 438, 194 S.W.2d 969 (1946); Fay v. Haven, 44 Mass. (3 Metc.) 109 (1841); Keenan v. Tonry, 91 N.H. 220, 16 A.2d 705 (1940); Wirgman v. Provident Life & Trust Co., 79 W.Va. 562, 92 S.E. 415 (1917); Restatement, Second, Conflict of Laws § 363 (1971).

allocation of judicial business. If in closing the ancillary administration, the balance of the assets are transmitted to the representative at the domicile of the decedent, that domiciliary representative must account for what is received.[4] The administration can be reopened in the state of principal administration, if necessary.[5]

After payment of claims and expenses of administration, the goods of one who died intestate are, by the general common law rule, distributed according to the rule of distribution of his domicile. If the decedent left a will, the domiciliary rule is usually the test of its validity.[6] The question then is raised whether the amount remaining, after payment of debts and expenses of ancillary administration, should be sent back to the principal administration for distribution. It is not necessary that distribution be made at the domicile just because that law is applied to determine how the distribution shall be made. If the general rule is not followed and assets are distributed according to the local rule and not that of the decedent's domicile, the balance probably will not be sent back to the domicile unless needed to pay debts.[7] Whether local distribution will be ordered or the balance sent to the place of principal administration is a question of judicial discretion in the individual case.[8] Ordinarily it will be ordered sent to the place of principal administration.[9] But if the legatees or distributees are local citizens and the principal administration is distant, the court will avoid needless expense

4. See In re Dana's Estate, 206 Misc. 408, 132 N.Y.S.2d 734 (Surr. 1954); In re Skeer's Estate, 249 Pa. 288, 95 A. 96 (1915); Conover & Co. v. Chapman, 2 Bailey 436 (S.C.App.1831). See also Jennison v. Hapgood, 27 Mass. (10 Pick.) 77 (1830). Cf. In re Patmore's Estate, 141 Cal.App.2d 416, 296 P.2d 863 (1956).

5. Leach v. Buckner, 19 W.Va. 36 (1881).

6. See supra §§ 20.3–20.4, 20.9–20.14.

7. Carroll v. McPike, 53 Miss. 569 (1876). Also proceeds of the sale of land need not be sent to the domicile for distribution. Smith v. Smith, 174 Ill. 52, 50 N.E. 1083 (1898).

8. Bedell v. Clark, 171 Mich. 486, 137 N.W. 627 (1912); Matter of Accounting of Hughes, 95 N.Y. 55 (1884); In re Bourne's Estate, 82 Misc.2d 824, 370 N.Y.S.2d 462 (1975); In re Meier's Estate, 33 Misc.2d 999, 226 N.Y.S.2d 733 (Surr. 1962); In re Radu's Estate, 35 Ohio App.2d 187, 301 N.E.2d 263 (1973); Restatement, Second, Conflict of Laws § 364 (1971). In Young v. Wittenmyre, 123 Ill. 303, 14 N.E. 869 (1888) it seems to be treated as obligatory. See Note, Disposal of Surplus Held by an Ancillary Administrator, 36 Harv. L. Rev. 608 (1923). The Uniform Probate Code provides:

Section 3–816. [Final Distribution to Domiciliary Representative.]

The estate of a non-resident decedent being administered by a personal representative appointed in this state shall, if there is a personal representative of the decedent's domicile willing to receive it, be distributed to the domiciliary personal representative for the benefit of the successors of the decedent unless (1) by virtue of the decedent's will, if any, and applicable choice-of-law rules, the successors are identified pursuant to the local law of this state without reference to the local law of the decedent's domicile; (2) the personal representative of this state, after reasonable inquiry, is unaware of the existence or identity of a domiciliary personal representative; or (3) the Court orders otherwise in a proceeding for a closing order under Section 3–1001 or incident to the closing of a supervised administration. In other cases, distribution of the estate of a decedent shall be made in accordance with the other Parts of this Article.

9. Lawrence v. Kitteridge, 21 Conn. 577, 56 Am. Dec. 385 (1852); In re Stacy's Estate, 131 Vt. 130, 300 A.2d 556 (1973).

and delay by allowing distributees[10] or legatees[11] their shares out of local assets. If the money is needed to pay creditors at the principal administration, local distribution will not be ordered.[12]

The testator's direction is usually deemed controlling should a preference be expressed for distribution in the state of ancillary or principal administration. Thus if the testator directs, the ancillary court will transmit to the domicile.[13] Likewise, the domiciliary court will transmit to an ancillary administration for distribution if so directed by the decedent.[14]

The greatest conflict-of-laws problem in administration of estates of decedents results from regarding administration in each state as separate. Even small estates can involve interests running across several state lines. Insistence upon the theory of the individual nature of administration in each state may increase administrative expenses wholly out of proportion to the size of the estate involved. The remedy would seem to lie in doing what the courts have already shown a disposition to do, i.e., to treat the estate as a whole wherever possible, and supplement this effort with statutory enactments from time to time, especially in the way of legislation securing uniformity in the rules of separate states.[15]

IV. GUARDIANS AND CONSERVATORS

A. IN GENERAL

§ 22.24   In the United States, the term "guardian" is sometimes used to denote both the individual who has custody and control of an

---

10. Harvey v. Richards, 11 F. Cas. 746, No. 6184 (D.Mass. 1818).

11. In re Meier's Estate, 33 Misc.2d 999, 226 N.Y.S.2d 733 (1962); Graveley v. Graveley, 25 S.C. 1, 60 Am.Rep. 478 (1886). Distribution may be made directly to foreign beneficiaries by transmitting funds to them. The so-called "Iron Curtain" statutes have purported to give the probate court power to refuse distribution to aliens resident in countries where the beneficiary may not receive the use of the funds. See In re Paroth's Estate, 72 Misc.2d 499, 340 N.Y.S.2d 433 (Surr. 1971); In re Sikorski's Estate, 54 Misc.2d 883, 283 N.Y.S.2d 794 (Surr. 1967). See also supra § 20.18; Evanoff, Payment of Estate Shares to Foreign Consuls, 52 Mich. St. B.J. 543 (1973).

12. In re Gable's Estate, 79 Iowa 178, 44 N.W. 352 (1890); In re Branholt's Estate, 9 Mich.App. 504, 157 N.W.2d 488 (1968).

13. See, e.g., Finch v. Reese, 28 Conn. Supp. 499, 268 A.2d 409 (1970).

14. See, e.g., Grasty v. Clare, 210 Va. 21, 168 S.E.2d 261 (1969).

15. See B. McDowell, Foreign Personal Representatives 187 (1957). This is the purpose of the Uniform Probate Code:

Section 1–102. [Purposes; Rule of Construction.]

(a) This Code shall be liberally construed and applied to promote its underlying purposes and policies.

(b) The underlying purposes and policies of this Code are:

(1) to simplify and clarify the law concerning the affairs of decedents, missing persons, protected persons, minors and incapacitated persons;

(2) to discover and make effective the intent of a decedent in the distribution of his property;

(3) to promote a speedy and efficient system for liquidating the estate of the decedent and making distribution to its successors;

(4) to facilitate use and enforcement of certain trusts;

(5) to make uniform the law among the various jurisdictions.

incapacitated or protected person, and the individual in whom is vested the management of the protected person's property. The preferred usage is to denote the latter as conservator of the protected person's property. Obviously the two functions are separate, and were so recognized by the common law. For instance, a parent as "natural" guardian of the person of a child is not, solely by virtue of parenthood, the guardian or conservator of the child's property.[1] It would be convenient if we kept separate the terms for the two functions, the conservator of the protected person's property, and the guardian of the person. Of course the same person may perform both functions. But it is possible and frequently desirable to place a person in need of protection in the custody and control of a relative, with a trust company or experienced business manager in charge of the protected person's property affairs.

The position of a guardian or conservator is in many respects similar to that of an administrator or executor. It is a fiduciary position and matters committed to the conservator's charge are handled for the benefit of another. But, while the administrator's duty is generally to close up the affairs of the decedent, pay off the debts, and distribute the remainder to those entitled, the conservator's function is to manage and conserve the property as trustee for the benefit of the protected person until such time as the latter is legally capable of conducting his own affairs.[2] Both are, in a sense, officers of the court.

B. CONSERVATORS

§ 22.25 Conflict-of-laws issues regarding the powers and liabilities of conservators are very similar to those involved in questions of powers and liabilities of representatives of decedents' estates, and this similarity is frequently pointed out and relied upon by courts as a basis of decision.

In absence of statute, a conservator or guardian of the property must be appointed for the personal property of the ward in each state where such property is situated.[1] The historical view, similar to the view regarding personal representatives, has been stated: "By the common law, a foreign guardian can exercise, as such, no rights, or powers, or functions over the property, real or personal, of his ward, which is situated in a different state or country from that in which he has

---

§ 22.24

1. See Fraser, Guardianship of the Person, 45 Iowa L. Rev. 239 (1960); Fratcher, Powers and Duties of Guardians of Property, 45 Iowa L. Rev. 264 (1960); Paulsen & Best, Appointment of a Guardian in the Conflict of Laws, 45 Iowa L. Rev. 212, 230 (1960).

2. See, e.g., U.P.C. § 5–420.

§ 22.25

1. See e.g. Matter of Klineman, 105 Misc.2d 896, 430 N.Y.S.2d 24 (Surr. 1980). See also Hoyt v. Sprague, 103 U.S. (13

Otto) 613, 26 L.Ed. 585 (1880); Kraft v. Wickey, 4 Gill & J. 332, 23 Am.Dec. 569 (Md.1832); In re Rice, 42 Mich. 528, 4 N.W. 284 (1880); Morrell v. Dickey, 1 Johns. Ch. 153 (N.Y. 1814). Cf. Lemoine v. Roberson, 366 So.2d 1009 (La.App.1978); Turner v. Turner, 637 S.W.2d 764 (Mo.App.1982) (for recognition of foreign guardian, Missouri statute required that both guardian and ward be nonresidents; where ward was Missouri resident, guardian appointed by Kansas court could not sue).

obtained his letters of guardianship. But he must obtain new letters of guardianship from the local tribunals, authorized to grant the same before he can exercise any rights, powers, or functions over the same."[2] Without a statute it has been generally assumed that there is no authority in a foreign conservator to manage or convey local land,[3] notwithstanding the similarity to trustees. These rules occasion much unnecessary expense and inconvenience and have been extensively modified by statute, either by conferring powers upon the foreign conservator, or in making easy his qualification locally.[4] The legislative coverage of the subject is sufficient so that the common law rules have been largely superseded and the problem has become one of investigating the particular statutes of each state involved in a transaction.

In the matter of litigation by and against foreign conservators, the rules governing administrators are also analogous. Often a foreign conservator cannot sue in his representative capacity,[5] nor can the conservator be sued outside the state of appointment.[6] However, the courts have made some exceptions to the traditional views even without statutory assistance.[7] For example, the conservator often may bring on the ward's behalf a petition in a foreign probate court,[8] or collect government insurance.[9] The conservator will be required to account in the state

---

2. Grimmett v. Witherington, 16 Ark. 377, 63 Am.Dec. 66 (1855). Many such statements may be found in the older cases. See Hoyt v. Sprague, 103 U.S. (13 Otto) 613, 631, 26 L.Ed. 585 (1880); Watts v. Wilson, 93 Ky. 495, 20 S.W. 505 (1892); Kraft v. Wickey, 4 Gill & J. 332, 23 Am.Dec. 569 (Md.1832); Jefferson v. Glover, 46 Miss. 510, 519 (1872); Morrell v. Dickey, 1 Johns. Ch. 153 (N.Y. 1814). See also In re Holquin's Estate, 101 Misc.2d 174, 420 N.Y.S.2d 670 (Surr.1979).

3. Smith's Executors v. Wiley, 22 Ala. 396, 58 Am.Dec. 262 (1853); McNeil v. First Congregational Society, 66 Cal. 105, 4 P. 1096 (1884); Watts v. Wilson, 93 Ky. 495, 20 S.W. 505 (1892); Adkins v. Loucks, 107 Wis. 587, 83 N.W. 934 (1900). Cf. Edmunds v. Equitable Savings & Loan Association, 223 A.2d 630 (D.C.App.1966); Russell v. Lovell, 362 Mass. 794, 291 N.E.2d 733 (1973); see supra § 21.5.

4. See Paulsen & Best, Appointment of a Guardian in the Conflict of Laws, 45 Iowa L. Rev. 212, 231 (1960). See also Obney v. Schmalzreid, 273 F.Supp. 373 (W.D.Pa. 1967); Miller v. Phoenix State Bank & Trust Co., 138 Conn. 12, 81 A.2d 444 (1951); Mercantile–Safe Deposit & Trust Co. v. Slater, 227 Md. 459, 177 A.2d 520 (1962); Layton v. Pribble, 200 Va. 405, 105 S.E.2d 864 (1958); U.P.C. §§ 5–410, 5–431.

The Uniform Probate Code, Article V, attempts to codify much of the law applicable to conservators and guardians and to integrate those provisions with the proce-

dures that relate primarily to the administration of decedents' estates.

5. Morgan v. Potter, 157 U.S. 195, 15 S.Ct. 590, 39 L.Ed. 670 (1895); Genesco, Inc. v. Cone Mills Corp., 604 F.2d 281 (4th Cir.1979); Greenstreet v. Simmons, 54 F.R.D. 554 (S.D.Ill.1972); Smith v. Madden, 78 Fed. 833 (N.D.Ohio 1896).

6. Jones v. Shields, 14 Ohio 359 (1846). But see In re Guardianship of Wonderly, 67 Ohio St.2d 178, 423 N.E.2d 420 (1981) (Ohio court not proper forum for guardianship termination proceedings where Indiana residents had been guardians for over nine years, notwithstanding fact that same Ohio court originally appointed foreign guardians).

7. See Note, The Incompetent and His Guardian in the Conflict of Laws, 49 Colum. L. Rev. 104 (1949). See also Vroon v. Templin, 278 F.2d 345 (4th Cir.1960); McLean v. American Security & Trust Co., 119 F.Supp. 405 (D.D.C.1954). Cf. Edmunds v. Equitable Savings & Loan Association, 223 A.2d 630 (D.C.App.1966). But see Mayer v. Willing, 196 Cal.App.2d 379, 16 Cal.Rptr. 476 (1961).

8. McCleary v. Menke, 109 Ill. 294 (1884); Earl v. Dresser, 30 Ind. 11, 95 Am. Dec. 660 (1868); In re Prouty's Estate, 101 Vt. 496, 144 A. 691 (1929). Cf. U.P.C. §§ 5–420, 5–424.

9. First National Bank of Colorado Springs, Colorado v. United States, 30

where appointed[10] for all assets collected in or out of the state of appointment.[11]

A minor or disabled person, upon removal of the disability or coming of age, has been allowed to sue the guardian where both were in another state from that in which the guardian was appointed.[12] This is analogous to those cases allowing suit against foreign administrators when equity so demands.[13]

It would seem that if property is taken into possession by a conservator the conservator may deal with it in whatever way the law prescribes for a trustee. Thus, if the conservator assigns a certificate of stock, the assignee is entitled to have his name entered as shareholder on the corporation's books.[14] An early case held, however, contrary to analogous authority, that a guardian of the property may not sue in another state for property wrongfully taken from his possession in the state of his appointment, the reason assigned being that, unlike the administrator, the guardian of the property has no title to the property.[15] It is submitted that this is incorrect; the conservator is essentially a trustee or at least a person in lawful possession, and like any other plaintiff whose lawful possession is interfered with, should be allowed an action against one who wrongfully interferes with that possession wherever the latter is subject to suit.

Assume the case of a minor with property scattered among several states for whose local property a conservator has been appointed at his domicile and for whose other property ancillary conservators have been appointed in the other states. It would seem that the estate should not be kept divided up, thus increasing the labor of administration in looking after investments, decreasing the opportunity for profitable handling of the property, and greatly increasing the expense of administration. The situation here is analogous to that in administration of decedents' estates, where the court ordinarily orders a balance remaining after debts and expenses are paid to be transmitted to the domiciliary representative for distribution. So here, if it appears for the best interests of the minor's estate, a court may order local property to be turned over to a foreign conservator, usually one at the minor's residence. The matter calls for the application of sound discretion,[16] and the property will not

F.Supp. 730 (D.D.C.1939). But cf. Matter of City Bank Farmers Trust Co., 11 Misc.2d 660, 174 N.Y.S.2d 544 (1958).

10. Burnet v. Burnet, 51 Ky. (12 B. Mon.) 323 (1851); Bell v. Suddeth, 10 Miss. (2 Smedes & M.) 532 (1844); In re Feltrinelli's Estate, 159 N.Y.S.2d 563, 575 (Surr. 1956). Cf. Anderson v. Story, 53 Neb. 259, 73 N.W. 735 (1898).

11. Cf. U.P.C. § 5–419.

12. Pickering v. De Rochemont, 45 N.H. 67 (1863). Cf. U.P.C. §§ 5–211, 5–413, 5–419.

13. See supra § 22.18.

14. Ross v. Southwestern Railroad Co., 53 Ga. 514 (1874).

15. Grist v. Forehand, 36 Miss. 69 (1858). Cf. Russell v. Lovell, 362 Mass. 794, 291 N.E.2d 733 (1973); Pfotenhauer v. Hunter, 536 P.2d 923 (Okla.1975).

16. Ponder v. Foster, 23 Ga. 489 (1857); Earl v. Dresser, 30 Ind. 11, 95 Am. Dec. 660 (1868); In re Wilson, 95 Mo. 184, 8 S.W. 369 (1888); Douglas v. Caldwell, 59 N.C. 20 (1860); Morrell v. Dickey, 1 Johns. Ch. 153 (N.Y. 1814); Ex parte Smith, 1 Hill.Eq. 140 (S.C.1833); Clendenning v. Conrad, 91 Va. 410, 21 S.E. 818 (1895); In re Chatard's Settlement [1899] 1 Ch. 712. Under the

be sent away if it appears inexpedient to do so.[17] Sometimes statutes provide for the transfer to the foreign conservator.[18] Such a statute, it has been held, does not affect the power of the court in its discretion to refuse the application.[19] If such property or fund is turned over to the foreign conservator, that conservator is accountable for it to the court in the state of appointment.[20] Where land belonging to the ward is sold or taken by eminent domain, some courts have held that the proceeds will be retained by the court, and only the income remitted for the use of the foreign ward.[21] This is based upon the theory that the fund partakes of the nature of realty. This is an inadequate reason for not unifying administration of the proceeds. The transfer should be made unless the best interests of the protected person require otherwise.

A choice-of-law issue is sometimes asserted regarding a conservator with reference to responsibility for management of the protected person's affairs. In the early case of *Lamar v. Micou*,[22] Mr. Justice Gray said: "The preference due to the law of the ward's domicile, and the importance of a uniform administration of his whole estate, require that, as a general rule, the management and investment of his property should be governed by the law of his domicile, . . . rather than by the law of any state in which a guardian may have been appointed or may have received some property of the ward." While the policies favoring unified administration may seem to support this view, the courts are likely to consider that the local law of the state of appointment is to control the details of administration for which the conservator or guardian of the property is to account. This power of the state where the property is located to fix its own rules governing administration of property by conservators or guardians has been recognized by the Supreme Court.[23]

If the property has, by order of the local court, been turned over to the conservator appointed at the protected person's domicile, then no doubt the conservator there is subject to the rules of the domiciliary state in its management.

Uniform Probate Code "Unitary management of the property is obtainable through easy transfer of proceedings (Section 1–303(b)) and easy collection of assets by foreign conservators (Section 5–431)."

17. In re Wilson, 95 Mo. 184, 8 S.W. 369 (1888); Wallis v. Brown, 63 N.J.Eq. 791, 52 A. 475 (1902); Douglas v. Caldwell, 59 N.C. 20 (1860).

18. Grimmett v. Witherington, 16 Ark. 377, 63 Am.Dec. 66 (1855); In re Benton, 92 Iowa 202, 60 N.W. 614 (1894); In re Cihlar, 216 Iowa 327, 249 N.W. 254 (1933) (bond required).

19. In re Wilson, 95 Mo. 184, 8 S.W. 369 (1888).

20. Jefferson v. Glover, 46 Miss. 510 (1872).

21. Clay v. Brittingham, 34 Md. 675 (1871); In re Department of Public Parks, 89 Hun. 529, 35 N.Y.S. 332 (1895). But see Johnson v. Avery, 11 Me. 99 (1833).

22. 112 U.S. 452, 5 S.Ct. 221, 28 L.Ed. 751 (1884).

23. Hoyt v. Sprague, 103 U.S. (13 Otto) 613, 26 L.Ed. 585 (1880). See also In re Feltrinelli's Estate, 159 N.Y.S.2d 563, 575 (Surr. 1956). This is the assumption of most statutes. See, e.g., U.P.C. §§ 5–413, 5–419, 5–420.

C. GUARDIANS OF THE PERSON

§ 22.26 The most common question arising in this connection has to do with disputes between persons, both of whom claim the custody of the ward, especially where the latter is a minor. If the object of the proceeding is to affect the permanent guardianship of the individual concerned, it should normally be made by the court of the state most concerned with his welfare. For most, but not all, cases, this will be the domicile of that person. This type of situation often arises where one of the points in controversy is the custody of children. As has before been stated, several states may have sufficient contact to exercise jurisdiction concerning a person's custody.[1]

However, any incapacitated person in need of protection may have someone appointed to provide care, if the local law so provides, wherever the incapacitated person may happen to be.[2] A person so appointed may be designated as a temporary guardian, or simply as guardian without distinction from one similarly appointed by the court at the domicile. Even so, the guardian appointed at the domicile usually is considered the principal guardian. Since the guardian of the person is concerned with the physical presence and well being of the incapacitated person, multiple appointments are rare.[3]

Ordinarily the authority of the domiciliary guardian will be recog-

§ 22.26

1. See supra §§ 15.39–15.41; Stumberg, The Status of Children in the Conflict of Laws, 8 U. Chi. L. Rev. 42 (1940); Stansbury, Custody and Maintenance Law Across State Lines, 10 Law & Contemp. Prob. 819 (1944); Ehrenzweig, Interstate Recognition of Custody Decrees, Law and Reason v. the Restatement, 51 Mich. L. Rev. 345 (1953); Rheinstein, Jurisdiction in Matters of Child Custody, An Analysis of the *Boardman* and *White* Cases, 26 Conn. B.J. 48 (1952); Paulsen and Best, Appointment of a Guardian in the Conflict of Laws, 45 Iowa L. Rev. 212 (1960); Ratner, Child Custody in a Federal System, 62 Mich. L. Rev. 795 (1964); Ratner, Legislative Resolution of the Interstate Child Custody Problem: A Reply to Professor Currie and a Proposed Uniform Act, 38 S. Calif. L. Rev. 183 (1965); Goodrich, Custody of Children in Divorce Suits, 7 Cornell L.Q. 1 (1921). See also Sampsell v. Superior Court, 32 Cal.2d 763, 197 P.2d 739 (1948); McDowell v. Gould, 166 Ga. 670, 144 S.E. 206 (1928) (noted 27 Mich. L. Rev. 338 (1929)); Casteel v. Casteel, 45 N.J.Super. 338, 132 A.2d 529 (App.Div.1957); Wallace v. Wallace, 63 N.M. 414, 320 P.2d 1020 (1958); In re Chase, 195 N.C. 143, 141 S.E. 471 (1928) (noted 6 N.C.L. Rev. 475 (1928)); Reed v. Reed, 11 Ohio Misc. 93, 229 N.E.2d 113 (1967); Restatement, Second, Conflict of Laws § 79 (1971). As to jurisdiction to appoint a guardian for an insane person,

see In re Estate of McCormick, 260 Ill.App. 36 (1931) (noted 44 Harv. L. Rev. 1138 (1931)), reversed 345 Ill. 461, 178 N.E. 195 (1931) (noted 27 Ill. L. Rev. 203 (1932); 80 U. Pa. L. Rev. 590 (1932)). See also Connell v. Guardianship of Connell, 476 So.2d 1381 (Fla.App.1985) (petition for restoration of competency could be decided by Florida court although woman adjudicated incompetent in Georgia; not a prerequisite that woman be bona fide resident of Florida).

2. See Shaw v. Shaw, 251 Ark. 665, 473 S.W.2d 848 (1971); Bliss v. Bliss, 133 Md. 61, 104 A. 467 (1918); In re Rice, 42 Mich. 528, 4 N.W. 284 (1880); Falco v. Grills, 209 Va. 115, 161 S.E.2d 713 (1968). See also Hartman v. Henry, 280 Mo. 478, 217 S.W. 987 (1919). See also Note, Jurisdiction to Appoint Guardians of the Person, 7 Colum. L. Rev. 348 (1907); U.P.C. § 5–302. But cf. Junco v. Suarez–Solis, 294 So.2d 334 (Fla. App.1974); In re Randell's Estate, 12 Ill. App.3d 640, 298 N.E.2d 735 (1973).

3. Cf. Restatement, Second, Conflict of Laws § 79, cmnt. (d) (1971). Johnson v. Melback, 5 Kan.App.2d 69, 612 P.2d 188 (1980). The Uniform Child Custody Jurisdiction Act requires that competing courts communicate with each other to resolve custody in the best interests of the child under supervision of the court best situated to supervise the custody. See In re Guard-

nized elsewhere.[4] The incapacitated person, for instance, may not sue the guardian for false imprisonment for exercising control over his person in a second state.[5] But the claim to the custody of the ward whether advanced by the domiciliary guardian or any other person is not one of absolute right. The best interests of the ward will be the paramount consideration, and custody awarded to the person by whom, in the opinion of the court, those interests will best be served.[6]

ianship of Donaldson, 178 Cal.App.3d 477, 223 Cal.Rptr. 707 (1986). See supra § 15.41 *et seq.*

4. Townsend v. Kendall, 4 Minn. 412, 77 Am.Dec. 534 (1860); Nugent v. Vetzera, L.R. 2 Eq. 704 (1866). Cf. Restatement, Second, Conflict of Laws § 79 (1971).

5. Townsend v. Kendall, 4 Minn. 412, 77 Am.Dec. 534 (1860); Alston v. Rains, 589 S.W.2d 481 (Tex.Civ.App.1979); In re Marriage of Saucido, 85 Wn.2d 653, 538 P.2d 1219 (1975); State ex rel. Klopotek v. District Court of Sheridan County, 621 P.2d 223 (Wyo.1980). Cf. In re Guardianship of

Arnold, 114 Ill.App.2d 68, 252 N.E.2d 398 (1969).

6. Kelsey v. Green, 69 Conn. 291, 37 A. 679 (1897); Woodworth v. Spring, 86 Mass. (4 Allen) 321 (1862); In re Rice, 42 Mich. 528, 4 N.W. 284 (1880); Falco v. Grills, 209 Va. 115, 161 S.E.2d 713 (1968). See New York Foundling Hospital v. Gatti, 9 Ariz. 105, 79 P. 231 (1905). See also supra n.1. Cf. Matter of Farrell, 97 Misc.2d 18, 410 N.Y.S.2d 775 (Surr.1978); Matter of Guardianship of Walling, 727 P.2d 586 (Okla. 1986); Pfotenhauer v. Hunter, 536 P.2d 923 (Okla.1975).

Chapter 23

═══════════════════════════════

CORPORATIONS, WINDING–
UP, AND BANKRUPTCY

Table of Sections

		Sections
I.	The Law Applicable to Corporations	23.1–23.11
A.	The Law of the Place of Incorporation	23.1–23.5
	1. The General Principle	23.1–23.2
	2. Special Choice–of–Law Rules	23.3
	3. Applications of the Incorporation–Rule	23.4–23.5
B.	Regulation of Foreign Corporations by the Forum	23.6–23.10
	1. Constitutional Limits	23.6
	2. Qualification Statutes	23.7–23.8
	3. Pseudo–Foreign Corporations	23.9
	4. Piercing the Corporate Veil	23.10
C.	Dissolution and Winding–Up	23.11
II.	Bankruptcy	23.12–23.20
A.	Introduction	23.12
B.	Interstate Bankruptcy	23.13–23.16
C.	International Bankruptcy	23.17
	1. Effect of Foreign Proceedings in the United States	23.18
	2. Effect of U.S. Proceedings Abroad	23.19
D.	Insolvency of Related and of Multinational Corporations	23.20

────────

I. THE LAW APPLICABLE TO CORPORATIONS

A. THE LAW OF THE PLACE OF INCORPORATION

1. *The General Principle*

§ 23.1 The activities of corporations in commerce[1] may give rise to a number of choice-of-law questions. An initial question may be whether

---

§ 23.1

1. This chapter deals only with private corporations engaged in commerce that are organized under state law and the law of the District of Columbia. Some private corporations, such as national banks, are incorporated under the law of the United States and are governed by the rules discussed in this chapter only to the extent

that state law applies to them. The chapter does not deal with public corporations, particularly those incorporated under the law of the United States (for instance, the Tennessee Valley Authority or the Resolution Trust or certain fraternal benefit societies to which special rules may apply): see Order of United Commercial Travelers of America v. Wolfe, 331 U.S. 586, 67 S.Ct. 1355, 91

an entity is a "corporation," in the sense that its officers and owners (stockholders) are entitled to claim limited liability. Other questions concern the law governing its dissolution,[2] the legal relationship between the stockholders and the corporation, the liability of directors and officers, and all the issues commonly regarded as relating to the "internal affairs" of the corporation: the validity of bylaws and of stock issues, the selection of officers, the validity of assessments, and the like.

Legal systems differ with respect to the connecting factors they use to determine the law applicable to corporations. English and American refer to the law of incorporation, as discussed in the next section below. In contrast, early suggestions in the French literature favored the use of the law of the place *"d'exploitation,"*[3] that is the place where the corporation has the center of its commercial activity. This reference resembles the American concept of a corporation's "principal place of business"[4] which will be considered below. French case law increasingly rejected the reference to the law of the place of principal commercial activity and instead adopted the reference to the corporation's seat (*"siège social"*).[5] This became the common rule on the Continent, except in Italy, the Netherlands, and the United Kingdom.[6] The "seat" of a corporation is where its principal administration or management is located or takes place.[7] The rationale for the reference to the place of the seat is that this will give greater protection to third parties[8] who deal with corporate management at the latter's "seat" than would a reference to the corporation's registered office or place of incorporations as in American law. Moreover, in cases in which the place of incorporation and the real seat are not the same, a reference to the place of incorporation may lead to the application of a law which has no territorial connection to the issues of the case.[9]

The reference to a corporation's seat, however, also has its problems. Thus, courts of different states may arrive at different conclusions on the facts, the "seat" may change over time,[10] and inconsistent results

L.Ed. 1687 (1947). In this respect, the coverage follows that of the Restatement, Second, Conflict of Laws, ch. 13, intro. note (1971).

2. This topic is treated infra § 23.10.

3. H. Batiffol & P. Lagarde, 1 Droit international privé no. 193, p. 337 (8th ed. 1993) (with references).

4. See infra §§ 23.3 (diversity jurisdiction) and 23.9 (pseudo-foreign corporations). Kegel's equation of the European concept of a corporations "seat" (*siège social*), see text immediately following, with the American concept of the "principal place of business" therefore seems inaccurate: Kegel & Schurig, Internationales Privatrecht 576 (9th ed. 2004).

5. Batiffol & Lagarde, supra n.3. The rule now appears in Art. 3 of the Law of

July 24, 1966, [1966] J.O. 642, [1966] D.S.L. 265.

6. See Ebke & Gockel, European Corporate Law, 24 Int'l Lawyer 54, 55 (1990).

7. Batiffol & Lagarde, supra n.3; Kegel & Schurig, supra n.4.

8. For this reason, the English *ultra vires* doctrine has been limited for the protection of third parties, who have dealt with a foreign corporation in good faith, upon accession of the United Kingdom to the European Communities. European Community Act § 9(1) (1972).

9. Kegel & Schurig, supra n.4, at 573–75.

10. Under German law, for instance, a corporation loses its corporate personality upon moving its seat abroad. See Kegel & Schurig, supra n.4, at 581–582, with refer-

may also occur when one state follows the seat theory while another looks to the place of incorporation.[11]

The European Communities' Convention on Jurisdiction and the Recognition of Judgments ("Brussels Convention") as well as the "Parallel" (Lugano) Convention among the EU and EFTA countries provide in Article 53(1) that, for jurisdictional purposes, a corporation's domicile is where its "seat" is. The provision leaves the determination of the seat to the respective forum's conflicts rules.[12] Regulation (EC) 44/2001, which substantially replaces the Brussels Convention, provides in Article 60 that a company is "domiciled" in the place of its "statutory seat, or ... central administration, or ... principal place of business."[13] Beyond jurisdiction, the European Union did not adopt a uniform rule. The decision of the European Court of Justice in the *Daily Mail* case had been interpreted (and criticized by some) as an endorsement of the seat theory. In fact, the Court's actual holding was much narrower. It confirmed that United Kingdom tax authorities could condition the newspaper's change of its corporate seat to the Netherlands on the satisfaction of its tax liability.[14]

More recently, the Court held in a series of cases that a corporation validly established in the state of incorporation, whether on the basis of the "incorporation" or "seat" rule, is entitled to recognition in all other

ences. However, within the European union the reference is now to incorporation. The seat principle German law thus now applies only with regard to non-European Union counties. Id. at 575, 577–78, 581–82; see infra n.15. See also Batiffol & Lagarde, supra n.3, at no. 194.

11. For instance, in a suit against a company incorporated in the United States with main offices in Hamburg, Germany, the German courts did not regard the company as an "American" company. Under the seat theory, the company was German and, having failed to comply with German law as to incorporation there, did not enjoy corporate personality. Consequently, German law with respect to non-incorporated associations applied, including the personal liability of officers, directors and shareholders. Judgment of March 31, 1904, 9 Deutsche Juristenzeitung 555. See also RGZ 73, 76 (1918); Hay, Internationales Privatrecht 358–59 (2d ed. 2002). However, current law within the European Union and in the relation of Germany to the United States now adopts the incorporation principle. See text at n. 15 et seq. infra. For French law see Batiffol & Lagarde, supra n.3, at no. 194, p. 338, with cases supra n.11. French law now permits a change of a corporation's seat from France to another country upon approval of an extraordinary stockholders' meeting on the condition of

the existence of a special convention between France and the transferee state. Ordinance of January 7, 1959, [1959] J.O. 640.

12. In England, Section 42 of the Civil Jurisdiction and Judgments Act of 1982 provides that a corporation's seat is in the state in which (a) it is incorporated *and* has its registered office or other official address or (b) in which its central management and control is exercised. If, in application of this test, the English court is referred to the law of another contracting state, the court inquires whether that law would also consider the corporation's seat in that state. If not, the corporation will be treated as domiciled outside the contracting states (and thus not entitled to the benefits of the conventions). For an application see Dicey & Morris, Conflict of Laws 287–88 (13th ed. by Collins et al. 2000).

13. Council Regulation (EC) No. 44/2001 on Jurisdiction and the Recognition of Judgments in Civil and Commercial Matters, [2002] O.J. L. 12/1. A special definition of "statutory seat" applies in the common-law jurisdictions of the United Kingdom and Ireland. There that term is expressly defined as "the registered office or, where there is no such office anywhere, the place of incorporation or, where there is no such place anywhere, the place under which the formation took place." Id art. 60(2).

14. Case 81/87, [1988] ECR 5483.

EC states in order to benefit from the EC Treaty's provisions on the right of establishment.[15] Indeed, the new state may not diminish the right of establishment of a company validly incorporated in another member state by requiring compliance with its stricter domestic rules, e.g., concerning capitalization or disclosure.[16]

In U.S. commercial treaties the potential conflict between the American incorporation theory and the civil law seat theory may be avoided through specific adoption of the former: "Companies constituted under the applicable laws and regulations within the territories of either Party shall be deemed companies thereof and shall have their juridical status recognized within the territories of the other Party."[17] The Treaty also provides for national and most-favored-nation treatment.[18] In a case involving a company incorporated in Florida with its administrative seat in Germany, the German Supreme Court (BGH) held that the clear language of treaty provisions cited, as well as the concept of the "right of establishment" as defined and applied in the decisions of the European Court, required recognition of the company according to the law of the state of incorporation.[19] Thus, within the European Union, as well as in the relationship between Germany and the United States, the "incorporation rule" has supplanted the "seat rule" for purposes of movement and establishment in another state. What remains of the "seat rule" is the power of a "seat" state to provide for the winding up and dissolution of a domestically incorporated company that moves its "seat" abroad: the right of establishment and the freedom of movement it affords inures to the benefit of the foreign company, but not to domestic corporations.

§ 23.2 Under English[1] and American law[2] the existence of a company, as well as its subsequent dissolution,[3] are governed by the law of incorporation. The same law also applies to most issues relating to the rights and liabilities of officers and stockholders and to the internal affairs of the corporation.

---

15. Case C–212/97 (*Centros*), [1999] ECR I–1459, with annotation by Behrens, 1999 IPRax 323; Case C–208/00 (*Überseering*), [2002] ECR I–9919; Case C–167/01 (*Inspire Art*), [2003] ECR I-; 2003 WL 102001.

16. *Inspire Art*, supra n. 15. Compare this result with the regulation of "pseudo-foreign corporations" in the United States. Infra § 23.9.

17. Art. XXV (5), Treaty of Friendship, Commerce and Navigation Between the United States of America and the Federal Republic of Germany, 7 U.S.T. 1840, T.I.A.S. 3593, 273 U.N.T.S. 3 entered into force July 14, 1956.

18. Art. XXV, para. 2, sentence 2.

19. Decision of the Bundesgerichtshof (BGH) of January 29 2003, Docket No. VIII ZR 155/02, 2003 Betriebsberater 810;

2003 IPRax 265. See also BGH Decision of March 13, 2003, Docket No. VII ZR 370/98, 58 Juristenzeitung 525 (2003) (Dutch company with "seat" in Germany. For comment see Weller, Das internationale Gesellschaftsrecht in der neuesten BGH–Rechtsprechung, 2003 IPRax 324; Weller, Einschränkungen der Gründungstheorie bei missbräuchlicher Auslandsgründung?, 2003 IPRax 520.

§ 23.2

1. Dicey & Morris, The Conflict of Laws 1101–32 (13th ed. by Collins 2000). But see National Bank of Greece v. Metliss, [1958] A.C. 509 (existence determined under the law of the alleged place of incorporation) and supra § 23.1 n.8.

2. Restatement, Second, Conflict of Laws § 297 (1971).

3. See infra § 23.10.

The internal affairs rule—application of the law of the state of incorporation to the corporation's internal affairs—has been virtually elevated to one of constitutional mandate by the U.S. Supreme Court in *CTS Corp. v. Dynamics Corp. of America*,[4] when it upheld the Indiana antitakeover statute against a commerce clause challenge. Although the statute applied to out-of-state securities transactions, the Court thus confirmed the exclusive authority of the state of incorporation over its corporations and thereby refused to adopt dicta in *Norlin Corp. v. Rooney, Pace Inc.*[5] to the effect that the state of incorporation is not necessarily an interested state.[6] To the extent that the Court considered full-faith-and-credit, due process and commerce clause issues in reaching its decision, it is now unclear whether state regulation of "pseudo-foreign" corporations will be affected by the decision.[7] Similarly, in American law, a corporation's "domicile" is said to be in the state of incorporation.[8] As applied to corporations, however, the domicile concept serves no useful purpose:[9] the reference to the law of incorporation is enough for most choice-of-law purposes, and special regulatory concerns, such as the exercise of judicial jurisdiction or the power to tax, can be put on other, more functional grounds, such as the corporation's particular activity.[10]

The reference to the law of incorporation is based on the theory that a corporation, being an artificial person, "can have existence only in that state [that created it]...."[11] Once validly organized under the law of the

4. 481 U.S. 69, 87–94, 107 S.Ct. 1637, 1648–52, 95 L.Ed.2d 67 (1987).

5. 744 F.2d 255 (2d Cir.1984).

6. See also In re ORFA Securities Litigation, 654 F.Supp. 1449, 1463–64 (D.N.J. 1987) and Haberman v. Washington Public Power Supply System, 109 Wn.2d 107, 744 P.2d 1032 (1987), opinion amended 109 Wn.2d 107, 750 P.2d 254 (1988) (both adopting a most-significant-relationship test); Becker v. PaineWebber, Inc., 962 F.2d 524, 526 (5th Cir.1992); Kafka v. Bellevue Corp., 999 F.2d 1117, 1121–22 (7th Cir. 1993).

7. See infra § 23.9.

8. See Johnson & Johnson v. Picard, 282 F.2d 386 (6th Cir.1960). Also, corporate "nationality" depends on the place of incorporation. See, e.g., Sumitomo Shoji America, Inc. v. Avagliano, 457 U.S. 176, 102 S.Ct. 2374, 72 L.Ed.2d 765 (1982), on remand 103 F.R.D. 562 (S.D.N.Y.1984). In that case, an employment discrimination suit, defendant, a New York corporation and wholly-owned subsidiary of a Japanese company, relied on Art. VIII(1) of the Treaty of Friendship, Commerce and Navigation between the U.S. and Japan (Apr. 2, 1953, [1953] 4 U.S.T. 2063, T.I.A.S. No. 2863), which provides that "[c]ompanies of either Party shall be permitted to engage, within

the territories of the other Party, [employees] of their choice." The Court held that the defendant was a U.S. company as a result of its New York incorporation (cf. Article XXII(3) of the Treaty), and thus not entitled to rely on the provisions of Art. VIII(1).

9. Restatement, Second, Conflict of Laws § 11, comment (l) (1971). For diversity of citizenship for purposes of federal jurisdiction see infra § 23.3.

10. See McDermott Inc. v. Lewis, 531 A.2d 206 (Del.1987) (extending the internal affairs rule to foreign-country corporations).

11. McDougal, Felix & Whitten, American Conflicts Law 827 (5th ed. 2001). The civil law does not share this logic. Approaching the problem more functionally, such as expectation of the parties, particularly of third parties, and the regulatory interests of the state where the corporation acts, civilians hold that just as an individual's center of existence is where he or she lives, a legal entity's center of existence is where its commercial activity is carried on.... A legal entity should therefore be governed by the law of its seat. Kegel & Schurig, Internationales Privatrecht 573 (9th ed. 2004). But see supra § 23.01 n.11–19. See also the concept of "pseudo-foreign"

state of incorporation,[12] it will generally be recognized by other states.[13] "Recognition" means merely that the entity's *legal status* will be recognized and not necessarily that it may engage in the same activities as in the state of incorporation: a corporation organized to engage in gambling operations is a good example.[14] The extent of permissible regulation by the second state is the subject of §§ 23.6–23.9, below. Similarly, a state may consider an entity to be a corporation within the meaning of a local statute or rule of law even though "the organization goes by some other name in the state of its formation. . . ."[15]

2. *Special Choice–of–Law Rules*

§ 23.3   Statutory provisions depart from the usual reference to the law of the place of incorporation in a few cases in order to address special problems. Thus, the incorporation theory could mean that a corporation organized and registered in X but solely or principally engaged in commercial activity in Y and, moreover, having as stockholders, directors and officers only residents of Y, could invoke the diversity jurisdiction of a federal court in Y in a suit against a Y resident. In order to avoid this result, the diversity statute provides that "a corporation shall be deemed a citizen of any State by which it has been incorporated and of the State where it has its principal place of business."[1] In the

corporations in American law, infra § 23.9. It is an interesting paradox that the seat theory of the civil law more closely resembles usual common law notions of domicile, while English and American law adopt a concept somewhat analogous to the usual civil law reference to the law of nationality as the "personal law" of an individual. Mann, Beiträge zum internationalen Privatrecht 55, 57 (1976).

12. Restatement, Second, Conflict of Laws § 296 (1971).

13. Id. § 296. See also Kozyris, The Limited Liability Company: Does It Exist Out of State? What Law Governs It?, 64 U. Cinn. L. Rev. 565 (1996).

14. McDougal et al., supra n.11, at 828. State regulation of a foreign corporation's activity is discussed further, infra §§ 23.6–23.9.

15. Restatement, Second, Conflict of Laws § 297, cmnt. (a) (1971). See State ex rel. Ferguson v. United Royalty Co., 188 Kan. 443, 363 P.2d 397 (1961) (Oklahoma "business trust" treated as a corporation in Kansas); Liverpool & London Life & Fire Insurance Co. v. Commonwealth of Massachusetts, 77 U.S. (10 Wall.) 566, 19 L.Ed. 1029 (1871) (Massachusetts may tax English joint stock company as a corporation). Cf. Note, Regulation of Foreign Limited Partnerships, 52 Boston U.L. Rev. 64 (1972).

§ 23.3

1. 28 U.S.C.A. § 1332(c). For comment see Moore & Weckstein, Corporations and Diversity of Citizenship: A Supreme Court Fiction Revisited, 77 Harv. L. Rev. 1426, 1431 et seq. (1964).

One question not directly answered by the section concerns the status of foreign-country corporations, having their principal place of business in the United States, with respect to diversity jurisdiction in the state of such place of business. The problem was considered in Eisenberg v. Commercial Union Assurance Co., 189 F.Supp. 500 (S.D.N.Y.1960) and in Jerguson v. Blue Dot Investment, Inc., 659 F.2d 31 (5th Cir. 1981), cert. denied 456 U.S. 946, 102 S.Ct. 2013, 72 L.Ed.2d 469 (1982). In *Eisenberg* the court concluded that the reference to the principal place of business applied only to corporations organized under the laws of another state of the Union and (dictum) to those foreign-country corporations whose only (worldwide) principal place of business is in the United States. In *Eisenberg,* the British defendant had its principal worldwide place of business in London and its principal American place of business in New York: § 1332(c) did not apply and diversity jurisdiction existed. See also Salomon Englander Y CIA LTDA v. Israel Discount Bank Ltd., 494 F.Supp. 914 (S.D.N.Y. 1980) (also reviewing other decisions). *Jer-*

foregoing example, the corporation would be deemed a "citizen" of both X and Y and the federal court in Y would not have jurisdiction in an action against a Y resident for lack of diversity of citizenship.[2] The

guson, takes a wider view: "Congress was endeavoring to define in which states *in the United States* a corporation would be deemed a citizen for purposes of diversity jurisdiction." *Jerguson,* 659 F.2d at 35 (original emphasis). According to this language, diversity would be destroyed even if the foreign corporation also had a place of business abroad. On the facts of the case, however, *Jerguson* does not go beyond *Eisenberg* because "Florida is not just Blue Dot's [a Panamanian corporation] principal place of business, it is its only place of business." Id. In accord with *Jerguson:* Rubinfeld v. Bahama Cruise Line, Inc., 613 F.Supp. 300 (S.D.N.Y.1985) (Bahamian corporation with offices in Tampa and Miami, Florida, and in New York, of which the last appeared to be the principal place of business worldwide). See also Barrantes Cabalceta v. Standard Fruit Co., 667 F.Supp. 833 (S.D.Fla.1987), affirmed in part, reversed in part 883 F.2d 1553 (11th Cir. 1989) (court applied "nerve center" test and found that a party with places of business in California, Florida, Ecuador, and Honduras was principally a "Latin American" and not a "Florida" corporation; diversity therefore was not destroyed). See also Bailey v. Grand Trunk Lines New England, 805 F.2d 1097, 1100 (2d Cir. 1986), cert. denied 484 U.S. 826, 108 S.Ct. 94, 98 L.Ed.2d 54 (1987). It seems generally accepted that the corporation must have its worldwide principal place of business in the United States as distinguished from being a principally foreign corporation with one or several places of business in the United States. 15 Moore's Federal Practice–Civil § 102.55 at n. 8 (2003). But see Note, The Application of 28 U.S.C. § 1332 (c) to Alien Corporations: A Dual Citizenship Analysis, 36 Va. J. Int'l L. 233 (1995) (surveying case law and urging the assignment of two citizenships for diversity purposes).

Plaintiffs have been uniformly unsuccessful in attempts to use an alter-ego theory to preserve diversity jurisdiction by ignoring the place of incorporation of a wholly-owned subsidiary and treating the latter as a citizen of the state of incorporation of the parent. Fritz v. American Home Shield Corp., 751 F.2d 1152 (11th Cir.1985) (interstate); Panalpina Welttransport GmBh v. Geosource, Inc., 764 F.2d 352 (5th Cir. 1985) (adding that the result might be different upon a showing that "Ucamar [the American defendant's subsidiary and a codefendant] was incorporated in the Cayman

Islands solely for purposes of diversity jurisdiction in a suit by an alien corporation.") Id. at 355. On the other hand, the *subsidiary's* place of incorporation may be imputed to the out-of-state parent on an alter-ego theory to destroy diversity. Freeman v. Northwest Acceptance Corp., 754 F.2d 553 (5th Cir.1985). "[I]n keeping with Congress' intendment to constrict the availability of diversity jurisdiction ... , the alter ego doctrine may be used to add places of citizenship to the abrogation of diversity jurisdiction but may not be used to extend such jurisdiction." *Panalpina,* supra, at 354–55. In keeping with this policy approach, it has been suggested that § 1332(c) should apply in suits between an American party and an alien corporation with a (not sole) place of business in the same state (thus destroying diversity). Note, Diversity Jurisdiction and Alien Corporations: The Application of Section 1332(c), 59 Ind. L.J. 659 (1984). The second suggestion (ibid.) that the section should not apply in suits between two alien corporations with principal places of businesses in different U.S. states because the section contemplates that a U.S. citizen (in contrast to the imputed citizenship of a state) be involved in the case, is less convincing. The functional view of corporate citizenship adopted by the cases for diversity purposes should accord diversity jurisdiction whenever corporations have *in fact* their principal U.S. (or worldwide) place of business in a state. See also generally Note, Diversity Jurisdiction over Alien Corporations, 50 U. Chi. L. Rev. 1458 (1983). As stated in the preceding paragraph of this note, these suggestions have not been adopted by the decisions.

28 U.S.C. § 1332 (a) confers diversity jurisdiction when the party is a "citizen of a foreign state or country." A corporation formed under the law of the British Virgin Islands, an Overseas Territory of the United Kingdom, was held to satisfy that requirement: JPMorgan Chase Bank v. Traffic Stream (BVI) Infrastructure, Ltd., 536 U.S. 88, 122 S.Ct. 2054, 153 L.Ed.2d 95 (2002).

2. See Campbell v. Triangle Corp., 336 F.Supp. 1002 (E.D.Pa.1972); John Mohr & Sons v. Apex Terminal Warehouses, Inc., 422 F.2d 638 (7th Cir.1970) (consolidated corporation may, under certain circumstances, have the citizenship of each of the separate, preconsolidation corporations so as to defeat diversity). See also Health

statute also provides that in direct actions against a liability insurer to which the insured is not joined as a party defendant, the insurer additionally shall be deemed a citizen of the state of which the insured is a citizen.[3] The purpose of the provision is to take away the diversity jurisdiction of federal courts, and thereby to relieve federal dockets, in cases in which a citizen of one state brings a direct action against the insurer of a fellow citizen for injuries caused by the latter.[4] The provision does not address the question of whether state courts may constitutionally exercise direct-action jurisdiction under these circumstances.[5]

The usual reference to the law of the place of incorporation may also be displaced by the second state's regulatory laws. Thus, when a corporation organized under the laws of X conducts all or a substantial part of its business in Y, the state of Y may choose to treat it for many purposes *as if* it were a Y corporation and subject it to aspects of its corporation law.[6] In effect, Y will treat the X corporation as a "pseudo-foreign corporation." This type of regulation thus seeks to substitute a "principal place of business" test for the incorporation-theory. "Pseudo-foreign corporations," as well as the more common form of regulation of foreign corporations by means of "qualifying statutes," are discussed subsequently.[7]

In addition to the reference to the place of incorporation or to the principal place of business, it might be thought that a corporation's "citizenship" could also be determined on the basis of the citizenship of

Group Management Co. v. Walker County Medical Center, Inc., 595 F.Supp. 381 (M.D.Tenn.1984) (under § 1332(c), *the* principal place of business, of which there is only one, and not "a" principal place of business, is determinative).

3. 28 U.S.C.A. § 1332(c) (proviso).

4. 1964 U.S. Code, Cong. & Admin. News 2778 (legislative history); Irvin v. Allstate Insurance Co., 436 F.Supp. 575 (W.D.Okla.1977); Aetna Casualty & Surety Insurance Co. v. Greene, 606 F.2d 123 (6th Cir.1979) (workers' compensation insurance is "liability insurance" within the meaning of the statute); Rosa v. Allstate Ins. Co., 981 F.2d 669 (2d Cir.1992). See also Northbrook National Ins. Co. v. Brewer, 493 U.S. 6, 110 S.Ct. 297, 107 L.Ed.2d 223 (1989). In this regard, compare Spooner v. Paul Revere Life Ins. Co., 578 F.Supp. 369 (E.D.Mich. 1984) and Estate of Zeiler v. Prudential Ins. Co. of America, 570 F.Supp. 627 (N.D.Ill. 1983) (holding that employee's suit on disability policy provided by employer is not within scope of the 28 U.S.C.A. § 1332(c) proviso, since such policies are not true liability insurance in that they do not protect an insured from an existing liability to a third person, but instead create a liability to the insured as a contractual matter) with Tyson v. Connecticut General Life Ins. Co.,

495 F.Supp. 240 (E.D.Mich.1980) (finding § 1332(c) applicable). See also Fortson v. St. Paul Fire and Marine Ins. Co., 751 F.2d 1157 (11th Cir.1985) (holding that Section 1332(c) proviso does not apply in suit by third party against insurer, based not on primary liability under policy but on insurer's failure to settle claim in good faith).

5. See Rush v. Savchuk, 444 U.S. 320, 100 S.Ct. 571, 62 L.Ed.2d 516 (1980) (invalidating the attachment procedure of the kind used in Seider v. Roth, 17 N.Y.2d 111, 269 N.Y.S.2d 99, 216 N.E.2d 312 (1966)). In *Seider*-type cases, the insured is not a citizen of the forum. Whether, for state court jurisdiction, sufficient contact exists between the forum and the defendant insurer to permit the exercise of direct-action jurisdiction over the defendant, then depends on the usual constitutional tests applicable to this problem.

6. But see supra § 23.2 n.5 and infra § 23.9 with respect to the impact of the U.S. Supreme Court's decision in CTS Corp. v. Dynamics Corp. of America, 481 U.S. 69, 107 S.Ct. 1637, 95 L.Ed.2d 67 (1987).

7. See infra §§ 23.9 and 23.7, respectively.

its owners. As a general reference, this idea has never taken hold, principally because a change in ownership of shares would result in changes in the applicable law. In Europe, moreover, where many or most stock certificates are issued in bearer form and not registered with the corporation, shareholders are often unknown; "citizenship" of the corporation therefore could not be determined.[8] The identity, and citizenship, of those holding ownership interests in a corporation are therefore considered only in one exceptional case: when a corporation organized under the laws of one state of the Union is owned by enemy aliens or by enemy-country corporations. Federal legislation, in furtherance of the President's war powers, has provided for the seizure of the property interests of such enemy aliens.[9] This practice, however, often does not constitute a piercing of the U.S. company's corporate veil inasmuch as it is the *alien's* property interest in the corporation that is seized under such legislation rather than the corporation itself (and its assets) as a consequence of alien ownership.[10]

3. *Applications of the Incorporation—Rule*

§ 23.4   The rights and duties of stockholders, that is, the legal

8.   Batiffol & Lagarde, Droit international privé n.3, no. 193, p. 337 (8th ed. 1973).

9.   55 Stat. § 301(1)(B) (1941) (amending the Trading with the Enemy Act of 1917, 40 Stat. § 415). In Kaufman v. Societe Internationale Pour Participations Industrielles Et Commerciales, S.A., 343 U.S. 156, 72 S.Ct. 611, 96 L.Ed. 853 (1952), the Supreme Court held that all corporate assets could be seized but emphasized the need to protect innocent, non-enemy stockholders. Similarly, in Uebersee Finanz–Korporation, A.G. v. McGrath, 343 U.S. 205, 72 S.Ct. 618, 96 L.Ed. 888 (1952), the Court held that non-enemy stockholders had a severable interest. In contrast, only specific shares of stock were seized in Silesian American Corp. v. Clark, 332 U.S. 469, 68 S.Ct. 179, 92 L.Ed. 81 (1947). However, the Court permitted extensive tracing of enemy interests, akin to a piercing of the corporate veil: the corporation was organized under the laws of Delaware and owned by a Swiss corporation which, in turn, was partially owned by a German corporation. Cf. Norem, Determination of Enemy Character of Corporations, 24 Am. J. Int'l L. 310 (1930). As a matter of international law, enemy-property legislation is regarded as an exception to the general principle that a corporation is an entity separate from its shareholders and is governed by the law (is a "citizen") of the state of incorporation. The Barcelona Traction, Light, and Power Co., [1970] I.C.J. 3, at ¶ 60 (International Court of Justice).

10.   In the reverse situation, the United States also pursues international claims on behalf of U.S. citizens for the protection of their overseas investments regardless of whether the investment takes the form of participation in a corporation organized under domestic or foreign-country law. See generally S. Rubin, Private Foreign Investment 32 et seq., 40 et seq. (1956); U.S. Dept State Press Rel. No. 630 on Foreign Investment and Nationalization (Dec. 30, 1975), 15 Int'l L. Mat. 186 (1976). For special choice-of-law problems with respect to multinational corporations and with respect to corporate takeovers and mergers (including the problem of minority shareholder protection) see Cassoni, Le droit international privé des groupes de sociétés— L'exemple italien pourrait-il devenir un modèle?, 75 Revue critique de droit international privé 633 (1986). For jurisdictional problems see Brilmayer & Paisley, Personal Jurisdiction and Substantive Legal Relations: Corporations, Conspiracies, and Agency, 74 Cal. L. Rev. 1 (1986).

In Sumitomo Shoji America, Inc. v. Avagliano, 457 U.S. 176, 102 S.Ct. 2374, 72 L.Ed.2d 765 (1982), the defendant, incorporated in New York, was the wholly-owned subsidiary of a Japanese corporation and, on that basis, sought to invoke rights under U.S.-Japanese Treaty of Friendship, Commerce and Navigation. Held: the defendant is a New York corporation and, as such, not entitled to rely on the Treaty. See also Kirmse v. Hotel Nikko, 51 Cal.App.4th 311, 59 Cal.Rptr.2d 96 (1996).

relationship between the stockholders and the corporation are usually[1] determined according to the law of the state of incorporation.[2] This "is practically a necessary rule. It would be intolerable for different holders of the same issue of stock to have different sets of rights and duties by reason of their stockholdings, perhaps according to the laws of the various places at which they acquired their stock. . . . The need for unity applies to such matters as the stockholder's right to dividends, his right to participate in the management of the corporation by voting at stockholders' meetings or otherwise, his liability on unpaid subscriptions, his subjection to assessments or double liability by reason of his being a shareholder, the existence and nature of possible preemptive rights in other stock or the properties of the corporation, and every other relational right and duty which grows out of the fact of his being a stockholder."[3] The law of the place of incorporation also determines when stock ownership passes from one person to another. Traditionally, many states provided for the passage of title only upon registration on the books of the corporation. By virtue of the universal adoption of the Uniform Commercial Code the rule now is that title to certified securities passes upon delivery of the certificate incorporating the right, title to the latter being governed by the law of the place where it is at the relevant time.[4] In the more common modern indirect holding system, the investor owns a "security entitlement" (not actual certificates), which is carried as his or her account on the books of the securities intermediary.[5]

Similarly, the liability of directors and officers is ordinarily determined by the law of the place of incorporation.[6] It is a different question whether the state of incorporation also has judicial jurisdiction to adjudicate the question of liability;[7] once validly imposed by the state of

---

§ 23.4

1. But see infra § 23.9 with respect to "pseudo-foreign corporations." Cf. DeMott, Perspectives on Choice of Law for Corporate Internal Affairs, 48 Law & Contemporary L. Probs. 161 (1985).

2. Restatement, Second, Conflict of Laws §§ 303, 304 (1971); Hausman v. Buckley, 299 F.2d 696, 93 A.L.R.2d 1340 (2d Cir. 1962), cert. denied 369 U.S. 885, 82 S.Ct. 1157, 8 L.Ed.2d 286 (1962); St. Louis Union Trust Co. v. Merrill Lynch, 412 F.Supp. 45, 56 (E.D.Mo.1976); Harrison v. NetCentric Corp., 433 Mass. 465, 744 N.E.2d 622 (Mass. 2001). General choice-of-law rules apply to a corporation's dealings with third parties. See Restatement, Second, Conflict of Laws §§ 301–302 (1971). See also Lewis v. Dicker, 118 Misc.2d 28, 459 N.Y.S.2d 215 (1982) (law of state of incorporation applied to question of whether demand must be made on corporate directors prior to bringing shareholders' derivative suit even though corporation had principal executive offices in New York).

3. McDougal, Felix & Whitten, American Conflicts Law 833 (5th ed. 2001).

4. See U.C.C. §§ 8–301(a)(1994 Revision, as amended 1999).

5. UCC § 8–501 et seq. (1994 Revision). See also infra at § 23.9 n. 5.

6. Restatement, Second, Conflict of Laws § 309 (1971). See, e.g., Smith v. Van Gorkom, 488 A.2d 858, 872 (Del.1985).

7. In Shaffer v. Heitner, 433 U.S. 186, 97 S.Ct. 2569, 53 L.Ed.2d 683 (1977), the U.S. Supreme Court held that Delaware lacked in personam jurisdiction, although both the majority (433 U.S. at 216, 97 S.Ct. at 2586) and the partial dissent (433 U.S. at 225 n.3, 97 S.Ct. at 2591 n.3) agreed that Delaware's law was probably applicable to the issue of the director's liability, citing to Restatement, Second, Conflict of Laws § 309 (1971). Delaware subsequently enacted a consent statute to permit its exercise of jurisdiction over persons accepting directorships in Delaware corporations. 10 Del. C., § 3114.

incorporation, however, the determination will usually be entitled to recognition elsewhere.[8]

The Supreme Court lent further support to the "internal affairs rule" when it held in a shareholders' derivative suit under the Investment Company Act that the "futility exception" is governed by the (state) law of incorporation and not by federal (common) law.[9]

§ 23.5 The concept of a corporation's "internal affairs" includes a variety of issues, such as the validity of stock issues and of corporate bylaws, the selection of directors and management, the declaration of assessments and dividends, as well as questions of management.[1] Early cases held that the forum court lacked power to entertain cases involving the internal affairs of a foreign corporation.[2] In *Rogers v. Guaranty Trust Co.*,[3] the Supreme Court also refused to hear such a case but put the decision on the twin grounds that uniformity required a decision by the state of incorporation and that a novel question of law, as in the case at bar, should be settled by the state of incorporation in the first place. In *Williams v. Green Bay & Wisconsin Railroad Co.*,[4] the Supreme Court adopted the viewpoint of the dissent in *Rogers* that uniformity or difficulties in the application of foreign law alone were not enough, but that the decision to entertain a case involving the internal affairs of a foreign corporation should be based on factors essentially the same as in the test for forum non conveniens. This has become the modern rule: courts do have jurisdiction to entertain an "internal affairs" action but may, in their discretion, elect not to do so when considerations of practicality and convenience suggest that litigation should more properly proceed elsewhere, particularly in the state of incorporation.[5] In addition to the usual factors that go into a determination of forum non conveniens,[6] "internal affairs" cases also raise the question of the efficacy of the resulting decree. Thus courts may wish to decline to exercise

---

8. See Restatement, Second, Conflict of Laws §§ 308, 310 (1971). Even when the liability imposed on a director or officer may be said to be in the nature of a penalty, a valid judgment will not be denied recognition for that reason elsewhere. Huntington v. Attrill, 146 U.S. 657, 13 S.Ct. 224, 36 L.Ed. 1123 (1892) (discussed supra § 3.17).

9. Kamen v. Kemper Financial Services, Inc., 500 U.S. 90, 111 S.Ct. 1711, 114 L.Ed.2d 152 (1991). See also infra § 23.6 at nn. 10–12.

§ 23.5

1. See, e.g., MHC Inv. Co. v. Racom Corp., 254 F. Supp. 2d 1090 (S.D. Iowa 2002)(internal affairs doctrine applicable to questions of fiduciary duty of corporation's board); In re Oracle Corp. Derivative Litig., 808 A.2d 1206, 1213 n.10 (Del. Ch. 2002).

2. Condon v. Mutual Reserve Fund Life Association, 89 Md. 99, 42 A. 944 (1899); State ex rel. Lake Shore Telephone & Tele-

graph Co. v. De Groat, 109 Minn. 168, 123 N.W. 417 (1909). For historical background see Note, 33 Colum. L. Rev. 492 (1933).

3. 288 U.S. 123, 53 S.Ct. 295, 77 L.Ed. 652 (1933).

4. 326 U.S. 549, 66 S.Ct. 284, 90 L.Ed. 311 (1946).

5. Restatement, Second, Conflict of Laws § 313 (1971), comment (c). See Novich v. Rojtman, 5 Misc.2d 1029, 161 N.Y.S.2d 817 (1957); Donna v. Abbotts Dairies, Inc., 399 Pa. 497, 161 A.2d 13 (1960); State ex rel. Starkey v. Alaska Airlines, Inc., 68 Wn.2d 318, 413 P.2d 352 (1966). See also Koster v. (American) Lumbermens Mutual Casualty Co., 330 U.S. 518, 67 S.Ct. 828, 91 L.Ed. 1067 (1947); Note, 42 Iowa L. Rev. 90 (1956).

6. See supra §§ 11.8–11.14.

jurisdiction in cases involving foreign corporations when the relief sought requires the exercise of supervisory powers by the court.[7]

B. REGULATION OF FOREIGN CORPORATIONS BY THE FORUM

1. *Constitutional Limits*

§ 23.6   Corporations are not "citizens" for purposes of the Privileges and Immunities Clause but are "persons" and as such protected by the Due Process and Equal Protection Clauses[1] as well as against impairment of their contracts.[2] Although it has been often stated that a state may exclude a foreign corporation altogether,[3] this power is very limited indeed in practice. On the one hand, a state may not exclude a corporation engaged in interstate commerce.[4] Regulation of foreign corporations engaged only in intrastate commerce in the forum, on the other hand, must not be unreasonable.[5] One recurring issue concerns a state's power to tax a foreign corporation and involves both the question of the required nexus of the corporation to the state[6] and the manner in which the tax is to be allocated to its intrastate and interstate activities.[7]

7. Lewald v. York Corp., 68 F.Supp. 386 (S.D.N.Y.1946); Koster v. (American) Lumbermens Mutual Casualty Co., 330 U.S. 518, 532, 67 S.Ct. 828, 835, 91 L.Ed. 1067 (1947) (Black, J., dissenting). See also infra § 23.6 n. 11.

§ 23.6

1. Supra §§ 3.32, 3.34.

2. U.S. Constitution Art. I, § 10; Bedford v. Eastern Building & Loan Association, 181 U.S. 227, 21 S.Ct. 597, 45 L.Ed. 834 (1901).

3. Restatement, Second, Conflict of Laws § 311, comnt. (b) (1971); Railway Express Agency v. Commonwealth of Virginia, 282 U.S. 440, 51 S.Ct. 201, 75 L.Ed. 450 (1931).

4. Allenberg Cotton Co. v. Pittman, 419 U.S. 20, 95 S.Ct. 260, 42 L.Ed.2d 195 (1974); Furst v. Brewster, 282 U.S. 493, 51 S.Ct. 295, 75 L.Ed. 478 (1931); Sioux Remedy Co. v. Cope, 235 U.S. 197, 35 S.Ct. 57, 59 L.Ed. 193 (1914); Unlaub Co., Inc. v. Sexton, 427 F.Supp. 1360, 1365 (W.D.Ark. 1977), affirmed 568 F.2d 72 (8th Cir.1977); Goodwin Brothers Leasing, Inc. v. Nousis, 373 Mass. 169, 366 N.E.2d 38, 42 (1977). Cf. Eli Lilly & Co. v. Sav–On–Drugs, Inc., 366 U.S. 276, 81 S.Ct. 1316, 6 L.Ed.2d 288 (1961).

5. McDougal, Felix & Whitten, American Conflicts Law 828–29 (5th ed. 2001) (citing cases). The requirement that a foreign corporation engaged in both interstate and intrastate business comply with a state

qualifying statute (infra § 23.7) is not an unreasonable burden on commerce. Eli Lilly & Co. v. Sav–On–Drugs, Inc., 366 U.S. 276, 81 S.Ct. 1316, 6 L.Ed.2d 288 (1961), rehearing denied 366 U.S. 978, 81 S.Ct. 1913, 6 L.Ed.2d 1268 (1961); Radio WHKW v. Ben Yarber, 838 F.2d 1439 (5th Cir.1988). See Hale, Unconstitutional Conditions and Constitutional Rights, 35 Colum. L. Rev. 321 (1935). Cf. Metropolitan Casualty Insurance Co. v. Brownell, 294 U.S. 580, 55 S.Ct. 538, 79 L.Ed. 1070 (1935). See also Schauer, Too Hard: Unconstitutional Conditions and the Chimera of Constitutional Consistency, 72 Denv.U.L.Rev. 989 (1995).

6. Northwestern States Portland Cement Co. v. Minnesota, 358 U.S. 450, 79 S.Ct. 357, 3 L.Ed.2d 421 (1959); Heublein, Inc. v. South Carolina Tax Commission, 409 U.S. 275, 93 S.Ct. 483, 34 L.Ed.2d 472 (1972). See also Netherlands Shipmortgage Corp. v. Madias, 717 F.2d 731 (2d Cir.1983) (overturning as "clearly erroneous" a decision upholding the New York qualification statute against a Bermuda company where transaction had both interstate (and international) and intrastate aspects.).

7. See Moorman Manufacturing Co. v. Bair, 437 U.S. 267, 98 S.Ct. 2340, 57 L.Ed.2d 197 (1978); J. Nowak & R. Rotunda, Constitutional Law 308 (6th ed. 2000). It was not a Constitutional violation for Wisconsin to require local incorporation for a company conducting local business in local markets: Alliant Energy Corp. v. Bie, 330 F.3d 904 (7th Cir. 2003), cert. denied

Rather than attempting to exclude foreign corporations, state legislation today usually takes the form of regulating their intrastate activities by means of "qualification statutes."

The validity of statutes purporting to regulate the internal affairs of foreign corporations is subject to scrutiny under the Commerce Clause. In *Edgar v. MITE Corp.*,[8] the Supreme Court struck down an Illinois anti-takeover statute which was applicable to, among others, foreign target corporations if 10% or more of the shares in question were owned by Illinois residents. While the target in *Edgar* was an Illinois corporation, the decision has potential implications for the regulation of pseudo-foreign corporations: The Court noted that Illinois's justification for the statute (its interest in regulating the internal affairs of Illinois corporations) was "somewhat incredible" in light of its applicability to foreign corporations under the circumstances noted above and that "Illinois has no interest in regulating the internal affairs of foreign corporations."[9]

In *CTS Corp. v. Dynamics Corp. of America*,[10] the Supreme Court upheld the Indiana anti-takeover statute that made the exercise of voting rights of transferred control stock in an Indiana corporation contingent on the approval of the disinterested shareholders. The Court distinguished *Edgar* on the ground, inter alia, that the Indiana statute, unlike the Illinois statute, applied only to Indiana corporations: "No principle of corporation law and practice is more firmly established than a State's authority to regulate domestic corporations, including the authority to define the voting rights of shareholders."[11] Some subsequent lower court decisions have sought to limit *CTS Corp.* to its Commerce Clause context and have allowed the application of forum law.[12]

2. *Qualification Statutes*

§ 23.7 Many states have legislation requiring foreign corporations to "qualify" before doing business within the state.[1] The requirement

___ U.S. ___, 124 S.Ct. 1047, 157 L.Ed.2d 890 (2004) and ___ U.S. ___, 124 S.Ct. 1077, 157 L.Ed.2d 890 (2004). For international implications, see Swaine, Negotiating Federalism: State Bargaining and the Dormant Treaty Power, 49 Duke L. J. 1127, 1146 (2000).

8. 457 U.S. 624, 102 S.Ct. 2629, 73 L.Ed.2d 269 (1982) (also discussed supra § 23.2 n.5).

9. Id. at 645–46, 102 S.Ct. at 2642.

10. 481 U.S. 69, 107 S.Ct. 1637, 95 L.Ed.2d 67 (1987).

11. Id. at 89, 107 S.Ct. at 1649 (citing to Restatement Second, Conflict of Laws § 304). For discussion see Kozyris, Some Observations on State Regulation of Multi-state Takeovers—Controlling Choice of Law Through the Commerce Clause, 14 Del. J. Corp. L. 499 (1989); Buxbaum, The Threat-

ened Constitutionalization of the Internal Affairs Doctrine in Corporation Law, 75 Cal. L. Rev. 29 (1987). See also Majchrzak, Corporate Chaos: Who Should Govern Internal Affairs?, 24 T.Jefferson L.Rev. 83 (2001).

12. See, e.g., A.S. Goldmen & Co. v. New Jersey Bureau of Securities, 163 F.3d 780 (3d Cir.) cert. denied, 528 U.S. 868, 120 S.Ct. 166, 145 L.Ed.2d 141 (1999) (application of forum state Blue Sky law to domestic corporation attempting to offer securities to out-of-state customers does not violate dormant commerce clause principles because adequate territorial nexus and state interests in regulation were established); Sadler v. NCR Corp., 928 F.2d 48 (2d Cir.1991) (application of New York law to order production of shareholder lists when no such remedy existed in the state of incorporation).

usually includes the filing of a copy of the articles of incorporation with the secretary of state and the designation of an agent for the receipt of service of process. Originally, a major purpose of these statutes was to facilitate the exercise of local jurisdiction over foreign corporations. This objective can now be attained by means of state long-arm statutes. It has therefore been suggested that qualification statutes have largely lost their usefulness and should be repealed,[2] and that they should be replaced by a "simpler system of interstate corporate recognition, perhaps reciprocal in nature, designed to facilitate rather than to limit corporate trade and commerce among the states...."[3]

States impose a wide range of sanctions when a foreign corporation fails to comply with the requirements of a qualification statute, including penalties and personal liability of directors and agents.[4] However, by far the most common consequence of a failure to qualify is the denial of access to the courts of the state[5] for the maintenance of actions on contracts[6] made by the foreign corporation in the state.[7] Subsequent compliance with the qualification statute may cure the defect and permit maintenance of the action.[8]

§ 23.7

1. See supra § 23.6, particularly nn.4–5, with respect to the regulation of interstate activity of foreign corporations. With respect to qualification of foreign trustees see supra § 21.5.

2. Walker, Foreign Corporation Laws: The Loss of Reason, 47 N.C. L. Rev. 1 (1968); Walker, Foreign Corporation Laws: A Current Account, 47 N.C. L. Rev. 733 (1969); Walker, Foreign Corporation Laws: Source and Support for Reform, 1969 Duke L.J. 1145.

3. McDougal, Felix & Leflar, American Conflicts Law 856 (5th ed. 2001).

4. See Note, Sanctions for Failure to Comply with Corporate Qualification Statutes: An Evaluation, 63 Colum. L. Rev. 117 (1963).

5. The non-access provisions also apply to the maintenance of actions in the federal courts of the state in diversity suits. Woods v. Interstate Realty Co., 337 U.S. 535, 69 S.Ct. 1235, 93 L.Ed. 1524 (1949). For criticism see Walker, Foreign Corporation Laws: Re–Examining *Woods v. Interstate Realty Co.* and Reopening the Federal Courts, 48 N.C. L. Rev. 56 (1969).

6. See, e.g., C & C Products, Inc. v. Premier Industries Corp., 290 Ala. 179, 275 So.2d 124 (1972), appeal after remand 292 Ala. 407, 295 So.2d 396 (1974), cert. denied 419 U.S. 1033, 95 S.Ct. 515, 42 L.Ed.2d 308 (1974); Boles v. Midland Guardian Company, 410 So.2d 82 (1982); Continental Tele-

phone Corp. v. Weaver, 410 F.2d 1196 (5th Cir.1969); Eastern Shore Marine, Inc. v. M/V Mistress, 717 F.Supp. 790 (1989). Such a provision, moreover, may not only bar the remedy but also the right, in the sense that an action may not be maintainable in a sister state as well. This may be the case if the contract is governed by the law of the state in which the corporation failed to comply with the qualification statute. Restatement, Second, Conflict of Laws § 312(2), comments (g), (h) (1971). A contract made in another state, on the other hand, may not be barred. Lee v. Great Northern Nekoosa Corp., 465 F.2d 1132 (5th Cir.1972); Linton & Company v. Robert Reid Engineers, 504 F.Supp. 1169 (1981). Restatement, Second, Conflict of Laws § 312(1) (1971). Nor do qualification statutes ordinarily prevent the enforcement of property and tort claims. 17 W. Fletcher, Private Corporations § 8508 (1987 rev.); but see Munday v. Wisconsin Trust Co., 252 U.S. 499, 40 S.Ct. 365, 64 L.Ed. 684 (1920). See also Netherlands Shipmortgage Corp. v. Madias, 717 F.2d 731 (2d Cir.1983) (overturning as "clearly erroneous" a decision upholding the New York qualification statute against a Bermuda company where transaction had both interstate and intra-state aspects).

7. For the distinction between intra and interstate business see supra § 23.6 nn.4–5. See also infra at § 23.8 n.1.

8. See Annot., 6 A.L.R.3d 326 (1966); but see Annot., 59 A.L.R.2d 1131 (1958).

§ 23.8   The requirements of the qualification statutes apply when a foreign corporation "does business" within a state and such transactions are not part of interstate commerce. There is no single definition of "doing business" for this purpose. However, § 15.01(b) of the Revised Model Business Corporation Act provides a useful list of activities which do *not* constitute "transacting business" within the meaning of its § 15.01(a), establishing the general qualification requirement.[1]

3. Pseudo–Foreign Corporations

§ 23.9   Issues relating to the "internal affairs" of a corporation are normally governed by the law of incorporation and a number of older decisions held that a court in another state also lacked jurisdiction to entertain actions dealing with such issues. The jurisdiction approach now follows principles of forum non conveniens,[1] and there have been similar departures from the uniform choice-of-law reference to the law of the place of incorporation in these cases. Thus, when a foreign corporation has its principal or a major place of business[2] in the forum, the local law of the forum may govern either in application of the forum's qualification statute[3] or, more generally, because the corporation is considered to be only a "pseudo-foreign corporation," with the result that, for some purposes, it may be treated as if it were a domestic corporation.[4]

California provides an example of legislative regulation of aspects of the internal affairs of pseudo-foreign corporations.[5] It provides for the

§ 23.8

1.   Among the excluded activities are the maintenance or defense of an action or administrative or arbitration proceeding or effecting the settlement of claims; the holding of meetings or conducting activities concerning its internal affairs; maintaining bank accounts; maintaining offices for the exchange of securities; creating instruments of indebtedness; effecting sales through independent contractors and conducting an isolated transaction. Model Business Corporation Act Ann. § 106(2). See also Charter Finance Co. v. Henderson, 60 Ill.2d 323, 326 N.E.2d 372 (1975).

§ 23.9

1.   Supra § 23.5.

2.   Cf. the European notion of a corporations seat, supra § 23.1 and Latty, Pseudo–Foreign Corporation, 65 Yale L.J. 137, 166 (1955).

3.   McCormick v. Statler Hotels Delaware Corp., 30 Ill.2d 86, 195 N.E.2d 172 (1963), transferred 55 Ill.App.2d 21, 203 N.E.2d 697 (1964). Cf. Toklan Royalty Corp. v. Tiffany, 193 Okla. 120, 141 P.2d 571 (1943).

4.   See State of Iowa ex rel. Weede v. Bechtel, 239 Iowa 1298, 31 N.W.2d 853 (1948), cert. denied sub nom. Bechtel v. Thatcher, 337 U.S. 918, 69 S.Ct. 1161, 93 L.Ed. 1728 (1949); Mansfield Hardwood Lumber Co. v. Johnson, 268 F.2d 317 (5th Cir.1959), cert. denied 361 U.S. 885, 80 S.Ct. 156, 4 L.Ed.2d 120 (1959); Latty, supra n.2; Note, The Pseudo–Foreign Corporation in California, 28 Hastings L.J. 119 (1976); Reese & Kaufman, The Law Governing Corporate Affairs: Choice of Law and the Impact of Full Faith and Credit, 58 Colum. L. Rev. 1118 (1958).

5.   Cal. Corp. Code § 2115(a). See also N.Y. Bus. Corp. Law §§ 1306, 1315–1320. The leading early California decision is Western Air Lines, Inc. v. Sobieski, 191 Cal.App.2d 399, 12 Cal.Rptr. 719 (1961). See also Western Air Lines, Inc. v. Schutzbank, 258 Cal.App.2d 218, 66 Cal.Rptr. 293 (1968); People v. Western Air Lines, Inc., 258 Cal.App.2d 213, 66 Cal.Rptr. 316 (1968).

U.C.C. § 8–110 (1994 Revision) distinguishes between direct and indirect holding of securities. In indirect holding, the investor is not registered on the corporation's books but has a claim against the "interme-

application of local law when both local ownership and the amount of business done in California exceed 50%, except when the foreign corporation's shares are listed on a national securities exchange.[6] A strict reading of *CTS Corp. v. Dynamics Corp. of America*,[7] invoking full faith and credit, due process, and commerce clause considerations to confirm a state's exclusive control over corporations created by it, may draw into question the continued validity of "pseudo-foreign corporation" legislation, at least to the extent that it has been applied broadly.[8] It would seem, however, that the forum must retain some measure of control over the activities of foreign, but essentially domestic corporations.[9]

4. *Piercing the Corporate Veil*

§ 23.10   The ability of plaintiffs to visit the sins of the parent upon its subsidiaries and vice versa is an important aspect of interstate and

diary," whose "jurisdiction" is defined by § 110 (e). For comment, see Schwarcz & Benjamin, Intermediary Risk in the Indirect Holding System for Securities, 12 Duke L.J.Comp. & Int'l L. 309 (2002).

The validity of statutes purporting to regulate the internal affairs of foreign corporations is subject to scrutiny under the Commerce Clause. In Edgar v. MITE Corp., 457 U.S. 624, 102 S.Ct. 2629, 73 L.Ed.2d 269 (1982), the Supreme Court struck down an Illinois anti-takeover statute which was applicable to, among others, foreign target corporations if 10% or more of the shares in question were owned by Illinois residents. While the target in *Edgar* was an Illinois corporation, the decision has potential implications for the regulation of pseudo-foreign corporations: The Court noted that Illinois' justification for the statute (its interest in regulating the internal affairs of Illinois corporations) was "somewhat incredible" in light of its applicability to foreign corporations under the circumstances noted above and that "Illinois has no interest in regulating the internal affairs of foreign corporations." Id. at 645–46, 102 S. Ct. at 2642. See also Kozyris, Corporate Wars and Choice of Law, 1985 Duke L.J. 1, 35 et seq. It appears, however, that a state's interest in regulating pseudo-foreign corporations would be stronger where the dominating contacts are local, with the exception of a foreign incorporation.

The California statute was most recently upheld in Wilson v. Louisiana–Pacific Resources, Inc., 138 Cal.App.3d 216, 187 Cal. Rptr. 852 (1982) and in Valtz v. Penta Investment Corp., 139 Cal.App.3d 803, 188 Cal.Rptr. 922 (1983). In Nedlloyd Lines B.V. v. Superior Court, 3 Cal.4th 459, 11 Cal.Rptr.2d 330, 351 n.13, 834 P.2d 1148, 1169 n.13 (1992) (Kennard, J., concurring

and dissenting) ("[internal affairs] doctrine's status in California is doubtful").

6. Cal. Corp. Code § 2115(e). Once listed on a national exchange, the corporation will be subject to federal securities and exchange rules and regulations and investors will enjoy protection similar to that sought to be achieved by the California legislation. Cf. Loss, The Conflict of Laws and the Blue Sky Laws, 71 Harv. L. Rev. 209 (1957).

7. 481 U.S. 69, 107 S.Ct. 1637, 95 L.Ed.2d 67 (1987) (discussed supra §§ 23.1 n.5 and 23.6 n.10).

8. In a case involving parallel litigation in Delaware and California and concerning a Delaware corporation, the Supreme Court of Delaware forcefully restated and confirmed the internal affairs doctrine (applicability of the law of the state of incorporation) and referred to its "constitutional underpinnings." Draper v. Paul N. Gardner Defined Plan Trust, 625 A.2d 859, 867 (Del. 1993).

The New York statute is found in N.Y. Bus. Corp. L. § 1320. It has been raised as a defense against indemnification of corporate employees: Stewart v. Continental Copper & Steel Industries, Inc., 67 A.D.2d 293, 414 N.Y.S.2d 910 (1979); Sierra Rutile Limited v. Katz, 1997 WL 431119 (S.D.N.Y. 1997).

9. See Haberman v. Washington Public Power Supply System, 109 Wn.2d 107, 744 P.2d 1032 (1987), opinion amended 109 Wn.2d 107, 750 P.2d 254 (1988), appeal dismissed 488 U.S. 805, 109 S.Ct. 35, 102 L.Ed.2d 15 (1988) (securities fraud claims adjudicated under Washington law in view of substantial relationship with Washington forum). See also Kozyris, Some Observations on State Regulation of Multistate Takovers—Controlling Choice of Law Through the Commerce Clause, 14 Del. J.Corp.L. 499, 519–25 (1989).

international enterprise liability. What law governs for jurisdictional or choice-of-law purposes whether the separate corporate identity of the units may be disregarded (piercing of the corporate veil)?

The great majority of cases, if not virtually all, will concern claims under federal law (e.g., for patent infringement, under RICO, and the like) or claims to which, under modern approaches to choice of law, forum law will apply. The issue will therefore usually concern jurisdiction. The context in which these cases arise no doubt influences the question as to the law applicable to "piercing."

The Second Restatement favors the application of the law of incorporation of the parent,[1] i.e. a traditional corporate law-approach, and that approach has support in the case law. However, when the claim arises from federal law or, if not, implicates interests of the forum, the question must naturally be whether federal common law applies in the former or the lex fori, as a result of interest analysis, in the latter case.

A federal common law test for piercing (in claims based on federal law) has not been adopted. The federal court either adopts the state test or frequently finds that there is no conflict between the laws of potentially interested states: there is thus no need to add another, a federal layer.[2]

In state courts, and in federal courts sitting in diversity, the applicability of forum law on the question of *substantive* liability will often answer the jurisdictional question. Contrary to the Second Restatement approach, the jurisdictional inquiry then answers both questions. Delaware, in particular, asserts adjudicatory and legislative jurisdiction when a Delaware parent or subsidiary is involved.[3] A recent federal court decision drew the line when none of the parties was from Delaware and jurisdiction over the out-of-state parent was sought to be established on the basis of contacts of the subsidiary which, under Delaware's statute, did not suffice for "general jurisdiction."[4]

C. DISSOLUTION AND WINDING–UP

§ 23.11 The dissolution of a corporation, just as its creation, is governed by the law of the state of incorporation and the termination of a corporation's existence by that state will be recognized by other states.[1]

§ 23.10

1. See Restatement, Second, Conflict of Laws § 303 et. seq. (1971). For an excellent discussion of piercing, see Craig v. Lake Asbestos of Quebec, Ltd., 843 F.2d 145 (3d Cir.1988).

2. See the much-cited decision in Mobil Oil Corp. v. Linear Films, Inc., 718 F.Supp. 260 (D.Del.1989).

3. See references in *Mobil Oil*, 718 F.Supp. 260 and in S. Bainbridge, Corporations Law and Economics § 4.3 at 165 (2002). The Restatement approach was fol-

lowed in a Texas diversity case: Alberto v. Diversified Group, Inc. 55 F.3d 201 (5th Cir. 1995) (Delaware law applied). The New York approach appears to be the same. Bainbridge, supra id.

4. C.R. Bard Inc. v. Guidant Corp. et al., 997 F.Supp. 556 (D.Del.1998).

§ 23.11

1. Restatement, Second, Conflict of Laws § 299 (1971); Bazan v. Kux Machine Co., 52 Wis.2d 325, 190 N.W.2d 521 (1971). See also 17 W. Fletcher, Private Corpora-

Dissolution of a corporation, or termination or suspension of its activities, however does not necessarily mean immediate cessation of all of its activities. Most states provide, by statute, for a limited time during which the corporation continues to exist for the purpose of winding-up its affairs.[2] When the time extension is provided by the law of the state of incorporation, it will ordinarily be recognized by other states as well.[3] In contrast, the time extension may be provided by the law of the forum for the convenience of local creditors in circumstances where the state of incorporation does not provide for such an extension. In such cases, an older decision of the United States Supreme Court has held that the resulting judgment need not be given full faith and credit by the state of incorporation.[4]

A state may also wind-up the local business of a foreign corporation in the absence of its dissolution in the state of incorporation to the extent that such action does not conflict with federal law, particularly the federal bankruptcy law. This power follows from the forum's authority to regulate the intrastate activities of foreign corporations.[5]

II. BANKRUPTCY

A. INTRODUCTION

§ 23.12   The amendments to the provisions of the Bankruptcy Code dealing with bankruptcy courts necessitated by the Supreme

tions § 8579 (1998 ed.); Annot., 19 A.L.R.3d (1968). For England, see Smart, International Insolvency: Ancillary Winding Up and the Foreign Corporation, 39 Int'l & Comp. L.Q. 827 (1990).

2. See 17 W. Fletcher, supra n.1, §§ 8582, 8583.

3. Restatement, Second, Conflict of Laws § 299, comnt. (e) (1971). The comment notes as one exception state statutory or constitutional provisions restricting the rights of foreign corporations to those enjoyed by domestic corporations. Such a provision may have the effect of denying recognition to the foreign time extension when domestic corporations do not benefit from a similar extension.

4. Pendleton v. Russell, 144 U.S. 640, 12 S.Ct. 743, 36 L.Ed. 574 (1892). In a number of cases, foreign-country corporations have been permitted to maintain local actions after dissolution in their respective country of incorporation. See Compania Ron Bacardi v. Bank of Nova Scotia, 193 F.Supp. 814 (S.D.N.Y.1961) (Cuban corporation may sue after termination by Cuban expropriation); A/S Merilaid & Co. v. Chase National Bank, 189 Misc. 285, 71 N.Y.S.2d 377 (1947) (Estonian corporation dissolved by Soviet decree); Vladikavzasky Railway

Co. v. New York Trust Co., 263 N.Y. 369, 189 N.E. 456 (1934) (Russian nationalization). The United States Supreme Court's adoption of the "Act of State Doctrine" in Banco Nacional de Cuba v. Sabbatino, 376 U.S. 398, 84 S.Ct. 923, 11 L.Ed.2d 804 (1964) now draws the continued validity of these decisions into question. See F. & H.R. Farman–Farmaian Consulting Engineers Firm v. Harza Engineering Co., 882 F.2d 281 (7th Cir.1989), cert. denied 497 U.S. 1038, 110 S.Ct. 3301, 111 L.Ed.2d 809 (1990). But see also 22 U.S.C.A. § 2370(e)(2) ("Hickenlooper amendment" to the Foreign Relations Act) which provides that the Act–of–State doctrine shall not apply when the foreign governmental act violates principles of international law.

5. Restatement, Second, Conflict of Laws § 300, cmnts. (a), (d) (1971). The rule is the same in England. Dicey & Morris, Conflict of Laws 1116 (13th ed. 2000 by Collins et al.).

The liability of a successor corporation for product liability claims against the predecessor is an issue of tort and not corporate law. See Ruiz v. Blentech Corp., 89 F.3d 320 (7th Cir.1996), cert. denied 519 U.S. 1077, 117 S.Ct. 737, 136 L.Ed.2d 677 (1997).

Court's decision in *Northern Pipeline Construction Co. v. Marathon Pipe Line Co.*[1] were enacted by Congress[2] and signed into law[3] in the summer of 1984. Between the expiration on December 24, 1982 of the stay of the Court's decision and the amendment of the Bankruptcy Code, bankruptcy courts operated under the Emergency Rule adopted by the district courts. The Emergency Rule provided for a blanket referral of bankruptcy cases from the district courts to the bankruptcy courts, with the proviso that in "related to" proceedings judgments would be rendered by the district courts upon proposed findings of fact and rulings by the bankruptcy courts.[4]

The amendments provide that *district courts,* as did the bankruptcy courts under the Bankruptcy Reform Act of 1978, have original and exclusive jurisdiction of all cases under title 11 of the U.S. Code (bankruptcy),[5] and "original but not exclusive jurisdiction of all *civil proceedings* arising under title 11, *or arising in or related to* cases under title 11."[6] However, the amendments contain novel discretionary and mandatory abstention provisions: A district court may, "in the interest of justice, or ... of comity with State courts or respect for State law," abstain from hearing such a proceeding.[7] Further, upon motion of a

§ 23.12

1. 458 U.S. 50, 102 S.Ct. 2858, 73 L.Ed.2d 598 (1982), judgment stayed 459 U.S. 813, 103 S.Ct. 199, 74 L.Ed.2d 160 (1982).

2. H.R. 5174, June 29, 1984.

3. Bankruptcy Amendments and Federal Judgeship Act of 1984, P.L. 98–353, July 10, 1984. For a discussion of the amendments, see, e.g., Chatz & Schumm, 1984 Bankruptcy Code Amendments—Fresh From the Anvil, 89 Com. L.J. 317 (1984); Taggart, The New Bankruptcy Court System, 30 Prac. L. 11 (1984); Cooper, Summary of the Bankruptcy Amendments and Federal Judgeship Act of 1984, 57 N.Y.St. B.J., April 1985, 29, May 1985, 29; Kamp, Court Structure under the Bankruptcy Code, 90 Com. L.J. 203 (1985); King, Jurisdiction and Procedure Under the Bankruptcy Amendments of 1984, 38 Vand. L. Rev. 675 (1985).

4. The constitutionality of this arrangement was upheld repeatedly. See, e.g., In re Lafayette Radio Electronics Corp., 761 F.2d 84 (2d Cir.1985); Oklahoma Health Services Federal Credit Union v. Webb, 726 F.2d 624 (10th Cir.1984). For a discussion of the *Marathon* decision, the Emergency Rule and the 1984 amendments, see Countryman, Scrambling to Refine Bankruptcy Jurisdiction: The Chief Justice, the Judicial Conference, and the Legislative Process, 22 Harv. J. on Legis. 1 (1985).

5. 28 U.S.C.A. § 1334(a).

6. 28 U.S.C.A. § 1334(b)(emphasis added). This is virtually the same jurisdiction granted bankruptcy courts under the Bankruptcy Reform Act of 1978. Note also Matter of Hudson Feather & Down Products, Inc., 36 B.R. 466 (E.D.N.Y.1984), holding that subject-matter jurisdiction over pending state claims did not terminate upon completion of a reorganization plan specifically providing for a retention of the bankruptcy court's jurisdiction in this respect.

7. 28 U.S.C.A. § 1334(c)(1). See, e.g., In re Weldpower Industries, Inc., 49 B.R. 46 (Bkrtcy.D.N.H.1985) (abstention ordered where same cause of action had previously been brought in state court, where it was dismissed for lack of *in personam* jurisdiction over defendant); Matter of Boughton, 49 B.R. 312 (Bkrtcy.N.D.Ill.1985) (no voluntary abstention on grounds of promotion of interests of justice and comity since matter did not involve "issues of State constitutional law, important State policy, or unsettled State law"); Macon Prestressed Concrete Co. v. Duke, 46 B.R. 727 (M.D.Ga. 1985) (no voluntary abstention where counterclaim "intimately connected" with debtor's petition for reorganization); State Bank of Lombard v. Chart House, Inc., 46 B.R. 468 (N.D.Ill.1985) (abstention ordered after breach of contract (subordination agreement) claim was removed from state court to federal district court and neither party was debtor in bankruptcy proceedings); In re Ghen, 45 B.R. 780 (Bkrtcy.E.D.Pa.1985) (abstention where pending state court breach of contract action would have no

party in interest, district courts must abstain from hearing any proceeding "based upon a State law claim or . . . cause of action, *related to* a case under title 11 but not arising under title 11 or arising in a case under title 11, with respect to which an action could not have been commenced in [federal] court absent [a bankruptcy filing]."[8]

Under the 1984 amendments, bankruptcy judges are appointed for judicial districts by the U.S. Court of Appeals for that circuit,[9] and will constitute a unit of the district court known as the bankruptcy court.[10] Each bankruptcy judge, as a judicial officer of the district court, may

bearing on administration of estate); In re DeLorean Motor Company, 49 B.R. 900 (Bkrtcy.E.D.Mich.1985) (existence of state law claims, inextricably tied to bankruptcy matters, and mere difficulty in ascertaining state law are insufficient basis for abstention given congressional interest in having all bankruptcy matters adjudicated in one forum); In re Schear & Associates, Inc., 47 B.R. 544 (Bkrtcy.S.D.Fla.1985) (action by trustee in bankruptcy to collect account receivable from California defendant dismissed without prejudice on grounds that (i) appropriate venue "probably" in federal district court sitting in California and (ii) this court is the busiest in the country and trustee "would be better served to refer this claim to California counsel for prosecution in either the state or federal court which is best equipped to provide prompt resolution").

8. 28 U.S.C.A. § 1334(c)(2) (emphasis added). However, personal injury tort and wrongful death claims against the estate are not subject to the mandatory abstention provisions. 28 U.S.C.A. § 157(b)(4).

For a discussion of the legislative history leading to the version of the mandatory abstention provision finally adopted, and of the meaning of the term "related to," see Kamp, supra n.3, at 206–208.

A number of courts have had occasion to deal with the abstention provisions and other 1984 revisions of the Bankruptcy Code, which are "confusing to say the least." In re White Motor Credit, et al., 761 F.2d 270 (6th Cir.1985). See also In re S.E. Hornsby & Sons Sand and Gravel Co., 45 B.R. 988 (Bkrtcy.M.D.La.1985). With respect to personal injury and wrongful death claims, supra, 11 U.S.C.A. § 157 further provides that "the district court shall order [such claims] to be tried in the *district court* in which the bankruptcy case is pending, or . . . arose." 28 U.S.C.A. § 157(b)(5) (emphasis added). While such claims are expressly exempt from the mandatory abstention provisions, the law is silent on the issue whether such cases are subject to the voluntary abstention provisions of 28 U.S.C.A.

§ 1334(c)(1). In this connection, see also In re Illinois–California Exp., Inc., 50 B.R. 232 (Bkrtcy.D.Colo.1985), where the court voluntarily abstained from hearing a matter which arose prior to the effective date of § 1334(c)(2), but with respect to which the prerequisites for mandatory abstention under that provision were met. In *White Motor Credit,* the court was confronted with the debtor's contention that § 157(b)(5) prevented district courts from leaving such cases in other courts for adjudication. Upon review of the legislative history, it held that bankruptcy courts *could* abstain from hearing such cases pursuant to § 1334(c)(1). Section 157(b)(5) would apply only absent such abstention, in which case trial in one of the district courts listed was required.

Abstention is only mandatory under 28 U.S.C.A. § 1334(c)(2) if the matter "can be timely adjudicated" in state courts. In this regard, see *Boughton,* 49 B.R. 312 ("lengthy" time lapse constituting "undue delay, seriously disrupting" estate administration is basis for denying application for abstention) and *DeLorean,* (earliest possible trial date 30–36 months hence is sufficient to decline abstention in order to prevent irreparable delay, and injury to interests of estate and creditors). Abstention is not mandatory under § 1334(c)(2) if, absent bankruptcy jurisdiction, the case could nevertheless have been brought in federal court, e.g., based on diversity: Matter of Republic Oil Corp., 51 B.R. 355 (Bkrtcy. W.D.Wis.1985); *Macon Prestressed Concrete,* 46 B.R. 727.

9. 28 U.S.C.A. § 152(a)(1). For a detailed discussion of the provisions relating to the bankruptcy courts, see 1 Collier on Bankruptcy, ch. 2 (King, ed., 1997).

10. 28 U.S.C.A. § 151. See also Borchers, Choice of Law Relative to Security Interest and Other Liens in International Bankruptcies, 46 Am. J. Comp. L. Supp. 165, 166 (1998).

exercise the powers conferred under Chapter 6 of Title 28, U.S.C.A.[11] This specifically includes the powers conferred by 28 U.S.C.A. § 157, pursuant to which district courts may make blanket referrals to bankruptcy judges of "all cases under title 11 and any or all proceedings arising under title 11 or arising in or related to a case under title 11."[12] Bankruptcy judges may hear and determine all cases under title 11 and all core proceedings[13] arising under title 11 or arising in a case under title 11.[14] The bankruptcy judge may hear non-core proceedings "related to a case under title 11," but must submit proposed findings of fact and conclusions of law to the district court, and any final order or judgment must be entered by the district judge,[15] unless all parties consent to a hearing and determination of the matter by the bankruptcy judge.[16]

The determination whether a proceeding is a core proceeding is made by the bankruptcy judge, and "shall not be made solely on the basis that its resolution may be affected by State law."[17]

Finally, the district court may on motion withdraw the reference of any case or proceeding for cause shown, and shall so withdraw a proceeding if it determines that resolution of the proceeding "requires consideration of both title 11 and other laws of the United States

---

11. 28 U.S.C.A. § 151.

12. 28 U.S.C.A. § 157(a).

13. As defined in 28 U.S.C.A. § 157(b)(2).

14. 28 U.S.C.A. § 157(b)(1). The constitutionality of this provision has been upheld in a number of recent decisions. See, e.g., In re Northwest Cinema Corp., 49 B.R. 479 (Bkrtcy.D.Minn.1985) (with further references).

15. 28 U.S.C.A. § 157(c)(1). The district court must review de novo all matters to which any party has made timely and specific objection.

Some of the issues that have arisen under 28 U.S.C.A. § 157(c)(1) include questions concerning the meaning of (i) a proceeding that is "not a core proceeding but is otherwise related to a case under title 11," and (ii) of a "final order or judgment." See, e.g., In re Bokum Resources Corp., 49 B.R. 854 (Bkrtcy.D.N.M.1985) (actions between debtor and third party which rely almost exclusively on state law for their resolution and must be resolved by an Article III court); UNR Industries, Inc. v. Continental Ins. Co., 623 F.Supp. 1319 (N.D.Ill.1985); In re Franklin Computer Corp., 50 B.R. 620 (Bkrtcy.E.D.Pa.1985) (accounts receivable litigation is core proceeding); In re Nell, 71 B.R. 305 (D.Utah 1987) (rejecting *Franklin,* preceding); In re Omega Equipment Corp., 51 B.R. 569 (D.D.C.1985) (power to issue contempt orders is reserved for Article III courts); Kellogg v. Chester, 71 B.R. 36

(N.D.Tex.1987) (rejecting *In re Omega,* preceding). See also, with respect to former 28 U.S.C.A. § 1471, In re Bobroff, 766 F.2d 797 (3d Cir.1985) ("related to" proceedings are those which could conceivably have an effect on the debtor's estate) and Matter of Colorado Energy Supply, Inc., 728 F.2d 1283 (10th Cir.1984) ("related" proceedings are "adversary cases ... triable only by Article III ... or state courts," "traditional state common-law claims").

For purposes of 28 U.S.C.A. § 157(c)(1), "final" orders which must be entered by the district court have been held not to include interlocutory orders of substantive or procedural import. In re Lion Capital Group, 46 B.R. 850 (Bkrtcy.S.D.N.Y.1985) rejected in *In re Nell.* The question arises whether an order to remand a suit among non-debtors to the state court can be entered by the bankruptcy court as an interlocutory order not affecting parties' potential claims against the debtor. While the court in In re Nilsson, 42 B.R. 587 (Bkrtcy. C.D.Cal.1984) refrained from entering such an order, submitting a proposal to the district court, the court in In re Kennedy, 48 B.R. 621 (Bkrtcy.D.Ariz.1985) denied defendant's objection to its grant of plaintiffs' motion to remand proceedings back to the state system.

16. 28 U.S.C.A. § 157(c)(2).

17. 28 U.S.C.A. § 157(b)(3). For elements affecting determination, see, e.g., *Bokum Resources Corp.*, 49 B.R. 854.

regulating organizations or activities affecting interstate commerce."[18] The district court will hear appeals from final judgments, orders and decrees, and, with leave of the court, from interlocutory orders and decrees of bankruptcy judges.[19]

B. INTERSTATE BANKRUPTCY

§ 23.13   The bankruptcy court has jurisdiction over civil claims "related" to the bankruptcy case, including, for instance, contract and tort claims in the hands of the trustee.[1] The substantive law governing

---

18. 28 U.S.C.A. § 157(d). With regard to the withdrawal of referred cases by the district court, see, e.g., In re DeLorean Motor Co., supra n.7, at 911, indicating that only substantial and material considerations of the laws mentioned would mandate such withdrawal. Congress intended to have bankruptcy proceedings adjudicated in bankruptcy court, necessitating withdrawal only if *essential* to preserve higher interests and overriding policy. The existence of state law issues by itself is not sufficient to justify withdrawal. See also *In re Nell,* 71 B.R. 305, 308 n.3 (D.Utah 1987).

19. 28 U.S.C.A. § 158(a).

§ 23.13

1. Under pre–1984 case law, "related" claims included, for instance: Action against non-debtor defendants for rescission of loan transaction which financed contract with debtor, In re Zamost, 7 B.R. 859 (Bkrtcy. S.D.Cal.1980); debtors' claim for pain and suffering and punitive damages as involving issues inextricably interrelated with debtors Section 1983 claim against landlord for post-petition eviction, Matter of Pickus, 8 B.R. 114 (Bkrtcy.Conn.1980), appeal after remand 26 B.R. 171 (D.Conn.1982); cross-claims in removed action when sufficiently related to main action, In re Robert Carnahan Griffith and Ruth Ina Griffith, 6 B.R. 750 (Bkrtcy.D.N.M.1980); the dischargeability of the debtor's ex-wife's debts for attorney fees in connection with her divorce and of an outstanding loan cosigned by her which debtor was ordered to pay under the divorce decree, In re Fontaine, 10 B.R. 175 (Bkrtcy.R.I.1981).

There has not been much case law under the 1984 amendments construing the meaning of the term "related to" in 28 U.S.C.A. § 1334(b). A suit by individual spouses against the trustee in bankruptcy for their estate seeking damages for an alleged breach of fiduciary duties by defendant, was found to have a "sufficient nexus" to the bankruptcy proceedings to constitute a related case under 28 U.S.C.A. § 1334(b).

Weaver v. Gillen, 49 B.R. 70 (W.D.N.Y. 1985). In an action by debtors against former president to collect on loans, defendant's counterclaims, including setoff, are "sufficiently connected to ... [d]ebtors and their affairs" to be considered "related to" proceedings under 28 U.S.C.A. § 1334(b). Baldwin–United Corp. et al. v. Thompson, 48 B.R. 49 (Bkrtcy.S.D.Ohio 1985), rejected in *In re Nell,* 71 B.R. 305 (D.Utah 1987). See also In re Apex Oil Co., 88 B.R. 968 (Bkrtcy.E.D.Mo.1988), Thomasson v. AmSouth Bank, N.A., 59 B.R. 997 (N.D.Ala. 1986).

In contrast, the bankruptcy court does not have jurisdiction over divorce petition: expanded jurisdiction does not encompass domestic relations which are peculiarly within the province of state law. In re Cunningham, 9 B.R. 70 (Bkrtcy.D.N.M.1981). An action among three entities claiming entitlement to the surplus from a Chapter 11 distribution relating to the validity of a post-petition compromise between two of the three and the alleged post-petition tortious interference with that compromise by the third was found to be "so tangential to the Chapter 11 case to fall outside the scope of 28 U.S.C.A. § 1334(b)." In re Nilsson, 42 B.R. 587, 589 (Bkrtcy.C.D.Cal.1984).

Similarly, 11 U.S.C.A. § 523(a)(5) expressly exempts support obligations from discharge in bankruptcy. However, it is often a difficult question whether an agreement between the spouses is one for support or a division of property to be effected over time, especially when such an agreement antedates, and therefore did not contemplate, the bankruptcy. Earlier decisions considered the issue to be one that should be determined with reference to state law. In re Waller, 494 F.2d 447 (6th Cir.1974). With the adoption of 11 U.S.C.A. § 523(a)(5), the federal court now makes an independent determination of whether the agreement or decree was intended for support or constitutes a property settlement. In re Boggess, 105 B.R. 470 (Bkrtcy.S.D.Ill.

these claims, theoretically, may be state or federal; in the case of the former, the question is: the law of which state? There are many additional provisions giving rise to the same question. Thus, for instance, "the estate shall have the benefit of any defense available to the debtor as against an entity other than the estate, including statutes of limitation, statutes of frauds, usury, and other personal defenses."[2]

These subject matter provisions, moreover, must be seen in the context of the bankruptcy court's judicial jurisdiction and the Act's venue provisions. Judicial jurisdiction in bankruptcy is nationwide.[3] Venue for cases "under title 11" properly lies at the "domicile, residence, principal place of business ... or principal assets in the United States;"[4] venue for a proceeding "arising under title 11 or arising in or related to a case under title 11" lies in the court in which the bankruptcy case is pending.[5] The procedure in the case of improper venue is not so clear as under the previous provisions, pursuant to which the court could transfer or retain the case. Under the 1984 amendments, a case

1989); In re Cartner, 9 B.R. 543, 546 (Bkrtcy.M.D.Ala.1981). Through its control over the debtor's assets, the bankruptcy court can in effect achieve a fair distribution as between the former spouse and creditors of the estate. See Matter of Lanham, 13 B.R. 45 (Bkrtcy.C.D.Ill.1981). While doing so technically does not discharge the support obligation for the future, or extinguish a claim for any arrearage, such action does affect the present amount recoverable by the obligee from the estate.

2. 11 U.S.C.A. § 558 (" ... any defense ... against *any* entity ... ") (emphasis added). Similarly, what law determines whether there was a fraudulent conveyance? See 11 U.S.C.A. § 544(b) ("The trustee may avoid any transfer ... that is voidable *under applicable law* ... ,") (emphasis added). Further instances include 11 U.S.C.A. § 365, relating to executory contracts and unexpired leases, and 11 U.S.C.A. § 522, relating to exemptions. In this regard, see also Countryman, The Use of State Law in Bankruptcy Cases, 47 N.Y.U. L. Rev. 407, 631 (1972).

3. Bankr. Rule 7004(d). For a complete discussion, see supra § 10.7. See also In re WWG Industries, Inc., 44 B.R. 287 (N.D.Ga. 1984) (stating that change of venue provisions should be used in proper cases to abrogate the debtor's power to "reel persons from all over the country into a single forum"). Cf. Hogue v. Milodon Engineering, Inc., 736 F.2d 989 (4th Cir.1984) (upholding jurisdiction of bankruptcy court under Bankruptcy Act of 1898) (pre-Bankruptcy Reform Act petition) to enjoin defendants resident out of its territorial district from

prosecuting action against debtor discharged in proceedings before it.

4. 28 U.S.C.A. § 1408(1). For a discussion of the venue provisions, see 1 Collier on Bankruptcy, ¶ 3.02 (King, ed., 1997). Note also In re Kava Bowl, 41 B.R. 244 (Bkrtcy.D.Haw. 1984), dismissing proceedings for lack of jurisdiction with respect to Chapter 11 petition of American Samoa corporation upon finding that (i) there is no bankruptcy remedy in American Samoa and (ii) the petitioner maintained its principal place of business and assets there, holding that the keeping of accounting records and some cash, and the collection of some accounts receivable, in Hawaii do not constitute sufficient venue for jurisdiction. See also In re Almeida, 37 B.R. 186 (Bkrtcy. E.D.Pa. 1984), granting motion to transfer proceedings to California where debtor resided for the ten years preceding his move to Pennsylvania less than four months prior to his filing of a Chapter 7 petition and where the vast majority of his creditors were located. And In re Garden Manor Associates, L.P., 99 B.R. 551 (Bkrtcy.S.D.N.Y. 1988) venue would not be transferred to Arizona from New York, even though debtor sole asset was located in Arizona, the New York partnerships now in bankruptcy had made most business decisions in New York and most bankruptcy plans would have to be executed in New York.

5. 28 U.S.C.A. § 1409(a). If the claim arises after the commencement of the bankruptcy case from the operation of the business of the debtor, venue lies in the court where venue lies under nonbankruptcy provisions or in the court in which the bankruptcy case is pending. 28 U.S.C.A. § 1409(d), (e).

"may" be transferred,[6] leaving open the question whether the case may also be retained or dismissed.[7] Additionally, a claim pending in a civil action may be removed to a bankruptcy court having *subject matter* jurisdiction (i.e., a "related claim"),[8] and a bankruptcy court may transfer both the bankruptcy case and a proceeding on a related claim to a bankruptcy court for another district "in the interest of justice and for the convenience of the parties."[9] The questions raised by the venue provisions are: does state or federal substantive law govern in "related cases;" if state law, is it determined with the aid of a federal conflicts rule or must the bankruptcy court apply the choice-of-law rule of the state in which it sits; and, if the latter, do the principles of Van Dusen v. Barrack[10] govern upon transfer, requiring the transferee court to apply the law that would have been applied by the transferor court?

§ 23.14   There appears to be no reason why the bankruptcy court's subject matter jurisdiction over "related claims" that do not arise under the Bankruptcy Act itself (e.g. avoidance of preferences[1]) should entail the creation of federal substantive law. No federal interest or concern is implicated and the policy of the bankruptcy law itself is one of "geographic uniformity," not substantive uniformity, as Justice Frankfurter wrote in *Vanston Bondholders*. The "Constitutional requirement of uniformity ... is wholly satisfied when existing obligations of a debtor are treated alike by the bankruptcy administration throughout the country, regardless of the State in which the bankruptcy court sits.... To establish uniform laws of bankruptcy does not mean wiping out the differences among the ... States in their laws governing commercial transactions. The Constitution did not intend that transactions that have different legal consequences because they took place in different States shall come out with the same result because they passed through a bankruptcy court.... These differences inherent in our federal scheme the day before a bankruptcy are not wiped out or transmuted the day after."[2] The situation is different when, as in *Vanston* itself, the issue relates directly to bankruptcy law and policy or if some other federal law or concern is implicated.[3]

6. 28 U.S.C.A. § 1412(a).

7. Cf. 1 Collier on Bankruptcy, ¶ 3.02[4][d][ii], [iii](King ed. 1997) (suggesting § 1412 should include only the ability to retain or transfer, but not to dismiss, cases in the event of improper venue).

8. 28 U.S.C.A. § 1452(a). For "related" claims see supra n.1. See also supra § 23.11.

9. 28 U.S.C.A. § 1412.

10. 376 U.S. 612, 84 S.Ct. 805, 11 L.Ed.2d 945 (1964) (discussed supra § 3.46). The language of the transfer provision (§ 1412) parallels the provision for federal transfer in 28 U.S.C.A. § 1404(a), except that the latter restricts a transfer to a court where the civil action originally "might have been brought." The limitation

is unnecessary in § 1412 given the courts' nationwide jurisdiction and the Act's wide venue provisions.

§ 23.14

1. 11 U.S.C.A. § 547.

2. Vanston Bondholders Protective Committee v. Green, 329 U.S. 156, 172–73, 67 S.Ct. 237, 244–45, 91 L.Ed. 162 (1946) (Frankfurter, J. concurring).

3. See Corbin v. Federal Reserve Bank of N.Y., 475 F.Supp. 1060, 1070 (S.D.N.Y. 1979), aff'd 629 F.2d 233 (2d Cir.1980), cert. denied 450 U.S. 970, 101 S.Ct. 1492, 67 L.Ed.2d 621 (1981) (in action by trustee of insolvent bank against Federal Reserve Bank of New York and Federal Deposit Insurance Corp. for reduction in interest

Vanston involved a claim in a reorganization proceeding for interest upon unpaid interest arising from a pre-insolvency agreement. The majority stated that whether "claims of creditors are valid and subsisting obligations against the bankrupt at the time a petition in bankruptcy is filed is a question which, in the absence of overruling federal law, is to be determined by reference to state law."[4] However, even if the claim is valid under state law, it must still be determined whether its allowance "would be compatible with the policy of the Bankruptcy Act.... In determining what claims are allowable ... , a bankruptcy court does not apply the law of the state where it sits. *Erie* ... has no such implications.... [B]ankruptcy courts must administer the Bankruptcy Act as interpreted by this Court ... to determine how and what claims shall be allowed under equitable principles.... The general rule in bankruptcy and in equity receivership has been that interest on the debtors' obligations ceases to accrue at the beginning of the proceedings."[5] The claim was disallowed. *Vanston* therefore cannot be read as sanctioning resort to federal common law for gap filling.[6] Instead, it *confirms* the applicability of state law unless displaced by a federal rule for reasons of federal law and policy.[7]

§ 23.15   If a claim is not governed by federal statutory law or by federal common law as a result of a federal policy or interest, what state law applies? Dictum by the majority in *Vanston* suggested that the "determination requires the exercise of an informed judgment in the balancing of all the interests of the states with the most significant contacts in order best to accommodate the equities among the parties to the policies of those states."[1] Justice Frankfurter, in his concurrence,

payable, "the rules of decision are to be sought first in the National Bank Act, ... the Federal Deposit Insurance Act, ... and the case law thereunder.... If federal law is silent ... , state law may be selected as the applicable federal rule.... See United States v. Little Lake Misere Land Co., 412 U.S. 580, 93 S.Ct. 2389, 37 L.Ed.2d 187 (1973))".

4. Vanston Bondholders Protective Committee v. Green, 329 U.S. 156, 161, 67 S.Ct. 237, 239, 91 L.Ed. 162 (1946).

5. 329 U.S. at 162–63, 67 S.Ct. at 240.

6. The case could also have been decided on the basis that the allowance of post-petition interest is a question of bankruptcy law. In this event, federal common law would supply the answer when the Act is silent. This does not appear to have been the approach taken by the majority: it did not *start* with federal law but *displaced* state law because of contrary federal policy.

7. Justice Frankfurter, in his concurrence, reached the same result by finding New York law applicable (under which a promise to pay interest upon interest is void) and therefore did "not reach consider-

ations of policy in bankruptcy administration ... " 329 U.S. at 171, 67 S.Ct. at 244.

The conclusion in the text is not changed by the fact that "courts of bankruptcy are essentially courts of equity, and their proceedings inherently proceedings in equity," Local Loan Co. v. Hunt, 292 U.S. 234, 240, 54 S.Ct. 695, 697, 78 L.Ed. 1230 (1934), and, that, consequently they have "full power to inquire into the validity of any claim asserted against the estate and to disallow it if it is ascertained to be without lawful existence." Pepper v. Litton, 308 U.S. 295, 305, 60 S.Ct. 238, 244, 84 L.Ed. 281 (1939). These powers give the court a corrective function and do not address the question as to the law applicable for the initial determination with respect to a claim, defense, or issue.

§ 23.15

1. 329 U.S. at 162, 67 S. Ct. at 239. The statement is dictum because the Court concluded its review of the contacts of the transaction with various states by stating: "For assuming, *arguendo*, that the obligation for interest on interest is valid under the law of New York, Kentucky, and the

concluded that New York law applied to the action which had been brought in Kentucky because the "covenant ... was entered into by the parties in New York [and] the dominant place of performance was also New York."[2] Both statements suggest that the determination of the applicable state law is made by the bankruptcy court itself and not on the basis of the conflicts rules of the state where it sits.

This approach has found acceptance. The two opinions of the Fifth Circuit in *Woods–Tucker Leasing Corp. v. Hutcheson–Ingram Development Co.*[3] are particularly instructive. A Mississippi corporation which had entered into a sale-leaseback transaction with the debtor sought reclamation of farm equipment. The debtor counterclaimed on the ground that the transaction was not a sale-leaseback but a usurious secured loan. The bankruptcy and federal district courts in Texas both had held, and the Fifth Circuit agreed, that the transaction was a loan and the question was whether the law of the forum or the law of Mississippi (which the parties had chosen in their agreement) should determine the consequences of usury. In its first review of the case, the Fifth Circuit reversed the district court's application of Mississippi law and held, on the authority of *Vanston,* that Texas had the most significant interest, that Texas law was protective of local borrowers, and that the choice-of-law clause was therefore invalid and Texas law applied.[4] Texas indeed appears to have had most of the contacts with the transaction. The court, however, did not address these contacts but based its conclusion mainly on the ground that "the transaction involved a Texas borrower for whose protection the Texas usury laws were enacted (the Mississippi usury laws were not enacted to protect Texas borrowers)."[5] It found support for its position in the fact that Texas, the forum, "sanctions the emphasis this Court places on interest analysis in choice of law."[6]

---

other states having some interest in the indenture transaction, we would still have to decide whether allowance of the claim would be compatible with the policy of the Bankruptcy Act." Id. It then proceeded to hold that the claim was not so compatible. Supra § 23.13 n.5.

2. 329 U.S. at 171, 67 S.Ct. at 244. See also infra n.15.

3. 626 F.2d 401 (5th Cir.1980), vacated 642 F.2d 744 (5th Cir.1981).

4. The court also quoted 1A Moore's Federal Practice ¶ 0.325 (1979) that "in federal matters ... , a federal court is not bound by the forum's conflicts rules and can apply whatever law in its independent judgment it deems applicable ... " 626 F.2d at 406. It then decided to apply Texas law on the basis that Texas had "the most significant contacts with the transaction." The reference to Moore was not entirely

apposite. The issues involved in the present discussion are state law issues "related to" a bankruptcy case; they are "federal matters" at best because of that "relation." The need for federal rules of choice, as distinguished from the use of those of the forum state, cannot simply be derived from a redefinition of what is federal; instead, it must also rest on the underlying policy of bankruptcy law for "geographic uniformity" (supra § 23.13, n.2 and infra n.16), the need for which, moreover, appears particularly strong because of the wide subject matter jurisdiction of bankruptcy courts and the venue provisions of bankruptcy law.

5. 626 F.2d at 406.

6. Id. at 409 (citing to Gutierrez v. Collins, 583 S.W.2d 312 (Tex.1979) in which the Texas Supreme Court abandoned the place-of-wrong rule in torts).

The partial dissent by Judge Tate clearly saw the majority's approach as forum-centered and oriented: "Might the result differ depending on whether the courts of Texas or of Mississippi were addressing the issue? ... [The majority] has settled upon a rationale that pits the parochial policies underlying the usury laws of a single jurisdiction irreconcilably against the policy of national uniformity embodied in the Uniform Commercial Code ... "[7] Judge Tate agreed that "Texas should provide the rule by which the choice of law should be made in the bankruptcy proceedings," again citing to *Vanston,* but thought that, in the interest of uniformity, the rule should be derived from the Texas version of the U.C.C. and not from Texas usury legislation.[8] Under the Code, the transaction had enough contact with Mississippi to validate the contractual choice of Mississippi law.[9]

On petition for rehearing, the Fifth Circuit withdrew and vacated its prior opinion and, upon further consideration of the parties' contractual choice of Mississippi law, affirmed the district court's decision.[10] Now writing for a unanimous panel, Judge Tate noted that the "threshold question ... is whether in resolving issues of state law arising in the context of a bankruptcy proceeding, a federal court must apply the choice of law rules of the forum state in which it sits ... or may exercise its independent judgment and choose whatever state's substantive law it deems appropriate in the context of the case before it...."[11] For purposes of the case at bar, the court did not resolve the issue because "Texas, by its adoption of the U.C.C., has provided a choice of law rule specifically directed to contractual choice of law ... [The U.C.C. was] adopted in identical versions in both Texas and Mississippi ... [and] we would likewise look to U.C.C. § 1–105(1) [if a federal rule were to be adopted].... We therefore conclude ... that the application of an independent federal choice of law rule and of the forum state's choice of law rule would lead to the same result, and thus 'we do not determine which road the trial court should have travelled to arrive at the common destination.' "[12] In essence, the case presented a false conflict: the choice-of-law rules of Texas and Mississippi as well as the rule that *might* have been applied as federal law all were the same. Since Mississippi bore a "reasonable relation" to the transaction within the meaning of U.C.C. § 1–105(1), the parties' stipulation of Mississippi law was valid.

In arriving at his conclusion, Judge Tate did, however, address the "threshold question" he had posed earlier. In deliberate dictum, he wrote: "If we *were* required to exercise independent federal judgment in choosing whether to apply Texas or Mississippi law to this U.C.C.-regulated transaction involving significant contacts with both Texas and Mississippi, we would likewise look to U.C.C. § 1–105(1) ... as part of a

7. Id. at 415 (Tate, J., concurring in part and dissenting in part).

8. Id. at 415–16.

9. U.C.C. § 1–105(1).

10. Woods-Tucker Leasing Corp. v. Hutcheson-Ingram Development Co., 30

U.C.C. Rep. Serv. 1505, 642 F.2d 744 (5th Cir.1981).

11. 642 F.2d at 748 (again citing to Moore, supra n.4).

12. Id. at 748–49 (quoting from Fahs v. Martin, 224 F.2d 387, 399 (5th Cir.1955)).

national effort to establish a nationally uniform law to govern the validity and effect of commercial transactions. . . . [The U.C.C.] 'should generally be considered as the federal law of commerce-including secured transactions.' "[13]Both the view that a federal court, in true conflict cases, should exercise its independent judgment in the formulation of a choice-of-law rule[14] and that such a rule may be derived from, or incorporate

13. Id. at 749, quoting from In re King–Porter Co., 446 F.2d 722, 732 (5th Cir.1971) (emphasis in original).

14. Judge Tate also quoted from Wallace Lincoln–Mercury Co., Inc. v. Gentry, 469 F.2d 396, 400 n.1 (5th Cir.1972): "In this federal bankruptcy case the District Court is not obliged to use the choice-of-law methodology of the forum state . . . " (642 F.2d at 748), but cautions that "there may nevertheless be issues which should be . . . resolved [under forum law]. . . . [Thus, as in the case under discussion] the determination of whether usury prevents enforcement of the claim should not vary depending upon whether the defense is raised in a state or instead a federal court of the forum. At bottom, the issue presents a question that is 'independent of bankruptcy and precedes it,' Vanston . . . 329 U.S. at 169, 67 S.Ct. at 243 (Frankfurter, J., concurring), and that should be resolved in a manner that is not inconsistent with the resolution that would have occurred had the bankruptcy proceeding not intervened." This caveat somewhat detracts from the dictum favoring the exercise of independent judgment by the federal court in making the choice-of-law decision and seems to emphasize the false-conflicts aspect of the case. Under the particular facts of *Woods–Tucker,* the caveat may be appropriate, although it may overemphasize the goal of intrastate uniformity which perhaps is best reserved for true diversity actions: see infra at § 23.15, nn.2–9. Even if arguably appropriate in the particular circumstances of *Woods–Tucker,* the caveat must be restricted to cases and issues which *could have been brought* in the state courts of the forum. Given the bankruptcy court's nationwide jurisdiction and the limits of state court jurisdiction, this will often not be the case. See also Matter of Eli Witt Co., 12 B.R. 757, 759 (Bkrtcy.M.D.Fla.1981): plaintiff "is in error in seeking to have this Court apply the law applicable in federal diversity jurisdiction cases following *Erie* . . . and its progeny. This case is a *bankruptcy case* and this Court is free to make determinations concerning property before the Court without reference to the specific conflict of law rules arising under the *Erie* . . . test."

The cases continue to be in doubt whether federal or state choice of law rules should be applied in bankruptcy. In Fox v. Peck Iron and Metal Co., Inc., 25 B.R. 674 (Bkrtcy.S.D.Cal.1982), the court, when faced with a sale/leaseback between a California debtor and a corporation located and conducting business in Virginia, held that California law applies to the transaction. The opinion discusses both approaches and notes that the "Supreme Court and various circuit courts have taken care to avoid resolving the question." Id. at 685. This court, finding no true conflict, also left the issue unresolved, since both an independent federal and the California choice of law rule would lead to the application of California law. Id., at 687. In re Kaiser Steel Corp., 87 B.R. 154 (Bkrtcy.D.Colo.1988). Compare In re L.M.S. Associates, Inc., 18 B.R. 425 (Bkrtcy.S.D.Fla.1982) (holding that the bankruptcy court is free to apply the state law of its choice) with In re New England Fish Co., 749 F.2d 1277, 1280–81 (9th Cir. 1984) (contractual dispute), In re Cochise College Park, Inc., 703 F.2d 1339, 1348 n. 4 (9th Cir.1983) (suit against bankruptcy trustee regarding liability for collecting payments under debtor's installment land contracts), and In re O.P.M. Leasing Services Inc., 40 B.R. 380 (Bkrtcy.S.D.N.Y.1984), order affirmed 44 B.R. 1023 (S.D.N.Y.1984) (state law and Bankruptcy Code fraudulent conveyance claims) (all holding the forum state choice-of-law rules to be applicable).

The U.S. Supreme Court held in Phillips Petroleum Co. v. Shutts, 472 U.S. 797, 105 S.Ct. 2965, 86 L.Ed.2d 628 (1985), that a court may not apply forum law to the claims of absent members of a plaintiff class when they or their claims have no connection with the forum. Unsecured creditors in bankruptcy are like absent members of plaintiff class inasmuch as their claims may be precluded by proceedings in a state with which they may not have had contact. Major bankruptcy cases like Manville and Dalkon Shield demonstrate the magnitude of the problem. Both the discussion in the text, main volume, and the decision in *Shutts* suggest that the bankruptcy court may not, without more, apply the *lex fori.* It must either make its own choice of law, consistent with constitutional require-

rules of state law designed to further national uniformity are an appropriate approach to, and resolution of the problem under discussion.

The test for choice of law suggested in *Vanston*—"balancing of all the interests of the states with the most significant contacts"[15] thus appears to permit different approaches, chiefly the formulation of a choice-of-law rule emphasizing the constitutional objective of "geographic uniformity"[16] or an approach focussed on interest analysis. The latter will tend to be forum-oriented, as it was in the first opinion in *Woods–Tucker*. As a result, the choice-of-law process employed by the bankruptcy court will parallel that of a federal court sitting in diversity.[17] Neither the *Vanston* majority nor concurrence had considered the substantive or conflicts law of the Kentucky forum. Both the majority's dictum and Justice Frankfurter proceeded on the assumption that the determination of the applicable law was for the federal court. Thus, while *Vanston* does not sanction *substantive* federal common law for gap filling, the decision does support a conclusion that the bankruptcy court may fashion its own choice-of-law rule. In doing so, it should emphasize objectives of uniformity in the administration of bankruptcy law and policy[18] rather than the local governmental interests of the particular forum state.

The conclusion is further strengthened by comparison of the policy objectives that underlie *Erie,* on the one hand, and the function of bankruptcy courts. *Erie,* its constitutional aspects aside,[19] sought to bring about in-state uniformity as between state and federal courts with essentially identical judicial and subject matter jurisdiction in diversity cases. Bankruptcy courts are not limited in their exercise of judicial jurisdiction, and state courts lack subject matter jurisdiction in bankruptcy. Intrastate forum-shopping therefore is not a problem except in cases of removal (considered below). Interstate forum-shopping remains possible after *Erie* and *Klaxon* in diversity and is the price for achieving intrastate uniformity. This price need not be paid in bankruptcy—when there cannot be intrastate forum-shopping—and the goal should therefore be to eliminate, or at least reduce, interstate forum-shopping, i.e. to achieve the "geographic uniformity" or which Justice Frankfurter wrote in *Vanston*. For this reason, recent authorities preponderate toward

ments, or require claims to be reduced to judgment elsewhere before filed before it. *Shutts* is discussed supra §§ 3.23, 10.10.

15. 329 U.S. at 162, 67 S.Ct. at 239. Justice Frankfurter apparently did not disagree with this test but considered it inapplicable because "This is not a case where damages are claimed, in the form of interest, for the detention of monies due. *In such a situation the right to interest and its measure become matters for judicial determination.* The claim here asserted is based solely on the terms of the *agreement.*" 329 U.S. at 171, 67 S.Ct. at 244, emphasis added. Writing in the days of the vested-rights approach of the First Restatement, he then concluded that the agreement, made and to

be performed in New York, was a New York agreement to be governed by that state's law.

16. See supra § 23.14 n.2.

17. See also supra n.14 and infra § 23.15 nn.2–10.

18. Cf. Hill, The *Erie* Doctrine in Bankruptcy, 66 Harv.L.Rev. 1013, 1050 (1953) ("In bankruptcy ... the power to override state law can be determined only by reference to bankruptcy objectives.... Once [these] are defined in a given situation, the equity jurisdiction of the bankruptcy courts affords a flexible and effective instrument for attaining them.").

19. See supra § 3.36.

rejecting *Klaxon* in the bankruptcy context, though as in *Woods–Tucker* in many cases the substantial uniformity achieved by the U.C.C. obviates the need to address the question.[20]

§ 23.16 A resolution of the choice-of-law problem in favor of federally articulated conflicts rules would also alleviate the problems associated with transfers.[1] At least for cases arising within the same judicial circuit, uniform rules could be established. Conflicts between or among circuits would still occur but do not raise problems different from those encountered in any other area of federal practice. Differences in choice of law, however, could potentially occur in cases of removal of bankruptcy-related claims from civil courts to bankruptcy courts.[2] Illustratively, this might have occurred if, in *Woods–Tucker*,[3] a Texas state court had applied the protective Texas law regarding usury while the federal court honored the parties' choice of Mississippi law.[4] Despite the fact that, in apparent conflict with *Erie/Klaxon* principles,[5] the same civil claim or issue may thus be treated differently with respect to choice of law by courts sitting in the same state, the result is justified. Removal to a bankruptcy court is permissible only if that court has subject matter jurisdiction over the claim or cause of action.[6] Jurisdiction exists only if the claim arises in, or is related to a bankruptcy case.[7] If the claim is so related to the bankruptcy case, it is then appropriate that it be treated as part of that case, even if another court, in a civil action, would have applied different rules of choice of law. Additionally, and as a safeguard,

20. See Borchers, Choice of Law Relative to Security Interests and Other Liens in International Bankruptcies, 46 Am. J. Comp. L. 165, 172–73 (1998); see also In re Lindsay, 59 F.3d 942, 948 (9th Cir.1995), cert. denied 516 U.S. 1074, 116 S.Ct. 778, 133 L.Ed.2d 730 (1996) (*Klaxon* not applicable in bankruptcy cases because "the risk of forum-shopping which is avoided by applying state law has not application, because the case can only be litigated in federal court."). For strong criticism of this decision and endorsement of the view advanced in the text, see Ralph Brubaker, Conflict of Laws in Bankruptcy: Choosing Applicable State Law and the Appropriate (State or Federal?) Choice–of–Law Rule, 21 Bankruptcy Law Letter No. 7, 1–6 (July 2001). But see In re Gaston & Snow, 243 F.3d 599 (2d Cir.2001), cert. denied Erkins v. Bianco, 534 U.S. 1042, 122 S.Ct. 618, 151 L.Ed.2d 540 (2001) (federal courts sitting in bankruptcy must apply forum state's conflicts rule).

§ 23.16

1. Supra § 23.13, nn.7–9.

2. Supra § 23.13, n.8.

3. Supra § 23.15, nn.10–14.

4. The U.S. Supreme Court's decision in M/S Bremen v. Zapata Off–Shore Co., 407 U.S. 1, 92 S.Ct. 1907, 32 L.Ed.2d 513 (1972), upheld a contractual choice-of-forum clause, in circumstances where it was clear that the chosen forum would apply its own law and validate an exculpatory clause. A federal bankruptcy court, applying federally articulated rules of choice-of-law, should honor the parties' contractual choice to further the objective of uniformity. It should disregard it only when the stipulated law would conflict with the provisions or policy of the bankruptcy law (as in *Vanston*) a result which still preserves uniformity.

5. Supra § 3.36.

6. 28 U.S.C.A. § 1452(a). See generally In re Brothers Coal Co., Inc., 6 B.R. 567 (Bkrtcy.W.D.Va.1980); Western Helicopters, Inc. v. Hiller Aviation, Inc., 97 B.R. 1 (E.D.Cal.1988).

7. 28 U.S.C.A. § 1334(b). Certain subject matter is expressly beyond the jurisdiction of bankruptcy courts, e.g. support obligations of the debtor: but see supra § 23.12 n.1, with respect to 11 U.S.C.A. § 523(a)(5). See also Northern Pipeline Construction Co. v. Marathon Pipe Line Co., 458 U.S. 50, 102 S.Ct. 2858, 73 L.Ed.2d 598 (1982); In re Apex Oil Co., 88 B.R. 968 (Bkrtcy.E.D.Mo. 1988).

the bankruptcy court has the power to abstain, "in the interest of justice,"[8] from hearing such a claim or, if the claim is pending before it as a result of removal, to remand it "on any equitable ground."[9] Finally, in proceedings based on state law claims, the court must under certain circumstances abstain from hearing the same.[10]

C. INTERNATIONAL BANKRUPTCY[1]

§ 23.17 Business enterprises engaged in international commerce will often have assets—and creditors—in several countries and potentially face insolvency proceedings at home, or abroad, or in both places. Effective for cases filed after October 7, 1984, "debtor" is defined as "a person that resides or has a domicile, a place of business, *or property* in the United States."[2]

An overriding concern in international bankruptcies is the just and equal treatment of unsecured creditors.[3] The protection of their interests will depend on the effect given to a local determination in the other jurisdiction. Basically, two models may be envisioned. One is *territorial;*

---

8. 28 U.S.C.A. § 1334(c)(1). See supra § 23.11 n.7.

9. 28 U.S.C.A. § 1452(b).

10. 28 U.S.C.A. §§ 1334(c)(2), 1452(b).

§ 23.17

1. For detailed analysis of the 1978 Act as it relates to international cases see Honsberger, Conflict of Laws and the Bankruptcy Reform Act of 1978, 30 Case Western Res. L. Rev. 631 (1980); see also Borchers, Choice of Law Relative to Security Interest and Other Liens in International Bankruptices, 46 Am. J. Comp. L. (Supp.) 165, 173–81 (1998); Trautman, Westbrook & Gaillard, Four Models for International Bankruptcy, 41 Am. J. Comp. L. 573 (1993); Westbrook, The Coming Encounter: International Arbitration and Bankruptcy, 67 Minn. L. Rev. 595 (1983).

See generally Nadelmann, Compositions—Reorganizations and Arrangements in the Conflict of Laws, 61 Harv. L. Rev. 804 (1948); The Recognition of American Arrangements Abroad, 90 U. Pa. L. Rev. 780 (1942); Becker, Transnational Insolvency Transformed, 29 Am. J. Comp. L. 706 (1981); Kozyris, Cross–Border Insolvency, 38 Am. J. Comp. L. (Supp.) 271 (1990).

From among the foreign literature, *see* Hanisch, Die Wende im deutschen internationalen Insolvenzrecht, 6 Zeitschrift für Wirtschaftsrecht 1233 (1985); Deutsches internationales Insolvenzrecht in Bewegung, 4 Zeitschrift für Wirtschaftsrecht 1289 (1983); Probleme des internationalen Insolvenzrechts, in: Probleme des international-

en Insolvenzrechts, (Frankfurt Symposium, 1981) (Marschall v. Bieberstein (Ed.) 1982) 9; Pielorz, Wende im deutschen internationalen Insolvenzrecht, 4 Praxis des internationalen Privat—und Verfahrensrechts 241 (1984); Riesenfeld, Probleme des internationalen Insolvenzrechts aus der Sicht des neuen Konkursreformgesetzes der Vereinigten Staaten, in: Probleme, supra, at 39; Schlosser, Europäsche Wege aus der Sackgasse des deutschen internationalen Insolvenzrechts, 29 Recht der internationalen Wirtschaft 473 (1983); Spennemann, Insolvenzverfahren in Deutschland—Vermögen in Amerika: Das Beispiel Herstatt—Fragen des internationalen Insolvenzrechts der Bundesrepublik Deutschland und der USA (1981); Bogdan, International Bankruptcy Law in Scandinavia, 34 Int'l & Comp. L.Q. 49 (1985); Livadas, The Winding–Up of Insolvent Companies in England and France (1984); Aerts, Belgium: Insolvency Proceedings, in: European Insolvency Practitioners' Handbook (Cork & Weiss (Ed.) 1984), p. 1; Weiss, England and Wales: Insolvency Proceedings, id. at 35; Pavec, France: Insolvency Proceedings, id. at 85; Pajardi, Italy: Insolvency Proceedings, id. at 161; Hamminga, Netherlands: Insolvency Proceedings, id. at 193. For an extensive bibliography, see also Kegel & Schwig, Internationals Privarecht 1041–43 (9th Cir. 2004).

2. 11 U.S.C.A. § 109(a) (emphasis added).

3. See 11 U.S.C.A. § 304(c)(1).

it restricts the effect of a determination to the rendering jurisdiction. As a result, creditors may pursue independent remedies in the second forum and, upon recovery, may not need to take a deduction for amounts recovered in the first proceeding. In such a race for the assets, some creditors may thus recover a higher percentage of their claims than they would have if the estate had been considered as a unit or if the second forum provided a system of set-offs. At the same time, debtors remain free to shift assets, prior to insolvency, to the second forum and to dispose of them there free from any effects of the first jurisdiction's determination until a second, local, proceeding has been commenced.[4]

A second model, followed in some countries including Belgium, Luxembourg and, to some extent, in isolated treaties,[5] adopts the "theory of *universality* (ubiquity)."[6] Under such a system, the forum gives effect to all foreign determinations, including the right of the foreign administrator to claim title to local property or to pursue other remedies provided by the foreign law. Most legal systems will not surrender their control over local assets in this fashion or leave local creditors without the protection of local law. Both models therefore have drawbacks. This has prompted some countries, including the United States, to explore intermediate approaches in order to accommodate the interests of local and foreign parties.

A fair number of countries have systems that are intermediate between the two poles. A report on the subject prepared by the International Academy of Comparative Law found Japan, the Netherlands and Sweden to be the strictest adherents to the territorial system, and found the British and American systems to evidence a mixed approach.[7]

1. *Effect of Foreign Proceedings in the United States*

§ 23.18 American bankruptcy jurisdiction extends to persons who have "property" in the United States regardless of their nationality,

4. See German Konkursordnung § 237(1). In the case of Germany, the principle of territoriality and the scope of Konkursordnung § 237(1) appear to have been limited by two decisions of the Bundesgerichtshof (BGH), adopting a more "universal" approach: In its decision of July 13, 1983, the BGH held that a German creditor of a German debtor was obligated to turn over to the German trustee in bankruptcy assets of the debtor which the creditor had recovered in independent proceedings in Switzerland. 4 Zeitschrift für Wirtschaftsrecht 961 (1983). See also Klöcker, Foreign Debtors and Creditors under United States and West German Bankruptcy Laws: An Analysis and Comparison, 20 Tex. Int'l L.J. 55, 57, 79–82 (1985). In its decision of July 11, 1985, the BGH overruled previous decisions and held that a Belgian trustee was entitled to recover assets located in Germany for purposes of equitable distribution among all creditors in the Belgian proceedings on the condition that (i) the foreign

court has jurisdiction and that (ii) German public policy is not violated by the recognition of and deference to the foreign proceedings. 6 Zeitschrift für Wirtschaftsrecht 944 (1985). This decision is discussed by Hanisch, Die Wende . . . , supra n.1. For Switzerland, see Hanisch, Wirkungen deutscher Insolvenzverfahren auf in der Schweiz befindliches Schuldnervermögen, 1988 Juristenzeitung 737. See also infra § 23.18 n.8.

5. Hanisch, Aktuelle Probleme des internationalen Insolvenzrechts, 36 Schweiz. Jahrbuch für intern. Recht 109, 115–16 (1980).

6. Nadelmann, The National Bankruptcy Act and the Conflict of Laws, 59 Harv. L.Rev. 1025, 1025 (1946) at 1025 (emphasis added). See also Aerts, Belgium . . . , supra n.1, at 25–26.

7. Watté, Rapport General de la mise en oeuvre des suretes dans le cadre d'une faillite internationale 11–12 (1998).

domicile, residence, or place of business.[1] While American law on the subject originally proceeded from a view of strict territoriality,[2] more recent cases and statutory developments have softened this approach in favor of a more universalist conception. The foreign representative of the estate in a foreign proceeding may commence an involuntary case against the debtor in the United States;[3] he may also commence "a case ancillary to a foreign proceeding."[4] Provided that certain conditions are met,[5] the bankruptcy court may enjoin the continuance of other proceedings in the United States and order the turnover of the property or its proceeds to the foreign representative;[6] it may also suspend or dismiss a local proceeding upon petition of the foreign representative because of the pendency of a foreign proceeding.[7] These provisions thus reduce the

§ 23.18

1. 11 U.S.C.A. § 109(a).

2. See Borchers, Choice of Law Relative to Security Interest and Other Liens in International Bankruptcies 46 Am. J.Comp.L. Supp. 165, 176–81 (collecting articles) (1998).

3. "Foreign proceeding" and "foreign representative" are defined in 11 U.S.C.A. § 101(20) and (21), respectively.

4. 11 U.S.C.A. § 304(a). Venue lies in the district where the debtor's principal assets are located. 28 U.S.C.A. § 1474. Venue of cases ancillary to foreign proceedings is governed by 28 U.S.C.A. § 1410: A case brought to enjoin the commencement or continuation of an action or proceeding in a State or Federal court, or the enforcement of a judgment, must be commenced in the district where such State or Federal court sits. § 28 U.S.C.A. § 1410(a). A case brought to enjoin the enforcement of a lien against property, or to require the turnover of property of an estate, must be brought in the district in which such property is located. 28 U.S.C.A. § 1410(b). All other cases must be brought in the district where the debtor's principal place of business or his principal assets are located. 28 U.S.C.A. § 1410(c). For discussion of remedies available to foreign creditors (remedies under state law, U.S. bankruptcy proceedings, and ancillary proceedings), see Boshkoff, United States Judicial Assistance in Cross–Border Insolvencies, 36 Int'l & Comp. L.Q. 729 (1987). For England see Woloniecki, Cooperation Between National Courts in International Insolvencies: Recent United Kingdom Legislation, 35 Int'l & Comp. L.Q. 644 (1986).

5. Among these are that there will be "just treatment of all holders of claims,"

"protection of claim holders in the United States against prejudice and inconvenience ... in the processing of claims in such foreign proceeding," "comity." 11 U.S.C.A. § 304(c). For "comity" see infra § 23.19 n.12.

6. 11 U.S.C.A. § 304(b). For venue see supra n.4.

7. 11 U.S.C.A. § 305(a), (b). Such an order is not reviewable by appeal. 11 U.S.C.A. § 305(c). The Act also provides for a limited appearance by a foreign representative for purposes of petitions under §§ 303–305. 11 U.S.C.A. § 306. See Kenner Products Co. v. Societe Fonciere et Financiere Agache–Willot, 532 F.Supp. 478 (S.D.N.Y.1982), granting motion to transfer guaranty claim to suspense docket in deference, under international comity, to pending bankruptcy proceeding in France. See also Matter of Culmer, 25 B.R. 621 (Bkrtcy. S.D.N.Y.1982), in which the court granted a motion to transfer to the Bahamas all of the assets of a Bahamian bank in voluntary liquidation in the Bahamas. After determining that application of Bahamian law would not be "wicked, immoral, or violate American law and public policy," the court found that the Bahamas had the greatest interest in the liquidation proceedings and that the granting of the motion would afford equality of distribution of the available assets. But see Matter of Toga Mfg. Ltd., 28 B.R. 165 (Bkrtcy.E.D.Mich.1983). There, the court denied the petition of the Canadian bankruptcy trustee of a Canadian debtor who sought to enjoin U.S. creditors from taking actions against the debtor or its assets in the United States. The court decided to retain the United States claims in U.S. courts since, under United States law, the creditor in question was a secured creditor

effect of a strictly territorial approach by treating the estate as a unit. American jurisdiction over local assets has not been diminished but foreign proceedings are given effect under the supervision, and in the discretion, of the bankruptcy court. Although a bankruptcy court has broad discretion under § 304(c) as to whether to apply foreign law, recent U.S. cases show a clear trend towards applying foreign law in cases in which the primary bankruptcy is open abroad and the debtor's principal offices are located in the country in which the proceeding is opened.[8] This is a highly desirable trend that is moving the U.S. towards a more universalist perspective and is helping to make possible more national and economically efficient disposition of the debtor's assets.[9]

One problem, however, remains. It concerns the equal treatment of U.S. creditors in circumstances in which a creditor has already participated in a foreign distribution and seeks to recover again—against U.S. assets—in a subsequent American proceeding. The 1978 Act seeks to assure equality in the treatment of creditors by allowing a subsequent recovery only after domestic claim holders have received compensation equal to that received by the claimant in the foreign proceeding.[10] However, it is conceivable that a claimant participated in the foreign proceeding because of the prospect of a *larger* recovery than what could be anticipated domestically and therefore will not file in the domestic proceeding. In these circumstances, the Act makes no provision for him to disgorge the surplus for the benefit of domestic creditors.

A potentially important development in this area is UNICTRAL Model Law on Cross–Border Insolvency.[11] This model law, drafted with the help of INSOL—an association of insolvency experts—is designed to improve cooperation in multinational defaults.[12] The law stresses primarily procedural matters rather than attempting to harmonize the diverse national insolvency laws.[13] Its primary aim is to improve judicial cooperation and to aid in the recognition of foreign insolvency proceedings. It provides also for equal treatment of creditors, special notice to foreign creditors, and adopts the so-called "hotchpot" principle requiring any nation enacting the law to take into account distributions to the same

---

entitled to preferential payment, while he would most likely be only an "ordinary creditor" under Canadian law. Thus, from his perspective, the distribution of proceeds under Canadian law would not be "substantially in accordance with the order prescribed by [Title 11 of the U.S. Code]" as required by 11 U.S.C.A. § 304(c)(4). Id. at 168–169. See also In re Gee, 53 B.R. 891 (Bkrtcy.S.D.N.Y.1985): Petition of Cayman Islands trustee under § 304 granted and competing Chapter 11 petition dismissed; In re Trakman, 33 B.R. 780 (Bkrtcy. S.D.N.Y.1983): Proceedings relating to petition of foreign representative suspended pending outcome of interpleader action relating to assets in question. See also Cunard Steamship Co. Ltd. v. Salen Reefer Services

AB, 773 F.2d 452 (2d Cir.1985) and Comment, 19 Vand. J. Trans. L. 911 (1986).

8. Borchers, supra n.2, at 176–81.

9. See Westbrook, The Lessons of Maxwell Communications, 64 Fordham L.Rev. 2531, 2535 (1996)(discussing extensive cooperation between U.S. and British courts "leading to perhaps the first world-wide plan of orderly liquidation ever achieved").

10. 11 U.S.C.A. § 508(a).

11. Uncitral Model Law on Cross–Border Insolvency, 36 I.L.M. 1386 (1997).

12. See Winship, Survey: International Commercial Transactions: 1997, 53 Bus. Law. 1521 (1998).

13. Winship, supra n.12.

creditor in foreign proceedings.[14] The Model Law is expected eventually to be enacted in the United States.[15]

2. *Effect of U.S. Proceedings Abroad*

§ 23.19 Under American law, the "estate" created by the commencement of a bankruptcy proceeding consists of the debtor's property "wherever located;"[1] the trustee is the "representative of the estate"[2] to whom property owing to the estate is to be delivered.[3] Contrary to the modification of the territorial approach to give some effect to foreign proceedings, American law claims universal applicability in cases of American proceedings. Recognition abroad of such a claim to title to property "wherever located" is, of course, another matter.[4] While Belgium, Luxembourg,[5] and—to some extent—the United Kingdom and the common law provinces of Canada[6] recognize the foreign determination, other countries do not[7] or interpose procedural requirements which delay the representative's access to local assets.[8] Most states will accord the

---

14. Winship, supra n.12.

15. Winship, supra n.12. It was introduced and passed in 1998 as part of Senate Bill 1301, but died along with much more controversial efforts and reforming domestic, consumer bankruptcy law in the United States.

§ 23.19

1. 11 U.S.C.A. § 541(a); 28 U.S.C.A. § 1334(d).

2. 11 U.S.C.A. § 323(a).

3. 11 U.S.C.A. § 542.

4. The question may arise in several ways. Illustratively, does the American trustee have "title" to the foreign assets, for instance in order to have them turned over to him or for the purpose that a package sale of assets made by him in the United States will be given effect abroad in favor of the "title" of purchasers? If he does not have "title" to foreign assets by virtue of his claim thereto under American law, does he have standing, as the representative of the American estate, at least to lay *claim* to such foreign assets under applicable foreign procedures? For a recent comparative study see Watte', Rapport General de la mise en oeuvre des suretes dons le cadre d'une faillite internationales (1998).

5. In both, the foreign adjudication must not violate the local *"ordre public"* and, at least in Belgium, must be rendered by a state which accords reciprocity. With respect to reciprocity see also infra n.12.

6. *United Kingdom* (recognition with respect to English movables if determination rendered by a court with personal jurisdic-

tion over the debtor): Galbraith v. Grimshaw, [1910] 1 K.B. 339, [1910] A.C. 508; Solomons v. Ross, [1764] 1 H.Bl. 131; Nadelmann, Solomons v. Ross and International Bankruptcy Law, 9 Mod. L. Rev. 154 (1946). *Canada:* J. Castel, Canadian Conflict of Laws 500 (2d ed.1986); for the Insolvency Act, Bill C–17, 2d Sess., 32d Parliament, 1st Reading January 31, 1984, see id. at 502 et seq. In *Austria,* foreign proceedings are recognized under certain circumstances, e.g. where treaties granting reciprocity exist. Austrian Bankruptcy Code § 180. With respect to amendments to the Austrian Bankruptcy Code, see also Lober, Corporate Law—New Developments—Austria, 11 Int'l Bus. L. 11 (December 1983); Corporate Law—Recent Developments—Austria, 12 Int'l Bus. L. 475 (1984). For recent *German* decisions, see supra § 23.17 n.4.

7. E.g., *Germany:* Konkursordnung § 237; BGH in 1960 Neue Juristische Wochenschrift 774 and 1962 id. 1511. For *Netherlands,* as well as for new *German* case law, see supra § 23.16 n.4. For *Scandinavia,* see supra § 23.16 n.1. For *Sweden,* see Nadelmann, Codification of Conflicts Rules for Bankruptcy, 30 Schweizerisches Jahrbuch für Internationales Recht 91 (1974).

8. For *France* and *Italy* see Nadelmann, supra n.7 at 92–94 (requirement of prior *exequatur* in many cases).

For *France,* see supra § 23.17 n.1.

The *Swiss* Federal Statute on Conflicts of Laws (1987, in force since 1989) provides in Art. 166 that a foreign bankruptcy order relating to foreign debtors will be recog-

American representative some standing to pursue a claim according to local procedures.[9] In addition, an American discharge in bankruptcy will not be recognized automatically in England, and has no effect—does not protect the debtor—in Germany and Switzerland.[10]

There is thus little certainty concerning the extent to which the American proceeding can reach foreign assets of the debtor. Reciprocity requirements in several foreign systems may prove helpful in the light of the revisions in favor of the position and powers of foreign representatives in the U.S. Bankruptcy Reform Act of 1978. However, it is doubtful whether the allusion to reciprocity in the American Act[11] will prompt reform or change in practices abroad.

American proceedings, and the interest of American creditors, may additionally be affected if the European Union's convention on Insolvency Proceedings[12] takes effect.[13] The United Kingdom, however, blocked ratification, rendering its future uncertain.[14]

D.   INSOLVENCY OF RELATED AND OF MULTINATIONAL CORPORATIONS[1]

§ 23.20   The domestic debtor may be a subsidiary of a foreign parent corporation; more complex, but analytically the same, the overall organization may be that of an international conglomerate. The insolvency of the domestic corporation draws into question the liability of the parent. Similarly, it may be the domestic parent that is insolvent; in this

nized by Swiss courts, provided that it is enforceable where issued, that it does not violate Swiss public policy, and that reciprocity exists. Upon recognition of the foreign order, the debtor's Swiss assets will be collected and transmitted to the foreign estate after satisfaction of local preferred creditors, provided that the foreign plan for distribution is found to be equitable (e.g., if it provides for a reasonable satisfaction of the claims of the remaining Swiss creditors). Arts. 172–73. For a general discussion, see v. Overbeck in 3 Praxis des internationalen Privat und Verfahrensrechts 49 (1983).

9. See supra nn.5–8.

10. Conflict of Laws and the Bankruptcy Reform Act of 1978, 30 Case W.L.Rev. 631, 665–66 (1981). For discussion of the effect given to foreign arrangements, see id. at 666 et seq.

11. 11 U.S.C.A. § 304(c)(5): "comity" as a criterion for relief under § 304(b), discussed supra § 23.17 n.5. It has been suggested that the inclusion of "comity" serves the purpose of giving the court "broad discretion so that it may order the appropriate relief under the circumstances of each case." Honsberger, supra n.10 at 655.

12. European Union: Convention on Insolvency Proceedings, Nov. 23, 1995, 35 I.C.MN. 1223 (1996).

13. For extensive commentary see Symposium, Bankruptcy in the Global Village, 23 Brooklyn J. Int'l L. 1 (1997)(contributions by Westbrook, Ziegel, Fletcher, Segal and Baltz); International Insolvencies: Colloquium, 64 Fordham L.Rev. 2507 (1997)(contributions by Hoffman, Felsenfeld and Burman).

14. Bankruptcy Deal Back on Cards, European Accounting Bull., p.2 (May 13, 1997).

§ 23.20

1. Compare Landers, A Unified Approach to Parent, Subsidiary and Affiliate Questions in Bankruptcy, 42 U. Chi. L. Rev. 589 (1975) with Posner, The Rights of Creditors of Affiliated Corporations, 43 U. Chi. L. Rev. 499 (1976); Kennedy, Insolvency and the Corporate Veil in the United States, in: Centre Canadien de Droit Comparé, Travaux du Huitième Colloque international de Droit Comparé 233 (1971); Nadelmann, Codification of Conflicts Rules for Bankruptcy, 30 Schweizerisches Jahrbuch für internationales Recht 61–62 (1974) (with references).

case the question arises whether its creditors can reach the assets of the subsidiary.

When parent and subsidiary have claims against each other, American courts have long undertaken to adjust the rights of competing creditors, for instance by subordinating the claims of the parent against the bankrupt subsidiary to those of the preferred stockholders of the debtor when the debtor had been under the substantial control of the parent and has engaged in various forms of inequitable conduct.[2] These are adjustments as *between* the corporations involved for the benefit of creditors; they do not yet involve the piercing of the corporate veil of one of the corporations in order to disregard its separate legal personality and to reach its assets. In the case of fraudulent transfers, it appears that the corporate veil will be pierced to allow creditors to reach the assets of the controlling stockholder or other entity.[3] The power of the bankruptcy court to pierce the corporate veil in these circumstances derives from its broad equity powers under the federal bankruptcy law.[4] The matter is less clear when fraud is not involved. Whether piercing is allowable and appropriate when the only purpose is to enlarge the estate by inclusion of the other corporation's assets may not be a matter of bankruptcy law but rather one of corporate law, to be governed by state

2. Taylor v. Standard Gas & Electric Co., 306 U.S. 307, 59 S.Ct. 543, 83 L.Ed. 669 (1939). See also Soviero v. Franklin National Bank of Long Island, 328 F.2d 446 (2d Cir.1964) which presents the reverse case: bankrupt parent deemed to be in possession of the assets of a number of controlled subsidiaries. For the formulation of the original "instrumentality test" see Powell, Parent and Subsidiary Corporations 8 (1931). For subordination under the bankruptcy law, see particularly 11 U.S.C.A. § 510(c). For a discussion of another approach, consolidation, see Landers, supra n.1, at 629 et seq. With respect to consolidation generally, see also Tatelbaum, The Multi–Tiered Corporate Bankruptcy and Substantive Consolidation—Do Creditors Lose Rights and Protection?, 89 Comm. L.J. 285 (1984) and Gilbert, Substantive Consolidation in Bankruptcy: A Primer, 43 Vand. L. Rev. 207 (1990); Weintraub & Resnick, Consolidation in Bankruptcy—Reorganization of Multitiered Corporations—Chemical v. Kheel, Revisited, 14 U.C.C. L.J. 177 (1981); Weintraub & Resnick, Bankruptcy Law Manual ¶ 8.16 (1980 & 1989 Cum. Supp.). With respect to consolidation of debtor and non-debtor corporations, see 5 Collier on Bankruptcy ¶ 1100.06[3] Kinjjed (1997).

3. See Kennedy, supra n.1, at 244 (citing to Sampsell v. Imperial Paper & Color Corp., 313 U.S. 215, 61 S.Ct. 904, 85 L.Ed.

1293 (1941)). However, a piercing of the corporate veil for purposes of consolidating debtor and non-debtor corporations "should be undertaken only in the most unusual circumstances," since the Bankruptcy Code provides specific remedies for creditors, for instance, in the event of fraudulent transfers. 5 Collier on Bankruptcy, supra n.2, ¶ 1100.06[3]. See also Funding Systems Railcars, Inc. v. Pullman Standard Inc., 34 B.R. 706 (N.D.Ill.1983), holding that bankruptcy court did not have authority to enjoin suit brought against wholly-owned subsidiary of debtor in another jurisdiction absent a showing that the subsidiary was a sham or alter ego of its parent.

4. Cf. Pepper v. Litton, 308 U.S. 295, 305, 60 S.Ct. 238, 244, 84 L.Ed. 281 (1939). See also Aronofsky, Piercing the Transnational Corporate Veil: Trends, Developments and the Need for Widespread Adoption of Enterprise Analysis, 10 N.C.J. Int'l L. & Com. Reg. 31 (1985); Easterbrook & Fischel, Limited Liability and the Corporation, 52 U. Chi. L. Rev. 89 (1985). A comparison of the principles applicable in a number of foreign jurisdictions is provided in Directors' Liability, Including Piercing the Corporate Veil Doctrine, 12 Int'l Bus. L. 511 (1984). Cf. Note, Piercing the Corporate Law Veil: The Alter Ego Doctrine Under Federal Common Law, 95 Harv. L. Rev. 853 (1982).

law.[5] Non-bankruptcy decisions under state law,[6] for instance for purposes of acquiring jurisdiction over a foreign corporation,[7] have frequently pierced the corporate veil. A functional, economic approach to the matter, rather than a continued focus on the separate legal personality of the entities involved, suggests that piercing is also appropriate for bankruptcy purposes.[8]

In the international context, when the object is to reach the foreign parent through its American subsidiary, the question may arise as to which substantive corporation law should determine the appropriateness of "piercing." It has been suggested that the reference should be to the law applicable to the subsidiary since the parent created it and creditors dealt with it under its law.[9] The wide definition, in the Bankruptcy Act, of a "debtor" as one who has "property" in the United States[10] also supports this view: the stock held by the parent in the U.S. subsidiary is

---

5. See Landers, supra n.1, at 616; Kennedy, supra n.1, at 240.

6. For the state law applicable to corporations see supra § 23.2.

7. See, e.g., in the interstate context: Rabinowitz v. Kaiser–Frazer Corp., 198 Misc. 707, 96 N.Y.S.2d 642 (1950) affirmed 302 N.Y. 892, 100 N.E.2d 177 (1951); in the international context: Boryk v. deHavilland Aircraft Co., 341 F.2d 666 (2d Cir.1965); Taca International Airlines, S.A. v. Rolls–Royce of England, Ltd., 15 N.Y.2d 97, 256 N.Y.S.2d 129, 204 N.E.2d 329 (1965), on remand 47 Misc.2d 771, 263 N.Y.S.2d 269 (1965); Regie Nationale des Usines Renault v. Superior Court, 208 Cal.App.2d 702, 25 Cal.Rptr. 530 (1962): Lamb v. Volkswagenwerk Aktiengesellschaft, 104 F.R.D. 95 (S.D.Fla.1985); Ex parte Volkswagenwerk Aktiengesellschaft, 443 So.2d 880 (Ala. 1983) (finding service on U.S. subsidiary sufficient to obtain jurisdiction over foreign parent as a result of degree of control exercised by parent over subsidiary) See also Volkswagenwerk Aktiengesellschaft v. Schlunk, 486 U.S. 694, 108 S.Ct. 2104, 100 L.Ed.2d 722 (1988) (discussed supra § 12.7). But see Richardson v. Volkswagenwerk, A.G., 552 F.Supp. 73 (W.D.Mo.1982) (holding plaintiff did not prove necessary control in order for service on subsidiary to justify exercise of jurisdiction over parent under alter-ego theory). In the bankruptcy context, there is growing authority supporting piercing. For an early decision see Henderson v. Rounds and Porter Lumber Co., 99 F.Supp. 376 (W.D.Ark.1951).

8. Diamond, Insolvency and the Corporate Veil in England, in: Centre Canadien, supra n.1, 265, 284 (citing to Barcelona Traction, Light & Power Co., Ltd., 1970 I.C.J. Reports 3, 131–32: "Although an independent juridical personality is conferred on a company, this personality does not present itself as an end, but simply as a means to achieve an economic purpose...." (Tanaka, J., dissenting)). See also Landers, supra n.1, at 652, who supports piercing: "[C]laims of parent companies are sometimes subordinated and sometimes not, parents sometimes must pay the whole bill for their bankrupt subsidiaries and sometimes may get by without contributing anything, and related bankrupts are sometimes treated as separate entities and are sometimes consolidated.... [T]he owners of an enterprise have numerous business incentives to operate it in a manner that maximizes the profits of the entire enterprise, without regard to the profitability of the individual components of that enterprise. A resolution of parent-subsidiary issues on the basis of the existence of *actual* harm or commingling of assets, of adequate recordkeeping or the observation of formalities of separate existence, is therefore inherently unrealistic...." emphasis added. See also: Aronofsky, supra n.4, at 33–34. For a decision holding another corporation to be an affiliate of the debtor corporation for venue purposes when the same individual was the sole owner of such affiliate as well as of a corporation specifically created to be the holding corporation of the debtor, see In re Petroleum Tank Lines, Inc., 10 B.R. 286 (Bkrtcy.W.D.N.Y.1981). For discussion of "piercing" from a European perspective, particularly with respect of entities incorporated under the law of Liechtenstein, see Hanisch, Internationalprivatrecht der Gläubigeranfechtung, 2 Zeitschrift für Wirtschaftsrecht und Insolvenzpraxis 569, 575–78 (1981).

9. See supra § 23.17 n.5 for references.

10. 11 U.S.C.A. § 109(a).

such "property."[11]

11. See In re Seatrade Corp., 255 F.Supp. 696 (S.D.N.Y.1966), affirmed sub nom. Chemical Bank New York Trust Co. v. Kheel, 369 F.2d 845 (2d Cir.1966); Soviero v. Franklin National Bank of Long Island, 328 F.2d 446 (2d Cir.1964).

Chapter 24

RECOGNITION AND ENFORCEMENT OF FOREIGN JUDGMENTS AND DECREES

Table of Sections

		Sections
I.	Preliminary Considerations	24.1–24.7
	A. The Policy of Preclusion	24.1
	B. Preclusion and the Enforcement of Interstate Judgments	24.2
	C. Preclusion and the Enforcement of International Judgments	24.3–24.4
	D. Methods of Enforcing Foreign Judgments	24.5–24.7
II.	Interstate Recognition of Judgments	24.8–24.32
	A. What Constitutes Enforceable Foreign Proceedings	24.8–24.11
	1. Finality	24.8
	2. Equity Decrees: Jurisdiction and Recognition	24.9
	3. Foreign Decrees Relating to Land	24.10
	4. Nature of the Proceeding	24.11
	B. Methods of Enforcing Interstate Judgments	24.12–24.13
	1. Full Faith and Credit	24.12
	2. Recognition and Enforcement by Registration or Summary Proceeding	24.13
	C. Defenses to Claim on Sister–State Judgments	24.14–24.32
	1. Lack of Jurisdiction of Rendering Court	24.14–24.16
	2. Judgment Obtained by Fraud; Equitable Defenses	24.17–24.18
	3. The Public Policy of the Forum, Penal Judgments, Tax Judgments, and Lack of a Competent Court	24.19
	a. Public Policy	24.20–24.21
	b. No Competent Court in Recognizing Forum	24.22
	c. Tax and Penal Judgments and Claims	24.23
	4. Foreign Judgment Not on the Merits	24.24–24.26
	5. Other Defenses	24.27–24.32
III.	International Recognition of Judgments	24.33–24.48
	A. Recognition and Enforcement	24.33–24.40
	1. Early Approaches and the *Hilton* Doctrine	24.33–24.34
	2. Recognition Practice After *Hilton* and *Erie*	24.35–24.37
	3. Foreign Approaches and Their Implications for U.S. Recognition Practice	24.38
	4. Federal Preemption by Recognition Treaty	24.39
	5. Valuation of Foreign Money–Judgments	24.40
	B. Defenses to Claim on Foreign–Country Judgment	24.41
	1. Jurisdiction	24.42
	2. Foreign Judgment for Taxes or Penalties	24.43
	3. Public Policy	24.44

    4. International Recognition Treaties and Preclusion 24.45

IV. Extralitigious Proceedings, Administrative Determinations, and Arbitral Awards................................... 24.46–24.48

I. PRELIMINARY CONSIDERATIONS

A. THE POLICY OF PRECLUSION

§ 24.1 When a court or another tribunal or officer exercising judicial functions[1] renders a decision, one question concerns the effect of the decision on subsequent disputes between the parties or even on disputes between one of the original litigants and a third party. For instance, may the unsuccessful plaintiff seek a second determination of his claim, or may the disappointed defendant resist the enforcement of the decision by invoking the same defenses as in the original trial or perhaps raise new and additional defenses? What, furthermore, should be the effect of the determination of a particular *issue* in one law suit on the same issue in subsequent litigation between one of the original litigants and a third party: may either rely on the earlier determination, using it as shield or sword, as the case may be?

There is a strong and pervasive policy in all legal systems to limit repetitive litigation of claims and issues. The U.S. Supreme Court's statement that "one trial of an issue is enough"[2] is a shorthand expression of the policy of *preclusion*. This policy seeks to protect party expectations resulting from previous litigation, to safeguard against the harassment of defendants, to insure that the task of courts not be increased by never-ending litigation of the same disputes, and–in a larger sense–to promote what Lord Coke, in *Ferrer's Case* (1599), stated to be the goal of all law: "rest and quietness."[3]

The concept of *res judicata* was known in Roman law, but its appearance in early English law probably had Germanic roots.[4] Today, *res judicata* (strictly defined) encompasses the *merger* of the plaintiff's cause of action in the judgment-that is, he may not relitigate the same claim-and the *bar* which the successful defendant may interpose against a second action on the same claim.[5] Merger and bar thus operate with respect to the same cause of action and as between or among the same

---

§ 24.1

1. The tribunal need not be a court but may be an administrative tribunal. See Thomas v. Washington Gas Light Co., 448 U.S. 261, 100 S.Ct. 2647, 65 L.Ed.2d 757 (1980); New York v. Shapiro, 129 F.Supp. 149 (D.Mass.1954); see infra § 24.46. It may also be an official exercising judicial functions. See infra § 24.15. For preclusion in the context of the administration of estates, see supra § 22.20.

2. Baldwin v. Iowa State Traveling Men's Association, 283 U.S. 522, 525, 51 S.Ct. 517, 75 L.Ed. 1244 (1931).

3. VI Coke 7, 77 Eng. Rep. 263 (K.B. 1599).

4. Millar, The Historical Relation of Estoppel by Record to Res Judicata, 35 Ill. L. Rev. 41 (1940); A.D. Vestal, Res Judicata/Preclusion 17–42 (1969).

5. Restatement, Judgments § 45 (1942); Restatement, Second, Judgments §§ 17–19 (1982).

parties[6] or their privies *("claim preclusion")*. *Collateral estoppel* extends the res judicata effect of a judgment to encompass the same issues arising in a different action *("issue preclusion"*[7]) and even to different parties[8] where the issue has been determined in prior litigation with adequate opportunity to be heard for the party to be precluded.

Despite these technical meanings of res judicata and collateral estoppel, it is important to emphasize that they are shorthand expressions of a *policy,* the application of which will necessarily vary with the

6. Irish Lesbian & Gay Org. v. Giuliani, 143 F.3d 638, 644, 646 n.2 (2d Cir.1998); Zoriano Sanchez v. Caribbean Carriers Ltd., 552 F.2d 70 (2d Cir.1977), cert. denied 434 U.S. 853, 98 S.Ct. 168, 54 L.Ed.2d 123 (1977); Weston Funding Corp. v. Lafayette Towers, Inc., 550 F.2d 710 (2d Cir.1977); Howerton v. Grace Hosp., Inc., 130 N.C.App. 327, 502 S.E.2d 659 (1998).

7. Migra v. Warren City School Dist. Bd. of Education, 465 U.S. 75, 104 S.Ct. 892, 79 L.Ed.2d 56 (1984) (in federal civil rights action state law determines preclusive effect of earlier state action); Marrese v. American Academy of Orthopaedic Surgeons, 470 U.S. 373, 380–381, 384, 105 S.Ct. 1327, 84 L.Ed.2d 274 (1985) (same, concerning federal antitrust claim) (see infra § 24.2 n.8); Parsons Steel, Inc. v. First Alabama Bank, 474 U.S. 518, 106 S.Ct. 768, 88 L.Ed.2d 877 (1986) and cases cited § 24.12 n.7; Shoup v. Bell & Howell Co., 872 F.2d 1178 (4th Cir.1989) (federal law determines preclusive effect of federal judgment); Whitehall Co., Ltd. v. Barletta, 404 Mass. 497, 536 N.E.2d 333, 336 (1989) (same).

Allen v. McCurry, 449 U.S. 90, 101 S.Ct. 411, 66 L.Ed.2d 308 (1980), on remand 647 F.2d 167 (8th Cir.1981), appeal after remand 688 F.2d 581 (1982) (collateral estoppel applies when a plaintiff seeks to relitigate, in a § 1983 civil rights action in federal court, issues decided against him in an earlier state criminal proceeding); Arthur v. Supreme Court of Iowa, 709 F.Supp. 157 (S.D.Iowa 1989) (applying Allen); Morris v. Stuyvesant Insurance Co., 449 F.Supp. 14 (S.D.N.Y.1978), affirmed 582 F.2d 1271 (2d Cir.1978) (state court decision on constitutionality of confession of judgment statute given estoppel and res judicata effect in federal civil rights action); Stericycle, Inc. v. City of Delavan, 120 F.3d 657 (7th Cir.1997) (circumstances under which declaratory judgment may operate as a bar); Universal Am. Mtge. Co. v. Bateman (In re Bateman), 331 F.3d 821 (11th Cir. 2003) (confirmation of a Chapter 13 plan–in bankruptcy– is res judicata as to issues that were or could have been revised). Restatement,

Second, Judgments § 27 (1982). See Weston Funding Corp. v. Lafayette Towers, Inc., 550 F.2d 710 (2d Cir.1977); Vestal supra n.4, at 15, 189 et seq. See also Note, The Collateral Estoppel Effect of Administrative Agency Actions in Federal Civil Litigation, 46 Geo. Wash. L. Rev. 65 (1977). On the effect of consent judgments as res judicata or collateral estoppel see Annot., 91 A.L.R.3d 1170 (1979) and 1990 supplement. See also Casad, Intersystem Issue Preclusion and the Restatement (Second) of Judgment, 66 Cornell L. Rev. 510 (1981); Erichson, Interjurisdictional Preclusion, 96 Mich. L. Rev. 945 (1998).

8. For applications see Davidson v. Lonoke Production Credit Ass'n, 695 F.2d 1115 (8th Cir.1982) (creditor of bankrupt farmer collaterally estopped from litigating issue formerly adjudicated in separate action between the same farmer and a different creditor); Jack Faucett Associates, Inc. v. American Telephone & Telegraph Co., 744 F.2d 118 (D.C.Cir.1984), cert. denied 469 U.S. 1196, 105 S.Ct. 980, 83 L.Ed.2d 982 (1985) (availability of new evidence that was not available in previous action rendered use of collateral estoppel inappropriate); Lane v. Sullivan, 900 F.2d 1247 (8th Cir.1990), cert. denied 498 U.S. 847, 111 S.Ct. 134, 112 L.Ed.2d 101 (1990) (estoppel effect of bankruptcy proceeding on legal malpractice suit); Winters v. Diamond Shamrock Chemical Co., 149 F.3d 387 (5th Cir.1998), cert. denied 526 U.S. 1034, 119 S.Ct. 1286, 143 L.Ed.2d 378 (1999). See also Jimenez v. Weinberger, 523 F.2d 689, 701 (7th Cir.1975), cert. denied 427 U.S. 912, 96 S.Ct. 3200, 49 L.Ed.2d 1204 (1976) (collateral estoppel to class action); Poster Exchange, Inc. v. National Screen Service Corp., 517 F.2d 117, 123 (5th Cir.1975), cert. denied 425 U.S. 971, 96 S.Ct. 2166, 48 L.Ed.2d 793 (1976) (estoppel effect of antitrust treble damage action); Note, Collateral Estoppel of Non-parties, 87 Harv. L. Rev. 1485 (1974); Semmel, Collateral Estoppel, Mutuality and Joinder, 68 Colum. L. Rev. 1457 (1968); Casad, supra n.7; Vestal, supra n.4, at 300, 320 et seq.

particular facts. Thus, with respect to collateral estoppel, for instance, a party may or may not be precluded concerning a particular issue, depending on whether there was a prior determination which afforded adequate opportunity to litigate[9] the issue or, conversely, whether it would be unfair to a party *not* to preclude the other.[10] As Justice White noted for a unanimous U.S. Supreme Court in 1971, the several considerations include "whether the party against whom an estoppel is asserted had a full and fair opportunity to litigate"[11] the issue because due process prohibits estoppel when a party never had an opportunity to present evidence, whether estoppel is invoked offensively or defensively,[12]

9. When a nonresident defendant did not appear in the first action, existence or lack of jurisdiction in the first court can still be litigated in a second (collateral) action (for instance, one which was brought to enforce a default judgment entered in the first). It follows that a default judgment entered in a state court action against a nonresident defendant does not have preclusive effect on a jurisdictional issue in a subsequent federal action. Duncan v. Peck, 752 F.2d 1135 (6th Cir.1985), appeal after remand 844 F.2d 1261 (6th Cir.1988).

10. "[T]he desire to deal justly with individual litigants is increasingly realized not to be a policy competing-or even conflicting-with the rationale of the doctrine of res judicata. Whether relitigation is unfair, however, is not to be determined only in the light of the assumed correctness and incorrectness of the prior judgment, but rather by evaluation of all relevant circumstances including the extent to which the parties in the prior action had a full opportunity there to litigate, and actually litigated, the issues of their concern." Smit, International Res Judicata and Collateral Estoppel in the United States, 9 U.C.L.A. Rev. 44, 59 (1962).

11. Blonder–Tongue Laboratories, Inc. v. University of Illinois Foundation, 402 U.S. 313, 329, 91 S.Ct. 1434, 1443, 28 L.Ed.2d 788 (1971), on remand 334 F.Supp. 47 (N.D.Ill.1971), judgment affirmed 465 F.2d 380 (7th Cir.1972), cert. denied 409 U.S. 1061, 93 S.Ct. 559, 34 L.Ed.2d 513 (1972); Montana v. United States, 440 U.S. 147, 99 S.Ct. 970, 59 L.Ed.2d 210 (1979); United States v. Stauffer Chemical Co., 464 U.S. 165, 174, 104 S.Ct. 575, 581, 78 L.Ed.2d 388 (1984) (White J., concurring); Harding v. Ramsay, Scarlett & Co., Inc. 599 F.Supp. 180 (D.Md.1984).

12. "[T]he authorities have been more willing to permit a defendant in a second suit to invoke an estoppel against a plaintiff who lost on the same claim in an earlier suit than they have been to allow a plaintiff in the second to use offensively a judgment obtained by a different plaintiff in a prior suit against the same defendant." *Blonder-Tongue,* 402 U.S. at 329–30. This quote illustrates the *policy* reasons underlying the traditional requirement and mutuality which several courts have now abandoned: see the *Bernhard* and *United Air Lines* decisions, supra n.8. The California Supreme Court in Bernhard v. Bank of America Nat. Trust & Savings Ass'n 19 Cal.2d 807, 813, 122 P.2d 892, 894 (1942) summarized the criteria for res judicata as follows: "In determining the validity of a plea of res judicata three questions are pertinent: Was the issue decided in the prior adjudication identical with the one presented in the action in question? Was there a final judgment on the merits? Was the party against whom the plea is asserted a party or in privity with a party to the prior adjudication?"

The non-mutual offensive use of collateral estoppel (as in *United Airlines*) was approved in Parklane Hosiery Co. v. Shore, 439 U.S. 322, 99 S.Ct. 645, 58 L.Ed.2d 552 (1979). See also Burlington N.R.R. Co. v. Hyundai Merchant Marine Co., 63 F.3d 1227 (3d Cir.1995); Louviere v. Shell Oil Co., 588 F.Supp. 95 (E.D.La.1984); Whitehall Co., Ltd. v. Barletta et al., 404 Mass. 497, 536 N.E.2d 333, 336 (1989). However, United States v. Mendoza, 464 U.S. 154, 104 S.Ct. 568, 78 L.Ed.2d 379 (1984), adopted an exception for cases in which such estoppel is sought to be asserted against the federal government. The reason for treating the government differently is that application of collateral estoppel would "[freeze] the first final decision rendered on a particular issue. Allowing only one final adjudication would deprive this Court of the benefit it receives from permitting several courts of appeal to explore a difficult question before this Court grants certiorari ... " 464 U.S. at 160, 104 S.Ct. at 572. Where mutuality is present (i.e., when the parties are the same), the government is estopped. United States v. Stauffer Chemical Co., 464 U.S. 165, 104 S.Ct. 575,

and the burden that relitigation of previously determined issues would impose on the courts.

B. PRECLUSION AND THE ENFORCEMENT OF INTERSTATE JUDGMENTS

§ 24.2 The policy of preclusion-to put an end to litigation-extends beyond the jurisdiction which rendered the first decision and which may be faced with a second action on the same claim or one involving the same issue. In the United States, the policy must also operate between and among the States in the interest of the unity of the Federation. Thus, a judgment creditor who is not able to satisfy the judgment where rendered will seek enforcement of the judgment elsewhere, usually in a place in which property of the judgment debtor can be found. In the jurisdiction in which enforcement of the judgment is sought the judgment is a *foreign* judgment, whether rendered in a foreign country or in a sister state. The judgment creditor therefore cannot enforce the judgment directly but must depend on the assistance of local courts. The issue of the preclusive effect of the original judgment now arises in the second court: it is further complicated-as the discussion in this and subsequent sections will detail-by differences in the law of the two jurisdictions as to what is precluded by the first determination. For instance, if the first jurisdiction provides for compulsory counterclaims but the second jurisdiction does not, may the judgment debtor invoke his counterclaim in the enforcement proceeding or is the claim precluded? Similarly, there may be differences among jurisdictions as to when a judgment is "on the merits" and therefore should be given preclusive effect.[1]

78 L.Ed.2d 388 (1984). For discussion of *Mendoza,* see Note, Collateral Estoppel and Nonacquiescence: Precluding Government Relitigation in the Pursuit of Litigant Equality, 99 Harv. L. Rev. 847 (1986). See also Lytle v. Household Mfg., Inc., 494 U.S. 545, 110 S.Ct. 1331, 108 L.Ed.2d 504 (1990): Axelrod v. Phillips Academy, 74 F.Supp.2d 106, 109 (D.Mass. 1999).

In a case of nationwide first impression, the New Jersey Supreme Court held in 1977 that the absence of mutuality in a criminal prosecution does not automatically preclude application of the doctrine of collateral estoppel: after co-defendant's successful motion to suppress evidence found in a search prior to the arrest in a proceeding to which the present defendant was not a party, the court held that basic fairness in the administration of justice required that the same evidence must similarly be suppressed in the defendant's own subsequent trial. State v. Gonzalez, 75 N.J. 181, 380 A.2d 1128 (1977); Woodrick v. Burke Real Estate, Inc., 306 N.J.Super. 61, 703 A.2d 306 (1997). This view was rejected in Reid

v. State, 719 N.E.2d 451, 456 (Ind.App. 1999), cert. denied 531 U.S. 995, 121 S.Ct. 489, 148 L.Ed.2d 461 (2000); Martin v. State 740 N.E.2d 137 (Ind. App. 2000).

§ 24.2

1. It is not always easy to determine whether the result of the first litigation was "on the merits." For instance: the first forum dismissed an action in application of its statute of limitations. A second forum does likewise but does so not in application of its own statute of limitation but rather because its "borrowing statute" directs it to the first jurisdiction's statute as a matter of choice of law. Was the second forum's decision "on the merits" and does it therefore preclude litigation of the claim in yet a third forum? Similarly, when a jurisdiction refuses to entertain certain claims and therefore dismisses an action brought on such a claim, is such a decision "on the merits" of the claim? Is it on the merits-and does it therefore bind a federal court sitting in diversity in the same jurisdiction-with respect to the question whether the

As among the States of the Union, Art. IV, § 1 of the federal Constitution requires each State to give "Full Faith and Credit . . . to the . . . Judicial Proceedings of every other State." The Judiciary Act of 1790 particularized that this language means "the same full faith and credit as . . . [the judicial proceedings] have by law or usage in the courts of such State . . . *from which they are taken.*"[2] This statement of the policy is clear enough: conclusiveness and, with it, claim and issue preclusion are to be tested by "the law and usage" of the jurisdiction which made the original determination.

Similarly, the Second Conflicts Restatement states that "the local law of the State where the judgment was rendered determines, subject to constitutional limitations, whether, and to what extent the judgment is conclusive as to the issues involved in a later suit between the parties, or their privies, upon a different claim or cause of action."[3] Another, not necessarily inconsistent, view suggests that the recognizing (second) forum may apply its own rules to determine the effect of a sister-state judgment,[4] among other reasons by urging use of the flexible standards of choice-of-law evident in such cases as *Babcock v. Jackson,*[5] by pointing to § 103 of the Second Restatement,[6] and by considering rules of res judicata and estoppel to be rules of law (not entitled to full faith and credit) rather than part of the judgment.[7] It would seem that the last point—res judicata as a rule of law and not part of the judgment—

state court, in the prior action, unconstitutionally closed its doors? For an affirmative answer, see Angel v. Bullington, 330 U.S. 183, 67 S.Ct. 657, 91 L.Ed. 832 (1947). Finally, it is often difficult to determine whether a determination is on the merits when the law of the two jurisdictions differs with respect to compulsory counterclaims or the two-dismissals-rule. For further discussion see infra § 24.24 nn.6–7.

In Semtek International Inc. v. Lockheed Martin Corp., 531 U.S. 497, 121 S.Ct. 1021, 149 L.Ed.2d 32 (2001) the United States Supreme Court faced a case much like this hypothetical. A complete discussion of this important case appears supra § 3.40. In that case, the federal court's (F–1's) dismissal was improperly characterized as being "on the merits." The Court held, however, that this did not preclude relitigation in F–2 (a Maryland state court), because "on the merits" in its narrowest sense simply precludes relitigation in F–1. Along the way the Court also made clear that, in diversity cases, the effect of F–1's judgment is usually determined by state, not federal, law. See Burbank, *Semtek*, Forum Shopping, and Federal Common Law, 77 Notre Dame L. Rev. 1027 (2002).

2. 28 U.S.C.A. § 1738 (emphasis added). See also infra § 24.12 n.7 and § 24.29 n.4. See also Conopco, Inc. v. Roll Int'l, 231 F.3d 82 (2d Cir.2000) (rendering court's rule that would preclude subsequent litigation of

claims that should have been raised by compulsory counterclaim bars litigation of those claims in a subsequent proceeding in another state).

3. Restatement, Second, Conflict of Laws § 95, comnt. (g) (1971).

4. Carrington, Collateral Estoppel and Foreign Judgments, 24 Ohio St. L.J. 381 (1963); Comment, If at First You do Succeed: Recognition of State Preclusive Laws in Subsequent Multistate Actions, 35 Villanova L. Rev. 253 (1990).

5. 12 N.Y.2d 473, 240 N.Y.S.2d 743, 191 N.E.2d 279 (1963). The case is discussed supra § 17.26.

6. "A judgment rendered in one State of the United States need not be recognized or enforced in a sister State if such recognition or enforcement is not required by the national policy of full faith and credit because it would involve an improper interference with important interests of the sister State." For critical discussion of § 103, see infra § 24.21.

7. Note, supra n.4, at 1595, citing to Clark v. Clark, 80 Nev. 52, 57, 389 P.2d 69, 71–72 (1964). See also Schlesinger, Jurisdictional Clauses in Consumer Transactions: A Multifaceted Problem of Jurisdiction and Full Faith and Credit, 29 Hastings L.J. 967, 982 et seq. (1978).

confuses the flexibility in choice of law, which results from the relatively few applicable constitutional constraints with the recognition of judgments which is constitutionally mandated. The extent of that mandate, as a matter of constitutional law, leaves no room for state-law preferences: the effect of judgments is to be that accorded by the state of rendition. It may be that the recognizing (second) forum may accord *additional* preclusive effect to the sister-state judgment under its own law to the extent that doing so would not violate due process; however, this matter is still unsettled and very much in doubt.[8]

With respect to preclusion under the law of the court of rendition, the broad reach of the policy is illustrated by the Supreme Court's holding that the principles of res judicata extend to *all* issues, including the first court's determination of its jurisdiction over the subject matter and over the parties.[9] The proper procedure to obtain review of a

8. See Hart v. American Airlines, Inc., 61 Misc.2d 41, 304 N.Y.S.2d 810 (1969) (offensive non-mutual estoppel allowed under New York law when state of rendition, Texas, required mutuality). Cf. Marrese v. American Academy of Ortho. Surgeons, 470 U.S. 373, 105 S.Ct. 1327, 84 L.Ed.2d 274 (1985) (state court preclusion law determines preclusive effect in federal court in subsequent federal question litigation involving the same issues and basic claims than in the court where rendered); Matsushita Electric Industrial Co. v. Epstein, 516 U.S. 367, 116 S.Ct. 873, 134 L.Ed.2d 6 (1996), on remand 126 F.3d 1235 (9th Cir. 1997), opinion withdrawn and superseded on rehearing 179 F.3d 641 (9th Cir.1999) (*Marrese* applied). See also infra § 24.12 n.7.

For extensive discussion see A.D. Vestal, Res Judicata/Preclusion, 478–483 (1969). See also Jackson, Full Faith and Credit– The Lawyer's Clause of the Constitution, 45 Colum. L. Rev. 1, 30 (1945). An analogy, noted by Vestal, supra, at 480, is the rule that the second forum may apply its own longer statute of limitations to a judgment already barred by the statute of limitations of the jurisdiction of rendition. See Union National Bank v. Lamb, 337 U.S. 38, 46, 69 S.Ct. 911, 915, 93 L.Ed. 1190 (1949) (Frankfurter, J., dissenting in part).

As Vestal, supra, at 482, points out, constitutional objections may prevent the second jurisdiction from attaching greater preclusive effect to the first forum's judgment than obtains there. Thus, if the first forum defines a cause of action narrowly, the second forum's refusal to entertain a related claim on the ground that, under its definition of the cause of action, the litigant is splitting his claim may be a deprivation of that claim without due process. "On the other hand, this argument would have little force when applied to a question of *issue preclusion* if the losing party had the opportunity and incentive to litigate the issue fully in the first action. Due process considerations should not prevent Forum II from holding the losing party bound on the issues when its public policy leads to this result." Id. at 482–83 (emphasis added). These considerations lead to the narrow conclusion that more extensive preclusive effect by the second jurisdiction may be limited to the area of issue preclusion and not extend to claim preclusion. See also Erichson, Interjurisdictional Preclusion, 96 Mich. L. Rev. 945 (1998); Brownewell, Rethinking the Restatement View (Again!): Multiple Independent Holdings and the Doctrine of Issue Preclusion 37 Val. U. L. Rev. 879 (2003). "Claim definition," for purposes of preclusive effects to be attached to the first judgment, is of particular importance in relation to foreign legal systems, in which "claim" may be defined quite differently from the way it is in American law: to attach American preclusion consequences to judgment rendered in such a system severely prejudice a party (e.g. the judgment creditor who only sued on part of his or her as permitted by foreign law). See infra § 24.3 n.13.

9. Baldwin v. Iowa State Traveling Men's Association, 283 U.S. 522, 51 S.Ct. 517, 75 L.Ed. 1244 (1931); Treinies v. Sunshine Mining Co., 308 U.S. 66, 60 S.Ct. 44, 84 L.Ed. 85 (1939). The rule is the same in the European Union under Regulation (EC) 44/2001 or the Brussels Convention (Denmark) or the Parallel (Lugano) Convention (Iceland, Norway, Switzerland). See infra §§ 24.7, 24.38. In England alone the rule is different with respect to non-Convention countries. See Lowenfeld, Conflict of Laws

judgment is to appeal it. The requirement of the Full Faith and Credit Clause, subject to exceptions to be noted subsequently, does not permit collateral review in the second jurisdiction beyond the review available in the jurisdiction rendering the decision.[10] The Full Faith and Credit Clause and its focus on the preclusive effect which attaches to a determination in the state of rendition thus serve as unifying elements for the recognition of judgments in our federal system. A particularly good illustration is the rule that the *last* judgment-of several and possibly inconsistent judgments-is the one entitled to Full Faith and Credit in subsequent litigation even if such a last judgment itself erroneously failed to accord Full Faith and Credit to an earlier judgment. Again, the proper remedy would have been appeal, not collateral attack.[11]

Subsequent sections will explore some of the technical difficulties that inhere in the application of the Full Faith and Credit Clause. Understanding its basic policy, especially in the context of the pervasive policy of preclusion, will aid in the resolution of many of the complex problems.

C. PRECLUSION AND THE ENFORCEMENT OF INTERNATIONAL JUDGMENTS

§ 24.3   The Full Faith and Credit Clause does not apply to foreign-country judgments. An early U.S. Supreme Court decision (*Hilton v. Guyot*[1])—from which a substantial number of states have now departed[2] —therefore concluded that such judgments were entitled to recognition only on the basis of comity.[3] Other courts approached the problem by holding that the foreign-country decision created an *obligation,* to be

English Style—Review Essay, 37 Am. J. Comp. L. 353, 367 (1989). In the case of a diversity court rendering a judgment, the Supreme Court in Semtek v. Lockheed, 531 U.S. 497, 121 S.Ct. 1021, 149 L.Ed.2d 32 (2001), held that, although federal common law determines the effect of such a judgment, the federal common law rule normally incorporates the forum state's rule of preclusion.

10. If the first forum provides procedures for reopening or vacating a judgment, or for its collateral impeachment-for instance, for fraud-, these may also be invoked in a second forum in an action for the recognition and enforcement of the judgment.

11. "Even where the decision against the validity of the original judgment is erroneous, it is a valid exercise of judicial power by the second court.... 'The principles of *res judicata* apply to questions of jurisdiction as well as to other issues,' as well to jurisdiction of the subject matter as of the parties." Treinies v. Sunshine Mining Co.,

308 U.S. 66, 78, 60 S.Ct. 44, 50–51, 84 L.Ed. 85 (1939); Durfee v. Duke, 375 U.S. 106, 84 S.Ct. 242, 11 L.Ed.2d 186 (1963). The principles of *Baldwin* and *Durfee* were reaffirmed in Underwriters National Assurance Co. v. North Carolina Life and Accident and Health Insurance Ass'n, 455 U.S. 691, 102 S.Ct. 1357, 71 L.Ed.2d 558 (1982), in which an Indiana court exercised subject matter jurisdiction over North Carolina trust fund in a proceeding in which claimants participated and the jurisdictional issue was fully and fairly litigated, the decision-"erroneous or not"-was res judicata as between the parties and it was error for North Carolina to refuse full faith and credit to the Indiana judgments. 455 U.S. at 713, 102 S.Ct. at 1370.

§ 24.3

1. 159 U.S. 113, 16 S.Ct. 139, 40 L.Ed. 95 (1895). The case is discussed infra § 24.34.

2. See infra § 24.35 nn.6–7.

3. See infra § 24.34 n.6.

enforced everywhere.[4] The notion of an "obligation" created by the judgment of course parallels the ideas of *res judicata* and preclusion, in the sense that something has been determined with finality and now binds the parties.

However, the extent to which foreign-country decisions should have preclusive effect has long been uncertain. Story took the position in his Commentaries[5] that the successful defendant could plead the foreign court's determination in bar to a subsequent action by the original plaintiff in the United States, but that the successful plaintiff's recovery was subject to an inquiry into the merits. The latter thought re-emerged in the Supreme Court's decision, noted above, that a personal judgment was entitled to recognition only on the basis of comity. A corollary of his view was that the successful plaintiff's judgment was said *not* to have merged the underlying cause of action, thus leaving him free to seek either recognition and enforcement of the judgment or to relitigate the original claim. The Second Restatement retains this option.[6] Arguments in support of the non-merger rule correctly state that foreign rules of *res judicata* are often quite different from those of the second forum[7] which would make their ascertainment difficult and costly if the merger rule were to obtain,[8] and that the plaintiff should have the option to seek a new judgment when currency fluctuations have devalued the original judgment.[9]

The non-merger rule has been subject to criticism[10] and indeed makes little sense today. Some of the case law guards against judgment devaluation by permitting recovery in either currency; the Uniform Foreign–Money Claims Act has the same objective.[11] The policies favoring the conclusive termination of litigation are the same in the international as in the interstate setting; the respect for the governmental and judicial acts of another jurisdiction that the Full Faith and Credit Clause addresses in the interstate context has its international counterpart in

---

4. See, e.g., Johnston v. Compagnie Generale Transatlantique, 242 N.Y. 381, 152 N.E. 121 (1926). This doctrine, which still underlies judgment-recognition practice in England, differs from the vested-rights theory in choice of law (supra § 2.5) in that the recognizing forum does not, without more, accept and enforce the obligation created by the foreign judgment but tests the foreign court's jurisdiction by its *own* jurisdictional standards and subjects the foreign judgment to additional, local law defenses such as fraud, violation of local public policy, and the like. Dicey & Morris, Conflict of Laws 474–483, 487–504 (13th ed. 2000 by Collins et al.). See also Weintraub, How Substantial Is Our Need For a Judgments–Recognition Convention and What Should We Bargain Away to Get It?, 24 Brooklyn J. Int'l L. 167, 180 (1998) (commenting on British recognition practice).

5. J. Story, Commentaries on the Conflict of Laws §§ 500, 508, 591–92, 598 (1834).

6. Restatement, Second, Conflict of Laws § 95, comment (c)(1) (1971).

7. See Millar, The Premises of the Judgment as Res Judicata in Continental and Anglo–American Law, 39 Mich. L. Rev. 1 (1940).

8. Nussbaum, Principles of Private International Law 245–46 (1943).

9. See A.A. Ehrenzweig & E. Jayme, 2 Private International Law 61 (1973).

10. See, e.g., Peterson, Foreign Country Judgments and the Second Restatement, 72 Colum. L. Rev. 219, 230–32 (1972).

11. See infra § 24.40.

the act-of-state doctrine;[12] and, while legal systems do differ, "the 'jurisdictional' limitations of adequate notice, opportunity to be heard and appropriateness of forum should . . . provide ample protection for parties in this shrinking world."[13]

In England, a foreign judgment that falls within the Foreign Judgments Act of 1933 has conclusive effect.[14] Beyond that, the possibility of issue preclusion (estoppel) has also been recognized recently.[15] The House of Lords, however, was careful to note that differences in procedures might make it difficult to determine whether an issue was actually decided, that policy reasons might exist against an estoppel effect to a default judgment,[16] and that there must be identity of parties or privity.[17]

§ 24.4 In the United States, the Second Conflicts Restatement cautiously suggests[1] that when a judgment creditor seeks enforcement of the foreign judgment rather than presenting his claim anew[2] an American court would "normally . . . apply the foreign rules [with respect to *res judicata* and estoppel] if these rules are substantially the same as the rules of the American court." This formulation permits the different treatment of a foreign-country determination, compared with a sister-state judgment, when the international context makes this particularly appropriate. For instance, a foreign court's determination with respect to its jurisdiction over the parties should not have a *res judicata* effect similar to that of a sister-state court[3] when the foreign jurisdictional basis did not satisfy U.S. due-process standards nor, by hypothesis, was appealable and reviewable on such grounds.[4] The Second Restatement's

---

12. Scoles, Interstate and International Distinctions in Conflict of Laws in the United States, 54 Cal. L. Rev. 1599, 1607 (1966). See also Casad, Issue Preclusion and Foreign Country Judgments: Whose Law?, 70 Iowa L. Rev. 53 (1984).

13. Scoles, supra n.12, at 1606. See also infra § 24.41. However, some care must be taken in the determination of what the cause of action was that the foreign judgment has merged, if the merger rule were to be applied. Under German law, for instance, a plaintiff may sue on a portion of the claim and, if successful, seek the balance or another portion of the claim in subsequent litigation. Since court costs and attorney's fees by statute bear a relationship to the amount in controversy and since the losing party pays the costs of both, testing the waters with the prosecution of part of the claim is common practice. Under U.S. motions of res judicata, this practice amounts to a "splitting of the cause of action." However, since German law in effect accords several causes of action, only the claim litigated should be considered merged and relitigation of it precluded. See Hay, Weintraub & Borchers, Conflict of Laws–Cases and Materials 726 (12th ed. 2004).

14. Black-Clawson International Ltd. v. Papierwerke Waldhof–Aschaffenburg A.G., [1974] 2 W.L.R. 789; [1975] 2 Lloyd's Rep. 11.

15. Carl Zeiss Stiftung v. Rayner & Keeler Ltd., [1967] 1 A.C. 853; Carl Zeiss Stiftung v. Rayner & Keeler Ltd. (No. 3), [1970] 1 Ch. 506; ED&F Man (Sugar) Ltd. v. Yani Haryanto (No. 2), [1991] 1 Lloyd's Rep. 429 (Q.B.) (res judicata applies not only to issues brought forward by the parties but also to those determined by the court to be property related to the subject of the litigation).

16. See also Restatement, Second, Conflict of Laws § 98, cmnt. (d) (1971).

17. See the excellent discussion and summary in R.H. Graveson, Conflict of Laws 597–98 (7th ed. 1974).

§ 24.4

1. Restatement, Second, Conflict of Laws § 98, cmnt. (f) (1971).

2. Supra § 24.3 n.6.

3. Infra at § 24.12 n.3.

4. Cf. Gorie v. Gorie, 26 A.D.2d 368, 274 N.Y.S.2d 985 (1st Dept.1966).

standard of substantial similarity to the forum's standards guards against these dangers. By like token, however, the use of forum standards may give the foreign judgment greater preclusive effect than it has where rendered, for instance by applying domestic concepts of privity.[5] A reformulation of the Restatement's rules should therefore abandon the nonmerger rule and provide, for the recognition of foreign-country judgments, that *res judicata* and estoppel effect will be accorded foreign-country determinations which have been finally litigated there,[6] have a like effect in the forum where rendered, and, except for *factual* determinations, do not go to the jurisdiction of the foreign court.[7]

The trend in the international area is to accord foreign-country judgments "the same degree of recognition to which sister State judgments are entitled."[8] A unification of the applicable rules by the U.S. Supreme Court, in the exercise of the federal foreign-commerce or foreign-relation powers,[9] however, would be preferable to the present state of the law. "The approach of leaving this problem to be decided by the states as part of their common law development, with their solutions to be applied by the federal courts under *Erie* and *Klaxon*, is anomalous."[10] Until uniform rules have emerged in the case law, recognition treaties may provide uniform approaches with respect to particular foreign legal systems. Thus far the U.S. has been unsuccessful in concluding any such treaties; the drafting of a multi-lateral jurisdictional and judgment-recognition treaty in the Hague Conference was initiated by the U.S., although these efforts have not produced a draft likely to be acceptable to American interests.[11]

5. Cf. Watts v. Swiss Bank Corp., 27 N.Y.2d 270, 317 N.Y.S.2d 315, 265 N.E.2d 739 (1970). See also supra §§ 24.2 n.8, 24.3 n.13.

6. See Bata v. Bata, 39 Del.Ch. 258, 163 A.2d 493 (1960), certiorari denied 366 U.S. 964, 81 S.Ct. 1926, 6 L.Ed.2d 1255 (1961). See also Carl Zeiss Stiftung v. V.E.B. Carl Zeiss, Jena, 293 F.Supp. 892 (S.D.N.Y. 1968), aff'd as modified 433 F.2d 686 (2d Cir.1970).

7. See also Smit, International Res Judicata and Collateral Estoppel in the United States, 9 U.C.L.A. Rev. 44 (1962) (advocating that *res judicata* and estoppel effects be accorded foreign status, in rem, quasi-in-rem and those in personam determinations in which the foreign forum was also the domicile of the parties or in which the plaintiff is also the present plaintiff). The suggestion appears unduly restrictive. What if the foreign legal system permits a plaintiff to "split the cause of action" for instance, to avoid court and attorney fees while "testing" the probable success of her cause of action? See Hay, Weintraub, Borchers, Conflict of Laws 726 (12th ed. 2004). For decisions giving collateral estoppel effect to a foreign country judgment, see In-Tech Marketing, Inc. v. Hasbro, Inc., 719 F.Supp. 312 (D.N.J.1989); Ma v. Continental Bank N.A., 905 F.2d 1073 (7th Cir. 1990), cert. denied 498 U.S. 967, 111 S.Ct. 430, 112 L.Ed.2d 414 (1990); Scheiner v. Wallace, 832 F.Supp. 687 (S.D.N.Y.1993); Seetransport Wiking Trader Schiffartgesellschaft m.b.H. and Co. v. Navimpex Centrala Navala, 837 F.Supp. 79 (S.D.N.Y. 1993), affirmed 29 F.3d 79 (2d Cir.1994). The decisions do not address whether the court is applying American principles of collateral estoppel or those of the rendering state. See again supra § 24.3 n. 13.

8. Restatement, Second, Conflict of Laws § 98, comnt. (b) (1971).

9. Hay, International versus Interstate Conflicts Law in the United States, 35 Rabels Zeitschrift 429, 487–489 (1971).

10. Scoles, supra § 24.3 n.12, at 1607. The *Erie* and *Klaxon* decision are discussed supra § 3.36 et seq.

11. Infra § 24.39. See generally Symposium, Enforcing Judgments Abroad: The Global Challenge, 24 Brooklyn J. Int'l L. 1 (1998).

D. METHODS OF ENFORCING FOREIGN JUDGMENTS[1]

§ 24.5 As noted earlier, a judgment rendered in another jurisdiction-whether in a sister-state or in a foreign country-will be regarded as a *foreign* judgment by the jurisdiction where its enforcement is sought. The judgment thus has no direct or automatic effect in the second jurisdiction. The judgment creditor must depend on the assistance of the local courts for the recognition and enforcement of the judgment.

At common law, the judgment creditor could bring an action on the foreign judgment, obtain a local judgment and then enforce the local judgment against local assets.[2] Although the constitutional authority of Congress under the Full Faith and Credit Clause has not been fully exercised,[3] to provide for direct enforcement of sister-state judgments, the Full Faith and Credit Clause does mandate the recognition of interstate judgments, thereby curtailing any state refusal or recognition to sister-state judgments. State legislation, including several uniform acts, often provides summary procedures for the recognition of sister-state judgments, and federal law provides for the registration "in any other district" of a federal court's judgment for the recovery of money or property.[4]

§ 24.6 Foreign-country judgments do not benefit from the Full Faith and Credit Clause but they have traditionally been accorded recognition and enforcement as a matter of "comity."[1] Most states accord foreign-country judgments essentially the same status as sister-

§ 24.5

1. The recognition of divorce and other decrees pertaining to status as well as of support orders is discussed supra Chapter 15.

2. See Restatement, Second, Conflict of Laws §§ 99–100 (1971); McElmoyle v. Cohen, 38 U.S. (13 Pet.) 312, 10 L.Ed. 177 (1839); Ostrom v. Ostrom, 231 F.2d 193 (9th Cir.1955); Lamberton v. Grant, 94 Me. 508, 48 A. 127 (1901); Eaton v. Hasty, 6 Neb. 419, 29 Am.Rep. 365 (1877); Anglo–American Provision Co. v. Davis Provision Co., No. 1, 169 N.Y. 506, 62 N.E. 587 (1902), aff'd 191 U.S. 373, 24 S.Ct. 92, 48 L.Ed. 225 (1903).

3. U.S. Const. Art. IV, § 1; Cook, The Powers of Congress under the Full Faith and Credit Clause, 28 Yale L. J. 421 (1919); Corwin, The Full Faith and Credit Clause, 81 U. Pa. L. Rev. 371 (1933). Widespread child snatching by the non-custodial parent prompted the adoption of the federal Parental Kidnapping Prevention Act of 1980, adding § 1738A to 28 U.S.C.A., prescribing full faith and credit to state court decisions complying, essentially, with the UCCJA. See supra § 15.46.

4. 28 U.S.C.A. § 1963. See Note, The New Federal Judgment Enforcement Procedure, 50 Colum. L. Rev. 971 (1950); Note, 42 Iowa L. Rev. 285 (1957). Federal law requires courts to give full faith and credit to the judgments of any "State, Territory or Possession:" 29 U.S.C.A. § 1738. The provision has been held to include a judgment of the District of Columbia: Washington Gas Light Co. v. Hsu, 478 F.Supp. 1262 (D.Md. 1979). The court in the state of registration need not have personal jurisdiction over the judgment debtor. Dichter v. Disco Corp., 606 F.Supp. 721 (S.D.Ohio 1984).

§ 24.6

1. Hilton v. Guyot, 159 U.S. 113, 16 S.Ct. 139, 40 L.Ed. 95 (1895). See Restatement, Second, Conflict of Laws § 98 (1971); Joiner, The Recognition of Foreign Country Money Judgments by American Courts, 34 Am. J. Comp. L. 193 (Supp. 1986); Peterson, Foreign Country Judgments and the Restatement, Second, Conflict of Laws, 72 Colum. L. Rev. 220 (1972); von Mehren & Trautman, Recognition of Foreign Adjudications: A Survey and a Suggested Approach, 81 Harv. L. Rev. 1601, 1607 (1968); von Mehren & Patterson, Recognition and Enforcement of Foreign Country Judgments in the United States, 6 Law & Policy in Int'l Bus. 37 (1974). For the history of the doc-

state judgments.[2] However, a few states, as had the U.S. Supreme Court's in its pre-*Erie* decision in *Hilton v. Guyot*,[3] still condition recognition on reciprocity.

Just as the Congress has not legislated in the field, the Executive had long refrained from employing the federal treaty power to provide for the uniform recognition of foreign-country judgments in the United States. A number of factors has now led to a change in position. These factors include that continued disparate state practice within the United States may be an obstacle to the recognition of American judgments in foreign countries still requiring reciprocity[4] and that adoption of bilateral and multilateral recognition treaties by foreign countries may make foreign-country judgments against Americans enforceable in other foreign countries even though they would not have been entitled to recogni-

trine of comity, see Yntema, The Comity Doctrine, 65 Mich. L. Rev. 9 (1966).

2. See Restatement, Second, Conflict of Laws, § 98 comnt. (f), § 100 comnt. (d) (1971); § 3, Uniform Foreign Money–Judgments Recognition Act, which makes foreign-country judgments enforceable on nearly the same basis as sister-state judgments are enforced in the United States. See Hay, On Comity, Reciprocity, and Public Policy in U.S. and German Judgments Recognition Practice, in Basedow et al. (eds.), Private Law in the International Arena–Liber Amicorum Kurt Siehr 237 (2000).

For applications of the Uniform Act (recognizing a Canadian default judgment and dismissing counterclaims) see Bank of Montreal v. Kough, 612 F.2d 467 (9th Cir. 1980); Chase Manhattan Bank, N.A. v. Hoffman, 665 F.Supp. 73 (D.Mass.1987); Dresdner Bank AG v. Edelmann, 129 Misc.2d 686, 493 N.Y.S.2d 703 (1985); Desjardins Ducharme v. Hunnewell, 411 Mass. 711, 585 N.E.2d 321 (1992). See also Brand, Enforcement of Judgments in the United States and Europe, 13 J. of Law and Commerce 193 (1994); Simeone, The Recognition and Enforceability of Foreign Country Judgments, 37 St. Louis U.L.J. 341 (1993). For an extensive bibliography, see Ebke & Parker, Foreign Country Money–Judgments and Arbitral Awards and the Restatement (Third) of the Foreign Relations Law of the United States: A Conventional Approach, 24 Int'l Lawyer 21 (1990).

3. 159 U.S. 113, 16 S.Ct. 139, 40 L.Ed. 95 (1895). The Supreme Court's decision in *Hilton* required reciprocity as a precondition for the recognition and enforcement of foreign judgments other than those *in rem* or relating to status. For a state decision following *Hilton* see Leo Feist, Inc. v. Deb-

mar Publication Co., 232 F.Supp. 623 (E.D.Pa.1964). Largely as a result of the decisions in Erie Railroad Co. v. Tompkins, 304 U.S. 64, 58 S.Ct. 817, 82 L.Ed. 1188 (1938) and Klaxon v. Stentor Electric Manufacturing Co., 313 U.S. 487, 61 S.Ct. 1020, 85 L.Ed. 1477 (1941), most states have departed from *Hilton* and treat foreign judgments like sister-state judgments. See, e.g., Johnston v. Compagnie Generale Transatlantique, 242 N.Y. 381, 152 N.E. 121 (1926), reargument denied 243 N.Y. 541, 154 N.E. 597 (1926); Bergman v. De Sieyes, 170 F.2d 360 (2d Cir.1948); Scott v. Scott, 51 Cal.2d 249, 331 P.2d 641 (1958) (especially the concurring opinion of Traynor, J., 51 Cal.2d 249, 254, 331 P.2d 641, 644); New Central Jute Mills Co., Ltd. v. City Trade and Industries, Ltd., 65 Misc.2d 653, 318 N.Y.S.2d 980 (1971). Seven states provide for reciprocity by statute. For discussion see infra §§ 24.35, 24.36 n.1.

For the use of the federal treaty power in this context see Hay, Unification of Law in the United States: Uniform State Laws, Treaties and Judicially Declared, Federal Common Law, in: J.N. Hazard & W.J. Wagner, eds., Legal Thought in the United States of America Under Contemporary Pressures 261, at 265–272, 290–292 (1970); see also infra nn.6, 7.

4. An extreme example is an older German Supreme Court decision requiring a showing of *actual* reciprocity and holding that a statutory provision for the recognition of foreign (including German) judgments alone was insufficient proof: RGZ 70, 434 (1901) with respect to California. Modern German case law is more liberal in finding the reciprocity requirement to be satisfied: BGHZ 42, 194 (1964); BGH judgment of 5 August 1968, [1968] Aussenwirtschaftsdienst des Betriebsberaters 229. For further discussion see infra at § 24.38 n.9.

tion and enforcement in the United States.[5] The United States initialed a first recognition treaty (with England) in 1977;[6] it failed to be ratified because of English concerns over high American damage awards in products liability cases and the wide American antitrust jurisdiction. At the initiative of the United States, the Hague Conference on Private International Law is considering the draft of a multilateral jurisdiction and judgments convention, with the Brussels Convention as a model. It would "blacklist" two bases of jurisdiction generally recognized in the United States-general (not claim-related) doing of business, and transient service-in the sense that judgments based on these jurisdictional grounds would not be entitled to recognition.[7] At present, however, it seems unlikely that the Hague Project will move forward.

§ 24.7 Some Commonwealth countries recognize money judgments from other Commonwealth countries on the basis of registration.[1] The

5. For instance, because the foreign judgment was based on jurisdiction considered "exorbitant" by American standards of due process. Such exorbitant jurisdictional bases include, for instance, French assertion of jurisdiction on the basis of the French or European Union nationality and domicile of *the plaintiff* (even in the absence of any connection of the defendant or the transaction to France) (Arts. 14, 15 French Civil Code) and the exercise of *in personam* jurisdiction by German courts when the defendant has assets in Germany (but not restricted to the value of the assets) (§ 23 German Code of Civil Procedure). See Nadelmann, Jurisdictionally Improper Fora, in: XXth Century Comparative and Conflicts Law, Legal Essays in Honor of Hessel E. Yntema 321 (1961). Modern German case law now requires, in addition to the presence of assets, that the case bear an appropriate relationship to Germany. See BGH NJW 1991, 3092; OLG Celle (1998), in IPRax 2001, 338. Assertion of jurisdiction on the basis of the defendant's mere presence by American courts, in turn, is considered "exorbitant" by Europeans and also criticized in the United States. See Winter, Excessive Jurisdiction in Private International Law, 19 Int'l & Comp. L.Q. 706 (1968); Ehrenzweig, The Transient Rule of Personal Jurisdiction, 65 Yale L.J. 289 (1956). Its constitutionality was upheld once again in Burnham v. Superior Court of California, 495 U.S. 604, 110 S.Ct. 2105, 109 L.Ed.2d 631 (1990). For critical comments see Borchers, The Death of the Constitutional Law of Personal Jurisdiction: From *Pennoyer* to *Burnham* and Back Again, 24 U.C. Davis L. Rev. 19 (1990); Hay, 1990 U. Ill. L. Rev. 593 (1990); Symposium, The Future of Personal Jurisdiction, 22 Rutgers L.J. 559 (1991); Lowenfeld, International Litigation and the Quest for

Reasonableness, Hague Academy, 245 Recueil des cours 9, 120 et seq. (1994–I).

6. For analysis see Hay & Walker, The Proposed Recognition-of-Judgments Convention Between the United States and the United Kingdom, 11 Tex. Int'l L.J. 421 (1976); Hay & Walker, Le projet anglo-americain de Convention sur la reconnaissance des décisions et la Convention Communautaire, [1977] Cahiers de droit européen 3.

7. See infra § 24.39 at n.11.

On earlier drafts, see von Mehren, Recognition and Enforcement of Foreign Judgments: A New Approach for the Hague Conference?, 57 Law & Contemp. Probs. 271 (Summer 1994); Lowenfeld, Thoughts About a Multilateral Judgments Convention: A Reaction to the von Mehren Report, id. 289. For a foreign perspective, see Schack, Perspektiven eines weltweiten Anerkennungs-und Vollstreckungsabkommens, 1 Zeitschrift für Europäisches Privatrecht 306 (1993); Schack, Entscheidungszuständigkeiten in einem weltweiten Gerichtsstands-und Vollstreckungsübereinkommen, 6 Zeitschrift für Europäisches Privatrecht 931 (1998).

§ 24.7

1. *Australia:* Service and Execution of Process Act 1992, Commonwealth of Australia 172/1992; Foreign Judgments Act 1991, Commonwealth of Australia 112/1991 (counterpart to the 1933 English Act, infra); *Canada:* Sharpe, The Enforcement of Foreign Judgments, in: Debtor–Creditor Law: Practice and Doctrine 641 (Springman & Gertner, eds., 1985); Canadian Reciprocal Enforcement of Judgments Act (1959); Castel, Canadian Conflict of Laws 301 *et seq.* (4th ed. 1997). *United Kingdom:* Administration of Justice Act 1920, 10 § 11 Geo. V,

British Foreign Judgments (Reciprocal Enforcement) Act of 1933[2] extends the same recognition to judgments rendered in foreign countries according similar treatment to British judgments.

In addition, many foreign countries have long provided for the recognition of foreign judgments by bilateral treaty.[3] Multilateral conventions, for instance, the Hague Convention of 1971,[4] have also been proposed. The most comprehensive and successful multilateral agreement was the European Community's (Brussels) Convention on Jurisdiction and the Recognition of Judgments in Civil and Commercial Matters, replaced in 2001, effective in 2002, by an EC Regulation, which is directly applicable law in all European Union States, except Denmark.[5] The Brussels Convention still continues in force among the former and the latter; and the Lugano Convention (below) applies among all of the foregoing and Iceland, Norway, and Switzerland. In 1988, the twelve members of the European Community and the (then) six members of the European Free Trade Association (Austria, Finland, Iceland, Norway, Sweden, and Switzerland) adopted the "Parallel Convention" (Lugano Convention),[6] essentially extending the application of the Brussels Con-

---

c. 81; Foreign Judgments (Reciprocal Enforcement) Act, 1933, 23 Geo. V, c. 13; see also Private International Law (Miscellaneous Provisions Act) of 1995 (c. 42). See infra § 24.38 n.4.

See also Dicey & Morris, Conflict of Laws 471 (13th ed. 2001 by Collins); Pryles, Internationalism in Australian Private Law, 12 Sydney L. Rev. 96 (1989); Stone, The Recognition and Enforcement in England of Foreign Personal and Proprietary Judgments, Lloyds Maritime and Commercial Law Quarterly 1 (Feb. 1983); Westin, Enforcing Foreign Commercial Judgments and Arbitral Awards in the United States, West Germany, and England, 19 Law and Policy in International Business 325 (1987); Woodward, Reciprocal Recognition and Enforcement of Civil Judgments in the United States, the United Kingdom, and the European Community, 8 N.C. J. of Int'l L. & Comm'l Regulation 299 (1983); Glick, Foreign Civil Judgment: Direct Enforcement Legislation in Australia, 49 A.L.J. 538 (1974); Hay, The Recognition and Enforcement of American Judgments in Germany, 40 Am. J. Comp. L. 729 (1992); Yntema, The Enforcement of Foreign Judgments in Anglo–American Law, 33 Mich. L. Rev. 1129 (1935); Lowenfeld, Conflicts of Laws English Style—Review Essay, 37 Am. J. Comp. L. 353, 366, (1989).

2. Supra n.1.

3. For examples and analysis see Weser, Convention communautaire sur la compétence judiciaire et l'exécution des décisions 147–195, 429–442, 617–678 (1975). For Ca-

nadian recognition treaties with the United Kingdom and France, see Castel, supra n.1, at 312–315.

4. Recueil des Conventions de La Haye 107 (1973 ed.), reprinted in 21 Am. J. Comp. L. 136 (1973). For discussion see Nadelmann, The Extraordinary Session of The Hague Conference on Private International Law, 60 Am. J. Int'l L. 803 (1966).

5. *Brussels Convention of 1968*: A consolidated version of the Convention is reproduced in [1998] Official Journal C 27/1. For discussion see Bartlett, Full Faith and Credit Comes to the Common Market, 24 Int. & Comp. L.Q. 44 (1975); Hay, The Common Market Preliminary Draft Convention on the Recognition and Enforcement of Judgments—Some Considerations of Policy and Interpretation, 16 Am. J. Comp. L. 149 (1968). *Directly Applicable Community Law: Council Regulation (EC) No. 44/2001* on Jurisdiction and the Recognition of Judgments in Civil and Commercial Matters, [2001] Official Journal L 012/1. The Regulation was adopted pursuant to new powers conferred on the Community by the Treaty of Amsterdam. That treaty permitted Denmark, Ireland, and the United Kingdom to opt out of legislation enacted under the new powers, and Denmark exercised that right concerning Regulation 44/2001. It remains bound by the Brussels Convention.

6. [1988] Official Journal No. L 319/9. For discussion see Droz, La Convention de Lugano parallèle la Convention de Brux-

vention to all eighteen countries. With the accession of Austria, Finland, and Sweden to the European Union in 1995, the Brussels Convention was amended to provide for membership of these countries. One important feature of these instruments is that they abolish nationally available exorbitant bases of jurisdiction in relations of member countries to each other but generalize the availability of all such bases in favor of domiciliaries of member states as against parties of third states. A resulting judgment is entitled to recognition in all member states. Thus, even when such a judgment would not be entitled to recognition in the United States,[7] an American judgment debtor may be exposed to liability-through enforcement of the judgment against him-in any E.V. member state in which he has assets. This danger makes it particularly important that the United States conclude recognition conventions with foreign countries in order to guard against such problems.

II.   INTERSTATE RECOGNITION OF JUDGMENTS

A.   WHAT CONSTITUTES ENFORCEABLE FOREIGN PROCEEDINGS

1.   Finality

§ 24.8   The Full Faith and Credit Clause refers to "judicial proceedings"[1] and, on its face, does not require "finality" in a sister-state decree as condition of enforcement.[2] As a result, a recognizing court might enforce a non-final judgment, for instance a judgment still modifiable or subject to appeal in the rendering state, and accord the same recognition to any subsequent modification decreed by the rendering state.[3] However, it is generally assumed that, except for support and similar orders, recognition in the interstate setting is constitutionally required only for *final* decrees and judgments.[4] The rationale is that a judgment will not be given greater effect in the recognizing than in the rendering state.[5] The local law of the rendering state thus determines

elles concernant la compétence judiciaire et l'exécution des décisions en matière civile et commerciale, 78 Revue critique de droit internationale privé 1 (1989).

7. Supra § 24.6 n.5. See also supra text at § 24.6 n.7 with regard to American bases of jurisdiction that are regarded as exorbitant by Europeans and would be blacklisted by a possible future Hague Convention.

§ 24.8

1. See also 28 U.S.C.A. § 1738.

2. Barber v. Barber, 323 U.S. 77, 87, 65 S.Ct. 137, 141, 89 L.Ed. 82 (1944) (Jackson, J., concurring).

3. 323 U.S. at 87, 65 S.Ct. at 141.

4. See Maner v. Maner, 412 F.2d 449 (5th Cir.1969); Vardon Golf Co., Inc. v. Kar-

sten Mfg. Corp., 294 F.3d 1330, 1334 (Fed. Cir. 2002); Pure Distributors, Inc. v. Baker, 285 F.3d 150, 157 (1st. Cir. 2002); Note, The Finality of Judgments in the Conflict of Laws, 41 Colum. L. Rev. 878 (1941); Restatement, Second, Conflict of Laws § 107 (1971). See also infra § 24.28.

5. The Full Faith and Credit for Child Support Orders Act, 28 U.S.C.A. § 1738B, calls for the interstate enforcement of a child support order "according to its terms," even if modifiable in the state of rendition. As such the statute, passed under the "effect" provision of the Full–Faith and Credit Clause goes beyond the constitutional mandate itself. For additional discussion of modifiable decrees for alimony and support, see supra §§ 15.33–15.38. See also supra § 24.2 n.8 and accompanying text.

the extent to which a judgment is conclusive, or final, and entitled to recognition in a sister state. In the early case of *Paine v. Schenectady Insurance Co.*,[6] the Rhode Island court was faced with conflicting judgments from Rhode Island and New York with appeals pending against both. Under Rhode Island law, the pendency of an appeal vacated the local judgment, while New York law did not have such an effect until the prior judgment was, in fact, reversed. Rhode Island consequently considered the New York judgment to be conclusive. Similarly, a federal appellate decision vacating a trial court's decision in a diversity case for an intervening change in state law[7] did not have the effect of depriving the original district court's judgment of its "finality" because Federal Rule 60(b)(6) provides this relief, just as for after-discovered evidence,[8] in the case of "final judgments."[9] It thus bears emphasis that the effect of appeals, interlocutory orders, stays and the like on the "finality" of a judgment depends on the law of the rendering state.[10] However, there is a strong presumption in interstate cases that a judgment is final unless the contrary has been clearly demonstrated and that uncertainties are to be resolved in favor of enforcement.[11]

Declaratory judgments are also conclusive as to the matters in issue. Thus, despite the fact that they may serve as the basis for further relief, for instance for money damages, they are also entitled to recognition.[12]

2. Equity Decrees: Jurisdiction and Recognition

§ 24.9 Related to the question of whether an equity decree rendered by a sister state is to be recognized is the question of whether the forum had jurisdiction to enter such a decree. Analytically, the entry of equity judgments presents no significantly different question from the entry of a judgment at law. If the court has personal jurisdiction over the defendant, a question examined at length elsewhere,[1] then it has jurisdic-

---

6. 11 R.I. 411 (1876).

7. Pierce v. Cook & Co., 518 F.2d 720 (10th Cir.1975), cert. denied 423 U.S. 1079, 96 S.Ct. 866, 47 L.Ed.2d 89 (1976). Taking a narrow view of *Pierce*: McGeshick v. Choucair, 72 F.3d 62 (7th Cir. 1995), cert. denied 517 U.S. 1212, 116 S.Ct. 1834, 134 L.Ed.2d 937 (1996) (also reviewing decisions of the Second, Fourth, and Fifth Circuits).

8. F.R.C.P. 60(b)(2).

9. See also infra at § 24.9 n.4. The pendency of a Rule 60(b)(6) motion seeking relief from a default judgment in the state of rendition does not deprive that judgment of its finality and therefore does not preclude its enforcement in another state. Irvin L. Young Foundation, Inc. v. Damrell, 607 F.Supp. 705 (D.Me.1985).

10. See infra § 24.28. The earlier proposal for a Convention on the Recognition

of Judgments between the U.S. and the U.K., infra § 24.38, had defined finality with greater specificity. Thus, on the one hand, interlocutory decrees would have been expressly excluded (Art. 2(2)(c)), but judgments entitled to recognition where rendered would have been entitled to recognition in the second state (Art. 4(2)) even if an appeal was pending in the state of rendition (Art. 4(1)(b)). The greater detail provided by the Convention resulted from the international setting in which it operated, as compared with the more homogeneous interstate context in the United States.

11. See Barber v. Barber, 323 U.S. 77, 65 S.Ct. 137, 89 L.Ed. 82 (1944).

12. See Note, The Res Judicata Effect of Declaratory Relief in the Federal Courts, 46 So. Cal. L. Rev. 803 (1973).

§ 24.9

1. See supra chs. 5–11.

tion to render a judgment, whether for money damages or an equitable decree, such as an injunction.[2] Courts thus do, in fact, order parties to act[3] and to refrain from acting[4] in other states. As long as the court has personal jurisdiction over the party so enjoined, whether by his appearance, in-state service of the summons, or his contacts with the forum, then it can enforce the order.[5]

There are practical considerations here, however. The defendant who leaves the state and, with it, the court's power to enforce can disregard the order, though he may face contempt charges if he returns to the forum state. A bond conditioned upon performance of the act may, however, provide the needed economic pressure to ensure compliance.[6]

There are also considerations of comity, which blend with the secondary question of whether the equity decree will be recognized by sister courts. Antisuit injunctions, for instance, represent the most difficult use of the court's equitable powers, and will generally be invoked only if the foreign action would result in fraud, gross wrong or oppression.[7] An injunction by a court to "protect its jurisdiction" suggests a provincial pride that is most unfortunate in a federal nation.[8] Moreover, such antisuit injunctions do not generally preclude the merits of the litigation in a sister forum.[9] State courts are effectively blocked from enjoining federal courts by the Supremacy Clause of the Constitu-

2. Restatement, Second, Conflict of Laws § 53 (1971).

3. See, e.g., Bethell v. Peace, 441 F.2d 495 (5th Cir.1971); Ryan v. Ryan, 278 A.2d 121 (D.C.App.1971); State ex rel. General Dynamics Corp. v. Luten, 566 S.W.2d 452 (Mo.1978). For commentary, see Welkowitz, Preemption, Extraterritoriality, and the Problem of State Antidilution Laws, 67 Tul. L. Rev. 1 (1993); Messner, Jurisdiction to Compel the Doing of Acts Outside the Forum State, 14 Minn.L.Rev. 494 (1930).

4. Cf. James v. Grand Trunk Western Railroad Co., 14 Ill.2d 356, 152 N.E.2d 858 (1958), cert. denied 358 U.S. 915, 79 S.Ct. 288, 3 L.Ed.2d 239 (1958).

5. Restatement, Second, Conflict of Laws § 53, cmnt. c (1971).

6. See Parrish v. Parrish, 116 Va. 476, 82 S.E. 119 (1914); cf. Societe Internationale v. Rogers, 357 U.S. 197, 78 S.Ct. 1087, 2 L.Ed.2d 1255 (1958).

7. See, e.g., Karaha Bodas Co. v. Negara, 335 F.3d 357 (5th Cir. 2003)(insufficient showing of oppression to justify injunction); Stonington Partners v. Lernout & Hauspie Speech Prods. N.V., 310 F.3d 118 (3d Cir. 2002)(failure to consider comity factors makes trial court's issuance of an antisuit injunction erroneous); St. Paul Surplus Lines Ins. Co. v. Mentor Corp., 503 N.W.2d 511 (Minn.App.1993); Pauley Petroleum Inc. v. Continental Oil Co., 43 Del.Ch. 516, 239 A.2d 629 (1968). In Advanced Bionics Corp. v. Medtronic, Inc., 29 Cal.4th 697, 59 P.3d 231, 128 Cal. Rptr.2d 172 (2002), the California Supreme Court reversed the lower courts' approval of an anti-suit injunction (actually styled as a temporary restraining order) against proceedings in Minnesota. The dispute, which centered on the enforceability of an employee non-compete clause, initially resulted for a time in conflicting anti-suit injunctions issued by Minnesota and California courts. Even though the California actions were the first filed, the California Supreme Court concluded that "comity and judicial restraint" required reversal of the lower court decrees approving the issuance of the injunction. See generally Price, Full Faith and Credit and the Equity Conflict, 84 Va. L.Rev. 747 (1998).

8. Cf. James v. Grand Trunk Western Railroad Co., 14 Ill.2d 356, 152 N.E.2d 858 (1958), cert. denied 358 U.S. 915, 79 S.Ct. 288, 3 L.Ed.2d 239 (1958). See also 152 N.E.2d at 868, in which the dissenting opinion cogently notes that: "The place to stop this unseemingly kind of judicial disorder is where it begins."

9. See Baker v. General Motors Corp., 522 U.S. 222, 236, 118 S.Ct. 657, 665, 139 L.Ed.2d 580 (1998) (citing Second Edition of this book with approval); see infra n.12 and § 24.21.

tion, and federal courts are under a statutory disability from enjoining litigants before state courts with limited exceptions, such as interpleader[10] and bankruptcy proceedings.[11]

Even more sensitive comity considerations are called for in light of the Supreme Court's decision in *Baker v. General Motors Corp.*[12] In that case, the Court noted that equity decrees are generally within the command of the Full Faith and Credit Clause, and thus must be honored by sister courts. Nonetheless, a majority of the court concluded that equity decrees that interfere with important interests of other states can be resisted. In that case, the Court concluded that Michigan injunction purporting to prevent an engineer from testifying against his former employer could not bind a Missouri court's decision as to whether to allow the engineer to testify because a rule requiring recognition would improperly interfere with the Missouri court's right to control its own internal judicial processes.

Even before *Baker*, it was recognized that equity decrees are equivalent to judgments at law and entitled to recognition. This is true particularly of divorce decrees[13] and of equity decrees for the payment of money.[14] However, the enforceability of other equity decrees has been a matter not always free from uncertainty. The question has centered on the remedial aspect of an equity decree as an obligation on the defendant. "The early conception of equity courts as acting only upon the person and his conscience, has yielded gradually to equity's expanding power over rights in rem and to the formal abolition of many distinctions between law and equity. The conflicts rule that an equity decree is a mere procedural device not 'merging' the claim, and thus not entitled to recognition, is a relic of the old doctrine and now generally considered indefensible."[15]

To some extent, in some instances, equity decrees of course do differ in nature from those at law. This is the case, for instance, when a decree orders acts or forbearance. In the majority of cases, however, a conclusion that a particular decree is not entitled to recognition derives from reasons other than that the decree is one in equity. Thus, lack of finality is sometimes asserted as a defense to the recognition of alimony and support decrees which are retroactively or prospectively subject to modification where rendered.[16] Decrees ordering acts or forbearance in a

---

10. 28 U.S.C.A. § 2361.

11. See 11 U.S.C.A. § 362; Local Loan Co. v. Hunt, 292 U.S. 234, 54 S.Ct. 695, 78 L.Ed. 1230 (1934). For antisuit injunctions in the international context, see Levy, Antisuit Injunctions in Multinational Cases, in D. Levy (ed.), International Litigation 163 (2003).

12. 522 U.S. 222, 118 S.Ct. 657, 139 L.Ed.2d 580 (1998).

13. Supra §§ 15.6, 15.8–15.13, 15.17–15.23.

14. Barber v. Barber, 323 U.S. 77, 65 S.Ct. 137, 89 L.Ed. 82 (1944); Sistare v. Sistare, 218 U.S. 1, 30 S.Ct. 682, 54 L.Ed. 905 (1910).

15. A.A. Ehrenzweig, Conflict of Laws 182 (rev. ed. 1962) (cited with approval in Baker v. General Motors Corp., 522 U.S. 222, 234, 118 S.Ct. 657, 664, 139 L.Ed.2d 580 (1998)). See also infra n.6 and § 24.10 n.4.

16. For more extensive discussion see supra at §§ 15.33–15.38.

sister state may offend the second forum's public policy[17] or attempt, albeit indirectly, to operate impermissibly on the second forum itself (e.g., when litigation in the second forum is sought to be enjoined[18]) or on subject matter within its exclusive jurisdiction, such as real property.

3. *Foreign Decrees Relating to Land*

§ 24.10   The court of the situs has exclusive subject matter jurisdiction with respect to land within its jurisdiction.[1] A foreign decree will therefore not operate directly on the land.[2] If, however, the parties to the foreign litigation complied with the foreign decree and executed a conveyance, such a conveyance will serve to affect the local real property notwithstanding that its execution resulted from the compulsion of foreign judicial authority.[3]

---

17. The recognizing state's public policy ordinarily does not bar the enforcement of a sister state's money judgment since the underlying cause of action which might raise the public policy concern (e.g., a gambling contract) is said to have merged in the money judgment. Fauntleroy v. Lum, 210 U.S. 230, 28 S.Ct. 641, 52 L.Ed. 1039 (1908); see infra § 24.20. Apart from the fact that, according to traditional doctrine, claims do not merge in the equitable decree (see supra at n.3), the *act or forbearance* ordered by the decree may itself violate local prohibitions or public policy in a way that a decree for money does not.

18. See James v. Grand Trunk Western Railroad Co., 14 Ill.2d 356, 152 N.E.2d 858 (1958), cert. denied 358 U.S. 915, 79 S.Ct. 288, 3 L.Ed.2d 239 (1958). While such an antisuit injunction technically binds the parties, its recognition under the Full Faith and Credit Clause would allow it to operate indirectly on the second court and its exercise of jurisdiction as well: "[T]his court need not, and will not, countenance having its right to try cases, of which it has proper jurisdiction, determined by the courts of other States, through their injunctive process." 14 Ill.2d at 372, 152 N.E.2d at 867.

The United States Supreme Court recently adopted this view: "[A] Michigan court cannot, by entering an injunction [to which a party before it had stipulated], dictate to a court in another jurisdiction that evidence relevant to [a] case—a controversy to which Michigan is foreign—shall be inadmissible.... Michigan ... cannot determine evidentiary issues in a law suit brought by parties who were not subject to the jurisdiction of the Michigan court." Baker v. General Motors Corp., 522 U.S. 222, 239, 118 S.Ct. 657, 667, 139 L.Ed.2d 580 (1998). It follows from the last sentence that an equity decree can produce preclusive effects for

parties before the rendering court: infra § 24.10 n.4. See also Cunningham v. Cunningham, 25 Conn.Supp. 221, 200 A.2d 734 (1964); Restatement, Second, Conflict of Laws § 103, comment (b) and Reporter's Note (1971).

§ 24.10

1. Fall v. Eastin, 215 U.S. 1, 30 S.Ct. 3, 54 L.Ed. 65 (1909); Fitch v. Huntington, 125 Wis. 204, 102 N.W. 1066 (1905); Buchanan v. Weber, 152 N.C.App. 180, 567 S.E.2d 413, writ of supersedeas denied 356 N.C. 433, 572 S.E.2d 427 (2002).

2. Id. The reason for excluding a *direct* effect of the foreign decree on local land is the concern for the integrity of the local recording system and the protection it affords to local parties. But see R.J. Weintraub, Commentary on the Conflict of Laws 500–517 (4th ed. 2001); Hancock, Full Faith and Credit to Foreign Laws and Judgments in Real Property Litigation: The Supreme Court and the Land Taboo, 18 Stan. L. Rev. 1299 (1966); Weintraub, An Inquiry into the Utility of "Situs" As A Concept in Conflict Analysis, 52 Cornell L.Q. 1 (1966). See also Hay, The Situs Rule in European and American Conflicts Law, in P. Hay and M. Hoeflich (eds.), Property Law and Legal Education–Essays in Honor of John E. Cribbet 109, 118–120 (1988).

3. TWE Retirement Fund Trust v. Ream, 198 Ariz. 268, 8 P.3d 1182 (Ariz.App. 2000)(decree ordering out-of-state party to execute a transfer of land with a situs outside the forum state is valid and entitled to full faith and credit); Steele v. Bryant, 132 Ky. 569, 116 S.W. 755 (1909). Cf. Fall v. Fall, 75 Neb. 104, 128, 113 N.W. 175, 178 (1907), aff'd 215 U.S. 1, 30 S.Ct. 3, 54 L.Ed. 65 (1909) (dictum) (quoted with approval by the Supreme Court in Fall v. Eastin, 215

Although the foreign decree does not operate directly upon the local land, it does represent an adjudication of the rights and obligations of the parties to the foreign litigation. Consistent with the policy of preclusion discussed in the preceding section, the foreign decree may therefore serve as the basis either for a local decree ordering the conveyance or for the issuance of a local order effecting a transfer of title.[4]

The preclusive effect of the first action on the *parties,* as distinguished from an *in rem* effect of the foreign decree on local land, is illustrated by the U.S. Supreme Court's decision in *Durfee v. Duke.*[5] In a Nebraska action to quiet title in the petitioners to certain bottom land situated on the Missouri River, the Nebraska court had held that the land was situated in Nebraska, had found for petitioners on the merits, and had ordered title to be quieted in them. The Missouri federal court had granted recognition to the Nebraska decree, but was reversed by the Court of Appeals. In reversing, in turn, the Court of Appeals' decision and affirming the District Court, the U.S. Supreme Court pointed to its decision in *Treinies,*[6] found that all issues had been litigated in Nebraska, and held that the Nebraska decision was therefore entitled to Full Faith and Credit. The decision carefully distinguished between the *in personam* and *in rem* effects of the Nebraska determination: "It is to be emphasized that all that was ultimately determined in the Nebraska litigation was title to the land in question as between the parties to the litigation there. Nothing there decided ... could bind either Missouri or Nebraska with respect to any controversy they might have, now or in the future, as to the location of the boundary between them, or as to their respective sovereignty over the land in question."[7] Similarly, it remains for the local law of the situs to define the effect of the foreign decree against *third* parties, for instance whether the successful plaintiff in the first action can enforce the equitable decree against a purchaser with notice from the defendant.[8]

U.S. 1, 30 S.Ct. 3, 54 L.Ed. 65 (1909)). See also supra § 19.8.

4. "We see no reason why the preclusive effects of an adjudication on parties and those 'in privity' with them, i.e. claim preclusion and issue preclusion (res judicata and collateral estoppel) should differ depending solely upon the type of relief sought...." Baker v. General Motors Corp., 522 U.S. 222, 234, 118 S.Ct. 657, 664, 139 L.Ed.2d 580, 593 (1998).

See cases collected in Reporter's Note to Comment (d), Restatement, Second, Conflict of Laws § 102 (1971); Higginbotham v. Higginbotham, 92 N.J.Super. 18, 222 A.2d 120, 126 (1966); Varone v. Varone, 359 F.2d 769 (7th Cir.1966) (full faith and credit to sister-state decree ordering conveyance of local land); Day v. Wiswall, 11 Ariz.App. 306, 464 P.2d 626, 632 (1970) (California judgment determining that plaintiff was entitled to a share of testatrix' estate entitled

to full faith and credit in Arizona, even to the extent that this required conveyance of land situated in Arizona), relief on in Jeffs v. Stubbs, 970 P.2d 1234 (Utah 1998) cert. denied sub nom. Fundamentalist Church of Jesus Christ of Latter–Day Saints v. Bradshaw, 526 U.S. 1130, 119 S.Ct. 1803, 143 L.Ed.2d 1007 (1999).

For general discussion of the problems raised in this and the previous subsections see Reese, Full Faith and Credit to Foreign Equity Decrees, 42 Iowa L. Rev. 183 (1957).

5. 375 U.S. 106, 84 S.Ct. 242, 11 L.Ed.2d 186 (1963).

6. Treinies v. Sunshine Mining Co., 308 U.S. 66, 60 S.Ct. 44, 84 L.Ed. 85 (1939); see supra § 24.2 nn.9, 11.

7. 375 U.S. at 115, 84 S.Ct. at 247, confirmed in Underwriters National Assurance v. North Carolina Life and Acc. and Health Insurance etc., 455 U.S. 691, 102 S.Ct. 1357, 71 L.Ed.2d 558 (1982).

A decision of the Iowa Supreme Court may serve to illustrate all of the foregoing principles.[9] In dissolving the marriage of the parties, the Missouri divorce court "set off [to the former wife] the farm located in Cedar County, Iowa, more fully described as...."[10] There was no provision that the husband execute a conveyance and none was executed. The former wife remarried and shortly thereafter died intestate. An action brought in Iowa by the former husband against the decedent's estate sought declaratory relief that the Missouri court had been without jurisdiction to affect title to Iowa real estate, that the farm therefore continued in joint tenancy, and that title to it enured to the former husband's benefit rather than to the decedent's estate. The Iowa court acknowledged that some courts will recognize only those foreign decrees that actually require the conveyance of local land but not those purporting to adjudicate title. However, it chose to adopt the "preferable" view espoused by § 43 of the Second Judgments Restatement that a "judgment in an action determining interests in real or personal property conclusively determines the claims of the parties...." The remaining question was whether the decedent's failure to have title put in her name alone prior to her death now entitled the former husband to claim the land as the surviving joint tenant. The court also rejected this argument. It treated the decedent's rights under the Missouri decree as a chose in action, to be used offensively or defensively against her former husband, by her during life and by her personal representative upon her death. The decision differs from *Durfee v. Duke*[11] inasmuch as the Missouri court never purported, even as between the parties, to find that it had *in rem* jurisdiction. The Iowa court's result is nevertheless correct, since as between the original parties and their representatives, the *in rem effect* can be achieved by way of the *in personam* adjudication of their respective equities. To accord full faith and credit to such a determination represents the modern trend.[12]

4. Nature of the Proceeding

§ 24.11 The judgment or decree sought to be enforced in the second forum must have been rendered by an impartial tribunal[1] that

---

8. Fall v. Eastin, 215 U.S. 1, 30 S.Ct. 3, 54 L.Ed. 65 (1909) (particularly Holmes, J., concurring).

9. Matter of Estate of Mack, 373 N.W.2d 97 (Iowa 1985).

10. Id. at 98.

11. 375 U.S. 106, 84 S.Ct. 242, 11 L.Ed.2d 186 (1963); see supra n.5.

12. See Weintraub, supra n.2, at 516–517; Note, Modernizing the Situs Rule for Real Property Conflicts, 65 Texas L. Rev. 585 (1987); Hay, supra n.2. But see Buchanan v. Weber, supra n.1 (portion of Kansas divorce decree purporting to affect title

to North Carolina land not entitled to full faith and credit).

§ 24.11

1. Russell v. Perry, 14 N.H. 152, 155 (1843). The tribunal need not be a court but, in the absence of constitutional restrictions, may be a legislative, executive or administrative body. Magnolia Petroleum Co. v. Hunt, 320 U.S. 430, 64 S.Ct. 208, 88 L.Ed. 149 (1943); New York v. Shapiro, 129 F.Supp. 149 (D.Mass.1954), (noted 69 Harv. L. Rev. 378 (1955)); see infra at § 24.46. See Schopflocher, The Doctrine of Res Judicata in Administrative Law, 1943 Wis. L.

had proper jurisdiction and gave the defendant reasonable notice and opportunity to be heard. These requirements form part of the larger concept of due process to which the defendant is entitled and will be considered further below in connection with other defenses to the enforcement of a foreign judgment.

B. METHODS OF ENFORCING INTERSTATE JUDGMENTS

1. *Full Faith and Credit*

§ 24.12   Any judgment not rendered within the territorial jurisdiction of a state of the United States is, strictly speaking, a "foreign judgment" to that state. To be enforced in a state other than where rendered, such a judgment must be "recognized" and "given effect" by the local authority of the forum. Usually this recognition is by the judiciary of the second state, but the judgment may also be enforced administratively. The Full Faith and Credit Clause of the federal Constitution[1] mandates such recognition and effect for interstate judgments.

Rev. 4. Thus, e.g., an assessment on a shareholder of a corporation, made by an administrative officer of the state of incorporation without a hearing has been recognized as a conclusive determination of its necessity and of the amount of liability. Hood v. Guaranty Trust Co. of New York, 270 N.Y. 17, 200 N.E. 55 (1936). See also Conopco, Inc. v. Roll Int'l, 231 F.3d 82 (2d Cir.2000)(alleged mistake by F–1 in not allowing amendment of pleadings does not constitute a due process violation and thus F–2 must enforce F–1's judgment of dismissal).

Procedures for the settlement of disputes may rest on private agreement as well as on governmental power. Thus, in commercial disputes, arbitration is frequently used in lieu of the judicial process. Res judicata concepts now extend also to arbitral awards. Thus to the extent that policies underlying res judicata result in an award being conclusive and enforceable in the first forum, the same effect should be accorded in the second forum. See OTV (France) v. Hilmarton (UK), 21 YbK. Comm. Arb'n 524 § 529 (Cour d'appel de Versailles, France 1996); T. Várady, J. Barceló, A. von Mehren, International Commercial Arbitration 609 et seq. passim (1999); Shell, Res Judicata and Collateral Estoppel Effects of Commercial Arbitration, 35 UCLA L. Rev. 623 (1988). See, in another context, Scherk v. Alberto–Culver Co., 417 U.S. 506, 94 S.Ct. 2449, 41 L.Ed.2d 270 (1974) (construing and applying § 2 of the federal Arbitration Act, 9 U.S.C.A. § 2, permitting arbitration clauses in maritime cases and in transactions in interstate and foreign commerce, in extension of The Bremen v. Zapata Off–

Shore Co., 407 U.S. 1, 92 S.Ct. 1907, 32 L.Ed.2d 513 (1972) (upholding a choice of foreign court clause). For further discussion see infra §§ 24.46–24.47. See generally Stern, The Conflict of Laws in Commercial Arbitration, 17 Law & Contemp. Prob. 567 (1952). See also Payne, Enforceability of Mediated Agreements, 1 Ohio State J. on Dispute Resolution 385 (1986).

§ 24.12

1. U.S. Const., Art. IV, § 1 ("Full Faith and Credit shall be given in each State to the public Acts, Records, and Judicial Proceedings of every other State. And the Congress may by general Laws prescribe the Manner in which such Acts, Records and Proceedings shall be proved, and the Effect thereof.").

For the history of the clause see Cook, The Powers of Congress Under the Full Faith and Credit Clause, 28 Yale L.J. 421 (1919); Corwin, The Full Faith and Credit Clause, 81 U. Pa. L. Rev. 371 (1933); Costigan, The History of the Adoption of Section 1 of Article IV, 4 Colum. L. Rev. 470 (1904); Jackson, Full Faith and Credit—The Lawyer's Clause of the Constitution, 45 Colum. L. Rev. 1 (1945); Moore & Oglebay, The Supreme Court and Full Faith and Credit, 29 Va. L. Rev. 557 (1943); Nussbaum, Jurisdiction and Foreign Judgments, 41 Colum. L. Rev. 221 (1941); Page, Full Faith and Credit, 1948 Wis. L. Rev. 265; Paulsen, Enforcing the Money Judgment of a Sister State, 42 Iowa L. Rev. 202 (1957); Reese & Johnson, The Scope of Full Faith and Credit to Judgments, 49 Colum. L. Rev. 153

Congress has specified that the "records and judicial proceedings of any court of any ... State, Territory or Possession" of the United States "shall have the same full faith and credit in every court ... as they have by law or usage in the courts of such State, Territory or Possession from which they are taken."[2] Further implementing legislation extends the full faith and credit-mandate to child custody and child support orders.[3]

Mandatory recognition of a judgment under the Clause presupposes a *valid* judgment of a sister state,[4] for instance, one based on proper jurisdiction[5] and not defective for other reasons, such as fraud.[6] The recognition requirement applies to state court judgments in the courts of sister states and in federal courts[7] as well as to the recognition of federal

(1949); Sumner, Full Faith and Credit to Judgments, 2 UCLA L. Rev. 441 (1955); Sumner, The Full Faith and Credit Clause, 34 Or. L. Rev. 224 (1955); Yntema, Enforcement of Foreign Judgments in Anglo–American Law, 33 Mich. L. Rev. 1129 (1935).

2. 28 U.S.C.A. § 1738 (originally enacted in 1790). See Washington Gas Light Co. v. Hsu, 478 F.Supp. 1262 (D.Md.1979) extending the provision to a judgment of the District of Columbia Superior Court. Cf. also Menzel v. County Utilities Corp., 501 F.Supp. 354, 357 (E.D.Va.1979) (federal court in a state must give a state court judgment the same res judicata effect as it has within the state system). The Supreme Court has only addressed in dicta whether Indian tribal court judgments are entitled to full faith and credit:

"Judgments of tribal courts, as to matters properly within their jurisdiction, have been regarded in some circumstances as entitled to full faith and credit in other courts."

Santa Clara Pueblo v. Martinez, 436 U.S. 49, 66 n. 21, 98 S.Ct. 1670, 56 L.Ed.2d 106 (1978). Compare Sheppard v. Sheppard, 104 Idaho 1, 655 P.2d 895 (1982) with Brown v. Babbitt Ford, Inc., 117 Ariz. 192, 571 P.2d 689 (Ariz.App. 1977). For discussion, see Clark, 23 Okla. City U. L. Rev. 353 (1998); Clinton, Tribal Courts and the Federal Union, 26 Willamette L. Rev. 841 (1990).

3. Parental Kidnapping Prevention Act of 1980, 28 U.S.C.A. § 1738A (discussed supra § 15.42); Full Faith and Credit for Child Support Orders Act of 1994, 28 U.S.C.A. § 1738B (discussed supra § 15.30). A fourth implementing statute (the "Defense of Marriage Act," DOMA), 28 U.S.C.A. § 1738C, authorizes the states *not* to recognize same-sex unions. See supra § 13.20.

4. See Restatement, Second, Conflict of Laws § 93 (1971). See also n.2 with respect to tribal courts.

5. The extent to which the rendering forum permissibly exercised jurisdiction is a federal question under the Constitution's Due Process provisions. See Shaffer v. Heitner, 433 U.S. 186, 97 S.Ct. 2569, 53 L.Ed.2d 683 (1977); World–Wide Volkswagen v. Woodson, 444 U.S. 286, 100 S.Ct. 559, 62 L.Ed.2d 490 (1980). Failure to accord full faith and credit to a sister-state judgment thus raises the (federal) question whether such refusal was justified in view of the Constitutional mandate which, in turn, calls for an evaluation of the first forum's compliance with Due Process standards in its exercise of jurisdiction. The separate, but inextricably connected, Constitutional Due Process standard for the exercise of jurisdiction explains why the question of the rendering forum's jurisdiction is not addressed in the Full Faith and Credit Clause. In contrast, when an integrated legal system lacks such constitutional delineation of jurisdiction, but nevertheless provides for mandatory recognition of judgments of its constituent units, specification of permissible bases for jurisdiction must then be part of, and incorporated in the "full faith and credit" requirement. An example is the European Community's Regulation on the Recognition of Judgments.

6. For discussion of defenses see infra § 24.14 et seq.

7. These judgments are covered by the language of 28 U.S.C.A. § 1738, reproduced supra at § 24.2 n.3. See Milwaukee County v. M.E. White Co., 296 U.S. 268, 56 S.Ct. 229, 80 L.Ed. 220 (1935); Huron Holding Corp. v. Lincoln Mine Operating Co., 312 U.S. 183, 61 S.Ct. 513, 85 L.Ed. 725 (1941); Hoffman v. National Equipment Rental, Limited, 643 F.2d 987 (4th Cir.1981), supra n.5. State court judgments can have collateral estoppel effect in a subsequent federal action under 42 U.S.C.A. § 1983 for violation of civil rights: Kremer v. Chemical Const. Corp., 456 U.S. 461, 102 S.Ct. 1883, 72 L.Ed.2d 262 (1982), Migra v. Warren

City School District Board of Educ., 465 U.S. 75, 104 S.Ct. 892, 79 L.Ed.2d 56 (1984); Kutzik v. Young, 730 F.2d 149 (4th Cir.1984); Anderson v. New York, 611 F.Supp. 481 (S.D.N.Y.1985). See also Marrese v. American Academy of Orthopaedic Surgeons, 470 U.S. 373, 105 S.Ct. 1327, 84 L.Ed.2d 274 (1985); Comment, 71 Iowa L. Rev. 609 (1986) (preclusive effect of state court judgment on subsequent federal antitrust litigation determined by state law). *Marrese* was applied in Matsushita Electric Industrial Co. v. Epstein, 516 U.S. 367, 116 S.Ct. 873, 134 L.Ed.2d 6 (1996) (Delaware settlement judgment held entitled to full faith and credit in federal court, despite the fact that it released claims within the exclusive jurisdiction of the federal courts).

The difficulty with *Marrese* and *Matsushita* is that the federal court must determine what state preclusion law is in circumstances when the federal claim that is now being raised could not have been raised in state court. Nonetheless, and however difficult in application, *Marrese* and *Matsushita* are consistent with the so-called "*Rooker-Feldman*-Doctrine." See Rooker v. Fidelity Trust Co., 263 U.S. 413, 44 S.Ct. 149, 68 L.Ed. 362 (1923); District of Columbia Court of Appeals v. Feldman, 460 U.S. 462, 103 S.Ct. 1303, 75 L.Ed.2d 206 (1983). Construing 28 U.S.C.A. § 1257 (granting the U.S. Supreme jurisdiction to review state court decisions) and § 1331 (granting original jurisdiction to federal district courts), the Court held that district courts lack original jurisdiction over federal claims that are inextricably bound up with a state law claim decided by a state court. To allow a district court to entertain such a claim would put it in a position "to sit in review of judgments entered by courts of equal–or even greater–authority." Martin v. Wilks, 490 U.S. 755, 784 n.21, 109 S.Ct. 2180, 104 L.Ed.2d 835 (1989)(Stevens, J., dissenting). Such review may be sought only from the Supreme Court. It is thus important to determine what the state court decided, including what questions are precluded under state law. The "*Rooker-Feldman*-Doctrine" has been criticized as unnecessarily duplicating other doctrines, such as general res judicata (preclusion) law and abstention. For comprehensive review, see Comment, The *Rooker-Feldman*-Doctrine: Toward a Workable Role, 149 U. Pa. L. Rev. 1555 (2001).

See also Parsons Steel, Inc. v. First Alabama Bank, 474 U.S. 518, 106 S.Ct. 768, 88 L.Ed.2d 877 (1986) (federal court must give the same preclusive effect to state-court judgments as another court of that state would give); Manji v. New York Life Ins. Co., 945 F.Supp. 919 (D.S.C.1996) (federal court must give full faith and credit to state court judgments in identical class action claims).

See generally Symposium, Preclusion in a Federal System, 70 Cornell L. Rev. 599 (1985). See also infra § 24.29 n.4. The extent of the preclusive effect is determined by the law of the state in which the judgment was rendered. See, e.g., *Anderson,* 611 F.Supp. 481 An example is the question whether preclusion requires identity of parties in the second action: compare *Trujillo,* 775 F.2d 1359 (identity required under California law) with Atchison v. Wyoming, 763 F.2d 388 (10th Cir.1985) (Wyoming law does not require mutuality of parties). Similarly, in application of *Marrese,* supra, it has been held that a federal antitrust suit was not precluded by prior litigation in a California state court when, under California law, there is no preclusive effect unless the first court had jurisdiction over the claim; antitrust claims are within the exclusive jurisdiction of the federal courts: Eichman v. Fotomat Corp., 759 F.2d 1434 (9th Cir.1985). The Full Faith and Credit statute does not apply to unreviewed findings of state administrative agencies. But those findings can preclude federal court actions under federal common-law rules of preclusion. Those rules of preclusion are appropriate and will be applied when the federal statute creating the cause of action indicates that Congress did not intend such findings to be given preclusive effect and when state courts would give preclusive effect to the findings of the state agency, so long as the agency acted in a judicial capacity and the parties had adequate opportunity to litigate. University of Tennessee v. Elliott, 478 U.S. 788, 106 S.Ct. 3220, 92 L.Ed.2d 635 (1986). Similarly, the matter is different when, as a matter of state law, the administrative agency has adjudicatory authority so that its determination rises to the level of a "judicial proceeding:" Zanghi v. Incorporated Village of Old Brookville, 752 F.2d 42 (2d Cir.1985). There is no res judicata effect when the state court judgment is not yet final: Cable Holdings of Battlefield, Inc. v. Cooke, 764 F.2d 1466, 1473 (11th Cir.1985); First Alabama Bank of Montgomery, N.A. v. Parsons Steel, Inc., 825 F.2d 1475 (11th Cir.1987), cert. denied 484 U.S. 1060, 108 S.Ct. 1015, 98 L.Ed.2d 980 (1988). When the prior decision was rendered by a federal tribunal, it is federal law and not state law which determines the preclusive effect of the decision in a second federal tribunal even when both courts sit pursuant to their diversity jurisdiction. Smith v. Safeco Ins. Co., 863 F.2d 403 (5th Cir.1989); Nichols v. Anderson, 788 F.2d

judgments in state courts.[8] The effect to be given the judgment is generally[9] determined by the local law of the rendering court.[10]

In addition to its application to judicial proceedings, the Full Faith and Credit Clause, by its terms, also applies to the "public acts and records" of the states. The effect of this language and of the Due Process Clause as establishing constitutional limits for the choice-of-law process are considered elsewhere.[11]

2. Recognition and Enforcement by Registration or Summary Proceeding

§ 24.13 By legislation[1] Congress has provided for the registration of federal court judgments in other federal districts. Registration is restricted, however, to federal judgments for the "recovery of money or property" and thus does not extend to other judgments or decrees, for instance, an injunction.[2]

1140 (5th Cir.1986), appeal after remand 837 F.2d 1372 (1988); Freeman v. Lester Coggins Trucking, Inc., 771 F.2d 860 (5th Cir.1985). For the federal common law of collateral estoppel see Holmes v. Jones, 738 F.2d 711, 713 (5th Cir.1984). On preclusion, see further supra §§ 24.2 n.8, 24.9 nn.3, 6, 24.10 n.4.

8. 28 U.S.C.A. § 1738 does not expressly provide for such recognition, but the Supreme Court so held in Stoll v. Gottlieb, 305 U.S. 165, 59 S.Ct. 134, 83 L.Ed. 104 (1938) rehearing denied 305 U.S. 675, 59 S.Ct. 250, 83 L.Ed. 437 (1938). However, at the time of this and other early decisions, § 1738 (as amended in 1804) extended to judgments of courts of any "country" subject to United States jurisdiction in addition to the courts of any "State, Territory or Possession." The reference to "country" was deleted in 1948, thus technically leaving the question in doubt since a federal court is not a court of a "State," strictly speaking. Yet federal courts are analogized to state courts when sitting in diversity. Guaranty Trust v. York, 326 U.S. 99, 108, 65 S.Ct. 1464, 1469, 89 L.Ed. 2079 (1945). As a matter of constitutional policy, perhaps even law, recognition of judgments of either kind of court in the other is therefore due. See D. Currie, H. Kay & L. Kramer, Conflict of Laws—Cases, Comments, Questions 454 (6th ed. 2001). See also supra n.4, with respect to the District of Columbia.

9. For defenses and limitations see infra § 24.14 et seq. For discussion of some areas where the preclusive effect of a judgment may be different in the recognizing than in

the rendering forum, supra § 24.2 n.8 and Averill, Choice of Law Problems Raised by Sister–State Judgments and the Full–Faith-and-Credit Mandate, 64 Nw. L. Rev. 686 (1969).

10. See Restatement, Second, Conflict of Laws § 93, comnt. (b) (1971).

11. See supra § 3.20 et seq. "The . . . Clause does not compel 'a state to substitute the statutes of another state for its own statutes dealing with a subject matter concerning which it is competent to legislate'." Baker v. General Motors Corp., 522 U.S. 222, 232, 118 S.Ct. 657, 663, 139 L.Ed.2d 580 (1998) (quoting from Pacific Employers Ins. Co. v. Industrial Accident Comm'n, 306 U.S. 493, 501, 59 S.Ct. 629, 632, 83 L.Ed. 940 (1939)).

§ 24.13

1. 28 U.S.C.A. § 1963. See also infra § 24.14 n.3 and supra § 24.5 n.4.

An uncontested default judgment, in which the amount of damages has been established by the court, is entitled to registration under § 1963. Herzfeld v. Parker, 100 F.R.D. 770 (D.Colo.1984).

There is no requirement that the court of registration have personal jurisdiction over the judgment debtor at the time of registration or that the debtor have property in the district. Dichter v. Disco Corp., 606 F.Supp. 721 (S.D.Ohio 1984). For a contrary view under the State Uniform Enforcement of Judgments Act see *Kohlbusch,* infra n.7.

2. Stiller v. Hardman, 324 F.2d 626 (2d Cir.1963).

The Full Faith and Credit Clause, taken alone, does not provide immediate enforcement of sister-state judgments, in the sense of obviating the need for an action on the judgment,[3] and congressional power to implement the Clause and provide for registration of sister-state judgments in a manner akin to the registration of federal judgments,[4] though urged,[5] has not been used. The Uniform Enforcement of Foreign Judgments Act[6] seeks to approximate the ease and convenience of the federal registration system by providing a summary proceeding for the enforcement of interstate judgments. The Act provides that, upon compliance with its filing and notice requirements, the interstate judgment "has the same effect and is subject to the same procedures, defenses and proceedings for reopening, vacating, or staying as a judgment of a [court] of this state and may be enforced or satisfied in like manner" (§ 2).[7] The preclusive effect of the judgment thus is measured by the standards of the *recognizing* forum, rather than those of the state of rendition as provided by the Full Faith and Credit Clause.[8] Since local law might

---

3. McElmoyle v. Cohen, 38 U.S. (13 Pet.) 312, 325, 10 L.Ed. 177 (1839).

4. Cook, The Powers of Congress Under the Full Faith and Credit Clause, 28 Yale L.J. 421 (1919). Compare §§ 21(2) and 24 of the Australian Service and Execution of Process Act (1901–1974) which provides for registration of Australian state court judgments in other Australian states. As in the United States, similar legislation is also lacking in the other major federal system in the common law world, Canada, where a Uniform Act has been proposed for adoption by the states (akin to similar acts in the United States, infra n.6), but in fact has only been adopted by New Brunswick and Saskatchewan. See J.-G. Castel, Canadian Conflict of Laws § 298 (4th ed. 1997).

5. B. Currie, Full Faith and Credit, Chiefly to Judgments: A Role for Congress, 1964 Sup. Ct. Rev. 89.

6. 13 U.L.A. 155 (1964 revision of the original 1948 Act). The Act is now in force in all but a handful of states. For the Uniform Foreign Money–Judgments Recognition Act, see infra § 24.36.

7. In Tanner v. Hancock, 5 Kan.App.2d 558, 619 P.2d 1177 (1980), the court was faced with the novel question whether a Kansas judgment, registered in Missouri, had, as a result of such registration, become a Missouri judgment and was entitled to registration and enforcement as such in Kansas under the Uniform Enforcement of Foreign Judgments Act. The court held that the Uniform Act provides only a method for the enforcement of foreign judgments so that the original Kansas judgment did not become a new Missouri judgment. "Registration of the Missouri judgment under the Kansas ... Act may not be deemed to cre-

ate a judgment conferring more benefits upon the judgment creditor in Kansas than the original Kansas judgment. The underlying Kansas judgment upon which the Missouri judgment was based simply cannot be ignored." Id., at 1182. This decision overlooks whether it is for Kansas or for Missouri to say what constitutes a *Missouri judgment.* See text following infra § 24.15 n.3. Except when the registration is used only as a means to levy on property, it is a "suit brought by summons." The Missouri general venue statute thus applied to the registration of foreign judgment. Registration in a court of a county without "jurisdiction over the person of the defendant" was therefore improper. Kohlbusch v. Eberwein, 642 S.W.2d 683 (Mo.App.1982).

The *Tanner* decision was relied upon in Reading & Bates Const. Co. v. Baker Energy Resources Corp., 976 S.W.2d 702 (Tex. App. 1998), however in a different context. The question was whether a foreign country was entitled to recognition "on the sole basis that it has been recognized and made executory by a sister state's judgment". The court gave a negative answer: To do so, would grant the foreign country recognition through the "back door." The court proceeded to examine for itself, under the Texas Uniform Foreign–Money Judgment Recognition Act (infra § 24.36), whether the Canadian judgment was entitled to recognition. It accorded recognition over objections on the grounds of public policy and lack of reciprocity.

8. An Illinois appellate decision, however, held that "the provision for counterclaims in ... the Act is not co-extensive with the word 'counterclaim' as used in ... the Illinois Civil Practice Act...." The

provide defenses unknown to the state of rendition, the Act expressly provides (§ 6)—as it must in order to conform to the Constitutional mandate—that the "right of a judgment creditor to bring an action to enforce his judgment [i.e., by invoking the Full Faith and Credit Clause] instead of proceeding under this Act remains unimpaired."

C. DEFENSES TO CLAIM ON SISTER–STATE JUDGMENTS

The present section discusses the defenses available in the second forum to the recognition and enforcement of judgments rendered in a sister state. The extent to which additional defenses may be available in the case of foreign-country judgments is the subject of another section. Both sections also deal incidentally with the extent to which these defenses may in turn be barred by the applicability of principles of res judicata or estoppel.

1. Lack of Jurisdiction of Rendering Court

§ 24.14   The older case law held that the Full Faith and Credit Clause of the Federal Constitution and the legislation thereunder do not preclude on inquiry into the jurisdiction of the first court to render the judgment sought to be enforced. If there was no jurisdiction, the judgment was said not to be entitled to full faith and credit.[1] It must be noted, however, that this rule-as well as many of the other defenses discussed subsequently-has been limited severely by the application of principles of res judicata.[2] The rule therefore remains categorically true

court enforced a Florida judgment, on full faith and credit principles, and did not permit the judgment debtor to raise a counterclaim collaterally. Thompson v. Safeway Enterprises, Inc., 67 Ill.App.3d 914, 24 Ill. Dec. 561, 385 N.E.2d 702 (1978). The court relied heavily on Purser v. Corpus Christi State National Bank, 256 Ark. 452, 508 S.W.2d 549 (1974) in which the court placed primary emphasis on the fact that the defenses could have been raised in the original proceedings: "We have long recognized that a judgment debtor has a right to defend against a foreign judgment ... but not on defenses that could have been made in the action in which the judgment was rendered." 508 S.W.2d at 553. Accord: Ace Metal Fabricating Co. v. Arvid C. Walberg & Co., 135 Ill.App.3d 452, 481 N.E.2d 1066 (1985) ("A judgment of a sister state [sought to be registered under the Uniform Act] is not subject to collateral attack in the Illinois court except for the defenses of fraud in the procurement of the judgment or lack of jurisdiction"); All Seasons Industries, Inc. v. Gregory, 174 Ill.App.3d 700, 124 Ill.Dec. 308, 529 N.E.2d 25 (1988). See also People of State of Wis. v. Ubrig, 128

Ill.App.3d 743, 83 Ill.Dec. 877, 470 N.E.2d 1297 (1984).

§ 24.14

1.   Grover & Baker Sewing Machine Co. v. Radcliffe, 137 U.S. 287, 11 S.Ct. 92, 34 L.Ed. 670 (1890); National Exchange Bank v. Wiley, 195 U.S. 257, 25 S.Ct. 70, 49 L.Ed. 184 (1904); Wheeler v. Stewart Mapping Service, 50 A.D.2d 308, 377 N.Y.S.2d 965 (1976), affirmed 42 N.Y.2d 847, 397 N.Y.S.2d 626, 366 N.E.2d 286 (1977). A recital of jurisdictional facts in the record does not conclude the point in the absence of an opportunity to litigate the issue. Thompson v. Whitman, 85 U.S. (18 Wall.) 457, 21 L.Ed. 897 (1873). See also Jackson v. FIE Corp., 302 F.3d 515 (5th Cir. 2002)(ex parte finding of jurisdiction does not preclude later motion by defendant to vacate the judgment on the grounds of a lack of jurisdiction, citing *Thompson v. Whitman* for the proposition that uncontested jurisdictional recitals cannot bind the judgment debtor).

2.   See also the discussion of the pervasive policy of preclusion, supra §§ 24.1–

only when the judgment debtor did not litigate the jurisdictional issue in the first forum or had no opportunity to do so *and* the first forum, on the facts of the case, lacked jurisdiction.

An attempt to render a judgment where there is no jurisdiction is a violation of due process. Such a judgment is void where rendered and not entitled to full faith and credit.[3] Some cases have questioned this interplay of due process and of the requirement of full faith and credit to judgments. Thus, in *Colby v. Colby*,[4] the Nevada Supreme Court refused to recognize a Maryland decree declaring a prior ex parte Nevada divorce void for lack of jurisdiction based on domicile. It based its refusal on the ground that the Full Faith and Credit Clause did not require it to give greater effect to a sister-state judgment than to its own prior judgment "lawfully entered."[5] The decision erroneously overlooks the fact that the Maryland decree had conclusively adjudicated that the prior Nevada decree had *not* been lawfully entered. Whether the Maryland decree itself was valid and conclusive depends on the Maryland court's own jurisdiction and the propriety of *its* refusal to accord full faith and credit to the ex parte Nevada divorce. The Maryland court's refusal was grounded on a finding of lack of jurisdiction in Nevada or, to put it differently, a finding that Nevada had impermissibly attempted to exercise jurisdiction in violation of the constraints imposed by Due Process. Herein then lies the interplay of the Due Process and Full Faith and Credit Clauses: unless overturned by the U.S. Supreme Court upon

24.2; Underwriters National Assurance Co. v. North Carolina Life and Accident and Health Insurance etc., 455 U.S. 691, 102 S.Ct. 1357, 71 L.Ed.2d 558 (1982) (discussed supra § 24.2 n.9).

3. See, e.g., Miserandino v. Resort Properties, Inc., 345 Md. 43, 691 A.2d 208, cert. denied 522 U.S. 953, 118 S.Ct. 376, 139 L.Ed.2d 292 (1997) (service of process by mail violated due process and ensuing judgment not entitled to full faith and credit); Bertke v. Cartledge, 597 F.Supp. 68 (N.D.Ga.1984) (Kentucky default judgment set aside for lack of jurisdiction in rendering court when enforcement was sought in Georgia); World–Wide Volkswagen Corp. v. Woodson, 444 U.S. 286, 100 S.Ct. 559, 62 L.Ed.2d 490 (1980); Shaffer v. Heitner, 433 U.S. 186, 97 S.Ct. 2569, 53 L.Ed.2d 683 (1977); Hanson v. Denckla, 357 U.S. 235, 78 S.Ct. 1228, 2 L.Ed.2d 1283 (1958); Copeland Planned Futures, Inc. v. Obenchain, 9 Wn. App. 32, 510 P.2d 654, 658 (1973) (New York judgment enforced after examination of New York court's jurisdiction); Ticketmaster–New York, Inc. v. Alioto, 26 F.3d 201 (1st Cir.1994) (defendant's contact so slight, burden of appearance so onerous and fundamentally unfair that court lacked personal jurisdiction); Restatement, Second,

Conflict of Laws §§ 92, 104 (1971); von Mehren & Trautman, Jurisdiction to Adjudicate, 79 Harv. L. Rev. 1121, 1126 (1966). A default judgment rendered by a federal district court and registered in another district pursuant to 28 U.S.C.A. § 1963 may be subject to review, by the registering court, of the rendering court's jurisdiction over the judgment debtor under Federal Rule 60(b): Donnely v. Copeland Intra Lenses, Inc., 87 F.R.D. 80 (E.D.N.Y.1980). However, a greater number of federal courts seem to defer to the rendering court and require the petitioner to seek relief there. See Fuhrman v. Livaditis, 611 F.2d 203, 55 A.L.R. Fed. 433 (7th Cir. 1979); Loader Leasing Corp. v. Penn Erection & Rigging Co., Inc., 566 F.Supp. 348, 36 Fed. R. Serv. 2d 175 (W.D.Pa.1982); Zdrok v. V Secret Catalogue Inc., 215 F.Supp.2d 510 (D.N.J. 2002); Annot., 55 A.L.R. Fed. 439 (1981); Annot., 59 A.L.R. Fed. 831 (1982).

4. 78 Nev. 150, 157, 369 P.2d 1019, 1023 (1962), cert. denied 371 U.S. 888, 83 S.Ct. 186, 9 L.Ed.2d 122 (1962).

5. See also Kessler v. Fauquier National Bank, 195 Va. 1095, 81 S.E.2d 440 (1954), cert. denied 348 U.S. 834, 75 S.Ct. 57, 99 L.Ed. 658 (1954); Pace v. Pace, 222 Va. 524, 281 S.E.2d 891 (1981).

direct review[6] or unless the Maryland court itself lacked jurisdiction, its decree is entitled to full faith and credit.[7] The Full Faith and Credit Clause, moreover, does not permit of comparative or relative standards. Rather, the *same* effect is due in the recognizing as in the forum of rendition.[8] The existence of a prior local judgment is thus irrelevant.[9] A contrary view would destroy the unifying effect which the Full Faith and Credit Clause is designed to foster; in the area of divorce recognition, as in *Colby,* this view would fail to prevent "limping marriages," that is marriages which one jurisdiction regards as still persisting while another regards them as dissolved.

§ **24.15** The determination of the jurisdiction of the rendering court by the recognizing forum raises special problems in the case of default judgments based on a warrant of attorney or cognovit note.[1] The United States Supreme Court's endorsed jurisdiction by consent and agency in an early decision.[2] Due-process concerns underlying cognovits were addressed in subsequent decisions that essentially upheld the validity of such warrants when contained in contracts of economically equal parties, while expressing reservation about the practice in the consumer context.[3]

6. See supra § 24.2 n.11.

7. See Sutton v. Leib, 342 U.S. 402, 72 S.Ct. 398, 96 L.Ed. 448 (1952) (discussed supra § 15.12); Sherrer v. Sherrer, 334 U.S. 343, 68 S.Ct. 1087, 92 L.Ed. 1429 (1948) (discussed supra § 15.9).

8. See supra § 24.2. See also Fungaroli v. Fungaroli, 53 N.C.App. 270, 280 S.E.2d 787 (1981) refusing full faith and credit to the annulment, by a Virginia court applying Virginia law, of a marriage contracted in North Carolina by North Carolina parties on the ground that the Virginia court's choice of its own law was "arbitrary, fundamentally unfair and violated Due Process." Id. at 793–94. Public policy notions such as the foregoing are impermissible grounds for the denial of full faith and credit if the court had jurisdiction. See, e.g., Baker v. General Motors, 522 U.S. 222, 233, 118 S.Ct. 657, 664, 139 L.Ed.2d 580 (1998) (there is no roving public policy exception to the full faith and credit due judgments). Arguably, personal and subject matter jurisdiction for annulment exists whenever there is jurisdiction for divorce: supra § 15.15 n.4. Both spouses seemed to have been before the court. A possibly "wrong" choice of law does not permit collateral attack under full faith and credit.

9. This aspect of the policy of preclusion, supra § 1, that there should be an end to litigation, also finds expression in the rule that, as between inconsistent judgments, the last judgment in time governs and is entitled to recognition under full faith and credit. Supra § 24.2 and infra

§ 24.29. But see Tanner v. Hancock, 5 Kan. App.2d 558, 619 P.2d 1177 (1980) (discussed in § 24.13 n.7).

§ 24.15

1. In a warrant of attorney or cognovit note, a party to an agreement authorizes the other to appoint an attorney for him who may enter an appearance upon default of the obligation and "confess judgment."

2. National Equipment Rental Ltd. v. Szukhent, 375 U.S. 311, 84 S.Ct. 411, 11 L.Ed.2d 354 (1964). See also Microfibres, Inc. v. McDevitt–Askew, 20 F.Supp.2d 316 (D.R.I.).

3. D.H. Overmyer Co., Inc. of Ohio v. Frick Co., 405 U.S. 174, 92 S.Ct. 775, 31 L.Ed.2d 124 (1972); Swarb v. Lennox, 405 U.S. 191, 92 S.Ct. 767, 31 L.Ed.2d 138 (1972), rehearing denied 405 U.S. 1049, 92 S.Ct. 1303, 31 L.Ed.2d 592 (1972). See also Fuentes v. Shevin, 407 U.S. 67, 92 S.Ct. 1983, 32 L.Ed.2d 556 (1972), rehearing denied 409 U.S. 902, 93 S.Ct. 177, 34 L.Ed.2d 165 (1972); Mitchell v. W. T. Grant Co., 416 U.S. 600, 94 S.Ct. 1895, 40 L.Ed.2d 406 (1974). Relying on the *Overmyer* decision, a Pennsylvania federal court held that " . . . parties entering into a commercial lease must be held to know that a sheriff's levy may accompany a confession of judgment and that, under Pennsylvania law, this levy cannot be removed. . . . A party to a confession of judgment clause waives its rights to object to these specific consequences." SMI Industries, Inc. v. Lanard & Axilbund, Inc.,

Because of the need to provide a mechanism for the joinder of multiple parties, a court entertaining a class action will have jurisdiction over, and thus the power to preclude, absent members of the plaintiff class over whom it lacks in personam jurisdiction in the traditional sense, so long as those parties received, or were attempted to be served with, notice and were given an opportunity to "opt out."[4]

§ 24.16 American cases have historically treated lack of competence of the court as an absence of jurisdiction over the subject matter. While there is a presumption that a court of record is a court of general jurisdiction,[1] proof to the contrary may be offered, namely that the law of the state of rendition had not authorized the rendering court to exercise jurisdiction and render a judgment in the matter.[2] However, in the situation in which there is constitutional authority for jurisdiction in the *state* of rendition generally, a collateral attack against a judgment on the ground that the *particular court* was not competent to render it under the law of that state will be permitted only if such a collateral attack is permissible under the law of the state of rendition. Thus, if the state of rendition would not permit a collateral attack but give conclusive effect to a judgment rendered by a court without initial competence, the same conclusive effect must be accorded in the recognizing state.[3] The availability of collateral attack under the law of the state of rendition will be determined by the recognizing court itself[4] or, when the law of the former so provides, by certification of the question by the latter to the highest court of the state of rendition.[5]

Errors of law or fact made by a court of rendition, which otherwise had and properly exercised jurisdiction over the matter and the parties, do not go to the court's competence and its judgment, although considered to be erroneous by the recognizing court, is entitled to full faith and credit in the interstate setting.[6] Again, the proper procedure would have

481 F.Supp. 459, 465 (E.D.Pa.1979). In 1991, the New York Court of Appeals departed from its decision in Atlas Credit Corp. v. Ezrine, 25 N.Y.2d 219, 303 N.Y.S.2d 382, 250 N.E.2d 474 (1969), and held that a Pennsylvania cognovit judgment is entitled to full faith and credit in New York: Fiore v. Oakwood Plaza Shopping Center, Inc., 78 N.Y.2d 572, 578 N.Y.S.2d 115, 585 N.E.2d 364 (1991). For an analysis of the Pennsylvania confession of judgment process, including res judicata effect, see Riverside Memorial Mausoleum, Inc. v. UMET Trust, 581 F.2d 62 (3d Cir.1978).

4. Phillips Petroleum Co. v. Shutts, 472 U.S. 797, 105 S.Ct. 2965, 86 L.Ed.2d 628 (1985).

§ 24.16

1. Hanley v. Donoghue, 116 U.S. 1, 6 S.Ct. 242, 29 L.Ed. 535 (1885).

2. Thompson v. Whitman, 85 U.S. (18 Wall.) 457, 21 L.Ed. 897 (1873). Upon proof

of lack of competence, the judgment would not be entitled to recognition. Restatement, Second, Conflict of Laws § 105 (1971).

3. Aldrich v. Aldrich, 378 U.S. 540, 84 S.Ct. 1687, 12 L.Ed.2d 1020 (1964). See also Restatement, Second, Conflict of Laws § 105 (1971); Dobbs, The Validation of Void Judgments: The Bootstrap Principle, 53 Va. L. Rev. 1003 (1967).

4. See Adam v. Saenger, 303 U.S. 59, 58 S.Ct. 454, 82 L.Ed. 649 (1938).

5. See Aldrich v. Aldrich, supra n.3, utilizing the certification procedure provided by Florida law, 31 F.S.A. Rule 4.61. See also the Uniform Certification of Questions of Law Act, 12 U.L.A. 81 (now in force in more than half the states).

6. Restatement, Second, Conflict of Laws § 106 (1971) states this well accepted rule. Comment (a) also generalizes the rule, by reference to § 98, to foreign country judgments. This generalization may not be

been to seek direct review of the erroneous judgment, not collateral attack.

2. *Judgment Obtained by Fraud; Equitable Defenses*

§ 24.17 It was established early in England[1] and in the United States[2] that a judgment procured by fraud may be impeached and denied effect in the second forum. In the United States, a distinction is usually[3] drawn between extrinsic and intrinsic fraud, although the distinction is often "shadowy, uncertain and somewhat arbitrary."[4] Extrinsic fraud is thought to go to the rendering court's jurisdiction,[5] making the resulting judgment unenforceable for that reason. This will be the case when the defendant was lured into the jurisdiction by false representations[6] or was prevented, by fraudulent acts, to present his case and to have a fair determination on the merits. Bribery of judges[7] or a false promise of a compromise are examples.[8]

Intrinsic fraud is the "ordinary garden variety of fraud"[9] practiced in the first proceeding, such as perjury, the use of false documents, or misrepresentation of evidence.[10] When intrinsic fraud prevented a fair trial of the issues,[11] the delineation between it and extrinsic fraud indeed becomes blurred. The party's right to due process will have been violated, the rendering court's jurisdiction will have been defective for that reason,[12] and the resulting judgment should not be entitled to recognition. When the fraud practiced in the first proceeding did not prevent a fair trial of the issues, intrinsic fraud may give rise to equitable defenses against the resulting judgment in the second forum. The availability of

accurate, however, in states adhering to the *Hilton* doctrine (infra § 24.35 n.8) which may result in a denial of conclusive effect and in a review of the foreign judgments. Errors of law or fact by the court of rendition would be relevant in the event of such review.

The rule is the same in England: a foreign judgment which is final and conclusive and was rendered by a court with competent jurisdiction. Godard v. Gray, (1870) L.R. 6 Q.B. 139; Dicey & Morris, The Conflict of Laws 512 et seq. (13th ed. 2000 by Collins et al.).

§ 24.17

1. Dicey & Morris, The Conflict of Laws 518 et seq. (13th ed. 2000 by Collins et al.) (with references).

2. Fisher v. Fielding, 67 Conn. 91, 34 A. 714 (1895). See also Christopher v. Christopher, 198 Ga. 361, 31 S.E.2d 818 (1944); In re Topcuoglu's Will, 11 Misc.2d 859, 174 N.Y.S.2d 260 (Surr. 1958).

3. But see Laun v. Kipp, 155 Wis. 347, 145 N.W. 183 (1914) which makes no distinction.

4. Howard v. Scott, 225 Mo. 685, 714, 125 S.W. 1158, 1166 (1910).

5. See Comment, Direct and Collateral Attack on Judgments, 66 Yale L.J. 526 (1957).

6. See Tootle v. McClellan, 7 Ind. T. 64, 103 S.W. 766 (1907).

7. See Vestal, A Study in Perfidy, 35 Ind. L.J. 18 (1959); Note, Res Judicata—The Effect of the Oklahoma Supreme Court Scandal, 5 Tulsa L.J. 71 (1968).

8. Flood v. Templeton, 152 Cal. 148, 92 P. 78 (1907). For more extensive discussion see A.D. Vestal, Res Judicata/Preclusion 417–22 (1969).

9. Auerbach v. Samuels, 10 Utah 2d 152, 155, 349 P.2d 1112, 1114 (1960).

10. Id.

11. See Reese, The Status in this Country of Judgments Rendered Abroad, 50 Colum. L. Rev. 783 (1950).

12. Supra n.5.

an equitable defense in the second forum, however, will parallel, and depend on the availability of such a defense against the judgment in the jurisdiction where rendered.[13] Furthermore, facts ordinarily giving rise to relief for fraud or to an equitable defense may become conclusive through prior litigation or opportunity for litigation,[14] even if fraud going to jurisdiction was involved but subsequent litigation addressed this issue, however erroneously.[15] This result is simply another aspect of the conclusiveness of an erroneous judgment which the parties have failed to correct by utilizing the review procedures available in the jurisdiction of rendition.[16]

§ 24.18   Since foreign-country judgments are not entitled to full-faith-and-credit protection of the Constitution, it is said that foreign notions of conclusiveness also will not apply and that a foreign-country judgment will be denied recognition and enforcement in the United States if equitable relief would be available in the recognizing state against a domestic judgment under similar circumstances.[1] The formulation of the rule seems overbroad, especially when applied to cases in which the issues were fully and fairly litigated. In such circumstances, collateral attack of a foreign-country judgment then should be precluded,[2] just as in the interstate setting, to the same extent that it is where rendered, always assuming that the recognizing state accords conclusive effect to foreign-country judgments at all, either by its own law or as a result of a federal-law mandate (e.g., a recognition treaty).[3]

3.   The Public Policy of the Forum, Penal Judgments, Tax Judgments, and Lack of a Competent Court

§ 24.19   In a case in which the seizure of a slave ship on the high seas was attempted to be justified on the grounds that "the vessel

---

13. See Levin v. Gladstein, 142 N.C. 482, 55 S.E. 371 (1906); Restatement, Second, Conflict of Laws § 115, cmnts. (b), (c) (1971).

14. See Sherrer v. Sherrer, 334 U.S. 343, 68 S.Ct. 1087, 92 L.Ed. 1429 (1948).

15. Treinies v. Sunshine Mining Co., 308 U.S. 66, 60 S.Ct. 44, 84 L.Ed. 85 (1939); Durfee v. Duke, 375 U.S. 106, 84 S.Ct. 242, 11 L.Ed.2d 186 (1963). For further discussion of the res judicata effect, see supra § 24.1.

16. Supra § 24.16 n.6.

§ 24.18

1. Restatement, Second, Conflict of Laws § 115, comment (f) (1971). See Schoenbrod v. Siegler, 20 N.Y.2d 403, 283 N.Y.S.2d 881, 230 N.E.2d 638 (1967).

2. See A.A. Ehrenzweig & E. Jayme, 2 Private International Law 88 (1973); von Mehren & Trautman, Recognition of Foreign Adjudications: A Survey and a Suggest-

ed Approach, 81 Harv. L. Rev. 1601, 1624–29 (1968). See also the much more cautious formulation, approaching the view stated in the text, in Restatement, Second, Conflict of Laws § 98, cmnt. (f) (1971). Comment (h) cross references to § 115, supra n.1, but does so only with reference to "fraud" and not to equitable defenses generally. See Arab Monetary Fund v. Hashim (In re Hashim), 213 F.3d 1169 (9th Cir. 2000) (foreign judgment meeting conditions of full and fair trial before a court of competent jurisdiction, notice and regular proceedings will be given same recognition as a sister-state judgment in Arizona); International Transactions, Ltd. v. Embotelladora Agral Regiomontana, SA de CV, 347 F.3d 589 (5th. Cir. 2003) (same with respect to Texas). See also Restatement, Second, Conflict of Laws § 104 (1971).

3. Infra § 24.23. Defenses to foreign-country judgments, including defenses available under recognition treaties, are treated further infra § 24.41.

belongs to a nation which has prohibited the [slave] trade," Chief Justice Marshall stated "The courts of no country execute the penal laws of another.... It follows, that a foreign vessel engaged in the African slave-trade, captured on the high seas, in time of peace, by an American cruiser, and brought in for adjudication, would be restored."[1] This statement by the Chief Justice in 1825, perhaps dictum even in the case in which it was made, was repeatedly lifted out of context and asserted as a rule applicable to the enforcement of judgments between states of the United States.[2] In both the United States and England the rule was extended to apply to tax judgments which were historically classified with penalties. Frequently the rule came to be stated that one state will not notice the penal or revenue laws of another.[3] As stated, the rule usually made little distinction between judgments or original claims involving foreign penal or fiscal statutes.[4] Apart from earlier rationales for this rule which were derived from notions of territoriality and sovereignty, these exceptions to judgment recognition are closely related to public policy concerns of the recognizing forum.[5] Local public policy, in addition, will also often underlie the contention that no competent court exists, or that local courts may not entertain actions for the recognition and enforcement of a particular foreign judgment. It is for these reasons that these defenses are treated here together.

§ 24.19

1. The Antelope, 23 U.S. (10 Wheat.) 66, 123, 6 L.Ed. 268 (1825). For an earlier English decision see Folliott v. Ogden, (1789) 1 Bl. H. 124, 135.

2. In what must be regarded as the best analysis of the American origins of this rule it was stated: "One trouble about a rule of law which everyone takes for granted is that no judge ever bothers to state the reasons for it. A natural consequence of this may be that the rule extends itself gradually, and finally is applied to many new sets of facts to which the reason for the rule, assuming that there is a reason for it, has no relation. During the century after the decision in The Antelope was written, suitors presenting many new sets of facts came to know the excluding power of the words, 'the courts of no country execute the penal laws of another.' Whether the reason for the old rule fits well the new facts was never asked. Sufficient was the rule." Leflar, Extra State Enforcement of Penal and Governmental Claims, 46 Harv. L. Rev. 193, 196 (1932).

3. "The doctrine that one state will not notice the penal laws, or revenue laws of another state, is however, to be understood with some limitation, and cannot be extended so far as sometimes supposed." Story, Conflict of Laws 815 (6th ed. 1865). With respect to foreign tax *claims*, the "revenue rule" was followed in The Attorney General of Canada v. R.J. Reynolds Tobacco Holdings, Inc., 103 F.Supp.2d 134 (N.D.N.Y. 2000), aff'd 268 F.3d 103 (2d Cir.2001) cert. denied 537 U.S. 1000, 123 S.Ct. 513, 154 L.Ed.2d 394 (2002). The case involved a RICO action by the Canadian government against American tobacco companies alleging a fraudulent scheme to evade Canadian tobacco taxes through a smuggling operation. The court dismissed the complaint relying on the revenue rule. Arguably, this result is inconsistent with American domestic policy, as expressed in the RICO legislation. See also infra § 24.23 n.7.

4. See generally Stoel, The Enforcement of Foreign Non–Criminal Penal and Revenue Judgments in England and the United States, 16 Int'l & Comp. L.Q. 663 (1967).

5. See R.H. Graveson, Conflict of Laws 632–33 (7th ed. 1974) (discussing these defenses under the common heading of "public policy").

a. Public Policy

§ 24.20 In *Fauntleroy v. Lum*,[1] an action was brought in Mississippi upon a Missouri judgment. It was alleged that the judgment was based on an underlying Mississippi transaction, involving gambling in cotton futures, that such a transaction was illegal and void in Mississippi, and that the trial court in Missouri had refused to allow the defendant to show the nature of the transaction (the suit in Missouri having been upon an arbitration award). It was held that the illegality of the original cause of action in Mississippi could not be relied upon as a ground for denying recovery upon a judgment of another state. The Court said: "But, as the jurisdiction of the Missouri court is not open to dispute, the judgment cannot be impeached in Mississippi even if it went upon a misapprehension of the Mississippi law."[2] The District of Columbia appellate court formulated similarly: "[A] judgment shall be accorded the same faith and credit in every court within the United States as it has ... in the state ... where it was originally rendered; and this is true, though the cause of action upon which the judgment was based is against the law and public policy of the state or territory in which enforcement is sought."[3] Section 117 of the Second Restatement adopts the same view. More recently, the Supreme Court stated unequivocally that there is "no moving 'public policy exception' to the full faith and credit due judgments."[4]

The rule is stated in terms of the full-faith-and-credit requirement to sister-state judgments. Similarly, the result can be explained on the basis of the universal rule of the common law that a cause of action for money "merges" in the judgment[5] and that a judgment for money—the underlying cause of action now having disappeared—cannot offend the local public policy of the recognizing jurisdiction. It is important to stress again, however, that "merger" is but a short-hand statement of the pervasive policy of preclusion. This policy, for the reasons examined in Part I above, demands an end to litigation when there was a full opportunity to litigate the issues in the first proceeding. The Full Faith

---

§ 24.20

1. 210 U.S. 230, 28 S.Ct. 641, 52 L.Ed. 1039 (1908) (noted 8 Colum. L. Rev. 569, 22 Harv. L. Rev. 51 (1908)). See also Union National Bank v. Lamb, 337 U.S. 38, 69 S.Ct. 911, 93 L.Ed. 1190 (1949); Roche v. McDonald, 275 U.S. 449, 48 S.Ct. 142, 72 L.Ed. 365 (1928). See Note, 17 U. Chi. L. Rev. 520 (1950). Cf. Morris v. Jones, 329 U.S. 545, 67 S.Ct. 451, 91 L.Ed. 488 (1947).

2. 210 U.S. at 237, 28 S.Ct. at 643. See also Connolly v. Bell, 309 N.Y. 581, 132 N.E.2d 852 (1956).

3. Hieston v. National City Bank of Chicago, 51 App.D.C. 394, 280 Fed. 525, 528 (1922). See also Beal v. Carpenter, 235 Fed. 273 (8th Cir.1916); Westwater v. Murray, 245 Fed. 427 (6th Cir.1917); Harrah v. Craig, 113 Cal.App.2d 67, 247 P.2d 855 (1952); Summers v. Summers, 69 Nev. 83, 241 P.2d 1097 (1952); Puzio v. Puzio, 57

N.J.Super. 557, 155 A.2d 115 (1959); Parker v. Hoefer, 2 N.Y.2d 612, 162 N.Y.S.2d 13, 142 N.E.2d 194 (1957), cert. denied 355 U.S. 833, 78 S.Ct. 51, 2 L.Ed.2d 45 (1957); Engineers National Bank v. Drew, 311 Pa. 59, 166 A. 376 (1933); Wallihan v. Hughes, 196 Va. 117, 82 S.E.2d 553 (1954); Miller v. Kingsley, 194 Neb. 123, 230 N.W.2d 472, 475 (1975).

4. Baker v. General Motors, 522 U.S. 222, 233, 118 S.Ct. 657, 664, 139 L.Ed.2d 580 (1998).

5. Restatement, Second, Judgments § 17, 18 (1982). Cf. Milwaukee County v. M. E. White Co., 296 U.S. 268, 56 S.Ct. 229, 80 L.Ed. 220 (1935). See Reese, The Status in this Country of Judgments Rendered Abroad, 50 Colum. L. Rev. 783, 784 (1950). Compare J.-G. Castel, Canadian Conflict of Laws § 148 (3d ed. 1994) (foreign judgments do not merge; see supra § 24.3 for U.S. approach).

and Credit Clause generalizes this preclusive effect as it exists under the law of the jurisdiction of rendition to sister states in the interests of national unity. The policy of preclusion thus explains better than a mere reference to the merger doctrine or even the short statement in *Fauntleroy*[6] why the public policy of the second state is generally no defense to recognition of a sister state judgment.

By focusing mainly on the policy of preclusion, the exceptions to the rule also become more readily understandable. Thus, the constitutional mandate of Full Faith and Credit is occasionally said not to extend to sister-state "judicial proceedings" which are not in the form of money judgments, for example, equity decrees ordering an extrastate act[7] or forbearance or modifiable support orders. Modifiable decrees lack the finality which the policy of preclusion and Full Faith and Credit require: the first jurisdiction's decree has only[8] the preclusive effect in the recognizing forum that it enjoys where rendered.

§ 24.21 Similarly, Section 103 of the Second Restatement is best understood in most cases in the context of the policy of preclusion. It states that a judgment need not be accorded interstate recognition if such "is not required by the national policy of full faith and credit because it would involve an improper interference with important interests of the sister state." The examples given in the comments to the Section illustrate its very limited scope. One of them, relating to custody decrees-because these ordinarily remain modifiable in the state of rendition-now seems inapposite in light of the adoption of the Uniform Child Custody Jurisdiction Act and the full-faith-and-credit requirement established by the federal Parental Kidnapping Prevention Act.[1] Similarly, the second forum's general ability to apply its own statute of limitations to a sister-state judgment derives neither from a public-policy exception nor from the related notion expressed in § 103 of the Second Restatement. On the one hand, limitations are usually, although not always,[2] considered to be procedural and subject to forum law. On the other hand, dismissal of a sister-state judgment on limitation grounds may not be a judgment "on the merits"[3] and, if not, would not impair the rights and obligations of the parties under the judgment. To state it differently, the preclusive effect of the first court's determination would not be affected. While, however, any such exception is narrow in scope, the Supreme Court's decision in *Baker v. General Motors*,[4] did countenance a right of a recognizing court to deny enforcement to an earlier decree that "purport[s] to accomplish an official act within the exclusive province [of

---

6. Supra nn.1–2.

7. See *Baker*, 522 U.S. 222, 118 S.Ct. 657, 139 L.Ed.2d 580, on remand 138 F.3d 1225 (8th Cir.1998) (equity decrees generally entitled to full faith and credit).

8. But see supra § 24.2 n.8 as well as supra §§ 15.30–15.36 *passim* with respect to support decrees under the UIFSA.

§ 24.21

1. For a discussion of custody problems see supra §§ 15.39–15.43.

2. See supra § 24.2 n.8 and §§ 3.9–3.12.

3. See supra § 24.2 and the discussion infra § 24.24.

4. 522 U.S. 222, 235, 118 S.Ct. 657, 665, 139 L.Ed.2d 580 (1998).

the recognizing court] or interfered with litigation over which [the rendering court] had no authority."

Injunctions against litigation in sister-states likewise are said not to be entitled to full faith and credit under the policy expressed in § 103. However, the reason, despite the broad language in much of the case law,[5] may again be found in the underlying preclusion policy. The first determination in anti-suit injunction cases does not address, and thus has no preclusive effect on, the merits of the litigation.[6] From this point of view alone, litigation in a second forum is not precluded.

A focus on the underlying policy of preclusion, stressed throughout the discussion of the problem of judgment recognition in this Chapter, thus leads to the conclusion that § 103 of the Second Restatement usually does not identify areas where local public policy may serve as a basis for the refusal to accord recognition to a sister-state judgment when such recognition is otherwise mandated under the Full Faith and Credit Clause of the Constitution.[7] No court should deny recognition to a sister-state decree on the basis of such an exception, except in the most unusual and extraordinary or circumstances.

The federal Defense of Marriage Act[8] now purports to give states authority not to recognize same-sex marriages performed in other states, and a large number of states have adopted legislation to this effect. The Act thus defines a possible public policy concern (in the sense of the Restatement's "improper interference" exception).

b. *No Competent Court in Recognizing Forum*

§ 24.22 Intimately related to the subject matter of the previous subsection is the question whether a state may close its courts to foreign

---

5. See James v. Grand Trunk Western Railroad Co., 14 Ill.2d 356, 152 N.E.2d 858 (1958), cert. denied 358 U.S. 915, 79 S.Ct. 288, 3 L.Ed.2d 239 (1958). While such an antisuit injunction technically binds the parties, its recognition under the Full Faith and Credit Clause would allow it to operate indirectly on the second court and its exercise of jurisdiction as well: "[T]his court need not, and will not, countenance having its right to try cases, of which it has proper jurisdiction, determined by the courts of other States, through their injunctive process." 14 Ill.2d at 372, 152 N.E.2d at 867. See also Cunningham v. Cunningham, 25 Conn.Supp. 221, 200 A.2d 734 (1964); Restatement, Second, Conflict of Laws § 103, comnt. (b) and Reporter's Note to Comment (b) at 314–15 (1971). See also Baker v. General Motors Corp., 522 U.S. 222, 118 S.Ct. 657, 139 L.Ed.2d 580 (1998); Price, supra n.4. But see Advanced Bionics Corp. v. Medtronic, Inc., 29 Cal.4th 697, 59 P.3d 231, 128 Cal.Rptr.2d 172 (2002) (principles of "comity and judicial restraint" counsel sparing use of such decrees).

6. See Baker v. General Motors Corp., 522 U.S. 222, 236, 118 S.Ct. 657, 665, 139 L.Ed.2d 580 (1998) (citing Second Edition of this book with approval).

7. For criticism of § 103, see Note, 54 Calif. L. Rev. 282 (1966). Professors Ehrenzweig and Louisell characterized § 103 as "totally unsupported . . . by authority, policy, or reason. . . ." A.A. Ehrenzweig & D.W. Louisell, Jurisdiction in a Nutshell 138 (3d ed. 1973). Similarly, Professor Reynolds asserts that all authorities cited as supporting § 103 can be explained on other grounds and that there is no generalized "improper-interference" exception to full faith and credit. Reynolds, The Iron Law of Full Faith and Credit, 53 Maryland L. Rev. 412, 436–49 (1994). But see text immediately following.

8. P.L. 104–199, 110 Stat. 2419, to be codified as 28 U.S.C.A. § 1738C. See supra § 13.70.

judgments based on causes of action which could not have been sued upon in the forum. An early decision in support was *Anglo-American Provision Co. v. Davis Provision Co.*[1] That decision upheld a dismissal by a New York court of a claim based on an extrastate judgment under a statute denying jurisdiction to entertain suits between foreign corporations upon a foreign cause of action. The dismissal was held not to be a denial of full faith and credit, Mr. Justice Holmes remarking: "If the plaintiff can find a court into which it has a right to come, then the effect of the judgment is fixed by the Constitution and the act in pursuance of it which Congress has passed.... But the Constitution does not require the state to provide such a court."[2]

The significance of the exception to full faith and credit set out in *Anglo-American* was considerably narrowed by subsequent decisions. In *Fauntleroy v. Lum*,[3] the Supreme Court noted the difference between statutes defining the court's jurisdiction and those involving substantive law. In holding that a Mississippi statute which prohibited gambling in futures did not excuse a Mississippi court from enforcing a judgment rendered in Missouri on a futures contract made and performed in Mississippi, the Court, again by Holmes, stated that the statute in question set out a rule of substantive law and therefore did not fall within the exception of the *Anglo-American* case.[4] Moreover, the Court indicated that this exception should be interpreted narrowly, at least when the court involved is one of general jurisdiction, so that only the most unambiguous statute shall be treated as one denying a court the competence to hear a claim on a judgment.[5]

In *Kenney v. Supreme Lodge of the World, Loyal Order of Moose*,[6] the refusal of an Illinois court to entertain a suit on an Alabama judgment, under an Illinois statute prohibiting actions for deaths occurring out-of-state, was held a denial of full faith and credit. A state cannot, said the Court, escape its constitutional obligations to give effect to the judgments of sister states by the simple devise of denying jurisdiction to otherwise competent courts to entertain suits on the judgments. *Anglo-American* was distinguished as involving the special case of foreign corporations.[7]

Nor may a state accomplish the same result by limiting the means of enforcement to a form of action so complex and expensive that resort to its courts would be practically impossible. In *Broderick v. Rosner*,[8] the New York superintendent of banks brought suit in New Jersey against certain stockholders of a closed New York bank to recover an assessment

§ 24.22

1. 191 U.S. 373, 24 S.Ct. 92, 48 L.Ed. 225 (1903).

2. 191 U.S. at 374, 24 S.Ct. at 93 (1903).

3. 210 U.S. 230, 28 S.Ct. 641, 52 L.Ed. 1039 (1908) (discussed also supra § 24.20 nn.1–2).

4. 210 U.S. at 235, 28 S.Ct. at 642 (1908).

5. Id.

6. 252 U.S. 411, 40 S.Ct. 371, 64 L.Ed. 638 (1920).

7. 252 U.S. at 414, 40 S.Ct. at 372 (1920).

8. 294 U.S. 629, 55 S.Ct. 589, 79 L.Ed. 1100 (1935). See also infra n. 9.

levied on them. The complaint was dismissed on the ground that under a New Jersey statute such a liability could be enforced only in an equitable accounting in which all of the creditors and all of the stockholders should be necessary parties. The Supreme Court pointed out that if this meant that no judgment could be rendered unless all the stockholders and depositors were within the jurisdiction of the New Jersey court the statute made enforcement of the right a legal impossibility since 420,000 of them were non-residents. If, on the other hand, even substituted service by publication were permitted, the cost would be prohibitive. The Court therefore held that the suits, which had been brought at law against individual defendants, should be entertained.

After *Fauntleroy, Kenney,* and *Broderick,* it would appear that the no-competent-court exception to the enforcement of sister-state judgments may operate only in a severely restricted area, perhaps only if the statute withdrawing the court's jurisdiction is one which involves limitations upon parties, as opposed to causes of action.[9] This conclusion also follows from the Supreme Court's extension of the cases reviewed above beyond recognition of judgments, that is, when it required a state to open its doors to statutory causes of action arising in sister states which would have been entertained if arising locally. The leading cases are *Hughes v. Fetter* and *First National Bank v. United Air Lines.*[10] Although the full-faith-and-credit theory underlying the decisions in these cases might support a conclusion that even more direct enforcement is required, the holding suggests that, at a minimum, states are precluded from discriminating against sister-state causes of action.[11] To the extent that the unavailability of a local forum or remedy therefore may not be invoked as a subterfuge for limiting access to otherwise competent courts in the interstate setting, it would seem that foreign-country judgments similarly may not be excluded on such grounds. In most cases, to do so would infringe the foreign-country plaintiff's right to access to American courts, guaranteed under all U.S. bilateral commercial treaties,[12] and, in

9. See Stumberg, Conflict of Laws 119–20 (3d ed. 1963). See also Weidman v. Weidman, 274 Mass. 118, 174 N.E. 206 (1931) (a Massachusetts court refused enforcement of a sister-state judgment of a wife against her husband because of Massachusetts statute denied jurisdiction to its courts over an action between spouses).

In Wilson v. Louisiana–Pacific Resources, Inc., 138 Cal.App.3d 216, 187 Cal.Rptr. 852, (1982), the court questioned (at p.224) whether "there (is) vitality left" in *Broderick* after Allstate Ins. Co. v. Hague, supra § 3.23. In any event, the court considered *Broderick* distinguishable on the ground that New Jersey, in *Broderick*, had no conflicting interests to New York's, while in the case at bar, California had an interest in regulating "pseudo-foreign" corporations. A state's freedom to concern itself with the "internal affairs" of a foreign corporation in turn is now in doubt: see supra

§§ 23.6–23.9 for the "internal affairs" rule, "pseudo-foreign corporations," and the U.S. Supreme Court's decision in *CTS*.

10. Hughes v. Fetter, 341 U.S. 609, 71 S.Ct. 980, 95 L.Ed. 1212 (1951) (action on sister-state's wrongful death statute), discussed supra § 3.25; First National Bank v. United Air Lines, 342 U.S. 396, 72 S.Ct. 421, 96 L.Ed. 441 (1952). On court closing rules see also supra § 3.40.

11. But see Watkins v. Conway, 385 U.S. 188, 87 S.Ct. 357, 17 L.Ed.2d 286 (1966) (forum may apply shorter statute of limitations to sister state judgments than it does to domestic judgments when limitation runs from time of revival of sister state judgment). For further discussion see infra § 24.32.

12. See, e.g., Art. VI(1) of the Treaty of Friendship, Commerce and Navigation Between the United States of America and the

a wider sense, perhaps also the foreign-country plaintiff's right to due process.

c. Tax and Penal Judgments and Claims

§ 24.23 As noted initially,[1] Anglo–American courts historically did not entertain tax and penal judgments or claims, both for reasons of territorial sovereignty and local public policy. In 1963, the Supreme Court of Canada still stated: "It is perfectly elementary that a foreign government cannot come here" to enforce a judgment for taxes.[2] However, as between the states of the United States, the U.S. Supreme Court decided in the early case of *Milwaukee County v. M.E. White Co.* that "a judgment is not to be denied full faith and credit merely because it is for taxes."[3] Today, this rule also extends to administrative determinations of taxes.[4]

The decision in *Milwaukee County* expressly left it open whether the enforcement of unadjudicated tax claims was similarly constitutionally required. However, state courts have tended to enforce interstate tax claims[5] and more than half of the states now provide for such enforcement by reciprocal statutes.[6] The courts, however, continue to deny recognition to foreign-nation tax claims and judgments although the policy considerations reviewed above support a broad view in favor of enforcement of both interstate and international claims.[7]

Federal Republic of Germany, 7 U.S.T. 1840, T.I.A.S. 3593, 273 U.N.T.S. 3 (entered into force July 14, 1956). On bilateral treaties see supra §§ 3.58–3.59.

§ 24.23

1. Supra § 24.19.

2. [1963] S.C.R. 366, 41 D.L.R.2d 721 (1963); see Note, 77 Harv. L. Rev. 1327 (1964).

3. 296 U.S. 268, 279, 56 S.Ct. 229, 235, 80 L.Ed. 220 (1935).

4. City of New York v. Shapiro, 129 F.Supp. 149 (D.Mass.1954) (noted in 69 Harv. L. Rev. 378 (1955)); State of Ohio v. Kleitch Bros., Inc. 357 Mich. 504, 98 N.W.2d 636 (1959).

5. E.g., City of Detroit v. Gould, 12 Ill.2d 297, 146 N.E.2d 61 (1957) (personal property tax); State ex rel. Oklahoma Tax Commission v. Rodgers, 238 Mo.App. 1115, 193 S.W.2d 919 (1946) (income tax); State Tax Commission v. Cord, 81 Nev. 403, 404 P.2d 422 (1965); Buckley v. Huston, 60 N.J. 472, 291 A.2d 129 (1972).

6. Local Enforcement of Foreign Tax Laws, 20 Real Property, Probate, and Trust J. 73 (1985).

7. See The Attorney General of Canada v. R.J. Reynolds Tobacco Holdings, Inc., 268

F.3d 103 (2d Cir. 2001), cert. denied 537 U.S. 1000, 123 S.Ct. 513, 154 L.Ed.2d 394 (2002), (holding that RICO does not countenance claims on behalf of the Canadian government for tax revenue lost due to alleged smuggling of cigarettes); Her Majesty the Queen in Right of Province of British Columbia v. Gilbertson, 433 F.Supp. 410 (D.Or.1977), affirmed 597 F.2d 1161 (9th Cir.1979) (refusal to enforce a British Columbia tax judgment against Oregon domiciliaries on the ground that one country does not recognize the tax claims or judgments of another). See Note, The Nonrecognition of Foreign Tax Judgments—International Tax Evasion, 1981 U. Ill. L. Rev. 241. But see Bullen et al. v. Her Majesty's Government of the United Kingdom, 553 So.2d 1344 (Fla.App.1989) (enforcing money judgment based on an underlying tax liability).

In United States v. Harden, 41 D.L.R.2d 721 (1963), Canada similarly refused to enforce a U.S. judgment based on a tax claim. But cf. Banco Frances e Brasileiro S.A. v. Doe, 36 N.Y.2d 592, 370 N.Y.S.2d 534, 331 N.E.2d 502 (1975), cert. denied 423 U.S. 867, 96 S.Ct. 129, 46 L.Ed.2d 96 (foreign currency regulation enforced, albeit in an action between private parties); Note, 77 Harv. L. Rev. 1327 (1964).

The modern trend is similarly toward the recognition and enforcement of judgments for penalties, although some older cases denied them recognition.[8] The case initiating the shift was *Huntington v. Attrill*,[9] involving liability of a director of a corporation to its creditors for a false affidavit as to the amount of capital stock paid in. The test, said the Court, is "whether it appears, to the tribunal which is called upon to enforce it, to be, in its essential character and effect, a punishment of an offense against the public, or a grant of a civil right to a private person."

Huntington v. Attrill held that if a sister-state judgment is not based on a penal claim, as defined by the Supreme Court, it must be enforced by a state court under the Full Faith and Credit Clause. The Court did not hold the converse of this, *viz.*, that if the judgment was given for a penalty, enforcement is not required. The latter proposition, however, was supposed to have been established in the earlier case of *State of Wisconsin v. Pelican Insurance Co.*[10] There, in holding that a fine imposed by Wisconsin upon a foreign corporation could not be enforced, the Court said that the rule that the courts of one state will not enforce the penalties of another "for the protection of its revenue or other municipal laws" is not affected by the Full Faith and Credit Clause of the Constitution. But in *Fauntleroy v. Lum* this language was said to be dictum, on the ground that the point actually decided was that the original jurisdiction of the Supreme Court was confined to controversies of a civil nature.[11] As yet, the Supreme Court has not squarely decided that full faith and credit precludes a court from looking behind a money judgment rendered in a sister-state and denying it recognition on the ground that the underlying cause of action was penal. However, its decisions in *Fauntleroy* and *Milwaukee County* support the expectation that penalties, like taxes, which have been reduced to judgment will be enforceable in the future. The judgment enforced in *Milwaukee County* did include an item for a two percent delinquency "penalty" and, indeed, the policy considerations relevant to the enforcement of penal and fiscal obligations are analogous: the "very purpose of the full faith and credit clause was to alter the statutes of the several states as independent foreign sovereignties, each free to ignore the obligations created under the laws or by the judicial proceedings of the others...."[12]

The conclusion that penalties may be entitled to interstate enforcement under the Full Faith and Credit Clause is particularly important

8. See State of Wisconsin v. Pelican Insurance Co., 127 U.S. 265, 8 S.Ct. 1370, 32 L.Ed. 239 (1888).

9. 146 U.S. 657, 13 S.Ct. 224, 36 L.Ed. 1123 (1892).

10. 127 U.S. 265, 8 S.Ct. 1370, 32 L.Ed. 239 (1888).

11. 210 U.S. 230, 236, 28 S.Ct. 641, 643, 52 L.Ed. 1039 (1908). See also State of Oklahoma ex rel. West v. Gulf, Colorado & Santa Fe Railway Co., 220 U.S. 290, 31 S.Ct. 437, 55 L.Ed. 469 (1911).

12. Milwaukee County v. M.E. White Co., 296 U.S. 268, 276–277, 56 S.Ct. 229, 234, 80 L.Ed. 220 (1935). See generally Michael Finch, Giving Full Faith and Credit to Punitive Damages Awards: Will Florida Rule the Nation?, 86 Minn. L. Rev. 497 (2002)(suggesting a re-examination of whether punitive damage awards might in some circumstances fall within the—penal—category, particularly where the state is the plaintiff).

with respect to the growing area of business regulation. Violation of regulatory statutes may lead to substantial penalties for pollution, antitrust activities, and the like.

Perhaps the only subject still excluded from the broad recognition policy which emerges from *Huntington v. Atrill* and from the other cases discussed above is that of criminal jurisdiction. It remains governed by the concept of exclusive jurisdiction in the place where the crime is charged. Even in this area, however, interstate extradition meets the need in the U.S. interstate setting.[13]

4. Foreign Judgment Not on the Merits

§ 24.24 The Full Faith and Credit Clause of the Constitution requires that the second jurisdiction accord the same effect to a sister-state judgment as it has in the state of rendition. As suggested earlier,[1] it is not always easy to determine whether the first judgment was "on the merits" and what preclusive effects therefore attach to it in the state of rendition which the second forum is constitutionally bound to recognize.[2]

The problem arises in many forms. Thus, a judgment dismissing a cause because of the local statute of limitations will not bar a subsequent action on the identical claim in the courts of a sister state.[3] On the other hand, the result may be different if the second forum applies the rendering forum's statute of limitations under a borrowing statute or

13. See Note, Interstate Rendition and the Fourth Amendment 24 Rut. L. Rev. 551 (1970). The plurality opinion in Thomas v. Washington Gas Light Co., 448 U.S. 261, 100 S.Ct. 2647, 65 L.Ed.2d 757 (1980) suggested that, at least in the context of worker compensation awards, the first forum lacked power to adjudicate claims that might exist under the legislation of a second state (for instance, for a supplemental award) and that the second state could therefore deny recognition to that portion of the first state's award. Both the concurrences and the dissents rejected such a balancing of state interests in the context of the recognition of judgments and awards under the Full Faith and Credit Clause. The dissent by Mr. Justice Rehnquist in particular rejected such " . . . 'interest analysis,' once removed from the statutory choice-of-law context . . . " and considered cases like *Huntington* to fall into the category of " . . . *exceptional* judgments that this Court has indicated . . . [as] not entitled to full faith and credit." 448 U.S. at 295, 100 S.Ct. at 2668. The decision in *Thomas* is considered in greater detail infra § 24.26.

§ 24.24

1. Supra § 24.2 n.1.

2. See Restatement, Second, Conflict of Laws § 110 (1971); Cheatham, Res Judicata and the Full Faith and Credit Clause, 44 Colum. L. Rev. 330 (1944); Reese & Johnson, The Scope of Full Faith and Credit to Judgments, 49 Colum. L. Rev. 152 (1949). Cf. Angel v. Bullington, 330 U.S. 183, 67 S.Ct. 657, 91 L.Ed. 832 (1947).

3. Brent v. Bank of Washington, 35 U.S. (10 Pet.) 596, 9 L.Ed. 547 (1936); Hartmann v. Time, 166 F.2d 127 (3d Cir.1947), cert. denied 334 U.S. 838, 68 S.Ct. 1495, 92 L.Ed. 1763 (1948), cert. denied 334 U.S. 838, 68 S.Ct. 1495, 92 L.Ed. 1763 (1948); Union National Bank v. Lamb, 337 U.S. 38, 46, 69 S.Ct. 911, 915, 93 L.Ed. 1190 (1949) (Frankfurter, J., dissenting in part); Burgess v. Cohen, 593 F.Supp. 1122 (E.D.Va. 1984).

A number of decisions now view the statute of limitations as substantive, to be governed by the law applicable to the principal issue. See Tomlin v. Boeing Co., 650 F.2d 1065 (9th Cir.1981); see also, with respect to the Uniform Act, supra § 3.11 n.8. A dismissal by the forum under its own statute of a claim it considers stale will not, in these circumstances, be a decision on the merits.

under its general choice-of-law rules. In these circumstances the first determination may indeed be considered as conclusive.[4] Similarly, a judgment for the defendant on the pleadings is no bar when the complaint in the second suit properly alleges a cause of action.[5] Again, however, in circumstances in which the first jurisdiction's law is applicable according to the second court's choice-of-law rules, the first court's determination under its law—considered applicable by both jurisdictions—may be conclusive.

Even though the cause of action was not actually litigated in the first jurisdiction, the first determination will still have been "on the merits" and have preclusive effect in circumstances when the action would be barred under a two-dismissal[6] or compulsory counterclaim rule[7] of the first jurisdiction or when the first action resulted in a default judgment.[8] In addition, the manner in which a matter was concluded procedurally in the first action may determine whether it was "on the merits" and precludes further litigation in a second forum. Thus, while a judgment on the pleadings may not preclude a second action, as discussed above, the granting of a motion for summary judgment dismissing the complaint will certainly have preclusive effect.

As the several examples in the preceding discussion show, the common denominator for a determination that the first action precludes further litigation of the claim or of the issues is whether the matter was litigated or, at least, that it is so unfair to the other party to permit relitigation, in circumstances where *an opportunity to litigate* the matter existed in the first action, that the matter will be treated *as if* it had

---

4. For a case involving a borrowing statute (applying to a claim, rather than a judgment, but in which the court nevertheless referred to the Restatement's section on vacated judgments) see Gates v. Trans World Airlines, 493 S.W.2d 668, 670 (Mo. App.1973). Nevertheless, the rule remains unaffected that, on principle, the second forum is free to entertain the action. For further discussion of judgments barred by the first forum's statute of limitations see infra § 24.32.

5. Continental-Midwest Corp. v. Hotel Sherman, Inc., 13 Ill.App.2d 188, 141 N.E.2d 400 (1957); Wilson Co. v. Hartford Fire Ins. Co., 300 Mo. 1, 254 S.W. 266 (1923). A dismissal for lack of subject matter jurisdiction in the first court does not bar a subsequent action in a court with proper jurisdiction: Miller v. United States Postal Service, 729 F.2d 1033 (5th Cir. 1984). See also Tucker v. Kenney, 994 F.Supp. 412 (S.D.N.Y.1998).

6. For discussion see A.D. Vestal, Res Judicata/Preclusion 181–85 (1969).

7. Id. at 163–64.

8. See also Annot., Modern Views of State Courts As To Whether Consent Judg-

ment Is Entitled To Res Judicata Or Collateral Estoppel Effect, 91 A.L.R.3d 1170 (1979). Consent decrees are generally considered as final judgments on the merits: United States v. Fisher, 864 F.2d 434 (7th Cir.1988); United States v. Athlone Industries, Inc., 746 F.2d 977 (3d Cir.1984); I.A.M. Nat. Pension Fund, Ben. Plan A v. Industrial Gear Mfg. Co., 723 F.2d 944 (D.C.Cir.1983). See also Baylor v. U.S. Dep't of Housing and Urban Dev., 913 F.2d 223 (5th Cir.1990) (a class action suit affirming that consent decrees to ban new lawsuits arising from the same dispute as originally litigated); Norman v. McDonald, 930 F.Supp. 1219 (N.D.Ill.1996) (holding that "even if jurisdiction had not been expressly retained", the court could enforce the relief contained within the consent order). But see, United States v. Martell, 887 F.Supp. 1183 (N.D.Ind.1995) (acknowledging that there are some circumstances in which "express reservations of rights in a consent decree" warrant an exception because the intent of the parties must be weighed since consent decrees are of a "contractual" nature).

been litigated. It is readily apparent that, whatever procedural problem is involved and technical label used, it is the underlying *policy of preclusion* which supplies the answer.[9] Thus, when the plaintiff has dismissed the action twice in a jurisdiction which has a two-dismissal rule, the second forum may not only be constitutionally required to give the same preclusive effect to these dismissals as would the first state but it would also be unfair to require the defendant to litigate anew in the second or any additional forum just because the latter does not have a two-dismissal rule. Likewise, a defendant against whom a default judgment has been entered by a court with competent jurisdiction and after proper notice, should not be able to resist enforcement in a second forum which, for instance, has a more restrictive policy with respect to default judgment. In both situations, the party had an opportunity to litigate in the first action but failed to exercise it. The policy of preclusion is pervasive in both claim and issue preclusion.

§ 24.25   Another example will further illustrate the matter, particularly with respect to issues that could have been, but in fact were not litigated in the first action. In *Angel v. Bullington*[1] the plaintiff sought to enforce a deficiency, after the sale of land in Virginia, against the defendant in a North Carolina state court. The North Carolina Supreme Court, on appeal, reversed the lower court's overruling of defendant's demurrer and dismissed plaintiff's complaint on the basis of a North Carolina statute which prohibited actions for deficiencies by mortgages after the sale of land. The plaintiff did not seek review in the U.S. Supreme Court but, instead, brought another action for the same deficiency in a North Carolina federal court. In the federal proceeding and, ultimately, before the U.S. Supreme Court the plaintiff argued that the first proceeding in the North Carolina state courts did not preclude the second action because North Carolina, in the first action, had unconstitutionally closed its court to him. The U.S. Supreme Court disagreed:

> "Since it was open for Bullington to come here to seek reversal of the decision of the North Carolina Supreme court shutting him out of the North Carolina courts and he chose not to do so, the decision of the North Carolina Supreme Court concluded an adjudication of a federal question even though it was not couched in those terms. . . . It is a misconception of res judicata to assume that the doctrine does not come into operation if a court has not passed on the 'merits' in the sense of the ultimate substantive issues of a litigation. An adjudication declining to reach such ultimate substantive issues may bar a second attempt in another court of the State. Such a situation is presented when the first decision is based not on the ground that the distribution of judicial power among the various courts of the State requires the suit to be brought in another court in the State,

but on the inaccessibility of all the courts of the State to such litigation."[2]

§ 24.26 In *Thomas v. Washington Gas Light Co.*,[1] the Supreme Court held that the District of Columbia could award the petitioner a supplemental workers' compensation award despite his receipt of an earlier award under the Virginia act which, under Virginia law, excluded any other recovery. The supplemental award did not violate the District's obligation under the Full Faith and Credit Clause. One reason for the Court's decision was that "a workmen's compensation tribunal may [typically] only apply its own State's law."[2] Therefore, the petitioner's claim under the District of Columbia's statute were not before the Virginia Commission and its award therefore extended only to the Virginia claim. In addition, however, the opinion of the plurality also suggested that Virginia law, and a Virginia proceeding and award, *could not* have precluded a second supplemental award elsewhere: "[T]he substantial interests of the second State in these circumstances [worker compensation] should not be overridden by another State through an unnecessarily aggressive application of the Full Faith and Credit Clause.... We therefore would hold that a State has no legitimate interest within the context of our federal system in preventing another State from granting a supplemental compensation award when that second State would have had the power to apply its workmen's compensation law in the first instance."[3] The three concurring Justices reached the same result on the basis of the first reason, namely that Virginia's law and award, by their own terms, did not preclude a supplemental award.[4]

2. 330 U.S. at 189–190, 67 S.Ct. at 661 (1947). But see the strong and well-reasoned dissents by Justices Reed and Rutledge, 330 U.S. 183, 193, 201, 67 S.Ct. 657, 91 L.Ed. 832. See also Chongris v. Board of Appeals of Andover, 614 F.Supp. 998 (D.Mass.1985), affirmed 811 F.2d 36 (1st Cir.1987), cert. denied 483 U.S. 1021, 107 S.Ct. 3266, 97 L.Ed.2d 765 (1987) (federal constitutional challenge barred by prior state court proceeding in which it could have been raised).

§ 24.26

1. 448 U.S. 261, 100 S.Ct. 2647, 65 L.Ed.2d 757 (1980).

2. 448 U.S. at 282, 100 S.Ct. at 2661.

3. Id. at 285–86, 100 S.Ct. at 2663.

4. Id. at 289–90, 100 S.Ct. at 2664–65 (concurring opinion). The three concurring Justices therefore would apply the test of Industrial Commission of Wisconsin v. McCartin, 330 U.S. 622, 67 S.Ct. 886, 91 L.Ed. 1140 (1947) which allowed a second award unless the first was based on a stat-

ute which in "unmistakable language" precluded this. The two dissenting Justices preferred to adhere to Magnolia Petroleum Co. v. Hunt, 320 U.S. 430, 64 S.Ct. 208, 88 L.Ed. 149 (1943), which gave conclusive effect to the first award (precluding a second) and to which *McCartin* had become a major exception. The result of the present case thus is that the plurality of four Justices wanted to overrule *Magnolia* (and, by implication, also *McCartin*), the dissent wanted to overrule *McCartin*, and that the concurring Justices reach the same substantive result as the plurality *by application* of *McCartin*. The wish to overrule *Magnolia* of course fell short of realization for lack of a majority. While both the plurality and the dissenters wanted to overrule *McCartin* (seven Justices) this result also was not achieved for failure to agree on a substitute. For the sounder approach see Semler v. Psychiatric Institute of Washington, D.C., 575 F.2d 922 (D.C.Cir.1978) (recovery under Virginia's exclusive wrongful death act precludes further action under more favorable District of Columbia law).

The plurality opinion's additional ground-although stated to be applicable only to awards by worker compensation boards[5]—raises troublesome questions as to the operation " ... of the principles of full faith and credit in many areas."[6] It undercuts the function of the Full Faith and Credit Clause " ... to act as a nationally unifying force"[7] by balancing state interests.[8] Both the concurrences and the dissents, representing the views of five Justices, agree, as put in Justice Rehnquist's dissent, that "the Full Faith and Credit Clause did not allot to this Court the task of 'balancing' interests where the 'public Acts, Records and Judicial proceedings' of a state were involved. It simply directed that they be given ... 'Full Faith and Credit'.... "[9]

5. *Other Defenses*

§ 24.27 A number of additional circumstances may have a bearing on the effect of a judgment in a second forum. A suggestion in the U.S. Supreme Court's plurality opinion in *Thomas v. Washington Gas Light Co.* that a workers' compensation award may not affect the interests of a second forum in giving a supplemental award was considered above. Both the concurrences and the dissents rejected the suggestion of a balancing of state interests in the context of the Full Faith and Credit Clause. Other defenses to the recognition of sister-state judgments are summarized in the present section. Foreign-country judgments will receive additional consideration in another section.

§ 24.28 *Non-final Judgments.* An earlier section recalled that the Full Faith and Credit Clause speaks of "judicial proceedings" and not of "final judgments" (as traditionally required by the case law as a precondition to recognition) and that, in increasing measure, some non-final judgments are recognized,[1] such as modifiable support orders. Judgments may also not be final in other respects and, if so, quite properly may be denied recognition in an appropriate case. This may be so when the judgment has been appealed, vacated, or its execution stayed in the rendering forum or when it is conditional by it own terms.[2]

---

5. 448 U.S. at 286, 289–90, 100 S.Ct. at 2664–65 (plurality opinion and White, J., concurring).

6. Id. at 288, 100 S.Ct. at 2663 (White, J., concurring).

7. Id. at 289, 100 S.Ct. at 2664 (White, J., concurring).

8. Id. at 289, 100 S.Ct. at 2664 (White, J., concurring); id. at 296 (Rehnquist, J., dissenting).

9. Id. at 296, 100 S.Ct. at 2668 (Rehnquist, J., dissenting). See also Sterk, Full Faith and Credit, More or Less, to Judgments: Doubts About *Thomas v. Washington Gas Light Co.*, 69 Geo. L.J. 1329 (1981). In United Airlines, Inc. v. Kozel, 33 Va.App. 695, 536 S.E.2d 473 (Va.App.2000), a settlement approved by the Illinois Industrial Commission explicitly purported to pre-clude the employee from receiving supplemental benefits under Virginia's worker's compensation law. The Virginia court held that it was not required to give full faith credit because "[t]he Illinois Commission did not purport to, and could not have adjudicated the appropriateness of the proposed settlement *under the laws of Virginia*," id. at 477 (emphasis added), and did not have power "to foreclose the claimant's right to seek further relief before the Virginia Commission." Id.

§ 24.28

1. See supra § 24.8.

2. *Appeal:* see Restatement, Second, Conflict of Laws §§ 107–108 (1971). If the appeal in the rendering forum does not operate to vacate the judgment under that

On the other hand, the possibility that a federal court's judgment in a diversity matter may be vacated for a subsequent change in the applicable state law[3] does not affect its finality before it is so vacated. The applicable Federal Rule of Civil Procedure (60(b)(6)), by its own terms, envisions relief from a "final judgment." In this sense, relief occasioned by a subsequent change in applicable state law therefore does not differ from similar relief in the event of after-discovered evidence.[4]

§ 24.29 *Injunctions Against Enforcement and Inconsistent Judgments.* A judgment creditor may be enjoined[1] from enforcing his judgment, either by the original rendering court or by another court, or either party may, in a second forum, obtain a judgment inconsistent from a prior judgment in favor of the respective other party. To the extent that the injunction operates as a total bar to the enforcement of a judgment under the law of the court issuing it, both cases represent forms of inconsistent subsequent judgments.[2] In both cases, the subsequent decree or judgment is entitled to full faith and credit,[3] under

forum's law, the recognizing court may entertain an action on the judgment or, more usually, stay its recognition and enforcement proceedings pending the determination of the appeal. See Nowell v. Nowell, 157 Conn. 470, 254 A.2d 889 (1969), cert. denied 396 U.S. 844, 90 S.Ct. 68, 24 L.Ed.2d 94 (1969); Bonate v. Bonate, 78 Ill.App.3d 164, 397 N.E.2d 88, 33 Ill.Dec. 755 (1979); Brawer v. Pinkins, 164 Misc.2d 1018, 626 N.Y.S.2d 674 (1995); Restatement, Judgments § 41 (1942); Restatement, Second, Judgments § 13, 16 (1982). *Conditional* judgments: Restatement, Second, Conflict of Laws § 111 (1971). *Vacated* judgments: id. § 112. See also id. § 107.

3. Pierce v. Cook & Co., 518 F.2d 720 (10th Cir.1975), cert. denied 423 U.S. 1079, 96 S.Ct. 866, 47 L.Ed.2d 89 (1976). For a narrower view, see McGeshick v. Choucair, 72 F.3d 62 (7th Cir. 1995), cert. denied 517 U.S. 1212, 116 S.Ct. 1834, 134 L.Ed.2d 937 (1996) (also reviewing case law of the Second, Fourth and Fifth Circuits). The case is also discussed supra §§ 3.47 n.8, 24.8.

4. F.R.C.P. 60(b)(2). The effect of the *Pierce* decision on the "binding" nature of a federal judgment in a diversity case is also important for purposes of possible future recognition-of-judgments conventions (infra at § 24.39), and is discussed, in that context, in Hay & Walker, The Proposed Recognition-of-Judgments Convention Between the United States and the United Kingdom, 11 Texas Int'l L.J. 421, 423–424 n.19 (1976). *Pierce* is noted in 42 U. Chi. L. Rev. 646 (1976); 124 U. Pa. L. Rev. 843 (1976); 62 Va. L. Rev. 414 (1976).

§ 24.29

1. This situation differs from the case in which a party to a local action is enjoined

from bringing another action elsewhere. Such an injunction need not be recognized by the second forum. Supra §§ 24.09 n.7 and 24.21 n.4. But see the power of federal courts in interpleader matters to enjoin actions and proceedings anywhere in the United States. Such a power formerly also existed in bankruptcy matters: 11 U.S.C.A. §§ 714, 814 (1973). It has been replaced by an automatic stay provision: 11 U.S.C.A. § 362 (1979).

2. The situation discussed here must also be distinguished from the case of parallel, *consistent* judgments. Examples of the latter situation are: a local judgment recognizing and enforcing an earlier sister-state or foreign-country judgment, in which case both remain in effect (and may form the basis of an action in a third forum) until one is satisfied; and a judgment rendered on a foreign-country cause of action despite the existence of an earlier foreign-country judgment on the same cause of action. Both illustration follow from a non-merger concept: in the first case, that a judgment does not merge a judgment; in the second, that a foreign-country judgment does not merge a cause of action. With respect to the non-merger of a foreign-country cause of action see infra § 24.41.

3. Restatement, Second, Conflict of Laws §§ 113–14 (1971). See also Restatement, Judgments § 42 (1942); Restatement, Second, Judgments § 15 (1982); Ginsburg, Judgments in Search of Full Faith and Credit: The Last-in-Time Rule for Conflicting Judgments, 82 Harv. L. Rev. 798 (1969).

principles of res judicata,[4] between States of the United States,[5] even if the second decree or judgment itself erroneously failed to accord full faith and credit to the first.[6] Comment (b) of Second Conflicts Restatement § 114 suggests that the "rule may be different" when the "losing party has been denied review of the later inconsistent judgment by the Supreme Court of the United States" because it might then be "inappropriate" to give conclusive effect under Full Faith and Credit to the inconsistent judgment. This assertion is contrary to the Supreme Court's decision in *Treinies*.[7] There the Court required Washington to recognize in Idaho judgment which had refused to give full faith and credit to a prior Washington judgment even though the Supreme Court had earlier denied certiorari to the Idaho judgment.[8]

§ 24.30 *Reversal of Prior Judgment.* The reversal of a judgment does not automatically invalidate or otherwise affect a judgment in another forum based on the original judgment recognizing and enforcing it. As among sister states, the full-faith-and-credit principle requires recognition of the second, now inconsistent judgment, in accordance with

---

4. The recognizing forum is bound to accord the inconsistent judgment the effect given it by the law of the forum rendering it. The rule therefore presupposes that the latter attributes to its decree of judgment an effect which supersedes the prior judgment, whether rendered in the same or another forum. When there were two consecutive and inconsistent state court decisions, the last judgment in time was entitled to full faith and credit and to preclusive effect in subsequent federal litigation: First Tennessee Bank N.A. Memphis v. Smith, 766 F.2d 255 (6th Cir.1985).

5. Since the Full Faith and Credit requirement does not apply to foreign-country judgments, United States courts are free to accord the inconsistent foreign judgment res judicata effect or to deny such an effect. But see infra § 24.41. The proposal for a recognition of judgments convention between the U.S. and the U.K. had provided expressly that recognition of a judgment "is not required" if it conflicts with a judgment rendered by the forum or by a third state. Art. 7(c)(i and iii). However, recognition could have been accorded beyond that required by the Convention. Art. 3. See also infra n.6 with respect to the *Perkins* cases.

6. Treinies v. Sunshine Mining Co., 308 U.S. 66, 60 S.Ct. 44, 84 L.Ed. 85 (1939); Sutton v. Leib, 342 U.S. 402, 72 S.Ct. 398, 96 L.Ed. 448 (1952); Durfee v. Duke, 375 U.S. 106, 84 S.Ct. 242, 11 L.Ed.2d 186 (1963); Porter v. Wilson, 419 F.2d 254 (9th Cir.1969), cert. denied 397 U.S. 1020, 90 S.Ct. 1260, 25 L.Ed.2d 531 (1970). For another application of *Treinies*, see also First Tennessee Bank N.A. v. Smith et al., 766 F.2d 255 (6th Cir. 1985).

In Perkins v. Benguet Consolidated Mining Co., 55 Cal.App.2d 720, 132 P.2d 70 (1942), cert. denied 319 U.S. 774, 63 S.Ct. 1435, 87 L.Ed. 1721 (1943). California gave full faith and credit to a New York judgment determining that a Philippine judgment had been obtained by fraud. New York subsequently gave effect to a second Philippine judgment which was consistent with the first and inconsistent with the earlier New York determination (and the California judgment based on it): Perkins v. De Witt, 279 App.Div. 903, 111 N.Y.S.2d 752 (1952). New York, in allowing the second Philippine judgment to operate as a bar, thus accorded it the same effect as a similar sister-state judgment.

7. Supra n.6. See also supra § 24.2 nn.9–11.

8. Mason v. Pelkes, 57 Idaho 10, 59 P.2d 1087 (1936). There is no newer authoritative case law departing from *Treinies* or otherwise supporting the proposed exception. Occasional state court decision take the position that the first court's judgment may be denied effect where it failed to give effect to an earlier forum court's judgment. An example is Colby v. Colby, 78 Nev. 150, 157, 369 P.2d 1019, 1023, cert. denied 371 U.S. 888, 83 S.Ct. 186, 9 L.Ed.2d 122 (1962). As explained in §§ 15.12 and 24.14 n. 4 et seq. supra, in the context of *Colby*, this position is based on the erroneous assumption that the full-faith-and-credit command is relative. See also Thomas v. Washington Gas Light Co., 448 U.S. 261, 296, 100 S.Ct. 2647, 2668, 65 L.Ed.2d 757 (1980) (Rehnquist, J., dissenting).

the law of the state of rendition, assuming that it itself was based on proper jurisdiction.[1] This is a rare case since the time for appeal of the original judgment will usually have expired or an appeal have been determined before the foreign enforcement occurs. However, the judgment creditor may need to move promptly in order to protect his priorities. But even in the rare case of a reversal of the original judgment after a second judgment enforcing it has been entered, the state of rendition of the second judgment will allow the interposition of equitable defenses against the enforcement of the second judgment or provide a procedure for reopening for the purpose of allowing the reversal to be given effect.[2] The availability of equitable defenses in the state of rendition will also permit the interposition of such defenses in a third forum.[3] Even if no defenses are available against the enforcement of the second judgment, the reversal of the prior judgment will have an effect on the rights and obligations of the parties which may give rise to restitutionary remedies to correct or to avoid the injustice occasioned by the technicalities of the multi-state procedures.[4]

§ **24.31** *Payment.* Full-faith-and-credit principles require the second forum to accord a judgment the same effect that it enjoys in the state of rendition, including its discharge, as provided by the latter's law, by payment, performance of a required act (for instance, conveyance), or by other means such as accord and satisfaction.[1] Thus, when under the law of rendition only full satisfaction of a judgment against one joint tortfeasor will operate as a bar against its enforcement against the other joint tortfeasors, a pro rata payment by one will not be accepted as satisfaction of the judgment in a second forum.[2] When a second judgment has been entered recognizing and enforcing a prior judgment before satisfaction of the latter, both remain in effect until one of them has been satisfied.[3] This rule is of particular importance when one of the judgments becomes barred by a statute of limitations.

The same rules apply, in principle, in the international setting, except perhaps in the case that a United States judgment is enforced in a foreign country and payment is made in that country's local currency in an amount less than the dollar value of the United States judgment. Doubt has been expressed that such payment would discharge the United States judgment,[4] despite an older decision to this effect.[5] Howev-

§ 24.30

1. See Restatement, Second, Conflict of Laws § 121 (1971); Restatement, Judgments § 44 (1942); Restatement, Second, Judgments § 16 (1982). See Robertson v. Bartels, 148 F.Supp.2d 443 n. 3 (D.N.J. 2001), aff'd 543 U.S. 1110, 122 S.Ct. 914, 151 L.Ed.2d 881 (2002).

2. See also F.R.C.P. 60(b)(5), (6).

3. See supra § 24.17.

4. See Restatement, Restitution § 74 (1937).

§ 24.31

1. Restatement, Second, Conflict of Laws § 116 (1971).

2. See Burkett v. McCaw, 9 Wn.App. 917, 515 P.2d 988, 990 (1973); Harris v. EMI Television Programs, Inc., 102 Cai. App.3d 214, 162 Cal.Rptr. 357 (1980).

3. See supra § 24.29 n.2.

4. See Reese, The Status in this Country of Judgments Rendered Abroad, 50 Colum. L. Rev. 783, 798–99 (1950).

5. In re James' Will, 248 N.Y. 1, 161 N.E. 201 (1928).

er, it is possible in American state courts,[6] as well as in federal courts sitting in diversity,[7] to express a judgment in local or the original currency. This has long been the practice in civil law countries and has also been adopted in England.[8] As the emerging rules regarding valuation become more generalized, different treatment of interstate and international situations with respect to payment operating as discharge would no longer be indicated. The valuation of foreign-country money judgments is the subject of § 24.40.

§ **24.32** *Statutes of Limitation*.[1] The second forum may apply its own *longer* statute of limitation to a judgment already barred by the statute of limitation of the state of rendition.[2] However, ordinarily a foreign judgment will not be enforced by the second forum after the expiration of the statute of limitations applicable to judgments of the state of rendition or of the recognizing forum.[3] The foreign judgment may be denied enforcement under the forum's *shorter* statute of limitations as long as the limitation provided applies equally to domestic and foreign judgments.[4] Some uncertainty exists whether revival of the original judgment in the state of rendition will serve to overcome the recognizing forum's shorter limitation on the original judgment, assuming that the revived judgment itself is not barred by the limitation. One view[5] distinguishes between revival prolonging the original judgment and revival having the effect of creating a new judgment: the former is said to continue to be barred by the shorter local statute, while the latter is entitled to full faith and credit. However, the implication in the U.S. Supreme Court's decision in *Watkins v. Conway* is that *any* revival of a judgment is entitled to full faith and credit.[6]

6. See U.C.C. § 1–201(24) which defines "money" as a "medium of exchange authorized or adopted by a domestic or foreign government as a part of its currency;" Becker, The Currency of Judgment, 25 Am. J. Comp. L. 152 (1977). In Barton v. National Life Assurance Co. of Canada, 98 Misc.2d 300, 413 N.Y.S.2d 807 (App. Term 1978), the court enforced a provision in an insurance contract calling for payment in Jamaican pounds.

7. 31 U.S.C.A. § 371, originally adopted in 1792, provides that "money of account of the United States shall be expressed in dollars." For an early view that the section does not prevent the expression of a judgment in a foreign currency equivalent see Becker, supra n.6, at 158. For discussion of current law see infra § 24.40.

8. See Schorsch Meier GmbH. v. Hennin, [1975] 1 All E.R. 152 (C.A.); Miliangos v. George Frank (Textiles) Ltd., [1975] 3 All E.R. 801 (H.L.); Cheshire & North, Private International Law 90 et seq. (13th ed. by

North & Fawcett 1999); Drobnig, American–German Private International Law 257 (1972). See also § 24.40; Schack, Internationales Zivilverfahrensrecht 232, 409–10 (3d ed. 2002).

§ 24.32

1. See also supra § 24.24.

2. See Union National Bank v. Lamb, 337 U.S. 38, 46, 69 S.Ct. 911, 915, 93 L.Ed. 1190 (1949), Cf. also Sun Oil Co. v. Wortman, 486 U.S. 717, 108 S.Ct. 2117, 100 L.Ed.2d 743 (1988) (discussed supra § 3.27).

3. See generally Restatement, Second, Conflict of Laws § 118(2) (1971).

4. See Restatement, Second, Conflict of Laws § 118, cmnt. (c) (1971).

5. Id.

6. 385 U.S. 188, 87 S.Ct. 357, 17 L.Ed.2d 286 (1966). The Court stated: "In the case at bar ... all appellant need do is return to Florida and *revive* his judgment."

To the extent that courts apply interstate rules to international cases, the foregoing is also true for foreign-country judgments.[7] However, since a foreign-judgment is said not to merge the cause of action,[8] a successful[9] plaintiff in the foreign action may disregard the foreign judgment and sue anew on the cause of action, for instance in order to gain a higher recovery, assuming that the forum's or another state's statute of limitations applicable to the cause of action has not yet run. However, the earlier discussion suggested that the policy of preclusion applies equally to interstate and international judgments and that reliance on the traditional technical non-merger rule obscures the objectives of this policy. It was also suggested there that the modern trend is toward equality of treatment of interstate and international judgments for purposes of preclusion when the judgment resulted from a fair trial and was entered by a court with competent jurisdiction.[10] Art. 10(a) of the proposal for a Recognition-of-Judgments Convention between the U.S. and the U.K. had expressly envisioned protection to defendants by providing for the recognition of the first forum's judgment by the second forum when the party or its "predecessor in interest brought the original proceeding."

---

385 U.S. at 189–90, 87 S.Ct. at 357–58 (emphasis added). It noted that "the Florida statute of limitations on domestic judgments is 20 years.... Thus, it appears that appellant still has ample time to *revive* his judgment and bring it back to Georgia." 385 U.S. at 190 n.2, 87 S.Ct. at 358 n.2 (emphasis added). Both statements are dictum since the Florida statute had been construed to apply to the date of revival but must also be read against the dictum at 385 U.S. at 191 n.4, 87 S.Ct. at 358 n.4: "If the appellant held a judgment from a State which did not consider its judgments to become dormant, so that no revival proceeding could be brought, we would be faced with a different case." It would appear that a state may apply a discriminatory shorter limitation only when there exists a possibility for revival in the original state and, in such a case, must—as Georgia in fact did in *Watkins*—apply the foreign limitation or its own shorter limitation from the date of revival.

7. Restatement, Second, Conflict of Laws § 118, cmnt. (c) (1971) favors this position.

The earlier proposal for a recognition-of-judgments convention between the U.S. and the U.K. had provided a rule designed to obviate the differences existing in the States of the Union which might adversely affect the enforcement of English judgments (or result in forum shopping): enforcement would be barred in the second state if barred in the state of rendition or if an application for enforcement had not been brought in the second state within six years from the original judgment (defined as either the original judgment or the final judgment after appeal in the state of origin). Art. 17(1).

8. Supra § 24.3.

9. The res judicata defense will generally protect defendants against relitigation of claims by unsuccessful plaintiffs. Reese, The Status in This Country of Judgments Rendered Abroad, 50 Colum. L. Rev. 783, 788 (1950). See also Art. 3 of the Uniform Foreign Money Judgments Recognition Act; Ingersoll Mill. Mach. Co. v. Granger, 833 F.2d 680 (7th Cir. 1987); supra § 24.18 n.2.

10. See Hay, On Merger and Preclusion (Res Judicata) in U.S. Foreign Judgments Recognition–Unresolved Doctrinal Problems, in: R. Schütze et al. (eds.), Festschrift für Reinhold Geimer 325 (2002).

1. *Early Approaches and the Hilton Doctrine*[1]

III. INTERNATIONAL RECOGNITION OF JUDGMENTS

A. RECOGNITION AND ENFORCEMENT

§ 24.33 In England, early decisions concerning the recognition of foreign-country judgments expressed divergent views, sometimes suggesting a difference between the foreign judgment when sued upon as a cause of action and when set up as a matter of defense.[2] In the important case of *Godard v. Gray*,[3] an action was brought in England on a French judgment. It appeared that the French court in rendering the judgment had made a mistake as to English law involved in the original cause of action, and it was claimed that because of this mistake there could not be recovery in England. It was nevertheless held that the judgment was conclusive. Lord Blackburn said: "But in England, and in those states which are governed by the common law, such judgments are enforced, not by virtue of any treaty, nor by virtue of any statutes, but upon a principle very well stated by Parke B., in *Williams v. Jones*, 13 M. & W. 633: 'Where a court of competent jurisdiction has adjudicated a certain sum to be due from one person to another, a legal obligation arises to pay that sum, on which an action of debt to enforce the judgment may be maintained....'" The court went on to explain that defenses may be offered to deny the existence of the legal obligation of the judgment. These defenses, however, are limited to proof that the court rendering the judgment lacked jurisdiction of the person of the defendant or of the subject matter, or that the judgment had been obtained by fraud. This represents the modern English doctrine.[4]

§ 24.34 In the United States a variety of opinions have been expressed. The following statement from Kent, C.J., perhaps represents much of the earlier view upon the question: "Foreign judgments are never reexamined unless the aid of our courts is asked to carry them into effect by a direct suit upon the judgment. The foreign judgment is then held to be only prima facie evidence of the demand; but when it comes in collaterally, or the defendant relies upon it under the exceptio rei judicatae, it is then received as conclusive."[1] The modern tendency in this country is more in accord with the English view expressed in *Godard v. Gray*, discussed above, that the judgment of the foreign court

---

§ 24.33

1. See also supra § 24.32 nn.7–9 and the introductory discussion of this subject matter in the context of the policy of preclusion, supra § 24.3.

2. The older authorities are reviewed in Story, Conflict of Laws § 598 (8th ed. 1883).

3. L.R. 6 Q.B. 139 (1870).

4. Dicey & Morris, Conflict of Laws 469, 487 et seq. (13th ed. 2000 by Collins et al.); Cheshire & North, Private International Law 337 et seq. (13th ed. by North and

Fawcett 1999). For defenses, see infra § 24.41 et seq.

§ 24.34

1. Smith v. Lewis, 3 Johns. 157, 169, 3 Am.Dec. 469 (N.Y.1808). Among cases treating a foreign judgment as prima facie valid only are Williams v. Preston, 26 Ky. 600, 3 J.J. Marsh. 600, 20 Am.Dec. 179 (Ky. 1830); Tremblay v. Aetna Life Insurance Co., 97 Me. 547, 55 A. 509 (1903); Buttrick v. Allen, 8 Mass. 273, 5 Am.Dec. 105 (1811).

having jurisdiction is, subject to the few exceptions noted hereafter, conclusive as to the rights of the plaintiff and obligations of the defendant.[2]

This doctrine was seemingly qualified by the U.S. Supreme Court in the early leading case of *Hilton v. Guyot*.[3] An action was brought in a federal court upon a judgment recovered against a defendant in France. The court in France had jurisdiction, and the defendant had been served and had appeared and defended. The Supreme Court, in reversing a judgment given in the court below in favor of the judgment creditor, recognized the general rule as to the conclusiveness of a foreign judgment. It was said: "[W]here there has been opportunity for a full and fair trial abroad before a court of competent jurisdiction, conducting the trial upon regular proceedings, after due citation or voluntary appearance of the defendant, and under a system of jurisprudence likely to secure an impartial administration of justice between the citizens of its own country and those of other countries, and there is nothing to show either prejudice in the court, or in the system of laws under which it was sitting, or fraud in procuring the judgment, or any other special reason why the comity of this nation should not allow it full effect, the merits of the case should not, in an action brought in this country upon the judgment, be tried afresh . . . ".[4]

The Court then went on to hold that " . . . there is a distinct and independent ground upon which we are satisfied that the comity of our nation does not require us to give conclusive effect to the judgments of the courts of France; and that ground is want of reciprocity, on the part of France, as to the effect to be given to the judgments of this and other foreign countries."[5] Because France at that time did not regard American and other foreign judgments as conclusive, French judgments were not to be taken as conclusive here.[6]

This doctrine that, as another court put it, "courts are required to do, not as justice and reason require, but as they are done by,"[7] met with vigorous dissent by four members of the Court, and it would seem that the criticism was well founded. It may be granted that the methods of enforcement of foreign judgments in civil law countries differ from our

---

2. Johnston v. Compagnie Generale Transatlantique, 242 N.Y. 381, 152 N.E. 121 (1926). See Nippon Emo–Trans Co. (NET) v. Emo–Trans, Inc. (ETI), 744 F.Supp. 1215 (E.D.N.Y. 1990) holding that objection to foreign country's jurisdiction precluded collaterally after participating. See Joiner, The Recognition of Foreign Country Money Judgments by American Courts, 34 Am. J. Comp. L. 193 (Supp. 1986).

3. 159 U.S. 113, 16 S.Ct. 139, 40 L.Ed. 95 (1895).

4. 159 U.S. at 202–203, 16 S.Ct. at 158 (1895).

5. 159 U.S. at 210, 16 S.Ct. at 161 (1895).

6. The French practice of *revision au fond,* both as to questions of law and of fact, has meanwhile been abandoned. See infra § 24.38 n.10.

For the history of the comity doctrine, see Yntema, 65 Mich. L. Rev. 9 (1966). Comity does not necessarily have to include the reciprocity requirement, but Justice Gray in *Hilton* assumed that it did, 159 U.S. at 226–228, 16 S.Ct. at 167–168 and there are also statements in the literature to that effect: Cheatham, American Theories of Conflict of Laws: Their Role and Utility, 58 Harv. L. Rev. 361, 374 (1945).

7. Parsons, J., in MacDonald v. Grand Trunk Railway Co., 71 N.H. 448, 456, 52 A. 982, 986 (1902).

own.[8] So do many other rules of law, both in the conflict of laws and in other areas. But a court normally does not make its own rule dependent upon what the doctrine of a foreign state on a point may be nor varies its own rule according to the foreign conflict-of-laws rule. The effect of lack of reciprocity seems a political rather than a legal question.[9] As Fuller, C.J., said in his dissenting opinion in *Hilton:* "The application of the doctrine of res judicata does not rest in discretion; and it is for the government, and not for its courts, to adopt the principle of retorsion, if deemed under any circumstances desirable or necessary."[10]

Although the *Hilton* case is known for the reciprocity concept, the *Hilton* opinion itself limits its application to a very narrow situation. The Court noted that any foreign judgment would be conclusive if *in rem* or over status; or if payment had been made thereunder; or if between citizens of the foreign country; or if a citizen of the foreign country had sued a non-citizen and lost. Only where a suit by a citizen of the foreign country against a non-citizen results in a judgment for the former will it be reviewed when reciprocity is lacking. This is the only situation in which fraud would appear as a possibility.

Even the reciprocity doctrine, however, does call for conclusive effect to be given to English judgments and those of other jurisdictions governed by English law, by which a foreign judgment is allowed full and conclusive effect. The Supreme Court so held with respect to an Ontario judgment decided at the same time as the *Hilton* case.[11]

2.   *Recognition Practice After Hilton and Erie*

§ 24.35   Even before the Supreme Court's decisions in *Erie* and *Klaxon*,[1] the New York Court of Appeals refused to apply the *Hilton* doctrine. Noting that the Supreme Court itself had said that fraud in the procurement of the French judgment would have been sufficient ground for disregarding it, the New York Court said that "the preceding fifty-four pages of the opinion may be regarded as magnificent dictum."[2]

---

8.   Infra § 24.38. For a comparative survey see Juenger, The Recognition of Money Judgments in Civil and Commercial Matters, 36 Am. J. Comp. L. 1 (Supp. 1988). See Nadelmann, The Recognition of American Arrangements Abroad, 90 U. Pa. L. Rev. 70 (1942).

9.   See Note, 9 Harv. L. Rev. 430 (1896). See Banque Libanaise Pour Le Commerce v. Khreich, 915 F.2d 1000 (5th Cir.1990) applied "reciprocity requirement" to deny enforcement to a foreign judgment.

10.   Hilton v. Guyot, 159 U.S. 113, 234, 16 S.Ct. 139, 171, 40 L.Ed. 95 (1895).

11.   Ritchie v. McMullen, 159 U.S. 235, 16 S.Ct. 171, 40 L.Ed. 133 (1895). Accord: Alaska Commercial Co. v. Debney, 144 Fed. 1 (9th Cir.1906) (English judgment); Cruz v. O'Boyle, 197 Fed. 824 (M.D.Pa.1912)

(Mexican judgment); Fisher v. Fielding, 67 Conn. 91, 34 A. 714 (1895) (English judgment).

§ 24.35

1.   Erie Railroad Co. v. Tompkins, 304 U.S. 64, 58 S.Ct. 817, 82 L.Ed. 1188 (1938); Klaxon Co. v. Stentor Electric Manufacturing Co., 313 U.S. 487, 61 S.Ct. 1020, 85 L.Ed. 1477 (1941), reaffirmed in Day & Zimmermann, Inc. v. Challoner, 423 U.S. 3, 96 S.Ct. 167, 46 L.Ed.2d 3 (1975).

2.   Johnston v. Compagnie Generale Transatlantique, 242 N.Y. 381, 388, 152 N.E. 121, 123 (1926) (American plaintiff suing French defendant in New York held barred by French judgment for defendant). See also Cowans v. Ticonderoga Pulp and Paper Co., 219 App.Div. 120, 219 N.Y.S. 284

Hilton, moreover, had come to the Supreme Court from a lower federal court sitting in diversity. The decision, not resting on a federal question, therefore was not conclusive upon state courts and, with respect to federal courts thus announced a rule of federal common law. In 1938, the Supreme Court held in *Erie Railroad Co. v. Tompkins*[3] that federal courts have the constitutional obligation to apply the state law of the state in which they sit in diversity cases. In view of the broad sweep of the *Erie* doctrine, as extended to conflicts law by *Klaxon,*[4] the *Hilton* decision therefore probably no longer binds federal courts in diversity cases[5] and its authority seems negligible. As a result, a number of federal courts[6] as well as state courts[7] have declined to follow *Hilton* and regularly accord recognition to foreign-country judgments on essentially the same basis as sister-state judgments. On the other hand, a few jurisdictions have continued to adhere to *Hilton.*[8]

(1927), affirmed 246 N.Y. 603, 159 N.E. 669 (1927) (recovery allowed in New York against New York defendant on Quebec judgment).

3. 304 U.S. 64, 58 S.Ct. 817, 82 L.Ed. 1188 (1938).

4. Klaxon Co. v. Stentor Electric Manufacturing Co., 313 U.S. 487, 61 S.Ct. 1020, 85 L.Ed. 1477 (1941). For further discussion see supra § 3.36 et seq.

5. The question has been raised whether the Supreme Court's view with respect to impermissible state "intrusion . . . into the field of foreign affairs." Zschernig v. Miller, 389 U.S. 429, 432, 88 S.Ct. 664, 19 L.Ed.2d 683 (1968) might not suggest that the recognition of foreign-country judgments equally raises (federal) questions of foreign relations, thus preventing the states from pursuing independent policies. This view has been adopted by comment (c) to § 98 of the Restatement, Second, Conflict of Laws (1986 Revisions). However, no case has so held; on the contrary, a number of federal decisions clearly regard *Erie* as calling for the adoption of state law even though it departs from *Hilton.* See n.6 infra. Similarly, most state courts have now also departed from *Hilton,* see infra nn.7–8. In fact, the U.S. Supreme Court's decision in *Zschernig,* supra this note, has also been cited in support of the view that state courts may no longer require reciprocity. Scoles & Aarnas, The Recognition of Foreign Nation Judgments: California, Oregon, and Washington, 57 Ore. L.R. 377, 381 (1978). This reading of *Zschernig* may be too extensive, since the decision, on its facts, only prohibited the states, by statute or case law, from making *political* evaluations of foreign legal systems, without affecting the *Erie/Klaxon* doctrine in other respects. Federal preemption of this area therefore may be expected to occur mainly

as a result of recognition treaties (infra § 24.39) and possibly, but only remotely, of Congressional legislation. The lack of clarity and uniformity is, of course, unfortunate (see supra § 24.4) and should be redressed through federal legislation or treaty-making.

6. E.g., The Society of Lloyd's v. Turner, 303 F.3d 325 (5th Cir. 2002)(recognizing an English judgment by applying Texas version of the Uniform Foreign–Country Money Judgment Act); Bergman v. De Sieyes, 170 F.2d 360 (2d Cir. 1948); Svenska Handelsbanken v. Carlson, 258 F.Supp. 448 (D.Mass.1966); Mpiliris v. Hellenic Lines, Ltd., 323 F.Supp. 865 (S.D.Tex.1969), affirmed 440 F.2d 1163 (5th Cir.1971); Toronto–Dominion Bank v. Hall, 367 F.Supp. 1009 (E.D.Ark.1973). For literature see n.8 infra.

7. E.g., Johnston v. Compagnie Generale Transatlantique, 242 N.Y. 381, 152 N.E. 121 (1926); Scott v. Scott, 51 Cal.2d 249, 331 P.2d 641 (1958); In re Christoff's Estate, 411 Pa. 419, 192 A.2d 737 (1963); Watts v. Swiss Bank Corp., 27 N.Y.S.2d 270, 317 N.Y.S.2d 315, 265 N.E.2d 739 (1970); New Central Jute Mills Co., Limited v. City Trade and Industries, Limited, 65 Misc.2d 653, 318 N.Y.S.2d 980 (1971). See also Davidson & Co., Limited v. Allen, 89 Nev. 126, 508 P.2d 6 (1973). For literature see n.8. See generally Annot., 13 A.L.R. 4th 1109 (1982).

8. Despite an early decision that the *Hilton* doctrine would not be applied to common law countries that accept American decisions (Ritchie v. McMullen, 159 U.S. 235, 16 S.Ct. 171, 40 L.Ed. 133 (1895)), the doctrine was applied with respect to an English judgment in Leo Feist, Inc. v. Debmar Publishing Co., 232 F.Supp. 623 (D.Pa.

Absent federal preemption, by treaty or legislation, the trend is clearly away from *Hilton* and toward recognition similar to that of sister-state judgments.[9]

§ 24.36 The Uniform Foreign Money–Judgments Recognition Act (1962), which is now in force in several states,[1] provides for the recogni-

1964). Since Pennsylvania state law is contrary (In re Christoff's Estate, supra n.7), the decision may be explained on the ground that the judgment in question concerned copyright infringement and not a diversity matter. See also Brinco Mining Ltd. v. Federal Ins. Co., 552 F.Supp. 1233 (D.D.C.1982); Tahan v. Hodgson, 662 F.2d 862 (D.C.Cir. 1981); Toronto–Dominion Bank v. Hall, 367 F.Supp. 1009 (E.D.Ark. 1973); Cherun v. Frishman, 236 F.Supp. 292 (D.D.C.1964); Cannistraro v. Cannistraro, 352 Mass. 65, 223 N.E.2d 692 (1967). Statutory requirements of reciprocity exist in seven states. See infra § 24.36 n.1. The literature in this area is extensive. See, e.g., R.B. von Mehren & Patterson, Recognition and Enforcement of Foreign Country Judgments in the United States, 6 Law and Policy in Int'l Bus. 37 (1974); Scoles & Aarnas, supra n.5; Joiner, supra § 24.34 n.2; Juenger, supra § 24.34 n.8; Restatement (Third) Foreign Relations Law of the United States § 481–86 (1987). For an evaluation, see Hay, On Comity, Reciprocity, and Public Policy in U.S. and German Judgments Recognition Practice, in: Private Law in the International Arena–Liber Americorum, Kurt Siehr, 237–49 (J. Basedow et. al. (eds.) 2000).

As a matter of procedure, earlier practice required "legalization" of a foreign country judgment before it could be introduced into evidence. Legalization consists of consecutive certificates of authenticity: by the foreign judge, the clerk of the foreign court, the highest foreign judicial administration (such as a ministry of justice), and finally by the United States embassy in the particular foreign country. To simplify the process, the United States has adhered to the 1961 Hague Convention Abolishing the Requirement of Legalisation for Foreign Public Documents: T.I.A.S. 10072, Fed.Rule Civ. Proc., Rule 44 (entered into force Oct. 15, 1981). The Convention provides, and prescribes, a single standardized form of a certificate. It is in force in: Albania, Andorra, Antigua & Barbuda, Argentina, Armenia, Australia, Austria, Azerbaijan, The Bahamas, Barbados, Belarus, Belgium, Belize, Bosnia–Herzegovina, Botswana, Brunei, Bulgaria, China (only Hong Kong SAR & Macao SAR), Colombia, Croatia, Cyprus, Czech Republic, Dominica, El Salvador, Estonia, Fiji, Finland, France, Germany (Fed.

Rep.), Greece, Grenada, Honduras, Hungary, Ireland, Israel, Italy, Japan, Kazakhstan, Latvia, Lesotho, Liberia, Liechtenstein, Lithuania, Luxembourg, Macedonia (The former Yugoslav Republic of), Malawi, Malta, Marshall Islands, Mauritius, Mexico, Monaco, Namibia, The Netherlands, New Zealand, Niue, Norway, Panama, Portugal, Romania, Russian Federation, St. Kitts & Nevis, St. Lucia, St. Vincent & the Grenadines, Samoa, San Marino, Seychelles, Slovak. Rep., Serbia & Montenegro, Slovenia, South Africa, Spain, Suriname, Swaziland, Sweden, Switzerland, Tonga, Trinidad & Tobago, Turkey, United Kingdom, Ukraine, United States of America, Venezuela. (Jan. 1, 2003), and Website of the Hague Conference on Private International Law http://www.hcch.net (last visited June 21, 2004).

9. For bibliography of primary and secondary sources, also arranged by states and by subject matter, see Lutz, Enforcement of Foreign Judgments, 27 Int'l Law. 471 (Part I) (1993) and id. No. 4 (Part II) (Winter 1993). See also Hay, On Comity, Reciprocity, and Public Policy in U.S. and German Judgments Recognition Practice, in: Basedow et al. (eds.), Private Law in the International Arena–Liber Amicorum Kurt Siehr 237 (2000).

§ 24.36

1. 13 U.L.A.39 (Part II). The Act is in force in slightly more than half the states. A few versions of the Act require reciprocity. See, e.g., Col. Rev. Stat. Ann. § 13–62–102(1); Fla.Sta. Ann. § 55.605(2)(g); O.C. Ga. Ann. § 9–12–114(10); Idaho Code § 10–1404(2)(g); Mass. Gen. Laws Ann. ch. 235, § 23A; N.C.G.S. § 1C-1804(b)(7). Tex. Civil Practice and Remedies Code §§ 36.005(b)(7). The Colorado provision would recognize decision from a foreign governmental that has a reciprocal agreement with the United States. There is none at present. New Hampshire provides by statute for the recognition of Canadian judgments on the basis of reciprocity. N.H. Rev. Stat. Ann. 524.11. In Texas, the defense of lack of reciprocity failed in the context of the enforcement of an *Australian* judgment: Dart v. Balaam, 953 S.W.2d 478 (Tex.App.1997); *Canadian* judgments: Norkan Lodge Co. Ltd. v. Gillum, 587 F.Supp. 1457 (N.D.Tex.1984); Reading & Bates Const. Co. v. Baker Energy Resources

tion and enforcement "in the same manner as the judgment of a sister state which is entitled to full faith and credit" (§ 3) of foreign-country judgments which grant or deny the recovery of a sum of money[2] and which fulfill certain conditions. The latter include (§ 4): that the judgment was rendered in a legal system providing impartial tribunals "or procedures compatible with the requirements of due process ... ",[3] that the foreign court had personal jurisdiction over the defendant[4] as well as jurisdiction over the subject matter (§ 4(a)). A judgment, furthermore need not be recognized if obtained by fraud, if the foreign court was a

Corp., 976 S.W.2d 702 (Tex.App. 1998). Accord, with respect to *England*: Hunt v. BP Exploration Co. (Libya) Ltd., 580 F.Supp. 304 (N.D.Tex.1984); with respect to *Australia*: Dart v. Balaam, 953 S.W.2d 478 (Tex. App.1997).

For the manner of proving the authenticity of a foreign country judgment see supra § 24.35 n.8. See also, Lowenfeld, Conflict of Laws English Style—Review Essay, 37 Am. J. Comp. L. 353 (1989).

2. For an illustration see La Societe Anonyme Goro v. Conveyor Accessories, Inc., 286 Ill.App.3d 867, 677 N.E.2d 30 (1997). In view of the language quoted in the text, Illinois permits registration under the Uniform Enforcement of Foreign Judgments Act (supra § 24.13): see id.

In addition to excluding non-money judgments, the Act also does not apply to judgments for taxes, fines or penalties, or support judgments in matrimonial or family matters (§ 1(2)). As to taxes, see supra §§ 24.20 n.3, 24.23 n.7.

3. Section 4 distinguishes between foreign country judgments that are not entitled to recognition and therefore *need* not be recognized. The latter category includes judgments rendered without sufficient notice to the defendant. (§ 4(k)(1)). In view of *Mullane*, supra § 5.16, recognition in these circumstances would seem to violate the judgment debtor's due process rights and therefore *must* be denied. See similarly in European law, Regulation (EC) 44/2001, [2001] Official Journal L 012/1, Art. 34, No.2.

The provision of § 4(a)(i) a "must"-provision calling for an assessment of the foreign legal system as one providing "impartial tribunals and procedures,"-presumably as tested by American due-process standards, is troublesome.

In Bridgeway Corp. v. Citibank, 45 F.Supp.2d 276, 288 (S.D.N.Y.1999), aff'd 201 F.3d 134 (2d Cir.2000), the district court had entered summary judgment in favor of Citibank after concluding that the courts of Liberia were dominated by the political branches and did not afford a "system ... [for the] impartial administration of justice." The Court of Appeals reviewed the propriety of the procedures followed below and affirmed. It did not address a question that, arguably, could also have been raised: Is it permissible for state courts (or federal courts sitting in diversity) to undertake such a review and arrive at a negative finding or would the latter infringe the federal foreign relations power? See Hay, Weintraub & Borchers, Conflict of Laws, 704–22 (12th ed. 2004) (especially Zschernig v. Miller). Does the following type of case raise the same problem or is it distinguishable? In Aguinda v. Texaco, Inc., 2000 WL 122143 (S.D.N.Y.2000), the court (in a Memorandum Order) sought further input from the parties on the question of whether alleged military control of the judiciary of Ecuador made that country an inadequate alternative forum for purposes of a forum-non-conveniens dismissal. The court ultimately granted the forum-non-conveniens motion. 142 F.Supp.2d 534 (S.D.N.Y.2001).

4. Sec. 5(a) details six jurisdictional bases and provides that a foreign judgment based on one of them "shall not be refused recognition." They are: personal service in the jurisdiction, voluntary appearance, consent to jurisdiction, domicile or incorporation in the foreign jurisdiction, maintenance of a business in the foreign state (provided the claim arose from a transaction done by that business office), and claims arising out of the operation of a motor vehicle or airplane. Quite clearly, the Acts jurisdictional bases are much more limited than those recognized under modern long-arm statutes in the interstate setting. Supra §§ 8.32–8.35. Subsection (b) therefore provides that "courts of this state may recognize other bases of jurisdiction." See Restatement (Third) of the Foreign Re-

seriously inconvenient forum,[5] if the judgment conflicts with another judgment, violates the public policy of the recognizing forum[6] or an agreement to arbitrate (§ 4(b)).

§ 24.37 The Second Restatement now also reflects the trend toward recognition, although the formulation (in § 98) is more cautious than the language of the Uniform Act and of some of the cases. According to the Section, a "valid" foreign-country judgment will be recognized in this country if rendered after "a fair trial in a contested proceeding," but only insofar "as the immediate parties and the underlying cause of action is concerned."[1] The requirement of "validity" parallels the provision for interstate judgments,[2] while the requirement of contested proceedings excludes—contrary to some case law[3]—default judgments.[4] The limitation with respect to the "immediate parties and the underlying cause of action" expresses a certain uneasiness about

lations Law of the United States § 482, Reporters' Note 2 (1987).

5. This is not a valid defense in the interstate recognition of judgments. Despite the clear definition of "foreign state" in § 1 of the Act as excluding states of the United States, an Illinois appellate court considered this provision (§ 4(b)(6)) applicable to a case involving the recognition of a Florida judgment in Illinois but dismissed the defense (that Florida had been an inconvenient forum) on the merits. Southern Bell Telephone & Telegraph Co. v. Woodstock, Inc., 34 Ill.App.3d 86, 339 N.E.2d 423, 426 (1975). At least one other Illinois court has similarly applied the Act to a sister-state judgment. Salisbury Plumbing and Heating Co. v. Carpenter, 131 Ill.App.3d 829, 476 N.E.2d 15 (1985) (Florida judgment). Neither case has been overruled, although both holdings have been questioned. See Van Kooten Holding B.V. v. Dumarco Corp., 670 F.Supp. 227 (N.D.Ill.1987).

6. The public-policy defense ordinarily, but not always, is construed narrowly. See infra § 24.44. A New York court, however, took a wide view of the defense in Stein v. Siegel, 50 A.D.2d 916, 377 N.Y.S.2d 580 (1975). The court refused to treat an Austrian decree of discontinuance containing a waiver of a claim as constituting a bar to a New York action on the same claim because, under New York law, "a discontinuance by any method is ordinarily without prejudice to the commencement of a new action" and "a foreign country judgment will not be recognized by our courts insofar as it contravenes the public policy of this State." 50 A.D.2d 916, 377 N.Y.S.2d 580, 582. Since the Austrian decree incorporated a waiver, it was therefore not a decree for the "recovery of money" and the Act did not apply. However, the court did not rely

on this exception (§ 4(b)(3)), but on general law, stating—inexplicably—that nonrecognition for violation of local public policy was "a matter of comity." Id. For further discussion of the public policy defense, see infra § 24.44 n.2.

§ 24.37

1. See also supra § 24.3 with respect to the preclusive effect of foreign-country judgments, and supra § 24.35 n.9.

2. Restatement, Second, Conflict of Laws § 93 (1971). Section 92 defines validity: the court rendering the judgment must have had jurisdiction, have been a "competent court" under the law of the rendering forum, have employed a reasonable method to give notice and afforded a reasonable opportunity to be heard, and have complied with any other requirements established by the law of the state of rendition.

3. E.g., Somportex Limited v. Philadelphia Chewing Gum Corp., 453 F.2d 435 (3d Cir.1971), cert. denied 405 U.S. 1017, 92 S.Ct. 1294, 31 L.Ed.2d 479 (1972); British Midland Airways Limited v. International Travel, Inc., 497 F.2d 869 (9th Cir.1974); Tahan v. Hodgson, 662 F.2d 862 (D.C.Cir. 1981) (Israeli default judgment). But see Koster v. Automark Industries, Inc., 640 F.2d 77 (7th Cir.1981) (denying recognition to a Dutch default judgment on the basis of insufficient contacts to confer jurisdiction and insufficient provisions for notice to the absent defendant); Restatement, Second, Conflict of Laws § 93, comnt. (d) (1971).

4. But Restatement, Second, Conflict of Laws, comnt. (d) (1971), approving the recognition of valid in rem or quasi in rem default judgments and expressing some uncertainty with respect to in personam judg-

automatic recognition of foreign notions of privity and collateral estoppel as well as the res judicata effect to be accorded a foreign finding of jurisdiction.[5] However, as discussed previously,[6] the modern trend supports the view that there is little reason why the concept of conclusive determination—as reflected in the doctrines of res judicata and preclusion by prior litigation—should not be applied to foreign litigation involving U.S. citizens absent a showing of lack of jurisdiction or of a fraudulent imposition of jurisdiction.[7]

3. *Foreign Approaches and Their Implications for U.S. Recognition Practice*

§ 24.38 *English common law,* like United States practice, envisions an action on the foreign judgment for the latter's recognition and enforcement. As in the United States, enforcement presupposes that the foreign court had jurisdiction according to English standards, that the judgment was not procured by fraud and does not violate English public policy.[1] Recognition by statute is available under the Administration of Justice Act of 1920 (reciprocal enforcement of United Kingdom and Commonwealth judgments[2]), the Foreign Judgments (Reciprocal Enforcement) Act of 1933, and the Civil Jurisdiction and Judgments Act of 1982. The 1933 Act applies to judgments of courts of Commonwealth and foreign nations specified by Order in Council. A number of countries, but not the United States, have been so specified.[3] The 1982 Act implemented[4] the Brussels Convention on Jurisdiction and the Enforcement of Judgments in Civil and Commercial Matters with respect to the member states of the European Communities and of the European Free Trade

ments. See n.3 supra. With respect to foreign quasi-in-rem judgments the comment may have to be reevaluated in the light of Shaffer v. Heitner, 433 U.S. 186, 97 S.Ct. 2569, 53 L.Ed.2d 683 (1977).

5. Restatement, Second, Conflict of Laws § 98, comment (f) (1971).

6. Supra §§ 24.3–24.4, especially also § 24.3 n.13.

7. See particularly Scoles, Interstate and International Distinctions in Conflict of Laws in the United States, 54 Cal. L. Rev. 1599, 1606 (1966); Blom, The Enforcement of Foreign Judgments in Canada, 57 Oregon L. Rev. 399 (1978). See also Hunt v. BP Exploration Co. (Libya), 580 F.Supp. 304 (N.D.Tex.1984). For a review of U.S. practice from a foreign perspective, see Quintin, La reconnaissance et l'exécution des jugements étrangers en droit américain, 74 Revue critique de droit international privé 433 (1985); Hay, On Comity, Reciprocity, and Public Policy in U.S. and German Judgments Recognition Practice, in: Basedow et al. (eds.), Private Law in the International

Arena–Liber Amicorum Kurt Siehr 237 (2000).

§ 24.38

1. Dicey & Morris, The Conflict of Laws 469 (13th ed. 2000 by Collins et al.); Graveson, Conflict of Laws 619–635 (7th ed. 1974).

2. Botswana, Cyprus, Falkland Islands, Ghana, Gibraltar, Jamaica, Kenya, Malawi, Malaysia, Malta, Newfoundland, New Zealand, Nigeria, Saskatchewan, Singapore, Sri Lanka, Trinidad, Tanzania, Uganda, Zambia, Zimbabwe.

3. Austria, Australia, Canada, Guernsey, India, Isle of Man, Israel, Jersey, Norway, and Pakistan. The Act no longer applies to Austria, Belgium, France, Germany, Italy, the Netherlands, Norway (see note 5 infra) (except as to matters outside the purview of the EEC ("Brussels I") Regulation and Lugano Conventions), Suriname, Tonga.

4. The Act also replaces the Judgments Extension Act of 1868 (which provided for

Association (the latter being included as a result of the "Parallel" (Lugano) Convention of 1988).[5] The 1920 and 1933 Acts contemplate money judgments (as does the Uniform Act in the United States) and reciprocity. However, the view has been expressed that foreign judgments "are in practice enforceable at common law much more easily than they are in many foreign countries,"[6] primarily because defenses— e.g., that enforcement would be contrary to public policy—are narrowly construed.

In response to growing concerns about U.S. antitrust jurisdiction and awards, the Protection of Trading Interests Act of 1980 denies recognition to antitrust judgments and, in certain circumstances, allows the defendant in the foreign proceeding to recover from the plaintiff's British assets any treble damages he has had to pay.[7] *Recognition treaties,* such as the treaty that had been proposed with the United States (discussed below), ensure more uniform and reciprocal recognition of judgments.

registration of judgments from Scotland and Northern Ireland).

5. The individual provisions of the Act came into force at various dates since 1982 as specified by commencement orders. An earlier order, the European Communities (Enforcement of Community Judgments) Order 1972, S.I. 1972, No. 1590, provided for the registration of judgments and awards of the institutions of the Communities but not, at that time, of national judgments. For the 2001 E.C. Regulation, see infra § 24.38.

For comprehensive treatment see Hartley, Civil Jurisdiction and Judgments (1984); Stone, The Civil Jurisdiction and Judgments Act 1982, 32 Int'l & Comp. L.Q. 477 (1983); Lipstein, Enforcement of Judgments Under the Jurisdiction and Judgments Convention: Safeguards, 36 Int'l & Comp. L.Q. 873 (1987). For the practice in Commonwealth countries see K.W. Patchett, Recognition of Commercial Judgments and Awards in the Commonwealth (1984). On the Lugano Convention, extending the then Brussels Convention to the members of EFTA, see Droz, La Convention de Lugano parallèle la Convention de Bruxelles concernant la compétence judiciaire et l'exécution des décisions en matière civile et commerciale, 78 Revue critique de droit internationale privé 1 (1989). For an evaluation of the substantive differences in the three Conventions, see A. Trunk, Die Erweiterung des EuGVÜ–Systems am Vorabend des Europäischen Binnenmarktes (1991). Selected problems are also treated in the Court of Justice of the European Communities (ed.), Civil Jurisdiction and Judgments in Europe (1992). The Brussels Convention was replaced by binding Euro-

pean Community Law in 2002. See infra n.18

6. Dicey & Morris, supra n.1, at 471. See also Briggs, Which Foreign Judgments Should We Recognize Today?, 36 Int'l & Comp. L.Q. 240 (1987); Campbell & Popat, Enforcing American Money Judgments in the United Kingdom and Germany, 18 S. Ill. U.L.J. 517 (1994).

7. 1980, c. 11. For comment see Lowe, Blocking Extraterritorial Jurisdiction: The British Protection of Trading Interests Act, 1980, 75 Am. J. Int'l L. 257 (1981); Lowenfeld, Sovereignty, Jurisdiction, and Reasonableness: A Reply to A.V. Lowe, 75 Am. J. Int'l L. 619 (1981); Note, Power to Reverse Foreign Judgments: The British Clawback Statute Under International Law, 81 Colum. L. Rev. 1097 (1981); Davidson, U.S. Secondary Sanctions: The U.K. and EU Response, 27 Stetson L. Rev. 1425 (1998). See also Price, Foreign Blocking Statutes and the GATT: State Sovereignty and the Enforcement of U.S. Economic Laws Abroad, 28 Geo. Wash. J. Int'l. L. & Econ. 315 (1995). The English statute now has counterparts in Australia and Canada: Foreign Proceedings (Excess of Jurisdiction) Act 1984 (Australia); Foreign Extraterritorial Measures Act (Canada, entered into force February 14, 1985). See also Drolshammer & Schärer, Die Verletzung des materiellen ordre public als Verweigerungsgrund bei der Vollstreckung eines amerikanischen "punitive damages"-Urteils, 1986 Schweizerische Juristenzeitung 305 (reporting decision refusing recognition, on public policy grounds, to U.S. decision awarding punitive damages).

In *Canada,* section 10(1) of the Reciprocal Enforcement of Judgments Act, which is in force in every territory and Province except Quebec, also requires reciprocity. In contrast, the Canadian Foreign Judgments Act, in force only in New Brunswick and Saskatchewan, does not require reciprocity. This Act is in accord with English *common law,* with respect to which it is said that "recognition and enforcement of a foreign judgment takes place *ex debito justitiae* and reciprocity has nothing to do with it."[8]

Civil law countries provide a procedure to give executory force (*exequatur*) to the foreign judgment as distinguished from the Anglo–American common law (but not statutory) practice of requiring an action on the judgment.[9] During the *exequatur* proceeding the judgment debtor may resist the enforcement of the foreign judgment on a number of grounds, among them lack of reciprocity[10] and violation of local public policy, a concept which has received an extensive interpretation and application in some countries.[11]

8. J.-G. Castel, Canadian Conflict of Laws 412 (1st ed. 1975) (citing Russel v. Smyth, (1842) 9 M. & W. 810, 819; Williams v. Jones, (1845) 13 M. & W. 628, 633). Compare also Castel, Canadian Conflict of Laws 301 (4th ed. 1997); Kennedy, Recognition of Judgments *in Personam:* The Meaning of Reciprocity, 35 Can. B. Rev. 123 (1957); Glenn, Foreign Judgments, the Common Law and the Constitution: De Savoye v. Morguard Investments Ltd., 37 McGill L.J. 537 (1992).

9. For description of the recognition practice of the six original European Community countries (Belgium, France, Germany, Italy, Luxembourg, and the Netherlands) see M. Weser, Convention communautaire sur la compétence judiciaire et l'exécution des décisions 131 et seq. (1975). In some countries recognition of foreign judgments is available only in few cases in the absence of a treaty. See Netherlands Wetboek van burgerlijke rechtsvordering Art. 431(1)-(2). For recognition practice in Central America, see R. Casad, Civil Judgment Recognition and the Integration of Multiple–State Associations 67–135 (1981).

10. See, e.g., German Code of Civil Procedure § 328(1), No. 5; for Italy, see Italian Code of Civil Procedure Art. 4(4). The older German case law, moreover, required actual rather than mere statutory guarantees of reciprocity. Thus, the German Supreme Court held in 1909 that the California provision ensuring recognition of foreign judgments (now West's Ann. Cal. Civ. Proc. Code § 1115) was not enough in the absence of evidence showing reciprocity in practice. RGZ 70, 434 (1909). The German Supreme Court still applied a strict test in

1969: BGHZ 52, 251 (1969) with respect to South Africa. For more liberal decisions, see BGHZ 50, 100 (1968) with respect to France, and in [1992] Wertpapiermitteilungen 1451, and discussion by Hay, 40 Am. J.Comp.L. 729 (1992).

11. French courts formerly subjected foreign judgments to a *"révision au fond,"* a review on the merits, but abandoned the practice in 1964. Munzer v. Jacoby–Munzer, [1964] Bull. des arrts de la Cour de Cass., ch. civ I, No. 15; Nadelmann, French Courts Recognize Foreign Money–Judgments–One Down and More To Go, 13 Am. J. Comp. L. 72 (1964). Nevertheless, the Cour de Cassation, in the *Munzer* decision above, still detailed five preconditions to recognition: jurisdiction of the foreign court, regularity of procedure adopted by that court, application of a law regarded as applicable by French conflicts law, compliance with international public policy, and absence of evasion of mandatory rules of law. The concept of public policy is quite broad; in fact, the Court of Appeal of Paris expressed the opinion in 1956 that the concept was broad enough to obviate the need for a separate *"révision au fond."* Charr v. Hazim Ulusahim, [1956] D. Jurisp. I, 61. But see Delaume, International Arbitration under French law, 37 Arbitration J. 38, 42 (1982): "The French courts . . . have significantly relaxed French notions of public policy concerning international transactions, and in particular arbitration. . . . French courts show great restraint in relying on public policy to deny recognition and enforcement to foreign arbitral awards." It is possible that stricter standards continue to apply with respect to foreign judgments which are not based on a consent to submit

The *German* Supreme Court has adopted a liberal attitude toward the recognition and enforcement of American money judgments in Germany.[12] It (a) readily acknowledged that the German requirement of reciprocity was satisfied (in this case in relation to California) and that (b) an award of damages for pain and suffering in an amount 11 times greater than a likely domestic award did not offend German public policy in circumstances where the tort had occurred in California and involved parties domiciled there at the relevant time. It left open how it would view such an award in a case bearing a closer factual connection to Germany. Expressing the traditional European distaste for U.S. punitive damages, the Court refused to recognize and enforcement that part of the American judgment but left open the possibility of recognizing such portions of punitive damage awards in the future that could be shown to have an identifiable compensatory aspect, for example, to shift the plaintiff's obligation for contingent attorneys' fees to the defendant.[13]

In relation with each other, civil-law countries have traditionally maintained an extensive network of bilateral and multilateral recognition-of-judgments treaties.[14]

to the foreign court's jurisdiction. With respect to judgments of courts of other states of the European Union, *révision au fond* is now proscribed. Regulation (EC) 44/2001, infra n. 18, Art. 36.

For Eastern Europe see also Seiffert, Anerkennung und Vollstreckung ausländischer Entscheidungen in Osteuropa (1994). For South America see Möllring, Anerkennung und Vollstreckung ausländischer Urteile in Südamerika (1985). For Mexico see Evans, Enforcement of U.S. Judgments in Mexico: Illusion or Reality, 64 Tex. B. J. 138 (2001).

12. Judgment of June 4, 1992, BGHZ 118, 328, [1992] Wertpapiermitteilungen 1451.

13. For comment see Hay, The Recognition and Enforcement of American Money–Judgments in Germany, 40 Am. J. Comp. L. 729 (1992); Schack, Annot., 106 Zeitschrift für Zivilprozeï 104 (1993); Bungert, Annot., [1992] Zeitschrift für Wirtschaftsrecht 1707.

In another recognition-favoring decision, the German Supreme Court went beyond what American law would require or even permit in interstate practice. It held that a U.S. federal court's default judgment in a diversity case would satisfy the German jurisdictional test of § 328 No. 1 ZPO (Code of Civil Procedure) for judgment recognition if the United States, as a whole, would have jurisdiction by German standards. It dismissed as irrelevant, for recognition purposes, the division of the United States into states. As a result, a federal court's default judgment, rendered without personal juris-

diction over the defendant (by American standards) might be entitled to recognition in Germany on the basis of the broader "national jurisdiction" view of German law. BGH, Judgment of April 22, 1999, 2001 IPRax 2001 230, 232, with comment by Haas (without reference to American literature) id. at 195. By American standards, this decision—however favorable to American judgments—is clearly wrong. For criticism, see Wazlawik, Anerkennung von US-amerikanischen Urteilen: Bundes-oder Gesamtstaat–wer ist Urteilsstaat im Rahmen von § 328 I Nr.1 ZPO?, [2002] IPRax 273. Indeed, enforcement of a judgment by a court without jurisdiction by American standards, would violate the judgment debtor's due-process rights and, in turn, support a claim for restitution and damages for amounts paid under foreign compulsion.

In a 1994 decision, the German Constitutional Court held that the possibility of punitive damages in an American civil suit did not bar German judicial assistance in serving the documents initiating suit. [1995] Neue Juristische Wochenschrift 649. However, in 2003, the Court issued a preliminary injunction against service of such documents in an American class action seeking in excess of $80 billion because it considered the amount sought to be totally unrelated to any actual damage suffered and the action therefore an abuse of judicial process to force a settlement. Decision of July 25, 2003, [2003] IPRax No.5 at vii-x. For punitive damages in the context of European Community law, see infra § 24–39 n.16.

14. See Jellinek, Die zweiseitigen Staatsverträge über Anerkennung ausländischer

The European Community countries participated in the most far-reaching of these Conventions ("Brussels Convention")[15] which was justly called Europe's "full faith and credit clause."[16] By means of the "Parallel" (Lugano) Convention of 1988, it was extended to the then members of the European Free Trade Association (Austria, Finland, Iceland, Norway, Sweden, and Switzerland).[17] With the accession of Austria, Finland and Sweden to the EU, these states became members of the Brussels Convention. Either directly, or by way of the Lugano Convention, the common provisions were thus in effect in eighteen countries. As of March 1, 2002, a Community Regulation (in effect, equivalent to a federal statute in the United States) replaced the Brussels Convention in all Member States, except Denmark, which exercised its right to opt out. The new entrants to the EU in 2004 are subject to the Regulation.[18]

Zivilurteile (= Beiträge zum ausländischen und internationalen Privatrecht 1963); Weser, supra n.9, at 145 et seq.

15. A revised and updated version of the Convention is reproduced in [1998] O.J. C 27/1. For analysis see the literature cited in n.5 supra and Weser, supra n.9. See also Hay, The Common Market Preliminary Draft Convention on the Recognition and Enforcement of Judgments—Some Considerations of Policy and Interpretation, 16 Am. J. Comp. L. 149 (1968). A less ambitious convention—but designed for wider acceptance—was proposed by the Hague Conference on Private International Law in 1966. 5 Int. Leg. Mat. 636 (1966), 15 Am. J. Comp. L. 362 (1967). The convention did not enter into effect for lack of the requisite number of ratifications. For comparative analysis of the Hague, EC, and the earlier proposal for a U.S.–U.K. convention see Hay & Walker, Le projet anglo-americain de Convention sur la reconnaissance des décisions et la Convention Communautaire, [1977] Cahiers de droit européen 3. For the project of a worldwide jurisdiction and recognition convention to draw on the experience with all of these see generally Symposium, Enforcing Judgments Abroad: The Global Challenge, 24 Brooklyn J. Int'l L. 1 (1998). The project is currently suspended.

The Organization of American States sponsored the Inter–American Convention on Extraterritorial Validity of Foreign Judgments and Arbitral Awards, 18 Int. Legal Mat. 1224 (1979) (in force in Argentina, Colombia, Ecuador, Mexico, Paraguay, Peru, Uruguay, and Venezuela). Unlike European Community law, the Inter–American convention does not provide uniform

rules of jurisdiction which, if satisfied, would ensure the recognition of a judgment in another contracting state. Instead, the convention provides for recognition when the rendering court exercised jurisdiction in a manner "substantially equivalent to that accepted by the law of the [recognizing state] . . . " Art. 2(e); see also Art. 2(d). For commentary see Casad, supra n.9, at 169–81.

16. Bartlett, Full Faith and Credit Comes to the Common Market: An Analysis of the Convention on Jurisdiction and Enforcement of Judgments in Civil and Commercial Matters, 24 Int'l & Comp. L.Q. 44 (1975).

17. Official Journal of the EC No. 88/L 319/9 (Nov. 25, 1988). For analysis see Droz, supra n.5.

18. Council Regulation (EC) No.44/2001 on Jurisdiction and the Recognition of Judgments in Civil and Commercial Matters, [2001] Official Journal L 012/1. The authority for the promulgation of such a regulation was conferred upon the Community by the revision of the European Union (and European Community) Treaties by the 1999 Treaty of Amsterdam. However, Denmark, Ireland, and the United Kingdom are not bound by measures adopted pursuant to the enlarged competences, unless they elect to "opt in." Ireland and the United Kingdom chose to opt into Council Regulation 44/2001, Denmark did not. As to Denmark, the Brussels Convention will continue in effect in its relations to the rest of the Community. The Lugano Convention, of course, continues in effect, as between the Brussels/Regulation area and countries not party to that area but party to the Lugano Convention, most importantly: Switzerland.

European Community law eliminates as to all members (except Denmark), all of such obstacles to recognition as, for instance, reciprocity and *"révision au fond."* These restrictions, of course, continue to be obstacles to the recognition of U.S. judgments in these countries. The diversity of recognition practices followed by the several states of the U.S. may contribute to the problem. For instance, when a foreign jurisdiction requires reciprocity, the foreign court must evaluate the law of the particular U.S. state of rendition in order to determine whether the requirement has been satisfied. For these reasons alone, it is desirable that the United States speak internationally with one voice rather than with more than 50. The conclusion of a jurisdiction and recognition convention with EU and EFTA states would also permit the United States to obtain agreement on the removal of exorbitant bases of jurisdiction.[19] Thus, in the 1984 Convention between Canada and the United Kingdom on the reciprocal recognition of judgments,[20] the United Kingdom undertook not to recognize judgments rendered against persons habitually resident in Canada that are based on specified exorbitant jurisdictional grounds.

The new law, known widely as the "Brussels I Regulation,"[21] mainly parallels the Brussels Convention, but does revise it in a number of important respects.

Substantively, the principal changes effected by the new Regulation are:

Contract claims. The difficult provision of prior law (Art. 5(1)) for specific jurisdiction for contracts (place of performance of the characteristic obligation, with place of performance to be determined by the applicable conflicts law) has been simplified for two types of contracts. For sales and service contracts, the applicable law (as that of the "closest connection") is the law of the place of actual (or stipulated) delivery of goods or of rendition of services. For all other contracts, the previous rules continue to apply. The two changes do provide clear guidance. However, the problem is that a vendee's place of business will now often have jurisdiction under these rules, while, substantively, it may be the vendor's law that might be applicable under the Vienna Convention on the International Sale of Goods[22] among participating states within the European Community, under the Rome Convention.[23] This falling apart of jurisdiction and applicable law may create some difficulties of practical application in cases involving a non-Community party whose national law

---

New members of the EU, for instance those states that joined the EU in 2004, must accept Community law as it exists at the time of accession, therefore including Regulation 44/2001.

19. Supra n.16 and infra § 24.39 n.4.

20. S.C. 1984, c. 32. For brief discussion of this Convention see Castel, Canadian Conflict of Laws 312–14 (4th ed. 1997).

21. "Brussels II" is a Regulation dealing with divorce and custody jurisdiction. See supra § 15.43 n.2.

22. Entered into force for U.S. by 52 Fed. Reg. 6262 (1987) 1987 WL 128849 (F.R.); 15 U.S.C.A. App. (2004).

23. See supra § 18.40.

may become applicable (and difficult to determine) in an action pending in a national court in the European Community.

Consumer contracts. The Brussels Convention provided for jurisdiction over consumers at their habitual residence if three conditions had been met. Two required specific forum contacts: solicitation (in general or consumer-directed) in the consumer's state, the other that the consumer concluded (took the last step toward conclusion of) the contract in his/her state of habitual residence. The new law (Regulation 44/2001) requires a much lower forum-nexus: the provider need only have directed business activity to the forum—"by any means" and not directed specifically at the plaintiff-consumer—and the latter need no longer have concluded the contract (through a particular act of acceptance) in his or her state.

The potentially extensive reach of these rules has raised widespread concern. What about offers via Internet websites, especially interactive ones? Consider this case: A consumer from country A acts on a website offer-available in countries A and B (the latter an EC country)-while in B, specifying delivery in C (another EC country). (1) Suit *by* the consumer: at his or her residence in all cases, provided that the offering company, if a non-EC company, at least maintains a branch in the EC: such a company will be deemed to be "domiciled" in the European Community for purposes of consumer suits. As outlined above, "any" activity in the EC by the defendant, including through the Internet will do; the fact that the consumer may have placed the order from outside his or her state of habitual residence makes no difference. No wonder that this provision was vigorously opposed prior to adoption. It remains to be seen whether any US-type due process/foreseeability ideas will applied by the European Court in the interpretation and application of these rules. Suits *against* consumers, as under the Brussels Convention, are largely limited to the place of their habitual residence.

Changes in technology. Art. 23 of the Regulation [which replaces Art. 17 of the Brussels Convention] deals with forum selection clauses and the prerequisites they must fulfill for their validity. One from among three, stated in the alternative, is a writing. Article 23(2) states: "Any communication by electronic means which provides a durable record of the agreement shall be equivalent to 'writing'."

Article 60. This Article of the Regulation narrows the choices for the determination of a legal person's "domicile" for jurisdictional purposes and, in doing so, more closely parallels the EC Treaty's own provision (in Art. 48). The divergence in national corporate law (seat theory vs. law of incorporation, see supra § 23.1) is not addressed by this provision.

Enforcement. Under the Brussels Convention recognition and enforcement took place—primarily—at the trial level. Defenses to recognition, for instance, lack of jurisdiction of the court of rendition, could and would be raised there. Under the new law (Regulation 44/2001), the trial court orders execution upon presentation of the rendering court's jurisdiction. Defenses can be raised only upon appeal. Arts. 41, 45.

In 1992, the United States proposed that the Hague Conference on Private International Law resume work toward the drafting of a recognition and enforcement of judgments convention that would be open for potentially worldwide acceptance. Because of considerable differences in national laws, progress was difficult and slow. While the Brussels Convention—now Regulation—could state clear jurisdictional rules and then mandate recognition of judgments based on these rules, the Hague proposals were more tentative, leaving some jurisdictional matters unresolved and, therefore, to the continued application of national law. In those cases (i.e., jurisdictional bases that were left unaddressed, the so-called "Grey list"—neither permitted, nor prohibited), recognition of judgments would not be mandated but likewise be left to national law.[24] Because of the considerable differences among national positions, negotiations stalled and are presently suspended.

4. Federal Preemption by Recognition Treaty

§ 24.39 Neither Congress nor the federal courts may be expected to federalize conflicts law in general.[1] However, with respect to international conflicts law, isolated decisions have established uniform rules[2] and, following the example of foreign countries, the federal government has considered the conclusion of bilateral[3] treaties for the reciprocal recognition of judgments. Such treaties would overcome the obstacles to the recognition of U.S. judgments abroad which were noted above and, in

---

24. For an evaluation, from the perspective of German law, of the problems (and opportunities) presented by such a project, see Schack, Perspektiven eines weltweiten Anerkennungs-und Vollstreckungsabkommen, 1 Zeitschrift für Europäisches Privatrecht 306 (1993). For an American view, see Silberman, Comparative Jurisdiction in the International Context: Will the Proposed Hague Judgments Convention be Stalled?, 52 DePaul L.Rev. 319 (2002). For the "White," "Black," and "Grey" lists, see infra § 24.39 nn.13–14.

§ 24.39

1. See Cheatham & Maier, Private International Law And Its Sources, 22 Vand. L. Rev. 27, 61 (1968); Hay, Unification of Law in the United States: Uniform State Laws, Treaties and Judicially Declared Federal Common Law, in: Legal Thought in the United States of America Under Contemporary Pressures 261, 290–92 (J. Hazard & W. Wagner, eds., 1970). See also supra §§ 3.49–3.55.

2. See Zschernig v. Miller, 389 U.S. 429, 88 S.Ct. 664, 19 L.Ed.2d 683 (1968).

3. The only multilateral convention presently open to adoption by the United States is the Hague Convention of 1966. See supra § 24.38 n.13. There is substantial agreement that the Hague Convention would not meet United States needs. See Nadelmann & von Mehren, The Extraordinary Session of the Hague Conference on Private International Law, 60 Am. J. Int'l L. 803 (1966); Nadelmann, The Common Market Judgment Convention and a Hague Conference Recommendation: What Steps Next?, 82 Harv. L. Rev. 1282 (1969); Nadelmann, Recommendation Relating to the Convention on Recognition of Judgments, 16 Am. J. Comp. L. 601 (1968). See generally Symposium, Enforcing Judgments Abroad: The Global Challenge, 24 Brooklyn J. Int'l L. 1 (1998). The current project for a worldwide convention has its origin in an initiative of the United States but thus far there is little to suggest that these efforts will produce a convention that the U.S. is likely to sign. See supra § 24.38 at n.25.

the case of the European Community, would neutralize the potentially adverse effects of intra-EU jurisdiction and recognition of judgments law.[4]

A first attempt at a bilateral treaty was initiated in 1977 between the United States and the United Kingdom. However, and despite several years of revisions and attempts at accommodation, it failed to be adopted. The main reason was increasing British reluctance to facilitate easy recognition of U.S. judgments in the United Kingdom, in part because of the high level of U.S. awards in products liability cases and because of the wide reach of U.S. antitrust jurisdiction (possibly leading to treble damages).[5] A brief review of the draft convention's provision may nevertheless be instructive because it illustrates how recognition practice could be structured and uniformity achieved by means of international agreements.

The convention would have excluded judgments relating to status and family law generally, maintenance claims, succession, bankruptcy, certain corporate matters, duties, taxes, punitive or multiple damages and non-binding judgments. For judgments to which it would have applied, mainly-but not exclusively-binding money judgments, the Convention established jurisdictional criteria which, if satisfied in the original proceeding, would have entitled the resulting judgment to recognition and enforcement in the other jurisdiction by the "most rapid procedure provided . . . for the enforcement of non-local judgments."[6] In its catalog of jurisdictional bases, the Convention broke new ground (as compared to the American Uniform Act and the English Judgments Act) by recognizing jurisdiction over certain subject matters as an acceptable ground separate from personal jurisdiction.[7] While the treaty partners were obligated to recognize judgments based on the jurisdictional

---

4. The EC and Parallel Conventions as well as the EC Regulation supra § 24.38 nn.13, 15, 18 generalize—in favor of any plaintiff domiciled in the contracting states—the "exorbitant bases of jurisdiction" available in any one of them (supra § 24.6 n.5) against nondomiciliary defendants, but excludes the use of such exorbitant jurisdiction against domiciliary defendants. The Conventions and the Regulation do permit Member States to conclude bilateral conventions with non-member states by which they undertake not to enforce judgments against nationals of the latter if such a judgment would not be enforceable against a local domiciliary. Supra § 24.38 n.16. The proposal for a convention between the United States and the United Kingdom took advantage of this option in its Article 18. See Hay & Walker, The Proposed Recognition-of-Judgments Convention Between the United States and the United Kingdom, 11 Tex. Int'l L.J. 421, 444 (1976).

5. See supra § 24.38 n.7; Schack, Entscheidungszuständigkeiten in einem weltweiten Gerichtsstands- und Vollstreckungsübereinkommen, 6 Zeitschrift für Europäisches Privatrecht 931 (1998).

6. Art. 16. In the case of the United States, this provision might have resulted in the application of the summary procedure available under the Uniform Enforcement of Foreign Judgments Act (supra § 24.13). Locally available defenses permitted under the Act, however, would not have been available against an English judgment: the Convention itself specified available defenses and provided in Art. 9 that "Except as permitted by this Convention, there shall be no review of the judgment. . . ." See Hay & Walker, supra n.4, at 448. This issue is again relevant in the context of the project of a worldwide convention.

7. Id. at 435–49.

grounds specified, they remained free to grant recognition to judgments based on other, additional grounds.[8]

The Convention contained the usual list of defenses to recognition.[9] Of particular interest was the provision of Article 8(4) that allowed denial of recognition if the court of rendition had failed to apply mandatory rules of law of the recognizing forum which would have been applicable to the case under the choice-of-law rules of the latter had the case first been litigated there. This provision served to safeguard, *inter alia,* mandatory provisions of the Uniform Commercial Code. Since the U.C.C. is state law, and since state law may differ as to which provisions of the particular state version of the U.C.C. are mandatory, this reference to the law of the recognizing forum potentially might have been the source of renewed lack of uniformity.[10]

The "Preliminary Draft Convention on Jurisdiction and Foreign Judgments in Civil and Commercial Matters" (1999) of the Hague Conference on Private International Law sought to deal with judgment recognition on a worldwide basis.[11] The United States participated in the drafting. At this point, however, differences in national positions have caused negotiations to be suspended and prospects seem dim for adoption and ratification of a convention.[12] Nevertheless, some of its features are nonetheless noteworthy even now because they may pave the way for future work.

In many important respects, the Preliminary Draft Convention paralleled, indeed borrowed verbatim from, the Brussels Convention, in at least one case also from the Rome Convention, and, in some cases, improved upon its models. In contrast, it obviously needed to take account of the fact that far less closely related legal systems might come

---

8. Art. 3. This provision parallels Art. 5(b) of the U.S. Uniform Foreign Money–Judgments Recognition Act. See supra § 24.36 n.3. For discussion of the general problem of whether an American court should recognize a foreign court's jurisdiction by application of its own jurisdictional standards to the *facts* of the case, even though the foreign court had invoked different and possibly unacceptable jurisdictional grounds, see Hay, International versus Interstate Conflicts Law in the United States, 35 Rabels Zeitschrift für ausländisches und internationales Privatrecht 429, 450 n.101 (1971) (in English). See Nippon Emo–Trans Co., Ltd. v. Emo–Trans, Inc., 744 F.Supp. 1215 (E.D.N.Y.1990) (Japan had jurisdiction by New York standards).

9. See infra §§ 24.41 et seq.

10. Hay & Walker, supra n.4, at 442, 450. For further discussion of the Convention see Smit, The Proposed United States–United Kingdom Convention on Recognition and Enforcement of Foreign Judg-

ments: A Prototype for the Future?, 17 Va. J. Int'l L. 443 (1977); Hay & Walker, The Proposed U.S.-U.K. Recognition-of-Judgments Convention: Another Perspective, 18 Va. J. Int'l L. 753 (1978).

11. Preparatory materials relative to the Preliminary Draft Convention, as well as its text, may be found on the Internet under: www.hcch.net/e/workprog/jdgm.html

12. See Silberman, Comparative Jurisdiction in the International Context: Will the Proposed Hague Judgments Convention be Stalled?, 52 DePaul L.Rev. 319 (2002). For a discussion of some of the difficulties and the U.S. State Department—opposition to pursuing anything like the draft convention, see von Mehren, Drafting a Convention on International Jurisdiction and the Effects of Foreign Judgments Acceptable World-wide: Can the Hague Conference Project Succeed?, 49 Am. J. Comp. L. 191 (2001) (especially at page 192 discussing a letter from U.S. Assistant Legal Adviser Kovar to the Secretary General of the Conference).

together as contracting states than under the Brussels Convention and that some national differences therefore would not be capable of being bridged.

The draft convention would have required member states to recognize decisions rendered by a court exercising jurisdiction on the basis of the Convention. That means the rendering court must have employed a required/permitted basis of jurisdiction ("White List") and not one prohibited by the Convention ("Black List"). National bases of jurisdiction that are neither required nor prohibited ("Grey List") could be exercised but would not benefit from the mandatory recognition requirement for white-listed judgments.[13] The "black-listed" jurisdictional bases for European countries were identical with those of EU law (Regulation 44/2001). For the United States, they were general (not claim-related) doing business (Art. 20(2)(e)) and jurisdiction based on transient service (Art. 20(2)(f)). Both would have significantly changed American jurisdictional practice whenever a case involved the possibility that an ensuing judgment would need to be enforced abroad. They would, of course, have left unaffected U.S. practice in purely interstate cases.[14]

The Convention would have applied mainly to *final* decisions, but also would have extended to decisions ordering "provisional and protective measures" (Art. 14).[15] The latter provision, however, would not have

13. These judgments would have remained subject to national recognition rules.

14. From among the acceptable ("White List") bases of jurisdiction, those for claims arising from tort and contract are of particular interest. For *tort* claims, jurisdiction would have existed in the state in which the "act or omission that caused injury" occurred *or* where "the injury arose." Art. 10(1). This parallels the European Court's approach under the Brussels Convention. However, jurisdiction based on the place of injury was limited to cases where the defendant could "reasonably have foreseen" that injury would arise in that state (Art. 10(1)(b)), a limitation reminiscent of Swiss law (Art. 133(2), Swiss Conflicts Statute). For *contract* claims, the Preliminary Draft Convention essentially adopted the "characteristic performance" test of the Rome Convention by providing for jurisdiction in the state where goods were supplied, services where rendered, or—in mixed contracts— where the principal obligation was to take place. Art. 6. Except for the last group of cases, the Draft avoided the need to determine the place of performance of the particular obligation in issue which had been a source of difficulty under Art. 5 No. 1 of the Brussels Convention, and, in some measure, continues to be under the Regulation. Supra § 24.38, following n. 22. Like the latter, and derived from it, the Preliminary Draft

contained special jurisdictional provisions protective of consumers (Art. 7). The only basis of *general jurisdiction* would be the "defendant's forum" (Art. 3), i.e. the state of a natural person's habitual residence or a legal person's state of incorporation, principal place of business, statutory seat, or place of management. Art. 4 dealt with *choice-of-court clauses* in a manner very similar to the EC Regulation Art. 23, including by addressing electronic communications in the context of the requirements as to form (" ... communication which renders information accessible so as to be usable for subsequent reference"). Art. 5 dealt with the defendant's *appearance*. New, from the perspective of American law, was the provision—narrower than in European law—for a suspension of proceedings because of proceedings elsewhere (*lis pendens*) (Art. 23); new from the perspective of European law was the (very limited) *forum non conveniens* provision of Art. 24: a court may decline jurisdiction ("in exceptional circumstances") when it is "clearly inappropriate" as a forum *and* another court has jurisdiction and is "clearly more appropriate" as a forum.

15. A court without jurisdiction with respect to the principal claim could order protective measures only with respect to the territory of its state, i.e. such a decision would not have been entitled to extraterritorial recognition. Art. 14(3).

extended to ex parte decisions, such as English *"Anton Piller* orders" because, like Art. 34 No. 2 of the EC Regulation, the Hague Preliminary Draft Convention listed as a ground for the refusal of recognition the non-observance of a party's right to be heard (Art. 27(1)(c)).

American awards of punitive damages or of large amounts for pain and suffering often have not been recognized abroad on public policy grounds.[16] The Preliminary Convention took a slightly more moderate approach. Punitive damages "shall be recognized at least to the extent that similar or comparable damages could have been awarded" in the recognizing state (Art. 32(1)). This will not often be the case. However, the provision also expressly directs the recognizing court to examine to what extent the award of non-compensatory damages might serve to cover costs or expenses (Art. 32(3)). More troublesome is the discretion given the recognizing court in Art. 32(2)(a) to reduce a damage award that it considers to be "grossly excessive."[17]

While the EC Regulation permits review of the first court's jurisdiction by the recognizing court only in a limited number of case situations (Art. 35(1)), the Hague Preliminary Convention permits "verification" of jurisdiction in all cases. However, and here adopting the EC law's approach, the recognizing court is bound by the first court's finding of jurisdictional facts, unless rendered in a default proceeding (Art. 27).

Whatever the fate of the Preliminary Draft Convention may be on its way to possible adoption in this or amended form, the work that went into it is a remarkable accommodation of civil law and common law notions on judicial jurisdiction and its limits, of judgment recognition, and on res judicata. As such it will no doubt influence future developments, perhaps even domestic practice in some countries.

5. *Valuation of Foreign Money–Judgments*

§ 24.40 Section 144 of the Second Conflicts Restatement adopts the rule that ". . . the forum will convert the currency . . . into local currency as of the date of the award." While stated primarily as applicable to foreign-based *claims,* the comments make it clear that the rule is intended to apply to foreign money-judgments as well.[1] The rule is

---

16. See supra § 24.38 n.13. It is a safe assumption that the award of punitive damages will be regarded as a violation of public policy by all EU countries. Thus, the Proposal for a Regulation on the Law Applicable to Non-Contractual Obligations provides in Art. 25: "The application of a provision of the law designated by this Regulation which has the effect of causing non-compensatory damages, such as exemplary or punitive damages, to be awarded shall be contrary to Community public policy." COM (2003) 0427 (final).

17. For another example of forum review of foreign damage levels, see the Ger-

man choice-of-law rule in tort (Art. 40(3) EGBGB), supra § 17.50. For a critique of the German rule, see Hay, Entschädigung und andere Zwecke–Zu Präventionsgedanken im deutschen Schadensrecht, punitive damages und Art.40 Abs.3 Nr.2 EGBGB, in: Hohloch et al. (eds.), Festschrift für Hans Stoll 521 (2001).

§ 24.40

1. Restatement, Second, Conflict of Laws § 144, cmnt. (g) and § 101, cmnt. (d) (1971). According to Sec. 2(3) of the English Foreign Judgments Act of 1933, English currency is to be awarded at the "exchange

said to derive from the fact "that an Anglo–American court may only render a judgment for money . . . in its own local currency."[2] For claims or foreign judgments expressed in foreign currency, conversion will be into dollars and will be calculated as of the date of the award.[3]

The traditional rule has been criticized in the United States[4] and it has long been suggested that judgments on foreign claims or enforcing foreign judgment, both in state and in federal courts, need not be restricted to United States currency.[5] The Uniform Foreign–Money Claims Act[6] permits the parties to stipulate the currency to be used to satisfy claims arising out of their transaction. In the absence of a stipulation, judgments on foreign money claims as well as those recognizing foreign judgments expressed in foreign money are to be stated in the foreign currency, but the judgment debtor may effect payment in dollars at the conversion rate in effect at the time of payment. "The principle of the Act is to restore the aggrieved party to the economic position it would have been in had the wrong not occurred."[7]

rate prevailing at the date of the judgment of the original court." For the conversion of gold francs as specified in the Warsaw Convention see supra § 17.44 n.14.

2. Restatement, Second, Conflict of Laws § 144, cmnt. (b) (1971).

3. Restatement, Second, Conflict of Laws (1971) § 144, cmnt. (g) (1971).

4. For a good comparative analysis see Becker, The Currency of Judgment, 25 Am. J. Comp. L. 152 (1977). For additional discussion see also supra § 24.31.

5. Becker, supra n.4, at 157–58, with references. Section 823 of Restatement (Third) of the Foreign Relations Law of the United States (1988) states that U.S. courts will ordinarily express judgments (on obligations or in enforcing foreign judgments) in United States dollars "but they are not precluded from giving judgment in the currency in which the obligation is denominated or the loss was incurred." For a decision enforcing a foreign arbitral award partly in dollars and partly in English pounds see Waterside Ocean Navigation Co., Inc. v. International Navigation Ltd., 737 F.2d 150 (2d Cir.1984). When sitting in diversity, federal courts follow state practice. In New York, it has been held that an English judgment which could have been satisfied by the debtor in English pounds was to be satisfied in dollars when it was brought to the United States for recognition and enforcement and resulted in a New York judgment. Competex, S.A. v. Labow, 613 F.Supp. 332 (S.D.N.Y.1985), affirmed 783 F.2d 333 (2d Cir.1986). In actions on original foreign-based *claims* (not yet reduced to judgment), it has similarly been

held that the foreign obligation must be converted into dollars and judgment expressed in dollars. Newmont Mines Ltd. v. Adriatic Ins. Co., 609 F.Supp. 295 (S.D.N.Y. 1985), affirmed 784 F.2d 127 (2d Cir.1986) (Canadian insurance claim). But see Barton v. National Life Assurance Co. of Canada, 98 Misc.2d 300, 413 N.Y.S.2d 807 (App. Term 1978) (enforcing insurance contract stipulating payment in Jamaican pounds). The Restatement provision (§ 823(2)) also provides that any conversion into dollars (of a judgment or obligation) should be made "at such a rate as to make the creditor whole and to avoid rewarding a debtor who has delayed in carrying out the obligation." As comment (c) explains, this rule should lead to the use of the breach-day-rule for conversion if the foreign currency has depreciated since the injury, breach, or foreign judgment and to the use of the (local) judgment-day-rule when the foreign currency has appreciated since the injury, breach, or foreign judgment. For discussion and further case reference see id., Reporter's Notes No. 4. While the result was dictated by New York law, the decisions in *Newmont Mines* and *Competex,* supra, are consistent with this approach. See also, Foreign Currency Judgments: 1985 Report of the Committee on Foreign and Comparative Law [of the Association of the Bar of the City of New York], 18 J. Int'l L. & Politics 791 (1986).

6. 13 U.L.A. 13 (Part II), now in force in almost half the states.

7. Id., Prefatory Note. It is doubtful whether a plaintiff will really be restored by receiving today's equivalent of a currency that may have depreciated severely during

In England, the Court of Appeal departed from the rule,[8] the House of Lords subsequently approved the change,[9] and the judgment debtor may now effect payment either in the *foreign currency* in the amount due or in local currency equivalent to the foreign currency on the date of payment. French and German law similarly permit the expression of a judgment in foreign currency.[10] In times of substantial currency fluctuation in the world, the English and Continental rule may be better designed to preserve the value of the creditor's judgment. The proposal for a U.S.-U.K. Judgments Convention of 1977[11] had also adopted this rule. Its Art. 17(5) provided that a money judgment entitled to enforcement under the Convention could be enforced "either in the currency specified in the judgment or in the local currency at the buying rate in the place where and on the date when enforcement is granted."[12]

B. DEFENSES TO CLAIM ON FOREIGN–COUNTRY JUDGMENT

§ **24.41** Traditionally, a foreign-country judgment was considered as not "merging" the underlying cause of action, thus leaving the successful plaintiff free to seek either recognition of his judgment or to

the course of litigation. Arguably, however, the successful plaintiff in domestic litigation faces similar dangers. The Restatement (Third) Foreign Relations Law of the United States § 823, comment (c), advocates conversion as of the breach day whenever the U.S. dollar has appreciated and conversion on judgment-day when the dollar has depreciated. See also Art. 6.1.9(1) and 4 of the UNIDROIT Principles of International Commercial Contracts (Institute for the Unification of Private Law, 1994), adopting essentially the same view. For a different view, see F.A. Mann, The Legal Aspect of Money 351 (5th ed. 1992), followed by Hay, Fremdwährungsansprüche und-urteile nach dem US-amerikanischen Act, [1995] Recht der Internationalen Wirtschaft 113, 115 n.35, 118 n.66: compensation for delay and ensuing loss due to currency fluctuation should be left to the law applicable to the claim or the judgment.

8. Schorsch Meier GmbH. v. Hennin, [1975] 1 All E.R. 152 (C.A.).

9. Miliangos v. George Frank (Textiles) Limited, [1975] 3 All E.R. 801 (H.L.). For comment see J.H.C. Morris, English Judgments in Foreign Currency: A "Procedural" Revolution, 41 Law & Contemp. Probs., No. 2, 44 (1977); Cheshire & North, Private International Law 90 et seq. (13th ed. by North and Fawcett 1999). See Dicey & Morris, Conflict of Laws 1605 et seq. (13th ed. by Collins et al. 2000) for discussion and subsequent legislation.

In contrast, the Civil Jurisdiction and Judgments Order 2001, SI 3929, Sch.1, provides in Art. 6 (1) that sums payable under a maintenance oder "shall be paid in the currency of the United Kingdom" and (Art. 6(2)) that conversion shall be on the basis of the exchange rate prevailing on the day of registration of the order. It will be remembered that the United Kingdom, while a member of the European Union, does not participate in the Euro currency system. This Order therefore affects all EU countries' maintenance decrees that are expressed in Euro.

10. Nussbaum, Money in the Law, National and International 371 (1950); Drobnig, American–German Private International Law 257 (1972). For the practice in Austria, Belgium, Brazil, and England, see Restatement (Third) of the Foreign Relations Law of the United States § 823, Reporters' Notes at No. 6 (1987); F.A. Mann, The Legal Aspect of Money 340 (4th ed. 1982). Cf. U.C.C. § 3–107(2) concerning commercial paper: "If . . . an instrument specifies a foreign currency as the medium of payment the instrument is payable in that currency."

11. Supra § 24.39.

12. To the extent that there may have been doubt with respect to the freedom of federal courts to depart from the traditional rule (supra § 24.31, n.7), the convention would have taken precedence with respect to English judgments.

relitigate his original claim in the United States.[1] The defendant in the original action, however, was protected against relitigation of a claim by a plaintiff who had lost in the original proceeding.[2] The last-mentioned rule addresses one of the policy concerns of the pervasive policy of preclusion:[3] to protect the defendant against harassment. It is readily apparent that the same concern applies equally to the first-mentioned rule. Other reasons originally advanced for the non-merger rule are no longer as important as they may once have been.[4] It is for these, and other, reasons that the earlier discussion suggested that the focus of the analysis should properly be on the policy of preclusion, rather than on short-hand technical labels which obscure the analysis, and that principles of preclusion should apply equally in the interstate and international settings. It is believed that this approach represents the modern trend.

Foreign-country judgments are subject to the same defenses that would preclude the enforcement of a sister-state judgment. In some respects, however, these defenses will be different in scope and, in that sense, unique to foreign-country judgments. This results, for instance, from differences in concepts of jurisdiction in the United States and in foreign legal systems, with the result that-since the Full Faith and Credit Clause does not apply to foreign-country judgments-due process considerations assume new relevance. The emergence of recognition treaties introduces another different dimension. The following sections address these problems.

1. *Jurisdiction*

§ 24.42 As in interstate cases, a foreign-country judgment must have been rendered by a court having jurisdiction. Jurisdiction, even though often expressed as "jurisdiction in the international sense,"[1] requires general satisfaction of U.S. due-process standards[2] to entitle a

---

§ 24.41

1. Supra § 24.3.

2. Supra § 24.32 n.9.

3. Supra §§ 24.1–24.4.

4. § 24.3 nn.6 et seq.

§ 24.42

1. "Jurisdiction in the international sense" concerns the relationship of the foreign nation to the occurrence and to the parties and inquiries whether *any* court of the foreign country had jurisdiction, not whether the particular court did, either as a matter of competence under the foreign country's internal laws or as a matter of procedural venue. J.-G. Castel, Canadian Conflict of Laws § 162 (4th ed. 1997) (discussing need for forum's "internal competence"). See also CIBC Mellon Trust Co. v. Mora Hotel Corp. N.V., 296 A.D.2d 81, 743 N.Y.S.2d 408 (2002), order aff'd 100 N.Y.2d 215, 762 N.Y.S.2d 5, 792 N.E.2d 155 (2003), cert. denied ___ U.S. ___, 124 S.Ct. 399, 157 L.Ed.2d 279 (2003) (discussing whether English court had jurisdiction under Order 11).

2. It is generally accepted, both here and abroad, that the required jurisdiction is determined by the law of the enforcing forum. See, e.g., Wimmer Canada, Inc. v. Abele Tractor & Equip. Co., 299 A.D.2d 47, 750 N.Y.S.2d 331 (2002) (Quebec judgment entitled to enforcement in the U.S. because Quebec court would have had jurisdiction under New York standards); see also R.H. Graveson and J.-G. Castel, supra n.1, § 145. The same is theoretically true in the U.S. interstate setting but far less important because of the unifying effect of the federal due process standard against which all exercise of state jurisdiction must be measured. See infra n.5. Department of Human Services v. Shelnut, 772 So.2d 1041

foreign-country judgment to recognition in the United States. The difference to interstate cases lies in the fact that no uniform standard of due process obtains abroad which would result in the confluence of due-process and full-faith-and-credit observed in the interstate setting.[3] Thus a foreign-country judgment may well be valid where rendered but not entitled to recognition in the United States. Examples are a French judgment based jurisdictionally on the French nationality or domicile of the plaintiff or a German judgment in personam, and not quasi-in-rem, based on the presence of assets in Germany.[4] Neither judgment would be entitled to recognition in the U.S. because of insufficient connection of the defendant with the rendering forum.[5]

It is still an open question to what extent, if at all, a U.S. court should give a foreign court the benefit of (constitutionally valid) domestic statutory bases for jurisdiction when the circumstances of the case indicate that such jurisdiction existed in fact but the foreign court relied on a different and impermissible jurisdictional ground. Illustratively, if an American defendant had been engaged in doing business in France (without being personally present or domiciled there) and the French court had exercised jurisdiction on the ground of the plaintiff's French domicile in an action arising from the business activity, should the U.S. court conclude that jurisdiction existed, even though not invoked by the rendering court, because "doing business" would have been a proper basis for jurisdiction under the local long-arm statute in the reverse case?[6] A policy common to all legal systems is to provide for the final resolution of disputes. This policy is furthered by each nation's adoption of a view of "jurisdiction in the international sense" which recognizes the foreign court's assertion of jurisdiction as satisfying its own notions of due process in circumstances in which it itself would have asserted jurisdiction.

(Miss.2000)(unsuccessful challenge in a Canadian court to that court's jurisdiction precludes later collateral attack in U.S. court when judgment-creditor seeks to enforce).

3. See supra § 24.14.

4. Supra § 24.6 n.5. A German judgment based on quasi-in-rem jurisdiction may violate U.S. concepts of due process as defined in the Supreme Court's decision in Shaffer v. Heitner, 433 U.S. 186, 97 S.Ct. 2569, 53 L.Ed.2d 683 (1977).

5. See Davidson & Co., Ltd. v. Allen, 89 Nev. 126, 508 P.2d 6 (1973) (recognition denied to Canadian default judgment; Canadian court lacked jurisdiction when defendant's contacts with foreign forum did not satisfy due process standards); Lugot v. Harris, 499 F.Supp. 1118 (D.Nev.1980) (recognition denied to Mexican ex parte divorce judgment: Mexican court lacked jurisdiction when absent spouse's contacts with forum

did not satisfy due process); Koster v. Automark Industries, Inc., 640 F.2d 77 (7th Cir. 1981) (insufficient contacts of Illinois corporation with the Netherlands to permit enforcement of a Dutch default judgment).

6. In Canada, the Supreme Court adopted as the jurisdictional test for the recognition of a provincial or territorial judgment whether there had been a real and substantial connection between the rendering court and the subject matter of the suit or the defendant. Morguard Investments Ltd. v. DeSavoye, [1990] 3 S.C.R. 1077, 76 D.L.R. (4th) 256. For discussion, see J.–G. Castel, Canadian Conflict of Laws 280–82 et seq. (4th ed. 1997). This test has also been applied to foreign-country judgments. Id. at 282 n. 53, listing cases. Australian practice is similar, see Crick v. Hennessy, [1973] W.A.R. 74, and In the Marriage of C R and J A Gilmore, 16 Fam LR 285 (Family Court of Australia 1992).

Recognition statutes and treaties provide some certainty by designating jurisdictional bases which, if satisfied in the rendering forum, entitle the judgment to recognition in the courts of the state or treaty partner,[7] while still permitting the courts of each state or treaty partner[8] to accord recognition in additional cases.[9] However, recognition statutes and treaties apply principally only to money judgments and, from among these, furthermore exclude judgments for support in family and matrimonial matters.[10] Recognition treaties also often exclude money judgments with respect to certain subject matters such as damages resulting from nuclear incidents.[11]

2. *Foreign Judgment for Taxes or Penalties*

§ 24.43   The traditional view which held, as discussed previously, that a foreign-country judgment did not merge the underlying cause of action, results in a denial of recognition of foreign-country *judgments* for

---

7. See also Hay, International versus Interstate Conflicts Law in the United States, 35 Rabels Zeitschrift 429, 450 n.101 (1971); Cherun v. Frishman, 236 F.Supp. 292 (D.D.C.1964).

8. Section 5 of the Uniform Foreign Money–Judgments Recognition Act, 13 .L.A. 73 (Part II), provides:

"(a) The foreign judgment shall not be refused recognition for lack of personal jurisdiction if

"(1) the defendant was served personally in the foreign state;

"(2) the defendant voluntarily appeared in the proceedings, other than for the purpose of protecting property seized or threatened with seizure in the proceedings or of contesting the jurisdiction of the court over him;

"(3) the defendant prior to the commencement of the proceedings had agreed to submit to the jurisdiction of the foreign court with respect to the subject matter involved;

"(4) the defendant was domiciled in the foreign state when the proceedings were instituted, or, being a body corporate had its principal place of business, was incorporated, or had otherwise acquired corporate status, in the foreign state;

"(5) the defendant had a business office in the foreign state and the proceedings in the foreign court involved a cause of action arising out of business done by the defendant through that office in the foreign state; or

"(6) the defendant operated a motor vehicle or airplane in the foreign state and the proceedings involved a cause of action arising out of such operation.

"(b) The courts of this State may recognize other bases of jurisdiction."

For discussion of earlier proposal for a U.S.-U.K. Convention, see Hay & Walker, supra § 24.38 n.12 and § 24.39 n.4.

9. See § 5(b), Uniform Foreign Money—Judgments Act, supra n.2; Art. 3, proposed U.S.-U.K. Recognition-of-Judgments Convention.

10. See §§ 1(2) and 3 of the Uniform Foreign–Money Judgments Recognition Act. The proposed U.S.—U.K. Recognition-of-Judgments Convention expressly excluded (see also infra n.11) judgments relating to status and family law, succession, existence and powers of legal persons, bankruptcy, matters relating to social security and public assistance, customs duties, taxes, and like charges. These exclusions are standard to most international recognition treaties. See M. Weser, Convention communautaire sur la compétence judiciaire et l'exécution des décisions 218, 220 *passim* (1975).

11. The exclusion of nuclear incidents in the proposed U.S.-U.K. Convention resulted in part from the Paris Convention on Third Party Liability in the Field of Nuclear Energy which was given effect in the United Kingdom by § 17(5) of the Nuclear Installations Act (1965). The effect of these provisions is to put liability for damages arising from nuclear incidents on the operator of the installation.

taxes and penalties when the recognizing court, under its law, would not have entertained an original action on such a *claim*.[1]

The proposal for a U.S.-U.K. Recognition-of-Judgments Convention had envisioned protection of defendants against renewed litigation of the same claim, but did not depart from the traditional approach to judgments for taxes and penalties. Instead, it had expressly and carefully preserved the exception.[2] Indeed, owing to the strong English view on the matter, the Convention had also excluded judgments for multiple damages (for instance, treble damages in antitrust) even though, in the American view, they may not be "penal" because they inure to the benefit of private litigants.[3] Earlier discussion[4] has shown that these

§ 24.43

1. Judgments based on *tax claims:* See supra § 24.23 n.7 (*The Attorney General of Canada*) and Johansson v. United States, 336 F.2d 809 (5th Cir.1964); In re Bliss' Trust, 26 Misc.2d 969, 208 N.Y.S.2d 725 (1960). Cf. Restatement, Second, Conflict of Laws § 120 (1971) (by implication). See United States v. Harden, (1963) 41 D.L.R.2d 721 (Canada). But see Bullen et al. v. Her Majesty's Government of the United Kingdom, 553 So.2d 1344 (Fla.App. 1989) (enforcing judgment in favor of the U.K. government for money collected as value added tax but fraudulently diverted).

Judgments based on *penalties:* Cf. Restatement, Second, Conflict of Laws § 120 (1971) (by implication). Judgments based on tax claims and penalties are also excluded by § 1(2) of the Uniform Foreign Money–Judgments Recognition Act.

For *English law,* which denies recognition and enforcement of a judgment, "either directly or indirectly, . . . ordering the payment of taxes, fines or other contributions or penalties," see Dicey & Morris, Conflict of Laws 476 (13th ed. by Collins et al. 2000); § 1(2)(b) English Foreign Judgments Act of 1933. See also Stoel, The Enforcement of Non–Criminal Penal and Revenue Judgments in England and the United States, 16 Int'l & Comp. L.Q. 663 (1967). For a more liberal *New Zealand* decision see Connor v. Connor, (1974) 1 N.Z.L.R. 632 (Supreme Court), holding that the enforcement of a judgment which would result in the reimbursement of a foreign state agency's public assistance fund was not contrary to public policy. For Canada, see United States v. Harden, supra this note, and J.-G. Castel, Canadian Conflict of Laws No. 166, p. 285 (4th ed. 1997). The special problems raised by exchange controls are addressed in Note, Enforcement of Foreign Exchange Control Regulations in Domestic Courts, 70 Am. J. Int'l L. 101, 104 n.13 (1976), collecting cases. For additional discussion see supra § 24.23 n.7.

2. Art. 2(2): ". . . [T]his Convention shall not apply to judgments: (a) for customs duties, taxes and other charges of like nature, (b) to the extent that they are for punitive or multiple damages. . . ." Bilateral tax treaties provide for intergovernmental cooperation in this area and therefore make the inclusion of the enforcement of tax claims in a general judgments-recognition convention unnecessary. See Surr, Intertax: Intergovernmental Cooperation in Taxation, 7 Harv. Int'l L. Club J. 179 (1966); Surrey, International Tax Conventions: How They Operate and What They Accomplish, 23 J. Taxation 364 (1965); van Hoorn & Wright, Taxation, in: 2 E. Stein & T.L. Nicholson, American Enterprise in the European Common Market: A Legal Profile 343 (1960). See also Taylor, U.S. Tax Treaties and Common Market Corporate Tax Systems, 28 Tax Lawyer 73 (1974).

3. The Convention's "punitive or multiple" damages exception was broader than the English Judgments Act's and the American Uniform Act's (supra n.1) exclusion of "penalties" if one accepts the U.S. Supreme Court's distinction in Huntington v. Attrill, 146 U.S. 657, 13 S.Ct. 224, 36 L.Ed. 1123 (1892) (discussed supra § 24.23 n.9). For the strong English position, see Dicey & Morris, supra n.1. It is unclear whether Art. 2(5) of the Convention, providing for the recognition and enforcement of a "severable part" of a judgment, was to serve to facilitate recognition of that part of a judgment representing the ordinary, compensatory part of the damage award, e.g. one-third of a treble damage award in antitrust. See Hay & Walker, The Proposed Recognition-of-Judgments Convention Between the United States and the United Kingdom, 11 Tex. Int'l L.J. 421, 424 n.21 (1976). But see supra § 24.38 n.7. Punitive and multiple damages will be of major concern in the negotiations for a worldwide convention. See generally Symposium, Enforcing Judgments Abroad: The Global Challenge, 24 Brooklyn J. Int'l L. 1 (1998). See supra § 24.39, nn. 11–14.

4. Supra § 24.23.

defenses are no longer available in U.S. interstate practice, except in the area of criminal jurisdiction. The same policy considerations support the view that they should be unavailable in international practice. The "non-merger" concept of the traditional doctrine is only a short-hand articulation of what matters should or should not be precluded as a result of prior litigation; it is not a rule of analysis. To the extent that a common policy of preclusion obtains in all legal systems, the U.S. interstate approach can readily be generalized to international judgments, including those for taxes and penalties. The partial departure from the non-merger doctrine (in another context) is illustrated by Art. 9 of the earlier proposal of a U.S.-U.K. Recognition Convention, discussed below.[5]

3. *Public Policy*

§ 24.44   Unlike the narrow (perhaps nonexistent) scope given public policy as a defense to the recognition of a sister-state judgment, especially one for money, in the United States,[1] the public policy defense serves as an umbrella for a variety of concerns in international practice which may lead to a denial of recognition. In England, the non-recognition of tax and penal judgments is sometimes considered to result from the public policy exception,[2] while the American exception is often said to be based on notions of territorial sovereignty.[3] Similarly, procedural defects, for instance lack of adequate notice or insufficient opportunity to be heard, are often viewed in public policy terms in England,[4] while the U.S. objection tends to be formulated in due process, and thus often in jurisdictional terms.[5]

---

5. Infra § 24.45.

§ 24.44

1. Supra § 24.20.

2. R.H. Graveson, Conflict of Laws 632 (7th ed. 1974). See generally Carter, Rejection of Foreign Law: Some Private International Law Inhibitions, 55 Brit. Ybk. Int'l L. 1984, 111 (1985).

3. See Leflar, Extrastate Enforcement of Penal and Governmental Claims, 46 Harv. L. Rev. 193 (1932); Note, 25 U. Chi. L. Rev. 187 (1957). See also supra § 24.19.

4. See R.H. Graveson, supra n.2, at 633–34 ("disregard of English ideas of natural justice," a concept that overlaps public policy).

5. In Koster v. Automark Industries, Inc., 640 F.2d 77, 81 n.3 (7th Cir.1981), the court suggested in dictum that the Dutch statute governing service of process on defendants residing in foreign countries provided insufficient assurance of actual notice to satisfy U.S. due process requirements. See also Hilkmann v. Hilkmann, 816 A.2d 242 (Pa. Super. 2003)(failure to take suffi-

cient testimony or receive other evidence deemed by the U.S. court to be probative on question of competency meant that the judgment violated public policy).

In an interstate case, it has been held that service of process by mail violated due process and that the ensuing judgment therefore was not entitled to full faith and credit. See Miserandino v. Resort Properties, Inc., 345 Md. 43, 691 A.2d 208, cert. denied 522 U.S. 953, 118 S.Ct. 376, 139 L.Ed.2d 292 (1997).

The proposal for a U.S.–U.K. Recognition-of-Judgments Convention had defined sufficient notice as actual notice in sufficient time to allow the defendant to present his case or constructive notice of a quality acceptable to the recognizing forum. Art. 8(1). The provision thus built in American due-process standards when the recognizing forum is in the U.S. and English natural-justice standards when England is the second forum.

The New York Court of Appeals refused to recognize a Mexican adoption in Barry E. (Anonymous) v. Ingraham, 43 N.Y.2d 87, 400 N.Y.S.2d 772, 371 N.E.2d 492 (1977) in

Article 34(1) of the Regulation (EC) (successor to Article 27 of the Brussels Convention) also contains a public policy exception. Its scope is intended to be narrow,[6] as illustrated by specific exceptions to the recognition requirement for a number of other reasons.[7] The European Court has also adopted a narrow interpretation[8] and this has been followed by national courts.[9] The Brussels Convention does not contain an exception for the disregard of mandatory rules of law of the recognizing state. This had been the case in the proposed U.S.–U.K. Convention (Art. 8(4)). A principal reason for its inclusion there had been the concern that sections 4 and 5 of the English Supply of Goods Act (1973), with respect to implied terms and warranties, and cogent provisions of American law, principally as contained in the U.C.C., should not be subject to avoidance by private agreement or by an incorrect choice-of-law by the rendering court.[10] Similar concerns may surface and may need to be addressed with respect to the current proposal for a worldwide jurisdiction and judgments-recognition convention.

circumstances where the adoptive parents, the child, and the natural mother were all New York domiciliaries; the natural father was unknown. In the Mexican adoption proceedings, the natural mother appeared by counsel but neither she nor the child was present in the jurisdiction and the Mexican court did not engage in the extensive review prescribed by New York statutory law for adoptions in New York. The Court of Appeals therefore held that the Mexican court had not been a "competent court." The lack of competency was found in the difference of the procedures and in the conclusion that recognition of the Mexican decree would violate New York public policy: "To lend an imprimatur to an adoption, predicated upon insufficient jurisdictional foundations and a questionable perfunctory examination into the interests of the child, would be an inexcusable abdication of the State's role as *parens patriae*. It could also, it is feared, open the door to mercenary trading of children...." 43 N.Y.2d at 89, 400 N.Y.S.2d at 774, 371 N.E.2d at 493. See also infra n.13.

6. Jenard Report on the Brussels Convention 1968, Official Journal of the European Community. 1979 C 59/1.

7. E.g., lack of opportunity to be heard (Art. 34 No. 2), the existence of an inconsistent decision of the forum or an earlier inconsistent decision of a non-contracting state (Art. Nos. 3 and 5), or the exercise of jurisdiction by the rendering state in violation of the provisions dealing with exclusive jurisdiction or jurisdiction in consumer and insurance matters (Art. 35(1)). Except for the limited cases mentioned in Art. 35(1), the second court may not examine the jurisdiction of the rendering court. Art. 35(3). Lest such a review were to be attempted by resort to the public policy exception, Art. 35(3) states further that the provisions on jurisdiction are not part of public policy within the meaning of Art. 34, No. 1.

8. Hoffmann v. Krieg (Case 145/86) [1988] ECR 645.

9. See Interdesco v. Nullifire, [1992] 1 Lloyd's Rep. 180 (Q.B.); Maronier v. Larmer [2002] EWCA Civ 774, [2003] QB 620 (Court of Appeal 2002).

With respect to non-contracting states, national public policy exceptions may be applied more readily. See e.g., the decision of the German Supreme Court denying recognition on public policy grounds to the portion of an American judgment awarding the plaintiff punitive damages. BGHZ 118, 312; Hay, The Recognition and Enforcement of American Money–Judgments in Germany, 40 Am. J. Comp. L. 1001 (1992). More recently, see German Constitutional Court (BVerfG) decision of July 25, 2003 (No. 2 BvR 1198/03), [2003] IPRax No. 5 at vii-x, with comment by Rothe in RIW 2003, 859 (no service, under Hague Service Convention) of documents initiating suit in New York, seeking very high punitive damages, because suit was considered designed to force settlement and thus to constitute abuse of legal process).

10. Hay & Walker, supra n.3 at 442, 450. One difficulty with the provision was that uncertainty exists with respect to some U.C.C. provisions as to whether they are mandatory. Moreover, since the U.C.C. is state law, different conclusions may be reached in different states, thus making the application of such a recognition treaty less than uniform. Id.

In general, it appears to be the modern trend that the public policy defense will lie only in exceptional cases,[11] similar to its narrow scope in the interstate setting. Thus, while comment (c) to § 117 of the Second Restatement still states that "enforcement will usually be accorded the [foreign nation] judgment except in situations where the original claim is repugnant to fundamental notions" of fairness and decency of the enforcing forum, modern decisions have enforced foreign judgments in circumstances when the original claim would not have been entertained.[12]

The same trend is discernible in England. There, courts are said to have "a residuary discretion in the recognition of foreign judgments ... based on the broad common law concept of substantial justice."[13] Thus, the Court of Appeal refused recognition to a Maltese decree of nullity of

11. See, e.g., In re Davis' Will, 31 Misc.2d 270, 219 N.Y.S.2d 533 (1961). In that case, a probate proceeding, the surrogate's court denied recognition to a foreign judgment entered after the defendant's death. The court based its decision on the statutory prohibition, under New York law (Civ. P. Act § 478), to enter a judgment against a party who has died prior to judgment. The case thus superficially resembles the provision of the U.S.–U.K. Convention draft, supra n.9, with respect to mandatory rules of law in the recognizing forum. It differs from that provision, however, and goes beyond it, in that the issue in the *Davis* case did not involve a matter of substantive law and in that there is no evidence that New York law was applicable but had been disregarded by the foreign court. See also Arab Monetary Fund v. Hashim, 213 F.3d 1169 (9th Cir.2000) (English judgment imposing $10 million in costs on family members of debtor is not "repugnant" to American conceptions of justice and thus must be enforced in U.S. proceeding); Society of Lloyd's v. Mullin, 255 F.Supp.2d 468 (E.D. Pa. 2003), affirmed 96 Fed.Appx. 100 (3d Cir.2004) (English judgment did not violate due process and must be enforced).

12. See, e.g., Neporany v. Kir, 5 A.D.2d 438, 173 N.Y.S.2d 146 (1958) (recognition of Canadian judgment for seduction and criminal conversation, although these actions had been abolished in New York by statute). See also Biggelaar v. Wagner, 978 F.Supp. 848 (N.D.Ind.1997), affirmed 159 F.3d 41 (2d Cir. 1998) (recognizing Dutch judgment); Chabert v. Bacquie, 694 So.2d 805 (Fla.App.1997); and Alfadda v. Fenn, 966 F.Supp. 1317 (S.D.N.Y. 1997), aff'd 159 F.3d 41 (2d Cir.1998) (recognizing French judgments); Roy v. Buckley, 698 A.2d 497 (Me.1997) (recognizing Quebec judgment).

In at least two decisions, courts refused recognition to English judgments for damages because English law applicable to the underlying liability for libel did not comport with U.S. First and Fourth Amendment standards. Matusevitch v. Telnikoff, 877 F.Supp. 1 (D.C.C.1995), affirmed 159 F.3d 636 (D.C.Cir.1998); Bachchan v. India Abroad Publications Inc., 154 Misc.2d 228, 585 N.Y.S.2d 661 (1992). The courts could consider the cause of action underlying the judgment (and the content of the law applicable to the cause of action) because a foreign judgment, contrary to interstate practice, traditionally does not merge the underlying claim. See supra §§ 24.1, 24.3. It was suggested at § 24.3 supra that this distinction is not supportable and should be abandoned. Even if the distinction is maintained, the conclusion reached in the English libel cases is questionable. The court in *Bachchan* explained that the main difference between English and American cases lies in the placement of the burden of proof: "how can such a difference be so repugnant to our sense of justice and decency?" Symeonides, Perdue & von Mehren, Conflict of Laws: American, Comparative, International—Cases and Materials 846, Note 2 (2d. ed. 2003). See generally Hay, On Comity, Reciprocity, and Public Policy in U.S. and German Judgments Recognition Practice, in: J. Basedow on et al.(eds.), Private Law in the International Arena–Liber Americorum Kurt Siehr 237–49 (2000). See also Yahoo! Inc. v. La Ligue Contre Le Racisme et L'Antisémitisme, 169 F.Supp.2d 1181 (N.D.Cal.2001) (non-recognition of French decree ordering internet provider to filter out information about Nazi memorabilia).

13. R.H. Graveson, supra n.2, at 634 and Dicey & Morris, The Conflict of Laws 527 (13th ed. 2000 by Collins et al.), (citing Pemberton v. Hughes, [1899] 1 Ch. 781.).

a marriage because of the hardship created thereby for the wife and children in England.[14] However, denial of recognition to a judgment or reopening of a proceeding on this ground is said to be "exceptional" and "unlikely to develop into a general practice ... such as exists under the Continental doctrine of exequatur."[15] In Canada, similarly, the scope of the doctrine of "natural justice" as a defense to the enforcement of a foreign judgment is construed narrowly. It remains largely restricted to procedural-jurisdictional defects in the original judgment.[16]

4. *International Recognition Treaties and Preclusion*

§ 24.45 In the U.S. interstate context, the Full Faith and Credit Clause generalizes the preclusive effect of a judgment by requiring the enforcing court to give the judgment the same effect as it enjoys where rendered. The absence of such a Constitutional mandate in the international setting permits U.S. courts to give a lesser preclusive effect or, to state it differently, to enlarge the defenses available against the recognition and enforcement of a foreign nation judgment. However, as the initial discussion in this chapter suggested,[1] the underlying policy objectives favoring preclusion are the same and the jurisdictional-procedural defenses ordinarily provide sufficient protection to the judgment debtor. The sections immediately preceding have shown that, despite the absence of a Constitutional mandate of recognition, foreign nation judgments receive recognition in practice and that defenses are analogized to those available in interstate practice.

This modern trend was made explicit in Article 9 of the earlier proposal for a U.S.–U.K. Recognition Convention which had provided that "except as permitted by this Convention,[2] there shall be no review of the judgment [by the second forum]." It is important to note that this language also precluded the kind of review otherwise permissible under state summary recognition and enforcement procedures.[3] The mandate which this provision incorporates thus parallels the Full Faith and Credit Clause and, as a treaty provision, would supersede contrary state law under the Supremacy Clause of the Constitution. Unlike the Full Faith and Credit Clause, however, the provision would not automatically incorporate the preclusive effect accorded the judgment by the law of the court of rendition. The preclusive effect of the original judgment was addressed in another provision. Article 13(2) limited the res judicata effect to parties or their successors "represented ... in the original proceeding," thus excluding a collateral estoppel effect on non-parties. Art. 13(1) adopted a dual test for the extent of the preclusive effect. It (a) restricted the preclusive effect to that accorded similar judgments ren-

14. Gray v. Formosa, [1963] P. 259.

15. R.H. Graveson, supra n.2, at 635.

16. J.–G. Castel, Canadian Conflict of Laws No. 168, p. 287 (4th ed. 1997).

§ 24.45

1. Supra §§ 24.3–24.4.

2. Exceptions are, for instance, the provision of Art. 8(4), discussed supra § 24.44 n.9, as well as jurisdictional defects in the original judgment.

3. Supra § 24.13.

dered by the recognizing forum but (b) permitted, and, if respondent requested, require the forum to accord the judgment the preclusive effects it has where rendered. The formulation under (a) corresponds to the Second Restatement approach,[4] while (b) protects the judgment debtor according to the law of the place of the original judgment.

IV. EXTRALITIGIOUS PROCEEDINGS, ADMINISTRATIVE DETERMINATIONS, AND ARBITRAL AWARDS

§ 24.46 Decisions, decrees and awards often result from proceedings which are not "judicial" or, at least, not adversary in nature. The former encompass administrative determinations and arbitral awards. The latter are the "extralitigious" proceedings primarily known to civil-law jurisdictions.[1] They include determinations, in a judicial but often nonadversary proceeding, of such matters as child custody, declarations of death, incompetence, and emancipation, and probate and bankruptcy decrees. In the United States, these subject matters will ordinarily arise in judicial proceedings much like any other[2] and thus be governed by the ordinary principles regarding recognition.[3] Misunderstanding of substantive-law issues-for instance, of the legal rights and position of the heirs versus the executor or administrator in succession matters in the civil and common law, respectively[4]—may often be the real reason for non-recognition in the international setting. This suggests that these problems should not be regarded as ordinary conflict-of-laws problems such as arise in the interstate setting. Rather, it is necessary to achieve an understanding of the differing legal concepts and to fashion a local remedy which *recognizes,* and is *functionally equivalent* to, the foreign

---

4. Restatement, Second, Conflict of Laws § 98, comment (f) (1971) ("normally, an American court would apply the foreign rules [with respect to *res judicata* and estoppel] if these rules are substantially the same as the rules of the American court."). For additional discussion see supra § 24.3 n.13.

§ 24.46

1. For more extensive and comparative treatment see 2 A.A. Ehrenzweig & E. Jayme, Private International Law 66 ff (1973). A.A. Ehrenzweig, Conflict of Laws 180 ff (rev. ed. 1962); H. Battifol & P. Lagarde, 2 Droit international privé No. 716 (7th ed. 1983). Extralitigious proceedings should be distinguished from informal acts, such as the religious divorce recognized by Jewish and Islamic law. See supra §§ 15.24–15.25. An extralitigious proceeding, unlike an informal divorce, is one be-

fore a judicial body but not arising from (adversary) litigation.

2. The procedure under the Uniform Child Custody Jurisdiction and Enforcement Act combines adversary litigation (in F–1) with inter-court cooperation (F–1 and F–2) as distinguished from resolution of the dispute through litigation and relitigation in diverse fora. See supra §§ 15.41–15.43. See also Levicky v. Levicky, 49 N.J.Super. 562, 140 A.2d 534 (1958) (custody decree made contingent on similar decree by cooperating French court); Alley v. Parker, 707 A.2d 77 (Me.1998) (Maine and California trial judges conferred and agreed on California as convenient forum for temporary custody decision).

3. For recognition of status and family-law related decrees see supra Chapter 15.

4. See P. Hay, Law of the United States no. 529, also nos. 546–50 (2002).

result and, in this manner, will carry forward the policies of both jurisdictions and of the purpose of the conflict of laws.[5]

Administrative acts often result from quasi-judicial proceedings and, as such, have been treated and recognized as judgments in the interstate setting.[6] The Second Restatement includes decisions of a state's "legislature ... executive and administrative agencies" when these bodies acted "judicially" in the definition of the term "judgment."[7] State statutes establishing administrative agencies frequently give agency decisions the effect of judgments; examples include agencies dealing with worker compensation and pollution control. Administrative acts of foreign nations, on the other hand, have generally not been treated as judgments[8] except when their review, and the local forum's freedom to alter their result, was precluded by supervening executive action[9] or such notions as the "act of state" doctrine.[10] The earlier proposal for a U.S.–U.K. Recognition-of-Judgments Convention, in addition to excluding certain subject matter often dealt with administratively,[11] would have expressly limited its application to "judgments"[12] of "courts."[13] The European Community law, in contrast, is slightly broader. It applies to decisions "in civil and commercial matters regardless of the nature of the jurisdiction" (Art. 1) thus including administrative tribunals of a judicial

---

5. For instance, a certificate of inheritance should be issued in Germany to the U.S. administrator, rather than to the heirs, of an American decedent with movable property in Germany, but—in the reverse case—the claims of German heirs should be postponed until after completion of administration in the particular U.S. state. Ibid.

6. Magnolia Petroleum Co. v. Hunt, 320 U.S. 430, 64 S.Ct. 208, 88 L.Ed. 149 (1943) (drawn into question in Thomas v. Washington Gas Light Co., 448 U.S. 261, 100 S.Ct. 2647, 65 L.Ed.2d 757 (1980)); Industrial Commission of Wisconsin v. McCartin, 330 U.S. 622, 67 S.Ct. 886, 91 L.Ed. 1140 (1947). The *Thomas* decision is discussed supra § 24.26. For extensive discussion of a related problem see also Note, The Collateral Estoppel Effect of Administrative Agency Actions in Federal Civil Litigation, 46 Geo. Wash. L. Rev. 65 (1977).

7. § 92, comnt. (a) (1971). See also Nadelmann, Full Faith and Credit to Judgments and Public Acts, 56 Mich. L. Rev. 33 (1957) (Full Faith and Credit Clause was meant to apply to legislative divorces).

8. See A.A. Ehrenzweig & E. Jayme, 2 Private International Law 72 (1973). But see Restatement, Second, Conflict of Laws § 98, comnt. (a) (1971) which, in announcing the general rule that "valid" foreign-country judgments will be recognized in the United States, cross references—without discussion of administrative acts—to § 92. See supra § 24.37. When the foreign administrative act is one for taxes or penalties, the exceptions pertaining to these, discussed apply. But see the protection afforded by bilateral tax treaties, supra § 24.43 n.2.

9. See United States v. Pink, 315 U.S. 203, 62 S.Ct. 552, 86 L.Ed. 796 (1942) (Litvinov agreement).

10. Banco Nacional de Cuba v. Sabbatino, 376 U.S. 398, 84 S.Ct. 923, 11 L.Ed.2d 804 (1964), on remand 272 F.Supp. 836 (S.D.N.Y.1965), judgment affirmed 383 F.2d 166 (2d Cir.1967), cert. denied 390 U.S. 956, 88 S.Ct. 1038, 19 L.Ed.2d 1151 (1968). See also First National City Bank v. Banco Nacional de Cuba, 406 U.S. 759, 92 S.Ct. 1808, 32 L.Ed.2d 466 (1972); Menendez v. Saks & Co., decided sub nom. Alfred Dunhill of London, Inc. v. Republic of Cuba, 425 U.S. 682, 96 S.Ct. 1854, 48 L.Ed.2d 301 (1976); W.S. Kirkpatrick & Co., Inc. v. Environmental Tectonics Corp., Int'l, 493 U.S. 400, 110 S.Ct. 701, 107 L.Ed.2d 816 (1990). See also Kirgis, Act of State Exceptions and Choice of Law, 44 U. Colo. L. Rev. 173 (1972).

11. E.g. social security and public assistance. Art. 2(3)(f).

12. However, "the name given to the judgment, such as order or decree" is not relevant. Art. 2(1).

13. "[C]ourts ... in the exercise of their civil or commercial jurisdiction ... " Art. 2(1).

nature.[14] While still more limited than a recognition practice which would also include decisions of administrative agencies, the Convention's approach as well as isolated cases here and abroad[15] may bear out, at least for the future, that "the distinction between judgments and administrative acts is generally losing ground together with its obsolescent rationale."[16]

§ 24.47 Similar to early reluctance to enforce prorogation clauses in favor of a foreign court by dismissing local actions brought in violation,[1] American courts were slow to honor arbitration agreements and resulting arbitral awards granted elsewhere. Both, prorogation clauses and agreements to arbitrate, were seen as attempts impermissibly to "oust" the jurisdiction of the local court.[2] Even the Uniform

---

14. See Europäische Wirtschaftsgemeinschaft, Kommission, Bericht über den Vorentwurf eines Übereinkommens über die gerichtliche Zuständigkeit, die Anerkennung und Vollstreckung von Entscheidungen in Zivil-und Handelssachen und die Vollstreckung öffentlicher Urkunden, P. Jenard, Reporter, 20 (1965); Jenard Report of the Brussels Convention 1968, Official Journal of the European Community 1979 C 59/1; Netherlands v. Rüffer (Case 814/79) (European Court). Current law—Regulation (EC) 44/2001—is identical.

15. See Johnson v. Berger, 51 Misc.2d 513, 273 N.Y.S.2d 484 (Fam.Ct. 1966), affirmed (recognizing Danish administrative paternity decree); H. Battifol & P. Lagarde, 2 Droit international privé § 714 n.6 (6th ed. 1976) (with regard to French recognition of administrative divorces).

16. 2 A.A. Ehrenzweig & E. Jayme, supra n.8, at 72.

§ 24.47

1. See supra § 11.3.

2. See A.A. Ehrenzweig, Conflict of Laws, at 193, 195 (rev. ed. 1962). See also, Note, The Recognition and Enforcement of Foreign Arbitral Awards in the United States: Defenses to Arbitrability, 37 S.C.L. Rev. 719 (1986).

In England, arbitration agreements and awards have been recognized longer and more readily, resulting no doubt in part from the fact that England's longstanding position as a center of world trade was reflected in the frequent designation of England as the place for arbitration. Today, a foreign award is enforceable in England, at common law, if the parties submitted to arbitration under a valid agreement and the award is valid and final where rendered. Dicey & Morris, Conflict of Laws 625 (13th ed. 2000 by Collins et al.).

In addition, recognition and enforcement of foreign arbitral awards is available under the Geneva Convention which was adopted by England as Part II of the Arbitration Act of 1950. See id. at 616 et seq. The Arbitration Act of 1975 gives substantial effect to the 1958 U.N. (New York) Convention and provides for the enforcement in England of awards made pursuant to the Convention. Id. at 622 et seq. For the New York Convention see infra § 24.48, n.3. The Arbitration Act of 1979 repealed § 21 of the Arbitration Act of 1950 and abolished the power of the High Court to set aside an award for errors of fact or law appearing on the face of the award, deals with the Court's limited power to review the award on questions of law, and delineates the extent to which the parties may exclude these powers by stipulation. The Arbitration (International Investment Disputes) Act of 1966 incorporates the 1964 Washington convention which established a Center for the Settlement of Investment Disputes between contracting states and nationals of other contracting states. Id. at 634. The United States is also a party to this convention: 17 UST 1270; TIAS 6090 (entered into force Oct. 14, 1966). See Dicey & Morris, Conflict of Laws 634 seq. (13th ed. by Collins et al. 2000).

The German Supreme Court has held that a New York Arbitration award, confirmed by a judgment by a New York court, was entitled to recognition and enforcement when the New York court had undertaken a review of the award. Contrary to the previously prevailing view, the Court concluded that the award had merged into the judgment. It was therefore the latter and not the former that was sought to be enforced. New York judgments, unlike arbitral awards, are conclusive and not subject to further review. Judgment of March 27, 1984, (1984) Recht der Internationalen Wirtschaft 557. See also BGH, Decision of February 22, 2001, NJW 2001, 1730 (foreign award was set judicially aside in the

Arbitration Act,[3] now in force in most states, provides only procedures for in-state arbitration, judicial review and enforcement, but not for recognition and enforcement of sister-state awards. Such recognition, unless the award has been reduced to judgment and, as a judgment, is then entitled to full faith and credit,[4] remains a matter of state common law. The Second, Restatement,[5] with growing adoption by the case law, supports the recognition of arbitration *awards* (beyond those already reduced to judgment) when the award is enforceable where rendered, the arbitration tribunal had personal jurisdiction over the defendant and afforded him or her a reasonable opportunity to be heard. It does, however, expressly, preserve as an exception that the award not be based on a cause of action "contrary to the strong public policy of the forum."[6]

country of origin and enforcement in Germany therefore denied; reversal of the foreign judgment resulted in re-instatement of the award and its recognition in Germany.

In France, the Decree No. 81–500 of May 12, 1981 codifies the rules on international arbitration and now constitutes Article 1492 to 1507 of the New Code of Civil Procedure. For a translation see 20 Int. Legal Mat. 917 (1961). According to these provisions, foreign awards are binding and enforceable in France subject only to these limitations: absence of a valid arbitration agreement, irregularities in the appointment of the arbitrators, lack of due process in the proceeding, or violation of French public policy. The last limitation is said not to constitute a significant obstacle: Delaume, International Arbitration under French Law, 37 Arbitration J. 38, 39 (1982), also with further references; Bellet and Mezger, L'arbitrage international dans le nouveau Code de procedure civile, 70 Revue critique de droit international privé 661 (1981). See Delaume, ICSID Arbitration and the Courts, 77 Am. J. Int'l L. 784 (1983); Delaume, ICSID Arbitration in Practice, 2 Int'l Tax & Bus. Lawyer 58 (1984).

3. 7 U.L.A. 1.

4. See Campanelli v. Conservas Altamira, S.A., 86 Nev. 838, 477 P.2d 870 (1970) (New York judgment in arbitration matter, entered pursuant to New York statutory arbitration procedure, entitled to full faith and credit in Nevada). See also, R.C. Johnson & Assoc. v. Smithers, dba Town & Country Drywall, 87 Nev. 301, 486 P.2d 481 (1971). Fauntleroy v. Lum, 210 U.S. 230, 28 S.Ct. 641, 52 L.Ed. 1039 (1908), discussed supra § 24.20, involved a Missouri arbitration award on a gambling debt, reduced to judgment in Missouri, and then sought to be enforced in Mississippi.

5. § 220(a). The leading early case is Gilbert v. Burnstine, 255 N.Y. 348, 174 N.E. 706 (1931). See also Standard Magnesium Corp. v. Fuchs, K.G., 251 F.2d 455 (10th Cir.1957); Oilcakes & Oilseeds Trading Co. v. Sinason Teicher Inter American Grain Corp., 9 Misc.2d 651, 170 N.Y.S.2d 378 (1958), affirmed 8 N.Y.2d 852, 203 N.Y.S.2d 904, 168 N.E.2d 708 (1960).

6. Restatement, Second, Conflict of Laws § 220(b) (1971). See Benton v. Singleton, 114 Ga. 548, 40 S.E. 811 (1902) (gambling contract). The award would be enforceable once reduced to judgment in the original state or a third state: Fauntleroy v. Lum, supra n.4. See generally, Stanger, Interstate Enforcement of Arbitration Awards and Judgments, 8 Clev.–Mar. L. Rev. 559 (1959); Note, 56 Colum. L. Rev. 902 (1956). Cf. Firedoor Corp. of America v. MacFarland Builders, Inc., 79 A.D.2d 356, 436 N.Y.S.2d 647 (1981) (arbitration award is res judicata as to claims of which defendant was or reasonably should have been aware at the time of arbitration).

With respect to the applicable law in arbitration, see Croff, The Applicable Law in International Commercial Arbitration: Is It Still a Conflict of Laws Problem?, 16 Int'l Lawyer 613 (1982); A.T. von Mehren, Limitations on Party Choice of the Governing Law: Do They Exist for International Commercial Arbitration?, Tel Aviv University Mortimer and Raymond Sackler Institute of Advanced Studies IAS 835–86 (1986); Várady, Barceló & von Mehren, International Commercial Arbitration 527 *et seq.* (1999) (with materials and references). See also Hobér, Das anzuwendende Recht beim internationalen Schiedsverfahren in Schweden, 1986 Recht der Internationalen Wirtschaft 685; Xiaowen Qiu, Enforcing Arbitral Awards Involving Foreign Parties: A Comparison of the United States and China, 11 Am. Rev. Int'l Arb. 607 (2000).

Bilateral commercial treaties with foreign nations frequently provide for the recognition of arbitration awards by the several states on the same basis as sister-state awards. To the extent that recognition of the latter is not assured at common law, foreign awards, despite the existence of an applicable bilateral treaty, theoretically are in no better position.[7] Foreign-country awards may, however, be entitled to recognition under the U.N. Convention (immediately following).

§ 24.48   Federal law, however, has long provided for the enforcement of arbitration agreements and the recognition and enforcement of resulting awards with respect to matters within the legislative competence of Congress (admiralty and interstate and foreign commerce).[1] Of particular importance for foreign-country arbitration is the U.S. Supreme Court's decision in *Scherk v. Alberto–Culver Co.*,[2] enforcing an agreement to arbitrate abroad, combined with the ratification by the United States of the 1958 United Nations Convention.[3] The Convention provides for the enforcement of an *agreement* to arbitrate[4] and for the recognition, in the United States, of arbitration *awards* rendered in

---

7. See Quigley, Accession by the United States to the United Nations Convention on the Recognition and Enforcement of Foreign Arbitral Awards, 70 Yale L.J. 1049, 1051 et seq. (1961). For comprehensive discussion see De Vries, International Commercial Arbitration: A Contractual Substitute for National Courts, 57 Tulane L. Rev. 42 (1982).

§ 24.48

1. See §§ 1 and 2 of the Arbitration Act of 1947, as amended 1970, 9 U.S.C.A. §§ 1 and 2, in turn based on the 1925 Act, 43 Stat. 883. For the constitutionality of the 1947 Act see Prima Paint Corp. v. Flood & Conklin Manufacturing Co., 388 U.S. 395, 87 S.Ct. 1801, 18 L.Ed.2d 1270 (1967). For the interplay between state law and the federal act, see Kress Corp. v. Edw. C. Levy Co., 102 Ill.App.3d 264, 58 Ill.Dec. 561, 430 N.E.2d 593 (1981) (critically discussed supra § 3.37 n.4). See Carbonneau, Arbitration and the U.S. Supreme Court: A Plea for Statutory Reform, 5 Ohio St. J. Dispute Resol. 231 (1990).

2. 417 U.S. 506, 94 S.Ct. 2449, 41 L.Ed.2d 270 (1974). See also Mitsubishi Motors Corp. v. Soler Chrysler–Plymouth, Inc., 473 U.S. 614, 105 S.Ct. 3346, 87 L.Ed.2d 444 (1985), (international antitrust claims are arbitrable pursuant to the Arbitration Act); Vimar Seguros y Reaseguros, S.A. v. M/V Sky Reefer, 515 U.S. 528, 115 S.Ct. 2322, 132 L.Ed.2d 462 (1995) (claims under Carriage of Goods by Sea Act are arbitrable). See also Richards v. Lloyd's of London, 135 F.3d 1289 (9th Cir.1998) (en banc), cert. denied 525 U.S. 943, 119 S.Ct. 365, 142 L.Ed.2d 301 (1998) (by analogy, choice-of-court and choice-of-law clauses do not violate anti-waiver provisions of federal securities law).

3. 21 U.S.T. 2517 (1970); T.I.A.S. 6997; entered into force for the United States December 29, 1970; implemented as domestic law by P.L. 91–368, 84 Stat. 692, adding chapter 2 to U.S. Arbitration Act. For reservations applying to the United States see n.5 infra. For discussion see Quigley, Convention on Foreign Arbitral Awards, 58 A.B.A.J. 821 (1972). In England, awards under the New York Convention are enforced according to the Arbitration Act 1996, see Dicey & Morris, Conflict of Laws 634 seq. (13th ed. by Collins et al. 2000). For the Convention on International Investment Disputes see supra § 24.47 n.2.

In 1990, the United States ratified the Inter–American Convention on International Commercial Arbitration, and Congress enacted implementing legislation which will appear as 9 U.S.C.A. §§ 301–307. The new legislation, amending the Federal Arbitration Act, authorizes U.S. courts to order arbitration anywhere in or outside the United States. When both the U.N. and the Inter–American Convention are applicable, the former applies unless a majority of the parties to the arbitration agreement are citizens of a state or states that belong(s) to the Organization of American States and has (have) ratified the Convention.

4. Art. II. See Ledee v. Ceramiche Ragno, 684 F.2d 184 (1st Cir.1982); McCreary Tire & Rubber Co. v. CEAT S.p.A., 501 F.2d 1032 (3d Cir.1974); Antco Shipping Co., Limited v. Sidermar, S.p.A., 417 F.Supp. 207 (D.C.N.Y.1976). See infra n.5.

other contracting states.[5] The provision, permitting a state to refuse recognition to an award which violates local public policy,[6] has received a narrow construction in the case law which, in the main, restricts the defense to procedural due process objections.[7] In view of these developments, the restrictive provisions in bilateral commercial treaties, noted above, lose much of their earlier significance. Arbitral awards rendered in nations adhering to the U.N. Convention will, under the terms of that convention and its preemptive effect under the Supremacy Clause of the Constitution, be entitled to recognition and enforcement in the states of the Union and, depending on the particular state law, possibly enjoy a better position than sister-state awards. Awards rendered in nations which do not adhere to the Convention but with which the United States maintains bilateral commercial treaties may also benefit form the Convention's provisions under most-favored-nation principles.[8]

5. Arts. III, V. The United States ratified the Convention subject to two reservations: reciprocity and that the subject matter of the arbitration is "considered as commercial under the national law of the United States." For decisions on the definition of commercial see *Antco,* supra n. 4, and Island Territory of Curacao v. Solitron Devices, Inc., 356 F.Supp. 1 (S.D.N.Y.1973), affirmed 489 F.2d 1313 (2d Cir.1973), certiorari denied 416 U.S. 986, 94 S.Ct. 2389, 40 L.Ed.2d 763 (1974). See also Beromun Aktiengesellschaft v. Societa Industriale Agricola, 471 F.Supp. 1163 (S.D.N.Y.1979); Lander Co., Inc. v. MMP Investments, Inc. 107 F.3d 476 (7th Cir. 1997), cert. denied 522 U.S. 811, 118 S.Ct. 55, 139 L.Ed.2d 19 (1997).

6. Art. V(2)(b).

7. Geotech Lizenz AG v. Evergreen Systems, Inc., 697 F.Supp. 1248 (E.D.N.Y. 1988); Brandeis Intsel Ltd. v. Calabrian Chemicals Corp., 656 F.Supp. 160 (S.D.N.Y. 1987); Ledee v. Ceramiche Ragno, 684 F.2d 184 (1st Cir.1982); Waterside Ocean Navigation Co. v. International Navigation Ltd., 737 F.2d 150 (2d Cir.1984) (narrow construction of public policy exception and award of post-award, pre-judgment interest); Fertilizer Corp. of India v. IDI Management, Inc., 517 F.Supp. 948 (S.D.Ohio 1981); Parsons & Whittemore Overseas Co., Inc. v. Societe Generale de L'Industrie du Papier (RAKTA), 508 F.2d 969 (2d Cir. 1974); Fotochrome, Inc. v. Copal Co., Limited, 517 F.2d 512 (2d Cir.1975); Biotronik Mess-und Therapiegeraete GmbH & Co. v. Medford Medical Instrument Co., 415 F.Supp. 133 (D.N.J.1976). For discussion see Note, The Public Policy Defense to Recognition and Enforcement of Foreign Arbitral Awards, 7 Calif. W. Int'l L.J. 228 (1977); Hóber, Defenses to Recognition and Enforcement of Foreign Arbitral Awards in

the United States, 48 Nordisk Tidsskrift for international Ret 38 (1979). See also Shell, Res Judicata and Collateral Estoppel Effects of Commercial Arbitration, 35 U.C.L.A. L. Rev. 623 (1988). See also Sampson, Staying the Enforcement of Foreign Commercial Arbitral Awards: A Federal Practice Contravening the Purposes of the New York Convention, 26 Brooklyn J. Int'l L. 1839 (2001).

8. See generally Delaume, L'arbitrage transnational et les tribunaux américains, 108 J. du droit international 788 (1981). For more comprehensive discussion see A. Redfern & M. Hunter, Law and Practice of International Commercial Arbitration *passim* (1986); Note, General Principles of Law in International Commercial Arbitration, 101 Harv. L. Rev. 1816 (1988).

The law of most states does not authorize arbitrators to order interim measures, for instance to attach property, in order to secure the future performance of an award. This raises the question whether national courts have jurisdiction to order such measures pending arbitration under the Convention. The Convention is silent on this point because its objective is to facilitate recognition of awards and not to effect changes in national procedural law. A. van den Berg, The New York Arbitration Convention of 1958 (1981) at 143, 144. While the courts of most Convention states remain competent to order interim measures, American courts are split. In Carolina Power & Light Co. v. Uranex, 451 F.Supp. 1044 (N.D.Cal.1977) the court ordered attachment pending arbitration and considered this to be consistent with the Convention and with the requirements of Due Process. See Note, Pre–Award Attachment under the U.N. Convention on the Recognition and Enforcement of Foreign Arbitral

Awards, 21 Va. J. Int'l L. 785 (1981). Other decisions point to Art. VI of the Convention which authorizes the suspension of the enforcement of an award and, in that context, the entry of an order requiring the other party to post security. This provision for security is then considered to be exclusive, thus not permitting additional remedies such as pre-award attachment. I.T.A.D. Associates, Inc. v. Podar Bros., 636 F.2d 75 (4th Cir.1981); Cooper v. Ateliers de la Motobecane, S.A., 57 N.Y.2d 408, 456 N.Y.S.2d 728, 442 N.E.2d 1239 (1982). At least *Cooper* is distinguishable from *Uranex* because arbitration there was resisted altogether and the court was primarily concerned with enforcing the arbitration agreement rather than permitting litigation. The rationale of *Uranex,* permitting pre-award attachment, should prevail, it seems, whenever this remedy is sought *in support of* arbitration. The argument with respect to Art. VI of the Convention seems inapposite: the Convention addresses the award and its enforcement; it does not speak to pre-award procedures. This conclusion is supported by E.A.S.T., Inc. v. M/V Alaia, 876 F.2d 1168 (5th Cir.1989) in which the court held that "prejudgment attachment under Section 8—as an aid to arbitration—is manifestly not inconsistent with the aims of the convention." It follows, of course, that there should be no parallel judicial proceedings. These would be "inconsistent with the aims of the convention." It is a more difficult question whether arbitral proceedings in one country should bar or suspend judicial proceedings in another convention state. For an affirmative answer see T. Várady, J.

Barceló & A.T. von Mehren, International Commercial Arbitration 608–09 (1999). See also R. Fouchard et al., Traité de l'arbitrage commercial international 416 et seq. (1996). For the issue preclusive effect of an award, see T. Várady et al., supra, at 609.

The U.N. Commission for International Trade Law (UNCITRAL) has promulgated a Model Law on International Commercial Arbitration. Unlike the U.N. Arbitration Convention, the Model Law seeks to unify national substantive and procedural law with respect to arbitration. U.N. Doc. A/CN. 9/246, Annex (March 8, 1984); Kerr, Arbitration and the Courts: The UNCITRAL Model, 34 Int'l & Comp. L.Q. 1 (1985). As of November 2003, legislation based on the UNCITRAL Model Law on International Commercial Arbitration has been enacted in Australia, Azerbaijan, Bahrain, Belarus, Bermuda, Bulgaria, Canada, Croatia, Cyprus, Egypt, Germany, Greece, Guatemala, Hong Kong Special Administrative Region of China, Hungary, India, Iran (Islamic Republic of), Ireland, Japan, Jordan, Kenya, Lithuania, Macau Special Administrative Region of China, Madagascar, Malta, Mexico, New Zealand, Nigeria, Oman, Paraguay, Peru, Republic of Korea, Russian Federation, Singapore, Sri Lanka, Tunisia, Ukraine, within the United Kingdom of Great Britain and Northern Ireland: Scotland; within the United States of America: California, Connecticut, Illinois, Oregon and Texas; Zambia, and Zimbabwe.

For Switzerland, see Honsell, Vogt, Schnyder & Berti, International Arbitration in Switzerland (2000).

*

Publisher's Appendix

RESEARCHING CONFLICT
OF LAWS

Analysis

Sec.
1. Introduction
2. Westlaw Databases
3. Retrieving a Document with a Citation: Find and Hypertext
    Links
    3.1 Find
    3.2 Hypertext Links
4. Searching with Natural Language
    4.1 Natural Language Search
    4.2 Browsing Search Results
5. Searching with Terms and Connectors
    5.1 Terms
    5.2 Alternative Terms
    5.3 Connectors
    5.4 Field Restrictions
    5.5 Date Restrictions
6. Searching with Topic and Key Numbers
    6.1 Custom Digest
    6.2 KeySearch®
7. Verifying Your Research with Citation Research Services
    7.1 KeyCite® for Cases
    7.2 KeyCite for Statutes and Regulations
    7.3 KeyCite for Administrative Materials
    7.4 KeyCite Alert
8. Researching with Westlaw: Examples
    8.1 Retrieving Law Review Articles
    8.2 Retrieving Case Law
    8.3 Retrieving Statutes and Regulations
    8.4 Using KeyCite
    8.5 Following Recent Developments

Section 1. Introduction

***Conflict of Laws*, Fourth Edition, provides a strong base for analyzing even the most complex problem involving conflict of laws. Whether your research requires examination of case law, administrative decisions, statutes, expert commentary, or other materials, West books and Westlaw are excellent sources of information.**

To keep you informed of current developments, Westlaw provides frequently updated databases. With Westlaw, you have unparalleled legal research resources at your fingertips.

Additional Resources

If you have not previously used Westlaw or if you have questions not covered in this appendix, call the West Reference Attorneys at 1–800–REF–ATTY (1–800–733–2889). The West Reference Attorneys are trained, licensed attorneys, available 24 hours a day to assist you with your Westlaw search questions. To subscribe to Westlaw, call 1–800–344–5008 or visit westlaw.com at **www.westlaw.com**.

Section 2. Westlaw Databases

Each database on Westlaw is assigned an abbreviation called an *identifier*, which you can use to access the database. You can find identifiers for Westlaw databases in the online Westlaw Directory and in the printed *Westlaw Database Directory*. When you need to know more detailed information about a database, use Scope. Scope contains coverage information, lists of related databases, and valuable search tips.

The following chart lists selected Westlaw databases that contain information pertaining to conflict of laws. For a complete list of databases, see the online Westlaw Directory or the printed *Westlaw Database Directory*. Because new information is continually being added to Westlaw, you should also check the tabbed Westlaw page and the online Westlaw Directory for new database information.

Selected Westlaw Databases

Database	Identifier	Coverage
State and Federal Case Law Combined		
Federal and State Case Law	ALLCASES	Begins with 1945
Federal and State Case Law–Before 1945	ALLCASES–OLD	1789–1944
Individual Circuit Federal and State Cases	CTAX–ALL (where X is a circuit's number or DC)	Varies by court
Individual State State and Federal Cases	XX–CS–ALL (where XX is a state's two-letter postal abbreviation)	Varies by court

Database	Identifier	Coverage
Federal Case Law		
Federal Case Law	ALLFEDS	Begins with 1945
Federal Case Law–Before 1945	ALLFEDS–OLD	1789–1944
U.S. Supreme Court Cases	SCT	Begins with 1945
U.S. Supreme Court Cases–Before 1945	SCT–OLD	1790–1944
U.S. Courts of Appeals Cases	CTA	Begins with 1945
U.S. Courts of Appeals Cases–Before 1945	CTA–OLD	1891–1944
U.S. Court of Appeals Cases, Individual Circuit	CTAX (where X is a circuit's number, DC, or F)	Begins with 1945
U.S. Court of Appeals Cases, Individual Circuit–Before 1945	CTAX–OLD (where X is a circuit's number, DC, or F)	1891–1944
U.S. District Courts Cases	DCT	Begins with 1945
U.S. District Courts Cases–Before 1945	DCT–OLD	1789–1944
U.S. District Court Cases, Individual State	DCTXX (where XX is a state's two-letter postal abbreviation)	Begins with 1945
U.S. District Court Cases, Individual State–Before 1945	DCTXX–OLD (where XX is a state's two-letter postal abbreviation)	Varies by state
State Case Law		
State Case Law	ALLSTATES	Begins with 1945
State Case Law–Before 1945	ALLSTATES–OLD	1821–1944
Individual State Cases	XX–CS (where XX is a state's two-letter postal abbreviation)	Varies by state
West's® Atlantic Reporter®	ATL	Varies by jurisdiction
West's North Eastern Reporter®	NE	Varies by jurisdiction
West's North Western Reporter®	NW	Varies by jurisdiction
West's Pacific Reporter®	PAC	Varies by jurisdiction
West's South Eastern Reporter®	SE	Varies by jurisdiction
West's Southern Reporter®	SO	Varies by jurisdiction
West's South Western Reporter®	SW	Varies by jurisdiction
Briefs, Pleadings, and Other Court Documents		
Andrews Underlying Court Documents	ANDREWS–DOC	Begins with May 1997
Briefs Multibase	BRIEF–ALL	Varies by court
State Briefs All	STATE–BRIEF–ALL	Begins with 1970
Trial Motions	MOTIONS	Begins with 2000
Trial Pleadings	PLEADINGS	Begins with 2000

Database	Identifier	Coverage
United States Supreme Court Briefs Multibase	SCT–BRIEF–ALL	Begins with 1870
United States Court of Appeals Briefs	CTA–BRIEF	Begins with 1972

Federal Statutes, Rules, and Regulations

United States Code Annotated®	USCA	Current data
United States Code	USC	Current data
Federal Rules	US–RULES	Current data
Federal Orders	US–ORDERS	Current data
Code of Federal Regulations	CFR	Current data
Federal Register	FR	Begins with July 1980
United States Public Laws	US–PL	Current data

State Statutes, Rules, and Regulations

State Statutes–Annotated	ST–ANN–ALL	Current data
Individual State Statutes–Annotated	XX–ST–ANN (where XX is a state's two-letter postal abbreviation)	Current data
State Statutes–Unannotated	STAT–ALL	Current data
Individual State Statutes–Unannotated	XX–ST (where XX is a state's two-letter postal abbreviation)	Current data
State Court Rules	RULES–ALL	Current data
Individual State Court Rules	XX–RULES (where XX is a state's two-letter postal abbreviation)	Current data
State Court Orders	ORDERS–ALL	Current data
Individual State Court Orders	XX–ORDERS (where XX is a state's two-letter postal abbreviation)	Current data
Multistate Administrative Codes– Academic Accounts	ADC–ACAD	Current data
Individual State Administrative Code	XX–ADC (where XX is a state's two-letter postal abbreviation)	Current data
Multistate Legislative Service	LEGIS–ALL	Current data
Individual State Legislative Service	XX–LEGIS (where XX is a state's two-letter postal abbreviation)	Current data

Legal Texts, Periodicals, and Practice Materials

Texts and Periodicals–All Law Reviews, Texts, and Bar Journals	TP–ALL	Varies by publication
Journals and Law Reviews	JLR	Varies by publication

Database	Identifier	Coverage
Individual State Journals and Law Reviews	XX–JLR (where XX is a state's two-letter postal abbreviation)	Varies by publication
American Jurisprudence 2d	AMJUR	Current data
American Law Reports	ALR	Current data
Corpus Juris Secundum®	CJS	Current data
Federal Practice and Procedure®	FPP	Current data
Restatement of the Law–Conflict of Laws	REST–CONFL	Current data
News and Information		
All News	ALLNEWS	Varies by source
Westlaw Bulletin	WLB	Current data
Directories		
West Legal Directory®	WLD	Current data

Section 3. Retrieving a Document with a Citation: Find and Hypertext Links

3.1 Find

Find is a Westlaw service that allows you to retrieve a document by entering its citation. Find allows you to retrieve documents from any page in westlaw.com without accessing or changing databases. Find is available for many documents, including case law (state and federal), the *United States Code Annotated*® (USCA®), state statutes, administrative materials, and texts and periodicals.

To use Find, simply type the citation in the *Find this document by citation* text box at the tabbed Westlaw page and click **GO**. The following list provides some examples:

To find this document:	Access Find and type:
Massachusetts Mut. Life Ins. Co. v. Ludwig,	**96 sct 2158** 96 S. Ct. 2158 (1976)
Garcia v. International Elevator Co., 358 F.3d 777 (10th Cir. 2004)	**358 f3d 777**
29 U.S.C.A. § 165	**29 usca 165**
13 C.F.R. § 120.554	**13 cfr 120.554**
Fed. R. Civ. P. 4	**frcp 4**
Cal. Corp. Code § 17450	**cal corp code s 17450**
Fla. Stat. Ann. § 413.203	**fl st s 413.203**

For a complete list of publications that can be retrieved with Find and their abbreviations, click **Find** on the toolbar and then click **Publications List**.

3.2 Hypertext Links

Use hypertext links to move from one location to another on Westlaw. For example, use hypertext links to go directly from the statute, case, or law review article you are viewing to a cited statute, case, or article; from a headnote to the corresponding text in the opinion; or from an entry in a statutes index database to the full text of the statute.

Section 4. Searching with Natural Language

Overview: With Natural Language, you can retrieve documents by simply describing your issue in plain English. If you are a relatively new Westlaw user, Natural Language searching can make it easier for you to retrieve cases that are on point. If you are an experienced Westlaw user, Natural Language gives you a valuable alternative search method to the Terms and Connectors search method described in Section 5.

When you enter a Natural Language description, Westlaw automatically identifies legal phrases, removes common words, and generates variations of terms in your description. Westlaw then searches for the concepts in your description. Concepts may include significant terms, phrases, legal citations, or topic and key numbers. Westlaw retrieves the documents that most closely match the concepts in your description, beginning with the document most likely to match.

4.1 Natural Language Search

Access a database, such as the Federal Case Law database (ALLFEDS). Click **Natural Language** and type the following description in the text box:

what minimum contacts are sufficient to establish jurisdiction

4.2 Browsing Search Results

Best Mode: To display the best portion (the portion that most closely matches your description) of each document in a Natural Language search result, click the **Best** arrows at the bottom of the right frame.

Term Mode: Click the **Term** arrows at the bottom of the right frame to display portions of the document that contain your search terms.

Previous/Next Document: Click the left or right **Doc** arrow at the bottom of the right frame to view the previous or the next document in the search result.

Section 5. Searching with Terms and Connectors

Overview: With Terms and Connectors searching, you enter a query consisting of key terms from your issue and connectors specifying the relationship between these terms.

Terms and Connectors searching is useful when you want to retrieve a document for which you know specific details, such as the title or the fact situation. Terms and Connectors searching is also useful when you want to retrieve all documents containing specific terms.

5.1 Terms

Plurals and Possessives: Plurals are automatically retrieved when you enter the singular form of a term. This is true for both regular and irregular plurals (e.g., **child** retrieves *children*). If you enter the plural form of a term, you will not retrieve the singular form.

If you enter the nonpossessive form of a term, Westlaw automatically retrieves the possessive form as well. However, if you enter the possessive form, only the possessive form is retrieved.

Compound Words and Abbreviations: When a compound word is one of your search terms, use a hyphen to retrieve all forms of the word. For example, the term **non-judicial** retrieves *non-judicial*, *nonjudicial*, and *non judicial*.

When using an abbreviation as a search term, place a period after each of the letters to retrieve any of its forms. For example, the term **u.c.c.** retrieves *UCC*, *U.C.C.*, *U C C*, and *U. C. C.* Note: The abbreviation does not retrieve the phrase *Uniform Commercial Code*, so remember to add additional alternative terms such as **"uniform commercial code"** to your query.

The Root Expander and the Universal Character: When you use the Terms and Connectors search method, placing the root expander (!) at the end of a root term generates all other terms with that root. For example, adding the ! to the root *enforc* in the query

enforc! /s contract

instructs Westlaw to retrieve such terms as *enforce*, *enforced*, *enforcing*, *enforcement*, and *enforceable*.

The universal character (*) stands for one character and can be inserted in the middle or at the end of a term. For example, the term

withdr*w

will retrieve *withdraw* and *withdrew*. Adding three asterisks to the root *elect*

elect* * *

instructs Westlaw to retrieve all forms of the root with up to three additional characters. Terms such as *elected* or *election* are retrieved by this query. However, terms with more than three letters following the root, such as *electronic*, are not retrieved. Plurals are always retrieved, even if the plural form of the term has more than three letters following the root.

Phrase Searching: To search for an exact phrase, place it within quotation marks. For example, to search for references to *forum non conveniens*, type **"forum non conveniens"**. When you are using the Terms and Connectors search method, you should use phrase searching only if you are certain that the terms in the phrase will not appear in any other order.

5.2 Alternative Terms

After selecting the terms for your query, consider which alternative terms are necessary. For example, if you are searching for the term *constitutional*, you might also want to search for the term *unconstitutional*. You should consider both synonyms and antonyms as alternative terms. You can also use the Westlaw thesaurus to add alternative terms to your query.

5.3 Connectors

After selecting terms and alternative terms for your query, use connectors to specify the relationship that must exist between search terms in your retrieved documents. The connectors are described below:

Type:	To retrieve documents with:	Example:
(and)	both terms	**jurisdiction & "minimum contact"**
a space (or)	either term or both terms	**domicile residence**
/p	search terms in the same paragraph	**contract /p choice-of-law**
/s	search terms in the same sentence	**foreign /s judgment**
+s	the first search term preceding the second within the same sentence	**erie +s tompkins**
/n	search terms within *n* terms of each other (where *n* is a number from 1 to 255)	**significant /5 relationship**
+n	the first search term preceding the second by *n* terms (where *n* is a number from 1 to 255)	**full +3 faith +3 credit**
" "	search terms appearing in the same order as in the quotation marks	**"quasi in rem"**

Type:	To exclude documents with:	Example:
(but not)	search terms following the SYMBOL	**long-arm 'personal injury"**

5.4 Field Restrictions

Overview: Documents in each Westlaw database consist of several segments, or *fields*. One field may contain the citation, another the title, another the synopsis, and so forth. Not all databases contain the same fields. Also depending on the database, fields with the same name may contain different types of information.

To view a list of fields and their contents for a specific database, see Scope for that database. Note that in some databases not every field is available for every document.

To retrieve only those documents containing your search terms in a specific field, restrict your search to that field. To restrict your search to a specific field, type the field name or abbreviation followed by your search terms enclosed in parentheses. For example, to retrieve a U.S. court of appeals case titled *Gilbert v. Seton Hall University*, access the U.S. Courts of Appeals Cases database (CTA) and search for your terms in the title field (ti):

ti(gilbert & "seton hall")

The fields discussed below are available in Westlaw case law databases you might use for researching issues related to conflict of laws.

Digest and Synopsis Fields: The digest (di) and synopsis (sy) fields summarize the main points of a case. The synopsis field contains a brief description of a case. The digest field contains the topic and headnote fields and includes the complete hierarchy of concepts used by West's editors to classify the headnotes to specific West digest topic and key numbers. Restricting your search to the synopsis and digest fields limits your result to cases in which your terms are related to a major issue in the case.

Consider restricting your search to one or both of these fields if

● you are searching for common terms or terms with more than one meaning, and you need to narrow your search; or

● you cannot narrow your search by using a smaller database.

For example, to retrieve Massachusetts state cases that discuss the enforcement of foreign judgments, access the Massachusetts Cases database (MA–CS) and type the following query:

sy,di(enforc! /p foreign /p judgment decree)

Headnote Field: The headnote field (he) is part of the digest field but does not contain the topic names or numbers, hierarchical classification information, or key numbers. The headnote field contains a one-sentence summary for each point of law in a case and any supporting citations given by the author of the opinion. A headnote field restriction is useful when you are searching for specific statutory sections or rule numbers. For example, to retrieve headnotes from federal cases that cite 28 U.S.C.A. § 1360, access the ALLFEDS database and type the following query:

he(28 + s 1360)

Topic Field: The topic field (to) is also part of the digest field. It contains the hierarchical classification information, including the West digest topic names and numbers and the key numbers. You should restrict search terms to the topic field in a case law database if

● a digest field search retrieves too many documents; or

● you want to retrieve cases with digest paragraphs classified under more than one topic.

For example, the topic Insurance has the topic number 217. To retrieve New York state cases that discuss choice of law in the context of insurance, access the New York Cases database (NY–CS) and type a query like the following:

to(217) /p choice /5 law

To retrieve cases classified under more than one topic and key number, search for your terms in the topic field. For example, to retrieve recent cases from state and federal courts in the Fifth Circuit discussing long-arm jurisdiction, which may be classified to such topics as Courts (106) or Federal Courts (170B), access the Fifth Circuit Federal and State Cases database (CTA5–ALL) and type a query like the following:

to(long-arm) & da(aft 2002)

For a complete list of West digest topics and their corresponding topic numbers, access the Custom Digest by choosing **Key Numbers and Digest** from the *More* drop-down list on the toolbar.

Prelim and Caption Fields: When searching in a database containing statutes, rules, or regulations, restrict your search to the prelim (pr) and caption (ca) fields to retrieve documents in which your terms are important enough to appear in a section name or heading. For example, to retrieve federal statutes regarding the enforcement of foreign arbitration awards, access the United States Code Annotated database (USCA) and type the following query:

pr,ca(enforc! & foreign & arbitra!)

5.5 Date Restrictions

You can use Westlaw to retrieve documents *decided* or *issued* before, after, or on a specified date, as well as within a range of dates. The following sample queries contain date restrictions:

da(2003) & conflict-of-law

da(aft 1998) & conflict-of-law

da(5/20/2004) & conflict-of-law

You can also search for documents *added to a database* on or after a specified date, as well as within a range of dates, which is useful for updating your research. The following sample queries contain added-date restrictions:

ad(aft 2002) & conflict-of-law

ad(aft 11/9/2001 & bef 6/23/2002) & conflict-of-law

Section 6. Searching with Topic and Key Numbers

To retrieve cases that address a specific point of law, use topic and key numbers as your search terms. If you have an on-point case, run a search using the topic and key number from the relevant headnote in an appropriate database to find other cases containing headnotes classified to that topic and key number. For example, to search for California state cases containing headnotes classified under topic 253 (Marriage) and key number 3 (What Law Governs), access the California Cases database (CA–CS) and type the following query:

253k3

For a complete list of West digest topics and their corresponding topic numbers, access the Custom Digest by choosing **Key Numbers and Digest** from the *More* drop-down list on the toolbar.

> *Note*: Slip opinions and cases from topical services do not contain West topic and key numbers.

6.1 Custom Digest

The Custom Digest contains the complete topic and key number outline used by West attorney-editors to classify headnotes. You can use the Custom Digest to obtain a single document containing all case law headnotes from a specific jurisdiction that are classified under a particular topic and key number.

Access the Custom Digest by choosing **Key Numbers and Digest** from the *More* drop-down list on the toolbar. Select up to 10 topics and key numbers from the easy-to-browse outline and click **Search selected**. Then follow the displayed instructions.

For example, to research issues involving the federal courts, scroll down the Custom Digest page until topic 170B, *Federal Courts*, is displayed. Click the plus symbols (+) to display key number information. Select the check box next to each key number you want to include in your search, then click **Search selected**. Select the jurisdiction from which you want to retrieve headnotes and, if desired, type additional search terms and select a date restriction. Click **Search**.

6.2 KeySearch

KeySearch is a research tool that helps you find cases and secondary sources in a specific area of the law. KeySearch guides you through the selection of terms from a classification system based on the West Key Number System® and then uses the key numbers and their underlying concepts to automatically supply a query for you.

To access KeySearch, click **KeySearch** on the toolbar. Then browse the list of topics and subtopics and select a topic or subtopic to search by clicking the hypertext links. For example, to search for cases that discuss conflict of laws in the area of products liability, click **Conflict of Laws** at the first KeySearch page. Then click **Products Liability** at the next page. Select the source from which you want to retrieve documents and, if desired, type additional search terms. Click **Search**.

Section 7. Verifying Your Research with Citation Research Services

Overview: A citation research service, such as KeyCite, is a tool that helps you ensure that your cases, statutes, regulations, and administrative decisions are good law; retrieve cases, legislation, articles, or other documents that cite them; and verify the spelling and format of your citations.

7.1 KeyCite for Cases

KeyCite for cases covers case law on Westlaw, including unpublished opinions. KeyCite for cases provides the following:

- direct appellate history of a case, including related references, which are opinions involving the same parties and facts but resolving different issues

- negative indirect history of a case, which consists of cases outside the direct appellate line that may have a negative impact on its precedential value

- the title, parallel citations, court of decision, docket number, and filing date of a case

- citations to cases, administrative decisions, secondary sources, and briefs on Westlaw that have cited a case

- complete integration with the West Key Number System so you can track legal issues discussed in a case

7.2 KeyCite for Statutes and Regulations

KeyCite for statutes and regulations covers the USCA, the *Code of Federal Regulations* (CFR), statutes from all 50 states, and regulations from selected states. KeyCite for statutes and regulations provides

- links to session laws or rules amending or repealing a statute or regulation

- statutory credits and historical notes

- citations to pending legislation affecting a statute

- citations to cases, administrative decisions, secondary sources, and briefs that have cited a statute or regulation

7.3 KeyCite for Administrative Materials

KeyCite for administrative materials includes the following:

- National Labor Relations Board decisions beginning with 1935
- Board of Contract Appeals decisions (varies by agency)
- Board of Immigration Appeals decisions beginning with 1940
- Comptroller General decisions beginning with 1921
- Environmental Protection Agency decisions beginning with 1974
- Federal Communications Commission decisions beginning with 1960
- Federal Energy Regulatory Commission (Federal Power Commission) decisions beginning with 1931
- Internal Revenue Service revenue rulings beginning with 1954
- Internal Revenue Service revenue procedures beginning with 1954

- Internal Revenue Service private letter rulings beginning with 1954

- Internal Revenue Service technical advice memoranda beginning with 1954

- *Public Utilities Reports* beginning with 1974

- U.S. Merit Systems Protection Board decisions beginning with 1979

- U.S. Patent and Trademark Office decisions beginning with 1984

- U.S. Tax Court (Board of Tax Appeals) decisions beginning with 1924

- U.S. patents beginning with 1976

7.4 KeyCite Alert

KeyCite Alert monitors the status of your cases, statutes, regulations, and administrative decisions and automatically sends you updates at the frequency you specify when their KeyCite information changes.

Section 8. Researching with Westlaw: Examples

8.1 Retrieving Law Review Articles

Recent law review articles are often a good place to begin researching a legal issue because law review articles serve as an excellent introduction to a new topic or review for an old one, providing terminology to help you formulate a query; as a finding tool for pertinent primary authority, such as cases, statutes, and rules; and in some instances, as persuasive secondary authority.

Suppose you need to gain background information on conflict of laws issues surrounding same-sex marriage.

Solution

- To retrieve law review articles relevant to your issue, access the Journals and Law Reviews database (JLR). Using the Natural Language search method, type a description like the following:

conflict of laws same-sex marriage

- If you have a citation to an article in a specific publication, use Find to retrieve it. For more information on Find, see Section 3.1 of this appendix. For example, to retrieve the article found at 3 Whittier J. Child & Fam. Advoc. 231, access Find and type

3 whittier j child & fam advoc 231

- If you know the title of an article but not the journal in which it was published, access the JLR database and search for key terms in the title field. For example, to retrieve the article "Same–Sex Unions and Conflicts of Law: When 'I Do' May Be Interpreted As 'No, You Didn't!'," type the following Terms and Connectors query:

ti(same-sex & union & conflict)

8.2 Retrieving Case Law

Suppose you need to retrieve federal cases discussing the 100–mile bulge rule, which extends jurisdiction of the federal district courts to any party served within 100 miles of the place from which the summons was issued.

Solution

- Access the ALLFEDS database. Type a Terms and Connectors query such as the following:

100 /s mile /s bulge

- When you know the citation for a specific case, use Find to retrieve it. For example, to retrieve *Quinones v. Pennsylvania General Ins. Co.*, 804 F.2d 1167 (10th Cir. 1986), access Find and type

804 f2d 1167

- If you find a topic and key number that is on point, run a search using that topic and key number to retrieve additional cases discussing that point of law. For example, to retrieve federal cases containing headnotes classified under topic 170B (Federal Courts) and key number 76.5 (Contacts with Forum State), access the ALLFEDS database and type the following query:

170bk76.5

- To retrieve cases written by a particular judge, add a judge field (ju) restriction to your query. For example, to retrieve federal court of appeals cases written by Judge Tacha that contain headnotes classified under topic 170B (Federal Courts), access the CTA database and type the following query:

ju(tacha) & to(170b)

- You can also use KeySearch and the Custom Digest to retrieve cases and headnotes that discuss the issue you are researching.

8.3 Retrieving Statutes and Regulations

Suppose you need to retrieve Nevada statutes dealing with the determination of domicile in the context of estate taxes.

Solution

- Access the West's Nevada Revised Statutes–Annotated database (NV–ST–ANN). Search for your terms in the prelim and caption fields using the Terms and Connectors search method:

pr,ca(domicile & estate /p tax!)

- When you know the citation for a specific statute or regulation, use Find to retrieve it. For example, to retrieve Nev. Rev. Stat. Ann. § 375A.645, access Find and type

nv st s 375a.645

• To look at surrounding sections, use the Table of Contents service. Click **Table of Contents** on the Links tab in the left frame. To display a section listed in the Table of Contents, click its hypertext link. You can also use Documents in Sequence to retrieve the sections following section 375A.645 even if the subsequent sections were not retrieved with your search or Find request. Choose **Documents in Sequence** from the Tools menu at the bottom of the right frame.

8.4 Using KeyCite

Suppose one of the cases you retrieve in your case law research is *A.M. Capen's Co. v. American Trading and Production Corp.*, 973 F. Supp. 247 (D. P.R. 1997).

Solution

• Use KeyCite to retrieve direct and negative indirect history for the case. Access KeyCite and type **973 fsupp 247**.

• Use KeyCite to display citing references for the case. Click **Citing References** on the Links tab in the left frame.

8.5 Following Recent Developments

If you are researching issues related to conflict of laws, it is important to keep up with recent developments. How can you do this efficiently?

Solution

One of the easiest ways to follow recent conflict of laws developments is to access the Westlaw Bulletin database (WLB). The WLB database contains summaries of recent federal and state judicial, legislative, and administrative activities. When you access the WLB database, you automatically retrieve a list of documents added to the database in the last two weeks.

You can use the WestClip® clipping service to stay informed of recent developments of interest to you. WestClip will run your Terms and Connectors queries on a regular basis and deliver the results to you automatically. You can run WestClip queries in legal and news and information databases.

*

Table of Restatement Citations

RESTATEMENT 2ND AGENCY

Sec.	This Work Page
208	1026

RESTATEMENT 1ST CONFLICT OF LAWS

Sec.	This Work Page
6	97
7(b)	990
132	582
311 et seq.	990
323	1048
332	989
332	990
333	989
358, Comment (b)	990
377	21
377	713
377	717
377	720
378	21
382(1)	717
382(2)	717
382(c)	715
382, Comment	715
384	21
387	715
387, Comment (a)	715
452	1048
453	719
453	1042
621—622	544

RESTATEMENT 2ND CONFLICT OF LAWS

Sec.	This Work Page
2	1
Ch. 3, Intro. Note	287
Ch. 3, Intro. Note	296
Ch. 3, Intro. Note	297
Ch. 3, Intro. Note	298
6	45
6	53
6	59
6	60
6	61
6	63
6	64

RESTATEMENT 2ND CONFLICT OF LAWS

Sec.	This Work Page
6	65
6	66
6	80
6	82
6	91
6	125
6	130
6	145
6	749
6	760
6	764
6	766
6	772
6	787
6	877
6	912
6	998
6	1001
6	1005
6	1007
6	1027
6(2)(b)	727
6(2)(b)	760
6(2)(b)	881
6(2)(c)	727
6(2)(c)	760
6(2)(d)	782
6(2)(d)	996
6, Comment (c)	60
6, Comment (c)	760
6, Comment (d)	60
6, Comment (e)	760
7	1056
7, Comment (b)	125
7, Comment (b)	726
7, Comment (c)	127
8	138
8	142
8(2)	140
8(2)	142
8(3)	140
Ch. 8, Intro. Note	1036
Ch. 9, Intro.	1056
Ch. 9, Intro.	1075
11	233
11	234
11	249
11	252
11, Comment (f)	283

RESTATEMENT 2ND CONFLICT OF LAWS

Sec.	This Work Page
11, Comment (g)	265
11, Comment (k)	244
11, Comment (l)	1222
11, Comment (o)	251
Ch. 11, Intro. Note	559
12	233
12	250
12	252
12, Comment (d)	266
13	236
13	239
13, Comment (b)	240
13, Comment (c)	240
13, Comment (c)	241
Ch. 13, Intro. Note	1219
14(1)	272
14(2)	272
15	252
16	253
16, Comment (c)	266
17	260
17, Comment (c)	263
17, Comment (d)	262
17, Comment (d)	631
17, Comment (e)	265
17, Comment (g)	265
18	252
18	255
18	256
18	258
18, Comment (e)	257
18, Comment (f)	259
18, Comment (h)	255
19	252
19	273
20, Comment (c)	260
21	270
22	274
22	275
22	276
22, Comment (b)	276
22, Comment (b)	278
22, Comment (b)	279
22, Comment (c)	276
22, Comment (d)	274
22, Comment (d)	278
22, Comment (f)	281
22, Comment (g)	277
22, Comment (h)	279
22, Comment (h)	280
22, Comment (i)	279
23	282
23, Comment (c)	282
23, Comment (f)	280
23, Comment (f)	282
23, Comment (f)	283
24	285
24	459
25	519
25, Comment (e)	520
28	300

RESTATEMENT 2ND CONFLICT OF LAWS

Sec.	This Work Page
29—31	234
29, Comment (c)	300
29, Comment (c)	343
30	345
30, Comment (b)	321
31, Comment (b)	344
32	300
32	451
33	346
33—34	300
34	334
35(3)	320
35(3)	354
35(3)	359
40	451
40	452
40, Comment (b)	451
40, Comment (d)	452
40, Comment (e)	452
41	453
42	454
48	456
53	1274
53, Comment (c)	1274
56	1080
58	335
59—63	296
69—79	299
70	233
70	235
71	235
71	299
72	632
73	239
73	639
74	638
74	655
76	648
76(b)	646
76(b)	647
77	299
78	700
79	299
79	681
79	1216
79	1217
79, Comment (d)	1216
83	508
83, Comment (b)	508
84	454
84	492
84, Comment (c)	495
84, Comment (e)	501
84, Comment (e)	509
84, Comment (f)	499
85	148
85	498
85, Comment (b)	498
87	375
89, Comment (a)	147
90, Comment (a)	144

RESTATEMENT 2ND CONFLICT OF LAWS

Sec.	This Work Page
90, Comment (c)	143
92	679
92	1285
92	1314
92, Comment (a)	1338
93	1280
93	1314
93, Comment (b)	1282
93, Comment (d)	1314
95, Comment (b)	148
95, Comment (c)(1)	1265
95, Comment (g)	1262
96	239
96	332
97	332
98	333
98	1268
98	1287
98	1314
98, Comment (a)	1338
98, Comment (b)	1267
98, Comment (c)	1311
98, Comment (d)	333
98, Comment (d)	1266
98, Comment (f)	1266
98, Comment (f)	1269
98, Comment (f)	1289
98, Comment (f)	1315
98, Comment (f)	1337
98, Comment (h)	1289
99—100	1268
100, Comment (d)	1269
101, Comment (d)	1326
102, Comment (d)	1277
103	1262
103	1292
103	1293
103, Comment (b)	1276
103, Comment (b)	1293
104	1285
104	1289
105	1287
106	1287
106, Comment (a)	1287
107	1272
107	1303
107—108	1302
109	679
109(2)	675
109, Comment (d)	679
111	1303
112	1303
113—114	1303
114, Comment (b)	1304
115	1289
115, Comment (b)	1289
115, Comment (c)	1289
115, Comment (f)	1289
116	1305
117	1291
117, Comment (c)	1335

RESTATEMENT 2ND CONFLICT OF LAWS

Sec.	This Work Page
118(2)	1306
118, Comment (c)	1306
118, Comment (c)	1307
120	1332
120, Comment (d)	146
121	1305
122 et seq.	128
122, Comment (b)	129
136, Comment (h)	551
136, Comment (h)	553
138	536
138	537
139	537
139(1)	537
139(1)	543
139(2)	538
139(2)	540
139(2)	543
139, Comment (c)	538
139, Comment (c)	543
139, Comment (d)	538
139, Comment (d)	539
139, Comment (d)	542
140	1034
140, Comment (c)	1034
141	128
141	1034
141, Comment (b)	1034
141, Comment (g)	1035
142	130
142	131
142	135
142	137
142	726
142—143	137
142, Comment (b)	135
142, Comment (d)	129
143, Comment (c)	129
143, Comment (c)	131
143, Comment (c)	132
144	1326
144, Comment (b)	1327
144, Comment (g)	1326
144, Comment (g)	1327
145	60
145	62
145	63
145	66
145	82
145	91
145	125
145	717
145	739
145	760
145	761
145	764
145	766
145	787
145	870
145	877
145	912

RESTATEMENT 2ND CONFLICT OF LAWS

Sec.	This Work Page
145	924
145	988
145	1031
145(1)	759
145(2)	66
145(2)	760
145(2)(d)	809
145, Comment (d)	61
145, Comment (d)	766
145, Comment (f)	870
146	61
146	82
146	91
146	760
146	761
146	764
146	787
146	846
146	924
146	925
146	930
146—151	63
146—147	867
148	127
148(1)	867
148(2)	867
148, Comment (h)	867
149	872
149, Comment (c)	872
150(2)	873
150(3)	873
152	63
152	872
153	874
153—155	63
154	717
154	871
156	63
156	761
157	63
157	761
158	63
158	761
158(1)	768
159	63
159	761
160	63
160	761
161	63
161	761
162	63
162	761
163	63
163	761
164	63
164	761
165	63
165	761
166	63
166	761
168	63

RESTATEMENT 2ND CONFLICT OF LAWS

Sec.	This Work Page
168	761
169	63
169	761
170	761
170	1031
170—171	63
170, Comment (f)	1155
171	761
172	63
172	761
172	1152
173	761
173	887
173—174	63
175	63
181(a)	885
181(b)	885
181(c)	886
181(e)	886
182	886
182, Comment (b)	887
183, Comment (c)	887
184	889
184(b)	887
187	13
187	62
187	82
187	95
187	96
187	102
187	810
187	954
187	955
187	959
187	979
187	980
187	981
187	986
187	1001
187	1039
187—188	1023
187—188	1034
187(1)	955
187(1)	956
187(1)	980
187(2)	94
187(2)	553
187(2)	955
187(2)	970
187(2)	971
187(2)	980
187(2)	981
187(2)	982
187(2)(a)	953
187(2)(a)	978
187(2)(a)	981
187(2)(b)	954
187(2)(b)	956
187(2)(b)	958
187(2)(b)	961
187(2)(b)	964

RESTATEMENT 2ND CONFLICT OF LAWS

Sec.	This Work Page
187(2)(b)	965
187(2)(b)	982
187(3)	1010
187, Comment (a)	949
187, Comment (a)	951
187, Comment (b)	955
187, Comment (b)	966
187, Comment (c)	955
187, Comment (c)	956
187, Comment (c)	980
187, Comment (d)	981
187, Comment (e)	947
187, Comment (e)	966
187, Comment (e)	983
187, Comment (f)	981
187, Comment (g)	959
187, Comment (g)	964
187, Comment (h)	949
187, Comment (i)	981
188	62
188	63
188	77
188	80
188	96
188	100
188	125
188	761
188	898
188	958
188	982
188	983
188	988
188	998
188	1000
188	1001
188	1005
188	1007
188	1009
188	1012
188	1014
188	1017
188	1020
188	1021
188	1023
188	1031
188	1032
188	1035
188	1036
188	1039
188(2)	66
188(2)	992
188(2)	998
188(2)	1005
188(3)	61
188(3)	996
188(3)	998
188(3)	1005
188, Comment (b)	949
188, Comment (c)	1005
188, Comment (d)	61
188, Comment (f)	1005

RESTATEMENT 2ND CONFLICT OF LAWS

Sec.	This Work Page
189	1006
189	1007
189	1039
189—193	63
189—199	1006
189, Comment (d)	1006
190	1006
190	1007
190	1063
190	1064
190	1070
190, Comment (a)	1007
191	1007
191	1008
191	1009
191	1039
191, Comment (a)	1006
192	127
192	1013
192, Comment (d)	1015
192, Comment (h)	968
192, Comment (h)	1013
193	93
193	94
193	1001
193	1004
193	1012
193	1013
193	1014
193	1015
193, Comment (d)	1015
194	992
194	1016
194	1017
194, Comment (b)	1016
195	998
195	1018
196	63
196	78
196	101
196	1019
196	1020
196	1021
196	1022
196	1033
196, Comment (a)	1019
197	1019
197	1021
197, Comment (a)	1021
197, Comment (b)	1021
198	63
198	998
198	1000
198, Comment (a)	955
199	63
199	1034
199(2)	1023
199(2)	1035
199, Comment (a)	955
199, Comment (c)	1023
199, Comment (c)	1035

RESTATEMENT 2ND CONFLICT OF LAWS

Sec.	This Work Page
200, Comment (a)	955
201	1035
202	1035
202(2)	1006
202(2)	1035
202, Comment (e)	1006
203	80
203	969
203	1018
203	1035
203, Comment (e)	982
204	1009
205	1035
205	1036
205, Comment (c)	1035
205, Comment (f)	1036
205, Comment (g)	1036
206	1036
207	1035
207, Comment (c)	1036
208	1033
208	1102
208—211	1033
209	1033
209	1104
209—211	1033
210	1033
211	1033
212(2)	1031
214	1102
215	1032
215(1)	1032
216	1103
216	1106
216	1107
218, Comment (b)	1039
220(a)	1340
220(b)	1340
221	1030
221	1043
221	1046
221	1048
221	1050
221	1051
221(1)(a)	1045
221(2)	66
221(2)	1047
221, Comment (c)	1051
221, Comment (d)	1043
221, Comment (d)	1046
221, Comment (d)	1047
221, Comment (d)	1050
222	1056
222, Comment (e)	1099
223	62
223	138
223	787
223	1006
223	1055
223	1056
223	1057

RESTATEMENT 2ND CONFLICT OF LAWS

Sec.	This Work Page
223	1059
223	1062
223 et seq.	127
223, Comment (d)	1059
224	1006
224, Comment (b)	1062
224, Comment (c)	1062
224, Comment (d)	1062
225—232	62
226	1006
227	1006
228	1006
228	1069
228	1070
229	1006
229	1069
229, Comment (e)	1072
230	1006
231—232	1006
233	597
233	603
233—234	1006
234	607
234	623
234, Comment (a)	604
235	1006
236	62
236	1006
236	1111
237, Comment (b)	1111
238	1006
238, Comment (b)	1111
239	1006
239	1118
239	1119
239—242	62
239, Comment (i)	1120
240	140
240	1123
240, Comment (c)	1123
240, Comment (e)	1123
240, Comment (f)	1125
241—242	1006
243	1006
244	1074
244	1077
244	1106
245	138
245	1080
245—255	62
246	1078
246, Comment (b)	1078
247	1080
250	1104
255	1156
256	1156
257	608
257, Intro. Note	597
258	233
258	622
258	623

RESTATEMENT 2ND CONFLICT OF LAWS

Sec.	This Work Page
259	610
259	612
260	127
260	138
260	139
260	233
260	1114
260	1133
260—265	62
260, Comment (a)	1116
263	138
263	233
263	1125
263	1132
263	1143
263, Comment (i)	1129
264, Comment (d)	1123
265	233
265	607
266	1117
267	1150
268(2)	1149
269	1143
269	1144
269	1156
269, Comment (k)	1155
270	1146
270	1147
270, Comment (c)	1147
270, Comment (c)(1)	1146
271	1152
271, Comment (g)	1153
272	1152
272, Comment (e)	1153
273, Comment (d)	1153
274	1158
274	1160
274, Comment (c)	1158
275	1162
276	1065
276	1150
278	1064
278	1143
278	1145
278	1155
278, Comment (d)	1143
278, Comment (d)	1145
278, Comment (e)	1007
279	1065
282	1157
283	569
283	570
283	580
283	582
283	583
283	648
283(1)	647
283(1)	648
283(2)	564
283(2)	647
283, Comment	568

RESTATEMENT 2ND CONFLICT OF LAWS

Sec.	This Work Page
283, Comment (c)	572
283, Comment (d)	572
283, Comment (i)	565
283, Comment (i)	568
283, Comment (j)	569
283, Comment (j)	572
283, Comment (j)	579
283, Comment (k)	574
283, Comment (k)	580
283, Comment (m)	560
284	591
284, Comment (c)	566
285	62
285	233
285	630
285, Comment (d)	645
286	62
286	647
286	648
287	694
287	695
287, Comment (b)	696
287, Comment (f)	695
287, Comment (g)	695
288, Comment (b)	696
288, Comment (d)	699
289	62
289	699
290	703
290, Comment (b)	703
290, Comment (c)	703
291	1023
291—293	1019
292	1023
292	1026
292, Comment (a)	1027
292, Comment (d)	1027
292, Comment (f)	1027
293(2)	1023
296	1223
297	1221
297, Comment (a)	1223
299	1234
299, Comment (e)	1235
300, Comment (a)	1235
300, Comment (d)	1235
301—302	1227
303	1107
303	1227
303 et seq.	1234
304	1227
304	1230
308	1228
309	67
309	1227
310	1228
311, Comment (b)	1229
312(1)	1231
312(2)	1231
312, Comment (g)	1231
312, Comment (h)	1231

RESTATEMENT 2ND CONFLICT OF LAWS

Sec.	This Work Page
313, Comment (c)	1228
314	1166
314	1171
314	1176
314(b)	1175
314, Comment (k)	1175
315	1171
315	1172
316	1172
317	1167
320	1173
320	1174
322	1191
323	1180
324	1182
325	1182
326	1179
327	1183
327	1191
329	1190
329, Comment (b)	1190
333	1182
333(3)	1192
333, Comment (c)	1192
338	1189
338	1194
340	1191
341	1194
342	1206
342	1207
344	1206
345	1206
346	1206
346i	1005
348	1207
352	1206
353	1201
353	1202
354	1185
355	1193
356	1199
356	1200
357	1205
358	1197
358(b)	1198
359	1193
359	1198
362	1209
363	1209
364	1171
364	1210
380a, Comment (a)	768
458, Comment (a)	678
603	129
604	129

RESTATEMENT 1ST CONTRACTS

Sec.	This Work Page
72(2)	1042

RESTATEMENT 2ND CONTRACTS

Sec.	This Work Page
69	1042
239	948

RESTATEMENT 2ND FOREIGN RELATIONS LAW

Sec.	This Work Page
40	536

RESTATEMENT 3RD FOREIGN RELATIONS LAW

Sec.	This Work Page
303	223
402	847
402	848
403	848
403	896
415	868
441	868
442	535
442	536
443	504
443	505
467 et seq.	508
481—486	1312
482	1314
823	1327
823	1328
823(2)	1327
823, Comment (c)	1327
823, Comment (c)	1328

RESTATEMENT 1ST JUDGMENTS

Sec.	This Work Page
41	1303
42	1303
44	1305
45	1258

RESTATEMENT 2ND JUDGMENTS

Sec.	This Work Page
8	298
8	1205
8, Comment (a)	298
8, Comment (a)	301
9	1205
13	1303
15	1303
16	1303
16	1305
17	1168
17	1291
17—19	1258
18	1291
27	1259

RESTATEMENT 2ND JUDGMENTS

Sec.	This Work Page
30	1167
30	1205
43	1278
60	452
60, Comment (a)	452
61	450
61	452

RESTATEMENT OF RESTITUTION

Sec.	This Work Page
19	1046

RESTATEMENT OF RESTITUTION

Sec.	This Work Page
46(c)	544
74	1305
112	1046
113—115	1041
117(2)	1046

RESTATEMENT 2ND TORTS

Sec.	This Work Page
568	379
577A	872
652A—652I	872

*

Table of Uniform Commercial Code Citations

UNIFORM COMMERCIAL CODE		UNIFORM COMMERCIAL CODE	
Sec.	This Work Page	Sec.	This Work Page
Art. 1	975	1–301(e)	963
Art. 1	985	1–301(e)	975
Art. 1	986	1–301(e)(1)	954
1–105	78	1–301(e)(1)	986
1–105	97	1–301(e)(2)	963
1–105	98	1–301(e)(2)	986
1–105	907	1–301(e)(2)(A)	986
1–105	954	1–301(e)(2)(B)	986
1–105	955	1–301(f)	958
1–105	962	1–301(f)	961
1–105	984	1–301(f)	963
1–105	985	1–301(f)	987
1–105	986	1–301(g)	963
1–105	997	1–301, Comment 2	987
1–105	1001	1–301, Comment 3	987
1–105	1003	1–301, Comment 6	960
1–105	1008	1–301, Comment 6	962
1–105	1081	1–301, Comment 6	963
1–105	1083	1–302	963
1–105	1087	1–302	987
1–105	1103	1–302, Comment 2	987
1–105(1)	13	2–103	1081
1–105(1)	898	2–105	1011
1–105(1)	983	2–302(1)	986
1–105(1)	984	2–318	1035
1–105(1)	987	2–318	1036
1–105(1)	1007	2–401	1007
1–105(1)	1008	2–401	1008
1–105(1)	1241	2–402	138
1–105(2)	949	2–402	949
1–105(2)	984	2–402	984
1–201(24)	1306	2–403	1078
1–301	158	Art. 2A	1030
1–301	159	Art. 2A	1031
1–301	960	2A–103(1)(e)	1031
1–301	962	2A–105	138
1–301	986	2A–105	949
1–301	987	2A–105	1031
1–301(a)	987	2A–106	949
1–301(c)	954	2A–106	978
1–301(c)	976	2A–106	984
1–301(c)	987	2A–106	1030
1–301(c)(1)	976	2A–106(1)	967
1–301(c)(1)	987	3–104	1179
1–301(c)(2)	976	3–107(2)	1328
1–301(c)(2)	987	3–202	1103
1–301(d)	987	3–202	1106
1–301(d)	1008	3–202	1179
1–301(e)	954	3–301 et seq.	1179
1–301(e)	961	3–603(2)	1046

UNIFORM COMMERCIAL CODE

Sec.	This Work Page
4–102	138
4–102	949
4–102	984
Art. 4A	1032
4A–407	1032
4A–507	976
4A–507(b)	984
4A–507(b)	1032
4A–507(c)	1032
4A–507(d)	1032
Art. 6	138
6–102	138
6–102	949
6–102	984
Art. 8	1098
8–102	1107
8–102	1181
8–102(1)(b)	1098
8–105	1181
8–106	138
8–106	949
8–106	984
8–106	1098
8–106	1107
8–110	1232
8–110(d)	1098
8–110(e)	1098
8–110(e)	1233
8–301(a)	1227
8–313	1107
8–313—8–317	1181
8–317	1182
8–501 et seq.	1227
Art. 9	997
Art. 9	1074
Art. 9	1082
Art. 9	1083
Art. 9	1084
Art. 9	1086
Art. 9	1087
Art. 9	1090
Art. 9	1091
Art. 9	1093
Art. 9	1095
Art. 9	1098
Art. 9	1099
Art. 9	1100
Art. 9	1106
9–102	984
9–102	997
9–102	1083
9–102(a)(44)	1094
9–102(a)(45)	1097
9–102(a)(45)	1098
9–103	138
9–103	949
9–103	984
9–103	997
9–103	1081
9–103	1083
9–103	1084
9–103	1098

UNIFORM COMMERCIAL CODE

Sec.	This Work Page
9–103	1104
9–103	1175
9–103(1)	1084
9–103(1)	1092
9–103(1)	1096
9–103(1)	1104
9–103(1)	1105
9–103(1)	1106
9–103(1)	1107
9–103(1)(b)	1084
9–103(1)(b)	1086
9–103(1)(c)	1085
9 103(1)(d)	1086
9–103(1)(d)	1087
9–103(2)	1084
9–103(2)	1090
9–103(2)	1092
9–103(2)(d)	1091
9–103(3)	1084
9–103(3)	1092
9–103(3)	1093
9–103(3)	1094
9–103(3)	1096
9–103(3)	1104
9–103(3)	1106
9–103(3)(a)	1095
9–103(3)(c)	1094
9–103(3)(d)	1095
9–103(3)(d)	1104
9–103(3)(e)	1093
9–103(4)	1084
9–103(4)	1096
9–103(4)	1106
9–103(5)	1084
9–103(5)	1097
9–103(6)	1084
9–103(6)	1098
9–103, Comment 5(a)	1092
9–103, Comment 5(b)	1092
9–103, Comment 5(c)	1093
9–103, Comment 5(f)	1101
9–103, Comment 7	1087
9–105	1096
9–106	1106
9–107	1086
9–109	1092
9–203(1)	1085
9–301	1084
9–301	1087
9–301—9–307	1099
9–301—9–308	1083
9–301(1)	1074
9–301(1)	1087
9–301(1)	1089
9–301(1)	1093
9–301(1)	1094
9–301(1)	1095
9–301(1)	1096
9–301(1)	1097
9–301(1)	1105
9–301(1)	1106
9–301(2)	1094

UNIFORM COMMERCIAL CODE

Sec.	This Work Page
9–301(2)	1097
9–301(2)	1107
9–301(3)	1089
9–301(3)	1094
9–301(3)	1096
9–301(3)	1097
9–301(3)	1106
9–301(3)(A)	1089
9–301(3)(C)	1089
9–301(4)	1106
9–301(5)	1097
9–301(6)	1097
9–301, Comment 2	1087
9–301, Comment 3	1099
9–301, Comment 5	1089
9–301, Comment 5	1094
9–301, Comment 6	1089
9–301, Comment 6	1093
9–301, Comment 6	1094
9–301, Comment 7	1089
9–301, Comment 7	1094
9–301, Comment 7	1096
9–301, Comment 7	1097
9–302	1085
9–303	1091
9–303(b)	1091
9–303(c)	1091
9–304	1085
9–304	1094
9–304(3)	1094
9–304(4)	1094
9–304(5)	1094

UNIFORM COMMERCIAL CODE

Sec.	This Work Page
9–305(a)(1)	1098
9–305(a)(2)	1098
9–305(a)(4)	1098
9–305(b)	1098
9–305(c)	1098
9–306	1085
9–307	1081
9–307	1087
9–307	1093
9–307	1096
9–307	1098
9–307(b)(1)	1087
9–307(b)(2)	1087
9–307(b)(3)	1088
9–307(c)	1096
9–307(e)	1088
9–307(f)	1088
9–307(g)	1088
9–307(h)	1088
9–307(i)	1088
9–307(j)	1088
9–308	1096
9–316(a)	1093
9–316(a)(2)	1089
9–316(a)(3)	1090
9–316(a)(3)	1093
9–316(b)	1090
9–316(f)(2)	1090
9–316, Comment 2	1093
9–702	1087
11–103, Comment 8	1097

*

Table of Uniform Probate Code Citations

UNIFORM PROBATE CODE

Sec.	This Work Page
1–102	1211
1–303	1172
Art. 2, Pt. 10	1138
2–109	698
2–109(b)	699
2–201	603
2–201	607
2–201	1113
2–202	603
2–202	1135
2–202	1136
2–204	621
2–502	241
2–503	241
2–506	241
2–506	245
2–506	1119
2–506	1121
2–506	1143
2–511	1152
2–602	1123
2–703	1123
2–703	1135
2–801	1156
2–804	1130
2–1002	1139
2–1003	1139
2–1004	1139
2–1005	1139
2–1006	1139
2–1009	1139
3–201	1177
3–201	1179
3–202	502
3–202	1166
3–203(g)	1186
3–307	1166
3–307	1172
3–309	1172
3–408	1168
3–408	1169
3–602	1186
3–602	1199
3–703	1185
3–703(c)	1186

UNIFORM PROBATE CODE

Sec.	This Work Page
3–703(c)	1199
3–704	1189
3–714	1192
3–803(a)	1202
3–803(a)	1206
3–803(a)(1)	133
3–816	1171
3–816	1210
3–913	1151
4–201	1186
4–201	1190
4–202	1190
4–204	1186
4–205	1185
4–205	1186
4–301	1186
4–301	1199
4–302	1199
4–401	1113
4–401	1199
4–401	1204
Art. 5	1213
5–203	281
5–206	281
5–209	283
5–211	1214
5–302	1216
5–312	283
5–410	281
5–410	1213
5–413	1214
5–413	1215
5–419	1214
5–419	1215
5–420	1212
5–420	1213
5–420	1215
5–424	1213
5–431	1213
Art. 7, Pt. 1	1150
7–105	1151
7–201(b)	1150
7–203	502
7–305	502
7–305	1154

*

1375

Table of Statutes and Rules

UNITED STATES

UNITED STATES CONSTITUTION

Art.	This Work Page
I, § 8	209
I, § 8, cl. 3	512
I, § 10	1229
III	208
III	326
III	440
III	532
III	1238
III, § 2	209
IV	285
IV	286
IV, § 1	2
IV, § 1	4
IV, § I	593
IV, § 1	1262
IV, § 1	1268
IV, § 1	1279
IV, § 2	134
IV, § 2	171
VI	503
VI, cl. 2	222

Amend.	
1	376
5	304
5	418
5	420
5	421
5	424
5	425
5	426
5	427
5	428
5	429
5	430
5	438
5	440
5	441
5	519
5	541
5	542
7	182
11	237
11	238
14	134
14	176
14	234
14	243

UNITED STATES CONSTITUTION

Amend.	This Work Page
14	285
14	288
14	289
14	304
14	317
14	420
14	424
14	425
14	427
14	429
14	435
14	438
14	440
14	509
14	519
14, § 1	171
14, § 1	176

UNITED STATES CODE ANNOTATED

1 U.S.C.A.—General Provisions

Sec.	This Work Page
7	602

5 U.S.C.A.—Government Organization and Employees

Sec.	This Work Page
8101	883

7 U.S.C.A.—Agriculture

Sec.	This Work Page
13a–1	324
13a–2(4)	324
18(d)	324

9 U.S.C.A.—Arbitration

Sec.	This Work Page
1	1341
1 et seq.	342
1 et seq.	481
2	1279
2	1341

UNITED STATES CODE ANNOTATED
9 U.S.C.A.—Arbitration

Sec.	This Work Page
201—208	985
301—307	1341

10 U.S.C.A.—Armed Forces

Sec.	This Work Page
1408	614
1408(c)(1)	614

11 U.S.C.A.—Bankruptcy

Sec.	This Work Page
Ch. 7	1240
Ch. 11	1239
Ch. 11	1240
Ch. 11	1251
Ch. 13	1259
101 et seq.	1104
101(20)	1250
101(21)	1250
109(a)	1248
109(a)	1250
109(a)	1255
157	1237
303—305	1250
304	1251
304(a)	1250
304(b)	1250
304(b)	1253
304(c)	1250
304(c)	1251
304(c)(1)	1248
304(c)(4)	1251
304(c)(5)	1253
305(a)	1250
305(b)	1250
305(c)	1250
306	1250
323(a)	1252
362	1275
362	1303
365	1240
508(a)	1251
510(c)	1254
522	1240
522(6)	1102
523(a)(5)	1239
523(a)(5)	1247
541(a)	1252
542	1252
544(b)	1240
547	1241
558	1240
714	1303
814	1303

UNITED STATES CODE ANNOTATED
12 U.S.C.A.—Banks and Banking

Sec.	This Work Page
1831(d)	1018
2503	1117

15 U.S.C.A.—Commerce and Trade

Sec.	This Work Page
22	324
22	419
22	425
22	433
45(a)(1)	869
78a—78jj	454
78aa	197
78aa	418
78aa	425
79y	197
80a—43	197
1051—1127	869
1125	869
1125(d)	302
1125(d)(1)(A)	303
1125(d)(2)	303
1125(d)(2)(A)(ii)	304
1125(d)(2)(D)(i)	303

17 U.S.C.A.—Copyrights

Sec.	This Work Page
101	1095
301	1095

18 U.S.C.A.—Crimes and Criminal Procedure

Sec.	This Work Page
1073	686
1151	510
1151	511
1151(a)	511
1151(b)	511
1151(c)	511
1162	515
1204	689
1204	690
1915(b)	421
1915(b)	425
1915(b)	433
1915(d)	425
1915(d)	433
1961—1968	421
1965(d)	421

22 U.S.C.A.—Foreign Relations and Intercourse

Sec.	This Work Page
1172	570

UNITED STATES CODE ANNOTATED
22 U.S.C.A.—Foreign Relations and Intercourse

Sec.	This Work Page
2370(e)(2)	210
2370(e)(2)	222
2370(e)(2)	504
2370(e)(2)	1235
6001	210
6021	210

24 U.S.C.A.—Hospitals, Asylums, and Cemeteries

Sec.	This Work Page
1983	687

25 U.S.C.A.—Indians

Sec.	This Work Page
331—358 et seq.	511
1321—1326	515
1725(g)	517
1803(1)	688
1901	688
1901—1963	516
1902	688
1911	516
1911	681
1911(a)	688
1911(b)	688
1911(d)	517
1911(d)	688
1919	681
1980(4)	688

28 U.S.C.A.—Judiciary and Judicial Procedure

Sec.	This Work Page
Ch. 6	1238
151	1237
151	1238
152(a)(1)	1237
157	1238
157(a)	1238
157(b)(1)	1238
157(b)(2)	1238
157(b)(3)	1238
157(b)(4)	1237
157(b)(5)	1237
157(c)(1)	1238
157(c)(2)	1238
157(d)	1239
158(a)	1239
1257	1281
1291	330
1295	412
1330	470
1331	326
1331	434

UNITED STATES CODE ANNOTATED
28 U.S.C.A.—Judiciary and Judicial Procedure

Sec.	This Work Page
1331	438
1331	466
1331	1281
1332	323
1332	327
1332	434
1332(a)	327
1332(a)	1224
1332(a)(1)	190
1332(c)	453
1332(c)	1223
1332(c)	1224
1332(c)	1225
1332(c)(1)	453
1333	327
1333	436
1333	437
1334(a)	1236
1334(b)	1236
1334(b)	1239
1334(b)	1247
1334(c)(1)	1236
1334(c)(1)	1237
1334(c)(1)	1248
1334(c)(2)	1237
1334(c)(2)	1248
1334(d)	1252
1335	196
1360	515
1367	197
1367	465
1367(a)	197
1367(b)	197
1367(c)	469
1367(d)	134
1391	327
1391	420
1391	442
1391	477
1391(a)(1)	328
1391(a)(2)	328
1391(a)(3)	328
1391(b)	198
1391(b)(1)	328
1391(b)(2)	328
1391(b)(3)	328
1391(c)	328
1391(d)	420
1391(e)	425
1397	324
1397	428
1400	412
1404	186
1404	486
1404	506
1404	507
1404(a)	186
1404(a)	198
1404(a)	201

UNITED STATES CODE ANNOTATED

28 U.S.C.A.—Judiciary and Judicial Procedure

Sec.	This Work Page
1404(a)	205
1404(a)	443
1404(a)	487
1404(a)	497
1404(a)	501
1404(a)	505
1404(a)	506
1404(a)	1241
1406	198
1406	466
1406	507
1406(a)	200
1406(a)	507
1407	200
1407	508
1407(a)	198
1408(1)	1240
1409(a)	1240
1409(d)	1240
1409(e)	1240
1410	1250
1410(a)	1250
1410(b)	1250
1410(c)	1250
1412	1241
1412(a)	1241
1441	466
1441(a)	442
1441(b)	442
1452(a)	1241
1452(a)	1247
1452(b)	1248
1471	198
1471 (former)	1238
1472	198
1473	198
1474	1250
1602—1611	469
1603(d)	470
1603(d)	472
1603(e)	470
1603(e)	471
1603(e)	473
1604	470
1605	508
1605(5)	471
1605(a)(1)	470
1605(a)(2)	470
1605(a)(3)	470
1605(a)(3)	471
1605(a)(3)	473
1605(a)(4)	470
1605(a)(5)	471
1605(a)(7)	475
1605(a)(7)	864
1605(a)(7)(A)	472
1605(a)(7)(A)	476
1605(a)(7)(B)(i)	476
1605(b)	471

UNITED STATES CODE ANNOTATED

28 U.S.C.A.—Judiciary and Judicial Procedure

Sec.	This Work Page
1605(c)	471
1606	470
1631	507
1652	179
1652	190
1652	208
1659	899
1696(a)	524
1738	588
1738	592
1738	594
1738	655
1738	1262
1738	1272
1738	1280
1738	1282
1738A	300
1738A	592
1738A	668
1738A	681
1738A	685
1738A	1268
1738A	1280
1738A(e)	686
1738A(g)	683
1738A(g)	686
1738B	592
1738B	671
1738B	677
1738B	1272
1738B	1280
1738C	517
1738C	592
1738C	594
1738C	655
1738C	1280
1738C	1293
1781	532
1781	533
1781	540
1782	529
1782	530
1782	531
1782	532
1782	533
1782(a)	531
1963	1268
1963	1282
1963	1285
2361	324
2361	1275
2680(a)	471
2680(k)	846

29 U.S.C.A.—Labor

Sec.	This Work Page
1001 et seq.	415

UNITED STATES CODE ANNOTATED
29 U.S.C.A.—Labor

Sec.	This Work Page
1001 et seq.	615
1132(e)	415
1132(e)(2)	425
1451(d)	415
1738	1268
1801 et seq.	884
1854	884

31 U.S.C.A.—Money and Finance

Sec.	This Work Page
371	1306

33 U.S.C.A.—Navigation and Navigable Waters

Sec.	This Work Page
901	883
1051—1094	896

35 U.S.C.A.—Patents

Sec.	This Work Page
1 et seq.	1095

42 U.S.C.A.—The Public Health and Welfare

Sec.	This Work Page
654	686
1983	176
1983	185
1983	215
1983	1239
1983	1259
1983	1280
2014(hh)	200
2651(a)	217
4332	406
6901—6921	406
9601—9675	406
9613(f)	406
9613(P)	425
11601—11610	224
11601—11610	688

43 U.S.C.A.—Public Lands

Sec.	This Work Page
1601—1628	511

UNITED STATES CODE ANNOTATED
45 U.S.C.A.—Railroads

Sec.	This Work Page
51	883

46 U.S.C.A.—Shipping

Sec.	This Work Page
183(b)	225
688	891
688(b)(1)—(b)(2)	891
740	436
761—767	890
761—768	896
911 et seq.	439
951	1100
951 et seq.	1095

46 U.S.C.A.App.—Shipping

Sec.	This Work Page
688	883

49 U.S.C.A.—Transportation

Sec.	This Work Page
120	1095
1301	217
1403(a)	1095
1403(c)	1095
14301	1095

STATUTES AT LARGE

Year	This Work Page
1789, Ch. 20	179
1790, Ch. 11	285
1790, Ch. 11	286
1860, Ch. 179	570
1920, Ch. 250	891
1925, Ch. 212	1341
1946, Ch. 521	225
1953, Ch. 505	515
1963, P.L. 88–244	224
1964, P.L. 88–619	524
1965, P.L. 89–171	210
1968, P.L. 90–296	200
1970, P.L. 91–368	1341
1978, P.L. 95–608	688
1980, P.L.96–611	686
1984, P.L. 98–353	1236
1984, P.L. 98–378	671
1984, P.L. 98–378	698
1984, P.L. 98–397	615
1992, P.L. 102–484	210
1993, P.L. 103–206	485
1996, P.L. 104–114	210
1996, P.L. 104–199	1293

POPULAR NAME ACTS

ARBITRATION ACT

	This Work
Sec.	Page
Ch. 2	1341
1	1341
2	1341

CIVIL RIGHTS ACT OF 1964

	This Work
Sec.	Page
Tit. VII	227

CLAYTON ACT

	This Work
Sec.	Page
12	419
12	420

FEDERAL ARBITRATION ACT

	This Work
Sec.	Page
2	1279

FEDERAL TRADE COMMISSION ACT

	This Work
Sec.	Page
5	869

LANHAM TRADEMARK ACT

	This Work
Sec.	Page
43(a)	869

MANDAMUS AND VENUE ACT

	This Work
Sec.	Page
2	425

MIGRANT AND SEASONAL AGRICULTURAL WORKER PROTECTION ACT

	This Work
Sec.	Page
2 et seq.	884
504	884

MODEL BUSINESS CORPORATIONS ACT ANNOTATED

	This Work
Sec.	Page
106(2)	1232

MODEL UNIFORM PRODUCT LIABILITY ACT

	This Work
Sec.	Page
103(a)	900

NATIONAL BANK ACT

	This Work
Sec.	Page
94	416

REVISED MODEL BUSINESS CORPORATION ACT

	This Work
Sec.	Page
15.01(a)	1232
15.01(b)	1232

SECURITIES ACT OF 1934

	This Work
Sec.	Page
27	418
27	425

UNIFORM ACTS

UNIFORM ADOPTION ACT

	This Work
Sec.	Page
3–101	701
4	701

UNIFORM CHILD CUSTODY JURISDICTION ACT

	This Work
Sec.	Page
3	501
3	682
3	685
3(a)(2)	685
3(a)(3)	684
7	501
8	684
14	682
14	685
23	690
23	691

UNIFORM DISPOSITION OF COMMUNITY PROPERTY RIGHTS AT DEATH ACT

	This Work
Sec.	Page
1	605
8	618

UNIFORM DIVORCE RECOGNITION ACT

Sec.	This Work Page
2(a)	640

UNIFORM ENFORCEMENT OF FOREIGN JUDGMENT ACT

Sec.	This Work Page
2	1283
6	1284

UNIFORM FOREIGN MONEY JUDGMENT RECOGNITION ACT

Sec.	This Work Page
1	1314
1(2)	148
1(2)	1313
1(2)	1331
1(2)	1332
3	1269
3	1313
3	1331
4	1313
4(a)	1313
4(a)(i)	1313
4(b)	1314
4(b)(3)	1314
4(b)(5)	492
4(b)(6)	1314
4(k)(1)	1313
5	1331
5(a)	1313
5(b)	1313
5(b)	1324
5(b)	1331

UNIFORM INTERSTATE AND INTERNATIONAL PROCEDURE ACT

Sec.	This Work Page
1.05	501
2.04	548
3.02	548
4.01	548
4.01—4.03	548
4.01—4.03	549
4.01—4.03	550
4.02	549
4.03	548
4.03	549
4.04	549
5.01—5.05	548

UNIFORM INTERSTATE FAMILY SUPPORT ACT

Sec.	This Work Page
303	670

UNIFORM INTERSTATE FAMILY SUPPORT ACT

Sec.	This Work Page
303	671
303	676
604	676

UNIFORM JUDICIAL NOTICE OF FOREIGN LAW ACT

Sec.	This Work Page
3	548
5	548

UNIFORM MARRIAGE AND DIVORCE ACT

Sec.	This Work Page
206	589
207(c)	591
208	579
208(3)	630
209	591
209	629
210	579
210	580
210	581
307	601
409	684

UNIFORM NEGOTIABLE INSTRUMENT ACT

Sec.	This Work Page
171—177	1046

UNIFORM PARTNERSHIP ACT

Sec.	This Work Page
9	451

UNIFORM RECIPROCAL ENFORCEMENT OF SUPPORT ACT

Sec.	This Work Page
7	993

UNIFORM TESTAMENTARY ADDITIONS TO TRUSTS ACT

Sec.	This Work Page
1	1152

STATE STATUTES

ALABAMA CODE

Sec.	This Work Page
5–18–2	1018
6–2–17	133
7–1–105	955
8–8	1018
8–19–5	869
17, § 18	255
17, § 19	255
25–5–1	885
25–5–14	884
25–5–52	884
26–10A–7	705
26–10A–21	702
2590	714
7540	714

ALASKA STATUTES

Sec.	This Work Page
09.10.220	133
23.30.011(b)	884
23.30.045(a)	888
23.30.055	884
45.45	1018
45.50.471	869

ARIZONA REVISED STATUTES

Sec.	This Work Page
8–106	705
12–506	133
12–506	135
23–1022	884
25–901 et seq.	583
25–901 et seq.	628
29–104	452

ARKANSAS CODE ANNOTATED

Sec.	This Work Page
9–11–801 et seq.	583
9–11–801 et seq.	628
11–9–410	885
16–4–101 to 16–4–108	548
16–40–14	547
23–89–202 to 23–89–208	875
27–2504	549

ARKANSAS STATUTES

Sec.	This Work Page
4–57	1018
73–1813 (repealed)	124

WEST'S ANNOTATED CALIFORNIA CONSTITUTION

Art.	This Work Page
15, § 1	1018

WEST'S ANNOTATED CALIFORNIA BUSINESS AND PROFESSIONS CODE

Sec.	This Work Page
10242	1018
16600	965
25602	748

WEST'S ANNOTATED CALIFORNIA CIVIL CODE

Sec.	This Work Page
197—198	277
204	281
946	1115
1115	1317
1189	1145
1916	1018
4512	573
4513	573
4530	245
4530	246

WEST'S ANNOTATED CALIFORNIA CODE OF CIVIL PROCEDURE

Sec.	This Work Page
86(a)(1)	326
185	527
388	450
395	327
410.10	322
410.10	424
410.10	429
413.10	527
415.30	527
583(b)	185

WEST'S ANNOTATED CALIFORNIA COMMERCIAL CODE

Sec.	This Work Page
1105	955
1105	984

WEST'S ANNOTATED CALIFORNIA CORPORATIONS CODE

Sec.	This Work Page
2115	454
2115(a)	1232

WEST'S ANNOTATED CALIFORNIA CORPORATIONS CODE

Sec.	This Work Page
2115(e)	1233

WEST'S ANNOTATED CALIFORNIA EVIDENCE CODE

Sec.	This Work Page
310	548
311(a)	556
452	547
452(f)	547

WEST'S ANNOTATED CALIFORNIA FAMILY CODE

Sec.	This Work Page
299.2	592

WEST'S ANNOTATED CALIFORNIA FINANCIAL CODE

Sec.	This Work Page
21200	1018

WEST'S ANNOTATED CALIFORNIA LABOR CODE

Sec.	This Work Page
3601	884
3852	885

WEST'S ANNOTATED CALIFORNIA PROBATE CODE

Sec.	This Work Page
66(a)	621
101	621
102	621
120	1135

CALIFORNIA RULES OF COURT

Rule	This Work Page
1464	705

WEST'S COLORADO REVISED STATUTES ANNOTATED

Sec.	This Work Page
8–41–203	885
10–4–701 to 10–4–723	875
10–4–707(1)(c)	878

WEST'S COLORADO REVISED STATUTES ANNOTATED

Sec.	This Work Page
10–4–711	967
13–1.5–104	1011
13–25–106	547
13–50–105	450
13–62–102(1)	1312
13–80–118	133

CONNECTICUT GENERAL STATUTES ANNOTATED

Sec.	This Work Page
5–3–104	1018
5–13–103	1018
37–4	1018
38a–363 et seq.	875
45–170(c)	1152
52–59b	376
52–163(a)	547
52–527d	718

CONNECTICUT PUBLIC ACTS

No.	This Work Page
93–297	878

DELAWARE CODE

Tit.	This Work Page
6, § 1–105	955
10, § 3114	1227
10, § 8121	133
19, § 2363	885
1504(a)	646

DELAWARE RULES OF EVIDENCE

Rule	This Work Page
202	547

DISTRICT OF COLUMBIA CODE

Sec.	This Work Page
13–421 to 13–434	548
28–3301	1018
35–2101 to 35–2114	875

WEST'S FLORIDA STATUTES ANNOTATED

Sec.	This Work Page
47.081	262
55.605(2)(g)	1312
61.021	245

WEST'S FLORIDA STATUTES ANNOTATED

Sec.	This Work Page
90.202	547
90.203	547
95.10	133
440.39	885
627.727	967
627.730 to 627.741	875
627.733(2)	882
671.1–105	955
671.1–105	984
687.01	1018

OFFICIAL CODE OF GEORGIA ANNOTATED

Sec.	This Work Page
7.4	1018
9–10–91	376
9–12–114(10)	1312
19–6–15	674
19–9–42(3)	702
24–1–4	547
74–108	281

HAWAII REVISED STATUTES

Sec.	This Work Page
386–8	885
431:10C–101 to 431:10C–121	875
478	1018
621–1	547
626–1(b)	547
657–9	133

HAWAII RULES OF EVIDENCE

Rule	This Work Page
202	547
202(c)(5)	547

IDAHO CODE

Sec.	This Work Page
10–1404(2)(g)	1312
15–2201	621
15–2202	621
28–42.201	1018
32–1101	703

IDAHO RULES OF CIVIL PROCEDURE

Rule	This Work Page
44(d)	547

ILLINOIS COMPILED STATUTES

Ch.	This Work Page
205 ILCS 670/1	1018
235 ILCS 5/6–21	875
735 ILCS 5/8–1003	547
735 ILCS 5/8–1007	548
735 ILCS 5/13–210	133
750 ILCS 5/216	648
750 ILCS 5/401	630
755 ILCS 5/2–1	1115
810 ILCS 5/1–105	955
815 ILCS 205/4	1018

ILLINOIS SMITH–HURD ANNOTATED

Ch.	This Work Page
6, para. 2	229
26, para. 1–105	984
68, § 16	277

ILLINOIS REVISED STATUTES

Ch.	This Work Page
110, para. 2–301(c)	347
110 1/2, para. 5–2	1177
110 1/2, § 7–6	1131

ILLINOIS PROBATE ACT

Sec.	This Work Page
12	698

WEST'S ANNOTATED INDIANA CODE

Sec.	This Work Page
24–4.5–3–104	1018
28–7–5–28	1018
34–3–2–1	547
34–11–4–2	133

INDIANA RULES OF TRIAL PROCEDURE

Rule	This Work Page
44.1	547

IOWA CODE ANNOTATED

Sec.	This Work Page
535	1018
554.1105	955
567.3	1141
595.1	558
599.1	281
614.7	133
614.7	135
668.1	277

KANSAS STATUTES ANNOTATED

Sec.	This Work Page
16a–2–401	1018
40–3101 to 40–3121	875
59–805	1177
59–3003	277
60–409	547
60–516	133
84–1–105	955
84–1–105	984

KENTUCKY REVISED STATUTES

Sec.	This Work Page
360	1018
381–290	1141
381–300	1141
413–320	133

LOUISIANA STATUTES ANNOTATED— REVISED STATUTES

Sec.	This Work Page
9:272 et seq.	583
9:307	628
22:611	967
22:655	967
22:1406(D)	967

LOUISIANA STATUTES ANNOTATED— CIVIL CODE

Art.	This Work Page
Ch. 3, Art. 37	999
10	636
39	280
3515	728
3515	749
3515	750
3519	728
3519	750
3526	621
3537	728
3537	750
3537	993
3537—3540	78
3537—3541	1004
3540	810
3540	948
3540	954
3540	961
3542	728
3542	750
3542	751
3542	781
3542	808
3542	819
3542	837
3542—3546	942
3543	751

LOUISIANA STATUTES ANNOTATED— CIVIL CODE

Art.	This Work Page
3543	792
3543	798
3543	850
3543—3546	752
3543(1)	847
3544	751
3544	781
3544	792
3544	798
3544	802
3544	819
3544	837
3544(1)	803
3544(1)	808
3544(2)(a)	733
3544(2)(a)	813
3544(2)(a)	819
3544(2)(a)	837
3544(2)(b)	819
3544(2)(b)	825
3545	751
3545	897
3545	925
3545	934
3545	935
3545	941
3545	942
3545(2)	825
3546	751
3546	854
3546	866
3547	751
3547	803
3547	813
3547	819
3547	837
3547	935
3548	752
3548	803
3548	808
3548	813
3548	819
3548	837
3549	130

LOUISIANA ACTS

No.	This Work Page
923	115

LOUISIANA EVIDENCE CODE

Art.	This Work Page
202	547

MAINE REVISED STATUTES ANNOTATED

Tit.	This Work Page
11, § 1–105	955

MAINE REVISED STATUTES ANNOTATED

Tit.	This Work Page
14, § 866	135
16, § 402	547

MARYLAND ANNOTATED CODE

Art.	This Work Page
48A, §§ 538 to 547	875

MARYLAND CODE, COURTS AND JUDICIAL PROCEEDINGS

Sec.	This Work Page
10–501	547
10–501 to 10–507	548

MARYLAND WORKMEN'S COMPENSATION ACT

Sec.	This Work Page
34:15–1 et seq.	884

MASSACHUSETTS GENERAL LAWS ANNOTATED

Ch.	This Work Page
85, § 5	246
90, § 34A	875
90, § 34D	875
90, § 34M	875
90, § 34N	875
90, § 34O	875
106, § 1–105	955
175, § 113B	875
207, § 10	648
210, § 2	705
223A, §§ 1—14	548
233, § 70	547
235, § 23A	1312
260, § 9	133
260, § 9	135

MICHIGAN COMPILED LAWS ANNOTATED

Sec.	This Work Page
5.18.2	246
324.1804	1011
438	1018
440.1105	955
500.3101	874
551.2	558
565.11	1145
600.1852	548
600.2114a	548

MICHIGAN COMPILED LAWS ANNOTATED

Sec.	This Work Page
600.2118a	548

MICHIGAN RULES OF EVIDENCE

Rule	This Work Page
202	547

MINNESOTA STATUTES ANNOTATED

Sec.	This Work Page
60A.08(4)	967
65B.41 to 65B.71	875
80C.21	974
334	1018
336.1–105	955
336.1–105	984
524.3–201(a)(2)	156
524.3–201(d)	156
543.19	376
599.04	547

MISSISSIPPI CODE

Sec.	This Work Page
13–1–149	547
15–1–65	133
15–1–65	135
15–1–65	507
75–1–105	955
75–67–101	1018
75–67–127	1018
75–67–205	1018
89–1–23	1140
91–1–1	1116
93–13–1	277

VERNON'S ANNOTATED MISSOURI STATUTES

Sec.	This Work Page
509.202	547
516.190	133

MONTANA CODE ANNOTATED

Sec.	This Work Page
T. 26, Ch. 10	547
27–5–14	489
32–5–302	1018
40–7–103(3)	702
41–4–101	703
42–4–302(2)	700
61–6–303	882
400.1–105	955

MONTANA RULES OF EVIDENCE

Rule	This Work Page
202	547

NEBRASKA REVISED STATUTES

Sec.	This Work Page
25–12	547
25–101	547
25–215	133
76–402	1140
76–403	1140
76–404	1140
76–405	1140

NEVADA REVISED STATUTES

Sec.	This Work Page
11.020	133
47.140	547
202.100 (repealed)	748
Ch. 604, § 8	748
662.245	1151
696B.020	1012

NEW HAMPSHIRE REVISED STATUTES ANNOTATED

Sec.	This Work Page
399–A:3	1018
399–A:4	1018
458–A:2(III)	702
463:4	277
524.11	1312

NEW HAMPSHIRE RULES OF EVIDENCE

Rule	This Work Page
201	547

NEW JERSEY STATUTES ANNOTATED

Sec.	This Work Page
2A:82–27 to 2A:82–33	548
12A:1–105	955
31.1	1018
39:6A–1 et seq.	875

NEW JERSEY RULES OF EVIDENCE

Rule	This Work Page
201	547

NEW MEXICO STATUTES ANNOTATED

Sec.	This Work Page
22–7–4	262
52–1–22	889
58–15	1018

NEW MEXICO RULES OF EVIDENCE

Rule	This Work Page
1–044	547

NEW YORK, MCKINNEY'S CONSTITUTION

Art.	This Work Page
I, § 9(1)	661

NEW YORK, MCKINNEY'S STATUTES

Sec.	This Work Page
352	547

NEW YORK, MCKINNEY'S BANKING LAW

Sec.	This Work Page
352	1018
353	1018

NEW YORK, MCKINNEY'S BUSINESS CORPORATION LAW

Sec.	This Work Page
27 (repealed)	227
1306	1232
1315—1320	1232
1320	1233

NEW YORK CIVIL PRACTICE ACT

Sec.	This Work Page
478	1335

NEW YORK, MCKINNEY'S CIVIL PRACTICE LAW AND RULES

Sec.	This Work Page
202	133
301	302
301	306
301	424
302	302
302	321
302	376

NEW YORK, MCKINNEY'S CIVIL PRACTICE LAW AND RULES

Sec.	This Work Page
302	424
302	429
307—316	326
320(c)	333
327	501
503	327
507	478
903	447
904	447
3211(e)	331
4511	548
5301	672
5501(c)	187

NEW YORK CODE OF CIVIL PROCEDURE

Sec.	This Work Page
432	320

NEW YORK, MCKINNEY'S DECEDENTS ESTATE LAW

Sec.	This Work Page
47	617

NEW YORK, MCKINNEY'S DOMESTIC RELATIONS LAW

Sec.	This Work Page
10	558
75–c(3)	702
81	275
111	705
250	653
253	659
253(3)	660
253(6)	660

NEW YORK, MCKINNEY'S ESTATES, POWERS AND TRUSTS LAW

Sec.	This Work Page
3–5.1	1120
3–5.1(b)(1)	1118
3–5.1(d)	1133
3–5.1(g)	1156
3–5.1(g)	1158
3–5.1(g)	1159
3–5.1(g)	1160
3–5.1(h)	1123
3–5.1(h)	1131
3–5.1(h)	1134
5–1.1(d)(7)	1134

NEW YORK, MCKINNEY'S ESTATES, POWERS AND TRUSTS LAW

Sec.	This Work Page
5–1.1(d)(8)	1134
5–1.1–A(c)(6)	1136
5–1.1–A(c)(7)	1127
5–1.1–A(c)(7)	1136
5–3.3	1118
10–9.2	1156

NEW YORK, MCKINNEY'S GENERAL BUSINESS LAW

Sec.	This Work Page
349	869

NEW YORK, MCKINNEY'S GENERAL OBLIGATIONS LAW

Sec.	This Work Page
5–1401	954
5–1401	976
5–1402	501
5–1402	976

NEW YORK, MCKINNEY'S INSURANCE LAW

Sec.	This Work Page
5101 to 5109	875

NEW YORK, MCKINNEY'S FAMILY COURT ACT

Sec.	This Work Page
466(c)	680

NEW YORK, MCKINNEY'S LABOR LAW

Sec.	This Work Page
240	797
240—241	797

NEW YORK, MCKINNEY'S PERSONAL PROPERTY LAW

Sec.	This Work Page
12–a	617

NEW YORK, MCKINNEY'S STATE LAW

Sec.	This Work Page
1848	347
1850	331

NEW YORK, MCKINNEY'S UNIFORM COMMERCIAL CODE

Sec.	This Work Page
1–105	955

NEW YORK LAWS

Year	This Work Page
1996, Ch. 635, § 90	783

NORTH CAROLINA GENERAL STATUTES

Sec.	This Work Page
1–21	133
1C–1804(b)(7)	1312
8–4	547
14–391	1018
24–8	1018
25–1–105	955
53–178	1018
58–3–1	967
58–3–1	1012

NORTH DAKOTA CENTURY CODE

Sec.	This Work Page
13–03.1–15.1	1018
26.1–41–01 to 26.1–41–19	875
31–10–03	547

OHIO REVISED CODE

Sec.	This Work Page
1321.01	1018
1321.02	1018
2305.20	134
2329.92(B)	1312

OHIO REVISED CIVIL RULES

Rule	This Work Page
44.1	547

OKLAHOMA STATUTES ANNOTATED

Tit.	This Work Page
10, § 7505–4.1	702
12, §§ 104—108	133
12, § 2201	547
12A, § 1–105	955
12A, § 9–302(3)	1090
12A, § 9–302(4)	1090
36, § 3636	967
47, § 7–601(2)	882
47, § 23.3	1090
60, § 121	1141

OKLAHOMA STATUTES ANNOTATED

Tit.	This Work Page
60, § 123	1141

OREGON REVISED STATUTES

Sec.	This Work Page
40.090	547
81.100 to 81.135	105
81.100 to 81.135	116
81.100—81.135	1004
81.105(2)	954
81.112	999
81.115	961
81.120	810
81.120	954
81.120(2)	948
81.125	961
81.125(1)	963
81.125(2)	963
81.135(2)(a)	1006
81.135(2)(e)	1023
109.030	275
109.030	277
109.520	281
114.105	1135
465.480(2)(a)	1011
742.001	967
742.001	1012
742.018	967
742.018	1012
743.800 et seq.	875

PENNSYLVANIA STATUTES

Tit.	This Work Page
15, § 1201	227
15, § 2852–201 (repealed)	227
40, § 1301.102	193

PENNSYLVANIA CONSOLIDATED STATUTES ANNOTATED

Tit.	This Work Page
13, § 1105	955
23, § 2711(a)(1)	705
40, § 1009.110(c)(1)	883
40, § 1009.201	883
42, §§ 5321—5329	548
42, § 5322(e)	502
42, § 5327	547
42, § 5521	133
75, § 1705(a)(1)	876

PENNSYLVANIA RULES OF CIVIL PROCEDURE

Rule	This Work Page
423	452

RHODE ISLAND GENERAL LAWS

Sec.	This Work Page
9–1–18	133
9–19–3	547
14.2	1018

SOUTH CAROLINA CODE

Sec.	This Work Page
19–3–120	547
34–29–140	1018
36–1–105	955
38–77–10 et seq.	875
361–105	984

SOUTH DAKOTA CODIFIED LAWS

Sec.	This Work Page
15–7–2(7)	669
19–8–1	547
54–6–22	1018

TENNESSEE CODE ANNOTATED

Sec.	This Work Page
28–1–112	133
28–1–112	135
47–1–105	955

TENNESSEE RULES OF EVIDENCE

Rule	This Work Page
202	547

VERNON'S ANNOTATED TEXAS CONSTITUTION

Art.	This Work Page
XVI, § 15	620

V.A.T.S., INSURANCE CODE

Sec.	This Work Page
21.42	967
21.42	1012

V.T.C.A., CIVIL PRACTICE AND REMEDIES CODE

Sec.	This Work Page
36.005(b)(7)	1312
71.051	502
73.031	133

V.T.C.A., FAMILY CODE

Sec.	This Work Page
3.63	619

TEXAS RULES OF CIVIL EVIDENCE

Rule	This Work Page
203	547
203	549

UTAH CODE ANNOTATED

Sec.	This Work Page
31A–22–309	875
78–12–45	133

VERMONT STATUTES ANNOTATED

Tit.	This Work Page
12, § 814	450
15, § 5	648
15, § 592	636
15, § 1201 et seq.	592
15, § 1201 et seq.	628
15, § 1204(a)	681
15, § 1204(c)	669
15, § 1204(d)	629
15, § 1204(d)	646
15, § 1204(d)	671
15, § 1204(d)	681
15, § 1204(e)(1)	602
15, § 1204(e)(2)	602
15, § 1204(e)(4)	681
15, § 1204(e)(4)	700
15, § 1204(e)(4)	705
15, § 1206	629
15, § 1206	636
15, § 1206	646

VERMONT RULES OF CIVIL PROCEDURE

Rule	This Work Page
44.1	547

VIRGINIA CODE

Sec.	This Work Page
8.1–105	955
8.01–247	133

VIRGIN ISLANDS CODE

Tit.	This Work Page
1, § 4	202
5, §§ 4901—4943	548

WEST'S REVISED CODE OF WASHINGTON ANNOTATED

Sec.	This Work Page
4.16.290	133
5.24.010	547
7.72.010 et seq.	900
26.09.010	636
26.16.220	621
26.16.230	621
26.16.240	621
62A.1–105	955
62A.1–105	984
765.04	648

WEST VIRGINIA CODE

Sec.	This Work Page
23–4–2(c)	92
23–4–15a	228
46–1–105	955
46A–3–105	1018
55–2–17	133
57–1–4	547

WISCONSIN STATUTES ANNOTATED

Sec.	This Work Page
299.33(4)	1011
401.105	984
632.09	967
765.03(2)	573
765.04	648
766.55(2)(cm)	626
766.58	622
767.37	573
893.07	133
902.02	547

WYOMING STATUTES ANNOTATED

Sec.	This Work Page
1–3–117	133
1–12–301	547
34–15–101	1141

FEDERAL RULES

FEDERAL RULES OF CIVIL PROCEDURE

Rule	This Work Page
3	184
3	185
3	186
3	187
3(b)	185
4	430
4	437

FEDERAL RULES OF CIVIL PROCEDURE

Rule	This Work Page
4	440
4	441
4(d)	326
4(d)(1)	183
4(e)	429
4(e)(2)	183
4(e) (former)	425
4(e) (former)	429
4(e) (former)	430
4(f)	431
4(f)	524
4(f)	525
4(f)	529
4(f)(1)	524
4(h)	525
4(h)(1)	432
4(i)	524
4(k)	323
4(k)	361
4(k)	418
4(k)	428
4(k)	429
4(k)	430
4(k)	431
4(k)	441
4(k)(1)	425
4(k)(1)(A)	323
4(k)(1)(A)	386
4(k)(1)(A)	430
4(k)(1)(A)	437
4(k)(1)(A)	441
4(k)(1)(A)	443
4(k)(1)(B)	197
4(k)(1)(B)	323
4(k)(1)(B)	431
4(k)(1)(B)	432
4(k)(1)(B)	443
4(k)(1)(C)	323
4(k)(1)(D)	324
4(k)(2)	324
4(k)(2)	418
4(k)(2)	425
4(k)(2)	433
4(k)(2)	434
4(k)(2)	435
4(k)(2)	438
4(k)(2)	441
4(k)(2)	443
4(k)(2)	464
6	185
12	329
12	346
12	347
12(b)	329
12(b)	443
12(b)(2)	329
12(b)(2)	330
12(b)(3)	329
12(b)(5)	329
12(b)(6)	330
12(d)	329
12(g)	329
12(g)	330

FEDERAL RULES OF CIVIL PROCEDURE

Rule	This Work Page
12(g)	331
12(g)	346
12(g)	347
12(g)	443
12(h)	443
12(h)(1)	326
12(h)(1)	329
12(h)(1)	346
12(h)(1)	347
12(h)(2)	330
12(h)(3)	327
12(h)(3)	330
14	432
15(a)	346
18	465
19	431
19	432
23	444
23	446
23	449
23(a)	444
23(b)(1)	446
23(b)(1)	447
23(b)(1)	449
23(b)(2)	444
23(b)(2)	447
23(b)(2)	449
23(b)(3)	447
23(b)(3)	448
23(b)(3)	449
23(c)(2)	447
23(c)(2)	449
26—37	529
28	536
28(b)	529
28(b)	536
28(b)(1)	536
37	348
41	187
41(b)	185
41(b)	191
41(b)	192
44.1	549
44.1	550
44.1	551
44.1	552
44.1	746
52(a)	552
60(b)	1285
60(b)(2)	1273
60(b)(2)	1303
60(b)(5)	1305
60(b)(6)	204
60(b)(6)	1273
60(b)(6)	1303
60(b)(6)	1305

FEDERAL RULES OF CIVIL PROCEDURE—SUPPLEMENTAL RULES

Rule	This Work Page

FEDERAL RULES OF CIVIL PROCEDURE—SUPPLEMENTAL RULES

Rule	This Work Page
B	438
B	439
B(1)	438
C	439
C(1)(a)	439

FEDERAL RULES OF CRIMINAL PROCEDURE

Rule	This Work Page
17(a)	184

FEDERAL RULES OF EVIDENCE

Rule	This Work Page
302	184
501	184
601	184
702	184
1101(b)	184

FEDERAL RULES OF APPELLATE PROCEDURE

Rule	This Work Page
38	186

BANKRUPTCY RULES OF PROCEDURE

Rule	This Work Page
7004	440
7004	441
7004(a)	440
7004(a)	441
7004(b)	440
7004(c)	440
7004(d)	441
7004(d)	1240
7004(f)	425
7004(f)	441
7004(f)	442

CODE OF FEDERAL REGULATIONS

Tit.	This Work Page
14, § 203.4(c)	225
22, § 52.1	570
22, § 52.2(b)	570

FEDERAL REGISTER

Vol.	This Work Page
44, p. 62714	900
52, p. 6262	224

FEDERAL REGISTER

Vol.	This Work Page
52, p. 6262	1009
52, p. 6262	1320

*

Table of Cases

A

A v. M, 74 N.J.Super. 104, 180 A.2d 541 (N.J.Co.Prob.Div.1962)—§ **4.37, n. 2**; § **16.5, n. 5.**

Aaron Ferer & Sons Ltd. v. Chase Manhattan Bank, Nat. Ass'n, 731 F.2d 112 (2nd Cir.1984)—§ **2.23, n. 8**; § **3.36, n. 1.**

Abadian v. Lee, 117 F.Supp.2d 481 (D.Md. 2000)—§ **17.55, n. 9.**

Abadou v. Trad, 624 P.2d 287 (Alaska 1981)—§ **11.5, n. 3.**

Abels v. State Farm Fire & Cas. Co., 596 F.Supp. 1461 (W.D.Pa.1984)—§ **2.9, n. 19.**

Abendschein v. Farrell, 382 Mich. 510, 170 N.W.2d 137 (Mich.1969)—§ **17.7, n. 10.**

Abercrombie v. Davies, 35 Del.Ch. 354, 118 A.2d 358 (Del.Ch.1955)—§ **5.22, n. 4.**

Abety v. Abety, 10 N.J.Super. 287, 77 A.2d 291 (N.J.Super.Ch.1950)—§ **12.11**; § **12.11, n. 7.**

ABKCO Industries, Inc. v. Lennon, 52 A.D.2d 435, 384 N.Y.S.2d 781 (N.Y.A.D. 1 Dept.1976)—§ **5.13, n. 27**; § **6.8, n. 7**; § **6.9, n. 23.**

Abogados v. AT&T, Inc., 223 F.3d 932 (9th Cir.2000)—§ **17.48, n. 9.**

Abou–Issa v. Abou–Issa, 229 Ga. 77, 189 S.E.2d 443 (Ga.1972)—§ **4.30, n. 8.**

About.Com, Inc. v. Targetfirst, Inc., 2002 WL 826953 (S.D.N.Y.2002)—§ **17.40, n. 28.**

Abrams v. Daffron, 155 Ga.App. 182, 270 S.E.2d 278 (Ga.App.1980)—§ **4.41, n. 2.**

A. C. Beals Co. v. Rhode Island Hospital, 110 R.I. 275, 292 A.2d 865 (R.I.1972)— § **2.21, n. 70**; § **18.21, n. 9.**

Accelerated Christian Educ., Inc. v. Oracle Corp., 925 S.W.2d 66 (Tex.App.-Dallas 1996)—§ **11.5, n. 6.**

Accuweather, Inc. v. Total Weather, Inc., 223 F.Supp.2d 612 (M.D.Pa.2002)— § **9.3, n. 7.**

Ace Metal Fabricating Co. v. Arvid C. Walberg & Co., 135 Ill.App.3d 452, 90 Ill. Dec. 266, 481 N.E.2d 1066 (Ill.App. 2 Dist.1985)—§ **24.13, n. 8.**

Achesor v. Dowell (Morgan Guaranty Trust Co., In re), 320 N.Y.S.2d 905, 269 N.E.2d 571 (N.Y.1971)—§ **21.12, n. 5.**

Achilles v. Hoopes, 40 Wash.2d 664, 245 P.2d 1005 (Wash.1952)—§ **14.16, n. 10.**

Acker v. Priest, 92 Iowa 610, 61 N.W. 235 (Iowa 1894)—§ **19.6, n. 1.**

Ackermann v. Levine, 788 F.2d 830 (2nd Cir.1986)—§ **12.7, n. 3.**

Ackermann v. Levine, 610 F.Supp. 633 (S.D.N.Y.1985)—§ **12.7, n. 3.**

Adam v. J.B. Hunt Transport, Inc., 130 F.3d 219 (6th Cir.1997)—§ **11.14, n. 18**; § **17.13, n. 1, 8.**

Adam v. Saenger, 303 U.S. 59, 58 S.Ct. 454, 82 L.Ed. 649 (1938)—§ **5.8, n. 3**; § **5.23, n. 4**; § **6.5, n. 1, 10**; § **10.10, n. 7**; § **22.20, n. 32**; § **24.16, n. 4.**

Adam Hat Stores v. Lefco, 134 F.2d 101 (3rd Cir.1943)—§ **17.7, n. 3.**

Adams v. Adams, 154 Mass. 290, 28 N.E. 260 (Mass.1891)—§ **16.1, n. 8.**

Adams v. Agnew, 860 F.2d 1093, 274 U.S.App.D.C. 1 (D.C.Cir.1988)—§ **18.27, n. 3.**

Adams v. Batcheldor, 173 Mass. 258, 53 N.E. 824 (Mass.1899)—§ **22.15, n. 4.**

Adams v. Buffalo Forge Co., 443 A.2d 932 (Me.1982)—§ **2.23, n. 1**; § **17.26, n. 1.**

Adams v. D'Hauteville, 72 R.I. 325, 51 A.2d 92 (R.I.1947)—§ **21.11, n. 5.**

Adams v. Fitchburg R. Co., 67 Vt. 76, 30 A. 687 (Vt.1894)—§ **3.17, n. 2.**

Adams v. Keystone Ins. Co., 264 N.J.Super. 367, 624 A.2d 1008 (N.J.Super.A.D.1993)—§ **17.58, n. 9.**

Adams v. Londeree, 139 W.Va. 748, 83 S.E.2d 127 (W.Va.1954)—§ **4.26, n. 1.**

Adams v. Robertson, 520 U.S. 83, 117 S.Ct. 1028, 137 L.Ed.2d 203 (1997)—§ **10.11**; § **10.11, n. 9.**

Adamsen v. Adamsen, 151 Conn. 172, 195 A.2d 418 (Conn.1963)—§ **12.15, n. 9.**

Adams Fruit Co., Inc. v. Barrett, 494 U.S. 638, 110 S.Ct. 1384, 108 L.Ed.2d 585 (1990)—§ **17.59, n. 3.**

Adams Laboratories, Inc. v. Jacobs Engineering Co., 486 F.Supp. 383 (N.D.Ill. 1980)—§ **18.37, n. 7.**

Adderson v. Adderson, 1987 WL 717400 (Alta. C.A.1987)—§ **14.13, n. 8.**

Addison v. Addison, 62 Cal.2d 558, 43 Cal. Rptr. 97, 399 P.2d 897 (Cal.1965)— § **14.9, n. 4, 14.**

Addressograph–Multigraph Corp. v. American Expansion Bolt & Mfg. Co., 124 F.2d 706 (7th Cir.1941)—§ **17.53, n. 8.**

Adger v. Kirk, 116 S.C. 298, 108 S.E. 97 (S.C.1921)—§ **21.11, n. 12.**

Adkins v. Antapara, 850 S.W.2d 148 (Tenn. Ct.App.1992)—§ **15.43, n. 8.**

Adkins v. Chicago, R. I. & P. R. Co., 54 Ill.2d 511, 301 N.E.2d 729 (Ill.1973)— § **11.11, n. 6.**

Adkins v. Loucks, 107 Wis. 587, 83 N.W. 934 (Wis.1900)—§ **22.25, n. 3.**

Adkins v. Sperry, 190 W.Va. 120, 437 S.E.2d 284 (W.Va.1993)—§ **2.17, n. 11;** § **2.23, n. 5;** § **18.21, n. 14.**

Admiral Ins. Co. v. Brinkcraft Development, Ltd., 921 F.2d 591 (5th Cir. 1991)—§ **18.5, n. 12.**

Adoption of (see name of party)

Advanced Bionics Corp. v. Medtronic, Inc., 128 Cal.Rptr.2d 172, 59 P.3d 231 (Cal. 2002)—§ **18.5;** § **18.5, n. 24, 28;** § **24.9, n. 7;** § **24.21, n. 5.**

Advanced Bionics Corp. v. Medtronic, Inc., 105 Cal.Rptr.2d 265 (Cal.App. 2 Dist. 2001)—§ **18.5, n. 29.**

Advanced Micro Devices, Inc. v. Intel Corp., 292 F.3d 664 (9th Cir.2002)—§ **12.8, n. 10.**

Advani Enterprises, Inc. v. Underwriters at Lloyds, 140 F.3d 157 (2nd Cir.1998)— § **18.7, n. 8.**

Aero–Fastener, Inc., In re, 177 B.R. 120 (Bkrtcy.D.Mass.1994)—§ **7.11, n. 1.**

Aerogroup Intern., Inc. v. Marlboro Footworks, Ltd., 956 F.Supp. 427 (S.D.N.Y. 1996)—§ **10.5, n. 16.**

Aetna Cas. & Sur. Co. v. Crowther, Inc., 221 Ill.App.3d 275, 163 Ill.Dec. 679, 581 N.E.2d 833 (Ill.App. 3 Dist.1991)—§ **9.5, n. 7.**

Aetna Cas. & Sur. Co. v. Dow Chemical Co., 883 F.Supp. 1101 (E.D.Mich.1995)— § **18.26, n. 12.**

Aetna Cas. & Sur. Co. v. Holland, 1997 WL 736518 (Mass.Super.1997)—§ **17.56, n. 18.**

Aetna Cas. & Sur. Co. v. Looney, 98 Ill. App.3d 1057, 54 Ill.Dec. 444, 424 N.E.2d 1347 (Ill.App. 4 Dist.1981)—§ **8.6, n. 1.**

Aetna Cas. & Sur. Ins. Co. v. Greene, 606 F.2d 123 (6th Cir.1979)—§ **23.3, n. 4.**

Aetna Life Ins. Co. v. Johnson, 206 F.Supp. 63 (N.D.Ill.1962)—§ **3.43, n. 3.**

Aetna Life Ins. Co. v. Schmitt, 404 F.Supp. 189 (M.D.Fla.1975)—§ **14.11, n. 2.**

Afflerbach v. Furry, 1993 WL 465609 (Conn.Super.1993)—§ **17.59, n. 11.**

Afflick's Estate, In re, 10 D.C. 95 (D.C.Sup. 1877)—§ **4.41, n. 7.**

Aganoor's Trusts, In re, 64 L.J.Ch. 521 (1895)—§ **20.4, n. 6.**

Agent Orange Product Liability Litigation, In re, 580 F.Supp. 690 (E.D.N.Y.1984)— § **2.11, n. 8.**

Agent Orange Product Liability Litigation, In re, 506 F.Supp. 737 (E.D.N.Y.1979)— § **3.55, n. 8.**

Agostini's Estate, In re, 311 Pa.Super. 233, 457 A.2d 861 (Pa.Super.1983)—§ **21.3, n. 17.**

Agricultural Services Ass'n, Inc. v. Ferry–Morse Seed Co., Inc., 551 F.2d 1057 (6th Cir.1977)—§ **18.21, n. 11.**

Aguinda v. Texaco, Inc., 2000 WL 122143 (S.D.N.Y.2000)—§ **24.36, n. 3.**

AG Volkswagen v. Valdez, 897 S.W.2d 458 (Tex.App.-Corpus Christi 1995)— § **12.17, n. 13.**

Aiello v. United Air Lines, Inc., 818 F.2d 1196 (5th Cir.1987)—§ **18.29, n. 3, 5.**

Aircraft Accident at Little Rock, Arkansas, June 1, 1999, In re, 231 F.Supp.2d 852 (E.D.Ark.2002)—§ **17.50, n. 33.**

Air Crash Disaster at Boston, Massachusetts on July 31, 1973, In re, 399 F.Supp. 1106 (D.Mass.1975)—§ **3.46, n. 7.**

Air Crash Disaster at Sioux City, Iowa, on July 19, 1989, In re, 734 F.Supp. 1425 (N.D.Ill.1990)—§ **17.50;** § **17.50, n. 42;** § **17.66, n. 3, 5;** § **17.69, n. 12.**

Air Crash Disaster at Stapleton Intern. Airport, Denver, Colo., on Nov. 15, 1987, In re, 720 F.Supp. 1445 (D.Colo.1988)— § **17.50;** § **17.50, n. 11.**

Air Crash Disaster at Washington, D.C. on Jan. 13, 1982, In re, 559 F.Supp. 333 (D.D.C.1983)—§ **17.50;** § **17.50, n. 34, 56.**

Air Crash Disaster Near Chicago, Illinois on May 25, 1979, In re, 644 F.2d 594 (7th Cir.1981)—§ **17.50;** § **17.50, n. 12, 32, 35, 43.**

Air Crash Disaster Near Chicago, Ill., on May 25, 1979, In re, 526 F.Supp. 226 (N.D.Ill.1981)—§ **3.39, n. 7;** § **3.46, n. 17;** § **3.47, n. 7;** § **3.53, n. 10.**

Air Crash Disaster Near Chicago, Ill., on May 25, 1979, In re, 500 F.Supp. 1044 (N.D.Ill.1980)—§ **3.46, n. 17.**

Air Crash Disaster Near Monroe, Mich. on January 9, 1997, In re, 20 F.Supp.2d 1110 (E.D.Mich.1998)—§ **17.50, n. 35.**

Air Crash Disaster Near New Orleans, La. on July 9, 1982, In re, 821 F.2d 1147 (5th Cir.1987)—§ **11.8, n. 6;** § **11.9, n. 6.**

Air Crash Off Long Island, New York, on July 17, 1996, In re, 209 F.3d 200 (2nd Cir.2000)—§ **17.63, n. 4.**

Air Economy Corp. v. Aero–Flow Dynamics, Inc., 122 N.J.Super. 456, 300 A.2d 856 (N.J.Super.A.D.1973)—§ **11.5, n. 3.**

Air Products & Chemicals, Inc. v. Fairbanks Morse, Inc., 58 Wis.2d 193, 206 N.W.2d 414 (Wis.1973)—§ **3.12, n. 5.**

Air Products & Chemicals, Inc. v. Lummus Co., 252 A.2d 543 (Del.Supr.1969)— § **11.10, n. 4.**

A.I.U. Ins. Co. v. Superior Court, 177 Cal. App.3d 281, 222 Cal.Rptr. 880 (Cal.App. 1 Dist.1986)—§ **8.2, n. 13.**

Akro Corp. v. Luker, 45 F.3d 1541 (Fed.Cir. 1995)—§ **9.4, n. 11.**

Alabama G.S.R. Co. v. Carroll, 97 Ala. 126, 11 So. 803 (Ala.1892)—§ **2.7, n. 19;** § **17.2;** § **17.2, n. 5;** § **17.48, n. 2.**

Alaska Airlines, Inc. v. Lockheed Aircraft Corp., 430 F.Supp. 134 (D.Alaska 1977)—§ **3.12, n. 6.**

Alaska Airlines, Inc., State ex rel. Starkey v., 68 Wash.2d 318, 413 P.2d 352 (Wash. 1966)—§ **23.5, n. 5.**

Alaska Commercial Co v. Debney, 144 F. 1 (9th Cir.1906)—§ **24.34, n. 11.**

Alaska Packers Ass'n v. Industrial Acc. Com'n, 294 U.S. 532, 55 S.Ct. 518, 79 L.Ed. 1044 (1935)—§ **3.24;** § **3.24, n. 4;** § **17.59, n. 10.**

Albanese v. Albanese, 1997 WL 1921071 (B.C. S.C.1997)—§ **14.9, n. 12.**

Albany Ins. Co. v. Anh Thi Kieu, 927 F.2d 882 (5th Cir.1991)—§ **17.63, n. 5.**

Albany Ins. Co. v. Wisniewski, 579 F.Supp. 1004 (D.R.I.1984)—§ **2.21, n. 73.**

Alberding v. Brunzell, 601 F.2d 474 (9th Cir.1979)—§ **3.11, n. 3, 4, 5.**

Albert v. McGrath, 278 F.2d 16, 107 U.S.App.D.C. 336 (D.C.Cir.1960)—§ **17.5, n. 6.**

Albert & Harlow Inc. v. Great Northern Oil Co., 283 Minn. 246, 167 N.W.2d 500 (Minn.1969)—§ **19.9, n. 9.**

Alberti v. Empresa Nicaraguense De La Carne, 705 F.2d 250 (7th Cir.1983)— § **11.15, n. 1.**

Alberti, In the Estate of, 1955 WL 16547 (PDAD 1955)—§ **20.6, n. 10.**

Alberto v. Diversified Group, Inc., 55 F.3d 201 (5th Cir.1995)—§ **23.10, n. 3.**

Albert Trostel & Sons Co. v. Employers Ins. of Wausau, 216 Wis.2d 382, 576 N.W.2d 88 (Wis.App.1998)—§ **18.26, n. 13.**

Albina Engine & Mach. Works v. O'Leary, 328 F.2d 877 (9th Cir.1964)—§ **13.6, n. 2.**

Albritton v. General Finance Corp., 204 F.2d 125 (5th Cir.1953)—§ **18.7, n. 12.**

Albro v. Manhattan Life Ins. Co., 119 F. 629 (C.C.D.Mass.1902)—§ **18.7, n. 11.**

Albuquerque Nat. Bank v. Citizens Nat. Bank in Abilene, 212 F.2d 943 (5th Cir. 1954)—§ **22.12, n. 3.**

Alburger v. Alburger, 138 Pa.Super. 339, 10 A.2d 888 (Pa.Super.1940)—§ **4.37, n. 2.**

Alcoa S. S. Co., Inc. v. M/V Nordic Regent, 654 F.2d 147 (2nd Cir.1980)—§ **11.11, n. 2;** § **11.12, n. 2.**

Alcock v. Smith, 1892 WL 9784 (CA 1892)— § **19.13, n. 3.**

Alcolac, Inc. v. St. Paul Fire and Marine Ins. Co., 716 F.Supp. 1541 (D.Md. 1989)—§ **18.26, n. 19.**

Alcorn v. Epler, 206 Ill.App. 140 (Ill.App. 4 Dist.1917)—§ **19.5, n. 10.**

Aldrich v. Aldrich, 378 U.S. 540, 84 S.Ct. 1687, 12 L.Ed.2d 1020 (1964)—§ **5.17, n. 7;** § **24.16, n. 3.**

Alexander v. Alexander, 357 So.2d 1260 (La.App. 2 Cir.1978)—§ **20.5, n. 6.**

Alexander v. General Motors Corp., 267 Ga. 339, 478 S.E.2d 123 (Ga.1996)—§ **2.21, n. 16;** § **17.8, n. 2;** § **17.71;** § **17.71, n. 9.**

Alexander v. General Motors Corp., 219 Ga. App. 660, 466 S.E.2d 607 (Ga.App. 1995)—§ **17.71, n. 11.**

Alexander v. Ling–Temco–Vought, Inc., 406 S.W.2d 919 (Tex.Civ.App.-Texarkana 1966)—§ **19.12, n. 4;** § **19.13, n. 4.**

Alexander Proudfoot Co. World Headquarters v. Thayer, 877 F.2d 912 (11th Cir. 1989)—§ **11.4, n. 15.**

Alfadda v. Fenn, 966 F.Supp. 1317 (S.D.N.Y.1997)—§ **24.44, n. 12.**

Al–Fassi v. Al–Fassi, 433 So.2d 664 (Fla. App. 3 Dist.1983)—§ **15.43, n. 8.**

Alfred Dunhill of London, Inc. v. Republic of Cuba, 425 U.S. 682, 96 S.Ct. 1854, 48 L.Ed.2d 301 (1976)—§ **18.44, n. 11;** § **24.46, n. 10.**

Algemene Bank Nederland, M.V. v. Mattox, 611 F.Supp. 144 (N.D.Ga.1985)—§ **18.1, n. 22.**

Algie v. Algie, 261 S.C. 103, 198 S.E.2d 529 (S.C.1973)—§ **17.7, n. 8.**

Alioto Fish Co. v. Alioto, 34 Cal.Rptr.2d 244 (Cal.App. 1 Dist.1994)—§ **5.20, n. 4.**

Alisandrelli v. Kenwood, 724 F.Supp. 235 (S.D.N.Y.1989)—§ **3.41, n. 15.**

Allan v. Brown & Root, Inc., 491 F.Supp. 398 (S.D.Tex.1980)—§ **17.63, n. 23.**

Allegheny County, Pa., United States v., 322 U.S. 174, 64 S.Ct. 908, 88 L.Ed. 1209 (1944)—§ **3.52, n. 2.**

Allen, Matter of Estate of, 237 Mont. 114, 772 P.2d 297 (Mont.1989)—§ **20.8, n. 12;** § **21.11, n. 2.**

Allen v. Allen, 484 So.2d 269 (La.App. 3 Cir.1986)—§ **14.11, n. 2.**

Allen v. Allen, 200 Or. 678, 268 P.2d 358 (Or.1954)—§ **4.37, n. 3;** § **4.40, n. 4.**

Allen v. Greyhound Lines, Inc., 583 P.2d 613 (Utah 1978)—§ **4.24, n. 4.**

Allen v. Harvey, 568 S.W.2d 829 (Tenn. 1978)—§ **16.2, n. 9.**

Allen v. Lloyd's of London, 94 F.3d 923 (4th Cir.1996)—§ **11.3, n. 33;** § **18.2, n. 11.**

Allen v. McCurry, 449 U.S. 90, 101 S.Ct. 411, 66 L.Ed.2d 308 (1980)—§ **24.1, n. 7.**

Allen v. Nessler, 247 Minn. 230, 76 N.W.2d 793 (Minn.1956)—§ **17.6, n. 6.**

Allen, People v., 336 Ill.App.3d 457, 271 Ill.Dec. 175, 784 N.E.2d 393 (Ill.App. 2 Dist.2003)—§ **12.11, n. 7.**

Allen v. Superior Court in and for Los Angeles County, 41 Cal.2d 306, 259 P.2d 905 (Cal.1953)—§ **6.4, n. 6, 22;** § **12.3, n. 2.**

Allen v. Thomason, 30 Tenn. 536 (Tenn. 1851)—§ **4.36, n. 11; § 4.37, n. 2.**

Allenberg Cotton Co., Inc. v. Pittman, 419 U.S. 20, 95 S.Ct. 260, 42 L.Ed.2d 195 (1974)—§ **23.6, n. 4.**

Allen's Estate, In re, 64 Misc.2d 920, 316 N.Y.S.2d 352 (N.Y.Sur.1970)—§ **22.10, n. 12.**

Allen's Estate, Matter of, 239 N.W.2d 163 (Iowa 1976)—§ **22.9, n. 1.**

Allerton v. State Dept. of Ins., 635 So.2d 36 (Fla.App. 1 Dist.1994)—§ **7.3, n. 10.**

Alley v. Parker, 707 A.2d 77 (Me.1998)— § **15.42, n. 1; § 24.46, n. 2.**

Allgood v. Williams, 92 Ala. 551, 8 So. 722 (Ala.1891)—§ **4.37, n. 2, 10.**

Alliant Energy Corp. v. Bie, 330 F.3d 904 (7th Cir.2003)—§ **23.6, n. 7.**

Allianz Versicherungs–Aktiengesellschaft v. Steamship Eskisehir, 334 F.Supp. 1225 (S.D.N.Y.1971)—§ **12.18, n. 5.**

Allied Bank Intern. v. Banco Credito Agricola de Cartago, 757 F.2d 516 (2nd Cir. 1985)—§ **11.13, n. 21.**

Allied–Bruce Terminix Companies, Inc. v. Dobson, 513 U.S. 265, 115 S.Ct. 834, 130 L.Ed.2d 753 (1995)—§ **6.3, n. 19.**

Allied Thermal Corp. v. James Talcott, Inc., 165 N.Y.S.2d 91, 144 N.E.2d 66 (N.Y. 1957)—§ **19.9, n. 9.**

Allied Towing Corp. v. Great Eastern Petroleum Corp., 642 F.Supp. 1339 (E.D.Va. 1986)—§ **9.2, n. 21.**

Allison v. ITE Imperial Corp., 928 F.2d 137 (5th Cir.1991)—§ **17.74, n. 20; § 17.78, n. 11.**

All Seasons Industries, Inc. v. Gregory, 174 Ill.App.3d 700, 124 Ill.Dec. 308, 529 N.E.2d 25 (Ill.App. 5 Dist.1988)— § **24.13, n. 8.**

Allstate Ins. Co. v. Hague, 449 U.S. 302, 101 S.Ct. 633, 66 L.Ed.2d 521 (1981)— § **2.10, n. 30; § 3.7, n. 5; § 3.16, n. 3; § 3.21, n. 12, 13; § 3.23; § 3.23, n. 1; § 3.26, n. 6; § 3.48; § 3.48, n. 2; § 5.1, n. 10; § 17.15, n. 16.**

Allstate Ins. Co. v. Wal–Mart, 2000 WL 388844 (E.D.La.2000)—§ **17.44, n. 9.**

Allstate Ins. Co. (Stolarz), In re, 597 N.Y.S.2d 904, 613 N.E.2d 936 (N.Y. 1993)—§ **2.25, n. 20; § 18.21, n. 15, 17; § 18.26, n. 6.**

Almeida, In re, 37 B.R. 186 (Bkrtcy.E.D.Pa. 1984)—§ **23.13, n. 4.**

Almodovar v. Almodovar, 55 Misc.2d 300, 284 N.Y.S.2d 910 (N.Y.Sup.1967)— § **13.9, n. 8.**

Alonzo v. ACF Property Management, Inc., 643 F.2d 578 (9th Cir.1981)—§ **3.39, n. 14.**

Alpert v. Thomas, 643 F.Supp. 1406 (D.Vt. 1986)—§ **19.12, n. 2; § 19.17, n. 6.**

Alropa Corp. v. Bloom, 311 Mass. 442, 42 N.E.2d 269 (Mass.1942)—§ **19.9, n. 3.**

Alston v. Rains, 589 S.W.2d 481 (Tex.Civ. App.-Texarkana 1979)—§ **22.26, n. 5.**

Alton v. Alton, 207 F.2d 667 (3rd Cir. 1953)—§ **4.7, n. 1; § 15.4, n. 2, 4; § 15.5, n. 6; § 15.14, n. 6.**

Aluminum Co. of America, United States v., 148 F.2d 416 (2nd Cir.1945)—§ **17.48, n. 27.**

Alvarez–Machain v. United States, 331 F.3d 604 (9th Cir.2003)—§ **17.48, n. 19.**

Alves v. Alves, 262 A.2d 111 (D.C.App. 1970)—§ **4.30, n. 5; § 4.31, n. 6.**

Alves v. Siegel's Broadway Auto Parts, Inc., 710 F.Supp. 864 (D.Mass.1989)— § **17.78, n. 7.**

Alvord & Alvord v. Patenotre, 196 Misc. 524, 92 N.Y.S.2d 514 (N.Y.Sup.1949)— § **4.36, n. 11.**

Ambach v. Norwick, 441 U.S. 68, 99 S.Ct. 1589, 60 L.Ed.2d 49 (1979)—§ **3.58, n. 9, 16, 18.**

Ambrose v. Vandeford, 277 Ala. 66, 167 So.2d 149 (Ala.1964)—§ **4.13, n. 11.**

Amchem Products, Inc. v. Windsor, 521 U.S. 591, 117 S.Ct. 2231, 138 L.Ed.2d 689 (1997)—§ **10.9, n. 4.**

Amdur v. Zim Israel Nav. Co., 310 F.Supp. 1033 (S.D.N.Y.1969)—§ **12.18, n. 8.**

Amerco Marketing Co. of Memphis, Inc. v. Myers, 494 F.2d 904 (6th Cir.1974)— § **18.27, n. 4.**

American Air Filter Co., Inc. v. McNichol, 361 F.Supp. 908 (E.D.Pa.1973)— § **18.12, n. 9.**

American Aviation, Inc. v. Aviation Ins. Managers, Inc., 244 Ark. 829, 427 S.W.2d 544 (Ark.1968)—§ **12.17, n. 13.**

American Banana Co. v. United Fruit Co., 213 U.S. 347, 29 S.Ct. 511, 53 L.Ed. 826 (1909)—§ **12.19, n. 13; § 17.7, n. 3; § 17.53, n. 1.**

American Bible Soc. v. Healy, 153 Mass. 197, 26 N.E. 404 (Mass.1891)—§ **20.9, n. 9; § 20.10, n. 2; § 20.12, n. 4.**

American Bible Soc. v. Pendleton, 7 W.Va. 79 (W.Va.1873)—§ **21.2, n. 12.**

American Directory Service Agency v. Beam, 131 F.R.D. 635 (D.D.C.1990)— § **10.17, n. 9.**

American Dredging Co. v. Miller, 510 U.S. 443, 114 S.Ct. 981, 127 L.Ed.2d 285 (1994)—§ **10.6, n. 22; § 11.8, n. 6.**

American Elec. Power Co., Inc. v. Westinghouse Elec. Corp., 418 F.Supp. 435 (S.D.N.Y.1976)—§ **18.24, n. 2.**

American Family Mut. Ins. Co. v. Farmers Ins. Exchange, 504 N.W.2d 307 (N.D. 1993)—§ **2.25, n. 14; § 18.21, n. 17.**

American Freehold Land & Mortgage Co. v. Jefferson, 69 Miss. 770, 12 So. 464 (Miss.1892)—§ **18.9, n. 12.**

American Heritage Life Ins. Co. v. Heritage Life Ins. Co., 494 F.2d 3 (5th Cir.1974)— § **17.53, n. 5.**

American Home Assur. Co. v. American Emp. Ins. Co., 384 F.Supp. 3 (E.D.Pa. 1974)—§ **18.21, n. 19.**

American Home Assur. Co. v. Insurance Corp. of Ireland Ltd., 603 F.Supp. 636 (S.D.N.Y.1984)—§ **11.10, n. 8.**

American Home Assur. Co. v. L & L Marine Service, Inc., 153 F.3d 616 (8th Cir. 1998)—§ **2.23, n. 8.**

American Home Assur. Co. v. Safway Steel Products Co., Inc., A Div. of Figgie Intern., Inc., 743 S.W.2d 693 (Tex.App.-Austin 1987)—§ **18.26, n. 19.**

American Home Assur. Co. v. Sport Maska, Inc., 808 F.Supp. 67 (D.Mass.1992)—§ **8.2, n. 12.**

American Houses v. Schneider, 211 F.2d 881 (3rd Cir.1954)—§ **3.52, n. 2.**

American Ins. Ass'n v. Garamendi, 539 U.S. 396, 123 S.Ct. 2374, 156 L.Ed.2d 376 (2003)—§ **3.56; § 3.56, n. 4; § 10.19, n. 59.**

American Motorists Ins. Co. v. ARTRA Group, Inc., 338 Md. 560, 659 A.2d 1295 (Md.1995)—§ **2.21; § 2.21, n. 58; § 3.13, n. 11; § 3.14, n. 3; § 17.8, n. 1; § 18.21, n. 7.**

American Nat. Fire Ins. Co. v. Farmers Ins. Exchange, 927 P.2d 186 (Utah 1996)—§ **2.17, n. 16; § 2.19, n. 16; § 2.23, n. 2; § 18.21, n. 14.**

American Nonwovens, Inc. v. Non Wovens Engineering, S.R.L., 648 So.2d 565 (Ala. 1994)—§ **2.21, n. 42; § 18.21, n. 3.**

American Optical Co. v. Curtiss, 56 F.R.D. 26 (S.D.N.Y.1971)—§ **18.37, n. 12; § 19.29, n. 3.**

American Overseas Marine Corp. v. Patterson, 632 So.2d 1124 (Fla.App. 1 Dist. 1994)—§ **6.9, n. 20.**

American Pipe & Steel Corp. v. Firestone Tire & Rubber Co., 292 F.2d 640 (9th Cir.1961)—§ **3.52, n. 5.**

American Sav. Bank, F.S.B. v. Cheshire Management Co., Inc., 693 F.Supp. 42 (S.D.N.Y.1988)—§ **7.6, n. 9.**

American State Bank v. White, 217 Kan. 78, 535 P.2d 424 (Kan.1975)—§ **19.18, n. 19.**

American Sur. Co. of New York v. Gainfort, 219 F.2d 111 (2nd Cir.1955)—§ **3.11, n. 3.**

American Surety Co. v. Baldwin, 287 U.S. 156, 53 S.Ct. 98, 77 L.Ed. 231 (1932)—§ **4.7, n. 4; § 15.6, n. 5.**

American Tel. & Tel. Co. v. Compagnie Bruxelles Lambert, 94 F.3d 586 (9th Cir. 1996)—§ **10.5, n. 8.**

American Training Service, Inc. v. Commerce Union Bank, 415 F.Supp. 1101 (M.D.Tenn.1976)—§ **18.28, n. 4.**

American Triticale, Inc. v. Nytco Services, Inc., 664 F.2d 1136 (9th Cir.1981)—§ **18.29, n. 3.**

American Trust Co., Inc. v. South Carolina State Bd. of Bank Control, 381 F.Supp. 313 (D.S.C.1974)—§ **21.5, n. 1.**

Amerige v. Attorney General, 324 Mass. 648, 88 N.E.2d 126 (Mass.1949)—§ **21.2, n. 14; § 21.3, n. 3; § 21.6, n. 4; § 21.9, n. 2.**

Ames v. Citizens' Nat. Bank of Independence, 105 Kan. 83, 181 P. 564 (Kan. 1919)—§ **22.11, n. 17; § 22.16, n. 4.**

Ames v. Duryea, 6 Lans. 155 (N.Y.Sup.Gen. Term 1871)—§ **4.26, n. 1.**

Ames v. Ideal Cement Co., 37 Misc.2d 883, 235 N.Y.S.2d 622 (N.Y.Sup.1962)—§ **18.33, n. 3.**

Ames v. McCamber, 124 Mass. 85 (Mass. 1878)—§ **19.13, n. 4.**

Ames Iron Works v. Warren, 76 Ind. 512 (Ind.1881)—§ **19.11, n. 7; § 19.13, n. 8.**

Amey v. Colebrook Guaranty Sav. Bank, 92 F.2d 62 (2nd Cir.1937)—§ **19.8, n. 2.**

Amica Mut. Ins. v. Bourgault, 263 Ga. 157, 429 S.E.2d 908 (Ga.1993)—§ **2.21, n. 44, 47; § 18.21, n. 5.**

Amin v. Bakhaty, 812 So.2d 12 (La.App. 1 Cir.2001)—§ **16.5, n. 9.**

Amin Rasheed Shipping Corp v. Kuwait Insurance Co (The Al Wahab), 1983 WL 216819 (HL 1983)—§ **18.1, n. 16.**

Amiot v. Ames, 166 Vt. 288, 693 A.2d 675 (Vt.1997)—§ **2.16, n. 21; § 2.17, n. 6; § 2.23, n. 1, 2; § 17.26, n. 1, 8; § 17.32, n. 16.**

Amoco Egypt Oil Co. v. Leonis Nav. Co., Inc., 1 F.3d 848 (9th Cir.1993)—§ **5.12, n. 7; § 5.13, n. 19; § 6.9, n. 20; § 7.2, n. 34.**

Amoco Overseas Oil Co. v. Compagnie Nationale Algerienne de Navigation ("C. N. A. N."), 605 F.2d 648 (2nd Cir.1979)—§ **10.6, n. 50.**

Amoco Rocmount Co. v. Anschutz Corp., 7 F.3d 909 (10th Cir.1993)—§ **2.21, n. 46; § 18.21, n. 13.**

Amon v. Grange Mut. Cas. Co., 112 Ohio App.3d 407, 678 N.E.2d 1002 (Ohio App. 11 Dist.1996)—§ **17.26, n. 1.**

Amoroso v. Burdette Tomlin Memorial Hosp., 901 F.Supp. 900 (D.N.J.1995)—§ **17.42, n. 13.**

Amsden v. Danielson, 19 R.I. 533, 35 A. 70 (R.I.1896)—§ **22.11, n. 15.**

Amtrol, Inc. v. Vent–Rite Valve Corp., 646 F.Supp. 1168 (D.Mass.1986)—§ **9.7, n. 3.**

Amusement Equipment, Inc. v. Mordelt, 779 F.2d 264 (5th Cir.1985)—§ **6.2, n. 13.**

Amusement Equipment, Inc. v. Mordelt, 595 F.Supp. 125 (E.D.La.1984)—§ **8.5, n. 8.**

Anas v. Blecker, 141 F.R.D. 530 (M.D.Fla. 1992)—§ **12.11, n. 7.**

Anbe v. Kikuchi, 141 F.R.D. 498 (D.Hawai'i 1992)—§ **12.7, n. 3.**

Anderson v. Anderson, 520 So.2d 1236 (La. App. 5 Cir.1988)—§ **14.11, n. 2.**

Anderson v. Anderson's Estate, 42 Vt. 350 (Vt.1869)—§ **4.19, n. 3.**

Anderson v. Century Products Co., 943 F.Supp. 137 (D.N.H.1996)—§ **10.18, n. 16.**

Anderson v. City of New York, 611 F.Supp. 481 (S.D.N.Y.1985)—§ **24.12, n. 7.**

Anderson v. First Commodity Corp. of Boston, 618 F.Supp. 262 (W.D.Wis.1985)—§ **18.5, n. 2.**

Anderson v. French, 77 N.H. 509, 93 A. 1042 (N.H.1915)—§ **20.3, n. 4.**

Anderson v. Louisville & N. R. Co., 210 F. 689 (6th Cir.1914)—§ **22.15, n. 16.**

Anderson v. Sonat Exploration Co., 523 So.2d 1024 (Miss.1988)—§ **7.7, n. 1.**

Anderson v. Story, 53 Neb. 259, 73 N.W. 735 (Neb.1898)—§ **22.25, n. 10.**

Anderson's Estate, Matter of, 571 P.2d 880 (Okla.App. Div. 1 1977)—§ **20.5, n. 2.**

Andrews v. Andrews, 188 U.S. 14, 23 S.Ct. 237, 47 L.Ed. 366 (1903)—§ **15.6, n. 7.**

Andrews v. Carr, 26 Miss. 577 (Miss.Err. & App.1853)—§ **22.17, n. 1.**

Andrews v. Pond, 38 U.S. 65, 10 L.Ed. 61 (1839)—§ **18.2, n. 1.**

Andrews v. Signal Auto Parts, Inc., 492 S.W.2d 222 (Tenn.1972)—§ **13.6, n. 2.**

Andrews University v. Robert Bell Industries, Ltd., 685 F.Supp. 1015 (W.D.Mich. 1988)—§ **8.5, n. 8.**

Angenieux v. Hakenberg, 13/73, [1973] E.C.R. 935—§ **4.14, n. 4.**

Angel v. Bullington, 330 U.S. 183, 67 S.Ct. 657, 91 L.Ed. 832 (1947)—§ **3.40;** § **3.40, n. 4;** § **19.10, n. 8;** § **24.2, n. 1;** § **24.24, n. 2;** § **24.25;** § **24.25, n. 1.**

Anglo–American Provision Co. v. Davis Provision Co., 191 U.S. 373, 24 S.Ct. 92, 48 L.Ed. 225 (1903)—§ **24.22;** § **24.22, n. 1.**

Anglo–American Provision Co. v. Davis Provision Co., 169 N.Y. 506, 62 N.E. 587 (N.Y.1902)—§ **24.5, n. 2.**

Ankenbrandt v. Richards, 504 U.S. 689, 112 S.Ct. 2206, 119 L.Ed.2d 468 (1992)—§ **15.42, n. 13.**

Annan v. Wilmington Trust Co., 559 A.2d 1289 (Del.Supr.1989)—§ **21.3, n. 9.**

Annesley, Re, 1 Ch. 692 (Ch.D.1926)—§ **3.13, n. 10;** § **4.8, n. 1.**

Annis v. Dewey County Bank, 335 F.Supp. 133 (D.S.D.1971)—§ **11.17, n. 23, 40.**

Anonymous v. Anonymous, 46 Del. 458, 85 A.2d 706 (Del.Super.1951)—§ **13.6, n. 8.**

Antares Aircraft, L.P. v. Federal Republic of Nigeria, 999 F.2d 33 (2nd Cir.1993)—§ **10.19, n. 41.**

Antco Shipping Co., Ltd. v. Sidermar S. p. A., 417 F.Supp. 207 (S.D.N.Y.1976)—§ **24.48, n. 4.**

Anthem Ins. Companies, Inc. v. Tenet Healthcare Corp., 730 N.E.2d 1227 (Ind. 2000)—§ **10.16, n. 8.**

Antonelli v. Antonelli, 16 N.J.Super. 439, 84 A.2d 753 (N.J.Super.A.D.1951)—§ **4.33, n. 3;** § **4.34, n. 3.**

Antosz (Jantosz) v. State Compensation Com'r, 130 W.Va. 260, 43 S.E.2d 397 (W.Va.1947)—§ **3.58, n. 20.**

Antypas v. Cia. Maritima San Basilio, S. A., 541 F.2d 307 (2nd Cir.1976)—§ **17.63, n. 23.**

Apex Oil Co., In re, 88 B.R. 968 (Bkrtcy. E.D.Mo.1988)—§ **23.13, n. 1;** § **23.16, n. 7.**

Apollo Sprinkler Co., Inc. v. Fire Sprinkler Suppliers & Design, Inc., 382 N.W.2d 386 (N.D.1986)—§ **2.17, n. 12.**

Appeal Enterprises Ltd. v. First National Bank of Chicago, 1984 WL 442443 (Ont. C.A.1984)—§ **12.13, n. 8.**

Appeal in Pima County Juvenile Action No. B–7087, Matter of, 118 Ariz. 437, 577 P.2d 723 (Ariz.App. Div. 2 1977)—§ **16.5, n. 5.**

Appeal in Pima County Juvenile Action No. S–903, Matter of, 130 Ariz. 202, 635 P.2d 187 (Ariz.App. Div. 2 1981)—§ **11.17, n. 41;** § **15.42, n. 15.**

Appeal of (see name of party)

Appelbaum v. Appelbaum, 9 Misc.2d 677, 168 N.Y.S.2d 970 (N.Y.Sup.1957)—§ **13.6, n. 7.**

Appelt v. Whitty, 286 F.2d 135 (7th Cir. 1961)—§ **4.43, n. 1;** § **4.44, n. 2.**

Apperson v. Bolton, 29 Ark. 418 (Ark. 1874)—§ **20.15, n. 5.**

Apple, In re, 66 Cal. 432, 6 P. 7 (Cal. 1885)—§ **20.3, n. 1.**

Applegate v. Smith, 31 Mo. 166 (Mo.1860)—§ **20.6, n. 15.**

Appleton's Estate, 81 D. & C. 85, 67 Montg. Co. L.Rep. 181 (Pa.1951)—§ **22.20, n. 34.**

Application Group, Inc. v. Hunter Group, Inc., 72 Cal.Rptr.2d 73 (Cal.App. 1 Dist. 1998)—§ **18.4, n. 7;** § **18.5;** § **18.5, n. 19.**

Application of (see name of party)

Apt (Otherwise Magnus) v. Apt, 1947 WL 10609 (PDAD 1947)—§ **13.6, n. 12.**

Arab Monetary Fund v. Hashim, 213 F.3d 1169 (9th Cir.2000)—§ **24.18, n. 2;** § **24.44, n. 11.**

Arams v. Arams, 182 Misc. 328, 45 N.Y.S.2d 251 (N.Y.Sup.1943)—§ **12.19, n. 8.**

Arbaugh v. District of Columbia, 176 F.2d 28, 85 U.S.App.D.C. 97 (D.C.Cir.1949)—§ **4.20, n. 4.**

Arbuthnot v. Allbright, 35 A.D.2d 315, 316 N.Y.S.2d 391 (N.Y.A.D. 3 Dept.1970)—§ **17.30, n. 10.**

Arcand v. Flemming, 185 F.Supp. 22 (D.Conn.1960)—§ **13.2, n. 1.**

Arcata Graphics Co. v. Heidelberg Harris, Inc., 874 S.W.2d 15 (Tenn.Ct.App. 1993)—§ **18.12, n. 1.**

Arcila v. Christopher Trucking, 195 F.Supp.2d 690 (E.D.Pa.2002)—§ **17.45;** § **17.45, n. 46.**

Ardasee Cursetjee v. Perozebove, 10 Moore P.C. 375 (1856)—§ **13.17, n. 3.**

Arendell v. Arendell, 10 La.Ann. 566 (La. 1855)—§ **14.8, n. 4.**

Ardoyno v. Kyzar, 426 F.Supp. 78 (E.D.La. 1976)—§ **17.14;** § **17.14, n. 14;** § **17.50, n. 22;** § **17.55, n. 9.**

Arendell v. Arendell, 10 La.Ann. 566 (La. 1855)—§ **14.8, n. 4.**

Argo Welded Products, Inc. v. J. T. Ryerson Steel & Sons, Inc., 528 F.Supp. 583 (E.D.Pa.1981)—§ **12.19, n. 6.**

Arguello v. Industrial Woodworking Mach. Co., 838 P.2d 1120 (Utah 1992)—§ **7.4, n. 7.**

A. R. Industries, Inc. v. Superior Court, Sacramento County, 268 Cal.App.2d 328, 73 Cal.Rptr. 920 (Cal.App. 3 Dist. 1968)—§ **7.2, n. 12.**

Aristech Chemical Intern. Ltd. v. Acrylic Fabricators Ltd., 138 F.3d 624 (6th Cir. 1998)—§ **5.12, n. 9;** § **8.5, n. 7.**

Armstead v. National R.R. Passenger Corp., 954 F.Supp. 111 (S.D.N.Y.1997)— § **17.46, n. 22.**

Armstrong v. Accrediting Council For Continuing Educ. & Training, Inc., 980 F.Supp. 53 (D.D.C.1997)—§ **18.6, n. 1.**

Armstrong v. Armstrong, 441 P.2d 699 (Alaska 1968)—§ **2.16, n. 8;** § **2.21, n. 14;** § **2.23, n. 1;** § **17.26, n. 1;** § **17.39, n. 9.**

Armstrong v. Manzo, 380 U.S. 545, 85 S.Ct. 1187, 14 L.Ed.2d 62 (1965)—§ **16.5;** § **16.5, n. 6.**

Armstrong Business Services, Inc. v. H & R Block, 96 S.W.3d 867 (Mo.App. W.D. 2002)—§ **18.9, n. 1.**

Arneil v. Ramsey, 550 F.2d 774 (2nd Cir. 1977)—§ **3.11, n. 6.**

Arnett v. Thompson, 433 S.W.2d 109 (Ky. 1968)—§ **2.23, n. 6;** § **17.13;** § **17.13, n. 3;** § **17.22, n. 5;** § **17.26, n. 6;** § **17.39, n. 21.**

Arnhold & S. Bleichroeder, Inc., United States v., 96 F.Supp. 240 (S.D.N.Y. 1951)—§ **19.31, n. 8.**

Arnold, In re Guardianship of, 114 Ill. App.2d 68, 252 N.E.2d 398 (Ill.App. 5 Dist.1969)—§ **22.26, n. 5.**

Arnold v. Potter, 22 Iowa 194 (Iowa 1867)— § **18.2, n. 1;** § **18.7, n. 8.**

Arrowsmith v. United Press Intern., 320 F.2d 219 (2nd Cir.1963)—§ **10.2, n. 4;** § **10.3, n. 1.**

Arsham v. Banci, 511 F.2d 1108 (6th Cir. 1975)—§ **18.38, n. 5.**

Arthur v. Supreme Court of Iowa, 709 F.Supp. 157 (S.D.Iowa 1989)—§ **24.1, n. 7.**

Art Students' League of New York v. Hinkley, 31 F.2d 469 (D.Md.1929)—§ **21.11, n. 4.**

Asahi Metal Industry Co., Ltd. v. Superior Court of California, Solano County, 480 U.S. 102, 107 S.Ct. 1026, 94 L.Ed.2d 92 (1987)—§ **3.26, n. 4;** § **3.27, n. 1;** § **5.4;** § **5.4, n. 26;** § **5.12;** § **5.12, n. 3;** § **6.6, n. 21;** § **7.1, n. 2;** § **7.2;** § **7.2, n. 24;** § **7.4;** § **7.4, n. 2, 4;** § **7.5;** § **7.5, n. 3;** § **7.9, n. 10;** § **7.12, n. 10;** § **8.1, n. 27;** § **9.2;** § **9.2, n. 14;** § **10.2, n. 14, 25;** § **10.15;** § **10.15, n. 17;** § **10.16, n. 5.**

Asarco, Inc. v. Glenara, Ltd., 912 F.2d 784 (5th Cir.1990)—§ **8.8, n. 8.**

Asbestos Removal Corp. of America, Inc. v. Guaranty Nat. Ins. Co., 48 F.3d 1215 (4th Cir.1995)—§ **18.26, n. 12.**

A.S. Goldmen & Co., Inc. v. New Jersey Bureau of Securities, 163 F.3d 780 (3rd Cir.1999)—§ **23.6, n. 12.**

Ashe, Matter of Estate of, 114 Idaho 70, 753 P.2d 281 (Idaho App.1988)—§ **14.9, n. 1.**

Ashland Chemical Co. v. Provence, 129 Cal. App.3d 790, 181 Cal.Rptr. 340 (Cal.App. 4 Dist.1982)—§ **3.9, n. 8;** § **18.27, n. 5.**

Ashland County v. Bayfield County, 244 Wis. 210, 12 N.W.2d 34 (Wis.1943)— § **4.13, n. 2.**

Ashland Oil, Inc. v. Miller Oil Purchasing Co., 678 F.2d 1293 (5th Cir.1982)— § **17.50, n. 48.**

Ashton Park Apartments, Ltd. v. Lebor, 252 F.Supp.2d 539 (N.D.Ohio 2003)—§ **7.3, n. 10.**

A/S Kreditt–Finans v. Cia Venetico De Navegacion S.A. of Panama, 560 F.Supp. 705 (E.D.Pa.1983)—§ **12.18, n. 11;** § **19.26, n. 6.**

ASM Communications, Inc. v. Allen, 656 F.Supp. 838 (S.D.N.Y.1987)—§ **11.2, n. 4.**

A/S Merilaid & Co. v. Chase Nat. Bank of City of New York, 189 Misc. 285, 71 N.Y.S.2d 377 (N.Y.Sup.1947)—§ **23.11, n. 4.**

Aspden v. Nixon, 45 U.S. 467, 4 How. 467, 11 L.Ed. 1059 (1846)—§ **22.20, n. 10.**

Aspinall's Club Ltd. v. Aryeh, 86 A.D.2d 428, 450 N.Y.S.2d 199 (N.Y.A.D. 2 Dept. 1982)—§ **12.7, n. 3.**

A.S. Rampell, Inc. v. Hyster Co., 165 N.Y.S.2d 475, 144 N.E.2d 371 (N.Y. 1957)—§ **18.4, n. 42;** § **18.5, n. 39.**

Assessors of Everett v. Albert N. Parlin House, Inc., 331 Mass. 359, 118 N.E.2d 861 (Mass.1954)—§ **22.14, n. 4.**

Assetta v. Safety Ins. Co., 43 Mass.App.Ct. 317, 682 N.E.2d 931 (Mass.App.Ct. 1997)—§ **17.56, n. 17.**

Associated Trade Development, Inc. v. Condor Lines, Inc., 590 F.Supp. 525 (S.D.N.Y.1984)—§ **7.6, n. 8, 9.**

Associates Commercial Corp. v. Lincoln General Ins. Co., 702 F.Supp. 104 (W.D.Pa.1988)—§ **10.4, n. 14.**

Associates Discount Corp. v. Palmer, 47 N.J. 183, 219 A.2d 858 (N.J.1966)— § **18.19, n. 12.**

Associates Realty Credit Ltd. v. Brune, 89 Wash.2d 6, 568 P.2d 787 (Wash.1977)— § **19.19, n. 6.**

Asta Medica, S.A., Application of, 981 F.2d 1 (1st Cir.1992)—§ **12.8, n. 10.**

Atchison v. Atchison, 256 Mich.App. 531, 664 N.W.2d 249 (Mich.App.2003)— § **16.5, n. 9.**

Atchison v. Wyoming, 763 F.2d 388 (10th Cir.1985)—§ **24.12, n. 7.**

Atherton v. Atherton, 181 U.S. 155, 21 S.Ct. 544, 45 L.Ed. 794 (1901)—§ **15.4, n. 5.**

Athlone Industries, Inc., United States v., 746 F.2d 977 (3rd Cir.1984)—§ **24.24, n. 8.**

Atkins v. Atkins, 623 So.2d 239 (La.App. 2 Cir.1993)—§ **15.42, n. 9.**

Atkins v. Atkins, 308 Ark. 1, 823 S.W.2d 816 (Ark.1992)—§ **15.42, n. 9.**

Atkinson v. Staigg, 13 R.I. 725 (R.I.1882)— § **20.13, n. 6.**

Atkinson v. Superior Court In and For Los Angeles County, 49 Cal.2d 338, 316 P.2d 960 (Cal.1957)—§ **3.43, n. 2.**

Atkinson Trading Co., Inc. v. Shirley, 532 U.S. 645, 121 S.Ct. 1825, 149 L.Ed.2d 889 (2001)—§ **11.17, n. 13.**

Atlanta, City of v. Morgan, 268 Ga. 586, 492 S.E.2d 193 (Ga.1997)—§ **15.1, n. 7.**

Atlantic Financial Federal v. Bruno, 698 F.Supp. 568 (E.D.Pa.1988)—§ **6.3, n. 11.**

Atlantic Mut. Ins. Co. v. Truck Ins. Exchange, 797 F.2d 1288 (5th Cir.1986)— § **18.21, n. 19.**

Atlantic Phosphate Co. v. Ely, 82 Ga. 438, 9 S.E. 170 (Ga.1889)—§ **19.12, n. 1.**

Atlas Credit Corp. v. Ezrine, 303 N.Y.S.2d 382, 250 N.E.2d 474 (N.Y.1969)— § **24.15, n. 3.**

A–T–O, Inc. v. Stratton & Co., Inc., 486 F.Supp. 1323 (N.D.Ga.1980)—§ **18.37, n. 7.**

Attorney General v. Johnson, 282 Md. 274, 385 A.2d 57 (Md.1978)—§ **3.41, n. 18.**

Attorney General, State ex rel. v. Wright, 194 Ark. 652, 109 S.W.2d 123 (Ark. 1937)—§ **22.3, n. 1.**

Attorney General of Canada v. R.J. Reynolds Tobacco Holdings, Inc., 268 F.3d 103 (2nd Cir.2001)—§ **3.17, n. 3, 5;** § **3.18, n. 8; 24.23, n. 7.**

Attorney General of Canada v. R.J. Reynolds Tobacco Holdings, Inc., 103 F.Supp.2d 134 (N.D.N.Y.2000)—§ **24.19, n. 3.**

A. Uberti and C. v. Leonardo, 181 Ariz. 565, 892 P.2d 1354 (Ariz.1995)—§ **5.12, n. 8;** § **7.2, n. 33, 35.**

Auerbach v. Kinley, 594 F.Supp. 1503 (N.D.N.Y.1984)—§ **4.21, n. 2.**

Auerbach v. Samuels, 10 Utah 2d 152, 349 P.2d 1112 (Utah 1960)—§ **24.17, n. 9.**

Augello v. 20166 Tenants Corp., 224 A.D.2d 73, 648 N.Y.S.2d 101 (N.Y.A.D. 1 Dept. 1996)—§ **17.48, n. 7.**

Aurora Nat. Bank v. Anderson, 132 Ill. App.2d 217, 268 N.E.2d 552 (Ill.App. 2 Dist.1971)—§ **3.13, n. 4.**

Austin v. Ryan's Family Steakhouses, 668 So.2d 806 (Ala.Civ.App.1995)—§ **17.59, n. 3.**

Austin, State v., 160 W.Va. 337, 234 S.E.2d 657 (W.Va.1977)—§ **13.2, n. 8;** § **13.5, n. 1.**

Austin, Succession of, 527 So.2d 483 (La. App. 5 Cir.1988)—§ **20.6, n. 11.**

Auten v. Auten, 308 N.Y. 155, 124 N.E.2d 99 (N.Y.1954)—§ **2.14, n. 18;** § **2.16, n. 6;** § **2.17;** § **2.17, n. 4;** § **14.15, n. 3;** § **17.1, n. 1;** § **17.29, n. 4;** § **18.17;** § **18.17, n. 1;** § **18.18, n. 4.**

Autrey v. Chemtrust Industries Corp., 362 F.Supp. 1085 (D.Del.1973)—§ **17.52, n. 2.**

Avantel, S.A., In re, 343 F.3d 311 (5th Cir.2003)—§ **12.18, n. 16.**

Avant Industries, Limited, Petition of, Misc. No. M12–329 (S.D.N.Y.1980)—§ **12.8, n. 1.**

AVC Nederland B.V. v. Atrium Inv. Partnership, 740 F.2d 148 (2nd Cir.1984)— § **6.3, n. 22;** § **11.3, n. 19, 21.**

Avery v. Bender, 126 Vt. 342, 230 A.2d 786 (Vt.1967)—§ **22.19, n. 7.**

Avery's Estate, Matter of, 176 N.J.Super. 469, 423 A.2d 994 (N.J.Super.A.D.1980)—§ **16.6, n. 4.**

Aviall, Inc. v. Ryder System, Inc., 913 F.Supp. 826 (S.D.N.Y.1996)—§ **18.5, n. 1.**

Aviation Credit Corp. v. Batchelor, 190 So.2d 8 (Fla.App. 3 Dist.1966)—§ **3.11, n. 4.**

Avigliano v. Sumitomo Shoji America, Inc., 638 F.2d 552 (2nd Cir.1981)—§ **3.58, n. 6.**

Aviles v. Kunkle, 978 F.2d 201 (5th Cir. 1992)—§ **5.10, n. 26.**

Aviles v. Port Authority of New York and New Jersey, 202 A.D.2d 45, 615 N.Y.S.2d 668 (N.Y.A.D. 1 Dept.1994)— § **17.37, n. 16.**

Avins v. Hannum, 497 F.Supp. 930 (E.D.Pa. 1980)—§ **4.4, n. 3.**

Avitzur v. Avitzur, 459 N.Y.S.2d 572, 446 N.E.2d 136 (N.Y.1983)—§ **15.24, n. 7.**

Avnet, Inc. v. Wyle Laboratories, Inc., 263 Ga. 615, 437 S.E.2d 302 (Ga.1993)— § **2.21, n. 15.**

Award Incentives, Inc. v. Van Rooyen, 263 F.2d 173 (3rd Cir.1959)—§ **18.33, n. 13.**

Awrey v. Progressive Cas. Ins. Co., 728 F.2d 352 (6th Cir.1984)—§ **3.47, n. 2.**

Axelrod v. Phillips Academy, 74 F.Supp.2d 106 (D.Mass.1999)—§ **24.1, n. 12.**

Ayer v. Weeks, 65 N.H. 248, 18 A. 1108 (N.H.1889)—§ **4.17, n. 4.**

Azriel v. Frigitemp Corp., 397 F.Supp. 871 (E.D.Pa.1975)—§ **18.21, n. 17.**

B

B aka L v. L, 65 N.J.Super. 368, 168 A.2d 90 (N.J.Super.Ch.1961)—§ **13.15, n. 4.**

B_____, In the Matter of, 1 I. & N. Dec. 677 (BIA 1943)—§ **15.18, n. 3.**

Babb v. Rand, 345 A.2d 496 (Me.1975)— § **20.8, n. 11.**

Babbitt Ford, Inc. v. Navajo Indian Tribe, 710 F.2d 587 (9th Cir.1983)—§ **11.17, n. 2.**

Babcock v. Jackson, 12 N.Y.2d 473, 240 N.Y.S.2d 743, 191 N.E.2d 279 (N.Y. 1963)—§ **2.7, n. 19;** § **2.16;** § **2.16, n. 6, 9;** § **17.11, n. 23;** § **17.22;** § **17.22, n. 3;** § **17.29;** § **17.29, n. 1;** § **17.32, n. 4;** § **17.36, n. 1;** § **17.83, n. 8;** § **24.2;** § **24.2, n. 5.**

Babcock's Estate, In re, 64 S.D. 283, 266 N.W. 420 (S.D.1936)—§ **4.33, n. 3.**

Babineaux v. Southeastern Drilling Corp., 170 So.2d 518 (La.App. 3 Cir.1965)— § **8.4, n. 2.**

Baby Boy C., In re Adoption of, 31 Wash. App. 639, 644 P.2d 150 (Wash.App. Div. 2 1982)—§ **16.5, n. 5.**

Baby Boy S., Matter of Adoption of, 22 Kan.App.2d 119, 912 P.2d 761 (Kan.App. 1996)—§ **3.23, n. 16.**

Baby Girl B., Matter of Adoption of, 19 Kan.App.2d 283, 867 P.2d 1074 (Kan. App.1994) —§ **16.5, n. 9.**

Baca v. New Prime, Inc., 763 N.E.2d 1014 (Ind.App.2002)—§ **17.48, n. 10.**

Bach, Estate of, 145 Misc.2d 945, 548 N.Y.S.2d 871 (N.Y.Sur.1989)—§ **14.6, n. 7.**

Bacharach v. Spriggs, 173 Ark. 250, 292 S.W. 150 (Ark.1927)—§ **22.18, n. 13.**

Bachchan v. India Abroad Publications Inc., 154 Misc.2d 228, 585 N.Y.S.2d 661 (N.Y.Sup.1992)—§ **24.44, n. 12.**

Bache v. Dixie–Ohio Exp. Co., 8 F.R.D. 159 (N.D.Ga.1948)—§ **17.6, n. 3.**

Bachleda, People ex rel. v. Dean, 48 Ill.2d 16, 268 N.E.2d 11 (Ill.1971)—§ **16.6, n. 6.**

Bader v. Purdom, 841 F.2d 38 (2nd Cir. 1988)—§ **7.5, n. 10;** § **17.3, n. 3;** § **17.42, n. 11;** § **17.43, n. 9;** § **17.44, n. 13.**

Bad Horse v. Bad Horse, 163 Mont. 445, 517 P.2d 893 (Mont.1974)—§ **11.17, n. 39.**

Baedke v. John Morrell & Co., 748 F.Supp. 700 (N.D.Iowa 1990)—§ **17.5, n. 5;** § **18.29, n. 3, 5.**

Baehr v. Lewin, 74 Haw. 530, 74 Haw. 645, 852 P.2d 44 (Hawai'i 1993)—§ **13.20, n. 2.**

Baffin Land Corp. v. Monticello Motor Inn, Inc., 70 Wash.2d 893, 425 P.2d 623 (Wash.1967)—§ **2.17, n. 6;** § **2.23, n. 2;** § **14.15, n. 3;** § **14.16, n. 14;** § **18.18, n. 12.**

Bagdon v. Philadelphia & Reading Coal & Iron Co., 217 N.Y. 432, 111 N.E. 1075 (N.Y.1916)—§ **10.14, n. 6.**

Bagley, In re, 6 B.R. 387 (Bkrtcy.N.D.Ga. 1980)—§ **18.27, n. 2.**

Bailey v. Bailey, 867 P.2d 1267 (Okla. 1994)—§ **5.23, n. 1.**

Bailey v. Grand Trunk Lines New England, 805 F.2d 1097 (2nd Cir.1986)—§ **23.3, n. 1.**

Bailey v. Skipperliner Industries, Inc., 278 F.Supp.2d 945 (N.D.Ind.2003)—§ **3.12, n. 6.**

Bain v. Honeywell Intern., Inc., 257 F.Supp.2d 872 (E.D.Tex.2002)—§ **17.77, n. 3.**

Baindail v. Baindail, (1946) P. 122 (CA 1946)—§ **13.17, n. 9.**

Bain's Estate, In re, 104 Misc. 508, 172 N.Y.S. 604 (N.Y.Sur.1918)—§ **4.8, n. 1.**

Bainum v. Roundy, 21 Ariz.App. 534, 521 P.2d 633 (Ariz.App. Div. 1 1974)— § **14.16, n. 16.**

Baker v. Continental Western Ins. Co., 748 F.Supp. 716 (D.S.D.1990)—§ **17.56, n. 17.**

Baker, Estate of, 105 Misc.2d 365, 432 N.Y.S.2d 78 (N.Y.Sur.1980)—§ **16.1, n. 7.**

Baker v. First Nat. Bank of Denver, 603 P.2d 397 (Wyo.1979)—§ **3.11, n. 4;** § **19.10, n. 2.**

Baker v. Gotz, 387 F.Supp. 1381 (D.Del. 1975)—§ **18.12, n. 9.**

Baker v. State, 170 Vt. 194, 744 A.2d 864 (Vt.1999)—§ **13.20, n. 3.**

Baker by Thomas v. General Motors Corp., 522 U.S. 222, 118 S.Ct. 657, 139 L.Ed.2d 580 (1998)—§ **15.12, n. 11;** § **19.1, n. 6;** § **19.7, n. 3;** § **19.8, n. 11;** § **20.2, n. 11;** § **22.4;** § **22.4, n. 11;** § **24.9;** § **24.9, n. 9, 12, 15, 18;** § **24.10, n. 4;** § **24.12, n. 11;** § **24.14, n. 8;** § **24.20, n. 4;** § **24.21;** § **24.21, n. 4, 5, 6.**

Baldwin v. Brown, 202 F.Supp. 49 (E.D.Mich.1962)—§ **3.10, n. 1.**

Baldwin v. Fish and Game Commission of Montana, 436 U.S. 371, 98 S.Ct. 1852, 56 L.Ed.2d 354 (1978)—§ **3.32, n. 9.**

Baldwin v. Iowa State Traveling Men's Ass'n, 283 U.S. 522, 51 S.Ct. 517, 75

L.Ed. 1244 (1931)—§ **4.7, n. 4; § 5.21,
n. 7; § 24.1, n. 2; § 24.2, n. 9.**

Baldwin–United Corp., Matter of, 48 B.R.
49 (Bkrtcy.S.D.Ohio 1985)—§ **23.13, n.
1.**

Balsys, United States v., 524 U.S. 666, 118
S.Ct. 2218, 141 L.Ed.2d 575 (1998)—
§ **12.13; § 12.13, n. 10.**

Baltimore and Ohio Chicago Terminal R.
Co. v. Soo Line R. Co., 646 F.Supp. 327
(N.D.Ill.1986)—§ **9.2, n. 21.**

Baltimore & O. R. Co. v. Kepner, 314 U.S.
44, 62 S.Ct. 6, 86 L.Ed. 28 (1941)—
§ **11.13, n. 4.**

Baltimore, Town of v. Town of Chester, 53
Vt. 315 (Vt.1881)—§ **4.27, n. 1.**

Balts v. Balts, 273 Minn. 419, 142 N.W.2d
66 (Minn.1966)—§ **2.21, n. 14; § 17.39,
n. 10.**

Bamberger v. Clark, 390 F.2d 485, 129
U.S.App.D.C.   70   (D.C.Cir.1968)—
§ **12.18, n. 6, 17.**

Banco Ambrosiano, S.P.A. v. Artoc Bank &
Trust Ltd., 476 N.Y.S.2d 64, 464 N.E.2d
432 (N.Y.1984)—§ **5.9; § 5.9, n. 8;
§ 5.22, n. 8; § 11.10, n. 1.**

Banco Frances e Brasileiro S. A. v. Doe, 370
N.Y.S.2d 534, 331 N.E.2d 502 (N.Y.
1975)—§ **24.23, n. 7.**

Banco Metropolitano, S.A. v. Desarrollo de
Autopistas y Carreteras de Guatemala,
Sociedad Anonima, Through Junta In-
terventora of Dag, 616 F.Supp. 301
(S.D.N.Y.1985)—§ **11.11, n. 12.**

Banco Nacional de Cuba v. Farr, 383 F.2d
166 (2nd Cir.1967)—§ **3.50, n. 5.**

Banco Nacional de Cuba v. Sabbatino, 376
U.S. 398, 84 S.Ct. 923, 11 L.Ed.2d 804
(1964)—§ **3.50, n. 5; § 3.56; § 3.56, n.
3; § 11.13, n. 19; § 23.11, n. 4; § 24.46,
n. 10.**

Bane v. Netlink, Inc., 925 F.2d 637 (3rd
Cir.1991)—§ **10.13, n. 1.**

Bangor v. Readfield, 32 Me. 60 (Me.1850)—
§ **4.37, n. 8.**

Bangs v. Inhabitants of Brewster, 111 Mass.
382 (Mass.1873)—§ **4.19, n. 3.**

Bankemper v. Boone County Aviation, Inc.,
435 S.W.2d 58 (Ky.1968)—§ **22.10, n.
16.**

Bankers Trust Co., Complaint of, 752 F.2d
874 (3rd Cir.1984)—§ **18.21, n. 17;
§ 18.33, n. 1.**

Bankers Trust Co., In re, 9 Misc.2d 927,
169 N.Y.S.2d 698 (N.Y.Sup.1957)—
§ **21.13, n. 4.**

Bankers Trust Co. v. Lee Keeling & Associates, Inc., 20 F.3d 1092 (10th Cir.
1994)—§ **17.32; § 17.32, n. 34; § 17.42,
n. 11; § 17.43, n. 9; § 17.44, n. 5, 11.**

Bank of America v. Saville, 416 F.2d 265
(7th Cir.1969)—§ **18.44, n. 9; § 18.47,
n. 6.**

Bank of America v. Whitney Cent. Nat.
Bank, 261 U.S. 171, 43 S.Ct. 311, 67
L.Ed. 594 (1923)—§ **10.14, n. 9.**

Bank of America, Nat. Trust & Sav. Ass'n
v. Horowytz, 104 N.J.Super. 35, 248
A.2d 446 (N.J.Co.1968)—§ **18.33, n. 1.**

Bank of America Nat. Trust & Sav. Ass'n v.
Parnell, 352 U.S. 29, 77 S.Ct. 119, 1
L.Ed.2d 93 (1956)—§ **3.51, n. 5; § 3.54,
n. 8.**

Bank of America Nat. Trust & Sav. Ass'n,
United States v., 288 F.Supp. 343
(N.D.Cal.1968)—§ **3.51, n. 7.**

Bank of Augusta v. Earle, 38 U.S. 519, 10
L.Ed. 274 (1839)—§ **10.13, n. 4;
§ 10.14, n. 2.**

Bank of Boston Intern. of Miami v. Arguello
Tefel, 626 F.Supp. 314 (E.D.N.Y.1986)—
§ **3.11, n. 4.**

Bank of Indiana, Nat. Ass'n v. Holyfield,
476 F.Supp. 104 (S.D.Miss.1979)—
§ **18.37, n. 1, 3.**

Bank of Lexington v. Jack Adams Aircraft
Sales, Inc., 570 F.2d 1220 (5th Cir.
1978)—§ **19.13, n. 4.**

Bank of Montreal v. Kough, 612 F.2d 467
(9th Cir.1980)—§ **24.6, n. 2.**

Bank of Phoebus v. Byrum, 110 Va. 708, 67
S.E. 349 (Va.1910)—§ **4.26, n. 1.**

Bank of United States v. Lee, 38 U.S. 107,
10 L.Ed. 81 (1839)—§ **14.6, n. 6.**

Banks v. Galbraith, 149 Mo. 529, 51 S.W.
105 (Mo.1899)—§ **13.18, n. 12.**

Banks v. Junk, 264 So.2d 387 (Miss.1972)—
§ **20.5, n. 6.**

Banks v. Virginia Elec. & Power Co., 205
F.3d 1332 (4th Cir.2000)—§ **17.60, n. 5;
§ 17.61, n. 4.**

Bankston v. Toyota Motor Corp., 889 F.2d
172 (8th Cir.1989)—§ **12.7, n. 3.**

Bannister v. Bannister, 181 Md. 177, 29
A.2d 287 (Md.1942)—§ **13.9, n. 5.**

Banque Libanaise Pour Le Commerce v.
Khreich, 915 F.2d 1000 (5th Cir.1990)—
§ **12.18, n. 16; § 24.34, n. 9.**

Barber v. Barber, 51 Cal.2d 244, 331 P.2d
628 (Cal.1958)—§ **19.3, n. 4.**

Barber v. Barber, 323 U.S. 77, 65 S.Ct. 137,
89 L.Ed. 82 (1944)—§ **15.31, n. 1;
§ 24.8, n. 2, 11; § 24.9, n. 14.**

Barbin v. Moore, 85 N.H. 362, 159 A. 409
(N.H.1932)—§ **19.29, n. 3.**

Barclift v. Treece, 77 Ala. 528 (Ala.1884)—
§ **22.11, n. 1; § 22.14, n. 5.**

Barger, In re, 365 S.W.2d 89 (Mo.App.
1963)—§ **12.4, n. 1.**

Barkanic v. General Admin. of Civil Aviation of the People's Republic of China,
923 F.2d 957 (2nd Cir.1991)—§ **17.42,
n. 4, 11, 18.**

Barker v. Iowa Mut. Ins. Co., 241 N.C. 397,
85 S.E.2d 305 (N.C.1955)—§ **4.13, n. 1.**

Barndt v. Barndt, 397 Pa.Super. 321, 580
A.2d 320 (Pa.Super.1990)—§ **15.42, n.
9.**

Barnes, Succession of, 490 So.2d 630 (La. App. 2 Cir.1986)—§ **4.24, n. 2.**

Barnett's Trust, In re, (1902) 1 Ch. 847— § **20.4, n. 6.**

Barnes Group, Inc. v. Harper, 653 F.2d 175 (5th Cir.1981)—§ **18.29, n. 3.**

Barney's Will, In re, 120 A. 513 (N.J.Prerog.1923)—§ **22.3, n. 16.**

Barr v. MacHarg, 203 Kan. 612, 455 P.2d 516 (Kan.1969)—§ **22.10, n. 13;** § **22.19, n. 12.**

Barrantes Cabalceta v. Standard Fruit Co., 667 F.Supp. 833 (S.D.Fla.1987)—§ **23.3, n. 1.**

Barrell v. Benjamin, 15 Mass. 354 (Mass. 1819)—§ **5.2, n. 18;** § **5.8, n. 2;** § **5.14, n. 1;** § **6.2, n. 6.**

Barrett v. Barrett, 878 P.2d 1051 (Okla. 1994)—§ **13.18, n. 8.**

Barrett v. Barrett's Adm'r, 170 Ky. 91, 185 S.W. 499 (Ky.1916)—§ **22.7, n. 1.**

Barrett v. Catacombs Press, 44 F.Supp.2d 717 (E.D.Pa.1999)—§ **7.8, n. 14, 16.**

Barrett v. Foster Grant Co., 450 F.2d 1146 (1st Cir.1971)—§ **17.48, n. 5.**

Barrie's Estate, In re, 240 Iowa 431, 35 N.W.2d 658 (Iowa 1949)—§ **20.6, n. 10;** § **22.4, n. 8.**

Barrons v. United States, 191 F.2d 92 (9th Cir.1951)—§ **13.2, n. 4;** § **13.6, n. 12;** § **13.15, n. 4.**

Barrow v. ATCO Mfg. Co., 524 N.E.2d 1313 (Ind.App. 1 Dist.1988)—§ **2.22, n. 5;** § **18.1, n. 18;** § **18.21, n. 15.**

Barry E. (Anonymous) v. Ingraham, 400 N.Y.S.2d 772, 371 N.E.2d 492 (N.Y. 1977)—§ **24.44, n. 5.**

Barry Gilberg, Ltd. v. Craftex Corp., Inc., 665 F.Supp. 585 (N.D.Ill.1987)—§ **17.26, n. 1;** § **18.2, n. 11.**

Barthel v. Johnston, 92 Idaho 94, 437 P.2d 366 (Idaho 1968)—§ **20.3, n. 1.**

Bartholomew v. Universe Tankships, Inc., 263 F.2d 437 (2nd Cir.1959)—§ **17.63, n. 22.**

Bartlett v. General Motors Corp., 36 Del. Ch. 131, 127 A.2d 470 (Del.Ch.1956)— § **19.32, n. 7.**

Barton v. Barton, 74 Ga. 761 (Ga.1885)— § **4.27, n. 1.**

Barton v. National Life Assur. Co. of Canada, 98 Misc.2d 300, 413 N.Y.S.2d 807 (N.Y.Sup.App.Term 1978)—§ **24.31, n. 6;** § **24.40, n. 5.**

Barton v. National Life Assur. Co. of Canada, 91 Misc.2d 951, 398 N.Y.S.2d 941 (N.Y.City Civ.Ct.1977)—§ **18.26, n. 9.**

Barton, In re, 348 Pa. 279, 35 A.2d 266 (Pa.1944)—§ **21.11, n. 17.**

Barton's Estate, In re, 196 Cal. 508, 238 P. 681 (Cal.1925)—§ **20.4, n. 2.**

Bartsch v. Bartsch, 636 N.W.2d 3 (Iowa 2001)—§ **16.5, n. 5.**

Bartsch v. Metro–Goldwyn–Mayer, Inc., 391 F.2d 150 (2nd Cir.1968)—§ **3.54, n. 5;** § **12.18, n. 19.**

Bartsch v. Metro–Goldwyn–Mayer, Inc., 270 F.Supp. 896 (S.D.N.Y.1967)—§ **12.18, n. 9.**

Base Metal Trading, Ltd. v. OJSC "Novo-kuznetsky Aluminum Factory", 283 F.3d 208 (4th Cir.2002)—§ **10.5, n. 18.**

Bassi's Estate, In re, 234 Cal.App.2d 529, 44 Cal.Rptr. 541 (Cal.App. 1 Dist. 1965)—§ **16.1, n. 9, 11;** § **16.2;** § **16.2, n. 7.**

Bastian v. Personnel Bd. of City of Chicago, 108 Ill.App.3d 672, 64 Ill.Dec. 213, 439 N.E.2d 142 (Ill.App. 1 Dist.1982)— § **4.13, n. 3.**

Bata v. Bata, 39 Del.Ch. 258, 163 A.2d 493 (Del.Supr.1960)—§ **24.4, n. 6.**

Bata v. Bata, 304 N.Y. 51, 105 N.E.2d 623 (N.Y.1952)—§ **11.8, n. 3;** § **11.11, n. 9.**

Batchelor v. Fulcher, 415 S.W.2d 828 (Ky. 1967)—§ **15.29;** § **15.29, n. 3.**

Bates, In re, No. CA 122–89 (High Court of Justice, Family Div'l Ct., Royal Courts of Justice, UK 1989)—§ **15.29;** § **4.14, n. 11.**

Batman v. Cameron, 413 F.2d 999 (5th Cir. 1969)—§ **19.3, n. 3.**

Baton Rouge Contracting Co. v. West Hatchie Drainage Dist. of Tippah County, Miss., 279 F.Supp. 430 (N.D.Miss. 1968)—§ **3.41, n. 1.**

Battell's Will, In re, 286 N.Y. 97, 35 N.E.2d 913 (N.Y.1941)—§ **20.13, n. 4.**

Battle v. Battjes, 282 Mich. 696, 276 N.W. 874 (Mich.1937)—§ **19.10, n. 8.**

Battle v. Battjes, 274 Mich. 267, 264 N.W. 367 (Mich.1936)—§ **19.10, n. 8.**

Batton v. Tennessee Farmers Mut. Ins. Co., 153 Ariz. 268, 736 P.2d 2 (Ariz.1987)— § **8.2, n. 10.**

Batton, Succession of v. Prince, 384 So.2d 506 (La.App. 2 Cir.1980)—§ **21.5, n. 1.**

Bauer v. Club Med Sales, Inc., 1996 WL 310076 (N.D.Cal.1996)—§ **17.36, n. 15;** § **17.40;** § **17.40, n. 8;** § **17.48, n. 5.**

Bauer's Trust, In re, 251 N.Y.S.2d 23, 200 N.E.2d 207 (N.Y.1964)—§ **21.3, n. 15;** § **21.12;** § **21.12, n. 1.**

Bauer's Trust, In re, 13 A.D.2d 369, 216 N.Y.S.2d 920 (N.Y.A.D. 1 Dept.1961)— § **21.11, n. 15.**

Baum v. Birchall, 150 Pa. 164, 24 A. 620 (Pa.1892)—§ **19.10, n. 5.**

Baxter v. Sturm, Ruger and Co., Inc., 230 Conn. 335, 644 A.2d 1297 (Conn.1994)— § **3.9, n. 4;** § **17.76, n. 25.**

Baxter Chrysler Plymouth, Inc., State ex rel. Miller v., 456 N.W.2d 371 (Iowa 1990)—§ **9.8, n. 9.**

Baybutt Const. Corp. v. Commercial Union Ins. Co., 455 A.2d 914 (Me.1983)— § **2.17, n. 11;** § **2.23, n. 2;** § **18.21, n. 14.**

Bayley v. Bailey, 59 Mass. 245 (Mass. 1849)—§ **20.6, n. 10.**

Baylor v. United States Dept. of Housing and Urban Development, 913 F.2d 223 (5th Cir.1990)—§ **24.24, n. 8.**

Bays v. Bays, 105 Misc. 492, 174 N.Y.S. 212 (N.Y.Sup.1918)—§ **13.6, n. 7, 9.**

Bazan v. Kux Mach. Co., 52 Wis.2d 325, 190 N.W.2d 521 (Wis.1971)—§ **23.11, n. 1.**

Beal v. Carpenter, 235 F. 273 (8th Cir. 1916)—§ **24.20, n. 3.**

Beale v. Beale, 807 So.2d 797 (Fla.App. 1 Dist.2002)—§ **19.6, n. 5.**

Beals v. Sicpa Securink Corp., 1994 WL 236018 (D.D.C.1994)—§ **17.50, n. 55; § 17.67, n. 2; § 17.69, n. 10.**

Beals v. State Street Bank & Trust Co., 367 Mass. 318, 326 N.E.2d 896 (Mass. 1975)—§ **21.10, n. 7.**

Bean Dredging Corp. v. Dredge Technology Corp., 744 F.2d 1081 (5th Cir.1984)— § **7.2, n. 19.**

Beard v. Beard, 21 Ind. 321 (Ind.1863)— § **5.3, n. 1.**

Beardsley v. Hall, 291 Mass. 411, 197 N.E. 35 (Mass.1935)—§ **19.6, n. 5.**

Bearry v. Beech Aircraft Corp., 818 F.2d 370 (5th Cir.1987)—§ **5.12, n. 7; § 5.13, n. 19, 22; § 6.9, n. 20, 21; § 7.2, n. 34.**

Beatty Caribbean, Inc. v. Viskase Sales Corp., 241 F.Supp.2d 123 (D.Puerto Rico 2003)—§ **18.5, n. 33.**

Beauchamp v. Bertig, 90 Ark. 351, 119 S.W. 75 (Ark.1909)—§ **19.5, n. 6.**

Beauchamp's Estate, In re, 23 Del.Ch. 377, 2 A.2d 900 (Del.Orph.1938)—§ **22.22, n. 6.**

Beaudoin v. Trudel, 1936 WL 27886 (Ont. C.A.1936)—§ **14.9, n. 6.**

Beaulieu v. Beaulieu, 265 A.2d 610 (Me. 1970)—§ **2.16, n. 12; § 2.23, n. 1; § 17.26, n. 1; § 17.39, n. 8.**

Beaumont, Re, 1893 WL 9340 (Ch D 1893)—§ **4.38, n. 3.**

Beaumont's Estate, In re, 216 Pa. 350, 65 A. 799 (Pa.1907)—§ **20.9, n. 5.**

Bechtel v. Bechtel, 101 Minn. 511, 112 N.W. 883 (Minn.1907)—§ **4.13, n. 11.**

Bechtel, State ex rel. Weede v., 239 Iowa 1298, 31 N.W.2d 853 (Iowa 1948)— § **23.9, n. 4.**

Becker v. Becker, 143 Misc.2d 500, 541 N.Y.S.2d 699 (N.Y.Sup.1989)—§ **15.20, n. 10.**

Becker v. Hooshmand, 841 So.2d 561 (Fla. App. 4 Dist.2003)—§ **7.8, n. 14.**

Becker v. Marketing and Research Consultants, Inc., 526 F.Supp. 166 (D.Colo. 1981)—§ **18.28, n. 4.**

Becker v. PaineWebber, Inc., 962 F.2d 524 (5th Cir.1992)—§ **23.2, n. 6.**

Beckman v. Thompson, 6 Cal.Rptr.2d 60 (Cal.App. 2 Dist.1992)—§ **7.11, n. 13.**

Beckmann v. Beckmann, 358 Mo. 1029, 218 S.W.2d 566 (Mo.1949)—§ **4.37, n. 2, 3.**

Beddow v. Beddow, 257 S.W.2d 45 (Ky. 1952)—§ **13.8, n. 3.**

Bedell v. Clark, 171 Mich. 486, 137 N.W. 627 (Mich.1912)—§ **22.23, n. 8.**

Bedford v. Eastern Bldg. & Loan Ass'n of Syracuse, N.Y., 181 U.S. 227, 21 S.Ct. 597, 45 L.Ed. 834 (1901)—§ **23.6, n. 2.**

Beers v. Shannon, 73 N.Y. 292 (N.Y.1878)— § **22.11, n. 1, 2.**

Behagen v. Amateur Basketball Ass'n of United States of America, 744 F.2d 731 (10th Cir.1984)—§ **6.9, n. 19.**

Beistle Co. v. Party U.S.A., Inc., 914 F.Supp. 92 (M.D.Pa.1996)—§ **9.3, n. 4.**

Bejarano, People ex rel. Dunbar v., 145 Colo. 304, 358 P.2d 866 (Colo.1961)— § **14.6, n. 4.**

Belanger v. Keydril Co., 596 F.Supp. 823 (E.D.La.1984)—§ **12.15, n. 9.**

Beldock v. Braun, N. A., 465 F.Supp. 466 (S.D.N.Y.1979)—§ **8.5, n. 8.**

Bell v. Alpha Tau Omega Fraternity, Eta Epsilon Chapter, 98 Nev. 109, 642 P.2d 161 (Nev.1982)—§ **17.19, n. 10.**

Bell v. Bell, 181 U.S. 175, 21 S.Ct. 551, 45 L.Ed. 804 (1901)—§ **15.6, n. 7.**

Bell v. Kennedy, 1 H.L.(Sc.) 307 (1868)— § **4.17, n. 4; § 4.28, n. 2; § 4.36, n. 3.**

Bell, State v., 66 Tenn. 9 (Tenn.1872)— § **13.10, n. 1.**

Bell v. Suddeth, 10 Miss. 532 (Miss.Err. & App.1844)—§ **22.25, n. 10.**

Bell v. Vecellio & Grogan, Inc., 197 W.Va. 138, 475 S.E.2d 138 (W.Va.1996)— § **2.21, n. 40.**

Bellamah Community Development, In re, 107 B.R. 337 (Bkrtcy.D.N.M.1989)— § **19.3, n. 13.**

Bellepointe, Inc. v. Kohl's Dept. Stores, Inc., 975 F.Supp. 562 (S.D.N.Y.1997)— § **9.3, n. 12.**

Belleville Toyota, Inc. v. Toyota Motor Sales, U.S.A., Inc., 199 Ill.2d 325, 264 Ill.Dec. 283, 770 N.E.2d 177 (Ill.2002)— § **17.40, n. 26; § 18.1, n. 17.**

Belmont v. Cornen, 48 Conn. 338 (Conn. 1880)—§ **19.10, n. 3.**

Belmont, United States v., 301 U.S. 324, 57 S.Ct. 758, 81 L.Ed. 1134 (1937)— § **11.13, n. 8, 11.**

Belsky v. Belsky, 324 So.2d 111 (Fla.App. 3 Dist.1975)—§ **19.8, n. 3.**

Benchmark Electronics, Inc. v. J.M. Huber Corp., 343 F.3d 719 (5th Cir.2003)— § **17.40, n. 28; § 18.1, n. 18.**

Benefit Assn. Internat., Inc. v. Superior Court, 54 Cal.Rptr.2d 165 (Cal.App. 1 Dist.1996)—§ **8.2, n. 10.**

Benitez–Allende v. Alcan Aluminio do Brasil, S.A., 857 F.2d 26 (1st Cir.1988)— § **5.12, n. 8; § 7.2, n. 33, 35.**

Benker v. Meyer, 154 F. 290 (8th Cir. 1907)—§ **22.19, n. 24; § 22.20, n. 29.**

Benner v. Wichman, 874 P.2d 949 (Alaska 1994)—§ **17.61, n. 1.**

Bennett, In re, 51 B.R. 619 (Bkrtcy.D.N.M. 1984)—§ **18.21, n. 8.**

Benoit v. Test Systems, Inc., 142 N.H. 47, 694 A.2d 992 (N.H.1997)—§ **17.21, n. 13; § 17.42, n. 16, 20; § 17.59, n. 15.**

Bense v. Interstate Battery System of America, Inc., 683 F.2d 718 (2nd Cir. 1982)—§ **11.3, n. 19; § 11.6, n. 4.**

Bensusan Restaurant Corp. v. King, 126 F.3d 25 (2nd Cir.1997)—§ **9.3, n. 7.**

Benton, In re, 92 Iowa 202, 60 N.W. 614 (Iowa 1894)—§ **4.37, n. 7; § 4.41, n. 2, 6; § 22.25, n. 18.**

Benton v. Safe Deposit Bank of Pottsville, Pa., 255 N.Y. 260, 174 N.E. 648 (N.Y. 1931)—§ **18.4, n. 47.**

Benton v. Singleton, 114 Ga. 548, 40 S.E. 811 (Ga.1902)—§ **24.47, n. 6.**

Benu, People v., 87 Misc.2d 139, 385 N.Y.S.2d 222 (N.Y.City Crim.Ct.1976)—§ **13.6, n. 3, 9.**

Berc v. Berc, 407 N.W.2d 131 (Minn.App. 1987)—§ **4.19, n. 5.**

Berchtold, In re, (1923) 1 Ch. 192—§ **20.7, n. 3.**

Bergen v. Bergen, 439 F.2d 1008 (3rd Cir. 1971)—§ **15.40, n. 5.**

Bergman v. De Sieyes., 170 F.2d 360 (2nd Cir.1948)—§ **24.6, n. 3; § 24.35, n. 6.**

Bergmann v. Lord, 194 N.Y. 70, 86 N.E. 828 (N.Y.1909)—§ **22.19, n. 18.**

Bergner & Engel Brewing Co. v. Dreyfus, 172 Mass. 154, 51 N.E. 531 (Mass. 1898)—§ **4.3, n. 2; § 4.15, n. 2.**

Berkovits v. Grinberg, 1995 WL 1083713 (Fam.Div. 1995)—§ **15.25, n. 1.**

Berkowitz, United States v., 328 F.2d 358 (3rd Cir.1964)—§ **3.46, n. 8.**

Berle v. Berle, 97 Idaho 452, 546 P.2d 407 (Idaho 1976)—§ **14.9, n. 1; § 14.13, n. 8.**

Bernal v. Fainter, 467 U.S. 216, 104 S.Ct. 2312, 81 L.Ed.2d 175 (1984)—§ **3.58, n. 14, 15, 18.**

Bernhard v. Bank of America Nat. Trust & Savings Ass'n, 19 Cal.2d 807, 122 P.2d 892 (Cal.1942)—§ **24.1, n. 12.**

Bernhard v. Harrah's Club, 16 Cal.3d 313, 128 Cal.Rptr. 215, 546 P.2d 719 (Cal. 1976)—§ **2.9, n. 28; § 2.24, n. 8; § 2.25, n. 8; § 17.5, n. 8; § 17.19; § 17.19, n. 1; § 17.43; § 17.43, n. 12; § 17.48; § 17.48, n. 32; § 18.33, n. 8.**

Bernhardt v. Polygraphic Co. of America, 350 U.S. 198, 76 S.Ct. 273, 100 L.Ed. 199 (1956)—§ **3.37, n. 5.**

Bernkrant v. Fowler, 55 Cal.2d 588, 12 Cal. Rptr. 266, 360 P.2d 906 (Cal.1961)— § **2.9, n. 32; § 18.15, n. 4; § 18.19; § 18.19, n. 7; § 18.20, n. 5; § 18.38, n. 8.**

Bernstein v. Fidelity Union Life Ins. Co., 449 F.Supp. 327 (E.D.Mo.1978)— § **18.21, n. 14.**

Beromun Aktiengesellschaft v. Societa Industriale Agricola "Tresse" Di Dr. Domenico E Dr. Antonio Dal Ferro, 471 F.Supp. 1163 (S.D.N.Y.1979)—§ **24.48, n. 5.**

Berrigan v. Southeast Health Plan, Inc., 676 F.Supp. 1062 (D.Kan.1987)—§ **8.4, n. 6.**

Berry v. Berry, 647 S.W.2d 945 (Tex. 1983)—§ **14.11, n. 3.**

Berry v. Smith, 85 Ga.App. 710, 70 S.E.2d 62 (Ga.App.1952)—§ **22.10, n. 11.**

Bersch v. Drexel Firestone, Inc., 519 F.2d 974 (2nd Cir.1975)—§ **9.6, n. 19.**

Bertke v. Cartledge, 597 F.Supp. 68 (N.D.Ga.1984)—§ **24.14, n. 3.**

Besse v. Pellochoux, 73 Ill. 285 (Ill.1874)— § **14.15, n. 9.**

Besser v. E.R. Squibb & Sons, Inc., 75 N.Y.2d 847, 552 N.Y.S.2d 923, 552 N.E.2d 171 (N.Y.1990)—§ **3.11, n. 4.**

Bethell, In re, 38 Ch.Div. 220 (1888)— § **13.17, n. 2, 8.**

Bethell v. Bethell, 92 Ind. 318 (Ind.1884)— § **19.8, n. 6.**

Bethell v. Bethell, 54 Ind. 428 (Ind.1876)— § **19.5, n. 8.**

Bethell v. Peace, 441 F.2d 495 (5th Cir. 1971)—§ **24.9, n. 3.**

Bethlehem Steel Corp. v. Board of Com'rs of Dept. of Water and Power of City of Los Angeles, 276 Cal.App.2d 221, 80 Cal. Rptr. 800 (Cal.App. 2 Dist.1969)— § **11.13, n. 15.**

Bethlehem Steel Corp. v. G.C. Zarnas and Co., Inc., 304 Md. 183, 498 A.2d 605 (Md.1985)—§ **2.21, n. 56; § 18.4, n. 44; § 18.21, n. 7.**

Bethune v. Bethune, 192 Ark. 811, 94 S.W.2d 1043 (Ark.1936)—§ **4.24, n. 3.**

Bettys v. Milwaukee & St. P. Ry. Co., 37 Wis. 323 (Wis.1875)—§ **3.17, n. 2.**

Beverly Hills Fan Co. v. Royal Sovereign Corp., 21 F.3d 1558 (Fed.Cir.1994)— § **7.2, n. 33; § 9.4, n. 5.**

Beverly Hills Nat. Bank & Trust Co. v. Compania De Navegacione Almirante S. A., Panama, 437 F.2d 301 (9th Cir. 1971)—§ **12.15, n. 15; § 18.44, n. 9; § 18.47, n. 5.**

B.E.W.G., In re Adoption of, 379 Pa.Super. 264, 549 A.2d 1286 (Pa.Super.1988)— § **16.5, n. 9.**

B & G Budget Plan of Portland, Or. v. Young, 368 F.2d 731 (9th Cir.1966)— § **19.15, n. 8.**

BHP Petroleum (Americas), Inc. v. Texaco Exploration and Production, Inc., 1 P.3d 1253 (Wyo.2000)—§ **2.21, n. 46; § 18.21, n. 13.**

Bianchi v. Scott, 363 So.2d 289 (Miss. 1978)—§ **19.8, n. 3.**

Bibie v. T. D. Pub. Corp., 252 F.Supp. 185 (N.D.Cal.1966)—§ **17.55, n. 4.**

Bice Const. Co., Inc. v. CIT Corp. of South, Inc., 700 F.2d 465 (8th Cir.1983)— § 18.5, n. 12.

Bickel v. Korean Air Lines Co., Ltd., 83 F.3d 127 (6th Cir.1996)—§ **2.23, n. 8.**

Bigelow v. Halloran, 313 N.W.2d 10 (Minn. 1981)—§ **2.13, n. 14;** § **17.21, n. 14, 27.**

Big Four Mills v. Commercial Credit Co., 307 Ky. 612, 211 S.W.2d 831 (Ky. 1948)—§ **18.4, n. 53;** § **18.5, n. 12;** § **18.7, n. 12.**

Biggelaar v. Wagner, 978 F.Supp. 848 (N.D.Ind.1997)—§ **24.44, n. 12.**

Biglan v. Biglan, 330 Pa.Super. 512, 479 A.2d 1021 (Pa.Super.1984)—§ **22.14, n. 13.**

Bilancia v. General Motors Corp., 538 F.2d 621 (4th Cir.1976)—§ **17.64, n. 10.**

Bils v. Bils, 200 Ariz. 45, 22 P.3d 38 (Ariz. 2001)—§ **7.3, n. 11.**

Bilyk v. Vessel Nair, 754 F.2d 1541 (9th Cir.1985)—§ **17.63, n. 22.**

Bing v. Halstead, 495 F.Supp. 517 (S.D.N.Y. 1980)—§ **2.26, n. 16;** § **3.14, n. 4.**

Bingham, Appeal of, 64 Pa. 345 (Pa.1870)— § **21.13, n. 4.**

Binkley Co. v. Teledyne Mid–America Corp., 333 F.Supp. 1183 (E.D.Mo. 1971)—§ **18.24, n. 8.**

Binkow's Estate, In re, 120 So.2d 15 (Fla. App. 3 Dist.1960)—§ **20.9, n. 11.**

Biospherics, Inc. v. Forbes, Inc., 989 F.Supp. 748 (D.Md.1997)—§ **17.55, n. 10.**

Biotronik Mess–Und Therapiegeraete GmbH & Co. v. Medford Medical Instrument Co., 415 F.Supp. 133 (D.N.J. 1976)—§ **24.48, n. 7.**

Bird v. Computer Technology, Inc., 364 F.Supp. 1336 (S.D.N.Y.1973)—§ **18.38, n. 3.**

Birdseye v. Baker, 82 Ga. 142, 7 S.E. 863 (Ga.1888)—§ **19.30, n. 7.**

Birger v. Tuner, 104 Misc.2d 63, 427 N.Y.S.2d 904 (N.Y.City Civ.Ct.1980)— § **18.28, n. 3.**

Bi–Rite Enterprises, Inc. v. Bruce Miner Co., Inc., 757 F.2d 440 (1st Cir.1985)— § **17.26, n. 1;** § **17.55, n. 9;** § **18.2, n. 11.**

Birkholz's Estate, In re, 197 N.W. 896 (Iowa 1924)—§ **22.20, n. 19.**

Birmingham Fire Ins. Co. of Pennsylvania v. Winegardner and Hammons, Inc., 714 F.2d 548 (5th Cir.1983)—§ **3.47, n. 2.**

Birmingham Waterworks Co. v. Hume, 121 Ala. 168, 25 So. 806 (Ala.1899)—§ **14.9, n. 13.**

Birnberg v. Milk St. Residential Associates Ltd. Partnership, 2003 WL 151929 (N.D.Ill.2003)—§ **17.40, n. 28;** § **18.1, n. 18.**

Birtwhistle v. Vardill, 1840 WL 4439 (Unknown Court 1840)—§ **16.2, 3;** § **20.2, n. 4.**

Biscoe v. Arlington County, 738 F.2d 1352, 238 U.S.App.D.C. 206 (D.C.Cir.1984)— § **17.43;** § **17.43, n. 17.**

Bish v. Bish, 181 Md. 621, 31 A.2d 348 (Md.1943)—§ **20.15, n. 4.**

Bishop v. Florida Specialty Paint Co., 389 So.2d 999 (Fla.1980)—§ **2.16, n. 16;** § **2.23, n. 1;** § **17.26, n. 1;** § **17.39, n. 8.**

Bishop v. Twiford, 317 Md. 170, 562 A.2d 1238 (Md.1989)—§ **2.21, n. 7;** § **17.8, n. 4;** § **17.60, n. 6.**

Bittner v. Little, 270 F.2d 286 (3rd Cir. 1959)—§ **17.25, n. 1.**

Bituminous Cas. Corp. v. St. Clair Lime Co., 69 F.3d 547 (10th Cir.1995)—§ **18.26, n. 12.**

Bituminous Cas. Corp. v. Wacht, 84 Ga. App. 602, 66 S.E.2d 757 (Ga.App. 1951)—§ **13.9, n. 5.**

Bivians' Estate, In re, 98 N.M. 722, 652 P.2d 744 (N.M.App.1982)—§ **13.6, n. 4.**

Bixby v. Bixby, 361 P.2d 1075 (Okla. 1961)—§ **4.18, n. 2;** § **4.20, n. 7.**

Bjornquist v. Boston & A.R. Co., 250 F. 929 (1st Cir.1918)—§ **4.37, n. 2;** § **4.41, n. 7;** § **4.43, n. 1.**

Black v. Acme Markets, Inc., 564 F.2d 681 (5th Cir.1977)—§ **9.7, n. 3.**

Black v. Bryant, 905 F.Supp. 1046 (M.D.Fla.1995)—§ **10.17, n. 8.**

Black v. J.W. Zacharie & Co., 44 U.S. 483, 3 How. 483, 11 L.Ed. 690 (1845)—§ **19.32, n. 6.**

Black v. Walker, 295 N.J.Super. 244, 684 A.2d 1011 (N.J.Super.A.D.1996)— § **18.18, n. 10.**

Black Clawson International Ltd v. Papierwerke Waldhof–Aschaffenburg AG, 1975 WL 45601 (HL 1975)—§ **24.3, n. 14.**

Black Clawson International Ltd v. Papierwerke Waldhof–Aschaffenburg AG, 1974 WL 41065 (CA 1974)—§ **24.3, n. 14.**

Black & Decker Disability Plan v. Nord, 538 U.S. 822, 123 S.Ct. 1965, 155 L.Ed.2d 1034 (2003)—§ **3.54, n. 1.**

Blackmer v. United States, 284 U.S. 421, 52 S.Ct. 252, 76 L.Ed. 375 (1932)—§ **5.8, n. 5;** § **6.4;** § **6.4, n. 16.**

Blackwell v. Blackwell, 606 So.2d 1355 (La. App. 2 Cir.1992)—§ **14.9, n. 1, 3.**

Blackwell v. Grant, 46 Ga.App. 241, 167 S.E. 333 (Ga.App.1933)—§ **20.9, n. 5.**

Blain, State ex rel. Ralston v., 189 Kan. 575, 370 P.2d 415 (Kan.1962)—§ **20.3, n. 9.**

Blaine v. Curtis, 59 Vt. 120, 7 A. 708 (Vt. 1887)—§ **3.17, n. 2.**

Blaine v. Murphy, 265 F. 324 (D.Mass. 1920)—§ **4.19, n. 4.**

Blair v. Blair, 199 Md. 9, 85 A.2d 442 (Md. 1952)—§ **4.33, n. 6.**

Blais v. Allied Exterminating Co., 198 W.Va. 674, 482 S.E.2d 659 (W.Va. 1996)—§ **2.21, n. 29.**

Blaisdell v. Bickum, 139 Mass. 250, 1 N.E. 281 (Mass.1885)—§ **13.8, n. 1.**

Blake v. McClung, 172 U.S. 239, 19 S.Ct. 165, 43 L.Ed. 432 (1898)—§ **3.32;** § **3.32, n. 4, 6, 9;** § **3.34, n. 5;** § **19.30, n. 9;** § **22.21, n. 5, 17.**

Blakesley v. Wolford, 789 F.2d 236 (3rd Cir.1986)—§ **17.42, n. 17, 18, 29.**

Blalack, Succession of, 209 So.2d 531 (La. App. 2 Cir.1968)—§ **22.14, n. 3.**

Blalock v. Perfect Subscription Co., 458 F.Supp. 123 (S.D.Ala.1978)—§ **18.4, n. 7;** § **18.5, n. 17.**

Blamey v. Brown, 270 N.W.2d 884 (Minn. 1978)—§ **17.48;** § **17.48, n. 39.**

Blanco's Estate, In re, 117 Mich.App. 281, 323 N.W.2d 671 (Mich.App.1982)— § **16.2, n. 5.**

Blandino v. Blandino, 52 Va. Cir. 572 (Va. Cir. Ct.1999)—§ **15.42, n. 15.**

Blank, Commonwealth ex rel. v. Rutledge, 234 Pa.Super. 339, 339 A.2d 71 (Pa.Super.1975)—§ **15.40, n. 7.**

Blankenship, In re, 133 B.R. 398 (Bkrtcy. N.D.Ohio 1991)—§ **15.16, n. 3.**

Blankenship's Estate, Matter of, 571 P.2d 874 (Okla.App. Div. 1 1977)—§ **20.5, n. 7.**

B & L Drilling Electronics v. Totco, 87 F.R.D. 543 (W.D.Okla.1978)—§ **12.8, n. 12.**

Blech v. Blech, 6 Ariz.App. 131, 430 P.2d 710 (Ariz.App.1967)—§ **15.28, n. 6.**

Bledsoe v. Crowley, 849 F.2d 639, 270 U.S.App.D.C. 308 (D.C.Cir.1988)— § **3.41, n. 19;** § **17.42;** § **17.42, n. 30;** § **17.43, n. 33.**

Blessley v. Blessley, 91 N.M. 513, 577 P.2d 62 (N.M.1978)—§ **15.5, n. 1.**

Bliss v. Bliss, 133 Md. 61, 104 A. 467 (Md. 1918)—§ **22.26, n. 2.**

Bliss' Trust, In re, 26 Misc.2d 969, 208 N.Y.S.2d 725 (N.Y.Sup.1960)—§ **24.43, n. 1.**

Bloch v. Bloch, 473 F.2d 1067 (3rd Cir. 1973)—§ **13.6, n. 2;** § **15.16, n. 4, 5.**

Blondell v. Blondell, 157 Md. 15, 145 A. 184 (Md.1929)—§ **22.21, n. 9.**

Blonder–Tongue Laboratories, Inc. v. University of Illinois Foundation, 402 U.S. 313, 91 S.Ct. 1434, 28 L.Ed.2d 788 (1971)—§ **24.1, n. 11.**

Blood v. Poindexter, 534 N.E.2d 768 (Ind. Tax 1989)—§ **20.8, n. 12.**

Bloomer v. Bloomer, 1853 WL 5935 (N.Y.Sur.1853)—§ **20.11, n. 1.**

Bloomfield v. City of St. Petersburg Beach, 82 So.2d 364 (Fla.1955)—§ **4.19, n. 3;** § **4.20, n. 1.**

Bloomgarden v. Coyer, 479 F.2d 201, 156 U.S.App.D.C. 109 (D.C.Cir.1973)— § **18.45, n. 4.**

Blount v. Bartholomew, 714 F.Supp. 252 (E.D.Ky.1988)—§ **17.13, n. 13.**

Blount v. Peerless Chemicals (P.R.) Inc., 316 F.2d 695 (2nd Cir.1963)—§ **10.16, n. 9.**

Blount v. Walker, 134 U.S. 607, 10 S.Ct. 606, 33 L.Ed. 1036 (1890)—§ **21.11, n. 2.**

Blue Ball Properties, Inc. v. McClain, 658 F.Supp. 1310 (D.Del.1987)—§ **8.6, n. 3.**

Blumenthal v. Drudge, 992 F.Supp. 44 (D.D.C.1998)—§ **7.8, n. 14, 16.**

Blusy v. Rugh, 476 N.E.2d 874 (Ind.App. 3 Dist.1985)—§ **22.14, n. 10.**

B.L.V.B., In re Adoption of, 160 Vt. 368, 628 A.2d 1271 (Vt.1993)—§ **16.4, n. 3.**

B. M. Heede, Inc. v. West India Machinery & Supply Co., 272 F.Supp. 236 (S.D.N.Y. 1967)—§ **18.4, n. 1, 8, 42, 45.**

BMW of North America, Inc. v. Gore, 517 U.S. 559, 116 S.Ct. 1589, 134 L.Ed.2d 809 (1996)—§ **3.23, n. 31;** § **17.50;** § **17.50, n. 44.**

Boan v. Watson, 281 S.C. 516, 316 S.E.2d 401 (S.C.1984)—§ **14.2, n. 1.**

Boardman v. Boardman, 135 Conn. 124, 62 A.2d 521 (Conn.1948)—§ **4.34, n. 3;** § **4.40, n. 1.**

Boardman v. United Services Auto. Ass'n, 470 So.2d 1024 (Miss.1985)—§ **2.17, n. 11;** § **2.23, n. 2.**

Boardman Petroleum, Inc. v. Federated Mut. Ins. Co., 135 F.3d 750 (11th Cir. 1998)—§ **18.26, n. 13.**

Boardman Petroleum, Inc. v. Federated Mut. Ins. Co., 926 F.Supp. 1566 (S.D.Ga. 1995)—§ **18.21, n. 5.**

Board of Medical Registration and Examination v. Turner, 241 Ind. 73, 168 N.E.2d 193 (Ind.1960)—§ **4.13, n. 2.**

Board of Regents of University of Minnesota v. Royal Ins. Co. of America, 503 N.W.2d 486 (Minn.App.1993)—§ **18.26, n. 12.**

Board of Trade of City of Chicago v. Dow Jones & Co., Inc., 108 Ill.App.3d 681, 64 Ill.Dec. 275, 439 N.E.2d 526 (Ill.App. 1 Dist.1982)—§ **17.53, n. 5.**

Boase v. Lee Rubber & Tire Corp., 437 F.2d 527 (3rd Cir.1970)—§ **18.5, n. 1, 2, 4.**

Boatland, Inc. v. Brunswick Corp., 558 F.2d 818 (6th Cir.1977)—§ **18.11, n. 5;** § **18.21, n. 11.**

Boat Town U.S.A., Inc. v. Mercury Marine Division Of Brunswick Corp., 364 So.2d 15 (Fla.App. 4 Dist.1978)—§ **18.21, n. 4;** § **18.24, n. 4.**

Boatwright v. Budak, 625 N.W.2d 483 (Minn.App.2001)—§ **2.13, n. 16, 24;** § **17.21, n. 27;** § **17.23, n. 6, 12, 14;** § **17.48, n. 12.**

Boaz v. Boyle & Co., 46 Cal.Rptr.2d 888 (Cal.App. 2 Dist.1995)—§ **6.9, n. 21.**

Bobb v. Secretary, Dept. of Health, Ed. and Welfare, 312 F.Supp. 225 (S.D.N.Y. 1970)—§ **13.6, n. 4.**

Bobroff, In re, 766 F.2d 797 (3rd Cir. 1985)—§ **23.12, n. 15.**

Bochan v. La Fontaine, 68 F.Supp.2d 692 (E.D.Va.1999)—§ **7.8, n. 14, 16.**

Boda, Estate of, 124 Misc.2d 464, 476 N.Y.S.2d 476 (N.Y.Sur.1984)—§ **22.8, n. 1.**

Bodea v. Trans Nat Express, Inc., 286 A.D.2d 5, 731 N.Y.S.2d 113 (N.Y.A.D. 4 Dept.2001)—§ **17.46;** § **17.46, n. 14.**

Bodzai v. Arctic Fjord, Inc., 990 P.2d 616 (Alaska 1999)—§ **17.40, n. 25.**

Boehm v. Rohlfs, 224 Iowa 226, 276 N.W. 105 (Iowa 1937)—§ **13.14, n. 5.**

Bogen v. Bogen, 261 N.W.2d 606 (Minn. 1977)—§ **13.5, n. 1;** § **13.9, n. 17.**

Boggess, In re, 105 B.R. 470 (Bkrtcy.S.D.Ill. 1989)—§ **23.13, n. 1.**

Boggs v. Boggs, 520 U.S. 833, 117 S.Ct. 1754, 138 L.Ed.2d 45 (1997)—§ **14.11, n. 1.**

Bohannan v. Allstate Ins. Co., 820 P.2d 787 (Okla.1991)—§ **2.17, n. 13;** § **18.21, n. 14.**

Bohrer–Reagan Corp. v. Modine Mfg. Co., 433 F.Supp. 578 (E.D.Pa.1977)— § **17.64, n. 10.**

Boissiere v. Nova Capital, LLC, 106 S.W.3d 897 (Tex.App.-Dallas 2003)—§ **7.4, n. 9.**

Bokum Resources Corp., In re, 49 B.R. 854 (Bkrtcy.D.N.M.1985)—§ **23.12, n. 15.**

Bolduc v. Bailey, 586 F.Supp. 896 (D.Colo. 1984)—§ **17.26, n. 1.**

Boles v. Midland Guardian Co., 410 So.2d 82 (Ala.Civ.App.1982)—§ **23.7, n. 6.**

Bolles v. Bolles, 364 So.2d 813 (Fla.App. 3 Dist.1978)—§ **4.34, n. 4.**

Bolling v. Bolling, 88 Va. 524, 14 S.E. 67 (Va.1891)—§ **20.8, n. 9.**

Bollinger v. Wilson, 76 Minn. 262, 79 N.W. 109 (Minn.1899)—§ **19.12, n. 1.**

Bolmer v. Edsall, 106 A. 646 (N.J.Ch. 1919)—§ **13.6, n. 18.**

Bolton v. Tulane University of Louisiana, 692 So.2d 1113 (La.App. 4 Cir.1997)— § **17.59, n. 10.**

Boman v. Gibbs, 443 S.W.2d 267 (Tex.Civ. App.-Amarillo 1969)—§ **20.2, n. 1.**

Bombardier Capital, Inc. v. Richfield Housing Center, Inc., 1994 WL 118294 (N.D.N.Y.1994)—§ **17.43, n. 9;** § **17.44, n. 12.**

Bomze v. Nardis Sportswear, 165 F.2d 33 (2nd Cir.1948)—§ **10.14, n. 13.**

Bonate v. Bonate, 78 Ill.App.3d 164, 33 Ill.Dec. 755, 397 N.E.2d 88 (Ill.App. 1 Dist.1979)—§ **24.28, n. 2.**

Bonati v. Welsch, 24 N.Y. 157 (N.Y.1861)— § **14.7, n. 2.**

Bond v. Oak Mfg. Co., 293 F.2d 752 (3rd Cir.1961)—§ **18.44, n. 9.**

Bond Leather Co., Inc. v. Q.T. Shoe Mfg. Co., Inc., 764 F.2d 928 (1st Cir.1985)— § **7.12, n. 9.**

Bonito Boats, Inc. v. Thunder Craft Boats, Inc., 489 U.S. 141, 109 S.Ct. 971, 103 L.Ed.2d 118 (1989)—§ **17.53, n. 3.**

Bonneau v. Russell, 117 Vt. 134, 85 A.2d 569 (Vt.1952)—§ **4.43, n. 1.**

Bonny v. Society of Lloyd's, 3 F.3d 156 (7th Cir.1993)—§ **11.3, n. 33.**

Bonti v. Ford Motor Co., 898 F.Supp. 391 (S.D.Miss.1995)—§ **3.10, n. 3;** § **17.78, n. 9.**

Bonwich v. Bonwich, 699 P.2d 760 (Utah 1985)—§ **16.6, n. 2.**

Booker, Matter of Marriage of, 833 P.2d 734 (Colo.1992)—§ **14.11, n. 2.**

Booker's Estate, Matter of, 27 Or.App. 779, 557 P.2d 248 (Or.App.1976)—§ **13.5, n. 1.**

Bookman v. KAH Incorporated, Inc., 614 So.2d 1180 (Fla.App. 1 Dist.1993)— § **8.2, n. 10.**

Boole v. Union Marine Ins. Co., 52 Cal.App. 207, 198 P. 416 (Cal.App. 1 Dist.1921)— § **18.3, n. 1.**

Boomsma v. Star Transp., Inc., 202 F.Supp.2d 869 (E.D.Wis.2002)—§ **17.45;** § **17.45, n. 37.**

Boone v. Boone, 345 S.C. 8, 546 S.E.2d 191 (S.C.2001)—§ **2.21;** § **2.21, n. 8;** § **17.7, n. 8;** § **17.8, n. 2.**

Boone v. Huntington and Guerry Elec. Co., 311 S.C. 550, 430 S.E.2d 507 (S.C. 1993)—§ **17.61, n. 2.**

Boone v. Wachovia Bank & Trust Co., 163 F.2d 809, 82 U.S.App.D.C. 317 (D.C.Cir. 1947)—§ **22.18, n. 8.**

Booth, Commonwealth v., 266 Mass. 80, 165 N.E. 29 (Mass.1929)—§ **4.33, n. 3.**

Borax' Estate v. Commissioner, 349 F.2d 666 (2nd Cir.1965)—§ **15.13;** § **15.13, n. 2.**

Borcherling, United States v., 185 U.S. 223, 37 Ct.Cl. 553, 22 S.Ct. 607, 46 L.Ed. 884 (1902)—§ **22.10, n. 2.**

Borer v. Chapman, 119 U.S. 587, 7 S.Ct. 342, 30 L.Ed. 532 (1887)—§ **22.20, n. 11;** § **22.21, n. 2.**

Borland v. City of Boston, 132 Mass. 89 (Mass.1882)—§ **4.13, n. 2;** § **4.17, n. 4;** § **4.19, n. 2.**

Boryk v. deHavilland Aircraft Co., 341 F.2d 666 (2nd Cir.1965)—§ **23.20, n. 7.**

Bos Material Handling, Inc. v. Crown Controls Corp., 137 Cal.App.3d 99, 186 Cal. Rptr. 740 (Cal.App. 3 Dist.1982)— § **11.5, n. 3;** § **18.5, n. 5.**

Boston Safe Deposit and Trust Co. v. Paris, 15 Mass.App.Ct. 686, 447 N.E.2d 1268 (Mass.App.Ct.1983)—§ **19.29, n. 3;** § **21.6, n. 7.**

Boston Safe Deposit & Trust Co. v. Fleming, 361 Mass. 172, 279 N.E.2d 342 (Mass.1972)—§ **20.13, n. 4.**

Boston Safe Deposit & Trust Co. v. Painter, 322 Mass. 362, 77 N.E.2d 409 (Mass. 1948)—§ **21.11, n. 14.**

Boston Safe Deposit & Trust Co. v. Prindle, 290 Mass. 577, 195 N.E. 793 (Mass. 1935)—§ **21.9, n. 1.**

Botefuhr, United States v., 309 F.3d 1263 (10th Cir.2002)—§ **10.18, n. 9, 32.**

Boudreau v. Baughman, 322 N.C. 331, 368 S.E.2d 849 (N.C.1988)—§ **2.17, n. 12; § 2.21, n. 24; § 2.22, n. 7; § 3.11, n. 4; § 17.64, n. 10; § 18.12, n. 10; § 18.21, n. 15.**

Boughton, Matter of, 49 B.R. 312 (Bkrtcy. N.D.Ill.1985)—§ **23.12, n. 7.**

Boulevard Airport v. Consolidated Vultee Aircraft Corp., 85 F.Supp. 876 (E.D.Pa. 1949)—§ **17.52, n. 2.**

Bouley v. City of Norwich, 222 Conn. 744, 610 A.2d 1245 (Conn.1992)—§ **17.56, n. 16.**

Bounty–Full Entertainment, Inc. v. Forever Blue Entertainment Group, Inc., 923 F.Supp. 950 (S.D.Tex.1996)—§ **7.11, n. 11.**

Bourelle v. Soo–Crete, Inc., 165 Neb. 731, 87 N.W.2d 371 (Neb.1958)—§ **13.6, n. 2.**

Bourestom v. Bourestom, 231 Wis. 666, 285 N.W. 426 (Wis.1939)—§ **11.8, n. 3.**

Bourne's Estate, In re, 82 Misc.2d 824, 370 N.Y.S.2d 462 (N.Y.Sur.1975)—§ **22.23, n. 8.**

Bourne's Estate, In re, 181 Misc. 238, 41 N.Y.S.2d 336 (N.Y.Sur.1943)—§ **4.29, n. 2.**

Bournias v. Atlantic Maritime Co., 220 F.2d 152 (2nd Cir.1955)—§ **3.10, n. 1, 5.**

Bowen v. Johnson, 5 R.I. 112 (R.I.1858)— § **22.3, n. 4; § 22.4, n. 6.**

Bowen v. United States, 570 F.2d 1311 (7th Cir.1978)—§ **3.53; § 3.53, n. 5.**

Bowers v. Wyoming State Treasurer ex rel. Workmen's Compensation Division, 593 P.2d 182 (Wyo.1979)—§ **13.6, n. 2.**

Bowles v. Zimmer Mfg. Co., 277 F.2d 868 (7th Cir.1960)—§ **17.77, n. 2; § 18.24, n. 7.**

Bowlin v. Bowlin, 55 N.C.App. 100, 285 S.E.2d 273 (N.C.App.1981)—§ **15.16, n. 5.**

Bowling v. Founders Title Co., 773 F.2d 1175 (11th Cir.1985)—§ **7.12, n. 8.**

Bowman v. Curt G. Joa, Inc., 361 F.2d 706 (4th Cir.1966)—§ **8.5, n. 5.**

Bowman v. DuBose, 267 F.Supp. 312 (D.S.C.1967)—§ **4.26, n. 1, 8.**

Bowman v. Koch Transfer Co., 862 F.2d 1257 (6th Cir.1988)—§ **17.26, n. 1; § 17.42, n. 12, 18.**

Bowmer v. Dettelbach, 109 Ohio App.3d 680, 672 N.E.2d 1081 (Ohio App. 6 Dist. 1996)—§ **18.28, n. 4.**

Boyd v. Curran, 166 F.Supp. 193 (S.D.N.Y. 1958)—§ **14.9, n. 13; § 14.10, n. 3; § 21.3, n. 13.**

Boyer v. Boyer, 73 Ill.2d 331, 22 Ill.Dec. 747, 383 N.E.2d 223 (Ill.1978)—§ **15.31, n. 2.**

Boyer v. Piper, Jaffray & Hopwood, Inc., 391 F.Supp. 471 (D.S.D.1975)—§ **18.4, n. 7; § 18.5, n. 17; § 18.7, n. 8.**

Boykin v. State Indus. Acc. Commission, 224 Or. 76, 355 P.2d 724 (Or.1960)— § **13.6, n. 2.**

Boyle v. United Technologies Corp., 487 U.S. 500, 108 S.Ct. 2510, 101 L.Ed.2d 442 (1988)—§ **3.53, n. 4.**

Boys v. Chaplin, 1968 WL 22954 (CA 1967)—§ **17.39, n. 50.**

Boys v. Chaplin, [1971] A.C. 356 (H.L.)— § **2.27, n. 4.**

BP Chemicals Ltd. v. Formosa Chemical & Fibre Corp., 229 F.3d 254 (3rd Cir. 2000)—§ **9.3, n. 12; § 17.48, n. 10.**

Brack's Estate, Matter of, 121 Mich.App. 585, 329 N.W.2d 432 (Mich.App.1982)— § **13.6, n. 4.**

Braddock v. Braddock, 91 Nev. 735, 542 P.2d 1060 (Nev.1975)—§ **14.13, n. 8.**

Braddock v. Taylor, 592 S.W.2d 40 (Tex.Civ. App.-Beaumont 1979)—§ **13.6, n. 4.**

Braden Copper Co. v. Industrial Acc. Commission, 147 Cal.App.2d 205, 305 P.2d 222 (Cal.App. 1 Dist.1956)—§ **6.5, n. 13.**

Bradford v. Young, 1885 WL 17684 (CA 1885)—§ **4.36, n. 8.**

Bradford Elec. Light Co. v. Clapper, 286 U.S. 145, 52 S.Ct. 571, 76 L.Ed. 1026 (1932)—§ **3.20, n. 5; § 3.24; § 3.24, n. 2.**

Bradley v. Bradley, 725 S.W.2d 503 (Tex. App.-Corpus Christi 1987)—§ **14.15, n. 10.**

Bradley v. Lowry, Speers, Eq. 1 (S.C.App. Eq.1842)—§ **4.18, n. 2.**

Brady v. Brady, 151 W.Va. 900, 158 S.E.2d 359 (W.Va.1967)—§ **15.28, n. 4.**

Brainard v. Canaday, 49 Del. 182, 112 A.2d 862 (Del.Super.1955)—§ **19.32, n. 7.**

Braithwaite v. Harvey, 14 Mont. 208, 36 P. 38 (Mont.1894)—§ **22.20, n. 1, 8.**

Bramble Transp., Inc. v. Sam Senter Sales, Inc., 294 A.2d 104 (Del.Supr.1972)— § **19.20, n. 13.**

Branch Metal Processing, Inc. v. Boston Edison Co., 952 F.Supp. 893 (D.R.I. 1996)—§ **9.2; § 9.2, n. 19.**

Brand Distributors, Inc. v. Insurance Co. of North America, 400 F.Supp. 1085 (E.D.Va.1974)—§ **18.21, n. 12; § 18.26, n. 12; § 18.39, n. 6.**

Brandeis Intsel Ltd. v. Calabrian Chemicals Corp., 656 F.Supp. 160 (S.D.N.Y.1987)— § **24.48, n. 7.**

Branden v. Driver, 293 F.Supp. 871 (N.D.Cal.1968)—§ **3.51, n. 10.**

Branholt's Estate, In re, 9 Mich.App. 504, 157 N.W.2d 488 (Mich.App.1968)— § **22.21, n. 11; § 22.23, n. 12.**

Branstetter, In re Marriage of, 508 N.W.2d 638 (Iowa 1993)—§ **14.11, n. 1; § 15.30, n. 1.**

Braun v. Braun, 116 N.H. 714, 366 A.2d 484 (N.H.1976)—§ **15.12, n. 12.**

Braune v. Abbott Laboratories, 895 F.Supp. 530 (E.D.N.Y.1995)—§ **3.11, n. 6;** § **17.64, n. 12.**

Braun, Estates of v. Cactus Pete's, Inc., 108 Idaho 798, 702 P.2d 836 (Idaho 1985)— § **17.48, n. 38.**

Brauns' Estate, In re, 276 Mich. 598, 268 N.W. 890 (Mich.1936)—§ **22.21, n. 15.**

Brause v. Bureau of Vital Statistics, 1998 WL 88743 (Alaska Super.1998)— § **13.20, n. 2.**

Brawer v. Pinkins, 164 Misc.2d 1018, 626 N.Y.S.2d 674 (N.Y.Sup.1995)—§ **15.15, n. 4;** § **15.16, n. 1;** § **24.28, n. 2.**

Braxton v. Anco Elec., Inc., 330 N.C. 124, 409 S.E.2d 914 (N.C.1991)—§ **2.21, n. 25;** § **17.8, n. 1;** § **17.60, n. 6;** § **17.61, n. 4.**

Bray v. Cox, 39 A.D.2d 299, 333 N.Y.S.2d 783 (N.Y.A.D. 4 Dept.1972)—§ **17.30, n. 10;** § **17.31, n. 6.**

Breece v. Jett, 556 S.W.2d 696 (Mo.App. 1977)—§ **17.54, n. 4.**

Breen v. Aetna Cas. & Sur. Co., 153 Conn. 633, 220 A.2d 254 (Conn.1966)— § **18.21, n. 19.**

Breese's Estate, In re, 51 Wash.2d 302, 317 P.2d 1055 (Wash.1957)—§ **22.10, n. 11.**

Breitenstine v. Breitenstine, 62 P.3d 587 (Wyo.2003)—§ **14.9, n. 13.**

Brengle v. Hurst, 408 S.W.2d 418 (Ky. 1966)—§ **15.39, n. 2.**

Brenholdt v. Brenholdt, 94 N.M. 489, 612 P.2d 1300 (N.M.1980)—§ **14.6, n. 2;** § **14.9, n. 1.**

Brent v. Bank of Washington, 35 U.S. 596, 9 L.Ed. 547 (1836)—§ **24.24, n. 3.**

Brickner v. Gooden, 525 P.2d 632 (Okla. 1974)—§ **2.16, n. 12;** § **2.23, n. 1;** § **17.26, n. 1;** § **17.39, n. 11.**

Bridas Corp. v. Unocal Corp., 16 S.W.3d 893 (Tex.App.-Hous. (14 Dist.) 2000)— § **17.48, n. 9.**

Bridgeman v. Gateway Ford Truck Sales, 296 F.Supp. 233 (E.D.Ark.1969)— § **12.17, n. 13.**

Bridge Products, Inc. v. Quantum Chemical Corp., 1990 WL 19968 (N.D.Ill.1990)— § **18.21, n. 14.**

Bridgeway Corp. v. Citibank, 45 F.Supp.2d 276 (S.D.N.Y.1999)—§ **24.36, n. 3.**

Brierley v. Commercial Credit Co., 43 F.2d 724 (E.D.Pa.1929)—§ **18.7, n. 9.**

Brignoli v. Balch, Hardy & Scheinman, Inc., 696 F.Supp. 37 (S.D.N.Y.1988)—§ **4.15, n. 3.**

Brinco Mining Ltd. v. Federal Ins. Co., 552 F.Supp. 1233 (D.D.C.1982)—§ **11.10, n. 8;** § **24.35, n. 8.**

Brinderson–Newberg Joint Venture v. Pacific Erectors, Inc., 690 F.Supp. 891 (C.D.Cal.1988)—§ **11.2, n. 6.**

Brine v. Hartford Fire Ins. Co., 96 U.S. 627, 24 L.Ed. 858 (1877)—§ **19.3, n. 17.**

Brinkley v. Attorney General, 1890 WL 10301 (PDAD 1890)—§ **13.17, n. 1.**

Brink's Ltd. v. South African Airways, 93 F.3d 1022 (2nd Cir.1996)—§ **18.7, n. 6.**

Brinson v. Martin, 220 Ga.App. 638, 469 S.E.2d 537 (Ga.App.1996)—§ **11.5, n. 3.**

British Midland Airways Limited v. International Travel, Inc., 497 F.2d 869 (9th Cir.1974)—§ **24.37, n. 3.**

Brittain, United States v., 319 F.Supp. 1058 (N.D.Ala.1970)—§ **13.10, n. 3.**

Britten v. Britten, 1983 WL 379431 (B.C. S.C.1983)—§ **14.9, n. 12.**

Broadfoot v. Everett, 270 N.C. 429, 154 S.E.2d 522 (N.C.1967)—§ **22.19, n. 12.**

Brock v. Entre Computer Centers, Inc., 740 F.Supp. 428 (E.D.Tex.1990)—§ **11.6, n. 7.**

Brockway v. Maloney, 102 Mass. 308 (Mass. 1869)—§ **19.12, n. 1.**

Broderick v. Pardue, 102 S.W.2d 252 (Tex. Civ.App.-San Antonio 1936)—§ **3.10, n. 4.**

Broderick v. Rosner, 294 U.S. 629, 55 S.Ct. 589, 79 L.Ed. 1100 (1935)—§ **3.25;** § **3.25, n. 3;** § **24.22;** § **24.22, n. 8.**

Brokemond v. Marshall Field & Co., 612 N.E.2d 143 (Ind.App. 3 Dist.1993)— § **7.4, n. 8.**

Brokenleg v. Butts, 559 S.W.2d 853 (Tex. Civ.App.-El Paso 1977)—§ **15.39, n. 1, 4.**

Bromley, State, Child Support Enforcement Div. v., 987 P.2d 183 (Alaska 1999)— § **15.35, n. 5.**

Bronislawa K. v. Tadeusz K., 90 Misc.2d 183, 393 N.Y.S.2d 534 (N.Y.Fam.Ct. 1977)—§ **13.5, n. 1;** § **15.16, n. 2;** § **15.24, n. 9.**

Bronson v. St. Croix Lumber Co., 44 Minn. 348, 46 N.W. 570 (Minn.1890)—§ **19.2, n. 7;** § **19.4, n. 1.**

Brook v. Van Nest, 33 A. 382 (N.J.Err. & App.1895)—§ **19.31, n. 8.**

Brooklyn Children's Aid Society, People ex rel. v. Hendrickson, 54 Misc. 337, 104 N.Y.S. 122 (N.Y.Sup.1907)—§ **4.37, n. 7.**

Brookman v. Durkee, 46 Wash. 578, 90 P. 914 (Wash.1907)—§ **14.6, n. 2.**

Brooks v. Carson, 166 Kan. 194, 200 P.2d 280 (Kan.1948)—§ **20.5, n. 7;** § **20.6, n. 17;** § **20.15, n. 3.**

Brooks v. Eastern Airlines, Inc., 634 So.2d 809 (Fla.App. 1 Dist.1994)—§ **17.59, n. 5, 16.**

Brooks v. National Bank of Topeka, 251 F.2d 37 (8th Cir.1958)—§ **3.11, n. 2.**

Brooks v. Titusville Trust Co., 328 Mass. 472, 104 N.E.2d 437 (Mass.1952)— § **22.12, n. 2.**

Brook v. Brook, 1861 WL 7358 (Unknown Court - UK 1861)—§ **13.11, n. 1.**

Brosnan, United States v., 363 U.S. 237, 80 S.Ct. 1108, 4 L.Ed.2d 1192 (1960)— **§ 3.51, n. 11.**

Brothers Coal Co., Inc., In re, 6 B.R. 567 (Bkrtcy.W.D.Va.1980)—**§ 23.16, n. 6.**

Brown, In re Marriage of, 126 Cal.Rptr. 633, 544 P.2d 561 (Cal.1976)— **§ 14.11, n. 1.**

Brown v. American Broadcasting Co., Inc., 704 F.2d 1296 (4th Cir.1983)—**§ 7.10, n. 4, 7.**

Brown v. Babbitt Ford, Inc., 117 Ariz. 192, 571 P.2d 689 (Ariz.App. Div. 1 1977)— **§ 24.12, n. 2.**

Brown v. Brown, 1997 WL 754545 (Conn.Super.1997)—**§ 17.56, n. 12.**

Brown v. Brown, 104 Mich.App. 621, 305 N.W.2d 272 (Mich.App.1981)—**§ 15.41, n. 1.**

Brown v. Brown, 71 Misc.2d 11, 335 N.Y.S.2d 846 (N.Y.Fam.Ct.1972)— **§ 15.38, n. 3.**

Brown v. Brown, 105 Ariz. 273, 463 P.2d 71 (Ariz.1969)—**§ 15.39, n. 4.**

Brown v. Brown, 35 Minn. 191, 28 N.W. 238 (Minn.1886)—**§ 22.19, n. 24.**

Brown v. Brown, 5 Ala. 508 (Ala.1843)— **§ 19.14, n. 1.**

Brown v. Church of Holy Name of Jesus, 105 R.I. 322, 252 A.2d 176 (R.I.1969)— **§ 17.23, n. 6.**

Brown v. Cosby, 433 F.Supp. 1331 (E.D.Pa. 1977)—**§ 3.11, n. 4.**

Brown v. Finley, 157 Ala. 424, 47 So. 577 (Ala.1908)—**§ 16.1, n. 12.**

Brown v. Fletcher's Estate, 210 U.S. 82, 28 S.Ct. 702, 52 L.Ed. 966 (1908)—**§ 22.20, n. 17.**

Brown v. Fletcher's Estate, 146 Mich. 401, 109 N.W. 686 (Mich.1906)—**§ 22.19, n. 3; § 22.20, n. 4, 9.**

Brown v. Globe Laboratories, Inc., 165 Neb. 138, 84 N.W.2d 151 (Neb.1957)— **§ 10.12, n. 16.**

Brown v. Harper, 231 A.D.2d 483, 647 N.Y.S.2d 245 (N.Y.A.D. 2 Dept.1996)— **§ 17.44, n. 10.**

Brown v. Inter–Ocean Ins. Co., 438 F.Supp. 951 (N.D.Ga.1977)—**§ 18.26, n. 9.**

Brown v. Merlo, 106 Cal.Rptr. 388, 506 P.2d 212 (Cal.1973)—**§ 17.17, n. 4.**

Brown v. Pyle, 310 F.2d 95 (5th Cir.1962)— **§ 3.38, n. 5.**

Brown v. Riner, 500 P.2d 524 (Wyo.1972)— **§ 17.50, n. 26.**

Brown v. San Francisco Gaslight Co., 58 Cal. 426 (Cal.1881)—**§ 22.12, n. 7.**

Brown v. Sheridan, 83 Ga.App. 725, 64 S.E.2d 636 (Ga.App.1951)—**§ 13.9, n. 7.**

Brown, State ex rel. v. Hamilton, 202 Mo. 377, 100 S.W. 609 (Mo.1907)—**§ 4.41, n. 7.**

Brown v. TranSouth Financial Corp., 897 F.Supp. 1398 (M.D.Ala.1995)—**§ 4.33, n. 3.**

Brown v. Valentine, 240 F.Supp. 539 (W.D.Va.1965)—**§ 18.38, n. 5.**

Brown v. Wieland, 116 Iowa 711, 89 N.W. 17 (Iowa 1902)—**§ 19.12, n. 1.**

Brown, Will of, 132 Misc.2d 811, 505 N.Y.S.2d 334 (N.Y.Sur.1986)—**§ 4.13, n. 4; § 15.18, n. 3.**

Brown, Will of, 120 Misc.2d 799, 466 N.Y.S.2d 988 (N.Y.Sur.1983)—**§ 21.11, n. 17.**

Brown, Jr., v. Smith, 101 Me. 545, 64 A. 915 (Me.1906)—**§ 22.15, n. 9; § 22.17, n. 3.**

B.R.T. v. Executive Director of Social Service Bd. North Dakota, 391 N.W.2d 594 (N.D.1986)—**§ 4.37, n. 3.**

Bruington's Estate, In re, 160 Misc. 34, 289 N.Y.S. 725 (N.Y.Sur.1936)—**§ 20.2, n. 4.**

Bruneau v. Bruneau, 3 Conn.App. 453, 489 A.2d 1049 (Conn.App.1985)—**§ 15.20, n. 9.**

Brunner's Estate, Matter of, 394 N.Y.S.2d 621, 363 N.E.2d 346 (N.Y.1977)—**§ 4.22, n. 2.**

Bruns v. Desoto Operating Co., 204 Cal. App.3d 876, 251 Cal.Rptr. 462 (Cal.App. 4 Dist.1988)—**§ 8.5, n. 9.**

Bruton v. Villoria, 138 Cal.App.2d 642, 292 P.2d 638 (Cal.App. 2 Dist.1956)—**§ 14.9, n. 1; § 17.6, n. 5.**

Bryan v. Itasca County, Minnesota, 426 U.S. 373, 96 S.Ct. 2102, 48 L.Ed.2d 710 (1976)—**§ 11.17, n. 36.**

Bryant v. Finnish Nat. Airline, 260 N.Y.S.2d 625, 208 N.E.2d 439 (N.Y. 1965)—**§ 5.10, n. 12.**

Bryant v. Seward, 490 S.W.2d 497 (Tenn. 1973)—**§ 17.59, n. 16.**

Bryant v. Silverman, 146 Ariz. 41, 703 P.2d 1190 (Ariz.1985)—**§ 17.26, n. 1; § 17.50, n. 36.**

Bryks v. Canadian Broadcasting Corp., 928 F.Supp. 381 (S.D.N.Y.1996)—**§ 17.55, n. 9.**

Bucca v. State, 43 N.J.Super. 315, 128 A.2d 506 (N.J.Super.Ch.1957)—**§ 13.11, n. 2, 3; § 13.15, n. 4.**

Bucci v. Kaiser Permanente Foundation Health Plan of Mid–Atlantic States, Inc., 278 F.Supp.2d 34 (D.D.C.2003)— **§ 17.42, n. 29.**

Buchanan v. Doe, 246 Va. 67, 431 S.E.2d 289 (Va.1993)—**§ 2.21, n. 4, 45; § 18.21, n. 12.**

Buchanan v. Weber, 152 N.C.App. 180, 567 S.E.2d 413 (N.C.App.2002)—**§ 24.10, n. 1.**

Buchholz v. Buchholz, 63 Wash. 213, 115 P. 88 (Wash.1911)—**§ 4.33, n. 3; § 4.34, n. 3.**

Buck v. Branson, 34 Okla. 807, 127 P. 436 (Okla.1912)—**§ 13.18, n. 9.**

Buckeye v. Buckeye, 203 Wis. 248, 234 N.W. 342 (Wis.1931)—**§ 17.8, n. 9.**

Buckeye Boiler Co. v. Superior Court of Los Angeles County, 71 Cal.2d 893, 80 Cal. Rptr. 113, 458 P.2d 57 (Cal.1969)— § 5.10, n. 12; § 7.2; § 7.2, n. 9; § 7.4, n. 6.

Buckingham Hotel Co. v. Kimberly, 138 Miss. 445, 103 So. 213 (Miss.1925)— § 22.20, n. 35.

Buckley, Estate of, 677 S.W.2d 946 (Mo. App. W.D.1984)—§ 20.13, n. 4.

Buckley v. Huston, 60 N.J. 472, 291 A.2d 129 (N.J.1972)—§ 24.23, n. 5.

Buckley v. New York Times Co., 338 F.2d 470 (5th Cir.1964)—§ 7.8, n. 2.

Budd, People ex rel. v. Holden, 28 Cal. 123 (Cal.1865)—§ 4.26, n. 1.

Budget Plan, Inc. v. Sterling A. Orr, Inc., 334 Mass. 599, 137 N.E.2d 918 (Mass. 1956)—§ 19.15, n. 13.

Budget Rent–A–Car v. Eighth Judicial Dist. Court In and For County of Clark, 108 Nev. 483, 835 P.2d 17 (Nev.1992)— § 7.4, n. 7.

Budget Rent–A–Car Corp. v. Martin, 855 P.2d 1377 (Colo.1993)—§ 17.56, n. 13.

Budgget Industries, Inc. v. Faber Engineering, L.L.C., 2003 WL 21087138 (Tex. App.-Hous. (14 Dist.) 2003)—§ 8.5, n. 8.

Buehl, Matter of Adoption of, 87 Wash.2d 649, 555 P.2d 1334 (Wash.1976)— § 15.23, n. 7.

Buffalo Sav. Bank, United States v., 371 U.S. 228, 83 S.Ct. 314, 9 L.Ed.2d 283 (1963)—§ 3.51, n. 11.

Buglioli v. Enterprise Rent–A–Car, 811 F.Supp. 105 (E.D.N.Y.1993)—§ 17.45, n. 23.

Buhl v. Biosearch Medical Products, Inc., 635 F.Supp. 956 (D.Mont.1985)—§ 3.10, n. 6.

Builders Supply Co. v. McCabe, 366 Pa. 322, 77 A.2d 368 (Pa.1951)—§ 17.6, n. 3.

Bull v. Fuller, 78 Iowa 20, 42 N.W. 572 (Iowa 1889)—§ 22.11, n. 15.

Bullen v. Her Majesty's Government of the United Kingdom, 553 So.2d 1344 (Fla. App. 4 Dist.1989)—§ 24.23, n. 7; § 24.43, n. 1.

Bullen v. Wisconsin, 240 U.S. 625, 36 S.Ct. 473, 60 L.Ed. 830 (1916)—§ 20.3, n. 2; § 20.14, n. 1.

Bullington v. Angel, 220 N.C. 18, 16 S.E.2d 411 (N.C.1941)—§ 19.10, n. 2.

Bullington v. Mize, 25 Utah 2d 173, 478 P.2d 500 (Utah 1970)—§ 19.10, n. 1, 3, 5.

Bullins v. City of Philadelphia, 516 F.Supp. 728 (E.D.Pa.1981)—§ 3.37, n. 5.

Bulova's Will, In re, 14 A.D.2d 249, 220 N.Y.S.2d 541 (N.Y.A.D. 1 Dept.1961)— § 18.19; § 18.19, n. 6, 9; § 19.11, n. 2; § 20.9, n. 14.

Bundy v. United States Trust Co. of New York, 257 Mass. 72, 153 N.E. 337 (Mass. 1926)—§ 21.11, n. 15.

Bunge Corp. v. Biglane, 418 F.Supp. 1159 (S.D.Miss.1976)—§ 18.21, n. 14; § 18.24, n. 2.

Bunker v. Bunker, 261 Ark. 851, 552 S.W.2d 641 (Ark.1977)—§ 15.28, n. 1; § 15.30, n. 2.

Buraczynski v. Eyring, 919 S.W.2d 314 (Tenn.1996)—§ 18.5, n. 1.

Burbank v. Ford Motor Co., 703 F.2d 865 (5th Cir.1983)—§ 18.5, n. 5.

Burch v. Burch, 195 F.2d 799 (3rd Cir. 1952)—§ 4.13, n. 11.

Burcl v. North Carolina Baptist Hosp., Inc., 306 N.C. 214, 293 S.E.2d 85 (N.C. 1982)—§ 22.14, n. 10.

Burdell v. Canadian Pacific Airlines, Civil No. 66L 10799, 8 Int'l Legal Mat. 83 (1969)—§ 3.57, n. 22.

Burdick v. Takushi, 504 U.S. 428, 112 S.Ct. 2059, 119 L.Ed.2d 245 (1992)—§ 3.58, n. 17.

Buresh v. First Nat. Bank, 10 Or.App. 463, 500 P.2d 1063 (Or.App.1972)—§ 20.9, n. 7, 9.

Burg v. Knox, 334 Mo. 329, 67 S.W.2d 96 (Mo.1933)—§ 17.6, n. 6.

Burgan v. Burgan, 207 La. 1057, 22 So.2d 649 (La.1945)—§ 4.26, n. 1.

Burge v. Mid–Continent Cas. Co., 123 N.M. 1, 933 P.2d 210 (N.M.1996)—§ 18.5, n. 8.

Burger King Corp. v. Rudzewicz, 471 U.S. 462, 105 S.Ct. 2174, 85 L.Ed.2d 528 (1985)—§ 5.10, n. 15; § 5.11; § 5.11, n. 25; § 5.12; § 5.12, n. 2; § 6.6; § 6.6, n. 20; § 7.11; § 7.11, n. 9; § 8.1; § 8.1, n. 13; § 8.3; § 8.3, n. 2; § 8.5; § 8.5, n. 1; § 8.6, n. 4; § 8.7; § 8.7, n. 2; § 18.1, n. 23.

Burgess v. Cohen, 593 F.Supp. 1122 (E.D.Va.1984)—§ 24.24, n. 3.

Burke, Re, 1927 WL 23786 (Sask. K.B. [In Chambers] 1927)—§ 20.7, n. 3.

Burkett v. McCaw, 9 Wash.App. 917, 515 P.2d 988 (Wash.App. Div. 1 1973)— § 24.31, n. 2.

Burkhardt v. Burkhardt, 38 Del. 492, 193 A. 924 (Del.Super.1937)—§ 4.34, n. 3.

Burleson v. Liggett Group Inc., 111 F.Supp.2d 825 (E.D.Tex.2000)—§ 17.77, n. 5.

Burlington Industries, United States v., 600 F.2d 517 (5th Cir.1979)—§ 19.21, n. 13.

Burlington Northern R. Co. v. Allianz Underwriters Ins. Co., 1994 WL 637011 (Del.Super.1994)—§ 18.1, n. 25, 27.

Burlington Northern R. Co. v. Hyundai Merchant Marine Co., Ltd., 63 F.3d 1227 (3rd Cir.1995)—§ 24.1, n. 12.

Burlington Northern R. Co. v. Woods, 480 U.S. 1, 107 S.Ct. 967, 94 L.Ed.2d 1 (1987)—§ 3.39; § 3.39, n. 20.

Burnet v. Burnet, 51 Ky. 323 (Ky.1851)—§ **22.25, n. 10.**

Burnett v. Trans World Airlines, Inc., 368 F.Supp. 1152 (D.N.M.1973)—§ **12.18, n. 1.**

Burnette–Carter Co., United States v., 575 F.2d 587 (6th Cir.1978)—§ **19.18, n. 19.**

Burney v. P V Holding Corp., 218 Mich. App. 167, 553 N.W.2d 657 (Mich.App. 1996)—§ **17.36, n. 15; § 17.48, n. 17.**

Burnham v. Superior Court of California, County of Marin, 495 U.S. 604, 110 S.Ct. 2105, 109 L.Ed.2d 631 (1990)—§ **2.10; § 2.10, n. 27; § 5.4, n. 30; § 5.7, n. 5; § 5.8, n. 1; § 5.9, n. 27; § 5.10, n. 10, 14; § 5.13; § 5.13, n. 25; § 6.2; § 6.2, n. 15; § 15.28, n. 1; § 24.6, n. 5.**

Burns v. Burns, 253 Ga.App. 600, 560 S.E.2d 47 (Ga.App.2002)—§ **13.20, n. 8.**

Burns v. Burns, 321 So.2d 293 (Miss. 1975)—§ **17.11, n. 22.**

Burns Bros. Plumbers, Inc. v. Groves Ventures Co., 412 F.2d 202 (6th Cir.1969)—§ **18.38, n. 3.**

Burr v. Beckler, 264 Ill. 230, 106 N.E. 206 (Ill.1914)—§ **19.3, n. 7.**

Burr v. Renewal Guaranty Corp., 105 Ariz. 549, 468 P.2d 576 (Ariz.1970)—§ **2.17, n. 10; § 2.23, n. 2; § 18.21, n. 14.**

Burrowes v. Goodman, 50 F.2d 92 (2nd Cir.1931)—§ **22.19, n. 4.**

Burrows' Estate, In re, 136 Cal. 113, 68 P. 488 (Cal.1902)—§ **14.6, n. 2.**

Burse v. American Intern. Airways, Inc., 262 Conn. 31, 808 A.2d 672 (Conn. 2002)—§ **17.59, n. 10, 11, 15.**

Burt v. Board of Regents of University of Nebraska, 757 F.2d 242 (10th Cir. 1985)—§ **7.8, n. 10; § 7.9, n. 8.**

Burtis v. Burtis, 161 Mass. 508, 37 N.E. 740 (Mass.1894)—§ **4.34, n. 1.**

Burton v. Burton, 23 Ariz.App. 159, 531 P.2d 204 (Ariz.App. Div. 2 1975)—§ **14.9, n. 1, 2, 13; § 14.13, n. 8.**

Burton v. Burton, 52 Tenn.App. 484, 376 S.W.2d 504 (Tenn.Ct.App.1963)—§ **15.28, n. 4.**

Busby v. Perini Corp., 110 R.I. 49, 290 A.2d 210 (R.I.1972)—§ **2.13, n. 14; § 17.61, n. 4.**

Busch v. Buchman, Buchman & O'Brien, Law Firm, 11 F.3d 1255 (5th Cir.1994)—§ **10.2, n. 15, 19.**

Bushel v. Commonwealth Insurance Co., 15 S & R 173 (Pa.1827)—§ **10.13, n. 3.**

Bushkin Associates, Inc. v. Raytheon Co., 393 Mass. 622, 473 N.E.2d 662 (Mass. 1985)—§ **2.17, n. 12; § 2.25, n. 12; § 3.8, n. 6; § 17.26, n. 1; § 18.21, n. 17; § 18.24, n. 9; § 18.38, n. 8.**

Busik v. Levine, 63 N.J. 351, 307 A.2d 571 (N.J.1973)—§ **3.12, n. 3.**

Business Incentives Co., Inc. v. Sony Corp. of America, 397 F.Supp. 63 (S.D.N.Y. 1975)—§ **18.4, n. 7; § 18.5, n. 2; § 18.7, n. 8.**

Buss' Estate, In re, 71 S.D. 529, 26 N.W.2d 700 (S.D.1947)—§ **22.20, n. 29.**

Bussing v. Hough, 237 Iowa 194, 21 N.W.2d 587 (Iowa 1946)—§ **21.13, n. 5.**

Butcher's Union Local No. 498, United Food and Commercial Workers v. SDC Inv., Inc., 788 F.2d 535 (9th Cir.1986)—§ **9.8, n. 7; § 10.2, n. 6.**

Butkera v. Hudson River Sloop Clearwater, Inc., 300 N.J.Super. 550, 693 A.2d 520 (N.J.Super.A.D.1997)—§ **17.37, n. 14; § 17.45, n. 19.**

Butler v. Wittland, 18 Ill.App.2d 578, 153 N.E.2d 106 (Ill.App. 3 Dist.1958)—§ **17.5, n. 7.**

Buttrick v. Allen, 8 Mass. 273 (Mass. 1811)—§ **24.34, n. 1.**

Byers v. Auto–Owners Ins. Co., 119 S.W.3d 659 (Mo.App. S.D.2003)—§ **18.26, n. 13.**

Byrd v. Blue Ridge Rural Elec. Co-op., Inc., 356 U.S. 525, 78 S.Ct. 893, 2 L.Ed.2d 953 (1958)—§ **3.38; § 3.38, n. 1; § 3.41, n. 7.**

Byrd v. Southern Ry. Co., 203 A.2d 37 (D.C.App.1964)—§ **11.9, n. 1.**

Byrd, United States v., 750 F.2d 585 (7th Cir.1984)—§ **12.11, n. 7.**

Byrn v. American Universal Ins. Co., 548 S.W.2d 186 (Mo.App.1977)—§ **17.26, n. 6.**

Byrnes v. Kirby, 453 F.Supp. 1014 (D.Mass. 1978)—§ **3.41, n. 15.**

Byron v. Byron, Cro. Eliz. 472 (1596)—§ **22.11, n. 2.**

Byron v. Great American Indem. Co., 54 R.I. 405, 173 A. 546 (R.I.1934)—§ **3.10, n. 4.**

C

C. v. S., [1990] 2 All E.R. 961 (H.L.1990)—§ **4.14; § 4.14, n. 10.**

Caban v. Mohammed, 441 U.S. 380, 99 S.Ct. 1760, 60 L.Ed.2d 297 (1979)—§ **16.5, n. 7.**

Cabanne v. Skinker, 56 Mo. 357 (Mo. 1874)—§ **22.15, n. 13.**

Cabell v. Chavez–Salido, 454 U.S. 432, 102 S.Ct. 735, 70 L.Ed.2d 677 (1982)—§ **3.58, n. 15.**

Cable v. Sahara Tahoe Corp., 93 Cal.App.3d 384, 155 Cal.Rptr. 770 (Cal.App. 2 Dist. 1979)—§ **17.19, n. 12.**

Cable Holdings of Battlefield, Inc. v. Cooke, 764 F.2d 1466 (11th Cir.1985)—§ **24.12, n. 7.**

Cable/Home Communication Corp. v. Network Productions, Inc., 902 F.2d 829 (11th Cir.1990)—§ **9.3, n. 4.**

Cable News Network, Inc. v. American Broadcasting Companies, Inc., 528

F.Supp. 365 (N.D.Ga.1981)—§ **3.45, n. 4.**

Cable Tel Services, Inc. v. Overland Contracting, Inc., 154 N.C.App. 639, 574 S.E.2d 31 (N.C.App.2002)—§ **18.6, n. 1.**

Cabral v. State Bd. of Control, 112 Cal. App.3d 1012, 169 Cal.Rptr. 604 (Cal. App. 2 Dist.1980)—§ **4.30, n. 8; § 4.31, n. 6.**

Cacdac v. Sweet, 761 F.Supp. 594 (S.D.Ind. 1989)—§ **7.9, n. 6.**

Cacho v. Prince of Fundy Cruises, Ltd., 722 A.2d 349 (Me.1998)—§ **17.63, n. 23.**

Caddie Homes, Inc. v. Falic, 211 Pa.Super. 333, 235 A.2d 437 (Pa.Super.1967)— § **19.28, n. 1.**

Cadwalader v. Howell, 1840 WL 2744 (N.J. 1840)—§ **4.1, n. 2.**

Cadwalader v. Pyle, 95 Kan. 337, 148 P. 655 (Kan.1915)—§ **4.45, n. 2.**

Cady, People v., 143 N.Y. 100, 37 N.E. 673 (N.Y.1894)—§ **4.27, n. 1.**

Caesars World, Inc. v. Caesars–Palace.Com, 112 F.Supp.2d 502 (E.D.Va.2000)— § **5.9, n. 17.**

Caeti's Will, In re, 207 Misc. 353, 138 N.Y.S.2d 496 (N.Y.Sur.1955)—§ **13.6, n. 7; § 13.9, n. 3.**

Cahill v. Kendall, 202 F.Supp.2d 1322 (S.D.Ala.2002)—§ **15.42, n. 11.**

Calder v. Jones, 465 U.S. 783, 104 S.Ct. 1482, 79 L.Ed.2d 804 (1984)—§ **5.4, n. 24; § 7.1, n. 2; § 7.3; § 7.3, n. 3, 12; § 7.8; § 7.8, n. 4; § 7.9, n. 4; § 7.10; § 7.10, n. 2; § 7.11; § 7.11, n. 2; § 7.12; § 7.12, n. 6; § 9.3; § 9.3, n. 2; § 10.17; § 10.17, n. 6.**

Caldwell v. Gore, 175 La. 501, 143 So. 387 (La.1932)—§ **19.7, n. 2.**

Caldwell v. Simms, 1995 WL 1727515 (B.C. S.C.1995)—§ **14.9, n. 12.**

Caldwell, Succession of, 114 La. 195, 38 So. 140 (La.1905)—§ **16.5, n. 3.**

Caldwell–Baker Co. v. Southern Illinois Railcar Co., 225 F.Supp.2d 1243 (D.Kan. 2002)—§ **10.17, n. 9.**

Calhoun v. Somogyi, 190 Ga.App. 502, 379 S.E.2d 595 (Ga.App.1989)—§ **4.13, n. 4.**

Calhoun v. Yamaha Motor Corp., U.S.A., 216 F.3d 338 (3rd Cir.2000)—§ **10.6, n. 14; § 17.50, n. 55; § 17.63, n. 5; § 17.73, n. 4; § 17.74, n. 20; § 17.78, n. 12.**

California v. Superior Court of California, San Bernardino County, 482 U.S. 400, 107 S.Ct. 2433, 96 L.Ed.2d 332 (1987)— § **15.42, n. 12.**

California v. Texas, 437 U.S. 601, 98 S.Ct. 3107, 57 L.Ed.2d 464 (1978)—§ **4.5; § 4.5, n. 10.**

California Federal Sav. and Loan Ass'n v. Bell, 6 Haw.App. 597, 735 P.2d 499 (Hawai'i App.1987)—§ **19.10, n. 4.**

California Franchise Tax Bd. v. Hyatt, 538 U.S. 488, 123 S.Ct. 1683, 155 L.Ed.2d 702 (2003)—§ **3.25; § 3.25, n. 6; § 3.30, n. 6; § 4.5, n. 6; § 17.43, n. 15.**

California State Bd. of Equalization v. Chemehuevi Indian Tribe, 474 U.S. 9, 106 S.Ct. 289, 88 L.Ed.2d 9 (1985)—§ **11.17, n. 14.**

California, State of v. Copus, 158 Tex. 196, 309 S.W.2d 227 (Tex.1958)—§ **3.10, n. 4.**

Calla v. Shulsky, 148 A.D.2d 60, 543 N.Y.S.2d 666 (N.Y.A.D. 1 Dept.1989)— § **17.37, n. 16.**

Calloway v. Doe ex dem. Joyes, 1825 WL 997 (Ind.1825)—§ **20.6, n. 1.**

Callwood v. Virgin Islands National Bank, 221 F.2d 770 (3rd Cir.1955)—§ **19.29, n. 3.**

Camacho v. Camacho, 617 So.2d 685 (Ala. Civ.App.1992)—§ **15.9, n. 7.**

Camden Safe Deposit & Trust Co. v. Barbour, 48 A. 1008 (N.J.Sup.1901)—§ **6.4, n. 22.**

Camelback Ski Corp. v. Behning, 312 Md. 330, 539 A.2d 1107 (Md.1988)—§ **5.10, n. 12.**

Camelback Ski Corp. v. Behning, 307 Md. 270, 513 A.2d 874 (Md.1986)—§ **5.13, n. 19, 22; § 6.9, n. 20, 21.**

Cameron v. Cameron, 641 S.W.2d 210 (Tex. 1982)—§ **14.6, n. 3; § 14.13, n. 3, 4, 6.**

Cameron v. Gunstock Acres, Inc., 370 Mass. 378, 348 N.E.2d 791 (Mass.1976)— § **18.5, n. 39; § 19.3, n. 13.**

Cameron v. Rowland, 215 La. 177, 40 So.2d 1 (La.1948)—§ **14.9, n. 13.**

Cameron v. Thornburgh, 983 F.2d 253, 299 U.S.App.D.C. 228 (D.C.Cir.1993)— § **10.18, n. 9.**

Cameron v. Vandegriff, 53 Ark. 381, 13 S.W. 1092 (Ark.1890)—§ **17.3, n. 1.**

Cameron v. Watson, 40 Miss. 191 (Miss.Err. & App.1866)—§ **20.9, n. 7.**

Cammell v. Sewell, 1860 WL 9701 (Unknown Court - UK 1860)—§ **19.13, n. 2.**

Camp v. Guercio, 464 F.Supp. 343 (W.D.Pa. 1979)—§ **9.5, n. 14.**

Camp v. Lockwood, 1 U.S. 393, 1 Dall. 393, 1 L.Ed. 192 (1788)—§ **2.7, n. 2.**

Camp v. Simon, 23 Utah 56, 63 P. 332 (Utah 1900)—§ **22.17, n. 3.**

Campanelli v. Conservas Altamira, S.A., 86 Nev. 838, 477 P.2d 870 (Nev.1970)— § **24.47, n. 4.**

Campbell, Matter of Estate of, 673 P.2d 645 (Wyo.1983)—§ **20.9, n. 6.**

Campbell v. Albers, 313 Ill.App. 152, 39 N.E.2d 672 (Ill.App. 2 Dist.1942)— § **21.6, n. 4.**

Campbell v. Brown, 64 Iowa 425, 20 N.W. 745 (Iowa 1884)—§ **22.11, n. 11.**

Campbell v. Campbell, 120 Idaho 394, 816 P.2d 350 (Idaho App.1991)—§ **14.9, n. 1.**

Campbell v. Coon, 149 N.Y. 556, 44 N.E. 300 (N.Y.1896)—§ **19.9, n. 9.**

Campbell v. Davis, 274 Ala. 187, 145 So.2d 725 (Ala.1962)—§ **22.10, n. 11.**

Campbell v. Hussey, 368 U.S. 297, 82 S.Ct. 327, 7 L.Ed.2d 299 (1961)—§ **3.50, n. 4.**

Campbell v. Jenne, 172 Mont. 219, 563 P.2d 574 (Mont.1977)—§ **15.36, n. 7.**

Campbell v. Sheldon, 30 Mass. 8 (Mass. 1832)—§ **22.19, n. 1.**

Campbell v. Tousey, 7 Cow. 64 (N.Y.Sup. 1827)—§ **22.15, n. 13.**

Campbell v. Triangle Corp., 336 F.Supp. 1002 (E.D.Pa.1972)—§ **23.3, n. 2.**

Campbell's Estate, In re, 260 Wis. 625, 51 N.W.2d 709 (Wis.1952)—§ **13.13, n. 4.**

Campbell's Estate, In re, 138 Misc. 800, 248 N.Y.S. 344 (N.Y.Sur.1930)—§ **21.13, n. 5.**

Canadian Northern Ry. Co. v. Eggen, 252 U.S. 553, 40 S.Ct. 402, 64 L.Ed. 713 (1920)—§ **3.11, n. 2;** § **3.33, n. 2.**

Canale v. People, 177 Ill. 219, 52 N.E. 310 (Ill.1898)—§ **13.6, n. 4.**

Canfield v. Scripps, 15 Cal.App.2d 642, 59 P.2d 1040 (Cal.App. 2 Dist.1936)— § **22.14, n. 4;** § **22.19, n. 4.**

Canipe v. Canipe, 918 F.2d 955 (4th Cir. 1990)—§ **15.42, n. 11.**

Cannelton Industries, Inc. v. Aetna Cas. & Sur. Co. of America, 194 W.Va. 186, 460 S.E.2d 1 (W.Va.1994)—§ **2.17, n. 11;** § **2.23, n. 5;** § **18.1, n. 26.**

Cannistraro v. Cannistraro, 352 Mass. 65, 223 N.E.2d 692 (Mass.1967)—§ **24.35, n. 8.**

Cannon v. Cannon, 228 N.C. 211, 45 S.E.2d 34 (N.C.1947)—§ **22.14, n. 3.**

Cannon Mfg. Co. v. Cudahy Packing Co., 267 U.S. 333, 45 S.Ct. 250, 69 L.Ed. 634 (1925)—§ **10.16;** § **10.16, n. 1, 8.**

Canon's Estate, In re, 221 Wis. 322, 266 N.W. 918 (Wis.1936)—§ **13.13, n. 4.**

Canterbury, Mayor, etc, of v. Wyburn, 1894 WL 9469 (Privy Council 1894)—§ **20.10, n. 2;** § **21.2, n. 5.**

Canty v. Canty, 392 Mass. 1004, 465 N.E.2d 770 (Mass.1984)—§ **15.31, n. 2.**

Capasso v. Colonna, 122 A. 378 (N.J.Ch. 1923)—§ **13.6, n. 8.**

Cape May & D.B. Nav. Co., In re, 16 A. 191 (N.J.Sup.1888)—§ **22.12, n. 7;** § **22.15, n. 3;** § **22.17, n. 3.**

Caperonis' Estate, Matter of, 95 Misc.2d 690, 408 N.Y.S.2d 231 (N.Y.Sur.1978)— § **22.11, n. 1.**

Carbotrade S.p.A. v. Bureau Veritas, 99 F.3d 86 (2nd Cir.1996)—§ **17.63, n. 32.**

Carden v. Arkoma Associates, 494 U.S. 185, 110 S.Ct. 1015, 108 L.Ed.2d 157 (1990)—§ **10.12, n. 9.**

Cardillo v. Liberty Mut. Ins. Co., 330 U.S. 469, 67 S.Ct. 801, 91 L.Ed. 1028 (1947)—§ **3.24, n. 10;** § **17.59, n. 13.**

Cardinal, United States v., 452 F.Supp. 542 (D.Vt.1978)—§ **12.19, n. 19.**

Carefirst Of Maryland, Inc. v. Carefirst Pregnancy Centers, Inc., 334 F.3d 390 (4th Cir.2003)—§ **9.3, n. 7.**

Carefree Vacations, Inc. v. Brunner, 615 F.Supp. 211 (W.D.Tenn.1985)—§ **18.12, n. 1.**

Carey v. Bahama Cruise Lines, 864 F.2d 201 (1st Cir.1988)—§ **12.18, n. 8;** § **18.27, n. 5.**

Carlberg v. Chrysler Motors Corp., 199 Ill. App.3d 127, 145 Ill.Dec. 382, 556 N.E.2d 1284 (Ill.App. 2 Dist.1990)—§ **11.8, n. 6.**

Carlenstolpe v. Merck & Co., Inc., 638 F.Supp. 901 (S.D.N.Y.1986)—§ **11.9, n. 5.**

Carl Hagenbeck & Great Wallace Show Co. v. Randall, 75 Ind.App. 417, 126 N.E. 501 (Ind.App. 1 Div.1920)—§ **18.4, n. 43.**

Carlson v. Reed, 249 F.3d 876 (9th Cir. 2001)—§ **4.31;** § **4.31, n. 2.**

Carlson, State ex rel. v. Hedberg, 192 Minn. 193, 256 N.W. 91 (Minn.1934)—§ **4.37, n. 10.**

Carlson v. Tandy Computer Leasing, 803 F.2d 391 (8th Cir.1986)—§ **19.11, n. 15;** § **19.13, n. 9.**

Carl Zeiss Stiftung v. V. E. B. Carl Zeiss, Jena, 293 F.Supp. 892 (S.D.N.Y.1968)— § **24.4, n. 6.**

Carl Zeiss Stiftung v. Rayner & Keeler Ltd. (Authority to Institute Proceedings: Issue Estoppel), 1966 WL 22122 (HL 1966)—§ **24.3, n. 15.**

Carl Zeiss Stiftung v. Rayner & Keeler Ltd. (Pleadings: Striking Out), 1969 WL 27095 (Ch D 1969)—§ **24.3, n. 15.**

Carnival Cruise Lines, Inc. v. Shute, 499 U.S. 585, 111 S.Ct. 1522, 113 L.Ed.2d 622 (1991)—§ **5.10, n. 17;** § **6.3;** § **6.3, n. 20;** § **6.7, n. 16;** § **8.8;** § **8.8, n. 4;** § **11.3;** § **11.3, n. 24;** § **11.5;** § **11.5, n. 7.**

Carnival Cruise Lines, Inc. v. Superior Court, 234 Cal.App.3d 1019, 286 Cal. Rptr. 323 (Cal.App. 2 Dist.1991)— § **11.5, n. 8.**

Carolina v. Romel Iron Works, 1994 WL 700424 (Conn.Super.1994)—§ **17.59, n. 11.**

Carolina Power & Light Co. v. Uranex, 451 F.Supp. 1044 (N.D.Cal.1977)—§ **5.22, n. 3;** § **24.48, n. 8.**

Carpenter v. Bell, 96 Tenn. 294, 34 S.W. 209 (Tenn.1896)—§ **20.5, n. 4.**

Carpenter v. Strange, 141 U.S. 87, 11 S.Ct. 960, 35 L.Ed. 640 (1891)—§ **22.20;** § **22.20, n. 14, 16.**

Carr v. Carr, 413 N.Y.S.2d 305, 385 N.E.2d 1234 (N.Y.1978)—§ **15.23, n. 4;** § **15.31, n. 2.**

Carr v. Carr, 60 A.D.2d 63, 400 N.Y.S.2d 105 (N.Y.A.D. 2 Dept.1977)—§ **15.5, n. 4.**

Carr v. Isaacs, 2002 WL 553715 (Ohio App. 12 Dist.2002)—**§ 17.56, n. 20.**

Carr v. Kupfer, 250 Ga. 106, 296 S.E.2d 560 (Ga.1982)—**§ 2.21, n. 44; § 18.21, n. 5; § 20.9, n. 1.**

Carr v. Prudential Life Ins. Co. of America, 27 N.Y.S.2d 349 (N.Y.City Ct.1940)— **§ 22.16, n. 2.**

Carrier Corp. v. Home Ins. Co., 43 Conn. Supp. 182, 648 A.2d 665 (Conn.Super.1994)—**§ 17.59, n. 10; § 18.1, n. 27.**

Carrington v. Rash, 380 U.S. 89, 85 S.Ct. 775, 13 L.Ed.2d 675 (1965)—**§ 4.26, n. 7; § 4.27, n. 4.**

Carroll v. Lanza, 349 U.S. 408, 75 S.Ct. 804, 99 L.Ed. 1183 (1955)—**§ 3.24; § 3.24, n. 11, 13; § 17.43, n. 15; § 17.60, n. 1.**

Carroll v. McPike, 53 Miss. 569 (Miss. 1876)—**§ 22.23, n. 7.**

Carson, United States v., 372 F.2d 429 (6th Cir.1967)—**§ 3.51, n. 10.**

Carter v. Davis, 275 Ala. 250, 154 So.2d 9 (Ala.1963)—**§ 22.4, n. 8.**

Carter v. Sommermeyer, 27 Wis. 665 (Wis. 1871)—**§ 4.18, n. 1.**

Carter v. Tillery, 257 S.W.2d 465 (Tex.Civ. App.-Amarillo 1953)—**§ 3.19, n. 6; § 18.48, n. 4.**

Carter v. United States, 333 F.2d 791 (7th Cir.2003)—**§ 17.42, n. 29.**

Carteret Sav. Bank, F.A. v. Shushan, 954 F.2d 141 (3rd Cir.1992)—**§ 7.3, n. 10.**

Carteret Sav. Bank, F.A. v. Shushan, 919 F.2d 225 (3rd Cir.1990)—**§ 5.19, n. 12.**

Carter's Estate, In re, 6 N.J. 426, 78 A.2d 904 (N.J.1951)—**§ 21.6, n. 4.**

Carter's Estate, In re, 20 D. & C. 91 (O.C. Pa. 1933)—**§ 20.13, n. 4.**

Cartner, In re, 9 B.R. 543 (Bkrtcy.M.D.Ala. 1981)—**§ 23.13, n. 1.**

Caruolo v. A C and S, Inc., 1998 WL 730331 (S.D.N.Y.1998)—**§ 17.43, n. 9; § 17.44, n. 10.**

Caruolo v. John Crane, Inc., 226 F.3d 46 (2nd Cir.2000)—**§ 17.32, n. 21.**

Caruso v. Caruso, 148 A. 882 (N.J.Err. & App.1930)—**§ 20.3, n. 1; § 20.9, n. 14.**

Caruso v. Italian Line, 184 F.Supp. 862 (S.D.N.Y.1960)—**§ 18.30, n. 4.**

Caruth v. Caruth, 128 Iowa 121, 103 N.W. 103 (Iowa 1905)—**§ 20.3, n. 8.**

Carver v. Schafer, 647 S.W.2d 570 (Mo.App. E.D.1983)—**§ 17.48, n. 38.**

Cary v. Cary, 937 S.W.2d 777 (Tenn. 1996)—**§ 14.15, n. 1.**

Casarotto v. Lombardi, 268 Mont. 369, 886 P.2d 931 (Mont.1994)—**§ 2.17, n. 16; § 2.23, n. 2; § 18.21, n. 14.**

Casas v. Thompson, 228 Cal.Rptr. 33, 720 P.2d 921 (Cal.1986)—**§ 14.11, n. 1.**

Casdagli v. Casdagli, [1919] A.C. 145 (1918)—**§ 4.32, n. 1.**

Casey v. Manson Const. & Engineering Co., 247 Or. 274, 428 P.2d 898 (Or.1967)— **§ 2.16, n. 8; § 17.5, n. 5; § 17.26, n. 1;**

§ 17.27; § 17.27, n. 1; § 17.42, n. 12; § 18.20, n. 11.

Caskie v. Webster, 5 F.Cas. 271 (C.C.E.D.Pa.1851)—**§ 19.30, n. 7.**

Casper v. Cunard Line, Ltd., 560 F.Supp. 240 (E.D.Pa.1983)—**§ 2.14, n. 16.**

Cassidy, Succession of, 5 So. 292 (La. 1888)—**§ 19.5, n. 7.**

Cassidy Commission Co. v. United States, 387 F.2d 875 (10th Cir.1967)—**§ 3.51, n. 10.**

Casteel v. Casteel, 45 N.J.Super. 338, 132 A.2d 529 (N.J.Super.A.D.1957)— **§ 22.26, n. 1.**

Castillo v. Santa Fe Shipping Corp., 827 F.Supp. 1269 (S.D.Tex.1992)—**§ 17.63, n. 24.**

Castro v. Illies, 22 Tex. 479 (Tex.1858)— **§ 14.9, n. 13; § 14.15, n. 4, 9.**

Casualty Assur. Risk Ins. Brokerage Co. v. Dillon, 976 F.2d 596 (9th Cir.1992)— **§ 7.8, n. 13.**

Catalano v. Catalano, 148 Conn. 288, 170 A.2d 726 (Conn.1961)—**§ 13.2, n. 10; § 13.11, n. 3; § 13.15, n. 4.**

Catchpole v. Narramore, 102 Ariz. 248, 428 P.2d 105 (Ariz.1967)—**§ 19.10, n. 2.**

Catlett v. Catlett, 412 P.2d 942 (Okla. 1966)—**§ 15.34, n. 1.**

Cato v. Cato, 27 Conn.App. 142, 605 A.2d 558 (Conn.App.1992)—**§ 15.28, n. 1.**

Caton v. Leach Corp., 896 F.2d 939 (5th Cir.1990)—**§ 17.40, n. 28.**

Caulfield v. Sullivan, 85 N.Y. 153 (N.Y. 1881)—**§ 20.13, n. 5.**

Cayce v. Carter Oil Co., 618 F.2d 669 (10th Cir.1980)—**§ 14.5, n. 1.**

C & C Products, Inc. v. Premier Indus. Corp., 290 Ala. 179, 275 So.2d 124 (Ala. 1972)—**§ 23.7, n. 6.**

CCR Data Systems, Inc. v. Panasonic Communications & Systems Co., 1995 WL 54380 (D.N.H.1995)—**§ 18.6, n. 1.**

Cearley v. Cearley, 544 S.W.2d 661 (Tex. 1976)—**§ 14.11, n. 1.**

Cecere v. Aetna Ins. Co., 145 N.H. 660, 766 A.2d 696 (N.H.2001)—**§ 17.56, n. 20; § 18.26, n. 6.**

Cellutech, Inc. v. Centennial Cellular Corp., 871 F.Supp. 46 (D.D.C.1994)—**§ 8.5, n. 5.**

Celotex Corp., In re, 124 F.3d 619 (4th Cir.1997)—**§ 10.7, n. 19.**

Celotex Corp., Matter of, 152 B.R. 652 (Bkrtcy.M.D.Fla.1993)—**§ 18.21, n. 4.**

Central Contracting Co. v. C. E. Youngdahl & Co., 418 Pa. 122, 209 A.2d 810 (Pa. 1965)—**§ 11.5, n. 3.**

Central Mfrs. Mut. Ins. Co. of Van Wert, Ohio v. Friedman, 213 Ark. 9, 209 S.W.2d 102 (Ark.1948)—**§ 4.13, n. 1.**

Central Standard Life Ins. Co. v. Gardner, 17 Ill.2d 220, 161 N.E.2d 278 (Ill. 1959)—**§ 19.6, n. 6.**

Central States, Southeast and Southwest Areas Pension Fund v. Brown, 587 F.Supp. 1067 (N.D.Ill.1984)—§ **11.14, n. 6.**

Central States Southeast and Southwest Areas Pension Fund v. Kraftco, Inc., 589 F.Supp. 1061 (M.D.Tenn.1984)— § **18.21, n. 11.**

Centronics Data Computer Corp. v. Mannesmann, A. G., 432 F.Supp. 659 (D.N.H.1977)—§ **9.7, n. 3.**

Cepeda v. Cohane, 233 F.Supp. 465 (S.D.N.Y.1964)—§ **12.11, n. 8.**

Cerro De Pasco Copper Corp. v. Knut Knutsen, O.A.S., 187 F.2d 990 (2nd Cir. 1951)—§ **11.2, n. 10;** § **11.3, n. 5.**

Certain Property Located in Borough of Manhattan, City, County and State of N. Y., United States v., 344 F.2d 142 (2nd Cir.1965)—§ **3.51, n. 10.**

Certain–Teed Products Corp. v. Second Judicial Dist. Court, 87 Nev. 18, 479 P.2d 781 (Nev.1971)—§ **5.14, n. 18.**

Chabert v. Bacquie, 694 So.2d 805 (Fla.App. 4 Dist.1997)—§ **24.44, n. 12.**

Chadwick's Estate, In re, 309 So.2d 587 (Fla.App. 2 Dist.1975)—§ **22.8, n. 1.**

Chalker v. Birmingham & N. W. Ry. Co., 249 U.S. 522, 39 S.Ct. 366, 63 L.Ed. 748 (1919)—§ **3.32, n. 5, 9.**

Challoner v. Day & Zimmermann, Inc., 546 F.2d 26 (5th Cir.1977)—§ **17.7, n. 15.**

Challoner v. Day & Zimmermann, Inc., 512 F.2d 77 (5th Cir.1975)—§ **3.36, n. 5;** § **3.47;** § **3.47, n. 4, 5;** § **3.48, n. 19.**

Chambco, Div. of Chamberlin Waterproofing & Roofing, Inc. v. Urban Masonry Corp., 338 Md. 417, 659 A.2d 297 (Md. 1995)—§ **2.21, n. 3;** § **17.8, n. 4.**

Chamberlain v. Chamberlain, 43 N.Y. 424 (N.Y.1871)—§ **20.7, n. 3;** § **20.9, n. 9;** § **21.2, n. 9.**

Chambers v. Baltimore & O.R. Co., 207 U.S. 142, 28 S.Ct. 34, 52 L.Ed. 143 (1907)—§ **3.32, n. 10.**

Chambers v. Chambers, 122 Misc.2d 671, 471 N.Y.S.2d 958 (N.Y.Sup.1983)— § **15.24, n. 7.**

Chambers v. Dakotah Charter, Inc., 488 N.W.2d 63 (S.D.1992)—§ **2.16, n. 21;** § **2.19, n. 18;** § **2.23, n. 1;** § **17.7, n. 7;** § **17.26, n. 1, 20;** § **17.39, n. 14.**

Champagnie v. W. E. O'Neil Const. Co., 77 Ill.App.3d 136, 32 Ill.Dec. 609, 395 N.E.2d 990 (Ill.App. 1 Dist.1979)— § **2.17, n. 10;** § **2.19, n. 10.**

Champlain Enterprises, Inc. v. United States, 945 F.Supp. 468 (N.D.N.Y. 1996)—§ **17.40, n. 28;** § **17.76, n. 31;** § **18.1, n. 18.**

Chan v. Korean Air Lines, Ltd., 490 U.S. 122, 109 S.Ct. 1676, 104 L.Ed.2d 113 (1989)—§ **3.57, n. 21.**

Chance v. E. I. Du Pont De Nemours & Co., Inc., 371 F.Supp. 439 (E.D.N.Y.1974)— § **3.14, n. 2;** § **17.32, n. 1.**

Chancellor v. Lawrence, 501 F.Supp. 997 (N.D.Ill.1980)—§ **3.46, n. 4.**

Chancey v. State, 141 Ga. 54, 80 S.E. 287 (Ga.1913)—§ **4.19, n. 4.**

Chandhary v. Chandhary, [1985] Fam. 19 (C.A.)—§ **15.24, n. 2.**

Chandler v. Humphrey, 177 Wash. 402, 31 P.2d 1012 (Wash.1934)—§ **3.10, n. 5.**

Chapman, In re, 466 N.E.2d 777 (Ind.App. 3 Dist.1984)—§ **15.42, n. 9.**

Chapman v. Chapman, 129 Ill. 386, 21 N.E. 806 (Ill.1889)—§ **4.34, n. 1.**

Chapman v. Chapman, 284 A.D. 504, 132 N.Y.S.2d 707 (N.Y.A.D. 3 Dept.1954)— § **12.4, n. 1.**

Chappell's Estate, In re, 124 Wash. 128, 213 P. 684 (Wash.1923)—§ **21.2, n. 11;** § **21.12, n. 3.**

Charash v. Oberlin College, 14 F.3d 291 (6th Cir.1994)—§ **19.14, n. 9.**

Charles L. Bowman & Co. v. Erwin, 468 F.2d 1293 (5th Cir.1972)—§ **18.39, n. 6.**

Charles T. Dougherty Co. v. Krimke, 144 A. 617 (N.J.Err. & App.1929)—§ **19.13, n. 11.**

Charnock v. Taylor, 223 N.C. 360, 26 S.E.2d 911 (N.C.1943)—§ **17.6, n. 3.**

Charr v. Hazim Ulusahim, [1956] D. Jurisp. I, 61—§ **24.38, n. 11.**

Chartener v. Kice, 270 F.Supp. 432 (E.D.N.Y.1967)—§ **3.11, n. 4.**

Charter Finance Co. v. Henderson, 60 Ill.2d 323, 326 N.E.2d 372 (Ill.1975)—§ **23.8, n. 1.**

Chase, In re, 195 N.C. 143, 141 S.E. 471 (N.C.1928)—§ **22.26, n. 1.**

Chase, Matter of Estate of, 127 A.D.2d 415, 515 N.Y.S.2d 348 (N.Y.A.D. 3 Dept. 1987)—§ **16.6, n. 3.**

Chase Commercial Corp. v. Owen, 32 Mass. App.Ct. 248, 588 N.E.2d 705 (Mass.App. Ct.1992)—§ **18.5, n. 2.**

Chase Manhattan Bank, N.A. v. CVE, Inc., 206 F.Supp.2d 900 (M.D.Tenn.2002)— § **3.4, n. 7.**

Chase Manhattan Bank, N.A. v. Greenbriar North Section II, 835 S.W.2d 720 (Tex. App.-Hous. (1 Dist.) 1992)—§ **18.27, n. 4.**

Chase Manhattan Bank, N.A. v. Hoffman, 665 F.Supp. 73 (D.Mass.1987)—§ **24.6, n. 2.**

Chatard's Settlement, Re, 1899 WL 11857 (Ch D 1899)—§ **22.25, n. 16.**

Chatham Steel Corp. v. Brown, 858 F.Supp. 1130 (N.D.Fla.1994)—§ **9.2, n. 5, 21.**

Chaudry v. Chaudry, 159 N.J.Super. 566, 388 A.2d 1000 (N.J.Super.A.D.1978)— § **15.24, n. 4.**

Cheang Thye Phin v. Tan Ah Loy (Deceased), 1919 WL 13679 (Privy Council 1919)—§ **13.17, n. 8.**

Checkers, Simon & Rosner v. Lurie Corp., 864 F.2d 1338 (7th Cir.1988)—§ **19.2, n. 1.**

Cheever v. Wilson, 76 U.S. 108, 19 L.Ed. 604 (1869)—§ **4.33, n. 3; § 4.34, n. 1.**

Chemung Canal Bank v. Lowery, 93 U.S. 72, 23 L.Ed. 806 (1876)—§ **3.33; § 3.33, n. 1.**

Chenery v. Inhabitants of Waltham, 62 Mass. 327 (Mass.1851)—§ **4.19, n. 4.**

Cherokee Laboratories, Inc. v. Rogers, 398 P.2d 520 (Okla.1965)—§ **17.9, n. 3.**

Cherokee Nation v. State of Ga., 30 U.S. 1, 8 L.Ed. 25 (1831)—§ **11.17, n. 11.**

Cherokee Pump & Equipment Inc. v. Aurora Pump, 38 F.3d 246 (5th Cir.1994)— § **18.4, n. 16.**

Cherry, Bekaert & Holland v. Brown, 582 So.2d 502 (Ala.1991)—§ **2.23, n. 9; § 18.21, n. 3.**

Cherry Creek Dodge, Inc. v. Carter, 733 P.2d 1024 (Wyo.1987)—§ **2.21, n. 46; § 18.21, n. 13.**

Chertok v. Chertok, 208 A.D. 161, 203 N.Y.S. 163 (N.Y.A.D. 1 Dept.1924)— § **15.24, n. 4.**

Cherun v. Frishman, 236 F.Supp. 292 (D.D.C 1964)—§ **5.21, n. 11; § 24.35, n. 8; § 24.42, n. 7.**

Chesapeake Utilities Corp. v. American Home Assur. Co., 704 F.Supp. 551 (D.Del.1989)—§ **18.1, n. 27.**

Chew v. Dietrich, 143 F.3d 24 (2nd Cir. 1998)—§ **5.10, n. 26.**

Chewning v. Chewning, 20 N.C.App. 283, 201 S.E.2d 353 (N.C.App.1973)—§ **17.7, n. 7.**

Chiasson v. R. E. A. Exp. Co., 269 F.Supp. 685 (D.N.H.1966)—§ **3.10, n. 3.**

Chicago & N.W.R. Co. v. Ohle, 117 U.S. 123, 6 S.Ct. 632, 29 L.Ed. 837 (1886)— § **4.20, n. 2.**

Chick Kam Choo v. Exxon Corp., 486 U.S. 140, 108 S.Ct. 1684, 100 L.Ed.2d 127 (1988)—§ **11.8, n. 6.**

Chicot County Drainage Dist. v. Baxter State Bank, 308 U.S. 371, 60 S.Ct. 317, 84 L.Ed. 329 (1940)—§ **5.17, n. 9; § 5.21, n. 6.**

Child by R.K., Matter of Adoption of, 303 N.J.Super. 182, 696 A.2d 116 (N.J.Super.Ch.1997)—§ **16.5, n. 7.**

Child by T.W.C., Matter of Adoption of, 270 N.J.Super. 225, 636 A.2d 1083 (N.J.Super.A.D.1994)—§ **16.5, n. 9.**

Childs' Estate, In re, 63 Misc.2d 470, 312 N.Y.S.2d 390 (N.Y.Sur.1970)—§ **20.13, n. 6.**

Chilean Line Inc. v. United States, 344 F.2d 757 (2nd Cir.1965)—§ **10.6, n. 34.**

Chilean Nitrate Corp. v. M/V HANS LEONHARDT, 810 F.Supp. 732 (E.D.La. 1992)—§ **12.7, n. 3.**

Chinchilla v. Foreign Tankship Corp., 195 Misc. 895, 91 N.Y.S.2d 213 (N.Y.City Ct.1949)—§ **2.14, n. 18; § 17.1, n. 1; § 18.1, n. 20.**

Chipman, Limited, v. Thomas B. Jeffrey Co., 251 U.S. 373, 40 S.Ct. 172, 64 L.Ed. 314 (1920)—§ **5.3, n. 18.**

Chisholm v. Chisholm, 105 Fla. 402, 141 So. 302 (Fla.1932)—§ **4.33, n. 3.**

Chlystek v. Kane, 540 F.2d 171 (3rd Cir. 1976)—§ **13.9, n. 1.**

Choate v. Ransom, 74 Nev. 100, 323 P.2d 700 (Nev.1958)—§ **12.15, n. 8; § 14.9, n. 1, 13.**

Choike v. City of Detroit, 94 Mich.App. 703, 290 N.W.2d 58 (Mich.App.1980)—§ **4.13, n. 2; § 4.22, n. 2.**

Chongris v. Board of Appeals of Town of Andover, 614 F.Supp. 998 (D.Mass. 1985)—§ **24.25, n. 2.**

Christensen v. Christensen, 121 R.I. 272, 397 A.2d 900 (R.I.1979)—§ **19.8, n. 5, 14.**

Christiansen v. Elwin G. Smith, Inc., 598 A.2d 176 (Me.1991)—§ **9.5, n. 7.**

Christner v. Chicago, R. I. & P. Ry. Co., 228 Mo.App. 220, 64 S.W.2d 752 (Mo.App. 1933)—§ **3.11, n. 2.**

Christoff's Estate, In re, 411 Pa. 419, 192 A.2d 737 (Pa.1963)—§ **16.5, n. 3; § 24.35, n. 7.**

Christopher v. Christopher, 198 Ga. 361, 31 S.E.2d 818 (Ga.1944)—§ **24.17, n. 2.**

Christus St. Joseph's Health Systems v. Witt Biomedical Corp., 805 So.2d 1050 (Fla.App. 5 Dist.2002)—§ **8.5, n. 5.**

Christy v. Vest, 36 Iowa 285 (Iowa 1873)— § **22.8, n. 1.**

Chrysler Corp. v. Batten, 264 Ga. 723, 450 S.E.2d 208 (Ga.1994)—§ **17.76, n. 2.**

Chrysler Corp. v. Skyline Indus. Services, Inc., 448 Mich. 113, 528 N.W.2d 698 (Mich.1995)—§ **2.17, n. 16; § 2.19, n. 17; § 2.23, n. 2, 6; § 18.21, n. 14.**

Chubbuck v. Holloway, 182 Minn. 225, 234 N.W. 314 (Minn.1931)—§ **17.6, n. 6.**

Chumos v. Chumos, 105 Kan. 374, 184 P. 736 (Kan.1919)—§ **4.41, n. 1.**

Church v. Hubbart, 6 U.S. 187, 2 L.Ed. 249 (1804)—§ **12.15, n. 3.**

Church v. Massey, 697 So.2d 407 (Miss. 1997)—§ **17.43, n. 16.**

Churchill v. Jackson, 132 Ga. 666, 64 S.E. 691 (Ga.1909)—§ **4.41, n. 6.**

Ciampittiello v. Campitello, 134 Conn. 51, 54 A.2d 669 (Conn.1947)—§ **3.15, n. 5.**

Cianci v. Nationwide Ins. Co., 659 A.2d 662 (R.I.1995)—§ **17.59, n. 3.**

Cianfrani v. Kalmar–Ac Handling Systems, Inc., 1995 WL 563289 (D.N.J.1995)— § **17.74, n. 20; § 17.78, n. 12.**

CIBC Mellon Trust Co. v. Mora Hotel Corp. N.V., 296 A.D.2d 81, 743 N.Y.S.2d 408 (N.Y.A.D. 1 Dept.2002)—§ **24.42, n. 1.**

Ciena Corp. v. Jarrard, 203 F.3d 312 (4th Cir.2000)—§ **8.4, n. 9; § 18.7, n. 9.**

Cihlar, In re, 216 Iowa 327, 249 N.W. 254 (Iowa 1933)—§ **22.25, n. 18.**

Cincinnati Ins. Co. v. Leeper, 1998 WL 123108 (Ohio App. 6 Dist.1998)— § **17.56, n. 9.**

Cincinnati Sub–Zero Products, Inc. v. Augustine Medical, Inc., 800 F.Supp. 1549 (S.D.Ohio 1992)—§ **10.17, n. 2.**

Cipolla v. Shaposka, 439 Pa. 563, 267 A.2d 854 (Pa.1970)—§ **2.16, n. 9; § 2.25, n. 15; § 17.12, n. 7, 12; § 17.13; § 17.13, n. 18; § 17.31, n. 7; § 17.37, n. 5; § 17.42; § 17.42, n. 2, 17; § 17.76, n. 21.**

Circus Circus Reno, Inc., State ex rel. v. Pope, 317 Or. 151, 854 P.2d 461 (Or. 1993)—§ **5.10, n. 34.**

Cissna v. Tennessee, 246 U.S. 289, 38 S.Ct. 306, 62 L.Ed. 720 (1918)—§ **3.50, n. 3.**

C. I. T. Corp. v. Edwards, 418 P.2d 685 (Okla.1966)—§ **12.19, n. 15.**

Citizens and Southern Nat. Bank v. Bruce, 420 F.Supp. 795 (E.D.Mo.1976)— § **18.21, n. 14; § 18.29, n. 3.**

Citizens Bank & Trust Co. v. Glaser, 70 N.J. 72, 357 A.2d 753 (N.J.1976)— § **4.13, n. 6; § 4.21, n. 1.**

Citizens First Bank v. Intercontinental Exp., Inc., 77 Or.App. 655, 713 P.2d 1097 (Or.App.1986)—§ **18.20, n. 11; § 18.37, n. 8.**

Citizens' Nat. Bank of Baltimore v. Sharp, 53 Md. 521 (Md.1880)—§ **22.16, n. 6.**

Citizens Nat. Bank of Orange, Va., v. Waugh, 78 F.2d 325 (4th Cir.1935)— § **18.4, n. 7.**

Citro Florida, Inc. v. Citrovale, S.A., 760 F.2d 1231 (11th Cir.1985)—§ **11.6, n. 2.**

Citrynell v. Citrynell, 86 Misc.2d 60, 382 N.Y.S.2d 256 (N.Y.Sup.1976)—§ **13.9, n. 5, 8.**

City Bank Farmers Trust Co., Application of, 9 Misc.2d 183, 166 N.Y.S.2d 772 (N.Y.Sup.1957)—§ **21.6, n. 4.**

City Bank Farmers Trust Co., Matter of, 11 Misc.2d 660, 174 N.Y.S.2d 544 (N.Y.Sup. 1958)—§ **22.25, n. 9.**

City Bank Farmers Trust Co. v. Cheek, 202 Misc. 303, 110 N.Y.S.2d 434 (N.Y.Sup. 1952)—§ **21.3, n. 17.**

City of (see name of city)

Cladis v. Cladis, 512 So.2d 271 (Fla.App. 4 Dist.1987)—§ **14.15, n. 1.**

Clagett v. King, 308 A.2d 245 (D.C.1973)— § **15.9, n. 6; § 15.21, n. 3.**

Clanton v. Barnes, 50 Ala. 260 (Ala.1874)— § **19.31, n. 8.**

Clark, In re Estate of, 288 N.Y.S.2d 993, 236 N.E.2d 152 (N.Y.1968)—§ **14.12, n. 9; § 17.30, n. 14; § 20.5, n. 7; § 20.9, n. 9; § 20.13, n. 2; § 20.14; § 20.14, n. 5, 7.**

Clark v. Allen, 331 U.S. 503, 67 S.Ct. 1431, 91 L.Ed. 1633 (1947)—§ **11.13, n. 8; § 20.17, n. 7.**

Clark v. Clark, 107 N.H. 351, 222 A.2d 205 (N.H.1966)—§ **2.13, n. 15; § 2.16, n. 10; § 2.23, n. 6; § 2.25, n. 3; § 3.13, n. 4, 5; § 17.21; § 17.21, n. 13, 22; § 17.39, n. 8.**

Clark v. Clark, 80 Nev. 52, 389 P.2d 69 (Nev.1964)—§ **24.2, n. 7.**

Clark v. Clark, 30 A. 81 (N.J.Ch.1894)— § **13.6, n. 2.**

Clark v. Eltinge, 29 Wash. 215, 69 P. 736 (Wash.1902)—§ **14.16, n. 10.**

Clark v. Favalora, 722 So.2d 82 (La.App. 1 Cir.1998)—§ **17.77, n. 3.**

Clark v. Gordon, 313 S.C. 240, 437 S.E.2d 144 (S.C.App.1993)—§ **16.5, n. 9.**

Clark v. Graham, 19 U.S. 577, 5 L.Ed. 334 (1821)—§ **19.2, n. 4.**

Clark v. Jelinek, 90 Idaho 592, 414 P.2d 892 (Idaho 1966)—§ **4.41, n. 1.**

Clark v. Jeter, 486 U.S. 456, 108 S.Ct. 1910, 100 L.Ed.2d 465 (1988)—§ **16.3, n. 10, 11.**

Clark v. Moran Towing & Transp. Co., Inc., 738 F.Supp. 1023 (E.D.La.1990)—§ **8.4, n. 2.**

Clark v. Robinson, 88 Ill. 498 (Ill.1878)— § **4.27, n. 11.**

Clark v. Rockwell, 190 W.Va. 49, 435 S.E.2d 664 (W.Va.1993)—§ **2.17, n. 11; § 2.23, n. 5; § 18.21, n. 14.**

Clark v. Tarbell, 58 N.H. 88 (N.H.1877)— § **19.13, n. 8.**

Clarke, Appeal of, 70 Conn. 483, 40 A. 111 (Conn.1898)—§ **20.7, n. 3.**

Clarke, Appeal of, 70 Conn. 195, 39 A. 155 (Conn.1898)—§ **20.13, n. 5.**

Clarke v. Clarke, 423 N.W.2d 818 (S.D. 1988)—§ **15.10, n. 2.**

Clarke v. Clarke, 178 U.S. 186, 20 S.Ct. 873, 44 L.Ed. 1028 (1900)—§ **20.2; § 20.2, n. 1, 6; § 22.4, n. 7.**

Clarke v. Sound Advice Live, Inc., 221 A.D.2d 227, 633 N.Y.S.2d 490 (N.Y.A.D. 1 Dept.1995)—§ **17.48, n. 11.**

Clark's Estate, In re, 495 F.2d 102, 161 U.S.App.D.C. 276 (D.C.Cir.1973)— § **21.6, n. 5.**

Clark's Estate, In re, 148 Cal. 108, 82 P. 760 (Cal.1905)—§ **22.2, n. 3; § 22.3, n. 15.**

Clarkson v. Finance Co. of America at Baltimore, 328 F.2d 404 (4th Cir.1964)— § **18.1, n. 3; § 18.5, n. 12; § 18.6, n. 4.**

Clarkson v. MFA Mut. Ins. Co., 413 S.W.2d 10 (Mo.App.1967)—§ **4.13, n. 1.**

Clarkson Co. Ltd. v. Shaheen, 660 F.2d 506 (2nd Cir.1981)—§ **12.18, n. 8.**

Clark's Will, In re, 59 N.M. 433, 285 P.2d 795 (N.M.1955)—§ **14.7, n. 3, 5.**

Clay v. Brittingham, 34 Md. 675 (Md. 1871)—§ **22.25, n. 21.**

Clay v. Sun Ins. Office, Limited, 377 U.S. 179, 84 S.Ct. 1197, 12 L.Ed.2d 229 (1964)—§ **3.22; § 3.22, n. 2, 4; § 18.26, n. 14, 16.**

Clayman v. Goodman Properties, Inc., 518 F.2d 1026, 171 U.S.App.D.C. 88 (D.C.Cir.1973)—§ **18.37, n. 14.**

Clearfield Trust Co. v. United States, 318 U.S. 363, 318 U.S. 744, 63 S.Ct. 573, 87 L.Ed. 838 (1943)—§ **3.51, n. 3; § 3.54, n. 7; § 3.55, n. 9.**

Clearwater Mercantile Co. v. Roberts, Johnson, Rand Shoe Co., 51 Fla. 176, 40 So. 436 (Fla.1906)—§ **10.13, n. 3.**

Clemens v. Kinsley, 72 Idaho 251, 239 P.2d 266 (Idaho 1951)—§ **4.37, n. 9; § 5.23, n. 1, 8.**

Clements v. Macaulay, 1866 WL 6415 (2 Div 1866)—§ **11.8, n. 2.**

Clendenning v. Conrad, 91 Va. 410, 21 S.E. 818 (Va.1895)—§ **22.25, n. 16.**

C & L Enterprises, Inc. v. Citizen Band Potawatomi Indian Tribe of Oklahoma, 532 U.S. 411, 121 S.Ct. 1589, 149 L.Ed.2d 623 (2001)—§ **11.17, n. 22.**

Clesas v. Hurley Mach. Co., 52 R.I. 69, 157 A. 426 (R.I.1931)—§ **10.15, n. 4.**

Cleveland v. United States Printing Ink, Inc., 218 Conn. 181, 588 A.2d 194 (Conn.1991)—§ **17.59, n. 9, 11, 16.**

Cleveland Trust Co. v. Shuman, 39 Ohio Misc. 136, 317 N.E.2d 256 (Ohio Com.Pl. 1974)—§ **21.13, n. 2.**

Click v. Thuron Industries, Inc., 475 S.W.2d 715 (Tex.1972)—§ **3.10, n. 3.**

Clinton v. Janger, 583 F.Supp. 284 (N.D.Ill. 1984)—§ **11.6, n. 8.**

Clopton v. Booker, 27 Ark. 482 (Ark. 1872)—§ **22.19, n. 18.**

Clouse v. Andonian, 189 F.Supp. 78 (N.D.Ind.1960)—§ **6.4, n. 6.**

Cloverleaf Cold Storage Co., United States v., 286 F.Supp. 680 (N.D.Iowa 1968)— § **3.51, n. 7.**

C.M.A., In re, 557 N.W.2d 353 (Minn.App. 1996)—§ **16.5, n. 1.**

CNA Ins. Co. v. Colman, 222 Conn. 769, 610 A.2d 1257 (Conn.1992)—§ **17.56, n. 16.**

Coakes v. Arabian American Oil Co., 831 F.2d 572 (5th Cir.1987)—§ **11.9, n. 5.**

Coastal Mall, Inc. v. Askins, 265 S.C. 307, 217 S.E.2d 725 (S.C.1975)—§ **7.7, n. 8.**

Coastal States Gas Corp. v. Atlantic Tankers, Ltd., 546 F.2d 15 (2nd Cir.1976)— § **18.1, n. 20.**

Coastal Steel Corp. v. Tilghman Wheelabrator Ltd., 709 F.2d 190 (3rd Cir.1983)— § **11.3, n. 19.**

Coats v. Chicago, R.I. & P. Ry. Co., 239 Ill. 154, 87 N.E. 929 (Ill.1909)—§ **18.4, n. 7.**

Coats v. Penrod Drilling Corp., 61 F.3d 1113 (5th Cir.1995)—§ **17.63, n. 22.**

Coats Co., Inc. v. Vulcan Equipment Co., Ltd., 459 F.Supp. 654 (N.D.Ill.1978)— § **9.7, n. 3.**

Coburn's Will, In re, 9 Misc. 437, 61 N.Y.St. Rep. 743, 30 N.Y.S. 383 (N.Y.Sur. 1894)—§ **20.12, n. 5, 6.**

Cochise College Park, Inc., In re, 703 F.2d 1339 (9th Cir.1983)—§ **23.15, n. 14.**

Cochran v. Benton, 126 Ind. 58, 25 N.E. 870 (Ind.1890)—§ **19.3, n. 1, 6.**

Cochran v. Cochran, 196 N.Y. 86, 89 N.E. 470 (N.Y.1909)—§ **4.44, n. 2.**

Cochran v. Ellsworth, 126 Cal.App.2d 429, 272 P.2d 904 (Cal.App. 2 Dist.1954)— § **2.21, n. 64.**

Cocke v. Duke University, 260 N.C. 1, 131 S.E.2d 909 (N.C.1963)—§ **21.6, n. 6.**

Codagnone v. Perrin, 351 F.Supp. 1126 (D.R.I.1972)—§ **4.26, n. 1, 4, 8.**

Coe v. Coe, 334 U.S. 378, 68 S.Ct. 1094, 92 L.Ed. 1451 (1948)—§ **4.7, n. 2; § 15.9, n. 4; § 15.17, n. 12.**

Coe's Estate, In re, 42 N.J. 485, 201 A.2d 571 (N.J.1964)—§ **20.13, n. 4.**

Coe's Estate, In re, 130 Iowa 307, 106 N.W. 743 (Iowa 1906)—§ **20.3, n. 9.**

Cofield v. Randolph County Com'n, 844 F.Supp. 1499 (M.D.Ala.1994)—§ **7.6, n. 10.**

Cohen v. Beneficial Indus. Loan Corp., 337 U.S. 541, 69 S.Ct. 1221, 93 L.Ed. 1528 (1949)—§ **3.37, n. 5.**

Cohen v. Hathaway, 595 F.Supp. 579 (D.Mass.1984)—§ **3.50, n. 3.**

Cohen v. United States, 297 F.2d 760 (9th Cir.1962)—§ **4.27, n. 1.**

Cohen's Estate, In re, 149 Misc. 765, 269 N.Y.S. 235 (N.Y.Sur.1933)—§ **22.21, n. 9.**

Cohn v. Heymann, 544 So.2d 1242 (La.App. 3 Cir.1989)—§ **20.14, n. 1.**

Colburn, Appeal of, 74 Conn. 463, 51 A. 139 (Conn.1902)—§ **19.29, n. 3.**

Colby v. Colby, 78 Nev. 150, 369 P.2d 1019 (Nev.1962)—§ **15.12; § 15.12, n. 2, 8; § 24.14; § 24.14, n. 4; § 24.29, n. 8.**

Cole v. Doe, 77 Mich.App. 138, 258 N.W.2d 165 (Mich.App.1977)—§ **7.9, n. 7.**

Cole v. Lee, 435 S.W.2d 283 (Tex.Civ.App.-Dallas 1968)—§ **19.3, n. 8.**

Cole v. Steinlauf, 144 Conn. 629, 136 A.2d 744 (Conn.1957)—§ **19.2, n. 5; § 19.4, n. 1.**

Coleman v. Coleman, 361 Pa.Super. 446, 522 A.2d 1115 (Pa.Super.1987)— § **15.28, n. 2.**

Colhoun v. Greyhound Lines, Inc., 265 So.2d 18 (Fla.1972)—§ **3.11, n. 4.**

Collins v. McCook, 17 La.App. 415, 136 So. 204 (La.App. 2 Cir.1931)—§ **5.23, n. 4.**

Collins v. Trius, Inc., 663 A.2d 570 (Me. 1995)—§ **2.23, n. 1; § 17.26; § 17.26, n. 1, 21; § 17.36, n. 15; § 17.39, n. 16, 34.**

Collins v. Yancey, 55 N.J.Super. 514, 151 A.2d 68 (N.J.Super.L.1959)—§ **4.1, n. 2.**

Collins, Royal Bk., etc., In re v. Kroogh, [1986] 1 All E.R. 611—§ **20.14, n. 1.**

Colodny v. Krause, 141 Ga.App. 134, 232 S.E.2d 597 (Ga.App.1977)—§ **19.10, n. 2.**

Colorado v. Harbeck, 232 N.Y. 71, 133 N.E. 357 (N.Y.1921)—§ **11.13, n. 7.**

Colorado Energy Supply, Inc., Matter of, 728 F.2d 1283 (10th Cir.1984)—§ **23.12, n. 15.**

Colpitt v. Cheatham, 267 P.2d 1003 (Okla. 1954)—§ **16.1, n. 11.**

Colt Plumbing Co., Inc. v. Boisseau, 435 Pa.Super. 380, 645 A.2d 1350 (Pa.Super.1994)—§ **8.4, n. 8.**

Columb v. Columb, 161 Vt. 103, 633 A.2d 689 (Vt.1993)—§ **15.42, n. 9.**

Columbia Nastri & Carta Carbone S/p/A v. Columbia Ribbon & Carbon Mfg. Co., 367 F.2d 308 (2nd Cir.1966)—§ **18.44, n. 9.**

Colvin v. Hutchison, 338 Mo. 576, 92 S.W.2d 667 (Mo.1936)—§ **20.6, n. 17;** § **20.15, n. 3.**

Colvin v. Reed, 55 Pa. 375 (Pa.1867)— § **4.34, n. 1.**

Combined Properties v. American Mfrs. Mut. Ins. Co., 986 F.2d 1412 (4th Cir. 1993)—§ **18.21, n. 12.**

Combs v. Combs, 249 Ky. 155, 60 S.W.2d 368 (Ky.1933)—§ **5.5, n. 11.**

Combustion, Inc., In re, 960 F.Supp. 1056 (W.D.La.1997)—§ **18.26, n. 13.**

Comer v. Comer, 195 Ga. 79, 23 S.E.2d 420 (Ga.1942)—§ **20.13, n. 6.**

Commerce Consultants Intern., Inc. v. Vetrerie Riunite, S.p.A., 867 F.2d 697, 276 U.S.App.D.C. 81 (D.C.Cir.1989)—§ **11.3, n. 22.**

Commercial Discount Corp. v. King, 552 F.Supp. 841 (N.D.Ill.1982)—§ **3.47, n. 2.**

Commercial Union Ins. Co. v. Porter Hayden Co., 116 Md.App. 605, 698 A.2d 1167 (Md.App.1997)—§ **3.14, n. 3;** § **17.56, n. 9;** § **18.26, n. 13.**

Commercial Union Ins. Co. v. Porter Hayden Co., 97 Md.App. 442, 630 A.2d 261 (Md.App.1993)—§ **18.26, n. 12.**

Commissioner of Immigration at Port of New York, United States v., 298 F. 103 (S.D.N.Y.1924)—§ **13.6, n. 12.**

Commissioner v. ———— (see opposing party)

Commissioner's Subpoenas, In re, 325 F.3d 1287 (11th Cir.2003)—§ **12.8, n. 14.**

Commonwealth v. ———— (see opposing party)

Commonwealth ex rel. v. ———— (see opposing party and relator)

Commonwealth of (see name of Commonwealth)

Community Credit Co. v. Gillham, 191 Neb. 198, 214 N.W.2d 384 (Neb.1974)— § **19.19, n. 8.**

Compagnie d'Armament Maritime S.A. v. Companie Tunisienne de Navigation S.A., [1970] 3 W.L.R. 389 (H.L.)—§ **18.1, n. 19.**

Compagnie De Reassurance D'Ile de France v. New England Reinsurance Corp., 57 F.3d 56 (1st Cir.1995)—§ **18.38, n. 8.**

Compagnie Generale Transatlantique v. Rivers, 211 F. 294 (2nd Cir.1914)— § **12.19, n. 8.**

Compagnie Nationale Air France, People ex rel. v. Giliberto, 74 Ill.2d 90, 23 Ill.Dec. 106, 383 N.E.2d 977 (Ill.1978)—§ **3.57, n. 22.**

Compania de Gas de Nuevo Laredo, S. A. v. Entex, Inc., 686 F.2d 322 (5th Cir. 1982)—§ **11.13, n. 21.**

Compania De Inversiones Internacionales v. Industrial Mortg. Bank of Finland, 269 N.Y. 22, 198 N.E. 617 (N.Y.1935)— § **18.4, n. 8.**

Compania Ron Bacardi v. Bank of Nova Scotia, 193 F.Supp. 814 (S.D.N.Y. 1961)—§ **23.11, n. 4.**

Compco Corp. v. Day–Brite Lighting, Inc., 376 U.S. 234, 84 S.Ct. 779, 11 L.Ed.2d 669 (1964)—§ **17.53, n. 3.**

Competex, S.A. v. Labow, 613 F.Supp. 332 (S.D.N.Y.1985)—§ **24.40, n. 5.**

Complaint of (see name of party)

Complete Auto Transit, Inc. v. Brady, 430 U.S. 274, 97 S.Ct. 1076, 51 L.Ed.2d 326 (1977)—§ **11.16, n. 6.**

Compton's Adm'r v. Borderland Coal Co., 179 Ky. 695, 201 S.W. 20 (Ky.1918)— § **22.16, n. 4.**

CompuServe, Inc. v. Patterson, 89 F.3d 1257 (6th Cir.1996)—§ **9.3, n. 6, 16.**

Concord v. Rumney, 45 N.H. 423 (N.H. 1864)—§ **4.45, n. 2, 4.**

Condon v. Mutual Reserve Fund Life Ass'n, 89 Md. 99, 42 A. 944 (Md.1899)—§ **23.5, n. 2.**

Condos v. Sun State Painting, Inc., 450 N.E.2d 86 (Ind.App. 2 Dist.1983)—§ **8.6, n. 3.**

Conille v. Secretary of Housing and Urban Development, 840 F.2d 105 (1st Cir. 1988)—§ **3.52, n. 2.**

Conklin v. Horner, 38 Wis.2d 468, 157 N.W.2d 579 (Wis.1968)—§ **3.13, n. 4, 6;** § **17.21, n. 15, 27;** § **17.22;** § **17.22, n. 1;** § **17.39, n. 21.**

Conley v. Conley, 324 Mass. 530, 87 N.E.2d 153 (Mass.1949)—§ **4.37, n. 6.**

Conley v. Mathieson Alkali Works, 190 U.S. 406, 23 S.Ct. 728, 47 L.Ed. 1113 (1903)—§ **5.3, n. 16.**

Conley v. Moe, 7 Wash.2d 355, 110 P.2d 172 (Wash.1941)—§ **14.7, n. 3.**

Conley v. Walden, 171 Mont. 58, 555 P.2d 960 (Mont.1976)—§ **16.6, n. 2.**

Conlin v. Hutcheon, 560 F.Supp. 934 (D.Colo.1983)—§ **17.26, n. 1.**

Conlon by Conlon v. Heckler, 719 F.2d 788 (5th Cir.1983)—§ **15.28, n. 1.**

Conn v. ITT Aetna Finance Co., 105 R.I. 397, 252 A.2d 184 (R.I.1969)—§ **10.16, n. 8.**

Connecticut General Life Ins. Co. v. Boseman, 84 F.2d 701 (5th Cir.1936)— **§ 18.4, n. 7.**

Connecticut General Life Ins. Co. v. Johnson, 303 U.S. 77, 58 S.Ct. 436, 82 L.Ed. 673 (1938)—**§ 3.34, n. 3.**

Connecticut Mut. Life Ins. Co. v. Wyman, 718 F.2d 63 (3rd Cir.1983)—**§ 3.47, n. 2.**

Connecticut Mut. Life Ins. Co. of Hartford, Conn. v. Hansell, 194 Minn. 41, 259 N.W. 390 (Minn.1935)—**§ 19.10, n. 3.**

Connell v. Francisco, 127 Wash.2d 339, 898 P.2d 831 (Wash.1995)—**§ 15.1, n. 7.**

Connell v. Guardianship of Connell, 476 So.2d 1381 (Fla.App. 1 Dist.1985)— **§ 22.26, n. 1.**

Conner v. Elliott, 59 U.S. 591, 18 How. 591, 15 L.Ed. 497 (1855)—**§ 3.32, n. 2, 10.**

Conner v. Spencer, 304 F.2d 485 (9th Cir. 1962)—**§ 3.11, n. 3.**

Connolly v. Bell, 309 N.Y. 581, 132 N.E.2d 852 (N.Y.1956)—**§ 24.20, n. 2.**

Connolly v. Woolrich, 3 Low. Can. L.J. 14 (1867)—**§ 13.18, n. 8, 10, 14.**

Connor v. Connor, (1974) 1 N.Z.L.R. 632 (Sup.Ct.)—**§ 24.43, n. 1.**

Connor v. Hauch, 50 Md.App. 217, 437 A.2d 661 (Md.App.1981)—**§ 17.60, n. 6.**

Connors v. Cunard S.S. Co., 204 Mass. 310, 90 N.E. 601 (Mass.1910)—**§ 22.6, n. 1.**

Conopco, Inc. v. Roll Intern., 231 F.3d 82 (2nd Cir.2000)—**§ 24.2, n. 2; § 24.11, n. 1.**

Conover & Co. v. Chapman, 1831 WL 1580 (S.C.App.1831)—**§ 22.23, n. 4.**

Conrad v. Conrad, 275 Ala. 202, 153 So.2d 635 (Ala.1963)—**§ 4.26, n. 6.**

Conseco, Inc. v. Hickerson, 698 N.E.2d 816 (Ind.App.1998)—**§ 7.8, n. 14.**

Consolidated Bathurst, Ltd. v. Rederiaktiebolaget Gustaf Erikson, 645 F.Supp. 884 (S.D.Fla.1986)—**§ 11.6, n. 8.**

Consolidated Gold Fields PLC v. Minorco, S.A., 871 F.2d 252 (2nd Cir.1989)— **§ 17.53, n. 1.**

Consolidated Jewelers, Inc. v. Standard Financial Corp., 325 F.2d 31 (6th Cir. 1963)—**§ 18.6, n. 1, 4; § 18.7, n. 8, 12.**

Consolidated Mut. Ins. Co. v. Radio Foods Corp., 108 N.H. 494, 240 A.2d 47 (N.H. 1968)—**§ 2.17, n. 6; § 2.23, n. 2, 6; § 18.26, n. 13.**

Consolidated Sun Ray, Inc. v. Oppenstein, 335 F.2d 801 (8th Cir.1964)—**§ 18.37, n. 2.**

Consul General of Yugoslavia at Pittsburgh v. Pennsylvania, 375 U.S. 395, 84 S.Ct. 452, 11 L.Ed.2d 411 (1964)—**§ 20.17, n. 6.**

Conti v. Pneumatic Products Corp., 977 F.2d 978 (6th Cir.1992)—**§ 8.4, n. 3.**

Continental Cas. Co. v. Diversified Industries, Inc., 884 F.Supp. 937 (E.D.Pa. 1995)—**§ 17.52, n. 2.**

Continental Coffee Co. v. Clark's Estate, 84 Nev. 208, 438 P.2d 818 (Nev.1968)— **§ 22.21, n. 4.**

Continental Grain Export Corp. v. Ministry of War–Etka Co. Ltd., 603 F.Supp. 724 (S.D.N.Y.1984)—**§ 11.3, n. 23.**

Continental Illinois Nat. Bank and Trust Co. of Chicago v. Stanley, 606 F.Supp. 558 (N.D.Ill.1985)—**§ 11.14, n. 6.**

Continental Ins. Co. v. McKain, 820 F.Supp. 890 (E.D.Pa.1993)—**§ 4.26, n. 5.**

Continental–Midwest Corp. v. Hotel Sherman, Inc., 13 Ill.App.2d 188, 141 N.E.2d 400 (Ill.App. 1 Dist.1957)—**§ 24.24, n. 5.**

Continental Oil Co. v. Lane Wood & Co., 443 S.W.2d 698 (Tex.1969)—**§ 19.13, n. 1.**

Continental Tel. Corp. v. Weaver, 410 F.2d 1196 (5th Cir.1969)—**§ 23.7, n. 6.**

Continental–Wirt Electronics Corp. v. Sprague Elec. Co., 329 F.Supp. 959 (E.D.Pa.1971)—**§ 18.24, n. 7.**

Contra Costa County ex rel. Petersen v. Petersen, 234 Neb. 418, 451 N.W.2d 390 (Neb.1990)—**§ 15.9, n. 6.**

Convergys Corp. v. Keener, 276 Ga. 808, 582 S.E.2d 84 (Ga.2003)—**§ 2.21; § 2.21, n. 48; § 18.2, n. 11; § 18.5, n. 27; § 18.21, n. 5.**

Conway v. Chemical Leaman Tank Lines, Inc., 540 F.2d 837 (5th Cir.1976)— **§ 3.39, n. 7.**

Conway v. Ogier, 115 Ohio App. 251, 184 N.E.2d 681 (Ohio App. 10 Dist.1961)— **§ 17.5, n. 4.**

Cook v. Cameron, 733 S.W.2d 137 (Tex. 1987)—**§ 14.13, n. 4.**

Cook v. Carolina Freight Carriers Corp., 299 F.Supp. 192 (D.Del.1969)—**§ 13.6, n. 2.**

Cook v. Cook, 342 U.S. 126, 72 S.Ct. 157, 96 L.Ed. 146 (1951)—**§ 4.7, n. 2; § 15.9; § 15.9, n. 8; § 15.11, n. 3; § 15.17, n. 12.**

Cook v. Frazier, 765 S.W.2d 546 (Tex.App.-Fort Worth 1989)—**§ 19.9, n. 10.**

Cook v. Goodhue, 842 F.Supp. 1509 (N.D.N.Y.1994)—**§ 17.46; § 17.46, n. 8, 21.**

Cook v. Pryor, 251 Md. 41, 246 A.2d 271 (Md.1968)—**§ 17.7, n. 7.**

Cook v. Todd's Estate, 249 Iowa 1274, 90 N.W.2d 23 (Iowa 1958)—**§ 20.3, n. 4.**

Cooke, People v., 150 Colo. 52, 370 P.2d 896 (Colo.1962)—**§ 21.10, n. 7.**

Cooke v. Yarrington, 62 N.J. 123, 299 A.2d 400 (N.J.1973)—**§ 6.4, n. 6, 22.**

Cook's Estate, In re, 204 Misc. 704, 123 N.Y.S.2d 568 (N.Y.Sur.1953)—**§ 20.13, n. 2.**

Cooney v. Osgood Machinery, Inc., 81 N.Y.2d 66, 595 N.Y.S.2d 919, 612 N.E.2d 277 (N.Y.1993)—**§ 2.25, n. 19; § 17.26, n. 10; § 17.32; § 17.32, n. 18; § 17.42, n. 11.**

Cooper v. American Exp. Co., 593 F.2d 612 (5th Cir.1979)—§ **17.50, n. 48.**

Cooper v. Ateliers de la Motobecane, S.A., 456 N.Y.S.2d 728, 442 N.E.2d 1239 (N.Y. 1982)—§ **24.48, n. 8.**

Cooper v. Atlantic Federal Sav. & Loan Ass'n of Fort Lauderdale, 249 Md. 228, 239 A.2d 89 (Md.1968)—§ **19.10, n. 2.**

Cooper v. Beers, 143 Ill. 25, 33 N.E. 61 (Ill.1892)—§ **4.28, n. 4;** § **22.10, n. 2;** § **22.11, n. 1.**

Cooper v. Cherokee Village Development Co., 236 Ark. 37, 364 S.W.2d 158 (Ark. 1963)—§ **19.9, n. 10.**

Cooper v. Molko, 512 F.Supp. 563 (N.D.Cal. 1981)—§ **7.3, n. 1.**

Cooper v. Reynolds, 77 U.S. 308, 19 L.Ed. 931 (1870)—§ **5.2;** § **5.2, n. 14, 20;** § **5.3, n. 9.**

Copeland Planned Futures, Inc., v. Obenchain, 9 Wash.App. 32, 510 P.2d 654 (Wash.App. Div. 1 1973)—§ **12.19, n. 6;** § **24.14, n. 3.**

Coppedge v. Clinton, 72 F.2d 531 (10th Cir.1934)—§ **4.27, n. 11;** § **4.45, n. 2.**

Copperweld Steel Co. v. Demag–Mannesmann–Boehler, 347 F.Supp. 53 (W.D.Pa. 1972)—§ **11.3, n. 22.**

Corbett v. Stergios, 257 Iowa 1387, 137 N.W.2d 266 (Iowa 1965)—§ **16.7, n. 12.**

Corbett v. Stergios, 381 U.S. 124, 85 S.Ct. 1364, 14 L.Ed.2d 260 (1965)—§ **20.17, n. 6.**

Corbett v. Stergios, 256 Iowa 12, 126 N.W.2d 342 (Iowa 1964)—§ **16.7, n. 12.**

Corbin v. Federal Reserve Bank of New York, 475 F.Supp. 1060 (S.D.N.Y. 1979)—§ **23.14, n. 3.**

Cordoba v. Wiswall, 7 Ariz.App. 144, 436 P.2d 922 (Ariz.App.1968)—§ **22.11, n. 11;** § **22.12, n. 8.**

Core–Vent Corp. v. Nobel Industries AB, 11 F.3d 1482 (9th Cir.1993)—§ **5.12, n. 7;** § **5.15, n. 6;** § **7.2, n. 34.**

Corfield v. Coryell, 6 F.Cas. 546 (C.C.E.D.Pa.1823)—§ **3.32;** § **3.32, n. 3.**

Cornelison v. Chaney, 127 Cal.Rptr. 352, 545 P.2d 264 (Cal.1976)—§ **5.10, n. 12.**

Cornell v. Burr, 32 S.D. 1, 141 N.W. 1081 (S.D.1913)—§ **20.6, n. 8, 21;** § **22.4, n. 7.**

Corning's Will, In re, 159 Mich. 474, 124 N.W. 514 (Mich.1910)—§ **22.2, n. 1.**

Corporacion Venezolana de Fomento v. Vintero Sales Corp., 629 F.2d 786 (2nd Cir.1980)—§ **2.23, n. 8;** § **3.36, n. 1.**

Corrigan v. Bjork Shiley Corp., 182 Cal. App.3d 166, 227 Cal.Rptr. 247 (Cal.App. 2 Dist.1986)—§ **11.9, n. 5.**

Cortes v. Ryder Truck Rental, Inc., 220 Ill.App.3d 632, 163 Ill.Dec. 50, 581 N.E.2d 1 (Ill.App. 1 Dist.1991)—§ **3.4, n. 5;** § **17.8, n. 7.**

Cory v. Shierloh, 174 Cal.Rptr. 500, 629 P.2d 8 (Cal.1981)—§ **17.19, n. 2.**

Cory v. White, 457 U.S. 85, 102 S.Ct. 2325, 72 L.Ed.2d 694 (1982)—§ **4.5, n. 12.**

Cosby v. Shackelford, 408 F.2d 1144 (10th Cir.1969)—§ **20.13, n. 4.**

Cosme v. Whitin Mach. Works, Inc., 417 Mass. 643, 632 N.E.2d 832 (Mass. 1994)—§ **17.76, n. 25.**

Cosmopolitan Equities, Inc. v. Pacific Seafarers, Inc., 41 Misc.2d 772, 246 N.Y.S.2d 412 (N.Y.Sup.1963)—§ **18.24, n. 9.**

Cosulich Societa Triestina Di Navigazione v. Elting, 66 F.2d 534 (2nd Cir.1933)—§ **13.6, n. 12.**

Cotting v. De Sartiges, 17 R.I. 668, 24 A. 530 (R.I.1892)—§ **21.8, n. 1;** § **21.13, n. 5.**

Cotton Petroleum Corp. v. New Mexico, 490 U.S. 163, 109 S.Ct. 1698, 104 L.Ed.2d 209 (1989)—§ **11.17, n. 2.**

Coulombre v. Board of Registrars of Voters of Worcester, 3 Mass.App.Ct. 206, 326 N.E.2d 360 (Mass.App.Ct.1975)—§ **4.27, n. 11.**

County Asphalt, Inc. v. Lewis Welding & Engineering Corp., 323 F.Supp. 1300 (S.D.N.Y.1970)—§ **18.6, n. 1;** § **18.7, n. 2, 5.**

Courtney v. Courtney, 40 N.C.App. 291, 253 S.E.2d 2 (N.C.App.1979)—§ **19.8, n. 14.**

Courtright v. Courtright, 11 Dec.Rptr. 413 (Ohio Com. Pl. 1899)—§ **13.12, n. 1.**

Couzado v. United States By and Through its Drug Enforcement Admin. of the Dept. of Justice, 105 F.3d 1389 (11th Cir.1997)—§ **17.48, n. 19.**

Cove Tankers Corp. v. United Ship Repair, Inc., 528 F.Supp. 101 (S.D.N.Y.1981)—§ **17.63, n. 2.**

Cowans v. Ticonderoga Pulp & Paper Co., 219 A.D. 120, 219 N.Y.S. 284 (N.Y.A.D. 3 Dept.1927)—§ **24.35, n. 2.**

Cowden v. Jacobson, 165 Mass. 240, 43 N.E. 98 (Mass.1896)—§ **22.20, n. 35;** § **22.21, n. 8.**

Cox v. Cox, 262 S.C. 8, 202 S.E.2d 6 (S.C. 1974)—§ **16.6, n. 5.**

Cox v. Crow, 336 F.Supp. 761 (N.D.Tex. 1972)—§ **22.19, n. 9.**

Cox v. Harrison, 535 S.W.2d 78 (Ky.1975)—§ **20.6, n. 11.**

Cox v. Kansas City, 86 Kan. 298, 120 P. 553 (Kan.1912)—§ **22.7, n. 5.**

Cox v. Morrow, 14 Ark. 603 (Ark.1854)—§ **12.15, n. 4.**

CPC Intern., Inc. v. Aerojet–General Corp., 825 F.Supp. 795 (W.D.Mich.1993)—§ **18.26, n. 12.**

CPC Intern., Inc. v. Northbrook Excess & Surplus Ins. Co., 46 F.3d 1211 (1st Cir. 1995)—§ **18.26, n. 13.**

Crabtree v. Academy Life Ins. Co., 878 F.Supp. 727 (E.D.Pa.1995)—§ **18.29, n. 5.**

Craig v. Bemis Co., Inc., 517 F.2d 677 (5th Cir.1975)—§ **18.7, n. 8.**

Craig v. Carrigo, 353 Ark. 761, 121 S.W.3d 154 (Ark.2003)—§ **22.4, n. 7.**

Craig v. Craig, 365 So.2d 1298 (La.1978)— § **4.33, n. 3;** § **4.34, n. 3.**

Craig v. Donovan, 63 Ind. 513 (Ind.1878)— § **19.5, n. 8.**

Craig v. Lake Asbestos of Quebec, Ltd., 843 F.2d 145 (3rd Cir.1988)—§ **23.10, n. 1.**

Craignish, Re, [1892] 3 Ch. 180 (CA 1892)— § **4.28, n. 3.**

Cramer v. Phoenix Mut. Life Ins. Co. of Hartford, Conn., 91 F.2d 141 (8th Cir. 1937)—§ **22.18, n. 3.**

Crandell v. Barker, 8 N.D. 263, 78 N.W. 347 (N.D.1898)—§ **20.13, n. 4.**

Crane v. Blackman, 126 Ill.App. 631 (Ill. App. 4 Dist.1906)—§ **19.5, n. 4, 10.**

Crane v. Carr, 814 F.2d 758, 259 U.S.App. D.C. 229 (D.C.Cir.1987)—§ **5.12, n. 7;** § **7.2, n. 34.**

Craven v. Craven, 27 Wis. 418 (Wis.1871)— § **4.34, n. 1.**

Crawford, In re, 68 Ohio St. 58, 67 N.E. 156 (Ohio 1903)—§ **22.23, n. 1.**

Crawford v. Seattle, R. & S. Ry. Co., 86 Wash. 628, 150 P. 1155 (Wash.1915)— § **18.6, n. 1;** § **18.7, n. 1;** § **18.11, n. 4.**

Craycroff v. Morehead, 67 N.C. 422 (N.C. 1872)—§ **14.8, n. 2.**

C.R. Bard, Inc. v. Guidant Corp., 997 F.Supp. 556 (D.Del.1998)—§ **23.10, n. 4.**

Creighton v. Murphy, Neal & Co., 8 Neb. 349, 1 N.W. 138 (Neb.1879)—§ **22.20, n. 4.**

Crescent City Ice Co. v. Stafford, 6 F.Cas. 804 (C.C.D.La.1877)—§ **22.9, n. 5.**

Crescent Corp. v. Protor & Gamble Corp., 627 F.Supp. 745 (N.D.Ill.1986)—§ **11.6, n. 8.**

Crescent Intern., Inc. v. Avatar Communities, Inc., 857 F.2d 943 (3rd Cir.1988)— § **11.6, n. 4.**

Cresswell v. Slack, 68 Iowa 110, 26 N.W. 42 (Iowa 1885)—§ **22.20, n. 1, 7.**

Cribb v. Augustyn, 696 A.2d 285 (R.I. 1997)—§ **2.13, n. 26;** § **2.19, n. 13;** § **17.21, n. 16, 18;** § **17.23, n. 6;** § **17.39, n. 15.**

Cribbs v. Floyd, 188 S.C. 443, 199 S.E. 677 (S.C.1938)—§ **4.41, n. 5.**

Crichton v. Succession of Crichton, 232 So.2d 109 (La.App. 2 Cir.1970)—§ **20.9, n. 9.**

Crichton's Estate, In re, 281 N.Y.S.2d 811, 228 N.E.2d 799 (N.Y.1967)—§ **14.9, n. 1;** § **14.12, n. 9;** § **17.30, n. 14;** § **20.9, n. 9.**

Crick v. Hennessy, 1973 WL 141508 (WASC 1973)—§ **24.40, n. 6.**

Crippen v. Dexter, 79 Mass. 330 (Mass. 1859)—§ **22.4;** § **22.4, n. 5.**

Crittenden, Estate of, 29 Or.App. 189, 562 P.2d 609 (Or.App.1977)—§ **13.5, n. 1, 2;** § **13.6, n. 9.**

Croll v. Croll, 229 F.3d 133 (2nd Cir. 2000)—§ **15.42, n. 17.**

Cromeens, Holloman, Sibert, Inc v. AB Volvo, 349 F.3d 376 (7th Cir.2003)—§ **18.5, n. 32.**

Crompton Corp. v. Clariant Corp., 221 F.Supp.2d 683 (M.D.La.2002)—§ **9.7, n. 3, 9.**

Cropp v. Interstate Distributor Co., 129 Or. App. 510, 880 P.2d 464 (Or.App.1994)— § **3.9, n. 7, 8;** § **17.36, n. 15.**

Crosby, United States v., 11 U.S. 115, 3 L.Ed. 287 (1812)—§ **19.2, n. 4.**

Cross v. Lightolier Inc., 395 N.W.2d 844 (Iowa 1986)—§ **8.4, n. 3.**

Cross v. United States Trust Co. of New York, 131 N.Y. 330, 30 N.E. 125 (N.Y. 1892)—§ **21.2, n. 13.**

Crossley v. Pacific Emp. Ins. Co., 198 Neb. 26, 251 N.W.2d 383 (Neb.1977)—§ **2.16, n. 16;** § **2.23, n. 1.**

Crosson v. Conlee, 745 F.2d 896 (4th Cir. 1984)—§ **22.2, n. 3;** § **22.19, n. 11.**

Crouch v. General Elec. Co., 699 F.Supp. 585 (S.D.Miss.1988)—§ **17.64, n. 11;** § **17.66, n. 5;** § **17.78, n. 7.**

Crowe v. Di Manno, 225 F.2d 652 (1st Cir. 1955)—§ **22.18, n. 3.**

Crowley v. Glaze, 710 F.2d 676 (10th Cir. 1983)—§ **3.36, n. 2.**

Crown Beverage Co., Inc. v. Cerveceria Moctezuma, S.A., 663 F.2d 886 (9th Cir. 1981)—§ **11.3, n. 19, 22;** § **11.6, n. 5.**

Crown Coach Co. v. Whitaker, 208 Ark. 535, 186 S.W.2d 940 (Ark.1945)—§ **17.6, n. 5.**

Cruickshank v. Cruickshank, 193 Misc. 366, 82 N.Y.S.2d 522 (N.Y.Sup.1948)—§ **13.6, n. 4.**

Crum, In re, 98 Misc. 160, 164 N.Y.S. 149 (N.Y.Sur.1916)—§ **21.2, n. 13.**

Crum v. Bliss, 47 Conn. 592 (Conn.1880)— § **20.10, n. 2.**

Cruse v. Chittum, [1974] 2 All E.R. 940 (Fam.Div.)—§ **4.14, n. 2, 5;** § **15.26;** § **15.26, n. 4.**

Crutchfield v. Landry, 778 So.2d 1249 (La. App. 4 Cir.2001)—§ **17.56, n. 19.**

Cruz v. Maritime Co. of Philippines, 549 F.Supp. 285 (S.D.N.Y.1982)—§ **17.63, n. 24.**

Cruz v. O'Boyle, 197 F. 824 (M.D.Pa. 1912)—§ **24.34, n. 11.**

Cryomedics, Inc. v. Spembly, Ltd., 397 F.Supp. 287 (D.Conn.1975)—§ **9.7, n. 3.**

Csulik v. Nationwide Mut. Ins. Co., 88 Ohio St.3d 17, 723 N.E.2d 90 (Ohio 2000)— § **18.26, n. 7.**

CSX Transp., Inc. v. Union Tank Car Co., 247 F.Supp.2d 833 (E.D.Mich.2002)— § **8.4, n. 6.**

CTB, Inc., Ex parte, 782 So.2d 188 (Ala. 2000)—§ **11.1, n. 4.**

CTS Corp. v. Dynamics Corp. of America, 481 U.S. 69, 107 S.Ct. 1637, 95 L.Ed.2d 67 (1987)—§ **3.24, n. 18;** § **3.32, n. 13;** § **23.2;** § **23.2, n. 4;** § **23.3, n. 6;** § **23.6;** § **23.6, n. 10;** § **23.9;** § **23.9, n. 7.**

Cuba R. Co. v. Crosby, 222 U.S. 473, 32 S.Ct. 132, 56 L.Ed. 274 (1912)—§ **12.19, n. 13.**

Cuevas v. Cuevas, 191 So.2d 843 (Miss. 1966)—§ **19.8, n. 14.**

Cuffe v. Sanders Const. Co., Inc., 748 P.2d 328 (Alaska 1988)—§ **17.61, n. 2;** § **17.62, n. 1.**

Culbertson v. Board of Com'rs of Floyd County, 52 Ind. 361 (Ind.1876)—§ **4.21, n. 2.**

Culley's Will, In re, 182 Misc. 998, 48 N.Y.S.2d 216 (N.Y.Sur.1944)—§ **20.12, n. 5.**

Culmer, Matter of, 25 B.R. 621 (Bkrtcy. S.D.N.Y.1982)—§ **23.18, n. 7.**

Culp and Evans v. White, 524 F.Supp. 81 (W.D.N.Y.1981)—§ **8.6, n. 1.**

Culpepper v. Daniel Industries, Inc., 500 S.W.2d 958 (Tex.Civ.App.-Hous. (1 Dist.) 1973)—§ **3.9, n. 6.**

Culver, Appeal of, 48 Conn. 165 (Conn. 1880)—§ **4.45, n. 2, 3.**

Cummings v. Bullock, 367 F.2d 182 (9th Cir.1966)—§ **18.37, n. 14.**

Cummings' Estate, In re, 153 Pa. 397, 25 A. 1125 (Pa.1893)—§ **20.15, n. 6.**

Cummins Engine Co. v. Hyundai MIPO Dockyard (Rationis Enterprises, Inc.), 210 F.Supp.2d 421 (S.D.N.Y.2002)— § **10.4, n. 14.**

Cummiskey v. Cummiskey, 259 Minn. 427, 107 N.W.2d 864 (Minn.1961)—§ **4.7, n. 4.**

Cunard S.S. Co. Ltd. v. Salen Reefer Services AB, 773 F.2d 452 (2nd Cir.1985)— § **23.18, n. 7.**

Cunningham, In re, 9 B.R. 70 (Bkrtcy. D.N.M.1981)—§ **23.13, n. 1.**

Cunningham v. Brown, 51 N.C.App. 264, 276 S.E.2d 718 (N.C.App.1981)— § **12.17, n. 3.**

Cunningham v. Cunningham, 25 Conn. Supp. 221, 200 A.2d 734 (Conn.Super.1964)—§ **24.9, n. 18;** § **24.21, n. 5.**

Cunningham v. Cunningham, 206 N.Y. 341, 99 N.E. 845 (N.Y.1912)—§ **13.8, n. 3;** § **13.12, n. 2.**

Cunningham v. PFL Life Ins. Co., 42 F.Supp.2d 872 (N.D.Iowa 1999)— § **17.50, n. 22;** § **17.52, n. 3.**

Curda–Derickson v. Derickson, 266 Wis.2d 453, 668 N.W.2d 736 (Wis.App.2003)— § **14.16, n. 19.**

Curles v. Curles, 136 F.Supp. 916 (D.D.C 1955)—§ **18.44, n. 9;** § **18.47, n. 7.**

Currier v. Tuck, 112 N.H. 10, 287 A.2d 625 (N.H.1972)—§ **18.28, n. 1;** § **19.10, n. 1.**

Curry v. McCanless, 307 U.S. 357, 59 S.Ct. 900, 83 L.Ed. 1339 (1939)—§ **4.5, n. 3.**

Curtis v. Curtis, 185 A.D. 391, 173 N.Y.S. 103 (N.Y.A.D. 1 Dept.1918)—§ **21.6, n. 7;** § **21.7, n. 2.**

Curtis 1000, Inc. v. Suess, 24 F.3d 941 (7th Cir.1994)—§ **18.5, n. 17.**

Curtis 1000, Inc. v. Youngblade, 878 F.Supp. 1224 (N.D.Iowa 1995)—§ **18.6, n. 1.**

Curtis Pub. Co. v. Cassel, 302 F.2d 132 (10th Cir.1962)—§ **7.8, n. 10.**

Custody and Control of Murphy, Matter of, 120 F.Supp.2d 517 (D.Virgin Islands 2000)—§ **15.43, n. 9.**

Custody of a Minor (No. 3), 392 Mass. 728, 468 N.E.2d 251 (Mass.1984)—§ **4.37, n. 3;** § **15.43;** § **15.43, n. 8, 11.**

Custody of Johnson, In the Matter of, 1985 WL 8382 (Ohio App. 6 Dist.1985)— § **15.29, n. 3.**

Custody of Sagan, In re, 261 Pa.Super. 384, 396 A.2d 450 (Pa.Super.1978)—§ **4.40, n. 4.**

Custom Products, Inc. v. Fluor Daniel Canada, Inc., 262 F.Supp.2d 767 (W.D.Ky. 2003)—§ **17.70;** § **17.70, n. 7.**

Cutler's Will, In re, 114 Misc. 203, 186 N.Y.S. 271 (N.Y.Sur.1921)—§ **20.12, n. 3.**

Cutrer v. State of Tennessee, 98 Miss. 841, 54 So. 434 (Miss.1911)—§ **22.19, n. 18, 19.**

CXY Chemicals U.S.A. v. Gerling Global General Ins. Co., 991 F.Supp. 770 (E.D.La.1998)—§ **18.26, n. 13.**

Cybersell, Inc. v. Cybersell, Inc., 130 F.3d 414 (9th Cir.1997)—§ **9.3, n. 7.**

Cycles, Ltd. v. W.J. Digby, Inc., 889 F.2d 612 (5th Cir.1989)—§ **7.6, n. 9.**

Cyr v. Walker, 29 Okla. 281, 116 P. 931 (Okla.1911)—§ **13.18, n. 13.**

Cytomedix v. Little Rock Foot, 287 B.R. 901 (N.D.Ill.2002)—§ **10.7, n. 19.**

D

Dabbs v. Silver Eagle Mfg. Co., Inc., 98 Or.App. 581, 779 P.2d 1104 (Or.App. 1989)—§ **17.75, n. 1;** § **17.76, n. 27.**

Da Costa Fonseca v. Frota Oceanica Brasileira, S. A., 67 A.D.2d 636, 412 N.Y.S.2d 145 (N.Y.A.D. 1 Dept.1979)—§ **11.11, n. 3;** § **11.12, n. 3, 4.**

Dagesse v. Plant Hotel N.V., 113 F.Supp.2d 211 (D.N.H.2000)—§ **5.10, n. 27;** § **5.11, n. 22.**

D'Agostino v. Johnson & Johnson, Inc., 133 N.J. 516, 628 A.2d 305 (N.J.1993)— § **17.48, n. 19.**

Dahlberg v. Brown, 198 S.C. 1, 16 S.E.2d 284 (S.C.1941)—§ **22.18, n. 3.**

Dailey v. Dallas Carriers Corp., 51 Cal. Rptr.2d 48 (Cal.App. 2 Dist.1996)— **§ 17.59, n. 7, 16.**

DaimlerChrysler AG Securities Litigation, In re, 247 F.Supp.2d 579 (D.Del.2003)— **§ 9.6, n. 20.**

Dakota Country Store Foods, Inc., In re, 107 B.R. 977 (Bkrtcy.D.S.D.1989)— **§ 18.24, n. 2.**

Dale System v. General Teleradio, 105 F.Supp. 745 (S.D.N.Y.1952)—**§ 17.55, n. 7.**

Dalip Singh Bir's Estate, In re, 83 Cal. App.2d 256, 188 P.2d 499 (Cal.App. 3 Dist.1948)—**§ 13.19, n. 3; § 20.5, n. 7.**

Dallas v. Whitney, 118 W Va. 106, 188 S.E. 766 (W.Va.1936)—**§ 17.3, n. 1.**

Dalpay, In re, 41 Minn. 532, 43 N.W. 564 (Minn.1889)—**§ 19.30, n. 7.**

Dalrymple v. Dalrymple, 2 Hagg. Cons. 54 (1811)—**§ 13.6, n. 1.**

Dalrymple v. Gamble, 68 Md. 523, 13 A. 156 (Md.1888)—**§ 22.3, n. 9.**

Dalton v. Murphy, 30 Miss. 59 (Miss.Err. & App.1855)—**§ 19.12, n. 4; § 19.13, n. 7.**

Dalton v. R & W Marine, Inc., 897 F.2d 1359 (5th Cir.1990)—**§ 5.12, n. 7; § 5.13, n. 19; § 6.9, n. 20; § 7.2, n. 34.**

Dalton v. Taliaferro, 101 Ill.App. 592 (Ill. App. 2 Dist.1902)—**§ 19.5, n. 2, 5.**

Damaskinos v. Societa Navigacion Interamericana, S.A., Panama, 255 F.Supp. 919 (S.D.N.Y.1966)—**§ 17.63, n. 31.**

Damato's Estate, In re, 86 N.J.Super. 107, 206 A.2d 171 (N.J.Super.A.D.1965)— **§ 3.13, n. 4, 7.**

Damigos v. Flanders Compania Naviera, S.A. Panama, 716 F.Supp. 104 (S.D.N.Y. 1989)—**§ 11.3, n. 22.**

Dammert v. Osborn, 140 N.Y. 30, 35 N.E. 407 (N.Y.1893)—**§ 20.9, n. 3; § 20.10, n. 2.**

Dana's Estate, In re, 206 Misc. 408, 132 N.Y.S.2d 734 (N.Y.Sur.1954)—**§ 22.23, n. 4.**

Danbury v. New–Haven, 5 Conn. 584 (Conn.1825)—**§ 4.38, n. 1.**

Dane v. Board of Registrars of Voters of Concord, 374 Mass. 152, 371 N.E.2d 1358 (Mass.1978)—**§ 4.27, n. 9.**

Danforth v. Nabors, 120 Ala. 430, 24 So. 891 (Ala.1898)—**§ 4.19, n. 4.**

D'Angelo, Estate of, 139 Misc.2d 5, 526 N.Y.S.2d 729 (N.Y.Sur.1988)—**§ 16.6, n. 2.**

Danielson v. National Supply Co., 670 N.W.2d 1 (Minn.App.2003)—**§ 17.66, n. 4; § 17.73, n. 6.**

Danner v. Brewer, 69 Ala. 191 (Ala.1881)— **§ 19.9, n. 6.**

Dansby v. North Carolina Mut. Life Ins. Co., 209 N.C. 127, 183 S.E. 521 (N.C. 1936)—**§ 10.14, n. 10.**

Danz' Estate, In re, 444 Pa. 411, 283 A.2d 282 (Pa.1971)—**§ 18.21, n. 17.**

D'Arcy v. Ketchum, 52 U.S. 165, 11 How. 165, 13 L.Ed. 648 (1850)—**§ 5.1, n. 7; § 5.2, n. 8, 23.**

Dardenne, State ex rel. Wooters v., 131 La. 109, 59 So. 32 (La.1912)—**§ 4.29, n. 2.**

Dart v. Balaam, 953 S.W.2d 478 (Tex.App.-Fort Worth 1997)—**§ 24.36, n. 1.**

Data Disc, Inc. v. Systems Technology Associates, Inc., 557 F.2d 1280 (9th Cir. 1977)—**§ 5.19, n. 2.**

Data General Corp. v. Digital Computer Controls, Inc., 357 A.2d 105 (Del.Ch. 1975)—**§ 17.53, n. 3, 5.**

Dauenhauer's Estate, In re, 167 Mont. 83, 535 P.2d 1005 (Mont.1975)—**§ 20.2, n. 4.**

Davenport v. Webb, 11 N.Y.2d 392, 230 N.Y.S.2d 17, 183 N.E.2d 902 (N.Y. 1962)—**§ 3.15, n. 8; § 17.9, n. 3.**

Davenport Mach. & Foundry Co., A Division of Middle States Corp. v. Adolph Coors Co., 314 N.W.2d 432 (Iowa 1982)—**§ 5.13, n. 22; § 6.9, n. 21.**

David v. Atlantic County Soc. for Prevention of Cruelty to Animals, 19 A.2d 896 (N.J.Ch.1941)—**§ 21.11, n. 5, 15.**

David B. Lilly Co., Inc. v. Fisher, 18 F.3d 1112 (3rd Cir.1994)—**§ 17.44, n. 11.**

Davidson v. Cao, 211 F.Supp.2d 264 (D.Mass.2002)—**§ 17.55, n. 10.**

Davidson v. Lonoke Production Credit Ass'n, 695 F.2d 1115 (8th Cir.1982)— **§ 24.1, n. 8.**

Davidson & Co., Ltd. v. Allen, 89 Nev. 126, 508 P.2d 6 (Nev.1973)—**§ 5.21, n. 11; § 24.35, n. 7; § 24.42, n. 5.**

David–Zieseniss v. Zieseniss, 205 Misc. 836, 129 N.Y.S.2d 649 (N.Y.Sup.1954)— **§ 15.5, n. 4.**

Davis v. American Family Mut. Ins. Co., 861 F.2d 1159 (9th Cir.1988)—**§ 8.2, n. 10.**

Davis v. Cayton, 214 S.W.2d 801 (Tex.Civ. App.-Amarillo 1948)—**§ 22.10, n. 11.**

Davis v. Davis, 305 U.S. 32, 59 S.Ct. 3, 83 L.Ed. 26 (1938)—**§ 4.7, n. 2; § 15.9; § 15.9, n. 1.**

Davis v. Farmers' Co-op. Equity Co., 262 U.S. 312, 43 S.Ct. 556, 67 L.Ed. 996 (1923)—**§ 11.16, n. 1.**

Davis v. Humble Oil & Refining Co., 283 So.2d 783 (La.App. 1 Cir.1973)—**§ 18.5, n. 10, 11.**

Davis v. Jointless Fire Brick Co., 300 F. 1 (9th Cir.1924)—**§ 18.4, n. 43, 46.**

Davis v. Jouganatos, 81 Nev. 333, 402 P.2d 985 (Nev.1965)—**§ 18.33, n. 2.**

Davis v. Mills, 194 U.S. 451, 24 S.Ct. 692, 48 L.Ed. 1067 (1904)—**§ 3.10, n. 4, 5, 6.**

Davis v. National Broadcasting Co., 320 F.Supp. 1070 (E.D.La.1970)—**§ 17.55, n. 4.**

Davis v. National Gypsum Co., 743 F.2d 1132 (5th Cir.1984)—**§ 17.26, n. 1.**

Davis v. Piper Aircraft Corp., 615 F.2d 606 (4th Cir.1980)—§ **22.14, n. 5.**

Davis v. P. R. Sales Co., 304 F.2d 831 (2nd Cir.1962)—§ **3.13, n. 4.**

Davis v. Shiley Inc., 75 Cal.Rptr.2d 826 (Cal.App. 4 Dist.1998)—§ **17.76, n. 27.**

Davis v. Upson, 230 Ill. 327, 82 N.E. 824 (Ill.1907)—§ **22.2, n. 1.**

Davis v. Zimmerman, 67 Pa. 70 (Pa.1871)— § **14.9, n. 1.**

Davis by Davis v. Maryland Cas. Co., 76 N.C.App. 102, 331 S.E.2d 744 (N.C.App. 1985)—§ **4.37, n. 3.**

Davis by Lane v. Schweiker, 553 F.Supp. 158 (D.Md.1982)—§ **16.1, n. 12.**

Davison v. Sinai Hospital of Baltimore, Inc., 462 F.Supp. 778 (D.Md.1978)—§ **3.41, n. 15, 18.**

Davis's Estate, In re, 100 Misc.2d 498, 419 N.Y.S.2d 827 (N.Y.Sur.1979)—§ **21.10, n. 7.**

Davis' Will, In re, 31 Misc.2d 270, 219 N.Y.S.2d 533 (N.Y.Sur.1961)—§ **24.44, n. 11.**

Davy, Application of, 281 A.D. 137, 120 N.Y.S.2d 450 (N.Y.A.D. 3 Dept.1952)— § **4.19, n. 3, 4.**

Dawes v. Head, 20 Mass. 128 (Mass.1825)— § **22.21, n. 10.**

Dawkins v. State, 306 S.C. 391, 412 S.E.2d 407 (S.C.1991)—§ **2.21, n. 9.**

Dawson v. Capital Bank & Trust Co. of Baton Rouge, 261 So.2d 727 (La.App. 1 Cir.1972)—§ **14.9, n. 2.**

Dawson v. Dawson, 241 S.W.2d 725 (Mo. App.1951)—§ **4.41, n. 6.**

Dawson–Austin v. Austin, 920 S.W.2d 776 (Tex.App.-Dallas 1996)—§ **14.9, n. 11, 13; § 14.13, n. 7.**

Day v. Day, 237 Md. 229, 205 A.2d 798 (Md.1965)—§ **15.10, n. 2.**

Day v. Temple Drilling Co., 613 F.Supp. 194 (S.D.Miss.1985)—§ **10.6, n. 51.**

Day v. Wiswall, 11 Ariz.App. 306, 464 P.2d 626 (Ariz.App. Div. 2 1970)—§ **19.8, n. 14; § 24.10, n. 4.**

Dayton v. Adkisson, 17 A. 964 (N.J.Ch. 1889)—§ **16.2, n. 5.**

Dayton, State ex rel. Ramey v., 77 Mo. 678 (Mo.1883)—§ **4.17, n. 4.**

Day & Zimmermann, Inc. v. Challoner, 423 U.S. 3, 96 S.Ct. 167, 46 L.Ed.2d 3 (1975)—§ **3.23, n. 16; § 3.36; § 3.36, n. 4, 19; § 3.47, n. 6; § 12.11, n. 7; § 17.7; § 17.7, n. 11; § 24.35, n. 1.**

DCA Food Industries Inc. v. Hawthorn Mellody, Inc., 470 F.Supp. 574 (S.D.N.Y. 1979)—§ **10.16, n. 10.**

Deal v. Deal, 496 So.2d 1175 (La.App. 5 Cir.1986)—§ **5.23, n. 1.**

Dean, People ex rel. Bachleda v., 48 Ill.2d 16, 268 N.E.2d 11 (Ill.1971)—§ **16.6, n. 6.**

DeAngelis v. Scott, 337 F.Supp. 1021 (W.D.Pa.1972)—§ **18.37, n. 12.**

Deary v. Evans, 570 F.Supp. 189 (D.Virgin Islands 1983)—§ **3.47, n. 2.**

Debbis v. Hertz Corp., 269 F.Supp. 671 (D.Md.1967)—§ **17.6, n. 7.**

DeBoer v. Schmidt, 442 Mich. 648, 502 N.W.2d 649 (Mich.1993)—§ **16.5, n. 9.**

De Camillis' Estate, In re, 66 Misc.2d 882, 322 N.Y.S.2d 551 (N.Y.Sur.1971)— § **22.9, n. 1.**

Decker v. Vreeland, 220 N.Y. 326, 115 N.E. 989 (N.Y.1917)—§ **20.9, n. 10.**

DeCoteau v. District County Court for Tenth Judicial Dist., 420 U.S. 425, 95 S.Ct. 1082, 43 L.Ed.2d 300 (1975)— § **11.17, n. 2, 35.**

Deemer v. Silk City Textile Machinery Co., 193 N.J.Super. 643, 475 A.2d 648 (N.J.Super.A.D.1984)—§ **17.78, n. 8.**

Deese v. Hundley, 232 F.Supp. 848 (W.D.S.C.1964)—§ **4.26, n. 3.**

De Fogassieras v. Duport, 11 L.R.Ir. 123 (1881)—§ **20.6, n. 20.**

DeFoor v. Lematta, 249 Or. 116, 437 P.2d 107 (Or.1968)—§ **17.27, n. 7.**

DeFrance v. DeFrance, 273 A.D.2d 468, 710 N.Y.S.2d 612 (N.Y.A.D. 2 Dept.2000)— § **14.12, n. 9.**

De Garza v. Chetister, 62 Ohio App.2d 149, 405 N.E.2d 331 (Ohio App. 6 Dist. 1978)—§ **22.14, n. 9.**

DeGrasse v. Sensenich Corp., 1989 WL 23775 (E.D.Pa.1989)—§ **17.76; § 17.76, n. 20.**

De Groat, State v., 109 Minn. 168, 123 N.W. 417 (Minn.1909)—§ **23.5, n. 2.**

Dehn's Will, In re, 75 Misc.2d 85, 347 N.Y.S.2d 821 (N.Y.Sur.1973)—§ **20.9, n. 4.**

Deitrick v. Greaney, 309 U.S. 190, 60 S.Ct. 480, 84 L.Ed. 694 (1940)—§ **3.51, n. 2.**

DeJames v. Magnificence Carriers, Inc., 654 F.2d 280 (3rd Cir.1981)—§ **10.3, n. 3; § 12.7, n. 5.**

DeKorwin v. First Nat. Bank of Chicago, 318 F.2d 176 (7th Cir.1963)—§ **19.29, n. 3.**

Delagi v. Volkswagenwerk A.G. of Wolfsburg, Germany, 328 N.Y.S.2d 653, 278 N.E.2d 895 (N.Y.1972)—§ **10.16; § 10.16, n. 6.**

De La Montanya v. De La Montanya, 112 Cal. 101, 44 P. 345 (Cal.1896)—§ **5.1, n. 9; § 5.3, n. 11; § 6.4, n. 3.**

De Lane v. Moore, 55 U.S. 253, 14 How. 253, 14 L.Ed. 409 (1852)—§ **14.6, n. 6.**

Delaney v. Delaney, 35 Conn.Supp. 230, 405 A.2d 91 (Conn.Super.1979)—§ **13.6, n. 2.**

De Lano's Estate, In re, 181 Kan. 729, 315 P.2d 611 (Kan.1957)—§ **22.11, n. 1.**

Delaware v. New York, 507 U.S. 490, 113 S.Ct. 1550, 123 L.Ed.2d 211 (1993)— § **20.4, n. 8.**

Delaware, L. & W. R. Co. v. Ashelman, 300 Pa. 291, 150 A. 475 (Pa.1930)—§ **11.11, n. 6.**

Delaware, L. & W.R. Co. v. Petrowsky, 250 F. 554 (2nd Cir.1918)—§ **4.37, n. 2, 10; § 4.41, n. 7; § 4.43, n. 1.**

Delhomme Industries, Inc. v. Houston Beechcraft, Inc., 669 F.2d 1049 (5th Cir. 1982)—§ **18.12, n. 10.**

DeLoach v. Alfred, 192 Ariz. 28, 960 P.2d 628 (Ariz.1998)—§ **3.9, n. 8; § 3.12, n. 9.**

DeLorean v. DeLorean, 211 N.J.Super. 432, 511 A.2d 1257 (N.J.Super.Ch.1986)— § **14.15, n. 2.**

DeLorean Motor Co., In re, 49 B.R. 900 (Bkrtcy.E.D.Mich.1985)—§ **23.12, n. 7.**

Deloro Smelting & Refining Co. v. Engelhard Minerals & Chemicals Corp., 313 F.Supp. 470 (D.N.J.1970)—§ **10.8, n. 15.**

Delta Bag Co. v. Frederick Leyland & Co., 173 Ill.App. 38 (Ill.App. 1 Dist.1912)— § **18.4, n. 8.**

Deluxe Ice Cream Co. v. R.C.H. Tool Corp., 726 F.2d 1209 (7th Cir.1984)—§ **5.10, n. 26; § 6.7, n. 20.**

Del Valle, Matter of Estate of, 126 Misc.2d 78, 481 N.Y.S.2d 232 (N.Y.Sur.1984)— § **16.1, n. 12; § 16.2, n. 5.**

Demas v. Harvouros, 1951 WL 3261 (Pa. Com.Pl.1951)—§ **12.16, n. 7.**

De Mateos v. Texaco Panama, Inc., 417 F.Supp. 411 (E.D.Pa.1976)—§ **17.63, n. 20.**

Demczuck's Estate, In re, 8 Pa. D. & C.2d 462, 6 Fiduc.Rep. 633 (Pa.Orph.1957)— § **12.17, n. 7.**

De Meli v. De Meli, 120 N.Y. 485, 24 N.E. 996 (N.Y.1890)—§ **4.13, n. 2.**

de Melo v. Lederle Laboratories, Div. of American Cyanamid Corp., 801 F.2d 1058 (8th Cir.1986)—§ **11.9, n. 5.**

Dempster v. Stephen, 63 Ill.App. 126 (Ill. App. 4 Dist.1896)—§ **14.9, n. 1.**

DeMyrick v. Guest Quarters Suite Hotels, 944 F.Supp. 661 (N.D.Ill.1996)—§ **17.48, n. 5.**

Denick's Estate, In re, 71 N.Y.St.Rep. 549, 36 N.Y.S. 518 (N.Y.Sup.Gen.Term 1895)—§ **6.4, n. 14.**

De Nicols v. Curlier (No.2), 1900 WL 30071 (Ch D 1900)—§ **14.9, n. 6.**

De Nicols v. Curlier (No.1), 1899 WL 11679 (HL 1899)—§ **14.9; § 14.9, n. 5.**

Denlinger v. Brennan, 87 F.3d 214 (7th Cir.1996)—§ **4.27, n. 1.**

Denlinger v. Chinadotcom Corp., 2 Cal. Rptr.3d 530 (Cal.App. 6 Dist.2003)— § **12.7, n. 3.**

Denman v. Snapper Div., 131 F.3d 546 (5th Cir.1998)—§ **17.78; § 17.78, n. 1.**

Denney v. Teel, 688 P.2d 803 (Okla.1984)— § **19.2, n. 1.**

Dennis v. State, 17 Fla. 389 (Fla.1879)— § **4.21, n. 2.**

Dennis Mitchell Industries, Inc., In re, 419 F.2d 349 (3rd Cir.1969)—§ **19.18, n. 12; § 19.20, n. 7.**

Denny v. American Tobacco Co., 308 F.Supp. 219 (N.D.Cal.1970)—§ **18.31, n. 5; § 18.38, n. 6, 9; § 18.44, n. 9.**

Denny v. Sumner County, 134 Tenn. 468, 184 S.W. 14 (Tenn.1916)—§ **4.13, n. 2; § 4.20, n. 3; § 4.36, n. 11.**

Dent–Air, Inc. v. Beech Mountain Air Service, Inc., 332 N.W.2d 904 (Minn. 1983)—§ **18.1, n. 22.**

De Paris v. Wilmington Trust Co., 30 Del. 178, 104 A. 691 (Del.Supr.1918)— § **22.18, n. 4.**

Department of Human Services v. Shelnut, 772 So.2d 1041 (Miss.2000)—§ **24.42, n. 2.**

Department of Public Parks, In re, 69 N.Y.St.Rep. 743, 35 N.Y.S. 332 (N.Y.Sup.Gen.Term 1895)—§ **22.25, n. 21.**

Depas v. Mayo, 11 Mo. 314 (Mo.1848)— § **14.6, n. 5; § 14.7, n. 2; § 19.6, n. 2.**

Deposit Guaranty Nat. Bank v. River Valley Co., 247 Ark. 226, 444 S.W.2d 880 (Ark. 1969)—§ **12.17, n. 13.**

De Potty v. De Potty, 226 Ark. 881, 295 S.W.2d 330 (Ark.1956)—§ **13.6, n. 9.**

Deprenyl Animal Health, Inc. v. University of Toronto Innovations Foundation, 297 F.3d 1343 (Fed.Cir.2002)—§ **9.4, n. 11, 12.**

de Reyes v. Marine Management and Consulting, Ltd., 586 So.2d 103 (La.1991)— § **5.12, n. 7; § 5.13, n. 20; § 6.9, n. 19; § 7.2, n. 34.**

De Sairigne v. Gould, 83 F.Supp. 270 (S.D.N.Y.1949)—§ **11.14, n. 8.**

DeSantis v. Wackenhut Corp., 793 S.W.2d 670 (Tex.1990)—§ **18.1, n. 3; § 18.2, n. 4; § 18.4, n. 1, 7; § 18.5, n. 16, 17; § 18.10, n. 2; § 18.21, n. 14; § 18.29, n. 5.**

DES Cases, In re, 789 F.Supp. 552 (E.D.N.Y.1992)—§ **6.6, n. 22; § 10.9; § 10.9, n. 16.**

DeShane v. Deere & Co., 726 F.2d 443 (8th Cir.1984)—§ **11.8, n. 4.**

Desjardins Ducharme v. Hunnewell, 411 Mass. 711, 585 N.E.2d 321 (Mass. 1992)—§ **24.6, n. 2.**

Desktop Technologies, Inc. v. Colorworks Reproduction & Design, Inc., 1999 WL 98572 (E.D.Pa.1999)—§ **5.11, n. 22; § 9.5, n. 7.**

Deslions v. La Compagnie Generale Transatlantique, 210 U.S. 95, 28 S.Ct. 664, 52 L.Ed. 973 (1908)—§ **17.63, n. 32.**

Despard v. Churchill, 53 N.Y. 192 (N.Y. 1873)—§ **21.2, n. 8.**

De Sylva v. Ballentine, 351 U.S. 570, 76 S.Ct. 974, 100 L.Ed. 1415 (1956)— § **3.54, n. 5.**

Det Bergenske Dampskibsselskab v. Sabre Shipping Corp., 341 F.2d 50 (2nd Cir. 1965)—§ **10.6, n. 35.**

Detrio v. United States, 264 F.2d 658 (5th Cir.1959)—§ **10.12, n. 14, 16.**

Detroit Auto. Inter–Insurance Exchange v. Feys, 205 F.Supp. 42 (N.D.Cal.1962)— § **4.26, n. 2.**

Detroit, City of v. Gould, 12 Ill.2d 297, 146 N.E.2d 61 (Ill.1957)—§ **24.23, n. 5.**

Detroit Greyhound Emp. Federal Credit Union v. Aetna Life Ins. Co., 7 Mich. App. 430, 151 N.W.2d 852 (Mich.App. 1967)—§ **19.28, n. 2.**

Deupree v. Le, 402 A.2d 428 (D.C.1979)— § **11.11, n. 2.**

De Villeneuve v. Morning Journal Ass'n, 206 F. 70 (S.D.N.Y.1913)—§ **12.6, n. 9.**

Devine v. Rook, 314 S.W.2d 932 (Mo.App. 1958)—§ **3.11, n. 3.**

DeVries v. Bankers Life Co., 128 Ill.App.3d 647, 83 Ill.Dec. 931, 471 N.E.2d 230 (Ill.App. 1 Dist.1984)—§ **11.8, n. 6;** § **11.11, n. 6.**

DeWeerth v. Baldinger, 38 F.3d 1266 (2nd Cir.1994)—§ **3.47, n. 9.**

Dewey, In re Estate of, 387 N.Y.S.2d 426, 355 N.E.2d 386 (N.Y.1976)—§ **20.5, n. 7.**

Dewey v. City of Des Moines, 173 U.S. 193, 19 S.Ct. 379, 43 L.Ed. 665 (1899)—§ **5.3, n. 12.**

Dewey v. Dewey, 745 S.W.2d 514 (Tex.App.-Corpus Christi 1988)—§ **14.11, n. 2;** § **14.15, n. 10.**

De Wolf v. Middleton, 18 R.I. 810, 31 A. 271 (R.I.1895)—§ **16.1, n. 8;** § **16.2, n. 5.**

De Wolf v. Middleton, 18 R.I. 810, 26 A. 44 (R.I.1893)—§ **16.1, n. 8;** § **16.2, n. 5.**

Dews v. Halliburton Industries, Inc., 288 Ark. 532, 708 S.W.2d 67 (Ark.1986)— § **18.44, n. 9.**

Dexter v. Berge, 76 Minn. 216, 78 N.W. 1111 (Minn.1899)—§ **22.16, n. 2.**

Deyo v. Jennison, 92 Mass. 410 (Mass. 1865)—§ **19.15, n. 5.**

DeYoung v. DeYoung, 27 Cal.2d 521, 165 P.2d 457 (Cal.1946)—§ **4.24, n. 3.**

D. H. Overmyer Co. Inc., of Ohio v. Frick Co., 405 U.S. 174, 92 S.Ct. 775, 31 L.Ed.2d 124 (1972)—§ **6.3, n. 10, 12;** § **12.5, n. 4;** § **24.15, n. 3.**

Dial v. Gary, 14 S.C. 573 (S.C.1881)— § **22.11, n. 1;** § **22.15, n. 9.**

Dialogue's Will, In re, 159 Misc. 18, 287 N.Y.S. 237 (N.Y.Sur.1936)—§ **20.8, n. 8.**

Diamond Mortg. Corp. of Illinois v. Sugar, 913 F.2d 1233 (7th Cir.1990)—§ **10.7, n. 19.**

DiAntonio v. Northampton–Accomack Memorial Hospital, 628 F.2d 287 (4th Cir. 1980)—§ **3.41, n. 15.**

Diaz v. Southeastern Drilling Co. of Argentina, S. A., 324 F.Supp. 1 (N.D.Tex. 1969)—§ **18.37, n. 12.**

Di Brigida v. Di Brigida, 116 N.J.Eq. 208, 172 A. 505 (N.J.Err. & App.1934)— § **4.24, n. 3.**

Dichter v. Disco Corp., 606 F.Supp. 721 (S.D.Ohio 1984)—§ **24.5, n. 4;** § **24.13, n. 1.**

Dick v. Motorists Ins. Cos., 103 Ohio App.3d 441, 659 N.E.2d 860 (Ohio App. 6 Dist.1995)—§ **17.56, n. 17.**

Dickerson v. Scott, 476 So.2d 524 (La.App. 1 Cir.1985)—§ **19.8, n. 14.**

Dicks v. Dicks, 177 Ga. 379, 170 S.E. 245 (Ga.1933)—§ **4.26, n. 1.**

Diederichs' Estate, In re, 255 Wis. 221, 38 N.W.2d 489 (Wis.1949)—§ **22.21, n. 9.**

Diehl v. Ogorewac, 836 F.Supp. 88 (E.D.N.Y.1993)—§ **17.40, n. 4;** § **17.46, n. 13, 22.**

Diehl v. United States, 438 F.2d 705 (5th Cir.1971)—§ **15.9, n. 6;** § **22.10, n. 2.**

Dierker v. Gypsum Transp., Ltd., 606 F.Supp. 566 (E.D.La.1985)—§ **17.63, n. 4.**

Dignam v. Shaff, 51 Wash. 412, 98 P. 1113 (Wash.1909)—§ **4.13, n. 2;** § **4.20, n. 8.**

Dillaplain v. Lite Industries, Inc., 788 S.W.2d 530 (Mo.App. W.D.1990)—§ **7.2, n. 33.**

Dillard v. McKnight, 34 Cal.2d 209, 209 P.2d 387 (Cal.1949)—§ **10.12, n. 14.**

Dillon v. Legg, 68 Cal.2d 728, 69 Cal.Rptr. 72, 441 P.2d 912 (Cal.1968)—§ **17.56, n. 5.**

Dillon v. Numismatic Funding Corp., 291 N.C. 674, 231 S.E.2d 629 (N.C.1977)— § **5.13, n. 22;** § **6.9, n. 21.**

DiMauro v. Pavia, 492 F.Supp. 1051 (D.Conn.1979)—§ **22.3, n. 1;** § **22.10, n. 2;** § **22.19, n. 20;** § **22.20, n. 26.**

Di Medio v. Port Norris Exp. Co., 71 N.J.Super. 190, 176 A.2d 550 (N.J.Super.L.1961)—§ **20.3, n. 9.**

Dimirsky's Estate, In re, 201 Misc. 118, 108 N.Y.S.2d 849 (N.Y.Sur.1951)—§ **20.3, n. 9.**

Diorinou v. Mezitis, 132 F.Supp.2d 139 (S.D.N.Y.2000)—§ **15.42, n. 17.**

Direction der Disconto–Gesellschaft v. United States Steel Corporation, 267 U.S. 22, 45 S.Ct. 207, 69 L.Ed. 495 (1925)— § **22.12, n. 10.**

Director, Office of Workers' Compensation Programs, United States Dept. of Labor v. National Van Lines, Inc., 613 F.2d 972, 198 U.S.App.D.C. 239 (D.C.Cir. 1979)—§ **17.59, n. 16.**

Director of Revenue, State of Colo. v. United States, 392 F.2d 307 (10th Cir. 1968)—§ **3.51, n. 10.**

Disaster at Detroit Metropolitan Airport on Aug. 16, 1987, In re, 750 F.Supp. 793 (E.D.Mich.1989)—§ **17.76, n. 16, 28;** § **17.79, n. 3.**

Disconto Gesellschaft v. Terlinden, 127 Wis. 651, 106 N.W. 821 (Wis.1906)—§ **11.8, n. 3.**

Distefano v. Carozzi North America, Inc., 286 F.3d 81 (2nd Cir.2001)—§ **9.5, n. 3.**

District Court of Ninth Judicial Dist., State ex rel. Peterson v., 617 P.2d 1056 (Wyo. 1980)—§ **11.17, n. 23.**

District Court of Sheridan County, State ex rel. Klopotek v., 621 P.2d 223 (Wyo. 1980)—§ **22.26, n. 5.**

District Court, State ex rel. Ruff v., 34 Mont. 96, 85 P. 866 (Mont.1906)— § **22.3, n. 1; § 22.4, n. 7.**

District of Columbia v. Coleman, 667 A.2d 811 (D.C.1995)—§ **17.36, n. 15; § 17.48, n. 8.**

District of Columbia v. Murphy, 314 U.S. 441, 62 S.Ct. 303, 86 L.Ed. 329 (1941)— § **4.20, n. 3, 4.**

District of Columbia v. Stackhouse, 239 F.2d 62, 99 U.S.App.D.C. 242 (D.C.Cir. 1956)—§ **4.45, n. 2.**

District of Columbia Court of Appeals v. Feldman, 460 U.S. 462, 103 S.Ct. 1303, 75 L.Ed.2d 206 (1983)—§ **24.12, n. 7.**

District of Columbia Ins. Guar. Ass'n v. Algernon Blair, Inc., 565 A.2d 564 (D.C. 1989)—§ **2.25, n. 11; § 18.21, n. 17; § 18.27, n. 3.**

Ditson v. Ditson, 4 R.I. 87 (R.I.1856)— § **4.34, n. 1; § 13.1, n. 2.**

Dix v. Pineda, 205 F.2d 957 (9th Cir. 1953)—§ **19.29, n. 3.**

Dixon v. Picopa Const. Co., 160 Ariz. 251, 772 P.2d 1104 (Ariz.1989)—§ **11.17, n. 39.**

Dixson v. Newsweek, Inc., 562 F.2d 626 (10th Cir.1977)—§ **17.55, n. 4.**

D. L. L., Matter of Guardianship of, 291 N.W.2d 278 (S.D.1980)—§ **4.37, n. 10.**

D.L. Peoples Group, Inc. v. Hawley, 804 So.2d 561 (Fla.App. 1 Dist.2002)— § **17.59, n. 10.**

Dobbins, In re, 371 F.Supp. 141 (D.Kan. 1973)—§ **19.20, n. 3.**

Dobbins v. Martin Buick Co., 216 Ark. 861, 227 S.W.2d 620 (Ark.1950)—§ **19.11, n. 1; § 19.13, n. 4; § 19.15, n. 6.**

Dobbs v. Chevron U.S.A., Inc., 39 F.3d 1064 (10th Cir.1994)—§ **9.5, n. 4.**

Dobesh v. Dobesh, 216 Neb. 196, 342 N.W.2d 669 (Neb.1984)—§ **15.11, n. 4.**

Doe v. National Medical Services, 974 F.2d 143 (10th Cir.1992)—§ **5.13, n. 19; § 6.9, n. 20.**

D'Oench, Duhme & Co. v. Federal Deposit Ins. Corporation, 315 U.S. 447, 62 S.Ct. 676, 86 L.Ed. 956 (1942)—§ **3.51, n. 2.**

Doering v. Copper Mountain, Inc., 259 F.3d 1202 (10th Cir.2001)—§ **7.4, n. 8.**

Dohm & Nelke, a div. of Cashin Systems Corp. v. Wilson Foods Corp., 531 N.E.2d 512 (Ind.App. 3 Dist.1988)—§ **2.22, n. 5; § 18.21, n. 15.**

Dolan v. Dolan, 259 A.2d 32 (Me.1969)— § **13.1, n. 2.**

Dolan v. Mutual Reserve Fund Life Ass'n, 173 Mass. 197, 53 N.E. 398 (Mass. 1899)—§ **18.2, n. 1; § 18.6, n. 3; § 18.7, n. 11.**

Dole Food Co. v. Patrickson, 538 U.S. 468, 123 S.Ct. 1655, 155 L.Ed.2d 643 (2003)—§ **10.19; § 10.19, n. 8.**

Dole Food Co., Inc. v. Watts, 303 F.3d 1104 (9th Cir.2002)—§ **7.3, n. 10; § 7.12, n. 8.**

Dollar Sav. & Trust Co. v. First Nat. Bank of Boston, 32 Ohio Misc. 81, 285 N.E.2d 768 (Ohio Com.Pl.1972)—§ **21.10, n. 7.**

Dolphin v. Robins, 7 H.L. Cas. 390 (1859)— § **4.33, n. 2.**

Dominion Caisson Corp. v. Clark, 614 A.2d 529 (D.C.1992)—§ **17.59, n. 9; § 17.60, n. 6; § 17.61, n. 2, 4.**

Dominion Nat. Bank v. Jones, 202 Va. 502, 118 S.E.2d 672 (Va.1961)—§ **22.11, n. 1; § 22.12, n. 2.**

Domtar, Inc. v. Niagara Fire Ins. Co., 533 N.W.2d 25 (Minn.1995)—§ **5.12, n. 8; § 7.2, n. 35; § 8.2, n. 13.**

Donahue v. United States Dept. of Justice, 751 F.Supp. 45 (S.D.N.Y.1990)—§ **17.48, n. 19.**

Donahue v. Warner Bros. Pictures, 194 F.2d 6 (10th Cir.1952)—§ **17.7, n. 2.**

Donaldson v. Greenwood, 40 Wash.2d 238, 242 P.2d 1038 (Wash.1952)—§ **19.8, n. 6.**

Donaldson, Guardianship of, 178 Cal. App.3d 477, 223 Cal.Rptr. 707 (Cal.App. 5 Dist.1986)—§ **22.26, n. 3.**

Donaldson v. United States, 634 F.Supp. 735 (S.D.Fla.1986)—§ **17.26, n. 1.**

Donatelli v. National Hockey League, 893 F.2d 459 (1st Cir.1990)—§ **5.19, n. 13.**

Donlay's Estate, In re, 280 A.D. 37, 111 N.Y.S.2d 253 (N.Y.A.D. 4 Dept.1952)— § **13.9, n. 11.**

Donna v. Abbotts Dairies, Inc., 399 Pa. 497, 161 A.2d 13 (Pa.1960)—§ **23.5, n. 5.**

Donnelly's Estates, In re, 81 Wash.2d 430, 502 P.2d 1163 (Wash.1972)—§ **16.6, n. 5.**

Donnely v. Copeland Intra Lenses, Inc., 87 F.R.D. 80 (E.D.N.Y.1980)—§ **24.14, n. 3.**

Doody v. John Sexton & Co., 411 F.2d 1119 (1st Cir.1969)—§ **17.52, n. 2.**

Doolittle v. Lewis, 7 Johns.Ch. 45, 2 N.Y. Ch. Ann. 215 (N.Y.Ch.1823)—§ **22.18, n. 12.**

Doppke v. American Bank & Trust Co., 402 S.W.2d 317 (Tex.Civ.App.-Houston 1966)—§ **19.12, n. 3.**

Dorado Beach Hotel Corp. v. Jernigan, 202 So.2d 830 (Fla.App. 1 Dist.1967)— § **3.15, n. 5.**

Dorey v. Dorey, 609 F.2d 1128 (5th Cir. 1980)—§ **15.34, n. 1.**

Dorman v. Emerson Elec. Co., 23 F.3d 1354 (8th Cir.1994)—§ **17.64, n. 11;** § **17.75, n. 3;** § **17.77;** § **17.77, n. 1.**

Dorothy K. Winston & Co. v. Town Heights Development, Inc., 376 F.Supp. 1214 (D.D.C.1974)—§ **18.35;** § **18.35, n. 1.**

Dorr v. Briggs, 709 F.Supp. 1005 (D.Colo. 1989)—§ **17.36, n. 15.**

Dorrance's Estate, In re, 116 N.J.Eq. 204, 172 A. 503 (N.J.Prerog.1934)—§ **4.23, n. 2.**

Dorrance's Estate, In re, 115 N.J.Eq. 268, 170 A. 601 (N.J.Prerog.1934)—§ **4.4, n. 2;** § **4.23, n. 2.**

Dorrance's Estate, In re, 309 Pa. 151, 163 A. 303 (Pa.1932)—§ **4.4, n. 2;** § **4.23, n. 1.**

Dosanjh v. Bhatti, 85 Wash.App. 769, 934 P.2d 1210 (Wash.App. Div. 3 1997)—§ **17.59, n. 3.**

Dotzler v. Perot, 899 F.Supp. 416 (E.D.Mo. 1995)—§ **7.10, n. 5.**

Douglas v. Caldwell, 59 N.C. 20 (N.C. 1860)—§ **22.25, n. 16, 17.**

Douglas v. New York, N.H. & H.R. Co., 279 U.S. 377, 49 S.Ct. 355, 73 L.Ed. 747 (1929)—§ **3.32, n. 9;** § **3.33;** § **3.33, n. 5;** § **11.11, n. 12.**

Doulgeris v. Bambacus, 203 Va. 670, 127 S.E.2d 145 (Va.1962)—§ **16.5, n. 1.**

Dow v. Lillie, 26 N.D. 512, 144 N.W. 1082 (N.D.1914)—§ **22.21, n. 13.**

Dow Chemical Co. v. Castro Alfaro, 786 S.W.2d 674 (Tex.1990)—§ **11.13;** § **11.13, n. 1.**

Dowell v. Beech Acceptance Corp., Inc., 91 Cal.Rptr. 1, 476 P.2d 401 (Cal.1970)—§ **19.21, n. 6.**

Dow Jones & Co Inc v. Gutnick, 2002 WL 31743880 (HCA 2002)—§ **17.55, n. 16.**

Downing v. Abercrombie & Fitch, 265 F.3d 994 (9th Cir.2001)—§ **17.48, n. 12.**

Downs v. American Mut. Liability Ins. Co., 19 A.D.2d 376, 243 N.Y.S.2d 640 (N.Y.A.D. 1 Dept.1963)—§ **19.28, n. 3.**

Dow's Estate, In re, 81 Misc.2d 506, 366 N.Y.S.2d 831 (N.Y.Sur.1975)—§ **20.13, n. 2.**

DP Aviation v. Smiths Industries Aerospace and Defense Systems Ltd., 268 F.3d 829 (9th Cir.2001)—§ **12.18, n. 4.**

Drago v. Home Ins. Co., 486 So.2d 940 (La.App. 1 Cir.1986)—§ **7.4, n. 8.**

Dragor Shipping Corp. v. Union Tank Car Co., 378 F.2d 241 (9th Cir.1967)—§ **6.5, n. 10.**

Drake v. Gordon, 848 F.2d 701 (6th Cir. 1988)—§ **17.56, n. 15;** § **17.58, n. 2.**

Drames v. Milgreva Compania Maritima, S.A., 571 F.Supp. 737 (E.D.Pa.1983)—§ **10.4, n. 10.**

Drapek v. Drapek, 399 Mass. 240, 503 N.E.2d 946 (Mass.1987)—§ **14.11, n. 1.**

Draper v. Draper, 107 Ohio App. 32, 151 N.E.2d 379 (Ohio App. 10 Dist.1958)—§ **4.26, n. 1.**

Draper v. Paul N. Gardner Defined Plan Trust, 625 A.2d 859 (Del.Supr.1993)—§ **23.9, n. 8.**

Dreisel v. Metropolitan Property and Cas. Ins. Co., 836 So.2d 347 (La.App. 1 Cir. 2002)—§ **17.56, n. 20.**

Dresdner Bank AG (New York Branch) v. Edelmann, 129 Misc.2d 686, 493 N.Y.S.2d 703 (N.Y.Sup.1985)—§ **24.6, n. 2.**

Dresser Industries, Inc. v. Sandvick, 732 F.2d 783 (10th Cir.1984)—§ **18.5, n. 16.**

Dreyfus v. First Nat. Bank of Chicago, 424 F.2d 1171 (7th Cir.1970)—§ **20.9, n. 9;** § **20.10, n. 1.**

Drinkall v. Used Car Rentals, Inc., 32 F.3d 329 (8th Cir.1994)—§ **17.44, n. 10.**

Driver v. Helms, 577 F.2d 147 (1st Cir. 1978)—§ **6.2, n. 13.**

Drudge v. Overland Plazas Co., 531 F.Supp. 210 (S.D.Iowa 1981)—§ **3.9, n. 8.**

Drumm, State ex rel. Rashid v., 824 S.W.2d 497 (Mo.App. E.D.1992)—§ **15.43, n. 8.**

Ducharme v. Ducharme, 316 Ark. 482, 872 S.W.2d 392 (Ark.1994)—§ **14.9, n. 14.**

Duckwall v. Lease, 106 Ind.App. 664, 20 N.E.2d 204 (Ind.App.1939)—§ **20.7, n. 3.**

Dudley v. Dudley, 151 Iowa 142, 130 N.W. 785 (Iowa 1911)—§ **13.9, n. 5.**

Duehay v. Acacia Mut. Life Ins. Co., 105 F.2d 768 (D.C.Cir.1939)—§ **22.21, n. 3.**

Dugan v. Mobile Medical Testing Services, Inc., 265 Conn. 791, 830 A.2d 752 (Conn.2003)—§ **17.42, n. 29, 35.**

Duggan, In re Marriage of, 659 N.W.2d 556 (Iowa 2003)—§ **14.11, n. 1.**

Duhon v. Union Pacific Resources Co., 43 F.3d 1011 (5th Cir.1995)—§ **17.45, n. 56;** § **17.60, n. 5;** § **17.61, n. 4.**

Duke v. Housen, 589 P.2d 334 (Wyo. 1979)—§ **3.11, n. 3, 4.**

Duke of Wellington, [1947] Ch. 506—§ **3.13, n. 10.**

Duley v. Duley, 151 A.2d 255 (D.C.Mun. App.1959)—§ **13.12, n. 1.**

Dumaine, In re, 135 N.H. 103, 600 A.2d 127 (N.H.1991)—§ **21.2, n. 14.**

Dumaresly v. Fishly, 10 Ky. 368 (Ky. 1821)—§ **13.6, n. 9.**

Dunavant Enterprises, Inc. v. Ford, 294 So.2d 788 (Miss.1974)—§ **19.12, n. 3.**

Dunbar, People ex rel. v. Bejarano, 145 Colo. 304, 358 P.2d 866 (Colo.1961)—§ **14.6, n. 4.**

Duncan v. Cessna Aircraft Co., 665 S.W.2d 414 (Tex.1984)—§ **2.17, n. 11;** § **2.23, n. 2;** § **14.12, n. 3.**

Duncan v. Peck, 752 F.2d 1135 (6th Cir. 1985)—§ **24.1, n. 9.**

Duncan v. Lawson, 1889 WL 10275 (Ch D 1889)—§ **19.2, n. 1.**

Dunes Hospitality, L.L.C. v. Country Kitchen Intern., Inc., 623 N.W.2d 484 (S.D. 2001)—§ **18.2, n. 14.**

Dunham v. Dunham, 602 So.2d 1139 (La. App. 1 Cir.1992)—§ **14.11, n. 2.**

Dunkin' Donuts Inc. v. Guang Chyi Liu, 2002 WL 31375509 (E.D.Pa.2002)— § **17.40, n. 26.**

Dunkley, In re Marriage of, 89 Wash.2d 777, 575 P.2d 1071 (Wash.1978)— § **11.11, n. 2.**

Dunkley v. Peoples Bank & Trust Co., 728 F.Supp. 547 (W.D.Ark.1989)—§ **21.3, n. 9.**

Dunlap by Wells v. Buchanan, 741 F.2d 165 (8th Cir.1984)—§ **4.2, n. 1; § 4.13, n. 4; § 4.37, n. 10.**

Dunlop Tire & Rubber Corp. v. Ryan, 171 Neb. 820, 108 N.W.2d 84 (Neb.1961)— § **18.4, n. 43; § 18.6, n. 3.**

Dunn v. A/S Em. Z. Svitzer, 885 F.Supp. 980 (S.D.Tex.1995)—§ **9.5, n. 4.**

Dunn v. Blumstein, 405 U.S. 330, 92 S.Ct. 995, 31 L.Ed.2d 274 (1972)—§ **4.20, n. 6.**

Dupasseur v. Rochereau, 88 U.S. 130, 22 L.Ed. 588 (1874)—§ **3.40; § 3.40, n. 15.**

Duplan Corp., In re, 455 F.Supp. 926 (S.D.N.Y.1978)—§ **19.18, n. 12.**

Duplan Corp. (Duplan Yarn Division) v. W. B. Davis Hosiery Mills, Inc., 442 F.Supp. 86 (S.D.N.Y.1977)—§ **18.7, n. 10.**

duPont v. Southern Nat. Bank of Houston, Texas, 575 F.Supp. 849 (S.D.Tex.1983)— § **19.2, n. 2.**

Dupree v. Virgil R. Coss Mortg. Co., 167 Ark. 18, 267 S.W. 586 (Ark.1924)— § **18.7, n. 12.**

Dupuy v. Wurtz, 53 N.Y. 556 (N.Y.1873)— § **4.21, n. 2.**

Duquesne's Estate, In re, 29 Utah 2d 94, 505 P.2d 779 (Utah 1973)—§ **20.2, n. 4.**

Durdahl v. National Safety Associates, Inc., 988 P.2d 525 (Wyo.1999)—§ **17.40, n. 25.**

Durfee v. Duke, 375 U.S. 106, 84 S.Ct. 242, 11 L.Ed.2d 186 (1963)—§ **4.7, n. 5; § 5.17, n. 9; § 5.21, n. 6; § 19.8; § 19.8, n. 12; § 20.2; § 20.2, n. 7, 8; § 20.6, n. 23; § 22.3, n. 13; § 22.20; § 22.20, n. 28; § 24.2, n. 11; § 24.10; § 24.10, n. 5, 11; § 24.17, n. 15; § 24.29, n. 6.**

Durfee v. Durfee, 293 Mass. 472, 200 N.E. 395 (Mass.1936)—§ **4.40, n. 2.**

Duro v. Reina, 495 U.S. 676, 110 S.Ct. 2053, 109 L.Ed.2d 693 (1990)—§ **11.17, n. 2.**

Dusenbery v. United States, 534 U.S. 161, 122 S.Ct. 694, 151 L.Ed.2d 597 (2002)— § **12.3, n. 7.**

Duskin v. Pennsylvania–Central Airlines Corp., 167 F.2d 727 (6th Cir.1948)— § **18.3, n. 1; § 18.7, n. 6.**

Dutcher v. Dutcher, 39 Wis. 651 (Wis. 1876)—§ **4.33, n. 1.**

Du Val v. Marshall, 30 Ark. 230 (Ark. 1875)—§ **22.17, n. 6.**

Duval's Estate, In re, 133 Vt. 197, 332 A.2d 802 (Vt.1975)—§ **20.7, n. 3; § 20.13, n. 4.**

Dworak v. Olson Const. Co., 191 Colo. 161, 551 P.2d 198 (Colo.1976)—§ **18.37, n. 6.**

Dworkin v. Hustler Magazine, Inc., 668 F.Supp. 1408 (C.D.Cal.1987)—§ **17.55, n. 11.**

Dwyer's Estate, In re, 159 Cal. 680, 115 P. 242 (Cal.1911)—§ **20.9, n. 10.**

Dyer v. National Steam Nav. Co., 118 U.S. 507, 6 S.Ct. 1174, 30 L.Ed. 153 (1886)— § **3.57, n. 16.**

Dyke v. Dyke, 227 F.2d 461 (6th Cir. 1955)—§ **3.54, n. 2.**

Dym v. Gordon, 262 N.Y.S.2d 463, 209 N.E.2d 792 (N.Y.1965)—§ **17.29, n. 9; § 17.30; § 17.30, n. 1.**

Dymond v. National Broadcasting Co., Inc., 559 F.Supp. 734 (D.Del.1983)—§ **3.11, n. 5.**

Dyszel v. Marks, 6 F.3d 116 (3rd Cir. 1993)—§ **17.58, n. 9.**

E

Eads v. Woodmen of the World Life Ins. Soc., 785 P.2d 328 (Okla.App. Div. 2 1989)—§ **11.5, n. 3.**

EA Oil Service, Inc. v. Mobil Exploration & Producing Turkmenistan, Inc., 2000 WL 552406 (Tex.App.-Hous. (14 Dist.) 2000)—§ **17.48, n. 9.**

Earl v. Dresser, 30 Ind. 11 (Ind.1868)— § **22.25, n. 8, 16.**

Earle v. Earle, 141 A.D. 611, 126 N.Y.S. 317 (N.Y.A.D. 1 Dept.1910)—§ **13.9, n. 3.**

Earnhardt v. Shattuck, 232 F.Supp. 845 (D.Vt.1964)—§ **3.10, n. 1, 6.**

East Denver Municipal Irr. Dist. v. Doherty, 293 F. 804 (S.D.N.Y.1923)—§ **10.12, n. 16.**

Easterly v. Goodwin, 35 Conn. 279 (Conn. 1868)—§ **4.21, n. 2.**

Eastern Shore Marine, Inc. v. M/V Mistress, 717 F.Supp. 790 (S.D.Ala.1989)—§ **23.7, n. 6.**

E.A.S.T., Inc. of Stamford, Conn. v. M/V Alaia, 876 F.2d 1168 (5th Cir.1989)— § **24.48, n. 8.**

East Montpelier v. City of Barre, 79 Vt. 542, 66 A. 100 (Vt.1906)—§ **4.19, n. 4.**

Eaton v. Eaton, 66 Neb. 676, 92 N.W. 995 (Neb.1902)—§ **13.9, n. 4.**

Eaton v. Hasty, 6 Neb. 419 (Neb.1877)— § **24.5, n. 2.**

E.B. & A.C. Whiting Co. v. Hartford Fire Ins. Co., 838 F.Supp. 863 (D.Vt.1993)— § **18.21, n. 14; § 18.26, n. 13.**

Echols v. Wells, 508 S.W.2d 118 (Tex.Civ. App.-Hous. (1 Dist.) 1973)—§ **19.2, n. 2.**

Eco Swiss China Time Ltd. v. Timex Corp., 944 F.Supp. 134 (D.Conn.1996)—§ **12.8, n. 9.**

Edelmann v. Chase Manhattan Bank, N.A., 861 F.2d 1291 (1st Cir.1988)—§ **2.23, n. 8.**

Edelson v. Soricelli, 610 F.2d 131 (3rd Cir. 1979)—§ **3.41**; § **3.41, n. 2, 18.**

ED&F Man (Sugar) Ltd v. Haryanto Yani (No.2), 1990 WL 753393 (CA 1990)— § **24.3, n. 15.**

Edgar v. MITE Corp., 457 U.S. 624, 102 S.Ct. 2629, 73 L.Ed.2d 269 (1982)— § **23.6**; § **23.6, n. 8**; § **23.9, n. 5.**

Edgerly v. Bush, 81 N.Y. 199 (N.Y.1880)— § **19.11, n. 12**; § **19.15, n. 7.**

Edmunds v. Equitable Sav. & Loan Ass'n, 223 A.2d 630 (D.C.App.1966)—§ **22.25, n. 3, 7.**

Edmundson, In re, 273 N.C. 92, 159 S.E.2d 509 (N.C.1968)—§ **22.10, n. 11**; § **22.19, n. 6.**

Edmundson v. Miley Trailer Co., 211 N.W.2d 269 (Iowa 1973)—§ **4.13, n. 3.**

EDO Corp. v. Newark Ins. Co., 1997 WL 76575 (D.Conn.1997)—§ **18.26, n. 13.**

Edrington v. Mayfield, 5 Tex. 363 (Tex. 1849)—§ **14.10, n. 3.**

Education Resouces Inst. v. Lipsky, 2002 WL 1463461 (Cal.App. 1 Dist.2002)— § **17.40, n. 26**; § **18.1, n. 17.**

Edward J. Moriarty & Co. v. General Tire & Rubber Co., 289 F.Supp. 381 (S.D.Ohio 1967)—§ **10.3, n. 8.**

Edwards v. Associated Press, 512 F.2d 258 (5th Cir.1975)—§ **17.55, n. 9.**

Edwards v. Edwards, 108 Okla. 93, 233 P. 477 (Okla.1924)—§ **14.6, n. 5.**

Edwards v. Pulitzer Pub. Co., 716 F.Supp. 438 (N.D.Cal.1989)—§ **7.10, n. 4.**

Edwards' Estate, In re, 87 Misc.2d 337, 385 N.Y.S.2d 253 (N.Y.Sur.1976)—§ **22.10, n. 2.**

Eells v. Holder, 12 F. 668 (C.C.D.Kan. 1880)—§ **22.11, n. 14, 17**; § **22.14, n. 3.**

E.E.O.C. v. Waffle House, Inc., 534 U.S. 279, 122 S.Ct. 754, 151 L.Ed.2d 755 (2002)—§ **11.6**; § **11.6, n. 11.**

Egan v. Kaiser Aluminum & Chemical Corp., 677 So.2d 1027 (La.App. 4 Cir. 1996)—§ **17.78, n. 8.**

Egan v. McNamara, 467 A.2d 733 (D.C. 1983)—§ **19.32, n. 3.**

Egbert v. Baker, 58 Conn. 319, 20 A. 466 (Conn.1890)—§ **19.30, n. 7.**

Eger v. E.I. Du Pont DeNemours Co., 110 N.J. 133, 539 A.2d 1213 (N.J.1988)— § **2.24, n. 6**; § **17.42**; § **17.42, n. 20, 23**; § **17.60, n. 5**; § **17.61, n. 4.**

E. Gerli and Co. v. Cunard S.S. Co., 48 F.2d 115 (2nd Cir.1931)—§ **18.2, n. 2.**

Eggemeyer v. Eggemeyer, 554 S.W.2d 137 (Tex.1977)—§ **14.13, n. 3.**

Ehler v. Ehler, 214 Iowa 789, 243 N.W. 591 (Iowa 1932)—§ **20.5, n. 6.**

Ehredt v. DeHavilland Aircraft Co. of Canada, Ltd., 705 P.2d 446 (Alaska 1985)— § **2.17, n. 16**; § **2.23, n. 1, 2**; § **17.26, n. 1**; § **18.21, n. 14.**

Ehrman v. Cook Elec. Co., 468 F.Supp. 98 (N.D.Ill.1979)—§ **18.38, n. 6.**

Eichman v. Fotomat Corp., 759 F.2d 1434 (9th Cir.1985)—§ **24.12, n. 7.**

Eikel v. Bristow Corp., 529 S.W.2d 795 (Tex.Civ.App.-Hous. (1 Dist.) 1975)— § **22.14, n. 5**; § **22.18, n. 4.**

Eikel v. Burton, 530 S.W.2d 907 (Tex.Civ. App.-Hous. (1 Dist.) 1975)—§ **22.14, n. 5.**

Eimers v. Honda Motor Co., Ltd., 785 F.Supp. 1204 (W.D.Pa.1992)—§ **17.44, n. 9**; § **17.70, n. 6.**

Einhorn v. Einhorn, (N.Y.Sup.Ct.1976)— § **15.21, n. 5.**

Eisel v. Secretary of the Army, 477 F.2d 1251, 155 U.S.App.D.C. 366 (D.C.Cir. 1973)—§ **4.26, n. 4.**

Eisenberg v. Commercial Union Assur. Co., 189 F.Supp. 500 (S.D.N.Y.1960)—§ **23.3, n. 1.**

Eisenberg's Estate, Matter of, 177 Misc. 655, 31 N.Y.S.2d 380 (N.Y.Sur.1941)— § **4.28, n. 4.**

Ela, Appeal of, 68 N.H. 35, 38 A. 501 (N.H. 1894)—§ **22.9, n. 1.**

El Al Israel Airlines, Ltd. v. Tsui Yuan Tseng, 525 U.S. 155, 119 S.Ct. 662, 142 L.Ed.2d 576 (1999)—§ **3.56, n. 2**; § **3.57, n. 23.**

Elam v. Maggard, 165 Ky. 733, 178 S.W. 1065 (Ky.1915)—§ **4.13, n. 2.**

Elbeco Inc. v. Estrella de Plato, Corp., 989 F.Supp. 669 (E.D.Pa.1997)—§ **10.17, n. 10.**

Eldon Industries, Inc. v. Paradies & Co., 397 F.Supp. 535 (N.D.Ga.1975)— § **18.37, n. 5.**

Eldridge v. Don Beachcomber, Inc., 342 Ill. App. 151, 95 N.E.2d 512 (Ill.App. 1 Dist. 1950)—§ **17.5, n. 7.**

Eleanor A., In re, 84 Cal.App.3d 184, 148 Cal.Rptr. 315 (Cal.App. 4 Dist.1978)— § **4.37, n. 10.**

Electrical Equipment Co. v. Daniel Hamm Drayage Co., 217 F.2d 656 (8th Cir. 1954)—§ **10.14, n. 10.**

Electrical Products Consolidated v. Bodell, 132 Mont. 243, 316 P.2d 788 (Mont. 1957)—§ **11.5, n. 3.**

El-Fadl v. Central Bank of Jordan, 75 F.3d 668, 316 U.S.App.D.C. 86 (D.C.Cir. 1996)—§ **11.10, n. 1.**

Elia Corp. v. Paul N. Howard Co., 391 A.2d 214 (Del.Super.1978)—§ **11.5, n. 3.**

Eliah v. Ucatan Corp., 433 F.Supp. 309 (W.D.N.Y.1977)—§ **17.55, n. 4, 9.**

Eli Lilly and Co. v. Home Ins. Co., 764 F.2d 876, 246 U.S.App.D.C. 243 (D.C.Cir. 1985)—§ **17.26, n. 1**; § **18.26, n. 12.**

Eli Lilly & Co. v. Sav–On–Drugs, Inc., 366 U.S. 276, 81 S.Ct. 1316, 6 L.Ed.2d 288 (1961)—§ **23.6, n. 4, 5.**

Eli Lilly & Co., Prozac Products Liability Litigation, In re, 789 F.Supp. 1448 (S.D.Ind.1992)—§ **17.75, n. 1; § 17.77, n. 3.**

Eli Witt Co., Matter of, 12 B.R. 757 (Bkrtcy. M.D.Fla.1981)—§ **23.15, n. 14.**

Elkind v. Byck, 68 Cal.2d 453, 67 Cal.Rptr. 404, 439 P.2d 316 (Cal.1968)—§ **15.33; § 15.33, n. 2.**

Elkins v. Moreno, 435 U.S. 647, 98 S.Ct. 1338, 55 L.Ed.2d 614 (1978)—§ **4.20, n. 5; § 4.31, n. 5; § 4.32, n. 2.**

Ellington v. Harris, 127 Ga. 85, 56 S.E. 134 (Ga.1906)—§ **14.6, n. 2.**

Elliot v. Lord Joicey, 1935 WL 25142 (HL 1935)—§ **12.16, n. 2.**

Elliott v. Day, 218 F.Supp. 90 (D.Or. 1962)—§ **22.10, n. 6.**

Elliott v. Hardcastle, 271 Ark. 90, 607 S.W.2d 381 (Ark.1980)—§ **15.9, n. 6.**

Elliott v. Johnston, 365 Mo. 881, 292 S.W.2d 589 (Mo.1956)—§ **11.8, n. 3.**

Elliott v. Krear, 466 F.Supp. 444 (E.D.Va. 1979)—§ **4.37, n. 10; § 4.40, n. 6.**

Elliott v. Peirsol's Lessee, 26 U.S. 328, 7 L.Ed. 164 (1828)—§ **5.1, n. 7; § 5.2, n. 8.**

Elliott v. Van Kleef, 830 So.2d 726 (Ala. 2002)—§ **7.4, n. 8.**

Elliott v. Wood, 45 N.Y. 71 (N.Y.1871)—§ **19.9, n. 7.**

Ellis v. Abbott, 69 Or. 234, 138 P. 488 (Or.1914)—§ **19.5, n. 4.**

Ellis v. Barto, 82 Wash.App. 454, 918 P.2d 540 (Wash.App. Div. 3 1996)—§ **17.36, n. 15; § 17.48, n. 6.**

Ellis v. Great Southwestern Corp., 646 F.2d 1099 (5th Cir.1981)—§ **3.46, n. 15.**

Ellis v. Southeast Const. Co., 260 F.2d 280 (8th Cir.1958)—§ **4.26, n. 2.**

Ellis, United States v., 714 F.2d 953 (9th Cir.1983)—§ **3.52, n. 3.**

Elmer v. Hall, 148 Pa. 345, 23 A. 971 (Pa. 1892)—§ **22.17, n. 7.**

El Paso Natural Gas Co. v. Neztsosie, 526 U.S. 473, 119 S.Ct. 1430, 143 L.Ed.2d 635 (1999)—§ **11.17; § 11.17, n. 33.**

Else v. Inflight Cinema Intern., Inc., 465 F.Supp. 1239 (W.D.Pa.1979)—§ **10.16, n. 8.**

Elson, In re Estate of, 120 Ill.App.3d 649, 76 Ill.Dec. 237, 458 N.E.2d 637 (Ill.App. 2 Dist.1983)—§ **22.6, n. 1.**

Elson v. Defren, 283 A.D.2d 109, 726 N.Y.S.2d 407 (N.Y.A.D. 1 Dept.2001)—§ **17.48, n. 12.**

Elston v. Industrial Lift Truck Co., 420 Pa. 97, 216 A.2d 318 (Pa.1966)—§ **18.46, n. 5.**

Embiricos v. Anglo Austrian Bank, 1905 WL 13494 (CA 1905)—§ **19.12, n. 3; § 19.31, n. 8.**

Embry v. Millar, 8 Ky. 300 (Ky.1818)—§ **22.9, n. 1.**

Emerson v. Cole, 847 So.2d 606 (Fla.App. 2 Dist.2003)—§ **7.8, n. 10.**

Emerson v. Falcon Mfg., Inc., 333 F.Supp. 888 (S.D.Tex.1971)—§ **3.45, n. 4.**

Emerson Elec. Co. v. Aetna Cas. & Sur. Co., 319 Ill.App.3d 218, 252 Ill.Dec. 761, 743 N.E.2d 629 (Ill.App. 1 Dist.2001)—§ **18.26, n. 12.**

Emery v. Batchelder, 132 Mass. 452 (Mass. 1882)—§ **22.23, n. 2.**

Emery v. Burbank, 163 Mass. 326, 39 N.E. 1026 (Mass.1895)—§ **18.15; § 18.15, n. 1; § 18.19, § 18.19, n. 1, 9.**

Emery v. Clough, 63 N.H. 552, 4 A. 796 (N.H.1886)—§ **19.13, n. 4.**

Emery v. Emery, 45 Cal.2d 421, 289 P.2d 218 (Cal.1955)—§ **17.8, n. 10; § 17.16; § 17.16, n. 5; § 17.39, n. 6.**

Emery v. Hildreth, 68 Mass. 228 (Mass. 1854)—§ **22.10, n. 2.**

Emery Transp. Co. v. Baker, 254 Iowa 744, 119 N.W.2d 272 (Iowa 1963)—§ **12.3, n. 6.**

Emhart Industries, Inc. v. Duracell Intern. Inc., 665 F.Supp. 549 (M.D.Tenn. 1987)—§ **18.2, n. 11.**

EMI Music Mexico, S.A. v. Rodriguez, 97 S.W.3d 847 (Tex.App.-Corpus Christi 2003)—§ **5.10, n. 26.**

E/M Lubricants, Inc. v. Microfral, S. A. R. L., 91 F.R.D. 235 (N.D.Ill.1981)—§ **11.15, n. 4.**

Emory v. Grenough, 3 U.S. 369, 3 Dall. 369, 1 L.Ed. 640 (1797)—§ **2.7, n. 5.**

Employers Ins. of Wausau v. Duplan Corp., 899 F.Supp. 1112 (S.D.N.Y.1995)—§ **18.26, n. 12.**

Engel v. Davenport, 194 Cal. 344, 228 P. 710 (Cal.1924)—§ **6.5, n. 11.**

Engin v. Engin, 1984 WL 6053 (Ohio App. 10 Dist.1984)—§ **15.29, n. 3.**

Engineering Equipment Co. v. S.S. Selene, 446 F.Supp. 706 (S.D.N.Y.1978)—§ **10.6, n. 50, 52.**

Engineers Nat. Bank v. Drew, 311 Pa. 59, 166 A. 376 (Pa.1933)—§ **24.20, n. 3.**

English v. McIntyre, 29 A.D. 439, 51 N.Y.S. 697 (N.Y.A.D. 1 Dept.1898)—§ **21.2, n. 5.**

English & Smith v. Metzger, 901 F.2d 36 (4th Cir.1990)—§ **8.4, n. 6.**

Enis v. State, 408 So.2d 486 (Miss.1981)—§ **13.6, n. 2.**

Enke, Application of, 129 Mont. 353, 287 P.2d 19 (Mont.1955)—§ **4.37, n. 3; § 4.40, n. 2.**

Ennis v. Smith, 55 U.S. 400, 14 How. 400, 14 L.Ed. 472 (1852)—§ **4.20, n. 4; § 4.27, n. 12; § 4.36, n. 3; § 20.3, n. 1.**

E.N.O. v. L.M.M., 429 Mass. 824, 711 N.E.2d 886 (Mass.1999)—§ **16.1, n. 13.**

Enriquez v. Superior Court, In and For Pima County, 115 Ariz. 342, 565 P.2d

522 (Ariz.App. Div. 2 1977)—§ **11.17, n. 21, 30.**

Ensley v. Hodgson, 212 Ala. 526, 103 So. 465 (Ala.1925)—§ **20.6, n. 11.**

Enterprises & Contracting Co. v. Plicoflex, Inc., 529 S.W.2d 805 (Tex.Civ.App.-Hous. (1 Dist.) 1975)—§ **12.15, n. 9.**

Entron, Inc. v. Affiliated FM Ins. Co., 749 F.2d 127 (2nd Cir.1984)—§ **3.8, n. 3.**

E.P. v. District Court of Garfield County, 696 P.2d 254 (Colo.1985)—§ **15.41, n. 2.**

EPIC Mortg. Ins. Litigation, In re, 701 F.Supp. 1192 (E.D.Va.1988)—§ **3.46, n. 7.**

Epperson v. Dixie Ins. Co., 461 So.2d 172 (Fla.App. 1 Dist.1984)—§ **17.58, n. 4.**

Epps v. Stewart Information Services Corp., 327 F.3d 642 (8th Cir.2003)—§ **10.16, n. 8.**

Equilease Corp. v. Belk Hotel Corp., 42 N.C.App. 436, 256 S.E.2d 836 (N.C.App. 1979)—§ **19.3, n. 14;** § **19.10, n. 1;** § **19.12, n. 3.**

Equitable Trust Co. v. Bratwursthaus Management Corp., 514 F.2d 565 (4th Cir. 1975)—§ **18.21, n. 12;** § **18.39, n. 6.**

Erdman's Estate, In re, 264 Cal.App.2d 335, 70 Cal.Rptr. 774 (Cal.App. 2 Dist. 1968)—§ **21.13, n. 5.**

Erie Ins. Exchange v. Shapiro, 248 Va. 638, 450 S.E.2d 144 (Va.1994)—§ **2.21, n. 45;** § **18.21, n. 12.**

Erie R. Co. v. Tompkins, 304 U.S. 64, 58 S.Ct. 817, 82 L.Ed. 1188 (1938)—§ **3.2, n. 5;** § **3.17, n. 11;** § **3.36;** § **3.36, n. 2;** § **3.49, n. 1;** § **10.6;** § **10.6, n. 6;** § **11.4, n. 1;** § **24.6, n. 3;** § **24.35;** § **24.35, n. 1, 3.**

Ernst v. Ernst, 722 F.Supp. 61 (S.D.N.Y. 1989)—§ **11.3, n. 22.**

Erny v. Estate of Merola, 171 N.J. 86, 792 A.2d 1208 (N.J.2002)—§ **17.45;** § **17.45, n. 9.**

Erny v. Russo, 333 N.J.Super. 88, 754 A.2d 606 (N.J.Super.A.D.2000)—§ **17.45, n. 10.**

Erwin v. Thomas, 264 Or. 454, 506 P.2d 494 (Or.1973)—§ **17.14;** § **17.14, n. 4;** § **17.27, n. 7;** § **17.45;** § **17.45, n. 2.**

ESAB Group, Inc. v. Centricut, Inc., 126 F.3d 617 (4th Cir.1997)—§ **9.8, n. 7;** § **10.2, n. 5;** § **10.18, n. 9.**

Escola v. Coca Cola Bottling Co. of Fresno, 24 Cal.2d 453, 150 P.2d 436 (Cal.1944)—§ **7.1, n. 3;** § **7.2, n. 1.**

Escoto v. United States Lending Corp., 675 So.2d 741 (La.App. 4 Cir.1996)—§ **9.6, n. 21.**

Escrow Service Co. v. Cressler, 59 Wash.2d 38, 365 P.2d 760 (Wash.1961)—§ **14.13, n. 2;** § **14.16, n. 10.**

Esenwein v. Commonwealth of Pennsylvania, 325 U.S. 279, 65 S.Ct. 1118, 89 L.Ed. 1608 (1945)—§ **15.6, n. 4;** § **15.27;** § **15.27, n. 2.**

Esfeld v. Costa Crociere, S.P.A., 289 F.3d 1300 (11th Cir.2002)—§ **3.41, n. 12.**

Eskofot A/S v. E.I. Du Pont De Nemours & Co., 872 F.Supp. 81 (S.D.N.Y.1995)—§ **10.5, n. 14;** § **10.6, n. 29.**

Espinosa v. Norfolk & W. Ry. Co., 86 Ill.2d 111, 56 Ill.Dec. 31, 427 N.E.2d 111 (Ill. 1981)—§ **11.8, n. 6.**

Esser v. Esser, 277 Ga. 97, 586 S.E.2d 627 (Ga.2003)—§ **15.33, n. 4.**

Esser v. McIntyre, 169 Ill.2d 292, 214 Ill. Dec. 693, 661 N.E.2d 1138 (Ill.1996)—§ **2.19, n. 17;** § **17.39, n. 15.**

Estabrook v. Wise, 506 S.W.2d 248 (Tex. Civ.App.-Tyler 1974)—§ **19.3, n. 12;** § **19.8, n. 3.**

Estate of (see name of party)

Esteve Bros. & Co. v. Harrell, 272 F. 382 (5th Cir.1921)—§ **10.12, n. 9.**

Estin v. Estin, 334 U.S. 541, 68 S.Ct. 1213, 92 L.Ed. 1561 (1948)—§ **3.28, n. 4;** § **5.7, n. 3;** § **15.12, n. 1;** § **15.27;** § **15.27, n. 3.**

Etheredge v. Genie Industries, Inc., 632 So.2d 1324 (Ala.1994)—§ **2.21, n. 1;** § **3.9, n. 4;** § **17.71;** § **17.71, n. 8.**

Ethridge v. Sullivan, 245 S.W.2d 1015 (Tex. Civ.App.-Amarillo 1951)—§ **12.15, n. 10.**

Eubank Heights Apartments, Ltd. v. Lebow, 615 F.2d 571 (1st Cir.1980)—§ **22.19, n. 12, 33;** § **22.20, n. 25.**

Eureka Federal Sav. and Loan Ass'n v. Kidwell, 672 F.Supp. 436 (N.D.Cal.1987)—§ **3.54, n. 2.**

Euromepa, S.A. v. R. Esmerian, Inc., 154 F.3d 24 (2nd Cir.1998)—§ **12.8, n. 10.**

Evans v. Beaver, 50 Ohio St. 190, 33 N.E. 643 (Ohio 1893)—§ **19.3, n. 6.**

Evans v. Evans, 668 F.Supp. 639 (M.D.Tenn.1987)—§ **15.42, n. 10.**

Evans v. Valley Forge Convention Center, 1996 WL 468688 (E.D.Pa.1996)—§ **17.42, n. 17.**

Evans v. Young, 201 Tenn. 368, 299 S.W.2d 218 (Tenn.1957)—§ **16.2, n. 5.**

Evansville Ice & Cold-Storage Co. v. Winsor (State Report Title: Evansville Ice & Cold Storage Co. v. Winsor), 148 Ind. 682, 48 N.E. 592 (Ind.1897)—§ **22.3, n. 1, 2.**

Everett v. Vendryes, 19 N.Y. 436 (N.Y. 1859)—§ **19.31, n. 8.**

Everett/Charles Contact Products, Inc. v. Gentec, S.A.R.L., 692 F.Supp. 83 (D.R.I. 1988)—§ **2.21, n. 73.**

Everson v. Everson, 264 Pa.Super. 563, 400 A.2d 887 (Pa.Super.1979)—§ **14.10, n. 3;** § **14.16, n. 17.**

Ewing v. Warren, 144 Miss. 233, 109 So. 601 (Miss.1926)—§ **20.4, n. 5.**

Examining Bd. of Engineers, Architects and Surveyors v. Flores de Otero, 426 U.S. 572, 96 S.Ct. 2264, 49 L.Ed.2d 65 (1976)—§ **3.58, n. 12;** § **20.17, n. 2.**

Executive Jet Aviation, Inc. v. City of Cleveland, Ohio, 409 U.S. 249, 93 S.Ct. 493, 34 L.Ed.2d 454 (1972)—§ **3.53, n. 10;** § **10.6;** § **10.6, n. 12;** § **17.63, n. 32.**

Exide Corp. v. Electro Services, Inc., 596 F.Supp. 1404 (E.D.Pa.1984)—§ **11.14, n. 6.**

Ex parte (see name of party)

Export Ins. Co. v. Mitsui S. S. Co., 26 A.D.2d 436, 274 N.Y.S.2d 977 (N.Y.A.D. 1 Dept.1966)—§ **11.5, n. 3.**

Exum v. Vantage Press, Inc., 17 Wash.App. 477, 563 P.2d 1314 (Wash.App. Div. 2 1977)—§ **11.5, n. 3.**

Exxon Corp., Ex parte, 725 So.2d 930 (Ala. 1998)—§ **2.21, n. 1.**

Exxon Co., U.S.A. v. Sofec, Inc., 517 U.S. 830, 116 S.Ct. 1813, 135 L.Ed.2d 113 (1996)—§ **7.4, n. 3.**

Ezell v. Hayes Oilfield Const. Co., Inc., 693 F.2d 489 (5th Cir.1982)—§ **17.40, n. 28;** § **18.1, n. 18.**

F

Fabbri's Will, In re, 159 N.Y.S.2d 184, 140 N.E.2d 269 (N.Y.1957)—§ **20.13, n. 4.**

Faber v. Althoff, 168 Ariz. 213, 812 P.2d 1031 (Ariz.App. Div. 1 1990)—§ **5.5, n. 7.**

Fabricius v. Horgen, 257 Iowa 268, 132 N.W.2d 410 (Iowa 1965)—§ **17.39, n. 12.**

Factors Etc., Inc. v. Pro Arts, Inc., 652 F.2d 278 (2nd Cir.1981)—§ **3.47, n. 7, 12;** § **17.55, n. 9.**

Factors Etc., Inc. v. Pro Arts, Inc., 496 F.Supp. 1090 (S.D.N.Y.1980)—§ **3.54, n. 5.**

Fadgen v. Lenkner, 469 Pa. 272, 365 A.2d 147 (Pa.1976)—§ **17.54, n. 1.**

Fagin's Estate, In re, 246 Iowa 496, 66 N.W.2d 920 (Iowa 1954)—§ **22.10, n. 11, 16.**

Fagone v. Fagone, 508 So.2d 644 (La.App. 2 Cir.1987)—§ **19.1, n. 3.**

Fahs v. Martin, 224 F.2d 387 (5th Cir. 1955)—§ **19.9, n. 10;** § **23.15, n. 12.**

Fairfield Lease Corp. v. Pratt, 6 Conn.Cir. Ct. 537, 278 A.2d 154 (Conn.Cir.Ct. 1971)—§ **18.5, n. 2;** § **18.11, n. 4;** § **18.12, n. 10, 14.**

Falco v. Grills, 209 Va. 115, 161 S.E.2d 713 (Va.1968)—§ **22.26, n. 2, 6.**

Falcon Tankers, Inc. v. Litton Systems, Inc., 300 A.2d 231 (Del.Super.1972)— § **18.3, n. 1;** § **18.12, n. 7.**

Falke v. Terry, 32 Colo. 85, 75 P. 425 (Colo.1903)—§ **22.19, n. 17, 18.**

Fall v. Eastin, 215 U.S. 1, 30 S.Ct. 3, 54 L.Ed. 65 (1909)—§ **19.8, n. 11;** § **20.2, n. 11;** § **24.10, n. 1, 3, 8.**

Fall v. Fall, 75 Neb. 104, 113 N.W. 175 (Neb.1907)—§ **24.10, n. 3.**

Faloona by Fredrickson v. Hustler Magazine, Inc., 799 F.2d 1000 (5th Cir. 1986)—§ **17.26, n. 1;** § **17.55, n. 11.**

Fangman v. Moyers, 90 Colo. 308, 8 P.2d 762 (Colo.1932)—§ **4.13, n. 2.**

Fanselow v. Rice, 213 F.Supp.2d 1077 (D.Neb.2002)—§ **17.50, n. 36.**

Fantome v. Frederick, 2003 WL 215812 (11th Cir.2003)—§ **17.63, n. 28.**

Fantome, S.A., In re Complaint of, 232 F.Supp.2d 1298 (S.D.Fla.2002)—§ **17.63;** § **17.63, n. 25.**

Farah v. Farah, 16 Va.App. 329, 429 S.E.2d 626 (Va.App.1993)—§ **15.16, n. 3.**

Farber v. Smolack, 282 N.Y.S.2d 248, 229 N.E.2d 36 (N.Y.1967)—§ **17.30, n. 12;** § **17.48, n. 17.**

Farbman v. Esskay Mfg. Co., 676 F.Supp. 666 (W.D.N.C.1987)—§ **8.4, n. 3.**

Farias v. Mattel, Inc., 153 Ariz. 113, 735 P.2d 143 (Ariz.App. Div. 2 1986)— § **17.60, n. 5.**

Farley v. Farley, 19 Utah 2d 301, 431 P.2d 133 (Utah 1967)—§ **19.8, n. 3.**

Farmer v. Standard Dredging Corp, 167 F.Supp. 381 (D.Del.1958)—§ **17.63, n. 22.**

Farmers' & Mechanics' Nat. Bank v. Loftus, 133 Pa. 97, 19 A. 347 (Pa.1890)— § **19.11, n. 12;** § **19.12, n. 4;** § **19.31, n. 8.**

Farmers' & Mechanics' Sav. Bank v. Brewer, 27 Conn. 600 (Conn.1858)—§ **21.6, n. 3.**

Farmers & Merchants Trust Co. v. Madeira, 261 Cal.App.2d 503, 68 Cal.Rptr. 184 (Cal.App. 5 Dist.1968)—§ **22.14, n. 4;** § **22.18, n. 7.**

Farmers State Bank v. Production Credit Ass'n of St. Cloud, 243 Kan. 87, 755 P.2d 518 (Kan.1988)—§ **19.18, n. 17.**

Farmland Industries, Inc. v. Frazier–Parrott Commodities, Inc., 806 F.2d 848 (8th Cir.1986)—§ **6.3, n. 22;** § **11.3, n. 21;** § **11.4, n. 15;** § **11.6, n. 8.**

Farnham v. Farnham, 80 Nev. 180, 391 P.2d 26 (Nev.1964)—§ **15.12, n. 9.**

Farnsworth's Estate, In re, 109 N.H. 15, 241 A.2d 204 (N.H.1968)—§ **21.5, n. 4;** § **21.6, n. 4.**

Farnum v. Pennsylvania Co. for Insurance on Lives and Granting Annuities, 99 A. 145 (N.J.Ch.1916)—§ **21.13, n. 10.**

Farrell, Matter of, 97 Misc.2d 18, 410 N.Y.S.2d 775 (N.Y.Sur.1978)—§ **22.26, n. 6.**

Farrell v. David Davis Enterprises, Inc., 1996 WL 21128 (E.D.Pa.1996)—§ **17.45;** § **17.45, n. 5.**

Farrell v. Farrell, 190 Iowa 919, 181 N.W. 12 (Iowa 1921)—§ **13.9, n. 5.**

Farrell v. Ford Motor Co., 199 Mich.App. 81, 501 N.W.2d 567 (Mich.App.1993)— § **17.74, n. 11;** § **17.76, n. 14;** § **17.77, n. 8.**

Farrier v. May Dept. Stores Co., Inc., 357 F.Supp. 190 (D.D.C.1973)—§ **3.12, n. 1.**

Farris v. ITT Cannon, a Div. of ITT Corp., 834 F.Supp. 1260 (D.Colo.1993)— § **18.29, n. 3, 5.**

Far West Capital, Inc. v. Towne, 46 F.3d 1071 (10th Cir.1995)—§ **7.3, n. 11;** § **8.7, n. 9.**

F. A. Straus & Co. v. Canadian Pac. R. Co., 254 N.Y. 407, 173 N.E. 564 (N.Y.1930)— § **18.4, n. 8;** § **18.5, n. 4.**

Fateh Muhammad v. Sardav Begum Suna, 1956 S.C. 367—§ **13.17, n. 3.**

Fattibene v. Fattibene, 183 Conn. 433, 441 A.2d 3 (Conn.1981)—§ **13.2, n. 10.**

Faulk v. Faulk, 255 Ala. 237, 51 So.2d 255 (Ala.1951)—§ **4.37, n. 3.**

Fauntleroy v. Lum, 210 U.S. 230, 28 S.Ct. 641, 52 L.Ed. 1039 (1908)—§ **3.40, n. 1;** § **15.12, n. 9;** § **15.30, n. 8;** § **24.9, n. 17;** § **24.20;** § **24.20, n. 1;** § **24.22;** § **24.22, n. 3;** § **24.23;** § **24.23;** § **24.23, n. 11;** § **24.47, n. 4.**

Fay v. Haven, 44 Mass. 109 (Mass.1841)— § **22.23, n. 3.**

Fay v. Parker, 53 N.H. 342 (N.H.1872)— § **17.50, n. 4, 72.**

FCE Transp., Inc. v. Ajayem Lumber Midwest Corp., 1988 WL 48018 (Ohio App. 10 Dist.1988)—§ **17.36, n. 15;** § **17.48, n. 6.**

F.D.I.C. v. Aaronian, 93 F.3d 636 (9th Cir. 1996)—§ **12.5, n. 4.**

Feder v. Evans–Feder, 63 F.3d 217 (3rd Cir.1995)—§ **4.14, n. 8;** § **15.42, n. 17.**

Federal Deposit Ins. Corp. v. Petersen, 770 F.2d 141 (10th Cir.1985)—§ **18.1, n. 17.**

Federal Ins. Co. v. Fries, 78 Misc.2d 805, 355 N.Y.S.2d 741 (N.Y.City Civ.Ct. 1974)—§ **2.9, n. 41.**

Feinberg v. Automobile Banking Corp., 353 F.Supp. 508 (E.D.Pa.1973)—§ **18.33, n. 3.**

Feinstein v. Massachusetts General Hospital, 643 F.2d 880 (1st Cir.1981)—§ **3.41, n. 15, 18.**

Feldman v. Acapulco Princess Hotel, 137 Misc.2d 878, 520 N.Y.S.2d 477 (N.Y.Sup. 1987)—§ **17.42, n. 11, 18.**

Fellows v. Miner, 119 Mass. 541 (Mass. 1876)—§ **20.10, n. 2.**

Felt, Estate of v. Commissioner, T.C. Memo. 1987-465 (U.S.Tax Ct.1987)— § **15.13, n. 8.**

Feltrinelli's Estate, In re, 159 N.Y.S.2d 563 (N.Y.Sur.1956)—§ **22.25, n. 10, 23.**

Fender v. St. Louis Southwestern Ry. Co., 49 Ill.2d 1, 273 N.E.2d 353 (Ill.1971)— § **11.11, n. 8.**

Fenn, State v., 47 Wash. 561, 92 P. 417 (Wash.1907)—§ **13.8, n. 5;** § **13.9, n. 4.**

Fennell v. Monongahela Power Co., 350 F.2d 867 (4th Cir.1965)—§ **22.14, n. 5.**

Ferdie Sievers and Lake Tahoe Land Co., Inc. v. Diversified Mortg. Investors, 95 Nev. 811, 603 P.2d 270 (Nev.1979)— § **19.10, n. 7.**

Ferens v. John Deere Co., 494 U.S. 516, 110 S.Ct. 1274, 108 L.Ed.2d 443 (1990)— § **3.9, n. 6;** § **3.46;** § **3.46, n. 9;** § **3.48;** § **3.48, n. 18;** § **7.4, n. 3;** § **11.14;** § **11.14, n. 12.**

Feres v. United States, 340 U.S. 135, 71 S.Ct. 153, 95 L.Ed. 152 (1950)—§ **3.53, n. 2.**

Ferguson v. Morris, 67 Ala. 389 (Ala. 1880)—§ **22.16, n. 2.**

Ferguson, State ex rel. v. United Royalty Co., 188 Kan. 443, 363 P.2d 397 (Kan. 1961)—§ **23.2, n. 15.**

Ferguson's Estate, In re, 25 Wis.2d 75, 130 N.W.2d 300 (Wis.1964)—§ **13.9, n. 14.**

Fernandes v. Fernandes, 275 A.D. 777, 87 N.Y.S.2d 707 (N.Y.A.D. 2 Dept.1949)— § **13.6, n. 12.**

Fernandez v. Casey, 77 Tex. 452, 14 S.W. 149 (Tex.1890)—§ **6.4, n. 2.**

Fernandez v. Fernandez, 208 Conn. 329, 545 A.2d 1036 (Conn.1988)—§ **11.15, n. 1.**

Ferrara v. Ibach, 285 F.Supp. 1017 (D.S.C. 1968)—§ **4.26, n. 4, 8;** § **15.5, n. 1.**

Ferreira v. Ferreira, 109 Cal.Rptr. 80, 512 P.2d 304 (Cal.1973)—§ **15.40, n. 2.**

Ferren v. General Motors Corp., Delco Battery Div., 137 N.H. 423, 628 A.2d 265 (N.H.1993)—§ **2.13, n. 14, 25;** § **17.21, n. 13, 28;** § **17.23, n. 13.**

Ferrer's Case, VI Coke 7, 77 Eng. Rep. 263 (K.B.1599)—§ **24.1, § 24.1, n. 3.**

Ferrofluidics Corp. v. Advanced Vacuum Components, Inc., 968 F.2d 1463 (1st Cir.1992)—§ **18.29, n. 3, 5.**

Ferry v. Spokane, P. & S. Ry. Co., 258 U.S. 314, 42 S.Ct. 358, 66 L.Ed. 635 (1922)— § **3.32, n. 2, 10.**

Fertilizer Corp. of India v. IDI Management, Inc., 517 F.Supp. 948 (S.D.Ohio 1981)—§ **24.48, n. 7.**

Fessenden v. Smith, 255 Iowa 1170, 124 N.W.2d 554 (Iowa 1963)—§ **17.5, n. 9.**

Fetters, In re Marriage of, 41 Colo.App. 281, 584 P.2d 104 (Colo.App.1978)— § **13.5, n. 1;** § **13.12, n. 1.**

Feuerstein v. Feuerstein, 37 Del. 414, 183 A. 705 (Del.Super.1936)—§ **4.34, n. 3.**

F. & H.R. Farman–Farmaian Consulting Engineers Firm v. Harza Engineering Co., 882 F.2d 281 (7th Cir.1989)— § **23.11, n. 4.**

Fickeisen v. Wheeling Electrical Co., 67 W.Va. 335, 67 S.E. 788 (W.Va.1910)— § **22.10, n. 9.**

Fidelity and Cas. Co. of New York v. Philadelphia Resins Corp., 766 F.2d 440 (10th Cir.1985)—§ **7.2, n. 20.**

Fidelity & Columbia Trust Co. v. Lucas, 66 F.2d 116 (6th Cir.1933)—§ **20.8, n. 8.**

Fidelity Union Trust Co. v. Caldwell, 44 A.2d 842 (N.J.Ch.1945)—§ **21.11, n. 15.**

Fields v. Ramada Inn, Inc., 816 F.Supp. 1033 (E.D.Pa.1993)—§ **5.13, n. 27;** § **5.15, n. 6;** § **6.8, n. 7;** § **6.9, n. 23.**

Figuero v. Figuero, 303 So.2d 801 (La.App. 3 Cir.1974)—§ **19.17, n. 6.**

Filetech S.A. v. France Telecom S.A., 157 F.3d 922 (2nd Cir.1998)—§ **17.48, n. 27.**

Films by Jove, Inc. v. Berov, 250 F.Supp.2d 156 (E.D.N.Y.2003)—§ **12.18, n. 11.**

Finance America Corp. v. Moyler, 494 A.2d 926 (D.C.1985)—§ **18.28, n. 4.**

Financial Bancorp, Inc. v. Pingree and Dahle, Inc., 880 P.2d 14 (Utah App. 1994)—§ **17.40, n. 26;** § **18.1, n. 17.**

Financial Trust Co., Inc. v. Citibank N.A., 268 F.Supp.2d 561 (D.Virgin Islands 2003)—§ **17.40, n. 28;** § **18.1, n. 18.**

Finch v. Reese, 28 Conn.Supp. 499, 268 A.2d 409 (Conn.Super.1970)—§ **22.23, n. 13.**

Fine v. Property Damage Appraisers, Inc., 393 F.Supp. 1304 (E.D.La.1975)—§ **18.4, n. 52;** § **18.5, n. 16, 17.**

Fineberg, In re, 202 B.R. 206 (Bkrtcy. E.D.Pa.1996)—§ **17.40, n. 26;** § **18.1, n. 17.**

Finkbiner v. Mullins, 532 A.2d 609 (Del.Super.1987)—§ **7.4, n. 7.**

Finnish Fur Sales Co., Ltd. v. Juliette Shulof Furs, Inc., 770 F.Supp. 139 (S.D.N.Y. 1991)—§ **18.5, n. 39.**

Fiore v. Oakwood Plaza Shopping Center, Inc., 578 N.Y.S.2d 115, 585 N.E.2d 364 (N.Y.1991)—§ **6.3, n. 12;** § **24.15, n. 3.**

Firedoor Corp. of America v. MacFarland Builders, Inc., 79 A.D.2d 356, 436 N.Y.S.2d 647 (N.Y.A.D. 1 Dept.1981)— § **24.47, n. 6.**

Fireman's Fund Am. Ins. Co. v. Boston Harbor Marina, Inc., 285 F.Supp. 36 (D.Mass.1968)—§ **3.50, n. 3.**

Fireman's Fund Ins. Companies, Inc., In re, 588 F.2d 93 (5th Cir.1979)—§ **11.2, n. 6.**

Firipis v. The Margaritis, 181 F.Supp. 48 (E.D.Va.1960)—§ **17.63, n. 20, 23.**

First Alabama Bank of Montgomery, N.A. v. Parsons Steel, Inc., 825 F.2d 1475 (11th Cir.1987)—§ **24.12, n. 7.**

First American First, Inc. v. National Ass'n of Bank Women, 802 F.2d 1511 (4th Cir.1986)—§ **7.8, n. 10;** § **7.10, n. 4.**

First–Central Trust Co. v. Claflin, 73 N.E.2d 388 (Ohio Com.Pl.1947)— § **21.11, n. 17.**

First Christian Church of Guthrie, Ky. v. Moneypenny, 59 Tenn.App. 229, 439 S.W.2d 620 (Tenn.Ct.App.1968)—§ **20.6, n. 1.**

First Commerce Realty Investors v. K–F Land Co., 617 S.W.2d 806 (Tex.Civ.App.-Hous. (14 Dist.) 1981)—§ **19.10, n. 5.**

First Nat. Bank v. Balcom, 35 Conn. 351 (Conn.1868)—§ **4.36, n. 11.**

First Nat. Bank v. Blessing, 231 Mo.App. 288, 98 S.W.2d 149 (Mo.App.1936)— § **22.20, n. 8.**

First Nat. Bank v. National Broadway Bank, 156 N.Y. 459, 51 N.E. 398 (N.Y. 1898)—§ **21.6, n. 7.**

First Nat. Bank, People v., 364 Ill. 262, 4 N.E.2d 378 (Ill.1936)—§ **21.6, n. 7.**

First Nat. Bank v. Sharpe, 12 Tex.Civ.App. 223, 33 S.W. 676 (Tex.Civ.App.1896)— § **13.18, n. 8.**

First Nat. Bank v. United States, 30 F.Supp. 730 (D.D.C 1939)—§ **22.25, n. 9.**

First Nat. Bank v. Walker, 61 Conn. 154, 23 A. 696 (Conn.1891)—§ **19.30, n. 6.**

First Nat. Bank in Fort Collins v. Rostek, 182 Colo. 437, 514 P.2d 314 (Colo. 1973)—§ **2.16, n. 12;** § **2.23, n. 1;** § **17.26, n. 1;** § **17.28;** § **17.28, n. 10;** § **17.32, n. 2;** § **17.39, n. 8.**

First Nat. Bank in Mitchell v. Daggett, 242 Neb. 734, 497 N.W.2d 358 (Neb.1993)— § **21.3, n. 1.**

First Nat. Bank of Ariz. v. British Petroleum Co., 324 F.Supp. 1348 (S.D.N.Y. 1971)—§ **12.18, n. 2.**

First Nat. Bank of Arizona v. First Nat. Bank of Birmingham, 348 So.2d 1041 (Ala.1977)—§ **21.13, n. 2.**

First Nat. Bank of Boston (Intern.) v. Banco Nacional de Cuba, 658 F.2d 895 (2nd Cir.1981)—§ **3.56, n. 3.**

First Nat. Bank of Chicago v. Ettlinger, 465 F.2d 343 (7th Cir.1972)—§ **21.13, n. 1.**

First Nat. Bank of Chicago v. United Air Lines, 342 U.S. 396, 72 S.Ct. 421, 96 L.Ed. 441 (1952)—§ **24.22;** § **24.22, n. 10.**

First Nat. Bank of Chicago, United States v., 699 F.2d 341 (7th Cir.1983)—§ **12.9, n. 16.**

First Nat. Bank of Mount Dora v. Shawmut Bank of Boston, 378 Mass. 137, 389 N.E.2d 1002 (Mass.1979)—§ **20.13, n. 6.**

First Nat. City Bank v. Banco Nacional de Cuba, 406 U.S. 759, 92 S.Ct. 1808, 32 L.Ed.2d 466 (1972)—§ **24.46, n. 10.**

First Nat. City Bank v. Compania de Aguaceros, S. A., 398 F.2d 779 (5th Cir. 1968)—§ **12.18, n. 6, 16.**

First Nat. City Bank v. Nanz, Inc., 437 F.Supp. 184 (S.D.N.Y.1975)—§ **11.2, n. 4.**

First Tennessee Bank N.A. Memphis v. Smith, 766 F.2d 255 (6th Cir.1985)— § **24.29, n. 4, 6.**

First Trust & Deposit Co. v. Goodrich, 165 N.Y.S.2d 510, 144 N.E.2d 396 (N.Y. 1957)—§ **4.37, n. 10;** § **4.42, n. 2.**

First Union Nat. Bank of Delaware v. Bankers Wholesale Mortg., LLC, 153 N.C.App. 248, 570 S.E.2d 217 (N.C.App. 2002)—§ **7.4, n. 9.**

Fischer v. Fischer, 254 N.Y. 463, 173 N.E. 680 (N.Y.1930)—§ **4.24, n. 3.**

Fischer v. Stuart, 138 A. 873 (N.J.Err. & App.1927)—§ **20.7, n. 1.**

Fischer's Estate, In re, 180 A. 633 (N.J.Prerog.1935)—§ **22.3, n. 9; § 22.20, n. 29.**

Fischl v. Chubb, 30 Pa. D. & C. 40 (Pa.Com. Pl.1937)—§ **17.3, n. 3.**

Fishbein v. Guerra, 131 Vt. 493, 309 A.2d 922 (Vt.1973)—§ **12.19, n. 19.**

Fisher v. Agios Nicolaos V, 628 F.2d 308 (5th Cir.1980)—§ **17.63, n. 23.**

Fisher v. Browning, 107 Miss. 729, 66 So. 132 (Miss.1914)—§ **16.5, n. 3; § 20.2, n. 4.**

Fisher v. District Court of Sixteenth Judicial Dist. of Montana, in and for Rosebud County, 424 U.S. 382, 96 S.Ct. 943, 47 L.Ed.2d 106 (1976)—§ **11.17, n. 2, 22.**

Fisher v. Fielding, 67 Conn. 91, 34 A. 714 (Conn.1895)—§ **24.17, n. 2; § 24.34, n. 11.**

Fisher v. Fisher, 250 N.Y. 313, 165 N.E. 460 (N.Y.1929)—§ **13.6, n. 18.**

Fisher v. Huck, 50 Or.App. 635, 624 P.2d 177 (Or.App.1981)—§ **2.11, n. 23; § 2.26, n. 7; § 17.14, n. 5, 8; § 17.27, n. 7.**

Fisher v. Parry, 68 Ind. 465 (Ind.1879)—§ **19.5, n. 5.**

Fisher, United States v., 864 F.2d 434 (7th Cir.1988)—§ **24.24, n. 8.**

Fisher v. Virginia Elec. and Power Co., 258 F.Supp.2d 445 (E.D.Va.2003)—§ **19.5, n. 4.**

Fisher v. Virginia Electric and Power Co., 243 F.Supp.2d 538 (E.D.Va.2003)—§ **5.18, n. 14; § 7.7, n. 6, 9.**

Fishman v. Keating, 542 S.W.2d 314 (Mo. App.1976)—§ **20.8, n. 8.**

Fitch v. Huff, 218 F. 17 (4th Cir.1914)—§ **4.34, n. 2.**

Fitch v. Huntington, 125 Wis. 204, 102 N.W. 1066 (Wis.1905)—§ **24.10, n. 1.**

Fitts v. Minnesota Min. & Mfg. Co., 581 So.2d 819 (Ala.1991)—§ **2.21, n. 1; § 17.79, n. 2.**

Fitzgerald v. Austin, 715 So.2d 795 (Ala. Civ.App.1997)—§ **2.21, n. 1; § 17.2, n. 8; § 17.56, n. 9.**

Fitzgerald v. Fitzgerald, 210 Wis. 543, 246 N.W. 680 (Wis.1933)—§ **13.8, n. 4.**

Fitzsimmons v. Barton, 589 F.2d 330 (7th Cir.1979)—§ **9.6, n. 19.**

Fitzsimmons v. Johnson, 90 Tenn. 416, 17 S.W. 100 (Tenn.1891)—§ **22.19, n. 20.**

5208 Los Franciscos Way, Los Angeles, Cal., United States v., 252 F.Supp.2d 1060 (E.D.Cal.2003)—§ **19.8, n. 8.**

F. Koechlin et Cie v. Kestenbaum Bros., 1927 WL 21931 (CA 1927)—§ **19.31, n. 8.**

Flagler's Will, In re, 4 Misc.2d 705, 158 N.Y.S.2d 941 (N.Y.Sur.1957)—§ **20.13, n. 6; § 21.13, n. 2.**

Flaherty v. Allstate Ins. Co., 822 A.2d 1159 (Me.2003)—§ **17.56, n. 20; § 18.26, n. 6.**

Flaherty v. Flaherty, 138 N.H. 337, 638 A.2d 1254 (N.H.1994)—§ **21.2, n. 14.**

Flaiz v. Moore, 353 S.W.2d 74 (Tex.Civ. App.-San Antonio 1962)—§ **18.48, n. 4.**

Flammia v. Mite Corp., 401 F.Supp. 1121 (E.D.N.Y.1975)—§ **18.18, n. 2; § 18.37, n. 4.**

Flanagan v. Marvel, 94 F.Supp. 145 (D.Minn.1950)—§ **22.11, n. 1.**

Flatow v. Islamic Republic of Iran, 999 F.Supp. 1 (D.D.C.1998)—§ **17.50; § 17.50, n. 63.**

Flaugher, State ex rel. v. Rogers, 226 Ind. 32, 77 N.E.2d 594 (Ind.1948)—§ **4.19, n. 4.**

Fleck v. Fleck, 79 N.D. 561, 58 N.W.2d 765 (N.D.1953)—§ **14.7, n. 2.**

Fleet Bank, United States v. (In re Calore Exp. Co., Inc.), 288 F.3d 22 (1st Cir. 2002)—§ **3.51, n. 12.**

Fleischmann Distilling Corp. v. Distillers Co. Ltd., 395 F.Supp. 221 (S.D.N.Y. 1975)—§ **12.18, n. 1.**

Fletcher, Ex parte, 225 Ala. 139, 142 So. 30 (Ala.1932)—§ **4.41, n. 5.**

Flexner v. Farson, 248 U.S. 289, 39 S.Ct. 97, 63 L.Ed. 250 (1919)—§ **5.3, n. 14, 18.**

Flexner's Trust, In re, 7 Misc.2d 621, 166 N.Y.S.2d 469 (N.Y.Sup.1957)—§ **21.7, n. 2.**

Fliehler v. Uninsured Employers Fund, 310 Mont. 99, 48 P.3d 746 (Mont.2002)—§ **17.59, n. 12.**

Flood v. Templeton, 152 Cal. 148, 92 P. 78 (Cal.1907)—§ **24.17, n. 8.**

Flores v. A.C., Inc., 2003 WL 1566507 (W.D.Tex.2003)—§ **8.4, n. 5.**

Flores v. Central American S.S. Agency Inc., 594 F.Supp. 735 (S.D.N.Y.1984)—§ **17.63, n. 24.**

Florey's Estate, In re, 212 Neb. 665, 325 N.W.2d 643 (Neb.1982)—§ **20.15, n. 2.**

Florida Evergreen Foliage v. E.I. Du Pont De Nemours, Co., 135 F.Supp.2d 1271 (S.D.Fla.2001)—§ **17.40, n. 28.**

Florida Lime & Avocado Growers, Inc. v. Paul, 373 U.S. 132, 83 S.Ct. 1210, 10 L.Ed.2d 248 (1963)—§ **3.50, n. 4.**

Florida State Bd. of Admin. v. Engineering and Environmental Services, Inc., 262 F.Supp.2d 1004 (D.Minn.2003)—§ **17.40, n. 26; § 18.1, n. 17.**

Flowers v. Carville, 310 F.3d 1118 (9th Cir. 2002)—§ **3.11, n. 2.**

Floyd v. Floyd, 95 N.J.Eq. 661, 124 A. 525 (N.J.Err. & App.1924)—§ **4.33, n. 3.**

Fluke Corp. v. Hartford Acc. & Indem. Co., 145 Wash.2d 137, 34 P.3d 809 (Wash. 2001)—§ **18.26, n. 19.**

FMC Finance Corp. v. Reed, 592 F.2d 238 (5th Cir.1979)—§ **18.21, n. 14.**

Foden v. Gianoli Aldunate, 3 F.3d 54 (2nd Cir.1993)—§ **12.8, n. 4, 9.**

Foley v. Connelie, 435 U.S. 291, 98 S.Ct. 1067, 55 L.Ed.2d 287 (1978)—§ **3.58, n. 15.**

Folk v. York–Shipley, Inc., 239 A.2d 236 (Del.Supr.1968)—§ **17.5, n. 4.**

Folliott v. Ogden, (1789) 1 Bl. H. 124— § **24.19, n. 1.**

Follansbee v. Wilbur, 14 Wash. 242, 44 P. 262 (Wash.1896)—§ **13.18, n. 10.**

Follweiler v. Lutz, 112 Pa. 107, 2 A. 721 (Pa.1886)—§ **4.19, n. 4.**

Fonseca v. Blumenthal, 620 F.2d 322 (2nd Cir.1980)—§ **12.8, n. 3.**

Fonseca v. Cunard S.S. Co., 153 Mass. 553, 27 N.E. 665 (Mass.1891)—§ **18.2, n. 1; § 18.4, n. 47.**

Fontaine, In re, 10 B.R. 175 (Bkrtcy.D.R.I. 1981)—§ **23.13, n. 1.**

Fontenot, In re Marriage of, 317 Mont. 298, 77 P.3d 206 (Mont.2003)—§ **16.5, n. 9.**

Forbes v. Cochrane, 2 B. and Cres. R. 448, 117 Eng. Rep. 450 (K.B. 1824)—§ **2.7, n. 6.**

Ford v. Brown, 319 F.3d 1302 (11th Cir. 2003)—§ **11.11, n. 5.**

Ford v. Ford, 276 Cal.App.2d 9, 80 Cal.Rptr. 435 (Cal.App. 1 Dist.1969)—§ **14.6, n. 2.**

Ford v. Ford, 80 Mich. 42, 44 N.W. 1057 (Mich.1890)—§ **20.7, n. 1, 5; § 20.8, n. 9; § 20.13, n. 5; § 21.2, n. 7; § 21.3, n. 4.**

Ford v. Ford, 72 Wis. 621, 40 N.W. 502 (Wis.1888)—§ **20.6, n. 18; § 20.7, n. 5.**

Ford v. Ford, 70 Wis. 19, 33 N.W. 188 (Wis.1887)—§ **20.6, n. 18; § 20.7, n. 5; § 20.8, n. 9.**

Ford v. Newman, 64 Ill.App.3d 528, 21 Ill. Dec. 283, 381 N.E.2d 392 (Ill.App. 4 Dist.1978)—§ **21.3, n. 10.**

Ford v. Pace, 672 S.W.2d 219 (Tenn.Ct.App. 1984)—§ **22.2, n. 3.**

Ford Motor Co. v. Aguiniga, 9 S.W.3d 252 (Tex.App.-San Antonio 1999)—§ **17.73, n. 4.**

Fore, Petition of, 151 N.E.2d 777 (Ohio App. 8 Dist.1958)—§ **4.41, n. 6.**

Foreman's Estate, In re, 16 Cal.App.2d 96, 60 P.2d 310 (Cal.App. 3 Dist.1936)— § **22.22, n. 7.**

Formant v. Bell, 250 A.2d 565 (D.C.App. 1969)—§ **19.3, n. 8.**

Forney Industries, Inc. v. Andre, 246 F.Supp. 333 (D.N.D.1965)—§ **18.4, n. 46; § 18.5, n. 16, 17.**

Forney's Estate, In re, 43 Nev. 227, 184 P. 206 (Nev.1919)—§ **20.3, n. 5; § 20.4, n. 6.**

Fornshill v. Ruddy, 891 F.Supp. 1062 (D.Md.1995)—§ **17.55, n. 9.**

Forrest v. Verizon Communications, Inc., 805 A.2d 1007 (D.C.2002)—§ **17.40, n. 28.**

Forsman v. Forsman, 779 P.2d 218 (Utah 1989)—§ **2.16, n. 16; § 2.19, n. 16; § 2.21, n. 14; § 2.23, n. 1; § 17.26, n. 1, 7; § 17.39, n. 9, 13.**

Forsman v. Forsman, 694 S.W.2d 112 (Tex. App.-San Antonio 1985)—§ **14.11, n. 1.**

Forsyth v. Cessna Aircraft Co., 520 F.2d 608 (9th Cir.1975)—§ **17.27, n. 7.**

Forsythe v. Saudi Arabian Airlines Corp., 885 F.2d 285 (5th Cir.1989)—§ **11.3, n. 22.**

Fort Howard Cup Corp. v. Quality Kitchen Corp., 1992 WL 207276 (Del.Super.1992)—§ **18.3, n. 1.**

Fortson v. St. Paul Fire and Marine Ins. Co., 751 F.2d 1157 (11th Cir.1985)— § **23.3, n. 4.**

Fortune Ins. Co. v. Owens, 351 N.C. 424, 526 S.E.2d 463 (N.C.2000)—§ **18.26, n. 6.**

Foshee v. Torch Operating Co., 763 So.2d 82 (La.App. 3 Cir.2000)—§ **17.60, n. 5; § 17.61, n. 4.**

Foster, Matter of Estate of, 180 W.Va. 250, 376 S.E.2d 144 (W.Va.1988)—§ **13.6, n. 2; § 15.16, n. 4.**

Foster v. Carlin, 200 F.2d 943 (4th Cir. 1952)—§ **4.45, n. 2.**

Foster v. Destin Trading Corp., 700 So.2d 199 (La.1997)—§ **10.6, n. 19.**

Foster v. Leggett, 484 S.W.2d 827 (Ky. 1972)—§ **2.24, n. 11; § 17.11; § 17.11, n. 25; § 17.13; § 17.13, n. 9; § 17.26, n. 6; § 17.42; § 17.42, n. 1; § 17.70, n. 9.**

Foster v. Stein, 183 Mich.App. 424, 454 N.W.2d 244 (Mich.App.1990)—§ **16.5, n. 9.**

Foster v. United States, 768 F.2d 1278 (11th Cir.1985)—§ **17.26, n. 1.**

Foster v. Waterman, 124 Mass. 592 (Mass. 1878)—§ **16.5, n. 4.**

Fotochrome, Inc. v. Copal Co., Ltd., 517 F.2d 512 (2nd Cir.1975)—§ **24.48, n. 7.**

Fouke v. Fleming, 13 Md. 392 (Md.1859)— § **19.13, n. 4.**

Four B Corp. v. Ueno Fine Chemicals Industry, Ltd., 241 F.Supp.2d 1258 (D.Kan.2003)—§ **7.2, n. 32.**

Four Star Aviation, Inc. v. United States, 409 F.2d 292 (5th Cir.1969)—§ **19.13, n. 4.**

Fowler, Appeal of, 125 Pa. 388, 17 A. 431 (Pa.1889)—§ **21.3, n. 10, 13.**

Fowler v. Fowler, 96 N.H. 494, 79 A.2d 24 (N.H.1951)—§ **12.15, n. 10.**

Fowler, State v., 196 Wis. 451, 220 N.W. 534 (Wis.1928)—§ **10.14, n. 6.**

Fox v. Carr, 1879 WL 9656 (N.Y.Sup.Gen. Term 1879)—§ **22.10, n. 3.**

Fox v. Morrison Motor Freight, Inc., 25 Ohio St.2d 193, 267 N.E.2d 405 (Ohio 1971)—§ **17.12, n. 12;** § **17.39, n. 11.**

Fox v. Peck Iron and Metal Co., Inc., 25 B.R. 674 (Bkrtcy.S.D.Cal.1982)— § **23.15, n. 14.**

Fox, United States v., 94 U.S. 315, 24 L.Ed. 192 (1876)—§ **20.6, n. 18.**

Fox–Greenwald Sheet Metal Co. v. Markowitz Bros., Inc., 452 F.2d 1346, 147 U.S.App.D.C. 14 (D.C.Cir.1971)— § **18.29, n. 3;** § **18.37, n. 12;** § **19.28, n. 2.**

Fox' Guardianship, In re, 212 Or. 80, 318 P.2d 933 (Or.1957)—§ **4.13, n. 2;** § **4.36, n. 1;** § **4.37, n. 2.**

F.P.P. Enterprises v. United States, 646 F.Supp. 713 (D.Neb.1986)—§ **19.2, n. 6;** § **19.3, n. 16;** § **19.6, n. 3;** § **21.3, n. 1.**

Frame v. Frame, 120 Tex. 61, 36 S.W.2d 152 (Tex.1931)—§ **14.7, n. 4.**

Frame v. Merrill Lynch, Pierce, Fenner & Smith, Inc., 20 Cal.App.3d 668, 97 Cal. Rptr. 811 (Cal.App. 1 Dist.1971)— § **18.5, n. 17.**

Frame v. Thormann, 102 Wis. 653, 79 N.W. 39 (Wis.1899)—§ **4.24, n. 1.**

Francesca M., Adoption of, 133 Misc.2d 152, 506 N.Y.S.2d 642 (N.Y.Sur.1986)— § **16.7, n. 4.**

Francis v. Herrin Transp. Co., 432 S.W.2d 710 (Tex.1968)—§ **3.10, n. 3.**

Francisco v. State of Arizona, 113 Ariz. 427, 556 P.2d 1 (Ariz.1976)—§ **11.17, n. 39.**

Francosteel Corp. v. M/V Charm, 825 F.Supp. 1074 (S.D.Ga.1993)—§ **8.8, n. 8.**

Franklin, Matter of, 709 F.Supp. 109 (E.D.Va.1989)—§ **3.43, n. 3.**

Franklin Computer Corp., In re, 50 B.R. 620 (Bkrtcy.E.D.Pa.1985)—§ **23.12, n. 15.**

Franklin Life Ins. Co. v. Falkingham, 229 F.2d 300 (7th Cir.1956)—§ **19.29, n. 3.**

Frank's Casing Crew & Rental Tools, Inc. v. PMR Technologies, Ltd., 292 F.3d 1363 (Fed.Cir.2002)—§ **5.23, n. 4.**

Fray, Matter of, 721 P.2d 1054 (Wyo. 1986)—§ **20.2, n. 2.**

Frazier v. Boggs, 37 Fla. 307, 20 So. 245 (Fla.1896)—§ **20.6, n. 15.**

Fred Briggs Distributing Co., Inc. v. California Cooler, Inc., 2 F.3d 1156 (9th Cir. 1993)—§ **18.5, n. 32.**

Fredericks v. Fredericks, 226 Cal.App.3d 875, 277 Cal.Rptr. 107 (Cal.App. 4 Dist. 1991)—§ **14.9, n. 4.**

Fred W. Beal, Inc. v. Allen, 287 F.Supp. 126 (D.Me.1968)—§ **3.51, n. 10.**

Free v. Bland, 369 U.S. 663, 82 S.Ct. 1089, 8 L.Ed.2d 180 (1962)—§ **3.51, n. 6.**

Free v. Bland, 368 U.S. 811, 82 S.Ct. 50, 7 L.Ed.2d 21 (1961)—§ **14.9, n. 4.**

Freedman v. Chemical Const. Corp., 401 N.Y.S.2d 176, 372 N.E.2d 12 (N.Y. 1977)—§ **18.5, n. 40.**

Freedom Finance Co., Inc. v. New Jersey Bell Tel. Co., 123 N.J.Super. 255, 302 A.2d 184 (N.J.Dist.Ct.1973)—§ **18.37, n. 12.**

Freeland v. Charnley, 80 Ind. 132 (Ind. 1881)—§ **19.2, n. 6.**

Freeman, In re, 489 F.2d 431 (9th Cir. 1973)—§ **19.28, n. 1.**

Freeman v. Lester Coggins Trucking, Inc., 771 F.2d 860 (5th Cir.1985)—§ **24.12, n. 7.**

Freeman v. Northwest Acceptance Corp., 754 F.2d 553 (5th Cir.1985)—§ **4.15, n. 2;** § **23.3, n. 1.**

Freeman v. World Airways, Inc., 596 F.Supp. 841 (D.Mass.1984)—§ **17.50, n. 43.**

Frees' Estate, In re, 187 Cal. 150, 201 P. 112 (Cal.1921)—§ **14.10, n. 2.**

Freiman v. Lazur, 925 F.Supp. 14 (D.D.C. 1996)—§ **10.4, n. 4.**

French v. Short, 207 Va. 548, 151 S.E.2d 354 (Va.1966)—§ **20.3, n. 1;** § **20.6, n. 1;** § **20.9, n. 4.**

Frericks v. General Motors Corp., 278 Md. 304, 363 A.2d 460 (Md.1976)—§ **19.12, n. 2;** § **19.13, n. 4.**

Freudensprung v. Offshore Technical Services, Inc., 186 F.Supp.2d 716 (S.D.Tex. 2002)—§ **8.4, n. 3.**

Frey v. Sargent's Estate, 533 S.W.2d 142 (Tex.Civ.App.-Amarillo 1976)—§ **18.18, n. 5;** § **20.13, n. 2.**

Frick v. Pennsylvania, 268 U.S. 473, 45 S.Ct. 603, 69 L.Ed. 1058 (1925)—§ **20.9, n. 2.**

Fricke v. Isbrandtsen Co., 151 F.Supp. 465 (S.D.N.Y.1957)—§ **18.1, n. 3;** § **18.4, n. 7;** § **18.5, n. 1, 4;** § **18.30, n. 4.**

Friedenberg v. Friedenberg, 136 A.D.2d 593, 523 N.Y.S.2d 578 (N.Y.A.D. 2 Dept. 1988)—§ **15.24, n. 7.**

Friedrich v. Friedrich, 983 F.2d 1396 (6th Cir.1993)—§ **4.14, n. 11.**

Frierson v. Williams, 57 Miss. 451 (Miss. 1879)—§ **19.3, n. 5.**

Fritz v. American Home Shield Corp., 751 F.2d 1152 (11th Cir.1985)—§ **23.3, n. 1.**

Frolova v. Union of Soviet Socialist Republics, 558 F.Supp. 358 (N.D.Ill.1983)— § **11.13, n. 21;** § **11.15, n. 1.**

Frontiero v. Richardson, 411 U.S. 677, 93 S.Ct. 1764, 36 L.Ed.2d 583 (1973)— § **14.8, n. 5.**

Frothingham v. Shaw, 175 Mass. 59, 55 N.E. 623 (Mass.1899)—§ **20.4, n. 1.**

Frugard v. Pritchard, 112 N.C.App. 84, 434 S.E.2d 620 (N.C.App.1993)—§ **17.59, n. 12.**

Fruin-Colnon Corp. v. Missouri Highway and Transp. Com'n, 736 S.W.2d 41 (Mo. 1987)—§ **2.17, n. 10;** § **2.23, n. 2.**

Frummer v. Hilton Hotels Intern., Inc., 281 N.Y.S.2d 41, 227 N.E.2d 851 (N.Y. 1967)—§ **10.16, n. 7.**

F.T.C. v. Jim Walter Corp., 651 F.2d 251 (5th Cir.1981)—§ **10.2, n. 15.**

Fuentes v. Shevin, 407 U.S. 67, 92 S.Ct. 1983, 32 L.Ed.2d 556 (1972)—§ **24.15, n. 3.**

Fuerste v. Bemis, 156 N.W.2d 831 (Iowa 1968)—§ **2.16, n. 8;** § **2.23, n. 1;** § **17.12, n. 13;** § **17.26, n. 1, 20;** § **17.39, n. 14.**

Fugate v. Moore, 86 Va. 1045, 11 S.E. 1063 (Va.1890)—§ **22.15, n. 13;** § **22.19, n. 22.**

Fuhrman v. Livaditis, 611 F.2d 203 (7th Cir.1979)—§ **24.14, n. 3.**

Fuller v. Greenup, 267 Cal.App.2d 10, 72 Cal.Rptr. 531 (Cal.App. 2 Dist.1968)— § **17.17, n. 4.**

Fuller Co. v. Compagnie Des Bauxites De Guinee, 421 F.Supp. 938 (W.D.Pa. 1976)—§ **18.12, n. 7, 11.**

Fuller's Will, In re, 72 N.Y.S.2d 498 (N.Y.Sur.1947)—§ **21.10, n. 2.**

Fulton, State v., 49 S.W. 297 (Tenn.Ch.App. 1898)—§ **22.20, n. 1.**

Funding Systems Leasing Corp. v. Diaz, 34 Conn.Supp. 99, 378 A.2d 108 (Conn. Com.Pl.1977)—§ **11.5, n. 3.**

Funding Systems Railcars, Inc. v. Pullman Standard Inc., 34 B.R. 706 (N.D.Ill. 1983)—§ **23.20, n. 3.**

Fungaroli v. Fungaroli, 53 N.C.App. 270, 280 S.E.2d 787 (N.C.App.1981)— § **24.14, n. 8.**

Furimsky, In re Marriage of, 122 Ariz. 385, 595 P.2d 177 (Ariz.App. Div. 1 1978)— § **15.30, n. 1.**

Furry v. First Nat. Monetary Corp., 602 F.Supp. 6 (W.D.Okla.1984)—§ **11.2, n. 4.**

Furst v. Brady, 375 Ill. 425, 31 N.E.2d 606 (Ill.1940)—§ **22.10, n. 11.**

Furst v. Brewster, 282 U.S. 493, 51 S.Ct. 295, 75 L.Ed. 478 (1931)—§ **23.6, n. 4.**

Fuss v. Fuss, 24 Wis. 256 (Wis.1869)— § **14.15, n. 4, 9.**

G

Gabisso, Succession of, 119 La. 704, 44 So. 438 (La.1907)—§ **13.9, n. 7;** § **13.10, n. 1.**

Gable's Estate, In re, 79 Iowa 178, 44 N.W. 352 (Iowa 1890)—§ **22.21, n. 11;** § **22.23, n. 12.**

Gaden v. Gaden, 323 N.Y.S.2d 955, 272 N.E.2d 471 (N.Y.1971)—§ **17.54, n. 1.**

Gadway, Matter of Estate of, 123 A.D.2d 83, 510 N.Y.S.2d 737 (N.Y.A.D. 3 Dept. 1987)—§ **4.21, n. 2;** § **22.7, n. 1.**

Gadzinski v. Chrysler Corp., 2001 WL 629336 (N.D.Ill.2001)—§ **17.50, n. 61;** § **17.67, n. 2;** § **17.69, n. 8.**

Gagne v. Berry, 112 N.H. 125, 290 A.2d 624 (N.H.1972)—§ **17.21, n. 13, 27.**

Gailey's Will, In re, 169 Wis. 444, 171 N.W. 945 (Wis.1919)—§ **20.6, n. 13.**

Gainer Bank, N.A. v. Jenkins, 284 Ill. App.3d 500, 219 Ill.Dec. 809, 672 N.E.2d 317 (Ill.App. 1 Dist.1996)—§ **18.28, n. 4.**

Gaines, Succession of, 14 So. 233 (La. 1893)—§ **22.3, n. 1.**

Gaither v. Myers, 404 F.2d 216, 131 U.S.App.D.C. 216 (D.C.Cir.1968)— § **17.12, n. 13;** § **17.48, n. 17.**

Galapagos Corporacion Turistica Galatours, S.A. v. Panama Canal Com'n., 190 F.Supp.2d 900 (E.D.La.2002)—§ **17.63, n. 32.**

Galard v. Winans, 111 Md. 434, 74 A. 626 (Md.1909)—§ **21.11, n. 15;** § **21.13, n. 4.**

Galbraith v. Grimshaw, 1909 WL 15719 (CA 1909)—§ **23.19, n. 6.**

Gall v. Robertson, 10 Wis.2d 594, 103 N.W.2d 903 (Wis.1960)—§ **20.3, n. 9.**

Gallagher v. Mazda Motor of America, Inc., 781 F.Supp. 1079 (E.D.Pa.1992)— § **12.7, n. 3.**

Gallagher v. Philadelphia Transp. Co., 185 F.2d 543 (3rd Cir.1950)—§ **4.33, n. 3.**

Gallagher's Estate, In re, 10 Misc.2d 422, 169 N.Y.S.2d 271 (N.Y.Sur.1957)— § **20.9, n. 14;** § **20.13, n. 6.**

Gallegos v. Wilkerson, 79 N.M. 549, 445 P.2d 970 (N.M.1968)—§ **13.6, n. 1, 2.**

Gallo, In re Marriage of, 752 P.2d 47 (Colo. 1988)—§ **14.11, n. 1.**

Galpin v. Page, 85 U.S. 350, 21 L.Ed. 959 (1873)—§ **5.2, n. 8;** § **5.3, n. 9;** § **5.14, n. 5.**

Galu v. Swissair: Swiss Air Transport Co., Ltd., 734 F.Supp. 129 (S.D.N.Y.1990)— § **12.18, n. 1, 11.**

Gamble v. Dawson, 67 Wash. 72, 120 P. 1060 (Wash.1912)—§ **22.12, n. 3.**

Gamer v. duPont Glore Forgan, Inc., 65 Cal.App.3d 280, 135 Cal.Rptr. 230 (Cal. App. 4 Dist.1976)—§ **18.4, n. 7;** § **18.5, n. 1, 12;** § **18.9, n. 5;** § **18.12, n. 16.**

Gamez v. Industrial Commission, 114 Ariz. 179, 559 P.2d 1094 (Ariz.App. Div. 1 1976)—§ **13.6, n. 4.**

Gandolfo v. Alford, 31 Conn.Supp. 417, 333 A.2d 65 (Conn.Super.1975)—§ **22.19, n. 14.**

Gantes v. Kason Corp., 145 N.J. 478, 679 A.2d 106 (N.J.1996)—§ **3.10, n. 3;** § **3.12, n. 5, 9;** § **17.67, n. 5;** § **17.75, n. 2;** § **17.76;** § **17.76, n. 1;** § **17.78, n. 8.**

Garcia v. American Airlines, Inc., 12 F.3d 308 (1st Cir.1993)—§ **17.60, n. 5;** § **18.29, n. 3.**

Garcia v. General Motors Corp., 195 Ariz. 510, 990 P.2d 1069 (Ariz.App. Div. 1 1999)—§ **17.78, n. 10.**

Garden Manor Associates, L.P., In re, 99 B.R. 551 (Bkrtcy.S.D.N.Y.1988)— § **23.13, n. 4.**

Gardner v. Best Western Intern., Inc., 929 S.W.2d 474 (Tex.App.-Texarkana 1996)—§ **12.17, n. 13;** § **12.18, n. 11.**

Gardner Hotel Supply of Houston v. Clark's Estate, 83 Nev. 388, 432 P.2d 495 (Nev. 1967)—§ **22.21, n. 4.**

Garland's Adm'r v. Garland's Adm'r, 84 Va. 181, 4 S.E. 334 (Va.1887)—§ **22.20, n. 14.**

Garrett v. Chapman, 252 Or. 361, 449 P.2d 856 (Or.1969)—§ **13.8, n. 4;** § **13.15, n. 3, 4.**

Garrick v. Chamberlain, 97 Ill. 620 (Ill. 1880)—§ **19.2, n. 5.**

Garver's Estate, Matter of, 135 N.J.Super. 578, 343 A.2d 817 (N.J.Super.A.D.1975)—§ **20.6, n. 10, 13;** § **20.12, n. 2, 3.**

Garvin v. Hyatt Corp., 2000 Mass.App.Div. 143 (Mass.App.Div.2000)—§ **17.48, n. 5.**

Garza v. Greyhound Lines, Inc., 418 S.W.2d 595 (Tex.Civ.App.-San Antonio 1967)—§ **3.19, n. 7.**

Gaskins v. Gaskins, 311 Ky. 59, 223 S.W.2d 374 (Ky.1949)—§ **22.22, n. 4.**

Gasper v. Wales, 223 A.D. 89, 227 N.Y.S. 421 (N.Y.A.D. 1 Dept.1928)—§ **4.24, n. 1.**

Gasperini v. Center for Humanities, Inc., 518 U.S. 415, 116 S.Ct. 2211, 135 L.Ed.2d 659 (1996)—§ **3.37, n. 6;** § **3.38, n. 3;** § **3.39;** § **3.39, n. 25.**

Gaston & Snow, In re, 243 F.3d 599 (2nd Cir.2001)—§ **23.15, n. 20.**

Gates v. Commissioner, 199 F.2d 291 (10th Cir.1952)—§ **4.20, n. 4.**

Gates v. P. F. Collier, Inc., 256 F.Supp. 204 (D.Hawai'i 1966)—§ **12.18, n. 6.**

Gates v. Trans World Airlines, 493 S.W.2d 668 (Mo.App.1973)—§ **24.24, n. 4.**

Gateway Western Ry. Co. v. Morrison Metalweld Process Corp., 46 F.3d 860 (8th Cir.1995)—§ **18.29, n. 3, 5.**

Gator.Com Corp. v. L.L. Bean, Inc., 341 F.3d 1072 (9th Cir.2003)—§ **5.13, n. 19.**

Gaulding v. Gaulding, 503 S.W.2d 617 (Tex. Civ.App.-Eastland 1973)—§ **14.11, n. 2.**

Gautier v. Pro-Football, Inc., 304 N.Y. 354, 107 N.E.2d 485 (N.Y.1952)—§ **17.7, n. 2.**

Gbye v. Gbye, 130 N.C.App. 585, 503 S.E.2d 434 (N.C.App.1998)—§ **2.21, n. 27;** § **17.7, n. 8.**

G. C. Murphy Co. v. Reserve Ins. Co., 444 N.Y.S.2d 592, 429 N.E.2d 111 (N.Y. 1981)—§ **22.21, n. 17.**

Gee, In re, 53 B.R. 891 (Bkrtcy.S.D.N.Y. 1985)—§ **23.18, n. 7.**

Geelhoed v. Jensen, 277 Md. 220, 352 A.2d 818 (Md.1976)—§ **6.4, n. 6, 22.**

Gehling v. St. George's School of Medicine, Ltd., 773 F.2d 539 (3rd Cir.1985)—§ **7.3, n. 10;** § **7.4, n. 8.**

Geier v. Mercantile–Safe Deposit & Trust Co., 273 Md. 102, 328 A.2d 311 (Md. 1974)—§ **20.13, n. 6.**

Geiger v. Keilani, 270 F.Supp. 761 (E.D.Mich.1967)—§ **12.18, n. 8.**

Geiser's Will, In re, 82 N.J.Eq. 311, 87 A. 628 (N.J.Prerog.1913)—§ **4.33, n. 3.**

Gelfand v. Tanner Motor Tours, Limited, 339 F.2d 317 (2nd Cir.1964)—§ **5.10, n. 34;** § **8.8, n. 7.**

Gelpi v. Burke, 364 So.2d 1064 (La.App. 4 Cir.1978)—§ **19.10, n. 5.**

General Adjustment Bureau, Inc. v. Fuess, 192 F.Supp. 542 (S.D.Tex.1961)—§ **17.53, n. 5.**

General Ceramics Inc. v. Firemen's Fund Ins. Companies, 66 F.3d 647 (3rd Cir. 1995)—§ **18.26, n. 13.**

General Conference Ass'n of Seventh–Day Adventists v. Michigan Sanitarium & Benevolent Ass'n, 166 Mich. 504, 132 N.W. 94 (Mich.1911)—§ **22.11, n. 11;** § **22.17, n. 1.**

General Dynamics Corp. v. Selb Mfg. Co., 481 F.2d 1204 (8th Cir.1973)—§ **17.52, n. 2.**

General Dynamics Corp., State ex rel. v. Luten, 566 S.W.2d 452 (Mo.1978)—§ **24.9, n. 3.**

General Elec. Co. v. Keyser, 166 W.Va. 456, 275 S.E.2d 289 (W.Va.1981)—§ **18.27, n. 3.**

General Elec. Credit Corp. v. Beyerlein, 55 Misc.2d 724, 286 N.Y.S.2d 351 (N.Y.Sup. 1967)—§ **18.11, n. 4, 5.**

General Elec. Credit Corp. v. Home Indem. Co., 168 Ga.App. 344, 309 S.E.2d 152 (Ga.App.1983)—§ **2.21, n. 44;** § **18.21, n. 5.**

General Elec. Credit Corp. v. Western Crane & Rigging Co., 184 Neb. 212, 166 N.W.2d 409 (Neb.1969)—§ **19.20, n. 11.**

General Engineering Corp. v. Martin Marietta Alumina, Inc., 783 F.2d 352 (3rd Cir.1986)—§ **11.4, n. 15.**

General Instrument Corp., F. W. Sickles Division v. Pennsylvania Pressed Metals, Inc., 366 F.Supp. 139 (M.D.Pa.1973)—§ **18.24, n. 2.**

General Motors Acceptance Corp. v. Robinson, 263 A.2d 302 (Del.Super.1970)—§ **19.12, n. 3;** § **19.13, n. 4.**

General Motors Acceptance Corp. v. Thomas, 15 Ohio Misc. 267, 237 N.E.2d 427 (Ohio Com.Pl.1968)—§ **12.3, n. 7.**

General Telephone Co. of Southeast v. Trimm, 252 Ga. 95, 311 S.E.2d 460 (Ga. 1984)—§ **2.21, n. 44, 47;** § **18.21, n. 5.**

General Telephone Co. of the Southeast v. Trimm, 706 F.2d 1117 (11th Cir.1983)—§ **18.27, n. 2.**

General Universal Trading Corp. v. Morgan Guaranty Trust Co., 936 F.2d 702 (2nd Cir.1991)—§ **12.8, n. 11.**

Genesco, Inc. v. Cone Mills Corp., 604 F.2d 281 (4th Cir.1979)—§ **22.25, n. 5.**

Genetic Implant Systems, Inc. v. Core–Vent Corp., 123 F.3d 1455 (Fed.Cir.1997)— § **9.4, n. 10.**

Gentle v. Western Union Tel. Co., 82 Ark. 96, 100 S.W. 742 (Ark.1907)—§ **3.4, n. 4.**

George v. George, 389 So.2d 1389 (Miss. 1980)—§ **13.6, n. 2.**

George Foreman Associates, Ltd. v. Foreman, 389 F.Supp. 1308 (N.D.Cal.1974)— § **18.11, n. 4.**

George Lombard & Lomar, Inc. v. Economic Development Admin. of Puerto Rico, 1995 WL 447651 (S.D.N.Y.1995)— § **17.50, n. 35.**

George's Estate, In re, 20 Ohio App.2d 87, 252 N.E.2d 176 (Ohio App. 3 Dist. 1969)—§ **22.10, n. 12.**

Georg's Estate, In re, 298 F.Supp. 741 (D.Virgin Islands 1969)—§ **20.6, n. 1.**

Geotech Lizenz AG v. Evergreen Systems, Inc., 697 F.Supp. 1248 (E.D.N.Y.1988)— § **24.48, n. 7.**

Gerling Global Reinsurance Corp. of America v. Low, 296 F.3d 832 (9th Cir. 2002)—§ **3.23, n. 21.**

Gertz v. Robert Welch, Inc., 418 U.S. 323, 94 S.Ct. 2997, 41 L.Ed.2d 789 (1974)— § **7.8, n. 1.**

G & H Const. Co., Inc. v. Daniels Flooring Co., Inc., 173 Ga.App. 181, 325 S.E.2d 773 (Ga.App.1984)—§ **8.6, n. 1.**

Ghen, In re, 45 B.R. 780 (Bkrtcy.E.D.Pa. 1985)—§ **23.12, n. 7.**

Ghilain v. Couture, 84 N.H. 48, 146 A. 395 (N.H.1929)—§ **22.10, n. 6.**

Giampalo v. Taylor, 335 Pa. 121, 6 A.2d 499 (Pa.1939)—§ **22.19, n. 24.**

Gianni v. Fort Wayne Air Service, Inc., 342 F.2d 621 (7th Cir.1965)—§ **3.12, n. 1.**

Giantvalley, In re, 14 B.R. 457 (Bkrtcy. D.Nev.1981)—§ **18.28, n. 5.**

Gibbons v. Udaras na Gaeltachta, 549 F.Supp. 1094 (S.D.N.Y.1982)—§ **11.15, n. 1.**

Gibbs–Brower Intern. v. Kirchheimer Bros. Co., 611 F.Supp. 122 (N.D.Ill.1985)— § **18.31, n. 5;** § **18.44, n. 9.**

Gibbs' Estate, In re, 73 Wyo. 425, 280 P.2d 556 (Wyo.1955)—§ **22.21, n. 14.**

Gibbs ex rel. Gibbs v. Carnival Cruise Lines, 314 F.3d 125 (3rd Cir.2002)— § **10.6, n. 14.**

Giblin, Petition of, 304 Minn. 510, 232 N.W.2d 214 (Minn.1975)—§ **15.40, n. 7;** § **15.42, n. 1.**

Gibson v. Boynton, 112 Kan. 173, 210 P. 648 (Kan.1922)—§ **19.4, n. 3.**

Gibson v. Gibson, 292 F. 657 (D.C.Cir. 1923)—§ **20.15, n. 6.**

Gibson v. Hughes, 192 F.Supp. 564 (S.D.N.Y.1961)—§ **13.2, n. 5;** § **13.6, n. 2;** § **13.15, n. 4.**

Gifford's Will, In re, 279 N.Y. 470, 18 N.E.2d 663 (N.Y.1939)—§ **22.3, n. 9.**

Gilbert v. Burnstine, 255 N.Y. 348, 174 N.E. 706 (N.Y.1931)—§ **24.47, n. 5.**

Gilbert v. David, 235 U.S. 561, 35 S.Ct. 164, 59 L.Ed. 360 (1915)—§ **4.20, n. 3.**

Gilbert v. Gilbert, 442 So.2d 1330 (La.App. 3 Cir.1983)—§ **14.9, n. 2, 3;** § **14.11, n. 2;** § **20.3, n. 1.**

Gilbert v. Seton Hall University, 332 F.3d 105 (2nd Cir.2003)—§ **17.46;** § **17.46, n. 5.**

Gilbert Spruance Co. v. Pennsylvania Mfrs. Ass'n Ins. Co., 134 N.J. 96, 629 A.2d 885 (N.J.1993)—§ **2.19, n. 17;** § **2.25, n. 10;** § **18.21, n. 17;** § **18.26, n. 13.**

Gil de Rebollo v. Miami Heat Associations, Inc., 137 F.3d 56 (1st Cir.1998)—§ **3.37, n. 6.**

Giliberto, People ex rel. Compagnie Nationale Air France v., 74 Ill.2d 90, 23 Ill. Dec. 106, 383 N.E.2d 977 (Ill.1978)— § **3.57, n. 22.**

Gillan v. Gillan, 236 Pa.Super. 147, 345 A.2d 742 (Pa.Super.1975)—§ **18.17, n. 2.**

Gillmore's Estate, In re, 101 N.J.Super. 77, 243 A.2d 263 (N.J.Super.A.D.1968)— § **4.13, n. 2.**

Gillock, United States v., 445 U.S. 360, 100 S.Ct. 1185, 63 L.Ed.2d 454 (1980)— § **3.50, n. 5.**

Gilman v. Gilman, 52 Me. 165 (Me.1863)— § **4.1, n. 2;** § **4.20, n. 8;** § **4.36, n. 4.**

Gilmer v. Interstate/Johnson Lane Corp., 500 U.S. 20, 111 S.Ct. 1647, 114 L.Ed.2d 26 (1991)—§ **6.3, n. 18.**

Gilmore, Estate of, 124 N.M. 119, 946 P.2d 1130 (N.M.App.1997)—§ **2.21, n. 21.**

Gilson v. Republic of Ireland, 682 F.2d 1022, 221 U.S.App.D.C. 73 (D.C.Cir. 1982)—§ **7.6, n. 11.**

Gimmestad v. Gimmestad, 451 N.W.2d 662 (Minn.App.1990)—§ **17.21, n. 14.**

Ginkowski v. Ginkowski, 28 Wis.2d 530, 137 N.W.2d 403 (Wis.1965)—§ **13.13, n. 5.**

Giorgio v. Nukem, Inc., 31 Conn.App. 169, 624 A.2d 896 (Conn.App.1993)—§ **18.21, n. 14.**

Girard Trust Co. v. United States, 149 F.2d 872 (3rd Cir.1945)—§ **3.52, n. 2.**

Gkiafis v. S. S. Yiosonas, 387 F.2d 460 (4th Cir.1967)—§ **12.18, n. 8.**

Gladwin v. Power, 21 A.D.2d 665, 249 N.Y.S.2d 980 (N.Y.A.D. 1 Dept.1964)— § **4.3, n. 3;** § **4.33, n. 6.**

Glaeske v. Shaw, 261 Wis.2d 549, 661 N.W.2d 420 (Wis.App.2003)—§ **21.3, n. 10.**

Glanding v. Industrial Trust Co., 29 Del.Ch. 517, 46 A.2d 881 (Del.Supr.1946)— § **20.2, n. 4.**

Glansman v. Ledbetter, 190 Ind. 505, 130 N.E. 230 (Ind.1921)—§ **4.38, n. 1.**

Glassford's Estate, In re, 114 Cal.App.2d 181, 249 P.2d 908 (Cal.App. 2 Dist. 1952)—§ **22.7, n. 1.**

Gleason v. Holman Contract Warehouse, Inc., 250 A.D.2d 339, 681 N.Y.S.2d 664 (N.Y.A.D. 3 Dept.1998)—§ **17.46, n. 21.**

Glencore Grain Rotterdam B.V. v. Shivnath Rai Harnarain Co., 284 F.3d 1114 (9th Cir.2002)—§ **10.5, n. 18.**

Glickman v. Mesigh, 200 Colo. 320, 615 P.2d 23 (Colo.1980)—§ **15.34, n. 7.**

Glickman v. United States, 626 F.Supp. 171 (S.D.N.Y.1985)—§ **17.48, n. 19.**

Global Servicios, S.A. v. Toplis & Harding, Inc., 561 So.2d 674 (Fla.App. 3 Dist. 1990)—§ **8.8, n. 6.**

Globe & Rutgers Fire Ins. Co., People v., 96 Cal.App.2d 571, 216 P.2d 64 (Cal.App. 1 Dist.1950)—§ **18.3, n. 1.**

Glona v. American Guarantee & Liability Ins. Co., 391 U.S. 73, 88 S.Ct. 1515, 20 L.Ed.2d 441 (1968)—§ **3.54, n. 5; § 16.3, n. 3.**

Gloucester Holding Corp. v. United States Tape and Sticky Products, LLC, 832 A.2d 116 (Del.Ch.2003)—§ **17.40, n. 28; § 18.1, n. 18.**

Glover v. Wells, 140 Ill. 102, 29 N.E. 680 (Ill.1892)—§ **19.29, n. 3.**

Glowski v. Allstate Ins. Co., 134 N.H. 196, 589 A.2d 593 (N.H.1991)—§ **18.21, n. 14.**

Glunt v. ABC Paving Co., Inc., 247 A.D.2d 871, 668 N.Y.S.2d 846 (N.Y.A.D. 4 Dept. 1998)—§ **17.43, n. 9; § 17.44, n. 13.**

Godard v. Gray, 1870 WL 11634 (QB 1870)—§ **24.16, n. 6; § 24.33; § 24.33, n. 3.**

Goddard, In re, 33 Mass. 504 (Mass.1835)—§ **4.13, n. 12.**

Gogan v. Jones, 197 Tenn. 436, 273 S.W.2d 700 (Tenn.1954)—§ **22.14, n. 3.**

Go Intern., Inc. v. Lewis, 601 S.W.2d 495 (Tex.Civ.App.-El Paso 1980)—§ **16.6, n. 6.**

Goldberg v. Goldberg, 57 Misc.2d 224, 291 N.Y.S.2d 482 (N.Y.Fam.Ct.1968)—§ **15.38, n. 2.**

Golden v. National Finance Adjusters, 555 F.Supp. 42 (E.D.Mich.1982)—§ **5.17, n. 8.**

Golden Plains Feedlot, Inc. v. Great Western Sugar Co., 588 F.Supp. 985 (D.S.D. 1984)—§ **18.24, n. 2.**

Golden Rule Ins. Co. v. Hopkins, 788 F.Supp. 295 (S.D.Miss.1991)—§ **18.24, n. 2.**

Goldey v. Morning News of New Haven, 156 U.S. 518, 15 S.Ct. 559, 39 L.Ed. 517 (1895)—§ **5.3, n. 15; § 5.15, n. 1; § 6.2; § 6.2, n. 20; § 10.8; § 10.8, n. 11.**

Goldfarb v. Goldfarb, 246 Ga. 24, 268 S.E.2d 648 (Ga.1980)—§ **15.29, n. 4.**

Goldin v. Goldin, 48 Md.App. 154, 426 A.2d 410 (Md.App.1981)—§ **13.6, n. 4.**

Golding v. Golding, 176 A.D.2d 20, 581 N.Y.S.2d 4 (N.Y.A.D. 1 Dept.1992)—§ **15.24, n. 7.**

Goldlawr, Inc. v. Heiman, 369 U.S. 463, 82 S.Ct. 913, 8 L.Ed.2d 39 (1962)—§ **9.7, n. 7.**

Goldsmith v. Allied Bldg. Components, Inc., 833 S.W.2d 378 (Ky.1992)—§ **17.61, n. 2.**

Goldsmith v. Goldsmith, 281 N.Y.S.2d 344, 228 N.E.2d 400 (N.Y.1967)—§ **15.11, n. 2.**

Goldsmith v. Salkey, 131 Tex. 139, 112 S.W.2d 165 (Tex.1938)—§ **4.37, n. 3.**

Goldsmith v. Salkey, 115 S.W.2d 778 (Tex. Civ.App.-San Antonio 1937)—§ **4.40, n. 4.**

Goldstein v. California, 412 U.S. 546, 93 S.Ct. 2303, 37 L.Ed.2d 163 (1973)—§ **17.53, n. 3.**

Goldstein v. Cox, 396 U.S. 471, 90 S.Ct. 671, 24 L.Ed.2d 663 (1970)—§ **11.13, n. 17.**

Goldwater, Estate of, 539 F.2d 878 (2nd Cir.1976)—§ **15.13; § 15.13, n. 6.**

Gomez v. ITT Educational Services, Inc., 348 Ark. 69, 71 S.W.3d 542 (Ark.2002)—§ **3.10, n. 6; § 3.12, n. 1.**

Gomez v. Karavias U.S.A. Inc., 401 F.Supp. 104 (S.D.N.Y.1975)—§ **17.63, n. 23.**

Gomez v. Perez, 409 U.S. 535, 93 S.Ct. 872, 35 L.Ed.2d 56 (1973)—§ **3.54, n. 5.**

Gonzales v. Harris, 514 F.Supp. 995 (E.D.Cal.1981)—§ **16.2, n. 6.**

Gonzalez v. Naviera Neptuno A.A., 832 F.2d 876 (5th Cir.1987)—§ **11.9, n. 6.**

Gonzalez, State v., 75 N.J. 181, 380 A.2d 1128 (N.J.1977)—§ **24.1, n. 12.**

Gonzalez–Gonzalez–Jimenez de Ruiz v. United States, 231 F.Supp.2d 1187 (M.D.Fla.2002)—§ **13.11, n. 4.**

Goodale, In re, 298 B.R. 886 (Bkrtcy. W.D.Wash.2003)—§ **14.4, n. 12.**

Goodall v. Marshall, 14 N.H. 161 (N.H. 1843)—§ **22.20, n. 34.**

Goodlett v. Anderson, 75 Tenn. 286 (Tenn. 1881)—§ **22.11, n. 8, 17.**

Goodman v. First Nat. Bank, 218 Ky. 229, 291 S.W. 54 (Ky.1927)—§ **22.16, n. 6.**

Goodman v. Nadler, 113 Ga.App. 493, 148 S.E.2d 480 (Ga.App.1966)—§ **19.10, n. 2.**

Goodman v. Winter, 64 Ala. 410 (Ala. 1879)—§ **22.3, n. 1.**

Goodman, In re Adoption of, 49 Del. 550, 121 A.2d 676 (Del.Orph.1952)—§ **16.5, n. 5.**

Goodman's Trusts, Re, 1881 WL 18546 (CA 1881)—§ **16.1, n. 8.**

Goodridge v. Department of Public Health, 440 Mass. 309, 798 N.E.2d 941 (Mass. 2003)—§ **13.20, n. 3, 4.**

Good's Will, In re, 304 N.Y. 110, 106 N.E.2d 36 (N.Y.1952)—§ **20.8, n. 10, 12.**

Goodwin v. Jones, 3 Mass. 514 (Mass. 1807)—§ **22.14, n. 3, 5.**

Goodwin v. Townsend, 197 F.2d 970 (3rd Cir.1952)—§ **3.10, n. 6.**

Goodwin v. Young, 34 Mun. 252 (N.Y. S.Ct. 1884)—§ **17.5, n. 7.**

Goodwin Bros. Leasing, Inc. v. H & B Inc., 597 S.W.2d 303 (Tenn.1980)—§ **2.19, n. 9.**

Goodwin Bros. Leasing, Inc. v. Nousis, 373 Mass. 169, 366 N.E.2d 38 (Mass.1977)—§ **23.6, n. 4.**

Gordon v. Clifford Metal Sales Co., Inc., 602 A.2d 535 (R.I.1992)—§ **2.21, n. 75;** § **18.7, n. 3;** § **18.21, n. 9.**

Gordon v. Gordon, 110 A.D.2d 623, 487 N.Y.S.2d 574 (N.Y.A.D. 2 Dept.1985)—§ **22.7, n. 1.**

Gordon v. Gordon, 369 So.2d 421 (Fla.App. 3 Dist.1979)—§ **4.34, n. 4.**

Gordon v. Gordon, 118 N.H. 356, 387 A.2d 339 (N.H.1978)—§ **3.9, n. 6;** § **17.17, n. 8.**

Gordon v. Gordon, 27 Misc.2d 948, 211 N.Y.S.2d 265 (N.Y.Sup.1960)—§ **13.6, n. 2.**

Gordon v. Holly Woods Acres, Inc., 328 F.2d 253 (6th Cir.1964)—§ **22.2, n. 3.**

Gordon v. Parker, 83 F.Supp. 40 (D.Mass. 1949)—§ **17.5, n. 6.**

Gordon v. Shea, 300 Mass. 95, 14 N.E.2d 105 (Mass.1938)—§ **22.10, n. 11.**

Gordon v. Yost, 140 F. 79 (C.C.N.D.W.Va. 1905)—§ **4.34, n. 2.**

Gordon's Will, In re, 26 A. 268 (N.J.Pre-rog.1893)—§ **22.2, n. 3.**

Gordy v. Daily News, L.P., 95 F.3d 829 (9th Cir.1996)—§ **7.8, n. 10.**

Gore v. Northeast Airlines, Inc., 373 F.2d 717 (2nd Cir.1967)—§ **17.17, n. 8.**

Gore v. United States Steel Corp., 15 N.J. 301, 104 A.2d 670 (N.J.1954)—§ **11.8, n. 3.**

Gorie v. Gorie, 26 A.D.2d 368, 274 N.Y.S.2d 985 (N.Y.A.D. 1 Dept.1966)—§ **24.4, n. 4.**

Gorun v. Fall, 393 U.S. 398, 89 S.Ct. 678, 21 L.Ed.2d 628 (1969)—§ **11.13, n. 17.**

Gorun v. Montana, 399 U.S. 901, 90 S.Ct. 2195, 26 L.Ed.2d 555 (1970)—§ **11.13, n. 17.**

Gosney v. Department of Public Welfare, 206 Neb. 137, 291 N.W.2d 708 (Neb. 1980)—§ **4.44, n. 7;** § **4.45, n. 1.**

Goss, Succession of, 304 So.2d 704 (La.App. 3 Cir.1974)—§ **13.6, n. 7;** § **20.5, n. 7;** § **20.9, n. 11.**

Gosschalk v. Gosschalk, 28 N.J. 73, 145 A.2d 327 (N.J.1958)—§ **4.20, n. 7;** § **4.30, n. 4.**

Gould v. Gould, 235 N.Y. 14, 138 N.E. 490 (N.Y.1923)—§ **15.17, n. 9;** § **15.24, n. 8.**

Gould Electronics Inc. v. United States, 220 F.3d 169 (3rd Cir.2000)—§ **3.1, n. 4;** § **3.13, n. 2;** § **17.32, n. 21;** § **17.45, n. 53;** § **17.46;** § **17.46, n. 19.**

Gould Inc. v. Continental Cas. Co., 822 F.Supp. 1172 (E.D.Pa.1993)—§ **18.26, n. 12.**

Goulding v. Sands, 237 F.Supp. 577 (W.D.Pa.1965)—§ **18.21, n. 17.**

Gould's Estate, In re, 140 N.E.2d 793 (Ohio Prob.1956)—§ **20.9, n. 13.**

Gourneau v. Smith, 207 N.W.2d 256 (N.D. 1973)—§ **11.17, n. 23.**

Gove v. Gove, 64 N.H. 503, 15 A. 121 (N.H. 1888)—§ **22.17, n. 1.**

Govett American Endeavor Fund Ltd. v. Trueger, 112 F.3d 1017 (9th Cir.1997)—§ **18.4, n. 43, 55.**

Go–Video, Inc. v. Akai Elec. Co., Ltd., 885 F.2d 1406 (9th Cir.1989)—§ **9.7, n. 3;** § **10.2, n. 15.**

Gower v. Carter, 195 N.C. 697, 143 S.E. 513 (N.C.1928)—§ **4.13, n. 2.**

Gowins v. Gowins, 466 So.2d 32 (La.1985)—§ **5.23, n. 1, 7;** § **15.5, n. 1.**

Grable v. City of Detroit, 48 Mich.App. 368, 210 N.W.2d 379 (Mich.App.1973)—§ **4.33, n. 6;** § **4.34, n. 3.**

Grace v. MacArthur, 170 F.Supp. 442 (E.D.Ark.1959)—§ **6.2, n. 8.**

Graduate Management Admission Council v. Raju, 241 F.Supp.2d 589 (E.D.Va. 2003)—§ **10.5, n. 18.**

Grady's Estate, In re, 79 Wash.2d 41, 483 P.2d 114 (Wash.1971)—§ **21.8, n. 2;** § **21.11, n. 7.**

Graham, Commonwealth v., 157 Mass. 73, 31 N.E. 706 (Mass.1892)—§ **4.44, n. 2.**

Graham v. General United States Grant Post No. 2665, V. F. W., 43 Ill.2d 1, 248 N.E.2d 657 (Ill.1969)—§ **2.10, n. 10;** § **17.5, n. 7.**

Graham v. Graham, 452 Pa. 404, 305 A.2d 48 (Pa.1973)—§ **22.19, n. 18.**

Graham v. Hamilton County, 224 Tenn. 82, 450 S.W.2d 571 (Tenn.1969)—§ **19.7, n. 4.**

Graham v. Wilkins, 145 Conn. 34, 138 A.2d 705 (Conn.1958)—§ **18.37, n. 3.**

Grand Bahama Petroleum Co., Ltd. v. Canadian Transp. Agencies, Ltd., 450 F.Supp. 447 (W.D.Wash.1978)—§ **10.6, n. 51.**

Grand Jury Proceedings, Yanagihara Grand Jury, Impanelled June 13, 1988, In re, 709 F.Supp. 192 (C.D.Cal.1989)—§ **12.9, n. 16.**

Grand Trunk Western R. Co. v. Chicago & Western Indiana R. Co., 131 F.2d 215 (7th Cir.1942)—§ **18.47, n. 4.**

Granite Equipment Leasing Corp. v. Hutton, 84 Wash.2d 320, 525 P.2d 223 (Wash.1974)—§ **18.27, n. 5.**

Granite & Quartzite Centre Inc. v. M/S Virma, 374 F.Supp. 1124 (S.D.Ga. 1974)—§ **8.8, n. 9.**

Grant v. McAuliffe, 41 Cal.2d 859, 264 P.2d 944 (Cal.1953)—§ **2.16;** § **2.16, n. 3;** § **3.4, n. 5;** § **17.10;** § **17.10, n. 1;** § **17.16;** § **17.16, n. 4;** § **17.43;** § **17.43, n. 5.**

Grant v. Rogers, 94 N.C. 755 (N.C.1886)— § **22.11, n. 1.**

Grant v. Superior Court In and For Pima County, 27 Ariz.App. 427, 555 P.2d 895 (Ariz.App. Div. 2 1976)—§ **13.6, n. 2, 4.**

Grasser v. Blakkolb, 12 Wash.App. 529, 530 P.2d 684 (Wash.App. Div. 3 1975)— § **22.20, n. 33.**

Grasty v. Clare, 210 Va. 21, 168 S.E.2d 261 (Va.1969)—§ **22.23, n. 14.**

Graumann v. Treitel, (1940) 2 All E.R. 188 (K.B.)—§ **4.27, n. 12.**

Graveley v. Graveley, 25 S.C. 1 (S.C.1886)— § **22.23, n. 11.**

Graves, State v., 228 Ark. 378, 307 S.W.2d 545 (Ark.1957)—§ **13.2;** § **13.2, n. 8;** § **13.9, n. 5;** § **13.12, n. 1, 5.**

Graves Motors, Inc. v. Docar Sales, Inc., 414 F.Supp. 717 (E.D.La.1976)— § **19.17, n. 6.**

Gravina v. Brunswick Corp., 338 F.Supp. 1 (D.R.I.1972)—§ **17.55, n. 9.**

Gravquick A/S v. Trimble Navigation Intern. Ltd., 323 F.3d 1219 (9th Cir. 2003)—§ **18.5, n. 32.**

Gray v. American Exp. Co., 743 F.2d 10, 240 U.S.App.D.C. 10 (D.C.Cir.1984)— § **3.36, n. 1.**

Gray v. American Radiator & Standard Sanitary Corp., 22 Ill.2d 432, 176 N.E.2d 761 (Ill.1961)—§ **7.1, n. 5;** § **7.2;** § **7.2, n. 3;** § **7.4, n. 6.**

Gray v. Busch Entertainment Corp., 886 F.2d 14 (2nd Cir.1989)—§ **17.48, n. 8.**

Gray v. Franks, 86 Mich. 382, 49 N.W. 130 (Mich.1891)—§ **22.14, n. 7.**

Gray v. Gray, 189 So.2d 735 (La.App. 1 Cir.1966)—§ **19.2, n. 8;** § **19.3, n. 3.**

Gray v. O'Banion, 23 Cal.App. 468, 138 P. 977 (Cal.App. 3 Dist.1913)—§ **4.19, n. 3, 4.**

Gray (Otherwise Formosa) v. Formosa, 1962 WL 21511 (CA 1962)—§ **24.44, n. 14.**

Gray's Estate, 116 Pa. 256, 11 A. 66 (Pa. 1887)—§ **22.16, n. 2.**

Grayson v. Robertson, 122 Ala. 330, 25 So. 229 (Ala.1899)—§ **22.12, n. 3;** § **22.15, n. 9.**

Great Am. Ins. Co. v. Hartford Acc. & Indem. Co., 519 S.W.2d 579 (Tenn.1975)— § **2.21, n. 77;** § **18.21, n. 11.**

Great Northern Ry. Co. v. Johnson, 254 F. 683 (8th Cir.1918)—§ **13.6, n. 10.**

Great Southern Life Ins. Co. v. Burwell, 12 F.2d 244 (5th Cir.1926)—§ **18.6, n. 3;** § **18.7, n. 11.**

Great West Cas. Co. v. Hovaldt, 603 N.W.2d 198 (S.D.1999)—§ **18.26, n. 6.**

Great–West Life Assurance Co. v. Guarantee Co. of North America, 205 Cal. App.3d 199, 252 Cal.Rptr. 363 (Cal.App. 2 Dist.1988)—§ **8.2, n. 10.**

Greaves v. Fogel, 12 N.J.Super. 5, 78 A.2d 719 (N.J.Super.A.D.1951)—§ **20.2, n. 4.**

Greco v. Anderson, 615 S.W.2d 429 (Mo. App. E.D.1980)—§ **17.54, n. 4.**

Greco v. Grand Casinos of Mississippi, Inc.– Gulfport, 1996 WL 617401 (E.D.La. 1996)—§ **17.48, n. 5.**

Green v. Alden, 92 Me. 177, 42 A. 358 (Me.1898)—§ **22.18, n. 13, 14.**

Green v. Clinic Masters, Inc., 272 N.W.2d 813 (S.D.1978)—§ **11.5, n. 3.**

Green v. Gross, 12 Neb. 117, 10 N.W. 459 (Neb.1881)—§ **19.2, n. 5.**

Green v. Rugely, 23 Tex. 539 (Tex.1859)— § **22.9, n. 1.**

Green v. Van Buskirk, 74 U.S. 139, 38 How. Pr. 52, 19 L.Ed. 109 (1868)—§ **19.11, n. 12.**

Green v. Van Buskirk, 72 U.S. 307, 18 L.Ed. 599 (1866)—§ **19.11, n. 12;** § **19.13;** § **19.13, n. 7.**

Greenberg v. Rothberg, 72 Ga.App. 882, 35 S.E.2d 485 (Ga.App.1945)—§ **12.17, n. 7.**

Greene v. Greene, 28 Mass. 410 (Mass. 1831)—§ **4.21, n. 2.**

Greene v. Lindsey, 456 U.S. 444, 102 S.Ct. 1874, 72 L.Ed.2d 249 (1982)—§ **12.3, n. 13.**

Greene v. Willis, 47 R.I. 375, 133 A. 651 (R.I.1926)—§ **4.41, n. 7.**

Green Giant Co. v. Tribunal Superior, 104 D.P.R. 489 (P.R.1975)—§ **2.17, n. 7;** § **2.22, n. 8;** § **18.21, n. 15.**

Greenhow v. James' Ex'r, 80 Va. 636 (Va. 1885)—§ **16.1, n. 8.**

Green Leaf Nursery v. E.I. DuPont De Nemours and Co., 341 F.3d 1292 (11th Cir.2003)—§ **17.40, n. 28;** § **18.1, n. 18.**

Greenman v. Yuba Power Products, Inc., 59 Cal.2d 57, 27 Cal.Rptr. 697, 377 P.2d 897 (Cal.1963)—§ **7.1, n. 3;** § **7.2, n. 1.**

Green Mountain Ins. Co. v. George, 138 N.H. 10, 634 A.2d 1011 (N.H.1993)— § **18.21, n. 14.**

Green Mountain Power Corp. v. Certain Underwriters at Lloyd's, London, 1995 WL 433597 (D.Vt.1994)—§ **18.26, n. 13.**

Greenough v. Osgood, 235 Mass. 235, 126 N.E. 461 (Mass.1920)—§ **21.6, n. 7;** § **21.11, n. 15.**

Greenray Industries, Inc. v. Charleswater Products, Inc., 1990 WL 26887 (D.Mass. 1990)—§ **18.12, n. 16.**

Greenstreet v. Simmons, 54 F.R.D. 554 (S.D.Ill.1972)—§ **22.25, n. 5.**

Greenwood v. Hildebrand, 357 Pa.Super. 253, 515 A.2d 963 (Pa.Super.1986)— § **4.16, n. 1;** § **4.17, n. 1, 4;** § **4.18, n. 4.**

Greenwood v. Page, 138 F.2d 921, 78 U.S.App.D.C. 166 (D.C.Cir.1943)— **§ 20.8, n. 8.**

Greenwood Trust Co. v. Commonwealth of Massachusetts., 776 F.Supp. 21 (D.Mass. 1991)—**§ 18.28, n. 1, 5.**

Greer v. Ferguson, 56 Ark. 324, 19 S.W. 966 (Ark.1892)—**§ 22.14, n. 5; § 22.19, n. 1, 3, 4.**

Gregg v. Louisiana Power and Light Co., 626 F.2d 1315 (5th Cir.1980)—**§ 4.36, n. 4; § 4.37, n. 1.**

Gregory v. Ashcroft, 501 U.S. 452, 111 S.Ct. 2395, 115 L.Ed.2d 410 (1991)— **§ 3.58, n. 15, 18.**

Grengs, State v., 253 Wis. 248, 33 N.W.2d 248 (Wis.1948)—**§ 13.9, n. 3.**

Greschler v. Greschler, 434 N.Y.S.2d 194, 414 N.E.2d 694 (N.Y.1980)—**§ 15.20, n. 6.**

Gribbel v. Henderson, 151 Fla. 712, 10 So.2d 734 (Fla.1942)—**§ 22.19, n. 18.**

Griesemer v. Mutual Life Ins. Co. of New York, 10 Wash. 202, 38 P. 1031 (Wash. 1894)—**§ 18.2, n. 1.**

Gries Sports Enterprises, Inc. v. Modell, 15 Ohio St.3d 284, 473 N.E.2d 807 (Ohio 1984)— **§ 2.17, n. 11; § 2.23, n. 2; § 18.21, n. 14.**

Griffin v. Griffin, 327 U.S. 220, 66 S.Ct. 556, 90 L.Ed. 635 (1946)—**§ 15.34, n. 1, 6.**

Griffin v. Griffin, 95 Or. 78, 187 P. 598 (Or.1920)—**§ 4.40, n. 2.**

Griffin v. McCoach, 313 U.S. 498, 61 S.Ct. 1023, 85 L.Ed. 1481 (1941)—**§ 3.43; § 3.43, n. 3.**

Griffin v. Summit Specialties, Inc., 622 So.2d 1299 (Ala.1993)—**§ 2.21, n. 1.**

Griffis v. Luban, 646 N.W.2d 527 (Minn. 2002)—**§ 7.8, n. 14.**

Griffith, In re, 6 B.R. 750 (Bkrtcy.D.N.M. 1980)—**§ 23.13, n. 1.**

Griffith v. Mitsubishi Aircraft Intern., Inc., 136 Ill.2d 101, 143 Ill.Dec. 274, 554 N.E.2d 209 (Ill.1990)—**§ 11.8, n. 6.**

Griffith v. United Air Lines, Inc., 416 Pa. 1, 203 A.2d 796 (Pa.1964)—**§ 2.16, n. 9; § 3.5; § 3.5, n. 5; § 3.12, n. 6; § 17.12; § 17.12, n. 4, 8; § 18.20, n. 1; § 18.21, n. 17; § 18.24, n. 2.**

Griffith v. White, 929 F.Supp. 755 (D.Vt. 1996)—**§ 17.26, n. 9.**

Griffiths, Application of, 413 U.S. 717, 93 S.Ct. 2851, 37 L.Ed.2d 910 (1973)— **§ 3.58, n. 11, 18.**

Griggs v. Riley, 489 S.W.2d 469 (Mo.App. 1972)—**§ 17.26, n. 6.**

Grigg's Estate, In re, 54 Pa. D. & C. 25 (Pa.Orph.1945)—**§ 20.5, n. 6.**

Grignon v. Shope, 100 Or. 611, 197 P. 317 (Or.1921)—**§ 22.11, n. 11.**

Griley v. Griley, 43 So.2d 350 (Fla.1949)— **§ 20.9, n. 11; § 20.15, n. 7.**

Grimes v. Vitalink Communications Corp., 17 F.3d 1553 (3rd Cir.1994)—**§ 10.11, n. 7.**

Grimmett v. Witherington, 16 Ark. 377 (Ark.1855)—**§ 22.25, n. 2, 18.**

Grist v. Forehand, 36 Miss. 69 (Miss.Err. & App.1858)—**§ 22.25, n. 15.**

Griswold v. Griswold, 23 Colo.App. 365, 129 P. 560 (Colorado App.1913)—**§ 13.9, n. 4, 9.**

Griswold's Trust, In re, 99 N.Y.S.2d 420 (N.Y.Sup.1950)—**§ 21.3, n. 13, 17.**

Grodzinsky, State ex rel. Miller v., 571 N.W.2d 1 (Iowa 1997)—**§ 9.8, n. 9.**

Groh v. Egan, 526 P.2d 863 (Alaska 1974)— **§ 4.26, n. 8; § 4.27, n. 13.**

Groome v. Freyn Engineering Co., 374 Ill. 113, 28 N.E.2d 274 (Ill.1940)—**§ 12.17, n. 7.**

Groome v. Leatherwood, 240 N.C. 573, 83 S.E.2d 536 (N.C.1954)—**§ 22.20, n. 34; § 22.23, n. 1.**

Groos, Re, 1915 WL 18812 (Ch D 1915)— **§ 20.9, n. 16.**

Groseclose v. Rice, 366 P.2d 465 (Okla. 1961)—**§ 4.45, n. 2.**

Gross v. Hocker, 243 Iowa 291, 51 N.W.2d 466 (Iowa 1952)—**§ 22.10, n. 6; § 22.15, n. 10.**

Gross v. McDonald, 354 F.Supp. 378 (E.D.Pa.1973)—**§ 3.11, n. 4.**

Grossen's Estate v. Vincent, 657 P.2d 1345 (Utah 1983)—**§ 20.6, n. 4.**

Gross Income Tax Division v. Bartlett, 228 Ind. 505, 93 N.E.2d 174 (Ind.1950)— **§ 19.2, n. 4.**

Grossman v. Citrus Associates of New York Cotton Exchange, Inc., 706 F.Supp. 221 (S.D.N.Y.1989)—**§ 11.6, n. 7.**

Grove v. Principal Mut. Life Ins. Co., 14 F.Supp.2d 1101 (S.D.Iowa 1998)— **§ 17.52, n. 3.**

Grover v. Isom, 137 Idaho 770, 53 P.3d 821 (Idaho 2002)—**§ 17.42; § 17.42, n. 34.**

Grover & Baker Sewing–Mach. Co. v. Radcliffe, 137 U.S. 287, 11 S.Ct. 92, 34 L.Ed. 670 (1890)—**§ 24.14, n. 1.**

Groves v. Barto, 109 Wash. 112, 186 P. 300 (Wash.1919)—**§ 4.40, n. 2.**

Groves v. Universe Tankships, Inc., 308 F.Supp. 826 (S.D.N.Y.1970)—**§ 17.63, n. 23.**

Grubel v. Nassauer, 210 N.Y. 149, 103 N.E. 1113 (N.Y.1913)—**§ 6.4, n. 15.**

GTE New Media Services Inc. v. BellSouth Corp., 199 F.3d 1343, 339 U.S.App.D.C. 332 (D.C.Cir.2000)—**§ 9.7, n. 3.**

Guaranty Trust Co., United States v., 293 U.S. 340, 55 S.Ct. 221, 79 L.Ed. 415 (1934)—**§ 19.31, n. 8.**

Guaranty Trust Co. of N.Y. v. Stevens, 28 N.J. 243, 146 A.2d 97 (N.J.1958)— **§ 21.3, n. 15; § 21.10, n. 6; § 21.11, n. 9, 12, 14; § 21.13, n. 2.**

Guaranty Trust Co. of N.Y. v. York, 326 U.S. 99, 65 S.Ct. 1464, 89 L.Ed. 2079 (1945)—§ **3.37, n. 1**; § **3.48, n. 17**; § **24.12, n. 8.**

Guardian Royal Exchange Assur., Ltd. v. English China Clays, P.L.C., 815 S.W.2d 223 (Tex.1991)—§ **5.12, n. 7**; § **7.2, n. 34.**

Guardianship of (see name of party)

Guerard v. Guerard, 73 Ga. 506 (Ga. 1884)—§ **20.8, n. 9.**

Guidi v. Inter–Continental Hotels Corp., 224 F.3d 142 (2nd Cir.2000)—§ **11.9, n. 7.**

Guidry v. Hardy, 254 So.2d 675 (La.App. 3 Cir.1971)—§ **20.6, n. 21.**

Guillander v. Howell, 35 N.Y. 657 (N.Y. 1866)—§ **19.13, n. 7.**

Guinness v. Miller, 291 F. 769 (S.D.N.Y. 1923)—§ **2.8, n. 5.**

Guinness Import Co. v. Mark VII Distributors, Inc., 153 F.3d 607 (8th Cir.1998)—§ **9.7, n. 10.**

Gulf, C. & S.F. Ry. Co. v. Lemons, 109 Tex. 244, 206 S.W. 75 (Tex.1918)—§ **4.43, n. 1.**

Gulf Life Ins. Co. v. Arnold, 809 F.2d 1520 (11th Cir.1987)—§ **9.5, n. 11.**

Gulf Offshore Co. v. Mobil Oil Corp., 453 U.S. 473, 101 S.Ct. 2870, 69 L.Ed.2d 784 (1981)—§ **3.39, n. 7.**

Gulf Oil Corp. v. Gilbert, 330 U.S. 501, 67 S.Ct. 839, 91 L.Ed. 1055 (1947)—§ **3.33, n. 4**; § **10.13, n. 9**; § **11.8**; § **11.8, n. 3, 5**; § **11.9, n. 1**; § **11.11**; § **11.11, n. 1, 6**; § **11.14**; § **11.14, n. 1, 9.**

Gulstine's Estate, In re, 166 Wash. 325, 6 P.2d 628 (Wash.1932)—§ **14.6, n. 8.**

Gunn v. Giraudo, 48 Cal.App.2d 622, 120 P.2d 177 (Cal.App. 4 Dist.1941)—§ **22.20, n. 34.**

Gurley v. Lindsley, 459 F.2d 268 (5th Cir. 1972)—§ **22.18, n. 10.**

Gursky v. Gursky, 39 Misc.2d 1083, 242 N.Y.S.2d 406 (N.Y.Sup.1963)—§ **16.1, n. 14.**

Gustafson v. Jensen, 515 So.2d 1298 (Fla. App. 3 Dist.1987)—§ **14.15, n. 2.**

Gutierrez v. Cayman Islands Firm of Deloitte & Touche, 100 S.W.3d 261 (Tex. App.-San Antonio 2002)—§ **7.6, n. 8**; § **9.6, n. 21.**

Gutierrez v. Collins, 583 S.W.2d 312 (Tex. 1979)—§ **2.16, n. 12**; § **2.23, n. 1**; § **3.19, n. 10**; § **17.26, n. 1**; § **17.39, n. 11**; § **23.15, n. 6.**

Gutierrez v. Givens, 989 F.Supp. 1033 (S.D.Cal.1997)—§ **10.9, n. 21.**

Gutillo v. Gutillo, 30 A.D.2d 484, 294 N.Y.S.2d 438 (N.Y.A.D. 4 Dept.1968)—§ **15.38, n. 1.**

Guy v. Liederbach, 501 Pa. 47, 459 A.2d 744 (Pa.1983)—§ **2.17, n. 12.**

Gyfteas' Estate, In re, 59 Misc.2d 977, 300 N.Y.S.2d 913 (N.Y.Sur.1968)—§ **22.3, n. 4.**

H

H. v. P., 90 A.D.2d 434, 457 N.Y.S.2d 488 (N.Y.A.D. 1 Dept.1982)—§ **16.1, n. 15.**

Haag v. Barnes, 216 N.Y.S.2d 65, 175 N.E.2d 441 (N.Y.1961)—§ **15.36, n. 4**; § **18.18**; § **18.18, n. 6.**

Haarhuis v. Kunnan Enterprises, Ltd., 177 F.3d 1007, 336 U.S.App.D.C. 174 (D.C.Cir.1999)—§ **12.18, n. 13.**

Haase v. Title Guarantee & Trust Co., 269 A.D. 319, 55 N.Y.S.2d 428 (N.Y.A.D. 1 Dept.1945)—§ **21.6, n. 6.**

Habeck, Application of, 75 S.D. 535, 69 N.W.2d 353 (S.D.1955)—§ **4.37, n. 6, 10.**

Haberman v. Washington Public Power Supply System, 109 Wash.2d 107, 744 P.2d 1032 (Wash.1987)—§ **23.2, n. 6**; § **23.9, n. 9.**

Hackettstown Bank v. Mitchell, 1860 WL 5240 (N.J.Sup.1860)—§ **4.33, n. 2.**

Haddock v. Haddock, 201 U.S. 562, 26 S.Ct. 525, 50 L.Ed. 867 (1906)—§ **5.7, n. 2**; § **15.4, n. 6.**

Hagen v. Utah, 510 U.S. 399, 114 S.Ct. 958, 127 L.Ed.2d 252 (1994)—§ **11.17, n. 49.**

Hagen v. Viney, 124 Fla. 747, 169 So. 391 (Fla.1936)—§ **11.8, n. 3.**

Hager v. Hager, 3 Va.App. 415, 349 S.E.2d 908 (Va.App.1986)—§ **13.5, n. 7**; § **13.6, n. 3.**

Haggart v. Morgan, 5 N.Y. 422 (N.Y. 1851)—§ **4.13, n. 2.**

Haggerty v. Cedeno, 279 N.J.Super. 607, 653 A.2d 1166 (N.J.Super.A.D.1995)—§ **17.48, n. 17.**

Hagle v. Leeder, 442 S.W.2d 908 (Tex.Civ. App.-Austin 1969)—§ **4.34, n. 3.**

Hague v. Allstate Ins. Co., 289 N.W.2d 43 (Minn.1978)—§ **2.17, n. 9**; § **2.25, n. 6**; § **17.21, n. 12, 14**; § **18.21, n. 16.**

Hague v. Committee for Indus. Organization, 307 U.S. 496, 59 S.Ct. 954, 83 L.Ed. 1423 (1939)—§ **3.32, n. 7.**

Haines v. Mid–Century Ins. Co., 47 Wis.2d 442, 177 N.W.2d 328 (Wis.1970)—§ **2.17, n. 7**; § **2.25, n. 7**; § **18.21, n. 16.**

Hainey v. World AM Communications, Inc., 263 F.Supp.2d 338 (D.R.I.2003)—§ **8.4, n. 3.**

Haisten v. Grass Valley Medical Reimbursement Fund, Ltd., 784 F.2d 1392 (9th Cir.1986)—§ **18.4, n. 1**; § **18.5, n. 9.**

Haldeman–Homme Mfg. Co. v. Texacon Industries, Inc., 236 F.Supp. 99 (D.Minn. 1964)—§ **7.2, n. 12.**

Hall, In re, 61 A.D. 266, 70 N.Y.S. 406 (N.Y.A.D. 3 Dept.1901)—§ **13.6, n. 4.**

Hall v. Coleman, 242 Ga.App. 576, 530 S.E.2d 485 (Ga.App.2000)—§ **16.1, n. 7.**

Hall v. Fall, 235 F.Supp. 631 (W.D.N.C. 1964)—§ **4.43, n. 1.**

Hall v. General Motors Corp., 229 Mich. App. 580, 582 N.W.2d 866 (Mich.App. 1998)—§ **17.17, n. 8; § 17.74, n. 9, 11; § 17.75, n. 4; § 17.76, n. 14; § 17.77; § 17.77, n. 8.**

Hall v. Hall, 25 Wis. 600 (Wis.1870)— § **4.20, n. 2.**

Hall v. Helicopteros Nacionales De Colombia, S.A. (Helicol), 638 S.W.2d 870 (Tex. 1982)—§ **5.10, n. 17, 18; § 5.14, n. 18.**

Hall v. Hoff, 295 Pa. 276, 145 A. 301 (Pa. 1929)—§ **19.9, n. 10; § 19.10, n. 6.**

Hall v. Industrial Commission, 165 Wis. 364, 162 N.W. 312 (Wis.1917)—§ **13.14, n. 3.**

Hall v. National Basketball Ass'n, 651 F.Supp. 335 (D.Kan.1987)—§ **8.4, n. 3.**

Hall v. Tucker, 414 S.W.2d 766 (Tex.Civ. App.-Eastland 1967)—§ **19.2, n. 8.**

Hall v. University of Nevada, 74 Cal.App.3d 280, 141 Cal.Rptr. 439 (Cal.App. 1 Dist. 1977)—§ **17.43, n. 11.**

Hallet v. Bassett, 100 Mass. 167 (Mass. 1868)—§ **4.13, n. 2.**

Hallett v. Collins, 51 U.S. 174, 10 How. 174, 13 L.Ed. 376 (1850)—§ **13.6, n. 1.**

Hall's Guardianship, In re, 235 N.C. 697, 71 S.E.2d 140 (N.C.1952)—§ **4.37, n. 2; § 4.41, n. 5, 6.**

Hall's Specialties, Inc. v. Schupbach, 758 F.2d 214 (7th Cir.1985)—§ **8.5, n. 8.**

Halpern v. Canada (Attorney General), [2003] O.J. No. 2268—§ **13.4, n. 6**

Halpern, In re Will of, 48 A.D.2d 776, 368 N.Y.S.2d 845 (N.Y.A.D. 1 Dept.1975)— § **20.5, n. 7.**

Halvey, Ex parte, 185 Misc. 52, 55 N.Y.S.2d 761 (N.Y.Sup.1945)—§ **4.40, n. 4.**

Ham v. La Cienega Music Co., 4 F.3d 413 (5th Cir.1993)—§ **9.3, n. 18.**

Hambrecht & Quist Venture Partners v. American Medical Internat., Inc., 46 Cal. Rptr.2d 33 (Cal.App. 2 Dist.1995)— § **17.40, n. 26; § 18.1, n. 17; § 18.7, n. 9.**

Hamill v. Talbott, 72 Mo.App. 22 (Mo.App. 1897)—§ **6.4, n. 14.**

Hamilton v. Accu–Tek, 47 F.Supp.2d 330 (E.D.N.Y.1999)—§ **17.32, n. 15; § 17.38, n. 1; § 17.44, n. 5.**

Hamilton v. Blackman, 915 P.2d 1210 (Alaska 1996)—§ **22.10, n. 11.**

Hamilton v. Roth, 624 F.2d 1204 (3rd Cir. 1980)—§ **3.41, n. 15.**

Hamilton v. Volkswagenwerk A.G., No. 81–01–L (D.N.H.1981)—§ **12.7, n. 6.**

Hamilton, State ex rel. Brown v., 202 Mo. 377, 100 S.W. 609 (Mo.1907)—§ **4.41, n. 7.**

Hamilton Bank, N.A. v. Kookmin Bank, 245 F.3d 82 (2nd Cir.2001)—§ **17.55, n. 10.**

Hamm v. Carson City Nugget, Inc., 85 Nev. 99, 450 P.2d 358 (Nev.1969)—§ **17.19, n. 3, 9.**

Hammack v. Wise, 158 W.Va. 343, 211 S.E.2d 118 (W.Va.1975)—§ **4.37, n. 5.**

Hammond v. Hernstrom, Civ. No. 80–2051 (N.D.Ill.1980)—§ **9.5, n. 14**

Hampshire v. Hampshire, 70 Idaho 522, 223 P.2d 950 (Idaho 1950)—§ **4.26, n. 1.**

Hampton v. McConnel, 16 U.S. 234, 4 L.Ed. 378 (1818)—§ **5.1, n. 7; § 5.2, n. 7; § 5.21, n. 2.**

Hampton v. Mow Sun Wong, 426 U.S. 88, 96 S.Ct. 1895, 48 L.Ed.2d 495 (1976)— § **20.17, n. 2.**

Hanau, Estate of v. Hanau, 730 S.W.2d 663 (Tex.1987)—§ **14.9, n. 3.**

Hanberry v. Hanberry, 29 Ala. 719 (Ala. 1857)—§ **4.34, n. 1.**

Hand v. Hand, 834 So.2d 619 (La.App. 1 Cir.2002)—§ **14.9, n. 2, 13.**

Handel v. Artukovic, 601 F.Supp. 1421 (C.D.Cal.1985)—§ **2.9, n. 19.**

Handelswekerij GJ Bier BV v. Mines de Potasse d'Alsace SA (21/76), 1976 WL 46534 (ECJ 1976)—§ **9.2, n. 11.**

Handley v. Palmer, 91 F. 948 (C.C.W.D.Pa. 1899)—§ **21.2, n. 5.**

Hanil Bank v. PT. Bank Negara Indonesia (Persero), 148 F.3d 127 (2nd Cir.1998)— § **10.19, n. 40.**

Hanley v. Donoghue, 116 U.S. 1, 6 S.Ct. 242, 29 L.Ed. 535 (1885)—§ **24.16, n. 1.**

Hanley v. Tribune Pub. Co., 527 F.2d 68 (9th Cir.1975)—§ **17.55, n. 9.**

Hanna v. Plumer, 380 U.S. 460, 85 S.Ct. 1136, 14 L.Ed.2d 8 (1965)—§ **3.37, n. 2; § 3.38; § 3.38, n. 2; § 3.39; § 3.39, n. 1; § 3.40, n. 20; § 3.41, n. 4; § 3.50, n. 8.**

Hanreddy's Estate, In re, 176 Wis. 570, 186 N.W. 744 (Wis.1922)—§ **22.21, n. 6, 14.**

Hansford v. District of Columbia, 84 Md. App. 301, 578 A.2d 844 (Md.App.1990)— § **7.4, n. 7.**

Hanson v. Denckla, 357 U.S. 235, 78 S.Ct. 1228, 2 L.Ed.2d 1283 (1958)—§ **2.14, n. 53; § 3.27, n. 1; § 5.4; § 5.4, n. 19; § 5.11; § 5.11, n. 8; § 7.4, n. 4; § 8.2; § 8.2, n. 8; § 8.5, n. 6; § 10.15, n. 8, 10; § 21.12, n. 6; § 24.14, n. 3.**

Hanson v. Hanson, 78 N.H. 560, 103 A. 307 (N.H.1918)—§ **4.13, n. 2.**

Hanson v. Hoffman, 150 Kan. 121, 91 P.2d 31 (Kan.1939)—§ **20.6, n. 12.**

Hansson v. Hansson, 1981 WL 306369 (B.C. S.C.1981)—§ **14.9, n. 12.**

Hapner v. Rolf Brauchli, Inc., 404 Mich. 160, 273 N.W.2d 822 (Mich.1978)— § **7.2, n. 13.**

Harbor Funding Corp. v. Kavanagh, 666 A.2d 498 (Me.1995)—§ **19.9, n. 7.**

Hardaway Constructors, Inc. v. Conesco Industries, Ltd., 583 F.Supp. 617 (D.N.J. 1983)—§ **18.28, n. 4.**

Harden, United States v., [1963] Can. Sup. Ct. 366, 41 Dom. L.R. 2d 721 (1963)—§ 3.18, n. 9; § 24.23, n. 7; § 24.43, n. 1.

Hardin v. McAvoy, 216 F.2d 399 (5th Cir. 1954)—§ 4.20, n. 3.

Hardin v. Straub, 490 U.S. 536, 109 S.Ct. 1998, 104 L.Ed.2d 582 (1989)—§ 3.54, n. 1.

Harding v. Ramsay, Scarlett & Co., Inc., 599 F.Supp. 180 (D.Md.1984)—§ 24.1, n. 11.

Harding v. Schapiro, 120 Md. 541, 87 A. 951 (Md.1913)—§ 20.13, n. 4.

Hardy v. Hardy, 181 Cal.App.2d 317, 5 Cal. Rptr. 110 (Cal.App. 3 Dist.1960)—§ 19.28, n. 1.

Hardy v. Hardy, 164 Cal.App.2d 77, 330 P.2d 278 (Cal.App. 3 Dist.1958)—§ 19.28, n. 1.

Hardy v. Monsanto Enviro–Chem Systems, Inc., 414 Mich. 29, 323 N.W.2d 270 (Mich.1982)—§ 18.11, n. 5.

Hardzynski v. ITT Hartford Ins. Co., 227 A.D.2d 449, 643 N.Y.S.2d 122 (N.Y.A.D. 2 Dept.1996)—§ 17.48, n. 11.

Hare v. O'Brien, 233 Pa. 330, 82 A. 475 (Pa.1912)—§ 22.18, n. 7, 9.

Hargrave v. Oki Nursery, Inc., 646 F.2d 716 (2nd Cir.1980)—§ 3.39, n. 6; § 3.40, n. 8.

Harlan v. Industrial Acc. Commission, 194 Cal. 352, 228 P. 654 (Cal.1924)—§ 4.41, n. 7.

Harlan Feeders, Inc. v. Grand Laboratories, Inc., 881 F.Supp. 1400 (N.D.Iowa 1995)—§ 17.50; § 17.50, n. 39; § 17.77, n. 24.

Harlow v. Duryea, 42 R.I. 234, 107 A. 98 (R.I.1919)—§ 21.13, n. 4.

Harlow, People v., 9 Cal.App.2d 643, 50 P.2d 1052 (Cal.App. 2 Dist.1935)—§ 4.24, n. 3.

Harmon, In re Marriage of, 184 Cal.App.3d 754, 217 Cal.Rptr. 329 (Cal.App. 4 Dist. 1985)—§ 14.11, n. 1.

Harmon v. Commissioner, 1 T.C. 40 (Tax Ct.1942)—§ 14.7, n. 4.

Harold M. Pitman Co. v. Typecraft Software Ltd., 626 F.Supp. 305 (N.D.Ill. 1986)—§ 6.2, n. 13.

Harper v. Silva, 224 Neb. 645, 399 N.W.2d 826 (Neb.1987)—§ 2.16, n. 16; § 2.23, n. 1; § 17.26, n. 1.

Harrah v. Craig, 113 Cal.App.2d 67, 247 P.2d 855 (Cal.App. 1 Dist.1952)—§ 24.20, n. 3.

Harral v. Harral, 39 N.J.Eq. 279 (N.J.Err. & App.1884)—§ 4.30, n. 3.

Harrall v. Wallis, 1883 WL 8006 (N.J.Ch. 1883)—§ 14.8, n. 2.

Harrelson Rubber Co. v. Dixie Tire and Fuels, Inc., 62 N.C.App. 450, 302 S.E.2d 919 (N.C.App.1983)—§ 8.3, n. 11.

Harrelson Rubber Co. v. Layne, 69 N.C.App. 577, 317 S.E.2d 737 (N.C.App. 1984)—§ 8.3, n. 12.

Harriman's Estate, In re, 124 Misc. 320, 208 N.Y.S. 672 (N.Y.Sur.1924)—§ 21.11, n. 15.

Harris v. Balk, 198 U.S. 215, 25 S.Ct. 625, 49 L.Ed. 1023 (1905)—§ 5.6; § 5.6, n. 2, 9; § 5.9, n. 5, 28; § 22.20, n. 31.

Harris v. Browning–Ferris Industries Chemical Services, Inc., 100 F.R.D. 775 (M.D.La.1984)—§ 12.7, n. 3.

Harris v. City of Memphis, Tenn., 119 F.Supp.2d 893 (E.D.Ark.2000)—§ 17.43, n. 16.

Harris v. EMI Television Programs, Inc., 102 Cal.App.3d 214, 162 Cal.Rptr. 357 (Cal.App. 2 Dist.1980)—§ 24.31, n. 2.

Harris v. Harris, 205 Iowa 108, 215 N.W. 661 (Iowa 1927)—§ 4.26, n. 1.

Harris v. Metropolitan Cas. Ins. Co. of New York, 156 Misc. 692, 282 N.Y.S. 449 (N.Y.Mun.Ct.1935)—§ 19.10, n. 3, 5.

Harris v. Polskie Linie Lotnicze, 820 F.2d 1000 (9th Cir.1987)—§ 2.23, n. 8; § 3.13, n. 9.

Harris v. Shuttleworth and Ingersoll, P.C., 831 So.2d 706 (Fla.App. 4 Dist.2002)—§ 7.4, n. 7.

Harris v. Trans Union, LLC, 197 F.Supp.2d 200 (E.D.Pa.2002)—§ 7.3, n. 11.

Harris Corp. v. Comair, Inc., 712 F.2d 1069 (6th Cir.1983)—§ 17.13, n. 1, 13.

Harrison v. Harrison, [1953] 1 W.L.R. 865—§ 4.36, n. 8.

Harrison v. Harrison, 1872 WL 14799 (CA in Chancery 1873)—§ 19.4, n. 17.

Harrison v. Insurance Co. of North America, 294 Ala. 387, 318 So.2d 253 (Ala. 1975)—§ 18.21, n. 3.

Harrison v. Moncravie, 264 F. 776 (8th Cir. 1920)—§ 20.2, n. 3.

Harrison v. NetCentric Corp., 433 Mass. 465, 744 N.E.2d 622 (Mass.2001)—§ 23.4, n. 2.

Harrison v. Nixon, 34 U.S. 483, 9 L.Ed. 201 (1835)—§ 20.13, n. 3, 4.

Harrison v. Rice, 89 Nev. 180, 510 P.2d 633 (Nev.1973)—§ 18.23, n. 5.

Harris Rutsky & Co. Ins. Services, Inc. v. Bell & Clements Ltd., 328 F.3d 1122 (9th Cir.2003)—§ 10.16, n. 8.

Harris Trust and Sav. Bank v. SLT Warehouse Co., Inc., 605 F.Supp. 225 (N.D.Ill.1985)—§ 11.14, n. 6.

Harrop v. Harrop, [1920] 3 K.B. 386—§ 15.37, n. 2.

Hart v. American Airlines, Inc., 61 Misc.2d 41, 304 N.Y.S.2d 810 (N.Y.Sup.1969)—§ 24.2, n. 8.

Hart, Estate of, 165 Cal.App.3d 392, 209 Cal.Rptr. 272 (Cal.App. 4 Dist.1984)—§ 16.6, n. 2.

Hart v. Horn, 4 Kan. 232 (Kan.1867)—§ 4.19, n. 3.

Hart v. Lindsey, 17 N.H. 235 (N.H.1845)—§ **4.1, n. 2.**

Harteau v. Harteau, 31 Mass. 181 (Mass. 1833)—§ **4.33, n. 1; § 4.34, n. 1.**

Hartford Accident & Indem. Co. v. American Red Ball Transit Co., Inc., 262 Kan. 570, 938 P.2d 1281 (Kan.1997)—§ **2.21, n. 6, 55; § 18.26, n. 19.**

Hartford Accident & Indemnity Co. v. Delta & Pine Land Co., 292 U.S. 143, 54 S.Ct. 634, 78 L.Ed. 1178 (1934)—§ **3.21; § 3.21, n. 11.**

Hartford Acc. & Indem. Co. v. Dana Corp., 690 N.E.2d 285 (Ind.App.1997)—§ **18.26, n. 13.**

Hartford, City of v. Champion, 58 Conn. 268, 20 A. 471 (Conn.1889)—§ **4.20, n. 4.**

Hartford Fire Ins. Co. v. California, 509 U.S. 764, 113 S.Ct. 2891, 125 L.Ed.2d 612 (1993)—§ **17.48; § 17.48, n. 25; § 17.53, n. 1.**

Hartford & N.H.R. Co. v. Andrews, 36 Conn. 213 (Conn.1869)—§ **22.10, n. 8.**

Hartley v. Hartley, 71 Kan. 691, 81 P. 505 (Kan.1905)—§ **20.3, n. 9, 10.**

Hartley v. Wheatherford Crane Co., 1986 WL 10643 (E.D.Pa.1986)—§ **12.7, n. 3.**

Hartman v. Hartman, 132 W.Va. 728, 53 S.E.2d 407 (W.Va.1949)—§ **4.28, n. 4.**

Hartman v. Henry, 280 Mo. 478, 217 S.W. 987 (Mo.1919)—§ **22.26, n. 2.**

Hartmann v. Time, Inc., 166 F.2d 127 (3rd Cir.1947)—§ **17.7, n. 1; § 24.24, n. 3.**

Hartman's Estate, In re, 70 N.J.Eq. 664, 62 A. 560 (N.J.Prerog.1906)—§ **4.33, n. 2.**

Hartsfield v. Lescher, 721 F.Supp. 1052 (E.D.Ark.1989)—§ **19.2, n. 7; § 19.3, n. 10; § 19.6, n. 3, 5; § 19.9, n. 1; § 21.6, n. 2.**

Haruye Masaoka v. People, 39 Cal.2d 883, 245 P.2d 1062 (Cal.1952)—§ **3.59, n. 3.**

Harvard College v. Gore, 22 Mass. 370 (Mass.1827)—§ **4.19, n. 2; § 4.36, n. 3, 4.**

Harvey v. Richards, 11 F.Cas. 746 (C.C.D.Mass.1818)—§ **22.23, n. 10.**

Hasling, Succession of, 114 La. 293, 38 So. 174 (La.1905)—§ **20.6, n. 1.**

Hassan v. Hassan, 2001 WL 1329840 (Conn.Super.2001)—§ **15.16, n. 2.**

Hastings, City of v. River Falls Golf Club, 187 F.3d 640 (8th Cir.1999)—§ **17.48, n. 38.**

Hastings Motor Truck Co., United States v., 460 F.2d 1159 (8th Cir.1972)—§ **18.38, n. 3.**

Hataway v. McKinley, 830 S.W.2d 53 (Tenn.1992)—§ **2.16, n. 21; § 2.19, n. 8, 16; § 2.21, n. 78; § 2.23, n. 1; § 17.26, n. 1, 20; § 17.39, n. 14; § 18.21, n. 11.**

Hatch v. Hatch, 15 N.J. Misc. 461, 192 A. 241 (N.J.Ch.1937)—§ **5.23, n. 8.**

Hatcher, In re Estate of, 439 So.2d 977 (Fla.App. 3 Dist.1983)—§ **20.9, n. 2; § 22.2, n. 3.**

Hatcher v. Anders, 117 Ill.App.3d 236, 72 Ill.Dec. 769, 453 N.E.2d 74 (Ill.App. 2 Dist.1983)—§ **4.18, n. 1.**

Hauch v. Connor, 295 Md. 120, 453 A.2d 1207 (Md.1983)—§ **2.21, n. 7; § 17.8, n. 4.**

Hauenstein & Bermeister, Inc. v. Met–Fab Industries, Inc., 320 N.W.2d 886 (Minn. 1982)—§ **11.5, n. 3.**

Haumschild v. Continental Cas. Co., 7 Wis.2d 130, 95 N.W.2d 814 (Wis.1959)—§ **2.16; § 2.16, n. 2; § 2.21, n. 14; § 3.4, n. 5; § 3.14, n. 3; § 17.8; § 17.8, n. 9; § 17.15, n. 24; § 17.39, n. 6.**

Hausman v. Buckley, 299 F.2d 696 (2nd Cir.1962)—§ **23.4, n. 2.**

Havenfield Corp. v. H & R Block, Inc., 509 F.2d 1263 (8th Cir.1975)—§ **18.31, n. 5.**

H.A.W. v. Manuel, 524 N.W.2d 10 (Minn. App.1994)—§ **7.4, n. 7.**

Hawes v. Club Ecuestre El Comandante, 598 F.2d 698 (1st Cir.1979)—§ **4.18, n. 2; § 4.24, n. 3.**

Hawkins v. Winstead, 65 Idaho 12, 138 P.2d 972 (Idaho 1943)—§ **4.26, n. 1.**

Hawley v. Beech Aircraft Corp., 625 F.2d 991 (10th Cir.1980)—§ **3.13, n. 4.**

Hawley & King v. James, 7 Paige Ch. 213, 4 N.Y. Ch. Ann. 129 (N.Y.Ch.1838)—§ **19.6, n. 2.**

Haws v. Haws, 96 Nev. 727, 615 P.2d 978 (Nev.1980)—§ **15.12, n. 9.**

Hayden v. Wheeler, 33 Ill.2d 110, 210 N.E.2d 495 (Ill.1965)—§ **22.10, n. 13; § 22.19, n. 9.**

Hayes v. Frey, 54 Wis. 503, 11 N.W. 695 (Wis.1882)—§ **22.18, n. 12.**

Hayner v. Weinberger, 382 F.Supp. 762 (E.D.N.Y.1974)—§ **18.48, n. 4.**

Haynes v. Carr, 379 A.2d 1178 (D.C.1977)—§ **15.35, n. 2.**

Haynes v. General Elec. Credit Corp., 432 F.Supp. 763 (W.D.Va.1977)—§ **19.21, n. 7.**

Haynie v. Hanson, 16 Wis.2d 299, 114 N.W.2d 443 (Wis.1962)—§ **17.8, n. 13.**

Hays and Co. v. Merrill Lynch, Pierce, Fenner & Smith, Inc., 885 F.2d 1149 (3rd Cir.1989)—§ **11.6, n. 8.**

H. B. Fuller Co. v. Hagen, 363 F.Supp. 1325 (W.D.N.Y.1973)—§ **18.7, n. 10.**

Headen v. Pope & Talbot, Inc., 252 F.2d 739 (3rd Cir.1958)—§ **13.2, n. 1, 3.**

Health Group Management Co. v. Walker County Medical Center, Inc., 595 F.Supp. 381 (M.D.Tenn.1984)—§ **23.3, n. 2.**

Healy v. Beer Institute, Inc., 491 U.S. 324, 109 S.Ct. 2491, 105 L.Ed.2d 275 (1989)—§ **3.31, n. 3; § 3.32; § 3.32, n. 14.**

Healy v. Carlson Travel Network Association, Inc., 227 F.Supp.2d 1080 (D.Minn. 2002)—§ **18.5, n. 33.**

Heard v. Heard, 323 Mass. 357, 82 N.E.2d 219 (Mass.1948)—§ **4.37, n. 6.**

Heartfield v. Heartfield, 749 F.2d 1138 (5th Cir.1985)—§ **15.42, n. 9.**

Heath v. Zellmer, 35 Wis.2d 578, 151 N.W.2d 664 (Wis.1967)—§ **2.16, n. 9; § 2.25, n. 5; § 17.21, n. 15.**

Heathmount A.E. Corp v. Technodome.com, 106 F.Supp.2d 860 (E.D.Va.2000)— § **5.9, n. 21.**

Heavner v. Uniroyal, Inc., 63 N.J. 130, 305 A.2d 412 (N.J.1973)—§ **3.12; § 3.12, n. 1; § 17.10, n. 3.**

Hedberg, State ex rel. Carlson v., 192 Minn. 193, 256 N.W. 91 (Minn.1934)—§ **4.37, n. 10.**

Hedenberg v. Hedenberg, 46 Conn. 30 (Conn.1878)—§ **22.19, n. 1.**

Hedrick v. Daiko Shoji Co., Ltd., Osaka, 715 F.2d 1355 (9th Cir.1983)—§ **7.2, n. 21.**

Hedrick v. Hedrick, 571 P.2d 1217 (Okla. 1977)—§ **15.40, n. 5.**

Heffernan, State ex rel. Merritt v., 142 Fla. 496, 195 So. 145 (Fla.1940)—§ **6.4, n. 22.**

Heine v. Mechanics' & Traders' Ins. Co., 13 So. 1 (La.1893)—§ **14.15, n. 7.**

Heinz' Will, In re, 50 Misc.2d 1072, 272 N.Y.S.2d 394 (N.Y.Sur.1966)—§ **22.2, n. 3.**

Helicopteros Nacionales de Colombia, S.A. v. Hall, 466 U.S. 408, 104 S.Ct. 1868, 80 L.Ed.2d 404 (1984)—§ **3.27, n. 2; § 5.10, n. 14; § 5.13; § 5.13, n. 12; § 6.6; § 6.6, n. 18; § 6.7; § 6.7, n. 10; § 6.9; § 6.9, n. 2, 3, 13; § 7.1, n. 2; § 8.8; § 8.8, n. 1; § 10.15; § 10.15, n. 16.**

Hellenic Lines, Limited v. Embassy of Pakistan, 307 F.Supp. 947 (S.D.N.Y.1969)— § **18.3; § 18.3, n. 1, 3.**

Hellenic Lines Ltd.v. Rhoditis, 398 U.S. 306, 90 S.Ct. 1731, 26 L.Ed.2d 252 (1970)—§ **17.63, n. 11, 30.**

Heller–Baghero, In re Will of, 26 N.Y.2d 337, 310 N.Y.S.2d 313, 258 N.E.2d 717 (N.Y.1970)—§ **3.19, n. 8.**

Helme v. Buckelew, 229 N.Y. 363, 128 N.E. 216 (N.Y.1920)—§ **22.19, n. 19; § 22.20, n. 13.**

Hemar Ins. Corp. of America v. Ryerson, 108 S.W.3d 90 (Mo.App. E.D.2003)— § **17.40, n. 26; § 18.1, n. 17.**

Hembree v. Tinnin, 807 F.Supp. 109 (D.Kan.1992)—§ **5.18, n. 16.**

Henderson v. Henderson, 199 Md. 449, 87 A.2d 403 (Md.1952)—§ **13.2, n. 6; § 13.9, n. 5.**

Henderson v. Rounds & Porter Lumber Co., 99 F.Supp. 376 (W.D.Ark.1951)— § **23.20, n. 7.**

Henderson v. Staniford, 105 Mass. 504 (Mass.1870)—§ **6.4, n. 2, 14.**

Henderson v. Usher, 125 Fla. 709, 170 So. 846 (Fla.1936)—§ **20.9, n. 11.**

Henderson's Will, In re, 40 N.J.Super. 297, 123 A.2d 78 (N.J.Super.Ch.1956)— § **21.2, n. 11; § 21.7, n. 2, 3.**

Hendrickson, In re, 40 S.D. 211, 167 N.W. 172 (S.D.1918)—§ **6.4, n. 2.**

Hendrickson, People ex rel. Brooklyn Children's Aid Society v., 54 Misc. 337, 104 N.Y.S. 122 (N.Y.Sup.1907)—§ **4.37, n. 7.**

Hendry v. Masonite Corp., 455 F.2d 955 (5th Cir.1972)—§ **4.4, n. 3; § 4.21, n. 3.**

Henningsen v. Bloomfield Motors, Inc., 32 N.J. 358, 161 A.2d 69 (N.J.1960)—§ **7.1, n. 3; § 7.2, n. 1.**

Henning's Estate, In re, 128 Cal. 214, 60 P. 762 (Cal.1900)—§ **4.37, n. 7; § 4.41, n. 2.**

Henrietta Min & Mill Co v. Johnson, 173 U.S. 221, 19 S.Ct. 402, 43 L.Ed. 675 (1899)—§ **10.14, n. 7.**

Henriksen v. Younglove Const., 540 N.W.2d 254 (Iowa 1995)—§ **17.59, n. 13.**

Henry v. S/S Bermuda Star, 863 F.2d 1225 (5th Cir.1989)—§ **12.18, n. 12.**

Henry v. Windjammer Barefoot Cruises, 851 So.2d 731 (Fla.App. 3 Dist.2003)— § **17.63, n. 23, 28.**

Hensley v. Rich, 191 Ind. 294, 132 N.E. 632 (Ind.1921)—§ **22.11, n. 11, 17.**

Hensley v. United States, 728 F.Supp. 716 (S.D.Fla.1989)—§ **17.73, n. 4.**

Henson v. East Lincoln Tp., 814 F.2d 410 (7th Cir.1987)—§ **10.9, n. 6, 20.**

Herbert v. Direct Wire and Cable, Inc., 694 F.Supp. 192 (E.D.Va.1988)—§ **8.4, n. 6.**

Hercules & Co., Ltd. v. Shama Restaurant Corp., 566 A.2d 31 (D.C.1989)—§ **18.24, n. 4.**

Herczog v. Herczog, 186 Cal.App.2d 318, 9 Cal.Rptr. 5 (Cal.App. 2 Dist.1960)— § **15.37, n. 12; § 15.38, n. 1.**

Her Majesty the Queen In Right of Province of British Columbia v. Gilbertson, 433 F.Supp. 410 (D.Or.1977)—§ **24.23, n. 7.**

Hermanson v. Hermanson, 110 Nev. 1400, 887 P.2d 1241 (Nev.1994)—§ **2.17, n. 15; § 2.22, n. 6; § 18.21, n. 15.**

Hernandez v. Aeronaves de Mexico, S.A., 583 F.Supp. 331 (N.D.Cal.1984)— § **17.50, n. 61.**

Hernandez, Succession of, 15 So. 461 (La. 1894)—§ **13.6, n. 8.**

Hernas v. City of Hickory Hills, 507 F.Supp. 103 (N.D.Ill.1981)—§ **3.39, n. 16.**

Herndon v. Herndon, 9 Misc.2d 1047, 174 N.Y.S.2d 568 (N.Y.Sup.1957)—§ **13.6, n. 4.**

Herrera v. Health and Social Services, 92 N.M. 331, 587 P.2d 1342 (N.M.App. 1978)—§ **14.9, n. 1.**

Herrmann v. Gleason, 126 F.2d 936 (6th Cir.1942)—§ **18.47, n. 1.**

Herzfeld v. Parker, 100 F.R.D. 770 (D.Colo. 1984)—§ **24.13, n. 1.**

Herzog v. Stern, 264 N.Y. 379, 191 N.E. 23 (N.Y.1934)—§ **11.13, n. 7; § 17.10, n. 2.**

Hesington v. Hesington's Estate, 640 S.W.2d 824 (Mo.App. S.D.1982)—§ **13.6, n. 4.**

Hesler v. Snyder, 422 P.2d 432 (Okla. 1967)—§ **22.2, n. 3; § 22.7, n. 1; § 22.10, n. 2.**

Heslinga v. Bollman, 482 N.W.2d 921 (Iowa 1992)—§ **7.6, n. 8, 10.**

Hess v. Pawloski, 274 U.S. 352, 47 S.Ct. 632, 71 L.Ed. 1091 (1927)—§ **5.3; § 5.3, n. 21; § 5.14, n. 6; § 5.16, n. 4; § 6.3, n. 3; § 12.3; § 12.3, n. 9; § 12.6, n. 4.**

Hess v. United States, 361 U.S. 314, 80 S.Ct. 341, 4 L.Ed.2d 305 (1960)— § **17.63, n. 32.**

Heublein, Inc. v. South Carolina Tax Commission, 409 U.S. 275, 93 S.Ct. 483, 34 L.Ed.2d 472 (1972)—§ **23.6, n. 6.**

Hewitt v. Cox, 55 Ark. 225, 15 S.W. 1026 (Ark.1891)—§ **20.3, n. 1.**

Hewitt v. Hollahan, 56 N.J.Super. 372, 153 A.2d 371 (N.J.Super.A.D.1959)—§ **12.4, n. 1.**

Heyward v. Williams, 57 S.C. 235, 35 S.E. 503 (S.C.1900)—§ **22.17, n. 3.**

Hicklin v. Orbeck, 437 U.S. 518, 98 S.Ct. 2482, 57 L.Ed.2d 397 (1978)—§ **3.32, n. 9.**

Hicklin Engineering, Inc. v. Aidco, Inc., 959 F.2d 738 (8th Cir.1992)—§ **7.8, n. 13.**

Hicks v. Fox, 81 Minn. 197, 83 N.W. 538 (Minn.1900)—§ **4.38, n. 3; § 4.40, n. 2.**

Hicks v. Pope, 8 La. 554 (La.1835)—§ **14.9, n. 13; § 14.10, n. 3.**

Hidden Brook Air, Inc. v. Thabet Aviation Intern. Inc., 241 F.Supp.2d 246 (S.D.N.Y.2002)—§ **12.18, n. 4.**

Hiestand v. Kuns, 1847 WL 2491 (Ind. 1847)—§ **4.41, n. 7.**

Hieston v. National City Bank of Chicago, 280 F. 525 (D.C.Cir.1922)—§ **24.20, n. 3.**

Higginbotham v. Higginbotham, 92 N.J.Super. 18, 222 A.2d 120 (N.J.Super.A.D.1966)—§ **19.8, n. 14; § 24.10, n. 4.**

Higginson v. United States, 384 F.2d 504 (6th Cir.1967)—§ **3.51, n. 10.**

Highsmith, In re Marriage of, 130 Ill. App.3d 725, 86 Ill.Dec. 1, 474 N.E.2d 915 (Ill.App. 3 Dist.1985)—§ **15.30, n. 2.**

Higinbotham v. Manchester, 113 Conn. 62, 154 A. 242 (Conn.1931)—§ **19.4, n. 3; § 20.8, n. 9.**

Hilkmann v. Hilkmann, 816 A.2d 242 (Pa.Super.2003)—§ **24.44, n. 5.**

Hill v. Barton, 194 Mo.App. 325, 188 S.W. 1105 (Mo.App.1916)—§ **22.18, n. 11.**

Hill v. Hill, 262 A.2d 661 (Del.Ch.1970)— § **19.3, n. 8, 12.**

Hill v. Martin, 296 U.S. 393, 56 S.Ct. 278, 80 L.Ed. 293 (1935)—§ **4.23, n. 2.**

Hill v. Tucker, 54 U.S. 458, 13 How. 458, 14 L.Ed. 223 (1851)—§ **22.20; § 22.20, n. 13, 15.**

Hill v. Upper Mississippi Towing Corp., 252 Minn. 165, 89 N.W.2d 654 (Minn. 1958)—§ **11.10, n. 2; § 11.12, n. 2.**

Hiller v. Burlington & M.R.R. Co., 70 N.Y. 223 (N.Y.1877)—§ **5.14, n. 5; § 6.2, n. 21.**

Hilliard v. Colclazier, 122 Colo. 60, 220 P.2d 353 (Colo.1950)—§ **22.21, n. 14.**

Hilliard v. Hilliard, 24 Misc.2d 861, 209 N.Y.S.2d 132 (N.Y.Sup.1960)—§ **13.6, n. 9; § 13.12, n. 1; § 13.15, n. 4.**

Hilton v. Guyot, 159 U.S. 113, 16 S.Ct. 139, 40 L.Ed. 95 (1895)—§ **24.3; § 24.3, n. 1; § 24.6; § 24.6, n. 1, 3; § 24.34; § 24.34, n. 3, 10.**

HIMC Inv. Co. v. Siciliano, 103 N.J.Super. 27, 246 A.2d 502 (N.J.Super.L.1968)— § **18.28, n. 4.**

Hime v. State Farm Fire & Cas. Co., 284 N.W.2d 829 (Minn.1979)—§ **17.21, n. 12; § 18.21, n. 16.**

Hinckley, Town of v. Kettle River R. Co., 70 Minn. 105, 72 N.W. 835 (Minn.1897)— § **10.13, n. 3.**

Hinderlider v. La Plata River & Cherry Creek Ditch Co., 304 U.S. 92, 58 S.Ct. 803, 82 L.Ed. 1202 (1938)—§ **3.36, n. 12; § 3.50, n. 3.**

Hinds v. Hinds, 1 Iowa 36 (Iowa 1855)— § **4.13, n. 2.**

Hines v. Elkhart General Hospital, 465 F.Supp. 421 (N.D.Ind.1979)—§ **3.41, n. 15.**

Hirsch's Estate, In re, 146 Ohio St. 393, 66 N.E.2d 636 (Ohio 1946)—§ **22.21, n. 3, 14.**

Hislop v. Taaffe, 141 A.D. 40, 125 N.Y.S. 614 (N.Y.A.D. 2 Dept.1910)—§ **4.13, n. 2.**

Hitt v. Nissan Motor Co., Ltd., 399 F.Supp. 838 (S.D.Fla.1975)—§ **10.16, n. 10.**

HM Holdings, Inc. v. Aetna Cas. & Sur. Co., 154 N.J. 208, 712 A.2d 645 (N.J.1998)— § **18.26, n. 13.**

Hoag v. Sweetwater Intern., 857 F.Supp. 1420 (D.Nev.1994)—§ **8.7, n. 5.**

Hobart v. Connecticut Turnpike Co., 15 Conn. 145 (Conn.1842)—§ **22.14, n. 3; § 22.20, n. 20.**

Hobbs v. Fireman's Fund American Ins. Companies, 339 So.2d 28 (La.App. 3 Cir. 1976)—§ **4.13, n. 1.**

Hobson v. Hale, 95 N.Y. 588 (N.Y.1884)— § **20.6, n. 18.**

Hodge v. Hodge, 621 F.2d 590 (3rd Cir. 1980)—§ **5.21, n. 6; § 19.8, n. 6.**

Hodges v. Kimball, 91 F. 845 (4th Cir. 1899)—§ **22.14, n. 7.**

Hoechst Celanese Corp. v. National Union Fire Ins. Co. of Pittsburgh, Pa., C.A. No.

89C–09–035 (Del.Super.1994)—§ **18.1, n. 27.**

Hoechst Celanese Corp. v. Nylon Engineering Resins, Inc., 896 F.Supp. 1190 (M.D.Fla.1995)—§ **7.3, n. 11.**

Hoeller v. Riverside Resort Hotel, 169 Ariz. 452, 820 P.2d 316 (Ariz.App. Div. 1 1991)—§ **17.48; § 17.48, n. 33.**

Hoes of America, Inc. v. Hoes, 493 F.Supp. 1205 (C.D.Ill.1979)—§ **2.26, n. 17.**

Hofferbert v. City of Knoxville, Tenn., 470 F.Supp. 1001 (E.D.Tenn.1979)—§ **4.21, n. 2.**

Hoffman v. Blaski, 363 U.S. 335, 80 S.Ct. 1084, 4 L.Ed.2d 1254 (1960)—§ **11.10, n. 2; § 11.14, n. 3.**

Hoffman v. National Equipment Rental, Ltd., 643 F.2d 987 (4th Cir.1981)— § **24.12, n. 7.**

Hoffmann v. Krieg (145/86), 1988 WL 623336 (ECJ 1988)—§ **24.44, n. 8.**

Hoffman's Estate, In re, 6 Ill.App.3d 438, 286 N.E.2d 103 (Ill.App. 1 Dist.1972)— § **22.10, n. 2.**

Hogan v. Johnson, 39 Wash.App. 96, 692 P.2d 198 (Wash.App. Div. 1 1984)— § **17.64, n. 15.**

Hogue v. Hogue, 242 S.W.2d 673 (Tex.Civ. App.-Dallas 1951)—§ **4.36, n. 5.**

Hogue v. Milodon Engineering, Inc., 736 F.2d 989 (4th Cir.1984)—§ **23.13, n. 3.**

Holbein v. Rigot, 245 So.2d 57 (Fla.1971)— § **3.18, n. 1.**

Holburn v. Pfanmiller's Adm'r, 114 Ky. 831, 71 S.W. 940 (Ky.1903)—§ **22.6, n. 1.**

Holdeen's Trust, In re, 58 Pa. D. & C.2d 602, 23 Fiduc.Rep. 70 (Pa.Com.Pl. 1972)—§ **21.6, n. 6.**

Holden v. Holden, 374 Pa.Super. 184, 542 A.2d 557 (Pa.Super.1988)—§ **7.3, n. 11.**

Holden, People ex rel. Budd v., 28 Cal. 123 (Cal.1865)—§ **4.26, n. 1.**

Holden's Estate, In re, 110 Vt. 60, 1 A.2d 721 (Vt.1938)—§ **22.2, n. 1.**

Holder v. Holder, 384 P.2d 663 (Okla. 1962)—§ **17.5, n. 10.**

Holdford v. Leonard, 355 F.Supp. 261 (W.D.Va.1973)—§ **3.10, n. 1.**

Holeman v. National Business Institute, Inc., 94 S.W.3d 91 (Tex.App.-Hous. (14 Dist.) 2002)—§ **18.5, n. 31.**

Holemar, Matter of Marriage of, 27 Or.App. 613, 557 P.2d 38 (Or.App.1976)—§ **13.6, n. 12.**

Holladay v. Fidelity Nat. Bank of Baton Rouge, 312 So.2d 883 (La.App. 1 Cir. 1975)—§ **21.5, n. 2.**

Holland v. Jackson, 121 Tex. 1, 37 S.W.2d 726 (Tex.1931)—§ **22.4, n. 6.**

Holland America Ins. Co. v. Rogers, 313 F.Supp. 314 (N.D.Cal.1970)—§ **13.2, n. 11, 14.**

Hollins v. Yellow Freight System, Inc., 590 F.Supp. 1023 (N.D.Ill.1984)—§ **3.11, n. 2.**

Hollister's Estate, In re, 274 N.Y.S.2d 585, 221 N.E.2d 376 (N.Y.1966)—§ **20.12, n. 3, 6.**

Hollowell v. Hux, 229 F.Supp. 50 (E.D.N.C. 1964)—§ **4.17, n. 2; § 4.43, n. 1.**

Holman v. Johnson, 1775 WL 22 (Unknown Court - UK 1775)—§ **2.1, n. 4.**

Holman v. McMullan Trucking, 684 So.2d 1309 (Ala.1996)—§ **2.21, n. 1.**

Holmes v. Adams, 110 Me. 167, 85 A. 492 (Me.1912)—§ **20.3, n. 5.**

Holmes v. Jones, 738 F.2d 711 (5th Cir. 1984)—§ **24.12, n. 7.**

Holmes v. Syntex Laboratories, Inc., 156 Cal.App.3d 372, 202 Cal.Rptr. 773 (Cal. App. 1 Dist.1984)—§ **11.9, n. 5.**

Holquin's Estate, In re, 101 Misc.2d 174, 420 N.Y.S.2d 670 (N.Y.Sur.1979)— § **22.25, n. 2.**

Holt v. Hendee, 248 Ill. 288, 93 N.E. 749 (Ill.1910)—§ **4.1, n. 2; § 4.18, n. 1.**

Holt Motors v. Casto, 136 W.Va. 284, 67 S.E.2d 432 (W.Va.1951)—§ **19.11, n. 1.**

Holzsager v. Valley Hospital, 646 F.2d 792 (2nd Cir.1981)—§ **10.8, n. 8.**

Home Indem. Co. of N. Y. v. Poladian, 270 F.2d 156 (4th Cir.1959)—§ **17.6, n. 3.**

Home Ins. Co. v. Dick, 281 U.S. 397, 50 S.Ct. 338, 74 L.Ed. 926 (1930)—§ **3.15; § 3.15, n. 6; § 3.21; § 3.21, n. 1, 8; § 3.26; § 3.26, n. 7; § 3.48; § 3.48, n. 1; § 18.26, n. 16.**

Home Ins. Co. of New York v. Morse, 87 U.S. 445, 22 L.Ed. 365 (1874)—§ **11.2, n. 8; § 11.3, n. 2.**

Home Owners Funding Corp. of America v. Century Bank, 695 F.Supp. 1343 (D.Mass.1988)—§ **7.12, n. 11.**

Homeside Lending, Inc., State v., 826 A.2d 997 (Vt.2003)—§ **10.10, n. 15.**

Honda Associates, Inc. v. Nozawa Trading, Inc., 374 F.Supp. 886 (S.D.N.Y.1974)— § **17.53, n. 6.**

Honda Motor Co. v. Superior Court, 12 Cal.Rptr.2d 861 (Cal.App. 6 Dist.1992)— § **12.7, n. 5.**

Hood v. Guaranty Trust Co. of New York, 270 N.Y. 17, 200 N.E. 55 (N.Y.1936)— § **24.11, n. 1.**

Hood v. Hood, 93 Mass. 196 (Mass.1865)— § **4.34, n. 3.**

Hood v. McGehee, 237 U.S. 611, 35 S.Ct. 718, 59 L.Ed. 1144 (1915)—§ **16.6, n. 2.**

Hooker v. Nationwide Mut. Ins. Co., 1997 WL 337623 (Ohio App. 8 Dist.1997)— § **17.56, n. 8, 9.**

Hooks v. Hooks, 771 F.2d 935 (6th Cir. 1985)—§ **15.42, n. 14.**

Hoopeston Canning Co. v. Cullen, 318 U.S. 313, 63 S.Ct. 602, 87 L.Ed. 777 (1943)— § **3.21, n. 10.**

Hoover, In re, 447 F.2d 195 (5th Cir. 1971)—**§ 19.17, n. 6.**

Hoover v. Recreation Equipment Corp., 792 F.Supp. 1484 (N.D.Ohio 1991)—**§ 17.44, n. 9; § 17.70, n. 6.**

Hope v. Brewer, 136 N.Y. 126, 48 N.Y.St. Rep. 834, 32 N.E. 558 (N.Y.1892)—**§ 20.7, n. 3; § 21.2, n. 9, 12; § 21.6, n. 4.**

Hopkins v. Grubb, 160 W.Va. 71, 230 S.E.2d 470 (W.Va.1977)—**§ 17.7, n. 7.**

Hopkins v. Lockheed Aircraft Corp., 201 So.2d 743 (Fla.1967)—**§ 17.6, n. 1, 8.**

Hopper v. Hopper, 125 N.Y. 400, 35 N.Y.St. Rep. 400, 26 N.E. 457 (N.Y.1891)—**§ 22.20, n. 15.**

Horak v. Argosy Gaming Co., 648 N.W.2d 137 (Iowa 2002)—**§ 17.63, n. 4.**

Horiba, Matter of Marriage of, 151 Or.App. 489, 950 P.2d 340 (Or.App.1997)—**§ 15.43, n. 8.**

Horne v. Adolph Coors Co., 684 F.2d 255 (3rd Cir.1982)—**§ 9.4, n. 7.**

Horne v. Horne, 31 N.C. 99 (N.C.1848)—**§ 4.1, n. 2; § 4.18, n. 2; § 4.19, n. 2.**

Horowitz v. Schneider Nat., Inc., 708 F.Supp. 1573 (D.Wyo.1989)—**§ 17.50; § 17.50, n. 24.**

Horton v. Jessie, 423 F.2d 722 (9th Cir. 1970)—**§ 3.12, n. 1.**

Horton's Will, In re, 217 N.Y. 363, 111 N.E. 1066 (N.Y.1916)—**§ 22.3, n. 1.**

Hossler v. Barry, 403 A.2d 762 (Me.1979)—**§ 3.9, n. 6; § 22.19, n. 12.**

Houghton v. Hughes, 108 Me. 233, 79 A. 909 (Me.1911)—**§ 20.8, n. 9; § 20.13, n. 4.**

Houghton v. May, 1911 WL 14082 (Ont. C.A.1911)—**§ 19.15, n. 5.**

Household Intern., Inc. v. Liberty Mut. Ins. Co., 321 Ill.App.3d 859, 255 Ill.Dec. 221, 749 N.E.2d 1 (Ill.App. 1 Dist.2001)—**§ 18.26, n. 12.**

Houston Fearless Corp. v. Teter, 318 F.2d 822 (10th Cir.1963)—**§ 10.14, n. 10.**

Houston Oil & Minerals Corp. v. SEEC, Inc., 616 F.Supp. 990 (W.D.La.1985)—**§ 3.46, n. 15.**

Hovav v. Hovav, 312 Pa.Super. 305, 458 A.2d 972 (Pa.Super.1983)—**§ 15.43, n. 8.**

Howard v. Howard, 499 So.2d 222 (La.App. 2 Cir.1986)—**§ 4.17, n. 4; § 14.9, n. 3.**

Howard v. Lyons, 360 U.S. 593, 79 S.Ct. 1331, 3 L.Ed.2d 1454 (1959)—**§ 3.50, n. 5.**

Howard v. Pulver, 329 Mich. 415, 45 N.W.2d 530 (Mich.1951)—**§ 22.10, n. 6.**

Howard v. Reynolds, 30 Ohio St.2d 214, 283 N.E.2d 629 (Ohio 1972)—**§ 20.3, n. 1; § 20.4, n. 2.**

Howard v. Scott, 225 Mo. 685, 125 S.W. 1158 (Mo.1910)—**§ 24.17, n. 4.**

Howard v. Skinner, 87 Md. 556, 40 A. 379 (Md.1898)—**§ 4.29, n. 2.**

Howard Fuel v. Lloyd's Underwriters, 588 F.Supp. 1103 (S.D.N.Y.1984)—**§ 12.18, n. 8.**

Howard Nat. Bank v. King, 10 Abb. N. Cas. 346 (N.Y.Sup.1881)—**§ 19.30, n. 7.**

Howard Sav. Inst. v. Baronych, 8 N.J.Super. 599, 73 A.2d 853 (N.J.Super.Ch.1950)—**§ 21.2, n. 14.**

Howells v. Limbeck, 172 Ohio St. 297, 175 N.E.2d 517 (Ohio 1961)—**§ 16.1, n. 8; § 16.2, n. 5; § 20.2, n. 4.**

Howerton v. Grace Hosp., Inc., 130 N.C.App. 327, 502 S.E.2d 659 (N.C.App. 1998)—**§ 24.1, n. 6.**

Howlett By and Through Howlett v. Rose, 496 U.S. 356, 110 S.Ct. 2430, 110 L.Ed.2d 332 (1990)—**§ 3.33; § 3.33, n. 10.**

Hoy v. Sears, Roebuck & Co., 861 F.Supp. 881 (N.D.Cal.1994)—**§ 18.5, n. 2.**

Hoyt v. Sprague, 103 U.S. 613, 26 L.Ed. 585 (1880)—**§ 22.25, n. 1, 2, 23.**

HRO v. Greenwich Catholic Elementary School System, Inc., 202 Conn. 609, 522 A.2d 785 (Conn.1987)—**§ 22.19, n. 11.**

Hrubec v. National R.R. Passenger Corp., 778 F.Supp. 1431 (N.D.Ill.1991)—**§ 7.10, n. 7.**

Hua, In re, 62 Ohio St.2d 227, 405 N.E.2d 255 (Ohio 1980)—**§ 12.17, n. 5.**

Hubbard, In re Succession of, 803 So.2d 1074 (La.App. 1 Cir.2001)—**§ 14.9, n. 2.**

Hubbard Mfg. Co., Inc. v. Greeson, 515 N.E.2d 1071 (Ind.1987)—**§ 2.16, n. 17; § 2.19, n. 15; § 2.22, n. 1; § 17.26, n. 1; § 17.39, n. 14; § 17.67, n. 2.**

Huber v. Steiner, [1835] 2 Bing. (N.C.) 202—**§ 2.7, n. 10.**

Huck, In re, 435 Pa. 325, 257 A.2d 522 (Pa.1969)—**§ 4.37, n. 10; § 4.41, n. 6.**

Huddy v. Fruehauf Corp., 953 F.2d 955 (5th Cir.1992)—**§ 17.17, n. 3; § 17.73; § 17.73, n. 2.**

Hudson v. Continental Bus System, Inc., 317 S.W.2d 584 (Tex.Civ.App.-Texarkana 1958)—**§ 3.19, n. 7.**

Hudson v. Hermann Pfauter GmbH & Co., 117 F.R.D. 33 (N.D.N.Y.1987)—**§ 12.9, n. 15.**

Hudson v. Kingston Contracting Co., 58 N.J.Super. 455, 156 A.2d 491 (N.J.Co. 1959)—**§ 17.59, n. 5.**

Hudson v. Von Hamm, 85 Cal.App. 323, 259 P. 374 (Cal.App. 1 Dist.1927)—**§ 11.13, n. 7.**

Hudson Feather & Down Products, Inc., Matter of, 36 B.R. 466 (E.D.N.Y.1984)—**§ 23.12, n. 6.**

Huff v. Director, United States Office of Personnel Management, 40 F.3d 35 (3rd Cir.1994)—**§ 15.1, n. 6.**

Huffman v. Huffman, 232 Neb. 742, 441 N.W.2d 899 (Neb.1989)—**§ 4.13, n. 4.**

Hugel v. McNell, 886 F.2d 1 (1st Cir. 1989)—**§ 7.3, n. 10; § 7.8, n. 10.**

Hugh, Adoption of, 35 Mass.App.Ct. 346, 619 N.E.2d 979 (Mass.App.Ct.1993)— § 16.5, n. 6.

Hughes, In re, 73 Ariz. 97, 237 P.2d 1009 (Ariz.1951)—§ 4.40, n. 2.

Hughes, In re, 95 N.Y. 55 (N.Y.1884)— § 22.9, n. 2; § 22.23, n. 8.

Hughes v. Fetter, 341 U.S. 609, 71 S.Ct. 980, 95 L.Ed. 1212 (1951)—§ 3.15, n. 4; § 3.25; § 3.25, n. 1; § 3.33, n. 7; § 3.40; § 3.40, n. 2; § 11.11, n. 12; § 16.6, n. 2; § 24.22; § 24.22, n. 10.

Hughes v. Hughes, 91 N.M. 339, 573 P.2d 1194 (N.M.1978)—§ 14.6, n. 1, 2; § 14.9, n. 2, 3, 13; § 14.13, n. 8.

Hughes v. Illinois Public Aid Commission, 2 Ill.2d 374, 118 N.E.2d 14 (Ill.1954)— § 4.13, n. 2.

Hughes v. Industrial Com'n, 69 Ariz. 193, 211 P.2d 463 (Ariz.1949)—§ 4.41, n. 7.

Hughes v. Prudential Lines, Inc., 425 Pa.Super. 262, 624 A.2d 1063 (Pa.Super.1993)—§ 3.5, n. 5; § 3.12, n. 6.

Hughes v. Wal–Mart Stores, Inc., 250 F.3d 618 (8th Cir.2001)—§ 17.21, n. 28; § 17.23, n. 11, 13; § 17.77, n. 7.

Hughes v. Winkleman, 243 Mo. 81, 147 S.W. 994 (Mo.1912)—§ 19.3, n. 17; § 19.9, n. 8.

Hughes Associates, Inc. v. Printed Circuit Corp., 631 F.Supp. 851 (N.D.Ala.1986)— § 18.2, n. 11.

Hughes Wood Products, Inc. v. Wagner, 18 S.W.3d 202 (Tex.2000)—§ 17.60, n. 6.

Huling v. Kaw Val. Ry. & Imp. Co., 130 U.S. 559, 9 S.Ct. 603, 32 L.Ed. 1045 (1889)—§ 12.3, n. 7.

Hulis v. M. Foschi & Sons, 124 A.D.2d 643, 507 N.Y.S.2d 898 (N.Y.A.D. 2 Dept. 1986)—§ 13.6, n. 2.

Humble v. Toyota Motor Co., Ltd., 727 F.2d 709 (8th Cir.1984)—§ 7.2, n. 23.

Humble Oil & Refining Co. v. Copeland, 398 F.2d 364 (4th Cir.1968)—§ 20.6, n. 20; § 20.7, n. 3; § 20.8, n. 11.

Humble Oil & Refining Co. v. DeLoache, 297 F.Supp. 647 (D.S.C.1969)—§ 18.37, n. 2.

Humphrey v. Langford, 246 Ga. 732, 273 S.E.2d 22 (Ga.1980)—§ 6.2, n. 13.

Hunker v. Royal Indem. Co., 57 Wis.2d 588, 204 N.W.2d 897 (Wis.1973)—§ 2.13, n. 14, 26; § 17.21, n. 15.

Hunt v. BP Exploration Co. (Libya) Ltd., 580 F.Supp. 304 (N.D.Tex.1984)— § 24.36, n. 1; § 24.37, n. 7.

Hunt v. Erie Ins. Group, 728 F.2d 1244 (9th Cir.1984)—§ 8.2, n. 10.

Hunter v. Derby Foods, 110 F.2d 970 (2nd Cir.1940)—§ 17.3, n. 1.

Hunter's Estate, In re, 125 Mont. 315, 236 P.2d 94 (Mont.1951)—§ 14.7, n. 2.

Huntington v. Attrill, 146 U.S. 657, 13 S.Ct. 224, 36 L.Ed. 1123 (1892)—§ 3.3, n. 1; § 3.17; § 3.17, n. 6; § 3.23; § 3.23, n. 30; § 23.4, n. 8; § 24.23; § 24.23, n. 9; § 24.43, n. 3.

Huntington v. Attrill, [1893] A.C. 150 (P.C. 1892)—§ 3.3, n. 1; § 3.17, n. 7.

Huntington's Estate, In re, 10 Misc.2d 932, 170 N.Y.S.2d 452 (N.Y.Sur.1957)— § 21.13, n. 2.

Hunt Wesson Foods, Inc. v. Supreme Oil Co., 817 F.2d 75 (9th Cir.1987)—§ 11.2, n. 4; § 11.6, n. 2.

Hupp v. Hupp, 239 Va. 494, 391 S.E.2d 329 (Va.1990)—§ 13.2, n. 6.

Hurlbut v. Hurlbut, 101 Misc.2d 571, 421 N.Y.S.2d 509 (N.Y.Sup.1979)—§ 15.30, n. 2.

Huron Holding Corporation v. Lincoln Mine Operating Co., 312 U.S. 183, 61 S.Ct. 513, 85 L.Ed. 725 (1941)—§ 24.12, n. 7.

Hurtado v. Superior Court, 114 Cal.Rptr. 106, 522 P.2d 666 (Cal.1974)—§ 17.14; § 17.14, n. 9; § 17.18; § 17.18, n. 2; § 17.37; § 17.37, n. 9; § 17.45; § 17.45, n. 42.

Husa v. Laboratoires Servier SA, 326 N.J.Super. 150, 740 A.2d 1092 (N.J.Super.A.D.1999)—§ 12.9, n. 11, 15.

Husband v. Pierce, 800 S.W.2d 661 (Tex. App.-Tyler 1990)—§ 13.12, n. 1.

Hussain (Aliya) v. Hussain (Shahid), 1982 WL 222403 (CA 1982)—§ 13.4, n. 4.

Hussey v. Sargent, 116 Ky. 53, 75 S.W. 211 (Ky.1903)—§ 21.2, n. 5.

Huston v. Colonial Trust Co., 266 S.W.2d 231 (Tex.Civ.App.-El Paso 1954)— § 14.6, n. 2; § 20.15, n. 3.

Huston v. Hayden Bldg. Maintenance Corp., 205 A.D.2d 68, 617 N.Y.S.2d 335 (N.Y.A.D. 2 Dept.1994)—§ 17.37, n. 16; § 17.48, n. 11.

Hutchins v. Bethel Methodist Home, 370 F.Supp. 954 (S.D.N.Y.1974)—§ 18.39, n. 6.

Hutchinson v. Chase & Gilbert, 45 F.2d 139 (2nd Cir.1930)—§ 10.14; § 10.14, n. 13, 15.

Hutchison v. Ross, 262 N.Y. 381, 187 N.E. 65 (N.Y.1933)—§ 14.12; § 14.12, n. 6; § 14.15, n. 3; § 21.3; § 21.3, n. 14.

Hutzell v. Boyer, 252 Md. 227, 249 A.2d 449 (Md.1969)—§ 2.21, n. 7.

Hyatt Intern. Corp. v. Coco, 302 F.3d 707 (7th Cir.2002)—§ 8.6, n. 5.

Hyde v. Hyde, 562 S.W.2d 194 (Tenn. 1978)—§ 15.20, n. 10; § 15.22, n. 5.

Hyder v. Hyder, 16 Tenn.App. 64, 66 S.W.2d 235 (Tenn.Ct.App.1932)—§ 4.36, n. 11; § 22.22, n. 5.

Hyde v. Hyde, 1866 WL 8213 (Divorce Ct 1866)—§ 13.17, n. 1, 3, 4.

Hydro Engineering v. Landa, Inc., 231 F.Supp.2d 1130 (D.Utah 2002)—§ 7.8, n. 14.

Hymowitz v. Eli Lilly and Co., 541 N.Y.S.2d 941, 539 N.E.2d 1069 (N.Y.1989)— § 10.9, n. 17.

I

IAC, Ltd. v. Princeton Porsche–Audi, 75 N.J. 379, 382 A.2d 1125 (N.J.1978)— **§ 19.19, n. 6.**

I.A.M. Nat. Pension Fund, Ben. Plan A v. Industrial Gear Mfg. Co., 723 F.2d 944, 232 U.S.App.D.C. 418 (D.C.Cir.1983)— **§ 24.24, n. 8.**

ICEE Distributors, Inc. v. J&J Snack Foods Corp., 325 F.3d 586 (5th Cir.2003)— **§ 9.3, n. 4.**

Idaho, State of v. M.A. Hanna Co., 819 F.Supp. 1464 (D.Idaho 1993)—**§ 9.2, n. 21.**

Ideal Structures Corp. v. Levine Huntsville Development Corp., 396 F.2d 917 (5th Cir.1968)—**§ 18.21, n. 3; § 18.37, n. 4.**

Illinois v. City of Milwaukee, Wis., 406 U.S. 91, 92 S.Ct. 1385, 31 L.Ed.2d 712 (1972)—**§ 3.49, n. 6; § 3.54; § 3.54, n. 16.**

Illinois–California Exp., Inc., In re, 50 B.R. 232 (Bkrtcy.D.Colo.1985)—**§ 23.12, n. 8.**

Illinois Dept. of Public Aid on Behalf of Washoe County, Nev. v. Peterson, 156 Ill.App.3d 657, 108 Ill.Dec. 720, 509 N.E.2d 146 (Ill.App. 4 Dist.1987)— **§ 15.36, n. 7.**

Illinois Farmers Ins. Co., State ex rel. v. Koehr, 834 S.W.2d 233 (Mo.App. E.D. 1992)—**§ 8.2, n. 10.**

Illinois Tool Works v. Sierracin Corp., 134 Ill.App.3d 63, 89 Ill.Dec. 40, 479 N.E.2d 1046 (Ill.App. 1 Dist.1985)—**§ 2.19, n. 10; § 18.24, n. 10.**

Ilsley v. Nichols, 29 Mass. 270 (Mass. 1831)—**§ 19.15, n. 5.**

Iman Din v. National Assistance Board, (1967) 2 Q.B. 213—**§ 13.17, n. 10.**

IMO Industries, Inc. v. Kiekert AG, 155 F.3d 254 (3rd Cir.1998)—**§ 7.11, n. 14.**

Inacom Corp. v. Sears, Roebuck and Co., 254 F.3d 683 (8th Cir.2001)—**§ 17.52, n. 1.**

Inamed Corp. v. Kuzmak, 249 F.3d 1356 (Fed.Cir.2001)—**§ 9.4, n. 12.**

Inconnu Lodge v. Commbine.com LLC, 214 F.Supp.2d 1204 (D.Utah 2002)—**§ 9.3, n. 8.**

Incuria v. Incuria, 155 Misc. 755, 280 N.Y.S. 716 (N.Y.Dom.Rel.Ct.1935)— **§ 13.11, n. 3.**

Independent Petrochemical Corp. v. Aetna Cas. and Sur. Co., 117 F.R.D. 292 (D.D.C.1987)—**§ 12.11, n. 7.**

Index Fund, Inc. v. Insurance Co. of North America, 580 F.2d 1158 (2nd Cir.1978)— **§ 18.31, n. 5.**

Indon Industries, Inc. v. Charles S. Martin Distributing Co., Inc., 234 Ga. 845, 218 S.E.2d 562 (Ga.1975)—**§ 3.10, n. 1.**

Industrial Commission of Wis. v. McCartin, 330 U.S. 622, 67 S.Ct. 886, 91 L.Ed.

1140 (1947)—**§ 17.59, n. 16; § 17.60, n. 2; § 24.26, n. 4; § 24.46, n. 6.**

Industrial Credit Co. v. J. A. D. Const. Corp., 29 A.D.2d 952, 289 N.Y.S.2d 243 (N.Y.A.D. 2 Dept.1968)—**§ 19.10, n. 1.**

Industrial Development Bank of Israel Ltd. v. Bier, 149 Misc.2d 797, 565 N.Y.S.2d 980 (N.Y.Sup.1991)—**§ 18.28, n. 5.**

Industrial Indem. Ins. Co. v. United States, 757 F.2d 982 (9th Cir.1985)—**§ 18.21, n. 14.**

Industrial Nat. Bank of Rhode Island v. Butler Aviation Intern., Inc., 370 F.Supp. 1012 (E.D.N.Y.1974)—**§ 19.21, n. 7.**

Indyka v. Indyka, 1967 WL 23373 (HL 1967)—**§ 15.5, n. 2.**

In–Flight Devices Corp. v. Van Dusen Air, Inc., 466 F.2d 220 (6th Cir.1972)— **§ 5.10, n. 26; § 6.7, n. 20.**

Infodek, Inc. v. Meredith–Webb Printing Co., Inc., 830 F.Supp. 614 (N.D.Ga. 1993)—**§ 9.3, n. 4.**

Info. Leasing Corp. v. Jaskot, 151 Ohio App.3d 546, 784 N.E.2d 1192 (Ohio App. 1 Dist.2003)—**§ 11.3, n. 21.**

Ingersoll v. Coram, 211 U.S. 335, 29 S.Ct. 92, 53 L.Ed. 208 (1908)—**§ 22.20, n. 10, 33.**

Ingersoll v. Klein, 46 Ill.2d 42, 262 N.E.2d 593 (Ill.1970)—**§ 2.16, n. 12; § 2.23, n. 1; § 17.26, n. 1, 20; § 17.39, n. 14; § 17.53, n. 5.**

Ingersoll Mill. Mach. Co. v. Granger, 833 F.2d 680 (7th Cir.1987)—**§ 24.32, n. 9.**

Ingersol's Estate, In re, 128 Mont. 230, 272 P.2d 1003 (Mont.1954)—**§ 4.17, n. 4.**

Ingraham v. Carroll, 665 N.Y.S.2d 10, 687 N.E.2d 1293 (N.Y.1997)—**§ 5.14, n. 15.**

Ingraham v. Williams, 173 F.Supp. 1 (N.D.Cal.1959)—**§ 3.51, n. 10.**

Ingrassia v. Shell Oil Co., 394 F.Supp. 875 (S.D.N.Y.1975)—**§ 18.39, n. 6.**

Inhabitants of Abington v. Inhabitants of North Bridgewater, 40 Mass. 170 (Mass. 1839)—**§ 4.3, n. 3; § 4.19, n. 4.**

Inhabitants of Hiram v. Pierce, 45 Me. 367 (Me.1858)—**§ 13.6, n. 9.**

Inhabitants of Medway v. Inhabitants of Needham, 16 Mass. 157 (Mass.1819)— **§ 13.10, n. 2.**

Inhabitants of Stockton v. Staples, 66 Me. 197 (Me.1877)—**§ 4.18, n. 2.**

Inhabitants of Topsham v. Inhabitants of Lewiston, 74 Me. 236 (Me.1882)—**§ 4.27, n. 1.**

Inhabitants of Town of Camden v. Inhabitants of Town of Warren, 160 Me. 158, 200 A.2d 419 (Me.1964)—**§ 4.43, n. 2.**

Inhabitants of West Cambridge v. Inhabitants of Lexington, 18 Mass. 506 (Mass. 1823)—**§ 13.8, n. 5.**

Inhabitants of Whately v. Inhabitants of Hatfield, 196 Mass. 393, 82 N.E. 48 (Mass.1907)—**§ 4.13, n. 2.**

In Interest of Gray, 131 Ill.App.3d 401, 86 Ill.Dec. 737, 475 N.E.2d 1116 (Ill.App. 4 Dist.1985)—§ **4.37, n. 3.**

Inland Revenue Commissioners v. Bullock, 1975 WL 45060 (CA 1976)—§ **4.36, n. 5.**

In re (see name of party)

Institutional Food Marketing Associates, Ltd. v. Golden State Strawberries, Inc., 747 F.2d 448 (8th Cir.1984)—§ **5.14, n. 12.**

Instituto Per Lo Sviluppo Economico Dell' Italia Meridionale v. Sperti Products, Inc., 323 F.Supp. 630 (S.D.N.Y.1971)— § **12.18, n. 1, 11.**

Instructional Systems, Inc. v. Computer Curriculum Corp., 130 N.J. 324, 614 A.2d 124 (N.J.1992)—§ **18.5, n. 34.**

Insurance Corp. of Ireland, Ltd. v. Compagnie des Bauxites de Guinee, 456 U.S. 694, 102 S.Ct. 2099, 72 L.Ed.2d 492 (1982)—§ **3.26, n. 12;** § **5.4, n. 23;** § **5.19, n. 17;** § **6.3, n. 9;** § **6.5;** § **6.5, n. 2, 21;** § **10.2;** § **10.2, n. 18;** § **10.3;** § **10.3, n. 9.**

Intamin, Inc. v. Figley Wright Contractors, Inc., 605 F.Supp. 707 (N.D.Ill.1985)— § **17.26, n. 1.**

In–Tech Marketing Inc. v. Hasbro, Inc., 719 F.Supp. 312 (D.N.J.1989)—§ **24.4, n. 7.**

Integral Development Corp. v. Weissenbach, 122 Cal.Rptr.2d 24 (Cal.App. 6 Dist.2002)—§ **7.3, n. 10.**

Integrated Container Service, Inc. v. Starlines Container Shipping, Ltd., 476 F.Supp. 119 (S.D.N.Y.1979)—§ **10.6, n. 35.**

Inter–City Products Corp. v. Insurance Co. of North America, 1993 WL 18948 (D.Del.1993)—§ **18.1, n. 27.**

Intercontinental Hotels Corp. (Puerto Rico) v. Golden, 15 N.Y.2d 19, 254 N.Y.S.2d 527, 203 N.E.2d 210 (N.Y.1964)—§ **3.15, n. 2, 5;** § **11.10, n. 7;** § **18.4, n. 48, 50, 52.**

Intercontinental Planning, Limited v. Daystrom, Inc., 300 N.Y.S.2d 817, 248 N.E.2d 576 (N.Y.1969)—§ **14.12, n. 8;** § **18.31;** § **18.31, n. 1.**

Interdesco SA v. Nullifire Ltd, 1991 WL 838094 (QBD (Comm Ct) 1991)— § **24.44, n. 9.**

Interest of M.L.K., Matter of, 13 Kan. App.2d 251, 768 P.2d 316 (Kan.App. 1989)—§ **16.5, n. 5.**

Interest of W.A., 63 P.3d 607 (Utah 2002)— § **15.29, n. 5.**

Interface Flooring Systems, Inc. v. Aetna Cas. and Sur. Co., 261 Conn. 601, 804 A.2d 201 (Conn.2002)—§ **18.26, n. 12.**

Interface Group–Massachusetts, LLC v. Rosen, 256 F.Supp.2d 103 (D.Mass.2003)— § **5.10, n. 27.**

Interlease Aviation Investors II (ALOHA) L.L.C. v. Vanguard Airlines, Inc., 262

F.Supp.2d 898 (N.D.Ill.2003)—§ **7.12, n. 8.**

International Aerial Tramway Corp. v. Konrad Doppelmayr and Sohn, 70 Cal.2d 400, 74 Cal.Rptr. 908, 450 P.2d 284 (Cal. 1969)—§ **10.12, n. 9.**

International Broth. of Teamsters, United States v., 945 F.Supp. 609 (S.D.N.Y. 1996)—§ **10.2, n. 15;** § **10.5, n. 15, 16.**

International Controls Corp. v. Vesco, 593 F.2d 166 (2nd Cir.1979)—§ **3.45, n. 4.**

International Harvester Co. of America v. Commonwealth of Kentucky, 234 U.S. 579, 34 S.Ct. 944, 58 L.Ed. 1479 (1914)—§ **5.3, n. 18;** § **10.14, n. 7.**

International Harvester Credit Corp. v. Pefley, 458 N.E.2d 257 (Ind.App. 2 Dist. 1983)—§ **19.18, n. 21.**

International Harvester Credit Corp. v. Ricks, 16 N.C.App. 491, 192 S.E.2d 707 (N.C.App.1972)—§ **18.24, n. 10.**

International Honeycomb Corp. v. Transtech Service Network, Inc., 742 F.Supp. 1011 (N.D.Ill.1990)—§ **11.14, n. 6.**

International Inv. and Equine Consultants, Inc. v. Jebrock, 573 F.Supp. 592 (W.D.Pa.1983)—§ **11.2, n. 6.**

International Mill. Co. v. Columbia Transp. Co., 292 U.S. 511, 54 S.Ct. 797, 78 L.Ed. 1396 (1934)—§ **11.16, n. 1.**

International Paper Co. v. Midvale–Heppenstall Co., 63 Pa. D. & C.2d 627 (Pa.Com. Pl.1973)—§ **18.3, n. 1.**

International Shoe Co. v. Hawkinson, 73 N.D. 677, 18 N.W.2d 761 (N.D.1945)— § **10.12, n. 15.**

International Shoe Co. v. State of Washington, Office of Unemployment Compensation and Placement, 326 U.S. 310, 66 S.Ct. 154, 90 L.Ed. 95 (1945)—§ **3.26, n. 5;** § **5.1, n. 3;** § **5.4;** § **5.4, n. 2;** § **5.10;** § **5.10, n. 1;** § **5.12, n. 1;** § **5.13;** § **5.13, n. 3;** § **5.14;** § **5.14, n. 7;** § **6.2, n. 1;** § **6.3, n. 4;** § **6.6;** § **6.6, n. 8;** § **6.7;** § **6.7, n. 2;** § **6.8;** § **6.8, n. 1;** § **6.9;** § **6.9, n. 1;** § **7.1;** § **7.1, n. 1;** § **7.2, n. 2;** § **8.1, n. 5;** § **8.8, n. 10;** § **9.1;** § **9.1, n. 2;** § **9.5;** § **9.5, n. 1;** § **10.1, n. 1;** § **10.15;** § **10.15, n. 1, 15.**

International Transactions, Ltd. v. Embotelladora Agral Regiomontana, SA de CV, 347 F.3d 589 (5th Cir.2003)— § **24.18, n. 2.**

International Truck and Engine Corp. v. Dawson International Inc., 216 F.Supp.2d 754 (N.D.Ind.2002)—§ **9.4, n. 5.**

Interpool Ltd. v. Through Transport Mut. Ins. Ass'n Ltd., 635 F.Supp. 1503 (S.D.Fla.1985)—§ **11.6, n. 8.**

Interstate Tire Co. v. United States, 1973 WL 537 (D.Ariz.1973)—§ **19.18, n. 12.**

Ioannidis/Riga v. M/V SEA CONCERT, 132 F.Supp.2d 847 (D.Or.2001)—§ **17.63, n. 24.**

Ionics, Inc. v. Elmwood Sensors, Inc., 896 F.Supp. 66 (D.Mass.1995)—§ **18.24, n. 8.**

Iowa v. Slimmer, 248 U.S. 115, 39 S.Ct. 33, 63 L.Ed. 158 (1918)—§ **22.11, n. 6.**

Iowa Mut. Ins. Co. v. LaPlante, 480 U.S. 9, 107 S.Ct. 971, 94 L.Ed.2d 10 (1987)— § **11.17, n. 32.**

Iragorri v. United Technologies Corp., 274 F.3d 65 (2nd Cir.2001)—§ **11.9, n. 7.**

Irish Lesbian and Gay Organization v. Giuliani, 143 F.3d 638 (2nd Cir.1998)— § **24.1, n. 6.**

Irons v. Irons, 242 Ind. 504, 180 N.E.2d 105 (Ind.1962)—§ **4.20, n. 3.**

Iroquois Energy Management, LLC, In re, 284 B.R. 28 (Bkrtcy.W.D.N.Y.2002)— § **19.20, n. 12; § 19.30, n. 2, 8.**

Irrigation & Indus. Development Corp. v. Indag S. A., 375 N.Y.S.2d 296, 337 N.E.2d 749 (N.Y.1975)—§ **11.11, n. 6.**

Irvin v. Allstate Ins. Co., 436 F.Supp. 575 (W.D.Okla.1977)—§ **23.3, n. 4.**

Irvin v. Irvin, 182 Kan. 563, 322 P.2d 794 (Kan.1958)—§ **4.17, n. 2.**

Irving v. Ford, 183 Mass. 448, 67 N.E. 366 (Mass.1903)—§ **16.1, n. 12.**

Irving v. Owens–Corning Fiberglas Corp., 864 F.2d 383 (5th Cir.1989)—§ **7.2, n. 32.**

Irving Trust Co. v. Maryland Casualty Co., 83 F.2d 168 (2nd Cir.1936)—§ **3.4, n. 5; § 19.3, n. 16, 21; § 19.8; § 19.8, n. 9.**

Irvin L. Young Foundation, Inc. v. Damrell, 607 F.Supp. 705 (D.Me.1985)—§ **24.8, n. 9.**

Irwin, Appeal of, 33 Conn. 128 (Conn. 1865)—§ **20.6, n. 3; § 20.12, n. 3.**

Isaacson v. Heffernan, 189 Misc. 16, 64 N.Y.S.2d 726 (N.Y.Sup.1946)—§ **4.13, n. 2.**

ISI Intern., Inc. v. Borden Ladner Gervais LLP, 256 F.3d 548 (7th Cir.2001)— § **10.2, n. 15; § 10.5, n. 15, 18; § 10.17, n. 8.**

I. S. Joseph Company, Inc. v. Toufic Aris & Fils, 54 A.D.2d 665, 388 N.Y.S.2d 1 (N.Y.A.D. 1 Dept.1976)—§ **18.12, n. 7, 15.**

Islamic Republic of Iran v. Pahlavi, 478 N.Y.S.2d 597, 467 N.E.2d 245 (N.Y. 1984)—§ **11.10, n. 1.**

Island v. Fireman's Fund Indem. Co., 30 Cal.2d 541, 184 P.2d 153 (Cal.1947)— § **4.26, n. 1.**

Island Territory of Curacao v. Solitron Devices, Inc., 356 F.Supp. 1 (S.D.N.Y. 1973)—§ **24.48, n. 5.**

Isley v. Capuchin Province, 878 F.Supp. 1021 (E.D.Mich.1995)—§ **17.50; § 17.50, n. 27.**

Isostatic Graphite Antitrust Litigation, In re, 2002 WL 31421920 (E.D.Pa.2002)— § **9.7, n. 3.**

Israel v. Allen, 195 Colo. 263, 577 P.2d 762 (Colo.1978)—§ **13.11, n. 5.**

Issendorf v. Olson, 194 N.W.2d 750 (N.D. 1972)—§ **2.16, n. 15; § 2.22, n. 2; § 17.26, n. 1, 20; § 17.39, n. 14.**

Istre v. Diamond M. Drilling Co., 226 So.2d 779 (La.App. 3 Cir.1969)—§ **3.10, n. 1.**

I. T. A. D. Associates, Inc. v. Podar Bros., 636 F.2d 75 (4th Cir.1981)—§ **24.48, n. 8.**

IUE AFL–CIO Pension Fund v. Herrmann, 9 F.3d 1049 (2nd Cir.1993)—§ **10.18, n. 9.**

Ives v. Salisbury's Heirs, 56 Vt. 565 (Vt. 1883)—§ **22.2, n. 2; § 22.3, n. 1, 2, 15; § 22.4, n. 8.**

Ivor B. Clark Co. v. Hogan, 296 F.Supp. 398 (S.D.N.Y.1968)—§ **18.37, n. 12.**

J

J., In re, [1990] 2 A.C. 562, [1990] 3 W.L.R. 492—§ **4.14, n. 10.**

Jack v. Enterprise Rent–A–Car Co. of Los Angeles, 899 P.2d 891 (Wyo.1995)— § **2.21, n. 5; § 3.4, n. 5.**

Jack Faucett Associates, Inc. v. American Tel. and Tel. Co., 744 F.2d 118, 240 U.S.App.D.C. 103 (D.C.Cir.1984)— § **24.1, n. 8.**

Jackson, Matter of, 592 S.W.2d 320 (Mo. App. S.D.1979)—§ **4.41, n. 1.**

Jackson v. Continental Southern Lines, Inc., 172 F.Supp. 809 (W.D.Ark.1959)— § **3.10, n. 6.**

Jackson v. FIE Corp., 302 F.3d 515 (5th Cir.2002)—§ **5.21, n. 4; § 24.14, n. 1.**

Jackson v. Green, 112 Ind. 341, 14 N.E. 89 (Ind.1887)—§ **19.5, n. 8.**

Jackson v. Hudspeth, 208 Ark. 55, 184 S.W.2d 906 (Ark.1945)—§ **19.2, n. 5.**

Jackson v. Johns–Manville Sales Corp., 750 F.2d 1314 (5th Cir.1985)—§ **3.55, n. 6.**

Jackson v. Koninklijke Luchtvaart Maatschappij N. V., 459 F.Supp. 953 (S.D.N.Y.1978)—§ **17.18, n. 14.**

Jackson v. National Semi–Conductor Data Checker/DTS, Inc., 660 F.Supp. 65 (S.D.Miss.1986)—§ **3.10, n. 1.**

Jackson v. North Bank Towing Corp., 213 F.3d 885 (5th Cir.2000)—§ **17.63, n. 6.**

Jackson v. North Bank Towing Corp., 742 So.2d 1 (La.App. 3 Cir.1999)—§ **17.63, n. 6.**

Jackson v. Travelers Ins. Co., 26 F.Supp.2d 1153 (S.D.Iowa 1998)—§ **17.50; § 17.50, n. 17.**

Jackson v. West Telemarketing Corp. Outbound, 245 F.3d 518 (5th Cir.2001)— § **3.46, n. 7, 11; § 3.47, n. 7.**

Jackson's Estate, Matter of, 48 Ill.App.3d 1035, 6 Ill.Dec. 972, 363 N.E.2d 919 (Ill.App. 4 Dist.1977)—§ **22.6, n. 1.**

Jackson & Sons v. Lumbermen's Mut. Cas. Co., 86 N.H. 341, 168 A. 895 (N.H. 1933)—§ **11.8, n. 3.**

Jacobs, In re Marriage of, 20 Wash.App. 272, 579 P.2d 1023 (Wash.App. Div. 3 1978)—§ **14.9, n. 1.**

Jacobs v. Jacobs, 82 Or.App. 333, 728 P.2d 89 (Or.App.1986)—§ **19.2, n. 7.**

Jacobs v. Jacobs, 130 Iowa 10, 104 N.W. 489 (Iowa 1905)—§ **4.43, n. 4.**

Jacobsen v. Bunker, 699 P.2d 1208 (Utah 1985)—§ **12.15, n. 9.**

Jacobsen v. Oliver, 201 F.Supp.2d 93 (D.D.C.2002)—§ **7.4, n. 9.**

Jacoubovitch v. Jacoubovitch, 279 A.D. 1027, 112 N.Y.S.2d 1 (N.Y.A.D. 2 Dept. 1952)—§ **4.27, n. 12.**

Jaeger v. Jaeger, 262 Wis. 14, 53 N.W.2d 740 (Wis.1952)—§ **14.9, n. 1, 13.**

Jaeglin v. Moakley, 236 Mo.App. 254, 151 S.W.2d 524 (Mo.App.1941)—§ **22.22, n. 6.**

Jaffrey v. McGough, 83 Ala. 202, 3 So. 594 (Ala.1888)—§ **14.8, n. 4; § 14.9, n. 3.**

Jagers v. Royal Indem. Co., 276 So.2d 309 (La.1973)—§ **2.16, n. 14; § 2.21, n. 14; § 3.12, n. 6; § 17.39, n. 10.**

Jambrone v. David, 16 Ill.2d 32, 156 N.E.2d 569 (Ill.1959)—§ **13.1, n. 1; § 13.6, n. 4.**

James v. Adams, 56 Okla. 450, 155 P. 1121 (Okla.1915)—§ **13.18, n. 13.**

James v. Grand Trunk Western R. Co., 14 Ill.2d 356, 152 N.E.2d 858 (Ill.1958)— § **24.9, n. 4, 8, 18; § 24.21, n. 5.**

James v. Powell, 279 N.Y.S.2d 10, 225 N.E.2d 741 (N.Y.1967)—§ **19.3, n. 20; § 19.8, n. 9.**

James' Will, In re, 248 N.Y. 1, 161 N.E. 201 (N.Y.1928)—§ **24.31, n. 5.**

Jamison v. Cooper, 754 F.2d 1568 (11th Cir.1985)—§ **3.12, n. 6.**

Janssen v. Janssen, 269 Ill.App. 233 (Ill. App. 3 Dist.1933)—§ **4.24, n. 3.**

Japan Petroleum Co. (Nigeria) Ltd. v. Ashland Oil, Inc., 456 F.Supp. 831 (D.Del. 1978)—§ **18.33, n. 3.**

Jaramillo v. Burkhart, 999 F.2d 1241 (8th Cir.1993)—§ **22.20, n. 30.**

Jaramillo v. McLoy, 263 F.Supp. 870 (D.Colo.1967)—§ **19.2, n. 4; § 19.3, n. 3, 18; § 19.9, n. 2.**

Jardine v. Superior Court in and for Los Angeles County, 213 Cal. 301, 2 P.2d 756 (Cal.1931)—§ **5.20, n. 8.**

Jarel v. Moon's Succession, 190 So. 867 (La.App. 2 Cir.1939)—§ **20.6, n. 17; § 20.15, n. 3.**

J.A.R., Inc. v. M/V Lady Lucille, 963 F.2d 96 (5th Cir.1992)—§ **10.6, n. 15.**

J. A. Thompson & Son, Inc., In re, 665 F.2d 941 (9th Cir.1982)—§ **19.20, n. 3.**

Jay v. Jay, 212 A.2d 331 (D.C.App.1965)— § **13.5, n. 1.**

J. C. Equipment, Inc. v. Sky Aviation, Inc., 498 S.W.2d 73 (Mo.App.1973)—§ **19.13, n. 4.**

Jefferson v. Beall, 117 Ala. 436, 23 So. 44 (Ala.1898)—§ **22.19, n. 1, 2, 5.**

Jefferson v. Glover, 46 Miss. 510 (Miss. 1872)—§ **22.25, n. 2, 20.**

Jefferson Parish Hosp. Service Dist. #2 v. W.R. Grace & Co., 1992 WL 167263 (E.D.La.1992)—§ **17.77, n. 3.**

Jeffersonville R. Co. v. Swayne's Adm'r, 26 Ind. 477 (Ind.1866)—§ **22.10, n. 8.**

Jeffs v. Stubbs, 970 P.2d 1234 (Utah 1998)—§ **24.10, n. 4.**

Jenkins, Matter of Estate of, 133 Misc.2d 420, 506 N.Y.S.2d 1009 (N.Y.Sur. 1986)—§ **13.6, n. 2.**

Jenkins v. Clark, 71 Iowa 552, 32 N.W. 504 (Iowa 1887)—§ **4.37, n. 10; § 4.41, n. 2.**

Jenness v. Jenness, 24 Ind. 355 (Ind. 1865)—§ **4.33, n. 1; § 4.34, n. 1.**

Jennings v. Boeing Co., 660 F.Supp. 796 (E.D.Pa.1987)—§ **11.9, n. 5.**

Jennings v. Jennings, 133 Ill.App.3d 753, 88 Ill.Dec. 806, 479 N.E.2d 419 (Ill.App. 5 Dist.1985)—§ **15.42, n. 7.**

Jennings v. Jennings, 20 Md.App. 369, 315 A.2d 816 (Md.App.1974)—§ **13.6, n. 2.**

Jennings v. Jennings, 21 Ohio St. 56 (Ohio 1871)—§ **20.8, n. 11.**

Jennison v. Hapgood, 27 Mass. 77 (Mass. 1830)—§ **22.23, n. 4.**

Jensen v. Barnes, 33 Colo.App. 333, 519 P.2d 1223 (Colo.App.1974)—§ **15.12, n. 2.**

Jensen v. Sorenson, 211 Iowa 354, 233 N.W. 717 (Iowa 1930)—§ **4.41, n. 7.**

Jepson v. General Cas. Co. of Wisconsin, 513 N.W.2d 467 (Minn.1994)—§ **2.13, n. 14, 19, 20, 23; § 3.23, n. 15; § 17.22, n. 7; § 17.23, n. 11; § 17.56, n. 11; § 18.21, n. 16.**

Jerguson v. Blue Dot Inv., Inc., 659 F.2d 31 (5th Cir.1981)—§ **23.3, n. 1.**

Jerome B. Grubart, Inc. v. Great Lakes Dredge & Dock Co., 513 U.S. 527, 115 S.Ct. 1043, 130 L.Ed.2d 1024 (1995)— § **17.63, n. 3.**

Jeske v. Jeske, 1982 WL 499637 (B.C. S.C. 1982)—§ **14.9, n. 12.**

Jesse v. Department of Revenue on Behalf of Robinson, 711 So.2d 1179 (Fla.App. 2 Dist.1998)—§ **15.38, n. 1.**

Jester v. Baltimore Steam Packet Co., 131 N.C. 54, 42 S.E. 447 (N.C.1902)—§ **5.1, n. 9; § 5.3, n. 16; § 6.2, n. 21.**

Jetco Electronic Industries v. Gardiner, 325 F.Supp. 80 (S.D.Tex.1971)—§ **12.18, n. 8.**

Jett v. Coletta, 2003 WL 22171862 (D.N.J. 2003)—§ **17.42, n. 29.**

Jett Racing & Sales, Inc. v. Transamerica Commercial Finance Corp., 892 F.Supp. 161 (S.D.Tex.1995)—§ **18.12, n. 2.**

Jet Wine & Spirits, Inc. v. Bacardi & Co., Ltd., 298 F.3d 1 (1st Cir.2002)—§ **7.11, n. 11.**

Jewish Defense Organization, Inc. v. Superior Court, 85 Cal.Rptr.2d 611 (Cal.App. 2 Dist.1999)—§ **7.8, n. 14, 16.**

Jim v. CIT Financial Services Corp., 87 N.M. 362, 533 P.2d 751 (N.M.1975)— § **15.23, n. 7.**

Jimenez v. American Airlines, Inc., 579 F.Supp. 631 (D.Puerto Rico 1983)— § **17.26, n. 1.**

Jimenez v. Weinberger, 523 F.2d 689 (7th Cir.1975)—§ **24.1, n. 8.**

Jim's Water Service v. Eayrs, 590 P.2d 1346 (Wyo.1979)—§ **13.6, n. 2.**

Jinks v. Richland County, 349 S.C. 298, 563 S.E.2d 104 (S.C.2002)—§ **3.11, n. 3.**

Jizmejian v. Jizmejian, 16 Ariz.App. 270, 492 P.2d 1208 (Ariz.App. Div. 2 1972)— § **14.9, n. 1; § 14.13, n. 8.**

J. Josephson, Inc. v. Crum & Forster Ins. Co., 293 N.J.Super. 170, 679 A.2d 1206 (N.J.Super.A.D.1996)—§ **18.26, n. 13.**

J.L.H., Matter of Adoption of, 737 P.2d 915 (Okla.1987)—§ **16.5, n. 5.**

J.M. Atherton Co. v. Ives, 20 F. 894 (C.C.D.Ky.1884)—§ **19.30, n. 6.**

J. M. S. v. H. A., 161 W.Va. 433, 242 S.E.2d 696 (W.Va.1978)—§ **4.37, n. 5.**

Joe v. Marcum, 621 F.2d 358 (10th Cir. 1980)—§ **11.17, n. 40.**

Johannsen v. Brown, 788 F.Supp. 465 (D.Or.1992)—§ **9.3, n. 4.**

Johansen v. Johansen, 305 N.W.2d 383 (S.D.1981)—§ **15.30, n. 2; § 15.31, n. 2.**

Johansson v. United States, 336 F.2d 809 (5th Cir.1964)—§ **24.43, n. 1.**

John Hancock Mut. Life Ins. Co. v. Yates, 299 U.S. 178, 57 S.Ct. 129, 81 L.Ed. 106 (1936)—§ **3.21, n. 2, 7.**

John Mohr and Sons v. Apex Terminal Warehouses, Inc., 422 F.2d 638 (7th Cir. 1970)—§ **23.3, n. 2.**

Johns v. Rozet, 770 F.Supp. 11 (D.D.C. 1991)—§ **10.17, n. 9.**

Johns Hopkins University v. Uhrig, 145 Md. 114, 125 A. 606 (Md.1924)— § **20.13, n. 6.**

John Simmons Co. v. Sloan, 104 N.J.L. 612, 142 A. 15 (N.J.Err. & App.1928)—§ **4.7, n. 4.**

Johnson, In re, 87 Iowa 130, 54 N.W. 69 (Iowa 1893)—§ **4.39, n. 2.**

Johnson, In re Adoption of, 399 Pa. 624, 161 A.2d 358 (Pa.1960)—§ **4.42, n. 2.**

Johnson v. Avery, 11 Me. 99 (Me.1833)— § **22.25, n. 21.**

Johnson v. Baker, 142 Or. 404, 20 P.2d 407 (Or.1933)—§ **13.6, n. 18.**

Johnson v. Berger, 51 Misc.2d 513, 273 N.Y.S.2d 484 (N.Y.Fam.Ct.1966)— § **24.46, n. 15.**

Johnson v. Bradbury, 233 N.J.Super. 129, 558 A.2d 61 (N.J.Super.A.D.1989)— § **7.3, n. 10.**

Johnson v. Capps, 415 N.E.2d 108 (Ind.App. 3 Dist.1981)—§ **16.5, n. 9.**

Johnson v. Chicago, B. & Q. R. Co., 243 Minn. 58, 66 N.W.2d 763 (Minn.1954)— § **11.8, n. 3; § 11.12, n. 1.**

Johnson v. Commissioner, 88 F.2d 952 (8th Cir.1937)—§ **14.7, n. 5.**

Johnson v. Ford Motor Co., Inc., 2003 WL 22317425 (N.D.Ill.2003)—§ **17.73, n. 4.**

Johnson v. Hertz Corp., 315 F.Supp. 302 (S.D.N.Y.1970)—§ **17.45, n. 20.**

Johnson v. Jackson, 56 Ga. 326 (Ga.1876)— § **22.19, n. 19, 21.**

Johnson v. Johnson, 605 So.2d 1157 (La. App. 2 Cir.1992)—§ **14.11, n. 2.**

Johnson v. Johnson, 115 Ga.App. 749, 156 S.E.2d 186 (Ga.App.1967)—§ **15.34, n. 7.**

Johnson v. Johnson, 57 Wash. 89, 106 P. 500 (Wash.1910)—§ **13.11, n. 3.**

Johnson v. Johnson's Adm'r, 30 Mo. 72 (Mo.1860)—§ **13.18, n. 10, 14.**

Johnson v. Knight, 459 F.Supp. 962 (N.D.Miss.1978)—§ **17.64, n. 10.**

Johnson v. La Grange State Bank, 73 Ill.2d 342, 22 Ill.Dec. 709, 383 N.E.2d 185 (Ill.1978)—§ **21.3, n. 17.**

Johnson v. LaGrange State Bank, 50 Ill. App.3d 830, 8 Ill.Dec. 670, 365 N.E.2d 1056 (Ill.App. 1 Dist.1977)—§ **20.9, n. 11; § 21.3, n. 7.**

Johnson v. Liberty Mut. Ins. Co., 297 So.2d 858 (Fla.App. 4 Dist.1974)—§ **17.58, n. 5.**

Johnson v. Lincoln Square Properties, Inc., 571 So.2d 541 (Fla.App. 2 Dist.1990)— § **13.6, n. 2.**

Johnson v. McKinnon, 129 Ala. 223, 29 So. 696 (Ala.1901)—§ **22.20, n. 1.**

Johnson v. Melback, 5 Kan.App.2d 69, 612 P.2d 188 (Kan.App.1980)—§ **22.26, n. 3.**

Johnson v. Muelberger, 340 U.S. 581, 71 S.Ct. 474, 95 L.Ed. 552 (1951)—§ **4.7, n. 2; § 15.11, n. 2.**

Johnson v. Ortiz, 244 Ill.App.3d 384, 185 Ill.Dec. 274, 614 N.E.2d 408 (Ill.App. 1 Dist.1993)—§ **7.4, n. 7.**

Johnson v. Pischke, 108 Idaho 397, 700 P.2d 19 (Idaho 1985)—§ **2.16, n. 16; § 2.23, n. 1; § 17.26, n. 1, 20; § 17.39, n. 14.**

Johnson v. Powers, 139 U.S. 156, 11 S.Ct. 525, 35 L.Ed. 112 (1891)—§ **22.14, n. 3; § 22.20, n. 1.**

Johnson v. Ranch Steamboat Condominium Assn., 1999 WL 184068 (N.D.Ill.1999)— § **17.71; § 17.71, n. 6.**

Johnson v. Rockefeller, 58 F.R.D. 42 (S.D.N.Y.1972)—§ **13.11, n. 5.**

Johnson v. Smith, 94 Ind.App. 619, 180 N.E. 188 (Ind.App.1932)—§ **4.41, n. 5.**

Johnson v. Spider Staging Corp., 87 Wash.2d 577, 555 P.2d 997 (Wash. 1976)—§ **2.16, n. 12;** § **2.23, n. 1;** § **17.26, n. 1, 5;** § **18.18, n. 12.**

Johnson v. Wachovia Bank & Trust Co., 22 N.C.App. 8, 205 S.E.2d 353 (N.C.App. 1974)—§ **22.14, n. 6.**

Johnson Controls, Inc. v. American Motorists Ins. Co., 719 F.Supp. 1459 (E.D.Wis. 1989)—§ **18.26, n. 19.**

Johnson & Johnson v. Picard, 282 F.2d 386 (6th Cir.1960)—§ **23.2, n. 8.**

Johnston v. Commercial Travelers Mut. Acc. Ass'n of America, 242 S.C. 387, 131 S.E.2d 91 (S.C.1963)—§ **18.4, n. 43;** § **18.5, n. 8.**

Johnston v. Compagnie Generale Transatlantique, 242 N.Y. 381, 152 N.E. 121 (N.Y.1926)—§ **24.3, n. 4;** § **24.6, n. 3;** § **24.34, n. 2;** § **24.35, n. 2, 7.**

Johnston v. Gawtry, 11 Mo.App. 322 (Mo. App.1882)—§ **19.3, n. 1, 5.**

Johnston v. State, 212 Ind. 375, 8 N.E.2d 590 (Ind.1937)—§ **21.5, n. 1.**

Johnston v. Wallis, 112 N.Y. 230, 19 N.E. 653 (N.Y.1889)—§ **22.18, n. 3;** § **22.19, n. 16.**

Johnston Jewels, Limited v. Leonard, 156 Conn. 75, 239 A.2d 500 (Conn.1968)—§ **19.13, n. 1.**

Joint Holdings & Trading Co. v. First Union Nat. Bk. of North Carolina, 50 Cal. App.3d 159, 123 Cal.Rptr. 519 (Cal.App. 2 Dist.1975)—§ **19.18, n. 14.**

Jolicoeur v. Mihaly, 5 Cal.3d 565, 96 Cal. Rptr. 697, 488 P.2d 1 (Cal.1971)—§ **4.9, n. 2;** § **4.13, n. 5.**

Jones v. Bradford, 353 So.2d 1348 (La.App. 3 Cir.1977)—§ **19.17, n. 6.**

Jones v. Burkett, 346 P.2d 338 (Okla. 1959)—§ **4.13, n. 2.**

Jones v. Habersham, 107 U.S. 174, 2 S.Ct. 336, 27 L.Ed. 401 (1883)—§ **20.7, n. 1.**

Jones v. Hadican, 552 F.2d 249 (8th Cir. 1977)—§ **4.27, n. 8, 10.**

Jones v. International Tel. & Tel. Corp., 462 So.2d 1348 (La.App. 3 Cir.1985)—§ **13.2, n. 10.**

Jones v. Jones, 402 N.W.2d 146 (Minn.App. 1987)—§ **4.33, n. 6.**

Jones v. Jones, 293 Ala. 39, 299 So.2d 729 (Ala.1974)—§ **19.2, n. 7;** § **19.9, n. 2.**

Jones v. Jones, 136 A.2d 580 (D.C.Mun.App. 1957)—§ **4.20, n. 3.**

Jones v. Jones, 301 S.W.2d 310 (Tex.Civ. App.-Texarkana 1957)—§ **22.3, n. 1.**

Jones v. Jones, 107 Ill.App. 464 (Ill.App. 1 Dist.1903)—§ **22.3, n. 14.**

Jones v. Layne, 144 N.C. 600, 57 S.E. 372 (N.C.1907)—§ **20.14, n. 1;** § **22.22, n. 5.**

Jones v. McKesson & Robbins, Inc., 237 F.Supp. 454 (D.N.D.1965)—§ **17.6, n. 2.**

Jones v. New York Life Ins. Co., 32 Okla. 339, 122 P. 702 (Okla.1912)—§ **18.5, n. 9.**

Jones v. R.S. Jones and Associates, Inc., 246 Va. 3, 431 S.E.2d 33 (Va.1993)—§ **2.21, n. 4.**

Jones v. Shields, 14 Ohio 359 (Ohio 1846)—§ **22.25, n. 6.**

Jones v. Southeastern Pa. Transp. Authority, 1993 WL 141646 (E.D.Pa.1993)—§ **17.67, n. 5;** § **17.69, n. 9.**

Jones, State v., 202 Neb. 488, 275 N.W.2d 851 (Neb.1979)—§ **4.34, n. 4.**

Jones v. Weibrecht, 901 F.2d 17 (2nd Cir. 1990)—§ **11.4, n. 15.**

Jones' Estate, In re, 192 Iowa 78, 182 N.W. 227 (Iowa 1921)—§ **3.6, n. 4;** § **4.3, n. 3;** § **4.36, n. 10, 11;** § **20.3, n. 5.**

Jones & McKnight Corp. v. Birdsboro Corp., 320 F.Supp. 39 (N.D.Ill.1970)—§ **18.12, n. 10.**

Jones Truck Lines v. Transport Ins. Co., 1989 WL 49517 (E.D.Pa.1989)—§ **18.26, n. 13.**

Jonnet v. Dollar Sav. Bank of City of New York, 530 F.2d 1123 (3rd Cir.1976)—§ **5.4, n. 32.**

Jordan v. Chicago & N.W.R. Co., 125 Wis. 581, 104 N.W. 803 (Wis.1905)—§ **22.10, n. 10.**

Jordan v. Fox, Rothschild, O'Brien & Frankel, 20 F.3d 1250 (3rd Cir.1994)—§ **12.5, n. 4.**

Jordan v. Missouri & Kansas Telephone Co., 136 Mo.App. 192, 116 S.W. 432 (Mo. App.1909)—§ **13.6, n. 4.**

Jordan v. States Marine Corp. of Del., 257 F.2d 232 (9th Cir.1958)—§ **17.5, n. 4.**

Jose v. M/V Fir Grove, 765 F.Supp. 1024 (D.Or.1991)—§ **17.63, n. 24.**

Joseph L. Wilmotte & Co. v. Rosenman Bros., 258 N.W.2d 317 (Iowa 1977)—§ **2.17, n. 10;** § **2.23, n. 2;** § **18.21, n. 14.**

Jovanopoulos' Will, In re, 51 Misc.2d 995, 274 N.Y.S.2d 249 (N.Y.Sur.1966)—§ **20.6, n. 18.**

Joy v. Heidrick & Struggles, Inc., 93 Misc.2d 818, 403 N.Y.S.2d 613 (N.Y.City Civ.Ct.1977)—§ **18.7, n. 10.**

JPMorgan Chase Bank v. Traffic Stream (BVI) Infrastructure Ltd., 536 U.S. 88, 122 S.Ct. 2054, 153 L.Ed.2d 95 (2002)—§ **23.3, n. 1.**

J.P. Morgan Delaware v, Henley–Paradis, 1993 WL 6866 (Del.Ch.1993)—§ **21.3, n. 10.**

JRT, Inc. v. TCBY Systems, Inc., 52 F.3d 734 (8th Cir.1995)—§ **18.5, n. 35;** § **18.7, n. 5.**

J.S. Alberici Const. Co., Inc. v. Mid–West Conveyor Co., Inc., 750 A.2d 518 (Del. Supr.2000)—§ **18.4, n. 7.**

Jucker v. Jucker, 190 Conn. 674, 461 A.2d 1384 (Conn.1983)—§ **15.10, n. 2.**

Judd v. J.W. Forsinger Co., 186 A. 525 (N.J.Sup.1936)—§ **19.30, n. 6.**

Juden v. Southeast Mo. Tel. Co., 361 Mo. 513, 235 S.W.2d 360 (Mo.1950)—§ **19.4, n. 3.**

Judge v. Pilot Oil Corp., 205 F.3d 335 (7th Cir.2000)—§ **17.48, n. 5.**

Judge Trucking Co., Inc. v. Estate of Cooper, 1994 WL 164519 (Del.Super.1994)—§ **17.32, n. 16.**

Judkins v. Reed, 48 Me. 386 (Me.1860)—§ **4.19, n. 4.**

Judy v. Evans, 109 Ill.App. 154 (Ill.App. 3 Dist.1903)—§ **19.15, n. 7.**

Judy v. Kelley, 11 Ill. 211 (Ill.1849)—§ **22.19, n. 1, 3, 4.**

Julen v. Larson, 25 Cal.App.3d 325, 101 Cal.Rptr. 796 (Cal.App. 2 Dist.1972)—§ **12.2, n. 2; § 12.4, n. 1; § 12.7, n. 5.**

Jump v. Goldenhersh, 619 F.2d 11 (8th Cir.1980)—§ **18.29, n. 3.**

Junco v. Suarez–Solis, 294 So.2d 334 (Fla. App. 3 Dist.1974)—§ **22.26, n. 2.**

Jungquist v. Sheikh Sultan Bin Khalifa Al Nahyan, 115 F.3d 1020, 325 U.S.App. D.C. 117 (D.C.Cir.1997)—§ **10.19, n. 34.**

Juodis v. Schule, 79 Misc.2d 955, 361 N.Y.S.2d 605 (N.Y.Sup.1974)—§ **17.32, n. 1.**

K

Kadjar's Estate, In re, 200 Misc. 268, 102 N.Y.S.2d 113 (N.Y.Sur.1950)—§ **20.13, n. 5.**

Kafka v. Bellevue Corp., 999 F.2d 1117 (7th Cir.1993)—§ **23.2, n. 6.**

Kahn v. Great–West Life Assur. Co., 61 Misc.2d 918, 307 N.Y.S.2d 238 (N.Y.Sup. 1970)—§ **18.5, n. 11.**

Kaho v. Ilchert, 765 F.2d 877 (9th Cir. 1985)—§ **12.18, n. 17.**

Kaiser v. Loomis, 391 F.2d 1007 (6th Cir. 1968)—§ **4.12, n. 3; § 4.17, n. 4.**

Kaiser–Georgetown Community Health Plan, Inc. v. Stutsman, 491 A.2d 502 (D.C.1985)—§ **2.24, n. 7; § 17.14; § 17.14, n. 11; § 17.42, n. 29; § 17.45; § 17.45, n. 7.**

Kaiser Steel Corp., In re, 87 B.R. 154 (Bkrtcy.D.Colo.1988)—§ **23.15, n. 14.**

Kaiser Steel Corp. v. Mullins, 455 U.S. 72, 102 S.Ct. 851, 70 L.Ed.2d 833 (1982)—§ **3.50, n. 5.**

Kajut, Estate of, 22 Pa. D. & C.3d 123 (Pa.Com.Pl.1981)—§ **16.1, n. 5.**

Kakarapis v. Kakarapis, 58 Misc.2d 515, 296 N.Y.S.2d 208 (N.Y.Fam.Ct.1968)—§ **15.20, n. 6.**

Kalhar v. Transamerica Ins. Co., 129 Or. App. 38, 877 P.2d 656 (Or.App.1994)—§ **17.56, n. 17.**

Kalmich v. Bruno, 553 F.2d 549 (7th Cir. 1977)—§ **3.10, n. 1, 5, 6.**

Kalmich v. Bruno, 404 F.Supp. 57 (N.D.Ill. 1975)—§ **3.11, n. 2.**

Kaltsas v. Kaltsas, 22 Mass.App.Ct. 689, 497 N.E.2d 26 (Mass.App.Ct.1986)—§ **22.9, n. 4; § 22.18, n. 10; § 22.19, n. 19, 22.**

Kam Chin Chun Ming v. Kam Hee Ho, 45 Haw. 521, 371 P.2d 379 (Hawai'i 1962)—§ **13.17, n. 8.**

Kamen v. Kemper Financial Services, Inc., 500 U.S. 90, 111 S.Ct. 1711, 114 L.Ed.2d 152 (1991)—§ **23.4, n. 9.**

Kandlbinder's Estate, In re, 183 Neb. 178, 159 N.W.2d 199 (Neb.1968)—§ **22.10, n. 11; § 22.19, n. 6.**

Kane v. New Jersey, 242 U.S. 160, 37 S.Ct. 30, 61 L.Ed. 222 (1916)—§ **5.3, n. 19.**

Kann's Estate, In re, 253 Cal.App.2d 212, 61 Cal.Rptr. 122 (Cal.App. 2 Dist. 1967)—§ **14.12, n. 7.**

Kansas City, Ft. S. & M. R. Co. v. Daughtry, 138 U.S. 298, 11 S.Ct. 306, 34 L.Ed. 963 (1891)—§ **10.13, n. 2.**

Kantlehner v. United States, 279 F.Supp. 122 (E.D.N.Y.1967)—§ **18.44, n. 9.**

Kantor v. Wellesley Galleries, Ltd., 704 F.2d 1088 (9th Cir.1983)—§ **3.36, n. 2; § 4.2, n. 1; § 4.9, n. 2; § 4.13, n. 4.**

Kanz v. Wilson, 703 So.2d 1331 (La.App. 1 Cir.1997)—§ **4.21, n. 3.**

Kapigian v. Der Minassian, 212 Mass. 412, 99 N.E. 264 (Mass.1912)—§ **13.19, n. 1.**

Kaplinsky v. Kaplinsky, 198 A.D.2d 212, 603 N.Y.S.2d 574 (N.Y.A.D. 2 Dept. 1993)—§ **15.24, n. 7.**

Karaha Bodas Co., L.L.C. v. Perusahaan Pertambangan Minyak Dan Gas Bumi Negara, 335 F.3d 357 (5th Cir.2003)—§ **24.9, n. 7.**

Karakatsanis v. Conquestador Cia. Nav., S.A., 247 F.Supp. 423 (S.D.N.Y.1965)—§ **17.63, n. 31.**

Karlberg European Tanspa, Inc. v. JK–Josef Kratz Vertriebsgeselischaft MbH, 699 F.Supp. 669 (N.D.Ill.1988)—§ **11.3, n. 22.**

Karlsen v. Hanff, 278 F.Supp. 864 (S.D.N.Y. 1967)—§ **10.4, n. 5.**

Karpo v. Deitsch, 196 So.2d 180 (Fla.App. 3 Dist.1967)—§ **22.18, n. 9.**

Karvelis v. Constellation Lines SA, 608 F.Supp. 966 (S.D.N.Y.1985)—§ **17.63, n. 23.**

Katz v. Goodyear Tire and Rubber Co., 737 F.2d 238 (2nd Cir.1984)—§ **4.4, n. 3.**

Kaufman v. Societe Internationale Pour Participations Industrielles Et Commerciales, S.A., 343 U.S. 156, 72 S.Ct. 611, 96 L.Ed. 853 (1952)—§ **23.3, n. 9.**

Kava Bowl, In re, 41 B.R. 244 (Bkrtcy.D.Hawai'i 1984)—§ **23.13, n. 4.**

Kaye–Martin v. Brooks, 267 F.2d 394 (7th Cir.1959)—§ **10.15, n. 5.**

Kazin v. Kazin, 81 N.J. 85, 405 A.2d 360 (N.J.1979)—§ **15.20, n. 9; § 15.22, n. 1.**

Kearney v. Savannah Foods & Industries, Inc., 350 F.Supp. 85 (S.D.Ga.1972)—§ 12.18, n. 8.

Kearney v. Todd L. Smith, P.A., 624 F.Supp. 1008 (S.D.N.Y.1985)—§ 7.9, n. 6.

Keatley v. Travelers' Ins. Co. of Hartford, Conn., 187 Pa. 197, 40 A. 808 (Pa. 1898)—§ 18.4, n. 43.

Keaty v. Freeport Indonesia, Inc., 503 F.2d 955 (5th Cir.1974)—§ 11.2, n. 4.

Keelean v. Central Bank of the South, 544 So.2d 153 (Ala.1989)—§ 11.4, n. 3.

Keenan v. Tonry, 91 N.H. 220, 16 A.2d 705 (N.H.1940)—§ 22.23, n. 3.

Keene Corp. v. Gardner, 837 S.W.2d 224 (Tex.App.-Dallas 1992)—§ 12.19, n. 19.

Keener v. Convergys Corp., 342 F.3d 1264 (11th Cir.2003)—§ 2.21, n. 48.

Keener v. Convergys Corp., 312 F.3d 1236 (11th Cir.2002)—§ 2.21, n. 48; § 18.5; § 18.5, n. 27.

Keener v. Convergys Corp., 205 F.Supp.2d 1374 (S.D.Ga.2002)—§ 2.21, n. 48; § 18.5, n. 25.

Keeton v. Hustler Magazine, Inc., 131 N.H. 6, 549 A.2d 1187 (N.H.1988)—§ 2.13; § 2.13, n. 21.

Keeton v. Hustler Magazine, Inc., 465 U.S. 770, 104 S.Ct. 1473, 79 L.Ed.2d 790 (1984)—§ 5.4, n. 24; § 5.10, n. 15; § 7.1, n. 2; § 7.3; § 7.3, n. 4, 9; § 7.8; § 7.8, n. 5; § 7.11; § 7.11, n. 3; § 7.12; § 7.12, n. 7; § 9.3; § 9.3, n. 1.

Keiningham v. Keiningham's Ex'r, 139 Ky. 666, 71 S.W. 497 (Ky.1903)—§ 22.19, n. 23.

Keith v. Eaton, 58 Kan. 732, 51 P. 271 (Kan.1897)—§ 19.4, n. 3; § 20.8, n. 9.

Keith v. Johnson, 97 Mo. 223, 10 S.W. 597 (Mo.1889)—§ 20.6, n. 1; § 22.4, n. 4, 7, 8.

Kell v. Henderson, 26 A.D.2d 595, 270 N.Y.S.2d 552 (N.Y.A.D. 3 Dept.1966)—§ 17.30, n. 10; § 17.31, n. 6.

Kell v. Henderson, 47 Misc.2d 992, 263 N.Y.S.2d 647 (N.Y.Sup.1965)—§ 3.16, n. 5.

Keller v. Department of Revenue, 292 Or. 639, 642 P.2d 284 (Or.1982)—§ 14.9, n. 1.

Keller v. Paine, 107 N.Y. 83, 13 N.E. 635 (N.Y.1887)—§ 19.13, n. 8.

Kelley v. Von Kuznick, 18 Cal.App.3d 805, 96 Cal.Rptr. 184 (Cal.App. 2 Dist. 1971)—§ 17.17, n. 4.

Kelley's Estate, In re, 210 Or. 226, 310 P.2d 328 (Or.1957)—§ 13.9, n. 4; § 13.15, n. 4.

Kellogg, In re, 113 F. 120 (W.D.N.Y.1902)—§ 19.9, n. 6.

Kellogg v. Chester, 71 B.R. 36 (N.D.Tex. 1987)—§ 23.12, n. 15.

Kellogg v. Miller, 13 F. 198 (C.C.D.Neb. 1881)—§ 18.2, n. 1; § 18.7, n. 8.

Kelly v. Davis, 1876 WL 8680 (La.1876)—§ 19.3, n. 1.

Kelly v. Ford Motor Co., 933 F.Supp. 465 (E.D.Pa.1996)—§ 17.50; § 17.50, n. 51; § 17.69; § 17.69, n. 1; § 17.76, n. 12.

Kelly's Will, In re, 174 Misc. 80, 20 N.Y.S.2d 6 (N.Y.Sur.1940)—§ 21.11, n. 4.

Kelly's Will, In re, 161 Misc. 255, 291 N.Y.S. 860 (N.Y.Sur.1936)—§ 21.13, n. 5.

Kelm v. Carlson, 473 F.2d 1267 (6th Cir. 1973)—§ 4.20, n. 5.

Kelsey v. Green, 69 Conn. 291, 37 A. 679 (Conn.1897)—§ 22.26, n. 6.

Kemart Corp. v. Printing Arts Research Lab., Inc., 269 F.2d 375 (9th Cir.1959)—§ 17.6, n. 2; § 17.55, n. 3.

Kem Mfg. Corp. v. Howland, 121 R.I. 601, 401 A.2d 1284 (R.I.1979)—§ 12.19, n. 19.

Kemp v. Pfizer, Inc., 947 F.Supp. 1139 (E.D.Mich.1996)—§ 17.50, n. 16; § 17.77; § 17.77, n. 19.

Kendrick v. Parker, 258 Ga. 210, 367 S.E.2d 544 (Ga.1988)—§ 4.20, n. 6; § 4.26, n. 3.

Kenji Namba v. McCourt, 185 Or. 579, 204 P.2d 569 (Or.1949)—§ 3.59, n. 3.

Kenna v. So–Fro Fabrics, Inc., 18 F.3d 623 (8th Cir.1994)—§ 2.13, n. 23, 26; § 17.21, n. 14; § 17.23, n. 11.

Kennedy, In re, 48 B.R. 621 (Bkrtcy.D.Ariz. 1985)—§ 23.12, n. 15.

Kennedy v. Dixon, 439 S.W.2d 173 (Mo. 1969)—§ 2.16, n. 8; § 2.23, n. 1; § 17.26; § 17.26, n. 1; § 17.39, n. 8.

Kennedy v. Hodges, 215 Mass. 112, 102 N.E. 432 (Mass.1913)—§ 22.12, n. 3.

Kennedy v. Kennedy, 87 Ill. 250 (Ill.1877)—§ 4.33, n. 2.

Kennedy v. Ryall, 67 N.Y. 379 (N.Y.1876)—§ 4.37, n. 2, 6.

Kennedy, State v., 76 N.C. 251 (N.C. 1877)—§ 13.10, n. 1.

Kennerly v. District Court of Ninth Judicial Dist. of Mont., 400 U.S. 423, 91 S.Ct. 480, 27 L.Ed.2d 507 (1971)—§ 11.17, n. 20, 23.

Kenner Products Co., a Division of CPG Products Corp. v. Societe Fonciere et Financiere Agache–Willot, 532 F.Supp. 478 (S.D.N.Y.1982)—§ 23.18, n. 7.

Kenney v. Kenney, 314 F.2d 268, 114 U.S.App.D.C. 263 (D.C.Cir.1963)—§ 22.18, n. 8.

Kenney v. Supreme Lodge of the World, Loyal Order of Moose, 252 U.S. 411, 40 S.Ct. 371, 64 L.Ed. 638 (1920)—§ 24.22; § 24.22, n. 6.

Kent v. Chase, 1 Kan.App.2d 251, 563 P.2d 1103 (Kan.App.1977)—§ 22.10, n. 13.

Kentucky Finance Corp. v. Paramount Auto Exch. Corp., 262 U.S. 544, 43 S.Ct. 636,

67 L.Ed. 1112 (1923)—§ **3.34**; § **3.34, n. 4.**

Kentucky Oaks Mall Co. v. Mitchell's Formal Wear, Inc., 53 Ohio St.3d 73, 559 N.E.2d 477 (Ohio 1990)—§ **8.7, n. 8.**

K.E. Pittman v. Kaiser Aluminum and Chemical Corp., 559 So.2d 879 (La.App. 4 Cir.1990)—§ **17.77, n. 3.**

Kerobo v. Southwestern Clean Fuels, Corp., 285 F.3d 531 (6th Cir.2002)—§ **11.4, n. 3.**

Kerr v. Dougherty, 79 N.Y. 327 (N.Y. 1880)—§ **20.10, n. 2.**

Kessler v. Fauquier Nat. Bank, 195 Va. 1095, 81 S.E.2d 440 (Va.1954)—§ **15.12, n. 2**; § **24.14, n. 5.**

Kessler's Estate, In re, 177 Ohio St. 136, 203 N.E.2d 221 (Ohio 1964)—§ **14.6, n. 4.**

Ketcham v. Hall Syndicate Inc., 19 A.D.2d 611, 242 N.Y.S.2d 182 (N.Y.A.D. 1 Dept. 1963)—§ **18.29.**

Ketcham v. Hall Syndicate, Inc., 37 Misc.2d 693, 236 N.Y.S.2d 206 (N.Y.Sup.1962)— § **18.29, n. 6.**

Kewanee Oil Co. v. Bicron Corp., 416 U.S. 470, 94 S.Ct. 1879, 40 L.Ed.2d 315 (1974)—§ **17.53, n. 3.**

Key Bank of Alaska v. Donnels, 106 Nev. 49, 787 P.2d 382 (Nev.1990)—§ **18.28, n. 5**; § **19.10, n. 7.**

Keys v. Pullman Co., 87 F.Supp. 763 (S.D.Tex.1949)—§ **3.10, n. 6.**

Khaury v. Playboy Publications, Inc., 430 F.Supp. 1342 (S.D.N.Y.1977)—§ **17.55, n. 4.**

Khotim, Matter of, 393 N.Y.S.2d 702, 362 N.E.2d 253 (N.Y.1977)—§ **20.4, n. 6**; § **21.2, n. 5.**

Kibbey v. Mercer, 11 Ohio App.2d 51, 228 N.E.2d 337 (Ohio App. 4 Dist.1967)— § **22.19, n. 7.**

Kiernan, In re, 38 Misc. 394, 77 N.Y.S. 924 (N.Y.Sur.1902)—§ **4.42, n. 4.**

Kilberg v. Northeast Airlines, Inc., 9 N.Y.2d 34, 211 N.Y.S.2d 133, 172 N.E.2d 526 (N.Y.1961)—§ **2.9, n. 14**; § **2.16**; § **2.16, n. 4**; § **3.4**; § **3.4, n. 6**; § **3.15, n. 8**; § **17.9**; § **17.9, n. 1**; § **17.16, n. 6**; § **17.29, n. 4**; § **17.32, n. 31**; § **17.42, n. 9.**

Kimball v. Plant, 14 La. 10 (La.1839)— § **19.30, n. 7.**

Kimbell v. Smith, 64 N.M. 374, 328 P.2d 942 (N.M.1958)—§ **22.10, n. 11.**

Kimbell Foods, Inc., United States v., 440 U.S. 715, 99 S.Ct. 1448, 59 L.Ed.2d 711 (1979)—§ **3.1, n. 3**; § **3.50, n. 7**; § **3.51, n. 9, 12**; § **19.21, n. 13.**

Kimmel's Estate, In re, 193 Minn. 233, 258 N.W. 304 (Minn.1935)—§ **20.9, n. 14.**

Kindler v. Kindler, 60 A.D.2d 753, 400 N.Y.S.2d 605 (N.Y.A.D. 4 Dept.1977)— § **19.8, n. 3.**

King v. Bruce, 145 Tex. 647, 201 S.W.2d 803 (Tex.1947)—§ **14.12, n. 3, 4, 7.**

King v. Foxwell, 1876 WL 18906 (Ch D 1876)—§ **4.36, n. 8.**

King v. King, 218 Ga. 534, 129 S.E.2d 147 (Ga.1962)—§ **21.3, n. 17.**

King v. King, 71 A. 687 (N.J.Err. & App. 1908)—§ **4.28, n. 6.**

King, Succession of, 201 So.2d 335 (La.App. 4 Cir.1967)—§ **20.2, n. 2.**

King–Porter Co., In re, 446 F.2d 722 (5th Cir.1971)—§ **3.51, n. 8**; § **23.15, n. 13.**

Kingsley and Keith (Canada) Ltd. v. Mercer Intern. Corp., 291 Pa.Super. 96, 435 A.2d 585 (Pa.Super.1981)—§ **8.8, n. 5.**

Kinkead's Estate, In re, 239 Minn. 27, 57 N.W.2d 628 (Minn.1953)—§ **13.9, n. 5.**

Kinney v. Commonwealth, 71 Va. 858 (Va. 1878)—§ **13.10, n. 1.**

Kinross–Wright v. Kinross–Wright, 248 N.C. 1, 102 S.E.2d 469 (N.C.1958)— § **14.15, n. 10.**

Kin Yong Lung Indus. Co., Ltd. v. Temple, 816 So.2d 663 (Fla.App. 2 Dist.2002)— § **7.2, n. 33.**

Kiowa Tribe of Oklahoma v. Manufacturing Technologies, Inc., 523 U.S. 751, 118 S.Ct. 1700, 140 L.Ed.2d 981 (1998)— § **11.17, n. 20.**

Kipin Industries, Inc. v. Van Deilen Intern., Inc., 182 F.3d 490 (6th Cir.1999)— § **18.11, n. 5.**

Kirby v. Lee, 1999 WL 562750 (E.D.Pa. 1999)—§ **17.48, n. 8.**

Kirkbride v. Hickok, 155 Ohio St. 293, 98 N.E.2d 815 (Ohio 1951)—§ **21.2, n. 7.**

Kirkby's Estate, In re, 57 Misc.2d 982, 293 N.Y.S.2d 1008 (N.Y.Sur.1968)—§ **20.2, n. 2**; § **20.3, n. 1.**

Kirkland v. Inhabitants of Whately, 86 Mass. 462 (Mass.1862)—§ **4.42, n. 3.**

Kirkpatrick v. Transtector Systems, 114 Idaho 559, 759 P.2d 65 (Idaho 1988)— § **4.15, n. 3.**

Kirmse v. Hotel Nikko, 59 Cal.Rptr.2d 96 (Cal.App. 1 Dist.1996)—§ **23.3, n. 10.**

Kirschbaum v. WRGSB Associates, 243 F.3d 145 (3rd Cir.2001)—§ **17.48, n. 5.**

Kirstein v. Kirstein, 64 N.C.App. 191, 306 S.E.2d 552 (N.C.App.1983)—§ **19.8, n. 14.**

Kitzman v. Kitzman, 167 Wis. 308, 166 N.W. 789 (Wis.1918)—§ **13.6, n. 4.**

Klaxon Co. v. Stentor Electric Mfg. Co., 313 U.S. 487, 61 S.Ct. 1020, 85 L.Ed. 1477 (1941)—§ **3.2, n. 5**; § **3.17, n. 11**; § **3.36**; § **3.36, n. 1**; § **10.18, n. 30**; § **11.4, n. 1**; § **24.6, n. 3**; § **24.35, n. 1, 4.**

Kleb v. Kleb, 62 A. 396 (N.J.Ch.1905)— § **14.15, n. 4, 11.**

Klehr v. A.O. Smith Corp., 521 U.S. 179, 117 S.Ct. 1984, 138 L.Ed.2d 373 (1997)—§ **9.8, n. 5.**

Klein v. French, 57 Miss. 662 (Miss.1880)—
§ **22.15, n. 4, 13.**

Klemp v. Franchise Tax Bd., 45 Cal.App.3d 870, 119 Cal.Rptr. 821 (Cal.App. 2 Dist. 1975)—§ **4.17, n. 4.**

KL Group v. Case, Kay & Lynch, 829 F.2d 909 (9th Cir.1987)—§ **17.19, n. 1.**

Kline v. Kline, 57 Iowa 386, 10 N.W. 825 (Iowa 1881)—§ **4.34, n. 1, 3;** § **4.40, n. 4.**

Klineman, Matter of, 105 Misc.2d 896, 430 N.Y.S.2d 24 (N.Y.Sur.1980)—§ **22.25, n. 1.**

Kling v. Sejour, 1849 WL 3848 (La.1849)—§ **19.5, n. 7.**

Klinger, Adoption of, 5 Pa. D. & C.2d 767, 6 Fiduc.Rep. 394 (Pa.Orph.1956)—§ **16.5, n. 5.**

Klippel v. U–Haul Co. of Northeastern Michigan, 759 F.2d 1176 (4th Cir. 1985)—§ **3.47, n. 2.**

Klipple's Estate, In re, 101 So.2d 924 (Fla. App. 3 Dist.1958)—§ **22.10, n. 11.**

Klondike Helicopters, Limited v. Fairchild Hiller Corp., 334 F.Supp. 890 (N.D.Ill. 1971)—§ **3.11, n. 4, 6.**

Klopotek, State ex rel. v. District Court of Sheridan County, 621 P.2d 223 (Wyo. 1980)—§ **22.26, n. 5.**

Klos v. Lotnicze, 133 F.3d 164 (2nd Cir. 1997)—§ **18.5, n. 1.**

Klutts v. Jones, 21 N.M. 720, 158 P. 490 (N.M.1916)—§ **4.20, n. 8.**

K Mart Corp. v. Gen–Star Industries Co., Ltd., 110 F.R.D. 310 (E.D.Mich.1986)—§ **11.15, n. 4.**

Knapp v. Knapp, 95 Mich. 474, 55 N.W. 353 (Mich.1893)—§ **20.3, n. 8.**

Knapp v. Lee, 42 Mich. 41, 3 N.W. 244 (Mich.1879)—§ **22.11, n. 13.**

Knapp v. State Farm Ins., 584 F.Supp. 905 (E.D.La.1984)—§ **4.33, n. 6.**

Knappenberger v. Bittner, 524 F.Supp. 777 (W.D.Pa.1981)—§ **17.59, n. 7.**

Kneeland v. Ensley, 19 Tenn. 620 (Tenn. 1839)—§ **14.8, n. 4.**

Knight v. Gallaway, 42 Wash. 413, 85 P. 21 (Wash.1906)—§ **16.5, n. 4.**

Knight v. Handley Motor Co., 198 A.2d 747 (D.C.App.1964)—§ **17.6, n. 4.**

Knight v. San Jacinto Club, Inc., 96 N.J.Super. 81, 232 A.2d 462 (N.J.Super.L.1967)—§ **7.3, n. 1.**

Knippel's Estate, In re, 7 Wis.2d 335, 96 N.W.2d 514 (Wis.1959)—§ **14.15, n. 3;** § **18.18, n. 5.**

Knoll v. Knoll, 104 Wash. 110, 176 P. 22 (Wash.1918)—§ **13.9, n. 3, 7.**

Knox v. Jones, 47 N.Y. 389 (N.Y.1872)—§ **19.6, n. 1.**

Knutson v. Rexair, Inc., 749 F.Supp. 214 (D.Minn.1990)—§ **11.6, n. 4.**

Kobogum v. Jackson Iron Co., 76 Mich. 498, 43 N.W. 602 (Mich.1889)—§ **13.17, n. 2;** § **13.18, n. 8.**

Koehler v. Koehler, 182 Misc.2d 436, 697 N.Y.S.2d 478 (N.Y.Sup.1999)—§ **14.6, n. 4.**

Koehr, State ex rel. Illinois Farmers Ins. Co. v., 834 S.W.2d 233 (Mo.App. E.D. 1992)—§ **8.2, n. 10.**

Kohlbusch v. Eberwein, 642 S.W.2d 683 (Mo.App. E.D.1982)—§ **24.13, n. 7.**

Kohler Co. v. Kohler Intern., Ltd., 196 F.Supp.2d 690 (N.D.Ill.2002)—§ **9.3, n. 4.**

Kohr v. Allegheny Airlines, Inc., 504 F.2d 400 (7th Cir.1974)—§ **3.53;** § **3.53, n. 7;** § **18.44, n. 9.**

Kokomo Times Pub. & Printing Corp., In re, 301 F.Supp. 529 (S.D.Ind.1968)—§ **19.25, n. 1.**

Kolentus v. Avco Corp., 798 F.2d 949 (7th Cir.1986)—§ **17.26, n. 1.**

Kolovrat v. Oregon, 366 U.S. 187, 81 S.Ct. 922, 6 L.Ed.2d 218 (1961)—§ **20.17, n. 7.**

Komlos v. Compagnie Nationale Air France, 209 F.2d 436 (2nd Cir.1953)—§ **22.10, n. 6.**

Komlos v. Compagnie Nationale Air France, 111 F.Supp. 393 (S.D.N.Y.1952)—§ **17.6, n. 9.**

Kopp v. Rechtzigel, 273 Minn. 441, 141 N.W.2d 526 (Minn.1966)—§ **17.5, n. 9.**

Korean Air Lines Disaster of Sept. 1, 1983, In re, 829 F.2d 1171, 265 U.S.App.D.C. 39 (D.C.Cir.1987)—§ **3.46, n. 20.**

Korean Air Lines Disaster of Sept. 1, 1983, In re, 664 F.Supp. 1478 (D.D.C.1986)—§ **3.46, n. 7;** § **11.14, n. 20.**

Korf v. Korf, 38 Wis.2d 413, 157 N.W.2d 691 (Wis.1968)—§ **13.6, n. 1;** § **13.9, n. 14;** § **13.13, n. 4, 5.**

Korn v. Korn, 398 F.2d 689 (3rd Cir. 1968)—§ **4.17, n. 4.**

Korsrud v. Korsrud, 242 Iowa 178, 45 N.W.2d 848 (Iowa 1951)—§ **15.7, n. 3.**

Kossick v. United Fruit Co., 365 U.S. 731, 81 S.Ct. 886, 6 L.Ed.2d 56 (1961)—§ **18.38, n. 9.**

Koster v. Lumbermens Mut.Cas. Co., 330 U.S. 518, 67 S.Ct. 828, 91 L.Ed. 1067 (1947)—§ **10.13, n. 9;** § **11.8, n. 3;** § **11.11, n. 10;** § **11.14, n. 1;** § **23.5, n. 5, 7.**

Koster v. Automark Industries, Inc., 640 F.2d 77 (7th Cir.1981)—§ **24.37, n. 3;** § **24.42, n. 5;** § **24.44, n. 5.**

Kotlisky v. Kotlisky, 195 Ill.App.3d 725, 142 Ill.Dec. 465, 552 N.E.2d 1206 (Ill.App. 1 Dist.1990)—§ **6.5, n. 15, 16.**

Koupetoris v. Konkar Intrepid Corp., 535 F.2d 1392 (2nd Cir.1976)—§ **17.63, n. 31.**

Kovacs v. Brewer, 356 U.S. 604, 78 S.Ct. 963, 2 L.Ed.2d 1008 (1958)—§ **15.39, n. 1.**

Kowalke's Guardianship, In re, 232 Minn. 292, 46 N.W.2d 275 (Minn.1950)— § **4.41, n. 2.**

Kowalski v. Wojtkowski, 19 N.J. 247, 116 A.2d 6 (N.J.1955)—§ **4.38, n. 1.**

Kraemer v. Kraemer, 52 Cal. 302 (Cal. 1877)—§ **14.9, n. 1.**

Kraemer's Estate, In re, 276 Cal.App.2d 715, 81 Cal.Rptr. 287 (Cal.App. 2 Dist. 1969)—§ **11.13, n. 15.**

Kraft v. Wickey, 1832 WL 1263 (Md.1832)— § **22.25, n. 1, 2.**

Kraham v. Kraham, 73 Misc.2d 977, 342 N.Y.S.2d 943 (N.Y.Sup.1973)—§ **15.22, n. 1.**

Krakow v. Department of Public Welfare, 326 Mass. 452, 95 N.E.2d 184 (Mass. 1950)—§ **4.38, n. 1.**

Kramer v. Bally's Park Place, Inc., 311 Md. 387, 535 A.2d 466 (Md.1988)—§ **18.4, n. 44.**

Kramer v. Kramer, 6 Conn.L.Rptr. 286 (Conn.Super.1992)—§ **15.38, n. 1.**

Kramer v. Showa Denko K.K., 929 F.Supp. 733 (S.D.N.Y.1996)—§ **17.43, n. 9;** § **17.44, n. 5;** § **17.50;** § **17.50, n. 49;** § **17.70;** § **17.70, n. 1.**

Kransco Mfg., Inc. v. Markwitz, 656 F.2d 1376 (9th Cir.1981)—§ **9.4, n. 10.**

Kranzler v. Austin, 189 Misc.2d 369, 732 N.Y.S.2d 328 (N.Y.Sup.App.Term 2001)—§ **17.42, n. 11.**

Krasnov v. Dinan, 465 F.2d 1298 (3rd Cir. 1972)—§ **4.27, n. 11.**

Krause v. Stroh Brewery Co., 240 F.Supp.2d 632 (E.D.Mich.2002)— § **17.40, n. 26.**

Krauss v. Manhattan Life Ins. Co. of New York, 643 F.2d 98 (2nd Cir.1981)— § **18.26, n. 10.**

Kremer v. Chemical Const. Corp., 456 U.S. 461, 102 S.Ct. 1883, 72 L.Ed.2d 262 (1982)—§ **24.12, n. 7.**

Kress Corp. v. Edw. C. Levy Co., 102 Ill. App.3d 264, 58 Ill.Dec. 561, 430 N.E.2d 593 (Ill.App. 3 Dist.1981)—§ **18.1, n. 19;** § **24.48, n. 1.**

Kreutter v. McFadden Oil Corp., 527 N.Y.S.2d 195, 522 N.E.2d 40 (N.Y. 1988)—§ **10.17, n. 4.**

Krey's Estate, In re, 183 Cal.App.2d 312, 6 Cal.Rptr. 804 (Cal.App. 4 Dist.1960)— § **14.9, n. 4.**

Krimsky v. Lombardi, 78 Misc.2d 685, 357 N.Y.S.2d 671 (N.Y.Sup.1974)—§ **22.19, n. 20;** § **22.20, n. 26.**

Krock v. Lipsay, 97 F.3d 640 (2nd Cir. 1996)—§ **17.40, n. 28;** § **18.1, n. 18.**

Kronovet v. Lipchin, 288 Md. 30, 415 A.2d 1096 (Md.1980)—§ **2.21, n. 57;** § **2.23, n. 9;** § **18.9, n. 7;** § **18.21, n. 7.**

Krumenacker v. Andis, 38 N.D. 500, 165 N.W. 524 (N.D.1917)—§ **22.22, n. 6.**

Kruse v. Kruse, 150 Kan. 946, 96 P.2d 849 (Kan.1939)—§ **4.40, n. 2.**

Kruskal v. United States, 178 F.2d 738 (2nd Cir.1950)—§ **22.18, n. 2, 4.**

Kubasko v. Kubasko, 2000 WL 1211219 (Del.Super.2000)—§ **17.60, n. 6.**

Kubeck v. Consolidated Underwriters, 267 Or. 548, 517 P.2d 1039 (Or.1974)— § **18.20, n. 11.**

Kubik v. Letteri, 532 Pa. 10, 614 A.2d 1110 (Pa.1992)—§ **5.14, n. 12.**

Kubis & Perszyk Associates, Inc. v. Sun Microsystems, Inc., 146 N.J. 176, 680 A.2d 618 (N.J.1996)—§ **18.4, n. 1, 44.**

Kuchenig v. California Co., 410 F.2d 222 (5th Cir.1969)—§ **16.2, n. 5;** § **19.2, n. 3;** § **20.2, n. 4.**

Kuchinic v. McCrory, 422 Pa. 620, 222 A.2d 897 (Pa.1966)—§ **17.12, n. 7.**

Kuehn v. Childrens Hosp., Los Angeles, 119 F.3d 1296 (7th Cir.1997)—§ **17.21, n. 15;** § **17.36, n. 15;** § **17.40, n. 28;** § **17.44;** § **17.44, n. 14;** § **18.1, n. 18.**

Kugler v. Haitian Tours, Inc., 120 N.J.Super. 260, 293 A.2d 706 (N.J.Super.Ch.1972)—§ **15.22, n. 1.**

Kuhn, State ex rel. v. Luchsinger, 231 Wis. 533, 286 N.W. 72 (Wis.1939)—§ **11.5, n. 3.**

Kula v. J.K. Schofield & Co., Inc., 668 F.Supp. 1126 (N.D.Ill.1987)—§ **3.47, n. 2.**

Kulko v. California Superior Court, 436 U.S. 84, 98 S.Ct. 1690, 56 L.Ed.2d 132 (1978)—§ **3.26, n. 2;** § **5.7, n. 5;** § **5.11;** § **5.11, n. 16;** § **15.22, n. 1;** § **15.28, n. 1;** § **15.30, n. 2;** § **15.31, n. 2.**

Kumar v. Superior Court, 186 Cal.Rptr. 772, 652 P.2d 1003 (Cal.1982)—§ **15.42, n. 9.**

Kupec v. Cooper, 593 So.2d 1176 (Fla.App. 5 Dist.1992)—§ **16.5, n. 1.**

Kurent v. Farmers Ins. of Columbus, 62 Ohio St.3d 242, 581 N.E.2d 533 (Ohio 1991)—§ **17.56, n. 16, 19.**

Kurtz v. Kurtz' Estate, 169 Md. 554, 182 A. 456 (Md.1936)—§ **22.3, n. 1.**

Kush v. Abbott Lab., 238 A.D.2d 172, 655 N.Y.S.2d 520 (N.Y.A.D. 1 Dept.1997)— § **17.44, n. 5.**

Kutzik v. Young, 730 F.2d 149 (4th Cir. 1984)—§ **24.12, n. 7.**

K & V Scientific Co., Inc. v. Bayerische Motoren Werke Aktiengesellschaft ("BMW"), 314 F.3d 494 (10th Cir. 2002)—§ **11.2, n. 4.**

Kyle, In re, 77 Cal.App.2d 634, 176 P.2d 96 (Cal.App. 1 Dist.1947)—§ **15.40, n. 3.**

Kyle v. Kyle, 128 So.2d 427 (Fla.App. 2 Dist.1961)—§ **19.3, n. 4.**

Kyser v. Board of Elections of Cuyahoga County, 36 Ohio St.2d 17, 303 N.E.2d 77 (Ohio 1973)—§ **4.29, n. 2.**

L

LaBeach v. Beatrice Foods Co., 461 F.Supp. 152 (S.D.N.Y.1978)—§ **18.7;** § **18.7, n. 7, 12.**

Labine v. Vincent, 401 U.S. 532, 91 S.Ct. 1017, 28 L.Ed.2d 288 (1971)—§ **3.54, n. 5;** § **16.3, n. 5.**

LaBounty v. American Ins. Co., 122 N.H. 738, 451 A.2d 161 (N.H.1982)—§ **2.13, n. 14.**

Labree v. Major, 111 R.I. 657, 306 A.2d 808 (R.I.1973)—§ **17.13, n. 23;** § **17.14, n. 2;** § **17.32, n. 2;** § **17.34, n. 10;** § **17.45;** § **17.45, n. 3.**

Laccetti v. Laccetti, 245 Md. 97, 225 A.2d 266 (Md.1967)—§ **13.6, n. 2.**

Lacey v. Cessna Aircraft Co., 932 F.2d 170 (3rd Cir.1991)—§ **17.76;** § **17.76, n. 22.**

LaChance v. Service Trucking Co., 215 F.Supp. 162 (D.Md.1963)—§ **17.6, n. 3.**

Laconis v. Burlington County Bridge Com'n, 400 Pa.Super. 483, 583 A.2d 1218 (Pa.Super.1990)—§ **17.43, n. 16.**

L & A Contracting Co. v. Southern Concrete Services, Inc., 17 F.3d 106 (5th Cir.1994)—§ **18.27, n. 3.**

Ladd v. Ladd, 265 Ark. 725, 580 S.W.2d 696 (Ark.1979)—§ **14.9, n. 3;** § **14.13, n. 8.**

LaFarge Corp. v. Travelers Indem. Co., 118 F.3d 1511 (11th Cir.1997)—§ **18.26, n. 13.**

Lafayette Ins. Co. v. French, 59 U.S. 404, 18 How. 404, 15 L.Ed. 451 (1855)— § **5.3, n. 17;** § **5.8, n. 4;** § **6.3, n. 2;** § **10.14, n. 4.**

Lafayette Radio Electronics Corp., In re, 761 F.2d 84 (2nd Cir.1985)—§ **23.12, n. 4.**

LaForge v. Normandin, 158 A.D.2d 990, 551 N.Y.S.2d 142 (N.Y.A.D. 4 Dept.1990)— § **17.45, n. 23.**

La Forte, People ex rel. v. Rubin, 98 N.Y.S. 787 (N.Y.Sup.1905)—§ **13.18, n. 8.**

La Framboise v. Day, 136 Minn. 239, 161 N.W. 529 (Minn.1917)—§ **13.18, n. 8, 9, 13.**

Laikola v. Engineered Concrete, 277 N.W.2d 653 (Minn.1979)—§ **13.6, n. 4;** § **13.9, n. 14;** § **15.16, n. 5.**

Laker Airways Ltd. v. Pan American World Airways, 103 F.R.D. 42 (D.D.C.1984)— § **12.9, n. 8.**

Lalli v. Lalli, 439 U.S. 259, 99 S.Ct. 518, 58 L.Ed.2d 503 (1978)—§ **16.3;** § **16.3, n. 8.**

La Luna Enterprises, Inc. v. CBS Corp., 74 F.Supp.2d 384 (S.D.N.Y.1999)—§ **17.55, n. 10.**

Lamar v. Micou, 114 U.S. 218, 5 S.Ct. 857, 29 L.Ed. 94 (1885)—§ **4.41, n. 6;** § **4.42, n. 1.**

Lamar v. Micou, 112 U.S. 452, 5 S.Ct. 221, 28 L.Ed. 751 (1884)—§ **4.41, n. 6;** § **4.42, n. 1, 3;** § **22.25;** § **22.25, n. 22.**

Lamb v. Volkswagenwerk Aktiengesellschaft, 104 F.R.D. 95 (S.D.Fla.1985)— § **12.7, n. 6;** § **23.20, n. 7.**

Lamberton v. Grant, 94 Me. 508, 48 A. 127 (Me.1901)—§ **24.5, n. 2.**

Lamb's Estate, Matter of, 99 N.M. 157, 655 P.2d 1001 (N.M.1982)—§ **13.6, n. 4;** § **15.16, n. 4.**

Lampert Through Thurston, Estate of v. Estate of Lampert Through Stauffer, 896 P.2d 214 (Alaska 1995)—§ **20.2, n. 10.**

Lance v. Lance, 195 Mont. 176, 635 P.2d 571 (Mont.1981)—§ **15.10, n. 2.**

Lancey's Guardianship, In re, 232 Iowa 191, 2 N.W.2d 787 (Iowa 1942)—§ **4.41, n. 7.**

Land v. Yamaha Motor Corp., 272 F.3d 514 (7th Cir.2001)—§ **17.78, n. 7.**

Lander Co., Inc. v. MMP Investments, Inc., 107 F.3d 476 (7th Cir.1997)—§ **24.48, n. 5.**

Landers v. Landers, 153 Conn. 303, 216 A.2d 183 (Conn.1966)—§ **17.5, n. 10.**

Landmark Land Co., Inc. v. Sprague, 529 F.Supp. 971 (S.D.N.Y.1981)—§ **3.7, n. 7.**

Landolfi, In re, 283 A.D.2d 497, 724 N.Y.S.2d 470 (N.Y.A.D. 2 Dept.2001)— § **13.11, n. 4.**

Landrum v. Board of Com'rs of Orleans Levee Dist., 758 F.Supp. 387 (E.D.La. 1991)—§ **7.10, n. 4.**

Landry, In re Marriage of, 103 Wash.2d 807, 699 P.2d 214 (Wash.1985)—§ **14.9, n. 2;** § **14.11, n. 2.**

Lane, Commonwealth v., 113 Mass. 458 (Mass.1873)—§ **13.9, n. 5, 8.**

Lane v. Lane, 20 Del. 368, 55 A. 184 (Del. Supr.1903)—§ **21.13, n. 4.**

Lane v. St. Louis Union Trust Co., 356 Mo. 76, 201 S.W.2d 288 (Mo.1947)—§ **20.9, n. 14.**

Lane v. Sullivan, 900 F.2d 1247 (8th Cir. 1990)—§ **24.1, n. 8.**

Lane–Burslem v. Commissioner, 659 F.2d 209, 212 U.S.App.D.C. 163 (D.C.Cir. 1981)—§ **14.9, n. 1.**

Lang v. Lang, 17 Utah 2d 10, 403 P.2d 655 (Utah 1965)—§ **22.18, n. 3.**

Langan v. St. Vincent's Hosp. of N.Y., 196 Misc.2d 440, 765 N.Y.S.2d 411 (N.Y.Sup. 2003)—§ **13.20, n. 9;** § **14.4, n. 13.**

Langdon v. New York, L.E. & W.R. Co., 58 Hun. 122, 11 N.Y.S. 514 (N.Y.Sup.Gen. Term 1890)—§ **3.17, n. 2.**

Langsam–Borenstein Partnership by Langsam v. NOC Enterprises, Inc., 137 F.R.D. 217 (E.D.Pa.1990)—§ **10.4, n. 10, 12, 14.**

Lang's Estate, In re, 301 Pa. 429, 152 A. 570 (Pa.1930)—§ **22.11, n. 7.**

Lanham, Matter of, 13 B.R. 45 (Bkrtcy. C.D.Ill.1981)—§ **23.13, n. 1.**

Lanham v. Lanham, 136 Wis. 360, 117 N.W. 787 (Wis.1908)—§ **13.9, n. 4, 7, 12.**

Lanier v. Union Mortg., Banking & Trust Co., 64 Ark. 39, 40 S.W. 466 (Ark. 1897)—§ **18.7, n. 8.**

Lans' Estate, In re, 29 Misc.2d 758, 210 N.Y.S.2d 611 (N.Y.Sur.1960)—§ **20.6, n. 13.**

Lansverk v. Studebaker–Packard Corp., 54 Wash.2d 124, 338 P.2d 747 (Wash. 1959)—§ **11.8, n. 3.**

Lapham v. Olney, 5 R.I. 413 (R.I.1858)— § **20.6, n. 1.**

Lapham–Hickey Steel Corp. v. Protection Mut. Ins. Co., 166 Ill.2d 520, 211 Ill.Dec. 459, 655 N.E.2d 842 (Ill.1995)—§ **2.21, n. 59;** § **18.26, n. 12.**

La Plante v. American Honda Motor Co., Inc., 27 F.3d 731 (1st Cir.1994)— § **17.21, n. 16, 18;** § **17.23, n. 6;** § **17.73, n. 4;** § **17.74, n. 2.**

Lappert v. Lappert, 283 N.Y.S.2d 26, 229 N.E.2d 599 (N.Y.1967)—§ **15.20, n. 6.**

Larch, In re, 872 F.2d 66 (4th Cir.1989)— § **15.42, n. 15.**

LaRose v. Sponco Mfg. Inc., 712 F.Supp. 455 (D.N.J.1989)—§ **7.2, n. 20.**

Larsen v. A.C. Carpenter, Inc., 620 F.Supp. 1084 (E.D.N.Y.1985)—§ **18.24, n. 2, 4.**

Larson, State ex rel. v. Larson, 190 Minn. 489, 252 N.W. 329 (Minn.1934)—§ **4.37, n. 3;** § **4.40, n. 4.**

La Salle Nat. Bank of Chicago v. Akande, 235 Ill.App.3d 53, 175 Ill.Dec. 780, 600 N.E.2d 1238 (Ill.App. 2 Dist.1992)— § **8.7, n. 5.**

La Selle v. Woolery, 14 Wash. 70, 44 P. 115 (Wash.1896)—§ **14.16, n. 12.**

La Selle v. Woolery, 11 Wash. 337, 39 P. 663 (Wash.1895)—§ **14.16, n. 10.**

Laskosky v. Laskosky, 504 So.2d 726 (Miss. 1987)—§ **5.21, n. 9.**

La Societe Anonyme Goro v. Conveyor Accessories, Inc., 286 Ill.App.3d 867, 222 Ill.Dec. 217, 677 N.E.2d 30 (Ill.App. 2 Dist.1997)—§ **24.36, n. 2.**

Lassin's Estate, In re, 33 Wash.2d 163, 204 P.2d 1071 (Wash.1949)—§ **4.21, n. 2.**

Lathrop's Estate, In re, 165 Cal. 243, 131 P. 752 (Cal.1913)—§ **20.9, n. 10;** § **20.10, n. 4.**

Latine v. Clements, 3 Ga. 426 (Ga.1847)— § **22.20, n. 14, 29.**

La Tourette v. McMaster, 248 U.S. 465, 39 S.Ct. 160, 63 L.Ed. 362 (1919)—§ **3.32;** § **3.32, n. 8.**

Latrobe Const. Co., United States v., 246 F.2d 357 (8th Cir.1957)—§ **3.51, n. 10.**

Laufer v. Ostrow, 449 N.Y.S.2d 456, 434 N.E.2d 692 (N.Y.1982)—§ **5.13, n. 20;** § **6.9, n. 19.**

Laughlin v. Solomon, 180 Pa. 177, 36 A. 704 (Pa.1897)—§ **22.19, n. 23.**

Laun v. Kipp, 155 Wis. 347, 145 N.W. 183 (Wis.1914)—§ **24.17, n. 3.**

Lauritzen v. Larsen, 345 U.S. 571, 73 S.Ct. 921, 97 L.Ed. 1254 (1953)—§ **2.14, n. 18;** § **2.16;** § **2.16, n. 5;** § **17.63, n. 10, 11, 22;** § **18.1, n. 3;** § **18.4, n. 7.**

Lauterbach v. Lauterbach, 392 P.2d 24 (Alaska 1964)—§ **4.26, n. 6;** § **15.5, n. 2;** § **15.19, n. 3.**

LaVallee v. Parrot–Ice Drink Products of America, Inc., 193 F.Supp.2d 296 (D.Mass.2002)—§ **7.12, n. 9.**

Lawlor v. Gallagher Presidents' Report, Inc., 394 F.Supp. 721 (S.D.N.Y.1975)— § **17.55, n. 3.**

Lawrence, Appeal of, 49 Conn. 411 (Conn. 1881)—§ **22.21, n. 8.**

Lawrence v. Kitteridge, 21 Conn. 577 (Conn.1852)—§ **20.3, n. 1, 7;** § **22.23, n. 9.**

Lawrence v. Lawrence, [1985] 3 W.L.R. 125, 2 All. E.R. 733 (CA)— § **13.9, n. 13;** § **15.26, 4.**

Lawrence v. Lawrence, [1985] 2 W.L.R. 86, 1 All. E.R. 506 (Fam.)—§ **13.4, n. 4;** § **13.9, n. 13.**

Lawrence v. Nelson, 143 U.S. 215, 12 S.Ct. 440, 36 L.Ed. 130 (1892)—§ **22.19, n. 24.**

Lawrence v. State Tax Commission of Mississippi, 286 U.S. 276, 52 S.Ct. 556, 76 L.Ed. 1102 (1932)—§ **4.30, n. 1.**

Lawson v. Morgan, 352 F.Supp. 282 (E.D.Pa.1973)—§ **4.17, n. 2.**

Lawton v. National Surety Co., 248 Mass. 440, 143 N.E. 333 (Mass.1924)—§ **22.23, n. 1.**

Layton v. Pribble, 200 Va. 405, 105 S.E.2d 864 (Va.1958)—§ **22.25, n. 4.**

Layton's Estate, In re, 217 Cal. 451, 19 P.2d 793 (Cal.1933)—§ **20.10, n. 4.**

Lazard Freres & Co. v. Protective Life Ins. Co., 108 F.3d 1531 (2nd Cir.1997)— § **18.4, n. 44.**

L.C. Jones Trucking Co. v. Superior Oil Co., 68 Wyo. 384, 234 P.2d 802 (Wyo.1951)— § **10.12, n. 9.**

Lea v. Dudley, 20 N.C.App. 702, 202 S.E.2d 799 (N.C.App.1974)—§ **19.8, n. 14.**

Lea v. Lea, 18 N.J. 1, 112 A.2d 540 (N.J. 1955)—§ **4.19, n. 3.**

Leach v. Buckner, 19 W.Va. 36 (W.Va. 1881)—§ **22.23, n. 5.**

Leach v. Leach, 238 Mass. 100, 130 N.E. 262 (Mass.1921)—§ **22.21, n. 2.**

Leahy v. Haworth, 141 F. 850 (8th Cir. 1905)—§ **22.14, n. 7.**

Leane v. Joseph Entertainment Group, Inc., 267 Ill.App.3d 1036, 204 Ill.Dec. 951, 642 N.E.2d 852 (Ill.App. 1 Dist.1994)— § **17.48, n. 5.**

Leary v. Gledhill, 8 N.J. 260, 84 A.2d 725 (N.J.1951)—§ **12.19, n. 9, 11.**

Leasco Data Processing Equipment Corp. v. Maxwell, 468 F.2d 1326 (2nd Cir. 1972)—§ **9.6, n. 19.**

Leasing Service Corp. v. Patterson Enterprises, Ltd., 633 F.Supp. 282 (S.D.N.Y. 1986)—§ **11.14, n. 6.**

Lebel v. Everglades Marina, Inc., 115 N.J. 317, 558 A.2d 1252 (N.J.1989)—§ **7.3, n. 10.**

Le Breton v. Miles, 8 Paige Ch. 261, 4 N.Y. Ch. Ann. 422 (N.Y.Ch.1840)—§ **14.15, n. 10.**

LeClair v. Powers, 632 P.2d 370 (Okla. 1981)—§ **11.17, n. 39.**

LeClert v. LeClert, 80 N.M. 235, 453 P.2d 755 (N.M.1969)—§ **14.13, n. 8.**

Lectric's & Inc. v. Power Controls, Inc., 1995 WL 809558 (Mass.Super.1995)— § **18.12, n. 1.**

Ledee v. Ceramiche Ragno, 684 F.2d 184 (1st Cir.1982)—§ **24.48, n. 4, 7.**

Lee v. Commissioner, 550 F.2d 1201 (9th Cir.1977)—§ **15.13, n. 8.**

Lee v. Great Northern Nekoosa Corp., 465 F.2d 1132 (5th Cir.1972)—§ **23.7, n. 6.**

Lee v. Ohio Cas. Ins. Co., 445 F.Supp. 189 (D.Del.1978)—§ **10.8, n. 15.**

Lee v. Saliga, 179 W.Va. 762, 373 S.E.2d 345 (W.Va.1988)—§ **2.17, n. 11; § 2.23, n. 5.**

Leeco Steel Products, Inc. v. Ferrostaal Metals Corp., 698 F.Supp. 724 (N.D.Ill. 1988)—§ **7.6, n. 8.**

Lees v. Harding, Whitman & Co., 60 A. 352 (N.J.Err. & App.1905)—§ **19.11, n. 7; § 19.13, n. 4, 9, 10.**

Lee, Town of v. Town of Lincoln, 351 A.2d 554 (Me.1976)—§ **21.3, n. 9.**

Leff v. Leff, 25 Cal.App.3d 630, 102 Cal. Rptr. 195 (Cal.App. 2 Dist.1972)— § **14.5, n. 2.**

Lefferts v. Lefferts, 263 N.Y. 131, 188 N.E. 279 (N.Y.1933)—§ **4.24, n. 3.**

Le Forest v. Tolman, 117 Mass. 109 (Mass. 1875)—§ **17.3, n. 5.**

Legel Braswell Government Securities Corp., In re, 695 F.2d 506 (11th Cir. 1983)—§ **19.18, n. 7.**

Legg v. Chopra, 286 F.3d 286 (6th Cir. 2002)—§ **3.39, n. 7.**

Lehman v. Dow Jones & Co., Inc., 606 F.Supp. 1152 (S.D.N.Y.1985)—§ **3.37, n. 5.**

Lehman Bros. Commercial Corp. v. Minmetals Intern. Non–Ferrous Metals Trading Co., 179 F.Supp.2d 118 (S.D.N.Y. 2000)—§ **18.4, n. 51.**

Lehmer v. Hardy, 294 F. 407 (D.C.Cir. 1923)—§ **4.41, n. 6, 7; § 4.42, n. 1.**

Lehr, In re Guardianship of, 249 Iowa 625, 87 N.W.2d 909 (Iowa 1958)—§ **4.41, n. 6.**

Lehr v. Robertson, 463 U.S. 248, 103 S.Ct. 2985, 77 L.Ed.2d 614 (1983)—§ **16.5, n. 7.**

Leighton v. Roper, 300 N.Y. 434, 91 N.E.2d 876 (N.Y.1950)—§ **22.19, n. 32.**

Leisure Group, Inc. v. Edwin F. Armstrong & Co., 404 F.2d 610 (8th Cir.1968)— § **18.33, n. 3.**

LeJeune v. Bliss–Salem, Inc., 85 F.3d 1069 (3rd Cir.1996)—§ **17.74, n. 20; § 17.78, n. 12.**

Lembcke v. United States, 181 F.2d 703 (2nd Cir.1950)—§ **13.9, n. 5.**

Lemley v. Barr, 176 W.Va. 378, 343 S.E.2d 101 (W.Va.1986)—§ **16.6, n. 2.**

Lemme v. Wine of Japan Import, Inc., 631 F.Supp. 456 (E.D.N.Y.1986)—§ **11.6, n. 8.**

Lemoine v. Roberson, 366 So.2d 1009 (La. App. 1 Cir.1978)—§ **22.25, n. 1.**

Lemonis v. Prudential–Grace Lines, Inc., 81 Misc.2d 614, 366 N.Y.S.2d 541 (N.Y.Sup. 1975)—§ **17.63, n. 31.**

Lenherr's Estate, In re, 455 Pa. 225, 314 A.2d 255 (Pa.1974)—§ **13.2, n. 10; § 13.6, n. 1; § 13.9, n. 15.**

Lenn v. Riche, 331 Mass. 104, 117 N.E.2d 129 (Mass.1954)—§ **22.7, n. 5.**

Leo Feist, Inc. v. Debmar Pub. Co., 232 F.Supp. 623 (E.D.Pa.1964)—§ **24.6, n. 3; § 24.35, n. 8.**

Leon v. Galceran, 78 U.S. 185, 20 L.Ed. 74 (1870)—§ **10.6, n. 18.**

Leon v. Numkena, 142 Ariz. 307, 689 P.2d 566 (Ariz.App. Div. 1 1984)—§ **2.7, n. 14.**

Leonard v. Johns–Manville Sales Corp., 309 N.C. 91, 305 S.E.2d 528 (N.C.1983)— § **2.21, n. 22.**

Leonard v. Paxson, 654 S.W.2d 440 (Tex. 1983)—§ **11.5, n. 6.**

Leonard v. Wharton, 268 F.Supp. 715 (D.Md.1967)—§ **3.10, n. 6; § 22.14, n. 9; § 22.20, n. 5, 11.**

Leroux v. Brown, 138 Eng.R. 1119 (C.P. 1852)—§ **3.3, n. 2.**

Leroy v. Great Western United Corp., 443 U.S. 173, 99 S.Ct. 2710, 61 L.Ed.2d 464 (1979)—§ **5.18, n. 8; § 9.6; § 9.6, n. 8.**

Le Roy Dyal Co., United States v., 186 F.2d 460 (3rd Cir.1950)—§ **3.52, n. 3.**

Leslie v. Construcciones Aeronauticas, S.A. (CASA), 896 F.Supp. 243 (D.Puerto Rico 1995)—§ **17.26, n. 1.**

Lessard v. Clarke, 143 N.H. 555, 736 A.2d 1226 (N.H.1999)—§ **2.13, n. 25; § 17.21, n. 13, 28; § 17.22, n. 3; § 17.23, n. 11, 13; § 17.39, n. 16.**

Lester v. Aetna Life Ins. Co., 433 F.2d 884 (5th Cir.1970)—§ **3.47; § 3.47, n. 3.**

LeSueur, In re, 53 B.R. 414 (Bkrtcy.D.Ariz. 1985)—§ **14.16, n. 16.**

Leszinske v. Poole, 110 N.M. 663, 798 P.2d 1049 (N.M.App.1990)—§ **13.11, n. 4; § 13.12, n. 4.**

Letter of Request for Judicial Assistance from Tribunal Civil de Port-au–Prince, Republic of Haiti, In re, 669 F.Supp. 403 (S.D.Fla.1987)—§ **12.8, n. 4.**

Letters of Request to Examine Witnesses from Court of Queen's Bench for Manitoba, Canada, In re, 59 F.R.D. 625 (N.D.Cal.1973)—§ **12.8, n. 6.**

Letters Rogatory from City of Haugesund, Norway, In re, 497 F.2d 378 (9th Cir. 1974)—§ **12.6, n. 9.**

Letters Rogatory from Tokyo Dist., Tokyo, Japan, In re, 539 F.2d 1216 (9th Cir. 1976)—§ **12.8, n. 4.**

Letters Rogatory Issued By Director of Inspection of Government of India, In re, 272 F.Supp. 758 (S.D.N.Y.1967)—§ **12.8; § 12.8, n. 2.**

Letters Rogatory out of First Civil Court of City of Mexico, In re, 261 F. 652 (S.D.N.Y.1919)—§ **12.6, n. 9.**

Levc v. Connors, 171 Mont. 1, 555 P.2d 750 (Mont.1976)—§ **20.17, n. 5.**

Levicky v. Levicky, 49 N.J.Super. 562, 140 A.2d 534 (N.J.Super.Ch.1958)—§ **15.43, n. 9; § 24.46, n. 2.**

Levie, Estate of, 50 Cal.App.3d 572, 123 Cal.Rptr. 445 (Cal.App. 1 Dist.1975)—§ **13.6, n. 3.**

Levin v. Gladstein, 142 N.C. 482, 55 S.E. 371 (N.C.1906)—§ **24.17, n. 13.**

Levine v. Levine, 95 Or. 94, 187 P. 609 (Or.1920)—§ **15.34, n. 1.**

Levy v. Daniels' U–Drive Auto Renting Co., 108 Conn. 333, 143 A. 163 (Conn. 1928)—§ **2.16; § 2.16, n. 1; § 3.4, n. 5; § 17.8; § 17.8, n. 5.**

Levy v. Downing, 213 Mass. 334, 100 N.E. 638 (Mass.1913)—§ **13.12, n. 1.**

Levy v. Levy, 185 A.D.2d 15, 592 N.Y.S.2d 480 (N.Y.A.D. 3 Dept.1993)—§ **15.28, n. 1.**

Levy v. Levy, 33 N.Y. 97 (N.Y.1865)—§ **19.6, n. 3.**

Levy v. Louisiana, 391 U.S. 68, 88 S.Ct. 1509, 20 L.Ed.2d 436 (1968)—§ **3.54, n. 5; § 16.3, n. 2.**

Levy v. Mutual Life Ins. Co. of N.Y., 56 N.Y.S.2d 32 (N.Y.Sup.1945)—§ **12.11; § 12.11, n. 4.**

Levy v. Steiger, 233 Mass. 600, 124 N.E. 477 (Mass.1919)—§ **3.8, n. 7.**

Lewald v. York Corp, 68 F.Supp. 386 (S.D.N.Y.1946)—§ **23.5, n. 7.**

Lewal's Settlement Trusts, In re, 2 Ch. 391 (1981)—§ **21.10, n. 11.**

Lewandowski v. National Grange Mut. Ins. Co., 149 N.J.Super. 591, 374 A.2d 489 (N.J.Super.L.1977)—§ **3.13, n. 4.**

Lewis v. Adams, 70 Cal. 403, 11 P. 833 (Cal.1886)—§ **22.18, n. 9; § 22.20, n. 38.**

Lewis v. American Family Ins. Group, 555 S.W.2d 579 (Ky.1977)—§ **2.17, n. 10; § 2.23, n. 2, 6; § 18.21, n. 14, 19.**

Lewis v. Dicker, 118 Misc.2d 28, 459 N.Y.S.2d 215 (N.Y.Sup.1982)—§ **23.4, n. 2.**

Lewis v. Doerle, 1897 WL 10661 (Ont. H.C. 1897)—§ **20.6, n. 18; § 20.7, n. 1.**

Lewis v. Fresne, 252 F.3d 352 (5th Cir. 2001)—§ **9.6, n. 21.**

Lewis v. Hanson, 36 Del.Ch. 235, 128 A.2d 819 (Del.Supr.1957)—§ **21.3; § 21.3, n. 16, 17; § 21.9, n. 2; § 21.11, n. 17.**

Lewis v. Johns, 24 Cal. 98 (Cal.1864)—§ **14.7, n. 3; § 14.10, n. 2.**

Lewis v. Lewis, 69 Haw. 497, 748 P.2d 1362 (Hawai'i 1988)—§ **2.17, n. 12; § 2.25, n. 13; § 14.15, n. 2; § 18.21, n. 17.**

Lewis v. Lewis, 471 S.W.2d 290 (Ky.1971)—§ **15.29, n. 3.**

Lewis v. Missouri, K. & T. Ry. Co., 82 Kan. 351, 108 P. 95 (Kan.1910)—§ **4.43, n. 1.**

Lewis–DeBoer v. Mooney Aircraft Corp., 728 F.Supp. 642 (D.Colo.1990)—§ **17.50, n. 16; § 17.76, n. 16, 29.**

Lewis Mfg. Co. v. Superior Court In and For Los AngelesCounty, 140 Cal.App.2d 245, 295 P.2d 145 (Cal.App. 2 Dist. 1956)—§ **10.12, n. 9.**

Lewis Tree Service, Inc. v. Lucent Technologies Inc., 239 F.Supp.2d 322 (S.D.N.Y. 2002)—§ **17.40, n. 28.**

Lexecon Inc. v. Milberg Weiss Bershad Hynes & Lerach, 523 U.S. 26, 118 S.Ct. 956, 140 L.Ed.2d 62 (1998)—§ **11.14, n. 19.**

Lexie v. State Farm Mut. Auto. Ins. Co., 251 Va. 390, 469 S.E.2d 61 (Va.1996)—§ **2.21, n. 45; § 18.21, n. 12.**

Lezine v. Security Pacific Financial, 58 Cal. Rptr.2d 76, 925 P.2d 1002 (Cal.1996)—§ **14.6, n. 6.**

LFC Lessors, Inc. v. Pacific Sewer Maintenance Corp., 739 F.2d 4 (1st Cir.1984)—§ **11.2, n. 6.**

Liaw Su Teng v. Skaarup Shipping Corp., 743 F.2d 1140 (5th Cir.1984)—§ **11.10, n. 8.**

Liberty Mut. Ins. Co. v. Triangle Industries, Inc., 182 W.Va. 580, 390 S.E.2d 562 (W.Va.1990)—§ **18.29, n. 4.**

Liberty Nat. Bank & Trust Co. v. United States, 867 F.2d 302 (6th Cir.1989)—§ **20.8, n. 8.**

Liberty Sales Associates, Inc. v. Dow Corning Corp., 816 F.Supp. 1004 (D.N.J. 1993)—§ **18.5, n. 32.**

Lichtenberger v. Graham, 50 Ind. 288 (Ind. 1875)—§ **14.9, n. 3.**

Lichter v. Fritsch, 77 Wis.2d 178, 252 N.W.2d 360 (Wis.1977)—§ **2.13, n. 14; § 2.16, n. 9; § 17.21, n. 15, 27.**

Lidoriki Maritime Corp., In re, 404 F.Supp. 1402 (E.D.Pa.1975)—§ **17.63, n. 31.**

Lieb v. Lieb, 53 A.D.2d 67, 385 N.Y.S.2d 569 (N.Y.A.D. 2 Dept.1976)—§ **15.28, n. 1.**

Lieblein v. Charles Chips, Inc., 32 A.D.2d 1016, 301 N.Y.S.2d 743 (N.Y.A.D. 3 Dept.1969)—§ **13.9, n. 5.**

Lieuallen v. Young, 115 Okla. 153, 241 P. 342 (Okla.1925)—§ **22.19, n. 24.**

Liew v. Official Receiver and Liquidator (Hong Kong), 685 F.2d 1192 (9th Cir. 1982)—§ **17.19, n. 1.**

Ligget v. Fidelity & Columbia Trust Co., 274 Ky. 387, 118 S.W.2d 720 (Ky. 1938)—§ **21.11, n. 2, 15.**

Liggett Group Inc. v. Affiliated FM Ins. Co., 788 A.2d 134 (Del.Super.2001)—§ **18.1, n. 27.**

Light v. Light, 12 Ill.2d 502, 147 N.E.2d 34 (Ill.1957)—§ **15.34, n. 7.**

Lilienthal v. Kaufman, 239 Or. 1, 395 P.2d 543 (Or.1964)—§ **2.9, n. 23; § 2.17, n. 8; § 2.24, n. 5; § 3.16, n. 5; § 3.28; § 3.28, n. 3; § 18.5, n. 40; § 18.20; § 18.20, n. 2; § 18.27, n. 5.**

Liljedahl v. Glassgow, 190 Iowa 827, 180 N.W. 870 (Iowa 1921)—§ **19.9, n. 11.**

Lillegraven v. Tengs, 375 P.2d 139 (Alaska 1962)—§ **3.10, n. 1, 5.**

Lily R., In re, 283 A.D.2d 901, 724 N.Y.S.2d 231 (N.Y.A.D. 4 Dept.2001)—§ **16.7, n. 9.**

LINC Finance Corp. v. Onwuteaka, 129 F.3d 917 (7th Cir.1997)—§ **8.7, n. 4.**

Lincoln v. Aldrich, 149 Mass. 368, 21 N.E. 671 (Mass.1889)—§ **20.8, n. 8; § 20.13, n. 4.**

Lincoln Nat. Life Ins. Co. v. NCR Corp., 603 F.Supp. 1393 (N.D.Ind.1984)—§ **3.8, n. 3.**

Lindsay, In re, 59 F.3d 942 (9th Cir.1995)—§ **2.23, n. 8; § 19.2, n. 3; § 23.15, n. 20.**

Lindsay v. Wilson, 103 Md. 252, 63 A. 566 (Md.1906)—§ **20.6, n. 3, 15.**

Lindsey v. Lindsey, 388 N.W.2d 713 (Minn. 1986)—§ **15.10, n. 2.**

Lindsley v. Patterson, 177 S.W. 826 (Mo. 1915)—§ **20.15, n. 4, 5.**

Ling v. Jan's Liquors, 237 Kan. 629, 703 P.2d 731 (Kan.1985)—§ **2.21, n. 2.**

Lingen v. Lingen, 45 Ala. 410 (Ala.1871)—§ **16.1, n. 12.**

Lingscheit, Matter of Estate of, 387 N.W.2d 738 (S.D.1986)—§ **20.14, n. 1.**

Linn v. Delaware Child Support Enforcement, 736 A.2d 954 (Del.Supr.1999)—§ **15.34, n. 8.**

Linton v. Moorhead, 209 Pa. 646, 59 A. 264 (Pa.1904)—§ **19.3, n. 1.**

Linton & Co., Inc. v. Robert Reid Engineers, Inc., 504 F.Supp. 1169 (M.D.Ala. 1981)—§ **23.7, n. 6.**

Linville v. Price, 572 F.Supp. 345 (S.D.W.Va.1983)—§ **4.37, n. 3; § 4.40, n. 6; § 4.43, n. 5.**

Linzer v. EMI Blackwood Music, Inc., 904 F.Supp. 207 (S.D.N.Y.1995)—§ **9.3, n. 5.**

Lion Capital Group, In re, 46 B.R. 850 (Bkrtcy.S.D.N.Y.1985)—§ **23.12, n. 15.**

Lisak v. Mercantile Bancorp, Inc., 834 F.2d 668 (7th Cir.1987)—§ **10.2, n. 15.**

Lisi v. Alitalia–Linee Aeree Italiane, S. p. A., 370 F.2d 508 (2nd Cir.1966)—§ **3.57, n. 21.**

Lister v. NationsBank of Delaware, N.A., 329 S.C. 133, 494 S.E.2d 449 (S.C.App. 1997)—§ **2.21, n. 53; § 18.21, n. 10.**

Lit v. Storer Broadcasting Co., 217 Pa.Super. 186, 269 A.2d 393 (Pa.Super.1970)—§ **10.16, n. 8.**

Little v. Little, 513 So.2d 464 (La.App. 2 Cir.1987)—§ **14.11, n. 2.**

Littlefield v. Inhabitants of Brooks, 50 Me. 475 (Me.1862)—§ **4.17, n. 4; § 4.19, n. 2.**

Littlefield v. Mobil Exploration and Producing, North America, Inc., 988 F.Supp. 1403 (D.Utah 1996)—§ **17.60, n. 5.**

Little Horn State Bank v. Stops, 170 Mont. 510, 555 P.2d 211 (Mont.1976)—§ **11.17, n. 40.**

Little Lake Misere Land Co., Inc., United States v., 412 U.S. 580, 93 S.Ct. 2389, 37 L.Ed.2d 187 (1973)—§ **3.50, n. 7; § 3.52, n. 2; § 3.54, n. 15; § 23.14, n. 3.**

Livermore v. Jenckes, 62 U.S. 126, 21 How. 126, 16 L.Ed. 55 (1858)—§ **19.30, n. 6.**

Liverpool & London Life & Fire Ins. Co. v. State of Massachusetts, 77 U.S. 566, 19 L.Ed. 1029 (1870)—§ **23.2, n. 15.**

Livingston v. Jefferson, 15 F.Cas. 660 (C.C.D.Va.1811)—§ **5.18; § 5.18, n. 13; § 7.7; § 7.7, n. 2.**

Lloyd v. Classic Motor Coaches, Inc., 388 F.Supp. 785 (N.D.Ohio 1974)—§ **19.12, n. 2.**

Lloyd v. Loeffler, 694 F.2d 489 (7th Cir. 1982)—§ **15.42, n. 13; § 18.1, n. 18.**

L. M. S. Associates, Inc., In re, 18 B.R. 425 (Bkrtcy.S.D.Fla.1982)—§ **23.15, n. 14.**

Loader Leasing Corp. v. Penn Erection & Rigging Co., Inc., 566 F.Supp. 348 (W.D.Pa.1982)—§ **24.14, n. 3.**

Local Loan Co. v. Hunt, 292 U.S. 234, 54 S.Ct. 695, 78 L.Ed. 1230 (1934)—§ **23.14, n. 7; § 24.9, n. 11.**

Local 1804–1, Intern. Longshoremen's Ass'n, AFL–CIO, United States v., 44 F.3d 1091 (2nd Cir.1995)—§ **12.5, n. 4.**

Locke v. McPherson, 163 Mo. 493, 63 S.W. 726 (Mo.1901)—§ **14.8, n. 5.**

Lockert v. Breedlove, 321 N.C. 66, 361 S.E.2d 581 (N.C.1987)—§ **6.2, n. 13.**

Locknane v. United States Savings & Loan Co., 103 Ky. 265, 44 S.W. 977 (Ky. 1898)—§ **18.7, n. 11.**

Lockwood v. M/S Royal Viking Star, 663 F.Supp. 181 (C.D.Cal.1986)—§ **17.63, n. 22.**

Lockwood v. United States Steel Corporation, 209 N.Y. 375, 103 N.E. 697 (N.Y. 1913)—§ **22.12, n. 8.**

Lockwood Corp., Matter of, 216 B.R. 628 (Bkrtcy.D.Neb.1997)—§ **10.7, n. 18.**

Loewenthal v. Mandell, 125 Fla. 685, 170 So. 169 (Fla.1936)—§ **22.3, n. 9.**

Loftin v. Carden, 203 Ala. 405, 83 So. 174 (Ala.1919)—§ **4.41, n. 7.**

Lofton v. Turbine Design, Inc., 100 F.Supp.2d 404 (N.D.Miss.2000)—§ **7.8, n. 14, 16.**

Loftus v. Lee, 308 S.W.2d 654 (Mo.1958)—§ **11.8, n. 3.**

Lohman v. Kansas City Southern Ry. Co., 326 Mo. 819, 33 S.W.2d 112 (Mo.1930)— § 22.12, n. 8.

Lommen v. City of East Grand Forks, 522 N.W.2d 148 (Minn.App.1994)—§ 2.13, n. 23; § 17.21, n. 14; § 17.23, n. 7, 11; § 17.43; § 17.43, n. 26.

London, Paris & American Bank v. Aronstein, 117 F. 601 (9th Cir.1902)— § 22.12, n. 3.

Londre by Long v. Continental Western Ins. Co., 117 Wis.2d 54, 343 N.W.2d 128 (Wis.App.1983)—§ 4.37, n. 3.

Long v. Hess, 154 Ill. 482, 40 N.E. 335 (Ill.1895)—§ 14.15, n. 4, 9.

Long v. Holland America Line Westours, Inc., 26 P.3d 430 (Alaska 2001)— § 17.40, n. 26; § 18.1, n. 17; § 18.4, n. 7.

Long v. Pan Am. World Airways, Inc., 266 N.Y.S.2d 513, 213 N.E.2d 796 (N.Y. 1965)—§ 17.30; § 17.30, n. 11.

Long v. Sears Roebuck & Co., 877 F.Supp. 8 (D.D.C.1995)—§ 17.50; § 17.50, n. 37; § 17.72; § 17.72, n. 2, 10.

Longines–Wittnauer Watch Co. v. Barnes & Reinecke, Inc., 261 N.Y.S.2d 8, 209 N.E.2d 68 (N.Y.1965)—§ 5.14, n. 15.

Longshore's Will, In re, 188 Iowa 743, 176 N.W. 902 (Iowa 1920)—§ 22.3, n. 15; § 22.4, n. 8.

Lopez v. Bonner, 439 P.2d 687 (Okla. 1967)—§ 13.5, n. 1.

Lops v. Lops, 140 F.3d 927 (11th Cir. 1998)—§ 15.42, n. 17.

Loranger v. Nadeau, 215 Cal. 362, 10 P.2d 63 (Cal.1932)—§ 17.5, n. 9.

Lord v. Maryland Auto. Ins. Fund, 38 Md. App. 374, 381 A.2d 23 (Md.App.1977)— § 17.58, n. 6.

Lord Cranstown v. Johnston, 3 Ves.Jr. 170 (1796)—§ 19.8, n. 1.

Lorenz v. Royer, 194 Or. 355, 241 P.2d 142 (Or.1952)—§ 4.37, n. 2, 6; § 4.40, n. 2.

Lorenz–Auxier Financial Group, Inc. v. Bidewell, 160 Ariz. 218, 772 P.2d 41 (Ariz.App. Div. 1 1989)—§ 14.13, n. 8.

Los Angeles Airways, Inc. v. Lummis, 603 S.W.2d 246 (Tex.Civ.App.-Hous. (14 Dist.) 1980)—§ 4.23, n. 3.

Losson v. Blodgett, 1 Cal.App.2d 13, 36 P.2d 147 (Cal.App. 2 Dist.1934)—§ 19.3, n. 9.

Loth v. Loth's Estate, 54 Colo. 200, 129 P. 827 (Colo.1913)—§ 13.9, n. 5.

Lotz v. Atamaniuk, 172 W.Va. 116, 304 S.E.2d 20 (W.Va.1983)—§ 20.14, n. 1.

Loucks v. Standard Oil Co. of New York, 224 N.Y. 99, 120 N.E. 198 (N.Y.1918)— § 2.21, n. 12; § 3.15; § 3.15, n. 2; § 3.17, n. 7; § 17.23, n. 1; § 17.32, n. 30; § 18.4, n. 9, 50.

Loughran v. Loughran, 292 U.S. 216, 54 S.Ct. 684, 78 L.Ed. 1219 (1934)—§ 13.9, n. 5.

Louis–Dreyfus v. Paterson Steamships, 43 F.2d 824 (2nd Cir.1930)—§ 18.14, n. 10, 14.

Louis Schlesinger Co. v. Kresge Foundation, 260 F.Supp. 763 (D.N.J.1966)—§ 18.33, n. 1.

Louisville, City of v. Sherley's Guardian, 80 Ky. 71 (Ky.1882)—§ 4.42, n. 2, 3.

Louisville & N.R. Co. v. Kimbrough, 115 Ky. 512, 74 S.W. 229 (Ky.1903)—§ 4.41, n. 4.

Louisville & N.R. Co. v. Mottley, 211 U.S. 149, 29 S.Ct. 42, 53 L.Ed. 126 (1908)— § 5.17, n. 5, 6; § 5.19, n. 15.

Louknitsky v. Louknitsky, 123 Cal.App.2d 406, 266 P.2d 910 (Cal.App. 1 Dist. 1954)—§ 12.15, n. 14.

Louviere v. Shell Oil Co., 588 F.Supp. 95 (E.D.La.1984)—§ 24.1, n. 12.

Lovett v. Wal–Mart Stores, Inc., 1993 WL 38001 (Tenn.Ct.App.1993)— § 18.21, n. 11.

Loving v. Virginia, 388 U.S. 1, 87 S.Ct. 1817, 18 L.Ed.2d 1010 (1967)—§ 13.9, n. 1; § 13.10, n. 3.

Lowe v. Plainfield Trust Co. of Plainfield, N.J., 216 A.D. 72, 215 N.Y.S. 50 (N.Y.A.D. 1 Dept.1926)—§ 20.7, n. 4.

Lowell v. Kowalski, 380 Mass. 663, 405 N.E.2d 135 (Mass.1980)—§ 16.3, n. 11.

Lowell, State v., 78 Minn. 166, 80 N.W. 877 (Minn.1899)—§ 4.44, n. 2.

Lowell Wiper Supply Co. v. Helen Shop, Inc., 235 F.Supp. 640 (S.D.N.Y.1964)— § 3.11, n. 3.

Lowe's Estate, In re, 155 Kan. 679, 127 P.2d 512 (Kan.1942)—§ 21.5, n. 4.

Lowham's Estate, In re, 30 Utah 436, 85 P. 445 (Utah 1906)—§ 22.10, n. 9.

Lowndes v. Cooch, 87 Md. 478, 39 A. 1045 (Md.1898)—§ 20.13, n. 9.

Lozier v. Lozier, 99 Ohio St. 254, 124 N.E. 167 (Ohio 1919)—§ 21.6, n. 3, 7.

L.R. Willson & Sons, Inc. v. PMA Group, 867 F.Supp. 335 (D.Md.1994)—§ 17.59, n. 9, 14, 16.

Lubbe v. Cape Plc (No.2), 2000 WL 976033 (HL 2000)—§ 11.11.

Lubbock Production Credit Ass'n v. Hubble, 599 P.2d 434 (Okla.App. Div. 1 1979)—§ 12.17, n. 13.

Luber, Estate of, 109 Misc.2d 1065, 441 N.Y.S.2d 612 (N.Y.Sur.1981)—§ 16.2, n. 2.

Luce v. Manchester & L. R. R., 63 N.H. 588, 3 A. 618 (N.H.1886)—§ 22.12, n. 7; § 22.15, n. 4; § 22.17, n. 1.

Luchsinger, State ex rel. Kuhn v., 231 Wis. 533, 286 N.W. 72 (Wis.1939)—§ 11.5, n. 3.

Lucky Five Min. Co. v. H. & H. Mines, Inc., 75 Idaho 423, 273 P.2d 676 (Idaho 1954)—§ 10.12, n. 9.

Lugot v. Harris, 499 F.Supp. 1118 (D.Nev. 1980)—§ 24.42, n. 5.

Lumb v. Cooper, 266 A.2d 196 (Del.Super.1970)—§ **22.14, n. 10.**

Lumbermens Mut. Cas. Co. v. Connecticut Bank & Trust Co., N.A., 806 F.2d 411 (2nd Cir.1986)—§ **18.26, n. 12.**

Lummis v. White, 629 F.2d 397 (5th Cir. 1980)—§ **4.5; § 4.5, n. 11.**

Lummus Company v. Commonwealth Oil Refining Co., 280 F.2d 915 (1st Cir. 1960)—§ **18.1, n. 19.**

Lund's Estate, In re, 26 Cal.2d 472, 159 P.2d 643 (Cal.1945)—§ **16.1, n. 9; § 16.2; § 16.2, n. 6.**

Lurie v. Blackwell, 51 P.3d 846 (Wyo. 2002)—§ **19.11, n. 12.**

Luten, State ex rel. General Dynamics Corp. v., 566 S.W.2d 452 (Mo.1978)—§ **24.9, n. 3.**

Luther v. Shaw, 157 Wis. 234, 147 N.W. 18 (Wis.1914)—§ **17.50, n. 4.**

Lutz, In re Marriage of, 74 Wash.App. 356, 873 P.2d 566 (Wash.App. Div. 1 1994)—§ **14.6, n. 6.**

Lyle Cashion Co. v. McKendrick, 227 Miss. 894, 87 So.2d 289 (Miss.1956)—§ **19.8, n. 2.**

Lynch v. Miller, 54 Iowa 516, 6 N.W. 740 (Iowa 1880)—§ **20.6, n. 1.**

Lynch v. Provisional Paraguay, 1869 WL 10351 (Ct of Probate 1871)—§ **20.4; § 20.4, n. 9.**

Lynde v. Lynde, 181 U.S. 183, 21 S.Ct. 555, 45 L.Ed. 810 (1901)—§ **15.31, n. 1.**

Lyndon Lumber Co. v. Sawyer, 135 Wis. 525, 116 N.W. 255 (Wis.1908)—§ **19.5, n. 4, 10.**

Lynn M., In re, 312 Md. 461, 540 A.2d 799 (Md.1988)—§ **16.5, n. 2.**

Lyon v. Knott, 26 Miss. 548 (Miss.Err. & App.1853)—§ **14.8, n. 2; § 14.9, n. 1.**

Lyon v. Ogden, 85 Me. 374, 27 A. 258 (Me.1893)—§ **20.6, n. 3.**

Lyons v. Egan, 107 Colo. 32, 108 P.2d 873 (Colo.1940)—§ **22.22, n. 3.**

Lyons v. Lyons, 2 Ohio St.2d 243, 208 N.E.2d 533 (Ohio 1965)—§ **17.5, n. 10.**

Lyons' Estate, In re, 175 Wash. 115, 26 P.2d 615 (Wash.1933)—§ **20.4, n. 7.**

Lytal v. Lytal, 818 So.2d 111 (La.App. 1 Cir.2001)—§ **14.9, n. 1.**

Lytle v. Household Mfg., Inc., 494 U.S. 545, 110 S.Ct. 1331, 108 L.Ed.2d 504 (1990)—§ **24.1, n. 12.**

M

Ma v. Continental Bank N.A., 905 F.2d 1073 (7th Cir.1990)—§ **24.4, n. 7.**

Ma v. Ma, 483 N.W.2d 732 (Minn.App. 1992)—§ **13.2, n. 4; § 13.6, n. 1; § 13.14, n. 6.**

Maag v. Voykovich, 46 Wash.2d 302, 280 P.2d 680 (Wash.1955)—§ **17.6, n. 5.**

Maas v. German Sav. Bank, 176 N.Y. 377, 68 N.E. 658 (N.Y.1903)—§ **22.16, n. 4.**

Mabry v. Fuller–Shuwayer Co., Ltd., 50 N.C.App. 245, 273 S.E.2d 509 (N.C.App. 1981)—§ **8.4, n. 2.**

MacDonald v. General Motors Corp., 110 F.3d 337 (6th Cir.1997)—§ **17.73, n. 1, 5.**

MacDonald v. Grand Trunk Ry. Co., 71 N.H. 448, 52 A. 982 (N.H.1902)—§ **24.34, n. 7.**

Mace v. Webb, 614 P.2d 647 (Utah 1980)—§ **16.4, n. 2.**

Macey v. Rozbicki, 274 N.Y.S.2d 591, 221 N.E.2d 380 (N.Y.1966)—§ **17.30; § 17.30, n. 9; § 17.39, n. 15.**

Machado–Miller v. Mersereau & Shannon, LLP, 180 Or.App. 586, 43 P.3d 1207 (Or.App.2002)—§ **18.4, n. 45.**

Machransky v. Machransky, 31 Ohio App. 482, 166 N.E. 423 (Ohio App. 8 Dist. 1927)—§ **15.24, n. 7.**

Machulsky v. Hall, 210 F.Supp.2d 531 (D.N.J.2002)—§ **7.8, n. 14, 16; § 7.11, n. 13.**

Mack, Matter of Estate of, 373 N.W.2d 97 (Iowa 1985)—§ **24.10, n. 9.**

Mackay v. Saint Mary's Church, 15 R.I. 121, 23 A. 108 (R.I.1885)—§ **22.17, n. 1; § 22.18, n. 6.**

MacKendrick v. Newport News Shipbuilding & Dry Dock Co., 59 Misc.2d 994, 302 N.Y.S.2d 124 (N.Y.Sup.1969)—§ **17.30, n. 12.**

Mackensworth v. American Trading Transp. Co., 367 F.Supp. 373 (E.D.Pa. 1973)—§ **8.8, n. 9.**

Mackenzie, Re, [1911] 1 Ch. 578 (1911)—§ **4.33, n. 2.**

Mackey & Nichols v. Pettijohn, 6 Kan.App. 57, 49 P. 636 (Kan.App.1897)—§ **19.13, n. 4.**

Macklin's Estate, In re, 82 Misc.2d 376, 371 N.Y.S.2d 238 (N.Y.Sur.1975)—§ **13.5, n. 1.**

Mack Trucks, Inc. v. Bendix–Westinghouse Automotive Air Brake Co., 372 F.2d 18 (3rd Cir.1966)—§ **3.11, n. 4; § 3.12, n. 6.**

MacLean's Estate, In re, 47 Wis.2d 396, 177 N.W.2d 874 (Wis.1970)—§ **12.4, n. 1.**

MacNamara v. Korean Air Lines, 863 F.2d 1135 (3rd Cir.1988)—§ **3.58, n. 6.**

Macon Prestressed Concrete Co. v. Duke, 46 B.R. 727 (M.D.Ga.1985)—§ **23.12, n. 7, 8.**

MacShannon v. Rockware Glass Ltd, 1978 WL 58340 (HL 1978)—§ **11.8, n. 2.**

Macurdy v. Sikov & Love, P.A., 894 F.2d 818 (6th Cir.1990)—§ **18.29, n. 3, 5.**

Madara v. Hall, 916 F.2d 1510 (11th Cir. 1990)—§ **6.8, n. 7; § 7.8, n. 11.**

Maddox v. American Airlines, Inc., 298 F.3d 694 (8th Cir.2002)—§ **17.40, n. 26.**

Madison Consulting Group v. State of S.C., 752 F.2d 1193 (7th Cir.1985)—§ **8.5, n. 7.**

Madrin v. Wareham, 344 F.Supp. 166 (W.D.Pa.1972)—§ **17.12, n. 7.**

Magnant v. Medtronic, Inc., 818 F.Supp. 204 (W.D.Mich.1993)—§ **17.76, n. 28.**

Magnetic Audiotape Antitrust Litigation, In re, 334 F.3d 204 (2nd Cir.2003)—§ **9.7, n. 9; § 10.2, n. 15.**

Magnolia Petroleum Co. v. Hunt, 320 U.S. 430, 64 S.Ct. 208, 88 L.Ed. 149 (1943)—§ **3.18, n. 1; § 24.11, n. 1; § 24.26, n. 4; § 24.46, n. 6.**

Maguire v. Exeter & Hampton Elec. Co., 114 N.H. 589, 325 A.2d 778 (N.H. 1974)—§ **2.13, n. 15; § 17.21, n. 13, 27.**

Mahmud v. Mahmud, 444 So.2d 774 (La. App. 4 Cir.1984)—§ **14.9, n. 2.**

Mahne v. Ford Motor Co., 900 F.2d 83 (6th Cir.1990)—§ **17.74, n. 11; § 17.75, n. 1; § 17.76; § 17.76, n. 26; § 17.77, n. 18.**

Mahoney v. Ronnie's Road Service, 122 N.C.App. 150, 468 S.E.2d 279 (N.C.App. 1996)—§ **17.67, n. 2; § 17.69, n. 11.**

Maine Surgical Supply Co. v. Intermedics Orthopedics, Inc., 756 F.Supp. 597 (D.Me.1991)—§ **18.29, n. 3, 5.**

Majot's Estate, In re, 199 N.Y. 29, 92 N.E. 402 (N.Y.1910)—§ **14.5, n. 1; § 14.9, n. 13.**

Maki v. George R. Cooke Co., 124 F.2d 663 (6th Cir.1942)—§ **3.10, n. 1, 5, 6.**

Maklad v. Maklad, 2001 WL 51662 (Conn.Super.2001)—§ **15.24, n. 4.**

Malaterre v. Malaterre, 293 N.W.2d 139 (N.D.1980)—§ **15.42, n. 15.**

Malatesta v. Mitsubishi Aircraft Intern., Inc., 275 Ill.App.3d 370, 211 Ill.Dec. 710, 655 N.E.2d 1093 (Ill.App. 1 Dist.1995)— § **17.56, n. 2; § 17.59, n. 12.**

Malaysia British Assur. v. El Paso Reyco, Inc., 830 S.W.2d 919 (Tex.1992)—§ **8.2, n. 10.**

Male Child Born July 15, 1985 To L.C., Matter of, 221 Mont. 309, 718 P.2d 660 (Mont.1986)—§ **16.6, n. 2.**

Malev Hungarian Airlines, Application of, 964 F.2d 97 (2nd Cir.1992)—§ **12.8, n. 9.**

Mallory Associates, Inc. v. Barving Realty Co., Inc., 300 N.Y. 297, 90 N.E.2d 468 (N.Y.1949)—§ **19.8, n. 9.**

Maly v. Genmar Industries, Inc., 1996 WL 28473 (N.D.Ill.1996)—§ **17.66, n. 6; § 17.78, n. 9.**

Mamlin v. Susan Thomas, Inc., 490 S.W.2d 634 (Tex.Civ.App.-Dallas 1973)— § **18.11, n. 4.**

Mandel–Mantello v. Treves, 103 Misc.2d 700, 426 N.Y.S.2d 929 (N.Y.Sup.1980)— § **15.31, n. 2.**

Maner v. Maner, 412 F.2d 449 (5th Cir. 1969)—§ **24.8, n. 4.**

Maner v. Maner, 401 F.2d 616 (5th Cir. 1968)—§ **15.34, n. 1.**

Manetti–Farrow, Inc. v. Gucci America, Inc., 858 F.2d 509 (9th Cir.1988)— § **11.4, n. 15.**

Mangrum v. Mangrum, 310 Ky. 226, 220 S.W.2d 406 (Ky.1949)—§ **13.12, n. 1.**

Manion v. Roadway Package System, Inc., 938 F.Supp. 512 (C.D.Ill.1996)—§ **17.40, n. 26; § 18.1, n. 17.**

Manion's Adm'rs v. Titsworth, 57 Ky. 582 (Ky.1857)—§ **22.19, n. 21.**

Manitowoc Western Co., Inc. v. Montonen, 250 Wis.2d 452, 639 N.W.2d 726 (Wis. 2002)—§ **11.15, n. 4.**

Manji v. New York Life Ins. Co., 945 F.Supp. 919 (D.S.C.1996)—§ **24.12, n. 7.**

Manley v. Engram, 755 F.2d 1463 (11th Cir.1985)—§ **5.18, n. 5; § 6.4, n. 20.**

Manley v. Nelson, 50 Haw. 484, 50 Haw. 524, 443 P.2d 155 (Hawai'i 1968)— § **12.3, n. 5; § 12.6, n. 4.**

Manlugon v. A/S Facto, 419 F.Supp. 550 (S.D.N.Y.1976)—§ **17.63, n. 31.**

Mann v. Frank Hrubetz & Co., Inc., 361 So.2d 1021 (Ala.1978)—§ **7.2, n. 13.**

Manndorff v. Dax, 13 Conn.App. 282, 535 A.2d 1324 (Conn.App.1988)—§ **15.15, n. 3.**

Manos v. Trans World Airlines, Inc., 295 F.Supp. 1170 (N.D.Ill.1969)—§ **3.11, n. 4.**

Manos v. Trans World Airlines, Inc., 295 F.Supp. 1166 (N.D.Ill.1968)—§ **18.37, n. 6.**

Manrique v. Fabbri, 493 So.2d 437 (Fla. 1986)—§ **11.5, n. 3.**

Mansfield v. McFarland, 202 Pa. 173, 51 A. 763 (Pa.1902)—§ **22.14, n. 3.**

Mansfield Hardwood Lumber Co. v. Johnson, 268 F.2d 317 (5th Cir.1959)— § **23.9, n. 4.**

Mantello v. Hall, 947 F.Supp. 92 (S.D.N.Y. 1996)—§ **9.3; § 9.3, n. 9.**

Manton v. J.F. Seiberling & Co., 107 Iowa 534, 78 N.W. 194 (Iowa 1899)—§ **19.3, n. 16.**

Manufacturers Finance Co. v. B. & L. Johnson & Co., 15 Tenn.App. 236 (Tenn.Ct. App.1931)—§ **18.7, n. 9.**

Manu Intern., S.A. v. Avon Products, Inc., 641 F.2d 62 (2nd Cir.1981)—§ **11.10, n. 2.**

Manz v. Continental American Life Ins. Co., 117 Or.App. 78, 843 P.2d 480 (Or.App. 1992)—§ **18.20, n. 11.**

Maple v. Maple, 566 P.2d 1229 (Utah 1977)—§ **12.15, n. 9.**

Maple Island Farm v. Bitterling, 196 F.2d 55 (8th Cir.1952)—§ **4.12, n. 3.**

Marathon County v. Milwaukee County, 273 Wis. 541, 79 N.W.2d 233 (Wis. 1956)—§ **4.27, n. 1.**

Marathon Oil Co. v. Ruhrgas, 145 F.3d 211 (5th Cir.1998)—§ **5.19, n. 16.**

Marchesani v. Pellerin–Milnor Corp., 269 F.3d 481 (5th Cir.2001)—§ **3.9, n. 8;** § **17.76, n. 27.**

Marcus v. Kane, 18 F.2d 722 (2nd Cir. 1927)—§ **3.4, n. 5.**

Marie v. Garrison, 13 Abb. N. Cas. 210 (N.Y.Super.1883)—§ **3.7, n. 1;** § **3.8, n. 5;** § **18.38;** § **18.38, n. 4.**

Marine Const. & Design Co. v. Vessel Tim, 434 P.2d 683 (Alaska 1967)—§ **3.10, n. 2.**

Marine Midland Bank, N.A. v. Miller, 664 F.2d 899 (2nd Cir.1981)—§ **10.17, n. 3.**

Marine Midland Bank, N.A. v. United Missouri Bank, N.A., 223 A.D.2d 119, 643 N.Y.S.2d 528 (N.Y.A.D. 1 Dept.1996)— § **18.12, n. 15, 16.**

Marino v. New York Telephone Co., 944 F.2d 109 (2nd Cir.1991)—§ **17.56, n. 11.**

Marion Power Shovel Co. v. Hargis, 698 So.2d 1246 (Fla.App. 3 Dist.1997)— § **17.42, n. 12, 20;** § **17.60, n. 5.**

Maritime Intern. Nominees Establishment v. Republic of Guinea, 693 F.2d 1094, 224 U.S.App.D.C. 119 (D.C.Cir.1982)— § **10.19, n. 37;** § **11.15, n. 1.**

Markakis v. SS Volendam, 475 F.Supp. 29 (S.D.N.Y.1979)—§ **12.18, n. 12.**

Markham v. City of Newport News, 292 F.2d 711 (4th Cir.1961)—§ **3.41, n. 1.**

Marks v. Marks, 75 F. 321 (C.C.D.Tenn. 1896)—§ **4.18, n. 3;** § **4.28, n. 5.**

Maronier v. Larmer (CA 2002)—§ **24.44, n. 9.**

Maroon v. State, Dept. of Mental Health, 411 N.E.2d 404 (Ind.App. 1 Dist.1980)— § **3.13, n. 4.**

Marquette Nat. Bank of Minneapolis v. First of Omaha Service Corp., 439 U.S. 299, 99 S.Ct. 540, 58 L.Ed.2d 534 (1978)—§ **18.28, n. 1.**

Marquez v. Hahnemann Medical College and Hospital of Philadelphia, 435 F.Supp. 972 (E.D.Pa.1976)—§ **3.40, n. 10;** § **3.41, n. 10.**

Marr v. Hendrix, 952 S.W.2d 693 (Ky. 1997)—§ **22.3, n. 15;** § **22.4, n. 12;** § **22.7, n. 4.**

Marra v. Bushee, 447 F.2d 1282 (2nd Cir. 1971)—§ **17.5, n. 6.**

Marra v. Bushee, 317 F.Supp. 972 (D.Vt. 1970)—§ **17.54, n. 2.**

Marrese v. American Academy of Orthopaedic Surgeons, 470 U.S. 373, 105 S.Ct. 1327, 84 L.Ed.2d 274 (1985)—§ **24.1, n. 7;** § **24.2, n. 8;** § **24.12, n. 7.**

Marrett, In re, 1887 WL 10886 (CA 1887)— § **4.36, n. 8.**

Marriage of (see name of party)

Marris v. Sockey, 170 F.2d 599 (10th Cir. 1948)—§ **13.18, n. 13;** § **15.24, n. 3.**

Marshall v. Geo. M. Brewster & Son, Inc., 37 N.J. 176, 180 A.2d 129 (N.J.1962)— § **3.10, n. 6;** § **3.12, n. 2.**

Marshall Contractors, Inc. v. Peerless Ins. Co., 827 F.Supp. 91 (D.R.I.1993)— § **18.27, n. 3.**

Marsland's Estate, In re, 142 Misc. 230, 254 N.Y.S. 293 (N.Y.Sur.1931)—§ **21.11, n. 11.**

Martell, United States v., 887 F.Supp. 1183 (N.D.Ind.1995)—§ **24.24, n. 8.**

Martin v. Battey, 87 Kan. 582, 125 P. 88 (Kan.1912)—§ **20.15, n. 3.**

Martin v. Choudhuri, 563 F.Supp. 207 (W.D.Wis.1983)—§ **3.41, n. 15.**

Martin v. Curran, 303 N.Y. 276, 101 N.E.2d 683 (N.Y.1951)—§ **10.12, n. 3.**

Martin v. Denver Juvenile Court, 177 Colo. 261, 493 P.2d 1093 (Colo.1972)— § **11.17, n. 39.**

Martin v. Eslick, 229 Miss. 234, 90 So.2d 635 (Miss.1956)—§ **20.8, n. 9.**

Martin v. Goodyear Tire & Rubber Co., 114 Wash.App. 823, 61 P.3d 1196 (Wash. App. Div. 1 2003)—§ **17.72, n. 3.**

Martin v. Haycock, 22 N.J. 1, 123 A.2d 223 (N.J.1956)—§ **21.7, n. 2.**

Martin v. Julius Dierck Equipment Co., 43 N.Y.2d 583, 403 N.Y.S.2d 185, 374 N.E.2d 97 (N.Y.1978)—§ **3.11, n. 3, 4.**

Martin v. Julius Dierck Equipment Co., 52 A.D.2d 463, 384 N.Y.S.2d 479 (N.Y.A.D. 2 Dept.1976)—§ **17.64, n. 9;** § **18.24, n. 5.**

Martin v. L. Potter & Co., 34 Vt. 87 (Vt. 1861)—§ **19.30, n. 7.**

Martin v. State, 740 N.E.2d 137 (Ind.App. 2000)—§ **24.1, n. 12.**

Martin v. Stovall, 103 Tenn. 1, 52 S.W. 296 (Tenn.1899)—§ **22.3, n. 1.**

Martin v. Wilks, 490 U.S. 755, 109 S.Ct. 2180, 104 L.Ed.2d 835 (1989)—§ **24.12, n. 7.**

Martineau v. Guertin, 170 Vt. 415, 751 A.2d 776 (Vt.2000)—§ **17.22, n. 5.**

Martinez v. Bynum, 461 U.S. 321, 103 S.Ct. 1838, 75 L.Ed.2d 879 (1983)—§ **4.37, n. 10.**

Martinez v. Dow Chemical Co., 219 F.Supp.2d 719 (E.D.La.2002)—§ **12.18, n. 10.**

Martinez v. Reed, 490 So.2d 303 (La.App. 4 Cir.1986)—§ **16.5, n. 2.**

Martino v. Cottman Transmission Systems, Inc., 218 Mich.App. 54, 554 N.W.2d 17 (Mich.App.1996)—§ **18.4, n. 1, 44.**

Maru Shipping Co., Inc. v. Burmeister & Wain American Corp., 528 F.Supp. 210 (S.D.N.Y.1981)—§ **3.50, n. 3.**

Marvin v. Marvin, 134 Cal.Rptr. 815, 557 P.2d 106 (Cal.1976)—§ **15.1, n. 7.**

Marvin Safe Co. v. Norton, 7 A. 418 (N.J.Sup.1886)—§ **19.13, n. 10.**

Maryland Cas. Co. v. Continental Cas. Co., 332 F.3d 145 (2nd Cir.2003)—§ **18.26, n. 12.**

Maryland Casualty Co. v. San Juan Racing Assoc., Inc., 83 P.R.R. 538, 83 D.P.R.

559 (P.R.1961)—§ **2.17, n. 7;** § **2.22, n. 8;** § **18.21, n. 15.**

Maryland, State of v. Eis Automotive Corp., 145 F.Supp. 444 (D.Conn.1956)—§ **3.10, n. 3.**

Maryland v. Capital Airlines, Inc., 280 F.Supp. 648 (S.D.N.Y.1964)—§ **18.44, n. 9.**

Mas v. Perry, 489 F.2d 1396 (5th Cir. 1974)—§ **4.33, n. 3.**

Mascarella v. Brown, 813 F.Supp. 1015 (S.D.N.Y.1993)—§ **17.42, n. 11, 29;** § **17.43, n. 9;** § **17.44, n. 13.**

Mason v. Fuller, 36 Conn. 160 (Conn. 1869)—§ **14.8, n. 2.**

Mason v. Homer, 105 Mass. 116 (Mass. 1870)—§ **4.33, n. 2;** § **14.8, n. 4.**

Mason v. Mason, 775 N.E.2d 706 (Ind.App. 2002)—§ **13.11, n. 4.**

Mason v. Pelkes, 57 Idaho 10, 59 P.2d 1087 (Idaho 1936)—§ **24.29, n. 8.**

Mason v. Southern New England Conference Ass'n of Seventh–Day Adventists of Town of South Lancaster, Com. of Massachusetts, 696 F.2d 135 (1st Cir. 1982)—§ **17.26, n. 1.**

Mason, State ex rel. Torres v., 315 Or. 386, 848 P.2d 592 (Or.1993)—§ **16.5, n. 9.**

Masonite Corp. Hardboard Siding Products Liability Litigation, In re, 21 F.Supp.2d 593 (E.D.La.1998)—§ **17.44, n. 9;** § **17.70, n. 6.**

Massachusetts, Commonwealth of v. State of Missouri, 308 U.S. 1, 60 S.Ct. 39, 84 L.Ed. 3 (1939)—§ **4.5, n. 9.**

Massachusetts Bay Ins. Co. v. Vic Koenig Leasing, Inc., 136 F.3d 1116 (7th Cir. 1998)—§ **2.19, n. 10.**

Massachusetts School of Law at Andover, Inc. v. American Bar Ass'n, 142 F.3d 26 (1st Cir.1998)—§ **9.7, n. 9.**

Massaglia, Estate of, 38 Cal.App.3d 767, 113 Cal.Rptr. 751 (Cal.App. 2 Dist. 1974)—§ **22.6, n. 5;** § **22.15, n. 13.**

Massey v. Parker, 369 So.2d 1310 (La. 1979)—§ **16.6, n. 6.**

Massey–Ferguson Credit Corp. v. Wells Motor Co., Inc., 374 So.2d 319 (Ala.1979)—§ **19.18, n. 21.**

Massie v. Watts, 10 U.S. 148, 3 L.Ed. 181 (1810)—§ **19.8;** § **19.8, n. 2, 4.**

Mata v. Moreno, 601 S.W.2d 58 (Tex.Civ. App.-Hous. (1 Dist.) 1980)—§ **16.1, n. 7.**

Matarese v. Calise, 111 R.I. 551, 305 A.2d 112 (R.I.1973)—§ **18.33, n. 2;** § **19.3, n. 12;** § **19.8;** § **19.8, n. 3.**

Mather v. Cunningham, 105 Me. 326, 74 A. 809 (Me.1909)—§ **4.30, n. 3;** § **4.32, n. 1.**

Mathews v. Lucas, 427 U.S. 495, 96 S.Ct. 2755, 49 L.Ed.2d 651 (1976)—§ **3.54, n. 5.**

Mathey v. United States, 491 F.2d 481 (3rd Cir.1974)—§ **12.18, n. 18.**

Matous' Estate, In re, 53 Misc.2d 255, 278 N.Y.S.2d 70 (N.Y.Sur.1967)—§ **20.4, n. 6.**

Matson by Kehoe v. Anctil, 7 F.Supp.2d 423 (D.Vt.1998)—§ **17.36, n. 15.**

Matson by Kehoe v. Anctil, 979 F.Supp. 1031 (D.Vt.1997)—§ **17.26, n. 19;** § **17.36, n. 15;** § **17.48, n. 8.**

Matson Navigation Co., Inc. v. Stal–Laval Turbin AB, 609 F.Supp. 579 (N.D.Cal. 1985)—§ **11.10, n. 8.**

Matsushita Elec. Indus. Co., Ltd. v. Epstein, 516 U.S. 367, 116 S.Ct. 873, 134 L.Ed.2d 6 (1996)—§ **24.2, n. 8;** § **24.12, n. 7.**

Mattel, Inc. v. Barbie–Club.com, 310 F.3d 293 (2nd Cir.2002)—§ **5.9, n. 20.**

Matter of (see name of party)

Mattes v. National Hellenic Am. Line, S.A., 427 F.Supp. 619 (S.D.N.Y.1977)—§ **17.63, n. 23.**

Matthews v. Matthews, 141 So.2d 799 (Fla. App. 1 Dist.1962)—§ **4.45, n. 3.**

Mattos v. Thompson, 491 Pa. 385, 421 A.2d 190 (Pa.1980)—§ **3.41, n. 2.**

Matusevitch v. Telnikoff, 877 F.Supp. 1 (D.D.C.1995)—§ **24.44, n. 12.**

Max Daetwyler Corp. v. R. Meyer, 762 F.2d 290 (3rd Cir.1985)—§ **9.4, n. 8.**

Maxfield v. Terry, 885 S.W.2d 216 (Tex. App.-Dallas 1994)—§ **22.3, n. 1.**

Maxus Exploration Co. v. Moran Bros., Inc., 817 S.W.2d 50 (Tex.1991)—§ **18.29, n. 3, 5.**

Maxwell v. Maxwell, 51 Misc.2d 687, 273 N.Y.S.2d 728 (N.Y.Sup.1966)—§ **13.6, n. 3, 9.**

Maxwell v. Ricks, 294 F. 255 (9th Cir. 1923)—§ **19.10, n. 2.**

Maxwell's Estate, In re, 55 Montg. Co. L.R. 154 (Pa. 1939)—§ **22.21, n. 14.**

May v. Anderson, 345 U.S. 528, 73 S.Ct. 840, 97 L.Ed. 1221 (1953)—§ **15.29;** § **15.29, n. 1;** § **15.39;** § **15.39, n. 9;** § **15.41, n. 3.**

May v. May, 169 L.T. 42 (1943)—§ **4.27 n. 12.**

May v. Mulligan, 36 F.Supp. 596 (W.D.Mich.1939)—§ **18.4, n. 1, 8, 43, 46.**

Mayberry v. Flowers, 347 Ark. 476, 65 S.W.3d 418 (Ark.2002)—§ **16.5, n. 6.**

Mayer v. Mayer, 66 N.C.App. 522, 311 S.E.2d 659 (N.C.App.1984)—§ **15.20, n. 5.**

Mayer v. Willing, 196 Cal.App.2d 379, 16 Cal.Rptr. 476 (Cal.App. 2 Dist.1961)—§ **22.25, n. 7.**

Mayer–Kolker v. Kolker, 359 N.J.Super. 98, 819 A.2d 17 (N.J.Super.A.D.2003)—§ **15.24, n. 7.**

Mayhew v. Mayhew, 205 W.Va. 490, 519 S.E.2d 188 (W.Va.1999)—§ **14.9, n. 1.**

Mayo v. Hartford Life Ins. Co., 354 F.3d 400 (5th Cir.2004)—§ **18.26, n. 9.**

Mayo v. Tillman Aero, Inc., 640 So.2d 314 (La.App. 3 Cir.1994)—§ **6.9, n. 21.**

Mays v. Laurant Pub., Ltd., 600 F.Supp. 29 (N.D.Ga.1984)—§ **7.10, n. 4.**

May's Estate, In re, 305 N.Y. 486, 114 N.E.2d 4 (N.Y.1953)—§ **13.2, n. 9; § 13.12, n. 4; § 13.15, n. 4.**

Mazza v. Mazza, 475 F.2d 385, 154 U.S.App.D.C. 274 (D.C.Cir.1973)— **§ 19.1, n. 3, 5.**

Mazzolini v. Mazzolini, 168 Ohio St. 357, 155 N.E.2d 206 (Ohio 1958)—§ **13.11, n. 2; § 13.15, n. 4.**

MBI Acquisition Partners, L.P. v. Chronicle Pub. Co., 2001 WL 1478812 (W.D.Wis. 2001)—§ **17.40, n. 28.**

McAndrews v. Krause, 245 Minn. 85, 71 N.W.2d 153 (Minn.1955)—§ **22.19, n. 18.**

McBride v. Minstar, Inc., 283 N.J.Super. 471, 662 A.2d 592 (N.J.Super.L.1994)— **§ 18.7, n. 3.**

McBride v. Whiting–Turner Contracting Co., 1993 WL 489487 (Del.Super.1993)— **§ 17.42, n. 12, 20; § 17.60, n. 5.**

McCabe, In re, 84 A.D. 145, 82 N.Y.S. 180 (N.Y.A.D. 3 Dept.1903)—§ **22.9, n. 6.**

McCampbell's Trust, In re, 36 Misc.2d 108, 232 N.Y.S.2d 522 (N.Y.Sup.1962)— **§ 21.3, n. 13; § 21.13, n. 4.**

McCann v. Somoza, 933 F.Supp. 362 (S.D.N.Y.1996)—§ **17.46, n. 21.**

McCarthy v. McCarthy, 361 Mass. 359, 280 N.E.2d 151 (Mass.1972)—§ **15.9, n. 7; § 15.20, n. 7.**

McCartney v. Osburn, 118 Ill. 403, 9 N.E. 210 (Ill.1886)—§ **20.8, n. 10; § 20.13, n. 5.**

McCarty v. Hall, 13 Mo. 480 (Mo.1850)— **§ 22.11, n. 11; § 22.17, n. 3.**

McCarty v. Herrick, 41 Idaho 529, 240 P. 192 (Idaho 1925)—§ **11.5, n. 5.**

McCarty v. McCarty, 453 U.S. 210, 101 S.Ct. 2728, 69 L.Ed.2d 589 (1981)— **§ 14.11, n. 1.**

McCasland v. McCasland, 506 N.Y.S.2d 329, 497 N.E.2d 696 (N.Y.1986)—§ **14.12, n. 5.**

McCaughna v. Bilhorn, 10 Cal.App.2d 674, 52 P.2d 1025 (Cal.App. 4 Dist.1935)— **§ 20.7, n. 3.**

McCausland's Estate, In re, 213 Pa. 189, 62 A. 780 (Pa.1906)—§ **16.1, n. 8.**

McClain, United States v., 545 F.2d 988 (5th Cir.1977)—§ **12.18, n. 12.**

McClanahan v. State Tax Commission of Arizona, 411 U.S. 164, 93 S.Ct. 1257, 36 L.Ed.2d 129 (1973)—§ **11.17, n. 10, 12, 14.**

McClaney v. Utility Equipment Leasing Corp., 560 F.Supp. 1265 (N.D.N.Y. 1983)—§ **18.26, n. 12.**

McCleary v. Menke, 109 Ill. 294 (Ill.1884)— **§ 22.25, n. 8.**

McCluney v. Joseph Schlitz Brewing Co., 649 F.2d 578 (8th Cir.1981)—§ **3.23, n. 16.**

McClure v. United States Lines Co., 368 F.2d 197 (4th Cir.1966)—§ **17.63, n. 22.**

McCluskey v. Rob San Services, Inc., 443 F.Supp. 65 (S.D.Ohio 1977)—§ **18.37, n. 6.**

McCollum v. Smith, 19 Tenn. 342 (Tenn. 1839)—§ **14.9, n. 13; § 19.2, n. 2.**

McCombs' Estate, In re, 80 N.E.2d 573 (Ohio Prob.1948)—§ **20.9, n. 14; § 22.22, n. 7.**

McConnell v. Kelley, 138 Mass. 372 (Mass. 1885)—§ **4.24, n. 1.**

McCord v. Smith, 43 So.2d 704 (Fla.1949)— **§ 22.20, n. 29; § 22.21, n. 6.**

McCord v. Thompson, 92 Ind. 565 (Ind. 1884)—§ **22.15, n. 9; § 22.18, n. 5; § 22.20, n. 6.**

McCorhill Pub., Inc., In re, 86 B.R. 783 (Bkrtcy.S.D.N.Y.1988)—§ **18.28, n. 5.**

McCormick v. Statler Hotels Delaware Corp., 30 Ill.2d 86, 195 N.E.2d 172 (Ill. 1963)—§ **23.9, n. 3.**

McCormick's Estate, In re, 260 Ill.App. 36 (Ill.App. 1 Dist.1931)—§ **22.26, n. 1.**

McCornick & Co., Bankers, v. Tolmie Bros., 46 Idaho 544, 269 P. 96 (Idaho 1928)— **§ 19.28, n. 6.**

McCraw v. Simpson, 208 Ark. 471, 187 S.W.2d 536 (Ark.1945)—§ **22.18, n. 9.**

McCreary's Estate, In re, 29 Pa. D. & C. 93 (Pa.Orph.1937)—§ **21.11, n. 15.**

McCreary Tire & Rubber Co. v. Ceat S. p. A., 501 F.2d 1032 (3rd Cir.1974)— **§ 24.48, n. 4.**

McCrossin v. Hicks Chevrolet, Inc., 248 A.2d 917 (D.C.App.1969)—§ **2.17, n. 8; § 2.24, n. 5.**

McCurdy v. McCallum, 186 Mass. 464, 72 N.E. 75 (Mass.1904)—§ **20.13, n. 7.**

McDaniel v. Ritter, 556 So.2d 303 (Miss. 1989)—§ **3.11, n. 5.**

McDermott Inc. v. Lewis, 531 A.2d 206 (Del.Supr.1987)—§ **23.2, n. 10.**

McDonald v. Hartford Trust Co., 104 Conn. 169, 132 A. 902 (Conn.1926)—§ **4.3, n. 3; § 4.20, n. 1.**

McDonald v. Mabee, 243 U.S. 90, 37 S.Ct. 343, 61 L.Ed. 608 (1917)—§ **6.2, n. 2; § 12.3, n. 3.**

McDonald v. McDonald, 6 Cal.2d 457, 58 P.2d 163 (Cal.1936)—§ **13.12, n. 1.**

McDonnell Douglas Corp. v. Islamic Republic of Iran, 758 F.2d 341 (8th Cir.1985)— **§ 11.3, n. 23.**

McDonnell–Douglas Corp. v. Lohn, 192 Colo. 200, 557 P.2d 373 (Colo.1976)— **§ 11.11, n. 2.**

McDougald v. Jenson, 596 F.Supp. 680 (N.D.Fla.1984)—§ **15.34, n. 1.**

McDougald's Estate, In re, 272 A.D. 176, 70 N.Y.S.2d 200 (N.Y.A.D. 3 Dept.1947)— **§ 22.21, n. 6.**

McDowell v. Gould, 166 Ga. 670, 144 S.E. 206 (Ga.1928)—§ **22.26, n. 1.**

McElhinney Jr., Benjamin H. v. Commissioner, 17 T.C. 7 (Tax Ct.1951)—§ **14.9, n. 13; § 14.10, n. 3.**

McElmoyle v. Cohen, 38 U.S. 312, 10 L.Ed. 177 (1839)—§ **24.5, n. 2; § 24.13, n. 3.**

McEwan v. Brown, 176 N.C. 249, 97 S.E. 20 (N.C.1918)—§ **22.3, n. 1.**

McFadden, In re Marriage of, 380 N.W.2d 6 (Iowa App.1985)—§ **6.5, n. 15.**

McFarland v. McFarland, 524 N.Y.S.2d 392, 519 N.E.2d 303 (N.Y.1987)—§ **15.20, n. 10.**

McGee v. International Life Ins. Co., 355 U.S. 220, 78 S.Ct. 199, 2 L.Ed.2d 223 (1957)—§ **5.11; § 5.11, n. 2; § 6.7, n. 6; § 7.2; § 7.2, n. 2, 5; § 7.11; § 7.11, n. 8; § 8.1; § 8.1, n. 7; § 8.2; § 8.2, n. 1; § 10.15; § 10.15, n. 5.**

McGehee v. McGehee, 152 Md. 661, 136 A. 905 (Md.1927)—§ **20.15, n. 8, 10.**

McGehee v. McGehee, 189 N.C. 558, 127 S.E. 684 (N.C.1925)—§ **20.15, n. 8.**

McGeshick v. Choucair, 72 F.3d 62 (7th Cir.1995)—§ **3.47, n. 9; § 24.8, n. 7; § 24.28, n. 3.**

McGill v. Hill, 31 Wash.App. 542, 644 P.2d 680 (Wash.App. Div. 1 1982)—§ **18.1, n. 16.**

McGinness v. Chambers, 156 Tenn. 404, 1 S.W.2d 1015 (Tenn.1928)—§ **20.15, n. 4, 5.**

McGirl v. Brewer, 132 Or. 422, 280 P. 508 (Or.1929)—§ **19.10, n. 2.**

McGonigle v. Penn–Central Transp. Co., 49 F.R.D. 58 (D.Md.1969)—§ **10.4, n. 14.**

McGoon v. Scales, 76 U.S. 23, 19 L.Ed. 545 (1869)—§ **19.2, n. 3, 7; § 19.3, n. 17; § 19.4, n. 1.**

McGovern v. Marriott Intern., Inc., 1996 WL 470643 (E.D.La.1996)—§ **17.48, n. 5.**

McGowan v. University of Scranton, 759 F.2d 287 (3rd Cir.1985)—§ **3.47, n. 2.**

McGrath v. Kristensen, 340 U.S. 162, 71 S.Ct. 224, 95 L.Ed. 173 (1950)—§ **4.13, n. 3; § 4.27, n. 12.**

McGrath v. Zander, 177 F.2d 649, 85 U.S.App.D.C. 334 (D.C.Cir.1949)— § **4.34, n. 4.**

McGuire v. Andre, 259 Ala. 109, 65 So.2d 185 (Ala.1953)—§ **20.7, n. 3.**

McIlvain v. Scheibley, 109 Ky. 455, 59 S.W. 498 (Ky.1900)—§ **13.8, n. 1.**

McIlvaine v. AmSouth Bank, N.A., 581 So.2d 454 (Ala.1991)—§ **16.1, n. 7.**

McIlvaine Trucking, Inc. v. W.C.A.B. (States), 570 Pa. 662, 810 A.2d 1280 (Pa.2002)—§ **17.59, n. 14.**

McIlvoy v. Alsop, 45 Miss. 365 (Miss. 1871)—§ **22.11, n. 15.**

McIndoo v. Burnett, 494 F.2d 1311 (8th Cir.1974)—§ **3.11, n. 5.**

McIntosh v. Maricopa County, 73 Ariz. 366, 241 P.2d 801 (Ariz.1952)—§ **4.19, n. 3.**

McIntyre v. Chappell, 4 Tex. 187 (Tex. 1849)—§ **14.8, n. 4.**

McKee v. Dodd, 152 Cal. 637, 93 P. 854 (Cal.1908)—§ **22.21, n. 6.**

McKenna v. McKenna, 282 Pa.Super. 45, 422 A.2d 668 (Pa.Super.1980)—§ **4.27, n. 8.**

McKenna v. Ortho Pharmaceutical Corp., 622 F.2d 657 (3rd Cir.1980)—§ **3.47; § 3.47, n. 10.**

McKenzie v. K. S. N. Co., 79 N.M. 314, 442 P.2d 804 (N.M.App.1968)—§ **22.10, n. 9.**

McKinney v. Fairchild Intern., Inc., 199 W.Va. 718, 487 S.E.2d 913 (W.Va. 1997)—§ **2.21; § 2.21, n. 28.**

McKinney v. McKinney, 1980 WL 258248 (B.C. S.C.1980)—§ **14.9, n. 12.**

McKinney v. S & S Trucking, Inc., 885 F.Supp. 105 (D.N.J.1995)—§ **17.48, n. 17.**

McKinnon v. F.H. Morgan & Co., Inc., 170 Vt. 422, 750 A.2d 1026 (Vt.2000)— § **17.78, n. 6.**

McLam v. McLam, 85 N.M. 196, 510 P.2d 914 (N.M.1973)—§ **19.8, n. 14.**

McLaughlin v. People, 403 Ill. 493, 87 N.E.2d 637 (Ill.1949)—§ **20.2, n. 4.**

McLean v. American Sec. & Trust Co., 119 F.Supp. 405 (D.D.C 1954)—§ **22.25, n. 7.**

McLennan v. American Eurocopter Corp., Inc., 245 F.3d 403 (5th Cir.2001)— § **17.76; § 17.76, n. 19, 28.**

McLennan v. McLennan, 31 Or. 480, 50 P. 802 (Or.1897)—§ **13.9, n. 4.**

McLeod v. Birnbaum, 14 N.J. Misc. 485, 185 A. 667 (N.J.Sup.1936)—§ **10.15, n. 4.**

McLeod v. Board, 30 Tex. 238 (Tex.1867)— § **14.15, n. 10.**

McLouth Steel Corp. v. Jewell Coal & Coke Co., 570 F.2d 594 (6th Cir.1978)— § **18.24, n. 11.**

McMillan v. McMillan, 219 Va. 1127, 253 S.E.2d 662 (Va.1979)—§ **2.21, n. 4; § 17.5, n. 10; § 17.7, n. 8.**

McMillen v. Winona Nat. & Sav. Bank, 279 Ark. 16, 648 S.W.2d 460 (Ark.1983)— § **2.19, n. 23; § 2.22, n. 4.**

McMorrow v. Rodman Ford Sales, Inc., 462 F.Supp. 947 (D.Mass.1979)—§ **18.33, n. 3.**

McMorrow v. Schweiker, 561 F.Supp. 584 (D.N.J.1982)—§ **13.5, n. 1.**

McMullin's Estate, In re, 490 Pa. 502, 417 A.2d 152 (Pa.1980)—§ **21.13, n. 2.**

McNamara v. McNamara, 303 Ill. 191, 135 N.E. 410 (Ill.1922)—§ **16.2, n. 5; § 16.4, n. 2.**

McNamara v. McNamara, 62 Ga. 200 (Ga. 1879)—§ **22.11, n. 8, 17.**

McNeil v. First Congregational Soc., 66 Cal. 105, 4 P. 1096 (Cal.1884)—§ **22.25, n. 3.**

McPike v. McPike, 111 Mo. 216, 20 S.W. 12 (Mo.1892)—§ **22.15, n. 15.**

McQuillan v. "Italia" Societa Per Azione Di Navigazione, 386 F.Supp. 462 (S.D.N.Y. 1974)—§ **18.4, n. 7;** § **18.5, n. 1.**

McRae v. Bandy, 270 Ala. 12, 115 So.2d 479 (Ala.1959)—§ **19.13, n. 4;** § **19.15, n. 6.**

M.C.S., Matter of, 504 N.W.2d 322 (S.D. 1993)—§ **16.5, n. 9.**

McSurely v. McClellan, 753 F.2d 88, 243 U.S.App.D.C. 270 (D.C.Cir.1985)— § **17.55, n. 3.**

McSwain v. McSwain, 420 Pa. 86, 215 A.2d 677 (Pa.1966)—§ **17.12, n. 7.**

McVickers v. Chesapeake & O. Ry. Co., 194 F.Supp. 848 (E.D.Mich.1961)—§ **17.5, n. 4.**

Meadow Gold Dairies v. Oliver, 535 P.2d 290 (Okla.1975)—§ **16.6, n. 6.**

Meadows v. Dominican Republic, 817 F.2d 517 (9th Cir.1987)—§ **10.19, n. 47.**

Meagher v. Harjo, 72 Okla. 206, 179 P. 757 (Okla.1919)—§ **13.18, n. 8.**

Mech v. Pullman Standard, 136 Ill.App.3d 939, 92 Ill.Dec. 45, 484 N.E.2d 776 (Ill. App. 1 Dist.1984)—§ **17.26, n. 1.**

Mechanics Laundry & Supply, Inc. v. Wilder Oil Co., Inc., 596 N.E.2d 248 (Ind. App. 5 Dist.1992)—§ **11.4, n. 4;** § **11.5, n. 8.**

Medical Mut. of Ohio v. deSoto, 245 F.3d 561 (6th Cir.2001)—§ **10.2, n. 15, 22.**

Medinah Mining, Inc. v. Amunategui, 237 F.Supp.2d 1132 (D.Nev.2002)—§ **7.8, n. 14, 16.**

Medline Industries Inc. v. Maersk Medical Ltd., 230 F.Supp.2d 857 (N.D.Ill.2002)— § **17.40, n. 28.**

Med–Tec Iowa, Inc. v. Computerized Imaging Reference Systems, Inc., 223 F.Supp.2d 1034 (S.D.Iowa 2002)—§ **9.4, n. 8.**

Medtronic, Inc. v. Advanced Bionics Corp., 630 N.W.2d 438 (Minn.App.2001)— § **18.5, n. 29;** § **18.29, n. 5.**

Meeker v. Lehigh Valley R Co, 236 U.S. 412, 35 S.Ct. 328, 59 L.Ed. 644 (1915)— § **3.41, n. 18.**

Meier's Estate, In re, 33 Misc.2d 999, 226 N.Y.S.2d 733 (N.Y.Sur.1962)—§ **22.23, n. 8, 11.**

Meijer, Inc. v. General Star Indem. Co., 826 F.Supp. 241 (W.D.Mich.1993)—§ **18.26, n. 19.**

Meir v. Auto Owners Ins. Co., 1989 WL 14913 (Minn.App.1989)—§ **2.13, n. 20.**

Meisenhelder v. Chicago & N. W. Ry. Co., 170 Minn. 317, 213 N.W. 32 (Minn. 1927)—§ **13.13, n. 5;** § **13.14, n. 4.**

Meister's Estate, Matter of, 71 Wis.2d 581, 239 N.W.2d 52 (Wis.1976)—§ **22.15, n. 14.**

Mell v. Goodbody & Co., 10 Ill.App.3d 809, 295 N.E.2d 97 (Ill.App. 1 Dist.1973)— § **18.7, n. 2;** § **18.12, n. 2, 10, 12, 15.**

Mellk v. Sarahson, 49 N.J. 226, 229 A.2d 625 (N.J.1967)—§ **2.16, n. 9;** § **2.24, n. 3;** § **17.36, n. 15;** § **17.39, n. 8.**

Mellon Nat. Bank & Trust Co. v. Commissioner of Corporations and Taxation, 327 Mass. 631, 100 N.E.2d 370 (Mass. 1951)—§ **4.20, n. 7;** § **4.21, n. 1.**

Melville v. American Home Assur. Co., 443 F.Supp. 1064 (E.D.Pa.1977)—§ **18.21, n. 17.**

Melvin v. Doe, 49 Va. Cir. 257 (Va. Cir. Ct.1999)—§ **7.8, n. 14.**

Memorial Hospital v. Maricopa County, 415 U.S. 250, 94 S.Ct. 1076, 39 L.Ed.2d 306 (1974)—§ **4.20, n. 6.**

Memphis Development Foundation v. Factors Etc., Inc., 616 F.2d 956 (6th Cir. 1980)—§ **3.47, n. 7.**

Memphis State University v. Agee, 566 S.W.2d 283 (Tenn.Ct.App.1977)—§ **20.9, n. 9;** § **20.10, n. 1.**

Mendoza, United States v., 464 U.S. 154, 104 S.Ct. 568, 78 L.Ed.2d 379 (1984)— § **24.1, n. 12.**

Menendez v. Perishable Distributors, Inc., 254 Ga. 300, 329 S.E.2d 149 (Ga.1985)— § **2.21, n. 15.**

Menendez v. Saks & Co., 485 F.2d 1355 (2nd Cir.1973)—§ **18.29, n. 3;** § **18.44, n. 11.**

Mennonite Bd. of Missions v. Adams, 462 U.S. 791, 103 S.Ct. 2706, 77 L.Ed.2d 180 (1983)—§ **5.5, n. 18;** § **12.3, n. 5, 14.**

Menschefrend's Estate, In re, 283 A.D. 463, 128 N.Y.S.2d 738 (N.Y.A.D. 1 Dept. 1954)—§ **20.4, n. 6.**

Menzel v. County Utilities Corp., 501 F.Supp. 354 (E.D.Va.1979)—§ **24.12, n. 2.**

Mercantile Financial Corp. v. Sea Work Marine Services, Inc., 403 F.Supp. 979 (E.D.La.1975)—§ **19.13, n. 4.**

Mercantile Nat. Bank at Dallas, State ex rel. v. Rooney, 402 S.W.2d 354 (Mo. 1966)—§ **22.14, n. 5;** § **22.19, n. 6.**

Mercantile–Safe Deposit & Trust Co. v. Slater, 227 Md. 459, 177 A.2d 520 (Md. 1962)—§ **22.25, n. 4.**

Merchants Distributors, Inc. v. Hutchinson, 16 N.C.App. 655, 193 S.E.2d 436 (N.C.App.1972)—§ **22.14, n. 10.**

Merchants' Loan & Trust Co. v. Northern Trust Co., 250 Ill. 86, 95 N.E. 59 (Ill. 1911)—§ **20.7, n. 2.**

Merchants Nat. Bank of Mobile, United States v., 261 F.2d 570 (5th Cir.1958)— § **21.13, n. 2.**

Mergenthaler Linotype Co. v. Leonard Storch Enterprises, Inc., 66 Ill.App.3d 789, 23 Ill.Dec. 352, 383 N.E.2d 1379 (Ill.App. 1 Dist.1978)—§ **11.11, n. 3;** § **11.12, n. 1.**

Merican, Inc. v. Caterpillar Tractor Co., 596 F.Supp. 697 (E.D.Pa.1984)—§ **12.18, n. 11.**

Merrill v. New England Mut. Life Ins. Co., 103 Mass. 245 (Mass.1869)—§ **22.13, n. 4.**

Merrion v. Jicarilla Apache Tribe, 455 U.S. 130, 102 S.Ct. 894, 71 L.Ed.2d 21 (1982)—§ **11.17, n. 12;** § **15.39, n. 4.**

Merritt v. Corties, 54 N.Y.St.Rep. 215, 24 N.Y.S. 561 (N.Y.Sup.Gen.Term 1893)— § **21.2, n. 5.**

Merritt, State ex rel. v. Heffernan, 142 Fla. 496, 195 So. 145 (Fla.1940)—§ **6.4, n. 22.**

Merritt Dredging Co., Inc., In re, 839 F.2d 203 (4th Cir.1988)—§ **18.12, n. 16;** § **18.24, n. 2;** § **19.17, n. 6.**

Mertz v. Mertz, 271 N.Y. 466, 3 N.E.2d 597 (N.Y.1936)—§ **3.15, n. 2.**

Mertz v. Pharmacists Mut. Ins. Co., 261 Neb. 704, 625 N.W.2d 197 (Neb.2001)— § **18.29, n. 3.**

Mescalero Apache Tribe v. Jones, 411 U.S. 145, 93 S.Ct. 1267, 36 L.Ed.2d 114 (1973)—§ **11.17, n. 18, 35.**

Mescalero Apache Tribe v. State of N. M., 630 F.2d 724 (10th Cir.1980)—§ **11.17, n. 13.**

Messenger v. Rutherford, 80 Ill.App.2d 25, 225 N.E.2d 94 (Ill.App. 1 Dist.1967)— § **22.21, n. 4.**

Messina (formerly Smith Otherwise Vervaeke) v. Smith (Messina Intervening), 1971 WL 36917 (PDAD 1971)—§ **15.20, n. 1.**

Metcalf v. Lowther's Ex'x, 56 Ala. 312 (Ala. 1876)—§ **4.37, n. 2, 6.**

Metcalf's Estate, In re, 93 Mont. 542, 19 P.2d 905 (Mont.1933)—§ **22.22, n. 3.**

Metropolitan Cas. Ins. Co. of New York v. Brownell, 294 U.S. 580, 55 S.Ct. 538, 79 L.Ed. 1070 (1935)—§ **23.6, n. 5.**

Metropolitan Life Ins. Co. v. Chase, 294 F.2d 500 (3rd Cir.1961)—§ **13.6, n. 2.**

Metropolitan Life Ins. Co. v. Holding, 293 F.Supp. 854 (E.D.Va.1968)—§ **13.6, n. 2.**

Metropolitan Life Ins. Co. v. Manning, 568 F.2d 922 (2nd Cir.1977)—§ **13.2, n. 3, 14;** § **13.3, n. 2;** § **13.14, n. 2.**

Metzger v. Metzger, 32 Ohio App. 202, 167 N.E. 690 (Ohio App. 4 Dist.1929)— § **15.27, n. 1.**

Meyer v. State Farm Fire and Cas. Co., 85 Md.App. 83, 582 A.2d 275 (Md.App. 1990)—§ **18.5, n. 5.**

MFA Life Ins. Co. v. Kyle, 630 F.2d 322 (6th Cir.1980)—§ **14.11, n. 2.**

M & G Convoy, Inc. v. Mauk, 85 Md.App. 394, 584 A.2d 101 (Md.App.1991)— § **17.59, n. 16.**

MGM Grand Hotel, Inc. v. Imperial Glass Co., 65 F.R.D. 624 (D.Nev.1974)— § **18.4, n. 7, 55;** § **18.5, n. 17;** § **18.7, n. 8.**

MGM Studios Inc. v. Grokster, Ltd., 243 F.Supp.2d 1073 (C.D.Cal.2003)—§ **5.10, n. 26.**

M & G Polymers USA v. CNC Containers Corp., 190 F.Supp.2d 854 (S.D.W.Va. 2002)—§ **8.5, n. 5.**

MHC Investment Co. v. Racom Corp., 254 F.Supp.2d 1090 (S.D.Iowa 2002)— § **23.5, n. 1.**

Mianecki v. Second Judicial Dist. Court, In and For Washoe County, 99 Nev. 93, 658 P.2d 422 (Nev.1983)—§ **17.43, n. 16.**

Michael v. S S Thanasis, 311 F.Supp. 170 (N.D.Cal.1970)— § **12.18, n. 8.**

Michaelesco, In re, 288 B.R. 646 (D.Conn. 2003)—§ **10.7, n. 19.**

Michael Schiavone & Sons, Inc. v. Securalloy Co., 312 F.Supp. 801 (D.Conn. 1970)—§ **18.24, n. 1.**

Michalik v. Michalik, 172 Wis.2d 640, 494 N.W.2d 391 (Wis.1993)—§ **15.42, n. 9.**

Michelson v. Exxon Research and Engineering Co., 578 F.Supp. 289 (W.D.Pa. 1984)—§ **4.9, n. 2.**

Michigan Trust Co. v. Chaffee, 73 N.D. 86, 11 N.W.2d 108 (N.D.1943)—§ **22.17, n. 1.**

Michigan Trust Co. v. Ferry, 228 U.S. 346, 33 S.Ct. 550, 57 L.Ed. 867 (1913)— § **5.23, n. 1;** § **22.19, n. 20, 32;** § **22.20, n. 26.**

Mick v. American Dental Ass'n, 49 N.J.Super. 262, 139 A.2d 570 (N.J.Super.A.D.1958)—§ **12.19, n. 15.**

Microfibres, Inc. v. McDevitt–Askew, 20 F.Supp.2d 316 (D.R.I.1998)—§ **24.15, n. 2.**

Micromedia v. Automated Broadcast Controls, 799 F.2d 230 (5th Cir.1986)— § **7.12, n. 8.**

Middlebrook v. Merchants' Bank of New York, 1866 WL 5751 (N.Y.1866)— § **22.12, n. 7.**

Middleton v. Luckenbach S.S. Co., 70 F.2d 326 (2nd Cir.1934)—§ **3.54, n. 4.**

Middleton v. Middleton, 227 Va. 82, 314 S.E.2d 362 (Va.1984)—§ **15.43, n. 8.**

Midland–Ross Corp. v. Sunbeam Equipment Corp., 316 F.Supp. 171 (W.D.Pa.1970)— § **17.53, n. 3.**

Midwest Mfg. Holding, L.L.C. v. Donnelly Corp., 975 F.Supp. 1061 (N.D.Ill.1997)— § **18.7, n. 8.**

Miedreich v. Lauenstein, 232 U.S. 236, 34 S.Ct. 309, 58 L.Ed. 584 (1914)—§ **12.3, n. 7.**

Migra v. Warren City School Dist. Bd. of Educ., 465 U.S. 75, 104 S.Ct. 892, 79 L.Ed.2d 56 (1984)—§ **24.1, n. 7;** § **24.12, n. 7.**

Mihalopoulos v. Westwind Africa Line, Ltd., 511 So.2d 771 (La.App. 5 Cir.1987)— § **17.63, n. 23.**

Milanovich v. Costa Crociere, S.p.A., 954 F.2d 763, 293 U.S.App.D.C. 332 (D.C.Cir.1992)—§ **18.5, n. 1.**

Milena Ship Management Co. v. Newcomb, 804 F.Supp. 859 (E.D.La.1992)— § **12.18, n. 17.**

Miles v. Illinois Cent. R. Co., 315 U.S. 698, 62 S.Ct. 827, 86 L.Ed. 1129 (1942)— § **11.13, n. 4.**

Milford, Town of v. Town of Greenwich, 126 Conn. 340, 11 A.2d 352 (Conn. 1940)—§ **4.43, n. 1.**

Miliangos v. George Frank (Textiles) Ltd (No.1), 1975 WL 45627 (HL 1975)— § **24.31, n. 8; § 24.40, n. 9.**

Milkovich v. Lorain Journal Co., 497 U.S. 1, 110 S.Ct. 2695, 111 L.Ed.2d 1 (1990)— § **7.8, n. 1.**

Milkovich v. Saari, 295 Minn. 155, 203 N.W.2d 408 (Minn.1973)—§ **2.13, n. 7; § 2.16, n. 13; § 2.25, n. 2; § 3.13, n. 4; § 3.16, n. 5; § 17.21, n. 23, 27; § 17.22; § 17.22, n. 2; § 17.34, n. 8; § 17.37, n. 12; § 17.39, n. 21.**

Millar–Mintz v. Abbott Laboratories, 268 Ill.App.3d 566, 206 Ill.Dec. 273, 645 N.E.2d 278 (Ill.App. 1 Dist.1994)— § **17.64, n. 12.**

Miller, In re, 31 Cal.2d 191, 187 P.2d 722 (Cal.1947)—§ **14.9, n. 4, 14.**

Miller, In re, 5 Dem. 381 (N.Y.1887)— § **22.13, n. 1.**

Miller v. American Dredging Co., 595 So.2d 615 (La.1992)—§ **11.13, n. 3.**

Miller v. A.N. Webber, Inc., 484 N.W.2d 420 (Minn.App.1992)—§ **12.19, n. 19.**

Miller v. Bode, 80 Ind.App. 338, 139 N.E. 456 (Ind.App. 2 Div.1923)—§ **4.39, n. 1.**

Miller v. Bombardier, Inc., 872 F.Supp. 114 (S.D.N.Y.1995)—§ **17.42, n. 11, 19.**

Miller v. Gay, 323 Pa.Super. 466, 470 A.2d 1353 (Pa.Super.1983)—§ **2.16, n. 9; § 17.45; § 17.45, n. 27; § 17.56, n. 7.**

Miller v. Hirschbach Motor Lines, Inc., 714 S.W.2d 652 (Mo.App. S.D.1986)— § **17.59, n. 9, 14.**

Miller v. Hoover, 121 Mo.App. 568, 97 S.W. 210 (Mo.App.1906)—§ **22.10, n. 4; § 22.14, n. 3; § 22.18, n. 9.**

Miller v. Kingsley, 194 Neb. 123, 230 N.W.2d 472 (Neb.1975)—§ **24.20, n. 3.**

Miller v. Lucks, 203 Miss. 824, 36 So.2d 140 (Miss.1948)—§ **13.10, n. 4.**

Miller v. Miller, 22 N.Y.2d 12, 290 N.Y.S.2d 734, 237 N.E.2d 877 (N.Y.1968)—§ **3.23, n. 10; § 17.11, n. 8; § 17.17, n. 8; § 17.30; § 17.30, n. 13; § 17.31, n. 6.**

Miller v. Miller, 247 Md. 358, 231 A.2d 27 (Md.1967)—§ **15.29, n. 4.**

Miller v. Miller, 205 N.C. 753, 172 S.E. 493 (N.C.1934)—§ **4.33, n. 3.**

Miller v. Miller, 67 Or. 359, 136 P. 15 (Or.1913)—§ **4.13, n. 2.**

Miller v. Miller, 91 N.Y. 315 (N.Y.1883)— § **16.2, n. 5.**

Miller v. Nelson, 160 Fla. 410, 35 So.2d 288 (Fla.1948)—§ **4.42, n. 6.**

Miller v. Northside Danzi Const. Co., 629 P.2d 1389 (Alaska 1981)—§ **17.61, n. 2.**

Miller v. Phoenix State Bank & Trust Co., 138 Conn. 12, 81 A.2d 444 (Conn. 1951)—§ **22.25, n. 4.**

Miller, State ex rel. v. Baxter Chrysler Plymouth, Inc., 456 N.W.2d 371 (Iowa 1990)—§ **9.8, n. 9.**

Miller, State ex rel. v. Grodzinsky, 571 N.W.2d 1 (Iowa 1997)—§ **9.8, n. 9.**

Miller v. State Farm Mut. Auto. Ins. Co., 87 F.3d 822 (6th Cir.1996)—§ **17.56, n. 11.**

Miller v. Trans World Airlines, Inc., 302 F.Supp. 174 (E.D.Ky.1969)—§ **10.16, n. 8.**

Miller v. United States Postal Service, 729 F.2d 1033 (5th Cir.1984)—§ **24.24, n. 5.**

Miller v. Wells Fargo Bank Intern. Corp., 406 F.Supp. 452 (S.D.N.Y.1975)— § **18.37, n. 12.**

Miller v. White, 167 Vt. 45, 702 A.2d 392 (Vt.1997)—§ **17.26; § 17.26, n. 8; § 17.36, n. 15; § 17.39, n. 15, 17; § 17.56, n. 10, 13, 20; § 17.57, n. 4, 8.**

Miller's Estate, In re, 239 Mich. 455, 214 N.W. 428 (Mich.1927)—§ **13.2, n. 10; § 13.11, n. 3.**

Miller's Estate v. Commissioner of Taxation, 240 Minn. 18, 59 N.W.2d 925 (Minn.1953)—§ **4.24, n. 1.**

Miller's Estate v. Executrix of Miller's Estate, 90 Kan. 819, 136 P. 255 (Kan. 1913)—§ **22.12, n. 1.**

Miller, Succession of v. Moss, 479 So.2d 1035 (La.App. 3 Cir.1985)—§ **19.8, n. 14.**

Milliken v. Meyer, 311 U.S. 457, 61 S.Ct. 339, 85 L.Ed. 278 (1940)—§ **4.3, n. 1; § 4.13, n. 4; § 4.30, n. 1; § 5.3, n. 11; § 5.4, n. 9; § 5.8, n. 5; § 5.13, n. 26; § 6.4; § 6.4, n. 4; § 11.7, n. 1.**

Milliken v. Pratt, 125 Mass. 374 (Mass. 1878)—§ **2.9, n. 14; § 18.14; § 18.14, n. 2.**

Milliken v. Tri–County Elec. Co-op., Inc., 254 F.Supp. 302 (D.S.C.1966)—§ **4.24, n. 1.**

Millikin Trust Co. v. Jarvis, 34 Ill.App.2d 180, 180 N.E.2d 759 (Ill.App. 3 Dist. 1962)—§ **14.5, n. 1; § 14.6, n. 2; § 14.7, n. 3, 5.**

Millipore Corp. v. Travelers Indem. Co., 115 F.3d 21 (1st Cir.1997)—§ **18.26, n. 13.**

Mills v. City of Philadelphia Acting Through Bd. of City Trusts, 52 N.J.Super. 52, 144 A.2d 728 (N.J.Super.Ch.1958)—§ **21.7, n. 2.**

Mills v. Duryee, 11 U.S. 481, 3 L.Ed. 411 (1813)—§ **5.1, n. 6; § 5.2, n. 4; § 5.8, n. 5; § 5.14, n. 3; § 6.5, n. 2.**

Mills v. Fogal, 4 Edw.Ch. 559, 6 N.Y. Ch. Ann. 975 (N.Y.Ch.1844)—§ **20.11, n. 1.**

Mills v. Habluetzel, 456 U.S. 91, 102 S.Ct. 1549, 71 L.Ed.2d 770 (1982)—§ **16.3, n. 9.**

Mills v. Howard, 228 S.W.2d 906 (Tex.Civ. App.-Amarillo 1950)—§ **4.40, n. 4.**

Mills v. Jacobs, 333 Pa. 231, 4 A.2d 152 (Pa.1939)—§ **19.32, n. 5.**

Mills v. Mills, 119 Conn. 612, 179 A. 5 (Conn.1935)—§ **4.24, n. 3.**

Mills v. Quality Supplier Trucking, Inc., 203 W.Va. 621, 510 S.E.2d 280 (W.Va. 1998)—§ **2.21; § 2.21, n. 31; § 17.8, n. 2.**

Mills v. State Farm Mut. Auto. Ins. Co., 827 F.2d 1418 (10th Cir.1987)—§ **13.3, n. 2, 3.**

Millsap v. Central Wis. Motor Transport Co., 41 Ill.App.2d 1, 189 N.E.2d 793 (Ill.App. 1 Dist.1963)—§ **17.6, n. 3.**

Mills' Guardian v. City of Hopkinsville, 11 S.W. 776 (Ky.1889)—§ **4.42, n. 2.**

Milton v. Escue, 201 Md. 190, 93 A.2d 258 (Md.1952)—§ **16.1, n. 8; § 16.2, n. 5.**

Milwaukee, City of v. Illinois and Michigan, 451 U.S. 304, 101 S.Ct. 1784, 68 L.Ed.2d 114 (1981)—§ **3.49, n. 7; § 3.50, n. 5; § 3.54, n. 17.**

Milwaukee Concrete Studios, Ltd. v. Fjeld Mfg. Co., Inc., 8 F.3d 441 (7th Cir. 1993)—§ **5.18, n. 10; § 9.3, n. 12.**

Milwaukee County v. M.E. White Co., 296 U.S. 268, 56 S.Ct. 229, 80 L.Ed. 220 (1935)—§ **3.17, n. 9; § 24.12, n. 7; § 24.20, n. 5; § 24.23; § 24.23, n. 3, 12.**

Mims v. Mims, 635 A.2d 320 (D.C.1993)—§ **4.37, n. 3.**

Miner v. Austin, 45 Iowa 221 (Iowa 1876)—§ **22.21, n. 6.**

Ministers & Missionaries Ben. Bd. v. McKay, 64 Misc.2d 231, 315 N.Y.S.2d 549 (N.Y.Sup.1970)—§ **21.2, n. 13.**

Minnesota v. Cuypers, 559 N.W.2d 435 (Minn.App.1997)—§ **17.56, n. 1.**

Minnesota Min. and Mfg. Co. v. Nishika Ltd., 953 S.W.2d 733 (Tex.1997)—§ **18.21, n. 14.**

Minnesota, State of v. United States, 305 U.S. 382, 59 S.Ct. 292, 83 L.Ed. 235 (1939)—§ **11.17, n. 16.**

Minnesota, State of, by Humphrey v. Granite Gate Resorts, Inc., 568 N.W.2d 715 (Minn.App.1997)—§ **9.8, n. 9.**

Minor v. Cardwell, 37 Mo. 350 (Mo.1866)—§ **19.2, n. 2.**

Minor, In re Adoption of, 191 Wash. 452, 71 P.2d 385 (Wash.1937)—§ **4.38, n. 2.**

Minton v. McManus, 9 Ohio App.3d 165, 458 N.E.2d 1292 (Ohio App. 9 Dist. 1983)—§ **15.43, n. 8.**

Minuteman Press Intern., Inc. v. Sparks, 782 S.W.2d 339 (Tex.App.-Fort Worth 1989)—§ **8.3, n. 11.**

Miracle v. New Yorker Magazine, 190 F.Supp.2d 1192 (D.Hawai'i 2001)—§ **17.55, n. 9.**

Miree v. DeKalb County, Ga., 433 U.S. 25, 97 S.Ct. 2490, 53 L.Ed.2d 557 (1977)—§ **3.50, n. 6, 9; § 3.53, n. 11; § 3.54; § 3.54, n. 6.**

Miserandino v. Resort Properties, Inc., 345 Md. 43, 691 A.2d 208 (Md.1997)—§ **24.14, n. 3; § 24.44, n. 5.**

Mission Ins. Co. v. Industrial Commission, 114 Ariz. 170, 559 P.2d 1085 (Ariz.App. Div. 1 1976)—§ **13.5, n. 1.**

Mission Ins. Co. v. Nethers, 119 Ariz. 405, 581 P.2d 250 (Ariz.App. Div. 2 1978)—§ **18.26, n. 12.**

Mississippi Band of Choctaw Indians v. Holyfield, 490 U.S. 30, 109 S.Ct. 1597, 104 L.Ed.2d 29 (1989)—§ **4.8, n. 1; § 4.9, n. 2; § 11.17, n. 2, 43.**

Missouri ex rel. Southern Ry. Co., State of v. Mayfield, 340 U.S. 1, 71 S.Ct. 1, 95 L.Ed. 3 (1950)—§ **3.32, n. 9; § 11.11, n. 11; § 11.13, n. 5.**

Missouri Farmers Ass'n, Inc., United States v., 764 F.2d 488 (8th Cir.1985)—§ **3.51, n. 11.**

Missouri Pac. R. Co. v. Bradley, 51 Neb. 596, 71 N.W. 283 (Neb.1897)—§ **22.10, n. 10.**

Missouri Pac. R. Co. v. Lewis, 24 Neb. 848, 40 N.W. 401 (Neb.1888)—§ **22.10, n. 8.**

Missouri Portland Cement Co. v. J. A. Jones Const. Co., 323 F.Supp. 242 (M.D.Tenn.1970)—§ **18.21, n. 11.**

Missouri State Life Ins. Co. v. Lovelace, 1 Ga.App. 446, 58 S.E. 93 (Ga.App.1907)—§ **18.5, n. 9.**

Missouri, State of v. Holland, 252 U.S. 416, 40 S.Ct. 382, 64 L.Ed. 641 (1920)—§ **3.56, n. 9.**

Mitchell v. Craft, 211 So.2d 509 (Miss. 1968)—§ **2.16, n. 8; § 2.23, n. 1; § 17.11, n. 22; § 17.26, n. 1; § 17.39, n. 12.**

Mitchell v. Lone Star Ammunition, Inc., 913 F.2d 242 (5th Cir.1990)—§ **17.76; § 17.76, n. 17.**

Mitchell v. Mackey, 915 F.Supp. 388 (M.D.Ga.1996)—§ **4.18, n. 1; § 4.19, n. 1.**

Mitchell v. State Farm Ins. Co., 315 Mont. 281, 68 P.3d 703 (Mont.2003)—§ **17.56, n. 19; § 18.26, n. 7.**

Mitchell v. W. T. Grant Co., 416 U.S. 600, 94 S.Ct. 1895, 40 L.Ed.2d 406 (1974)—§ **24.15, n. 3.**

Mitsubishi Motors Corp. v. Soler Chrysler–Plymouth, Inc., 473 U.S. 614, 105 S.Ct. 3346, 87 L.Ed.2d 444 (1985)—§ **3.59, n. 13; § 11.6, n. 4, 6; § 24.48, n. 2.**

Mitsui & Co. (U.S.A.) Inc. v. Puerto Rico Water Resources Authority, 79 F.R.D. 72 (D.Puerto Rico 1978)—§ **12.11, n. 3, 7.**

Mitsui Manufacturers Bank v. Tucker, 152 Cal.App.3d 428, 199 Cal.Rptr. 517 (Cal. App. 4 Dist.1984)—§ **22.19, n. 14.**

Mittenthal v. Mascagni, 183 Mass. 19, 66 N.E. 425 (Mass.1903)—§ **18.4, n. 42.**

MM, In re Adoption of, 652 P.2d 974 (Wyo. 1982)—§ **16.5, n. 5.**

M.M.D., In re, 662 A.2d 837 (D.C.1995)— § **16.4, n. 3.**

Mobil Oil Corp. v. Linear Films, Inc., 718 F.Supp. 260 (D.Del.1989)—§ **23.10, n. 2.**

Mobil Tankers Co., S. A. v. Mene Grande Oil Co., 363 F.2d 611 (3rd Cir.1966)— § **11.9, n. 1.**

Mocher v. Rasmussen–Taxdal, 180 So.2d 488 (Fla.App. 2 Dist.1965)—§ **15.36, n. 2.**

Modern Computer Corp. v. Ma, 862 F.Supp. 938 (E.D.N.Y.1994)—§ **9.3, n. 17.**

Modern Computer Systems, Inc. v. Modern Banking Systems, Inc., 871 F.2d 734 (8th Cir.1989)—§ **18.5, n. 37.**

Modern Computer Systems, Inc. v. Modern Banking Systems, Inc., 858 F.2d 1339 (8th Cir.1988)—§ **18.5; § 18.5, n. 36.**

Modern Woodmen of America v. Hester, 66 Kan. 129, 71 P. 279 (Kan.1903)—§ **4.37, n. 2, 7, 10.**

Modianos, United States ex rel. v. Tuttle, 12 F.2d 927 (E.D.La.1925)—§ **13.6, n. 12.**

Modnick, In re Marriage of, 191 Cal.Rptr. 629, 663 P.2d 187 (Cal.1983)—§ **15.10, n. 2.**

Moe v. Confederated Salish and Kootenai Tribes of Flathead Reservation, 425 U.S. 463, 96 S.Ct. 1634, 48 L.Ed.2d 96 (1976)—§ **11.17, n. 7.**

Moe v. Shaffer, 150 Minn. 114, 184 N.W. 785 (Minn.1921)—§ **3.11, n. 2.**

Moen v. Moen, 16 S.D. 210, 92 N.W. 13 (S.D.1902)—§ **20.2, n. 4.**

Mohamed v. Knott, 1968 WL 23095 (DC 1968)—§ **13.17, n. 10.**

Mohn v. Tingley, 191 Cal. 470, 217 P. 733 (Cal.1923)—§ **13.9, n. 5.**

Molzen's Will, In re, 72 Misc.2d 46, 338 N.Y.S.2d 189 (N.Y.Sur.1972)—§ **22.10, n. 12.**

Monarch Ins. Co. of Ohio v. Spach, 281 F.2d 401 (5th Cir.1960)—§ **3.38, n. 5.**

Moncada v. Lemuria Shipping Corp., 491 F.2d 470 (2nd Cir.1974)—§ **17.63, n. 23.**

Mon Chi Heung Au v. Lum, 360 F.Supp. 219 (D.Hawai'i 1973)—§ **4.18, n. 2.**

Monroe v. Jackson, 55 Me. 55 (Me.1867)— § **4.45, n. 6.**

Monroe v. Numed Inc., 250 A.D.2d 20, 680 N.Y.S.2d 707 (N.Y.A.D. 3 Dept.1998)— § **17.43, n. 9; § 17.44, n. 10.**

Monsanto Co. v. Aetna Cas. & Sur. Co., C.A. No. 88C–01–118 (Del.Super. Jan.19, 1991)—§ **18.1, n. 27.**

Montana v. United States, 440 U.S. 147, 99 S.Ct. 970, 59 L.Ed.2d 210 (1979)— § **24.1, n. 11.**

Montgomery v. Farmers Texas County Ins. Co., 786 So.2d 306 (La.App. 2 Cir. 2001)—§ **17.56, n. 20.**

Montgomery v. National Sav. & Trust Co., 356 F.2d 806, 123 U.S.App.D.C. 53 (D.C.Cir.1966)—§ **22.2, n. 3; § 22.7, n. 1.**

Montpetit v. Allina Health System, Inc., 2000 WL 1486581 (Minn.App.2000)— § **17.23, n. 14.**

Montreal Trust Co., United States v., 358 F.2d 239 (2nd Cir.1966)—§ **10.17, n. 3; § 22.19, n. 10.**

Mooar v. Harvey, 128 Mass. 219 (Mass. 1880)—§ **4.26, n. 1.**

Moon v. Moon, 265 Ark. 310, 578 S.W.2d 203 (Ark.1979)—§ **4.24, n. 1; § 4.34, n. 3.**

Moore, Matter of, 129 Misc.2d 639, 493 N.Y.S.2d 924 (N.Y.Sup.1985)—§ **21.3, n. 17; § 21.9, n. 1; § 21.11, n. 6, 17; § 21.13, n. 1.**

Moore v. Church, 70 Iowa 208, 30 N.W. 855 (Iowa 1886)—§ **19.3, n. 16.**

Moore v. Fields, 42 Pa. 467 (Pa.1862)— § **22.18, n. 10.**

Moore v. Greene, 431 F.2d 584 (9th Cir. 1970)—§ **17.55, n. 9.**

Moore v. KLLM, Inc., 673 So.2d 1268 (La. App. 5 Cir.1996)—§ **17.59, n. 10.**

Moore v. Kraft, 179 F. 685 (7th Cir.1910)— § **22.18, n. 8.**

Moore v. Livingston, 148 Ind.App. 275, 265 N.E.2d 251 (Ind.App. 1 Div.1970)— § **19.4, n. 3; § 20.7, n. 3; § 21.2, n. 8.**

Moore v. Montes, 22 Ariz.App. 562, 529 P.2d 716 (Ariz.App. Div. 1 1974)— § **22.10, n. 16.**

Moore v. Moore, 430 S.W.2d 247 (Tex.Civ. App.-Dallas 1968)—§ **22.22, n. 2.**

Moore v. Owens–Corning, 528 U.S. 1005, 120 S.Ct. 500, 145 L.Ed.2d 386 (1999)— § **3.32, n. 9.**

Moore v. Pywell (D.C.Cir.1907)—§ **17.5, n. 3.**

Moore v. Wa-me-go, 72 Kan. 169, 83 P. 400 (Kan.1905)—§ **13.18, n. 8, 14.**

Moore & Ferrie, In re Marriage of, 18 Cal. Rptr.2d 543 (Cal.App. 1 Dist.1993)— § **14.9, n. 2, 3.**

Moore's Estate, In re, 68 Wash.2d 792, 415 P.2d 653 (Wash.1966)—§ **4.38, n. 1; § 4.41, n. 7.**

Moorman Mfg. Co. v. Bair, 437 U.S. 267, 98 S.Ct. 2340, 57 L.Ed.2d 197 (1978)— § **23.6, n. 7.**

Moragne v. States Marine Lines, Inc., 398 U.S. 375, 90 S.Ct. 1772, 26 L.Ed.2d 339 (1970)—§ **17.63, n. 2.**

Morales v. Navieras de Puerto Rico, 713 F.Supp. 711 (S.D.N.Y.1989)—§ **11.14, n. 6.**

Morefield v. Harris, 126 N.C. 626, 36 S.E. 125 (N.C.1900)—§ **22.9, n. 1; § 22.18, n. 9.**

Moreno v. Milk Train, Inc., 182 F.Supp.2d 590 (W.D.Tex.2002)—§ **8.4, n. 2.**

Moreno v. Toll, 489 F.Supp. 658 (D.Md. 1980)—§ **4.31, n. 6.**

Moretti & Perlow Law Offices v. Aleet Associates, 668 F.Supp. 103 (D.R.I.1987)— § **11.6, n. 8.**

Moretti's Estate, In re, 16 Pa. D. & C. 715 (Pa.Orph.1932)—§ **16.1, n. 12.**

Morewitz v. Andros Compania Maritima, S. A., 614 F.2d 379 (4th Cir.1980)— § **17.63, n. 24.**

Morgan v. Biro Mfg. Co., Inc., 15 Ohio St.3d 339, 474 N.E.2d 286 (Ohio 1984)— § **2.16, n. 16;** § **2.23, n. 1;** § **17.26, n. 1.**

Morgan v. Mar–Bel, Inc., 614 F.Supp. 438 (N.D.Ga.1985)—§ **18.21, n. 5.**

Morgan v. McGhee, 24 Tenn. 13 (Tenn. 1844)—§ **13.18, n. 8, 10.**

Morgan v. Potter, 157 U.S. 195, 15 S.Ct. 590, 39 L.Ed. 670 (1895)—§ **22.25, n. 5.**

Morgan v. South Bend Community School Corp., 797 F.2d 471 (7th Cir.1986)— § **3.51, n. 12.**

Morgan Guaranty Trust Co. of New York v. Huntington, 149 Conn. 331, 179 A.2d 604 (Conn.1962)—§ **21.11, n. 17;** § **21.13, n. 2.**

Morgan Guar. Trust Co. v. Hellenic Lines Ltd., 621 F.Supp. 198 (S.D.N.Y.1985)— § **19.26, n. 6.**

Morgan Walton Properties, Inc. v. International City Bank & Trust Co., 404 So.2d 1059 (Fla.1981)—§ **18.5, n. 12.**

Morguard Investments Ltd. v. De Savoye (S.C.C.1990)—§ **24.40, n. 6.**

Morisette v. Canadian Pac. Ry. Co., 76 Vt. 267, 56 A. 1102 (Vt.1904)—§ **17.6, n. 2.**

Morrell v. Dickey, 1 Johns.Ch. 153, 1 N.Y. Ch. Ann. 96 (N.Y.Ch.1814)—§ **22.25, n. 1, 2, 16.**

Morris, Matter of, 30 F.3d 1578 (7th Cir. 1994)—§ **19.3, n. 1, 8.**

Morris v. Barkbuster, Inc., 923 F.2d 1277 (8th Cir.1991)—§ **5.10, n. 34;** § **5.13, n. 19;** § **6.9, n. 20.**

Morris v. Garmon, 291 Ark. 67, 722 S.W.2d 571 (Ark.1987)—§ **22.6, n. 4.**

Morris v. Gilmer, 129 U.S. 315, 9 S.Ct. 289, 32 L.Ed. 690 (1889)—§ **4.24, n. 1, 2.**

Morris v. Jones, 329 U.S. 545, 67 S.Ct. 451, 91 L.Ed. 488 (1947)—§ **22.20, n. 28;** § **22.21, n. 17;** § **24.20, n. 1.**

Morris v. Stuyvesant Ins. Co., 449 F.Supp. 14 (S.D.N.Y.1978)—§ **24.1, n. 7.**

Morris v. Watsco, Inc., 385 Mass. 672, 433 N.E.2d 886 (Mass.1982)—§ **18.12, n. 16;** § **18.39, n. 3, 7.**

Morrison v. Bershire Loan & Trust Co., 229 Mass. 519, 118 N.E. 895 (Mass.1918)— § **22.16, n. 3.**

Morrison v. Hass, 229 Mass. 514, 118 N.E. 893 (Mass.1918)—§ **22.2, n. 3.**

Morris Plan Co. of Cal. v. Converse, 15 Cal.App.3d 399, 93 Cal.Rptr. 103 (Cal. App. 4 Dist.1971)—§ **13.5, n. 7.**

Morris Plan Indus. Bank of N.Y. v. Richards, 131 Conn. 671, 42 A.2d 147 (Conn. 1945)—§ **3.10, n. 1.**

Morse v. King, 63 A. 986 (N.J.Err. & App. 1906)—§ **22.18, n. 2.**

Morse Electro Products Corp. v. S.S. Great Peace, 437 F.Supp. 474 (D.N.J.1977)— § **11.3, n. 22;** § **12.18, n. 3.**

Morson v. Second Nat. Bank of Boston, 306 Mass. 588, 29 N.E.2d 19 (Mass.1940)— § **19.32, n. 9.**

Mortenson v. Mortenson, 409 N.W.2d 20 (Minn.App.1987)—§ **14.11, n. 1.**

Mortenson's Estate, In re, 83 Ariz. 87, 316 P.2d 1106 (Ariz.1957)—§ **13.11, n. 4;** § **13.13, n. 5.**

Morton v. Environmental Land Systems, Ltd., 55 Ill.App.3d 369, 13 Ill.Dec. 79, 370 N.E.2d 1106 (Ill.App. 1 Dist.1977)— § **10.12, n. 8.**

Morton v. Mancari, 417 U.S. 535, 94 S.Ct. 2474, 41 L.Ed.2d 290 (1974)—§ **11.17, n. 10, 11.**

Morton Internatl., Inc. v. Aetna Cas. & Sur. Co., 106 Ohio App.3d 653, 666 N.E.2d 1163 (Ohio App. 1 Dist.1995)—§ **18.26, n. 13.**

Mostyn v. Fabrigas, 1775 WL 17 (Unknown Court 1775)—§ **12.15, n. 2.**

Motenko v. MGM Dist., Inc., 112 Nev. 1038, 921 P.2d 933 (Nev.1996)—§ **2.16, n. 20;** § **2.24, n. 13;** § **17.15;** § **17.15, n. 21;** § **17.42, n. 15, 19.**

Motorcity of Jacksonville, Ltd. By and Through Motorcity of Jacksonville, Inc. v. Southeast Bank, N.A., 83 F.3d 1317 (11th Cir.1996)—§ **3.51, n. 2.**

Motor Club of America Ins. Co. v. Hanifi, 145 F.3d 170 (4th Cir.1998)—§ **3.47, n. 2.**

Motschenbacher v. R. J. Reynolds Tobacco Co., 498 F.2d 821 (9th Cir.1974)— § **17.55, n. 9.**

Mott v. Duncan Petroleum Trans., 434 N.Y.S.2d 155, 414 N.E.2d 657 (N.Y. 1980)—§ **13.6, n. 2.**

Moultrie v. Hunt, 23 N.Y. 394 (N.Y.1861)— § **20.12, n. 3.**

Mount v. Tuttle, 183 N.Y. 358, 76 N.E. 873 (N.Y.1906)—§ **20.7, n. 1, 5.**

Mountaire Feeds, Inc. v. Agro Impex, S. A., 677 F.2d 651 (8th Cir.1982)—§ **8.5, n. 7.**

Mounteer v. Bayly, 86 A.D.2d 942, 448 N.Y.S.2d 582 (N.Y.A.D. 3 Dept.1982)— § **10.12, n. 3.**

Mowry v. Latham, 17 R.I. 480, 23 A. 13 (R.I.1891)—§ **4.45, n. 3.**

Moye v. Palma, 263 N.J.Super. 287, 622 A.2d 935 (N.J.Super.A.D.1993)— § **17.36, n. 15;** § **17.48, n. 8.**

Moyer v. Citicorp Homeowners, Inc., 799 F.2d 1445 (11th Cir.1986)—§ **18.11, n. 4;** § **19.11, n. 15.**

Mozes v. Mozes, 239 F.3d 1067 (9th Cir. 2001)—§ **4.14;** § **4.14, n. 9.**

Mpiliris v. Hellenic Lines, Ltd., 323 F.Supp. 865 (S.D.Tex.1969)—§ **13.8, n. 6;** § **13.15, n. 3, 4;** § **17.63, n. 23;** § **24.35, n. 6.**

M.T.C. v. J.M.M., 60 Mass.App.Ct. 1106, 799 N.E.2d 606 (Mass.App.Ct.2003)— § **16.3, n. 11.**

Muckle v. Superior Court, 125 Cal.Rptr.2d 303 (Cal.App. 4 Dist.2002)—§ **15.28, n. 1.**

Mueller v. Mueller, 127 Ala. 356, 28 So. 465 (Ala.1900)—§ **14.15, n. 10.**

Mueller, State v., 44 Wis.2d 387, 171 N.W.2d 414 (Wis.1969)—§ **13.9, n. 14.**

Mullane v. Central Hanover Bank & Trust Co., 339 U.S. 306, 70 S.Ct. 652, 94 L.Ed. 865 (1950)—§ **5.5, n. 17;** § **5.16;** § **5.16, n. 1, 6;** § **6.6, n. 3;** § **10.9;** § **10.9, n. 7;** § **12.3, n. 1, 4;** § **22.3, n. 6;** § **22.21, n. 2.**

Muller v. Reagh, 148 Cal.App.2d 157, 306 P.2d 593 (Cal.App. 1 Dist.1957)—§ **5.20, n. 8.**

Mullins v. M.G.D. Graphics Systems Group, 867 F.Supp. 1578 (N.D.Ga.1994)— § **17.79, n. 2.**

Mulvihill v. Furness, Withy & Co, 136 F.Supp. 201 (S.D.N.Y.1955)—§ **18.30, n. 4.**

Munday v. Baldwin, 79 Ky. 121 (Ky.1880)— § **4.41, n. 7.**

Munday v. Wisconsin Trust Co., 252 U.S. 499, 40 S.Ct. 365, 64 L.Ed. 684 (1920)— § **23.7, n. 6.**

Munford v. Maclellan, 258 Ga. 679, 373 S.E.2d 368 (Ga.1988)—§ **21.5, n. 1.**

Muns v. Muns, 567 S.W.2d 563 (Tex.Civ. App.-Dallas 1978)—§ **14.13, n. 4.**

Munson v. Exchange Nat. Bank, 19 Wash. 125, 52 P. 1011 (Wash.1898)—§ **22.17, n. 1.**

Munson v. Johnston, 16 N.J. 31, 106 A.2d 1 (N.J.1954)—§ **4.41, n. 6.**

Munzer v. Jacoby–Munzer, [1964] Bull. des arrts de la Cour de Cass., ch. civ. I, No. 15—§ **24.38, n. 11.**

Murdoch, Appeal of, 81 Conn. 681, 72 A. 290 (Conn.1909)—§ **22.4, n. 8.**

Murdock v. Volvo of America Corp., 403 F.Supp. 55 (N.D.Tex.1975)—§ **10.16, n. 8.**

Murnion, Matter of Estate of, 212 Mont. 107, 686 P.2d 893 (Mont.1984)—§ **13.2, n. 2.**

Murphy v. Acme Markets, Inc., 650 F.Supp. 51 (E.D.N.Y.1986)—§ **17.46, n. 22.**

Murphy v. Crouse, 135 Cal. 14, 66 P. 971 (Cal.1901)—§ **22.12, n. 3, 4;** § **22.15, n. 4;** § **22.17, n. 6.**

Murphy v. Erwin–Wasey, Inc., 460 F.2d 661 (1st Cir.1972)—§ **17.52, n. 2.**

Murphy v. F.D.I.C., 61 F.3d 34, 314 U.S.App.D.C. 24 (D.C.Cir.1995)—§ **3.51, n. 2.**

Murphy v. Murphy, 380 Mass. 454, 404 N.E.2d 69 (Mass.1980)—§ **4.40, n. 2.**

Murphy v. Murphy, 125 Fla. 855, 170 So. 856 (Fla.1936)—§ **20.9, n. 11;** § **20.15, n. 7.**

Murphy v. Thornton, 746 So.2d 575 (Fla. App. 1 Dist.1999)—§ **17.48, n. 5.**

Murray v. British Broadcasting Corp., 81 F.3d 287 (2nd Cir.1996)—§ **11.9, n. 5, 6.**

Murry v. Sheahan, 991 F.Supp. 1052 (N.D.Ill.1998)—§ **3.47, n. 2.**

Murty v. Aga Khan, 92 F.R.D. 478 (E.D.N.Y.1981)—§ **11.11, n. 1.**

Muscillo, In re Estate of, 139 A.D.2d 429, 527 N.Y.S.2d 20 (N.Y.A.D. 1 Dept. 1988)—§ **22.19, n. 11, 31.**

Musgrave v. HCA Mideast, Ltd., 856 F.2d 690 (4th Cir.1988)—§ **18.1, n. 24.**

Mutual Life Ins. Co. of New York v. Liebing, 259 U.S. 209, 42 S.Ct. 467, 66 L.Ed. 900 (1922)—§ **3.21, n. 10.**

Mutual Life Ins. Co. of New York v. Mullen, 107 Md. 457, 69 A. 385 (Md.1908)— § **18.4, n. 43.**

Mutual Reserve Fund Life Ass'n v. Phelps, 190 U.S. 147, 23 S.Ct. 707, 47 L.Ed. 987 (1903)—§ **10.14, n. 10.**

Muus v. Muus, 29 Minn. 115, 12 N.W. 343 (Minn.1882)—§ **14.9, n. 13.**

Myers v. Alvey–Ferguson Co., 331 F.2d 223 (6th Cir.1964)—§ **3.10, n. 5.**

Myers v. Cessna Aircraft Corp., 275 Or. 501, 553 P.2d 355 (Or.1976)—§ **3.12, n. 5.**

Myers v. Columbus Sales Pavilion, Inc., 575 F.Supp. 805 (D.Neb.1983)—§ **19.13, n. 1.**

Myers v. Gaither, 232 A.2d 577 (D.C.App. 1967)—§ **2.16, n. 8.**

Myers v. Hayes Intern. Corp., 701 F.Supp. 618 (M.D.Tenn.1988)—§ **17.56, n. 8.**

Myers v. Langlois, 168 Vt. 432, 721 A.2d 129 (Vt.1998)—§ **17.26, n. 20;** § **17.36, n. 15;** § **17.39, n. 16.**

Myers v. Myers, 341 Ill.App. 406, 94 N.E.2d 100 (Ill.App. 1 Dist.1950)—§ **5.22, n. 4.**

Myrick v. Superior Court of State, 256 P.2d 348 (Cal.App. 1 Dist.1953)—§ **4.13, n. 4;** § **6.4, n. 22.**

N

Nachimson v. Nachimson, 1930 WL 7903 (CA 1930)—§ **13.17, n. 3.**

Nadler v. Liberty Mut. Fire Ins. Co., 188 W.Va. 329, 424 S.E.2d 256 (W.Va. 1992)—§ **2.17, n. 11;** § **2.23, n. 5;** § **18.21, n. 14.**

Naghiu v. Inter–Continental Hotels Group, Inc., 165 F.R.D. 413 (D.Del.1996)— **§ 17.48, n. 5.**

Nagy v. Nagy–Horvath, 273 S.C. 583, 257 S.E.2d 757 (S.C.1979)—**§ 4.13, n. 2; § 4.18, n. 3.**

Nahar v. Nahar, 656 So.2d 225 (Fla.App. 3 Dist.1995)—**§ 14.9, n. 3; § 21.3, n. 10.**

Najarian v. National Amusements, Inc., 768 A.2d 1253 (R.I.2001)—**§ 2.13, n. 25, 26; § 2.19, n. 13; § 17.21, n. 18, 28; § 17.23, n. 14; § 17.48, n. 5.**

Nakhleh v. Chemical Const. Corp., 359 F.Supp. 357 (S.D.N.Y.1973)—**§ 18.1, n. 8; § 18.5, n. 39; § 18.6, n. 2.**

Naphtali v. Lafazan, 8 A.D.2d 22, 186 N.Y.S.2d 1010 (N.Y.A.D. 2 Dept.1959)— **§ 17.5, n. 9.**

Napletana v. Hillsdale College, 385 F.2d 871 (6th Cir.1967)—**§ 4.33, n. 3.**

Narco Avionics, Inc. v. Sportsman's Market, Inc., 792 F.Supp. 398 (E.D.Pa.1992)— **§ 12.7, n. 5.**

Nardi v. Segal, 90 Ill.App.2d 432, 234 N.E.2d 805 (Ill.App. 2 Dist.1967)— **§ 15.24, n. 7; § 15.37, n. 14.**

Nasco, Inc. v. Gimbert, 239 Ga. 675, 238 S.E.2d 368 (Ga.1977)—**§ 18.4, n. 7; § 18.5, n. 17; § 18.29, n. 3.**

Nash v. Benari, 117 Me. 491, 105 A. 107 (Me.1918)—**§ 22.20; § 22.20, n. 1, 2, 7.**

Natchez v. Minor, 17 Miss. 544 (Miss.Err. & App.1848)—**§ 19.9, n. 15.**

National Bank of Greece v. Metliss, [1958] A.C.509—**§ 23.2, n. 1.**

National Bank of Washington v. Equity Investors, 81 Wash.2d 886, 506 P.2d 20 (Wash.1973)—**§ 22.19, n. 7.**

National Bellas Hess, Inc. v. Department of Revenue of State of Ill., 386 U.S. 753, 87 S.Ct. 1389, 18 L.Ed.2d 505 (1967)— **§ 11.16, n. 5.**

National City Bank of N.Y. v. Beebe, 131 N.Y.S.2d 67 (N.Y.Sup.1954)—**§ 21.6, n. 4; § 21.7, n. 2.**

National Equipment Rental, Limited v. Szukhent, 375 U.S. 311, 84 S.Ct. 411, 11 L.Ed.2d 354 (1964)—**§ 6.3; § 6.3, n. 7; § 11.2; § 11.2, n. 7; § 12.5; § 12.5, n. 2; § 24.15, n. 2.**

National Exchange Bank v. Wiley, 195 U.S. 257, 25 S.Ct. 70, 49 L.Ed. 184 (1904)— **§ 24.14, n. 1.**

National Farmers Union Ins. Companies v. Crow Tribe of Indians, 471 U.S. 845, 105 S.Ct. 2447, 85 L.Ed.2d 818 (1985)— **§ 11.17, n. 32.**

National Glass, Inc. v. J.C. Penney Properties, Inc., 336 Md. 606, 650 A.2d 246 (Md.1994)—**§ 2.21, n. 57; § 2.23, n. 9; § 18.21, n. 7.**

National Indus. Sand Ass'n v. Gibson, 897 S.W.2d 769 (Tex.1995)—**§ 6.9, n. 20.**

National Iranian Oil Co. v. Ashland Oil, Inc., 817 F.2d 326 (5th Cir.1987)— **§ 11.3, n. 23.**

National Lead Co., United States v., 63 F.Supp. 513 (S.D.N.Y.1945)—**§ 17.53, n. 1.**

National Life Ins. Co., In re, 247 F.Supp.2d 486 (D.Vt.2002)—**§ 10.10, n. 16.**

National Metropolitan Bank v. United States, 323 U.S. 454, 65 S.Ct. 354, 89 L.Ed. 383 (1945)—**§ 3.51, n. 4.**

National Shawmut Bank v. Cumming, 325 Mass. 457, 91 N.E.2d 337 (Mass.1950)— **§ 21.2, n. 14; § 21.3, n. 7.**

National Starch and Chemical Corp. v. Newman, 577 S.W.2d 99 (Mo.App. 1978)—**§ 2.17, n. 10; § 18.29, n. 8.**

National Sur. Corp. v. Inland Properties, Inc., 286 F.Supp. 173 (E.D.Ark.1968)— **§ 18.1, n. 3; § 18.4, n. 44; § 18.5, n. 12; § 18.6, n. 1, 3; § 18.7, n. 2.**

National Trailer Convoy Co. v. Mount Vernon Nat. Bank & Trust Co. of Fairfax County, 420 P.2d 889 (Okla.1966)— **§ 19.15, n. 3.**

National Transp. Co. v. J. E. Faltin Motor Transp. Co., 109 N.H. 446, 255 A.2d 606 (N.H.1969)—**§ 12.15, n. 8.**

National Union Fire Ins. Co. of Pittsburgh, Pa. v. D & L Const. Co., 353 F.2d 169 (8th Cir.1965)—**§ 3.52, n. 5.**

Nationwide Resources Corp. v. Massabni, 143 Ariz. 460, 694 P.2d 290 (Ariz.App. Div. 2 1984)—**§ 14.11, n. 2.**

Natural Footwear Ltd. v. Hart, Schaffner & Marx, 579 F.Supp. 543 (D.N.J.1983)— **§ 17.53, n. 3.**

Natus Corp. v. United States, 178 Ct.Cl. 1, 371 F.2d 450 (Ct.Cl.1967)—**§ 3.51, n. 8.**

Naylor v. Conroy, 46 N.J.Super. 387, 134 A.2d 785 (N.J.Super.A.D.1957)—**§ 18.4, n. 42, 49.**

Neal v. Boykin, 132 Ga. 400, 64 S.E. 480 (Ga.1909)—**§ 22.9, n. 1, 4.**

Neal v. Butler Aviation Intern., Inc., 460 F.Supp. 98 (E.D.N.Y.1978)—**§ 3.14, n. 2.**

Neal v. Janssen, 270 F.3d 328 (6th Cir. 2001)—**§ 7.12, n. 8.**

Neal v. Neal, 116 Ariz. 590, 570 P.2d 758 (Ariz.1977)—**§ 15.30, n. 1.**

Neal, United States v., 443 F.Supp. 1307 (D.Neb.1978)—**§ 3.14, n. 3.**

Nebraska v. Iowa, 406 U.S. 117, 92 S.Ct. 1379, 31 L.Ed.2d 733 (1972)—**§ 19.2, n. 3; § 19.7, n. 3.**

Nederland Life Ins. Co. v. Meinert, 127 F. 651 (7th Cir.1904)—**§ 18.5, n. 9.**

Nedlloyd Lines B.V. v. Superior Court, 3 Cal.4th 459, 11 Cal.Rptr.2d 330, 834 P.2d 1148 (Cal.1992)—**§ 2.23, n. 9; § 2.25, n. 9; § 17.40, n. 28; § 18.1, n. 18; § 18.4, n. 7, 42; § 18.7, n. 9, 13; § 18.10, n. 2; § 23.9, n. 5.**

Neely v. Club Med Management Services, Inc., 63 F.3d 166 (3rd Cir.1995)— **§ 17.63; § 17.63, n. 22, 33.**

Negri v. Schering Corp., 333 F.Supp. 101 (S.D.N.Y.1971)— **§ 17.55, n. 9.**

Nehemiah v. Athletics Congress of U.S.A., 765 F.2d 42 (3rd Cir.1985)—**§ 6.2, n. 13.**

Nell, In re, 71 B.R. 305 (D.Utah 1987)— **§ 23.12, n. 15, 18; § 23.13, n. 1.**

Nelson v. Aetna Life Ins. Co., 359 F.Supp. 271 (W.D.Mo.1973)—**§ 18.5, n. 8, 11; § 18.21, n. 14; § 18.26, n. 10.**

Nelson v. American Employers' Ins. Co., 258 Wis. 252, 45 N.W.2d 681 (Wis. 1951)—**§ 14.9, n. 1, 13.**

Nelson v. Chicago, B. & Q.R. Co., 225 Ill. 197, 80 N.E. 109 (Ill.1906)—**§ 10.13, n. 3.**

Nelson v. Dubois, 232 N.W.2d 54 (N.D. 1975)—**§ 11.17, n. 21.**

Nelson v. Hix, 122 Ill.2d 343, 119 Ill.Dec. 355, 522 N.E.2d 1214 (Ill.1988)—**§ 2.19, n. 17; § 17.26, n. 1, 7; § 17.39, n. 15.**

Nelson v. Miller, 201 F.2d 277 (9th Cir. 1952)—**§ 4.5, n. 1.**

Nelson v. Nationwide Mortg. Corp., 659 F.Supp. 611 (D.D.C.1987)—**§ 18.28, n. 4.**

Nelson v. Nelson, 61 Wash.2d 608, 379 P.2d 717 (Wash.1963)—**§ 14.13, n. 8.**

Nelson v. Quimby Island Reclamation Dist. Facilities Corp., 491 F.Supp. 1364 (N.D.Cal.1980)—**§ 9.6, n. 20.**

Nelson v. R. Greenspan & Co., Inc., 613 F.Supp. 342 (E.D.Mo.1985)—**§ 10.18, n. 16.**

Nelson v. Sandoz Pharmaceuticals Corp., 288 F.3d 954 (7th Cir.2002)—**§ 17.70, n. 6.**

Nelson, Will of, 125 Misc.2d 451, 475 N.Y.S.2d 194 (N.Y.Sur.1984)—**§ 22.7, n. 1.**

Nelson v. World Wide Lease, Inc., 110 Idaho 369, 716 P.2d 513 (Idaho App.1986)— **§ 6.3, n. 5; § 6.5, n. 10; § 6.9, n. 22.**

Nemariam v. Federal Democratic Republic of Ethiopia, 315 F.3d 390, 354 U.S.App. D.C. 309 (D.C.Cir.2003)—**§ 11.10, n. 5.**

Neporany v. Kir, 5 A.D.2d 438, 173 N.Y.S.2d 146 (N.Y.A.D. 1 Dept.1958)— **§ 24.44, n. 12.**

Nesladek v. Ford Motor Co., 46 F.3d 734 (8th Cir.1995)—**§ 17.17, n. 8; § 17.77, n. 7, 9.**

Nesladek v. Ford Motor Co., 876 F.Supp. 1061 (D.Minn.1994)—**§ 2.13, n. 25; § 17.21, n. 28; § 17.23, n. 13.**

Ness v. Commissioner of Corporations and Taxation, 279 Mass. 369, 181 N.E. 178 (Mass.1932)—**§ 4.36, n. 11.**

Ness v. Ford Motor Co., 1993 WL 996164 (N.D.Ill.1993)—**§ 17.79; § 17.79, n. 4.**

Netherlands Shipmortgage Corp., Ltd. v. Madias, 717 F.2d 731 (2nd Cir.1983)— **§ 23.6, n. 6; § 23.7, n. 6.**

Netherlands v. Ruffer (C814/79), 1980 WL 148835 (ECJ 1980)—**§ 24.46, n. 14.**

Neto v. Thorner, 718 F.Supp. 1222 (S.D.N.Y.1989)—**§ 3.13, n. 4; § 21.3, n. 17.**

Netting v. Strickland, 1899 WL 633 (Ohio Cir.1899)—**§ 22.19, n. 24.**

Net2Phone, Inc. v. Superior Court, 135 Cal. Rptr.2d 149 (Cal.App. 2 Dist.2003)— **§ 11.6, n. 12.**

Neumeier v. Kuehner, 31 N.Y.2d 121, 335 N.Y.S.2d 64, 286 N.E.2d 454 (N.Y. 1972)—**§ 2.14, n. 12; § 2.26; § 2.26, n. 19; § 17.13, n. 28; § 17.18, n. 16; § 17.26, n. 6; § 17.28; § 17.28, n. 12; § 17.31; § 17.31, n. 1; § 17.45; § 17.45, n. 1, 21.**

Nevada v. Hall, 440 U.S. 410, 99 S.Ct. 1182, 59 L.Ed.2d 416 (1979)—**§ 3.24, n. 9, 13; § 3.30, n. 6; § 4.5, n. 6; § 17.43; § 17.43, n. 10.**

Nevada v. Hicks, 533 U.S. 353, 121 S.Ct. 2304, 150 L.Ed.2d 398 (2001)—**§ 11.17; § 11.17, n. 26.**

Nevarez v. Bailon, 287 S.W.2d 521 (Tex.Civ. App.-El Paso 1956)—**§ 13.1, n. 2; § 13.6, n. 2; § 13.17, n. 3.**

Neville Chemical Co. v. Union Carbide Corp., 422 F.2d 1205 (3rd Cir.1970)— **§ 17.77, n. 2; § 18.24, n. 7.**

Nevin v. Nevin, 88 R.I. 426, 149 A.2d 722 (R.I.1959)—**§ 4.20, n. 3.**

Nevins v. Nevins, 129 Cal.App.2d 150, 276 P.2d 655 (Cal.App. 2 Dist.1954)—**§ 14.5, n. 1.**

New v. Tac & C Energy, Inc., 177 W.Va. 648, 355 S.E.2d 629 (W.Va.1987)— **§ 2.17, n. 11; § 2.23, n. 5.**

Newark Sav. Inst. v. Jones' Ex'rs, 1882 WL 8382 (N.J.Ch.1882)—**§ 22.19, n. 4, 24.**

Newark Shoe Stores, In re, 2 F.Supp. 384 (D.Md.1933)—**§ 19.2, n. 1.**

New Britain, Conn., City of, United States v., 347 U.S. 81, 74 S.Ct. 367, 98 L.Ed. 520 (1954)—**§ 3.51, n. 11.**

New Central Jute Mills Co. v. City Trade and Industries, Limited, 65 Misc.2d 653, 318 N.Y.S.2d 980 (N.Y.Sup.1971)— **§ 24.6, n. 3; § 24.35, n. 7.**

Newcomb v. Newcomb, 108 Ky. 582, 57 S.W. 2 (Ky.1900)—**§ 22.3, n. 14.**

Newcomb's Estate, In re, 192 N.Y. 238, 84 N.E. 950 (N.Y.1908)—**§ 4.24, n. 1.**

Newcomer v. Orem, 2 Md. 297 (Md.1852)— **§ 14.5, n. 1, 2; § 14.9, n. 1.**

Newco Mfg. Co., Inc., Ex parte, 481 So.2d 867 (Ala.1985)—**§ 5.13, n. 20; § 6.9, n. 19.**

New England Fish Co., In re, 749 F.2d 1277 (9th Cir.1984)—**§ 17.26, n. 1; § 23.15, n. 14.**

New England Merchants Nat. Bank v. Rosenfield, 679 F.2d 467 (5th Cir.1982)— **§ 18.27, n. 3.**

New England Merchants Nat. Bank of Boston v. Mahoney, 356 Mass. 654, 255 N.E.2d 592 (Mass.1970)—§ **21.3, n. 10;** § **21.9, n. 2.**

New England Mut. Life Ins. Co. v. Olin, 114 F.2d 131 (7th Cir.1940)—§ **18.6, n. 3;** § **18.7, n. 11.**

New England Mut. Life Ins. Co. v. Spence, 104 F.2d 665 (2nd Cir.1939)—§ **19.29, n. 3.**

New England Mut. Life Ins. Co. v. Woodworth, 111 U.S. 138, 4 S.Ct. 364, 28 L.Ed. 379 (1884)—§ **22.13, n. 2.**

New Jersey Mfrs. Ins. Co. v. MacVicar, 307 N.J.Super. 507, 704 A.2d 1343 (N.J.Super.A.D.1998)—§ **17.56, n. 11.**

Newman v. Graham, 82 Idaho 90, 349 P.2d 716 (Idaho 1960)—§ **4.20, n. 5.**

Newman v. Newman, 558 So.2d 821 (Miss. 1990)—§ **15.5, n. 1.**

New Mexico Federation of Labor, United Food and Commercial Workers Union Local 1564 v. City of Clovis, N.M., 735 F.Supp. 999 (D.N.M.1990)—§ **18.29, n. 3.**

Newmont Mines Ltd. v. Adriatic Ins. Co., 609 F.Supp. 295 (S.D.N.Y.1985)— § **24.40, n. 5.**

Newport v. Newport, 219 Va. 48, 245 S.E.2d 134 (Va.1978)—§ **15.27, n. 5.**

Newsday, United States ex rel. Sabella v., 315 F.Supp. 333 (E.D.N.Y.1970)— § **3.11, n. 3.**

Newsom v. Langford, 174 S.W. 1036 (Tex. Civ.App.-Amarillo 1915)—§ **19.5, n. 5, 7.**

Newspaper Readers Service v. Canonsburg Pottery Co., 146 F.2d 963 (3rd Cir. 1945)—§ **19.28, n. 2.**

Newton v. National Broadcasting Co., Inc., 109 F.R.D. 522 (D.Nev.1985)—§ **12.11, n. 7.**

Newton v. Newton, 13 N.J. Misc. 613, 179 A. 621 (N.J.Ch.1935)—§ **4.24, n. 3.**

Newton v. Porter, 69 N.Y. 133 (N.Y.1877)— § **18.42, n. 3.**

New York v. Shapiro, 129 F.Supp. 149 (D.Mass.1954)—§ **24.1, n. 1;** § **24.11, n. 1;** § **24.23, n. 4.**

New York Breweries Co. Ltd. v. Attorney General, 1897 WL 11492 (CA 1897)— § **22.15, n. 13.**

New York, City of v. Pullman Inc., 477 F.Supp. 438 (S.D.N.Y.1979)—§ **11.2, n. 6.**

New York Foundling Hospital v. Gatti, 9 Ariz. 105, 79 P. 231 (Ariz.Terr.1905)— § **22.26, n. 6.**

New York Life Ins. Co. v. Dodge, 246 U.S. 357, 38 S.Ct. 337, 62 L.Ed. 772 (1918)— § **3.21, n. 10.**

New York Life Ins. Co. v. Dunlevy, 241 U.S. 518, 36 S.Ct. 613, 60 L.Ed. 1140 (1916)—§ **5.23, n. 3.**

New York Life Ins. Co. v. Head, 234 U.S. 149, 34 S.Ct. 879, 58 L.Ed. 1259 (1914)—§ **3.21, n. 10.**

New York Life Ins. Co. v. Smith, 67 F. 694 (9th Cir.1895)—§ **22.13, n. 2.**

New York Life Ins. & Trust Co., In re, 209 N.Y. 585, 103 N.E. 315 (N.Y.1913)— § **21.13, n. 4.**

New York Life Insurance Co v. Public Trustee, 1924 WL 19794 (CA 1924)—§ **22.13, n. 2.**

New York Times Co. v. Connor, 365 F.2d 567 (5th Cir.1966)—§ **7.8, n. 2.**

New York Times Co. v. Sullivan, 376 U.S. 254, 84 S.Ct. 710, 11 L.Ed.2d 686 (1964)—§ **7.8, n. 1.**

Nez v. Forney, 109 N.M. 161, 783 P.2d 471 (N.M.1989)—§ **17.40, n. 26;** § **18.1, n. 17.**

Ng Suey Hi v. Weedin, 21 F.2d 801 (9th Cir.1927)—§ **13.19, n. 1.**

Nguyen v. Lewis/Boyle, Inc., 899 F.Supp. 58 (D.R.I.1995)—§ **18.5, n. 5.**

Niccum v. Lawrence, 186 Kan. 223, 350 P.2d 133 (Kan.1960)—§ **4.37, n. 3;** § **4.40, n. 2.**

Nicholas' Will, In re, 50 Misc.2d 76, 269 N.Y.S.2d 623 (N.Y.Sur.1966)—§ **21.11, n. 5.**

Nichols v. Anderson, 788 F.2d 1140 (5th Cir.1986)—§ **24.12, n. 7.**

Nichols v. G.D. Searle & Co., 991 F.2d 1195 (4th Cir.1993)—§ **6.9, n. 19.**

Nichols v. Marshall, 491 F.2d 177 (10th Cir.1974)—§ **22.10, n. 13.**

Nichols v. Mase, 94 N.Y. 160 (N.Y.1883)— § **19.13, n. 1.**

Nichols' Estate, In re, 24 Pa. D. & C.2d 247, 11 Fiduc.Rep. 163 (Pa.Orph.1961)— § **22.12, n. 8.**

Nicole Santos, In re Estate of, 648 So.2d 277 (Fla.App. 4 Dist.1995)—§ **14.9, n. 3.**

Nicol's Trust, In re, 3 Misc.2d 898, 148 N.Y.S.2d 854 (N.Y.Sup.1956)—§ **21.3, n. 13.**

Nicosia v. De Rooy, 72 F.Supp.2d 1093 (N.D.Cal.1999)—§ **7.8, n. 14.**

Nieman v. Press & Equipment Sales Co., 588 F.Supp. 650 (S.D.Ohio 1984)— § **3.10, n. 5.**

Nikimiha Securities Ltd. v. Trend Group Ltd., 646 F.Supp. 1211 (E.D.Pa.1986)— § **12.18, n. 8.**

Nikiporez's Estate, Matter of, 19 Wash.App. 231, 574 P.2d 1204 (Wash.App. Div. 3 1978)—§ **22.22, n. 2.**

Niles v. Niles, 35 Del.Ch. 106, 111 A.2d 697 (Del.Ch.1955)—§ **20.2, n. 4.**

Nilsson, In re, 42 B.R. 587 (Bkrtcy.C.D.Cal. 1984)—§ **23.12, n. 15;** § **23.13, n. 1.**

93.970 Acres of Land, United States v., 360 U.S. 328, 79 S.Ct. 1193, 3 L.Ed.2d 1275 (1959)—§ **3.51, n. 10;** § **3.55, n. 9.**

Nippon Emo–Trans Co., Ltd. v. Emo–Trans, Inc., 744 F.Supp. 1215 (E.D.N.Y.1990)— **§ 24.34, n. 2; § 24.39, n. 8.**

Nippon Paper Industries Co., Ltd., United States v., 109 F.3d 1 (1st Cir.1997)— **§ 17.48; § 17.48, n. 28.**

NL Industries, Inc. v. Commercial Union Ins. Co., 154 F.3d 155 (3rd Cir.1998)— **§ 18.26, n. 13.**

Noble v. Noble, 26 Ariz.App. 89, 546 P.2d 358 (Ariz.App. Div. 1 1976)— **§ 12.15, n. 9.**

Nobuo Hiramatsu v. Phillips, 50 F.Supp. 167 (S.D.Cal.1943)— **§ 4.27, n. 1.**

Nodak Mut. Ins. Co. v. American Family Mut. Ins. Co., 604 N.W.2d 91 (Minn. 2000)— **§ 2.13, n. 25, 26; § 2.19, n. 13; § 17.21, n. 14, 20, 28; § 17.23, n. 13, 14; § 17.45; § 17.45, n. 31; § 18.21, n. 16; § 18.26, n. 7.**

Noel v. Airponents, Inc., 169 F.Supp. 348 (D.N.J.1958)— **§ 2.14, n. 18; § 17.1, n. 1; § 17.63, n. 32.**

Noel v. Metropolitan Property & Liability Ins. Co., 41 Mass.App.Ct. 593, 672 N.E.2d 119 (Mass.App.Ct.1996)— **§ 17.56, n. 17.**

Noel v. St. Johnsbury Trucking Co., 147 F.Supp. 432 (D.Conn.1956)— **§ 22.14, n. 3.**

Nolan v. Boeing Co., 919 F.2d 1058 (5th Cir.1990)— **§ 3.37, n. 7.**

Nolan v. Borger, 203 N.E.2d 274 (Ohio Prob.1963)— **§ 3.13, n. 4, 10.**

Nolan v. Transocean Air Lines, 276 F.2d 280 (2nd Cir.1960)— **§ 2.19, n. 4.**

Nolan's Estate, In re, 135 Cal.App.2d 16, 286 P.2d 899 (Cal.App. 1 Dist.1955)— **§ 20.4, n. 7.**

Noonan, People ex rel. v. Wingate, 376 Ill. 244, 33 N.E.2d 467 (Ill.1941)— **§ 4.41, n. 5.**

Noonan v. Winston Co., 135 F.3d 85 (1st Cir.1998)— **§ 7.8, n. 12.**

Nora v. Nora, 494 So.2d 16 (Ala.1986)— **§ 4.26, n. 2; § 15.5, n. 1; § 20.3, n. 1.**

Nordmark Presentations, Inc. v. Harman, 557 So.2d 649 (Fla.App. 2 Dist.1990)— **§ 8.4, n. 9.**

Norfolk Shipbuilding & Drydock Corp. v. Garris, 532 U.S. 811, 121 S.Ct. 1927, 150 L.Ed.2d 34 (2001)— **§ 10.6, n. 4.**

Norfolk Southern Corp. v. California Union Ins. Co., 859 So.2d 167 (La.App. 1 Cir. 2003)— **§ 18.1, n. 27.**

Norfolk & W. Ry. Co. v. Liepelt, 444 U.S. 490, 100 S.Ct. 755, 62 L.Ed.2d 689 (1980)— **§ 3.39, n. 7; § 3.53, n. 8.**

Norgaard v. DePuy Orthopaedics, Inc., 121 F.3d 1074 (7th Cir.1997)— **§ 3.47, n. 9.**

Norkan Lodge Co. Ltd. v. Gillum, 587 F.Supp. 1457 (N.D.Tex.1984)— **§ 24.36, n. 1.**

Norlin Corp. v. Rooney, Pace Inc., 744 F.2d 255 (2nd Cir.1984)— **§ 23.2; § 23.2, n. 5.**

Norman v. Baldwin, 152 Va. 800, 148 S.E. 831 (Va.1929)— **§ 3.10, n. 4, 6.**

Norman v. McDonald, 930 F.Supp. 1219 (N.D.Ill.1996)— **§ 24.24, n. 8.**

Norman v. Norman, 121 Cal. 620, 54 P. 143 (Cal.1898)— **§ 13.6, n. 16, 18.**

Normann v. Johns–Manville Corp., 406 Pa.Super. 103, 593 A.2d 890 (Pa.Super.1991)— **§ 17.78, n. 8.**

Norrie v. Kansas City Southern Ry. Co., 7 F.2d 158 (S.D.N.Y.1925)— **§ 22.12, n. 8.**

Norrie v. Lohman, 16 F.2d 355 (2nd Cir. 1926)— **§ 22.12, n. 8.**

Norris v. Loyd, 183 Iowa 1056, 168 N.W. 557 (Iowa 1918)— **§ 20.7, n. 5.**

Norris v. Taylor, 460 So.2d 151 (Ala. 1984)— **§ 2.21, n. 1.**

North American Bank, Ltd. v. Schulman, 123 Misc.2d 516, 474 N.Y.S.2d 383 (N.Y.Co.Ct.1984)— **§ 18.28, n. 5.**

North American Philips Corp. v. Aetna Cas. and Sur. Co., 1994 WL 555399 (Del.Super.1994)— **§ 18.1, n. 27.**

North Bergen Rex Transport, Inc. v. Trailer Leasing Co., a Div. of Keller Systems, Inc., 158 N.J. 561, 730 A.2d 843 (N.J. 1999)— **§ 2.23, n. 9; § 17.40, n. 26.**

Northbrook Nat. Ins. Co. v. Brewer, 493 U.S. 6, 110 S.Ct. 297, 107 L.Ed.2d 223 (1989)— **§ 23.3, n. 4.**

Northern Pipeline Const. Co. v. Marathon Pipe Line Co., 458 U.S. 50, 102 S.Ct. 2858, 73 L.Ed.2d 598 (1982)— **§ 10.7; § 10.7, n. 4; § 23.12; § 23.12, n. 1; § 23.16, n. 7.**

Northern Trust Co. v. Randolph C. Dillon, Inc., 558 F.Supp. 1118 (N.D.Ill.1983)— **§ 8.7, n. 9.**

Northwest Airlines v. State of Minnesota, 322 U.S. 292, 64 S.Ct. 950, 88 L.Ed. 1283 (1944)— **§ 3.53, n. 8.**

Northwest Airlines, Inc. v. Friday, 617 N.W.2d 590 (Minn.App.2000)— **§ 7.8, n. 14.**

Northwest Cinema Corp., In re, 49 B.R. 479 (Bkrtcy.D.Minn.1985)— **§ 23.12, n. 14.**

Northwestern Mortg. & Sec. Co. v. Noel Const. Co., 71 N.D. 256, 300 N.W. 28 (N.D.1941)— **§ 4.19, n. 2.**

Northwestern Mut. Life Ins. Co. v. Wender, 940 F.Supp. 62 (S.D.N.Y.1996)— **§ 17.50, n. 22.**

Northwestern Nat. Ins. Co. v. Donovan, 916 F.2d 372 (7th Cir.1990)— **§ 11.3, n. 21; § 11.4, n. 15.**

Northwestern National Casualty Co. v. Davis, 90 Cal.App.3d 782, 153 Cal.Rptr. 556 (Cal.App. 2 Dist.1979)— **§ 4.13, n. 2; § 4.26, n. 2; § 4.43, n. 4.**

Northwestern States Portland Cement Co. v. State of Minnesota, 358 U.S. 450, 79 S.Ct. 357, 3 L.Ed.2d 421 (1959)— **§ 23.6, n. 6.**

Northwest Healthcare Alliance Inc. v. Healthgrades.Com, Inc., 50 Fed.Appx. 339 (9th Cir.2002)—§ **7.8, n. 14, 16.**

Northwest Pipe Co. v. Eighth Judicial Dist. Court ex rel. County of Clark, 118 Nev. 133, 42 P.3d 244 (Nev.2002)—§ **2.24, n. 13; § 17.15; § 17.15, n. 26.**

North Yarmouth, Town of v. Town of West Gardiner, 58 Me. 207 (Me.1870)—§ **4.13, n. 2.**

Norton v. Cobb, 744 F.Supp. 798 (N.D.Ohio 1990)—§ **15.42, n. 14.**

Norwegian Cruise Line, Ltd. v. Clark, 841 So.2d 547 (Fla.App. 2 Dist.2003)— § **11.3, n. 21.**

Norwood v. Kirkpatrick, 349 U.S. 29, 75 S.Ct. 544, 99 L.Ed. 789 (1955)—§ **11.14, n. 6; § 11.16, n. 1.**

Noto v. Cia Secula di Armanento, 310 F.Supp. 639 (S.D.N.Y.1970)—§ **12.18, n. 11.**

Nott v. Nott, 111 La. 1028, 36 So. 109 (La.1904)—§ **14.5, n. 1.**

Novack, In re, 88 B.R. 353 (Bkrtcy. N.D.Okla.1988)—§ **19.11, n. 15; § 19.13, n. 1.**

Nova Ribbon Products, Inc. v. Lincoln Ribbon, Inc., 1992 WL 392614 (E.D.Pa. 1992)—§ **18.12, n. 7.**

Novich v. Rojtman, 5 Misc.2d 1029, 161 N.Y.S.2d 817 (N.Y.Sup.1957)—§ **23.5, n. 5.**

Nowak v. Tak How Investments, Ltd., 94 F.3d 708 (1st Cir.1996)—§ **5.10, n. 26, 34.**

Nowell v. Nowell, 157 Conn. 470, 254 A.2d 889 (Conn.1969)—§ **24.28, n. 2.**

Nowotny v. L & B Contract Industries, Inc., 933 P.2d 452 (Wyo.1997)—§ **3.11, n. 3.**

NRM Corp. v. Hercules, Inc., 758 F.2d 676, 244 U.S.App.D.C. 356 (D.C.Cir.1985)— § **3.52, n. 4.**

Nuclear Corp. of America v. Hale, 355 F.Supp. 193 (N.D.Tex.1973)—§ **19.9, n. 9.**

Nugent v. Vetzera, 1866 WL 8223 (Ct of Chancery 1866)—§ **22.26, n. 4.**

Nunez v. Hunter Fan Co., 920 F.Supp. 716 (S.D.Tex.1996)—§ **18.29, n. 4.**

Nuovo Pignone, SpA v. Storman Asia M/V, 310 F.3d 374 (5th Cir.2002)—§ **12.7, n. 3.**

Nursing Home Consultants, Inc. v. Quantum Health Services, Inc., 926 F.Supp. 835 (E.D.Ark.1996)—§ **18.2, n. 11.**

Nute v. Hamilton Mut. Ins. Co., 72 Mass. 174 (Mass.1856)—§ **11.2, n. 8; § 11.3, n. 2.**

Nye v. A/S D/S Svendborg, 358 F.Supp. 145 (S.D.N.Y.1973)—§ **17.63, n. 22.**

Nyquist v. Mauclet, 432 U.S. 1, 97 S.Ct. 2120, 53 L.Ed.2d 63 (1977)—§ **3.58, n. 13.**

Nytco Leasing, Inc. v. Dan–Cleve Corp., 31 N.C.App. 634, 230 S.E.2d 559 (N.C.App. 1976)—§ **18.37, n. 1.**

O

Oakes v. Oxygen Therapy Services, 178 W.Va. 543, 363 S.E.2d 130 (W.Va. 1987)—§ **2.21, n. 29.**

Oakland, State v., 129 Mont. 347, 287 P.2d 39 (Mont.1955)—§ **3.59, n. 3.**

Oakley v. National Western Life Ins. Co., 294 F.Supp. 504 (S.D.N.Y.1968)— § **18.26, n. 10.**

Oasis Corp. v. Judd, 132 F.Supp.2d 612 (S.D.Ohio 2001)—§ **7.8, n. 14, 16.**

Oates v. Morningside College, 217 Iowa 1059, 252 N.W. 783 (Iowa 1934)— § **22.21, n. 2.**

Ober v. Bounds, 528 So.2d 247 (La.App. 3 Cir.1988)—§ **4.26, n. 2, 4; § 14.9, n. 1; § 14.11, n. 1.**

Obici's Estate, In re, 373 Pa. 567, 97 A.2d 49 (Pa.1953)—§ **4.21, n. 2.**

Obney v. Schmalzreid, 273 F.Supp. 373 (W.D.Pa.1967)—§ **22.25, n. 4.**

O'Brien v. Shearson Hayden Stone, Inc., 90 Wash.2d 680, 586 P.2d 830 (Wash. 1978)—§ **18.4, n. 7; § 18.5, n. 13.**

Occidental Fire and Cas. Co. of North Carolina v. Bankers and Shippers Ins. Co. of New York, 564 F.Supp. 1501 (W.D.Va. 1983)—§ **18.21, n. 12.**

Oceanic Steam Nav. Co. v. Corcoran, 9 F.2d 724 (2nd Cir.1925)—§ **18.4, n. 7, 8.**

Oceanic Sun Line Special Shipping Company Inc. v. Fay, 1988 WL 624640 (HCA 1988)—§ **2.12, n. 8.**

O'Connell v. Hamm, 267 N.W.2d 839 (S.D. 1978)—§ **11.17, n. 16, 20.**

O'Connor v. O'Connor, 201 Conn. 632, 519 A.2d 13 (Conn.1986)—§ **2.16, n. 16; § 2.19, n. 15, 17; § 2.23, n. 1; § 17.26, n. 1, 7, 16; § 17.39, n. 12; § 17.56, n. 11, 20; § 17.57, n. 4, 7.**

O'Connor v. United States Fencing Ass'n, 260 F.Supp.2d 545 (E.D.N.Y.2003)— § **17.40, n. 7; § 17.46; § 17.46, n. 11, 22.**

O'Connor's Estate, In re, 218 Cal. 518, 23 P.2d 1031 (Cal.1933)—§ **14.13, n. 2; § 20.9, n. 14.**

Oddi v. Mariner–Denver, Inc., 461 F.Supp. 306 (S.D.Ind.1978)—§ **10.16, n. 8.**

O'Donnell v. O'Donnell, 22 Mass.App.Ct. 936, 493 N.E.2d 889 (Mass.App.Ct. 1986)—§ **15.31, n. 2.**

O'Donnell v. St. Luke's Episcopal Presbyterian Hospitals, 800 F.2d 739 (8th Cir. 1986)—§ **18.21, n. 14.**

Oetiker v. Jurid Werke, G. m. b. H., 556 F.2d 1, 181 U.S.App.D.C. 124 (D.C.Cir. 1977)—§ **10.18, n. 9.**

Official Airlines Schedule Information Service, Inc. v. Eastern Air Lines, Inc., 333 F.2d 672 (5th Cir.1964)—§ **18.46, n. 4.**

Offshore Logistics, Inc. v. Bell Helicopter Textron, 1995 WL 555593 (E.D.La. 1995)—§ **17.50, n. 16; § 17.76, n. 31.**

Offshore Rental Co. v. Continental Oil Co., 22 Cal.3d 157, 148 Cal.Rptr. 867, 583 P.2d 721 (Cal.1978)—§ **2.9, n. 28; § 2.24, n. 8; § 2.25, n. 8; § 17.19; § 17.19, n. 12; § 17.32, n. 28.**

Ogdon v. Gianakos, 415 Ill. 591, 114 N.E.2d 686 (Ill.1953)—§ **6.4, n. 6.**

Oglevie v. Stasser, 1 Kan.App.2d 315, 564 P.2d 563 (Kan.App.1977)—§ **22.15, n. 14.**

O'Guin v. Estate of Pikul, 153 Misc.2d 526, 581 N.Y.S.2d 976 (N.Y.Sup.1991)—§ **7.4, n. 7.**

Ohayon v. Safeco Ins. Co. of Illinois, 91 Ohio St.3d 474, 747 N.E.2d 206 (Ohio 2001)—§ **17.56, n. 20; § 18.26, n. 6.**

Ohio v. Wyandotte Chemicals Corp., 401 U.S. 493, 91 S.Ct. 1005, 28 L.Ed.2d 256 (1971)—§ **9.2; § 9.2, n. 9.**

Ohio, Dept. of Taxation, State of v. Kleitch Bros., Inc., 357 Mich. 504, 98 N.W.2d 636 (Mich.1959)—§ **24.23, n. 4.**

Ohio Southern Exp. Co. v. Beeler, 110 Ga. App. 867, 140 S.E.2d 235 (Ga.App. 1965)—§ **12.19, n. 6.**

Ohlquist v. Nordstrom, 143 Misc. 502, 257 N.Y.S. 711 (N.Y.Sup.1932)—§ **5.23, n. 5.**

Oilcakes & Oilseeds Trading Co. v. Sinason Teicher Inter Am. Grain Corp., 9 Misc.2d 651, 170 N.Y.S.2d 378 (N.Y.Sup. 1958)—§ **24.47, n. 5.**

O'Keeffe v. Bry, 456 F.Supp. 822 (S.D.N.Y. 1978)—§ **18.38, n. 6.**

O'Keeffe v. Snyder, 83 N.J. 478, 416 A.2d 862 (N.J.1980)—§ **3.12; § 3.12, n. 3, 4; § 19.14, n. 3, 7.**

Oklahoma ex rel. West v. Gulf, C. & S. F. R. Co., 220 U.S. 290, 31 S.Ct. 437, 55 L.Ed. 469 (1911)—§ **24.23, n. 11.**

Oklahoma Health Services Federal Credit Union v. Webb, 726 F.2d 624 (10th Cir. 1984)—§ **23.12, n. 4.**

Oklahoma Tax Commission, State ex rel. v. Rodgers, 238 Mo.App. 1115, 193 S.W.2d 919 (Mo.App.1946)—§ **24.23, n. 5.**

Olcott, Ex parte, 55 A.2d 820 (N.J.Ch. 1947)—§ **4.43, n. 1.**

Old Colony Trust Co. v. Penrose Industries Corp., 280 F.Supp. 698 (E.D.Pa.1968)— § **18.7, n. 8.**

Old Republic Ins. Co. v. Christian, 389 F.Supp. 335 (E.D.Tenn.1975)—§ **13.6, n. 2.**

Oldtown v. Inhabitants of Falmouth, 40 Me. 106 (Me.1855)—§ **4.37, n. 9.**

Old Wayne Mut. Life Ass'n v. McDonough, 204 U.S. 8, 27 S.Ct. 236, 51 L.Ed. 345 (1907)—§ **5.3, n. 18.**

Oliner v. Canadian Pacific Railway Company, 318 N.Y.S.2d 745, 267 N.E.2d 480 (N.Y.1970)—§ **19.32, n. 4.**

Oliver v. Oliver, 741 S.W.2d 225 (Tex.App.-Fort Worth 1987)—§ **14.13, n. 4.**

Oliver v. Robertson, 41 Tex. 422 (Tex. 1874)—§ **14.10, n. 2.**

Oliver B. Cannon and Son, Inc. v. Dorr-Oliver, Inc., 394 A.2d 1160 (Del. Supr.1978)—§ **2.17, n. 10; § 2.23, n. 2.**

Oliver Gintel, Inc. v. Koslow's, Inc., 355 F.Supp. 236 (N.D.Tex.1973)—§ **17.53, n. 5.**

Olivet v. Whitworth, 82 Md. 258, 33 A. 723 (Md.1896)—§ **21.11, n. 1.**

Olivier v. Townes, 1824 WL 1736 (La. 1824)—§ **19.13, n. 9.**

Olmstead v. Anderson, 428 Mich. 1, 400 N.W.2d 292 (Mich.1987)—§ **2.24, n. 12; § 17.8, n. 14; § 17.15, n. 7; § 17.56, n. 11; § 17.57, n. 1.**

Olmsted v. Olmsted, 216 U.S. 386, 30 S.Ct. 292, 54 L.Ed. 530 (1910)—§ **16.2; § 16.2, n. 1.**

Olney v. Angell, 5 R.I. 198 (R.I.1858)— § **22.3, n. 4.**

Olsen v. Celano, 234 Ill.App.3d 1045, 175 Ill.Dec. 799, 600 N.E.2d 1257 (Ill.App. 2 Dist.1992)—§ **2.19, n. 10.**

Olsen v. Olsen, 27 Misc.2d 555, 209 N.Y.S.2d 503 (N.Y.Sup.1960)—§ **13.9, n. 8.**

Olshen v. Kaufman, 235 Or. 423, 385 P.2d 161.(Or.1963)—§ **3.28, n. 5; § 18.20, n. 4.**

Olson v. Empire Dist. Elec. Co., 14 S.W.3d 218 (Mo.App. S.D.2000)—§ **17.48, n. 5.**

Olson v. Preferred Auto. Ins. Co., 259 Mich. 612, 244 N.W. 178 (Mich.1932)— § **22.10, n. 13.**

Olympic Sports Products, Inc. v. Universal Athletic Sales Co., 760 F.2d 910 (9th Cir.1985)—§ **3.39, n. 15.**

Oman v. Johns–Manville Corp., 764 F.2d 224 (4th Cir.1985)—§ **17.63, n. 4.**

Omega Equipment Corp., In re, 51 B.R. 569 (D.D.C.1985)—§ **23.12, n. 15.**

O'Melveny & Myers v. F.D.I.C., 512 U.S. 79, 114 S.Ct. 2048, 129 L.Ed.2d 67 (1994)—§ **3.51; § 3.51, n. 13; § 3.53; § 3.53, n. 12; § 3.55, n. 7.**

OMI Holdings, Inc. v. Royal Ins. Co. of Canada, 149 F.3d 1086 (10th Cir.1998)— § **5.12, n. 7; § 8.2, n. 10.**

Ommang's Estate, In re, 183 Minn. 92, 235 N.W. 529 (Minn.1931)—§ **13.9, n. 14; § 13.14, n. 5.**

Omni Capital Intern., Ltd. v. Rudolf Wolff & Co., Ltd., 484 U.S. 97, 108 S.Ct. 404, 98 L.Ed.2d 415 (1987)—§ **5.15; § 5.15, n. 2, 15; § 9.6; § 9.6, n. 11; § 10.2, n. 14; § 10.3; § 10.3, n. 13; § 10.5; § 10.5, n. 2; § 10.18; § 10.18, n. 25.**

O'Neal v. National Cylinder Gas Co., 103 F.Supp. 720 (N.D.Ill.1952)—§ **3.10, n. 3, 5.**

O'Neal v. Warmack, 250 Ark. 685, 466 S.W.2d 913 (Ark.1971)—§ **12.17, n. 13.**

O'Neill v. Barnett Bank of Jacksonville, N. A., 360 So.2d 150 (Fla.App. 1 Dist. 1978)—§ **19.21, n. 6.**

O'Neill v. Dent, 364 F.Supp. 565 (E.D.N.Y. 1973)—§ **13.11, n. 5.**

O'Neill v. Henderson, 15 Ark. 235 (Ark. 1854)—§ **14.6, n. 6.**

One Lucite Ball Containing Lunar Material, United States v., 252 F.Supp.2d 1367 (S.D.Fla.2003)—§ **12.18, n. 14.**

One 1953 Ford Victoria, People v., 48 Cal.2d 595, 311 P.2d 480 (Cal.1957)— § **2.9, n. 32; § 17.19, n. 6.**

1700 Ocean Ave. Corp. v. GBR Associates, 354 F.2d 993 (9th Cir.1965)—§ **12.15, n. 11.**

Oney v. Ferguson, 41 W.Va. 568, 23 S.E. 710 (W.Va.1895)—§ **22.19, n. 22.**

O.P.M. Leasing Services, Inc., In re, 40 B.R. 380 (Bkrtcy.S.D.N.Y.1984)—§ **23.15, n. 14.**

Opperman v. Sullivan, 330 N.W.2d 796 (Iowa 1983)—§ **15.31, n. 2.**

Oracle Corp. Derivative Litigation, In re, 808 A.2d 1206 (Del.Ch.2002)—§ **23.5, n. 1.**

Order of United Commercial Travelers of America v. Wolfe, 331 U.S. 586, 67 S.Ct. 1355, 91 L.Ed. 1687 (1947)—§ **3.24, n. 18; § 23.1, n. 1.**

O'Reilly v. Curtis Pub. Co., 31 F.Supp. 364 (D.Mass.1940)—§ **17.7, n. 1; § 17.55, n. 4.**

ORFA Securities Litigation, In re, 654 F.Supp. 1449 (D.N.J.1987)—§ **23.2, n. 6.**

Orland Properties, Inc. v. Broderick, 94 N.J.Super. 307, 228 A.2d 95 (N.J.Super.Ch.1967)—§ **19.3, n. 8.**

Orleans Parish School Bd. v. United States Gypsum Co., 1993 WL 205091 (E.D.La. 1993)—§ **17.77, n. 3.**

Orlich v. Helm Bros., Inc., 160 A.D.2d 135, 560 N.Y.S.2d 10 (N.Y.A.D. 1 Dept. 1990)—§ **12.13, n. 2.**

O'Rourke v. Colonial Ins. Co. of California, 624 So.2d 84 (Miss.1993)—§ **17.26, n. 1.**

Orr v. Ahern, 107 Conn. 174, 139 A. 691 (Conn.1928)—§ **17.6, n. 6.**

Orr v. Bowen, 648 F.Supp. 1510 (D.Nev. 1986)—§ **13.6, n. 2.**

Orr v. Orr, 440 U.S. 268, 99 S.Ct. 1102, 59 L.Ed.2d 306 (1979)—§ **14.2, n. 1; § 15.30, n. 1.**

Orr v. Sasseman, 239 F.2d 182 (5th Cir. 1956)—§ **17.5, n. 6.**

Ortiz's Estate, In re, 86 Cal. 306, 24 P. 1034 (Cal.1890)—§ **22.15, n. 13.**

Ortley v. Ross, 78 Neb. 339, 110 N.W. 982 (Neb.1907)—§ **13.18, n. 8.**

Osborn v. Bank of United States, 22 U.S. 738, 6 L.Ed. 204 (1824)—§ **5.17, n. 5.**

Osborn v. Kinnington, 787 S.W.2d 417 (Tex.App.-El Paso 1990)—§ **17.60, n. 6.**

Osborn v. Osborn, 10 Ohio Misc. 171, 226 N.E.2d 814 (Ohio Com.Pl.1966)— § **18.18, n. 5.**

Osborne, People v., 170 Mich. 143, 135 N.W. 921 (Mich.1912)—§ **4.20, n. 8.**

Osborn's Estate, In re, 151 Misc. 52, 270 N.Y.S. 616 (N.Y.Sur.1934)—§ **20.8, n. 11.**

Oshiek v. Oshiek, 244 S.C. 249, 136 S.E.2d 303 (S.C.1964)—§ **17.5, n. 10.**

OSI Industries, Inc. v. Carter, 834 So.2d 362 (Fla.App. 5 Dist.2003)—§ **7.12, n. 8.**

Osoinach v. Watkins, 235 Ala. 564, 180 So. 577 (Ala.1938)—§ **13.11, n. 3.**

Ossorio v. Leon, 705 S.W.2d 219 (Tex.App.-San Antonio 1985)—§ **14.12, n. 3.**

Ostrom v. Greene, 161 N.Y. 353, 55 N.E. 919 (N.Y.1900)—§ **10.12, n. 3, 19.**

Ostrom v. Ostrom, 231 F.2d 193 (9th Cir. 1955)—§ **24.5, n. 2.**

Otis v. City of Boston, 66 Mass. 44 (Mass. 1853)—§ **4.20, n. 2.**

Otis v. Gregory, 111 Ind. 504, 13 N.E. 39 (Ind.1887)—§ **19.2, n. 4.**

Otto v. Otto, 80 N.M. 331, 455 P.2d 642 (N.M.1969)—§ **14.11, n. 2.**

Overbaugh v. Strange, 254 Kan. 605, 867 P.2d 1016 (Kan.1994)—§ **17.58, n. 1.**

Overby v. Gordon, 177 U.S. 214, 20 S.Ct. 603, 44 L.Ed. 741 (1900)—§ **22.3, n. 10, 14.**

Owego Community Consol. School Dist. No. 434 v. Goodrich, 28 Ill.App.2d 407, 171 N.E.2d 816 (Ill.App. 2 Dist.1960)— § **4.17, n. 4.**

Owen v. Moody, 29 Miss. 79 (Miss.Err. & App.1855)—§ **22.11, n. 11, 17.**

Owen v. Owen, 444 N.W.2d 710 (S.D. 1989)—§ **17.7, n. 7; § 17.8, n. 2.**

Owen v. Owen, 427 A.2d 933 (D.C.1981)— § **2.25, n. 11; § 18.21, n. 17.**

Owen v. Owen, 178 Wis. 609, 190 N.W. 363 (Wis.1922)—§ **13.14, n. 5; § 13.15, n. 4.**

Owen v. Stewart, 111 N.H. 350, 283 A.2d 492 (N.H.1971)—§ **19.8, n. 3.**

Owen J. Roberts School Dist. v. HTE, Inc., 2003 WL 735098 (E.D.Pa.2003)— § **17.40, n. 28; § 18.1, n. 18.**

Owens v. Ford, 451 So.2d 796 (Ala.1984)— § **22.6, n. 5.**

Owens v. Hagenbeck–Wallace Shows Co., 58 R.I. 162, 192 A. 158 (R.I.1937)—§ **2.21, n. 68; § 18.6, n. 1, 4.**

Owens v. Saville's Estate, 409 S.W.2d 660 (Mo.1966)—§ **3.11, n. 2; § 22.21, n. 2.**

Owens v. Superior Court of Los Angeles County, 52 Cal.2d 822, 345 P.2d 921 (Cal.1959)—§ **6.4, n. 6.**

Owens Corning v. Carter, 997 S.W.2d 560 (Tex.1999)—§ **3.32, n. 9.**

Owens' Estate, Matter of, 89 N.M. 420, 553 P.2d 700 (N.M.1976)—§ **22.10, n. 12;** § **22.19, n. 6.**

Ownby v. Dies, 337 F.Supp. 38 (E.D.Tex. 1971)—§ **4.9, n. 2.**

Owners of the Las Mercedes v. Owners of the Abidin Daver, 1984 WL 282847 (HL 1984)—§ **11.8, n. 2.**

Owsley v. Bowden, 161 Ga. 884, 132 S.E. 70 (Ga.1926)—§ **22.21, n. 2, 10.**

Owsley v. Central Trust Co. of New York, 196 F. 412 (S.D.N.Y.1912)—§ **22.20, n. 14, 29.**

Owsley's Estate, In re, 122 Minn. 190, 142 N.W. 129 (Minn.1913)—§ **20.15, n. 5.**

Oxley v. Oxley, 159 F.2d 10, 81 U.S.App. D.C. 346 (D.C.Cir.1946)—§ **4.33, n. 3;** § **4.34, n. 3;** § **4.37, n. 3;** § **4.40, n. 4.**

Oyama v. California, 332 U.S. 633, 68 S.Ct. 269, 92 L.Ed. 249 (1948)—§ **3.59, n. 3.**

Ozias' Estate, In re, 29 S.W.2d 240 (Mo. App.1930)—§ **4.1, n. 2.**

P

Paccar Financial Corp., Inc. v. J.L. Healy Const. Co., 561 F.Supp. 342 (D.S.D. 1983)—§ **19.18, n. 21.**

Pace v. Pace, 222 Va. 524, 281 S.E.2d 891 (Va.1981)—§ **24.14, n. 5.**

Pacific Employers Ins. Co. v. Industrial Accident Commission of State of California, 306 U.S. 493, 59 S.Ct. 629, 83 L.Ed. 940 (1939)—§ **3.24;** § **3.24, n. 8;** § **17.59, n. 9;** § **24.12, n. 11.**

Pacific etc. Conference of United Methodist Church v. Superior Court, 82 Cal.App.3d 72, 147 Cal.Rptr. 44 (Cal.App. 4 Dist. 1978)—§ **5.20, n. 8.**

Pacific Gamble Robinson Co. v. Lapp, 95 Wash.2d 341, 622 P.2d 850 (Wash. 1980)—§ **14.16, n. 4, 16;** § **18.28, n. 4.**

Pacific States Cut Stone Co. v. Goble, 70 Wash.2d 907, 425 P.2d 631 (Wash. 1967)—§ **14.16;** § **14.16, n. 8, 14, 15;** § **18.18, n. 12.**

Pack v. Beech Aircraft Corp., 50 Del. 413, 132 A.2d 54 (Del.Supr.1957)—§ **3.10, n. 3, 6;** § **17.6, n. 7.**

Packaging Store, Inc. v. Leung, 917 P.2d 361 (Colo.App.1996)—§ **8.3, n. 1.**

Packard's Estate, In re, 223 A.D. 491, 228 N.Y.S. 591 (N.Y.A.D. 4 Dept.1928)— § **4.36, n. 3.**

Padula v. Lilarn Properties Corp., 620 N.Y.S.2d 310, 644 N.E.2d 1001 (N.Y. 1994)—§ **17.36;** § **17.36, n. 10;** § **17.37;** § **17.37, n. 17;** § **17.48, n. 11;** § **17.50, n. 2.**

Page v. Cameron Iron Works, Inc., 259 F.2d 420 (5th Cir.1958)—§ **3.10, n. 6.**

Page v. Page, 189 Mass. 85, 75 N.E. 92 (Mass.1905)—§ **15.34, n. 1.**

Page v. Something Weird Video, 908 F.Supp. 714 (C.D.Cal.1995)—§ **17.55, n. 11.**

Page Const. Co. v. Perini Const., 712 F.Supp. 9 (D.R.I.1989)—§ **11.2, n. 6.**

Pain v. United Technologies Corp., 637 F.2d 775, 205 U.S.App.D.C. 229 (D.C.Cir. 1980)—§ **11.11, n. 2.**

Paine v. Schenectady Ins. Co., 11 R.I. 411 (R.I.1876)—§ **24.8;** § **24.8, n. 6.**

Paley v. Bank of America Nat. Trust and Sav. Ass'n, 159 Cal.App.2d 500, 324 P.2d 35 (Cal.App. 2 Dist.1958)—§ **14.9, n. 4.**

Pallavicini v. International Tel. & Tel. Corp., 41 A.D.2d 66, 341 N.Y.S.2d 281 (N.Y.A.D. 1 Dept.1973)—§ **18.31, n. 2.**

Palmer v. Beverly Enterprises, 823 F.2d 1105 (7th Cir.1987)—§ **17.52, n. 2.**

Palmer v. Hoffman, 318 U.S. 109, 63 S.Ct. 477, 87 L.Ed. 645 (1943)—§ **3.37, n. 4.**

Palmer v. L. E. Leach Co., Inc., 60 F.R.D. 602 (D.Vt.1973)—§ **22.19, n. 6.**

Palmer v. Palmer, 654 So.2d 1 (Miss. 1995)—§ **14.6, n. 5.**

Palmer G. Lewis Co., Inc. v. ARCO Chemical Co., 904 P.2d 1221 (Alaska 1995)— § **2.17, n. 16;** § **2.19, n. 16;** § **2.23, n. 2;** § **18.21, n. 14.**

Palmer's Estate, In re, 192 Misc. 385, 79 N.Y.S.2d 404 (N.Y.Sur.1948)—§ **13.6, n. 8.**

Palmieri v. Ahart, 111 Ohio App. 195, 167 N.E.2d 353 (Ohio App. 4 Dist.1960)— § **3.11, n. 3.**

Palmisano v. News Syndicate Co., 130 F.Supp. 17 (S.D.N.Y.1955)—§ **17.7, n. 1;** § **17.55, n. 7.**

Panalpina Welttransport GmBh v. Geosource, Inc., 764 F.2d 352 (5th Cir. 1985)—§ **23.3, n. 1.**

Panama Processes, S.A. v. Cities Service Co., 796 P.2d 276 (Okla.1990)—§ **5.21, n. 10.**

Panchal v. Ethen, 648 So.2d 245 (Fla.App. 4 Dist.1994)—§ **7.3, n. 2.**

Pandazopoulos v. Universal Cruise Line, Inc., 365 F.Supp. 208 (S.D.N.Y.1973)— § **17.63, n. 20, 23.**

Panhandle Eastern Corp., United States v., 693 F.Supp. 88 (D.Del.1988)—§ **12.18, n. 1.**

Papandreou, In re, 139 F.3d 247, 329 U.S.App.D.C. 210 (D.C.Cir.1998)— § **10.19, n. 37.**

Param Petroleum Corp. v. Commerce and Industry Ins. Co., 296 N.J.Super. 164, 686 A.2d 377 (N.J.Super.A.D.1997)— § **18.4, n. 1, 7, 44;** § **18.5, n. 8;** § **18.26, n. 13.**

Pardey v. Boulevard Billiard Club, 518 A.2d 1349 (R.I.1986)—§ **17.23, n. 6;** § **17.48, n. 12.**

Parentage of M.J., In re, 203 Ill.2d 526, 272 Ill.Dec. 329, 787 N.E.2d 144 (Ill.2003)— § **16.1, n. 15.**

Paribas Properties, Inc. v. Benson, 146 A.D.2d 522, 536 N.Y.S.2d 1007 (N.Y.A.D. 1 Dept.1989)—§ **18.5, n. 39.**

Parish v. B. F. Goodrich Co., 395 Mich. 271, 235 N.W.2d 570 (Mich.1975)—§ **3.11, n. 4, 6.**

Parish v. Minvielle, 217 So.2d 684 (La.App. 3 Cir.1969)—§ **13.6, n. 2.**

Park Bank–West v. Mueller, 151 Wis.2d 476, 444 N.W.2d 754 (Wis.App.1989)— § **14.16, n. 8.**

Parker v. Hoefer, 162 N.Y.S.2d 13, 142 N.E.2d 194 (N.Y.1957)—§ **24.20, n. 3.**

Parkey v. Baker, 254 Ark. 283, 492 S.W.2d 891 (Ark.1973)—§ **19.8, n. 3.**

Parkhurst v. Roy, 1882 WL 18302 (Unknown Court - Canada 1882)—§ **19.6, n. 3; § 21.6, n. 4.**

Parklane Hosiery Co., Inc. v. Shore, 439 U.S. 322, 99 S.Ct. 645, 58 L.Ed.2d 552 (1979)—§ **24.1, n. 12.**

Parkwood, Inc., In re, 461 F.2d 158, 149 U.S.App.D.C. 67 (D.C.Cir.1971)—§ **19.3, n. 11; § 19.9, n. 2.**

Paroth's Estate, In re, 72 Misc.2d 499, 340 N.Y.S.2d 433 (N.Y.Sur.1971)—§ **20.3, n. 1; § 22.23, n. 11.**

Parra v. Larchmont Farms, Inc., 942 S.W.2d 6 (Tex.App.-El Paso 1996)— § **17.60, n. 6.**

Parrett v. Palmer, 8 Ind.App. 356, 35 N.E. 713 (Ind.App.1893)—§ **4.33, n. 2; § 14.8, n. 4.**

Parrish v. Parrish, 116 Va. 476, 82 S.E. 119 (Va.1914)—§ **24.9, n. 6.**

Parry v. Ernst Home Center Corp., 779 P.2d 659 (Utah 1989)—§ **5.12, n. 7; § 7.2, n. 32, 34.**

Parson v. United States, 460 F.2d 228 (5th Cir.1972)—§ **14.11, n. 2.**

Parsons v. Chesapeake & O. Ry. Co., 375 U.S. 71, 84 S.Ct. 185, 11 L.Ed.2d 137 (1963)—§ **11.11, n. 8; § 11.14, n. 5.**

Parsons v. City of Bangor, 61 Me. 457 (Me. 1872)—§ **4.18, n. 2.**

Parsons v. Lyman, 20 N.Y. 103, 18 How. Pr. 193 (N.Y.1859)—§ **22.15, n. 15.**

Parsons Steel, Inc. v. First Alabama Bank, 474 U.S. 518, 106 S.Ct. 768, 88 L.Ed.2d 877 (1986)—§ **24.1, n. 7; § 24.12, n. 7.**

Parsons & Whittemore Overseas Co., Inc. v. Societe Generale De L'Industrie Du Papier (RAKTA), 508 F.2d 969 (2nd Cir. 1974)—§ **24.48, n. 7.**

Partee v. Kortrecht, 54 Miss. 66 (Miss. 1876)—§ **20.4, n. 5.**

Pascente v. Pascente, 1993 WL 43502 (S.D.N.Y.1993)—§ **17.42, n. 11, 22.**

Paschal v. Acklin, 27 Tex. 173 (Tex.1863)— § **20.9, n. 10.**

Pascoe v. Keuhnast, 642 S.W.2d 37 (Tex. App.-Waco 1982)—§ **14.9, n. 3.**

Pasqualone v. Pasqualone, 63 Ohio St.2d 96, 406 N.E.2d 1121 (Ohio 1980)— § **15.29, n. 3; § 15.39, n. 9.**

Patch v. Stanley Works (Stanley Chemical Co. Division), 448 F.2d 483 (2nd Cir. 1971)—§ **3.13, n. 4.**

Patchen & Patchen v. Wilson, 4 Hill 57 (N.Y.1842)—§ **22.18, n. 11.**

Patience, Re, 29 Ch.Div. 976 (Ch.D.1885)— § **4.28, n. 3.**

Patmore, In re Estate of, 141 Cal.App.2d 416, 296 P.2d 863 (Cal.App. 2 Dist. 1956)—§ **20.15, n. 5, 6, 9; § 22.23, n. 4.**

Patrick v. Bank of Tupelo, 169 Miss. 157, 152 So. 838 (Miss.1934)—§ **4.34, n. 3.**

Patten v. General Motors Corp., Chevrolet Motor Div., 699 F.Supp. 1500 (W.D.Okla.1987)—§ **17.64, n. 11.**

Patterson's Estate, In re, 64 Cal.App. 643, 222 P. 374 (Cal.App. 2 Dist.1923)— § **20.12, n. 1, 3, 5.**

Patton v. Carnrike, 510 F.Supp. 625 (N.D.N.Y.1981)—§ **17.48, n. 16.**

Paul v. International Precious Metals Corp., 613 F.Supp. 174 (S.D.Miss.1985)— § **7.12, n. 11.**

Paul v. National Life, 177 W.Va. 427, 352 S.E.2d 550 (W.Va.1986)—§ **2.21, n. 32.**

Paul v. State of Virginia, 75 U.S. 168, 19 L.Ed. 357 (1868)—§ **3.32, n. 4.**

Pauley Petroleum Inc. v. Continental Oil Co., 43 Del.Ch. 516, 239 A.2d 629 (Del. Supr.1968)—§ **10.16, n. 9; § 24.9, n. 7.**

Paul Revere Protective Life Ins. Co. v. Weis, 535 F.Supp. 379 (E.D.Pa.1981)— § **18.27, n. 2.**

Paulson v. Shapiro, 490 F.2d 1 (7th Cir. 1973)—§ **18.38, n. 6, 9.**

Pavlou v. Ocean Traders Marine Corp., 211 F.Supp. 320 (S.D.N.Y.1962)—§ **17.63, n. 23.**

Pavlovich v. Superior Court, 127 Cal. Rptr.2d 329, 58 P.3d 2 (Cal.2002)— § **5.11, n. 22; § 7.3, n. 11; § 7.11, n. 13; § 9.3, n. 8, 12.**

Payne v. Kirchwehm, 141 Ohio St. 384, 48 N.E.2d 224 (Ohio 1943)—§ **3.11, n. 3.**

Payne v. Motorists' Mut. Ins. Companies, 4 F.3d 452 (6th Cir.1993)—§ **8.2, n. 10, 12.**

Pazzi v. Taylor, 342 N.W.2d 481 (Iowa 1984)—§ **16.6, n. 4.**

Peabody v. Kent, 153 A.D. 286, 138 N.Y.S. 32 (N.Y.A.D. 2 Dept.1912)—§ **21.3, n. 3.**

Peacock v. Bradshaw, 145 Tex. 68, 194 S.W.2d 551 (Tex.1946)—§ **4.41, n. 1.**

Peacock v. Retail Credit Co., 302 F.Supp. 418 (N.D.Ga.1969)—§ **17.55, n. 4.**

Peanut Corp. of America v. Hollywood Brands, Inc., 696 F.2d 311 (4th Cir. 1982)—§ **8.5, n. 9.**

Pearce v. E.F. Hutton Group, Inc., 664 F.Supp. 1490 (D.D.C.1987)—§ **2.9, n. 19; § 17.26, n. 1; § 17.55, n. 9, 11.**

Pearce v. Pearce, 281 Ill. 194, 118 N.E. 84 (Ill.1917)—§ **20.15, n. 10.**

Peare v. Griggs, 201 N.Y.S.2d 326, 167 N.E.2d 734 (N.Y.1960)—§ **22.19, n. 32;** § **22.20, n. 29.**

Pearl v. Hansborough, 28 Tenn. 426 (Tenn. 1848)—§ **14.10, n. 3.**

Pearsall v. Dwight, 2 Mass. 84 (Mass. 1806)—§ **3.9, n. 2.**

Pearson v. Erb, 82 N.W.2d 818 (N.D. 1957)—§ **17.5, n. 9.**

Pearson v. Friedman, 112 So.2d 894 (Fla. App. 3 Dist.1959)—§ **6.3, n. 11.**

Pearson v. Northeast Airlines, Inc., 309 F.2d 553 (2nd Cir.1962)—§ **3.15;** § **3.15, n. 8;** § **3.27, n. 1;** § **17.9, n. 3.**

Peart's Estate, In re, 277 A.D. 61, 97 N.Y.S.2d 879 (N.Y.A.D. 1 Dept.1950)— § **13.2, n. 3;** § **13.9, n. 3, 4, 5, 8, 13.**

Pecheur Lozenge Co. v. National Candy Co., 315 U.S. 666, 62 S.Ct. 853, 86 L.Ed. 1103 (1942)—§ **17.53, n. 3.**

Peck's Estate, In re, 80 N.M. 290, 454 P.2d 772 (N.M.1969)—§ **4.45, n. 1.**

Pecorino's Estate, Matter of, 64 A.D.2d 711, 407 N.Y.S.2d 550 (N.Y.A.D. 2 Dept. 1978)—§ **13.2, n. 10.**

Pederson, In re, 105 B.R. 622 (Bkrtcy. D.Colo.1989)—§ **19.30, n. 9.**

Peebles v. Murray, 411 F.Supp. 1174 (D.Kan.1976)—§ **18.39, n. 6.**

Peet v. Peet, 229 Ill. 341, 82 N.E. 376 (Ill.1907)—§ **20.8, n. 11.**

Peffley–Warner v. Bowen, 113 Wash.2d 243, 778 P.2d 1022 (Wash.1989)—§ **13.6, n. 2, 11.**

Pegler v. Sullivan, 6 Ariz.App. 338, 432 P.2d 593 (Ariz.App.1967)—§ **7.10, n. 4.**

Peirce v. Peirce, 379 Ill. 185, 39 N.E.2d 990 (Ill.1942)—§ **16.1, n. 8.**

Pelican Point Operations, L.L.C. v. Carroll Childers Co., 807 So.2d 1171 (La.App. 1 Cir.2002)—§ **17.43, n. 30.**

Pelleport Investors, Inc. v. Budco Quality Theatres, Inc., 741 F.2d 273 (9th Cir. 1984)—§ **11.3, n. 22.**

Pemberton v. Colonna, 290 F.2d 220 (3rd Cir.1961)—§ **4.12, n. 3.**

Pemberton v. OvaTech, Inc., 669 F.2d 533 (8th Cir.1982)—§ **7.4, n. 9.**

Pembina Consol. Silver Mining & Milling Co. v. Commonwealth of Pennsylvania, 125 U.S. 181, 8 S.Ct. 737, 31 L.Ed. 650 (1888)—§ **3.34, n. 3.**

Pendleton v. Russell, 144 U.S. 640, 12 S.Ct. 743, 36 L.Ed. 574 (1892)—§ **23.11, n. 4.**

Penfield v. Tower, 1 N.D. 216, 46 N.W. 413 (N.D.1890)—§ **19.6, n. 3;** § **20.7, n. 3.**

Penn v. Lord Baltimore, 1750 WL 6 (Ct of Chancery 1750)—§ **19.8, n. 2.**

Pennegar v. State, 87 Tenn. 244, 10 S.W. 305 (Tenn.1889)—§ **13.9, n. 7, 8.**

Pennington's Trust, In re, 421 Pa. 334, 219 A.2d 353 (Pa.1966)—§ **20.13, n. 4;** § **21.3, n. 9.**

Pennoyer v. Neff, 95 U.S. 714, 24 L.Ed. 565 (1877)—§ **2.14, n. 53;** § **5.1, n. 9;** § **5.2,** n. 6; § **5.3;** § **5.3, n. 3;** § **5.5, n. 14;** § **5.6, n. 1;** § **5.7;** § **5.7, n. 6;** § **5.14, n. 2, 3;** § **5.16, n. 2;** § **5.21, n. 4;** § **6.2;** § **6.2, n. 7;** § **6.3;** § **6.3, n. 1;** § **6.5, n. 3.**

Pennsylvania v. New York, 407 U.S. 206, 92 S.Ct. 2075, 32 L.Ed.2d 693 (1972)— § **3.24, n. 18.**

Pennsylvania Fire Ins. Co. of Philadelphia v. Gold Issue Min. & Mill. Co., 243 U.S. 93, 37 S.Ct. 344, 61 L.Ed. 610 (1917)— § **10.14, n. 5.**

Pennsylvania R. Co. v. Levine, 263 F. 557 (2nd Cir.1920)—§ **20.3, n. 9.**

Pennzoil Products Co. v. Colelli & Associates, Inc., 149 F.3d 197 (3rd Cir.1998)— § **7.2, n. 33.**

Penry v. Wm. Barr, Inc., 415 F.Supp. 126 (E.D.Tex.1976)—§ **3.10, n. 3.**

Penwest Development Corp. Ltd. v. Dow Chemical Co., 667 F.Supp. 436 (E.D.Mich.1987)—§ **11.14, n. 8.**

People v. ———— (see opposing party)

People ex rel. v. ———— (see opposing party and relator)

People of State of New York ex rel. Cohn v. Graves, 300 U.S. 308, 57 S.Ct. 466, 81 L.Ed. 666 (1937)—§ **4.30, n. 1.**

People of State of Wisconsin v. Ubrig, 128 Ill.App.3d 743, 83 Ill.Dec. 877, 470 N.E.2d 1297 (Ill.App. 2 Dist.1984)— § **24.13, n. 8.**

Peoples Bank and Trust Co. v. Piper Aircraft Corp., 598 F.Supp. 377 (S.D.Fla. 1984)—§ **17.26, n. 1.**

Peplin v. Bruyere, [1900] 2 Ch. 504— § **20.6, n. 20.**

Pepper v. Litton, 308 U.S. 295, 60 S.Ct. 238, 84 L.Ed. 281 (1939)—§ **23.14, n. 7;** § **23.20, n. 4.**

Pepper's Estate, In re, 158 Cal. 619, 112 P. 62 (Cal.1910)—§ **14.7, n. 3.**

Peregrine Myanmar Ltd. v. Segal, 89 F.3d 41 (2nd Cir.1996)—§ **11.9, n. 6.**

Perez v. Alcoa Fujikura, Ltd., 969 F.Supp. 991 (W.D.Tex.1997)—§ **18.21, n. 14;** § **18.29, n. 3.**

Perez v. Finch, 320 F.Supp. 787 (E.D.Wash. 1970)—§ **13.2, n. 10.**

Perez v. Lippold, 32 Cal.2d 711, 198 P.2d 17 (Cal.1948)—§ **13.10, n. 3.**

Perez & Compania (Cataluna), S.A. v. M/V Mexico I, 826 F.2d 1449 (5th Cir.1987)— § **12.18, n. 16.**

Perez' Estate, In re, 98 Cal.App.2d 121, 219 P.2d 35 (Cal.App. 2 Dist.1950)—§ **13.6, n. 1.**

Pericles, In re Estate of, 266 Ill.App.3d 1096, 204 Ill.Dec. 51, 641 N.E.2d 10 (Ill.App. 1 Dist.1994)—§ **20.5, n. 7;** § **20.14, n. 3.**

Perin v. McMicken's Heirs, 1860 WL 5534 (La.1860)—§ **19.6, n. 3.**

Perito v. Perito, 756 P.2d 895 (Alaska 1988)—§ **4.18, n. 3;** § **4.20, n. 4;** § **15.5, n. 2.**

Perkins v. Benguet Consol. Min. Co., 158 Ohio St. 145, 107 N.E.2d 203 (Ohio 1952)—**§ 6.9, n. 9.**

Perkins v. Benguet Consol. Min. Co., 342 U.S. 437, 72 S.Ct. 413, 96 L.Ed. 485 (1952)—**§ 3.48; § 3.48, n. 14; § 5.10, n. 11, 16; § 5.13; § 5.13, n. 7; § 6.7, n. 8; § 6.9; § 6.9, n. 4.**

Perkins v. Benguet Consol. Min. Co., 55 Cal.App.2d 720, 132 P.2d 70 (Cal.App. 1 Dist.1942)—**§ 24.29, n. 6.**

Perkins v. CCH Computax, Inc., 333 N.C. 140, 423 S.E.2d 780 (N.C.1992)—**§ 11.5, n. 3.**

Perkins v. Clark Equipment Co., Melrose Div., 823 F.2d 207 (8th Cir.1987)—**§ 3.12, n. 5.**

Perkins v. De Witt, 279 A.D. 903, 111 N.Y.S.2d 752 (N.Y.A.D. 1 Dept.1952)—**§ 24.29, n. 6.**

Perkins v. Philadelphia Life Ins. Co., 586 F.Supp. 296 (W.D.Mo.1984)—**§ 18.26, n. 10.**

Perl v. Perl, 126 A.D.2d 91, 512 N.Y.S.2d 372 (N.Y.A.D. 1 Dept.1987)—**§ 15.24, n. 7.**

Perlman v. Great States Life Ins. Co., 164 Colo. 493, 436 P.2d 124 (Colo.1968)—**§ 10.16, n. 8.**

Perlman v. Perlman, 113 N.J.Eq. 3, 165 A. 646 (N.J.Ch.1933)—**§ 4.24, n. 3.**

Perlmuter Printing Co. v. Strome, Inc., 436 F.Supp. 409 (N.D.Ohio 1976)—**§ 18.29, n. 4; § 18.38, n. 5.**

Perloff v. Symmes Hospital, 487 F.Supp. 426 (D.Mass.1980)—**§ 3.23, n. 10; § 17.17, n. 8.**

Perlstein v. Perlstein, 152 Conn. 152, 204 A.2d 909 (Conn.1964)—**§ 5.5, n. 7.**

Permacel v. American Ins. Co., 299 N.J.Super. 400, 691 A.2d 383 (N.J.Super.A.D.1997)—**§ 18.26, n. 13.**

Perotti v. Perotti, 78 Misc.2d 131, 355 N.Y.S.2d 68 (N.Y.Sup.1974)—**§ 4.37, n. 4.**

Perrin v. Perrin, 408 F.2d 107 (3rd Cir. 1969)—**§ 15.20, n. 7.**

Perrin v. Perrin, 140 Misc. 406, 250 N.Y.S. 588 (N.Y.Sup.1931)—**§ 4.1, n. 2.**

Perry v. Ponder, 604 S.W.2d 306 (Tex.Civ. App.-Dallas 1980)—**§ 15.29, n. 2.**

Perry v. Richardson, 336 F.Supp. 451 (E.D.Pa.1972)—**§ 13.2, n. 10.**

Perry v. St. Joseph & W. R. Co., 29 Kan. 420 (Kan.1883)—**§ 22.10, n. 8.**

Perry's Estate, In re, 480 S.W.2d 893 (Mo. 1972)—**§ 14.9, n. 3; § 20.3, n. 1.**

Persson v. Dukes, 280 Md. 194, 372 A.2d 240 (Md.1977)—**§ 20.13, n. 9.**

Perusahaan Umum Listrik Negara Pusat v. M/V Tel Aviv, 711 F.2d 1231 (5th Cir. 1983)—**§ 11.10, n. 4, 8.**

Pescatore v. Pan American World Airways, Inc., 97 F.3d 1 (2nd Cir.1996)—**§ 17.44, n. 5.**

Peters v. Haley, 762 So.2d 695 (La.App. 1 Cir.2000)—**§ 14.9, n. 1.**

Peters v. Peters, 63 Haw. 653, 634 P.2d 586 (Hawai'i 1981)—**§ 2.16, n. 19; § 2.17, n. 12; § 2.25, n. 13; § 17.39, n. 5, 7; § 18.21, n. 17.**

Petersen v. Chemical Bank, 32 N.Y. 21, 29 How. Pr. 240 (N.Y.1865)—**§ 22.15, n. 6; § 22.17, n. 3.**

Petersen v. Ogden Union Ry. & Depot Co., 110 Utah 573, 175 P.2d 744 (Utah 1946)—**§ 11.5, n. 6.**

Petersen Towing Corp. v. Capt. Abrams, Inc., 388 F.Supp. 1166 (E.D.N.Y.1975)—**§ 10.6, n. 42.**

Peterson v. State of Texas, 635 P.2d 241 (Colo.App.1981)—**§ 17.43, n. 16.**

Peterson v. Warren, 31 Wis.2d 547, 143 N.W.2d 560 (Wis.1966)—**§ 18.21, n. 19.**

Peterson, Wyoming ex rel. v. District Court of Ninth Judicial Dist., 617 P.2d 1056 (Wyo.1980)—**§ 11.17, n. 23.**

Peterson's Guardianship, In re, 119 Neb. 511, 229 N.W. 885 (Neb.1930)—**§ 4.41, n. 1.**

Petition of (see name of party)

Petranek, In re Marriage of, 255 Mont. 458, 843 P.2d 784 (Mont.1992)—**§ 15.36, n. 7.**

Petrasek's Estate, In re, 191 Misc. 9, 79 N.Y.S.2d 561 (N.Y.Sur.1948)—**§ 20.3, n. 9.**

Petri v. Rhein, 162 F.Supp. 834 (N.D.Ill. 1957)—**§ 19.32, n. 5.**

Petroleo Brasileiro, S. A., Petrobras v. Ameropan Oil Corp., 372 F.Supp. 503 (E.D.N.Y.1974)—**§ 18.24, n. 2.**

Petroleum Helicopters, Inc. v. Avco Corp., 804 F.2d 1367 (5th Cir.1986)—**§ 5.15, n. 6; § 7.2, n. 19.**

Petroleum Tank Lines, Inc., In re, 10 B.R. 286 (Bkrtcy.W.D.N.Y.1981)—**§ 23.20, n. 8.**

Pettie v. Roberts, 214 Ga. 750, 107 S.E.2d 657 (Ga.1959)—**§ 5.23, n. 3.**

Pettit v. Pettit, 105 A.D. 312, 93 N.Y.S. 1001 (N.Y.A.D. 3 Dept.1905)—**§ 13.9, n. 3.**

Pettit, Estate of v. Levine, 657 S.W.2d 636 (Mo.App. E.D.1983)—**§ 22.7, n. 1; § 22.9, n. 7.**

Pevoski v. Pevoski, 371 Mass. 358, 358 N.E.2d 416 (Mass.1976)—**§ 2.16, n. 14; § 2.21, n. 14; § 17.39, n. 9; § 17.56, n. 18.**

Pfau v. Moseley, 9 Ohio St.2d 13, 222 N.E.2d 639 (Ohio 1966)—**§ 20.5, n. 6; § 20.15, n. 3.**

Pfau v. Trent Aluminum Co., 55 N.J. 511, 263 A.2d 129 (N.J.1970)—**§ 3.14, n. 1; § 17.12, n. 13.**

Pfeifer v. Wright, 41 F.2d 464 (10th Cir. 1930)—**§ 16.1, n. 11.**

Pfizer, Inc. v. Employers Ins. of Wausau, 154 N.J. 187, 712 A.2d 634 (N.J.1998)—**§ 18.26, n. 13.**

Pfotenhauer v. Hunter, 536 P.2d 923 (Okla. 1975)—**§ 22.25, n. 15; § 22.26, n. 6.**

Pharmaceutical Research and Mfrs. of America v. Walsh, 538 U.S. 644, 123 S.Ct. 1855, 155 L.Ed.2d 889 (2003)—**§ 3.32, n. 15.**

Phelan, Matter of Estate of, 235 Mont. 257, 766 P.2d 876 (Mont.1988)—**§ 22.6, n. 4.**

Phelps v. Decker, 10 Mass. 267 (Mass. 1813)—**§ 19.3, n. 4.**

Philadelphia, City of v. Cohen, 15 A.D.2d 464, 222 N.Y.S.2d 226 (N.Y.A.D. 1 Dept. 1961)—**§ 3.17, n. 3.**

Philadelphia, City of v. Williamson, 1873 WL 11503 (Pa.Quar.Sess.1873)—**§ 13.8, n. 1.**

Philadelphia Newspapers, Inc. v. Hepps, 475 U.S. 767, 106 S.Ct. 1558, 89 L.Ed.2d 783 (1986)—**§ 7.8, n. 1.**

Philadelphia & R. Ry. Co. v. McKibbin, 243 U.S. 264, 37 S.Ct. 280, 61 L.Ed. 710 (1917)—**§ 10.14, n. 9.**

Philip Morris Inc. v. Angeletti, 358 Md. 689, 752 A.2d 200 (Md.2000)—**§ 17.2, n. 3; § 17.64, n. 13.**

Philips Credit Corp. v. Regent Health Group, Inc., 953 F.Supp. 482 (S.D.N.Y. 1997)—**§ 18.21, n. 17; § 18.28, n. 4.**

Phillips, In re Marriage of, 274 Kan. 1049, 58 P.3d 680 (Kan.2002)—**§ 16.1, n. 7.**

Phillips v. Amoco Trinidad Oil Co., 632 F.2d 82 (9th Cir.1980)—**§ 17.63, n. 21.**

Phillips v. Anchor Hocking Glass Corp., 100 Ariz. 251, 413 P.2d 732 (Ariz.1966)—**§ 7.2, n. 13.**

Phillips v. Englehart, 437 S.W.2d 158 (Mo. App.1968)—**§ 19.12, n. 3.**

Phillips v. General Motors Corp., 298 Mont. 438, 995 P.2d 1002 (Mont.2000)—**§ 2.16, n. 7, 21; § 2.23, n. 1; § 17.26, n. 1; § 17.32, n. 33; § 17.50; § 17.50, n. 59; § 17.74; § 17.74, n. 1.**

Phillips v. Iowa Dist. Court for Johnson County, 380 N.W.2d 706 (Iowa 1986)—**§ 15.31, n. 2.**

Phillips v. Phillips, 213 Ala. 27, 104 So. 234 (Ala.1925)—**§ 20.6, n. 14.**

Phillips v. South Carolina Ins. Co., 607 F.Supp. 593 (M.D.Ga.1985)—**§ 18.26, n. 15.**

Phillips Petroleum Co. v. Shutts, 472 U.S. 797, 105 S.Ct. 2965, 86 L.Ed.2d 628 (1985)—**§ 3.9, n. 6; § 3.16, n. 3; § 3.23; § 3.23, n. 17; § 3.26; § 3.26, n. 8; § 3.43, n. 6; § 5.1, n. 10; § 5.4, n. 24; § 10.10; § 10.10, n. 8; § 10.11, n. 1; § 23.15, n. 14; § 24.15, n. 4.**

Philp v. Macri, 261 F.2d 945 (9th Cir. 1958)—**§ 12.19, n. 5.**

Phil Phillips Ford, Inc. v. St. Paul Fire & Marine Ins. Co., 465 S.W.2d 933 (Tex. 1971)—**§ 19.19, n. 8.**

Phoenix Arbor Plaza, Ltd. v. Dauderman, 163 Ariz. 27, 785 P.2d 1215 (Ariz.App. Div. 1 1989)—**§ 18.27, n. 3.**

Phoenix Canada Oil Co. Ltd. v. Texaco Inc., 560 F.Supp. 1372 (D.Del.1983)—**§ 18.44, n. 7.**

Picarella v. Picarella, 20 Md.App. 499, 316 A.2d 826 (Md.App.1974)—**§ 13.6, n. 3, 9.**

Pickard v. Pickard, 241 Iowa 1307, 45 N.W.2d 269 (Iowa 1950)—**§ 13.9, n. 5.**

Pickering v. De Rochemont, 45 N.H. 67 (N.H.1863)—**§ 22.25, n. 12.**

Pickus, Matter of, 8 B.R. 114 (Bkrtcy. D.Conn.1980)—**§ 23.13, n. 1.**

Piekarski v. Home Owners Sav. Bank, 743 F.Supp. 38 (D.D.C.1990)—**§ 11.14, n. 6.**

Pierburg GmbH & Co. Kg. v. Superior Court, 137 Cal.App.3d 238, 186 Cal.Rptr. 876 (Cal.App. 2 Dist.1982)—**§ 12.9, n. 7.**

Pierce v. Board of County Com'rs of Leavenworth County, 200 Kan. 74, 434 P.2d 858 (Kan.1967)—**§ 12.3, n. 5.**

Pierce v. Cook & Co., Inc., 518 F.2d 720 (10th Cir.1975)—**§ 3.47, n. 9; § 24.8, n. 7; § 24.28, n. 3.**

Pierce v. Globemaster Baltimore, Inc., 49 F.R.D. 63 (D.Md.1969)—**§ 10.4, n. 12.**

Pierce v. Pierce, 58 Wash. 622, 109 P. 45 (Wash.1910)—**§ 13.8, n. 5.**

Pierce v. Serafin, 787 S.W.2d 705 (Ky.App. 1990)—**§ 7.10, n. 4.**

Piercy, In re, [1895] 1 Ch. 83—**§ 20.7, n. 1.**

Pierrakos v. Pierrakos, 148 N.J.Super. 574, 372 A.2d 1331 (N.J.Super.A.D.1977)—**§ 19.8, n. 14.**

Pilcher v. Paulk, 228 So.2d 663 (La.App. 3 Cir.1969)—**§ 19.2, n. 4, 7.**

Pillsbury Co. v. Delta Boat & Barge Rental, Inc., 72 F.R.D. 630 (E.D.La.1976)—**§ 10.4, n. 12, 14.**

Pimental v. Cherne Industries, Inc., 46 Conn.App. 142, 698 A.2d 361 (Conn.App. 1997)—**§ 17.59, n. 11.**

Pimental v. Cherne Industries, Inc., 1996 WL 456373 (Conn.Super.1996)—**§ 17.59, n. 11.**

Pines v. Warnaco, Inc., 706 F.2d 1173 (11th Cir.1983)—**§ 18.21, n. 3.**

Pingpank, Matter of, 134 A.D.2d 263, 520 N.Y.S.2d 596 (N.Y.A.D. 2 Dept.1987)—**§ 4.18, n. 1; § 22.7, n. 1.**

Pink, United States v., 315 U.S. 203, 62 S.Ct. 552, 86 L.Ed. 796 (1942)—**§ 11.13, n. 8, 10; § 24.46, n. 9.**

Pinker v. Roche Holdings Ltd., 292 F.3d 361 (3rd Cir.2002)—**§ 9.6, n. 20; § 10.2, n. 22.**

Pinney v. McGregory, 102 Mass. 186 (Mass. 1869)—**§ 22.9, n. 9; § 22.10, n. 2.**

Pinney v. Providence Loan & Investment Co., 106 Wis. 396, 82 N.W. 308 (Wis. 1900)—**§ 10.13, n. 3.**

Pinorsky v. Pinorsky, 217 Ill.App.3d 165, 160 Ill.Dec. 169, 576 N.E.2d 1123 (Ill. App. 5 Dist.1991)—§ **17.26, n. 1.**

Pintlar Corp., In re, 133 F.3d 1141 (9th Cir.1998)—§ **10.7, n. 11, 17.**

Pioneer Credit Corp. v. Carden, 127 Vt. 229, 245 A.2d 891 (Vt.1968)—§ **2.17, n. 6; § 2.23, n. 2; § 12.19, n. 19.**

Pioneer Credit Corp. v. Morency, 122 Vt. 463, 177 A.2d 368 (Vt.1962)—§ **19.11, n. 2.**

Piper Aircraft Co. v. Reyno, 454 U.S. 235, 102 S.Ct. 252, 70 L.Ed.2d 419 (1981)— § **3.46, n. 6; § 11.9; § 11.9, n. 2; § 11.10, n. 5; § 11.11; § 11.11, n. 2, 4, 6; § 11.14, n. 8; § 17.76, n. 15.**

Pirkle v. Cassity, 104 F.Supp. 318 (E.D.Tex. 1952)—§ **22.21, n. 6.**

Pisacane v. Italia Societa Per Azioni Di Navigazione, 219 F.Supp. 424 (S.D.N.Y. 1963)—§ **18.11, n. 4.**

Pitman v. Pitman, 314 Mass. 465, 50 N.E.2d 69 (Mass.1943)—§ **21.11, n. 5.**

Pittman v. Maldania, Inc., 2001 WL 1221704 (Del.Super.2001)—§ **17.36, n. 15; § 17.48, n. 18.**

Pitts v. First Union Nat'l Bank, 262 F.Supp.2d 593 (D.Md.2003)—§ **21.4, n. 2.**

Pittston Co. v. Sedgwick James of New York, Inc., 971 F.Supp. 915 (D.N.J. 1997)—§ **17.10, n. 3.**

Pizarro v. Hoteles Concorde Intern., C.A., 907 F.2d 1256 (1st Cir.1990)—§ **5.10, n. 27, 34; § 6.7, n. 22.**

Place v. Norwich & N.Y. Transp. Co., 118 U.S. 468, 6 S.Ct. 1150, 30 L.Ed. 134 (1886)—§ **3.57, n. 16.**

Plant v. Harrison, 36 Misc. 649, 74 N.Y.S. 411 (N.Y.Sup.1902)—§ **4.24, n. 2; § 4.36, n. 11.**

Plante v. Columbia Paints, 494 N.W.2d 140 (N.D.1992)—§ **17.26, n. 1.**

Platano v. Norm's Castle, Inc., 830 F.Supp. 796 (S.D.N.Y.1993)—§ **17.48, n. 12.**

Platner v. Vincent, 187 Cal. 443, 202 P. 655 (Cal.1921)—§ **19.5, n. 3, 5, 10.**

Plazza's Estate, In re, 34 Colo.App. 296, 526 P.2d 155 (Colo.App.1974)—§ **20.5, n. 6, 7; § 22.22, n. 2, 4, 8.**

Pleasonton's Estate, In re, 45 N.J.Super. 154, 131 A.2d 795 (N.J.Super.A.D.1957)—§ **20.13, n. 6.**

Plum v. Tampax, Inc., 402 Pa. 616, 168 A.2d 315 (Pa.1961)—§ **11.8, n. 3.**

Plum Tree, Inc. v. N. K. Winston Corp., 351 F.Supp. 80 (S.D.N.Y.1972)—§ **18.37, n. 2.**

Plybon, In re, 157 W.Va. 366, 201 S.E.2d 315 (W.Va.1973)—§ **22.7, n. 5.**

Pochop v. Toyota Motor Co., Ltd., 111 F.R.D. 464 (S.D.Miss.1986)—§ **12.7, n. 3.**

Point Landing, Inc. v. Omni Capital Intern., Ltd., 795 F.2d 415 (5th Cir.1986)— § **10.3, n. 14.**

Polacke v. Superior Court In and For County of Maricopa, 170 Ariz. 217, 823 P.2d 84 (Ariz.App. Div. 1 1991)—§ **5.6, n. 7; § 5.9, n. 3.**

Poling v. Poling, 116 W.Va. 187, 179 S.E. 604 (W.Va.1935)—§ **11.13, n. 7.**

Pollack v. Bridgestone/Firestone, Inc., 939 F.Supp. 151 (D.Conn.1996)—§ **17.73, n. 4.**

Pollard, Ex parte, Mont. & C. 239 (1840)— § **19.8, n. 6.**

Pollock, Matter of Adoption of, 293 Ark. 195, 736 S.W.2d 6 (Ark.1987)—§ **16.5, n. 4.**

Pollux Holding Ltd. v. Chase Manhattan Bank, 329 F.3d 64 (2nd Cir.2003)— § **11.11, n. 2.**

Polson v. Stewart, 167 Mass. 211, 45 N.E. 737 (Mass.1897)—§ **19.3, n. 3; § 20.5, n. 5.**

Polydore v. Prince, 19 F.Cas. 950 (D.Me. 1837)—§ **13.19, n. 2.**

Pond v. Makepeace, 43 Mass. 114 (Mass. 1840)—§ **22.14, n. 4.**

Pond v. Porter, 141 Conn. 56, 104 A.2d 228 (Conn.1954)—§ **21.3, n. 3.**

Ponder v. Foster, 23 Ga. 489 (Ga.1857)— § **22.25, n. 16.**

Ponina v. Leland, 85 Nev. 263, 454 P.2d 16 (Nev.1969)—§ **13.6, n. 1; § 13.18, n. 11.**

Poor v. Poor, 381 Mass. 392, 409 N.E.2d 758 (Mass.1980)—§ **15.20, n. 10; § 15.21, n. 3.**

Pope v. Atlantic Coast Line R. Co., 345 U.S. 379, 73 S.Ct. 749, 97 L.Ed. 1094 (1953)—§ **11.13, n. 4.**

Pope v. Pope, 520 S.W.2d 634 (Mo.App. 1975)—§ **13.6, n. 2.**

Pope, State ex rel. Circus Circus Reno, Inc. v., 317 Or. 151, 854 P.2d 461 (Or. 1993)—§ **5.10, n. 34.**

Pope v. Terre Haute Car and Mfg. Co., 87 N.Y. 137 (N.Y.1881)—§ **6.2, n. 21; § 10.8, n. 12.**

Pope v. Terre Haute Car & Manufacturing Co., 107 N.Y. 61, 13 N.E. 592 (N.Y. 1887)—§ **5.3, n. 16.**

Popkin & Stern, In re, 292 B.R. 910 (8th Cir.2003)—§ **14.9, n. 13; § 14.13, n. 8.**

Porsche Cars North America, Inc. v. Porsche.Net, 302 F.3d 248 (4th Cir. 2002)—§ **5.9, n. 17, 20, 24.**

Porter v. LSB Industries, Inc., 192 A.D.2d 205, 600 N.Y.S.2d 867 (N.Y.A.D. 4 Dept. 1993)—§ **10.16, n. 8.**

Porter v. Wilson, 419 F.2d 254 (9th Cir. 1969)—§ **24.29, n. 6.**

Porterfield v. City of Augusta, 67 Me. 556 (Me.1877)—§ **4.19, n. 5.**

Portnoy v. Portnoy, 81 Nev. 235, 401 P.2d 249 (Nev.1965)—§ **15.28, n. 6.**

Portwood v. Portwood, 109 S.W.2d 515 (Tex.Civ.App.-Eastland 1937)—§ **13.6, n. 7, 9.**

Post v. First Nat. Bank, 138 Ill. 559, 28 N.E. 978 (Ill.1891)—§ **19.3, n. 1, 6.**

Poster Exchange, Inc. v. National Screen Service Corp., 517 F.2d 117 (5th Cir. 1975)—§ **24.1, n. 8.**

Potlatch No. 1 Federal Credit Union v. Kennedy, 76 Wash.2d 806, 459 P.2d 32 (Wash.1969)—§ **18.18, n. 12; § 18.27, n. 5.**

Potter v. St. Louis–San Francisco Ry. Co., 622 F.2d 979 (8th Cir.1980)—§ **17.8, n. 14.**

Potts v. Potts, 142 Md.App. 448, 790 A.2d 703 (Md.App.2002)—§ **14.11, n. 1; § 15.30, n. 1.**

Pound v. Insurance Co. of North America, 439 F.2d 1059 (10th Cir.1971)—§ **18.21, n. 8.**

Poust v. Huntleigh Healthcare, 998 F.Supp. 478 (D.N.J.1998)—§ **17.44, n. 9.**

Powell v. American Charter Federal Sav. and Loan Ass'n, 245 Neb. 551, 514 N.W.2d 326 (Neb.1994)—§ **2.17, n. 16; § 2.19, n. 16; § 2.23, n. 2; § 18.21, n. 14.**

Powell v. Erb, 349 Md. 791, 709 A.2d 1294 (Md.1998)—§ **2.21, n. 7; § 17.8, n. 4; § 17.60, n. 6.**

Powell v. McDermott Intern., Inc., 588 So.2d 84 (La.1991)—§ **17.63, n. 22.**

Powell v. McKee, 1849 WL 3840 (La. 1849)—§ **19.15, n. 5.**

Powell v. Sappington, 495 So.2d 569 (Ala. 1986)—§ **2.21, n. 1; § 17.59, n. 9.**

Power v. Plummer, 93 N.H. 37, 35 A.2d 230 (N.H.1943)—§ **22.7, n. 5; § 22.8, n. 2; § 22.10, n. 11.**

Power Mfg. Co. v. Saunders, 274 U.S. 490, 47 S.Ct. 678, 71 L.Ed. 1165 (1927)—§ **3.35, n. 1.**

Power Motive Corp. v. Mannesmann Demag Corp., 617 F.Supp. 1048 (D.Colo.1985)—§ **18.21, n. 14.**

Powers v. Powers, 105 Nev. 514, 779 P.2d 91 (Nev.1989)—§ **14.9, n. 1.**

Power & Telephone Supply Co., Inc. v. Harmonic, Inc., 268 F.Supp.2d 981 (W.D.Tenn.2003)—§ **18.5, n. 33.**

Poyner v. Erma Werke Gmbh, 618 F.2d 1186 (6th Cir.1980)—§ **10.16, n. 7.**

Poyner v. Lear Siegler, Inc., 542 F.2d 955 (6th Cir.1976)—§ **10.16, n. 8.**

Prack v. Weissinger, 276 F.2d 446 (4th Cir. 1960)—§ **11.14, n. 8.**

Practical Concepts, Inc. v. Republic of Bolivia, 811 F.2d 1543, 258 U.S.App.D.C. 354 (D.C.Cir.1987)—§ **5.17, n. 8; § 5.21, n. 5.**

Prakash v. American University, 727 F.2d 1174, 234 U.S.App.D.C. 75 (D.C.Cir. 1984)—§ **4.2, n. 1; § 4.13, n. 4.**

Pratt, In re, 219 Minn. 414, 18 N.W.2d 147 (Minn.1945)—§ **4.37, n. 10; § 4.41, n. 5; § 4.42, n. 2, 4.**

Pratt v. Douglas, 1884 WL 426 (N.J.Err. & App.1884)—§ **20.6, n. 16; § 22.2, n. 2.**

Pratt v. Hawley, 297 Ill. 244, 130 N.E. 793 (Ill.1921)—§ **22.4, n. 8.**

Pratt v. United Arab Shipping Co., 585 F.Supp. 1573 (E.D.La.1984)—§ **17.63, n. 24.**

Pratt's Trust, In re, 5 A.D.2d 501, 172 N.Y.S.2d 965 (N.Y.A.D. 1 Dept.1958)—§ **21.3, n. 9; § 21.11; § 21.11, n. 16.**

Pray v. Pray, 5 Fam. Law Rep. 2945 (D.C. Super. Ct. Fam. Div.1979)—§ **15.30, n. 2.**

Precision Mach. Works v. King, 1986 WL 6955 (N.D.Ill.1986)—§ **12.7, n. 3.**

Precision Screen Machines Inc. v. Elexon, Inc., 1996 WL 495564 (N.D.Ill.1996)—§ **17.40, n. 28; § 18.1, n. 18.**

Precision Tune Auto Care, Inc. v. Radcliffe, 815 So.2d 708 (Fla.App. 4 Dist.2002)—§ **17.40, n. 26.**

Preferred RX, Inc. v. American Prescription Plan, Inc., 46 F.3d 535 (6th Cir.1995)—§ **5.19, n. 10; § 6.5, n. 9.**

Prejean v. Sonatrach, Inc., 652 F.2d 1260 (5th Cir.1981)—§ **5.10, n. 26; § 6.7, n. 20.**

Premix–Marbletite Mfg. Corp. v. SKW Chemicals, Inc., 145 F.Supp.2d 1348 (S.D.Fla.2001)—§ **17.64, n. 10.**

Prentice v. Parker, 376 So.2d 568 (La.App. 4 Cir.1979)—§ **16.6, n. 6.**

Presbyterian University Hosp. v. Wilson, 337 Md. 541, 654 A.2d 1324 (Md.1995)—§ **5.10, n. 12, 26; § 6.7, n. 20.**

Pres–Kap, Inc. v. System One, Direct Access, Inc., 636 So.2d 1351 (Fla.App. 3 Dist.1994)—§ **8.7, n. 9.**

Preston's Estate, In re, 193 Kan. 145, 392 P.2d 922 (Kan.1964)—§ **22.10, n. 13.**

Prettyman v. Conaway, 14 Del. 221, 32 A. 15 (Del.Super.1891)—§ **4.36, n. 4.**

Price v. Atchison, T. & S. F. Ry. Co., 42 Cal.2d 577, 268 P.2d 457 (Cal.1954)—§ **11.8, n. 3.**

Price v. Brown Group, Inc., 206 A.D.2d 195, 619 N.Y.S.2d 414 (N.Y.A.D. 4 Dept. 1994)—§ **18.1, n. 26.**

Price v. Howard County General Hosp., 950 F.Supp. 141 (D.Md.1996)—§ **12.12, n. 1.**

Price v. International Tel. and Tel. Corp., 651 F.Supp. 706 (S.D.Miss.1986)—§ **18.12, n. 16.**

Price v. Johnson, 78 N.M. 123, 428 P.2d 978 (N.M.1967)—§ **20.5, n. 6.**

Price v. Litton Systems, Inc., 784 F.2d 600 (5th Cir.1986)—§ **3.10, n. 1, 3; § 17.26, n. 1; § 17.79, n. 3.**

Price v. Price, 156 Pa. 617, 27 A. 291 (Pa. 1893)—§ **4.18, n. 2; § 4.19, n. 2; § 4.20, n. 4; § 4.36, n. 3.**

Price v. Socialist People's Libyan Arab Jamahiriya, 294 F.3d 82, 352 U.S.App.D.C. 284 (D.C.Cir.2002)—§ **7.3, n. 10;** § **10.19, n. 50.**

Price v. Sommermeyer, 195 Colo. 285, 577 P.2d 752 (Colo.1978)—§ **22.10, n. 11;** § **22.19, n. 6.**

Price and Sons v. Second Judicial Dist. Court of State, In and For County of Washoe, 108 Nev. 387, 831 P.2d 600 (Nev.1992)—§ **7.2, n. 20, 33.**

Pridemore, In re Marriage of, 146 Ill.App.3d 990, 100 Ill.Dec. 640, 497 N.E.2d 818 (Ill.App. 4 Dist.1986)—§ **6.2, n. 13.**

Priebe & Sons v. United States, 332 U.S. 407, 68 S.Ct. 123, 92 L.Ed. 32 (1947)— § **3.52, n. 3.**

Prima Paint Corp. v. Flood & Conklin Mfg. Co., 388 U.S. 395, 87 S.Ct. 1801, 18 L.Ed.2d 1270 (1967)—§ **3.37, n. 5;** § **24.48, n. 1.**

Prince's Estate, In re, 49 Misc.2d 219, 267 N.Y.S.2d 138 (N.Y.Sur.1964)—§ **20.14, n. 11.**

Pritchard v. Norton, 106 U.S. 124, 1 S.Ct. 102, 27 L.Ed. 104 (1882)—§ **18.1, n. 7;** § **18.2, n. 1;** § **18.14;** § **18.14, n. 5;** § **18.18, n. 2.**

Probate Court In and For Hennepin County, State v., 149 Minn. 464, 184 N.W. 43 (Minn.1921)—§ **22.10, n. 9.**

Process and Storage Vessels, Inc. v. Tank Service, Inc., 541 F.Supp. 725 (D.Del. 1982)—§ **11.6, n. 8.**

Proctor v. Clark, 154 Mass. 45, 27 N.E. 673 (Mass.1891)—§ **20.13, n. 10.**

Proctor v. Frost, 89 N.H. 304, 197 A. 813 (N.H.1938)—§ **19.3, n. 4;** § **19.9, n. 4, 5;** § **20.5, n. 5.**

Production of Records to Grand Jury, In re, 618 F.Supp. 440 (D.Mass.1985)— § **12.11, n. 7.**

Professional Ins. Corp. v. Sutherland, 700 So.2d 347 (Ala.1997)—§ **11.4, n. 3;** § **11.5, n. 4.**

Propst v. Fisher, 313 F.2d 248 (6th Cir. 1963)—§ **22.19, n. 31, 32;** § **22.21, n. 2.**

Prosser, State ex rel. Van Loh v., 78 S.D. 35, 98 N.W.2d 329 (S.D.1959)—§ **4.41, n. 6.**

Prouty's Estate, In re, 101 Vt. 496, 144 A. 691 (Vt.1929)—§ **22.25, n. 8.**

Provident Sav. Bank & Trust Co. v. Steinmetz, 270 N.Y. 129, 200 N.E. 669 (N.Y. 1936)—§ **19.10, n. 3, 5.**

Prows v. Pinpoint Retail Systems, Inc., 868 P.2d 809 (Utah 1993)—§ **2.23, n. 9;** § **11.5, n. 6;** § **18.9, n. 11;** § **18.21, n. 14.**

Proyecfin de Venezuela, S.A. v. Banco Industrial de Venezuela, S.A., 760 F.2d 390 (2nd Cir.1985)—§ **11.11, n. 12.**

Prudential Ins. Co. of America v. Lewis, 306 F.Supp. 1177 (N.D.Ala.1969)—§ **4.26, n. 1.**

Prudential Ins. Co. of America v. O'Grady, 97 Ariz. 9, 396 P.2d 246 (Ariz.1964)— § **12.15, n. 8.**

Prudential Lines, Inc. v. General Tire Intern. Co., 440 F.Supp. 556 (S.D.N.Y. 1977)—§ **12.18, n. 1.**

Prudential Resources Corp. v. Plunkett, 583 S.W.2d 97 (Ky.App.1979)—§ **11.5, n. 3;** § **18.21, n. 14.**

Pruitt v. Levi Strauss & Co., 932 F.2d 458 (5th Cir.1991)—§ **18.29, n. 3, 5.**

Pryor v. Swarner, 445 F.2d 1272 (2nd Cir. 1971)—§ **17.31, n. 7.**

P & S Business Machines, Inc. v. Canon USA, Inc., 331 F.3d 804 (11th Cir. 2003)—§ **11.4, n. 13.**

P. S. & E., Inc. v. Selastomer Detroit, Inc., 470 F.2d 125 (7th Cir.1972)—§ **18.33, n. 4.**

PT United Can Co. Ltd. v. Crown Cork & Seal Co., Inc., 138 F.3d 65 (2nd Cir. 1998)—§ **9.8, n. 7;** § **10.2, n. 6;** § **10.8, n. 5.**

Public Adm'r of New York County v. Angela Compania Naviera, S.A., 592 F.2d 58 (2nd Cir.1979)—§ **17.63, n. 23.**

Publications Intern., Ltd. v. Simon & Schuster, Inc., 763 F.Supp. 309 (N.D.Ill. 1991)—§ **9.3;** § **9.3, n. 14.**

Publicker's Estate, In re, 385 Pa. 403, 123 A.2d 655 (Pa.1956)—§ **4.17, n. 2.**

Public Parks Amusement Co. v. Embree–McLean Carriage Co., 64 Ark. 29, 40 S.W. 582 (Ark.1897)—§ **19.13, n. 10.**

Public Service Coordinated Transport v. Marlo Trucking Co., 108 N.J.Super. 232, 260 A.2d 855 (N.J.Super.A.D.1970)— § **12.17, n. 10.**

Pucci v. Litwin, 828 F.Supp. 1285 (N.D.Ill. 1993)—§ **3.11, n. 2.**

Puerto Rico, Commonwealth of v. SS Zoe Colocotroni, 628 F.2d 652 (1st Cir. 1980)—§ **8.2, n. 13.**

Puerto Rico, Commonwealth of v. SS Zoe Colocotroni, 456 F.Supp. 1327 (D.Puerto Rico 1978)—§ **17.63, n. 32.**

Pugh's Estate, In re, 22 Wash.2d 83, 154 P.2d 308 (Wash.1944)—§ **22.22, n. 7.**

Pullis Bros. Iron Co. v. Parish of Natchitoches, 26 So. 402 (La.1899)—§ **19.9, n. 9.**

Purdon v. Pavey, 26 Can. 412 (1896)— § **19.6, n. 3.**

Pure Distributors, Inc. v. Baker, 285 F.3d 150 (1st Cir.2002)—§ **24.8, n. 4.**

Purnell, In re Estate of, 482 So.2d 438 (Fla.App. 5 Dist.1986)—§ **22.9, n. 3.**

Purser v. Corpus Christi State Nat. Bank, 256 Ark. 452, 508 S.W.2d 549 (Ark. 1974)—§ **24.13, n. 8.**

Putnam v. Johnson, 10 Mass. 488 (Mass. 1813)—§ **4.20, n. 4, 8.**

Putnam Resources v. Pateman, 958 F.2d 448 (1st Cir.1992)—§ **12.18, n. 3, 19.**

Puzio v. Puzio, 57 N.J.Super. 557, 155 A.2d 115 (N.J.Super.A.D.1959)—§ **24.20, n. 3.**

Pyles v. Russell, 36 S.W.3d 365 (Ky.2000)— **§ 20.3, n. 1.**

Pyrenee, Ltd. v. Wocom Commodities, Ltd., 984 F.Supp. 1148 (N.D.Ill.1997)—**§ 10.5, n. 15.**

Pytlik v. Professional Resources, Ltd., 887 F.2d 1371 (10th Cir.1989)—§ **9.5, n. 8.**

Q

Quackenbush v. Allstate Ins. Co., 517 U.S. 706, 116 S.Ct. 1712, 135 L.Ed.2d 1 (1996)—§ **11.14, n. 7.**

Quade v. Quade, 238 Mich.App. 222, 604 N.W.2d 778 (Mich.App.1999)—§ **14.15, n. 1.**

Quarl v. Abbott, 102 Ind. 233, 1 N.E. 476 (Ind.1885)—§ **5.2, n. 15.**

Quazi v. Quazi, 1979 WL 69220 (HL 1979)—§ **15.24, n. 2.**

Quenzer v. Quenzer, 653 P.2d 295 (Wyo. 1982)—§ **15.42, n. 5.**

Quill Corp. v. North Dakota By and Through Heitkamp, 504 U.S. 298, 112 S.Ct. 1904, 119 L.Ed.2d 91 (1992)— **§ 11.16; § 11.16, n. 2.**

Quilloin v. Walcott, 434 U.S. 246, 98 S.Ct. 549, 54 L.Ed.2d 511 (1978)—§ **4.37, n. 5; § 16.5, n. 7.**

Quinn v. St. Charles Gaming Co., Inc., 815 So.2d 963 (La.App. 3 Cir.2002)—§ **17.63, n. 4.**

Quinones v. Pennsylvania General Ins. Co., 804 F.2d 1167 (10th Cir.1986)—§ **10.4, n. 14.**

Quin's Estate, In re, 77 Misc.2d 1077, 354 N.Y.S.2d 561 (N.Y.Sur.1974)—§ **20.8, n. 3, 8.**

Quintana v. Ordono, 195 So.2d 577 (Fla. App. 3 Dist.1967)—§ **14.9, n. 3; § 18.44, n. 9.**

Qureshi v. Qureshi, 1970 WL 29460 (PDAD 1970)—§ **15.25, n. 1.**

R

R. v. Nagib, [1917] 1 K.B. 359—§ **12.19, n. 14.**

Rabbani v. Rabbani, 178 A.D.2d 637, 578 N.Y.S.2d 213 (N.Y.A.D. 2 Dept.1991)— **§ 15.20, n. 10.**

Rabe v. McAllister, 177 Md. 97, 8 A.2d 922 (Md.1939)—§ **20.11, n. 1.**

Rabinowitz v. Kaiser–Frazer Corp., 198 Misc. 707, 96 N.Y.S.2d 642 (N.Y.Sup. 1950)—§ **23.20, n. 7.**

Rabun v. Rabun, 1860 WL 5647 (La.1860)— **§ 19.13, n. 5.**

Rackemann v. Taylor, 204 Mass. 394, 90 N.E. 552 (Mass.1910)—§ **22.2, n. 1.**

Radioactive, J.V. v. Manson, 153 F.Supp.2d 462 (S.D.N.Y.2001)—§ **18.9, n. 9.**

Radio WHKW, Inc. v. Yarber, 838 F.2d 1439 (5th Cir.1988)—§ **23.6, n. 5.**

Radu's Estate, In re, 35 Ohio App.2d 187, 301 N.E.2d 263 (Ohio App. 8 Dist. 1973)—§ **22.21, n. 14; § 22.23, n. 8.**

Ragan v. Merchants Transfer & Warehouse Co., 337 U.S. 530, 69 S.Ct. 1233, 93 L.Ed. 1520 (1949)—§ **3.37, n. 5; § 3.39; § 3.39, n. 9.**

Raher v. Raher, 150 Iowa 511, 129 N.W. 494 (Iowa 1911)—§ **5.3, n. 11; § 6.4, n. 3.**

Railway Co. v. Whitton, 80 U.S. 270, 20 L.Ed. 571 (1871)—§ **3.41; § 3.41, n. 14, 17.**

Railway Express Agency v. Commonwealth of Virginia, 282 U.S. 440, 51 S.Ct. 201, 75 L.Ed. 450 (1931)—§ **23.6, n. 3.**

Rainbow Travel Service, Inc. v. Hilton Hotels Corp., 896 F.2d 1233 (10th Cir. 1990)—§ **7.12, n. 8.**

Raines v. Browning–Ferris Industries of Alabama, Inc., 638 So.2d 1334 (Ala.Civ. App.1993)—§ **17.59, n. 3.**

Rainy Day Books, Inc. v. Rainy Day Books & Cafe, L.L.C., 186 F.Supp.2d 1158 (D.Kan.2002)—§ **9.3, n. 4.**

Raisor v. Chicago & A.R. Co., 215 Ill. 47, 74 N.E. 69 (Ill.1905)—§ **3.17, n. 2.**

Ralston, State ex rel. v. Blain, 189 Kan. 575, 370 P.2d 415 (Kan.1962)—§ **20.3, n. 9.**

Ramey v. Rockefeller, 348 F.Supp. 780 (E.D.N.Y.1972)—§ **4.20, n. 6.**

Ramey, State ex rel. v. Dayton, 77 Mo. 678 (Mo.1883)—§ **4.17, n. 4.**

Ramey v. Wal–Mart, Inc., 967 F.Supp. 843 (E.D.Pa.1997)—§ **17.48, n. 5.**

Ramirez v. Autobuses Blancos Flecha Roja, S.A. De C.V., 486 F.2d 493 (5th Cir. 1973)—§ **12.18, n. 13; § 18.48, n. 4.**

Ramsay v. Boeing Co., 432 F.2d 592 (5th Cir.1970)—§ **12.18, n. 12, 16.**

Ramsey v. Ramsey, 196 Ill. 179, 63 N.E. 618 (Ill.1902)—§ **22.21, n. 12.**

Rand v. Hubbard, 45 Mass. 252 (Mass. 1842)—§ **22.11, n. 11.**

Randall v. Arabian American Oil Co., 778 F.2d 1146 (5th Cir.1985)—§ **12.18, n. 16.**

Randall v. Randall, 216 Neb. 541, 345 N.W.2d 319 (Neb.1984)—§ **13.5, n. 7; § 13.9, n. 3.**

Randell's Estate, In re, 12 Ill.App.3d 640, 298 N.E.2d 735 (Ill.App. 5 Dist.1973)— **§ 22.26, n. 2.**

Randolph's Estate, In re, 175 Kan. 685, 266 P.2d 315 (Kan.1954)—§ **20.14, n. 1.**

Rannels v. Rowe, 166 F. 425 (8th Cir. 1908)—§ **20.15, n. 4.**

Rano v. Sipa Press, Inc., 987 F.2d 580 (9th Cir.1993)—§ **9.3, n. 13.**

Raphael J. Musicus, Inc. v. Safeway Stores, Inc., 743 F.2d 503 (7th Cir.1984)—§ **7.7, n. 8.**

Rapoport's Estate, In re, 317 Mich. 291, 26 N.W.2d 777 (Mich.1947)—§ **20.4, n. 6.**

RAR, Inc. v. Turner Diesel, Ltd., 107 F.3d 1272 (7th Cir.1997)—§ **5.10, n. 27.**

Rashid, State ex rel. v. Drumm, 824 S.W.2d 497 (Mo.App. E.D.1992)—§ **15.43, n. 8.**

Raskin v. Allison, 30 Kan.App.2d 1240, 57 P.3d 30 (Kan.App.2002)—§ **2.21, n. 6.**

Raskulinecz v. Raskulinecz, 141 N.J.Super. 148, 357 A.2d 330 (N.J.Super.L.1976)— § **3.12, n. 3.**

Raspa v. Raspa, 207 N.J.Super. 371, 504 A.2d 683 (N.J.Super.Ch.1985)—§ **15.20, n. 9.**

Rau v. Rau, 6 Ariz.App. 362, 432 P.2d 910 (Ariz.App.1967)—§ **14.6, n. 2; § 14.9, n. 2, 3, 13; § 14.13, n. 8.**

Raygor v. Regents of University of Minnesota, 534 U.S. 533, 122 S.Ct. 999, 152 L.Ed.2d 27 (2002)—§ **3.11, n. 3.**

Raymond AA v. Doe, 217 A.D.2d 757, 629 N.Y.S.2d 321 (N.Y.A.D. 3 Dept.1995)— § **16.5, n. 7.**

Raymond, Colesar, Glaspy & Huss, P.C. v. Allied Capital Corp., 761 F.Supp. 423 (E.D.Va.1991)—§ **8.4, n. 6.**

Raynor v. Stockton Sav. & Loan Bank, 165 Cal.App.2d 715, 332 P.2d 416 (Cal.App. 3 Dist.1958)—§ **4.7, n. 4.**

RCA Corp. v. Tucker, 696 F.Supp. 845 (E.D.N.Y.1988)—§ **19.29, n. 3.**

RCA Mfg. Co. v. Whiteman, 114 F.2d 86 (2nd Cir.1940)—§ **17.53, n. 1.**

R. C. Johnson and Associates v. Smithers, 87 Nev. 301, 486 P.2d 481 (Nev.1971)— § **24.47, n. 4.**

Reach v. Pearson, 860 F.Supp. 141 (S.D.N.Y.1994)—§ **17.40, n. 3; § 17.57, n. 7.**

Reading & Bates Const. Co. v. Baker Energy Resources Corp., 976 S.W.2d 702 (Tex.App.-Hous. (1 Dist.) 1998)— § **24.13, n. 7; § 24.36, n. 1.**

Reagan v. McGee Drilling Corp., 123 N.M. 68, 933 P.2d 867 (N.M.App.1997)— § **2.21, n. 53; § 18.21, n. 8.**

Reagan, United States v., 453 F.2d 165 (6th Cir.1971)—§ **12.8; § 12.8, n. 12.**

Reale by Reale v. Herco, Inc., 183 A.D.2d 163, 589 N.Y.S.2d 502 (N.Y.A.D. 2 Dept. 1992)—§ **17.45, n. 23.**

Reasor–Hill Corp. v. Harrison, 220 Ark. 521, 249 S.W.2d 994 (Ark.1952)—§ **7.7, n. 8.**

Reaves v. Reaves, 15 Okla. 240, 82 P. 490 (Okla.Terr.1905)—§ **13.6, n. 9.**

Reconstruction Finance Corp. v. Mercury Realty Co., 97 F.Supp. 491 (E.D.Mich. 1951)—§ **19.10, n. 5.**

Red Fox, Matter of Marriage of, 23 Or.App. 393, 542 P.2d 918 (Or.App.1975)—§ **2.7, n. 14; § 13.18, n. 6.**

Red Sea Insurance Co Ltd v. Bouygues SA (Privy Council 1994)—§ **17.39, n. 50.**

Redwing Carriers, Inc. v. Foster, 382 So.2d 554 (Ala.1980)—§ **11.4, n. 3.**

Red Wing Shoe Co., Inc. v. Hockerson–Halberstadt, Inc., 148 F.3d 1355 (Fed.Cir. 1998)—§ **9.4, n. 10.**

Reed, Matter of Estate of, 768 P.2d 566 (Wyo.1989)—§ **20.6, n. 21; § 22.3, n. 1; § 22.4, n. 4; § 22.7, n. 2.**

Reed v. American Airlines, Inc., 197 Mont. 34, 640 P.2d 912 (Mont.1982)—§ **6.9, n. 21.**

Reed, Appeal of, 71 Pa. 378 (Pa.1872)— § **4.36, n. 11.**

Reed v. Campbell, 476 U.S. 852, 106 S.Ct. 2234, 90 L.Ed.2d 858 (1986)—§ **16.3, n. 6.**

Reed v. General Motors Corp., 773 F.2d 660 (5th Cir.1985)—§ **3.39, n. 7.**

Reed v. Reed, 404 U.S. 71, 92 S.Ct. 251, 30 L.Ed.2d 225 (1971)—§ **14.2, n. 1.**

Reed v. Reed, 11 Ohio Misc. 93, 229 N.E.2d 113 (Ohio Com.Pl.1967)—§ **22.26, n. 1.**

Reed v. University of North Dakota, 543 N.W.2d 106 (Minn.App.1996)—§ **17.42, n. 16.**

Reed's Estate, Matter of, 233 Kan. 531, 664 P.2d 824 (Kan.1983)—§ **20.6, n. 1, 21; § 22.3, n. 14.**

Reed's Marriage, In re, 226 N.W.2d 795 (Iowa 1975)—§ **13.5, n. 1; § 13.6, n. 4; § 15.16, n. 4.**

Reeves v. Chem Indus. Co., 262 Or. 95, 495 P.2d 729 (Or.1972)—§ **11.5, n. 3.**

Reeves v. Schulmeier, 303 F.2d 802 (5th Cir.1962)—§ **14.5, n. 2; § 14.9, n. 1, 13; § 14.10, n. 3; § 14.16, n. 20; § 17.6, n. 5.**

Reger v. National Ass'n of Bedding Mfrs. Group Ins. Trust Fund, 83 Misc.2d 527, 372 N.Y.S.2d 97 (N.Y.Sup.1975)—§ **18.4, n. 7, 54; § 18.5, n. 10, 11; § 18.7, n. 8; § 18.9, n. 5; § 18.12, n. 16; § 18.26, n. 10.**

Regie Nationale des Usines Renault v. Superior Court, 208 Cal.App.2d 702, 25 Cal.Rptr. 530 (Cal.App. 3 Dist.1962)— § **23.20, n. 7.**

Reich v. Purcell, 67 Cal.2d 551, 63 Cal.Rptr. 31, 432 P.2d 727 (Cal.1967)—§ **2.16, n. 9; § 2.24, n. 1; § 3.23, n. 10; § 17.11, n. 12; § 17.12, n. 13; § 17.17; § 17.17, n. 1.**

Reichelderfer v. Illinois Cent. Gulf R. R., 513 F.Supp. 189 (N.D.Miss.1981)— § **3.41, n. 15.**

Reichhold Chemicals, Inc. v. Hartford Acc. and Indem. Co., 243 Conn. 401, 703 A.2d 1132 (Conn.1997)—§ **18.26, n. 13.**

Reichhold Chemicals, Inc. v. Hartford Accident and Indemnity Co., 252 Conn. 774, 750 A.2d 1051 (Conn.2000)—§ **18.26, n. 13.**

Reid v. Hansen, 440 N.W.2d 598 (Iowa 1989)—§ **17.60, n. 6.**

Reid v. Reid, 72 Misc. 214, 129 N.Y.S. 529 (N.Y.Sup.1911)—§ **13.12, n. 1.**

Reid v. State, 719 N.E.2d 451 (Ind.App. 1999)—§ **24.1, n. 12.**

Reidling v. Meacham, 148 Ohio App.3d 86, 772 N.E.2d 163 (Ohio App. 6 Dist. 2002)—§ **17.56, n. 20.**

Reif v. Reif, 86 Ohio App.3d 804, 621 N.E.2d 1279 (Ohio App. 2 Dist.1993)—§ **20.9, n. 1;** § **22.6, n. 2.**

Reighard's Estate, Matter of, 381 Pa. 304, 113 A.2d 305 (Pa.1955)—§ **4.20, n. 7;** § **4.24, n. 2.**

Reik v. Reik, 112 N.J.Eq. 234, 163 A. 907 (N.J.Err. & App.1933)—§ **4.24, n. 3.**

Reilly, Matter of Estate of, 137 Misc.2d 780, 522 N.Y.S.2d 809 (N.Y.Sur.1987)—§ **20.14, n. 1.**

Reimonenq v. Foti, 72 F.3d 472 (5th Cir. 1996)—§ **18.5, n. 2.**

Reinsurance Co. of America, Inc. v. Administratia Asigurarilor de Stat (Admin. of State Ins.), 902 F.2d 1275 (7th Cir. 1990)—§ **12.9, n. 16.**

Reisch v. McGuigan, 745 F.Supp. 56 (D.Mass.1990)—§ **17.26, n. 16;** § **17.57, n. 7.**

Reisig v. Associated Jewish Charities of Baltimore, 182 Md. 432, 34 A.2d 842 (Md. 1943)—§ **12.15, n. 11.**

Renard, Estate of, 108 Misc.2d 31, 437 N.Y.S.2d 860 (N.Y.Sur.1981)—§ **20.14;** § **20.14, n. 8.**

Renard, Estate of, 100 Misc.2d 347, 417 N.Y.S.2d 155 (N.Y.Sur.1979)—§ **20.9, n. 9;** § **21.12, n. 4.**

Renshaw v. Heckler, 787 F.2d 50 (2nd Cir. 1986)—§ **13.5, n. 1.**

Republic Intern. Corp. v. Amco Engineers, Inc., 516 F.2d 161 (9th Cir.1975)—§ **8.6, n. 5;** § **11.3, n. 22.**

Republic Nat. Bank of Miami v. United States, 506 U.S. 80, 113 S.Ct. 554, 121 L.Ed.2d 474 (1992)—§ **5.2, n. 14;** § **5.23, n. 1.**

Republic of Argentina v. Weltover, Inc., 504 U.S. 607, 112 S.Ct. 2160, 119 L.Ed.2d 394 (1992)—§ **10.19;** § **10.19, n. 1, 20.**

Republic of Panama v. BCCI Holdings (Luxembourg) S.A., 119 F.3d 935 (11th Cir. 1997)—§ **9.8, n. 7;** § **10.2;** § **10.2, n. 17, 20.**

Republic Oil Corp., Matter of, 51 B.R. 355 (Bkrtcy.W.D.Wis.1985)—§ **23.12, n. 8.**

Request for Assistance from Ministry of Legal Affairs of Trinidad and Tobago, In re, 848 F.2d 1151 (11th Cir.1988)—§ **12.8, n. 7, 10.**

Request for Intern. Judicial Assistance (Letter Rogatory) from the Federative Republic of Brazil, In re, 687 F.Supp. 880 (S.D.N.Y.1988)—§ **12.8;** § **12.8, n. 3, 7.**

Residential Indus. Loan Co. v. Brown, 559 F.2d 438 (5th Cir.1977)—§ **18.21, n. 5;** § **18.28, n. 3.**

Resolution Trust Corp. v. Atchity, 259 Kan. 584, 913 P.2d 162 (Kan.1996)—§ **19.9, n. 8;** § **19.10, n. 3, 4.**

Resolution Trust Corp. v. Cityfed Financial Corp., 57 F.3d 1231 (3rd Cir.1995)—§ **3.50, n. 3.**

Resorts Intern., Inc. v. Zonis, 577 F.Supp. 876 (N.D.Ill.1984)—§ **3.15, n. 5.**

Response Reward Systems, L.C. v. Meijer, Inc., 189 F.Supp.2d 1332 (M.D.Fla. 2002)—§ **9.4, n. 8.**

Rettig's Estate, In re, 8 Ohio Misc. 38, 216 N.E.2d 924 (Ohio Prob.1964)—§ **22.3, n. 2;** § **22.20, n. 5, 11.**

Revell v. Lidov, 317 F.3d 467 (5th Cir. 2002)—§ **7.8, n. 14, 15, 16.**

Reyes–Gaona v. North Carolina Growers Ass'n, 250 F.3d 861 (4th Cir.2001)—§ **17.53, n. 1.**

Reyno v. Piper Aircraft Co., 630 F.2d 149 (3rd Cir.1980)—§ **17.76;** § **17.76, n. 23.**

Reynolds v. International Amateur Athletic Federation, 23 F.3d 1110 (6th Cir. 1994)—§ **7.3, n. 11;** § **7.8, n. 12.**

Reynolds v. McMullen, 55 Mich. 568, 22 N.W. 41 (Mich.1885)—§ **22.17, n. 3.**

Reynolds v. Reynolds, 21 Cal.2d 580, 134 P.2d 251 (Cal.1943)—§ **5.23, n. 7.**

Reynolds Publishers, Inc. v. Graphics Financial Group, Ltd., 938 F.Supp. 256 (D.N.J.1996)—§ **8.7, n. 5;** § **18.2, n. 11.**

Reysa v. Reysa, 521 S.W.2d 746 (Tex.Civ. App.-Texarkana 1975)—§ **15.34, n. 1.**

R. Griggs Group Ltd. v. Filanto Spa, 920 F.Supp. 1100 (D.Nev.1996)—§ **12.7, n. 10.**

Rhoades, Matter of Estate of, 160 Misc.2d 262, 607 N.Y.S.2d 893 (N.Y.Sup.1994)—§ **20.14, n. 9.**

Rhode Island Hospital Trust Co. v. Dunnell, 34 R.I. 394, 83 A. 858 (R.I.1912)—§ **21.13, n. 4.**

Rhode Island Hospital Trust Co. v. Hail, 47 R.I. 64, 129 A. 832 (R.I.1925)—§ **20.6, n. 12.**

Rhode Island Hospital Trust Co. v. Votolato, 102 R.I. 467, 231 A.2d 491 (R.I. 1967)—§ **20.13, n. 4.**

Rhodes v. McAfee, 224 Tenn. 495, 457 S.W.2d 522 (Tenn.1970)—§ **13.5, n. 5, 7.**

Rhodes v. Superior Investigative Services, Inc., 437 F.Supp. 1012 (E.D.Pa.1977)—§ **18.24, n. 4;** § **18.39, n. 6.**

Riblet Products Corp. v. Nagy, 191 A.D.2d 626, 595 N.Y.S.2d 228 (N.Y.A.D. 2 Dept. 1993)—§ **8.4, n. 8.**

Ricard v. Birch, 529 F.2d 214 (4th Cir. 1975)—§ **22.14, n. 3, 6.**

Ricci v. Alternative Energy Inc., 211 F.3d 157 (1st Cir.2000)—§ **17.42, n. 12, 20;** § **17.60, n. 5.**

Ricci v. Superior Court of Alameda County, 107 Cal.App. 395, 290 P. 517 (Cal.App. 1 Dist.1930)—**§ 4.42, n. 4.**

Ricci's Estate, In re, 201 Cal.App.2d 146, 19 Cal.Rptr. 739 (Cal.App. 3 Dist.1962)—**§ 13.19, n. 8.**

Rice, In re, 42 Mich. 528, 4 N.W. 284 (Mich. 1880)—**§ 22.25, n. 1; § 22.26, n. 2, 6.**

Rice v. Dow Chemical Co., 124 Wash.2d 205, 875 P.2d 1213 (Wash.1994)—**§ 17.77, n. 9.**

Rice v. Metropolitan Life Ins. Co., 152 Ark. 498, 238 S.W. 772 (Ark.1922)—**§ 22.13, n. 2.**

Rice v. Nova Biomedical Corp., 38 F.3d 909 (7th Cir.1994)—**§ 10.17, n. 5, 9; § 10.18, n. 6; § 17.50, n. 29.**

Rice v. Nova Biomedical Corp., 763 F.Supp. 961 (N.D.Ill.1991)—**§ 9.5, n. 3.**

Rice v. Peteet, 66 Tex. 568, 1 S.W. 657 (Tex.1886)—**§ 5.2, n. 15.**

Rice v. Rice, 222 Ark. 639, 262 S.W.2d 270 (Ark.1953)—**§ 5.23, n. 1, 7.**

Rice v. Rice, 336 U.S. 674, 69 S.Ct. 751, 93 L.Ed. 957 (1949)—**§ 4.7, n. 1.**

Rice v. United Mercantile Agencies of Louisville, Ky., 395 Ill. 512, 70 N.E.2d 618 (Ill.1946)—**§ 4.21, n. 1.**

Rich v. Rich, 93 Misc.2d 409, 402 N.Y.S.2d 767 (N.Y.Sup.1978)—**§ 15.30, n. 2; § 15.31, n. 2.**

Rich v. Rosenshine, 131 W.Va. 30, 45 S.E.2d 499 (W.Va.1947)—**§ 4.13, n. 12.**

Richards v. Blaisdell, 12 Cal.App. 101, 106 P. 732 (Cal.App. 2 Dist.1909)—**§ 22.20, n. 1.**

Richards v. Huff, 146 Okla. 108, 293 P. 1028 (Okla.1930)—**§ 4.1, n. 2.**

Richards v. Lloyd's of London, 135 F.3d 1289 (9th Cir.1998)—**§ 11.3, n. 33; § 24.48, n. 2.**

Richards v. Lloyd's of London, 107 F.3d 1422 (9th Cir.1997)—**§ 11.3, n. 33.**

Richards v. United States, 369 U.S. 1, 82 S.Ct. 585, 7 L.Ed.2d 492 (1962)—**§ 3.1, n. 4; § 3.13, n. 2; § 3.24, n. 17; § 3.53; § 3.53, n. 6; § 17.48, n. 19.**

Richardson v. Busch, 198 Mo. 174, 95 S.W. 894 (Mo.1906)—**§ 22.12, n. 3, 4.**

Richardson v. De Giverville, 107 Mo. 422, 17 S.W. 974 (Mo.1891)—**§ 14.15, n. 7.**

Richardson v. Michelin North America, Inc., 1998 WL 135804 (W.D.N.Y.1998)—**§ 17.48, n. 10.**

Richardson v. Neblett, 122 Miss. 723, 84 So. 695 (Miss.1920)—**§ 20.4, n. 5; § 22.16, n. 2, 7.**

Richardson v. Volkswagenwerk, A.G., 552 F.Supp. 73 (W.D.Mo.1982)—**§ 12.7, n. 3, 6; § 23.20, n. 7.**

Richardson v. Watkins Bros. Memorial Chapels, Inc., 527 S.W.2d 19 (Mo.App. 1975)—**§ 3.11, n. 5, 6.**

Richardson v. Wilson, 16 Tenn. 67 (Tenn. Err. & App.1835)—**§ 15.27, n. 1.**

Richardson Engineering Co. v. International Business Machines Corp., 554 F.Supp. 467 (D.Vt.1981)—**§ 11.6, n. 8.**

Richland Development Co. v. Staples, 295 F.2d 122 (5th Cir.1961)—**§ 18.29, n. 4.**

Richter v. Harmon, 243 N.C. 373, 90 S.E.2d 744 (N.C.1956)—**§ 4.37, n. 6.**

Ricks v. Goodrich, 1848 WL 3758 (La. 1848)—**§ 19.9, n. 7.**

Ridgell v. Ridgell, 960 S.W.2d 144 (Tex. App.-Corpus Christi 1997)—**§ 14.7, n. 1.**

Riesenberg's Estate, In re, 116 Mo.App. 308, 90 S.W. 1170 (Mo.App.1905)—**§ 20.13, n. 4.**

Riffe v. Magushi, 859 F.Supp. 220 (S.D.W.Va.1994)—**§ 12.15, n. 10.**

Riffe Petroleum Co. v. Cibro Sales Corp., 601 F.2d 1385 (10th Cir.1979)—**§ 10.6, n. 40.**

Rigdon v. Pittsburgh Tank & Tower Co., Inc., 682 So.2d 1303 (La.App. 1 Cir. 1996)—**§ 17.59, n. 3.**

Riggle's Estate, In re, 226 N.Y.S.2d 416, 181 N.E.2d 436 (N.Y.1962)—**§ 22.10, n. 11.**

Riley v. Burroughs, 41 Neb. 296, 59 N.W. 929 (Neb.1894)—**§ 19.5, n. 3.**

Riley v. Moseley, 44 Miss. 37 (Miss.1870)—**§ 22.7, n. 1; § 22.10, n. 3; § 22.11, n. 10.**

Riley v. New York Trust Co., 315 U.S. 343, 62 S.Ct. 608, 86 L.Ed. 885 (1942)—**§ 22.3, n. 10; § 22.20, n. 27.**

Ringen, Succession of, 521 So.2d 587 (La. App. 1 Cir.1988)—**§ 22.6, n. 5.**

Rini v. New York Cent. R. Co., 429 Pa. 235, 240 A.2d 372 (Pa.1968)—**§ 11.11, n. 2, 3.**

Rinsley v. Brandt, 446 F.Supp. 850 (D.Kan. 1977)—**§ 17.55, n. 4.**

Risch v. Risch, 395 S.W.2d 709 (Tex.Civ. App.-Houston 1965)—**§ 4.34, n. 3.**

Risdal & Anderson, Inc., In re Petition of, 266 F.Supp. 157 (D.Mass.1967)—**§ 3.54, n. 4.**

Risher v. American Surety Co., 227 Wis. 104, 277 N.W. 160 (Wis.1938)—**§ 20.13, n. 2; § 21.5, n. 4; § 21.6, n. 4.**

Ritcher v. Childers, 2 Conn.App. 315, 478 A.2d 613 (Conn.App.1984)—**§ 12.17, n. 4.**

Ritchie v. Carvel Corp., 714 F.Supp. 700 (S.D.N.Y.1989)—**§ 6.3, n. 22; § 11.3, n. 19, 21; § 11.4, n. 15.**

Ritchie v. McMullen, 159 U.S. 235, 16 S.Ct. 171, 40 L.Ed. 133 (1895)—**§ 24.34, n. 11; § 24.35, n. 8.**

Ritenour v. Creamery Service, 19 N.J. Misc. 82, 17 A.2d 283 (N.J.Dept.of Labor 1941)—**§ 17.59, n. 5.**

Rittenhouse v. Mabry, 832 F.2d 1380 (5th Cir.1987)—**§ 5.15, n. 6.**

Ritzmann v. Weekly World News, Inc., 614 F.Supp. 1336 (N.D.Tex.1985)—**§ 17.26, n. 1; § 17.55, n. 9.**

Rivas, Matter of Estate of, 233 Kan. 898, 666 P.2d 691 (Kan.1983)—§ **20.9, n. 1.**

Rivendell Forest Products, Ltd. v. Canadian Pacific Ltd., 2 F.3d 990 (10th Cir. 1993)—§ **3.40, n. 12.**

Rivera, State v., 95 Wash.App. 961, 977 P.2d 1247 (Wash.App. Div. 3 1999)— § **13.5, n. 3.**

Rivera v. Taylor, 61 Ill.2d 406, 336 N.E.2d 481 (Ill.1975)—§ **22.19, n. 12.**

Riverside & Dan River Cotton Mills v. Menefee, 237 U.S. 189, 35 S.Ct. 579, 59 L.Ed. 910 (1915)—§ **5.1, n. 9; § 5.3, n. 12, 16; § 5.14, n. 4; § 6.2, n. 22.**

Riverside Memorial Mausoleum, Inc. v. UMET Trust, 581 F.2d 62 (3rd Cir. 1978)—§ **24.15, n. 3.**

Roach v. Jurchak, 182 Md. 646, 35 A.2d 817 (Md.1944)—§ **22.4, n. 8.**

Roadway Exp., Inc. v. Warren, 163 Ga.App. 759, 295 S.E.2d 743 (Ga.App.1982)— § **17.59, n. 16.**

Robards v. Marley, 80 Ind. 185 (Ind.1881)— § **19.2, n. 7.**

Robbins v. Chamberlain, 297 N.Y. 108, 75 N.E.2d 617 (N.Y.1947)—§ **4.20, n. 4; § 4.24, n. 1.**

Robbins v. National Bank of Georgia, 241 Ga. 538, 246 S.E.2d 660 (Ga.1978)— § **20.4, n. 3; § 22.10, n. 2.**

Roberson v. Queen, 87 Tenn. 445, 11 S.W. 38 (Tenn.1889)—§ **19.2, n. 4.**

Roberson v. U–Bar Ranch, Inc., 303 F.Supp. 730 (D.N.M.1968)—§ **17.6, n. 5.**

Robert Half of Iowa, Inc. v. Citizens Bank of Newburg, 453 N.W.2d 236 (Iowa App. 1990)—§ **8.4, n. 3.**

Robert M. Neff, Inc. v. W.C.A.B. (Burr), 155 Pa.Cmwlth. 44, 624 A.2d 727 (Pa. Cmwlth.1993)—§ **17.59, n. 14.**

Roberts v. Chase, 25 Tenn.App. 636, 166 S.W.2d 641 (Tenn.Ct.App.1942)—§ **20.9, n. 12.**

Roberts v. Energy Development Corp., 235 F.3d 935 (5th Cir.2000)—§ **18.4, n. 7.**

Roberts v. Northern Trust Co., 550 F.Supp. 729 (N.D.Ill.1982)—§ **21.9, n. 2; § 21.11, n. 5.**

Roberts v. Robben, 188 Kan. 217, 362 P.2d 29 (Kan.1961)—§ **4.37, n. 9; § 4.41, n. 1.**

Roberts' Estate, In re, 509 P.2d 495 (Okla. App. Div. 1 1972)—§ **20.9, n. 1; § 21.2, n. 5.**

Robertson v. Bartels, 148 F.Supp.2d 443 (D.N.J.2001)—§ **24.30, n. 1.**

Robertson v. Hert's Adm'rs, 312 Ky. 405, 227 S.W.2d 899 (Ky.1950)—§ **21.6, n. 6.**

Robertson v. McKnight's Estate, 609 S.W.2d 534 (Tex.1980)—§ **17.26, n. 1.**

Robertson v. Pickrell, 109 U.S. 608, 3 S.Ct. 407, 27 L.Ed. 1049 (1883)—§ **20.6, n. 1; § 22.4, n. 7.**

Robertson v. Railroad Labor Board, 268 U.S. 619, 45 S.Ct. 621, 69 L.Ed. 1119 (1925)—§ **5.15, n. 2.**

Robinson v. American Marine Holdings, Inc., 2002 WL 873185 (E.D.La.2002)— § **17.64, n. 10.**

Robinson v. Bland, 1760 WL 14 (Unknown Court - UK 1760)—§ **2.1, n. 4.**

Robinson v. Gaines, 331 S.W.2d 653 (Mo. 1960)—§ **17.5, n. 10.**

Robinson v. Robinson, 778 So.2d 1105 (La. 2001)—§ **14.9, n. 13; § 15.11, n. 4; § 18.6, n. 1.**

Robinson v. Suburban Brick Co., 127 F. 804 (4th Cir.1904)—§ **19.5, n. 9.**

Roboz v. Kennedy, 219 F.Supp. 892 (D.D.C 1963)—§ **4.27, n. 12.**

Roby v. Bailey, 856 P.2d 1013 (Okla.App. Div. 1 1993)—§ **18.21, n. 14.**

Roby v. Corporation of Lloyd's, 996 F.2d 1353 (2nd Cir.1993)—§ **11.3, n. 33; § 17.40, n. 28.**

Roche v. McDonald, 275 U.S. 449, 48 S.Ct. 142, 72 L.Ed. 365 (1928)—§ **24.20, n. 1.**

Roche v. Washington, 19 Ind. 53 (Ind. 1862)—§ **13.18, n. 8, 11.**

Roche's Estate, In re, 16 N.J. 579, 109 A.2d 655 (N.J.1954)—§ **22.10, n. 13.**

Rock v. W.C.A.B. (Youngstown Cartage Co.), 92 Pa.Cmwlth. 491, 500 A.2d 183 (Pa.Cmwlth.1985)—§ **17.59, n. 14.**

Rockwell Intern. Systems, Inc. v. Citibank, N.A., 719 F.2d 583 (2nd Cir.1983)— § **11.3, n. 23.**

Rocky Mountain Helicopters, Inc. v. Bell Helicopter Textron, Inc., 24 F.3d 125 (10th Cir.1994)—§ **17.64, n. 8; § 18.7, n. 5.**

Rodgers, State ex rel. Okl. Tax Commission v., 238 Mo.App. 1115, 193 S.W.2d 919 (Mo.App.1946)—§ **24.23, n. 5.**

Rodrigue v. Rodrigue, 218 F.3d 432 (5th Cir.2000)—§ **14.11, n. 1.**

Rodriguez de Quijas v. Shearson/American Exp., Inc., 490 U.S. 477, 109 S.Ct. 1917, 104 L.Ed.2d 526 (1989)—§ **11.6, n. 6.**

Rodriguez–Diaz v. Sierra–Martinez, 853 F.2d 1027 (1st Cir.1988)—§ **4.9, n. 2; § 4.24, n. 2.**

Rodriguez Diaz v. Sierra Martinez, 665 F.Supp. 96 (D.Puerto Rico 1987)— § **3.36, n. 2; § 4.9, n. 2.**

Roebling v. Office of Personnel Management, 788 F.2d 1544 (Fed.Cir.1986)— § **14.9, n. 4.**

Roecker v. United States, 379 F.2d 400 (5th Cir.1967)—§ **3.54, n. 3.**

Roesgen v. American Home Products Corp., 719 F.2d 319 (9th Cir.1983)—§ **2.9, n. 28.**

Rogers v. Grimaldi, 875 F.2d 994 (2nd Cir. 1989)—§ **3.47, n. 7; § 12.15, n. 9.**

Rogers v. Guaranty Trust Co. of New York, 288 U.S. 123, 53 S.Ct. 295, 77 L.Ed. 652 (1933)—§ **23.5; § 23.5, n. 3.**

Rogers, State ex rel. Flaugher v., 226 Ind. 32, 77 N.E.2d 594 (Ind.1948)—§ **4.19, n. 4.**

Rogers' Estate, In re, 164 Kan. 492, 190 P.2d 857 (Kan.1948)—§ **22.10, n. 13.**

Rogers' Estate, Matter of, 569 P.2d 536 (Okla.App. Div. 1 1977)—§ **13.9, n. 7, 10.**

Rohm and Haas Co. v. Adco Chemical Co., 689 F.2d 424 (3rd Cir.1982)—§ **17.53, n. 3.**

Roll v. Tracor, Inc., 140 F.Supp.2d 1073 (D.Nev.2001)—§ **17.71;** § **17.71, n. 5.**

Roller v. Holly, 176 U.S. 398, 20 S.Ct. 410, 44 L.Ed. 520 (1900)—§ **12.4, n. 2.**

Rolls Royce (Canada), Ltd. v. Cayman Airways, Ltd., 617 F.Supp. 17 (S.D.Fla. 1985)—§ **11.10, n. 8;** § **11.11, n. 6.**

Romani v. Cramer, Inc., 992 F.Supp. 74 (D.Mass.1998)—§ **17.74, n. 20;** § **17.78, n. 11.**

Romann v. Geissenberger Mfg. Corp., 865 F.Supp. 255 (E.D.Pa.1994)—§ **6.9, n. 19;** § **8.4, n. 7.**

Romero, In re, 56 Misc. 319, 107 N.Y.S. 621 (N.Y.Sup.1907)—§ **12.6, n. 9.**

Romero v. International Terminal Operating Co., 358 U.S. 354, 79 S.Ct. 468, 3 L.Ed.2d 368 (1959)—§ **17.63, n. 11.**

Romero v. Shumate Constructors, Inc., 119 N.M. 58, 888 P.2d 940 (N.M.App. 1994)—§ **17.61, n. 2.**

Ronar, Inc. v. Wallace, 649 F.Supp. 310 (S.D.N.Y.1986)—§ **11.3, n. 22.**

Rong Yao Zhou v. Jennifer Mall Restaurant, Inc., 534 A.2d 1268 (D.C.1987)—§ **2.24, n. 2;** § **17.12, n. 1;** § **17.26, n. 1;** § **17.36, n. 15;** § **17.48;** § **17.48, n. 14.**

Roofing & Sheet Metal Services, Inc. v. La Quinta Motor Inns, Inc., 689 F.2d 982 (11th Cir.1982)—§ **3.46, n. 13.**

Rooker v. Fidelity Trust Co., 263 U.S. 413, 44 S.Ct. 149, 68 L.Ed. 362 (1923)—§ **24.12, n. 7.**

Rooney, State ex rel. Mercantile Nat. Bank at Dallas v., 402 S.W.2d 354 (Mo.1966)—§ **22.14, n. 5;** § **22.19, n. 6.**

Roorda v. Volkswagenwerk, A. G., 481 F.Supp. 868 (D.S.C.1979)—§ **4.24, n. 2.**

Roquette America, Inc. v. Gerber, 651 N.W.2d 896 (Iowa App.2002)—§ **7.3, n. 11.**

Rosa v. Allstate Ins. Co., 981 F.2d 669 (2nd Cir.1992)—§ **23.3, n. 4.**

Rose v. K. K. Masutoku Toy Factory Co., 597 F.2d 215 (10th Cir.1979)—§ **3.11, n. 6.**

Rose v. Rambo, 120 Miss. 305, 82 So. 149 (Miss.1919)—§ **19.4, n. 3.**

Rose v. Rose, 483 So.2d 181 (La.App. 2 Cir.1986)—§ **14.11, n. 2.**

Rose v. Rose, 132 Minn. 340, 156 N.W. 664 (Minn.1916)—§ **20.12, n. 2.**

Rose v. State Farm Mut. Auto. Ins. Co., 821 P.2d 1077 (Okla.App. Div. 1 1991)—§ **17.56, n. 17.**

Rose v. St. Louis Union Trust Co., 43 Ill.2d 312, 253 N.E.2d 417 (Ill.1969)—§ **20.9, n. 11;** § **21.3, n. 6, 7.**

Rosemont Enterprises, Inc. v. Lummis, 596 S.W.2d 916 (Tex.Civ.App.-Hous. (14 Dist.) 1980)—§ **22.11, n. 5, 7.**

Rosenbaum v. Garrett, 41 A. 252 (N.J.Ch. 1898)—§ **20.13, n. 4, 8;** § **21.2, n. 5;** § **21.6, n. 3.**

Rosenbaum v. Rosenbaum, 309 N.Y. 371, 130 N.E.2d 902 (N.Y.1955)—§ **15.23, n. 3.**

Rosenberg Bros. & Co. v. Curtis Brown Co., 260 U.S. 516, 43 S.Ct. 170, 67 L.Ed. 372 (1923)—§ **5.13, n. 15;** § **10.14, n. 9.**

Rosenblum v. Judson Engineering Corp., 99 N.H. 267, 109 A.2d 558 (N.H.1954)—§ **10.12, n. 9.**

Rosenfeld v. Hotel Corp. of America, 281 N.Y.S.2d 308, 228 N.E.2d 374 (N.Y. 1967)—§ **22.19;** § **22.19, n. 8.**

Rosengarten v. Downes, 71 Conn.App. 372, 802 A.2d 170 (Conn.App.2002)—§ **13.20, n. 8.**

Rosenstiel v. Rosenstiel, 262 N.Y.S.2d 86, 209 N.E.2d 709 (N.Y.1965)—§ **15.20, n. 3.**

Rosenthal v. Fonda, 862 F.2d 1398 (9th Cir.1988)—§ **2.9, n. 28;** § **3.8, n. 6.**

Rosenthal v. Renick, 44 Ill. 202 (Ill.1867)—§ **22.21, n. 8.**

Rosenthal v. Warren, 475 F.2d 438 (2nd Cir.1973)—§ **17.32, n. 1;** § **17.42;** § **17.42, n. 28.**

Ross, In re, [1930] 1 Ch. 377—§ **3.13, n. 10;** § **20.9, n. 9.**

Ross v. Bryant, 90 Okla. 300, 217 P. 364 (Okla.1923)—§ **13.12, n. 2.**

Ross v. Eaton, 90 N.H. 271, 6 A.2d 762 (N.H.1939)—§ **20.3, n. 9.**

Ross v. Pick, 199 Md. 341, 86 A.2d 463 (Md.1952)—§ **4.37, n. 3, 9;** § **4.40, n. 2.**

Ross v. Southwestern R. Co., 53 Ga. 514 (Ga.1874)—§ **22.25, n. 14.**

Ross, State v., 76 N.C. 242 (N.C.1877)—§ **13.15, n. 4.**

Rostad v. On–Deck, Inc., 372 N.W.2d 717 (Minn.1985)—§ **7.2, n. 21.**

Rotary Club of Tucson v. Chaprales Ramos de Pena, 160 Ariz. 362, 773 P.2d 467 (Ariz.App. Div. 2 1989)—§ **5.21, n. 11.**

Rothstein v. Rothstein, 272 A.D. 26, 68 N.Y.S.2d 305 (N.Y.A.D. 1 Dept.1947)—§ **18.48, n. 4.**

Rougeron's Estate, In re, 270 N.Y.S.2d 578, 217 N.E.2d 639 (N.Y.1966)—§ **20.9, n. 9.**

Rouse Co. v. Federal Ins. Co., 991 F.Supp. 460 (D.Md.1998)—§ **2.21, n. 60.**

Rousseau v. United States Trust Co. of New York, 422 F.Supp. 447 (S.D.N.Y.1976)—§ **21.4, n. 3.**

Routh v. Routh, 9 Rob. 224, 41 Am.Dec. 326 (La.1844)—§ **14.8, n. 4.**

Roy v. Buckley, 698 A.2d 497 (Me.1997)—§ **24.44, n. 12.**

Roy v. Star Chopper Co., Inc., 442 F.Supp. 1010 (D.R.I.1977)—§ **2.21, n. 73.**

Royal v. Cudahy Packing Co., 195 Iowa 759, 190 N.W. 427 (Iowa 1922)—§ **13.19, n. 1.**

Royal Baking Powder Co. v. Hessey, 76 F.2d 645 (4th Cir.1935)—§ **19.13, n. 4.**

Royce v. Denby's Estate, 117 N.H. 893, 379 A.2d 1256 (N.H.1977)—§ **20.13, n. 6.**

Roy Export Co. Establishment of Vaduz, Liechtenstein v. Columbia Broadcasting System, Inc., 672 F.2d 1095 (2nd Cir. 1982)—§ **17.53, n. 3.**

Rozan v. Rozan, 49 Cal.2d 322, 317 P.2d 11 (Cal.1957)—§ **14.9, n. 13; § 14.10, n. 2.**

R–Square Investments, Inc. v. Teledyne Industries, Inc., 1997 WL 436245 (E.D.La. 1997)—§ **17.44, n. 9; § 17.64, n. 10.**

Rubert, In re Estate of, 139 N.H. 273, 651 A.2d 937 (N.H.1994)—§ **22.3, n. 9.**

Rubin v. Irving Trust Co., 305 N.Y. 288, 113 N.E.2d 424 (N.Y.1953)—§ **18.19; § 18.19, n. 2, 9.**

Rubin, People ex rel. La Forte v., 98 N.Y.S. 787 (N.Y.Sup.1905)—§ **13.18, n. 8.**

Rubinfeld v. Bahama Cruise Line, Inc., 613 F.Supp. 300 (S.D.N.Y.1985)—§ **23.3, n. 1.**

Ruding v. Smith, 1821 WL 2128 (Unknown Court - UK 1821)—§ **13.6, n. 7.**

Rudow v. Fogel, 12 Mass.App.Ct. 430, 426 N.E.2d 155 (Mass.App.Ct.1981)—§ **21.3, n. 4.**

Rufer v. Abbott Laboratories, 118 Wash. App. 1080 (Wash.App. Div. 1 2003)—§ **17.50, n. 16.**

Ruff v. St. Paul Mercury Ins. Co., 393 F.2d 500 (2nd Cir.1968)—§ **12.18, n. 3, 19.**

Ruff, State ex rel. v. District Court, 34 Mont. 96, 85 P. 866 (Mont.1906)—§ **22.3, n. 1; § 22.4, n. 7.**

Ruffin–Steinback v. dePasse, 267 F.3d 457 (6th Cir.2001)—§ **17.55, n. 9.**

Ruhrgas AG v. Marathon Oil Co., 526 U.S. 574, 119 S.Ct. 1563, 143 L.Ed.2d 760 (1999)—§ **5.15, n. 4.**

Ruiz v. Blentech Corp., 89 F.3d 320 (7th Cir.1996)—§ **17.76, n. 30; § 23.11, n. 5.**

Rungee v. Allied Van Lines, Inc., 92 Idaho 718, 449 P.2d 378 (Idaho 1968)—§ **2.17, n. 6; § 2.23, n. 2; § 18.21, n. 14; § 18.30, n. 2.**

Runnels v. TMSI Contractors, Inc., 764 F.2d 417 (5th Cir.1985)—§ **8.4, n. 2.**

Running v. Southwest Freight Lines, Inc., 227 Ark. 839, 303 S.W.2d 578 (Ark. 1957)—§ **11.8, n. 3.**

Rush v. Savchuk, 444 U.S. 320, 100 S.Ct. 571, 62 L.Ed.2d 516 (1980)—§ **3.21, n. 2; § 3.23, n. 11; § 3.26, n. 4; § 5.6;**
§ **5.6, n. 18; § 7.1, n. 2; § 10.15, n. 9; § 22.10; § 22.10, n. 15; § 23.3, n. 5.**

Russel v. Smyth, (1842) 9 M. & W. 810—§ **24.38, n. 8.**

Russell v. Bush & Burchett, Inc., 210 W.Va. 699, 559 S.E.2d 36 (W.Va.2001)—§ **2.21; § 2.21, n. 33; § 17.59, n. 3.**

Russell v. Grigsby, 168 F. 577 (6th Cir. 1909)—§ **19.29, n. 3.**

Russell v. Hooker, 67 Conn. 24, 34 A. 711 (Conn.1895)—§ **22.12, n. 1.**

Russell v. Joys, 227 Mass. 263, 116 N.E. 549 (Mass.1917)—§ **21.11, n. 2.**

Russell v. Lovell, 362 Mass. 794, 291 N.E.2d 733 (Mass.1973)—§ **22.25, n. 3, 15.**

Russell v. Madden, 95 Ill. 485 (Ill.1880)—§ **20.3, n. 1.**

Russell v. Perry, 14 N.H. 152 (N.H.1843)—§ **24.11, n. 1.**

Russell v. Shapleigh, 275 Mass. 15, 175 N.E. 100 (Mass.1931)—§ **20.15, n. 3, 6.**

Russell v. State, 62 Neb. 512, 87 N.W. 344 (Neb.1901)—§ **4.43, n. 1.**

Russell v. Wachovia Bank, N.A., 353 S.C. 208, 578 S.E.2d 329 (S.C.2003)—§ **21.3, n. 9; § 21.6, n. 7; § 21.13, n. 1.**

Rustad v. Rustad, 61 Wash.2d 176, 377 P.2d 414 (Wash.1963)—§ **19.2, n. 4.**

Rusty Eck Ford–Mercury Corp. of Leavenworth v. American Custom Coachworks, Ltd., 184 F.Supp.2d 1138 (D.Kan. 2002)—§ **8.5, n. 7.**

Rutas Aereas Nacionales, S. A. v. Robinson, 339 F.2d 265 (5th Cir.1964)—§ **18.29, n. 8.**

Ruth v. Ruth, 158 N.C.App. 123, 579 S.E.2d 909 (N.C.App.2003)—§ **16.5, n. 9.**

Rutherford, Commonwealth v., 160 Va. 524, 169 S.E. 909 (Va.1933)—§ **4.33, n. 3, 6; § 4.34, n. 3.**

Rutherford v. Goodyear Tire and Rubber Co., 943 F.Supp. 789 (W.D.Ky.1996)—§ **17.64, n. 11; § 17.66, n. 6; § 17.70, n. 8; § 17.75, n. 1; § 17.77; § 17.77, n. 25.**

Rutherford v. Gray Line, Inc., 615 F.2d 944 (2nd Cir.1980)—§ **3.13, n. 4; § 18.37, n. 6.**

Ruth F. v. Robert B., 456 Pa.Super. 398, 690 A.2d 1171 (Pa.Super.1997)—§ **16.5, n. 2.**

Rutledge, Commonwealth ex rel. Blank v., 234 Pa.Super. 339, 339 A.2d 71 (Pa.Super.1975)—§ **15.40, n. 7.**

Rutledge v. Rockwells of Bedford, Inc., 200 A.D.2d 36, 613 N.Y.S.2d 179 (N.Y.A.D. 2 Dept.1994)—§ **17.48, n. 12.**

Rutter v. BX of Tri–Cities, Inc., 60 Wash. App. 743, 806 P.2d 1266 (Wash.App. Div. 3 1991)—§ **18.21, n. 14.**

Ryals v. State Farm Mut. Auto. Ins. Co., 134 Idaho 302, 1 P.3d 803 (Idaho 2000)—§ **18.26, n. 6.**

Ryan v. Ford Motor Co., 334 F.Supp. 674 (E.D.Mich.1971)—§ **17.6, n. 1.**

Ryan v. Ryan, 278 A.2d 121 (D.C.1971)—
§ 24.9, n. 3.

Rydder v. Rydder, 49 F.3d 369 (8th Cir.
1995)—**§ 15.42, n. 17.**

Rye v. Atlas Hotels, Inc., 30 Mass.App.Ct.
904, 566 N.E.2d 617 (Mass.App.Ct.
1991)—**§ 7.3, n. 10; § 7.4, n. 8.**

Rylands v. Fletcher, 1868 WL 9885 (HL
1868)—**§ 7.5; § 7.5, n. 7.**

Rymanowski v. Rymanowski, 105 R.I. 89,
249 A.2d 407 (R.I.1969)—**§ 12.19, n. 19.**

S

Sabella, United States ex rel. v. Newsday,
315 F.Supp. 333 (E.D.N.Y.1970)—
§ 3.11, n. 3.

Sack v. Low, 478 F.2d 360 (2nd Cir.1973)—
§ 3.11, n. 4, 6.

Sackett, Chapman, Brown & Cross v. Osgood, 149 F.2d 825, 80 U.S.App.D.C. 99
(D.C.Cir.1945)—**§ 22.21, n. 14.**

Sadat v. Mertes, 615 F.2d 1176 (7th Cir.
1980)—**§ 4.12, n. 3.**

Sadat v. Mertes, 464 F.Supp. 1311
(E.D.Wis.1979)—**§ 4.12, n. 3.**

Sadler v. Boston & Bolivia Rubber Co., 202
N.Y. 547, 95 N.E. 1139 (N.Y.1911)—
§ 6.2, n. 21.

Sadler v. Boston & Bolivia Rubber Co., 140
A.D. 367, 125 N.Y.S. 405 (N.Y.A.D. 1
Dept.1910)—**§ 5.1, n. 9.**

Sadler v. NCR Corp., 928 F.2d 48 (2nd
Cir.1991)—**§ 23.6, n. 12.**

Saenz v. Roe, 526 U.S. 489, 119 S.Ct. 1518,
143 L.Ed.2d 689 (1999)—**§ 3.11, n. 2.**

Safeco Ins. Co. of America v. Allen, 262
Kan. 811, 941 P.2d 1365 (Kan.1997)—
§ 2.21, n. 6, 55; § 18.21, n. 6.

Safeco Ins. Co. of America v. Criterion Inv.
Corp., 732 F.Supp. 834 (E.D.Tenn.
1989)—**§ 18.27, n. 2.**

Sain v. City of Bend, 309 F.3d 1134 (9th
Cir.2002)—**§ 3.39, n. 14.**

Salazar v. Coastal Corp., 928 S.W.2d 162
(Tex.App.-Hous. (14 Dist.) 1996)—
§ 18.29, n. 4.

Salem Independent School Dist. v. Kiel, 206
Iowa 967, 221 N.W. 519 (Iowa 1928)—
§ 4.1, n. 2.

Salgado v. Les Nouvelles Esthetiques, 218
F.Supp.2d 203 (D.Puerto Rico 2002)—
§ 7.8, n. 12; § 7.10, n. 5.

Salisbury Plumbing & Heating Co. v. Carpenter, 131 Ill.App.3d 829, 86 Ill.Dec.
839, 476 N.E.2d 15 (Ill.App. 5 Dist.
1985)—**§ 24.36, n. 5.**

Sall v. G.H. Miller & Co., 612 F.Supp. 1499
(D.Colo.1985)—**§ 11.2, n. 4; § 18.5, n. 5.**

Salomon Englander Y CIA, Ltda v. Israel
Discount Bank, Ltd., 494 F.Supp. 914
(S.D.N.Y.1980)—**§ 23.3, n. 1.**

Salsman v. Barden & Robeson Corp., 164
A.D.2d 481, 564 N.Y.S.2d 546 (N.Y.A.D.

3 Dept.1990)—**§ 17.37, n. 16; § 17.48,
n. 11.**

Salucco v. Alldredge, 17 Mass.L.Rep. 498
(Mass.Super.2004)—**§ 13.20, n. 8.**

Salyer v. Mason Technologies, Inc., 690
So.2d 1183 (Miss.1997)—**§ 17.61, n. 2.**

Sami v. United States, 617 F.2d 755, 199
U.S.App.D.C. 173 (D.C.Cir.1979)—
§ 17.48, n. 19.

Sampsell v. Imperial Paper & Color Corp.,
313 U.S. 215, 61 S.Ct. 904, 85 L.Ed.
1293 (1941)—**§ 23.20, n. 3.**

Sampsell v. Superior Court in and for Los
Angeles County, 32 Cal.2d 763, 197 P.2d
739 (Cal.1948)—**§ 5.23, n. 1, 8; § 15.39;
§ 15.39, n. 5; § 22.26, n. 1.**

Samson Plastic Conduit and Pipe Corp. v.
Battenfeld Extrusionstechnik GMBH,
718 F.Supp. 886 (M.D.Ala.1989)—
§ 11.3, n. 22.

Samuelson v. Susen, 576 F.2d 546 (3rd Cir.
1978)—**§ 3.47, n. 7; § 12.11, n. 8.**

Sanborn v. Perry, 86 Wis. 361, 56 N.W. 337
(Wis.1893)—**§ 22.20, n. 34.**

Sanchez v. Sanchez De Davila, 547 So.2d
943 (Fla.App. 3 Dist.1989)—**§ 21.3, n.
17.**

Sanchez ex rel. Estate of Galvan v. Brownsville Sports Center, Inc., 51 S.W.3d 643
(Tex.App.-Corpus Christi 2001)—
§ 17.72; § 17.72, n. 1.

Sanders v. Doe, 831 F.Supp. 886 (S.D.Ga.
1993)—**§ 18.24, n. 9.**

Sanders v. M. D. Aircraft Sales, Inc., 575
F.2d 1086 (3rd Cir.1978)—**§ 19.21, n. 7.**

Sanders v. Robinson, 864 F.2d 630 (9th
Cir.1988)—**§ 15.24, n. 3.**

Sanders' Estate, In re, 147 Cal.App.2d 450,
305 P.2d 655 (Cal.App. 4 Dist.1957)—
§ 13.9, n. 8.

San Diego County Dep't of Social Services
v. Delay, 199 Cal.App.3d 1031, 245 Cal.
Rptr. 216 (Cal.App. 4 Dist.1988)—
§ 5.20, n. 9.

Sandoval, United States v., 231 U.S. 28, 34
S.Ct. 1, 58 L.Ed. 107 (1913)—**§ 11.17, n.
2.**

Sandoval v. Valdez, 91 N.M. 705, 580 P.2d
131 (N.M.App.1978)—**§ 18.21, n. 8.**

Sandstrom v. ChemLawn Corp., 904 F.2d
83 (1st Cir.1990)—**§ 5.13, n. 19; § 6.9,
n. 20, 22.**

Sanford v. McCreedy, 28 Wis. 103 (Wis.
1871)—**§ 22.11, n. 13.**

Sangamo Weston, Inc. v. National Sur.
Corp., 307 S.C. 143, 414 S.E.2d 127 (S.C.
1992)—**§ 2.21, n. 53; § 18.21, n. 10.**

San Juan Dupont Plaza Hotel Fire Litigation, In re, 745 F.Supp. 79 (D.Puerto
Rico 1990)—**§ 17.50, n. 35.**

San Patricio County v. Nueces County
Hosp. Dist., 721 S.W.2d 375 (Tex.App.-
Corpus Christi 1986)—**§ 4.13, n. 12.**

San Rafael Compania Naviera, S. A. v. American Smelting & Refining Co., 327 F.2d 581 (9th Cir.1964)—§ **12.15, n. 9.**

Sanson v. Sanson, 466 N.E.2d 770 (Ind.App. 4 Dist.1984)—§ **15.34, n. 7;** § **15.37, n. 12.**

Santa Clara Pueblo v. Martinez, 436 U.S. 49, 98 S.Ct. 1670, 56 L.Ed.2d 106 (1978)—§ **24.12, n. 2.**

Santamauro v. Taito do Brasil Industria E Comercia Ltda., 587 F.Supp. 1312 (E.D.La.1984)—§ **11.3, n. 22.**

Santa Rosa Band of Indians v. Kings County, 532 F.2d 655 (9th Cir.1975)—§ **11.17, n. 15.**

Santoli v. Louisville Trust Co., 550 S.W.2d 182 (Ky.App.1977)—§ **20.13, n. 4.**

Santos v. Figueroa, 87 N.J.Super. 227, 208 A.2d 810 (N.J.Super.A.D.1965)—§ **11.15, n. 2.**

Santovincenzo v. Egan, 284 U.S. 30, 52 S.Ct. 81, 76 L.Ed. 151 (1931)—§ **3.56, n. 8.**

Saporita v. Litner, 371 Mass. 607, 358 N.E.2d 809 (Mass.1976)—§ **22.19, n. 13, 14;** § **22.20, n. 25.**

Sarbacher v. McNamara, 564 A.2d 701 (D.C.1989)—§ **14.16, n. 10.**

Sarraf v. Szunics, 132 Misc.2d 97, 503 N.Y.S.2d 513 (N.Y.City Civ.Ct.1986)—§ **4.13, n. 2.**

Sarrica v. Sarrica, 41 A.D.2d 613, 340 N.Y.S.2d 568 (N.Y.A.D. 1 Dept.1973)—§ **19.6, n. 3.**

Sasse v. Sasse, 41 Wash.2d 363, 249 P.2d 380 (Wash.1952)—§ **4.26, n. 1.**

Satellite Financial Planning Corp. v. First Nat. Bank of Wilmington, 633 F.Supp. 386 (D.Del.1986)—§ **18.2, n. 11.**

Saucido's Marriage, In re, 85 Wash.2d 653, 538 P.2d 1219 (Wash.1975)—§ **15.40, n. 7;** § **22.26, n. 5.**

Saudi Arabia v. Nelson, 507 U.S. 349, 113 S.Ct. 1471, 123 L.Ed.2d 47 (1993)—§ **10.19;** § **10.19, n. 24.**

Saul v. His Creditors, 1827 WL 1936 (La. 1827)—§ **14.9, n. 13, 14.**

Saunders v. Weston, 74 Me. 85 (Me.1882)—§ **22.10, n. 3.**

Savage Arms, Inc. v. Western Auto Supply Co., 18 P.3d 49 (Alaska 2001)—§ **3.5, n. 2;** § **17.44, n. 9;** § **17.70, n. 6.**

Savannah Bank & Trust Co. of Savannah v. Shuman, 250 S.C. 344, 157 S.E.2d 864 (S.C.1967)—§ **19.3, n. 8, 15;** § **19.9, n. 2.**

Savannah Sugar Refining Corp. v. S. S. Hudson Deep, 288 F.Supp. 181 (S.D.N.Y. 1968)—§ **12.18, n. 8.**

Sayre's Ex'rs. v. Helme's Ex'rs., 61 Pa. 299 (Pa.1869)—§ **22.10, n. 2;** § **22.14, n. 3.**

SBKC Service Corp. v. 1111 Prospect Partners, L.P., 153 F.3d 728 (10th Cir. 1998)—§ **2.23, n. 9.**

S.B. Schmidt Paper Co. v. A to Z Paper Co., Inc., 452 N.W.2d 485 (Minn.App.1990)—§ **8.5, n. 5.**

Schacht v. Schacht, 435 S.W.2d 197 (Tex. Civ.App.-Dallas 1968)—§ **12.15, n. 9.**

Schaeffer v. Village of Ossining, 58 F.3d 48 (2nd Cir.1995)—§ **11.14, n. 18.**

Schaffer v. Krestovnikow, 102 A. 246 (N.J.Ch.1917)—§ **13.8, n. 1.**

Schaheen v. Schaheen, 17 Mich.App. 147, 169 N.W.2d 117 (Mich.App.1969)—§ **19.8, n. 3.**

Schalk v. Dickinson, 89 S.D. 263, 232 N.W.2d 140 (S.D.1975)—§ **20.5, n. 6.**

Schantz v. White Lightning, 502 F.2d 67 (8th Cir.1974)—§ **11.17, n. 21, 30.**

Schaub v. Schaub (B.C. S.C.1984)—§ **14.9, n. 12.**

Schear & Associates, Inc., In re, 47 B.R. 544 (Bkrtcy.S.D.Fla.1985)—§ **23.12, n. 7.**

Schechter v. Tauck Tours, Inc., 17 F.Supp.2d 255 (S.D.N.Y.1998)—§ **17.48, n. 5.**

Schecter v. Superior Court, 49 Cal.2d 3, 314 P.2d 10 (Cal.1957)—§ **14.9, n. 13.**

Scheer v. Rockne Motors Corporation, 68 F.2d 942 (2nd Cir.1934)—§ **3.28, n. 2;** § **17.4;** § **17.4, n. 2.**

Scheer v. Scheer, 881 P.2d 479 (Colo.App. 1994)—§ **17.26, n. 1.**

Scheerer v. Hardee's Food Systems, Inc., 92 F.3d 702 (8th Cir.1996)—§ **17.48, n. 5.**

Scheiner v. Wallace, 832 F.Supp. 687 (S.D.N.Y.1993)—§ **24.4, n. 7.**

Schenk v. Piper Aircraft Corp., 377 F.Supp. 477 (W.D.Pa.1974)—§ **3.11, n. 4, 6.**

Scherer v. Scherer, 405 N.E.2d 40 (Ind.App. 4 Dist.1980)—§ **15.20, n. 10.**

Scherk v. Alberto–Culver Co., 417 U.S. 506, 94 S.Ct. 2449, 41 L.Ed.2d 270 (1974)—§ **3.59, n. 13;** § **11.3, n. 4, 20;** § **24.11, n. 1;** § **24.48;** § **24.48, n. 2.**

Schertenleib v. Traum, 589 F.2d 1156 (2nd Cir.1978)—§ **11.10, n. 2.**

Schewe v. Bentsen, 424 F.2d 60 (5th Cir. 1970)—§ **19.9, n. 12.**

Schiereck v. Schiereck, 14 Mass.App.Ct. 378, 439 N.E.2d 859 (Mass.App.Ct. 1982)—§ **5.21, n. 9.**

Schiff v. Mazda Motor of America, Inc., 102 F.Supp.2d 891 (S.D.Ohio 2000)—§ **17.52, n. 2.**

Schlanger v. Seamans, 401 U.S. 487, 91 S.Ct. 995, 28 L.Ed.2d 251 (1971)—§ **4.26, n. 4.**

Schlawig v. De Peyster, 83 Iowa 323, 49 N.W. 843 (Iowa 1891)—§ **4.13, n. 2.**

Schlemmer v. Fireman's Fund Ins. Co., 292 Ark. 344, 730 S.W.2d 217 (Ark.1987)—§ **2.13, n. 14;** § **17.21, n. 17, 19;** § **17.26, n. 1.**

Schley, Estate of, 11 Phila. 139 (Pa. 1876)—§ **22.9, n. 6.**

Schlinder v. Schlinder, 107 Wis.2d 695, 321 N.W.2d 343 (Wis.App.1982)—**§ 15.21, n. 3.**

Schlosser v. Allis–Chalmers Corp., 86 Wis.2d 226, 271 N.W.2d 879 (Wis. 1978)—**§ 2.17, n. 7; § 2.25, n. 7; § 18.21, n. 16; § 18.29, n. 4.**

Schlueter v. Schlueter, 975 S.W.2d 584 (Tex.1998)—**§ 14.13, n. 4.**

Schlunk v. Volkswagenwerk Aktiengesellschaft, 145 Ill.App.3d 594, 105 Ill.Dec. 39, 503 N.E.2d 1045 (Ill.App. 1 Dist.1986)—**§ 12.7; § 12.7, n. 7.**

Schmidt v. de Lottman, 428 So.2d 1056 (La.App. 1 Cir.1983)—**§ 19.8, n. 14.**

Schmidt v. Driscoll Hotel, Inc., 249 Minn. 376, 82 N.W.2d 365 (Minn.1957)—**§ 17.5, n. 7; § 17.12; § 17.12, n. 1; § 17.34; § 17.34, n. 1; § 17.48; § 17.48, n. 13.**

Schmidt v. Duo–Fast, Inc., 1995 WL 422681 (E.D.Pa.1995)—**§ 17.74, n. 20; § 17.78, n. 12.**

Schmidt, People v., 228 Mich.App. 463, 579 N.W.2d 431 (Mich.App.1998)—**§ 15.1, n. 6.**

Schmidt v. Perkins, 67 A. 77 (N.J.Err. & App.1907)—**§ 19.11, n. 7; § 19.13, n. 8.**

Schmidt v. Schmidt, 291 Ala. 543, 283 So.2d 601 (Ala.1973)—**§ 12.3, n. 6.**

Schneider v. Laffoon, 4 Ohio St.2d 89, 212 N.E.2d 801 (Ohio 1965)—**§ 21.10, n. 7.**

Schneider v. Schneider, 110 N.H. 70, 260 A.2d 97 (N.H.1969)—**§ 17.21, n. 29.**

Schneider's Estate, In re, 198 Misc. 1017, 96 N.Y.S.2d 652 (N.Y.Sur.1950)—**§ 4.10, n. 3; § 20.14, n. 11.**

Schneller v. Vance, 8 La. 506 (La.1835)—**§ 22.21, n. 9, 12.**

Schoeberle v. United States, 2000 WL 1868130 (N.D.Ill.2000)—**§ 17.50; § 17.50, n. 30.**

Schoenberg v. Exportadora de Sal, S.A. de C.V., 930 F.2d 777 (9th Cir.1991)—**§ 2.23, n. 8; § 10.19, n. 57.**

Schoenbrod v. Siegler, 283 N.Y.S.2d 881, 230 N.E.2d 638 (N.Y.1967)—**§ 13.6, n. 3; § 24.18, n. 1.**

Schoenfeld v. Marsh, 418 Pa.Super. 469, 614 A.2d 733 (Pa.Super.1992)—**§ 15.34, n. 7.**

Scholes v. Murray Iron–Works Co., 44 Iowa 190 (Iowa 1876)—**§ 4.19, n. 5.**

School Dist. Board, State ex rel. v. Thayer, 74 Wis. 48, 41 N.W. 1014 (Wis.1889)—**§ 4.13, n. 2.**

Schorsch Meier GmbH v. Hennin, 1974 WL 41393 (CA 1974)—**§ 24.31, n. 8; § 24.40, n. 8.**

Schrader v. Smith, 10 Misc.2d 475, 169 N.Y.S.2d 797 (N.Y.Sup.1958)—**§ 19.28, n. 1.**

Schram's Estate, In re, 132 Neb. 268, 271 N.W. 694 (Neb.1937)—**§ 22.22, n. 4.**

Schreiber v. Allis–Chalmers Corp., 611 F.2d 790 (10th Cir.1979)—**§ 3.9, n. 6; § 3.48, n. 13.**

Schreiber v. Allis–Chalmers Corp., 448 F.Supp. 1079 (D.Kan.1978)—**§ 3.10, n. 2; § 3.11, n. 7; § 3.46, n. 4, 5; § 3.47, n. 12; § 3.48; § 3.48, n. 6; § 6.2, n. 13; § 12.11, n. 7.**

Schroeder v. City of New York, 371 U.S. 208, 83 S.Ct. 279, 9 L.Ed.2d 255 (1962)—**§ 5.16, n. 9.**

Schulke Radio Productions, Ltd. v. Midwestern Broadcasting Co., 6 Ohio St.3d 436, 453 N.E.2d 683 (Ohio 1983)—**§ 18.29, n. 3.**

Schultz v. Boy Scouts of America, Inc., 491 N.Y.S.2d 90, 480 N.E.2d 679 (N.Y. 1985)—**§ 2.1, n. 14; § 17.32; § 17.32, n. 3; § 17.36, n. 7; § 17.37, n. 14; § 17.39, n. 2, 16, 31; § 17.46; § 17.46, n. 4.**

Schultz v. Tecumseh Products, 310 F.2d 426 (6th Cir.1962)—**§ 19.12, n. 2.**

Schutt, People ex rel. v. Siems, 198 Ill.App. 342 (Ill.App. 1 Dist.1916)—**§ 13.11, n. 4; § 13.15, n. 4.**

Schwartz v. Consolidated Freightways Corp. of Delaware, 300 Minn. 487, 221 N.W.2d 665 (Minn.1974)—**§ 17.21, n. 31.**

Schwartz v. Schwartz, 103 Ariz. 562, 447 P.2d 254 (Ariz.1968)—**§ 2.16, n. 8; § 2.21, n. 14; § 2.23, n. 1; § 17.26, n. 1; § 17.36, n. 15; § 17.39, n. 9, 13.**

Schwebel v. Ungar, 1963 WL 21408 (Ont. C.A.1963)—**§ 15.24, n. 7.**

Schweitzer v. Bean, 154 Ark. 228, 242 S.W. 63 (Ark.1922)—**§ 22.3, n. 1.**

Scoggins v. Pollock, 727 F.2d 1025 (11th Cir.1984)—**§ 4.4, n. 3; § 4.21, n. 3.**

Scoggins v. Scoggins, 382 Pa.Super. 507, 555 A.2d 1314 (Pa.Super.1989)—**§ 15.28, n. 1.**

Scott v. Attorney General, 1886 WL 14697 (PDAD 1886)—**§ 13.8, n. 5.**

Scott v. Furrow, 141 Conn. 113, 104 A.2d 224 (Conn.1954)—**§ 4.40, n. 5.**

Scott v. Key, 1856 WL 4520 (La.1856)—**§ 16.2, n. 5.**

Scott v. Nesbitt, 14 Ves. 438 (1808)—**§ 19.8, n. 6.**

Scott v. Perlee, 39 Ohio St. 63 (Ohio 1883)—**§ 18.2, n. 1.**

Scott v. Pilot Corp., 205 Wis.2d 738, 557 N.W.2d 257 (Wis.App.1996)—**§ 17.48, n. 5.**

Scott v. Scott, 51 Cal.2d 249, 331 P.2d 641 (Cal.1958)—**§ 15.20, n. 3; § 15.23, n. 5; § 24.6, n. 3; § 24.35, n. 7.**

Scott v. Scott, 153 Neb. 906, 46 N.W.2d 627 (Neb.1951)—**§ 13.9, n. 3.**

Scott, United States v., 472 F.Supp. 1073 (N.D.Ill.1979)—**§ 4.13, n. 3.**

Scott by Ricciardi v. First State Ins. Co., 155 Wis.2d 608, 456 N.W.2d 152 (Wis. 1990)—**§ 3.11, n. 5.**

Scottish Air Intern., Inc. v. British Caledonian Group, PLC, 81 F.3d 1224 (2nd Cir.1996)—§ **11.9, n. 6.**

Scribner v. Scribner, 556 So.2d 350 (Miss. 1990)—§ **15.9, n. 6.**

Scripps v. Durfee, 131 Mich. 265, 90 N.W. 1061 (Mich.1902)—§ **22.3, n. 15.**

S & D Foods, Inc., In re, 144 B.R. 121 (Bkrtcy.D.Colo.1992)—§ **7.11, n. 1.**

SD Leasing, Inc. v. Al Spain and Associates, Inc., 277 Ark. 178, 640 S.W.2d 451 (Ark. 1982)—§ **18.1, n. 23.**

S. D. Sales Corp. v. Doltex Fabrics Corp., 92 N.J.Super. 586, 224 A.2d 345 (N.J.Super.L.1966)—§ **11.11, n. 7.**

Seaboard Coast Line R. Co. v. Swain, 362 So.2d 17 (Fla.1978)—§ **11.11, n. 2.**

Sea–Gate Tire & Rubber Co. v. Moseley, 161 Okla. 256, 18 P.2d 276 (Okla. 1933)—§ **19.15, n. 5.**

Sea–Land Service, Inc. v. Director, Office of Workers' Compensation Programs, United States Dept. of Labor, 540 F.2d 629 (3rd Cir.1976)—§ **17.63, n. 4.**

Sea–Land Service, Inc. v. Workers' Comp. Appeals Bd., 42 Cal.Rptr.2d 865 (Cal. App. 1 Dist.1995)—§ **17.59, n. 1.**

Seale's Marriage Settlement, In re, [1961] Ch. 574—§ **21.6, n. 2.**

Sealey v. United States, 7 F.Supp. 434 (E.D.Va.1934)—§ **4.27, n. 11.**

Sealord Marine Co., Ltd. v. American Bureau of Shippins, 220 F.Supp.2d 260 (S.D.N.Y.2002)—§ **17.63, n. 32.**

Seaman v. Cook, 14 Ill. 501 (Ill.1853)—§ **19.6, n. 2.**

Sears v. City of Boston, 42 Mass. 250 (Mass. 1840)—§ **4.21, n. 2.**

Sears, Roebuck & Co. v. Stiffel Co., 376 U.S. 225, 84 S.Ct. 784, 11 L.Ed.2d 661 (1964)—§ **17.53, n. 3.**

Seatrade Corp., In re, 255 F.Supp. 696 (S.D.N.Y.1966)—§ **23.20, n. 11.**

Seawind Compania, S. A. v. Crescent Line, Inc., 320 F.2d 580 (2nd Cir.1963)—§ **10.6, n. 34, 35.**

S.E.C. v. Blazon Corp., 609 F.2d 960 (9th Cir.1979)—§ **6.5, n. 1.**

S.E.C. v. Elmas Trading Corp., 683 F.Supp. 743 (D.Nev.1987)—§ **18.11, n. 4.**

S.E.C. v. Infinity Group Co., 27 F.Supp.2d 559 (E.D.Pa.1998)—§ **17.52, n. 3.**

S.E.C. v. Steadman, 798 F.Supp. 733 (D.D.C.1991)—§ **9.6, n. 21.**

Second Bank–State St. Trust Co. v. Weston, 342 Mass. 630, 174 N.E.2d 763 (Mass. 1961)—§ **20.13, n. 4.**

Second Nat. Bank of Ashland v. Thomson, 455 S.W.2d 51 (Ky.1970)—§ **22.4, n. 7.**

Securities and Exchange Commission v. National Securities, Inc., 393 U.S. 453, 89 S.Ct. 564, 21 L.Ed.2d 668 (1969)—§ **10.13, n. 10.**

Securities Inv. Co. v. Finance Acceptance Corp., 474 S.W.2d 261 (Tex.Civ.App.-Hous. (1 Dist.) 1971)—§ **18.7, n. 12.**

Securities Investor Protection Corp. v. Vigman, 764 F.2d 1309 (9th Cir.1985)—§ **9.6, n. 19.**

Security Trust Co. v. Hanby, 32 Del.Ch. 70, 79 A.2d 807 (Del.Ch.1951)—§ **20.15, n. 3.**

Security Trust & Safe Deposit Co. v. Ward, 10 Del.Ch. 408, 93 A. 385 (Del.Ch. 1915)—§ **21.11, n. 2.**

Seeley v. Bedillion, 23 Ohio Misc. 4, 260 N.E.2d 639 (Ohio Com.Pl.1969)—§ **20.13, n. 6.**

Seeman v. Philadelphia Warehouse Co., 274 U.S. 403, 47 S.Ct. 626, 71 L.Ed. 1123 (1927)—§ **18.5, n. 12;** § **18.6, n. 1;** § **18.7, n. 2.**

Seetransport Wiking Trader Schiffartgesellschaft, MBH & Co. v. Navimpex Centrala Navala, 837 F.Supp. 79 (S.D.N.Y. 1993)—§ **24.4, n. 7.**

Segal v. Greater Val. Terminal Corp., 83 N.J.Super. 120, 199 A.2d 48 (N.J.Super.A.D.1964)—§ **18.37, n. 2;** § **19.5, n. 10.**

Seguros Banvenez, S.A. v. S/S Oliver Drescher, 761 F.2d 855 (2nd Cir.1985)—§ **10.6, n. 39.**

S.E. Hornsby & Sons Sand and Gravel Co., Inc. (E.I. No. 72–0792818), In re, 45 B.R. 988 (Bkrtcy.M.D.La.1985)—§ **23.12, n. 8.**

Seibold v. Wahl, 164 Wis. 82, 159 N.W. 546 (Wis.1916)—§ **4.13, n. 2.**

Seider v. Roth, 269 N.Y.S.2d 99, 216 N.E.2d 312 (N.Y.1966)—§ **5.6;** § **5.6, n. 11;** § **5.9, n. 5;** § **23.3, n. 5.**

Sei Fujii v. State, 38 Cal.2d 718, 242 P.2d 617 (Cal.1952)—§ **3.59, n. 3.**

Seizer v. Sessions, 132 Wash.2d 642, 940 P.2d 261 (Wash.1997)—§ **14.9, n. 1.**

Sell v. Miller, 11 Ohio St. 331 (Ohio 1860)—§ **19.3, n. 1.**

Selle v. Pierce, 494 N.W.2d 634 (S.D. 1993)—§ **2.19, n. 16, 18;** § **17.50, n. 55.**

Selle v. Rapp, 143 Ark. 192, 220 S.W. 662 (Ark.1920)—§ **20.6, n. 21;** § **22.4, n. 7.**

Selleck v. Rusco, 46 Conn. 370 (Conn. 1878)—§ **22.16, n. 2.**

Seminole Nation v. United States, 316 U.S. 286, 62 S.Ct. 1049, 86 L.Ed. 1480, 86 L.Ed. 1777 (1942)—§ **11.17, n. 11.**

Semler v. Psychiatric Institute of Washington, D. C., Inc., 575 F.2d 922, 188 U.S.App.D.C. 41 (D.C.Cir.1978)—§ **24.26, n. 4.**

Semtek Intern. Inc. v. Lockheed Martin Corp., 531 U.S. 497, 121 S.Ct. 1021, 149 L.Ed.2d 32 (2001)—§ **3.39;** § **3.39, n. 23;** § **3.40;** § **3.40, n. 13;** § **24.2, n. 1, 9.**

Senac, Succession of, 1842 WL 1673 (La. 1842)—§ **20.12, n. 6.**

Seneca Falls Mach. Co. v. McBeth, 368 F.2d 915 (3rd Cir.1966)—§ **18.33, n. 4.**

Sentinel Industrial Contracting Corp. v. Kimmins Industrial Service Corp., 743 So.2d 954 (Miss.1999)—§ **18.6, n. 1.**

Seoane v. Ortho Pharmaceuticals, Inc., 472 F.Supp. 468 (E.D.La.1979)—§ **3.41, n. 15.**

Sequa Corp. v. Aetna Cas. and Sur Co., 1995 WL 465192 (Del.Super.1995)— § **18.26, n. 12.**

Sequa Corp. v. Aetna Cas. & Sur. Co., 1990 WL 123006 (Del.Super.1990)—§ **18.1, n. 27.**

Sequa Corp. v. Lititech, Inc., 780 F.Supp. 1349 (D.Colo.1992)—§ **18.29, n. 3, 5.**

Seren v. Douglas, 30 Colo.App. 110, 489 P.2d 601 (Colo.App.1971)—§ **4.31, n. 3.**

Service Lines, Inc. v. Mitchell, 419 S.W.2d 525 (Ky.1967)—§ **22.10, n. 12.**

Servicios Comerciales Andinos, S.A. v. General Elec. Del Caribe, Inc., 145 F.3d 463 (1st Cir.1998)—§ **3.37, n. 6.**

Servo Instruments, Inc. v. Fenway Mach. Co., 92 Ill.App.3d 509, 47 Ill.Dec. 309, 415 N.E.2d 34 (Ill.App. 3 Dist.1980)— § **8.5, n. 5.**

Sestito v. Knop, 297 F.2d 33 (7th Cir. 1961)—§ **17.5, n. 4.**

Seubert Excavators, Inc. v. Anderson Logging Co., 126 Idaho 648, 889 P.2d 82 (Idaho 1995)—§ **17.59, n. 12.**

Sewall v. Haymaker, 127 U.S. 719, 8 S.Ct. 1348, 32 L.Ed. 299 (1888)—§ **19.2, n. 5.**

Sewall v. Wilmer, 132 Mass. 131 (Mass. 1882)—§ **21.11, n. 1, 12; § 21.13, n. 4.**

Seward v. Devine, 888 F.2d 957 (2nd Cir. 1989)—§ **11.6, n. 5.**

Sewart's Estate, In re, 342 Mich. 491, 70 N.W.2d 732 (Mich.1955)—§ **20.13, n. 2.**

Sexton v. Ryder Truck Rental, Inc., 413 Mich. 406, 320 N.W.2d 843 (Mich. 1982)—§ **2.16, n. 18; § 2.23, n. 6; § 2.24, n. 12; § 17.15, n. 7; § 17.39, n. 12; § 17.48, n. 17.**

Seymour v. Parke, Davis & Co., 423 F.2d 584 (1st Cir.1970)—§ **6.9, n. 12.**

Seymour v. Superintendent of Washington State Penitentiary, 368 U.S. 351, 82 S.Ct. 424, 7 L.Ed.2d 346 (1962)— § **11.17, n. 2.**

Sfiridas v. Santa Cecelia Co. S.A., 358 F.Supp. 108 (E.D.Pa.1973)—§ **17.63, n. 24.**

Shacklett v. Polk, 51 Miss. 378 (Miss. 1875)—§ **19.3, n. 5.**

Shaffer v. Heitner, 433 U.S. 186, 97 S.Ct. 2569, 53 L.Ed.2d 683 (1977)—§ **2.10, n. 28; § 2.13, n. 10; § 2.14, n. 53; § 3.23, n. 2; § 3.26, n. 1; § 3.27, n. 3; § 3.43, n. 2; § 4.3, n. 1; § 5.4, n. 30; § 5.5; § 5.5, n. 2; § 5.6; § 5.6, n. 14; § 5.9; § 5.9, n. 2, 4; § 5.11; § 5.11, n. 13; § 5.13; § 5.13, n. 24; § 5.22; § 5.22, n. 5; § 6.2; § 6.2, n. 11; § 6.3, n. 6; § 6.6; § 6.6, n.** 15; § **6.8, n. 4; § 9.1; § 9.1, n. 16; § 10.2, n. 2; § 10.6; § 10.6, n. 46; § 10.15, n. 4, 13; § 11.17, n. 40; § 15.7, n. 8; § 15.10, n. 4; § 15.27, n. 7; § 15.29, n. 5; § 15.30; § 15.30, n. 2; § 15.31, n. 2; § 22.7; § 22.7, n. 7; § 22.8, n. 2; § 22.10; § 22.10, n. 14; § 22.20, n. 31; § 23.4, n. 7; § 24.12, n. 5; § 24.14, n. 3; § 24.37, n. 4; § 24.42, n. 4.**

Shah v. Nu–Kote Intern., Inc., 898 F.Supp. 496 (E.D.Mich.1995)—§ **8.4, n. 2, 6.**

Shahid v. A/S J. Ludwig Mowinckels Rederi, 236 F.Supp. 751 (S.D.N.Y.1964)— § **17.63, n. 31.**

Shames v. Nebraska, 323 F.Supp. 1321 (D.Neb.1971)—§ **20.17, n. 5.**

Shanahan v. George B. Landers Const. Co., 266 F.2d 400 (1st Cir.1959)—§ **19.13, n. 1.**

Shanks v. Treadway, 110 S.W.3d 444 (Tex. 2003)—§ **14.13, n. 3.**

Shannon v. Irving Trust Co., 275 N.Y. 95, 9 N.E.2d 792 (N.Y.1937)—§ **21.3, n. 10, 17; § 21.12, n. 3.**

Shannon v. Irving Trust Co., 246 A.D. 280, 285 N.Y.S. 478 (N.Y.A.D. 1 Dept.1936)— § **21.2, n. 13; § 21.3, n. 15.**

Shannon v. White, 109 Mass. 146 (Mass. 1872)—§ **20.14, n. 1.**

Shapiro v. Marcus, 211 Md. 83, 124 A.2d 846 (Md.1956)—§ **4.1, n. 2.**

Shapiro v. Shapiro, 168 A.D.2d 491, 562 N.Y.S.2d 733 (N.Y.A.D. 2 Dept.1990)— § **15.24, n. 7.**

Shapiro v. Shapiro, 110 Misc.2d 726, 442 N.Y.S.2d 928 (N.Y.Sup.1981)—§ **15.24, n. 4, 7.**

Shapiro v. State Tax Commission, 67 A.D.2d 191, 415 N.Y.S.2d 282 (N.Y.A.D. 3 Dept.1979)—§ **4.17, n. 1.**

Shapiro v. Thompson, 394 U.S. 618, 89 S.Ct. 1322, 22 L.Ed.2d 600 (1969)— § **4.20, n. 6.**

Sharon's Estate, In re, 179 Cal. 447, 177 P. 283 (Cal.1918)—§ **16.5, n. 4.**

Sharp v. Johnson, 248 Minn. 518, 80 N.W.2d 650 (Minn.1957)—§ **17.5, n. 9.**

Sharp v. Sharp, 830 So.2d 328 (La.App. 4 Cir.2002)—§ **14.9, n. 1.**

Sharpe v. Crispen, L.R. 1 Prob. & Div. 610 (1869)—§ **4.45, n. 6.**

Shasta Livestock Auction Yard, Inc. v. Bill Evans Cattle Management Corp., 375 F.Supp. 1027 (D.Idaho 1974)—§ **18.34; § 18.34, n. 1.**

Shattuck v. Bates, 92 Wis. 633, 66 N.W. 706 (Wis.1896)—§ **19.2, n. 4.**

Shattuck, State v., 69 Vt. 403, 38 A. 81 (Vt.1897)—§ **13.9, n. 5.**

Shaw v. Goebel Brewing Co., 202 F. 408 (6th Cir.1913)—§ **19.32, n. 6.**

Shaw v. Gould, 3 H.L. 55 (1868)—§ **16.1, n. 8.**

Shaw v. Rivers White Water Rafting Resort, 2002 WL 31748919 (E.D.Mich.2002)— **§ 17.40, n. 26; § 18.1, n. 17.**

Shaw v. Shaw, 251 Ark. 665, 473 S.W.2d 848 (Ark.1971)—**§ 22.26, n. 2.**

Shaw v. Shaw, 98 Mass. 158 (Mass.1867)— **§ 4.19, n. 2.**

Shaw v. Stutchman, 105 Nev. 128, 771 P.2d 156 (Nev.1989)—**§ 22.19, n. 24.**

Shearer, United States v., 473 U.S. 52, 105 S.Ct. 3039, 87 L.Ed.2d 38 (1985)— **§ 3.53, n. 4.**

Shearson Lehman Bros., Inc. v. M & L Investments, 10 F.3d 1510 (10th Cir. 1993)—**§ 18.21, n. 14.**

Sheehan v. Scott, 145 Cal. 684, 79 P. 350 (Cal.1905)—**§ 4.18, n. 1; § 4.19, n. 3.**

Shehady v. Richards, 83 N.M. 311, 491 P.2d 528 (N.M.1971)—**§ 16.6, n. 5.**

Shelby v. Creighton, 65 Neb. 485, 91 N.W. 369 (Neb.1902)—**§ 22.8, n. 1.**

Shelby v. Guy, 24 U.S. 361, 6 L.Ed. 495 (1826)—**§ 19.14, n. 1.**

Sheldon v. PHH Corp., 135 F.3d 848 (2nd Cir.1998)—**§ 17.46, n. 22.**

Sheldon–Claire Co. v. Judson Roberts Co., 88 F.Supp. 120 (S.D.N.Y.1949)—**§ 17.7, n. 1.**

Shelley v. Trafalgar House Public Ltd. Co., 918 F.Supp. 515 (D.Puerto Rico 1996)— **§ 17.40, n. 28; § 18.1, n. 18.**

Shenton v. Abbott, 178 Md. 526, 15 A.2d 906 (Md.1940)—**§ 4.26, n. 1.**

Sheppard v. Sheppard, 104 Idaho 1, 655 P.2d 895 (Idaho 1982)—**§ 24.12, n. 2.**

Sherburne, Town of v. Town of Hartland, 37 Vt. 528 (Vt.1865)—**§ 4.43, n. 1.**

Sherif v. Sherif, 76 Misc.2d 905, 352 N.Y.S.2d 781 (N.Y.Fam.Ct.1974)— **§ 15.24, n. 3, 8.**

Sherman v. Sherman, 213 N.Y.S.2d 216 (N.Y.Sup.1961)—**§ 13.9, n. 3.**

Sherman's Estate, In re, 76 Misc.2d 551, 351 N.Y.S.2d 570 (N.Y.Sur.1974)— **§ 20.3, n. 1, 5, 9.**

Sherrer v. Sherrer, 334 U.S. 343, 68 S.Ct. 1087, 92 L.Ed. 1429 (1948)—**§ 4.7, n. 2; § 6.5, n. 1; § 15.9; § 15.9, n. 3; § 15.17, n. 12; § 15.28, n. 1; § 15.30, n. 3; § 24.14, n. 7; § 24.17, n. 14.**

Sherrer v. Sherrer, 334 U.S. 343, 68 S.Ct. 1097, 92 L.Ed. 1429 (1948)—**§ 15.22, n. 3.**

Sherrill's Estate, In re, 92 Ariz. 39, 373 P.2d 353 (Ariz.1962)—**§ 4.45, n. 3.**

Shikoh v. Murff, 257 F.2d 306 (2nd Cir. 1958)—**§ 15.24, n. 4.**

Shima v. Shima, 130 F.2d 809, 75 U.S.App. D.C. 370 (D.C.Cir.1942)—**§ 15.15, n. 3.**

Shimshak v. Cox, 166 La. 102, 116 So. 714 (La.1928)—**§ 22.3, n. 1.**

Shinn v. Kreul, 311 S.C. 94, 427 S.E.2d 695 (S.C.App.1993)—**§ 15.31, n. 2.**

Shinn's Estate, In re, 166 Pa. 121, 30 A. 1026 (Pa.1895)—**§ 22.15, n. 13.**

Shippy, In re Estate of, 37 Wash.App. 164, 678 P.2d 848 (Wash.App. Div. 2 1984)— **§ 13.5, n. 3; § 13.9, n. 4.**

Shirk v. City of La Fayette, 52 F. 857 (C.C.D.Ind.1892)—**§ 21.5, n. 1.**

Shoei Kako Co. v. Superior Court, 33 Cal. App.3d 808, 109 Cal.Rptr. 402 (Cal.App. 1 Dist.1973)—**§ 12.7, n. 5.**

Shoemaker, Commonwealth ex rel. v. Shoemaker, 211 Pa.Super. 188, 235 A.2d 455 (Pa.Super.1967)—**§ 15.43, n. 9.**

Shoemaker, Commonwealth ex rel. Shoemaker v., 211 Pa.Super. 188, 235 A.2d 455 (Pa.Super.1967)—**§ 15.43, n. 9.**

Sholes v. Agency Rent–A–Car, Inc., 76 Ohio App.3d 349, 601 N.E.2d 634 (Ohio App. 8 Dist.1991)—**§ 17.26, n. 1.**

Shonac Corp. v. AMKO Intern., Inc., 763 F.Supp. 919 (S.D.Ohio 1991)—**§ 12.18, n. 8.**

Shope v. State Farm Ins. Co., 122 N.M. 398, 925 P.2d 515 (N.M.1996)—**§ 2.21, n. 53; § 17.56, n. 18; § 18.21, n. 8.**

Shorewood Packaging Corp. v. Commercial Union Ins. Co., 865 F.Supp. 1577 (N.D.Ga.1994)—**§ 2.21, n. 15; § 18.21, n. 5.**

Shotwell v. Dairymen's League Co-op. Ass'n, 22 N.J. Misc. 171, 37 A.2d 420 (N.J.Dist.Ct.1944)—**§ 18.6, n. 4.**

Shoup v. Bell & Howell Co., 872 F.2d 1178 (4th Cir.1989)—**§ 24.1, n. 7.**

Shuder v. McDonald's Corp., 859 F.2d 266 (3rd Cir.1988)—**§ 17.42, n. 17, 22.**

Shull v. Dain, Kalman & Quail Inc., 201 Neb. 260, 267 N.W.2d 517 (Neb.1978)— **§ 2.17, n. 16; § 2.23, n. 2.**

Shultz v. Pulver, 3 Paige Ch. 182, 3 N.Y. Ch. Ann. 107 (N.Y.Ch.1832)—**§ 22.15, n. 13.**

Shultz' Estate, In re, 180 Kan. 444, 304 P.2d 539 (Kan.1956)—**§ 22.7, n. 1.**

Shun T. Takahashi's Estate, In re, 113 Mont. 490, 129 P.2d 217 (Mont.1942)— **§ 13.10, n. 2.**

Shute v. Carnival Cruise Lines, 897 F.2d 377 (9th Cir.1990)—**§ 5.10; § 5.10, n. 17, 24; § 6.7; § 6.7, n. 9, 14, 19.**

Shute v. Sargent, 67 N.H. 305, 36 A. 282 (N.H.1893)—**§ 4.33, n. 3; § 4.34, n. 2.**

Shutts v. Phillips Petroleum Co., 235 Kan. 195, 679 P.2d 1159 (Kan.1984)—**§ 3.23, n. 18.**

Siata Intern. U.S.A. Inc. v. Insurance Co. of North America, 362 F.Supp. 1355 (E.D.Pa.1973)—**§ 18.27, n. 4.**

Sibaja v. Dow Chemical Co., 757 F.2d 1215 (11th Cir.1985)—**§ 3.37, n. 7; § 3.40, n. 12; § 11.11, n. 6.**

Sidis v. F–R Pub. Corporation, 113 F.2d 806 (2nd Cir.1940)—**§ 17.7, n. 2.**

Siegelman v. Cunard White Star Limited, 221 F.2d 189 (2nd Cir.1955)—**§ 18.1, n. 3; § 18.2, n. 2, 16; § 18.5, n. 1, 4.**

Siegmann v. Meyer, 100 F.2d 367 (2nd Cir. 1938)—§ **17.4, n. 4.**

Siemens Medical Systems, Inc. v. Nuclear Cardiology Systems, Inc., 945 F.Supp. 1421 (D.Colo.1996)—§ **18.12, n. 1;** § **18.21, n. 14.**

Siems, People ex rel. Schutt v., 198 Ill.App. 342 (Ill.App. 1 Dist.1916)—§ **13.11, n. 4;** § **13.15, n. 4.**

Sierra Diesel Injection Service v. Burroughs Corp., Inc., 648 F.Supp. 1148 (D.Nev. 1986)—§ **3.11, n. 3.**

Sierra Rutile Limited v. Katz, 1997 WL 431119 (S.D.N.Y.1997)—§ **23.9, n. 8.**

Sikorski's Estate, In re, 54 Misc.2d 883, 283 N.Y.S.2d 794 (N.Y.Sur.1967)—§ **22.23, n. 11.**

Silent Drive, Inc. v. Strong Industries, Inc., 326 F.3d 1194 (Fed.Cir.2003)—§ **9.4, n. 10.**

Siler v. Storey, 587 F.Supp. 986 (N.D.Tex. 1984)—§ **15.42, n. 5.**

Silesian Am. Corp. v. Clark, 332 U.S. 469, 68 S.Ct. 179, 92 L.Ed. 81 (1947)—§ **23.3, n. 9.**

Silva v. Tillinghast, 36 F.2d 801 (D.Mass. 1929)—§ **13.6, n. 12.**

Silver v. Great Am. Ins. Co., 328 N.Y.S.2d 398, 278 N.E.2d 619 (N.Y.1972)— § **11.11, n. 2.**

Silverman, Matter of, 15 B.R. 843 (Bkrtcy. S.D.N.Y.1981)—§ **20.2, n. 2.**

Silverman, United States v., 745 F.2d 1386 (11th Cir.1984)—§ **3.39, n. 7.**

Silver Surprize, Inc. v. Sunshine Min. Co., 74 Wash.2d 519, 445 P.2d 334 (Wash. 1968)—§ **19.8, n. 6.**

Simler v. Conner, 372 U.S. 221, 83 S.Ct. 609, 9 L.Ed.2d 691 (1963)—§ **3.38, n. 4;** § **3.41, n. 18.**

Simmons v. Rosenberg, 572 F.Supp. 823 (E.D.N.Y.1983)—§ **4.12, n. 3.**

Simmons v. Skyway of Ocala, 592 F.Supp. 356 (S.D.Ga.1984)—§ **4.2, n. 1;** § **4.13, n. 4.**

Simmons v. State, 206 Mont. 264, 670 P.2d 1372 (Mont.1983)—§ **3.30, n. 6.**

Simms, Succession of, 250 La. 177, 195 So.2d 114 (La.1965)—§ **20.5, n. 6;** § **20.6, n. 20.**

Simon v. Simon, 478 F.Supp. 548 (E.D.Pa. 1979)—§ **19.8, n. 14.**

Simon v. United States, 805 N.E.2d 798 (Ind.2004)—§ **2.22, n. 1.**

Simonds v. Simonds, 154 F.2d 326, 81 U.S.App.D.C. 50 (D.C.Cir.1946)—§ **4.41, n. 1.**

Simons v. Marriott Corp., 1993 WL 410457 (S.D.N.Y.1993)—§ **17.46, n. 21.**

Simons v. Miami Beach First Nat. Bank, 381 U.S. 81, 85 S.Ct. 1315, 14 L.Ed.2d 232 (1965)—§ **15.28;** § **15.28, n. 4.**

Simpson v. Cornish, 196 Wis. 125, 218 N.W. 193 (Wis.1928)—§ **22.4, n. 8.**

Simpson v. Cureton, 97 N.C. 112, 2 S.E. 668 (N.C.1887)—§ **22.22, n. 4.**

Simpson v. Kelly Services, Inc., 339 So.2d 490 (La.App. 2 Cir.1976)—§ **18.5, n. 16.**

Simpson v. Simpson, 267 A.2d 891 (Del.Super.1970)—§ **19.8, n. 14.**

Sims v. Mack Trucks, Inc., 444 F.Supp. 1277 (E.D.Pa.1978)—§ **17.53, n. 7.**

Sims Snowboards, Inc. v. Kelly, 863 F.2d 643 (9th Cir.1988)—§ **18.20, n. 11.**

Sinatra v. National Enquirer, Inc., 854 F.2d 1191 (9th Cir.1988)—§ **5.12, n. 8;** § **7.2, n. 35.**

Singer v. Lexington Ins. Co., 658 F.Supp. 341 (N.D.Tex.1986)—§ **18.1, n. 27.**

Singh v. Singh, 213 Conn. 637, 569 A.2d 1112 (Conn.1990)—§ **13.5, n. 1.**

Singleton v. St. Louis Union Trust Co., 191 S.W.2d 143 (Tex.Civ.App.-Waco 1945)— § **14.6, n. 3.**

Sioux Remedy Co. v. Cope, 235 U.S. 197, 35 S.Ct. 57, 59 L.Ed. 193 (1914)—§ **23.6, n. 4.**

Sirois v. Sirois, 94 N.H. 215, 50 A.2d 88 (N.H.1946)—§ **13.6, n. 8.**

Sisal Sales Corp., United States v., 274 U.S. 268, 47 S.Ct. 592, 71 L.Ed. 1042 (1927)—§ **17.53, n. 1.**

Sistare v. Sistare, 218 U.S. 1, 30 S.Ct. 682, 54 L.Ed. 905 (1910)—§ **15.31, n. 1;** § **15.32, n. 2;** § **24.9, n. 14.**

Sivalls v. United States, 205 F.2d 444 (5th Cir.1953)—§ **4.36, n. 3.**

Skaggs, Commissioner v., 122 F.2d 721 (5th Cir.1941)—§ **14.7, n. 3, 5.**

Skandia America Reinsurance Corp. v. Schenck, 441 F.Supp. 715 (S.D.N.Y. 1977)—§ **18.31, n. 5.**

Skeer's Estate, In re, 249 Pa. 288, 95 A. 96 (Pa.1915)—§ **22.23, n. 4.**

Skillsoft Corp. v. Harcourt General, Inc., 146 N.H. 305, 770 A.2d 1115 (N.H. 2001)—§ **8.4, n. 7.**

Skinner v. Brunsen, 69 R.I. 159, 32 A.2d 263 (R.I.1943)—§ **20.13, n. 4.**

Skinner v. Tober Foreign Motors, Inc., 345 Mass. 429, 187 N.E.2d 669 (Mass. 1963)—§ **18.19, n. 12.**

Skinner's Guardianship, In re, 230 Iowa 1016, 300 N.W. 1 (Iowa 1941)—§ **4.41, n. 1.**

Skipper v. Prince George's County, 637 F.Supp. 638 (D.D.C.1986)—§ **17.43, n. 25.**

Skiriotes v. Florida, 313 U.S. 69, 61 S.Ct. 924, 85 L.Ed. 1193 (1941)—§ **6.4, n. 18.**

Ski Train Fire In Kaprun, Austria on Nov. 11, 2000, In re, 257 F.Supp.2d 717 (S.D.N.Y.2003)—§ **6.9, n. 20, 21.**

Skolnik v. Rose, 449 N.Y.S.2d 182, 434 N.E.2d 251 (N.Y.1982)—§ **21.3, n. 9.**

Slagenweit v. Slagenweit, 63 F.3d 719 (8th Cir.1995)—§ **3.57, n. 7.**

Slater v. Mexican Nat. R. Co., 194 U.S. 120, 24 S.Ct. 581, 48 L.Ed. 900 (1904)—§ **2.7,**

n. 17; § 3.2, n. 4; § 3.19; § 3.19, n. 4; § 11.10, n. 7; § 12.19, n. 13; § 17.2, n. 1; § 18.48, n. 4.

Slater v. Stoffel, 313 F.2d 175 (7th Cir. 1963)—§ 22.21, n. 2.

Slattery v. Hartford–Connecticut Trust Co., 115 Conn. 163, 161 A. 79 (Conn.1932)—§ 16.6, n. 2; § 20.3, n. 4.

Slaughter v. Garland, 40 Miss. 172 (Miss. Err. & App.1866)—§ 20.15, n. 5.

Sleeper v. Pennsylvania R. Co., 100 Pa. 259 (Pa.1882)—§ 19.13, n. 5.

Slessinger v. Secretary of Health and Human Services, 835 F.2d 937 (1st Cir. 1987)—§ 15.11, n. 4; § 15.22, n. 1.

Sloan v. Jones, 192 Tenn. 400, 241 S.W.2d 506 (Tenn.1951)—§ 14.12, n. 7.

Sloan's Estate, In re, 7 Cal.App.2d 319, 46 P.2d 1007 (Cal.App. 2 Dist.1935)—§ 21.11, n. 11.

Slocum v. DeWitt, 374 So.2d 755 (La.App. 3 Cir.1979)—§ 4.22, n. 1.

Small v. Carey, 269 Or. 35, 522 P.2d 1202 (Or.1974)—§ 19.8, n. 14.

Small v. Small, 96 Misc.2d 469, 409 N.Y.S.2d 379 (N.Y.Sup.1978)—§ 4.34, n. 3.

Smallwood v. Bickers, 139 Ga.App. 720, 229 S.E.2d 525 (Ga.App.1976)—§ 13.9, n. 5.

SmarTalk Teleservices Securities, Inc. Litigation, In re, 124 F.Supp.2d 505 (S.D.Ohio 2000)—§ 17.52, n. 2.

Smart's Trust, In re, 15 Misc.2d 906, 181 N.Y.S.2d 647 (N.Y.Sup.1958)—§ 21.7, n. 2.

SMI Industries, Inc. v. Lanard & Axilbund, Inc., 481 F.Supp. 459 (E.D.Pa.1979)—§ 24.15, n. 3.

Smith, Ex parte, 1833 WL 1625 (S.C.App. 1833)—§ 22.25, n. 16.

Smith v. Anderson, 821 So.2d 323 (Fla.App. 2 Dist.2002)—§ 13.6, n. 4; § 13.11, n. 4.

Smith v. Babbitt, 96 F.Supp.2d 907 (D.Minn.2000)—§ 13.18, n. 3.

Smith v. Basin Park Hotel, Inc., 178 F.Supp.2d 1225 (N.D.Okla.2001)—§ 5.11, n. 22.

Smith v. Carter, 545 F.2d 909 (5th Cir. 1977)—§ 4.12, n. 3.

Smith v. Cessna Aircraft Corp., 428 F.Supp. 1285 (N.D.Ill.1977)—§ 3.53, n. 9.

Smith v. Colloty, 55 A. 805 (N.J.Err. & App.1903)—§ 5.1, n. 9.

Smith v. Croom, 7 Fla. 81 (Fla.1857)—§ 4.3, n. 3; § 4.19, n. 2.

Smith v. Daimlerchrysler Corp., 2002 WL 31814534 (Del.Super.2002)—§ 17.71; § 17.71, n. 2.

Smith v. Dravo Corp., 203 F.2d 369 (7th Cir.1953)—§ 17.53, n. 5.

Smith v. Florida Gulf Airlines, Inc., 1996 WL 156859 (E.D.La.1996)—§ 17.48, n. 5.

Smith v. Howard, 86 Me. 203, 29 A. 1008 (Me.1894)—§ 22.22, n. 3, 4.

Smith v. Ingram, 132 N.C. 959, 44 S.E. 643 (N.C.1903)—§ 19.3, n. 3, 4; § 19.5, n. 6.

Smith v. Ingram, 130 N.C. 100, 40 S.E. 984 (N.C.1902)—§ 19.2, n. 8.

Smith v. Lewis, 3 Johns. 157 (N.Y.Sup. 1808)—§ 24.34, n. 1.

Smith v. Madden, 78 F. 833 (C.C.N.D.Ohio 1896)—§ 22.25, n. 5.

Smith v. Mercantile Trust Co. of Baltimore, 199 Md. 264, 86 A.2d 504 (Md.1952)—§ 21.6, n. 4.

Smith v. Normart, 51 Ariz. 134, 75 P.2d 38 (Ariz.1938)—§ 22.11, n. 9.

Smith v. Peters, 482 F.2d 799 (6th Cir. 1973)—§ 3.39, n. 10; § 3.46, n. 4, 8.

Smith v. Safeco Ins. Co., 863 F.2d 403 (5th Cir.1989)—§ 24.12, n. 7.

Smith v. Sands Hotel & Casino, 1997 WL 162156 (D.N.J.1997)—§ 9.8, n. 10.

Smith v. Smith, [1962] 3 S.A. 930—§ 4.31, n. 3.

Smith v. Smith, 99 N.H. 362, 111 A.2d 531 (N.H.1955)—§ 13.13, n. 5.

Smith v. Smith, 174 Ill. 52, 50 N.E. 1083 (Ill.1898)—§ 22.22, n. 4; § 22.23, n. 7.

Smith v. Smith, 84 Ga. 440, 11 S.E. 496 (Ga.1890)—§ 13.12, n. 2.

Smith v. Smith, 15 D.C. 255 (D.C.Sup. 1885)—§ 4.34, n. 3.

Smith v. Turner, 91 N.H. 198, 17 A.2d 87 (N.H.1940)—§ 3.10, n. 3.

Smith v. Union Bank of Georgetown, 30 U.S. 518, 8 L.Ed. 212 (1831)—§ 22.21, n. 5.

Smith, United States v., 398 F.2d 173 (3rd Cir.1968)—§ 12.3, n. 7.

Smith v. Van Gorkom, 488 A.2d 858 (Del. Supr.1985)—§ 23.4, n. 6.

Smith v. Young, 136 Mo.App. 65, 117 S.W. 628 (Mo.App.1909)—§ 4.41, n. 6.

Smith Kline & French Laboratories Ltd. v. Bloch (Interlocutory Injunction), 1982 WL 222260 (CA 1982)—§ 11.9, n. 4.

Smith's Estate, In re, 2 Misc.2d 755, 153 N.Y.S.2d 110 (N.Y.Sur.1956)—§ 21.5, n. 3.

Smith's Estate, In re, 182 Misc. 711, 48 N.Y.S.2d 631 (N.Y.Sur.1944)—§ 20.9, n. 13.

Smith's Estate, In re, 55 Wyo. 181, 97 P.2d 677 (Wyo.1940)—§ 20.12, n. 5.

Smith's Ex'rs v. Wiley, 22 Ala. 396 (Ala. 1853)—§ 22.25, n. 3.

Smolik v. Philadelphia & Reading Coal & Iron Co., 222 F. 148 (S.D.N.Y.1915)—§ 10.14; § 10.14, n. 12.

Snider v. Lone Star Art Trading Co., Inc., 659 F.Supp. 1249 (E.D.Mich.1987)—§ 11.6, n. 9.

Snider Bros., Inc. v. Heft, 271 Md. 409, 317 A.2d 848 (Md.1974)—§ 18.33, n. 3.

Snow v. Admiral Ins. Co., 612 F.Supp. 206 (W.D.Ark.1985)—§ 18.26, n. 12.

Soar v. National Football League Players' Ass'n, 550 F.2d 1287 (1st Cir.1977)—§ **2.21, n. 74.**

Societe du Gaz de Paris v. Societe Anonyme de Navigation 'Les Armateurs Francais', 1925 WL 23137 (HL 1925)—§ **11.8, n. 2.**

Societe Internationale Pour Participations Industrielles Et Commerciales, S. A. v. Rogers, 357 U.S. 197, 78 S.Ct. 1087, 2 L.Ed.2d 1255 (1958)—§ **24.9, n. 6.**

Societe Jean Nicolas Et Fils v. Mousseux, 123 Ariz. 59, 597 P.2d 541 (Ariz.1979)—§ **11.5, n. 3.**

Societe Nationale Industrielle Aerospatiale v. United States Dist. Court for Southern Dist. of Iowa, 482 U.S. 522, 107 S.Ct. 2542, 96 L.Ed.2d 461 (1987)—§ **2.7, n. 15; § 12.9; § 12.9, n. 9.**

Society of Lloyd's v. Mullin, 255 F.Supp.2d 468 (E.D.Pa.2003)—§ **24.44, n. 11.**

Society of Lloyd's v. Turner, 303 F.3d 325 (5th Cir.2002)—§ **24.35, n. 6.**

Society of Mount Carmel v. National Ben Franklin Ins. Co. of Illinois, 268 Ill. App.3d 655, 205 Ill.Dec. 673, 643 N.E.2d 1280 (Ill.App. 1 Dist.1994)—§ **2.19, n. 10.**

Sohnlein v. Winchell, 230 Cal.App.2d 508, 41 Cal.Rptr. 145 (Cal.App. 4 Dist. 1964)—§ **13.5, n. 1.**

Sokolowski v. Flanzer, 769 F.2d 975 (4th Cir.1985)—§ **3.10, n. 5.**

Solomon R. Guggenheim Foundation v. Lubell, 567 N.Y.S.2d 623, 569 N.E.2d 426 (N.Y.1991)—§ **19.14, n. 4.**

Solomons v. Ross, [1764] 1 H.Bl. 131—§ **23.19, n. 6.**

Soltex Polymer Corp. v. Fortex Industries, Inc., 590 F.Supp. 1453 (E.D.N.Y.1984)—§ **10.17, n. 3.**

Somerville Container Sales v. General Metal Corp., 39 N.J.Super. 348, 120 A.2d 866 (N.J.Super.A.D.1956)—§ **12.19, n. 15.**

Somerville v. Somerville, 5 Ves. Jr. 750 (1801)—§ **4.36, n. 4.**

Sommers v. 13300 Brandon Corp., 712 F.Supp. 702 (N.D.Ill.1989)—§ **17.48, n. 38.**

Sommerville, United States v., 324 F.2d 712 (3rd Cir.1963)—§ **3.51, n. 10.**

Somportex Limited v. Philadelphia Chewing Gum Corp., 453 F.2d 435 (3rd Cir. 1971)—§ **24.37, n. 3.**

Sondergard v. Miles, Inc., 985 F.2d 1389 (8th Cir.1993)—§ **6.9, n. 22.**

Sonnenberg, In re, 256 Minn. 571, 99 N.W.2d 444 (Minn.1959)—§ **4.43, n. 2.**

Sood, Application of, 208 Misc. 819, 142 N.Y.S.2d 591 (N.Y.Sup.1955)—§ **13.19, n. 5.**

Sorensen, People v., 68 Cal.2d 280, 66 Cal. Rptr. 7, 437 P.2d 495 (Cal.1968)—§ **16.1, n. 15.**

Sorenson v. Sorenson, 122 Misc. 196, 202 N.Y.S. 620 (N.Y.Sup.1924)—§ **15.24, n. 3.**

Sorsby, In re, 210 W.Va. 708, 559 S.E.2d 45 (W.Va.2001)—§ **19.19, n. 13.**

Sortwell v. Hughes, 22 F.Cas. 801 (C.C.D.N.H.1852)—§ **19.12, n. 1.**

Sosa v. M/V Lago Izabal, 736 F.2d 1028 (5th Cir.1984)—§ **17.63, n. 23.**

Sosna v. Iowa, 419 U.S. 393, 95 S.Ct. 553, 42 L.Ed.2d 532 (1975)—§ **4.13, n. 2, 10; § 4.18, n. 4; § 15.5, n. 5; § 15.7; § 15.7, n. 1; § 15.22, n. 1.**

Sousa v. Freitas, 10 Cal.App.3d 660, 89 Cal.Rptr. 485 (Cal.App. 1 Dist.1970)—§ **13.19, n. 8.**

Southard v. Southard, 305 F.2d 730 (2nd Cir.1962)—§ **15.12, n. 2.**

South Burlington, Town of v. Town of Cambridge, 77 Vt. 289, 59 A. 1013 (Vt. 1905)—§ **4.37, n. 8.**

South Carolina v. Katzenbach, 383 U.S. 301, 86 S.Ct. 803, 15 L.Ed.2d 769 (1966)—§ **10.19; § 10.19, n. 44.**

South Carolina Insurance Co. v. Assurantie Maatshappij De Zeven Provincien NV, 1985 WL 311424 (CA 1985)—§ **12.9, n. 14.**

South Dakota v. Bourland, 508 U.S. 679, 113 S.Ct. 2309, 124 L.Ed.2d 606 (1993)—§ **11.17, n. 17.**

Southeast Bank, N.A. v. Lawrence, 498 N.Y.S.2d 775, 489 N.E.2d 744 (N.Y. 1985)—§ **20.3, n. 1.**

Southeastern Express Systems v. Southern Guaranty Ins. Co., 40 Cal.Rptr.2d 216 (Cal.App. 1 Dist.1995)—§ **8.2, n. 13.**

Southern Bell Tel. & Tel. Co. v. Woodstock, Inc., 34 Ill.App.3d 86, 339 N.E.2d 423 (Ill.App. 1 Dist.1975)—§ **24.36, n. 5.**

Southern Cross S. S. Co. v. Firipis, 285 F.2d 651 (4th Cir.1960)—§ **17.63, n. 20, 23.**

Southern Farm Bureau Cas. Ins. Co. v. Craven, 79 Ark.App. 423, 89 S.W.3d 369 (Ark.App.2002)—§ **17.56, n. 20.**

Southern Intern. Sales Co., Inc. v. Potter & Brumfield Division of AMF Inc., 410 F.Supp. 1339 (S.D.N.Y.1976)—§ **18.2, n. 11; § 18.5, n. 17; § 18.18, n. 2; § 18.33, n. 3.**

Southern Pac. Co. v. Jensen, 244 U.S. 205, 37 S.Ct. 524, 61 L.Ed. 1086 (1917)—§ **3.50, n. 3.**

Southwestern Greyhound Lines v. Crown Coach Co., 178 F.2d 628 (8th Cir. 1949)—§ **17.6, n. 3.**

Soviero v. Franklin Nat. Bank of Long Island, 328 F.2d 446 (2nd Cir.1964)—§ **23.20, n. 2, 11.**

Spalding v. Commissioner, 537 F.2d 666 (2nd Cir.1976)—§ **13.5, n. 2; § 15.13, n. 4.**

Spano's Estate, In re, 49 N.J. 263, 229 A.2d 645 (N.J.1967)—§ **16.1, n. 12; § 20.2, n. 4.**

Sparks v. Green, 259 Or. 93, 485 P.2d 400 (Or.1971)—§ **19.3, n. 13.**

Sparling v. Hoffman Const. Co., Inc., 864 F.2d 635 (9th Cir.1988)—§ **6.3, n. 22; § 11.3, n. 21.**

Spatz v. Nascone, 364 F.Supp. 967 (W.D.Pa. 1973)—§ **11.6, n. 3.**

Speckine v. Stanwick Intern., Inc., 503 F.Supp. 1055 (W.D.Mich.1980)—§ **8.4, n. 3.**

Spence v. Hughes, 485 So.2d 903 (Fla.App. 5 Dist.1986)—§ **17.58, n. 5.**

Spence v. Spence, 239 Ala. 480, 195 So. 717 (Ala.1940)—§ **20.5, n. 6.**

Spencer v. Myers, 150 N.Y. 269, 44 N.E. 942 (N.Y.1896)—§ **19.29, n. 3.**

Spencer v. People, 133 Colo. 196, 292 P.2d 971 (Colo.1956)—§ **13.12, n. 1.**

Spencer v. Wolf, 49 Neb. 8, 67 N.W. 858 (Neb.1896)—§ **22.7, n. 1.**

Sperry Rand Corp. v. Industrial Supply Corp., 337 F.2d 363 (5th Cir.1964)—§ **18.24, n. 6, 8.**

Spicer v. New York Life Ins. Co., 237 Mo. App. 725, 167 S.W.2d 457 (Mo.App. 1942)—§ **21.6, n. 6.**

Spiegel v. Rabinovitz, 121 F.3d 251 (7th Cir.1997)—§ **13.2, n. 4; § 13.6, n. 2.**

Spiess v. C. Itoh & Co. (America), Inc., 643 F.2d 353 (5th Cir.1981)—§ **3.58, n. 6.**

Spiliada Maritime Corp. v. Cansulex Ltd. (The Spiliada) (HL 1986)—§ **11.8, n. 2.**

Spinozzi v. ITT Sheraton Corp., 174 F.3d 842 (7th Cir.1999)—§ **17.37, n. 4; § 17.48, n. 5.**

Spooner v. Paul Revere Life Ins. Co., 578 F.Supp. 369 (E.D.Mich.1984)—§ **23.3, n. 4.**

Sporn v. Celebrity, Inc., 129 N.J.Super. 449, 324 A.2d 71 (N.J.Super.L.1974)—§ **12.17, n. 10.**

Spradlin v. State Compensation Com'r, 145 W.Va. 202, 113 S.E.2d 832 (W.Va. 1960)—§ **13.2, n. 10.**

Spragins v. Louise Plantation, Inc., 391 So.2d 97 (Miss.1980)—§ **2.17, n. 11; § 2.23, n. 2.**

Sprayberry v. Culberson, 32 Ga. 299 (Ga. 1861)—§ **22.7, n. 2.**

Spreckels v. Spreckels, 116 Cal. 339, 48 P. 228 (Cal.1897)—§ **14.7, n. 3.**

Sprick v. Sprick, 25 S.W.3d 7 (Tex.App.-El Paso 1999)—§ **14.16, n. 8.**

Springfield Oil Services, Inc. v. Costello, 941 F.Supp. 45 (E.D.Pa.1996)—§ **17.40, n. 26; § 18.1, n. 17.**

Springfield Rare Coin Galleries, Inc. v. Johnson, 115 Ill.2d 221, 104 Ill.Dec. 743, 503 N.E.2d 300 (Ill.1986)—§ **11.13, n. 16.**

Sprow v. Hartford Ins. Co., 594 F.2d 412 (5th Cir.1979)—§ **10.4, n. 12, 14.**

Spurgeon v. Mission State Bank, 151 F.2d 702 (8th Cir.1945)—§ **4.37, n. 10; § 4.43, n. 1.**

Squire v. Vazquez, 52 Ga.App. 712, 184 S.E. 629 (Ga.App.1936)—§ **4.36, n. 1.**

Squire v. Vazquez, 52 Ga.App. 215, 183 S.E. 127 (Ga.App.1935)—§ **20.3, n. 1.**

Squires, United States v., 378 F.Supp. 798 (S.D.Iowa 1974)—§ **19.18, n. 21.**

S & S Chopper Service, Inc. v. Scripter, 59 Ohio App.2d 311, 394 N.E.2d 1011 (Ohio App. 6 Dist.1977)—§ **18.29, n. 3.**

Stabile, In re, 348 Pa. 587, 36 A.2d 451 (Pa.1944)—§ **4.13, n. 2.**

Stabilisierungsfonds Fur Wein v. Kaiser Stuhl Wine Distributors Pty. Ltd., 647 F.2d 200, 207 U.S.App.D.C. 375 (D.C.Cir.1981)—§ **9.3, n. 4.**

Stacy v. St. Charles Custom Kitchens of Memphis, Inc., 284 Ark. 441, 683 S.W.2d 225 (Ark.1985)—§ **2.19, n. 23.**

Stacy v. Thrasher for Use of Sellers, 47 U.S. 44, 6 How. 44, 12 L.Ed. 337 (1848)— § **22.20, n. 1, 6, 8.**

Stacy's Estate, In re, 131 Vt. 130, 300 A.2d 556 (Vt.1973)—§ **20.3, n. 5; § 22.23, n. 9.**

Staedler v. Staedler, 6 N.J. 380, 78 A.2d 896 (N.J.1951)—§ **15.10, n. 2.**

Stafford v. Briggs, 444 U.S. 527, 100 S.Ct. 774, 63 L.Ed.2d 1 (1980)—§ **10.2; § 10.2, n. 8.**

Stafford v. People, 144 Cal.App.2d 79, 300 P.2d 231 (Cal.App. 2 Dist.1956)—§ **5.20, n. 5.**

Stagg v. Green, 47 Mo. 500 (Mo.1871)— § **22.20, n. 19.**

Staigg v. Atkinson, 144 Mass. 564, 12 N.E. 354 (Mass.1887)—§ **20.6, n. 17; § 20.8, n. 9.**

Standal v. Armstrong Cork Co., 356 N.W.2d 380 (Minn.App.1984)—§ **17.76, n. 30.**

Standard Leasing Corp. v. Schmidt Aviation, Inc., 264 Ark. 851, 576 S.W.2d 181 (Ark.1979)—§ **2.17, n. 9; § 2.19, n. 23; § 2.22, n. 4.**

Standard Magnesium Corp. v. Fuchs, 251 F.2d 455 (10th Cir.1957)—§ **24.47, n. 5.**

Standard Oil Co. of Cal., United States v., 332 U.S. 301, 67 S.Ct. 1604, 91 L.Ed. 2067 (1947)—§ **3.51, n. 9; § 3.53, n. 1.**

Stanley v. Illinois, 405 U.S. 645, 92 S.Ct. 1208, 31 L.Ed.2d 551 (1972)—§ **16.5, n. 7.**

Stanton v. St. Jude Medical, Inc., 340 F.3d 690 (8th Cir.2003)—§ **7.2, n. 33.**

Stark Carpet Corp. v. M–Geough Robinson, Inc., 481 F.Supp. 499 (S.D.N.Y.1980)— § **6.9, n. 21; § 7.6, n. 9.**

Starkenstein v. Merrill Lynch Pierce Fenner & Smith Inc., 572 F.Supp. 189 (M.D.Fla.1983)—§ **18.21, n. 4.**

Starkey, State ex rel. v. Alaska Airlines, Inc., 68 Wash.2d 318, 413 P.2d 352 (Wash.1966)—§ **23.5, n. 5.**

Star–Kist Foods, Inc. v. County of Los Angeles, 227 Cal.Rptr. 391, 719 P.2d 987 (Cal.1986)—§ **11.13, n. 15.**

Starkweather v. American Bible Soc., 72 Ill. 50 (Ill.1874)—§ **20.6, n. 19.**

Starns v. Malkerson, 326 F.Supp. 234 (D.Minn.1970)—§ **4.13, n. 10.**

Starry v. Central Dakota Printing, Inc., 530 N.W.2d 323 (N.D.1995)—§ **2.25, n. 14;** § **18.21, n. 17.**

State v. _____ (see opposing party)

State Bank of Lombard v. Chart House, Inc., 46 B.R. 468 (N.D.Ill.1985)— § **23.12, n. 7.**

State by Van Riper v. American Sugar Refining Co., 20 N.J. 286, 119 A.2d 767 (N.J.1956)—§ **20.4, n. 6.**

State Election Bd. v. Bayh, 521 N.E.2d 1313 (Ind.1988)—§ **4.15, n. 3.**

State ex rel. v. _____ (see opposing party and relator)

State Farm Fire & Cas. Co. v. Tashire, 386 U.S. 523, 87 S.Ct. 1199, 18 L.Ed.2d 270 (1967)—§ **3.43, n. 6;** § **5.15, n. 10;** § **5.17, n. 5.**

State Farm Mut. Auto. Ins. Co. v. Baker, 14 Kan.App.2d 641, 797 P.2d 168 (Kan.App. 1990)—§ **18.5, n. 9.**

State Farm Mut. Auto. Ins. Co. v. Ballard, 132 N.M. 696, 54 P.3d 537 (N.M.2002)— § **17.56, n. 19;** § **18.26, n. 7.**

State Farm Mut. Auto. Ins. Co. v. Boury, 289 Ill.App.3d 903, 224 Ill.Dec. 677, 682 N.E.2d 238 (Ill.App. 1 Dist.1997)— § **17.56, n. 10.**

State Farm Mut. Auto. Ins. Co. v. Campbell, 538 U.S. 408, 123 S.Ct. 1513, 155 L.Ed.2d 585 (2003)—§ **3.17, n. 12;** § **3.23;** § **3.23, n. 26;** § **17.50, n. 3, 44.**

State Farm Mut. Auto. Ins. Co. v. Feldman, 359 N.W.2d 57 (Minn.App.1984)— § **17.58, n. 3.**

State Farm Mut. Auto. Ins. Co. v. Gillette, 251 Wis.2d 561, 641 N.W.2d 662 (Wis. 2002)—§ **2.13, n. 23, 26;** § **17.21, n. 15, 21;** § **17.56, n. 20;** § **18.26, n. 6.**

State Farm Mut. Auto. Ins. Co. v. Simmons' Estate, 84 N.J. 28, 417 A.2d 488 (N.J. 1980)—§ **2.17, n. 12.**

State Farm Mut. Auto. Ins. Co. v. Tennessee Farmers Mut. Ins. Co., 645 N.W.2d 169 (Minn.App.2002)—§ **8.2, n. 10.**

State Farm Mut. Ins. Co. v. Conyers, 109 N.M. 243, 784 P.2d 986 (N.M.1989)— § **18.21, n. 8.**

State in Interest of I., 68 N.J.Super. 598, 173 A.2d 457 (N.J.Juv. & Dom.Rel. 1961)—§ **13.12, n. 2.**

State of (see name of state)

State Securities, Inc. v. Anderson, 84 N.M. 629, 506 P.2d 786 (N.M.1973)—§ **11.17, n. 39.**

State Street Capital Corp. v. Dente, 855 F.Supp. 192 (S.D.Tex.1994)—§ **8.3, n. 11.**

State Tax Commission v. Cord, 81 Nev. 403, 404 P.2d 422 (Nev.1965)—§ **24.23, n. 5.**

State Tax Commission of Utah v. Aldrich, 316 U.S. 174, 62 S.Ct. 1008, 86 L.Ed. 1358 (1942)—§ **4.5, n. 3.**

Stathis v. National Car Rental Systems, Inc., 109 F.Supp.2d 55 (D.Mass.2000)— § **17.48, n. 17.**

Stauffer Chemical Co., United States v., 464 U.S. 165, 104 S.Ct. 575, 78 L.Ed.2d 388 (1984)—§ **24.1, n. 11, 12.**

Stavriotis v. Litwin, 710 F.Supp. 216 (N.D.Ill.1988)—§ **3.11, n. 2.**

Stawski Distributing Co., Inc. v. Browary Zywiec S.A., 349 F.3d 1023 (7th Cir. 2003)—§ **18.5, n. 33.**

St. Charles Land Trust, Achille Guibet v. St. Amant, 253 La. 243, 217 So.2d 385 (La.1968)—§ **22.4, n. 1.**

St. Clair v. Cox, 106 U.S. 350, 1 S.Ct. 354, 27 L.Ed. 222 (1882)—§ **10.14, n. 2, 4, 11.**

Stearns v. Burnham, 5 Me. 261 (Me.1828)— § **22.11, n. 11;** § **22.17, n. 3.**

Stearns v. Wright, 51 N.H. 600 (N.H. 1872)—§ **22.9, n. 1, 9.**

Steele v. Bryant, 132 Ky. 569, 116 S.W. 755 (Ky.1909)—§ **24.10, n. 3.**

Steele v. Connecticut General Life Ins. Co., 31 A.D. 389, 52 N.Y.S. 373 (N.Y.A.D. 4 Dept.1898)—§ **22.13, n. 4.**

Steele v. G. D. Searle & Co., 428 F.Supp. 646 (S.D.Miss.1977)—§ **3.9, n. 6.**

Steere, People v., 184 Mich. 556, 151 N.W. 617 (Mich.1915)—§ **13.8, n. 5;** § **13.14, n. 4.**

Steffke, Estate of, 538 F.2d 730 (7th Cir. 1976)—§ **15.13, n. 7.**

Steger v. Egyud, 219 Md. 331, 149 A.2d 762 (Md.1959)—§ **17.6, n. 3.**

Stein v. Fleischmann Co., 237 F. 679 (S.D.N.Y.1916)—§ **4.36, n. 11.**

Stein v. Siegel, 50 A.D.2d 916, 377 N.Y.S.2d 580 (N.Y.A.D. 2 Dept.1975)—§ **12.15, n. 9;** § **12.19, n. 19;** § **24.36, n. 6.**

Stein v. Stein, 641 S.W.2d 856 (Mo.App. W.D.1982)—§ **13.6, n. 4.**

Stein v. Welch, 78 Wash.App. 251, 896 P.2d 740 (Wash.App. Div. 2 1995)—§ **22.2, n. 1;** § **22.6, n. 1.**

Stell v. Firestone Tire & Rubber Co., 306 F.Supp. 17 (W.D.N.C.1969)—§ **3.11, n. 4.**

Stem v. Ahearn, 908 F.2d 1 (5th Cir. 1990)—§ **15.42, n. 14.**

Stencel Aero Engineering Corp. v. United States, 431 U.S. 666, 97 S.Ct. 2054, 52 L.Ed.2d 665 (1977)—§ **3.53, n. 4.**

Stenzel v. State Farm Mut. Auto. Ins. Co., 379 N.W.2d 674 (Minn.App.1986)— § **2.13, n. 20.**

Stephens v. Entre Computer Centers, Inc., 696 F.Supp. 636 (N.D.Ga.1988)—§ **6.3, n. 22;** § **11.3, n. 21;** § **11.6, n. 7.**

Stephens v. Household Finance Corp., 566 P.2d 1163 (Okla.1977)—§ **3.12, n. 6.**

Stephenson v. Stephenson, 41 Tenn.App. 659, 298 S.W.2d 36 (Tenn.Ct.App. 1956)—§ **13.9, n. 5.**

Stericycle, Inc. v. City of Delavan, 120 F.3d 657 (7th Cir.1997)—§ **24.1, n. 7.**

Sterling v. Blackwelder, 302 F.Supp. 1125 (E.D.Va.1968)—§ **19.2, n. 2, 7; § 19.9, n. 2, 6.**

Sterling Finance Management, L.P. v. UBS PaineWebber, Inc., 336 Ill.App.3d 442, 270 Ill.Dec. 336, 782 N.E.2d 895 (Ill. App. 1 Dist.2002)—§ **12.11, n. 7.**

Sterling Forest Associates, Ltd. v. Barnett-Range Corp., 673 F.Supp. 1394 (E.D.N.C.1987)—§ **11.4, n. 15.**

Sternberg v. St. Louis Union Trust Co., 394 Ill. 452, 68 N.E.2d 892 (Ill.1946)— § **20.6, n. 11.**

Sternhagen v. Dow Co., 282 Mont. 168, 935 P.2d 1139 (Mont.1997)—§ **17.74, n. 15.**

Stetson v. Morgan Guaranty Trust Co. of N. Y., 22 Conn.Supp. 158, 164 A.2d 239 (Conn.Super.1960)—§ **21.3, n. 13.**

Steven A. v. Rickie M. v. Kari S., 1 Cal.4th 816, 4 Cal.Rptr.2d 615, 823 P.2d 1216 (1992)—§ **16.5, n. 7.**

Steven C., In re, 169 Wis.2d 727, 486 N.W.2d 572 (Wis.App.1992)—§ **16.5, n. 9.**

Stevens v. Allen, 139 La. 658, 71 So. 936 (La.1916)—§ **4.34, n. 1.**

Stevens v. Larwill, 110 Mo.App. 140, 84 S.W. 113 (Mo.App.1904)—§ **4.20, n. 4; § 4.34, n. 1.**

Stevens v. Meaut, 264 F.Supp.2d 226 (E.D.Pa.2003)—§ **7.3, n. 10.**

Stevens v. Shields, 131 Misc.2d 145, 499 N.Y.S.2d 351 (N.Y.Sup.1986)—§ **17.45, n. 23.**

Stevenson v. Lima Locomotive Works, 180 Tenn. 137, 172 S.W.2d 812 (Tenn. 1943)—§ **18.6, n. 1.**

Stewart v. Commissioner, 95 F.2d 821 (5th Cir.1938)—§ **14.10, n. 2.**

Stewart v. Commissioner, 35 B.T.A. 406 (B.T.A.1937)—§ **14.7, n. 4.**

Stewart v. Continental Copper and Steel Industries, Inc., 67 A.D.2d 293, 414 N.Y.S.2d 910 (N.Y.A.D. 1 Dept.1979)— § **23.9, n. 8.**

Stewart v. Litchenberg, 148 La. 195, 86 So. 734 (La.1920)—§ **11.8, n. 3.**

Stewart v. Stewart, 32 Idaho 180, 180 P. 165 (Idaho 1919)—§ **20.12, n. 2.**

Stewart Organization, Inc. v. Ricoh Corp., 487 U.S. 22, 108 S.Ct. 2239, 101 L.Ed.2d 22 (1988)—§ **3.39; § 3.39, n. 17; § 3.40, n. 20; § 11.4; § 11.4, n. 5.**

Stewart, Matter of, 11 Paige Ch. 398, 5 N.Y. Ch. Ann. 175 (N.Y.Ch.1845)—§ **20.9, n. 7; § 21.11, n. 11.**

Stich, In re Marriage of, 169 Cal.App.3d 64, 214 Cal.Rptr. 919 (Cal.App. 1 Dist. 1985)—§ **15.23, n. 5.**

Stier, In re Marriage of, 178 Cal.App.3d 42, 223 Cal.Rptr. 599 (Cal.App. 4 Dist. 1986)—§ **14.9, n. 1.**

Stifel v. Hopkins, 477 F.2d 1116 (6th Cir. 1973)—§ **4.27; § 4.27, n. 3.**

Stiller v. Hardman, 324 F.2d 626 (2nd Cir. 1963)—§ **24.13, n. 2.**

Stillman v. Nickel Odeon, S.A., 608 F.Supp. 1050 (S.D.N.Y.1985)—§ **18.30, n. 1.**

Stine v. Moore, 213 F.2d 446 (5th Cir. 1954)—§ **4.4, n. 3; § 4.15, n. 2; § 4.21, n. 3.**

Stinson v. Geer, 42 Kan. 520, 22 P. 586 (Kan.1889)—§ **19.2, n. 5.**

St. John v. Hodges, 68 Tenn. 334 (Tenn. 1878)—§ **22.11, n. 15, 17.**

St. John's Episcopal Mission Center v. South Carolina Dept. of Social Services, 276 S.C. 507, 280 S.E.2d 207 (S.C. 1981)—§ **11.5, n. 3.**

St. Jude Medical, Inc. v. Lifecare Intern., Inc., 250 F.3d 587 (8th Cir.2001)—§ **8.5, n. 7, 10.**

St. Louis–San Francisco Ry. Co. v. Gitchoff, 68 Ill.2d 38, 11 Ill.Dec. 598, 369 N.E.2d 52 (Ill.1977)—§ **5.13, n. 20; § 6.9, n. 19.**

St. Louis Union Trust Co. v. Merrill Lynch, Pierce, Fenner & Smith, Inc., 412 F.Supp. 45 (E.D.Mo.1976)—§ **17.52, n. 2; § 23.4, n. 2.**

St. Mary's Franco–American Petroleum Co. v. State of West Virginia, 203 U.S. 183, 27 S.Ct. 132, 51 L.Ed. 144 (1906)— § **10.13, n. 3.**

Stober, Estate of, 108 Cal.App.3d 591, 166 Cal.Rptr. 628 (Cal.App. 4 Dist.1980)— § **21.10, n. 1.**

Stockmen's Livestock Exchange v. Thompson, 520 N.W.2d 255 (S.D.1994)—§ **2.17, n. 16; § 2.19, n. 16, 18; § 2.23, n. 2; § 18.21, n. 14.**

Stoddard v. Thomas, 60 Pa.Super. 177 (Pa.Super.1915)—§ **18.7, n. 9.**

Stoll v. Gottlieb, 305 U.S. 165, 59 S.Ct. 134, 83 L.Ed. 104 (1938)—§ **4.7, n. 4; § 24.12, n. 8.**

Stonewall Surplus Lines Ins. Co. v. Johnson Controls, Inc., 17 Cal.Rptr.2d 713 (Cal. App. 4 Dist.1993)—§ **18.26, n. 19.**

St. Onge v. McNeilus Truck and Mfg., Inc., 645 F.Supp. 280 (D.Minn.1986)—§ **4.18, n. 3.**

Stonington Partners, Inc. v. Lernout & Hauspie Speech Products N.V., 310 F.3d 118 (3rd Cir.2002)—§ **24.9, n. 7.**

Stoot v. Fluor Drilling Services, Inc., 851 F.2d 1514 (5th Cir.1988)—§ **18.11, n. 5.**

Store Decor Div. of Jas Intern., Inc. v. Stylex Worldwide Industries, Ltd., 767 F.Supp. 181 (N.D.Ill.1991)—§ **9.3, n. 4.**

Stork v. First Nat. Bank of South Carolina, 281 S.C. 515, 316 S.E.2d 400 (S.C. 1984)—§ **14.15, n. 2.**

St. Paul Fire and Marine Ins. Co. v. Jacobson, 826 F.Supp. 155 (E.D.Va.1993)—§ **18.21, n. 12.**

St. Paul Surplus Lines Ins. Co. v. Cannelton Industries, Inc., 828 F.Supp. 498 (W.D.Mich.1993)—§ **8.2, n. 13.**

St. Paul Surplus Lines Ins. Co. v. International Playtex, Inc., 245 Kan. 258, 777 P.2d 1259 (Kan.1989)—§ **2.21, n. 6, 54;** § **18.21, n. 6;** § **18.26, n. 19.**

St. Paul Surplus Lines Ins. Co. v. Mentor Corp., 503 N.W.2d 511 (Minn.App. 1993)—§ **24.9, n. 7.**

Strait v. Laird, 406 U.S. 341, 92 S.Ct. 1693, 32 L.Ed.2d 141 (1972)—§ **4.26, n. 4.**

Strang v. Strang, 258 Ark. 139, 523 S.W.2d 887 (Ark.1975)—§ **19.8, n. 3.**

Strassberg v. New England Mut. Life Ins. Co., 575 F.2d 1262 (9th Cir.1978)—§ **18.26, n. 9.**

Strassheim v. Daily, 221 U.S. 280, 31 S.Ct. 558, 55 L.Ed. 735 (1911)—§ **17.48, n. 24.**

Strate v. A–1 Contractors, 520 U.S. 438, 117 S.Ct. 1404, 137 L.Ed.2d 661 (1997)—§ **11.17;** § **11.17, n. 21, 25.**

Straub v. A P Green, Inc., 38 F.3d 448 (9th Cir.1994)—§ **10.19, n. 47.**

Straub v. Lyman Land & Investment Co., 30 S.D. 310, 138 N.W. 957 (S.D.1912)—§ **10.13, n. 3.**

Strauss v. Phillips, 189 Ill. 9, 59 N.E. 560 (Ill.1901)—§ **22.20, n. 1.**

Strauss' Estate, In re, 75 Misc.2d 454, 347 N.Y.S.2d 840 (N.Y.Sur.1973)—§ **19.2, n. 4, 7;** § **20.7, n. 1.**

Strawbridge v. Curtiss, 7 U.S. 267, 2 L.Ed. 435 (1806)—§ **5.17, n. 5.**

Strickland Ins. Group v. Shewmake, 642 So.2d 1159 (Fla.App. 5 Dist.1994)—§ **8.2, n. 10.**

Stringer v. Stringer, 689 So.2d 194 (Ala.Civ. App.1997)—§ **15.1, n. 6.**

Strom v. Montana Cent. R. Co., 81 Minn. 346, 84 N.W. 46 (Minn.1900)—§ **5.2, n. 15.**

Stromberg Metal Works, Inc. v. Press Mechanical, Inc., 77 F.3d 928 (7th Cir. 1996)—§ **18.7, n. 12.**

Strubbe v. Sonnenschein, 299 F.2d 185 (2nd Cir.1962)—§ **18.26, n. 9.**

Structural Dynamics Research Corp. v. Engineering Mechanics Research Corp., 401 F.Supp. 1102 (E.D.Mich.1975)—§ **18.29;** § **18.29, n. 7.**

Struebin v. State, 322 N.W.2d 84 (Iowa 1982)—§ **17.43, n. 16.**

Stuart v. Colorado Interstate Gas Co., 271 F.3d 1221 (10th Cir.2001)—§ **17.60, n. 5;** § **17.61, n. 4.**

Stull's Estate, In re, 183 Pa. 625, 39 A. 16 (Pa.1898)—§ **13.9, n. 7.**

Stults, In re, 65 B.R. 652 (Bkrtcy.W.D.Mich. 1986)—§ **19.19, n. 8.**

Stumpf v. Hallahan, 101 A.D. 383, 91 N.Y.S. 1062 (N.Y.A.D. 1 Dept.1905)—§ **19.10, n. 4.**

Sturgeon v. Korte, 34 Ohio St. 525 (Ohio 1878)—§ **4.27, n. 11.**

Sturgis v. State of Wash., 368 F.Supp. 38 (W.D.Wash.1973)—§ **4.13, n. 10.**

Sturiano v. Brooks, 523 So.2d 1126 (Fla. 1988)—§ **2.19, n. 6;** § **2.21, n. 43;** § **2.23, n. 6;** § **18.21, n. 4.**

Stutsman v. Kaiser Foundation Health Plan of Mid–Atlantic States, Inc., 546 A.2d 367 (D.C.1988)— § **2.24, n. 7;** § **13.3, n. 2;** § **17.45, n. 8, 24.**

Subacz v. Town Tower Motel Corp., 567 F.Supp. 1308 (N.D.Ind.1983)—§ **3.46, n. 14.**

Succession of (see name of party)

Sudler v. Sudler, 121 Md. 46, 88 A. 26 (Md.1913)—§ **4.37, n. 2, 7;** § **4.41, n. 2, 7.**

Sugarman v. Dougall, 413 U.S. 634, 93 S.Ct. 2842, 37 L.Ed.2d 853 (1973)—§ **3.58, n. 10, 17.**

Sugg v. Thornton, 132 U.S. 524, 10 S.Ct. 163, 33 L.Ed. 447 (1889)—§ **6.5, n. 1;** § **10.12, n. 9.**

Suglove v. Oklahoma Tax Commission, 605 P.2d 1315 (Okla.1979)—§ **4.17, n. 4;** § **4.36, n. 4.**

Suisse Atlantique Societe d'Armament Maritime S.A. v. N.V. Rotterdamsch Kolen Centrale, [1967] 1 A.C. 361—§ **18.2, n. 4.**

Suitt Const. Co., Inc. v. Seaman's Bank for Sav., 30 N.C.App. 155, 226 S.E.2d 408 (N.C.App.1976)—§ **18.28, n. 4.**

Sullivan v. American Bridge Co., 115 Pa.Super. 536, 176 A. 24 (Pa.Super.1935)—§ **13.6, n. 7.**

Sullivan v. Burkin, 390 Mass. 864, 460 N.E.2d 572 (Mass.1984)—§ **14.4, n. 8;** § **20.14, n. 12.**

Sullivan v. Savin Business Machines Corp., 560 F.Supp. 938 (N.D.Ind.1983)—§ **18.5, n. 5.**

Sulz v. Mutual Reserve Fund Life Ass'n, 145 N.Y. 563, 65 N.Y.St.Rep. 513, 40 N.E. 242 (N.Y.1895)—§ **22.13, n. 3.**

Sumitomo Shoji America, Inc. v. Avagliano, 457 U.S. 176, 102 S.Ct. 2374, 72 L.Ed.2d 765 (1982)—§ **23.2, n. 8;** § **23.3, n. 10.**

Summers v. Interstate Tractor & Equipment Co., 466 F.2d 42 (9th Cir.1972)—§ **17.27, n. 7.**

Summers v. Summers, 69 Nev. 83, 241 P.2d 1097 (Nev.1952)—§ **24.20, n. 3.**

Sumwalt v. Allstate Ins. Co., 12 Ohio St.3d 294, 466 N.E.2d 544 (Ohio 1984)—§ **17.56, n. 17.**

Sun First Nat. Bank of Orlando v. Miller, 77 F.R.D. 430 (S.D.N.Y.1978)—§ **10.16, n. 10.**

Sungard Data Systems, Inc. v. Central Parking Corp., 214 F.Supp.2d 879 (N.D.Ill.2002)—§ **8.2, n. 10.**

Sun Ins. Office Limited v. Clay, 265 F.2d 522 (5th Cir.1959)—§ **3.22, n. 6.**

Sun Oil Co. v. Wortman, 486 U.S. 717, 108 S.Ct. 2117, 100 L.Ed.2d 743 (1988)—§ **3.9, n. 6; § 3.10, n. 6; § 3.23, n. 24; § 3.27, n. 4; § 3.37, n. 3; § 3.48; § 3.48, n. 16; § 24.32, n. 2.**

Sunrise Indus. Joint Venture v. Ditric Optics, Inc., 873 F.Supp. 765 (E.D.N.Y. 1995)—§ **8.7, n. 5.**

Sun World Lines, Ltd. v. March Shipping Corp., 801 F.2d 1066 (8th Cir.1986)—§ **11.3, n. 22.**

Superfos Investments Ltd. v. FirstMiss Fertilizer, Inc., 809 F.Supp. 450 (S.D.Miss. 1992)—§ **18.4, n. 44.**

Superior Coal Co. v. Ruhrkohle, A.G., 83 F.R.D. 414 (E.D.Pa.1979)—§ **10.16, n. 8.**

Superior Court In and For Maricopa County, United States v., 144 Ariz. 265, 697 P.2d 658 (Ariz.1985)—§ **11.17, n. 39.**

Supreme Court of New Hampshire v. Piper, 470 U.S. 274, 105 S.Ct. 1272, 84 L.Ed.2d 205 (1985)—§ **3.32, n. 9.**

Susi v. Belle Acton Stables, Inc., 360 F.2d 704 (2nd Cir.1966)—§ **19.12, n. 2; § 19.20, n. 11.**

Suter v. Suter, 72 Miss. 345, 16 So. 673 (Miss.1895)—§ **4.34, n. 3.**

Sutherland v. Kennington Truck Service, Ltd., 454 Mich. 274, 562 N.W.2d 466 (Mich.1997)—§ **2.19, n. 25; § 2.24, n. 12; § 17.15; § 17.15, n. 6.**

Sutton v. Hollywood Entertainment Corp., 181 F.Supp.2d 504 (D.Md.2002)—§ **17.40, n. 30; § 18.1, n. 18.**

Sutton v. Leib, 342 U.S. 402, 72 S.Ct. 398, 96 L.Ed. 448 (1952)—§ **15.12; § 15.12, n. 4, 6; § 15.13; § 15.13, n. 1; § 15.15, n. 2, 7; § 15.28; § 15.28, n. 5; § 24.14, n. 7; § 24.29, n. 6.**

Sutton v. Leib, 188 F.2d 766 (7th Cir. 1951)—§ **15.12, n. 5; § 15.13.**

Suydam v. Suydam, 404 F.2d 1332, 131 U.S.App.D.C. 355 (D.C.Cir.1968)—§ **22.21, n. 11.**

Suzanna, Ex parte, 295 F. 713 (D.Mass. 1924)—§ **13.6, n. 12.**

Svege v. Mercedes Benz Credit Corp., 182 F.Supp.2d 226 (D.Conn.2002)—§ **17.36, n. 15; § 17.48, n. 11.**

Svenska Handelsbanken v. Carlson, 258 F.Supp. 448 (D.Mass.1966)—§ **24.35, n. 6.**

Svoboda v. Svoboda, 61 Tenn.App. 444, 454 S.W.2d 722 (Tenn.Ct.App.1969)—§ **22.2, n. 1.**

Swain v. Swain, 339 So.2d 453 (La.App. 1 Cir.1976)—§ **19.8, n. 14.**

Swancy v. Scott, 28 Tenn. 327 (Tenn. 1848)—§ **22.10, n. 4; § 22.15, n. 8.**

Swank v. Hufnagle, 111 Ind. 453, 12 N.E. 303 (Ind.1887)—§ **19.3, n. 1, 2; § 19.9, n. 4.**

Swann v. Swann, 21 F. 299 (C.C.E.D.Ark. 1884)—§ **18.4, n. 42.**

Swanson v. Image Bank, Inc., 206 Ariz. 264, 77 P.3d 439 (Ariz.2003)—§ **18.9, n. 2.**

Swanson v. Image Bank, Inc., 202 Ariz. 226, 43 P.3d 174 (Ariz.App. Div. 2 2002)—§ **18.9, n. 1.**

Swanson v. United–Greenfield Corp., 239 F.Supp. 299 (D.Conn.1965)—§ **18.5, n. 39.**

Swarb v. Lennox, 405 U.S. 191, 92 S.Ct. 767, 31 L.Ed.2d 138 (1972)—§ **6.3, n. 12; § 12.5, n. 4; § 24.15, n. 3.**

Swartz v. McNabb, 830 So.2d 1093 (La.App. 3 Cir.2002)—§ **17.56, n. 20.**

Sweitzer, In re, 111 B.R. 792 (Bkrtcy. W.D.Wis.1990)—§ **14.16, n. 16.**

Swetland v. Swetland, 149 A. 50 (N.J.Ch. 1930)—§ **21.6, n. 3.**

Swiss American Bank, Ltd., United States v., 274 F.3d 610 (1st Cir.2001)—§ **7.3, n. 11.**

Swiss American Bank, Ltd., United States v., 191 F.3d 30 (1st Cir.1999)—§ **10.5, n. 8.**

Swope v. Mitchell, 324 So.2d 461 (La.App. 3 Cir.1975)—§ **14.9, n. 1; § 14.11, n. 2.**

Sworoski v. Sworoski, 75 N.H. 1, 70 A. 119 (N.H.1908)—§ **4.34, n. 1.**

Sybron Transition Corp. v. Security Ins. Co. of Hartford, 107 F.3d 1250 (7th Cir. 1997)—§ **18.7, n. 8.**

Sylvane v. Whelan, 506 F.Supp. 1355 (E.D.N.Y.1981)—§ **3.55, n. 8.**

Sylvester v. Sylvester, 723 P.2d 1253 (Alaska 1986)—§ **19.3, n. 16.**

Sylvestri v. Warner & Swasey Co., 398 F.2d 598 (2nd Cir.1968)—§ **3.39, n. 10.**

Symonette Shipyards, Limited v. Clark, 365 F.2d 464 (5th Cir.1966)—§ **17.63, n. 22.**

Syndicate 420 at Lloyd's London v. Early American Ins. Co., 796 F.2d 821 (5th Cir.1986)—§ **11.9, n. 5.**

Syntex Ophthalmics, Inc. v. Novicky, 745 F.2d 1423 (Fed.Cir.1984)—§ **17.53, n. 5.**

System Operations, Inc. v. Scientific Games Development Corp., 555 F.2d 1131 (3rd Cir.1977)—§ **17.53, n. 4.**

Systems Designs, Inc. v. New Customware Co., Inc., 248 F.Supp.2d 1093 (D.Utah 2003)—§ **9.3, n. 8.**

Szollosy v. Hyatt Corp., 208 F.Supp.2d 205 (D.Conn.2002)—§ **17.63, n. 4.**

Szumlicz v. Norwegian America Line, Inc., 698 F.2d 1192 (11th Cir.1983)—§ **17.63, n. 23.**

T

Tabas v. Crosby, 444 A.2d 250 (Del.Ch. 1982)—§ **22.19, n. 12.**

Tabbagh's Estate, In re, 167 Misc. 156, 3 N.Y.S.2d 542 (N.Y.Sur.1938)—§ **21.6, n. 4.**

Taca Intern. Airlines, S. A. v. Rolls–Royce of England, Limited, 256 N.Y.S.2d 129, 204 N.E.2d 329 (N.Y.1965)—§ **23.20, n. 7.**

Ta-cha-na-tah, State v., 64 N.C. 614 (N.C. 1870)—§ **13.18, n. 11.**

Taggart & Taggart Seed, Inc. v. First Tennessee Bank Nat. Ass'n, 684 F.Supp. 230 (E.D.Ark.1988)—§ **19.3, n. 11; § 19.10, n. 6.**

Tahan v. Hodgson, 662 F.2d 862, 213 U.S.App.D.C. 306 (D.C.Cir.1981)—§ **24.35, n. 8; § 24.37, n. 3.**

Tal v. Tal, 158 Misc.2d 703, 601 N.Y.S.2d 530 (N.Y.Sup.1993)—§ **15.24, n. 7.**

Talbot v. Chamberlain, 149 Mass. 57, 20 N.E. 305 (Mass.1889)—§ **4.45, n. 2, 3.**

Tallant v. State, 658 S.W.2d 828 (Tex.App.-Fort Worth 1983)—§ **12.15, n. 9.**

Talley v. Commonwealth, 127 Va. 516, 103 S.E. 612 (Va.1920)—§ **4.13, n. 2.**

Talmadge's Adm'r v. Talmadge, 66 Ala. 199 (Ala.1880)—§ **4.18, n. 1; § 4.19, n. 2; § 4.20, n. 2.**

Talmage v. Chapel, 16 Mass. 71 (Mass. 1819)—§ **22.18, n. 9.**

Talmudical Academy of Baltimore v. Harris, 238 So.2d 161 (Fla.App. 3 Dist.1970)—§ **18.38, n. 5.**

Tang, Application of, 39 A.D.2d 357, 333 N.Y.S.2d 964 (N.Y.A.D. 1 Dept.1972)—§ **4.13, n. 3.**

Tanges v. Heidelberg North America, Inc., 93 N.Y.2d 48, 687 N.Y.S.2d 604, 710 N.E.2d 250 (N.Y.1999)—§ **3.9, n. 4, 8; § 17.74, n. 20; § 17.78, n. 11.**

Tanner v. Hancock, 5 Kan.App.2d 558, 619 P.2d 1177 (Kan.App.1980)—§ **24.13, n. 7; § 24.14, n. 9.**

Tannerfors v. American Fidelity Fire Ins. Co., 535 F.2d 1247 (3rd Cir.1976)—§ **19.29, n. 3.**

Tannerfors v. American Fidelity Fire Ins. Co., 397 F.Supp. 141 (D.N.J.1975)—§ **18.37, n. 12.**

Taormina v. Taormina Corp., 35 Del.Ch. 17, 109 A.2d 400 (Del.Ch.1954)—§ **21.2, n. 5.**

Tapley v. Proctor, 150 Ga.App. 337, 258 S.E.2d 25 (Ga.App.1979)—§ **22.18, n. 9.**

Tapp's Estate, Matter of, 569 S.W.2d 281 (Mo.App.1978)—§ **16.6, n. 5.**

Tart v. Prescott's Pharmacies, Inc., 118 N.C.App. 516, 456 S.E.2d 121 (N.C.App. 1995)—§ **7.12, n. 8.**

Tate v. Tate, 149 W.Va. 591, 142 S.E.2d 751 (W.Va.1965)—§ **4.34, n. 3.**

Tatum v. Tatum, 241 F.2d 401 (9th Cir. 1957)—§ **13.6, n. 4.**

Taubenfeld v. Taubenfeld, 276 A.D. 873, 93 N.Y.S.2d 757 (N.Y.A.D. 2 Dept.1949)—§ **4.27, n. 12.**

Taubler v. Giraud, 655 F.2d 991 (9th Cir. 1981)—§ **7.11, n. 11.**

Taussig v. Wellington Fund, Inc., 187 F.Supp. 179 (D.Del.1960)—§ **17.53, n. 3.**

Taylor v. Barron, 35 N.H. 484 (N.H.1857)—§ **22.20, n. 34, 36.**

Taylor v. Bullock, 111 N.H. 214, 279 A.2d 585 (N.H.1971)—§ **17.21, n. 13.**

Taylor v. Canady, 536 A.2d 93 (D.C.1988)—§ **17.11, n. 8.**

Taylor, Estate of, 480 Pa. 488, 391 A.2d 991 (Pa.1978)—§ **20.5, n. 3.**

Taylor v. Milam, 89 F.Supp. 880 (W.D.Ark. 1950)—§ **4.21, n. 2.**

Taylor v. Murray, 231 Ga. 852, 204 S.E.2d 747 (Ga.1974)—§ **3.10, n. 1.**

Taylor v. Rorke, 279 N.J.Super. 63, 652 A.2d 207 (N.J.Super.A.D.1995)—§ **17.58, n. 9.**

Taylor v. Security Nat. Bank, 20 Ariz.App. 504, 514 P.2d 257 (Ariz.App. Div. 1 1973)—§ **18.21, n. 14.**

Taylor v. Standard Gas & Elec. Co., 306 U.S. 307, 306 U.S. 618, 59 S.Ct. 543, 83 L.Ed. 669 (1939)—§ **23.20, n. 2.**

Taylor v. State Farm Mut. Auto. Ins. Co., 248 La. 246, 178 So.2d 238 (La.1965)—§ **4.37, n. 2, 8.**

Taylor v. Taylor, 105 Nev. 384, 775 P.2d 703 (Nev.1989)—§ **14.11, n. 2.**

Taylor v. Taylor, 160 W.Va. 124, 230 S.E.2d 924 (W.Va.1976)—§ **13.5, n. 1.**

Taylor, United States v., 333 F.2d 633 (5th Cir.1964)—§ **3.52, n. 5.**

Taylor–Segan v. Rajagopal, 275 N.J.Super. 286, 645 A.2d 1272 (N.J.Super.A.D.1994)—§ **17.58, n. 9.**

Taylor's Estate, In re, 5 Ariz.App. 144, 424 P.2d 186 (Ariz.App.1967)—§ **20.13, n. 2.**

T. B. Harms Co. v. Eliscu, 339 F.2d 823 (2nd Cir.1964)—§ **3.54, n. 5.**

Teague v. Bad River Band of Lake Superior Tribe of Chippewa Indians, 265 Wis.2d 64, 665 N.W.2d 899 (Wis.2003)—§ **15.23, n. 7.**

Teamsters Local 639 Employer's Pension Trust v. Johnson, 1992 WL 200075 (D.D.C.1992)—§ **13.6, n. 9.**

Teas v. Kimball, 257 F.2d 817 (5th Cir. 1958)—§ **18.5, n. 40; § 18.37, n. 4.**

Teitelbaum, Commonwealth v., 160 Pa.Super. 286, 50 A.2d 713 (Pa.Super.1947)—§ **4.39, n. 1.**

TELCO Communications v. An Apple A Day, 977 F.Supp. 404 (E.D.Va.1997)—§ **7.8, n. 14, 16.**

Telectronics Pacing Systems, Inc., In re, 953 F.Supp. 909 (S.D.Ohio 1997)—§ **10.5, n. 11.**

Teledyne, Inc. v. Kone Corp., 892 F.2d 1404 (9th Cir.1989)—§ **5.12, n. 7; § 5.15, n. 6; § 7.2, n. 34.**

Telemedia Partners Worldwide Ltd. v. Hamelin Ltd., 1996 WL 41818 (S.D.N.Y. 1996)—§ **17.40, n. 28; § 18.1, n. 18.**

Teller v. Kaufman, 426 F.2d 128 (8th Cir. 1970)—§ **20.13, n. 4.**

Temple v. Synthes Corp., Ltd., 498 U.S. 5, 111 S.Ct. 315, 112 L.Ed.2d 263 (1990)— **§ 10.4, n. 4.**

Templeton v. Witham, 595 F.Supp. 770 (S.D.Cal.1984)—§ **15.42, n. 8.**

Tenna Mfg. Co., Inc. v. Columbia Union Nat. Bank and Trust Co., 484 F.Supp. 1214 (W.D.Mo.1980)—§ **18.38, n. 5.**

Tennessee Carolina Transp., Inc. v. Strick Corp., 16 N.C.App. 498, 192 S.E.2d 702 (N.C.App.1972)—§ **17.64, n. 10.**

Tercero v. Roman Catholic Diocese of Norwich, Connecticut, 132 N.M. 312, 48 P.3d 50 (N.M.2002)—§ **7.4, n. 8.**

Terenzio v. Nelson, 107 N.J.Super. 223, 258 A.2d 20 (N.J.Super.A.D.1969)—§ **3.17, n. 5.**

Terjen, Commonwealth v., 197 Va. 596, 90 S.E.2d 801 (Va.1956)—§ **14.9, n. 3.**

Terkel v. Hearth Rooms, Inc., 410 F.Supp. 1160 (W.D.Pa.1976)—§ **18.37, n. 1.**

Terlizzi v. Brodie, 38 A.D.2d 762, 329 N.Y.S.2d 589 (N.Y.A.D. 2 Dept.1972)— **§ 11.15, n. 3.**

Terrell v. Terrell, 578 S.W.2d 637 (Tenn. 1979)—§ **15.20, n. 10;** § **15.28, n. 2.**

Teseniar v. Spicer, 74 P.3d 910 (Alaska 2003)—§ **15.34, n. 8.**

Testa v. Katt, 330 U.S. 386, 67 S.Ct. 810, 91 L.Ed. 967 (1947)—§ **11.13;** § **11.13, n. 6.**

Texair Flyers, Inc. v. District Court, First Judicial Dist., 180 Colo. 432, 506 P.2d 367 (Colo.1973)—§ **22.10, n. 10;** § **22.19, n. 10.**

Texas v. Fasken, (unreported)—§ **3.59, n. 3.**

Texas v. New Jersey, 379 U.S. 674, 85 S.Ct. 626, 13 L.Ed.2d 596 (1965)—§ **3.24, n. 18;** § **3.50, n. 3;** § **20.4, n. 8.**

Texas City Refining, Inc. v. Grand Bahama Petroleum Co., Ltd., 347 A.2d 657 (Del. Supr.1975)—§ **11.11, n. 2.**

Texas Commerce Bank Nat. Ass'n v. Interpol '80 Ltd. Partnership, 703 S.W.2d 765 (Tex.App.-Corpus Christi 1985)— **§ 18.14, n. 10;** § **18.23, n. 6.**

Texas & P. Ry. Co. v. Humble, 181 U.S. 57, 21 S.Ct. 526, 45 L.Ed. 747 (1901)— **§ 17.6, n. 5.**

Texas, State of v. State of Florida, 306 U.S. 398, 59 S.Ct. 563, 83 L.Ed. 817 (1939)— **§ 4.5;** § **4.5, n. 8;** § **4.17, n. 2;** § **4.22, n. 1.**

Texas, State of v. Pankey, 441 F.2d 236 (10th Cir.1971)—§ **3.49, n. 7;** § **3.50, n. 3, 5.**

Texas Tunneling Co. v. City of Chattanooga, Tenn., 204 F.Supp. 821 (E.D.Tenn. 1962)—§ **17.52, n. 1.**

Textile Workers Union of America v. Lincoln Mills of Ala., 353 U.S. 448, 77 S.Ct. 912, 1 L.Ed.2d 972 (1957)—§ **3.50, n. 2.**

T. G. I. Friday's, Inc. v. International Restaurant Group, Inc., 569 F.2d 895 (5th Cir.1978)—§ **17.53, n. 5.**

Thayer v. City of Boston, 124 Mass. 132 (Mass.1878)—§ **4.24, n. 1.**

Thayer, State ex rel. School Dist. Board v., 74 Wis. 48, 41 N.W. 1014 (Wis.1889)— **§ 4.13, n. 2.**

Thayer v. Thayer, 187 N.C. 573, 122 S.E. 307 (N.C.1924)—§ **4.38, n. 1.**

The Admiral Peoples, 295 U.S. 649, 55 S.Ct. 885, 79 L.Ed. 1633 (1935)—§ **10.6, n. 9.**

The Antelope, 23 U.S. 66, 6 L.Ed. 268 (1825)—§ **3.17, n. 1, 4;** § **24.19, n. 1.**

The Atlantic Star, [1974] A.C. 436—§ **11.8, n. 2.**

The Belgenland, 114 U.S. 355, 5 S.Ct. 860, 29 L.Ed. 152 (1885)—§ **17.63, n. 32.**

The Bremen v. Zapata Off-Shore Co., 407 U.S. 1, 92 S.Ct. 1907, 32 L.Ed.2d 513 (1972)—§ **2.26, n. 17;** § **3.39, n. 18;** § **6.3;** § **6.3, n. 14, 22;** § **11.2, n. 11;** § **11.3, n. 6;** § **11.5;** § **11.5, n. 2;** § **18.5, n. 4;** § **18.9, n. 12;** § **23.16, n. 4;** § **24.11, n. 1.**

The Genesee Chief, 53 U.S. 443, 12 How. 443, 13 L.Ed. 1058 (1851)—§ **10.6, n. 8.**

The Harrisburg, 119 U.S. 199, 7 S.Ct. 140, 30 L.Ed. 358 (1886)—§ **3.10, n. 1, 3.**

The Jefferson, 61 U.S. 393, 20 How. 393, 15 L.Ed. 961 (1857)—§ **10.6, n. 16.**

The Kensington, 183 U.S. 263, 22 S.Ct. 102, 46 L.Ed. 190 (1902)—§ **18.4, n. 43.**

The Miguel di Larrinaga, 217 F. 678 (S.D.N.Y.1914)—§ **18.4, n. 7.**

Theodoropoulos, Estate of, 93 Misc.2d 551, 402 N.Y.S.2d 927 (N.Y.Sur.1978)— **§ 22.3, n. 4.**

Theo. H. Davies & Co., Ltd. v. Republic of Marshall Islands, 174 F.3d 969 (9th Cir. 1998)—§ **10.19, n. 47.**

Thera-Kinetics, Inc. v. Managed Home Recovery, Inc., 1997 WL 610305 (N.D.Ill. 1997)—§ **17.26, n. 1;** § **18.4, n. 45.**

Theunissen v. Matthews, 935 F.2d 1454 (6th Cir.1991)—§ **5.12, n. 8;** § **7.2, n. 35.**

Thibodeaux v. King-Wilkinson, Inc., 386 So.2d 189 (La.App. 3 Cir.1980)—§ **8.4, n. 3.**

Thiele v. Northern Mut. Ins. Co., 36 F.Supp.2d 852 (E.D.Wis.1999)—§ **17.50, n. 61.**

Thigpen v. Greyhound Lines, Inc., 11 Ohio App.2d 179, 229 N.E.2d 107 (Ohio App. 10 Dist.1967)—§ **3.11, n. 6.**

Third Nat. Bank in Nashville v. WEDGE Group Inc., 882 F.2d 1087 (6th Cir. 1989)—§ **5.15, n. 6.**

Thomas v. Fidelity Brokerage Services, Inc., 977 F.Supp. 791 (W.D.La.1997)—§ **18.1, n. 18.**

Thomas v. Hanmer, 109 A.D.2d 80, 489 N.Y.S.2d 802 (N.Y.A.D. 4 Dept.1985)— **§ 17.56, n. 20;** § **17.57, n. 4.**

Thomas v. Price, 631 F.Supp. 114 (S.D.N.Y. 1986)—§ **11.6, n. 8.**

Thomas v. Thomas, 58 Wash.2d 377, 363 P.2d 107 (Wash.1961)—§ **4.26, n. 1.**

Thomas v. United Air Lines, Inc., 301 N.Y.S.2d 973, 249 N.E.2d 755 (N.Y. 1969)—§ **17.63, n. 4.**

Thomas v. Washington Gas Light Co., 448 U.S. 261, 100 S.Ct. 2647, 65 L.Ed.2d 757 (1980)—§ **17.59, n. 16;** § **17.60, n. 2;** § **24.1, n. 1;** § **24.23, n. 13;** § **24.26;** § **24.26, n. 1;** § **24.29, n. 8;** § **24.46, n. 6.**

Thomas Iron Co. v. Ensign–Bickford Co., 131 Conn. 665, 42 A.2d 145 (Conn 1945)—§ **3.10, n. 5.**

Thomas J.R., In re, 262 Wis.2d 217, 663 N.W.2d 734 (Wis.2003)—§ **15.29, n. 5.**

Thomason v. Chemical Bank, 234 Conn. 281, 661 A.2d 595 (Conn.1995)—§ **6.9, n. 21.**

Thomasson v. AmSouth Bank, N.A., 59 B.R. 997 (N.D.Ala.1986)—§ **23.13, n. 1.**

Thommessen v. Whitwill, 118 U.S. 520, 6 S.Ct. 1172, 30 L.Ed. 156 (1886)—§ **3.57, n. 16.**

Thompson v. Board of Regents of University of Nebraska, 187 Neb. 252, 188 N.W.2d 840 (Neb.1971)—§ **4.13, n. 10.**

Thompson v. Chrysler Motors Corp., 755 F.2d 1162 (5th Cir.1985)—§ **5.14, n. 12;** § **7.2, n. 19.**

Thompson v. Doe, 596 So.2d 1178 (Fla.App. 5 Dist.1992)—§ **7.4, n. 7.**

Thompson v. International Business Machines Corp., 862 F.Supp. 79 (S.D.N.Y. 1994)—§ **17.37, n. 16;** § **17.48, n. 7.**

Thompson v. Ketcham, 8 Johns. 189 (N.Y.Sup.1811)—§ **18.2, n. 1.**

Thompson v. Love, 42 Ohio St. 61 (Ohio 1884)—§ **4.33, n. 2;** § **4.34, n. 3.**

Thompson v. Nesheim, 280 Minn. 407, 159 N.W.2d 910 (Minn.1968)—§ **19.8, n. 6.**

Thompson v. Parnell, 81 Kan. 119, 105 P. 502 (Kan.1909)—§ **22.2, n. 3;** § **22.4, n. 1.**

Thompson v. Safeway Enterprises, Inc., 67 Ill.App.3d 914, 24 Ill.Dec. 561, 385 N.E.2d 702 (Ill.App. 1 Dist.1978)— § **24.13, n. 8.**

Thompson v. Thompson, 484 U.S. 174, 108 S.Ct. 513, 98 L.Ed.2d 512 (1988)— § **15.42;** § **15.42, n. 11.**

Thompson v. Whitman, 85 U.S. 457, 21 L.Ed. 897 (1873)—§ **24.14, n. 1;** § **24.16, n. 2.**

Thomson v. Continental Ins. Co., 66 Cal.2d 738, 59 Cal.Rptr. 101, 427 P.2d 765 (Cal. 1967)—§ **11.11, n. 2.**

Thomson v. Kyle, 39 Fla. 582, 23 So. 12 (Fla.1897)—§ **19.2, n. 3;** § **19.3, n. 6;** § **19.9, n. 4.**

Thorlin, In re Marriage of, 155 Ariz. 357, 746 P.2d 929 (Ariz.App. Div. 1 1987)— § **15.30, n. 1.**

Thorman v. Broderick, 27 So. 735 (La. 1900)—§ **22.11, n. 8.**

Thorne, In re, 240 N.Y. 444, 148 N.E. 630 (N.Y.1925)—§ **4.41, n. 1.**

Thornton v. Cessna Aircraft Co., 886 F.2d 85 (4th Cir.1989)—§ **3.9, n. 4;** § **17.64, n. 10;** § **17.79, n. 2.**

Thornton v. Sea Quest, Inc., 999 F.Supp. 1219 (N.D.Ind.1998)—§ **17.78, n. 10.**

Thornton's Estate, In re, 1 Cal.2d 1, 33 P.2d 1 (Cal.1934)—§ **14.6, n. 4;** § **14.9, n. 4.**

Three Affiliated Tribes of Fort Berthold Reservation v. Wold Engineering (Wold II), 476 U.S. 877, 106 S.Ct. 2305, 90 L.Ed.2d 881 (1986)—§ **11.17;** § **11.17, n. 28, 37.**

Three Affiliated Tribes of Fort Berthold Reservation v. Wold Engineering, P.C. (Wold I), 467 U.S. 138, 104 S.Ct. 2267, 81 L.Ed.2d 113 (1984)—§ **11.17;** § **11.17 n. 28.**

3D Systems, Inc. v. Aarotech Laboratories, Inc., 160 F.3d 1373 (Fed.Cir.1998)— § **9.4, n. 3.**

Threlkeld v. Worsham, 30 Ark.App. 251, 785 S.W.2d 249 (Ark.App.1990)—§ **2.19, n. 23;** § **17.21, n. 17.**

Thurber v. Carpenter, 18 R.I. 782, 31 A. 5 (R.I.1895)—§ **22.18, n. 12.**

Thurman v. Kyle, 71 Ga. 628 (Ga.1884)— § **19.9, n. 9.**

Thyssen Steel Co. v. M/V Kavo Yerakas, 911 F.Supp. 263 (S.D.Tex.1996)— § **12.18, n. 2.**

Ticketmaster–New York, Inc. v. Alioto, 26 F.3d 201 (1st Cir.1994)—§ **24.14, n. 3.**

Ticknor v. Choice Hotels Intern., Inc., 265 F.3d 931 (9th Cir.2001)—§ **18.4, n. 7;** § **18.5, n. 33.**

Ticor Title Ins. Co. v. Brown, 511 U.S. 117, 114 S.Ct. 1359, 128 L.Ed.2d 33 (1994)— § **10.11;** § **10.11, n. 8.**

Tidewater Oil Co. v. Waller, 302 F.2d 638 (10th Cir.1962)—§ **12.19, n. 8.**

Tiernan v. Westext Transport, Inc., 295 F.Supp. 1256 (D.R.I.1969)—§ **17.21, n. 16.**

Tillett v. J.I. Case Co., 580 F.Supp. 1276 (E.D.Wis.1984)—§ **17.21, n. 12.**

Tilt v. Kelsey, 207 U.S. 43, 28 S.Ct. 1, 52 L.Ed. 95 (1907)—§ **22.3, n. 5, 10, 13.**

Timken Roller Bearing Co. v. United States, 341 U.S. 593, 71 S.Ct. 971, 95 L.Ed. 1199 (1951)—§ **17.53, n. 1.**

Timmons v. Garrison, 23 Tenn. 148 (Tenn. 1843)—§ **19.15, n. 5.**

Tiner v. State, 279 Ala. 126, 182 So.2d 859 (Ala.1966)—§ **12.19, n. 7.**

Tingley Systems, Inc. v. CSC Consulting, Inc., 152 F.Supp.2d 95 (D.Mass.2001)— § **17.52, n. 3.**

Tirado v. Tirado, 357 S.W.2d 468 (Tex.Civ. App.-Texarkana 1962)—§ **14.10, n. 2.**

Tischendorf v. Tischendorf, 321 N.W.2d 405 (Minn.1982)—§ **15.43, n. 9.**

Tisdale v. Shell Oil Co., 723 F.Supp. 653 (M.D.Ala.1987)—§ **11.3, n. 22.**

TJN, Inc., In re, 207 B.R. 502 (Bkrtcy. D.S.C.1996)—§ **10.7, n. 19.**

Tkaczevski v. Ryder Truck Rental, Inc., 22 F.Supp.2d 169 (S.D.N.Y.1998)—§ **17.48, n. 6.**

T.M. Hylwa, M.D., Inc. v. Palka, 823 F.2d 310 (9th Cir.1987)—§ **8.4, n. 9; § 9.5, n. 11.**

TMI, In re, 89 F.3d 1106 (3rd Cir.1996)— § **3.46, n. 12.**

Toanone v. Williams, 405 F.Supp. 36 (E.D.Pa.1975)—§ **17.55, n. 4.**

Tod v. Mitchell, 228 Mass. 541, 117 N.E. 899 (Mass.1917)—§ **22.21, n. 14.**

Todd v. Armour, 1882 WL 18961 (Unknown Court - UK 1882)—§ **19.15, n. 7.**

Toga Mfg. Ltd., Matter of, 28 B.R. 165 (Bkrtcy.E.D.Mich.1983)—§ **23.18, n. 7.**

Tohato, Inc. v. Pinewild Management, Inc., 128 N.C.App. 386, 496 S.E.2d 800 (N.C.App.1998)—§ **18.7, n. 12.**

Toklan Royalty Corp. v. Tiffany, 193 Okla. 120, 141 P.2d 571 (Okla.1943)—§ **23.9, n. 3.**

Toledo Soc. for Crippled Children v. Hickok, 152 Tex. 578, 261 S.W.2d 692 (Tex. 1953)—§ **20.6, n. 20; § 20.7, n. 3, 4; § 20.14, n. 13; § 21.2, n. 7.**

Toledo Soc. for Crippled Children v. Hickok, 252 S.W.2d 739 (Tex.Civ.App.-Eastland 1952)—§ **14.6, n. 2.**

Toledo Traction Co. v. Cameron, 137 F. 48 (6th Cir.1905)—§ **4.40, n. 2.**

Toledo Trust Co. v. Santa Barbara Foundation, 32 Ohio St.3d 141, 512 N.E.2d 664 (Ohio 1987)—§ **20.8, n. 8; § 21.11, n. 5; § 21.13, n. 2.**

Toler's Estate, In re, 325 S.W.2d 755 (Mo. 1959)—§ **4.17, n. 2.**

Toll v. Moreno, 284 Md. 425, 397 A.2d 1009 (Md.1979)—§ **4.31, n. 6.**

Tolofson v. Jensen, [1994] 3 S.C.R. 1022 (S.C.C.1994)—§ **3.9, n. 2; § 17.7, n. 9; § 17.15, n. 19; § 17.26, n. 16; § 17.57, n. 6.**

Tolson v. Arden, 89 Wash.App. 21, 947 P.2d 1242 (Wash.App. Div. 2 1997)—§ **4.7, n. 2.**

Tolson v. Hodge, 411 F.2d 123 (4th Cir. 1969)—§ **22.19, n. 11.**

Tomczak v. Erie Ins. Exchange, 268 F.Supp. 185 (W.D.Pa.1967)—§ **22.14, n. 9.**

Tomlin v. Boeing Co., 650 F.2d 1065 (9th Cir.1981)—§ **24.24, n. 3.**

Toncray v. Toncray, 123 Tenn. 476, 131 S.W. 977 (Tenn.1910)— § **15.27, n. 1.**

Toner v. Conqueror Trust Co., 131 Kan. 651, 293 P. 745 (Kan.1930)—§ **22.11, n. 7.**

Tonetti's Will, In re, 53 Misc.2d 501, 279 N.Y.S.2d 299 (N.Y.Sur.1967)—§ **20.8, n. 8.**

Tooker v. Lopez, 24 N.Y.2d 569, 301 N.Y.S.2d 519, 249 N.E.2d 394 (N.Y. 1969)—§ **2.11, n. 23; § 2.14, n. 12; § 17.30; § 17.30, n. 3, 15; § 17.39, n. 15.**

Toomer v. Witsell, 334 U.S. 385, 68 S.Ct. 1156, 92 L.Ed. 1460 (1948)—§ **3.31, n. 3; § 3.32, n. 9.**

Tootle v. McClellan, 7 Ind.T. 64, 103 S.W. 766 (Indian Terr.1907)—§ **24.17, n. 6.**

Topcuoglu's Will, In re, 11 Misc.2d 859, 174 N.Y.S.2d 260 (N.Y.Sur.1958)—§ **24.17, n. 2.**

Torah Soft Ltd. v. Drosnin, 224 F.Supp.2d 704 (S.D.N.Y.2002)—§ **12.19, n. 1.**

Torlonia v. Torlonia, 108 Conn. 292, 142 A. 843 (Conn.1928)—§ **4.8, n. 1; § 20.12, n. 2.**

Toronto–Dominion Bank v. Hall, 367 F.Supp. 1009 (E.D.Ark.1973)—§ **24.35, n. 6, 8.**

Torres v. State, 119 N.M. 609, 894 P.2d 386 (N.M.1995)—§ **2.21, n. 18; § 17.8, n. 2.**

Torres, State ex rel. v. Mason, 315 Or. 386, 848 P.2d 592 (Or.1993)—§ **16.5, n. 9.**

Torres v. Torres, 144 N.J.Super. 540, 366 A.2d 713 (N.J.Super.Ch.1976)—§ **13.6, n. 12.**

Torrey v. Bruner, 60 Fla. 365, 53 So. 337 (Fla.1910)—§ **22.3, n. 9; § 22.4, n. 8.**

Torrington Co. v. Stutzman, 46 S.W.3d 829 (Tex.2000)—§ **17.76, n. 31.**

Tortuguero Logging Operation, Limited v. Houston, 349 S.W.2d 315 (Tex.Civ.App.-San Antonio 1961)—§ **12.15, n. 13.**

Total Oilfield Services, Inc. v. Garcia, 711 S.W.2d 237 (Tex.1986)—§ **3.19, n. 10.**

Toter v. Knight, 278 Pa.Super. 547, 420 A.2d 676 (Pa.Super.1980)—§ **17.58, n. 8.**

Tourton v. Flower, 3 P.Wms. 369 (1735)— § **22.14, n. 3.**

Toutant, In re Estate of, 247 Wis.2d 400, 633 N.W.2d 692 (Wis.App.2001)—§ **13.6, n. 9.**

Tower v. Tower, 120 Vt. 213, 138 A.2d 602 (Vt.1958)—§ **4.13, n. 2.**

Townes v. Durbin, 60 Ky. 352 (Ky.1861)— § **14.8, n. 4.**

Town of (see name of town)

Townsend v. Kendall, 4 Minn. 412 (Minn. 1860)—§ **22.26, n. 4, 5.**

Traglio v. Harris, 104 F.2d 439 (9th Cir. 1939)—§ **17.6, n. 5.**

Trailways, Inc. v. Clark, 794 S.W.2d 479 (Tex.App.-Corpus Christi 1990)—§ **3.19, n. 6, 10.**

Train v. Kendall, 137 Mass. 366 (Mass. 1884)—§ **19.30, n. 6.**

Trakman, In re, 33 B.R. 780 (Bkrtcy. S.D.N.Y.1983)—§ **23.18, n. 7.**

Trammell v. Kansas Compensation Bd., 142 Kan. 329, 46 P.2d 867 (Kan.1935)— **§ 4.37, n. 2.**

Tramontana v. S. A. Empresa De Viacao Aerea Rio Grandense, 350 F.2d 468, 121 U.S.App.D.C. 338 (D.C.Cir.1965)— **§ 3.14, n. 3.**

Trans–Asiatic Oil Ltd., S.A. v. Apex Oil Co., 604 F.Supp. 4 (D.Puerto Rico 1983)— **§ 10.6, n. 51.**

Transatlantic Cement, Inc. v. Lambert Freres et Cie., 462 F.Supp. 363 (S.D.N.Y.1978)—**§ 18.37, n. 4.**

Trask v. Karrick, 94 Vt. 70, 108 A. 846 (Vt.1920)—**§ 4.13, n. 2.**

Travelers Health Ass'n v. Virginia, 339 U.S. 643, 70 S.Ct. 927, 94 L.Ed. 1154 (1950)—**§ 7.12; § 7.12, n. 2; § 9.1; § 9.1, n. 8; § 9.6; § 9.6, n. 1; § 10.14, n. 1.**

Travelers Indem. Co. v. Allied–Signal, Inc., 718 F.Supp. 1252 (D.Md.1989)—**§ 18.27, n. 2.**

Travelers Indem. Co. v. Calvert Fire Ins. Co., 798 F.2d 826 (5th Cir.1986)— **§ 5.13, n. 19, 22; § 6.9, n. 20, 21.**

Travelers Indem. Co. v. Lake, 594 A.2d 38 (Del.Supr.1991)—**§ 2.16, n. 21; § 2.23, n. 1; § 17.26, n. 1, 7; § 17.39, n. 12; § 17.56, n. 20; § 18.21, n. 14.**

Travelers Ins. Co. v. Fields, 451 F.2d 1292 (6th Cir.1971)—**§ 18.37, n. 12.**

Travelers Ins. Co. v. Workmen's Compensation Appeals Bd., 68 Cal.2d 7, 64 Cal. Rptr. 440, 434 P.2d 992 (Cal.1967)— **§ 2.17, n. 8; § 2.24, n. 5.**

Travenol Laboratories, Inc. v. Zotal, Ltd., 394 Mass. 95, 474 N.E.2d 1070 (Mass. 1985)—**§ 18.24, n. 9.**

Traversi's Estate, In re, 189 Misc. 251, 64 N.Y.S.2d 453 (N.Y.Sur.1946)—**§ 20.6, n. 10, 13; § 20.11, n. 3; § 20.12, n. 3.**

Travis v. Anthes Imperial Limited, 473 F.2d 515 (8th Cir.1973)—**§ 10.9, n. 21.**

Travis v. Yale & Towne Mfg. Co., 252 U.S. 60, 40 S.Ct. 228, 64 L.Ed. 460 (1920)— **§ 3.32, n. 5, 9.**

Traylor v. Grafton, 273 Md. 649, 332 A.2d 651 (Md.1975)—**§ 18.23, n. 5.**

Treinies v. Sunshine Mining Co., 308 U.S. 66, 60 S.Ct. 44, 84 L.Ed. 85 (1939)— **§ 4.7, n. 4; § 15.6, n. 5; § 15.12, n. 7; § 22.3, n. 8, 13, 17; § 22.20, n. 27; § 24.2, n. 9, 11; § 24.10, n. 6; § 24.17, n. 15; § 24.29, n. 6.**

Tremblay v. Aetna Life Ins. Co., 97 Me. 547, 55 A. 509 (Me.1903)—**§ 24.34, n. 1.**

Triad International Maintenance Corp. v. Guernsey Air Leasing, Ltd., 178 F.Supp.2d 547 (M.D.N.C.2001)— **§ 19.26, n. 7.**

Triangle Underwriters, Inc. v. Honeywell, Inc., 457 F.Supp. 765 (E.D.N.Y.1978)— **§ 18.24, n. 7.**

Trigg's Estate, In re, 3 Ariz.App. 385, 414 P.2d 988 (Ariz.App.1966)—**§ 13.6, n. 2.**

Trilogy Development Group, Inc. v. Teknowledge Corp., 1996 WL 527325 (Del.Super.1996)—**§ 18.3, n. 1; § 18.12, n. 15.**

Trimble v. Gordon, 430 U.S. 762, 97 S.Ct. 1459, 52 L.Ed.2d 31 (1977)—**§ 3.54, n. 5; § 4.38, n. 4; § 13.19, n. 7; § 16.3; § 16.3, n. 6; § 20.2, n. 4.**

Trinh v. Citibank, N.A., 623 F.Supp. 1526 (E.D.Mich.1985)—**§ 3.36, n. 1.**

Tripp v. Tripp, 240 S.C. 334, 126 S.E.2d 9 (S.C.1962)—**§ 22.3, n. 1.**

Trippodo's Estate, Matter of, 161 Misc. 542, 292 N.Y.S. 296 (N.Y.Sur.1936)—**§ 4.33, n. 3.**

Tri–State Crematory Litigation, In re, 215 F.R.D. 660 (N.D.Ga.2003)—**§ 2.21, n. 15.**

Tri–State Loan & Trust Co. v. Lake Shore & M. S. Ry. Co., 76 Ind.App. 141, 131 N.E. 523 (Ind.App. 2 Div.1921)— **§ 22.10, n. 10.**

Trivette's Estate v. Trivette, 564 S.W.2d 672 (Tenn.Ct.App.1977)—**§ 19.8, n. 3.**

T.R.M., Matter of Adoption of, 525 N.E.2d 298 (Ind.1988)—**§ 4.15, n. 3.**

Trojan Engineering Corp. v. Green Mountain Power Corp., 293 Mass. 377, 200 N.E. 117 (Mass.1936)—**§ 11.16, n. 1.**

Trotter v. Trotter, 503 So.2d 1160 (La.App. 3 Cir.1987)—**§ 14.11, n. 2.**

Trotter v. Van Pelt, 144 Fla. 517, 198 So. 215 (Fla.1940)—**§ 20.6, n. 8.**

Trowbridge's Estate, In re, 266 N.Y. 283, 194 N.E. 756 (N.Y.1935)—**§ 4.5, n. 4.**

Troxel v. A.I. Dupont Institute, 450 Pa.Super. 71, 675 A.2d 314 (Pa.Super.1996)— **§ 17.42, n. 45; § 17.44, n. 24.**

Troxel v. A.I. duPont Institute, 431 Pa.Super. 464, 636 A.2d 1179 (Pa.Super.1994)—**§ 17.36, n. 15; § 17.42; § 17.42, n. 17, 39; § 17.44; § 17.44, n. 19.**

Trump v. Eighth Judicial Dist. Court of State of Nev. In and For County of Clark, 109 Nev. 687, 857 P.2d 740 (Nev. 1993)—**§ 5.14, n. 12; § 7.3, n. 10.**

Trussell v. United Underwriters, Limited, 236 F.Supp. 801 (D.Colo.1964)—**§ 3.45, n. 4.**

Trustees of Jesse Parker Williams Hospital v. Nisbet, 189 Ga. 807, 7 S.E.2d 737 (Ga.1940)—**§ 2.21, n. 15.**

Trusts Created by Agreement with Harrington, In re, 311 Minn. 403, 250 N.W.2d 163 (Minn.1977)—**§ 20.13, n. 4.**

TRWL Financial Establishment v. Select Intern., Inc., 527 N.W.2d 573 (Minn. App.1995)—**§ 8.5, n. 10; § 11.6, n. 10.**

Trzecki v. Gruenewald, 532 S.W.2d 209 (Mo.1976)—**§ 3.11, n. 5.**

Tsakonites v. Transpacific Carriers Corp., 246 F.Supp. 634 (S.D.N.Y.1965)— **§ 17.63, n. 23.**

Tschira v. Willingham, 135 F.3d 1077 (6th Cir.1998)—§ **12.18, n. 11**; § **18.7, n. 12.**

Tsilidis v. Pedakis, 132 So.2d 9 (Fla.App. 1 Dist.1961)—§ **16.6, n. 2.**

Tubos de Acero de Mexico, S.A. v. American Intern. Inv. Corp., Inc., 292 F.3d 471 (5th Cir.2002)—§ **17.50, n. 61.**

Tucci v. Club Mediterranee, S.A., 107 Cal. Rptr.2d 401 (Cal.App. 2 Dist.2001)— § **17.42**; § **17.42, n. 14, 20, 25**; § **17.60, n. 5.**

TUC Electronics, Inc. v. Eagle Telephonics, Inc., 698 F.Supp. 35 (D.Conn.1988)— § **11.4, n. 15**; § **11.6, n. 3.**

Tucker v. Kenney, 994 F.Supp. 412 (E.D.N.Y.1998)—§ **24.24, n. 5.**

Tucker v. Norfolk & W. R. Co., 403 F.Supp. 1372 (E.D.Mich.1975)—§ **17.8, n. 14.**

Tudor v. Vail, 195 Mass. 18, 80 N.E. 590 (Mass.1907)—§ **21.13, n. 4.**

Tuggle v. Helms, 231 Ga.App. 899, 499 S.E.2d 365 (Ga.App.1998)—§ **17.7, n. 7.**

Tuition Plan, Inc. v. Zicari, 70 Misc.2d 918, 335 N.Y.S.2d 95 (N.Y.Dist.Ct.1972)— § **18.28, n. 4.**

Tulsa Professional Collection Services, Inc. v. Pope, 485 U.S. 478, 108 S.Ct. 1340, 99 L.Ed.2d 565 (1988)—§ **5.16, n. 10**; § **12.3, n. 5, 12**; § **22.21, n. 2.**

Tune v. Philip Morris Inc., 766 So.2d 350 (Fla.App. 2 Dist.2000)—§ **17.44, n. 9**; § **17.64, n. 13**; § **17.70, n. 6.**

Turkey Exp., Inc. v. Skelton Motor Co., 246 Ark. 739, 439 S.W.2d 923 (Ark.1969)— § **12.17, n. 13.**

Turley v. Dreyfus, 1881 WL 8753 (La. 1881)—§ **22.20, n. 14.**

Turley v. Griffin, 508 S.W.2d 764 (Ky. 1974)—§ **15.42, n. 1.**

Turnbull v. Cole, 70 Colo. 364, 201 P. 887 (Colo.1921)—§ **19.15, n. 7.**

Turner v. Aldens, Inc., 179 N.J.Super. 596, 433 A.2d 439 (N.J.Super.A.D.1981)— § **18.4, n. 1.**

Turner v. Alton Banking & Trust Co., 166 F.2d 305 (8th Cir.1948)—§ **22.18, n. 2, 7.**

Turner v. Ford Motor Co., 81 Mich.App. 521, 265 N.W.2d 400 (Mich.App.1978)— § **12.17, n. 13.**

Turner v. Turner, 637 S.W.2d 764 (Mo.App. S.D.1982)—§ **22.25, n. 1.**

Turtur v. Rothschild Registry Intern., Inc., 26 F.3d 304 (2nd Cir.1994)—§ **17.40, n. 28.**

Tuthill Finance v. Cartaya, 133 A.D.2d 343, 519 N.Y.S.2d 243 (N.Y.A.D. 2 Dept. 1987)—§ **19.3, n. 11.**

Tuttle, United States ex rel. Modianos v., 12 F.2d 927 (E.D.La.1925)—§ **13.6, n. 12.**

Tutty, State v., 41 F. 753 (C.C.S.D.Ga. 1890)—§ **13.10, n. 1.**

Tutules' Estate, In re, 204 Cal.App.2d 481, 22 Cal.Rptr. 427 (Cal.App. 2 Dist. 1962)—§ **19.2, n. 2.**

Tutu Wells Contamination Litigation, In re, 846 F.Supp. 1243 (D.Virgin Islands 1993)—§ **7.5, n. 11, 13.**

TWE Retirement Fund Trust v. Ream, 198 Ariz. 268, 8 P.3d 1182 (Ariz.App. Div. 1 2000)—§ **24.10, n. 3.**

Twinlab Corp. v. Paulson, 283 A.D.2d 570, 724 N.Y.S.2d 496 (N.Y.A.D. 2 Dept. 2001)—§ **17.40, n. 28.**

Two Children by H.N.R., Matter of Adoption of, 285 N.J.Super. 1, 666 A.2d 535 (N.J.Super.A.D.1995)—§ **16.4, n. 3.**

Twohy v. First Nat. Bank of Chicago, 758 F.2d 1185 (7th Cir.1985)—§ **12.18, n. 17**; § **17.40, n. 28**; § **18.1, n. 18.**

Tyler v. Judges of the Court of Registration, 175 Mass. 71, 55 N.E. 812 (Mass.1900)— § **5.5, n. 6.**

Tyler v. Thompson, 44 Tex. 497 (Tex. 1876)—§ **22.21, n. 6.**

Tyma v. Montgomery County, 369 Md. 497, 801 A.2d 148 (Md.2002)—§ **15.1, n. 7.**

Tyrone v. Kelley, 21 Cal.App.3d 817, 99 Cal.Rptr. 290 (Cal.App. 1 Dist.1971)— § **18.33, n. 3.**

Tyson v. Connecticut General Life Ins. Co., 495 F.Supp. 240 (E.D.Mich.1980)— § **23.3, n. 4.**

U

Udny v. Udny, 1 H.L.(Sc.) 441 (1869)— § **4.28, n. 2**; § **4.36, n. 1, 8.**

Uebersee Finanz–Korporation, A.G. v. McGrath, 343 U.S. 205, 72 S.Ct. 618, 96 L.Ed. 888 (1952)—§ **23.3, n. 9.**

Uhrig v. Pulliam, 713 S.W.2d 649 (Tenn. 1986)—§ **14.15, n. 1.**

Uihlein's Estate, In re, 269 Wis. 170, 68 N.W.2d 816 (Wis.1955)—§ **16.6, n. 5.**

Umana v. SCM, 291 A.D.2d 446, 737 N.Y.S.2d 556 (N.Y.A.D. 2 Dept.2002)— § **12.9, n. 15.**

Umbenhauer v. Woog, 969 F.2d 25 (3rd Cir.1992)—§ **5.16, n. 11.**

Unanue v. Unanue, 141 A.D.2d 31, 532 N.Y.S.2d 769 (N.Y.A.D. 2 Dept.1988)— § **4.13, n. 11.**

Uncle Henry's Inc. v. Plaut Consulting Inc., 240 F.Supp.2d 63 (D.Me.2003)—§ **17.52, n. 2.**

Underhill v. Hernandez, 168 U.S. 250, 18 S.Ct. 83, 42 L.Ed. 456 (1897)—§ **11.13, n. 18.**

Underwriters Nat. Assur. Co. v. North Carolina Life and Acc. and Health Ins. Guaranty Ass'n, 455 U.S. 691, 102 S.Ct. 1357, 71 L.Ed.2d 558 (1982)—§ **22.20, n. 28**; § **22.21, n. 17**; § **24.10, n. 7**; § **24.14, n. 2.**

Uni–Bond, Ltd. v. Schultz, 607 F.Supp. 1361 (E.D.Wis.1985)—§ **8.5, n. 9.**

Unigard Ins. Group v. Royal Globe Ins. Co., 100 Idaho 123, 594 P.2d 633 (Idaho 1979)—§ **18.21, n. 14.**

Union Carbide Corp. v. Aetna Cas. and Sur. Co., 212 Conn. 311, 562 A.2d 15 (Conn. 1989)—§ **18.26, n. 13.**

Union Carbide Corp. Gas Plant Disaster at Bhopal, India in Dec., 1984, In re, 809 F.2d 195 (2nd Cir.1987)—§ **11.8, n. 6; § 11.9, n. 6.**

Union Nat. Bank v. Hartwell, 84 Ala. 379, 4 So. 156 (Ala.1888)—§ **19.32, n. 8.**

Union Nat. Bank of Wichita, Kan. v. Lamb, 337 U.S. 38, 69 S.Ct. 911, 93 L.Ed. 1190 (1949)—§ **24.2, n. 8; § 24.20, n. 1; § 24.24, n. 3; § 24.32, n. 2.**

Union Oil Co. of California v. John Brown E&C, 1994 WL 535108 (N.D.Ill.1994)—§ **17.40, n. 28.**

Union Planters Nat. Bank of Memphis v. ABC Records, Inc., 82 F.R.D. 472 (W.D.Tenn.1979)—§ **12.11, n. 7.**

Union Sav. Bank v. DeMarco, 105 R.I. 592, 254 A.2d 81 (R.I.1969)—§ **19.3, n. 8; § 19.9, n. 5, 10.**

Unisys Corp. v. Insurance Co. of North America, 154 N.J. 217, 712 A.2d 649 (N.J.1998)—§ **18.26, n. 13.**

United Airlines, Inc. v. Kozel, 33 Va.App. 695, 536 S.E.2d 473 (Va.App.2000)—§ **24.26, n. 9.**

United Bank Ltd. v. Cosmic Intern., Inc., 542 F.2d 868 (2nd Cir.1976)—§ **19.31, n. 2.**

United Broth. of Carpenters and Joiners of America, AFL–CIO, Ex parte, 688 So.2d 246 (Ala.1997)—§ **5.13, n. 22.**

United Coal Companies v. Powell Const. Co., 839 F.2d 958 (3rd Cir.1988)—§ **12.11, n. 7.**

United Counties Trust Co. v. Mac Lum, Inc., 643 F.2d 1140 (5th Cir.1981)—§ **18.12, n. 1.**

United Divers Supply Co. v. Commercial Credit Co., 289 F. 316 (5th Cir.1923)—§ **18.6, n. 4; § 18.7, n. 9.**

United Elec., Radio and Mach. Workers of America v. 163 Pleasant Street Corp., 960 F.2d 1080 (1st Cir.1992)—§ **10.3, n. 3.**

United Food & Commercial Workers Intern. Union–Industry Pension Fund v. Spartan Stores, Inc., 1992 WL 309545 (N.D.Ill.1992)—§ **9.5, n. 13.**

United Mine Workers of America v. Coronado Coal Co., 259 U.S. 344, 42 S.Ct. 570, 66 L.Ed. 975 (1922)—§ **10.12, n. 9.**

United Mine Workers of America v. Gibbs, 383 U.S. 715, 86 S.Ct. 1130, 16 L.Ed.2d 218 (1966)—§ **3.45; § 3.45, n. 1; § 10.18, n. 5.**

United Rope Distributors, Inc. v. Seatriumph Marine Corp., 930 F.2d 532 (7th Cir.1991)—§ **8.8, n. 8.**

United Royalty Co., State ex rel. Ferguson v., 188 Kan. 443, 363 P.2d 397 (Kan. 1961)—§ **23.2, n. 15.**

United States v. _____ (see opposing party)

United States ex rel. v. _____ (see opposing party and relator)

United States Fidelity and Guar. Co. v. Preston, 26 S.W.3d 145 (Ky.2000)—§ **18.26, n. 6.**

United States Fire Ins. Co. v. Goodyear Tire & Rubber Co., 726 F.Supp. 740 (D.Minn. 1989)—§ **3.48, n. 22.**

United States Gypsum Co. v. Admiral Ins. Co., 268 Ill.App.3d 598, 205 Ill.Dec. 619, 643 N.E.2d 1226 (Ill.App. 1 Dist.1994)—§ **18.26, n. 19.**

United States Inv. Co. v. Phelps & Bigelow Windmill Co., 54 Kan. 144, 37 P. 982 (Kan.1894)—§ **19.9, n. 9.**

United States Leasing Corp. v. Keiler, 290 So.2d 427 (La.App. 4 Cir.1974)—§ **18.12, n. 10; § 18.37, n. 1.**

United States S.E.C. v. Carrillo, 115 F.3d 1540 (11th Cir.1997)—§ **10.2, n. 15.**

United States Trust Co. v. Bohart, 197 Conn. 34, 495 A.2d 1034 (Conn.1985)—§ **21.3, n. 9.**

United States Trust Co. of New York v. Wood, 146 A.D. 751, 131 N.Y.S. 427 (N.Y.A.D. 1 Dept.1911)—§ **20.7, n. 5.**

Universal Adjustment Corp. v. Midland Bank, Ltd., of London, England, 281 Mass. 303, 184 N.E. 152 (Mass.1933)—§ **11.8, n. 3; § 11.11, n. 6, 8.**

Universal Am. Mtge. Co. v. Bateman (In re Bateman), 331 F.3d 821 (11th Cir. 2003)—§ **24.1, n. 7.**

Universe Sales Co., Ltd. v. Silver Castle, Ltd., 182 F.3d 1036 (9th Cir.1999)—§ **12.18, n. 11.**

University of Tennessee v. Elliott, 478 U.S. 788, 106 S.Ct. 3220, 92 L.Ed.2d 635 (1986)—§ **24.12, n. 7.**

Unlaub Co., Inc. v. Sexton, 427 F.Supp. 1360 (W.D.Ark.1977)—§ **23.6, n. 4.**

UNR Industries, Inc. v. Continental Ins. Co., 623 F.Supp. 1319 (N.D.Ill.1985)—§ **23.12, n. 15.**

Uppgren v. Executive Aviation Services, Inc., 326 F.Supp. 709 (D.Md.1971)—§ **17.64, n. 10.**

Urhammer v. Olson, 39 Wis.2d 447, 159 N.W.2d 688 (Wis.1968)—§ **2.17, n. 7.**

Ury v. Jewelers Acceptance Corp., 227 Cal. App.2d 11, 38 Cal.Rptr. 376 (Cal.App. 1 Dist.1964)—§ **18.4, n. 44, 52; § 18.5, n. 1, 12, 15; § 18.7, n. 5, 12.**

Usatorre v. The Victoria, 172 F.2d 434 (2nd Cir.1949)—§ **12.18, n. 6.**

US Telecom, Inc. v. Hubert, 678 F.Supp. 1500 (D.Kan.1987)—§ **10.18, n. 3.**

Utah Farm Production Credit Ass'n v. Dinner, 302 F.Supp. 897 (D.Colo.1969)—**§ 19.18, n. 17.**

Utassi's Will, In re, 261 N.Y.S.2d 4, 209 N.E.2d 65 (N.Y.1965)—**§ 20.4, n. 6, 7.**

V

Vaage v. Lewis, 29 A.D.2d 315, 288 N.Y.S.2d 521 (N.Y.A.D. 2 Dept.1968)—**§ 11.11, n. 7.**

Valente's Will, In re, 18 Misc.2d 701, 188 N.Y.S.2d 732 (N.Y.Sur.1959)—**§ 13.6, n. 12; § 15.16, n. 3.**

Valentine v. Duke, 128 Wash. 128, 222 P. 494 (Wash.1924)—**§ 22.15, n. 4; § 22.17, n. 3.**

Valentine v. Elliott (Delaney, In re Estate of), 819 A.2d 968 (D.C.2003)—**§ 22.2, n. 1.**

Val Leasing, Inc. v. Hutson, 674 F.Supp. 53 (D.Mass.1987)—**§ 10.18, n. 6.**

Valley Juice Ltd., Inc. v. Evian Waters of France, Inc., 87 F.3d 604 (2nd Cir. 1996)—**§ 17.40, n. 28; § 18.1, n. 18; § 18.2, n. 11.**

Valley Nat. Bank of Phoenix v. Siebrand, 74 Ariz. 54, 243 P.2d 771 (Ariz.1952)—**§ 22.20, n. 29.**

Vallimont, Application of, 182 Kan. 334, 321 P.2d 190 (Kan.1958)—**§ 4.41, n. 1.**

Valtz v. Penta Investment Corp., 139 Cal. App.3d 803, 188 Cal.Rptr. 922 (Cal.App. 4 Dist.1983)—**§ 23.9, n. 5.**

Value House, Inc. v. MCI Telecommunications Corp., 917 F.Supp. 5 (D.D.C. 1996)—**§ 17.52, n. 2.**

Van Bokkelen's Estate, In re, 282 N.Y. 687, 26 N.E.2d 814 (N.Y.1940)—**§ 22.21, n. 14.**

Vance v. Vance, 286 Md. 490, 408 A.2d 728 (Md.1979)—**§ 16.1, n. 7.**

Vandelune v. 4B Elevator Components Unlimited, 148 F.3d 943 (8th Cir.1998)—**§ 7.2, n. 35.**

Vanderbilt v. Vanderbilt, 354 U.S. 416, 77 S.Ct. 1360, 1 L.Ed.2d 1456 (1957)—**§ 15.27; § 15.27, n. 5.**

Vanderpoel v. O'Hanlon, 53 Iowa 246, 5 N.W. 119 (Iowa 1880)—**§ 4.13, n. 2.**

Vandever v. Industrial Com'n of Arizona, 148 Ariz. 373, 714 P.2d 866 (Ariz.App. Div. 1 1985)—**§ 13.5, n. 1; § 15.16, n. 5.**

Van Dusen v. Barrack, 376 U.S. 612, 84 S.Ct. 805, 11 L.Ed.2d 945 (1964)—**§ 3.11, n. 7; § 3.46; § 3.46, n. 3; § 11.11, n. 6; § 11.14, n. 10, 14; § 23.13; § 23.13, n. 10.**

Van Dyke, Appeal of, 60 Pa. 481 (Pa. 1869)—**§ 20.15, n. 4, 6, 7, 8.**

Vangrack, Axelson & Williamowsky, P.C. v. Estate of Abbasi, 261 F.Supp.2d 352 (D.Md.2003)—**§ 22.2, n. 1; § 22.14, n. 13.**

Van Grutten v. Digby, 31 Beav. 561 (1862)—**§ 21.3, n. 13.**

Van Horn v. Van Horn, 107 Iowa 247, 77 N.W. 846 (Iowa 1899)—**§ 20.2, n. 4.**

Vanity Fair Mills, Inc. v. T. Eaton Co., 234 F.2d 633 (2nd Cir.1956)—**§ 11.14, n. 8; § 17.7, n. 3; § 17.53, n. 8.**

Van Kooten Holding B.V. v. Dumarco Corp., 670 F.Supp. 227 (N.D.Ill.1987)—**§ 24.36, n. 5.**

Van Loan v. Van Loan, 116 Ariz. 272, 569 P.2d 214 (Ariz.1977)—**§ 15.30, n. 1.**

Van Loh, State ex rel. v. Prosser, 78 S.D. 35, 98 N.W.2d 329 (S.D.1959)—**§ 4.41, n. 6.**

Van Matre v. Sankey, 148 Ill. 536, 36 N.E. 628 (Ill.1893)—**§ 4.37, n. 7; § 4.41, n. 2; § 16.5, n. 3.**

Vanneck v. Vanneck, 427 N.Y.S.2d 735, 404 N.E.2d 1278 (N.Y.1980)—**§ 15.42, n. 1.**

Vanquelin v. Bouard, 15 C.B., N.S., 341 (1863)—**§ 22.18, n. 15.**

Van Rensselaer v. General Motors Corp., 223 F.Supp. 323 (E.D.Mich.1962)—**§ 18.44, n. 9; § 18.46, n. 4.**

Van Rensselaer v. Van Rensselaer, 103 N.H. 23, 164 A.2d 244 (N.H.1960)—**§ 4.34, n. 3.**

Vansant v. Roberts, 3 Md. 119 (Md.1852)—**§ 21.2, n. 12.**

Vanston Bondholders Protective Committee v. Green, 329 U.S. 156, 67 S.Ct. 237, 91 L.Ed. 162 (1946)—**§ 23.14, n. 2, 4.**

Van Trump's Estate v. National Ins. Underwriters, 517 P.2d 856 (Colo.App.1973)—**§ 22.10, n. 11.**

Van Vliet v. Blatt, 51 Pa. D. & C. 182 (Pa.Com.Pl.1944)—**§ 4.27, n. 12.**

Van Vonno v. Hertz Corp., 120 Wash.2d 416, 841 P.2d 1244 (Wash.1992)—**§ 18.27, n. 5.**

Van Voorhis v. Brintnall, 86 N.Y. 18 (N.Y. 1881)—**§ 13.9, n. 5, 8.**

Van Wickle v. Van Wickle, 44 A. 877 (N.J.Ch.1899)—**§ 20.6, n. 12.**

Vardon Golf Co., Inc. v. Karsten Manufacturing Corp., 294 F.3d 1330 (Fed.Cir. 2002)—**§ 24.8, n. 4.**

Vargas v. A. H. Bull S. S. Co., 25 N.J. 293, 135 A.2d 857 (N.J.1957)—**§ 11.12, n. 3.**

Vargas v. A. H. Bull S. S. Co., 44 N.J.Super. 536, 131 A.2d 39 (N.J.Super.L.1957)—**§ 11.10, n. 2, 4.**

Vargas v. M/V Mini Lama, 709 F.Supp. 117 (E.D.La.1989)—**§ 11.8, n. 6.**

Vargus v. Pitman Mfg. Co., 675 F.2d 73 (3rd Cir.1982)—**§ 3.47, n. 2.**

Varone v. Varone, 359 F.2d 769 (7th Cir. 1966)—**§ 24.10, n. 4.**

Vasquez v. Bridgestone/Firestone, Inc., 325 F.3d 665 (5th Cir.2003)—**§ 11.11, n. 5.**

Vaughan v. Nationwide Mut. Ins. Co., 702 A.2d 198 (D.C.1997)—**§ 17.56, n. 10, 20.**

Vaughan v. Northup, 40 U.S. 1, 10 L.Ed. 639 (1841)—**§ 22.19, n. 1.**

Vaughn v. Barret, 5 Vt. 333 (Vt.1833)—§ **22.16, n. 2.**

Veasley v. CRST Intern., Inc., 553 N.W.2d 896 (Iowa 1996)—§ **2.19, n. 17; § 17.26, n. 1; § 17.36, n. 15; § 17.48, n. 17.**

Veba–Chemie A.G. v. M/V Getafix, 711 F.2d 1243 (5th Cir.1983)—§ **11.10, n. 4.**

Vecchio v. Rye Brook Obstetrics–Gynecology, P.C., 2003 WL 22482046 (Conn.Super.2003)—§ **17.42, n. 29, 35.**

Veile v. Koch, 27 Ill. 129 (Ill.1862)—§ **20.14, n. 1.**

Velandra v. Regie Nationale des Usines Renault, 336 F.2d 292 (6th Cir.1964)—§ **10.16, n. 8.**

Vennard, Succession of, 11 So. 705 (La. 1892)—§ **4.37, n. 7.**

Venturini v. Worldwide Marble & Granite Corp., 1995 WL 606281 (S.D.N.Y. 1995)—§ **17.32, n. 34; § 17.42, n. 11; § 17.43, n. 9; § 17.44, n. 13.**

Verizon Online Services, Inc. v. Ralsky, 203 F.Supp.2d 601 (E.D.Va.2002)—§ **7.12, n. 8.**

Verlinden B.V. v. Central Bank of Nigeria, 461 U.S. 480, 103 S.Ct. 1962, 76 L.Ed.2d 81 (1983)—§ **10.19, n. 10.**

Vermeulen v. Renault, U.S.A., Inc., 985 F.2d 1534 (11th Cir.1993)—§ **5.12, n. 8; § 7.2, n. 35.**

Versatile Plastics, Inc. v. Sknowbest! Inc., 247 F.Supp.2d 1098 (E.D.Wis.2003)—§ **9.4, n. 10.**

Vertner v. Humphreys, 22 Miss. 130 (Miss. Err. & App.1850)—§ **14.5, n. 1, 2.**

Vervaeke v. Smith, [1983] 1 A.C. 145 (HL 1982)—§ **13.4, 1; § 15.20, n. 1.**

Vesely v. Sager, 95 Cal.Rptr. 623, 486 P.2d 151 (Cal.1971)—§ **17.19, n. 2.**

Vespe Contracting Co. v. Anvan Corp., 433 F.Supp. 1226 (E.D.Pa.1977)—§ **10.12, n. 9.**

Vest v. St. Albans Psychiatric Hosp., Inc., 182 W.Va. 228, 387 S.E.2d 282 (W.Va. 1989)—§ **2.21, n. 29; § 17.42, n. 31.**

Vestal v. Shiley Inc., 1997 WL 910373 (C.D.Cal.1997)—§ **17.76, n. 14; § 17.77, n. 8.**

Vetrotex Certainteed Corp. v. Consolidated Fiber Glass Products Co., 75 F.3d 147 (3rd Cir.1996)—§ **8.5, n. 5.**

V.H. v. Estate of Birnbaum, 543 N.W.2d 649 (Minn.1996)—§ **22.19, n. 11.**

Viam Corp. v. Iowa Export–Import Trading Co., 84 F.3d 424 (Fed.Cir.1996)—§ **9.4, n. 3.**

Vick v. Cochran, 316 So.2d 242 (Miss. 1975)—§ **3.9, n. 6; § 3.11, n. 4, 5; § 17.11, n. 22.**

Vickery v. Garretson, 527 A.2d 293 (D.C. 1987)—§ **5.5, n. 7.**

Victor v. Sperry, 163 Cal.App.2d 518, 329 P.2d 728 (Cal.App. 4 Dist.1958)—§ **17.6, n. 1; § 17.16; § 17.16, n. 1; § 17.18; § 17.18, n. 3.**

Victor v. Victor, 177 Ariz. 231, 866 P.2d 899 (Ariz.App. Div. 1 1993)—§ **13.17, n. 3.**

Victoria v. Smythe, 703 A.2d 619 (R.I. 1997)—§ **2.13, n. 14, 18; § 17.21, n. 16; § 17.23, n. 6.**

Vidal v. South American Securities Co., 276 F. 855 (2nd Cir.1921)—§ **4.12, n. 3.**

Viditz v. O'Hagan, 1899 WL 11989 (Ch.D. 1899)—§ **21.3, n. 13.**

Vien, Re, 1988 WL 865962 (Ont. C.A. 1988)—§ **14.15, n. 2.**

Viernes v. District Court In and For Fourth Judicial Dist., El Paso County, 181 Colo. 284, 509 P.2d 306 (Colo.1973)—§ **15.5, n. 2.**

Vigen Const. Co. v. Millers Nat. Ins. Co., 436 N.W.2d 254 (N.D.1989)—§ **18.26, n. 12.**

Viking Dodge Inc. v. Hoffman, 147 Ill. App.3d 203, 101 Ill.Dec. 33, 497 N.E.2d 1346 (Ill.App. 3 Dist.1986)—§ **4.21, n. 2.**

Vilas' Estate, In re, 166 Or. 115, 110 P.2d 940 (Or.1941)—§ **22.10, n. 11.**

Villaman v. Schee, 15 F.3d 1095 (9th Cir. 1994)—§ **17.14, n. 10; § 17.45; § 17.45, n. 44; § 17.50, n. 25.**

Villar v. Crowley Maritime Corp., 990 F.2d 1489 (5th Cir.1993)—§ **6.9, n. 20.**

Villar v. Crowley Maritime Corp., 782 F.2d 1478 (9th Cir.1986)—§ **17.63, n. 24.**

Vimar Seguros y Reaseguros, S.A. v. M/V SKY REEFER, 515 U.S. 528, 115 S.Ct. 2322, 132 L.Ed.2d 462 (1995)—§ **24.48, n. 2.**

Vincent's Estate, In re, 189 Misc. 489, 71 N.Y.S.2d 165 (N.Y.Sur.1947)—§ **20.2, n. 4.**

Violet v. Picillo, 613 F.Supp. 1563 (D.R.I. 1985)—§ **9.2; § 9.2, n. 7, 16.**

Virgil v. Virgil, 55 Misc.2d 64, 284 N.Y.S.2d 568 (N.Y.Sup.1967)—§ **15.11, n. 3.**

Vishay Intertechnology, Inc. v. Delta Intern. Corp., 696 F.2d 1062 (4th Cir. 1982)—§ **7.11, n. 11.**

Vishipco Line v. Chase Manhattan Bank, N.A., 660 F.2d 854 (2nd Cir.1981)—§ **12.18, n. 8, 9.**

Vita Food Products Inc. v. Unus Shipping Co., [1939] A.C. 277 (Privy Council 1939)—§ **12.19, n. 4; § 18.2, n. 4.**

Vladikavkazsky R. Co. v. New York Trust Co., 263 N.Y. 369, 189 N.E. 456 (N.Y. 1934)—§ **23.11, n. 4.**

Vlandis v. Kline, 412 U.S. 441, 93 S.Ct. 2230, 37 L.Ed.2d 63 (1973)—§ **4.13, n. 10; § 4.30, n. 2.**

VMS/PCA Ltd. Partnership v. PCA Partners Ltd. Partnership, 727 F.Supp. 1167 (N.D.Ill.1989)—§ **10.18, n. 9.**

Volkswagen of America, Inc. v. Young, 272 Md. 201, 321 A.2d 737 (Md.1974)—§ **18.24, n. 6.**

Volkswagenwerk Aktiengesellschaft, Ex parte, 443 So.2d 880 (Ala.1983)—§ **12.7, n. 6; § 23.20, n. 7.**

Volkswagenwerk Aktiengesellschaft v. Schlunk, 486 U.S. 694, 108 S.Ct. 2104, 100 L.Ed.2d 722 (1988)—§ **12.6, n. 14;** § **23.20, n. 7.**

Volyrakis v. M/V Isabelle, 668 F.2d 863 (5th Cir.1982)—§ **17.63, n. 24.**

V–1 Oil Co. v. Ranck, 767 P.2d 612 (Wyo. 1989)—§ **22.10, n. 4;** § **22.19, n. 33;** § **22.20, n. 25;** § **22.21, n. 7.**

Von Gontard's Trust, In re, 36 Misc.2d 529, 233 N.Y.S.2d 30 (N.Y.Sup.1962)— § **21.11, n. 17.**

Vons Companies, Inc. v. Seabest Foods, Inc., 58 Cal.Rptr.2d 899, 926 P.2d 1085 (Cal.1996)—§ **7.11, n. 11.**

Vorhees v. Fischer & Krecke, 697 F.2d 574 (4th Cir.1983)—§ **12.7, n. 3.**

Voss v. Shalala, 32 F.3d 1269 (8th Cir. 1994)—§ **22.3, n. 10.**

Vroon v. Templin, 278 F.2d 345 (4th Cir. 1960)—§ **22.25, n. 7.**

VTT Vulcan Petroleum, S.A. v. Langham– Hill Petroleum, Inc., 684 F.Supp. 389 (S.D.N.Y.1988)—§ **10.6, n. 35.**

Vulcanized Rubber & Plastics Co. v. Scheckter, 400 Pa. 405, 162 A.2d 400 (Pa.1960)—§ **12.15, n. 15;** § **12.19, n. 2;** § **18.44, n. 9;** § **18.47, n. 6.**

W

Wachs v. Winter, 569 F.Supp. 1438 (E.D.N.Y.1983)—§ **12.18, n. 8.**

Waddoups v. Amalgamated Sugar Co., 54 P.3d 1054 (Utah 2002)—§ **17.45;** § **17.45, n. 25.**

Wadsworth, Inc. v. Schwarz–Nin, 951 F.Supp. 314 (D.Puerto Rico 1996)— § **17.52, n. 2.**

Waeltz v. Delta Pilots Retirement Plan, 301 F.3d 804 (7th Cir.2002)—§ **9.5, n. 14.**

Wagner, In re Estate of, 50 Wash.App. 162, 748 P.2d 639 (Wash.App. Div. 1 1987)— § **16.6, n. 3.**

Wagner v. Duncan's Estate, 546 S.W.2d 859 (Tex.Civ.App.-Dallas 1977)—§ **22.2, n. 1.**

Wagner v. Islamic Republic of Iran, 172 F.Supp.2d 128 (D.D.C.2001)—§ **17.50;** § **17.50, n. 66.**

Wagner v. Miskin, 660 N.W.2d 593 (N.D. 2003)—§ **7.8, n. 14, 16.**

Wagner, Petition of, 381 Pa. 107, 112 A.2d 352 (Pa.1955)—§ **4.41, n. 1.**

Wagoner v. Wagoner, 294 Ark. 82, 740 S.W.2d 915 (Ark.1987)—§ **14.10, n. 2.**

Wahl v. Pan Am. World Airways, Inc., 227 F.Supp. 839 (S.D.N.Y.1964)—§ **11.11, n. 3.**

Wailes v. Curators of Central College, 363 Mo. 932, 254 S.W.2d 645 (1953)—§ **16.6, n. 5.**

Wainwright's Vacations, LLC v. Pan American Airways Corp., 130 F.Supp.2d 712 (D.Md.2001)—§ **17.55, n. 9.**

Waite, In re, 190 Iowa 182, 180 N.W. 159 (Iowa 1920)—§ **4.42, n. 4.**

Waldoborough v. Friendship, 87 Me. 211, 32 A. 880 (Me.1895)—§ **4.39, n. 1.**

Waldron v. Armstrong Rubber Co., 54 Mich. App. 154, 220 N.W.2d 738 (Mich.App. 1974)—§ **3.11, n. 4.**

Walker v. Armco Steel Corp., 446 U.S. 740, 100 S.Ct. 1978, 64 L.Ed.2d 659 (1980)— § **3.37, n. 5;** § **3.39;** § **3.39, n. 11.**

Walker v. City of Hutchinson, Kan., 352 U.S. 112, 77 S.Ct. 200, 1 L.Ed.2d 178 (1956)—§ **5.5, n. 16;** § **5.16, n. 9;** § **12.3, n. 5.**

Walker v. Hildenbrand, 243 Or. 117, 410 P.2d 244 (Or.1966)—§ **13.6, n. 2, 4.**

Walker v. Newgent, 442 F.Supp. 38 (S.D.Tex.1977)—§ **10.16, n. 7.**

Walker v. Yarbrough, 257 Ark. 300, 516 S.W.2d 390 (Ark.1974)—§ **13.6, n. 2.**

Walkes v. Walkes, 465 F.Supp. 638 (S.D.N.Y.1979)—§ **17.32, n. 1.**

Wall v. Williamson, 8 Ala. 48 (Ala.1845)— § **13.18, n. 8, 13.**

Wallace v. Herron, 778 F.2d 391 (7th Cir. 1985)—§ **7.3, n. 11.**

Wallace v. Smith, 238 A.D. 599, 265 N.Y.S. 253 (N.Y.A.D. 1 Dept.1933)—§ **10.15, n. 4.**

Wallace v. Wallace, 63 N.M. 414, 320 P.2d 1020 (N.M.1958)—§ **4.26, n. 6;** § **15.5, n. 2;** § **22.26, n. 1.**

Wallace v. Wallace, 371 Pa. 404, 89 A.2d 769 (Pa.1952)—§ **4.26, n. 1.**

Wallace Lincoln–Mercury Co., Inc. v. Gentry, 469 F.2d 396 (5th Cir.1972)— § **23.15, n. 14.**

Wallack v. Wallack, 211 Ga. 745, 88 S.E.2d 154 (Ga.1955)—§ **14.9, n. 3.**

Waller, In re, 494 F.2d 447 (6th Cir.1974)— § **23.13, n. 1.**

Wallihan v. Hughes, 196 Va. 117, 82 S.E.2d 553 (Va.1954)—§ **24.20, n. 3.**

Walling, Matter of Guardianship of, 727 P.2d 586 (Okla.1986)—§ **22.26, n. 6.**

Wallis v. Brown, 52 A. 475 (N.J.Err. & App.1902)—§ **22.25, n. 17.**

Wallis v. Mrs. Smith's Pie Co., 261 Ark. 622, 550 S.W.2d 453 (Ark.1977)—§ **2.16, n. 13;** § **2.25, n. 1;** § **17.21, n. 19.**

Wallis v. Pan Am. Petroleum Corp., 384 U.S. 63, 86 S.Ct. 1301, 16 L.Ed.2d 369 (1966)—§ **3.50, n. 9;** § **3.52, n. 6;** § **3.54, n. 9;** § **3.55, n. 5.**

Walls v. General Motors, Inc., 906 F.2d 143 (5th Cir.1990)—§ **17.77, n. 3.**

Walls v. Quick & Reilly, Inc., 824 So.2d 1016 (Fla.App. 5 Dist.2002)—§ **17.40, n. 26.**

Wal–Mart Stores, Inc. v. Manning, 788 So.2d 116 (Ala.2000)—§ **17.48, n. 5.**

Walter v. Netherlands Mead N. V., 514 F.2d 1130 (3rd Cir.1975)—§ **12.18, n. 8.**

Walter E. Heller & Co. v. James Godbe Co., 601 F.Supp. 319 (N.D.Ill.1984)—§ **11.2, n. 4.**

Walters, In re Marriage of, 220 Cal.App.3d 1062, 269 Cal.Rptr. 557 (Cal.App. 4 Dist. 1990)—§ **14.11, n. 1; § 15.30, n. 1.**

Walters v. Maren Engineering Corp., 246 Ill.App.3d 1084, 186 Ill.Dec. 931, 617 N.E.2d 170 (Ill.App. 1 Dist.1993)— § **17.77, n. 3; § 17.79, n. 10.**

Walton v. Arabian American Oil Company, 233 F.2d 541 (2nd Cir.1956)—§ **12.15, n. 17; § 12.19, n. 5, 10; § 19.8, n. 5.**

Walton v. Hall's Estate, 66 Vt. 455, 29 A. 803 (Vt.1894)—§ **22.3, n. 14.**

Walton v. Walton, 925 F.Supp. 453 (S.D.Miss.1996)—§ **4.14; § 4.14, n. 7.**

Wang v. Marziani, 885 F.Supp. 74 (S.D.N.Y. 1995)—§ **17.50, n. 25.**

Wangler v. Harvey, 41 N.J. 277, 196 A.2d 513 (N.J.1963)—§ **11.15, n. 2.**

Waples–Platter Companies v. General Foods Corp., 439 F.Supp. 551 (N.D.Tex. 1977)—§ **17.53, n. 5.**

Ward v. Boyce, 152 N.Y. 191, 46 N.E. 180 (N.Y.1897)—§ **22.20, n. 31.**

Ward v. Formex, Inc., 27 Ill.App.3d 22, 325 N.E.2d 812 (Ill.App. 2 Dist.1975)—§ **8.5, n. 7.**

Ward v. Nationwide Mut. Auto. Ins. Co., 328 Md. 240, 614 A.2d 85 (Md.1992)— § **18.4, n. 44.**

Ward v. Stanard, 82 A.D. 386, 81 N.Y.S. 906 (N.Y.A.D. 2 Dept.1903)—§ **21.11, n. 12.**

Ward v. Ward, 272 Kan. 12, 30 P.3d 1001 (Kan.2001)—§ **16.5, n. 9.**

Ward v. Ward, 115 W.Va. 429, 176 S.E. 708 (W.Va.1934)—§ **4.24, n. 3.**

Ward's Estate, Matter of, 168 Mont. 396, 543 P.2d 382 (Mont.1975)—§ **4.13, n. 6.**

Ware v. Ware, 302 Ky. 438, 194 S.W.2d 969 (Ky.1946)—§ **22.23, n. 3.**

Ware v. Wisner, 50 F. 310 (C.C.D.Iowa 1883)—§ **20.6, n. 11.**

Warn v. M/Y Maridome, 169 F.3d 625 (9th Cir.1999)—§ **17.63, n. 24.**

Warn v. M/Y Maridome, 961 F.Supp. 1357 (S.D.Cal.1997)—§ **10.5, n. 8.**

Warner, Matter of Estate of, 687 S.W.2d 686 (Mo.App. E.D.1985)—§ **15.21, n. 3.**

Warner v. Auberge Gray Rocks, Inn, Ltee., 827 F.2d 938 (3rd Cir.1987)—§ **3.12, n. 5.**

Warner v. Florida Bank & Trust Co., at West Palm Beach, 160 F.2d 766 (5th Cir.1947)—§ **21.3, n. 6.**

Warner v. Kressly, 9 Wash.App. 358, 512 P.2d 1116 (Wash.App. Div. 3 1973)— § **18.33; § 18.33, n. 5.**

Warner v. Warner, 14 Ark.App. 257, 687 S.W.2d 856 (Ark.App.1985)—§ **20.9, n. 8.**

Warner & Swasey Co. v. Salvagnini Transferica S.p.A., 633 F.Supp. 1209 (W.D.N.Y.1986)—§ **11.3, n. 22.**

Warren v. Eddy, 13 Abb.Pr. 28, 32 Barb. 664 (N.Y.Sup.Gen.Term 1860)—§ **22.14, n. 6.**

Warren v. Foster, 450 So.2d 786 (Miss. 1984)—§ **16.6, n. 4.**

Warren v. Warren, 622 So.2d 864 (La.App. 4 Cir.1993)—§ **15.28, n. 1.**

Warren v. Warren, 127 Cal.App. 231, 15 P.2d 556 (Cal.App. 3 Dist.1932)—§ **4.24, n. 3.**

Warrender v. Warrender, 79 N.J.Super. 114, 190 A.2d 684 (N.J.Super.A.D.1963)—§ **15.20, n. 8.**

Warren Trading Post Co. v. Arizona State Tax Commission, 380 U.S. 685, 85 S.Ct. 1242, 14 L.Ed.2d 165 (1965)—§ **11.17, n. 12.**

Warter v. Warter, 1890 WL 10066 (PDAD 1890)—§ **13.9, n. 3.**

Wasche v. Wasche, 268 N.W.2d 721 (Minn. 1978)—§ **11.11, n. 3.**

Washburn v. White, 140 Mass. 568, 5 N.E. 813 (Mass.1886)—§ **4.39, n. 1.**

Washburn's Estate, In re, 45 Minn. 242, 47 N.W. 790 (Minn.1891)—§ **22.7, n. 1; § 22.15, n. 2, 4, 5, 12, 13.**

Washburn's Estate, In re, 32 Minn. 336, 20 N.W. 324 (Minn.1884)—§ **20.15, n. 4.**

Washington v. Confederated Tribes of Colville Indian Reservation, 447 U.S. 134, 100 S.Ct. 2069, 65 L.Ed.2d 10 (1980)— § **11.17, n. 14.**

Washington v. Washington, 486 S.W.2d 668 (Mo.App.1972)—§ **13.1, n. 2.**

Washington v. Superior Court, 289 U.S. 361, 53 S.Ct. 624, 77 L.Ed. 1256 (1933)—§ **10.14, n. 10; § 12.6, n. 4.**

Washington Gas Light Co. v. Hsu, 478 F.Supp. 1262 (D.Md.1979)—§ **24.5, n. 4; § 24.12, n. 2.**

Washington Statewide Organization of Stepparents v. Smith, 85 Wash.2d 564, 536 P.2d 1202 (Wash.1975)—§ **13.1, n. 2.**

Washington Tp. v. Beaver Tp., 1842 WL 4765 (Pa.1842)—§ **4.43, n. 1; § 4.45, n. 6.**

Wasserman v. Wasserman, 671 F.2d 832 (4th Cir.1982)—§ **15.42, n. 13.**

Waste Management of Wisconsin, Inc. v. Uniroyal, Inc., 1992 WL 227379 (W.D.Wis.1992)—§ **9.2, n. 7.**

Waste Recovery Corp. v. Mahler, 566 F.Supp. 1466 (S.D.N.Y.1983)—§ **4.27, n. 10.**

Waters v. Barton, 41 Tenn. 450 (Tenn. 1860)—§ **19.14, n. 1.**

Waterside Ocean Nav. Co., Inc. v. International Nav. Ltd., 737 F.2d 150 (2nd Cir. 1984)—§ **24.40, n. 5; § 24.48, n. 7.**

Watertown, Town of v. Greaves, 112 F. 183 (1st Cir.1901)—§ **4.34, n. 2.**

Watkins v. Conway, 385 U.S. 188, 87 S.Ct. 357, 17 L.Ed.2d 286 (1966)—§ **3.33, n. 3; § 24.22, n. 11; § 24.32; § 24.32, n. 6.**

Watkins v. Watkins, 160 Tenn. 1, 22 S.W.2d 1 (Tenn.1929)—§ **19.6, n. 2.**

Watson v. Collins' Adm'r, 37 Ala. 587 (Ala. 1861)—§ **22.6, n. 1.**

Watson v. Employers Liability Assur. Corp., 348 U.S. 66, 75 S.Ct. 166, 99 L.Ed. 74 (1954)—§ **3.22; § 3.22, n. 1.**

Watson v. Merrell Dow Pharmaceuticals, Inc., 769 F.2d 354 (6th Cir.1985)— § **11.10, n. 8.**

Watts v. Swiss Bank Corp., 317 N.Y.S.2d 315, 265 N.E.2d 739 (N.Y.1970)—§ **24.4, n. 5; § 24.35, n. 7.**

Watts v. Wilson, 93 Ky. 495, 20 S.W. 505 (Ky.1892)—§ **22.25, n. 2, 3.**

Watts' Estate, In re, 341 N.Y.S.2d 609, 294 N.E.2d 195 (N.Y.1973)—§ **13.6, n. 2.**

Way v. Sears, Roebuck, 1993 WL 540205 (Conn.Super.1993)—§ **17.59, n. 11.**

Wayman v. Southard, 23 U.S. 1, 6 L.Ed. 253 (1825)—§ **18.1, n. 3, 7; § 18.2, n. 1.**

Wayne v. Tennessee Valley Authority, 730 F.2d 392 (5th Cir.1984)—§ **17.56, n. 8.**

Wayne Pigment Corp. v. Halox, 220 F.Supp.2d 931 (E.D.Wis.2002)—§ **9.4, n. 5.**

Ways' Marriage, In re, 85 Wash.2d 693, 538 P.2d 1225 (Wash.1975)—§ **15.5, n. 2.**

W.C. Richards Co., Inc. v. Hartford Acc. and Indem. Co., 289 Ill.App.3d 207, 224 Ill. Dec. 659, 682 N.E.2d 220 (Ill.App. 1 Dist.1997)—§ **18.26, n. 13.**

Weatherby Associates, Inc. v. Ballack, 783 So.2d 1138 (Fla.App. 4 Dist.2001)— § **17.40, n. 26.**

Weaver v. Gillen, 49 B.R. 70 (W.D.N.Y. 1985)—§ **23.13, n. 1.**

Webber v. Webber, 32 N.C.App. 572, 232 S.E.2d 865 (N.C.App.1977)—§ **15.28, n. 1.**

Webb's Adoption, In re, 65 Ariz. 176, 177 P.2d 222 (Ariz.1947)—§ **4.37, n. 9; § 4.40, n. 6.**

Webco Industries, Inc. v. Thermatool Corp., 278 F.3d 1120 (10th Cir.2002)—§ **3.37, n. 5.**

Weber v. Aetna Cas. & Sur. Co., 406 U.S. 164, 92 S.Ct. 1400, 31 L.Ed.2d 768 (1972)—§ **3.54, n. 5.**

Weber v. Weber, 200 Neb. 659, 265 N.W.2d 436 (Neb.1978)—§ **13.8, n. 3; § 15.11, n. 4; § 15.20, n. 10.**

Webster v. Modern Woodmen of America, 192 Iowa 1376, 186 N.W. 659 (Iowa 1922)—§ **13.8, n. 5.**

Webster v. Sun Co., Inc., 790 F.2d 157, 252 U.S.App.D.C. 335 (D.C.Cir.1986)— § **12.12, n. 3.**

Weddington v. Jackson, 331 F.Supp. 1271 (E.D.Pa.1971)—§ **18.37, n. 6.**

Wedemann v. United States Trust Co. of New York, 258 N.Y. 315, 179 N.E. 712 (N.Y.1932)—§ **22.21, n. 7.**

Weede, State ex rel. v. Bechtel, 239 Iowa 1298, 31 N.W.2d 853 (Iowa 1948)— § **23.9, n. 4.**

Weeks' Will, In re, 294 N.Y. 516, 63 N.E.2d 85 (N.Y.1945)—§ **14.15, n. 3.**

Wegematic Corp., United States v., 360 F.2d 674 (2nd Cir.1966)—§ **3.51, n. 8.**

Wehr's Estate, In re, 96 Mont. 245, 29 P.2d 836 (Mont.1934)—§ **16.1, n. 7.**

Weidman v. Weidman, 274 Mass. 118, 174 N.E. 206 (Mass.1931)—§ **24.22, n. 9.**

Weinberger v. Salfi, 422 U.S. 749, 95 S.Ct. 2457, 45 L.Ed.2d 522 (1975)—§ **4.31, n. 1.**

Weinstein, In re Marriage of, 87 Ill.App.3d 101, 42 Ill.Dec. 243, 408 N.E.2d 952 (Ill.App. 1 Dist.1980)—§ **15.42, n. 1.**

Weinstein v. Freyer, 93 Ala. 257, 9 So. 285 (Ala.1891)—§ **19.13, n. 10.**

Weinstein v. Medical Center Hospital of Vermont, Inc., 358 F.Supp. 297 (D.Vt. 1972)—§ **22.14, n. 5, 10.**

Weisberg v. Layne–New York Co., Inc., 132 A.D.2d 550, 517 N.Y.S.2d 304 (N.Y.A.D. 2 Dept.1987)—§ **17.46, n. 21.**

Weiss v. Hunna, 312 F.2d 711 (2nd Cir. 1963)—§ **12.19, n. 5.**

Weissfeld v. Herman Miller, Inc., 293 F.Supp. 995 (W.D.Mich.1968)—§ **22.14, n. 10.**

Weiss' Will, In re, 64 N.Y.S.2d 331 (N.Y.Sur.1946)—§ **20.9, n. 11.**

Welch v. Trustees of Robert A. Welch Foundation, 465 S.W.2d 195 (Tex.Civ.App.-Hous. (1 Dist.) 1971)—§ **19.6, n. 2.**

Weldpower Industries, Inc., In re, 49 B.R. 46 (Bkrtcy.D.N.H.1985)—§ **23.12, n. 7.**

Weller v. Cromwell Oil Co., 504 F.2d 927 (6th Cir.1974)—§ **10.17, n. 2.**

Wellmark, Inc. v. Deguara, 257 F.Supp.2d 1209 (S.D.Iowa 2003)—§ **9.5, n. 13.**

Wells v. Liddy, 186 F.3d 505 (4th Cir. 1999)—§ **17.55, n. 9.**

Wells v. 10–X Mfg. Co., 609 F.2d 248 (6th Cir.1979)—§ **18.29, n. 4.**

Wells, United States v., 403 F.2d 596 (5th Cir.1968)—§ **3.51, n. 10.**

Wells v. Wells, 230 Ala. 430, 161 So. 794 (Ala.1935)—§ **4.24, n. 3.**

Wells Fargo & Co. v. Wells Fargo Exp. Co., 556 F.2d 406 (9th Cir.1977)—§ **10.3, n. 8.**

Wells Fargo & Co. v. Wells Fargo Exp. Co., 358 F.Supp. 1065 (D.Nev.1973)— § **17.53, n. 2.**

Wendel v. Hoffman, 258 A.D. 1084, 259 A.D. 732, 18 N.Y.S.2d 96 (N.Y.A.D. 2 Dept.1940)—§ **11.12, n. 2.**

Wendelken v. Superior Court In and For Pima County, 137 Ariz. 455, 671 P.2d 896 (Ariz.1983)—§ **17.39, n. 15.**

Wendt v. Osceola County, Iowa, 289 N.W.2d 67 (Minn.1979)—§ **17.43, n. 16.**

Werner v. Werner, 84 Wash.2d 360, 526 P.2d 370 (Wash.1974)—§ **2.16, n. 12;** § **2.23, n. 1;** § **17.26, n. 1;** § **19.3, n. 19.**

Wessling v. Paris, 417 S.W.2d 259 (Ky. 1967)—§ **2.16, n. 8;** § **2.23, n. 6;** § **17.13;** § **17.13, n. 2;** § **17.39, n. 8.**

West v. Conrail, 481 U.S. 35, 107 S.Ct. 1538, 95 L.Ed.2d 32 (1987)—§ **3.39, n. 14.**

West v. Fitz, 109 Ill. 425 (Ill.1884)—§ **20.6, n. 16.**

West Africa Trading & Shipping Co. v. London Intern. Group, 968 F.Supp. 996 (D.N.J.1997)—§ **10.5, n. 14;** § **10.6, n. 29.**

Westbury Union Free School Dist., Towns of North Hempstead and Hempstead v. Amityville Union Free School Dist., 106 Misc.2d 189, 431 N.Y.S.2d 641 (N.Y.Sup. 1980)—§ **4.27, n. 2.**

West Chester Borough School Directors v. James, 1841 WL 4230 (Pa.1841)— § **4.42, n. 2.**

Westerman v. Schwab, 43 Sc.L.R. 161 (1905)—§ **20.12, n. 6.**

Westerman v. Sears, Roebuck & Co., 577 F.2d 873 (5th Cir.1978)—§ **17.77, n. 2;** § **18.24, n. 7.**

Western Air Lines, Inc., People v., 258 Cal. App.2d 213, 66 Cal.Rptr. 316 (Cal.App. 2 Dist.1968)—§ **23.9, n. 5.**

Western Air Lines, Inc. v. Schutzbank, 258 Cal.App.2d 218, 66 Cal.Rptr. 293 (Cal. App. 2 Dist.1968)—§ **23.9, n. 5.**

Western Air Lines, Inc. v. Sobieski, 191 Cal.App.2d 399, 12 Cal.Rptr. 719 (Cal. App. 2 Dist.1961)—§ **23.9, n. 5.**

Western Equities, Ltd. v. Hanseatic, Ltd., 956 F.Supp. 1232 (D.Virgin Islands 1997)—§ **10.5, n. 14;** § **10.6, n. 29.**

Western Group Nurseries, Inc. v. Ergas, 211 F.Supp.2d 1362 (S.D.Fla.2002)— § **17.40, n. 26;** § **18.1, n. 17.**

Western Helicopters, Inc. v. Hiller Aviation, Inc., 97 B.R. 1 (E.D.Cal.1988)—§ **23.16, n. 6.**

Western Nat. Mut. Ins. Co. v. State Farm Ins. Co., 374 N.W.2d 441 (Minn.1985)— § **17.58, n. 3.**

Western Union Tel. Co. v. Pennsylvania, 368 U.S. 71, 82 S.Ct. 199, 7 L.Ed.2d 139 (1961)—§ **20.4, n. 8.**

Western Union Telegraph Co. v. Chilton, 100 Ark. 296, 140 S.W. 26 (Ark.1911)— § **3.4, n. 4.**

Western Union Telegraph Co. v. Flannagan, 113 Ark. 9, 167 S.W. 701 (Ark.1914)— § **3.4, n. 5.**

Western Union Telegraph Co. v. Griffin, 92 Ark. 219, 122 S.W. 489 (Ark.1909)— § **3.4, n. 5.**

Western Union Telegraph Co. v. Way, 83 Ala. 542, 4 So. 844 (Ala.1887)—§ **12.15, n. 12.**

Western United Nurseries, Inc., In re v. Estate of Adams, 191 B.R. 820 (Bkrtcy. D.Ariz.1996)—§ **17.40, n. 26;** § **18.1, n. 17.**

Westinghouse Elec. Corp. v. Liberty Mut. Ins. Co., 233 N.J.Super. 463, 559 A.2d 435 (N.J.Super.A.D.1989)—§ **18.26, n. 12.**

Westinghouse Electric Corp Uranium Contract Litigation MDL Docket 235 (No.2), 1977 WL 58879 (HL 1977)—§ **12.9, n. 6;** § **12.13, n. 9;** § **12.14, n. 10.**

Weston Funding Corp. v. Lafayette Towers, Inc., 550 F.2d 710 (2nd Cir.1977)— § **18.33;** § **18.33, n. 10;** § **24.1, n. 6, 7.**

Westpfal, Matter of Estate of, 140 Misc.2d 487, 531 N.Y.S.2d 81 (N.Y.Sur.1988)— § **21.5, n. 4.**

West Virginia Pulp & Paper Co. v. Miller, 176 F. 284 (4th Cir.1909)—§ **20.7, n. 5;** § **21.3, n. 4.**

Westwater v. Murray, 245 F. 427 (6th Cir. 1917)—§ **24.20, n. 3.**

Wetherell Bros. Co. v. United States Steel Co., 105 F.Supp. 81 (D.Mass.1952)— § **19.28, n. 2.**

Wexler v. Metropolitan Life Ins. Co., 38 N.Y.S.2d 889 (N.Y.City Ct.1942)— § **12.11, n. 4.**

Weyrich v. New Republic, Inc., 235 F.3d 617, 344 U.S.App.D.C. 245 (D.C.Cir. 2001)—§ **17.55, n. 9.**

Whalley v. Lawrence's Estate, 93 Vt. 424, 108 A. 387 (Vt.1919)—§ **20.9, n. 10;** § **20.15, n. 6, 8;** § **22.21, n. 14.**

Whatley v. Clark, 482 F.2d 1230 (5th Cir. 1973)—§ **4.20, n. 6.**

W.H. Barber Co. v. Hughes, 223 Ind. 570, 63 N.E.2d 417 (Ind.1945)—§ **2.14, n. 18;** § **2.16, n. 6;** § **2.17;** § **2.17, n. 1;** § **2.22, n. 5;** § **17.1, n. 1;** § **18.21, n. 15;** § **18.28, n. 3.**

Whealton v. Whealton, 67 Cal.2d 656, 63 Cal.Rptr. 291, 432 P.2d 979 (Cal.1967)— § **15.15, n. 3, 4;** § **15.16, n. 1.**

Wheat v. Fidelity & Cas. Co. of N. Y., 128 Colo. 236, 261 P.2d 493 (Colo.1953)— § **22.10, n. 11.**

Wheat v. Wheat, 229 Ark. 842, 318 S.W.2d 793 (Ark.1958)—§ **4.26, n. 6.**

Wheeler v. District Court In and For City and County of Denver, 186 Colo. 218, 526 P.2d 658 (Colo.1974)—§ **15.42, n. 1.**

Wheeler v. Hollis, 19 Tex. 522 (Tex.1857)— § **4.38, n. 3;** § **4.42, n. 4.**

Wheeler v. Shoemaker, 78 F.R.D. 218 (D.R.I.1978)—§ **3.41, n. 15, 18.**

Wheeler v. Southwestern Greyhound Lines, 207 Ark. 601, 182 S.W.2d 214 (Ark. 1944)—§ **17.6, n. 7.**

Wheeler v. Stewart Mapping Service, 50 A.D.2d 308, 377 N.Y.S.2d 965 (N.Y.A.D. 3 Dept.1976)—§ **24.14, n. 1.**

Wheeling Steel Corp. v. Glander, 337 U.S. 562, 69 S.Ct. 1291, 93 L.Ed. 1544 (1949)—§ **3.34, n. 3.**

Wheelock v. Freiwald, 66 F.2d 694 (8th Cir.1933)—§ **13.9, n. 5.**

Whelchel, In re Marriage of, 476 N.W.2d 104 (Iowa App.1991)—§ **14.12, n. 9.**

Whipple v. Fowler, 41 Neb. 675, 60 N.W. 15 (Neb.1894)—§ **19.3, n. 17.**

Whirlpool Financial Corp. v. Sevaux, 96 F.3d 216 (7th Cir.1996)—§ **12.18, n. 4.**

Whitaker v. DeVilla, 147 N.J. 341, 687 A.2d 738 (N.J.1997)—§ **17.58, n. 9.**

Whitaker v. Harvell–Kilgore Corp., 418 F.2d 1010 (5th Cir.1969)—§ **17.64, n. 10;** § **18.24, n. 1.**

Whitaker v. Spiegel Inc., 95 Wash.2d 408, 623 P.2d 1147 (Wash.1981)—§ **18.5, n. 12.**

White, Matter of Estate of, 133 Misc.2d 971, 509 N.Y.S.2d 252 (N.Y.Sur.1986)—§ **21.5, n. 1.**

White v. All America Cable & Radio, Inc., 642 F.Supp. 69 (D.Puerto Rico 1986)—§ **4.17, n. 5;** § **4.19, n. 2.**

White v. Archbill, 34 Tenn. 588 (Tenn. 1855)—§ **22.20, n. 14.**

White v. Blake, 859 S.W.2d 551 (Tex.App.-Tyler 1993)—§ **16.5, n. 9.**

White v. Brown, 29 F.Cas. 982 (C.C.E.D.Pa. 1848)—§ **4.36, n. 3.**

White v. Ford Motor Co., 312 F.3d 998 (9th Cir.2002)—§ **3.23, n. 31;** § **17.50, n. 50.**

White v. Glover, 116 N.Y.S. 1059 (N.Y.Sup. 1909)—§ **4.34, n. 2.**

White v. Govatos, 40 Del. 349, 10 A.2d 524 (Del.Super.1939)—§ **3.10, n. 1, 4.**

White v. Howard, 38 Conn. 342 (Conn. 1871)—§ **20.6, n. 19.**

White v. I.N.S., 75 F.3d 213 (5th Cir. 1996)—§ **4.24, n. 3;** § **4.30, n. 6;** § **4.31, n. 4.**

White v. Keller, 68 F. 796 (5th Cir.1895)— § **20.13, n. 5.**

White v. Lavigne, 741 F.2d 229 (8th Cir. 1984)—§ **3.41, n. 2.**

White v. Marlin Firearms Co., 1996 WL 704378 (Conn.Super.1996)—§ **17.56, n. 8.**

White v. Tennant, 31 W.Va. 790, 8 S.E. 596 (W.Va.1888)—§ **4.18, n. 3;** § **4.19, n. 1;** § **20.3, n. 1.**

White v. United States, 680 F.2d 1156 (7th Cir.1982)—§ **21.13, n. 2.**

White v. United States, 511 F.Supp. 570 (S.D.Ind.1981)—§ **20.8, n. 8.**

White v. White, 94 Idaho 26, 480 P.2d 872 (Idaho 1971)—§ **12.15, n. 8.**

White v. White, 77 N.H. 26, 86 A. 353 (N.H.1913)—§ **4.37, n. 2.**

Whitehall Co., Ltd. v. Barletta, 404 Mass. 497, 536 N.E.2d 333 (Mass.1989)— § **24.1, n. 7, 12.**

Whitehorn v. Dickerson, 419 S.W.2d 713 (Mo.App.1967)—§ **18.37, n. 2.**

White Motor Credit, In re, 761 F.2d 270 (6th Cir.1985)—§ **23.12, n. 8.**

White Mountain Apache Tribe v. Bracker, 448 U.S. 136, 100 S.Ct. 2578, 65 L.Ed.2d 665 (1980)—§ **11.17, n. 12, 13.**

Whiteside v. New Castle Mut. Ins. Co., 595 F.Supp. 1096 (D.Del.1984)—§ **18.26, n. 12.**

White–Spunner Const., Inc. v. Cliff, 588 So.2d 865 (Ala.1991)—§ **11.5, n. 4.**

White's Will, In re, 112 Misc. 433, 183 N.Y.S. 129 (N.Y.Sur.1920)—§ **20.12, n. 6.**

Whitley, In re Marriage of, 775 P.2d 95 (Colo.App.1989)—§ **15.34, n. 7.**

Whitley v. Hartford Acc. and Indem. Co., 532 F.Supp. 190 (N.D.Tex.1981)— § **3.10, n. 4.**

Whitley v. Whitley, 778 S.W.2d 233 (Mo. App. W.D.1989)—§ **13.6, n. 2.**

Whitmer v. Whitmer, 243 Pa.Super. 462, 365 A.2d 1316 (Pa.Super.1976)—§ **19.8, n. 14.**

Whitmore v. Mitchell, 152 Ariz. 425, 733 P.2d 310 (Ariz.App. Div. 2 1987)— § **14.15, n. 1.**

Whitney v. Dodge, 105 Cal. 192, 38 P. 636 (Cal.1894)—§ **19.11, n. 12;** § **21.2, n. 5.**

Whitney v. Madden, 400 Ill. 185, 79 N.E.2d 593 (Ill.1948)—§ **11.8, n. 3.**

Whittington v. McCaskill, 65 Fla. 162, 61 So. 236 (Fla.1913)—§ **13.10, n. 4.**

Wichita Federal Sav. and Loan Ass'n v. Landmark Group, Inc., 674 F.Supp. 321 (D.Kan.1987)—§ **17.52, n. 2.**

Wickware v. Session, 538 S.W.2d 466 (Tex. Civ.App.-Tyler 1976)—§ **16.1, n. 8.**

Widmer v. Wood, 243 Ark. 457, 420 S.W.2d 828 (Ark.1967)—§ **19.8, n. 10.**

Widmeyer, Matter of Estate of, 741 S.W.2d 758 (Mo.App. S.D.1987)—§ **22.9, n. 1.**

Widow of Fornaris v. American Surety Co. of N.Y., 93 D.P.R. 29, 93 P.R.R. 28 (1966)—§ **2.16, n. 11;** § **2.22, n. 3;** § **17.39, n. 11.**

Wiel v. Curtis, Mallet–Prevost, Colt and Mosle, 66 Misc.2d 466, 321 N.Y.S.2d 250 (N.Y.Sup.1970)—§ **22.18, n. 7.**

Wiener King Systems, Inc. v. Brooks, 628 F.Supp. 843 (W.D.N.C.1986)—§ **8.3, n. 11.**

Wiggins v. New York Life Ins. Co., 2 F.Supp. 365 (E.D.Ky.1932)—§ **4.43, n. 1;** § **4.44, n. 2.**

Wiggins v. Rush, 83 N.M. 133, 489 P.2d 641 (N.M.1971)—§ **14.16, n. 2.**

Wilbur's Estate v. Bingham, 8 Wash. 35, 35 P. 407 (Wash.1894)—§ **13.10, n. 2.**

Wilcox v. District Court of Salt Lake County, 2 Utah 2d 227, 272 P.2d 157 (Utah 1954)—§ **22.14, n. 3.**

Wilcox v. Wilcox, 26 Wis.2d 617, 133 N.W.2d 408 (Wis.1965)—§ **2.13, n. 26;** § **2.16, n. 9;** § **17.39, n. 8.**

Wilcox v. Wilcox, 10 N.Y.St.Rep. 746 (N.Y.Sup.Gen.Term 1887)—§ **13.6, n. 8.**

Wilcoxen v. United States, 310 F.Supp. 1006 (D.Kan.1969)—§ **20.5, n. 3.**

Wildcatt v. Smith, 69 N.C.App. 1, 316 S.E.2d 870 (N.C.App.1984)—§ **11.17, n. 40.**

Wilder v. Absorption Corp., 107 S.W.3d 181 (Ky.2003)—§ **11.5, n. 8.**

Wilder v. Placid Oil Co., 611 F.Supp. 841 (W.D.La.1985)—§ **17.63, n. 2.**

Wilkins v. Bentley, 385 Mich. 670, 189 N.W.2d 423 (Mich.1971)—§ **4.13, n. 5;** § **4.20, n. 5.**

Wilkins v. Ellett, 108 U.S. 256, 2 S.Ct. 641, 27 L.Ed. 718 (1883)—§ **22.15, n. 1, 2;** § **22.16, n. 3.**

Wilkins v. Ellett, 76 U.S. 740, 19 L.Ed. 586 (1869)—§ **22.16, n. 2.**

Wilkins v. Zelichowski, 26 N.J. 370, 140 A.2d 65 (N.J.1958)—§ **13.2;** § **13.2, n. 7;** § **13.6, n. 8;** § **13.12, n. 2, 5.**

Wilkins v. Zelichowski, 43 N.J.Super. 598, 129 A.2d 459 (N.J.Super.A.D.1957)— § **13.2, n. 3.**

Wille v. Farm Bureau Mut. Ins. Co., 432 N.W.2d 784 (Minn.App.1988)—§ **2.13, n. 20.**

Willenbrock v. Rogers, 255 F.2d 236 (3rd Cir.1958)—§ **4.13, n. 2;** § **4.24, n. 2;** § **4.26, n. 2.**

Willets, Appeal of, 50 Conn. 330 (Conn. 1882)—§ **22.3, n. 9.**

Willey v. Willey, 22 Wash. 115, 60 P. 145 (Wash.1900)—§ **13.9, n. 4.**

William B. Tanner Co., Inc. v. WIOO, Inc., 528 F.2d 262 (3rd Cir.1975)—§ **18.33, n. 4;** § **18.39, n. 6.**

Williams, Matter of, 608 F.2d 1015 (5th Cir.1979)—§ **19.17, n. 6.**

Williams v. Carr, 263 Ark. 326, 565 S.W.2d 400 (Ark.1978)—§ **17.21, n. 19.**

Williams v. City of Roxbury, 78 Mass. 21 (Mass.1858)—§ **4.20, n. 2.**

Williams v. Cruise Ships Catering, 299 F.Supp.2d 1273 (S.D.Fla.2003)—§ **17.63, n. 23.**

Williams v. Curtiss–Wright Corp., 694 F.2d 300 (3rd Cir.1982)—§ **11.13, n. 21.**

Williams v. Green Bay & W.R. Co., 326 U.S. 549, 66 S.Ct. 284, 90 L.Ed. 311 (1946)— § **23.5;** § **23.5, n. 4.**

Williams v. Jeffs, 57 P.3d 232 (Utah App. 2002)—§ **17.54, n. 1, 5.**

Williams v. Jones, (1845) 13 M. & W. 628— § **24.38, n. 8.**

Williams v. Knott, 690 S.W.2d 605 (Tex. App.-Austin 1985)—§ **16.5, n. 9.**

Williams v. Lee, 358 U.S. 217, 79 S.Ct. 269, 3 L.Ed.2d 251 (1959)—§ **11.17;** § **11.17, n. 19, 20, 22.**

Williams v. North Carolina, 325 U.S. 226, 65 S.Ct. 1092, 89 L.Ed. 1577 (1945)— § **4.7, n. 1, 5;** § **4.9;** § **4.9, n. 1;** § **15.4, n. 4;** § **15.6;** § **15.6, n. 2, 6;** § **15.7, n. 8;** § **15.8, n. 3;** § **15.11, n. 1;** § **15.12, n. 12.**

Williams v. North Carolina, 317 U.S. 287, 63 S.Ct. 207, 87 L.Ed. 279 (1942)—§ **4.7, n. 3;** § **5.7, n. 2;** § **15.4, n. 7;** § **15.6, n. 1;** § **15.12, n. 1;** § **15.27;** § **15.27, n. 4.**

Williams v. Pope Mfg. Co., 27 So. 851 (La. 1900)—§ **14.9, n. 1.**

Williams v. Preston, 26 Ky. 600 (Ky.1830)— § **24.34, n. 1.**

Williams v. Rawlings Truck Line, Inc., 357 F.2d 581, 123 U.S.App.D.C. 121 (D.C.Cir.1965)—§ **17.12, n. 13.**

Williams v. State, 76 Wash.App. 237, 885 P.2d 845 (Wash.App. Div. 2 1994)— § **17.26, n. 1.**

Williams v. State Farm Mut. Auto. Ins. Co., 229 Conn. 359, 641 A.2d 783 (Conn. 1994)—§ **2.17, n. 16;** § **2.19, n. 17;** § **2.23, n. 2;** § **17.26, n. 1;** § **17.56, n. 19;** § **18.21, n. 14;** § **18.26, n. 7.**

Williams v. State Farm Mut. Auto. Ins. Co., 737 F.2d 741 (8th Cir.1984)—§ **17.26, n. 1.**

Williams v. United States, 71 F.3d 502 (5th Cir.1995)—§ **17.55, n. 9.**

Williams v. White Mountain Const. Co., Inc., 749 P.2d 423 (Colo.1988)—§ **17.61, n. 1.**

Williams v. Williams, 1993 WL 331874 (Del. Fam.Ct.1993)—§ **15.23, n. 5.**

Williams v. Williams, 390 A.2d 4 (D.C. 1978)—§ **19.8, n. 3.**

Williams v. Williams, 328 F.Supp. 1380 (D.Virgin Islands 1971)—§ **4.30, n. 4, 8.**

Williams v. Zachary, 463 P.2d 343 (Okla. App.1969)—§ **22.11, n. 5, 13.**

Williams Elec. Co., Inc. v. Honeywell, Inc., 854 F.2d 389 (11th Cir.1988)—§ **7.3, n. 10.**

Williams' Estate, In re, 71 Misc.2d 243, 335 N.Y.S.2d 950 (N.Y.Sur.1972)—§ **22.3, n. 5.**

Williams' Estate, In re, 130 Iowa 558, 107 N.W. 608 (Iowa 1906)—§ **22.7, n. 1;** § **22.15, n. 4;** § **22.16, n. 2.**

Williamson v. Osenton, 232 U.S. 619, 34 S.Ct. 442, 58 L.Ed. 758 (1914)—§ **4.20, n. 3;** § **4.24, n. 1;** § **4.33, n. 1, 6;** § **4.34, n. 2.**

William Whitman Co. v. Universal Oil Products Co., 125 F.Supp. 137 (D.Del.1954)— § **18.6, n. 1.**

Willis v. Westin Hotel Co., 651 F.Supp. 598 (S.D.N.Y.1986)—§ **4.17, n. 4;** § **4.21, n. 2;** § **4.28, n. 3;** § **4.29, n. 2.**

Willitt v. Purvis, 276 F.2d 129 (5th Cir. 1960)—§ **12.10, n. 4.**

Willmore v. Willmore, 273 Minn. 537, 143 N.W.2d 630 (Minn.1966)—§ **4.37, n. 4;** § **4.40, n. 1.**

Will of (see name of party)

Willys Overland Co. v. Evans, 104 Kan. 632, 180 P. 235 (Kan.1919)—§ **19.15, n. 7.**

Wilmington Trust Co. v. Sloane, 30 Del.Ch. 103, 54 A.2d 544 (Del.Ch.1947)—§ **21.7, n. 2;** § **21.11, n. 17.**

Wilmington Trust Co. v. Wilmington Trust Co., 26 Del.Ch. 397, 24 A.2d 309 (Del. Supr.1942)—§ **21.3, n. 9;** § **21.7, n. 1;** § **21.11, n. 17;** § **21.12, n. 3.**

Wilmington Trust Co. v. Wilmington Trust Co., 21 Del.Ch. 188, 186 A. 903 (Del.Ch. 1936)—§ **21.11, n. 15;** § **21.13, n. 4.**

Wilson, In re, 95 Mo. 184, 8 S.W. 369 (Mo. 1888)—§ **22.25, n. 16, 17, 19.**

Wilson v. Belin, 20 F.3d 644 (5th Cir. 1994)—§ **5.13, n. 19, 27;** § **6.8, n. 7;** § **6.9, n. 20, 23.**

Wilson v. Butler, 513 So.2d 304 (La.App. 1 Cir.1987)—§ **4.15, n. 3.**

Wilson v. Cook, 256 Ill. 460, 100 N.E. 222 (Ill.1912)—§ **13.9, n. 7.**

Wilson v. Cox, 49 Miss. 538 (Miss.1873)— § **20.15, n. 3, 5.**

Wilson v. Faull, 27 N.J. 105, 141 A.2d 768 (N.J.1958)—§ **17.27, n. 5;** § **18.46, n. 5.**

Wilson v. Hartford Fire Ins. Co., 164 F. 817 (8th Cir.1908)—§ **22.20, n. 11.**

Wilson v. League General Ins. Co., 195 Mich.App. 705, 491 N.W.2d 642 (Mich. App.1992)—§ **17.57, n. 3.**

Wilson v. Louisiana–Pacific Resources, Inc., 138 Cal.App.3d 216, 187 Cal.Rptr. 852 (Cal.App. 1 Dist.1982)—§ **23.9, n. 5;** § **24.22, n. 9.**

Wilson v. Massengill, 124 F.2d 666 (6th Cir.1942)—§ **3.10, n. 3.**

Wilson v. Omaha Indian Tribe, 442 U.S. 653, 99 S.Ct. 2529, 61 L.Ed.2d 153 (1979)—§ **3.50, n. 7.**

Wilson v. Slatalla, 970 F.Supp. 405 (E.D.Pa. 1997)—§ **17.55, n. 9.**

Wilson v. Willard, 183 Ga.App. 204, 358 S.E.2d 859 (Ga.App.1987)—§ **4.4, n. 4;** § **4.8, n. 1.**

Wilson By and Through Wilson v. Kimble, 573 F.Supp. 501 (D.Colo.1983)—§ **3.36, n. 2.**

Wilson & Co. v. Hartford Fire Ins. Co., 300 Mo. 1, 254 S.W. 266 (Mo.1923)—§ **24.24, n. 5.**

Wilson's Estate, In re, 127 N.Y.S.2d 772 (N.Y.Sur.1953)—§ **22.12, n. 2.**

Wilson's Estate v. National Bank of Commerce, 364 So.2d 1117 (Miss.1978)— § **22.20, n. 11;** § **22.21, n. 2.**

Wilson's Will, In re, 60 Misc.2d 290, 302 N.Y.S.2d 910 (N.Y.Sur.1969)—§ **20.6, n. 3.**

Wimbush's Estate, Matter of, 41 Colo.App. 289, 587 P.2d 796 (Colo.App.1978)— § **20.6, n. 11;** § **20.12, n. 4, 5.**

Wimmer v. Koenigseder, 108 Ill.2d 435, 92 Ill.Dec. 233, 484 N.E.2d 1088 (Ill. 1985)—§ **17.5, n. 8.**

Wimmer Canada, Inc. v. Abele Tractor & Equipment Co., Inc., 299 A.D.2d 47, 750 N.Y.S.2d 331 (N.Y.A.D. 3 Dept.2002)— § **24.42, n. 2.**

Wimpfheimer v. Goldsmith, 298 A.2d 778 (Del.Ch.1972)—§ **22.21, n. 2.**

Winans v. Attorney General (No.1), 1904 WL 13000 (HL 1904)—§ **4.36, n. 5.**

Winans v. Winans, 205 Mass. 388, 91 N.E. 394 (Mass.1910)—§ **4.18, n. 2;** § **4.20, n. 3, 4;** § **4.28, n. 6.**

Windbourne v. Eastern Air Lines, Inc., 479 F.Supp. 1130 (E.D.N.Y.1979)—§ **22.8, n. 1;** § **22.10, n. 7;** § **22.14, n. 10;** § **22.15, n. 16.**

Winder's Estate, In re, 98 Cal.App.2d 78, 219 P.2d 18 (Cal.App. 1 Dist.1950)— § **13.9, n. 5.**

Winer Motors, Inc. v. Jaguar Rover Triumph, Inc., 208 N.J.Super. 666, 506 A.2d 817 (N.J.Super.A.D.1986)—§ **18.4, n. 45.**

Wingate, People ex rel. Noonan v., 376 Ill. 244, 33 N.E.2d 467 (Ill.1941)—§ **4.41, n. 5.**

Winger, People ex rel. v. Young, 78 Ill. App.3d 512, 33 Ill.Dec. 920, 397 N.E.2d 253 (Ill.App. 2 Dist.1979)—§ **15.36, n. 7.**

Winger v. Pianka, 831 S.W.2d 853 (Tex. App.-Austin 1992)—§ **14.15, n. 10.**

Winkworth v. Christie Manson & Woods Ltd, 1979 WL 68486 (Ch.D.1979)— § **19.15, n. 8.**

Winn v. United Press Intern., 938 F.Supp. 39 (D.D.C.1996)—§ **17.55, n. 9.**

Winslow's Estate, In re, 138 Misc. 672, 247 N.Y.S. 506 (N.Y.Sur.1930)—§ **20.13, n. 4.**

Winsor v. United Air Lines, Inc., 52 Del. 161, 154 A.2d 561 (Del.Super.1958)— § **11.8, n. 3.**

Winters v. Diamond Shamrock Chemical Co., 149 F.3d 387 (5th Cir.1998)— § **24.1, n. 8.**

Winter's Estate, In re, 40 A.2d 648 (N.J.Err. & App.1945)—§ **22.21, n. 14.**

Winter Storm Shipping, Ltd. v. TPI, 310 F.3d 263 (2nd Cir.2002)—§ **10.6, n. 32, 51.**

Wipfler, In re, 45 F.Supp. 171 (D.Mass. 1942)—§ **22.16, n. 10.**

Wireless Distributors, Inc. v. Sprintcom, Inc., 2003 WL 22175607 (N.D.Ill.2003)— § **17.40, n. 28;** § **18.1, n. 18.**

Wirgman v. Provident Life & Trust Co., 79 W.Va. 562, 92 S.E. 415 (W.Va.1917)— § **22.23, n. 3.**

Wisconsin, State of v. Pelican Ins. Co., 127 U.S. 265, 8 S.Ct. 1370, 32 L.Ed. 239 (1888)—§ **3.17, n. 10;** § **24.23;** § **24.23, n. 8, 10.**

Wiseman v. Wiseman, 216 Tenn. 702, 393
S.W.2d 892 (Tenn.1965)—§ **4.13, n. 2.**

Wit v. Berman, 306 F.3d 1256 (2nd Cir.
2002)—§ **4.13, n. 1;** § **4.20, n. 6.**

Witt v. Realist, Inc., 18 Wis.2d 282, 118
N.W.2d 85 (Wis.1962)—§ **19.29, n. 3.**

Witt v. Reynolds Metals Co., 240 Va. 452,
397 S.E.2d 873 (Va.1990)—§ **6.9, n. 12.**

Witter v. Torbett, 604 F.Supp. 298 (W.D.Va.
1984)—§ **3.8, n. 3;** § **18.21, n. 12.**

Wiwa v. Royal Dutch Petroleum Co., 226
F.3d 88 (2nd Cir.2000)—§ **11.9, n. 7.**

Wm. H. Muller & Co. v. Swedish American
Line Ltd., 224 F.2d 806 (2nd Cir.1955)—
§ **11.3, n. 5.**

Wm. T. Thompson Co. v. General Nutrition
Corp., Inc., 671 F.2d 100 (3rd Cir.
1982)—§ **3.39, n. 7;** § **12.11, n. 7.**

WNS, Inc. v. Farrow, 884 F.2d 200 (5th
Cir.1989)—§ **7.3, n. 10.**

WOCO v. Benjamin Franklin Corp., 1976
WL 23632 (D.N.H.1976)—§ **18.9, n. 12.**

Woessner v. Air Liquide Inc., 242 F.3d 469
(3rd Cir.2001)—§ **17.69, n. 11.**

Wo-gin-up's Estate, In re, 57 Utah 29, 192
P. 267 (Utah 1920)—§ **13.18, n. 8, 14.**

Wolcott v. Holcomb, 97 Mich. 361, 56 N.W.
837 (Mich.1893)—§ **4.27, n. 11.**

Wolf, Appeal of, 13 A. 760 (Pa.1888)—
§ **16.5, n. 2.**

Wolfe v. Bank of Anderson, 123 S.C. 208,
116 S.E. 451 (S.C.1923)—§ **22.16, n. 3,
6.**

Wolman, In re, 314 F.Supp. 703 (D.Md.
1970)—§ **19.9, n. 2, 3, 9.**

Wolpert v. North Shore University Hosp.,
231 N.J.Super. 378, 555 A.2d 729
(N.J.Super.A.D.1989)—§ **7.3, n. 10.**

Wonderlic Agency, Inc. v. Acceleration
Corp., 624 F.Supp. 801 (N.D.Ill.1985)—
§ **18.33, n. 2.**

Wonderly's Guardianship, In re, 67 Ohio
St.2d 178, 423 N.E.2d 420 (Ohio 1981)—
§ **22.25, n. 6.**

Wondsel v. Commissioner, 350 F.2d 339
(2nd Cir.1965)—§ **15.13, n. 2.**

Wood v. Johnson, 117 Minn. 267, 135 N.W.
746 (Minn.1912)—§ **19.9, n. 13.**

Wood v. The Wilmington, 48 F. 566 (D.Md.
1880)—§ **10.6, n. 41.**

Wood v. Wheeler, 111 N.C. 231, 16 S.E. 418
(N.C.1892)—§ **19.3, n. 2.**

Wood v. Wood, 159 Tex. 350, 320 S.W.2d
807 (Tex.1959)—§ **4.26, n. 6;** § **15.5, n.
2.**

Wood Bros. Homes, Inc. v. Walker Adjustment Bureau, 198 Colo. 444, 601 P.2d
1369 (Colo.1979)—§ **2.17, n. 10;** § **2.23,
n. 2;** § **18.21, n. 14;** § **18.29, n. 3.**

Woodfield Ford, Inc. v. Akins Ford Corp.,
77 Ill.App.3d 343, 32 Ill.Dec. 750, 395
N.E.2d 1131 (Ill.App. 1 Dist.1979)—
§ **8.5, n. 5.**

Woodfin v. Curry, 228 Ala. 436, 153 So. 620
(Ala.1934)—§ **10.12, n. 9.**

Woodrick v. Jack J. Burke Real Estate, Inc.,
306 N.J.Super. 61, 703 A.2d 306
(N.J.Super.A.D.1997)—§ **24.1, n. 12.**

Woodrow v. Colt Industries Inc., 565
N.Y.S.2d 755, 566 N.E.2d 1160 (N.Y.
1991)—§ **10.11, n. 7.**

Woodruffe v. DeMola, 146 N.J.Super. 51,
368 A.2d 967 (N.J.Super.Ch.1976)—
§ **19.8, n. 14.**

Woods v. Interstate Realty Co., 337 U.S.
535, 69 S.Ct. 1235, 93 L.Ed. 1524
(1949)—§ **3.37, n. 5;** § **3.40, n. 10;**
§ **3.41;** § **3.41, n. 10, 13;** § **11.17, n. 31;**
§ **23.7, n. 5.**

Wood & Selick v. Compagnie Generale
Transatlantique, 43 F.2d 941 (2nd Cir.
1930)—§ **3.10, n. 6.**

Wood's Estate, In re, 137 Cal. 129, 69 P.
900 (Cal.1902)—§ **13.9, n. 4.**

Woods–Tucker Leasing Corp. of Georgia v.
Hutcheson–Ingram Development Co.,
642 F.2d 744 (5th Cir.1981)—§ **3.51, n.
8;** § **23.15, n. 10.**

Woods–Tucker Leasing Corp. of Georgia v.
Hutcheson–Ingram Development Co.,
626 F.2d 401 (5th Cir.1980)—§ **18.5, n.
12;** § **23.15;** § **23.15, n. 3.**

Woodward v. Blake, 38 N.D. 38, 164 N.W.
156 (N.D.1917)—§ **13.9, n. 5.**

Woodward v. Brooks, 128 Ill. 222, 20 N.E.
685 (Ill.1889)—§ **19.30, n. 6.**

Woodward v. Stewart, 104 R.I. 290, 243
A.2d 917 (R.I.1968)—§ **2.16, n. 10;**
§ **2.19, n. 3;** § **2.21, n. 69;** § **2.25, n. 4;**
§ **17.21, n. 16;** § **17.23, n. 6;** § **17.36, n.
15;** § **17.39, n. 8;** § **18.21, n. 9.**

Woodward v. Woodward, [1981] 30 B.C.L.R.
351 (S.C.)—§ **14.9, n. 12;** § **4.42, n. 3.**

Woodward v. Woodward, 117 Ariz. 148, 571
P.2d 294 (Ariz.App. Div. 1 1977)—
§ **14.11, n. 2, 3.**

Woodward v. Woodward, 87 Tenn. 644, 11
S.W. 892 (Tenn.1889)—§ **4.39, n. 2;**
§ **4.42, n. 3.**

Woodworth v. Spring, 86 Mass. 321 (Mass.
1862)—§ **22.26, n. 6.**

Woolridge v. McKenna, 8 F. 650
(C.C.W.D.Tenn.1881)—§ **4.43, n. 1.**

Woolums v. Simonsen, 214 Kan. 722, 522
P.2d 1321 (Kan.1974)—§ **20.8, n. 12.**

Wooters, State ex rel. v. Dardenne, 131 La.
109, 59 So. 32 (La.1912)—§ **4.29, n. 2.**

Worcester County Trust Co. v. Riley, 302
U.S. 292, 58 S.Ct. 185, 82 L.Ed. 268
(1937)—§ **4.4, n. 4;** § **4.5;** § **4.5, n. 5, 7;**
§ **15.6, n. 11.**

Worcester North Sav. Institution v. Somerville Mill. Co., 101 N.H. 307, 141 A.2d
885 (N.H.1958)—§ **19.2, n. 3;** § **19.9, n.
7.**

Worden v. Mercer County Bd. of Elections,
61 N.J. 325, 294 A.2d 233 (N.J.1972)—
§ **4.13, n. 5.**

Workgroup Technology Corp. v. MGM Grand Hotel, LLC, 246 F.Supp.2d 102 (D.Mass.2003)—§ **9.8, n. 9.**

World Tanker Carriers Corp. v. M/V Ya Mawlaya, 99 F.3d 717 (5th Cir.1996)—§ **10.5;** § **10.5, n. 12;** § **10.6, n. 29.**

World–Wide Volkswagen Corp. v. Woodson, 444 U.S. 286, 100 S.Ct. 559, 62 L.Ed.2d 490 (1980)—§ **2.10, n. 28;** § **3.26, n. 3;** § **3.36, n. 16;** § **5.4;** § **5.4, n. 21;** § **5.11;** § **5.11, n. 18;** § **7.1, n. 2;** § **7.2;** § **7.2, n. 12, 14;** § **7.4;** § **7.4, n. 1, 4, 5;** § **7.5;** § **7.5, n. 2;** § **7.6, n. 1;** § **7.9, n. 10;** § **7.12, n. 10;** § **9.2;** § **9.2, n. 12;** § **10.2;** § **10.2, n. 12;** § **10.9;** § **10.9, n. 13;** § **10.15;** § **10.15, n. 11;** § **10.18;** § **10.18, n. 20;** § **15.10, n. 4;** § **24.12, n. 5;** § **24.14, n. 3.**

Worley v. Hineman, 6 Ind.App. 240, 33 N.E. 260 (Ind.App.1893)—§ **19.5, n. 5.**

Worthley v. Rockville Leasecar, Inc., 328 F.Supp. 185 (D.Md.1971)—§ **22.19, n. 12.**

Worthley v. Worthley, 44 Cal.2d 465, 283 P.2d 19 (Cal.1955)—§ **15.34;** § **15.34, n. 5;** § **15.35, n. 1;** § **15.37, n. 13.**

Wortman v. Sun Oil Co., 241 Kan. 226, 755 P.2d 488 (Kan.1987)—§ **3.23;** § **3.23, n. 23.**

WPMK Corp., In re, 59 B.R. 991 (D.Hawai'i 1986)—§ **19.2, n. 2.**

W.R. Grace & Co. v. Hartford Acc. and Indem. Co., 407 Mass. 572, 555 N.E.2d 214 (Mass.1990)—§ **18.1, n. 27.**

Wright, Matter of Estate of, 637 A.2d 106 (Me.1994)—§ **3.13, n. 9;** § **3.14, n. 4;** § **20.14, n. 11.**

Wright v. Brown, 528 N.E.2d 824 (Ind.App. 2 Dist.1988)—§ **15.34, n. 1.**

Wright v. Fireman's Fund Ins. Co., 522 F.2d 1376 (5th Cir.1975)—§ **3.12, n. 6.**

Wright v. Kroeger, 219 Or. 102, 345 P.2d 809 (Or.1959)—§ **13.9, n. 11, 14.**

Wright v. Rains, 106 S.W.3d 678 (Tenn.Ct. App.2003)—§ **21.3, n. 9;** § **21.6, n. 7;** § **21.13, n. 1.**

Wright v. Roberts, 116 Ga. 194, 42 S.E. 369 (Ga.1902)—§ **22.22, n. 5.**

Wright, State ex rel. Attorney General v., 194 Ark. 652, 109 S.W.2d 123 (Ark. 1937)—§ **22.3, n. 1.**

Wright–Moore Corp. v. Ricoh Corp., 908 F.2d 128 (7th Cir.1990)—§ **18.4, n. 1, 46;** § **18.5, n. 34.**

Wrigley v. Wrigley, 99 Wis.2d 802, 300 N.W.2d 81 (Wis.App.1980)—§ **15.15, n. 2, 7.**

W.S. Kirkpatrick & Co., Inc. v. Environmental Tectonics Corp., Intern., 493 U.S. 400, 110 S.Ct. 701, 107 L.Ed.2d 816 (1990)—§ **24.46, n. 10.**

Wuchter v. Pizzutti, 276 U.S. 13, 48 S.Ct. 259, 72 L.Ed. 446 (1928)—§ **5.14, n. 6;** § **5.16, n. 5;** § **12.3;** § **12.3, n. 8;** § **12.5, n. 1;** § **12.6, n. 4.**

WWG Industries, Inc., In re, 44 B.R. 287 (N.D.Ga.1984)—§ **23.13, n. 3.**

Wyatt v. Fulrath, 264 N.Y.S.2d 233, 211 N.E.2d 637 (N.Y.1965)—§ **14.12, n. 5;** § **18.4, n. 8;** § **18.7, n. 1;** § **18.9, n. 12.**

Wyatt v. Fulrath, 38 Misc.2d 1012, 239 N.Y.S.2d 486 (N.Y.Sup.1963)—§ **3.13, n. 4.**

Wyatt v. Kaplan, 686 F.2d 276 (5th Cir. 1982)—§ **7.9, n. 7.**

Wylie v. Speyer, 62 How. Pr. 107 (N.Y.Sup. 1881)—§ **19.15, n. 7.**

Wyman v. Newhouse, 93 F.2d 313 (2nd Cir.1937)—§ **11.15, n. 3.**

Wynne v. Wynne, 23 Miss. 251 (Miss.Err. & App.1852)—§ **20.6, n. 15.**

Wysong and Miles Co. v. Employers of Wausau, 4 F.Supp.2d 421 (M.D.N.C.1998)—§ **18.26, n. 13.**

X

X v. Y, [1994] H.J. (1493) 71 (S.Ct.)—§ **3.13, n. 10.**

Xanadu of Cocoa Beach, Inc. v. Zetley, 822 F.2d 982 (11th Cir.1987)—§ **19.3, n. 14.**

Xuncax v. Gramajo, 886 F.Supp. 162 (D.Mass.1995)—§ **17.55, n. 9.**

Y

Yahoo!, Inc. v. La Ligue Contre Le Racisme et L'Antisemitisme, 169 F.Supp.2d 1181 (N.D.Cal.2001)—§ **24.44, n. 12.**

Yakima Joe v. To–Is–Lap, 191 F. 516 (C.C.D.Or.1910)—§ **13.18, n. 8, 14.**

Yarborough v. Yarborough, 290 U.S. 202, 54 S.Ct. 181, 78 L.Ed. 269 (1933)—§ **15.32;** § **15.32, n. 1;** § **15.33, n. 1.**

Yarbrough v. Prentice Lee Tractor Co., 252 Ark. 349, 479 S.W.2d 549 (Ark.1972)—§ **12.17, n. 13.**

Yarbrough v. United States, 169 Ct.Cl. 589, 341 F.2d 621 (Ct.Cl.1965)—§ **13.7, n. 1.**

Yarbrough's Estate, In re, 126 Wash. 85, 216 P. 889 (Wash.1923)—§ **22.10, n. 9.**

Yazell, United States v., 382 U.S. 341, 86 S.Ct. 500, 15 L.Ed.2d 404 (1966)—§ **3.51, n. 9, 11.**

Yellow Cab Co., United States v., 340 U.S. 543, 71 S.Ct. 399, 95 L.Ed. 523 (1951)—§ **3.53, n. 3.**

Yiatchos v. Yiatchos, 376 U.S. 306, 84 S.Ct. 742, 11 L.Ed.2d 724 (1964)—§ **3.51, n. 6;** § **14.9, n. 4.**

Yick Wo v. Hopkins, 118 U.S. 356, 6 S.Ct. 1064, 30 L.Ed. 220 (1886)—§ **3.34, n. 3.**

Yocum v. Oklahoma Tire & Supply Co., 191 Ark. 1126, 89 S.W.2d 919 (Ark.1936)—§ **10.15, n. 4.**

Yoder v. Nu–Enamel Corp., 140 Neb. 585, 300 N.W. 840 (Neb.1941)—§ **10.14, n. 10.**

Yoder v. Yoder, 31 Conn.Supp. 345, 330 A.2d 825 (Conn.Super.1974)—§ **2.7, n. 14;** § **15.20, n. 9.**

Yoerg v. Northern N. J. Mortg. Associates, 44 N.J.Super. 286, 130 A.2d 392 (N.J.Super.A.D.1957)—§ **18.33, n. 1.**

York v. Bank of Commerce & Trust Co., 19 Tenn.App. 594, 93 S.W.2d 333 (Tenn.Ct. App.1936)—§ **22.19, n. 32.**

York v. Texas, 137 U.S. 15, 11 S.Ct. 9, 34 L.Ed. 604 (1890)—§ **5.8, n. 3;** § **6.5;** § **6.5, n. 19.**

York's Estate, In re, 95 N.H. 435, 65 A.2d 282 (N.H.1949)—§ **21.6, n. 5.**

Youn v. Track, Inc., 324 F.3d 409 (6th Cir.2003)—§ **8.3, n. 11.**

Young v. Fulton Iron Works Co., 709 S.W.2d 927 (Mo.App. S.D.1986)—§ **17.67, n. 2.**

Young v. Garcia, 172 So.2d 243 (Fla.App. 3 Dist.1965)—§ **13.5, n. 1.**

Young v. Masci, 289 U.S. 253, 53 S.Ct. 599, 77 L.Ed. 1158 (1933)—§ **3.28;** § **3.28, n. 1;** § **17.4;** § **17.4, n. 5.**

Young v. Mobil Oil Corp., 85 Or.App. 64, 735 P.2d 654 (Or.App.1987)—§ **17.40, n. 28;** § **18.20, n. 11.**

Young v. New Haven Advocate, 315 F.3d 256 (4th Cir.2002)—§ **5.11, n. 22;** § **7.8, n. 14, 15.**

Young v. O'Neal, 35 Tenn. 55 (Tenn. 1855)—§ **22.11, n. 10, 16;** § **22.15, n. 9.**

Young v. Pattridge, 40 F.R.D. 376 (N.D.Miss.1966)—§ **22.14, n. 10.**

Young, People ex rel. Winger v., 78 Ill. App.3d 512, 33 Ill.Dec. 920, 397 N.E.2d 253 (Ill.App. 2 Dist.1979)—§ **15.36, n. 7.**

Young v. Players Lake Charles, L.L.C., 47 F.Supp.2d 832 (S.D.Tex.1999)—§ **17.63, n. 4.**

Young v. Pollak, 85 Ala. 439, 5 So. 279 (Ala.1888)—§ **4.24, n. 1.**

Young v. Wittenmyre, 123 Ill. 303, 14 N.E. 869 (Ill.1888)—§ **22.23, n. 8.**

Young v. W.S. Badcock Corp., 222 Ga.App. 218, 474 S.E.2d 87 (Ga.App.1996)— § **17.40, n. 28;** § **18.1, n. 18.**

Younger v. Gianotti, 176 Tenn. 139, 138 S.W.2d 448 (Tenn.1940)—§ **4.34, n. 3.**

Youngstown Sheet & Tube Co. v. Westcott, 147 F.Supp. 829 (W.D.Okla.1957)— § **19.28, n. 6.**

Your Const. Center, Inc. v. Dominion Mortg. and Realty Trust (Dominion), 402 F.Supp. 757 (S.D.Fla.1975)—§ **19.9, n. 2, 5.**

Yousafzai v. Hyundai Motor America, 27 Cal.Rptr.2d 569 (Cal.App. 2 Dist.1994)— § **5.17, n. 3.**

Ytuarte v. Gruner & Jahr Printing and Pub. Co., 935 F.2d 971 (8th Cir.1991)— § **6.9, n. 22.**

Z

Zablocki v. Redhail, 434 U.S. 374, 98 S.Ct. 673, 54 L.Ed.2d 618 (1978)—§ **13.9, n. 1, 14.**

Zacaria v. Gulf King 35, Inc., 31 F.Supp.2d 560 (S.D.Tex.1999)—§ **17.63, n. 21.**

Zachariah K., Adoption of, 8 Cal.Rptr.2d 423 (Cal.App. 2 Dist.1992)—§ **16.5, n. 9.**

Zamost, In re, 7 B.R. 859 (Bkrtcy.S.D.Cal. 1980)—§ **23.13, n. 1.**

Zanghi v. Incorporated Village of Old Brookville, 752 F.2d 42 (2nd Cir.1985)— § **24.12, n. 7.**

Zangiacomi v. Saunders, 714 F.Supp. 658 (S.D.N.Y.1989)—§ **17.37, n. 16;** § **17.48, n. 11.**

Zanzonico v. Neeld, 17 N.J. 490, 111 A.2d 772 (N.J.1955)—§ **16.5, n. 3.**

Zapata Marine Service v. O/Y Finnlines, Ltd., 571 F.2d 208 (5th Cir.1978)— § **11.2, n. 1.**

Zdrok v. V Secret Catalogue, Inc., 215 F.Supp.2d 510 (D.N.J.2002)—§ **24.14, n. 3.**

Zeidner v. Wulforst, 197 F.Supp. 23 (E.D.N.Y.1961)—§ **3.41, n. 1.**

Zeiler, Estate of v. Prudential Ins. Co. of America, 570 F.Supp. 627 (N.D.Ill. 1983)—§ **23.3, n. 4.**

Zelinger v. State Sand & Gravel Co., 38 Wis.2d 98, 156 N.W.2d 466 (Wis.1968)— § **17.8, n. 13;** § **17.21, n. 15.**

Zendman v. Harry Winston, Inc., 305 N.Y. 180, 111 N.E.2d 871 (N.Y.1953)— § **19.13;** § **19.13, n. 4, 12;** § **19.15, n. 11.**

Zepeda v. Zepeda, 41 Ill.App.2d 240, 190 N.E.2d 849 (Ill.App. 1 Dist.1963)— § **16.1, n. 1.**

Ziady v. Curley, 396 F.2d 873 (4th Cir. 1968)—§ **4.37, n. 4;** § **4.41, n. 1.**

Zicherman v. Korean Air Lines Co., Ltd., 516 U.S. 217, 116 S.Ct. 629, 133 L.Ed.2d 596 (1996)—§ **17.63, n. 4.**

Ziemer v. Crucible Steel Co., 99 A.D. 169, 90 N.Y.S. 962 (N.Y.A.D. 1 Dept.1904)— § **22.10, n. 9.**

Zimmerman v. Board of Publications of Christian Reformed Church, Inc., 598 F.Supp. 1002 (D.Colo.1984)—§ **18.29, n. 3.**

Zimmerman v. Zimmerman, 175 Or. 585, 155 P.2d 293 (Or.1945)—§ **4.26, n. 1.**

Zimmerman Metals, Inc. v. United Engineers & Constructors, Inc., Stearns-Roger Div., 720 F.Supp. 859 (D.Colo. 1989)—§ **11.2, n. 6.**

Zimmerman's Estate, In re, 195 Minn. 38, 261 N.W. 467 (Minn.1935)—§ **22.22, n. 6.**

Zinsler v. Marriott Corp., 605 F.Supp. 1499 (D.Md.1985)—§ **11.11, n. 6.**

Zions First Nat. Bank v. Allen, 688 F.Supp. 1495 (D.Utah 1988)—§ **11.2, n. 4.**

Zipcey v. Thompson, 67 Mass. 243 (Mass. 1854)—§ **19.30, n. 7.**

Zippo Mfg. Co. v. Zippo Dot Com, Inc., 952 F.Supp. 1119 (W.D.Pa.1997)—§ **5.11, n. 22; § 7.8, n. 16.**

Zisblatt v. Zisblatt, 693 S.W.2d 944 (Tex. App.-Fort Worth 1985)—§ **14.11, n. 3.**

Zivalich v. International Broth. of Teamsters, Chauffeurs, Warehousemen and Helpers of America, 662 So.2d 62 (La. App. 4 Cir.1995)—§ **6.9, n. 19.**

Zobel v. Williams, 457 U.S. 55, 102 S.Ct. 2309, 72 L.Ed.2d 672 (1982)—§ **3.31, n. 3; § 3.32, n. 9; § 3.34, n. 3.**

Zogg v. Penn Mut. Life Ins. Co., 276 F.2d 861 (2nd Cir.1960)—§ **18.26, n. 9.**

Zombro v. Moffett, 329 Mo. 137, 44 S.W.2d 149 (Mo.1931)—§ **20.8, n. 9.**

Zoriano Sanchez v. Caribbean Carriers Ltd., 552 F.2d 70 (2nd Cir.1977)—§ **24.1, n. 6.**

Zorick v. Jones, 193 So.2d 420 (Miss. 1966)—§ **19.8, n. 14.**

Zschernig v. Miller, 389 U.S. 429, 88 S.Ct. 664, 19 L.Ed.2d 683 (1968)—§ **3.36, n. 16; § 3.50, n. 4; § 3.56; § 3.56, n. 2; § 3.59, n. 4; § 10.19, n. 59; § 11.13; § 11.13, n. 12; § 20.17; § 20.17, n. 9; § 24.35, n. 5; § 24.39, n. 2.**

Zumbro, Inc. v. California Natural Products, 861 F.Supp. 773 (D.Minn.1994)—§ **9.3, n. 18.**

Zurich Ins. Co. v. Shearson Lehman Hutton, Inc., 618 N.Y.S.2d 609, 642 N.E.2d 1065 (N.Y.1994)—§ **18.26, n. 19.**

Zuviceh v. Nationwide Ins. Co., 786 So.2d 340 (La.App. 1 Cir.2001)—§ **17.56, n. 20.**

Zwerling v. Zwerling, 167 Misc.2d 782, 636 N.Y.S.2d 595 (N.Y.Sup.1995)—§ **15.25, n. 2.**

Zwerling v. Zwerling, 270 S.C. 685, 244 S.E.2d 311 (S.C.1978)—§ **13.5, n. 1.**

Zygmuntowicz v. Hospitality Investments, Inc., 828 F.Supp. 346 (E.D.Pa.1993)—§ **17.48, n. 38.**

*

Index

References are to Sections

ACCESS TO COURTS
Erie doctrine, 3.36.
Foreign nationals under bilateral treaties, 3.58.
Privileges and immunities, 3.32, 3.33.
Public policy of the forum, 3.15, 3.25, 3.40, 24.40, 24.44.

ADMINISTRATION OF DECEDENTS' ESTATES
See also Probate; Succession.
Accounting and distribution, 22.23.
Actions against foreign representatives, 22.17.
Actions by personal representative outside state of appointment, 22.19.
Assignment of intangible by personal representative, 22.17.
Claims of creditors, 22.21.
Commercial paper, 22.11.
Conservators and guardians, 22.24, 22.25.
Corporate stock, 22.12.
Creditors,
  Claims, 22.21.
  Proof and payment of claims, 22.21.
Debtor's payments to foreign representatives, 22.16.
Distribution, 22.24.
Ecclesiastic courts, 22.5.
Executor, privity between foreign executors, 22.19.
Family allowances, 22.22.
Foreign assets, taking possession, 22.15.
Guardian and conservators, 22.24, 22.25.
Guardians of the person, 22.26.
Insolvent estates, rights of creditors, 22.21.
Intangible assets, 22.10.
Judgments, enforcement by personal representative, 22.18.
Judgments against foreign representatives, 22.19.
Jurisdiction over foreign representatives, 22.19.
Law suits arising out of administration, 22.18.
Life insurance, 22.13.
Long-arm jurisdiction over personal representatives, 22.19.
Payment to foreign representative, 22.16.

ADMINISTRATION OF DECEDENTS' ESTATES—Cont'd
Post-death move of assets, 22.9.
Place of administration, 22.6.
Situs of assets, 22.7.
Temporary presence of assets, 22.8.
Personal representative,
  Jurisdiction over and power to sue, 22.14, 22.15.
  Payment to foreign representative, 22.16.
  Suits arising out of administration, 22.18.
  Title to assets, 22.15.
  Transfer of claims, 22.17.
Preclusion by prior litigation between foreign personal representatives, 22.20.
Privity between foreign representatives, 22.20.
Protected persons, 22.24.
Res judicata as between foreign personal representatives, 22.19.
Spousal and family allowances, 22.22.
Taxation of succession, 22.7.
Title of personal representative, 22.15.
Transfer of claim by personal representatives, 22.17.
Universal successor, suit by, 22.18.

ADMINISTRATIVE DETERMINATIONS
See also Judgments; Workers' Compensation.
In foreign recognition practice, 24.46.
Recognition of, 24.46.

ADMIRALTY, 3.50, 17.49
Jurisdiction, 10.6.
Tort Choice of Law, 17.63.

ADOPTION
Applicable law, 16.4, 16.5.
Extrastate consequences, 16.6.
Hague Convention on Adoption, 16.8.
Hague Convention on the Protection of Children and Cooperation in Respect of lntercountry Adoptions, 16.9.
History, 16.4.
Inheritance rights as related to, 16.2, 16.3.
International adoptions and bilateral treaties, 16.7.
Jurisdiction for, 16.5.

ADOPTION—Cont'd
Legitimation, 16.1.

AGENCY, 18.32, 18.36

AIRCRAFT
Chattel security, 19.20, 19.26.
Convention on international recognition of
  rights in aircraft, 19.26.

ALIENATION OF AFFECTIONS, 17.54

ANNULMENT
Celebration state, defects in marriage,
  15.16.
Divisible divorce concept and, 15.14, 15.15.
Jurisdiction to grant, 15.15.
Law applicable to, 15.15, 15.16.
Relation to divorce, 15.2, 15.15.
Uniform Marriage Evasion Act, 15.16.

ANTISUIT INJUNCTIONS, 24.9, 24.21

ARBITRATION
Clauses, 6.3.
Enforcement of awards,
  Under bilateral treaty, 24.48.
  Under common law or full faith & cred-
    it, 24.47.
  Under federal law, 24.47, 24.48.
Geneva Convention, 24.46, 24.47.
International Investment Disputes Conven-
  tion, 24.47.
Non-parties, 11.6.
U.N. (New York) Convention, 24.47, 24.48.
Uniform Arbitration Act, 24.47.

ATTACHMENT
See Jurisdiction, Quasi in rem.

BANKRUPTCY
Bankruptcy court, jurisdiction of, 23.12.
Claims "related" to bankruptcy,
  Applicable conflicts law, 23.13, 23.14,
    23.15, 23.16.
  Applicable substantive law, 23.13, 23.14,
    23.15.
  Federal common law, 23.14.
European Communities' Preliminary Draft
  Convention on Bankruptcy, 23.19.
International bankruptcies,
  Foreign proceeding, effect in United
    States, 23.18.
  United States proceeding, effect abroad,
    23.19.
Personal Jurisdiction, 10.7.
Piercing the corporate veil, 23.70.
Related and multinational corporations,
  23.19.
Support obligation, effect on, 23.13.
Transfer, 23.16.
  And federal conflicts rules, 23.16.
Venue, 23.13.

BEALE, JOSEPH H., 2.7

**BETTER LAW APPROACH, SEE ALSO
  LEFLAR, ROBERT**
In conflicts theory, 2.13.

**BETTER LAW APPROACH, SEE ALSO
  LEFLAR, ROBERT**—Cont'd
In tort conflicts, 17.21.

BORROWING STATUTES, 3.11

**"BRUSSELS I" AND "BRUSSELS II" REG-
  ULATIONS SEE EUROPEAN UNION**

BUSINESS ASSOCIATIONS
See Corporations.

CANADA
Foreign Judgments Act, 24.38.
Reciprocal Enforcement of Judgments Act,
  24.38.

CAVERS, DAVID F., 2.8, 2.12, 17.38, 17.40,
  17.42–17.44, 17.48–17.49, 17.81

CHARACTERIZATION
Doctrinal context, 3.2, 3.4–3.12.
Domicile, 4.8–4.10.
In marital property, 14.13, 14.14.
In tort cases, 17.8.
Issue identification in contract cases, 18.17.
  Of state law in federal court, see *Erie*
    doctrine.
Penal Statutes, 3.17.
Statute of frauds, 3.8.
Statute of limitations,
  As procedural, 3.3, 3.9, 3.10.
  As substantive, 3.8, 3.9–3.12.
  Borrowing statutes, 3.11.
  Built-in limitations, 3.10.
  In wrongful death acts, 3.10.
Subject matter,
  And false conflicts, 3.2, 3.5.
  Connecting factors, 3.6.
  Under First Restatement, 3.4–3.6.
  Under modern approaches, 3.2, 3.4, 3.5,
    3.7, 3.8.
Substance/procedure,
  In general, 3.2, 3.4, 3.5, 3.8.
  Statute of frauds as substantive under
    Restatement Second, 3.8.
  Statute of limitations, 3.8, 3.10.

CHILD SUPPORT
See Dissolution of Marriage; Hague Convention on; United Nations.

CHOICE OF FORUM CLAUSES, 11.1, 11.8,
  18.1

CHOICE OF LAW
  See also Choice of Law Approaches;
    Choice of Law Rules; Constitu-
    tional Limitations; *Erie* Doctrine;
    particular subject matter (Con-
    tracts, Torts, etc.).
Characterization, 3.2–3.5, 17.8.
Connecting Factors, 3.7, 3.8.
Local Remedy, 3.19.
Post-occurrence change of domicile, effect
  of, 3.23.
Public Policy Exception, 3.2, 3.15, 3.16.

CHOICE OF LAW—Cont'd
Renvoi, 3.2, 3.13.
Substance and Procedure, 3.8–3.10.

CHOICE OF LAW APPROACHES
Beale, Joseph H., 2.7.
Better law approach, see also Leflar, R.A., 2.13, 17.21.
California approach, 17.16–17.19.
Cavers, David F., 2.8, 2.12.
Comity, 2.5, 2.7.
Comparative Impairment, 2.9, 7.16–17.20.
Cook, Walter Wheeler, 2.8.
Currie, Brainerd, 2.9, 17.11.
Eclecticism, 2.19, 17.1.
Ehrenzweig, A.E., 2.10.
Forum law preference, 2.10, 2.24, 17.15.
Functional analyses, 2.11.
Interest analysis, 2.9, 2.24, 17.11–17.20.
Leflar, R.A., 2.13, 17.21.
Lex fori, 2.10, 2.24, 17.15.
Lex loci delicti, 17.2–17.6, 17.33.
Louisiana approach, 17.20, 17.39.
Most-significant relationship, 2.22, 17.24–17.28.
Neumeier rules, 17.31, 17.32, 17.39, 17.42, 17.43.
Policy analysis, 17.34.
Restatement, Second, 2.14, 2.23, 17.24–17.28.
State methodologies, 2.18–2.25.
Traditional approaches, 2.7, 2.16, 2.17, 2.21, 17.2.
Value oriented approaches, 2.12, 2.13.

CHOICE OF LAW CLAUSES
See also Contracts; Wills.
Interpretation, 18.3.
Succession, 20.8.
Public Policy Limits, 18.4, 18.5, 18.10.
Under Uniform Commercial Code, 18.12.
Relational requirements, 18.6–18.9.
Restatement Second approach, 18.8–18.11.
Torts, 17.40.
Trusts, 21.3.

CHOICE OF LAW RULES
See also Codifications.
As a goal in American law, 2.26, 17.33, 17.35, 17.81.
Emerging from American cases, 17.39–17.50, 17.81.
In other countries, 2.27, 17.39, 17.47, 17.49, 17.80.
In products liability, 17.80–17.82.
Louisiana rules, see Louisiana codification.
Neumeier rules, 17.31, 17.32, 17.39, 17.42, 17.43.

CIVIL UNIONS, 13.90
See also Domestic Relationships and Dissolution of Domestic Relationships

CODIFICATIONS
Louisiana, See Louisiana Codification.

CODIFICATIONS—Cont'd
In other countries, 2.27, 17.39, 17.47, 17.49, 17.80.

COGNOVIT NOTES
And jurisdiction, 6.3.
Recognition of judgments based on, 24.15.

COMITY
See also Judgments; Privileges and Immunities Clause.
In conflicts theory, 2.7.

COMMERCIAL PAPER
Assignability, 19.27.

COMMUNITY PROPERTY
See Matrimonial Property.

COMPARATIVE IMPAIRMENT, 17.16–17.20
California approach, 17.16–17.19.
Louisiana approach, 17.20, 17.39.

CONDUCT REGULATION IN TORTS, 17.36–17.38, 17.48–17.49

CONFESSION OF JUDGMENTS
Jurisdiction based on cognovit, 6.3.
Recognition of judgments based on, 24.15.

CONFLICT OF LAWS
Defined, 1.1.
Scope, 1.2.

CONFLICTS THEORY, GENERALLY
Ancient Greece, 2.2.
Bartolus, 2.3.
Beale, Joseph H., 2.7.
Cavers, David F., 2.8, 2.12.
Comity, 2.5, 2.7.
Comparative impairment, 2.9, 17.16–17.20.
Contracts theory, 2.14, 2.22.
Cook, Walter Wheeler, 2.8.
Carrie, Brainerd, 2.9, 17.11.
Dutch school, 2.5.
Ehrenzweig, A.E., 2.10.
Forum law preference, 2.10, 2.24, 17.15.
French statutists, 2.4.
Functional analyses, 2.11.
Huber, Ulrich, 2.5.
Interest analysis, 2.9, 2.24, 17.11–17.20.
Italian statutists, 2.3.
Leflar, R.A., 2.13, 17.21.
Louisiana approach, 2.27, 17.20.
Restatement, Second, 2.14, 2.23.
Restatement, Third, proposals, 2.14.
Savigny, Friedrich Carl von, 2.6.
State methodologies, 2.18–2.25.
Story, Joseph, 2.7.
Traditional approaches, 2.7, 2.16, 2.17, 2.21, 17.2.
von Mohren & Trautmon, 2.11.
Wächter, Carl Georg, 2.6.
Weintraub, Russell, 2.11.

CONSERVATORS AND GUARDIANS, 22.24–22.26

CONSTITUTIONAL LIMITATIONS
See also Access to Courts; Direct Action; *Erie* Doctrine; Jurisdiction.
And *Klaxon* doctrine, 3.36, 3.47.
Contacts test, 3.23, 3.26, 3.29.
Due process and fairness to the defendant, 3.20, 3.25, 3.27.
Equal protection, 3.24, 3.30, 3.31, 3.34, 3.35.
Federal Court application, 3.48.
On choice of law,
Balancing state interests, 3.21, 3.24, 3.30.
Due process limitations, 3.21, 3.30.
Full faith and credit limitations, 3.20, 3.24, 3.30.
Matrimonial property, 14.14.
Relation of due process and full faith and credit, 3.20, 3.24.
Requirement of significant relationship, 3.21, 3.22, 3.23, 3.24, 3.35.
Workers' compensation, 17.60, 17.61.
On choice of law in federal court, 3.48.
Privileges and immunities, 3.22, 3.31.
Refusal to entertain cause of action, 3.25.

CONTRACTS
Accord and satisfaction, 18.37.
Adhesion contracts, 18.5.
Agency, 18.32, 18.33, 18.34, 18.35, 18.36.
Assignability of intangible, 19.28.
Assignments, 18.37.
Bailments, 18.45.
Case categories, 18.3, 18.17.
Characteristic performance, 18.22.
Chattels, 18.24–18.35.
Checks and notes, 18.37.
Choice of law, in general, 18.13.
By party stipulation, 18.1–18.12.
Modern approaches, overview of, 18.16–18.21.
Place of contracting, 18.14.
Place of performance, 18.14.
Choice of law, modern approaches in the courts, 18.21.
Classic Approach, 18.14, 18.15.
Construction contracts, 18.29.
Covenants in land, 18.23, 19.3, 19.9.
Covenants no to compete, 18.7.
Damages, 18.39.
Discharge, 18.37.
Employment contracts, 18.29–18.31.
Equitable remedies and quasi-contract, 18.47, 18.48.
European Communities Convention, 18.17, 18.40.
Family law aspects, 18.17, 18.18.
For rendition of services, 18.29.
For repayment of money lent, 18.28.
Funds transfers, 18.37.

CONTRACTS—Cont'd
Governmental interest analysis, 18.20.
Judicial decisions summarized, 18.21.
Hague Convention on the Law Applicable to Agency, 18.36.
Hague Convention relating to a Uniform Law on the International Sale of Goods, 18.25.
Illegality, 18.39.
Implied warranty, 18.25.
Insurance contracts, 18.5, 18.26.
Integrated in a writing, 18.38.
Inter–American Convention on Law Applicable to International Contracts, 2.27, 18.4, 18.6, 18.21.
Interest in chattels, 18.24.
Interests in land, 18.23.
Joint ventures, 18.37.
Leases, 18.37.
Leflar approach, 18.11, 18.16.
Lex loci contractus, 18.14, 18.15.
Loan repayment, 18.28.
Measure of recovery, 18.23, 18.48.
Modern approaches, 18.16.
Options, 18.37.
Oregon codification, 18.16, 18.23, 18.29, 18.32.
Party autonomy, 11.2, 18.1, 18.2.
Adhesion contracts, 18.5.
Choice-of-court clauses, 18.1.
Construction and interpretation of choice-of-law clauses, 10.3.
Covenants not to compete, 18.7.
"Floating" clauses, 18.02 n. 11, 18.7.
Insurance contracts, 18.5.
Place of contracting rule, 18.14, 18.15.
Personal property, 18.14.
Public policy limitation, 18.2, 18.4, 18.5, 18.10.
In specific contracts, 18.5.
Purpose of the contract, 18.18, 18.21, 18.39, 18.41.
Characterization, 18.16.
Restatement (First), 18.14, 18.15.
Characterization, 18.14.
Reasonable basis for choice, 18.9.
Restatement (Second), 18.2, 18.5, 18.8, 18.9, 18.10, 18.11.
Substantial relationship requirement, 18.6, 18.7, 18.9.
UCC, 18.2, 18.5, 18.6, 18.10, 18.12.
Usury, 18.5.
Validation principle, 18.11.
Quasi-contract, 18.42.
Real Estate, 18.37.
Releases, 18.37.
Restatement (First), 18.14, 18.15.
Restatement (Second), 18.2, 18.5, 18.8, 18.9, 18.10.
Rome Convention, 2.27, 18.4, 18.5, 18.6, 18.40.
Sale of goods, international, 18.1, 18.25.
Sales of chattels, 18.24, 18.25.
Service contracts, 18.29.

CONTRACTS—Cont'd
Statute of frauds, 18.38.
Succession law aspects, 18.19.
Summary of current approaches, 18.21.
Suretyship, 10.2, 18.27.
Traditional approach, 18.14, 18.15.
Transportation contracts, 18.30, 18.31.
UNICTRAL Convention for the International Sale of Goods (Vienna Sales Convention), 18.1, 18.25.
Undue influence, 18.39.
Unjust enrichment, 18.39, 18.42, 18.43, 18.44, 18.45, 18.46.
Usury, 18.5, 18.39.
Validation rule, 18.16, 18.20, 18.28.
Vienna Sales Convention, 18.1, 18.25.

CONVENTIONS
See European Communities; Hague Convention On; International Treaties; United Nations; subject matter entries.

CORPORATIONS
See also Bankruptcy; Jurisdiction, Jurisdiction over things.
Agency, 18.32–18.36.
Constitutional protection, 23.6.
Corporate stock, assignment of, 19.23, 23.4.
Directors, rights and duties of, 23.4.
Dissolution, 23.11.
Diversity jurisdiction, 23.3.
Domicile, analogous relationship, 4.46.
Enemy corporations, 23.3.
European Community, recognition of foreign, 23.1, 23.2.
Foreign corporations, regulation of,
Constitutional limits, 23.4, 23.6.
Pseudo-foreign corporations, 23.9.
Qualification statutes, 23.7, 23.9.
Forum, regulation by, 23.6.
In United States bilateral treaties, 23.2.
Incorporation, reference to law of, 23.2.
Inter–American Recognition Convention, 23.1.
Internal affairs, 23.4, 23.5, 23.6, 23.9.
Jurisdiction, 6.3.
Consent, 6.3.
Continuous and systematic contracts, 6.9.
Corporate employees, 10.17.
Domestic corporations, 10.13.
Foreign corporations, 10.14, 10.15.
Foreign State caps–owned corporations, 10.19.
Parents & subsidiaries, 10.16.
Model Business Corporation Act, 23.8.
Piercing the corporate veil, 23.10, 23.20.
Principal place of business, reference to, 23.3, 23.4.
Pseudo-foreign corporations, 23.3, 23.9.
Qualification statutes, 23.7, 23.8.
Seat concept in European law, 23.1.
Stockholders, rights and duties of, 23.4.

CORPORATIONS—Cont'd
Winding-up, 23.11.

COVENANT MARRIAGE, 13.16, 15.3

CURRIE, BRAINERD
See also Governmental Interests.
Conflicts Theory, 2.9.
Theory in contract cases, 18.16.
Theory in tort cases, 17.1, 17.2.

CUSTODY
"Clean hands" doctrine, 15.39, 15.41.
European Union, EC Regulation No. 2201/2003, 11.10, 15.43, 24.38.
Forum non conveniens, 11.10.
Full faith and credit, 24.12.
Hague Convention on Civil Aspects of International Child Abduction, 15.42, 15.43.
Hague Convention on Protection of Minors, 15.43.
Indian tribes, jurisdiction of, 15.42.
International Parental Kidnapping Act of 1993, 15.42.
International recognition and modification, 15.42, 15.43.
Interstate recognition and modification, 15.40.
Jurisdiction, 15.39, 15.42.
Parental Kidnaping Prevention Act, 15.39, 15.40, 15.42.
Uniform Child Custody Jurisdiction Act, 15.39, 15.41, 15.43.

DAMAGES
Characterization in tort, 17.9.
For breach of contract, 18.38, 18.39.
Valuation under Warsaw Convention, 17.44.

DECEDENTS' ESTATES
See Administration of Decedents' Estates; Probate; Succession.

DEFAMATION
Choice of Law, 17.55.
Jurisdiction, 7.8–7.10.

DEFENSE OF MARRIAGE ACT (DOMA), 13.19, 15.17, 15.30

DÉPEÇAGE, 18.38, 24.39

DIRECT ACTION
Constitutional limitations on, 3.23.

DISCOVERY
See Evidence, Foreign Law, Proof of.

DISINTERESTED THIRD STATE
And Restatement (Second), 2.14.
Case application, 17.17.
In Currie's theory, 2.19.

DISSOLUTION OF DOMESTIC RELATIONSHIPS
See also Annulment.
Bigamy, 15.11.

**DISSOLUTION OF DOMESTIC RELATION-
SHIPS**—Cont'd
Child custody, see Custody.
Collateral determination of invalidity,
    15.12, 15.13.
Covenant marriage, 15.1–15.3.
Dissolution of civil union and same-sex
    marriage, 13.20, 15.17.
Divisible divorce concept, 15.27.
    Annulment, 15.2.
    Custody, 15.27, 15.29, 15.39.
    Support, 15.28, 15.29.
Divorce and annulment compared, 15.01,
    15.2, 15.15
Divorce jurisdiction and preclusion,
    15.08–15.11.
Divorce jurisdiction in the European Union,
    15.5, 15.17, 24.38.
Divorce jurisdiction not at domicile,
    Generally, 15.5, 15.7.
In inter partes divorce, 15.8.
"Domesticating" foreign country divorces,
    15.20.
Domicile and divorce jurisdiction,
    Generally, 15.4.
    Domicile as federal question, 15.6.
    Ex parte divorces, 15.6, 15.11.
    In recognition of foreign-country di-
        vorce, 15.17–15.23.
    Service personnel statutes, 15.5.
Dominican Republic divorces, 15.20, 15.22.
Durational residence requirements, 15.7,
    15.14, 15.20.
Enforcement and modification of Support
    Decrees, 15.31.
    International recognition, 15.37.
    Uniform Reciprocal Enforcement of Sup-
        port Act, 15.30, 15.34, 15.36.
Ex parte divorce, 15.6, 15.11.
Hague Convention on the Recognition of
    Divorces and Legal Separations,
    15.26.
Haitian divorces, 15.20, 15.22.
Inter parties divorce, 15.8–15.11, 15.21.
Jewish law, 15.24.
Islamic law, 15.25.
Law applicable to divorce, 15.4, 15.15.
Limited divorce, 15.1, 15.2.
Mexican divorces, 15.20–15.22.
Military personnel, 15.5.
No-fault divorce, 15.1–15.3.
Non-judicial divorces, recognition of, 15.24.
Recognition of foreign-country consensual
    divorces in United States,
    15.17–15.23.
Recognition of foreign-country judicial di-
    vorces in United States, 15.14–15.22.
Recognition of United States divorces
    abroad, 15.26.
Renvoi, 15.17.
Sham proceedings, 15.10, 15.20.
Sherrer doctrine, 15.9, 15.14, 15.23.
Support obligations, 15.30.
    Choice of law, 15.35.

**DISSOLUTION OF DOMESTIC RELATION-
SHIPS**—Cont'd
Support obligations—Cont'd
    Enforcement and modification of, 15.31,
        15.34.
    Forum shopping, 15.33.
    International recognition, 15.37.
    Lump-sum claims, 15.32.
Talaq, 15.24, 15.25.
Uniform Divorce Recognition Act, 15.11.
Uniform Interstate Family Support Act,
    15.30.
Uniform Marriage and Divorce Act, 15.2.
Uniform Reciprocal Enforcement of Sup-
    port Act, 15.30.

DIVISIBLE DIVORCE
See Dissolution of Domestic Relationships.

DIVORCE
See Dissolution of Domestic Relationships.

DOCUMENTS
Hague Convention on Service, 12.7, 12.8.
Legalization for international use, 12.7,
    24.35.
Service abroad, 12.6–12.8.

DOMA
See Defense of Marriage Act.

**DOMESTIC CORPORATIONS, JURISDIC-
TION OVER,** 10.13

DOMESTIC RELATIONSHIPS
    Generally, 13.01–13.21.
    See Civil Union, Marriage, Same-sex
        Marriage, Dissolution of Domestic
        Relationships. For other partner-
        ships, see 13.21.
See also Adoption, Custody, Dissolution.

DOMICILE
Adopted children, 4.39.
Aliens, 4.30, 4.31.
Armed service personnel, 4.26.
Capacity to acquire, 4.45.
Characterization by forum, 4.8, 4.9.
Children,
    Adopted, 4.39.
    Emancipated, 4.44.
    On death of parent, 4.33.
    Power of guardian to change, 4.37.
Children born out of wedlock, 4.38.
Children of separated parents, 4.40.
Choice of law significance in torts, 4.1,
    17.39, 17.40–17.45.
Citizenship compared in products, 4.12,
    17.65.
Constitutional control, 4.8, 4.12.
Continues once acquired, 4.21.
Convicts, 4.27.
Corporations, analogous relationship, 4.46.
Death taxes,
    Compromise, 4.4.

DOMICILE—Cont'd
Death taxes—Cont'd
    Multiple domicile, 4.4.
Defined, 4.15.
Derivative domicile,
    Children,
        Illegitimate, 4.38.
        Legitimate, 4.37.
        Origin, domicile of, 4.36.
Determination by law of forum, 4.8.
Different findings by different courts, 4.4, 4.6, 4.7.
Diplomatic personnel, 4.32.
Divorce jurisdiction and choice of law, 15.4.
Divorce procedural determination, 4.4, 4.7.
Domicile of choice,
    Abandonment, 4.19.
    Acquisition, 4.17.
    Duration of presence, 4.18.
    Evidence of intent, 4.18, 4.19.
    Freedom of choice, 4.25.
    Intent, distinguished from motive, 4.24.
    Intent to acquire, 4.18, 4.19.
    Presence requirement, 4.18.
Family member as evidencing "presence", 4.19.
Foreign law as controlling, 4.10.
Forum defines, 4.8, 4.9.
Geographic boundaries of, 4.28.
Governmental privileges based on, 4.19, 4.31.
Habitual residence compared, 4.11, 4.13, 4.14.
Home, equivalent to, 4.15.
Homes, multiple, 4.4.
In foreign law, 4.11.
Incompetent persons, 4.45.
Institutionalized persons, 4.45.
Intent, 4.20.
Itinerants, 4.29.
Jurisdiction, domicile as a factor, 6.4.
Married minors, 4.44.
Married persons, 4.33–4.35.
    English approach, 4.35.
Military personnel, 15.5.
Minors, 4.36, 4.37.
Mobile home occupants, 4.29.
Motive, distinguished from intent, 4.24.
Multiple domicile, 4.5.
Multiple homes, 4.21–4.23.
Nationality compared, 4.11.
Nationality in federal system, 4.11.
Origin, domicile of, 4.36.
Preclusion by prior litigation, 4.4.
Prisoners, 4.27.
Religious orders, member of, 4.27.
Residence as meaning domicile, 4.13.
Spouses, 4.33–4.35.
State citizenship compared, 4.28.
Status, effect of, 4.30.
Tax liability based on, 4.4–4.6.
Territorial extent, 4.28.
Treaty arrangements, 4.32.
Unitary concept, 4.16.

DOMICILE—Cont'd
Variation, 4.4, 4.6.
Vicarious presence, 4.19.
Visa, nature of as affecting domicile, 4.30–4.32.

DUE PROCESS
See also Constitutional Limitations, On choice of law.
And notice, 12.2, 12.3.
And opportunity to be heard, 12.2, 12.4.

EHRENZWEIG, ALBERT A.
Choice-of-law theory, 2.10.

EMPLOYMENT CONTRACTS, 18.29

EQUAL PROTECTION CLAUSE
And choice of law, 3.31, 3.34.

EQUITY DECREES
Recognition and enforcement of, 24.9.

ERIE DOCTRINE
Alternative dispute resolution, 3.41.
Choice of law in federal courts, 3.36–3.48.
Court closing rules, 3.40.
Determining state law, 3.47.
Federal common law, 3.49, 3.50.
Federal Rules of Civil Procedure, 3.38, 3.39.
Federal Rules of Evidence, 3.39.
Federal transfers, 3.46, 3.48.
Interpleader, 3.43.
Interstate forum shopping, 3.42, 3.43.
Involuntary Dismissals, 3.40, 24.2, 24.11.
Not applicable in bankruptcy, 23.14.
100–mile bulge rule, 3.44.
Outcome-determinative test, 3.37, 3.38.
Policy of *Erie* and *Klaxon*, 3.36.
Practical issues, 3.37.
Preclusion rules, 3.40, 24.2, 24.11.
Supplemental jurisdiction, 3.45.
Testimonial privileges, 12.10.
Tort obligations, 3.53.
Uniform Certification of Questions of Law Act, 3.47.
When forum is disinterested, 3.47.

EUROPEAN UNION
"Brussels I," see Regulation No. 44/2201 below.
"Brussels II," see Regulation No. 2201/2003 below.
Convention on Jurisdiction and Recognition of Judgments, 24.38.
Convention on Law Applicable to Contractual Obligations ("Rome I"), 2.27, 17.39, 18.1, 18.2, 18.4–18.7, 18.12, 18.20, 18.21, 18.23, 18.28, 18.30, 18.40.
Forum non conveniens, 11.10, 11.11.
Forum selection clauses, 11.2.
Law Applicable to Tort, Proposal for a Regulation ("Rome I"), 2.27, 3.13, 17.36, 17.39, 17.40, 17.49, 17.50, 17.55, 17.80, 17.82.
Lis pendens, 11.10.
Notice, as a condition for judgment recognition, 12.2.
Party autonomy, 11.2.

EUROPEAN UNION—Cont'd
Regulation No. 44/2001 on Jurisdiction and
    Judgment Recognition.
    In Civil and Commercial Matters
        ("Brussels I"), 2.27, 12.2, 12.4,
        14.28, 14.38, 24.38.
Regulation No. 2201/2003 on Jurisdiction
    and Judgment.
    Recognition in Matrimonial and Child
        Custody Matters ("Brussels II"),
        2.27, 11.10, 15.6.
Regulation No. 1348/2000 on Service of
    Documents, 12.7.
Regulation No. 1206/2001 on Taking of Evi-
    dence, 12.9.

EVIDENCE
    See also Foreign Law, Proof of.
Admissibility, 12.10.
European Community, Regulation No.
    1206/2001, 12.9.
Hague Convention on Taking Evidence
    Abroad, 12.09, 12.8, 12.9.
Intent in domicile, 4.17, 4.19.
International conflicts, 12.13.
Interstate conflicts, 12.11, 12.13, 12.14.
Letters rogatory, 12.08, 12.8.
Taking abroad of, 12.08, 12.8.
Under European Community Regulation,
    12.9.
Testimonial privilege,
    In United States law, 12.10.
    Under Hague Convention, 12.13, 12.14.
U.S. discovery in aid of foreign proceedings,
    12.8.

FALSE CONFLICTS
    In general, 2.9.
Renvoi, 3.13, 3.14.
Tort, 17.12, 17.32, 17.39–17.40.

FAMILY PROPERTY
    See Matrimonial Property; Property; Suc-
        cession; Trusts; Wills.

FEDERAL COMMON LAW, 3.49, 3.50
And Supremacy Clause, 3.36.
Contractual obligations, 3.52.
Federal interest defined, 3.51.
In bankruptcy, 23.15, 23.16.
Governmental obligations, 3.51.
Standard for, 3.49, 3.50.
To prevent interstate forum shopping, 3.46.
Tort obligations, 3.53.

FEDERAL COURTS
    See Admiralty; Bankruptcy; *Erie* Doctrine.

FEDERAL INTERPLEADER
Erie doctrine, 3.43.
Estate tax claims by different states, 4.5.

FEDERAL RULES OF CIVIL PROCEDURE
Erie doctrine, 3.38, 3.39.

FEDERAL RULES OF EVIDENCE
Erie doctrine, 3.39.

FEDERAL TRANSFERS, 11.14
Erie doctrine, 3.46.
Generally, 11.14.

FOREIGN LAW, PROOF OF
Common law, 12.15.
European Convention on Information on
    Foreign Law, 12.16.
Failure of proof, 12.19.
Federal practice, 12.18.
Foreign country approaches to, 12.16.
Judicial notice, 12.16, 12.17.
Presumptions, 12.15.
State statutes and uniform laws, 12.17.

FOREIGN RELATIONS POWER, 3.56
See International Treaties.

FORUM NON CONVENIENS, 5.18,
    11.8–11.13
See also Jurisdiction, Limitations on exer-
    cise.

FORUM SELECTION CLAUSES, 6.3, 11.2,
    11.8

FRAUD, 17.37

FULL FAITH AND CREDIT
See Constitutional Limitations on choice of
    law; Defense of Marriage Act
    (DOMA); Dissolution of Marriage;
    Judgments; Workers' Compensation.

GARNISHMENT
See Jurisdiction, Quasi in rem.

GOVERNMENTAL INTERESTS
    In general, 2.9.
And homeward trend, 2.13.
In contract choice of law, 18.20.
    In Currie's analysis, 2.9.
    In tort choice of law, 17.11–17.15.

GUARDIANS AND CONSERVATORS,
    22.24, 22.25

GUARDIAN OF THE PERSON, 22.26

HAGUE CONVENTION ON
Abolishing the Requirement of Legalization
    for Foreign Public documents, 24.35.
Agency, applicable law, 18.26, 18.36.
Civil Aspects of International Child Abduc-
    tion, 15.42, 15.43.
Civil procedure, 12.6.
Decedents Estates, applicable law, 20.14,
    20.16.
Intercountry adoptions, 16.9.
International Sale of Goods, 18.25.
Jurisdiction, applicable law and recognition
    of decrees relating to adoption, 16.8.
Jurisdiction and recognition of judgments
    in civil and commercial matters
    (draft), 24.38, 24.39.

HAGUE CONVENTION ON—Cont'd
Legalization, 12.7, 24.35.
Maintenance obligations, applicable law, 15.30, 15.37.
Obligation to support minor children, applicable law, 16.09, 16.9.
Products liability, applicable law, 17.36, 17.39, 17.74, 17.76.
Protection of minors, 15.43.
Recognition and enforcement of decisions relating to adoption, 16.8.
Recognition and enforcement of decisions relating to maintenance obligations, 15.37.
Recognition and enforcement of decisions involving obligations to support minor children, 16.8.
Recognition of divorces and legal separations, 15.26.
Service abroad of documents, 12.7, 12.8.
Taking of evidence abroad, 12.9.

HUBER, ULRICH, 2.5

ILLEGITIMACY
And Uniform Parentage Act, 16.3.
Common law, 16.01, 16.1, 16.3.
Inheritance rights, 16.03, 16.2, 16.3.

INCIDENTAL QUESTION
Marital status as, 13.3.

INDIAN TRIBES
Judgments, 24.12.
Jurisdiction of in child custody matters, 15.42.
Jurisdiction over Indian country, 11.17, 11.19.

INSURANCE CONTRACTS
Choice of law, 18.26.
Jurisdiction, 8.2.
Party autonomy, 18.5, 18.76.

INTERNATIONAL TREATIES, 3.52
See also European Unions; Hague Convention On; United Nations; subject matter entries.
Bilateral, 3.58, 3.59.
Convention on International Wills, 20.16.
Multilateral, 3.57.

INTERNET
Active websites, jurisdiction, 5.22.
Cybersquatting, 5.9.
Defamation, jurisdiction, 7.8.
Passive websites, jurisdiction, 5.22.
Trade secrets, 7.11.
Zippo test, 5.22.

INTERPLEADER
Erie doctrine and, 3.47.
Garnishment alternative, 7.17.
Personal jurisdiction, 10.2.

INVASION OF PRIVACY, 17.40

JUDGMENTS
See also Administrative Determinations; Arbitration; Bankruptcy; Dissolution of Marriage.
Antisuit injunctions, 24.9, 24.21.
British Foreign Judgments Act, 24.7.
Brussels and Lugano Convention, 24.6, 24.7.
Class Actions, 24.15.
Child Support, 24.8, 24.12.
Collateral estoppel, 24.1.
Comity, 24.6, 24.12.
Confession of judgments, 6.3, 24.15.
Custody decrees, see Custody.
Default judgments, 24.15.
Defenses to enforcement of foreign-country judgments, 24.41.
Defenses to enforcement of sister state judgments,
    Competent court, 24.16, 24.18, 24.19, 24.22.
    Equitable defenses, 24.17.
    Finality, lack of, 24.28.
    Fraud, 24.17.
    Inconsistent judgments, 24.29.
    Injunctions against enforcement, 24.29.
    Lack of jurisdiction, 24.14, 24.42.
    Limitations, statute of, 24.32.
    Not on the merits, 24.24, 24.25.
    Payment, 24.31.
    Penal judgments, 3.18, 24.18, 24.19, 24.23.
    Public policy, 24.19, 24.20, 24.44.
    Reversal of prior judgment, 24.30.
    Rome Convention, 3.9.
    Tax judgments, 24.23.
    Worker's Compensation, 24.26.
Deficiency, 19.10.
Equity decrees, 24.9.
For penalties, 3.18, 24.19, 24.23.
For taxes, 24.23.
Foreign approaches to recognition, 24.38, 24.39, 24.78.
Full faith and credit, generally, 24.2, 24.8, 24.12.
Hague Convention (Draft), 24.39.
Inconsistent judgments, 24.29.
Indian tribes, 24.12.
Injunctions against enforcement of, 24.29.
Inter–American Recognition Convention, 24.38.
International judgments,
    See also Jurisdiction of rendering court, this entry; Recognition, this entry.
    Antisuit injunctions, 24.9, 24.21.
    British Foreign Judgments Act, 24.7.
    British Practice, 24.38.
    Canadian Foreign Judgments Act, 24.38.
    Canadian Reciprocal Enforcement of Judgments Act, 24.30.
    Comity, 24.6, 24.12, 24.33, 24.34.
    Defenses to recognition of, 24.18, 24.41.
    Enforcement of, 24.4, 24.5.

JUDGMENTS—Cont'd

International judgments—Cont'd

English Foreign Judgments Act, 24.38.

European Community Recognition of Judgments Regulation, 12.2, 14.28, 14.38, 24.38.

German practice, 24.38.

Hague Conference on PIL, 24.6, 24.7, 24.38.

Hilton doctrine, 24.3, 24.6, 24.33, 24.34, 24.35.

Jurisdiction in Non-merger rule, 24.3.

Non-merger rule, 24.3.

Penal Judgments, 24.40.

Preclusion, 24.3, 24.4.

Public policy, 24.44.

Reciprocity, 24.34, 24.35.

State Law, 24.35.

Taxes, 24.43.

Uniform Foreign Money–Judgments Recognition Act, 24.36.

Valuation of, 24.40.

Jurisdiction of rendering court,

Equity decrees, 24.9.

Exorbitant bases of jurisdiction, 24.4.

Nature of the proceeding, 24.7.

Land, regarding title of, 24.10.

Limitation, statute of, 24.32.

Nature of proceeding, 24.11.

Notice, 12.2.

"On the merits", 24.2, 24.24, 24.60.

Payment, 24.31.

Preclusion, policy of, 24.1, 24.3, 24.4.

Public policy defenses, 3.15, 24.20, 24.44.

Real property, decrees affecting, 24.10.

Reciprocity in international recognition, 24.36, 24.38.

Recognition and enforcement of,

At common law, 24.5.

By bilateral treaty, 24.7, 24.39, 24.45.

Decrees relating to land, 24.3, 24.10.

Defenses,

International judgments, 24.41.

Sister state judgments, 24.14.

Equity decrees, 24.9, 24.10.

Finality, requirement for, 24.28.

Foreign approaches, 24.38, 24.39.

Foreign country judgments, 24.3, 24.33.

Full faith and credit, 24.8, 24.12.

Opportunity to be heard, 12.4.

Registration as Summary proceeding, 24.13.

Recognition Convention (Hague Draft), 24.39.

Recognition Convention between United States and U.K. (proposed), 24.6, 24.32, 24.40, 24.43, 24.44, 24.45, 24.46.

Recognition of judgments for penalties and taxes, 24.23, 24.43.

Registration in federal courts, 24.13.

Res judicata, 24.1.

Restatement, Second, Conflict of Laws approach, 24.37.

Reversal of prior judgment, 24.30.

JUDGMENTS—Cont'd

Treaty Power, 24.6.

Uniform Enforcement of Foreign Judgments Act, 24.13.

Uniform Foreign Money–Judgments Recognition Act, 24.36.

Valuation of, 24.40.

Workers' Compensation, 24.26.

JURISDICTION

See also Dissolution of Domestic Relationships, Judgments.

Admiralty, 10.6.

Agents, appointment of, 6.9.

Antitrust actions, 9.7.

Associations, unincorporated, 10.12.

Bankruptcy, 10.7.

Brussels I Convention, 24.38.

Brussels I Regulation, 24.38.

Carriage contracts, 8.8.

Clayton Act, 9.7.

Collateral attack, 5.21.

Competence of court, in general, 5.17.

Conversion actions, 7.6.

Copyright actions, 9.2.

Consent as a basis, 6.3.

Construction contracts, 8.6.

Continuing jurisdiction, 5.23.

Contract actions, 8.1.

Corporate shield doctrine, 10.17.

Corporations, domestic, 10.13.

Decree to be performed outside forum, 24.9.

Direct attack, 5.19.

Divorce, 5.7, 15.4.

Domestic corporations, 10.13.

Employment litigation, 8.4, 9.5.

Enjoining foreign acts, 24.9.

Environmental litigation, 9.2.

Equity decrees, 24.9.

ERISA, 9.5.

Exorbitant bases for, 6.2.

Family law, 5.23.

Fiduciary shield doctrine, 10.17.

Field Code, 5.20.

Fifth Amendment, 10.2.

Foreign corporations,

Corporations alien to United States, 10.14–10.35.

Economic activities of subsidiary, 10.16.

Parent-subsidiary relationships, 10.16.

Foreign states, 10.19.

Franchise contracts, 8.3.

Fraud actions, 9.8.

Garnishment,

See also Jurisdiction quasi in rem, this entry.

Federal interpleader, 10.2.

Historical development, 5.2–5.4.

In rem, in general, 5.2, 5.5.

Admiralty, 10.6.

In personam, in general, 5.2, 5.8.

Insurance contracts, 7.11.

Interference with contract, 7.11.

Internet, 9.3.

JURISDICTION—Cont'd
Jurisdiction, personal,
    100–mile bulge rule, 5.15, 10.4.
    Choice of forum clauses, 6.3.
    Citizenship or allegiance, 6.4.
    Class actions, 10.9–10.11.
    Cognovit notes, 6.3.
    Common law bases, 5.3.
    Confession notes, clauses, 6.3.
    Consent,
        In general, 6.3.
        Adequacy, 6.3.
        Adhesion contracts, 6.3.
        Appearance or waiver, 6.5.
        By operation of law, 6.3.
        Choice of forum clauses, 6.3.
        Prior, 6.3.
        Prior as within due process, 6.3.
    Continuous and systematic contacts, 6.9.
    Defamation actions, 7.8, 7.9.
    Domicile as basis, 6.4.
    Due process requirements, 5.1, 5.3.
    Exorbitant jurisdiction, 6.2.
    Federal courts, 5.15.
    Federal statutes, 5.15.
    Full Faith and Credit Clause, 5.1, 5.2.
    International cases, 5.12.
    Libel actions, 7.8.
    Litigation unrelated to activities with in forum, 5.13.
    Local action rule, 7.7.
    Long-arm statutes, 5.14.
    Maximum judicial authority, 5.14.
    Minimum contacts test, 5.4.
    Motorists, non-resident, 5.3, 5.16.
    Nationwide service statutes, 10.2.
    Necessity for statute, 5.14, 5.15.
    Partnerships, 10.12.
    Patent infringement actions, 9.4.
    Pendent personal jurisdiction, 10.18.
    Personal service within the forum, 6.2.
    Preclusion by prior litigation, 5.12.
    Presence, 6.2.
    Prior consent, 6.3.
    Privacy, invasion of, actions for, 10.14.
    Purposeful availment, 5.11.
    Real property actions, 7.7.
    Reasonableness, 5.12.
    Removal of actions to federal court, 10.8.
    Residence or habitual residence, 6.4.
    RICO actions, 9.8.
    Sales contract actions, 8.5.
    Securities litigation, 9.6.
    Sovereignty theory, 5.4.
    Strict liability claims, 7.5.
    Subject matter jurisdiction compared, 5.17.
    Transient jurisdiction, 6.2.
    Trespass to chattels, 7.6.
    Venue compared, 5.18.
    Web pages as contacts, 9.3.
Jurisdiction, quasi in rem,
    Admiralty actions, 10.6.
    Compared to in rem, 5.6.

JURISDICTION—Cont'd
Jurisdiction—Cont'd
    Constitutionality, 5.9.
    Garnishment, 5.6.
    Limited appearance, 5.22.
    Removal of res, 5.23.
Limitations on exercise,
    Choice of forum clauses, 11.2–11.7.
    Commerce clause, 11.16.
    Contract limitations, 11.2–11.7.
        Federal courts, 11.3, 11.4.
        Interpretation of clauses, 11.6.
        Judgment recognition, 11.7.
        Limitations on exercise, 11.3.
        State courts, 11.5.
    Derogation by contract, 11.2–11.7.
    Federal law, 11.16.
    Federal transfers for trial, 11.14.
    Foreign relations, 11.13.
    Forum non conveniens, 11.8.
        Application of doctrine, 11.8.
        Availability of other forum, 11.10.
        Factors, other, 11.11.
        Federal transfers for trial, 11.14.
        Methods, 11.12.
        Preference for chosen forum, 11.9.
        State court application, 11.13.
    Forum selection clauses, 11.2.
    Indian country limitations, 11.17.
    Iron curtain statutes, 11.13.
    Native American limitations, 11.17.
    Ouster of jurisdiction by contract, 11.12.
Limited appearance, 5.22.
Notice and opportunity to appear, 5.16.
Ordering acts outside forums, 24.9.
Partnership, 10.12.
Presence as a basis, 6.2.
Quasi in rem, in general, 5.6.
Restraining foreign litigation, 24.9.
Specific performance of foreign land, 24.10.
Status determinations, 5.7, 5.9, 15.4.
Venue statutes, 11.1.

KEGEL, GERHARD, 2.13

KLAXON DOCTRINE
    See also *Erie* Doctrine.
And constitutional limitations, 3.48.
And testimonial privileges, 12.10.
Foreign Sovereign Immunities Act, application in, 10.19.
In bankruptcy, 23.13, 23.15.

LEASES, 18.37

LEFLAR, ROBERT A.
Conflicts theory, 2.12–2.14, 17.21–17.23.

LEGALIZATION OF DOCUMENTS AND JUDGMENTS IN INTERNATIONAL PRACTICE, 12.7, 24.35

LEGITIMATION, 16.1
Inheritance rights, 16.02, 16.2, 16.3.

LETTERS ROGATORY, 12.08

LEX FORI APPROACH, 2.10

LEX LOCI, 2.16, 2.17
English and Scottish Law Commission,
17.30.

LIS PENDENS, 11.11, 24.39

LOSS ALLOCATION IN TORTS,
17.36–17.47

LOUISIANA CODIFICATION, 2.27, 17.11,
17.13, 17.20, 17.32, 17.36, 17.37, 17.39,
17.40, 17.42–17.46, 17.49, 17.50, 17.74

MARRIAGE
    See also Domestic Relationships; Disso-
        lution of Domestic Relationships.
Breach of promise, 18.18.
Civil unions, 13.19.
Contract or status, 13.1.
Consent, 13.2.
Covenant marriage, 13.16, 15.1, 15.3.
Defense of Marriage Act, 13.19.
Dissolution, see Dissolution of Marriage.
Domicile versus nationality, 13.4.
Evasion statutes, 13.13.
Form and capacity, 13.7.
Incest, 13.2.
Incidental question, 13.3.
Indian custom marriages, 13.17.
Miscegenation, 13.10.
Non-age, 13.2.
Parental consent, 13.12.
Parties with different domiciles, 13.15.
Policies, 13.2.
Polygamy, 13.9, 13.16.
Progressive polygamy, 13.9, 13.16.
Property rights, see Matrimonial Property.
Recognition of,
    Celebration, place of, 13.2, 13.5, 13.6.
    Domicile, prohibitions by, 13.7, 13.8.
    Domicile, validation by, 13.6.
    Evasion statutes, 13.7.
    Form and capacity, 13.7.
    In third state when void at domicile,
        13.14.
    Incest, 13.2, 13.11.
    Law of vessel's flag, 13.6.
    Miscegenation, 13.10.
    Non-age, 13.12.
    Parties with different domiciles, 13.17.
    Place of celebration, 13.2, 13.5, 13.6.
    Polygamous marriages, 13.9, 13.17.
    Progressive polygamy, 13.9, 13.16.
    Remarriage after divorce, 13.9.
    Substantive prohibition, 13.8.
    Unusual marriages, 13.17.
Remarriage after divorce, 13.9.
Same-sex marriages, 13.20.
Substantive limitation, 13.8.
Unusual marriages, 13.16–13.18.

MATRIMONIAL PROPERTY
Acquired after marriage, 14.4, 14.6, 14.9.
Assets moved to other states, 14.12.
At time of marriage, 14.4, 14.5, 14.8.
Common law property states, 14.2.
Community property states, 14.3.
Contract obligations, 14.15.
Contractual modifications of marital re-
    gime, 14.15.
Creditors' claims, 14.16.
Debts, 14.16.
Income from, 14.7, 14.10.
Introduction, 14.1.
Land, 14.5, 14.6.
Movables,
    Accrual values, 14.11.
    Acquired after marriage, 14.9.
    At time of marriage, 14.8.
    Change of domicile, 14.9.
    Income from, 14.10.
    Insurance, 14.11.
    Intentional transfers, 14.12.
    Mutation, 14.11.
    Pensions, 14.11.
    Transactions after acquisition, 14.11.
Multi-state problems, 14.4.
Quasi-community property, 14.13, 14.15.
Separate property, 14.13.
Tort liability, 14.6.
Tracing rules, 14.15.

MISREPRESENTATION, 17.37

**MODEL UNIFORM PRODUCT LIABILITY
ACT,** 17.41

MOST SIGNIFICANT RELATIONSHIP
See Restatement (Second).

NEGOTIABLE INSTRUMENTS
Assignment, 19.3.

NEUTRAL FORUM
See Disinterested Third State

NO–FAULT LIABILITY, 17.42

NOTICE, 5.16, 12.2
Method of giving, 5.16, 12.3.
Requirement of, 5.16, 12.13.
Waiver of, 12.5.

PARTNERSHIP, JURISDICTION, 10.12

PARTY AUTONOMY, 18.1, 18.2
See also Contracts.

PENAL CLAIMS
    See also Judgments, Public Policy.
Defined, 3.17.

PENDENT JURISDICTION
And *Erie* Doctrine, 3.45.
Pendent Personal Jurisdiction, 10.18.

POWERS OF APPOINTMENT
Capacity of donee, 21.11.
Exercise, by residuary clause, 21.13.

POWERS OF APPOINTMENT—Cont'd
General power, exercise of, 21.11.
Nature and scope, 21.10.
Rule against perpetuities, 21.12.
Special power, exercise of, 21.11.
Theoretical analysis, 21.8.
Validity, 21.9, 21.11.

PRECLUSION BY PRIOR LITIGATION, POLICY OF, 24.1
See also Judgments.

PRINCIPLES OF PREFERENCE
See Cavers, David F.

PRIVATE INTERNATIONAL LAW, 1.1

PRIVILEGES AND IMMUNITIES CLAUSE
And choice of law, 3.32, 3.33, 3.35.

PROBATE
See also Administration of Decedents' Estates.
Collection of assets, 22.15.
Distribution, 22.15.
Foreign probate, recognition of, 22.3.
Historical problems, 22.5.
Land-probate of will of, 22.4.
Contest, 22.4.
Full faith and credit, 22.4.
Preclusion by prior litigation, 22.4.
Movables, probate of will, 22.2.
Personal representatives-powers outside state of appointment,
Full faith and credit, 22.14.
Other acts, 22.15.
Power to sue, 22.14.
Standing to sue, 22.14.
Place of administration,
Chattels moved after death, 22.9.
Chattels temporarily within state, 22.8.
Commercial payee, 22.11.
Corporate stock, 22.12.
Domicile, 22.6.
Intangibles, 22.10.
Land, 22.7.
Life insurance, 22.13.
Negotiable instruments, 22.11.
Situs of tangibles, 22.7.
Probate of will of movable, 22.2.

PRODUCTS LIABILITY
Choice of law generally, 17.64 17.67.
Choice-of-law rules, 17.80–17.82.
Common denominations in choice of law, 17.65–17.67.
Defendant-favoring case law, 17.69, 17.77.
Jurisdiction, 7.2.
Hague Convention, 17.80.
Louisiana Statute, 17.80.
Plaintiff-favoring case law, 17.70, 17.76.
Puerto Rico draft statute, 17.80.
True conflicts, 17.68–17.74.
Pertinent contacts, 17.66.
Proposed rules, 17.81.
Unprovided for cases, 17.75–17.79.

PROOF OF FOREIGN LAW
See Foreign Law, Proof of.

PROPERTY
Community, see Matrimonial Property.
Contracts concerning, see Contracts.
Corporate stock, 19.32.
Decedents' estates, see Administration of Decedents' Estates; Probate.
Intangibles,
Assignment of commercial paper, 19.29.
Assignments, 19.29.
Assignments for benefit of creditors, 19.30.
Assignability, 19.28.
Commercial assignments, 19.31.
Commercial paper assignability, 19.29.
Stock-assignment, 19.32.
Situs, 19.27.
Transfer, 19.27.
Interests in land, 19.1.
Intestate succession, see Succession.
Land,
See also Matrimonial Property.
Capacity to contract or convey, 19.3.
See also Contracts.
Capacity to hold, 19.3.
Commercial transactions, 19.2.
Contract and conveyance distinctions, 19.3.
Constructive Trust, 19.8.
Covenants, 19.5.
Covenants running with land, 19.5.
Conveyances, 19.2, 19.4.
Deficiency judgments, 19.10.
Encumbrances, 19.9.
Equitable decree by non-situs court, 19.8.
Equitable interests, 19.6.
Equitable remedies, 19.8.
Equitable servitudes, 19.7.
Foreclosure, 19.9, 19.10.
Formalities of transfer, 19.5.
Fraudulent conveyances, 19.3, 19.8.
Interests in, 19.2.
Intestate succession, 20.2.
Jurisdiction in rem, 5.5.
Matrimonial property, see Matrimonial Property.
Mechanics lien, 19.9.
Minerals, 19.23.
Mortgage, 19.10.
Mortgage assumption, 19.10.
Personal covenants, 19.5.
Purchase money mortgages, 19.10.
Real covenants, 19.5.
Renvoi, 19.2.
Secured creditor, 19.9.
Situs rule, 19.1, 19.2.
Spousal transfer, 19.3.
Succession, 20.2, 20.5.
Testate succession, 20.5.
Whole law, 19.2.
Land use, 19.1.

PROPERTY—Cont'd
Matrimonial, see Matrimonial Property.
Movables, trusts of, 21.1.
Powers of appointment, 21.8–21.13.
Rule against perpetuities, powers of appointment, 21.17.
Succession to tangibles, see Succession.
Tangibles,
    Adverse possession, 19.14.
    Chattel paper, 19.22.
    Chattel security, 19.16.
        Accounts, general intangibles, and mobile goods, 19.20.
        Certificate of title, 19.19.
        Commodities, Accounts, 19.24.
        Documents, 19.18.
        Deposit accounts, 19.20.
        Hague Convention on Law Applicable to sale of goods, 19.26.
        Instruments, 19.18.
        International transactions, 19.21.
        Minerals, 19.23.
        Possessory security interest, 19.20.
        Renvoi, 19.25.
        Treaties, 19.26.
        Uncertificated securities, 19.24.
        Uniform Commercial Code, 19.17.
    Chattel transfers, 19.11, 19.12, 19.13.
    Debtor location, 19.18.
    Domiciliary nexus, 19.11.
    Gratuitous transaction, 19.1.
    Intervivos transfers, 19.11.
    Mobilia sequuntur personam, 19.11.
    Policy considerations, 19.11.
    Prescription, 19.14.
    Purchasers without notice, 19.13.
    Removal from state, 19.15.
    Situs and market policies, 19.13.
    Title transfer, 19.3.
Testamentary succession, see Succession.
Trusts, see Trusts.
Wills, see Succession.

PROTECTED PERSONS
See Guardian and Conservators.

PUBLIC POLICY
Access to courts, 3.40.
Adhesion contracts, 18.5.
Applicable law and, 3.15.
As defense to enforcement of foreign claims, 3.2, 3.15, 3.28.
As defense to enforcement of foreign judgments, 24.20, 24.44.
Availability of local remedy, 3.19.
Governmental claims, 3.17.
Judgment recognition and, 3.15, 24.20, 24.21, 24.44.
Party autonomy, 18.4, 18.5.
Penal claims, 3.17.
Punitive damages, European view of, 24.39.
Tax claims, 3.18.

PUERTO RICO
Choice of law in products liability, 17.74.

PUERTO RICO—Cont'd
Draft statute codifying choice of law, 2.27, 17.20, 17.24, 17.36, 17.39.

PUNITIVE DAMAGES, 17.10, 17.50, 24.23
European view of, 24.39.

QUALIFICATION
In choice of law, see Characterization.
Corporations, qualification statutes, 23.7.

QUASI-COMMUNITY PROPERTY, 14.14
See also Matrimonial Property.

QUASI-CONTRACT, 18.42

RECIPROCITY, 24.33, 24.36

RECOGNITION OF JUDGMENTS, 24.1
See also Judgments; Dissolution of Marriage.

RENVOI
And false conflicts, 3.13, 3.14.
And recognition of foreign country divorces, 15.17.
Foreign court theory, 3.13.
Hidden, 3.14, 15.17.
In choice of law relating to property, 19.2, 19.25.
In English conflicts theory, 2.5.
Remission, 3.13.
Restatement (Second), 3.14.
Transmission, 3.13.

RES JUDICATA, 24.1
See also Dissolution of Marriage; Judgments.

RESIDENCE
See Domicile.

RESIDUARY LAW OF FORUM
And "better law" theory, 2.13.
In Ehrenzweig's theory, 2.10.

RESTATEMENT FIRST
    See also subject matter entries.
Torts, approach to, 17.21.

SALE OF GOODS
See Contracts; Property.

SAVIGNY, FRIEDRICH CARL VON, 2.6, 2.12

SERVICE
    See also Notice, Jurisdiction.
Hague Convention on the Service of Documents Abroad, 12.6, 12.7.
Immunities from, 11.15.
United States practice in international cases, 12.6.

STATUTE OF FRAUDS
Characterization, 3.8.
Contracts, 18.39.

STATUTE OF LIMITATIONS
Borrowing statutes, 3.11.
Characterization, 3.9.
Judgments, 24.32.

STATUTISTS
Conflicts theory of, 2.3, 2.4.

STORY, JOSEPH
Commentaries, 2.7.

SUCCESSION
    See also Administration of Decedents'
        Estates; Probate.
Alien, Devises to, 20.17.
Convention on International Wills, 20.16.
Election, 20.15.
    Equitable conversion, 20.2.
Family protection, 20.14.
Forced share, 20.14.
Hague Convention on the Law Applicable to
    Trusts, 20.16, 21.3.
Hague Convention on Law Applicable to
    Decedents Estates, 20.14, 20.16.
International wills, 20.17.
    Uniform Act, 20.17.
Intestate succession,
    Land, interests in, 20.2.
    Movables, 20.3, 20.4.
    Policy considerations, 20.1.
Spousal election, 20.16.
Testamentary, 20.5.
    Alien devises, 20.18.
    Devises to aliens, 20.18
    Formal validity, 20.6
    Iron curtain statutes, 20.18.
    Land,
        Choice of law clause, 20.8.
        Trust validity, 20.7.
        Trusts, change of investment, 20.7.
        Will construction, 20.8.
        Will of land, formal validity, 20.6.
        Wills of and revocation, 20.6.
    Lord Kingsdown Act, 20.6.
    Movables,
        Charitable gifts, 20.10.
        Estate as a unit, 20.3, 20.4.
        Revocation by instrument, 20.11.
        Revocation by operation of law,
          20.12.
        Revocation by physical act, 20.11.
        Situs as controlling, 20.4.
        Trusts, validity, 20.13.
        Validity of wills, 20.9.
        Will construction, 20.13.
        Wills, 20.9.
    Validity references, 20.13.
Wills of land, 20.6–20.8.

**SUPPLEMENTAL JURISDICTION AND
ERIE DOCTRINE**, 3.45

SUPPORT
See Dissolution of Marriage; Hague Con-
    vention On; United Nations.

SURETYSHIP, 18.27

TAX CLAIMS
Judgments, enforcement, 24.19, 24.33.
Tax treaties, 3.18, 3.58.

TESTIMONIAL PRIVILEGE, 12.10–12.14

TORTS
Admiralty, 17.49, 17.63.
Alienation of affections, 17.39, 17.54.
And public policy, 17.8.
    Characterization, 17.8–17.10.
Approaches to choice of law generally, 17.2,
    17.26.
    "Better law", 17.18, 17.21, 17.68.
    California approach, 17. 16–17.19.
    Characterization, 17.8–17.10.
    Comparative impairment, 17.14, 17.16.
    Eclecticism, 2.19, 17.1.
    Interest analysis, generally, 17.11.
    Lex fori, 17.15.
    Lex loci delicti, 17.2–17.6, 17.33.
    Exceptions, 17.5.
    Most-significant relationship, 17.21,
        17.24–17.28.
    Neumeier rules, 17.30–17.32, 17.39,
        17.42, 17.43.
    Policy analysis, 17.34.
    Principled rules, 17.35–17.37,
        17.74–17.76.
    Statutory rules, 17.74.
Choice of law by the parties, 17.40, 18.01.
Conduct regulation and loss allocation,
    17.36–17.39, 17.47–17.49.
Defamation, 17.55.
Dramshop acts, 17.5, 17.48.
False conflicts, 17.12.
Federal common law, 3.53.
Fraud and misrepresentation, 17.7, 17.52.
Guest statute cases, 17.7, 17.26.
Interest analysis, 17.11.
    And false conflicts, 17.13, 17.32.
    In California, 17.14.
Invasion of privacy, 17.55.
Jurisdiction, 7.1.
Law favorable to plaintiff, 17.34, 17.41,
    17.55, 17.70.
Leflar approach, 17.21, 17.68.
Lex fori, 17.15.
Louisiana approach, 17.11, 17.13, 17.20,
    17.32, 17.36, 17.37, 17.39, 17.40,
    17.42–17.46, 17.49, 17.50, 17.74.
No-fault liability, 17.56–17.58.
Non-physical injuries, 17.7.
Place of tort defined, 17.2.
Post-accident change of domicile, 3.23,
    17.16.
Procedural characterization, 17.9, 17.10.
Products liability, 17.64–17.82.
Public policy exception, 17.23.
Punitive damages, 17.50, 17.68.
Restatement, (Second) approach,
    17.24–17.28.
Seduction, 17.54.

TORTS—Cont'd
Split-domicile cases, 17.41–17.47.
Spousal immunity, 17.7.
True conflicts, 2.9, 17.13, 17.42–17.44, 17.68–17.74.
Unfair competition, 17.7, 17.53.
Uniform Motor Vehicle Accident Reparations Act, 17.42.
Uniform Single Publication Act, 17.55.
Unprovided-for cases, 17.14, 17.45, 17.77–17.79.
Vicarious liability, 17.4.
    See also Agency.
Warsaw Convention, 3.57.
Workers' compensation, 17.59–17.62.

TRANSPORTATION CONTRACTS, 18.30

TRAUTMAN, DONALD T.
Conflicts theory, 2.8, 2.11.

TREATIES, BILATERAL AND MULTILATERAL, 3.57–3.60
    Limitations on state conflicts law, 3.56.
See also European Communities; Hague Convention On; International Treaties; United Nations; subject matter entries.

TRUE CONFLICTS
In general, 2.9.
In torts, 17.13, 17.42–17.44.
In products liability, 17.68–17.74.

TRUSTS
Administration, 21.5, 21.6.
Foreign trustees, qualification, 21.5.
Hague Convention in Law Applicable Trust, 21.3.
Inter vivos, validity, 21.3.
Land,
    Inter vivos, 21.3.
    Validity, 21.2.
Movables, inter vivos, 21.3.
    Validity, 21.2, 21.3.
Powers of appointment, 21.8.
Resiluory clause, 21.13.
Rule Against Perpetuities, 21.12.
    Nature and Scope, 21.10.
    Validity, 21.9.
Settlers intention, policy of giving effect to, 21.1.
Testamentary, 21.2.
    Lord Kingsdown Act, 21.2.
    Validity, 21.2.
Testamentary of land, 21.2.
Trustees,
    Powers, 21.6.
    Qualification, 21.5.
Validity, 21.2.
Wills,
    See also Succession, Testamentary.
    Probate, see Administration of Decedents' Estates; Probate.

TRUSTS—Cont'd
Wills—Cont'd
UNCITRAL CONVENTION ON THE INTERNATIONAL SALE OF GOODS, 18.25

UNFAIR COMPETITION, 17.38

UNIFORM ARBITRATION ACT, 24.47

UNIFORM CERTIFICATION OF QUESTIONS OF LAW ACT, 3.47

UNIFORM CHILD CUSTODY JURISDICTION ACT, 15.39, 15.41

UNIFORM COMMERCIAL CODE
See separate Table

UNIFORM DISPOSITION OF COMMUNITY PROPERTY AT DEATH ACT, 14.6

UNIFORM DIVORCE RECOGNITION ACT, 15.11

UNIFORM FOREIGN MONEY–JUDGMENTS RECOGNITION ACT, 24.36

UNIFORM INTERSTATE AND INTERNATIONAL PROCEDURE ACT, 12.17

UNIFORM INTERSTATE FAMILY SUPPORT ACT, 15.30

UNIFORM JUDICIAL NOTICE OF FOREIGN LAW ACT, 12.17

UNIFORM MARRIAGE AND DIVORCE ACT, 15.02

UNIFORM MARRIAGE EVASION ACT, 15.16

UNIFORM MOTOR VEHICLE ACCIDENT REPARATION ACT, 17.42

UNIFORM PARENTAGE ACT, 16.4

UNIFORM PROBATE ACT
See separate Table

UNIFORM RECIPROCAL ENFORCEMENT OF SUPPORT ACT, 15.30

UNIFORM SINGLE PUBLICATION ACT, 17.40

UNITED KINGDOM
Return to lex loci rule in tort, 17.31.
Proposed recognition-of-judgments convention with United States, 24.39.

UNITED NATIONS
Arbitration Conventions (New York Conventions), 24.47.
Recovery abroad of maintenance, 15.37.

UNCITRAL Convention for the International Sale of Goods, 18.25

UNJUST ENRICHMENT, 18.32

UNPROVIDED FOR CASES, 2.9, 17.14, 17.45, 17.75–17.79

USURY
And choice of law clauses, 18.5, 18.28.

VALUATION
Gold francs in Warsaw Convention, 17.44, 24.40.

VENUE, 5.18
Federal court transfer of, 5.18.
Forum non conveniens, 5.18.

VIENNA CONVENTION ON THE INTERNA- TIONAL SALE OF GOODS, 18.01, 18.25

VON MEHREN, A.T.
Conflicts theory, 2.8, 2.11.

WACHTER, CARL GEORG VON, 2.6

WARRANTY IMPLIED, 18.25

WARSAW CONVENTION, 3.57

WASHINGTON CONVENTION OF 1973
Concerning international wills, 3.57, 20.16.

WEINTRAUB, R.J.
Conflicts theory, 2.11.
Products liability choice of law, 17.81.

WILLS
    See Administration of Decedents' Es-
        tates; Probate; Succession.
International Wills, 3.57, 20.16.
Powers of appointment, 21.8.

WORKER'S COMPENSATION, 17.59

WRONGFUL DEATH
    See Torts
Statutory limitations as substantive, 3.10.
    As procedural, 17.9.

†